Herbert Bucksch · Dictionary of Construction Law, Land Law and Regional Policy 2

IN MEMORIAM

MEINER FRAU ELLA BUCKSCH GEWIDMET

DEDICATED TO MY LATE, BELOVED WIFE

HERBERT BUCKSCH

Dictionary of Construction Law Land Law and Regional Policy

English – German

Englisch – Deutsch

2

Wörterbuch für Baurecht Grundstücksrecht und Raumordnung

BAUVERLAG GMBH · WIESBADEN UND BERLIN

CIP-Kurztitelaufnahme der Deutschen Bibliothek

Bucksch, Herbert:
Wörterbuch für Baurecht, Grundstücksrecht und
Raumordnung = Dictionary of construction law,
land law, and regional policy / Herbert Bucksch.
— Wiesbaden; Berlin: Bauverlag
NE: HST
2. English-German. — 1986.
ISBN 3-7625-2071-2

Das Werk ist urheberrechtlich geschützt.
Die dadurch begründeten Rechte, insbesondere die der Übersetzung,
des Nachdruckes, der Entnahme von Abbildungen, der Funksendung,
der Wiedergabe auf fotomechanischem oder ähnlichem Wege
(Fotokopie, Mikrokopie) und der Speicherung in Datenverarbeitungsanlagen,
bleiben, auch bei nur auszugsweiser Verwertung, vorbehalten.

© 1986 Bauverlag GmbH, Wiesbaden und Berlin
Druck: A. Sutter Druckerei GmbH, Essen
Einband: C. Fikentscher, Darmstadt

ISBN 3-7625-2071-2

PREFACE

The present work is a valuable contribution to the bilingual literature concerning land law, construction law, and regional policy. The difficulties which the author faced were awesome: For one, he not only had to deal with a very complex group of subjects, but he also had to compare legal systems which are basically different in their approach to many questions, particularly in the case of real estate. However, while American real property law is derived from the ancient feudal law of England, the modern terminology in Great Britain and the USA is often quite different. This book in itself is again proof of the phrase that Great Britain and the USA are two countries divided by a common language. This also applies to German which is also spoken and written in Switzerland and Austria. The equivalent terms had to be selected with this difficulty in mind.

The next problem, of course, is that the legal philosophy and its accompanying terminology are so very different between the civil law and the common law. However, the author has to be congratulated that he has tried to cover these differences and to explain them. For that reason, this volume will be helpful to practitioners in all the fields touching upon these areas of law.

No such book will ever be complete, nor will it ever be totally up-to-date, because the natural evolution of the law and the natural evolution of society brings constant changes which find their way into dictionaries, encyclopedias and glossaries many years later. Nevertheless, this book covers the subject as thoroughly as anybody could reasonably demand. To the person who is familiar only with one of the two legal systems involved, there will still be problems because at least a passing acquaintance with the other legal system is necessary for full understanding of the concepts and words. Nevertheless, this work will be an invaluable aid to people working in the fields it covers.

>
> Ernest A. Seemann, J. D., LL. M.
> Partner,
> Spencer, Bernstein, Seemann, Klein & Perlstein
> Attorneys at Law,
> 1901 Ponce de Leon Boulevard,
> Coral Gables, Miami, Florida 33134, USA

VORWORT

Dieses Wörterbuch ist ein wertvoller Beitrag zur zweisprachigen Literatur über Grundstücksrecht, Baurecht und Raumordnung. Der Autor hatte beträchtliche Schwierigkeiten zu überwinden, weil er es nicht nur mit vielschichtigen Themengruppen zu tun hatte, sondern auch mit zwei in ihrer Anlage verschiedenen Rechtssystemen, besonders beim Grundstücksrecht. Obgleich das Grundstücksrecht in den USA sich aus dem mittelalterlichen englischen Feudalrecht herleitet, ist die heutige Terminologie auf diesem Gebiet in Großbritannien und den USA sehr unterschiedlich. Dieses Buch ist wieder ein Beweis für die These, daß Großbritannien und die USA zwei durch eine gemeinsame Sprache getrennte Länder sind. Dies gilt auch für Deutsch, das auch in Österreich und der Schweiz gesprochen und geschrieben wird. Die sich deckenden Benennungen mußten unter diesem Gesichtspunkt erarbeitet werden.

Eine weitere Schwierigkeit war, daß die Rechtsphilosophie und ihr Wortschatz auf den Gebieten des bürgerlichen und des gemeinen Rechtes sehr verschieden sind. Dem Autor gebührt Anerkennung, daß er diese Schwierigkeiten durch Erklärungen überwunden hat. Aus diesem Grund ist dieses Wörterbuch vor allem für Praktiker auf den oben genannten Gebieten eine wertvolle Unterstützung.

Ein solches Buch wird natürlich nie vollständig sein und dem letzten Stand der Dinge entsprechen, weil die natürliche Entwicklung des Rechts und der menschlichen Gesellschaft einem ständigen Wandel unterworfen ist und die sich daraus ergebenden Tatsachen in Wörterbüchern, Enzyklopädien und Glossaren erst Jahre später ihren Niederschlag finden. Dieses Buch deckt den Themenbereich aber so sorgfältig wie nur möglich ab. Allerdings wird es für jemanden, der sich nur in einem der beiden Rechtssysteme auskennt, immer noch offene Fragen geben, weil zum vollen Verständnis der Begriffe und Benennungen in der einen oder anderen Sprache das Verständnis des anderen Rechtssystems erforderlich ist.

Dieses Wörterbuch kann allen sich in Deutsch und Englisch mit Baurecht, Grundstücksrecht und Raumordnung befassenden Fachleuten, aber auch dem interessierten Laien, empfohlen werden.

        Ernest A. Seemann, J. D., LL. M.
        Partner,
        Spencer, Bernstein, Seemann, Klein & Perlstein
        Attorneys at Law,
        1901 Ponce de Leon Boulevard,
        Coral Gables, Miami, Florida 33134, USA

INTRODUCTION

Brackets are used:

a) Square brackets:

   1. Description or definition, e.g.   Bewerber *m* *[Person, die sich um den Ersterwerb eines Kaufeigenheimes, einer Trägerkleinsied(e)lung oder einer Kaufeigentumswohnung oder um die erstmalige mietweise Überlassung einer neugeschaffenen Miet- oder Genossenschaftswohnung bewirbt]*

   2. Particular field, e.g.   Beschneideformat *n*, Beschnittformat *[Kartographie]*

b) Round brackets:

   3. Omissions, e.g.   Besucher(an)zahl *f* = Besucherzahl

   4. Abbreviations   (Brit.) = Großbritannien
                              (US)   = USA

The Comma separates synonymous words.

The Semicolon separates words of a concept, which are differently used in various countries.

The gender of the German words is indicated by:

m   = masculine
f   = feminine
n   = neuter
mpl = the term is given in its plural form, with the singular being masculine; *fpl* and *npl* apply accordingly.

EINFÜHRUNG

Anwendung der Klammern:
a) Eckige Klammern:
 1. Beschreibung oder Definition, z. B. Bewerber *m* *[Person, die sich um den Ersterwerb eines Kaufeigenheimes, einer Trägerkleinsied(e)lung oder einer Kaufeigentumswohnung oder um die erstmalige mietweise Überlassung einer neugeschaffenen Miet- oder Genossenschaftswohnung bewirbt]*
 2. Bestimmung des Sachgebiets, z. B. Beschneideformat *n*, Beschnittformat *[Kartographie]*

b) Runde Klammern:
 3. Auslassungen, z. B. Besucher(an)zahl *f* = Besucherzahl
 4. Abkürzungen (Brit.) = Großbritannien
 (US) = USA

Das Komma teilt Synonyme.

Das Semikolon teilt die in verschiedenen Ländern verwendeten Wörter für einen Begriff.

Das Geschlecht der deutschen Wörter ist wie folgt angegeben:
m = männlich
f = weiblich
n = sächlich
mpl = Das Wort ist in der Mehrzahl angegeben, wobei die Einzahl männlich ist. Dementsprechend sind *fpl* und *npl* zu verstehen.

A

(ab)alienability · Veräußerbarkeit f, Veräußerlichkeit

(ab)alienable, disposable · veräußerlich, veräußerbar

(ab)alienable fief, disposable fief; feudum alienabile, feodum alienabile [*Latin*] · veräußerliches Leh(e)n, veräußerbares Leh(e)n n

to (ab)alienate, to dispose of; to dispone [*Scots law*] · veräußern

(ab)alienated in mortmain, conveyed to mortmain, amortized, amortised, held in mortmain · veräußert an die tote Hand

to (ab)alienate in mortmain, to convey to mortmain, to amortize, to amortise · veräußern an die tote Hand

(ab)alienating in mortmain, amortizing, admortizing, amortising, conveying to mortmain · Veräußern n an die tote Hand

(ab)alienation, disposal [*In real property law, the transfer of property and possession of land(s) and other things from one person to another*] · Veräußerung f

(ab)alienation against anticipation, disposal of anticipation, (ab)alienation restraint, disposal restraint, restraint on (ab)alienation, restraint on disposal · Veräußerungsverbot n

(ab)alienation authority, authority of disposal, authority of (ab)alienation, disposal authority · Veräußerungsvollmacht f, Veräußerungsvertretungsmacht

(ab)alienation by juridic(al) act(ion), (ab)alienation by juristic act(ion) · rechtsgeschäftliche Veräußerung f

(ab)alienation contract, disposal contract, contract of (ab)alienation, contract of disposal · Veräußerungsvertrag m

(ab)alienation deed, disposal deed, deed of (ab)alienation, deed of disposal · Veräußerungsurkunde f

(ab)alienation duty, disposal duty, duty of (ab)alienation, duty of disposal · Veräußerungspflicht f

(ab)alienation in fee simple · Veräußerung f von Allodi(aleigent)um

(ab)alienation in mortmain; amortizatio [*Latin*]; amortization, amortisation, amortizement, amortisement [*The action of (ab)alienating land(s) or tenements in mortmain*] · Veräußerung f an die tote Hand

(ab)alienation mode, disposal mode, mode of (ab)alienation, mode of disposal · Veräußerungsweise f

(ab)alienation obligation, disposal obligation, obligation of (ab)alienation, obligation of disposal · Veräußerungsbindung f, Veräußerungsgebundenheit f, Veräußerungsverpflichtung f, Veräußerungsverbindlichkeit f

(ab)alienation of building land · Baulandveräußerung f

(ab)alienation of (real) estate, (ab)alienation of (real) property, (ab)alienation of land, (ab)alienation of realty, disposal of land, land disposal, land (ab)alienation · Grund(stücks)veräußerung f, Landveräußerung, Bodenveräußerung, Liegenschaftsveräußerung

(ab)alienation period, disposal period, period of (ab)alienation, period of disposal · Veräußerungsfrist f

(ab)alienation permission, disposal permission, permission of (ab)alienation, permission of disposal · Veräußerungsgenehmigung f, Veräußerungserlaubnis f

(ab)alienation power, disposal power, right of (ab)alienation, power of (ab)alienation, right of disposal, power of disposal, (ab)alienation right · Veräußerungsbefugnis f, Veräußerungsrecht n

(ab)alienation restraint, disposal restraint, restraint on (ab)alienation, restraint on disposal, (ab)alienation against anticipation, disposal of anticipation · Veräußerungsverbot n

(ab)alienation right, (ab)alienation power, disposal power, right of (ab)alienation, power of (ab)alienation, right of disposal, power of disposal · Veräußerungsbefugnis f, Veräußerungsrecht n

(ab)alienee, possessory successor, successor in possession · Besitznachfolger m, Veräußerungsbegünstigte

(ab)alienor, grantor [*He who makes a grant, transfer of title, conveyance, or (ab)alienation*] · Veräußerer m

to abandon, to stop, to cease · einstellen [*Arbeit(en)*]

to abandon · auflassen [*Bergrecht*]

to abandon, to desert, to give up, to leave (to itself), to forsake, to let go [*place*] · aufgeben, preisgeben, verlassen

to abandon, to relinquish, to remise, to forsake, to give up, to renounce, to disclaim [*To relinquish with intent of never again resuming one's right or interest*] · aufgeben, preisgeben, Verzicht leisten, verzichten, ausschlagen, entsagen, derelinquieren

to abandon [*vehicle*] · aussetzen, stehen lassen [*Fahrzeug*]

abandoned, derelict, forsaken, cast off, derserted, cast away, thrown away [*Personal property abandoned or thrown away by the owner in such manner as to indicate that he intends to make no further claim thereto*] · herrenlos, aufgegeben

abandoned, given up, left (to itself), forsaken, let gone, deserted, idle [*place*] · aufgegeben, verlassen, preisgegeben

abandoned · auflässig, aufgelassen [*Bergrecht*]

abandoned, relinquished, renounced, remised, forsaken, given up, waived, disclaimed · aufgegeben, preisgegeben, Verzicht geleistet, verzichtet, ausgeschlagen, entsagt, derelinquiert

abandoned, ceased, stopped · eingestellt [*Arbeiten*]

abandoned vehicle · ausgesetztes Fahrzeug *n*, herrenloses Fahrzeug *n*, stehengelassenes Fahrzeug *n*

abandonee [*A party to whom a right or property is abandoned by another*] · Verzicht(leistungs)nehmer *m*

abandoner, forsaker · Verzichtende *m*

abandoning, giving up, renouncing, relinquishing, forsaking · Aufgeben *n*, Preisgeben *n*, Verzichten *n*

abandoning, letting go, abandoning, deserting, giving up, leaving (a thing) (to itself) · Aufgeben *n*, Verlassen *n* [*Gebäude; Betrieb; Flußbett usw.*]

abandonment, relinquishment, renunciation, renouncement, disclaimer, waiver [*It includes the intention, and also the external act(ion) by which it is carried into effect*] · Aufgabe *f*, Preisgabe *f*, Verzicht(leistung) *m*, *(f)*, Entsagung, Ausschlagung

abandonment, abandoning, forsaking, dereliction [*The act of abandoning a chattel or mov(e)able*] · Aufgabe *f*, Preisgabe *f*, Verzicht(leistung) *m*, *(f)*

abandonment deed, deed of dereliction, dereliction deed, deed of abandonment · Aufgabeerklärung *f*, Preisgabeerklärung *f*, Verzichterklärung *f*

abandonment of a chattel, dereliction of a chattel · Fahrnisaufgabe *f*, Fahrnispreisgabe, Fahrnisdereliktion *f*, Fahrnisverzicht(leistung) *m*, *(f)*, Fahrhabepreisgabe, Fahrhabeaufgabe, Fahrhabedereliktion, Fahrhabeverzicht(leistung)

abandonment of easement(s) [*An easement may be lost by abandonment, of which non-use for twenty years may be sufficient evidence*] · Grunddienstbarkeitsaufgabe *f*, Grunddienstbarkeitsverzicht *m*

abandonment of (general) property, dereliction of proprietorship, abandonment of proprietorship, dereliction of ownership (of property), abandonment of ownership (of property), dereliction of (general) property · Eigentumsaufgabe *f*, Eigentumspreisgabe, Eigentumsverzicht(leistung) *m*, *(f)*

abandonment of inheritance, abandonment of heirship, relinquishment of inheritance, relinquishment of heirship, renunciation of heirship, renunciation of inheritance, renouncement of heirship, renouncement of inheritance · Erbaufgabe *f*, Erbentsagung *f*, Erbpreisgabe, Erbverzicht(leistung) *m*, *(f)*, Erbausschlagung

abandonment of light, relinquishment of light, renunciation of light, renouncement of light · Lichtrechtaufgabe *f*, Lichtrechtverzicht *m*, Lichtrechtpreisgabe

abandonment of possession, dereliction of possession · Besitzaufgabe *f*, Besitzpreisgabe, Besitzverzicht(leistung) *m*, *(f)*

abandonment of work(s), stop(ping) of work(s), cessation of work(s) [*Cessation of operation and intent(ion) of owner and contractor to cease operations permanently*] · Einstellung *f* der Arbeit(en), Arbeitseinstellung

abandonment of work(s), discontinuance of work(s), cessation of work(s) [*Cessation of operation for a definite period*] · Arbeitsunterbrechung *f*, Unterbrechung *f* der Arbeiten

abandonment presumption, presumption of abandonment · Aufgabevermutung *f*, Preisgabevermutung *f*, Verzichtsvermutung *f*

ab antiquo [*Latin*]; from old times · seit alter Zeit, von altersher

to abate, to deprive of operation, to rescind, to nullify, to annul, to repeal, to overrule, to cancel, to abrogate, to abolish (by authority), to do away with · abschaffen, aufheben, rückgängig machen, annullieren, außer Kraft setzen, löschen, abbauen

to abate, to deduct, to strike off a part, to subtract, to make an abatement from · abstreichen, abziehen

to abate, to break down, to destroy, to remove [*To abate a structure is to beat it down*] · zerstören

to abate, to beat down · schleifen [*Festungsmauer; Stadtmauer*]

to abate, to lessen, to reduce · reduzieren, mindern, herabsetzen, verringern

to abate , to bring to an end [*(court) action*] · erlöschen [*Klage*]

to abate · widerrechtlich Besitz ergreifen, widerrechtlich (in) Besitz nehmen [*Beim Tode einer Person*]

to abate [*To enter without right upon a tenement after the death of the last possessor and before the heir or devisee takes possession*] · widerrechtlich belegen

abated, brought to an end [*(court) action*] · erloschen [*Klage*]

abated, annulled, nullified, abolished (by authority), rescinded, overruled, done away with, deprived of operation, repealed, cancelled, abrogated · aufgehoben, annulliert, rückgängig gemacht, außer Kraft gesetzt, abgeschafft, gelöscht, abgebaut

abatement, removal [*nuisance*] · Aufhebung *f*, Beseitigung, Entfernung, Abstellung [*Immission*]

abatement, rebate [*A proportionate reduction of a payment allowed for special reasons, e.g. for prompt payment*] · Abzug *m*, Rabatt *m*

abatement, abolishment (by authority), annulment, nullification, rescission, avoidance, repeal, abrogation, cancellation, abolition · Annullierung *f*, Rückgängigmachung, Aufhebung, Abschaffung, Abbau *m*, Löschung

abatement, reduction · Verringerung *f*, Minderung, Reduzierung, Herabsetzung

abatement of (court) action, abatement of (law)suit, abatement of cause, abatement of plea · Erlöschen *n* einer Klage, Klageerlöschen

abatement of debts and legacies, reduction of debts and legacies · Herabsetzung *f* der Schuldforderungen und Vermächtnisse nach Maßgabe des Mankos am hinterlassenen Vermögen, Reduzierung der Schuldforderungen und Vermächtnisse nach Maßgabe des Mankos am hinterlassenen Vermögen, Minderung der Schuldforderungen und Vermächtnisse nach Maßgabe des Mankos am hinterlassenen Vermögen, Verringerung der Schuldforderungen und Vermächtnisse nach Maßgabe des Mankos am hinterlassenen Vermögen

abatement of pecuniary legacy, abatement of pecuniary bequest [*A proportional diminution of a pecuniary legacy, when the funds or assets out of which such legacy is payable are not sufficient to pay it in full*] · Geldvermächtnisherabsetzung *f*, Geldlegatherabsetzung

abatement plea, plea of abatement · Antrag *m* auf Niederschlagung

abating, lessening, reducing · Verringern *n*, Herabsetzen, Mindern, Reduzieren

abating, rendering null and void, doing away with, nullifying, rescinding, making void, annulling, (a)voiding, repealing, abolishing, abrogating, cancelling, overruling · Aufheben *n*, Rückgängigmachen *n*, Annullieren *n*, Abschaffen *n*, Löschen *n*, Abbauen *n*

abator, abater [*In real property law, a stranger who, having no right of entry, contrives to get possession of an estate of freehold, to the prejudice of the heir or devisee, before the latter can enter, after the ancestor's death*] · widerrechtlicher Besitzergreifer *m*, widerrechtlicher Besitznehmer

abbas [*Ang. Sax.*]; aestruarium [*Latin*]; abb(e)y-land(s) [*Estates of an abb(e)y*] · Abteiland *n*, Abteiboden *m*, Abteiländereien *f pl*

Abbé-Helmert criterion · Abbé-Helmertsches Kriterium *n* [*Statistik*]

abetter, abettor · Anstifter *m*

ab extra, from outside · von außen

abeyance, condition of abeyance, state of abeyance, state of suspension, abeyancy, temporary nonexistence, expectancy of law, contemplation of law; abeyantia [*Latin*] [*In the law of real estate. Where there is no person in existence in whom an inheritance can vest, it is said to be in abeyance, that is, in expectation; the law considering is as always potentially existing, and ready to vest when ever a proper owner appears*] · Schwebe(zustand) *f*, *(m)*

abeyance of seisin, abeyance of freehold possession [*Interruption of the tenancy of a freehold. Forbidden under early law, so that every transfer of land had to be open and necessitated public delivery of seisin*] · Schwebe(zustand) *f*, *(m)* einer Gewere

abeyant, in abeyance, dormant · in der Schwebe (sein), schwebend, noch nicht entschieden, unentschieden

ability, qualification, capability, capacity · (Leistungs)Fähigkeit *f*, (Leistungs)Vermögen *n*

ability for being cultivated, capacity for being cultivated, capability for being cultivated, qualification for being cultivated · Anbaufähigkeit *f*, Anbaubarkeit, Anbaueignung *f*, Kultivierbarkeit

ability for performing legal acts, qualification for performing legal acts, capability for performing legal acts, capacity for performing legal acts · Handlungsfähigkeit *f*, Handlungseignung *f*

ability of being controlled, ability of being re-examined, ability of being checked, capability of being checked, capability of being controlled, capability of being re-examined, capacity of being checked, capacity of being re-examined, capacity of being controlled, qualification of being re-examined, qualification of being checked, qualification of being controlled · Nachprüfbarkeit *f*, Kontrollierbarkeit

ability of earning a living, capacity of earning a living, capability of earning a living

ability tax — able to contract

· Erwerbsfähigkeit *f*, Erwerbsvermögen *n*

ability tax · Wohnhaussteuer *f* [*In Tasmanien 1904 eingeführt*]

ability to be a party, capacity to be a party, capability to be a party, qualification to be a party · Parteifähigkeit *f*

ability to be approved, approvable quality, approbativeness, quality of being approbative, approvableness, worthiness of approval · Zulassungswürdigkeit *f*, Zustimm(ungs)würdigkeit, Zulassungsfähigkeit, Zustimm(ungs)fähigkeit

ability to buy, ability to purchase, capacity to buy, capacity to purchase, capability to buy, capability to purchase, qualification to purchase, qualification to buy · Kauffähigkeit *f*, Kaufeignung *f*

ability to commit crime, capacity to commit crime, capability to commit crime, qualification to commit crime · (kriminelle) Schuldfähigkeit *f*, (kriminelle) Schuldeignung *f*

ability to deal with land, capacity to deal with land, qualification to deal with land, capability to deal with land · Bodenverkehrsfähigkeit *f*, Bodenverkehrseignung *f*, Grundstücksverkehrsfähigkeit, Grundstücksverkehrseignung, Immobiliarverkehrsfähigkeit, Immobiliarverkehrseignung, Immobilienverkehrsfähigkeit, Immobilienverkehrseignung, Liegenschaftsverkehrsfähigkeit, Liegenschaftsverkehrseignung

ability to earn profits, capacity to earn profits, capability to earn profits, qualification to earn profits · Gewinneignung *f*, Gewinnfähigkeit *f*, Profiteignung, Profitfähigkeit

ability to inherit, capacity to inherit, qualification to inherit, capability to inherit · (aktive) Erbfähigkeit *f*, (aktive) Erbeignung *f*

ability to make payments → capacity to pay

ability to pay, capability to pay, capacity to make payments, ability to make payments, capability to make payments, solvency, soundness, trustworthiness, capacity to pay · Zahlungsfähigkeit *f*, Zahlungsvermögen *n*, Bonität *f*, Kreditfähigkeit, Kreditwürdigkeit

ability-to-pay principle · Zahlungsfähigkeitsgrundsatz *m*, Zahlungsfähigkeitsprinzip *n*

ab initio [*Latin*]; from the beginning · von Anfang an

ab intestato, from an intestate [*Succession ab intestato refers to succession to property of a person who has not disposed of it by will*] · nichttestamentarisch, ohne Testament

abjuration → abjuring

abjuration oath, oath of abjuration · Abschwörungseid *m* der Leh(e)n(s)treue

abjuration of the realm · Schwur *m* das Königreich zu verlassen

to abjure, to forswear, to renounce by oath, to renounce (up)on oath · abschwören

abjurer · Abschwörende *m*

able, capable, qualified · (leistungs)fähig

able-bodied, fit for work · arbeitsfähig

able-bodied (person) · Arbeitsfähige *m*

able of being checked, able of being controlled, able of being re-examined, qualified of being checked, qualified of being controlled, qualified of being re-examined, capable of being checked, capable of being controlled, capable of being re-examined · kontrollierbar, nachprüfbar

able of being revoked, able of revocation, qualified of being revoked, qualified of revocation, during pleasure, revocable, at will, revokable, ambulatory, capable of being revoked, capable of revocation · auf Widerruf, widerruflich, widerrufbar, einvernehmlich geduldet

able of being tested, qualified of being tested, capable of being tested · prüfungsfähig, prüfungsreif, prüfungsgeeignet

able of contracting, qualified of contracting, capable to contract, able to contract, qualified to contract, competent to contract, capable of contracting · vertragsfähig, vertragsgeeignet

able of earning, qualified of earning, capable of earning, able to earn, capable to earn, qualified to earn · erwerbsgeeignet, erwerbsfähig

able of revocation, qualified of being revoked, qualified of revocation, during pleasure, revocable, at will, revokable, ambulatory, capable of being revoked, capable of revocation, able of being revoked · auf Widerruf, widerruflich, widerrufbar, einvernehmlich geduldet

able to be approved, approbative, approvable [*Worthy or deserving of approval*] · zulassungswürdig, zustimm(ungs)fähig

able to be compared, capable of comparison (with), comparable, comparative · vergleichbar

able to buy, able to purchase, capable to buy, capable to purchase, qualified to buy, qualified to purchase · kauffähig, kaufgeeignet

able to contract, qualified to contract, competent to contract, capable of contracting, able of contracting, qualified of contracting, capable to contract · vertragsfähig, vertragsgeeignet

able to earn, capable to earn, qualified to earn, able of earning, qualified of earning, capable of earning · erwerbsgeeignet, erwerbsfähig

able to make a will, capable to make a will, qualified to make a will, able of making a will, qualified of making a will, capable of making a will · testierfähig, testiergeeignet, testamentsfähig, testamentsgeeignet

able to pay, trust(worth)y, solvent, financially able, sound, capable to pay · zahlungsfähig, flüssig, kreditfähig, kreditwürdig

able to purchase, capable to buy, capable to purchase, qualified to buy, qualified to purchase, able to buy · kauffähig, kaufgeeignet

ablocation; locatio [Latin]; letting · Vermietung f

abnegation oath, oath of abnegation · Ableugnungseid m

abnormal hazard, abnormal risk · Ausfallrisiko n, Ausfallwagnis n

abnormality · Anormalität f

abnormality index, index of abnormality · Anormalitätsindex m

abnormal person · Person f mit geminderter Geschäftsfähigkeit

abnormal risk, abnormal hazard · Ausfallrisiko n, Ausfallwagnis n

abode → (place of) abode

to abolish (by authority), to do away with, to abate, to deprive of operation, to rescind, to nullify, to annul, to repeal, to overrule, to cancel, to abrogate · abschaffen, aufheben, rückgängig machen, annullieren, außer Kraft setzen, löschen, abbauen

abolished (by authority), rescinded, overruled, done away with, deprived of operation, repealed, cancelled, abrogated, abated, annulled, nullified · aufgehoben, annulliert, rückgängig gemacht, außer Kraft gesetzt, abgeschafft, gelöscht, abgebaut

abolishing, abrogating, cancelling, overruling, abating, rendering null and void, doing away with, nullifying, rescinding, making void, annulling, (a)voiding, repealing · Aufheben n, Rückgängigmachen n, Annullieren n, Abschaffen n, Löschen n, Abbauen n

abolishment (by authority), annulment, nullification, rescission, avoidance, repeal, abrogation, cancellation, abolition, abatement · Annullierung f, Rückgängigmachung, Aufhebung, Abschaffung, Abbau m, Löschung

abolition, abatement, abolishment (by authority), annulment, nullification, rescission, avoidance, repeal, abrogation, cancellation · Annullierung f, Rückgängigmachung, Aufhebung, Abschaffung, Abbau m, Löschung

aborigine · Ureinwohner m

above-average, more-than-average · überdurchschnittlich

above-ceiling salary, above-scale salary · überhöhtes Gehalt n

above-ceiling wage, above-scale wage · überhöhter Lohn m

above-grade entrance [e.g. to an underground railway] · oberirdischer Eingang m, Übertageeingang

abridgement · Rechtsfallsammlung f

abrocator [Latin] → ((real) estate) broker

abrogatable, rescindable, annullable, defeasible · annullierbar, aufhebbar, löschbar, abschaffbar, abbaubar

to abrogate, to abolish (by authority), to do away with, to abate, to deprive of operation, to rescind, to nullify, to annul, to repeal, to overrule, to cancel · abschaffen, aufheben, rückgängig machen, annullieren, außer Kraft setzen, löschen, abbauen

abrogated, abated, annulled, nullified, abolished (by authority), rescinded, overruled, done away with, deprived of operation, repealed, cancelled · aufgehoben, annulliert, rückgängig gemacht, außer Kraft gesetzt, abgeschafft, gelöscht, abgebaut

abrogating, cancelling, overruling, abating, rendering null and void, doing away with, nullifying, rescinding, making void, annulling, (a)voiding, repealing, abolishing · Aufheben n, Rückgängigmachen n, Annullieren n, Abschaffen n, Löschen n, Abbauen n

abrogation, cancellation, abolition, abatement, abolishment (by authority), annulment, nullification, rescission, avoidance, repeal · Annullierung f, Rückgängigmachung, Aufhebung, Abschaffung, Abbau m, Löschung

to abscond, to hide away [To depart secretly or to hide oneself from the jurisdiction of the court so as to avoid legal process. It may amount to an act of bankruptcy] · flüchtig sein

abscondence, hiding · Flüchtigsein n

absconder, runaway from justice · Flüchtige m

absconding debtor, hiding debtor · flüchtiger Schuldner m, flüchtig gewordener Schuldner

absence · Abwesenheit f

absence from the job · Arbeits(ver)säumnis f, n, (f)

absence of defect — absolute conveyance

absence of defect · Baumangelfreiheit f, (Sach)Mangelfreiheit, Nachbesserungsfreiheit

absence of defects · Baumängelfreiheit f, (Sach)Mängelfreiheit, Nachbesserungsfreiheit

absence of defects · Mängelfreiheit f

absence of doubt, distinctness, certainty, clearness of statement, definiteness · Bestimmtheit f, Klarheit, Gewißheit

absence of errors · Fehlerlosigkeit f

absence of quorum, lack of quorum · Beschlußunfähigkeit f [Wenn über einen Beschluß abgestimmt werden muß]

absence of segmentation with factor proportions variable · Produktionsfunktion f vom Typ A nach Gutenberg [Ein bestimmter Produktionsfaktor oder eine bestimmte Produktionsfaktorgruppe, die kontant ist, läßt sich mit jeder beliebigen Menge eines anderen Produktionsfaktors oder einer anderen Produktionsfaktorgruppe kombinieren]

absent · abwesend, nicht anwesend

absentee · abwesende Person f

absentee [A landed proprietor who (1) resides away from his estate, or (2) from his country] · nichtansässiger (Grund)Besitzer m, nichtansässiger Grundstücksbesitzer

absenteeism, absenteeship · Absentismus m, Nichtansässigkeit f [Der in gewohnheitsmäßiger Abwesenheit zu Tage tretende Mangel aller persönlichen Beziehungen der Landeigentümer zum Boden und seinen Bebauern. Die Verwaltung und Bewirtschaftung bleibt Verwaltern und Pächtern überlassen]

absentee voter · Briefwähler m

absentmindedness · Geistesabwesenheit f

absolute, total, unrestricted, unlimited, irrebuttable, unconditional · absolut, unbeschränkt, uneingeschränkt, unbedingt, unbegrenzt, bedingungslos

absolute; al(l)odian [obsolete]; odhal [In old English law]; al(l)odial · absolut, leh(e)n(s)frei, allodial, erbeigen, unbeschränkt, zinsfrei [Im freien, eigentümlichen Besitz nach römischem Recht]

absolute · rechtskräftig [Urteil]

absolute, complete, unconditional · bedingungslos, absolut, vollständig

absolute (ab)alienation (of land) with back-bond, absolute disposal (of land) with back-bond · Bodenveräußerung f mit Rückübereignung, Landveräußerung mit Rückübereignung, Grund(stücks)veräußerung mit Rückübereignung

absolute acceptance of a bill (of exchange), general acceptance of a bill (of exchange) · allgemeine Wechselannahme f

absolute and unqualified gift · unbedingte und unbeschränkte Schenkung f

absolute assignment, absolute cession, absolute assignation · absolute Abtretung f, absolute Zession f

absolute bequest, absolute legacy [One given without condition and intended to vest immediately] · absolutes (Fahrnis)Legat n, absolutes (Fahrnis)Vermächtnis n

absolute binding authority of precedents, total binding authority of precedents, unrestricted binding authority of precedents, unlimited binding authority of precedents, irrebuttable binding authority of precedents · absolute Bindungswirkung f, unbeschränkte Bindungswirkung, unbegrenzte Bindungswirkung, uneingeschränkte Bindungswirkung, unbedingte Bindungswirkung

absolute cession, absolute assignation, absolute assignment · absolute Abtretung f, absolute Zession f

absolute chattel, allodial ownership, absolute ownership, al(l)odium; franc-al(l)eu [French law]; al(l)odial estate, al(l)odial property, al(l)odial chattel, absolute estate, absolute property [An estate held without service or acknowledg(e)ment of any superior, as among the early Teutonic peoples, opposed to feud(um)] · Allodialgut n, allodiales Eigentum n, allodiales Erbgut, allodiales Eigengut, leh(e)n(s)freies Eigentum, leh(e)n(s)freies Erbgut, leh(e)n(s)freies Eigengut, absolutes Eigentum, absolutes Erbgut, absolutes Eigengut, erbeigenes Erbgut, erbeigenes Eigengut, unbeschränktes Erbgut, unbeschränktes Eigentum, unbeschränktes Eigengut, (zins)freies Erbgut, (zins)freies Eigentum, (zins)freies Eigengut, uneingeschränktes Erbgut, uneingeschränktes Eigentum, uneingeschränktes Eigengut, unbegrenztes Erbgut, unbegrenztes Eigentum, unbegrenztes Eigengut, Allodialeigentum, Allodialvermögen n, Al(l)odium n, Alodis n, Alode f, Alodus m, Alaudium n, Vollgut, echtes Eigen(gut) n, lediges Eigen(gut), Ludeigen(gut), Alleingut

absolute conveyance (of land), absolute land conveyance [A conveyance by which the right or property of land is transferred, free of any condition, or qualification, by which it might be defeated, or changed; as an ordinary deed of lands, in contradistinction to a mortgage, which is a conditional conveyance] · absolute (Land)Übertragung f, unbeschränkte (Land)Übertragung, uneingeschränkte (Land)Übertragung, unbedingte (Land)Übertragung, unbegrenzte (Land)Übertragung

absolute discretion — absolute land conveyance

absolute discretion · freies Ermessen *n*

absolute disposal (of land) with backbond, absolute (ab)alienation (of land) with back-bond · Bodenveräußerung *f* mit Rückübereignung, Landveräußerung mit Rückübereignung, Grund(stücks)- veräußerung mit Rückübereignung

(absolute) divorce; divortium [*Latin*] · (Ehe)Scheidung *f*

absolute estate, absolute property, absolute chattel, allodial ownership, absolute ownership, al(l)odium; franc-al(l)eu [*French law*]; al(l)odial estate, al(l)odial property, al(l)odial chattel [*An estate held without service or acknowledg(e)ment of any superior, as among the early Teutonic peoples, opposed to feud(um)*] · Allodialgut *n*, allodiales Eigentum *n*, allodiales Erbgut, allodiales Eigentum, leh(e)n(s)freies Eigentum, leh(e)n(s)freies Erbgut, leh(e)n(s)freies Eigentum, absolutes Eigentum, absolutes Erbgut, absolutes Eigengut, erbeigenes Eigentum, erbeigenes Erbgut, unbeschränktes Erbgut, unbeschränktes Eigentum, unbeschränktes Eigengut, (zins)freies Erbgut, (zins)freies Eigengut, uneingeschränktes Erbgut, uneingeschränktes Eigentum, uneingeschränktes Eigengut, unbegrenztes Erbgut, unbegrenztes Eigentum, unbegrenztes Eigengut, Allodialeigentum, Allodialvermögen *n*, Al(l)odium *n*, Alodis *n*, Alode *f*, Alodus *m*, Alaudium *n*, Vollgut, echtes Eigen(gut) *n*, lediges Eigen(gut), Ludeigen(gut), Alleingut

absolute estate for years, absolute estate of years, absolute lease(hold) tenure, absolute (good) lease(hold) title, absolute tenancy of years, absolute tenancy for years · absolutes (Besitz)Recht *n* auf Zeit, absolutes (Besitz)Recht auf Jahre, absolutes Grundbesitzrecht auf Zeit, absolutes Grundbesitzrecht auf Jahre, absoluter (Grund)Besitz(stand) *m* auf Zeit, absoluter (Grund)Besitz(stand) auf Jahre

absolute failure to perform, unrestricted failure to perform, unlimited failure to perform, irrebuttable failure to perform, total failure to perform · absolute Nichterfüllung *f*, uneingeschränkte Nichterfüllung, unbeschränkte Nichterfüllung, unbedingte Nichterfüllung, unbegrenzte Nichterfüllung

absolute (fee simple) title [*Title that is unqualified; best title one can obtain*] · absoluter (Rechts)Titel *m*

absolute freehold title · absolut freier (Grund)Besitztitel *m*

absolute frequency · absolute Häufigkeit *f*

absolute gift, irrevocable gift, gift inter vivos [*A gift made by one living person to another, as opposed to a gift by will*] · Schenkung *f* unter Lebenden

absolute (good) lease(hold) title, absolute tenancy of years, absolute tenancy for years, absolute estate for years, absolute estate of years, absolute lease(hold) tenure · absolutes (Besitz)Recht *n* auf Zeit, absolutes (Besitz)Recht auf Jahre, absolutes Grundbesitzrecht auf Zeit, absolutes Grundbesitzrecht auf Jahre, absoluter (Grund)Besitz(stand) *m* auf Zeit, absoluter (Grund)Besitz(stand) auf Jahre

absolute guaranty, absolute guarantee, absolute garantie · Bürgschaft *f* ohne Einrede der Vorausklage

absolute heiress, exclusive heiress, sole heiress, absolute heir female, exclusive heir female, sole heir female · absolute Erbin *f*, unbegrenzte Erbin, unbedingte Erbin, uneingeschränkte Erbin, unbeschränkte Erbin, Alleinerbin, Vollerbin

absolute heir (male), sole heir (male), exclusive heir (male) · absoluter Erbe *m*, unbeschränkter Erbe, uneingeschränkter Erbe, unbedingter Erbe, unbegrenzter Erbe, Alleinerbe, Vollerbe

absolute in authority, autocratic · selbstherrlich

absolute interest, exclusive interest, sole interest, exclusive ownership (of property), sole ownership (of property), unlimited ownership (of property); dominium plenum, dominium perpetuum [*Latin*]; absolute ownership (of property), sole property, sole proprietorship [*In English law absolute ownership can only exist in chattels, as all land is subject theoretically to the obligations of tenure; but practically the fee simple in land gives absolute ownership*] · absolutes Eigentum *n*, uneingeschränktes Eigentum, unbeschränktes Eigentum, unbegrenztes Eigentum, ausschließliches Eigentum, unbedingtes Eigentum, Alleineigentum

absolute jurisdiction, unrestricted jurisdiction, irrebuttable jurisdiction, total jurisdiction, unlimited jurisdiction · absolute Gerichtsbarkeit *f*, uneingeschränkte Gerichtsbarkeit, unbeschränkte Gerichtsbarkeit, unbedingte Gerichtsbarkeit, unbegrenzte Gerichtsbarkeit, absolute Rechtspflege(funktion) *f*, uneingeschränkte Rechtspflege(funktion), unbeschränkte Rechtspflege(funktion), unbedingte Rechtspflege(funktion), unbegrenzte Rechtspflege(funktion)

absolute land conveyance, absolute conveyance (of land) [*A conveyance by which the right or property of land is transferred, free of any condition, or qualification, by which it might be defeated, or changed; as an ordinary deed of lands, in contradistinction to a mortgage, which is a conditional conveyance*] · absolute (Land)Übertra-

absolute (land) owner — absolute property 8

gung f, unbeschränkte (Land)Übertragung, uneingeschränkte (Land)Übertragung, unbedingte (Land)Übertragung, unbegrenzte (Land)Übertragung

absolute (land) owner, exclusive (land) owner, absolute proprietor, exclusive proprietor, al(l)odial proprietor, free man, holder of an allodium; liber homo, homo liber [*Latin*]; allodiary, allodialist, al(l)odial (land) owner · absoluter Eigentümer m, unbeschränkter Eigentümer, Alleineigentümer, Freiguteigentümer, Allodialeigentümer, freier Mann m, Freie m

absolute lease(hold) tenure, absolute (good) lease(hold) title, absolute tenancy of years, absolute tenancy for years, absolute estate for years, absolute estate of years · absolutes (Besitz)Recht n auf Zeit, absolutes (Besitz)Recht auf Jahre, absolutes Grundbesitzrecht auf Zeit, absolutes Grundbesitzrecht auf Jahre, absoluter (Grund)Besitz(stand) m auf Zeit, absoluter (Grund)Besitz(stand) auf Jahre

absolute legacy, absolute bequest [*One given without condition and intended to vest immediately*] · absolutes (Fahrnis)Legat n, absolutes (Fahrnis)Vermächtnis n

absolute liability, strict liability · Gefährdungshaftung f, Gefährdungshaftpflicht f, Haftung ohne Verschulden, Haftpflicht ohne Verschulden, Gefährdungshaftbarkeit f, Haftbarkeit ohne Verschulden

absolute mandamus → absolute (writ of) mandamus

absolute necessity, natural necessity, unlimited necessity, unrestricted necessity, irrebuttable necessity, total necessity · absolute Notwendigkeit f, unbedingte Notwendigkeit, unbegrenzte Notwendigkeit, uneingeschränkte Notwendigkeit, unbeschränkte Notwendigkeit

absoluteness · Absolutheit f

absolute ownership, al(l)odium; franc-al(l)eu [*French law*]; al(l)odial estate, al(l)odial property, al(l)odial chattel, absolute estate, absolute property, absolute chattel, allodial ownership [*An estate held without service or acknowledg(e)ment of any superior, as among the early Teutonic peoples, opposed to feud(um)*] · Allodialgut n, allodiales Eigentum n, allodiales Erbgut, allodiales Eigengut, leh(e)n(s)freies Eigentum, leh(e)n(s)freies Erbgut, leh(e)n(s)freies Eigengut, absolutes Eigentum, absolutes Erbgut, absolutes Eigengut, erbeigenes Eigentum, erbeigenes Eigengut, erbeigenes Erbgut, unbeschränktes Erbgut, unbeschränktes Eigentum, unbeschränktes Eigengut, (zins)freies Erbgut, (zins)freies Eigentum, (zins)freies Eigengut, uneingeschränktes Erbgut, uneingeschränktes Eigen-

tum, uneingeschränktes Eigengut, unbegrenztes Erbgut, unbegrenztes Eigentum, unbegrenztes Eigengut, Allodialeigentum, Allodialvermögen n, Al(l)odium n, Alodis n, Alode f, Alodus m, Alaudium n, Vollgut, echtes Eigen(gut) n, lediges Eigen(gut), Ludeigen(gut), Alleingut

absolute ownership land, alody, inheritable land, al(l)odial land, free land, land held in absolute ownership · allodiales Land n, erbeigenes Land, leh(e)n(s)-freies Land, absolutes Land, unbeschränktes Land, uneingeschränktes Land, unbegrenztes Land, zinsfreies Land, Allodialland

absolute ownership of land, fee simple (absolute) [*Largest estate or ownership in real property; free from all manner of conditions or encumbrances*] · absolutes Grund(stücks)eigentum n

absolute ownership (of property), absolute interest, exclusive interest, sole interest, exclusive ownership (of property), sole ownership (of property), unlimited ownership (of property); dominium plenum, dominium perpetuum [*Latin*]; sole property, sole proprietorschip [*In English law absolute ownership can only exist in chattels, as all land is subject theoretically to the obligations of tenure; but practically the fee simple in land gives absolute ownership*] · absolutes Eigentum n, uneingeschränktes Eigentum, unbeschränktes Eigentum, unbegrenztes Eigentum, ausschließliches Eigentum, unbedingtes Eigentum, Alleineigentum, Volleigentum

absolute possession, exclusive possession, sole possession · absoluter Besitz m, unbegrenzter Besitz, uneingeschränkter Besitz, unbeschränkter Besitz, ausschließlicher Besitz, Alleinbesitz, Vollbesitz

absolute possessor, sole possessor, exclusive possessor · Alleinbesitzer m

absolute presumption, unrestricted presumption, total presumption, unlimited presumption, irrebuttable presumption · absolute Rechtsvermutung f, unbeschränkte Rechtsvermutung, unbegrenzte Rechtsvermutung, uneingeschränkte Rechtsvermutung, unbedingte Rechtsvermutung

absolute property, absolute chattel, allodial ownership, absolute ownership, al(l)odium; franc-al(l)eu [*French law*]; al(l)odial estate, al(l)odial property, al(l)odial chattel, absolute estate [*An estate held without service or acknowledg(e)ment of any superior, as among the early Teutonic peoples, opposed to feud(um)*] · Allodialgut n, allodiales Eigentum n, allodiales Erbgut, allodiales Eigengut, leh(e)n(s)freies Eigentum, leh(e)n(s)freies Erbgut, leh(e)n(s)freies Eigengut, absolutes Eigentum, absolutes Erbgut, absolutes Eigengut, erbei-

absolute proprietary right — abstract right of property

genes Eigentum, erbeigenes Eigengut, erbeigenes Erbgut, unbeschränktes Erbgut, unbeschränktes Eigentum, unbeschränktes Eigentum, (zins)freies Erbgut, (zins)freies Eigentum, uneingeschränktes Erbgut, uneingeschränktes Eigentum, uneingeschränktes Eigengut, unbegrenztes Erbgut, unbegrenztes Eigentum, unbegrenztes Eigengut, Allodialeigentum, Allodialvermögen *n*, Al(l)odium *n*, Alodis *n*, Alode *f*, Alodus *m*, Alaudium *n*, Vollgut, echtes Eigen(gut) *n*, lediges Eigen(gut), Ludeigen(gut); Alleingut

absolute proprietary right (of land), sole proprietary right (of land), exclusive proprietary right (of land) · Alleinbesitzanspruch *m*, Alleinbesitz(an)recht *n* [*Grundstück*]

absolute proprietor → allodiary

absolute remedy, sole remedy, exclusive remedy · ausschließlicher Rechtsbehelf *m*, alleiniger Rechtsbehelf *m*

absolute right, exclusive right, sole right [*A right which only the grantee thereof can exercise, and from which all others are prohibited or shut out*] · Alleinrecht *n*, Ausschließlichkeitsrecht, absolutes (subjektives) Recht, subjektives absolutes Recht

absolute tenancy of years, absolute tenancy for years, absolute estate for years, absolute estate of years, absolute lease(hold) tenure, absolute (good) lease(hold) title · absolutes (Besitz)Recht *n* auf Zeit, absolutes (Besitz)Recht *n* auf Jahre, absolutes Grundbesitzrecht auf Zeit, absolutes Grundbesitzrecht auf Jahre, absoluter (Grund)Besitz(stand) *m* auf Zeit, absoluter (Grund)Besitz(stand) auf Jahre

absolute title → absolute (fee simple) title

absolute unbiased estimator · absolut nichtverzerrende Schätzfunktion *f*, stets erwartungstreue Schätzfunktion [*Statistik*]

absolute value · Absolutwert *m*

absolute (writ of) mandamus, peremptory (writ of) mandamus [*A (writ of) mandamus which absolutely requires an act to be done, without any alternative of showing cause against it. Usually granted on the return of an alternative mandamus, where such return is found insufficient in law or false in fact*] · absolutes gerichtliches Mandat *n*, zwingendes gerichtliches Mandat, gerichtliches absolutes Mandat, gerichtliches zwingendes Mandat

absolved from, set free, discharged · entbunden von (Verpflichtungen)

to absolve from, to acquit, to pronounce not guilty, to discharge · freisprechen

to absolve from, to set free, to discharge · entbinden von (Verpflichtungen)

absolving from (an) office · Entbinden *n* von einem Amt

absorbed, extinguished, merged, sunk, drowned · untergegangen [*Wenn sich z. B. Eigentum und Pfandrecht in einer Hand vereinigen, geht das kleinere im größeren unter*]

absorbed cost(s), full cost(s) · Vollkosten *f*

absorbing barrier · absorbierender Rand *m* [*Statistik*]

absorption, extinguishment, merger, drowning, sinking [*Of one estate in another*] · Untergang *m*

absorption account, adjunct account · Vollkostenkonto *n*

absorption (cost(s)) accounting, full (cost(s)) accounting, actual cost(s) system, absorption costing, full costing [*The practice of charging all cost(s), both variable and fixed, to products, processes or services*] · Vollkostenkalkulation *f*, Voll(kosten)rechnung *f*, Vollkostenermitt(e)lung, Vollkostenberechnung

absorption of immigrants, assimilation of immigrants, integration of immigrants, immigrant absorption, immigrant assimilation, immigrant integration · Einwandereingliederung *f*, Einwandererintegration *f*

absorption of surplus money, adjustment levy · Abschöpfung *f*

absorptive capacity [*market*] · Aufnahmefähigkeit *f*, Aufnahmevermögen *n*

absque impetitione vasti [*Latin*]; without impeachment of waste · ohne Haftung *f* für Substanzveränderung, ohne Haftpflicht *f* für Substanzveränderung, ohne Haftbarkeit *f* für Substanzveränderung [*Ein einem lebenslänglichen Pächter eingeräumtes Recht auf Abnützung ohne Schadenersatz*]

abstract, extract, excerpt · Auszug *m*

abstract economic order · reine Wirtschaftsordnung *f*

abstract (of account), account statement, account abstract, bank statement, bank abstract, statement (of account) · (Konto)Auszug *m*

abstract of title [*It must be supplied by a landowner to a purchaser under contract of sale, of documents and events affecting title. The abstract states the history of title; the epitome is a schedule of documents going back to the root of title*] · Auszug *m*, Grundbuchauszug, (Rechts)Titelauszug, (Rechts)-Titelbeschreibung *f*

abstract right of property, mere right; merum jus [*Latin*] [*The mere right of*

absurd — acceptance duty

property in land, without either possession or even the right of possession] · Besitzrecht *n* ohne Nießbrauch

absurd, unreasonable, opposed to sound reason · sinnwidrig, unvernünftig

absurdity, absurdness, unreasonable sense · Sinnwidrigkeit *f*, Unvernunft *f*

abuse of contract, misuser of contract · Vertragsmißbrauch *m*, Vertragsüberschreitung *f*

abuse of discretion, misuser of discretion · Ermessensmißbrauch *m*, Ermessensüberschreitung *f*

abuse of process, misuser of process · Mißbrauch *m* der prozessualen Formen, Überschreitung *f* der prozessualen Formen, prozessualer Formenmißbrauch, prozessuale Formenüberschreitung *[Um einen Vorteil über einen Gegner zu erlangen]*

abuse of right(s), misuser of right(s) · Rechtsmißbrauch *m*, Rechtsüberschreitung

to abut, to reach, to touch, abuttare *[Latin]* · angrenzen *[(Grundstücks)-Enden]*

abuttal, lot line; bonda, bunda, bonna *[In old English law]* boundary (line) *[A legally defined line dividing one lot of property from another]* · Grund(stücks)grenze *f*

abutting, reaching, contiguous, touching · angrenzend *[(Grundstücks)Enden]*

accelerated depreciation; amortization (US) *[Depreciation at a larger than usual rate]* · beschleunigte Abschreibung *f*

accelerated public works legislation, accelerated public works lawmaking · Arbeitsbeschaffungsgesetzgebung *f*

acceleration *[Shortening of a time for the vesting of an expected interest, performance on a contract, or payment of a note]* · Beschleunigung *f*

acceleration bonus, bonus (for early completion), bonus of early completion, completion bonus · Beschleunigungsvergütung *f*, (Leistungs)Prämie *f*

acceleration claim, acceleration demand, claim for early completion, demand for early completion · Beschleunigungsvergütungsforderung *f*, Beschleunigungsvergütungsverlangen, (Leistungs)Prämienforderung, (Leistungs)Prämienverlangen *n*

acceleration clause *[Clause in a mortgage, land purchase contract, or lease stating that upon default of a payment due, the balance of the obligation should at once become due and payable]* · Fälligkeitsklausel *f*, Verfallsklausel

acceleration (of work), acceleration of performance, early completion · Beschleunigung *f* *[Fertigstellung der Arbeit(en) vor der gesetzten Frist]*

to accept *[(construction) work(s)]* · abnehmen *[Bauarbeit(en)]*

to accept · annehmen

acceptability, readiness for acceptance · Abnahmefähigkeit *f*, Abnahmereife *f*, Bauabnahmefähigkeit, Bauabnahmereife

acceptability · Annahmefähigkeit *f* *[Wechsel]*

acceptability · Annehmbarkeit *f*

acceptable, ready for acceptance · abnahmefähig, abnahmereif, bauabnahmefähig, bauabnahmereif

acceptable · annehmbar

acceptable · annahmefähig *[Wechsel]*

acceptance *[This term is frequently used to denote the bill of exchange itself, and it is then synonymous with "bill of exchange"]* · Akzept *n*, Annahmeerklärung *f*, Annahme(vermerk) *f*, *(m)* *[auf einem Wechsel]*

acceptance *[The taking and receiving of anything in good part]* · Annahme *f*

acceptance boundary · Annahmegrenze *f* *[Statistik]*

acceptance certificate, certificate of acceptance (of (the) work(s)) · Abnahmeattest *n*, Abnahmebescheinigung *f*, Abnahmeschein *m*, Bauabnahmeattest, Bauabnahmeschein, Bauabnahmebescheinigung

acceptance company · Kundenfinanzierungsgesellschaft *f*

acceptance contract, contract of acceptance · Annahmevertrag *m*

acceptance credit · Akzeptkredit *m*, Annahmekredit

acceptance date, date of acceptance (of (the) work(s)) · Abnahmedatum *n*, Abnahmetermin *m*, Bauabnahmedatum, Bauabnahmetermin

acceptance declaration, declaration of acceptance · Annahmeerklärung *f*

acceptance declaration, declaration of acceptance (of (the) work(s)) · Abnahmeerklärung *f*, Bauabnahmeerklärung

acceptance delay, delay of acceptance · Abnahmeverzug *m*, Bauabnahmeverzug

acceptance delay, delay of acceptance · Annahmeverzug *m*

acceptance duty, duty of acceptance (of (the) work(s)) · Abnahmepflicht *f*, Bauabnahmepflicht

acceptance duty, duty of acceptance · Annahmepflicht *f*

acceptance fee — access

acceptance fee · Abnahmegebühr f, Bauabnahmegebühr

acceptance (fixed) period (of time) → acceptance time (allowed)

acceptance house · Wechselbank f

acceptance inspection · Abnahmeprüfung f [Statistik]

acceptance letter, letter of acceptance, notice of acceptance, letter of award of contract, letter of letting of contract, notice of award of contract, notice of letting of contract, letter of award, notice of award · Auftragsschreiben n, Zuschlag(s)schreiben n

acceptance line · Annahmelinie f [Statistik]

acceptance minutes, minutes of acceptance (of (the) work(s)) · Abnahmeniederschrift f, Abnahmeprotokoll n, Bauabnahmeniederschrift, Bauabnahmeprotokoll

acceptance number, number of acceptance · Annahmezahl f [Statistik]

acceptance of a bill (of exchange) [An engagement to pay a bill in money when due] · Wechselannahme f

acceptance of (bid) proposal (US) → acceptance of offer

acceptance of building level · Sockelabnahme f [Eine Prüfung aufgrund älteren Rechts, ob die festgelegte Höhenlage eines Gebäudes eingehalten ist]

acceptance of carcass, acceptance of fabric; acceptance of shell [Canada] · Rohbauabnahme f

acceptance of contract, contract acceptance · Vertragsannahme f

acceptance of credit, credit acceptance · Kreditnahme f, Kreditaufnahme

acceptance of fabric; acceptance of shell [Canada]; acceptance of carcass · Rohbauabnahme f

acceptance official, acceptance officer · Abnahmebeamte m, Bauabnahmebeamte

acceptance of floor reinforcement · Deckenabnahme f [Prüfung der Deckenbewehrung]

acceptance of offer, acceptance of tender, acceptance of bid; acceptance of (bid) proposal (US) · Angebotsannahme f

acceptance of part of (the) works, partial acceptance (of (the) work(s)) · Teilabnahme f, Teilbauabnahme

acceptance of payment, payment acceptance · Zahlungsannahme f

acceptance of shell [Canada]; acceptance of carcass, acceptance of fabric · Rohbauabnahme f

acceptance of state of construction · Bauzustandsabnahme f [Es gibt: Rohbauabnahme, Gebrauchsabnahme und Schlußabnahme]

acceptance (of (the) work(s)) · (Bau)Abnahme f, Abnahme zur Erfüllung; Kollaudierung f [Schweiz] [Die körperliche Hinnahme der vollendeten Bauleistung und deren Billigung als eine wenigstens in der Hauptsache vertragsgemäße Bauleistung]

acceptance (of (the) work(s)) by inspection · Abnahme f durch Augenschein, Bauabnahme durch Augenschein; Kollaudierung f durch Augenschein [Schweiz]

acceptance (of (the) work(s)) by use · Abnahme f durch Benutzung, Bauabnahme durch Benutzung; Kollaudierung f durch Benutzung [Schweiz]

acceptance (of (the) work(s)) (up)on condition, conditional acceptance (of work(s)) · Abnahme f unter Vorbehalt, Vorbehaltabnahme, bedingte Abnahme [Bauarbeiten]

acceptance provision, provision of acceptance · (Bau)Abnahmebestimmung f

acceptance region · Gutbereich m [Statistik]

acceptance request · Aufforderung f zur (Bau)Abnahme

acceptance supra protest, collateral acceptance · Ehrenakzept n, Ehrenannahme(vermerk) f, (m), Ehrenannahmeerklärung f [auf einem Wechsel]

acceptance test, test of acceptance (of (the) work(s)) · Abnahmeprüfung f, Abnahmeprobe f, Abnahmeversuch m, Bauabnahmeprüfung, Bauabnahmeprobe, Bauabnahmeversuch

acceptance time (allowed), acceptance time period, acceptance term, acceptance (fixed) period (of time), (fixed) period (of time) for acceptance · Annahmefrist f, (bestimmter) Annahmezeitraum m, (bestimmte) Annahmezeit f

acceptance (up)on condition, conditional acceptance · Annahme f unter Vorbehalt, Vorbehaltannahme, bedingte Annahme

to accept as law · annehmen als Recht

accepted · abgenommen [Bauleistung]

accepted proposition of law, accepted law proposition, accepted rule · feststehender Rechtssatz m

acceptor, accepter [A person who accepts a bill of exchange] · Annehmer m, Akzeptant m, Wechselnehmer f, Wechselakzeptant

access, vehicular drive · Zufahrt f

access · Zutritt m, Zulaß m [*Zu Gerichtsverhandlungen, Akten, Kindern, deren Erziehung bei geschiedenen Gatten dem anderen Teil anvertraut ist, usw.*]

access, right to enter and leave over the land(s) of another, way right, right-of-way, wayleave, ingress · Durchgangsrecht n, Wegerecht

access agreement, agreement of access · Betretungsabmachung f, Zugangsabmachung, Betretungsvereinbarung, Zugangsvereinbarung, Betretungsabkommen, Zugangsabkommen n, Zutrittsabkommen, Zutrittsabmachung, Zutrittsvereinbarung

accessary, accessory · Beihelfer m [*Teilnehmer an einem nicht in seiner Gegenwart verübten schweren Verbrechen vor oder nach der Tat*]

access for vehicles, way right for vehicles, right-of-way for vehicles, wayleave for vehicles, ingress for vehicles · Fahrzeugwegerecht n

accessibility · Zugänglichkeit f

accessibility [*The quality of being accessible, or of admitting approach*] · Wegsamkeit f, Zugänglichkeit

accessibility index, index of accessibility · Wegsamkeitsindex m, Zugänglichkeitsindex

accessibility to markets, market accessibility · Marktzugänglichkeit f

accessible, admitting approach · wegsam, zugänglich

accessible · zugänglich

accession, accretion, addition [*Increase in economic worth from any cause; as, the growth of timber, the aging of wines, the increase of flocks and herds, etc.*] · Zuwachs m, Zunahme f

accession · Nebensache f [*Jede Sache, welche zu einer anderen Sache in einem Abhängigkeitsverhältnis steht. Dieser Begriff und diese Benennung sind allerdings wegen ihrer Unbestimmtheit juristisch unbrauchbar*]

accession · Erlangung f [*Amt; Recht*]

accession, adherence [*The unconditional acceptance by a country of a treaty already concluded between other countries*] · Beitritt m [*zu einem Staatsvertrag*]

accession → (artificial) accession (of property)

accession of an office · Amtserlangung f

accession of a right · Rechtserlangung f

accession (of property), addition of property, augmentation of property, increase of property · Besitznahme f, Besitzzuwachs m, Besitzerhöhung f, Besitzsteigerung

accession (of property) → (artificial) accession (of property)

accession principle, principle of accession · Grundsatz m vom wesentlichen Bestandteil, Prinzip n vom wesentlichen Bestandteil

accession rate, accretion rate, rate of accession, rate of addition, rate of accretion, addition rate · Zunahmerate f, Zuwachsrate, Zunahmesatz, Zuwachssatz m

accessless, inaccessible, without access · ohne Zugang, unzugänglich, zuganglos

accessories of a plot (of land), appurtenances of a plot (of land) · Grund(stücks)zubehör n

accessory, extra, additional; additionary [*obsolete*] · zusätzlich

accessory, accessary · Beihelfer m [*Teilnehmer an einem nicht in seiner Gegenwart verübten schweren Verbrechen vor oder nach der Tat*]

accessory after the fact, accessary after the fact · Beihelfer m nach der Tat

accessory agreement, additional agreement, extra agreement · Zusatzabkommen n, Zusatzabmachung f, Zusatzvereinbarung

accessory before the fact, accessary before the fact · Beihelfer m vor der Tat [*Derjenige der Täter (principal) herbeischafft (procures), berät (counsels), oder anstiftet (abets)*]

accessory bequest → accessory legacy

accessory capital, additional capital, extra capital · Zusatzkapital n, zusätzliches Kapital

accessory clause, additional clause, extra clause · Zusatzklausel f

accessory condition, extra condition, additional condition · Zusatzbedingung f

accessory contract, additional contract, extra contract [*Such a contract is made for assuring the performance of a prior contract, either by the same parties or by others; such as suretyship, mortgage, and pledge*] · Zusatzvertrag m

accessory contract condition, additional contract condition, extra contract condition · zusätzliche Vertragsbedingung f

accessory cost(s), additional cost(s), extra cost(s) · zusätzliche Kosten f, Zusatzkosten

accessory income, additional income, extra income · Zusatzeinkommen n

accessory item, extra item, additional item · Zusatzposition f

accessory legacy, accessory bequest, additional legacy, aditional bequest, extra legacy, extra bequest

· Zusatz(fahrnis)legat n, Zusatz(fahrnis)vermächtnis n

accessory loan, additional loan, extra loan · Zusatzdarleh(e)n n

accessory mortgage, extra mortgage, additional mortgage · Zusatzhypothek f

accessory obligation, supplemental obligation, supplementary obligation · Zusatzverpflichtung f, Zusatzverbindlichkeit f, Zusatzgebundenheit, Zusatzbindung, Ergänzungsverpflichtung, Ergänzungsverbindlichkeit, Ergänzungsgebundenheit, Ergänzungsbindung

accessory payment, additional payment, extra payment · Nachzahlung f, zusätzliche Zahlung, Zusatzzahlung

accessory reimbursement, additional reimbursement, extra reimbursement · Vergütung f aus einem Zusatzauftrag, zusätzliche Vergütung

accessory right · akzessorisches Recht n, hinzutretendes Recht

accessory tax, extra tax, surtax, additional tax · Zusatzsteuer f

accessory (technical) spec(ification)(s), additional (technical) spec(ification)(s), extra (technical) spec(ification)(s) · zusätzliche technische Vorschriften fpl

accessory trust, active trust [Scots law] · aktive Treuhand f

accessory trustee [Scots law]; active trustee · aktiver Treuhänder m, handelnder Treuhänder

accessory use [The use of real property for other than its principal purpose] · Nebennutzung f, Nebengebrauch m

accessory value, added value, additional value, extra value · Zusatzwert m, Mehrwert

access right, access power, admittance, right of access, power of access · Betretungsbefugnis f, Betretungsrecht n, Zutrittsbefugnis, Zutrittsrecht, Zugangsbefugnis, Zugangsrecht

access to a plot, plot access · Grundstückszufahrt f

access to open country [That means access to mountain, moor, heath, down, cliff, foreshore, etc.] · Zugang m zu offenem Land

access to the project [The professional or his representatives have the prerogative to enter the project during the progress of the work for any purpose that will benefit the project] · Zugangsvorrecht n, Zutrittsvorrecht

accidement, undulation (of the ground) · Bodenwelle f, (Gelände)Welle

accident · Unfall m

accidental · zufällig

accidental, by chance, fortuitous, unforeseen, occasional · unvorhergesehen

accidental ignorance, nonessential ignorance · unwesentliche Unkenntnis f

accidented · wellig [Gelände]

accident frequency · Unfallhäufigkeit f

accident insurance · Unfallversicherung f

accident prevention regulations, accident prevention control(s) · Unfallverhütungsvorschriften fpl, Unfallverhütungsregelung f

accident risk, accident hazard · Unfallrisiko n, Unfallwagnis n

to accommodate, to house · unterbringen

accommodated party [One to whom the credit of the accommodation party is loaned, and is not necessarily the payee, since the inquiry always is as to whom did the maker of the paper loan his credit as a matter of fact] · Begünstigte m

accommodating, housing · Unterbringen n

accommodation, lodging, shelter, quarter · Unterkunft f

accommodation, relief [Pecuniary aid in an emergency] · Unterstützung f

accommodation, mutual agreement, accord, amicable composition (of differences), (amicable) arrangement, mutuality, (pacific) settlement · Einigung f, Willenseinigung, gütliche Regelung, Einvernehmen n, gütliche Einigung, Vergleich m, Konsensus m, Übereinstimmung, Einverständnis n

accommodation acceptance · Gefälligkeitsakzept n, Gefälligkeitsannahme(vermerk) f, (m), Gefälligkeitsannahmeerklärung f [auf einem Wechsel]

accommodation agency · Wohnungsvermitt(e)lungsbüro n

accommodation bill, fictitious bill, feint bill, faint bill, feigned bill, pretended bill; windmill, kite (Brit.) · Freundschaftswechsel m, Gefälligkeitswechsel, Kellerwechsel, Reitwechsel, Schornsteinwechsel, Scheinwechsel

accommodation contract · Gefälligkeitsvertrag m

accommodation for homeless persons · Obdachlosenunterkunft f

accommodation highway, accommodation road · Bequemlichkeitsstraße f

accommodation indorsement, accommodation endorsement · Gefälligkeitsindossament n

accommodation maker [One who puts his name to a note without any considera-

accommodation note — account abstract

tion with the intention of lending his credit to the accommodated party] · Gefälligkeitsaussteller *m*

accommodation note, accommodation paper · Gefälligkeitsakzept *n*

accommodation of homeless persons, housing of homeless persons · Obdachlosenunterbringung *f*, Unterbringung von Obdachlosen

accommodation paper, accommodation note · Gefälligkeitsakzept *n*

accommodation party · Gefälligkeitspartei *f*

accommodation rent · Gefälligkeitsmiete *f*, Gefälligkeits(miet)zins *m*

accommodation road, accommodation highway · Bequemlichkeitsstraße *f*

accommodation work, accommodation structure, accommodation physical facility · Bequemlichkeitsbau(werk) *m*, *(n)* [*Ein Bauwerk welches eine Eisenbahngesellschaft im Interesse der Nachbarn errichten muß, z. B. Brücke, Zaun usw.*]

accompanying condition, incident · Begleitbedingung *f*, unentziehbare Eigenschaft *f*, Attribut *n*

accompt, account [*Record of debts and credits, or items to be balanced*] · Konto *n*

accomptant [*French*]; accountant [*One whose business it is to compute, adjust, and range in due order accounts or to audit accounts*] · Rechnungsprüfer *m*

to accord, to agree · übereinstimmen

accord [*A satisfaction agreed upon between the party injuring and the party injured which, when performed, is a bar to all actions upon this account*] · Erlaßabrede *f*

accord, amicable composition (of differences), (amicable) arrangement, mutuality, (pacific) settlement, accommodation, mutual agreement · Einigung *f*, Willenseinigung, gütliche Regelung, Einvernehmen *n*, gütliche Einigung, Vergleich *m*, Konsensus *m*, Übereinstimmung, Einverständnis *n*

accordable, agreeable · übereinstimmbar

accord and satisfaction [*An agreement between two persons, one of whom has a right of action against the other, that the latter should do or give, and the former accept, something in satisfaction of the right of action different from, and usually less than, what might be legally enforced. When the agreement is executed, and satisfaction has been made, it is called "accord and satisfaction"*] · Hingabe *f* erfüllungshalber, Vergleich *m* und Befriedigung *f*, vergleichsweise Erfüllung

accordant, consistent, not contradictory, concurrent, agreeing with, according to, consonant, conformable [*Having agreement with itself or something else*] · gemäß, nicht gegenteilig, konform mit, übereinstimmend, gerecht mit

accordant frontiers · übereinstimmende Grenzen *f pl*

according to, consonant, conformable, accordant, consistent, not contradictory, concurrent, agreeing with [*Having agreement with itself or something else*] · gemäß, nicht gegenteilig, konform mit, übereinstimmend, gerecht mit

according to civil law · zivilrechtlich

according to drawing(s) · zeichnungsgemäß, zeichnungsgerecht, zeichnungskonform

according to law, at law, by law, for law, in law · nach dem Gesetz, dem Gesetz nach

according to law and equity · nach Recht und Billigkeit

according to plan(s) · plangemäß, plangerecht, plankonform

according to Roman law · römisch-rechtlich

according to the constitution · verfassungsrechtlich

accord without satisfaction · Vergleich *m* ohne Befriedigung

account [*The amount owing by one person to another, often evidenced by a statement showing details*] · Schuldbetrag *m*, Forderungsbetrag

account, accompt [*Record of debts and credits, or items to be balanced*] · Konto *n*

accountability, responsibility · Verantwortung *f*, Rechenschaftspflicht *f*, Verantwortlichkeit *f*, Verpflichtung

accountable → responsible

accountable condition, answerable condition, responsible condition [*A condition giving rise to a transaction, and requiring recognition*] · rechenschaftspflichtige Bedingung *f*, verantwortliche Bedingung

accountable event, answerable event, responsible event [*An event giving rise to a transaction, and requiring recognition*] · rechenschaftspflichtiges Ereignis *n*, verantwortliches Ereignis

accountable person, answerable person, responsible person · verantwortliche Person *f*, rechenschaftspflichtige Person

account abstract, bank statement, bank abstract, statement (of account), abstract (of account), account statement · (Konto)Auszug *m*

accountancy — account of settlement

accountancy, accounting · Rechnungswesen *n*

accountancy entry, posting, accounting entry [*Entering a business transaction in the books of account*] · Buchung *f*, (Buch)Eintrag(ung) *m*, *(f)*

accountancy period, accounting period · Buchungszeitraum *m*, Rechnungszeitraum

accountant · Wirtschaftsprüfer *m*

accountant · Oberbuchhalter *m*, Rechnungsbeamte [*Bank*]

accountant · Buchhalter *m*, Rechnungsführer

accountant; accomptant [*French*] [*One whose business it is to compute, adjust, and range in due order accounts or to audit accounts*] · Rechnungsprüfer *m*

accountant in bankruptcy, assignee in bankruptcy, referee in bankruptcy, trustee in bankruptcy, commissioner in bankruptcy · (Konkurs)Masse(n)kurator *m*, Konkursverwalter *m*, Kurator

accountant's (audit) certificate · Prüfvermerk *m*, Richtigkeitsvermerk

(account) balance [*The equality of the total debit balances and the total credit balances of the accounts in a ledger*] · (Konto)Ausgleich *m*

account current, demand account, continuing account, running account, open account · laufendes Konto *n*, Kontokorrent *n*

account duty [*This was the duty imposed by the Customs and Inland Revenue Act, 1881, ss. 38, 39 (as amended by the Customs and Inland Revenue Act, 1889, s. 11), in connection with deaths after May 31, 1881, upon personal property above the value of £ 100 passing at death by way of donatio mortis causa, joint investment, voluntary settlement, or under a policy of life insurance kept up for a donee, or passing by voluntary disposition within three years before death. It was meant to apply to property which was not subject to probate duty. The rate of the duty varied with the value of the property from 2 per cent to 3 per cent. The duty is not payable, in respect of deaths since August 1, 1894, upon any property upon which estate duty (q.v.) is payable (Finance Act, 1894, s. 1, Sched. I, para 2*] · Steuer *f* zur Vermeidung der Umgehung der Erbschaftssteuer durch Weggabe von Werten vor dem Tode

account form · Kontoform *f*

account form · Kontoformular *n*

account holder · Kontoinhaber *m*

accounting, accountment · Rechnungslegung *f*

accounting, accountancy · Rechnungswesen *n*

accounting · Gesamtrechnung *f*

accounting → costing

accounting approach · buchtechnische Kostenauflösung *f*

accounting code → costing code

accounting entry, accountancy entry, posting [*Entering a business transaction in the books of account*] · Buchung *f*, (Buch)Eintrag(ung) *m*, *(f)*

accounting for the flow of funds, statement of (sources and applications of) funds, funds statement, summary of financial operations; capital-reconciliation statement (Brit.) · Kapitalzuflußrechnung *f*, Finanzierungsrechnung, Finanzflußrechnung, Bewegungsbilanz *f*, Mittelherkunft- und -verwendungsrechnung

accounting method → costing method

accounting office, general accounting office (US); audit office, audit department, commissioners of audit (Brit.) [*It is entrusted with the audit and control of public accounts*] · (Rechnungs)-Prüfungsbehörde *f*, (Rechnungs)-Revisionsbehörde, Rechnungshof *m*, Oberrechnungskammer *f*

accounting ordinance → costing ordinance

accounting period, accountancy period · Buchungszeitraum *m*, Rechnungszeitraum

accounting records · Rechnungsaufzeichnungen *fpl*

accounting (reference) period, accountment (reference) period · Bilanzziehungsfrist *f*, Rechnungsfrist

accounting statement · Rechnungsaufstellung *f*

accounting technique → costing technique

accounting theory → costing theory

accountless, free from accountableness, irresponsible · nicht verantwortlich, nicht rechenschaftspflichtig

accountment, accounting · Rechnungslegung *f*

accountment (reference) period, accounting (reference) period · Bilanzziehungsfrist *f*, Rechnungsfrist

account money, money of account · Rechengeld *n*, Schuldwährung *f*

account of lading · Frachtdeklaration *f*

account of settlement, settlement account · Saldierungsrechnung *f*

account payable — accrued income

account payable [*An amount owing to a creditor, generally on open account, as the result of delivered goods or completed services; distinguished from accruals and other current liabilities not arising out of every day transactions*] · Verbindlichkeitsbetrag *m*

account receivable [*An amount of a claim against a debtor, generally an open account, its application usually limited to uncollected amounts of completed sales of goods and services; distinguished from deposits, accruals, and other items not arising out of every day transactions*] · Forderungsbetrag *m*

account rendered · Rechenschaftsbericht *m*

account sales, A/S · Verkaufsabrechnung *f*, Abrechnung des Verkaufskommissionärs

account stated, stated account [*An account (Forderungsbetrag) the balance of which, as determined by the creditor, has been accepted as correct, sometimes implicitly, by the debtor*] · Buchschuldbetrag *m*, Buchforderungsbetrag

account statement, account abstract, bank statement, bank abstract, statement (of account), abstract (of account) · (Konto)Auszug *m*

to accredit · akkreditieren

to accrete by alluvion, to accrete by alluvium · anschwemmen, anwachsen [*Land*]

to accrete by dereliction · anwachsen durch Meeresspiegelsenkung, gewinnen durch Meeresspiegelsenkung, anwachsen durch zurückweichendes Wasser, gewinnen durch zurückweichendes Wasser

accretion, addition, accession [*Increase in economic worth from any cause; as, the growth of timber, the aging of wines, the increase of flocks and herds, etc.*] · Zuwachs *m*, Zunahme *f*

(accretion by) dereliction (of land), land dereliction · (Land)Anwachs(ung) *m*, *(f)* durch Meeresspiegelsenkung, (Land)-Zuwachs durch Meeresspiegelsenkung, (Land)Anwachs(ung) durch zurückweichendes Wasser, (Land)Zuwachs durch zurückweichendes Wasser, (Land)Gewinnung durch zurückweichendes Wasser

accretion (of land), land accretion, alluvion, alluvium · (Land)Anschwemmung *f*, (Land)Anschutt *m*, (Land)Akkreszenz *f*, (Land)Gewinnung durch Anschwemmung, Alluvion *n*, Alluvium *n*, Zulandung

accretion rate, rate of accession, rate of addition, rate of accretion, addition rate, accession rate · Zunahmerate *f*, Zuwachsrate, Zunahmesatz, Zuwachssatz *m*

accretive · anwachsend, gewinnend [*Land*]

accrual, accruement, accrued amount [*The amount that accrues*] · aufgelaufener Betrag *m*, Auflaufbetrag *m*

accrual, accruing, accruement, accruer, running up, growing to · Auflaufen *n* [*Betrag*]

accrual · Abgrenzungsposten *m* [*Buchführung*]

accrual accounting · Abgrenzung *f* [*Buchführungssystem*]

accrual by inheritance, accruer by inheritance, inheritance accrual, inheritance accruer · Erbzuwachs *m*, Erbzunahme *f*

accrual date, maturity date, expiry date, expiration date, due date, termination date, falling in date, running out date · Fälligkeitsdatum *n*, Fälligkeitstag *m*, Verfalldatum, Verfalltermin *m*, (Frist)-Ablauftermin, (Frist)Ablaufdatum, Fälligkeitstermin, Verfalltag, (Frist)Ablauftag

accrual method · Gewinnermitt(e)lung *f* durch Betriebsvermögensvergleich

to accrue, to grow · (an)wachsen, zuwachsen

to accrue, to be added to [*As a thing or right passes from one person to another*] · zufallen

to accrue, to increase · zunehmen

to accrue, to arise to have a legal existence, to begin to have a legal existence [*For instance, an action accrues when the plaintiff has a right to commence it*] · gesetzlich entstehen

to accrue, to become due, to mature, to fall due [*As rent or interest*] · fällig werden, verfallen

to accrue, to run up, to grow to, to accumulate · auflaufen, anwachsen, zuwachsen, aufhäufen, anhäufen [*Betrag*]

accrued, run up, grown to, accumulated · angewachsen, angehäuft, zugewachsen, aufgehäuft, aufgelaufen

accrued amount → accrual

accrued charges, accrued expenses · antizipative Passiva *f* [*Noch nicht bezahlte Aufwendungen*]

accrued depreciation [*Total depreciation accumulated in a property up to the present*] · Gesamtabschreibung *f*

accrued depreciation [*Difference between the cost(s) or replacement new as of the date of the appraisal and the present appraisal value*] · Abschreibungsreserve *f*

accrued income · antizipative Aktiva *f* [*Noch nicht eingenommene Erträge*]

accrued interest, run up interest, accumulated interest, undistributed interest · aufgelaufene Zinsen f, Stückzinsen f, angehäufte Zinsen, angewachsene Zinsen, aufgehäufte Zinsen, zugewachsene Zinsen, Vorzugszinsen

accrued item · antizipativer Posten m, vorweggenommener Posten

accrued liability, (liability) reserve · Rückstellung f

accrued price reduction · abgegrenzte Preisermäßigung f

accruement, accruer, running up, growing to, accrual, accruing · Auflaufen n [Betrag]

accruement, accrued amount, accrual [The amount that accrues] · aufgelaufener Betrag m, Auflaufbetrag m

accruer, running up, growing to, accrual, accruing, accruement · Auflaufen n [Betrag]

accruer by inheritance, inheritance accrual, inheritance accruer, accrual by inheritance · Erbzuwachs m, Erbzunahme f

accruing, accruement, accruer, running up, growing to, accrual · Auflaufen n [Betrag]

accruing, accumulating · Anwachsen n, Zuwachsen n, Ansammeln n, Anhäufen n, Aufhäufen n

acculturation · Kulturguterwerbung f

to accumulate · horten [Land]

to accumulate, to accrue, to run up, to grow to · auflaufen, anwachsen, zuwachsen, aufhäufen, anhäufen [Betrag]

accumulated, accrued, run up, grown to · angewachsen, angehäuft, zugewachsen, aufgehäuft, aufgelaufen

accumulated cost(s), undistributed cost(s) · angesammelte Kosten f, unverteilte Kosten, aufgelaufene Kosten

accumulated deviation · aufsummierte Abweichung f [Statistik]

accumulated dividend, dividends in arrears [The amount of undeclared dividends accumulated on cumulative preferred stock] · angesammelte Dividende f, angehäufte Dividende, aufgehäufte Dividende

accumulated interest, undistributed interest, accrued interest, run up interest · aufgelaufene Zinsen f, Stückzinsen f, angehäufte Zinsen, angewachsene Zinsen, aufgehäufte Zinsen, zugewachsene Zinsen, Vorzugszinsen

accumulating, accruing · Anwachsen n, Zuwachsen n, Ansammeln n, Anhäufen n, Aufhäufen n

accumulation [The putting by of incomes of any kind and converting them into principal by investing them, and again investing the income arising from the new principal, and so on] · Ansammlung f, Anhäufung, Aufhäufung

accumulation of capital, capital accumulation, creation of capital, capital creation, capital formation, formation of capital · Kapitalschöpfung f, Kapitalbildung

accumulation of land(s), land(s) accumulation · Bodenhortung f, Landhortung

accumulation plan, plan of accumulation · Ansammlungsplan m, Anhäufungsplan, Aufhäufungsplan

accumulation schedule, table of accumulation, schedule of accumulation, accumulation table · Ansammlungstabelle f, Anhäufungstabelle, Aufhäufungstabelle

accumulation trust, institutional investor, investing institution · Kapitalsammelstelle f [Ein Institut, welches nach Gesetz oder Satzung langfristig ausleihbares Kapital ansammelt. §§ 103 und 104 des II. WoBauG]

accumulative [characterized by accumulation] · anwachsend, zuwachsend

accumulative interest rate, accumulative rate of interest · anwachsender Zinssatz m

accumulative voting, proxy-voting · Logenabstimmung f [z. B. bei den Bergarbeitern in Northumberland]

accusation; accusement [obsolete]; accusing [The action of charging with an offense] · Anklagen n, Beschuldigen

to accuse, to charge (with an offence) · beschuldigen, anklagen

accused, charged (with an offence) · angeklagt, beschuldigt

accused (person) · Beschuldigte m, Angeklagte

accusing, accusation; accusement [obsolete] [The action of charging with an offense] · Anklagen n, Beschuldigen

ac etiam [Latin]; and also [The introduction to the statement of the real cause of action in cases where it was necessary to allege a fictitious cause in order to give the court jurisdiction] · und auch

achievement-orientation, striving for success (in achievement), status striving · Erfolgsstreben n

to acknowledge, to concede, to admit · einräumen, zugestehen, anerkennen

to acknowledge · bestätigen, bescheinigen [Erhalt eines Schriftstückes]

to acknowledge, to certify in legal form, to attest legally · (amtlich) beurkunden

acknowledg(e)able, certifiable in legal form · (amtlich) beurkundbar

acknowledg(e)ment [*Signed form that acknowledges that the bidder has received the proper bidding documents*] · Erhaltsbestätigung *f* über Ausschreibungsunterlagen

acknowledg(e)ment, acknowledg(e)ment upon record, recognition, recognisance; recognitio [*Latin*] · Rekognition *f*, Anerkenntnis *f*, Anerkennung *f* [*Die Anerkennung der Identität einer Person, einer Sache oder einer Urkunde vor einem Gericht oder Notar*]

acknowledg(e)ment, concession, admission [*Made by a party of the existence of certain facts*] · Einräumung *f*, Zugeständnis *n*, Anerkennung

acknowledg(e)ment, legal attestation · (amtliche) Beurkundung *f*

acknowledg(e)ment certificate, certificate of acknowledg(e)ment · Rekognitionsbescheinigung *f*, Rekognitionsschein *m*, Rekognitionsattest *n* [*Bescheinigung einer in ein öffentliches Buch erfolgten Eintragung*]

acknowledg(e)ment certificate, certificate of acknowledg(e)ment · Grundschuldbrief *m*

acknowledg(e)ment fee, fee of acknowledg(e)ment, acknowledg(e)ment money, money of acknowledg(e)ment [*A sum of money paid by copyhold tenants, in some parts of England, on the death of their landlords, as an acknowledg(e)ment of their new lords*] · Anerkennungsgeld *n*, Rekognitionsgeld, Anerkennungsgebühr *f*, Rekognitionsgebühr

acknowledg(e)ment money, money of acknowledg(e)ment, acknowledg(e)ment fee, fee of acknowledg(e)ment [*A sum of money paid by copyhold tenants, in some parts of England, on the death of their landlords, as an acknowledg(e)ment of their new lords*] · Anerkennungsgeld *n*, Rekognitionsgeld, Anerkennungsgebühr *f*, Rekognitionsgebühr

acknowledg(e)ment of married women · gerichtliche Anerkennung *f* von Urkunden durch Ehefrauen

acknowledg(e)ment of money debt, acknowledg(e)ment of debt (of money) · (Geld)Schuldanerkenntnis *n*, *f*

acknowledg(e)ment of reception · Empfangsbestätigung *f* [*schriftlich (Quittung) oder mündlich*]

acknowledg(e)ment under seal, legal attestation under seal · Beurkundung *f* unter Siegel, gesiegelte Beurkundung

acknowledg(e)ment ((up)on record), recognition, recognisance; recognitio [*Latin*] · Rekognition *f*; Anerkenntnis *f* [*im Rechtswesen: n*]; Anerkennung *f* [*Die Anerkennung der Identität einer Person, einer Sache oder einer Urkunde vor einem Gericht oder Notar*]

to acknowledge ((up)on record); recognoscere [*Latin*]; to recognize [*The authority or claim of*] · anerkennen

acoustic(al) environment · Schallumgebung *f*

acquiescence · Nichtgeltendmachung *f* von Rechten [*Obwohl jemand nach Treu und Glauben verpflichtet ist, um andere vor Schaden zu bewahren, dieselben geltend zu machen*]

acquiescence · Schweigen *n*

acquirable · beschaffbar, erwerbbar, erstehbar

to acquire · beschaffen, erwerben, erstehen

to acquire afterwards · nachträglich erwerben, nacherwerben, nachträglich beschaffen

to acquire by demise, to acquire by tenancy, to acquire by lease · beschaffen durch Pacht, erwerben durch Pacht, erstehen durch Pacht

to acquire by exchange · beschaffen durch Tausch, erwerben durch Tausch, erstehen durch Tausch

to acquire by lease, to acquire by demise, to acquire by tenancy · beschaffen durch Pacht, erwerben durch Pacht, erstehen durch Pacht

to acquire by purchase · beschaffen durch Kauf, erwerben durch Kauf, erstehen durch Kauf

to acquire by tenancy, to acquire by lease, to acquire by demise · beschaffen durch Pacht, erwerben durch Pacht, erstehen durch Pacht

to acquire compulsorily · zwangsweise beschaffen, zwangsweise erwerben, zwangsweise erstehen

acquired allegiance, acquired liegance, acquired lawful obedience · naturalisationsbedingter gesetzmäßiger Gehorsam *m*, naturalisationsbedingter rechtmäßiger Gehorsam

acquired goods, onerous goods · erworbene Güter *n pl*, beschaffte Güter, erstandene Güter

acquired lawful obedience, acquired allegiance, acquired liegance · naturalisationsbedingter gesetzmäßiger Gehorsam *m*, naturalisationsbedingter rechtmäßiger Gehorsam, erworbener gesetzmäßiger Gehorsam, erworbener rechtmäßiger Gehorsam

acquirer · Beschaffer *m*, Erwerber, Ersteher

acquirer by juristic act(ion), acquirer by juridic(al) act(ion) · rechtsgeschäftlicher Erwerber *m,* Erwerber durch Rechtsgeschäft

acquirer in good conscience · redlicher Erwerber *m*

acquirer of an inheritance · Erberwerber *m,* Erbschaftserwerber

acquirer of (building) land, acquirer of (building) (land) area · (Bau)Bodenbeschaffer *m,* (Bau)Landbeschaffer, (Bau)- Bodenerwerber, (Bau)Landerwerber, (Bau)Flächenbeschaffer, (Bau)Flächenerwerber

acquirer of (real) estate, acquirer of (real) property, acquirer of realty, acquirer of land · Grund(stücks)erwerber *m,* Landerwerber, Bodenerwerber, Liegenschaftserwerber

acquiring; acquiry [*obsolete*]; acquisition [*The action of gaining or obtaining for oneself*] · Beschaffen *n,* Erwerben, Erstehen

acquiring authority, acquisition authority · Beschaffungsbehörde *f,* Erwerbsbehörde

acquiry [*obsolete*]; acquisition, acquiring [*The action of gaining or obtaining for oneself*] · Beschaffen *n,* Erwerben, Erstehen

acquisition [*The result of acquiring for oneself. The term "acquirement" is also used, but it usually means a personal attainment of body or mind*] · Erwerb(ung) *m, (f),* Beschaffung, Sachübernahme *f*

acquisition, acquiring; acquiry [*obsolete*] [*The action of gaining or obtaining for oneself*] · Beschaffen *n,* Erwerben, Erstehen

acquisition [*A thing obtained or gained for oneself*] · beschafftes Gut *n,* erworbenes Gut, erstandenes Gut

acquisition appraisal, acquisition appraisement, acquisition (e)valuation, acquisition val. · Beschaffungs(ab)schätzung *f,* Erwerbs(ab)schätzung, Erwerbsbewertung, Beschaffungsbewertung

acquisition authority, acquiring authority · Beschaffungsbehörde *f,* Erwerbsbehörde

acquisition by juristic act(ion), acquisition by juridic(al) act(ion) · Erwerb *m* durch Rechtsgeschäft, rechtsgeschäftlicher Erwerb, Erwerbung *f* durch Rechtsgeschäft, rechtsgeschäftliche Erwerbung

acquisition by purchase · Kauferwerb *m,* Kaufbeschaffung *f*

acquisition contract · Beschaffungsvertrag *m,* Erwerbsvertrag

acquisition cost(s), cost(s) of acquisition · Beschaffungskosten *f,* Erwerbskosten

acquisition duty, duty of acquisition, duty to acquire · Beschaffungspflicht *f,* Erwerbspflicht

acquisition (e)valuation, acquisition val., acquisition appraisal, acquisition appraisement · Beschaffungs(ab)schätzung *f,* Erwerbs(ab)schätzung, Erwerbsbewertung, Beschaffungsbewertung

acquisition mortis causa · Erwerb *m* von Todes wegen, Erwerbung *f* von Todes wegen

acquisition notice, acquisition notification · Beschaffungsanzeige *f,* Erwerbsanzeige, Beschaffungsmitteilung *f,* Erwerbsmitteilung, Beschaffungsbenachrichtigung, Erwerbsbenachrichtigung

acquisition of (building) (land) area, acquisition of (building) land, acquisition of (building) space, (building) space acquisition, (building) land acquisition, (building) (land) area acquisition · (Bau)Bodenbeschaffung *f,* (Bau)Bodenerwerb *m,* (Bau)Flächenbeschaffung, (Bau)Flächenerwerb, (Bau)Landerwerb, (Bau)Landbeschaffung

acquisition of estate → (real) property acquisiton

acquisition office · Beschaffungsamt *n*

acquisition of (general) property, acquisition of proprietorship, acquisition of ownership (of property) · Eigentumserwerb *m,* Eigentumsbeschaffung *f*

acquisition of (general) property by servitude, acquisition of ownership (of property) by servitude, acquisition of proprietorship by servitude · Eigentumserwerb *m* durch Dienstbarkeit, Eigentumsbeschaffung *f* durch Dienstbarkeit

acquisition (of land) by compulsion, purchase (of land) by compulsion, compulsory purchase (of land), compulsory acquisition (of land) · Landzwangsbeschaffung *f,* (Boden)Zwangsbeschaffung, (Boden)Zwangserwerb *m,* (Boden)Zwangskauf *m,* Landzwangserwerb, Landzwangskauf, (Boden)Enteignung gegen Entschädigung, Landenteignung gegen Entschädigung

acquisition of land(s) → (real) property acquisition

acquisition of possession, possession acquisition · Besitzerwerb *m,* Besitzbeschaffung *f*

acquisition of property, property acquisition · Vermögenserwerb *m,* Vermögensbeschaffung *f*

acquisition of (real) estate → (real) property acquisition

acquisition of (real) property → (real) property acquisition

acquisition of substitute land — act for the conservation

acquisition of substitute land · Ersatzlandbeschaffung f, Ersatzlanderwerb m, Ersatzbodenbeschaffung, Ersatzbodenerwerb

acquisition price · Beschaffungspreis m, Erwerbspreis

acquisition prohibition, prohibition of acquisition · Beschaffungsverbot n, Erwerbsverbot

acquisition right, right to acquisition · Beschaffungsrecht n, Erwerbsrecht

acquisition val., acquisition appraisal, acquisition appraisement, acquisition (e)valuation · Beschaffungs(ab)schätzung f, Erwerbs(ab)schätzung, Erwerbsbewertung, Beschaffungsbewertung

acquisitive business · Erwerbsgeschäft n

acquisitiveness · Erwerbssucht f

acquisitive prescription, positive prescription, prescription of incorporeal hereditament(s), prescription of not tangible hereditament(s) [*Acquisition of a right. See remark under "incorporeal hereditament". In international law "aquisitive" or "positive" prescription means title to territory based on uninterrupted and uncontested occupation over a reasonably long period*] · Ersitzung f nichtkörperlichen Erbgutes, Ersitzung unkörperlichen Erbgutes, Ersitzung immateriellen Erbgutes

acquisitive society · erwerbssüchtige Gesellschaft f

to acquit, to pronounce not guilty, to discharge, to absolve from · freisprechen

to acquit, to discharge, to set free; to release [*Required to be under seal*] · freistellen, entlasten, befreien, freigeben, dispensieren

acquittal, discharge, acquittance, receipt · Quittung f, Empfangsbestätigung

acquittal, discharge [*A judicial deliverance from an accusation (of guilt)*] · Freispruch m, Freisprechung f

acquittal [*Exemption from entry and molestation by a superior lord, for services issuing out of lands*] · Besitzergreifungsverzicht m

acquittal in deed, discharge in deed · ausdrücklicher Freispruch m, ausdrückliche Freisprechung f

acquittal in law, discharge in law · selbstverständlicher Freispruch m, selbstverständliche Freisprechung f

acquittance · (Schuld)Begleichung f

acquittance, receipt, acquittal, discharge · Quittung f, Empfangsbestätigung

acquittance [*A written discharge, whereby one is freed from an obligation to pay money or perform a duty. It differs from a "release" in not requiring to be under seal*] · Entlastungsbestätigung f, Freistellungsbestätigung, Dispens(ierungs)bestätigung, Freigabebestätigung, Befreiungsbestätigung, (Schuld)Begleichungsbestätigung

acquittance, acquitting, setting free, discharging; releasing [*Required to be under seal*] [*The act by which a discharge in writing is effected*] · Befreien n, Freistellen, Freigeben, Entlasten, Dispensieren

acquitted, discharged, set free; released [*Required to be under seal*] [*From debt, obligation, duty, etc.*] · befreit, entlastet, freigestellt, freigegeben, dispensiert

acreage swell, swell of acreage, swell of land, addition of acreage, acreage addition, addition of land, land addition, land swell [*of a real estate*] · Landzuwachs m, Flächenzuwachs, Bodenzuwachs, Landzunahme f, Bodenzunahme, Flächenzunahme

acred [*Possessing acres, or landed estates*] · grund(stücks)besitzend, landbesitzend, bodenbesitzend, liegenschaftsbesitzend

acre-land [*obsolete*] → arable field

acreman [*obsolete*]; cultivator of the ground · Anbauer m

acre strip, day's work (at ploughing), daywere; diurnalis [*Latin*] [*In old English law. A term applied to land, and signifying as much arable ground as could be ploughed up in one day's work*] · Tag(e)werk n; Tagwan n, Tagwen n [*In den Alpen*]

to act · handeln

act → Act of Parliament

act, action · Akt m, Handlung f

act and law, statute and law · Gesetz n und Recht n

act concerning unfair competition, statute concerning unfair competition, law concerning unfair competition · Gesetz n gegen unlauteren Wettbewerb

act for execution, statute for execution, law for execution · Ausführungsgesetz n

act for public utility housing, statute for public utility housing, law for public utility housing · Wohnungsgemeinnützigkeitsgesetz n

act for the conservation of monuments, law for the conservation of monuments, statute for the conservation of monuments, act for the preservation of monuments, law for the preservation of monuments, statute for the preservation of monuments · Denkmalpflegegesetz n, Denkmalerhaltungsgesetz, Denkmalschutzgesetz

to act fraudulently — action of injunction

to act fraudulently · arglistig handeln, betrügerisch handeln

acting · aktiv, handelnd

acting · amtierend

actio ex delicto [*Latin*] · Klage *f* wegen erlittener Unbill

actio mixta, actio mista [*Latin*]; mixed (court) action, mixed cause, mixed (law-)suit, mixed plea [*An action partaking of the nature of real and personal actions, by which some property is demanded and also damages for a wrong sustained*] · gemischte Klage *f*, Mischklage

act(ion) · Akt *m*, Handlung *f*

action → (court) action

actionare [*Latin*]; to bring an action (against), to file a bill, to file a (law)suit, to file an action, to sue · einreichen (einer Klage), erheben (einer Klage), klagen

action area · Baugebiet *n* [*Im Flächennutzungsplan ausgewiesenes Gebiet, das grundsätzlich bebaut werden darf. Art und Maß der baulichen Nutzung werden im Bebauungsplan festgesetzt*]

action at common law → (court) action at common law

action(-at-law) [*In English law. Before the Judicature Acts, 1873—1875, "action(-at-law)" generally meant a proceeding in a common law court, as opposed to a suit in equity*] · Prozeß *m* bei einem gemeinrechtlichen Gericht

action de bonis asportatis → (court) action de bonis asportatis

actio negatoria [*Latin*] · Eigentumsfreiheitsklage *f*, Klage zur Abwehr von Eingriffen, Klage auf Beseitigung und Unterlassung

action for an account → (court) action for an account

action for breach of contract → (court) action for breach of contract

action for delivery → (court) action for delivery

action for exemption from liability → (court) action for exemption from liability

action for intrusion → (court) action for trespass

action for money had and received → (court) action for money had and received

action for payment → (court) action for payment

action for proving a will in solemn form, action for propounding the will · Testamenteinweisungsantrag *m* in feierlicher Form

action for redemption → (court) action for redemption

action for refunding → (court) action for reimbursement

action for removal → (court) action for removal

action for specific performance → (court) action for specific performance

action for the recovery of land → (court) action for the recovery of land

action for trespass → (court) action for trespass

action for unjust detainer → (court) action for unjust detention

action founded on tort → (court) action founded on tort

action in error → (court) action in error

action of account → (court) action for account

action of advowson → (court) action of advowson

act(ion) of (a) party, party act(ion) · Parteihandlung *f*, Parteiakt *m*

action of assumpsit → · (court) action of assumpsit

act(ion) of bankruptcy · Konkursvoraussetzung *f*

act(ion) of commission, commission act(ion) · Funktionsakt *m*, Funktionshandlung *f*

action of contestation → (court) action of contestation

action of contravention → violation (of law)

action of debt → (court) action of debt

action of deceit → (court) action of deceit

action of detinue → (court) action for unjust detention

action of devastation → (court) action of devastation

action of equity → (court) action of equity

action of estrepement → (court) action of estrepement

action of eviction → (court) action of eviction

action of giving assent, sanctioning, approbating, approving, consenting, assenting · Billigen *n*, Einwilligen, Zustimmen

act(ion) of granting, granting act(ion) · Überlassungsakt *m*, Überlassungshandlung *f*

action of injunction → (court) action of injunction

action of mistake — activity variance

action of mistake → (court) action of mistake

action of patronage → (court) action of patronage

action of possessory right → (court) action of possessory right

action of replevin → (court) action of replevin

act(ion) of the will, volition, exercise of the will · Willensakt *m*, Willensausübung *f*, Willenshandlung, Wollen *n*

action of transumpt → (court) action of transumpt

action on personam → personal (court) action

action on the case → (court) action on the case

action per se → (court) action per se

action personal → (court) action personal

action plan · Aktionsplan *m*

action realizable · zielverfügbare Aktion *f*

action real (of the common law) [*The proceedings at common law by means of which a freeholder could recover his land(s). This action was displaced by the action of ejectment*] · dingliche Landklage *f* nach gemeinem Recht

action required · zielnotwendige Aktion *f*

action research · Aktionsforschung *f*

action set, set of actions · Aktionsfolge *f*, Handlungsfolge

action space, activity space · Aktionsraum *m*, Aktivraum

action space plan, action spatial plan · Aktivraumplan *m*

action spatial planning, action space planning · Aktivraumplanung *f*

action sphere, sphere of action · Aufgabenbereich *m*

action to gain an injunction, cause to gain an injunction, (law)suit to gain an injunction, plea to gain an injunction · Unterlassungsklage *f*

action to quiet title → (court) action to quiet title

actio publiciana [*Latin*] · Klage *f* aus früherem Besitz, publizianische Klage

actio quanti minoris [*Latin*] · (Kaufpreis)Minderungsklage *f*

actio revocatoria [*Latin*] · Revokatorienklage *f*, revokatorische Klage, Rückrufklage

actio spolii [*Latin*] · Spolienklage *f*

active, laborious, diligent, steadily applied · aktiv, unermüdlich, fleißig

active balance of payments, active balance of trade · aktive Handelsbilanz *f*

active concealment · aktive Unterdrückung *f* der Wahrheit

active estate of a bankrupt, active property of a bankrupt, estate, bankrupt's property, bankrupt's estate [*The assets and liabilities of a bankrupt person*] · Konkursmasse *f*, Fallitmasse, Konkursvermögen *n*, Konkursgut *n*, Konkurshabe *f*

active legitimation, capacity to sue, capability to sue, qualification to sue, standing to sue · Aktivlegitimation *f* [*Zur gerichtlichen Geltendmachung von Ansprüchen*]

active misconduct → misfeasance

activeness at location, location(al) activity, location(al) activeness, activity at location · standortmäßige Aktivität *f*

active partner · tätiger Gesellschafter *m*, tätiger Teilhaber

active property of a bankrupt, estate, bankrupt's property, bankrupt's estate, active estate of a bankrupt [*The assets and liabilities of a bankrupt person*] · Konkursmasse *f*, Fallitmasse, Konkursvermögen *n*, Konkursgut *n*, Konkurshabe *f*

active trust; accessory trust [*Scots law*] · aktive Treuhand *f*

active trustee; accessory trustee [*Scots law*] · aktiver Treuhänder *m*, handelnder Treuhänder

activity · Betätigung *f*

activity at location, activeness at location, location(al) activity, location(al) activeness · standortmäßige Aktivität *f*

activity in private practice, free-lance activity · freiberufliche Tätigkeit *f*, freischaffende Tätigkeit

activity model · Tätigkeitsmodell *n*

activity pattern, activity scheme, pattern of activities, scheme of activities · Tätigkeitsmuster *n*, Tätigkeitsschema *n*, Tätigkeitenmuster, Tätigkeitenschema

activity space, action space · Aktionsraum *m*

activity submodel · Tätigkeitsuntermodell *n*

activity variance, volume variance, capacity variance · Beschäftigungsabweichung *f* (im engeren Sinne) [*Diese Abweichung wird von der Kapazitätsabweichung nicht streng unterschieden*]

activity variance, volume variance, capacity variance · Kapazitätsabweichung *f*, Produktions(volumen)grad *m*, Volumenabweichung bei Kapazitätsplanung, Produktionshöhenabweichung [*Sie stellt die nicht gedeckten Plankosten dar*]

to act judicially · richterlich handeln

act number, statute number, law number · Gesetz(es)nummer f

(act of) advancing money · Bevorschussen n, Vorschießen, Vorstrecken, Vorauszahlen, Pränumerieren

act of banking, bank(ing) law, bank(ing) statute, bank(ing) act, law of banking, statute of banking · Kreditwesengesetz n

act of (building) (land) area replotting, law of (building) (land) area replotting, statute of (building) (land) area replotting · (Bau)Landumlegungsgesetz n, (Bau)-Bodenumlegungsgesetz, (Bau)Flächenumlegungsgesetz

act of building lines, statute of building lines, building line act, building line law, building line statute, law of building lines · Flucht(linien)gesetz n, Bauflucht(linien)gesetz

act of contravention → violation (of law)

act of disappeared persons, law of missing persons, act of missing persons, statute of missing persons, statute of disappeared persons, law of disappeared persons · Verschollenheitsgesetz n

(act of) fixing the value date, valuation · Valutierung f, Wertstellung

act of fraud, law of fraud, statute of fraud · Betrugsgesetz n

act of fraudulent bankruptcy, fraudulent bankruptcy [*An act done or suffered by a trader, tending to defraud his creditors, by which he becomes a bankrupt, within the meaning of the bankrupt laws, and liable to be proceeded against as such*] · betrügerischer Bank(e)rott m, Konkursbetrug m, böswilliger Bank(e)-rott

act of God; actus Dei [*Latin*] [*A direct, violent, sudden and irresistible act of nature, which could not have been foreseen or resisted*] · Naturgewaltereignis n

act of inheritance, statute of inheritance, inheritance act, inheritance law, inheritance statute, law of inheritance · Erb(schafts)gesetz n

Act of King, Statute of King, Law of King · Königsgesetz n

act of (land) area replotting → act of (building) (land) area replotting

act of land (possession) → law of land (possession)

act of limitation, limitation statute, limitation law, limitation act, statute of limitation, law of limitation · Verjährungsgesetz n

act of missing persons, statute of missing persons, statute of disappeared persons, law of disappeared persons, act of disappeared persons, law of missing persons · Verschollenheitsgesetz n

Act of Parliament, enabling act, law made by Parliament, act, statute; statutum, actus [*Latin*] · formelles Gesetz n, parlamentarisches Gesetz, (Parlaments)Gesetz

(act of) pawning, (act of) pledging · Pfandbestellung f, Verpfänden n

act of possession → law of possession

act of settlement, statute of settlement, law of settlement · Ortsangehörigkeitsgesetz n [*In England. Die Arbeiter mußten an dem Ort wo sie heimatberechtigt waren bleiben, um zu verhüten, daß eine Gemeinde die Armen einer anderen unterstützen müßte*]

act of the country, law of the country, statute of the country, national act, national law, national statute · Landesgesetz n, Nationalgesetz, Staatsgesetz

act of unearthing, unearthing law, unearthing statute, unearthing act, statute of unearthing, law of unearthing · Ausgrabungsgesetz n

act of wills, law of wills, wills act, wills statute, wills law, statute of wills · Testamentsgesetz n

act on inspection of insurance, statute on inspection of insurance, law on inspection of insurance · Versicherungsaufsichtsgesetz n

act on rights in registered ships, statute on rights in registered ships, law on rights in registered ships · Schiffsrechtegesetz n

actor [*Latin*]; plaintiff, plainant · Kläger m, Zivilprozeßkläger

actor in a real action; petens [*Latin*]; demandant · Grundstücksprozeßkläger m

Act relating to Protection against Environmental Hazards and Pollution · Bundesimmissionsschutzgesetz n, BImSchG [*Bundesrepublik Deutschland*]

act relating to protection against notice to terminate, law relating to protection against notice to terminate, statute relating to protection against notice to terminate · Kündigungsschutzgesetz n

act relating to protection against notice to terminate residential leases, law relating to protection against notice to terminate residential leases, statute relating to protection against notice to terminate residential leases · Mieterkündigungsschutzgesetz n

actual, de facto · tatsächlich, wirklich

actual aggregate loss, actual total loss · tatsächlicher Gesamtverlust m, wirklicher Gesamtverlust

actual (construction) period (of time),
actual (construction) time period · tatsächliche Baufrist *f*, wirkliche Baufrist, tatsächliche Zeit *f* des Bauablaufes, wirkliche Zeit des Bauablaufes

actual costing, historic(al) costing, actual cost(s) accounting, historic(al) cost(s) accounting [*The ascertainment of cost(s) after they have been incurred*] · Istkostenrechnung *f*

actual cost(s), historic(al) cost(s) · tatsächliche Kosten *f*, wirkliche Kosten, historische Kosten, Istkosten, wirklicher Anschaffungswert, tatsächlicher Anschaffungswert, historischer Anschaffungswert, Istanschaffungswert *m*

actual cost(s) system, absorption costing, full costing, absorption (cost(s)) accounting, full (cost(s)) accounting [*The practice of charging all cost(s), both variable and fixed, to products, processes or services*] · Vollkostenkalkulation *f*, Voll(kosten)rechnung *f*, Vollkostenermitt(e)lung, Vollkostenberechnung

actual delivery (of possession) · tatsächliche (Besitz)Ableitung *f*, tatsächlicher (Besitz)Übergang *m* [*bewegliche Sache(n)*]

actual demand · Istnachfrage *f*, tatsächliche Nachfrage

actual entry [*A person has made an actual entry on land as soon as he has any part of his body thereon*] · tatsächliche Grund(stücks)besitzergreifung *f*, tatsächliche Grund(stücks)(in)besitznahme *f*

actual fraud · tatsächlicher Betrug *m*, wirklicher Betrug

actual grant · (dingliche) Überlassung *f*, dinglicher Vertrag *m* durch welchen ein neues Recht geschaffen wird

actual income, net income · Reineinkommen *n*, Nettoeinkommen

actualized · aktualisiert

actually executed [*deed*] · gesiegelt und übergeben [*Urkunde*]

actual (management) fee, (management) fee based on the actual cost of the work · festgesetzter Zuschlag *m* [*Selbstkostenerstattungsvertrag*]

actual notice · tatsächliche Kenntnis *f*

actual period (of time) → actual (construction) period (of time)

actual physical control (over a thing), potential physical control (over a thing), actual possession, physical possession, de facto possession · tatsächliche Sachherrschaft *f*, tatsächliche Beherrschung *f* einer Sache, unmittelbarer Besitz *m*, wirklicher Besitz, tatsächlicher Besitz, wirkliche Sachherrschaft, wirkliche Beherrschung einer Sache, unmittelbare Sachherrschaft, unmittelbare Beherrschung einer Sache

actual physical existence · tatsächliches physisches Dasein *n*

actual population, existing population, real population · tatsächliche Bevölkerung *f*, wirkliche Bevölkerung, Istbevölkerung

actual possession, physical possession, de facto possession, actual physical control (over a thing), potential physical control (over a thing) · tatsächliche Sachherrschaft *f*, tatsächliche Beherrschung *f* einer Sache, unmittelbarer Besitz *m*, wirklicher Besitz, tatsächlicher Besitz, wirkliche Sachherrschaft, wirkliche Beherrschung einer Sache, unmittelbare Sachherrschaft, unmittelbare Beherrschung einer Sache

actual quantity produced · Istproduktionsmenge *f*

actual regional policy [*As opposed to the theory of regional policy*] · praktische Raumordnung *f* [*Sie ist die Aufgabe des Staates und seiner Gebietskörperschaften*]

actual seisin, seisin in deed [*Seisin acquired by purchase*] · Kaufgewere *f*

actual situation, established facts, ascertained facts, case facts, situation of facts, state of facts · Sachlage *f*, Sachverhalt *m*, Tatbestand *m*

actual time period → actual (construction) period (of time)

actual total loss, actual aggregate loss · tatsächlicher Gesamtverlust *m*, wirklicher Gesamtverlust

actual traffic volume · Verkehrsaufkommen *n*

actual words · Wortlaut *m*

actuarial · versicherungsmathematisch

actuarial · statistikmathematisch

actuarius, notary (public) · Notar *m*

actuary [*One skilled in insurance mathematics*] · Versicherungsmathematiker *m*

actuary [*One skilled in statistics*] · Statistiker *m*

actus [*A servitude of footway and horseway*] · Fuß- und Reitwegservitut *n*, (*f*)

actus, faldagium [*Latin*]; frank-fold, faldage, right of drove, drove right, feldage · Triftrecht *n*, Treibrecht

actus [*Latin*] → Act of Parliament

actus Dei [*Latin*]; act of God [*A direct, violent, sudden and irresistible act of nature, which could not have been foreseen or resisted*] · Naturgewaltereignis *n*

to act with perfect good faith · handeln in Treu und Glauben

to adapt, to suit, to make suitable [*To fit a person or thing to another, to or for a purpose*] · anpassen

adaptability, adaptableness, adaptiveness, adaptedness, suitableness, suitability, fitness, flexibility · Anpassungsvermögen *n*, Anpassungsfähigkeit *f*

adaptable, flexible [*Capable of being adapted or of adapting oneself*] · anpassungsfähig

adap(ta)tion effect, adapting effect, fitting effect, suiting effect · Anpassungswirkung *f*

adapted, fit(ted) · angepaßt

adaptive; adaptorial [*obsolete*] [*Characterized by, or given to, adaptation*] · anpassend

to addecimate, to take tithes · einnehmen von Zehnten

added value, additional value, extra value, accessory value · Zusatzwert *m*, Mehrwert

addendum, supplement [*Revised, changed, or corrected document or addition to the contract documents*] · Ergänzung *f*, Nachtrag *m*

addendum bill of quantities · Nachtragsleistungsverzeichnis *n*, Nachtrags-L.V.

addition, extension, enlargement [*structure*] · Erweiterung *f* [*Bauwerk*]

addition · Zusatz *m*

addition, markup, surcharge [*That which is added to price(s) or cost(s)*] · Zuschlag *m*, Aufschlag [*Preis; Kosten*]

addition, accession, accretion [*Increase in economic worth from any cause; as, the growth of timber, the aging of wines, the increase of flocks and herds, etc.*] · Zuwachs *m*, Zunahme *f*

addition · Prädikat *n* [*Zusatz zum Namen von Stand und Wohnort*]

additional; additionary [*obsolete*]; accessory, extra · zusätzlich

additional agreement, extra agreement, accessory agreement · Zusatzabkommen *n*, Zusatzabmachung *f*, Zusatzvereinbarung

additional amount · Mehrbetrag *m*, Zusatzbetrag

additional bequest → additional legacy

additional capital, extra capital, accessory capital · Zusatzkapital *n*, zusätzliches Kapital

additional clause, extra clause, accessory clause · Zusatzklausel *f*

additional condition, accessory condition, extra condition · Zusatzbedingung *f*

additional contract, extra contract, accessory contract [*Such a contract is made for assuring the performace of a prior contract, either by the same parties or by others; such as suretyship, mortgage, and pledge*] · Zusatzvertrag *m*

additional contract condition, extra contract condition, accessory contract condition · zusätzliche Vertragsbedingung *f*

additional cost(s), extra cost(s), accessory cost(s) · zusätzliche Kosten *f*, Zusatzkosten

additional dividend · Zusatzdividende *f*

additional dividend · Zusatzverzinsung *f* [*bei Renten*]

additional income, extra income, accessory income · Zusatzeinkommen *n*

additional item, accessory item, extra item · Zusatzposition *f*

additional legacy, aditional bequest, extra legacy, extra bequest, accessory legacy, accessory bequest · Zusatz(fahrnis)legat *n*, Zusatz(fahrnis)vermächtnis *n*

additional loan, extra loan, accessory loan · Zusatzdarleh(e)n *n*

additional mortgage, accessory mortgage, extra mortgage · Zusatzhypothek *f*

additional payment, extra payment, accessory payment · Nachzahlung *f*, zusätzliche Zahlung, Zusatzzahlung

additional premium · Extraprämie *f*

additional reimbursement, extra reimbursement, accessory reimbursement · Vergütung *f* aus einem Zusatzauftrag, zusätzliche Vergütung

(additional) respite, prolongation of a term · Nachfrist *f*

additional services · Nebenleistungen *f pl*

additional succession duty [*Abolished in England by the Finance Act 1894*] · Nachfolgesteuerzuschlag *m*

additional tax, accessory tax, extra tax, surtax · Zusatzsteuer *f*

additional (technical) spec(ification)(s), extra (technical) spec(ification)(s), accessory (technical) spec(ification)(s) · zusätzliche technische Vorschriften *f pl*

additional value, extra value, accessory value, added value · Zusatzwert *m*, Mehrwert

additional work(s) · Nebenarbeit(en) *f (pl)*

addition for resumption of work, markup for resumption of work, surcharge for resumption of work · Wiederaufnahmezuschlag *m*, Wiederaufnahmeaufschlag

addition of dwelling rent, (residential) rent addition, dwelling rent addition, addition

addition of land — adjoining beneficiary

of (residential) rent · (Wohnungs)Mietzuschlag *m*

addition of land, land addition, land swell, acreage swell, swell of acreage, swell of land, addition of acreage, acreage addition [*of a real estate*] · Landzuwachs *m*, Flächenzuwachs, Bodenzuwachs, Landzunahme *f*, Bodenzunahme, Flächenzunahme

addition of property, augmentation of property, increase of property, accession of property · Besitzzunahme *f*, Besitzzuwachs *m*, Besitzerhöhung *f*, Besitzsteigerung

addition of (residential) rent, addition of dwelling rent, (residential) rent addition, dwelling rent addition · (Wohnungs)Mietzuschlag *m*

addition rate, accession rate, accretion rate, rate of accession, rate of addition, rate of accretion · Zunahmerate *f*, Zuwachsrate, Zunahmesatz, Zuwachssatz *m*

addition rate, markup rate, surcharge rate · Aufschlag(s)rate *f*, Zuschlag(s)rate

addition to contract amount [*Addition to the contractor's basic proposal(s), either in the form of an accepted additive alternate, or as a change order amending the contract*] · Zusatzbetrag *m*

addition to wage(s) · Lohnzulage *f*

additive algorism · additiver Algorithmus *m*, Additionsalgorithmus

address commission · Vollchartergebühr *f*

to adeem [*legacy*] · widerrufen [*Vermächtnis*]

ademption of legacy, revocation of legacy, ademption of bequest, revocation of bequest, legacy ademption, bequest ademption, legacy revocation, bequest revocation; ademptio legati [*Latin*] [*It occurs where a legacy does not take effect owing to some act on the part of a testator not affecting the validity of the will*] · (Fahrnis)Legatrücknahme *f*, (Fahrnis)Legatentziehung *f*, (Fahrnis)Vermächtnisrücknahme, (Fahrnis)Vermächtnisentziehung, Fahrhabelegatrücknahme, Fahrhabelegatentziehung, Fahrhabevermächtnisrücknahme, Fahrhabevermächtnisentziehung

adequacy · Angemessenheit *f*

ad-exposure · Exposition *f* einer Anzeige

to adhere [*Of a court, to affirm the judg(e)ment of a lower court*] · bestätigen eines Urteils

adherence, accession [*The unconditional acceptance by a country of a treaty already concluded between other countries*] · Beitritt *m* [*zu einem Staatsvertrag*]

adhesion contract, contract of adhesion · einseitig vorformulierter Vertrag *m*

adhesion contract, government contract, contract of adhesion, contract by regulation [*As opposed to a private contract*] · (Beschaffungs)Vertrag *m* mit einer Regierung, Vertrag durch Beitritt

adhesion contract provisions, general contract provisions, standard form contract provisions · allgemeine Geschäftsbestimmungen *fpl*

adjacency matrix · Knotenmatrix *f*, Adjazenzmatrix [*Graphentheorie*]

adjacent, near; neighbouring (Brit.); neighboring (US) · benachbart

adjacent area; neighbouring area (Brit.); neighboring area (US); vicinage · Nachbarfläche *f*, benachbarte Fläche

adjacent area, adjacent territory; neighbouring area (Brit.); neighbouring territory (Brit.); neighboring area, neighboring territory (US) · Nachbargebiet *n*

adjacent community; neighbouring community (Brit.); neighboring community (US) · Nachbargemeinde *f*, Nachbarkommune *f*

adjacent coverage · Anschlußbebauung *f*; Anschlußüberbauung *f* [*Schweiz*]

adjacent plot, adjacent parcel; neighbouring plot, neighbouring parcel (Brit.); neighboring plot, neighboring parcel (US) · Nachbargrundstück *n*

adjacent (property) owner; neighbouring (property) owner (Brit.); neighboring (property) owner (US) · Nachbar(eigentümer) *m*

adjective law, remedial law, procedural law, procedure law, law of (court) procedure (and practice) [*Law consisting of rules of conduct prescribed by substantive law, and enforced by adjective law. In other words, substantive law is administered by the courts and deals with rights and duties, whereas adjective law relates to practice and procedure and deals with remedies. "Substantive law" and "adjective law" were first used by Bentham (2 works, 6) and are now generally adopted, notwithstanding Austin's criticism of them (2 Jurisprudence, 788—789)*] · Formalrecht *n*, formelles Recht, Verfahrensrecht, Prozeßrecht

to adjoin, to lie (up)on, to border (up)on, to be co(n)terminous with · angrenzen

adjoining, co(n)terminous with, lying (up)on, bordering (up)on [*The term "adjoining" also sometimes means "near" or "neighbo(u)ring"*] · angrenzend [*(Grundstücks)Seiten*]

adjoining beneficiary, adjoining occupier · angrenzender Nutznießer *m*, angrenzender Nießbraucher

adjoining land — (ad)measurement mistake

adjoining land · angrenzendes Land *n*, angrenzender Grund *m*

adjoining owner, adjoining proprietor · angrenzender Eigentümer *m* angrenzender Eigner

adjoining possessor · angrenzender Besitzer *m*

adjoining property · angrenzendes Grundeigentum *n*

to adjourn · vertagen

adjourned · vertagt

adjourning, adjournment · Vertagen *n*

adjournment [*The state of being adjourned*] · Vertagung *f*

to adjourn sine die, to adjourn without a day fixed · unbestimmt vertagen

to adjudge, to sentence judicially, to condemn [*Any one to a penalty, or to do or suffer something*] · verurteilen

adjudged, forfeited, confiscated · eingezogen, konfisziert

to adjudicate → to decide

to adjudicate to be a bankrupt · sich bank(e)rott erklären, sich für bank(e)rott erklären

adjudicated, decided, tried, ruled · entschieden [*(Rechts)Fall*]

adjudication · Zuerkennung *f*

adjudication · Verfügungserlaßverfahren *n*

adjudication, (legal) judg(e)ment [*abbreviated: judgt.*], judg(e)ment (at law), decree (at law), judg(e)ment of a court [*The words "judg(e)ment" and "decree" are often used synonymously; especially now that the codes have abolished the distinction between "law" and "equity". But of the two terms "judg(e)ment" (Urteil) is the more comprehensive, and includes "decree" (Erlaß)*] · gerichtliches Urteil *n*, (Gerichts)Urteil, Rechtsspruch *m*, Erkenntnis *f* eines Gerichts(hofes)

adjudication of bankruptcy · (definitive) (Konkurs)Eröffnung *f*

adjudication of disputes, declaration of the law; jurisdictio [*Latin*]; administration of justice, jurisdiction, use of (the) law · Rechtsprechung *f*, Entscheidung von Einzelfällen, Justizausübung, Rechtspflege

adjudication order *f* [*A court order declaring a debtor to be a bankrupt and putting his property under the control of a trustee in bankruptcy*] · Bank(e)rottverfügung *f*, Konkurseröffnungsverfügung

adjunct account, absorption account · Vollkostenkonto *n*

to adjust, to compromise, to settle [*difference; conflicting claims; etc.*] · beilegen

to adjust [*(real) estate value*] · fortschreiben [*Grund(stücks)wert*]

adjustment [*general average*] · Dispache *f* [*große Havarie*]

adjustment [*(real) estate value*] · Fortschreibung *f* [*Grund(stücks)wert*]

adjustment · Bereinigung *f* [*Korrektur oder Modifizierung von Geschäftsvorgängen, um besondere Umstände oder Abweichungen zu berücksichtigen*]

adjustment, engineering of consent · Herbeiführung *f* von Übereinstimmungen

adjustment board (US) · paritätischer Schlichtungsausschuß *m*

adjustment clause · Gleitklausel *f*, Wertsicherungsklausel

adjustment levy, absorption of surplus money · Abschöpfung *f*

adjustment of condition clause · Konditionsanpassungsklausel *f*

adjustment of debt(s), debt(s) adjustment · Schuld(en)regulierung *f*

adjustment of (lot) boundaries, boundary replotting, confusion of (lot) boundaries [*The title of that branch of equity jurisdiction which relates to the discovery and settlement of conflicting, disputed, or uncertain boundaries*] · Grenzregelung *f*, Grenzausgleich *m*, Miniaturumlegung

adjustment of rent(s) · Mietenanpassung *f*

adjustment register, adjustment registry · Fortschreitungsprotokoll *n*

adjutorium, subsidium, auxidium [*Latin*]; aid [*In feudal law. A kind of pecuniary tribute paid by a vassal to his lord, on occasions of peculiar emergency, and which was one of the incidents of tenure in chivalry, or by knight's service*] · Hilfsgeld *n*

(ad)measured price · aufgemessener Preis *m*, Aufmaßpreis

(ad)measured work(s) · aufgemessene Arbeit(en) *f(pl)*

(ad)measurement book, book of (ad)measurement · Aufmaßbuch *n*

(ad)measurement document, document of (ad)measurement · Aufmaßurkunde *f*

(ad)measurement engineer · Aufmaßingenieur *m*

(ad)measurement error, error of (ad)measurement · Aufmaßfehler *m*

(ad)measurement method, method of (ad)measurement · Aufmaßmethode *f*, Aufmaßverfahren *n*

(ad)measurement mistake, mistake of (ad)measurement · Aufmaßirrtum *m*

(ad)measurement (of (the) work(s)) — administration letters

(ad)measurement (of (the) work(s)) · Aufmaß *n* (der Arbeit(en))

(ad)measurement prescription, prescription of (ad)measurement · Aufmaßvorschrift *f*

(ad)measurement provision, provision of (ad)measurement · Aufmaßbestimmung *f*

(ad)measurement record, record of (ad)measurement · Aufmaßaufzeichnung *f*

to (ad)measure together · gemeinsam aufmessen

to (ad)measure (up) · aufmessen

(ad)measuring (up) · Aufmessen *n*

to administer · verwalten

to administer, to operate, to manage · handhaben, verwalten, durchführen [*Vertrag*]

administered price, support price · Stütz(ungs)preis *m*

administered price · Monopolpreis *m*

administering, managing, operating · Durchführen *n*, Verwalten, Handhaben [*Vertrag*]

administering of oath, administration of oath, (oath) administration · Eidabnahme *f*, Eidesleistung *f*, Beeidigung, Abnahme, Schwören *n*

administration · Verwaltung *f*

administration → (oath) administration

administration (US); government (Brit.) · Regierung *f*

administration ad litem, administration for the (law)suit · Erb(schafts)verwaltung *f* zum Zwecke der Prozeßführung, Nachlaßverwaltung zum Zwecke der Prozeßführung

administration body, administrative body · Verwaltungsorgan *n*, Verwaltungskörper *m*

administration bond · Nachlaßverwaltungsbürgschaft *f*, Erbschaftsverwaltungsbürgschaft

administration building · Verwaltungsgebäude *n*

administration cost(s) · Verwaltungskosten *f*

administration court jurisdiction, administration tribunal jurisdiction · Verwaltungsrechtsprechung *f*, verwaltungsgerichtliche Rechtsprechung, verwaltungsgerichtliche Entscheidung von Einzelfällen, verwaltungsgerichtliche Justizausübung [*Jurisdiktion über subjektive Ansprüche aus Verwaltungsrecht. Im englischen Rechtsleben verfassungswidrig*]

administration cum testamento annexo · Erb(schafts)verwaltung *f* im Falle eines Testaments ohne Ernennung eines Testamentvollstreckers, Nachlaßverwaltung im Falle eines Testaments ohne Ernennung eines Testamentvollstreckers

administration de bonis non (administratis) · Einweisung *f* in bezug auf den unverteilten Nachlaß

administration district, administrative district · Verwaltungsbezirk *m*

administration durante absentia · Erb(schafts)verwaltung *f* während Abwesenheit, Nachlaßverwaltung während Abwesenheit, Erb(schafts)verwaltung für einen Abwesenden, Nachlaßverwaltung für einen Abwesenden

administration durante dementia, administration for the use and benefit of the lunatic · Erb(schafts)verwaltung *f* während Geisteskrankheit, Nachlaßverwaltung während Geisteskrankheit

administration durante minore aetate · Erb(schafts)verwaltung *f* während der Minderjährigkeit eines Beteiligten, Nachlaßverwaltung während der Minderjährigkeit eines Beteiligten

administration expert · Verwaltungsfachmann *m*

administration for the (law)suit, administration ad litem · Erb(schafts)verwaltung *f* zum Zwecke der Prozeßführung, Nachlaßverwaltung zum Zwecke der Prozeßführung

administration for the use and benefit of the lunatic, administration durante dementia · Erb(schafts)verwaltung *f* während Geisteskrankheit, Nachlaßverwaltung während Geisteskrankheit

administration for trust property, trust property administration · Erb(schafts)verwaltung *f* für Treuhandvermögen, Nachlaßverwaltung für Treuhandvermögen

administration game, administrative game · Verwaltungsplanspiel *n*

administration in bankruptcy of estate of a person dying insolvent · konkursartige Nachlaßverwaltung *f*, konkursartige Erb(schafts)verwaltung, konkursartige erbrechtliche Verwaltung

administration judg(e)ment · Urteil *n* welches die Verwaltung eines Nachlasses oder eines Fideikommisses gerichtlicher Aufsicht unterstellt

administration (law)suit · Nachlaßprozeß *m*, Nachlaßverwaltungsprozeß, Erb(schafts)(verwaltungs)prozeß

administration letters, letters of administration [*A document issued to an probate administrator granting his author-*

administration level — administrative contracting officer

ity] · Bestellungsdekret *n*, Bestellungserlaß *m*, Erbschaftsverwalterdekret, Erbschaftsverwaltererlaß, Nachlaßverwalterdekret, Nachlaßverwaltererlaß

administration level, level of administration · Verwaltungsstufe *f*, Verwaltungsebene *f*

administration of a (construction) project · Verwaltung *f* eines (Bau)Vorhabens

administration of (a) contract, contract management, contract operation, contract administration, management of (a) contract, operation of (a) contract · Durchführung *f* eines Vertrages, Handhabung eines Vertrages, Verwaltung eines Vertrages, Vertragsdurchführung, Vertragshandhabung, Vertragsverwaltung

administration of active estate of a bankrupt, administration of bankrupt's estate · (Konkurs)Masse(n)verwaltung, Fallitmasse(n)verwaltung *f*

administration (of assets) cost(s), administration of estate(s) cost(s) · Erb(schafts)verwaltungskosten *f*, Nachlaßverwaltungskosten

administration (of estate), administration of asset, administration of property, personal representation, estate administration, asset administration · erbrechtliche Verwaltung *f*, Nachlaßverwaltung, Erb(schafts)verwaltung

administration (of estate(s)) pendente lite, administration (of estate(s)) during the litigation [*The administrator has all the powers of a general administrator except that he cannot distribute the property among the beneficiaries*] · anhängige Erb(schafts)verwaltung *f*, anhängige Nachlaßverwaltung, Nachlaßverwaltung während eines Prozesses, Erb(schafts)verwaltung während eines Prozesses, anhängige erbrechtliche Verwaltung während eines Prozesses

administration of justice, jurisdiction, use of (the) law, adjudication of disputes, declaration of the law; jurisdictio [*Latin*] · Rechtsprechung *f*, Entscheidung von Einzelfällen, Justizausübung, Rechtspflege *f*

administration of land(ed) proprietorship, administration of land(ed) ownership, administration of proprietorship of land, administration of ownership of land, administration of landed property · erbrechtliche Verwaltung *f* für Grundstückseigentum, erbrechtliche Verwaltung für Bodeneigentum, erbrechtliche Verwaltung für Landeigentum, Erb(schafts)verwaltung für Grund(stücks)eigentum, Erb(schafts)verwaltung für Landeigentum, Erb(schafts)verwaltung für Bodeneigentum, Nachlaßverwaltung für Grund(stücks)eigentum, Nachlaßverwaltung für Bodeneigentum, Nachlaßverwaltung für Landeigentum

administration of mov(e)ables · Fahrniserbschaftsverwaltung *f*, Fahrnisnachlaßverwaltung

administration of oath, (oath) administration, administering of oath · Eidabnahme *f*, Eidesleistung *f*, Beeidigung, Abnahme, Schwören *n*

administration of planning, planning administration · Planungshandhabung *f*

administration of trust(s), trust(s) administration · Treuhandverwaltung *f*

administration science, science of administration · Verwaltungswissenschaft *f*

administration zone, zone of administration · Verwaltungszone *f*

administrative action → administrative (court) action

administrative affair · Verwaltungsangelegenheit *f*

administrative agreement · Verwaltungsabkommen *n*

administrative appeal · „klassische" Berufung *f*

administrative area, administrative territory · Verwaltungsgebiet *n*

administrative (area) map, administrative territory map · Verwaltungs(gebiet)karte *f*

administrative authority · Verwaltungsbehörde *f*

administrative authority, administrative power · Verwaltungshoheit *f*, Verwaltungskompetenz *f*, Verwaltungsmacht *f*, Verwaltungsgewalt *f*

administrative behaviour (Brit.); administrative behavior (US) · Verwaltungshandeln *n*

administrative board · Verwaltungsamt *n*

administrative body, administration body · Verwaltungsorgan *n*, Verwaltungskörper *m*

administrative border · Verwaltungsgrenze *f*

administrative branch · Verwaltungszweig *m*

administrative budget · Verwaltungshaushalt *m*

administrative business · Verwaltungsgeschäft *n*

administrative cause, administrative court action, administrative (law)suit, administrative plea · Verwaltungsklage *f*

administrative committee · Verwaltungsausschuß *m*

administrative contracting officer, administrative contracting official · (Beschaf-

administrative county — administrative plea of assets

fungs)Beamte *m* für die Verwaltung von (Beschaffungs)Verträgen mit einer Regierung

administrative county · Verwaltungsgrafschaft *f*

administrative county council · Verwaltungsgrafschaftsrat *m*

administrative court, administrative tribunal, court for matters in public administration, tribunal for matters in public administration · Verwaltungsgericht *n*, VG

administrative (court) action, administrative (law-)suit, administrative cause, administrative plea · Verwaltungsklage *f*

administrative (court) action (of estate(s)), administrative (court) action of assets, administrative (law)suit (of estate(s)), administrative (law)suit of assets, administrative cause of assests, administrative cause (of estate(s)), administrative plea of assets, administrative plea (of estate(s)) · Erb(schafts)verwaltungsklage *f*, Nachlaßverwaltungsklage

administrative court judge · Verwaltungsrichter *m*

administrative court proceeding · Verwaltungsgerichtverfahren *n*

administrative courts code · Verwaltungsgerichtsordnung *f*

administrative decision · Verwaltungsentscheid(ung) *m*, *(f)*

administrative discretion · Verwaltungsermessen *n*

administrative discretion in the interpretation of statutes · Verwaltungsermessen *n* bei der Gesetz(es)auslegung

administrative district, administration district · Verwaltungsbezirk *m*

administrative division · Verwaltungsteil *m*

administrative effectiveness · Leistungsstärke *f* der Verwaltung

administrative entity · Verwaltungsganze *n*

administrative expenses · Verwaltungsaufwand *m*

administrative facility · Verwaltungseinrichtung *f*

administrative feasibility · Verwaltungsdurchführbarkeit *f*

administrative fee · Verwaltungsgebühr *f*

administrative function · Verwaltungsfunktion *f*, verwaltende Funktion

administrative game, administration game · Verwaltungsplanspiel *n*

administrative history · Verwaltungsgeschichte *f*

administrative law · Verwaltungsrecht *n*

administrative lawmaking, administrative legislation · Verwaltungsgesetzgebung *f*, untergeordnete Gesetzgebung

administrative law science, administrative legal science, administrative jurisprudence · Verwaltungsrechtlehre *f*, Verwaltungsrechtswissenschaft *f*, Verwaltungsjurisprudenz *f*, Lehre der allgemeinen Verwaltungsrechtsfragen

administrative (law)suit, administrative cause, administrative plea, administrative (court) action · Verwaltungsklage *f*

administrative (law)suit (of estate(s)), administrative (law)suit of assets, administrative cause of assests, administrative cause (of estate(s)), administrative plea of assets, administrative plea (of estate(s)), administrative (court) action (of estate(s)), administrative (court) action of assets · Erb(schafts)verwaltungsklage *f*, Nachlaßverwaltungsklage

administrative legal authority, administrative legal power, jurisdiction · Verwaltungsgerichtsbarkeit *f*

administrative legislation, administrative lawmaking · Verwaltungsgesetzgebung *f*, untergeordnete Gesetzgebung

administrative machine(ry) · Verwaltungsmechanismus *m*

administrative management · Verwaltungsführung *f*, Verwaltungsleitung

administrative map → administrative (area) map

administrative measure · Verwaltungsmaßnahme *f*

administrative officer, administrative official · Verwaltungsbeamte *m*

administrative order · Verwaltungsakt *m*, Verwaltungshandlung *f* [*Verwaltungsakte sind behördliche Verfügungen, Bescheide, Beschlüsse, Anordnungen, Genehmigungen und Feststellungen*]

administrative organization · Verwaltungsorganisation *f*

administrative overhead(s), administrative overhead cost(s) · Verwaltungsgemeinkosten *f*, Verwaltungsgeneralkosten

administrative personnel, administrative staff · Verwaltungspersonal *n*

administrative planning · Verwaltungsplanung *f*

administrative plea, administrative cause, administrative court action, administrative (law)suit · Verwaltungsklage *f*

administrative plea of assets, administrative plea (of estate(s)), administrative (court) action (of estate(s)), administra-

administrative policy — admission

tive (court) action of assets, administrative (law)suit (of estate(s)), administrative (law)suit of assets, administrative cause of assests, administrative cause (of estate(s)) · Erb(schafts)verwaltungsklage f, Nachlaßverwaltungsklage

administrative policy · Verwaltungspolitik f

administrative power, administrative authority · Verwaltungshoheit f, Verwaltungskompetenz f, Verwaltungsmacht f, Verwaltungsgewalt f

administrative prescription, administrative regulation, administrative rule · Verwaltungsvorschrift f

administrative procedure, administrative process · Verwaltungsverfahren n

administrative procedure act, administrative procedure law, administrative procedure statute, administrative process act, administrative process law, administrative process statute · Verwaltungsverfahrensgesetz n

administrative procedure legislation, administrative procedure lawmaking, administrative process legislation, administrative process lawmaking · Verwaltungsverfahrensgesetzgebung f

administrative process law, law of administrative process, law of administrative procedure, administrative procedure law · Verwaltungsverfahrensrecht n

administrative provision · Verwaltungsbestimmung f

administrative quarter · Verwaltungsquartier n, Verwaltungsviertel n

administrative redress, administrative remedy · Verwaltungsabhilfe f, Verwaltungsbehelf m

administrative reform · Verwaltungsreform f

administrative region · Verwaltungsregion f

administrative regulation, administrative rule, administrative prescription · Verwaltungsvorschrift f

administrative remedy, administrative redress · Verwaltungsabhilfe f, Verwaltungsbehelf m

administrative reorganization · Verwaltungsumbildung f

administrative rule, administrative prescription, administrative regulation · Verwaltungsvorschrift f

administrative service · Verwaltungsdienst m

administrative simplification, simplification of administration · Verwaltungsvereinfachung f

administrative staff, administrative personnel · Verwaltungspersonal n

administrative structure · Verwaltungsgefüge n, Verwaltungsstruktur f, Verwaltungsaufbau m, Verwaltungszusammensetzung f

administrative system · Verwaltungsapparat m

administrative territory, administrative area · Verwaltungsgebiet n

administrative territory map, administrative (area) map · Verwaltungs(gebiet)karte f

administrative tribunal, court for matters in public administration, tribunal for matters in public administration, administrative court · Verwaltungsgericht n, VG

administrative work(s) · Verwaltungsarbeit(en) f (pl)

administrator [A manager or conductor of affairs, especially the affairs of another, in his name or behalf] · Verwalter m

administrator → (probate) administrator

administrator de bonis non (administratis) → (probate) administrator de bonis non (administratis)

administrator durante minore aetate → (probate) administrator durante minore aetate

administrator during the litigation → (probate) administrator during the litigation

administrator of justice · Rechtsverwalter m

administrator of the unadministered estate → (probate) administrator de bonis non (administratis)

administrator's oath · Nachlaßverwaltereid m, Erbschaftsverwaltereid

administrator with the will annexed → (probate) administrator with the will annexed

administratrix → female administrator

Admiralty chart [Great Britain]; nautical chart · See(navigations)karte f [Mit nautischen Angaben versehene Karte der Küstengebiete und Meere]

admiralty jurisdiction · Seegerichtsbarkeit f

Admiralty Law [Great Britain]; maritime law · Seerecht n

admissibility · Zulässigkeit f

admissibility of proof, admissibility of evidence · Beweiszulässigkeit f

admissible building area, permissible building area · zulässige Grundfläche f

admission, approval, sanction · Zulassung f

admission — adult population

admission, acknowledg(e)ment, concession [*Made by a party of the existence of certain facts*] · Einräumung f, Zugeständnis n

admission, number of visitors · Besucher(an)zahl f

admission · Anerkennung f

admission, commission, order, installation, vesting · (Amts)Einsetzung f, (Amts)-Bestallung

admission against interest · Eintrag(ung) m, (f) gegen das Interesse des Eintragenden [*Beweisrecht*]

admission fee, entrance fee · Eintrittsgeld n

admission of guilt, confession · Eingeständnis n, Geständnis, Schuld(ein)geständnis, Schuldbekenntnis

admission test · Zulassungsprüfung f

admission to the bar, call to the bar · Zulassung f zur (Rechts)Anwaltschaft

admission waiting list, waiting list for admission · Anwartschaftsliste f [*z. B. für den Bezug einer Wohnung*]

to admit, to confess, to avow, to make a confession [*To admit the truth of what is charged*] · (ein)gestehen, bekennen, zugeben, geständig sein [*Schuld*]

to admit · feierlich auflassen, übertragen einer Gewere [*Schrift(sassen)gut*]

to admit, to acknowledge, to concede · einräumen, zugestehen

to admit, to instal · einsetzen, bestallen

admittance [*In English law. The form of giving seisin(a) of a copyhold estate, corresponding with livery of seisin(a) of a freehold; one of the formalities necessary for the conveyance of copyhold, the other two being surrender, and presentment*] · feierliche Auflassung f für ein Schrift(sassen)gut, Gewereübertragung für ein Schrift(sassen)gut

admittance, right of access, power of access, access right, access power · Betretungsbefugnis f, Betretungsrecht n, Zutrittsbefugnis, Zutrittsrecht, Zugangsbefugnis, Zugangsrecht

admitting approach, accessible · wegsam, zugänglich

admixture of fluids, confusion (of goods); confusio [*Latin*] · (Sach)Vermischung f [*Unfeste Körper werden so untereinander gebracht, daß sie nicht mehr einzeln, sondern nur noch als Masse gelten*]

admixture of solids, commixture, commixtion, commixtio [*Latin*] · Vermengung f [*Feste Körper werden so untereinander gebracht, daß sie nicht mehr einzeln, sondern nur als Masse gelten*]

adolescence · jugendliches Alter n

adolescent · Heranwachsende m, Jugendliche

to adopt a contract, to make a contract, to contract, to settle a contract, to conclude a contract · abschließen eines Vertrages, vertraglich vereinbaren

adopting a contract, contracting, settling a contract, concluding a contract, making a contract · Abschließen n eines Vertrages

adoption inheritance, inheritance by adoption · Adoptiverbe n, Adoptiverbschaft f

adoption law, law of adoption · Adoptionsrecht n

adoption of (a) resolution · Beschlußfassung f

adoption of referee's report · Genehmigung f des Berichtes des Einzelrichters

adoptive Act of Parliament [*England*] · Parlamentsgesetz n dessen Annahme in das Belieben der Lokalbehörden gestellt ist

ad opus, ad usum [*Latin*]; to the use(r) of · zu Nutzen und Besten, zum Besten

to adorn, to beautify, to embellish · verschönern

adpage audience · Leserschaft f einer Anzeigenseite

ad-page-exposure days · Expositionstage m pl einer Anzeigenseite

adpromissio [*Latin*] · Stipulationsbürgschaft f

adstipulator [*Latin*] · Nebengläubiger m

adult age · Erwachsenenalter n

adult death rate · Erwachsenensterberate f

adulted [*obsolete*]; grown to maturity, matured · erwachsen

adult education · Erwachsenenbildung f

adulteration of drugs · Medikamenten(ver)fälschung f

adulteration of food, food adulteration · Nahrungsmittel(ver)fälschung f

adultery [*The intrusion of a person into a bishopric during the former bishop's life. The reason of the appellation is that a bishop is supposed to contract a sort of spiritual marriage with his church*] · geistlicher Ehebruch m

adult man, male adult · Erwachsene m, erwachsener Mann m

adult (person) · erwachsene Person f, Erwachsene m

adult population · erwachsene Bevölkerung f

adult woman, female adult · Erwachsene *f*, erwachsene Frau

ad usum [*Latin*]; to the use(r) of; ad opus [*Latin*] · zu Nutzen und Besten, zum Besten

ad valorem [*Latin*]; proportional to value, in proportion to value · wertverhältnismäßig

ad valorem (customs) duty, customs duty ad valorem · Wertzoll *m*

ad valorem tax · Wertsteuer *f*

ad valorem taxation · Wertbesteuerung *f*

to advance a date, to antedate · vordatieren

advanced capital · Vorschußkapital *n*

advanced fee · Gebührenvorschuß *m*, Gebührenvorauszahlung *f*, Gebührenvorstreckung, Gebührenbevorschussung, Honorarvorschuß, Honorarvorauszahlung, Honorarbevorschussung, Honorarvorstreckung

advanced member → borrower

advanced permission · Vorwegerlaubnis *f*, Vorweggenehmigung *f*

advanced society, developed society · entwickelte Gesellschaft *f*

advance factory [*A factory built in advance of demand*] · Standardfabrik *f* [*In einem indischen Gewerbepark*]

advance financing, prefinancing, preliminary financing · Vorfinanzierung *f*

advancement · vermögensrechtlicher Vorteil *m*, Schenkung *f* [*Einem Erbberechtigten von jemandem bei dessen Lebzeiten zugewendet. Stirbt der Erblasser intestat, so wird dieser Vorteil von dem Erbteil des früher Bedachten abgezogen*]

advancement · Schenkungsgut *n* [*An einen Erbberechtigten bei Lebzeiten eines Erblassers*]

advancement, promotion · Beförderung *f* [*In eine höhere Stellung oder ein höheres Amt*]

advance(ment) (of money), money advance(ment), cash advance(ment) · Vorschuß *m*

advancement presumption, presumption of advancement [*It means that a gift was intended and arises where a voluntary conveyance has been made to the wife or child of the donor or to a person to whom he stands in loco parentis*] · Schenkungsvermutung *f*

to advance (money) · bevorschussen, vorschießen, vorstrecken, vorauszahlen, pränumerieren

advance payment invoice, prepayment invoice · Vorauszahlungsrechnung *f*

advance performance · Vorleistung *f*

advance planning, planning from-the-top-down, forward planning · Vorausplanung *f*, Planung von oben

advances, business of lending against collateral, deposit and loan business · Lombardgeschäft *n*

advancing money → advance(ment) (of money)

advantage, benefit · Nutzen *m*, Vorteil *m*

advantage → (common) advantage

advantage principle, principle of advantage · Vorteilsgrundsatz *m*, Vorteilsprinzip *n*

adventure, speculation · Spekulation *f*

adventure aversion, risk aversion, hazard aversion · Risikoabneigung *f*, Wagnisabneigung

adventure in stocks · Aktienunternehmen *n*, Aktienunternehmung *f*

adventure playground · Abenteuerspielplatz *m*

adventurer, gambler, speculator · Spekulant *m*

adventurer, mine operator · Bergwerk(be)treibende *m*, Bergwerkbetreiber, Bergbau(be)treibende, Bergbaubetreiber

adversary, contested, undecided, contentious, unsettled, controversial, moot [*Litigated between adverse parties*] · streitig, strittig

adversary, opposing party, adverse party, opposite party, opponent (party) · Prozeßgegner *m*, Gegenpartei *f*

adversary system [*As opposed to the accusatorial system*] · System *n* der Prozeßgegnerschaft [*Des streitigen Parteivortrags im Gegensatz zum Anklageprinzip*]

adverse · passiv [*Bilanz*]

adverse, wrongful, inconsistent with possessory right · entgegenstehend, fehlerhaft, entgegen dem Recht, rechtswidrig [*(subjektives) Besitzrecht*]

adverse balance · passive Bilanz *f*

adverseness of possession, adversity of possession · Besitzfehlerhaftigkeit *f*, Fehlerhaftigkeit des Besitzes

adverse occupation, incroachment, incroaching, trespass, intrusion, encroaching, encroachment · (Beeinträchtigung *f* durch) Eindringen *n*, Verletzung durch Eindringen, Störung durch Eindringen, Besitzverletzung durch Eindringen, Besitzstörung durch Eindringen, Besitzbeeinträchtigung durch Eindringen

adverse party, opposite party, opponent (party), adversary, opposing party · Prozeßgegner *m*, Gegenpartei *f*

adverse physical conditions (on the site) · negative Bedingungen *fpl* (auf der Baustelle), negative Verhältnisse *fpl* (auf der Baustelle)

adverse possession, wrongful possession [*An occupation of realty inconsistent with the right of the true owner*] · entgegenstehender (Land)Besitz *m*, entgegenstehender Bodenbesitz, entgegenstehender Grund(stücks)besitz, fehlerhafter (Land)Besitz, fehlerhafter Grund(stücks)besitz, fehlerhafter Bodenbesitz, rechtswidriger Bodenbesitz, rechtswidriger (Land)Besitz, rechtswidriger Grund(stücks)besitz

adverse possessor [*An occupier of realty inconsistent with the right of the true owner*] · rechtswidriger (Land)Besitzer *m*, rechtswidriger Bodenbesitzer, rechtswidriger Grund(stücks)besitzer, entgegenstehender (Land)Besitzer, entgegenstehender Bodenbesitzer, entgegenstehender Grund(stücks)besitzer, fehlerhafter (Land)Besitzer, fehlerhafter Bodenbesitzer, fehlerhafter Grund(stücks)besitzer

adverse report · negativer Bericht *m*

adverse weather, bad weather · Schlechtwetter *n*

adverse-weather conditions, bad-weather conditions · Schlechtwetterverhältnisse *f*, Schlechtwetterbedingungen *fpl*

adverse-weather construction, bad-weather construction · Schlechtwetterbau *m*

adverse-weather day, bad-weather day · Schlechtwettertag *m*

adversity of possession, adverseness of possession · Besitzfehlerhaftigkeit *f*, Fehlerhaftigkeit des Besitzes

to advertise a project · öffentlich ausschreiben

advertisement; advertizement (US) · Reklame *f*, Werbung *f*

advertisement control, control of advertisements · Überwachung *f* des Reklamewesens, Reklameüberwachung

advertisement dangerous to traffic, traffic-endangering advertisement · verkehrsgefährdende Werbung *f*, verkehrsgefährdende Reklame *f*

advertisement facility · Werbeeinrichtung *f*, Reklameeinrichtung

advertisement for bids, advertisement for tenders · Submissionsanzeige *f*

(advertisement) hoarding, billboard · Werbetafel *f*, Reklametafel

advertisement media research, advertising units research, advertisement units research, advertising media research · Werbemittelforschung *f*, Reklamemittelforschung

advertisement media research, advertisement vehicles research, advertising media research, advertising vehicles research · Werbeträgerforschung *f*, Reklameträgerforschung

advertisement medium, advertising medium, advertisement unit, advertising unit · Werbemittel *n*, Reklamemittel

advertisement medium, advertisement vehicle, advertising medium, advertising vehicle · Werbeträger *m*, Reklameträger

advertisement of a project, project advertisement, public tendering (out), public tender(ing) action, public bidding (action), public invitation to tender, open tendering, open bidding, open competition · öffentliche Ausschreibung *f*, öffentliche Aufforderung (zur Angebotsabgabe), offenes Verfahren *n*, offener Wettbewerb *m*, Ausschreibung der öffentlichen Hand [*Bauleistungen werden im vorgeschriebenen Verfahren nach öffentlicher Aufforderung einer unbeschränkten Zahl von Unternehmern zur Einreichung von Angeboten vergeben*]

advertisement planning, planning for advertisements · Werbungsplanung *f*, Reklameplanung

advertisement posting · Anschlagen *n* von Reklame, Anschlagen *n* von Werbung

advertisement prohibition, prohibition of advertisement · Werbeverbot *n*, Reklameverbot

advertisement sign · Reklameschild *n*

advice, information · Information *f*, Ankündigung *f*

advice, counsel, consultancy, consultation · Beratung *f*

advice note · Avis *n*

advisability · Ratsamkeit *f*

advisable · ratsam

to advise, to consult, to give advice, to counsel · beraten

to advise, to inform, to notify, to give notice · anzeigen, benachrichtigen, mitteilen, informieren

to advise [*Scots law*]; to take into avizandum · prüfen [*Urteil*]

adviser, consultant, advisor · Berater *m*

adviser-designed project, consultant-designed project · Beraterentwurfsprojekt *n*

advising, counsel(l)ing, consulting · Beraten *n*

advising activity, consulting activity, consultative activity, advisory activity, counsel(l)ing activity · beratende Tätigkeit *f,* Beratungstätigkeit

advising bank · avisierende Bank *f,* anzeigende Bank [*Akkreditiv*]

advising combine, advisory combine, consulting combine, consultative combine · Beratungs-Arbeitsgemeinschaft *f*

advising committee, counsel(l)ing committee, advisory committee, consultative committee, consulting committee · beratender Ausschuß *m,* Beratungsausschuß

advising duty, advisory duty, counsel(l)ing duty, consulting duty, duty to consult, consultative duty · Beratungspflicht *f*

advisory activity, counsel(l)ing activity, advising activity, consulting activity, consultative activity · beratende Tätigkeit *f,* Beratungstätigkeit

advisory board [*U.S. Investment Company Act 1940/1970*] · Anlageberatungsausschuß *m*

advisory council, advisory panel · Beirat *m*

advisory council for Land planning, advisory panel for Land planning, advisory Land planning council, advisory Land planning panel, Land planning advisory council, Land planning advisory panel · Landesplanungsbeirat *m* [*Bundesrepublik Deutschland*]

advisory opinion, expertise, survey · Gutachten *n,* Sachverständigenbericht *m*

advisory planning association · Landschaftsverband *m* [*Bundesrepublik Deutschland*]

advisory planning council, advisory planning panel, planning advisory council, planning advisory panel · Planungsbeirat *m*

advisory service, consultation service, consultancy service, consultant service · Beratungsdienst *m*

advocacy · Advokatur *f,* Befürwortung *f*

advocacy, advocateship [*The function of an advocate*] · Advokatur *f*

advocacy planner, advocate planner · Anwaltplaner *m*

advocacy planning, advocate planning [*The use of experts by neighbo(u)rhood organizations and other interest groups to make their case and articulate their needs and desires*] · Advokatenplanung *f,* Anwaltplanung *f,* advozierende Planung

to advocate [*To speak or write in support of; to be in favour of*] · verfechten

advocate [*A person who speaks or writes in support of something*] · Verfechter *m*

advocate [*A person who pleads another's cause, as a lawyer*] · Advokat *m*

advocate-general, Queen's advocate, King's advocate [*England*] · Kronjurist *m* für See- und Kriegsrecht

advocate of choice [*In Scotland*]; barristor of choice, barrister of choice · Vertrauensanwalt *m,* Vertrauensadvokat *m* [*Als plädierender (Rechts)Anwalt*]

advocate planner, advocacy planner · Anwaltplaner *m*

advocateship , advocacy [*The function of an advocate*] · Advokatur *f*

advocating · Verfechten *n*

advocatio [*Latin*] · Vogtei *f,* Amt *n,* Drostei *f*

advocatus [*Latin*]; a(d)vowee · Kirchenpatron *m,* Inhaber des Präsentationsrechts einer Pfründe

advocatus ecclesiae [*Latin*] · Kirchenvogt *m*

advowee paramount, avowee paramount · höchster Kirchenpatron *m*

advowson; jus patronatus [*Latin*]; (right of) patronage [*The right of presentation, i.e. the right of appointing a parson to a rectory, vicarage or other ecclesiastic(al) benefice*] · Patronat(srecht) *n,* Präsentation(srecht) *f, (n)* [*Ein dauerndes Präsentationsrecht zu einer geistlichen Pfründe*]

advowson appendant, advowson incident, patronage appendant, patronage incident [*An advowson annexed to a manor, and passing with it, as incident or appendant to it, by a grant of the manor only, without adding any other words*] · Grundbesitzpatronat(srecht) *n,* ununterbrochene Präsentation *f,* ununterbrochenes Präsentationsrecht *n,* ununterbrochenes Patronat(srecht) *n,* Grundbesitzpräsentationsrecht, Patronat(srecht) mit Grundbesitz, Präsentationsrecht mit Grundbesitz

advowson collative, collative advowson · Patronat(srecht) *n* bei dem der Bischof der Patron ist, Präsentation(srecht) bei dem der Bischof der Patron ist

advowson donative, donative advowson, (right of) patronage donative · Patronat(srecht) *n* bei dem der Patron ohne Inanspruchnahme eines Bischofs jemanden zum Inhaber einer geistlichen Pfründe ernennen konnte, Präsentation(srecht) bei dem der Patron ohne Inanspruchnahme eines Bischofs jemanden zum Inhaber einer geistlichen Pfründe ernennen konnte

advowson in gross, advowson at large, patronage in gross, patronage at large · losgelöste Präsentation *f,* persönliche Präsentation, losgelöstes Präsentationsrecht *n*, persönliches Präsentationsrecht, losgelöstes Patronat(srecht) *n*, persönliches Patronat(srecht)

advowson presentative, (right of) patronage presentative · Patronat(srecht) *n* wenn der Patron das Recht hat eine geeignete Person für die erledigte Pfründe dem Bischof zu präsentieren, und der letztere verpflichtet ist, die Investitur sowohl mit den Spiritualien als auch mit den Temporalien vorzunehmen

aerial colour photography (Brit.); aerial color photography (US) · Luft-Buntphotographie *f*, Bunt-Luftphotographie

aerial geography · Luft(bild)geographie *f*, Luftaufnahmegeographie

aerial navigation right, navigation right [*Right to use the air above the land for aerial navigation*] · Überflugrecht *n*

aerial photogrammetry, air surveying, air photogrammetry, aerial surveying · Luftbildmessung *f*, Luftbildtechnik *f*, Aerophotogrammetrie *f*, Luftphotogrammetrie, Luftvermessung

aerial photo(graph), air photo(graph), flight photo(graph) · Luftbild *n*, Luftaufnahme *f*, Luftphoto *n*

aerial photographer, air photographer · Luftphotograph *m*

aerial photograph(ic) interpretation, interpretation of aerial photography, airphoto interpretation · Luftbildauswertung *f*, Luftaufnahmeauswertung, Luftphotoauswertung

aerial photograph interpreter, airphoto interpreter · Luftbildauswerter *m*, Luftaufnahmeauswerter, Luftphotoauswerter

aerial photograph research, airphoto research · Luftbildforschung *f*, Luftaufnahmeforschung

aerial photography, air photography, aerophotography · Luftphotographie *f*

aerial (picture) map · Luft(bild)karte *f*

aerial survey camera, air survey camera · Luftmeßbildkamera *f*

aerial surveying, aerial photogrammetry, air surveying, air photogrammetry · Luftbildmessung *f*, Luftbildtechnik *f*, Aerophotogrammetrie *f*, Luftphotogrammetrie, Luftvermessung

aerial topography, air topography, aerotopography · Lufttopographie *f*

aerodrome city, airport town, airport city, aerodrome town · Flughafenstadt *f*

aerodrome planning, airport planning · Flughafenplanung *f*

aerodrome umland, airport umland · Flughafenumland *n*

aeronautical chart, air navigation chart · Luftfahrtkarte *f*, Luftnavigationskarte [*zivil*]

aeronautical chart, air chart · Fliegerkarte *f* [*militärisch*]

aeronautical information overprint · aeronautischer Überdruck *m* [*Kartographie*]

aerophotography, aerial photography, air photography · Luftphotographie *f*

aerotopography, aerial topography, air topography · Lufttopographie *f*

aesnetia, eisnetia, enitia pars, dignitas primogeniti [*Latin*]; right of primogeniture, right of the eldest, right of the first born · (männliches) Erstgeburtsrecht *n*, Primogenitur *f*, Vorrecht des Erstgeborenen

(a)esthetical disturbance · ästhetische Störung *f*

(a)esthetical perception · ästhetisches Empfinden *n*, ästhetische Wahrnehmung *f*

aestruarium [*Latin*]; abb(e)y-land(s); abbas [*Ang. Sax.*] [*Estates of an abb(e)y*] · Abteiland *n*, Abteiboden *m*, Abteiländerei(en) *f (pl)*

affair, matter · Angelegenheit *f*, Sache *f*

affected with public interest · mit öffentlichem Interesse behaftet

affeeror, taxator [*A officer who was sworn by the steward of the court of a manor or hundred to assess the amerciaments imposed by the court, if the amount thereof was not fixed by custom or statute. Affeerors seem also to have been employed to assess the damages in cases brought in the inferior courts*] · Geschworene *m* als Schätzer

affidavit, statutory declaration, statutory statement, declaration on the oath, statement on the oath [*A written statement sworn on oath which may be used in certain cases as evidence*] · Erklärung *f* an Eidesstatt, Versicherung an Eidesstatt, eidesstattliche Erklärung, eidesstattliche Versicherung, schriftlicher Eid *m*

affidavit of service · eidliche Versicherung *f* der Zustellung durch den Kläger

affiliate(d) company), allied company, associated company · verbundene Gesellschaft *f* [*Eine Gesellschaft, die eine verbundene Person ist*]

affiliated group member · Konzernunternehmen *n*, Konzernunternehmung *f*

affiliated group of enterprises, affiliated group of undertakings, trust · Konzern *m*

affiliated person · verbundene Person *f* [*Eine mit einer anderen Person verbundene Person*]

affiliation — age composition

affiliation, twinning of cities, twinning of towns · Verschwisterung *f*

affiliation [*An affiliation exists between a holding or parent company and its subsidiary, or between two corporations or other organizations owned or controlled by a third*] · Angliederung *f*

affiliation proceeding · Vaterschaftsverfahren *n*

to affirm, to make firm, to confirm; affirmare [*Latin*] · bestätigen

affirmation · Festhalten *n* des vertragstreuen Partners am Vertrag

affirmation, solemn declaration without oath · Gelöbnis *n*, feierliche Erklärung *f*

affirmation, confirmation · Bestätigung *f*

affirmation notice, affirmation notification, notice of confirmation, notice of affirmation, notification of confirmation, notification of affirmation, confirmation notice, confirmation notification · Bestätigungsmitteilung *f*, Bestätigungsanzeige *f*, Bestätigungsbenachrichtigung

affirmation of order, confirmation of order · Auftragsbestätigung *f*

affirmation of sale, confirmation of sale · Verkaufsbestätigung *f*

affirmative easement, positive easement [*The servient owner allows the dominant owner to perform a certain act or certain acts upon the servient tenement*] · positive Grunddienstbarkeit *f*

affirmatory letter, letter of confirmation, letter of affirmation, confirmatory letter · Bestätigungsschreiben *n*

affirming, confirming · Bestätigen *n*

to affirm on appeal, to confirm on appeal [*judg(e)ment*] · bestätigen in der Berufung [*Urteil*]

to affirm solemnly [*Instead of taking an oath*] · feierlich versichern

affluence · Zustrom *m*

affluent; branch (US); tributary · Nebenfluß *m*

affluent society · Überflußgesellschaft *f*

affordable · erschwinglich

affording compensation, compensative, compensating, serving to compensate, compensatory · entschädigend

to afforest · aufforsten

afforestation · Aufforstung *f*

afforestation act, afforestation law, afforestation statute; Forestry Act [*England*] · Aufforstungsgesetz *n*

afforestation land, land for afforestation · Aufforstungsland *n*, Aufforstungsboden *m*, Aufforstungsfläche *f*

afforestation of fallow land, fallow land afforestation · Brachlandaufforstung *f*

afforested [*Converted into forest*] · aufgeforstet

afforesting · Aufforsten *n*

affray · Einschüchterung *f*

affreightment, charter party [*A contract for transporting goods by sea*] · Seefrachtvertrag *m*, Charterpartie *f*, Chartervertrag, Charterurkunde, Seefrachtpartie, Seefrachturkunde *f*

aforethought, evil mind; mens vea, malitia (praecogitata) [*Latin*]; malice (prepense) · Dolus *m*, Vorsatz *m*, krimineller Wille *m*

after-acquired [*Acquired after a particular date or event. Thus, a judgment is a lien on after-acquired realty, i.e. land(s) acquired by the debtor after entry of the judgment*] · nacherworben, nachträglich erworben

after-acquired clause [*mortgage*] · Nachverpfändungsklausel *f*

after-care · Schulentlassenenfürsorge *f*, Jugendfürsorge

after guarantor · Afterbürge *m*, Nachbürge

after-heiress, substitute heiress, after female heir, substitute female heir · Aftererbin *f*, Nacherbin, Ersatzerbin

after-heir (male), second heir (male), revisionary heir (male), substitute · Aftererbe *m*, Nacherbe *m*, Substitut *m*, Ersatzerbe [*Derjenige, der nach einem ernannten Erben als Erbe in einem Testament ernannt ist, wenn der erste Erbe die Erbschaft nicht erwerben würde*]

after sight · auf Sicht [*Wechsel*]

against all the world, against the whole world · gegen jedermann

against evidence, against proof, contrary to evidence, contrary to proof · beweiswidersprechend

against good morals; contra bonos mores [*Latin*] · gegen die guten Sitten

against law → nonlegal

against one's will · wider Willen

against the plan(s) · planfremd, planwidrig

against the whole world, against all the world · gegen jedermann

age bracket · Altersspanne *f*

age class · Altersklasse *f*

age composition, age structure · Altersaufbau *m*, Altersstruktur *f*, Alterszusammensetzung *f*, Altersgefüge *n*

age distribution · Altersverteilung f

aged persons' home, old people's home, old persons' home, aged people's home · Altenheim n, Altersheim

age group · Altersgruppe f

ageing population · Bevölkerung f mit steigendem Altenanteil

age-life method, straight line method · lineare Abschreibung f

agency [*The relation created between principal (constituent) and agent*] · (Stell)Vertretung f

agency → (official) agency

agency contract, contract of agency · (Stell)Vertretungsvertrag m

agency from necessity, agency of necessity · Not(stell)vertretung f

agency with agent contracting as such for unnamed principal · halbverdeckte (Stell)Vertretung f [*Der Vertreter gibt sich als solcher zu erkennen, nennt aber nicht den Auftraggeber*]

agenda · Tagesordnung f

agenda topic · Tagesordnungspunkt m

agent → (authorized) agent

agent → ((real) estate) broker

agent authorized to effect sales · Abschlußvertreter m

agent by statute → (authorized) agent by statute

agent for a person in a (law)suit · Vertreter m einer Person in einem Prozeß

agent for levying distress; bailiff [*Low Latin*]; distrainer, distrainor, distreinor · Privatpfänder m von beweglichen Sachen, eigenmächtiger Pfänder von beweglichen Sachen

agent (on site), supervisor (on site), site agent, site supervisor · Bauleiter m, Bauleitung f, Baustellenleiter, Baustellenleitung, örtlicher Bauleiter, örtliche Bauleitung [*des Unternehmers*]

age of consent, mature years, statutory age, legal age, full age, (age of (legal)) majority [*The age fixed by law at which a person's consent to certain acts is valid in law*] · Majorennität f, Volljährigkeit(salter) f, (n)

age of Enlightenment [*The age of Frederick the Great, Voltaire and the Encyclopaedists*] · Zeitalter n der Aufklärung

(age of (legal)) minority, non-age · Minderjährigkeit f

age pyramid · Alterspyramide f

ager publicus [*Latin*]; land of the people, folkland, folcland, falk-land; terra popularis [*Latin*]; [*Anglo-Saxon land law. Folcland was held by customary law, without written title. Inheritance depended on custom. It could not be (ab)alienated without the consent of those who had some interest in it*] · Volksland n

age selection · Altersauslese f

age-specific · altersspezifisch

age-specific headship rate [*The headship rate for a particular age group*] · altersspezifische Haushaltvorstandsziffer f

age-specific migration · altersspezifische Wanderung f

age-specific mortality · altersspezifische Sterblichkeit f

age-specific mortality rate · altersspezifische Sterblichkeitsziffer f, altersspezifische Sterberate f

age-specific vital rate [*It is calculated for particular age groups*] · altersspezifische Bevölkerungsziffer f

age structure, age composition · Altersaufbau m, Altersstruktur f, Alterszusammensetzung f, Altersgefüge n

agglomerated settlement, cluster settlement, nucleated settlement with an irregular street-plan · Haufen(an)sied(e)lung f, unregelmäßig zusammengewachsene (An)Sied(e)lung, Gruppen(an)sied(e)lung mit unregelmäßigem Grundriß

agglomerating · Verdichten n, Ballen, Agglomerieren

agglomeration · Verdichtung f, Ballung, Agglomeration f, allgemeine Konzentration, räumliche Konzentration [*Die zunehmende Anzahl der auf eine bestimmte Fläche bezogenen Einheiten*]

agglomeration area, agglomeration territory · Verdichtungsraum n, Verdichtungsraum m, Ballungsgebiet n, Ballungsraum, Agglomerationsgebiet, Agglomerationsraum, Ballungsbereich, Verdichtungsbereich, Agglomerationsbereich n

agglomeration axis, axis of agglomeration · Verdichtungsachse f, Ballungsachse, Agglomerationsachse, allgemeine Konzentrationsachse

agglomeration core · Ballungskern m, Verdichtungskern, Agglomerationskern, allgemeiner Konzentrationskern

agglomeration economies · Agglomerationsvorteile m pl, Standortgunst f

agglomeration-orien(ta)ted, agglomeration-related · agglomerationsbezogen, agglomerationsorientiert

agglomeration territory, agglomeration area · Verdichtungsgebiet n, Verdich-

agglomeration through interrelationship — agiotage

tungsraum m, Ballungsgebiet n, Ballungsraum, Agglomerationsgebiet, Agglomerationsraum, Ballungsbereich, Verdichtungsbereich, Agglomerationsbereich m

agglomeration through interrelationship · verbundene Häufung f

aggravated compensation, aggravated indemnification, aggravated indemnity, aggravated damages · erhöhte Entschädigung f, erhöhter Schadenersatz m

aggravating circumstance, aggravation, handicap · erschwerender Umstand m, Erschwerung f, Erschwernis f

aggregate, mass [*A collection of individuals, units, or things, in order to form a whole*] · Masse f

aggregate acreage, total acreage · Totalfläche f, Gesamtfläche

aggregate agency, total authority, aggregate authority, total agency · Gesamtvertretungsmacht f, Gesamtvollmacht

aggregate amount, total amount · Gesamtbetrag m, Totalbetrag

aggregate assets, whole assets, total assets · Gesamtaktiva f, Totalaktiva

aggregate building cost(s), whole building cost(s), total construction cost(s), aggregate construction cost(s), whole construction cost(s), total building cost(s) · Gesamtherstellungskosten f, Gesamtbaukosten, Totalbaukosten, Totalherstellungskosten

aggregate density, overall density, total density · Gesamtdichte f

aggregate freight, total freight, whole freight · Gesamtfracht f

aggregate gain, whole gain, total profit, aggregate profit, whole profit, total gain · Gesamtgewinn m, Totalgewinn, Gesamtprofit, Totalprofit m

aggregate grossed-up amount, total grossed-up amount [*An amount to be charged for carrying out the whole quantity of an item*] · Gesamtbetrag m, Totalbetrag [*Spalte in einem L.V.*]

aggregate hazard, total risk, total hazard, aggregate risk · Gesamtrisiko n, Gesamtwagnis n, Totalrisiko, Totalwagnis

aggregate index · Aggregatform f des zusammengesetzten Index [*Statistik*]

aggregate interest rate, total interest rate, whole interest rate · Gesamtzinsfuß m

aggregate loss, total loss · Gesamtverlust m, Totalverlust

aggregate meeting · Gesamtversammlung f

aggregate of rights, total of rights, property · Masse f von (subjektiven) Rechten, Menge f von (subjektiven) Rechten

aggregate planning, whole planning, total planning · Totalplanung f, Gesamtplanung

aggregate population, whole population, total population · Gesamtbevölkerung f

aggregate production cost(s), whole production cost(s), total production cost(s) · Totalherstellungskosten, Gesamtherstellungskosten f

aggregate profit, whole profit, total gain, aggregate gain, whole gain, total profit · Gesamtgewinn m, Totalgewinn, Gesamtprofit, Totalprofit m

aggregate rights of building, total rights of building, aggregate superficies, total superficies · Gesamtbaurecht n [*Es erstreckt sich über mehrere Liegenschaften*]

aggregate risk, aggregate hazard, total risk, total hazard · Gesamtrisiko n, Gesamtwagnis n, Totalrisiko, Totalwagnis

aggregate stock, total stock · Gesamtbestand m

aggregate superficies, total superficies, aggregate rights of building, total rights of building · Gesamtbaurecht n [*Es erstreckt sich über mehrere Liegenschaften*]

aggregate supply function, total supply function · Gesamtangebotsfunktion f, aggregierte Angebotsfunktion, Funktion des gesamten Angebots [*Nach der keynesianischen Theorie ist es eine funktionale Beziehung zwischen dem gewinnmaximalen Wert der Produktion und dem entsprechenden Einsatz an Arbeit*]

aggregate usable space, total usable space, whole usable space · gesamte Nutzfläche f [*Summe von Wohn- und Nutzfläche der Räume eines Gebäudes*]

aggregate value, total value · Gesamtwert m

aggregation [*Adding together all property passing at death in one estate for the purposes of ascertaining the rate of estate duty*] · Zusammenlegung f

aggregation of titles, title amalgamation, title aggregation, title concentration, amalgamation of titles, concentration of titles · (Rechts)Titelzusammenlegung f

aggregative model · zusammengesetztes Modell n [*Statistik*]

agio, premium [*A charge made for exchanging the currency of one country for that of another*] · Agio n, Aufgeld n, Übersatz m, Aufschlag m

agiotage [*Speculation in foreign exchange or stock exchange securities*] · Agio-

tage f, Börsenspiel n, Börsengeschäft n, Börsenspekulation [*unter Ausnutzung des Agios*]

agister · Weideaufseher m

agistment · Weidegeld n, Viehweidegeld

agistment of sea banks · Deichsteuer f

A.G.M., (annual) general meeting, yearly general meeting · (Jahres)Hauptversammlung f

agnate · vaterseitiger Verwandter m

agnation [*Kinship by the father's side*] · vaterseitige Verwandtschaft f

agnomination, surname, family name, last name · Nachname m, Familienname

agrarian act, agrarian statute, agriculture law, agriculture act, agriculture statute, agrarian law · Agrargesetz n, Landwirtschaftsgesetz, landwirtschaftliches Gesetz

agrarian aid, agrarian help, agricultural aid, agricultural help · Agrarhilfe f, Landwirtschaftshilfe, landwirtschaftliche Hilfe

agrarian area, agrarian territory, agricultural area, farming area, agricultural territory, farming territory, cultivation area, cultivation territory · Agrarfläche f, Agrargebiet n, landwirtschaftliche Fläche, landwirtschaftliches Gebiet, Anbaufläche, Anbaugebiet

agrarian atlas, agricultural atlas · Agraratlas m, Landwirtschaftsatlas, landwirtschaftlicher Atlas

agrarian authority, agricultural authority · Agrarbehörde f, Landwirtschaftsbehörde, landwirtschaftliche Behörde

agrarian bank, land bank, agricultural bank · Landwirtschaftsbank f

agrarian belt, agriculture belt, agricultural belt · Landwirtschaftsgürtel m, landwirtschaftlicher Gürtel, Agrargürtel

agrarian civilization, agricultural civilization · Agrarzivilisation f, Landwirtschaftszivilisation, landwirtschaftliche Zivilisation

agrarian code, agricultural code · Landwirtschaftsordnung f

agrarian commodity, agricultural commodity · landwirtschaftliches Handelsgut n, Agrarhandelsgut

agrarian community, agricultural community · Agrargemeinde f, Landwirtschaftsgemeinde, landwirtschaftliche Gemeinde, Bauerngemeinde

agrarian composition, agricultural structure, agrarian structure, agricultural composition · Landwirtschaftsstruktur f, Agrarstruktur, landwirtschaftsgefüge n, Agrargefüge, Landwirtschaftszusammensetzung f, Agrarzusammensetzung [*Die Gesamtheit der strukturellen Gegebenheiten die die Wirtschafts-, Arbeits- und Lebensbedingungen der Landwirtschaft eines Gebietes auch in Verflechtung mit außerlandwirtschaftlichen Bereichen bestimmen*]

agrarian cooperative warehouse society, agricultural cooperative warehouse society · Lagergenossenschaft f

agrarian court, agricultural court · Ackergericht n, Flurgericht, Agrargericht, Landwirtschaftsgericht, landwirtschaftliches Gericht

agrarian credit, agricultural credit · Landwirtschaftskredit m, Agrarkredit

agrarian depression, agricultural depression · landwirtschaftlicher Notstand m

agrarian development, agricultural development · Agrarentwick(e)lung f, landwirtschaftliche Entwick(e)lung

agrarian engineering, agricultural engineering · (Landes)Kulturtechnik f

agrarian fixture, agricultural fixture · landwirtschaftlicher (Grundstücks)Bestandteil m

agrarian geography, agricultural geography · Agrargeographie f, Landwirtschaftsgeographie, landwirtschaftliche Geographie

agrarian help, agricultural aid, agricultural help, agrarian aid · Agrarhilfe f, Landwirtschaftshilfe, landwirtschaftliche Hilfe

agrarian hinterland, agricultural hinterland · landwirtschaftliches Hinterland n, Agrarhinterland, Agrohinterland

agrarian inheritance law, agrarian law of inheritance, agricultural inheritance law, agricultural law of inheritance · Agrarerbrecht n, landwirtschaftliches Erbrecht

agrarianism, agrarian reform, agricultural reform [*The principle of an equal division of agricultural land(s)*] · agrarische Bodenreform f, landwirtschaftliche Bodenreform, Agrarreform, Landwirtschaftsreform

agrarianism · Bodenreformlehre f, Landreformlehre

to agrarianize [*To imbue with the ideas of agrarianism*] · erfüllen mit bodenreformerischen Gedanken

agrarian landowner, agricultural landowner, farming landowner, farmland owner · Agrarlandeigentümer m, Kulturlandeigentümer, Kulturbodeneigentümer, Agrarlandeigner, Kulturlandeigner, Kulturbodeneigner

agrarian land rent, agrarian rent of land, (agricultural) land rent, (agricultural) rent of land · landwirtschaftliche Rente f, Bodenrente [*J. H. von Thünen zerlegt diese Rente in „Landrente" (= Lagerente) und „Gutsrente"*]

agrarian law — agrarian society

agrarian law, agrarian act, agrarian statute, agriculture law, agriculture act, agriculture statute, agricultural law, agricultural act, agricultural statute · Agrargesetz *n*, Landwirtschaftsgesetz, landwirtschaftliches Gesetz

agrarian law, agricultural law · Agrarrecht *n*, Landwirtschaftsrecht, landwirtschaftliches Recht, Bauernrecht [*Das auf den land- und forstwirtschaftlich nutzbaren Boden bezogene Recht, das unmittelbar oder mittelbar die Bodenbenutzung beeinflußt*]

agrarian law of inheritance, agricultural inheritance law, agricultural law of inheritance, agrarian inheritance law · Agrarerbrecht *n*, landwirtschaftliches Erbrecht

agrarian location, agrarian site, agricultural location, agricultural site · Agrarstandort *m*, Landwirtschaftsstandort, landwirtschaftlicher Standort

agrarian lot, agricultural lot · landwirtschaftliches Grundstück *n* (im katastertechnischen Sinne), landwirtschaftliches Katastergrundstück, landwirtschaftliches Kartengrundstück, landwirtschaftliches Flurstück, landwirtschaftliche (Kataster)Parzelle *f*

agrarian outrage [*An act of violence originating in discord between bordage lords and tenants*] · Gewalttat *f* gegen den Gutsherren

agrarian overpopulation, agricultural overpopulation · landwirtschaftliche Überbevölkerung *f*, Agrarüberbevölkerung

agrarian planning, agricultural planning · Agrarplanung *f*, Landwirtschaftsplanung, landwirtschaftliche Planung

agrarian policy, agricultural policy · Agrarpolitik *f*, Landwirtschaftspolitik, landwirtschaftliche Politik

agrarian possession, agricultural possession · Agrargrundbesitz *m*, landwirtschaftlicher Grundbesitz

agrarian price, agricultural price · Agrarpreis *m*, Landwirtschaftspreis, landwirtschaftlicher Preis

agrarian problem area, agricultural problem area · agrarisches Problemgebiet *n*, landwirtschaftliches Problemgebiet

agrarian reform, agricultural reform, agrarianism [*The principle of an equal division of agricultural land(s)*] · agrarische Bodenreform *f*, landwirtschaftliche Bodenreform, Agrarreform, Landwirtschaftsreform

agrarian reform authority, land(s) reform authority · Bodenreformbehörde *f*, Landreformbehörde

agrarian (reformer), land(s) reformer [*One in favour of a redistribution of landed property*] · Bodenreformer *m*, Landreformer

agrarian reform law, law of land(s) reform, law of agrarian reform, land(s) reform law · Bodenreformrecht *n*, Landreformrecht

agrarian reform law, agrarian reform act, agrarian reform statute, land(s) reform statute, land(s) reform act, land(s) reform law · Bodenreformgesetz *n*, Landreformgesetz

agrarian reform legislation, land(s) reform lawmaking, agrarian reform lawmaking, land(s) reform legislation · Bodenreformgesetzgebung *f*, Landreformgesetzgebung

agrarian reform plan, land(s) reform plan · Bodenreformplan *m*, Landreformplan

agrarian region, agricultural region, farming region · Agrarregion *f*, Landwirtschaftsregion, Agrarraum *m*, Landwirtschaftsraum, landwirtschaftliche Region, landwirtschaftlicher Raum, Anbauraum, Anbauregion

agrarian rent of land, (agricultural) land rent, (agricultural) rent of land, agrarian land rent · landwirtschaftliche Rente *f*, Bodenrente [*J. H. von Thünen zerlegt diese Rente in „Landrente" (= Lagerente) und „Gutsrente"*]

agrarian rent (received), agricultural rent (received) · Gutsrente *f* [*nach v. Thünen*]; Landrente [*nach Ad. Smith*] [*Eine Rente welche ein Gutsherr von einem verpachteten Gut bezieht*]

agrarian school, agricultural school · Landwirtschaftsschule *f*

agrarian sector, agricultural sector · Agrarsektor *m*, landwirtschaftlicher Sektor, Landwirtschaftssektor [*Er ist nahbezugstätig und fernbedarfstätig*]

agrarian settlement, agricultural settlement · Agrarsied(e)lung *f*, landwirtschaftliche (An)Sied(e)lung [*Das Ergebnis landwirtschaftlichen (An)Siedelns*]

agrarian settlement, agricultural settling, agrarian settling · landwirtschaftliches (An)Siedeln *n*

agrarian settlement law, agricultural settlement law · Agrar(an)sied(e)lungsrecht *n*, landwirtschaftliches (An)Sied(e)lungsrecht

agrarian settling, agrarian settlement, agricultural settling, agricultural settlement · landwirtschaftliches (An)Siedeln *n*

agrarian site, agricultural location, agricultural site, agrarian location · Agrarstandort *m*, Landwirtschaftsstandort, landwirtschaftlicher Standort

agrarian society, agricultural society · Landwirtschaftsgesellschaft *f*

agrarian sociology — agreement of tenancy

agrarian sociology, agricultural sociology · Agrarsoziologie *f*, Landwirtschaftssoziologie, landwirtschaftliche Soziologie

agrarian statute, agriculture law, agriculture act, agriculture statute, agrarian law, agrarian act · Agrargesetz *n*, Landwirtschaftsgesetz, landwirtschaftliches Gesetz

agrarian structure, agricultural composition, agrarian composition, agricultural structure · Landwirtschaftsstruktur *f*, Agrarstruktur, Landwirtschaftsgefüge *n*, Agrargefüge, Landwirtschaftszusammensetzung *f*, Agrarzusammensetzung [*Die Gesamtheit der strukturellen Gegebenenheiten die die Wirtschafts-, Arbeits- und Lebensbedingungen der Landwirtschaft eines Gebietes auch in Verflechtung mit außerlandwirtschaftlichen Bereichen bestimmen*]

agrarian structure improvement, agricultural structure improvement · Agrarstrukturverbesserung *f*

agrarian territory, agricultural area, farming area, agricultural territory, farming territory, cultivation area, cultivation territory, agrarian area · Agrarfläche *f*, Agrargebiet *n*, landwirtschaftliche Fläche, landwirtschaftliches Gebiet, Anbaufläche, Anbaugebiet

agrarian underpopulation, agricultural underpopulation · landwirtschaftliche Unterbevölkerung *f*, Agrarunterbevölkerung

agrarian unit, agricultural unit · landwirtschaftliche Wirtschaftseinheit *f*, Agrarwirtschaftseinheit

agrarian village, agricultural village, agro-village, peasant village · Agrardorf *n*, Bauerndorf, Landwirtschaftsdorf, landwirtschaftliches Dorf

agrarian water use, agricultural water use · landwirtschaftliche Wassernutzung *f*

agrarian work, agricultural work, farm work · Landarbeit *f*, Agrararbeit

agrarian worker, farm worker; labourer (Brit.); agricultural worker · Landarbeiter *m*

agrarian zone, agricultural zone · Agrarzone *f*, Landwirtschaftszone, landwirtschaftliche Zone

to agree, to accord · übereinstimmen

agreeable, accordable · übereinstimmbar

agreed (building society) sum · Vertragssumme *f* [*Bausparkasse*]

agreed judg(e)ment, contradictory judg(e)ment, judg(e)ment after trial, judg(e)ment agreed (up)on · kontradiktorisches Urteil *n*, vereinbartes Urteil, abgemachtes Urteil

agreed (local) venue · vereinbarter Gerichtsstand *m*, vereinbarter Gerichtsort *m*

(agreed) settlement, compromise [*Settlement out of court of claims in dispute. The term implies some element of accommodation on each side*] · Vergleich *m*, (Streit)Beilegung *f*

agreed ((up)on), contradictory · vereinbart, kontradiktorisch, abgemacht, übereingekommen

agreeing with, according to, consonant, conformable, accordant, consistent, not contradictory, concurrent [*Having agreement with itself or something else*] · gemäß, nicht gegenteilig, konform mit, übereinstimmend, gerecht mit

agreement · Abmachung *f* im Rechtssinn, Abkommen *n* im Rechtssinn, Übereinkommen *n* im Rechtssinn, Übereinkunft *f* im Rechtssinn, Vereinbarung *f* im Rechtssinn, Willenseinigung *f* im Rechtssinn [*Die rechtlichen Verhältnisse der Parteien müssen berührt werden*]

agreement by word of mouth, agreement by parol(s), parol(e) agreement, verbal agreement, oral agreement · mündliches Abkommen *n*, mündliche Vereinbarung *f*, mündliche Abmachung

agreement of access, access agreement · Betretungsabmachung *f*, Zugangsabmachung, Betretungsvereinbarung, Zugangsvereinbarung, Betretungsabkommen, Zugangsabkommen *n*, Zutrittsabkommen, Zutrittsabmachung, Zutrittsvereinbarung

agreement of demise → agreement of tenancy

agreement of imperfect obligation, unenforceable contract · materiell unantastbarer Vertrag *m*

agreement of lease(hold) → agreement of tenancy

agreement of management, management agreement · Betreuungsabkommen *n*, Betreuungsabmachung *f*, Betreuungsvereinbarung

agreement of opinion, consent of opinion, unanimity, consension, consensus of opinion, unity of opinion · Meinungsgleichheit *f*, Einstimmigkeit, Übereinstimmung *f*

agreement of satisfaction, satisfaction agreement · Befriedigungsabkommen *n*, Befriedigungsabmachung *f*, Befriedigungsvereinbarung

agreement of tenancy, agreement of demise, agreement of lease(hold), agreement of tenure, tenancy agreement, demise agreement, lease(hold) agreement, tenure agreement · Pachtabkommen *n*, Pachtabmachung *f*, Pachtvereinbarung, Nutzungsrechtabkommen, Nutzungsrechtvereinbarung, Nutzungsrechtabmachung, Verpachtungsabkommen, Verpachtungsvereinbarung, Verpachtungsabmachung

agreement on proviso, agreement on reservation · Vorbehaltabkommen *n*, Vorbehaltabmachung *f*, Vorbehaltvereinbarung

agreement to sell ascertained goods, agreement to sell specific goods · Speziesverkaufsabmachung *f*, Speziesverkaufsabkommen *n*, Speziesverkaufsvereinbarung

agreement tripartite, tripartite agreement · Dreiecksabkommen *n*, Dreiecksabmachung *f*, Dreiecksvereinbarung

to agree ((up)on) · abmachen, übereinkommen, vereinbaren, abschließen (einer Abmachung)

agricultural zone, agrarian zone · Agrarzone *f*, Landwirtschaftszone, landwirtschaftliche Zone

agricultural act → agrarian law

agricultural aid, agricultural help, agrarian aid, agrarian help · Agrarhilfe *f*, Landwirtschaftshilfe, landwirtschaftliche Hilfe

agricultural area, farming area, agricultural territory, farming territory, cultivation area, cultivation territory, agrarian area, agrarian territory · Agrarfläche *f*, Agrargebiet *n*, landwirtschaftliche Fläche, landwirtschaftliches Gebiet, Anbaufläche, Anbaugebiet

agricultural atlas, agrarian atlas · Agraratlas *m*, Landwirtschaftsatlas, landwirtschaftlicher Atlas

agricultural authority, agrarian authority · Agrarbehörde *f*, Landwirtschaftsbehörde, landwirtschaftliche Behörde

agricultural bank, agrarian bank, land bank · Landwirtschaftsbank *f*

agricultural belt, agrarian belt, agriculture belt · Landwirtschaftsgürtel *m*, landwirtschaftlicher Gürtel, Agrargürtel

agricultural building · landwirtschaftliches Betriebsgebäude *n*

agricultural city → agricultural town

agricultural civilization, agrarian civilization · Agrarzivilisation *f*, Landwirtschaftszivilisation, landwirtschaftliche Zivilisation

agricultural code, agrarian code · Landwirtschaftsordnung *f*

agricultural commodity, agrarian commodity · landwirtschaftliches Handelsgut *n*, Agrarhandelsgut

agricultural community, agrarian community · Agrargemeinde *f*, Landwirtschaftsgemeinde, landwirtschaftliche Gemeinde, Bauerngemeinde

agricultural composition, agrarian composition, agricultural structure, agrarian structure · Landwirtschaftsstruktur *f*, Agrarstruktur, Landwirtschaftsgefüge *n*, Agrargefüge, Landwirtschaftszusammensetzung *f*, Agrarzusammensetzung [*Die Gesamtheit der strukturellen Gegebenheiten die die Wirtschafts-, Arbeits- und Lebensbedingungen der Landwirtschaft eines Gebietes auch in Verflechtung mit außerlandwirtschaftlichen Bereichen bestimmen*]

agricultural contributing population · Agrarerwerbsbevölkerung *f*, landwirtschaftliche Erwerbsbevölkerung

agricultural control, control of agriculture · Landwirtschaftslenkung *f*, Agrarlenkung, landwirtschaftliche Lenkung

agricultural cooperative warehouse society, agrarian cooperative warehouse society · Lagergenossenschaft *f*

agricultural country, agricultural land [*A state exporting products of the soil*] · Bodenland *n*

agricultural court, agrarian court · Ackergericht *n*, Flurgericht, Agrargericht, Landwirtschaftsgericht, landwirtschaftliches Gericht

agricultural credit, agrarian credit · Landwirtschaftskredit *m*, Agrarkredit

agricultural crew, agricultural team, agricultural party, agricultural gang · Landarbeiterkolonne *f*, Landarbeitertrupp *m*

agricultural depression, agrarian depression · landwirtschaftlicher Notstand *m*

agricultural development, agrarian development · Agrarentwick(e)lung *f*, landwirtschaftliche Entwick(e)lung

agricultural engineering, agrarian engineering · (Landes)Kulturtechnik *f*

agricultural fixture, agrarian fixture · landwirtschaftlicher (Grundstücks)Bestandteil *m*

agricultural gang, agricultural crew, agricultural team, agricultural party · Landarbeiterkolonne *f*, Landarbeitertrupp *m*

agricultural geography, agrarian geography · Agrargeographie *f*, Landwirtschaftsgeographie, landwirtschaftliche Geographie

agricultural help, agrarian help, agricultural aid, agrarian aid · Agrarhilfe *f*, Landwirtschaftshilfe, landwirtschaftliche Hilfe

agricultural hinterland, agrarian hinterland · landwirtschaftliches Hinterland *n*, Agrarhinterland, Agrohinterland

agricultural holdings act, agricultural holdings statute, agricultural holdings law · landwirtschaftliches Pachtlandgesetz *n*

agricultural homestead · (landwirtschaftliche) Wirtschaftsheimstätte *f* [*Ein landwirtschaftliches Anwesen, zu dessen*

agricultural housing sector — agricultural poverty

Bewirtschaftung eine Familie unter regelmäßigen Verhältnissen keiner ständigen fremden Arbeitskraft bedarf]

agricultural housing sector, agricultural housing field, farm housing sector, farm housing field · landwirtschaftlicher Wohnungssektor *m*

agricultural improvement, soil improvement, land melioration, land improvement, agricultural melioration · (Boden)Melioration *f*, landwirtschaftliche Verbesserung *f*, Landmelioration [Maßnahmen zur Verbesserung der Standortbedingungen für die Kulturpflanzen]

agricultural inheritance law, agricultural law of inheritance, agrarian inheritance law, agrarian law of inheritance · Agrarerbrecht *n*, landwirtschaftliches Erbrecht

(agricultural) labourer's house (Brit.); (agricultural) laborer's house (US) · Leutehaus *n*

agricultural land, farming land, land agricultural in character, farmland, improved land, farmed land, agriculturally used land, crop land [Land may be assessable as "agricultural land" though it be covered by timber and underbrush, grass and weeds] · landwirtschaftlicher Boden *m*, landwirtschaftlich genutzter Boden, landwirtschaftliches Land *n*, landwirtschaftlich genutztes Land, Kulturland, Kulturboden, Agrarland, landwirtschaftlich genutzte Fläche *f*, LN, landwirtschaftliche Nutzfläche, Fruchtland, Agrarnutzfläche

agricultural land, agricultural country [A state exporting products of the soil] · Bodenland *n*

agricultural land law, farmland law · Kulturlandrecht *n*, Kuturbodenrecht

agricultural landowner, farming landowner, farmland owner, agrarian landowner · Agrarlandeigentümer *m*, Kulturlandeigentümer, Kulturbodeneigentümer, Agrarlandeigner, Kulturlandeigner, Kulturbodeneigner

(agricultural) land rent, (agricultural) rent of land, agrarian land rent, agrarian rent of land · landwirtschaftliche Rente *f*, Bodenrente [J. H. von Thünen zerlegt diese Rente in „Landrente" (= Lagerente) und „Gutsrente"]

agricultural landscape · Agrarlandschaft *f*

agricultural law → agrarian law

agricultural law of inheritance, agrarian inheritance law, agrarian law of inheritance, agricultural inheritance law · Agrarerbrecht *n*, landwirtschaftliches Erbrecht

agricultural loan bank · Landschaftsbank *f*

agricultural location, agricultural site, agrarian location, agrarian site · Agrarstandort *m*, Landwirtschaftsstandort, landwirtschaftlicher Standort

agricultural lot, agrarian lot · landwirtschaftliches Grundstück *n* (im katastertechnischen Sinne), landwirtschaftliches Katastergrundstück, landwirtschaftliches Kartengrundstück, landwirtschaftliches Flurstück, landwirtschaftliche (Kataster)Parzelle *f*

agriculturally used · landwirtschaftlich genutzt, landwirtschaftlich bebaut

agriculturally zoned land, agriculturally used land, crop land, agricultural land, farming land, land agricultural in character, farmland, improved land, farmed land [Land may be assessable as "agricultural land" though it be covered by timber and underbrush, grass and weeds] · landwirtschaftlicher Boden *m*, landwirtschaftlich genutzter Boden, landwirtschaftliches Land *n*, landwirtschaftlich genutztes Land, Kulturland, Kulturboden, Agrarland, landwirtschaftlich genutzte Fläche *f*, LN, landwirtschaftliche Nutzfläche, Fruchtland, Agrarnutzfläche

agricultural melioration, agricultural improvement, soil improvement, land melioration, land improvement · (Boden)Melioration *f*, landwirtschaftliche Verbesserung *f*, Landmelioration [Maßnahmen zur Verbesserung der Standortbedingungen für die Kulturpflanzen]

agricultural mutual loan association, agricultural mutual loan society · landwirtschaftliche Kreditgenossenschaft *f*, landwirtschaftlicher Vorschuß- und Kreditverein *m*

agricultural overpopulation, agrarian overpopulation · landwirtschaftliche Überbevölkerung *f*, Agrarüberbevölkerung

agricultural party, agricultural gang, agricultural crew, agricultural team · Landarbeiterkolonne *f*, Landarbeitertrupp *m*

agricultural physical facilities, agricultural structures, agricultural works · landwirtschaftliche Bauten *f*, landwirtschaftliche Baulichkeiten *fpl*, landwirtschaftliche (Bau)Werke *npl*, landwirtschaftliche (bauliche) Anlagen, landwirtschaftliche Bauanlagen *fpl*

agricultural planning, agrarian planning · Agrarplanung *f*, Landwirtschaftsplanung, landwirtschaftliche Planung

agricultural policy, agrarian policy · Agrarpolitik *f*, Landwirtschaftspolitik, landwirtschaftliche Politik

agricultural possession, agrarian possession · Agrargrundbesitz *m*, landwirtschaftlicher Grundbesitz

agricultural poverty · landwirtschaftliche Armut *f*

agricultural price — agricultural value

agricultural price, agrarian price · Agrarpreis *m*, Landwirtschaftspreis, landwirtschaftlicher Preis

agricultural problem area, agrarian problem area · agrarisches Problemgebiet *n*, landwirtschaftliches Problemgebiet

agricultural reform, agrarianism, agrarian reform [*The principle of an equal division of agricultural land(s)*] · agrarische Bodenreform *f*, landwirtschaftliche Bodenreform, Agrarreform, Landwirtschaftsreform

agricultural region, farming region, agrarian region · Agrarregion *f*, Landwirtschaftsregion, Agrarraum *m*, Landwirtschaftsraum, landwirtschaftliche Region, landwirtschaftlicher Raum, Anbauraum, Anbauregion

(agricultural) rent of land, agrarian land rent, agrarian rent of land, (agricultural) land rent · landwirtschaftliche Rente *f*, Bodenrente [*J. H. von Thünen zerlegt diese Rente in „Landrente" (= Lagerente) und „Gutsrente"*]

agricultural rent (received), agrarian rent (received) · Gutsrente *f* [*nach v. Thünen*]; Landrente [*nach Ad. Smith*] [*Eine Rente welche ein Gutsherr von einem verpachteten Gut bezieht*]

agricultural school, agrarian school · Landwirtschaftsschule *f*

agricultural sector, agrarian sector · Agrarsektor *m*, landwirtschaftlicher Sektor, Landwirtschaftssektor [*Er ist nahbezugstätig und fernbedarfstätig*]

agricultural serfdom · Gutsuntertänigkeit *f*

agricultural settlement, agrarian settlement · Agrarsied(e)lung *f*, landwirtschaftliche (An)Sied(e)lung [*Das Ergebnis landwirtschaftlichen (An)Siedelns*]

agricultural settlement, agrarian settling, agrarian settlement, agricultural settling · landwirtschaftliches (An)Siedeln *n*

agricultural settlement law, agrarian settlement law · Agrar(an)sied(e)lungsrecht *n*, landwirtschaftliches (An)- Sied(e)lungsrecht

agricultural settling, agrarian settlement, agrarian settling, agrarian settlement · landwirtschaftliches (An)Siedeln *n*

agricultural site, agrarian location, agrarian site, agricultural location · Agrarstandort *m*, Landwirtschaftsstandort, landwirtschaftlicher Standort

agricultural society, agrarian society · Landwirtschaftsgesellschaft *f*

agricultural sociology, agrarian sociology · Agrarsoziologie *f*, Landwirtschaftssoziologie, landwirtschaftliche Soziologie

agricultural statute → agrarian law

agricultural structure, agrarian structure, agricultural composition, agrarian composition · Landwirtschaftsstruktur *f*, Agrarstruktur, Landwirtschaftsgefüge *n*, Agrargefüge, Landwirtschaftszusammensetzung *f*, Agrarzusammensetzung [*Die Gesamtheit der strukturellen Gegebenenheiten die die Wirtschafts-, Arbeits- und Lebensbedingungen der Landwirtschaft eines Gebietes auch in Verflechtung mit außerlandwirtschaftlichen Bereichen bestimmen*]

agricultural structure improvement, agrarian structure improvement · Agrarstrukturverbesserung *f*

agricultural structures, agricultural works, agricultural physical facilities · landwirtschaftliche Bauten *f*, landwirtschaftliche Baulichkeiten *fpl*, landwirtschaftliche (Bau)Werke *fpl*, landwirtschaftliche (bauliche) Anlagen, landwirtschaftliche Bauanlagen *fpl*

agricultural system (US); type of farming (Brit.) · Landwirtschaftssystem *n*, Agrarsystem

agricultural team, agrarian party, agricultural gang, agricultural crew · Landarbeiterkolonne *f*, Landarbeitertrupp *m*

agricultural territory, farming territory, cultivation area, cultivation territory, agrarian area, agrarian territory, agricultural area, farming area · Agrarfläche *f*, Agrargebiet *n*, landwirtschaftliche Fläche, landwirtschaftliches Gebiet, Anbaufläche, Anbaugebiet

agricultural town, agricultural city, agrotown, agro-city, peasant-city, peasanttown, rural agglomeration, farmer-town, farmer-city · Agrarstadt *f*, Agrostadt, Landwirtschaftsstadt [*Landwirtschaftliche Groß(an)sied(e)lung mit weiterverarbeitender Industrie und ausgebautem Dienstleistungsnetz*]

agricultural underpopulation, agrarian underpopulation · landwirtschaftliche Unterbevölkerung *f*, Agrarunterbevölkerung

agricultural unit, agrarian unit · landwirtschaftliche Wirtschaftseinheit *f*, Agrarwirtschaftseinheit

agricultural use, cultivation (of land), cultivation of fields, cultivation of soil, land cultivation, field cultivation, farming, soil cultivation · Anbau *m*, Bodenkultivierung *f*, Landkultivierung, Bodenkultur *f*, Feldbau

agricultural value [*The value which an agricultural property would have if it were subject to a perpetual covenant prohibiting its use otherwise than as agricultural property decreased by the value of any timber, trees or underwood growing thereon*] · Agrarwert *m*, landwirtschaftlicher Wert

**agricultural village, **agro-village, peasant village, agrarian village · Agrardorf *n*, Bauerndorf, Landwirtschaftsdorf, landwirtschaftliches Dorf

**agricultural water use, **agrarian water use · landwirtschaftliche Wassernutzung *f*

**agricultural work, **farm work, agrarian work · Landarbeit *f*, Agrararbeit

**agricultural worker, **agrarian worker, farm worker; labourer (Brit.) · Landarbeiter *m*

**agricultural works, **agricultural physical facilities, agricultural structures · landwirtschaftliche Bauten *f*, landwirtschaftliche Baulichkeiten *fpl*, landwirtschaftliche (Bau)Werke *npl*, landwirtschaftliche (bauliche) Anlagen, landwirtschaftliche Bauanlagen *fpl*

agriculture · Landwirtschaft *f*

agri deserti [*Latin*] · Ödländereien *fpl*

agrimensor [*Latin*] · römischer Feldmesser *m*

agro-town → agricultural town

**agro-village, **peasant village, agrarian village, agricultural village · Agrardorf *n*, Bauerndorf, Landwirtschaftsdorf, landwirtschaftliches Dorf

**aid, **help · Hilfe *f*

**aid; **auxidium, adjutorium, subsidium [*Latin*] [*In feudal law. A kind of pecuniary tribute paid by a vassal to his lord, on occasions of peculiar emergency, and which was one of the incidents of tenure in chivalry, or by knight's service*] · Hilfsgeld *n*

**AIDA, **analysis of interconnected decision areas · Analyse *f* verknüpfter Entscheidungsbereiche, Untersuchung *f* verknüpfter Entscheidungsbereiche

aided self-help · unterstützte Selbsthilfe *f*

aided self-help housing [*Utilizing leisure time when some form of aid from the community and other source so that men may improve his shelter*] · subventionierte Bauselbsthilfe *f*, subventionierte bauliche Selbsthilfe, subventionierte Selbsthilfe im Wohn(ungs)bau

aider · Helfershelfer *m*

air advertisement · Luftwerbung *f*, Luftreklame *f*

**air bill of lading, **air waybill, air consignment note · Luftfrachtbrief *m*

air brush · Luftpinsel *m* [*Kartographie*]

**air chart, **aeronautical chart · Fliegerkarte *f* [*militärisch*]

**air city, **air town · flugzeuggerechte Stadt *f*

air commuter · Flugpendler *m*

air commuting · Flugpendeln *n*

air-conditioning contractor · Klimaanlagenunternehmer *m*

**air consignment note, **air bill of lading, air waybill · Luftfrachtbrief *m*

**air contamination, **atmospheric pollution, atmospheric contamination, air pollution · Luftverunreinigung *f*, Luftverseuchung, Luftverschmutzung [*Das Einfallen fester, flüssiger und/oder gasförmiger luftfremder Stoffe in Bodennähe*]

air corporation → air(ways) corporation

air corridor · Luftkorridor *m*

aircraft noise · Fluglärm *m*

**aircraft noise law, **aircraft noise statute, aircraft noise act · Fluglärmgesetz *n*

**air domain, **air space · Luftgebiet *n*, Luftraum *f*

**air domain law, **air space law · Luftrecht *n*

**air domain sovereignty, **air space sovereignty · Lufthoheit *f*

**air freedom, **freedom of the air · Luftfreiheit *f*, Freiheit des Luftraumes, Freiheit des Luftgebietes

airfreight broker · Luftfrachtmakler *m*

air in-commuter · Flugeinpendler *m*, Flugzupendler

air in-commuting · Flugeinpendeln *n*, Flugzupendeln

**air navigation chart, **aeronautical chart · Luftfahrtkarte *f*, Luftnavigationskarte [*zivil*]

air obstruction · Luftentziehung *f*

air out-commuter · Flugauspendler *m*, Flugwegpendler

air out-commuting · Flugauspendeln *n*, Flugwegpendeln

**air photogrammetry, **aerial surveying, aerial photogrammetry, air surveying · Luftbildmessung *f*, Luftbildtechnik *f*, Aerophotogrammetrie *f*, Luftphotogrammetrie, Luftvermessung

**air photo(graph), **flight photo(graph), aerial photo(graph) · Luftbild *n*, Luftaufnahme *f*, Luftphoto *n*

**air photographer, **aerial photographer · Luftphotograph *m*

**air photography, **aerophotography, aerial photography · Luftphotographie *f*

**airphoto interpretation, **aerial photograph(ic) interpretation, interpretation of aerial photography · Luftbildauswertung *f*, Luftaufnahmeauswertung, Luftphotoauswertung

**airphoto interpreter, **aerial photograph interpreter · Luftbildauswerter *m*, Luftaufnahmeauswerter, Luftphotoauswerter

**airphoto research, **aerial photograph research · Luftbildforschung *f*, Luftaufnahmeforschung

air pollution, air contamination, atmospheric pollution, atmospheric contamination · Luftverunreinigung f, Luftverseuchung, Luftverschmutzung [*Das Einfallen fester, flüssiger und/oder gasförmiger luftfremder Stoffe in Bodennähe*]

air pollution control, air pollution prevention, atmospheric pollution control, atmospheric pollution prevention, air quality control, clean air control · Luftreinhaltung f

air pollution prevention → air quality control

airport planning, aerodrome planning · Flughafenplanung f

airport town, airport city, aerodrome town, aerodrome city · Flughafenstadt f

airport umland, aerodrome umland · Flughafenumland f

air quality act, air quality statute, air quality law, clean air statute, clean air law, clean air act · Luftreinhaltungsgesetz n

air quality code, clean air code · Luftreinhaltungsordnung f

air quality control, clean air control, air pollution control, air pollution prevention, atmospheric pollution control, atmospheric pollution prevention · Luftreinhaltung f

air quality law, clean air law · Luftreinhaltungsrecht n

air quality legislation, air quality lawmaking, clean air legislation, clean air lawmaking · Luftreinhaltungsgesetzgebung f

air quality plan, clean air plan · Luftreinhaltungsplan m, Luftreinhalteplan

air quality territory, air quality area, clean air area, clean air territory · Luftreinhaltungsgebiet n, Luftreinhaltegebiet

air renewal · Lufterneuerung f

air sampling · Luftprobe(n)nahme f

air shelter gallery · Luftschutzstollen m

air space, air domain · Luftgebiet n, Luftraum m

air space law, air domain law · Luftrecht n

air space sovereignty, air domain sovereignty · Lufthoheit f

air supply, supply of air · Luftversorgung f

air survey camera, aerial survey camera · Luftmeßbildkamera f

air surveying, air photogrammetry, aerial surveying, aerial photogrammetry · Luftbildmessung f, Luftbildtechnik f, Aerophotogrammetrie f, Luftphotogrammetrie, Luftvermessung

air topography, aerotopography, aerial topography · Lufttopographie f

air town, air city · flugzeuggerechte Stadt f

air traffic, air transport(ation) · Luftverkehr m

air traffic act, air traffic statute, air traffic law, air transport(ation) statute, air transport(ation) law, air transport(ation) act · Luftverkehrsgesetz n

air traffic law, air transport(ation) law · Luftverkehrsrecht n

air traffic safety · Flugsicherheit f

air transport(ation), air traffic · Luftverkehr m

air travel spatial structure, air travel space structure · Luftreisen-Raumstruktur f

air waybill, air consignment note, air bill of lading · Luftfrachtbrief m

air(ways) corporation · Luftfahrtgesellschaft f

aisiamentum, aysiamentum [*Latin*]; aise(ment) [*Norman French*]; easement · Grunddienstbarkeit f [*Ein Grundstück kann zugunsten der jeweiligen Eigentümers eines anderen Grundstücks in der Weise belastet werden, daß dieser das Grundstück in einzelnen Beziehungen benutzen darf oder daß auf dem Grundstück gewisse Handlungen nicht vorgenommen werden dürfen oder daß die Ausübung eines Rechtes ausgeschlossen ist, das sich aus dem Eigentum an dem belasteten Grundstück dem anderen Grundstück gegenüber ergibt*]

albom, redditus albi [*Latin*]; blanch holding, blanch farm, blench holding, blanch firme, blanch rent, blanch fe(a)rme, white farm, white rent, white fe(a)rme, white rent; alba firma, firma blanca, firma alba [*Latin*]; [*Rent payable in silver, or white money, as distinguished from that which was anciently paid in corn or provisions, called black mail, or black rent*] · Silberpacht(zins) f, (m), Silberzins, Bodenzins in Silbergeld

alderman · (Gemeinde)Älteste m, Ratsherr, Magistratsrat

aldermanry · Wahlbezirk m eines Ratsherren

aleatory contract, risky contract, uncertain contract · zufallabhängiger Vertrag m, ungewisser Vertrag, riskanter Vertrag

aleatory variable, random variable, stochastic variable, variate · stochastische Variable f, Zufallsvariable

ale-bedrip, ale-bidrip(e), ale-bed(e)repe, ale-bedrape, ale-bidrepe · befohlene Ernearbeit f bei der Bier verabreicht wurde [*Fronhofarbeit*]

ale-kenner — allied company

ale-kenner; gustator cerevisiae [*Latin*]; ale-taster, ale-conner, ale-founder [*This was the title of an officer formerly appointed under the Assize of Bread and Ale (1267) to inspect the quality and regulate the sale of those commodities in every borough and manor*] · Bierkoster *m*, Bieraufseher, Bierprober

Alemannic law · alemannisches Recht *n*

alien · Ausländer *m*

alienability → (ab)alienability

alienable → (ab)alienable

alien ami, alien friend, alien amy · Freundausländer *m*

to alien(ate) → to (ab)alienate

alienation → (ab)alienation

alienation against anticipation → (ab)alienation against anticipation

alienation authority → (ab)alienation authority

alienation contract → (ab)alienation contract

alienation deed → (ab)alienation deed

alienation duty → (ab)alienation duty

alienation in fee simple → (ab)alienation in fee simple

alienation in mortmain → (ab)alienation in mortmain

alienation mode → (ab)alienation mode

alienation obligation → (ab)alienation obligation

alienation period → (ab)alienation period

alienation permission → (ab)alienation permission

alienation power → (ab)alienation power

alienation restraint → (ab)alienation restraint

alienation right → (ab)alienation right

alien by birth · Ausländer *m* von Geburt

alien certificate of inheritance, alien inheritance certificate · Fremdenrechtserbschein *m*, Fremdenrechtserbattest *n*, Fremdenrechtserbbescheinigung *f*

alienee → (ab)alienee

alien enemy, enemy alien, alien enemi; hostile foreigner [*India*] · Feindausländer *m*, feindlicher Ausländer

alien friend, alien amy, alien ami · Freundausländer *m*

alien inheritance certificate, alien certificate of inheritance · Fremdenrechtserbschein *m*, Fremdenrechtserbattest *n*, Fremdenrechtserbbescheinigung *f*

alien law, law applied to aliens, law of aliens, law on aliens · Ausländerrecht *n*, Fremdenrecht *n* [*Rechtssätze, die einen Ausländer anders behandeln als einen Inländer*]

alien law, alien act, alien statute · Ausländergesetz *n*, Fremdengesetz *n*

alienor → (ab)alienor

alien property administration · Feindvermögensverwaltung *f*, Verwaltung feindlichen Vermögens

alien property custodian, custodian of enemy property · Feindvermögensverwahrer *m*, Verwahrer feindlichen Vermögens, Verwahrer feindlichen Eigentums, Feindeigentumsverwahrer

alien without a home country · heimatloser Ausländer *m*

alimony; aliment [*Scots law*] [*The allowance which is made to a woman for her support out of her husband's estate when she is under the necessity of living apart from him*] · Unterhalt *m*

all-age school · Gesamtschule *f*

all charges deducted, deducting all charges · abzüglich aller Unkosten, alle Unkosten abgezogen

all-day parker, long-term parker · Dauerparker *m*

allegation, averment, assertion [*A statement of fact made in any proceeding, as, for instance, in a pleading, particularly a statement of charge which is, as yet, unproved*] · Behauptung *f*, Bekräftigung

to allege, to aver, to assert [*To prove or justify a plea; to make an averment*] · behaupten

allegiance, feudality; fidelitas feudalis [*Latin*]; fealty, fidelity, feodality [*It was due by feudal tenants to their lords*] · Leh(e)n(s)treue *f*

allegiance, lawful obedience, legal obedience · gesetzmäßiger Gehorsam *m*

alleging, averring, asserting · Behaupten *n*

all-embracing law · allumfassendes Recht *n*

all-embracing liability · Haftpflicht *f* für alle Wagnisse, Haftpflicht für alle Risiken, Haftung *f* für alle Wagnisse, Haftung für alle Risiken, Haftbarkeit *f* für alle Wagnisse, Haftbarkeit für alle Risiken

alleviation of poverty, poverty alleviation · Linderung *f* der Armut

alley (US) · Hintergasse *f*

allied company, associated company, affiliate(d company) · verbundene Gesellschaft *f* [*Eine Gesellschaft, die eine verbundene Person ist*]

all-in bid, all-in offer, all-in tender, turnkey bid, turnkey offer, turnkey tender; all-in (bid) proposal, turnkey (bid) proposal (US) · Angebot *n* für Entwurf und Bau

all-in service contract, turnkey contract [*The contractor carries out design and construction*] · Vertrag *m* für schlüsselfertige Erstellung

all-integer algorism · Algorithmus *m* II von Gomory

allmend, common field, commonable land, commonable field, public land, community land, communal land, mark; county (US); waste of the manor, (manorial) waste [*obsolete*]; common (land), corporate land · Al(l)mend(e) *f,* Allmeind *f,* Allmid *f,* Allmein(i) *f,* Allmen *f,* Allmig *f,* Allmand(e) *f,* Allmat *f,* All(ge)meinde *f,* Allmandgut *n,* Allmente *f,* (Feld)Mark *f,* Gemarkung *f,* Kommunalboden *m,* Gemeindeboden *m,* Bürgerland *n,* bürgerliches Nutzungsland *n,* Gemeindeland *n,* Gemeinheit(sland) *f, (n),* Kommunalland *n,* unverteilter Gemeindegrund *m,* ländliches Gemeingut, Gemein(de)anger *m,* Gemeindeimmobilien *fpl*; Korporationsland *n* [*Schweiz*]

all-negro town, all-negro city · Negerstadt *f*

to allocate · zuweisen

allocation · Zuweisung *f*

allocation equilibrium, equilibrium of allocation · Zuweisungsgleichgewicht *n*

allocation mechanism · Zuweisungsmechanismus *m*

allocation of fund, fund allocation · Mittelzuweisung *f,* Geldzuweisung, Finanzzuweisung, Fondszuweisung

allocation of space, space allocation · Raumzuweisung *f*

allocation of urban land, urban land allocation · Stadtlandzuweisung *f*

allocation process · Zuweisungsvorgang *m*

allocation theory · Zuweisungstheorie *f*

al(l)odial, absolute; al(l)odian [*obsolete*]; odhal [*In old English law*] · absolut, leh(e)n(s)frei, allodial, erbeigen, unbeschränkt, zinsfrei [*Im freien, eigentümlichen Besitz nach römischem Recht*]

al(l)odial castle · allodiale Burg *f,* Allodialburg

al(l)odial chattel, absolute estate, absolute property, absolute chattel, al(l)odial ownership, absolute ownership, al(l)odium; franc-al(l)eu [*French law*]; al(l)odial estate, al(l)odial property [*An estate held without service or acknowledg(e)ment of any superior, as among the early Teutonic peoples, opposed to feud(um)*] · Allodialgut *n,* allodiales Eigentum *n,* allodiales Erbgut, allodiales Eigengut, leh(e)n(s)freies Eigentum, leh(e)n(s)freies Erbgut, leh(e)n(s)freies Eigentum, absolutes Eigentum, absolutes Erbgut, absolutes Eigengut, erbeigenes Eigentum, erbeigenes Eigengut, erbeigenes Erbgut, unbeschränktes Erbgut, unbeschränktes Eigentum, unbeschränktes Eigengut, (zins)freies Erbgut, (zins)freies Eigentum, (zins)freies Eigengut, uneingeschränktes Erbgut, uneingeschränktes Eigentum, uneingeschränktes Eigengut, unbegrenztes Erbgut, unbegrenztes Eigentum, unbegrenztes Eigengut, Allodialeigentum, Allodialvermögen *n,* Al(l)odium *n,* Alodis *n,* Alode *f,* Alodus *m,* Alaudium *n,* Vollgut, echtes Eigen(gut) *n,* lediges Eigen(gut), Ludeigen(gut)

al(l)odial heiress, al(l)odial heir female · Allodialerbin *f*

al(l)odial heir (male) · Allodialerbe *m*

allodialism, al(l)odial system [*As opposed to the feudal system*] · Allodialsystem *n*

allodialist → allodiary

allodiality, al(l)odial tenure [*The quality of being al(l)odial, of holding or being held in free ownership*] · Leh(e)n(s)freiheit *f*

al(l)odial land, free land, land held in absolute ownership, absolute ownership land, alody, inheritable land, al(l)odium · allodiales Land *n,* erbeigenes Land, leh(e)n(s)freies Land, absolutes Land, unbeschränktes Land, uneingeschränktes Land, unbegrenztes Land, (zins)freies Land, Allodialland

al(l)odial (land) owner → allodiary

al(l)odial proprietor → allodiary

al(l)odial system, allodialism [*As opposed to the feudal system*] · Allodialsystem *n*

al(l)odial tenure, allodiality [*The quality of being al(l)odial, of holding or being held in free ownership*] · Leh(e)n(s)freiheit *f*

al(l)odian [*obsolete*] → al(l)odial

allodiary, allodialist, al(l)odial (land) owner, absolute (land) owner, exclusive (land) owner, absolute proprietor, exclusive proprietor, al(l)odial proprietor, free man, holder of an allodium; liber homo, homo liber [*Latin*] · absoluter Eigentümer *m,* unbeschränkter Eigentümer, Alleineigentümer, Freigutentümer, Allodialeigentümer, freier Mann, Freie, uneingeschränkter Eigentümer

allodification · Allodialisierung *f,* Allodifizierung, Allodifikation *f* [*Umwandlung von Leh(e)n(s)gütern in Freigüter*]

al(l)odium; franc-al(l)eu [*French law*]; al(l)odial estate, al(l)odial property, al(l)odial chattel, absolute estate, absolute property, absolute chattel, allodial

al(l)odium — alms-giving 50

ownership, absolute ownership [*An estate held without service or acknowledg(e)ment of any superior, as among the early Teutonic peoples, opposed to feud(um)*] · Allodialgut *n*, allodiales Eigentum *n*, allodiales Erbgut, allodiales Eigengut, leh(e)n(s)freies Eigentum, leh(e)n(s)freies Erbgut, leh(e)n(s)freies Eigengut, absolutes Eigentum, absolutes Erbgut, absolutes Eigengut, erbeigenes Eigentum, erbeigenes Eigengut, erbeigenes Erbgut, unbeschränktes Erbgut, unbeschränktes Eigentum, unbeschränktes Eigengut, (zins)freies Erbgut, (zins)freies Eigentum, (zins)freies Eigengut, uneingeschränktes Erbgut, uneingeschränktes Eigentum, uneingeschränktes Eigengut, unbegrenztes Erbgut, unbegrenztes Eigentum, unbegrenztes Eigengut, Allodialeigentum, Allodialvermögen *n*, Al(l)odium *n*, Alodis *n*, Alode *f*, Alodus *m*, Alaudium *n*, Vollgut, echtes Eigen(gut) *n*, lediges Eigen(gut), Ludeigen(gut), Alleingut

al(l)odium → al(l)odial land

allonge · Allonge *f* [*Wechsel*]

all or nothing allotment, all or nothing apportionment [*transportation planning*] · Alles-oder-nichts-Zuteilung *f*

to allot, to apportion, to portion out [*To divide and distribute proportionally or according to a plan*] · zuteilen

allotable, apportionable · zuteilbar

alloted proportion · Anteilziffer *f*

allotment · Verteilung *f* durch Los, Verlosung, Auslosung

allotment, apportionment · Zuteilung *f*

allotment · Kontingent *n*

allotment certificate, apportionment certificate · Zuteilungsbescheinigung *f*, Zuteilungsschein *m*, Zuteilungsattest *n*

allotment garden, small garden · Kleingarten *m*, Schrebergarten

allotment holder, occupier of a small portion of land [*A cultivator who, while he has some spare time and money to cultivate land, is partially employed in some other occupation or business*] · (landwirtschaftlicher) Parzellenbesitzer *m*

allotment letter, letter of allotment, scrip (certificate) · Interimsschein *m* [*Für neuausgegebene Wertpapiere*]

allotment of land use, land use apportionment, apportionment of land use, land use allotment · Flächenzuteilung *f*, Bodenzuteilung, Landzuteilung

allotment of space, apportionment of space, space apportionment, space allotment · Raumzuteilung *f*

allotment of water, apportionment of water, water allotment, water apportionment · Wasserzuteilung *f*

allotment planning, apportionment planning · Zuteilungsplanung *f*

Allotments Act · Kleinparzellengesetz *n* [*England*]

allotment system → (garden) allotment system

to allow [*appeal*] · stattgeben [*Berufung*]

allowance, bonus · Zulage *f*, Zuschlag *m*, Sondervergütung *f*

allowance · Zuschuß *m*

allowance, subvention · Beihilfe *f*, Subvention *f*

allowance for bad debt(s) · Forderungswertberichtigung *f*

allowance for children, children allowance, family bonus, family allowance · Kindergeld *n*, Kinderbeihilfe *f*

allowance for risk, discount for risk · Gewißheitsäquivalent *n*, Sicherheitsabschlag *m* bei Marktdaten

allowance of wood, wood right, wood interest, wood allowance · Holzberechtigung *f*, Holz(bezugs)recht *n*

allowance plan, subvention plan · Subventionsplan *m*, Beihilfeplan

all-purpose open space · Allgemeinfläche *f*

all-purpose zone, zone of mixed functions · Mischgebiet *n*, Mischbaugebiet, gemischte Baufläche *f* [*Es dient dem Wohnen und der Unterbringung von Gewerbebetrieben, die das Wohnen nicht wesentlich stören*]

all-risks insurance → (contractor's) all-risks insurance

all-risks policy → (contractor's) all-risks policy

all-the-year-round camping site, all-the-year-round caravan site, permanent camping site, permanent caravan site · Dauercampingplatz *m*

alluvion, alluvium, accretion (of land), land accretion · (Land)Anschwemmung *f*, (Land)Anschutt *m*, (Land)Akkreszenz *f*, (Land)Gewinnung durch Anschwemmung, Alluvion *n*, Alluvium *n*, Zulandung

alm [*In old English law*] · kirchliches Eigen *n*

almoner, poor law overseer, poor law guardian, parish officer, overseer (of the poor), guardian (of the poor) · Armenvater *m*, Armenaufseher *m*, Armenpfleger *m*

almonry of a city, almshouse of a city, city almshouse, city almonry, poorhouse of a city, city poorhouse · städtisches Armenhaus *n*

alms-giving · Almosenspenden *n*

almshouse, almonry poorhouse [*A house given by charitable person(s) for poor persons to live in free of charge*] · Armenspital *n*, Spital für Arme, privates Armenhaus *n*

almshouse-rate · (örtliche) Armenhaussteuer *f*, gemeindliche Armenhaussteuer, kommunale Armenhaussteuer, lokale Armenhaussteuer

alms tenure (of land) → (free) alms tenure (of land)

alod, family land, heir land, ethel(-land), erf-land · Erbland *n*, erbliches Land

alody → al(l)odial land

alone, sole, single, not married · ledig

alta tenura [*Latin*]; highest tenure · höchstes Leh(e)n *n*

to alter, to convert · umbauen

alterable, convertible · umbaubar

alterable, changeable, variable · (ab)änderungsfähig, umänderungsfähig

alterable will, changeable will · (ab)änderungsfähiges Testament *n*, umänderungsfähiges Testament

to alterate, to vary, to change · (ab)ändern, umändern, verändern

alterated, varied, changed · (ab)geändert, umgeändert

alteration, variation, change · (Ab)Änderung *f*, Umänderung, Veränderung

alteration → (building) alteration

alteration by equity, variation by equity, change by equity · Umänderung *f* durch Billigkeit, (Ab)Änderung durch Billigkeit, Veränderung durch Billigkeit

alteration clause, variation clause, change clause · (Ab)Änderungsklausel *f*, Umänderungsklausel, Veränderungsklausel

alteration contract, contract of variation, contract of alteration, contract of change, change contract, variation contract · (Ab)Änderungsvertrag *m*, Umänderungsvertrag, Veränderungsvertrag

alteration list, alteration register, alteration registry, change list, change register, change registry, variation list, variation register, variation registry · Veränderungsliste *f*, Veränderungsverzeichnis *n*, (Ab)Änderungsliste, (Ab)Änderungsverzeichnis, Umänderungsliste, Umänderungsverzeichnis

alteration markup, markup for conversion, markup for alteration, conversion markup · Umbauzuschlag *m*

alteration of building lines, variation of building lines, change of building lines · (Bau)Fluchtlinien(ab)änderung *f*

alteration of law, law change, law variation, law alteration, change of law, variation of law · Rechts(ab)änderung *f*, Rechtsumänderung, Rechtsveränderung

alteration of structural design, structural design variation, structural design alteration, structural design change, variation of structural design, change of structural design · (Ab)Änderung *f* des Bauentwurfs, Umänderung des Bauentwurfs, Veränderung des Bauentwurfs, Bauentwurfs(ab)änderung, Bauentwurfsumänderung, Bauentwurfsveränderung

alteration of (the) design, change of (the) design, design change, design alteration, design variation, variation of (the) design · Entwurfs(ab)änderung *f*, Entwurfsveränderung, Entwurfsumänderung, (Ab)Änderung des Entwurfs, Umänderung des Entwurfs, Veränderung des Entwurfs

alteration register, alteration registry, change list, change register, change registry, variation list, variation register, variation registry, alteration list · Veränderungsliste *f*, Veränderungsverzeichnis *n*, (Ab)Änderungsliste, (Ab)Änderungsverzeichnis, Umänderungsliste, Umänderungsverzeichnis

altered, converted · umgebaut

altered dwelling unit, converted dwelling unit, altered housing unit, converted housing unit, altered living unit, converted living unit, altered apartment, converted apartment (US); altered dwelling, converted dwelling, altered tenement, converted tenement, altered residence, converted residence · Umbauwohnung *f*, umgebaute Wohnung

altering, converting · Umbauen *n*

alternate bid, alternate offer, alternate tender; alternate (bid) proposal (US) · Alternativangebot *n*

alternate member · Ersatzmitglied *n*

alternative accommodation · Ersatzunterkunft *f*

alternative approach · Alternativansatz *m*

alternative attraction · Alternativanziehung *f*

alternative bequest, alternative legacy · Auswahl(fahrnis)vermächtnis *n*, Auswahl(fahrnis)legat *n*, Auswahlfahrhabevermächtnis, Auswahlfahrhabelegat

alternative clause · Alternativklausel *f*

alternative contract [*A contract whose terms allow of performance by the doing of either one of several acts at the election of the party from whom performance is due*] · Alternativvertrag *m*

alternative cost(s), opportunity cost(s) · Schattenkosten *f*, Alternativkosten, Opportunitätskosten [*Kosten die nicht*

alternative date — ami

oder nicht sofort als solche entstehen, sondern ihren Ausdruck in der verpaßten Gelegenheit einer noch vorteilhafteren Gestaltung finden]

alternative date · Ausweichtermin *m*, Ausweichdatum *n*, Ersatztermin, Ersatzdatum

alternative hypothesis, non-null hypothesis · Gegenhypothese *f* [*Statistik*]

alternative item · Alternativposition *f*, Wahlposition

alternative obligation · Alternativverpflichtung *f*

alternative plan · Alternativplan *m*

alternative planning · Alternativplanung *f*

alternative proposal · Alternativvorschlag *m*

alternative scheme · Wahlprojekt *n*, Wahlvorschlag *m* [*Ideenwettbewerb*]

alternative time period, alternative time (allowed), alternative term, alternative (fixed) period (of time) · (bestimmte) Alternativzeit *f*, (bestimmter) Alternativzeitraum *m*, Alternativfrist *f*

to alter slightly, to change slightly, to vary slightly, to modify · geringfügig (ab)ändern, geringfügig umändern, geringfügig verändern

altum mare [*Latin*]; high sea · hohe See *f*

alveus derelictus [*Latin*]; derelict stream bed · verlassenes Flußbett *n*

amalgamation (of companies) · Zusammenschluß *m* von Firmen, Firmenzusammenschluß

amalgamation of contractors · Unternehmerzusammenschluß *m*

amalgamation of titles, concentration of titles, aggregation of titles, title amalgamation, title aggregation, title concentration · (Rechts)Titelzusammenlegung *f*

ambience, surroundings · Umgebung *f*

ambient noise · Umgebungslärm *m*

ambiguity, obscure meaning, doubtfulness of meaning, uncertainty of meaning, obscurity of meaning, uncertain meaning, doubtful meaning · unklare Bedeutung *f*, Zweideutigkeit *f*

ambit [*A space surrounding a house, castle, town, etc.*] · Umkreis *m*

ambit [*The limits or circumference of a power or jurisdiction*] · Zuständigkeitsumfang *m*

ambulatory, capable of being revoked, capable of revocation, able of being revoked, able of revocation, qualified of being revoked, qualified of revocation, during pleasure, revocable, at will, revokable · auf Widerruf, widerruflich, widerrufbar, einvernehmlich geduldet

ameliorating waste [*Alteration which improves the land, such as converting dilapidated store buildings into dwellings or a farm into a market-garden, constitutes what is paradoxically termed ameliorating waste*] · werterhöhende Substanzveränderung *f*

amenability, liability to answer to law, amenableness [*The quality of being amenable*] · Verantwortlichkeit *f* vor dem Gesetz, Rechenschaftspflicht *f* vor dem Gesetz

amenable, subject to answer to law, liable to answer to law, responsible to law, answerable to law, liable to be brought before any jurisdiction · verantwortlich vor dem Gesetz, rechenschaftspflichtig vor dem Gesetz

to amend [*To correct a defect in a writ or pleadings, or in criminal proceedings*] · berichtigen, korrigieren, verbessern, richtigstellen, (ab)ändern

amendment · Zusatzartikel *m*, Ergänzung *f*

amendment [*Correction of a defect in a writ or pleadings, or in criminal proceedings*] · Berichtigung *f*

amendment [*A revision or change proposed or made in a bill or law*] · Abänderung *f*, Novelle *f*

amendment act, amendment law, amendment statute · Änderungsgesetz *n*, Novellengesetz

amendment column · (Ab)Änderungsgesetzspalte *f* [*Grundbuch*]

amendment document · (Ab)Änderungsurkunde *f* [*Hypothek*]

amendments and supplements to the general conditions · Zusätze *mpl* und Ergänzungen *fpl* der allgemeinen Bedingungen

amenities, modern conveniences, mode cons · Wohnkomfort *m*

amenity · Erhaltung *f* der natürlichen Umwelt, natürliche Umwelterhaltung

amenity, convenience [*In real property law, such circumstances, in regard to situation, outlook, access to a water course, or the like, as enhance the pleasantness or desirability of an estate for purposes of residence, or contribute to the pleasure and enjoyment of the occupants, rather than to their indispensable needs*] · Annehmlichkeit *f*

amenity area, amenity territory · Gebiet *n* von landschaftlichem Reiz

amenity need, amenity requirement · Wohnkomfortbedürfnis *n*

amenity resource · Wohlstandsbaustein *m*

American Title Association · (Bundes)Verband *m* der Eigentumsprüfer der USA

ami → (prochein) amy

amicable compositeur — amount of restitution

amicable compositeur, conciliator · Schlichter *m*

amicable composition (of differences), (amicable) arrangement, mutuality, (pacific) settlement, accommodation, mutual agreement, accord · Einigung *f*, Willenseinigung, gütliche Regelung, Einvernehmen *n*, gütliche Einigung, Vergleich *m*, Konsensus *m*, Übereinstimmung, Einverständnis *n*

amortization, amortisation, amortizement, amortisement, (ab)alienation in mortmain; amortizatio [*Latin*] [*The action of (ab)alienating land(s) or tenements in mortmain*] · Veräußerung *f* an die tote Hand

amortization, amortisation [*The extinction of a debt, or of any pecuniary liability, especially by means of a sinking fund*] · Amortisation *f*, Tilgung *f*

amortization (US); accelerated depreciation [*Depreciation at a larger than usual rate*] · beschleunigte Abschreibung *f*

amortization act, amortization law, amortization statute · Amortisationsgesetz *n*, Tilgungsgesetz

amortization bill, amortizing bill, bill of amortization · Amortisationsbescheinigung *f*, Tilgungsbescheinigung, Tilgungsschein *m*, Amortisationsschein, Amortisationsattest *n*, Tilgungsattest

amortization credit, amortisation credit · Tilgungskredit *m*, Amortisationskredit

amortization debt, sinking fund debt, debt redeemable in instal(l)ments · Tilgungsschuld *f*, Amortisationsschuld

amortization land charge, amortisation land charge · Amortisationsgrundschuld *f*, Tilgungsgrundschuld

amortization law, amortization statute, amortization act · Amortisationsgesetz *n*, Tilgungsgesetz

amortization mortgage, amortizing mortgage, annuity mortgage, amortisation mortgage, amortising mortgage · Amortisationshypothek *f*, Tilgungshypothek, Annuitätenhypothek, Annuitätshypothek

amortization schedule, amortization table, amortisation schedule, amortisation table · Amortisationstabelle *f*, Tilgungstabelle

amortization schedule, amortizing plan, amortizing schedule, amortization plan, amortisation schedule, amortisation plan · Amortisationsplan *m*, Tilgungsplan

amortization statute, amortization act, amortization law · Amortisationsgesetz *n*, Tilgungsgesetz

to amortize, to amortise, to (ab)alienate in mortmain, to convey to mortmain · veräußern an die tote Hand

amortized, amortised, held in mortmain, (ab)alienated in mortmain, conveyed to mortmain · veräußert an die tote Hand

amortizing, amortising, conveying to mortmain, (ab)alienating in mortmain · Veräußern *n* an die tote Hand

amortizing bill, bill of amortization, amortization bill, amortisation bill · Amortisationsbescheinigung *f*, Tilgungsbescheinigung, Tilgungsschein *m*, Amortisationsschein, Amortisationsattest *n*, Tilgungsattest

amortizing loan, amortization loan, amortisation loan · Amortisationsdarlehe(e)n *n*

amortizing plan, amortizing schedule, amortization plan, amortization schedule, amortisation schedule, amortisation plan · Amortisationsplan *m*, Tilgungsplan

amotion, removal; amotio [*Latin*] · Absetzung *f*, Entsetzung, Enthebung, Untersagung, Entziehung, Ausschluß *m*

amotion, wrongful taking of personal chattels; amotio [*Latin*] · widerrechtliche Fahrnisentziehung *f*, widerrechtlicher Fahrnisentzug, widerrechtlicher Fahrhabeentzug *m*

amotion from (a) membership, removal from (a) membership · Mitgliedschaftsausschluß *m*, Mitgliedschaftsentziehung *f*

amotion from (an) office, deprivation of office, removal from (an) office · Amtsabsetzung *f*, Amtsenthebung, Amtsentsetzung, Amtsentziehung, Amtsausschluß *m*, Amtsuntersagung

amount in controversy, amount in dispute, value in dispute, disputed value; jurisdictional amount (US) · Streitwert *m*

amount of cost(s), cost(s) amount · Kostenbetrag *m*

amount of gain, amount of profit · Gewinnbetrag *m*, Profitbetrag

amount of indemnification, amount of compensation, amount of damages, amount of indemnity · Entschädigungsbetrag *m*, Schadenersatzbetrag

amount of liability, scope of liability · Haftungsumfang *m*

amount of light, light quantity, light quantum, light amount, quantum of light, quantity of light · Lichtmenge *f*

amount of money, money amount · Geldbetrag *m*

amount of profit, amount of gain · Gewinnbetrag *m*, Profitbetrag

amount of property · Vermögensbestand *m*

amount of restitution, amount of reimbursement, amount of refunding,

amount usually put to sinking fund — animal ecology 54

amount of recovery · Ersetzungsbetrag m, Erstattungsbetrag, Abgeltungsbetrag, Vergütungsbetrag

amount usually put to sinking fund, yearly instal(l)ment of redemption, annual instal(l)ment of redemption · jährliche Tilgungsrate f, jährliche Tilgungsquote, jährliche Amortisationsrate, jährliche Amortisationsquote

to amove, to remove; amovere [Latin]; to depose [From membership or office] · absetzen, entsetzen, entheben, untersagen, entziehen, ausschließen

to amove, to remove from (a) membership; amovere [Latin] · ausschließen [von einer Mitgliedschaft]

amply · umfassend

amusement arcade (Brit.); penny arcade (US) · Spielhalle f

amy → (prochein) amy

analysis, study · Analyse f, Untersuchung f

analysis of cost(s) variances, study of cost(s) variances · Kostenabweichungsanalyse f, Kostenabweichungsuntersuchung f

analysis of environment, study of environment, environmental study environmental analysis · Umweltanalyse f, Umweltuntersuchung

analysis of interconnected decision areas, AIDA, study of interconnected decision areas · Analyse f verknüpfter Entscheidungsbereiche, Untersuchung f verknüpfter Entscheidungsbereiche

analysis of migration, study of migration, migration analysis, migration study · Wanderungsanalyse f, Wanderungsuntersuchung f

analysis of regression, regression analysis, study of regression, regression study · Regressionsanalyse f, Regressionsuntersuchung f

analysis of site, study of site, site analysis, site study, analysis of location, study of location, location(al) analysis, location(al) study [The evaluation of the qualities of a site by comparison with those of other comparable sites] · Standortanalyse f, Standortuntersuchung f

analytic(al) jurisprudence · analytische Jurisprudenz f, analytische Rechtslehre [Sie behandelt die Grundlehren und Grundbegriffe des Rechts]

analytic(al) optimizing model · analytisches Optimierungsmodell n

analytic(al) regression · analytische Regression f

analytic(al) technique · Analysentechnik f

ancestry, lineage, descent · Abstammung f

ancestor, progenitor, ascendant [Not to be confused with "predecessor" = Vorgänger] · Vorfahre m, Ahn m

anchorage → (duty of) anchorage

ancient custom · alter Brauch m

ancient demesne, copyhold tenure by custom of ancient demesne; dominium antiquum, antiquum dominicum, vetus patrimonium domini [Latin]; customary freehold [Such land(s) as were entered by William I., in Doomesday-book, under the title "De Terra Regis"; and which were held later by a species of copyhold tenure] · altes Krongut(leh(e)n) n

ancient house [A house which has stood so long as to acquire the privilege of support from that of another adjoining it; so that the owner of the latter cannot excavate his ground to its injury] · stützberechtigtes Haus n, stützwürdiges Haus

ancient light(s), ancient windows, servitude not to hinder lights; servitus ne luminibus officiatur [Latin]; right of light, right to light, light right · Lichtrecht n, Abwehrrecht des Fenstereigentümers gegen den Nachbarn [Schutz gegen Verbauung des Lichteinfalls durch den Grundstücksnachbarn]

ancillary, paravail, subordinate, inferior · nachgeordnet, untergeordnet

ancillary administration (of estate(s)) · Erb(schafts)verwaltung f in dem Land oder den Ländern in welchem oder welchen sich zum Nachlaß gehörige Vermögenswerte befunden haben, Nachlaßverwaltung in dem Land oder den Ländern in welchem oder welchen sich zum Nachlaß gehörige Vermögenswerte befunden haben

ancillary administrator · Nebennachlaßverwalter m, Nebenerb(schafts)verwalter

ancillary guardianship · Nebenvormundschaft f

ancillary industrial estate · Zulieferer-Gewerbepark m

ancillary restraint · wettbewerbsbeschränkende Nebenabrede f

and also; ac etiam [Latin] [The introduction to the statement of the real cause of action in cases where it was necessary to allege a fictitious cause in order to give the court jurisdiction] · und auch

Anglo-Saxon land law · angelsächsisches Bodenrecht n, angelsächsisches Landrecht

angular line village · Winkelzeilendorf n

angular row village · Winkelreihendorf n

animal breeding · Tierzucht f

animal ecology · Tierökologie f

animal husbandry — annual audit

animal husbandry · Haustierwirtschaft *f*

animal industry · Viehwesen *n*

animal keeper · Tierhalter *m*

animal migration · Tierwanderung *f*

animal population · Tierbestand *m*

animal-raising farm · Viehzuchtgut *n*

animal sanctuary · Tierschutzgebiet *n*

animal shelter · Tierunterkunft *f*

animal that has strayed away, wandering beast, estray [*Any beast, not wild, found within any lordship, and not owned by any man*] · herrenloses Tier *n*, verlaufenes Tier

animal tithe · Blutzehnt *m*, Fleischzehnt, Viehzehnt, lebendiger Zehnt

animated cartography · Filmkartographie *f*

animus manendi [*Latin*]; intent(ion) to establish a permanent residence, intent(ion) of remaining · Absicht *f* sich dauernd in einem Rechtsgebiet niederzulassen und dort einen Wohnsitz zu erlangen, Absicht zum Bleiben

animus possidendi [*Latin*]; intention of possession, possessory intention · Besitzabsicht *f*

to annex, to municipalize, to communalize, to incorporate · eingemeinden, einbezirken, vereinigen, verschmelzen, ausbezirken, umbezirken, inkorporieren, angemeinden

annexation [*Appropriation of territory, usually by war*] · rechtswidrige Landnahme *f*, Landraub *m*, unrechtmäßige Landnahme

annexation, communalization, municipalization, suburbanization, incorporation · Einbezirkung *f*, Vereinigung, Eingemeindung, Fusion(ierung) *f*, Verschmelzung, Ausbezirkung, Umbezirkung, Einverleibung, Inkorporation *f*, Inkommunalisation *f*, Inkommunalisierung, Angemeindung, Ausgemeindung, Umgemeindung [*Der rechtliche Vorgang einer organischen Verbindung mehrerer Gemeinden oder Gemeindeteile*]

annexation contract, communalization contract, municipalization contract, incorporation contract, suburbanization contract · Angemeindungsvertrag *m*, Eingemeindungsvertrag, Einbezirkungsvertrag, Vereinigungsvertrag, Verschmelzungsvertrag, Fusion(ierung)svertrag, Ausbezirkungsvertrag, Umbezirkungsvertrag, Einverleibungsvertrag, Inkorporationsvertrag, Inkommunalisationsvertrag, Ausgemeindungsvertrag, Umgemeindungsvertrag

to annihilate · vernichten

anniversary day · Gedenktag *m*

annona [*Latin*] · Getreideabgabe *f*

annonae civiles [*Rents paid to monasteries*] · Klosterpachtgelder *n pl*

annotated · annotiert, kommentiert, (schriftlich) angemerkt

annotated statutes, statutes annotated · annotierte Gesetzessammlung *f*

annotation [*A note which describes, explains, comments on, or sets out additional information or detail*] · (schriftliche) Anmerkung *f*, Kommentar *m*, Annotation *f*

to announce, to promulgate, to publicize, to publish · bekanntgeben, veröffentlichen, verbreiten, öffentlich bekanntgeben, (öffentlich) bekanntmachen

announcement, publication, promulgation · Bekanntmachung *f*, Bekanntgabe *f*, Veröffentlichung *f*, Kundmachung, Verlautbarung, Verbreitung

announcement by (the) bulletin board, promulgation by (the) bulletin board, publication by (the) bulletin board, publicity by (the) bulletin board · Aushängung *f*, Bekanntgabe *f* durch Aushang, Bekanntmachung *f* durch Aushang, Veröffentlichung *f* durch Aushang, Kundmachung *f* durch Aushang, Verbreitung durch Aushang

announcement of bidding, announcement of tendering [*General announcement to the various trade periodicals, bidders, and material suppliers that bids will be received from a selected list of bidders on a specific job, or that the project was open to all bidders*] · Ausschreibungsbekanntmachung *f*

announcement posting, publication posting, promulgation posting, publicity posting, public notice by poster · Anschlagung *f*, Bekanntmachung *f* durch Anschlag, Veröffentlichung *f* durch Anschlag, Bekanntgabe *f* durch Anschlag, Kundmachung *f* durch Anschlag, Verbreitung durch Anschlag

announcing, publicizing, promulgating · Bekanntgeben *n*, Bekanntmachen, Veröffentlichen, Kundmachen, Verbreiten

announcing by ringing a bell, publicizing by ringing a bell, promulgating by ringing a bell · Ausklingeln *n*, Ausschellen

annual, from year to year, yearly · auf unbestimmte Zeit, von Jahr zu Jahr [*Land(besitz)recht*]

annual accounts → annual (statement of) accounts

annual amount, yearly amount · Jahresbetrag *m*

annual audit, yearly audit · Jahresbuchprüfung *f*

annual auditor, balance(-sheet) auditor, yearly auditor · Abschlußprüfer *m*

annual average, yearly average · Jahresdurchschnitt *m*, Jahresmittel *n*

annual balance(-sheet), yearly balance(-sheet) · Jahresbilanz *f*

annual cost(s) of operation, yearly cost(s) of operation, annual operating cost(s), yearly operating cost(s) · Jahresbetriebskosten *f*

annual gain, yearly profit, yearly gain, annual profit · Jahresgewinn *m*

(annual) general meeting, yearly general meeting, A.G.M. · (Jahres)Hauptversammlung *f*

annual gross income, yearly gross income, gross annual income, gross yearly income · Bruttojahreseinkommen *n*, Jahresbruttoeinkommen

annual gross value, yearly gross value, gross annual value, gross yearly value · Bruttoertragswert *m* [*Liegenschaft*]

annual instal(l)ment of redemption, amount usually put to sinking fund, yearly instal(l)ment of redemption · jährliche Tilgungsrate *f*, jährliche Tilgungsquote, jährliche Amortisationsrate, jährliche Amortisationsquote

annual insurance, yearly insurance · Jahresversicherung *f*

annual net income, yearly net income, net annual income, net yearly income · Jahresnettoeinkommen *n*, Nettojahreseinkommen

annual operating cost(s), yearly operating cost(s), annual cost(s) of operation, yearly cost(s) of operation · Jahresbetriebskosten *f*

annual payment, yearly payment · Jahreszahlung *f*, jährliche Zahlung

annual production, yearly production · Jahresleistung *f*

annual profit, annual gain, yearly profit, yearly gain · Jahresgewinn *m*

annual rent, yearly rent · Jahresmiete *f*

annual rent, yearly rent [*Yearly interest on a loan of money*] · jährlich abgerechnete Darleh(e)nszinsen *f*

annual report, annual return, yearly report, yearly return · Jahresbericht *m*

annual running cost(s), yearly running cost(s) · jährliche laufende Kosten *f*, laufende jährliche Kosten

annual (statement of) accounts, yearly (statement of) accounts · Jahresabschluß *m*

annual stockturn, yearly turnover, yearly stockturn, annual turnover · Jahresumsatz *m*

annual sum, yearly sum · Jahressumme *f*

annual value, yearly value · Jahreswert *m*

annual wage, yearly wage · Jahreslohn *m*

annuitant · Annuitätenempfänger *m*, Annuitätsempfänger

annuity · Annuität *f*

annuity, pension [*A periodic payment to a retired employ(e)e*] · Pension *f*, Rente *f*

annuity agreement, guaranteed bond, money-back annuity, annuity bond, annuity certificate, annuity contract · Renten(versicherungsspar)brief *m*, Renten(versicherungsspar)schein *m*

annuity bank · Rentenbank *f*

annuity benefit, tontine · Leibrente *f*

annuity certain · Zeitrente *f*, Rente mit bestimmter Laufzeit

annuity charge, annuity encumbrance, annuity burden, annuity incumbrance, annuity load · Annuitätenbelastung *f*, Annuitätenlast *f*, Annuitätsbelastung, Annuitätslast

annuity contract · Annuitätsvertrag *m*, Annuitätenvertrag, (privater) Rentenversicherungsvertrag

annuity due [*An annuity where payment is made at the beginning of each period; the opposite of "ordinary annuity"*] · vorschüssige Rente *f*

annuity for life, life annuity [*The payments cease at the death of the investor*] · lebenslange Annuität *f*, lebenslängliche Annuität, Annuität auf Lebensdauer

annuity for terms of years, terminable annuity [*The payments cease after a specified number of years*] · Jahresannuität *f*

annuity for 49 years [*In England*] · kurze Annuität *f*

annuity for 99 years [*in England*] · lange Annuität *f*

annuity fund [*The amount resulting from the accumulation of periodic payments of annuities*] · angesammelte Annuitäten *fpl*, angehäufte Annuitäten, aufgehäufte Annuitäten

annuity fund; bond fund (US) [*The fund created as the result of an annuity agreement*] · Rentenfonds *m*

annuity given by will, annuity transmitted by will · Testamentsannuität *f*

annuity incumbrance → annuity charge

annuity in perpetuity, perpetual annuity [*The payments cease only on repayment of the principal*] · immerwährende Annuität *f*, Dauerannuität, dauernde Annuität, ewige Annuität, Ewigannuität

annuity insurance — antichrese

annuity insurance · Annuitätenversicherung f, Annuitätsversicherung

annuity loan · Annuitätendarleh(e)n n, Annuitätsdarleh(e)n

annuity mortgage, amortisation mortgage, amortising mortgage, amortization mortgage, amortizing mortgage · Amortisationshypothek, Tilgungshypothek, Annuitätenhypothek, Annuitätshypothek

annuity payment · Annuitätenzahlung f, Annuitätszahlung

annuity put off, deferred annuity, postponed annuity, reversionary annuity · aufgeschobene Annuität f, Zukunftsannuität, Anwartschaftsannuität

annuity register, annuity registry, register of annuities, registry of annuities · Annuitätenregister n, Annuitätenverzeichnis n, Annuitätenliste f

annuity society · Rentenkasse f

annuity subsidy, annuity subvention · Annuitätensubvention f, Annuitätssubvention [Sammelbezeichnung für Darleh(e)n und Zuschuß zur Deckung einer Annuität]

annuity table · Annuitätstabelle f, Annuitätentabelle

annuity transmitted by will, annuity given by will · Testamentsannuität f

to annul, to repeal, to overrule, to cancel, to abrogate, to abolish (by authority), to do away with, to abate, to deprive of operation, to rescind, to nullify · abschaffen, aufheben, rückgängig machen, annullieren, außer Kraft setzen, löschen, abbauen

to annul, to avoid, to invalidate, to make void · ungültig machen, für ungültig erklären

annullable, defeasible, abrogatable, rescindable · annullierbar, aufhebbar, löschbar, abschaffbar, abbaubar

annulled, made void, avoided, cancelled, invalidated · ungültig gemacht, für ungültig erklärt

annulled, nullified, abolished (by authority), rescinded, overruled, done away with, deprived of operation, repealed, cancelled, abrogated, abated · aufgehoben, annulliert, rückgängig gemacht, außer Kraft gesetzt, abgeschafft, gelöscht, abgebaut

annulling, (a)voiding, repealing, abolishing, abrogating, cancelling, overruling, abating, rendering null and void, doing away with, nullifying, rescinding, making void · Aufheben n, Rückgängigmachen n, Annullieren n, Abschaffen n, Löschen n, Abbauen n

annulment, nullification, rescission, avoidance, repeal, abrogation, cancellation, abolition, abatement, abolishment (by authority) · Annullierung f, Rückgängigmachung, Aufhebung, Abschaffung, Abbau m, Löschung

answer → (defendant's) answer

answerable → responsible

answerable condition, responsible condition, accountable condition [A condition giving rise to a transaction, and requiring recognition] · rechenschaftspflichtige Bedingung f, verantwortliche Bedingung

answerable event, responsible event, accountable event [An event giving rise to a transaction, and requiring recognition] · rechenschaftspflichtiges Ereignis n, verantwortliches Ereignis

answerable person, responsible person, accountable person · verantwortliche Person f, rechenschaftspflichtige Person

answerable to law, liable to be brought before any jurisdiction, amenable, subject to answer to law, liable to answer to law, responsible to law · verantwortlich vor dem Gesetz, rechenschaftspflichtig vor dem Gesetz

antecedent negotiations · Anbahnung f

antecedent negotiations for a contract · Vertragsanbahnung f

to antedate, to advance a date · vordatieren

ante-nuptial, before marriage · vor der Eheschließung, vorehelich

ante-nuptial contract, ante-nuptial settlement, contract before marriage, settlement before marriage, marriage settlement [A contract or agreement between a man and a woman before marriage, but in contemplation and generally in consideration of marriage, whereby the property rights and interests of either the prospective husband or wife, or both of them, are determined, or where property is secured to either or both of them, or to their children] · Ehevertrag m, Ehestiftung f

antichrese, antichresis [This covenant was allowed by the Romans, among whom usury was prohibited; it was afterwards called "mortgage" to distinguish it from a simple engagement, where the fruits of the ground were not alienated, which was called vif-gage, i.e. vivum vadium. The obsolete Welsh mortgage bears a resemblance to the antichresis] · Antichrese f, Nutzpfandrecht n (an Grundstücken), Grundpfandrecht n mit Sachherrschaft des Gläubigers und Nutzung, Nutzungspfand n (an Grundstücken), antichretisches Pfandrecht [Ein Vertrag, durch den der Gläubiger zur Sicherung seiner Forderung das Recht erlangt, die Früchte des ihm übergebenen Grundstücks zu ziehen, sie aber auf

antichresis by implication — apparent authority

die geschuldeten Zinsen, im übrigen auf das Kapital anrechnen muß]

antichresis by implication, tacit antichresis, implied antichresis; antichresis tacita [*Latin*] · stillschweigende Antichrese *f*

antichresis pledge · antichresisches Pfand *n*

to anticipate, to deal with beforehand · vorwegnehmen

anticipation [*Act of doing or taking a thing before its proper time. In conveyancing, the act of assigning, charging, or otherwise dealing with income before it becomes due*] · Vorwegnahme *f*

anticipatory breach of contract [*A breach committed before there is a present duty of performance, and is the outcome of words evincing intention to refuse performance in the future*] · vorweggenommene Erfüllungs(ver)weigerung *f*, vorweggenommener Bruch *m*

anticipatory restraint, restraint on anticipation · Beschränkung *f* der Ehefrau in der Verfügungsfreiheit über ihr Vorbehaltgut, Verbot *n* einer Verfügung im voraus

anti-dumping certificate [*USA*] · Bescheinigung *f* über die Richtigkeit der Preise im Verhältnis zu den Weltmarktpreisen

antinomy [*A contradiction between two laws or an opposition to an express law, by disobedience or by a directly contrary practice*] · Antinomie *f*, Widerspruch *m*, Gesetz(es)widerspruch, Gegensatz *m*

antipollution authority, environmental protection authority, environmental control authority, environmental prevention authority, pollution control authority, pollution prevention authority · Umweltschutzbehörde *f*

antipollution board, pollution control board, pollution prevention board, environmental control board, environmental protection board, environmental prevention board, PCB · Umweltschutzamt *n*

antipollution policy, environmental policy · Umweltpolitik *f*

anti-poverty programme; anti-poverty program (US) · Armenhilfsprogramm *n*

antiquated, grown out of use, disused, obsolete · außer Gebrauch, nicht mehr verwendet

antiquity article, article of antiquity · Altertumsgegenstand *m*, Altertumsfund *m*

antiquum dominicum, vetus patrimonium domini [*Latin*]; customary freehold, ancient demesne, copyhold tenure by custom of ancient demesne; dominicum antiquum [*Such land(s) as were entered by William I., in Doomesday-book, under the title "De Terra Regis"; and which were held later by a species of copyhold tenure*] · altes Krongut(leh(e)n) *n*

antisocial · asozial

antitheoretical nature · Theoriewidrigkeit *f*

anti-urban · antistädtisch, städtefeindlich

AONB, area of (outstanding) natural beauty, territory of (outstanding) natural beauty · Naturschönheitsgebiet *n*

AOQ, average outgoing quality [*The quality of material ultimately passed into stock by an inspection procedure that enforces good 100 per cent inspection of each rejected lot to remove therefrom all defective items, which — in theory at least — are then replaced by good items*] · Durchschnittsgüte *f* der geprüften Liefermengen

AOQ limit, average outgoing quality limit · Durchschnittsgütehöchstwert *m* der geprüften Liefermengen

appealable · berufungsfähig, appellationsfähig

apartment (Brit.) [*archaic*]; tenement, residence, dwelling; dwelling unit, DU, du, living unit, LU, lu, housing unit, unit of housing, apartment (US) · Wohnung *f*

apartment (Brit.); bachelor apartment (US) [*Apartment designed for occupancy by one or more persons, primarily limited in area and containing one large room for sleeping, cooking, eating, and living with bathroom facilities and closet space*] · Einzimmerwohnung *f*, Einraumwohnung

apartment hotel (US); service flats (Brit.) · Wohnhotel *n*, Wohnhaus *n* mit Bedienung

apartment house, tenement (house) [*A building used as a dwelling for several families, each living separate and apart*] · Mietwohn(ungs)haus *n*, Mehrwohn(ungs)haus, Mehrfamilien(wohn)haus, Mehrparteien(wohn)haus, Miethaus, Vielwohn(ungs)haus, Familienhaus, Vermietungshaus, Zinshaus

apparator, apparitor [*An officer of a church court who serves summons, etc.*] · Diener *m* eines geistlichen Gerichts

apparent, presumptive, presumed, reputed, ostensible · angeblich, anscheinend, scheinbar, mutmaßlich, vermutlich, vermeintlich

apparent authority, ostensible authority, authority by estoppel · Scheinvollmacht *f*, Scheinvertretungsmacht, Anscheinvollmacht, allgemeine Vollmacht, allgemeine Vertretungsmacht, Vollmacht kraft Rechtsschein, Vertretungsmacht kraft Rechtsschein, Vollmacht kraft Partnerstellung, Vertretungsmacht kraft Partnerstellung

apparent evidence, apparent proof, prima facie evidence, prima facie proof · Anscheinsbeweis *m*, widerlegbarer Beweis, Beweis des ersten Anscheins

apparent owner, presumptive owner, presumed owner, apparent proprietor, presumptive proprietor, presumed proprietor, reputed owner, reputed proprietor · angeblicher Eigentümer *m*, vermutlicher Eigentümer, anscheinender Eigentümer, mutmaßlicher Eigentümer, scheinbarer Eigentümer, vermeintlicher Eigentümer

apparent ownership, apparent proprietorship, apparent property, presumptive ownership, presumptive proprietorship, presumptive property, reputed ownership, reputed property, reputed proprietorship, presumed ownership, presumed proprietorship, presumed property · angebliches Eigentum *n*, mutmaßliches Eigentum, scheinbares Eigentum, vermutliches Eigentum, anscheinendes Eigentum, vermeintliches Eigentum, Vermögen *n* Dritter in einer Konkursmasse

apparent partner, ostensible partner [*If a man holds himself out to the world as a partner, or permits others to hold him out as a partner, when in fact he is not, he is called an ostensible partner or apparent partner*] · Scheinpartner *m*, Partner kraft Rechtsschein, Anscheinspartner

apparilor → apparator

App. Div., Appellate Division · Sammlung *f* von Entscheidungen der Bezirksberufungsgerichte des Staates New York

appeal; appellatio [*Latin*] [*The judicial examination by a higher court of the decision of an inferior court*] · Appellation *f*, Berufung *f*

appeal · Privatklage *f*

appealability, appellancy · Appellationseignung *f*, Appellationsfähigkeit *f*, Berufungseignung, Berufungsfähigkeit

to appeal (against), to lodge an appeal · einlegen [*Berufung*]

appeal at law, reference to a court · Anruf(ung) *m*, (*f*) eines Gerichtes

appeal authority · (Gerichts)Instanz *f*

appeal circuit, circuit (of appeal) · Berufungs(gerichts)sprengel *m*, Appellations(gerichts)sprengel

appeal committee · Appellationsausschuß *m*, Berufungsausschuß *m*

appealer, appellant, appealing party, plaintiff in appeal; appelator [*Latin*] · Appellant *m*, Appellationskläger *m*, Berufungskläger *m*

appeal instrument, instrument of appeal · Berufungsinstitut *n*, Appellationsinstitut

appeal judg(e)ment, judg(e)ment of appeal · Berufungsurteil *n*, Appellationsurteil

appeal motion, motion of appeal · Berufungsantrag *m*, Appellationsantrag

appeal period (of time) → time (allowed) for appeal

appeal right, right of appeal · Appellationsrecht *n*, Berufungsrecht *n*, subjektives Appellationsrecht *n*, subjektives Berufungsrecht *n*

appeals court, C.A., court of (error and) appeal, court of review (of errors and appeal), appellate court · Appellationsgericht *n* für Zivilsachen, Berufungsgericht *n* für Zivilsachen

appearance · Erscheinen *n* [*bei Gericht*]

appearance · Einlassung *f* (des Beklagten)

appearance, pretext, pretence; colour (Brit.); color (US) [*A fictitious allegation of a right. A person is said to have no colour of title when he has not even a prima facie title*] · Deckmantel *m*, Vorwand *m*, Anschein *m*

appearance notice, notification of appearance, appearance notification, notice of appearance [*A notice given by defendant for a plaintiff that he appears in the action in person or by attorney*] · Einlassungsmitteilung *f*, Einlassungsanzeige *f*, Einlassungsbenachrichtigung

appearance of justice, appearance of right · Rechtsschein *m*, Rechtsanschein

appellancy, appealability · Appellationseignung *f*, Appellationsfähigkeit *f*, Berufungseignung *f*, Berufungsfähigkeit *f*

appellant → appealer

appellate court, appeals court, C.A., court of (error and) appeal, court of review (of errors and appeal) · Appellationsgericht *n* für Zivilsachen, Berufungsgericht *n* für Zivilsachen

Appellate Division, App. Div. · Sammlung *f* von Entscheidungen der Bezirksberufungsgerichte des Staates New York

Appellate Division of the Supreme Court [*In New York*] · Appellationsgericht *n*, Berufungsgericht *n*

appellate judge, appellate justice; judex ad quem [*Latin*]; justice of appeal, judge of appeal [*A judge to whom an appeal is made*] · Appellationsrichter *m*, Berufungsrichter *m*

appellate jurisdiction [*A court is said to have appellate jurisdiction when it can only go into the matter on appeal after it has been adjudicated on by a court of first instance*] · Berufungszuständigkeit *f* [*Siehe Anmerkung unter „Zuständigkeit"*]

appellate notice — application for registration

appellate notice, notice of appeal · Appellationsanmeldung *f*, Berufungsanmeldung

appellate procedure · Appellationsverfahren *n*, Berufungsverfahren *n*

appellate ruling · Appellationsentscheid(ung) *m, (f)*, Berufungsentscheid(ung) *m, (f)*

Appellate Term of the Supreme Court [*In New York*] · Beschwerdegericht *n*

appellatio [*Latin*]; appeal [*The judicial examination by a higher court of the decision of an inferior court*] · Appellation *f*, Berufung *f*

appellee, defendant in court of appeal · Appellat *m*, Berufungsverklagter *m*, Berufungsbeklagter *m*

appendage, appurtenance; appertinance [*obsolete*]; pertinent, pertinance [*Scots law*]; appenditia [*Latin*]; thing of an accessory character, appurtenant [*A thing belonging to another thing. Things appendant can be claimed only by prescription, while things appurtenant can be claimed either by prescription or by express grant*] · Zubehör *n*, Dazugehöriges *n*, Pertinenz *f*; Zugehör *n* [*Schweiz*]

appendant, appurtenant (to), attached, belonging to [*Things appendant can be claimed only by prescription, while things appurtenant can be claimed either by prescription or by express grant*] · anhaftend, zugehörig

applicability · Anwendbarkeit *f*

applicable · diesbezüglich

applicable · anwendbar

applicant, person invited to tender, prospective bidder, prospective tenderer, prospective offeror, prospective competitor, prospective tendering contractor, prospective competing contractor · Bewerber *m* [*Ein Bauunternehmer, der sich um eine Bauleistung bewirbt, aber noch kein Angebot auf diese Bauleistung abgegeben hat*]

applicant · Antragsteller *m*, Gesuchsteller *m*

applicant company · Gesuchstellerin *f*, Antragstellerin, gesuchstellende Firma *f*, antragstellende Firma

application, request · Antrag *m*, Gesuch *n*, Ersuchen *n*

application · Anwendung *f*

application blank (form), request blank (form), blank (form) of request, blank (form) of application · Gesuchsformular *n*, Gesuchsmuster *n*, Antragsformular, Antragsmuster, Antragsformblatt *n*, Antragsblankett, Antragsvordruck *m*, Gesuchsformblatt, Gesuchsblankett *n*, Gesuchsvordruck

application case · Antragsfall *m*

application date, request date, date of filing, date of application, date of request, filing date · Antragsdatum *n*, Gesuchsdatum *n*

application en parte, en parte application · einseitiger Zwischenantrag *m*

application fee, request fee, fee of request, fee of application · Antragsgebühr *f*, Gesuchsgebühr

application for building permit, application for construction permit · Bauantrag *m*, Baugesuch *n* [*Förmlicher Antrag auf eine Baugenehmigung*]

application for cancelling, request for cancelling, application for ruling through, request for ruling through · Löschungsantrag *m*, Löschungsgesuch *n*, Löschungsersuchen *n* [*Löschung im Grundbuch*]

application for demolition, application for wrecking, request for pulling down, application for pulling down, application for razing, request for razing, request for demolition, request for wrecking · Abbruchantrag *m*, Abbruchgesuch *n*, Abrißantrag, Abrißgesuch, Einreißantrag, Einreißgesuch, Abreißantrag, Abreißgesuch

application for licence, license application, application for license, licence application · Lizenzgesuch *n*, Lizenzantrag *m*

application for payment, payment application, payment request [*Statement of amounts on proper acceptables or forms claimed by the contractor as payment due on account of work performed or materials stored*] · Zahlungsantrag *m*, Zahlungsgesuch *n*, Zahlungsersuchen *n*

application for planning permission, request for planning permission, planning permission application, planning permission request · Planungserlaubnisantrag *m*, Planungserlaubnisgesuch *n*, Planungsgenehmigungsantrag, Planungsgenehmigungsgesuch

application for priority, request for priority, priority application, priority request · Dringlichkeitsantrag *m*, Dringlichkeitsgesuch *n*, Dringlichkeitsersuchen

application for pulling down → application for demolition

application for razing → application for demolition

application for registration, request for registration, application for recording, request for recording, application for recordation, request for recordation · Buchungsgesuch *n*, Buchungsantrag *m*, Eintragungsantrag, Eintragungsgesuch,

application for ruling through — appointment of an heir

Registrierungsantrag, Registrierungsgesuch, Eintragungsersuchen *n*, Registrierungsersuchen, Buchungsersuchen

application for ruling through, request for ruling through, application for cancelling, request for cancelling · Löschungsantrag *m*, Löschungsgesuch *n* [*Löschung im Grundbuch*]

application for the summons, request for the summons · Ladungsantrag *m*, Ladungsgesuch *n*, Ladungsersuchen *n*

application for wrecking → application for demolition

application of motion, request of motion · Initiativantrag *m*, Initiativgesuch *n*, Initiativersuchen *n*

application of profit, application of gain · Gewinnvermehrung *f*, Profitvermehrung

application of (the) law · Rechtsanwendung *f*

application of (the) law · Gesetz(es)anwendung *f*

application prerequisite, prerequisite for application · Anwendungsvoraussetzung *f*

application principle, principle of application · Anwendungsgrundsatz *m*, Anwendungsprinzip *n*

application procedure, request procedure · Antragsverfahren *n*, Gesuchsverfahren

application to record, application to register · Eintragungsanmeldung *f*

application to record a resolution, application to register a resolution · Beschlußanmeldung *f*, Entschließungsanmeldung

application to reverse (a judg(e)ment), application to set aside (a judg(e)ment), motion to set aside (a judg(e)ment), request to set aside (a judg(e)ment), motion to reverse (a judg(e)ment), request to reverse (a judg(e)ment) · Aussetzungsantrag *m*, Aussetzungsgesuch *n* [*Urteil*]

applied cost(s) [*Cost that has been allocated to a product or activity*] · verrechnete Gemeinkosten *f*

applied economics · angewandte Volkswirtschaftslehre *f*

applied geography · angewandte Geographie *f*, Landeskunde *f*

to apply · beantragen

to apply retrospectively, to apply retroactively · rückwirkend wirksam werden

to appoint, to nominate · benennen, nominieren, namhaft machen, ernennen

to appoint · geben [*Verfügungsbefugnis*]

to appoint a contractor, to let a contract, to contract, to award (a contract), to let (out), to commission a project · zuschlagen, erteilen eines Auftrages

appointed day, key day, cut-off-date, effective date · Stichtag *m*

appointed day of appraisal, key-day of appraisal, (e)valuation cut-off-date, (e)valuation key-day, appointed day of (e)valuation, effective date of appraisal, cut-off date of appraisal · Bewertungsstichtag *m*, Wertermitt(e)lungsstichtag, Taxierungsstichtag, (Ab)Schätzungsstichtag

appointed guardianship → (court)-appointed guardianship

appointed sub(contractor), nominated sub(contractor) · ernannter Nachunternehmer *m*, ernannter Subunternehmer, bauseitiger Nachunternehmer, bauseitiger Subunternehmer, benannter Nachunternehmer, benannter Subunternehmer, nominierter Nachunternehmer, nominierter Subunternehmer

appointed supplier, nominated supplier · bauseitiger Lieferant *m*, ernannter Lieferant, benannter Lieferant, nominierter Lieferant [*Von der Bauherrschaft ernannter Lieferant*]

appointee, nominee · Benannte *m*, Ernannte, Nominierte

appointing, nominating · Benennen *n*, Ernennen, Nominieren, Namhaftmachen

appointing party, nominating party · benennende Partei *f*, nominierende Partei *f*, ernennende Partei *f*

appointment, nomination · Benennung *f*, Nominierung, Namhaftmachung, Ernennung

appointment by implication, implied appointment, tacit appointment · stillschweigende Benennung *f*, stillschweigende Ernennung, stillschweigende Namhaftmachung, stillschweigende Nominierung, gefolgerte Benennung, gefolgerte Ernennung, gefolgerte Namhaftmachung, gefolgerte Nominierung, konkludente Benennung, konkludente Ernennung, konkludente Namhaftmachung, konkludente Nominierung

appointment certificate, certificate of appointment · Ernennungszeugnis *n* [*Konkursverwalter*]

appointment committee, nomination committee · Benennungsausschuß *m*, Ernennungsausschuß, Nominierungsausschuß

appointment contract, contract to nominate, contract to appoint, nomination contract · Benennungsvertrag *m*, Ernennungsvertrag, Nominierungsvertrag

appointment of an heir, institution · Erbenernennung *f*

appointment to view — appraisal (of value)

appointment to view · Besichtigungstermin *m* [*Wohnung*]

to apportion, to portion out, to allot [*To divide and distribute proportionally or according to a plan*] · zuteilen

apportionable, allotable · zuteilbar

apportioned operating cost(s) · Umlage *f* [*Umlagen sind auf die Mieter umgelegte und im allgemeinen mit der Miete erhobene Betriebskosten*]

apportioned tax, rated tax · Umlegesteuer *f*, Repartitionssteuer, Repartierungssteuer, Kontigentierungssteuer, Verteilungssteuer

apportionment, allotment · Zuteilung *f*

apportionment certificate, allotment certificate · Zuteilungsbescheinigung *f*, Zuteilungsschein *m*, Zuteilungsattest *n*

apportionment of land use → allotment of land use

apportionment of space, space apportionment, space allotment, allotment of space · Raumzuteilung *f*

apportionment of water, water allotment, water apportionment, allotment of water · Wasserzuteilung *f*

apportionment planning, allotment planning · Zuteilungsplanung *f*

appraisable · (ab)schätzbar, bewertbar, taxierbar

appraisal, appraised price, estimated price · (Ab)Schätzungspreis *m*

appraisal basis, appraisement basis, (e)valuation basis · Bewertungsgrundlage *f*, Wertermitt(e)lungsgrundlage

appraisal by adding together · Kalkulationsverfahren *n* [*Verkehrswertberechnung eines Grundstückes*]

appraisal by capitalization, capitalization appraisal, capitalized value appraisal [*Estimate of value by capitalization of productivity and income*] · Ertragswertverfahren *n*, Ertragsberechnung *f*

appraisal by comparison, comparative appraisal, comparative method [*Estimate of value by comparison with the sales prices of other similar properties*] · Vergleichswertverfahren *n*, Vergleichsberechnung *f*

appraisal by summation, summation appraisal [*Adding together of parts of a property separately appraised to form the whole. For example, the value of the land considered as vacant is added to the cost(s) of reproduction of the building less depreciation*] · Sachwertverfahren *n*, Sachberechnung *f*

appraisal clause, appraisement clause, evaluative clause, weighting clause, (e)valuation clause · (Ab)Schätzungsklausel *f*, Bewertungsklausel, Taxierungsklausel, Wertermitt(e)lungsklausel

appraisal council, appraisal panel, appraisement council, appraisement panel, evaluative council, evaluative panel, (e)valuation council, (e)valuation panel · (Ab)Schätzungsbeirat *m*, Bewertungsbeirat, Taxierungsbeirat, Wertermitt(e)lungsbeirat

appraisal factor → factor of (e)valuation

appraisal guide lines, appraisement guide lines, evaluative guide lines, weighting guide lines, (e)valuation guide lines · (Ab)Schätzungsrichtlinien *f pl*, Wertermitt(e)lungsrichtlinien, Bewertungsrichtlinien, Taxierungsrichtlinien

appraisal index, appraisement index, (e)valuation index, weighting index · Schätzungsindex *m*, Bewertungsindex, Taxierungsindex, Wertermitt(e)lungsindex, Abschätzungsindex

appraisal method, appraisement method, (e)valuation method · Bewertungsverfahren *n*, (Ab)Schätzungsverfahren, Wertermitt(e)lungsverfahren, Taxierungsverfahren

appraisal of (building) (land) area, appraisement of (building) (land) area, (e)valuation of (building) (land) area, appraisement of (building) land, (e)valuation of (building) land, appraisal of (building) land · (Bau)Bodenbewertung *f*, (Bau)Landbewertung, (Bau)Flächenbewertung, (Bau)Flächen(ab)schätzung, (Bau)Bodenabschätzung, (Bau)Land(ab)schätzung, (Bau)Bodentaxierung, (Bau)Landtaxierung

appraisal of estate → (real) property (e)valuation

appraisal officer, appraisal official, appraisement officer, appraisement official, (e)valuation officer, (e)valuation official · Schätzungsbeamte *m*

appraisal of land(s) → (real) property (e)valuation

appraisal of property → (real) property (e)valuation

appraisal of (real) estate → (real) property (e)valuation

appraisal of (real) property → (real) property (e)valuation

appraisal of urban land(s) and urban houses and urban buildings, (e)valuation of urban land(s) and urban houses and urban buildings · städtische Grundstücks- und Gebäude(ab)schätzung *f*

appraisal (of value), appraisement (of value), assessment (of value), (e)valuation, val. [*The determined or estimated value or price*] · (Ab)Schätzung *f*, Taxierung, Wertermitt(e)lung *f*, Bewertung

appraisal ordinance — appropriateness

appraisal ordinance, weighting ordinance, appraisement ordinance, (e)valuation ordinance · Bewertungsverordnung *f*, (Ab)Schätzungsverordnung, Taxierungsverordnung, Wertermitt(e)lungsverordnung

appraisal panel → appraisal council

appraisal planning, appraisement planning, (e)valuation planning, evaluative planning · Bewertungsplanung *f*, Wertermitt(e)lungsplanung, Taxierungsplanung, (Ab)Schätzungsplanung

appraisal prescription, appraisement prescription, evaluative prescription, weighting prescription, weighting regulation, appraisal regulation, (e)valuation regulation, appraisement regulation, evaluative regulation, (e)valuation prescription · (Ab)Schätzungsvorschrift *f*, Bewertungsvorschrift, Wertermitt(e)lungsvorschrift, Taxierungsvorschrift

appraisal scheme, appraisement scheme, evaluative scheme, weighting scheme, (e)valuation scheme · (Ab)Schätzungsrahmen *m*, Bewertungsrahmen, Taxierungsrahmen, Wertermitt(e)lungsrahmen

appraisal theory, appraisement theory, (e)valuation theory, theory of appraisal, theory of appraisement, theory of (e)valuation · Bewertungstheorie *f*, Wertermitt(e)lungstheorie, Taxierungstheorie, (Ab)Schätzungstheorie

appraisal value, estimated value · (ab)geschätzter Wert *m*, (Ab)Schätzungswert, Taxierungswert, ermittelter Wert

to appraise, to evaluate, to value [*To estimate the value or amount of; to determine the worth of*] · (ab)schätzen, (be)werten, taxieren, ermitteln eines Wertes

appraised price, estimated price, appraisal · (Ab)Schätzungspreis *m*, Taxierungspreis, ermittelter Preis, (ab)geschätzter Preis

appraiser → valuer

appraising, (e)valuating [*The action of setting a price or value on*] · (Be)Werten *n*, (Ab)Schätzen, Taxieren, Ermitteln *n* eines Wertes

appreciation → (capital) appreciation

apprehension [*The capture of a person upon a criminal charge*] · Festnahme *f*, Ergreifung *f*

apprehension warrant, warrant of apprehension · Vorführungsorder *f*, Vorführungsauftrag *m*, Vorführungsdekret *n*

apprentice · Lehrling *m*

apprenticeship, training of apprentices, apprentice training · Lehrlingsausbildung *f*, Lehre *f*

to approach · ansetzen

approach · Ansatz *m*

approach · Kostenauflösung *f*

approach, connection · Anknüpfung *f*

approach, means of approaching, (means of) access · Zugang *m*

approachability, approachableness · Ansatzfähigkeit *f*

approachable · ansatzfähig

approaching, approachment [*Drawing near in circumstantial relation*] · Ansetzen *n*

approaching attraction · (An)Näherungsanziehung *f*

approach in planning, planning approach · Planungsansatz *m*

approach in stages, step-by-step approach · stufenweise Kostenauflösung *f*, Stufenkostenauflösung

approachless, unapproachable · nicht ansatzfähig

approachment, approaching [*Drawing near in circumstantial relation*] · Ansetzen *n*

approach of cost(s), cost(s) approach · Kostenansatz *m*

approach step · Ansatzstufe *f*

to approbate, to approve, to assent, to consent, to sanction · billigen, einwilligen, zustimmen

approbated, approved, assented, consented, sanctioned · gebilligt, eingewilligt, zugestimmt

approbating, approving, consenting, assenting, action of giving assent, sanctioning · Billigen *n*, Einwilligen, Zustimmen

approbation, consensus, approval, assent, consent, sanction · Billigung *f*, Einwilligung, Zustimmung, Konsens *m*

approbative, approvable, able to be approved [*Worthy or deserving of approval*] · zulassungswürdig, zustimm(ungs)fähig

approbativeness, quality of being approbative, approvableness, worthiness of approval, ability to be approved, approvable quality · Zulassungswürdigkeit *f*, Zustimm(ungs)würdigkeit, Zulassungsfähigkeit, Zustimm(ungs)fähigkeit

appropriate, fit (for a particular purpose) · geeignet

appropriated surplus, (surplus) reserve [*Earned surplus earmarked on the books of account and in financial statements for some specific or general purposes*] · Rücklage *f*

appropriateness, fitness (for a particular purpose) · Eignung *f*

appropriateness — approved society

appropriateness, special fitness, suitableness, suitability · Zweckmäßigkeit f

to appropriate (to oneself) · (sich) aneignen

to appropriate to the contract · zuführen dem Vertragszweck [Güter]

appropriating · Aneignen n, (In)Besitznehmen

appropriation · Willenserklärung f zum Eigentumsübergang [Waren]

appropriation, occupancy; occupatio [Latin] [The taking of the first possession by any one, of a thing of which there is no owner] · tatsächliche Besitznahme f, Besitzergreifung f, (In)Besitznahme, Aneignung, Besitznehmung

appropriation → appropriation (of funds)

appropriation account [In governmental accounting. The account of a government agency to which the amount of a legislative appropriation is credited; it is eventually offset by expenditure or by a cancellation, return, or lapsing of any remaining balance] · (Mittel)Bewilligungskonto n

appropriation account (Brit.) [The account to which the profit-and-loss balance for the year is carried and taxes and dividends are charged, the balance being transferred to revenue reserves] · Rückstellungskonto n

appropriation law, appropriation statute, appropriation act · (Mittel)Bewilligungsgesetz n

appropriation law · Aneignungsrecht n

appropriation (of funds) · (Mittel)Bewilligung f

appropriation of loss(es) · Verlustzuweisung f

appropriation of retained earnings · Einstellung f auf die Rücklage(n)

appropriation period · (Mittel)Bewilligungszeitraum m

appropriation refund [In governmental accounting. The return of an advance or the recovery of an improper disbursement, regarded as a full or partial cancellation of the original expenditure and hence available for reobligation or reexpenditure] · Mittelrückführung f, Mittelrückgabe f

appropriations bill · (Mittel)Bewilligungsvorlage f

appropriations committee · (Mittel)Bewilligungsausschuß m

appropriations doctrine · Zuteilungsdoktrin f [Wasserwirtschaft]

appropriation statute, appropriation act, appropriation law · (Mittel)Bewilligungsgesetz n

appropriative · aneignend

approvable, able to be approved, approbative [Worthy or deserving of approval] · zulassungswürdig, zustimm(ungs)fähig

approvableness, worthiness of approval, ability to be approved, approvable quality, approbativeness, quality of being approbative · Zulassungswürdigkeit f, Zustimm(ungs)würdigkeit, Zulassungsfähigkeit, Zustimm(ungs)fähigkeit

approval, sanction, admission · Zulassung f

approval, assent, consent, approbation, consensus · Billigung f, Einwilligung, Zustimmung, Konsens m

approval in writing, written assent, written approval, written consent, written sanction, consent in writing, assent in writing, sanction in writing · schriftliche Billigung f, schriftliche Einwilligung, schriftliche Zustimmung, schriftlicher Konsens m

approval to assignment, approval to cession, assent to assignment, assent to cession, consent to assignment, consent to cession, sanction to assignment, sanction to cession · Abtretungseinwilligung f, Abtretungszustimmung, Abtretungsbilligung, Zessionseinwilligung, Zessionszustimmung, Zessionsbilligung

to approve [To enclose for the purpose of cultivation] · abfrieden zum Kultivieren, einhegen zum Kultivieren, umfrieden zum Kultivieren, einfrieden zum Kultivieren, abschließen zum Kultivieren

to approve, to assent, to consent, to approbate · billigen, einwilligen, zustimmen

approved, assented, consented, approbated · gebilligt, eingewilligt, zugestimmt

approved bidder, low responsible bidder, successful bidder, approved tenderer, low responsible tenderer, successful tenderer, successful contractor, approved contractor, low responsible contractor [He is not necessarily the bidder whose bid is the lowest. "Responsible" means that the bid is taken together with the bidders financial ability, reputation and past performance] · Auftragnehmer m, AN

(approved) course of instruction · Schullehrplan m

approved equal [Term used to indicate that the material, equipment, or product finally supplied or installed must be equal to that specified and approved by the owner or his duly authorized representative and acceptable to the former] · anerkannt gleichwertig

approved society · staatlich zugelassene Sozialversicherungsgesellschaft f

approvement, enclosure (for the purpose of cultivation); approveamentum, appruvamentum [*Latin*] · Einfried(ig)ung *f* zum Kultivieren, Abfried(ig)ung zum Kultivieren, Einhegung zum Kultivieren, Abschließung zum Kultivieren, Umfried(ig)ung zum Kultivieren, Kultivierungseinhegung, Kultivierungseinfried(ig)ung, Kultivierungsabfried(ig)ung, Kultivierungsumfried(ig)ung, Kultivierungsabschließung

approver · Kronzeuge *m*

approving, sanctioning, confirming (authoritatively) · Zulassen *n*

approving, consenting, assenting, action of giving assent, sanctioning, approbating · Billigen *n*, Einwilligen, Zustimmen

approving authority, sanctioning authority · Zulassungsbehörde *f*

approximate(d) quantity · angenäherte Menge *f*, (An)Näherungsmenge

approximate estimate, shortcut estimate [*The owner's or his architect/engineer's project estimate, made prior to awarding the project contract, is approximate, since it is not based on a detailed costing of the project work quantities*] · Preisvorstellung *f*

appurtenances of a plot (of land), accessories of a plot (of land) · Grund(stücks)zubehör *n*

appurtenant, appendage, appurtenance; appertinance [*obsolete*]; pertinent, pertinance [*Scots law*]; appenditia [*Latin*]; thing of an accessory character [*A thing belonging to another thing. Things appendant can be claimed only by prescription, while things appurtenant can be claimed either by prescription or by express grant*] · Zubehör *n*, Dazugehörige *n*, Pertinenz *f*; Zugehör *n* [*Schweiz*]

appurtenant (to), attached, belonging to, appendant [*Things appendant can be claimed only by prescription, while things appurtenant can be claimed either by prescription or by express grant*] · anhaftend, zugehörig

apron-string tenure; feudum femineum successivum, feodum femineum successivum [*Latin*] [*Tenure of property in virtue of one's wife, or during her lifetime only*] · Frauenleh(e)n *n*

aquage, aquagium [*Latin*]; watercourse · Wasserlauf *m*

aquage, aquagium [*Latin*]; ewage [*In old English law. Toll paid for water passage*] · Wasserdurchleitungsgebühr *f*, Wasser-(transport)zoll *m*

aquatic right, water right, right of water [*Right to the use of sea, rivers, streams, lakes, ponds and canals, for the purpose of fishing and navigation, and also to the soil of them*] · (subjektives) Wasserrecht *n*

arable, fit for tillage; capable of being ploughed (Brit.); capable of being plowed (US) · pflügbar, beackerbar

arable → arable field

arable farming, arable husbandry, tillage · Ackerbau *m*

arable farming food, field food · Ackernahrung *f*

arable farming system, arable husbandry system, tillage system · Ackerbausystem *n*, Betriebssystem, Wirtschaftssystem

arable field, arable ground, tilled land, tilled ground, tilled field, tillage ground, tillage land, tillage field, aralia; acre-land [*obsolete*]; arable (land) · Acker-(boden) *m*, Acker(bau)land *n*, Ackerfeld, Artland, Aracker, Pflugland

arable field except from tithes and socage · Freiacker *m*

arable land which can be owned separately from the common land of a commune · walzender Acker *m*, Wandelakker

arable-pastoral system; co-ploughing of the waste (Brit.); co-plowing of the waste (US) [*An agricultural system in which the land is divided into arable and pasture, the arable going to grass as soon as it is exhausted and the pasture then being ploughed up in its stead*] · Feldgraswirtschaft *f*; Koppelwirtschaft [*Schleswig-Holstein*], Egartenwirtschaft [*In süddeutschen Gebirgsgegenden*]

aralia → arable field

ArbAct, arbitration act, arbitration law, arbitration statute · Schieds(gerichts)gesetz *n*

arbiter [*This term is rarely used*]; arbiter compromissarius [*Latin*]; arbitrator · Schiedsrichter *m*, Spruchrichter

arbitrability · Schiedsgerichtsbarkeit *f*

arbitrable dispute · Schiedsstreit(igkeit) *m*, (*f*), Schiedsgerichtsstreit(igkeit)

arbitrage [*The principle of profiting from the difference which the same thing may have in different places at the same time, achieved by buying in the one place (the cheaper) and selling in another simultaneously; applied to foreign exchange, and securities; a broker engaging in such transactions is called an arbitrager*] · Arbitrage *f*

arbitrager, dealer in arbitrage · Arbitrageur *m*

arbitral · schiedsgerichtlich, schiedsrichterlich

arbitral award, arbitrator's award; arbitrament [*obsolete*]; arbitrium [*Latin*]; (arbitration) award · Schiedsgerichtsspruch *m*, (Schieds)Spruch

arbitral board — arbitration tribunal

arbitral board, board of arbitration, arbitration board · Schiedsstelle *f*

arbitral capability, arbitral capacity · Schieds(gerichts)vermögen *n*, Schieds(gerichts)eigenschaft *f*, Schieds(gerichts)fähigkeit

arbitral clause, arbitration clause · Schiedsklausel *f*, Schiedsgerichtsklausel

arbitral code, code of arbitration, arbitration code · Schiedsordnung *f*, Schiedsgerichtsordnung

arbitral committee, arbitration committee · Ausschuß *m* für Schiedsgerichtswesen

arbitral contract, arbitration contract · Schiedsvertrag *m*, Schiedsgerichtsvertrag

arbitral court → court of arbitration

arbitral party, party to an arbitration, arbitration party · Schiedspartei *f*

arbitral proceeding, arbitration proceeding · Schieds(gerichts)verfahren *n*, schiedsgerichtliches Verfahren, schiedsrichterliches Verfahren, Spruchverfahren [*Es entscheidet einen Rechtsstreit anstelle eines Staatsgerichtes*]

arbitral provision, arbitration provision · Schieds(gerichts)bestimmung *f*

arbitrament, arbitration · Schiedssprechung *f*, Schiedsgerichtssprechung

arbitrament [*obsolete*]; arbitrium [*Latin*]; (arbitration) award, arbitral award, arbitrator's award · Schiedsgerichtsspruch *m*, (Schieds)Spruch

arbitrament as to defects, arbitration as to defects · Mängelschieds(gerichts)sprechung *f*

arbitrar(il)y; arbitrarious(ly) [*obsolete*] · eigenmächtig, willkürlich

arbitrariness; arbitrariousness [*obsolete*] [*Conduct or acts based alone upon one's will, and not upon any course of reasoning and exercise of judgement*] · eigenmächtiges Handeln *n*, willkürliches Handeln

arbitrary origin · willkürlicher Nullpunkt *m* [*Statistik*]

arbitrary power [*Power to act according to one's own will; especially applicable to power conferred on an administrative officer, who is not furnished any adequate determining principle*] · Eigenmächtigkeit *f*, Willkür *f*

arbitrary situation · Willkürlage *f*

to arbitrate · schiedssprechen

arbitration, arbitrament · Schiedssprechung *f*, Schiedsgerichtssprechung

arbitration act, arbitration law, arbitration statute, ArbAct · Schieds(gerichts)gesetz *n*

arbitration agreement · Schiedsabkommen *n*, Schiedsabmachung *f*, Schiedsvereinbarung

arbitration appeals board · Oberschiedsgericht *n*

arbitration as to defects, arbitrament as to defects · Mängelschieds(gerichts)sprechung *f*

(arbitration) award, arbitral award, arbitrator's award; arbitrament [*obsolete*]; arbitrium [*Latin*] · Schiedsgerichtsspruch *m*, (Schieds)Spruch

(arbitration) award void on the face of it · (Schieds)Spruch *m* nichtig in sich selbst

arbitration board, arbitral board, board of arbitration · Schiedsstelle *f*

arbitration code, arbitral code, code of arbitration · Schiedsordnung *f*, Schiedsgerichtsordnung

arbitration committee, arbitral committee · Ausschuß *m* für Schiedsgerichtswesen

arbitration contract, arbitral contract · Schiedsvertrag *m*, Schiedsgerichtsvertrag

arbitration court → court of arbitration

arbitration law, arbitration statute, ArbAct, arbitration act · Schieds(gerichts)gesetz *n*

arbitration law, law of arbitration · Schiedsrecht *n*, Schiedsgerichtsrecht

arbitration legislation, lawmaking of arbitration, arbitration lawmaking, legislation of arbitration · Schieds(gerichts)gesetzgebung *f*

arbitration on documents · Schiedssprechung *f* auf der Grundlage von Urkunden

arbitration party, arbitral party, party to an arbitration · Schiedspartei *f*

arbitration place, place of arbitration · Schiedsort *m*, Schiedsgerichtsort

arbitration practice · Schieds(gerichts)wesen *n*

arbitration proceeding, arbitral proceeding · Schieds(gerichts)verfahren *n*, schiedsgerichtliches Verfahren, schiedsrichterliches Verfahren, Spruchverfahren [*Es entscheidet einen Rechtsstreit anstelle eines Staatsgerichtes*]

arbitration provision, arbitral provision · Schieds(gerichts)bestimmung *f*

arbitration rule, arbitration prescription, arbitration regulation · Schiedsgerichtsvorschrift *f*

arbitration statute, ArbAct, arbitration act, arbitration law · Schieds(gerichts)gesetz *n*

arbitration tribunal → court of arbitration

arbitrator; arbiter [*This term is rarely used*]; arbiter compromissarius [*Latin*] · Schiedsrichter *m*, Spruchrichter

arbitrator appointed by court; judex [*Latin*]; (official) referee · gerichtlich ernannter Schiedsrichter *m*

arbor finalis [*Latin*]; boundary tree [*A tree used for marking a bound(ary) (line)*] · Grenzbaum *m*

arboriculture · Baumzucht *f*

arbor(icultur)ist · Baumzüchter *m*

Arches-Court, Court of Arches · geistlicher Appellhof *m* unter dem Erzbischof von Canterbury

archetype, original copy · Originalausfertigung *f*, Urausfertigung

archiepiscopal court, provincial court [*In English law. The courts in the two ecclesiastic(al) provinces of England*] · erzbischöfliches Gericht *n*

archiepiscopal land · erzbischöfliches Land *n*

architect · Architekt *m*, A.

architect → (supervising) architect

architect-engineer [*An individual offering professional services as architect and/or engineer*] · Architekt-Ingenieur *m*

architect-engineers, engineer-architects [*A firm offering professional services as architect and/or engineer*] · Architekt-Ingenieur-Gruppe *f*, Ingenieur-Architekt-Gruppe

architect-in-charge, supervising architect, principal architect · ausführender Architekt *m*, (bau)leitender Architekt

architect in charge of planning and supervision · Bauanwalt *m* [*Ein Architekt, der mit Planung und Bauleitung betraut ist*]

architect in private practice · freiberuflicher Architekt *m*, frei(schaffend)er Architekt

architectonic design · künstlerische Gestaltung *f*, künstlerischer Entwurf *m*

architectonic general supervision, architectonic general superintendence · künstlerische Oberleitung *f* [*Künstlerische Oberleitung umfaßt die Überwachung der Herstellung des Werkes hinsichtlich der Einzelheiten der Gestaltung. (Auf diese Teilaufgabe entfallen 15% der Gesamtsumme)*]

architectress, female architect · Architektin *f*

architects' advisory panel, architects' advisory council · Architektenbeirat *m*

architect's certificate · Architektenattest *n*, Architektenbescheinigung *f*, Architektenschein *m*

architects' code · Architektenordnung *f*

architect's contract · Architektenvertrag *m*, Architektenwerkvertrag *m*, A-(Werk)Vertrag *m*

architect's duty · Architektenpflicht *f*

architect's fee · Architektenhonorar *n*, Architektengebühr *f*, A-Honorar *n*, A-Gebühr *f*

architect's indemnity insurance, architect's liability insurance, architect's third-party insurance · Architekten-Haftpflichtversicherung *f*

architect's interest, architect's right · Architektenrecht *n*, subjektives Architektenrecht *n*

architects' joint venture, joint-venture of architects · Architekten(arbeits)gemeinschaft *f*, Architektenarge *f* [*Zwei oder mehrere Architekten schließen sich zur Planung und/oder Leitung eines Bauvorhabens zusammen*]

architects' law · Architektenrecht *n*, objektives Architektenrecht *n*

architects' law → architects' (registration) act

architect's liability · Architektenhaftung *f*, Architektenhaftpflicht *f*, Architektenhaftbarkeit *f*

architect's liability insurance, architect's third-party insurance, architect's indemnity insurance · Architekten-Haftpflichtversicherung *f*

architect's model contract · Architekten-Mustervertrag *m*, Architekten-Formularvertrag *m*, Muster-Architektenvertrag *m*, Formular-Architektenvertrag *m*, A-Formularvertrag *m*, A-Mustervertrag *m*, Einheits-Architektenvertrag *m*, A-Einheitsvertrag *m*, Architekten-Einheitsvertrag *m*

architect's office · Architektenbüro *n*, Architekturbüro

architect's pre-planning contract · Architekten-Vorplanungsvertrag *m*

architects' (registration) act, architects' (registration) law, architects' (registration) statute · ArchG *n*, Architektengesetz *n*

architect's right, architect's interest · Architektenrecht *n*, subjektives Architektenrecht *n*

architect's satisfaction [*In regard of the qualities and standards of materials and workmanship*] · Architekteneinverständnis *n*

architect's third-party insurance, architect's indemnity insurance, architect's liability insurance · Architekten-Haftpflichtversicherung *f*

architect's work(s) · Architektenarbeit(en) *f(pl)*, A-Werk *n*, Architekten-

architectural adviser — area lease(hold)

werk *n*, A-Leistung(en) *f(pl)*, Architektenleistung(en), A-Arbeit(en)

architectural adviser, architectural consultant · beratender Architekt *m*

architectural guide · Architekturführer *m*

architectural history · Architekturgeschichte *f*

architectural historian · Architekturhistoriker *m*

architectural plan · Bebauungsentwurf *m* mit Darstellung der Bauobjekte im technischen Sinn

architectural practice · Architektenwesen *n*

architectural superintendence, architectural supervision · Ausbauaufsicht *f*, Ausbauüberwachung *f*

archives · Archiv *n*

archivist · Archivar *m*

area, territory · Gebiet *n*, Territorium *n*

area [*The superficial content of any figure*] · Fläche *f*

area → (building) (land) area

area acquisition → (building) land acquisition

area analysis → land analysis

area-bound · bereichsgebunden, flächengebunden

area boundary → area(l) boundary

area category, territory category · Gebietskategorie *f*, Territorialkategorie

area comparability factor · Flächenvergleichsfaktor *m*

area condemnation (US); area expropriation · Flächenenteignung *f* [*Gegensatz: Einzelenteignung*]

area consumption, consumption of land, consumption of area, land consumption · Bodenbeanspruchung *f*, Landbeanspruchung, Flächenbeanspruchung, Flächenverbrauch *m*, Bodenverbrauch, Landverbrauch

area corridor → area(l) corridor

area demise → (building) (land) area tenancy

area development law, area development statute, area development act, town and country planning act, town and country planning law, town and country planning statute · Bauleitplanungsgesetz *n*

area development plan, town and country plan, (physical) development plan, plan for (physical) development · Bauleitplan *m* [*Förmlicher Plan einer Gemeinde zur Ordnung ihrer gemeindlichen Entwick(e)lung (§ 1 Abs. 1 BBauG). Bauleitpläne unterscheiden sich mit unterschiedlicher Genauigkeit und Verbindlichkeit in: 1.) Flächennutzungsplan = vorbereitender Bauleitplan und 2.) Bebauungsplan = verbindlicher Bauleitplan*]

area development plan, territorial development plan · Gebietsentwick(e)lungsplan *m*, Territorialentwick(e)lungsplan

area development planning, (physical) development planning, planning for (physical) development, town and country planning · Bauleitplanung *f*

area development planning, territorial development planning · Gebietsentwick(e)lungsplanung *f*, Territorialentwick(e)lungsplanung

area division → area (sub)division

area estimate [*Approximation of probable project construction cost(s) based on assumed unit cost(s) per square foot or square metre*] · Baukostenschätzung *f* nach Fläche

area expropriation; area condemnation (US) · Flächenenteignung *f* [*Gegensatz: Einzelenteignung*]

area for a public utility, utility area · Versorgungsfläche *f*, Fläche für Versorgungsanlage [*Eine Grundstücksfläche für die öffentliche Versorgung; z. B. für Wasserwerk, Gaswerk, E-Werk, Trafohaus usw.*]

area for (a) secondary structure · Nebenanlagenfläche *f*, Fläche für Nebenanlagen

area for common facilities, area for public facilities, area to satisfy common needs, area to satisfy public needs, area for common needs, area for public needs · Gemeinbedarfsfläche *f*

area forecast, territory forecast · Gebietsvorhersage *f*

area for mixed development → (building) land for mixed development

area for (public) high speed transit · Schnellverkehrsfläche *f*, öffentliche Schnellverkehrsfläche

area improvement loan → (building) (land) area improvement loan

areal · flächenhaft

area(l) boundary, territorial boundary · Gebietsgrenze *f*, Territorialgrenze

area(l) corridor, (territorial) corridor · (Gebiets)Streifen *m*, Territorialstreifen

area(l) data · Flächendaten *f*

area(l) diagram map · Gebietsdiagrammkarte *f*, Territorialdiagrammkarte

area lease(hold) → (building) (land) area tenancy

area(l) extent · Flächenausdehnung *f*

area(l) natural monument · Flächennaturdenkmal *n*

area(l) network, territorial network · Gebietsnetz *n*, Territorialnetz

area(l) overlapping, overlapping of areas, overlapping of territories, territorial overlapping · Gebietsüberlagerung *f*, Gebietsüberschneidung, territoriale Überlagerung, territoriale Überschneidung

area(l) pattern, area(l) scheme, territorial pattern, territorial scheme · Gebietsmuster *n*, Gebietsschema *n*, Territorialmuster, Territorialschema

area(l) pattern, land pattern, land scheme, area(l) scheme · Bodenmuster *n*, Bodenschema *n*, Flächenmuster, Flächenschema, Landmuster, Landschema

area(l) percentage · Flächenanteil *m*, Flächenprozentsatz *m*

area(l) position map, position map of an area · Gebietslagekarte *f*, Lagekarte eines Gebietes; Mosaikkarte [*nach Imhof*]

area(l) production · Erzeugung *f* auf einer Fläche, Herstellung auf einer Fläche, Produktion *f* auf einer Fläche, Fertigung auf einer Fläche

area(l) scheme, territorial pattern, territorial scheme, area(l) pattern · Gebietsmuster *n*, Gebietsschema *n*, Territorialmuster, Territorialschema

area(l) system, territorial system · Gebietssystem *n*, Territorialsystem

area(l) unit · Flächeneinheit *f*

area(l) unit, territorial unit · Gebietseinheit *f*, Territorialeinheit

area(l) value · Arealitätsziffer *f*, Flächendichte *f* [*früher: Flächenausstattungsziffer*]

area map, territory map · Gebietskarte *f*

area market → (building) (land) area market

area monopoly → (building) (land) area monopoly

area natural monument → area(l) natural monument

area need → (building) (land) area need

area network → area(l) network

area not covered by a detailed local plan but which has already been developed without plan · im Zusammenhang bebauter Ortsteil *m*

area of comprehensive development, territory of comprehensive development, C.D.A., comprehensive development area, comprehensive development territory · Generalbebauungsgebiet *n*

area of comprehensive redevelopment, comprehensive redevelopment area (Brit.); redevelopment area, area of redevelopment (US) · Wiederbebauungsgebiet *n*; Wiederüberbauungsgebiet [*Schweiz*]

area of coverage, coverage area · Bebauungsfläche *f*; Überbauungsfläche [*Schweiz*]

area of demolition and rebuilding → area of wrecking and rebuilding

area of depopulation, depopulation area, depopulation territory, territory of depopulation · Aushöhlungsgebiet *n*, Entleerungsgebiet *n*

area of destination, territory of destination · Zielgebiet *n*, Bestimmungsgebiet

area of distribution of the individual groups of elements, area of the earth's surface, individual land area [*Climate; water; land; plants and cultural phenomena*] · Erdraum *m*

area of ground, terrain area, area of terrain, ground area · Geländefläche *f*, Terrainfläche

area of land, land area · Landfläche *f* [*im Gegensatz zur Meeresfläche*]

area of (outstanding) natural beauty, territory of (outstanding) natural beauty, AONB · Naturschönheitsgebiet *n*

area of poverty, territory of poverty, poverty area, poverty territory · Armutsgebiet *n*

area of preference, preference territory, preference area, territory of preference · Vorranggebiet *n*

area of problems, territory of problems, problem area, problem territory · Problemgebiet *n*

area of redevelopment (US) → area of comprehensive redevelopment

area of special control, territory of special control [*In an area of special control, where it is usual for no advertisements to be allowed, those that are permitted are agreed exceptions to the rule*] · reklamearmes Gebiet *n*

area of terrain, ground area, area of ground, terrain area · Geländefläche *f*, Terrainfläche

area of the earth's surface, individual land area, area of distribution of the individual groups of elements [*Climate; water; land; plants and cultural phenomena*] · Erdraum *m*

area of validity · Geltungsgebiet *n*

area of validity of prohibition · Veränderungssperregebiet *n*

area of water, water area · Wasserfläche *f*

area of wrecking and rebuilding, territory of demolition and rebuilding, territory of wrecking and rebuilding, wrecking and rebuilding territory, razing and rebuilding territory, demolition and rebuilding area, demolition and rebuilding territory, wrecking and rebuilding area, area of demolition and rebuilding · Abbruch- und Wiederaufbaugebiet *n*, Abriß- und Wiederaufbaugebiet, Abreiß- und Wiederaufbaugebiet

area overlapping → area(l) overlapping

area owner → (building) (land) area owner

area planning, territorial planning · Gebietsplanung *f*, Territorialplanung

area planning commission, territorial planning commission · Gebietsplanungskommission *f*, Territorialplanungskommission

area proprietor → (building) (land) area proprietor

area protection, territory protection, protection of area, protection of territory · Gebietsschutz *m*

area quality → (building) (land) area quality

area-related, area-orien(ta)ted · flächenbezogen, flächenorientiert

area-related, territory-orien(ta)ted, area-orien(ta)ted, territory-related · gebietsbezogen, gebietsorientiert, territorialbezogen, territorialorientiert

area reserved for handling of aircrafts · Luftverkehrsfläche *f*

area scarcity factor, land(s) scarcity factor · Bodenknappheitsgrad *m*, Landknappheitsgrad, Flächenknappheitsgrad

area scheme → area(l) pattern

area size, size of area · Flächengröße *f*

area speculation → (building) (land) area speculation

area (sub)division · Flächengliederung *f*, Landgliederung, Bodengliederung, Flächenaufteilung, Bodenaufteilung, Landaufteilung

area (sub)division plan · Flächenaufteilungsplan *m*, Flächengliederungsplan, Landaufteilungsplan, Landgliederungsplan, Bodenaufteilungsplan, Bodengliederungsplan

area subject to one sovereign power, territory subject to one sovereign power, state area, state territory · Staatsgebiet *n*, Hoheitsgebiet

area subject to one system of law; territorium legis [*Latin*]; territory subject to one system of law · Rechtsgebiet *n*

area supply → (building) (land) area supply

area system → area(l) system

area tax → (building) (land) area tax

area to satisfy common needs, area to satisfy public needs, area for common needs, area for public needs, area for common facilities, area for public facilities · Gemeinbedarfsfläche *f*

area to satisfy public needs → area to satisfy common needs

area under crops and grass, cultivated area · Kulturfläche *f*

area use → (land) area use

area use regulation → (land) area use regulation

areawide · flächendeckend

arguing, reasoning [*The drawing of inferences or conclusions from known or assumed facts*] · Argumentieren *n*

argumentation, use of reason · Argumentation *f*

argumentum · Analogieschluß *m*

argumentum a contrario [*Latin*] · Umkehrschluß *m*, Gegenschluß

argumentum a fortiori [*Latin*] · Analogieschluß *m* vom Stärkeren auf das Schwächere

argumentum a majus ad minore [*Latin*] · Analogieschluß *m* vom Größeren auf das Kleinere

argumentum a minore ad majus [*Latin*] · Analogieschluß *m* vom Kleineren auf das Größere

arid zone soil · Trockenzonenboden *m*

to arise to have a legal existence, to begin to have a legal existence, to accrue [*For instance, an action accrues when the plaintiff has a right to commence it*] · gesetzlich entstehen

aristocracy, nobles · Hochadel *m*

arithmetical check · rechnerische Nachprüfung *f*

arithmetical error · Rechenfehler *m*

arithmetic mean, average · arithmetisches Mittel *n*

arles, erles, arrha(bo), handmoney, handsel, earnest (money) [*A sum paid to bind a bargain*] · Angeld *n*, Kaufschilling *m*, Handgeld, D(a)rauf(gabe)geld, D(a)raufgabe *f*, Haftgeld, Mietstaler *m* [*Wenn Angeld gegeben wird, so gilt dies nach dem Gesetz als ein Zeichen, daß ein Vertrag abgeschlossen wurde*]

armory · Zeughaus *n*

arraignment · Versetzung *f* in den Anklagezustand [*Gefängnisinsasse*]

arrangement · Vorkehrung *f*

arrangement · Anordnung *f*, Aufbau *m* [*System*]

arrangement → amicable composition (of differences)

arrangement by multiple nuclei; multi(ple)-centered pattern, multi(ple)-centered scheme (US) · Mehrkernschema *n*, Vielkernschema, Mehrkernmuster *n*, Vielkernmuster

arrangement deed, deed of arrangement · Akkord *m*, Nachlaßvertrag *m* [*Der Vertrag, vermöge dessen dem Schuldner ein Teil der Schuld von den Gläubigern erlassen wird*]

arrangement (in bankruptcy), composition (in bankruptcy) [*An agreement between debtor and creditor, by which the latter agrees to discharge the former on payment of a certain sum*] · (Gläubiger)Vergleich *m*, Konkursakkord *m*, Akkord im Konkurs

arrangement of streets, street arrangement · Stadtstraßenanordnung *f*

arrangement scheme, scheme of arrangement · Nachlaßvertrag *m* mit Vermögensabtretung, Akkord *m* mit Vermögensabtretung

arrangement scheme, scheme of composition, scheme of arrangement, composition scheme · (Gläubiger)Vergleichsvorschlag *m*, Konkursakkordvorschlag

array · Anordnung *f* [*Berechnung einer Determinante*]

arrearage [*Money remaining unpaid after the agreed time for payment*] · Rückstand *m*

arrearage of dwelling rent → residential rent in arrear(age)

arrear(age) of interest, interest arrear(age) · Zinsrückstand *m*

arrear(age) of rent, rent in arrear(age) · Mietrückstand *m*

arrear(age) of residential rent → residential rent in arrear(age)

arrear(age)s [*Monies remaining unpaid after the agreed time for payment*] · Rückstände *mpl*

arrendare [*Latin*]; to let land(s) yearly · verpachten von Land jährlich

arrest book · Arrestbuch *n*

arresting process [*Scots law*], attachment process · Beschlagnahmeverfahren *n*, Pfändungsverfahren, dingliches Arrestverfahren

arrestment [*Scots law*], attachment [*The act or process of taking, apprehending, or seizing property, by virtue of a writ, summons, or other judicial order, and bringing the same into the custody of the law*] · Beschlagnahme *f*, Pfändung *f*, dinglicher Arrest *m*

arrestment of debt(s), attachment of debt(s) [*Scots law*] · (Geld)Schuldenpfändung *f*, (Geld)Forderungspfändung, Pfändung von (Geld)Forderungen, Pfändung von (Geld)Schulden, dinglicher Arrest *m* von (Geld)Forderungen

arrestment order, order of attachment, order of arrestment, attachment order [*Scots law*] · Beschlagnahmebefehl *m*, Pfändungsbefehl, dinglicher Arrestbefehl, Beschlagnahmeverfügung *f*, Pfändungsverfügung, dingliche Arrestverfügung

arrest of judg(e)ment [*The act of staying a judgment, or refusing to render judgment in an action at law, after verdict, of some matter intrinsic appearing on the face of the record, which would render the judgment, if given, erroneous or reversible*] · Urteilsaussetzung *f*, Urteilsaufschiebung, Urteilsaufschub *m*, Unterbleiben *n* des Urteils, Aussetzung des Urteils, Aufschub des Urteils, Aufschiebung des Urteils

arrha(bo), handmoney, handsel, earnest (money), arles, erles [*A sum paid to bind a bargain*] · Angeld *n*, Kaufschilling *m*, Handgeld, D(a)rauf(gabe)geld, D(a)raufgabe *f*, Haftgeld, Mietstaler *m* [*Wenn Angeld gegeben wird, so gilt dies nach dem Gesetz als ein Zeichen, daß ein Vertrag abgeschlossen wurde*]

arriere fief, arriere fee, arriere tenure, mesne fief, mesne fee, mesne tenure, mean fief, mean fee, mean tenure, middle fief, middle fee, middle tenure, intermediate fief, intermediate fee, intermediate tenure [*A fief dependent on a superior one; an inferior fief granted by a vassal of the king, out of the fief held by him*] · Afterleh(e)n *n*

arriere lord, mesne lord, mean lord, middle lord; tenente in capite [*Latin*], intermediate lord · (feudaler) Belehner *m* von Aftervasallen, Feudalherr von Aftervasallen, Leh(e)n(s)herr von Aftervasallen, Leh(e)n(s)gutgeber von Aftervasallen, mittlerer Leh(e)n(s)herr, mittlerer Feudalherr, Vasall *m* der Krone, Kronvasall, Afterleh(e)nsherr

arriere tenant, mean tenant, middle tenant, intermediate tenant, mesne tenant · Afterleh(e)n(s)mann *m*

arriere vassal, under-feudatory, vassal of a vassal · Aftervasall *m*

arrival date [*event*] · Eintrittsdatum *n* [*Ereignis*]

arrow symbol · Pfeilkartenzeichen *n*, Pfeilsignatur *f*

arrow (symbol) map · Pfeillinienkarte *f*

arson · Brandstiftung *f*

art exhibition, exhibition of works of art · Kunstausstellung *f*

article, fixture, component, object affixed to a structure · Bestandteil *m*, Grund-

article attached by the tenant — ascertainment error

stücksbestandteil, (grundstücks)verbundene Sache f, Sache mit einem Grundstück verbunden

article attached by the tenant, fixture attached by the tenant, component attached by the tenant · Mieter-(Grundstücks)Bestandteil m

article attached by the owner, fixture attached by the proprietor, component attached by the proprietor, article attached by the proprietor, fixture attached by the owner, component attached by the owner · Eigentümer-(Grundstücks)Bestandteil m

articled clerk · angehender Geschäftsanwalt m, Geschäftsanwaltlehrling m

article of antiquity, antiquity article · Altertumsgegenstand m, Altertumsfund m

article of confederation, confederation article · Konföderationsartikel m

article pawned, article pledged, object pawned, object pledged, pawn, vadium, pledged article, pledged object, pawned article, pawned object · Pfand n, Pfandstück n, verpfändeter Gegenstand m, gegebenes (Mobiliar)Pfand, Pfandsache f

articles of apprenticeship · Lehr(lings)vertrag m

articles (of association) · Beilagen f pl zur Gründungsurkunde, Beilagen zur Satzung, Beilagen zum Gründungsvertrag, Beilagen zum Gesellschaftsvertrag

articles of incorporation (US); social contract, partnership contract, memorandum (of association), deed of partnership, partnership deed; deed of settlement [*obsolete*] [*Business corporations are now usually created under a general statute which permits a specified number of persons to form a corporation by preparing and filing with the proper public official, usually the secretary of state, a document known as the articles of incorporation*] · Gründungsurkunde f, Gründungssatzung f, Gesellschaftsvertrag m, Gründungsvertrag, Gesellschaftsurkunde [*1.) Körperschaft, Korporation; 2.) (Kapital)Gesellschaft; 3.) vereinsähnliche Gemeinschaft*]

(artificial) accession (of property), (artificial) addition of property, artificial augmentation of property, artificial increase of property [*Addition to property by artificial improvement; which becomes the property of the owner of that which receives the addition, who is said to acquire the proprietorship thereof by accession*] · künstliche Besitzzunahme f, künstlicher Besitzzuwachs m, künstliche Besitzerhöhung, künstliche Besitzsteigerung

artificial environment, man-made environment · künstliche Umwelt f

artificial evidence, artificial proof · künstlicher Beweis m

artificial fruits [*Such as by metaphor or analogy are likened to the fruits of the earth. Interest on money is an example*] · künstliche Früchte f pl

artificial landmark, artificial monument, man-made land mark, man-made monument · künstliche Landmarke f, künstliches festes Seezeichen n

artificial (land) surface form, man-made (land) surface form · anthropogene (Land)Oberflächenform f, künstliche (Land)Oberflächenform f

artificial monument, man-made land mark, man-made monument, artificial landmark · künstliche Landmarke f, künstliches festes Seezeichen n

artificial obstacle, artificial obstruction, artificial hindrance · künstliches Hindernis n

artificial person, legal person · juristische Person f, Rechtsperson, J. P.

artificial proof, artificial evidence · künstlicher Beweis m

artificial reason of law · richterliche Vernunft f und Erfahrung f

artificial variable · künstliche Variable f

artisan, (hand) craftsman · Handwerker m

art of government · Staatskunst f

A/S, account sales · Verkaufsabrechnung f, Abrechnung des Verkaufskommissionärs

as-built drawing, as-constructed drawing, 'work as executed' drawing, as-completed drawing · (Bau)Bestandsplan m, (Bau)Bestandszeichnung f

as-built state, as-completed state, "work as executed" state, as-constructed state · Ausbauzustand m, Bestandszustand m

ascendant, ancestor, progenitor [*Not to be confused with "predecessor" = Vorgänger*] · Vorfahre m, Ahn m

ascertained facts, case facts, situation of facts, state of facts, actual situation, established facts · Sachlage f, Sachverhalt m, Tatbestand m

ascertained goods, specific goods · Spezieswaren f pl

ascertained person · bestimmte Person f

ascertaining facts, establishing facts · Feststellung f des Lebenssachverhalts zum juristischen Sachverhalt, Fixierung des Lebenssachverhalts zum juristischen Sachverhalt [*In Deutschland im Urteil unter dem Titel „Tatbestand" zusammengefaßt*]

ascertainment error, error of observation, error of ascertainment, observation error · Beobachtungsfehler m [*Statistik*]

ascertainment of facts — assent in writing

ascertainment of facts · Tatsachenermitt(e)lung *f*

as-completed drawing, as-built drawing, as-constructed drawing, 'work as executed' drawing · (Bau)Bestandsplan *m*, (Bau)Bestandszeichnung *f*

as-completed state, "work as executed" state, as-constructed state, as-built state · Ausbauzustand *m*, Bestandszustand *m*

ascription · Zuschreibung *f* [*Gegensatz: Leistungsorientierung*]

as-fitted drawing · Montageplan *m*, Montagezeichnung *f*

asked [*price*] · angeboten, gefordert [*Börsenausdruck*]

asked price [*The price at which a dealer or specialist in securities will sell shares of stock out of inventory*] · Inventarwert *m*, geforderter Preis *m*, angebotener Preis, Angebot *n*, Verkaufspreis, Briefkurs *m* [*Börsenausdruck*]

aspiration level · Anspruchsniveau *n*, Zufriedenheitsniveau

asportation · widerrechtliche Wegschaffung *f* einer fremden Sache

as prescribed, in due form · vorschriftsmäßig, wie vorgeschrieben, vorschriftsgemäß

to assart, to essart; exartare [*Low Latin*] [*This, in the ancient forest laws of England, meant to stub up trees and bushes in a forest so that they could not grow again*] · ausholzen, ausreuten, roden

assart [*A clearing in a forest*] · (Wald)Lichtung *f*

assartare [*Latin*] · to assart

assarting; disbocatio, essartum [*Latin*]; [*Grubbing up trees and bushes from forest-land, so as to make it arable*] · Ausholzen *n*, Ausreuten *n*, Roden *n*

assault and battery · tätlicher Angriff *m*

assedation, tack [*Scots law*]; estate less than freehold, lease(hold), tenure, leasehold estate, demise, tenancy; demissio, dimissio [*Latin*] [*Holding of real estate under a lease. Such an estate continues for a fixed or determinable period of time but not for a lifetime. It is a conveyance of land whereby the owner of landed property, called the lessor, grants the possession and use of his landed property to another party, called the lessee, in consideration of a sum of money, called the rent*] · Bodenpacht *f*, Landpacht, Bodennutzungsrechtvergabe *f*, Landnutzungsrechtvergabe, Bodenverpachtung *f*, Landverpachtung, (Boden)Nutzungsrecht *n*

assedation law [*Scots law*] → law of estates less than freehold

assemblage, plottage, assembling real properties, assembling (real) estates, assembling lands, assembling realties · Grund(stücks)zusammenschreibung *f*, Bodenzusammenschreibung, (Land)-Zusammenschreibung

to assemble · zusammenschreiben [*Land*]

to assemble, to convene [*To meet together, usually for a common purpose*] · zusammenkommen, sich versammeln

assembling a bid, assembling a tender, assembling an offer; assembling a (bid) proposal (US) · Angebotsausarbeitung *f*

assembling real properties, assembling (real) estates, assembling lands, assembling realties, assemblage, plottage · Grund(stücks)zusammenschreibung *f*, Bodenzusammenschreibung, (Land)-Zusammenschreibung

assembly · Versammlung *f*

assembly, composite article [*A combination of parts and possibly raw materials put together*] · Verbunderzeugnis *n*, Verbundprodukt *n*

assembly · Wahlkammer *f* [*Kronkolonie*]

assembly · Zusammenrottung *f*

assembly freedom, freedom of assembly · Versammlungsfreiheit *f*

assembly of condo(minium) owners (US); assembly of private flat owners (Brit.) · Wohnungseigentümerversammlung *f*

assembly of works council members, assembly of workers' council members, assembly of workmen's council members · Betriebsräteversammlung *f*

assembly plant · Montageanlage *f*, Montagewerk *n*, Montagefabrik *f*

to assent, to consent, to approbate, to approve · billigen, einwilligen, zustimmen

assent, consent, approbation, consensus, approval · Billigung *f*, Einwilligung, Zustimmung, Konsens *m*

assent to assignment, assent to cession, consent to assignment, consent to cession, sanction to assignment, sanction to cession, approval to assignment, approval to cession · Abtretungseinwilligung *f*, Abtretungszustimmung, Abtretungsbilligung, Zessionseinwilligung, Zessionszustimmung, Zessionsbilligung

assented, consented, approbated, approved · gebilligt, eingewilligt, zugestimmt

assenting, action of giving assent, sanctioning, approbating, approving, consenting · Billigen *n*, Einwilligen, Zustimmen

assent in writing, sanction in writing, approval in writing, written assent, writ-

to assert — assignation

ten approval, written consent, written sanction, consent in writing · schriftliche Billigung f, schriftliche Einwilligung, schriftliche Zustimmung, schriftlicher Konsens m

to assert, to allege, to aver [*To prove or justify a plea; to make an averment*] · behaupten

to assert, to lay claim to, to defend a right, to maintain a right · beanspruchen, geltend machen [*Forderung; Recht*]

asserting, alleging, averring · Behaupten n

assertion, allegation, averment [*A statement of fact made in any proceeding, as, for instance, in a pleading, particularly a statement of charge which is, as yet, unproved*] · Behauptung f, Bekräftigung

assertion · Geltendmachung f, Beanspruchung [*Forderung*]

to assess, to rate · anteil(mäß)ig festsetzen, bemessen, einstufen, einschätzen, festsetzen eines Satzes [*z. B. ein Bauwerk für Versicherungszwecke; Steuern*]

assessable for tax(ation) (purposes), assessible for tax(ation) (purposes), taxable, subject to tax(ation), rat(e)able · veranlagbar, steuerlich einstufbar, besteuerbar, versteuerbar

assessable value [*deprecated*]; reduced net annual value, reduced rat(e)able value, rat(e)able value · reduzierter Nettoertragswert m [*Die landwirtschaftlich genutzten Grundstücke werden mit einem herabgesetzten Nettoertragswert zur Steuer eingeschätzt*]

assessed value, rated value, taxable value [*The value of property as appraised for taxation*] · bemessener Wert m, eingestufter Wert, festgesetzter Wert, veranlagter Wert

to assess for (land-)tax, to register for (land-)tax · katastrieren

to assess (for rating purposes), to rate · veranlagen, steuerlich einstufen

assessing, rating · anteiliges Festsetzen n, anteilmäßiges Festsetzen n, Einstufen n, Bemessen n, Festsetzen n eines Satzes

assessment, rating · (anteilige) Festsetzung f, anteilmäßige Festsetzung f, Bemessung f, Einstufung f, Einschätzung f, Festsetzung f eines Satzes, Satzfestsetzung

assessment → assessment (of value)

assessment area · Steuer(einschätzungs)bezirk m [*Umfaßt mehrere "rating areas"*]

assessment committee → (tax) assessment committee

74

assessment insurance · Versicherung f nach dem Umlage- oder Aufwanddeckungsverfahren

assessmentism · (Ab)Schätzungswesen n, Tax(ierungs)wesen, Wertermitt(e)lungswesen, Bewertungswesen

assessment of damage, damage assessment · Schadensbemessung f

assessment of indemnification, assessment of compensation, assessment of damages, assessment of indemnity · Entschädigungsbewertung f

assessment of property · Vermögensbewertung

assessment (of value), (e)valuation, val., appraisal (of value), appraisement (of value) [*The determined or estimated value or price*] · (Ab)Schätzung f, Taxierung, Wertermitt(e)lung f, Bewertung

assessment rate, rate of assessment · Bemessungssatz m, Festsetzungssatz

assessor, rating officer, rating official [*A public official who evaluates property for the purposes of taxation*] · Veranlagungsbeamte m, Steuerveranlagungsbeamte

assessor [*One who sits as assistant or adviser to a judge or magistrate and is competent to advise on technical points of law, commercial usage, etc.*] · Schiedsgutachter m, Schiedssachverständige

assessor · Beisitzer m

Assessors for the Land Valuation · staatliche Landabschätzungskommission f [*In Schottland*]

asset, valuable thing, property · geldwerter Gegenstand m, Vermögensgegenstand, Vermögenssache f, geldwerte Sache, Vermögensding n, geldwertes Ding, Vermögensrechtsobjekt n, geldwertes Rechtsobjekt

asset administration, administration (of estate), administration of asset, administration of property, personal representation, estate administration · erbrechtliche Verwaltung f, Nachlaßverwaltung, Erb(schafts)verwaltung

assets · Aktiva f, Guthaben n

assets and liabilities · Aktiva f und Passiva

to assign, to cede · abtreten, zedieren

assignability · Abtretbarkeit f, Zedierbarkeit

assignable · abtretbar, zedierbar

assignably [*In a manner capable of being assigned*] · abtretungsweise

assignate; assigned [*obsolete*] · abgetreten, zediert

assignation, summons to appear in court · (Gerichts)Vorladung f

assignation — assistance hous(ebuild)ing institution

assignation, assignment, cession · (dingliche) Abtretung f, (dingliche) Zession f

assigned; assignate [obsolete] · abgetreten, zediert

assigned counsel, court-appointed counsel · Pflichtanwalt m

assigned defender, court-appointed defender · Pflichtverteidiger m

assign(ee); cessionary [Scots law] [One to whom a property or right is legally transferred or made over] · Abtretungsempfänger m, Forderungsübernehmer, Zessionar, Zessionär

assignee in bankruptcy, referee in bankruptcy, trustee in bankruptcy, commissioner in bankruptcy, accountant in bankruptcy · (Konkurs)Masse(n)kurator m, Konkursverwalter m, Kurator

assignee in law · gesetzlicher Kurator m, gesetzlicher Konkursverwalter, gesetzlicher (Konkurs)Masse(n)verwalter, gesetzlicher Zwangsverwalter

assigning · Abtreten n, Zedieren

assignment, cession, assignation · (dingliche) Abtretung f, (dingliche) Zession f

assignment · Festsetzung f

assignment by operation of law, cession by operation of law, assignation by operation of law · Abtretung f auf Grund von Rechtsvorschriften, Zession f auf Grund von Rechtsvorschriften

assignment clause, cession clause, assignation clause · Abtretungsklausel f, Zessionsklausel

assignment contract, cession contract, contract of assignation, assignation contract, contract of assignment, contract of cession · Abtretungsvertrag m, Zessionsvertrag

assignment declaration, cession declaration, assignment statement, cession statement, assignation statement, assignation declaration, statement of assignment, declaration of assignment, declaration of cession, statement of cession, declaration of assignation, statement of assignation · Abtretungserklärung f, Zessionserklärung

assignment deed, cession deed, assignation deed, deed of assignation, deed of cession, deed of assignment · Abtretungsurkunde f, Zessionsurkunde

assignment law, cession law, law of assignation, assignation law, law of cession, law of assignment · Abtretungsrecht n, Zessionsrecht

assignment notice, assignment notification, cession notice, cession notification, notice of assignment, notice of cession, notification of assignment, notification of cession · Zessionsanzeige f, Zessionsmitteilung f, Abtretungsanzeige, Abtretungsmitteilung

assignment of dower · Festsetzung f des Witwenanteils am Immobiliarvermögen des Gatten

assignment of errors · Festsetzung f von Gründen weshalb ein Urteil kassiert werden soll

assignment of land, cession of land, land assignment, land cession, assignation of land, land assignation · Bodenabtretung f, Landabtretung, Grund(stücks)abtretung, Grund(stücks)zession f, Bodenzession, Landzession

assignment of lease(hold), assignment of demise, assignment of tenancy, lease(hold) cession, lease(hold) assignment, demise cession, demise assignment, tenancy cession, tenancy assignment, cession of lease(hold), cession of demise, cession of tenancy · Pachtabtretung f, Pachtzession f

assignment of possession, cession of possession, possession assignment, possession cession, assignation of possession, possession assignation · Besitzabtretung f, Besitzzession f

assignment of right, assignation of right, cession of right [A transfer of an existing right from one person to another] · Rechtsabtretung f, Rechtszession f

assignment practice, cession practice, assignation practice · Abtretungswesen n, Zessionswesen

assignment statement, cession statement, assignation statement, assignation declaration, statement of assignment, declaration of assignment, declaration of cession, statement of cession, declaration of assignation, statement of assignation, assignment declaration, cession declaration · Abtretungserklärung f, Zessionserklärung

assignor, assigner, grantor; cedent [Scots law] [A person who assigns a claim, right, property, etc.] · Abtreter m, Geber, Zedent m

assimilation of immigrants, integration of immigrants, immigrant absorption, immigrant assimilation, immigrant integration, absorption of immigrants · Einwandererangliederung f, Einwandererintegration f

assise → assize

assise of bread, assize of bread; assisa panis [Latin] · Brottaxe f

assise of darrein presentment → (petty) assise of darrein presentment

assise of last presentation → (petty) assise of last presentation

assise of mort d'ancestor → (petty) assise of mort d'ancestor

assistance hous(ebuild)ing institution, sponsoring hous(ebuid)ing institution,

assistance of export — association of architects

promotion(al) hous(ebuild)ing institution · Wohn(ungs)bauförderungsanstalt f

assistance of export, sponsoring of export, export promotion, export assistance, promotion of export · Ausfuhrförderung f, Exportförderung

assistance of homebuilding · Eigenheimförderung f, Eigenhausförderung

assistant-barrister · Hilfsrichter m des königlichen Stadtrichters von London

assistant clerk · Bürobeamte m, Hilfsschreiber m [Grafschaftsgericht in England]

assistant commissioner · Kommissarsgehilfe m

assistant-judge [At a borough or local court] · Hilfsrichter m

assistant judge · rechtsgelehrter Richter m

assistant-overseer · besoldeter Armenaufseher m

assistant professor, lecturer · (Privat)-Dozent m

assistant professor in law, lecturer in law · Rechtsdozent m

assistant solicitor · Stadtrechtsrat m

assisted hous(ebuild)ing, promotion(al) hous(ebuild)ing, sponsoring hous(e-build)ing · geförderter Wohn(ungs)-bau m, Wohn(ungs)bauförderung f

assisting individual system, individual promotion(al) system, individual sponsoring system, individual assistance system, promotion(al) individual system, sponsoring individual system · Individualförderungssystem n

assize, assise [These terms anciently signified a legislative enactment] · Assise f

assize, judicial inquest, assise · richterliche Untersuchung f

assize, jury trial, trial by jury [A trial in which sworn assessors or jurymen decide questions of fact] · Gerichtsverhandlung f vor Geschworenen, (Haupt)-Verhandlung vor Geschworenen, Geschworenen(haupt)verhandlung, Geschworenengerichtsverhandlung, Schwurgerichtsverfahren n, Geschworenenverfahren, Schwurgerichtsverhandlung

assize court, court of assize, assise court, court of assise [England] · Geschworenengericht n [Es wird in jeder Grafschaft periodisch von den Richtern des High Court und sonstigen beauftragten Personen mindestens zweimal jährlich abgehalten]

assize of bread and ale, assise of bread and ale · Brot- und Biertaxe f

Assize of Weights and Measures · Maß- und Gewichtsordnung f, Maß- und Gewichtstaxe f [In England im Jahre 1197 veröffentlicht]

associate · Richtergehilfe m

associate, member · Mitglied n

associate · Genosse m

associate [obsolete]; master of the supreme court [England] · richterlicher Hilfsbeamter m eines gemeinrechtlichen Gerichtes

associate certificate [obsolete]; master's certificate · Zeugnis n des richterlichen Hilfsbeamten über das vom Richter bei der Assisenverhandlung gefällte Urteil zur Registrierung beim Hohen Justizhof [An Stelle des ehemaligen „postea"]

associated · unselbständig [Wohnung. Die Insassen benutzen Spülküche und/oder Abort mit anderen]

associated activity · gemeinschaftliche Anstrengung f, gemeinsame Anstrengung

associate(d) architect [Architect working with another architect in a temporary agreement or partnership · Architektengenosse m

associated company · Beteiligungsgesellschaft f mit höchstens 50% Beteiligung

associated company, affiliate(d company), allied company · verbundene Gesellschaft f [Eine Gesellschaft, die eine verbundene Person ist]

associate(d) judge · beigeordneter Richter m

association, society, institution [An establishment, specially one of public character or one affecting a community] · (Personen)Verein(igung) m, (f)

association, commercial corporation · Handelsgesellschaft f

association · engerer Verband m [Im Sinne von Otto Gierke]

association coefficient, coefficient of association · Assoziationskoeffizient m

association corporate, membership corporation · rechtsfähiger Verein m, Verein mit Korporationsrecht, eingetragener Verein, e.V.

association for providing settlers with land, land settlement association · Landlieferungsverband m

association movement → (building and loan) association movement

association of architects, society of architects, institution of architects · Architektenverein(igung) m, (f)

Association of Architects — atmospheric pollution

Association of Architects of the Federal Republic of Germany, Society of Architects of the Federal Republic of Germany, Institution of Architects of the Federal Republic of Germany · Bundesarchitektenkammer *f*

association of borrowers, institution of borrowers, federation of borrowers, society of borrowers · landwirtschaftlicher Kreditverein *m*, Landschaft *f*, landwirtschaftliche Kreditvereinigung *f*

association of building contractors, society of construction contractors, society of building contractors, institution of construction contractors, institution of building contractors, federation of construction contractors, federation of building contractors, association of construction contractors · Bauunternehmerverein(igung) *m*, *(f)*

association of civil engineers, society of civil engineers, institution of civil engineers · Bauingenieurverein(igung) *m*, *(f)*

association of contractors, institution of contractors, contractors' association, contractors' institution, contractors' society, society of contractors · Unternehmerverein(igung) *m*, *(f)*

association of credit, popular bank, credit association · Vorschußverein *m*

association of engineering unions, institution of engineering unions, society of engineering unions, federation of engineering unions · Verein(igung) *m*, *(f)* der Ingenieurverbände

association of landlords, society of landlords · Haus- und Grundeigentümerverein *m*

association of landowners, landowners' association · Grundeigentümergenossenschaft *f*, Genossenschaft von Grundeigentümern

association of tenants, society of tenants · Mieterverein *m*

association of urban landowners, urban landowners' association [*They procure money on the security of their estates*] · Stadtschaft *f*, Genossenschaft von städtischen Grundeigentümern, städtische Grundeigentümergenossenschaft

association unincorporate, membership association · Verein *m* ohne Korporationsrecht, nicht eingetragener Verein, nicht rechtsfähiger Verein

assumed fact · unterstellte Tatsache *f*

assumpsit → (court) action of assumpsit

assumpsit [*Latin*] [*obsolete*]; promise, undertaking · (Leistungs)Versprechen *n*, Naturalversprechen

assumption of loan, loan assumption · Darleh(e)nsübernahme *f*

assumption of risk · Einwilligung *f* des Verletzten

assurable [*deprecated*]; insurable · versicherungsfähig, versicherbar

assurance, commitment, engagement · Zusage *f* [*Bindende Verpflichtung für ein künftiges Verhalten*]

assurance, conveyance · dingliche Übertragung *f*, Übertragung eines dinglichen Rechtes

assurance [*deprecated*]; insurance · Versicherung *f*, Assekuranz *f*

assurance (on conveyance of land) → (common) assurance (on conveyance of land)

to assure, to insure · versichern

to assure, to commit, to engage · zusagen

to assure [*To declare or promise confidently*] · zusichern

to assure · dinglich übertragen

to assure, to convince [*To make (a person) sure of something*] · überzeugen

assured (party), insuree, insured (party) · Versicherte *m*, Assekurat, Versicherungsnehmer

assurement · Friedensgelöbnis *n* [*Feudalrecht*]

assurer (Brit.); insurer · Versicherer *m*, Assekurant *m*

asylum board · Amt *n* für Hospitalwesen

asymptotically efficient estimator · asymptotisch wirksame Schätzfunktion *f* [*Statistik*]

asymptotic distribution · Grenzverteilung *f* [*Statistik*]

asymptotic efficiency · asymptotische Leistungsfähigkeit *f* [*Statistik*]

ath [*Saxon*]; oath; othe [*old English*]; juramentum, jus jurandum, sacramentum [*Latin*] · Eid *m*

athletic club · Sportverein *m*

at insured exchange · ohne Kursrisiko, mit gesichertem Kurs [*Pensionsgeschäft*]

atlas of diseases · Krankheitenatlas *m*

atlas of mineral resources · Mineralstättenatlas *m*

at law, by law, for law, in law, according to law · nach dem Gesetz, dem Gesetz nach

atmospheric pollution, atmospheric contamination, air pollution, air contamination · Luftverunreinigung *f*, Luftverseuchung, Luftverschmutzung [*Das Einfallen fester, flüssiger und/oder gasförmiger luftfremder Stoffe in Bodennähe*]

atmospheric pollution control, atmospheric pollution prevention, air quality control, clean air control, air pollution control, air pollution prevention · Luftreinhaltung *f*

atomic law, nuclear law · Atomrecht *n*, Kernrecht *n*

atomic station, nuclear plant, atomic plant, nuclear station · Atomanlage *f*, Kernanlage *f*

at one's pleasure · nach freiem Belieben

atrium house · Atriumhaus *n*

ats, a.t.s., at the suit of · auf die Klage von

at sufferance, by sufferance · geduldet [*Besitz(stand)*]

to attach · beschlagnahmen, pfänden, dinglich arrestieren

attached, belonging to, appendant, appurtenant (to) [*Things appendant can be claimed only by prescription, while things appurtenant can be claimed either by prescription or by express grant*] · anhaftend, zugehörig

attached building [*A building that has any part of its exterior or bearing walls in common with another building or which is connected to another building by a roof*] · (Gebäude)Anbau *m*

attachment · Personalarrest *m* [*Als Strafe für Ungehorsam gegen eine gerichtliche Verfügung oder wegen Unterlassung einer durch die Prozeßordnung gebotenen Obliegenheit*]

attachment; arrestment [*Scots law*] [*The act or process of taking, apprehending, or seizing property, by virtue of a writ, summons, or other judicial order, and bringing the same into the custody of the law*] · Beschlagnahme *f*, Pfändung *f*, dinglicher Arrest *m*

attachment [*The act or process of taking, apprehending, or seizing persons, by virtue of a writ, summons, or other judicial order, and bringing the same into the custody of the law*] · Arrest *m*, Personalarrest

attachment of debt(s), arrestment of debt(s) [*Scots law*] · (Geld)Schuldenpfändung *f*, (Geld)Forderungspfändung, Pfändung von (Geld)Forderungen, Pfändung von (Geld)Schulden, dinglicher Arrest *m* von (Geld)Forderungen

attachment order, order of attachment · Arrestbefehl *m*, Personalarrestbefehl

attachment order, order of attachment, order of arrestment, arrestment order [*Scots Law*] · Beschlagnahmebefehl *m*, Pfändungsbefehl, dinglicher Arrestbefehl, Beschlagnahmeverfügung *f*, Pfändungsverfügung, dingliche Arrestverfügung

attachment process, arresting process [*Scots law*] · Beschlagnahmeverfahren *n*, Pfändungsverfahren, dingliches Arrestverfahren

attachment writ, writ of attachment · Personalarrestdekret *n*, Arrestdekret

attainment level, level of attainment, target · Programmziel *n*

attempt [*An act done with intent to commit a crime and forming part of a series of acts which would constitute its actual commission if it were not interrupted*] · strafrechtlicher Versuch *m*

attendance book · Anwesenheitsbuch *n*

at term · für einen bestimmten Pachtzins

to attermin, to respite a payment, to grant respite for a payment [*To allow time for the payment of a debt*] · stunden, Zahlungsaufschub bewilligen, Zahlungsfrist gewähren, Zahlungsfrist bewilligen, Zahlungsaufschub gewähren

atterminated · gestundet [*Schuld*]

attermination, atterminement, respite of payment [*Adjournment of the payment of a debt to a fixed future date*] · Zahlungsaufschub *m*, Stundung *f* [*Schuld*]

to attest; certificare [*Latin*]; to certify, to testify in writing, to give a certificate · bescheinigen

attestation [*The verification of a document by the signature of a witness or witnesses who were present at the time of its execution*] · Unterschriftsbeglaubigung *f*

attestation, certifying, testifying in writing, giving a certificate, attesting · Bescheinigen *n*

attestation, certificate [*A written assurance, or official representation, that some act has or has not been done, or some event occurred, or some legal formality been complied with*] · Attest *n*, Bescheinigung *f*, Schein *m*

attestation clause [*The usual clause is: "Signed before me" (US): "N.N."*] · Beglaubigungsformel *f*

attestation of completion, final certificate, final attestation, completion certificate, completion attestation, certificate of completion · Endbescheinigung *f*, Endschein *m*, Endattest *n*, Schlußbescheinigung, Schlußschein, Schlußattest [*Über die Beendigung der Bauarbeiten*]

attested by a notary (public) · notariell beglaubigt

attesting witness, subscribing witness · Unterschriftszeuge *m*

to attest legally, to acknowledge, to certify in legal form · (amtlich) beurkunden

at the right time, on time, in due time, duly · rechtzeitig

at the suit of, ats, a.t.s. · auf die Klage von

at (the) will (of the lord), non-free, unfree, customary · unfrei, nichtfrei, zugestanden, prekarisch, auf Ruf und Widerruf, willkürlich aufkündbar [*Leh(e)n*]

Attic law · attisches Recht *n*

attitude rating · Rangskala *f* über Verhaltensweisen [*Umfragetechnik*]

attitude scale · Verhaltensskala *f*

to attorn, to transfer, to turn over [*To another money or goods*] · übertragen

to attorn [*To agree to become tenant to one of an estate previously held of another, or to agree to recognize a new owner of a property or estate and promise payment of rent to him*] · anerkennen

attornable, transferable, capable of being turned over · übertragbar

attorned, transferred, turned over · übertragen

attorney, policitor, proctor, procurator [*A manager of another person's affair*] · Prokurator *m*

attorney · Parteiberater *m*

attorney by statute, representative by statute, legal representative, legal agent, legal attorney, (authorized) agent by statute · gesetzlicher Verteter *m*

attorney-general · Generalstaatsanwalt *m*

attorney general · Justizminister *m* [*USA-Bundesstaat*]

Attorney-General (of England) [*The principal counsel of the Crown. He is appointed by patent and holds at the pleasure of the Crown*] · Kronanwalt *m*

attorney in fact · Gechäftsführer *m*

attorney (in fact), representative, delegate, proxy, (authorized) agent [*A person either actually or by law held to be authorized and employed by one person to bring him into contractual or other legal relations with a third party*] · Beauftragte *m*, Bevollmächtigte, Sachwalter, (Stell)Vertreter, Agent *m*

attorney in law · Rechtsanwalt *m* bei den gemeinrechtlichen Gerichten

attorney's code of ethics · Grundsätze *m pl* des (rechts)anwaltlichen Standesrechts, Prinzipien *f pl* des (rechts)anwaltlichen Standesrechts

attorneys' ethics · (rechts)anwaltliches Standesrecht *n*

attorneyship · Sachwalterschaft *f*

attorney warrant, warrant of attorney · (Rechts)Anwaltsvollmacht *f* [*Unwiderrufliche Prozeßvollmacht durch welche ein Anwalt von seinem Mandanten zur Erklärung eines Anerkenntnisses vor Gericht ermächtigt wird*]

attornment; attornamentum, attornatio [*Latin*] [*In feudal and old English law. A turning over or transfer by a lord of the services of his tenant to the grantee of his seigniory*] · Leh(e)n(s)übertragung *f*

attornment clause · Anerkennungsklausel *f* [*Mit dieser Klausel erkennt in einer Hypothekenurkunde zur Sicherheit für die Zinszahlung der Schuldner den Gläubiger als Grundherrn an*]

attracting power, (force of) attraction, drawing power, attractiveness · Anziehung(skraft) *f*, Attraktivität *f*

attractiveness measure, measure of attractiveness · Anziehungsmaß *n*, Attraktivitätsmaß *n*

attribute · homogrades Merkmal *n*, qualitatives Merkmal, Gütemerkmal [*Statistik*]

at will, revokable, ambulatory, capable of being revoked, capable of revocation, able of being revoked, able of revocation, qualified of being revoked, qualified of revocation, during pleasure, revocable · auf Widerruf, widerruflich, widerrufbar, einvernehmlich geduldet

auction → (sale by) auction

to auction(eer), to sell at public auction; subhastare [*Latin*] · versteigern, meistbietend verkaufen

auctioneer · Auktionator *m*, Versteigerer *m*

auctioneering · Versteigern *n*

auction proceeds · Versteigerungserlös *m*, Auktionserlös

auction without reserve · Versteigerung *f* ohne Vorbehalt, Auktion *f* ohne Vorbehalt

auctor · Gewährer *m*

audience claims · Angaben *f pl* und Behauptungen *f pl* von Versuchspersonen [*Umfragetechnik*]

auditable invoice · prüfungsfähige Rechnung *f*

audit certificate, audit report · Buchprüfungsbericht *m*, Revisionsbericht

audit day · Rechnungstag *m* [*Termin für Pacht- und Mietzahlungen*]

audit guideline · Buchprüfungsrichtlinie *f*

audi(ting) of cash in hand, cash in hand audit(ing) · Kassen(bestand)revision *f*

audit office, audit department, commissioners of audit (Brit.); accounting office, general accounting office (US) [*It is entrusted with the audit and control of public accounts*] · (Rechnungs)-

auditor — authority constraint

Prüfungsbehörde f, (Rechnungs)Revisionsbehörde, Rechnungshof m, Oberrechnungskammer f

auditor · Buchprüfer m, (Bücher)Revisor

auditor general · Präsident m der Oberrechnungskammer

audit(orial investigation) · (Bücher)Revision f, Buchprüfung f, Buchrevision

auditorium building → (city) auditorium building

auditorship [*The office or position of auditor*] · (Bücher)Revisoramt n, Buchprüferamt

audit report, audit certificate · Buchprüfungsbericht m, Revisionsbericht

audit year · Buchprüfungsjahr n, Revisionsjahr

augmentation, increase · Steigerung f, Zunahme f, Erhöhung

augmentation of property, increase of property, accession of property, addition of property · Besitzzunahme f, Besitzzuwachs m, Besitzerhöhung f, Besitzsteigerung

augmentation rate, rate of increase, rate of augmentation, increase rate · Steigerungssatz m, Erhöhungssatz, Steigerungsrate, Erhöhungsrate f

Augustinian canon, regular canon · regulierter Kanoniker m, Augustiner

aulnager [*An officer appointed by the King, whose business it was to measure all woollen-cloth made for sale, that the Crown might not be defrauded of customs and duties*] · Ellenwart m

a use cannot be engendered of a use · eine Nutzung kann nicht aus einer Nutzung hervorgehen

to authenticate · amtlich beglaubigen

to authenticate by document(s), to make authentic by document(s), to prove (authentic) by document(s) · belegen

authenticated · amtlich beglaubigt

authentication [*Certification of a document by the signature of an officer whose seal is usually affixed to validate the procedure*] · amtliche Beglaubigung f

authenticity, truth in substance · Echtheit f, Authentie f, Authentizität f

authentic wording, authentic text, overruling wording, overruling text · maßgebender Text m, maßgebender Wortlaut m

author index · Autorenverzeichnis n, Autorenregister n

authoritarian socialism · Staatssozialismus m

authoritative, commanding, binding · bindend, verbindlich, geltend

authoritative force (of decided cases), binding authority (of precedents), principle of stare decisis, binding effect, binding force (of decided cases) · bindende Kraft f (der Präjudizien), verbindliche Kraft (der Präjudizien), Bindkraft (der Präjudizien), Bindungswirkung f (der Präjudizien), Prinzip n der bindenden Kraft gerichtlicher Entscheidungen, Beharren n auf der gefällten Entscheidung, Grundsatz m der bindenden Kraft gerichtlicher Entscheidungen

authoritative precedent · bindender Präzedenzfall m, verbindlicher Präzedenzfall, geltender Präzedenzfall [*Bindend ist das der Entscheidung zugrundeliegende Rechtsprinzip, sofern es als die unentbehrliche Grundlage derselben erscheint*]

authoritative source of law, authoritative fountain of law, binding source of law, binding fountain of law, commanding source of law, commanding fountain of law · geltende Rechtsquelle f, verbindliche Rechtsquelle, bindende Rechtsquelle

authoritative text statement · kurze begründende Ausführung f [*In einer Rechtsenzyklopädie der USA*]

authority, majesty, pre-eminence; majestas [*Latin*]; sovereign power, sovereign right, sovereign dominion, sovereignty, liberty, supremacy · Hoheitsrecht n, Hoheitsbefugnis f, hoheitliches Recht, hoheitliche Befugnis, Souveränität f, Oberhoheit f, Hoheitsmacht f, vollziehende Gewalt f

authority [*The right, ability, or faculty of doing something which the grantor might himself lawfully perform*] · Vertretungsmacht f, Vollmacht

authority · Behörde f

authority · Belegstelle f, Rechtserkenntnisquelle f

authority [*The body or persons exercising power or command*] · Obrigkeit f

authority, power · Gewalt f, Hoheit f, Macht f, Kompetenz f

authority administering funds of a Land · Landesmittelbehörde f [*Bundesrepublik Deutschland*]

authority by estoppel, apparent authority, ostensible authority · Scheinvollmacht f, Scheinvertretungsmacht, Anscheinvollmacht, allgemeine Vollmacht, allgemeine Vertretungsmacht, Vollmacht kraft Rechtsschein, Vertretungsmacht kraft Rechtsschein, Vollmacht kraft Partnerstellung, Vertretungsmacht kraft Partnerstellung

authority constraint · territorialherrschaftliche Begrenzung f [*nach Hägerstrand*]

authority for common assurance (on conveyance of land) · Auflassungsvertretungsmacht *f*, Verfügungsvertretungsmacht *f*, Auflassungsvollmacht *f*, Verfügungsvollmacht *f*

authority for performing legal acts · Handlungsvollmacht *f*, Handlungsvertretungsmacht

authority for perpetuities · Familienfideikommißbehörde *f*

authority from necessity · notwendige Vollmacht *f*, notwendige Vertretungsmacht

authority implied, authority in law, implied authority, tacit authority · gefolgerte Vollmacht *f*, gefolgerte Vertretungsmacht, konkludente Vollmacht, konkludente Vertretungsmacht, stillschweigende Vollmacht, stillschweigende Vertretungsmacht

authority of control, authority of checking, control authority, check(ing) authority, review(ing) authority, re-examination authority · Kontrollvollmacht *f*, Nachprüf(ungs)vollmacht

authority of disposal, authority of (ab)alienation, disposal authority, (ab)alienation authority · Veräußerungsvollmacht *f*, Veräußerungsvertretungsmacht

authority of disposition [*Every authority of disposition is deemed absolute, by means of which the donee of such authority is enabled in his lifetime to dispose of the entire for his own benefit*] · Verfügungsvollmacht *f*

authority of incorporation, power of incorporation · Inkorporierungsmacht *f*, Inkorporierungshoheit *f*, Inkorporierungsgewalt *f*, Inkorporierungskompetenz *f*

authority of sale · Verkaufsvollmacht *f*

authority of supervision, authority of superintendence, supervising authority, superintending authority · Aufsichtsvollmacht *f*, Beaufsichtigungsvollmacht *f*, Überwachungsvollmacht *f*, Aufsichtsvertretungsmacht, Überwachungsvertretungsmacht, Beaufsichtigungsvertretungsmacht

authority of surveyors · (Bau)Aufsichtsbehörde *f*

authority-owned · behördeneigen

authority(-owned) (building) (land) area, authority(-owned) land · Behörden(bau)land *n*, Behörden(bau)fläche *f*, Behörden(bau)boden *m* [*Unbebautes Behördenland, das nach dem Flächennutzungsplan und der Bauordnung bebaut werden darf*]

authority's district · Behördenbezirk *m*

authority's property · Behördenbesitz *m*

authority to give ordinances, power to give ordinances · Verordnungsgewalt *f*, Verordnungskompetenz *f*, Verordnungshoheit *f*, Verordnungsmacht *f*

authority to inspect building lines · Fluchtliniengenehmigungsbehörde *f*, Fluchtlinienaufsichtsbehörde [*frühere Benennung: Fluchtlinienpolizei f*]

authority to legislate, legislative authority, legislative power, legislature, jurisdiction; jurisdictio [*Latin*]; power to make law, authority to make law, power to legislate · gesetzgebende Gewalt *f*, gesetzgebende Hoheit, gesetzgebende Macht, gesetzgebende Kompetenz, Gesetzgebungsgewalt, Gesetzgebungskompetenz, Gesetzgebungsmacht, Gesetzgebungshoheit

authority to pay · Tratteneinlösungsvollmacht *f*

authority under seal, power of attorney [*Where the authority is given formally by deed, it is called a power of attorney*] · gesiegelte Vollmacht *f*, unter Siegel erteilte Vollmacht, unter Siegel verliehene Vollmacht

authorization · Vollmachterteilung *f*

authorization · Betriebserlaubnis *f* [*Für ein öffentliches Versorgungsunternehmen*]

authorization by the board of surveyors · bauaufsichtliche Zulassung *f*, bauaufsichtliche Einführung

authorization procedure · Betriebserlaubnisverfahren *n* [*Für ein öffentliches Versorgungsunternehmen*]

authorization to sell, listing · Verkaufsauftrag *m* [*Grundstücksmakler*]

to authorize · bevollmächtigen

authorized, endowed with authority, placed in authority · bevollmächtigt

(authorized) agent, representative (in fact), representative, delegate, proxy [*A person either actually or by law held to be authorized and employed by one person to bring him into contractual or other legal relations with a third party*] · Beauftragte *m*, Bevollmächtigte, Sachwalter, (Stell)Vertreter, Agent *m*

(authorized) agent by statute, attorney by statute, representative by statute, legal representative, legal agent, legal attorney · gesetzlicher Verteter *m*

authorized broker · bevollmächtigter Makler *m*

authorized by building law(s), authorized by construction law(s) · baurechtlich zugelassen, baurechtlich eingeführt

authorized by the board of surveyors · bauaufsichtlich zugelassen, bauaufsichtlich eingeführt

authorized capital, registered capital, nominal capital, original capital [*When a* company is formed its application for registration is accompanied by a statement indicating the amount of capital with which it purposes to be registered] · Grundkapital n [Nicht verwechseln mit der deutschen Benennung „genehmigtes (Aktien)Kapital"; denn dieses ist ein durch Beschluß der Hauptversammlung festgesetzter Betrag, um den der Vorstand während einer bestimmten Zeit das Grundkapital erhöhen kann]

(authorized) capital (stock), stated capital [The number of shares and usually the par or stated value of the capital (stock) that may be issued by a corporation under its articles of incorporation. In some instances the stockholders or directors may determine the stated value per share] · Grundkapital n, Stammkapital, (genehmigtes) (Aktien)-Kapital

authorized dealer · Vertragshändler m

authors' index · Verfasserregister n

autocorrelation · Eigenkorrelation f

autocracy, self-sustained power, independent power · Selbstherrlichkeit f

autocratic, absolute in authority · selbstherrlich

automated cartography · automatische Kartographie f

automated mapping · automatische Kartierung f

automatic debit transfer, direct debiting service · Einziehung f, rückläufige Überweisung f

automobile disposal, disposal of automobile bulks · Autowrackbeseitigung f

automobile ferry · Autofähre f

automobile law, motor vehicle law · Kfz.-Recht n, Kraftfahrzeugrecht

automobile row, auto row group · Einkaufszeile f für Kraftfahrzeuge

automobile traffic, motor traffic · Autoverkehr m

automobilized population · motorisierte Bevölkerung f

autonomous administrative statute · autonome Satzung f [Eine von einer Verwaltungsstelle erlassene Rechtsnorm, auf deren Erlaß der betreffenden Behörde ein Recht zusteht]

autonomous lawmaking, independent legislation, independent lawmaking, autonomous legislation · autonome Gesetzgebung f, unabhängige Gesetzgebung

autonomy · Selbständigkeit f

autoregression · Eigenregression f

auto row group, automobile row · Einkaufszeile f für Kraftfahrzeuge

autumn population, fall population · Herbstbevölkerung f

auxidium, adjutorium, subsidium [Latin]; aid [In feudal law. A kind of pecuniary tribute paid by a vassal to his lord, on occasions of peculiar emergency, and which was one of the incidents of tenure in chivalry, or by knight's service] · Hilfsgeld n

auxiliary contour · Hilfshöhenlinie f, Hilfsisohypse f

auxiliary enterprise, auxiliary undertaking · Hilfsbetrieb m, Hilfsunternehmen n, Hilfsunternehmung f

auxiliary (land) expropriation; auxiliary (land) condemnation (US) · Hilfs(land)-enteignung f, Hilfsbodenenteignung [z. B. Ersatzlandenteignung]

auxiliary occupations, service activity, nonbasic activity, nonbasic employment · Nahversorgungstätigkeit f, Folgeleistung, Befriedigung f der örtlichen Nachfrage, Versorgung der Bevölkerung der eigenen Stadt, sekundäre Aktivität f [Eine innerhalb der Region abgesetzte wirtschaftliche Leistung]

auxiliary plan · Hilfsplan m

auxiliary undertaking, auxiliary enterprise · Hilfsbetrieb m, Hilfsunternehmen n, Hilfsunternehmung f

auxiliary use · Hilfsbenutzung f, Hilfsgebrauch m

availability · Verfügbarkeit f

availability of judicial review · Verfahrensvoraussetzung f für eine richterliche Nachprüfung

available [Capable of being employed with advantage or turned to account] · verfügbar

available act(ion) of bankruptcy · wirksame Konkurshandlung f

available assets [Assets, including available cash, free for any general use, unencumbered, and not serving as collateral] · verfügbare Aktiva f

available (earned) surplus, earned surplus, cash flow, retained earnings, retained income [The spendable income from an investment after paying all expenses, such as operating expenses and debt service] · Gewinneinbehalt m, Profiteinbehalt, einbehaltener Gewinn m, einbehaltener Profit

avenue [USA] · Stadtstraße f in Nord-Süd-Richtung

to aver, to assert, to allege [To prove or justify a plea; to make an averment] · behaupten

average, arithmetic mean · arithmetisches Mittel *n*

average · Havarie *f*, Havarei *f*, Beschädigung *f* [*Seeversicherung*]

average, mean · Durchschnitt *m*

average bond · Havarieschein *m*, Havareischein

average building site wage → average site wage

average construction site wage → average site wage

average cost(s) in the long run, long-run average cost(s), LRAC · langfristige Durchschnittskosten *f*

average cost(s) in the short run, short-run average cost(s), SRAC · kurzfristige Durchschnittskosten *f*

average crowding, mean crowding · wahrscheinlichkeitstheoretische Häufung *f* [*Besied(e)lung*]

average deviation, mean deviation [*A measure of the variation of a group of numerical data from a designated point*] · durchschnittliche Abweichung *f*

average dwelling rent, mean dwelling rent, average (residential) rent, mean (residential) rent · Durchschnittswohnungsmiete *f*, Durchschnittswohnungs-(miet)zins *m*, mittlere Wohnungsmiete, mittlerer Wohnungs(miet)zins

average earner, mean earner · Durchschnittsverdiener *m*, mittlerer Verdiener

average earning, mean earning · Durchschnittsverdienst *m*, mittlerer Verdienst

average expectation of life, mean expectation of life · durchschnittliche voraussichtliche Lebensdauer *f*, voraussichtliche durchschnittliche Lebensdauer

average income, mean income · Durchschnittseinkommen *n*, mittleres Einkommen

average length of life, mean length of life · durchschnittliches Lebensalter *n*, Lebensalterdurchschnitt *m*

average life, mean life [*The estimated useful-life expectancy of a group of assets subject to depreciation*] · durchschnittliche Nutzungsdauer *f*, durchschnittliche Lebensdauer

average number, mean number · Durchschnittszahl *f*, mittlere Zahl

average outgoing quality, AOQ [*The quality of material ultimately passed into stock by an inspection procedure that enforces good 100 per cent inspection of each rejected lot to remove therefrom all defective items, which — in theory at least — are then replaced by good items*] · Durchschnittsgüte *f* der geprüften Liefermengen

average outgoing quality limit, AOQ limit · Durchschnittsgütehöchstwert *m* der geprüften Liefermengen

average price, mean price · Durchschnittspreis *m*, mittlerer Preis

average quality, mean standard, mean quality, average standard · Durchschnittsgüte *f*, mittlere Güte

average rate, mean rate · Durchschnittssatz *m*, mittlerer Satz

average rent, mean rent · Durchschnittsmiete *f*, mittlere Miete

average (residential) rent, mean (residential) rent, average dwelling rent, mean dwelling rent · Durchschnittswohnungsmiete *f*, Durchschnittswohnungs-(miet)zins *m*, mittlere Wohnungsmiete, mittlerer Wohnungs(miet)zins

average shipment distance · durchschnittliche Entfernung *f* zwischen einem Liefersektor und allen Empfangssektoren

average site wage, mean site wage, average construction site wage, mean construction site wage, average building site wage, mean building site wage, average job (site) wage, mean job (site) wage · Bau(stellen)-Mittellohn *m*

average standard, average quality, mean standard, mean quality · Durchschnittsgüte *f*, mittlere Güte

average value, mean value · Durchschnittswert *m*, Mittelwert, mittlerer Wert

averagium, summagium [*Latin*]; carting · Fuhrdienst *m* [*Fronhofarbeit*]

averge adjuster · Dispacheur *m*

averment, assertion, allegation [*A statement of fact made in any proceeding, as, for instance, in a pleading, particularly a statement of charge which is, as yet, unproved*] · Behauptung *f*, Bekräftigung

averring, asserting, alleging · Behaupten *n*

to avoid, to invalidate, to make void, to annul · ungültig machen, für ungültig erklären

avoidance, nullity, invalidity · Nichtigkeit *f*, Ungültigkeit

avoidance, repeal, abrogation, cancellation, abolition, abatement, abolishment (by authority), annulment, nullification, rescission · Annullierung *f*, Rückgängigmachung, Aufhebung, Abschaffung, Abbau *m*, Löschung

avoidance, rendering void, rendering of no effect · Ungültigmachen *n*, Nichtigmachen

avoided, cancelled, invalidated, annulled, made void · ungültig gemacht, für ungültig erklärt

(a)voiding, repealing, abolishing, abrogating, cancelling, overruling, abating, rendering null and void, doing away with, nullifying, rescinding, making void, annulling · Aufheben *n*, Rückgängigmachen *n*, Annullieren *n*, Abschaffen *n*, Löschen *n*, Abbauen *n*

to avow, to make a confession, to admit, to confess [*To admit the truth of what is charged*] · (ein)gestehen, bekennen, zugeben, geständig sein [*Schuld*]

avowant · Beklagte *m* der gesteht Vermögensobjekte des Klägers auf Grund seines Pfändungsrechtes weggenommen zu haben

avowee paramount, advowee paramount · höchster Kirchenpatron *m*

avulsion [*Removal of land from one owner to another when a stream or river suddenly changes its direction of flow*] · Avulsion *f*, Abtrieb *m*, Abriß *m*

award · zuerkannte Summe *f*

award → (arbitration) award

award → (contract) award

to award (a contract), to let (out), to commission a project, to appoint a contractor, to let a contract, to contract · zuschlagen, erteilen eines Auftrages

award date, letting date, date of award, date of letting · Auftragsdatum *n*, Zuschlag(s)datum *n*, Auftragstermin *m*, Zuschlag(s)termin *m*

award(ing) of a contract, letting of a contract, letting out, (contract) award, (contract) letting, contracting · Zuschlag *m*, Auftragserteilung *f*

award negotiation → (final) award negotiation

award void on the face of it → (arbitration) award void on the face of it

awareness of space, spatial awareness · Raumbewußtsein *n*

away-going crop · Ernte *f* die nicht zur Pachtzeit des Aussäenden reif wird

axial development theory, theory of axial development, sector(ial) theory · Grundsatz *m* der sektoralen Differenzierung einer Stadt, Prinzip *n* der sektoralen Differenzierung einer Stadt, Sektortheorie *f*, Sektorentheorie *f*

axiomatic foundation of accountancy · Axiomatik *f* des Rechnungswesens

axiom of independence, independence axiom · Axiom *n* der Unabhängigkeit, Unabhängigkeitsaxiom

axiom of unequal probability, unequal probability axiom · Axiom *n* der ungleichen Wahrscheinlichkeit, ungleiches Wahrscheinlichkeitsaxiom

axis of agglomeration, agglomeration axis · Verdichtungsachse *f*, Ballungsachse, Agglomerationsachse, allgemeine Konzentrationsachse

B

B/Dft., bank(ers') draft · Banktratte *f*

B/L, bill of lading · Konnossement *n*, Ladeschein *m*, Verladungsschein

bachelor apartment (US); apartment (Brit.) [*Apartment designed for occupancy by one or more persons, primarily limited in area and containing one large room for sleeping, cooking, eating, and living with bathroom facilities and closet space*] · Einzimmerwohnung *f*, Einraumwohnung

backbencher · Hinterbänkler *m* [*Parlament*]

backer, supporter · Unterstützende *m* [*z. B. Kreditgeber*]

back freight, return freight, home freight · Rückfracht *f*

back garden (Brit.); dooryard (US); house garden, domestic garden · Hausgarten *m*

backing [*Support for a country's note issue*] · Deckung *f*

backing, indorsing, endorsing · Indossieren *n*, Girieren, Begeben

back letter · Verpflichtungsschein *m*

backlog, back orders · Auftragsbestand *m*, Auftragspolster *n* [*Österreich: m*]

back order [*An order against stock which cannot be met until a replenishment quantity is received*] · rückständiger Auftrag *m*

to back out, to withdraw (oneself) from an enterprise · zurückziehen, sich zurückziehen

to back out [*To refuse to keep a promise or engagement*] · nicht einhalten

back pay · (Lohn)Nachzahlung *f*

back-to-back credit, countervailing credit · Ausgleichskredit *m*, Kompensationskredit

back-to-back houses · Häuser *npl* mit aneinanderstoßenden rückwärtigen Mauern, rückwärts an(einander)gebaute Häuser

backward area, backward territory · zurückgebliebenes Gebiet *n*

backwardation — bailment

backwardation, carry-over [*London Stock Exchange*]. *The fee, including interest, paid by a speculator for the delayed delivery of stock he has sold, pending what he hopes will be a decline in its price*] · Prolongationsgebühr *f*, Kostgeld *n*, Kursabschlag *m*, Deport *m*

backwardation business · Deportgeschäft *n*, Kostgeschäft

backwardation rate, carry-over rate · Prolongations(gebühr)satz *m*, Kostgeldsatz, Deportsatz, Kursabschlagsatz

backward integration · vertikaler Zusammenschluß *m* einer Unternehmung mit ihr vorgelagerten Unternehmungsstufen

backward linkage · Rückwärtsverflechtung *f*, Rückwärtskopplung [*Industriezweig*]

backwardness · Rückständigkeit *f*

backward planning, planning from-the-bottom-up, planning from below · Planung *f* von unten

backward territory → backward area

backwash · Entzug *m* [*räumliches Entwick(e)lungsgefälle*]

backwash effect, polarization · Entzugswirkung *f*, Konterwirkung [*räumliches Entwick(e)lungsgefälle*]

backwoodsman · Hinterwäldler *m*

bad, irrecoverable, unobtainable, desperate, hopeless, non collectable, noncollectible, nonrecoverable, nonobtainable, uncollectable, unrecoverable, uncollectible · nicht beitreibbar, nicht einziehbar, nicht eintreibbar, uneinziehbar, uneintreibbar, uneinbringlich, unbeitreibbar [*Schuld*]

bad debt · dubiose Forderung *f*, zweifelhafte Forderung, dubioser Außenstand *m*, zweifelhafter Außenstand

bad debt allowance · Wertberichtigung *f* auf Forderungen

bad debts reserve · Rückstellung *f* zweifelhafter Forderungen

bad faith; mala fides [*Latin*] · böser Glaube *m*

bad finance · schwindelhafte Finanzoperation *f*

badlands; barren region (Brit.) · bizarr erodiertes Ödland *n*, Erosionslandschaft *f*

bad money, hot money · heißes Geld *n*, Fluchtgeld [*Devisenbörse*]

bad weather, adverse weather · Schlechtwetter *n*

bad-weather conditions, adverse-weather conditions · Schlechtwetterverhältnisse *f*, Schlechtwetterbedingungen *f pl*

bad-weather construction, adverse-weather construction · Schlechtwetterbau *m*

bad-weather day, adverse-weather day · Schlechtwettertag *m*

bag village · Sackdorf *n*

to bail [*To set at liberty a person arrested or imprisoned, on security being taken for his appearance on a day and at a place certain, which security is called bail*] · freilassen

bail [*A security being given for a person arrested or imprisoned to be set at liberty*] · Kaution *f*

bail · strafrechtlicher Bürge *m*, Strafrechtsbürge

bailable · kautionsfähig

bailable · vercharterungsfähig

bailable · pfandfähig

bailable · besitzübertragungsfähig

bailee → protector

bailer → bailor

bailiff · Stadtrichter *m* [*Scotland*]

bailiff, (land) steward, steward of manor [*A person that has administration and charge of lands, goods and chattels to make the best benefit for the owner*] · Amtmann *m*, (Guts)Verwalter *m*, Gutsschulze *m*, Vogt *m*, Rentenmeister *m*, Haushofmeister

bailiff · Gerichtsvollzieherassistent *m* eines Grafschaftsgerichts [*England*]

bailiff [*Low Latin*] → protector

bailiff [*Low Latin*] · distrainer, distrainor, distreinor, agent for levying distress · Privatpfänder *m* von beweglichen Sachen, eigenmächtiger Pfänder von beweglichen Sachen

bailiff of a franchise · Verwaltungsbeamte *m* an der Spitze eines von der Verwaltung eines Sheriff eximierten Distrikts

bailiff of a hundred · Distriktbote *m* [*Diener eines Sheriffs um Strafen einzukassieren, Geschworene zu berufen und den Friedens- und Assisenrichtern zu helfen*]

bail jumping · Flucht *f* bei Haftkaution

bailment [*The transfer of the possession of personal property without a transfer of ownership, with the understanding that the personal property will be returned to the owner when the purpose of the transfer has been completed. Bailments are concerned only with personal property and not with land*] · Besitzübertragung *f*

bailment · anvertrautes Gut *n*

bailment · Freilassung *f* gegen Kaution

bailment for reward — banishment

bailment for reward, hire of custody · Deponieren *n* gegen Entgelt durch eine Bank, entgeltliche Deponierung *f* durch eine Bank

bailor, bailer · anvertrauender Geber *m*, Anvertrauende, Geber anvertrauten Gutes

bajulus [*Latin*] → protector

to balance · bilanzieren

to balance · ausgleichen, saldieren

balance → (account) balance

balance → balance(-sheet)

balance account · Bilanzkonto *n*

balance amount · Saldobetrag *m*

balance auditor → balance(-sheet) auditor

balance claim, balance demand · Saldoforderung *f*, Saldoverlangen *n*

balanced bond, umbrella fund, managed fund, mixed bond, selective bond, three-way fund · gemischter Versicherungsfonds *m*

balanced bond certificate, three-way fund certificate, managed fund certificate, mixed bond certificate, umbrella fund certificate · gemischtes Versicherungsfondszertifikat *n*

balanced budget · ausgeglichener Haushalt *m*

balanced city, balanced town · gewerbliche Wohnstadt *f*

balanced confounding · ausgewogenes Vermengen *n*, ausgeglichenes Vermengen, gleichgewichtiges Vermengen [*Statistik*]

balanced economy → balanced (natural) economy

balance demand, balance claim · Saldoforderung *f*, Saldoverlangen *n*

balanced fund · gemischter Fonds *m* [*In den USA Aktien und Rentenpapiere*]

balanced fund · gemischter Fonds *m* mit Lebensversicherungsdeckung [*In Großbritannien Wertpapiere und Immobilien*]

balanced growth · ausgewogenes Wachstum *n*, gleichgewichtiges Wachstum *n*, ausgeglichenes Wachstum

balanced lattice square · ausgewogenes Gitterquadrat *n*, ausgeglichenes Gitterquadrat, gleichgewichtiges Gitterquadrat, ausgewogenes quadratisches Gitter *n*, ausgeglichenes quadratisches Gitter, gleichgewichtiges quadratisches Gitter [*Statistik*]

balanced (natural) economy · ausgeglichene (Volks)Wirtschaft *f*

balanced neighbourhood (Brit.); balanced neighborhood (US) · Gleichgewicht *n* [*Stadtsoziologie*]

balanced town, balanced city · gewerbliche Wohnstadt *f*

balance due, debit balance · Debitsaldo *m*

balance of accounts, trade balance, visible balance, balance of payments, balance of trade · Zahlungsbilanz *f*, Handelsbilanz

balance of interest, interest balance · Zins(en)saldo *m*

balance of nature, natural balance, ecosystem · Naturhaushalt *m*

balance of payments, balance of trade, balance of accounts, trade balance, visible balance · Zahlungsbilanz *f*, Handelsbilanz

balance of power, power balance · Machtgleichgewicht *n*

balance of trade, balance of accounts, trade balance, visible balance, balance of payments · Zahlungsbilanz *f*, Handelsbilanz

balance on current account · Leistungsbilanz *f*, Bilanz der laufenden Posten

balance(-sheet), statement of financial position, statement of financial condition, position of the company, statement of assets and liabilities; inventory (US) · Bilanz *f*

balance(-sheet) audit · Bilanzprüfung *f*, Abschlußprüfung

balance(-sheet) auditor, annual auditor · Abschlußprüfer *m*, Bilanzprüfer

balance sum · Saldosumme *f*

balancing · Bilanzieren *n*

balancing item · Restposten *m*

balancing with money · Geldausgleich *m* [*Flurbereinigung. Unvermeidbare Mehr- oder Minderausweisungen von Land sind in Geld auszugleichen*]

balley [*Manx*]; tref [*Welsh*]; ker [*Brittanic*]; clachan [*Galic*]; bally [*Irish*] · Drubbel *m*; Eschdorf *n* [*nach Rothert 1924*]; Eschweiler *m* [*nach Helbok 1938*]

balloon photogrammetry · Ballonphotogrammetrie *f*

ballot, secret voting · geheime Abstimmung *f*

ballot paper, voting paper [*Used in secret voting*] · Wahlzettel, Stimmzettel *m*

bally [*Irish*]; balley [*Manx*], tref [*Welsh*], ker [*Brittanic*]; clachan [*Galic*] · Drubbel *m*; Eschdorf *n* [*nach Rothert 1924*]; Eschweiler *m* [*nach Helbok 1938*]

to banish from court, to exclude from court, to expel from court · ausschließen vom Gericht

banishment · Verbannung *f*, Deportation *f*, Zwangsverschickung

bank · Bank f

bankable · bankfähig, diskontierbar

bank abstract, statement (of account), abstract (of account), account statement, account abstract, bank statement · (Konto)Auszug m

bank account, cash-in-bank account · Bankkonto n [*Ein Konto der betrieblichen Buchführung welches Soll- und Habenbestände eines Kontos bei einer Bank ausweist*]

bank act → bank(ing) law

bank acting as central bank to the saving banks · Girozentrale f

bank bill → bank(er's) bill

bank bill (US); (bank) note · (Bank)Note f

bank bill circulation (US); bank note circulation · (Bank)Notenumlauf m

bank bill issue (US); (bank) note issue · (Bank)Notenausgabe f

bank-book, pass-book, banker's book [*A book furnished by a banker to a customer, containing a transcript of his account in the bank ledger*] · Bankeinlagebuch n

bank cashier · Bankkassierer m

bank chain, bank group · Bankenkette f, Bankengruppe f

bank charges, bank commission · Kontoführungskosten f

bank creditor · Bankgläubiger m

(bank) deposit · (Bank)Einlage f, Bankdepot n

bank discount, simple discount [*The charge by a bank for discounting a note or bill of exchange*] · Bankdiskont m

bank discount rate, simple discount rate · Bankdiskontsatz m

bank draft → bank(er's) draft

banker [*Das Wort "banker" bedeutet auch eine Bankgeschäfte betreibende, inkorporierte oder andere Personenvereinigung*] · Bankier m

bank(er's) acceptance · Bankakzept n

bankers and commission merchant · Bankierkommissionär m

bank(er's) bill, finance bill (of exchange) · Bankwechsel m, Finanzwechsel [*Wechsel, welchen eine Bank auf eine andere zieht*]

banker's book, bank-book, pass-book [*A book furnished by a banker to a customer, containing a transcript of his account in the bank ledger*] · Bankeinlagebuch n

bank(er's) credit · Bankkredit m

(banker's) discretion · Bankgeheimnis n

bank(er's) draft, B/Dft. · Banktratte f

bank financing · Bankfinanzierung f

bank financing promoting company · Gründungsbank f

bank for the protection of mortgagors [*A bank which guarantees the capital and amortisation of mortgages against the payment of interest*] · Hypothekenschutzbank f

bank giro · Sammelscheckϋberweisung f

bank group, bank chain · Bankenkette f, Bankengruppe f

bank guaranty, bank guarantee, bank guarantie · Bankbürgschaft f

banking business, business of banking · Bankgeschäft n

banking department [*Bank of England*] · Bankabteilung f

banking house · Bankhaus n

banking industry · Bankwirtschaft f

bank(ing) law, law of banking · Kreditwesenrecht n

bank(ing) law, bank(ing) statute, bank(ing) act, law of banking, statute of banking, act of banking · Kreditwesengesetz n

bank(ing) legislation, bank(ing) lawmaking · Kreditwesengesetzgebung f

banking place · Bankplatz m

banking practice, practice of banking · Bankwesen n

bank money · Bankgeld n

bank mortgage · Bankhypothek f

(bank) note; bank bill (US) · (Bank)Note f

bank note circulation; bank bill circulation (US) · (Bank)Notenumlauf m

(bank) note issue; bank bill issue (US) · (Bank)Notenausgabe f

bank of circulation · Girobank f

bank of deposit, deposit bank · Depositenbank f

bank of discount, discount bank, discount house, discount company · Diskontbank f, Diskonthaus n, Geldmarktbank

Bank of Germany · Reichsbank f

bank of issue, house of issue, issuing house, issuing bank, issuing firm, issue house, issue firm, issue bank · Notenbank f, Emissionsbank, Zettelbank, Emissionshaus n

(bank) overdraft, running account credit · Überziehung(skredit) f, (m), Kontokredit

bank paper · Bankpapier n

bank post bill — bar association

bank post bill · Wechsel m der Bank of England auf 7 Tage Sicht ausgegeben [*Wert 7£ bis 1,000£*]

bank reconciliation · Kontenabstimmung f, Kontoabstimmung

bank report, bank return · Bankbericht m

Bank Restriction Period [*The period 1796—1819 during which Bank of England notes were not convertible for gold on demand*] · Einlösungseinschränkungszeitraum m

bankrupt commission · Massekuratoren mpl

bankruptcy; bankrupting, bankruptism, bankruptship, bankrupture [*obsolete terms*] · Konkurs m

bankruptcy act, bankruptcy law, bankruptcy statute · Konkursgesetz n

bankruptcy amendment act, bankruptcy amendment law, bankruptcy amendment statute · Konkursänderungsgesetz n

bankruptcy application, bankruptcy request · Konkursantrag m, Konkursgesuch n

bankruptcy code, code of bankruptcy · Konkursordnung f, KO

bankruptcy court, court of bankruptcy · Konkursgericht n

bankruptcy declaration, declaration of bankruptcy, statement of bankruptcy, bankruptcy statement · Konkurserklärung f

(bankruptcy) discharge, discharge of a bankrupt [*Freeing of a bankrupt from debts and liabilities, by order of discharge*] · Entlassung f aus dem Konkurs, Konkursentlassung, (Konkurs)Entlastung, Entlastung eines Gemeinschuldners [*Nach englischem Konkursrecht werden nach Abschluß des Verfahrens dem Gemeinschuldner die Restschulden erlassen, vorausgesetzt, daß er sich nichts hat zuschulden kommen lassen. Nach deutschem Konkursrecht haftet er noch 30 Jahre lang für nicht befriedigte Forderungen*]

(bankruptcy) discharge resolution, resolution of (bankruptcy) discharge · Entlassungsbeschluß m, Entlassungsentschließung f, Entlastungsbeschluß, Entlastungsentschließung, Konkursentlassungsbeschluß, Konkursentlastungsbeschluß, Konkursentlassungsentschließung, Konkursentlastungsentschließung

bankruptcy law, law of bankruptcy · Konkursrecht n

bankruptcy law, bankruptcy statute, bankruptcy act · Konkursgesetz n

bankruptcy petition · Antrag m auf Eröffnung eines Konkursverfahrens, Gesuch n auf Eröffnung eines Konkursverfahrens, (Konkurs)Eröffnungsgesuch n, (Konkurs)Eröffnungsantrag m, Konkursantrag m, Konkursgesuch n

bankruptcy request, bankruptcy application · Konkursantrag m, Konkursgesuch n

bankruptcy statement, bankruptcy declaration, declaration of bankruptcy, statement of bankruptcy · Konkurserklärung f

bankruptcy statute, bankruptcy act, bankruptcy law · Konkursgesetz n

bankrupt(ed) · bank(e)rott, pleite

bankrupting, bankruptism, bankruptship, bankrupture [*obsolete terms*]; bankruptcy · Konkurs m

bankrupt person · Bank(e)rotteur m, Insolvent m, Konkursschuldner, Fallit m [*Derjenige, über dessen Vermögen das Konkursverfahren eröffnet wurde*]

bankrupt's estate, active estate of a bankrupt, active property of a bankrupt, estate, bankrupt's property, bankrupt's assets [*The assets and liabilities of a bankrupt person*] · Konkursmasse f, Fallitmasse, Konkursvermögen n, Konkursgut n, Konkurshabe, Aktivmasse f

bank share · Bankanteil m

bank statement, bank abstract, statement (of account), abstract (of account), account statement, account abstract · (Konto)Auszug m

bank statute → bank(ing) law

bank stock · Aktie f der Bank of England

bank transfer · Banküberweisung f

banlieue · Außenrandzone f [*Stadt*]

banns (of marriage) · Eheaufgebot n, (Heirats)Aufgebot

baptismal register, baptismal registry · Taufregister n

to bar · aufheben, sperren [*(subjektives) Recht*]

to bar · (ver)hindern

bar · Hindernis n, Schranke f, Sperre f

bar · Hinderung f, Sperrung, Verhinderung

bar · Gerichtsschranke f

bar · Anwaltstand m, Rechtsanwaltstand m, (Rechts)Anwaltschaft f [*in England*]

to bar an entail, to destroy an entail, to disentail · aufheben der gebundenen (Land)Erbfolge(ordnung)

bar association, bar society, bar institution · (Rechts)Anwaltsverein(igung) m, (f)

bar chart [*A statistical series, such as a frequency distribution, represented by means of relative or absolute heights of a group of rectangles*] · Balkenplan *m*, Balkendarstellung *f*

bare majority · knappe Mehrheit *f*

bare naked bailment, depositum · Deponierung *f*

bare trustee · weisungsabhängiger Treuhänder *m* [*Er hat nur die Pflicht über das Treuhandvermögen nach den Weisungen der Benefiziare zu verfügen*]

bar examination · Juraprüfung, juristische Prüfung *f*

to bargain · aushandeln von Preisen, feilschen

bargain [*A transaction on the stock exchange*] · Abschluß *m*

bargain for cash · Kassageschäft *n* [*Wertpapierbörse*]

bargain for the account · Termingeschäft *n* [*Wertpapierbörse*]

bargaining, haggling, higgling [*Bargaining over prices as an alternative to fixed prices for commodities*] · Aushandeln *n* von Preisen, Feilschen

bargaining · Wertpapierhandel *m* [*Börse*]

bar institution → bar association

baron [*Title of a judge of the Court of Exchequer*] · Schatzkammerrichter *m*, Richter (bei) der Schatzkammer

baronady [*obsolete*]; baronage, baron(r)y [*The rank or dignity of baron*] · Baronswürde *f*, Freiherrenwürde

baronage [*The relation of a baron to his lord superior*] · Baronsleh(e)n(s)verhältnis *n*, Freiherrenleh(e)n(s)verhältnis

baronage [*obsolete*]; baron(r)y, domain of a baron · Baronsgut *n*, Freiherrengut, Baronshof *m*, Freiherrenhof

baron(-bailie) court, court-baron (proper), court of (the) manor, freeholders' court baron; curia legalis [*Latin*]; manor(ial) court, feudal court, feodal court, feuda(to)ry court, court of the baron, court of the lord [*The court of justice held by a baron or his steward in the presence of the freehold tenants of the manor. In modern times lawyers have distinguished between court(-baron) which was the court of the freehold tenants, and the customary court-baron which was the court of the copy-hold tenants. The early history of this distinction is obscure*] · Feudalgericht *n*, grundherrliches Gericht, Leh(e)n(s)herrengericht, Hofgericht, Patrimonialgericht, feudales Gutsgericht

baron by tenure, king's baron [*One who held by military or other honourable service, directly from the king, and at length mostly applied to the grantor of these (the Great Barons) who personally attended the Great Council, or, from the time of Henry III, were summoned by writ to Parliament (barons by writ)*] · Baron *m* mit Leh(e)n(s)pflicht dem König zugetan, Freiherr *m* mit Leh(e)n(s)pflicht dem König zugetan, Leh(e)n(s)baron, Leh(e)n(s)freiherr

baron by writ · Leh(e)n(s)baron *m* mit Parlamentssitz, Leh(e)n(s)freiherr *m* mit Parlamentssitz

baronet · Kleinbaron *m*, Kleinfreiherr *m*

baronetage [*The body of baronets collectively*] · Kleinbaronie *f*, Kleinfreiherrentum *n*

baronetage, baronethood, baronetcy, baronetship [*The rank or dignity of baronet*] · Kleinbaronswürde *f*, Kleinfreiherrenwürde

baronial jurisdiction · Freiherrengerichtsbarkeit *f*, Baronsgerichtsbarkeit

baronial system, baronism · Baronsherrschaft *f*, Freiherrenherrschaft

baron(r)y, domain of a baron; baronage [*obsolete*] · Baronsgut *n*, Freiherrengut, Baronshof *m*, Freiherrenhof

baron(r)y; baronady [*obsolete*]; baronage [*The rank or dignity of baron*] · Baronswürde *f*, Freiherrenwürde

baron(r)y by (king's) tenure, baron(r)y held directly from the king · Freiherrschaft *f* [*Nur dem König oder Kaiser und dem Reich mit Leh(e)n(s)pflicht zugetan*]

baronship [*The office or position of a baron; e.g. of Baron of the Exchequer*] · Baronsamt *n*, Freiherrenamt

barony, baronship [*The office of Baron of the Exchequer*] · Schatzkammeramt *n*

barony [*Scotland*]; manor, large freehold estate [*It is called so even though the proprietor is a simple commoner*] · Herr(e)ngut *n*, Herr(e)nhof *m*

baroque town, baroque city · Barockstadt *f*

barrable · aufhebbar, sperrbar [*(subjektives) Recht*]

barred · aufgehoben, gesperrt [*(subjektives) Recht*]

barren [*Applied in North America to elevated plains on which grow small trees, but no timber, classed as oak-barrens, pine-barrens, etc.*] · Hochebene *f* ohne Nutzholz

barren land · unfruchtbares Land *n*, unbrauchbares Land [*zu Ackerzwecken*]

barrenness · Unfruchtbarkeit *f* [*Land*]

barren region (Brit.); badlands · bizarr erodiertes Ödland *n*, Erosionslandschaft *f*

barren rent, dry rent, rent-seck; redditius siccus [*Latin*] [*A rent not supported by a right of distress. Ceased to exist after the Landlord and Tenant Act 1730*] · Rente f ohne Pfändungsrecht, trockene Rente

barrier [*In continental towns: The gate at which custom duties were collected*] · Zolltor n

barring · Hindern n, Sperren, Verhindern

barring · Aufheben n [*(subjektives) Recht*]

barring act, barring law, barring statute · hinderndes Gesetz n, schrankensetzendes Gesetz, sperrendes Gesetz, verhinderndes Gesetz

barring law · hinderndes Recht n, schrankensetzendes Recht, sperrendes Recht

barrister-client privilege · (Rechts)Anwaltgeheimnis n [*plädierender (Rechts)-Anwalt*]

barrister of choice; advocate of choice [*In Scotland*]; barristor of choice · Vertrauensanwalt m, Vertrauensadvokat m [*Als plädierender (Rechts)Anwalt*]

barrow-boy, costermonger, street trader · Straßenhändler m

bar scale, graphic scale · Linearmaßstab m, Maßstableiste f

bar society → bar association

barter [*Exchange of wares for wares*] · Waren(aus)tausch m, Tauschhandel m

barter · Tausch m

barter economy, non-monetary economy, natural economy [*Goods are exchanged for goods*] · Tauschwirtschaft f

barter of land for land, exchange of realty, realty exchange, exchange of land(s), exchange of (real) estate, exchange of (real) property, (real) estate exchange, (real) property exchange, land(s) exchange · Boden(aus)tausch m, Land-(aus)tausch, Grund(stücks)(aus)tausch, Liegenschafts(aus)tausch, Immobiliar-(aus)tausch, Immobilien(aus)tausch, Flächen(aus)tausch

barter-of-land-for-land plan, (real) property exchange plan, (real) estate exchange plan, realty exchange plan · Grund(stücks)tauschplan m, (Boden)-Tauschplan, Landtauschplan

barter term · Verhältnis n des Ausfuhrpreises zum Einfuhrpreis

barter-trade, counter-trade · Kompensationsgeschäft n

bar trial, trial at bar [*A trial which takes place before all the judges, at the bar of the court in which the action is brought*] · (Haupt)Verhandlung f vor allen Richtern, Gerichtsverhandlung vor allen Richtern, Prozeß m vor versammeltem Gericht, (Haupt)Verhandlung vor einem Gericht(shof) [*Anstatt vor einem Assisenrichter*]

base bid, base offer, base tender; base (bid) proposal (US) [*A bid before alternates are considered*] · Grundangebot n

base bid documents, base offer documents, base tender documents; base (bid) proposal documents (US) · Grundangebotsunterlagen fpl

base bid (price), base tender price, base offer price; base (bid) proposal price (US) [*Bidder quoted price or monetary consideration for the base bid*] · Grundangebotssumme f, Grundangebotspreis m

base-court [*An inferior court of justice, one that is not a court of record*] · Untergericht n

base dwelling rent, base (residential) rent [*The minimum amount of rent payable under the terms of a percentage lease*] · Mindestwohn(ungs)miete f

base estate, (estate in) base fee, (estate in) qualified fee, (estate in) determinable fee, (estate in) fee simple defeasible [*An estate or fee which has a qualification subjoined thereto, and which must be determined wherever the qualification annexed to it is at an end*] · beschränkte (Grund)Besitzdauer f

base file · Basisdatei f, Grunddatei

base in law, basis in law, lawful base, lawful basis, legal base, legal basis · rechtliche Grundlage f

baseless · grundlos

base map, basic map, fundamental map · Grund(land)karte f

basement ownership · Kellereigentum n

base-metal money; hard money (US); coins · Metallgeld n, Hartgeld, Münzen fpl, Münzgeld

base period · Basiszeitraum m, Grundzeitraum

base (residential) rent, base dwelling rent [*The minimum amount of rent payable under the terms of a percentage lease*] · Mindestwohn(ungs)miete f

base salary, basic salary, fundamental salary · Grundgehalt n

base tenure, bassa tenura [*Latin*] [*A holding by ville(i)nage, or other customary service; opposed to alta tenura, the highest tenure in capite, or by military service*] · niedrigstes Leh(e)n n

base weight, original weight · Ausgangsgewicht n, Originalgewicht, Ursprungsgewicht

base year · Basisjahr n, Grundjahr

basic, fundamental · grundlegend

basic, non-service · fest [*Von der Bevölkerungsverteilung unabhängiger Standort*]

basic activity, economic base, primary occupations, basic employment · Fernversorgungstätigkeit *f*, Erzeugung *f* von Ausfuhrgütern, Grundleistung, Originärbeschäftigung, Exportaktivität *f*, Ausfuhraktivität, primäre Aktivität [*Eine der Ausfuhr aus einer Region dienende Leistung*]

basic amount, fundamental amount · Grundbetrag *m*, Basisbetrag

basic central community, fundamental central community · Grundzentrum *n*, Basiszentrum

basic composition, fundamental composition, basic structure, fundamental structure · Grundgefüge *n*, Grundaufbau *m*, Grundstruktur *f*, Grundzusammensetzung *f*

basic cost(s), fundamental cost(s) · Grundkosten *f*

basic data, fundamental data · Ausgangsdaten *f*, Basisdaten *f*, grundlegende Daten *f*, Grunddaten *f*

basic design, fundamental design · Ausgangsentwurf *m*, Grundentwurf *m*

basic dimension · Grundabmessung *f*

basic dwelling rent, fundamental dwelling rent, dwelling basic rent, dwelling fundamental rent · Wohnungskostenmiete *f*, Wohnungskosten(miet)zins *m*

basic employment, basic activity, economic base, primary occupations · Fernversorgungstätigkeit *f*, Erzeugung *f* von Ausfuhrgütern, Grundleistung, Originärbeschäftigung, Exportaktivität *f*, Ausfuhraktivität, primäre Aktivität [*Eine der Ausfuhr aus einer Region dienende Leistung*]

basic employment range [*Concept of base ratios*] · Grundleistungsbereich *m*

basic error, fundamental error · Grundfehler *m*

basic fact, fundamental fact · Grundtatsache *f*

basic fee, fundamental fee · Grundgebühr *f*, Grundhonorar *n*

basic fee rate, fundamental fee rate · Grundgebührensatz *m*, Grundhonorarsatz

basic floor area (US); floor area ratio, F.A.R., floor space index, F.S.I. (Brit.) [*The square-foot amount of total floor area (all stories) for each square foot of land area of a property*] · Geschoßflächenzahl *f*, GFZ, Geschoßflächendichte *f*, GFD; Ausnutzungsziffer *f* [*frühere Benennung*]

basic form, basic shape, fundamental form, fundamental shape · Grundgestalt *f*, Grundform *f*

basic function, fundamental function · Grundfunktion *f*

basic goal (of policy), basic target goal, basic policy goal · Grundzielnorm *f*, Grundoberziel *n*, übergeordnetes Grundziel

basic human function, human basic function · Daseinsgrundfunktion *f*

basic industry, primary industry, fundamental industry · Grundindustrie *f*

basic law, constitutional law, fundamental law, organic law of a state [*The law which determines the constitution of government in a state, and prescribes and regulates the manner of its exercise*] · Grundgesetz *n*

basic map, fundamental map, base map · Grund(land)karte *f*

basic mapping · Grund(land)kartenwerk *n* [*für Folgemaßstäbe*]

basic measure, fundamental measure · Grundmaßnahme *f*

basic mistake, fundamental mistake · Grundirrtum *m*

basic motion time · Vorgabezeit *f* aus überbetrieblich ermittelter Normalzeit abgeleitet

basic need for shelter · Obdachgrundrecht *n*

basic norm, fundamental norm · Grundnorm *f*

basic objective · (strukturpolitisches) Grundentwick(e)lungsziel *n*

basic obligation, fundamental obligation · Grundverpflichtung *f*, Kardinalverpflichtung

basic order, fundamental order · Grundauftrag *m*

basic plan, fundamental plan · Grundplan *m*

basic policy goal, basic goal (of policy), basic target goal · Grundzielnorm *f*, Grundoberziel *n*, übergeordnetes Grundziel

basic price, fundamental price · Grundpreis *m*

basic rate, fundamental rate · Grundtarif *m*

basic rent, fundamental rent [*Rent on which calculations for other rents are based*] · Grundrente *f*, Basisrente

basic research, fundamental research · Grundlagenforschung *f*

basic rule, fundamental rule · Ausgangsregel *f*, Grundregel *f*

basic salary, fundamental salary, base salary · Grundgehalt n

basic scale · Grund(land)kartenmaßstab m, Maßstab des Grund(land)kartenwerks

basic sector · Originärsektor m

basic service(s) · Hauptleistung(en) f (pl)

basic shape, fundamental form, fundamental shape, basic form · Grundgestalt f, Grundform f

basic social spatial and functional unity, basic sociospatial and functional unity · sozialräumlich-funktionale Grundeinheit f

basic solution, b.s., fundamental solution · Grundlösung f

basic standard, frozen standard · Plankostenverrechnungssatz m nicht an Tagespreisen orientiert

basic standard cost(s), bogey standard cost(s), measure standard cost(s), fixed standard cost(s) · Maßstandardkosten f, Standardkosten 2. Art, Grundstandardkosten

basic structure, fundamental structure, basic composition, fundamental composition · Grundgefüge n, Grundaufbau m, Grundstruktur f, Grundzusammensetzung f

basic target goal, basic policy goal, basic goal (of policy) · Grundzielnorm f, Grundoberziel n, übergeordnetes Grundziel

basic value, fundamental value · Ausgangswert m, Grundwert m

basic variable, fundamental variable · Grundvariable f

basic wage, fundamental wage · Ausgangslohn m, Grundlohn m, Ecklohn m

basic work(s), main work(s), principal work(s) · Hauptarbeit(en) f (pl)

basic work(s) · fernbedarfstätige Arbeit(en) f(pl), fernbedarfstätige Leistung(en)

basic work(s) · Grundleistung(en) f (pl), Grundarbeit(en) f (pl) [Im Gegensatz zu „besonderen Leistungen'']

basis in law, lawful base, lawful basis, legal base, legal basis, base in law · rechtliche Grundlage f

basis of contract, contract basis, foundation of contract, contract foundation · Vertragsgrundlage f, Vertragsbasis f

basis of prices, price basis · Preisgrundlage f

basis of validity of law · Rechtsgeltungsgrund m

basket purchase, lump-sum purchase · Pauschalkauf m

basket-tenure, basket-tenancy, basketfief, basket-fee, basket-feud, basketfeod, basket tenement [Lands held by the service of making the king's baskets] · Korbleh(e)n n

bassa tenura [Latin]; base tenure [A holding by ville(i)nage, or other customary service; opposed to alta tenura, the highest tenure in capite, or by military service] · niedrigstes Leh(e)n n

batable ground [Land that is debated, i.e. the subject of dispute] · umstrittenes Land n

batch-module · Stapelbetrieb m [Verfahren zur Durchführung von Programmmodulgruppen]

bathing facility · Badeeinrichtung f

bathing place · Badeplatz m [Freifläche am Ufer eines für das Baden freigegebenen Gewässers, die mit den für einen Badebetrieb erforderlichen Einrichtungen ausgestattet ist]

bathymetric chart · Tiefenlinienkarte f, bathymetrische Karte

bathymetric contour, depth contour · Tiefenlinie f, Isobathe f

"battle of forms" · ,,Formularkrieg" m

ba(u)lk · niedriger Wall m [Um ein eisenzeitliches kleines Feld]

ba(u)lk [A strip of ground left unploughed as a boundary line between two ploughed portions] · Grenzrain m, Grasrain, ungepflügter Grasstreifen m, unbeackerter Grasstreifen, unbestellter Grasstreifen

to be added to, to accrue [As a thing or right passes from one person to another] · zufallen

beadle, bedell [obsolete]; crier [1. A crier or usher of a law court, 2. a town crier] · Ausrufer m

beadle, bedell; bedellus [Latin]; beodan, bydel [Anglo-Saxon]; parish constable [A common law parish officer whose office dates from time immemorial. He is chosen by, and holds office at the pleasure of, the vestry; he gives notice to parishioners of the meetings of the vestry and attends the meetings; and he sometimes summons jurors for coroners' inquests] · Ratsdiener m, Pedell m

to be adverse, to be wrongful, to be inconsistent with possessory right · entgegenstehen [(subjektives) Besitzrecht]

to be applicable, to be proper to be used, to lie [An action is said to lie in a case in which it may properly be brought] · anwendbar sein

bear · Baissespekulant m, Börsenspekulant ,,a la baisse", Baissier

bearer — to begin to have legal existence

bearer [*He who carries or brings*] · Überbringer *m*

bearer, holder [*The possessor of any personal endowment or quality; the holder of rank or office*] · Träger *m*, Inhaber

bearer · Vorzeiger *m* [*Wechsel*]

bearer cheque (Brit.); bearer check (US) · Inhaberscheck *m*

bearer in fact, holder in fact · tatsächlicher Inhaber *m*, tatsächlicher Träger, wirklicher Inhaber, wirklicher Träger

bearer of title, title bearer · Titelträger *m*, Titelinhaber

bearer policy, holder policy · Inhaberpolice *f*, Trägerpolice

bearer(-)security, negotiable instrument (payable to bearer), negotiable instrument payable to order · begebbares Papier *n*, umlauffähiges Papier, indossables Papier, Handelspapier, Orderpapier, umlaufbares Papier

bearer stock, share warrant to bearer · Inhaberaktie *f*

bearing of interests, interest yield(ing), interest bearing, interest return, returning of interests, yielding of interests · Verzinsung *f*

bear point · Baissemoment *n*

bearsmuck · Torf-Ton-Gemisch *n*, Torf-Ton-Mischung *f*

bear speculation · Baissespekulation *f*

to bear witness, to testify · bezeugen

beast of plough (Brit.); beast of plow (US) · Pflugtier *n*

beasts of the chase → (wild) beasts of the chase

beat [*The round or couse habitually traversed by a watchman, sentinel, or constable on duty*] · Patrouillenbezirk *m*

to beat down · abhandeln [*Preis*]

to beat down, to abate · schleifen [*Festungsmauer; Stadtmauer*]

to beautify, to embellish, to adorn · verschönern

to be beneficially interested, to be interested beneficially · faktisches Eigentumsrecht haben

to be cast in cost(s) · verurteilt werden Kosten zu tragen

to become bankrupt, to break · in Konkurs geraten, in Konkurs gehen, pleite gehen, pleite machen, Konkurs machen, fallieren

to (become) corrupt · bestechlich werden

to become due, to mature, to fall due, to accrue [*As rent or interest*] · fällig werden, verfallen

to become to have effect → to come into existence

to become invalid, to stand void · ungültig werden

to become obsolete · veralten

to become operative → to come into existence

becoming binding · Verbindlichwerden *n*

becoming due, maturity, maturation · Fälligkeit *f*, Verfall *m*

becoming invalid, standing void · Ungültigwerden *n*

to be consistent with, to be non-adverse, to be non-wrongful · nicht entgegenstehen [*(subjektives) Besitzrecht*]

to be co(n)terminous with, to adjoin, to lie (up)on, to border (up)on · angrenzen

bedell → beadle

bedell [*obsolete*]; crier, beadle [*1. A crier or usher of a law court, 2. a town crier*] · Ausrufer *m*

bedrip, bidrip(e), bed(e)repe, bedrape, bidrepe [*Reaping the lord's corn for one, two, or three days*] · befohlene Erntearbeit *f* [*Fronhofarbeit*]

bedroom community, dormitory community · Schlafgemeinde *f*, Auspendlergemeinde, reine Wohngemeinde

bedroom suburb(an place) (Brit.); dormitory suburb(an place) · Schlafvorort *m*, Auspendlervorort, reiner Wohnvorort

to be entitled beneficially, to be beneficially entitled · faktisch berechtigt sein

to be exposed to an ad(vertisement) · ausgesetzt sein [*einer Werbung gegenüber*]

to be favoured by law · auf gesetzlicher Bestimmung (be)ruhend

before/after circulation · vor/nach Beginn *m* der Verbreitung, vor/nach Beginn der Streuung, vor/nach Erscheinen *n* der Streuung, vor/nach Erscheinen der Verbreitung [*Umfragetechnik*]

before completion · vorzeitig [*Grund(stücks)(in)besitznahme und Grund(stücks)Besitzeinweisung*]

before marriage, ante-nuptial · vor der Eheschließung, vorehelich

beggar able to labour (Brit.); beggar able to labor (US); valiant beggar · arbeitsfähiger Bettler *m*

to begin, to open, to commence [*trial of a cause*] · eröffnen, anfangen, beginnen

to begin to have a legal existence, to accrue, to arise to have a legal existence [*For instance, an action accrues when the plaintiff has a right to commence it*] · gesetzlich entstehen

beginning of execution of (the) work(s) — beneficial interest 94

beginning of execution of (the) work(s) · Ausführungsbeginn *m*

beginning of liability, commencement of liability · Haftpflichtbeginn *m*, Haftungsbeginn, Haftbarkeitsbeginn

beginning of (the) limitation period, commencement of (the) limitation period · Verjährungsanfang *m*, Verjährungseintritt *m*

beginning of the liquidation, commencement of the winding(-)up, beginning of the winding(-)up, commencement of the liquidation · Liquidationseröffnung *f*

beginning of (the) work(s), commencement of (the) work(s) · Aufnahme *f* der Arbeiten, Beginn *m* der Arbeiten, Arbeitsbeginn *m*, (Bau)Beginn *m*

beginning of (the) year, BOY · Jahresanfang *m*

beginning (of validity), coming into operation, coming into being, coming into existence, commencement (of validity) · Inkrafttreten *n*, Wirksamwerden

behaviour (Brit.) → (personal) behaviour

behavio(u)ral scientist · Verhaltenswissenschaftler *m*

behaviour pattern, behaviour scheme (Brit.); behavior pattern, behavior scheme (US) · Verhaltensmuster *n*, Verhaltensschema *n*

behaviour setting (Brit.); behavior setting (US) · Mensch-Umwelt-Interaktion *f*

behaviour towards risks, behaviour towards hazards (Brit.); behavior towards risks, behavior towards hazards (US) · Risikoverhalten *n*, Wagnisverhalten

behind-closed-doors · hinter verschlossenen Türen *fpl*

to be immune from · befreit sein von, Immunität genießen

to be inconsistent with possessory right, to be adverse, to be wrongful · entgegenstehen [*(subjektives) Besitzrecht*]

to be in mercy · bußfällig sein

to be interested beneficially, to be beneficially interested · faktisches Eigentumsrecht haben

belief statement, statement of belief · gutgläubige Aussage *f*, gutgläubige Angabe

belonging to shore, lit(t)oral · litoral

belonging to, appandant, appurtenant (to), attached [*Things appendant can be claimed only by prescription, while things appurtenant can be claimed either by prescription or by express grant*] · anhaftend, zugehörig

below average, substandard, less-than-average · unterdurchschnittlich

below par · unter Pari

belt formation, formation of belt(s) · Gürtelbildung *f*

belt line · Gürtellinie *f*

belt of chemical plants · Chemiegürtel *m*

belt of industry, industrial belt, industry belt · Industriegürtel *m*

belt of meadows · Wiesengürtel *m*

belt of sea, sea belt [*In political sense*]; coast(al) waters [*In geographic and nautical sense*]; territorial waters, territorial sea, maritime belt · Küstengewässer *n*, Küstenmeer *n*, Territorialgewässer, Hoheitsgewässer, Meeresstreifen *m*, Hoheitsmeer, Territorialmeer

belt of trees, tree belt · Baumgürtel *m*

belt of woodland, woodland belt · Waldgürtel *m*, Waldparkgürtel

bench [*The judges collectively*] · Richtertum *n*

benefice; beneficium [*Latin*] · Pfründe *f*

benefice of a canon, canonry · kanonische Pfründe *f*

beneficia [*Latin*] [*For some time after the Norman Conquest "beneficia" meant lands given by feudal superiors to their followers upon consideration of their swearing fealty and performing military service*] · Treu(e)leh(e)n *n*

beneficial, bonitarian, bonitary [*Having possession with all its benefits, but without a legal title*] · bonitarisch, benefiziarisch, voll, im eigenen Interesse, nicht treuhänderisch

beneficial, enjoying the usufruct; beneficient [*obsolete*] [*Of or pertaining to the usufruct of property*] · nutznießend

beneficial demise, beneficial lease · Verpachtung *f* auf Jahre bei der der Pächter nach Vorwegzahlung der Pachtsumme den Pachtbesitz übernahm, Nutzungsrechtvergabe *f* auf Jahre bei der der Pächter nach Vorwegzahlung der Pachtsumme den Pachtbesitz übernahm [*Englisches mittelalterliches Recht*]

beneficial dominion, ownership in land(s); dominium utile [*Latin*] [*In der englischen Umgangssprache und in einigen Parlamentsgesetzen werden vielfach die Benennungen "landowner" und "ownership in land(s)" an Stelle von "tenant or holder of land" und "estate in land(s)" gebracht. In diesem Falle ist zu beachten, daß unter "ownership in land(s)" nur das "dominium utile" und nicht das "dominium directum" gemeint ist*] · Nutzeigentum *n*, Untereigentum, leh(e)n(s)rechtliches Nutzungsrecht *n*

beneficial interest · Nutzungsrecht *n* des wirtschaftlichen Eigentümers, Ge-

beneficial lease — benefit club

brauchsrecht des wirtschaftlichen Eigentümers

beneficial lease, beneficial demise · Verpachtung f auf Jahre bei der der Pächter nach Vorwegzahlung der Pachtsumme den Pachtbesitz übernahm, Nutzungsrechtvergabe f auf Jahre bei der der Pächter nach Vorwegzahlung der Pachtsumme den Pachtbesitz übernahm [Englisches mittelalterliches Recht]

(beneficial) occupant, (beneficial) occupier, beneficial owner, tenant, user, usufructuary, beneficiary; cestui (à) que use, cestui à l'use de qui, cestui (à) que trust, cestuy que trust [Norman French]; usufructarius [Latin] [He to whose use another is enfeoffed of lands or tenements. The substantial and beneficial owner, as distinguished from the feoffee to uses] · Nutznießer m, faktischer Eigentümer, Nehmer, Empfänger eines benefiziarischen Nutzungsrechts, Benefiziar, Besitznehmer, Usufruktuar, Fruchtnießer, Nießbraucher

(beneficial) occupation, (beneficial) occupancy · Nutz(nieß)ung f [Nutzbares Innehaben von ertragsfähigem Realbesitz]

(beneficial) occupation (up)on an occupation, (beneficial) occupancy (up)on an occupancy · Nutz(nieß)ung f auf einer Nutz(nieß)ung

(beneficial) occupation without transmutation of possession at common law, (beneficial) occupancy without transmutation of possession at common law · Nutz(nieß)ung f ohne Wechsel des gemeinrechtlichen Besitzes

beneficial owner → (beneficial) occupant

beneficial ownership, bonitary ownership, bonitarian ownership [The benefit accruing to a tenant whose rent is less than the net annual value of the property which he occupies] · benefiziarisches Eigentum n, wirtschaftliches Eigentum, Volleigentum, Eigentum im eigenen Interesse, nicht treuhänderisches Eigentum, bonitarisches Eigentum

beneficial purpose · nutzbringender Zweck m, nützlicher Zweck

beneficial rate, renumerative rate [Terms used by Alfred Marshall for local rates where the money is spent on lighting, drainage, etc., the services so provided being regarded as a net benefit to the people paying the rates, in contrast to onerous rates which yield no compensating benefit to the ratepayer] · nutzbringende Kommunalabgabe f, nutzbringende Gemeindeabgabe

beneficiary, feudal, feodal, feuda(to)ry, manorial [Relating to feuds or feudal tenures. Held by feudal service] · feudal, grundherr(schaft)lich, zu einer Grundherrschaft gehörig

beneficiary [One who receives benefits or favours] · Begünstigte m

beneficiary, holder of a feudal benefice, land tenant, (feudal) tenant, manorial tenant, feudal bondman, vassal, tenant of land, feeholder, holder of a fee, holder of a fief, fief-tenant, feoda(to)ry, feuda(to)ry; homo pertinens [Latin] [A tenant or vassal who held his estate by feudal service] · Leh(e)n(s)mann m, Leh(e)n(s)träger m, Gefolgsmann, Gutszinsmann, Vasall m

beneficiary → (beneficial) occupant

beneficient [obsolete]; beneficial, enjoying the usufruct [Of or pertaining to the usufruct of property] · nutznießend

beneficium [Latin]; benefice · Pfründe f

beneficium abstinendi [Latin] · Ausschlagsrecht n [römisches Recht]

beneficium castrale, feudum castrense, peculium castrense [Latin] · Burgleh(e)n n, Burggut n [Es wurde jemandem gegeben mit der Bedingung eine Burg zu schützen]

beneficium divisionis [Latin] · Teilschuld f

beneficium excussionis, beneficium ordinis, beneficium discussionis [Latin] [A privilege given to sureties in the later Roman law, which enabled them to postpone the payment of the guaranteed debt until the principal debtor had been sued for the amount] · Einrede f der Vorausklage

beneficium inventarii [Latin] [When an heir male had recorded an inventory of the estate he was liable only to the extent of the estate for the obligations of the deceased] · Gestaltungsrecht n [Mit dem Gestaltungsrecht beschränkte der Erbe seine Haftung durch ein Inventar]

benefit [The advantage of belonging to a privileged order which was exempted from the jurisdiction or sentence of the ordinary courts of law] · Standesprivileg n

benefit, advantage · Nutzen m, Vorteil m

benefit [A natural advantage or "gift"] · natürliche Gabe f

benefit, pecuniary advange · Geldvorteil m

benefit analysis, utility analysis, worth analysis · Nutz(ungs)wertanalyse f, NWA

benefit building society (Brit.); non-incorporated (building and loan) association, benefit (building and loan) association (US); non-incorporated building society · nichteingetragene Bausparkasse f

benefit club, benefit society, friendly society [A society whose members, by the regular payment of small sums, are *entitled to pecuniary help in time of age or sickness*] · Hilfskasse *f*, Selbsthilfeorganisation *f*, Unterstützungsverein *m*, Förderungsverein(igung) *m, (f)*, Unterstützungskasse

benefit-cost(s) analysis, CBA, cost(s)-benefit analysis [*A systematic comparison between the cost(s) of carrying out a service or activity and the value of that service or activity, quantified as far as possible, all costs and benefits (direct and indirect, financial and social) being taken into account*] · Kosten-Nutzen-Analyse *f*, Nutzen-Kosten-Analyse, Kosten-Nutzen-Untersuchung *f*, Nutzen-Kosten-Untersuchung, NKA

benefit-cost(s) ratio, cost(s)-benefit ratio · Kosten-Nutzen-Verhältnis *n*, Nutzen-Kosten-Verhältnis, NKA-Verhältnis

benefit housing association, cooperative housing association, hous(e build)ing cooperative, benefit housing society, cooperative housing society · Wohnungsgenossenschaft *f* [*Fehlbenennungen: (Wohnungs)Baugenossenschaft*] [*Wohnungsunternehmen in der Rechtsform der eingetragenen Genossenschaft, deren Zweck der Bau, die Bewirtschaftung und/oder die Verwaltung von Wohnungen und deren Überlassung zur Nutzung oder zu Eigentum an die Mitglieder ist. Die häufig verwendeten Benennungen „(Wohnungs)Baugenossenschaft" sind begrifflich insofern irreführend, als die deutschen Wohnungsgenossenschaften keine Produktivgenossenschaften (Bauunternehmen) sind; zutreffender ist daher die Benennung „Wohnungsgenossenschaft"*]

benefit of fall-clause · Baisseklausel *f*, Preissturzklausel

benefit of (his) clergy, (his) clergy [*Old Law. Originally the privilege of exemption from trial by a secular court, allowed to or claimed by clergymen arraigned for felony; in later times the privilege of exemption from the sentence, which in the case of certain offences might be pleaded on his first conviction by every one who could read. Abolished in England, after various earlier modifications, in 1827*] · Besserstellung *f* der Geistlichkeit, Kirchenasyl *n*

benefit plan, retirement plan, pension plan · (Alters)Versorgungsplan *m*, Pensionsplan

benefit society, friendly society, benefit club [*A society whose members, by the regular payment of small sums, are entitled to pecuniary help in time of age or sickness*] · Hilfskasse *f*, Selbsthilfeorganisation *f*, Unterstützungsverein *m*, Förderungsverein(igung) *m, (f)*, Unterstützungskasse

benevolence · freiwillig angebotene Geldsumme *f*

benevolence, charity, charitableness · Wohltätigkeit *f*

benevolence organization, charity organization, charitable organization, benevolent organization · Wohltätigkeitsorganisation *f*

benevolent, charitable; charitative [*obsolete*] · wohltätig, karitativ

benevolent institution, charitable institution · Wohltätigkeitsanstalt *f*

benevolent organization, benevolence organization, charity organization, charitable organization · Wohltätigkeitsorganisation *f*

to be non-adverse, to be non-wrongful, to be consistent with · nicht entgegenstehen [*(subjektives) Besitzrecht*]

beodan → beadle

bēodland · Tafelgut *n* des Kathedralstiftes, Tafelgut des Klosterklerus

to be proper to be used, to lie, to be applicable [*An action is said to lie in a case in which it may properly be brought*] · anwendbar sein

to bequeath · (testamentarisch) vermachen, testamentarisch verfügen, letztwillig vermachen, letztwillig verfügen [*Fahrnis*]

bequeathable, capable of being bequeathed · (testamentarisch) vermachbar, letztwillig verfügbar, letztwillig vermachbar, testamentarisch verfügbar [*Fahrnis*]

bequeathed · letztwillig verfügt, letztwillig vermacht, testamentarisch verfügt, (testamentarisch) vermacht [*Fahrnis*]

bequeathed annuity · (Fahrnis)Vermächtnisannuität *f*, Fahrhabevermächtnisannuität

bequeather, legator [*One who makes a will, and leaves legacies*] · (Fahrnis)Legatgeber *m*, (Fahrnis)Vermächtnisgeber, Fahrhabelegatgeber, Fahrhabevermächtnisgeber

bequeathing, bequeathment, bequeathal · (testamentarisches) Vermachen *n*, letztwilliges Vermachen, testamentarisches Verfügen, letztwilliges Verfügen [*Fahrnis*]

bequest, legacy [*A gift made by will of money or mov(e)able things*] · Legat *n*, Vermächtnis *n*, Fahrnisvermächtnis, Fahrnislegat, Fahrhabevermächtnis, Fahrhabelegat

bequest ademption, legacy revocation, bequest revocation; ademptio legati [*Latin*]; ademption of legacy, revocation of legacy, ademption of bequest, revocation of bequest, legacy ademption [*It occurs where a legacy does not take effect owing to some act on the part of* a testator not affecting the validity of the will] · (Fahrnis)Legatrücknahme f, (Fahrnis)Legatentziehung f, (Fahrnis)-Vermächtnisrücknahme, (Fahrnis)Vermächtnisentziehung, Fahrhabelegatrücknahme, Fahrhabelegatentziehung, Fahrhabevermächtnisrücknahme, Fahrhabevermächtnisentziehung

bequest by particular title, legacy by particular title · Einzelvermächtnis n einer beweglichen Sache, Einzellegat n einer beweglichen Sache, Einzel(fahrnis)vermächtnis, Einzel(fahrnis)legat

bequest duty, legacy duty, legacy tax, bequest tax · (Fahrnis)Vermächtnissteuer f, (Fahrnis)Legatsteuer, (Fahrnis)Erb(schafts)steuer, Fahrhabelegatsteuer, Fahrhabeerb(schafts)steuer, Fahrhabevermächtnissteuer

bequest revocation; ademptio legati [*Latin*]; ademption of legacy, revocation of legacy, ademption of bequest, revocation of bequest, legacy ademption, bequest ademption, legacy revocation [*It occurs where a legacy does not take effect owing to some act on the part of a testator not affecting the validity of the will*] · (Fahrnis)Legatrücknahme f, (Fahrnis)Legatentziehung f, (Fahrnis)Vermächtnisrücknahme, (Fahrnis)Vermächtnisentziehung, Fahrhabelegatrücknahme, Fahrhabelegatentziehung, Fahrhabevermächtnisrücknahme, Fahrhabevermächtnisentziehung

bequest tax, bequest duty, legacy duty, legacy tax · (Fahrnis)Vermächtnissteuer f, (Fahrnis)Legatsteuer, (Fahrnis)Erb(schafts)steuer, Fahrhabelegatsteuer, Fahrhabeerb(schafts)steuer, Fahrhabevermächtnissteuer

Bernoulli trials · Bernoullischema n [*Statistik*]

to be silent as to · nichts aussagen über

bespeaking the judg(e)ment · Abfassung f des Urteils, Urteilsabfassung

best evidence rule · Regel f des besten Beweismittels

to bestow a fee, to bestow a fief, to bestow a feud; feoffare, infeodare, infeudare [*Latin*]; to invest [*old Scots law*]; to give possession of land(s), to give a seisin of land(s), to (give a) feud, to infeft, to infeoff, to enfeoff · belehnen, feudal belehnen

to bestow by will, to give by will, to dispose by will, to leave by will · (testamentarisch) vermachen, letztwillig verfügen, testamentarisch verfügen, letztwillig vermachen

bestowed by will, given by will, disposed by will, left by will · letztwillig verfügt, letztwillig vermacht, (testamentarisch) vermacht, testamentarisch verfügt

bestower of a fee → liege-lord

to better · steigern des Wertes, verbessern des Wertes [*Grundbesitz*]

better equity · stärkere Billigkeit f

better law · besseres Recht n

better law approach · Wahl f des besseren Rechts

betterment, (capital) appreciation, increase of value, value increase, (prospective) development value [*An improvement which adds to the cost(s) of a property. Distinguished from a repair or replacement*] · Wertverbesserung f, Wertzuwachs m, Wertsteigerung, Wertzunahme f, Werterhöhung

betterment clause, value increase clause, (prospective) development value clause, increase of value clause, (capital) appreciation clause · Werterhöhungsklausel f, Wertsteigerungsklausel, Wertzuwachsklausel, Wertzunahmeklausel, Wertverbesserungsklausel

betterment duty, betterment rate, betterment levy, betterment tax · Wertzuwachsabgabe f, Wertzunahmeabgabe, Wertverbesserungsabgabe, Werterhöhungsabgabe, Wertsteigerungsabgabe, Wertzunahmesteuer, Wertzuwachssteuer f, Werterhöhungssteuer, Wertsteigerungssteuer, Wertverbesserungssteuer, Steuer auf den unverdienten Wertzuwachs

better rule approach · Vorzug m der materiell beseren Lösung kollidierender Rechtsordnungen

better rule of law · bessere Sachnorm f

betting office · Wettbüro n

betting tax · Wettsteuer f

between parties who are alive, between persons who are alive, between living people, between living persons; inter vivos [*Latin*] · unter Lebenden

to be worked at a profit, to be worked at a gain · gewinnbringend betreiben

to be wrongful, to be inconsistent with possessory right, to be adverse · entgegenstehen [*(subjektives) Besitzrecht*]

beyond repair → not capable of repair

beyond the control of the contractor · vom Unternehmer nicht zu vertreten

beyond the law, more than the law requires; extra jus [*Latin*] · übergesetzlich

beyond the power(s), beyond the capacity, beyond the capacities; ultra vires [*Latin*] · gewaltüberschreitend, hoheit(s)überschreitend, kompetenzüberschreitend, machtüberschreitend

bias · systematischer Fehler m [*demoskopische Forschung*]

bias · Nicht-Erwartungstreue f [*in der Schätztheorie*]

bias · Voreingenommenheit f, Parteilichkeit f, Befangenheit

biased, unduly influenced, unfair influenced · voreingenommen, parteiisch, befangen

biased estimator · verzerrende Schätzfunktion f, nichterwartungstreue Schätzfunktion, nichttendenzfreie Schätzfunktion [*Statistik*]

bicycle trail, biking path, bicycle path, biking trail · Rad(fahr)weg m

bid · Nachfrage f, Geld n [*Fonds. Gegensatz: Inventarwert, Angebot, Brief = asked price*]

bid; (bid) proposal (US); tender, offer · Angebot n

bid (US) → bid sum

bid analysis; (bid) proposal analysis (US); tender analysis, offer analysis · Angebotsanalyse f, Angebotsuntersuchung f

bid and asked · angeboten und gefragt, Brief m und Geld n

bid (blank) form, offer (blank) form, form of offer, form of offer, form of bid, bid(ding) form; (bid) proposal form, form of (bid) proposal, (bid) proposal blank (form) (US); tender (blank) form · Angebotsblankett n, Angebotsformular n, Angebotsvordruck m

bid bond, tender bond, offer bond; (bid) proposal bond (US) [*A bid guarantee by bond. The function of a bid bond is to guarantee the good faith of the bidder, so that if awarded the contract within the time stipulated, he will enter into the contract and furnish the prescribed performance and payment bonds*] · Bietungsgarantie f [*Eine Bietungssicherheit durch beurkundete Schuldforderung*]

bid collusion, rigging bids, collusion among(st) bidders, collusion among(st) offerers, collusion among(st) tenderers, price taking, collusive agreement, combining to eliminate competition, restrictive covenant, restrictive tendering agreement, taking a price, collusive tendering, collusive bidding, (collusive) price fixing, bid-rigging [*The frequently heavy cost of tendering sometimes leads contractors to put forward tenders which are not genuine, in the sense that, rather than refuse to make a tender when invited to do so, the contractor tenders a price higher than that "taken" from another contractor who does desire to obtain the contract, thus avoiding expense and leading the employer to believe that he has had genuine competitive tenders for the work*] · Abrede f unter Bietern, Absprache f unter Bietern, Preisabrede, Preisabsprache, Submissionsabrede, Submissionsabsprache, Konkurrenzvereinbarung f, Verständigung f unter Bietern, Angebotsabsprache

to bid competitively, to offer competitively, to tender competitively, to submit a competitive bid · abgeben n eines Wettbewerbsangebotes, einreichen eines Wettbewerbsangebotes, anbieten im Wettbewerb, submittieren im Wettbewerb

bid conditions, offer conditions, tender conditions; conditions of the (bid) proposal, (bid) proposal conditions (US); conditions of the bid, conditions of the offer, conditions of the tender · Angebotsbedingungen f pl

bid covering letter, offer covering letter; (bid) proposal covering letter (US), tender covering letter · Angebots-(an)schreiben n, Angebotsbegleitschreiben

bid date → closing date (for receipt of tenders)

bidder, tenderer, offeror, competitor, tendering contractor, competing contractor · (an)bietende Firma f, (An)Bieter m, Angebotsabgeber

bidder at a sale; licitator [*Latin*] · Versteigerungsbieter m, Auktionsbieter

bidder's list, tenderer's list, competitor's list, tendering contractor's list, competiting contractor's list · Ausschreibungsliste f, (An)Bieterliste f

bidder's prequalifications, tenderer's prequalifications · Bietereignung f

bidding (action), tender(ing) action, tendering (out) · Ausschreibung f, Angebotseinholung, Einholung f von Angeboten

bidding authority, tendering authority · ausschreibende Behörde f

bidding combination, tendering combination, bidding partnership, tendering partnership · Bietergemeinschaft f

bidding cost(s), cost(s) of tendering, cost(s) of bidding, tendering cost(s) [*The cost(s) to the contractor of preparing his tender, including any amended tender necessitated by bona fide alterations in the bill of quantities and plans*] · Bieterkosten f, Blankettkosten, Bietungskosten, Angebots(abgabe)kosten

bid(ding) date, closing date for bids, date of receipt of bids, tendering date, closing date (for receipt of tenders), closing time (for receipt of bids) · (Angebots)Abgabedatum n, (Angebots)Abgabetermin m, Einreich(ungs)datum, Einreich(ungs)termin, Angebotstermin, Angebotsdatum

bid(ding) document, offer document; (bid) proposal document (US); tendering

bidding error — (bid) proposal conditions (US)

bidding document · Ausschreibungsunterlage *f*, Ausschreibungsdokument *n* [*Fehlbenennungen: Angebotsunterlage, Angebotsdokument*]

bidding error, tendering error · Angebotsfehler *m*, Bietungsfehler

bid(ding) form; (bid) proposal form, form of (bid) proposal, (bid) proposal blank (form) (US); tender (blank) form, bid (blank) form, offer (blank) form, form of tender, form of offer, form of bid · Angebotsblankett *n*, Angebotsformular *n*, Angebotsvordruck *m*

bidding invitation, invitation to (submit a) bid, request for tender, request for offer, request for bid, call for tender, call for offer, call for bid; request for (bid) proposal, call for (bid) proposal (US); tendering invitation, invitation to tender, invitation to bid · (Angebots)Aufforderung *f*, Aufforderung zur Angebotsabgabe

bidding partnership, tendering partnership, bidding combination, tendering combination · Bietergemeinschaft *f*

bidding period, bidding time, period of tendering, time of tendering, period of bidding, time of bidding, tendering period, tendering time · Angebotsfrist *f*, Angebotszeitraum *m*, Ausschreibungsfrist, Ausschreibungszeitraum

bidding procedure, tendering procedure · Ausschreibungsverfahren *n*

bidding result, tendering result · Ausschreibungsergebnis *n*

bidding sheet, tendering sheet, estimating sheet, calculation sheet · Angebotsbogen *m*, Kalkulationsbogen

bidding stage, stage of tendering, stage of bidding, tendering stage [*The stage in which a suitable contractor is selected and an acceptable offer obtained*] · Ausschreibungsstadium *n*, Ausschreibungsstufe *f*, Stadium *n* der Angebotseinholung, Stufe *f* der Angebotseinholung, Stufe *f* der Ausschreibung, Stadium *n* der Ausschreibung, Angebotseinholungsstufe *f*, Angebotseinholungsstadium *n*

bidding time, period of tendering, time of tendering, period of bidding, time of bidding, tendering period, tendering time, bidding period · Angebotsfrist *f*, Angebotszeitraum *m*, Ausschreibungsfrist, Ausschreibungszeitraum

bid drawing → tender drawing

bid estimate, (bid) proposal estimate (US); tender estimate, offer estimate · Angebotsvoranschlag *m*

bid figure → bid sum

bid form → bid (blank) form

bid guarantee, bid guarantie, bid guaranty, bid security, tender guarantie, tender guarantee, tender guaranty, tender security, offer guarantee, offer guarantie, offer guaranty, offer security; (bid) proposal guarantee, (bid) proposal guarantie, (bid) proposal guaranty, (bid) proposal security (US) [*Deposit for cash, check, money order, or bid bond when the bid is submitted by the bidder to guarantee that he will sign the contract and furnish the required surety if awarded*] · Bietungsbürgschaft *f*, Bietungssicherheit *f*

bid guarantee by cashier's cheque → bid security by cashier's cheque

bid guarantee by certified cheque → bid security by certified cheque

bid item, tender item, offer item; (bid) proposal item (US) · Angebotsposition *f*

bid opening, tender opening, offer opening; (bid) proposal opening, opening of (bid) proposal (US); opening of tenders, opening of offers, opening of bids · Angebotseröffnung *f*, Submission *f*

(bid) opening date; (bid) proposal opening date (US); submission date, date of submission, date set for the opening of tenders, deadline for submission of bids, date of opening · (Angebots)Eröffnungstermin *m*, (Angebots)Eröffnungsdatum *n*, Submissionstermin, Submissionsdatum

(bid) opening time, tender opening time · Submissionszeit *f*

bid prescriptions, bid regulations; (bid) proposal prescriptions, (bid) proposal regulations (US); tender prescriptions, tender regulations, offer prescriptions, offer regulations · Angebotsvorschriften *fpl*

bid price [*The price at which a jobber is willing to buy*] · Geldkurs *m*

bid price, offer(ed) price · Ausgabepreis *m*, Rücknahmepreis, Rückkaufpreis [*Investmentanteil*]

bid (price) → bid sum

(bid) proposal (US); tender, offer, bid · Angebot *n*

(bid) proposal blank (form) (US); tender (blank) form, bid (blank) form, offer (blank) form, form of tender, form of offer, form of bid, bid(ding) form; (bid) proposal form, form of (bid) proposal (US) · Angebotsblankett *n*, Angebotsformular *n*, Angebotsvordruck *m*

(bid) proposal conditions (US); conditions of the bid, conditions of the offer, conditions of the tender, bid conditions, offer conditions, tender conditions; conditions of the (bid) proposal (US) · Angebotsbedingungen *fpl*

(bid) proposal estimate (US); tender estimate, offer estimate, bid estimate · Angebotsvoranschlag *m*

(bid) proposal opening, opening of (bid) proposal (US); opening of tenders, opening of offers, opening of bids, bid opening, tender opening, offer opening · Angebotseröffnung *f*, Submission *f*

(bid) proposal prescriptions, (bid) proposal regulations (US), tender prescriptions, tender regulations, offer prescriptions, offer regulations, bid prescriptions, bid regulations · Angebotsvorschriften *fpl*

bid rate → tender rate

bid regulations → bid prescriptions

bidrepe → bedripe

bid request; (bid) proposal request (US); tender request, offer request · Angebotsanforderung *f*

bid request form, tender request form, offer request form; (bid) proposal request form (US) · Angebotsanforderungsformular *n*

bid-rigging, bid collusion, rigging bids, collusion among(st) bidders, collusion among(st) offerers, collusion among(st) tenderers, price taking, collusive agreement, combining to eliminate competition, restrictive covenant, restrictive tendering agreement, taking a price, collusive tendering, collusive bidding, (collusive) price fixing [*The frequently heavy cost of tendering sometimes leads contractors to put forward tenders which are not genuine, in the sense that, rather than refuse to make a tender when invited to do so, the contractor tenders a price higher than that "taken" from another contractor who does desire to obtain the contract, thus avoiding expense and leading the employer to believe that he has had genuine competitive tenders for the work*] · Abrede *f* unter Bietern, Absprache *f* unter Bietern, Preisabrede, Preisabsprache, Submissionsabrede, Submissionsabsprache, Konkurrenzvereinbarung *f*, Verständigung *f* unter Bietern, Angebotsabsprache

bidrip(e) → bedripe

bid security → bid guarantee

bid security by cashier's cheque, bid guarantee by cashier's cheque (Brit.); bid security by cashier's check, bid guarantee by cashier's check (US) · Bietungsbürgschaft *f* durch Selbstscheck, Bietungssicherheit *f* durch Selbstscheck

bid security by certified cheque, bid guarantee by certified cheque (Brit.); bid security by certified check, bid guarantee by certified check (US) · Bietungsbürgschaft *f* durch beglaubigten Scheck, Bietungssicherheit *f* durch beglaubigten Scheck

bid sum, tender(ed) figure, offer figure, bid figure; (bid) proposal sum, (bid) proposal figure, (bid) proposal price (US); tender(ed) price, offer price, bid price, tender(ed) sum, offer sum [*Amount stated in the bid as the sum for which the bidder offers to perform the work*] · Angebotspreis *m*, Angebotssumme *f*

bid total, offer total; (bid) proposal total (US); tender total [*The total of the priced bill of quantities at the date of acceptance of the contractor's tender for the works*] · Angebotsendsumme *f*, Angebotsendpreis *m*

bifactor model · Doppelfaktorenmodell *n*

bifocal [*e.g. interpretation*] · doppelt [*z. B. Auslegung*]

big bailiff [*England*] · Gerichtsvollzieher *m* eines Grafschaftsgerichts

big city, great city · Großstadt *f*

big city dweller, great city inhabitant, big city inhabitant, great city dweller · Großstadteinwohner *m*, Großstadtbewohner

big city life, great city life · Großstadtleben *n*

big city population, great city population · Großstadtbevölkerung *f*, großstädtische Bevölkerung

big game · Großwild *n*

big group city, big group town, large group city, large group town · Gruppengroßstadt *f*

big village, great village · Großdorf *n*

biking trail, bicycle trail, biking path, bicycle path · Rad(fahr)weg *m*

bilateral [*In the law of contract, executory on both sides*] · beid(er)seitig, zweiseitig

bilateral duties · beid(er)seitige Pflichten *fpl*, zweiseitige Pflichten

bilateral error · beid(er)seitiger Fehler *m*, zweiseitiger Fehler

bilateral legal act(ion) · zweiseitige Rechtshandlung *f*, zweiseitiger Rechtsakt *m*, beid(er)seitige Rechtshandlung, beid(er)seitiger Rechtsakt

bilateral mistake · beid(er)seitiger Irrtum *m*, zweiseitiger Irrtum

bilateral monopoly · beid(er)seitiges Monopol *n*, zweiseitiges Monopol

bilateral treaty · zweiseitiger völkerrechtlicher Vertrag *m*, beid(er)seitiger völkerrechtlicher Vertrag

bill, list, schedule, tabulation, index, registry, register · Verzeichnis *n*, Liste *f*, Aufstellung *f*, Register *n*

bill, invoice · Rechnung *f*

bill [*A formal declaration of particular things in writing*] · (Rechts)Schrift *f*

bill, poster, placard, placart · Plakat *n*

bill → bill (of exchange)

bill account · Wechselkonto *n*

bill at usance · Handelsbrauchwechsel *m*, Usowechsel, Usanzwechsel

billboard · Plakatierwand *f*

billboard, (advertisement) hoarding · Werbetafel *f*, Reklametafel

bill broker · Wechselmäkler *m*, Wechselhändler; Wechselagent *m* [*Fehlbenennung*] [*Es handelt sich um einen Wechselhändler im eigenen Namen*]

bill contract, contract for measure and value, unit-price contract, measurement contract, measured contract, measure-and-value contract · Einheits(preis)vertrag *m* [*Ein Vertrag zu Einheitspreisen für technisch und wirtschaftlich einheitliche Teilleistungen, deren Menge nach Maß, Gewicht oder Stückzahl vom Auftraggeber in den Verdingungsunterlagen angegeben ist*]

bill debt · Wechselschuld *f*

bill-doer, bill-jobber · Diskonteur *m*, Wechselreiter, Wechselspekulant *m*

bill due · fälliger Wechsel *m*

billet · Quartier *n*

billeting · Einquartieren *n*

billet-master · Quartiermeister *m*

billhead (US) · Rechnungsformular *n*

bill holder · Wechselinhaber *m*, Wechselgläubiger

billing · Inrechnungstellen, Fakturieren

billion, million millions [*Great Britain*] · (eine) Million Millionen

billion, 1,000 million [*USA*] · (ein)tausend Millionen

bill-jobber, bill-doer · Diskonteur *m*, Wechselreiter, Wechselspekulant *m*

bill market, discount market, Lombard Street · Diskontmarkt *m*

bill of amortization, amortization bill, amortizing bill · Amortisationsbescheinigung *f*, Tilgungsbescheinigung, Tilgungsschein *m*, Amortisationsschein, Amortisationsattest *n*, Tilgungsattest

bill of cost(s) [*A certified, itemized statement of the amount of cost(s) in an action of suit*] · Kostenrechnung *f*

bill of delivery, delivery order, order of delivery, delivery bill · Lieferschein *m*

bill of (en)feoffment, bill of infeftment, (en)feoffment bill, infeftment bill · Leh(e)n(s)brief *m*

bill of exceptions, certificate of evidence, statement of case [*A formal statement in writing of the objections or exceptions taken by a party during the trial of a cause to the decisions, rulings, or instructions of the trial judge, stating the objections, with the facts and circumstances on which it is founded, and, in order to attest its accuracy, signed and sealed by the judge; the object being to put the controverted rulings or decisions upon the record for the information of the appellate court when the ends of justice require it, the terms "bill of exceptions" and "statement of case" are regarded as synonymous*] · Niederschrift *f* der Beweisverhandlung, Aufzeichnung *f* der Beweisverhandlung

bill (of exchange) · Wechsel *m* [*Im anglo-amerikanischen Wechselrecht ist „bill of exchange" die Sammelbenennung für Wechsel und Scheck, in der kaufmännischen Praxis wird aber nur der Wechsel als „ bill of exchange" bezeichnet*]

bill (of exchange) after date, bill (of exchange) with exact expiry, time bill (of exchange), date draft · Datowechsel *m*, Zeitwechsel, Zielwechsel [*Die Zahlungszeit ist auf eine bestimmte Zeit nach dem Tage der Ausstellung festgesetzt*]

bill (of exchange) deposited as security · Depotwechsel *m*, Kautionswechsel, Sicherheitswechsel

bill (of exchange) payable at a named fair · Messewechsel *m*

bill (of exchange) payable at a named market · Marktwechsel *m*

bill of health, health bill · Gesundheitspaß *m*

bill of lading, B/L · Konnossement *n*, Ladeschein *m*, Verladungsschein

bill of lading contract · Stückgütervertrag *m* [*Seefrachtgeschäft*]

bill (of law) · Gesetz(es)antrag *m*, Gesetz(es)vorlage *f*, Gesetz(es)vorschlag *m* [*Im Parlament eingebracht*]

bill of mortality [*Abolished in England in 1842, as the modern system of registration of births, deaths and marriages made the bills of mortality unnecessary*] · Sterbetafel *f*

bill of parcels · Faktura *f*, spezifizierte Warenrechnung *f*

bill of quantities, itemized quotation · Leistungsbeschreibung *f* mit Mengenansätzen, Leistungsverzeichnis *n*, LV

bill of quantities, spec(ification) · Mengenverzeichnis *n*

bill of sale [*A written agreement by the terms of which the title or other interest of one person in goods is transferred or assigned to another*] · Kaufbrief *m*,

bill of sight — biological spatial research

Übertragungsurkunde f, Mobiliarschuldverschreibung f

bill of sight · Zollerlaubnisschein m, vorläufiger Zolleinfuhrschein

bill of store, store bill · Wiedereinfuhrschein m

bill of sufferance, sufferance bill · Freihandelsschein m, Passierschein [*Erlaubnisschein Güter zollfrei zu versenden*]

bill of tonnage, tonnage bill · Meßbrief m [*Schiff*]

bill payable · Schuldwechsel m

(bill-)posting, placard-posting, bill sticking, placard sticking, poster sticking · Plakatankleben, Plakatanschlagen

bill price, itemized price · L.V.-Preis m, Leistungsverzeichnispreis

bill receivable · Rimesse f, Besitzwechsel m, ausstehender Wechsel

bill to peace · Zusammenlegung f im Billigkeitsverfahren

bi-margin map · (Land)Karte f mit zwei Anschnittkanten

bi-metallic system of currency, bi-metallism [*The employment of two metals, to form at the same time, in combination with each other, the standard of value*] · Doppel(metall)währung f, Zweimetallwährung, Bimetallismus n

bi-monthly · zweimonatlich

binary choice model, model of binary choice · Modell n der dualen Entscheidung, Verkehrsmodell der dualen Entscheidung, duales Entscheidungs(verkehrs)modell

to bind · binden

bind day, boon-day, reaping day, precaria [*The day (up)on which a tenant was required to perform the service of bedrip*] · befohlener Erntearbeitstag m, Frontag auf besonderes Begehr

binder (US) [*1. Agreement by which the buyer and seller tentatively agree on the terms of a contract. In some states, if for some valid reason the contract cannot be drawn, the agreement is no longer enforceable. 2. Agreement to cover a down payment for the purchase of real estate as evidence of good faith on the part of the purchaser; in insurance a temporary agreement given to one having an insurable interest and who desires insurance subject to the same conditions that will apply if, as, and when a policy is issued*] · Deckungszusage f

binding, authoritative, commanding · bindend, verbindlich, geltend

binding · Bindung f, Gebundenheit f

binding to a plan · Planbindung f

binding clause · Bindeklausel f, Bindungsklausel

binding declaration · Gebundenheitserklärung f

binding effect → binding force (of decided cases)

binding force (of decided cases), authoritative force (of decided cases), binding authority (of precedents), principle of stare decisis, binding effect · bindende Kraft f (der Präjudizien), verbindliche Kraft f (der Präjudizien), Bindekraft (der Präjudizien), Bindungswirkung f (der Präjudizien), Prinzip n der bindenden Kraft gerichtlicher Entscheidungen, Beharren n auf der gefällten Entscheidung, Grundsatz m der bindenden Kraft gerichtlicher Entscheidungen

binding fountain of law, commanding source of law, commanding fountain of law, authoritative source of law, authoritative fountain of law, binding source of law · geltende Rechtsquelle f, verbindliche Rechtsquelle, bindende Rechtsquelle

binding in law, having the force of law, having effect in law, legally binding · rechtsverbindlich

binding of price(s) · Preisgebundenheit f, Preisbindung f

binding option · bindende Option f

binding period, binding time, period of binding, time of binding · Bindungsfrist f, Bindefrist [*Die Zeit, in welcher der Bieter an sein Angebot gegenüber dem Auftraggeber gebunden ist*]

binding settlement of property · vollwirksame Vermögensstiftung f

binding source of law, binding fountain of law, commanding source of law, commanding fountain of law, authoritative source of law, authoritative fountain of law · geltende Rechtsquelle f, verbindliche Rechtsquelle, bindende Rechtsquelle

binding to employ a certain engineer · Ingenieurbindung f

binding to employ a certain architect · Architektenbindung f

to bind oneself · sich binden

to bind over · durch Bürgschaft verpflichten

biological architecture · Bioarchitektur f

biological environment · biologische Umwelt f

biological spatial research, biological space research · biologische Raumforschung f [*Raumforschung über die Wechselwirkungen der Naturerscheinungen*]

bipartite, of two parts · zweiteilig

biproportional approach · biproportionaler Ansatz *m*

bird sanctuary · Vogelschutzgebiet *n*

birds of game, fowls of warren · Jagdgeflügel *n*, Jagdvögel *mpl*

birth and means · Geburtsadel *m* und Wohlstand *m*

birth certificate, certificate of birth · Geburtsurkunde *f*

birth control, family planning · Familienplanung *f*, Geburtenbegrenzung, Geburteneinschränkung, Geburtenbeschränkung

birth place, place of birth · Geburtsort *m*

birth rate, rate of birth · Geborenenziffer *f*, Geburtenziffer

birth-rate fluctuation · Geborenenzifferschwankung *f*, Geburtenzifferschwankung

birthright · Geburtsrecht *n*, Erbanwartschaftsrecht

Bishops Court; Commissariat [*Scots law*]; Commissary Court [*The supreme court established in Edinburgh in 1563, in which matters of probate and divorce, previously under the jurisdiction of the bishop's commissary, were decided; it was absorbed by the Court of Session in 1836*] · Bischofsgericht *n* in Edinburgh

bissextile day, intercalary day, double sextile day · Schalttag *m* [*29. Februar*]

bivariate normal distribution · zweidimensionale Normalverteilung *f* [*Statistik*]

BL, frontage line, building line · (Bau)Fluchtlinie *f* [*Die amtlich festgesetzte Linie, allgemein parallel zur Straße, über die nicht hinaus gebaut werden darf und die die vordere Gebäudekante festlegt*]

black-box · Lücke *f* [*Zwischen abhängigem und unabhängigem variablen Konsumverhaltensmodell*]

black game · Schwarzwild *n*

blackleg [*A person who makes his living by betting and playing at cards*] · Spieler *m*

blackleg (Brit.); scab (US); strike-breaker · Streikbrecher *m*

black letter prevailing rule · fettgedruckte leitsatzartige Zusammenfassung *f* [*In einer Rechtsenzyklopädie der USA*]

black market · Schwarzmarkt *m*

black marketing · Schwarzmarkthandel *m*

black market price · Schwarzmarktpreis *m*

black migration, negro migration · Negerwanderung *f*

black money, dirty money · Schmutzgeld *n* [*Vergütung für schmutzige Arbeiten*]

black population, negro population · Negerbevölkerung *f*

black (real) estate market, black (real) property market, black realty market · schwarzer Grundstücksmarkt *m*, schwarzer Bodenmarkt, schwarzer Landmarkt

blamelessness · Unbescholtenheit *f*

blanch holding, blanch farm, blench holding, blanch firme, blanch rent, blanch fe(a)rme, white farm, white rent, white fe(a)rme, white rent; alba firma, firma blanca, firma alba, albom, redditus albi [*Latin*] [*Rent payable in silver, or white money, as distinguished from that which was anciently paid in corn or provisions, called black mail, or black rent*] · Silberpacht(zins) *f*, *(m)*, Silberzins, Bodenzins in Silbergeld

blank [*A void space in writing; a part of a deed, record, or other instrument not written upon, or filled up*] · leerer Raum *m* [*Schriftstück*]

blank → blank (form)

blank bar, common bar [*In pleading. The old name of a plea in bar, put in in an action of trespass, to oblige the plaintiff to assign the certain place where the trespass was committed*] · Rechtseinwand *m* des Ortsnachweises

blank cheque (Brit.); blank check (US) · Blankoscheck *m*

blank date · Blankotermin *m*, Blankodatum *n*

blank endorsement, blank indorsement, endorsement in blank, indorsement in blank · Blankoindossament *n*, Blankogiro *n*

blanket coverage · Pauschaldeckung *f*

blanket insurance [*An insurance relating to any class of property; the number of items covered may fluctuate from time to time*] · Kollektivversicherung *f*

blanket mortgage · Gesamthypothek *f*, Globalhypothek [*Jedes Grundstück haftet für die gesamte Forderung, der Gläubiger darf aber nur einmal den Schuldbetrag eintreiben*]

blanket primary (election), wide-open primary (election) [*USA*] · weit-offene Vorwahl *f*, weit-offene Erstwahl, weit-offene Urwahl [*Der Vorwahlteilnehmer kann für jedes Wahlamt seinen Kandidaten benennen ohne daß alle Kandidaten derselben Partei angehören müssen*]

blank (form) (US); form · Blankett *n*, Muster *n*, Formblatt *n*, Formular *n*, Vordruck *m*

blank (form) of application, application blank (form), request blank (form), blank (form) of request · Gesuchsformular *n*, Gesuchsmuster *n*, Antragsformular, Antragsmuster, Antragsformblatt *n*, Antragsblankett, Antragsvordruck *m*, Gesuchsformblatt, Gesuchsblankett *n*, Gesuchsvordruck

blank (form) of contract, form of contract, contract blank (form) · Vertragsmuster *n*, Vertragsformular *n*, Vertragsformblatt *n*, Vertragsblankett *n*, Vertragsvordruck *m*

blank indorsement, endorsement in blank, indorsement in blank, blank endorsement · Blankoindossament *n*, Blankogiro *n*

bled edge, bleed(ing edge) · Anschnittkante *f*, Stoßkante, randlose Kartenseite *f*

blench holding → blanch holding

blind alley hamlet · Sackgassenweiler *m*

blind alley (occupation) [*An occupation which offers no future prospects*] · chancenloser Beruf *m*, brotloser Beruf

blind alley village · Sackgassendorf *n*, Sackstraßendorf

blind settlement · Stiel(an)sied(e)lung *f*, Stielort *m* [*nach M. Sidaritsch, 1925*]

blister, border break · Randüberzeichnung *f*

blitzed area, blitzed territory · zerbombtes Gebiet *n*

blitzed site, war-damaged site · (Kriegs)-Trümmergrundstück *n*, (Kriegs)Schuttgrundstück

blitzed site clearance act, blitzed site clearance law, blitzed site clearance statute · Enttrümmerungsgesetz *n*, Schutträumungsgesetz, Trümmerräumungsgesetz

blitzed site clearance law · Enttrümmerungsrecht *n*, Schutträumungsrecht, Trümmerräumungsrecht

BL law, law of building lines, building line law · (Bau)Fluchtlinienrecht *n* [*Es betrifft die Anlegung und Veränderung von Straßen und Plätzen in Gemeinden aller Art*]

to block, to freeze · sperren [*Guthaben*]

block [*Land area shaped in a square or rectangular form that is a portion of a city, town or village, enclosed by streets and alleys*] · (Straßen)Block *m*

block building, rockery house · Miet(s)kaserne *f*, Wohnkaserne, Massenmiet(s)haus *n*

block coverage · Blockbebauung *f*; Blocküberbauung [*Schweiz*]

block density (US); net density (Brit.) [*Density relating to a block area*] · Blockdichte *f*

block diagram · Blockbild *n*, Blockdiagramm *n*

blocked account, frozen account, blocked balance, frozen balance · Sperrkonto *n*

blocked exchange · nicht frei konvertierbare Währung *f*

block field pattern · Blockflur *f*

block grant · ungebundener Regierungszuschuß *m* an eine Gemeinde

blocking of assets, freezing of assets · Guthabensperre *f*, Sperren *n* von Guthaben

blocking of property, freezing of property, property freezing, property blocking · Vermögenssperre *f*, Sperren *n* von Vermögen

block lot · Blockparzelle *f*

block lot bundle, bundle of block lots · Block(parzellen)verband *m*

block of grouped shops, shopping district, shop(ping) centre (Brit.); shop(ping) center (US) · D-Zentrum *n*, Ladengruppe *f*, Wohnbezirkszentrum, Ladenzentrum, (Ein)Kaufzentrum

blood feud · Blutrache *f*

blood relation(ship), consanguinity, relation(ship) by blood · Blutsbande *f*, Blutsverwandtschaft *f*, Verwandtschaft durch gleiche Abstammung

blood relative → next of blood

blue collar worker, laborer (US); worker, workman, operative; labourer (Brit.) [*A wage-earning worker, skilled or semiskilled, whose work is characterized largely by physical exertion*] · Arbeiter *m*

blue key · Blaukopie *f* [*Kartographie*]

blue law · Sonntagsgesetz *n*, Gesetz gegen die Entheiligung des Sonntags

blueprint planning · starre Planung *f*

blue sky law · Wertpapiermißbrauchgesetz *n* [*USA. Einzelstaatliches Wertpapiergesetz zum Schutz der Anlagen*]

blue sky permit [*USA*] · Wertpapierzulassungserlaubnis *f*, Wertpapierzulassungsgenehmigung *f*

board [*An official or representative body organized to perform a trust or to execute official or representative functions or having the management of a public office or department exercising administrative or governmental functions*] · Amt *n*

board · Beköstigung *f*

boarder [*One who has his food, or food and lodging, at the house of another for compensation*] · Kostgänger *m*

boarding house [*A house in which persons board*] · Pension(shaus) *f, (n)*

boarding school; board school [*obsolete*] · Internat *n*

board of almoners, board of overseers, board of guardians [*England. Under the Poor Law Amendment Act of 1834 parishes were grouped together in unions which had to provide workhouses. The administration of the unions was placed under Boards of Guardians*] · Armen(pflege)rat *m*

board of appeal; housing appeals board (US) · Appellationsamt *n*, Berufungsamt *n* [*Es behandelt Einsprüche von Eigentümern, denen eine Bauerlaubnis versagt wurde*]

board of arbitration, arbitration board, arbitral board · Schiedsstelle *f*

board of commissioners of works and public buildings · Staatsbauamt *n*

board of commissioners of woods and forests and land revenues (of the Crown) · (königliches) Amt *n* für Domänen und Forsten

board of conciliation, board of mediation, mediation board, conciliation board · Schlichtungsamt *n*

board of control, control board · Kontrollamt *n*

board of directors · Verwaltungsausschuß *m* [*Genossenschaft in den USA*]

board of directors, committee of management, executive board, managing board · Vorstand *m*, Verwaltungsrat *m*, Direktorium *n*

board of education, education(al) board · Bildungsamt *n*

board of guardians, poor law guardians, poor board · (Orts)Armenamt *n*

board of guardians, board of almoners, board of overseers [*England. Under the Poor Law Amendment Act of 1834 parishes were grouped together in unions which had to provide workhouses. The administration of the unions was placed under Boards of Guardians*] · Armen(pflege)rat *m*

board of inquiry, board of enquiry · Disziplinarkammer *f*

board of mediation → board of conciliation

board of ordinance, ordinance board · Arsenalamt *n*

board of overseers, board of guardians, board of almoners [*England. Under the Poor Law Amendment Act of 1834 parishes were grouped together in unions which had to provide workhouses. The administration of the unions was placed under Boards of Guardians*] · Armen(pflege)rat *m*

board of studies · Fakultät *f*

board of surveyors, construction authority, building authority · Baubehörde *f*, Baugenehmigungsbehörde, (Bau)Aufsichtsbehörde [*früher: Baupolizei f*] [*Behörde für die Genehmigung und Überwachung von Bauvorhaben bis zu deren Abnahme. Die Behörden sind dafür verantwortlich, daß die baurechtlichen Vorschriften eingehalten werden*]

board of surveyors' act, board of surveyors' law, board of surveyors' statute · Aufsichtsgesetz *n*, Bauaufsichtsgesetz *n*

board of surveyors' fee code · (Bau)Aufsichtsgebührenordnung *f* [*früher: Baupolizeigebührenordnung*]

board of surveyors' notice, board of surveyors' notification · (bau)aufsicht(sbehörd)liche Anzeige *f*, (bau)aufsicht(sbehörd)liche Mitteilung *f*, (Bau)Aufsichtsanzeige, (Bau)Aufsichtsmitteilung [*früher: baupolizeiliche Anzeige, baupolizeiliche Mitteilung*]

board of surveyors' order · (Bau)Aufsichtsanordnung *f*, (Bau)Aufsichtsbefehl *m*, (Bau)Aufsichtsgebot *n*, (Bau)Aufsichtsverfügung, (bau)aufsicht(sbehörd)liche Anordnung [*früher: baupolizeiliche Anordnung*]

board of surveyors' ordinance · (Bau)Aufsichtsverordnung *f*, (bau)aufsicht(sbehörd)liche Verordnung [*früher: Baupolizeiverordnung*]

board of surveyors' permission · (bau)aufsicht(sbehörd)liche Erlaubnis *f*, (bau)aufsicht(sbehörd)liche Genehmigung, (Bau)Aufsichtserlaubnis, (Bau)Aufsichtsgenehmigung *f* [*früher: baupolizeiliche Erlaubnis, baupolizeiliche Genehmigung*]

board of surveyors' prescription, board of surveyors' regulation, board of surveyors' rule · (Bau)Aufsichtsvorschrift *f*, (bau)aufsicht(sbehörd)liche Vorschrift [*früher: baupolizeiliche Vorschrift*]

board of surveyors' provision · (Bau)Aufsichtsbestimmung *f*, (bau)aufsicht(sbehörd)liche Bestimmung [*früher: baupolizeiliche Bestimmung*]

board of surveyors' regulation, board of surveyors' rule, board of surveyors' prescription · (Bau)Aufsichtsvorschrift *f*, (bau)aufsicht(sbehörd)liche Vorschrift [*früher: baupolizeiliche Vorschrift*]

board of surveyors' statute → board of surveyors' act

Board of Trade · Wirtschaftsministerium *n* [*England*]

board of weights and measures — bona fide possessor

board of weights and measures, weights and measures board · Eichamt *n*

to board out · in Pflege geben [*Kind*]

board school · Schule *f* aus öffentlichen Geldern erhalten

board school [*obsolete*] → boarding school

board school (Brit.); elementary school, common school (US); day school, primary school · Elementarschule, Grundschule, Volksschule *f*

board (type) game · nichtrollenspezifisches Spiel *n*

boating · Bootssport *m*

boating activity · Bootssportbetätigung *f*

boating lake, lake for boating · Bootsteich *m*

boating place · Bootsstadt *f*

boat sheet · Arbeitskarte *f* [*Seevermessung*]

bockland, charter-land; terra haereditaria, terra libraria [*Latin*]; bócland, bookland [*Land which, in pre-Norman Conquest time, was held by charter, handbook, or other written title*] · Buchland *n*

bodily female heir → heiress

bodily harm, personal harm, personal injury, trespass to the person, bodily injury · Körperverletzung *f* [*Jeder äußere Eingriff in die körperliche Unversehrtheit*]

bodily heiress, bodily heir female, bodily female heir; heiress of line, heir female of line [*Scots law*], female heir of the blood, female heir of the body, female heir of line, heiress of the blood, heiress of the body, heir female of the blood, heir female of the body [*A woman who succeeds lineally by right of blood*] · Blutserbin *f*, Leibeserbin, natürliche Erbin, leibliche Erbin

bodily heir (male), natural heir (male); heir (male) of line [*Scots law*], heir (male) of the body, heir (male) of the blood [*An heir (male) begotten or borne by the person referred to, or a child of such heir; any lineal descendant, excluding a surviving husband or wife, adopted children, and collateral relations*] · Leibeserbe *m*, leiblicher Erbe, Blutserbe, natürlicher Erbe

bodily injury, bodily harm, personal harm, personal injury, trespass to the person · Körperverletzung *f* [*Jeder äußere Eingriff in die körperliche Unversehrtheit*]

body · Organ *n*

body at large, whole body (of the corporators), whole corporation · Gesamtkörperschaft *f*, Gesamtkorporation *f*, Gesamtheit *f* der Korporationsgenossen, Körperschaft im ganzen, Korporation im ganzen

body corporate, corporat(iv)e body, (private) corporation aggregate; corpus corporatum [*Latin*] [*An incorporated group of coexisting persons*] · Körperschaft *f* mit Personenmehrheit, Korporation *f* mit Personenmehrheit, inkorporierte Körperschaft

body corporate constituted by the incorporation of the inhabitants of a community · Einwohnergemeinde *f*, Einwohnerkommune *f*

body of accountants · Wirtschaftsprüfungsorganisation *f*

(body of) citizens, citizenhood, citizenry · Bürgerschaft *f*, Bürgerstand *m*, Stand der Bürger

body of commoners; commonance [*misnomer*]; communance · Markgenossen *m pl*, Al(l)mend(e)genossen

body of law, law body, jurisprudence · Rechtskomplex *m*

body of rules · Gesamtheit *f* von Regeln, Regelgesamtheit

body of the map, face of the sheet, body of the sheet, face of the map · Kartenfeld *n*

body of trustees · Kuratorium *n*

body politic, political corporation · politische Körperschaft *f*, politische Korporation *f*

body politic, nation · Nation *f*

bogey standard cost(s), measure standard cost(s), fixed standard cost(s), basic standard cost(s) · Maßstandardkosten *f*, Standardkosten 2. Art, Grundstandardkosten

bogus firm · Schwindelfirma *f*

bomb-damaged · ausgebombt, zerbombt, bombengeschädigt

bomb shelter · Luftschutzbunker *m*

bon · Gutschein *m*

bona fide [*Latin*]; in good faith, of good faith, innocent, honestly, without fraud · aufrichtig, in gutem Glauben, ehrlich, gutgläubig

bona fide acquisition · gutgläubiger Erwerb *m*, gutgläubige Erwerbung *f*

bona fide bid, bona fide offer, bona fide tender; bona fide (bid) proposal (US) · gutgläubiges Angebot *n*

bona fide holder, holder in good faith · gutgläubiger Inhaber *m*

bona fide possessor; possessor non vitiosus [*Latin*] · gutgläubiger Besitzer *m*

bona fides [*Latin*]; good faith, loyalty and faith, honesty, sincerity · Aufrichtigkeit *f*, Ehrlichkeit *f*, guter Glaube *m*, Treu' *f* und Glauben *m*

bond · Versicherungsfondszertifikat *n*

bond, medium-dated stock [*Between five and ten years until maturity*] · mittelfristige Staatsschuldverschreibung *f*, mittelfristige Staatsobligation *f* [*in Großbritannien*]

bond [*A deed, by which A (known as the obligor) binds himself, his heirs, executors, or assigns to pay a certain sum of money to B (known as the obligee), or his heirs, etc.*] · beurkundete Schuldforderung *f*, gesiegeltes Schuldversprechen *n*, gesiegelte Schuldurkunde *f*, Garantie *f*

bond [*USA*]; stock [*Great Britain*] [*The term "bond" designates in Great Britain short- and medium-dated stocks, that means stocks up to ten years until maturity*] · Schuldverschreibung *f*, Obligation *f* [*nicht von einer privaten Kapitalgesellschaft*]

bond, short-dated stock [*Up to five years until maturity*] · kurzfristige Staatsschuldverschreibung *f*, kurzfristige Staatsobligation [*in Großbritannien*]

bond → surety bond

bond → bond (fund)

bonda [*old English law*] → boundary (line)

bondage (on an estate), serfdom (on an estate), villanage, ville(i)nage; nativitas [*Latin*]; servile status, villein status, villain status, status of a serf, (pr(a)edial) bondage [*Called by Britton "naifte"*] · Hörigenstatus *m*, Leibeigenschaft *f*, Grundhörigkeit *f*, (Grund)Untertänigkeit, Bauerndienst *m*

bondager, bond(s)man, culvert, serf; villarus [*Latin*]; regardant (to the manor), bond tenant, villain (tenant), villein (tenant) [*Strictly a man of servile condition holding usually one virgate of land, this is the fourth part of a hide, in the common fields of a manor by base services; but the term is sometimes applied to one of free status who holds land by servile tenure*] · Leibeigene, unfreier Bauer, Dienstbauer *m*, Hörige, Unfreie, Knechtsleh(e)n(s)mann

bondage service, villenage service · Dienstbauernleistung *f*

bondage tenure, villenage tenure, tenure in villenage, tenure in bondage, tenure in bond service, tenure of bond-land [*A distinct sort of copyhold*] · Dienstbauernleh(e)n *n*

bondage to a particular manor · Gutspflichtigkeit *f*

bond and disposition in security · dingliche Pfandsicherung *f* des Gläubigers, dingliche Gläubigerpfandsicherung

bond broker · Rentenmakler *m*

bonded debt, documentary debt, debt secured by a document · Briefschuld *f*

bonded factory (Brit.); bonded manufacturing warehouse (US) · Fabrik *f* unter Zollverschluß

bonded mortgage, indenture of mortgage, mortgage secured by a document, documentary mortgage · Briefhypothek *f* [*Neben einer Eintragung der Hypothek in das Grundbuch besteht auch eine Brieferteilung an den Gläubiger*]

bonded warehouse, bonding warehouse · Zollspeicher *m*, Zollniederlage *f*, Zollager *n*

bonded warehouse, sufferance warehouse · Freilager *n*, Freihafenniederlage *f*

bond for construction, bond for building, construction bond, building bond [*A bond to guarantee the good faith of the builder or contractor*] · Baugarantie *f*

bond (fund) · Versicherungsfonds *m*

bond fund [*A fund established by a municipality or other government agency for the receipt and disbursement of the proceeds of a bond issue*] · Obligationenfonds *m*

bond fund (US) [*The fund created as the result of an annuity agreement*]; annuity fund · Rentenfonds *m*

bond group · Versicherungsfondskonzern *m*

bond hamlet [*A hamlet in medieval Wales, deemed in law to contain only nine houses*] · Weiler *m* mit neun Häusern

bondholder · Obligationeninhaber *m*, Obligationär *m*

bond indebtedness · Obligationsverschuldung *f*

bonding underwriter · Übernahmekonsortium *n* für Obligationen

bonding warehouse, bonded warehouse · Zollspeicher *m*, Zollniederlage *f*, Zollager *n*

bond issue · Obligationenemission *f*, Obligationenausgabe *f*

bondly [*obsolete*]; servilely · knechtisch, unterwürfig

bond market · Obligationenmarkt *m*

bond note, bond warrant · Zollbegleitschein *m*

bond of completion, bond of performance, completion bond, performance bond [*Bond given by the contractor to the owner and lending institution guaranteeing that the work will be completed* *and that funds will be provided for that purpose*] · Fertigstellungsgarantie f, Ausführungsgarantie

bond premium · Obligationsagio n

bond return, bond yield · Obligationenrendite f, Obligationsrendite

bond(s)man, culvert, serf; villarus [*Latin*]; regardant (to the manor), bond tenant, villain (tenant), villein (tenant), bondager [*Strictly a man of servile condition holding usually one virgate of land, this is the fourth part of a hide, in the common fields of a manor by base services; but the term is sometimes applied to one of free status who holds land by servile tenure*] · Leibeigene, unfreier Bauer, Dienstbauer m, Hörige, Unfreie, Knechtsleh(e)n(s)mann

bond(s)man [*One who is seized as security*] · Leibesbürge m

bond(s)man · gewerblicher Bürgschaftssteller m

bond(s)woman · Dienstbäuerin f

bond tenant → copiholder

bond warrant, bond note · Zollbegleitschein m

bond with a condition, double bond, conditional bond · gesiegeltes Schuldversprechen n mit Strafklausel, gesiegelte Schuldurkunde f mit Strafklausel, beurkundete Schuldforderung f mit Strafklausel

bond yield, bond return · Obligationenrendite f, Obligationsrendite

bonitarian ownership → beneficial ownership

bonitary, beneficial, bonitarian [*Having possession with all its benefits, but without a legal title*] · bonitarisch, benefiziarisch, voll, im eigenen Interesse, nicht treuhänderisch

bonna [*old English law*] → boundary (line)

bonus, allowance · Zulage f, Zuschlag m, Sondervergütung f

bonus, extra wage, extra pay · Lohnzuschlag m, Bonus m

bonus and penalty clause, bonus-penalty provision [*Not to be confused with the bonus for early completion. In the bonus-penalty provision the project completion was geared to an estimated completion date, and the parties to the contract would agree that if the project was completed a certain number of days later, the owner would, in effect, suffer liquidated damages; by the same token, if the job was completed sooner, the owner would be benefited and should pay for the early completion by the specific sum per day agreed upon*] · Prämien- und Konventionalstrafenklausel f

bonus (for early completion), bonus of early completion, completion bonus, acceleration bonus · Beschleunigungsvergütung f, (Leistungs)Prämie f

bonus on shares, extra dividend · Dividendenbonus m, Extradividende f, Superdividende

bonus payment · Bonuszahlung f

bonus schedule for early completion, bonus scheme for early completion · Beschleunigungsvergütungsplan m, (Leistungs)Prämienplan

bonus scheme, bonus schedule · Bonusplan m

bonus stock · Freiaktie f [*In den USA. Ohne Gegenleistung als Geschenk oder Prämie ausgegeben. Nach deutschem Aktienrecht nicht zulässig*]

booking · verbuchter Auftrag m, Bestellung f

to book · buchen

book [*bócland*] · Beurkundung f, Urkunde f [*Buchland*]

bookdebt, contract money, outstanding money, outstanding debt · Außenstand m, (Geschäfts)Forderung f

bookkeeping · Buchführung f, Buchhaltung

bookkeeping entry · Buchhaltungseintrag(ung) m, (f)

bookland, bockland, charter-land; terra haereditaria, terra libraria [*Latin*]; bócland [*Land which, in pre-Norman Conquest time, was held by charter, handbook, or other written title*] · Buchland n

book-learned; booklered [*obsolete*] · buchgelehrt

booklearnedness · Buchgelehrtheit f

book of (ad)measurement, (ad)measurement book · Aufmaßbuch n

book of authority · Standardbuch n

book of certificate · Nachweisbuch n [*Zunft*]

book of servitudes, servitude book · Dienstbarkeitsbuch n, Gerechtigkeitsbuch, Servitutenbuch

book of spec(ification)s [*A bound volume describing the work containing the bidding documents, sample contract forms, or sections alluding to recommended contract forms*] · Lastenheft n

book seller · Sortimenter m

bookstall · Bücherkiosk m

book value, carrying value [*The amount at which a property is recorded on the books, net of depreciation, if any*] · Buchwert m

Boolean method — bord service

Boolean method · Verfahren *n* auf der Grundlage Boolescher Algebra

boom town, boom city · Stadt *f* mit bedeutendem Wachstum und hohem sozioökonomischen Status

boon-day, reaping day, precaria, bind day [*The day (up)on which a tenant was required to perform the service of bedrip*] · befohlener Erntearbeitstag *m*, Frontag auf besonderes Begehr

boon-man · Fronarbeiter *m*

boon-work; boonage [*obsolete*] · Fronarbeit *f*

boot → bot(e)

bordage fee (tenure) (of land), bordage (tenure); bordagium [*Latin*] [*In old English law. A species of base tenure by which certain lands were anciently held in England, the tenants being termed bordmen*] · Frondienstleh(e)n *n*, Fronbauernleh(e)n

bordage lord · Frond(dienst)herr *m*, Gutsherr, Herr der Gutsherrlichkeit

bordage manor Frongut *n*, Fronhof *m*, Gutsherrschaft *f*, Gutsherrlichkeit *f* [*Im Mittelalter und danach vornehmlich im Osten Deutschlands. Die abhängigen Bauern zahlten Zins und Pacht, aber sie waren hauptsächlich Arbeitskräfte für die Bewirtschaftung der Hofländereien*]

bordage manor district · Gutsbezirk *m*

bordage (tenure); bordagium [*Latin*]; bordage fee (tenure) (of land) [*In old English law. A species of base tenure by which certain lands were anciently held in England, the tenants being termed bordmen*] · Frondienstleh(e)n *n*, Fronbauernleh(e)n

bordar, bordman, tenant in bordage, bordage tenant; bordarius [*Latin*]; bordmannus [*Old Gallic*] · Fronbauer *m*, Frondienstmann *m*, gutsherrlicher Bauer

border, frontier · Grenze *f*

border area, border territory, frontier area, frontier territory · Grenzgebiet *n*

border area, border territory · Randgebiet *n*

border break, blister · Randüberzeichnung *f*

border-crossing, transfrontier · grenzüberschreitend, grenzüberquerend

border data, border information, marginal data, marginal information · Blattrandangaben *f pl*, Randausstattung *f*, Randangaben, Blattrandausstattung [*Alle Angaben im Kartenrand und im Kartenrahmen*]

border gardening, border cultivation · Beetanbau *m*, Beetkultur *f*

bordering (up)on, adjoining, co(n)terminous with, lying (up)on [*The term "adjoining" also sometimes means "near" or "neighbo(u)ring"*] · angrenzend [*(Grundstücks)Seiten*]

border lake · Grenzsee *m*

borderland, frontier land · Grenzland *n*

borderline case · Grenzfall *m*

border margin, margin of border · Bauabstand *m*, (Bau)Wich *m*, Reihe *f*, Schupf *m*, Grenzabstand *m* [*Bei der Errichtung von Gebäuden sind in voller Tiefe des Grundstücks von den seitlichen Grundstücksgrenzen Bauwiche von baulichen Anlagen freizuhalten, soweit nicht an die Grundstücksgrenze gebaut werden darf (geschlossene Bauweise). Von der hinteren Grundstücksgrenze ist ein Abstand freizuhalten, der der Breite des Bauwichs entspricht (hinterer Grenzabstand)*]

border region, frontier region · Grenzregion *f*

border stream · Grenzfluß *m*

border territory, frontier area, frontier territory, border area · Grenzgebiet *n*

border territory, border area · Randgebiet *n*

to border (up)on, to be co(n)terminous with, to adjoin, to lie (up)on · angrenzen

border wasteland · Grenzöde *f*

border watercourse · Grenzwasserlauf *m*

bordland, table demesne, home farm (of the lord of the manor), demesnial settlement; terra indominicata, terra dominica [*Latin*]; demain (land), demeyne (land), demeine (land), demesne (land), inland, land in (the lord's) demesne [*Those lands of a manor not granted out in tenancy, but reserved by the lord for his own use and occupation. The opposite of "tenemental lands"*] · Hoffeld *n*, Salland *n*, grundherrliches Eigenland, Hofländerei *f*, Hofland, grundherrschaftliches Eigenland

bordland, land(s) of a manor, manorial land(s) [*Land held by a bordar in bordage tenure*] · Herr(e)ngutland *n*, Fron(dienst)land, Frongutland, Fronbauernland, Herr(e)nhofland

bord-lode [*In the feudal system, the service required of the tenants, to carry timber out of the woods of the lord to his house*] · Holzfrondienst *m*

bord service [*A tenure under which tenants of the temporalities of a fee sometimes held at a rent payable towards the support of the bishop's table. The tenure existed in respect of some lands in Fulham in Middlesex in favour of the Bishop of London*] · kirchlicher Frondienst *m*, kirchliche Fron(d)e *f*

borough — boundary (line)

borough, territorial fraction of a city [*in American law*] · (Stadt)Bezirk *m*, Verwaltungsbezirk

borough [*Scotland*]; burgh [*A town possessing a municipal corporation and special privileges conferred by royal charter*] · kreisfreie Stadt *f*

borough · Bezirk *m* [*In New York. Es gibt fünf Bezirke in New York*]

borough → (municipal) borough

borough (civil) court → (municipal) borough (civil) court

borough council → (municipal) borough council

borough election → (municipal) borough election

borough English → borow English

borough fund → (municipal) borough fund

Borough Funds Act, Leeman's Act [*in England. 1872 and 1903*] · Munizipalstadtkassengesetz *n*

boroughholder [*One holding by burgage tenure*] · Bürgerleh(e)n(s)mann *m*

borough president [*in American law*] · (Stadt)Bezirksbürgermeister *m*, Verwaltungsbezirksbürgermeister

borough quarter session · städtische Quartalsitzung *f*

borough rate → (municipal) borough rate

borough's ealder, borough's ealdor, parochial constable, borsholder, headborough, tithing-man · Polizeischulze *m*

boroughship · Stadtbezirk *m* integriert durch kleine Zentren

borough surveyor · Stadtbauamtleiter *m*

borow English, borough tenure, borough kind; tenure en Burgh Engloys [*Anglo-French*]; burg(h) English, borough English, burg(h) Engloys, cradle-holding; postremo-geniture [*Latin*] [*Ancient mode of descent by which land descended to the youngest son. Abolished under the A.E.A. 1925*] · Wiegengut *n*, Minorat *n*, Leh(e)n(s)recht *n* des Jüngeren

to borrow · (ab)borgen [*Unter Bürgschaft oder Rückgabeversprechen abnehmen*]

borrowed capital, outside capital, debt capital · Fremdkapital *n*, Schuldenkapital

borrower; commodatarius [*Latin*] · Entlehner *m* [*unentgeltliche Entlehnung*]

borrower · Entleiher *m* [*bewegliche Sache*]

borrower, borrowing member, advanced member [*A member having obtained advances from the building society*] · borgendes Mitglied *n*, Bausparer *m* [*Bausparkasse*]

borrower (of money), money-borrower · Kreditnehmer *m*, Geldnehmer

borrowing · Schuld(en)aufnahme *f*

borrowings, loan debt · Darleh(e)nsschuld *f*

borsholder, head-borough, tithing-man, borough's ealder, borough's ealdor, parochial constable · Polizeischulze *m*

boscage, browse-wood, mast; boscagium [*Latin*] [*In English law. The food which wood and trees yield to cattle*] · Viehfutter *n* von Bäumen und Sträuchern

boscage, boskage, thicket, bosket, bosquet · Dickicht *n*

botanical garden · botanischer Garten *m*

bot(e), boot, bota, estouvier, estover, profit (à prendre) of estover [*The right to take wood from the land of another as hay-bote, house-bote or plough-bote*] · Holzzubuße *f*, Holzentnahme *f*

botel [*A facility providing lodging and other services for boat travel(l)ers*] · Bootshotel *n*

bothagium [*Latin*]; stallage, boothage [*Customary dues paid to the lord of a manor or soil, for the pitching or standing of booths in fairs or markets*] · Budenzins *m*, Standgeld *n*

bottom paging · Seitennumerierung *f* am unteren Seitenrand

bought note · Kaufnota *f*, Kaufzettel *m* [*Handelsmakler*]

bought off, portioned off, portioned out · ausgezahlt [*Erb(schafts)anteil*]

bounce [*colloquial term*]; dishonoured cheque, dishonoured check · geplatzter Scheck *m*

bound · gebunden

boundary [*That which indicates or fixes some limit, e.g. a fence, wall*] · Grenzvorrichtung *f*

boundary → boundary (line)

boundary commission · Grenzregelungskommission *f*, Grenzausgleichskommission

boundary community · Randgemeinde *f*

boundary delimitation, delimitation by boundary marks, separation by boundary marks · Abmark(ier)ung *f* [*§ 919. BGB. Kenntlichmachung von Grundstücksgrenzen durch Grenzzeichen*]

boundary dispute · Grenzstreit(igkeit) *m*, *(f)*

boundary, (line), abuttal, lot line; bonda, bunda, bonna [*In old English law*] [*A legally defined line dividing one lot of property from another*] · Grund(stücks)grenze *f*

boundary map · Grenzenkarte f [Karte mit Darstellung politischer Grenzen und Verwaltungsgrenzen]

boundary mark · Grenzzeichen n

boundary masonry wall · Grenzmauer f

boundary of a field, field boundary · Feldmarkung f, Feldgrenze f

boundary of coverage, coverage boundary · Bebauungsgrenze f; Überbauungsgrenze [Schweiz]

boundary of planning area · Plangrenze f

boundary replotting, confusion of (lot) boundaries, adjustment of (lot) boundaries [The title of that branch of equity jurisdiction which relates to the discovery and settlement of conflicting, disputed, or uncertain boundaries] · Grenzregelung f, Grenzausgleich m, Miniaturumlegung

boundary river · Grenzstrom m

boundary stream · Grenzfluß m

boundary survey [A mathematically perfect closed diagram of the complete peripheral boundary of a site, provided by the owner] · Baustellendiagramm n

boundary tree; arbor finalis [Latin] [A tree used for marking a bound(ary) (line)] · Grenzbaum m

boundary wall · Grenzwand f

boundary zone · Grenzstreifen m

bound bailiff; bum bailiff [popular name] · Distriktbote m [Diener eines Sheriffs für die Zustellung von Erlassen und Ausführung von Vollstreckungen]

bound currency, fixed currency [Currency fixed or bound to a special metal] · gebundene Währung f

bounding charter [A charter which defines the land comprised in it by description of the boundaries] · Grundstücksgrenzurkunde f

bound to the soil, living in serfdom on an estate · grunduntertänig

bourgage tenure, bourgage tenancy · städtisches Hausleh(e)n n

bout, end, head, front, butt(al) · Ende n, Grundstücksende

bovate, oxgang (of land), oxgate (of land), osken (of land); bovata terrae [Latin] [An oxgang, or as much land as one ox could plough in a year; one-eighth of a carucate or plough-land; varying in amount from 10 to 18 acres according to the system of tillage] · Flächeneinheit f des Domesday (Book) zwischen 10 und 18 acres

BOY, beginning of (the) year · Jahresanfang m

boy clerk · Lehrling m [Im Staatsdienst und öffentlichen Dienst in England]

bracket of cost(s), cost(s) bracket · Kostenspanne f

Bractonian gage · Bracton'sches (Verfalls)Pfand n

Bractonian gage for years · Bracton'sches (Verfalls)Pfand n auf Jahre

Bractonian lease for years · Bracton'sche Verpachtung f auf Jahre

bragbote, brugbote, brigbote, bruckbote [The liability to contribute to the cost(s) of maintaining bridges, walls and castles, which in Anglo-Saxon time were attached to land and might not be remitted] · Brücken-, Mauer- und Burgzubuße f

brain drain · Abwanderung f hochqualifizierter im Inland ausgebildeter Arbeitskräfte

branch, sector, province, division, department [public administration] · Abteilung f, Referat n, Dezernat n, Ressort n

branch · Außenstelle f [Behörde]

branch (US); tributary, affluent · Nebenfluß m

branch-and-bound method · Enumerationsverfahren n [Zur Bestimmung der optimalen Lösung einer ganzzahligen linearen Programmierungsaufgabe]

branch bank · Filialbank f, Zweigbank, Branchenbank

branch banking · Branchenbankwesen n, Zweigbankwesen, Filialbankwesen

branch line · Zweiglinie f

branch (office) · Zweigstelle f, Filiale f, Zweigniederlassung f

branch of industry, industrial branch · Industriezweig m

brassage, mintcharge [A charge made by a mint for the minting of coins] · Prägegebühr f

brazen law · ehernes Gesetz n

to breach · brechen

breach, violation of a duty · Pflichtvergehen n

breach, performance refusal, refusal of performance · Bruch m, Erfüllungs(ver)weigerung f

breach → invasion of right

breach by anticipation · Vertragsbruch m vor Fälligkeit

breach of a principle · Grundsatzbruch m, Prinzipbruch

breach of close [The unlawful or unwarrantable entry on another person's soil, land, or close] · widerrechtliches Betreten n fremder Grundstücke

breach of confidence, breach of faith · Vertrauensbruch *m*

breach of contract, contract breach · Vertragsbruch *m*

breach of duty, duty breach · Pflichtverstoß *m*, Pflichtverletzung *f*

breach of duty to exercise due care and skill, breach of duty to take care, failure to exercise care, negligence, negligent performance of the contract, failure to use ordinary care · Verletzung *f* der Sorgfaltspflicht, Verstoß *m* gegen die Sorgfaltspflicht, Sorgfalts(pflicht)verletzung, Sorgfalts(pflicht)verstoß *m*

breach of faith, breach of confidence · Vertrauensbruch *m*

breach of law · Rechtsbruch *m*

breach of law, breach of act, breach of statute · Gesetz(es)bruch *m*

breach of planning control [*Development of land without appropriate planning permission*] · Vergehen *n* gegen die Planungslenkung

breach of pound, pound breach; parci fractio [*Latin*]; pundbreach [*Saxon*] [*The offence of breaking a pound, for the purpose of taking out the cattle and/or goods impounded*] · Einbruch *m* in einen Pfandstall

breach of prison, prison-breach [*An escape by a prisoner lawfully in prison*] · Strafanstaltsflucht *f*

breach of promise to marry · Eheversprechensbruch *m*, Heiratsversprechensbruch, Bruch des Eheversprechens, Bruch des Heiratsversprechens

breach of public peace · Störung *f* der öffentlichen Ruhe und Ordnung

breach of right, invasion of right · Störung *f* eines subjektiven Rechts, Behinderung eines subjektiven Rechts

breach of sub-contract, sub-contract breach · Nachunternehmervertragsbruch *m*, Subunternehmervertragsbruch, Unterunternehmervertragsbruch; Unterakkordantenvertragsbruch [*Schweiz*]

breach of the peace · Friedensbruch *m*, Störung *f* der öffentlichen Ruhe (und Ordnung), Ruhestörung

breach of trust, trust breach · Pflichtverletzung *f* eines Treuhänders, Treubruch *m* [*Abweichung von den Bestimmungen der Treuhand*]

breach of warranty, warranty breach · Garantiebruch *m*

breadwinner, earner · Verdiener *m*

to break, to become bankrupt · in Konkurs geraten, in Konkurs gehen, pleite gehen, pleite machen, Konkurs machen, fallieren

breakage insurance · Bruchversicherung *f*

to break down, to destroy, to remove, to abate [*To abate a structure is to beat it down*] · zerstören

breakdown, make-up, (sub)division · (Auf)Gliederung *f*, Aufschlüsselung

breakdown of cost(s), make-up of cost(s), subdivision of cost(s), cost(s) breakdown, cost(s) make-up, cost(s) subdivision · Kosten(auf)gliederung *f*, Kostenaufschlüsselung

breaker → (house)breaker

break even · Abschluß *m* ohne Gewinn und Verlust

break-even-analysis [*This term may be interpreted in its broad or narrow sense. Taken in its narrow sense, it refers to a system of determining that level of operations where total revenues equal total expenses. In its broad sense, it refers to a system of analysis that can be used to determine the probable profit at any level of operations. This type of analysis is extremely useful for forecasting purposes as well as for judging the results of operations*] · Deckungspunktanalyse *f*, Deckungspunktuntersuchung *f*

break-even chart [*It graphically depicts the nature of break-even analysis*] · Deckungspunktanalysenschaubild *n*, Deckungspunktdiagramm *n*

break-even point, crisis point [*It represents the volume of sales at which total cost(s) equal total revenues, that is, profits equal zero. The firm neither makes a profit nor suffers a loss*] · Deckungspunkt *m*, Gewinnschwelle *f*, Kostendeckungspunkt, toter Punkt, Nutzschwelle

breaking · Bank(e)rottwerden *n*, Fallieren, Bank(e)rottgehen *n*

breaking down, failing, crashing, dropping to pieces, collapsing · Einstürzen *n*, Einfallen

breaking up value · Zerschlagungswert *m* des Betriebes [*Einzelverkaufswert sämtlicher Aktien abzüglich Verpflichtungen und Liquidationskosten*]

break in prices · Preiseinbruch *m*

to break into · angreifen [*Vorrat*]

to break off · abbrechen [*Geschäftsverbindung; Beziehung*]

breeder of cattle, cattle breeder · Rindviehzüchter *m*

breeder of (live)stock, (live)stock breeder · Viehzüchter *m*

breeding of cattle, raising of cattle, cattle breeding, cattle raising · Rindvieh(auf)zucht f

breeding of (live)stock, raising of (live)stock, (live)stock breeding, (live)stock raising · Vieh(auf)zucht f

breeding small animals · Kleintierzucht f

brehon [*In old Irish law before the conquest by Henry II*] · Richter m

breve [*Latin*]; writ [*A document under the seal of the Crown, a court or an a officer of the Crown, commanding the person to whom it is addressed to do or forbear from doing some act*] · Dekret n, (Hof)Rescript n

breve de errore [*Latin*]; motion in arrest of judg(e)ment, writ of error [*In criminal cases the accused may at any time between conviction and sentence move an arrest of judg(e)ment — that is to say, move that judgment be not pronounced — because of some defect in the indictment which is more than a mere formal defect and which has not been amended or used by verdict*] · Formfehlergesuch n, Gesuch daß ein Urteil nicht auf einen Geschworenenspruch gegründet wird

breve de nova desaisina [*Latin*]; writ of (assize of) novel disseisin · Klage f zur Wiedererlangung entzogenen Grundbesitzes, Klage zum Schutz vor eigenmächtiger Entwerung

breve de recto [*Latin*]; writ of right · Eigentumsklage f [*Liegenschaft. Formell beseitigt durch 3 und 4 W.IV. c 77*]

breve donationis, commemoratorium, notifia donationis [*Latin*] · (schlichte) Schenkungsurkunde f [*Urkunde, in welcher die stattgehabte Schenkung als eine geschehene Tatsache beurkundet wird*]

breve originale [*Latin*]; original (writ) [*In English practice. A writ issuing out of chancery, and so called because it anciently gave origin and commencement to an action at common law. In modern practice, the use of an original (writ) is confined to real actions exclusively. In American practice, original writs have been employed to some extent, but are now in general superseded by other forms of process*] · prozeßeinleitende Kabinettorder f [*Hofgericht*]

brewer for sale · gewerblicher Brauer m

bribable · bestechungsfähig

to bribe · bestechen

bribe [*A consideration voluntarily offered to corrupt a person and induce him or her to act in the interest of the giver*] · Bestechungsmittel n

bribe money; "palm oil" (Brit.); graft (US); financial bribe · Bestechungsgeld n, Schmiergeld

briber [*One who offers or gives a bribe*] · Bestecher m

briberess [*A woman who bribes*] · Bestecherin f

bribery [*The act or practice of giving or accepting a bribe or bribes*] · Bestechung f

bribe-service [*A service done for a bribe*] · Bestechungsdienst m

bribe-taker · Bestochene m

bribe-taking · Bestechungsannahme f

bribing, corrupting by bribe(s) · Bestechen n

brick-and-mortar unit, natural city, natural town · Städteregion f, Städtezusammenschluß m, Städtezone f, Stadtverband m, Regionalstadt f

bridge authority · Brückenbehörde f

bridge board · Brückenamt n

bridge committee · Gemeindebrückenausschuß m, Kommunalbrückenausschuß

bridgehead settlement · Brückenkopf(an)sied(e)lung f

bridge master · Brückenmeister m

bridge toll · Brückengeld n, Brückenzoll m, Brücken(benutzungs)gebühr f; Brückenmaut f [*Österreich*]

bridge ward · Brückenbezirk m [*in London*]

bridge ward without (the walls) · Brückenbezirk m außerhalb [*in London*]

bridging credit · Überbrückungskredit m

bridging loan · Überbrückungsdarleh(e)n n

briefs and arguments · Rechtsausführungen fpl

brief stage [*The stage in which the client's requirements are established*] · Sachdarstellungsstadium n

brigancy; her(d)ship [*Scots law*] [*The crime of driving away cattle by force*] · Rindviehraub m

brigbote, bruckbote, bragbote, brugbote [*The liability to contribute to the cost(s) of maintaining bridges, walls and castles, which in Anglo-Saxon time were attached to land and might not be remitted*] · Brücken-, Mauer- und Burgzubuße f

to bring an action (against), to file a bill, to file a (law)suit, to file an action, to sue; actionare [*Latin*] · einreichen (einer Klage), erheben (einer Klage), klagen

to bring an action for damages, to sue for damages · klagen auf Schadenersatz

**to bring down, **to cut (down), to lower ·
ermäßigen

to bring in [*bill*] · einbringen, vorlegen
[*Gesetz(es)vorlage*]

to bring in gain, to bring in profit · abfallen
[*bei einem Geschäft*]

bringing down, cutting (down), lowering ·
Ermäßigen *n*, Ermäßigung *f*

bringing to an end, terminating · Beenden *n*

to bring into litigation, to engage in litigation, to claim by action, to dispute by action, to litigate, to go to law, to carry on a (law)suit [*Latin: litigare*] · prozessieren, einen Rechtsstreit austragen, einen Prozeß anhängig machen, rechtshängig werden lassen

to bring to an end, to abate [*(court) action*] · erlöschen [*Klage*]

British fund, Government stock [*There are short-dated stocks (up to five years until maturity), medium-dated stocks (between five and ten years until maturity) and long-dated stocks (over ten years until maturity)*] · Staatsschuldverschreibung *f*, Staatsobligation *f* [*Ein festverzinsliches Wertpapier der britischen Regierung oder der verstaatlichten Industrien*]

broad strip field system · Gelängeflur *f*

broc(c)arius [*Latin*] → ((real) estate) broker

broccator [*Latin*] → ((real) estate) broker

broker → (stock)broker

broker → ((real) estate) broker

brokerage → (real) estate broking

brok(er)age, brocage; (a)brocagium [*Latin*] · Maklergebühr *f*, Maklerprovision *f*, Courtage *f*

broker agency → (land) broking company

broker authorized to effect sales ·
Abschlußmakler *m*

broker-bank · Kreditinstitut *n* für Wertpapiergeschäfte

broker's commission · Abschlußprovision *f*

broker's loan · Maklerdarleh(e)n *n*

brokers' ordinance · Maklerverordnung *f*

broker-system · Trennung *f* des Wertpapierhandels von Kreditgeschäft und sonstigem Bankgeschäft

broking → (real) estate broking

broking company → (land) broking company

brood of speculators · Nachkommenschaft *mpl*, (*f*) der Spekulanten

brother architect · Architektenkollege *m*

brotherhood, brotherly union, confraternity · Verbrüderung *f*, Konfraternität *f*

brought to an end, abated [*(court) action*] · erloschen [*Klage*]

browse-wood, mast; boscagium [*Latin*]; boscage [*In English law. The food which wood and trees yield to cattle*] · Viehfutter *n* von Bäumen und Sträuchern

bruarium, bruyrium [*Latin*]; heath ground · Heideland *n*

bruckbote, bragbote, brugbote, brigbote [*The liability to contribute to the cost(s) of maintaining bridges, walls and castles, which in Anglo-Saxon time were attached to land and might not be remitted*] · Brücken-, Mauer- und Burgzubuße *f*

brutum fulmen [*Latin*]; empty thread · leere Drohung *f*

b.s., fundamental solution, basic solution · Grundlösung *f*

bucket shop [*The business for providing means for speculation in stocks and shares, carried on by an "outside broker", i.e. a broker who is not a member of a recognized stock exchange, and who is not therefore subject to the rules and regulations of such a body*] · Winkelbörsentätigkeit *f*

budellus [*Latin*] · Büttel *m*

budget account; charge account (US) · Kundenkreditkonto *n* [*Der monatliche Schuldsaldo ist in Raten zu zahlen*]

budget and accounting act, budget and accounting law, budget and accounting statute · Haushalt- und Rechnungsprüfungsgesetz *n*

budget(ary) control [*Allocating financial limits to component parts of individual enterprises and accounting for outlays in such a way as to provide continuous comparisons between actual and forecast results so that, if remedial action is necessary, it may be at an early stage or alternatively the objectives may be reviewed*] · Haushalt(s)lenkung *f*

budget(ary) law, law of budget(s) · Haushalt(s)recht *n*

budget(ary) plan), plan of income and expenditure · Wirtschaftsplan *m*, Haushalt(s)plan *m*, Budget *n*

budget balancing · Haushalt(s)ausgleich *m*

budget constraint · Plafond *n* [*Aufstellen von mehrjährigen Finanzplänen*]

budget cost(s), budgets · Budgetkosten *f*, Prognosekosten, Sollkosten der Betriebsabteilungen, budgetierte Kosten [*Plankosten im Sinne vorausberechneter Istkosten für bestimmte Bereiche der Unternehmung in einer Zeitspanne*]

budget deficiency — building arrangement drawing

budget deficiency, deficiency of budget · Haushalt(s)defizit *n*

budget discussion, discussion of the budget · Haushalt(s)beratung *f*

budget for construction project, budget for building project, construction project budget, building project budget [*The total sum established by the owner for the project*] · Baukostenhaushalt *m*

budgeting · Budgetierung *f*, Kostenplanung

budget(ing) committee · Kostenplanungsausschuß *m*, Budget(ierungs)ausschuß

budget manual · Budgethandbuch *n*

budgets, budget cost(s) · Budgetkosten *f*, Prognosekosten, Sollkosten der Betriebsabteilungen, budgetierte Kosten [*Plankosten im Sinne vorausberechneter Istkosten für bestimmte Bereiche der Unternehmung in einer Zeitspanne*]

budget variance, spending variance, controllable variance · (Mengen)Verbrauchsabweichung *f*, Abweichung (des effektiven) vom geplanten (Mengen)Verbrauch, Budgetabweichung [*Der Unterschied zwischen den Soll- und Istkosten einer Kostenart oder Kostenstelle*]

budget year, financial year · Haushalt(s)jahr *n*

buffer district · Pufferbezirk *m*

buffer employment · Notstandsbeschäftigung *f*

buffer stock · Pufferbestand *m*

buffer zone · Pufferzone *f*

to build · bauen [*Hochbau*]

to build, to construct · bauen

to build a design · umsetzen [*Entwurf in bauliche Anlage(n)*]

builder, building (construction) contractor · Hochbauunternehmer *m*

builder [*A person who is employed to build or to execute work to, in, or upon a structure. Definition according to the London Building Acts (Amendment Act) 1939*] · Bauausführende *m*

builder → developer

builder-developer contract [*i.e. where there is no architect or engineer*] · Vertrag *m* zwischen Bauausführendem und Bauträger

builders' debris · Bauschutt *m*

builder's law → developer's law

building → building (construction)

building · Bauen *n* [*Hochbau*]

building → constructing

building, construction · Bau *m*

building · Gebäude *n*

building accessories · Gebäudezubehör *n*

building accounting, building accountancy, construction accounting, construction accountancy · Baurechnungswesen *n*

building act, construction law, construction statute, construction act, building law, building statute · Baugesetz *n*

building act → building (construction) act

building activity → building (construction) activity

building activity, construction activity · Bautätigkeit *f*

building administration, construction administration · Bauverwaltung *f*

building administration → building (construction) administration

building agreement → building (construction) agreement

building along a public road, building along a public highway · Anbauen *n* an einer öffentlichen Straße

(building) alteration, (building) conversion, structural alteration, structural conversion · (Gebäude)Umbau *m*

building and construction contract rules committee, committee for contract procedure in the building and construction industry · Verdingungsausschuß *m* (für Bauleistungen), Verdingungsausschuß für das Bauwesen

building (and loan) association (US) → building society

building (and loan) association law, law of building (and loan) associations (US); building society law (Brit.) · Bauspar(kassen)recht *n*

building (and loan) association mortgage (US); building society mortgage (Brit.) · Bauspar(kassen)hypothek *f*

(building (and loan)) association movement (US); building society movement (Brit.) · Bausparbewegung *f*

building (and loan) company (US) → building society

building area · Gebäudefläche *f*

building area [*The area of a plot which is covered by a building or buildings as measured on a horizontal plane*] · Grundfläche *f* [*Gebäude*]

building arrangement · Gebäudeanordnung *f*

building arrangement drawing · Aufteilungsplan *m* [*Eine von der Baubehörde mit Unterschrift und Siegel oder Stem-*

building association — building competition

pel zu versehende Bauzeichnung, aus der die Aufteilung des Gebäudes sowie die Lage und Größe der im Sondereigentum und der im gemeinschaftlichen Eigentum stehenden Gebäudeteile ersichtlich ist]

building association (US) → building society

building association mortgage (US) → building (and loan) association mortgage

building authority, board of surveyors, construction authority · Baubehörde *f*, Baugenehmigungsbehörde, (Bau)Aufsichtsbehörde [*früher: Baupolizei f*] [*Behörde für die Genehmigung und Überwachung von Bauvorhaben bis zu deren Abnahme. Die Behörden sind dafür verantwortlich, daß die baurechtlichen Vorschriften eingehalten werden*]

building bid → building (construction) tender

building board → building (construction) board

building bond, bond for construction, bond for building, construction bond [*A bond to guarantee the good faith of the builder or contractor*] · Baugarantie *f*

building bookkeeping, construction bookkeeping · Baubuchführung *f*

building bulk, building dimensions [*The height, depth, density, and width of a building*] · Gebäudeabmessungen *f pl*

building bulk · Gebäudeumfang *m*

building business, construction business · Bauwirtschaft *f* [*Wirtschaftszweig, der die der Bauproduktion, d. h. der Errichtung, dem Ausbau und der Reparatur von baulichen Anlagen dienenden Betriebe und freischaffenden Berufstätigen umfaßt*]

building by(e)-law → (local) building by(e)-law

building capital, construction capital · Baukapital *n*

building case, construction case · Baufall *m*

building census, census of buildings, count of buildings, building count · Gebäudezählung *f*

(building) certificate [*A statement signed by the architect (or engineer) that the builder is entitled to an instal(l)ment on work done. Certificates are usually completed and paid monthly during the progress of construction*] · Bescheinigung *f* für Abschlagzahlung

building charge, construction requirement, construction charge, building requirement · Bauauflage *f*, Bauanforderung *f*

building chart, building schedule, construction chart, construction schedule, outline of construction procedure, (contractor's) completion schedule, working chart, working schedule [*Written or graphically explained, the procedure of construction prepared by the contractor, usually by a bar chart of scheduled dates by trades or a critical path chart*] · (Ausführungs)Fristenplan *m*, Baufristenplan

building claim, construction claim · Bauforderung *f*

building client → building (construction) client

building club, terminating building society (Brit.); terminating (building (and loan)) association (US) · Bausparkasse *f* auf Zeit gegründet, aufhörende Bausparkasse [*Sie stellt ihre Tätigkeit ein, sobald alle Mitglieder ihre Bausparsummen erhalten haben*]

building code, construction code · Bauordnung *f*, BauO [*früher: Baupolizeiordnung*] [*Sie regelt die baurechtlichen Vorgänge auf Grundstücken und Baustellen sowie die Bauarbeit(en) und die Zulassung von Baustoffen und Bauteilen und bestimmt die Aufgaben der Bauaufsichtsbehörden, des Bauherrn und aller am Bau Beteiligten*]

building code → building (construction) code

building code law, construction code law · Bauordnungsrecht *n*, (Bau)Aufsichtsrecht [*früher: Baupolizeirecht*] [*Manchmal werden „Bauordnungsrecht" nur auf die materiell(rechtlich)en und „Bauaufsichtsrecht" nur auf die verfahrensrechtlichen Vorschriften bezogen. Diese Unterscheidung ist aber nicht begründet. Das Bauordnungsrecht regelt die Ausführungen der Bauwerke auf einem Grundstück*]

building code law general clause, construction code law general clause · bauordnungsrechtliche Generalklausel *f*, (bau)aufsicht(srecht)liche Generalklausel

building code provision, construction code provision · Bauordnungsbestimmung *f*

building company, construction firm, building firm, contracting firm, contracting company, construction company · Bauunternehmen *n*, Baugesellschaft *f*, Bauunternehmung *f*, Baubetrieb *m*, Baufirma *f*

building company (US) → building society

building competition, construction competition · Bauwettbewerb *m*

building component · Gebäudebestandteil *m*

building condition, construction condition · Baubedingung *f*

building condition → building (construction) condition

building conservation, conservation of buildings, preservation of buildings, building preservation · Gebäudeerhaltung *f*, Gebäudepflege *f*

building (construction) [*It is usually designed by architectural firms*] · Hochbau *m*

building (construction) act, building (construction) law, building (construction) statute · Hochbaugesetz *n*

building (construction) activity, building (construction) operations [*It includes rebuilding operations, structural alterations of or additions to buildings and other operations normally undertaken by a person carrying on business as a builder*] · Hochbautätigkeit *f*

building (construction) administration · Hochbauverwaltung *f*

building (construction) agreement [*It is part of a building (construction) contract*] · Hochbauvertrag *m* [*Der Vertrag als Vertragsbestandteil; andere Vertragsbestandteile sind Zeichnungen, Angebot, Garantie usw.*]

building (construction) board · Hochbauamt *n*

building (construction) capital, construction capital · Baukapital *n*

building (construction) client, building (construction) employer, building (constuction) promoter, building (construction) owner · Hochbauauftraggeber *m*, Hochbaubesteller, Hochbau-Bauherr(schaft) *m, (f)*

building (construction) code · Hochbauordnung *f*

building (construction) condition · Hochbaubedingung *f*

building (construction) contract · Hochbauvertrag *m* [*Der Vertrag und alle Vertragsbestandteile zusammen*]

building (construction) contracting practice · Hochbauvergabewesen *n*

building (construction) contractor, builder · Hochbauunternehmer *m*

building (construction) cost(s) · Hochbaukosten *f*

building (construction) cost(s) index · Hochbau(kosten)index *m* [*Die Kennziffer für die Höhe der Hochbaukosten, jeweils im Vergleich zu einer festgesetzten Basis auf Grund bestimmter Berechnungen aus der Praxis ermittelt*]

building (construction) department · Hochbauabteilung *f*

building (construction) drawing, building (construction) plan · Hochbauplan *m*, Hochbauzeichnung *f*

building (construction) drawing · Hochbauzeichnen *n*

building (construction) employer, building (constuction) promoter, building (construction) owner, building (construction) client · Hochbauauftraggeber *m*, Hochbaubesteller, Hochbau-Bauherr(schaft) *m, (f)*

building (construction) engineer · Hochbauingenieur *m*

building (construction) engineering · Hochbautechnik *f* [*als Wissenschaft*]

building (construction) engineer's contract · Hochbauingenieurvertrag *m*

building (construction) expert · Hochbausachverständige *m*

building (construction) expertise · Hochbaugutachten *n*

building (construction) field, building (construction) sector · Hochbausektor *m*

building (construction) financing · Hochbaufinanzierung *f*

building (construction) industry · Hochbauindustrie *f*

building (construction) law, building (construction) act, building (construction) statute · Hochbaugesetz *n*

building (construction) law · (objektives) Hochbaurecht *n*

building (construction) legislation, building (construction) lawmaking · Hochbaugesetzgebung *f*

building (construction) measure · Hochbaumaßnahme *f*

building (construction) operations, building (construction) activity [*It includes rebuilding operations, structural alterations of or additions to buildings and other operations normally undertaken by a person carrying on business as a builder*] · Hochbautätigkeit *f*

building (construction) order · Hochbauauftrag *m*

building (construction) ordinance · Hochbauverordnung *f*

building (construction) owner, building (construction) client, building (construction) employer, building (constuction) promoter · Hochbauauftraggeber *m*, Hochbaubesteller, Hochbau-Bauherr(schaft) *m, (f)*

building (construction) plan, building (construction) drawing · Hochbauplan *m*, Hochbauzeichnung *f*

building (construction) planning · Hochbauplanung *f*

building (construction) practice · Hochbauwesen *n*

building (construction) price · Hochbaupreis *m*

building (construction) project · Hochbauvorhaben *n*, Hochbauprojekt *n*

building (construction) promoter, building (construction) owner, building (construction) client, building (construction) employer · Hochbauauftraggeber *m*, Hochbaubesteller, Hochbau-Bauherr-(schaft) *m*, *(f)*

building (construction) proposal (US) → building (construction) tender, building (construction) provision · Hochbaubestimmung *f*

building (construction) sector, building (construction) field · Hochbausektor *m*

building (construction) sub-contract · Nachunternehmervertrag *m* im Hochbau, Subunternehmervertrag im Hochbau, Unterunternehmervertrag im Hochbau; Unterakkordantenvertrag im Hochbau [*Schweiz*]

building (construction) sub(contractor) · Hochbaunachunternehmer *m*, Hochbausubunternehmer; Hochbauunterakkordant *m* [*Schweiz*]

building (construction) sum, sum of building (construction) · Herstellungssumme *f*, Bausumme [*Hochbau*]

building (construction) surveyor · Hochbaubeamte *m*

building (construction) technique · Hochbautechnik *f* [*als betriebstechnische Anwendung*]

building (construction) tender, building (construction) offer, building (construction) bid; building (construction) (bid) proposal (US) · Hochbauangebot *n*

building (construction) time · Hochbauzeit *f*

building (construction) trades, (structural) trades, construction trades · Bauhandwerk *n* [*Die Gesamtheit der sich mit Bauarbeiten befassenden Handwerkszweige*]

building (construction) volume · Hochbauvolumen *n*

building (construction) worker · Hochbauarbeiter *m*

building consulting agency, building consulting office, construction consulting agency, construction consulting office · Bauberatungsstelle *f*

building consulting service, construction consulting service · Bauberatung *f*

building contract, (construction) contract [*It means the conditions of contract, specification, drawings, priced bill of quantities, schedule of rates (if any), tender, letter of acceptance and the contract agreement (if completed). It is a contract for the building of anything — not necessarily a house, but any structure*] · (Bau)Vertrag *m* (im weiteren Sinne)

building contract → building (construction) contract

building contract according to the German Civil Code, (construction) contract according to the German Civil Code · BGB-(Bau)Vertrag *m* (im weiteren Sinne)

building contract agreement, (construction) contract agreement · (Bau)Vertrag *m* im engeren Sinne

building (contract) documents, construction (contract) documents · Bau(vertrags)unterlagen *f pl*

building contracting practice, construction contracting practice · Bauvergabewesen *n*

building contract law, construction contract law · Bauvertragsrecht *n*

building contractor → (civil) engineering contractor

building contractor, building construction contractor · Hochbauunternehmer *m*

building contractor practice, construction contractor practice · Bauunternehmerwesen *n*

(building) conversion, structural alteration, structural conversion, (building) alteration · (Gebäude)Umbau *m*

building cost(s), construction cost(s) · Herstellungskosten *f*, Baukosten [*Steuerliche Bezeichnung der Gesamtkosten der Bauherrn*]

building cost(s) → building (construction) cost(s)

building cost(s) · Gebäudekosten *f*

building cost(s) allowance, construction cost(s) allowance · Baukostenzuschuß *m*

building cost(s) estimate, construction cost(s) estimate · Bau(kosten)(vor)-anschlag *m*

building cost(s) index, construction cost(s) index · Baukostenindex *m*

building cost(s) index → building (construction) cost(s) index

building count, building census, census of buildings, count of buildings · Gebäudezählung *f*

building coverage — building financing

building coverage · Bebauung *f* mit Gebäuden, Gebäudebebauung; Überbauung mit Gebäuden, Gebäudeüberbauung [*Schweiz*]

(building) coverage map, building scheme map · Bebauungskarte *f*; Überbauungskarte [*Schweiz*]

building credit, construction credit · Baukredit *m*

building credit law, construction credit law · Baukreditgesetz *n*

building damage · Gebäudeschaden *m*

building delay, delay of construction, delay of building, construction delay · Bauverzug *m*

building density · Gebäudedichte *f*

building depth, depth of a building · Gebäudetiefe *f*, Bautiefe

building dimensions, building bulk [*The height, depth, density, and width of a building*] · Gebäudeabmessungen *fpl*

building dispensation · Baudispensierung *f*, Baufreigabe *f*, Baubefreiung

building dispensation agreement · Baudispens(ierungs)vertrag *m*, Baubefreiungsvertrag, Baufreigabevertrag [*In ihm verpflichtet sich eine Gemeinde zur Erteilung eines Dispenses zugunsten des Bauherrn, und der Bauherr übernimmt dafür Verpflichtungen hinsichtlich des Baugrundstücks oder/und zu sonstigen Gegenleistungen*]

building dispute, construction dispute · Baustreit(igkeit) *m*, (*f*), Baurechtsstreit

building distance · Gebäudeabstand *m*

building district, construction district · Baubezirk *m*

building documents, construction documents, work(ing) documents · Arbeitsunterlagen *fpl*, Bauunterlagen *fpl*, (Bau)Ausführungsunterlagen *fpl*

building document (to be presented), construction document (to be presented) · Bauvorlage *f*

building drawing → plan

building drawing → building (construction) plan

building easement · Gebäudegrunddienstbarkeit *f*

building emergency tax, construction emergency tax · Baunotabgabe *f*

building employer → building (construction) owner

building employment, employment in the building industry, employment in the construction industry, construction employment · Beschäftigung *f* in der Bauindustrie

building engineer → building (construction) engineer

building engineering → building (construction) engineering

building engineering, construction engineering · Bautechnik [*als Wissenschaft*]

building engineer's contract → building (construction) engineer's contract

building enlargement, building extension · Gebäudeerweiterung *f*

building environment, construction environment · Bauumwelt *f*

building erection, erection of building(s) · Gebäudeerrichtung *f*, Gebäudeerstellung

building (estate) lot · Bauparzelle *f*, Bauflurstück *n*, Baugrundstück im katastertechnischen Sinne

building (estate) parcel, building (estate) plot, building property parcel, building property plot, building realty parcel, building realty plot, building estate, plot of building land · Baugrundstück *n* [*Ein Grundstück, das nach öffentlich-rechtlichen Vorschriften mit Gebäuden bebaubar oder bebaut ist (nach § 2 Abs. 1 MuBO). Ein Baugrundstück hat im allgemeinen eine bebaute und eine unbebaute Fläche*]

building estimate, construction estimate · Bauvoranschlag *m*

building exhibition, construction exhibition · Bauausstellung *f*

building expert → building (construction) expert

building expert, construction expert · Bausachverständiger *m*, Baugutachter

building expertise → building (construction) expertise

building extension, building enlargement · Gebäudeerweiterung *f*

building fabric [*It has buildings as its constituent form elements*] · Gebäudenetz *n*

building fair, construction fair · Baumesse *f*

building fee, construction fee · Baugebühr *f*, Bauhonorar *n*

building field → building (construction) sector

building field, construction sector, building sector, construction field · Bausektor *m*

building files, construction files · Bauakten *f*

building financing, construction financing · Baufinanzierung *f*

building financing — (building) (land) area acquisition 120

building financing → building (construction) financing

building fire insurance · Gebäude-Feuerversicherung *f*, Gebäude-Brandversicherung

building firm, contracting firm, contracting company, construction company, building company, construction firm · Bauunternehmen *n*, Baugesellschaft *f*, Bauunternehmung *f*, Baubetrieb *m*, Baufirma *f*

building for disabled persons · Bauen *n* für Behinderte

building for social needs, social building · Sozialbau *m*

building freeze, construction freeze · Bausperre *f* [*Wenn eine Veränderungssperre nach § 14 BBauG nicht beschlossen wird, obwohl die Voraussetzungen gegeben sind, so kann im Einzelfall die Baugenehmigungsbehörde auf Antrag der Gemeinde das Baugesuch eines Bauherrn für einen Zeitraum bis zu 12 Monaten zurückstellen wenn zu befürchten ist, daß die Planungsdurchführung durch das beabsichtigte Vorhaben unmöglich gemacht oder doch wesentlich erschwert werden würde (§ 15 BBauG)*]

building gross return multiplier, building gross yield multiplier · Gebäuderohrenditevervielfältiger, Gebäudebruttorenditevervielfältiger *m*

building group, group of buildings · Gebäudegruppe *f*

building hazard, building risk, construction hazard, construction risk · Baurisiko *n*, Bauwagnis *n*

building height, height of (a) building · Gebäudehöhe *f*

building hindrance, construction hindrance · Baubehinderung *f*

building industry → building (construction) industry

building industry and trades, construction industry and trades, construction trades and industry, building trades and industry · Baugewerbe *n* [*Sammelbenennung für das handwerklich und industriell betriebene Bauen*]

building industry code of practice, code of practice for the construction industry, code of practice for the building industry, construction industry code of practice · Baumerkblatt *n*

building inspection, construction inspection · Aufsicht *f*, Bauaufsicht, (Bau)-Überwachung *f*, (Bau)Kontrolle *f*

building inspector, construction inspector · Baukontrolleur *m*

building instal(l)ment, construction instal(l)ment · Abschlag *m* für Bauarbeiten

building instal(l)ment (payment) certificate, construction instal(l)ment (payment) certificate · Abschlags(zahlungs)schein *m* für Bauarbeiten

building insurance · Gebäudeversicherung *f*

building insurance, (contractor's) all-risks insurance, construction insurance · Bau(wesen)versicherung *f*

building interest, interest on building loan(s), interest on construction loan(s), construction interest · Bauzinsen *f*

building investment, construction investment · Bauinvestition *f*

building jobs, construction jobs · Sekundärsektor *m*

building (job) site, (construction) job site, (construction) site · Baustelle *f*

building (job) site land, (construction) job site land, (construction) site land · Baustellenland *n*

(building) land, (building) space, (building) (land) area · (Bau)Boden *m*, (Bau)Fläche *f*, (Bau)Land *n* [*Unbebautes Land, das nach dem Flächennutzungsplan und der Bauordnung bebaut werden darf*]

(building) land acquisition, (building) (land) area acquisition, acquisition of (building) (land) area, acquisition of (building) land, acquisition of (building) space, (building) space acquisition · (Bau)Bodenbeschaffung *f*, (Bau)Bodenerwerb *m*, (Bau)Flächenbeschaffung, (Bau)Flächenerwerb, (Bau)Landerwerb, (Bau)Landbeschaffung

(building) land acquisition law, (building) land acquisition act, (building) land acquisition statute · (Bau)Bodenbeschaffungsgesetz *n*, (Bau)Landbeschaffungsgesetz, (Bau)Landerwerbsgesetz, (Bau)Bodenerwerbsgesetz, (Bau)Flächenbeschaffungsgesetz, (Bau)Flächenerwerbsgesetz

(building) land acquisition tax · (Bau)Landerwerb(s)steuer *f*, (Bau)Bodenerwerb(s)steuer

(building) land act, (building) land law, (building) land statute · (Bau)Bodengesetz *n*, (Bau)Landgesetz

building land affair · Baulandsache *f*, Baubodensache, Baulandangelegenheit *f*, Baubodenangelegenheit

(building) (land) area, (building) land, (building) space · (Bau)Boden *m*, (Bau)Fläche *f*, (Bau)Land *n* [*Unbebautes Land, das nach dem Flächennutzungsplan und der Bauordnung bebaut werden darf*]

(building) (land) area acquisition, acquisition of (building) (land) area, acquisition of (building) land, acquisition of (building) space, (building) space acquisition, (building) land acquisition · (Bau)Bodenbeschaffung *f*, (Bau)Bodenerwerb *m*, (Bau)Flächenbeschaffung, (Bau)-Flächenerwerb, (Bau)Landerwerb, (Bau)Landbeschaffung

(building) (land) area demise → (building) (land) area tenancy

(building) (land) area for mixed development, mixed building land (area), (building) land for mixed development · gemischte (Bau)Fläche, *f*, gemischter (Bau)Boden *m*, gemischtes (Bau)-Land *n*, Misch(bau)boden, Misch(bau)fläche, Misch(bau)land

(building) (land) area improvement loan, (building) land improvement loan · (Bau)Landerschließungsdarleh(e)n *n*, (Bau)Bodenerschließungsdarleh(e)n, (Bau)Flächenerschließungsdarleh(e)n, Erschließungsdarleh(e)n

(building) (land) area lease(hold) → (building) (land) area tenancy

(building) (land) area market, (building) land market, (real) estate market, (real) property market, market in (building) land · (Bau)Bodenmarkt *m*, (Bau)Landmarkt, (Bau)Grundstücksmarkt

(building) (land) area monopoly, (building) land monopoly · (Bau)Bodenmonopol *n*, (Bau)Landmonopol, (Bau)Flächenmonopol

(building) (land) area need, (building) land need · (Bau)Bodenbedarf *m*, (Bau)Flächenbedarf, (Bau)Landbedarf

(building) (land) area owner, (building) (land) (area) proprietor, (building) land owner, proprietor of (the) (building) land, owner of (the) (building) land, landed proprietor, landed owner, (building) land proprietor · (Bau)Bodeneigentümer *m*, (Bau)Flächeneigentümer, (Bau)Landeigentümer, (Bau)Landherr, (Bau)Bodeneigner, (Bau)Flächeneigner, (Bau)Landeigner

(building) (land) (area) proprietor, (building) land owner, proprietor of (the) (building) land, owner of (the) (building) land, landed proprietor, landed owner, (building) land proprietor, (building) land area owner · (Bau)Bodeneigentümer *m*, (Bau)Flächeneigentümer, (Bau)Landeigentümer, (Bau)Landherr, (Bau)Bodeneigner, (Bau)Flächeneigner, (Bau)Landeigner

(building) (land) area quality, (building) land quality · (Bau)Bodengüte *f*, (Bau)Flächengüte, (Bau)Landgüte

(building) (land) area replotting · (Bau)Landumlegung *f*, (Bau)Bodenumlegung, (Bau)Flächenumlegung

(building) (land) area speculation, (building) land speculation, speculation in (building) (land) area, speculation in (building) land · (Bau)Bodenspekulation *f*, (Bau)Landspekulation, (Bau)Flächenspekulation

(building) (land) area supply, (building) land supply · (Bau)Bodenangebot *n*, (Bau)Landangebot, (Bau)Landbereitstellung *f*, (Bau)Bodenbereitstellung, (Bau)Flächenangebot, (Bau)Flächenbereitstellung

(building) (land) area tax · (Bau)Landsteuer *f*, (Bau)Bodensteuer, (Bau)-Flächensteuer

(building) (land) area tenancy, (building) (land) area lease(hold), (building) (land) area demise, (building) land tenancy, (building) land lease(hold), (building) land demise, tenancy of (building) (land) area, lease(hold) of (building) (land) area, demise of (building) (land) area, tenancy of (building) land, lease(hold) of (building) land · (Bau)Landpacht *f*, (Bau)Bodenpacht, (Bau)Flächenpacht, (Bau)Flächennutzungsrecht *n*, (Bau)Bodennutzungsrecht, (Bau)Landnutzungsrecht, Pacht von (Bau)Boden, Nutzungsrecht von (Bau)Boden, Pacht von (Bau)Land, Nutzungsrecht von (Bau)Land, Pacht von (Bau)Flächen, Nutzungsrecht von (Bau)Flächen

(building) land clearance, clearance of (the) (building) land · (Bauland)Freilegung *f*, Landfreilegung, (Bau)Bodenfreilegung

(building) land clearance cost(s), cost(s) for clearance of (the) (building) land · (Bauland)Freilegungskosten *f*, Landfreilegungskosten, (Bau)Bodenfreilegungskosten

(building) land code · (Bau)Bodenordnung *f*, (Bau)Landordnung [*als Vorschrift*]

(building) land code law · (Bau)Bodenordnungsrecht *n*, (Bau)Landordnungsrecht

building land cooperative [*It enables a group of prospective home owners to buy raw land and develop it according to their own design and ideas without the profit margin which goes to the individual land developer*] · Baulandgenossenschaft *f*

(building) land court · Baulandgericht *n*, (Bau)Bodengericht

(building) land demise → (building) (land) area tenancy

(building) land for mixed development, (building) (land) area for mixed development, mixed building land (area) · gemischte (Bau)Fläche, *f*, gemischter (Bau)Boden *m*, gemischtes (Bau)-Land *n*, Misch(bau)boden, Misch(bau)fläche, Misch(bau)land, M

building land improvement, improvement to land, installation of improvements, (land) improvement [*Facilities, usually public utilities, such as sidewalks or*

(building) land improvement loan — building legislation

sewers, added to land which increase its usefulness] · Erschließung, (Bau)-Landerschließung, (Bau)Bodenerschließung, (Bau)Flächenerschließung, (Bau)Geländeerschließung, (Bau)-Terrainerschließung, Baureifmachung, Zuwegung

(building) land improvement loan, (building) (land) area improvement loan · (Bau)Landerschließungsdarleh(e)n *n*, (Bau)Bodenerschließungsdarleh(e)n, (Bau)Flächenerschließungsdarleh(e)n, Erschließungsdarleh(e)n

(building) land improvement provision, provision for (building) land improvement · (Bau)Landerschließungsbestimmung *f*, (Bau)Bodenerschließungsbestimmung, (Bau)Flächenerschließungsbestimmung

(building) land law, (building) land statute, (building) land act · (Bau)Bodengesetz *n*, (Bau)Landgesetz

(building) land law · (Bau)Bodenrecht *n*, (Bau)Landrecht

(building) land legislation, (building) land lawmaking · Bodengesetzgebung *f*, (Bau)Landgesetzgebung, Baubodengesetzgebung

(building) land market, (real) estate market, (real) property market, market in (building) land, (building) (land) area market · (Bau)Bodenmarkt *m*, (Bau)-Landmarkt, (Bau)Grundstücksmarkt

(building) land monopoly, (building) (land) area monopoly · (Bau)Bodenmonopol *n*, (Bau)Landmonopol, (Bau)Flächenmonopol

(building) land need → (building) (land) area need

(building) land owner, proprietor of (the) (building) land, owner of (the) (building) land, landed proprietor, landed owner, (building) land proprietor, (building) (land) area owner, (building) (land) (area) proprietor · (Bau)Bodeneigentümer *m*, (Bau)Flächeneigentümer, (Bau)-Landeigentümer, (Bau)Landherr, (Bau)-Bodeneigner, (Bau)Flächeneigner, (Bau)Landeigner

building land parcel, building land plot · Baulandgrundstück *n* (im tatsächlichen Sinne)

(building) land policy · (Bau)Bodenpolitik *f*, (Bau)Landpolitik

building land proceeding · Baulandverfahren *n*, Baubodenverfahren, Landverfahren, Bodenverfahren

(building) land proprietor, (building) (land) area owner, (building) (land) (area) proprietor, (building) land owner, proprietor of (the) (building) land, owner of (the) (building) land, landed proprietor, landed owner · (Bau)Bodeneigentümer *m*, (Bau)Flächeneigentümer, (Bau)-Landeigentümer, (Bau)Landherr, (Bau)-Bodeneigner, (Bau)Flächeneigner, (Bau)Landeigner

(building) land purchase, purchase of (real) estate, purchase of (real) property, purchase of (building) land, (real) estate purchase, (real) property purchase · Grund(stücks)kauf *m*, (Bau)-Landkauf, (Bau)Bodenkauf, Liegenschaftskauf [*Österreich: Grundeinlösung f*]

(building) land quality, (building) (land) area quality · (Bau)Bodengüte *f*, (Bau)Flächengüte, (Bau)Landgüte

building land replotting, replotting of building land · Baulandumlegung *f*, Baubodenumlegung, Bauflächenumlegung [*Die Zusammenfassung und Neuverteilung benachbarter Grundstücke zu Zwecken der Bebauung*]

(building) land speculation, speculation in (building) (land) area, speculation in (building) land, (building) (land) area speculation · (Bau)Bodenspekulation *f*, (Bau)Landspekulation, (Bau)Flächenspekulation

(building) land statute, (building) land act, (building) land law · (Bau)Bodengesetz *n*, (Bau)Landgesetz

(building) land strip, strip of (building) land · (Bau)Landstreifen *m*, (Bau)Bodenstreifen

(building) land supply, (building) (land) area supply · (Bau)Bodenangebot *n*, (Bau)Landangebot, (Bau)Landbereitstellung *f*, (Bau)Bodenbereitstellung, (Bau)Flächenangebot, (Bau)Flächenbereitstellung

(building) land tenancy → (building) (land) area tenancy

building land turnover · Baulandumsatz *m*

building law, construction law · Baurecht *n*

building law, building statute, building act, construction law, construction statute, construction act · Baugesetz *n*

building law → building (construction) act

building lawmaking, construction legislation, building legislation, construction lawmaking · Baugesetzgebung *f*

building-lease, ninety-nine years lease · (Bau)Pacht(vertrag) *f*, *(m)* für 99 Jahre

building lease · (Bau)Pacht(vertrag) *f*, *(m)*

building-lease law, 99 years lease law · (Bau)Pachtrecht *n* auf 99 Jahre

building legislation, construction lawmaking, building lawmaking, construction legislation · Baugesetzgebung *f*

building legislation → building (construction) legislation

building limiting line · Baulinie f [*Sie schreibt verbindlich vor, an welcher Stelle genau eine Gebäudekante zu errichten ist*]

building line, BL, frontage line · (Bau)Fluchtlinie f [*Die amtlich festgesetzte Linie, allgemein parallel zur Straße, über die nicht hinaus gebaut werden darf und die die vordere Gebäudekante festlegt*]

building line act, building line law, building line statute, law of building lines, act of building lines, statute of building lines · Fluchtliniengesetz n, Bauflucht(linien)gesetz

building line law, building line statute, law of building lines, act of building lines, statute of building lines, building line act · Fluchtliniengesetz n, Bauflucht(linien)gesetz

building line law, BL law, law of building lines · (Bau)Fluchtlinienrecht n [*Es betrifft die Anlegung und Veränderung von Straßen und Plätzen in Gemeinden aller Art*]

building line plan, plan of building lines · Fluchtlinienplan m, Baufluchtlinienplan

building litigation, construction litigation · Bauprozeß m

building loan, construction loan · Baudarleh(e)n n

building loan lender, building loaner, construction loaner, building moneylender, construction loan lender · Baudarleh(e)n(s)geber m

building lot → building estate lot

building maintenance · Gebäudeunterhaltung f

building maintenance cost(s) · Gebäudeunterhaltungskosten f

building management, management of construction, management of project, management of building, construction management, project management · (Bau)Betreuung f, Betreuung von Bauvorhaben [*Die technische und wirtschaftliche Vorbereitung und Überwachung eines Bauvorhabens in fremdem Namen und für fremde Rechnung*]

building management, construction management, project management, management of construction, management of project, management of building · Bau(betriebs)führung f [*Die technische und wirtschaftliche Vorbereitung und Überwachung eines Bauvorhabens in eigenem Namen*]

building management agent, project management agent, construction management agent [*Er bereitet ein Bauvorhaben im Namen und für Rechnung des Betreuten (= Bauherrn) vor und/oder führt es durch. Der Umfang der Betreuung und der Vollmacht wird in einem Betreuungsvertrag vereinbart*] · (Bau)Betreuer m

building management contract, construction management contract · (Bau)Betreuungsvertrag m

building management law, project management law, construction management law · (Bau)Betreuungsrecht n

building management law, construction management law, project management law · Baubetriebsrecht n

building management plan, construction management plan · (Bau)Betreuungsplan m

building market, construction market · Baumarkt m [*Der Teilmarkt einer Volkswirtschaft, auf dem sich die Preise für bauliche Leistungen aller Art nach den Gesetzen von Angebot und Nachfrage bilden*]

(building) material(s) supplier, construction material(s) supplier · (Bau)Stofflieferant m

building materials supplied by owner, owner-furnished (construction) materials, owner-furnished building materials, (construction) materials supplied by owner · (Bau)Stoffe mpl vom Bauherrn, (Bau-)Materialien npl vom Bauherrn, bauseits gestellte (Bau)Stoffe, bauseits gestellte (Bau)Materialien

(building) material testing standard, construction material testing standard · (Bau)Stoffprüfnorm f

building measure, construction measure · Baumaßnahme f

building measure, building construction measure · Hochbaumaßnahme f

(building) mechanic · Bauhandwerker m

(building) mechanic's lien [*A lien in favour of unpaid mechanics who have performed labour on buildings or in favour of those who have furnished material for the structures*] · (Bau)Handwerkereinbehaltungsrecht n, (Bau)Handwerkerretentionsrecht, (Bau)Handwerker(zu)rück(be)haltungsrecht

building method, construction method · Bauweise f, Bauverfahren n [*Art der Bauausführung*]

building moneylender, construction loan lender, building loan lender, building loaner, construction loaner, construction moneylender · Baudarleh(e)n(s)geber m

building mortgage, construction mortgage · Bauhypothek f [*Nicht verwechseln mit „Baugeld(er)hypothek"*]

building neighbour's law — building practice

building neighbour's law (Brit.); building neighbor's law (US) · Baunachbarrecht *n*, objektives Baunachbarrecht

building neighbour's right (Brit.); building neighbor's right (US) · Baunachbarrecht *n*, subjektives Baunachbarrecht

building noise, construction noise · Baulärm *m*

building notice, construction notice, building notification, construction notification · Baumitteilung *f*, Bauanzeige *f* [*Für Bauvorhaben untergeordneter Bedeutung, z. B. Gartenlaube, für die ein Bauantrag nicht vorgeschrieben ist*]

building notice procedure, building notification procedure, construction notice procedure, construction notification procedure · Bauanzeigeverfahren *n*, Baumitteilungsverfahren

building of architectural interest · Gebäude *n* von künstlerischer Bedeutung

building of a structure, erection of a structure, construction of a structure · Bauwerkerrichtung *f*, Bauwerkerstellung

building offer → building (construction) tender

building of flats · Geschoßwohn(ungs)bau *m*, Etagenwohn(ungs)bau, Stockwerkwohn(ungs)bau

building of sewers, construction of sewers · (Abwasser)Kanalbau *m*

building of small-sized housing, construction of small-sized housing · Kleinwohn(ungs)bau *m*

building of theory, formulation of theory, theory building, theory formulation · Theoriegestaltung *f*, Theorieformulierung

building operations → building (construction) works

building order, construction order · Bauauftrag *m*

building order → building (construction) order

building ordinance → building (construction) ordinance

(building) owner, construction owner, project owner, client, employer, promoter [*In Great Britain, the term "employer" is preferred since this is used in both the RIBA and ICE standard forms of contract*] · Bauherr(schaft) *m*, *(f)*, Auftraggeber *m*, BH *f*, AG *m* [*im Sinne der VOB*]; Besteller [*im Sinne des BGB*] [*Nach geläufiger Fachsprache ist „Bauherr" stets der „Letzt-Besteller" eines Bauwerkes (oder Bauwerk-Teils), also nicht der Unternehmer, der einen Subunternehmer bezieht. Dieser „Letzt-Besteller" ist Bauherr im engen (und eigentlichen) Sinne des Wortes. In einem übertragenen (nicht geläufigen) Sinne aber kann „Bauherr" auch ein Unternehmer sein, der übernommene Bauarbeiten durch Abschluß eines Bauvertrages an einen Subunternehmer weitervergibt. In diesem übertragenen Sinne muß das Wort dann verstanden werden, wenn die SIA-Norm 118 (Schweiz) auf den Bauvertrag zwischen Unternehmer und Subunternehmer zur Anwendung kommt. Im Verhältnis Unternehmer/Subunternehmer ist alsdann der erstere „Bauherr" im Sinne der Norm, der andere „Unternehmer"*]

building owner · Gebäudeeigentümer *m*, Gebäudeeigner

building ownership · Gebäudeeigentum *n*

building parcel → building (estate) parcel

building participant, construction participant · Baubeteiligte *m*

building permission, construction permission, permission to construct, permission to build · (Bau)Genehmigung *f*, (Bau)Erlaubnis *f*, Ausführungsgenehmigung, Ausführungserlaubnis [*Entscheidung einer Baugenehmigungsbehörde über die Zulässigkeit eines Vorhabens auf einem bestimmten Grundstück (§ 36 BBauG)*]

building permission authority, construction permission authority · Baugenehmigungsbehörde *f*

(building) permit, construction permit · (Bau)Erlaubnisbescheinigung *f*, (Bau)-Genehmigungsbescheinigung, (Bau)-Erlaubnisschein *m*, (Bau)Genehmigungsschein, Bauschein, Baukonsens *m*

(building) permit fee, construction permit fee · Bauscheingebühr *f*

building plan, construction plan · Aufbauplan *m* [*Plan mit verbindlichen Anforderungen für die Gestaltung einer baulichen Anlage*]

building plan, construction plan · Bauplan *m* [*Er stellt ein gestalterisches Ziel, also einen Endzustand dar*]

building planning, construction planning · Bauplanung *f* [*Zur Durchführung eines Bauvorhabens*]

building planning → building (construction) planning

building planning law, construction planning law · Bauplanungsrecht *n*

building plot → building (estate) parcel

building policy, construction policy · Baupolitik *f*

building practice, construction practice · Bauwesen *n*

building practice → building (construction) practice

building preparation — building scheme design

building preparation, preparation of construction, preparation of building, construction preparation · Bauvorbereitung *f*

building prescription, construction regulation, construction prescription, construction rule, building regulation, building rule · Bauvorschrift *f*, baurechtliche Vorschrift

building preservation, building conservation, conservation of buildings, preservation of buildings · Gebäudeerhaltung *f*, Gebäudepflege *f*

building price, construction price · Baupreis *m*

building price index, construction price index · Baupreisindex *m* [*Fehlbenennung: Baukostenindex*]

building price law, construction price law · Baupreisrecht *n*

building price ordinance, construction price ordinance · Baupreisverordnung *f*, BaupreisVO

building progress, progress of the work(s), construction progress, (job) progress · Baufortschritt *m*, Arbeitsfortschritt

building progress photograph, construction progress photograph · Baufortschrittfoto *n*, Arbeitsfortschrittfoto

building project, construction project · Bauvorhaben *n*, Bauprojekt *n*

building project → building (construction) project

building project budget, budget for construction project, budget for building project, construction project budget [*The total sum established by the owner for the project*] · Baukostenhaushalt *m*

building promoter → building (construction) client

building promotion, promotion of construction, promotion of building, construction promotion · Bauförderung *f*

building promotion fund, construction promotion fund · Bauförderungsmittel *f*, Bauförderungsfonds *m*

building property parcel → building (estate) parcel

building property plot → building (estate) parcel

building proposal (US) → building (construction) tender

building protection, protection of buildings · Gebäudeschutz *m*

building provision, construction provision · Baubestimmung *f*

building provision → building (construction) provision

building realty parcel → building (estate) parcel

building realty plot → building (estate) parcel

building regulation, building rule, building prescription, construction regulation, construction prescription, construction rule · Bauvorschrift *f*, baurechtliche Vorschrift

building release ordinance, construction release ordinance · Baufreistellungsverordnung *f*, BauFreiVO

building remnant, remnant of a building · Gebäuderest *m*

building renewal · Gebäudeerneuerung *f*

building rent · Gebäuderente *f*

building requirement, building charge, construction requirement, construction charge · Bauauflage *f*, Bauanforderung *f*

building research, construction research · Bauforschung *f*

building research institute, construction research institute · Bauforschungsinstitut *n*, Institut für Bauforschung

building residual technique · Gebäuderestwertverfahren *n*

building residual value · Gebäuderestwert *m*

building restriction, construction restriction · Baubeschränkung *f*, Baueinschränkung

building retardation, retardation of construction, retardation of building, construction retardation · Bauverzögerung *f*

building risk, construction hazard, construction risk, building hazard · Bausiko *n*, Bauwagnis *n*

building rule, building prescription, construction regulation, construction prescription, construction rule, building regulation · Bauvorschrift *f*, baurechtliche Vorschrift

building safety code, site safety code, construction safety code · Bau(stellen)sicherheitsordnung *f*

building schedule → building chart

building scheme, (detailed) local (development) plan, coverage scheme, detailed local plan · Bebauungsplan *m*, qualifizierter Bebauungsplan, verbindlicher Bauleitplan; Überbauungsplan [*Schweiz*] [*Der Bebauungsplan steht zwischen dem Bauplan und dem Flächennutzungsplan*]

building scheme design, (detailed) local (development) plan design, coverage scheme design · Bebauungsplanentwurf *m*, verbindlicher Bauleitplanentwurf; Überbauungsplanentwurf [*Schweiz*]

building scheme law — building site organization

building scheme law, (detailed) local (development) plan law, coverage scheme law · Bebauungsrecht *n*; Überbauungsrecht [*Schweiz*]

building scheme law, building scheme act, building scheme statute · Bebauungsgesetz *n*; Überbauungsgesetz [*Schweiz*]

building scheme map, (building) coverage map · Bebauungskarte *f*; Überbauungskarte [*Schweiz*]

building scheme proceeding · Bebauungsplanverfahren *n*, Überbauungsplanverfahren [*Schweiz*]

building scheme proposal, (detailed) local (development) plan proposal, coverage scheme proposal · Bebauungsvorschlag *m*; Überbauungsvorschlag [*Schweiz*]

building sector → building (construction) sector

building shell insurance · Rohbauversicherung *f*

building site → building (job) site

building site accident, (job) site accident, construction site accident · Bau(stellen)unfall *m*

building site accident damage, construction site accident damage, job site accident damage, site accident damage · Bauunfallschaden *m*

building site bookkeeping, site bookkeeping, job site bookkeeping, construction site bookkeeping · Baustellenbuchführung *f*

building site checking, building site control, job site checking, job site control, site checking, site control, construction site checking, construction site control · Baustellenkontrolle *f* [*Aufsuchen der Baustelle in Zeitabständen zur Prüfung der Arbeiten des Bauunternehmers*]

building site clearance cost(s), job site clearance cost(s), construction site clearance cost(s), site clearance cost(s) · Baustellenräumungskosten *f*

building site conditions, job site conditions, (construction) site conditions · Bau(stellen)verhältnisse *f*, Verhältnisse (auf) der Baustelle

building site diary, construction site daily record, building site daily record, (job)-site diary, (job)site daily record, job (daily) record, job diary, construction site diary · Bau(stellen)tagebuch *n*, Bau(stellen)buch

building site examination, examination of site, visit of site, inspection of site, site inspection, site visit, site examination, construction site visit, construction site examination, construction site inspection, building site visit, building site inspection · Baustellenbesichtigung *f*, (Baustellen)Begehung, Ortsbesichtigung [*Vor Abgabe eines Angebotes*]

building site facilities, job site facilities, site facilities, construction site facilities · Bau(stellen)einrichtung *f* [*Alle Maschinen und Geräte einer Baustelle*]

building site facilities cost(s), construction site facilities cost(s), job site facilities cost(s), site facilities cost(s) · Bau(stellen)einrichtungskosten *f*

building site facilities plan, (construction) site facilities plan, job (site) facilities plan · Bau(stellen)ordnungsplan *m* [*Fehlbenennungen: Bau(stellen)einrichtungsplan*]

building site fence, site fence, job site fence, construction site fence · Bau(stellen)zaun *m*

building site inspection, building site examination, examination of site, inspection of site, site inspection, site visit, site examination, construction site visit, construction site examination, construction site inspection, building site visit · Baustellenbesichtigung *f*, (Baustellen)Begehung, Ortsbesichtigung [*Vor Abgabe eines Angebotes*]

building site land → building (job) site land

building site lighting, building site illumination, construction site lighting, construction site illumination, job site lighting, job site illumination, site lighting, site illumination · Bau(stellen)beleuchtung *f*

building site limit, construction site limit, job site limit, site limit · Baustellengrenze *f*

building site management, site management, job site management, construction site management · Bau(stellen)führung *f*, örtliche Bauaufsicht *f*

building site manager, job site manager, manager on site, site manager, construction site manager · Baustellenführer *m*, örtlicher Bauführer [*des Unternehmers*]

building site meeting, job site meeting, job (progress) meeting, (construction) site meeting · Bau(stellen)besprechung *f*

building site meeting minutes, job site meeting minutes, site meeting minutes, construction site meeting minutes · Bau(stellen)besprechungsprotokoll *n*

building site operations, construction site operations, job operations, (job) site operations · Bau(stellen)betrieb *m*

building site organization, job site organization, site organization, construction site organization · Bau(stellen)organisation *f*

building site planning, construction site planning, job site planning, site planning · Baustellenplanung *f*

building site safety, safety of job site, job site safety, safety of (construction) site, safety of building site, (construction) site safety · Baustellensicherheit *f*

building site salary, site salary, job site salary, construction site salary · Bau(stellen)gehalt *n*

(building) site sign → site sign

building site supervision, supervision of site(s), superintendence of site(s), site supervision, site superintendence, construction site supervision, construction site superintendence, job site supervision, job site superintendence, building site superintendence · Bau(stellen)aufsicht *f*, Bau(stellen)überwachung *f*, Objektaufsicht, Objektüberwachung

building site turnover, job (site) turnover, (construction) site turnover · Bau(stellen)umsatz *m*

building site visit, building site inspection, building site examination, examination of site, visit of site, inspection of site, site inspection, site visit, site examination, construction site visit, construction site examination, construction site inspection · Baustellenbesichtigung *f*, (Baustellen)Begehung, Ortsbesichtigung [*Vor Abgabe eines Angebotes*]

building (site) wage, job (site) wage; construction labour wage (Brit.); construction labor wage (US); site wage, construction (site) wage · Bau(stellen)lohn *m*

building site water supply, job (site) water supply, (construction) site water supply · Bau(stellen)wasserversorgung *f*

Building Societies Association · Bausparkassenverband *m* [*Great Britain*]

building society (Brit.); building (and loan) association, mortgage bank, building (and loan) company, savings and loan company (US); co-operative bank [*Massachusetts*] [*An institution organized to make real estate loans with the funds received from depositors, paying interest to the latter for use of their money*] · Bausparkasse *f* [*Fehlbenennungen: Bau(kredit)genossenschaft, Bausparegenossenschaft f*]

building society law (Brit.); building (and loan) association law, law of building (and loan) associations (US) · Bauspar(kassen)recht *n*

building society law, building society act, building society statute (Brit.); building (and loan) association law (US) · Bauspargesetz *n*, Bausparkassengesetz

building society mortgage (Brit.); building (and loan) association mortgage (US) · Bauspar(kassen)hypothek *f*

building society movement (Brit.); (building (and loan)) association movement (US) · Bausparbewegung *f*

(building) space, (building) (land) area, (building) land · (Bau)Boden *m*, (Bau)Fläche *f*, (Bau)Land *n* [*Unbebautes Land, das nach dem Flächennutzungsplan und der Bauordnung bebaut werden darf*]

(building) space acquisition, (building) land acquisition, (building) (land) area acquisition, acquisition of (building) (land) area, acquisition of (building) land, acquisition of (building) space · (Bau)Bodenbeschaffung *f*, (Bau)Bodenerwerb *m*, (Bau)Flächenbeschaffung, (Bau)Flächenerwerb, (Bau)Landerwerb, (Bau)Landbeschaffung

building speculation, construction speculation · Bauspekulation *f*

building sponsoring, construction sponsoring · (Bau)Trägerschaft *f*, Baubetreuung *f* im weiteren Sinne

building stage, construction stage, stage of building, stage of construction · Baustadium *n*, Baustufe *f*

building statute, building act, construction law, construction statute, construction act, building law · Baugesetz *n*

building statute → building (construction) act

building stock, construction stock · Bauaktie *f*

building sub-contract → building (construction) sub-contract

building sub(contractor) → building (construction) sub(contractor)

building sum, production sum, sum of construction, sum of building, sum of production, construction sum · Bausumme *f*, Herstellungssumme

building surveyor, construction surveyor · Baubeamte *m*, (Bau)Aufsichtsbeamte; Baupolizeibeamte [*frühere Benennung*]

building surveyor → building (construction) surveyor

building technique, construction technique · Bautechnik *f* [*Als betriebstechnische Anwendung*]

building technique → building (construction) technique

building technology, construction technology · Bautechnologie *f*

building tender → building (construction) tender

building terrain. construction terrain · Baugelände *n* [*In der Gesetzgebung nicht mehr verwendete Benennung für Bauland, Baufläche und Baugebiet*]

**building time, ** time of construction, time of building, time for completion, construction time · Bau(fertigstellungs)zeit *f*

building time → building (construction) time

building to be demolished · Abbruchgebäude *n*, Abrißgebäude, Einreißgebäude

building to be preserved, building to be conserved, listed building · erhaltungswürdiges Gebäude *n*, erhaltenswertes Gebäude

(building) trade, structural trade, craft, construction trade [*Classification or type of work done by workers who restrict themselves to this type of work, established by jurisdictional agreements*] · (Bau)Gewerk *n*

building trades → building (construction) trades

building trades and industry, building industry and trades, construction industry and trades, construction trades and industry · Baugewerbe *n* [*Sammelbenennung für das handwerklich und industriell betriebene Bauen*]

building used for trade purposes · gewerblich genutztes Gebäude *n*

building value · Gebäudewert *m*

building value approach · Gebäudewertansatz *m*

building value computation, building value calculation · Gebäudewertberechnung *f*

building value table · Gebäudewerttabelle *f*

building volume, cubage, enclosed space, space enclosed, cube, cubic(al) capacity, (cubic(al)) content, structural volume, cubic extent, cubing, walled-in space [*Enclosed total volume measurements of a structure*] · Baumasse *f*, umbauter Raum *m*, Rauminhalt *m*

building volume → building (construction) volume

building wage → building (site) wage

building waste · Gebäudevernachlässigung *f*

building without permission, constructing without permission · Bauen *n* ohne Genehmigung, Schwarzbauen

building worker → building (construction) worker

building worker, construction worker · Bauarbeiter *m*

building workers, construction workers · Bauarbeiter(schaft) *m pl*, *(f)*

building workers' strike, construction workers' strike · Bau(arbeiter)streik *m*

building work(s), (construction) work(s) · (Bau)Arbeit(en) *f (pl)*, (Bau)Leistung(en) *f (pl)*

building work(s) → building (construction) work(s)

building yield, yield of building · Gebäudeertrag *m*

building yield tax, tax on yield of a building · Gebäudeertrag(s)steuer *f*, Gebäuderenditesteuer

building zone, construction zone · Bauzone *f*

to build (up)on, to construct (up)on, to cover · bebauen; überbauen [*Schweiz*]

built-in [*An appliance included in the construction of a property by the nature of its installation*] · Einbau(teil) *m*

built-in, fixed, in-place · eingebaut

built-in life cover · automatischer Lebensversicherungsschutz *m* [*Versicherungsfonds*]

built-up, covered, built (up)on · bebaut; überbaut [*Schweiz*]

built-up area, covered land, built-up land, covered territory, built-up territory, covered area · bebautes Gebiet *n*; überbautes Gebiet [*Schweiz*]

bulk cargo, unpackaged cargo · Massengutladung *f*

bulk sales law · Gesamtverkaufsgesetz *n*

bull [*One who endeavours by speculative purchase(s), or ortherwise, to raise the price of stocks. "Bull" was originally a speculative purchase for a rise*] · Haussier *m*, Haussespekulant

bulletin board, notice-board · Anschlagbrett *n*, schwarzes Brett, Aushangbrett

bum bailiff [*popular name*]; bound bailiff · Distriktbote *m* [*Diener eines Sheriffs für die Zustellung von Erlassen und Ausführung von Vollstreckungen*]

bunda [*In old English law*] → boundary (line)

bunder [*Anglo-Indian*]; custom-house · Zollhaus *n*

bunder [*Anglo-Indian*]; landing (place) [*A place on a navigable water for loading and unloading goods, or for the reception and delivery of passengers*] · Landestelle *f*, Schiff(s)anlegestelle

bundle of block and strip lots · Block/Streifen-Verband *m*, Streifen/Block-Verband

bundle of block lots, block lot bundle · Block(parzellen)verband *m*

bundle of legal rights [*Rights that establish real estate ownership and consist of the rights to sell, to mortgage, to lease, to will, to regain possession at the end* of a lease (reversion), to build and remove improvements, and to control use within the law] · Grundstücksrechte n pl

bundle of long strip lots within a pattern of consolidated holdings · Langstreifeneinödverband m

bundle of long strip lots within a pattern of fragmented holdings · Langstreifengemengeverband m

bundle of lots, lot bundle · Parzellenverband m

bundle of narrow strip lots within a pattern of consolidated holdings · Schmalstreifeneinödverband m

bundle of narrow strip lots within a pattern of fragmented holdings · Schmalstreifengemengeverband m

bundle of short strip lots within a pattern of consolidated holdings · Kurzstreifeneinödverband m

bundle of short strip lots within a pattern of fragmented holdings · Kurzstreifengemengeverband m

bundle of strip lots, strip lot bundle · Streifen(parzellen)verband m

bundle of wide strip lots within a pattern of consolidated holdings · Breitstreifeneinödverband m

bundle of wide strip lots within a pattern of fragmented holdings · Breitstreifengemengeverband m

to burden, to incumber, to load, to encumber, to charge · belasten, dinglich belasten

burden, incumbrance; incumbramentum [*Latin*]; charge, encumbrance, load [*A claim or lien attached to property as a mortgage*] · (dingliche) Belastung f, (dingliche) Last f

burdenable [*obsolete*]; capable of bearing a burden, chargeable · belastbar

burdened, charged, imperfect, encumbered, incumbered, loaded · belastet, dinglich belastet

burdened by law, encumbered by law, incumbered by law, charged by law, loaded by law · gesetzlich belastet

burdened by mortgage(s), charged by mortgage(s), encumbered by mortgage(s), incumbered by mortgage(s), loaded by mortgage(s) · hypothek(en)belastet

burdened with lease(hold), encumbered with lease(hold), incumbered with lease(hold), loaded with lease(hold), charged with lease(hold) · erbbaurechtbelastet, platzrechtbelastet

burdening, incumbering, encumbering, loading, charging · (dingliches) Belasten n

burdenless, unburdened, uncharged, not imperfect, unencumbered, unloaded, unincumbered, without a burden, without a load · (dinglich) unbelastet, (dinglich) nicht belastet

burden of easement, charge of easement, encumbrance of easement, incumbrance of easement, load of easement · Grunddienstbarkeitslast f

burden of national debt, encumbrance of national debt, incumbrance of national debt, load of national debt · Staatsschuldenlast f

burden of proof, onus of proof, burden of evidence, onus of evidence, burden of proving, onus of proving; onus probandi [*Latin*] · Beweislast f

burden of the poor rates, encumbrance of the poor rates, incumbrance of the poor rates, charge of the poor rates, load of the poor rates · Armenlast f

burden on capital, charge on capital, encumbrance on capital, incumbrance on capital, capital charge, capital burden, capital encumbrance, capital incumbrance · Kapitaldienst m, Kapitallast f

burden on personal property, charge on personal property, encumbrance on personal property, incumbrance on personal property, load (up)on personal property · Fahrnislast f, Fahrhabelast, Mobiliarlast, Mobilienlast

burden prohibition, charge prohibition, load prohibition, encumbrance prohibition, incumbrance prohibition · Belastungsverbot n, Lastenverbot

burden rate, encumbrance rate, incumbrance rate, charge rate, load rate · Belastungssatz m

burdensome proprietorship, burdensome (general) property, burdensome ownership (of property) [*Under bankruptcy laws the trustee is not required to take title of property that is unprofitable or subject to excessive liens and may obtain release from this property upon action by the court*] · lästiges Eigentum n

bureaucratic rule · bürokratische Herrschaft f

Bureau of Litigation [*USA*] · Rechtsverfolgungsabteilung f

Bureau of the Census [*USA*] · statistisches Bundesamt n

burgage-holder, burgage-tenant · Bürgerleh(e)n(s)inhaber m, Stadtleh(e)n(s)inhaber

burgage-house [*A house held by burgage (tenure)*] · Bürgerleh(e)n(s)haus n, Stadtleh(e)n(s)haus

burgage-land · Bürgerleh(e)n(s)land n, Stadt(leh(e)n(s)land

burgagium — business document

burgagium, feudum burgense, feudum urbanum, feodum burgense, feodum urbanum [*Latin*]; tenure of burgage, burgage (tenure), burgage tenancy, burgage-holding, tenure in burgage, tenancy in burgage, tenancy of burgage, burgage tenement, tenement in burgage [*A tenure whereby lands or houses in cities and towns were held of the king or queen or other lord, for a certain yearly rent*] · Bürgerleh(e)n *n*, Stadtleh(e)n, städtischer Freibesitz *m* (an Häusern und Land)

burg and land [*Scotland*]; town and country, city and country · Stadt *f* und Land *n*

burgeoning industry · (auf)blühende Industrie *f*

burgess, freeman of a borough, townman; cityman [*obsolete*]; urban resident, town resident, city resident, urban inhabitant, town inhabitant, city inhabitant, urban dweller, town dweller, city dweller, urbanite, citizen · Stadtbewohner *m*, Stadteinwohner, Städter, Stadtbürger

burgess [*In England. One selected to represent his fellow-citizens in parliament*] · städtischer Parlamentsabgeordneter *m*, Stadtparlamentsabgeordnete, Parlamentsabgeordnete einer Stadt

burgess [*A member of the governing body of a town. Used as an official title (with varying signification) in certain English boroughs before the Municipal Reform Act of 1835; magistrate*] · Magistratsperson *f*

burgh, borough [*Scotland*] [*A town possessing a municipal corporation and special privileges conferred by royal charter*] · kreisfreie Stadt *f*

burg(h)bote [*In old English law. A tribute or contribution towards the repairing of castles, walls of defence, boroughs, or cities*] · Burgzubuße *f*, Steuer *f* zur Erhaltung befestigter Plätze

burg(h) English → borow English

burgh of barony [*In Scotland. The charter is derived from a baron*] · Stadt *f* mit Freiherrnstadtrecht

burgh school · städtische Schule *f* [*Schottland*]

burglar; burglator [*Latin*]; nocturnal (house)breaker · Einbrecher *m* in der Nacht, Einbrecher zur Nacht, Nachteinbrecher

burglary, nocturnal (house)breaking · Einbrechen *n* zur Nachtzeit, Einbruch *m* zur Nachtzeit, Einbruch in der Nacht, Nachteinbruch, Einbrechen in der Nacht

burglary insurance, nocturnal (house)-breaking insurance · Nachteinbruchversicherung *f*

Burgundian law; lex burgundiorum [*Latin*] [*The law of the Burgundians, first compiled and published by Gundebald, one of the last of their kings, about A.D. 500*] · Burgundisches Recht *n*

burial board, cemetery board · Friedhofsamt *n*

burial-ground → burial-yard

burial-place, burying-place · Begräbnisstätte *f*, Begräbnisstelle *f*, Grabstätte, Grabstelle

burial rate · (örtliche) Begräbnissteuer *f*, (örtliche) Beerdigungssteuer, kommunale Begräbnissteuer, kommunale Beerdigungssteuer, gemeindliche Begräbnissteuer, gemeindliche Beerdigungssteuer, lokale Begräbnissteuer, lokale Beerdigungssteuer

burial society [*An insurance society for providing money for the expenses of burial*] · Sterbekasse *f*

burial-yard, grave-yard, cemetery, burying ground, burial-ground · Friedhof *m*

burned down · abgebrannt, niedergebrannt

burning to ashes, incinerating, cremation [*The act of reducing a corpse by means of fire*] · Einäschern *n*

business [*This term has no definite or legal meaning; it may be an uncertain one*] · Geschäft *n*

business administration · Betriebsverwaltung *f*

business area, business territory · Geschäftsgebiet *n*

business building · Geschäftsgebäude *n*, Geschäftshaus *n*

business capacity, business capability · Geschäftstüchtigkeit *f*

business client · Geschäftsmandant *m*

business cluster · Geschäftsanhäufung *f*

business concern · Geschäftsbelang *m*

business condition · Geschäftsbedingung *f*

business core, central business district, CBD · Geschäftszentrum *n*, funktioneller Stadtkern *m*, Hauptgeschäftsbezirk *m*

business corporation [*USA*] · gewinnorientierte (Kapital)Gesellschaft *f*, gewinnbezogene (Kapital)Gesellschaft

business decline · Konjunkturrückgang *m*

business development, development of business · Geschäftsentwick(e)lung *f*

business district · Geschäftsbezirk *m*, Geschäftsgegend *f*

business document · Geschäftsurkunde *f*

business economics · Betriebswirtschaft *f*

business exodus, exodus of business firms · Geschäftsflucht *f*

(business) failure [*Condition when a business has terminated with a loss to creditors*] · (Geschäfts)Pleite *f*

business game, management game, managing game, managerial game · Unternehmungs(plan)spiel *n*

business hour · Geschäftsstunde *f*

business income · Geschäftseinkommen *n*

business insurance · Geschäftsversicherung *f*

business interest, share in a business, interest in a business, business share · Geschäftsanteil *m*

business journey, business trip, business travel · Geschäftsreise *f*

business law, law merchant; lex mercatoria [*Latin*]; merchant law, mercantile law, commercial law · Handelsrecht *n*

business loss · Geschäftsverlust *m*

business mistake · Geschäftsirrtum *m*

business name · Geschäftsname *m*

business of banking, banking business · Bankgeschäft *n*

business of grazing, grazing business, grass farming, pastoral economy · Graswirtschaft *f*, (Vieh)Weidewirtschaft

business of issue, issue business · Emissionsgeschäft *n*

business of lending against collateral, deposit and loan business, advances · Lombardgeschäft *n*

business organization, business unit · Unternehmensform *f*, Rechtsform eines Unternehmens

business place, place of business · Geschäftsort *m*

(business) premises [*They form part of a building*] · Geschäftsräume *mpl*

(business) premises · Geschäftsanwesen *n*

business quarter · Geschäftsquartier *n*, Geschäftsviertel *n*

business report · Geschäftsbericht *m*

business risk · Geschäftsrisiko *n*, Geschäftswagnis *n*

business room · Geschäftsraum *m*, Geschäftslokal *n*

business sale · kaufmännisches Geschäft *n*

business secret · Geschäftsgeheimnis *n*

business share, business interest, share in a business, interest in a business · Geschäftsanteil *m*

business street · Geschäftsstraße *f*

business structure, structure of business · Geschäftsaufbau *m*, Geschäftsgefüge *n*, Geschäftsstruktur *f*, Geschäftszusammensetzung *f*

business territory, business area · Geschäftsgebiet *n*

business travel, business journey, business trip · Geschäftsreise *f*

business trust, common law trust, Massachusetts trust [*A business organization wherein property is conveyed to trustees and managed for benefit of holders of certificates like corporate stock certificates*] · treuhänderisch geleitetes Unternehmen *n*, treuhänderisch geleitete Unternehmung *f*

business unit, business organization · Unternehmensform *f*, Rechtsform eines Unternehmens

business visitor · geschäftlicher Besucher *m*, Geschäftsbesucher

business year · Geschäftsjahr *n*

bus service · (Auto)Busbetrieb *m*, Omnibusbetrieb

butt; head-rig [*Scotch*]; pen tir [*Welsh*]; forera, terra capitalis, caput terrae, caputium, chevitia, forlandum, versura [*Latin*]; headland, foreland, forebalk, foreherda [*The slip of unploughed land left at the head or end of a ploughed field on which the plough is turned*] · Anwende *f*, Voracker *m*, Vorwart *f*, Anwänder *m*

butt(al), bout, end, head, front · Ende *n*, Grundstücksende

to buy back, to repurchase · zurückkaufen

buy back agreement, repurchase agreement · Rückkaufabkommen *n*, Rückkaufabmachung *f*, Rückkaufvereinbarung

buy back value, repurchase value · Rückkaufwert *m*

buyer, purchaser, vendee · Käufer *m*

buyer for value, purchaser for value · entgeltlicher Käufer *m*

buyer of (real) estate, buyer of (real) property, vendee of (real) estate, vendee of (real) property, purchaser of realty, vendee of realty, buyer of realty, land buyer, land purchaser, purchaser of (real) estate, purchaser of (real) property · Grund(stücks)käufer *m*, Bodenkäufer, Liegenschaftskäufer, Landkäufer, Immobilienkäufer, Immobiliarkäufer

buyers' guide, trade directory · Bezugsquellennachweis *m*

buyer's market, purchaser's market, vendee's market · Käufermarkt *m*

buying ability, purchasing power, buying power, purchasing ability · Kaufkraft *f*

buying back, repurchasing · Rückkaufen *n*

buying behaviour (Brit.); purchasing behavior, buying behavior (US); purchasing behaviour · Kaufverhalten *n*

buying habit, purchasing habit · Kaufgewohnheit *f*

buying of landed estate on time bargains, purchasing of landed estate on time bargains · Protokollhandel *m*

buying policy, purchasing policy · Kaufpolitik *f*

buying power, purchasing ability, buying ability, purchasing power · Kaufkraft *f*

buying power flow, buying power stream, purchasing power stream, purchasing power flow · Kaufkraftstrom *m*

buying trap, purchasing trap · Kauffalle *f*

to buy off, to portion out, to portion off · auszahlen [*Erb(schafts)anteil*]

by-bidder, by-tenderer, mock bidder, mock tenderer [*One employed by the seller or his agent to bid on property with no purpose to become a purchaser, so that bidding thereon may be stimulated in others who are bidding in good faith*] · Scheinbieter *m*

by-bidding, by-tendering, mock bidding, mock tendering · Scheinbieten *n*

by chance, fortuitous, unforeseen, occasional, accidental · unvorhergesehen

by construction of law · aus objektivem Recht gefolgert

by custom, common, customary · gewohnheitsrechtlich

bydel [*Anglo-Saxon*] → beadle

by description · nach Angabe

by devise · im Wege der testamentarischen Erbfolge

bye-election · Nachwahl *f*

by(e)-law, statute · Satzung *f*, Statut *n*, autonomes Recht *n* einer Körperschaft, Rechtsnorm *f* einer Körperschaft mit Personenmehrheit [*Im internen materiellen Recht*]

by(e)-law → communal by(e)-law

by gift · durch Schenkung

by implication, implied, tacit · stillschweigend

by inadvertence, by oversight, inadvertently, from inadvertence, from oversight · versehentlich

by inheritance · im Wege der Intestaterbfolge

by law, for law, in law, according to law, at law · nach dem Gesetz, dem Gesetz nach

by lawful means · auf recht(mäßig)em Wege

by oversight, inadvertently, from inadvertence, from oversight, by inadvertence, by inadvertency · versehentlich

by-pass road, by-pass highway · Umgehungsstraße *f*

by return of post · postwendend

by sufferance, at sufferance · geduldet [*Besitz(stand)*]

by-tenderer, mock bidder, mock tenderer, by-bidder [*One employed by the seller or his agent to bid on property with no purpose to become a purchaser, so that bidding thereon may be stimulated in others who are bidding in good faith*] · Scheinbieter *m*

by-tendering, by-bidding, mock bidding, mock tendering · Scheinbieten *n*

by the court; per curiam, per cur. [*Latin*] · durch das Gericht

by (virtue of) · kraft

by (virtue of) operation of law, by (virtue of) strength of law, by (virtue of) force of law · kraft Rechtssatz(es), kraft Rechtsvorschrift, kraft Gesetzes, von Rechts wegen, von Gesetzes wegen

by virtue of the office; ex officio [*Latin*]; in the regular course · von Amts wegen

by way of conditional proposition, conditionally, by way of hypothesis · hypothetischerweise

by way of lease, by way of tenancy, by way of demise, on demise, on lease, on tenancy · pachtweise

by will, testamentary · testamentarisch, durch Testament

by word of mouth, verbal, oral, parol [*In early times few persons could write, and therefore when a document was required to record a transaction the parties put their seals to it and made it a deed. Transactions of less importance were testified by word of mouth or by parol, and this use of "parol", to signify the absence of a deed, remained after simple writing without sealing had come into use*] · mündlich

C

C.A., court of (error and) appeal, court of review (of errors and appeal), appellate court, appeals court · Appellationsgericht *n* für Zivilsachen, Berufungsgericht *n* für Zivilsachen

cable clause · Kabelklausel *f*

cable damage · Kabelschaden *m*

cable transfer, C.T. · telegraphische Auszahlung *f*

cablish, windfall(-wood), wind-fallen wood · Windbruchholz *n*, Windfallholz

cabotage, coastwise navigation, coasting, coast(al) navigation · Küstenschiffahrt *f*

cad, cash against documents · Kasse *f* gegen Dokumente, Barzahlung *f* gegen Dokumente

cadaster → cadastre

cadastral act, cadastral statute, cadastral law · Katastergesetz *n*

cadastral authority · Katasterbehörde *f*

cadastral board · Katasteramt *n*

cadastral book · Flurbuch *n*

cadastral code · Katasterordnung *f*

cadastral district · Gemarkung *f*, Katasterbezirk *m* [*frühere Benennungen: Feldmark f, Steuergemeinde f, Katastergemeinde, Vermessungsbezirk*]

cadastral fee, cadastral charge · Katastergebühr *f*

cadastral field sheet · Katasterriß *m*

cadastral hand drawing · Katasterhandzeichnung *f*

cadastral law · Katasterrecht *n*

cadastral law → cadastral act

cadastral practice · Katasterwesen *n* [*Es dient der Beschaffung von Grundlagen für eine gerechte Bodenbesteuerung*]

cadastral resurvey(ing), recadastration · Katasternachvermessung *f*, Katasternachaufnahme *f*

cadastral survey(ing), cadastration [*a. Strictly, a survey of land(s) for the purposes of a cadastre; b. Loosely, a survey on a scale sufficiently large to show accurately the extent and measurements of every field and other plot of land*] · Katastervermessung *f*, Katasteraufnahme *f*

cadastre, cadaster; capitastrum [*Latin*] · Kataster *n*, Bodenregister *n* [*Ein Grundstücksverzeichnis zum Zwecke der Besteuerung. Es besteht aus Gemarkungskarten und Liegenschaftsbüchern*]

calculability · Berechenbarkeit *f*, Kalkulierbarkeit

calculable, computable · berechenbar, kalkulierbar

calculable interest, imputed interest, calculatory interest · kalkulatorische Zinsen *f*

to calculate, to compute · berechnen, kalkulieren

to calculate cost(s), to cost · kalkulieren von Kosten

calculated in value(s), computed in value(s) · wertmäßig

calculated risk, calculated hazard · bewußtes Risiko *n*, bewußtes Wagnis *n*

calculation, computation · Berechnung *f*, Kalkulation *f*

calculation balance, computation balance · Berechnungsausgleich *m*, Kalkulationsausgleich

calculation documents, computation documents · Berechnungsunterlagen *fpl*, Kalkulationsunterlagen

calculation error, computation error · Berechnungsfehler *m*, Kalkulationsfehler

calculation mistake, computation mistake · Berechnungsirrtum *m*, Kalkulationsirrtum

calculation of a parcel fragment, calculation of a plot fragment, computation of a plot fragment · Abschnittsberechnung *f*, Klassenabschnittsberechnung

calculation of burden(s), calculation of encumbrance(s), calculation of incumbrance(s), computation of burden(s), computation of encumbrance(s), computation of incumbrance(s), calculation of charge(s), computation of charge(s) · Belastungsberechnung *f*, Lastenberechnung, Belastungskalkulation *f*, Lastenkalkulation, Belastungsermitt(e)lung, Lastenermitt(e)lung

calculation of cost(s), computation of cost(s), cost(s) calculation, cost(s) computation, costing, (cost(s)) accounting · Kostenrechnung *f*, Kostenkalkulation *f*, (Kostenbe)Rechnung, Kostenermitt(e)lung

calculation of damage, computation of damage, damage calculation, damage computation · Schadensberechnung *f*, Schadenskalkulation *f*

calculation of fee(s) — call loan

calculation of fee(s), computation of fee(s), fee calculation, fee computation · Gebührenberechnung *f*, Honorarberechnung

calculation of (fixed) period (of time), computation of (fixed) period (of time), calculation of time (allowed), computation of time (allowed), calculation of period, computation of period, calculation of term, computation of term · Fristberechnung *f*

calculation of lot widths, computation of lot widths · Breitenberechnung *f*, Breitenkalkulation *f*

calculation of (residential) rent prices · (Wohnungs)Miet(preis)bildung *f*, (Wohnungs)Miet(preis)berechnung

calculation ordinance, computation ordinance · Berechnungsverordnung *f*, Kalkulationsverordnung

calculation period, computation period · Berechnungszeitraum *m*, Kalkulationszeitraum

calculation rate, computation rate · Berechnungssatz *m*, Kalkulationssatz

calculation risk, computation risk · Berechnungsrisiko *n*, Berechnungswagnis *n*, Kalkulationswagnis, Kalkulationsrisiko

calculation sheet, bidding sheet, tendering sheet, estimating sheet · Angebotsbogen *m*, Kalkulationsbogen

calculator, computer, reckoner, estimator [*A person who calculates*] · Kalkulator *m*

calculatory interest, calculable interest, imputed interest · kalkulatorische Zinsen *f*

calendar month, solar month · Kalendermonat *m*

call [*An option to buy (or call) a share of stock at a specified price within a specified period*] · Aktieneinzahlung *f*, Einzahlung (auf Aktien)

call [*The process of redeeming a bond or preferred stock issue before its normal maturity*] · Einlösung *f*

call · Abruf *m* [*Geld; gekaufte Ware*]

call · Zubuße *f*

call [*In conveyancing. A visible natural object or landmark designated in a patent, entry, grant, or other conveyance of land(s), as a limit or boundary to the land described, with which the points of surveying must correspond. Also the courses and distances designated*] · natürliches Grenzzeichen *n*

call, demand · Nachfrage *f*

call, option · Bezugsoption *f*, Empfangsoption, Prämiengeschäft *n* auf Nehmen [*Börse*]

call · Vorprämie *f* [*Wertpapierhandel in den USA*]

call · Einforderung *f* [*Konkurs*]

callable debenture, redeemable debenture [*Great Britain*]; redeemable corporate bond, callable corporate bond [*USA*] · (vorzeitig) kündbare Schuldverschreibung *f*, (vorzeitig) kündbare Obligation *f*, Obligation mit Tilgungsverpflichtung, Schuldverschreibung mit Tilgungsverpflichtung [*private Kapitalgesellschaft*]

call and supply, supply and demand, supply and call, market forces, demand and supply · Angebot *n* und Nachfrage *f*, Nachfrage und Angebot

to call back; to revocate [*obsolete*]; to revoke, to recall · widerrufen, rückgängig machen

call-back · Ansprechwiederholung *f* [*Statistik*]

call control, demand control · Nachfragelenkung *f*

call curve, demand curve · Nachfragekurve *f*

call deposit · Spareinlage *f* mit gesetzlicher Kündigungsfrist

called, cited, summoned · (vor)geladen, aufgeboten [*vor Gericht*]

call fluctuation, fluctuation of call, fluctuation of demand, demand fluctuation · Nachfrageschwankung *f*

call for bid; request for (bid) proposal, call for (bid) proposal (US); tendering invitation, invitation to tender, invitation to bid, bidding invitation, invitation to (submit a) bid, request for tender, request for offer, request for bid, call for tender, call for offer · (Angebots)Aufforderung *f*, Aufforderung zur Angebotsabgabe

call for (building) (land) area, call for (building) land, demand for (building) land, demand for (building) (land) area · (Bau)Bodennachfrage *f*, (Bau)Landnachfrage, (Bau)Flächennachfrage

call for housing, housing demand, housing call, demand for housing · Wohnungsnachfrage *f*

call function, demand function · Nachfragefunktion *f*

to call in · kündigen [*Hypothek*]

calling in a lawyer · Zuziehung *f* eines (Rechts)Anwalts

calling to meeting · Einberufung *f* [*Versammlung*]

call level, level of demand, level of call, demand level · Nachfragestand *m*

call loan [*A loan terminable at will by either party. The term is confined mostly to loans made by banks to*

call money — canon law

stockbrokers] · Darleh(e)n n jederzeit rückzahlbar, jederzeit rückzahlbares Darleh(e)n

call money, demand money, money at call and short notice · tägliches Geld n, Tagesgeld, sofort abrufbares Geld

call price, demand price · Nachfragepreis m

to call to account, to make responsible, to hold accountable · verantwortlich machen, rechenschaftspflichtig machen

call to the bar, admission to the bar · Zulassung f zur (Rechts)Anwaltschaft

calumnia [Latin]; calumny · wissentliches Unrecht n, subjektives Unrecht

cambia sicca [Latin] · trockener Wechsel m

cameralistics [Relating to the management of the state property in Germany] · Kameralistik f

camera stellata [Latin]; star chamber [The court called by this name is commonly regarded as being the Aula Regis, sitting in the star chamber, a room at Westminster] · Sternkammer f [in England]

camping site, caravan site, camping ground, caravan ground · Campingplatz m, Wohnwagenplatz

camp of refuge, refuge camp · Fluchtburg f

campus, university quarter · Universitätsviertel n

campus maii [Latin]; field of May · Maifeld n

campus martii [Latin]; field of March · Märzfeld n

canon of construction, canon of interpretation, rule of interpretation, rule of construction [Canons of construction are the system of fundamental rules and maxims which are recognized as governing the construction or interpretation of written instruments] · Auslegungsregel f, Deutungsregel f

to cancel, to abrogate, to abolish (by authority), to do away with, to abate, to deprive of operation, to rescind, to nullify, to annul, to repeal, to overrule · abschaffen, aufheben, rückgängig machen, annullieren, außer Kraft setzen, löschen, abbauen

to cancel, to rule through · löschen [im Grundbuch]

to cancel [debt(s)] · erlassen [Schuld(en)]

to cancel, to rule through, to strike out · ausstreichen, durchstreichen

to cancel [contract] · auflösen [Vertrag]

to cancel [certificate] · entziehen [Zeugnis]

cancel and endorse plan · Tilgungs- und Indossamentplan m [Bausparkasse]

cancellation, ruling through, cancelling · (Amts)Löschung f [im Grundbuch]

cancellation [debt(s)] · Erlassen n [Schuld(en)]

cancellation, abolition, abatement, abolishment (by authority), annulment, nullification, rescission, avoidance, repeal, abrogation · Annullierung f, Rückgängigmachung, Aufhebung, Abschaffung, Abbau m, Löschung

cancelled, invalidated, annulled, made void, avoided · ungültig gemacht, für ungültig erklärt

cancelled, abrogated, abated, annulled, nullified, abolished (by authority), rescinded, overruled, done away with, deprived of operation, repealed · aufgehoben, annulliert, rückgängig gemacht, außer Kraft gesetzt, abgeschafft, gelöscht, abgebaut

cancelling, cancellation, ruling through · (Amts)Löschung f [im Grundbuch]

cancelling, striking out, ruling through · Durchstreichen n, Ausstreichen

cancelling, overruling, abating, rendering null and void, doing away with, nullifying, rescinding, making void, annulling, (a)voiding, repealing, abolishing, abrogating · Aufheben n, Rückgängigmachen n, Annullieren n, Abschaffen n, Löschen n, Abbauen n

cancelling declaration, ruling through declaration · Löschungsbewilligung f [Erklärung eines Berechtigten zur Löschung eines in einem Grundbuch eingetragenen Rechts]

cannibalizing of goods · Ausschlachtung f von Gütern, Güterauschlachtung

canoeing map · Kanu(ten)karte f

canon · Domherr m, Kanonikus, Kanoniker, Chorherr

canon · Erbpacht(gut)abgabe f

canon, rule, regulator · Regel f, Regulativ n

canoness [A woman holding a canonry] · Kanonissin f

canonist, canon lawyer; canonistre, canoneer [obsolete] · Kanonist m

canonistic(al) doctrine · kanonische Lehre f

canonizing, canonization · Kanonisierung f, Kanonisation f, Kanonisieren n

canon law, the canons, canonry; jus canonicum [Latin] [Formerly: law canon. It is laid down in decrees of the pope *and statutes of councils. Not to be confused with "jus ecclesiasticum'*]; canons collectively · kanonisches Recht *n,* geistliches Recht

canon lawyer → canonist

canon of ethics, ethical rules, disciplinary rules (US); etiquette (Brit) [*The forms established by convention or prescribed by social arbiters for behavio(u)r in polite society*] · Standesrecht *n*

canon of formation, canon of drafting, canon of construing, canon of phrasing, canon of wording, canon of construction, canon of drawing up, canon of setting up, rule of formation, rule of construing, rule of drafting, rule of phrasing, rule of wording, rule of construction, rule of drawing up, rule of setting up [*Canon of arranging or marshalling words*] · Entwurfsregel *f,* Gestaltungsregel, Abfassungsregel, Ausarbeitungsregel

canon of interpretation, rule of interpretation, rule of construction, canon of construction [*Canons of construction are the system of fundamental rules and maxims which are recognized as governing the construction or interpretation of written instruments*] · Auslegungsregel *f,* Deutungsregel *f*

canonry; jus canonicum [*Latin*] [*Formerly: law canon. It is laid down in decrees of the pope and statutes of councils. Not to be confused with "jus ecclesiasticum'*]; canons collectively, canon law, the canons · kanonisches Recht *n,* geistliches Recht

canonry, benefice of a canon · kanonische Pfründe *f*

canonry [*The status, dignity or office of a canon*] · Kanonikat *n* [*Stelle, Würde oder Amt eines Kanonikers*]

canons collectively, canon law, the canons, canonry; jus canonicum [*Latin*] [*Formerly: law canon. It is laid down in decrees of the pope and statutes of councils. Not to be confused with "jus ecclesiasticum'*] · kanonisches Recht *n,* geistliches Recht

canons of inheritance, canons of descent, rules of inheritance, rules of descent [*The legal rules by which inheritances are regulated, and according to which estates are transmitted by descent from the ancestor to the heir*] · Erbordnung *f,* Erbschaftsordnung, Regeln *f pl* der Abstammungserbfolge

cantonal council · Landrat *m* [*Schweiz*]

canvasser [*One who canvasses electors for votes*] · Wahlwerber *m*

canvasser [*A salesman who calls upon his customers with samples and takes orders. He is usually paid a commission on sales*] · (Handels)Vertreter *m*

capability, capacity, ability, qualification · (Leistungs)Fähigkeit *f,* (Leistungs)Vermögen *n*

capability constraint · Reichweitenbegrenzung *f* [*Nach Hägerstrand, physiologische und technische Reichweitenbegrenzung. Hägerstrands Leitidee ist es, die Umwelt sowie die Handlungsspielräume der Individuen von ihren restriktiven Determinanten, von ihren räumlich-zeitlichen Begrenzungen her zu erfassen*]

capability for being cultivated, qualification for being cultivated, ability for being cultivated, capacity for being cultivated · Anbaufähigkeit *f,* Anbaubarkeit, Anbaueignung *f,* Kultivierbarkeit

capability for performing legal acts, capacity for performing legal acts, ability for performing legal acts, qualification for performing legal acts · Handlungsfähigkeit *f,* Handlungseignung *f*

capability of being checked, capability of being controlled, capability of being re-examined, capacity of being checked, capacity of being re-examined, capacity of being checked, qualification of being re-examined, qualification of being checked, qualification of being controlled, ability of being controlled, ability of being re-examined, ability of being checked · Nachprüfbarkeit, Kontrollierbarkeit *f*

capability of being examined, capacity of being examined, examinable capability, examinable capacity · Prüfbarkeit *f*

capability of being substituted → capacity of being substituted

capability of earning a living, ability of earning a living, capacity of earning a living · Erwerbsfähigkeit *f,* Erwerbsvermögen *n*

capability of having interests → capacity of having rigths

capability of having rights → capacity of having rights

capability of the testator → testamentary capacity

capability to be a party, qualification to be a party, ability to be a party, capacity to be a party · Parteifähigkeit *f*

capability to buy, capability to purchase, qualification to purchase, qualification to buy, ability to buy, ability to purchase, capacity to buy, capacity to purchase · Kauffähigkeit *f,* Kaufeignung *f*

capability to commit crime, qualification to commit crime, ability to commit crime, capacity to commit crime · (kriminelle) Schuldfähigkeit *f,* (kriminelle) Schuldeignung *f*

capability to deal with land, ability to deal with land, capacity to deal with land,

capability to earn profits — capable to make a will

qualification to deal with land · Bodenverkehrsfähigkeit f, Bodenverkehrseignung f, Grundstücksverkehrsfähigkeit, Grundstücksverkehrseignung, Immobiliarverkehrsfähigkeit, Immobiliarverkehrseignung, Immobilienverkehrsfähigkeit, Immobilienverkehrseignung, Liegenschaftsverkehrsfähigkeit, Liegenschaftsverkehrseignung

capability to earn profits, qualification to earn profits, ability to earn profits, capacity to earn profits · Gewinneignung f, Gewinnfähigkeit f, Profiteignung, Profitfähigkeit

capability to finance, qualification to finance, capacity to finance, financing ability, financing capacity, financing qualification, financing capability, ability to finance · Finanzierungseignung f, Finanzierungsfähigkeit f

capability to inherit, ability to inherit, capacity to inherit, qualification to inherit · (aktive) Erbfähigkeit f, (aktive) Erbeignung f

capability to make payments → capacity to pay

capability to pay, capacity to make payments, ability to make payments, capability to make payments, solvency, soundness, trustworthiness, capacity to pay, ability to pay · Zahlungsfähigkeit f, Zahlungsvermögen n, Bonität f, Kreditfähigkeit, Kreditwürdigkeit

capability to purchase, capability to buy, capacity to purchase, ability to purchase, qualification to purchase · Kaufeignung f, Kauffähigkeit

capability to sue, qualification to sue, standing to sue, active legitimation, capacity to sue · Aktivlegitimation f [Zur gerichtlichen Geltendmachung von Ansprüchen]

capable, qualified, able · (leistungs)fähig

capable of bearing a burden, chargeable; burdenable [obsolete] · belastbar

capable of being bequeathed, bequeathable · (testamentarisch) vermachbar, letztwillig verfügbar, letztwillig vermachbar, testamentarisch verfügbar [Fahrnis]

capable of being checked, capable of being controlled, capable of being re-examined, able of being checked, able of being controlled, able of being re-examined, qualified of being checked, qualified of being controlled, qualified of being re-examined · kontrollierbar, nachprüfbar

capable of being ploughed (Brit.); capable of being plowed (US); arable, fit for tillage · pflügbar, beackerbar

capable of being recorded → capable of registration

capable of being revoked, capable of revocation, able of being revoked, able of revocation, qualified of being revoked, qualified of revocation, during pleasure, revocable, at will, revokable, ambulatory · auf Widerruf, widerruflich, widerrufbar, einvernehmlich geduldet

capable of being tested, able of being tested, qualified of being tested · prüfungsfähig, prüfungsreif, prüfungsgeeignet

capable of being turned over → attornable

capable of breaking down, capable to fail, collapsible, collapsable, capable of collapsing · einsturzgefährlich, einfallgefährlich [Bauwerk]

capable of comparison (with), comparable, comparative, able to be compared · vergleichbar

capable of contracting, able of contracting, qualified of contracting, capable to contract, able to contract, qualified to contract, competent to contract · vertragsfähig, vertragsgeeignet

capable of earning, able to earn, capable to earn, qualified to earn, able of earning, qualified of earning · erwerbsgeeignet, erwerbsfähig

capable of registration, capable of recordation, capable of recording, registrable, recordable, capable of being recorded, capable of being registered · eintragungsfähig, registrierfähig, buchungsfähig, registrierbar, eintragungsreif, buchungsreif, registrierreif

capable of repair, repairable · reparierbar

capable of revocation, able of being revoked, able of revocation, qualified of being revoked, qualified of revocation, during pleasure, revocable, at will, revokable, ambulatory, capable of being revoked · auf Widerruf, widerruflich, widerrufbar, einvernehmlich geduldet

capable to buy, capable to purchase, qualified to buy, qualified to purchase, able to buy, able to purchase · kauffähig, kaufgeeignet

capable to contract, able to contract, qualified to contract, competent to contract, capable of contracting, able of contracting, qualified of contracting · vertragsfähig, vertragsgeeignet

capable to earn, qualified to earn, able of earning, qualified of earning, capable of earning, able to earn · erwerbsgeeignet, erwerbsfähig

capable to fail, collapsible, collapsable, capable of collapsing, capable of breaking down · einsturzgefährlich, einfallgefährlich [Bauwerk]

capable to make a will, qualified to make a will, able of making a will, qualified of

capable to pay — capias utlagatium

making a will, capable of making a will, able to make a will · testierfähig, testiergeeignet, testamentsfähig, testamentsgeeignet

capable to pay, able to pay, trust(worth)y, solvent, financially able, sound · zahlungsfähig, flüssig, kreditfähig, kreditwürdig

capable to purchase, qualified to buy, qualified to purchase, able to buy, able to purchase, capable to buy · kauffähig, kaufgeeignet

capacity, ability, qualification, capability · (Leistungs)Fähigkeit *f*, (Leistungs)Vermögen *n*

capacity effect of investments · Kapazitätswirkung *f* von Investitionen

capacity for being built on along a public road, capacity for being built on along a public highway · Anbaufähigkeit *f*, Anbaubarkeit [*Eines unmittelbar an eine öffentliche Straße grenzenden Grundstückes*]

capacity for being cultivated, capability for being cultivated, qualification for being cultivated, ability for being cultivated · Anbaufähigkeit *f*, Anbaubarkeit, Anbaueignung *f*, Kultivierbarkeit

capacity for performing legal acts, ability for performing legal acts, qualification for performing legal acts, capability for performing legal acts · Handlungsfähigkeit *f*, Handlungseignung *f*

capacity load · Auslastung *f*

capacity of being checked, capacity of being re-examined, capacity of being controlled, qualification of being re-examined, qualification of being checked, qualification of being controlled, ability of being controlled, ability of being checked, capability of being checked, capability of being controlled, capability of being re-examined · Nachprüfbarkeit, Kontrollierbarkeit

capacity of earning a living, capability of earning a living, ability of earning a living · Erwerbsfähigkeit *f*, Erwerbsvermögen *n*

capacity of land(s), land(s) capacity · Bodenkapazität *f*, Landkapazität, Flächenkapazität

capacity of the testator, capability of the testator, qualification of the testator, testamentary capacity, disposing capacity, disposing capability, testamentary capability, testamentary qualification, disposing qualification · Testierfähigkeit *f*, Testiereignung *f*, Testamentsfähigkeit, Testamentseignung

capacity planning · Kapazitätsplanung *f*

capacity ratio [*The ratio of actual to maximum possible output*] · Leistungsverhältnis *n*

capacity to be a party, capability to be a party, qualification to be a party, ability to be a party · Parteifähigkeit *f*

capacity to buy, capacity to purchase, capability to buy, capability to purchase, qualification to purchase, qualification to buy, ability to buy, ability to purchase · Kauffähigkeit *f*, Kaufeignung *f*

capacity to commit crime, capability to commit crime, qualification to commit crime, ability to commit crime · (kriminelle) Schuldfähigkeit *f*, (kriminelle) Schuldeignung *f*

capacity to deal with land, qualification to deal with land, capability to deal with land, ability to deal with land · Bodenverkehrsfähigkeit *f*, Bodenverkehrseignung *f*, Grundstücksverkehrsfähigkeit, Grundstücksverkehrseignung, Immobiliarverkehrsfähigkeit, Immobiliarverkehrseignung, Immobilienverkehrsfähigkeit, Immobilienverkehrseignung, Liegenschaftsverkehrsfähigkeit, Liegenschaftsverkehrseignung

capacity to earn profits, capability to earn profits, qualification to earn profits, ability to earn profits · Gewinneignung *f*, Gewinnfähigkeit *f*, Profiteignung, Profitfähigkeit

capacity to finance, financing ability, financing capacity, financing qualification, financing capability, ability to finance, capability to finance, qualification to finance · Finanzierungseignung *f*, Finanzierungsfähigkeit *f*

capacity to inherit, qualification to inherit, capability to inherit, ability to inherit · (aktive) Erbfähigkeit *f*, (aktive) Erbeignung *f*

capacity to make payments → capacity to pay

capacity to pay, ability to pay, capability to pay, capacity to make payments, ability to make payments, capability to make payments, solvency, soundness, trustworthiness · Zahlungsfähigkeit *f*, Zahlungsvermögen *n*, Bonität *f*, Kreditfähigkeit, Kreditwürdigkeit

capacity variance, activity variance, volume variance · Beschäftigungsabweichung *f* (im engeren Sinne) [*Diese Abweichung wird von der Kapazitätsabweichung nicht streng unterschieden*]

capacity variance, activity variance, volume variance · Kapazitätsabweichung *f*, Produktions(volumen)grad *m*, Volumenabweichung bei Kapazitätsplanung, Produktionshöhenabweichung [*Sie stellt die nicht gedeckten Plankosten dar*]

capias → (writ of) capias

capias utlagatium → (writ of) capias utlagatium

capiat vadium [*Latin*]; genime wed · Viehpfändungsakt *m*

capital · Hauptstadt *f*

capital → (authorized) capital stock

capital accumulation, creation of capital, capital creation, capital formation, formation of capital, accumulation of capital · Kapitalschöpfung *f*, Kapitalbildung

(capital) appreciation, increase of value, value increase, (prospective) development value, betterment [*An improvement which adds to the cost(s) of a property. Distinguished from a repair or replacement*] · Wertverbesserung *f*, Wertzuwachs *m*, Wertsteigerung, Wertzunahme *f*, Werterhöhung

(capital) appreciation clause, betterment clause, value increase clause, (prospective) development value clause, increase of value clause · Werterhöhungsklausel *f*, Wertsteigerungsklausel, Wertzuwachsklausel, Wertzunahmeklausel, Wertverbesserungsklausel

capital assets · Kapitalguthaben *n*

capital balance · Bilanzsaldo *m*

capital bonus (Brit.); stock dividend (US) · Aktiendividende *f*, Dividende in Form von jungen Aktien der gleichen Art, Dividende in Aktien statt in bar, Gratisaktie *f*

capital budget [*Municipal accounting. A plan of municipal improvements including the method of financing them*] · Investitionsplan *m*

capital burden, capital encumbrance, capital incumbrance, burden on capital, charge on capital, encumbrance on capital, incumbrance on capital, capital charge · Kapitaldienst *m*, Kapitallast *f*

capital call, capital demand · Kapitalnachfrage *f*

capital charge, capital burden, capital encumbrance, capital incumbrance, burden on capital, charge on capital, encumbrance on capital, incumbrance on capital · Kapitaldienst *m*, Kapitallast *f*

capital compensation for an annuity · Kapitalabfindung *f*

capital composition, capital structure · Kapitalgefüge *n*, Kapitalzusammensetzung *f*, Kapitalstruktur *f*, Kapitalaufbau *m*

capital consisting of stocks and shares · Finanzkapital *n* [*Kapital welches im Wege des Effektenwesens die Organisation des Wirtschaftslebens betreibt*]

capital consolidation, capital merger, capital fusion, fusion of capitals, merger of capitals, consolidation of capitals · Kapitalverschmelzung *f*, Kapitalkonsolidation *f*, Kapitalfusion

capital-contributing partner according to German law · stiller Gesellschafter *m*, stiller Teilhaber [*§§ 335—342 HGB. Er beteiligt sich nur mit einer Einlage (= capital contribution), die in das Vermögen des tätigen Teilhabers oder der tätigen Teilhaber übergeht. Er ist am Gewinn beteiligt, haftet nicht und hat einen schuldrechtlichen Anspruch auf Rückerstattung seiner Einlage*]

capital contribution · Kapitaleinlage *f*

capital creation, capital formation, formation of capital, accumulation of capital, capital accumulation, creation of capital · Kapitalschöpfung *f*, Kapitalbildung

capital demand, capital call · Kapitalnachfrage *f*

capital differential rent · Kapitaldifferentialrente *f*, Intensitätsrente

capital dividend [*A dividend charged to and hence demanded to be paid from paid-in capital*] · Kapitaldividende *f*

capital duty · Kapitalsteuer *f*

capital earning, capital rent, rent earned by capital · Kapitalrente *f*

capital employed · genutztes Kapital *n*

capital encumbrance, capital incumbrance, burden on capital, charge on capital, encumbrance on capital, incumbrance on capital, capital charge, capital burden · Kapitaldienst *m*, Kapitallast *f*

capital estate, income property, capital property [*Property that is expected to produce an income to its owner from rents or leases*] · Kapitalvermögen *n*

capital expansion · Kapitalausbreitung *f*

capital expenditure, capital outlay · Kapitalaufwand *m*, Kapitalverausgabung *f*

capital export · Kapitalausfuhr *f*

capital fee (tenure) → knight's fee (tenure)

capital flight, flight of capital · Kapitalflucht *f*

capital formation, formation of capital, accumulation of capital, capital accumulation, creation of capital, capital creation · Kapitalschöpfung *f*, Kapitalbildung

capital fusion, fusion of capitals, merger of capitals, consolidation of capitals, capital consolidation, capital merger · Kapitalverschmelzung *f*, Kapitalkonsolidation *f*, Kapitalfusion

capital gain, capital profit [*It occurs when stock exchange securities are sold at higher prices than were paid for it*] · Kursgewinn *m*, Kursprofit *m*

capital gain, capital profit · Kapitalgewinn *m*, Kapitalprofit *m*

capital gains tax — capital merger

capital gains tax, capital profits tax · Kursgewinnsteuer *f*, Kursprofitsteuer, Spekulationsgewinnsteuer, Spekulationsprofitsteuer, Steuer auf Spekulationsgewinne, Steuer auf Kursgewinne, Steuer auf Spekulationsprofite, Steuer auf Kursprofite

capital goods, producers' goods, producers' capital [*Capital used to further production. These terms may also refer to the material forms of producers' goods, such as machines, equipment, etc.*, in contact with capital values, the monetary measures of such goods] · Produktionsmittel *n pl*

capital growth · Kapitalwachstum *n*

capital import · Kapitaleinfuhr *f*

capital improvement budget · Investitionsplan *m* zur Entwick(e)lung einer Gemeinde

capital income · Kapitalertrag *m*

capital increase, increase of capital · Aufstockung *f*, Kapitalaufstockung

capital increase against contributions of assets · Kapitalerhöhung *f* mit Sacheinlagen

capital incumbrance, burden on capital, charge on capital, encumbrance on capital, incumbrance on capital, capital charge, capital burden, capital encumbrance · Kapitaldienst *m*, Kapitallast *f*

capital insurance, insurance of capital · Kapitalversicherung *f*

capital intensive · kapitalintensiv

(capital) investment · Anlage *f*, Geldanlage, Kapitalanlage, Investition *f*

(capital) investment surplus · Investitionsüberhang *m*

capital investor, investor (of capital) · Anleger *m*, Geldanleger, Kapitalanleger, Investitionsträger, Anlagesuchende

capitalis justitiarius [*Latin*]; Land Lieutenant [*In the British Empire*] · Statthalter *m*

capitalis plegius [*Latin*] · Zehntschaftsführer *m*

capital issue · Kapitalemission *f*

capital issues committee · Emissions-Genehmigungsausschuß *m*

capitalistic · kapitalistisch

capitalization [*Conversion of investments in property, stock, or other holdings into money or profit or ultimate value*] · Kapitalisierung *f*

capitalization appraisal, capitalized value appraisal, appraisal by capitalization [*Estimate of value by capitalization of productivity and income*] · Ertragswertverfahren *n*, Ertragsberechnung *f*

capitalization interest rate · Kapitalisierungszinsfuß *m*

capitalization of reserves · Kapitalerhöhung *f* aus Gesellschaftsmitteln, Umwandlung von offenen Rücklagen in Grundkapital

capitalization rate, capitalizing rate [*Rate used as factor in determining the value of an asset based on the net annual earning to be produced by the asset*] · Kapitalisierungssatz *m*

capitalization table · Kapitalisierungstabelle *f*

to capitalize · kapitalisieren, aktivieren, umwandeln in Kapital

to capitalize · übernehmen auf Kapitalkonto

capitalized earnings · kapitalisierter Ertrag *m* [*Grundstück*]

capitalized expense(s) · Ausgaben *f pl* auf Kapitalkonto übernommen, kapitalisierte Ausgaben

capitalized surplus · kapitalisierter Überschuß *m*

capitalized value, income value · Ertragswert *m*

capitalized value appraisal, appraisal by capitalization, capitalization appraisal, income value appraisal [*Estimate of value by capitalization of productivity and income*] · Ertragswertverfahren *n*, Ertragsberechnung *f*

capitalized value of a building, income value of a building · Gebäudeertragswert *m*

capitalizing · Kapitalisieren *n*

capitalizing rate, capitalization rate [*Rate used as factor in determining the value of an asset based on the net annual earning to be produced by the asset*] · Kapitalisierungssatz *m*

capital lengthening · Verlängerung *f* der Lebensdauer der Kapitalgüter

capital levy [*A tax on privately owned wealth*] · (Privat)Vermögensabgabe *f*

capital market, money market · Geldmarkt *m*, Kapitalmarkt, Markt für kurzfristige Kredite

capital market loan · Kapitalmarktdarleh(e)n *n*, Geldmarktdarleh(e)n

capital merger, capital fusion, fusion of capitals, merger of capitals, consolidation of capitals, capital consolidation · Kapitalverschmelzung *f*, Kapitalkonsolidation *f*, Kapitalfusion

capital messuage — capitatio terrena

capital messuage, principal mansion (house), chief mansion (house) [*The only one mansion (house) on settled land*] · alleiniges Gutshaus *n*, alleiniges Herrschaftshaus, alleiniger Herrensitz *m*

capital migration, migration of capital · Kapitalwanderung *f*

capital movements · Kapitalverkehr *m*

capital outlay, capital expenditure · Kapitalaufwand *m*, Kapitalverausgabung *f*

capital paid in, capital paid up, paid-up capital, paid-in capital · einbezahltes Kapital *n*, eingezahltes Kapital

capital producing industry, instrumental industry [*The capital is instrumental to the production of goods*] · Ertragsgüterindustrie *f*

capital profit, capital gain [*It occurs when stock exchange securities are sold at higher prices than were paid for it*] · Kursgewinn *m*, Kursprofit *m*

capital profit, capital gain · Kapitalgewinn *m*, Kapitalprofit *m*

capital profits tax → capital gains tax

capital property, capital estate, income property [*Property that is expected to produce an income to its owner from rents or leases*] · Kapitalvermögen *n*

capital punishment · Todesstrafe *f*

capital-reconciliation statement (Brit.); accounting for the flow of funds, statement of (sources and applications of) funds, funds statement, summary of financial operations · Kapital(zu)flußrechnung *f*, Finanzierungsrechnung, Finanz(zu)flußrechnung, Bewegungsbilanz *f*, Mittelherkunft- und -verwendungsrechnung

capital redemption reserve fund · Kapitalrückerwerbsrücklage *f*

capital rent, rent earned by capital, capital earning · Kapitalrente *f*

capital rent(s) tax, tax on rent(s) earned by capital, tax on capital earning(s) · Kapitalrentensteuer *f*

capital reserve [*That portion, or any detail thereof, of the net worth or total equity of an enterprise consisting of such items as premium on capital stock, revaluation surplus, reserve for the retirement of capital stock, and sometimes capital gains and other items, all of which is regarded as unavailable for withdrawal by proprietors; contrasts with revenue reserve*] · Kapitalreserve *f*

capital return → capital yield

capital scarcity, capital shortage · Kapitalknappheit *f*, Kapitalmangel *m*, Kapitalverknappung *f*, Kapitalklemme *f*, Kapitalnot *f*

capital (stock) → (authorized) capital (stock)

capital stock association, guaranty building (and loan) association (US); guaranty building society (Brit.); guaranty stock association, permanent stock association · Bausparkasse *f* mit Eigenkapital, kapitalistische Bausparkasse

capital structure, capital composition · Kapitalgefüge *n*, Kapitalzusammensetzung *f*, Kapitalstruktur *f*, Kapitalaufbau *m*

capital sum, original amount, principal [*The total amount of capital of an estate, fund, mortgage, bond, note, or other form of financial investment, together with accretions not yet recognized as income*] · Kapitalsumme *f*, Hauptsumme

capital surplus, paid-in surplus, paid-up surplus · eingezahlte Rücklage(n) *f (pl)*

capital transfer tax · Vermögensübertragungssteuer *f*

capital turnover · Kapitalumschlag *m*

capital use, use of capital · Kapitalnutzung *f*

capital value, true (cash) value, fair (cash) value [*The value of land imputed from the annual rent. Determined by dividing the annual rent specified in the lease agreement by the previously concurred-in current annual rate of rent. The capital value must be not less than the fair value of the land in fee at the time of the lease. The capital value of the annual rent determined in this way provides a valid basis for comparing the proposed lease with offers to purchase*] · Kapitalwert *m*

capital value [*The investment in capital goods (= fixed assets), measured in terms of cost(s) or other value*] · Kapitalwert *m*

capital yield, capital return, investment yield, investment return, ROI, return on investment, yield on investment, return on capital, yield on capital · Kapitalrendite *f* [*Verhältnis von erzielten Gewinn zum eingesetzten Kapital*]

capitastrum [*Latin*]; cadastre, cadaster · Kataster *n*, Bodenregister *n* [*Ein Grundstücksverzeichnis zum Zwecke der Besteuerung. Es besteht aus Gemarkungskarten und Liegenschaftsbüchern*]

capitation tax, poll-tax, head tax [*A tax on each person in consideration of his labour, office, rank, etc.*] · Kopfsteuer *f*

capitatio terrena [*Latin*]; realty tax, tax on realty, tax on (real) estate, tax on land(s), tax on (real) property, (real) estate tax, (real) property tax, land(s) tax · Grund(besitz)steuer *f*, Grundstückssteuer

capitular — carriage contract

capitular [*A member of an ecclesiastic(al) chapter*] · Kirchenkapitelmitglied *n*

capitulary [*A collection of ordinances (called "capitula" in modern Latin), especially those made on their own authority by the Frankish Kings*] · Kapitularien *f pl*

caption [*That part of a legal instrument, as a commission, indictment, etc., which shows where, when, and by what authority it is taken, found, or executed*] · einleitende Formel *f*

caption, heading, title, headline · Überschrift *f*

caput terrae, forera, terra capitalis, caputium, chevitia, forlandum, versura [*Latin*]; headland, foreland, forebalk, foreherda, butt; head-rig [*Scotch*]; pen tir [*Welsh*] [*The slip of unploughed land left at the head or end of a ploughed field on which the plough is turned*] · Anwende *f*, Voracker *m*, Vorwart *f*, Anwänder *m*

caravan, housing-type trailer, (travel) trailer, mobile home · Wohnwagen *m*, Wagenhim *m*

caravaning · Autowohnen *n*

caravan route · Karawanenweg *m*

caravan site, camping ground, caravan ground, camping site · Campingplatz *m*, Wohnwagenplatz

caravan site for gipsies, gipsy caravan site · Zigeunerlager *n*

carcass, fabric; shell [*Canada*] · Rohbau *m*

carcass acceptance certificate, fabric acceptance certificate; shell acceptance certificate [*Canada*] · Rohbauschein *m*, Rohbauabnahmeschein, Rohbau(abnahme)bescheinigung *f*

carcass contractor, fabric contractor; shell contractor [*Canada*] · Rohbauunternehmer *m*

carcass insurance, fabric insurance; shell insurance [*Canada*] · Rohbauversicherung *f*

cardinal change, cardinal variation, cardinal alteration [*A change which is clearly outside the scope of the contract is a cardinal change and a breach of contract*] · vertragswidrige (Ab)Änderung *f*, vertragswidrige Umänderung, vertragswidrige Veränderung

card of accounts, chart of accounts · Kontenplan *m*, Kontenrahmen *m*

care, diligence · Sorgfalt *f*

careers guidance, occupational consulting service, vocational consulting service, occupational (guidance) service, occupational advisory service, vocational (guidance) service, vocational guidance, occupational guidance · Berufsberatung *f*

care for surviving dependants, care for surviving dependents · Hinterbliebenenfürsorge *f*

careless, reckless, negligent, without care [*With an indifference whether anything is true or false*] · leichtsinnig, fahrlässig, nachlässig, leichtfertig

careless conduct, negligent conduct, reckless conduct, negligence, carelessness, recklessness · Fahrlässigkeit *f*, Nachlässigkeit, Leichtfertigkeit, Leichtsinnigkeit

carelessly fraudulent (mis)representation, recklessly fraudulent (false) representation, negligently fraudulent (false) representation, carelessly fraudulent (false) representation, recklessly fraudulent (false) recital, negligently fraudulent (false) recital, carelessly fraudulent (false) recital, recklessly fraudulent (mis)representation, negligently fraudulent (mis)representation · fahrlässige betrügerische (Falsch)Darstellung *f*, fahrlässige betrügerische (Falsch)Erklärung, fahrlässige arglistige (Falsch)Darstellung, fahrlässige arglistige (Falsch)Erklärung

carelessly untrue, carelessly false, carelessly not true, negligently false, negligently untrue, negligently not true, recklessly untrue, recklessly false, recklessly not true · leichtsinning unwahr, leichtsinnig falsch, leichtfertig unwahr, leichtfertig falsch, fahrlässig unwahr, fahrlässig falsch, nachlässig unwahr, nachlässig falsch

carelessness, recklessness, careless conduct, negligent conduct, reckless conduct, negligence · Fahrlässigkeit *f*, Nachlässigkeit, Leichtfertigkeit, Leichtsinnigkeit

care of existence, existence care · Daseinsvorsorge *f*

care-taker · Hausmeister *m*, Hauswart *m*

cargo liner · Linienfrachter *m*, Frachtlinienschiff *n*

car owner · PKW-Halter *m*

car ownership · PKW-Haltung *f*

carpet (pattern) coverage · Teppich(haus)bebauung *f*, verdichteter Flachbau *m*, Teppichbauweise *f* [*Überwiegend erdgeschossige Häuser sind schachbrettartig einander zugeordnet*]

carriage · Beförderung *f*, Güterbeförderung

carriage contract, contract of carriage · Beförderungsvertrag *m*, Güterbeförderungsvertrag, Frachtvertrag

carriage forward · unter Frachtnachnahme, frachtunfrei

carriage of goods by rail · Gütertransport *m* auf Schienen

carriage of passengers by rail · Personenbeförderung *f* auf Schienen

carriage paid, carriage free, free of carriage, freight free, freight paid, free of freight · frachtfrei, Fracht bezahlt

carriage-way, cartway · Fuhrweg *m*

carrier · Verkehrsmittel *n*

carrier · Sektor *m* der genau einen Lieferstrom empfängt und von dem auch nur einer ausgeht [*Graphentheorie*]

carrier → (public) carrier

carrier · Spediteur *m* [*Er unterliegt den „Allgemeine Deutsche Spediteurbedingungen" = ADSp*]

carrier · Transporteur *m* [*Er unterliegt dem „Güterkraftverkehrsgesetz" und dem „Güterfernverkehrsgesetz"*]

carrier · Reeder *m*

carrier industry, export industry · Exportindustrie *f*, Ausfuhrindustrie *f*

carrier (of goods) [*A person who has received goods for the purpose of carrying them from one place to another for hire, under a special contract or in the course of his business as a common carrier*] · Frachtführer *m*, Verfrachter, Vercharterer

carrier (of goods) by sea · Verfrachter *m* zur See, Seeverfrachter, Frachtführer zur See, Seefrachtführer

carriers' business · Frachtgeschäft *n*

carriers' law · Frachtführergesetz *n*, Verfrachtergesetz, Verchartergesetz

car(r)ucage [*A tax levied on the car(r)ucage, the measure of land cultivated by one plough with its team of eight oxen in a year*] · Pflugsteuer *f*

car(r)ucate, plough-land, caruk; ploughgate [*Scotland*] [*A measure of land, varying with the nature of the soil etc., being as much as could be tilled with one plough with its team of 8 oxen in a year*] · Pflugland *n*

carryback [*Federal income taxes in USA. The amount of the net (operating) loss for a given year of an individual, corporation, or other taxpayer carrying on a business, subject to certain adjustments, that may be deducted from the net income of the preceding years; if not thus fully absorbed, the balance may be treated as a carryover*] · Verlustrücktrag *m*

to carry forward [*To transfer the total of a column of figures to another column or to another page, especially where a column or a page has been filled with entries or postings*] · übertragen

carry-forward · Übertrag *m*, (Saldo)Vortrag

carry-forward provision · Vortragsbestimmung *f*

carrying charges, recurrent cost(s), taxes and mortgage interest on (real) estate · wiederkehrende Grundstückskosten *f*, Grundstücksspesen *f*

carrying charges, recurrent cost(s) [*A recurring cost incident to the possession or ownership of property, usually regarded as a current expense but occasionally added to the cost of an asset held for ultimate disposition where the market or likely disposal proceeds are judged to be sufficient to absorb the cost thus enhanced*] · wiederkehrende Kosten *f*, Spesen *f*

carrying charges, recurrent cost(s) for storage and insurance on merchandise · wiederkehrende Lagerkosten *f*, Lagerspesen *f*

carrying charges, interest charged by brokers on margin accounts · wiederkehrende Prolongationskosten *f*, Prolongationsspesen *f*

carrying contour · tragende Höhenlinie *f*, Ersatzlinie für sich überdeckende Höhenlinien

carrying cost(s), freight cost(s) · Frachtkosten *f*

carrying cost(s) [*A term used by Lord Keynes and others. It refers to the fact that assets, other than money, decline in value with the passage of time, and this is their carrying cost(s)*] · Wertminderungskosten *f*

carrying trade · Frachtwesen *n*

carrying value, book value [*The amount at which a property is recorded on the books, net of depreciation, if any*] · Buchwert *m*

to carry into effect, to give effect (to) · wirksam machen

to carry on [*business*] · betreiben [*Geschäft*]

to carry on a (law)suit, to bring into litigation, to engage in litigation, to claim by action, to dispute by action, to litigate, to go to law [*Latin: litigare*] · prozessieren, einen Rechtsstreit austragen, einen Prozeß anhängig machen, rechtshängig werden lassen

to carry out, to perform, to execute · ausführen, durchführen, erbringen [*Arbeit(en)*]

carry-over, backwardation [*London Stock Exchange. The fee, including interest, paid by a speculator for the delayed*

carryover file — caseworker

delivery of stock he has sold, pending what he hopes will be a decline in its price] · Prolongationsgebühr *f*, Kostgeld *n*, Kursabschlag *m*, Deport *m*

carryover file, permanent file [*Auditing. Papers and schedules kept in a separate file for use in succeeding audits*] · Buchprüfungsunterlagen *f pl*

carry-over rate → backwardation rate

to carry the bonds · käuflich die gesamten Effekten übernehmen [*kleines (Emissions)Übernahmesyndikat*]

car survey · PKW-Enquête *f*, Personen(kraft)wagenenquête

carta donationis, cartula donationis, epistola donationis, testamentum [*Latin*] · (dispositive) Schenkungsurkunde *f* [*Urkunde, in welcher ein Schenker erklärt die Schenkung vorzunehmen oder vorgenommen zu haben*]

cart-cote · Beholzungsrecht *n* für Wagenbau, Holzbezugsrecht für Wagenbau, Wagenzubuße *f*

cartel [*A group of separate business organizations that has agreed to institute measures to control competition*] · Kartell *n*

Cartesian co-ordinate system [*A co-ordinate system, with uniformly scaled axes at right angles to each other, devised by René Descartes (1596—1650) as a means of solving algebraic and geometric problems*] · kartesianisches Koordinatensystem *n*

carting; averagium, summagium [*Latin*] · Fuhrdienst *m* [*Fronhofarbeit*]

cartographer → c(h)artographer

cartographic compilation, chartographic compilation · Kartenentwurfbearbeitung *f*

cartographic representation, chartographic representation · kartographische Ausdrucksform *f*

cartography → c(h)artography

cartology · Kartologie *f*

cartometric scaling · Abgreifen *n* [*Koordination aus einer Karte*]

cartometric scaling · Kartieren *n* [*Punkte in einer Karte*]

cartometry · Kartometrie *f*

cartula donationis, epistola donationis, testamentum, carta donationis [*Latin*] · (dispositive) Schenkungsurkunde *f* [*Urkunde, in welcher ein Schenker erklärt die Schenkung vorzunehmen oder vorgenommen zu haben*]

cartway, carriage-way · Fuhrweg *m*

carucae, pratum bovis [*Latin*] [*A meadow for oxen employed in tillage*] · Ochsenwiese *f*

caruk, car(r)ucate, plough-land; ploughgate [*Scotland*] [*A measure of land, varying with the nature of the soil etc., being as much as could be tilled with one plough with its team of 8 oxen in a year*] · Pflugland *n*

cascade process · Schauerprozeß *m* [*Statistik*]

case · (Einzel)Fall *m*

case → (legal) case

case and controversy rule · Rechtsstreitregel *f*

case book · Gerichtsentscheidungssammlung *f*

case distinguishing · Fallunterscheiden *n*

case facts, situation of facts, state of facts, actual situation, established facts, ascertained facts · Sachlage *f*, Sachverhalt *m*, Tatbestand *m*

case in equity, equity case · Billigkeitsfall *m*

case in law, (legal) case · Fall *m*, Rechtsfall

case law, judicial law, judge-made law · richterliches Recht *n*, gerichtliches Recht, Richterrecht, Fallrecht, Spruchrecht, Präzedenzienrecht

case of deprivation, deprivation case · Entziehungsfall *m*

case of emergency, emergency case, extraordinary occasion · Notfall *m*

case of exception, exceptional case · Ausnahmefall *m*

case of extra profit analogous to rent, rent of ability, profits partaking of the nature of rent, conjuncture-profit, entrepreneur's rent · Unternehmerpension *f*, Seltenheitsprämie *f*

case of first impression · unbekannter Fall *m*

case of hardship, hardship case · Härtefall *m*

case of inheritance, inheritance case · Erbfall *m*

case of the facts, statement of the facts · Darlegung *f* eines Tatbestandes, Tatbestanddarlegung

case principle, principle of the case · Fallgrundsatz *m*, Fallprinzip *n*

case study · Fallstudie *f*

casework, social work · Sozialarbeit *f*, Sozialfürsorge *f*

caseworker, social worker, community worker, communal worker · Sozialarbeiter *m*, Sozialfürsorger

cash, ready money · Bargeld n, Barschaft f, bares Geld

cash account · Kassakonto n

cash advance(ment), advance(ment) (of money), money advance(ment) · Vorschuß m

cash against documents → cad

cash allowance · Barzuschuß m

cash asset(s), cash resources [*Cash and any asset(s) which may be converted immediately into cash without upsetting day-to-day operations; marketable securities are excluded*] · Bargeld n und Vermögensgegenstände m pl

cash bond · Kassaobligation f

cashbook, cash journal [*A book of original entry for cash receipt, disbursements, or both*] · Kassabuch n, Kassajournal n

cash budget [*An estimate of cash receipts and disbursements for a future period, cash requirements at various points within the period, and cash on hand at the end of the period*] · Kassenvorschau f

cash deposit · Bardepot n

cash disbursement · Barauszahlung f, Kassenauszahlung, Barausgang, Kassenausgang m

cash-disbursement journal · Kassenausgangsbuch n, Kassenauszahlungsbuch, Barausgangsbuch, Barauszahlungsbuch

cash discount, ready-money discount · Barzahlungsrabatt m, Kassaskonto n, Kassarabatt, Bargeldskonto, Barbezahlungsrabatt

cash dividend · Bardividende f

cash (down), ready-money payment, cash payment, payment in cash · Bar(be)zahlung f

cash earnings [*misnomer*] → fund (generated) from operation(s)

cash flow, retained earnings, retained income, available (earned) surplus, earned surplus [*The spendable income from an investment after paying all expenses, such as operating expenses and debt service*] · Gewinneinbehalt m, Profiteinbehalt, einbehaltener Gewinn, einbehaltener Profit

cash flow · Aktienanalyse f zur Ertragsbeurteilung

cash flow [*misnomer*] → cash profit

cash flow (from operations), cash income (from operations), cash earnings (from operations), cash generation (from operations) · Geld(rück)fluß m

cash-flow (of an investment) [*According to Blohm/Lüder und Kern. Diese Summe als "cash-flow (of an investment)" zu bezeichnen ist problematisch*] · Summe f von pagatorischem Gewinn und Abschreibungen des Projekts

cash fund · Geldmittel f

cash-grain farm · Getreidebaubetrieb m

cashier, teller · Kassierer m, Kassenführer

cashier (US); general bank manager, chief bank officer · Bankdirektor m

cashier's check, cashier's cheque · Selbstscheck m

cash-in-bank account, bank account · Bankkonto n [*Ein Konto der betrieblichen Buchführung welches Soll- und Habenbestände eines Kontos bei einer Bank ausweist*]

cash in bank, cash on hand (US); cash in vaults, fund in the treasury · Bankbarbestand m, Bankkassenbestand

cash(ing)-in value, surrender value · Rückkaufwert m, Rückkaufkurs m [*Versicherungsfondsanteil; Sparbrief; Police*]

cash in hand, cash on hand · Kassenbestand m, Barbestand

cash in hand audit(ing), audi(ting) of cash in hand · Kassen(bestand)revision f

cash in transit · durchlaufendes Geld n, durchlaufende Gelder n pl

cash in vaults, fund in the treasury; cash on hand, cash in bank (US) · Bankbarbestand m, Bankkassenbestand

cash item · Kassenposten m

cash journal, cashbook [*A book of original entry for cash receipt, disbursements, or both*] · Kassabuch n, Kassajournal n

cashless, without cash · bargeldlos, ohne Bargeld

cash on delivery price, COD price, cash price · Barpreis m, Effektivpreis

cash on hand, cash in bank (US); cash in vaults, fund in the treasury · Bankbarbestand m, Bankkassenbestand

cash on hand, cash in hand · Kassenbestand m, Barbestand

cash outlay · Barauslage f

cash payment, payment in cash, cash (down), ready-money payment · Bar(be)zahlung f

cash payment clause · Bar(be)zahlungsklausel f

cash payment plan · Plan m mit sofortiger Auszahlung

cash price, cash on delivery price, COD price · Barpreis m, Effektivpreis

cash price, spot price · Kaufpreis m

cash profit, fund provided by profit, fund made available from operation(s), fund provided by operation(s); cash flow, cash earnings [*misnomers*]; fund (generated) from operation(s), earnings from operation(s) · Geldgewinn *m* aus (Betriebs)Umsatz, Fondsbeitrag *m* aus (Betriebs)Umsatz, Fondszufluß *m* aus (Betriebs)Umsatz, Nettofondszugang *m* aus (Betriebs)Umsatz, Kapitalzufluß aus Betriebstätigkeit, Fondszuwachs *m* aus Betriebsleistungen, Zugang an flüssigen Mitteln aus Betriebstätigkeit, finanzwirtschaftlicher Überschuß *m*, Umsatzüberschuß, Fondszugang aus Betriebstätigkeit

cash purchase, ready-money purchase · Barkauf *m*

cash receipt · Bareinnahme *f*, Kasseneinnahme, Bareingang, Kasseneingang *m*

cash-receipts journal · Kasseneingangsbuch *n*, Kasseneinnahmebuch, Bareingangsbuch, Bareinnahmebuch

cash records [*The records and evidences of the receipt, disbursement, deposit, and withdrawal of cash*] · Kassenunterlagen *fpl*

cash reimbursement, ready-money reimbursement · Barvergütung *f*

cash requirement · Barbedarf *m*

cash reserve · Barreserve *f*

cash resources, cash asset(s) [*Cash and any asset(s) which may be converted immediately into cash without upsetting day-to-day operations; marketable securities are excluded*] · Bargeld *n* und Vermögensgegenstände *mpl*

cash transaction, spot transaction · Kassageschäft *n*

cash value, ready-money value · Barwert *m*

cash with order · Kasse *f* bei Auftragserteilung

cassation · Kassation *f*, Aufhebung *f* eines vorinstanzlichen Urteils

cassation [*A decision in the last resort*] · Entscheidung *f* der letzten Instanz

cassation [*A making null and void any unjust or illegal act or decision*] · Ungültigkeitserklärung *f*

to cast [*vote*] · abgeben [*Stimme*]

to cast a vote, to poll · abstimmen

cast away, thrown away, abandoned, derelict, forsaken, cast off, derserted [*Personal property abandoned or thrown away by the owner in such manner as to indicate that he intends to make no further claim thereto*] · herrenlos, aufgegeben

castellain; castellanus [*Latin*] [*The governor or constable of a castle*] · Burgvogt *m*, Kastellan *m*, Burggraf *m*

castellany [*The jurisdiction of a castellan*] · Burggrafgerichtsbarkeit *f*, Burgvogtgerichtsbarkeit, Kastellangerichtsbarkeit

castellany [*The office of a castellan*] · Burggrafenamt *n*, Burgvogtamt, Kastellanamt

castellany; castlory, castelry [*obsolete*] [*The district belonging to a castle*] · Burgbezirk *m*

casting (of) votes, polling · Abstimmen *n*

casting vote · entscheidende Stimme *f*, zweite Stimme, ausschlaggebende Stimme [*Bei Stimmengleichheit vom Vorsitzenden abgegeben*]

casting voting · Stichentscheid *m*

castle, castel [*A large building or group of buildings fortified with thick walls, battlements, and often, a moat*] · Burg *f*

castle-g(u)ard, castleward, castle-yard [*In the feudal system a kind of knight-service, whereby a feudal tenant was bound, when required, to defend the lord's castle*] · Burgritterdienst *m*

castle-hamlet · Burgweiler *m*

castle rock · Schloßfelsen *m*

castlory [*obsolete*] → castellany

cast off, derserted, cast away, thrown away, abandoned, derelict, forsaken [*Personal property abandoned or thrown away by the owner in such manner as to indicate that he intends to make no further claim thereto*] · herrenlos, aufgegeben

cast value of the incumbrance, cast value of the encumbrance, present value of the incumbrance, present value of the encumbrance · Barwert *m* der Belastung [*z. B. durch Wegerecht*]

casual · Wanderarme *m*

casual · gelegentlich

casual ejector · zufälliger (Besitz)Entzieher *m*, zufälliger (Besitz)Entsetzer

casual evidence, casual proof · zufälliger Beweis *m*

casual labour (Brit.); casual labor (US) · Gelegenheitsarbeit *f*

casual labourer (Brit.); casual laborer (US); casual worker, casual workman · Gelegenheitsarbeiter *m*

casual ward · Obdachstätte *f*

catching bargain · Wuchergeschäft *n*

catching up function, filling in function, pressure-relieving function · Nachholfunktion *f* [*Funktion des Staates für die Infrastruktur*]

catchman, dayman, oddman · (landwirtschaftlicher) Gelegenheitsarbeiter *m*, Gelegenheitslandarbeiter

catchment area, catchment territory, tributary area, tributary territory, tributary land, outlay territory, hinterland, catchment land · Hinterland *n*, Einzugsgebiet *n*, Einzugsbereich *m*

category · Merkmalklasse *f*, Kategorie *f*

category analysis · Kategorienanalyse *f*, Kategorienuntersuchung *f*

cathedral chancellor, chancellor of a cathedral · Domstiftkanzler *m*

cathedral city, cathedral town · Domstadt *f*

cathedral immunity, right of immunity · Domfreiheit *f*

cathedral quarter · Domviertel *n*

cattle breeder, breeder of cattle · Rindviehzüchter *m*

cattle breeding, cattle raising, breeding of cattle, raising of cattle · Rindvieh(auf)zucht *f*

cattle dealer · Rindviehhändler *m*

cattle farm · Rindviehbetrieb *m*

cattle farmer, cattle holder, cattle man · Rindviehhalter *m*

cattle farming, cattle husbandry · Rindviehhaltung *f*

cattle insurance · Rindviehversicherung *f*

cattle larceny, stealing of cattle, larceny of cattle, cattle-stealing · Rindviehdiebstahl *m*

cattle market · Rindviehmarkt *m*

cattle raising → cattle breeding

cattle ranch · Rindviehzuchtgut *n*

cattle size · Rindviehbesatz *m*

cattle-stealing, cattle larceny, stealing of cattle, larceny of cattle · Rindviehdiebstahl *m*

cattle stock, stock of cattle · Rindviehbestand *m*

cattle that has strayed away, estray, wandering cattle · herrenloses Rindvieh *n*, verlaufenes Rindvieh, eingeschüttetes Rindvieh

cattle yard · Rindviehhof *m*

caucus, primary assembly · Vorversammlung *f*, Urversammlung, Erstversammlung [*Vorwahlen in den USA*]

causa finalis [*Latin*] · Zweckursache *f*

causality, causation · Ursächlichkeit *f*

causal loop diagram · Wirkungsgefüge *n* [*In einem Wirkungsgefüge werden die Variablen und ihre Wirkungsbezüge untereinander dargestellt*]

causal relation(ship) · sächliche Beziehung *f*, Kausalbeziehung, Kausalverhältnis *n*

cause, matter of law, legal affair, lawful affair · Rechtsangelegenheit *f*, Rechtssache *f*

cause; writ, (court) action, (law)suit, plea [*In old English law, "writ" is used as equivalent to "action", hence writs are sometimes divided into real, personal, and mixed. It is not uncommon to call a proceeding in a common law court an action(-at-law), and one in an equity court a (law)suit, but this is not a necessary distinction*] · (Gerichts)Klage *f*

cause, ground, reason · Grund *m*

cause at common law, (law)suit at common law, plea at common law, common law (court) action, common law (law)suit, common law cause, common law plea, (court) action at common law · Klage *f* nach gemeinem Recht, gemeinrechtliche Klage

cause book, register of pleading actions, judg(e)ment docket, judg(e)ment book, plea list, plea book, cause list · Klagenverzeichnis *n*, Klagenregister *n*, Prozeßverzeichnis, Prozeßregister

cause de bonis asportatis, plea de bonis asportatis, (court) action de bonis asportatis, (law)suit de bonis asportatis · Klage *f* wegen rechtswidriger (Besitz)Entziehung einer beweglichen Sache

cause for an account, plea for an account, (court) action for an account, (law)suit for an account · Abrechnungsklage *f*, Klage auf Abrechnung [*Billigkeitsrecht*]

cause for breach of contract, plea for breach of contract, (court) action for breach of contract, (law)suit for breach of contract · Vertragsbruchklage *f*

cause for delivery, plea for delivery, (court) action for delivery, (law)suit for delivery · Nichtlieferungsklage *f*, Klage wegen Nichtlieferung

cause for dissolution, plea for dissolution, (law)suit for dissolution, (court) action for dissolution · Auflösungsklage *f*

cause for exemption from liability, plea for exemption from liability, (court) action for exemption from liability, (law)suit for exemption from liability · negative Feststellungsklage *f*

cause for intrusion → cause for trespass

cause for money had and received, plea for money had and received, (court) action for money had and received, (law)suit for money had and received · Geldrückerstattungsklage *f*

cause for payment, plea for payment, (court) action for payment, (law)suit for payment · Zahlungsklage *f*

cause for recovery, plea for recovery, (law)suit for recovery, cause for reimbursement, cause for restitution, cause for refunding, plea for reimbursement, plea for refunding, plea for restitution, (law)suit for reimbursement, (law)suit for refunding, (law)suit for restitution, (court) action for reimbursement, (court) action for restitution, (court) action for refunding, (court) action for recovery · Abgeltungsklage *f*, Ersetzungsklage, Erstattungsklage, Vergütungsklage

cause for redemption, (law)suit for redemption, plea for redemption, (court) action for redemption · Klage *f* auf Freigabe von Sicherheiten, Sicherheit(en)freigabeklage

cause for reimbursement, cause for restitution, cause for refunding, plea for reimbursement, plea for refunding, plea for restitution, (law)suit for reimbursement, (law)suit for refunding, (law)suit for restitution, (court) action for reimbursement, (court) action for restitution, (court) action for refunding, (court) action for recovery, cause for recovery, plea for recovery, (law)suit for recovery · Abgeltungsklage *f*, Ersetzungsklage, Erstattungsklage, Vergütungsklage

cause for removal, plea for removal, (court) action for removal, (law)suit for removal · Beseitigungsklage *f*

cause for specific performance, plea for specific performance, (court) action for specific performance, (law)suit for specific performance, (court) action for completion of contract, (law)suit for completion of contract, cause for completion of contract, plea for completion of contract · (Vertrags)Erfüllungsklage *f*, Naturalerfüllungsklage

cause for the recovery of land, plea for the recovery of land, (court) action for the recovery of land, (law)suit for the recovery of land [*The mixed action at common law to recover the possession of land (which is real), and damages and cost(s) for the wrongful withholding of the land (which are personal)*] · (Immobilien)Besitzklage *f*, Liegenschaftsbesitzklage, Immobiliarbesitzklage, Grund(stücks)besitzklage, eigentliche Besitzklage, Klage aus (widerrechtlicher) Besitzentziehung, (D)Ejektionsklage, possessorische Klage in bezug auf Immobilien, Delogierungsklage [*Als uneigentliche Besitzklage kann diese Klage auch als Räumungsklage des Vermieters gegen den Mieter angewendet werden*]

cause for (the tort of) deceit, plea for (the tort of) deceit, (court) action for (the tort of) deceit, (law)suit for (the tort of) deceit · Betrugsklage *f*

cause for tort, cause in tort, plea for tort, plea in tort, (court) action for tort, (court) action in tort, (law)suit for tort, (law)suit in tort · Deliktklage *f*

cause for trespass, cause for intrusion, (law)suit for trespass, (law)suit for intrusion, plea for trespass, plea for intrusion, (court) action for trespass, (court) action for intrusion · (Besitz)Verletzungsklage *f* wegen Eindringen, (Besitz)Störungsklage wegen Eindringen, (Besitz)Beeinträchtigungsklage wegen Eindringen

cause for unjust detention, cause for unjust retention, cause for unjust detainment, cause for unjust detainer, (law)suit for unjust detention, (law)suit for unjust retention, (law)suit for unjust detainment, (law)suit for unjust detainer, (court) action of detinue, plea of detinue, (law)suit of detinue, cause of detinue, (court) action for unjust detention, (court) action for unjust retention, (court) action for unjust detainment, (court) action for unjust detainer, plea for unjust detention, plea for unjust retention, plea for unjust detainment, plea for unjust detainer · Klage *f* wegen ungerechtfertigter Vorenthaltung, Klage wegen ungerechtfertigter Zurück(be)haltung, Klage wegen ungerechtfertigter Einbehaltung, Klage wegen ungerechtfertigter Retention, Klage wegen ungerechtfertigtem Einbehalt, Klage wegen ungerechtfertigtem Vorenthalt

cause founded on contract, plea founded on contract, (court) action founded on contract, (law)suit founded on contract · Entschädigungsklage *f* ex contractu vel quasi, Schadenersatzklage ex contractu vel quasi, Forderungsklage ex contractu vel quasi, Personenklage ex contractu vel quasi; Personalklage ex contractu vel quasi [*Fehlbenennung*]

cause founded on tort, plea founded on tort, (court) action founded on tort, (law)suit founded on tort · Entschädigungsklage *f* im engeren Sinne, Schadenersatzklage im engeren Sinne, Forderungsklage im engeren Sinne, Personenklage im engeren Sinne; Personalklage im engeren Sinne [*Fehlbenennung*]

cause in error, plea in error, (court) action in error, (law)suit in error · Nichtigkeitsklage *f*, Revisionsklage

cause in personam → personal (court) action

cause in tort, plea for tort, plea in tort, (court) action for tort, (court) action in tort, (law)suit for tort, (law)suit in tort, cause for tort · Deliktklage *f*

cause list, cause book, register of pleading actions, judg(e)ment docket, judg(e)ment book, plea list, plea book · Klagenverzeichnis n, Klagenregister n, Prozeßverzeichnis, Prozeßregister

cause of account, (law)suit of account, plea of account, (court) action of account · Klage f auf Rechnungslegung, Rechnungslegungsklage

cause of advowson, plea of patronage, plea of advowson, (court) action of advowson, (law)suit of patronage, (law)suit of advowson, cause of patronage · Patronats(recht)klage f

cause of assumpsit, (plea of) assumpsit, (court) action of assumpsit, (law)suit of assumpsit · Nichteinhaltungsklage f, Nichterfüllungsklage [*Schadenersatzklage wegen schuldhafter Nichterfüllung eines formlosen mündlich oder schriftlich gegebenem Versprechen*]

cause of contract, (law)suit of contract, (court) action of contract, plea of contract · Vertragsklage f

cause of (court) action, cause of (law)suit, cause of plea · Klagegrund m

cause of debt, (law)suit of debt, plea of debt, (court) action of debt · Schuld(en)klage f [*Zur Einklagung einer Schuld*]

cause of deceit, plea of deceit, (court) action of deceit, (law)suit of deceit · Klage f wegen Täuschung, Täuschungsklage

cause of detinue, plea of detinue, (law)suit of detinue, (court) action of detinue [*An action by a plaintiff who seeks to recover goods in specie, or on failure thereof the value, and also damages for the detention*] · Klage f auf Wiedererlangung einer beweglichen Sache und Schadenersatz, Klage auf Herausgabe einer beweglichen Sache und Schadenersatz

cause of equity, (law)suit of equity, equitable plea, plea of equity, equitable (court) action, equitable (law)suit, equitable cause, (court) action of equity · Billigkeitsklage f, Billigkeitsrechtklage, Klage nach Billigkeit(srecht)

cause of estrepement, cause of devastation, plea of estrepement, plea of devastation, (court) action of estrepement, (court) action of devastation, (law)suit of estrepement, (law)suit of devastation · Verwüstungsklage f

cause of eviction, plea of eviction, (court) action of eviction, (law)suit of eviction · Grund(stücks)besitzklage f wegen Grund(stücks)besitzentziehung

cause of injunction, plea of injunction, (court) action of injunction, (law)suit of injunction · Verfügungsklage f

cause of mistake, plea of mistake, (court) action of mistake, (law)suit of mistake · Irrtumsklage f

cause of patronage, cause of advowson, plea of patronage, plea of advowson, (court) action of patronage, (court) action of advowson, (law)suit of patronage, (law)suit of advowson · Patronats(recht)klage f

cause of possessory right, plea of possessory right, (court) action of possessory right, (law)suit of possessory right · Besitzrechtklage f

cause of replevin, plea of replevin, (court) action of replevin, (law)suit of replevin · Klage f auf Wiedererlangung einer beweglichen Sache und Schadenersatz bei unzulässiger Selbstpfändung, Klage auf Rückgabe einer selbstgepfändeten Sache

cause of transumpt, (law)suit of transumpt, transumpt, (court) action of transumpt, plea of transumpt [*Scots law. An action brought for the purpose of obtaining transumpt(s)*] · Klage f auf Schriftstückabschrift

cause of trover (and conversion), (law-)suit of trover (and conversion), plea of trover (and conversion), (court) action of trover (and conversion) · Bereicherungsklage f, Schatzfundklage, Deliktsklage wegen Unterschlagung, Unterschlagungsklage [*Klage auf Schadenersatz für die Besitzentziehung von beweglichen Sachen (= goods)*]

cause on the case, plea on the case, (law)suit on the case, (court) action on the case · tatsächlich angestellte Klage f

cause on trespass, (court) action on trespass, (law)suit on trespass, plea on trespass · Rechtsverletzungsklage f, Klage wegen Rechtsverletzung

cause per se, (law)suit per se, plea per se, (court) action per se · Klage f die nicht von einem Schadensnachweis abhängt

cause personal, plea personal, personal (court) action, personal plea, personal (law)suit, personal cause; personal writ [*In old English law*], (court) action personal, (law)suit personal · Entschädigungsklage f, Schadenersatzklage, Forderungsklage, Personenklage [*Fehlbenennung: Personalklage*]

cause to gain an injunction, (law)suit to gain an injunction, plea to gain an injunction, (court) action to gain an injunction · Unterlassungsklage f

cause to quiet title, plea to quiet title, (court) action to quiet title, (law)suit to quiet title · Klage f nach § 256 ZPO, Feststellungsklage

caution [*In ecclesiastic(al) law, a caution is a security for the performance of a duty*] · Sicherheit f für eine Pflichterfüllung [*Kirchenrecht*]

caution — ceding insurer

caution [*An accused person must be cautioned by examining justices that he need not say anything in answer to a charge but that if he does his statement will be taken down and may be used in evidence upon his trial*] · Aussagebelehrung *f*

caution [*In Scotland*]; security, deposit · Deckung *f*, (Bar)Sicherheit *f*, Unterlage *f*, Sicherung, Kaution *f*

cautionary [*Scots law. The obligation by which a person becomes a surety for another*] · Bürgschaftsleistung *f*

cautioner, pledge, surety, insurer of a debt, guarantor [*The party who expresses his willingness to answer for the debt, default, or obligation of another. The word "surety" is sometimes used interchangeably for the word "guarantor"; but, strictly speaking, a "surety" is one who is bound with the principal debtor upon the original contract, the same as if he had made the contract himself, while a "guarantor" is bound upon a separate contract to make good in case the principal debtor fails. The guarantor is therefore an insurer of the solvency of the debtor. A surety is held primarily liable on an instrument while a guarantor is held secondarily liable on it; that is, the surety agrees that he will pay the obligation in any event, while the guarantor merely agrees that he will pay the obligation if the principal debtor fails to pay*] · Bürge *m*

cautioner of collection, collection surety, collection cautioner, collection guarantor, guarantor of collection, surety of collection · Ausfallbürge *m*, Rückbürge, Schad(los)bürge

cautioner right, right of the surety, right of the guarantor, right of the cautioner, right of the insurer of a debt, surety right, guarantor right · Bürgenrecht *n*, subjektives Bürgenrecht

caveat · Einweisungseinspruch *m*

caveat emptor · Gewährleistungsausschluß *m*

caveat emptor [*Latin*]; let the buyer beware, let the buyer take care · ohne Gewähr für die Mängelfreiheit, Risiko *n* trägt der Käufer, Wagnis *n* trägt der Käufer, Käufer *m* trägt die Mängelgefahr

caveator · Einsprucherhebende *m* gegen eine Einweisung

CBA, cost(s)-benefit analysis, benefit-cost(s) analysis [*A systematic comparison between the cost(s) of carrying out a service or activity and the value of that service or activity, quantified as far as possible, all costs and benefits (direct and indirect, financial and social) being taken into account*] · Kosten-Nutzen-Analyse *f*, Nutzen-Kosten-Analyse, Kosten-Nutzen-Untersuchung *f*, Nutzen-Kosten-Untersuchung, NKA

CBD, business core, central business district · Geschäftszentrum *n*, funktioneller Stadtkern *m*, Hauptgeschäftsbezirk *m*

CBD frame, transition zone, central belt (area) · innenstadtnahe Wohn- und Gewerbeviertel *npl*, Ergänzungsraum *m* der Innenstadt

CBHI, central business height index · zentraler Geschäftshöhenindex *m*

CBI, central business index · zentraler Geschäftsindex *m*

CBII, central business intensity index · zentraler Geschäftsintensitätsindex *m*

C.C., Coroners Court · Feststellungskommission *f* bei Mordsachen [*In England*]

C.C.A., court of criminal appeal · Appellationsgericht *n* für Kriminalsachen, Appellationsgericht für Strafsachen, Berufungsgericht für Kriminalsachen, Berufungsgericht für Strafsachen [*In England*]

CCC/Works/1 [*deprecated*]; general conditions of government contracts for building and civil engineering works, GC/Works/1 [*Great Britain*] · Vertragsbedingungen *fpl* für staatliche Bauten

CCM map, country-cross-movement map · militärgeographische Karte *f* mit Darstellung der Geländebefahrbarkeit

CD, community development [*The process of applying the physical, social, human, financial, or other particular resources of a community toward its improvement*] · Gemeinwesenentwick(e)lung *f*, Gemeinwesenarbeit *f*

C.D.A., comprehensive development area, comprehensive development territory, area of comprehensive development, territory of comprehensive development · Generalbebauungsgebiet *n*

to cease; to fall in (Brit.); to expire, to end, to terminate, to lapse, to run out · ablaufen, verfristen

to cease, to abandon, to stop · einstellen [*Arbeit(en)*]

cease and desist order · Unterlassungsverfügung *f*

ceased, stopped, abandoned · eingestellt [*Arbeiten*]

to cease to have effect · unwirksam werden, wirkungslos werden

ceasing to have effect · Unwirksamwerden *n*, Wirkungsloswerden

to cede, to assign · abtreten, zedieren

cedent [*Scots law*]; assignor, assigner, grantor [*A person who assigns a claim, right, property, etc.*] · Abtreter *m*, Geber, Zedent *m*

ceding insurer · Erstversicherer *m*

ceiling — centrality

ceiling, income (admission) limit · Einkommensgrenze *f* (für Sozialwohnungsmieter)

ceiling, maximum limit, upper limit · Höchstgrenze *f*, Obergrenze

ceiling price [*Maximum price imposed under a system of price control*] · Grenzpreis *m*

cellar below (a) street · Straßenkeller *m*

cell frequency · Besetzungszahl *f* eines Tabellenfeldes [*Statistik*]

cell(ular) cluster village · Zellenhaufendorf *n*

Celtic (farming) system · Innenfeld-Außenfeld-System *n*

Celtic field · Kammerparzelle *f*, Kammerflur *f*

cemetery, burying ground, burial-ground, burial-yard, grave-yard · Friedhof *m*

cemetery board, burial board · Friedhofsamt *n*

cemetery keeper · Friedhofsaufseher *m*

censor [*Domesday book*] · Zinsmann *m*

censored distribution · abgeschnittene Verteilung *f* mit bekanntem Restumfang [*Statistik*]

census, count · Zählung *f*

census district, count tract, count district, census tract, census sub-county, count sub-county · (statistischer) Zählbezirk *m*

census feudalis [*Latin*] → copyhold

census hereditarius, gabella hereditaria, quindena, detractus realis [*Latin*] · Abschoß *m*, Erb(schafts)geld *n*

census nemorum [*Latin*] · Waldzins *m*

census of buildings, count of buildings, building count, building census · Gebäudezählung *f*

census of job sites and employed people, count of job sites and employed people · Arbeitsstätten- und Beschäftigtenzählung *f*, AZ

census of population, count of population, population census, population count · Bevölkerungszählung *f*, Volkszählung

census promobilis [*Latin*] · Rutscherzins *m*

census reliability, count reliability · Zählungsverläßlichkeit *f*

census sub-county, census district, count tract, count district, census tract, count sub-county · (statistischer) Zählbezirk *m*

center-of-gravity-approach (US); most-significant-relation(ship) test; centre-of-gravity-approach (Brit.) · Schwerpunkt-Anknüpfungsregel *f* [*Bestimmung des maßgeblichen Rechts durch Feststellung des Schwerpunktes des Rechtsverhältnisses im Wege einer objektiven, individualisierenden Methode*]

centile · Prozentstelle *f*

central administrative district · Verwaltungszentrum *n*, Hauptverwaltungsbezirk *m*

central agency, central office · Zentralstelle *f*

central area · Stadtmitte *f* [*Oberbegriff für Stadtkern im physiognomischen und Stadtzentrum im funktionalen Sinn*]

central audit authority · Zentralbuchprüfungsbehörde *f*, Zentralrevisionsbehörde

central authority · Zentralbehörde *f*

central belt (area), CBD frame, transition zone · innenstadtnahe Wohn- und Gewerbeviertel *npl*, Ergänzungsraum *m* der Innenstadt

central business district, CBD, business core · Geschäftszentrum *n*, funktioneller Stadtkern *m*, Hauptgeschäftsbezirk *m*

central business height index, CBHI · zentraler Geschäftshöhenindex *m*

central business index, CBI · zentraler Geschäftsindex *m*

central business intensity index, CBII · zentraler Geschäftsintensitätsindex *m*

central city → metropolitan city

Central Committee for the Territorial Organization of the Reich [*Established in 1920*] · Zentralstelle *f* für Gliederung des Reiches [*Deutschland*]

central cooperative agricultural bank · landwirtschaftliche Zentralgenossenschaftsbank *f*

central density · Zentraldichte *f*

central depopulation · Aushöhlung *f* der Innenstadt, Entleerung *f* der Innenstadt

central district · Zentralbezirk *m*

Central Electricity Generating Board · Stromerzeugungsbehörde *f* für England und Wales

central facility · zentrale Einrichtung *f*

central function · zentrale Funktion *f*, Zentralfunktion

central government [*England*] · Zentralverwaltung *f*

Central Imperial Court [*Established in 1495*] · Reichskammergericht *n*

centrality, hierarchy of central places, nodality, central place hierarchy · Zentralität *f*, Hierarchie *f* zentraler Orte,

centrality characteristic — centre (of gravity) of (the) population

Bedeutungsüberschuß *m*, Zentralorthierarchie, zentralörtliche Bedeutung *f*, Knotenpunktlage *f*, Zentralitätsgrad *m* [*Ein Ort versorgt sich und seine ländliche Umgebung mit Gütern und Dienstleistungen. Die Zentralität ist gleich seinem Bedeutungsüberschuß, d. h. gleich der relativen Bedeutung in bezug auf ein ihm zugehöriges Gebiet definiert*]

centrality characteristic, characteristic of centrality · Zentralitätsmerkmal *n*

centrality concept, concept of centrality · Zentralitätsbegriff *m*

centrality model · Zentralitätsmodell *n*

centrality research · Zentralitätsforschung *f*

centralization · Zentralisation *f*, Zentrenbildung *f* [*Dieser Begriff gibt bestimmte städtebauliche und wirtschaftliche Folgen der Konzentration wieder: Die räumliche Auskristallisation bestimmter Funktionen (z. B. zentrale Dienstleistungen, Gewerbe, Wohnung) oder deren räumliche Streuung im Falle der Dezentralisation (z. B. Gemengelage)*]

centralized accountancy, centralized accounting · Zentralrechnungswesen *n*

centralized activity · zentrale Aktivität *f*

central(ized) planning · Zentralplanung *f*

central Land bank, Land central bank [*The Deutsche Bundesbank delegates its function of "lender of last resort" to the branches of the Landeszentralbanken, with which it is essential to maintain a balance if a German bank wishes to borrow from the central bank*] · Landeszentralbank *f*

central management function, CMF · zentrale Führungsfunktion *f*

central metrics · Zentralmetrik *f*

central office · Zentralbüro *n*

Central Office · Zentralbüro *n* [*In London für alle Abteilungen des Supreme Court*]

central office, central agency · Zentralstelle *f*

central open space · zentrale Freifläche *f*

central place · Zentralort *m*, zentraler Ort [*Gemeinden sind zentrale Orte, wenn ihre sozialen, wirtschaftlichen und kulturellen Einrichtungen nicht nur der örtlichen Bevölkerung sondern auch den Einwohnern anderer Ortschaften dienen*]

central place concept, concept of central place · Zentralortbegriff *m*

central place function · zentralörtliche Funktion *f*

central place hierarchy, centrality, hierarchy of central places, nodality · Zentralität *f*, Hierarchie *f* zentraler Orte, Bedeutungsüberschuß *m*, Zentralorthierarchie, zentralörtliche Bedeutung *f*, Knotenpunktlage *f*, Zentralitätsgrad *m* [*Ein Ort versorgt sich und seine ländliche Umgebung mit Gütern und Dienstleistungen. Die Zentralität ist gleich seinem Bedeutungsüberschuß, d. h. gleich der relativen Bedeutung in bezug auf ein ihm zugehöriges Gebiet definiert*]

central place pattern, central place scheme · Zentralortschema *n*, Zentralortmuster *n*

central place research, research of central places · Forschung *f* der zentralen Orte, Forschung zentraler Orte, zentralörtliche Forschung

central place system, system of central places · zentralörtliches System *n*, System der zentralen Orte, System zentraler Orte, Zentralortsystem, zentralörtliche Gliederung *f* von Gemeinden

central place theory, theory of central places · Theorie *f* der zentralen Orte, Theorie zentraler Orte, zentralörtliche Theorie, Zentralorttheorie, Mittelzentrumtheorie

central planning authority · Zentralplanungsbehörde *f*

central point · Mittelpunkt *m*

central rate · Leitkurs *m* einer Währung gegenüber dem US-Dollar

central school · Mittelpunktschule *f*

central settlement · Kern(an)sied(e)lung *f*, Zentral(an)sied(e)lung

central site · Zentralörtlichkeit *f*

central statistical office, general register office · statistisches Zentralbüro *n*

central town → metropolitan city

central unit · Zentrale *f*

central village · zentrales Dorf *n*, Zentraldorf

centre of development, development centre (Brit.); development center, center of development (US) · Entwick(e)lungszentrum *n*, Entwick(e)lungsschwerpunkt *m*, Mittelbereichszentrum, Sied(e)lungsschwerpunkt

centre-of-gravity-approach (Brit.); center-of-gravity-approach (US); most-significant-relation(ship) test · Schwerpunkt-Anknüpfungsregel *f* [*Bestimmung des maßgeblichen Rechts durch Feststellung des Schwerpunktes des Rechtsverhältnisses im Wege einer objektiven, individualisierenden Methode*]

centre (of gravity) of (the) population (Brit.); center (of gravity) of (the) population (US) · Bevölkerungsmittelpunkt *m*, Bevölkerungsschwerpunkt, Bevölkerungszentrum *n*

centripetal migrant · Randwanderer *m*

centripetal migration, rush to sub(urb)s · Randwanderung *f*

ceorl, churl, ye(o)man(-farmer) [*An Old English freeman of the lowest class, opposed on one side to a thane or nobleman, on the other to the servile classes*] · Gemeinfreie *m*

certainty · Rechtssicherheit *f*, Rechtsgewißheit

certainty, clearness of statement, definiteness, absence of doubt, distinctness · Bestimmtheit *f*, Klarheit, Gewißheit

certainty to a certain intent · relative Bestimmtheit *f*

certifiable in legal form, acknowledg(e)able · (amtlich) beurkundbar

certificare [*Latin*]; to certify, to testify in writing, to give a certificate, to attest · bescheinigen

certificate · Zeugnis *n*

certificate, attestation [*A written assurance, or official representation, that some act has or has not been done, or some event occurred, or some legal formality been complied with*] · Attest *n*, Bescheinigung *f*, Schein *m*

certificated bankrupt · Gemeinschuldner *m* mit Entlastungsschein, Gemeinschuldner mit Entlastungsattest, Gemeinschuldner mit Entlastungsbescheinigung

certificate for payment, payment certificate · Zahlungsbescheinigung *f*, Zahlungsattest *n*, Zahlungsschein *m*

certificate for right to a dwelling · Wohnberechtigungsbescheinigung *f*, Wohnberechtigungsattest *n*, Wohnberechtigungsschein *m*

certificate of ability to marry · Ehefähigkeitszeugnis *n*

certificate of absence of defects · Mängelfreiheitsbescheinigung *f*, Mängelfreiheitsschein *m*, Mängelfreiheitsattest *n*

certificate of acceptance (of (the) work(s)), acceptance certificate · Abnahmeattest *n*, Abnahmebescheinigung *f*, Abnahmeschein *m*, Bauabnahmeattest, Bauabnahmeschein, Bauabnahmebescheingung

certificate of acknowledg(e)ment, acknowledg(e)ment certificate · Grundschuldbrief *m*

certificate of acknowledg(e)ment, acknowledg(e)ment certificate · Rekognitionsbescheinigung *f*, Rekognitionsschein *m*, Rekognitionsattest *n* [*Bescheinigung einer in ein öffentliches Buch erfolgten Eintragung*]

certificate of appointment, appointment certificate · Ernennungszeugnis *n* [*Konkursverwalter*]

certificate of birth, birth certificate · Geburtsurkunde *f*, Geburtsschein *m*

certificate of capacity, certificate of fitness, certificate of capability · Befähigungsschein *m*, Befähigungsbescheinigung *f*, Befähigungsattest *n*, Befähigungsnachweis *m*

certificate of citizenship, citizenship certificate, certificate of nationality, nationality certificate · Staatsangehörigkeitsausweis *m*

certificate of citizenship (US); certificate of naturalization (Brit.) · Bürgerbrief *m*

certificate of completion, attestation of completion, final certificate, final attestation, completion certificate, completion attestation · Endbescheinigung *f*, Endschein *m*, Endattest *n*, Schlußbescheinigung, Schlußschein, Schlußattest [*Über die Beendigung der Bauarbeiten*]

certificate of completion by stages, certificate for stage-wise completion · Bescheinigung *f* für abschnittsweise Fertigstellung, Schein *m* für abschnittsweise Fertigstellung, Attest *n* für abschnittsweise Fertigstellung

certificate of completion of making good defects · (Sach)Mängelbeseitigungsattest *n*, Baumängelbeseitigungsattest

certificate of conformity, conformity certificate · Entlastungsattest *n* für einen Gemeinschuldner, Entlastungsschein *m* für einen Gemeinschuldner, Entlastungsbescheinigung *f* für einen Gemeinschuldner

certificate of contribution, contribution certificate · Beitragsbescheinigung *f*, Beitragsattest *n*, Beitragsschein *m*

certificate of employment, employment certificate · Arbeitsnachweis *m*, Arbeitszeugnis *n*

certificate of evidence, statement of case, bill of exceptions [*A formal statement in writing of the objections or exceptions taken by a party during the trial of a cause to the decisions, rulings, or instructions of the trial judge, stating the objections, with the facts and circumstances on which it is founded, and, in order to attest its accuracy, signed and sealed by the judge; the object being to put the controverted rulings or decisions upon the record for the information of the appellate court when the ends of justice require it, the terms "bill of exceptions" and "statement of case" are regarded as synonymous*] · Niederschrift *f* der Beweisverhandlung, Aufzeichnung *f* der Beweisverhandlung

certificate of executorship — certified accountant

certificate of executorship, letter of executorship · (Testaments)Vollstreckerzeugnis n

certificate of fitness → certificate of capacity

certificate of incorporation [*The instrument by which a private corporation is legally formed and in which are specified name, location, principle, and purpose(s) of the incorporators in compliance with some designated public office, usually the state. It served as evidence of the corporation's existence*] · staatliche Gründungsbescheinigung f, staatlicher Gründungsschein m, staatliches Gründungsattest n, Inkorporierungsbescheinigung, Inkorporierungsattest, Inkorporierungsschein

certificate of indebtedness [*An obligation sometimes issued by corporations having practically the same force and effect as a bond, though not usually secured on any specific property*] · Schatzanweisung f

certificate of inheritance, inheritance certificate · Erbschein m, Erbzeugnis n, Erbbescheinigung f, Erbattest n

certificate of inheritance confined to definite assets, inheritance certificate confined to definite assets · gegenständlich beschränkter Erbschein m, gegenständlich beschränkte Erbbescheinigung f, gegenständlich beschränktes Erbattest n, gegenständlich beschränktes Erbzeugnis n

certificate of legality, legality certificate · Rechtskraftattest n, Rechtskraftbescheinigung f, Rechtskraftschein m, Legalitätsattest, Legalitätsbescheinigung, Legalitätsschein

certificate of loan, loan certificate · Darleh(e)nsschein m

certificate of maintenance, maintenance certificate · Unterhaltungsschein m, Unterhaltungsbescheinigung f, Unterhaltungsattest n, Instandhaltungsschein, Instandhaltungsbescheinigung, Instandhaltungsattest

certificate of nationality, nationality certificate, certificate of citizenship, citizenship certificate · Staatsangehörigkeitsausweis m

certificate of naturalization (Brit.); certificate of citizenship (US) · Bürgerbrief m

certificate of nomination, paper of nomination, nomination paper, nomination certificate, declaration of candidacy, nomination petition [*USA*] · Vorwahlvorschlag m

certificate of noncompletion · Nichtfertigstellungsbescheinigung f, Nichtfertigstellungsschein m, Nichtfertigstellungsattest n

certificate of nonobjection, nonobjection certificate, negative certificate · Unbedenklichkeitsattest n, Unbedenklichkeitsbescheinigung f, Unbedenklichkeitsschein m, Bodenverkehrszeugnis n, Negativattest, Negativbescheinigung, Negativschein

certificate of occupancy, occupancy certificate [*Certificate issued by governmental authority certifying that all or a designated portion of a building complies with the provisions of applicable statutes and regulations*] · Gebäudeabnahmezeugnis n

certificate of occupancy, occupancy certificate [*Certificate issued by the governing authority granting permission to occupy a project for a specific use. It is procured by the prime contractor*] · Übergabezeugnis n

certificate of occupancy, occupancy certificate · Beziehbarkeitsbescheinigung f [*Wohnraum*]

certificate of origin · Ursprungszeugnis n

certificate (of ownership), ownership certificate · Einlageschein m [*gemischte Bürgschaftsbausparkasse*]

certificate of possession, possession certificate · Besitzzeugnis n

certificate of purchase, certificate of sale [*A certificate issued by public officer to successful bidder at a judicial sale (such as a tax sale), which will entitle him to a deed upon confirmation of sale by the court, or (as the case may be) if the land is not redeemed within the time limited*] · Bodenkaufattest n, Bodenkaufbescheinigung f, Bodenkaufschein m, Bodenverkaufsattest n, Bodenverkaufsbescheinigung, Bodenverkaufsschein, Grunderwerbsattest, Grunderwerbsschein, Grunderwerbsbescheinigung

certificate of quality, quality certificate · Gütezeugnis n

certificate of registration, registration certificate · Beurkundung f über Grund(stücks)rechte [*Torrens-System*]

certificate of residence, residence certificate · Heimatbescheinigung f, Heimatschein m, Heimatattest n

certificate of satisfaction, satisfaction certificate · Befriedigungsattest n, Befriedigungsschein m, Befriedigungsbescheinigung f, Befriedigungsnachweis m

certificate with annuity coupons · Berechtigungsschein m mit Rentenschein

certification document, document of certification · Bestätigungsunterlage f

certified accountant, chartered accountant [*In Great Britain*] · Wirtschaftsprüfer m

certified public accountant [*In the USA*] · Wirtschaftsprüfer *m*

certified public accountant [*A trained accountant who examines the books of accounts of corporations and others and reports upon them*] · amtlich zugelassener Rechnungsprüfer *m*, amtlicher Rechnungsprüfer

certified transcript, exemplification; exemplificatio [*Latin*] · rechtsgültige Abschrift *f*, rechtsgültige Kopie *f*

certifier → valuer

to certify, to testify in writing, to give a certificate, to attest; certificare [*Latin*] · bescheinigen

certifying, testifying in writing, giving a certificate, attesting, attestation · Bescheinigen *n*

to certify in legal form, to attest legally, to acknowledge · (amtlich) beurkunden

certiorari [*Latin*]; writ of certiorari [*An original writ which issued out of the Crown side of the Queen's Bench Division addressed to judges or officers of inferior courts, commanding them to certify or to return the records of a cause depending before them, to the end that justice might be done. By the Administration of Justice (Miscellaneous Provisions) Act, 1938, S. 7, the writ of certiorari was abolished, but the High Court now has the power to make an order of certiorari*] · Abberufungsdekret *n*, Abberufungsschreiben *n*

certiorari denied · Revisionsantrag *m* abgelehnt

cessation of work(s), abandonment of work(s), stop(ping) of work(s) [*Cessation of operation and intent(ion) of owner and contractor to cease operations permanently*] · Einstellung *f* der Arbeit(en), Arbeitseinstellung

cessation of work(s), abandonment of work(s), discontinuance of work(s) [*Cessation of operation for a definite period*] · Arbeitsunterbrechung *f*, Unterbrechung *f* der Arbeiten

cessio bonorum [*Latin*] [*In early days the insolvent debtor in Scotland was treated practically as a criminal, and was subject to the penalties of rebellion against a command from the Crown enjoining him to pay his creditor. From the Roman law there was, however, borrowed, a process of relief — the cessio bonorum — under which he gave up all his property and thus secured liberation and immunity from imprisonment on the ground of his debt, but was not discharged*] · Güterabtretung *f*, Güterzession *f*

cessio legis [*Latin*] · Abtretung *f* kraft Gesetz(es)

cession, assignation, assignment · (dingliche) Abtretung *f*, (dingliche) Zession *f*

cessionary [*Scots law*]; assign(ee) [*One to whom a property or right is legally transferred or made over*] · Abtretungsempfänger *m*, Forderungsübernehmer, Zessionar, Zessionär

cession by operation of law, assignation by operation of law, assignment by operation of law · Abtretung *f* auf Grund von Rechtsvorschriften, Zession *f* auf Grund von Rechtsvorschriften

cession clause, assignation clause, assignment clause · Abtretungsklausel *f*, Zessionsklausel

cession contract, contract of assignation, assignation contract, contract of assignment, contract of cession, assignment contract · Abtretungsvertrag *m*, Zessionsvertrag

cession declaration, assignment statement, cession statement, assignation statement, assignation declaration, statement of assignment, declaration of assignment, declaration of cession, statement of cession, declaration of assignation, statement of assignation, assignment declaration · Abtretungserklärung *f*, Zessionserklärung

cession deed, assignation deed, deed of assignation, deed of cession, deed of assignment, assignment deed · Abtretungsurkunde *f*, Zessionsurkunde

cession law, law of assignation, assignation law, law of cession, law of assignment, assignment law · Abtretungsrecht *n*, Zessionsrecht

cession notice, cession notification, notice of assignment, notice of cession, notification of assignment, notification of cession, assignment notice, assignment notification · Zessionsanzeige *f*, Zessionsmitteilung *f*, Abtretungsanzeige, Abtretungsmitteilung

cession of land, land assignment, land cession, assignation of land, land assignation, assignment of land · Bodenabtretung *f*, Landabtretung, Grund(stücks)abtretung, Grund(stücks)zession *f*, Bodenzession, Landzession

cession of lease(hold), cession of demise, cession of tenancy, assignment of lease(hold), assignment of demise, assignment of tenancy, lease(hold) cession, lease(hold) assignment, demise cession, demise assignment, tenancy cession, tenancy assignment · Pachtabtretung *f*, Pachtzession *f*

cession of possession, possession assignment, possession cession, assignation of possession, possession assignation, assignment of possession · Besitzabtretung *f*, Besitzzession *f*

cession of right, assignment of right, assignation of right [*A transfer of an existing right from one person to another*] · Rechtsabtretung *f*, Rechtszession *f*

cession practice, assignation practice, assignment practice · Abtretungswesen *n*, Zessionswesen

cession statement, assignation statement, assignation declaration, statement of assignment, declaration of assignment, declaration of cession, statement of cession, declaration of assignation, statement of assignation, assignment declaration, cession declaration, assignment statement · Abtretungserklärung *f*, Zessionserklärung

cesspit emptying service, (leaching) cesspool emptying service, pervious cesspool emptying service · Senkgrubenentleerungsdienst *m*

cestui (à) que use, cestui à l'use de qui, cestui (à) que trust, cestuy que trust [*Norman French*]; usufructarius [*Latin*]; (beneficial) occupant, (beneficial) occupier, beneficial owner, tenant, user, usufructuary, beneficiary [*He to whose use another is enfeoffed of lands or tenements. The substantial and beneficial owner, as distinguished from the feoffee to uses*] · Nutznießer *m*, faktischer Eigentümer, Nehmer, Empfänger eines benefiziarischen Nutzungsrechts, Benefiziar, Besitznehmer, Usufruktuar, Fruchtnießer, Nießbraucher

cestui que vie · Person *f* mit deren Tod der Heimfall des Grundstückes eintritt

chain discount · Stufenrabatt *m*, Listenpreisabschlag *m*

chain of command · Weisungsweg *m*

chain of liability, liability chain · Haftpflichtkette *f*, Haftungskette

chain of representation, representation chain · Kette *f* der Rechtsnachfolge, Rechtsnachfolgekette

chain of title(s) to land(s), title chain [*A term applied to the past series of transactions and documents affecting the title to a particular tract of land*] · (Rechts)Titelkette *f*, Rechtskette, Kette von (Rechts)Titeln, Kette von Rechten [*Eintragung in Landregister in den USA*]

chain-relative · Verkettungsmeßziffer *f* [*Statistik*]

chain settlement · Ketten(an)sied(e)lung *f*

chain store · Filialgeschäft *n*, Kettenladen *m*

chain stores, multiple shops · Kettenläden *m pl*, Filialgeschäfte *n pl*

chair · Lehrstuhl *m*

challenge, provocation · Herausforderung *f*

challenge method · Einwendungsverfahren *n*, Ablehnungsverfahren [*Es dient dazu Parteinominierungen auf Parteianhänger zu beschränken*]

to challenge the array · ablehnen der Geschworenenliste

challenge to the array · Ablehnung *f* der Geschworenenliste

challenge (to the array) for cause · begründete Ablehnung *f* der Geschworenenliste

challenge to the favour (Brit.); challenge to the favor (US) · Ablehnung *f* von Geschworenen auf Grund subjektiver Vermutungen

challenge to the polls · Ablehnung *f* einzelner Geschworener

chamber · Kammer *f*

chamber → (judge) chamber

chamber-letter [*One who lets rooms for hire*] · Zimmervermieter *m*

chamber of agriculture · Landwirtschaftskammer *f*

chamber of commerce, commercial chamber · Handelskammer *f*

champarty, champerty [*The illegal proceeding, whereby a party not naturally concerned in a suit engages to help the plaintiff or defendant to prosecute it, on condition that, if it be brought to a successful issue, he is to receive a share of the property in dispute*] · Prozeßkauf *m*

champertor · Prozeßkäufer *m*

chance agglomeration · zufällige Häufung *f*

chance bargain · Gelegenheitskauf *m*

chancellor of a bishop, chancellor of a diocese · Diözesankanzler *m*

chancellor of a cathedral, cathedral chancellor · Domstiftkanzler *m*

Chancellor of the Exchequer · Schatzkanzler *m*

chancellorship · Kanzlerschaft *f*

chance move · Zufallszug *m*

to change, to alterate, to vary · (ab)ändern, umändern, verändern

change, alteration, variation · (Ab)Änderung *f*, Umänderung, Veränderung

changeability, variability · (Ab)Änderungsfähigkeit *f*, Umänderungsfähigkeit, (Ab)Änderungsvermögen *n*, Umänderungsvermögen, Veränderungsfähigkeit, Veränderungsvermögen

changeable, variable, alterable · (ab)änderungsfähig, umänderungsfähig, veränderungsfähig

changeable will, alterable will · (ab)änderungsfähiges Testament n, umänderungsfähiges Testament, veränderungsfähiges Testament

change agent · Entwick(e)lungshelfer m

change by equity, alteration by equity, variation by equity · Umänderung f durch Billigkeit, (Ab)Änderung durch Billigkeit, Veränderung durch Billigkeit

change clause, alteration clause, variation clause · (Ab)Änderungsklausel f, Umänderungsklausel, Veränderungsklausel

change contract, variation contract, alteration contract, contract of variation, contract of alteration, contract of change · (Ab)Änderungsvertrag m, Umänderungsvertrag, Veränderungsvertrag

changed, altered, varied · (ab)geändert, umgeändert, verändert

change in property, property change · Vermögenswechsel m

change in zoning, rezoning [*Action by a governing body changing the zoning classification of a land area to another classification*] · Baunutzungswechsel m, veränderte (bauliche) Nutzung f, veränderte Baunutzung, Umzonung

change in zoning (up)on condition, conditional rezoning, conditional change in zoning, rezoning (up)on condition · bedingter Baunutzungswechsel m, Baunutzungswechsel mit Vorbedingung, Baunutzungswechsel unter Vorbehalt

change list, change register, change registry, variation list, variation register, variation registry, alteration list, alteration register, alteration registry · Veränderungsliste f, Veränderungsverzeichnis n, (Ab)Änderungsliste, (Ab)Änderungsverzeichnis, Umänderungsliste, Umänderungsverzeichnis

change of building lines, alteration of building lines, variation of building lines · (Bau)Fluchtlinien(ab)änderung f

change of domicil(e) · Domizilwechsel m

change of law, variation of law, alteration of law, law change, law variation, law alteration · Rechts(ab)änderung f, Rechtsumänderung, Rechtsveränderung

change of name; mutatio nominis [*Latin*] · Namenswechsel m

change of ownership (of property), change of proprietorship, change of (general) property · Eigentumswechsel m

change of population, population change · Bevölkerungszahlwechsel m, Bevölkerungsstandwechsel

change of possession · Besitzwechsel m

change of structural design, alteration of structural design, structural design variation, structural design alteration, structural design change, variation of structural design · (Ab)Änderung f des Bauentwurfs, Umänderung des Bauentwurfs, Veränderung des Bauentwurfs, Bauentwurfs(ab)änderung, Bauentwurfsumänderung, Bauentwurfsveränderung

change of (the) design, design change, design alteration, design variation, variation of (the) design, alteration of (the) design · Entwurfs(ab)änderung f, Entwurfsveränderung, Entwurfsumänderung, (Ab)Änderung des Entwurfs, Umänderung des Entwurfs, Veränderung des Entwurfs

change of use of land, land use change · Landnutzungswechsel m, Bodennutzungswechsel

change of value, value change · Wertveränderung f

change of venue (of court) · Gerichtsstandwechsel m, Gerichtsortwechsel

change order [*Revision to the contract after it has been officially awarded*] · Vertragsänderung f

change order [*Work order, usually prepared by the contractor, submitted to the agent of the owner, and signed by the owner or his agent, authorizing a change, revision, or addition*] · Änderungsauftrag m

change-over trial, switch-back design, cross-over design · Gruppenwechselplan m [*Statistik*]

change register, change registry, variation list, variation register, variation registry, alteration list, alteration register, alteration registry, change list · Veränderungsliste f, Veränderungsverzeichnis n, (Ab)Änderungsliste, (Ab)Änderungsverzeichnis, Umänderungsliste, Umänderungsverzeichnis

change room, workmen's shanty · Bauarbeiterbude f

to change slightly, to vary slightly, to modify, to alter slightly · geringfügig (ab)ändern, geringfügig umändern, geringfügig verändern

to change the wording of, to state again in other words, to express again in other words, to restate, to reword · umschreiben, neugestalten, neuschreiben, umgestalten [*Text*]

changing the wording, stating again in other words, expressing again in other words, changing the text, rewording · Textumschreibung f, Textgestaltung, Textneugestaltung, Textneuschreibung

chantry certificate · (Seelen)Meßstiftungsurkunde f

chapel of ease — charge rate

chapel of ease [*A chapel built for the convenience of parishioners who live far from the main parish church*] · Nebenkirche *f*, Andachtskapelle *f*

chapter [*A congregation of ecclesiastic(al) persons in a cathedral church*] · (Dom)Kapitel *n*, Bischofssenat *m*, Senat des Bischofs [*Kirchenrecht*]

chapter [*English law*] · Gesetz(es)kapitel *n*, Kapitel, Einzelgesetz *n*

characteristic · Merkmal *n*

characteristic of centrality, centrality characteristic · Zentralitätsmerkmal *n*

characteristic of mobility, mobility characteristic · Beweglichkeitsmerkmal *n*, Mobilitätsmerkmal

characteristic of well-being, characteristic of prosperity · Wohlstandsmerkmal *n*

characteristic root · Eigenwert *m* [*Statistik*]

to charge → to place to account

to charge, to burden, to incumber, to load, to encumber · belasten, dinglich belasten

to charge · pfandrechtlich belasten

charge [*in common-law practice*] · (Richter)Schlußrede *f*

charge [*A security for the payment of a debt or performance of an obligation. It is a general term, and therefore includes mortgages, liens, writs of execution, etc., but is also applied in a restricted sense to cases where the security has no special name, and where there is not necessarily a personal debt*] · Pfandlast *f*, Pfandbelastung *f*

charge, duty [*Charged in payment of services rendered by the state or public authority*] · Gebühr *f*

charge · Beschuldigung *f*

charge · Belehrung *f* der Anklagejury [*Durch den präsidierenden Richter bevor sich die Jury zur Beratung zurückzieht*]

charge, encumbrance, load, burden, incumbrance; incumbramentum [*Latin*] [*A claim or lien attached to property as a mortgage*] · (dingliche) Belastung *f*, (dingliche) Last *f*

charge · Vorwurf *m*

chargeable · anrechenbar

chargeable; burdenable [*obsolete*]; capable of bearing a burden · belastbar

charge account (US); budget account · Kundenkreditkonto *n* [*Der monatliche Schuldsaldo ist in Raten zu zahlen*]

charge customer (US) · Kredit-Einzelhandelskunde *m*

charged · pfandrechtlich belastet

charged, imperfect, encumbered, incumbered, loaded, burdened · belastet, dinglich belastet

chargé d'affaires · Geschäftsträger *m*

charged by law, loaded by law, burdened by law, encumbered by law, incumbered by law · gesetzlich belastet

charged by mortgage(s), encumbered by mortgage(s), incumbered by mortgage(s), loaded by mortgage(s), burdened by mortgage(s) · hypothek(en)belastet

charged property · belastetes Vermögen *n*

charged (with an offence), accused · angeklagt

charged with lease(hold), burdened with lease(hold), encumbered with lease(hold), incumbered with lease(hold), loaded with lease(hold) · erbbaurechtbelastet, platzrechtbelastet

charge for use, use charge, use duty, duty for use · Benutzungsgebühr *f*, Gebrauchsgebühr

charge of contribution(s), contribution(s) charge, contribution(s) load, load of contribution(s) · Beitragslast *f*

charge of easement, encumbrance of easement, incumbrance of easement, load of easement, burden of easement · Grunddienstbarkeitslast *f*

charge of the poor rates, load of the poor rates, burden of the poor rates, encumbrance of the poor rates, incumbrance of the poor rates · Armenlast *f*

charge on capital, encumbrance on capital, incumbrance on capital, capital charge, capital burden, capital encumbrance, capital incumbrance, burden on capital · Kapitaldienst *m*, Kapitallast *f*

charge on personal property, encumbrance on personal property, incumbrance on personal property, load (up)on personal property, burden on personal property · Fahrnislast *f*, Fahrhabelast, Mobiliarlast, Mobilienlast

charge plate (US) · Kundenkreditausweis *m*

charge prohibition, load prohibition, encumbrance prohibition, incumbrance prohibition, burden prohibition · Belastungsverbot *n*, Lastenverbot

charge rate, rate of charge, duty rate, rate of duty · Gebührensatz *m*

charge rate, load rate, burden rate, encumbrance rate, incumbrance rate · Belastungssatz *m*

charge rate, rate of charge · Abgabensatz *m*

charge register, charge registry, charge sheet · Angeklagtenliste *f*

charges · Unkosten *f*

charge scale, charge schedule, scale of duties, schedule of duties, duty schedule, duty scale, scale of charges, schedule of charges · Gebührentabelle *f*, Gebührentafel

charge sheet · Anklageformular *n*

charges register, charges registry · Lastenregister *n*, (Grundbuch)Abteilung III *f*

to charge (with an offence), to accuse · beschuldigen, anklagen

charging, placing to account, putting to account · Anrechnung *f*

charging, burdening, incumbering, encumbering, loading · (dingliches) Belasten *n*

charging order, order of distringas [*obsolete*] · Befehl *m* zur Pfändung von Anteilsrechten

charitable; charitative [*obsolete*]; benevolent · wohltätig, karitativ

charitable bequest, charitable legacy · karitatives (Fahrnis)Vermächtnis *n*, karitatives (Fahrnis)Legat *n*, wohltätiges (Fahrnis)Vermächtnis, wohltätiges (Fahrnis)Legat

charitable corporation, eleemosinary corporation · wohltätige Körperschaft *f*, wohltätige Korporation, karitative Körperschaft, karitative Korporation, Almosenkörperschaft, Almosenkorporation

charitable gift · karitative Schenkung *f*, wohltätige Schenkung

charitable institution, benevolent institution · Wohltätigkeitsanstalt *f*

charitableness, benevolence, charity · Wohltätigkeit *f*

charitable object, charitable purpose · Wohltätigkeitszweck *m*, wohltätiger Zweck

charitable organization, benevolent organization, benevolence organization, charity organization · Wohltätigkeitsorganisation *f*

charitable trustee, trustee of a charity · Stiftungstreuhänder *m*

Charitable Trusts Act 1853 · Stiftungstitelgesetz *n* [*England*]

Charity Commission(ers) [*England and Wales*] · Aufsichtsbehörde *f* für milde Stiftungen, Kommission *f* für milde Stiftungen

charity land(s) · Stiftungsland *n*, Länderei(en) *f (pl)* einer milden Stiftung, Gut *n* einer milden Stiftung, Stiftungsgut

charity organization, charitable organization, benevolent organization, benevolence organization · Wohltätigkeitsorganisation *f*

charity work, work of charity · mildtätiges Werk *n*

chart · Kurskarte *f*, Navigationskarte

chart → (navigation(al)) chart

charter · Verleihungsurkunde *f*

charter · Miete *f* [*Überlassung eines Gegenstandes auf Zeit*]

charter · Frachtvertrag *m* [*Überlassung eines Schiffes oder Flugzeuges samt Mannschaft*]

charter · Werkvertrag *m* [*Eine Sache wird einem bestimmten Personenkreis oder einer bestimmten Person auf bestimmte Dauer zur Verfügung gestellt*]

charter [*A document delivered by the sovereign or legislature granting privileges or recognizing rights or creating a borough, university, company, or other corporation*] · Freibrief *m*

charter [*obsolete*]; deed (under seal); sealed instrument, document under seal · Siegelurkunde *f*, gesiegelte Urkunde, Urkunde unter Siegel

charter contract (of a corporation) [*USA*] · Statut *n*, Korporationscharter *f*

chartered accountant, certified accountant [*In Great Britain*] · Wirtschaftsprüfer *m*

chartered accountant · konzessionierter Rechnungsprüfer *m*

chartered auditor · konzessionierter Buchprüfer *m*, konzessionierter (Bücher)Revisor

chartered town · privilegierte Stadt *f*

charter government · Freibriefregierung *f*

charter granted to a province · Landhandfeste *f* [*Österreich*]

charter-land; terra haereditaria, terra libraria [*Latin*]; bócland, bookland, bockland [*Land which, in pre-Norman Conquest time, was held by charter, handbook, or other written title*] · Buchland *n*

charter of (en)feoffment, charter of infeftment, feudal charter, feuda(to)ry charter, feodal charter, manorial charter · Belehnungs(frei)brief *m*, Leh(e)n(s)(frei)brief

charter party, affreightment [*A contract for transporting goods by sea*] · Seefrachtvertrag *m*, Charterpartie *f*, Chartervertrag, Charterurkunde, Seefrachtpartie, Seefrachturkunde f

Charter Rolls · Grundregister n für den Landesadel [*Am englischen Königshof im 13. Jahrhundert*]

charter service · Charterdienst m

chartist movement, Chartism [*Its aims were social and industrial amelioration*] · Chartistenbewegung f, Chartismus m

chart of accounts, card of accounts · Kontenrahmen m, Kontenplan m

c(h)artographer, c(h)artographist · Kartograph m

c(h)artography [*The drawing of charts and maps*] · Kartographie f

chart reference · Indexangabe f [*Seekarte*]

to chase, to hunt; fugare [*Latin*] · jagen

chase, hunting ground [*District of land priveleged for wild beasts of chase, with the exclusive right of hunting therein*] · Jagdrevier n

chase, hunting right [*The right of hunting over a tract of country; also, that of keeping beasts of the chase therein*] · Jagdrecht n, subjektives Jagdrecht

chase beasts, game, wild animals, (wild) beasts of the chase · (Jagd)Wild n, jagdbare Tiere n pl

chasing · Antreiben n [*zur Arbeit*]

chasing, hunting · Jagen n

chattel → personal estate

chattel interest in land(s) → interest in (real) estate

chattel law → property law

chattel mortgage [*Mortgage or loan on chattel (personal) as contrasted to a real estate mortgage*] · Mobiliarhypothek f, Fahrnishypothek, Fahrhabehypothek

chattel (personal) → personal estate

chattel real → interest in (real) estate

chattels personal, mov(e)able properties, (goods and) chattels · bewegliche Güter n pl, Mobilien f pl, Mobiliar n, bewegliche Sachen f pl, bewegliche Gegenstände m pl

chattels vegetable · pflanzliche Erzeugnisse n pl eines Grundstücks, pflanzliche Produkte n pl eines Grundstücks

cheating · Betrügen n

to check, to control, to-examine, to review · kontrollieren, nachprüfen

check (US); cheque (Brit.) · Scheck m

check, control, to-examination, review · Kontrolle f, Nachprüfung f

check and voucher trading (US); cheque and voucher · Warengutscheinhandel m

check bearer, check holder (US); holder for value; holding (Brit.); cheque bearer, cheque holder (Brit.) · Scheckinhaber m, Scheckträger

check-book (US); cheque-book (Brit.) · Scheckbuch n

check calculation, check computation · Kontrollrechnung f

checkerboard pattern, checkerboard plan, checkerboard scheme, checkerboard layout, grid (iron) pattern, grid (iron) scheme, grid (iron) plan, grid (iron) layout, chessboard pattern, chessboard scheme, chessboard plan, chessboard layout · Gitternetzmuster n, Schachbrettmuster, Gitternetzschema n, Schachbrettschema, Gitternetzgrundriß m, Schachbrettgrundriß

checking, controlling, re-examining · Kontrollieren n, Nachprüfen

checking account · Scheck-Konto n

check(ing) authority, review(ing) authority, re-examination authority, authority of control, authority of checking, control authority · Kontrollvollmacht f, Nachprüf(ungs)vollmacht

check(ing) duty, duty to review, review(ing) duty, duty to check, duty to control, duty to re-examine, checking duty, control duty, re-examination duty · Nachprüfungspflicht f, Kontrollpflicht

check(ing) measure, control measure, re-examination measure · Nachprüfungsmaßnahme f, Kontrollmaßnahme f

checking of bid, checking of tender, checking of offer; checking of (bid) proposal (US) · Angebotsprüfung f

checking of cost(s), cost(s) checking · Kostenfeststellung f, Kostennachkalkulation f, Kostenkontrolle f

checking-off, ticking [*item*] · Abhaken n [*Position*]

checking of plan(s) · Plankontrolle f

check list, list to be ticked · Abhakliste f

check list · Prüfliste f

checkman, inspector · Kontrolleur m

to check off, to tick [*item*] · abhaken [*Position*]

check presentor (US); cheque presentor (Brit.) · Scheckübelbringer m

checks and balances · wechselseitige Beaufsichtigung f der (Staats)Gewalt(en)träger, Gewaltenhemmung und Gewaltenkontrolle f [*Jeder Gewaltenträger ist in der Lage die beiden anderen dadurch zu kontrollieren, daß ihm gewisse Funktionen übertragen sind, die eigentlich in den Bereich der oder des anderen gehören*]

chemical complex · Chemiekomplex m

cheque (Brit.); check (US) · Scheck m

cheque bearer, cheque holder (Brit.); check bearer, check holder (US); holder for value · Scheckinhaber m, Scheckträger

cheque-book — childrens' playground

cheque-book (Brit.); check-book (US) · Scheckbuch *n*

cheque law, cheque statute, cheque act (Brit.); check law, check act, check statute (US) · Scheckgesetz *n*

chessboard pattern, chessboard scheme, chessboard plan, chessboard layout, checkerboard pattern, checkerboard plan, checkerboard scheme, checkerboard layout, grid (iron) pattern, grid (iron) scheme, grid (iron) plan, grid (iron) layout · Gitternetzmuster *n*, Schachbrettmuster, Gitternetzschema *n*, Schachbrettschema, Gitternetzgrundriß *m*, Schachbrettgrundriß

chevitia, forlandum, versura, forera, terra capitalis, caput terrae, caputium [*Latin*]; headland, foreland, forebalk, foreherda, butt; head-rig [*Scotch*]; per tir [*Welsh*] [*The slip of unploughed land left at the head or end of a ploughed field on which the plough is turned*] · Anwende *f*, Voracker *m*, Vorwart *f*, Anwänder *m*

chief accountant · Rechnungsdirektor *m*

chief bank officer; cashier (US); general bank manager · Bankdirektor *m*

chief Baron [*The president of the Court of Exchequer*] · Schatzkammervorsitzende *m*, Schatzkammeroberrichter, Schatzkammerpräsident, Vorsitzende der Schatzkammer, Präsident der Schtzkammer, Oberrichter der Schatzkammer

chief cashier · (Gemeinde)Kassenverwalter *m*

Chief Clerk (of the Central Office) [*In London*] · Zentralbürovorsteher *m*

chief commissary → commissary general

chief constable → chief (parochial) constable

chief education officer · Leiter *m* des Unterrichtswesens [*Stadtbeamte*]

chief executive · Verwaltungschef *m* [*öffentliche Verwaltung*]

chief lord, possessory lord, liege-lord, over lord, lord of (the) mayor; supreme owner, landlord, grantor, feoffor, feoffer, manor lord, langeman, bestower of a fee, feudal chief; dominus directus, feoffator [*Latin*]; (feudal) lord, superior lord · Leh(e)n(s)herr *m*, Feudalherr, (feudaler) Belehner, Leh(e)n(s)gutgeber, Obereigentümer, Landübertragende, Übertragende von Land

chief mansion (house) capital messuage, principal mansion (house) [*The only one mansion (house) on settled land*] · alleiniges Gutshaus *n*, alleiniges Herrschaftshaus, alleiniger Herrensitz *m*

chief office, leading office, principal office, main office · Hauptbüro *n*

chief of state, head of state, state head, state chief · Staatsoberhaupt *n*

chief (parochial) constable, high (parochial) constable · Oberpolizeischulze *m*

chief rate clerk · oberster Gemeindesteuerbeamter *m*, höchster Gemeindesteuerbeamter

chief-rent, rent charge, quit-rent, fee farm (rent); quieti reditus, reditus quieti [*Latin*]; forgavel [*In old English law*] [*An annual or periodical sum issuing out of land, payable by holders of land in a manor to the lord. Some writters use "fee farm" to signify not only the estate itself, but the rent reserved on it, taking the word "farm" itself in the sense of rent. This practice should, however, be deprecated*] · Erbzins *m*, Befreiungszins, Leh(e)n(s)zins

chief-rent law, quit-rent law, fee farm (rent) law · Befreiungszinsrecht *n*, Erbzinsrecht, objektives Befreiungszinsrecht, objektives Erbzinsrecht

chief-rent roll, quit-rent roll, fee farm (rent) roll · Erbzinsbuch, Befreiungszinsbuch *n*

chief warden of the forests, master of the woods, master of the forests, chief warden of the woods, keeper of the woods, keeper of the forests [*In old English law. An officer who had the principal government of all things relating to the forest, and the control of all officers belonging to the same*] · Waldbewahrer *m*, Forstbewahrer, Oberforstmeister

chief whip · erster Parteieinpeitscher *m* [*Parteiorganisation im englischen Parlament*]

child benefit act, child benefit law, child benefit statute · Kindergeldgesetz *n*

child by adoption · adoptiertes Kind *n*, Adoptivkind

child by birth, natural child [*A child distinguished from a child by adoption*] · leibliches Kind *n*

child en ventre sa mère · Leibesfrucht *f*

childless, without issue, without child(ren), issueless · kinderlos, ohne Nachkommenschaft

child of tender age, child of tender years · Kleinkind *n*

child-orien(ta)ted, child-related · kinderbezogen, kinderorientiert

child population · Kinderanteil *m* [*An der Bevölkerung*]

children allowance, family bonus, family allowance, allowance for children · Kindergeld *n*, Kinderbeihilfe *f*

childrens' playground · Kinderspielplatz *m*

child's property — church-building

child's property · Kindesvermögen n

child's property mortgage · Kindergeldhypothek f [zur Sicherstellung von Kindesvermögen]

child's share · Kindesanteil m

child welfare · Kinderfürsorge f

child-woman ratio, fecundity [The ratio which the number of births per annum bears to the number of persons of reproductive age, or of women of reproductive age; or of married persons, or wives only, at that age] · Fruchtbarkeitsziffer f, Fruchtbarkeitsrate f

chiminage, pedagium [Toll due by custom for having a way through a forest] · Waldgebühr f, Waldzoll m

chimney acceptance · Schornsteinabnahme f

chimney sweeper charge · Kehrgebühr f, Schornsteinfegergebühr

chirograph (of debt) [An obligation or bond given in one's own handwriting] · handschriftliche Schuldurkunde f

Chi square distribution · Chi-Quadrat-Verteilung f

Chi square statistic · Chi-Quadrat-Maßzahl f

Chi statistic · Chi-Maßzahl f

chivalry, knighthood [The position and character of a knight] · Ritterschaft f

chivalry [The knightly system of feudal times with its religious, moral, and social code and practices] · Rittertum n

chloropleth map · Wertflächenkarte f, Flächenkartogramm f, Chloroplethenkarte, Gebiets(dichte)stufenkarte; Dichtemosaikkarte [nach Imhof]

choice → (freedom of) choice

choice investment · erstklassige Investition f, erstklassige (Kapital)Anlage, erstklassige Geldanlage

choice-of-design function · Funktion f zur Auswahl der Faktorintensitäten

choice-of-law, election-of-law, law choice, law election · Rechtswahl f

choice-of-law rule, choice-of-law norm, law choice rule, law choice norm, law election rule, election-of-law rule, law election norm, election-of-law norm · Rechtswahlnorm f

choice of location for an economic unit, choice of site for an economic unit · betriebswirtschaftliche Standortwahl f

choice of location restricted by source of supply · lagergebundene Standortwahl f

choice of space, spatial choice · Raumwahl f

choice theory · Theorie f der Wahlakte, Wahlaktetheorie

choking up · Verschlammung f

chorographic(al) · raumbeschreibend [Darstellung]

chose, physical thing, thing corporeal, corporeal chattel (personal); res corporales, res singula [Latin]; corporeal thing, tangible thing [A thing that affects the senses and may be seen and handled] · (Einzel)Sache f, körperliches Rechtsobjekt n, materielles Rechtsobjekt, körperliches Ding n, materielles Ding, körperlicher (Rechts)Gegenstand m, materieller (Rechts)Gegenstand [Ausgenommen lebender menschlicher Körper. Unter den Sachbegriff fallen nicht die Rechte, die Sachgesamtheiten, d. h. Mehrheiten von Sachen, die eine besondere Benennung haben, z. B. Bücherei, Warenlager usw. und die Inbegriffe von Sachen und Rechten, z. B. Erbschaftsvermögen usw. Im Preußischen Allgemeinen Landrecht von 1794 (A.L.R.) ist (Einzel)Sache allerdings alles, was Gegenstand eines Rechtes oder einer Verbindlichkeit sein kann (§ 1.I.2)]

chose in possession, corporeal chattel in the possession of the owner · körperlich bewegliche Sache f im Besitz des Eigentümers

chose local, local chose; immov(e)able [International Private Law]; immov(e)able, thing, real thing, thing immov(e)able, thing real · Immobilie f, unbeweglicher Gegenstand m, unbewegliche (Einzel)Sache f, unbewegliches Ding n, unbewegliches Rechtsobjekt n

choses local, local choses; immov(e)ables [International Private Law]; things immov(e)able, things real, real things, immov(e)able things · Immobilien f pl, unbewegliche (Einzel)Sache f pl, unbewegliche Dinge n pl, unbewegliche Gegenstände m pl, unbewegliche Rechtsobjekte n pl

chose transitory · Mobil n

Christian Law of Nature · christliches Naturgesetz n

chronic unemployment, persistent unemployment · Dauerarbeitslosigkeit f, Dauererwerbslosigkeit

chunk sampling · Raffprobe f [Statistik]

church administration · Kirchenverwaltung f, kirchliche Verwaltung

church-ale [Periodical festive gathering held in connexion with a local parish church] · Kirchweih(fest) f, (n)

church-building · Kirchenbau m

church-building [*The material edifice of the church*] · Kirche *f* [*als Gebäude*]

church-building (US); ecclesiastic(al) building [*A building for meetings, etc., adjoining a church*] · Kirchengebäude *n*, kirchliches Gebäude

church centre (Brit.); church center (US) · Kirchenzentrum *n*

church corporation, religious house, acclesiastic(al) corporation, spiritual corporation · geistliche Körperschaft *f*, geistliche Korporation, kirchliche Korporation, kirchliche Körperschaft

church-court, court Christian, consistory court; commissary court [*Scotland*]; spiritual court, ecclesiastic(al) court, consistorial court · geistliches Gericht *n*, Kirchengericht, Konsistorialgericht, kirchliches Gericht [*Die schottischen ,,ecclesiastic(al) courts" haben nur eine Jurisdiktion über Fragen der Doktrin, des Gottesdienstes, der Sakramente und der Disziplin der Geistlichen*]

churchdom, ecclesiastic(al) status; churchship [*obsolete*] · Kirchenstatus *m*

church estate, spiritual estate, ecclesiastic(al) estate, church property, spiritual property, ecclesiastic(al) property · Kirchenvermögen *n*, Kirchengut *n*, Kirchenhabe *f*

church farm · Kirchenlandgut *n*

church-garth [*dialect*]; church yard · Kirchhof *m*

church hamlet · Kirchweiler *m*

church-land, spiritual land, ecclesiastic(al) land · Kirchenland *n*, Kirchenboden *m*

church master [*obsolete*]; warden, church warden; church reeve [*In England. A lay honorary officer of a parish or district church, elected to assist the incumbent in the discharge of his administrative duties, to manage such various parochial offices as by custom or legislation devolve upon him, and generally to act as the lay representative of the parish in matters of church-organization*] · Kirchenvorsteher *m*

Church of England as by law established · anglikanische Staatskirche *f*

church property, spiritual property, ecclesiastic(al) property, church estate, spiritual estate, ecclesiastic(al) estate · Kirchenvermögen *n*, Kirchengut *n*, Kirchenhabe *f*

church province, ecclesiastic(al) province, spiritual province · Kirchenprovinz *f*

church-rate [*A rate upon the assessed property within a parish, in England and Ireland, levied by resolution of the vestry, for the maintenance of the church and its services. In 1868 the compulsory rate was abolished, except in cases, where, though bearing this name, it had been mortgaged or was applied to secular purposes*] · (örtliche) Kirchensteuer *f*, gemeindliche Kirchensteuer, lokale Kirchensteuer, kommunale Kirchensteuer

church record of baptisms and burials · (kirchles) Tauf- und Sterberegister *n*

churchship [*obsolete*] → churchdom

church vassal, homo ecclesiasticus [*Latin*] · Kirchenvasall *m*

church village, large village · Kirchdorf *n*

church warden; church reeve, church master [*obsolete*]; warden [*In England. A lay honorary officer of a parish or district church, elected to assist the incumbent in the discharge of his administrative duties, to manage such various parochial offices as by custom or legislation devolve upon him, and generally to act as the lay representative of the parish in matters of church-organization*] · Kirchenvorsteher *m*

churchwardenship [*The office or position of a churchwarden*] · Kirchenvorsteheramt *n*

churchway · Kirchweg *m*

church-work [*Work at the edifice of a church*] · Kirchenarbeit(en) *f (pl)*

church-work [*Work on behalf of, or in connection with, the church as an institution*] · Kirchenarbeit *f*

church-worker · Kirchenarbeiter *m*

church yard; church-garth [*dialect*] · Kirchhof *m*

churl, ye(o)man(-farmer), ceorl [*An Old English freeman of the lowest class, opposed on one side to a thane or nobleman, on the other to the servile classes*] · Gemeinfreie *m*

cinema construction code · Lichtspieltheaterbauordnung *f*, Kinobauordnung

circuit [*In English law. A portion of the country, appointed for a particular judge to visit for the trial of causes or for the administration of justice*] · Assisensprengel *m*, Gerichtssprengel

circuit court of appeal [*USA*] · Bezirksappellationsgericht *n*, Bezirksberufungsgericht

Circuit Court of Appeals [*USA*] · Bundesobergericht *n*

Circuit Court of the United States [*USA*] · Kreisgerichtshof *m*

circuit judge, itinerant judge, justice in eyre, justice in eire, justice itinerant, circuit justice, itinerant justice · Sendrichter *m*, Umgangsrichter, reisender Richter

circuit (of appeal) — citizen initiative

circuit (of appeal), appeal circuit · Berufungs(gerichts)sprengel *m*, Appellations(gerichts)sprengel

circuit of the United States [*USA*] · Gerichtskreis *m*

circuit system · Assisengerichtsbarkeit *f*

circular city, circular town, round city, round town · Rundstadt *f*

circular letter (of credit) [*A letter of credit addressed by a banker to several other bankers, in favour of a person named therein*] · Zirkularkreditbrief *m*

circular market area, circular market territory · kreisförmiges Marktgebiet *n*

circular order · Rundverfügung *f*, Rundanordnung, Rundgebot *n*, Rundbefehl *m*

circular test · Interkalationsprüfung *f* [*Statistik*]

circular village, ring-fence village, round village · Rundling *m*

circular (zone) theory, concentric circle theory, concentric (zone) theory · Kreistheorie *f*, Theorie der ringförmigen Anordnung (der sozialökonomischen Stadtviertel)

circulating capital, working capital, floating capital [*Capital available for the purpose of meeting current expenditure*] · Betriebskapital *n*

circulation · Verbreitung *f*, Streuung [*Umfragetechnik*]

circumstance, state of matters, condition · Umstand *m*, Lage *f*

circumstantial evidence, circumstantial proof, presumptive evidence, presumptive proof [*"Circumstantial evidence" and "circumstantial proof" haben auch einen besonderen juristischen Sinn und bezeichnen denjenigen indirekten Beweis, welcher nach dem positiven Recht eines Landes ausreicht, um zur Grundlage gerichtlicher Entscheidungen zu dienen. Beide Benennungen werden aber auch ganz allgemein als Gegensatz zu Zeugen und Urkunden gebraucht. Wo eine philosophische oder historische Wahrheit durch Schlußfolgerungen aus entfernt liegenden Momenten oder durch Analogie dargetan wird kann man wohl nicht von circ. ev. und circ. proof reden. Im Deutschen würde „Anzeigebeweis" dafür gewiß nicht gebraucht werden*] · indirekter Beweis *m*, Beweis *m*, durch Nebenumstände, Indizienbeweis *m*

citation [*A passage cited, a quotation*] · Zitat *n*

citation, citing · Zitieren *n*

citation [*The written form of summons, or the document containing it*] · Aufgebotsschreiben *n*, (Vor)Ladungsschreiben

citation, citing, summons, summoning [*The operation of calling upon a person who is not a party to an action or proceeding to appear before the court in that action or proceeding; applied particularly to process in the probate, spiritual and matrimonial courts*] · Aufgebot *n*, Aufbieten *n*, (Vor)Ladung *f*

citation book, citor · Zitierbuch *n*

citation form, form of citation; style (US) · Zitierform *f*

citation method, method of citation · Zitierweise *f*

citation order, order of citation · Zitierfolge *f*

citation rule, rule of citation, rule as to citation · Zitierregel *f*

to cite · zitieren

cited, summoned, called · (vor)geladen, aufgeboten [*vor Gericht*]

citied, civicized, urbanized [*Made into or like a city*] · verstädtert

cities-within-cities · Stadtsystem(e) *n (pl)*

citing → citation

citizen, burgess, freeman of a borough, townman; cityman [*obsolete*]; urban resident, town resident, city resident, urban inhabitant, town inhabitant, city inhabitant, urban dweller, town dweller, city dweller, urbanite · Stadtbewohner *m*, Stadteinwohner *m*, städter, Stadtbürger

citizen · Bürger *m*

citizen control, public participation, participation of citizens, citizen involvement, involvement of citizens, citizen participation · Bürgerbeteiligung *f*, Bürgermitwirkung *f*, Bürgerteilnahme *f*, bürgerschaftliche Beteiligung, bürgerschaftliche Mitwirkung, bürgerschaftliche Teilnahme [*z. B. an der Bauleitplanung*]

citizen(ess), female citizen, citizette · Bürgerin *f*

citizen hearing, hearing of citizens, public hearing · Bürgeranhörung *f*, öffentliche Anhörung

citizenhood, citizenry, (body of) citizens · Bürgerschaft *f*, Bürgerstand *m*, Stand der Bürger

citizenship, citizenship [*The position or status of being a citizen with its rights and privileges*] · Bürgerschaft *f*, Bürgerstatus *m*

citizen initiative · Bürgerbegehren *n*, Bürgerinitiative *f* [*Nicht verwechseln mit Bürgerinitiative als kommunalpolitische handelnde Bürgergruppe*]

citizen involvement, involvement of citizens, citizen participation, citizen control, public participation, participation of citizens · Bürgerbeteiligung *f*, Bürgermitwirkung, Bürgerteilnahme *f*, bürgerschaftliche Beteiligung, bürgerschaftliche Mitwirkung, bürgerschaftliche Teilnahme [*z. B. an der Bauleitplanung*]

citizenism, principle of citizenship, principle of citizenhood · Bürgerschaftsprinzip *n*, Bürgerschaftsgrundsatz *m*

to citizenize [*To make a citizen, naturalize as a citizen*] · einbürgern

citizen of the world, citizen of the nature, cosmopolitan · Weltbürger *m*

citizen participation, citizen control, public participation, participation of citizens, citizen involvement, involvement of citizens · Bürgerbeteiligung *f*, Bürgermitwirkung, Bürgerteilnahme *f*, bürgerschaftliche Beteiligung, bürgerschaftliche Mitwirkung, bürgerschaftliche Teilnahme [*z. B. an der Bauleitplanung*]

citizen participation in planning, public participation in planning · Bürgerbeteiligung *f* an der Planung, Partizipation *f* an der Planung

citizen referendum · Bürgerentscheid *m*

citizenry, (body of) citizens, citizenhood · Bürgerschaft *f*, Bürgerstand *m*, Stand der Bürger

citizenship, nationality [*human being*] · Staatsangehörigkeit *f*

citizenship, citizenhood [*The position or status of being a citizen with its rights and privileges*] · Bürgerschaft *f*, Bürgerstatus *m*

citizenship act, citizenship law, citizenship statute, nationality act, nationality law, nationality statute · Staatsangehörigkeitsgesetz *n*

citizenship certificate, certificate of nationality, nationality certificate, certificate of citizenship · Staatsangehörigkeitsausweis *m*

citizenship law, nationality law · Staatsangehörigkeitsrecht *n*

citizenship legislation, citizenship lawmaking, nationality legislation, nationality lawmaking · Staatsangehörigkeitsgesetzgebung *f*

citizens' organization · Bürgerorganisation *f*

citizette → citizen(ess)

citor, citation book · Zitierbuch *n*

city, town [*These terms may be generally used, especially in combinations, although they have different meanings in one or the other English-speaking country*] · Stadt *f* [*Eine räumliche Konzentration von Wohn- und Arbeitsstätten und Menschen mit vorwiegend tertiär- und sekundärwirtschaftlicher Betätigung, mit innerer Differenzierung und vielfältigen Verkehrsströmen zwischen ihren Teilräumen und solchen, die auf sie insgesamt als Verkehrsmittelpunkt gerichtet sind, deren Wachstum großenteils auf Wanderungsgewinn beruht und die einen erweiterten Bereich mit Gütern und Dienstleistungen versorgt.*]

city, incorporated municipality, incorporated city, incorporated community [*USA*] · Stadt(gemeinde) *f* erster Ordnung [*In den USA ist eine corporate oder legal city eine verhältnismäßig große Stadt mit höherem gebietskörperschaftlichem Status als eine town*]

city · Innenstadt *f*

city accountant, town accountant, urban accountant · Stadtbuchhalter *m*

city acreage, urban acreage, town acreage · Stadtflächeninhalt *m*

city administrative region, urban administrative region, town administrative region · Stadtgebiet *n* [*Die Fläche der Verwaltungseinheit ,,Stadt", unabhängig von städtischer Bebauung und städtischer Funktion*]

city affair, town affair, urban affair · städtische Angelegenheit *f*

city agency, urban agency, urban office, town agency, town office, city office · städtische Dienststelle *f*

city air, urban air, town air · Stadtluft *f*

city alderman, urban alderman, town alderman · Stadtälteste *m*

city and country; burg and land [*Scotland*]; town and country · Stadt *f* und Land *n*

city area, urban area, town area · Stadtfläche *f*, städtische Fläche

city area, city territory, urban area, urban territory, town area, town territory · städtisches Gebiet *n* [*Ein Gebiet, welches im funktionalen und physiognomischen Sinne vorrangig durch städtische Funktionen geprägt ist*]

city area use, town area use, urban land(s) use, city land(s) use, town land(s) use, urban area use · städtische Bodennutzung *f*, städtische Landnutzung, städtische Flächennutzung, Stadtbodennutzung, Stadtlandnutzung, Stadtflächennutzung

city atlas, town atlas, urban atlas · Stadtatlas *m*

(city) auditorium building, town auditorium building, urban auditorium building · Stadthalle *f*

city authority — city construction project

city authority, urban authority, town authority · Stadtbehörde *f*, städtische Behörde

"city beautiful" movement · Stadtverschönerungsbewegung *f*

city block, town block, urban block · Baublock *m*

city board, urban board, town board · Stadtamt *n*, städtisches Amt

city border area, city border territory · Innenstadtrandgebiet *n*

city boundary, urban boundary, town boundary · Stadtgrenze *f*

city builder, urban builder, town builder · Städtebauer *m*, Stadtbauer

city building, city construction, urban building, urban construction, town building, town construction · Städtebau *m*

city building board, city construction board, urban construction board, urban building board, town building board, town construction board · Stadtbauamt *n*, städtisches Bauamt

city building code, city construction code, town building code, town construction code, urban building code, urban construction code · städtische Bauordnung *f*, Stadtbauordnung

city building (construction), urban building (construction), town building (construction) · städtischer Hochbau *m*

city building project, urban construction project, urban building project, town construction project, town building project, city construction project · städtebauliches Vorhaben *n*, städtebauliches Projekt *n*

city by(e)-law, city ordinance, urban statute, urban by(e)-law, urban ordinance, town statute, town by(e)-law, town ordinance, city statute · Stadtsatzung *f*, Stadtstatut *n*, Stadtgesetz *n*

city cartography, urban cartography, town cartography · Stadtkartographie *f*

city cemetery, urban cemetery, town cemetery · Stadtfriedhof *m*

city centre (Brit.); urban center, town center, city center, downtown (area) (US); urban centre, town centre · Stadtzentrum *n*, Innenstadt *f*, Stadtinnere *n* [*im funktionalen Sinne*]

(city) charter · Stadtfreiheitsbrief *m*, Stadtrecht *n*

city child, town child, urban child · Stadtkind *n*

city church, urban church, town church · Stadtkirche *f*

city civil engineer, town civil engineer, urban civil engineer · Stadtbauingenieur *m*

city (civil) engineering, urban (civil) engineering, town (civil) engineering · städtischer Tiefbau *m*

city civilization, urban civilization, town civilization · Stadtzivilisation *f*, städtische Zivilisation

city classification, urban classification, town classification · Städtetypisierung *f*

city cleansing board, town cleansing board · Stadtreinigungsamt *n*

city climate, urban climate, town climate · Stadtklima *n*

city code, urban code, town code · Städteordnung *f*

city commissioners of sewers · Kanalausschuß *m*, Kanalisierungsausschuß

city community, urban community, town community · Stadtgemeinde *f*, Stadtkommune *f*, städtische Gemeinschaft *f*, städtische Kommune, städtische Gemeinde [*Als Organisationsform*]

city composition, town structure, city structure, urban structure, town composition, urban composition · Stadtstruktur *f*, Stadtzusammensetzung *f*, Stadtgefüge *n*, Stadtaufbau *m*, städtische Struktur, städtische Zusammensetzung, städtischer Aufbau, städtisches Gefüge

city composition planning, urban structure planning, urban composition planning, town structure planning, town composition planning, city structure planning · Stadtaufbauplanung *f*, Stadtstrukturplanung, Stadtgefügeplanung, Stadtzusammensetzungsplanung

city conservation, city preservation, urban conservation, urban preservation, town conservation, town preservation · Stadtpflege *f*, Stadterhaltung *f*

city constitution, urban constitution, town constitution · Stadtverfassung *f*

city construction, urban building, urban construction, town building, town construction, city building · Städtebau *m*

city construction board, urban construction board, urban building board, town building board, town construction board, city building board · Stadtbauamt *n*, städtisches Bauamt

city construction code, town building code, town construction code, urban building code, urban construction code, city building code · städtische Bauordnung *f*, Stadtbauordnung

city construction project, city building project, urban construction project, urban building project, town construction project, town building project · städtebauliches Vorhaben *n*, städtebauliches Projekt *n*

city construction theory, urban construction theory, town construction theory · Städtebautheorie *f*

city conversion, town conversion, urban conversion · Stadtumbau *m*

city core, core of the city, core of the town, urban core, town core · Stadtkern *m* [*im physiognomischen Sinn*]

city council, town council, urban council · (Stadt)Rat *m*, Stadtvertretung *f*, Stadtparlament *n*, städtischer Gemeinderat, Stadtgemeinderat

city councillor, town councillor, urban councilman, town councilman, city councilman, town council member, city council member, urban council member, urban councillor · (Stadt)Verordnete *m*, (Stadt)Rat(smitglied) *m*, *(n)*

city-court [*A judicial court held in a city by the city magistrates; in the USA the municipal court of a city, consisting of the mayor or recorder and aldermen*] · Stadtgericht *n*

city culture, town culture, urban culture · Stadtkultur *f*

city design, urban design, town design · dreidimensionale Stadtplanung *f*, räumliche Stadtplanung, Stadtgestaltung [*Dieser Zweig liegt zwischen Stadtplanung und Architektur und schafft Leitbilder stadträumlicher Gestaltung*]

city design team, city design group, urban design team, urban design group, town design team, town design group · Städtebau(arbeits)gruppe *f*

city development, urban development, town development · städtische Entwick(e)lung *f*, städtebauliche Entwick(e)lung, Stadtentwick(e)lung

city development area, urban development area, town development area · städtische Bebauuungsfläche *f*

city development assistance, urban development assistance, town development assistance · Städtebauförderung *f*

city development corporation, urban development corporation, town development corporation · Stadtentwick(e)lungskorporation *f*, Stadtentwick(e)lungskörperschaft *f*

city development land, urban development land, town development land · städtebaulicher Entwick(e)lungsbereich *m*

city development measure, urban development measure, town development measure · städtebauliche Entwick(e)lungsmaßnahme *f*

city development plan, urban development plan, town development plan · Stadtentwick(e)lungsplan *m*

city development planning, urban development planning, town development planning · Stadtentwick(e)lungsplanung *f*

city development programme; town development program, urban development program, city development program (US); town development programme, urban development programme · Stadtentwick(e)lungsprogramm *n*

city development simulation, urban development simulation, town development simulation · Stadtentwick(e)lungssimulation *f*

city district, town district, urban district [*A densely settled area within the city or town limits*] · Stadtbezirk *m*

city drainage scheme, urban drainage scheme, town drainage scheme · Stadtentwässerungsplan *m*

city dweller, urbanite, citizen, burgess, freeman of a borough, townman; cityman [*obsolete*]; urban resident, town resident, city resident, urban inhabitant, town inhabitant, city inhabitant, urban dweller, town dweller · Stadtbewohner *m*, Stadteinwohner, Städter, Stadtbürger

city ecology, ecology of the town, ecology of the city, urban ecology, town ecology · Stadtökologie *f*

city economist, urban economist, town economist · Stadtwirtschaftler *m*

city economy, urban economy, town economy · Stadtwirtschaft *f*

city educational officer, city educational official, urban educational officer, urban educational official, town educational officer, town educational official · Stadtschulrat *m*

city element, town element, urban element · Stadtfliese *f*

city engineer, town engineer, urban engineer · Stadtingenieur *m*

city engineering, urban engineering, town engineering · Stadtbautechnik *f*, Städtebautechnik

city enlargement, city extension, urban enlargement, urban extension, town enlargement, town extension · Stadterweiterung *f*

city enlargement plan, city extension plan, urban enlargement plan, urban extension plan, town enlargement plan, town extension plan · Stadterweiterungsplan *m*

city enlargement planning → urban enlargement planning

city environment, urban environment, town environment · Stadtumwelt *f*

city environmental factor, urban environmental factor, town environmental factor · Stadtumweltfaktor *m*

city exchequer — city land

city exchequer, office of municipal finances, town exchequer · Stadtkämmerei *f*

city extension, urban enlargement, urban extension, town enlargement, town extension, city enlargement · Stadterweiterung *f*

city extension area, city extension territory, urban extension area, urban extension territory, town extension area, town extension territory · Stadtneubaugebiet *n*, Stadterweiterungsgebiet

city extension plan, urban enlargement plan, urban extension plan, town enlargement plan, town extension plan, city enlargement plan · Stadterweiterungsplan *m*

city extension planning → urban enlargement planning

city family, urban family, town family · Stadtfamilie *f*

city father, town father, urban father · Stadtvater *m*

city filler, town filler · Städtefüller *m* [*Handwerk; Dienstleistungsbetriebe usw.*]

city forest, urban forest, town forest · Stadtwald *m*

city form, urban form, town form · Stadtform *f*

city-forming, town-forming · städtebildend

city-forming industry, sporadic industry, town-forming industry · stadtbildende Industrie *f*

city fortification, urban fortification, town fortification · Stadtbefestigung *f*

city founder, town founder · Stadtgründer *m*, Städtegründer, Stadterbauer, Städteerbauer

city freeman · Stadtbürger *m* von London

city fringe, urban fringe, town fringe · Vorstadtgelände *n*, Bannmeile *f*, Stadtrandzone *f*

city function, urban function, town function · städtische Funktion *f*, Stadtfunktion

city garden, urban garden, town garden · Stadtgarten *m*

city gate, urban gate, town gate · Stadttor *n*

city geography, urban geography, geography of towns, geography of cities, town geography · Stadtgeographie *f*, Städtegeographie

city (ground) plan, urban layout, town layout, city layout, urban (ground) plan, town (ground) plan · Stadtgrundriß *m*

city growth pattern, town growth pattern, urban growth pattern · Stadtwachstumsmuster *n*, Städtewachstumsmuster, Stadtwachstumsschema, Städtewachstumsschema

city-hall, town-hall, moot-house, moot-hall · Stadthaus *n*, Rathaus

city history research, urban history research, town history research · Stadtgeschichtsforschung *f*

city hous(ebuild)ing, urban hous(ebuild)ing, town hous(ebuild)ing · Stadtwohn(ungs)bau *m*, städtischer Wohn(ungs)bau

city hous(ebuild)ing practice, urban hous(ebuild)ing practice, town hous(ebuild)ing practice · Stadtwohn(ungs)wesen *n*, städtisches Wohn(ungs)wesen

city hous(ebuild)ing sector, urban hous(ebuild)ing field, town hous(ebuild)ing field, city hous(ebuild)ing field, urban hous(ebuild)ing sector, town hous(ebuild)ing sector · Stadtwohn(ungs)sektor *m*, städtischer Wohn(ungs)sektor [*als Tätigkeitsgebiet*]

city housing, town housing, urban housing · Stadtwohnungen *f pl*, städtische Wohnungen

city housing land (area), urban residential land (area), urban housing land (area), town residential land (area), town housing land (area), city residential land (area) · städtischer Wohn(ungs)(bau)boden *m*, städtisches Wohn(ungs)(bau)land *n*, städtische Wohn(ungs)(bau)fläche *f*

city improvement planner, urban improvement planner, town improvement planner · Stadterschließungsplaner *m*

city improvement planning, urban improvement planning, town improvement planning · Stadterschließungsplanung *f*, städtische Erschließungsplanung

city infrastructure, urban infrastructure, town infrastructure · Stadtinfrastruktur *f*

city inhabitant, urban dweller, town dweller, city dweller, urbanite, citizen, burgess, freeman of a borough, townman; cityman [*obsolete*]; urban resident, town resident, city resident, urban inhabitant, town inhabitant · Stadtbewohner *m*, Stadteinwohner, Städter, Stadtbürger

city interspersed with green areas, town interspersed with green areas · durchgrünte Stadt *f*

city land, town land, urban land · städtischer Bereich *m* [*Im planerischen Sinne*]

city land — city planning administration

city land, urban land, town land · städtischer Boden *m*, städtisches Land *n*, Stadtboden, Stadtland, Stadtgrund, städtischer Grund *m*

city land rent, urban land rent, town land rent · städtische Grundrente *f*

city land(s) use, town land(s) use, urban area use, city area use, town area use, urban land(s) use · städtische Bodennutzung *f*, städtische Landnutzung, städtische Flächennutzung, Stadtbodennutzung, Stadtlandnutzung, Stadtflächennutzung

city land(s) use density, urban land(s) use density, town land(s) use density · städtische Flächennutzungsdichte *f*, städtische Bodennutzungsdichte, städtische Landnutzungsdichte

city land(s) use plan, urban land(s) use plan, town land(s) use plan · Stadtflächennutzungsplan *m*

city land(s) use planning, urban land(s) use planning, town land(s) use planning · Stadtflächennutzungsplanung *f*

city land(s) value, urban land value, town land value · städtischer Landwert *m*, städtischer Bodenwert, Stadtlandwert, Stadtbodenwert

city law, urban law, town law · Stadtrecht *n* [*Das in einer Stadt geltende Recht*]

city layout, urban (ground) plan, town (ground) plan, city (ground) plan, urban layout, town layout · Stadtgrundriß *m*

city life, urban life, town life · städtisches Leben *n*, Stadtleben [*Summe der in einer Stadt sinnfällig werdenden Tätigkeiten, Verkehrsbewegungen und Einrichtungen, die der materiellen und kulturellen Bedarfsdeckung der Stadtbewohner, gegebenenfalls auch der Bewohner eines Hinterlandes dienen*]

city location, town location, urban site, town site, city site, urban location · Stadtstandort *m*, städtischer Standort

city lot, urban lot, town lot · städtisches Katastergrundstück *n*, städtisches Grundstück (im katastertechnischen Sinne), städtisches Kartengrundstück, städtisches Flurstück, städtische (Kataster)Parzelle *f*, Stadtgrundstück (im katastertechnischen Sinne), Stadtkatastergrundstück, Stadt-Kartengrundstück, Stadt(kataster)parzelle, Stadtflurstück

cityman [*obsolete*]; urban resident, town resident, city resident, urban inhabitant, town inhabitant, city inhabitant, urban dweller, town dweller, city dweller, urbanite, citizen, burgess, freeman of a borough, townman · Stadtbewohner *m*, Stadteinwohner, Städter, Stadtbürger

city (masonry) wall, urban (masonry) wall, town (masonry) wall · Stadtmauer *f*

city master plan, urban master plan, town master plan · Stadtgeneralplan *m*

city middle class, urban middle class, town middle class · städtische Mittelschicht *f*

city migrant, urban migrant, town migrant · Stadtwanderer *m*

city moat, urban moat, town moat · Stadtgraben *m*

city model, urban model, town model · Stadtmodell *n*

city morphology, town morphology, urban morphology · Stadtmorphologie *f*

city network, urban network, town network · städtisches Netz *n*, Stadtnetz

city noise, urban noise, town noise · Stadtlärm *m*

city of bureaucracy, town of bureaucracy · Verwaltungsstadt *f*

city office, city agency, urban agency, urban office, town agency, town office · städtische Dienststelle *f*

city officer, city official, urban officer, urban official, town officer, town official · Stadtbeamte *m*, städtischer Beamte

city ordinance, urban statute, urban by(e)-law, urban ordinance, town statute, town by(e)-law, town ordinance, city statute, city by(e)-law · Stadtsatzung *f*, Stadtstatut *n*, Stadtgesetz *n*

city-owned, town-owned · stadteigen

city-owned land(s), town-owned land(s) · stadteigenes Land *n*, stadteigener Boden *m*, stadteigener Grund *m*

city parish, urban parish, town parish · städtisches Kirchspiel *n*

city park, urban park, town park · Stadtpark *m*

city pattern, urban pattern, town pattern · Stadtmuster *n*, Stadtschema *n*

city plan, urban plan, town plan · städtebaulicher Plan *m*, Städtebauplan

city plan → city (ground) plan

city planner, town planner, urban planner · Stadtplaner *m*, Städteplaner

city planning, town planning, urban planning · Städte(bau)planung *f*, Stadt(bau)planung, städtebauliche Planung

city planning act → city planning law

city planning administration, town planning administration, urban planning administration · Stadtplanungsverwaltung *f*

city planning area — city renewal

city planning area, urban planning area, town planning territory, city planning territory, urban planning territory, town planning area · Stadtplanungsgebiet *n*

city planning authority, urban planning authority, town planning authority · Stadtplanungsbehörde *f*

city planning board, urban planning board, town planning board · Stadtplanungsamt *n*

city planning commission, urban planning commission, town planning commission · Stadtplanungsausschuß *m*

city planning consultant, urban planning consultant, town planning consultant · Stadtplanungsberater *m*

city planning data, urban planning data, town planning data · städtebauliche Planungsgrundlagen *f pl*

city planning education, urban planning education, town planning education · Stadtplanerausbildung *f*

city planning ideas competition, urban planning ideas competition, town planning ideas competition · städtebaulicher Ideenwettbewerb *m*

city planning institute, urban planning institute, town planning institute · Institut für Städtebau, Städtebauinstitut *n*

city planning law, urban planning law, town planning law · Stadtplanungsrecht *n*, städtisches Planungsrecht, städtebauliches Planungsrecht

city planning law, city planning statute, city planning act, urban planning act, urban planning law, urban planning statute, town planning law, town planning act, town planning statute · Stadtplanungsgesetz *n*, städtisches Planungsgesetz, städtebauliches Planungsgesetz

city planning model, urban planning model, town planning model · städtebauliches Leitbild *n*

city planning office, urban planning office, town planning office · Stadtplanungsstelle *f*

city planning officer, town planning officer, urban planning officer · Stadtplanungsbeamte *m*

city planning organization, urban planning organization, town planning organization · Stadtplanungsorganisation *f*

city planning practice, urban planning practice, town planning practice · Stadtplanungswesen *n*

city planning science, urban planning science, town planning science · Stadtplanungswissenschaft *f*

city planning statute → city planning law

city planning survey, urban planning survey, town planning survey · städtebauliche Enquête *f*, Stadtplanungsenquête, städtische Planungsenquête

city planning task, urban planning task, town planning task · städtebauliche Aufgabe *f*

city planning territory, urban planning territory, town planning area, city planning area, urban planning area, town planning territory · Stadtplanungsgebiet *n*

city poorhouse → almonry of a city

city population, urban population, town population · Stadtbevölkerung *f*, städtische Bevölkerung, Stadtvolk *n*

city population density, urban population density, town population density · Stadtbevölkerungsdichte *f*

city population structure, urban population structure, town population structure · Stadtbevölkerungsstruktur *f*, Stadtbevölkerungsgefüge *n*, Stadtbevölkerungszusammensetzung *f*, Stadtbevölkerungsaufbau *m*

city preservation, urban conservation, urban preservation, town conservation, town preservation, city conservation · Stadtpflege *f*, Stadterhaltung *f*

city prison, urban prison, town prison · Stadtgefängnis *n*

city protection, town protection, urban protection · Stadtschutz *m*

city quarter, local community, urban quarter, town quarter · Stadtviertel *n*, Stadtteil *m, n*, Stadtquartier *n*

city railway, urban railway, town railway (Brit.); urban railroad, town railroad, city railroad (US) · Stadtbahn *f*

city rate, town rate, urban rate · städtische Steuer *f*, Stadtsteuer

city (real) estate, city (real) property, city realty, urban (real) estate, urban realty, urban (real) property, town (real) estate, town (real) property, town realty · städtischer Bodenbesitz *m*, städtischer Grund(stücks)besitz, städtischer Landbesitz, Stadtbodenbesitz, Stadtlandbesitz, Stadt-Grund(stücks)besitz, Grund(stücks)besitz in der Stadt, städtischer Besitz, Besitz in der Stadt

city rebuilding, town reconstruction, town rebuilding, urban reconstruction, urban rebuilding, city reconstruction · Stadtwiederaufbau *m*

(city) recorder, town recorder, urban recorder · (Stadt)Syndikus *m*

city renewal, urban renewal, town renewal, city revival, urban revival, town revival [*The adjustment of obsolete parts of the urban structure to meet anticipated future demand*] · Stadterneuerung *f*

city renewal area — city structure planning

city renewal area, city revival area, urban renewal area, urban revival area, town renewal area, town revival area · Stadterneuerungsfläche f

city renewal legislation, city renewal lawmaking, town renewal legislation, town renewal lawmaking, urban renewal legislation, urban renewal lawmaking, city revival legislation, town revival legislation, urban revival legislation, city revival lawmaking, town revival lawmaking, urban revival lawmaking · Stadterneuerungsgesetzgebung f

city renewal specialist, city revival specialist, urban renewal specialist, urban revival specialist, town renewal specialist, town revival specialist · Stadterneuerungsfachmann m

city re-planning, urban re-planning, town re-planning · Stadtumplanung f

city resident, urban inhabitant, town inhabitant, city inhabitant, urban dweller, town dweller, city dweller, urbanite, citizen, burgess, freeman of a borough, townman; cityman [*obsolete*]; urban resident, town resident · Stadtbewohner m, Stadteinwohner m, Städter, Stadtbürger

city residential environment, urban residential environment, town residential environment · städtische Wohnumwelt f

city residential land (area), city housing land (area), urban residential land (area), urban housing land (area), town residential land (area), town housing land (area) · städtischer Wohn(ungs)(bau)boden m, städtisches Wohn(ungs)(bau)land n, städtische Wohn(ungs)(bau)fläche f

city revival area, urban renewal area, urban revival area, town renewal area, town revival area, city renewal area · Stadterneuerungsfläche f

cityscape → civicized landscape

city scene, urban scene, town scene · Stadtprofil n

city selection, town selection, urban selection · Stadtauslese f

city service, urban service, town service · städtische Dienstleistung f

city serving industry, ubiquitous industry, town serving industry · stadtführende Industrie f

city setting, urban setting, town setting · städtische Umgebung f

city settlement, urban settlement, town settlement · Stadt(an)sied(e)lung f, städtische (An)Sied(e)lung

city settlement area [*According to Dickinson "the urban tract" (verstädtertes Gebiet) und the rural urban fringe (ländlicher Gürtel)*], metropolitan region, metropolitan area [*Metropolis together with a surrounding area which is strongly influenced by and dependent on the metropolis, as evidenced by activities which would not be there but for the proximity of the metropolis*] · Metropolenregion f, Stadt f und (ihr) Hinterland

city sewage, urban sewage, town sewage · städtisches Abwasser n, Stadtabwasser

city site, urban location, city location, town location, urban site, town site · Stadtstandort m, städtischer Standort

city size, town size · Stadtgröße f

city size distribution, distribution of town size, distribution of city size, town size distribution · Stadtgrößenverteilung f

city social system, urban social system, town social system · städtisches Sozialsystem n

city sociologist, urban sociologist, town sociologist · Stadtsoziologe m

city sociology, urban sociology, town sociology · Stadtsoziologie f, städtische Soziologie

city space, urban space, town space · Stadtraum m, städtischer Raum

city space organization → city spatial organization

city space structure, town spatial structure, town space structure, urban spatial structure, urban space structure, city spatial structure · städtische Raumstruktur f, städtische Raumzusammensetzung f, städtisches Raumgefüge n, städtischer Raumaufbau m

city state, town state, urban state · Stadtstaat m

city statistic(s), town statistic(s), urban statistic(s) · Städtestatistik f

city statute, city by(e)-law, city ordinance, urban statute, urban by(e)-law, urban ordinance, town statute, town by(e)-law, town ordinance · Stadtsatzung f, Stadtstatut n, Stadtgesetz n

city store, town store, urban store · Zentral(laden)geschäft n, zentripetales (Laden)Geschäft

city street grid → urban street grid

city structure, urban structure, town composition, urban composition, city composition, town structure · Stadtstruktur f, Stadtzusammensetzung f, Stadtgefüge n, Stadtaufbau m, städtische Struktur, städtische Zusammensetzung, städtischer Aufbau, städtisches Gefüge

city structure planning, city composition planning, urban structure planning, urban composition planning, town structure planning, town composition planning · Stadtaufbauplanung f, Stadtstrukturplanung, Stadtgefügeplanung, Stadtzusammensetzungsplanung

city surface, urban surface, town surface · Stadtoberfläche f

city surveyor, urban surveyor, town surveyor · Stadtbaumeister m

city surveyor-general, urban surveyor-general, town surveyor-general · Stadtoberbaurat m

city territory, urban area, urban territory, town area, town territory, city area · städtisches Gebiet n [*Ein Gebiet, welches im funktionalen und physiognomischen Sinne vorrangig durch städtische Funktionen geprägt ist*]

city trade, urban trade, town trade · Stadtgewerbe n, städtisches Gewerbe

city trade area, urban trade area, town trade area · Stadtgewerbegebiet n

city traffic, town traffic, urban traffic · Stadtverkehr m

city transport(ation) network, urban transport(ation) network, urban transit network, town transit network, town transport(ation) network, city transit network · städtisches (Massen)Verkehrsnetz n

city transport(ation) planning, urban transport(ation) planning, urban transit planning, town transit planning, town transport(ation) planning, city transit planning · städtische (Massen)Verkehrsplanung f

city treasurer, urban treasurer, town treasurer · Stadtkämmerer m

city treasury, town treasury, municipal treasury · Stadtkasse f

city uglification, town uglification, urban uglification · Stadtverschandelung f

city umland, urban umland, town umland · Stadtumland n

city-village, urban village [*According to Dickinson*]; mere urban tract [*According to Wooldridge and East*]; town-village · Pseudostadt f, unechte Stadt, Stadtdorf n

cityward migration, townward migration · Stadt(zu)wanderung f

cityward(s), townward(s) [*Toward, or in the direction of, the city. Also capable of being used attributively or as adjective, as in "the cityward view, course, route, etc."*] · stadtwärts

city with municipal charter, town with municipal charter · Stadt f mit Municipium

civic; civical [*obsolete*] [*Of, pertaining, or proper to citizens*] · bürgerlich

civically [*In a civic manner or sense*] · bürgerlicherweise

civic amenities law, nature conservation law · Landeskulturrecht n

civic amenities law, civic amenities act, civic amenities statute, nature conservation law, nature conservation act, nature conservation statute · Landeskulturgesetz n

civic duty · Bürgerpflicht f

civic enterprise, neighbourhood council (Brit.); neighborhood council (US); citizen group [*The citizens of a city cooperate to promote the common good and general welfare of the people of the city*] · Bürgerinitiative f, Interessengruppe f, Einwohnerinitiative, Bürgergruppe f

civicism [*Civic system or organization*] · Bürgersystem n

civicism [*The principle that all citizens have equal rights and duties*] · Bürgergleichheit f

to civicize, to make urban, to urbanize · verstädtern

to civicize [*To make civic*] · verbürgerlichen

civicized, urbanized, citied [*Made into or like a city*] · verstädtert

civicized · verbürgerlicht

civicized landscape, cityscape, townscape, urban agglomeration; conurbation (Brit); urban tract [*According to Dickinson*]; urban(ized) landscape [*An area occupied by a continuous series of dwellings, factories and other buildings, harbour and docks, urban parks and playing fields, etc., which are not separated from each other by rural land; though in many cases such an urban area includes enclaves of rural land which is still in agricultural occupation*] · Stadtlandschaft f, Städtelandschaft, verstädterte Landschaft, Städteschar f, Städteagglomeration f, Zusammenstädterung f

civics [*The theory of the rights and duties of citizenship*] · Bürgerrechtslehre f, Bürgerkunde f

civic spirit, public spirit, sense of citizenship · Bürgersinn m

civil [*Opposite sense of criminal and military*] · zivil

civil action → civil (court) action

civil aeronautics authority · Zivilluftfahrtbehörde f

civil case · Zivil(rechts)fall m

civil cause, civil (court) action, civil plea, civil (law)suit · Zivil(gerichts)klage f

civil code — (civil) engineering geology

civil code, code of civil law · bürgerliches Gesetzbuch n, BGB

(civil) commotion · (Bürger)Unruhe f

civil corporation [z. B. die Bürgerschaft einer Gemeinde] · weltliche Körperschaft f, weltliche Korporation f, bürgerliche Körperschaft, bürgerliche Korporation

civil court · Zivilgericht n

civil (court) action, civil plea, civil (law-)suit, civil cause · Zivil(gerichts)klage f

civil death; mors civilis [Latin] [That change of a person's civil condition which is produced by certain acts or offences on his part; and which extinguishes his civil rights and capacities, just as natural death extinguishes his bodily existence] · bürgerlicher Tod m

civil disorder game · Notsituationsspiel n, Notstandsspiel

(civil) engineer, construction engineer · Bauingenieur m

(civil) engineer contract, construction engineer contract · Bauingenieurvertrag m

(civil) engineering, (engineering) construction, construction engineering [It involves construction which is planned and designed by professional (civil) engineers. It is often divided into highway construction (= Straßenbau) and heavy construction (= Tiefbau)] · Ingenieurbau m

(civil) engineering activity, (engineering) construction activity, construction engineering activity · Ingenieurbautätigkeit f

(civil) engineering administration, (engineering) construction administration, construction engineering administration · Ingenieurbauverwaltung f

(civil) engineering agreement, (engineering) construction agreement, construction engineering agreement [It is a part of a construction contract] · Ingenieurbauvertrag m [Der Vertrag als Vertragsbestandteil; andere Vertragsbestandteile sind Zeichnungen, Angebot, Garantie usw.]

(civil) engineering board, (engineering) construction board, construction engineering board · Ingenieurbauamt n

(civil) engineering code of practice, (engineering) construction code of practice, construction engineering code of practice · Ingenieurbaumerkblatt n

(civil) engineering condition, (engineering) construction condition, construction engineering condition · Ingenieurbaubedingung f

(civil) engineering contract, (engineering) construction contract, construction engineering contract · Ingenieurbauvertrag m [Der Vertrag und alle Vertragsbestandteile zusammen]

(civil) engineering contractor, (engineering) construction contractor, construction engineering contractor, building contractor · Ingenieurbauunternehmer m, Bauunternehmer, BU

(civil) engineering cost(s), (engineering) construction cost(s), construction engineering cost(s) · Ingenieurbaukosten f

(civil) engineering cost(s) index, (engineering) construction cost(s) index, construction engineering cost(s) index · Ingenieurbau(kosten)index m [Die Kennziffer für die Höhe der Ingenieurbaukosten, jeweils im Vergleich zu einer festgesetzten Basis auf Grund bestimmter Berechnungen aus der Praxis ermittelt]

(civil) engineering department, (engineering) construction department, construction engineering department · Ingenieurbauabteilung f

(civil) engineering drawing, (engineering) construction drawing, construction engineering drawing · Ingenieurbauzeichnen n

(civil) engineering drawing, (civil) engineering plan, (engineering) construction drawing, (engineering) construction plan, construction engineering drawing, construction engineering plan · Ingenieurbauzeichnung f, Ingenieurbauplan m

(civil) engineering expert, (engineering) construction expert, construction engineering expert · Ingenieurbausachverständige m

(civil) engineering expertise, (engineering) construction expertise, construction engineering expertise · Ingenieurbaugutachten n

(civil) engineering field, (engineering) construction sector, construction field, construction engineering sector, construction engineering field, (civil) engineering sector · Ingenieurbausektor m

(civil) engineering financing, (engineering) construction financing, construction engineering financing · Ingenieurbaufinanzierung f

(civil) engineering geologist, (engineering) construction geologist, construction engineering geologist, heavy construction geologist · Tiefbaugeologe m, Bau(grund)geologe

(civil) engineering geology, (engineering) construction geology, construction engineering geology, heavy construction geology, heavy construction geology · Bau(grund)geologie f, Tiefbaugeologie

(civil) engineering geology expertise, construction geology expertise, heavy construction geology expertise, heavy construction geology expertise · Baugrundgutachten n

(civil) engineering industry, (engineering) construction industry, construction engineering industry · Ingenieurbauindustrie f

(civil) engineering legislation, (civil) engineering lawmaking, (engineering) construction legislation, (engineering) construction lawmaking, construction engineering legislation, construction engineering lawmaking · Ingenieurbaugesetzgebung f

(civil) engineering operations, (civil) engineering work(s), (engineering) construction operations, (engineering) construction work(s), construction engineering operations, construction engineering work(s) · Ingenieurbauarbeit(en) f (pl), Ingenieurbauleistung(en) f (pl)

(civil) engineering plan, (engineering) construction drawing, (engineering) construction plan, construction engineering drawing, construction engineering plan, (civil) engineering drawing · Ingenieurbauzeichnung f, Ingenieurbauplan m

(civil) engineering practice, (engineering) construction practice, construction engineering practice · Ingenieurbauwesen n

(civil) engineering price, (engineering) construction price, construction engineering price · Ingenieurbaupreis m

(civil) engineering provision, (engineering) construction provision, construction engineering provision · Ingenieurbaubestimmung f

(civil) engineering sector, (civil) engineering field, (engineering) construction sector, (engineering) construction field, construction engineering sector, construction engineering field · Ingenieurbausektor m

(civil) engineering sub-contract, (engineering) construction sub-contract, construction engineering sub-contract · Nachunternehmervertrag m im Ingenieurbau, Subunternehmervertrag im Ingenieurbau, Unterunternehmervertrag im Ingenieurbau, Unterakkordantenvertrag im Ingenieurbau [Schweiz]

(civil) engineering sub(contractor), (engineering) construction sub(contractor), construction engineering sub(contractor) · Ingenieurbaunachunternehmer m, Ingenieurbausubunternehmer; Ingenieurbauunterakkordant m [Schweiz]

(civil) engineering technique, (engineering) construction technique, construction engineering technique · Ingenieurbautechnik f, Ingenieurbaupraxis f [als betriebstechnische Anwendung]

(civil) engineering tender, (civil) engineering offer, (civil) engineering bid, (engineering) construction tender, (engineering) construction offer, (engineering) construction bid, construction engineering tender, construction engineering offer, construction engineering bid; (civil) engineering (bid) proposal, (engineering) construction (bid) proposal, construction engineering (bid) proposal (US) · Ingenieurbauangebot n

(civil) engineering volume, (engineering) construction volume, construction engineering volume · Ingenieurbauvolumen n

(civil) engineering worker, (engineering) construction worker, construction engineering worker · Ingenieurbauarbeiter m

(civil) engineer in private practice, construction engineer in private practice, consulting (civil) engineer, consulting construction engineer · beratender Bauingenieur m, Beratungsbauingenieur

civil government · Zivilregierung f

civilian, nonmilitary person · Zivilist m, Zivilperson f

civilian [One who makes or has made civil law the object of his study; a practitioner, doctor, professor, or student of civil law, a writer or authority on civil law] · Zivilrechtfachmann m

civilian population; non-combatants [French] · Zivilbevölkerung f

civilis possessio, corporalis possessio [Latin] · genießliche Gewere f, hebbende Gewere, nützliche Gewere, Eigengewere, titellose Gewere, brukerode Gewere, eigentliche Gewere

civil judg(e)ment · Zivilurteil n

civil law; jus civile, corpus juris civilis [Latin] · (objektives) Zivilrecht n, bürgerliches Recht

(civil) law of Rome, Roman (civil) law; jus civile Romanum [Latin] [As distinguished from the English law] · römisches Recht n [„Civil law" ist die englische Sammelbezeichnung für die im römischen Recht wurzelnden Rechtsordnungen]

civil law partnership · Gesellschaft f bürgerlichen Rechts, BGB-Gesellschaft

civil (law)suit, civil cause, civil (court) action, civil plea · Zivil(gerichts)klage f

civil law with reference to construction · bauliches Zivilrecht n

civil liability · zivilrechtliche Haftbarkeit f, zivilrechtliche Haftung f, zivilrechtliche Haftpflicht f

civil liberty, civil rights · (subjektive) Grundrechte npl, (subjektive) Zivilrechte

civilly dead · bürgerlich tot [z. B. ein Geächteter]

civil matter · Zivilsache f

civil parish · Kirchspiel n zur Durchführung der Lokalverwaltung, (Pfarr)Sprengel m zur Durchführung der Lokalverwaltung, kirchlicher Sprengel zur Durchführung der Lokalverwaltung, Parochie f zur Durchführung der Lokalverwaltung

civil plea, civil (law)suit, civil cause, civil (court) action · Zivil(gerichts)klage f

civil procedure rules, Code of Civil Procedure, rules of civil procedure · ZPO f, Zivilprozeßordnung

civil proceeding · zivilprozessualisches Verfahren n

civil registrar, registrar (of births and marriages and deaths) · Zivilstandsbeamte m, Standesbeamte

civil right · (subjektives) Grundrecht n, (subjektives) Zivilrecht

civil rights, civil liberty · (subjektive) Grundrechte npl, (subjektive) Zivilrechte

civil servant, clerk · Bedienstete m [*Im Staatsdienst und öffentlichen Dienst*]

civil service · öffentlicher Dienst m

civil service · Zivildienst m

Civil Service Commission [*USA*] · Bundespersonalamt n

civil service worker · Arbeiter m im öffentlichen Dienst

civil side · zivilrechtliche Seite f

civil status → lawful ability

civil suit → civil (law)suit

(civil) wrong → violation (of law)

clachan [*Galic*]; bally [*Irish*]; balley [*Manx*]; tref [*Welsh*]; ker [*Brittanic*] · Drubbel m; Eschdorf n [*nach Rothert 1924*]; Eschweiler m [*nach Helbok 1938*]

to claim, to demand (as one's own) · verlangen, fordern

claim, demand · Forderung f, Verlangen n

claim → (mining) claim

claimant · Fordernde m, Forderungsberechtigte, Beanspruchende, Forderer

to claim back, to demand back, to reclaim · zurückfordern, zurückverlangen

to claim by action, to dispute by action, to litigate, to go to law, to carry on a (law)suit, to bring into litigation, to engage in litigation [*Latin: litigare*] · prozessieren, einen Rechtsstreit austragen, einen Prozeß anhängig machen, rechtshängig werden lassen

claim debtor, claim obligor, demand debtor, demand obligor · Forderungsschuldner m, Verlangensschuldner

claim for additional payment, demand for additional payment · Nachforderung f, Nachverlangen n

claim for compensation for efforts · Ausgleichsanspruch m, Ausgleichsforderung f, Ausgleichsverlangen n

claim for early completion, demand for early completion, acceleration claim, acceleration demand · Beschleunigungsvergütungsforderung f, Beschleunigungsvergütungsverlangen, (Leistungs)Prämienforderung, (Leistungs)Prämienverlangen n

claim for indemnification, claim for indemnity, claim for compensation, claim for damages, compensation claim, indemnity claim, indemnification claim, damages claim · Entschädigungsforderung f, Schadenersatzforderung, Entschädigungsverlangen n, Schadenersatzverlangen

claim for making good of defect, demand for remedying of defect, demand for making good of defect · Baumangelbeseitigungsforderung f, Baumangelbeseitigungsverlangen n, (Sach)Mangelbeseitigungsverlangen, Nachbesserungsverlangen, (Sach)Mangelbeseitigungsforderung, Nachbesserungsforderung

claim for payment, payment demand, payment claim, demand for payment · Zahlungsverlangen n, Zahlungsforderung f

claim from having found a mine · (Gruben)Fundrecht n

claim in rem, real claim, demand in rem, real demand · dingliche Forderung f, dingliches Verlangen n

claim in tort, demand in tort, tort claim, tort demand · Forderung f aus unerlaubter Handlung, Verlangen n aus unerlaubter Handlung

claim obligor, demand debtor, demand obligor, claim debtor · Forderungsschuldner m, Verlangensschuldner

claim of a cause, demand of a cause, claim of a plea, demand of a plea, claim of a (law)suit, demand of a (law)suit, claim of a court action, claim of an action, demand of an action · Klageforderung f, Klageverlangen n

claim of contribution, demand of contribution, contribution claim, contribution demand · Beitragsforderung *f*, Beitragsverlangen *n*

claim of harmonization, harmonization demand, demand of harmonization, harmonization claim · Übereinstimmungsforderung *f*, Übereinstimmungsverlangen *n*

claim of privilege [*Claim entitling a person to refuse the production of documents for inspection*] · Vorlageverweigerung *f*, Einsichtnahmeverweigerung

claim of right, demand of right · Rechtsforderung *f*, Rechtsverlangen *n*

claim of title, demand of title, title claim, title demand · Titelforderung *f*, Titelverlangen *n*, Freigabeforderung, Freigabeverlangen

claim period, demand period, period of claim, period of demand · Forderungsfrist *f*, Verlangensfrist

claim to compensation for tort, claim to damages for tort, claim to indemnity for tort, claim to indemnification for tort · Schadenersatzforderung *f* für unerlaubte Handlung, Entschädigungsforderung für unerlaubte Handlung, Schadensersatzverlangen *n* für unerlaubte Handlung, Entschädigungsverlangen für unerlaubte Handlung

claim to inheritance, inheritance claim, demand to inheritance, inheritance demand · Erb(schafts)forderung *f*, Erb(schafts)verlangen *n*

claim to money, demand to money, money demand, pecuniary demand, pecuniary claim, money claim · Geldforderung *f*, Geldverlangen *n*

clan · Sippe *f*

clan hamlet · Sippenweiler *m*

clan settlement · Sippen(an)sied(e)lung *f*

clan village · Sippendorf *n*

clarification · Aufklärung *f*, Klarstellung

clarification, disclosure · Aufklärung *f*, (Beweis)Offenlegung, Offenbarung, Auskunft *f*, Vorlage *f*

clarification duty, duty of disclosure, duty of clarification, disclosure duty · Aufklärungspflicht *f*, Offenbarungspflicht, (Beweis)Offenlegungspflicht, Auskunftspflicht, Vorlagepflicht

to clarify, to free from secrecy, to free from ignorance, to lay bare, to disclose, to reveal, to knowledge, to make known · aufklären, enthüllen, offenbaren, offenlegen, offen darlegen, preisgeben, kundtun, vorlegen

clarify of form(s) · Formenklarheit

class-consciousness · Klassenbewußtsein *n*

class (court) action, class plea, class (law-)suit, class cause · Gruppenklage *f*

class distinction · Klassendünkel *m*

classical English mortgage · resolutiv bedingte Übereignung *f*

classical heavy construction work(s), classical heavy construction operation(s) [*As opposed to heavy construction works associated with building construction*] · eigentliche Tiefbauarbeit(en) *f (pl)*, eigentliche Tiefbauleistung(en) *f (pl)*

classification → (zoning) classification

classification of functions, functional classification · Funktions(auf)gliederung *f*

classification of land(ed) property according to soil quality · Bonitierung *f* [*Bodengüte*]

classification of land(s) use, land(s) use classification · Bodennutzungseinteilung *f*, Flächennutzungseinteilung, Landnutzungseinteilung

classification of zoning, (zoning) classification · (Auf)Gliederung *f* [*Baunutzungsverordnung*]

classification survey · Klassifizierungsaufnahme *f*

classification table for arable land · Ackerschätzungsrahmen *m*

classificatory variable · Klass(ifiz)ierungsveränderliche *f*

classified highway, classified road · klassifizierte Straße *f*

to classify land(ed) property according to soil quality · bonitieren [*Bodengüte*]

class lawmaking, class legislation · Klassengesetzgebung *f*

classless society · klassenlose Gesellschaft *f*

class of population, population class · Bevölkerungsklasse *f*

class of property, property class · Vermögensklasse *f*

class of stock, stock class · Aktiengattung *f*

class structure · Klassenaufbau *m*, Klassenzusammensetzung *f*, Klassengefüge *n*, Klassenstruktur *f*

class struggle, class warfare · Klassenkampf *m*

clause [*A paragraph or subdivision of a legal document*] · Klausel *f*

claused bill of lading, foul bill of lading, foul B/L, dirty bill of lading · unreines Konnossement *n*

clause of defeasance — clearance of slums

clause of defeasance · Annullierungsklausel f

clause of execution, execution clause · Vollstreckungsklausel f

clause of hardship, hardship clause · Härteklausel f

clause of interpretation, clause of construction, interpretation clause, construction clause · Auslegungsklausel f, Deutungsklausel f

clause of re-entry, re-entry clause · (Besitz)Wiederübernahmeklausel f, Wiederinbesitznahmeklausel, Wiedereintrittklausel

clause of weighing the facts · Abwägungsklausel f

clause reference · Klauselbezug m

clause-riddled · verklausuliert

Clauses Consolidations Act 1847 · Konsolidierungsgesetz n [England] [Die in vielen „Local Acts" zur Anwendung gelangten Rechtsgrundsätze für die innere Verwaltung werden systematisch in je einem Gesetz, entsprechend dem Hauptgegenstand, zusammengefaßt]

clause(s) prohibition · Klauselverbot n

clause stipulating insurance, insurance clause · Versicherungsklausel f

Clawson approach, user-benefit approach · Clawson-Ansatz m [Zum Messen des primären Nutzens aus einem Erholungsakt über die Schätzung einer Erholungsnachfragekurve]

clean air area, clean air territory, air quality territory, air quality area · Luftreinhaltungsgebiet n, Luftreinhaltegebiet

clean air code, air quality code · Luftreinhaltungsordnung f

clean air control, air pollution control, air pollution prevention, atmospheric pollution control, atmospheric pollution prevention, air quality control · Luftreinhaltung f

clean air law, air quality law · Luftreinhaltungsrecht n

clean air legislation, clean air lawmaking, air quality legislation, air quality lawmaking · Luftreinhaltungsgesetzgebung f, Luftreinhaltegesetzgebung

clean air plan, air quality plan · Luftreinhaltungsplan m, Luftreinhalteplan

clean air statute, clean air law, clean air act, air quality act, air quality statute, air quality law · Luftreinhaltungsgesetz n, Luftreinhaltegesetz

clean bill of lading, clean B/L · reines Konossement n

clean draft · ungesicherte Tratte f, nichtdokumentäre Tratte

clean hands · einwandfreies Verhalten n

clean(s)ing department, clean(s)ing division · Reinigungsabteilung f

clean(s)ing duty of (the) tenant · Reinigungspflicht f des Mieters

clean(s)ing of ditches · Grabenreinigung f

clean(s)ing of sewers, sewer clean(s)ing · (Abwasser)Kanalreinigung f

clean(s)ing of (the) air · Luftreinigung f

clear, sal(e)able, perfect, good, marketable · frei, vollgültig [(Rechts)Titel]

clear, perfect, free from load(s), unloaded, not imperfect, without a burden, without a load, burdenless, free from encumbrance(s), free from charge(s), free from incumbrance(s), free from burden(s), uncharged, unburdened, unencumbered, unincumbered · entschuldet, lastenfrei, (dinglich) unbelastet, (dinglich) nicht belastet

clearance, clearing (up) [The clearing of land(s) from any obstructions] · Aufräumen n

clearance → (slum) clearance

clearance area → (slum) clearance area

clearance authority → (slum) clearance authority

clearance builder → (slum) clearance builder

clearance card [A letter given to an employe(e) by his employer, at the time of his discharge or end of service, showing the cause of such discharge or voluntary quittance, the length of time of service, his capacity, and such other facts as would give to those concerned information of his former employment] · Dienstzeugnis n

clearance committee → (slum) clearance committee

clearance corporation → (slum) clearance corporation

clearance cost(s) → (slum) clearance cost(s)

clearance gain → (slum) clearance profit

clearance hamlet · Rodeweiler m

clearance law → (slum) clearance law

clearance loss → (slum) clearance loss

clearance measure → (slum) clearance measure

clearance of site (on completion), site clearance (on completion) · Baustellenräumung f

clearance of slums, eradication of slums, demolition of slums, (slum) clearance, slum eradication, slum demolition ·

Elendsviertelbeseitigung f [1. Entkernung; 2. Totalsanierung]

clearance of (the) (building) land, (building) land clearance · (Bauland)Freilegung f

clearance order → (slum) clearance order

clearance parcel → (slum) clearance parcel

clearance plan → (slum) clearance plan

clearance planning → (slum) clearance planning

clearance plot → (slum) clearance plot

clearance procedure → (slum) clearance procedure

clearance profit → (slum) clearance profit

clearance resolution → (slum) clearance resolution

clearance sale · Räumungsverkauf m

clearance sale → (slum) clearance sale

clearance site → (slum) clearance site

clearance village · Rodedorf n

clearance work(s), clearing (up) work(s) · Aufräumungsarbeit(en) f(pl)

clear annuity [*The devise of an annuity "clear" means an annuity free from taxes*] · steuerfreie Annuität f

to clear away · wegräumen

cleared · geräumt

cleared · saniert

cleared site value · Grund(stücks)wert m nach Räumung

clear evidence, clear proof [*Evidence which is positive, precise and explicit, which tends directly to establish the point to which it is adduced and is sufficient to make out a prima facie case*] · einwandfreier Beweis m

clear gain, clear profit, net gain, net profit, pure gain, pure profit · Reingewinn m, Reinprofit m, Nettogewinn, Nettoprofit

clearing · Abrechnung f, Skontration f, Saldierung, Liquidation, Kompensation, Skontrierung [*Eine organisierte Ausgleichung von Zahlungen bzw. Forderungen und Gegenforderungen unter mehr als zwei Personen*]

clearing · Geldausgleich m, Abrechnungsverkehr m [*zwischen Banken*]

clearing-house · Abrechnungsstelle f

clearing process · Abrechnungsvorgang m [*Skontration von bankmäßigen Zahlungen*]

clearing (up), clearance [*The clearing of land(s) from any obstructions*] · Aufräumen n

clearing (up) gang · Aufräumungskolonne f

clearing (up) work(s), clearance work(s) · Aufräumungsarbeit(en) f(pl)

clearly erroneous · offensichtlich falsch

clearly proved · klar bewiesen

clearness of statement, definiteness, absence of doubt, distinctness, certainty · Bestimmtheit f, Klarheit, Gewißheit

clear profit → clear gain

clear proof, clear evidence [*Evidence which is positive, precise and explicit, which tends directly to establish the point to which it is adduced and is sufficient to make out a prima facie case*] · einwandfreier Beweis m

clear residue [*Addition of income from funds, used to pay decedent's debts, administration expenses, and general legacies, to residue of estate*] · reiner Nachlaß m

clear to the understanding, evident, obvious, manifest · augenscheinlich, offensichtlich

to clear (up) · aufräumen

clergy fee, fee of clergy · Stolgebühr f

clerical error, writing error · Schreibfehler m

clerical error correction, writing error correction · Schreibfehlerberichtigung f

clerical error made in good faith, writing error made in good faith · unabsichtlicher Schreibfehler m, unbeabsichtigter Schreibfehler

clerical labour, office labour (Brit.); office labor, clerical labor (US) · Büroarbeitskräfte fpl

clerical mistake, writing mistake · Schreibirrtum m

clerical personnel, clerical staff, office staff, office personnel · Büropersonal n

clericus [*Latin*]; clerk (in holy orders) · Geistliche m

clerk, civil servant · Bedienstete m [*Im Staatsdienst und öffentlichen Dienst*]

clerk in consular office · Konsularsekretär m

clerk (in holy orders); clericus [*Latin*] · Geistliche m

clerk of justices · Bezirkssekretär m [*Sekretär der Petty und Special Sessions. Er ist in der Regel ein studierter Jurist, der nebenbei eine anwaltschaftliche Praxis betreibt*]

clerk of magistrates — closed-end fund

clerk of magistrates · Friedensrichtersekretär *m*

clerk of the council, council clerk · Kanzleivorsteher *m* [*Beamter einer Distriktstadt in England*]

clerk of (the) court), court clerk · Gerichtsschreiber *m*, Aktuar *m*, Gerichtskanzlist *m*

clerk of the Crown [*England*] · Kronsekretär *m*

clerk of the market, market clerk · Marktschreiber *m*

clerk of the peace · Friedenssekretär *m*, Grafschaftssekretär, ständiger Sekretär der Quartalsitzungen, Leiter der Kanzlei der Friedensgerichte, Generalsekretär [*England*]

clerk of the (poor law) union, (poor law) union clerk [*In England*] · Armen(pflege)verbandvorsteher *m*

clerk of the works, on-site clerk · Baustellenverwaltungsangestellte *m*

clerk to the guardians · Armenratsekretär *m*, Sekretär *m* des Armenamtes

client, employer, promoter, (building) owner, construction owner, project owner [*In Great Britain, the term "employer" is preferred since this is used in both the RIBA and ICE standard forms of contract*] · Bauherr(schaft) *m*, (*f*), Auftraggeber *m*, BH *f*, AG *m* [*im Sinne der VOB*]; Besteller [*im Sinne des BGB*] [*Nach geläufiger Fachsprache ist „Bauherr" stets der „Letzt-Besteller" eines Bauwerkes (oder Bauwerk-Teils), also nicht der Unternehmer, der einen Subunternehmer bezieht. Dieser „Letzt-Besteller" ist Bauherr im engen (und eigentlichen) Sinne des Wortes. In einem übertragenen (nicht geläufigen) Sinne aber kann „Bauherr" auch ein Unternehmer sein, der übernommene Bauarbeiten durch Abschluß eines Bauvertrages an einen Subunternehmer weitervergibt. In diesem übertragenen Sinne muß das Wort dann verstanden werden, wenn die SIA-Norm 118 (Schweiz) auf den Bauvertrag zwischen Unternehmer und Subunternehmer zur Anwendung kommt. Im Verhältnis Unternehmer/Subunternehmer ist alsdann der erstere „Bauherr" im Sinne der Norm, der andere „Unternehmer"*]

client · Kunde *m*

client · Mandant *m*

client-designed project, employer-designed project, promoter-designed project, owner-designed project · Bauherrenentwurfsprojekt *n*, Bauherrschaftsentwurfsprojekt

client's delay, employer's delay, promoter's delay, owner's delay · bauseitiger Verzug *m*

client's design, employer's design, promoter's design, owner's design · Ausschreibungsentwurf *m*, Bauherrenentwurf *m*

client's liability, employer's liability, owner's liability, promoter's liability · Bauherrenhaftpflicht *f*, Bauherrenhaftung *f*, Bauherrenhaftbarkeit *f*

client's liability insurance, employer's liability insurance, promoter's liability insurance, owner's liability insurance · Bauherrenhaftpflichtversicherung *f*, Bauherrschaftshaftpflichtversicherung

client's risk, employer's risk, promoter's risk, owner's risk · Bauherrenrisiko *n*, Bauherrenwagnis *n*, Bauherrschaftsrisiko, Bauherrschaftswagnis

climate geography · Klimageographie *f*

climatic belt · Klimagürtel *m*

climatic map · Klimakarte *f*

climatic planning · Klimaplanung *f*

climatic zone · Klimazone *f*

climatological atlas · Klimaatlas *m*

clogging the (equity of) redemption · Verhinderung *f* der (Pfand)Einlösung

to close · abschließen [*Verkauf; Kauf*]

to close · schließen [*z. B. Grundbuchblatt*]

close, closing [*An assembly of the parties in a real estate transaction, at which purchaser and seller execute appropriate documents referring title from the seller to the purchaser*] · Abschluß *m* [*Kauf; Verkauf*]

close, paddock, intake · (Tier)Gehege *n*

close → closing

to close an account, to state an account, to settle an account · abschließen [*Konto*]

close company · Gesellschaft *f* [*Im Besitz von nur wenigen Personen und nicht börseneingeführt*]

closed · abgeschlossen [*Hypothek*]

closed, stated, settled · abgeschlossen [*Konto*]

closed area, closed territory, prohibited area, prohibited territory · Sperrgebiet *n*

closed development, closed (block) system · geschlossene Bauweise *f*, Blockbebauung [*Der Baublock hat eine allseitige Randbebauung*]

closed-end fund, closed-end investment trust · geschlossener (Investment)Fonds *m*, Investmentfonds mit begrenzter Stückzahl der auszugebenden Anteile für die keine Rücknahmeverpflichtung besteht

**closed-end fund, **closed-end company · Investmentfonds *m* mit beschränkter Emissionshöhe von Anteilen, Investmentgesellschaft *f* mit beschränkter Emissionshöhe von Anteilen

closed pound, covert pound · geschlossener Pfandstall *m*

closed primary (election) [*USA*] · geschlossene Vorwahl *f*, geschlossene Erstwahl, geschlossene Urwahl [*Der Vorwahlteilnehmer muß seine Parteizugehörigkeit aufdecken und gegebenenfalls nachweisen*]

(closed) scholarship, fellowship · Stipendium *n*, Freistelle *f*

closed sequential model · abgeschlossenes sequentielles Modell *n* [*Statistik*]

closed shop [*England*] · Betrieb *m* mit nur Gewerkschaftsmitgliedern, Unternehmen *n* mit nur Gewerkschaftsmitgliedern, Unternehmung *f* mit nur Gewerkschaftsmitgliedern

closed-shop agreement · Abkommen *n* nur Gewerkschaftsmitglieder zu beschäftigen, Abmachung *f* nur Gewerkschaftsmitglieder zu beschäftigen, Vereinbarung nur Gewerkschaftsmitglieder zu beschäftigen

close-in space [*A space immediately surrounding an urban settlement*] · Nahraum *m*

close of pleadings · Schließung *f* des Schriftsatzwechsels, Schriftsatzwechselschluß *m*

close season, prohibited month; (de)fence month (Brit.); defense month (US) [*A period of thirty-one days in the year, during which time it is unlawful for anybody to hunt in the forest*] · Schonzeit *f*, Hegezeit, Setzzeit

close statement → closing statement

closing, close [*An assembly of the parties in a real estate transaction, at which purchaser and seller execute appropriate documents referring title from the seller to the purchaser*] · Abschluß *m* [*Kauf; Verkauf*]

closing date (for receipt of tenders), closing time (for receipt of bids), bid(ding) date, closing date for bids, date of receipt of bids, tendering date · (Angebots)Abgabedatum *n*, (Angebots)Abgabetermin *m*, Einreich(ungs)datum, Einreich(ungs)termin, Angebotstermin, Angebotsdatum

closing order [*Order for closing part or the whole of a building which is unfit for human habitation*] · Räumungsbefehl *m*, Räumungsgebot *n*, Räumungsanordnung *f*, Räumungsverfügung

closing speech · Schlußrede *f*, Schlußwort *n*, Schlußansprache *f*

closing statement, close statement [*Accounting of funds in a real estate sale made by a broker to the seller and buyer, respectively*] · Abschluß(konto)auszug *m*

closing time · Schlußzeit *f*

closing time (for receipt of bids), bid(ding) date, closing date for bids, date of receipt of bids, tendering date, closing date (for receipt of tenders) · (Angebots)Abgabedatum *n*, (Angebots)Abgabetermin *m*, Einreich(ungs)datum, Einreich(ungs)termin, Angebotstermin, Angebotsdatum

cloth hall · Gewandhaus *n*

cloud interpretation · Wolkenauswertung *f*

cloud on (the) title · (Rechts)Titelbelastung *f*, (Rechts)Titelmangel *m*

cluster · gedrängte Mittelpunkte *m pl* [*flächenförmige (Standort)Ballung*]

cluster development [*Development of a land tract in a cluster(ing) pattern*] · Zellenbebauung *f*

cluster(ing) scheme, cluster(ing) pattern · Zellenmuster *n*, Zellenschema *n* [*Stadtplanung*]

cluster of trees, tree cluster · Baumgruppe *f*

cluster road village, irregular nucleated road village · (Haufen)Wegedorf *n*, (Haufen)Straßendorf

cluster sampling · Klumpenauswahlverfahren *n* [*Statistik*]

cluster settlement, nucleated settlement with an irregular street-plan, agglomerated settlement · Haufen(an)sied(e)lung *f*, unregelmäßig zusammengewachsene (An)Sied(e)lung, Gruppen(an)sied(e)lung mit unregelmäßigem Grundriß

cluster village, irregular nucleated village · Haufendorf *n*

CMF, central management function · zentrale Führungsfunktion *f*

co-administration, joint administration · Mit(nachlaß)verwaltung *f*, erbrechtliche Mitverwaltung, Erb(schafts)mitverwaltung, gerichtliche (Nachlaß)Mitverwaltung

co-administrator → (probate) co-administrator

co-aid, joint aid, co-help, joint help · Mithilfe *f*

coaling harbour (Brit.); coaling harbor (US) · Bekohlungshafen *m*

coalition · Interessengemeinschaft *f*

coal miners' settlement · Kohlenbergarbeiter(an)sied(e)lung *f*, Zechenarbeiter(an)sied(e)lung

coal mining enterprise, coal mining undertaking · Kohlenbergbauunternehmen *n*, Kohlenbergbaubetrieb *m*, Kohlenbergbauunternehmung *f*

coal mining servitude · Kohlenabbaugerechtigkeit *f*, Kohlenabbaudienstbarkeit, Kohlenabbauservitut *n*, *f*, (servitutisches) Kohlenabbaurecht *n*

coal tithe · Kohlenzehnt *m*

coarse tithe, great tithe, large tithe [*A chief predial tithe, as corn, hay, wood and fruit*] · großer Zehnt *m*

co-assign(ee), co-cessionary, joint assign(ee), joint cessionary · Mitzessionar *m*, Mitzessionär

coast(al) area, coastline · Küstengebiet *n*

coast(al) belt · Küstengürtel *m*

coast(al) city → coast(al) town

coast(al) ecology · Küstenökologie *f*

coast(al) environment · Küstenumwelt *f*

coast(al) fishery, coast(al) fishing · Küstenfischerei *f*

coast(al) forest · Küstenwald *m*

coast(al) green belt · Küstengrüngürtel *m*

coast(al) highway, coast(al) road · Küstenstraße *f*

coast(al) landscape · Küstenlandschaft *f*

coast(al) low land, low coast(al) land · Küstentiefland *n*, Küstentiefebene *f*

coast(al) mapping · Küstenkartierung *f*

coast(al) metropolis · Küstenmetropole *f*

coast(al) navigation, cabotage, coastwise navigation, coasting · Küstenschiffahrt *f*

coast(al) plan · Küstenplan *m*

coast(al) protection · Küstenschutz *m*

coast(al) protection act, coast(al) protection law, coast(al) protection statute · Küstenschutzgesetz *n*

coast(al) protection area, coast(al) protection territory · Küstenschutzgebiet *n*

coast(al) protection authority · Küstenschutzbehörde *f*

coast(al) protection law · Küstenschutzrecht *n*

coast(al) province · Küstenprovinz *f*

coast(al) resort, sea resort · Seebad(eort) *n*, *(m)*

coast(al) road → coast(al) highway

coast(al) state, maritime state · Küstenstaat *m*

coast(al) stretch, stretch of coast · Küstenstreifen *m*

coast(al) town, coast(al) city · Küstenstadt *f*

coast(al) waters [*In geographic and nautical sense*], territorial waters, territorial sea, maritime belt, belt of sea, sea belt [*In political sense*] · Küstengewässer *n*, Küstenmeer *n*, Territorialgewässer, Hoheitsgewässer, Meeresstreifen *m*, Hoheitsmeer, Territorialmeer

coast blockade · Küstenblockade *f*

coasting, coast(al) navigation, cabotage, coastwise navigation · Küstenschiffahrt *f*

coastline, coast(al) area · Küstengebiet *n*

coast-man · Küstenbewohner *m*

coastward(s) · küstenwärts

coastwise navigation, coasting, coast(al) navigation, cabotage · Küstenschiffahrt *f*

co-buyer, joint purchaser, joint buyer, co-purchaser · Mitkäufer *m*

co-cessionary, joint assign(ee), joint cessionary, co-assign(ee) · Mitzessionar *m*, Mitzessionär

co-contractor, joint contractor · Mitunternehmer *m*

co-creditor, co-promisee, co-debtee, fellow creditor, fellow promisee, fellow debtee, joint creditor, joint promisee, joint debtee · Mitgläubiger *m*, Mitversprechensempfänger, Gesamtgläubiger, Gesamtversprechensempfänger

code, codification [*The collection of all the principles of any system of law into one body after the manner of the Codex Justinianus and other codes*] · Kodifikation *f*, Kodifizierung, Gesetzeszusammenfassung *f*

code [*A system or collection of rules or regulations on any subject*] · Ordnung *f*

code administration, code enforcement [*The regulation by an official agency of the adherence to a governmental entity's codes by those subject to its provisions; usually refers to the administration or enforcement of minimum standards of occupancy*] · Ordnungsdurchführung *f*

co-debtee, fellow creditor, fellow promisee, fellow debtee, joint creditor, joint promisee, joint debtee, co-creditor, co-promisee · Mitgläubiger *m*, Mitversprechensempfänger, Gesamtgläubiger, Gesamtversprechensempfänger

co-debtor, co-obligor, fellow debtor, fellow obligor, joint debtor, joint obligor · Mitschuldner *m*, Gesamtschuldner

code enforcement, code administration [*The regulation by an official agency of the adherence to a governmental*

code of arbitration — co-executor

entity's codes by those subject to its provisions; usually refers to the administration or enforcement of minimum standards of occupancy] · Ordnungsdurchführung *f*

code of arbitration, arbitration code, arbitral code · Schiedsordnung *f*, Schiedsgerichtsordnung

code of bankruptcy, bankruptcy code · Konkursordnung *f*, KO

code of civil law, civil code · bürgerliches Gesetzbuch *n*

Code of Civil Procedure, rules of civil procedure, civil procedure rules · ZPO *f*, Zivilprozeßordnung

code of condominium owners (US); code of private flat owners (Brit.) · Gemeinschaftsordnung *f*, Miteigentumsordnung [*Wohnungseigentümergemeinschaft*]

code of (court) procedure, (court) procedure code, rules of (court) practice, rules of (court) procedure, (general) (standing) rules of court, court (practice) rules, procedural code · Prozeßregeln *fpl*, Prozeßordnung *f*, Gerichtsverfahrensregeln, Gerichtsverfahrensordnung, (gerichtliche) Verfahrensregeln, (gerichtliche) Verfahrensordnung

code of criminal procedure, criminal procedure code · Strafprozeßordnung *f*, StPO

code of ethics · Berufsehrenordnung *f*

code of factory discipline · Arbeitsordnung *f*

code of flotsams, code of jetsams · Strandungs(gut)ordnung *f*, Strandgutordnung

code of honour (Brit.); code of honor (US) · Ehrenkodex *m*

code of land(s) management, land(s) management code · Bodenbewirtschaftungsordnung *f*, Landbewirtschaftungsordnung

code (of law), codex [*A systematic collection or digest of the laws of a country, or those relating to a particular subject*] · Gesetzbuch *n*, Kodex *m*

code of ownership (of property), code of proprietorship, code of (general) property · Eigentumsordnung *f*

code of practice · Merkblatt *n*

code of practice for the construction industry, code of practice for the building industry, construction industry code of practice, building industry code of practice · Baumerkblatt *n*

code of prescriptions, code of regulations, code of rules · (Rechts)Vorschriftenordnung *f*

code relating to industry and business · Gewerbeordnung *f*, GewO

codetermination, industrial democracy [*An economic system in which the workers have a share in the management of industry*] · Mitbestimmung *f*

codetermination · Mitspracherecht *n*

codex, code (of law) [*A systematic collection or digest of the laws of a country, or those relating to a particular subject*] · Gesetzbuch *n*, Kodex *m*

codicil; codicillus [*Latin*] [*A supplement or addition made to a will by the testator*] · Kodizill *n*, Testamentsanhang *m*, Testamentsnachtrag *m*, Testamentszusatz *m*

codification, code [*The collection of all the principles of any system of law into one body after the manner of the Codex Justinianus and other codes*] · Kodifikation *f*, Kodifizierung, Gesetzeszusammenfassung *f*

codification guide line · Kodifizierungsrichtlinie *f*, Kodifikationsrichtlinie

codification of mercantile law · Kodifikation *f* des Handelsrechts, Kodifizierung *f* des Handelsrechts

codified law, digested law · kodifiziertes Recht *n*

codifier [*One who codifies*] · Kodifizierer *m*

to codify, to digest, to reduce (laws) to a code · kodifizieren

codifying statute · Rechtsregel *f* aus richterlicher Praxis gewonnen

coding · Kodierung *f*

COD price, cash price, cash on delivery price · Barpreis *m*, Effektivpreis

coefficient of association, association coefficient · Assoziationskoeffizient *m*

coefficient of correlation, correlation coefficient · Korrelationskoeffizient *m*

coefficient of geographical association, coefficient of linkage, linkage coefficient · Koeffizient *m* der räumlichen Verflechtung

coefficient of localization, localization coefficient · Lokalisierungskoeffizient *m*

coefficient of (value added by) manufacture, form-value [*Manufacturing in the process of giving "form" to coarse materials*] · Formkoeffizient *m*

coercion · Zwang *m*

coerci(ti)ve detention · Beugehaft *f*

coerci(ti)ve measure, measure of coercion · Zwangsmaßnahme *f*

co-executor · Mit(testaments)vollstrecker *m*

co-executor dative [*Scotland*] → (probate) co-administrator

cognates [*Those related on the mother's side*] · mutterseitige Verwandtschaft *f*, Verwandtschaft mütterlicherseits

cognition and volition · Wissen *n* und Wollen *n*

cognitive mapping · subjektive Kartierung *f* [*Landkartenerstellung nach kognitiven Repräsentationen einer bestimmten Umwelt beim Individuum*]

cognovit [*An acknowledg(e)ment by a defendant that the plaintiff's cause is just, in which case the defendant, to save expense, suffers judg(e)ment to be entered against him without trial*] · Anerkenntnis *n* des Beklagten

coguarantee, coguaranty, coguarantie · Mitbürgschaft *f*

coguarantor · Mitbürge *m*

cohabitation, community of life [*Living together as husband and wife; often with the implication of not being married*] · Lebensgemeinschaft *f*

co-heir, fellow-heir, joint-heir, co(in)heritor, joint inheritor, (co)parcener; coparticeps [*In old English law*] · Anteilerbe, Miterbe *m*, Erbgenosse *m*, (Bruch)Teilerbe

co-heiress, fellow-heiress, joint-heiress · Miterbin *f*, Erbgenossin

co-help, joint help, co-aid, joint aid · Mithilfe *f*

coheritor → co-heir

coinage right, right of coinage · Münzrecht *n*

coined money, milled money · Münzgeld *n*

to co-inhere, to inhere together · miterben

co-inheritance, (estate in) (co)parcenary, joint heirship · Anteilerbschaft *f*, Anteilerbe *n*, (Bruch)Teilerbschaft, (Bruch)-Teilerbe, Miterbschaft, Miterbe

co(in)heritor → co-heir

coin minting · Münzprägen *n*

coin-operated machine · Münzautomat *m*

coins, base-metal money; hard money (US) · Metallgeld *n*, Hartgeld, Münzen *fpl*

coinsurance · Mitversicherung *f*

coinsuree · Mitversicherte *m*

coinsurer · Mitversicherer *m*

co-judge, joint judge · Mitrichter *m*

coke-town [*in England*]; large industrial town, large industrial city · Industriegroßstadt *f*, industrielle Großstadt

cold timber line · Höhenbaumgrenze *f*, Baumgrenze

co-legatary, joint legatary · Mitvermächtnisnehmer *m*

co-lessee, joint lessee · Mitpächter *m*

co-lessor, joint lessor · Mitverpächter *m*, Mitpachtherr

colibert, tenant of socage-land, socageland tenant, socage tenant, gainor, sok(e)man, socman, socheman, socager, tenant by socage, tenant in socage, tenant in ancient demesne, servant · freier weltlicher Leh(e)n(s)besitzer *m*, (weltlicher) Freigutbesitzer

collapse, crash · Einsturz *m* [*Bauwerk*]

collapse danger, crash danger, failure danger · Einsturzgefahr *f*, Einfallgefahr

collapsible, collapsable, capable of collapsing, capable of breaking down, capable to fail · einsturzgefährlich, einfallgefährlich [*Bauwerk*]

collapsing, breaking down, failing, crashing, dropping to pieces · Einstürzen *n*, Einfallen

collateral [*Belonging to the common ancestral stock, although not in direct line of descent*] · in Seitenlinie, seitenlinienverwandt

collateral acceptance, acceptance supra protest · Ehrenakzept *n*, Ehrenannahme(vermerk) *f*, *(m)*, Ehrenannahmeerklärung *f* [*auf einem Wechsel*]

collateral agreement · nebensächliche Vereinbarung *f*, nebensächliche Abmachung, nebensächliches Abkommen *n*

collateral assurance [*Assurance made over and above a principal deed*] · Ehrenversprechen *n*

collateral consanguinity · Seitenlinien-Blutsverwandtschaft *f*

collateral contract · Nebenvertrag *m*

collateral estoppel · Widerspruch *m* zu eigenem Verhalten

collateral estoppel [*Conclusiveness of judg(e)ment in prior action where subsequent action is upon a different cause of action*] · Feststellung *f* eines früheren Urteils

collateral fact [*A fact outside the controversy, or not directly connected with the principal matter or issue in dispute*] · Nebentatsache *f*

collateral guaranty, collateral guarantee, collateral guarantie · Gesamtbürgschaft *f*, Solidarbürgschaft

collateral heiress, collateral heir female, heiress collateral, heir female collateral · Seitenlinienerbin *f*

collateral heir (male) — collection cautioner

collateral heir (male), heir (male) collateral · Seitenlinienerbe *m*

collateral (hereditary) descent, collateral (hereditary) succession, collateral succession by inheritance, collateral heirdom · Erbfolge *f* in der Seitenlinie, Erbgang *m* in der Seitenlinie, erbrechtliche Nachfolge in der Seitenlinie

collateral kinsman · Seitenlinienverwandte *m*

collateral liability · akzessorische Obligation *f*

collateral line of descent · Seiten(abstammungs)linie *f*

collateral loan · Nebensicherheitsdarleh(e)n *n* [*Ein durch eine Nebensicherheit gedecktes Darleh(e)n*]

collateral negligence · positive Vertragsverletzung *f*, pVV, positive Forderungsverletzung [*Dem Bauherrn entsteht ein Schaden oder entstehen Schäden dadurch, daß der Architekt eine sich aus dem Vertrag ergebende Nebenpflicht schuldhaft verletzt. Sie verpflichtet den Architekten zu Schadenersatz. Die Benennung ,,positive Forderungsverletzung" ist juristisch besser als die andere*]

collateral (promissory) note [*A promissory note to which is added a description of the property which has been pledged by the maker as security that the note will be paid at maturity*] · Eigenwechsel *m* durch Sicherheiten gedeckt

collateral security [*It is given in addition to the principal security. Thus, a person who borrows money on mortgage (which is the principal security) may deposit an insurance policy or shares with the lender as collateral security*] · Nebendeckung *f*, Nebensicherung, Nebensicherheit *f*, Nebenunterlage *f*, mittelbare Deckung, mittelbare Sicherheit, mittelbare Sicherung, mittelbare Unterlage

collateral succession by inheritance, collateral heirdom, collateral (hereditary) descent, collateral (hereditary) succession · Erbfolge *f* in der Seitenlinie, Erbgang *m* in der Seitenlinie, erbrechtliche Nachfolge in der Seitenlinie

collateral trust bond (US) [*These bonds are secured by securities deposited with a trustee*] · treuhänderisch gesicherte Schuldverschreibung *f*, treuhänderisch gesicherte Obligation *f*, Schuldverschreibung durch Wertpapiere gesichert, Obligation durch Wertpapiere gesichert

collatio bonorum [*Latin*]; hotchpot(ch), collation [*In Roman and Scots law. The throwing together of the possessions of several persons, in order to an equal division of the whole stock*] · Besitzzusammenlegung *f* zwecks gleichmäßiger Verteilung, Gemengsel *n*, Farrago *n*

collation of seals [*In ancient deeds, when one seal was set on the back of another, upon the same ribbon, or label*] · Siegelvergleich *m*

collation of texts, textural comparison, collation of wordings [*Of different copies of a document*] · Textvergleich *m*

collative advowson, advowson collative · Patronat(srecht) *n* bei dem der Bischof der Patron ist, Präsentation(srecht) bei dem der Bischof der Patron ist

to collect, to get renewed possession of, to get again, to obtain again, to recover, to win back, to regain · zurückerhalten, wiedererlangen, wiedererhalten, zurückgewinnen, zurückbekommen

to collect, to obtain, to recover, to enforce payment [*amount*] · beitreiben, eintreiben, einziehen [*Betrag*]

to collect, to gather, to procure, to raise [*money, etc.*] · erheben

collecta [*Latin*] → petitio

collectable, obtainable, recoverable, collectible · beitreibbar, eintreibbar, einziehbar

collecting, gathering, procuring, raising · Erheben *n*

collecting, obtaining, recovering, enforcing payment · Beitreiben *n*, Eintreiben, Einziehen [*Betrag*]

collecting agency, collection agency · Inkassostelle *f*

collecting agent, collection agent · Inkassobevollmächtigte *m*, Inkassovertreter

collecting charitable corporation, collecting charitable corporate body, collecting charitable body corporate · Sammlung *f* von juristischen Personen mit wohltätigen oder gemeinnützigen Zwecken

collecting charity · Sammelvermögen *n*

collection, collectorate [*A district under the jurisdiction of a collector of customs, taxes, etc.*] · Erhebungsbezirk *m*, Einziehungsbezirk, Eintreibungsbezirk [*Steuern; Zölle; usw.*]

collection · Sammlung *f*

collection, raise, procurement, procuration · Erhebung *f*

collection, recovery, enforcement of payment [*amount*] · Beitreibung *f*, Eintreibung, Einziehung [*Betrag*]

collection agency, collecting agency · Inkassostelle *f*

collection agent → collecting agent

collection cautioner, collection guarantor, guarantor of collection, surety of collection, cautioner of collection, collection

collection loss — collective system

surety · Ausfallbürge *m*, Rückbürge, Schad(los)bürge

collection loss, vacancy loss · Mietausfall *m*, Mietverlust *m*

collection loss decline, vacancy (loss) decline · Mietausfallrückgang *m*, Mietverlustrückgang

collection loss risk, collection loss hazard, vacancy (loss) risk, vacancy (loss) hazard · Mietausfallwagnis *n*, Mietausfallrisiko *n*, Mietverlustwagnis, Mietverlustrisiko

collection of contribution(s) · Beitragserhebung *f*

collection of documentary drafts · Dokumententratteninkasso *n*

collection of duties, collection of statutory charges, collection of legal charges · Abgabenerhebung *f*, Erhebung von Abgaben

collection of natural persons, collection of human beings · Zusammenfassung *f* von Menschen, Zusammenfassung von natürlichen Personen

collection of property, property collection · Zusammenfassung *f* von Besitzen, Besitzzusammenfassung

collection of rates, rate collection · Gemeindesteuereinziehung *f*, Gemeindesteuererhebung, Gemeindesteuereintreibung

collection of rights · Rechtsgesamtheit *f*

collection surety, collection cautioner, collection guarantor, guarantor of collection, surety of collection, cautioner of collection · Ausfallbürge *m*, Rückbürge, Schad(los)bürge

(collective) bargaining [*Negotiations relating to the conditions and terms of employment carried on between trade unions and employers or their associations*] · Tarif(partner)verhandlung *f*, Tarifrunde *f*

collective facility · Gemeinschaftseinrichtung *f* [*Eine von mehr als einem Berechtigten zu nutzende Einrichtung, z. B. eine Gemeinschaftsgarage*]

collective (farm) · landwirtschaftliches Kollektiv *n*, Kolchose *f*

collective farming settlement · kollektivwirtschaftliche (An)Sied(e)lung *f*, Kollektiv(an)sied(e)lung

collective garage (building) · Sammelgarage *f*

collective item, omnibus item · Gesamtposition *f*, Sammelposition

collective lease(hold), concurrent lease(hold), joint lease(hold) · Teilerbbaurecht *n*, gemeinsames Erbbaurecht, gemeinschaftliches Erbbaurecht, Gemeinerbbaurecht, Bruchteilerbbaurecht, Mehrheitserbbaurecht, Miterbbaurecht, Anteilerbbaurecht [*Bruchteil eines mehreren Personen gemeinschaftlich zustehenden Erbbaurechts, welcher in der Weise beschränkt ist, daß jedem der Mitberechtigten das Sondereigentum an nicht zu Wohnzwecken dienenden bestimmten Räumen in einem aufgrund des Erbbaurechts errichteten oder zu errichtenden Gebäuden eingeräumt wird. (§ 30 Abs. 1 WoEigG)*]

collective life, communal living [*A style of living that occurs in a commune-like setting*] · gemeinschaftliches Leben *n*, Gemeinschaftsleben, gemeinsames Leben

collectively bargained [*Conditions and terms of employment negotiated between trade unions and employers or their associations*] · tariflich (ausgehandelt)

collectively bargained bonus · tarifliche Gratifikation *f*

collective possession, concurrent possession · Bruchteilbesitz *m*, Anteilsbesitz, Gemeinbesitz, Mehrheitsbesitz, Mitbesitz, Vielherrlich-Besitz, gesamthänderischer Besitz, Gesamt(hand)besitz, vielherrlicher Besitz, gemeinschaftlicher Besitz, gemeinsamer Besitz

collective property, collective ownership (of property), collective proprietorship, co-ownership (of property), concurrent interests, co-proprietorship, co-property, tenancy in common [*The German terms are stronger in the sense of having less flavour of individual rights than the English terms*] · Bruchteileigentum *n*, Anteileigentum, Gemeineigentum, Mehrheitseigentum, Miteigentum, Vielherrlich-Eigentum, gesamthänderisches Eigentum, Gesamthandschaft *f*, vielherrliches Eigentum, Gesamthand(eigentum) *f, (n)*, gemeinschaftliches Eigentum, gemeinsames Eigentum, Gesamteigentum, Quoteneigentum

collective purchase · Sammelkauf *m*

collective responsibility · Kollektivverantwortung *f*

collective short-distance transit, collective short-distance transport(ation), short-distance passenger transit, short-distance mass transit, short-distance passenger transport(ation), short-distance mass transport(ation), short-distance collective transit, short-distance collective transport(ation), (public) short-distance transit, (public) short-distance transport(ation) · (öffentlicher) (Personen)Nahverkehr *m*, ÖPNV

collective system, collectivism · Kollektivsystem *n*

collective task — color (US)

collective task, common task · Gemeinschaftsaufgabe *f*

collective transit, passenger transit, mass transit, collective transport(ation), passenger transport(ation), mass transport(ation), (public) transit, (public) transport(ation) · Massenverkehr *m*, Personen(massen)verkehr, (öffentlicher) Massentransport *m*, öffentlicher Massenverkehr, (öffentliche) Massenbeförderung *f*, öffentliche Beförderung, Personen(massen)transport, Personen(massen)beförderung, Kollektiv(personen)transport, Kollektiv(personen)verkehr, Kollektiv(personen)beförderung

collectivism, collective system · Kollektivsystem *n*

collectivization of farms · Kolchosierung *f*

collector (US); official receiver · gerichtlicher Zwangsverwalter *m*, gerichtlicher Empfänger, gerichtlicher Masse(n)verwalter, gerichtlicher Kurator [*Er nimmt das Eigentum des Schuldners bis zur Ernennung eines Treuhänders in Empfang*]

collector [*One who collects money; an officer employed to collect or receive money due, as taxes, customs, etc.*] · Erheber *m*, Eintreiber, Einzieher, Einkassierer

collectorate, collection [*A district under the jurisdiction of a collector of customs, taxes, etc.*] · Erhebungsbezirk *m*, Einziehungsbezirk, Eintreibungsbezirk [*Steuern; Zölle; usw.*]

collector of alms · Almosensammler *m*

collector of customs, customer · Zollbeamte *m*, Zöllner

collector of rates, rate collector · Gemeindesteuererheber *m*, Gemeindesteuereintreiber, Gemeindesteuereinzieher

collector of taxes · Steuereinzieher *m*, Steuereintreiber, Steuererheber

collector of tithes, tithe-man, tithing-man, tithe-gatherer, tithe-collector · Zehnt(en)mann *m*

college for administrative civil service · Verwaltungsakademie *f*

College of Justice · Korporation *f* der Richter des höchsten schottischen Zivilgerichtshofes [*gegründet 1537*]

collegiate church, collegiate chapter [*A collegiate church is one built and endowed for a society, or body corporate, consisting of a college or chapter with a dean, or president and canons, or prebendaries*] · Kollegiatkirche *f*, Stiftskirche

colliery spoilheap · Zechenabfallhalde *f*

collusion [*Agreement, usually secret, for some deceitful or unlawful purpose*] · betrügerische Abrede *f*, betrügerische Absprache

collusion affidavit → (non-)collusion affidavit

collusion among(st) bidders, collusion among(st) offerers, collusion among(st) tenderers, price taking, collusive agreement, combining to eliminate competition, restrictive covenant, restrictive tendering agreement, taking a price, collusive tendering, collusive bidding, (collusive) price fixing, bid-rigging, bid collusion, rigging bids [*The frequently heavy cost of tendering sometimes leads contractors to put forward tenders which are not genuine, in the sense that, rather than refuse to make a tender when invited to do so, the contractor tenders a price higher than that "taken" from another contractor who does desire to obtain the contract, thus avoiding expense and leading the employer to believe that he has had genuine competitive tenders for the work*] · Abrede *f* unter Bietern, Absprache *f* unter Bietern, Preisabrede, Preisabsprache, Submissionsabrede, Konkurrenzvereinbarung *f*, Verständigung unter Bietern, Angebotsabsprache

(collusive) fee agreement, (collusive) fee fixing · Gebührenabrede *f*, Honorarabrede, Gebührenabsprache *f*, Honorarabsprache

collusive permission → feigned permission

colonat partiaire, share-tenancy, share-tenure, metayage, metayer system [*Under this system land is divided in small farms, among single families, the landlord generally supplying the stock and receiving, in lieu of rent a fixed proportion of the produce. This proportion, which is generally paid in kind, is usually one-half*] · Halbscheidwirtschaft *f*, Halbpacht *f*

colonial green village, colonial plaza village · Kolonisationsangerdorf *n*, Kolonisationsplatzdorf

colonial regime · Kolonialherrschaft *f*

colonial third culture · Überlappung *f* der ursprünglichen Kultur der Einheimischen mit der ursprünglichen Kultur der fremden Elite [*Kolonialstadt*]

colonial town, colonial city · Kolonialstadt *f*

colonization within a State's own territory, settlement within a State's own territory, home colonization, home settlement · (B)Innenkolonisation *f*, innere Kolonisation

color (US); appearance, pretext, pretence; colour (Brit.) [*A fictitious allegation of a right. A person is said to have no colour* of title when he has not even a prima facie title] · Deckmantel m, Vorwand m, Anschein m

colour (Brit.); color (US); appearance, pretext, pretence [A fictitious allegation of a right. A person is said to have no colour of title when he has not even a prima facie title] · Deckmantel m, Vorwand m, Anschein m

colourable claim (Brit.); colorable claim (US) [In bankruptcy law, a claim made by one holding the property as an agent or bailee of the bankrupt; a claim in which as a matter of law, there is no adverseness] · aussonderungsberechtigte Forderung f, Aussonderungsforderung

colourable imitation (Brit.); colorable imitation (US) [In the law of trademarks, this phrase denotes such a close or ingenious imitation as to be calculated to deceive ordinary persons] · Warenzeichenfälschung f

colourable transaction (Brit.); colorable transaction (US) · Scheintransaktion f

colour filling (Brit.); color filling (US) · Farbfüllung f [Kartographie]

colour jet plotter (Brit.); color jet plotter (US); ink jet plotter · Farbbildschreiber m, Tintenstrahlplotter, Tintenstrahlzeichenautomat m

colour of right (Brit.); color of right (US) [Some claim, not necessary legal or official, indicating one's right to ownership of property] · angebliches (An)Recht n, angeblicher Anspruch m

colour of title (Brit.); color of title (US) · Schein m der Rechtmäßigkeit

colour tab (Brit.); color tab (US) · Andruckfarbskala f [Kartographie]

colour wedge (Brit.); color wedge (US) · (Karten)Farbstufenskala f

column · Spalte f

column for remarks, remarks column · Bemerkungsspalte f

combining to eliminate competition, restrictive covenant, restrictive tendering agreement, taking a price, collusive tendering, collusive bidding, (collusive) price fixing, bid-rigging, bid collusion, rigging bids, collusion among(st) bidders, collusion among(st) offerers, collusion among(st) tenderers, price taking, collusive agreement [The frequently heavy cost of tendering sometimes leads contractors to put forward tenders which are not genuine, in the sense that, rather than refuse to make a tender when invited to do so, the contractor tenders a price higher than that "taken" from another contractor who does desire to obtain the contract, thus avoiding expense and leading the employer to believe that he has had genuine competitive tenders for the work] · Abrede f unter Bietern, Absprache f unter Bietern, Preisabrede, Preisabsprache, Submissionsabrede, Submissionsabsprache, Konkurrenzvereinbarung f, Verständigung f unter Bietern, Angebotsabsprache

Combination Laws · Gesetze npl gegen Arbeiterverbindung [England]

combined land (area), combined area, combined territory · gemeinsames Gebiet n, überörtliches Gebiet, gemeinschaftliches Gebiet [Gebietsplan]

to come into existence, to come into operation, to come into being, to take effect, to become to have effect, to inure, to become operative, to enure, to operate · wirksam werden, in Kraft treten

to come to a conclusion, to conclude, to prove, to infer · folgern, ableiten, schließen (von etwas auf etwas)

to (come to an) end, to terminate (automatically), to determine (automatically) [In a certain event] · auslaufen [Frist]

to come to one's own · großjährig werden, volljährig werden

to come to terms about, to come to terms by mutual concession, to settle by mutual concession · einigwerden

to come to terms by mutual concession, to settle by mutual concession, to come to terms about · einigwerden

comfort · Behaglichkeit f

comfort · Gütergenuß m

comfort standard; level of living, living level (US); standard of living, standard of comfort, living standard · Lebensstandard m, Lebensniveau n, Lebenshaltung f

comfort zone · Behaglichkeitszone f

coming into operation, coming into being, coming into existence, commencement (of validity), beginning (of validity) · Inkrafttreten n, Wirksamwerden

comitatus, pagus · Gau m [Im fränkischen Reich]

committee of inspection, inspection committee · Gläubigerausschuß m

comity of nations · internationale Courtoisie f

commanding, binding, authoritative · bindend, verbindlich, geltend

commanding fountain of law, authoritative source of law, authoritative fountain of law, binding source of law, binding fountain of law, commanding source of law · geltende Rechtsquelle f, verbindliche Rechtsquelle, bindende Rechtsquelle

commandite partnership — commercial freshwater fishing

commandite partnership, (private) partnership with limited liability, limited (private) partnership · Kommanditgesellschaft *f*, KG [*Sie besteht aus Gesellschaftern, von denen mindestens einer, der Komplementär, den Gläubigern unbeschränkt haftet, und auch mindestens einer, der Kommanditist, nur mit dem Betrag seiner Einlage*]

commemoratorium, notilia donationis, breve donationis [*Latin*] · (schlichte) Schenkungsurkunde *f* [*Urkunde, in welcher die stattgehabte Schenkung als eine geschehene Tatsache beurkundet wird*]

to commence, to initiate · einleiten [*Verfahren*]

to commence, to begin, to open [*trial of a cause*] · eröffnen, anfangen, beginnen

commencement, institution, initiation [*The commencement of an action or prosecution; as, A. has instituted an action against B. to recover damages for trespass*] · Einleitung *f*

commencement date, date of commencement · Anfangsdatum *n*, Anfangstermin *m*, Anfangstag *m*

commencement of liability, beginning of liability · Haftpflichtbeginn *m*, Haftungsbeginn, Haftbarkeitsbeginn

commencement of (the) limitation period, beginning of (the) limitation period · Verjährungsanfang *m*, Verjährungseintritt *m*

commencement of (the) liquidation, beginning of (the) liquidation, commencement of (the) winding(-)up, beginning of (the) winding(-)up · Liquidationseröffnung *f*

commencement of (the) work(s), beginning of (the) work(s) · Aufnahme *f* der Arbeiten, Beginn *m* der Arbeiten, Arbeitsbeginn, (Bau)Beginn

commencement (of validity), beginning (of validity), coming into operation, coming into being, coming into existence · Inkrafttreten *n*, Wirksamwerden

commencing party, initiating party · einleitende Partei *f*

commendation [*In feudal law, was where an owner of land placed himself and his land under the protection of a lord, so as to constitute himself a vassal or feudal tenant*] · Kommendation *f*

comment(ary) on legal points · Rechtskommentar *m*

commerce power · Handelsgewalt *f*

commercial agency, mercantile agency, credit enquiry agency · Handelsauskunftei *f*

commercial agent, mercantile agent · Handelsagent *m*

commercial arbitrability · Handelsschiedsgerichtsbarkeit *f*

commercial arbitration, commercial arbitrament · Handelsschieds(gerichts)sprechung *f*

commercial arbitration field, field of commercial arbitration · Handelsschieds(gerichts)wesen *n*

commercial bank, credit bank · Kreditbank *f*

commercial bank (US); merchant bank (Brit.) [*Sometimes known as "accepting house", such a bank owes its name to the fact that in most cases the banking and financial sides of its business originally developed as a sideline to its trading activities*] · Handelsbank *f*, Geschäftsbank

commercial bill (of exchange) · Handelswechsel *m*, Warenwechsel

commercial branch · Handelszweig *m*

commercial broker, mercantile broker · Handelsmakler *m*

commercial cause · Handelssache *f*

commercial chamber, chamber of commerce · Handelskammer *f*

commercial city, commercial town · Handelsstadt *f*

commercial code · Handelsgesetzbuch *n*

commercial contract, mercantile contract · Handelsvertrag *m*

commercial corporation · Laienkörperschaft *f* mit wirtschaftlichem Geschäftsbetrieb, Laienkörperschaft *f* mit wirtschaftlichem Geschäftsbetrieb

commercial corporation, association · Handelsgesellschaft *f*

commercial court · Handelsgericht *n*

commercial credit · Handelskredit *m*

commercial depression · Handelsnotstand *m*

commercial enterprise, commercial undertaking · Handelsunternehmen *n*, Handelsunternehmung *f*, Handelsbetrieb *m*

commercial forest · Wirtschaftswald *m*, Forst *m*, Holzfabrik *f*, Holzacker *m*, Stangenacker [*Hauptkennzeichen ist die durch Anpflanzung und Pflege erreichte Einheitlichkeit des Bestandes und des Alters der Bäume innerhalb bestimmter Flächen*]

commercial freshwater fishing, commercial freshwater fishery · berufsmäßige Binnenfischerei *f*, Erwerbsbinnenfischerei

commercial fruit-culture, commercial fruit-growing, market fruit-culture, market fruit-growing · Erwerbsobst(an)bau m, Handelsobst(an)bau

commercial garden (Brit.); truck garden, truck farm (US), market garden · Garten(bau)betrieb m, Handelsgärtnerei f, (Erwerbs)Gärtnerei, gärtnerischer Betrieb

commercial garden area (Brit.); truck garden area, truck farm area (US); market garden area · gartenbaulich genutzte Fläche f, Gartenbaufläche

commercial gardener (Brit.); truck farmer (US); market gardener · Erwerbsgärtner m, Handelsgärtner

commercial gardening (Brit.); truck farming (US); market gardening · Erwerbsgartenbau m, Handelsgartenbau

commercial garden produce (Brit.); truck garden produce (US); market garden produce · Garten(bau)erzeugnisse n pl

commercial geography · Handelsgeographie f

commercial insurance, private insurance · Privatversicherung f

commercial insurance law, private insurance law · Privatversicherungsrecht n

commercial land(s) use, commercial use of land(s) · geschäftliche Flächennutzung f

commercial law, business law, law merchant; lex mercatoria [Latin]; merchant law, mercantile law · Handelsrecht n

commercial letter of credit · Handelskreditbrief m

commercially operative bank · Handelsbank f

commercial property [stores; malls; merchandise markets; supermarkets; etc.] · Eigentum n für Verkaufszwecke, Verkaufseigentum

commercial prosperity · Handelsblüte f

commercial research, advertising research · wissenschaftliche Marktforschung f

commercial route, trade route · Handelsweg m

commercial science · Handelswissenschaft f

commercial seat, seat of commerce · Handelssitz m

commercial settlement · Erwerbs-(an)sied(e)lung f

commercial standard · Handelsnorm f

commercial strip, strip commercial · Handelszeile f [Aufreihung von Tankstellen, Garagen, Restaurants, Läden und anderer vom Auto aus zu benutzender Einrichtungen (drive-in facilities) entlang einer städtischen Ausfallstraße]

commercial suburb(an place) · Erwerbsvorort m

commercial system · Handelssystem n

commercial town, commercial city · Handelsstadt f

commercial trade · Warenhandel m

commercial traveller · Handelsreisende m, Handlungsreisende, Geschäftsreisende

commercial treaty, mercantile treaty · Handelsvertrag m [zwischen Nationen]

commercial undertaking, commercial enterprise · Handelsunternehmen n, Handelsunternehmung f, Handelsbetrieb m

commercial use of land(s), commercial land(s) use · geschäftliche Flächennutzung f

commercial use of residential property, commercial use of dwelling property, commercial use of residential plot(s), commercial use of dwelling plot(s), commercial use of residential parcel(s), commercial use of dwelling parcel(s) · geschäftliche Nutzung f von Wohn(ungs)grundstücken

commercial value, mint price, mint rate, mint value · Münzwert m

commercial vehicle survey · Nutzfahrzeugenquête f

commercial vehicle trip generation, commercial vehicle journey generation, commercial vehicle travel generation · Nutzfahrzeug-Fahrtenerzeugung f

commercial work(ing) place · Handelsarbeitsplatz m

commercial zone · Handelszone f

commingled benefit fund · Investment-Versorgungsfonds m

commissariat [That department of the military service which is charged with the duty of providing food for the armed forces] · (Militär)Intendantur f, Verpflegungskommissariat n

commissariat, commissaryship [The office or position of a commissary] · Kommissariat n

Commissariat [Scots law]; Commissary Court, Bishops Court [The supreme court established in Edinburgh in 1563, in which matters of probate and divorce, previously under the jurisdiction of the bishop's commissary, were decided; it was absorbed by the Court of Session in 1836] · Bischofsgericht n in Edinburgh

commissary [*In Scotland. The judge in a commissary or bishops court*] · geistlicher Richter *m*, bischöflicher Richter

commissary [*In Scotland. The sheriff of each county acting in the commissary court*] · Richter *m* bei einem Testamentsvollstreckergericht

commissary [*One to whom a special duty or charge is committed by a superior power; one commissioned to act as a representative*] · Kommissar *m*

commissary court [*Scotland. A sheriff or county court which appoints and confirms executors of deceased persons leaving personal property in Scotland*] · Testamensvollstreckergericht *n*

commissary court [*Scotland*]; spiritual court, ecclesiastic(al) court, consistorial court, church-court, court Christian, consistory court · geistliches Gericht *n*, Kirchengericht, Konsistorialgericht, kirchliches Gericht [*Die schottischen „ecclesiastic(al) courts" haben nur eine Jurisdiktion über Fragen der Doktrin, des Gottesdienstes, der Sakramente und der Disziplin der Geistlichen*]

commissary general · Musterungskommissar *m*

commissary general, chief commissary, head commissary [*One appointed to act as a supreme representative of a superior power*] · Generalkommissar *m*

commissaryship → commissariat

to commission → to instal

commission [*A warrant or instrument conferring a commission of the peace*] · Friedensrichteramtvollmacht *f*

commission, order, installation, vesting, admission · (Amts)Einsetzung *f*, (Amts)Bestallung

commission [*Authoritative charge or direction to act in a prescribed manner*] · Kommission *f*

commission [*A percentage of the sales price of a property paid as a fee to a broker who arranges for sale*] · Kommission *f*

commission [*A group of persons established to perform a public function*] · Kommission *f*

commission act(ion), act(ion) of commission · Funktionsakt *m*, Funktionshandlung *f*

commission agent · (Einkaufs)Kommissionär *m*

to commission a project, to appoint a contractor, to let a contract, to contract, to award (a contract), to let (out) · zuschlagen, erteilen eines Auftrages

commission-business · Kommissionsgeschäft *n*

commission dealing with objections · Widerspruchausschuß *m*

commissioner [*A member of a commission*] · Kommissionsmitglied *n*

commissioner for oaths [*A solicitor who administers oaths, e.g., to those making affidavits*] · Eidabnahmeanwalt *m*

commissioner in bankruptcy, accountant in bankruptcy, assignee in bankruptcy, referee in bankruptcy, trustee in bankruptcy · (Konkurs)Masse(n)kurator *m*, Konkursverwalter *m*, Kurator

commissionership; commissionship [*misnomer*] [*The office of a commissioner*] · Kommissionsmitgliedschaft *f*

Commissioners of Assize · Reisegericht *n* [*England*]

commissioners of audit (Brit.); accounting office, general accounting office (US); audit office, audit department [*It is entrusted with the audit and control of public accounts*] · (Rechnungs)Prüfungsbehörde *f*, (Rechnungs)Revisionsbehörde, Rechnungshof *m*, Oberrechnungskammer *f*

Commissioners of His (or Her) Majesty's Board of Works · königliches Hofbauamt *n*

commissioning, putting into service, putting into operation · Inbetriebnahme *f*, Ingebrauchnahme

commission merchant, factor, consignee [*He receives goods and sells them for a commission or on a percentage basis*] · (Verkaufs)Kommissionär *m*, Konsignatär *m*

Commission of Assize and of Nisi Prius · Ermächtigung *f* für zivilrechtliche Gerichtsbarkeit [*Assisengerichtshof*]

commission of inquiry, inquiry commission · Untersuchungskommission *f*

Commission of Oyer and Terminer and of Gaol Delivery · Ermächtigung *f* für Strafrechtspflege [*Assisengerichtshof*]

commission of the peace [*The authority given under the Great Seal empowering certain persons to act as Justices of the Peace in a specified district*] · Friedensrichteramt *n*

commission payment, payment of commission · Kommissionszahlung *f*

commissionship [*misnomer*] → commissionership

commissive waste · Beschädigung *f* [*Pachtland*]

to commit, to engage, to assure · zusagen

commitment, committal, confinement · Haft *f*, Inhaftierung *f*

commitment — commodity substitution rate

commitment, engagement, assurance · Zusage f [*Bindende Verpflichtung für ein künftiges Verhalten*]

commitment, committal, confining, committing to confinement · Inhaftieren n, Inhaftnahme f

commitment, financial liability · geldliche Verpflichtung f

commitment, pledge, promise · Versprechen n, Verpflichtung f

commitment charge · Bereitstellungsprovision f

commitment for trial, committal for trial · Verweisung f eines Angeklagten vor ein Schwurgericht

commitment interests · Bereitstellungszinsen f [*Für die Bereitstellung der Mittel für die Zeit von der Zusage bis zur Auszahlung des Darleh(e)ns berechnete Zinsen*]

committal, confinement, commitment · Haft f, Inhaftierung f

committal, confining, committing to confinement, commitment · Inhaftieren n, Inhaftnahme f

committal writ, commitment writ, confinement writ, warrant, (writ of) capias, writ of committal, writ of commitment, writ of confinement [*A writ commanding the officer to take the body of the person named in that, that is, to arrest him*] · Haftbefehl m

committed to confinement, confined · inhaftiert

committee · Kurator m

committee, select body · Ausschuß m

committee for contract procedure in the building and construction industry, building and construction contract rules committee · Verdingungsausschuß m (für Bauleistungen), Verdingungsausschuß für das Bauwesen

committeeing [*The procedure of a committee*] · Ausschußverfahren n

committeeism · Ausschußwesen n

committee-man, committee member · Ausschußmitglied n

committee meeting, committee session · Ausschußsitzung f

committee of a lunatic · Kurator m eines Geisteskranken

committee of experts, experts committee · Gutachterausschuß m, Sachverständigenausschuß

committee of inquiry, inquiry committee · Untersuchungsausschuß m

committee of management, executive committee, management committee · geschäftsführender Auschuß m, Geschäftsführungsausschuß

committee of management → board of directors

committee of the Privy Council · Kronratausschuß m

committee of vice-chancellors and principals [*England*] · Rektorenkonferenz f [*Universität*]

committee on expenditures in the executive departments · Finanz- und Verwaltungskontrollausschuß m

Committee on Rules [*Constitution of the USA*] · Geschäftsordnungsausschuß m

committee on the judiciary, law committee · Rechtsausschuß m

committee room · Parteilokal n [*Wahlpartei in England*]

committee session → committee meeting

committing to confinement, commitment, committal, confining · Inhaftieren n, Inhaftnahme f

to commit (to confinement), to confine · inhaftieren

commixture, commixtion; commixtio [*Latin*]; admixture of solids · Vermengung f [*Feste Körper werden so untereinander gebracht, daß sie nicht mehr einzeln, sondern nur als Masse gelten*]

commodatarius [*Latin*]; borrower · Entlehner m [*unentgeltliche Entlehnung*]

to commodate · entlehnen

commodatum · Entlehnung f

commodities, goods · Güter npl, Waren fpl

commodities handling, handling of goods, goods handling, handling of commodities · Güterumschlag m, Warenumschlag

commodities market equilibrium, goods market equilibrium · Gütermarktgleichgewicht n

commodity arbitrability · Branchen-Schiedsgerichtsbarkeit f

commodity clause · Güterklausel f

commodity contract · Warenbörsenvertrag f

commodity flow · Güterstrom m

commodity flow gravity model · Gravitationsmodell n für Güterströme

commodity market, goods market · Gütermarkt m, Warenmarkt

commodity money, natural money · Naturalgeld n, Nutzgeld

commodity substitution rate, rate of commodity substitution · (marginale) Substitutionsrate f

common — common certificate of heirship

common, (village) plaza, (village) green · Anger *m*, Dorfplatz *m*, Dorfplan *m*, Platz (eines Dorfes)

common, usual, customary, ordinary · herkömmlich, üblich

common, union of communities · Kommunalverband *m*, Gemeindeverband

common, customary, by custom · gewohnheitsrechtlich

common → (in) common

common → allmend

common → common (law)

commonable cattle [*Cattle that may be pastured on common land*] · Al(l)mend(e)rindvieh *n*

commonable field → common (land)

common(able) fields · Feldgemeinschaft *f*

commonable land → common (land)

commonable right to land, right of commonage, commonage right · Al(l)mend(e)recht *n*, Markrecht, subjektives Al(l)mend(e)recht, subjektives Markrecht

(common) advantage, common benefit, joint benefit · gemeinsamer Nutzen *m*, gemeinsamer Vorteil, gemeinschaftlicher Nutzen, gemeinschaftlicher Vorteil

commonage, common right; jus pascendi, communis pasturae, herbagium [*Latin*]; (right of) pastur(ag)e, (right of) grazing, pastoral right, herbage, grazing right, shack, common pastur(ag)e · Angerrecht *n*, Hütungsrecht, Atzung *f*, Ätzung, (Vieh)Weiderecht, (Vieh)Weideberechtigung

commonage right, commonable right to land, right of commonage · Al(l)mend(e)recht *n*, Markrecht, subjektives Al(l)mend(e)recht, subjektives Markrecht

commonance [*misnomer*] → communance

common annexed to a person, common in gross, common at large · gemeinheitliches Personalrecht *n*

common appendant · Gemeinheitsrecht *n* auf unbebautes Land innerhalb des Gutsbezirks

common appurtenant · Gemeinheitsrecht *n* auf Ländereien anderer Gutsbezirke als dem in welchem der Berechtigte (commoner) ansässig ist

common arable field · offener Acker *m*

common assumpsit, indebted assumpsit; indebitatus assumpsit [*Latin*]; general assumpsit · ausdrückliches Schuldtilgungsversprechen *n*

(common) assurance (on conveyance of land) · Auflassung *f*, Grundstücksauflassung [*Die Erklärungen, die der Veräußerer und der Erwerber eines Grundstükkes vor einer zuständigen Stelle (Gericht, Notar usw.) abgeben müssen, damit das Grundstück auf den Erwerber übertragen wird (§ 925 in Verbindung mit § 873 BGB)*]

common at large, common annexed to a person, common in gross · gemeinheitliches Personalrecht *n*

common averment · Behauptung *f* durch gewöhnliche Beweismittel, Bekräftigung durch gewöhnliche Beweismittel [*Vor einem Geschworenengericht*]

common bar, blank bar [*In pleading. The old name of a plea in bar, put in in an action of trespass, to oblige the plaintiff to assign the certain place where the trespass was committed*] · Rechtseinwand *m* des Ortsnachweises

common bargain · Geschäft *n* für gemeinsame Rechnung

common benefit, joint benefit, (common) advantage · gemeinsamer Nutzen *m*, gemeinsamer Vorteil, gemeinschaftlicher Nutzen, gemeinschaftlicher Vorteil

common carrier, public traffic carrier, common traffic carrier, (public) carrier · (öffentlicher) (Massen)Verkehrsträger *m*, (öffentlicher) (Massen)Beförderungsträger

common carrier (by water) · Wasserfrachtführer *m*

common carrier (of goods) [*It is a person or company who is engaged in the business of transporting goods, for a remuneration, for any and all persons who may apply*] · gewerbsmäßiger Frachtführer *m*, öffentlicher Frachtführer, gewerbsmäßiger Verfrachter, öffentlicher Verfrachter, gewerbsmäßiger Vercharterer, öffentlicher Vercharterer

common carrier (of goods) by land · gewerbsmäßiger Landfrachtführer *m*, öffentlicher Landfrachtführer, gewerbsmäßiger Frachtführer zu Lande, öffentlicher Frachtführer zu Lande

common carrier (of goods) by sea · öffentlicher Frachtführer *m* zur See, öffentlicher Verfrachter zur See, gewerbsmäßiger Verfrachter zur See, gewerbsmäßiger Frachtführer zur See, öffentlicher Seeverfrachter, gewerbsmäßiger Seeverfrachter, öffentlicher Seefrachtführer, gewerbsmäßiger Seefrachtführer

common certificate of heirship, common certificate of inheritance, common heirship certificate, common inheritance certificate · gemeinsamer Erbschein *m*, gemeinschaftlicher Erbschein, gemeinschaftliches Erbzeugnis *n*, gemeinsames Erbzeugnis

common city land, common town land, urban common (land) · Stadtgemarkung f, Stadtal(l)mend(e) f

common conditions, concurrent conditions, mutual conditions, reciprocal conditions · gegenseitige Bedingungen fpl, Zug-um-Zug-Bedingungen [*Bedingungen, daß die Parteien die Leistungen Zug um Zug erfüllen*]

common contract, reciprocal contract, mutual contract · gegenseitiger Vertrag m [*Ein beide Teile verpflichtender Vertrag, bei dem wenigstens einige der beiderseitigen Leistungspflichten dadurch miteinander verbunden sind, daß die Leistungen des einen nach dem Willen beider Parteien die Gegenleistung, das Entgelt, für die des anderen darstellt*]

common convenience, good of the community, public interests, common wellbeing, general good, prosperity of the community, public welfare, public weal, public good, public necessity, public convenience, common welfare, common weal, common good, common necessity · Gemeinwohl n, öffentliches Wohl, öffentliches Interesse n, allgemeines Wohl, allgemeines Interesse, Allgemeinwohl, öffentliche Belange mpl

common councilman (of the ward), common councillor (of the ward), common council member (of the ward), commoner · Stadtbezirksrat m, Stadtbezirksverordnete m [*in London*]

common credits, mutual credits, reciprocal credits [*In bankruptcy law. Credits which must, from their nature, terminate in debts; as where a debt is due from one party, and credit given by him on the other for a sum of money payable at a future day, and which will then become a debt; or where there is a debt on one side; and a delivery of property with directions to turn it into money on the other*] · gegenseitige Guthaben npl, gegenseitige Gutschriften fpl,

common crier · öffentlicher Ausrufer m

(common) custom, universal custom of the realm, custom which runs through the whole land (Brit.); jus commune [*Latin*]; common (law), general customs, customary law · gemeines Recht n, objektives gemeines Recht, (objektives) Gemeinrecht, Präjudizienrecht, (gemeines) Gewohnheitsrecht [*England. Das gemeine Recht, das von reisenden Richtern ("itinerant justices" oder "justices in eyre") des königlichen Gerichts zu Westminster gebildet wurde. Neben der Gegenüberstellung "common law" (oder "law") — "equity" (= „strenges Recht — Billigkeitsrecht") wird "common law" noch stellvertretend für das gesamte case law und das anglo-amerikanische Rechtssystem verwandt: "common law — statute law" (= „Richterrecht — Gesetzesrecht"), bzw. "common law — civil law" (anglo-amerikanisches Recht im Gegensatz zum kontinentaleuropäischen Recht)*]

common debt, mutual debt, reciprocal debt · Gegenschuld f

common debtor · Gemeinschuldner m, gemeinsamer Schuldner, gemeinschaftlicher Schuldner

common drove · Gemeintrift f, Koppeltrift

common duties, duties in common, joint duties · gemeinschaftliche Pflichten fpl, gemeinsame Pflichten

common employment · Beschäftigung f beim gleichen Dienstherrn [*Der Dienstherr haftet einem Dritten gegenüber für den Schaden, den sein Arbeitnehmer schuldhafterweise anrichtet, nicht, wenn der Dritte ein Arbeitnehmer desselben Dienstherrn in demselben Betrieb ist*]

commoner, sharer, participator [*One who shares or takes part in anything*] · Gemeinberechtigte m, Gemeinheitsgenosse m

commoner [*One who has a joint right in common land*] · Markgenosse m, Al(l)mend(e)genosse

commoner [*A person below the rank of a peer*] · Bürgerliche m

commoner → common councilman (of the ward)

common facilities, public facilities · Gemeinbedarf m, Gemeineinrichtungen fpl [*Die der Allgemeinheit dienenden baulichen Anlagen und Einrichtungen (§ 5 Abs. 2 Nr. 2, § 9, Abs. 1 Nr. 1 Buchst. f BBauG)*]

common facilities plan, public facilities plan · Plan m der öffentlichen Standorte, Plan der Gemeineinrichtungen, Gemeinbedarfsplan

common factor space · Raum m der gemeinsamen Faktoren

common farming system, common field system · Feldgemeinschaftssystem n

common field → common (land)

common fixed cost(s) · allgemeine Festkosten f, allgemeine Fixkosten

common form · gewöhnliche Form f

common form business · freiwillige Gerichtsbarkeit f in Nachlaßsachen

common fund · gemeinsamer Fonds m, gemeinschaftlicher Fonds

common gain, common profit · Gemeingewinn m, Gemeinprofit m

common geese pasture, mutual geese pasture · Gänseanger m, Gänseweide f

common (general) property — common law fee simple (absolute)

common (general) property, common proprietorship, common ownership (of property) · Eigentumsgemeinschaft *f*

common good, common necessity, common convenience, good of the community, public interests, common wellbeing, general good, prosperity of the community, public welfare, public weal, public good, public necessity, public convenience, common welfare, common weal · Gemeinwohl *n*, öffentliches Wohl, öffentliches Interesse *n*, allgemeines Wohl, allgemeines Interesse, Allgemeinwohl, öffentliche Belange *mpl*

common guardian, customary guardian, guardian by custom · gewohnheitsrechtlicher Vormund *m*

common guardianship, customary guardianship, guardianship by custom · gewohnheitsrechtliche Vormundschaft *f*

common heir (male), heir (male) by custom, customary heir (male) [*A man whose right of inheritance depends upon a particular and local custom, such as gavelkind, or borough English*] · gewohnheitsrechtlicher Erbe *m*

common heirship certificate, common inheritance certificate, common certificate of heirship, common certificate of inheritance · gemeinsamer Erbschein *m*, gemeinschaftlicher Erbschein, gemeinschaftliches Erbenzeugnis *n*, gemeinsames Erbenzeugnis

common in gross, common at large, common annexed to a person · gemeinheitliches Personalrecht *n*

common inheritance contract, mutual inheritance contract, reciprocal inheritance contract · gegenseitiger Erb(schafts)vertrag *m*, gemeinsamer Erb(schafts)vertrag

common intention · gemeinsame Absicht *f*, gemeinschaftliche Absicht

common jury book · allgemeine Geschworenenliste *f*

common (land), corporate land, allmend, common field, commonable land, commonable field, public land, community land, communal land, mark; county (US); waste of the manor, (manorial) waste [*obsolete*] · Al(l)mend(e) *f*, Allmeind *f*, Allmid *f*, Allmein(i) *f*, Allmen *f*, Allmig *f*, Allmand(e) *f*, Allmat *f*, All(ge)meinde *f*, Allmandgut *n*, Allmente *f*, (Feld)Mark *f*, Gemarkung *f*, Kommunalboden *m*, Gemeindeboden *m*, Bürgerland *n*, bürgerliches Nutzungsland *n*, Gemeindeland *n*, Gemeinheit(sland) *f*, *(n)*, Kommunalland *n*, unverteilter Gemeindegrund *m*, ländliches Gemeingut, Gemein(de)anger *m*, Gemeindeimmobilien *fpl*; Korporationsland *n* [*Schweiz*]

common (law), general customs, customary law, (common) custom, universal custom of the realm, custom which runs through the whole land (Brit.); jus commune [*Latin*] · gemeines Recht *n*, objektives gemeines Recht, (objektives) Gemeinrecht, Präjudizienrecht, (gemeines) Gewohnheitsrecht [*England. Das gemeine Recht, das von reisenden Richtern ("itinerant justices" oder "justices in eyre") des königlichen Gerichts zu Westminster gebildet wurde. Neben der Gegenüberstellung "common law" (oder "law") — "equity" (= „strenges Recht — Billigkeitsrecht") wird "common law" noch stellvertretend für das gesamte case law und das anglo-amerikanische Rechtssystem verwandt: "common law — statute law" (= „Richterrecht — Gesetzesrecht"), bzw. "common law — civil law" (anglo-amerikanisches Recht im Gegensatz zum kontinentaleuropäischen Recht)*]

common law cause, common law plea, (court) action at common law, cause at common law, (law)suit at common law, plea at common law, common law (court) action, common law (law)suit · Klage *f* nach gemeinem Recht, gemeinrechtliche Klage

common law corporation, corporation at common law · Körperschaft *f* nach gemeinem Recht, Korporation *f* nach gemeinem Recht

common law court, court of common law · Gericht *n* des gemeinen Rechts, gemeinrechtliches Gericht

common law (court) action, common law (law)suit, common law cause, common law plea, (court) action at common law, cause at common law, (law)suit at common law, plea at common law · Klage *f* nach gemeinem Recht, gemeinrechtliche Klage

common law debt, legal debt · gemeinrechtliche Schuld *f*

common law easement, legal easement [*As opposed to an equitable easement*] · Grunddienstbarkeit *f* nach gemeinem Recht, gemeinrechtliche Grunddienstbarkeit

common law estate tail, common law restricted fee, (estate in) legal fee tail, legal restricted fee, legal estate tail, common law fee tail · beschnittenes Leh(e)n *n* nach gemeinem Recht, eingeschränktes Leh(e)n nach gemeinem Recht, begrenztes Leh(e)n nach gemeinem Recht, beschränktes Leh(e)n nach gemeinem Recht, gebundenes Leh(e)n nach gemeinem Recht

common law fee simple (absolute) (in possession), ((freehold) estate in) legal fee simple (absolute) (in possession) · absolutes Bodenbesitzrecht *n* nach gemeinem Recht, absolutes Landbesitzrecht nach gemeinem Recht, immerwährendes Landbesitzrecht nach gemeinem Recht, immerwährendes Bodenbesitzrecht nach gemeinem Recht, gemeinrechtliches absolutes Bodenbesitzrecht, gemeinrechtliches absolutes Landbesitzrecht, gemeinrechtliches immerwährendes Bodenbesitzrecht, gemeinrechtliches immerwährendes Landbesitzrecht

common law fee tail, common law estate tail, common law restricted fee, (estate in) legal fee tail, legal restricted fee, legal estate tail · beschnittenes Leh(e)n *n* nach gemeinem Recht, eingeschränktes Leh(e)n nach gemeinem Recht, begrenztes Leh(e)n nach gemeinem Recht, beschränktes Leh(e)n nach gemeinem Recht, gebundenes Leh(e)n nach gemeinem Recht

common law history, history of the common law · Gemeinrechtsgeschichte *f*

common law judge, common law justice · gemeinrechtlicher Richter *m*

common law (law)suit, common law cause, common law plea, (court) action at common law, cause at common law, (law)suit at common law, plea at common law, common law (court) action · Klage *f* nach gemeinem Recht, gemeinrechtliche Klage

common law liability, general customs liability, customary law liability · gemeinrechtliche Haftung *f*, gemeinrechtliche Haftpflicht *f*, gemeinrechtliche Haftbarkeit *f*

common law lien · gemeinrechtliches Sicherheitsrecht *n*, gemeinrechtliches Sicherungsrecht

common law mortgage, legal mortgage, conventional mortgage [*In the USA, "conventional mortgage" means a mortgage that is not insured by the Federal Housing Administration or guaranteed by the Veterans Administration*] · Verkehrshypothek *f*, gewöhnliche Hypothek [*Der Gläubiger erteilt über sein Pfandrecht als Urkunde einen vom Grundbuchamt ausgestellten Hypothekenbrief*]

common law parish · Kirchspiel *n* nach gemeinem Recht, (Pfarr)Sprengel *m* nach gemeinem Recht, kirchlicher Sprengel *m* nach gemeinem Recht, Parochie *f* nach gemeinem Recht

common law plea, (court) action at common law, cause at common law, (law)suit at common law, plea at common law, common law (court) action, common law (law)suit, common law cause · Klage *f* nach gemeinem Recht, gemeinrechtliche Klage

common law power of appointment, common law right of appointment, common law power of disposition, common law right of disposition [*It allows the donee to pass the legal estate*] · gemeinrechtliche Verfügungbefugnis *f*, gemeinrechtliche Bestimmungsbefugnis, gemeinrechtliches Verfügungsrecht *n*, gemeinrechtliches Bestimmungsrecht

common law prescription · Ersitzung *f* nach gemeinem Recht

common law prescriptive right, common law prescriptive interest · gemeinschaftliches (subjektives) Ersitzungsrecht *n*, gemeinsames (subjektives) Ersitzungsrecht

common law restricted fee, (estate in) legal fee tail, legal restricted fee, legal estate tail, common law fee tail, common law estate tail · beschnittenes Leh(e)n *n* nach gemeinem Recht, eingeschränktes Leh(e)n nach gemeinem Recht, begrenztes Leh(e)n nach gemeinem Recht, beschränktes Leh(e)n nach gemeinem Recht, gebundenes Leh(e)n nach gemeinem Recht

common (law) right · subjektives gemeines Recht *n*, gemeines subjektives Recht

common law right of appointment, common law power of disposition, common law right of disposition, common law power of appointment [*It allows the donee to pass the legal estate*] · gemeinrechtliche Verfügungbefugnis *f*, gemeinrechtliche Bestimmungsbefugnis, gemeinrechtliches Verfügungsrecht *n*, gemeinrechtliches Bestimmungsrecht

common law rule · gemeinrechtliche Regel *f*, Regel nach Gemeinrecht, Regel nach gemeinem Recht

common law tenure → simple fee

common law theory of possession · gemeinrechtliche Besitztheorie *f*, Besitztheorie des gemeinen Rechts

common law trade-mark · nicht eingetragenes Warenzeichen *n*

common law trust, Massachusetts trust, business trust [*A business organization wherein property is conveyed to trustees and managed for benefit of holders of certificates like corporate stock certificates*] · treuhänderisch geleitetes Unternehmen *n*, treuhänderisch geleitete Unternehmung *f*

common lodging-house, doss lodging-house (Brit.); common rooming house (US) · allgemeines Logierhaus *n*, öffentliches Logierhaus, Armenherberge *f*

common lodging houses act, common lodging houses law, common lodging houses statute · Gesetz *n* zur Überwachung öffentlicher Herbergen

common mistake, reciprocal mistake, mutual mistake · gegenseitiger Irrtum *m*, gemeinsamer Irrtum

common mowing ground · Gemeinwiese *f*

common necessity — common rooming house (US)

common necessity, common convenience, good of the community, public interests, common well-being, general good, prosperity of the community, public welfare, public weal, public good, public necessity, public convenience, common welfare, common weal, common good · Gemeinwohl *n*, öffentliches Wohl, öffentliches Interesse *n*, allgemeines Wohl, allgemeines Interesse, Allgemeinwohl, öffentliche Belange *mpl*

common need, public need · öffentlicher Bedarf *m*

commonness [*The state or quality of being common to, or shared by, more than one*] · Gemeinberechtigung *f*

common occupant, general occupant [*At common law where a man was tenant pur autre vie, or had an estate granted to himself only (without mentioning his heirs) for the life of another man, and died without alienation during the life of cestuy que vie, or him by whose life it was holden, he that could first enter on the land(s) might lawfully retain the possession, so long as cestuy que vie lived, by right of occupancy, and was hence termed a general or common occupant*] · Besitzergreifende *m* von nicht erblichem Leh(e)n beim Tode des Vasallen

common of estover, common of estouvier · gemeinschaftliches Holzfällrecht *n*, gemeinheitliches Holzfällrecht, gemeinsames Holzfällrecht

common (of) fishery, common (of) piscary; communis piscaria [*Latin*] [*The liberty of fishing in another man's water in common with other person*] · gemeinschaftliches Fischereirecht *n*, gemeinheitliches Fischereirecht, gemeinsames Fischereirecht

common of pannage, common of pawnes, common pannage [*The right of feeding swine on mast, acorns, etc. at certain seasons in a commonable wood or forest*] · gemeinschaftliches Recht *n* auf Waldfrüchte als Schweinefutter, gemeinheitliches Recht auf Waldfrüchte als Schweinefutter, gemeinsames Recht auf Waldfrüchte als Schweinefutter

common (of) pastur(ag)e sans nombre, common (of) pastur(ag)e without stint · Angerrecht *n* mit unbeschränkter Anzahl von Tieren, Hütungsrecht mit unbeschränkter Anzahl von Tieren, (Vieh)Weiderecht mit unbeschränkter Anzahl von Tieren, Atzung *f* mit unbeschränkter Anzahl von Tieren, Ätzung mit unbeschränkter Anzahl von Tieren

common of turbary; communia turbariae [*Latin*] · gemeinschaftliches Torfstichrecht *n*, gemeinheitliches Torfstichrecht, gemeinsames Torfstichrecht

common ownership (of property), common (general) property, common proprietorship · Eigentumsgemeinschaft *f*

common pannage, common of pannage, common of pawnes [*The right of feeding swine on mast, acorns, etc. at certain seasons in a commonable wood or forest*] · gemeinschaftliches Recht *n* auf Waldfrüchte als Schweinefutter, gemeinheitliches Recht auf Waldfrüchte als Schweinefutter, gemeinsames Recht auf Waldfrüchte als Schweinefutter

common pastur(ag)e, commonage, common right; jus pascendi, communis pasturae, herbagium [*Latin*]; (right of) pastur(ag)e, (right of) grazing, pastoral right, herbage, grazing right, shack · Angerrecht *n*, Hütungsrecht, Atzung *f*, Ätzung, (Vieh)Weiderecht, (Vieh)Weideberechtigung

common pasture, mutual pasture · Gemeinweide *f*, Koppelweide, Gemeinanger *m*

common port authority · Hafengemeinschaft *f*

common porter · Transporteur *m*

common pour cause de vicinage, right pour cause de vicinage · Vizinitätsrecht *n*

common profit, common gain · Gemeingewinn *m*, Gemeinprofit *m*

common proprietorship, common ownership (of property), common (general) property · Eigentumsgemeinschaft *f*

common recovery [*Mode of barring estate tail by a collusive action, abolished by the Fines and Recoveries Act 1833. Process comprised the following steps: (1) Friendly plaintiff A, brings action against tenant in tail B; (2) B conveys life estate to "tenant to the preaecipe" C; (3) C vouches B to warranty; (4) B vouches the common vouches (a court official), D, on fiction that D had conveyed land to B with warranty of title; (5) D admits fiction and leaves court; (6) Judg(e)ment is given against D, so that the land is held to belong to A, and D must give land of equal value to C; (7) No land is given by D, and B's land goes to A under the judg(e)ment, the land now being rid of the estate tail; (8) A conveys land back to B in fee simple*] · gemeinrechtliche Wiedereinsetzung *f* in Land

common right; jus pascendi, communis pasturae, herbagium [*Latin*]; (right of) pastur(ag)e, (right of) grazing, pastoral right, herbage, grazing right, shack, common pastur(ag)e, commonage · Angerrecht *n*, Hütungsrecht, Atzung *f*, Ätzung, (Vieh)Weiderecht, (Vieh)Weideberechtigung

common right → common (law) right

common rooming house (US); common lodging-house, doss lodging-house

commons — communal autonomy

(Brit.) · allgemeines Logierhaus *n*, öffentliches Logierhaus, Armenherberge *f*

commons · Gemeindeländerei(en) *f (pl)*

common school (US); day school, primary school, board school (Brit.); elementary school · Elementarschule, Grundschule, Volksschule *f*

common seal · gemeinsames Siegel *n*, gemeinschaftliches Siegel, Gemeinschaftssiegel

common share, ordinary share · Stammanteil *m*

common stock, ordinary stock · Stammaktie *f*

common stock, partnership stock · (Gesellschafts)Stammvermögen *n*, gemeinsames Betriebskapital *n*

common-stock fund, ordinary-stock fund · Stammaktienfonds *m*, Fonds für Stammaktienwerte

common task, collective task · Gemeinschaftsaufgabe *f*

common tenant, tenant by custom, customary tenant · gewohnheitsrechtlicher Leh(e)n(s)mann *m*, Werkmann [*In England im 14., 15. und 16. Jahrhundert*]

common tenure, tenure by custom, customary tenure [*Examples were gavelkind and borough English*] · gewohnheitsrechtliches Leh(e)n *n*

common to both parties, mutual, interchangeable, reciprocal · gegenseitig, wechselseitig

common to pasture geese · gemeinschaftliches Gänseweiderecht *n*, gemeinheitliches Gänseweiderecht, gemeinsames Gänseweiderecht

common to pasture goats · gemeinschaftliches Ziegenweiderecht *n*, gemeinheitliches Ziegenweiderecht, gemeinsames Ziegenweiderecht

common town land, urban common (land), common city land · Stadtgemarkung *f*, Stadtal(l)mend(e) *f*

common traffic carrier, (public) carrier, common carrier, public traffic carrier · (öffentlicher) (Massen)Verkehrsträger *m*, (öffentlicher) (Massen)Beförderungsträger

common use · Gemeinbenutzung *f*, Gemeingebrauch *m*

common use facility, facility for common use · Gemeingebrauchseinrichtung *f* [*Öffentliche Grünflächen, Spielplätze und öffentliche Verkehrseinrichtungen*]

common ville(i)nage → copyhold

common well-being, general good, prosperity of the community, public welfare, public weal, public good, public necessity, public convenience, common welfare, common weal, common good, common necessity, common convenience, good of the community, public interests, · Gemeinwohl *n*, öffentliches Wohl, öffentliches Interesse *n*, allgemeines Wohl, allgemeines Interesse, Allgemeinwohl, öffentliche Belange *mpl*

common will · Gemeinwille *m*

common will, reciprocal will, mutual will, double will, counter will · gegenseitiges Testament *n*

commorients [*Persons dying together on the same occasion at the same time*] · Personen *fpl* die zum gleichen Zeitpunkt sterben

commotion → (civil) commotion

commot(ion)er · Unruhestifter *m*

communal, local [*Belonging to a place having the right of local government; belonging to, or affecting a particular state or separate community*] · gemeindlich, kommunal, örtlich

communal advisory council, local advisory panel, communal advisory panel, local advisory council · Ortsbeirat *m*, Gemeindebeirat, Kommunalbeirat

communal affair, local affair, community affair · Gemeindeangelegenheit *f*, Kommunalangelegenheit, Ortsangelegenheit

communal agency, communal office, local agency, local office, community agency, community office · kommunale Dienststelle *f*, Kommunaldienststelle, Gemeindedienststelle, gemeindliche Dienststelle, Ortsdienststelle

communal arable field · Gemein(de)acker *m*, Ortsacker, Kommunalacker

communal area, communal territory, community area, community territory, incorporated area, incorporated territory, local area, local territory · Gemeindegebiet *n*, gemeindliches Gebiet, Kommunalgebiet, kommunales Gebiet, Ortsgebiet

communal authority, community power, community authority, communal power · gemeindliche Macht *f*, kommunale Macht, gemeindliche Hoheit, kommunale Hoheit, gemeindliche Kompetenz, kommunale Kompetenz, gemeindliche Gewalt, kommunale Gewalt

communal authority, community authority, local authority · Gemeindebehörde *f*, Ortsbehörde, Kommunalbehörde, kommunale Behörde, örtliche Behörde

communal autonomy · gemeindliche Selbständigkeit *f*, kommunale Selbständigkeit

communal body — communal (government) election

communal body, local body, community body · Gemeindeorgan *n*, Ortsorgan, Kommunalorgan

communal border, community border · Gemeindegrenze *f*, Kommunalgrenze, Ortsgrenze

communal boundary map, community boundary map, local boundary map, community border map, communal border map, local border map · Gemeindegrenzenkarte *f*, Ortsgrenzenkarte, Kommunalgrenzenkarte

communal budget, community budget, local budget · Gemeindehaushalt *m*, Kommunalhaushalt

communal budget law, community budget law, local budget law · Gemeindehaushaltsrecht *n*, Kommunalhaushaltsrecht

communal budget ordinance, local budget ordinance, community budget ordinance · Gemeindehaushaltsordnung *f*, Kommunalhaushaltsordnung

communal building, communal construction, community building, community construction, local building, local construction · Gemeindebau *m*

communal building (construction), community building (construction), local building (construction) · Gemeinde(hoch)bau *m*, gemeindlicher (Hoch)Bau, örtlicher (Hoch)Bau, kommunaler (Hoch)Bau

communal by(e)-law → (local) by(e)-law

communal by(e)-law, communal ordinance, communal statute, community by(e)-law, community ordinance, community statute, (local) by(e)-law, local ordinance, local statute · Gemeindegesetz *n*, Ortsgesetz, Ortsstatut *n*, Ortssatzung *f*, kommunales Gesetz, örtliches Gesetz, gemeindliches Gesetz, Kommunalgesetz, Kommunalsatzung, Kommunalstatut, Gemeindestatut, Gemeindesatzung, gemeindliche Satzung, gemeindliches Statut, kommunale Satzung, kommunales Statut, örtliche Satzung, örtliches Statut

communal code, local code, community code · Gemeindeordnung *f*, Kommunalordnung

communal construction, community building, community construction, local building, local construction, communal building · Gemeindebau *m*

communal core, community core, core of (a) community · Gemeindekern *m*, Ortskern

communal development, local development, community development · Gemeindeentwick(e)lung *f*, Kommunalentwick(e)lung, Ortsentwick(e)lung, kommunale Entwick(e)lung

communal development model, community development model · Gemeinwesenentwick(e)lungsmodell *n*, Gemeinwesenarbeitsmodell

communal development planning, community developement planning, local development planning · Gemeindeentwick(e)lungsplanung *f*, Ortsentwick(e)lungsplanung, kommunale Entwick(e)lungsplanung, Kommunalentwick(e)lungsplanung

communal (development) share, community's (development) share · Gemeindeanteil *m*, Kommunalanteil, gemeindlicher Anteil, kommunaler Anteil [*Anteil einer Gemeinde an den Erschließungskosten*]

communal district, local district, community district · Gemeindebezirk *m*, Ortsbezirk, Kommunalbezirk

communal earnings, community earnings · Gemeindeeinkünfte *f*, Kommunaleinkünfte

communal education(al) authority, community education(al) authority, local eduction(al) authority · Gemeindeschulbehörde *f*, Kommunalschulbehörde

communal enterprise, communal undertaking, community enterprise, community undertaking · Kommunalbetrieb *m*, Kommunalunternehmen, Kommunalunternehmung *f*, Gemeindebetrieb, Gemeindeunternehmen, Gemeindeunternehmung, kommunaler Betrieb, kommunales Unternehmen, kommunale Unternehmung, gemeindlicher Betrieb, gemeindliches Unternehmen, gemeindliche Unternehmung

communal facility, community facility, local facility · Gemeindeeinrichtung *f*, Kommunaleinrichtung, gemeindliche Einrichtung, kommunale Einrichtung, öffentlicher Standort *m*

communal finance reform, community finance reform, local finance reform · Gemeindefinanzreform *f*, Kommunalfinanzreform, Ortsfinanzreform, gemeindliche Finanzreform, kommunale Finanzreform

communal finance system, community finance system · Kommunalfinanzsystem *n*, Gemeindefinanzsystem

communal forest, community forest · Gemeindewald *m*, Kommunalwald, gemeindlicher Wald, kommunaler Wald

communal forum, community forum · Bürgerforum *n*, Einwohnerforum, Gemeindeforum

communal garage, community garage · Gemeindegarage *f*, Kommunalgarage

communal (government) election, local (government) election · Gemeindewahl *f*, Kommunalwahl

communal growth, community growth · Gemeindewachstum *n*, kommunales Wachstum, gemeindliches Wachstum

communal health authority, communal sanitary authority, community health authority, community sanitary authority, local health authority, local sanitary authority · örtliche Gesundheitsbehörde *f*, kommunale Gesundheitsbehörde, gemeindliche Gesundheitsbehörde, Ortsgesundheitsbehörde, Gemeindegesundheitsbehörde, Kommunalgesundheitsbehörde

communal health service, community health service · Gemeindegesundheitsdienst *m*, Kommunalgesundheitsdienst, gemeindlicher Gesundheitsdienst, kommunaler Gesundheitsdienst

communal hous(ebuild)ing · kommunaler Wohn(ungs)bau *m*, gemeindlicher Wohn(ungs)bau

communal housing authority, community housing authority, local housing authority · Ortswohn(ungs)behörde *f*, Gemeindewohn(ungs)behörde, Kommunalwohn(ungs)behörde

communal housing code, local housing code · Gemeindewohn(ungs)ordnung *f*, Kommunalwohn(ungs)ordnung

communality · Gemeinsamkeitsgrad *m* [*Statistik*]

communalization, municipalization, suburbanization, incorporation, annexation · Einbezirkung *f*, Vereinigung, Eingemeindung, Fusion(ierung) *f*, Verschmelzung, Ausbezirkung, Umbezirkung, Einverleibung, Inkorporation *f*, Inkommunalisation *f*, Inkommunalisierung, Angemeindung, Ausgemeindung, Umgemeindung [*Der rechtliche Vorgang einer organischen Verbindung mehrerer Gemeinden oder Gemeindeteile*]

communalization contract, municipalization contract, incorporation contract, suburbanization contract, annexation contract · Angemeindungsvertrag *m*, Eingemeindungsvertrag, Einbezirkungsvertrag, Vereinigungsvertrag, Verschmelzungsvertrag, Fusion(ierung)svertrag, Ausbezirkungsvertrag, Umbezirkungsvertrag, Einverleibungsvertrag, Inkorporationsvertrag, Inkommunalisationsvertrag, Inkommunalisierungsvertrag, Ausgemeindungsvertrag, Umgemeindungsvertrag

to communalize, to incorporate, to annex, to municipalize · eingemeinden, einbezirken, vereinigen, verschmelzen, ausbezirken, umbezirken, inkorporieren, angemeinden

communal land → common (land)

communal land law, community land law, local land law · Gemeindelandrecht *n*, Kommunallandrecht, Gemeindebodenrecht, Kommunalbodenrecht

communal (land) parcel, communal plot, community plot, community (land) parcel · Kommunalgrundstück *n*, Gemeindegrundstück

communal land policy, local land policy, community land policy · kommunale Bodenpolitik *f*, gemeindliche Bodenpolitik, Kommunalbodenpolitik, Kommunallandpolitik, Gemeindebodenpolitik, Gemeindelandpolitik

communal land reform, local land reform, community land reform · gemeindliche Bodenreform *f*, kommunale Bodenreform, gemeindliche Landreform, kommunale Landreform

communal land statute, communal land act, communal land law, community land act, community land law, community land statute · Gemeindelandgesetz *n*, Gemeindebodengesetz, Kommunallandgesetz, Kommunalbodengesetz

communal law, community law, local law · Gemeinderecht *n*, Kommunalrecht, Ortsrecht, Lokalrecht

communal lawmaking, community legislation, community lawmaking, communal legislation · Gemeindegesetzgebung *f*, Kommunalgesetzgebung, Ortsgesetzgebung

communal legislation, communal lawmaking, community legislation, community lawmaking · Gemeindegesetzgebung *f*, Kommunalgesetzgebung, Ortsgesetzgebung

communal legislator, community lawmaker, community legislator, local lawmaker, local legislator, communal lawmaker · Ortsgesetzgeber *m*, Gemeindegesetzgeber, Kommunalgesetzgeber

communal level, local level, community level · Gemeindeebene *f*, lokale Ebene, örtliche Ebene, Kommunalebene

communal living, collective life [*A style of living that occurs in a commune-like setting*] · gemeinschaftliches Leben *n*, Gemeinschaftsleben, gemeinsames Leben

communal map, community map · Gemeinde(land)karte *f*, Kommunal(land)karte

communal mortgage bank, community mortgage bank · Hypothekenamt *n*

communal office, local agency, local office, community agency, community office, communal agency · kommunale Dienststelle *f*, Kommunaldienststelle, Gemeindedienststelle, gemeindliche Dienststelle, Ortsdienststelle

communal officer, communal official · Gemeindebeamte *m*, Kommunalbeamte, kommunaler Beamter

communal option, community option, local option · Gemeindebestimmungsrecht *n*, Kommunalbestimmungsrecht

communal ordinance → communal by(e)-law

communal organization, community organization, local organization · Gemeindeorganisation *f*, Kommunalorganisation

communal park, community park, local park · Gemeindepark *m*, Kommunalpark

communal pasture, community pasture, local pasture · Gemeindeweide *f*, Kommunalweide, Ortsweide

communal planning, community planning, local planning · gemeindliche Planung *f*, örtliche Planung, kommunale Planung, lokale Planung, Gemeindeplanung, Ortsplanung, Kommunalplanung, Lokalplanung

communal planning authority, local planning authority, community planning authority · Gemeindeplanungsbehörde *f*, Ortsplanungsbehörde, gemeindliche Planungsbehörde, örtliche Planungsbehörde, kommunale Planungsbehörde, Kommunalplanungsbehörde

communal (planning) game, community (planning) game · kommunales (Plan)Spiel *n*, gemeindliches (Plan)Spiel

communal planning law, local planning law, community planning law · Ortsplanungsgesetz *n*, Gemeindeplanungsgesetz, Kommunalplanungsgesetz, örtliches Planungsgesetz, gemeindliches Planungsgesetz, kommunales Planungsgesetz

communal planning office, community planning office, local planning office · Ortsplanungsstelle *f*, Gemeindeplanungsstelle, Kommunalplanungsstelle

communal planning policy, local planning policy, community planning policy · Gemeindeplanungspolitik *f*, Kommunalplanungspolitik, Ortsplanungspolitik

communal plot, community plot, community (land) parcel, communal (land) parcel · Kommunalgrundstück *n*, Gemeindegrundstück

communal police (authority), local police (authority), community police (authority) · Ortspolizei(behörde) *f*, Kommunalpolizei(behörde), Gemeindepolizei(behörde)

communal policy, community policy · Gemeindepolitik *f*, Kommunalpolitik, Ortspolitik

communal power, communal authority, community power, community authority · gemeindliche Macht *f*, kommunale Macht, gemeindliche Hoheit, kommunale Hoheit, gemeindliche Kompetenz, kommunale Kompetenz, gemeindliche Gewalt, kommunale Gewalt

communal power structure, community power structure · Gemeindemachtstruktur *f*, gemeindliche Machtstruktur, kommunale Machtstruktur

communal prescription, communal regulation, community prescription, community regulation, local prescription, local regulation · gemeindliche Vorschrift *f*, kommunale Vorschrift, Ortsvorschrift, Gemeindevorschrift, örtliche Vorschrift, Kommunalvorschrift

(communal) primary equipment, primary communal equiqment, primary community equipment · Erstausstattung *f*, kommunale Erstausstattung, gemeindliche Erstausstattung

communal property, community property · Gemeindevermögen *n*, Kommunalvermögen

communal reapportionment → communal reorganization

communal reform, local reform, community reform · Gemeindereform *f*, Kommunalreform, Ortsreform

communal regulation, community prescription, community regulation, local prescription, local regulation, communal prescription · gemeindliche Vorschrift *f*, kommunale Vorschrift, Ortsvorschrift, Gemeindevorschrift, örtliche Vorschrift, Kommunalvorschrift

communal renewal, community renewal · Gemeindeerneuerung *f*, Ortserneuerung

communal reorganization, communal reapportionment, community reorganization, community reapportionment, local reorganization, local reapportionment · gemeindliche Neugliederung *f*, kommunale Neugliederung, gemeindliche Neuordnung, kommunale Neuordnung, gemeindliche Gebietsreform, kommunale Gebietsreform

communal research, community research · Gemeindeforschung *f*, Kommunalforschung

communal sanitary authority, community health authority, community sanitary authority, local health authority, local sanitary authority, communal health authority · örtliche Gesundheitsbehörde *f*, kommunale Gesundheitsbehörde, gemeindliche Gesundheitsbehörde, Ortsgesundheitsbehörde, Gemeindegesundheitsbehörde, Kommunalgesundheitsbehörde

communal science · Kommunalwissenschaft *f*, Gemeindewissenschaft

communal self-administration, community self-administration, local self-administration · kommunale Selbstverwaltung *f*, gemeindliche Selbstverwaltung, Gemeindeselbstverwaltung, Ortsselbstverwaltung, Kommunalselbstverwaltung

communal self-government · kommunale Selbstverwaltung *f* [*Bundesrepublik*

communal service — community affair

Deutschland. Kommunale Selbstverwaltung entspricht mehr dem US-Begriff „municipal government and administration" als dem englischen Begriff „local government"]

communal service, community service · Gemeindedienst *m*, Kommunaldienst

communal servitude · Gemeindedienstbarkeit *f*, Gemeindeservitut *n*, *f*, Gemeindegerechtigkeit *f*, (servitutisches) Gemeinderecht *n* [*Für die Gemeinde als juristische Person, aber mit Sonderrechten für das Gemeindemitglied*]

communal share → communal (development) share

communal sociologist, community sociologist, local sociologist · Gemeindesoziologe *m*, Kommunalsoziologe

communal sociology, local sociology, community sociology · Gemeindesoziologie *f*, Kommunalsoziologie

communal statistics, community statistics, local statistics · Gemeindestatistik *f*, Kommunalstatistik

communal statute → (local) by(e)-law

communal structure, community structure · gemeindliche Struktur *f*, kommunale Struktur *f*, gemeindlicher Aufbau *m*, kommunaler Aufbau, gemeindliches Gefüge *n*, kommunales Gefüge, gemeindliche Zusammensetzung *f*, kommunale Zusammensetzung

communal taxation, community taxation, local taxation · Gemeindebesteuerung *f*, Kommunalbesteuerung

communal territory, community area, community territory, incorporated area, incorporated territory, local area, local territory, communal area · Gemeindegebiet *n*, gemeindliches Gebiet, Kommunalgebiet, kommunales Gebiet, Ortsgebiet

communal (territory) reorganization, local (territorial) reorganization, local (territorial) reapportionment, community (territorial) reorganization, community (territorial) reapportionment, communal (territory) reapportionment · Gemeindeneugliederung *f*, kommunale Neugliederung, Gemeindegebietsreform *f*, (territoriale) Gemeindeneuordnung

communal undertaking → communal enterprise

communal unit, CU, community unit, local unit · lokale Einheit *f*, örtliche Einheit, gem- eindliche Einheit, Gemeindeeinheit, Ortseinheit

communal use zoning → communal zoning

communal worker, caseworker, social worker, community worker · Sozialarbeiter *m*, Sozialfürsorger

communal worker, community worker · Kommunalarbeiter *m*, Gemeindearbeiter

communal zoning, community zoning, local (land) use zoning, communal (land) use zoning, community (land) use zoning, local zoning · gemeindliche Baunutzung, kommunale Baunutzung, örtliche Baunutzung, gemeindliche bauliche Nutzung, kommunale bauliche Nutzung, örtliche bauliche Nutzung, lokale Baunutzung, lokale bauliche Nutzung *f*

communance, body of commoners; commonance [*misnomer*] · Markgenossen *m pl*, All(I)mend(e)genossen

commune, [*obsolete*]; community · Gemeinde *f*, Kommune *f*

communia turbariae [*Latin*]; common of turbary · gemeinschaftliches Torfstichrecht *n*, gemeinheitliches Torfstichrecht, gemeinsames Torfstichrecht

communio incidens [*Latin*]; privity, participation in interest, (legal) succession, succession in title, title sucession [*A successive relationship to or mutual interest in the same property, etc., established by law or legalized by contract, as between a testator and legatee, lessor and lessee, etc.*] · Rechtsgemeinschaft *f*, rechtliche Beteiligung *f*, Rechtsbeziehung, Rechtsverhältnis *n*, Rechtsnachfolge *f*

communis pasturae, herbagium [*Latin*]; (right of) pastur(ag)e, (right of) grazing, pastoral right, herbage, grazing right, shack, common pastur(ag)e, commonage, common right; jus pascendi · Angerrecht *n*, Hütungsrecht, Atzung *f*, Ätzung, (Vieh)Weiderecht, (Vieh)Weideberechtigung

communis piscaria [*Latin*]; common (of) fishery, common (of) piscary [*The liberty of fishing in another man's water in common with other person*] · gemeinschaftliches Fischereirecht *n*, gemeinheitliches Fischereirecht, gemeinsames Fischereirecht

community, human community [*A group of people living or working close to one another and sharing common interests*] · Gemeinschaft *f*, Gemeinwesen *n*, Gemeinde *f*

community; commune [*obsolete*] · Gemeinde *f*, Kommune *f*

community · Gesellschaft *f*

community account, joint (bank) account [*A bank account of separate and community funds commingled in such manner that neither can be distinguished from the other*] · gemeinsames Konto *n*, Gemeinschafts(bank)konto, gemeinschaftliches Konto

community affair, communal affair, local affair · Gemeindeangelegenheit *f*, Kommunalangelegenheit, Ortsangelegenheit

**community agency, **community office, communal agency, communal office, local agency, local office · kommunale Dienststelle f, Kommunaldienststelle, Gemeindedienststelle, gemeindliche Dienststelle, Ortsdienststelle

**community appearance, **scenery of the locality · Gemeindebild n, Ortsbild

**community area, **community territory, incorporated area, incorporated territory, local area, local territory, communal area, communal territory · Gemeindegebiet n, gemeindliches Gebiet, Kommunalgebiet, kommunales Gebiet, Ortsgebiet

**community authority, **communal power, communal authority, community power · gemeindliche Macht f, kommunale Macht, gemeindliche Hoheit, kommunale Hoheit, gemeindliche Kompetenz, kommunale Kompetenz, gemeindliche Gewalt, kommunale Gewalt

**community authority, **local authority, communal authority · Gemeindebehörde f, Ortsbehörde, Kommunalbehörde, kommunale Behörde, örtliche Behörde

**community background **· Rückhalt m in der Öffentlichkeit

**community balance **· Ausgewogenheit f einer Gemeinde

**community board, **local board · Gemeindeamt n, Kommunalamt, Ortsamt

**community body, **communal body, local body · Gemeindeorgan n, Ortsorgan, Kommunalorgan

**community border, **communal border · Gemeindegrenze f, Kommunalgrenze, Ortsgrenze

**community border map, **communal border map, local border map, communal boundary map, community boundary map, local boundary map · Gemeindegrenzenkarte f, Ortsgrenzenkarte, Kommunalgrenzenkarte

**community budget, **local budget, communal budget · Gemeindehaushalt m, Kommunalhaushalt

**community budget law, **local budget law, communal budget law · Gemeindehaushaltsrecht n,Kommunalhaushaltsrecht

**community budget ordinance, **communal budget ordinance, local budget ordinance · Gemeindehaushaltsordnung f, Kommunalhaushaltsordnung

**community building, **community construction, local building, local construction, communal building, communal construction · Gemeindebau m

**community building (construction), **local building (construction), communal building (construction) ·
Gemeinde(hoch)bau m, gemeindlicher (Hoch)Bau, örtlicher (Hoch)Bau, kommunaler (Hoch)Bau

**community burden, **community encumbrance, community incumbrance, community charge · Kommunallast f, Kommunalbelastung f, Gemeindelast, Gemeindebelastung

**community by(e)-law, **community ordinance, community statute, (local) by(e)-law, local ordinance, local statute, communal by(e)-law, communal ordinance, communal statute · Gemeindegesetz n, Ortsgesetz, Ortsstatut n, Ortssatzung f, kommunales Gesetz, örtliches Gesetz, gemeindliches Gesetz, Kommunalgesetz, Kommunalsatzung, Kommunalstatut, Gemeindestatut, Gemeindesatzung, gemeindliche Satzung, gemeindliches Statut, kommunale Satzung, kommunales Statut, örtliche Satzung, örtliches Statut

**community centre (Brit.); **community center (US) · Gemeinschaftszentrum n

**community charge, **community burden, community encumbrance, community incumbrance · Kommunallast f, Kommunalbelastung f, Gemeindelast, Gemeindebelastung

**community chest (organization) **· Finanz(ierungs)gemeinschaft f des sozialen Dienstes, soziale Finanz(ierungs)gemeinschaft, Gemeindesozialfonds m

**community citizen **· Gemeindebürger m, Kommunalbürger

**community classification **· Gemeindetypisierung f

**community code, **communal code, local code · Gemeindeordnung f, Kommunalordnung

**community construction, **local building, local construction, communal building, communal construction, community building · Gemeindebau m

**community control **[*Authority of the members of a community to oversee the planning and/or implementation of a facility or a service*] · Bürgermitspracherecht n

**community core, **core of (a) community, communal core · Gemeindekern m, Ortskern

**(community) council, **(court of) common council, local council · Kommunalrat m, Ortsrat, (Gemeinde)Rat, (Gemeinde)Vertretung f, Kommunalvertretung, Ortsvertretung, Vertretungskörperschaft f

**community debt **[*One chargeable to the community (of husband and wife) rather than to either of the parties individually*] · Gemeinschaftsschuld f

community development, CD [*The process of applying the physical, social, human, financial, or other particular resources of a community toward its improvement*] · Gemeinwesenentwick(e)lung *f*, Gemeinwesenarbeit *f*

community development, communal development, local development · Gemeindeentwick(e)lung *f*, Kommunalentwick(e)lung, Ortsentwick(e)lung, kommunale Entwick(e)lung

community development model, communal development model · Gemeinwesenentwick(e)lungsmodell *n*, Gemeinwesenarbeitsmodell

community developement planning, local development planning, communal development planning · Gemeindeentwick(e)lungsplanung *f*, Ortsentwick(e)lungsplanung, kommunale Entwick(e)lungsplanung, Kommunalentwick(e)lungsplanung

community district, communal district, local district · Gemeindebezirk *m*, Ortsbezirk, Kommunalbezirk

community earnings, communal earnings · Gemeindeeinkünfte *f*, Kommunaleinkünfte

community education(al) authority, local eduction(al) authority, communal education(al) authority · Gemeindeschulbehörde *f*, Kommunalschulbehörde

community encumbrance, community incumbrance, community charge, community burden · Kommunallast *f*, Kommunalbelastung *f*, Gemeindelast, Gemeindebelastung

community enterprise → communal enterprise

community facility, local facility, communal facility · Gemeindeeinrichtung *f*, Kommunaleinrichtung, gemeindliche Einrichtung, kommunale Einrichtung, öffentlicher Standort *m*

community finance reform, local finance reform, communal finance reform · Gemeindefinanzreform *f*, Kommunalfinanzreform, Ortsfinanzreform, gemeindliche Finanzreform, kommunale Finanzreform

community finances · Gemeindefinanzen *f*, Kommunalfinanzen

community finance system, communal finance system · Kommunalfinanzsystem *n*, Gemeindefinanzsystem

community forest, communal forest · Gemeindewald *m*, Kommunalwald, gemeindlicher Wald, kommunaler Wald

community formation → (human) community formation

community forum, communal forum · Bürgerforum *n*, Einwohnerforum, Gemeindeforum

community garage, communal garage · Gemeindegarage *f*, Kommunalgarage

community growth, communal growth · Gemeindewachstum *n*, kommunales Wachstum, gemeindliches Wachstum

community health authority, community sanitary authority, local health authority, local sanitary authority, communal health authority, communal sanitary authority · örtliche Gesundheitsbehörde *f*, kommunale Gesundheitsbehörde, gemeindliche Gesundheitsbehörde, Ortsgesundheitsbehörde, Gemeindegesundheitsbehörde, Kommunalgesundheitsbehörde

community health service, communal health service · Gemeindegesundheitsdienst *m*, Kommunalgesundheitsdienst, gemeindlicher Gesundheitsdienst, kommunaler Gesundheitsdienst

community housing authority, local housing authority, communal housing authority · Ortswohn(ungs)behörde *f*, Gemeindewohn(ungs)behörde, Kommunalwohn(ungs)behörde

community incumbrance, community charge, community burden, community encumbrance · Kommunallast *f*, Kommunalbelastung *f*, Gemeindelast, Gemeindebelastung

community land → common (land)

community land act, community land law, community land statute, communal land statute, communal land act, communal land law · Gemeindelandgesetz *n*, Gemeindebodengesetz, Kommunallandgesetz, Kommunalbodengesetz

community land law, local land law, communal land law · Gemeindelandrecht *n*, Kommunallandrecht, Gemeindebodenrecht, Kommunalbodenrecht

community (land) parcel, communal (land) parcel, communal plot, community plot · Kommunalgrundstück *n*, Gemeindegrundstück

community land policy, communal land policy, local land policy · kommunale Bodenpolitik *f*, gemeindliche Bodenpolitik, Kommunalbodenpolitik, Kommunallandpolitik, Gemeindebodenpolitik, Gemeindelandpolitik

community land reform, communal land reform, local land reform · gemeindliche Bodenreform *f*, kommunale Bodenreform, gemeindliche Landreform, kommunale Landreform

community (land) use zoning → communal zoning

community law, local law, communal law · Gemeinderecht n, Kommunalrecht, Ortsrecht, Lokalrecht

community lawmaker, community legislator, local lawmaker, local legislator, communal lawmaker, communal legislator · Ortsgesetzgeber m, Gemeindegesetzgeber, Kommunalgesetzgeber

community legislation, community lawmaking, communal legislation, communal lawmaking · Gemeindegesetzgebung f, Kommunalgesetzgebung, Ortsgesetzgebung

community level, communal level, local level · Gemeindeebene f, lokale Ebene, örtliche Ebene, Kommunalebene

community map, communal map · Gemeinde(land)karte f, Kommunal(land)karte

community member · Gemeindemitglied n

community membership · Gemeindemitgliedschaft f

community mortgage bank, communal mortgage bank · Hypothekenamt n

community office, communal agency, communal office, local agency, local office, community agency · kommunale Dienststelle f, Kommunaldienststelle, Gemeindedienststelle, gemeindliche Dienststelle, Ortsdienststelle

community of goods · Gütergemeinschaft f

community of heirs, plurality of heirs · Erbengemeinschaft f

community of interests [Term as applied to relation of joint adventure means interest common to both or all parties] · gemeinsame Interessen n pl, gemeinschaftliche Interessen

community of life, cohabitation [Living together as husband and wife; often with the implication of not being married] · Lebensgemeinschaft f

community of origin, origin community · Ausgangsgemeinde f

community of possession, possessory community · Besitzgemeinschaft f

community option, local option, communal option · Gemeindebestimmungsrecht n, Kommunalbestimmungsrecht

community ordinance → communal by(e)-law

community organization · Gemeinschaftsarbeit f [Arbeit zur Erreichung bestimmter Ziele in einer Gemeinde]

community organization, local organization, communal organization · Gemeindeorganisation f, Kommunalorganisation

community organization → (human) community organization

community organization (for social welfare), community welfare organization · Wohlfahrtsarbeit f

community organization and planning · Wohlfahrtsarbeit f und -planung f

community organization planning · Wohlfahrtsplanung f

community organizer (for social welfare) · Wohlfahrtsarbeiter m

community-owned · gemeindeeigen

community park, local park, communal park · Gemeindepark m, Kommunalpark

community pasture, local pasture, communal pasture · Gemeindeweide f, Kommunalweide, Ortsweide

community physician, communal physician · Gemeindearzt m, Kommunalarzt

community planning, local planning, communal planning · gemeindliche Planung f, örtliche Planung, kommunale Planung, lokale Planung, Gemeindeplanung, Ortsplanung, Kommunalplanung, Lokalplanung

community planning authority, communal planning authority, local planning authority · Gemeindeplanungsbehörde f, Ortsplanungsbehörde, gemeindliche Planungsbehörde, örtliche Planungsbehörde, kommunale Planungsbehörde, Kommunalplanungsbehörde

community (planning) game, communal (planning) game · kommunales (Plan)Spiel n, gemeindliches (Plan)Spiel

community planning law, communal planning law, local planning law · Ortsplanungsgesetz n, Gemeindeplanungsgesetz, Kommunalplanungsgesetz, örtliches Planungsgesetz, gemeindliches Planungsgesetz, kommunales Planungsgesetz

community planning office, local planning office, communal planning office · Ortsplanungsstelle f, Gemeindeplanungsstelle, Kommunalplanungsstelle

community planning policy, communal planning policy, local planning policy · Gemeindeplanungspolitik f, Kommunalplanungspolitik, Ortsplanungspolitik

community plot, community (land) parcel, communal (land) parcel, communal plot · Kommunalgrundstück n, Gemeindegrundstück

community police (authority), communal police (authority), local police (authority) · Ortspolizei(behörde) f, Kommunalpolizei(behörde), Gemeindepolizei(behörde)

community policy, communal policy · Gemeindepolitik f, Kommunalpolitik, Ortspolitik

community power — community structure

community power, community authority, communal power, communal authority · gemeindliche Macht *f*, kommunale Macht, gemeindliche Hoheit, kommunale Hoheit, gemeindliche Kompetenz, kommunale Kompetenz, gemeindliche Gewalt, kommunale Gewalt

community power structure, communal power structure · Gemeindemachtstruktur *f*, gemeindliche Machtstruktur, kommunale Machtstruktur, Kommunalmachtstruktur

community prescription, community regulation, local prescription, local regulation, communal prescription, communal regulation · gemeindliche Vorschrift *f*, kommunale Vorschrift, Ortsvorschrift, Gemeindevorschrift, örtliche Vorschrift, Kommunalvorschrift

community property, communal property · Gemeindevermögen *n*, Kommunalvermögen

community property → (marital) community property

community reapportionment → community reorganization

community reform, communal reform, local reform · Gemeindereform *f*, Kommunalreform, Ortsreform

community-regulated cultivation, community-regulated work, uniform cultivation of land, compulsory crop-raising under the common field system [*Compulsion on all the members of a village community to raise the same crops, so that all should sow and reap at the same time*] · Flurzwang *m*

community regulation, local prescription, local regulation, communal prescription, community prescription · gemeindliche Vorschrift *f*, kommunale Vorschrift, Ortsvorschrift, Gemeindevorschrift, örtliche Vorschrift, Kommunalvorschrift

community renewal, communal renewal · Gemeindeerneuerung *f*, Ortserneuerung

community renewal programme, community revival programme, CRP; community renewal program, community revival program (US) · Gemeindeerneuerungsprogramm *n*

community reorganization, community reapportionment, local reorganization, local reapportionment, communal reorganization, communal reapportionment · gemeindliche Neugliederung *f*, kommunale Neugliederung, gemeindliche Neuordnung, kommunale Neuordnung, gemeindliche Gebietsreform, kommunale Gebietsreform

community research, communal research · Gemeindeforschung *f*, Kommunalforschung

community response game, disaster game · Katastrophenspiel *n*

community sanitary authority, local health authority, local sanitary authority, communal health authority, communal sanitary authority, community health authority · örtliche Gesundheitsbehörde *f*, kommunale Gesundheitsbehörde, gemeindliche Gesundheitsbehörde, Ortsgesundheitsbehörde, Gemeindegesundheitsbehörde, Kommunalgesundheitsbehörde

community's (development) share, communal (development) share · Gemeindeanteil *m*, Kommunalanteil, gemeindlicher Anteil, kommunaler Anteil [*Anteil einer Gemeinde an den Erschließungskosten*]

community self-administration, local self-administration, communal self-administration · kommunale Selbstverwaltung *f*, gemeindliche Selbstverwaltung, Gemeindeselbstverwaltung, Ortsselbstverwaltung, Kommunalselbstverwaltung

community sense, togetherness, sense of community · Zusammengehörigkeitsbewußtsein *n*, Gemeinschaftssinn *m*

community service, communal service · Gemeindedienst *m*, Kommunaldienst

community service charge, community service burden, community service encumbrance, community service incumbrance · Gemeindedienstleistungslast *f*, Gemeindedienstleistungsbelastung *f*, Kommunaldienstleistungslast, Kommunaldienstleistungsbelastung

community settlement · Gemeinschafts(an)sied(e)lung *f*

community sociologist, local sociologist, communal sociologist · Gemeindesoziologe *m*, Kommunalsoziologe

community sociology, communal sociology, local sociology · Gemeindesoziologie *f*, Kommunalsoziologie

community statistics, local statistics, communal statistics · Gemeindestatistik *f*, Kommunalstatistik, Ortsstatistik

community statute → communal by(e)-law

(community) street land · (Kommunal)Straßenland *n*, Gemeindestraßenland, Ortsstraßenland

(community) street map · (Gemeinde)Straßenkarte *f*, Kommunalstraßenkarte, Ortsstraßenkarte

community structure, communal structure · gemeindliche Struktur *f*, kommunale Struktur, gemeindlicher Aufbau *m*, kommunaler Aufbau, gemeindliches Gefüge *n*, kommunales Gefüge, gemeindliche Zusammensetzung *f*, kommunale Zusammensetzung

community supervising authority — companies act

community supervising authority · Gemeindeaufsichtsbehörde *f*, Kommunalaufsichtsbehörde

community taxation, local taxation, communal taxation · Gemeindebesteuerung *f*, Kommunalbesteuerung

community (territorial) reorganization, community (territorial) reapportionment, communal (territory) reapportionment, communal (territory) reorganization, local (territorial) reorganization, local (territorial) reapportionment · Gemeindeneugliederung *f*, kommunale Neugliederung, Gemeindegebietsreform *f*, (territoriale) Gemeindeneuordnung

community territory, incorporated area, incorporated territory, local area, local territory, communal area, communal territory, community area · Gemeindegebiet *n*, gemeindliches Gebiet, Kommunalgebiet, kommunales Gebiet, Ortsgebiet

community that has retained all the rights over the common (land) · Realgemeinde *f*

community tie · Ortsbindung *f*, Ortsverbundenheit *f*

community undertaking → communal enterprise

community unit, local unit, communal unit, CU · lokale Einheit *f*, örtliche Einheit, gemeindliche Einheit, Gemeindeeinheit, Ortseinheit

community use zoning → communal zoning

community welfare organization, community organization (for social welfare) · Wohlfahrtsarbeit *f*

community-wide · gemeindeumfassend

community-wide zoning, comprehensive zoning · General(bau)nutzung *f*

community worker, communal worker, caseworker, social worker · Sozialarbeiter *m*, Sozialfürsorger

community worker, communal worker · Kommunalarbeiter *m*, Gemeindearbeiter

community zoning → communal zoning

communization [*The making of anything the public property of a community*] · Kommunalisierung *f*

communization of land(s), land(s) communization · Landkommunalisierung *f*, Bodenkommunalisierung, Kommunalisierung des Bodens, Kommunalisierung des Landes

to communize · kommunalisieren

commutation ticket, periodical ticket · Abonnementsbillet *n*, Zeit(fahr)karte *f*

commutative contract [*One in which each of the contracting parties gives and receives an equivalent; e.g. the contract of sale*] · wechselseitiger Vertrag *m*

commuter · pendelnde Person *f*

commuter area · Pendlereinzugsgebiet *n*

commuter catchment area, commuter catchment territory · Pendlereinzugsgebiet *n*

commuter field, commuting sector, commuting field, commuter sector · Pendlersektor *m*, Pendelsektor

commuter parking · Pendlerparken *n*

commuter-shed · Pendlerscheide *f*

commuter town, commuter city · Pendlerstadt *f*

commuter traffic · Pendlerverkehr *m*

commuter trip, commuter journey, commuter travel · Pendelfahrt *f*, Pendlerfahrt

commuter zone · Pendlerzone *f*, Pendelzone

commuting [*Travel(l)ing to and from work, usually over a fairly long distance*] · Pendeln *n*; Pendelwanderung *f* [*Fehlbenennung, weil es sich nicht um Wanderung, d. h. gezielten Ortswechsel handelt, sondern um regelmäßigen, meistens täglichen Verkehr zwischen Standort und Wohnort*]

commuting area, commuting territory · Pendelgebiet *n*

commuting distance · Pendelentfernung *f*

commuting pattern, commuting scheme, pattern of commuting, scheme of commuting · Pendler(verkehrs)muster *n*, Pendler(verkehrs)schema *n*

commuting practice · Pendlerwesen *n*

commuting quote · Pendlerquote *f*

commuting ratio · Pendelfaktor *m*

commuting stream, stream of commuters · Pendlerstrom *m*

co-mortgagee · Mithypothekengläubiger *m*, Mithypothekar *m*

compact cluster village, compact irregular nucleated village · kompaktes Haufendorf *n*

compact geographical unit · Teillandschaft *f*

compact holding · Einödflur *f*

compact irregular nucleated village, compact cluster village · kompaktes Haufendorf *n*

companies act, companies law, companies statute · Aktiengesetz *n* [*Fehlbenennung: Vereinsgesetz*]

companies law, company law · (Kapital)Gesellschaftsrecht n

companies statute, company law, company act, company statute, companies law, companies act · (Kapital)Gesellschaftsgesetz n

company · (Kapital)Gesellschaft f [*In Deutschland ist eine Kapitalgesellschaft eine Gesellschaft mit eigener Rechtspersönlichkeit und ohne persönliche Haftung der Gesellschafter. Eine „company" kann jedoch auch eine unbeschränkte Haftung haben*]

company · Innung f

company, gilda [*Latin*]; g(u)ild · Verband m, Gilde f

company · Gesellschaft f [*großer Personenkreis*]

company act, company statute, companies law, companies act, companies statute, company law · (Kapital)Gesellschaftsgesetz n

company benefit plan → company pension plan

company bond · Gesellschaftsobligation f

company committee · Innungsausschuß m

company for guaranteering mortgages, mortgage guaranteering company, mortgage insurance company · Hypothekenversicherungsgesellschaft f

company formation, formation of company · Gründung f einer Kapitalgesellschaft im engeren Sinne [*Sie ist mit der Erlangung der Rechtsfähigkeit beendet*]

company formation · Gesellschaftsgründung f

company formation tax · Gesellschaftssteuer f

company health insurance · betriebliche Krankenversicherung f

company law, company act, company statute, companies law, companies act, companies statute · (Kapital)Gesellschaftsgesetz n

company law, companies law · (Kapital)Gesellschaftsrecht n

company lease contract · Betriebspachtvertrag m

company limited by guarantee → (joint stock) company limited by guarantee

company merchant, merchant g(u)ild, merchant company, g(u)ild merchant · Kaufmannsgilde f, Kaufmannsverband m

company name · Kapitalgesellschaftsname m

company of carpenters · Zimmermannsgilde f

company pension plan, occupational pension plan, company benefit plan, occupational benefit plan, company retirement plan, occupational retirement plan · betrieblicher Pensionsplan m, betrieblicher (Alters)Versorgungsplan

company secretary · Geschäftsführer m einer Kapitalgesellschaft

company shop · Fabrikgewerkschaft f

company statute, companies law, companies act, companies statute, company law, company act · (Kapital)Gesellschaftsgesetz n

company surrender contract · Betriebsüberlassungsvertrag m

company town [*A town or town area owned principally by the employer of the persons living in that town*] · Werkansied(e)lung f

company union [*A trade union, membership of which is confined specifically to a firm's employe(e)s*] · Arbeiterverband m einer Firma, Firmenarbeiterverband m

company welfare work · Betriebsfürsorge f

company with limited liability, private company · Gesellschaft f mit beschränkter Haftung, GmbH

comparability, comparativeness, comparative quality · Vergleichbarkeit f

comparable, comparative, able to be compared, capable of comparison (with) · vergleichbar

comparably, in a comparable manner, comparatively, comparingly, in the way of comparison · vergleichsweise

comparative, able to be compared, capable of comparison (with), comparable · vergleichbar

comparative [*Of or pertaining to comparison; that compares or involves comparison*] · vergleichend; Vergleichs...

comparative analysis · Vergleichsanalyse f, vergleichende Analyse

comparative appraisal, comparative method, appraisal by comparison [*Estimate of value by comparison with the sales prices of other similar properties*] · Vergleichswertverfahren n, Vergleichsberechnung f

comparative approach · Vergleichsansatz m, vergleichender Ansatz

comparative balance sheet · Vergleichsbilanz f

comparative carelessness, comparative negligence, comparative careless conduct, comparative negligent conduct · geteilte Fahrlässigkeit f, geteilte Nachlässigkeit

comparative (construction) project · Vergleichsbauvorhaben *n*, vergleichendes Bauvorhaben

comparative cost(s) · Vergleichskosten *f*

comparative history of law, comparative law history, comparative legal history · vergleichende Rechtsgeschichte *f*, Vergleichsrechtsgeschichte, historische Rechtsvergleichung, geschichtliche Rechtsvergleichung *f*

comparative law · Vergleichsrecht *n*, vergleichendes Recht

comparative law in legal education, teaching of comparative law · Rechtsunterrichtsvergleichung *f*

comparative legal history [*Hug*]; comparative nomothetics [*Wigmore*] [*Not to be confused with "comparative history of law"*] · Analyse *f* verschiedener Rechtseinrichtungen

comparative legal method · vergleichendes Rechtsverfahren *n*, vergleichende Rechtsmethode *f*, Vergleichsrechtsverfahren, Vergleichsrechtsmethode

comparative legal research · vergleichende Rechtsforschung *f*, Vergleichsrechtsforschung

comparatively, comparingly, in the way of comparison, comparably, in a comparable manner · vergleichsweise

comparative method, appraisal by comparison, comparative appraisal [*Estimate of value by comparison with the sales prices of other similar properties*] · Vergleichswertverfahren *n*, Vergleichsberechnung *f*

comparative negligence · mitwirkendes Verschulden *n*

comparativeness, comparative quality, comparability · Vergleichbarkeit *f*

comparative nomothetics [*Wigmore*]; comparative legal history [*Hug*] [*Not to be confused with "comparative history of law"*] · Analyse *f* verschiedener Rechtseinrichtungen

comparative price · Vergleichspreis *m*, vergleichender Preis

comparative quality, comparability, comparativeness · Vergleichbarkeit *f*

comparative regional geography · vergleichende Länderkunde *f*, Vergleichsländerkunde

comparative research · Vergleichsforschung *f*, vergleichende Forschung

comparative (residential) rent · Vergleichs(wohnungs)miete *f*, vergleichende (Wohnungs)Miete

comparative sale · Vergleichsverkauf *m*, vergleichender Verkauf

comparative socioecology · vergleichende Sozialökologie *f*, Vergleichssozialökologie

comparative statement [*A statement of assets and liabilities, operations, or other data, giving figures in comparative form for more than one date or period or organization*] · Vergleichsaufstellung *f*

comparative survey · Vergleichsenquête *f*, vergleichende Enquête

comparative technique, comparison technique · Vergleichstechnik *f*, vergleichende Technik

comparative value · Vergleichswert *m*, vergleichender Wert

(comparative) value analysis [*The comparison of the cost(s) of an object with the value obtained from it, to determine whether the value justifies the expenditure*] · Wertanalyse *f* am vorhandenen Erzeugnis

comparative value theory · Wertvergleichstheorie *f*

to compare · vergleichen

compareless [*obsolete*]; incomparable, without comparison · unvergleichbar, unvergleichlich

comparingly, in the way of comparison, comparably, in a comparable manner, comparatively · vergleichsweise

comparison · Vergleich *m*

comparison of cadastral maps with actual state of soil · Feldvergleichung *f* [*Als Vorbereitung für die Bodenschätzung werden die Katasterkarten sowie sie hinsichtlich der Kulturartenveränderungen nicht fortgeführt worden sind, in dem erforderlichen Umfang mit der Örtlichkeit verglichen. Die festgestellten Abweichungen werden in die Liegenschaftskataster übernommen*]

comparison of cost(s), cost(s) comparison · Kostenvergleich *m*

comparison of handwritings · Schriftvergleich *m*

comparison of law, law comparison · Rechtsvergleich(ung) *m, (f)*

comparison of prices · Preisvergleich(ung) *m, (f)*

comparison of values · Wertvergleich(ung) *m, (f) m*

comparison technique, comparative technique · Vergleichstechnik *f*, vergleichende Technik

comparison unit, unit of comparison · Vergleichseinheit *f*

to compart, to (sub)divide (into compartments) · aufteilen, zerlegen [*Grund(stück)*]

compartition — compensation in lieu of injunction

compartition, comparting, (sub)dividing (into compartments) · Aufteilen *n*, Zerlegen [*Grund(stück)*]

compartment · (Wahl)Zelle *f*

compartmented, (sub)divided (into compartments) · (auf)geteilt, zerlegt [*Grund(stück)*]

compartmented land, (sub)divided land · (auf)geteiltes Land *n*

compatibility · Verträglichkeit *f*

compatibility of goals (of policy), compatibility of target goals, compatibility of policy goals · Ziel(norm)verträglichkeit *f*, Oberzielverträglichkeit, Ziel(norm)konformität *f*, Oberzielkonformität

compatibility of interregional policy goals, compatibility of interregional target goals, compatibility of interregional goals (of policy), compatibility of intraregional goals (of policy) · Verträglichkeit *f* zwischenregionaler Zielnormen, Verträglichkeit zwischenregionaler Oberziele, Verträglichkeit zwischenregionaler übergeordneter Ziele, Konformität *f* zwischenregionaler Zielnormen, Konformität zwischenregionaler Oberziele, Konformität zwischenregionaler übergeordneter Ziele, Verträglichkeit intraregionaler Zielnormen

compatible · verträglich

compensable · entschädigungsreif

compensable, entitling to compensation · entschädigungsfähig

compensable regulation(s), compensative regulation(s) [*Usually, zoning regulation(s), the enforcement of which places a hardship on the property owner affected, for which he may be entitled to compensation*] · Entschädigungsregelung(en) *f (pl)*, Schadensersatzregelung(en)

to compensate, to indemnify · entschädigen

compensated [*suretyship*] · bezahlt [*Bürgschaft*]

compensating, serving to compensate, compensatory, affording compensation, compensative · entschädigend

compensating, indemnifying · Entschädigen *n*

compensating mistake · ausgleichender Irrtum *m*

compensation, damages, indemnity, indemnification [*"Compensation" is distinguishable from "damages" inasmuch as the former may mean the sum which will remunerate an owner for land actually taken, while the latter signifies an allowance made for injury to the residue; but such destinction is not ordinarily observed*] · Entschädigung *f*, Schadensersatz *m, (f)*

compensation · Abfindung *f*

compensation amount, amount of compensation · Ausgleichsbetrag *m*

compensation claim, indemnity claim, indemnification claim, damages claim, claim for indemnification, claim for indemnity, claim for compensation, claim for damages · Entschädigungsforderung *f*, Schadenersatzforderung, Entschädigungsverlangen *n*, Schadenersatzverlangen

compensation clause, indemnity clause, indemnification clause, damages clause · Entschädigungsklausel *f*, Schadenersatzklausel

compensation for breach of contract, indemnification for breach of contract, indemnity for breach of contract, damages for breach of contract · Entschädigung(sleistung) *f* wegen Vertragsbruch, Schadenersatz(leistung) *m, (f)* wegen Vertragsbruch

compensation for delay, damages for delay, indemnity for delay, indemnification for delay · Schadenersatz *m* bei Verzug, Entschädigung *f* bei Verzug

compensation for (land) expropriation, indemnification for (land) expropriation, indemnity for (land) expropriation, damages for (land) expropriation; compensation for (land) condemnation, indemnification for (land) condemnation, indemnity for (land) condemnation, damages for (land) condemnation (US) · Bodenenteignungsentschädigung *f*, (Land)Enteignungsentschädigung, (Land)Enteignungsschadenersatz *m*, Bodenenteignungsschadenersatz

compensation for negligence, indemnification for negligence, indemnity for negligence, damages for negligence · Entschädigung *f* für Fahrlässigkeit, Schadenersatz *m* für Fahrlässigkeit

compensation for nonperformance, indemnification for nonperformance, indemnity for nonperformance, damages for nonperformance · Schadenersatz *m* wegen Nichterfüllung, Entschädigung *f* wegen Nichterfüllung

compensation in cash, monetary compensation · Geldabfindung *f*

compensation in land, indemnity in land, indemnification in land, damages in land · Entschädigung *f* in Land, Schadenersatz *m* in Land, Landentschädigung, Landschadenersatz, Landabfindung

compensation in lieu of injunction, indemnification in lieu of injunction, indemnity in lieu of injunction, damages in lieu of injunction · Entschädigung *f* für richterlich privilegierten Eingriff, Schadenersatz *m* für richterlich privilegierten Eingriff

compensation law, indemnity law, indemnification law, damages law · (objektives) Entschädigungsrecht *n*, (objektives) Schadenersatzrecht,

compensation measure, measure of damages, measure of compensation, measure of indemnification, measure of indemnity, indemnifying measure, damages measure, indemnification measure, indemnity measure · Entschädigungsmaßnahme *f*, Schadenersatzmaßnahme

compensation of unemployment, relief of unemployment, out-of-work-pay, out-of-work-benefit, unemployment relief, unemployment benefit, donation money, idle money, unemployment compensation · Arbeitslosengeld *n*, Arbeitslosenunterstützung *f*, Erwerbslosengeld *n*, Erwerbslosenunterstützung

compensation (paid) in kind, damages (paid) in kind, indemnification (paid) in kind, indemnity (paid) in kind, in-kind compensation, in-kind indemnification, in-kind damages, in-kind indemnity · Entschädigung *f* in Natur, Schadenersatz *m* in Natur, Natural(schaden)ersatz, Naturalentschädigung

compensation (paid) in money, indemnity (paid) in money, money indemnity, payment of damages, money damages, pecuniary damages, pecuniary compensation, pecuniary indemnification, money compensation, money indemnification, indemnification (paid) in money, damages (paid) in money · Entschädigung *f* in Geld, Schadenersatz *m* in Geld, Geldentschädigung, Geld(schaden)ersatz, Schadenersatzzahlung, Entschädigungszahlung

compensation under public law, indemnification under public law, indemnity under public law, damages under public law · öffentlich-rechtliche Entschädigung *f*, öffentlich-rechtlicher Schadenersatz *m*

compensation water, water of compensation [*Water which any water authority or statutory water company are under an obligation to discharge into a river, stream, brook or other running water or into a canal as a condition of carrying on their undertaking*] · Ausgleichswasser *n*

compensative, compensating, serving to compensate, compensatory, affording compensation · entschädigend

compensative regulation(s), compensable regulation(s) [*Usually, zoning regulation(s), the enforcement of which places a hardship on the property owner affected, for which he may be entitled to compensation*] · Entschädigungsregelung(en) *f (pl)*, Schadenersatzregelung(en)

compensatory, affording compensation, compensative, compensating, serving to compensate · entschädigend

compensatory · ausgleichend [*Schadenersatz*]

compensatory; compenser [*obsolete*]; male indemnitor [*The male person who is bound, by an indemnity contract, to indemnify or protect the other*] · Entschädigende *m*, Entschädigungsleistende, Schadenersatzleistende, Schadenersatzpflichtige, Entschädigungspflichtige

competence, competency · Zuständigkeit *f* (im nicht erweiterten Sinne) [*Die Machtvollkommenheit eines Gerichts zur Entscheidung. Häufig wird allerdings von „Zuständigkeit" im erweiterten Sinne gesprochen (= jurisdiction), der die Gerichtsbarkeit (= jurisdiction) in sich schließt. Im Englischen ist es umgekehrt; das Wort „jurisdiction" (= Zuständigkeit im erweiterten Sinne) welches im erweiterten Sinne gebraucht wird und das Wort „competence" im Sinne von Zuständigkeit (im nicht erweiterten Sinne) ist verhältnismäßig selten*]

competency [*In the law of evidence. The presence of those characteristics, or the absence of those disabilities, which render a witness legally fit and qualified to give testimony in a court of justice; — applied, in the same sense, to documents and other written evidence*] · Tauglichkeit *f*

competency → competence

competent agency, competent office, responsible agency, responsible office · zuständige Stelle *f*

competent authority, responsible authority · zuständige Behörde *f*

competent court, responsible court · zuständiges Gericht *n*

competent office, responsible agency, responsible office, competent agency · zuständige Stelle *f*

competent to contract, capable of contracting, able of contracting, qualified of contracting, capable to contract, able to contract, qualified to contract · vertragsfähig, vertragsgeeignet

competent to inherit, entitled to take under the statute of descent and distribution · erbberechtigt

competent to make a resolution · beschlußfähig

competing contractor, bidder, tenderer, offeror, competitor, tendering contractor · (an)bietende Firma *f*, (An)Bieter *m*, Angebotsabgeber

competing contractor's list, bidder's list, tenderer's list, competitor's list, tendering contractor's list · Ausschreibungsliste *f*, (An)Bieterliste *f*

competing migrant · konkurrierender Wanderer *m*

competition · Wettbewerb *m*

competition drawing · Wettbewerbszeichnung *f*

competition for prizes, contest for prizes, prize competition, prize contest · Preiswettbewerb *m*

competition law, law of competition · Wettbewerbsrecht *n*

competition method · Wettbewerbsverfahren *n*

competitive · wettbewerbsfähig

competitive ability, competitive capacity, competitive capability, competitive qualification · Wettbewerbseignung *f*, Wettbewerbsfähigkeit *f*

competitive bid → competitive tender

competitive call, competitive demand · Konkurrenznachfrage *f*

competitive condition · Wettbewerbsbedingung *f*

competitive economy · Wettbewerbswirtschaft *f*

competitive equilibrium · Wettbewerbsgleichheit *f*, Wettbewerbsgleichgewicht *n*

competitive growth · Wachstum *n* einer Region auf Kosten einer anderen

competitive location, competitive site · konkurrierender Standort *m*, Konkurrenzstandort

competitive price · Wettbewerbspreis *m* [*Im Wettbewerb zustandegekommener und deshalb preisrechtlich zulässiger Preis. Hier gibt es keine Kostenfrage*]

competitive situation · Konkurrenzlage *f*

competitive solution · konkurrierende Lösung *f*

competitive strength · Wettbewerbsstärke *f*

competitive tender, competitive bid, competitive offer; competitive (bid) proposal (US) · Wettbewerbsangebot *n*, Gegenangebot

competitive tender(ing) action, competitive bidding (action), competitive tendering (out) · Wettbewerbsausschreibung *f*

competitive transport(ation) [*Transport(ation) which, as to anyone carrier, originates at a point served also by another carrier, which other carrier handles the traffic at equal line-haul rates from origin to destination*] · Konkurrenzmassenbeförderung *f*, Konkurrenzmassenverkehr *m*

competitor, tendering contractor, competing contractor, bidder, tenderer, offeror · (an)bietende Firma *f*, (An)Bieter *m*, Angebotsabgeber

competitor's list, tendering contractor's list, competing contractor's list, bidder's list, tenderer's list · Ausschreibungsliste *f*, (An)Bieterliste *f*

compilation scale, plotting scale · Zeichenmaßstab *m*, Arbeitsmaßstab [*Kartographie*]

compiled map · Folgemaßstab(land)karte *f*

complainant; querens [*Latin*] · Beschwerdeführer *m*

complaint · Beschwerde *f*

complaint [*In the proceedings before justices of the peace to obtain an order for the payment of money or otherwise, the proceedings are commenced by a complaint, which is a statement of the facts of the case made by the complainant or person aggrieved, sometimes in writing and sometimes verbally*] · Klagebegründung *f* [*Friedensrichterverfahren*]

complaint-book · Beschwerdebuch *n*

complaint case · Beschwerdefall *m*

complaints committee · Beschwerdeausschuß *m*

complementary intensity · Ergänzungsstärke *f*

complementary land · Ergänzungsbereich *m*, Komplementärbereich [*Er ergänzt eine Stadt zur Stadt-Umland-Einheit in ihrer materiell-immateriellen Komplexität, wobei nach der Methode der synthetischen Abgrenzung vorgegangen wird*]

complementary unit · Ergänzungseinheit *f*

to complete, to finish · fertigstellen

to complete, to mortgage (Brit.); to hypothecate (US) · bestellen, hypothekieren, hypothekarisch belasten

to complete, to perform [*contract*] · ausführen, durchführen, erfüllen [*Vertrag*]

complete, unconditional, absolute · bedingungslos, absolut, vollständig

to complete an act, to perform · leisten

complete and full right, full and complete right, real right; jus in re [*Latin*] [*A right existing or subject of property, inherent in his relation to it, implying complete ownership with possession*] · (dingliches) Recht *n* auf Beherrschung einer Sache im ganzen, volles Recht zu einer Sache, volles Recht zur Sache

complete audit [*An audit of all transactions, often made for limited periods, for special transactions, or for small concerns*] · Schlußbuchprüfung *f*

completed — component attached by the owner 212

completed, finished · fertig(gestellt)

complete discretion · volles Ermessen *n*

complete gift · rechtsgültige Schenkung *f*

complete in itself [*Of a legislative act, covering entire subject; not amendatory*] · in sich geschlossen

complete merchant · Vollkaufmann *m*

to complete on schedule · fristgemäß fertigstellen, fristgerecht fertigstellen

complete-ordering axiom · Axiom *n* der vollständigen Ordnung

completion bond, performance bond, bond of completion, bond of performance [*Bond given by the contractor to the owner and lending institution guaranteeing that the work will be completed and that funds will be provided for that purpose*] · Fertigstellungsgarantie *f*, Ausführungsgarantie

completion bonus, acceleration bonus, bonus (for early completion), bonus of early completion · Beschleunigungsvergütung *f*, (Leistungs)Prämie *f*

completion by stages → sectional completion

completion certificate, completion attestation, certificate of completion, attestation of completion, final certificate, final attestation · Endbescheinigung *f*, Endschein *m*, Endattest *n*, Schlußbescheinigung, Schlußschein, Schlußattest [*Über die Beendigung der Bauarbeiten*]

completion date, date of completion · Fertigstellungsdatum *n*, Fertigstellungstermin *m*, Fertigstellungstag *m*

completion delay, delay in completion · Fertigstellungsverzug *m*

completion in stages, completion in sections, completion by stages, stagewise completion, completion by sections, sectionwise completion, sectional completion, stage completion · abschnittsweise Fertigstellung *f*, etappenweise Fertigstellung, stufenweise Fertigstellung

completion of compulsory purchase (of land) · Vervollständigung *f* des Zwangskauftatbestandes

completion of contract, specific performance, contract completion · Naturalerfüllung *f*, Vertragserfüllung, Realerfüllung, vertragsgemäße Erfüllung, vertragsmäßige Erfüllung

completion of sale and purchase · Kaufvertragsabschluß *m*, Kaufvertragserfüllung *f*

completion (of (the) work(s)) · (Bau)Fertigstellung *f*, (Bau)Vollendung

completion on schedule, timely completion · fristgerechte Fertigstellung *f*, fristgemäße Fertigstellung

completion record, record of completion · Fertigstellungsniederschrift *f*

completion schedule → (contractor's) completion schedule

completion time, time of completion [*Number of calendar or working days or the actual date by which the work is required to be completed*] · Fertigstellungsfrist *f*

complex analysis · Verflechtungsanalyse, Komplexanalyse *f*

complexity axiom · Axiom *n* der Komplexität, Komplexitätsaxiom

complex of coverage, coverage complex · Bebauungskomplex *m*; Überbauungskomplex [*Schweiz*]

complex of premises · Hausstättenkomplex *m*, Anwesenkomplex

compliance, fulfilment, discharge, execution, performance [*The pursuance or carrying forth of the provisions of a plan or contract*] · Ausführung *f*, Vollzug *m*, Erbringung *f*, Vollziehung *f*, Erfüllung *f*, Leistung

compliance bond, discharge bond, performance bond, fulfilment bond, execution bond · Erfüllungsgarantie *f*, Vollzugsgarantie, Vollziehungsgarantie, Erbringungsgarantie, Leistungsgarantie, Ausführungsgarantie

compliance duty, duty of fulfilment, duty of execution, duty of compliance, duty of performance, performance duty, fulfilment duty, execution duty · Erfüllungspflicht *f*, Vollziehungspflicht, Ausführungspflicht, Vollzugspflicht, Erbringungspflicht

compliance period, execution period, fulfilment period, performance period · Ausführungsfrist *f*, Vollzugsfrist *f*, Erfüllungsfrist *f*, Vollziehungsfrist *f*, Erbringungsfrist *f*

to comply with, to fulfill, to discharge [*contract*] · erfüllen, vollziehen, nachkommen [*Vertrag*]

component, part [*An uniquely identifiable product that is considered indivisible for a particular planning or control purpose. NOTE. A part for one organizational group may be the final assembly of another group, e.g. an electric motor*] · (Bestand)Teil *m*

component, object affixed to a structure, article, fixture · Bestandteil *m*, Grundstücksbestandteil, (grundstücks)verbundene Sache *f*, Sache mit einem Grundstück verbunden

component attached by the owner, article attached by the owner, fixture attached by the proprietor, component attached by the proprietor, article attached by the proprietor, fixture attached by the owner · Eigentümer-(Grundstücks)-Bestandteil *m*

component attached by the tenant, article attached by the tenant, fixture attached by the tenant · Mieter-(Grundstücks)Bestandteil *m*

component depreciation, fixture depreciation [*Depreciation, for tax purposes, of the individual components of a structure*] · Bestandteilabschreibung *f*

component industry · Wirtschaftsgruppe *f*

component ownership (of property), fixture ownership (of property), component (general) property, fixture (general) property, component proprietorship, fixture proprietorship · Bestandteileigentum *n*

composite article, assembly [*A combination of parts and possibly raw materials put together*] · Verbunderzeugnis *n*, Verbundprodukt *n*

composite contract · gemischter Vertrag *m*, Mischvertrag

composite-function rule · Funktionskettenregel *f*, Kettenregel für Funktionen

composite household [*It is a household containing one or more hidden households*] · zusammengesetzter Haushalt *m*

composite-life method (of depreciation) [*Depreciation computed on the depreciation base of a fixed-asset group considered as a whole*] · Gruppenabschreibung *f*

composite map · Mehrthemen(land)karte *f*, Vielthemen(land)karte

composite (print) · Kombinationsdruck *m*, Kombinationskopie *f* [*einfarbig*] [*Kartographie*]

composite rent · zusammengesetzte Rente *f*

composite unit · komplexes Gebilde *n*

composite variance, incidental variance · Abweichung *f* 2. Grades [*Sie errechnet sich theoretisch aus dem Produkt der Mengenabweichung der Preisabweichung, d. h. die Abweichung 2. Grades ist die mit der Preisabweichung bewertete Mengenabweichung*]

composition, structure · Aufbau *m*, Zusammensetzung *f*, Gefüge *n*, Struktur *f*

composition → (real) composition

composition → composition (in bankruptcy)

composition by deed of arrangement, out-of-court settlement · außergerichtlicher (Gläubiger)Vergleich *m*

composition characteristic, structure characteristic · Aufbaumerkmal *n*, Gefügemerkmal *n*, Strukturmerkmal *n*, Zusammensetzungsmerkmal *n*

composition data, structure data · Strukturdaten *f*

composition deed, deed of composition · (Gläubiger)Vergleichsurkunde *f*

composition dividend, dividend of composition · Vergleichsquote *f*

composition (in bankruptcy), arrangement (in bankruptcy) [*An agreement between debtor and creditor, by which the latter agrees to discharge the former on payment of a certain sum*] · (Gläubiger)Vergleich *m*, Konkursakkord *m*, Akkord im Konkurs

composition plan, structure plan · Strukturplan *m*

composition procedure · Vergleichsverfahren *n*

composition proposal, proposal of composition · Vergleichsvorschlag *m*

composition resolution · Prozentvergleichbeschluß *m*

composition scheme, arrangement scheme, scheme of composition, scheme of arrangement · (Gläubiger)Vergleichsvorschlag *m*, Konkursakkordvorschlag

composition sum [*Sum of money accepted by creditor(s) in satisfaction of debt(s)*] · (Gläubiger)Vergleichssumme *f*

compos mentis [*Latin*]; mentally capable by law, mentally qualified by law, mentally competent by law, of sound mind · zurechnungsfähig

compossessor; compossessioner [*obsolete*]; co-possessor · Mitbesitzer *m*

to compound [*To settle or adjust by agreement, e.g., by accepting a composition*] · akkordieren

compound [*An enclosure containing house and grounds*] · bebautes eingefriedetes (Bau)Grundstück *n*, eingefriedetes bebautes (Bau)Grundstück

compound accumulation · Anhäufung *f* der Zinseszinsen

compound discount [*The excess of a payment or a series of payments to be made in the future over their present value*] · Zinsvermehrung *f* einer Zahlung

compound growth · Anlageergebnis *n* [*Kapitalwachstum unter Berücksichtigung der reinvestierten Kapitalerträge*]

compounding of rates, compounding the rates · Steuerzahlung *f* durch den Hauswirt [*In England. Eine auf gesetzlicher Grundlage oder freiwilliger Übereinkunft*

compound interest — compulsorily acquired

beruhende Steuerzahlung durch den Hauswirt für die Wohnungsinhaber. Die Steuer kann ein Teil des Mietpreises sein oder selbständig entrichtet werden]

compound interest, interest upon interest · Zinseszinsen f

compound interest account [National City Bank]; thrift account [Chase National Bank]; deposit account (Brit.); saving account [Saving banks in the USA] · Sparkonto n [In den USA dürfen die Sparkonten nur von den „saving banks" als „saving accounts" bezeichnet werden]

compound property settlement, compound settlement (of property) [The settlement formed by a series of separate instruments, e.g., as in the case of the original settlement, disentailing instrument and resettlement] · Vermögensbindung f mit mehreren Rechtsinstituten

comprehensive (development) analysis, general (development) analysis · Generalbebauungsanalyse f, Generalbebauungsuntersuchung f

comprehensive development area, comprehensive development territory, area of comprehensive development, territory of comprehensive development, C.D.A. · Generalbebauungsgebiet n

comprehensive (development) plan, structure (development) plan, three-dimensional master (development) plan, general (development) plan, master (development) plan [A long-range plan officially recognized as a guide for the physical growth and development of a community, together with the basic regulatory and administrative controls needed to attain the physical objectives] · General(bebauungs)plan m

comprehensive (development) planning, three-dimensional master planning, structure planning, general (development) planning, master (development) planning · General(bebauungs)planung f

comprehensive general liability insurance · allgemeine Haftpflichtversicherung f

comprehensive planning legislation, comprehensive planning lawmaking, three-dimensional master legislation, three-dimensional master lawmaking, structure planning legislation, structure planning lawmaking, general planning legislation, general planning lawmaking, master planning legislation, master planning lawmaking · Generalplanungsgesetzgebung f

comprehensive policy · Pauschalpolice f [Export-Kreditversicherung]

comprehensive redevelopment (Brit.),; redevelopment (US) · Wiederbebauung f, Wiederbebauen n (einer Fläche); Wiederüberbauen (einer Fläche), Wiederüberbauung (einer Fläche) [Schweiz]

comprehensive redevelopment area, area of comprehensive redevelopment (Brit.); redevelopment area, area of redevelopment (US) · Wiederbebauungsgebiet n; Wiederüberbauungsgebiet [Schweiz]

comprehensive redevelopment area map, (Brit.); redevelopment area map (US) · Wiederbebauungsgebietskarte f; Wiederüberbauungsgebietskarte [Schweiz]

comprehensive zoning, community-wide zoning · General(bau)nutzung f

compressed regional center, condensed regional center (US); compressed regional centre, condensed regional centre (Brit.) · eingeengtes regionales Zentrum n

to compromise, to settle, to adjust [difference; conflicting claims; etc.] · beilegen

compromise, (agreed) settlement [Settlement out of court of claims in dispute. The term implies some element of accommodation on each side] · Vergleich m, (Streit)Beilegung f

comptroller · Stapelaufseher m

comptroller [misnomer]; controller [An officer who has the inspection, examination or controlling of the accounts of other officers] · hoher Rechnungsbeamter m, Kämmerer, Finanzdezernent

Comptroller of the Currency · Bundeskontrolleur m [USA. Er übt die Bundesaufsicht über die Nationalbanken aus]

compulsion of connection, connection compulsion · (Leitungs)Anschlußzwang m

compulsion of correction, compulsion of rectification · Berichtigungszwang m, Korrekturzwang, Verbesserungszwang, Richtigstellungszwang

compulsion of registration, compulsion of recordation, compulsion of recording, compulsion of entry · Buchungszwang m, Registrierungszwang, Eintragungszwang

compulsion of use · Benutzungszwang m, Gebrauchszwang, Nutzungszwang [Durch Ortsstatut auferlegte Verpflichtung zur Benutzung einer bestimmten öffentlichen, in der Regel kommunalen, Einrichtung, unter Umständen verbunden mit Anschlußzwang]

compulsion to contribute · Beitragszwang m

compulsorily acquired · zwangsweise erworben, zwangsweise beschafft, zwangsweise erstanden, zwangserworben, zwangsbeschafft, zwangserstanden

compulsorily dischargeable, compulsorily redeemable · zwangseinlösbar, zwangsauslösbar, zwangsablösbar

compulsory, forced · zwangsweise

compulsory acquisition · Zwangserwerb *m*, Zwangsbeschaffung *f*

compulsory acquisition (of land), acquisition (of land) by compulsion, purchase (of land) by compulsion, compulsory purchase (of land) · Landzwangsbeschaffung *f*, (Boden)Zwangsbeschaffung, (Boden)Zwangserwerb *m*, (Boden)Zwangskauf *m*, Landzwangserwerb, Landzwangskauf, (Boden)Enteignung gegen Entschädigung, Landenteignung gegen Entschädigung

compulsory acquisition of (real) estate, compulsory purchase of (real) property, compulsory acquisition of (real) property, compulsory purchase of realty, compulsory acquisition of realty, compulsory purchase of (real) estate · Grund(stücks)enteignung *f* gegen Entschädigung, Grund(stücks)zwangsbeschaffung gegen Entschädigung, Grund(stücks)zwangserwerb *m* gegen Entschädigung

compulsory arbitration, compulsory arbitrament · Zwangsschieds(gerichts)sprechung *f*

compulsory assignment, compulsory cession · Zwangszession *f*, Zwangsabtretung *f*

compulsory assignment law, compulsory cession law · Zwangsabtretungsrecht *n*, Zwangszessionsrecht

compulsory auction law · Zwangsversteigerungsgesetz *n*, ZVG

compulsory auction of land(s) · Grund(stücks)zwangsversteigerung *f*

compulsory authority · Zwangsvollmacht *f*, Zwangsvertretungsmacht

compulsory cession, compulsory assignment · Zwangszession *f*, Zwangsabtretung *f*

compulsory cession law, compulsory assignment law · Zwangsabtretungsrecht *n*, Zwangszessionsrecht

compulsory clause (for registration of land charges) · (Grundbuch)Zwangsklausel *f*

compulsory condition · Zwangsbedingung *f*

compulsory connection · Zwangsanschluß *m*, Pflichtanschluß [*Leitung*]

compulsory contribution · Pflichtbeitrag *m*, Zwangsbeitrag

compulsory correction, compulsory rectification · Zwangsberichtigung *f*

compulsory crop-raising under the common field system, community-regulated cultivation, community-regulated work, uniform cultivation of land [*Compulsion on all the members of a village community to raise the same crops, so that all should sow and reap at the same time*] · Flurzwang *m*

compulsory demise → (en)forced lease(hold)

compulsory direction · Betriebsaufsicht *f*

compulsory discharge, compulsory redemption · Zwangseinlösung *f*, Zwangsauslösung, Zwangsablösung

compulsory evacuation · Zwangsräumung *f*

compulsory insurance act, compulsory insurance law, compulsory insurance statute · Pflichtversicherungsgesetz *n*, Zwangsversicherungsgesetz

compulsory insurance law · Pflichtversicherungsrecht *n*, Zwangsversicherungsrecht

compulsory land charges registration, compulsory land charges recordation, compulsory land charges recording, compulsory registration of land charges, compulsory recordation of land charges, compulsory recording of land charges · Grundbuchzwang *m*

compulsory (land) purchase order, (land) expropriation order, declaratory order; (land) condemnation order (US) · Bodenenteignungsanordnung *f*, Bodenenteignungsverfügung, Bodenenteignungsbefehl *m*, Bodenenteignungsgebot *n*, (Land)Enteignungsanordnung, (Land)Enteignungsverfügung, (Land)Enteignungsbefehl, (Land)Enteignungsgebot

compulsory lease(hold) → (en)forced lease(hold)

compulsory letting (of rooms), (en)forced letting (of rooms) · Zwangsvermietung *f* (von Räumen)

compulsory loan · Zwangsanleihe *f*, Pflichtanleihe

compulsory means, means of coercion · Zwangsmittel *n*

compulsory member · Pflichtmitglied *n*, Zwangsmitglied

compulsory membership · Pflichtmitgliedschaft *f*, Zwangsmitgliedschaft

compulsory money · Zwangsgeld *n*

compulsory mortgage · Zwangshypothek *f*, Pflichthypothek

compulsory on sale · obligatorisch beim Verkauf

compulsory payment · Pflichtzahlung *f*, Zwangszahlung

compulsory payment — computation of cost(s) 216

compulsory payment of legal cost(s) in advance · Vorschußpflichtzahlung f, Vorschußzwangszahlung

compulsory power · Zwangsenteignungsmacht f

compulsory prescription, compulsory regulation, compulsory rule · Mußvorschrift f, zwingende Vorschrift

compulsory process to obtain evidence, compulsory process to obtain proof · zwangsweise Beweissicherstellung f

compulsory purchase (of land), compulsory acquisition (of land), acquisition (of land) by compulsion, purchase (of land) by compulsion · Landzwangsbeschaffung f, (Boden)Zwangsbeschaffung, (Boden)Zwangserwerb m, (Boden)Zwangskauf m, Landzwangserwerb, Landzwangskauf, (Boden)Enteignung gegen Entschädigung, Landenteignung gegen Entschädigung

compulsory purchase (of land) order · Zwangs(an)kaufbefehl m, Zwangs(an)kaufanordnung f, Zwangs(an)kaufverfügung, Zwangs(an)kaufgebot n

compulsory purchase of (real) estate, compulsory acquisition of (real) estate, compulsory purchase of (real) property, compulsory acquisition of (real) property, compulsory purchase of realty, compulsory acquisition of realty · Grund(stücks)enteignung f gegen Entschädigung, Grund(stücks)zwangsbeschaffung gegen Entschädigung, Grund(stücks)zwangserwerb m gegen Entschädigung

compulsory purchase proceeding · Zwangs(an)kaufvertag n

compulsory rectification, compulsory correction · Zwangsberichtigung f

compulsory redemption, compulsory discharge · Zwangseinlösung f, Zwangsauslösung, Zwangsablösung

compulsory registration, compulsory recordation, compulsory recording · Zwangseintrag(ung) m, (f), Zwangsregistrierung, Zwangsbuchung [Grundstück]

compulsory registration of land charges, compulsory recordation of land charges, compulsory recording of land charges, compulsory land charges registration, compulsory land charges recordation, compulsory land charges recording · Grundbuchzwang m

compulsory school attendance · Schulzwang m

compulsory taking · Zwangswegnahme f

compulsory tenancy → (en)forced lease(hold)

compulsory tenant · Zwangsmieter m

compulsory tenure → (en)forced lease(hold)

compulsory winding(-)up by the court [Procedure whereby a company is wound up if, for instance, it has passed a special resolution to wind up, or it is unable to pay its debts or it has failed to commence operations within a year of incorporation or the court believes it equitable that it should be wound up] · Zwangsliquidation f

compupil · Mitschüler m

compurgation [Procedure whereby an accused person made a sworn denial of the accusation and brought together 12 persons who swore an oath to the validity of his statement. See King Williams (1824) 2 B & C 538. Abolished by the Civil Procedure Act 1833] · Beweis m durch Eideshilfe

compurgator, oath-helper · Eideshelfer m [Einer Prozeßpartei im Mittelalter in England]

compurgatrix, female oath-helper · Eideshelferin f [Einer Prozeßpartei im Mittelalter in England]

computable, calculable · berechenbar, kalkulierbar

computation, calculation · Berechnung f, Kalkulation f

computation balance, calculation balance · Berechnungsausgleich m, Kalkulationsausgleich

computation documents, calculation documents · Berechnungsunterlagen f pl, Kalkulationsunterlagen

computation error, calculation error · Berechnungsfehler m, Kalkulationsfehler

computation mistake, calculation mistake · Berechnungsirrtum m, Kalkulationsirrtum

computation of a plot fragment, calculation of a parcel fragment, calculation of a plot fragment · Abschnittsberechnung f, Klassenabschnittsberechnung

computation of burden(s), computation of encumbrance(s), computation of incumbrance(s), calculation of charge(s), computation of charge(s), calculation of burden(s), calculation of encumbrance(s), calculation of incumbrance(s) · Belastungsberechnung f, Lastenberechnung, Belastungskalkulation f, Lastenkalkulation, Belastungsermitt(e)lung, Lastenermitt(e)lung

computation of cost(s), cost(s) calculation, cost(s) computation, costing, (cost(s)) accounting, calculation of cost(s) · Kostenrechnung f, Kostenkalkulation f, (Kostenbe)Rechnung, Kostenermitt(e)lung

computation of damage, damage calculation, damage computation, calculation of damage · Schadensberechnung f, Schadenskalkulation f

computation of fee(s), fee calculation, fee computation, calculation of fee(s) · Gebührenberechnung f, Honorarberechnung

computation of (fixed) period (of time), calculation of time (allowed), computation of time (allowed), calculation of period, computation of period, calculation of term, computation of term, calculation of (fixed) period (of time) · Fristberechnung f

computation of lot widths, calculation of lot widths · Breitenberechnung f, Breitenkalkulation f

computation of period, calculation of term, computation of term, calculation of (fixed) period (of time), computation of (fixed) period (of time), calculation of time (allowed), computation of time (allowed), calculation of period · Fristberechnung f

computation ordinance, calculation ordinance · Berechnungsverordnung f, Kalkulationsverordnung

computation period, calculation period · Berechnungszeitraum m, Kalkulationszeitraum

computation rate, calculation rate · Berechnungssatz m, Kalkulationssatz

computation risk, calculation risk · Berechnungsrisiko n, Berechnungswagnis n, Kalkulationswagnis, Kalkulationsrisiko

to compute, to calculate · berechnen, kalkulieren

computed in value(s), calculated in value(s) · wertmäßig

computer, reckoner, estimator, calculator [*A person who calculates*] · Kalkulator m

computer(-aided) cartography, machine(-aided) cartography, machine-assisted cartography, computer-assisted cartography · Rechnerkartographie f, rechnergestützte Kartographie

computer(-aided) digitization of boundary networks, machine(-aided) digitization of boundary networks, computer-assisted digitization of boundary networks, machine-assisted digitization of boundary networks · Digitalisierung f flächenbezogener Netzwerke, Übertragung von Flächengrenzen in maschinenlesbare Form

computer-aided mapping · rechnergestützte Kartierung f

computer game · Rechnerspiel n

computer graphic technique · graphische Rechnertechnik f

computerization · Rechnerunterstützung f

computer map · Rechnerkarte f

computer security, safeguarding of data, data protection · Datenschutz m

computer simulation · Rechnersimulation f

to conceal, to hide, to secrete · verbergen

concealed, hidden · verborgen

concealed defect, latent defect, hidden defect · verborgener (Sach)Mangel m, verborgener Baumangel, verdeckter (Sach)Mangel, verdeckter Baumangel

concealed fraud, fraudulent concealment [*Designed fraud by which a party knowing to whom the right belongs, conceals the cirumstances giving that right, and, by means of such concealment, enables himself to enter and hold the land*] · arglistiges Verschweigen n, betrügerisches Verschweigen

concealed household, hidden household, potential household [*It consists of a family living with relatives or other people because they are unable to obtain a separate dwelling*] · statistisch nicht erfaßbarer Haushalt m

concealed household, hidden household, potential household · Gemeinschaftshaushalt m

concealed land(s) [*England. Land privily held from the King by a person having no title thereto; used especially of land(s) that had been monastic property between the Reformation*] · unrechtmäßig gehaltenes Land n, gesetz(es)widrig gehaltenes Land

concealed unemployment, hidden unemployment · verdeckte Arbeitslosigkeit f

to conceal fraudulently · arglistig verschweigen, betrügerisch verschweigen

concealment, non-disclosure [*The intentional suppression of truth or fact known, to the injury or prejudice of another*] · Verschweigung f, Verheimlichung, Unterdrückung der Wahrheit

to concede [*To allow formally for the sake of argument*] · zugeben

to concede, to admit, to acknowledge · einräumen, zugestehen

conceivable, imaginable, supposable · denkbar, vorstellbar

concentration of titles, aggregation of titles, title amalgamation, title aggregation, title concentration, amalgamation of titles · (Rechts)Titelzusammenlegung f

concentration of wealth, wealth concentration · Reichtumsballung *f*

concentric circle theory, concentric (zone) theory, circular (zone) theory · Kreistheorie *f*, Theorie der ringförmigen Anordnung (der sozialökonomischen Stadtviertel)

concept of centrality, centrality concept · Zentralitätsbegriff *m*

concept of central place, central place concept · Zentralortbegriff *m*

concept of disfigurement · Verschandelungsbegriff *m*, Verunstaltungsbegriff

concept of (legal) validity, law(ful) concept, legal concept, concept of law · Rechtsbegriff *m*, (Rechts)Geltungsbegriff, Legalbegriff

concept of region, region concept · Regionsbegriff *m*

concept of risk, concept of hazard, hazard concept, risk concept · Interessenabwägung *f*

concept of space, space concept, spatial concept · Raumbegriff *m*

concept of value · Wertbegriff *m*

conceptual analysis · Begriffsanalyse *f*

conceptual frame(work) · begrifflicher Rahmen *m*, Begriffsrahmen

concert, consent [*Agreement by a number of persons as to a course of action*] · Handlungszustimmung *f*, Handlungseinwilligung, Handlungsbilligung, Handlungskonsens *m*

concerted action [*Action that has been planned, arranged, adjusted, agreed on and settled between parties acting together pursuant to some design or scheme*] · konzertierte Aktion *f*

concession, admission, acknowledg(e)ment [*Made by a party of the existence of certain facts*] · Einräumung *f*, Zugeständnis *n*

concessionary fare · verbilligter Fahrpreis *m*

concessor [*In old English law*]; grantor, donor [*The person by whom a grant is made*] · Überlassende *m*, Überlasser

conciliation, mediation · Schlichtung *f*, Vermitt(e)lung bei Streitigkeiten

conciliation board → board of conciliation

conciliation code, mediation code · Schlichtungsordnung *f*

conciliator, amicable compositeur · Schlichter *m*

to conclude, to prove, to infer, to come to a conclusion · folgern, ableiten, schließen (von etwas auf etwas)

to conclude a contract, to adopt a contract, to make a contract, to contract, to settle a contract · abschließen eines Vertrages, vertraglich vereinbaren

concluder (of (a) contract) · Vertragschließende *m*

concluding a contract, making a contract, adopting a contract, contracting, settling a contract · Abschließen *n* eines Vertrages

concludingly [*obsolete*]; conclusively; concludently · schlüssigerweise

conclusion of a contract, contract conclusion, settlement of a contract, contract settlement · Abschluß *m* eines Vertrages, Vertragsabschluß

conclusion of fact [*An inference drawn from the subordinate or evidentiary facts*] · Tatsachenfolgerung *f*, Tatsachenschluß *m*

conclusion of peace, peace conclusion · Friedensschluß *m*

conclusive force, conclusory force · Folgerungskraft *f*, Schlußkraft, Ableitungskraft

conclusively; concludently, concludingly [*obsolete*] · schlüssigerweise

conclusiveness, decisiveness; concludency [*obsolete*] [*The quality of being conclusive*] · Schlüssigkeit *f*

conclusive presumption, conclusory presumption; presumptio juris et de jure [*Latin*] · schlüssige Vermutung *f*, gefolgerte Vermutung, abgeleitete Vermutung

conclusive proof, conclusory proof, conclusive evidence, conclusory evidence · schlüssiger Beweis *m*, gefolgerter Beweis, abgeleiteter Beweis

concrescence; growth by assimilation [*obsolete*]; concretion, growing together, uniting in one mass · Zusammenwachsen *n*

concrete contractor · Betonbauunternehmer *m*

"concrete desert" · ,,Betonwüste" *f*

concretion, growing together, uniting in one mass, concrescence; growth by assimilation [*obsolete*] · Zusammenwachsen *n*

concurrence, concurrency [*Pursuit of the same object*] · Interessengleichheit *f*, Interesseneinheit

concurrent · interessengleich

concurrent · gleichartig

concurrent, co-operating, operating on the same subject · zusammenarbeitend

concurrent [*Having the same authority*] · mitbestimmend

concurrent, contributory [*Contributing to the same event*] · mitwirkend

concurrent [*Acting in conjunction*] · gleichhandeln

concurrent, running together · gleichlaufend

concurrent, existing together · gleichzeitig bestehend, simultan bestehend

concurrent, agreeing with, according to, consonant, conformable, accordant, consistent, not contradictory [*Having agreement with itself or something else*] · gemäß, nicht gegenteilig, konform mit, übereinstimmend, gerecht mit

concurrent community → concurrent (interest(s)) community

concurrent conditions, mutual conditions, reciprocal conditions, common conditions · gegenseitige Bedingungen *fpl*, Zug-um-Zug-Bedingungen [*Bedingungen, daß die Parteien die Leistungen Zug um Zug erfüllen*]

concurrent demise, concurrent lease, concurrent tenancy [*A lease created out of a reversion on an existing lease and existing concurrently with another lease*] · mitbestimmende Pacht *f*, nicht ausschließliche Pacht

concurrent deviation, concurrent divergence · gleichsinnige Abweichung *f* [*Statistik*]

concurrent divergence, concurrent deviation · gleichsinnige Abweichung *f* [*Statistik*]

concurrent expression of intent(ion) · übereinstimmender Willensausdruck *m*

concurrent interest, concurrent right [*Interests in land held at one and the same time, by two or more persons*] · Bruchteil *m*, Mitrecht *n*

concurrent interests → collective property

concurrent (interest(s)) community, tenants in common · Bruchteilgemeinschaft *f*

concurrent lease, concurrent tenancy, concurrent demise [*A lease created out of a reversion on an existing lease and existing concurrently with another lease*] · mitbestimmende Pacht *f*, nicht ausschließliche Pacht

concurrent lease(hold), joint lease(hold), collective lease(hold) · Teilerbbaurecht *n*, gemeinsames Erbbaurecht, gemeinschaftliches Erbbaurecht, Gemeinerbbaurecht, Bruchteilerbbaurecht, Mehrheitserbbaurecht, Miterbbaurecht, Anteilerbbaurecht [*Bruchteil eines mehreren Personen gemeinschaftlich zustehenden Erbbaurechts, welcher in der Weise beschränkt ist, daß jedem der Mitberechtigten das Sondereigentum an nicht zu Wohnzwecken dienenden bestimmten Räumen in einem aufgrund des Erbbaurechts errichteten oder zu errichtenden Gebäuden eingeräumt wird. (§ 30 Abs. 1 WoEigG)*]

concurrent opinion · mitbestimmende Meinung *f*, nicht ausschließliche Meinung

concurrent possession, collective possession · Bruchteilbesitz *m*, Anteilbesitz, Gemeinbesitz, Mehrheitsbesitz, Mitbesitz, Vielherrlich-Besitz, gesamthänderischer Besitz, Gesamt(hand)besitz, vielherrlicher Besitz, gemeinschaftlicher Besitz, gemeinsamer Besitz

concurrent right, concurrent interest [*Interests in land held at one and the same time, by two or more persons*] · Bruchteil *m*, Mitrecht *n*

concurrent tenancy, concurrent demise, concurrent lease [*A lease created out of a reversion on an existing lease and existing concurrently with another lease*] · mitbestimmende Pacht *f*, nicht ausschließliche Pacht

concurrent writ · (Prozeß) Ladungsduplikat *n*

concurring opinion · Zusatzvotum *n*

to condemn, to adjudge, to sentence judicially [*Any one to a penalty, or to do or suffer something*] · verurteilen

to condemn (US); to expropriate · enteignen

condemnation [*Declaration that a property is unfit for occupancy because it does not meet requirements of codes*] · Unbewohnbarkeitserklärung *f*

condemnation [*A sentence or judg(e)ment which condemns some one to do, to give, or to pay something, or which declares that his claim or pretensions are unfounded*] · Verurteilung *f*

condemnation (US) → land condemnation

condemnation act (US) → (land) expropriation act

condemnation authority (US) → land condemnation authority

condemnation by zone(s) (US); expropriation by zone(s) · Zonenenteignung *f*

condemnation for opening up (US) → (land) condemnation for opening up

condemnation for substitute land (US); expropriation for substitute land · Ersatzlandenteignung *f*, Ersatzbodenenteignung [*Enteignung von Grundstücken zur Entschädigung in Land*]

condemnation for substitute right → (land) condemnation for substitute right

condemnation law (US) → (land) expropriation act

condemnation legislation — conditional devise

condemnation legislation → (land) condemnation legislation

condemnation (money) [*The damages which the party failing in an action is adjudged (= condemned) to pay*] · Schadenersatzgeld *n* auf Grund eines Urteils

condemnation order (US) → (land) condemnation order

condemnation plan (US) → (land) condemnation plan

condemnation procedure (US) → (land) condemnation procedure

condemnation statute (US) → (land) expropriation act

condemnation theory (US) → (land) condemnation theory

condemnation (US); expropriation · Enteignung *f*, enteignender Eingriff *m* [*Zugunsten der öffentlichen Hand*]

condemned (US); expropriated · enteignet

condensed balance sheet · Bilanzauszug *m*

condensed regional center, compressed regional center (US); compressed regional centre, condensed regional centre (Brit.) · eingeengtes regionales Zentrum *n*

condition, circumstance, state of matters · Umstand *m*, Lage *f*

condition [*Something that must exist or be present if something else is to be or take place; that on which anything else is contingent*] · Bedingung *f*

condition, nature, state, position, mode of being · Beschaffenheit *f*

condition, state [*A particular mode of being of a thing*] · Zustand *m*

condition, social position, rank [*A position with reference to the grades of society*] · Stellung *f*, Rang *m*

condition [*A particular mode of being of a person*] · Personenstand *m*

condition · Hauptpflicht *f* [*Liefervertrag*]

conditional; conditionary [*obsolete*]; hypothetical · hypothetisch

conditional, not absolute, contingent ((up)on), depending (up)on [*Operative only (up)on an uncertain event*] · bedingt durch, abhängig von, abhängend von

conditional, (up)on condition; conditionary [*obsolete*] · bedingt, unter Vorbehalt, mit Vorbedingung

conditional, rebuttable · widerlegbar, widerleglich

conditional acceptance, acceptance upon condition · Annahme *f* unter Vorbehalt, Vorbehaltannahme, bedingte Annahme

conditional acceptance of a bill (of exchange), qualified acceptance of a bill (of exchange) · bedingte Wechselannahme *f*

conditional acceptance (of work(s)), acceptance (of work(s)) (up)on condition · Abnahme *f* unter Vorbehalt, Vorbehaltabnahme, bedingte Abnahme [*Bauarbeiten*]

conditional agreement, dependent agreement, reciprocal agreement, mutual agreement, dependant agreement · gegenseitiges Abkommen *n*, gegenseitige Abmachung *f*, gegenseitige Vereinbarung

conditional and suspensive discharge, suspensive and conditional discharge · bedingte und suspensive Entlastung *f*, suspensive und bedingte Entlastung

conditional authority of precedents, contingent authority of precedents · bedingte Bindungswirkung *f*, abhängige Bindungswirkung [*Das Gericht kann von einem früheren Präzedenzfall abweichen*]

conditional bequest, conditional legacy, contingent bequest, contingent legacy [*A legacy given to a person at a future uncertain time, that may or may not arrive; as "at his age of twenty-one"*] · bedingtes (Fahrnis)Legat *n*, bedingtes (Fahrnis)Vermächtnis *n*, Bedingungs-(fahrnis)vermächtnis, Bedingungs(fahrnis)legat

conditional bill of sale · Sicherungsübereignungsurkunde *f*

conditional bond, bond with a condition, double bond · gesiegeltes Schuldversprechen *n* mit Strafklausel, gesiegelte Schuldurkunde *f* mit Strafklausel, beurkundete Schuldforderung *f* mit Strafklausel

conditional buyer, conditional purchaser, conditional vendee · Vorbehaltkäufer *m*

conditional change in zoning, rezoning (up)on condition, change in zoning (up)on condition, conditional rezoning · bedingter Baunutzungswechsel *m*, Baunutzungswechsel mit Vorbedingung, Baunutzungswechsel unter Vorbehalt

conditional contract [*An executory contract the performance of which depends upon a condition*] · Vorbehaltvertrag *m*

conditional covenant, contingent covenant · bedingter Formalvertrag *m*

conditional devise, contingent devise [*The vesting of any estate in the devisee is made to depend upon some future event, in which case, if the event never* occurs, or until it does occur, no estate vests under the devise] · bedingtes (Land)Vermächtnis *n*, bedingtes (Land)Legat, Bedingungs(land)vermächtnis, Bedingungs(land)legat *n*

conditional discharge, contingent discharge · bedingte Entlastung *f*, abhängige Entlastung [*Sie tritt sofort in Wirksamkeit, erzeugt aber nicht den völligen Untergang der Schulden des Konkursschuldners, sondern legt ihm die Verpflichtung auf, in einer vom Gericht zu bezeichnenden Weise für weitere Befriedigung der Gläubiger zu sorgen*]

conditional (en)feoffment, conditional infeudation, contingent (en)feoffment, contingent infeudation · bedingte Belehnung *f*, Belehnung unter Resolutivbedingung, abhängige Belehnung

conditional event · bedingendes Ereignis *n*

conditional grant · Verwendungsauflage *f*, Zweckzuwendung *f*

conditional indorsement, conditional endorsement · bedingtes Indossament *n* [*Nach deutschem Recht gelten Bedingungen bei Indossamenten als nicht geschrieben*]

conditional infeudation, contingent (en)feoffment, contingent infeudation, conditional (en)feoffment · bedingte Belehnung *f*, Belehnung unter Resolutivbedingung, abhängige Belehnung

conditional interest, conditional right [*An interest on condition subsequent*] · auflösendes Recht *n*, resolutives Recht *n*, Resolutivrecht *n*

conditionality · Bedingtheit *f*

to condition(alize), to stipulate · (aus)bedingen, konditionieren

conditional judg(e)ment · bedingtes Urteil *n*

conditional (land) use zoning, special (land) use zoning, conditional zoning, special zoning · bedingte (bauliche) Nutzung *f*, bedingte Baunutzung, bedingte Bauzonenfestlegung

conditional legacy → conditional bequest

conditional liability, contingent liability · bedingte Haftpflicht *f*, bedingte Haftung *f*, abhängige Haftpflicht, abhängige Haftung, bedingte Haftbarkeit, abhängige Haftbarkeit

conditionally [*In a conditional manner*] · bedingungsweise

conditionally, by way of hypothesis, by way of conditional proposition · hypothetischerweise

conditional (money) debt, contingent (money) debt · bedingte (Geld)Schuld *f*, abhängige (Geld)Schuld

conditional payment · bedingte Zahlung *f*

conditional presumption, rebuttable presumption · widerlegliche Vermutung *f*, widerlegbare Vermutung

conditional promise, dependent promise, reciprocal promise, mutual promise, double promise, counter-promise, dependant promise · gegenseitiges Versprechen *n*

conditional proposition · Bedingungsvorschlag *m*

conditional proprietorship, contingent ownership (of property), contingent (general) property, contingent proprietorship · bedingtes Eigentum *n*, unvollkommenes Eigentum

conditional purchaser, conditional vendee, conditional buyer · Vorbehaltkäufer *m*

conditional regression, regression (up)on condition · bedingte Regression *f*, Regression mit Vorbedingung, Regression unter Vorbehalt

conditional remainder (land(ed)) estate, executory remainder (land(ed)) estate, possibility of (a) future (land(ed)) estate; spes successionis [*Latin*]; contingent remainder (land(ed)) estate [*The remainder is contingent if the person who is to have the remainder is not yet living or if his identity is uncertain, or if the event which is to bring the remainder into existence is uncertain. The remainder becomes vested when such person is ascertained or upon the happening of the event*] · bedingter anwartschaftlicher Bodenbesitz(stand) *m*, möglicher anwartschaftlicher Bodenbesitz(stand), ungewisser anwartschaftlicher Bodenbesitz(stand)

conditional rezoning, conditional change in zoning, rezoning (up)on condition, change in zoning (up)on condition · bedingter Baunutzungswechsel *m*, Baunutzungswechsel mit Vorbedingung, Baunutzungswechsel unter Vorbehalt

conditional right → conditional interest

conditional sale [*A sale with the provision that the vendor may resume proprietorship on certain conditions or a certain condition*] · Kauf *m* unter Eigentumsvorbehalt, Kauf mit aufschiebender Bedingung

conditional seller, conditional vendor · Vorbehaltverkäufer *m*

conditional testament, conditional will [*A will executed with the intention that it shall be rendered operative only on the occurrence of a specified event*] · Vorbehalttestament *n*

conditional vendee, conditional buyer, conditional purchaser · Vorbehaltkäufer *m*

conditional vendor — conditions

conditional vendor, conditional seller · Vorbehaltverkäufer *m*

conditional zoning, special zoning, conditional (land) use zoning, special (land) use zoning · bedingte (bauliche) Nutzung *f*, bedingte Baunutzung, bedingte Bauzonenfestlegung

conditionary [*obsolete*]; hypothetical, conditional · hypothetisch

conditionary [*obsolete*]; conditional, (up)on condition · bedingt, unter Vorbehalt, mit Vorbedingung

condition as to time · Zeitbedingung *f*

conditionate, conditioned, stipulated · ausbedungen

condition implied, implied condition, tacit condition · konkludente Bedingung *f*, gefolgerte Bedingung, stillschweigende Bedingung

condition imposed by an authority, official condition · behördliche Bedingung *f*, amtliche Bedingung

condition in deed, condition in fact [*A condition expressed in a deed, as a feoffment, lease, or grant, in plain words, or legal terms of law*] · urkundliche Bedingung *f*

condition inherent, inherent condition [*One attaching to the tenure of property, and descending therewith to the inheritor*] · anhaftende Bedingung *f*, inbegriffene Bedingung

condition in law, legal condition [*In a legal instrument, e.g. a will, or contract, a provision on which its legal force or effect is made to depend*] · Rechtsbedingung *f*

condition in life, rank in life, social rank, social state, social condition, state in life · soziale Stellung *f*

condition in restraint of marriage · Bedingung *f* zur Verhinderung einer Verehelichung

condition of abeyance, state of abeyance, state of suspension, abeyancy, temporary nonexistence, expectancy of law, contemplation of law; abeyantia [*Latin*]; abeyance [*In the law of real estate. Where there is no person in existence in whom an inheritance can vest, it is said to be in abeyance, that is, in expectation; the law considering is as always potentially existing, and ready to vest when ever a proper owner appears*] · Schwebe(zustand) *f, (m)*

condition of a citizen, rank of a citizen, status of a citizen · Bürgerstand *m*, Bürgerstatus *m*

condition of being gilt-edged, rank of being gilt-edged · Mündelsicherheit *f*

condition of carriage · Beförderungsbedingung *f*

condition of compliance → condition of performance

condition of contract, (contract) fundamental term, contract condition [*Term of fundamental importance in a contract*] · Vertragsbedingung *f*

condition of discharge → condition of performance

condition of equity, equitable condition · Billigkeits(recht)bedingung *f*

condition of execution → condition of performance

condition of fulfil(l)ment → condition of performance

condition of lease, condition of tenancy, lease condition, tenancy condition · Pachtbedingung *f*

condition of payment, payment condition · Zahlungsbedingung *f*

condition of performance, condition of execution, condition of compliance, condition of fulfil(l)ment, condition of discharge · Ausführungsbedingung *f*, Erfüllungsbedingung *f*, Vollzugsbedingung *f*, Vollziehungsbedingung *f*, Erbringungsbedingung *f*

condition of society · Gesellschaftszustand *m*

condition of tenancy, lease condition, tenancy condition, condition of lease · Pachtbedingung *f*

condition on the mere arbitrary will of the promisor · Wollensbedingung *f*

condition precedent, condition suspensive, suspensive condition, precedent condition · Anfangsbedingung *f*, Suspensivbedingung, suspensive Bedingung, aufschiebende Bedingung, hinausschiebende Bedingung, verschiebende Bedingung

condition previously necessary, preliminary condition, prerequisite, precondition · Voraussetzung *f*, Vorbedingung

condition reduced to a mere warranty, warranty ex post facto · Bedingung *f* mit Verzicht auf die Rechtsfolgen eines Bedingungsbruches

condition resolutive, resolutory condition, condition subsequent · auflösende Bedingung *f*, resolutive Bedingung *f*, Endbedingung *f*, Resolutivbedingung *f* [*Die Wirkung des Geschäftes tritt sofort ein und endigt mit dem Eintritt des künftigen ungewissen Umstandes*]

conditions [*The whole affecting circumstances under which a being exists*] · Verhältnisse *f*

conditions for supply and installation, conditions for supply and erection, conditions for supply and assembly · Liefer- und Montagebedingungen *fpl*

condition sine qua non · unerläßliche Bedingung *f*

conditions of engagement, engagement conditions · Einstellungsbedingungen *fpl*

conditions of the bid, conditions of the offer, conditions of the tender, bid conditions; offer conditions, tender conditions; conditions of the (bid) proposal, (bid) proposal conditions (US) · Angebotsbedingungen *fpl*

condition subsequent, condition resolutive, resolutory condition · auflösende Bedingung *f*, resolutive Bedingung *f*, Endbedingung *f*, Resolutivbedingung *f* [*Die Wirkung des Geschäftes tritt sofort ein und endigt mit dem Eintritt des künftigen ungewissen Umstandes*]

condition suspensive, suspensive condition, precedent condition, condition precedent · Anfangsbedingung *f*, Suspensivbedingung, suspensive Bedingung, aufschiebende Bedingung, hinausschiebende Bedingung, verschiebende Bedingung

condominium (Brit.); joint sovereignty, joint rule · gemeinsame hoheitliche Befugnis *f*, gemeinschaftliche hoheitliche Befugnis, gemeinschaftliche Hoheitsbefugnis, gemeinsame Hoheitsbefugnis, gemeinschaftliches hoheitliches Recht *n*, gemeinschaftliches Hoheitsrecht, gemeinsames Hoheitsrecht, gemeinschaftliches Hoheitsrecht

condo(minium) (US); private flat, owner-occupied dwelling (Brit.) [*Form of complete ownership by which the buyer has the entire undivided interest in an apartment or dwelling as opposed to ownership of the land on which the apartment or dwelling sits*] · Wohnungseigentum *n*, WE, Stockwerkeigentum, Geschoßeigentum, Etageneigentum, EW, Eigen(tums)wohnung *f* [*Das Sondereigentum an einer Wohnung in Verbindung mit dem Miteigentumsanteil am zugehörigen gemeinschaftlichen Eigentum*]

condo(minium) fee (US); private dwelling fee · Hausgeld *n* [*Bewirtschaftung und Verwaltung von Eigentumswohnungen*]

condo(minium) law, condo(minium) act, condo(minium) statute (US); private flat law, private flat act, private flat statute (Brit.) · Wohnungseigentumsgesetz *n*, WEG

condo(minium) owner (US); private flat owner (Brit.) · Wohnungseigentümer *m*, WEer

conducive to industries · industriefördelich, industriefreundlich

conducive to mobility · beweglichkeitsfreundlich, mobilitätsförderlich, mobilitätsfreundlich, beweglichkeitsförderlich

conducive to motor traffic · autofreundlich

conducive to pedestrians · fußgängerfreundlich

conducive to the environment · umweltfreundlich

conduct; (personal) behavior (US); (personal) behaviour (Brit.) · Führung *f*, (persönliches) Verhalten *n*

conduct money (Brit.) · Zeugengebühr *f*

conduct of another's affairs; negotiorum gestio [*Latin*] · Geschäftsführung *f* ohne Auftrag

conductor, hirer [*The goods or chattels are left for hire with the bailee to be used by him*] · (Sach)Mieter *m*

conduct rule, rule of conduct · Verhaltensnorm *f*

confederation [*A number of states united by a league; a body of states united for certain common purposes*] · Konföderation *f*, Staatenbund *m*

confederation article, article of confederation · Konföderationsartikel *m*

to confess, to avow, to make a confession, to admit [*To admit the truth of what is charged*] · (ein)gestehen, bekennen, zugeben, geständig sein [*Schuld*]

to confess and avoid [*To admit a charge, but show it to be invalid in law*] · vorbringen neuer Tatsachen, einreden

confidence, trust · Vertrauen *n*

confidence belt, confidence interval, confidence region · Vertrauensbereich *m*, Vertrauensgürtel *m*, Vertrauensintervall *n* [*Statistik*]

confidence coefficient · statistische Sicherheit *f*

confidence limit, fiducial limit · Mutungsgrenze *f* [*Statistik*]

confidential information · vertrauliche Mitteilung *f*

confidential relation(ship) · Vertrauensverhältnis *n*, Vertrauensbeziehung *f*

confidential treatment, non-disclosure · vertrauliche Behand(e)lung *f*, Unterlassung einer Mitteilung

to confine, to commit (to confinement) · inhaftieren

confined, committed to confinement · inhaftiert

confinement — confraternity

confinement, commitment, committal · Haft f, Inhaftierung f

confinement writ, warrant, (writ of) capias, writ of committal, writ of commitment, writ of confinement, committal writ, commitment writ [*A writ commanding the officer to take the body of the person named in that, that is, to arrest him*] · Haftbefehl m

confining, committing to confinement, commitment, committal · Inhaftieren n, Inhaftnahme f

to confirm; affirmare [*Latin*]; to affirm, to make firm · bestätigen

confirmation, affirmation · Bestätigung f

confirmation notice, confirmation notification, affirmation notice, affirmation notification, notice of confirmation, notice of affirmation, notification of confirmation, notification of affirmation · Bestätigungsmitteilung f, Bestätigungsanzeige f, Bestätigungsbenachrichtigung

confirmation of order, affirmation of order · Auftragsbestätigung f

confirmation of sale, affirmation of sale · Verkaufsbestätigung f

confirmatory evidence, confirmatory proof, corroborating evidence, corroborative evidence, strengthening evidence, corroborating proof, corroborative proof, strengthening proof · bekräftigender Beweis m

confirmatory letter, affirmatory letter, letter of confirmation, letter of affirmation · Bestätigungsschreiben n

confirmed (letter of) credit, irrevocable (letter of) credit · unwiderrufliches Akkreditiv n

confirming, affirming · Bestätigen n

confirming (authoritatively), approving, sanctioning · Zulassen n

confirming bank · bestätigende Bank f [*Akkreditiv*]

to confirm on appeal, to affirm on appeal [*judg(e)ment*] · bestätigen in der Berufung [*Urteil*]

to confiscate [*To deprive of property by seizure*] · einziehen, konfiszieren

confiscated, adjudged, forfeited · eingezogen, konfisziert

confiscation [*In international law, is where a State seizes property belonging to another State, or to its subjects, and appropriates it*] · Einziehung f, Konfiskation f, Beschlagnahme f, Enteignung

confiscation act, confiscation law, confiscation statute · Konfiskationsgesetz n, Einziehungsgesetz, Beschlagnahmegesetz, Enteignungsgesetz

confiscator · Einzieher m, Konfiskator

confiscatory [*Of the nature of, or tending to, confiscation*] · konfiszierbar, einziehbar

conflict [*The clashing or variance of opposed principles, statements, arguments, etc.*] · Gegensatz m, Widerspruch m, Kollision f, Widerstreit m

conflict, interlock, (over)lap, interference, lappage · Überschneidung f, Überlagerung

conflicting decisions of co-ordinate courts · gegensätzliche Entscheidungen fpl gleichrangiger Gerichtsbarkeit, Widerspruch m der Entscheidungen gleichrangiger Gerichtsbarkeit, widersprechende Entscheidungen gleichrangiger Gerichtsbarkeit, Gegensatz m der Entscheidungen gleichrangiger Gerichtsbarkeit

conflict of interests · Interessengegensatz m, Interessenkollision f, Interessenwiderspruch m, Interessenwiderstreit m

conflict of laws; conflictus legum [*Latin*] · Kollision f, Rechtskollision, Rechtswiderspruch m

conflict of laws, law of conflicts, Private International Law, conflicts law, International Private Law, IPL · Außenprivatrecht n, Kollisionsrecht, zwischenstaatliches (Privat)Recht n, Internationales Privatrecht n, IPR n, Zwischenprivatrecht n, Grenzrecht n

conflict rule, rule of conflict of laws · Kollisionsregel f

conflictus legum [*Latin*]; conflict of laws · Kollision f, Rechtskollision, Rechtswiderspruch m

conformable, accordant, consistent, not contradictory, concurrent, agreeing with, according to, consonant [*Having agreement with itself or something else*] · gemäß, nicht gegenteilig, konform mit, übereinstimmend, gerecht mit

conforming to truth, just · wahrheits(ge)treu

conformity certificate, certificate of conformity · Entlastungsattest n für einen Gemeinschuldner, Entlastungsschein m für einen Gemeinschuldner, Entlastungsbescheinigung f für einen Gemeinschuldner

conformity to truth, justness · Wahrheitstreue f

confounding [*Mixing up or mingling so that the elements become difficult to distinguish or impossible to separate*] · Vermengen n, Konfundieren

confraternity, brotherhood, brotherly union · Verbrüderung f, Konfraternität f

confused condition, disordered condition · verworrene Lage f, verworrener Zustand m

confusing, throwing into disorder · Verwirren n, Bestürzen

confusingly [*In a confusing manner*] · verwirrenderweise, bestürzenderweise

confusion, disorder · Verwirrung f, Bestürzung

confusion of debts [*A mode of extinguishing a debt, by the concurrence in the same person of two qualities or adverse rights to the same thing which mutually destroy each other*] · Schuldausgleich m, Konfusion f

confusion (of goods); confusio [*Latin*]; admixture of fluids · (Sach)Vermischung f [*Unfeste Körper werden so untereinander gebracht, daß sie nicht mehr einzeln, sondern nur noch als Masse gelten*]

confusion of (lot) boundaries, adjustment of (lot) boundaries, boundary replotting [*The title of that branch of equity jurisdiction which relates to the discovery and settlement of conflicting, disputed, or uncertain boundaries*] · Grenzregelung f, Grenzausgleich m, Miniaturumlegung

confusion of property, property confusion · Güterzusammenschluß m

congested area, congested territory · überentwickeltes Gebiet n

congestion · Überentwick(e)lung f [*Gebiet*]

conglomerate · Mischkonzern m

conglomerate, multi(ple)-company · Konglomeratfirma f

conjugal right, matrimonial right · eheliches Recht n

conjugal rights, matrimonial rights [*The privilege which husband and wife have of each other's society, comfort, and affection (Wharton)*] · eheliche Rechte n pl, Eherechte

conjugate ranking · konjugierte Rangordnung f [*Statistik*]

conjuncture-profit, entrepreneur's rent; case of extra profit analogous to rent, rent of ability, profits partaking of the nature of rent · Unternehmerpension f, Seltenheitsprämie f

conjuratio pro libertate [*For instance in Cologne 1112*] · Schwurgenossenschaft f

connecting agreement, approach agreement, connection agreement · Anknüpfungsvereinbarung f, Anknüpfungsabkommen n, Anknüpfungsabmachung

connection · Anschluß m [*Von Grundstükken und (baulichen) Anlagen an öffentliche Erschließungsanlagen*]

connection, approach · Anknüpfung f

connection agreement, connecting agreement, approach agreement · Anknüpfungsvereinbarung f, Anknüpfungsabkommen n, Anknüpfungsabmachung

connection compulsion, compulsion of connection · Anschlußzwang m [*Leitung*]

connection contribution · Anschlußbeitrag m [*Leitung*]

connection cost(s) · Anschlußkosten f [*Der öffentlich-rechtliche Kostenerstattungsanspruch der Gemeinde gegenüber dem Grundstückseigentümer auf Ersatz jener Aufwendungen, die die Herstellung der Grundstückszuleitung (Stichleitung) von der Straßensammelleitung bis zur Grundstücksgrenze tatsächlich verursacht haben*]

connection duty, duty of connection, duty to connect · Anschlußpflicht f

connection fee · Anschlußgebühr f [*Leitung*]

consanguinity, relation(ship) by blood, blood relation(ship) · Blutsbande f, Blutsverwandtschaft f, Verwandtschaft durch gleiche Abstammung

conscience clause · Gewissensklausel f

consecutive numbering · Durchnumerieren n, fortlaufendes Numerieren

consecutive thought, line of thought, thoughtway · Gedankenfolge f, Gedankengang m

consension, consensus of opinion, unity of opinion, agreement of opinion, consent of opinion, unanimity · Meinungsgleichheit f, Einstimmigkeit

consensus of opinion, unity of opinion, agreement of opinion, consent of opinion, unanimity, consension · Meinungsgleichheit f, Einstimmigkeit

consent, concert [*Agreement by a number of persons as to a course of action*] · Handlungszustimmung f, Handlungseinwilligung, Handlungsbilligung, Handlungskonsens m

to consent, to approbate, to approve, to assent · billigen, einwilligen, zustimmen

consent, approbation, consensus, approval, assent · Billigung f, Einwilligung, Zustimmung, Konsens m

consented, approbated, approved, assented · gebilligt, eingewilligt, zugestimmt

consenting, assenting, action of giving assent, sanctioning, approbating, approving · Billigen n, Einwilligen, Zustimmen

**consent in writing, ** assent in writing, sanction in writing, approval in writing, written assent, written approval, written consent, written sanction · schriftliche Billigung f, schriftliche Einwilligung, schriftliche Zustimmung

consent of opinion, unanimity, consension, consensus of opinion, unity of opinion, agreement of opinion · Meinungsgleichheit f, Einstimmigkeit

consent principle, principle of coincidence of intent(ion), principle of consent · Bewilligungsprinzip n, Bewilligungsgrundsatz m, Einigungsprinzip, Einigungsgrundsatz, Konsensprinzip, Konsensgrundsatz [Grundbuchrecht]

consent to cession, sanction to assignment, sanction to cession, approval to assignment, approval to cession, assent to assignment, assent to cession, consent to assignment · Abtretungseinwilligung f, Abtretungszustimmung, Abtretungsbilligung, Zessionseinwilligung, Zessionszustimmung, Zessionsbilligung

consent to judge's order · Zustimmung f des Beklagten, daß der Richter die Eintragung eines Urteils für den Kläger verfüge

consent value [The value of the land with permission to carry out the proposed works or change of use] · Grund(stücks)wert m mit Planungsgenehmigung

consequential cost(s) · Folgekosten f

consequential damage from defect · Baumangelfolgeschaden m, (Sach)Mangelfolgeschaden

consequential damages, consequential indemnity, consequential compensation, consequential compensative, consequential indemnification · Folgeentschädigung(sleistung) f, Folgeschadenersatz(leistung) m, (f)

consequential gain, consequential profit · Folgegewinn m, Folgeprofit m

consequentiality; consequentialness [obsolete] [Logical sequence and consistency of thought] · Folgerichtigkeit f, Schlußrichtigkeit

consequential load, consequential burden, consequential encumbrance, consequential incumbrance · Folgelast f

consequential loss [The indirect loss arising out of fire or other insured period] · Folgeverlust m, mittelbarer Verlust [Versicherung]

consequential profit → consequential gain

conservable, preservable · erhaltbar, pflegbar

conservation, preservation · Erhaltung f, Pflege f, Substanzerhaltung, Substanzpflege

conservation · Instandhaltung f

conservation [The official care and protection of natural resources, as forests] · Naturschutz m, Naturpflege f, Naturerhaltung f

conservation [A forest, fishery, etc., or a part of one, under official supervision] · Schutzgebiet n

conservation area, conservation territory, preservation area, preservation territory [An area of special architectural or historic interest the character or appearance of which it is desirable to preserve or enhance] · Denkmalpflegegebiet n, Denkmalerhaltungsgebiet

conservation duty, preservation duty, duty of preservation, duty of conservation · Erhaltungspflicht f, Pflegepflicht [Bauwerk]

conservationist [A person who advocates conservation of the natural resources of a country or regions] · Naturschützer m

conservation of art, preservation of art · Kunstpflege f, Kunsterhaltung f

conservation of buildings, preservation of buildings, building preservation, building conservation · Gebäudeerhaltung f, Gebäudepflege f

conservation of energy, energy conservation · Energieeinsparung f

conservation of environment, preservation of environment · Umwelterhaltung f, Umweltpflege f

conservation of forests, forest preservation, forest conservation, preservation of forests · Walderhaltung f, Waldpflege f, Forsterhaltung, Forstpflege

conservation of land, land preservation, land conservation, preservation of land · Landeserhaltung f, Landespflege f

conservation of monuments, preservation of monuments, historic preservation, historic conservation · Denkmalerhaltung f, Denkmalpflege f, Denkmalschutz m

conservation of soil, preservation of soil, soil conservation, soil preservation · Bodenerhaltung f, Bodenpflege f

conservation of structures, preservation of structures · Bau(werk)erhaltung f, Bau(werk)pflege f

conservation of the historic(al) core, preservation of the historic(al) core · Altstadterhaltung f, Altstadtpflege f

conservation of the peace, police power, peace conservation [The power that enables the legislature to pass laws for the protection of the public health, morals, and safety, or laws which are other-

wise very clearly for the general welfare] · Ordnungsrecht *n*, Friedensbewahrung *f* [*Mit dem deutschen Wort „Polizeigewalt", auch der älteren Zeit, läßt sich dieses Institut „police power" kaum vergleichen. Es dient viel zu einseitig nur der Rechtfertigung der gesetzgeberischen Maßnahmen der Staatsgewalt*]

conservation of trees, tree conservation, tree preservation, preservation of trees · Baumerhaltung *f*, Baumpflege *f*

conservation territory, preservation area, preservation territory, conservation area [*An area of special architectural or historic interest the character or appearance of which it is desirable to preserve or enhance*] · Denkmalpflegegebiet *n*, Denkmalerhaltungsgebiet

conservator of the peace [*A preserver or keeper of the public peace*] · Ordnungshüter *m*, Friedensbewahrer

conserving of energy · Energiesparen *n*

consideration · Verpflichtungsgrund *m*, Rechtfertigungsgrund eines Versprechens

consideration · Valuta *f*

consideration · Überlegung *f*

consideration · Erwägung *f*

consideration · Gegenleistung *f*

consideration in money, money consideration, monetary consideration · Gegenleistung *f* in Geld, geldliche Gegenleistung

consideration principle, principle of consideration · Gegenleistungsgrundsatz *m*, Gegenleistungsprinzip *n*

consideration (up)on request · Gegenleistung *f* auf Aufforderung

considered judg(e)ment, reserved judg(e)ment · Urteil *n* nach vertagter Verkündung

consignee, commission merchant, factor [*He receives goods and sells them for a commission or on a percentage basis*] · (Verkaufs)Kommissionär *m*, Konsignatär *m*

consigner, consignor · Warenabsender *m*, Konsignant *m*

consignment · (Waren)Sendung *f*, Gütersendung

consignment note [*Not to be confused with "bill of lading"*] · Ladeschein *m*

consignment stock · Konsignationslager *n*

consistent, not contradictory, concurrent, agreeing with, according to, consonant, conformable, accordant [*Having agreement with itself or something else*] · gemäß, nicht gegenteilig, konform mit, übereinstimmend, gerecht mit

consistent decision · übereinstimmende Entscheidung *f*, übereinstimmender Entscheid *m* [*Sie stimmt mit einer anderen Entscheidung überein*]

consistent estimator · asymptotisch treffende Schätzfunktion *f* [*Statistik*]

consistent with, non-adverse, non-wrongful · nicht entgegenstehend, nicht entgegen dem Recht [*(subjektives) Besitzrecht*]

consistorial court, church-court, court Christian, consistory court; commissary court [*Scotland*]; spiritual court, ecclesiastic(al) court · geistliches Gericht *n*, Kirchengericht, Konsistorialgericht, kirchliches Gericht [*Die schottischen „ecclesiastic(al) courts" haben nur eine Jurisdiktion über Fragen der Doktrin, des Gottesdienstes, der Sakramente und der Disziplin der Geistlichen*]

to consolidate, to group together · zusammenfassen, verbinden [*Klagen; Sicherheiten*]

to consolidate · zusammenschreiben [*Hypotheken*]

consolidated block lot · Blockeinödparzelle *f*

consolidated farm, outlying farm, relocated farm · Einödhof *m*, Einöde *f*, Aussiedlerhof

consolidated goodwill, consolidation excess [*That portion of the amount paid by a parent or holding company for its investment in a subsidiary company attritubale to unusual earning power or other intangible value not recorded in the subsidiary's books*] · Fusionsüberschuß *m*

consolidated profit and loss account · zusammengezogene Gewinn- und Verlustrechnung *f*, zusammengezogene Bilanz *f*

consolidated shipment · Sammelladung *f*

consolidated strip lot · Streifeneinödparzelle *f*

consolidated surplus, retained earnings [*The combined surplus accounts of all companies whose accounts are consolidated, after deducting minority stockholders' interests therein, the interest acquired by the parent company in the subsidiary companies' surpluses existing at the date of their acquisition, and intercompany eliminations*] · Konzernüberschuß *m*

consolidating, fusioning, uniting · Konsolidieren *n*, Fusionieren, Verschmelzen

consolidatio fructus et proprietatis [*Latin*]; unity of possession [*The joint possession of two rights by several titles*] ·

consolidation — constitutional fact

Besitzeinheit *f*, gleiches Besitzrecht *n*, Einheit des Besitzes, Gleichzeitigkeit *f* des Besitzes

consolidation · Zusammenfassung *f*, Verbindung [*Klagen; Sicherheiten*]

consolidation, fusion, merger [*In the civil law, the uniting of possession, occupancy, profits, etc., of land(s) with property, and vice versa*] · Konsolidation *f*, Verschmelzung *f*, Fusion *f*

consolidation → (land) consolidation

Consolidation Act (Brit.) [*An act which repeals or re-enacts or collects in a single statute previous enactments relating to a topic. Acts of this nature may be passed without customary debate in Parliament: Consolidation of Enactments (Procedure) Act 1949*] · Zusammenfassungsgesetz *n*

consolidation excess, consolidated goodwill [*That portion of the amount paid by a parent or holding company for its investment in a subsidiary company attritutable to unusual earning power or other intangible value not recorded in the subsidiary's books*] · Fusionsüberschuß *m*

consolidation lawmaking → (land) consolidation legislation

consolidation ledger, eliminations ledger · Hilfsbuch *n* für Konzernbilanz

consolidation of capitals, capital consolidation, capital merger, capital fusion, fusion of capitals, merger of capitals · Kapitalverschmelzung *f*, Kapitalkonsolidation *f*, Kapitalfusion

consolidation of corporations · Zusammenfassung *f* von Körperschaften, Zusammenfassung von Korporationen

consolidation of (court) actions, consolidation of (law)suits, consolidation of causes, consolidation of pleas · Klagenzusammenfassung *f*, Klagenverbindung, Zusammenfassung von Klagen, Verbindung von Klagen

consolidation of mortgages, tacking (of) mortgages · Hypothekenvereinigung *f*, Hypothekenzusammenrechnung, Hypothekenzusammenschreibung [*Vereinigung einer nachstehenden (meist dritten) mit einer früheren (meist ersten) Hypothek zum Nachteil der dazwischenstehenden (meist zweiten) Hypothek, von der der Gläubiger der dritten Hypothek keine Kenntnis hatte*]

consolidation of securities · Sicherheitenverbindung *f*, Sicherheitenzusammenfassung

consolidation of valid federal law · Sammlung *f* des Bundesrechts, Bundesrechtsammlung

consolidation right, right of consolidation, right to consolidate · (subjektives) Verbindungsrecht *n*

consonant, conformable, accordant, consistent, not contradictory, concurrent, agreeing with, according to [*Having agreement with itself or something else*] · gemäß, nicht gegenteilig, konform mit, übereinstimmend, gerecht mit

conspicuous consumption [*The use of consumer goods in such a way as to create a display for the purpose of impressing others rather than for the satisfaction of a normal consumer demand*] · Geltungsverbrauch *m*

conspiracy doctrine · Verschwörungslehre *f*

constable, policeman · Polizist *m*, Polizeibeamte *m*; Schutzmann *m* [*volkstümlich*]

constabulary · Polizeitruppe *f*

constant of regression, regression constant · Regressionskonstante *f*

constituent company · Konzerngesellschaft *f*

constituent state [*USA*]; Land [*Federal Republic of Germany*], (federal) state · Staat *m* [*USA*]; (Bundes)Land *n* [*Bundesrepublik Deutschland*]

constituting document, document of incorporation, instrument incorporation, incorporation document, incorporation instrument, constituting instrument · Inkorporierungsurkunde *f*

constituting evidence, evidentiary, evidencing · beweiskräftig, beweisrechtlich

constituting instrument, constituting document, document of incorporation, instrument incorporation, incorporation document, incorporation instrument · Inkorporierungsurkunde *f*

constitution · Verfassung *f*

constitutional · verfassungsgemäß, verfassungskonform, verfassungsmäßig

constitutional act, constitutional law, constitutional statute · Verfassungsgesetz *n*

constitutional amendment · Verfassungs(ab)änderung *f*, Verfassungsnovelle *f*, Verfassungszusatzartikel *m*

constitutional complaint · Verfassungsbeschwerde *f*

constitutional contract · Verfassungsvertrag *m*

constitutional convention · verfassungsgebende Versammlung *f*

constitutional court · verfassungsrechtliches Gericht *n*

constitutional fact · verfassungsrechtlicher Tatbestand *m*

constitutional freedom — construction administration

constitutional freedom, constitutional liberty · Verfassungsfreiheit *f*

constitutional history · Verfassungsgeschichte *f*

constitutionality · Verfassungsmäßigkeit *f*

constitutional jurisdiction · ordentliche Gerichtsbarkeit *f*, allgemeine Zivil- und Strafgerichtsbarkeit

constitutional law, law of (the) constitution · Verfassungsrecht *n*

constitutional law, law of constitution; jus publicum [*Latin*]; public law [*The law concerned with the rights and duties of the state. It is contrasted with private law, which deals with the rights and duties of subjects inter se*] · öffentliches Recht

constitutional law, fundamental law, organic law of a state, basic law [*The law which determines the constitution of government in a state, and prescribes and regulates the manner of its exercise*] · Grundgesetz *n*

constitutional law → constitutional act

constitutional law concerning the economy · Wirtschaftsverfassungsrecht *n*

constitutional liberty, constitutional freedom · Verfassungsfreiheit *f*

constitutional limitation of legislative power · apriorische Begrenzung *f* der gesetzgebenden Gewalt

constitutional monarchy, limited monarchy · konstitutionelle Monarchie *f*

constitutional norm · Verfassungsnorm *f*

constitutional oath · Verfassungseid *m*, Eid auf die Verfassung

constitutional provision · Verfassungsbestimmung *f*

constitutional reality · Verfassungswirklichkeit *f*

constitutional right · verfassungsmäßiges Recht *n*

constitutional statute → constitutional act

constitutional structure · Verfassungsstruktur *f*, Verfassungsaufbau *m*, Verfassungsgefüge *n*, Verfassungszusammensetzung *f*

constitutional theory · Verfassungslehre *f*

Constitution of the United States of America · Bundesverfassung *f* der USA

constitutum possessorium [*Latin*]; constructive possession, indirect possession · (Besitz)Konstitut *n*, Besitzauftragung *f*, mittelbarer Besitz *m*, verdeckter Besitz, indirekter Besitz, vergeistigte Sachherrschaft *f* [*Der unmittelbare Besitzer macht einen anderen zum mittelbaren Besitzer und behält selbst unmittelbaren Besitz*]

to constrain, to restrict, to limit, to restrain · begrenzen, beschränken, einschränken

constrained maxima and minima · Maxima *npl* und Minima *npl* mit Nebenbedingungen

constraint, limitation, restriction, restraint · Begrenzung *f*, Einschränkung, Beschränkung

to construct, to draw up, to set up, to construe, to phrase, to word, to form, to draft [*To arrange or marshal words*] · abfassen, gestalten, entwerfen, ausarbeiten, formulieren

to construct, to build · bauen

to construct, to construe, to interpret [*To ascertain the meaning of language by a process of arrangement and interference*] · auslegen, deuten [*Text*]

to construct, to construe, to draw up, to set up, to work out, to form, to draft · ausarbeiten, abfassen, gestalten, entwerfen [*Schriftstück*]

constructing, building · Bauen *n*

constructing without permission, building without permission · Bauen *n* ohne Genehmigung, Schwarzbauen

construction, drawing-up, setting up, construing, phrasing, wording, formulation, formation, drafting [*Arranging or marshalling words*] · Abfassung *f*, Entwurf *m*, Gestaltung, Ausarbeitung, Formulierung

construction, drawing up, setting up, formation, drafting · Entwurf *m*, Gestaltung *f*, Abfassung, Ausarbeitung [*Schriftstück*]

construction, building · Bau *m*

construction, interpretation [*wording*] · Auslegung *f*, Deutung [*Text*]

construction → (civil) engineering

construction accounting, construction accountancy, building accounting, building accountancy · Baurechnungswesen *n*

construction act, building law, building statute, building act, construction law, construction statute · Baugesetz *n*

construction activity, building activity · Bautätigkeit *f*

construction activity → (civil) engineering activity

construction administration, building administration · Bauverwaltung *f*

construction administration → (civil) engineering administration

construction agreement → (civil) engineering agreement

construction authority, building authority, board of surveyors · Baubehörde *f*, Baugenehmigungsbehörde, (Bau)Aufsichtsbehörde [*früher: Baupolizei f*] [*Behörde für die Genehmigung und Überwachung von Bauvorhaben bis zu deren Abnahme. Die Behörden sind dafür verantwortlich, daß die baurechtlichen Vorschriften eingehalten werden*]

construction board → (civil) engineering board

construction bond, building bond, bond for construction, bond for building [*A bond to guarantee the good faith of the builder or contractor*] · Baugarantie *f*

construction bookkeeping, building bookkeeping · Baubuchführung *f*

construction business, building business · Bauwirtschaft *f* [*Wirtschaftszweig, der die der Bauproduktion, d. h. der Errichtung, dem Ausbau und der Reparatur von baulichen Anlagen dienenden Betriebe und freischaffenden Berufstätigen umfaßt*]

construction by(e)-law → (local) construction by(e)-law

construction by implication, interpretation by implication, implied construction, tacit construction, implied interpretation, tacit interpretation · stillschweigende Deutung *f*, stillschweigende Auslegung

construction capital, building capital · Baukapital *n*

construction case, building case · Baufall *m*

construction charge, building requirement, building charge, construction requirement · Bauauflage *f*, Bauanforderung *f*

construction chart, construction schedule, outline of construction procedure, (contractor's) completion schedule, working chart, working schedule, building chart, building schedule [*Written or graphically explained, the procedure of construction prepared by the contractor, usually by a bar chart of scheduled dates by trades or a critical path chart*] · (Ausführungs)Fristenplan *m*, Baufristenplan

construction clause, clause of interpretation, clause of construction, interpretation clause · Auslegungsklausel *f*, Deutungsklausel *f*

construction code, building code · Bauordnung *f*, BauO [*früher: Baupolizeiordnung*] [*Sie regelt die baurechtlichen Vorgänge auf Grundstücken und Baustellen sowie die Bauarbeit(en) und die Zulassung von Baustoffen und Bauteilen und bestimmt die Aufgaben der Bauaufsichtsbehörden, des Bauherrn und aller am Bau Beteiligten*]

construction code → (local) construction code

construction code law, building code law · Bauordnungsrecht *n*, (Bau)Aufsichtsrecht [*früher: Baupolizeirecht*] [*Manchmal werden ,,Bauordnungsrecht" nur auf die materiell(rechtlich)en und ,,Bauaufsichtsrecht" nur auf die verfahrensrechtlichen Vorschriften bezogen. Diese Unterscheidung ist aber nicht begründet. Das Bauordnungsrecht regelt die Ausführungen der Bauwerke auf einem Grundstück*]

construction code law general clause, building code law general clause · bauordnungsrechtliche Generalklausel *f*, (bau)aufsicht(srechtl)iche Generalklausel

construction code of practice → (civil) engineering code of practice

construction code provision, building code provision · Bauordnungsbestimmung *f*

construction company, building company, construction firm, building firm, contracting firm, contracting company · Bauunternehmen *n*, Baugesellschaft *f*, Bauunternehmung *f*, Baubetrieb *m*, Baufirma *f*

construction competition, building competition · Bauwettbewerb *m*

construction condition, building condition · Baubedingung *f*

construction condition → (civil) engineering condition

construction consulting agency, construction consulting office, building consulting agency, building consulting office · Bauberatungsstelle *f*

construction consulting service, building consulting service · Bauberatung *f*

(construction) contract, building contract [*It means the conditions of contract, specification, drawings, priced bill of quantities, schedule of rates (if any), tender, letter of acceptance and the contract agreement (if completed). It is a contract for the building of anything — not necessarily a house, but any structure*] · (Bau)Vertrag *m* (im weiteren Sinne)

(construction) contract agreement, building contract agreement · (Bau)Vertrag *m* im engeren Sinne

construction contract → (civil) engineering contract

(construction) contract according to the German Civil Code, building contract according to the German Civil Code · BGB-(Bau)Vertrag *m* (im weiteren Sinne)

construction (contract) documents — construction engineering

construction (contract) documents, building (contract) documents · Bau(vertrags)unterlagen *f pl*

construction contracting practice, building contracting practice · Bauvergabewesen *n*

construction contract law, building contract law · Bauvertragsrecht *n*

construction contractor → (civil) engineering contractor

construction contractor practice, building contractor practice · Bauunternehmerwesen *n*

construction cost(s), building cost(s) · Herstellungskosten *f*, Baukosten [*Steuerliche Bezeichnung der Gesamtkosten der Bauherrn*]

construction cost(s) → (civil) engineering cost(s)

construction cost(s) allowance, building cost(s) allowance · Baukostenzuschuß *m*

construction cost(s) estimate, building cost(s) estimate · Bau(kosten)(vor)anschlag *m*

(construction) cost(s) estimating, pricing (construction work), estimating (construction) cost(s) · (Bau)Kostenkalkulation *f*

construction cost(s) index, building cost(s) index · Baukostenindex *m*

construction cost(s) index → (civil) engineering cost(s) index

construction credit, building credit · Baukredit *m*

construction credit law, building credit law · Baukreditgesetz *n*

construction delay, building delay, delay of construction, delay of building · Bauverzug *m*, Bauverzögerung *f*

construction department → (civil) engineering department

construction dispute, building dispute · Baustreit(igkeit) *m*, *(f)*, Baurechtsstreit *m*

construction district, building district · Baubezirk *m*

construction documents, work(ing) documents, building documents · Arbeitsunterlagen *f pl*, Bauunterlagen *f pl*, (Bau)Ausführungsunterlagen *f pl*

construction document (to be presented), building document (to be presented) · Bauvorlage *f*

construction drawing → (civil) engineering drawing

construction emergency tax, building emergency tax · Baunotabgabe *f*

construction employment, building employment, employment in the building industry, employment in the construction industry · Beschäftigung *f* in der Bauindustrie

construction engineer, (civil) engineer · Bauingenieur *m*

construction engineer contract, (civil) engineer contract · Bauingenieurvertrag *m*

construction engineering, (civil) engineering, (engineering) construction [*It involves construction which is planned and designed by professional (civil) engineers. It is often divided into highway construction (= Straßenbau) and heavy construction (= Tiefbau)*] · Ingenieurbau *m*

construction engineering, building engineering · Bautechnik *f* [*als Wissenschaft*]

construction engineering activity, (civil) engineering activity, (engineering) construction activity · Ingenieurbautätigkeit *f*

construction engineering administration, (civil) engineering administration, (engineering) construction administration · Ingenieurbauverwaltung *f*

construction engineering agreement, (civil) engineering agreement, (engineering) construction agreement [*It is a part of a construction contract*] · Ingenieurbauvertrag *m* [*Der Vertrag als Vertragsbestandteil; andere Vertragsbestandteile sind Zeichnungen, Angebot, Garantie usw.*]

construction engineering board, (civil) engineering board, (engineering) construction board · Ingenieurbauamt *n*

construction engineering code of practice, (civil) engineering code of practice, (engineering) construction code of practice · Ingenieurbaumerkblatt *n*

construction engineering condition, (civil) engineering condition, (engineering) construction condition · Ingenieurbaubedingung *f*

construction engineering contract, (civil) engineering contract, (engineering) construction contract · Ingenieurbauvertrag *m* [*Der Vertrag und alle Vertragsbestandteile zusammen*]

construction engineering contractor, (civil) engineering contractor, (engineering) construction contractor · Ingenieurbauunternehmer *m*

construction engineering cost(s), (civil) engineering cost(s), (engineering) construction cost(s) · Ingenieurbaukosten *f*

construction engineering cost(s) index, (civil) engineering cost(s) index,

construction engineering — (construction) equipment list 232

(engineering) construction cost(s) index
· Ingenieurbau(kosten)index *m* [*Die
Kennziffer für die Höhe der Ingenieurbaukosten, jeweils im Vergleich zu einer
festgesetzten Basis auf Grund bestimmter Berechnungen aus der Praxis ermittelt*]

construction engineering department,
(civil) engineering department,
(engineering) construction department ·
Ingenieurbauabteilung *f*

construction engineering drawing, (civil)
engineering drawing, (engineering) construction drawing · Ingenieurbauzeichnen *n*

construction engineering drawing, construction engineering plan, (civil)
engineering drawing, (civil) engineering
plan, (engineering) construction drawing, (engineering) construction plan ·
Ingenieurbauzeichnung *f*, Ingenieurbauplan *m*

construction engineering expert, (civil)
engineering expert, (engineering) construction expert · Ingenieurbausachverständiger *m*

construction engineering expertise, (civil)
engineering expertise, (engineering)
construction expertise · Ingenieurbaugutachten *n*

construction engineering field, (civil)
engineering sector, (civil) engineering
field, (engineering) construction sector,
(engineering) construction field, construction engineering sector · Ingenieurbausektor *m*

construction engineering financing, (civil)
engineering financing, (engineering)
construction financing · Ingenieurbaufinanzierung *f*

construction engineering geologist, heavy
construction geologist, (civil) engineering geologist, (engineering) construction geologist · Tiefbaugeologe *m*,
Bau(grund)geologe

construction engineering geology, (civil)
engineering geology, (engineering) construction geology · Bau(grund)geolo-
gie *f*, Tiefbaugeologie

construction engineering industry, (civil)
engineering industry, (engineering) construction industry · Ingenieurbauindustrie *f*

construction engineering legislation, construction engineering lawmaking, (civil)
engineering legislation, (civil) engineering lawmaking, (engineering) construction legislation, (engineering) construction lawmaking · Ingenieurbaugesetzgebung *f*

construction engineering offer → (civil)
engineering tender

construction engineering plan, (civil)
engineering drawing, (civil) engineering
plan, (engineering) construction drawing, (engineering) construction plan,
construction engineering drawing ·
Ingenieurbauzeichnung *f*, Ingenieurbauplan *m*

construction engineering practice, (civil)
engineering practice, (engineering) construction practice · Ingenieurbauwesen *n*

construction engineering price, (civil)
engineering price, (engineering) construction price · Ingenieurbaupreis *m*

construction engineering provision, (civil)
engineering provision, (engineering)
construction provision · Ingenieurbaubestimmung *f*

construction engineering sector, construction engineering field, (civil)
engineering sector, (civil) engineering
field, (engineering) construction sector,
(engineering) construction field · Ingenieurbausektor *m*

construction engineering sub-contract,
(civil) engineering sub-contract,
(engineering) construction sub-contract
· Nachunternehmervertrag *m* im Ingenieurbau, Subunternehmervertrag im
Ingenieurbau, Unterunternehmervertrag
im Ingenieurbau; Unterakkordantenvertrag im Ingenieurbau [*Schweiz*]

construction engineering sub(contractor),
(civil) engineering sub(contractor),
(engineering) construction sub(contractor) · Ingenieurbaunachunternehmer *m*,
Ingenieurbausubunternehmer; Ingenieurbauunterakkordant *m* [*Schweiz*]

construction engineering technique, (civil)
engineering technique, (engineering)
construction technique · Ingenieurbautechnik *f*, Ingenieurbaupraxis *f* [*als
betriebstechnische Anwendung*]

construction engineering volume, (civil)
engineering volume, (engineering) construction volume · Ingenieurbauvolumen *n*

construction engineering worker, (civil)
engineering worker, (engineering) construction worker · Ingenieurbauarbeiter *m*

construction engineer in private practice,
consulting (civil) engineer, consulting
construction engineer, (civil) engineer in
private practice · beratender Bauingenieur *m*, Beratungsbauingenieur

construction environment, building environment · Bauumwelt *f*

(construction) equipment department,
(construction) machinery (and equipment) department, mechanical department · (Bau)Geräteabteilung *f*

(construction) equipment list · (Bau)Gerä-
teliste *f*, (Bau)Geräteverzeichnis *n*

(construction) equipment insurance, insurance of (construction) equipment · (Bau)Geräteversicherung

construction estimate, building estimate · Bauvoranschlag *m*

construction exhibition, building exhibition · Bauausstellung *f*

construction expert → (civil) engineering expert

construction expertise → (civil) engineering expertise

construction ex visceribus actus, interpretation ex visceribus actus, interpretation on all parts together · Auslegung *f* aus dem Zusammenhang des Ganzen heraus, Deutung *f* aus dem Zusammenhang des Ganzen heraus

construction fair, building fair · Baumesse *f*

construction fee, building fee · Baugebühr *f*, Bauhonorar *n*

construction field, building field, construction sector, building sector · Bausektor *m*

construction field → (civil) engineering sector

construction files, building files · Bauakten *f*

construction financing, building financing · Baufinanzierung *f*

construction financing → (civil) engineering financing

construction firm, building firm, contracting firm, contracting company, construction company, building company · Bauunternehmen *n*, Baugesellschaft *f*, Bauunternehmung *f*, Baubetrieb *m*, Baufirma *f*

construction freeze, building freeze · Bausperre *f* [*Wenn eine Veränderungssperre nach § 14 BBauG nicht beschlossen wird, obwohl die Voraussetzungen gegeben sind, so kann im Einzelfall die Baugenehmigungsbehörde auf Antrag der Gemeinde das Baugesuch eines Bauherrn für einen Zeitraum bis zu 12 Monaten zurückstellen wenn zu befürchten ist, daß die Planungsdurchführung durch das beabsichtigte Vorhaben unmöglich gemacht oder doch wesentlich erschwert werden würde (§ 15 BBauG)*]

construction geology expertise, (civil) engineering geology expertise · Baugrundgutachten *n*

construction geology map · Baugrundkarte *f*

construction hazard, construction risk, building hazard, building risk · Baurisiko *n*, Bauwagnis *n*

construction hindrance, building hindrance · Baubehinderung *f*

construction illegality, construction unlawfulness · Baurechtswidrigkeit *f*, Baugesetzwidrigkeit, Bauwiderrechtlichkeit

construction industry → (civil) engineering industry

construction (industry) contract, owner-contractor contract · Bauvertrag *m*, Unternehmervertrag [*Auf Bauleistungen gerichteter Werkvertrag*]

construction industry and trades, construction trades and industry, building trades and industry, building industry and trades · Baugewerbe *n* [*Sammelbenennung für das handwerklich und industriell betriebene Bauen*]

construction industry arbitration tribunal · Schiedsgericht *n* für das Bauwesen

construction industry arbitration rules, construction industry arbitral rules · Schieds(gerichts)ordnung *f* für das Bauwesen

construction industry code of practice, building industry code of practice, code of practice for the construction industry, code of practice for the building industry · Baumerkblatt *n*

construction inspection, building inspection · Aufsicht *f*, Bauaufsicht, (Bau)Überwachung *f*, (Bau)Kontrolle *f*

construction inspector, building inspector · Baukontrolleur *m*

construction instal(l)ment, building instal(l)ment · Abschlag *m* für Bauarbeiten

construction instal(l)ment (payment) certificate, building instal( )ment (payment) certificate · Abschlags(zahlungs)schein *m* für Bauarbeiten

construction insurance, building insurance, (contractor's) a l-risks insurance · Bau(wesen)versicherung *f*

construction interest, building interest, interest on building loan(s), interest on construction loan(s) · Bauzinsen *f*

construction investment, building investment · Bauinvestition *f*

construction jobs, building jobs · Sekundärsektor *m*

(construction) job site, (construction) site, building (job) site · Baustelle *f*

(construction) job site land, (construction) site land, building (job) site land · Baustellenland *n*

construction labour wage (Brit.); construction labor wage (US); site wage, construction (site) wage, building (site) wage, job (site) wage · Bau(stellen)lohn *m*

construction law — construction of contract(s)

construction law, building law · Baurecht *n*

construction law, construction statute, construction act, building law, building statute, building act · Baugesetz *n*

construction lawmaking, building lawmaking, construction legislation, building legislation · Baugesetzgebung *f*

construction litigation, building litigation · Bauprozeß *m*

construction loan, building loan · Baudarleh(e)n *n*

construction loan lender, building loan lender, building loaner, construction loaner, construction moneylender, building moneylender · Baudarleh(e)n(s)geber *m*

(construction) machinery (and equipment) department → (construction) equipment department

construction management, project management, building management, management of construction, management of project, management of building · (Bau)Betreuung *f*, Betreuung von Bauvorhaben [*Die technische und wirtschaftliche Vorbereitung und Überwachung eines Bauvorhabens in fremdem Namen und für fremde Rechnung*]

construction management, project management, management of construction, management of project, management of building, building management · Bau(betriebs)führung *f* [*Die technische und wirtschaftliche Vorbereitung und Überwachung eines Bauvorhabens in eigenem Namen*]

construction management agent, building management agent, project management agent [*Er bereitet ein Bauvorhaben im Namen und für Rechnung des Betreuten (= Bauherrn) vor und/oder führt es durch. Der Umfang der Betreuung und der Vollmacht wird in einem Betreuungsvertrag vereinbart*] · (Bau)Betreuer *m*

construction management contract, building management contract · (Bau)Betreuungsvertrag *m*

construction management law, project management law, building management law · Baubetriebsrecht *n*

construction management law, building management law, project management law · (Bau)Betreuungsrecht *n*

construction management plan, building management plan · (Bau)Betreuungsplan *m*

construction market, building market · Baumarkt *m* [*Der Teilmarkt einer Volkswirtschaft, auf dem sich die Preise für bauliche Leistungen aller Art nach den Gesetzen von Angebot und Nachfrage bilden*]

(construction) materials supplied by owner, building materials supplied by owner, owner-furnished (construction) materials, owner-furnished building materials · (Bau)Stoffe *mpl* vom Bauherrn, (Bau)Materialien *npl* vom Bauherrn, bauseits gestellte (Bau)Stoffe, bauseits gestellte (Bau)Materialien *npl*

construction material(s) supplier, (building) material(s) supplier · (Bau)Stofflieferant *m*

(construction) material(s) supply by owner, building material(s) supply by owner · (Bau)Materialbeistellung *f*, (Bau)Stoffbeistellung

construction material testing standard, (building) material testing standard · (Bau)Stoffprüfnorm *f*

construction measure, building measure · Baumaßnahme *f*

construction method, building method · Bauweise *f*, Bauverfahren *n* [*Art der Bauausführung*]

construction moneylender, building moneylender, construction loan lender, building loan lender, building loaner, construction loaner · Baudarleh(e)n(s)geber *m*

construction mortgage, building mortgage · Bauhypothek *f* [*Nicht verwechseln mit „Baugeld(er)hypothek"*]

construction noise, building noise · Baulärm *m*

construction notice, building notification, construction notification, building notice · Baumitteilung *f*, Bauanzeige *f* [*Für Bauvorhaben untergeordneter Bedeutung, z. B. Gartenlaube, für die ein Bauantrag nicht vorgeschrieben ist*]

construction notice procedure, construction notification procedure, building notice procedure, building notification procedure · Bauanzeigeverfahren *n*, Baumitteilungsverfahren

construction of act(s), construction of law(s), construction of statute(s), interpretation of act(s), interpretation of law(s), interpretation of statute(s) · Gesetz(es)auslegung *f*, Gesetz(es)deutung

construction of a structure, building of a structure, erection of a structure · Bauwerkerrichtung *f*, Bauwerkerstellung

construction of contract, interpretation of contract · Vertragsauslegung *f*, Vertragsdeutung

construction of contract(s), drafting of contract(s), drawing up of contract(s), setting up of contract(s), formation of contract(s) · Vertragsgestaltung *f*, Vertragsausarbeitung, Vertragsabfassung, Vertragsentwurf *m*, Vertragsbildung

construction of law · Regel *f* mit zwangsläufigem Ergebnis [*Das aus dieser Regel fließende Ergebnis ist zwangsläufig ganz gleich was die Absicht der Parteien und/oder die Verhältnisse waren*]

construction of law(s) → construction of act(s)

construction of public works · Ausführung *f* öffentlicher Arbeiten

construction of sewers, building of sewers · (Abwasser)Kanalbau *m*

construction of small-sized housing, building of small-sized housing · Kleinwohn(ungs)bau *m*

construction of statute(s) → construction of act(s)

construction of (the) works, execution (of (the) work(s)), performance (of (the) work(s)) · Arbeitsausführung *f*, Bau *m* (der Anlagen), Bauausführung *f*, Ausführung *f* (der (Bau)Arbeiten)

construction order, building order · Bauauftrag *m*

construction owner, project owner, client, employer, promoter, (building) owner [*In Great Britain, the term "employer" is preferred since this is used in both the RIBA and ICE standard forms of contract*] · Bauherr(schaft) *m*, *(f)*, Auftraggeber *m*, BH *f*, AG *m* [*im Sinne der VOB*]; Besteller [*im Sinne des BGB*] [*Nach geläufiger Fachsprache ist „Bauherr" stets der „Letzt-Besteller" eines Bauwerkes (oder Bauwerk-Teils), also nicht der Unternehmer, der einen Subunternehmer bezieht. Dieser „Letzt-Besteller" ist Bauherr im engen (und eigentlichen) Sinne des Wortes. In einem übertragenen (nicht geläufigen) Sinne aber kann „Bauherr" auch ein Unternehmer sein, der übernommene Bauarbeiten durch Abschluß eines Bauvertrages an einen Subunternehmer weitervergibt. In diesem übertragenen Sinne muß das Wort dann verstanden werden, wenn die SIA-Norm 118 (Schweiz) auf den Bauvertrag zwischen Unternehmer und Subunternehmer zur Anwendung kommt. Im Verhältnis Unternehmer/Subunternehmer ist alsdann der erstere „Bauherr" im Sinne der Norm, der andere „Unternehmer"*]

construction participant, building participant · Baubeteiligte *m*

construction permission, permission to construct, permission to build, building permission · (Bau)Genehmigung *f*, (Bau)Erlaubnis *f*, Ausführungsgenehmigung, Ausführungserlaubnis *f* [*Entscheidung einer Baugenehmigungsbehörde über die Zulässigkeit eines Vorhabens auf einem bestimmten Grundstück (§ 36 BBauG)*]

construction permission authority, building permission authority · Baugenehmigungsbehörde *f*

construction permit, (building) permit · (Bau)Erlaubnisbescheinigung *f*, (Bau)Genehmigungsbescheinigung, (Bau)Erlaubnisschein *m*, (Bau)Genehmigungsschein, Bauschein, Baukonsens *m*

construction permit fee, (building) permit fee · Bauscheingebühr *f*

construction plan, building plan · Aufbauplan *m* [*Plan mit verbindlichen Anforderungen für die Gestaltung einer baulichen Anlage*]

construction plan, building plan · Bauplan *m* [*Er stellt ein gestalterisches Ziel, also einen Endzustand dar*]

construction plan → (civil) engineering plan

construction planning, building planning · Bauplanung *f* [*Zur Durchführung eines Bauvorhabens*]

construction planning law, building planning law · Bauplanungsrecht *n*

construction policy, building policy · Baupolitik *f*

construction practice, building practice · Bauwesen *n*

construction practice → (civil) engineering practice

construction preparation, building preparation, preparation of construction, preparation of building · Bauvorbereitung *f*

construction prescription, construction rule, building regulation, building rule, building prescription, construction regulation · Bauvorschrift *f*, baurechtliche Vorschrift

construction price, building price · Baupreis *m*

construction price → (civil) engineering price

construction price index, building price index · Baupreisindex *m* [*Fehlbenennung: Baukostenindex*]

construction price law, building price law · Baupreisrecht *n*

construction price ordinance, building price ordinance · Baupreisverordnung *f*, BaupreisVO

construction progress, (job) progress, building progress, progress of the work(s) · Baufortschritt *m*, Arbeitsfortschritt

construction progress photograph, building progress photograph · Baufortschrittfoto *n*, Arbeitsfortschrittfoto

construction project, building project · Bauvorhaben *n*, Bauprojekt *n*

construction project budget — construction site facilities plan

construction project budget, building project budget, budget for construction project, budget for building project [*The total sum established by the owner for the project*] · Baukostenhaushalt *m*

construction promotion, building promotion, promotion of construction, promotion of building · Bauförderung *f*

construction promotion fund, building promotion fund · Bauförderungsmittel *f*, Bauförderungsfonds *m*

construction provision, building provision · Baubestimmung *f*

construction provision → (civil) engineering provision

construction rate, progress rate, speed of progress, progress speed, construction speed, speed rate, speed of construction, rate of construction, rate of progress · Baugeschwindigkeit *f*, Bautempo *n*, (Bau)Fortschrittstempo, (Bau)Fortschrittgeschwindigkeit

construction regulation, construction prescription, construction rule, building regulation, building rule, building prescription · Bauvorschrift *f*, baurechtliche Vorschrift

construction release ordinance, building release ordinance · Baufreistellungsverordnung *f*, BauFreiVO

construction report, work(s) report, site report, job report · Arbeitsbericht *m*, Bau(stellen)bericht *m*

construction requirement, construction charge, building requirement, building charge · Bauauflage *f*, Bauanforderung *f*

construction research, building research · Bauforschung *f*

construction research institute, building research institute · Bauforschungsinstitut *n*, Institut für Bauforschung

construction restriction, building restriction · Baubeschränkung *f*, Baueinschränkung

construction retardation, building retardation, retardation of construction, retardation of building · Bauverzögerung *f*

construction risk, building hazard, building risk, construction hazard · Baurisiko *n*, Bauwagnis *n*

construction rule, building regulation, building rule, building prescription, construction regulation, construction prescription · Bauvorschrift *f*, baurechtliche Vorschrift

construction safety code, building safety code, site safety code · Bau(stellen)sicherheitsordnung *f*

construction schedule → construction chart

construction sector, building sector, construction field, building field · Bausektor *m*

construction sector → (civil) engineering sector

(construction) site, building (job) site, (construction) job site · Baustelle *f*

construction site checking, construction site control, building site checking, building site control, job site checking, job site control, site checking, site control · Baustellenkontrolle *f* [*Aufsuchen der Baustelle in Zeitabständen zur Prüfung der Arbeiten des Bauunternehmers*]

construction site accident, building site accident, (job) site accident · Bau(stellen)unfall *m*

construction site accident damage, job site accident damage, site accident damage, building site accident damage · Bauunfallschaden *m*

construction site bookkeeping, building site bookkeeping, site bookkeeping, job site bookkeeping · Baustellenbuchführung *f*

construction site clearance cost(s), site clearance cost(s), building site clearance cost(s), job site clearance cost(s) · Baustellenräumungskosten *f*

(construction) site conditions, building site conditions, job site conditions · Bau(stellen)verhältnisse *f*, Verhältnisse (auf) der Baustelle

construction site diary, building site diary, construction site daily record, building site daily record, (job-)site diary, (job-)site daily record, job (daily) record, job diary · Bau(stellen)tagebuch *n*, Bau(stellen)buch

construction site examination, construction site inspection, building site visit, building site inspection, building site examination, examination of site, visit of site, inspection of site, site inspection, site visit, site examination, construction site visit · Baustellenbesichtigung *f*, (Baustellen)Begehung, Ortsbesichtigung [*Vor Abgabe eines Angebotes*]

construction site facilities, building site facilities, job site facilities, site facilities · Bau(stellen)einrichtung *f* [*Alle Maschinen und Geräte einer Baustelle*]

construction site facilities cost(s), job site facilities cost(s), site facilities cost(s), building site facilities cost(s) · Bau(stellen)einrichtungskosten *f*

construction site facilities plan, job (site) facilities plan, (building) site facilities plan · Bau(stellen)ordnungsplan *m* [*Fehlbenennungen: Bau(stellen)einrichtungsplan*]

construction site fence — construction technique

construction site fence, building site fence, site fence, job site fence · Bau(stellen)zaun *m*

construction site inspection, building site visit, building site inspection, building site examination, examination of site, visit of site, inspection of site, site inspection, site visit, site examination, construction site visit, construction site examination · Baustellenbesichtigung *f*, (Baustellen)Begehung, Ortsbesichtigung [*Vor Abgabe eines Angebotes*]

(construction) site land, building (job) site land, (construction) job site land · Baustellenland *n*

construction site lighting, construction site illumination, job site lighting, job site illumination, site lighting, site illumination, building site lighting, building site illumination · Bau(stellen)beleuchtung *f*

construction site limit, job site limit, site limit, building site limit · Baustellengrenze *f*

construction site management, building site management, site management, job site management · Bau(stellen)führung *f*, örtliche Bauaufsicht *f*

construction site manager, building site manager, job site manager, manager on site, site manager · Baustellenführer *m*, örtlicher Bauführer [*des Unternehmers*]

(construction) site meeting, building site meeting, job site meeting, job (progress) meeting · Bau(stellen)besprechung *f*

construction site meeting minutes, building site meeting minutes, job site meeting minutes, site meeting minutes · Bau(stellen)besprechungsprotokoll *n*

construction site operations, job operations, (job) site operations, building site operations · Bau(stellen)betrieb *m*

construction site organization, building site organization, job site organization, site organization · Bau(stellen)organisation *f*

construction site planning, job site planning, site planning, building site planning · Baustellenplanung *f*

(construction) site safety, building site safety, safety of job site, job site safety, safety of (construction) site, safety of building site · Baustellensicherheit *f*

construction site salary, building site salary, site salary, job site salary · Bau(stellen)gehalt *n*

(construction) site sign → site sign

construction site supervision, construction site superintendence, job site supervision, job site superintendence, building site superintendence, building site supervision, supervision of site(s), superintendence of site(s), site supervision, site superintendence · Bau(stellen)aufsicht *f*, Bau(stellen)überwachung *f*, Objektaufsicht, Objektüberwachung

(construction) site turnover, building site turnover, job (site) turnover · Bau(stellen)umsatz *m*

construction site visit, construction site examination, construction site inspection, building site visit, building site inspection, building site examination, examination of site, visit of site, inspection of site, site inspection, site visit, site examination · Baustellenbesichtigung *f*, (Baustellen)Begehung, Ortsbesichtigung [*Vor Abgabe eines Angebotes*]

construction (site) wage, building (site) wage, job (site) wage; construction labour wage (Brit.); construction labor wage (US); site wage · Bau(stellen)lohn *m*

(construction) site water supply, building site water supply, job (site) water supply · Bau(stellen)wasserversorgung *f*

construction speculation, building speculation · Bauspekulation *f*

construction speed, speed rate, speed of construction, rate of construction, rate of progress, construction rate, progress rate, speed of progress, progress speed · Baugeschwindigkeit *f*, Bautempo *n*, (Bau)Fortschrittempo, (Bau)Fortschrittgeschwindigkeit *f*

construction sponsoring, building sponsoring · (Bau)Trägerschaft *f*, Baubetreuung *f* im weiteren Sinne

construction stage, stage of building, stage of construction, building stage · Baustadium *n*, Baustufe *f*

construction statute, construction act, building law, building statute, building act, construction law · Baugesetz *n*

construction stock, building stock · Bauaktie *f*

construction sub-contract → (civil) engineering construction sub-contract

construction sub(contractor) → (civil) engineering sub(contractor)

construction sum, building sum, production sum, sum of construction, sum of building, sum of production · Bausumme *f*, Herstellungssumme

construction surveyor, building surveyor · Baubeamte *m*, (Bau)Aufsichtsbeamte; Baupolizeibeamte [*frühere Benennung*]

construction technique, building technique · Bautechnik *f* [*Als betriebstechnische Anwendung*]

construction technique → (civil) engineering technique

construction technology, building technology · Bautechnologie *f*

construction tender → (civil) engineering tender

construction terrain, building terrain · Baugelände *n* [*In der Gesetzgebung nicht mehr verwendete Benennung für Bauland, Baufläche und Baugebiet*]

construction time, building time, time of construction, time of building, time for completion · Bau(fertigstellungs)zeit *f*

construction trade, (building) trade, structural trade, craft [*Classification or type of work done by workers who restrict themselves to this type of work, established by jurisdictional agreements*] · (Bau)Gewerk *n*

construction trades, building (construction) trades, (structural) trades · Bauhandwerk *n* [*Die Gesamtheit der sich mit Bauarbeiten befassenden Handwerkszweige*]

construction trades and industry, building trades and industry, building industry and trades, construction industry and trades · Baugewerbe *n* [*Sammelbenennung für das handwerklich und industriell betriebene Bauen*]

construction unlawfulness, construction illegality · Baurechtswidrigkeit *f*, Baugesetzwidrigkeit, Bauwiderrechtlichkeit

construction (up)on the equity of the statute, interpretation (up)on the equity of the statute · Gesetz(es)auslegung *f* auf Grund der ratio legis, Gesetz(es)deutung auf Grund der ratio legis

construction volume → (civil) engineering volume

construction wage → construction (site) wage

construction worker, building worker · Bauarbeiter *m*

construction worker → (civil) engineering worker

construction workers, building workers · Bauarbeiter(schaft) *m pl*, *(f)*

(construction) work(s), building work(s) · (Bau)Arbeit(en) *f (pl)*, (Bau)Leistung(en) *f (pl)*

construction workers' strike, building workers' strike · Bau(arbeiter)streik *m*

construction work(s) → (civil) engineering operations

construction year, building year, year of construction, year of building · Baujahr *m*

construction zone, building zone · Bauzone *f*

constructive [*This word denotes that a right, liability or status has been created by the law without reference to the intention of the parties, as in the case of a constructive trust or constructive notice, or that a transaction or operation has not really taken place, but that something equivalent has*] · mittelbar, verdeckt

constructive delivery (of possession) [*e.g. by a bill of lading*] · symbolische (Besitz)Ableitung *f*, symbolischer (Besitz)Übergang *m* [*bewegliche Sache(n)*]

constructive notice · mittelbare Kenntnis *f*, verdeckte Kenntnis, zugerechnete Kenntnis

constructive possession, indirect possession; constitutum possessorium [*Latin*] · (Besitz)Konstitut *n*, Besitzauftragung *f*, mittelbarer Besitz *m*, verdeckter Besitz, indirekter Besitz, vergeistigte Sachherrschaft *f* [*Der unmittelbare Besitzer macht einen anderen zum mittelbaren und behält selbst unmittelbaren Besitz*]

constructive possessor, indirect possessor · indirekter Besitzer *m*, mittelbarer Besitzer, verdeckter Besitzer

constructive taking · ideelle Wegnahme *f*

to construct (up)on, to cover, to build (up)on · bebauen; überbauen [*Schweiz*]

to construe, to phrase, to word, to form, to draft, to construct, to draw up, to set up [*To arrange or marshal words*] · abfassen, gestalten, entwerfen, ausarbeiten, formulieren

to construe, to interpret, to construct [*To ascertain the meaning of language by a process of arrangement and interference*] · auslegen, deuten [*Text*]

to construe, to draw up, to set up, to work out, to form, to draft, to construct · ausarbeiten, abfassen, gestalten, entwerfen [*Schriftstück*]

construed, interpreted · ausgelegt, gedeutet [*Text*]

construing, phrasing, wording, formulation, formation, drafting, construction, drawing-up, setting up [*Arranging or marshalling words*] · Abfassung *f*, Entwurf *m*, Gestaltung, Ausarbeitung, Formulierung

construing, interpreting [*wording*] · Auslegen *n*, Deuten *n* [*Text*]

construing against title, flyspecking · übervorsichtige (Rechts)Titelprüfung *f*, übervorsichtige (Rechts)Titelbegutachtung

consular agent · Konsularagent *m*

consular assistent · Konsularassistent *m*

consular court · Konsulargericht *n*

consular officer, consular official · Konsularbeamte *m*

consular post · Konsularposten *m*, konsularische Vertretung *f*

consular service · Konsulardienst *m*

consul-general · Generalkonsul *m*

consul-general at large · Konsularinspektor *m*

to consult, to give advice, to counsel, to advise · beraten

consultancy, consultation, advice, counsel · Beratung *f*

consultancy fee, consultation fee, consulting fee · Beratungshonorar *n*, Beratungsgebühr *f*

consultancy service, consultant service, advisory service, consultation service · Beratungsdienst *m*

consultant, adviser, advisor · Berater *m*

consultant-designed project, adviser-designed project · Beraterentwurfsprojekt *n*

consultant service, advisory service, consultation service, consultancy service · Beratungsdienst *m*

consultation, advice, counsel, consultancy · Beratung *f*

consultation fee, consulting fee, consultancy fee · Beratungshonorar *n*, Beratungsgebühr *f*

consultation of organization · Organisationsberatung *f*

consultative activity, advisory activity, counsel(l)ing activity, advising activity, consulting activity · beratende Tätigkeit *f*, Beratungstätigkeit

consultative combine, advising combine, advisory combine, consulting combine · Beratungs-Arbeitsgemeinschaft *f*

consultative committee, consulting committee, advising committee, counsel(l)ing committee, advisory committee · beratender Ausschuß *m*, Beratungsausschuß

consultative duty, advising duty, advisory duty, counsel(l)ing duty, consulting duty, duty to consult · Beratungspflicht *f*

consulting, advising, counsel(l)ing · Beraten *n*

consulting activity, consultative activity, advisory activity, counsel(l)ing activity, advising activity · beratende Tätigkeit *f*, Beratungstätigkeit

consulting (civil) engineer, consulting construction engineer, (civil) engineer in private practice, construction engineer in private practice · beratender Bauingenieur *m*, Beratungsbauingenieur

consulting combine, consultative combine, advising combine, advisory combine · Beratungs-Arbeitsgemeinschaft *f*

consulting committee, advising committee, counsel(l)ing committee, advisory committee, consultative committee · beratender Ausschuß *m*, Beratungsausschuß

consulting construction engineer, (civil) engineer in private practice, construction engineer in private practice, consulting (civil) engineer · beratender Bauingenieur *m*, Beratungsbauingenieur

consulting duty, duty to consult, consultative duty, advising duty, advisory duty, counsel(l)ing duty · Beratungspflicht *f*

consulting engineer → consulting (civil) engineer

consulting fee, consultancy fee, consultation fee · Beratungshonorar *n*, Beratungsgebühr *f*

consumer · Verbraucher *m*

consumer attractiveness, consumer attraction · Verbraucheranziehung *f*, Verbraucherattraktivität *f*

consumer behaviour (Brit.); comsumer behavior (US) · Verbraucherverhalten *n*

consumer centre (Brit.); consumer center (US) · Verbrauchszentrum *n*, Verbrauchercherzentrum

consumer expectation · Verbrauchererwartung *f*

consumer goods · Verbrauchsgüter *n pl*

consumer journey, consumer trip, consumer travel · Verbraucherfahrt *f*

consumer journey pattern → consumer travel pattern

consumer journey scheme → consumer travel pattern

consumer location, consumption location · Verbrauchsstandort *m*

consumer-orien(ta)ted industry, consumer-related industry · Konsumgüterindustrie *f*

consumer protection · Verbraucherschutz *m*

consumer sale · Konsumentengeschäft *n*, Verbrauchergeschäft

consumer's connection · Abnehmeranschluß *m*, Verbraucheranschluß [*Gas; Strom; Wasser*]

consumers' co-operative (society), retail co-operative (society), provident co-operative (society), provident society · Konsumverein *m*, Konsumgenossenschaft *f*, Verbrauchergenossenschaft

consumers' goods — contiguous

consumers' goods, consumption goods, goods of the first order [*These goods satisfy wants directly*] · Verkaufsgüter *n pl*

consumer's market building · Verbrauchermarkt *m* [*als bauliche Anlage*]

consumer society · Verbrauchsgesellschaft *f*

consumer sovereignty [*The dominant role of the consumer in determining the types, qualities, and quantities of goods produced by an economic system*] · Konsumfreiheit *f*, Konsumhoheit, Verbraucherfreiheit, Verbraucherhoheit, Verbraucherunabhängigkeit *f*

consumer's rent, consumer's surplus · Verbraucherüberschuß *m*, Verbraucherrente *f*, Konsumentenüberschuß, Konsumentenrente, Rente des Verbrauchers, Rente des Konsumenten

consumer's want · Verbraucherbedürfnis *n*

consumer travel, consumer journey, consumer trip · Verbraucherfahrt *f*

consumer travel pattern, consumer travel scheme, consumer trip pattern, consumer trip scheme, consumer journey pattern, consumer journey scheme · Verbraucherfahrtmuster *n*, Verbraucherfahrtschema *n*

consumer trip, consumer travel, consumer journey · Verbraucherfahrt *f*

consumption curve, curve of consumption · Verbrauchskurve *f*

consumption economy · Verbrauchswirtschaft *f*, Aufwandswirtschaft

consumption goods, goods of the first order, consumers' goods [*These goods satisfy wants directly*] · Verkaufsgüter *n pl*

consumption location, consumer location · Verbrauchsstandort *m*

consumption of area, land consumption, area consumption, consumption of land · Bodenbeanspruchung *f*, Landbeanspruchung, Flächenbeanspruchung, Flächenverbrauch *m*, Bodenverbrauch, Landverbrauch

consumption of land, consumption of area, land consumption, area consumption · Bodenbeanspruchung *f*, Landbeanspruchung, Flächenbeanspruchung, Flächenverbrauch *m*, Bodenverbrauch, Landverbrauch

consumption product · Verbrauchsgut *n*

consumption tax, tax on articles of consumption, excise(-duty) · Verbrauchssteuer *f*

contact to forum · Binnenbeziehung *f*

contagious disease of animals legislation · Veterinärgesetzgebung *f*

containment policy · Eindämmungspolitik *f*

contemplation of flight, intent(ion) to abscond; meditatio fugae [*Latin*] · Verdunkelungsgefahr *f*

contemplation of law; abeyantia [*Latin*]; abeyance, condition of abeyance, state of abeyance, abbayance, state of suspension, abeyancy, temporary nonexistence, expectancy of law [*In the law of real estate. Where there is no person in existence in whom an inheritance can vest, it is said to be in abeyance, that is, in expectation; the law considering is as always potentially existing, and ready to vest when ever a proper owner appears*] · Schwebe(zustand) *f*, *(m)*

contemporary logic · moderne Logik *f*

contempt of court · Mißachtung *f* des Gerichts, Ungebühr *f* gegen das Gericht, Ungebühr vor Gericht, Widersetzlichkeit *f* gegenüber dem Gericht

content · Inhalt *m*

contention, contentious issue, issue (of fact), point in dispute · Streitfrage *f*, Streitpunkt *m*

contentious, unsettled, controversial, moot, adversary, contested, undecided [*Litigated between adverse parties*] · streitig, strittig

contentious business · streitiges Nachlaßverfahren *n*

contentious issue, issue (of fact), point in dispute, contention · Streitfrage *f*, Streitpunkt *m*, strittiger Punkt

(contentious) litigation, process (in law), judicial contest, judicial controversy [*Contest in a court of justice for the purpose of enforcing a right*] · Prozeß *m*

content of plan, plan content · Planinhalt *m*

co(n)terminous with, lying (up)on, bordering (up)on, adjoining [*The term "adjoining" also sometimes means "near" or "neighbo(u)ring"*] · angrenzend [*(Grundstücks)Seiten*]

contestation of an election · Wahlanfechtung *f*

contested, undecided, contentious, unsettled, controversial, moot, adversary [*Litigated between adverse parties*] · streitig, strittig

contest for prizes, prize competition, prize contest, competition for prizes · Preiswettbewerb *m*

contesting in a court of justice, litigating · Prozessieren *n*

context · Sinnzusammenhang *m*

context of actions · Aktionsrahmen *m*, Handlungsrahmen

contiguous, touching, abutting, reaching · angrenzend [*(Grundstücks)Enden*]

continental line · nach dem Festland gerichtete (Eisen)Bahnlinie [*in England*]

continental shelf · Festlandschelf *n*

contingency · ungewisse Verbindlichkeit *f*

contingency allowance [*Established amount of money included in the contract to cover unpredictable small changes in work due to site conditions during construction. It is not intended to cover additions that increase the scope of the job*] · Eventualbetrag *m*

contingency cost(s) [*The contractor's estimate of the amount of risk, involved in a particular project*] · Kosten *f* für Unvorhergesehenes

contingency item · Eventualposition *f*

contingency sum · Summe *f* für Unvorhergesehenes

contingency table [*Statistics. A table constructed for the purpose of analyzing or discovering associations between qualitative characteristics (= attributes)*] · Kontingenztafel *f*

contingent · ungewiß [*Schuld*]

contingent · bedingt [*Fachausdruck bei nicht feststehenden Bilanzposten*]

contingent annuity · bedingte Annuität *f*, abhängige Annuität, Annuität mit unbestimmter Laufzeit

contingent asset [*An asset that may be realized if and/or when something occurs or does not occur*] · potentieller Aktivposten *m*

contingent authority of precedents, conditional authority of precedents · bedingte Bindungswirkung *f*, abhängige Bindungswirkung [*Das Gericht kann von einem früheren Präzedenzfall abweichen*]

contingent bequest, contingent legacy, conditional bequest, conditional legacy [*A legacy given to a person at a future uncertain time, that may or may not arrive; as "at his age of twenty-one"*] · bedingtes (Fahrnis)Legat *n*, bedingtes (Fahrnis)Vermächtnis *n*, Bedingungs(fahrnis)vermächtnis, Bedingungs(fahrnis)legat

contingent charge · Eventuallast *f*

contingent cost(s) · Eventualkosten *f*

contingent covenant, conditional covenant · bedingter Formalvertrag *m*

contingent debt → contingent (money) debt

contingent devise, conditional devise [*The vesting of any estate in the devisee is made to depend upon some future event, in which case, if the event never occurs, or until it does occur, no estate vests under the devise*] · bedingtes (Land)Vermächtnis *n*, bedingtes (Land)Legat, Bedingungs(land)vermächtnis, Bedingungs(land)legat *n*

contingent discharge, conditional discharge · bedingte Entlastung *f*, abhängige Entlastung [*Sie tritt sofort in Wirksamkeit, erzeugt aber nicht den völligen Untergang der Schulden des Konkursschuldners, sondern legt ihm die Verpflichtung auf, in einer vom Gericht zu bezeichnenden Weise für weitere Befriedigung der Gläubiger zu sorgen*]

contingent (en)feoffment, contingent infeudation, conditional (en)feoffment, conditional infeudation · bedingte Belehnung *f*, Belehnung unter Resolutivbedingung, abhängige Belehnung

contingent expense · Eventualaufwand *m*

contingent fee, fee contingent on success · Erfolgshonorar *n*, Erfolgsgebühr *f*

contingent gain, contingent profit [*Profit the realization of which is dependent on an uncertain future event or condition*] · möglicher Gewinn *m*, möglicher Profit *m*

contingent (general) property, contingent proprietorship, conditional proprietorship, contingent ownership (of property) · bedingtes Eigentum *n*, unvollkommenes Eigentum

contingent infeudation, conditional (en)feoffment, conditional infeudation, contingent (en)feoffment · bedingte Belehnung *f*, Belehnung unter Resolutivbedingung, abhängige Belehnung

contingent legacy → contingent bequest

contingent liability, conditional liability · bedingte Haftpflicht *f*, bedingte Haftung *f*, abhängige Haftpflicht, abhängige Haftung, bedingte Haftbarkeit, abhängige Haftbarkeit

contingent (money) debt, conditional (money) debt · bedingte (Geld)Schuld *f*, abhängige (Geld)Schuld

contingent ownership (of property), contingent (general) property, contingent proprietorship, conditional proprietorship · bedingtes Eigentum *n*, unvollkommenes Eigentum

contingent profit, contingent gain [*Profit the realization of which is dependent on an uncertain future event or condition*] · möglicher Gewinn *m*, möglicher Profit *m*

contingent proprietorship, conditional proprietorship, contingent ownership (of property), contingent (general) property · bedingtes Eigentum *n*, unvollkommenes Eigentum

contingent remainder [*Misnomers: possibility of future (landed) estate*]; spes successionis [*Latin*] · Anwartschaftsmöglichkeit *f*, bedingtes Anwartschaftsrecht *n*

contingent remainder (land(ed)) estate, conditional remainder (land(ed)) estate, executory remainder (land(ed)) estate, possibility of (a) future (land(ed)) estate; spes successionis [*Latin*] [*The remainder is contingent if the person who is to have the remainder is not yet living or if his identity is uncertain, or if the event which is to bring the remainder into existence is uncertain. The remainder becomes vested when such person is ascertained or upon the happening of the event*] · bedingter anwartschaftlicher Bodenbesitz(stand) *m*, möglicher anwartschaftlicher Bodenbesitz(stand), ungewisser anwartschaftlicher Bodenbesitz(stand)

contingent right · geburtsbedingtes Recht *n*, geburtsabhängiges Recht

contingent ((up)on), depending (up)on, conditional, not absolute [*Operative only (up)on an uncertain event*] · bedingt durch, abhängig von, abhängend von

continuance · Fortbestand *m*, Fortführung *f*, Stetigkeit *f* [*Gesetz; Ordnung; Richtlinie usw.*]

continuance of income · Einkommensstetigkeit *f*

continuation bid → continuation tender

continuation contract, subsequent contract, follow-on contract, continuity contract · Anschlußvertrag *m*, Folgevertrag *m*

continuation of contract · Vertragsfortsetzung *f*

continuation of work · Weiterarbeit *f*

continuation order, follow-on order, subsequent order, continuity order · Anschlußauftrag *m*, Folgeauftrag *m*

continuation school · Fortbildungsschule *f*

continuation tender, continuity tender, subsequent offer, follow-on offer, continuation offer, continuity offer, subsequent bid, follwo-on bid, continuity bid, continuation bid; subsequent (bid) proposal, follow-on (bid) proposal, continuation (bid) proposal, continuity (bid) proposal (US); subsequent tender, follow-on tender · Folgeangebot *n*, Anschlußangebot

continued application · Fortgeltung *f*

continued education · Fortbildung *f*

continuing, enduring · fortsetzend

continuing account → open account

continuing consideration [*It is in part executed, but still continues*] · fortsetzende Gegenleistung *f*

continuing contract · (obligatorischer) Vertrag *m* mit wiederkehrenden Ansprüchen und Verpflichtungen, Legalversprechen *n* mit wiederkehrenden Ansprüchen und Verpflichtungen, Schuldvertrag *m* mit wiederkehrenden Ansprüchen und Verpflichtungen

continuing guaranty, continuing guarantee, continuing guarantie; mandatum qualificatum [*Latin*] [*It is an agreement to be responsible for money, goods, or services to be furnished by the creditor to the principal debtor from time to time in the future*] · Kreditbürgschaft *f*, Kreditauftrag *m*, Dauerbürgschaft

continuity axiom · Axiom *n* der Kontinuität, Kontinuitätsaxiom

continuity bid → continuation tender

continuity contract → continuation contract

continuity of building scheme, continuity of (detailed) local (development) plan, continuity of coverage scheme · Bebauungszusammenhang *m*; Überbauungszusammenhang [*Schweiz*] [*Die Kurzfassung der für die Abgrenzung zwischen Außenbereich und unbeplantem Innenbereich wesentlichen Tatbestandsmerkmale „im Zusammenhang bebaut"*]

continuity offer → continuation tender

continuity of settlement, settlement continuity · (An)Sied(e)lungskontinuität *f*

continuity order → continuation order

continuity proposal (US) → continuation tender

continuity tender → continuation tender

continuous, uninterrupted, unbroken · laufend, ständig, ununterbrochen, stetig

continuous audit · laufende Buchprüfung *f*

continuous inventory · laufende Bestandsaufnahme *f*

continuous landed servitude, continuous rural servitude, continuous pr(a)edial servitude, continuous (real) servitude · ständige Dienstbarkeit *f*, ständige (Real)Servitut *f*, ständiges (Real)Servitut *n*

continuous organization · zeitlich unbefristete Organisation *f*

continuous privity, continuous succession · fortgesetzte Nachfolge *f*

continuous (real) servitude, continuous landed servitude, continuous rural servitude, continuous pr(a)edial servitude · ständige Dienstbarkeit *f*, ständige (Real)Servitut *f*, ständiges (Real)Servitut *n*

continuous right of redemption, continuous right to redeem, unbroken right of redemption, unbroken right to redeem, uninterrupted right to redeem, uninterrupted right of redemption · laufendes Auslös(ungs)recht *n*, laufendes Einlösungsrecht, ständiges Auslös(ungs)recht, ständiges Einlösungsrecht, stetiges Auslös(ungs)recht, stetiges Einlösungsrecht, ununterbrochenes Auslös(ungs)recht, ununterbrochenes Einlösungsrecht

continuous servitude → continuous (real) servitude

continuous succession, continuous privity · fortgesetzte Nachfolge *f*

contour · Höhenlinie *f*, Isohypse *f*

contour farming · Feldbestellung *f* entlang waag(e)rechter Geländelinien

contour interval, vertical interval · Äquidistanz *f*

contour map, contoured map · Höhenkurvenkarte *f*, Höhen(schicht)linienkarte, Isohypsenkarte

contour map smoothing · Technik *f* des lokalen gewichteten Durchschnitts [*Konstruktion von regulär vernetzten Höhenpunkten*]

contour ploughing (Brit.); contour plowing (US) · isohypsenparalleles Pflügen *n* [*Es hindert den hangab gerichteten Wasserabfluß und fördert das Eindringen des Wassers in den Boden*]

contra account · Gegenkonto *n*

contra bonos mores [*Latin*]; against good morals · gegen die guten Sitten

to contract, to award (a contract), to let (out), to commission a project, to appoint a contractor, to let a contract · zuschlagen, erteilen eines Auftrages

to contract, to settle a contract, to conclude a contract, to adopt a contract, to make a contract · abschließen eines Vertrages, vertraglich vereinbaren

to contract [*one's service*] · verdingen [*seine Leistung*]

contract, legally binding promise, legally binding agreement [*It is that form of agreement which directly contemplates and creates an obligation and is enforceable at law*] · (obligatorischer) Vertrag *m*, Legalversprechen *n*, Schuldvertrag [*Ein zweiseitiges Rechtsgeschäft, welches auf Begründung eines Schuldverhältnisses gerichtet ist*]

contract → (construction) contract

contract acceptance, acceptance of contract · Vertragsannahme *f*

contract according to the German Civil Code → (construction) contract according to the German Civil Code

contract according to the German Federal Contract Procedure in the Building and Construction Industry · VOB-Vertrag *m*

contract administration, management of (a) contract, operation of (a) contract, administration of (a) contract, contract management, contract operation · Durchführung *f* eines Vertrages, Handhabung eines Vertrages, Verwaltung eines Vertrages, Vertragsdurchführung, Vertragshandhabung, Vertragsverwaltung

contract advance for plant and move-in · Vorschuß *m* für Baustelleneinrichtung

contract agreement → (construction) contract agreement

contract appendix · Vertragsanhang *m*

contract arrangement · Vertragsaufbau *m*, Vertragsanordnung *f*

contract authority [*The total money limit that a government agency can commit under a contract with a developer or other constituent for a given program(me)*] · Auftragsvergabegrenze *f*

contract authorization (US) [*A congressional enactment permitting federal agencies to incur obligations prior to actual appropriation by congress of funds to cover such obligations; usually followed by an appropriation to liquidate contract authorization*] · Auftragsvergabebevollmacht *f*

(contract) award, (contract) letting, contracting, award(ing) of a contract, letting of a contract, letting out · Zuschlag *m*, Auftragserteilung *f*

contract award negotiations, contracting negotiations, letting out negotiations, contract letting negotiations · Auftragsverhandlungen *f pl*

contract basis, foundation of contract, contract foundation, basis of contract · Vertragsgrundlage *f*

contract before marriage, settlement before marriage, marriage settlement, ante-nuptial contract, ante-nuptial settlement [*A contract or agreement between a man and a woman before marriage, but in contemplation and generally in consideration of marriage, whereby the property rights and interests of either the prospective husband or wife, or both of them, are determined, or where property is secured to either or both of them, or to their children*] · Ehevertrag *m*, Ehestiftung *f*

contract bill [*It describes the quality and quantity of work included in the contract sum*] · Leistungsverzeichnis *n*, L.V.

contract blank (form), blank (form) of contract, form of contract · Vertragsmuster *n*, Vertragsformular *n*, Vertragsformblatt *n*, Vertragsblankett *n*, Vertragsvordruck *m*

contract bond [*Guarantee of the faithful performance of a contract. The bond provides indemnity against failure of a contractor to comply with the terms of his contract*] · Vertragsgarantie *f*

contract bond, performance bond, contract surety, performance surety [*It is a guarantee of contractor performance and is the instrument by which a corporate surety company (the guarantor) guarantees the owner of a construction project (the obligee) that the contractor to whom a construction contract has*

contract breach — contract content

been awarded (the principal) will fulfil the contract in accordance with the plans and specifications and with all attendant financial obligations having been paid in full. The bond is not a contract of insurance and, unless specially conditioned and certainly in its standard forms most frequently encountered, will not cover all the contingencies which can occur on a construction project.] · Ausführungsbürgschaft *f*

contract breach, breach of contract · Vertragsbruch *m*

contract-breaker · Vertragsbrecher *m*

contract-breaking, defaulting · vertragsbrüchig, säumig

contract-breaking party, defaulting party · vertragsbrüchige Partei, säumige Partei *f*

contract building works, contract works (of construction) · vertragliche (bauliche) Anlagen *fpl*, vertragliche Bauten *f*

contract burden, contract encumbrance, contract incumbrance, contract load, contract charge · Vertragslast *f*

contract by deed, covenant in deed, covenant in fact, special(ty) contract, contract in sealed writing, sealed contract, (contract by) specialty, contract under seal, contract by seal [*Contracts under seal, such as deeds and bonds, are instruments which are not rarely in writing, but which are sealed by the party bound thereby, and delivered by him to, or for the benefit of, the person to whom the liability is thereby incurred*] · (schriftlicher) gesiegelter Vertrag *m*, gesiegelter schriftlicher Vertrag, Formalvertrag unter Siegel, Vertrag mit Siegel, förmlicher Vertrag unter Siegel

contract by implication, implied contract, tacit contract · stillschweigender Vertrag *m*

contract by regulation, adhesion contract, government contract, contract of adhesion [*As opposed to a private contract*] · (Beschaffungs)Vertrag *m* mit einer Regierung, Vertrag durch Beitritt

contract by seal, contract by deed, covenant in deed, covenant in fact, special(ty) contract, contract in sealed writing, sealed contract, (contract by) specialty, contract under seal [*Contracts under seal, such as deeds and bonds, are instruments which are not rarely in writing, but which are sealed by the party bound thereby, and delivered by him to, or for the benefit of, the person to whom the liability is thereby incurred*] · (schriftlicher) gesiegelter Vertrag *m*, gesiegelter schriftlicher Vertrag, Formalvertrag unter Siegel, Vertrag mit Siegel, förmlicher Vertrag unter Siegel

(contract by) specialty, contract under seal, contract by seal, contract by deed, covenant in deed, covenant in fact, special(ty) contract, contract in sealed writing, sealed contract [*Contracts under seal, such as deeds and bonds, are instruments which are not rarely in writing, but which are sealed by the party bound thereby, and delivered by him to, or for the benefit of, the person to whom the liability is thereby incurred*] · (schriftlicher) gesiegelter Vertrag *m*, gesiegelter schriftlicher Vertrag, Formalvertrag unter Siegel, Vertrag mit Siegel, förmlicher Vertrag unter Siegel

contract by unsealed writing, simple contract, unsealed contract, parol contract, (written) contract not under seal, (written) contract without seal [*A simple contract made by writing without seal. By a strange misuse of language, both kinds of simple contract (1. The simple contract made by word of mouth and 2. The simple contract made by writing without seal) are frequently spoken of in English law as parol contracts notwithstanding that the term "parol", both etymologically and in general parlance, means "by word of mouth"*] · nicht gesiegelter (schriftlicher) Vertrag *m*, ungesiegelter (schriftlicher) Vertrag, nicht formeller Vertrag, nicht notarieller Vertrag, (schriftlicher) Vertrag ohne Siegel, schriftlicher ungesiegelter Vertrag

contract charge, contract burden, contract encumbrance, contract incumbrance, contract load · Vertragslast *f*

contract claim → contract(ual) claim

Contract Clause · Vertragsklausel *f*, Verbot *n* des Erlassens von Staatsgesetzen die die bindende Kraft von Verträgen beeinträchtigen [*USA*]

contract completion, completion of contract, specific performance · Naturalerfüllung *f*, Vertragserfüllung, Realerfüllung, vertragsgemäße Erfüllung

contract completion date · Vertragsenddatum *n*

contract complied with, executed contract, performed contract, fulfilled contract · ausgeführter Vertrag *m*, erfüllter Vertrag *m*, erbrachter Vertrag *m*, vollzogener Vertrag *m*

contract conclusion, settlement of a contract, contract settlement, conclusion of a contract · Abschluß *m* eines Vertrages, Vertragsabschluß

contract condition, condition of contract, (contract) fundamental term [*Term of fundamental importance in a contract*] · Vertragsbedingung *f*

contract consideration · Vertragsgegenleistung *f*

contract content · Vertragsinhalt *m*

contract contravention — contracting

contract contravention, contravention of contract, infringement of contract, default of contract, contract violation, contract default, contract infringement · Vertragswidrigkeit *f*, Vertragsverletzung *f*

contract date · Vertragsdatum *n*

contract debt, debt by simple contract · Vertragsschuld *f*

contract design · Vertragsentwurf *m* [*Die Bauarbeiten werden nach ihm ausgeführt*]

(contract) deviation [*Departure from the method of performance agreed in a contract*] · (Vertrags)Abweichung *f*

contract discharge, discharge of contract · Vertragsauflösung *f*

contract documentation · Vertragsdokumentation *f*

contract documents [*The contract documents in the construction industry consists of the signed agreement, the general conditions of contract, the plans and the specifications*] · Vertragsdokumente *npl*, Vertragsschriftstücke *npl*, Vertragsunterlagen *fpl*

contract draftsman, contract drafter, contract draughtsman · Vertragsentwerfer *m*, Vertragsgestalter, Vertragsausarbeiter, Vertragsaufsteller

contract draftsmanship · Vertragsgestaltungswesen *n*

contract drawing · Vertragszeichnung *f*

contract(ed) rate, rate of contract [*for services*] · Vertragssatz *m*

contract element, element of contract · Vertragsbestandteil *m*

contract encumbrance, contract incumbrance, contract load, contract charge, contract burden · Vertragslast *f*

contract evidenced by writing, written contract, contract in writing · schriftlicher Vertrag *m*, schriftlich abgefaßter Vertrag

contract executory · obligatorische Verpflichtung *f*

contract file · Vertragsakte *f*

contract for a settlement · Stiftungsvertrag *m*

contract for equipment hire, equipment hire contract · Baugerätemietvertrag *m*, (Geräte)Mietvertrag

contract for hire-purchase, contract for lease-purchase, hire-purchase contract, lease-purchase contract · Mietkaufvertrag *m*

contract for marine insurance, contract for sea insurance · Seeversicherungsvertrag *m*

contract for measure and value, unit-price contract, measurement contract, measured contract, measure-and-value contract, bill contract · Einheits(preis)vertrag *m* [*Ein Vertrag zu Einheitspreisen für technisch und wirtschaftlich einheitliche Teilleistungen, deren Menge nach Maß, Gewicht oder Stückzahl vom Auftraggeber in den Verdingungsunterlagen angegeben ist*]

contract for necessaries · Vertrag *m* für notwendigen Unterhalt

contract for personal service, contract of (personal) service, contract of master and servant, personal service contract, master-and-servant contract · Dienst(leistungs)vertrag *m*

contract for purchase of (real) estate → (real) property (purchase) contract

contract for sale of land(s), land(s) sale contract · Bodenverkaufsvertrag *m*, Landverkaufsvertrag

contract for sea insurance, contract for marine insurance · Seeversicherungsvertrag *m*

contract for the benefit of third party, third party beneficiary contract · Vertrag *m* zugunsten Dritter

contract for the sale of unascertained goods · Genuskaufvertrag *m*

contract for the sale of specific goods, contract for the sale of ascertained goods · Spezieskaufvertrag *m*

contract for use · Nutzungsvertrag *m*

contract for work and labour and materials [*A contract by which the contractor undertakes to make an article from material which he himself supplies using his own labour*] · Werklieferungsvertrag *m*

contract foundation, basis of contract, contract basis, foundation of contract · Vertragsgrundlage *f*, Vertragsbasis *f*

(contract) fundamental term, contract condition, condition of contract [*Term of fundamental importance in a contract*] · Vertragsbedingung *f*

contract gap · Vertragslücke *f*

contract incumbrance, contract load, contract charge, contract burden, contract encumbrance · Vertragslast *f*

contract infringement, contract contravention, contravention of contract, infringement of contract, default of contract, contract violation, contract default · Vertragswidrigkeit *f*, Vertragsverletzung *f*

contracting, settling a contract, concluding a contract, making a contract, adopting a contract · Abschließen *n* eines Vertrages, Vertragsabschluß *m*

contracting → (contract) letting

contracting combine, partnership, contractor combination, contracting group, joint venture (firm) · Arbeitsgemeinschaft *f*, Arge, Baufirmengruppe *f*, Partnerschaftsfirma *f* [*Ein Zusammenschluß von Unternehmern auf vertraglicher Grundlage mit dem Zweck, meist große Bauaufträge der gleichen oder verschiedenen Fachrichtungen gemeinsam durchzuführen*]

contracting company, construction company, building company, construction firm, building firm, contracting firm · Bauunternehmen *n*, Baugesellschaft *f*, Bauunternehmung *f*, Baubetrieb *m*, Baufirma *f*

contract(ing) documents · Vergabeunterlagen *fpl*, Verdingungsunterlagen [*Sie umfassen Leistungsbeschreibung, Vertragsbedingungen und Vorbemerkungen*]

contracting firm, contracting company, construction company, building company, construction firm, building firm · Bauunternehmen *n*, Baugesellschaft *f*, Bauunternehmung *f*, Baubetrieb *m*, Baufirma *f*

contracting group, joint venture (firm), contracting combine, partnership, contractor combination · Arbeitsgemeinschaft *f*, Arge, Baufirmengruppe *f*, Partnerschaftsfirma *f* [*Ein Zusammenschluß von Unternehmern auf vertraglicher Grundlage mit dem Zweck, meist große Bauaufträge der gleichen oder verschiedenen Fachrichtungen gemeinsam durchzuführen*]

contracting measures · Vergabe *f*, Verdingung *f* [*Die Gesamtheit der zum Vertragsabschluß führenden Maßnahmen des Auftraggebers*]

contracting method · Vergabeverfahren *n*, Verdingungsverfahren

contracting negotiations, letting out negotiations, contract letting negotiations, contract award negotiations · Auftragsverhandlungen *fpl*

contracting officer, contracting official · Beschaffungsbeamte *m*

contracting out [*Persons for whose benefit a statute has been passed may usually contract with others in such a manner as to deprive themselves of the benefit of the statute*] · Freizeichnen *n*, Freikontrahieren

contract(ing) party, contract(ing) partner, contractant, contractee, contractor [*A person who is a party to a contract*] · Vertragspartei *f*, Vertragspartner *m*, Vertragsbeteiligte *m*, Vertragskontrahent *m*, Vertrags(ab)schließende *m*

contracting power, contracting right, contractual power, contractual right, power of contract(ing), right of contract(ing) · Vertragsbefugnis *f*, Vertragsrecht *n*

contracting practice · Vergabewesen *n*, Verdingungswesen

contracting right, contractual power, contractual right, power of contract(ing), right of contract(ing), contracting power · Vertragsbefugnis *f*, Vertragsrecht *n*

contracting state · Vertragsstaat *m*

contract in sealed writing, sealed contract, (contract by) specialty, contract under seal, contract by seal, contract by deed, covenant in deed, covenant in fact, special(ty) contract [*Contracts under seal, such as deeds and bonds, are instruments which are not rarely in writing, but which are sealed by the party bound thereby, and delivered by him to, or for the benefit of, the person to whom the liability is thereby incurred*] · (schriftlicher) gesiegelter Vertrag *m*, gesiegelter schriftlicher Vertrag, Formalvertrag unter Siegel, Vertrag mit Siegel, förmlicher Vertrag unter Siegel

contract in trust, contract on trust, contract under trusteeship, trustee(ship) contract, fiduciary contract, fiducial contract · Treuhandvertrag *m*, Treuhändervertrag

contract in writing, contract evidenced by writing, written contract · schriftlicher Vertrag *m*, schriftlich abgefaßter Vertrag

contract language, contract phraseology · Vertragssprache *f*

contract law, conventional law, law of contract; lex loci (contractus) [*Latin*] [*The law of the place of a contract; the law of the place where a contract is made, or is to be performed*] · Vertragsrecht *n*, Recht des Vertragsschlusses

contract length, contract time, time of contract, full life of contract, length of contract · Vertrags(lauf)zeit *f*, Vertragsdauer *f*

(contract) letting, contracting, award(ing) of a contract, letting of a contract, letting out, (contract) award · Zuschlag *m*, Auftragserteilung *f*

contract letting negotiations, contract award negotiations, contracting negotiations, letting out negotiations · Auftragsverhandlungen *fpl*

contract load, contract charge, contract burden, contract encumbrance, contract incumbrance · Vertragslast *f*

contract management, contract operation, contract administration, management of (a) contract, operation of (a) contract, administration of (a) contract · Durchführung *f* eines Vertrages, Handhabung eines Vertrages, Verwaltung eines Vertrages, Vertragsdurchführung, Vertragshandhabung, Vertragsverwaltung

contract money, outstanding money, outstanding debt, bookdebt · Außenstand *m*, (Geschäfts)Forderung *f*

contract negotiation · Vertragsverhandlung *f*

contract negotiation → (final) contract negotiation

contract note [*A document sent by a stockbroker to his client stating the terms on which he has bought or sold stocks or shares on his behalf. It also shows the stockbroker's commission, or brokerage, and the amount of stamp duty and any other charges payable*] · Schlußschein *m*, Schlußnota *f*, Schlußzettel *m*

contract of (ab)alienation, contract of disposal, (ab)alienation contract, disposal contract · Veräußerungsvertrag *m*

contract of acceptance, acceptance contract · Annahmevertrag *m*

contract of adhesion, adhesion contract · einseitig vorformulierter Vertrag *m*

contract of adhesion, contract by regulation, adhesion contract, government contract [*As opposed to a private contract*] · (Beschaffungs)Vertrag *m* mit einer Regierung, Vertrag durch Beitritt

contract of agency, agency contract · (Stell)Vertretungsvertrag *m*

contract of alteration → contract of variation

contract of assignment, contract of cession, assignment contract, cession contract, contract of assignation, assignation contract · Abtretungsvertrag *m*, Zessionsvertrag

contract of benevolence, deed poll, contract without consideration, gratuitous contract, nude contract, one-sided contract, unilateral contract · einseitiger Vertrag *m*, Vertrag ohne Gegenleistung

contract of carriage, carriage contract · Beförderungsvertrag *m*, Güterbeförderungsvertrag, Frachtvertrag

contract of cession, assignment contract, cession contract, contract of assignation, assignation contract, contract of assignment · Abtretungsvertrag *m*, Zessionsvertrag

contract of change → contract of variation

contract of condition precedent · aufschiebend-bedingter Vertrag *m*

contract of demise, contract of lease(hold), contract of tenure, tenancy contract, tenure contract, lease(hold) contract, demise contract, contract of tenancy · Pachtvertrag *m*, Nutzungsrechtvertrag, Verpachtungsvertrag

contract of development, development contract · Entwick(e)lungsvertrag *m*

contract of disposal, (ab)alienation contract, disposal contract, contract of (ab)alienation · Veräußerungsvertrag *m*

contract of employment → contract of service

contract of engagement · Zusagevertrag *m*

contract of government, government(al) contract · Herrschaftsvertrag *m*

contract of guaranty, contract of guarantee, guaranty contract, guarantee contract, contract of guarantie, guarantie contract · Bürgschaftsvertrag *m*

contract of hire, hire contract, hiring contract [*A contract by which one person grants to another either the enjoyment of a thing or the use of the labour and industry, either of himself, or his servant, during a certain time, for a stipulated compensation, or by which one contracts for the labour or services of another about a thing bailed to him for a specific purpose*] · Mietvertrag *m*

contract of hiring, hiring contract, hire contract [*A contract by which one person grants to another the use of the labour and industry, either of himself or his servant*] · Verdingungsvertrag *m*

(contract of) hiring, hire contract, hiring contract [*A contract by which one person grants to another the enjoyment of a thing*] · Sachmietvertrag *m*

contract of inheritance, inheritance contract · Erb(schafts)vertrag *m*, Erbeinsetzungsvertrag, Vermächtnisvertrag

contract of insurance, insurance contract · Versicherungsvertrag *m*

contract of job → contract of service

contract of lease(hold), contract of tenure, tenancy contract, tenure contract, lease(hold) contract, demise contract, contract of tenancy, contract of demise · Pachtvertrag *m*, Nutzungsrechtvertrag, Verpachtungsvertrag

contract of loan (of money), loan contract · Darleh(e)nsvertrag *m*

contract of mandate, mandate contract · Mandatsvertrag *m*

contract of pawn, contract of pledge, pledge contract, pawn contract · Pfandvertrag *m*

contract of (personal) service, contract of master and servant, personal service contract, master-and-servant contract, contract for personal service · Dienst(leistungs)vertrag *m*

contract of pledge, pledge contract, pawn contract, contract of pawn · Pfandvertrag *m*

contract of record · amtlich registrierter Vertrag *m*

contract of renewal, contract of revival, renewal contract, revival contract · Erneuerungsvertrag *m*

contract of renunciation of heirship, contract of renunciation of inheritance ·

Erbverzichtsvertrag m, Erbentsagungsvertrag

contract of sale, sale contract · Verpflichtungsvertrag m [*Übertragung von Grundstücksrechten*]

contract of sale, sale contract, contract to sell · Verkaufsvertrag m

contract of service → contract of (personal) service

contract of service, contract of employment, contract of job, contract of work, service contract, employment contract, job contract, work contract · Arbeitsvertrag m

contract of tenancy, contract of demise, contract of lease(hold), contract of tenure, tenancy contract, tenure contract, lease(hold) contract, demise contract · Pachtvertrag m, Nutzungsrechtvertrag, Verpachtungsvertrag

contract of use, use contract · Benutzungsvertrag m, Gebrauchsvertrag

contract of variation, contract of alteration, contract of change, change contract, variation contract, alteration contract · (Ab)Änderungsvertrag m, Umänderungsvertrag, Veränderungsvertrag

contract of warranty, warranty contract · Garantievertrag m

contract of work → contract of service

to contract (oneself) out of, to repudiate liability for · freizeichnen, sich freizeichnen

contract on trust, contract under trusteeship, trustee(ship) contract, fiduciary contract, fiducial contract, contract in trust · Treuhandvertrag m, Treuhändervertrag

contract operation, contract administration, management of (a) contract, operation of (a) contract, administration of (a) contract, contract management · Durchführung f eines Vertrages, Handhabung eines Vertrages, Verwaltung eines Vertrages, Vertragsdurchführung, Vertragshandhabung, Vertragsverwaltung

contractor → contract(ing) party

contractor combination, contracting group, joint venture (firm), contracting combine, partnership · Arbeitsgemeinschaft f, Arge, Baufirmengruppe f, Partnerschaftsfirma f [*Ein Zusammenschluß von Unternehmern auf vertraglicher Grundlage mit dem Zweck, meist große Bauaufträge der gleichen oder verschiedenen Fachrichtungen gemeinsam durchzuführen*]

contractor-financed project · unternehmerseitig finanziertes Projekt n

contractor practice · Unternehmerwesen n

(contractor's) all-risks insurance, construction insurance, building insurance · Bau(wesen)versicherung f

(contractor's) all-risks policy, construction insurance policy, building insurance policy · Bau(wesen)versicherungspolice f

contractors' association, contractors' institution, contractors' society, society of contractors, association of contractors, institution of contractors · Unternehmerverein(igung) m, (f)

contractor's claim, contractor's demand · Unternehmerforderung f, Unternehmerverlangen n

(contractor's) completion schedule, working chart, working schedule, building chart, building schedule, construction chart, construction schedule, outline of construction procedure [*Written or graphically explained, the procedure of construction prepared by the contractor, usually by a bar chart of scheduled dates by trades or a critical path chart*] · (Ausführungs)Fristenplan m, Baufristenplan

(contractor's) control of site, (contractor's) site control · Beherrschung f der Baustelle

contractor's (cost(s)) estimate, detailed (cost(s)) estimate, firm (cost(s)) estimate · detaillierter KV m, detaillierter (Bau)Kosten(vor)anschlag

contractor's demand, contractor's claim · Unternehmerforderung f, Unternehmerverlangen n

contractor's gain, contractor's profit · Unternehmergewinn m, Unternehmerprofit m

contractor's hazard, entrepreneurial hazard, entrepreneurial risk, contractor's risk · Unternehmerrisiko n, Unternehmerwagnis n

contractor's indemnity insurance, contractor's liability insurance, contractor's third-party insurance · Bauunternehmerhaftpflichtversicherung f

contractors' institution, contractors' society, society of contractors, association of contractors, institution of contractors, contractors' association · Unternehmerverein(igung) m, (f)

contractor's insurance · Unternehmerversicherung f

contractor's labour contract [*A contract by which the contractor undertakes to manufacture (or sometimes to alter) a specified object. It is distinct from the contract for work and labour and materials in that the ordering party supplies the material*] · Werkvertrag m

contractor's law · Unternehmerrecht n

contractor's liability insurance, contractor's third-party insurance, contractor's indemnity insurance · Bauunternehmerhaftpflichtversicherung f

contractor's own sub-contractor · unternehmerseitiger Nachunternehmer m, unternehmerseitiger Subunternehmer, unternehmerseitiger Unterunternehmer; unternehmerseitiger Unterakkordant m [Schweiz]

contractors' partnership · Unternehmergemeinschaft f

contractor's payment · Werklohn m, Unternehmerlohn

contractor's performance · Unternehmerleistung f

contractor's profit, contractor's gain · Unternehmergewinn m, Unternehmerprofit m

contractor's public liability insurance · Betriebshaftpflichtversicherung f

contractor's right to payment · Unternehmervergütungsrecht n

contractor's risk, contractor's hazard, entrepreneurial hazard, entrepreneurial risk · Unternehmerrisiko n, Unternehmerwagnis n

contractor's road · Unternehmerstraße f

(contractor's) site control, (contractor's) control of site · Beherrschung f der Baustelle

contractors' society, society of contractors, association of contractors, institution of contractors, contractors' association, contractors' institution · Unternehmerverein(igung) m, (f)

(contractor's) superintendent · Gesamtbauleiter m, Oberbauleiter [Der Vertreter des Auftragnehmers für die Leitung der Bauausführung im Gegensatz zu Aufsichtspersonen des Auftragnehmers mit begrenzten Tätigkeitsbereichen, z. B. Poliere, Meister, Bauführer]

contractor's third-party insurance, contractor's indemnity insurance, contractor's liability insurance · Bauunternehmerhaftpflichtversicherung f

contract payment · Vertragszahlung f

contract penalty, penalty for breach of contract, penalty for non-performance of contract, (conventional) penalty · Konventionalstrafe f, Vertragsstrafe

contract phraseology, contract language · Vertragssprache f

contract place, place of contract · Vertragsort m

contract precedent, precedent contract · früherer Vertrag m

contract price · Vertragspreis m

contract rate of interest · vereinbarter Zinsfuß m

contract rent [The rent income stipulated by contract — that is, under the terms of a lease] · Vertragsmiete f, vertragliche Miete, ausbedungene Miete, vertraglicher (Miet)Zins m, ausbedungener (Miet)Zins

contract rule · Vertragsvorschrift f

contract scope, scope of contract · Vertragsumfang m

contract to sell, contract of sale, sale contract · Verkaufsvertrag m

contract service · Vertragsleistung f

contract settlement, conclusion of a contract, contract conclusion, settlement of a contract · Abschluß m eines Vertrages, Vertragsabschluß

contract stamp · Schlußscheinstempel m

contract starting date · Vertragsbeginndatum n

contract subject(-matter), subject(-matter) of (a) contract · Vertragsgegenstand m

contract sum [The sum to be ascertained and paid in accordance with the provisions for the construction, completion and maintenance of the works in accordance with the contract] · Vertragssumme f

contract surety, performance surety, contract bond, performance bond [It is a guarantee of contractor performance and is the instrument by which a corporate surety company (the guarantor) guarantees the owner of a construction project (the obligee) that the contractor to whom a construction contract has been awarded (the principal) will fulfil the contract in accordance with the plans and specifications and with all attendant financial obligations having been paid in full. The bond ist not a contract of insurance and, unless specially conditioned and certainly in its standard forms most frequently encountered, will not cover all the contingencies which can occur on a construction project.] · Ausführungsbürgschaft f

(contract) term, term of contract [Not to be confused with "contract condition" which is a "fundamental (contract) term"] · (Vertrags)Nebenbedingung f

contract termination, termination of (the) contract · Vertragsbeend(ig)ung f

contract text, contract wording · Vertragstext m

contract theory · Vertragstheorie f

contract time, time of contract, full life of contract, length of contract, contract length · Vertrags(lauf)zeit f, Vertragsdauer f

contract to appoint, nomination contract, appointment contract, contract to nominate · Benennungsvertrag *m,* Ernennungsvertrag

contract to construct along a highway, contract to construct along a street; contract to construct along a road · Anbauvertrag *m*

contract to exchange · Tauschvertrag *m*

contract to make a will · Vertrag *m* ein Testament zu machen

contract to nominate, contract to appoint, nomination contract, appointment contract · Benennungsvertrag *m,* Ernennungsvertrag

contract to transfer profit, contract to transfer gain · Gewinnabführungsvertrag *m,* Profitabführungsvertrag

contractual, persuant to contract, subject to contract · vertragsgemäß, vertragsmäßig, vertraglich

contractual building term, contractual construction term · Vertragsfrist *f* für die Bauarbeiten, vertragliche Zeit *f* des Bauablaufes, vertragliche Bauzeit

contractual capacity, contractual capability, contractual standing · Vertragsfähigkeit *f*

contractual caveat emptor · vertraglicher Gewährleistungsausschluß *m*

contractual claim, contractual demand · Vertragsforderung *f,* Vertragsverlangen *n*

contractual construction term, contractual building term · Vertragsfrist *f* für die Bauarbeiten, vertragliche Zeit *f* des Bauablaufes, vertragliche Bauzeit

contractual date · vertragliches Datum *n*

contractual demand → contractual claim

contractual determination · vertragliche Festlegung *f*

contractual duty · Vertragspflicht *f,* vertragliche Pflicht

contractual duty of care · vertragliche Sorgfaltspflicht *f*

contractual force · Vertragskraft *f*

contractual interest rate · Vertragszinssatz *m*

contractual item · Vertragsposition *f*

contractual joint obligations · vertragliche Gesamtschuldhaftung *f*

contractual liability · vertragliche Haftung *f,* vertragliche Verbindlichkeit *f,* Vertragshaftung

contractual limitation, contractual restriction · vertragliche Einschränkung *f,* vertragliche Beschränkung

contractual matters · Vertragsangelegenheiten *f pl*

contractual payment · vertragliche Zahlung *f*

contractual pitfall · Vertragsfalle *f*

contractual plan, front-end load plan · Nennwert-Gebühren-Vorabzugs-Plan *m,* Vertragsplan, Anlageplan, Anlageprogramm *n,* Sparplan, Sparprogramm [*Investmentfonds*]

contractual position · Vertragsstellung *f*

contractual power, contractual right, power of contract(ing), right of contract(ing), contracting power, contracting right · Vertragsbefugnis *f,* Vertragsrecht *n*

contractual practice · Vertragswesen *n*

contractual principle · Vertragsgrundsatz *m,* Vertragsprinzip *n*

contractual protection · vertraglicher Schutz *m*

contractual provision · Vertragsbestimmung *f*

contractual public international law · Völkervertragsrecht *n*

contractual regime · vertragsmäßiges Güterrecht *n*

contractual relation(ship) · Vertragsverhältnis *n,* vertragliches Verhältnis, Vertragsbeziehung, vertragliche Beziehung *f*

contractual (residential) tenancy · vertragliches (Wohnungs)Mietverhältnis *n*

contractual responsibility · vertragliche Verpflichtung *f*

contractual restriction, contractual limitation · vertragliche Einschränkung *f,* vertragliche Beschränkung

contractual right, power of contract(ing), right of contract(ing), contracting power, contracting right, contractual power · Vertragsbefugnis *f,* Vertragsrecht *n*

contractual savings scheme · Vertragssparsystem *n*

contractual standing, contractual capacity, contractual capability · Vertragsfähigkeit *f*

contractual tenancy · vertragliches Mietsverhältnis *n*

contractual term · Vertragsfrist *f*

contractual use · ertragsmäßiger Gebrauch *m*

contractual variation · vertragliche (Ab)Änderung f

contractual work(s) · vertragliche (Bau)Arbeit(en) f (pl), vertragliche (Bau)Leistung(en) f (pl), vertraglich vereinbarte (Bau)Arbeit(en), vertraglich vereinbarte (Bau)Leistung(en), Vertrags(bau)arbeit(en), Vertrags(bau)leistung(en)

contract under seal, contract by seal, contract by deed, covenant in deed, covenant in fact, special(ty) contract, contract in sealed writing, sealed contract, (contract by) specialty [*Contracts under seal, such as deeds and bonds, are instruments which are not rarely in writing, but which are sealed by the party bound thereby, and delivered by him to, or for the benefit of, the person to whom the liability is thereby incurred*] · (schriftlicher) gesiegelter Vertrag m, gesiegelter schriftlicher Vertrag, Formalvertrag unter Siegel, Vertrag mit Siegel, förmlicher Vertrag unter Siegel

contract under trusteeship, trustee(ship) contract, fiduciary contract, fiducial contract, contract in trust, contract on trust · Treuhandvertrag m, Treuhändervertrag

contractus bilateralis aequalis · vollkommen zweiseitiger Vertrag m

contractus bilateralis inaequalis · unvollkommen zweiseitiger Vertrag m

contractus consensus [*Latin*]; rescission contract · Aufhebungsvertrag m

contractus sui generis [*Latin*] · Innominatvertrag m

contract validity, validity of a contract · Vertragsgültigkeit f

contract value · Auftragswert m, Vertragswert m

contract violation, contract default, contract infringement, contract contravention, contravention of contract, infringement of contract, default of contract · Vertragswidrigkeit f, Vertragsverletzung f

contract with an authority · Behördenvertrag m

contract with arbitrator(s) · Schiedsrichtervertrag m [*Mit Schiedsrichtern geschlossener Vertrag*]

contract without consideration, gratuitous contract, nude contract, one-sided contract, unilateral contract, contract of benevolence, deed poll · einseitiger Vertrag m, Vertrag ohne Gegenleistung

contract wording, contract text · Vertragstext m

contract works (of construction), contract building works · vertragliche (bauliche) Anlagen f pl, vertragliche Bauten f

contradictory, agreed ((up)on) · vereinbart, kontradiktorisch, abgemacht, übereingekommen

contradictory evidence, contradictory proof, rebutting testimony, disproof, counter-evidence, counter-proof, evidence to the contrary, proof to the contrary · Gegenbeweis m, gegenteiliger Beweis

contradictory judg(e)ment, judg(e)ment after trial, judg(e)ment (up)on, agreed judg(e)ment · kontradiktorisches Urteil n, vereinbartes Urteil

contra entry · Gegenbuchung f

contrahent → contract(ing) partner

contrariety opinion, contrary opinion · abweichende Meinung f, Meinungsverschiedenheit f, unterschiedliche Meinung

contrary · widrig

contrary to evidence, contrary to proof, against evidence, against proof · beweiswidersprechend

contrary to law → nonlegal

contrary to reason, irrational · verstandeswidrig, vernunftwidrig, vernunftlos

contrary view · gegenteilige Ansicht f

contravention → violation (of law)

contravention of contract, infringement of contract, default of contract, contract violation, contract default, contract infringement, contract contravention · Vertragswidrigkeit f, Vertragsverletzung f

contributability · Beitragsfähigkeit f, Beitragsvermögen n, Beitragseignung f

contributable · beitragsfähig, beitragsgeeignet

to contribute · beisteuern, beitragen

contributed capital · eingezahltes Grundkapital n

contributing, contributive, contributory · beisteuernd, beitragend

contributing payment, contribution payment, contributory payment, payment of contribution · Beitragszahlung f

contributing person, working member (of the population), employed person, working person · erwerbstätige Person f, beschäftigte Person, arbeitende Person, berufstätige Person, Beschäftigte m, Erwerbstätige m

contributing population, employed population, working population · erwerbstätige Bevölkerung f, beschäftigte Bevölkerung, arbeitende Bevölkerung, berufstätige Bevölkerung

contributing rate — control

contributing rate, contribution rate, rate of contribution, contributory rate · Beitragssatz *m*

contribution · Beitrag *m*

contribution certificate, certificate of contribution · Beitragsbescheinigung *f*, Beitragsattest *n*, Beitragsschein *m*

contribution claim, contribution demand, claim of contribution, demand of contribution · Beitragsforderung *f*, Beitragsverlangen *n*

contribution duty, duty to contribute, liability to contribute, contribution liability · Beitragspflicht *f*

contribution margin, marginal revenue, marginal balance, marginal income, variable gross margin, profit contribution · Deckungsbeitrag *m*, Beitragsüberschuß *m*, Überschußsaldo *m*, Erfolgsbeitrag, variabler Bruttoüberschuß, Grenzerfolg *m*, (Kosten)Deckungszuschlag *m*

contribution of (land) area, contribution of land · Flächenbeitrag *m*, Bodenbeitrag, Landbeitrag [*Die bei der Flächenumlegung nach dem Bundesbaugesetz auf Verlangen der Gemeinde von den eingeworfenen Grundstücken abgezogene Fläche, mit der die Vorteile ausgeglichen werden, die durch die Umlegung erwachsen. Der Flächenbeitrag darf in Gebieten, die erstmalig erschlossen werden nur bis 30%, in anderen Gebieten nur bis 10% der eingeworfenen Fläche betragen. Anstelle des Flächenbeitrages kann ganz oder teilweise ein entsprechender Geldbetrag erhoben werden*]

contribution-paying member · (beitrag)zahlendes Mitglied *n*

contribution payment, contributory payment, payment of contribution, contributing payment · Beitragszahlung *f*

contribution per unit of limiting factor · Deckungsbeitrag *m* pro Engpaßeinheit

contribution rate, rate of contribution, contributory rate, contributing rate · Beitragssatz *m*

contribution reduction, reduction of contribution · Beitragsermäßigung *f*

contribution right, right of contribution · Beitrags(an)recht *n*, Beitragsanspruch *m*

contribution(s) charge, contribution(s) load, load of contribution(s), charge of contribution(s) · Beitragslast *f*

contribution(s) load, load of contribution(s), charge of contribution(s), contribution(s) charge · Beitragslast *f*

contribution to administrative cost(s) · Verwaltungskostenbeitrag *m*

contribution to savings scheme · vermögenswirksame Leistung *f*

contributive, contributory, contributing · beisteuernd, beitragend

contributor, fellow (worker), co-worker · Mitarbeiter *m*

contributory, concurrent [*Contributing to the same event*] · mitwirkend

contributory · leistungspflichtig, nachschußpflichtig

contributory [*A member liable to help make up a deficiency in the assets of a company being dissolved*] · Leistungspflichtige *m*, Nachschußpflichtige [*Zwangsabwick(e)lung*]

contributory [*A person who, on the winding up of a company, is bound to contribute to its assets for the payment of its debts*] · haftbarer Teilhaber *m*, haftender Teilhaber

contributory, contributing, contributive · beisteuernd, beitragend

contributory, liable to contribution(s), subject to contribution(s) · beitragspflichtig

contributory · Beitragspflichtige *m*

contributory act(ion) · Mitwirkungshandlung *f*, Mitwirkungsakt *m*

contributory carelessness, co-operative carelessness, contributory negligence, co-operative negligence · Mitfahrlässigkeit *f*

contributory duty · Mitwirkungspflicht *f*

contributory fault · Mitverschulden *n*, mitwirkendes Verschulden

contributory mortgage [*A mortgage in which the mortgage money is contributed by two or more persons in separate amounts*] · Hypothek *f* für mehrere Gläubiger

contributory negligence, co-operative negligence, contributory carelessness, co-operative carelessness · Mitfahrlässigkeit *f*

contributory payment, payment of contribution, contributing payment, contribution payment · Beitragszahlung *f*

contributory plan · Plan *m* mit gemeinsamer Beitragszahlung [*durch Arbeitgeber und Arbeitnehmer*]

contributory rate, contributing rate, contribution rate, rate of contribution · Beitragssatz *m*

to control, to re-examine, to review, to check · kontrollieren, nachprüfen

control · Herrschaft *f* [*über eine Sache*]

control · Lenkung *f*

control, re-examination, review, check · Kontrolle *f*, Nachprüfung *f*

control — convalescent home

control → (physical) control (over a thing)

control account → control(ling) account

control authority, check(ing) authority, review(ing) authority, re-examination authority, authority of control, authority of checking · Kontrollvollmacht *f*, Nachprüf(ungs)vollmacht

control authority → control(ling) authority

control board, board of control · Kontrollamt *n*

control committee · Lenkungsausschuß *m*

control company → control(ling) company

control contract · Beherrschungsvertrag *m* [*Konzern*]

control duty, re-examination duty, check(ing) duty, duty to review, review(ing) duty, duty to check, duty to control, duty to re-examine, check(ing) duty · Nachprüfungspflicht *f*, Kontrollpflicht

control function · Lenkungsfunktion *f*

control group · Lenkungsgruppe *f*

controllable cost(s) · beeinflußbare Kosten *f*

controllable variance, budget variance, spending variance · (Mengen)Verbrauchsabweichung *f*, Abweichung (des effektiven) vom geplanten (Mengen)Verbrauch, Budgetabweichung [*Der Unterschied zwischen den Soll- und Istkosten einer Kostenart oder Kostenstelle*]

control law · Lenkungsrecht *n*

control law, control act, control statute · Lenkungsgesetz *n*

controlled economy, directed economy, planned economy · Planwirtschaft *f*

controlled enterprise, controlled undertaking · abhängiges Unternehmen *n*, abhängige Unternehmung *f*

controlled out-migration · gelenkte Abwanderung *f*

controlled rent · preisgebundene Miete *f*

controller; comptroller [*misnomer*] [*An officer who has the inspection, examination or controlling of the accounts of other officers*] · hoher Rechnungsbeamter *m*, Kämmerer, Finanzdezernent

controller · Geschäftsaufseher *m*

controlling · Erfolgs- und Liquiditätsrechnung *f* [*Unternehmen*]

controlling, re-examinating, checking, reviewing · Kontrollieren *n*, Nachprüfen

control(ling) account · Kontrollkonto *n*, Nachprüf(ungs)konto

control(ling) authority · Aufsichtsbehörde *f*, Überwachungsbehörde *f*

control(ling) company [*It may be either a holding company or a parent company*] · Kontrollgesellschaft *f*

control(ling) enterprise, control(ling) undertaking · herrschendes Unternehmen, herrschende Unternehmung *f*, herrschender Betrieb *m*

control measure, re-examination measure, check(ing) measure, review(ing) measure · Nachprüfungsmaßnahme, Kontrollmaßnahme

control of advertisements, advertisement control · Überwachung *f* des Reklamewesens, Reklameüberwachung

control of agriculture, agricultural control · Landwirtschaftslenkung *f*, Agrarlenkung, landwirtschaftliche Lenkung

control of development, development control · Entwick(e)lungslenkung *f*

control of economic cycles · Konjunkturlenkung

control of economy, economy control · Wirtschaftslenkung *f*

control of housing, housing control · Wohn(ungs)zwangswirtschaft *f*, Wohnraumbewirtschaftung *f*

control of land use, land use control, planning and zoning · Flächennutzungslenkung *f*, Bodennutzungslenkung, Landnutzungslenkung

control of property by receiver · Zwangsverwaltung *f*

control of trips, control of travels, control of journeys · Fahrt(en)steuerung *f*

control (over a thing) → (physical) control (over a thing)

control principle, principle of control · Lenkungsgrundsatz *m*, Lenkungsprinzip *n*

control system · Lenkungssystem *n*

controversial, moot, adversary, contested, undecided, contentious, unsettled [*Litigated between adverse parties*] · streitig, strittig

conurbation (Brit); urban tract [*According to Dickinson*]; urban(ized) landscape, civicized landscape, cityscape, townscape, urban agglomeration [*An area occupied by a continuous series of dwellings, factories and other buildings, harbour and docks, urban parks and playing fields, etc., which are not separated from each other by rural land; though in many cases such an urban area includes enclaves of rural land which is still in agricultural occupation*] · Stadtlandschaft *f*, Städelandschaft, verstädterte Landschaft, Städteschar *f*, Städteagglomeration *f*, Zusammenstädterung *f*

convalescent home · Genesungsheim *n*

to convene — converted dwelling unit

to convene [*To cause to meet together*] · einberufen

to convene, to assemble [*To meet together, usually for a common purpose*] · zusammenkommen, sich versammeln

to convene before a court of law → to subp(o)ena

convener [*A person appointed to call a group together for meetings*] · Einberufer *m*

convenience · Belieben *n*

convenience, amenity [*In real property law, such circumstances, in regard to situation, outlook, access to a water course, or the like, as enhance the pleasantness or desirability of an estate for purposes of residence, or contribute to the pleasure and enjoyment of the occupants, rather than to their indispensable needs*] · Annehmlichkeit *f*

convenience clause, termination for convenience (of the government) clause · Vertragsbeend(ig)ungsklausel *f* [*(Beschaffungs)Vertrag mit einer Regierung*]

convenience commodities, convenience goods [*Those consumers' goods which the customer usually purchases frequently, immediately, and with the minimum of effort*] · Güter *npl* des täglichen Bedarfs, Waren *fpl* des täglichen Bedarfs

convenience store · Ergänzungsbedarfladen *m*

convenient · gelegen

convention · Verfassungsbrauch *m*, ungeschriebenes Verfassungsrecht *n*, verfassungsrechtliche Gewohnheitsrechtsregel *f*

conventional · vereinbarungsgemäß

conventional · rechtsgeschäftlich

conventional loan · Darleh(e)n *n* ohne staatliche Garantie zum Zwecke der Finanzierung bestehender Gebäude [*USA*]

conventional mortgage, common law mortgage, legal mortgage [*In the USA, "conventional mortgage" means a mortgage that is not insured by the Federal Housing Administration or guaranteed by the Veterans Administration*] · Verkehrshypothek *f*, gewöhnliche Hypothek [*Der Gläubiger erteilt über sein Pfandrecht als Urkunde einen vom Grundbuchamt ausgestellten Hypothekenbrief*]

(conventional) penalty, contract penalty, penalty for breach of contract, penalty for nonperformance of contract · Konventionalstrafe *f*, Vertragsstrafe

conventional project [*Low-rent public housing project developed by a local housing authority, as distinguished from a turnkey project*] · nicht schlüsselfertiges Bauvorhaben *n*

conventional value, declared value, official value · Wert *m* für Zollzwecke deklariert

conventions of the constitution · konstitutionelles Herkommen *n* [*englische Verfassung*]

convergence in probability, stochastic convergence · stochastische Konvergenz *f*

conversion · unbefugte Aneignung *f*, (diebische) Aneignung, unerlaubte Vermögensverwendung, eigennützige Verwendung fremden Gutes

conversion · Konvertierung *f*

conversion → (building) conversion

conversion coefficient · Umrechnungskoeffizient *m*

conversion factor, factor of conversion · Umrechnungsfaktor *m*

conversion figure · Umrechnungsziffer *f*

conversion markup, alteration markup, markup for conversion, markup for alteration · Umbauzuschlag *m*

conversion number · Umrechnungszahl *f*

conversion of debt, debt conversion · Umschuldung *f*

Conversion Office for German External Debts · Konversionskasse *f* für Deutsche Auslandsschulden

conversion of stock, stock conversion · Konvertierung *f* einer Anleihe durch Herabsetzung des Zinsfußes

conversion of title, title conversion · (Rechts)Titelumwandlung *f*

conversion value [*Value created by changing from one state, character, form, or use to another*] · Umwandlungswert *m*

to convert · konvertieren

to convert, to alter · umbauen

converted · konvertiert

converted, altered · umgebaut

converted [*Changed from one state, character, form, or use to another*] · umgewandelt

converted dwelling unit, altered dwelling unit, altered housing unit, converted housing unit, altered living unit, converted living unit, altered apartment, converted apartment (US); altered dwelling, converted dwelling, altered tenement, converted tenement, altered residence, converted residence · Umbauwohnung *f*, umgebaute Wohnung

convertibility · Umwandelbarkeit *f*

convertibility · Umbaubarkeit *f*

convertibility · Konvertierbarkeit *f*

convertible · umwandelbar

convertible, alterable · umbaubar

convertible · konvertierbar

convertible debenture [*Great Britain*]; convertible corporate bond [*USA*] [*Such debentures may, at the option of the bearer, be exchanged for a definite number of shares within a stated period of time*] · Wandelschuldverschreibung *f*, Wandelobligation *f* [*private Kapitalgesellschaft*]

converting, altering · Umbauen *n*

to convey, to transfer voluntarily · freiwillig übertragen

conveyance, voluntary transfer · freiwillige Übertragung *f*

conveyance, assurance · dingliche Übertragung *f*, Übertragung eines dinglichen Rechtes

conveyance [*Obgleich diese Benennung im engeren Sinne nur einen „entgeltlichen dinglichen Vertrag" bezeichnet, wird sie vielfach ganz allgemein für jeden dinglichen Vertrag im Sinne des deutschen Rechts gebraucht. So bestimmt beispielsweise der § 2 der Conveyancing Act von 1881 (44 and 45 Vict. c. 41), daß unter „conveyance" verstanden werden solle:* "assignment, appointment, lease, settlement, or other assurance, and covenant to surrender, made by deed, on a sale mortgage, demise, or settlement of any property, or on any other dealing with or for any property"] · dinglicher Vertrag *m* [*Ein unmittelbar auf Begründung, Übertragung oder Belastung eines dinglichen Rechts gerichteter Vertrag, ein familienrechtlicher Vertrag und ein erbrechtlicher Vertrag. Solche Verträge sind nach englischem Recht keine „contracts". Für den deutschen Begriff „dinglicher Vertrag" kennt das englische Recht eine Reihe von Benennungen, je nachdem es sich um eine entgeltliche oder unentgeltliche dingliche Rechtshandlung oder um die Neubegründung eines dinglichen Rechts oder um die Übertragung eines schon bestehenden dinglichen Rechts handelt*]

conveyance clause, voluntary transfer clause · freiwillige Übertragungsklausel *f*

conveyance law, land conveyance law, law of conveyances (of land), law of land conveyances, law of voluntary transfer, voluntary transfer law · freiwilliges Übertragungsrecht *n*

conveyance (of land), voluntary transfer (of land), voluntary land transfer, land conveyance · freiwillige Übertragung (von Land), freiwillige Landübertragung, freiwillige Bodenübertragung

conveyance (of (real) estate), conveyance of (real) property, conveyance of realty, conveyance of land(s), voluntary transfer of (real) estate, voluntary transfer of (real) property, voluntary transfer of realty · Grund(stücks)übertragung *f*, Liegenschaftsübertragung, Immobilienübertragung

conveyance parcels, parcels of conveyance [*The technical term for the description of the property dealt with by a conveyance*] · Grund(stücks)beschreibung *f*

conveyancer, land barrister, conveyancing barrister, (real) property barrister, (real) estate barrister, realty barrister · Grundstücksspezialist *m*, Grundstücksadvokat

conveyancer, conveyancing party · freiwillige Übertragende, freiwillige Übertragungspartei *f*

conveyancing, transferring voluntarily · freiwilliges Übertragen *n*

conveyancing party, conveyancer · freiwillig Übertragende, freiwillige Übertragungspartei *f*

conveyancing practice, voluntary transfer practice · freiwilliges Übertragungswesen *n*

conveyed, transferred, turned over, attorned · übertragen

conveyed, voluntarily transferred · freiwillig übertragen

conveyed · aufgelassen

conveyed to mortmain, amortized, amortised, held in mortmain, (ab)alienated in mortmain · veräußert an die tote Hand

conveying to mortmain, (ab)alienating in mortmain, amortizing, admortizing, amortising · Veräußern *n* an die tote Hand

to convey to mortmain, to amortize, to amortise, to (ab)alienate in mortmain · veräußern an die tote Hand

conviction [*It is where a person is found guilty of an offence*] · Verurteilung *f*

conviction · Polizeibuße *f*

conviction · Ordnungsstrafspruch *m*, Strafurteil *n*

convict prison, penitentiary(-house) · Zuchthaus *n*

to convince, to assure [*To make (a person) sure of something*] · überzeugen

convincing evidence, convincing proof · schlagender Beweis *m*

convocation · Kirchenparlament *n*, Synode *f*, geistliches Parlament

convocation · gesetzgebende Körperschaft f der Universität Oxford

convolution · Faltung f [*Statistik*]

co-obligor → co-debtor

co-operating, operating on the same subject, concurrent · zusammenarbeitend

co-operation, mutuality · genossenschaftliches Prinzip n

co-operation, co-operative (societies) system · Genossenschaftswesen n

cooperation in examining witnesses in lieu of a commission · Rechtshilfeverkehr m

co-operative → co-operative (society)

cooperative, coöperative, co-operative, mutual · genossenschaftlich, kooperativ

co-operative advertising · Gemeinschaftswerbung f

co-operative agricultural enterprise → co-operative (society) farm

co-operative agriculture, co-operative farming · genossenschaftliche Landwirtschaft

co-operative apartment → co-operative (society) dwelling unit

co-operative bank [*Massachusetts*] → building society

cooperative building and loan association, mutual building and loan association (US); mutual building society, cooperative building society (Brit.) · genossenschaftliche Bausparkasse f, Genossenschaftsbausparkasse

co-operative carelessness, contributory negligence, co-operative negligence, contributory carelessness · Mitfahrlässigkeit f

cooperative chantry · genossenschaftliche (Seelen)Meßstiftung f

cooperative competition · konkurrierende Zusammenarbeit f

co-operative credit → co-operative (society) credit

co-operative dwelling (unit) → co-operative (society) dwelling (unit)

co-operative enterprise → co-operative (society) undertaking

co-operative facility → co-operative (society) facility

co-operative farm → co-operative (society) farm

co-operative farming, co-operative agriculture · genossenschaftliche Landwirtschaft

co-operative game · kooperatives Spiel n

co-operative hous(ebuild)ing → co-operative (society) hous(ebuild)ing

cooperative housing association, hous(ebuild)ing cooperative, benefit housing society, cooperative housing society, benefit housing association · Wohnungsgenossenschaft f [*Fehlbenennungen: (Wohnungs)Baugenossenschaft*] [*Wohnungsunternehmen in der Rechtsform der eingetragenen Genossenschaft, deren Zweck der Bau, die Bewirtschaftung und/oder die Verwaltung von Wohnungen und deren Überlassung zur Nutzung oder zu Eigentum an die Mitglieder ist. Die häufig verwendeten Benennungen „(Wohnungs)Baugenossenschaft" sind begrifflich insofern irreführend, als die deutschen Wohnungsgenossenschaften keine Produktivgenossenschaften (Bauunternehmen) sind; zutreffender ist daher die Benennung „Wohnungsgenossenschaft"*]

co-operative housing estate → co-operative (society) housing estate

co-operative housing practice → co-operative (society) housing practice

cooperative housing society, benefit housing association, cooperative housing cooperative, benefit housing society · Wohnungsgenossenschaft f [*Fehlbenennungen: (Wohnungs)Baugenossenschaft*] [*Wohnungsunternehmen in der Rechtsform der eingetragenen Genossenschaft, deren Zweck der Bau, die Bewirtschaftung und/oder die Verwaltung von Wohnungen und deren Überlassung zur Nutzung oder zu Eigentum an die Mitglieder ist. Die häufig verwendeten Benennungen „(Wohnungs)Baugenossenschaft" sind begrifflich insofern irreführend, als die deutschen Wohnungsgenossenschaften keine Produktivgenossenschaften (Bauunternehmen) sind; zutreffender ist daher die Benennung „Wohnungsgenossenschaft"*]

co-operative housing unit → co-operative (society) dwelling unit

co-operative living unit → co-operative (society) dwelling unit

co-operative movement → co-operative (society) movement

co-operative negligence, contributory carelessness, co-operative carelessness, contributory negligence · Mitfahrlässigkeit f

cooperative savings bank, mutual savings bank [*A bank organized by depositors, whose interest is shown by certificates of deposit, for the purpose of furnishing a safe depository for money of members. It need not be incorporated or under supervision unless state law so requires*] · genossenschaftliche Sparkasse f, kooperative Sparkasse, Sparkasse auf Gegenseitigkeit

co-operative self-help erection of dwellings, co-operative self-help production of dwellings, co-operative self-help hous(e)build)ing · genossenschaftliche Eigenhilfe-Wohnungserstellung *f*, genossenschaftliche Eigenhilfe-Wohnungsproduktion, genossenschaftlicher Eigenhilfe-Wohnungsbau

co-operative (societies) system, co-operation · Genossenschaftswesen *n*

co-operative (society) [*A business enterprise owned and operated by voluntary association of persons or organizations*] · Genossenschaft *f*

co-operative (society) agricultural enterprise, co-operative (society) farm · genossenschaftlicher Agrarbetrieb *m*, landwirtschaftlicher Genossenschaftsbetrieb, genossenschaftlicher Landwirtschaftsbetrieb

co-operative (society) credit · Genossenschaftskredit *m*

co-operative (society) dwelling unit, co-operative (society) housing unit, co-operative (society) living unit, co-operative (society) apartment (US); co-operative (society) dwelling · Genossenschaftswohnung *f*

co-operative (society) enterprise, co-operative (society) undertaking · Genossenschaftsunternehmen *n*, Genossenschaftsunternehmung *f*

co-operative (society) facility · genossenschaftliche Einrichtung *f*, Genossenschaftseinrichtung

co-operative (society) farm, co-operative (society) agricultural enterprise · genossenschaftlicher Agrarbetrieb *m*, landwirtschaftlicher Genossenschaftsbetrieb, genossenschaftlicher Landwirtschaftsbetrieb

co-operative (society) hous(e)build)ing · genossenschaftlicher Wohn(ungs)bau *m*, Genossenschaftswohn(ungs)bau

co-operative (society) housing estate · Genossenschaftssied(e)lung *f*

co-operative (society) housing · Genossenschaftswohnungen *f pl*

co-operative (society) housing practice [*Housing in which different persons, usually stockholders in a co-operation, hold title to the property*] · Genossenschaftswohnungswesen, Genossenschaftswohnungswirtschaft *f*

co-operative (society) housing programme; co-operative (society) housing program (US) · Genossenschaftswohnungsprogramm *n*

co-operative (society) movement · Genossenschaftsbewegung *f*

co-operative (society) undertaking, co-operative (society) enterprise · Genossenschaftsunternehmen *n*, Genossenschaftsunternehmung *f*

co-operative system → co-operation

co-operative task · Gemeinschaftsaufgabe *f*

co-operative wholesale society · Einkaufsgenossenschaft *f* [*von Konsumgenossenschaften*]

co-operator · Genossenschaftsmitglied *n*, Genossenschaftler *m*

co-ordinate, equal, of the same rank · gleichgestellt, gleichrangig

co-ordinate (mapping) method · Koordinatenmethode *f*

co-ordinating planning, co-ordination planning, co-ordinative planning · Koordinierungsplanung *f*, Koordinationsplanung

co-ordinating unit, co-ordinative unit, co-ordination unit · Koordinierungseinheit *f*, Koordinationseinheit

co-ordination duty, co-ordinative duty, duty to co-ordinate, duty of co-ordination · Koordinationspflicht *f*, Koordinierungspflicht

coordination of planning, planning coordination · Planungskoordination *f*

co-ordination task, co-ordinating task, task to co-ordinate, co-ordinative task · Koordinationsaufgabe *f*, Koordinierungsaufgabe

co-ordinative planning, co-ordinating planning, co-ordination planning · Koordinierungsplanung *f*, Koordinationsplanung

co-owner, co-proprietor, part-owner, part-proprietor, fellow-owner, fellow-proprietor · Anteileigentümer *m*, Miteigentümer, (Bruch)Teileigentümer

co-owner antichresis, co-proprietor antichresis, co-owner Welsh mortgage, co-proprietor Welsh mortgage · Bruchteileigentümerantichrese *f*, Bruchteileigentümernutzpfandrecht *n*, Miteigentümerantichrese, Miteigentümernutzpfandrecht

co-owner mortgage · Miteigentümergrundpfandrecht *n* mit Gläubigersachherrschaft in Form einer bedingten Eigentumsübertragung

co-ownership (of property) → collective property

co-owners of a real estate, co-owners of a (real) property, co-owners of a realty, co-owners of an estate · gemeinsame Eigentümer *m pl* eines Rechts an einem Grundstück

co-owner Welsh mortgage, co-proprietor Welsh mortgage, co-owner antichresis,

(co)parcenary — copyhold (tenement)

co-proprietor antichresis · Bruchteileigentümerantichrese f, Bruchteileigentümernutzpfandrecht n, Miteigentümerantichrese, Miteigentümernutzpfandrecht

(co)parcenary → (estate in) (co)parcenary

(co)parcener → co-heir

coparticeps [*In old English law*] → co-heir

co-partnership · Teilhaberschaft f

(co)partnership [*"(Co)Partnership" ist das Verhältnis zwischen in Gewinnabsicht ein Unternehmen betreibenden Personen (the relation which subsists between persons carrying on a "business with a view to profit"). Soweit das "business with a view to profit" ein Handelsgewerbe ist, entspricht "(co)partnership" ungefähr der deutschen offenen Handelsgesellschaft. Da aber nach § 45 des Partnership Act von 1980 "business" weitgehendst "every trade occupation, or profession" umfaßt, ist unter "(co)partnership" eine Gesellschaft zu verstehen deren Zweck auf den Betrieb eines Gewerbes unter gemeinschaftlicher Firma gerichtet ist, und deren Mitglieder den Gesellschaftsgläubigern gegenüber unbeschränkt haften*] · offene Handelsgesellschaft f, offene Erwerbsgesellschaft, OHG

co-perception, joint perception · Mitwahrnehmung f

copihold → copyhold

copiholder, tenant (holding) by copy of court roll, bond tenant, copyholder · Hintersasse m, Schriftsasse, Laßbesitzer, Besitzer eines Schriftsassenleh(e)ns, Zinsbauer, Zins(bauernguts)pächter, unfreier bäuerlicher Pächter

copihold inclusure and tithe commission, land commissioners for England, copyhold inclusure and tithe commission · Zehnt- und Einfriedungskommission f

copihold land, land held by copy of court roll, land held by copi of court roll, copyhold land · Hintersassenland n, Regalland, Schriftsassenland, Schriftgutland

co-plaintiff, joint plaintiff · Mitkläger m

co-ploughing of the waste (Brit.); co-plowing of the waste (US); arable-pastoral system [*An agricultural system in which the land is divided into arable and pasture, the arable going to grass as soon as it is exhausted and the pasture then being ploughed up in its stead*] · Feldgraswirtschaft f; Koppelwirtschaft [*Schleswig-Holstein*]; Egartenwirtschaft [*In süddeutschen Gebirgsgegenden*]

co-possession, joint possession · Mitbesitz(stand) m

co-possessor, compossessor; compossessioner [*obsolete*] · Mitbesitzer m

coppice; sub-boscus [*Latin*]; woody undergrowth, underwood, copse · Niederwald m, Holzung f, Unterholz n

co-promisee, co-debtee, fellow creditor, fellow promisee, fellow debtee, joint creditor, joint promisee, joint debtee, co-creditor · Mitgläubiger m, Mitversprechensempfänger, Gesamtgläubiger, Gesamtversprechensempfänger

co-promisor → co-debtor

co-property → collective property

co-proprietor, part-owner, part-proprietor, fellow-owner, fellow-proprietor, co-owner · Anteileigentümer m, Miteigentümer, (Bruch)Teileigentümer

co-proprietorship → collective property

co-proprietor Welsh mortgage, co-owner antichresis, co-proprietor antichresis, co-owner Welsh mortgage · Bruchteileigentümerantichrese f, Bruchteileigentümernutzpfandrecht n, Miteigentümerantichrese, Miteigentümernutzpfandrecht

copse, coppice; sub-boscus [*Latin*]; woody undergrowth, underwood · Niederwald m, Holzung f, Unterholz n

Coptic law · koptisches Recht n

co-purchaser, co-buyer, joint purchaser, joint buyer · Mitkäufer m

copy · Inserattextblock m

copyholder → copiholder

copyhold inclusure and tithe commission, copihold inclusure and tithe commission, land commissioners for England · Zehnt- und Einfriedungskommission f

copyhold land, copihold land, land held by copy of court roll, land held by copi of court roll · Hintersassenland n, Regalland, Schriftsassenland, Schriftgutland

copyhold (tenement), copihold (tenement), copyhold tenure, copihold tenure, (common) ville(i)nage, villein tenure, villein tenement, villain tenement, villain tenure, servile tenure, servile tenement, serf tenure, serf tenement, unfree (feodal) tenement, non-free (feodal) tenement, non-free fee (tenure), unfree fee (tenure), non-free fief, unfree fief, villain tenancy, villein tenancy, unfree tenancy, non-free tenancy, non-free (feodal) tenure, unfree (feodal) tenure; feudum censiticum, feodum censiticum, feudum censuale, feodum censuale, feudum persionarium, census feudalis [*Latin*] [*Tenure of (land(ed)) property proved by a written transcript or record in the roll of a manorial court. Abolished in 1922*] · Hintersassengut n, Hintersassenleh(e)n n, Schriftsassenleh(e)n, Schriftsassengut, Hörigenleh(e)n, Hörigengut, Leibeigenschaftsleh(e)n, Leibeigenschaftsgut, lassitisches (Bauern)-

Leh(e)n, lassitisches (Bauern)Gut, unfreies Leh(e)n, unfreies Gut, Zinsleh(e)n, Zinsgut

copyhold tenure by custom of ancient demesne; dominicum antiquum, antiquum dominicum, vetus patrimonium domini [*Latin*]; customary freehold, ancient demesne [*Such land(s) as were entered by William I., in Doomesdaybook, under the title "De Terra Regis"; and which were held later by a species of copyhold tenure*] · altes Krongut(leh(e)n) *n*

copyhold (tenure) by custom of the manor · Schriftsassenleh(e)n *n* nach Herrensitz-Gewohnheitsrecht

copying clerk · Kanzlist *m*, Schreiber *m* [*Im Staatsdienst und öffentlichen Dienst*]

copy of court roll · Hofesrollenabschrift *f*, Abschrift aus der Hofesrolle

copy of the court · Liste *f* der gutshörigen Bauern

copy original, duplicate original [*e.g. if the authenticity of a carbon copy is fully conceded*] · Duplikatoriginal *n*

copy research · Werbetextforschung *f*

copyright · Urheberrecht *n*

copyright in designs · Musterschutz *m*

core city → metropolitan city

core crystal, hard core, crystal of the core · harter Kern *m*, Kern im Kern [*Stadt*]

core-fringe gradient · Kern-Rand-Gefälle *n*, Kern-Rand-Gegensatz *m*

core land · Kernbereich *m* [*Im planerischen Sinn*]

core location, core site · Kernlage *f*, Kernstandort *m*

core of (a) community, communal core, community core · Gemeindekern *m*, Ortskern

core of the city, core of the town, urban core, town core, city core · Stadtkern *m* [*im physiognomischen Sinn*]

core of village, village core · Dorfkern *m*

core-satellite regional plan, multiple centers plan, satellite cities greenbelt plan · Plan *m* der neben der zentral in der Stadtregion gelegenen Kernstadt die Herausbildung mehrerer Großstädte zwischen 500 000 und 1 Mio. Einwohnern innerhalb derselben im Abstand von etwa 50 km oder mehr vom Zentrum der Kernstadt anstrebt

co-responsibility · Mitverantwortung *f*

core structure · Kernaufbau *m*, Kerngefüge *n*, Kernstruktur *f*, Kernzusammensetzung *f*

core town → metropolitan city

core zone · Kerngebiet *n*, MK [*Es dient vorwiegend der Unterbringung von Handelsbetrieben (Geschäften) sowie den zentralen Einrichtungen, aber auch dem Wohnen*]

cornage · Leh(e)n *n* mit Wachepflicht [*Der Leh(e)n(s)mann mußte an der Grenze nach Schottland Wache halten und in sein Horn blasen wenn Feinde nach England eindrangen oder eindringen wollten*]

to corner · (auf)schwänzen, kornern [*Spekulanten zwingen teuer zu kaufen*]

corner · Schwanz *m*, Korner *m* [*Börse*]

corner [*The action of a dealer in a commodity market who has obtained possession of almost the entire supply of a commodity available at a particular time*] · Kornern *n*, Aufschwänzen [*Ware*]

corner influence [*The effect upon the value of a property by virtue of its location on a corner lot*] · Einfluß *m* der Ecklage

corner lot [*A lot abutting upon two or more streets at their intersection*] · Eckflurstück *n*, Eckparzelle *f*, Eck-Katastergrundstück

(corner) mark, (corner) tick, register mark, register tick, registration mark, registration tick · Passermarke *f* [*Kartographie*]

corner plot (of land), corner plot of ground, corner parcel (of land), corner parcel of ground · Eckgrundstück *n*

corner solution · Ecklösung *f*

(corner) tick, register mark, register tick, registration mark, registration tick, (corner) mark · Passermarke *f* [*Kartographie*]

corn-exchange · Getreidebörse *f*

Corn Laws · Korngesetze *n pl* [*in England*]

corn tithe, tithe of corn (Brit.); grain tithe, tithe of grain · Getreidezehnt *m*, Kornzehnt [*altdeutsch: Kornzehent, Kornzehend*]

coroner [*In old English law*]; coronator [*Latin*] · Todesermitt(e)lungsbeamte, Totenschau(richt)er *m*, (kronamtlicher) Leichenbeschauer

Coroners Court, C.C. [*England*] · Feststellungskommission *f* bei Mordsachen

coroner's inquest · Totenschauvornahme *f*

corporalis possessio, civilis possessio [*Latin*] · genießliche Gewere *f*, hebende Gewere, nützliche Gewere, Eigengewere, titellose Gewere, brukerode Gewere, eigentliche Gewere

corporate bond [*A fixed-interest security issued by stock corporations in the USA*]; debenture [*A fixed-interest security issued by British joint-stock com-*

corporate bond holder — corporat(iv)e city 260

panies] · Schuldverschreibung *f*, Obligation *f* [*private Kapitalgesellschaft*]

corporate bond holder, corporate bond bearer [*USA*]; debenture holder, debenture bearer [*Great Britain*] · Schuldverschreibungsinhaber *m*, Obligationsinhaber [*private Kapitalgesellschaft*]

corporate estate → corporat(iv)e estate

corporate farm · landwirtschaftlicher Betrieb *m* in Gesellschaftsbesitz

corporate land → common (land)

corporate planning · Kommunalplanung *f* in bezug auf Verwaltung einer Gemeinde

corporate property → corporat(iv)e property

corporate title · Körperschaftstitel *m*, Korporationstitel

corporate trustee · Treuhänder *m* für Körperschaften, Körperschaftstreuhänder

corporation · (Kapital)Gesellschaft *f*; vereinsähnliche Gemeinschaft; Körperschaft, Korporation *f* [*In den USA ist „corporation" ein Oberbegriff für Personenmehrheiten mit juristischen Persönlichkeiten und umfaßt Kapitalgesellschaften im kontinental-europäischen Sinne, öffentlich-rechtliche Körperschaften und vereinsähnliche Gemeinschaften. „Partnerships" fallen aber nicht unter diesen Begriff*]

corporation aggregate → (private) corporation aggregate

corporation at common law, common law corporation · Körperschaft *f* nach gemeinem Recht, Korporation *f* nach gemeinem Recht

corporation bond, local authority bond [*Great Britain*]; short-dated municipal bond [*USA*] · kurzfristige Kommunalschuldverschreibung *f*, kurzfristige Kommunalobligation *f*

corporation borough [*England*] · Stadt *f* in der die Stadtverordneten das aktive Wahlrecht hatten

corporation by prescription, prescription corporation · Körperschaft *f* durch Vermutung, Korporation *f* durch Vermutung [*Inkorporierung auf Grund einer vermuteten Vollmacht*]

corporation constitution · Körperschaftsverfassung *f*, Korporationsverfassung

corporation embezzlement · aktienrechtliche Veruntreuung *f*, aktienrechtliche Unterschlagung

corporation estate, corporat(iv)e property, corporat(iv)e estate, corporation property · Körperschaftsvermögen *n*, Körperschaftsgut *n*, Korporationsvermögen, Korporationsgut, Körperschaftshabe *f*, Korporationshabe

corporation forest · Körperschaftswald *m*, Korporationswald

(corporation) headquarters · (Firmen)Hauptverwaltung *f*

corporation income tax law · Körperschaftssteuerrecht *n*, Korporationssteuerrecht

corporation income tax statute, corporation income tax law, corporation income tax act · Körperschaftssteuergesetz *n*, Korporationssteuergesetz

corporation interest, corporation right · (subjektives) Körperschaftsrecht *n*, (subjektives) Korporationsrecht

corporation law, law of corporations · (objektives) Körperschaftsrecht *n*, (objektives) Korporationsrecht

corporation of standing, Korporation *f* mit Berufsethos, Körperschaft *f* mit Berufsethos

corporation property, corporation estate, corporat(iv)e property, corporat(iv)e estate · Körperschaftsvermögen *n*, Körperschaftsgut *n*, Korporationsvermögen, Korporationsgut, Körperschaftshabe *f*, Korporationshabe

corporation right, corporation interest · (subjektives) Körperschaftsrecht *n*, (subjektives) Korporationsrecht

corporation's (common) seal · Körperschaftssiegel *n*, körperschaftliches Siegel, Korporationssiegel

corporation sole [*An incorporated series of successive persons*] · Ein-Mann-Körperschaft *f*, Ein-Mann-Korporation *f*, Körperschaft mit Einheit der Person, Korporation mit Einheit der Person

corporation sole at common law · Ein-Mann-Körperschaft *f* nach gemeinem Recht, Ein-Mann-Korporation *f* nach gemeinem Recht, gemeinrechtliche Ein-Mann-Körperschaft, gemeinrechtliche Ein-Mann-Korporation

corporation stock, local authority stock [*Great Britain*]; municipal bond [*USA*] · Kommunalschuldverschreibung *f*, Kommunalobligation *f*

corporat(iv)e act(ion) · Korporationshandlung *f*, Körperschaftshandlung, korporative (Begehungs)Handlung, korporativer (Begehungs)Akt *m*, Korporationsakt, Körperschaftsakt

corporat(iv)e body, (private) corporation aggregate; corpus corporatum [*Latin*]; body corporate [*An incorporated group of coexisting persons*] · Körperschaft *f* mit Personenmehrheit, Korporation *f* mit Personenmehrheit, inkorporierte Körperschaft

corporat(iv)e city, legal city · korporierte Stadt *f* [*USA. Eine Stadt die nach Erreichen einer Mindesteinwohnerzahl, im*

Staate Pennsylvania etwa 10 000 Menschen, im Staate Kansas dagegen bereits ab 1000 Menschen, auf Antrag und durch Beschluß der einzelstaatlichen Regierung eine City Charter verliehen bekommen hat]

corporat(iv)e industry · Korporativindustrie f

corporat(iv)e property, corporat(iv)e estate, corporation property, corporation estate · Körperschaftsvermögen n, Körperschaftsgut n, Korporationsvermögen, Korporationsgut, Körperschaftshabe f, Korporationshabe

corporator [*A member of a corporation aggregate*] · Körperschaftsgenosse m, Korporationsgenosse, Korporator

corporeal, physical, tangible [*Admitting of physical possession*] · physisch, körperlich, stofflich

corporeal asset, physical asset, tangible asset [*Asset for which a value can be established, e.g. real estate, equipment, furniture, inventories*] · stoffliche Aktiva f, körperliche Aktiva, physische Aktiva

corporeal chattel in the possession of the owner, chose in possession · körperlich bewegliche Sache f im Besitz des Eigentümers

corporeal chattel (personal); res corporales, res singula [*Latin*]; corporeal thing, tangible thing, chose, physical thing, thing corporeal [*A thing that affects the senses and may be seen and handled*] · (Einzel)Sache f, körperliches Rechtsobjekt n, materielles Rechtsobjekt, körperliches Ding n, materielles Ding, körperlicher (Rechts)Gegenstand m, materieller (Rechts)Gegenstand [*Ausgenommen lebender menschlicher Körper. Unter den Sachbegriff fallen nicht die Rechte, die Sachgesamtheiten, d. h. Mehrheiten von Sachen, die eine besondere Benennung haben, z. B. Bücherei, Warenlager usw. und die Inbegriffe von Sachen und Rechten, z. B. Erbschaftsvermögen usw. Im Preußischen Allgemeinen Landrecht von 1794 (A.L.R.) ist (Einzel)Sache allerdings alles, was Gegenstand eines Rechtes oder einer Verbindlichkeit sein kann (§ 1. l. 2)*]

corporeal chattel (personal), corporeal personal estate, corporeal personal property, corporeal personal chattel, corporeal personalty · körperliche Fahrnis f, körperliche Fahrhabe f, körperliche Mobilie f

corporeal inheritance, tangible inheritance, corporeal hereditament, tangible hereditament [*These two terms were used in old books. "Tangible" means the same thing as "land"*] · körperliches Erbgut n

corporeal interest, corporeal right · körperliches Recht n

corporeal property, tangible property, choses in possession [*Property that by its nature is susceptible to the senses. Generally, it includes the land, fixed improvements, furnishings, merchandise, and cash*] · körperliches Vermögen n

corporeal right, corporeal interest · körperliches Recht n

corporeal seisin · körperliche Gewere f

corporeal service incident to the tenure · körperlicher Dienst m zusammenhängend mit dem Grundbesitz

corporeal thing, tangible thing, chose, physical thing, thing corporeal, corporeal chattel (personal); res corporales, res singula [*Latin*] [*A thing that affects the senses and may be seen and handled*] · (Einzel)Sache f, körperliches Rechtsobjekt n, materielles Rechtsobjekt, körperliches Ding n, materielles Ding, körperlicher (Rechts)Gegenstand m, materieller (Rechts)Gegenstand [*Ausgenommen lebender menschlicher Körper. Unter den Sachbegriff fallen nicht die Rechte, die Sachgesamtheiten, d. h. Mehrheiten von Sachen, die eine besondere Benennung haben, z. B. Bücherei, Warenlager usw. und die Inbegriffe von Sachen und Rechten, z. B. Erbschaftsvermögen usw. Im Preußischen Allgemeinen Landrecht von 1794 (A.L.R.) ist (Einzel)Sache allerdings alles, was Gegenstand eines Rechtes oder einer Verbindlichkeit sein kann (§ 1. l. 2)*]

corpus · Stamm m, Vermögensstamm

corpus corporatum [*Latin*]; body corporate, corporat(iv)e body, (private) corporation aggregate [*An incorporated group of coexisting persons*] · Körperschaft f mit Personenmehrheit, Korporation f mit Personenmehrheit, inkorporierte Körperschaft

corpus juris civilis, jus civile [*Latin*]; civil law · (objektives) Zivilrecht n, bürgerliches Recht

to correct, to put right, to rectify · verbessern, richtigstellen, korrigieren, berichtigen, (ab)ändern [*Z. B. Fehler oder Irrtum in einer Rechnung*]

correctarius [*Latin*] → ((real) estate) broker

correct cost(s), true cost(s) · Plankosten f, geplante Kosten, planmäßige Kosten [*Die auf dem Planbeschäftigungsgrad basierenden Normkosten mit Konstanz für längere Zeit, deren mengen- als auch wertmäßiger Faktor durch wissenschaftliche Analyse ermittelt wird und volle Maßstäblichkeit in sich trägt. In der Praxis werden Plankosten oft mit Standardkosten gleichgesetzt*]

correction — costing theory

correction, rectification · (Ab)Änderung f, Richtigstellung, Korrektur f, Berichtigung, Verbesserung [z. B. Fehler oder Irrtum in einer Rechnung]

correction for grouping, grouping correction · Gruppierungskorrektur f [Statistik]

correction in the land register, correction in the land registry, correction in the register of land(s), correction in the registry of land(s) · Berichtigung f des Grundbuches, Grundbuchberichtigung

correction notification, correction notice · Berichtigungsanzeige f, Berichtigungsmitteilung f

correction of error(s), rectification of error(s) · Fehlerberichtigung f, Fehlerkorrektur f, Fehlerverbesserung, Fehlerrichtigstellung

correction sheet, rectification sheet · Berichtigungsblatt n, Korrekturblatt, Verbesserungsblatt, Richtigstellungsblatt

correlation attenuation · Korrelationsschwächung f

correlation coefficient, coefficient of correlation · Korrelationskoeffizient m

correlation matrix · Korrelationsmatrix f

correlation ratio · Korrelationsverhältnis n

correlation table · Korrelationstabelle f, Korrelationstafel f

correspondence/mail credit · Postlaufakkreditiv n (zwischen Banken)

corridor → (territorial) corridor

corridor (of cities), strip cities, semicontinuous cities, linear cities, ribbon cities · Städteband n

to corroborate, to strengthen · bekräftigen

corroborating evidence, corroborative evidence, strengthening evidence, corroborating proof, corroborative proof, strengthening proof, confirmatory evidence, confirmatory proof · bekräftigender Beweis m

corrupted person · bestochene Person f

corruptibility · Bestechlichkeit f

corruptible · bestechlich, korrupt [passive Bestechung]

corrupting by bribe(s), bribing · Bestechen n

corrupt practice (in election(s)) · Wahlfälschung f, Wahldelikt n

corrupt practices act, corrupt practices law, corrupt practices statute · Korruptionsgesetz n

corsepresent; mortuarium [Latin]; soulscot [So called in the laws of King Canute]; mortuary · Vermächtnis n an eine Kirche

cosmopolitan, citizen of the world, citizen of the nature · Weltbürger m

cosponsor · Mitförderer m, Mitträger

to cost, to calculate cost(s) · kalkulieren von Kosten

cost → cost(s)

cost accountant → cost(s) accountant

cost allocation → cost(s) allocation

cost analysis → cost(s) analysis

cost awareness → cost(s) consciousness

cost breakdown → cost(s) breakdown

cost consciousness → cost(s) consciousness

cost control → cost(s) control

cost determination → cost(s) determination

cost effectiveness → cost(s) consciousness

costermonger, street trader, barrow-boy · Straßenhändler m

cost estimate → cost(s) estimate

cost finding → cost(s) finding

costing, (cost(s)) accounting, calculation of cost(s), computation of cost(s), cost(s) calculation, cost(s) computation · Kostenrechnung f, Kostenkalkulation f, (Kostenbe)Rechnung, Kostenermitt(e)lung

costing code, (cost(s)) accounting code · (Kosten)Rechnungsordnung f, Kostenkalkulationsordnung, Kostenermitt(e)lungsordnung, Kostenberechnungsordnung

costing method, (cost(s)) accounting method · Kostenrechnungsverfahren n, Kostenrechnungsmethode f

costing ordinance, (cost(s)) accounting ordinance · (Kosten)Rechnungsverordnung f, Kostenkalkulationsverordnung, Kostenberechnungsverordnung, Kostenermitt(e)lungsverordnung

costing pain · Arbeitsleid n [Die Mühe, der man sich unterzieht um eine Verwendung von Kosten zu sichern]

costing system, (cost(s)) accounting system · (Kosten)Rechnungssystem n, Kostenkalkulationssystem, Kostenermitt(e)lungssystem, Kostenberechnungssystem

costing technique, (cost(s)) accounting technique · Kostenrechnungstechnik f

costing theory, (cost(s)) accounting theory · Kostenrechnungstheorie f, Theorie der Kostenrechnung

cost investigation → cost(s) investigation

cost make-up → cost(s) make-up

cost of building (estate) parcel → cost(s) of building (estate) parcel

cost of living allowance, subsistence allowance (Brit.); subsistence, living allowance (US); separating allowance, separation allowance · Auslösung *f,* Trennungsgeld *n,* Trennungsentschädigung [*Ein Arbeitnehmer, der auf einer Baustelle außerhalb des Betriebssitzes arbeitet, erhält eine Auslösung, wenn die tägliche Rückkehr zum Wohnort nicht zumutbar ist*]

cost-of-living index · Lebenshaltungsindex *m*

cost of reproduction less depreciation → cost(s) of reproduction less depreciation

cost overrun → cost(s) overrun

cost-plus fee contract · Selbstkostenerstattungsvertrag *m* mit Zuschlag, Selbstkostenerstattungsvertrag mit Aufschlag

cost-plus-fixed fee contract, fixed fee/ prime cost(s) contract, prime cost plus fixed fee contract [*A contractual arrangement whereby a contractor is paid the prime cost(s) and a fixed fee calculated in relation to the estimated amount of the prime cost*] · Selbstkostenerstattungsvertrag *m* mit begrenztem Zuschlag, Selbstkostenerstattungsvertrag mit begrenztem Aufschlag

cost-plus percentage contract → (prime) cost plus percentage contract

cost-plus pricing → cost(s)-plus pricing

cost reimbursement (type of) contract · Selbstkostenerstattungsvertrag *m* [*Es werden die bei der Vertragsdurchführung entstehenden Kosten ersetzt. Hinsichtlich des Gewinns können vereinbart werden: 1. Ein im voraus bestimmter fester Betrag (cost(s) plus fixed fee); 2. der Gewinn kann entfallen (cost(s) no fee); 3. es wird ein geringerer Teil als die vollen Kosten ersetzt (cost(s) sharing); 4. der Zuschlag wird geschätzt (estimated fee); 5. der Zuschlag ist veränderlich (variable fee); 6. der Zuschlag wird festgestellt (actual fee)*]

cost(s) [*Value when acquired or purchased*] · Anschaffungswert *m*

cost(s) [*Cost is the amount, measured in money, of cash expended or other property transferred, capital stock issued, services performed, or a liability. Incurred, in consideration of goods or services received or to be received*] · Aufwand *m*, Kosten *f* [*Im Gegensatz zur europäischen Literatur wird der Kostenbegriff in den USA kaum je so definiert, daß er nur die betriebsprozeßbedingten Güter- und Leistungsabgänge umfassen würde. Unter ,,cost(s)" sind die mit der Beschaffung von Wirtschaftsgütern aller Art verbundenen Wertabgänge zu verstehen. ,,Cost(s)" deckt sich also mit ,,Aufwand". Kosten im Sinne der Kostenlehre sind also nicht Kosten im Sinne des allgemeinen Sprachgebrauchs; nicht das, was etwas gekostet hat, sind Kosten. Obwohl also das Wort ,,Kosten" in der Kostenlehre erhebliche Mängel besitzt, wird es mit Rücksicht auf den Sprachgebrauch der Praxis benutzt. Kosten = Aufwand sind die in der Kostenrechnung anzusetzenden Werte der für Leistungen verzehrten Güter*]

cost(s)/output curve · Kosten/Ausbringungskurve *f*

cost(s) accountant · Kalkulator *m,* Kostenrechner

(cost(s)) accounting, calculation of cost(s), computation of cost(s), cost(s) calculation, cost(s) computation, costing · Kostenrechnung *f,* Kostenkalkulation *f,* (Kostenbe)Rechnung, Kostenermitt(e)lung

(cost(s)) accounting code, costing code · (Kosten)Rechnungsordnung *f,* Kostenkalkulationsordnung, Kostenermitt(e)lungsordnung, Kostenberechnungsordnung

(cost(s)) accounting method, costing method · Kostenrechnungsverfahren *n,* Kostenrechnungsmethode *f*

(cost(s)) accounting ordinance, costing ordinance · (Kosten)Rechnungsverordnung *f,* Kostenkalkulationsverordnung, Kostenberechnungsverordnung, Kostenermitt(e)lungsverordnung

(cost(s)) accounting system, costing system · (Kosten)Rechnungssystem *n,* Kostenkalkulationssystem, Kostenermitt(e)lungssystem, Kostenberechnungssystem

(cost(s)) accounting technique, costing technique · Kostenrechnungstechnik *f*

(cost(s)) accounting theory, costing theory · Kostenrechnungstheorie *f,* Theorie der Kostenrechnung

cost(s) advisor, cost(s) adviser, cost(s) consultant · Kostenberater *m*

cost(s) allocation · Kostenzuweisung *f*

cost(s) amount, amount of cost(s) · Kostenbetrag *m*

cost(s) analysis · Kostenanalyse *f,* Kostenuntersuchung

cost(s) approach, approach of cost(s) · Kostenansatz *m*

cost(s) as between party and party · absolut notwendige Gerichtskosten *f*

cost(s) awareness, cost(s) effectiveness, cost(s) consciousness [*The awareness of cost(s) during the process of decision-taking and subsequently, to ensure that cost(s) are not incurred unnecessarily and that maximum value is obtained from those cost(s) which are incurred*] · Kostenbewußtsein *n*

cost(s)-bearing duty · Kostentragungspflicht *f*

cost(s)-benefit analysis, benefit-cost(s) analysis, CBA [*A systematic comparison between the cost(s) of carrying out a service or activity and the value of that service or activity, quantified as far as possible, all costs and benefits (direct and indirect, financial and social) being taken into account*] · Kosten-Nutzen-Analyse *f*, Nutzen-Kosten-Analyse, Kosten-Nutzen-Untersuchung *f*, Nutzen-Kosten-Untersuchung, NKA

cost(s)-benefit ratio, benefit-cost(s) ratio · Kosten-Nutzen-Verhältnis *n*, Nutzen-Kosten-Verhältnis, NKA-Verhältnis

cost(s) bookkeeping [*USA*] · Monismus *m*, monistisches System *n* [*Rechnungswesen*]

cost(s)-book mining company · Bergbaugesellschaft *f* nach dem Kuxensystem

cost(s) bracket, bracket of cost(s) · Kostenspanne *f*

cost(s) breakdown, cost(s) make-up, cost(s) subdivision, breakdown of cost(s), make-up of cost(s), subdivision of cost(s) · Kosten(auf)gliederung *f*, Kostenaufschlüsselung

cost(s) calculation, cost(s) computation, costing, (cost(s)) accounting, calculation of cost(s), computation of cost(s) · Kostenrechnung *f*, Kostenkalkulation *f*, (Kostenbe)Rechnung, Kostenermitt(e)lung

cost(s) centre (Brit.); cost(s) center (US) · Organisationseinheit *f* eines divisional organisierten Unternehmens

cost(s) change, cost(s) variation · Kostenänderung *f*, Kostenabänderung

cost(s) checking, checking of cost(s) · Kostenfeststellung *f*, Kostennachkalkulation *f*, Kostenkontrolle *f*

cost(s) classification · Kostenklassifizierung *f*

cost(s) code, cost(s) types · Baukostenplan *m*, BKP, Kostenarten *fpl*

cost(s) comparison, comparison of cost(s) · Kostenvergleich *m*

cost(s) component · Kostenbestandteil *m*

cost(s) computation, costing, (cost(s)) accounting, calculation of cost(s), computation of cost(s), cost(s) calculation · Kostenrechnung *f*, Kostenkalkulation *f*, (Kostenbe)Rechnung, Kostenermitt(e)lung

cost(s) conscious [*Evidencing awareness of the need for keeping cost(s) under a specified ceiling or at the lowest possible level consistent with the performance of a specified task; endeavouring to incur a minimum of cost(s)*] · kostenbewußt

cost(s) consciousness, cost(s) awareness, cost(s) effectiveness [*The awareness of cost(s) during the process of decision-taking and subsequently, to ensure that cost(s) are not incurred unnecessarily and that maximum value is obtained from those cost(s) which are incurred*] · Kostenbewußtsein *n*

cost(s) consultancy · Kostenberatung *f*

cost(s) consultant, cost(s) advisor, cost(s) adviser · Kostenberater *m*

cost(s) control · Kostenüberwachung *f*

cost(s) cover, cover for cost(s) · Kostendeckung *f*

cost(s)-curve · Kostenkurve *f*

cost(s) decision · Kostenentscheid(ung) *m*, (*f*)

cost(s) depletion · Absetzung *f* nach Maßgabe der aufgewandten Kosten

cost(s) determination, determination of cost(s) · Kostenanschlag *m* [*Möglichst genaue Ermitt(e)lung der Kosten*]

cost(s) distribution · Kostenverteilung *f*

cost(s) distribution sheet · Betriebsabrechnungsbogen *m*

cost(s) division, division of cost(s), cost(s) splitting, splitting (up) of cost(s) · Kostenspaltung *f*, Kostentrennung

cost(s) effectiveness, cost(s) consciousness, cost(s) awareness [*The awareness of cost(s) during the process of decision-taking and subsequently, to ensure that cost(s) are not incurred unnecessarily and that maximum value is obtained from those cost(s) which are incurred*] · Kostenbewußtsein *n*

cost(s)-effectiveness analysis · Kosten-Wirksamkeitsanalyse *f*, KWA

cost(s) element, element of cost(s) · Kostenelement *n*

cost-sensitive activity · kostenabhängiger Produktionszweig *m*

cost(s) estimate, estimate of cost(s) · Kostenvoranschlag *m* [*Er ist die Vorstufe für einen Kostenanschlag*]

cost(s) estimating → (construction) cost(s) estimating

cost(s) (e)valuation · Kostenauswertung *f*

cost(s) finding · Kostenfestsetzung *f*, Kostenbestimmung, Kostenerfassung

cost(s) for clearance of (the) (building) land, (building) land clearance cost(s) · (Bauland)Freilegungskosten *f*

cost(s) for remedial work(s) · Baumängelbeseitigungskosten *f*, (Sach-)Mängelbeseitigungskosten, Nachbesserungskosten

cost(s) for the carcass, cost(s) for the fabric; cost(s) for the shell [*Canada*] · Rohbaukosten *f*

cost(s) function · Kostenfunktion *f*

cost(s) funding · Kostenzuordnung *f* auf die Betriebsleistung

cost(s) group · Kostengruppe *f*

cost(s) incidental to salaries · Gehaltsnebenkosten *fpl*

cost(s) index, index of cost(s) · Kostenindex *m*

cost(s) intensive · kostenintensiv

cost(s) investigation, cost(s) study · Kostenstudie *f*, Kostenuntersuchung *f*

cost(s)-kiting · Kostentreiberei *f*

cost(s) law · Kostenrecht *n*

cost(s) limit · Kostengrenze *f*

cost(s) make-up, cost(s) subdivision, breakdown of cost(s), make-up of cost(s), subdivision of cost(s), cost(s) breakdown · Kosten(auf)gliederung *f*, Kostenaufschlüsselung

cost(s) matrix · Kostenmatrix *f*

cost(s) minimization · Kostenminimierung *f*

cost(s) negotiation · Kostenverhandlung *f*

cost(s) of acquisition, acquisition cost(s) · Beschaffungskosten *f*, Erwerbskosten

cost(s) of bidding → cost(s) of tendering

cost(s) of building (estate) parcel · Baugrundstückskosten *f*

cost(s) of depreciation, depreciation cost(s) · Abschreibungskosten *f*

cost(s) of equivalent reinstatement · Kosten *f* für gleichwertige Wiederherstellung

cost(s) of idleness, cost(s) of unused capacity, idleness cost(s) · Leerkosten *f*, ungedeckte Fixkosten, ungedeckte Festkosten, nicht ausgenutzter Teil *m* der Fixkosten, Kosten der ungenutzten Kapazität [*Die anteiligen Fixkosten der nicht genutzten Kapazität einer Kostenstelle. Nach Plaut sind „Leerkosten" in der Grenzplankostenrechnung nicht nur die ungedeckten Fixkosten, sondern der gesamte Block der Fixkosten*]

cost(s) of (land) improvement, (land) improvement cost(s) · (Land)Erschließungskosten *f*

cost(s) of living, living cost(s) · Lebenshaltungskosten *f*

cost(s) of management, management cost(s) · Bewirtschaftungskosten *f*

cost(s) of money, interest on loan (capital), loan (capital) interest · Darleh(e)nszinsen *f*

cost(s) of opening up, opening-up cost(s) · Aufschließungskosten *f*

cost(s) of production, production cost(s) · Erzeugungskosten *f*, Herstellungskosten, Produktionskosten, Fertigungskosten

cost(s) of registration, cost(s) of recordation, cost(s) of recording · Eintragungskosten *f*

cost(s) of tendering, cost(s) of bidding, tendering cost(s), bidding cost(s) [*The cost(s) to the contractor of preparing his tender, including any amended tender necessitated by bona fide alterations in the bill of quantities and plans*] · Bieterkosten *f*, Blankettkosten, Bietungskosten, Angebots(abgabe)kosten

cost(s) of unused capacity, idleness cost(s), cost(s) of idleness · Leerkosten *f*, ungedeckte Fixkosten, ungedeckte Festkosten, nicht ausgenutzter Teil *m* der Fixkosten, Kosten der ungenutzten Kapazität [*Die anteiligen Fixkosten der nicht genutzten Kapazität einer Kostenstelle. Nach Plaut sind „Leerkosten" in der Grenzplankostenrechnung nicht nur die ungedeckten Fixkosten, sondern der gesamte Block der Fixkosten*]

cost(s) overrun, overrun of cost(s) · Kostenüberschreitung *f*

cost(s)-plus pricing · Preiskalkulation *f* mit Gewinnzuschlag auf Herstellungskosten

cost(s) policy · Kostenpolitik *f*

cost(s) price · Einstandspreis *m*, (Selbst)Kostenpreis

cost(s) push · Kostendruck *m*

cost(s) rate · Kostensatz *m*

cost(s) research · Kostenforschung *f*

cost(s)-revenue relation(ship) · Kosten-Einkünfte-Verhältnis *n*

cost(s) shifting · Kostenverschiebung *f*

cost(s)-space · Kostenraum *m*

cost(s) splitting, splitting (up) of cost(s), cost(s) division, division of cost(s) · Kostenspaltung *f*, Kostentrennung

cost(s) standard (value) · Kostenrichtwert *m*

cost(s) statement, statement of cost(s) · Kostenaufstellung *f*

cost(s) study — counsel(l)ing activity

cost(s) study, cost(s) investigation · Kostenstudie *f*, Kostenuntersuchung *f*

cost(s) subdivision, breakdown of cost(s), make-up of cost(s), subdivision of cost(s), cost(s) breakdown, cost(s) make-up · Kosten(auf)gliederung *f*, Kostenaufschlüsselung

cost(s) survey · Kostenübersicht *f*

cost(s) survey · Kostenenquête *f*

cost(s) theory, theory of cost(s) · Theorie *f* der Kostenabhängigkeiten; Kostentheorie [*Fehlbenennung*]

cost(s) to open up (for inspection) [*works covered up*] · Bloßlegungskosten *f*, Freimachungskosten, Freilegungskosten

cost(s) trend · Kostenentwick(e)lung *f*

cost study → cost(s) study

cost(s)-type · Kostenart *f*

cost(s) types, cost(s) code · Baukostenplan *m*, BKP, Kostenarten *fpl*

cost subdivision → cost(s) subdivision

cost(s) underrun, underrun of cost(s) · Kostenunterschreitung *f*

cost(s) value theory, theory of cost(s) value · Kostenwerttheorie *f*

cost(s) variance, variance of cost(s) · Kostenabweichung *f*

cost(s) variation, cost(s) change · Kostenänderung *f*, Kostenabänderung

cost(s)-volume-profit analysis · Kostenanalyse *f* über die Beziehung zwischen Kosten und Produktionsanlage(n) und Gewinn

cost(s) yardstick · Kostenmaßstab *m*

cost-value · Aufwandswert *m*

coterminous with → co(n)terminous with

cot for sheep, sheep-cot, sheep-pen, fold, pen for sheep · (Schaf)Pferch *m*

cotman, cottager, cotter, cosset, cot dweller; cottier, peasant-tenant [*Ireland*]; cotset(h)us [*Latin*] · (freier) Tagelöhner *m*, besitzloser Tagelöhner, (Leer)Häusler, Kotter, Kätner, Kossat

co-trustee, joint trustee · Mittreuhänder *m*, Mittreuhandverwalter

cottage · Kate *f*

cottage (Brit.); one-family house, single-family house, one-dwelling house, single-dwelling house · Einfamilienhaus *n*, Einwohnungshaus

cottage-flat (Brit.), two-family house, two-dwelling family house · Zweifamilienhaus *n*, Zweiwohnungshaus, Doppelfamilienhaus, Doppelwohnungshaus

cottage garden (Brit.); single-family house garden, one-family house garden · Einfamilienhausgarten *m*

cottage industry, financed work, sweated industry, domestic industry, domestic system, home(-work) industry · Hausindustrie *f*, Verlagssystem *n*, Heim(arbeits)industrie, Verlag *m*

cottar → cotman

cotton belt · Baumwollgürtel *m*

cotton grower · Baumwollpflanzer *m*

council, panel · Rat *m*

council → (community) council

council-board system · Magistratsverfassung *f*

council clerk, clerk of the council · Kanzleivorsteher *m* [*Beamter einer Distriktstadt in England*]

council elementary school, provided school · Gemeindeschule *f*

council-mayor-director system · Ratsverfassung *f*

council member, councilman, councillor · Gemeinderat(smitglied) *m*, *(n)*, (Gemeinde)Verordnete, Rat(smitglied), Gemeindevertreter

council of condo(minium) owners (US); council of private flat owners (Brit.) · Verwaltungsbeirat *m* [*Er ist ein Bindeglied zwischen der Gesamtheit der Wohnungseigentümer und der Verwaltung*]

council of judges, panel of judges · Richterkollegium *n*

council of social agencies, welfare council · Planungsgemeinschaft *f* des sozialen Dienstes, soziale Planungsgemeinschaft

Council of State Governments · Arbeitsgemeinschaft *f* der (Einzel)Staaten, Rat *m* der (Einzel)Staaten [*USA*]

council of tenants · Mieterbeirat *m*

council system; municipal charter (US) · Gemeindeverfassung *f*, (Gemeinde-)Hauptsatzung, Ortsverfassung, Ortshauptsatzung, Kommunalverfassung, Kommunalhauptsatzung

to counsel, to advise, to consult, to give advice · beraten

counsel, consultancy, consultation, advice · Beratung *f*

counsel · Justitiar *m*

counsel(l)ing, consulting, advising · Beraten *n*

counsel(l)ing activity, advising activity, consulting activity, consultative activity, advisory activity · beratende Tätigkeit *f*, Beratungstätigkeit

counsel(l)ing a legally-aided party, granting (free) legal aid · Armenvertretung *f* [*(Rechts)Anwalt*]

counsel(l)ing committee, advisory committee, consultative committee, consulting committee, advising committee · beratender Ausschuß *m*, Beratungsausschuß

counsel(l)ing duty, consulting duty, duty to consult, consultative duty, advising duty, advisory duty · Beratungspflicht *f*

counsel(l)or-at-law, legal counsel(l)or, legal counsel · Rechtsberater *m*, Rechtskonsulent

counsel's brief · schriftlich erteilte Instruktion *f* an den (Rechts)Anwalt für die Verhandlung

to count · zählen

to count, to declare, to recite, to state a case [*To narrate the facts constituting a plaintiff's cause of action*] · vorbringen einer Klage

count, census · Zählung *f*

count [*In civil procedure, the declaration in a real action*] · Realklageschrift *f*

count · ausländischer Graf *m*

count [*In a personal action, if the plaintiff included several causes of action in the same declaration, each section of the declaration was called a count*] · Klageschriftsatz *m*

count · Klageabschnitt *m*

count district, census tract, census subcounty, census district, count tract · (statistischer) Zählbezirk *m*

counter bid → counter offer

counter-cause, counter-plea, counter-(law)suit, counter (court) action, cross (court) action, cross cause, cross (law-) suit, cross plea · Gegenklage *f*, Widerklage

to counterclaim · gegenfordern, stellen einer Gegenforderung

counterclaim [*A claim presented by a defendant in opposition to or deduction from the claim of the plaintiff*] · Gegenanspruch *m*, Gegenforderung *f*

counter (court) action, cross (court) action, cross cause, cross (law)suit, cross plea, counter-cause, counter-plea, counter-(law)suit · Gegenklage *f*, Widerklage

countercurrent method · Gegenstromverfahren *n*

counter-evidence, counter-proof, evidence to the contrary, proof to the contrary, contradictory evidence, contradictory proof, rebutting testimony, disproof · Gegenbeweis *m*, gegenteiliger Beweis

to counterfeit, to make (something) false, to forge · (ver)fälschen, nachahmen, imitieren

counterfeit, not genuine, false · gefälscht, imitiert, nachgemacht, falsch

counterfeiting [*The making of a false or spurious thing to resemble a genuine thing with the intent to defraud*] · (Ver)Fälschung *f*, Nachahmung, Imitation *f*

counterfeit money · Falschgeld *n*

counterfoil · Kontrollkupon *m*

counter-inflation act, counter-inflation law, counter-inflation statute · Antiinflationsgesetz *n*, Inflationsbekämpfungsgesetz

counter-inflation measure · antiinflationäre Maßnahme *f*, inflationsbekämpfende Maßnahme

counter-(law)suit, counter (court) action, cross (court) action, cross cause, cross (law)suit, cross plea, counter-cause, counter-plea · Gegenklage *f*, Widerklage

counter-notice, counter-notification · Gegenmitteilung *f*, Gegenanzeige *f*, Gegenbenachrichtigung

counter-obligation · Gegenverpflichtung *f*

counterpart · Gegenstück *n*

counterpart-fund · Gegenwertfonds *m*, Gegenwertmittel

counter-promise, dependant promise, conditional promise, dependent promise, reciprocal promise, mutual promise, double promise · gegenseitiges Versprechen *n*

counter-proof, evidence to the contrary, proof to the contrary, contradictory evidence, contradictory proof, rebutting testimony, disproof, counter-evidence · Gegenbeweis *m*, gegenteiliger Beweis

counterproposal · Gegenvorschlag *m*

counter-seal · Gegensiegel *n*

to countersign [*To sign (a document) opposite to, alongside of, or in addition to, another signature; to add one's signature to a document already signed by another for authentication or confirmation*] · gegenzeichnen, gegenunterschreiben

countersignature [*A signature added to another person's signature on a document, for authentication or confirmation*] · Gegenunterschrift *f*, Gegenzeichnung *f*

countersigning · Gegenzeichnen *n*, Gegenunterschreiben

counter trade, barter-trade · Kompensationsgeschäft *n*

counterurbanization — country land in possession

counterurbanization, deurbanization · Entstädterung f

to counterurbanize, to deurbanize · entstädtern

counterurbanized, deurbanized · entstädtert

counterurbanized zone, deurbanized zone · entstädterte Zone f

countervailing credit, back-to-back credit · Ausgleichskredit m, Kompensationskredit

countervailing duty [*A duty or surtax imposed on imported goods in order to place them on an equal footing with articles of the same class manufactured at home, and liable to excise or other inland revenue duties*] · Ausgleichszoll m, Antidumpingzoll, Kompensationszoll

countervalue, equivalent value · Gegenwert m

counter will, common will, reciprocal will, mutual will, double will · gegenseitiges Testament n

countess · Gräfin f

count of buildings, building count, building census, census of buildings · Gebäudezählung f

count of job sites and employed people, census of job sites and employed people · Arbeitsstätten- und Beschäftigtenzählung f, AZ

count of population, population census, population count, census of population · Bevölkerungszählung f, Volkszählung

count reliability, census reliability · Zählungsverläßlichkeit f

country area, country territory, rural area, rural territory · ländliches Gebiet n, Landgebiet [*Phänomenologisch in der Regel ein Gebiet in welchem Bodennutzung und (An)Sied(e)lung vorherrschend von der Land- und Forstwirtschaft bestimmt werden. Eine genaue Begriffsabgrenzung ist aber besonders bei dem in den Randgebieten der Verdichtungsräume vorhandenen Kontinuum kaum möglich; ebenso ist wegen der verschiedenen sied(e)lungsgeschichtlichen und natürlichen Gegebenheiten eine innergebietliche Unterscheidung sehr schwierig*]

country authority, rural authority · ländliche Behörde f, Landbehörde

country bank · Provinzbank f [*Bank in Großbritannien außerhalb Londons*]

country belt, rural belt · ländlicher Gürtel m

country city, rural town, rural city, country town · Landstadt f

country-clearing [*Dem Londoner country-clearing entsprach die „Scheckaustauschstelle" in Berlin*] · Abrechnung f von Schecks in London auf englische Provinzbanken soweit diese eines der 10 Mitglieder des clearing-house als "clearing-agents" ernannt haben

country composition → rural composition

country-cross-movement map, CCM map · militärgeographische Karte f mit Darstellung der Geländebefahrbarkeit

country cultural life, rural cultural life · ländliches Kulturleben n

country development, rural development · ländliche Entwick(e)lung f

country estate in possession → country land in possession

country estate landscape · Adelslandschaft f

country estate market → rural (real) estate market

country family, rural family · Landfamilie f

country form of settlement, country settlement form, rural settlement form, rural form of settlement · ländliche (An)Sied(e)lungsform f, Land(an)sied(e)lungsform

country gentleman [*A man of some wealth who lives on a country estate*] · Landherr m

country geography, rural geography · ländliche Geographie f

country home → country(side) home

country homestead, rural homestead · ländliche Heimstätte f

country house · Landhaus n

country house possession, rural house possession · ländlicher Hausbesitz m

country house possessor, rural house possessor · ländlicher Hausbesitzer m

country improvement, rural improvement · ländliche Erschließung f

country improvement planning, rural improvement planning · ländliche Erschließungsplanung f

country-inn · Landwirtshaus n

country land, rural land · ländlicher Bereich m [*Im planerischen Sinne*]

country land, rural land [*Sometimes, by local usage also called "landed estate" and "landed property" as distinguished from (real) estate situated in a city*] · ländlicher Grund m, ländlicher Boden m, ländliches Land n, Landgrund, Landboden

country land in possession, rural (real) estate in possession, country (real) estate in possession, rural (real) property in possession, rural realty in possession, country (real) property in possession, country realty in possession, rural land in possession · ländlicher Grund(stücks)besitz *m*, ländlicher Bodenbesitz, ländlicher Landbesitz

country land law, rural land law · ländliches Landrecht *n*, ländliches Bodenrecht

country land market → rural (real) estate market

country landowner · Land-Grund(stücks)besitzer *m*, Grund-(stücks)besitzer auf dem Lande

country land possessor → rural land possessor

country land price, country realty price, rural (real) estate price, rural (real) property price, rural land price, rural realty price, country (real) estate price, country (real) property price · ländlicher Grundstückspreis *m*, ländlicher Bodenpreis, ländlicher Landpreis

country land reform, rural land reform · ländliche Bodenreform *f*, ländliche Landreform

country landscape, rural landscape · ländliche Landschaft *f* [*im Gegensatz zur „Stadtlandschaft"*]

country land(s) use, use of rural land(s), use of country land(s), rural land(s) use · ländliche Landnutzung *f*, ländliche Bodennutzung, ländliche Flächennutzung

country land(s) use density, rural land(s) use density · ländliche Landnutzungsdichte *f*, ländliche Bodennutzungsdichte, ländliche Flächennutzungsdichte

country land(s) use plan, rural land(s) use plan · Landflächennutzungsplan *m*

country land(s) use planning, rural land(s) use planning · Landflächennutzungsplanung *f*

country (lands) use zoning, rural zoning, country zoning, rural (lands) use zoning · ländliche Baunutzung *f*, ländliche bauliche Nutzung

country life, rural life · Landleben *n*, ländliches Leben

country local government, rural local government · ländliche Gemeindeverwaltung *f*

country locality, rural locality · ländlicher Ort *m*

country location, rural site, rural location, country site · ländlicher Standort *m*

countryman · Landbewohner *m*

country of destination, destination country · Bestimmungsland *n*

country officer, country official, rural officer, rural official · Landbeamter *m*

country outdoor recreation, rural outdoor recreation · ländliche Außenerholung *f*

country parish, rural parish · ländliches Kirchspiel *n*

country park · Naherholungsgebiet *n*

country place of work, country place of employment, rural place of work, rural place of employment · ländlicher Arbeitsort *m*

country planner, rural planner · Landplaner *m* [*Im Gegensatz zum Stadtplaner, die Benennung „Landesplaner" sollte hier nicht verwendet werden um Verwechselungen mit einem Landesplaner eines Landes der Bundesrepublik Deutschland zu vermeiden*]

country planning (advisory) panel, country planning (advisory) council, rural planning (advisory) panel, rural planning (advisory) council · Landplanungsbeirat *m*, ländlicher Planungsbeirat

country planning assistance, country planning sponsoring, country planning promotion, rural planning assistance, rural planning sponsoring, rural planning promotion · ländliche Planungsförderung *f*

country planning committee, rural planning committee · Landplanungsausschuß *m*, ländlicher Planungsausschuß

country planning law, rural planning law · Landplanungsrecht *n*, ländliches Planungsrecht

country planning law, country planning act, country planning statute, rural planning law, rural planning act, rural planning statute · Landplanungsgesetz *n*, ländliches Planungsgesetz

country planning office, rural planning office · Landplanungsstelle *f*, ländliche Planungsstelle

country planning organization, rural planning organization · Landplanungsorganisation *f*, ländliche Planungsorganisation

country planning practice, rural planning practice · Landplanungswesen *n*, ländliches Planungswesen

country planning promotion → country planning assistance

country planning science, rural planning science · Landplanungswissenschaft *f*, ländliche Planungswissenschaft

country planning sponsoring → country planning assistance

country plot, rural plot · ländliches Katastergrundstück *n*, ländliches Grundstück (im katastertechnischen Sinne), ländliches Kartengrundstück, ländliches Flurstück, ländliche (Kataster)Parzelle *f*, Landgrundstück (im katasterkechni-

country population — country zone

schen Sinne), Landkatastergrundstück, Land-Kartengrundstück, Land(kataster)parzelle, Landflurstück

country population, rural population · ländliche Bevölkerung *f*, Landbevölkerung *f*, Landvolk *n*

country poverty, rural poverty · Armut *f* auf dem Lande, Landarmut *f*

country property market → rural (real) estate market

country rate, rural rate · ländliche Steuer *f*

country (real) estate, country (real) property, country realty · Land-Grund-(stücks)besitz *m*, Grund(stücks)besitz auf dem Lande

country (real) estate in possession → country land in possession

country (real) estate market → rural (real) estate market

country (real) estate price, country (real) property price, country land price, country realty price, rural (real) estate price, rural (real) property price, rural land price, rural realty price · ländlicher Grundstückspreis *m*, ländlicher Bodenpreis, ländlicher Landpreis

country (real) property market → rural (real) estate market

country (real) property price, country land price, country realty price, rural (real) estate price, rural (real) property price, rural land price, rural realty price, country (real) estate price · ländlicher Grundstückspreis *m*, ländlicher Bodenpreis, ländlicher Landpreis

country realty in possession → country land in possession

country realty market → rural (real) estate market

country realty price, rural (real) estate price, rural (real) property price, rural land price, rural realty price, country (real) estate price, country (real) property price, country land price · ländlicher Grundstückspreis *m*, ländlicher Bodenpreis, ländlicher Landpreis

country region, rural region · ländlicher Raum *m*, Landraum, ländliche Region *f*, Landregion

country regional planning, rural regional planning · ländliche Regionalplanung *f*

country-residence, country-seat · Landsitz *m*

country residential place, rural residential place · ländlicher Wohnplatz *m*

country seat, hall · Schloß *n*, Herrensitz *m*

country setting, rural surrounding, rural setting, country surrounding · ländliche Umgebung *f*

country settlement, rural settlement · ländliche (An)Sied(e)lung *f*, Land(an)sied(e)lung

country settlement form, rural settlement form, rural form of settlement, country form of settlement · ländliche (An)Sied(e)lungsform *f*, Land(an)sied(e)lungsform

country settlement geography, geography of rural settlements, geography of country settlements, rural settlement geography · ländliche (An)Sied(e)lungsgeographie *f*

countryside, tract of land, land tract, country tract, tract of country [*It has a kind of natural unity*] · Landtrakt *m*, Landstrich *m*

country(side) home, rural home · Landeigenheim *n*, Landeigenhaus *n*

country(side) recreation · außerstädtische Erholung *f*, Erholung auf dem Lande

country site, country location, rural site, rural location · ländlicher Standort *m*

country social system, rural social system · ländliches Sozialsystem *n*

country sociology, rural sociology · ländliche Soziologie *f*

country structure → rural structure

country surrounding, country setting, rural surrounding, rural setting · ländliche Umgebung *f*

country territory, rural area, rural territory, country area · ländliches Gebiet *n*, Landgebiet [*Phänomenologisch in der Regel ein Gebiet in welchem Bodennutzung und (An)Sied(e)lung vorherrschend von der Land- und Forstwirtschaft bestimmt werden. Eine genaue Begriffsabgrenzung ist aber besonders bei den in den Randgebieten der Verdichtungsräume vorhandenen Kontinuum kaum möglich; ebenso ist wegen der verschiedenen sied(e)lungsgeschichtlichen und natürlichen Gegebenheiten eine innergebietliche Unterscheidung sehr schwierig*]

country town [*A town which forms the centre of a rural district*] · Kreisstadt *f*

country town, country city, rural town, rural city · Landstadt *f*

country tract, tract of country, countryside, tract of land, land tract [*It has a kind of natural unity*] · Landtrakt *m*, Landstrich *m*

country trade, rural trade · Landgewerbe *n*, ländliches Gewerbe

country use zoning → country zoning

country woman · Landbewohnerin *f*

country zone, rural zone · ländliche Zone *f*

country zoning, rural (land) use zoning, country (land) use zoning, rural zoning · ländliche Baunutzung f, ländliche bauliche Nutzung

count tract, count district, census tract, census sub-county, census district · (statistischer) Zählbezirk m

county, shire; scyran [*Saxon*] · Grafschaft f

county (US); waste of the manor, (manorial) waste [*obsolete*]; common (land), corporate land, allmend, common field, commonable land, commonable field, public land, community land, communal land, mark · Al(l)mend(e) f, Allmeind f, Allmid f, Allmein(i) f, Allmen f, Allmig f, Allmand(e) f, Allmat f, All(ge)meinde f, Allmandgut n, Allmente f, (Feld)Mark f, Gemarkung f, Kommunalboden m, Gemeindeboden, Bürgerland n, bürgerliches Nutzungsland, Gemeindeland, Gemeinheit(sland) f, (n), Kommunalland, unverteilter Gemeindegrund m, ländliches Gemeingut, Gemein(de)anger m, Gemeindeimmobilien fpl; Korporationsland [*Schweiz*]

county [*USA*] [*A political subdivision of a state empowered by the state to have jurisdiction over certain transactions and activities within its area*] · Bezirk m [*Diese ,,counties" greifen teilweise stark in die Verwaltung der ,,cities" ein, weil, von einigen Ausnahmen abgesehen, ,,Kreisfreiheit" in den USA unbekannt ist*]

county administration · Grafschaftsverwaltung f

county alderman · Grafschaftsälteste m

county authority · Grafschaftsbehörde f

county boundary · Grafschaftsgrenze f

county bridge · Grafschaftsbrücke f

county business · Verwaltungsgeschäft n eines Friedensrichters

county council [*A council which conducts the affairs of a county; in England, since the Local Government Act of 1888, the representative governing body, consisting of aldermen and councillors, of an administrative county; in Canada, a feature of the local government of longer standing*] · Grafschaftsrat m, Grafschaftsausschuß m

county council association · Grafschaftsratvereinigung f

county court · Gericht n innerhalb eines Selbstverwaltungsbezirkes [*in den USA*]

county court, shiremote, C. [*An assembly of the county or the shire at the assizes, etc.*] · Grafschaftsgericht n für mittlere Zivilsachen, Zivilgericht einer Grafschaft

county court judge · Grafschaftsrichter m

county court judge (Brit.) · Amtsrichter m [*Richter an einem örtlichen erstinstanzlichen Zivilgericht*]

county district · Verwaltungsbereich m einer Sanitätsbehörde [*England*]

county election · Grafschaftswahl f

county elector, county voter · Grafschaftswähler m

county gaol (Brit.); county jail, county prison · Grafschaftsgefängnis n

county hall · Grafschaftsgerichtsgebäude m

county hall rate, shire hall rate · Steuer f zur baulichen Verbesserung und den Bau von Grafschaftsgerichtsgebäuden

county jail, county prison; county gaol (Brit.) · Grafschaftsgefängnis n

county map · Grafschaftskarte f

county member · Grafschafts-Parlamentsmitglied n

County of London · Grafschaft f London

county palatin(at)e, palatin(at)e county · Pfalzgrafschaft f

county planning department · Grafschaftsplanungsabteilung f

county planning officer, county planning official · Grafschaftsplanungsbeamte m

county police · Grafschaftspolizei f, grafschaftliche Polizei

county police rate · Grafschaftspolizeisteuer f

county prison; county gaol (Brit.); county jail · Grafschaftsgefängnis n

county rate · Grafschaftssteuer f

county rate act, county rate statute, county rate law · Grafschaftssteuergesetz n

county session, quarter session · Vierteljahresversammlung f der Grafschaftsrichter, Quartalversammlung der Grafschaftsrichter, (Grafschafts)Quartalsitzung

county session(s) court, court of (quarter) session(s), court of county session(s), quarter session(s) court · Vierteljahresgericht n, Quartalgericht

county stock · Grafschafts-Nominalanleihe f, Grafschafts-Nominalrententitel m, Grafschafts-Stammvermögen n

county taxation · Grafschaftsbesteuerung f

county town [*The chief town of a county, formerly called "shire-town"*] · Grafschaftshauptstadt f

county treasure, public stock of the county · Grafschaftskasse f

county treasurer · Grafschaftseinnehmer m [*englisches Grundsteuersystem*]

county voter, county elector · Grafschaftswähler m

coupling constraint — (court) action for specific performance 272

coupling constraint · Koppelungsbegrenzung f [nach Hägerstrand]

coupon → (dividend) coupon

coupon bond [USA]; debenture to bearer, debenture to holder [Great Britain] · Inhaberschuldverschreibung f, Inhaberobligation f [private Kapitalgesellschaft]

coupon certificate · Einlegeschein m mit Coupon, Couponeinlegeschein [kapitalistische Bausparkasse]

coupon rate (of interest) · Nominalzinssatz m

course of business · Geschäftsverlauf m

course of fold, fold course, faldsoke; faldsoca [Saxon law]; falda libera, cursus faldae [Latin]; frank fold, free fold [The privilege of setting up and moving about in a field a fold, for the purpose of manuring the ground, which several lords anciently reserved to themselves in any fields within their manors, not only with their own but their tenants sheep] · (Schaf)Pferchrecht n

course of instruction → (approved) course of instruction

course of law, law course · Rechtsweg m

court · Hauptversammlung f [Universität]

court; forum [Latin] · Gericht n

court above · nächst(höher)e Instanz f

(court) action, (law-) suit, plea, cause; writ [In old English law, "writ" is used as equivalent to "action", hence writs are sometimes divided into real, personal, and mixed. It is not uncommon to call a proceeding in a common law court an action(-at-law), and one in an equity court a (law-)suit, but this is not a necessary distinction] · (Gerichts)Klage f

(court) action at common law, cause at common law, (law)suit at common law, plea at common law, common law (court) action, common law (law)suit, common law cause, common law plea · Klage f nach gemeinem Recht, gemeinrechtliche Klage

(court) action de bonis asportatis, (law)suit de bonis asportatis, cause de bonis asportatis, plea de bonis asportatis · Klage f wegen rechtswidriger (Besitz)Entziehung einer beweglichen Sache

(court) action for an account, (law)suit for an account, cause for an account, plea for an account · Abrechnungsklage f, Klage auf Abrechnung [Billigkeitsrecht]

(court) action for breach of contract, (law)suit for breach of contract, cause for breach of contract, plea for breach of contract · Vertragsbruchklage f

(court) action for delivery, (law)suit for delivery, cause for delivery, plea for delivery · Nichtlieferungsklage f, Klage wegen Nichtlieferung

(court) action for dissolution, cause for dissolution, plea for dissolution, (law)suit for dissolution · Auflösungsklage f

(court) action for exemption from liability, (law)suit for exemption from liability, cause for exemption from liability, plea for exemption from liability · negative Feststellungsklage f

(court) action for instrusion → (court) action for trespass

(court) action for money had and received, (law)suit for money had and received, cause for money had and received, plea for money had and received · Geldrückerstattungsklage f

(court) action for payment, (law)suit for payment, cause for payment, plea for payment · Zahlungsklage f

(court) action for recovery, cause for recovery, plea for recovery, (law)suit for recovery, cause for reimbursement, cause for restitution, cause for refunding, plea for reimbursement, plea for refunding, plea for restitution, (law)suit for reimbursement, (law)suit for refunding, (law)suit for restitution, (court) action for reimbursement, (court) action for restitution, (court) action for refunding · Abgeltungsklage f, Ersetzungsklage, Erstattungsklage, Vergütungsklage

(court) action for redemption, cause for redemption, (law)suit for redemption, plea for redemption · Klage f auf Freigabe von Sicherheiten, Sicherheit(en)freigabeklage

(court) action for reimbursement, (court) action for restitution, (court) action for refunding, (court) action for recovery, cause for recovery, plea for recovery, (law)suit for recovery, cause for reimbursement, cause for restitution, cause for refunding, plea for reimbursement, plea for refunding, plea for restitution, (law)suit for reimbursement, (law)suit for refunding, (law)suit for restitution · Abgeltungsklage f, Ersetzungsklage, Erstattungsklage, Vergütungsklage

(court) action for removal, (law)suit for removal, cause for removal, plea for removal · Beseitigungsklage f

(court) action for specific performance, (law)suit for specific performance, (court) action for completion of contract, (law)suit for completion of contract, cause for completion of contract, plea for completion of contract, cause for specific performance, plea for specific performance · (Vertrags)Erfüllungsklage f, Naturalerfüllungsklage

(court) action for the recovery of land, (law)suit for the recorvery of land, cause for the recovery of land, plea for the recovery of land [*The mixed action at common law to recover the possession of land (which is real), and damages and cost(s) for the wrongful withholding of the land (which are personal)*] · (Immobilien)Besitzklage f, Liegenschaftsbesitzklage, Immobiliarbesitzklage, Grund(stücks)besitzklage, eigentliche Besitzklage, Klage aus (widerrechtlicher) Besitzentziehung, (D)Ejektionsklage, possessorische Klage in bezug auf Immobilien, Delogierungsklage [*Als uneigentliche Besitzklage kann diese Klage auch als Räumungsklage des Vermieters gegen den Mieter angewendet werden*]

(court) action for (the tort of) deceit, (law)suit for (the tort of) deceit, cause for (the tort of) deceit, plea for (the tort of) deceit · Betrugsklage f

(court) action for tort, (court) action in tort, (law)suit for tort, (law)suit in tort, cause for tort, cause in tort, plea for tort, plea in tort · Deliktklage f

(court) action for trespass, (court) action for intrusion, cause for trespass, cause for intrusion, (law)suit for trespass, (law)suit for intrusion, plea for trespass, plea for intrusion · (Besitz)Verletzungsklage f wegen Eindringen, (Besitz)Störungsklage wegen Eindringen, (Besitz)Beeinträchtigungsklage wegen Eindringen

(court) action for unjust detention, (court) action for unjust retention, (court) action for unjust detainment, (court) action for unjust detainer, plea for unjust detention, plea for unjust retention, plea for unjust detainment, plea for unjust detainer, cause for unjust detention, cause for unjust retention, cause for unjust detainment, cause for unjust detainer, (law)suit for unjust detention, (law)suit for unjust retention, (law)suit for unjust detainment, (law)suit for unjust detainer, (court) action of detinue, plea of detinue, (law)suit of detinue, cause of detinue · Klage f wegen ungerechtfertigter Vorenthaltung, Klage wegen ungerechtfertigter Zurück(be)haltung, Klage wegen ungerechtfertigter Einbehaltung, Forderungsklage wegen ungerechtfertigter Retention, Klage wegen ungerechtfertigtem Einbehalt, Klage wegen ungerechtfertigtem Vorenthalt

(court) action founded on contract, (law)suit founded on contract, cause founded on contract, plea founded on contract · Entschädigungsklage f ex contractu vel quasi, Schadenersatzklage ex contractu vel quasi, Forderungsklage ex contractu vel quasi, Personenklage ex contractu vel quasi; Personalklage ex contractu vel quasi [*Fehlbenennung*]

(court) action founded on tort, (law)suit founded on tort, cause founded on tort, plea founded on tort · Entschädigungsklage f im engeren Sinne, Schadenersatzklage im engeren Sinne, Forderungsklage im engeren Sinne, Personenklage im engeren Sinne; Personalklage im engeren Sinne [*Fehlbenennung*]

(court) action in error, (law)suit in error, cause in error, plea in error · Nichtigkeitsklage f, Revisionsklage

(court) action in personam → personal (court) action

(court) action in tort, (law)suit for tort, (law)suit in tort, cause for tort, cause in tort, plea for tort, plea in tort, (court) action for tort · Deliktklage f

(court) action of account, cause of account, (law)suit of account, plea of account · Klage f auf Rechnungslegung, Rechnungslegungsklage

(court) action of advowson, (law)suit of patronage, (law)suit of advowson, cause of patronage, cause of advowson, plea of patronage, plea of advowson, (court) action of patronage · Patronats(recht)klage f

(court) action of assumpsit, (law)suit of assumpsit, cause of assumpsit, (plea of) assumpsit · Nichteinhaltungsklage f, Nichterfüllungsklage [*Schadenersatzklage wegen schuldhafter Nichterfüllung eines formlosen mündlich oder schriftlich gegebenem Versprechen*]

(court) action of debt, cause of debt, (law)suit of debt, plea of debt · Schuld(en)klage f [*Zur Einklagung einer Schuld*]

(court) action of deceit, (law)suit of deceit, cause of deceit, plea of deceit · Klage f wegen Täuschung, Täuschungsklage

(court) action of detinue → (court) action for unjust detention

(court) action of devastation, (law)suit of estrepement, (law)suit of devastation, cause of estrepement, cause of devastation, plea of estrepement, plea of devastation, (court) action of estrepement · Verwüstungsklage f

(court) action of equity, cause of equity, (law)suit of equity, equitable plea, plea of equity, equitable (court) action, equitable (law)suit, equitable cause · Billigkeitsklage f, Billigkeitsrechtklage, Klage nach Billigkeit(srecht)

(court) action of estrepement, (court) action of devastation, (law)suit of estrepement, (law-)suit of devastation, cause of estrepement, cause of devastation, plea of estrepement, plea of devastation · Verwüstungsklage f

(court) action of eviction — courthouse

(court) action of eviction, (law)suit of eviction, cause of eviction, plea of eviction · Grund(stücks)besitzklage *f* wegen Grund(stücks)besitzentziehung

(court) action of injunction, (law)suit of injunction, cause of injunction, plea of injunction · Verfügungsklage *f*

(court) action of mistake, (law)suit of mistake, cause of mistake, plea of mistake · Irrtumsklage *f*

(court) action of patronage, (court) action of advowson, (law)suit of patronage, (law)suit of advowson, cause of patronage, cause of advowson, plea of patronage, plea of advowson · Patronats(recht)klage *f*

(court) action of possessory right, (law)suit of possessory right, cause of possessory right, plea of possessory right · Besitzrechtklage *f*

(court) action of replevin, (law)suit of replevin, cause of replevin, plea of replevin · Klage *f* auf Wiedererlangung einer beweglichen Sache und Schadenersatz bei unzulässiger Selbstpfändung, Klage auf Rückgabe einer selbstgepfändeten Sache

(court) action of transumpt, plea of transumpt cause of transumpt, (law)suit of transumpt, transumpt [*Scots law. An action brought for the purpose of obtaining transumpt(s)*] · Klage *f* auf Schriftstückabschrift

(court) action of trover (and conversion), cause of trover (and conversion), (law)suit of trover (and conversion), plea of trover (and conversion) · Bereicherungsklage *f*, Schatzfundklage, Deliktsklage wegen Unterschlagung, Unterschlagungsklage [*Klage auf Schadenersatz für die Besitzentziehung von beweglichen Sachen (= goods)*]

(court) action on the case, cause on the case, plea on the case, (law)suit on the case · tatsächlich angestellte Klage *f*

(court) action on trespass, (law)suit on trespass, plea on trespass, cause on trespass · Rechtsverletzungsklage *f*, Klage wegen Rechtsverletzung

(court) action per se, cause per se, (law)suit per se, plea per se · Klage *f* die nicht von einem Schadensnachweis abhängt

(court) action personal, (law)suit personal, cause personal, plea personal, personal (court) action, personal plea, personal (law)suit, personal cause; personal writ [*In old English law*] · Entschädigungsklage *f*, Schadenersatzklage, Forderungsklage, Personenklage [*Fehlbenennung: Personalklage*]

(court) action to quiet title, (law)suit to quiet title, cause to quiet title, plea to quiet title · Klage *f* nach § 256 ZPO, Feststellungsklage

court-appointed counsel, assigned counsel · Pflichtanwalt *m*

court-appointed defender, assigned defender · Pflichtverteidiger *m*

(court-)appointed guardianship, guardianship by appointment (of court), guardianship by judicial appointment · gerichtlich ernannte Vormundschaft *f*, gerichtliche Vormundschaft

(court-)appointed guardian, guardian by judicial appointment, guardian by appointment (of court) · gerichtlich ernannter Vormund *m*, gerichtlicher Vormund

court-baron (proper), court of (the) manor, freeholders' court baron; curia legalis [*Latin*]; manor(ial) court, feudal court, feodal court, feudary court, court of the baron, court of the lord, baron(-bailie) court [*The court of justice held by a baron or his steward in the presence of the freehold tenants of the manor. In modern times lawyers have distinguished between court-baron which was the court of the freehold tenants, and the customary court(-baron) which was the court of the copyhold tenants. The early history of this distinction is obscure*] · Feudalgericht *n*, grundherrliches Gericht, Leh(e)n(s)herrengericht, Hofgericht, Patrimonialgericht, feudales Gutsgericht

court brief · Pflichtmandat *n*

court Christian, consistory court; commissary court [*Scotland*]; spiritual court, ecclesiastical court, consistorial court, church-court · geistliches Gericht *n*, Kirchengericht, Konsistorialgericht, kirchliches Gericht [*Die schottischen „ecclesiastic(al) courts" haben nur eine Jurisdiktion über Fragen der Doktrin, des Gottesdienstes, der Sakramente und der Disziplin der Geistlichen*]

court clerk, clerk (of (the) court) · Gerichtsschreiber *m*, Aktuar, Gerichtskanzlist

court cost(s) · Gerichtskosten *f*

court day; lage day, lagh day [*Latin*]; doomsday [*In old English law*]; dies juridicus [*Latin*]; juridic(al) day, law day · Gerichtstag *m*

(court) department, panel · Senat *m*, Gerichtsabteilung *f*

court fee · Gerichtsgebühr *f*

court files · Gerichtsakten *f pl*

court for matters in public administration, tribunal for matters in public administration, administrative court, administrative tribunal · Verwaltungsgericht *n*, VG

court-hand · gotische Kanzleischrift *f*

courthouse · Gerichtsgebäude *n*

courthouse square — court of probate

courthouse square · Gerichtsgebäudeplatz *m*

court in banc, sittings in banc [*England*] · Gerichtssitzung *f* von mindestens zwei Mitgliedern des Hohen Justizhofes, gesessenes Gericht *n* [*Im Gegensatz zum Einzelrichter bei den Assisen*]

court-leet · Ortspolizeigericht *n* [*Im mittelalterlichen England*]

court messenger · Gerichtsbote *m*

court not of record · nichtprotokollierendes Gericht *n*

Court of Aldermen · Magistratskollegium *n*, Ältestenrat *m* [*In London durch die lebenslänglichen Vorsteher (aldermen) der Stadtbezirke (wards) gebildet*]

court of appeal · Oberlandesgericht *n*

court of appeal → court of (error and) appeal

court of appeal in chancery · Appellationsgericht *n* für das Billigkeitsrecht, Berufungsgericht für das Billigkeitsrecht

Court of Appeals of New York · höchster Gerichtshof *m* des Staates New York, oberster Gerichtshof des Staates New York

court of arbitration, arbitral court, arbitration court, arbitration tribunal · Spruchkammer *f*, Spruchsenat *m*, Schiedsgericht *n*

Court of Arches, Arches-Court · geistlicher Appellhof *m* unter dem Erzbischof von Canterbury

court of assistants · Zunftgericht *n*, Zunftrat *m*

court of assize, assise court, court of assise, assize court [*England*] · Geschworenengericht *n* [*Es wird in jeder Grafschaft periodisch von den Richtern des High Court und sonstigen beauftragten Personen mindestens zweimal jährlich abgehalten*]

court of bankruptcy, bankruptcy court · Konkursgericht *n*

court of cassation · Kassationsgericht *n*, Kassationshof *m*

court of certiorari · Abberufungsgericht *n*

(Court of) Chancery → Chancery Division

Court of Claims · Gericht *n* für Klagen gegen die Union [*USA*]

(court of) common council, local council, (community) council · Kommunalrat *m*, Ortsrat, (Gemeinde)Rat, (Gemeinde)Vertretung *f*, Kommunalvertretung, Ortsvertretung, Vertretungskörperschaft *f*

Court of Common Council · Londoner Stadtrat *m*

court of common law, common law court · Gericht *n* des gemeinen Rechts, gemeinrechtliches Gericht

court of conscience, police court, P., petty court, summary court, registrar's court, court of summary jurisdiction, court of request, registrary's court · Bagatellgericht *n*, Friedensgericht für kleine Straf- und Zivilsachen, Polizeigericht, Ortsgericht für gering(fügig)e Schuldklagen [*in England*]

court of county session(s), quarter session(s) court, county session(s) court, court of (quarter) session(s) · Vierteljahresgericht *n*, Quartalgericht

court of criminal appeal, C.C.A. · Appellationsgericht *n* für Kriminalsachen, Appellationsgericht für Strafsachen, Berufungsgericht für Kriminalsachen, Berufungsgericht für Strafsachen [*In England*]

court of equity, equity court · Billigkeitsgericht *n*

court of (error and) appeal, court of review (of errors and appeal), appellate court, appeals court, C.A. · Appellationsgericht *n* für Zivilsachen, Berufungsgericht für Zivilsachen

Court of Errors of Connecticut · oberster Gerichtshof *m* des Staates Connecticut, höchster Gerichtshof des Staates Connecticut

Court of Exchequer, Exchequer of Pleas · Schatzkammergericht *n*, Schatzamtgericht [*England*]

court officer, court official · Gerichtsbeamte *m*

court of first instance · erstinstanzliches Gericht *n*

Court of General Surveyor of the lands belonging to the Crown · Generalinspektion *f* der Domänen [*England*]

court of honour (Brit.); court of honor (US) · Ehrengericht *n*

court of justice, law court, court of law [*As opposed to a "court of equity"*] · rechtsprechendes Gericht *n*

Court of Justiciary · höchstes Strafgericht *n* in Schottland

court of last resort [*A court from which there is no appeal*] · letztinstanzliches Gericht *n*

court of pie-powder, piepowder court [*So genannt wegen der staubigen Füße der Rechtsuchenden*] · Messegericht *n*, Gastgericht [*Im mittelalterlichen England*]

court of probate; surrogate's court, orphan's court; probate court [*A court in which wills are probated, or proved. Called "orphans" court in a few states of the USA*] · Nachlaßgericht *n*, Erb(schafts)gericht

court of probate act, court of probate law, court of probate statute · Nachlaßgerichtsgesetz n, Erb(schafts)gerichtsgesetz

court of (quarter) session(s), court of county session(s), quarter session(s) court, county session(s) court · Vierteljahresgericht n, Quartalgericht

court of record [*Das englische Recht definiert diese Zentralbehörde als ordentlichen, durch Parlamentsakt konstituierten Gerichtshof*] · Zentralbehörde f [*In England. Sie hat das Recht, alle Staatsbürger und alle lokalen Verwaltungsbehörden einzuvernehmen, Berichte von ihnen einzufordern und eventuell Zeugenschaft unter Eid zu verlangen*]

court of record · Protokollgericht n

court of request, registrary's court, court of conscience, police court, P., petty court, summary court, registrar's court, court of summary jurisdiction · Bagatellgericht n, Friedensgericht für kleine Straf- und Zivilsachen, Polizeigericht, Ortsgericht für gering(fügig)e Schuldklagen [*in England*]

court of review (of errors and appeal), appellate court, appeals court, C.A., court of (error and) appeal · Appellationsgericht n für Zivilsachen, Berufungsgericht n für Zivilsachen

Court of Session [*It is divided into the Inner House and the Outer House*] · höchster schottischer Zivilgerichtshof m [*gegründet am 17. Mai 1532*]

Court of Session Cases · schottische Entscheidungssammlung f

court of summary jurisdiction, court of request, registrary's court, court of conscience, police court, P., petty court, summary court, registrar's court · Bagatellgericht n, Friedensgericht für kleine Straf- und Zivilsachen, Polizeigericht, Ortsgericht für gering(fügig)e Schuldklagen [*in England*]

court of the baron, court of the lord, baron(-bailie) court, court-baron (proper), court of (the) manor, freeholders' court baron; curia legalis [*Latin*]; manor(ial) court, feudal court, feodal court, feuda(to)ry court [*The court of justice held by a baron or his steward in the presence of the freehold tenants of the manor. In modern times lawyers have distinguished between court-baron which was the court of the freehold tenants, and the customary court-baron which was the court of the copyhold tenants. The early history of this distinction is obscure*] · Feudalgericht n, grundherrliches Gericht, Leh(e)n(s)herrengericht, Hofgericht, Patrimonialgericht, feudales Gutsgericht

court of the duchy chamber · herzogliches Kammergericht n

court of the lord → court of the baron

court of (the) manor, freeholders' court baron; curia legalis [*Latin*]; manor(ial) court, feudal court, feodal court, feuda(to)ry court, court of the baron, court of the lord, baron(-bailie) court, court-baron (proper) [*The court of justice held by a baron or his steward in the presence of the freehold tenants of the manor. In modern times lawyers have distinguished between court-baron which was the court of the freehold tenants, and the customary court-baron which was the court of the copyhold tenants. The early history of this distinction is obscure*] · Feudalgericht n, grundherrliches Gericht, Leh(e)n(s)herrengericht, Hofgericht, Patrimonialgericht, feudales Gutsgericht

court of the staple, staple court · Stapelmarktgericht n, Stapelplatzgericht

court order, writ, order of (the) court [*A mandatory precept issuing from court of justice*] · Gerichtsverfügung f, Gerichtsgebot n, Gerichtsanordnung, Gerichtsbefehl m, (gerichtliche) Verfügung, gerichtliche Anordnung, gerichtliches Gebot, gerichtlicher Befehl, Mandat n

court order of execution, writ of execution · (Zwangs)Vollstreckungsmandat n, (Zwangs)Vollstreckungsbefehl m, (Zwangs)Vollstreckungsverfügung f, (Zwangs)Vollstreckungsanordnung, (Zwangs)Vollstreckungsgebot n

court physician · Gerichtsarzt m

court practice, practice of the courts · Prozeßwesen n, Gerichtswesen

court (practice) rules, procedural code, code of (court) procedure, (court) procedure code, rules of (court) practice, rules of (court) procedure, (general) (standing) rules of court · Prozeßregeln fpl, Prozeßordnung f, Gerichtsverfahrensregeln, Gerichtsverfahrensordnung, (gerichtliche) Verfahrensregeln, (gerichtliche) Verfahrensordnung

(court) procedure code, rules of (court) practice, rules of (court) procedure, (general) (standing) rules of court, (court) (practice) rules, procedural code, code of (court) procedure · Prozeßregeln fpl, Prozeßordnung f, Gerichtsverfahrensregeln, Gerichtsverfahrensordnung, (gerichtliche) Verfahrensregeln, (gerichtliche) Verfahrensordnung

court record · Gerichtsprotokoll n

court reporter (US) · Eidabnehmer m

court roll, roll of a manorial court [*A book in which an account of all the proceedings and transactions of the customary court of a manor was entered by a person duly authorized*] · Hofsrolle f, Gutsherrenregister n, Leh(e)n(s)herrenregister, Stammrolle des Herrenhofs

court roll — covenant to pay rent

court roll · Gerichtsrolle f

court room [A room in which a court is regularly held] · Sitzungssaal m

court rule, rule of court · Gerichtsentscheid(ung) m, (f) [z. B. einen Schiedsvertrag vor einem Gericht zu Protokoll geben um ihn zum Gerichtsentscheid erheben zu lassen]

court seal · Gerichtssiegel n

court service · Justizdienst m [Staatsanwälte und Richter]

court term, term (of court) · Gerichtsperiode f

court ward, ward of court · Gerichtsmündel m

co-use, joint use · Mitbenutzung f, Mitgebrauch m

covariance analysis · Kovarianzanalyse f, Kovarianzuntersuchung

covariance matrix, dispersion matrix · Dispersionsmatrix f, Kovarianzmatrix [Statistik]

covariation · Mitveränderlichkeit f

to covenant · urkundlich vereinbaren

covenant [An undertaking contained in a document, especially in a deed or lease] · Klausel f, (urkundliche) Vertragsklausel

covenant [A promise usually contained in a deed. No technical words are necessary to constitute a covenant] · Formalvertrag m

covenant by implication, implied covenant, tacit covenant, covenant in law · stillschweigender Formalvertrag m

covenant complied with, executed covenant, fulfilled covenant, performed covenant · ausgeführter Formalvertrag m, erfüllter Formalvertrag, vollzogener Formalvertrag, erbrachter Formalvertrag

covenant deed, deed of covenant · (gesiegelte) Nebenverpflichtungsurkunde f

covenantee, promisee · Vertragsgläubiger m, Vertragsempfänger, Versprechensgläubiger, Versprechensempfänger [Durch Vertrag berechtigte Person]

covenant for convenants performed · (Vertrags)Klausel f über die Erfüllung aller vorhergehenden (Vertrags)Klauseln [Auflassung]

covenant for freedom from charges, covenant for freedom from burdens, covenant for freedom from encumbrances, covenant for freedom from incumbrances · Formalvertrag m für Belastungsfreiheit

covenant for further assurance · (Vertrags)Klausel f zur Lösung aller einer Titelauflassung entgegenstehenden Rechte

covenant for quiet enjoyment, covenant for quiet exercise of a right · Formalvertrag m auf ungestörte (subjektive) Rechtsausübung, Formalvertrag auf ungestörte Ausübung eines (subjektiven) Rechts

covenant for right to convey · Auflassungsrechtklausel f

covenant for seisin · (Grund)Besitzeinweisungsurkunde f

covenant for title · (Rechts)Titelverpflichtung f, rechtsbegründender Formalvertrag m

covenant for validity of lease · (Vertrags)Klausel f für Haftung des Verkäufers für Pachtvertraggültigkeit

covenant giving the right of distress · Selbstpfändungsklausel f

covenant in deed, covenant in fact, special(ty) contract, contract in sealed writing, sealed contract, (contract by) specialty, contract under seal, contract by seal, contract by deed [Contracts under seal, such as deeds and bonds, are instruments which are not rarely in writing, but which are sealed by the party bound thereby, and delivered by him to, or for the benefit of, the person to whom the liability is thereby incurred] · (schriftlicher) gesiegelter Vertrag m, gesiegelter schriftlicher Vertrag, Formalvertrag unter Siegel, Vertrag mit Siegel, förmlicher Vertrag unter Siegel

covenant in law, covenant by implication, implied covenant, tacit covenant · stillschweigender Formalvertrag m

covenant in restraint of trade · Konkurrenzklausel f, Wettbewerbsklausel

covenant not to sue · Formalvertrag m den Schuldner nicht zu verklagen

covenantor, obligor, promisor, principal [One bound by an obligation. Under a bond both the "principal" and "surety" are "obligors"] · Versprechensgeber m, Versprechende, Verpflichtete

covenant running with the land · Klausel f die auf den Käufer übergeht, Vertragsklausel die auf den Käufer übergeht [Landkauf]

covenant that purchaser shall have quiet enjoyment, covenant that purchaser shall have quiet possession · (Vertrags)Klausel f für ungestörten Genuß des Käufers am Grundstück

covenant that vendor has a good right to convey · (Vertrags)Klausel f daß der Verkäufer ein Auflassungsrecht hat

covenant to insure, insurance covenant · gesiegeltes Versicherungsversprechen n

covenant to pay rent · gesiegeltes Mietzahlungsversprechen n, Mietzahlungsversprechen unter Siegel

covenant to pay the debt · Zahlungsversprechen *n* unter Siegel

covenant to repair, repairing covenant · gesiegeltes Reparaturversprechen *n*

co-venture (housing) cooperative (US) · Wohnungs(bau)genossenschaft *f*; Baugenossenschaft [*Fehlbennung*] [*Die Anteilseigner handeln als Mitglieder einer Gemeinschaft nur bei bestimmten Teilaktionen des Wohnungsbaus, wie etwa beim Kauf und der Aufschließung von Land oder selbst beim Bau der Häuser*]

to cover, to build (up)on, to construct (up)on · bebauen; überbauen [*Schweiz*]

coverage · Erfassung *f* [*Statistik*]

coverage, covering · Bebauen *n* (einer Fläche), Bebauung *f*; Überbauung, Überbauen (einer Fläche) [*Schweiz*]

coverage · Bebauung *f*; Überbauung [*Schweiz*] [*Das Ergebnis des Bebauens einer Fläche*]

coverage area, area of coverage · Bebauungsfläche *f*; Überbauungsfläche [*Schweiz*]

coverage boundary, boundary of coverage · Bebauungsgrenze *f*; Überbauungsgrenze [*Schweiz*]

coverage complex, complex of coverage · Bebauungskomplex *m*; Überbauungskomplex [*Schweiz*]

coverage density, density of coverage · Bebauungsdichte *f*, Baudichte; Überbauungsdichte [*Schweiz*]; Baudichtigkeit *f*, Bebauungsdichtigkeit *f* [*Fehlbenennungen*] [*Das Verhältnis der bebauten zur unbebauten Fläche*]

coverage depth, depth of coverage · Bebauungstiefe *f*; Überbauungstiefe [*Schweiz*] [*Im Bebauungsplan festgesetzte Tiefe der überbaubaren Fläche (§ 23 Abs. 4 BauNVo)*]

coverage design · Bebauungsentwurf *m*; Überbauungsentwurf [*Schweiz*]

coverage direction, direction of coverage · Bebauungsrichtung *f*; Überbauungsrichtung [*Schweiz*]

coverage height, height of coverage · Bebauungshöhe *f*; Überbauungshöhe [*Schweiz*]

coverage map → (building) coverage map

coverage provision, provision of coverage · Bebauungsbestimmung *f*; Überbauungsbestimmung [*Schweiz*]

coverage right, right of coverage · Bebauungsanspruch *m*, Bebauungs(an)recht *n*; Überbauungsanspruch, Überbauungs(an)recht [*Schweiz*]

coverage scheme, detailed local plan, building scheme, (detailed) local (development) plan · Bebauungsplan *m*, qualifizierter Bebauungsplan, verbindlicher Bauleitplan; Überbauungsplan [*Schweiz*] [*Der Bebauungsplan steht zwischen dem Bauplan und dem Flächennutzungsplan*]

coverage scheme design, building scheme design, (detailed) local (development) plan design · Bebauungsplanentwurf *m*, verbindlicher Bauleitplanentwurf; Überbauungsplanentwurf [*Schweiz*]

coverage scheme law, building scheme law, (detailed) local (development) plan law · Bebauungsrecht *n*; Überbauungsrecht [*Schweiz*]

coverage scheme proposal, building scheme proposal, (detailed) local (development) plan proposal · Bebauungsvorschlag *m*; Überbauungsvorschlag [*Schweiz*]

coverage type, type of coverage · Bauweise *f*, Bebauungsart *f*, Bebauungsweise; Überbauungsweise, Überbauungsart [*Schweiz*] [*Benennung einer Bebauung nach Größe und Form der Baukörper. „Bauweise" ist eine planungsrechtliche, nicht dem Bauordnungsrecht zugehörige Benennung*]

covered, built (up)on, built-up · bebaut; überbaut [*Schweiz*]

covered area, built-up area, covered land, built-up land, covered territory, built-up territory · bebautes Gebiet *n*; überbautes Gebiet [*Schweiz*]

cover for cost(s), cost(s) cover · Kostendeckung *f*

covering, coverage · Bebauen *n* (einer Fläche), Bebauung *f*; Überbauung, Überbauen (einer Fläche) [*Schweiz*]

covering letter · Anschreiben *n*, Begleitbrief *m*, Begleitschreiben

cover note · Deckungsnote *f*

covert pound, closed pound · geschlossener Pfandstall *m*

coverture · Personenstand *m* einer verheirateten Frau

co-worker, contributor, fellow (worker) · Mitarbeiter *m*

cradle-holding → borow English

craft, construction trade, (building) trade, structural trade [*Classification or type of work done by workers who restrict themselves to this type of work, established by jurisdictional agreements*] · (Bau)Gewerk *n*

craft code → (hand) craft code

craft g(u)ild, craft company · Handwerkergilde *f*, Handwerkerverband *m*

craft g(u)ild corporate, occupation corporate, craft company corporat(iv)e · kor-

craft line — credit letter

porierte (Handwerker)Zunft f, korporiertes Gewerk n

craft line → (hand) craft line

craftsman → (hand) craftsman

craftsman's town · Handwerkerstadt f

cranage · Winden- und Krangelder npl

crash, collapse · Einsturz m [Bauwerk]

crash danger, failure danger, collapse danger · Einsturzgefahr f, Einfallgefahr

crashing, dropping to pieces, collapsing, breaking down, failing · Einstürzen n, Einfallen

to create, to register · bestellen [Grundschuld]

to create an estate tail, to settle the succession to (real) property, to limit the succession to (real) property, to entail · beschränken, beschneiden [Vererbung von Grundstücken]

created annuity · General(fahrnis)legatannuität f, General(fahrnis)vermächtnisannuität

created by law · erzeugt vom Gesetz, geschaffen vom Gesetz, vom Gesetz erzeugt, vom Gesetz geschaffen

created by (the) parties · erzeugt von den Parteien, geschaffen von den Parteien

creating, registering · Bestellen n [Grundschuld]

creation of capital, capital creation, capital formation, formation of capital, accumulation of capital, capital accumulation · Kapitalschöpfung f, Kapitalbildung

creation of employment → creation of work

creation of new capital, formation of new capital · Kapitalneubildung f

creation of work, creation of jobs, creation of employment, job creation, work creation, employment creation · Arbeitsbeschaffung f

credibility, credibleness [Not to be confused with "competency". "Competency" is a question which arises before considering the evidence given by the witness; "credibility" concerns the degree of credit to be given to his story] · Glaubwürdigkeit f, Glaubhaftigkeit

credibility of evidence, credibility of proof · Beweiswürdigung f

credible, faithful, trust(worth)y · glaubwürdig, glaubhaft, vertrauenswürdig

credibleness, credibility [Not to be confused with "competency". "Competency" is a question which arises before considering the evidence given by the witness; "credibility" concerns the degree of credit to be given to his story] · Glaubwürdigkeit f, Glaubhaftigkeit

credible witness, suitor; sectator [Latin] · glaubwürdiger Zeuge m

credit acceptance, acceptance of credit · Kreditnahme f, Kreditaufnahme

credit association, association of credit, popular bank · Vorschußverein m

credit bank, commercial bank · Kreditbank f

credit broker · Kreditvermittler m

credit charge, finance charge · Finanzierungsaufschlag m

credit commissioner · Kreditüberwacher m

credit control · Kreditüberwachung f

credit cost(s) · Kreditkosten f

credit curb · Kreditrestriktion f, Kreditbeschränkung, Krediteinschränkung f

credit deficiency, deficiency of credit, shortage of credit, scarcity of credit, stringency of credit, credit scarcity, credit stringency, credit shortage · Kreditknappheit f, Kreditklemme f, Kreditnot f, Kreditmangel m, Kreditverknappung f, Kreditdefizit n

credit document · Krediturkunde f

credit economy · Kreditwirtschaft f

credit enquiry agency, commercial agency, mercantile agency · Handelsauskunftei f

credit for old building materials, credit for old construction materials · Gutschrift f für Altbaustoffe

credit granted against deposited securities · Lombardkredit m

credit granted to a manager · Organkredit m

credit hazard, credit risk · Kreditrisiko n, Kreditwagnis n, Delkredererisiko, Delkrederewagnis

credit in foreign exchange · Währungskredit m

credit institution for gentlemen-farmers · ritterschaftliche Kreditanstalt f, Ritterkreditanstalt

credit institution trading in commodities · Kreditinstitut n mit Warengeschäft

credit instrument · Kreditpapier n [Scheck; Wechsel]

credit insurance · Kreditversicherung f, Delkredereversicherung

credit insurer · Ratenversicherer m

credit interest · Habenzinsen f

credit investigation · Kreditprüfung f

credit-issuing bank · Akkreditivbank f

credit letter, letter of credit · Akkreditiv n, Kreditbrief m

credit limit · Kreditgrenze f

credit loss, loss of credit · Kreditverlust m

credit market · Kreditmarkt m

credit money, fiducial money · Kreditgeld n

credit mortgage · Kredithypothek f

credit note · Kreditnote f

credit note · Impressum n [Kartographie]

credit on open account, open book credit · offenes Ziel n

credit operation, credit transactions · Kreditverkehr m

creditor, debtee · Gläubiger m

creditor nation, debtee nation · Gläubigernation f

creditor (probate) administrator, debtee (probate) administrator, creditor trustee for sale, debtee trustee for sale · Gläubiger-Nachlaßverwalter m, Gläubiger-Erb(schafts)verwalter

creditor's default, debtee's default · Gläubiger(ver)säumnis f, n, (f)

creditor's delay, debtee's delay · Gläubigerverzug m, Annahmeverzug

creditor security, debtee security · Gläubigerpapier n

creditors' meeting, debtees' meeting · Gläubigerversammlung f

creditor trustee for sale, debtee trustee for sale, creditor (probate) administrator, debtee (probate) administrator · Gläubiger-Nachlaßverwalter m, Gläubiger-Erb(schafts)verwalter

creditor under a rent charge, rent-charger, debtee under a rent charge · Rentengläubiger m

credit period · Zahlungsziel n

credit practice · Kreditwesen n

credit reference agency · Kreditwürdigkeitsauskunftei f

creditress, creditrix, female creditor · Gläubigerin f

credit risk, credit hazard · Kreditrisiko n, Kreditwagnis n, Delkredererisiko, Delkrederewagnis

credit (risk(s)) security, security against risks in granting credit(s) [e.g. by means of an inquiry office] · Kreditsicherung f, Kreditdeckung

creditrix, female creditor, creditress · Gläubigerin f

credit sale · Kreditverkauf m

credit sale agreement · Kreditverkaufsabkommen n, Kreditverkaufsabmachung f, Kreditverkaufsvereinbarung

credit scarcity, credit stringency, credit shortage, credit deficiency, deficiency of credit, shortage of credit, scarcity of credit, stringency of credit · Kreditknappheit f, Kreditklemme f, Kreditnot f, Kreditmangel m, Kreditverknappung f, Kreditdefizit n

credit standing, credit status · Kreditwürdigkeit f

credit token · Kreditzeichen n

credit-token agreement · Kreditzeichenvereinbarung f, Kreditzeichenabkommen n, Kreditzeichenabmachung

credit transactions, credit operation · Kreditverkehr m

credit union · Kreditgenossenschaft f

credulity · Leichtgläubigkeit f

creeping inflation, persistent inflation · schleichende Inflation f

cremation, burning to ashes, incinerating [The act of reducing a corpse by means of fire] · Einäschern n

cremation [The practice of reducing a corpse by means of fire] · Einäscherung f, Feuerbestattung

cremation certificate [A sworn statement by a trustee or other appointed agent that reacquired and retired securities have been destroyed] · Vernichtungszeugnis n

cremation law, cremation act, cremation statute · Feuerbestattungsgesetz n, Einäscherungsgesetz

crescent · kurze gewundene Stadtstraße f mit Abschlußziel

crescent · organisch gewachsen

crier; beadle, bedell [obsolete] [1. A crier or usher of a law court, 2. a town crier] · Ausrufer m

crime · Verbrechen n

crime committed in public office · Amtsverbrechen n, Verbrechen im Amt

crime of violence · Gewaltverbrechen n

criminal intent(ion) · strafbare Absicht f, subjektives Verbrechenselement n

criminal investigation department · Kriminalabteilung f

criminal law, penal law [That portion of the law which relates to the definition of crimes and to their punishment] · Strafrecht n

criminal lawyer · Straf(prozeß)anwalt m

criminal liability · strafrechtliche Haftbarkeit f, strafrechtliche Haftung f, strafrechtliche Haftpflicht f

criminal occurrence book · Buch n der strafbaren Handlungen einer Polizeistation

criminal offence — crosstown location

criminal offence · Straftat *f*

criminal procedure code, code of criminal procedure · Strafprozeßordnung *f*, StPO

criminal profiteering law · Preis(treiberei)strafrecht *n*, Preiswucherstrafrecht

crippling, physical disability · Versehrtheit *f*

crisis point, break-even point [*It represents the volume of sales at which total cost(s) equal total revenues, that is, profits equal zero. The firm neither makes a profit nor suffers a loss*] · Deckungspunkt *m*, Gewinnschwelle *f*, Kostendeckungspunkt, toter Punkt, Nutzschwelle

criterion of decision, decision criterion · Entscheidungskriterium *n*

criterion of maximum profit, criterion of maximum gain · Höchstgewinnkriterium *n*, Maximalgewinnkriterium

critic · Kritiker *m*

critical region · Verwertungsbereich *m* [*Statistik*]

crofter [*Scottish term*] · Kleinpächter *m*

crofting agriculture · Kleinpächterlandwirtschaft *f*

crofting community · Kleinpächtergemeinde *f*

crofting tenancy [*Scottish term*] · Kleinpachtung *f*

crop · Feldfrucht *f*

crop combination · Anbaukombination *f*

crop land, agricultural land, farming land, land agricultural in character, farmland, improved land, farmed land, agriculturally zoned land, agriculturally used land [*Land may be assessable as "agricultural land" though it be covered by timber and underbrush, grass and weeds*] · landwirtschaftlicher Boden *m*, landwirtschaftlich genutzter Boden, landwirtschaftliches Land *n*, landwirtschaftlich genutztes Land, Kulturland, Kulturboden, Agrarland, landwirtschaftlich genutzte Fläche *f*, LN, landwirtschaftliche Nutzfläche, Fruchtland, Agrarnutzfläche

cropping freedom, freedom of cultivation, freedom of cropping, cultivation freedom · (Boden)Kultivierungsfreiheit *f*, Anbaufreiheit

crop-raising farm · Ackergut *n*, Ackerhof *m*

crop rotation, rotating crops, rotation of crops · Fruchtwechsel *m*, Fruchtfolge *f*

cross-acceptance, jobbing-in-bills, cross-drawing · Wechselreiterei *f*

cross action → cross cause

cross bill · Rückwechsel *m*

cross cause, cross (law)suit, cross plea, counter-cause, counter-plea, counter-(law)suit, counter (court) action, cross (court) action · Gegenklage *f*, Widerklage

to cross-check · gegenkontrollieren

cross-check(ing) · Gegenkontrolle *f*

cross-claims · Gegenansprüche *m pl* bei mehreren beklagten Parteien

cross (court) action, cross cause, cross (law)suit, cross plea, counter-cause, counter-plea, counter-(law)suit, counter (court) action · Gegenklage *f*, Widerklage

cross default · wechselseitige Verschulden *n*, gegenseitige Verschulden

cross-default clause · wechselseitige Verschuldensklausel *f*, gegenseitige Verschuldensklausel

cross-defendant · Widerbeklagte *m*

cross-drawing, cross-acceptance, jobbing-in-bills · Wechselreiterei *f*

crossed cheque, crossed check · gekreuzter Scheck *m*, Verrechnungsscheck

crossed-weight index number · gekreuzter Index *m* [*Statistik*]

cross examination · Kreuzverhör *n* durch die Gegenpartei

cross examination interrogatories · Kreuzverhörfragen *f pl*

crosshatched · kreuzschraffiert

crossing · Kreuzen *n*, Sperren, Vinkulieren [*Scheck*]

crossing [*USA*] · Vorwahlwechsel *m*

cross-land [*1568. Land belonging to the church in the Irish counties palatine*] · Kirchengüter *n pl* in Irland

cross (law)suit, cross plea, counter-cause, counter-plea, counter-(law)suit, counter (court) action, cross (court) action, cross cause · Gegenklage *f*, Widerklage

cross motion · Gegenantrag *m*

cross-over design, change-over trial, switch-back design · Gruppenwechselplan *m* [*Statistik*]

cross-rate · Usance-Kurs *m*

cross-roads village · Kreuzwegdorf *n*

cross-shaped row village · Kreuzreihendorf *n*

cross-street cluster settlement, cross-street irregular nucleated settlement · kreuzwegige Haufen(an)sied(e)lung *f*

crosstown location, crosstown site · Standort *m* am anderen Stadtende

to crowd — cultivation (of land)

to crowd [*To crowd many people in or on*] · voll belegen

crowded art · einengender Stand *m* der Technik [*Patentrecht*]

crowding · Häufung *f* [*Besied(e)lung*]

crowding · Beengtsein *n*, Enge *f*

Crown demesne land(s) held in socage, Crown lands, royal demesne (lands), royal demeine (lands), royal demain (lands), demesne (lands) of the Crown · Kronländer(eien) *n pl (f pl)*, Krongüter *n pl*, Länder(eien) der Krone, Domänen *f pl* der Krone, Güter der Krone, königliche Domänen, königliche Länder(eien), königliche Güter, Krondomänen, Land der Krone, Kronland *n*

(Crown) land(s) revenues, royal demesne revenues [*Income derived from Crown land(s) in Great Britain*] · Kronguteinkünfte *f pl*, Kronlandeinkünfte, Kronländerei(en)einkünfte

Crown law officer, law officer of the Crown · Kronjurist *m*

Crown office · Kronamt *n*

Crown's prerogative right, purveyance · königliches Vorkaufsrecht *n*, Vorkaufsrecht der Krone

Crown tenant, peasant of Crown land · Kronbauer *m*

croy, mere [*In old English law*]; marsh(y) ground, marsh(y) land · Marschland *n*

cruelty to animals · Tierquälerei *f*

crystal of the core, core crystal, hard core · harter Kern, Kern im Kern [*Stadt*]

C.T., cable transfer · telegraphische Auszahlung *f*

CU, community unit, local unit, communal unit · lokale Einheit *f*, örtliche Einheit, gem- eindliche Einheit, Gemeindeeinheit, Ortseinheit

cube, cubic(al) capacity, (cubic(al)) content, structural volume, cubic extent, cubing, walled-in space, building volume, cubage, enclosed space, space enclosed [*Enclosed total volume measurements of a structure*] · Baumasse *f*, umbauter Raum *m*, Rauminhalt *m*

cubic extent ratio, cubic extent index, cubing ratio, cubic index · Baumassenzahl *f*, BMZ [*Sie wird ausschließlich für Industriegebiete angewendet, da hier nicht wie bei Wohnhäusern mit normalen Geschoßhöhen, sondern mit Kubikmetern umbauten Raumes gerechnet wird. Sie gibt an, wieviel Kubikmeter Baumasse je Quadratmeter Grundstücksfläche zulässig sind (m^3/m^2). § 21 BauNVO*]

cubic metre · Kubikmeter *n*, *m*

cubing, walled-in space, building volume, cubage, enclosed space, space enclosed, cube, cubic(al) capacity, (cubic(al)) content, structural volume, cubic extent [*Enclosed total volume measurements of a structure*] · Baumasse *f*, umbauter Raum *m*, Rauminhalt *m*

cubing ratio, cubic index, cubic extent ratio, cubic extent index · Baumassenzahl *f*, BMZ [*Sie wird ausschließlich für Industriegebiete angewendet, da hier nicht wie bei Wohnhäusern mit normalen Geschoßhöhen, sondern mit Kubikmetern umbauten Raumes gerechnet wird. Sie gibt an, wieviel Kubikmeter Baumasse je Quadratmeter Grundstücksfläche zulässig sind (m^3/m^2). § 21 BauNVO*]

to cull out; to garble [*In old English statutes*], to sort out [*The good from the bad*] · aussortieren

culpability, culpableness · Schuldhaftigkeit *f*

culpable · schuldhaft

culpable ignorance · schuldhafte Unkenntnis *f*

culpable necessity, unfortunate necessity; necessitas culpabilis [*Latin*] [*A necessity which, while it excuses the act done under its compulsion, does not leave the doer entirely free from blame*] · schuldhafter Aggressivnotstand *m*

culpa in contrahendo [*Latin*] · gesetzliches Schuldverhältnis *n*, Verschulden *n* bei Vertragsanbahnung

culpa in eligendo [*Latin*] · Verschulden *n* des Geschäftsherren

cultiva(ta)ble · anbaufähig, kultivierbar, kultivierfähig, anbaubar

to cultivate, to produce by tillage, to raise by tillage, to farm · kultivieren, anbauen

cultivated area, area under crops and grass · Kulturfläche *f*

cultivation area, cultivation territory, agrarian area, agrarian territory, agricultural area, farming area, agricultural territory, farming territory · Agrarfläche *f*, Agrargebiet *n*, landwirtschaftliche Fläche, landwirtschaftliches Gebiet, Anbaufläche, Anbaugebiet

cultivation freedom, cropping freedom, freedom of cultivation, freedom of cropping · (Boden)Kultivierungsfreiheit *f*, Anbaufreiheit

cultivation of a single crop, single crop cultivation · Monokultur *f*

cultivation (of land), cultivation of fields, cultivation of soil, land cultivation, field cultivation, farming, soil cultivation, agricultural use · Anbau *m*, Bodenkultivierung *f*, Landkultivierung, Bodenkultur *f*, Feldbau

cultivation territory — currency note

cultivation territory, agrarian area, agrarian territory, agricultural area, farming area, agricultural territory, farming territory, cultivation area · Agrarfläche *f*, Agrargebiet *n*, landwirtschaftliche Fläche, landwirtschaftliches Gebiet, Anbaufläche, Anbaugebiet

cultivator of the ground; acreman [*obsolete*] · Anbauer *m*

cultura [*Latin*]; parcel of arable land, plot of arable land · Ackerstück *n*

cultural · kulturlich

cultural area, unit defined on the basis of cultural criteria, unit defined on the basis of human criteria · Kulturraum *m*

cultural facility · Kultureinrichtung *f*

cultural geography · Kulturgeographie *f*

cultural institution · Kulturinstitut *n*

cultural landscape, man-made landscape · Kulturlandschaft *f*, Sied(e)lungslandschaft

cultural poverty · Kulturarmut *f*

cultural stratum · Kulturschicht *f*

culvert, serf; villarus [*Latin*]; regardant (to the manor), bond tenant, villain (tenant), villein (tenant), bondager, bond(s)man [*Strictly a man of servile condition holding usually one virgate of land, this is the fourth part of a hide, in the common fields of a manor by base services; but the term is sometimes applied to one of free status who holds land by servile tenure*] · Leibeigene, unfreier Bauer, Dienstbauer *m*, Hörige, Unfreie, Knechtsleh(e)n(s)mann

culvertage, villanage, ville(i)nage; culvertagium [*Latin*] · Leibeigentum *n*

cum dividend, with dividend · mit Dividende, einschließlich Dividende

cumulant, half-invariant · Kumulante *f* [*Statistik*]

cumulative annual pocket part · Ergänzungsbändchen *n* [*Es wird am Buchende jährlich eingeheftet*]

cumulative frequency, sum(mation) frequency · Summenhäufigkeit *f*

cumulative voting · Verhältniswahl *f*

cumulative voting · Stimmenhäufung *f* in der Hauptversammlung

curate; curator [*Latin*] · Kurator *m*, (Nachlaß)Pfleger

curatel · Kuratel *f*

curate of an absentee; curator absentis [*Latin*] · Abwesenheitskurator *m*, Abwesenheits(nachlaß)pfleger

curateship · Kuratie *f*, (Nachlaß)Pflegschaft *f*

curative statute, validating statute · Formmängelgesetz *n* [*Es berichtigt Formmängel in Verfügungsurkunden (deeds of conveyance) um älteren, wegen Verstoßes gegen Formvorschriften nichtigen Verfügungen nachträglich zur Wirksamkeit zu verhelfen*]

curator [*Latin*]; curate · Kurator *m*, (Nachlaß)Pfleger

curator absentis [*Latin*]; curate of an absentee · Abwesenheitskurator *m*, Abwesenheits(nachlaß)pfleger

curatrix [*Latin*]; female curate · Kuratorin *f*, (Nachlaß)Pflegerin

curb market (US) · Straßenbörse *f*

curb parking (US); kerb(stone) parking (Brit.) · Bordsteinparken *n*

curia advisari vult, cur. adv. vult, c.a.v. [*Latin*] [*The court wishes to consider the matter*] [*When this term is placed before the judg(e)ment in the report of a case, it means that judg(e)ment was not delivered immediately. The judg(e)ment when delivered is then said to be a considered or reserved judg(e)ment*] · Vertagen *n* einer Urteilsverkündung

curia hundredi [*Latin*]; hundred court [*In old English law. A larger court baron, being held for all the inhabitants of a particular hundred, instead of a manor. This is not to be confounded with the hundred court of the Saxon times, called hundred gemote*] · Hundertgericht *n*

curia legalis [*Latin*]; manor(ial) court, feudal court, feodal court, feuda(to)ry court, court of the baron, court of the lord, baron(-bailie) court, court-baron (proper), court of (the) manor, freeholders' court baron [*The court of justice held by a baron or his steward in the presence of the freehold tenants of the manor. In modern times lawyers have distinguished between court-baron which was the court of the freehold tenants, and the customary court-baron which was the court of the copyhold tenants. The early history of this distinction is obscure*] · Feudalgericht *n*, grundherrliches Gericht, Leh(e)n(s)herrengericht, Hofgericht, Patrimonialgericht, feudales Gutsgericht

Curia Regis [*Latin*]; King's Court · Königsgericht *n*, königliches Gericht

currency, life, term · Dauer *f*, (Lauf)Zeit *f* [*z. B. eines Vertrages*]

currency area, currency territory · Währungsgebiet *n*

currency-convertibility clause · Konvertierbarkeitsklausel *f*

currency draft · Währungstratte *f*

currency note · Staatsnote *f*

currency notes · Staatspapiergeld *n*

currency reform, monetary reform · Währungsreform *f*

currency territory, currency area · Währungsgebiet *n*

current asset, quick asset [*An asset that can be converted readily into cash, e.g. stocks, notes, inventory*] · kurzfristiger Aktivposten *m*, kurzfristig realisierbarer Vermögensteil *m*

current assets → (total) current assets

current assets minus current liabilities, net current assets, net quick assets, (net) working capital [*The term "working capital" has two meanings. It may refer to the total current assets or to the difference between current assets and current liabilities*] · Nettoumlaufvermögen *n*, Nettoumlaufmittel *f*, Reinumlaufvermögen, Reinumlaufmittel

current liability · kurzfristig fällige Verbindlichkeit *f*, kurzfristig fällige Schuld *f*, kurzfristige Verbindlichkeit, kurzfristige Schuld, laufende Schuld, laufende Verbindlichkeit

current maintenance, permanent maintenance, ordinary maintenance · planmäßige Unterhaltung *f*, Routineunterhaltung

current of (migration) movement, stream of (migration) movement, flow of (migration) movement, (migration) movement current, (migration) movement stream, (migration) movement flow, migration flow, migration stream · Bewegungsstrom *m*, Wanderungsstrom

current opinion, leading opinion · Verkehrsauffassung *f*, Verkehrsmeinung, herrschende Meinung, herrschende Auffassung

current price, present price · gegenwärtiger Preis *m*

current ratio · Verhältnis *n* von Umlaufvermögen zu kurzfristigem Fremdkapital

current standard · angepaßter Verrechnungssatz *m*

current standard cost(s), ideal standard cost(s) · Soll(standard)kosten *f*, Standardkosten 1. Art

current year [*The year now running*] · laufendes Jahr *n*

cursus [*Latin*]; running-ground, drive · Trift *f*

cursus faldae [*Latin*]; frank fold, free fold, course of fold, fold course, faldsoke; faldsoca [*Saxon law*]; falda libera [*Latin*] [*The privilege of setting up and moving about in a field a fold, for the purpose of manuring the ground, which several lords anciently reserved to themselves in any fields within their manors, not only with their own but their tenants sheep*] · (Schaf)Pferchrecht *n*

curtailed inspection · abgebrochene Prüfung *f* [*Statistik*]

curtailment, cut · Beschneiden *n* [*Kosten*]

curtailment of service, service curtailment · Absperren *n* [*Gas, Wasser oder Strom bei Nichtzahlung der Gebühren*]

curtesy; jus curialitatis Angliae [*Latin*] · Witwergut *n*, Wittumsrecht *n* des Ehemannes

curtesy and dower, dower and curtesy · eheliches Güterrecht *n*

curtilage [*A courtyard adjoining a messuage*] · Wohnhaushof *m*

curtis episcopi [*Latin*] · Domhof *m*

curtis presbyter [*Latin*] · Pfarrhof *m*

curve of consumption, consumption curve · Verbrauchskurve *f*

curve of equidetectability, equidetectability curve · Kurve *f* gleicher Schärfe [*Statistik*]

curve of localization, localization curve · Lokalisierungskurve *f*

curvilinear regression, nonlinear regression, skew regression · nichtlineare Regression *f*

cushion [*Amount included in a contractor's bid to protect himself against contingencies*] · Betrag *m* für Unvorhergesehenes

custodia castrensis [*Latin*] · Burghude *f*, Burghute

custodia legis [*Latin*]; custody of the law · gesetzliche Verwahrung *f*, gesetzlicher Gewahrsam *m*, Rechtsgewahrsam, Rechtsverwahrung

custodian of enemy property, alien property custodian · Feindvermögenswahrer *m*, Verwahrer feindlichen Vermögens, Verwahrer feindlichen Eigentums, Feindeigentumsverwahrer

custodian trustee, passive trustee [*The custodian trustee holds the trust property as if it were sole trustee, but, except as regards that matter, the appointment of a custodian trustee does not effect the powers and duties of the ordinary trustees*] · passiver Treuhänder *m*

custody · Aufsicht *f*, Hut *f*, Personensorge *f*

custody, keeping safe · Gewahrsam *m*, Verwahrung *f*

custody and expenditure of the rate · (Steuer)Kassenverwaltung *f*

custody and tuition · Gewahrsam *m* und Erziehung *f* [*Mündel*]

custody of drawings · Aufbewahren n von Zeichnungen

custody of the law; custodia legis [*Latin*] · gesetzliche Verwahrung f, gesetzlicher Gewahrsam m, Rechtsgewahrsam, Rechtsverwahrung

custody prior to deportation · Abschiebungshaft f

custom, usage, habit, mode [*Uniform course of dealing in a particular trade*] · Brauch m, Üblichkeit f, Gepflogenheit f, Gewohnheit

custom · Außenzoll m

custom (Brit.) → common (law)

customary, at (the) will (of the lord), nonfree, unfree · unfrei, nichtfrei, zugestanden, prekarisch, auf Ruf und Widerruf, willkürlich aufkündbar [*Leh(e)n*]

customary, ordinary, common, usual · herkömmlich, üblich

customary, by custom, common · gewohnheitsrechtlich

customary factum, typical acknowledged experience, usual factum · typischer Sachverhalt m

customary freehold, ancient demesne, copyhold tenure by custom of ancient demesne; dominicum antiquum, antiquum dominicum, vetus patrimonium domini [*Latin*] [*Such land(s) as were entered by William I., in Doomesdaybook, under the title "De Terra Regis"; and which were held later by a species of copyhold tenure*] · altes Krongut(leh(e)n) n

customary guardian, guardian by custom, common guardian · gewohnheitsrechtlicher Vormund m

customary guardianship, guardianship by custom, common guardianship · gewohnheitsrechtliche Vormundschaft f

customary heir (male), common heir (male), heir (male) by custom [*A man whose right of inheritance depends upon a particular and local custom, such as gavelkind, or borough English*] · gewohnheitsrechtlicher Erbe m

customary international law, international customary law · Völkergewohnheitsrecht n, VGR

customary in the place, usual in the place · ortsüblich

customary law, (common) custom, universal custom of the realm, custom which runs through the whole land (Brit.); jus commune [*Latin*]; common (law), general customs · gemeines Recht n, objektives gemeines Recht, (objektives) Gemeinrecht, Präjudizienrecht, (gemeines) Gewohnheitsrecht [*England. Das gemeine Recht, das von reisenden Richtern ("itinerant justices" oder "justices in eyre") des königlichen Gerichts zu Westminster gebildet wurde. Neben der Gegenüberstellung "common law" (oder "law") — "equity" (= „strenges Recht — Billigkeitsrecht") wird "common law" noch stellvertretend für das gesamte case law und das anglo-amerikanische Rechtssystem verwandt: "common law — statute law" (= „Richterrecht — Gesetzesrecht"), bzw. "common law — civil law" (anglo-amerikanisches Recht im Gegensatz zum kontinentaleuropäischen Recht)*]

customary law liability, common law liability, general customs liability · gemeinrechtliche Haftung f, gemeinrechtliche Haftpflicht f, gemeinrechtliche Haftbarkeit f

customary practice · üblicher Brauch m

customary tenant, common tenant, tenant by custom · gewohnheitsrechtlicher Leh(e)n(s)mann m, Werkmann [*In England im 14., 15. und 16. Jahrhundert*]

customary tenure, common tenure, tenure by custom [*Examples were gavelkind and borough English*] · gewohnheitsrechtliches Leh(e)n n

customer, collector of customs · Zollbeamte m, Zöllner

customer parking · Käuferparken n, Kundenparken

customer's complaint, notice of defect, notification of defect · Baumangelbenachrichtigung f, Baumangelmitteilung, Baumangelanzeige f, (Sach)Mangelanzeige, (Sach)Mangelmitteilung, Nachbesserungsanzeige, Nachbesserungsmitteilung, Nachbesserungsbenachrichtigung, (Sach)Mangelbenachrichtigung, (Sach)Mangelrüge f, Baumängelrüge

customer's complaints, notice of defects, notification of defects · Baumängelanzeige f, Baumängelmitteilung f, (Sach)Mängelanzeige, (Sach)Mängelmitteilung, Nachbesserungsanzeige, Baumängelbenachrichtigung, (Sach)Mängelbenachrichtigung, (Sach)Mängelmitteilung, Nachbesserungsmitteilung, Nachbesserungsbenachrichtigung, (Sach)Mängelrüge f, Baumängelrüge

custom-house; bunder [*Anglo-Indian*] · Zollhaus n

customhouse broker, customs broker · Zollagent m

custom house quay · Zollkai m

custom of ancient demesne → ancient demesne

custom of the country · Landesbrauch m

custom of the merchants · Handelsgewohnheitsrecht n

customs and excise taxation · Verbrauchsbesteuerung f

customs attorney · Zoll(rechts)anwalt m

customs broker, customhouse broker · Zollagent *m*

customs clearance · Zollabfertigung *f*

(customs) debenture · Rück(zoll)schein *m* [*Versprechen des Zollamtes, den gezahlten Zoll bei Wiedereinführung der verzollten Ware zurückzugeben*]

customs drawback · Zoll(rück)vergütung *f*, Rückzoll *m*, Zollerstattung

(customs) duty · Zoll(abgabe) *m, f*

customs duty ad valorem, ad valorem (customs) duty · Wertzoll *m*

customs enclave · Zolleinschluß *m*

custom's entry · Zollanmeldung *f*, Zolldeklaration *f*

customs examination · Zollbeschau *f*, Zollrevision *f*

customs exclave · Zollausschluß *m*

customs invoice · Zollfaktura *f*, Zollrechnung *f*

customs lead, customs seal · Zollblei *n*

customs of the law merchant · Gebräuche *mpl* des Handelsrechts

customs supervision, customs superintendence · Zollaufsicht *f*, Zollüberwachung *f*

customs warehouse · staatliche Zollniederlage *f*

custom which runs through the whole land (Brit.); jus commune [*Latin*]; common (law), general customs, customary law, (common) custom, universal custom of the realm · gemeines Recht *n*, objektives gemeines Recht, (objektives) Gemeinrecht, Präjudizienrecht, (gemeines) Gewohnheitsrecht [*England. Das gemeine Recht, das von reisenden Richtern ("itinerant justices" oder "justices in eyre") des königlichen Gerichts zu Westminster gebildet wurde. Neben der Gegenüberstellung "common law" (oder "law") — "equity" (= „strenges Recht — Billigkeitsrecht") wird "common law" noch stellvertretend für das gesamte case law und das anglo-amerikanische Rechtssystem verwandt: "common law — statute law" (= „Richterrecht — Gesetzesrecht"), bzw. "common law — civil law" (anglo-amerikanisches Recht im Gegensatz zum kontinentaleuropäischen Recht)*]

custos rotulorum [*Latin*]; keeper of the rolls · Rollenbewahrer *m*, Rollenarchivar, aktenbewahrender Friedensrichter

cut, curtailment · Beschneiden *n* [*Kosten*]

to cut down [*expenses*] · abbauen [*Ausgaben*]

to cut (down), to lower, to bring down · ermäßigen

cut-off · Abbrechen *n*, Abbruch *m* [*statistische Erhebung*]

cut-off-date, effective date, appointed day, key day · Stichtag *m*

cut-off date of appraisal, appointed day of appraisal, key-day of appraisal, (e)valuation cut-off-date, (e)valuation key-day, appointed day of (e)valuation, effective date of appraisal · Bewertungsstichtag *m*, Wertermitt(e)lungsstichtag, Taxierungsstichtag, (Ab)Schätzungsstichtag

cut(-throat) competition, rate war, ruinous competition · ruinöser Wettbewerb *m*

cut(-throat) price, slaughtered price, price below cost price, ruinous price · Schleuderpreis *m*

cutting (down), lowering, bringing down · Ermäßigen *n*, Ermäßigung *f*

cutting of peat, digging of peat, peat-cutting, peat-digging · Torfgraben *n*, Torfstechen

cyclical unemployment · zyklische Arbeitslosigkeit *f*

D

D/A, documents against acceptance · Dokumente *n pl* gegen Akzept

d/a, documents against cash, d/C, documents against acceptance · Aushändigung *f* der Dokumente gegen Annahme der Tratte durch den Importeur

daily activity, daily work · tägliche Arbeit *f*

daily commuter · Tagespendler *m*, täglicher Pendler

daily commuting · Tagespendeln *n*, tägliches Pendeln

daily equipment card · Gerätetageskarte *f*

daily equipment report · Gerätetagesbericht *m*

daily need, daily requirement · Tagesbedarf *m*, täglicher Bedarf

daily population movement · tägliche Bevölkerungsbewegung *f*

daily rate, day rate · Tagessatz *m*

daily wage, day wage, daywork(s) wage, jobbing wage · Tagelohn *m*

daily wage rate, jobbing rate, daywork(s) rate, day wage rate · Tagelohnsatz *m*

daily work · Tagefronarbeit *f*, Tag(e)werk *n*

daily work — damages measure

daily work, daily activity · tägliche Arbeit f

dairy belt · Milchwirtschaftsgürtel m

dairying · Molkereiwesen n

dairy inspector · Molkereiinspektor m

to damage · beschädigen

damage · Schaden m

damage · Beschädigung f

damageable · schadanfällig

damage assessment, assessment of damage · Schadensbemessung f

damage by fire, fire damage · Brandschaden m, Feuerschaden

damage by game, ravage of game · Wildschaden m

damage by storm, storm damage · Gewitterschaden m

damage calculation, damage computation, calculation of damage, computation of damage · Schadensberechnung f, Schadenskalkulation f

damage caused by occupation(al) forces · Besatzungsschaden m

damage computation, calculation of damage, computation of damage, damage calculation · Schadensberechnung f, Schadenskalkulation f

damaged, injuriously affected [*Made less valuable, less useful, or less desirable*] · beschädigt

damage done by riot(s) · Tumultschaden m

damage due to mining, mining damage · Bergschaden m

damage feasant [*Said of stranger's cattle, found trespassing, and doing damage, as by feeding, etc.*] · Beschädigung f durch fremdes Vieh

damage from defect · Baumangelschaden m, (Sach)Mangelschaden

damage in residential building → (structural) damage in residential building

damage in transit · Transportschaden m

damage of severance, severance damage · (Ab)Trennungsschaden m

damage of structures, damage of a structure · Bauschaden m [*Ein Bauschaden entsteht nach Fertigstellung infolge einer äußeren Einwirkung, z. B. durch Holzbefall, Bergsenkung, Hochwasser und dgl.*]

damages, indemnity, indemnification, compensation [*"Compensation" is distinguishable from "damages" inasmuch as the former may mean the sum which will remunerate an owner for land actually taken, while the latter signifies an allowance made for injury to the residue; but such destinction is not ordinarily observed*] · Entschädigung f, Schadenersatz m, (f)

damages claim, claim for indemnification, claim for indemnity, claim for compensation, claim for damages, compensation claim, indemnity claim, indemnification claim · Entschädigungsforderung f, Schadenersatzforderung, Entschädigungsverlangen n, Schadenersatzverlangen

damages clause, compensation clause, indemnity clause, indemnification clause · Entschädigungsklausel f, Schadenersatzklausel

damages for breach of contract, compensation for breach of contract, indemnification for breach of contract, indemnity for breach of contract · Entschädigung(sleistung) f wegen Vertragsbruch, Schadenersatz(leistung) m, (f) wegen Vertragsbruch

damages for condemnation (US) → compensation for (land) expropriation

damages for delay, indemnity for delay, indemnification for delay, compensation for delay · Schadenersatz m bei Verzug, Entschädigung f bei Verzug

damages for (land) condemnation (US) → compensation for (land) expropriation

damages for (land) expropriation → compensation for (land) expropriation

damages for negligence, compensation for negligence, indemnification for negligence, indemnity for negligence · Entschädigung f für Fahrlässigkeit, Schadenersatz m für Fahrlässigkeit

damages for nonperformance, compensation for nonperformance, indemnification for nonperformance, indemnity for nonperformance · Schadenersatz m wegen Nichterfüllung, Entschädigung f wegen Nichterfüllung

damages in land, compensation in land, indemnity in land, indemnification in land · Entschädigung in Land, Schadenersatz m in Land, Landentschädigung, Landschadenersatz, Landabfindung

damages in lieu of injunction, compensation in lieu of injunction, indemnification in lieu of injunction, indemnity in lieu of injunction · Entschädigung f für richterlich privilegierten Eingriff, Schadenersatz m für richterlich privilegierten Eingriff

damages law, compensation law, indemnity law, indemnification law · (objektives) Entschädigungsrecht n, (objektives) Schadenersatzrecht,

damages measure, indemnification measure, indemnity measure, compensation measure, measure of damages, meas-

damages (paid) in kind — date of receipt of bids

ure of compensation, measure of indemnification, measure of indemnity, indemnifying measure · Entschädigungsmaßnahme f, Schadenersatzmaßnahme

damages (paid) in kind, indemnification (paid) in kind, indemnity (paid) in kind, in-kind compensation, in-kind indemnification, in-kind damages, in-kind indemnity, compensation (paid) in kind · Entschädigung f in Natur, Schadenersatz m in Natur, Natural(schaden)ersatz, Naturalentschädigung

damages (paid) in money, compensation (paid) in money, indemnity (paid) in money, money indemnity, payment of damages, money damages, pecuniary damages, pecuniary compensation, pecuniary indemnification, money compensation, money indemnification, indemnification (paid) in money · Entschädigung f in Geld, Schadenersatz m in Geld, Geldentschädigung, Geld(schaden)ersatz, Schadenersatzzahlung, Entschädigungszahlung

damages under public law, compensation under public law, indemnification under public law, indemnity under public law · öffentlich-rechtliche Entschädigung f, öffentlich-rechtlicher Schadenersatz m

dame president · Präsidentin f

damnum absque injuria, damnum sine injuria [*Latin*] [*Damage without wrong, for instance, damage for which no action can be maintained*] · Schadenzufügung f ohne Rechtsverletzung, Schadenzufügung nicht zum Ersatz verpflichtend, Schädigung nicht zum Ersatz verpflichtend

damnum corpori datum [*Latin*]; material damage · Sachschaden m, Sachbeschädigung f

danger area, danger territory · Gefahrengebiet n

danger bonus · Gefahrenzuschlag m

dangerous place · Gefahrenstelle f

danger prevention · Gefahrenverhütung f, Gefahrenabwehr f

danger protection · Gefahrenschutz m

danger zone · Gefahrenzone f

dasymetric map · geographisch überarbeitete Dichtekarte f, dasymmetrische Karte

data bank · Datenbank f

data collection · Datensammlung f, Datenerhebung

data processing · Datenverarbeitung f

data protection, computer security, safeguarding of data · Datenschutz m

data punching procedure · Datenlochungsverfahren n

data sequence, sequence of data · Datenfolge f

date · Datum n, Termin m

to date back · zurückdatieren

date draft, bill (of exchange) after date, bill (of exchange) with exact expiry, time bill (of exchange) · Datowechsel m, Zeitwechsel, Zielwechsel [*Die Zahlungszeit ist auf eine bestimmte Zeit nach dem Tage der Ausstellung festgesetzt*]

date of acceptance (of (the) work(s)), acceptance date · Abnahmedatum n, Abnahmetermin m, Bauabnahmedatum, Bauabnahmetermin

date of application, date of request, filing date, application date, request date, date of filing · Antragsdatum n, Gesuchsdatum

date of award, date of letting, award date, letting date · Auftragsdatum n, Zuschlag(s)datum, Auftragstermin m, Zuschlag(s)termin

date of commencement, commencement date · Anfangsdatum n, Anfangstermin m, Anfangstag m

date of completion, completion date · Fertigstellungsdatum n, Fertigstellungstermin m, Fertigstellungstag m

date of drawing, drawing date · Ausstellungsdatum n, Wechselausstellungsdatum

date of filing, date of application, date of request, filing date, application date, request date · Antragsdatum n, Gesuchsdatum

date of handing over, date of handover, date of (de)livery, date of surrender, handing over date, surrender date, handover date, (de)livery date · Aushändigungstermin m, Übergabetermin m, Aushändigungsdatum n, Übergabedatum

date of hearing, hearing date · Anhörungstermin m, Anhörungsdatum n

date of issue, issue date · Ausfertigungsdatum n, Ausstellungsdatum [*Bescheinigung*]

date of letting, award date, letting date, date of award · Auftragsdatum n, Zuschlag(s)datum, Auftragstermin m, Zuschlag(s)termin

date of payment, payment date · Zahlungstermin m, Zahlungsdatum n

date of posting, posting date · Aufgabedatum n [*Postsendung*]

date of receipt of bids → date of opening

date of request, filing date, application date, request date, date of filing, date of application · Antragsdatum *n*, Gesuchsdatum

date of service, service date · Zustellungstermin *m*, Zustellungsdatum *n*

date of submission, date set for the opening of tenders deadline for submission of bids, date of opening, (bid) opening date; (bid) proposal opening date (US); submission date · (Angebots)Eröffnungstermin *m*, (Angebots)Eröffnungsdatum *n*, Submissionstermin, Submissionsdatum

date of supply, supply date · Liefertag *m*, Lieferdatum *n*, Liefertermin *m*

date of surrender → date of handing over

date set for the opening of tenders deadline for submission of bids, date of opening, (bid) opening date; (bid) proposal opening date (US); submission date, date of submission · (Angebots)Eröffnungstermin *m*, (Angebots)Eröffnungsdatum *n*, Submissionstermin, Submissionsdatum

to date wrongly, to misdate · falsch datieren, unrichtig datieren

dathe · Gau *m*, Kreis *m* [*In der Grafschaft Kent, drei von vier ,,hundreds" umfassend*]

day continuation school · Berufsschule *f*, Zwangsfortbildungsschule

day (house)breaker · Einbrecher *m* am Tage

day (house)breaking · Einbruch *m* am Tage, Einbruch zur Tageszeit

day-labourer (Brit.); day-laborer (US) · Tagelöhner *m*

day lettergram (US); letter telegram sent during the day · Tag-Brieftelegramm *n*

daylight period · Tageslicht *n*

daylight saving time · Sommerzeit *f*

dayman, oddman, catchman · (landwirtschaftlicher) Gelegenheitsarbeiter *m*, Gelegenheitslandarbeiter

day nursery · (Kinder)Tagesstätte *f*

day of grace, grace day · Respekttag *m*

day of judg(e)ment, judg(e)ment day [*The day fixed by statute, rule, or custom of a court on which judg(e)ments are pronounced or entered upon the court records*] · Urteilstag *m*

day of rest · Ruhetag *m*

day order · Börsenauftrag *m* für einen Tag gültig

day population → day(time) population

day rate, daily rate · Tagessatz *m*

day return-ticket · Tagesrückfahrkarte *f*

day school, primary school, board school (Brit.); elementary school, common school (US) · Elementarschule, Grundschule, Volksschule *f*

day school · Externat *n*

day's work (at ploughing), daywere; diurnalis [*Latin*]; acre strip [*In old English law. A term applied to land, and signifying as much arable ground as could be ploughed up in one day's work*] · Tag(e)werk *n*; Tagwan *n*, Tagwen *n* [*In den Alpen*]

daytime poaching, poaching in daytime · Tagwilddieberei *f*, Tagwildfrevel *m*

day(time) population · Tagbevölkerung *f* [*Wohnbevölkerung ± Pendlersaldo*]

day-to-day · tagtäglich

day-to-day administration · laufende Verwaltung *f*

day-to-day money · Taggeld *n*

Dayton permanent (building and loan) association (US); permanent building society (Brit.) · Realkreditinstitut *n* für langfristige Baudarleh(e)n, Realkreditverein *m* für langfristige Baudarleh(e)n [*Fehlbenennungen: dauernde Bausparkasse, permanente Bausparkasse. Diese Institute bauen nicht selbst und geben ihr Darleh(e)n nicht nur an ihren Sparerkeis*]

Dayton permanent plan, optional payment plan, Ohio plan · individueller unregelmäßiger Plan *m* [*Eine dauernde Form einer amerikanischen Bausparkasse*]

day wage → daily wage

day wage rate, daily wage rate, jobbing rate, daywork(s) rate · Tagelohnsatz *m*

daywere; diurnalis [*Latin*]; acre strip, day's work (at ploughing) [*In old English law. A term applied to land, and signifying as much arable ground as could be ploughed up in one day's work*] · Tag(e)werk *n*; Tagwan *n*, Tagwen *n* [*In den Alpen*]

daywork(s) · Tagelohnarbeit(en) *f (pl)*

daywork(s) contract, jobbing contract · Tagelohnvertrag *m*

daywork(s) interim payment, jobbing interim payment · Tagelohnabschlagszahlung *f*

daywork(s) invoice · Tagelohnrechnung *f*

daywork(s) rate, day wage rate, daily wage rate, jobbing rate · Tagelohnsatz *m*

daywork(s) schedule, daywork(s) scheme, jobbing schedule, jobbing scheme · Tagelohnplan *m*

daywork(s) scheme, jobbing schedule, jobbing scheme, daywork(s) schedule · Tagelohnplan *m*

daywork(s) sheet — death rate

daywork(s) sheet · Tagelohnliste f, Tagelohnzettel m

daywork(s) wage → daily wage

DBDL (US), displaced business disaster loan · Darleh(e)n n für planungsverdrängte Gewerbetreibende

demise, decease · Ableben n, Hingang m

decentralization, formation of sub(urb)s, suburban process, suburban urbanization, (urban) spread, (urban) sprawl, outward spread, outward sprawl, suburban spread, suburban sprawl, spread(ing) of cities, sprawl of cities, spread(ing) of towns, sprawl of towns, suburbanization · Sied(e)lungsbrei m, Dezentralisation f, Ausufern n, Zersied(e)lung f, Überwucherung des städtischen Raumes, Dezentralisierung f

deacon convener · zusammenberufender Zunftmeister m

dead assets · totes Guthaben n, tote Aktiva f

deadfreight · Faustfracht f

dead hand, mortmain [*French*]; manus mortua [*Latin*]; mortification [*Scots law*] [*A condition of property in which it is held without the power of change or (ab)alienation*] · tote Hand f

dead letter · unbestellbarer Brief m, unzustellbarer Brief

deadline date, target date · Endtermin m, Enddatum n [*Der Zeitpunkt, bis zu dem der Auftragnehmer die vertraglich vereinbarte Bauleistung zu erbringen hat*]

deadlock · Entscheidungsunfähigkeit f

dead pledge, mortgage [*A thing put into the hands of a creditor*] · totes Pfand n

dead use, future use · (zu)künftige Benutzung f, (zu)künftiger Gebrauch m

dead wood · abgestorbenes Holz n, totes Holz

dealer [*In the popular sense, one who buys to sell, not one who buys to keep, or makes to sell*] · Händler m

dealer · Devisendisponent m, Händler

dealer → (securities) dealer

dealer → ((real) estate) broker

dealer in arbitrage, arbitrager · Arbitrageur m

dealer in secondhand books; secondhand bookseller [*misnomer*] · Antiquar m

dealer's store · Händlerlager m

dealing with authorities · Verkehr m mit Behörden

dealing with land(s), realty transactions, (real) estate transactions, (real) property transactions, land(s) transactions [*Acquiring, holding and disposing of land*] · Bodenverkehr m, Grundstücksverkehr, Liegenschaftsverkehr, Immobiliarverkehr, Immobilienverkehr

dealing with rural land(s) → rural (real) property transactions

dealing with urban land(s), urban (real) property transactions, urban (real) estate transactions, urban land(s) transactions · städtischer Grundstücksverkehr m, städtischer Bodenverkehr, städtischer Immobiliarverkehr, städtischer Immobilienverkehr, städtischer Liegenschaftsverkehr

to deal with beforehand, to anticipate · vorwegnehmen

dean · Dekan m, Dompropst m

dean of g(u)ild, dean of company · Gildenobermeister m

dean of peculiars · eximierter Dekan m, eximierter Dompropst

dear housing · Wohnungsteuerung f

dear money, tight money · knappes Geld n, teures Geld

dear money policy, tight money policy · Politik f des knappen Geldes, Politik des teuren Geldes

dearth of land(s), land(s) shortage, land(s) scarcity, shortage of land(s), scarcity of land(s), land(s) dearth · Bodenknappheit f, Landknappheit, Bodenverknappung f, Landverknappung, Bodenmangel m, Landmangel

deathbed declarations, dying declarations · Erklärungen fpl auf dem Sterbebett

death benefit, death grant · Sterbegeld n

death claim · Lebensversicherungsanspruch m, Lebensversicherungs(an)recht n

death declaration, declaration of disappearance, declaration of death, disappearance declaration · Todeserklärung f, Verschollenheitserklärung

death duty, inheritance duty [*England*]; inheritance tax [*USA*]; death tax [*USA*]; estate duty [*The duty payable on the devolution of property at death. The one now commonly payable is estate duty. Legacy duty and succession duty were abolished in England by the Finance Act, 1949, ss. 27, 28*] · Erb(schafts)steuer f, Nachlaßsteuer, Vermächtnissteuer

death grant, death benefit · Sterbegeld n

death presumption, presumption of death · Todesvermutung f

death rate, rate of death · Sterbeziffer f, Sterberate f

deaths at the same point of time · Gleichzeitigkeit *f* des Todes mehrerer Personen

death tax, inheritance tax [*USA*]; estate duty, death duty, inheritance duty [*England*]; [*The duty payable on the devolution of property at death. The one now commonly payable is estate duty. Legacy duty and succession duty were abolished in England by the Finance Act, 1949, ss. 27, 28*] · Erb(schafts)steuer *f*, Nachlaßsteuer, Vermächtnissteuer

to debar from an inheritance, to put out of an inheritance, to exclude from inheriting, to disinherit; to exheredate [*Scots law*], to deprive of an inheritance · enterben

debarment by force of law, debarment by strength of law, exclusion by force of law, exclusion by strength of law · Ausschließung *f* kraft Gesetzes, Ausschluß *m* kraft Gesetzes

debarring from an inheritance, excluding from an inheritance; exheredating [*Scots law*], disinheriting, depriving of an inheritance, putting out of an inheritance · Enterben *n*

debating society · Redeverein *m*

debenture [*A fixed-interest security issued by British joint-stock companies*]; corporate bond [*A fixed-interest security issued by stock corporations in the USA*] · Schuldverschreibung *f*, Obligation *f* [*private Kapitalgesellschaft*]

debenture (corporate) bond, plain corporate bond [*USA*]; naked debenture, simple debenture, unsecured debenture [*Great Britain*]; unsecured corporate bond [*USA*] · ungesicherte Schuldverschreibung *f*, ungesicherte Obligation *f* [*private Kapitalgesellschaft*]

debentured goods · Rückzollgüter *npl*

debenture holder, debenture bearer [*Great Britain*]; corporate bond holder, corporate bond bearer [*USA*] · Schuldverschreibungsinhaber *m*, Obligationsinhaber [*private Kapitalgesellschaft*]

debenture stock, loan stock, debentures · Schuldverschreibungen *fpl*

debenture to bearer, debenture to holder [*Great Britain*]; coupon bond [*USA*] · Inhaberschuldverschreibung *f*, Inhaberobligation *f* [*private Kapitalgesellschaft*]

to debit · belasten [*Konto*]

debit balance, balance due · Debitsaldo *m*

debitum [*Latin*]; debt [*That which is due from one person to another, whether money, goods, or services*] · Schuld *f*

de bonis non (administratis) [*Latin*]; of goods not yet administered, relating to assets which have not been administered [*A grant "de bonis non administratis", or more shortly "de bonis non", is made where an executor dies intestate or an administrator dies, in either case without having fully administered*] · von nicht verwalteten Nachlaßgegenständen

debris heap, heap of debris · Schutthalde *f*

debt; debitum [*Latin*] [*That which is due from one person to another, whether money, goods, or services*] · Schuld *f*

debt agreement · Schuldenvereinbarung *f*, Schuldenabkommen *n*, Schuldenabmachung

debt burden, debt encumbrance, debt incumbrance, debt charge · Schuld(en)belastung *f*, Schuld(en)last *f*

debt by deed, deed debt · (gesiegelte) Urkundenschuld *f*

debt by simple contract, contract debt · Vertragsschuld *f*

debt by specialty · Schuld *f* auf Grund eines feierlichen Vertrages

debt capacity · Kreditkapazität *f*

debt capital, borrowed capital, outside capital · Fremdkapital *n*, Schuldenkapital

debt charge, debt burden, debt encumbrance, debt incumbrance · Schuld(en)belastung *f*, Schuld(en)last *f*

debt claim · Schuldenforderung *f*

debt collecting · Schuldeneintreibung *f*

debt conversion, conversion of debt · Umschuldung *f*

debt counsel(l)ing · Schuldenberatung *f*

debt delinquency · Schuldvergehen *n*

debtee, creditor · Gläubiger *m*

debtee-executor, creditor-executor · Gläubiger *m* vom Schuldner als (Testaments)Vollstrecker bestellt

debtee nation, creditor nation · Gläubigernation *f*

debtee (probate) administrator, creditor trustee for sale, debtee trustee for sale, creditor (probate) administrator · Gläubiger-Nachlaßverwalter *m*, Gläubiger-Erb(schafts)verwalter

debtee's default, creditor's default · Gläubiger(ver)säumnis *f, n, (f)*

debtee's delay, creditor's delay · Gläubigerverzug *m*, Annahmeverzug

debtees' meeting, creditors' meeting · Gläubigerversammlung *f*

debtee trustee for sale, creditor (probate) administrator, debtee (probate) administrator, creditor trustee for sale · Gläubiger-Nachlaßverwalter *m*, Gläubiger-Erb(schafts)verwalter

debt encumbrance, debt incumbrance, debt charge, debt burden · Schuld(en)belastung *f*, Schuld(en)last *f*

debt in rem, real debt · dingliche Schuld *f*

debt-interest, interest on debt · Schuldzins *m*

debt-laden, indebted · verschuldet

debt-limit, limit of indebtedness [*Legally fixed limit on the amount of money a governmental entity may borrow*] · Verschuldungsgrenze *f*

debt (of money), money debt [*A sum of money due by certain and express agreement*] · (Geld)Schuld *f*

debt of priority, priority debt · Vorrangschuld *f*, Vorrechtschuld

debt of record, judg(e)ment debt · Prozeßschuld *f*, Judikatschuld, Urteilsschuld

debt of record, record debt · gerichtlich festgestellte Schuld *f*, tituliere Schuld

debt of the deceased (person) · Nachlaßschuld *f*

debtor-executor, obligor-executor · Schuldner *m* vom Gläubiger als (Testaments)Vollstrecker bestellt

debtor nation · Schuldnernation *f*

debtor's assets · Schuldnerguthaben *n*

debtor's default, obligor's default · Schuldner(ver)säumnis *f*, *n*, *(f)* [*Es liegt vor, wenn die vertraglich vereinbarte Leistung nach Eintritt der Fälligkeit trotz Mahnung nicht erbracht wird*]

debtor's delay, obligor's delay · Schuldnerverzug *m*

debtor's land, obligor's land · Schuldnerland *n*, Schuldnerboden *m*

debtor's summons, obligor's summons · Zahlungsaufforderung *f* [*Aufforderung an einen Schuldner durch ein Konkursgericht die im Schriftstück genannte Summe an den darin genannten Gläubiger zu zahlen oder Einspruch zu erheben, andernfalls über ihn das Konkursverfahren verhängt wird*]

debt provable in bankruptcy · Schuld *f* im Konkursverfahren berücksichtigt

debt redeemable in instal(l)ments, amortization debt, sinking fund debt · Tilgungsschuld *f*, Amortisationsschuld

debt reduction · Schuldenabbau *m*

debt(s) adjustment, adjustment of debt(s) · Schuld(en)regulierung *f*

debt(s) amortization rate, rate of amortization of debt(s) · Schuldentilgungsrate *f*

debt secured by a document, bonded debt, documentary debt · Briefschuld *f*

debt service cost(s) · Schuldendienstkosten *f*

debts provable, provable debts · Konkursforderung *f*

debt(s) service · Schuldendienst *m*

debt sum, indebtedness sum · Schuldensumme, Verschuldungssumme *f*

decartelization · Entkartellisierung *f*

to decartelize · entkartellisieren

decease, demise · Ableben *n*, Hingang *m*

deceased debtor, deceased obligor · Nachlaßschuldner *m*

deceased (person), decedent · Verstorbene *m*, verstorbene Person *f*

deceit, fraud · Arglist *f*, Betrug *m*

decentralization · Dezentralisation *f*

to decentralize, to disperse, to resite, to relocate, to resettle, to displace, to transfer from congested areas · aussiedeln, umsiedeln, verlegen, verändern des Standortes, umsetzen

to decentralize · entzentralisieren, dezentralisieren

decentralized · entzentralisiert, dezentralisiert

decentralized concentration · dezentrale Konzentration *f*

deceptive · täuschend

deceptive character · Täuschungscharakter *m*

decidability · Entscheidbarkeit *f*

decidable · entscheidbar

to decide, to try, to rule, to adjudicate [*To settle by authoritative sentence*] · entscheiden [*(Rechts)fall]*]

decided, adjudicated, tried, ruled · entschieden [*(Rechts)Fall*]

decidedly bound · unbedingt gebunden

decision · abschließendes Ergebnis *n* der Tatsachenermitt(e)lung und der Rechtsfindung

decision → (managerial) decision

decision(al) aid · Entscheidungshilfe *f*

decision(al) analysis · Entscheidungsanalyse *f*, Entscheidungsuntersuchung

decision(al) environment · Entscheidungsklima *n*

decision(al) framework, framework for decision · Entscheidungsrahmen *m*

decision(al) model · Entscheidungsmodell *n*

decision(al) pattern, decision(al) scheme · Entscheidungsmuster n, Entscheidungsschema n

decision(al) ripeness · Entscheidungsreife f

decision(al) space · Entscheidungsraum m

decision(al) technique · Entscheidungstechnik f

decision(al) theory · Entscheidungstheorie f

decision(al) variable · Entscheidungsveränderliche f

decision box · Entscheidungsblock m [*In einem Netzwerk*]

decision costing, decision (cost(s)) accounting · Kostenrechnung f als Entscheidungsgrundlage, Kostenkalkulation f als Entscheidungsgrundlage, Kostenermitt(e)lung als Entscheidungsgrundlage, (Kostenbe)Rechnung als Entscheidungsgrundlage

decision (cost(s)) accounting, decision costing · Kostenrechnung f als Entscheidungsgrundlage, Kostenkalkulation f als Entscheidungsgrundlage, Kostenermitt(e)lung als Entscheidungsgrundlage, (Kostenbe)Rechnung als Entscheidungsgrundlage

decision criterion, criterion of decision · Entscheidungskriterium n

decision ex aequo et bondo, discretionary decision · Ermessensentscheid(ung) m, (f), Entscheid(ung) nach Ermessen

decision in equity, equity decision, equitable decision · Billigkeitsentscheid(ung) m, (f)

decision maker, decision taker · Entscheidungsträger m

decision(-making) group, decision-taking group · Entscheidungsträgergruppe f

decision(-making) process, decision-taking process · Entscheidungsvorgang m

decision(-making) strategy, strategy of decision(-making), strategy of decision-taking, decision-taking strategy · Entscheidungsstrategie f

decision(-making) structure, decision-taking structure · Entscheidungsträgerstruktur f

decision simulation → (management) decision simulation

decision taker, decision maker · Entscheidungsträger m

decision-taking group, decision-making group · Entscheidungsträgergruppe f

decision-taking process, decision-making process · Entscheidungsvorgang m

decision-taking strategy, decision(-making) strategy, strategy of decision(-making) · Entscheidungsstrategie f

decision-taking structure, decision(-making) structure · Entscheidungsträgerstruktur f

decision to migrate, decision to move · Wanderungsentscheidung f

decision tree · Entscheidungshierarchie f

decisiveness; concludency [*obsolete*]; conclusiveness [*The quality of being conclusive*] · Schlüssigkeit f

declaration, statement · Erklärung f

declaration [*obsolete*], information [*It is in the nature of pleading. It is the step by which several civil and criminal proceedings are commenced*] · Klageschrift f, Klagebegründung(sschrift) f

declaration [*obsolete*]; statement of cleim · Klageschrift f [*Zivilprozeß*]

declaration in lieu of prospectus, statement in lieu of prospectus · Erklärung f an Prospektes statt

declaration mistake, statement mistake · Erklärungsirrtum m

declaration of acceptance, acceptance declaration · Annahmeerklärung f

declaration of acceptance (of (the) work(s)), acceptance declaration · Abnahmeerklärung f, Bauabnahmeerklärung

declaration of assignation, statement of assignation, assignment declaration, cession declaration, assignment statement, cession statement, assignation statement, assignation declaration, statement of assignment, declaration of assignment, declaration of cession, statement of cession · Abtretungserklärung f, Zessionserklärung

declaration of bankruptcy, statement of bankruptcy, bankruptcy statement, bankruptcy declaration · Konkurserklärung f

declaration of candidacy, nomination petition, certificate of nomination, paper of nomination, nomination paper, nomination certificate [*USA*] · Vorwahlvorschlag m

declaration of cession, statement of cession, declaration of assignation, statement of assignation, assignment declaration, cession declaration, assignment statement, cession statement, assignation statement, assignation declaration, statement of assignment, declaration of assignment · Abtretungserklärung f, Zessionserklärung

declaration of compliance · Erklärung f über die Einhaltung der Gründungsvorschriften [*Gesellschaft*]

declaration of co-ownership (of property) · Gemeineigentumerklärung f, Anteileigentumerklärung, Bruchteileigentumerklärung

declaration of disappearance, declaration of death, disappearance declaration, death declaration · Todeserklärung f, Verschollenheitserklärung

declaration of dividend · Quotenerklärung f [Konkurs]

declaration of exemption, declaration of discharge, declaration of release, declaration of dispensation · Befreiungserklärung f, Entlastungserklärung, Dispens(ierungs)erklärung, Freistellungserklärung, Erlaßerklärung [Der Globalgläubiger verpflichtet sich das Grundstück nach Eingang des gemäß Kaufvertrag zu zahlenden Betrages von der dinglichen Belastung freizustellen]

declaration of exercise of pre-emptive rights · Bezugserklärung f [AG]

declaration of guaranty, declaration of guarantee, garantie declaration, declaration of guarantie, guaranty declaration, guarantee declaration · Bürgschaftserklärung f

declaration of homestead, homestead declaration · Heimstättenerklärung f

declaration of immediate execution, statement of immediate execution · Erklärung f zur sofortigen Zwangsvollstreckung, Unterwerfungsklausel f

declaration of intent(ion) · Absichtserklärung f

declaration of invalidity, invalidity declaration · Kraftloserklärung f, Mortifikation f; Amortisation [Fehlbenennung]

declaration of law; jurisdiction

declaration of majority, majority declaration · Volljährigkeitserklärung f

declaration of trust, statement of trust, trust declaration, trust statement [The act by which the person who holds the legal title to property or an estate acknowledges and declares that he holds the same in trust to the use of another person or for certain specified purposes] · einseitige Erklärung f, treuhänderische Übertragung, Kundgabe f eines Treuhandverhältnisses

declaration on the oath, statement on the oath, affidavit, statutory declaration, statutory statement [A written statement sworn on oath which may be used in certain cases as evidence] · Erklärung f an Eidesstatt, Versicherung an Eidesstatt, eidesstattliche Erklärung, eidesstattliche Versicherung, schriftlicher Eid m

declaratory, declarative · deklaratorisch

declaratory (court) action, declaratory (law)suit, declaratory cause, declaratory plea [An action wherein the right of the pursuer is craved to be declared, but nothing claimed to be done by the defender. Scots law] · Feststellungsklage f

declaratory judg(e)ment [One which simply declares the rights of the parties or expresses the opinion of the court on a question of law without ordering anything to be done] · Feststellungsurteil n

declaratory order; (land) condemnation order (US), compulsory (land) purchase order, (land) expropriation order · Bodenenteignungsanordnung f, Bodenenteignungsverfügung, Bodenenteignungsbefehl m, Bodenenteignungsgebot n, (Land)Enteignungsanordnung, (Land)Enteignungsverfügung, (Land)Enteignungsbefehl, (Land)Enteignungsgebot

declaratory resolution · Feststellungsbeschluß m, Feststellungsentschließung f

declaratory resolution for claim of compensation, declaratory resolution for claim of damages, declaratory resolution for claim of indemnification, declaratory resolution for claim of indemnity, declaratory resolution for damages claim, declaratory resolution for indemnification claim, declaratory resolution for compensation claim, declaratory resolution for indemnity claim · Entschädigungsfeststellungsbeschluß m, Schadenersatzfeststellungsbeschluß, Entschädigungsfeststellungsentschließung f, Schadenersatzfeststellungsentschließung

to declare, to state · erklären

to declare, to recite, to state a case, to count [To narrate the facts constituting a plaintiff's cause of action] · vorbringen einer Klage

declared value, official value, conventional value · Wert m für Zollzwecke deklariert

declination → disaffirmation

to decline, to disaffirm, to refuse, to repudiate, to reject · ablehnen, versagen, verweigern, zurückweisen

decline · Niedergang m

declined, disaffirmed, refused, repudiated, rejected · abgelehnt, versagt, verweigert, zurückgewiesen

"decline of morals" · „Asphaltkultur" f

declining payment plan · degressiver (Darleh(e)ns)Rückzahlungsplan m

decomposition · Aufspaltung f [Statistik]

decomposition algorism · Zerlegungsalgorithmus m

to deconcentrate — to dedicate

to deconcentrate, to decongest · auflockern, entflechten, auslagern, entballen, deglomerieren

deconcentration, decongestion; overspill [*misnomer*] · Auflockerung *f*, Deglomeration *f*, Auslagerung, Entballung, Entflechtung

deconcentration · Entflechtung *f*

deconcentration of functions, functional deconcentration · Funktionsentflechtung *f*

to decongest, to deconcentrate · auflockern, entflechten, auslagern, entballen, deglomerieren

decongestion; overspill [*misnomer*]; deconcentration · Auflockerung *f*, Deglomeration *f*, Auslagerung *f*, Entballung *f*, Entflechtung *f*

decontrol · Abbau *m* der Zwangswirtschaft, Zwangswirtschaftsabbau

decorative fixture, ornamental object fixed to a building, decorative object fixed to a building, ornamental fixture · Dekor(ations)einrichtung *f*, Schmuckeinrichtung, Ziereinrichtung, dekorativer (Grundstücks)Bestandteil *m*

decorative object fixed to a building, ornamental fixture, decorative fixture, ornamental object fixed to a building · Dekor(ations)einrichtung *f*, Schmuckeinrichtung, Ziereinrichtung, dekorativer (Grundstücks)Bestandteil *m*

decorative repair · Schmuckreparatur *f*

decoy pond [*A pond used for the breeding and maintenance of water-fowl*] · Wassergeflügelteich *m*

to decrease · abnehmen

decrease · Abnahme *f*

decreased commercial value, inferior commercial value · merkantiler Minderwert *m* [*Die Minderung des Verkaufswertes einer Sache, die trotz völliger und ordnungsmäßiger Instandsetzung deshalb verbleibt, weil vor allem wegen des Verdachts verborgen gebliebener Schäden, eine den Preis beeinflussende Abneigung gegen den Erwerb besteht*]

decreased value, inferior value · Minderwert *m*

decrease of value · Wertabnahme *f*, Wertschwund *m*

decreasing · Abnehmen *n*

decreasing city, decreasing town · Stadt *f* mit Bevölkerungsabnahme, Stadt mit abnehmender Bevölkerung, Stadt mit Bevölkerungsschwund

decree · Erlaß *m*

decree absolute → final judg(e)ment (at law)

decree (at law), judg(e)ment of a court, adjudication, (legal) judg(e)ment, judg(e)ment (at law) [*abbreviated: judgt.*], [*The words "judg(e)ment" and "decree" are often used synonymously; especially now that the codes have abolished the distinction between "law" and "equity". But of the two terms "judg(e)ment" (Urteil) is the more comprehensive, and includes "decree" (Erlaß)*] · gerichtliches Urteil *n*, (Gerichts)Urteil, Rechtsspruch *m*, Erkenntnis *f* eines Gerichts(hofes)

decree dative [*In Scotch law. An order of a probate court appointing an administrator*] · Erb(schafts)verwalterbenennungsurteil *n*, Nachlaßverwalterbenennungsurteil

decree (in equity); decretum [*Latin*]; judg(e)ment of a court of equity [*The judg(e)ment of a court of equity, answering for most purposes to the judg(e)ment of a court of common law*] · Billigkeits(recht)urteil *n*, Urteil nach Billigkeit(srecht), Billigkeitsgerichtsurteil

decree in respect of taxation of (property) builders · Bauherrenerlaß *m* [*Bundesrepublik Deutschland*]

decree nisi [*Mainly used in matrimonial suits*] · provisorisches Urteil *n*

decree of constitution [*Scots law. A decree by which a debt is ascertained*] · Schuld(en)feststellungsurteil *n*

decree of distribution [*Scots law. An instrument by which heirs receive property of a deceased. It is a final determination of the parties to a proceeding*] · Nachlaßverteilungsurteil *n*

decree of foreclosure [*Decree by a court upon the completion of foreclosure of a mortgage, lien, or contract*] · Verfallserklärungsurteil *n*

decree of insolvency, insolvency decree [*Scots law. One entered in a probate court, declaring the estate in question to be insolvent, that is, that the assets are not sufficient to pay the debts in full*] · Vergleichsverfahrensurteil *n*

decree to build along a road, decree to build along a highway, decree to build along a street · Anbauerlaß *m*

decretum [*Latin*]; judg(e)ment of a court of equity, decree (in equity) [*The judg(e)ment of a court of equity, answering for most purposes to the judg(e)ment of a court of common law*] · Billigkeits(recht)urteil *n*, Urteil nach Billigkeit(srecht), Billigkeitsgerichtsurteil

decursive · nachschüssig [*Zinsberechnung*]

to dedicate · widmen, zueignen

dedicated land — deed of settlement

dedicated land [*Land dedicated for public use*] · Widmungsland *n*

dedication [*The allocation by a landowner of a certain land area for public use or common use, such as for a street, park, parking lot, way, etc.*] · Widmung, Zueignung *f*

dedication of way · Privatwegzueignung *f*, Privatwegwidmung [*Überlassung eines Privatweges an eine Gemeinde*]

de die in diem [*Latin*]; from day to day · von Tag zu Tag

to deduct, to strike off a part, to subtract, to make an abatement from, to abate · abstreichen, abziehen

to deduct, to set off · aufrechnen, abziehen, abrechnen, kompensieren; verrechnen [*Schweiz*] [*Gegenforderung*]

deductible · abziehbar

deductible amount · Selbstbehaltbetrag *m*

deductible clause · Selbstbehaltklausel *f*

deducting all charges, all charges deducted · abzüglich aller Unkosten, alle Unkosten abgezogen

deduction, setting off; setoff (Brit.); offset (US) · Anrechnung *f*, Kompensation *f*, Saldierung *f*, Abziehung *f*, Aufrechnung *f*, Abrechnung *f*, Abzug *m*; Verrechnung *f* [*Schweiz*] [*Gegenforderung*]

deduction of (land) area, deduction of land · Bodenabzug *m*, Flächenabzug, Landabzug [*Die Verminderung der Flächen aller in eine Umlegung eingeworfenen Grundstücke zur Deckung des Unterschiedes zwischen neuen und alten örtlichen Verkehrs- und/oder Grünflächen*]

deductive alternate [*An alternate listed in the documents that results in a deduction from the bidder's base bid*] · Abzugsalternative *f*

deed box · Urkundenkassette *f*

deed debt, debt by deed · (gesiegelte) Urkundenschuld *f*

deed indented; scriptum indentatum [*Latin*]; indenture [*A deed to which two or more persons are parties, and in which these enter into reciprocal and corresponding grants or obligations towards each other*] · gesiegelte mehrseitige Urkunde *f*, mehrseitige gesiegelte Urkunde, zahnförmig ausgeschnittene gesiegelte mehrseitige Urkunde, zahnförmig ausgeschnittene mehrseitige gesiegelte Urkunde

deed memorial, memorial of deed · Auszug *m* einer gesiegelten Urkunde zum Registrieren

deed of (ab)alienation, deed of disposal, (ab)alienation deed, disposal deed · Veräußerungsurkunde *f*

deed of abandonment, abandonment deed, deed of dereliction, dereliction deed · Aufgabeerklärung *f*, Preisgabeerklärung *f*, Verzichterklärung *f*

deed of appointment, deed of nomination · Benennungsurkunde *f*, Ernennungsurkunde

deed of apprenticeship, indenture · Lehrbrief *m*

deed of arrangement, arrangement deed · Akkord *m*, Nachlaßvertrag *m* [*Der Vertrag, vermöge dessen dem Schuldner ein Teil der Schuld von den Gläubigern erlassen wird*]

deed of assignation, deed of cession, deed of assignment, assignment deed, cession deed, assignation deed · Abtretungsurkunde *f*, Zessionsurkunde

deed of composition, composition deed · (Gläubiger)Vergleichsurkunde *f*

deed of co-ownership (of property) · Gemeineigentumurkunde *f*, Anteileigentumurkunde, Bruchteileigentumurkunde

deed of covenant, covenant deed · (gesiegelte) Nebenverpflichtungsurkunde *f*

deed of dereliction, dereliction deed, deed of abandonment, abandonment deed · Aufgabeerklärung *f*, Preisgabeerklärung *f*, Verzichterklärung *f*

deed of disposal, (ab)alienation deed, disposal deed, deed of (ab)alienation · Veräußerungsurkunde *f*

deed of entail, entail deed · Fideikommißurkunde *f*, Majoratsurkunde

deed of grant, grant deed · Überlassungsurkunde *f*

deed of grant, grant deed · Bewilligungsurkunde *f* [*Grundstückskaufvertrag*]

deed of nomination, deed of appointment · Benennungsurkunde *f*, Ernennungsurkunde

deed of participation, participation deed · Beteiligungsurkunde *f*

deed of release, release deed · formelle Freigabeerklärung *f*, förmliche Freigabeerklärung, Rückauflassung an den Schuldner

deed of sale, sale deed · Verkaufsurkunde *f*

deed of settlement [*obsolete*]; articles of incorporation (US); social contract, partnership contract, memorandum (of association), deed of partnership, partnership deed [*Business corporations are now usually created under a general statute which permits a specified number of persons to form a corporation by preparing and filing with the proper public official, usually the secretary of state, a document known as the articles*

deed of title — default judg(e)ment

of incorporation] · Gründungsurkunde *f*, Gründungssatzung *f*, Gesellschaftsvertrag *m*, Gründungsvertrag, Gesellschaftsurkunde [*1.) Körperschaft, Korporation; 2.) (Kapital)Gesellschaft; 3.) vereinsähnliche Gemeinschaft*]

deed of title → title-deed

deed of trust, trust deed [*A deed that establishes a trust*] · Treuhanderrichtungsurkunde *f*

deed of warranty, warranty deed · Garantieurkunde *f*

deed-poll · einseitig verpflichtende (gesiegelte) Urkunde *f*, (gesiegelte) Urkunde über ein Rechtsgeschäft [*Urkunde mit glattem Rand im Gegensatz zur zahnförmig ausgeschnittenen Urkunde (= indenture)*]

deed poll, contract without consideration, gratuitous contract, nude contract, one-sided contract, unilateral contract, contract of benevolence · einseitiger Vertrag *m*, Vertrag ohne Gegenleistung

deed recording, deed recordation, deed registration, registration of deeds, recordation of deeds, recording of deeds · Urkundeneintrag(ung) *m*, *(f)*, Urkundenregistrierung

deeds register, deeds registry · Urkundenregister *n*

deed (under seal), sealed instrument, document under seal; charter [*obsolete*] · Siegelurkunde *f*, gesiegelte Urkunde, Urkunde unter Siegel

deepening of land(s), land(s) deepening · Grund(stücks)vertiefung *f*

deep sea fishery, deep sea fishing · Hochseefischerei *f*

to deface, to mar, to disfigure · beeinträchtigen, verschandeln, entstellen, verunstalten, verunzieren [*Ortsbild*]

defacing, marring, disfiguring · Beeinträchtigen *n*, Verschandeln, Verunstalten, Entstellen, Verunzieren [*Ortsbild*]

de facto, actual · tatsächlich, wirklich

de facto population, present-in-area population · ortsanwesende Bevölkerung *f*

de facto possession, actual physical control (over a thing), potential physical control (over a thing), actual possession, physical possession · tatsächliche Sachherrschaft *f*, tatsächliche Beherrschung *f* einer Sache, unmittelbarer Besitz *m*, tatsächlicher Besitz, tatsächlicher Besitz, wirkliche Sachherrschaft, wirkliche Beherrschung einer Sache, unmittelbare Sachherrschaft, unmittelbare Beherrschung einer Sache

defamation · Diffamierung *f*, Ehrenkränkung, Ehrenbeleidigung

defamation by writing; libellus [*Latin*]; libel, written defamation · schriftliche Ehrenkränkung *f*, Schmähschrift *f*

defamatory words · ehrenkränkende Worte *npl*, diffamierende Worte

default, neglect, failure, omission, omittance, forbearance, negligence, negative act(ion) [*Omission of that which a person ought to do*] · (Ver)Säumnis *f*, *n*, *(f)*, Vernachlässigung *f*, Unterlassung(shandlung), Nichtleistung, Unterlassungsakt *m*, negativer Akt, negative Handlung

default, dishonesty · Unehrlichkeit *f*

default · Verfehlung *f*

default, nonconformity, nonfeasance, nonperformance, noncompliance [*An omission of that which ought to be done. Specifically, the omission or failure to perform a legal duty*] · Nichtbefolgung *f*, Nichteinhaltung, Nichterfüllung, technisches Versäumnis *n*, Nichtausführung

default → violation (of law)

default at the trial · Säumnis *f*, *n* wegen Fernbleibens von der Hauptverhandlung, Versäumnis *f* wegen Fernbleibens von der Hauptverhandlung

default clause, termination for default (of government) clause · (Ver)Säumnisbeend(ig)ungsklausel *f* [*(Beschaffungs)Vertrag mit einer Regierung*]

defaulted mortgage · notleidende Hypothek *f*

defaulter [*One who misappropriates money held by him in an official or fiduciary character, or fails to account for such money*] · Veruntreuer *m*

defaulter's book · Disziplinarstrafbuch *n*

defaulting, contract-breaking · vertragsbrüchig, säumig

defaulting party, contract-breaking party · vertragsbrüchige Partei, säumige Partei *f*

defaulting residential tenant, defaulting dwelling tenant · Wohnungsmietschuldner *m*

defaulting tenant · Mietschuldner *m*

default in issuing summons for directions · Antrags(ver)säumnis *n*, *f*, *(f)* auf Erlaß des Vorverhandlungsbeschlusses

default in setting down for trial · Antrags(ver)säumnis *n*, *f*, *(f)* auf Anberaumung der Hauptverhandlung, Antrags(ver)säumnis auf Ansetzen der Hauptverhandlung

default judg(e)ment, judg(e)ment by default [*It is obtained when one party neglects to take a certain step in the action within the proper time*] · (Ver)Säumnisurteil *n*

default notice — (de)fence month (Brit.)

default notice, default notification, notice of default, notification of default · Anzeige *f* der Vertragsverletzung, Mitteilung *f* der Vertragsverletzung, Benachrichtigung der Vertragsverletzung, Vertragsverletzungsanzeige, Vertragsverletzungsmitteilung, Vertragsverletzungsbenachrichtigung

default of appearance, nonappearance · Kontumaz *f* [*Nichterscheinen einer Prozeßpartei bei einer gerichtlichen Verhandlung*]

default of appearance, nonappearance · Nichterscheinen *n*, Fernbleiben, Wegbleiben

default of contract, contract violation, contract default, contract infringement, contract contravention, contravention of contract, infringement of contract · Vertragswidrigkeit *f*, Vertragsverletzung *f*

default of defense (US); default of defence (Brit.) · Klagebeantwortungs(ver)säumnis *f, n, (f)*, Klageerwiderungs(ver)säumnis

default of payment, nonpayment, halted payment · Nicht(be)zahlung *f*

default of pleading, pleading default · Säumnis *f, n* wegen unterlassener Klagebegründung, Versäumnis *f* wegen unterlassener Klagebegründung, (Ver-)Säumnis wegen Nichtablieferung einer Klagebegründung

default of reply to defens (US); default of reply to defence (Brit.) · (Ver)Säumnis *f, n, (f)* wegen unterlassener Entgegnung auf die Klagebeantwortung(sschrift)

defeasance, [*A condition relating to a deed, such as an obligation, recognizance, statute or the like, but contained in a separate instrument, whether entered into at the same time as the deed itself, or afterwards*] · Annullierung *f*, Aufhebung

defeasible, abrogatable, rescindable, annullable · annullierbar, aufhebbar, löschbar, abschaffbar, abbaubar

to defeat · prellen [*einen Gläubiger*]

defect · Baumangel *m*, (Sach)Mangel

defect check(ing) · Baumangelprüfung *f*, (Sach)Mangelprüfung

defect in a structure, structural defect · Bauwerkmangel *m*

defect in design · Konstruktionsmangel *m*

defect (in law) · Mangel *m*, Rechtsmangel

defective, improper · mangelhaft, nachbesserungsbedürftig

defective, faulty · fehlerhaft

defectiveness · Mangelhaftigkeit *f*, Nachbesserungsbedürftigkeit

defective organization, faulty organization · Organisationsmangel *m*

defective performance, improper performance, defective work, improper work · mangelhafte Leistung *f*, nachbesserungsbedürftige Leistung, nachbesserungsbedürftige Arbeit *f*, mangelhafte Arbeit

defective work, improper work, defective performance, improper performance · mangelhafte Leistung *f*, nachbesserungsbedürftige Leistung, nachbesserungsbedürftige Arbeit *f*, mangelhafte Arbeit

defect of (legal) form, want of (legal) form, formal defect, informality, irregularity in matter of form · Formfehler *m*, Formmangel *m*

defect of performance · Leistungsmangel *m*

defect of substance [*It consists in the omission of something which is essential to be set forth in a plea, contract, indictment, etc.*] · Auslassungsfehler *m*

defects · Baumängel *mpl*, (Sach)Mängel

defects clause · Baumängelklausel *f*, (Sach)Mängelklausel, Nachbesserungsklausel

defects law · Baumängelrecht *n*, (Sach)Mängelrecht, Nachbesserungsrecht

defects liability · Baumängelhaftung *f*, (Sach)Mängelhaftung, Nachbesserungshaftung

defects process · Baumängelprozeß *m*, (Sach)Mängelprozeß, Nachbesserungsprozeß

defence (Brit.); defense (US); issue · Verteidigung *f*

defence (Brit.); defense (US); (defendant's) answer [*A pleading by which defendant in suit at law endeavo(u)rs to resist the plaintiff's demand by an allegation of facts, either denying allegations of plaintiff's complaint or confessing them and alleging new matter in avoidance, which defendant alleges should prevent recovery on facts alleged by plaintiff*] · Klageverneinung *f*, Klagebeantwortung, Klageerwiderung

defence to counterclaim (Brit.); defense to counterclaim (US) · Erwiderung *f* auf eine Widerklage, Widerklageerwiderung

defence housing (Brit.); defense housing (US) · Rüstungsarbeiterwohnungen *fpl*

defence industry (Brit.); defense industry (US) · Rüstungsindustrie *f*

(de)fence month (Brit.); defense month (US); close season, prohibited month [*A*

defendant — deficiency mortgage

period of thirty-one days in the year, during which time it is unlaw-ful for anybody to hunt in the forest], · Schonzeit f, Hegezeit, Setzzeit

defendant; defender [Scots law] · Beklagte m, beklagte Partei f [Zivilprozeß]

defendant · Angeklagte m [im Strafprozeß]

defendant alleging counterclaim · Widerkläger m

defendant in court of appeal, appellee · Appellat m, Berufungsverklagte, Berufungsbeklagte

(defendant's) answer; defence (Brit.); defense (US) [A pleading by which defendant in suit at law endeavo(u)rs to resist the plaintiff's demand by an allegation of facts, either denying allegations of plaintiff's complaint or confessing them and alleging new matter in avoidance, which defendant alleges should prevent recovery on facts alleged by plaintiff] · Klageverneinung f, Klagebeantwortung, Klageerwiderung

(defendant's) rejoinder; rejunctio [Latin] [In pleading. A defendant's answer of fact to a plaintiff's replication. Corresponding to the duplicatio of the civil law, and the triplicatio of Bracton] · Duplik f, zweite Gegenschrift f, Gegenerwiderung f

to defend a right, to maintain a right, to assert, to lay claim to · beanspruchen, geltend machen [Forderung; Recht]

defender · Verteidiger m

defender [Scots law], defendant · Beklagte m, beklagte Partei f [im Zivilprozeß]

defense (US); issue, defence (Brit.) · Verteidigung f

defense (US); (defendant's) answer; defence (Brit.) [A pleading by which defendant in suit at law endeavo(u)rs to resist the plaintiff's demand by an allegation of facts, either denying allegations of plaintiff's complaint or confessing them and alleging new matter in avoidance, which defendant alleges should prevent recovery on facts alleged by plaintiff] · Klageverneinung f, Klagebeantwortung, Klageerwiderung

defense housing (US), defence housing (Brit.) · Rüstungsarbeiterwohnungen fpl

defense industry (US); defence industry (Brit.) · Rüstungsindustrie f

defensive profile · Portefeuillemischung f widerstandsfähig gegen Kursrückgänge [Versicherungsfonds]

defensive village · Wehrdorf n

deferment, putting off, postponement, suspension · Aufschub m, Aufschiebung f, Hinausschiebung f, Verschiebung f

deferred annuity, postponed annuity, reversionary annuity, annuity put off · aufgeschobene Annuität f, Zukunftsannuität, Anwartschaftsannuität

deferred charge · Rechnungsabgrenzungsposten m [auf der Aktivseite]

deferred creditor · Nachzugsgläubiger m

deferred debt · nachgehende Konkursforderung f

deferred debt · aufgehobene Schuld f, ausgestellte Schuld, tote Schuld

deferred distribution profit sharing plan · Gewinnbeteiligungsplan m mit späterer Ausschüttung, Profitbeteiligungsplan mit späterer Ausschüttung

deferred full vesting · spätere volle Verfügung f über erworbene Pensionsansprüche, spätere volle Anrechnung

deferred income · Rechnungsabgrenzungsposten m [auf der Passivseite]

deferred item · transitorischer Posten m

deferred maintenance · aufgeschobene Unterhaltung f

deferred partial vesting, deferred graded vesting · spätere teilweise Verfügung f über erworbene Pensionsansprüche, spätere teilweise Anrechnung

deferred payment credit · strapazierter Dokumenten-Akkreditiv m

deferred payment plan · (Pensions)Plan m mit späterer Auszahlung, (Alters)Versorgungsplan mit späterer Auszahlung

deferred rebate · Treurabatt m, zurückgestellter Rabatt

deferred vested retirement benefit, deferred vested pension · Pensionsanspruch m bei vorzeitigem Ausscheiden aus dem Betrieb

to defeudalize · entfeudalisieren

defeudalizing · Entfeudalisieren n

deficiency, scarcity, shortage, stringency · Knappheit f, Verknappung f, Mangel m, Klemme f, Not f

deficiency account [A statement prepared by or for a bankrupt showing how the deficiency revealed in the statement of affairs arose] · Verlustübersicht f, Verlustbericht m

deficiency judg(e)ment [Difference between the indebtedness sued upon and the sale price or market value of the real estate at the foreclosure sale] · Ausfallurteil n

deficiency mortgage, mortgage against loss · Ausfallsicherungshypothek f

deficiency of budget, budget deficiency · Haushalt(s)defizit *n*

deficiency of credit, shortage of credit, scarcity of credit, stringency of credit, credit scarcity, credit stringency, credit shortage, credit deficiency · Kreditknappheit *f*, Kreditklemme *f*, Kreditnot *f*, Kreditmangel *m*, Kreditverknappung *f*, Kreditdefizit *n*

deficiency of housing, house-famine, housing shortage, housing deficiency, housing stringency, housing scarcity, shortage of housing, stringency of housing, scarcity of housing · Wohnungsbedarf *m*, Wohnungsfehlbestand *m*, Wohnraumfehlbestand, Wohnungsmangel *m*, Wohnraummangel, Wohnungsknappheit *f*, Wohnraumknappheit, Wohnungsdefizit *n*, Wohnraumdefizit, Wohnungsnot *f*, Wohnungsverknappung *f*, Wohnraumverknappung, Wohnraumklemme *f*, Wohnraumnot, Wohnungsklemme, Wohnraumbedarf [*Die sich aus der zahlenmäßigen Gegenüberstellung von Haushalten und Normalwohnungen in abgegrenzten Gebieten oder Bereichen ergebende Zahl fehlender Wohnungen*]

deficiency of money → shortage of money

deficient · unergiebig [*Grund und Boden*]

deficient in (legal) form · formfehlerhaft, formmangelhaft

deficit · Defizit *n*, Ausfall *m*, Fehlbetrag *m*

deficit region · Zuschußregion *f*

deficit spending · Ausgaben *f pl* als Gegenmaßnahme eines Konjunkturabschwunges [*Nicht mit Mitteln des ordentlichen Haushaltes bestritten*]

defining boundaries [*e.g. of an urban economy*] · Grenzfindung *f*

defining facts by law, singling out facts by law · Tatbestandsetzung *f*

definite (cost(s)) estimate (US); project central (cost(s)) estimate · genereller KV *m*, genereller (Bau)Kosten(vor)anschlag

definiteness, absence of doubt, distinctness, certainty, clearness of statement · Bestimmtheit *f*, Klarheit, Gewißheit

definite standard · sicherer Maßstab *m* [*Zur Messung einer (richterlichen) Entscheidung*]

definite term mortgage, terminable mortgage, straight mortgage · kündbare Hypothek *f*

definition · Begriffsbestimmung *f*, Definition *f*

definition of natural areas on the basis of physical criteria · naturräumliche Gliederung *f* [*Abgrenzung von Landschaften nach naturgegebenen Merkmalen*]

definitive sale · abgeschlossener Verkauf *m*

to deforce; deforciare [*Latin*] [*To withhold the possession of land(s) from one who is lawfully entitled to it or them*] · gewaltsam vorenthalten, widerrechtlich vorenthalten [*Land*]

deforcement; deforciamentum [*Latin*] · gewaltsame (Besitz)Vorenthaltung *f*, widerrechtliche (Besitz)Vorenthaltung [*Land*]

deforciant · gewaltsamer (Besitz)Vorenthalter *m*, widerrechtlicher (Besitz)Vorenthalter

deforciare [*Latin*]; to deforce [*To withhold the possession of land(s) from one who is lawfully entitled to it or them*] · gewaltsam vorenthalten, widerrechtlich vorenthalten [*Land*]

to defray [*expenses*] · bestreiten [*Ausgaben*]

defunct · abgestorben [*Korporation*]

defunct, late · verstorben

degradation · Abwertung *f*

degradation · Verschlechterung *f*

degree (in life) · Rang *m* [*Person*]

degree of danger · Gefahrenstufe *f*

degree of density, density degree · Dichtegrad *m*

degree of employment, employment degree · Arbeitsgrad *m*, Beschäftigungsgrad *m*

degree of homogeneity, homogeneity degree · Homogenitätsgrad *m*, Einheitlichkeitsgrad

degree of (land) improvement · (Land)Erschließungsgrad *m*

degree of risk · Wagnisstufe *f*, Risikostufe

degree of scarcity, shortage degree, scarcity degree, degree of shortage · Verknappungsgrad *m*, Mangelgrad, Knappheitsgrad

degressive allowance · degressiver Zuschuß *m*

degressive depletion for wear (and tear) · degressive Absetzung *f* für Abnutzung, degressive AfA [*Der Wert des abnutzbaren Wirtschaftsguts wird auf die Gesamtzeit seiner Verwendung oder Nutzung in fallenden Jahresbeiträgen verteilt*]

de-jure population, resident(ial) population, permanent population · Wohnbevölkerung *f*, De-jure-Bevölkerung, wohnberechtigte Bevölkerung

delay · Verzug *m*

delay claim · Verzugsforderung *f*

delay damage · Verzugsschaden *m*

delayed completion · verspätete Fertigstellung *f*

delay in completion, completion delay · Fertigstellungsverzug *m*

delay in execution, execution delay, delay in performance, performance delay · Ausführungsverzug *m*, Vollziehungsverzug *m*, Erbringungsverzug *m*, Erfüllungsverzug *m*

delay of acceptance, acceptance delay · Abnahmeverzug *m*, Bauabnahmeverzug

delay of acceptance, acceptance delay · Annahmeverzug *m*

delay of building, construction delay, building delay, delay of construction · Bauverzug *m*

delay of payment, payment delay · Zahlungsverzug *m*

delay of performance, performance delay · Leistungsverzug *m*

delay period, period of delay · Verzugsfrist *f*

delegate, proxy, (authorized) agent, attorney (in fact), representative *[A person either actually or by law held to be authorized and employed by one person to bring him into contractual or other legal relations with a third party]* · Beauftragte *m*, Bevollmächtigte, Sachwalter, (Stell)Vertreter, Agent

delegated · abgetreten, übertragen *[Vertragspflicht; Aufgabe]*

delegated law, subordinate law · Verordnungsrecht *n*

delegated law, subordinate act, delegated act, subordinate statute, delegate statute, subordinate law · Verordnungsgesetz *n*

delegated lawmaking, subordinate legislation, subordinate lawmaking, delegated legislation · Gesetzgebung *f* auf dem Verordnungsweg, Verordnungsgesetzgebung, nachgeordnete Gesetzgebung

delegation of function(s) · Funktionsübertragung *f*

delegation of power, power delegation · Ermächtigungsübertragung *f*

delegation of powers · (Staats)Gewaltenübertragung *f*

de lege ferenda *[Latin]* · nach künftig geltendem Recht

de lege lata *[Latin]* · nach geltendem Recht

deliberately untrue, designedly untrue, intentionally untrue, knowingly false, deliberately false, designedly false, intentionally false, knowingly not true, deliberately not true, designedly not true, intentionally not true, knowingly untrue · absichtlich unwahr, wissentlich unwahr, bewußt unwahr, absichtlich falsch, bewußt falsch, wissentlich falsch

deliberation · Vorbedacht *m*

deliberatio seisinae *[Latin];* (formal) livery of seisin · (feierliche) Gewereübergabe *f,* (feierliche) Übergabe der Gewere, (formelle) leh(e)n(s)rechtliche Besitzeinweisung *f,* formelle Auflassung

delictum *[Latin]* → violation (of law)

to delimit, to demarcate · abgrenzen

delimitation, demarcation; demarkation (US) *[The act of setting and marking limits or boundaries]* · Abgrenzen *n*

delimitation by boundary marks, separation by boundary marks, boundary delimitation · Abmark(ier)ung *f* *[§ 919. BGB. Kenntlichmachung von Grundstücksgrenzen durch Grenzzeichen]*

to delimit by boundary marks, to separate by boundary marks · abmark(ier)en

delimiting by boundary marks, separating by boundary marks · Abmark(ier)en *n*

delineation of regions, regional delineation · Abgrenzung *f* von Regionen

deliverable state · lieferbarer Zustand *m*

delivered (up), surrendered, handed over · ausgehändigt, übergeben

to deliver (up), to hand over, to surrender · aushändigen, übergeben

delivery · Lieferung *f*

(de)livery, tradition; traditio *[Latin];* handing over, handover · Aushändigung *f,* Übergabe *f,* Aushändigen *n,* Übergeben, Tradition *f*

delivery and shipping provisions · Lieferungs- und Versandbestimmungen *fpl*

delivery bill, bill of delivery, delivery order, order of delivery · Lieferschein *m*

(de)livery date, date of handing over, date of handover, date of (de)livery, date of surrender, handing over date, surrender date, handover date · Aushändigungstermin *m*, Übergabetermin *m*, Aushändigungsdatum *n*, Übergabedatum *n*

(de)livery duty, duty to hand over, duty to deliver, handing over duty, handover duty · Aushändigungspflicht *f*, Übergabepflicht *f*

delivery of drawings · Zeichnungsübergabe *f*

delivery of ownership (of property), delivery of proprietorship, delivery of (general) property · Eigentumsübergang *m*

delivery of pleadings · (formeller) Schriftsatzwechsel *m*, förmlicher Schriftsatzwechsel, Wechsel der (formellen)

delivery (of possession) — demand in rem

Schriftsätze, Wechsel der förmlichen Schriftsätze

delivery (of possession) [*The voluntary transfer of possession, i.e., the putting of property into the legal possession of another*] · (Besitz)Ableitung *f*, (Besitz)Übergang *m* [*bewegliche Sache(n)*]

delivery of title certificates, delivery of title deeds · Übergabe *f* von (Rechts)Titelurkunden

delivery order, order of delivery, delivery bill, bill of delivery · Lieferschein *m*

delivery order · Konnossementteilschein *m*

delivery period · Lieferfrist *f*

delivery program (US); delivery programme, delivery scheme · Lieferprogramm *n*

delivery up · Herausgabe *f*

delivery writ, writ of delivery (of possession) · (Besitz)Ableitungsdekret *n*, (Besitz)Übergangsdekret [*bewegliche Sachen*]

Delphi method, Delphi technique · Delphi-Verfahren *n*, Delphi-Methode *f* [*Ein iteratives Verfahren bei dem durch systematische Annäherung an das Optimum Antworten auf Fragen nach sozialen, technischen und wirtschaftlichen Entwick(e)lungsrichtungen gefunden werden*]

demain (land), demeyne (land), demeine (land), demesne (land), inland, land in (the lord's) demesne, bordland, table demesne, home farm (of the lord of the manor), demesnial settlement; terra indominicata terra dominica [*Latin*] [*Those lands of a manor not granted out in tenancy, but reserved by the lord for his own use and occupation. The opposite of "tenemental lands"*] · Hoffeld *n*, Salland *n*, grundherrliches Eigenland, Hofländerei *f*, Hofland, grundherrschaftliches Eigenland

demand, call · Nachfrage *f*

demand, claim · Verlangen *n*, Forderung *f*

demand → demand note

demanda [*Latin*] → petitio

demand account, continuing account, running account, open account, account current · laufendes Konto *n*, Kontokorrent *n*

demand and supply, call and supply, supply and demand, supply and call, market forces · Angebot *n* und Nachfrage *f*, Nachfrage und Angebot

demandant, actor in a real action; petens [*Latin*] · Grundstücksprozeßkläger *m*

to demand (as one's own), to claim · verlangen, fordern

to demand back, to reclaim, to claim back · zurückfordern, zurückverlangen

demand control, call control · Nachfragelenkung

demand curve, call curve · Nachfragekurve *f*

demand debtor, demand obligor, claim debtor, claim obligor · Forderungsschuldner *m*, Verlangensschuldner

demand deposit · Sichteinlage *f*

demand deposits · Sichtgelder *n pl* [*Depositenbank*]

demanded in writing · schriftlich verlangt

demand factor of location, demand factor of site, location(al) factor, site factor · Standortfaktor *m*, Lagefaktor

demand fluctuation, call fluctuation, fluctuation of call, fluctuation of demand · Nachfrageschwankung *f*

demand for additional payment, claim for additional payment · Nachforderung *f*

demand for (building) (land) area, call for (building) (land) area, call for (building) land, demand for (building) land · (Bau)Bodennachfrage *f*, (Bau)Landnachfrage, (Bau)Flächennachfrage

demand for early completion, acceleration claim, acceleration demand, claim for early completion · Beschleunigungsvergütungsforderung *f*, Beschleunigungsvergütungsverlangen, (Leistungs)Prämienforderung, (Leistungs)Prämienverlangen *n*

demand for housing, call for housing, housing demand, housing call · Wohnungsnachfrage *f*

demand for making good of defect, claim for making good of defect, demand for remedying of defect · Baumangelbeseitigungsforderung *f*, Baumangelbeseitigungsverlangen *n*, (Sach)Mangelbeseitigungsverlangen, Nachbesserungsverlangen, (Sach)Mangelbeseitigungsforderung, Nachbesserungsforderung

demand for money · Geldnachfrage *f*

demand for payment, claim for payment, payment demand, payment claim · Zahlungsverlangen *n*, Zahlungsforderung *f*

demand for remedying of defect, demand for making good of defect, claim for making good of defect · Baumangelbeseitigungsforderung *f*, Baumangelbeseitigungsverlangen *n*, (Sach)Mangelbeseitigungsverlangen, Nachbesserungsverlangen, (Sach)Mangelbeseitigungsforderung, Nachbesserungsforderung

demand function, call function · Nachfragefunktion *f*

demand in rem, real demand, claim in rem, real claim · dingliche Forderung *f*, dingliches Verlangen *n*

demand in tort, tort claim, tort demand, claim in tort · Forderung *f* aus unerlaubter Handlung, Verlangen *n* aus unerlaubter Handlung

demand level, call level, level of demand, level of call · Nachfragestand *m*

demand money, money at call and short notice, call money · tägliches Geld *n*, Tagesgeld, sofort abrufbares Geld

demand note, demand notification, reminder (of debt due), letter demanding payment, (formal) demand, prompt note, prompt notification [*Slang: dunning letter*] · Mahnbrief *m*, Mahnschreiben *n*, Mahnung *f*

demand obligor, claim debtor, claim obligor, demand debtor · Forderungsschuldner *m*, Verlangensschuldner

demand of a cause, claim of a plea, demand of a plea, claim of a (law)suit, demand of a (law)suit, claim of a court action, demand of a court action, claim of an action, demand of an action, claim of a cause · Klageforderung *f*, Klageverlangen *n*

demand of contribution, contribution claim, contribution demand, claim of contribution · Beitragsforderung *f*, Beitragsverlangen *n*

demand of harmonization, harmonization claim, claim of harmonization, harmonization demand · Übereinstimmungsforderung *f*, Übereinstimmungsverlangen *n*

demand of right, claim of right · Rechtsforderung *f*, Rechtsverlangen *n*

demand of title, title claim, title demand, claim of title · Titelforderung *f*, Titelverlangen *n*, Freigabeforderung, Freigabeverlangen

demand period, period of claim, period of demand, claim period · Forderungsfrist *f*

demand price, call price · Nachfragepreis *m*

demand rate · Sichtkurs *m*

demand-related industry, demand-orien(ta)ted industry · nachfragebezogene Industrie *f*, nachfrageorientierte Industrie

demand to inheritance, inheritance demand, claim to inheritance, inheritance claim · Erb(schafts)forderung *f*, Erb(schafts)verlangen *n*

demand to money, money demand, pecuniary demand, pecuniary claim, money claim, claim to money · Geldforderung *f*, Geldverlangen *n*

to demarcate, to delimit · abgrenzen

demercation · vermarkte Abgrenzung *f*

demarcation; demarkation (US); delimitation [*The act of setting and marking limits or boundaries*] · Abgrenzen *n*

demesne · Kammergut *n*

demesne (lands) of the Crown, Crown demesne land(s) held in socage, Crown lands, royal demesne (lands), royal demeine (lands), royal demain (lands) · Kronländer(eien) *pl*, Krongüter *n pl*, Länder(eien) der Krone, Domänen *f pl* der Krone, Güter der Krone, königliche Domänen, königliche Länder(eien), königliche Güter, Krondomänen, Land der Krone, Kronland *n*

demesne lord · Grundherr *m*

demesnial settlement; terra indominicata, terra dominica [*Latin*] demain (land), demeyne (land), demeine (land), demesne (land), inland, land in (the lord's) demesne, bordland, table demesne, home farm (of the lord of the manor) [*Those lands of a manor not granted out in tenancy, but reserved by the lord for his own use and occupation. The opposite of "tenemental lands"*] · Hoffeld *n*, Salland *n*, grundherrliches Eigenland, Hofländerei *f*, Hofland, grundherrschaftliches Eigenland

demisability, leasability · Verpachtbarkeit *f*

demisable, leasable · verpachtbar

to demise, to let; demittere dimittere [*Latin*]; to lease · verpachten

demise, tenancy; demissio; dimissio [*Latin*]; assedation, tack [*Scots law*], estate less than freehold, lease(hold), tenure, leasehold estate [*Holding of real estate under a lease. Such an estate continues for a fixed or determinable period of time but not for a lifetime. It is a conveyance of land whereby the owner of landed property, called the lessor, grants the possession and use of his landed property to another party, called the lessee, in consideration of a sum of money, called the rent*] · Bodenpacht *f*, Landpacht, Bodennutzungsrechtvergabe *f*, Landnutzungsrechtvergabe, Bodenverpachtung *f*, Landverpachtung, (Boden)Nutzungsrecht *n*

demise, lease(hold), tenure; demissio dimissio [*Latin*]; tenancy · Pacht *f*, Nutzungsrechtvergabe *f*, Verpachtung *f*

demise agreement → agreement of tenancy

demise cession, demise assignment, tenancy cession, tenancy assignment, cession of lease(hold), cession of demise, cession of tenancy, assignment of lease(hold), assignment of demise, assignment of tenancy, lease(hold) cession, lease(hold) assignment · Pachtabtretung *f*, Pachtzession *f*

demise contract, contract of tenancy, contract of demise, contract of lease(hold), contract of tenure, tenancy contract, tenure contract, lease(hold) contract · Pachtvertrag *m*, Nutzungsrechtvertrag, Verpachtungsvertrag

demised — demographic characteristic

demised, leased · verpachtet

demise(d) housing, leased housing · Pachtwohnungen *fpl*

demise(d) housing without rehabilitation, leased housing without rehabilitation · Pachtwohnungen *fpl* ohne Instandsetzung

demise(d) housing with rehabilitation, leased housing with rehabilitation · Pachtwohnungen *fpl* mit Instandsetzung

demise(d) lot, leasing lot, tenancy lot, lease(hold) lot, leased lot · Pachtflurstück *n*, Pachtparzelle *f*

demise(d) plot (of land), demise(d) plot of ground, demise(d) piece of land, demise(d) piece of ground, demise(d) parcel (of land), demise(d) parcel of ground, lease(hold) plot (of land), lease(hold) plot of ground, lease(hold) piece of land, lease(hold) piece of ground, lease(hold) parcel (of land), lease(hold) parcel of ground, leasing plot (of land), leasing plot of ground, leasing piece of land, leasing piece of ground, leasing parcel (of land), leasing parcel of ground, tenancy plot (of land), tenancy plot of ground, tenancy piece of land, tenancy piece of ground, tenancy parcel (of land), tenancy parcel of ground, leased plot (of land), leased plot of ground, leased piece of land, leased piece of ground, leased parcel (of land), leased parcel of ground · Pachtgrundstück *n* (im tatsächlichen Sinne)

demise(d) value, leased value, lease(hold) value, tenancy value · Pachtwert

demise for 3,000 years → tenancy for 3,000 years

demise for life → tenancy for life

demise from year to year → tenancy from year to year

demise law → law of estates less than freehold

demise matters (in general), lease(hold) practice, tenancy practice, demise practice, lease(hold) matters (in general), tenancy matters (in general) · Pachtwesen *n*

demise of land(s) at will → tenancy of land(s) at will

demise of property without destroying its substance, tenancy of property without destroying its substance, lease(hold) of property without destroying its substance; jus utendi [*Latin*] · Pacht *f* ohne Zerstörung, Nutzungsrecht *n* ohne Zerstörung

demise of (real) estate → (real) estate lease(hold)

demise of (real) property → (real) estate lease(hold)

demise option, tenancy option, lease(hold) option · Pachtoption *f*

demise practice, lease(hold) matters (in general), tenancy matters (in general), demise matters (in general), lease(hold) practice, tenancy practice · Pachtwesen *n*

demise protection code, lease(hold) protection code, tenancy protection code · Pachtschutzordnung *f*

demise right → lease(hold) right

demise to a third party, tenancy to a third party, third party lease(hold), third party tenancy, third party demise, lease(hold) to a third party · Zwischenpacht *f*

demise with an option to purchase, demise with an option to buy, lease(hold) with an option to purchase, lease(hold) with an option to buy, tenancy with an option to purchase, tenancy with an option to buy · Kaufoptionspacht *f*, Pacht mit Kaufoption

demising, leasing, letting (out on lease) · Vergeben *n* von Nutzungsrecht(en), Verpachten

demising of land, leasing of space, leasing of land, demising of space · Pachten *n* von Land, Pachten von Boden

demising of space, demising of land, leasing of space, leasing of land · Pachten *n* von Land, Pachten von Boden

demissio, dimissio [*Latin*]; assedation, tack [*Scots law*], estate less than freehold, lease(hold), tenure, leasehold estate, demise, tenancy [*Holding of real estate under a lease. Such an estate continues for a fixed or determinable period of time but not for a lifetime. It is a conveyance of land whereby the owner of landed property, called the lessor, grants the possession and use of his landed property to another party, called the lessee, in consideration of a sum of money, called the rent*] · Bodenpacht *f*, Landpacht, Bodennutzungsrechtvergabe *f*, Landnutzungsrechtvergabe, Bodenverpachtung *f*, Landverpachtung, (Boden)Nutzungsrecht

demissio, dimissio [*Latin*]; tenancy, demise, lease(hold), tenure · Pacht *f*, Nutzungsrechtvergabe *f*, Verpachtung *f*

demissio regis [*Latin*] · Ableben *n* des Herrschers, Hingang *m* des Herrschers

demittere, dimittere [*Latin*]; to lease, to demise, to let · verpachten

demographic approach · demographischer Ansatz *m*

demographic boom, population boom · Bevölkerungsaufschwung *m*

demographic characteristic, population characteristic · Bevölkerungsmerkmal *n*

demographic c(h)artography, population c(h)artography · Bevölkerungskartographie *f*

demographic development, population development · Bevölkerungsentwick(e)lung *f*

demographic dynamics, population dynamics · Bevölkerungsdynamik *f*

demographic equilibrium, population equilibrium · Bevölkerungsgleichgewicht *n*

demographic explosion, population explosion · Bevölkerungsexplosion *f*, schneller Bevölkerungszuwachs *m*, demographischer Drang *m*, Bevölkerungsdrang, demographische Explosion

demographic geography, population geography · Bevölkerungsgeographie *f*

demographic growth rate, demographic increase rate, rate of population growth, rate of population increase, population growth rate, population increase rate · Bevölkerungswachstumsrate *f*, Bevölkerungszunahmerate

demographic history, population history · Bevölkerungsgeschichte *f*

demographic increase rate → demographic growth rate

demographic level, level of population, population level · Bevölkerungsstand *m*

demographic policy, population policy · Bevölkerungspolitik *f*

demographic pressure, population pressure · Bevölkerungsdruck *m* [*Er entsteht, wenn die einer Bevölkerung zur Verfügung stehenden Unterhaltsmittel im Verhältnis zur Bevölkerungszahl zu klein werden*]

demographic principle, population principle · Bevölkerungsprinzip *n*, Bevölkerungsgrundsatz *m*

demographic pyramid, population pyramid · Bevölkerungspyramide *f*

demographic stagnation, stagnation of population, population stagnation · Bevölkerungsstagnation *f*, Bevölkerungsstillstand *m*, Bevölkerungsstockung *f*

demographic subregion, population subregion · Bevölkerungsteilregion *f*, Bevölkerungsteilraum *m*

demographic succession, population succession · Bevölkerungsfolge *f*

demographic time series · demographische Zeitreihe *f*

demographic variable, population variable · Bevölkerungsvariable *f*

to demolish, to wreck, to pull down, to raze · abbrechen, abreißen, einreißen [*Bauwerk*]

to demolish fortifications · entfestigen

demolishing, wrecking, pulling down, razing · Abbrechen *n*, Abreißen, Einreißen, Niederreißen

demolition, wrecking, pulling down, razing · Abbruch *m*, Abriß *m*, Bauabbruch, Bauabriß

demolition and rebuilding area, demolition and rebuilding territory, wrecking and rebuilding area, area of demolition and rebuilding, area of wrecking and rebuilding, territory of demolition and rebuilding, territory of wrecking and rebuilding, wrecking and rebuilding territory, razing and rebuilding territory · Abbruch- und Wiederaufbaugebiet *n*, Abriß- und Wiederaufbaugebiet, Abreiß- und Wiederaufbaugebiet, Einreiß- und Wiederaufbaugebiet

demolition area, demolition territory, wrecking area, wrecking territory, pulling down area, pulling down territory, razing territory · Abbruchgebiet *n*, Einreißgebiet, Abrißgebiet, Abreißgebiet

demolition certificate, demolition certificate, pulling down certificate, razing certificate · Abbruchbescheinigung *f*, Abbruchschein *m*, Einreißschein, Abreißschein, Abrißschein, Einreißbescheinigung, Abreißbescheinigung, Abrißbescheinigung

demolition contract, wrecking contract, pulling down contract, razing contract · Abbruchvertrag *m*, Abrißvertrag, Einreißvertrag, Abreißvertrag

demolition contractor, wrecking contractor, pulling down contractor, razing contractor · Abbruchunternehmer *m*

demolition cost(s), wrecking cost(s), pulling down cost(s), razing cost(s) · Abbruchkosten *f*, Abreißkosten, Einreißkosten, Abrißkosten

demolition enterprise, demolition undertaking · Abbruchunternehmen *n*, Abbruchunternehmung *f*

demolition of fortifications · Entfestigung *f*

demolition of slums, (slum) clearance, slum eradication, slum demolition, clearance of slums, eradication of slums · Elendsviertelbeseitigung *f* [*1. Entkernung; 2. Totalsanierung*]

demolition operation, wrecking operation, pulling down operation, razing operation · Abbruchvorgang *m*, Abrißvorgang, Einreißvorgang, Abreißvorgang

demolition operations → demolition work(s)

demolition order, wrecking order, pulling down order · (Bau)Abbruchanordnung *f*, (Bau)Abbruchverfügung, (Bau)Abbruchgebot *n*, (Bau)Abbruchbefehl *m*, (Bau)Einreißverfügung, (Bau)Einreißanordnung, (Bau)Einreißbefehl, (Bau)Ein-

demolition ordinance — density of coverage

reißgebot, (Bau)Abrißanordnung, (Bau)Abrißverfügung, (Bau)Abrißbefehl, (Bau)Abrißgebot, (Bau)Abreißanordnung, (Bau)Abreißverfügung, (Bau)Abreißgebot, (Bau)Abreißbefehl [*In den Landesbauordnungen einiger Länder der Bundesrepublik Deutschland und in § 19 des Städtebauförderungsgesetzes*]

demolition ordinance, wrecking ordinance, pulling down ordinance · (Bau)Abbruchverordnung *f*, (Bau)Einreißverordnung, (Bau)Abrißverordnung, (Bau)Abreißverordnung

demolition permission, wrecking permission, pulling down permission, razing permission · Abbrucherlaubnis *f*, Abbruchgenehmigung *f*, Einreißerlaubnis, Einreißgenehmigung, Abrißerlaubnis, Abrißgenehmigung, Abreißgenehmigung, Abreißerlaubnis

demolition plot, wrecking plot, pulling down plot, demolition parcel, pulling down parcel, wrecking parcel, razing parcel · Abbruchgrundstück *n*, Einreißgrundstück, Abreißgrundstück, Abrißgrundstück

demolition stop, wrecking stop, pulling down stop, razing stop, prohibition of demolition, prohibition of wrecking, prohibition of pulling down · Abbruchverbot *n*, Abrißverbot, Einreißverbot, Abreißverbot

demolition territory, wrecking area, pulling down area, pulling down territory, razing territory, demolition area · Abbruchgebiet *n*, Einreißgebiet, Abrißgebiet, Abreißgebiet

demolition work(s), demolition operations, wrecking work(s), wrecking operations, pulling down work(s), pulling down operations, razing operations, razing work(s) · Abbrucharbeit(en) *f (pl)*, Abrißarbeit(en), Einreißarbeit(en), Abreißarbeit(en)

demonstration city, demonstration town · Beispielstadt *f*

demonstration commune [*obsolete*]; demonstration community · Beispielgemeinde *f*, Beispielkommune *f*

demonstration grant · Beispielprogrammzuschuß *m*

demonstration programme; demonstration program (US) · Beispielprogramm *n*

demonstration town, demonstration city · Beispielstadt *f*

demonstrative · hinweisend [*Legat (im engeren Sinne)*]

demonstrative bequest, demonstrative legacy · Geldlegat *n* aus einem bestimmten Fonds, Geldvermächtnis *n* aus einem bestimmten Fonds

to demur [*To enter a demurrer*] · einreden

demurrage · Liegegeld *n*

demurral, demur(rer) [*An objection raised or exception taken*] · Einrede *f*

demurral, demurring · Einreden *n*

demurrer [*Before the Judicature Acts 1873*] · Verteidigungsschrift *f* [*Die Tatsachen werden zugestanden, aber die behauptete Rechtsfolgerung wird bestritten*]

demurrer [*A person who demurs*] · Einreder *m*

demurrer (to a lawsuit), objection in point of law [*A kind of pause or stop put to an action, and usually in the pleadings, upon a point of difficulty which must be determined by the court before any further proceeding can be had*] · Rechtseinrede *f*, Prozeßeinrede, Bestreiten *n* der Schlüssigkeit der Klage

demurring, demurral · Einreden *n*

to denationalize · reprivatisieren

denial, disavowal, disclaimer · Leugnung *f*, Abstreitung, Abrede *f*, Wegrede, Ableugnung

denomination, nominal value, face value, par value [*The value mentioned on the face of a security as distinguished from the market value*] · Nennwert *m*, Nominalwert

denomination (of securities) · Stückelung *f*

to denote in money · angeben in Geld

densely populated, densely peopled, thickly peopled, thickly settled, thickly populated, densely settled · dicht bevölkert, dicht besiedelt

density [*The relation between two units of measurement, the first referring to use and the second to land area*] · Dichte *f*

density decay → (population) density decay

density degree, degree of density · Dichtegrad *m*

density function · Dichtefunktion *f*

density gradient, gradient of density · Dichtegradient *m*

density gradient → (population) density gradient

density map → (population) density map

density of cities, urban mesh density, density of the urban mesh, density of towns · Städtedichte *f*

density of coverage, coverage density · Bebauungsdichte *f*, Baudichte; Überbauungsdichte [*Schweiz*]; Baudichtigkeit *f*, Bebauungsdichtigkeit [*Fehlbenennungen*] [*Das Verhältnis der bebauten zur unbebauten Fläche*]

density of daytime population · Tagesbevölkerungsdichte *f*

density of de jure population, density of resident(ial) population, density of permanent population · Wohnbevölkerungsdichte *f*, De-jure-Bevölkerungsdichte, Dichte der wohnberechtigten Bevölkerung

density of dwelling units (US); density of dwellings · Wohnungsdichte *f* [*Wohnungen je ha Nettobauland*]

density of employment, density of work, work density, employment density · Arbeitsdichte *f*, Beschäftigungsdichte *f*

density of inhabitants · Einwohnerdichte *f*

density of land use, land use density · Bodennutzungsdichte *f*, Landnutzungsdichte, Flächennutzungsdichte

density of occupancy, occupancy density · (Wohnungs)Belegungsdichte *f* [*qm Bruttogeschoßfläche je Bewohner*]

density of overnight population, overnight population density · Nachtbevölkerungsdichte *f*

density of population, population density · (Be)Sied(e)lungsdichte *f*, Volksdichte, Bevölkerungsdichte, Menschenausstattung *f* einer Fläche, Ansied(e)lungsdichte

density of resident(ial) population, density of permanent population, density of de jure population · Wohnbevölkerungsdichte *f*, De-jure-Bevölkerungsdichte, Dichte der wohnberechtigten Bevölkerung

density of the urban mesh, density of towns, density of cities, urban mesh density · Städtedichte *f*

density of towns, density of cities, urban mesh density, density of the urban mesh · Städtedichte *f*

density of traffic, traffic density · Verkehrsdichte *f*

density of work, work density, employment density, density of employment · Arbeitsdichte *f*, Beschäftigungsdichte *f*

density pattern, density scheme, pattern of density, scheme of density · Dichteschema *n*, Dichtemuster *n*

density value · Dichtewert *m*

to deny, to traverse [*in pleading*] · bestreiten, leugnen

deodand · Gottespfand *n*

department · Zentralbehörde *f* [*Eines Einzelstaates der USA*]

department [*USA*]; ministry · Ministerium *n*

department, branch, sector, province, division [*public administration*] · Abteilung *f*, Referat *n*, Dezernat *n*, Ressort *n*

Department of Defence [*USA*] · Verteidigungsministerium *n*

department of hous(eubuild)ing (US); ministry of hous(e build)ing (Brit.) · Wohn(ungs)bauministerium *n*

Department of Housing and Urban Development [*USA*] · Ministerium *n* für Wohnungswesen und Stadtentwick(e)lung

Department of Labor · Arbeitsministerium *n*, Bundesarbeitsministerium [*USA*]

department of law, law division, law department, legal department, division of law · Rechtsabteilung *f*

department of public welfare · Wohlfahrtsressort *n*

department of reconstruction (US); ministry of reconstruction (Brit.) · Aufbauministerium *n*, Wiederaufbauministerium *n*

department of the environment · Umweltschutzministerium *n*

Department of the Interior [*USA*] · Innenministerium *n*

Department of Trade [*Great Britain*] · Handelsministerium *n*

department store, universal provider · Warenhaus *n*

department store building code, department store construction code · Warenhausbauordnung *f*

department store plot, universal provider plot · Warenhausgrundstück *n*

departure; departura, decessus [*Latin*] [*In pleading. The abandonment of the ground of a former pleading, and the adoption of another*] · Klageänderung *f*

departure in despite of court [*In old English practice, was when the tenant in a real action, after once appearing and being present in court, failed to appear upon demand*] · vorsätzliches Nichterscheinen *n* vor Gericht

dependence · Abhängigkeit *f*

dependency privilege · Schachtelprivileg *n*

dependent agreement, reciprocal agreement, mutual agreement, dependant agreement, conditional agreement · gegenseitiges Abkommen *n*, gegenseitige Abmachung *f*, gegenseitige Vereinbarung

dependent condition · abhängige Bedingung *f*

dependent person; person not sui juris [*Latin*] [*The English law has two types of dependent persons, viz. minors and married women*] · abhängige Person *f* [*Eine Person, die rechtlich unfähig ist einen Wohnsitzwechsel selbständig vorzunehmen*]

dependent promise — depreciation

dependent promise, reciprocal promise, mutual promise, double promise, counter-promise, dependant promise, conditional promise · gegenseitiges Versprechen *n*

dependent relative revocation · abhängiger Widerruf *m*

depending (up)on, conditional, not absolute, contingent ((up)on) [*Operative only (up)on an uncertain event*] · bedingt durch, abhängig von, abhängend von

depletion of value · Werterschöpfung *f*

deponent · Deponent *m*, Erklärende, Aussageperson *f*, Aussagende [*Jemand, der eine beeidete schriftliche Erklärung abgibt*]

deponent (US); witness · Zeuge *m*

to depopulate [*community*] · entleeren, aushöhlen

depopulation · Aushöhlung *f*, Entleerung

depopulation area, depopulation territory, territory of depopulation, area of depopulation · Aushöhlungsgebiet *n*, Entleerungsgebiet *n*

deportation [*Expulsion, as of an undesirable alien, from a country*] · Abschiebung *f*

to depose, to amove, to remove; amovere [*Latin*] [*From membership or office*] · absetzen, entsetzen, entheben, untersagen, entziehen, ausschließen

to deposit · einzahlen [*Bank*]

to deposit · deponieren, hinterlegen

deposit · Einzahlung *f* [*Bank*]

deposit · Deposit(um) *n*, Deponierung *f*, Depot *n*, Hinterlegung *f* [*Die Hingabe einer Sache zur unentgeltlichen Aufbewahrung*]

deposit; caution [*In Scotland*]; security · Deckung *f*, (Bar)Sicherheit *f*, Unterlage *f*, Sicherung, Kaution *f*

deposit → deposit(ing)

deposit → (bank) deposit

deposit account · Einlagekonto *n*

deposit account (Brit.); saving account [*Saving banks in the USA*]; compound interest account [*National City Bank*]; thrift account [*Chase National Bank*] · Sparkonto *n* [*In den USA dürfen die Sparkonten nur von den „saving banks" als „saving accounts" bezeichnet werden*]

deposit amount → deposit(ing) amount

deposit and loan business, advances, business of lending against collateral · Lombardgeschäft *n*

deposit bank, bank of deposit · Depositenbank *f*

deposit business · Depositengeschäft *n*

deposit contract · Verwahrungsvertrag *m*, Hinterlegungsvertrag

deposit(ed) money, deposit(ed) currency · Buchgeld *n*, Giralgeld, Verwahrgeld, bankdeponiertes Geld, Buchbeträge im bargeldlosen Zahlungsverkehr [*Bankguthaben für bargeldlosen Zahlungsverkehr*]

depositing · Hinterlegen *n*, Deponieren

deposit(ing), payment, submission · Erstattung *f* [*Für den Erhalt von Ausschreibungsunterlagen*]

deposit(ing) amount, submission amount, payment amount · Erstattungsbetrag *m* [*Betrag für den Erhalt von Ausschreibungsunterlagen*]

deposit insurance · Depositenversicherung *f*, Einlagenversicherung

deposition [*Testimony, given under oath, which is reduced to writing for use in the trial of a case*] · (mündliche) protokollierte eidliche Aussage *f*, Aussageprotokoll *n*

deposit loan, loan against security, loan against deposit, security loan · Sicherungsdarleh(e)n *n*, Sicherheitsdarleh(e)n

deposit money → deposit(ed) money

deposit of securities · Hinterlegung *f* von Wertpapieren, Wertpapierhinterlegung

deposit of title-deed [*A method of pledging real property as security for a loan, by placing the title-deed of the land in the keeping of the lender as pledgee*] · Hinterlegung *f* einer (Rechts)Titelurkunde

depositor · Einzahler *m*, Einleger [*bei einer Bank*]

depositor [*One who makes a deposit*] · Hinterleger *m*, Deponent *m*

deposit rate, rate of deposit · Lombardsatz *m*

deposit receipt, D/R · Einzahlungsbeleg *m*

deposit sum · Hinterlegungssumme *f*

depositum, bare nuked bailment · Deponierung *f*

depositum irregulare [*Latin*] · Sammelverwahrung *f* [*Wertpapierdepot der Banken*]

depositum regulare [*Latin*] · Sonderverwahrung *f*, Streifbanddepot *n* [*Depotgeschäft der Banken*]

depreciable cost(s) · Abschreibungsgrundwert *m*

depreciation · Abschreibung *f*

depreciation — derangement of intellect

depreciation, diminution of value, reduction of value · Wertminderung f, Wertherabsetzung, Wertverringerung, Wertreduzierung

depreciation · Kursrückgang m, Kursverlust m, De-facto-Abwertung f auf den Devisenmärkten

depreciation allowance [*Allowance that permits the owner of real property to shelter all or part of his income so that he pays no current tax on it*] · Abschreibungsfreiheit f

depreciation amount, depreciation charge · Abschreibungsbetrag m

depreciation by evaporation · „radioaktiver" Kapitalzerfall m

depreciation cost(s), cost(s) of depreciation · Abschreibungskosten f

depreciation income · Abschreibungseinnahme f

depreciation rate, rate of depreciation · Abschreibungssatz m

depredator [*In old English statutes, certain depredators from Redesdale, on the northern border of England, who made incursions into Scotland, and brought back to their accomplices at home — called intakers — any booty they had taken, were called "outparters"*] · Plünderer m

depressed agricultural area, distressed agricultrual area, less prosperous agricultural area, special agricultural area · landwirtschaftliches Notstandsgebiet n, landwirtschaftliches Passivgebiet

depressed area, distressed area, special area, less prosperous area, depressed territory, special territory, distressed territory, less prosperous territory · Notstandsgebiet n, Passivgebiet, Sondergebiet, SO

depressed community, distressed community, special community, less prosperous community · Notstandsgemeinde f, Passivgemeinde, Notstandskommune f, Passivkommune

depression · Notstand m, Stockung f [*wirtschaftlich gesehen*]

depression period, depression time, time of depression, period of depression · (wirtschaftliche) Notzeit f

depression pump-priming measure · Notstandsmaßnahme f, Wirtschaftsbelebungsmaßnahme, konjunkturelle Maßnahme

deprivation case, case of deprivation · Entziehungsfall m

deprivation of a right · Entrechtung f

deprivation of (legal) capacity · Entmündigung f

deprivation of office, removal from (an) office, amotion from (an) office · Amtsabsetzung f, Amtsenthebung, Amtsentsetzung, Amtsentziehung, Amtsausschluß m, Amtsuntersagung

deprived of operation, repealed, cancelled, abrogated, abated, annulled, nullified, abolished (by authority), rescinded, overruled, done away with · aufgehoben, annulliert, rückgängig gemacht, außer Kraft gesetzt, abgeschafft, gelöscht, abgebaut

to deprive of an inheritance, to debar from an inheritance, to put out of an inheritance, to exclude from inheriting, to disinherit; to exheredate [*Scots law*] · enterben

to deprive of a right · entrechten

to deprive of operation, to rescind, to nullify, to annul, to repeal, to overrule, to cancel, to abrogate, to abolish (by authority), to do away with, to abate · abschaffen, aufheben, rückgängig machen, annullieren, außer Kraft setzen, löschen, abbauen

to deprive of seisin, to disseise, to disseize · entweren

depriving of an inheritance, putting out of an inheritance, debarring from an inheritance, excluding from an inheritance; exheredating [*Scots law*], disinheriting · Enterben n

depth contour, bathymetric contour · Tiefenlinie f, Isobathe f

depth number · Tiefenlinienzahl f

depth of a building, building depth · Gebäudetiefe f, Bautiefe

depth of a house, house depth · Haustiefe f

depth of coverage, coverage depth · Bebauungstiefe f; Überbauungstiefe [*Schweiz*] [*Im Bebauungsplan festgesetzte Tiefe der überbaubaren Fläche (§ 23 Abs. 4 BauNVo)*]

deputy governor · Gouverneurstellvertreter m

deputy keeper of the public records · Staatsarchivar m

Deputy Keeper of the Signet · stellvertretender Siegelbewahrer m

deputy of a provincial diet · Landstand m

deputy steward (of manor), understeward (of manor) · Unteramtmann m, Untervogt m, Unter-(Guts)Verwalter m, Unter-Gutsschulze m

deranged; insanus [*Latin*]; unsound in mind, disordered in mind, diseased in mind, of unsound mind, non-sane, insane · geistesgestört, geisteskrank

derangement of intellect, mental unsoundness, mental alienation, mental disorder,

deratting — description

mental derangement, insanity, unsoundness of mind, madness [*Lunacy is properly a species of insanity, although the terms are frequently used as synonyms*] · Geisteskrankheit *f*, Geistesgestörtheit

deratting, rat control · Entrattung *f*, Rattenbekämpfung

derelict, forsaken, cast off, derserted, cast away, thrown away, abandoned [*Personal property abandoned or thrown away by the owner in such manner as to indicate that he intends to make no further claim thereto*] · herrenlos, aufgegeben

derelict · herrenloses Gut *n*

derelict, ship deserted at sea, unclaimed wreck · herrenloses Wrack *n*

derelict, remiss, neglectful of duty · pflichtvergessen, pflichtuntreu

derelict [*A person neglectful of duty or trust*] · Pflichtvergessene *m*

dereliction, abandonment, abandoning, forsaking [*The act of abandoning a chattel or mov(e)able*] · Aufgabe *f*, Preisgabe *f*, Verzicht(leistung) *m*, *(f)*

dereliction deed, deed of abandonment, abandonment deed, deed of derelicition · Aufgabeerklärung *f*, Preisgabeerklärung *f*, Verzichterklärung *f*

dereliction of a chattel, abandonment of a chattel · Fahrnisaufgabe *f*, Fahrnispreisgabe, Fahrnisdereliktion *f*, Fahrnisverzicht(leistung) *m*, *(f)*, Fahrhabepreisgabe, Fahrhabeaufgabe, Fahrhabedereliktion, Fahrhabeverzicht(leistung)

dereliction (of duty), neglect of duty [*Any culpable omission of a positive duty*] · Pflichtvergessenheit *f*, Pflichtvernachlässigung *f*, Pflicht(ver)säumnis *f*, *n*, *(f)*

dereliction of (general) property, abandonment of (general) property, dereliction of proprietorship, abandonment of proprietorship, dereliction of ownership (of property), abandonment of ownership (of property) · Eigentumsaufgabe *f*, Eigentumspreisgabe, Eigentumsverzicht(leistung) *m*, *(f)*

dereliction (of land) → (accreation by) dereliction (of land)

dereliction of possession, abandonment of possession · Besitzaufgabe *f*, Besitzpreisgabe, Besitzverzicht(leistung) *m*, *(f)*

derelict (land) · Anlandung *f* [*Durch Zurückweichen von Wasser gewonnenes Land*]

derelict stream bed; alveus derelictus [*Latin*] · verlassenes Flußbett *n*

derelict village · verlassenes Dorf *n*

derequisition · Freigabe *f* [*Wohnung*]

derivation · Ableitung *f*, Derivation *f* [*Modellfunktion. Vorgang der Transformation eines im Modell beinhalteten Gegenstandsbereiches und der Ableitung eines anderen Gegenstandsbereiches daraus*]

derivative acquisition · abgeleitete (Eigentums)Beschaffung *f*, abgeleiteter (Eigentums)Erwerb *m*

derivative possession · vermuteter Besitz *m*

derived call, derived demand · abgeleitete Nachfrage *f*

derived possession · abgeleiteter Besitz *m*

to derogate, to hurt, to harm, to prejudice · beeinträchtigen, schmälern

derogation, hurt, harm · Abbruch *m*, Beeinträchtigung *f*, Schmälerung, Schädigung

derserted, cast away, thrown away, abandoned, derelict, forsaken, cast off [*Personal property abandoned or thrown away by the owner in such manner as to indicate that he intends to make no further claim thereto*] · herrenlos, aufgegeben

to descend, to pass down from generation to generation · abstammen

descendant, issue, offspring · Abkömmling *m*, Nachkomme *m*, Deszendent *m*

descendant in tail, issue in tail, offspring in tail · sukzessionsberechtigter Nachkomme *m*, sukzessionsberechtigter Abkömmling *m*, sukzessionsberechtigter Deszendent *m*

descendants, succeeding generation(s), posterity · Nachkommenschaft *f*

descent, ancestry, lineage · Abstammung *f*

descent → (hereditary) descent

descent according to foreign law → (hereditary) descent according to foreign law

descent in direct line, lineal consanguinity, lineal descent · lineare Blutsverwandschaft *f*

descent per capita → (hereditary) descent per capita

to descent (to), to pass by succession · anheimfallen, übergehen (auf), zufallen [*Erbschaft*]

descent which tolls entry → (hereditary) descent which tolls entry

to describe wrongly, to misdescribe · falsch beschreiben, unrichtig beschreiben

description · Angabe *f*, Beschreibung [*Waren*]

description · Beschreibung *f*

description of (the) work(s), description of work(s) (content), work(s) description, spec(ification)(s) · Arbeitsbeschreibung *f*, (Bau)Leistungsbeschreibung *f*, Baubeschreibung *f*, Darstellung *f* der Bauaufgabe, Darstellung *f* der (Bau)Leistungen, Vorschreibung *f*

description of (the) work(s) with bill of quantities, description of (the) work(s) with specification · Leistungsbeschreibung *f* mit L.V. [*Die geforderte Bauleistung wird in einem in Teilleistungen gegliederten L.V. beschrieben*]

descriptive documents, descriptive matter · Beschreibungsunterlagen *fpl*

descriptive error, error in description · Beschreibungsfehler *m*

descriptive mistake, mistake in description · Beschreibungsirrtum *m*

descriptive model · beschreibendes Modell *n*

descriptive ratio · Regel *f* nach welcher der Fall entschieden wird [*Doppelnatur des tragenden Urteilsgrundes*]

descriptive sale of goods, sale of goods by description · Verkauf *m* beweglicher Sachen nach Angabe, Verkauf beweglicher Sachen nach Beschreibung, Warenverkauf nach Angabe, Warenverkauf nach Beschreibung

to desert, to give up, to leave (to itself), to forsake, to let go, to abandon [*place*] · aufgeben, preisgeben, verlassen

deserted, idle, abandoned, given up, left (to itself), forsaken, let gone [*place*] · aufgegeben, verlassen, preisgegeben

deserted city, lost town, lost city, deserted town · wüste Stadt *f*

deserted community, lost community · wüste Gemeinde *f*, wüste Kommune *f*

deserted land, lost land · wüste Flur *f*, wüstes Land *n*, wüster Boden *m*, Wüstland

deserted locality, lost locality · wüste Ortschaft *f*, wüster Ort *m*

deserted locality research, lost locality research, desertion research · Wüstungsforschung *f*

Deserted Medi(a)eval Village Research Group, D.M.V.R.G. · Forschungsgruppe *f* für mittelalterliche Wüstungen [*In England. Gegründet 1952*]

deserted village, lost village · wüstes Dorf *n*

desert environment · Wüstenumwelt *f*

deserting, giving up, leaving (a thing) (to itself), abandoning, letting go · Aufgeben *n*, Verlassen *n* [*Gebäude; Betrieb; Flußbett usw.*]

desertion · Wüstung *f*

desertion double farm, double farm by desertion · Wüstungsdoppelhof *m*

desertion of land, land desertion · Flurwüstung *f*

desertion of the early modern times · frühneuzeitliche Wüstung *f*

desertion pattern, desertion scheme · Wüstungsmuster *n*, Wüstungsschema *n*

desertion process · Wüstungsvorgang *m*

desertion research, deserted locality research, lost locality research · Wüstungsforschung *f*

desertion without cause for two years and upwards · unbegründetes mehr als zweijähriges Verlassen *n* [*Eheleute*]

design alteration, design variation, variation of (the) design, alteration of (the) design, change of (the) design, design change · Entwurfs(ab)änderung *f*, Entwurfsveränderung, Entwurfsumänderung, (Ab)Änderung des Entwurfs, Umänderung des Entwurfs, Veränderung des Entwurfs

design and construct contract, design and build contract, package deal [*The contractor carries out, in addition to building the works, some or all of the duties of architect, engineer or even surveyor*] · Entwurfs- und Bauauftrag *m*

design and construction time → (overall) design and construction time

design architect [*The architect who prepares the design plans and specifications for a construction project; distinguished from a supervising architect, although they are often one and the same*] · Entwurfsarchitekt *m*

designated land, land designated for expropriation; land designated for condemnation (US) · enteignungsbestimmter Boden *m*, enteignungsbestimmtes Land *n*

designation · Kenntlichmachung *f*

designation of an office · Amtsbezeichnung *f*

designation of land as subject to compulsory purchase · Bestimmung *f* von Land zur Enteignung

designation of merchandise · Warenbezeichnung *f*

design-build (joint) venture, design-construct (joint) venture · Arge *f* für Konstruktion und Bau, Arbeitsgemeinschaft für Konstruktion und Bau

design change, design alteration, design variation, variation of (the) design, alteration of (the) design, change of (the) design · Entwurfs(ab)änderung *f*, Entwurfsveränderung, Entwurfsumänderung, (Ab)Änderung des Entwurfs, Umänderung des Entwurfs, Veränderung des Entwurfs

design contest · Entwurfswettbewerb *m*

design cost(s) · Entwurfskosten *f*

design defect · Konstruktionsmangel *m*

design documents · Entwurfsunterlagen *f pl*

design duty · Entwurfspflicht *f*

designedly, scienter, knowingly · bewußt, wissentlich

designedly untrue, intentionally untrue, knowingly false, deliberately false, designedly false, intentionally false, knowingly not true, deliberately not true, designedly not true, intentionally not true, knowingly untrue, deliberately untrue · absichtlich unwahr, wissentlich unwahr, bewußt unwahr, absichtlich falsch, bewußt falsch, wissentlich falsch

designer · Entwurfsverfasser *m*

design error, error of design · Entwurfsfehler *m*

designing department · Konstruktionsabteilung *f*

design personnel, design staff · Entwurfspersonal *n*

design ready for execution, design ready for performance · ausführungsreifer Entwurf *m*

design stage · Entwurfsstadium *n*

design team · Entwurfsbearbeitungsgruppe *f*

design variation, variation of (the) design, alteration of (the) design, change of (the) design, design change, design alteration · Entwurfs(ab)änderung *f*, Entwurfsveränderung, Entwurfsumänderung, (Ab)Änderung des Entwurfs, Umänderung des Entwurfs, Veränderung des Entwurfs

design work(s) · Entwurfsarbeit(en) *f (pl)*

desirability · Erwünschtheit *f*

desk calculator · Tischrechner *m*

desk jobber, drop shipper (US) · Streckengeschäft-Großhändler *m*

desk research · sekundäre Marktforschung *f*

desocialization · Entsozialisierung *f*

desparate, hopeless, non collectable, noncollectible, nonrecoverable, nonobtainable, uncollectable, unrecoverable, uncollectible, bad, irrecoverable, unobtainable · nicht beitreibbar, nicht einziehbar, nicht eintreibbar, uneinziehbar, uneintreibbar, uneinbringlich, unbeitreibbar [*Schuld*]

despatch goods, dispatch goods · Eilgut *n*

despatch money, dispatch money · Eilgeld *n*

despatch note, dispatch note [*A document recording that products are available for despatch and authorizing arrangement for delivery*] · Versandanzeige *f*, Versandzettel *m*

to despoil, to lay waste, to devastate, to estrepe, to strip [*To commit waste upon a real estate, as by cutting down trees, removing buildings, etc. To injure the value of a reversionary interest by stripping the (real) estate*] · verschlechtern, verwüsten, mißbrauchen, über(be)nutzen, vernachlässigen

despoiling, devastating, stripping, laying waste, estreping [*Committing waste upon a real estate*] · Verwüsten *n*, Mißbrauchen, Über(be)nutzen, Verschlechtern, Vernachlässigen (der Instandhaltung), Deteriorieren, Depravieren

destination country, country of destination · Bestimmungsland *n*

destination-end → (trip) destination-end

destination of traffic, traffic destination · Verkehrsziel *n*

destination place, place of destination · Bestimmungsort *m*

destination station, station of destination · Bestimmungsstation *f*, Bestimmungsbahnhof *m*, Zielstation, Zielbahnhof

destitute, unpropertied · vermögenslos, ohne Vermögen

destitute · mittellos, notleidend

destitute · Notleidende *m*, Mittellose

destitute houseless pauper · obdachloser wandernder Armer *m*

destitution · Mittellosigkeit *f*

to destroy, to remove, to abate, to break down [*To abate a structure is to beat it down*] · zerstören

to destroy an entail, to disentail, to bar an entail · aufheben der gebundenen (Land)Erbfolge(ordnung)

destruction; destructio [*Latin*] · Zerstörung *f*

destruction by fire · Brandzerstörung *f*

destruction by natural event · Untergang *m* durch Naturereignis

destruction of fish, fish destruction · Fischsterben *n*

destruction of value · Wertzerstörung *f*

detached building, isolated building [*Building surrounded by open space*] · freistehendes Gebäude *n*

detached single-family house, free-standing single-family house, isolated single-family house · freistehendes Einfamilienhaus *n*

detail, particular · Einzelheit *f*

detail · graphischer Teil *m* des Karteninhalts

detailed, in particular · ausführlich

detailed building scheme · ausführlicher Bebauungsplan *m*, ausführlicher verbindlicher Bauleitplan *m*; ausführlicher Überbauungsplan *m* [*Schweiz*]; ausführlicher Bauplan *m* [*Fehlbenennung*]

detailed (cost(s)) estimate, firm (cost(s)) estimate, contractor's (cost(s)) estimate · detaillierter KV *m*, detaillierter (Bau)Kosten(vor)anschlag

detail(ed) drawing · Detailzeichnung *f*

(detailed) local (development) plan, coverage scheme, detailed local plan, building scheme · Bebauungsplan *m*, qualifizierter Bebauungsplan, verbindlicher Bauleitplan; Überbauungsplan [*Schweiz*] [*Der Bebauungsplan steht zwischen dem Bauplan und dem Flächennutzungsplan*]

(detailed) local (development) plan design, coverage scheme design, building scheme design · Bebauungsplanentwurf *m*, verbindlicher Bauleitplanentwurf; Überbauungsplanentwurf [*Schweiz*]

(detailed) local (development) plan law, coverage scheme law, building scheme law · Bebauungsrecht *n*; Überbauungsrecht [*Schweiz*]

(detailed) local (development) plan proposal, coverage scheme proposal, building scheme proposal · Bebauungsvorschlag *m*; Überbauungsvorschlag [*Schweiz*]

detailed local plan, building scheme, (detailed) local (development) plan, coverage scheme · Bebauungsplan *m*, qualifizierter Bebauungsplan, verbindlicher Bauleitplan; Überbauungsplan [*Schweiz*] [*Der Bebauungsplan steht zwischen dem Bauplan und dem Flächennutzungsplan*]

detail(ed) map · Detailkarte *f*

detail(ed) study · Durcharbeitung *f*

details, particulars · Angaben *fpl*, Einzelheiten *fpl*

to detain, to retain, to withhold · einbehalten, zurück(be)halten, vorenthalten

detainer; retentio [*Latin*]; retention, detention, detainment [*The act of keeping back or withholding, either accidentally or by design, a person or thing*] · Rückbehalt *m*, Retention *f*, Zurück(be)haltung *f*, Einbehalt(ung), Vorenthalt(ung)

detainer money, detainment money, retention money, detention money · Einbehaltungsgeld *n*, (Zu)Rück(be)haltungsgeld, Retentionsgeld

detaining, retaining, withholding · Einbehalten *n*, Zurück(be)halten, Vorenthalten

detainment, detainer; retentio [*Latin*]; retention, detention [*The act of keeping back or withholding, either accidentally or by design, a person or thing*] · Rückbehalt *m*, Retention *f*, Zurück(be)haltung *f*, Einbehalt(ung), Vorenthalt(ung)

detention book · Polizeigewahrsamsbuch *n*

detention camp · Internierungslager *n*

detention colony · Strafkolonie *f*

deteriorated · mäßig [*Bauwerkszustand*]

deteriorating [*structure*] · verfallend, verfallnähernd [*Bauwerk*]

deterioration [*of construction materials furnished*] · Verschlechterung *f* [*beigestellte Baustoffe*]

deterioration · Wertverschlechterung *f*, Wertrückgang *m*

deterioration of land(s), deterioration of real property, deterioration of realty · Grund(stücks)verschlechterung *f*

(de)terminable · kündbar, zeitlich begrenzt

(de)terminable [*Liable to be brought to an end upon the happening of a certain contingency*] · beendbar

(de)terminable · auflösbar

(de)terminable at will · aufkündbar

(de)terminable fee → (estate in) (de)terminable fee

(de)terminable mortgage, straight mortgage, definite term mortgage · kündbare Hypothek *f*

determinant · Bestimmungsfaktor *m*

determinate; perimere [*Latin*]; irrevocable, peremptory, final · bestimmt, endgültig, unwiderruflich

determination · Bestimmung *f*, Festsetzung *f*, Feststellung *f*

determination; determinatio [*Latin*] · Beendigung *f*

determination by assignee in bankruptcy, determination by trustee in bankruptcy, determination by referee in bankruptcy · Beendigung *f* durch Konkursverwalter

determination by referee in bankruptcy, determination by assignee in bankruptcy, determination by trustee in bankruptcy · Beendigung *f* durch Konkursverwalter

determination due to delay — developer's law 314

determination due to delay · Auftragsbeendigung f bei Verzug

determination of building lines · (Bau)Fluchtlinienfestsetzung f, (Bau-)Fluchtlinienbestimmung, (Bau)Fluchtlinienfeststellung

determination of cost(s), cost(s) determination · Kostenanschlag m [*Möglichst genaue Ermitt(e)lung der Kosten*]

(de)termination (of employment) by contractor · Auftragsbeendigung f seitens des Unternehmers

determination of ground value, determination of land value · Bodenwertermitt(e)lung f, Landwertermitt(e)lung, Grund(stücks)wertermitt(e)lung, Bodenbewertung, Landbewertung, Grund(stücks)bewertung

determination of maxima · Maximafestsetzung, Maximafeststellung, Maximabestimmung f

determination of minima, minima determination · Minimafestsetzung, Minimafeststellung, Minimabestimmung f

determination of need, determination of wants · Bedürfnisbestimmung f, Bedürfnisfestsetzung, Bedürfnisfeststellung

determination of policy goal importance, determination of target goal importance · Zielgewichtung f

determination of will · Willensentschluß m

determinations letter, letter ruling · verbindliche Auskunft f [*Steuerfestsetzung in den USA*]

determination subject to arbitration · Beendigung f durch Schiedsspruch

determinative clause, overriding clause, repealing clause · Aufhebungsklausel f

detinue [*It consists of the wrongful retention of the possession of goods, as where A lends B a car which B refuses to return*] · widerrechtliche Vorenthaltung f

detoxification centre (Brit.); detoxification center (US) · Entwöhnungsanstalt f

detractus personalis, gabella emigrationis [*Latin*] · Abfahrtsgeld n, Abzugsgeld, Auswanderungsgebühr f, Emigrationsgebühr [*Eine Abgabe welche früher von einem Auswanderer an den Staat oder die Gemeinde, welcher derselbe angehörte, zu entrichten war*]

detractus realis, census hereditarius, gabella hereditaria, quindena [*Latin*] · Abschoß m, Erb(schafts)geld n

detriment, disadvantage · Nachteil m

detrimental to cultivation · kulturschädlich

detrimental to health, offensive, unsanitary, prejudicial to health · gesundheitsschädlich, gesundheitsgefährdend

deurbanization, counterurbanization · Entstädterung f

to deurbanize, to counterurbanize · entstädtern

deurbanized, counterurbanized · entstädtert

deurbanized zone, counterurbanized zone · entstädterte Zone f

to devaluate · abwerten durch Paritätsveränderung

devaluation (of money), money devaluation · Geldabwertung, Abwertung f (durch Paritätsveränderung)

to devastate, to estrepe, to strip, to despoil, to lay waste [*To commit waste upon a real estate, as by cutting down trees, removing buildings, etc. To injure the value of a reversionary interest by stripping the (real) estate*] · verschlechtern, verwüsten, mißbrauchen, über(be)nutzen, vernachlässigen

devastating, stripping, laying waste, estreping, despoiling [*Committing waste upon a real estate*] · Verwüsten n, Mißbrauchen, Über(be)nutzen, Verschlechtern, Vernachlässigen (der Instandhaltung), Deteriorieren, Depravieren

devastation, estrepement [*real estate*] · Vernachlässigung f (der Instandhaltung), Verschlechterung, Verwüstung, technische Wertminderung, Depravierung, Deteriorierung, Über(be)nutzung

to develop, to make active · aktivieren

to develop · nutzbar machen

to develop · entwickeln

developed area · nutzbar gemachte Fläche f, Nutzfläche

developed ground-water · nutzbar gemachtes Grundwasser n, Nutzgrundwasser

developed land · nutzbar gemachtes Land n, Nutzland, Nutzboden m, nutzbar gemachter Boden

developed society, advanced society · entwickelte Gesellschaft f

developer → (land(s)) developer

developer, builder, promoter, (real) property developer, (real) estate promoter, (real) property builder, (real) estate builder, (real) property promoter, (real) estate developer, realty builder, realty developer, realty promoter [*A person who builds either on his own or another's land for profit*] · spekulierender Bauauftraggeber m, (Bau)Träger

developer's law, promoter's law, builder's law, (real) property builder's law, (real) property developer's law, (real) property promoter's law, (real) estate builder's

developing contacts — development value

law, (real) estate developer's law, (real) estate promoter's law, realty builder's law, realty developer's law, realty promoter's law · (Bau)Trägerrecht *n*

developing contacts · Kontaktpflege *f*

development · Entwick(e)lung *f*, Inwertsetzung

development → (land(s)) development

development approval · Bebauungsgenehmigung *f*, Bebauungserlaubnis *f*; Überbauungsgenehmigung, Überbauungserlaubnis [*Schweiz*]

development area, development territory · Bundesbaugebiet *n* [*Bundesrepublik Deutschland*]

development area · Entwick(e)lungsfläche *f*

development axis; development centre line (Brit.); development center line (US) · Entwick(e)lungsachse *f*

development centre, centre of development (Brit.); development center, center of development (US) · Entwick(e)lungszentrum *n*, Entwick(e)lungsschwerpunkt *m*, Mittelbereichszentrum, Sied(e)lungsschwerpunkt

development centre (Brit.); development center (US) · Bundesbauort *m* [*Bundesrepublik Deutschland*]

development charge · Entwick(e)lungsabgabe *f*

development company · Entwick(e)lungsgesellschaft *f*

development company (Brit.); development corporation (US) · (Bau)Trägergesellschaft *f*

development contract, contract of development · Entwick(e)lungsvertrag *m*

development control, control of development · Entwick(e)lungslenkung *f*, Entwick(e)lungssteuerung

development corporation (US); development company (Brit.) · (Bau)Trägergesellschaft *f*

development district · Entwick(e)lungsbezirk *m*

development expenditure · erstmaliger Aus- und Vorrichtungsaufwand *m* [*Bergwerk*]

development fee · Entwick(e)lungsgebühr *f*, Entwick(e)lungshonorar *n*

development freeze, prohibition on all development · Veränderungssperre *f* [*Wenn für ein Gebiet ein Bebauungsplan aufgestellt werden soll, können Neu- und Umbauten und Nutzungsanlagen auf den dort gelegenen Grundstücken nach dem BBauG §§ 14—18 befristet verboten werden, höchstens für 2 bis 4 Jahre*]

development gains tax, development profits tax [*A tax on the disposal of land(s)*] · Landveräußerungssteuer *f*

development land · Entwick(e)lungsbereich *m* [*Im planerischen Sinn*]

development measure, measure of development · Entwick(e)lungsmaßnahme *f*

development of business, business development · Geschäftsentwick(e)lung *f*

development opportunity · Entwick(e)lungsförderung *f*

development order · Entwick(e)lungsbefehl *m*, Entwick(e)lungsgebot *n*, Entwick(e)lungsanordnung *f*, Entwick(e)lungsverfügung

development ordinance · Entwick(e)lungsverordnung *f*

development ordinance → (physical) development ordinance

development permission, permission to develop · Entwick(e)lungserlaubnis *f*, Entwick(e)lungsgenehmigung *f*

development place · Entwick(e)lungsort *m*

development plan · Entwick(e)lungsplan *m*

development plan → (physical) development plan

development planning · Entwick(e)lungsplanung *f*

development pole · Entwick(e)lungspol *m*

development policy · Entwick(e)lungspolitik *f*

development policy goal, development (target) goal · Entwick(e)lungszielnorm *f*, Entwick(e)lungsoberziel, übergeordnetes Entwick(e)lungsziel *n*

development profits tax, development gains tax [*A tax on the disposal of land(s)*] · Landveräußerungssteuer *f*

development ribbon · Entwick(e)lungsband *n*

development right, right of development · Entwick(e)lungs(an)recht *n*, Entwick(e)lungsanspruch *m*

development (target) goal, development policy goal · Entwick(e)lungszielnorm *f*, Entwick(e)lungsoberziel, übergeordnetes Entwick(e)lungsziel *n*

development territory, development area · Bundesbaugebiet *n* [*Bundesrepublik Deutschland*]

development trend · Entwick(e)lungsrichtung *f*

development value → (prospective) development value

development via excess · Infrastrukturüberschuß *m*

development via shortage · Infrastrukturengpaß *m*

to deviate, to diverge, to vary [*from a norm*] · abweichen

deviation, variation, divergence [*from a norm*] · Abweichung *f*

deviation → (contract) deviation

devisable · (testamentarisch) vermachbar, testamentarisch verfügbar, letztwillig vermachbar, letztwillig verfügbar [*Liegenschaft(en)*]

devisare [*Latin*]; to make a will of land(s), to devise · vermachen, testamentarisch vermachen, letztwillig verfügen, testamentarisch verfügen [*Liegenschaft(en)*]

to devise; devisare [*Latin*]; to make a will of land(s) · vermachen, testamentarisch vermachen, letztwillig verfügen, testamentarisch verfügen [*Liegenschaft(en)*]

devise [*A testamentary disposition of land(s)*] · Bodenvermächtnis *n*, (Land)Vermächtnis, Grund(stücks)vermächtnis, Immobilienvermächtnis, Immobiliarvermächtnis, Bodenlegat *n*, (Land)Legat, Grund(stücks)legat, Immobilienlegat, Immobiliarlegat, Liegenschaftslegat, Liegenschaftsvermächtnis

devised · (testamentarisch) vermacht, testamentarisch verfügt, letztwillig vermacht, letztwillig verfügt [*Liegenschaft(en)*]

devisee · Bodenvermächtnisnehmer *m*, Landvermächtnisnehmer, (Grund(stücks))Vermächtnisnehmer, Vermächtnisnehmer von Immobiliarvermögen, Bedachter, Nachlaßnehmer, Testamentserbe *m* von Immobiliarvermögen, testamentarischer Grund(stücks)erbe, Liegenschaftserbe, Grundbesitzerbe

devise of usufruct, usufruct devise · Nießbrauchlegat *n*, Nießbrauchvermächtnis *n*, (Frucht)Genußlegat, (Frucht-)Genußvermächtnis, Nutzgewaltlegat, Nutzgewaltvermächtnis [*Liegenschaft*]

devisibility · Teilbarkeit *f*

devisor of land(s), testator of land(s) [*A giver of land(s) by will; the maker of a will of land(s)*] · Bodenerblasser *m*, Landerblasser, Grund(stücks)erblasser

devolution [*The transmission of an interest in property from one person to another by operation of law*] · Devolution *f*

devolution of an office · Amtsübergang *m*

devolution of a right · Rechtsübergang *m*

devolution of powers · Dezentralisierung *f* der inneren Verwaltung

to devolve [*To pass or be transferred from one person to another*] · übergehen [*Recht*]

diagonal regression · Diagonalregression *f*

diagonal street · Diagonalstraße *f*, Schrägstraße

diagram map · Diagrammkarte *f*

diagrammatic map · Kartogramm *n*

diary · Tagebuch *n*

diary note · Tagebucheintrag(ung) *m*, *(f)*

dictum [*An observation by a judge on a matter arising during the hearing of a case*] · richterliche Ansicht *f*

to die intestate · ohne letztwillige Verfügung sterben

dies juridicus [*Latin*]; juridic(al) day, law day, court day; lage day, lagh day [*Latin*]; doomsday [*In old English law*] · Gerichtstag *m*

dies non (juridicus) [*Latin*] · gerichtsfreier Tag *m*

to die without descendant, to die without offspring, to die without issue · ohne Nachkommen sterben

diffamatory representation · üble Nachrede *f*

difference between registered and true area · Besitzabweichung *f*

difference in values · Wertunterschied *m*

difference (of opinion) · Meinungsverschiedenheit *f*

differentiability · Unterscheidbarkeit *f*

differential equation · Differentialgleichung *f*

differential growth · unterschiedliches Wachstum *n*, Wachstumsunterschied *m*

differential net shift [*shift analysis*] · DS *f*, Standortkomponente *f*, Standortfaktor *m*

differential-piece-rate plan · Zwei-Akkordsatzsystem *n*

differential rent · Differenzrente *f*, Differentialrente, differentielle Rente; relative Grundrente [*nach Meinhold*]

diffidatio [*Latin*] · Treuaufsage *f*

diffusion process · räumlicher Ausbreitungsvorgang *m*

to digest, to reduce (laws) to a code, to codify · kodifizieren

digested law, codified law · kodifiziertes Recht *n*

digest of laws · Rechtssammlung *f*

digging of peat, peat-cutting, peat-digging, cutting of peat · Torfgraben *n*, Torfstechen

digging right — direct debiting service

digging right · Graberecht *n*

digital image processing · digitale Bildverarbeitung *f*

digital mapping · digitale Kartierung *f*, Digitalkartierung

digitization · Digitalisierung *f*

digitized array · Raumzelle *f* [*digitalisierte Karte*]

digitized array map · digitalisierte Karte *f*, Raumzellenkarte

dignitary · Prälat *m*, Geistlicher *m* mit Jurisdiktion

dignitas primogeniti [*Latin*]; right of primogeniture, right of the eldest, right of the first born; aesnetia, eisnetia, enitia pars [*Latin*] · (männliches) Erstgeburtsrecht *n*, Primogenitur *f*, Vorrecht des Erstgeborenen

to dig sand, to excavate sand · aussanden

dike law, dyke law · Deichrecht *n*

dike ownership (of property), dike (general) property, dike proprietorship, dyke ownership (of property), dyke (general) property, dyke proprietorship · Deicheigentum *n*

dike-reeve, dike-reed, dyke-reeve, dyke-reed · Deichhauptmann *m*, Deichvogt *m*

dike union, dyke union · Deichverband *m*

dilapidated housing district · Baufälligkeitsbezirk *m*, Verfallbezirk

dilapidation, (physical) deterioration, (physical) decay [*A state of disrepair, relating to structures where legal liability is imposed on those responsible*] · Baufälligkeit *f*, (baulicher) Verfall *m*

dilatory · aufschiebend, dilatorisch

dilatory plea · dilatorische Einrede *f*, aufschiebende Einrede, Fristgesuch *n*

diligence, care · Sorgfalt *f*

diligence, prudence, vigilant activity · Wachsamkeit *f*

diligent, steadily applied, active, laborious · aktiv, unermüdlich, fleißig

dimensional motion time · Vorgabezeit *f* auf überbetrieblicher Normalzeit

dimensions, size · Abmessungen *f pl*, Größe *f*

diminishing return, diminishing yield · abnehmende Rendite *f*, fallende Rendite

diminution, incompleteness [*It signifies that the record sent up from an inferior to a superior court for review is incomplete, or not fully certified. In such case the party may suggest a "diminution of the record", which may be rectified by a certiorari*] · Unvollständigkeit *f*, Abbrüchigkeit

diminution of value, reduction of value, depreciation · Wertminderung *f*, Wertherabsetzung, Wertverringerung, Wertreduzierung

dimissio, demissio [*Latin*]; assedation, tack [*Scots law*], estate less than freehold, lease(hold), tenure, leasehold estate, demise, tenancy [*Holding of real estate under a lease. Such an estate continues for a fixed or determinable period of time but not for a lifetime. It is a conveyance of land whereby the owner of landed property, called the lessor, grants the possession and use of his landed property to another party, called the lessee, in consideration of a sum of money, called the rent*] · Bodenpacht *f*, Landpacht, Bodennutzungsrechtvergabe *f*, Landnutzungsrechtvergabe, Bodenverpachtung *f*, Landverpachtung, (Boden)Nutzungsrecht *n*

dimissio [*Latin*]; tenancy, demise, lease(hold), tenure; demissio · Pacht *f*, Nutzungsrechtvergabe *f*, Verpachtung *f*

dimittere [*Latin*]; to lease, to demise, to let; demittere · verpachten

diplomatic privilege · diplomatischer Schutz *m*

direct appeal, leapfrogging, leapfrog procedure · Sprungappellation *f*, Sprungberufung *f*

direct comparison · Direktvergleich *m*

direct contract, prime contract · Direktvertrag *m*, direkter Vertrag

direct contractor, prime contractor [*A contractor having a contract with the owner*] · Direktunternehmer *m*

direct correlation · positive Korrelation *f*

direct costing · Deckungsbeitragsrechnung *f*

direct costing [*The practice of charging all direct cost(s) to products, processes and services, leaving all other cost(s) to be written-off against profits in the period in which they arise*] · Direktkostenrechnung *f* [*Dieses in den USA entwickelte Kostenrechnungsverfahren müßte richtiger „variable costing" heißen, weil es auf der Trennung von fixen und den als variabel angesehenen Kosten beruht. Direkte Kosten und variable Kosten sind nicht identisch*]

direct cost(s) · direkte Kosten *f*, spezifizierte Kosten, Direktkosten [*Kosten, die der Betriebsleistung (dem Kostenträger) direkt zugerechnet werden können (Einzelkosten) oder Kosten, die der Kostenstelle direkt zugerechnet werden können (Kostenstellen-Einzelkosten)*]

direct debiting service, automatic debit transfer · Einziehung *f*, rückläufige Überweisung *f*

direct dominion — disability

direct dominion; nuda proprietas, dominium feudi [*Latin*]; ultimate ownership (of property), strict ownership (of property) [*The nominal or bare right of ownership remaining in an owner who has granted the exclusive right of enjoyment and of limited or unlimited disposition over the thing to another person*] · Obereigentum *n* (der Krone), Eigentumsrecht *n* des Leh(e)n(s)herrn, Leh(e)n(s)herrlichkeit *f* [*Das Eigentum an Land ruht in England in allen Fällen unbedingt und ausnahmslos beim Thron. Diese Tatsache ist eine der wichtigsten Unterschiede zwischen dem englischen Mobiliar- und Immobiliarsachenrecht und findet ihren Ausdruck in der Rechtsdoktrin: "Land is, and goods are not, the subject of tenure"*]

directed economy, planned economy, controlled economy · Planwirtschaft *f*

directed graph · gerichteter Graph *m*, Diagraph

direct evidence, direct proof · direkter Beweis *m*, Direktbeweis

direct examination, examination-in-chief · erste Zeugenvernehme *f* durch die benennende Partei

direct interdependency, nonmarket interdependency · Wirkung *f* die nicht über den Marktmechanismus gesteuert wird

direction of coverage, coverage direction · Bebauungsrichtung *f*; Überbauungsrichtung [*Schweiz*]

direction power, power of direction · Leitungsmacht *f*

directions → (practice) directions

direct labour (Brit.); direct labor (US) · Regiearbeitskräfte *f pl*

direct labour wages (Brit.); direct labor wages (US) · Fertigungslöhne *m pl*

direct labour work (Brit.); direct labor work (US); force(-)account (construction), force(-)account work [*A public authority designs and builds*] · Regiearbeit(en) *f (pl)*, Regieleistung(en) *f (pl)*

direct labour work sheet (Brit.); direct labor work sheet (US) · Regie(arbeits)-zettel *m*, Regieleistungszettel

direct line, right line; linea (di)recta [*Latin*] [*The direct line of ascendants and descendants*] · direkte (Abstammungs)-Linie *f*, direkte (Abstammungs)Folge *f*

direct loss · direkter Verlust *m*

direct-mail shot, unaddressed printed papers · Postwurfsendung *f*

direct material(s) · Fertigungsmaterial(ien) *n (pl)*

directness · Unmittelbarkeit *f*

directness principle, principle of directness · Grundsatz *m* der Unmittelbarkeit, Prinzip *n* der Unmittelbarkeit, Unmittelbarkeitsprinzip, Unmittelbarkeitsgrundsatz

director, managing board member, executive board member · Vorstandsmitglied *n*, Direktor *m*, Verwaltungsratmitglied

director, mandator · Mandatsgeber *m*

director of public prosecutions · Vertreter *m* des Staatsanwaltes

directory · Adreßbuch *n*

directory · reglementarisch

directory trust [*One which is not completely and finally settled by the instrument of creating it, but only defined in its general purpose and to be carried into detail according to later specific directions*] · Treuhand *f* in Grundzügen bestimmt

direct personnel, permanent staff, permanent personnel, direct staff · Stammbelegschaft *f*, Stammpersonal *n*

(direct) primary (election) [*USA*] · (unmittelbare) Vorwahl *f*, (unmittelbare) Erstwahl, (unmittelbare) Urwahl [*Ein der allgemeinen Wahl angeglichenes Verfahren zur Kandidatenaufstellung für öffentliche Wahlämter unmittelbar durch die Wahlberechtigten*]

direct proof, direct, evidence · direkter Beweis *m*, Direktbeweis

direct real evidence, direct real proof, real direct evidence, real direct proof · unmittelbarer Realbeweis *m*

direct reduction · direkte Tilgung *f*, direkte Abzahlung [*Bausparhypothek*]

direct reduction plan · direkter Abzahlungsplan *m* [*Bausparkasse*]

direct sale · Direktverkauf *m*

direct service · persönliche Dienstleistung *f*

direct staff, direct personnel, permanent staff, permanent personnel · Stammbelegschaft *f*, Stammpersonal *n*

dirty bill of lading, claused bill of lading, foul bill of lading, foul B/L · unreines Konnossement *n*

dirty money, black money · Schmutzgeld *n* [*Vergütung für schmutzige Arbeiten*]

disability, inability, incapacity, incapability · Unvermögen *n*, Unfähigkeit *f*

disability, incapability, inability, incapacity [*The want of legal capability to perform an act*] · (Geschäfts)Unvermögen *n*, (Geschäfts)Unfähigkeit *f*

disability · Arbeitsunfähigkeit *f*, Invalidität *f*

disability benefit, disablement benefit · Invalidenrente *f*, Invaliditätsrente

disability insurance · Invalidenversicherung *f*

disability of infancy, incapacity of infancy, incapability of infancy, inability of infancy · (Geschäfts)Unvermögen *n* als Minderjähriger, (Geschäfts)Unfähigkeit *f* als Minderjähriger

disability supervening, inability supervening, incapacity supervening, incapability supervening · (Geschäfts)Unvermögen *n* nach Beginn der Verjährungsfrist, (Geschäfts)Unfähigkeit *f* nach Beginn der Verjährungsfrist

disability to perform official duties, incapacity to perform official duties, incapability to perform official duties · Amtsunfähigkeit *f*, Amtsunvermögen *n*

disabled person · Invalide *m*, Erwerbsunfähige *m*

disable (for work), incapable of working, unfit for work, · arbeitsunfähig

disablement benefit, disability benefit · Invalidenrente *f*, Invaliditätsrente

to disadvantage, to discriminate · benachteiligen

disadvantage, detriment · Nachteil *m*

disadvantage in law · Rechtsnachteil *m*

to disaffirm, to refuse, to repudiate, to reject, to decline · ablehnen, versagen, verweigern, zurückweisen

disaffirmation, disaffirmance, refusal, rejection, repudiation, declination · Ablehnung *f*, Zurückweisung, (Ver)Weigerung, Versagung, Aufsage *f*

disaffirmed, refused, repudiated, rejected, declined · abgelehnt, versagt, verweigert, zurückgewiesen

to dis(af)forest · entwalden

disagio, discount · Damnum *n*, Disagio *n*, Abschlag *m* [*Unterschiedsbetrag zwischen dem Nennwert (100%) und dem Auszahlungskurs einer Hypothek*]

to disallow · beanstanden, bemängeln

disallowance · Beanstandung *f*, Bemängelung

disappearance · Verschollensein *n*

disappearance declaration, death declaration, declaration of disappearance, declaration of death · Todeserklärung *f*, Verschollenheitserklärung

disappeared person, missing person · Verschollene *m*

disappeared persons' service, missing persons' service · Suchdienst *m*

disapproval · Mißbilligung *f*

to disapprove · mißbilligen

disapproved clause · mißbilligte Klausel *f*

disaster · Katastrophe *f*

disaster game, community response game · Katastrophenspiel *n*

disaster insurance · Katastrophenversicherung *f*

disaster plan · Katastrophenplan *m*

disaster service · Katastrophendienst *m*

disavowal, disclaimer, denial · Leugnung *f*, Abstreitung, Abrede *f*, Wegrede, Ableugnung

to disbar [*barrister*] · ausstoßen, ausschließen [*Aus einem Inn of Court*]; entziehen der Berechtigung zu plädieren

disbocatio [*Latin*]; essartum, assarting [*Grubbing up trees and bushes from forest-land, so as to make it arable*] · Ausholzen *n*, Ausreuten *n*, Roden *n*

to disburden, to free of incumbrance(s), to free of encumbrance(s), to disencumber · entlasten, entschulden, lastenfrei machen, schuldenfrei machen [*Grundstück*]

to disburse, to pay out, to pay down · auszahlen

disbursement · Auslage(betrag) *f*, *(m)*, verauslagter Betrag

disbursement · Auszahlung *f*

discard zone, zone of discard · heruntergekommene Randzone *f* eines Geschäftsviertels

to discharge, to redeem · ablösen, einlösen, auslösen [*Einen Gegenstand durch Zahlung der Gläubigerforderung*]

to discharge, to liquidate, to settle, to redeem, to pay off [*indebtedness*] · tilgen, begleichen, abbezahlen, rückzahlen

to discharge, to absolve from, to acquit, to pronounce not guilty · freisprechen

to discharge, to set free; to release, to acquit [*Required to be under seal*] · freistellen, entlasten, befreien, freigeben, dispensieren

to discharge, to comply with, to fulfill [*contract*] · erfüllen, vollziehen, nachkommen [*Vertrag*]

to discharge, to absolve from, to set free · entbinden von (Verpflichtungen)

discharge, redemption · Ablösung *f*, Auslösung, Einlösung [*Einen Gegenstand durch Zahlung der Gläubigerforderung*]

discharge, acquittance, receipt, acquittal · Quittung *f*, Empfangsbestätigung

discharge, acquittal [*A judicial deliverance from an accusation (of guilt)*] · Freispruch *m*, Freisprechung *f*

discharge — discharge price

discharge · Entlassung *f*

discharge, release, dispensation, immunity, exemption [*Relaxation of the law in a particular case by competent authority*] · Befreiung *f*, Freistellung, Entlastung, Freigabe *f*, Erlaß *m*, Dispens(ierung) *m*, (*f*), Dispensation *f*, Ausnahmebewilligung

discharge, execution, performance, compliance, fulfilment [*The pursuance or carrying forth of the provisions of a plan or contract*] · Ausführung *f*, Vollzug *m*, Erbringung *f*, Vollziehung *f*, Erfüllung *f*, Leistung

discharge → (bankruptcy) discharge

dischargeable, redeemable · ablösbar, auslösbar, einlösbar [*Einen Gegenstand durch Zahlung der Gläubigerforderung*]

dischargeable right, redeemable right [*A right which returns to the conveyor or disposer of land, etc., upon payment of the sum for which such right was granted*] · einlösbares Recht *n*, auslösbares Recht, ablösbares Recht

discharge application, release application, dispensation application, immunity application, exemption application · Befreiungsantrag *m*, Dispens(ier)ungsantrag, Freistellungsantrag, Entlastungsantrag, Freigabeantrag, Dispensationsantrag

discharge bond, performance bond, fulfilment bond, execution bond, compliance bond · Erfüllungsgarantie *f*, Vollzugsgarantie, Vollziehungsgarantie, Erbringungsgarantie, Leistungsgarantie, Ausführungsgarantie

discharged, performed, fulfilled, executed · erfüllt, ausgeführt, vollzogen, erbracht, nachgekommen

discharged, absolved from, set free · entbunden von (Verpflichtungen)

discharged, set free; released [*Required to be under seal*]; acquitted [*From debt, obligation, duty, etc.*] · befreit, entlastet, freigestellt, freigegeben, dispensiert

discharge duration → discharge period

discharge fee, redemption fee · Ablösungsgebühr *f*, Auslösungsgebühr, Einlösungsgebühr

discharge in deed, acquittal in deed · ausdrücklicher Freispruch *m*, ausdrückliche Freisprechung *f*

discharge in law, acquittal in law · selbstverständlicher Freispruch *m*, selbstverständliche Freisprechung *f*

discharge loan, redemption loan · Ablösungsdarleh(e)n *n*, Einlösungsdarleh(e)n, Auslösungsdarleh(e)n

discharge method, method of discharge, redemption method, method of redemption · Ablösungsverfahren *n*, Auslösungsmethode *f*, Ablösungsmethode, Einlösungsmethode, Auslösungsverfahren, Einlösungsverfahren

discharge of a bankrupt, (bankruptcy) discharge [*Freeing of a bankrupt from debts and liabilities, by order of discharge*] · Entlassung *f* aus dem Konkurs, Konkursentlassung, (Konkurs)Entlastung, Entlastung eines Gemeinschuldners [*Nach englischem Konkursrecht werden nach Abschluß des Verfahrens dem Gemeinschuldner die Restschulden erlassen, vorausgesetzt, daß er sich nichts hat zuschulden kommen lassen. Nach deutschem Konkursrecht haftet er noch 30 Jahre lang für nicht befriedigte Forderungen*]

discharge of a debt, settlement of a debt, redemption of a debt, liquidation of a debt · Tilgung *f*, Schuldrückzahlung

discharge of cautioner, release of cautioner, discharge of insurer of a debt, release of insurer of a debt, discharge of guarantor, release of guarantor, discharge of surety, release of surety · Bürgenbefreiung *f*, Bürgenfreistelllung

discharge of contract, contract discharge · Vertragsauflösung *f*

discharge of gas, gas discharge · Gasaustritt *m*

discharge of insurer of a debt, release of insurer of a debt, discharge of guarantor, release of guarantor, discharge of surety, release of surety, discharge of cautioner, release of cautioner · Bürgenbefreiung *f*, Bürgenfreistellung

discharge of (real) estate from debt, discharge of (real) property from debt, discharge of realty from debt · Grund(stücks)entschuldung *f*, Landentschuldung, Bodenentschuldung, Liegenschaftsentschuldung, Immobilienentschuldung

discharge order, order of discharge · Entlastungsverfügung *f*

discharge order → (bankruptcy) discharge order

discharge other than by performance · Rückabwick(e)lung *f*

discharge period, discharge duration, discharge term, period of discharge, term of discharge, duration of discharge, period of redemption, term of redemption, duration of redemption, redemption period, redemption term, redemption duration · Auslösungsfrist *f*, Einlösungsfrist *f*, Ablösungsfrist *f*

discharge price, price of redemption, price of discharge, redemption price · Ablösungspreis *m*, Einlösungspreis, Auslösungspreis

discharge right, right of discharge, right to discharge, redemption right, right of redemption, right to redeem, right to regain property, right to reclaim property · Ablösungsrecht *n*, Einlösungsrecht, Auslösungsrecht

discharge sum, sum of discharge, redemption sum, sum of redemption · Ablösungssumme *f*, Auslösungssumme, Einlösungssumme

discharge term → discharge period

discharging; releasing [*Required to be under seal*]; acquittance, acquitting, setting free [*The act by which a discharge in writing is effected*] · Befreien *n*, Freistellen, Freigeben, Entlasten, Dispensieren

disciplinarian · Disziplinarvorgesetzte *m*

disciplinary authority · Disziplinarbehörde *f*

disciplinary authority, disciplinary power · Disziplinargewalt *f*, Disziplinarmacht *f*, Disziplinarhoheit *f*, Disziplinarkompetenz *f*

disciplinary rules, canon of ethics, ethical rules (US); etiquette (Brit.) [*The forms established by convention or prescribed by social arbiters for behavio(u)r in polite society*] · Standesrecht *n*

discipline committee · Disziplinarausschuß *m*

discipline-orien(ta)ted, discipline-related · fachwissenschaftlich orientiert, fachwissenschaftlich bezogen

to disclaim, to abandon, to relinquish, to remise, to forsake, to give up, to renounce [*To relinquish with intent of never again resuming one's right or interest*] · aufgeben, preisgeben, Verzicht leisten, verzichten, ausschlagen, entsagen, derelinquieren

disclaimed, abandoned, relinquished, renounced, remised, forsaken, given up, waived · aufgegeben, preisgegeben, Verzicht geleistet, verzichtet, ausgeschlagen, entsagt, derelinquiert

disclaimer, denial, disavowal · Leugnung *f*, Abstreitung, Abrede *f*, Wegrede, Ableugnung

disclaimer, waiver, abandonment, relinquishment, renunciation, renouncement [*It includes the intention, and also the external act(ion) by which it is carried into effect*] · Aufgabe *f*, Preisgabe *f*, Verzicht(leistung) *m*, (*f*), Entsagung, Ausschlagung

disclaimer · Ableugnung *f* einer angeblichen Verpflichtung, Ableugnung eines Rechtsverhältnisses

to disclose, to reveal, to knowledge, to make known, to clarify, to free from secrecy, to free from ignorance, to lay bare · aufklären, enthüllen, offenbaren, offenlegen, offen darlegen, preisgeben, kundtun

disclosed (surplus) reserve · offene Rücklage *f*

disclosure, clarification · Aufklärung *f*, (Beweis)Offenlegung, Offenbarung

disclosure duty, clarification duty, duty of disclosure, duty of clarification · Aufklärungspflicht *f*, Offenbarungspflicht, (Beweis)Offenlegungspflicht, Auskunftspflicht, Vorlagepflicht

disclosure of all documents relating to a case, discovery of documents · Offenlegung *f* der Prozeßakten vor dem Verfahren, Urkundenvorlegung, Vorzeigung durch gerichtliche Verfügung, prozessuale Aufklärung

discomfort index · Unbehaglichkeitsindex *m*

to discommon [*To deprive commonable lands of their commonable quality, by inclosing and appropriating or improving them*] · parzell(is)ieren [*Gemein(frei)flächen*]

discontinuance of an action; nolle prosequi [*Latin*] · Klagezurücknahme *f* vor Abgabe des Wahrspruches [*Zivilprozeß. Nicht verwechseln mit „nonsuit" in der Hauptverhandlung*]

discontinuance of work(s), cessation of work(s), abandonment of work(s) [*Cessation of operation for a definite period*] · Arbeitsunterbrechung *f*, Unterbrechung der Arbeiten

to discontinue, to interrupt · unterbrechen [*Arbeit(en)*]

discontinued, interrupted · unterbrochen [*Arbeit(en)*]

discontinued prescription, interrupted prescription · unterbrochene Ersitzung *f*

discontinuous · nichtständig [*Dienstbarkeit*]

discontinuous segmentation · stufenförmige Anpassung *f* [*Bestimmte Faktoreinsatzmengen sind nicht frei variierbar, was immer dann zu einem stufenförmigen Verlauf der Gesamtkostenkurve führt, wenn nicht alle Faktoreinsatzmengen pro Einheiten der unabhängigen Variablen voll anpaßbar sind*]

discordant frontiers · nichtübereinstimmende Grenzen *fpl*

to discount · abzinsen, diskontieren

discount [*Foreign exchange. The difference if the forward rate is below the spot rate*] · Abschlag *m*, Deport *m*

discount · Abzinsung *f*, Diskont *m*

discount, disagio · Damnum *n*, Disagio *n*, Abschlag *m* [*Unterschiedsbetrag zwischen dem Nennwert (100%) und dem Auszahlungskurs einer Hypothek*]

discount bank — discriminatory land use practice

discount bank, discount house, discount company, bank of discount · Diskontbank *f*, Diskonthaus *n*, Geldmarktbank

discount factor, present-value factor · Abzinsungsfaktor *m*, AbF [*Er zinst einen nach soundsoviel Jahren fälligen Geldbetrag unter Berücksichtigung von Zins und Zinseszins auf einen jetzt fälligen Geldbetrag ab*]

discount for risk, allowance for risk · Gewißheitsäquivalent *n*, Sicherheitsabschlag *m* bei Marktdaten

discount house, discount shop · Diskontgeschäft *n*, Diskontladen *m*

discount market, Lombard Street, bill market · Diskontmarkt *m*

discount rate, rate of discount · Diskontsatz *m*

discount supermarket · Diskontsupermarkt *m*

to discover, to produce, to file, to submit, to present · abgeben, einreichen, vorlegen, enthüllen [*Mitteilen von Tatsachen oder Vorlegen von Schriftstücken an den Prozeßgegner*]

to discover by survey, to locate · auffinden

discovery, production, submission, presentation, filing · Abgabe *f*, Einreichung *f*, Vorlage *f*, Vorlegung, Edition *f*, Enthüllung [*Mitteilung von Tatsachen oder Vorlegung von Schriftstücken an den Prozeßgegner*]

discovery by interrogatories, submission by interrogatories, presentation by interrogatories, production by interrogatories, filing by interrogatories · Abgabe *f* von Tatsachen, Einreichung *f* von Tatsachen, Vorlage *f* von Tatsachen, Vorlegung von Tatsachen, Edition *f* von Tatsachen, Enthüllung von Tatsachen [*An den Prozeßgegner*]

discovery of documents, filing of documents, production of documents, submission of documents, presentation of documents · Abgabe *f* von Schriftstücken, Vorlage *f* von Schriftstücken, Einreichung *f* von Schriftstücken, Vorlegung von Schriftstücken, Enthüllung von Schriftstücken, Edition *f* von Schriftstücken [*An den Prozeßgegner*]

discovery of documents, disclosure of all documents relating to a case · Offenlegung *f* der Prozeßakten vor dem Verfahren, Urkundenvorlegung, Vorzeigung durch gerichtliche Verfügung, prozessuale Aufklärung

discreditable · abträglich

discretely · umsichtig

discretion · Ermessen *n*

discretion → (banker's) discretion

discretionary act(ion) · Ermessenshandlung *f*, Ermessensakt *m*

discretionary case · Kannfall *m*, Ermessensfall

discretionary clause · Ermessensklausel *f*, Kannklausel

discretionary consideration · Ermessenserwägung *f*

discretionary decision, decision ex aequo et bondo · Ermessensentscheid(ung) *m*, *(f)*, Entscheid(ung) nach Ermessen

discretionary error · Ermessensfehler *m*

discretionary freedom, freedom of discretion · Ermessensfreiheit *f*

discretionary mistake · Ermessensirrtum *m*

discretionary planning · Planungsermessen *n*

discretionary prescription, discretionary regulation, discretionary rule · Ermessensvorschrift *f*, Kannvorschrift

discretionary purchase · Ermessenskauf *m*

discretionary regulation → discretionary prescription

discretionary remedy, discretionary redress · Ermessensbehelf *m*, Ermessensabhilfe *f*

discretionary right, discretionary power · Ermessensbefugnis *f*, Ermessensrecht *n*

discretionary rule → discretionary prescription

discretionary sale, sale of discretion · Ermessensverkauf *m*

to discriminate, to disadvantage · benachteiligen

to discriminate, to exclude, to shut out · ausschließen, nicht zulassen

to discriminate · begünstigen [*Steuerwesen*]

discriminating duty · Differentialzoll *m*

discriminating tariff · Differentialtarif, Staffeltarif *m*

discrimination [*In real estate, prejudice or refusal to rent or sell to a person because of race, colo(u)r, religion, or ethnic origin*] · Benachteiligung *f*

discrimination · Begünstigung *f* [*Steuerwesen*]

discrimination in housing, housing discrimination · Wohn(ungs)benachteiligung *f*

discriminatory land use practice, snob zoning, exclusionary zoning, discriminatory zoning, spot zoning, exclusionary land use practice [*A land use restraint which has the effect of barring prospective lower income or minority residents*]

· diskriminierende (Bau)Nutzung f, diskriminierende (bauliche) Nutzung, Ausschluß(bau)nutzung

discussion of the budget, budget discussion · Haushalt(s)beratung f

diseased in mind, of unsound mind, nonsane, insane, deranged; insanus [*Latin*]; unsound in mind, disordered in mind · geistesgestört, geisteskrank

disembodied technical progress · nicht kapitalgebundener technischer Fortschritt m

to disencumber, to disburden, to free of incumbrance(s), to free of encumbrance(s) · entlasten, entschulden, lastenfrei machen, schuldenfrei machen [*Grundstück*]

dis(en)franchise · Entziehung f eines Sonderrechts, Entzug m eines Sonderrechts

disenfranchised · unterprivilegiert

dis(en)franchisement · Wahlrechtverlust m, Wahlrechtentzug m, Wahlrechtentziehung f

to disentail, to bar an entail, to destroy an entail · aufheben der gebundenen (Land)Erbfolge(ordnung)

disentailing deed, disentailment deed [*An assurance by which a tenant in tail bars the entail so as to convert it into a fee simple or a base fee*] · Aufhebungsurkunde f [*Erbfolgeordnung*]

disentail(ment) · Beschränkung f in der Erbfolge(ordnung), Begrenzung in der Erbfolge(ordnung), Einschränkung in der Erbfolge(ordnung), Aufhebung

disfiguration, disfigurement · Beeinträchtigung f, Entstellung, Verunstaltung, Verschandelung, Verunzierung [*Ortsbild*]

to disfigure, to deface, to mar · beeinträchtigen, verschandeln, entstellen, verunstalten, verunzieren [*Ortsbild*]

disfigurement law, disfigurement act, disfigurement statute · Verunstaltungsgesetz n, Verschandelungsgesetz, Verunzierungsgesetz

disfigurement prohibition · Verschandelungsverbot n, Verunstaltungsverbot

disfiguring, defacing, marring · Beeinträchtigen n, Verschandeln, Verunstalten, Entstellen, Verunzieren [*Ortsbild*]

disgraceful · entehrend

dishonest, false · unehrlich, falsch

dishonest abstraction of electricity · Stromdiebstahl m

dishonesty, default · Unehrlichkeit f

dishonoured bill (of exchange) (Brit.); dishonored bill (of exchange) (US) · notleidender Wechsel m

dishonoured cheque, dishonoured check; bounce [*colloquial term*] · geplatzter Scheck m

dis(in)herison; exhaeredatio [*Latin*]; disinheritance · Enterbung f

to disinherit; to exheredate [*Scots law*], to deprive of an inheritance, to debar from an inheritance, to put out of an inheritance, to exclude from inheriting · enterben

disinheritance, dis(in)herison; exhaeredatio [*Latin*] · Enterbung f

disinherited female person · Enterbte f

disinherited male person · Enterbte m

disinherited person; exhaeres [*Latin*] · enterbte Person f

disinheriting, depriving of an inheritance, putting out of an inheritance, debarring from an inheritance, excluding from an inheritance; exheredating [*Scots law*] · Enterben n

to disinter, to exhume, to unbury · exhumieren

disinterment, unburying, exhumation · Exhumierung f

disinvestment · Investitionsrückgang m per Saldo, (Kapital)Anlagerückgang per Saldo, Geldanlagerückgang per Saldo

disinvestment (by bondholders) · Rückgabe f von Versicherungsfondsanteilen

disjointed incrementalism · rationaldeduktive Planungsentscheidung f, schrittweise Planungsentscheidung, zusammenhanglose Planungsentscheidung

dislocated exchange · zerrüttete Währung f

disloyalty to contract · Vertragsuntreue f, Vertragsbrüchigkeit f

dismantling of scaffold(ing)s · Abbau m von Gerüsten, Gerüstabbau

to dismiss, to nonsuit, to strike out · abweisen [*Klage*]

to dismiss · entlassen [*aus einem Beschäftigungsverhältnis*]

dismissal · Entlassung f [*aus einem Beschäftigungsverhältnis*]

dismissal of (court) action, dismissal of plea, dismissal of (law)suit, dismissal of cause, nonsuit [*An order or judg(e)ment finally disposing of an action, suit, motion, etc., by sending it out of court, though without a trial of the issues involved*] · Abweisung f, Klageabweisung

dismissal of officers, dismissal of officials · Beamtenabbau m

dismissed · abgewiesen [*Klage*]

to dismiss with cost(s) · kostenpflichtig abweisen

disobedience → violation (of law)

disorder, confusion · Verwirrung *f*, Bestürzung

disordered condition, confused condition · verworrene Lage *f*, verworrener Zustand *m*

disordered in mind, diseased in mind, of unsound mind, non-sane, insane, deranged; insanus [*Latin*]; unsound in mind · geistesgestört, geisteskrank

disorderly · unordentlich

disorderly growth · wildes Wachstum *n*

disparity, inequality · Disparität *f*, Ungleichheit *f*

dispatch goods, despatch goods · Eilgut *n*

dispatch money, despatch money · Eilgeld *n*

dispatch note, despatch note [*A document recording that products are available for despatch and authorizing arrangement for delivery*] · Versandanzeige *f*, Versandzettel *m*

to dispauper(ize) · streichen aus der Armen(recht)liste

dispensation, immunity, exemption, discharge, release [*Relaxation of the law in a particular case by competent authority*] · Befreiung *f*, Freistellung, Entlastung, Freigabe *f*, Erlaß *m*, Dispens(ierung) *m*, (*f*), Dispensation *f*, Ausnahmebewilligung

dispensation application, immunity application, exemption application, discharge application, release application · Befreiungsantrag *m*, Dispens(ier)ungsantrag, Freistellungsantrag, Entlastungsantrag, Freigabeantrag, Dispensationsantrag

dispensing authority, dispensing power · Befreiungskompetenz *f*, Befreiungsmacht *f*, Befreiungsgewalt *f*, Befreiungshoheit *f*, Dispens(ierungs)macht, Dispens(ierungs)hoheit, Dispens(ierungs)gewalt, Dispens(ierungs)kompetenz *f*

to disperse, to resite, to relocate, to resettle, to displace, to transfer from congested areas, to decentralize · aussiedeln, umsiedeln, verlegen, verändern des Standortes, umsetzen

dispersed, scattered · gestreut, dekonzentriert, verstreut [*Raumordnung*]

dispersed city · Kleinstadtgruppe *f* [*Mehrere benachbarte Kleinstädte, die bei Abwesenheit eines Zentrums wie eine große Stadt wirken und sich mit ihren unterschiedlichen Funktionen in die Bedienung eines gemeinsamen Umlandes teilen*]

dispersed development, noncompact development, sporadic development, scattered development [*Developments occurring here and there without any co-ordinating feature to lick them or give them identity*] · Splitterbebauung *f*, Streubebauung, wilde Bebauung; Splitterüberbauung, Streuüberbauung, wilde Überbauung [*Schweiz*]

dispersed function, scattered function, noncentral function · disperse Funktion *f*, nichtzentrale Funktion, Streufunktion

dispersed hamlet · Streuweiler *m*

dispersed land(ed) estate, noncompact land(ed) estate, scattered land(ed) estate · Streu(land)besitz *m*, disperser (Land)Besitz, Streubodenbesitz, disperser Bodenbesitz

dispersed landscape, scattered landscape, noncompact landscape · Streulandschaft *f*, disperse Landschaft

dispersed location, scattered location, noncompact location · Streulage *f*, disperse Lage

dispersed lot · Streuparzelle *f*, Streuflurstück *n*

dispersed pattern, scattered pattern, noncompact pattern, dispersed scheme, scattered scheme, noncompact scheme · Streumuster *n*, Streuschema *n*, disperses Muster, disperses Schema

dispersed population, noncentral population, scattered population · nichtzentrale Bevölkerung *f*, disperse Bevölkerung, Streubevölkerung

dispersed regional city plan, spread city plan · Plan *m* punkthafter Verdichtungszonen in weiter Streuung über eine Stadtregion

dispersed settlement, dispersed settling, scattered settlement, scattered settling, noncompact settlement, noncompact settling · Streubesied(e)lung, Splitter-(be)sied(e)lung, Streu(an)sied(e)lung, Splitteransied(e)lung, Streusiedeln, Splittersiedeln, Streubesiedeln, Splitterbesiedeln *n* [*Tätigkeit, die zum Entstehen einer Streuansied(e)lung führt*]

dispersed settlement combined with small nucleated units, swarm-like settlement · Schwarm(an)sied(e)lung *f*

dispersed-site housing; noncompact site housing [*Housing units dispersed, usually by a local housing authority, in small numbers on numerous, noncontiguous sites throughout a community*], scattered-site housing · Streuwohnungen *fpl*

dispersed territorial domain, scattered territorial domain, noncompact territorial domain · Streugrundherrschaft *f*, disperse Grundherrschaft

dispersion — disposal period

dispersion, scatter · Dekonzentration f, (Ver)Streuung f [Raumordnung]

dispersion factor · Dispersionsfaktor m

dispersion matrix, covariance matrix · Dispersionsmatrix f, Kovarianzmatrix [Statistik]

dispersion of authority · Aufsplitterung f der Verwaltung auf örtlicher Ebene

dispersion of industries, industrial dispersion · Industriestreuung f

dispersion of population, scatter of population, population dispersion, population scatter · Bevölkerungsstreuung f

to displace, to transfer from congested areas, to decentralize, to disperse, to resite, to relocate, to resettle · aussiedeln, umsiedeln, verlegen, verändern des Standortes, umsetzen

displaced, resettled, relocated, resited · ausgesiedelt, planungsverdrängt, umgesetzt, verlegt, umgesiedelt

displaced business disaster loan, DBDL (US) · Darleh(e)n n für planungsverdrängte Gewerbetreibende

displaced family, relocated family, resettled family, resited family · Aussied(e)lerfamilie f, Umsied(e)lerfamilie, umgesiedelte Familie, ausgesiedelte Familie, verlegte Familie, umgesetzte Familie, planungsverdrängte Familie

displaced individual, displaced person, relocated person, relocated individual, resettled person, resettled individual, resited person, resited individual, displacee · Aussied(e)ler m, Aussied(e)lerperson f, Umsied(e)lerperson f, Umsied(e)ler, Umgesiedelte, Ausgesiedelte

displacement, rehousing, resettlement, transfer from congested areas, (tenant) relocation [Of persons from land acquired or appropriated for planning purposes] · Aussied(e)lung f, Umsied(e)lung, Standortveränderung, Verlegung, Umsetzung, Wiederunterbringung, Lageveränderung

displacement of industry, transfer of industry, relocation of industry, industrial resettlement, industrial relocation, industrial shifting, resettlement of industry · Industrieaussied(e)lung f, Industrieumsied(e)lung, Industrieumsetzung, Industrieverlegung, industrielle Standortveränderung, Industrieverlagerung

display device [For stock exchange quotations] · Kursanzeigegerät n, Kursanzeiger m

displayed advertisement · Großanzeige f, Schlagzeilenwerbung f

display of advertisements, outdoor advertisement, openair advertisement, exter-nal advertisement, exterior advertisement · Außenwerbung f, Außenreklame f

to dispone [Scots law]; to (ab)alienate, to dispose of · veräußern

disposable, (ab)alienable · veräußerlich, veräußerbar

disposable fief; feudum alienabile, feodum alienabile [Latin]; (ab)alienable fief · veräußerliches Leh(e)n, veräußerbares Leh(e)n n

disposable income [The gross income less various deductions for income tax, rent, dependents and other matters] · verfügbares Einkommen n [Einkommen zum Bestreiten der Lebenshaltungskosten]

disposal, (ab)alienation [In real property law, the transfer of property and possession of land(s) and other things from one person to another] · Veräußerung f

disposal, removal · Beseitigung f, Wegschaffung [z. B. Abfall]

disposal area, sewage land · Rieselfeld n

disposal authority, (ab)alienation authority, authority of disposal, authority of (ab)alienation · Veräußerungsvollmacht f, Veräußerungsvertretungsmacht

disposal contract, contract of (ab)alienation, contract of disposal, (ab)alienation contract · Veräußerungsvertrag m

disposal deed, deed of (ab)alienation, deed of disposal, (ab)alienation deed · Veräußerungsurkunde f

disposal duty, duty of (ab)alienation, duty of disposal, (ab)alienation duty · Veräußerungspflicht f

disposal mode, mode of (ab)alienation, mode of disposal, (ab)alienation mode · Veräußerungsweise f

disposal obligation, obligation of (ab)alienation, obligation of disposal, (ab)alienation obligation · Veräußerungsbindung f, Veräußerungsgebundenheit f, Veräußerungsverpflichtung, Veräußerungsverbindlichkeit f

disposal of anticipation, (ab)alienation restraint, disposal restraint, restraint on (ab)alienation, restraint on disposal, (ab)alienation against anticipation · Veräußerungsverbot n

disposal of automobile bulks, automobile disposal · Autowrackbeseitigung f

disposal of land → (ab)alienation of (real) estate

disposal of uncollected goods, sale of uncollected goods · Verkauf m nicht eingelöster Pfandgüter

disposal period, period of (ab)alienation, period of disposal, (ab)alienation period · Veräußerungsfrist f

disposal permission — to disprove

disposal permission, permission of (ab)alienation, permission of disposal, (ab)alienation permission · Veräußerungsgenehmigung *f*, Veräußerungserlaubnis *f*

disposal power, right of (ab)alienation, power of (ab)alienation, right of disposal, power of disposal, (ab)alienation right, (ab)alienation power · Veräußerungsbefugnis *f*, Veräußerungsrecht *n*

disposal restraint, restraint on (ab)alienation, restraint on disposal, (ab)alienation against anticipation, disposal of anticipation, (ab)alienation restraint · Veräußerungsverbot *n*

to dispose [*issue*] · begeben [*Emission*]

to dispose by will, to leave by will, to bestow by will, to give by will · (testamentarisch) vermachen, letztwillig verfügen, testamentarisch verfügen, letztwillig vermachen

disposed by will, left by will, bestowed by will, given by will · letztwillig verfügt, letztwillig vermacht, (testamentarisch) vermacht, testamentarisch verfügt

to dispose of; to dispone [*Scots law*]; to (ab)alienate · veräußern

disposing capacity, disposing capability, testamentary capability, testamentary qualification, disposing qualification, capacity of the testator, capability of the testator, qualification of the testator, testamentary capacity · Testierfähigkeit *f*, Testiereignung *f*, Testamentsfähigkeit, Testamentseignung

disposing mind · Zurechnungsfähigkeit *f* [*Testamentserrichtung*]

disposition mortis causa, testamentary disposition · Verfügung *f* von Todes wegen, Rechtsgeschäft *n* von Todes wegen, letzte Verfügung

disposition of improved land · Verteilung *f* aufgeschlossener Grundstücke

disposition (over a thing) · Verfügung *f*, Disposition *f*, Herrschaftsmacht *f* [*Das Wesen einer Verfügung besteht im Eintritt einer unmittelbaren Rechtsänderung. Wer das Eigentum an einer Sache überträgt, eine Sache mit einem Pfandrecht belastet, trifft damit eine Verfügung*]

disposition power, power of disposition · Verfügungsermächtigung *f*

disposition price, re-use value [*The price a local public agency places on land, cleared through the urban renewal process, to be sold to a redeveloper, based upon a re-use appraisal*] · Wiedernutzungswert *m*

disposition re-use, re-use appraisal, re-use (e)valuation, re-use appraisement [*An appraisal of re-use value*] · Wiedernutzungs(ab)schätzung *f*, Wiedernutzungsbewertung

disposition usufruct, usufruct of disposition · Dispositionsnießbrauch *m*, Nießbrauch der freien Verfügung

to dispossess, to turn a tenant out of his farm, to evict a tenant from his farm · abmei(g)ern

to dispossess, to oust, to evict · widerrechtlich entheben, widerrechtlich entziehen, widerrechtlich aberkennen [*Grundbesitz*]

to dispossess by equity · abbilligen [*Grundbesitz*]

to dispossess by legal process, to legally oust from the land, to evict, to dispossess by process of law [*To recover (real) property through court judgment or superior claim*] · entziehen, entheben, aberkennen [*Grundbesitz*]

dispossession, expulsion from a farm, distraint, turning a tenant out of his farm, evicting a tenant from his farm · Abmei(g)erung *f* [*In den Zeiten der feudalen Grund- und Gutsherrschaft das Recht des Grundherren, einem Bauern die Bauernstelle wegen Pflichtverletzung zu entziehen*]

dispossession, ouster, eviction · widerrechtliche Entziehung *f*, widerrechtliche Enthebung, widerrechtliche Aberkennung

dispossession by equity · Abbilligung *f* [*Grundbesitz*]

dispossession by legal process, dispossession by process of law, eviction, legal ousting from the land, removal from possession of (real) property [*Act of depriving a person of the possession of land that he has held in pursuance of the judgment of a court. "Eviction" is not necessarily accomplished by legal process, nor does it always compel removal*] · Enthebung *f*, Entziehung, Aberkennung [*Grundbesitz*]

dispossession by process of law → dispossession by legal process

disproof, counter-evidence, counterproof, evidence to the contrary, proof to the contrary, contradictory evidence, contradictory proof, rebutting testimony · Gegenbeweis *m*, gegenteiliger Beweis

disproportion · Mißverhältnis *n*

disproportionately, unproportionately · unverhältnismäßig

disproportion of value · Wertmißverhältnis *n*

to disprove, to prove (to be) false, to prove (to be) erroneous, to prove (to be) untrue, to prove (to be) unfounded, to falsify · widerlegen

to dispute — distinctness principle rules

to dispute · streiten

dispute · Auseinandersetzung *f*, Streit(igkeit) *m*, *(f)*

dispute · Rechtsstreit *m*

dispute as to terms of tenancy, dispute as to terms of tenure · Mietstreit(igkeit) *m*, *(f)*, Mietauseinandersetzung *f*

to dispute by action, to litigate, to go to law, to carry on a (law)suit, to bring into litigation, to engage in ligation, to claim by action [*Latin: litigare*] · prozessieren, einen Rechtsstreit austragen, einen Prozeß anhängig machen, rechtshängig werden lassen

dispute clause · (Vertrags)Streit(igkeits)klausel *f*

disputed matter, disputed subject, matter in dispute, matter in issue, matter in litigation, subject of issue, subject of dispute, subject of litigation · (Rechts)Streitsache *f*

disputed object · Streitobjekt *n*

disputed subject → disputed matter

disputed value; jurisdictional amount (US); amount in controversy, amount in dispute, value in dispute · Streitwert *m*

dispute of inheritance, inheritance dispute, heirship dispute, dispute of heirship · Erbauseinandersetzung *f*, Erbstreit(igkeit) *m*, *(f)*

dispute settlement · Beilegung *f* von Streitigkeiten

dispute settlement procedure · Streitbeilegungsverfahren *n*

disqualifications · Minderung *f* öffentlicher Rechte [*Schuldner*]

to disseise, to disseize, to deprive of seisin · entweren

disseised, disseized · entwert

disseisee; disseysitus [*Latin*] [*The party who is disseised, or put out of possession or seisin of the freehold*] · Gewereentsetzte *m*

disseisin, disseizin; disseisina, disseysina, dissaisina [*Latin*] · Entwerung *f*

disseisitrix, disseisoress, female disseisor · Gewereentsetzerin *f*

disseisor; disseysitor [*Latin*] [*One who puts another out of the possession of his land(s) wrongfully. A settled trespasser on the land(s) of another*] · Gewereentsetzer *m*, widerrechtlicher Landergreifer

disseized, disseised · entwert

dissenting opinion · Minderheitsgutachten *n* [*Abweichende Auffassung eines Richters in einem Spruchkörper eines Gerichts*]

dissolution · Auflösung *f*

dissolution by efflux of time · Auflösung *f* durch Zeitablauf [*Gesellschaft*]

dissolution instrument, instrument of dissolution · Auflösungsinstitut *n* [*Gesellschaft*]

dissolution of marriage, marriage dissolution · Eheauflösung *f*

dissolution of (private) partnership · Personalgesellschaftsauflösung *f*

to dissolve · auflösen

dissolved · aufgelöst

distance area, distance space · Abstandfläche *f* [*Die Abstandflächen werden von den Gebäuden zu den Grundstücksgrenzen freigehalten um Belichtung und Belüftung der Wohnungen zu sichern*]

distance between windows · Fensterabstand *m*

distance from boundaries, distance from boundary · Abstand *m* von der Grenze, Grenzabstand

distance of move, migration distance · Wanderungsentfernung *f*

distance rule, rule of distance · Abstandregel *f*

distance separation [*Open space between buildings or between a building and an interior lot line, which is provided to prevent the spread of fire*] · Brandraum *m*

distance space, distance area · Abstandfläche *f* [*Die Abstandflächen werden von den Gebäuden zu den Grundstücksgrenzen freigehalten um Belichtung und Belüftung der Wohnungen zu sichern*]

distance space ordinance, distance area ordinance · Abstandflächenverordnung *f*

distance variable · Entfernungsvariable *f*

distant space [*A space not immediately surrounding an urban settlement*] · Fernraum *m*

distinctness, certainty, clearness of statement, definiteness, absence of doubt · Bestimmtheit *f*, Klarheit, Gewißheit

distinctness · Bestimmtheit *f*, Spezialität *f* [*Grundbuchrecht*]

distinctness principle, distinctness doctrine, doctrine of distinctness, principle of distinctness · Bestimmtheitsgrundsatz *m*, Bestimmtheitsprinzip *n*, Spezialitätsgrundsatz, Spezialitätsprinzip [*Grundbuchrecht*]

distinctness principle rules, rules of principle of distinctness · formell(rechtlich)er Bestimmtheitsgrundsatz *m*, formell(rechtlich)er Spezialitätsgrundsatz, formell(rechtlich)es Bestimmtheitsprinzip *n*, formell(rechtlich)es Spezialitätsprinzip [*Grundbuchrecht*]

to distinguish — distribution modelling

to distinguish · differenzieren, unterscheiden

distinguishing · Unterscheiden *n*

distinguishing characteristic · Unterscheidungsmerkmal *n*

distortion · Verzerrung *f*

distortion of area, distortion of territory · Gebietsverzerrung *f*

distortion of competition · Wettbewerbsverzerrung *f*

distortion of facts, distortion of truth · Tatsachenverdrehung *f*, Wahrheitsverdrehung

distortion of the market, market distortion · Marktverzerrung *f*

distortion of truth, distortion of facts · Tatsachenverdrehung *f*, Wahrheitsverdrehung

to distrain, to levy a distress (upon), to execute a distress (upon) · (privat)pfänden

distrainable · selbstpfändbar

distrainer, distrainor, distreinor, agent for levying distress; bailiff [*Low Latin*] · Privatpfänder *m* von beweglichen Sachen, eigenmächtiger Pfänder von beweglichen Sachen

distraint, turning a tenant out of his farm, evicting a tenant from his farm, dispossession, expulsion from a farm · Abmei(g)erung *f* [*In den Zeiten der feudalen Grund- und Gutsherrschaft das Recht des Grundherren, einem Bauern die Bauernstelle wegen Pflichtverletzung zu entziehen*]

distraint, distress · Not *f*

distraint, distress [*A taking (away), without legal process, of a personal chattel from the possession of a wrongdoer into the hands of a party grieved, as a pledge for redressing an injury, the performance of a duty, or the satisfaction of a demand*] · eigenmächtige Pfändung *f* beweglicher Sachen, Privatpfändung beweglicher Sachen, Selbstpfändung beweglicher Sachen

distraint (for) damage feasant, distraint of cattle, distress of cattle, distress (for) damage feasant · Viehpfändung *f*, (Vieh)Schüttung [*Sie besteht in der Beschlagnahme von Rindern, welche sich widerrechtlicherweise auf einem fremden Grundstück befinden und die als Sicherheit für die Schadensvergütung dienen*]

distraint infinite, distress infinite · unbegrenzte wiederholte Privatpfändung *f* beweglicher Sachen, unbegrenzte wiederholte Selbstpfändung beweglicher Sachen, unbegrenzte wiederholte eigenmächtige Pfändung beweglicher Sachen

distress, distraint · Not *f*

distress, distraint [*A taking (away), without legal process, of a personal chattel from the possession of a wrongdoer into the hands of a party grieved, as a pledge for redressing an injury, the performance of a duty, or the satisfaction of a demand*] · eigenmächtige Pfändung *f* beweglicher Sachen, Privatpfändung beweglicher Sachen, Selbstpfändung beweglicher Sachen

distressed agricultral area, less prosperous agricultural area, special agricultural area, depressed agricultural area · landwirtschaftliches Notstandsgebiet *n*, landwirtschaftliches Passivgebiet

distressed area, special area, less prosperous area, depressed territory, special territory, distressed territory, less prosperous territory, depressed area · Notstandsgebiet *n*, Passivgebiet, Sondergebiet, SO

distressed community, special community, less prosperous community, depressed community · Notstandsgemeinde *f*, Passivgemeinde, Notstandskommune *f*, Passivkommune

distress (for) damage feasant, distraint (for) damage feasant, distraint of cattle, distress of cattle · Viehpfändung *f*, (Vieh)Schüttung [*Sie besteht in der Beschlagnahme von Rindern, welche sich widerrechtlicherweise auf einem fremden Grundstück befinden und die als Sicherheit für die Schadensvergütung dienen*]

distress for nonpayment of rent · Mietpfändung *f*

distress infinite, distraint infinite · unbegrenzte wiederholte Privatpfändung *f* beweglicher Sachen, unbegrenzte wiederholte Selbstpfändung beweglicher Sachen, unbegrenzte wiederholte eigenmächtige Pfändung beweglicher Sachen

distributee · Letztbegünstigte *m*

distributee [*One of the persons who are entitled, under the statute of distributions, to the personal estate of one who is dead intestate*] · Intestat-Fahrniserbe *m*, Zuteilungsberechtigte, Intestat-Fahrhabeerbe, Intestat-Mobilienerbe, Intestat-Mobiliarerbe

distribution · Verteilung *f*

distribution(al) pattern, distribution(al) scheme · Verteilungsmuster *n*, Verteilungsschema *n*

distribution area map, pseudo area map · Arealkarte *f*, Pseudogebietskarte, Verbreitungskarte

distribution modelling · Verteilungsmodellierung *f*

distribution of city size, town size distribution, city size distribution, distribution of town size · Stadtgrößenverteilung *f*

distribution of income, income distribution · Einkommensverteilung *f*

distribution of industry policy · Industrieansied(e)lungspolitik *f*

distribution of industry act, distribution of industry law, distribution of industry statute · Gesetz *n* über die räumliche Verteilung von Industrien, Industrieansied(e)lungsgesetz

distribution of industry act, distribution of industry law, distribution of industry statute · Industriedezentralisierungsgesetz *n*, Industrieaussied(e)lungsgesetz

distribution of land(s), land(s) distribution · Bodenverteilung *f*, Landverteilung

distribution of migration(s), migration distribution · Wanderungsverteilung *f*

distribution of ownership (of property), distribution of (general) property, distribution of proprietorship · Eigentumsverteilung *f*

distribution of population, population distribution · Bevölkerungsverteilung *f*

distribution of possession(s) · Besitzverteilung *f*

distribution of powers, power distribution, power separation, separation of powers · (Staats)Gewaltentrennung *f*, (Staats-) Gewaltenteilung

distribution of risk(s), distribution of hazard(s), sharing of risk(s), sharing of hazard(s), splitting (up) of risk(s), splitting (up) of hazard(s), hazard distribution, risk distribution, risk sharing, hazard sharing · Verteilung *f* des Risikos, Verteilung des Wagnisses, Risikoverteilung, Wagnisverteilung

distribution of tasks, task distribution · Aufgabenverteilung *f*

distribution of town size, distribution of city size, town size distribution, city size distribution · Stadtgrößenverteilung *f*

distribution scale, scale of distribution · Verteilungsmaßstab *m*, Maßstab *m* der Verteilung

distribution theory, theory of distribution(s) · Verteilungstheorie *f*

distributive finding (of the issue), distributive verdict · Wahrspruch *m* für und gegen beide Parteien, Verdikt *n* für und gegen beide Parteien

distributive verdict, distributive finding (of the issue) · Wahrspruch *m* für und gegen beide Parteien, Verdikt *n* für und gegen beide Parteien

district, division [*A specific portion of a larger area, such as of a city*] · Bezirk *m*

district → (court) district

district board, sanitary board [*England. A board constituted under the Metropolis Management Act, 1855, for the management of the sanitary affairs of groups of parishes as were formed into districts*] · Sanitätsamt *n*

district building ordinance, district construction ordinance · Bezirksbauverordnung *f*

district-cartel [*Cartel which assigns to its members the monopoly of a certain district or market*] · Gebietskartell *n*, Rayonierungskartell

district centre (Brit.); district center (US) · Bezirkszentrum *n*

district committee · Bezirksausschuß *m*

district construction ordinance, district building ordinance · Bezirksbauverordnung *f*

district council, sanitary authority [*In den inkorporierten Städten Englands übt die Stadtverwaltung zugleich die Funktionen einer „sanitary authority" aus und somit bildet eine solche Stadt zugleich einen „county district" (= Verwaltungsbereich einer Sanitätsbehörde) und die Stadtverwaltung ist ein „district council" doch mit dem Unterschied von anderen „district councils", daß ihr Name und ihre Verfassung ihr gewahrt bleiben*] · Sanitätsbehörde *f*

district council → (urban) district council

district councillor, sanitary councillor · Rat *m* des Verwaltungsbereiches einer Sanitätsbehörde

district court · erstinstanzliches Bundesgericht *n* [*USA*]

district court · Landgericht *n*, LG [*Bundesrepublik Deutschland*]

District Court of the United States · Unterkreisgerichtshof *m* [*USA*]

district fund · Distriktkasse *f*

district institution · Distriktanstalt *f*

district labour court (Brit.); district labor court (US) · Landesarbeitsgericht *n*, LAG

district level · Bezirksebene *f*, Bezirksstufe *f*

district medical officer, district medical official · Bezirksarmenarzt *m*

District of Columbia · Bundesdistrikt *m* [*USA*]

district parish [*England. A parish may be districted into two or more district parishes with the consent of the bishop of the diocese, when it has become so thickly populated as to become unworkable as a single parish (New Parishes Acts, 1843 and 1844; New Parishes*

district period cost(s) — divine judg(e)ment

Measure, 1943)] · Kirchspieldistrikt *m*, Parochialdistrikt, (Pfarr)Sprengeldistrikt, kirchlicher Sprengeldistrikt

district period cost(s) · Bereichsfixkosten *f*, Bereichsfestkosten

district planning · Bezirksplanung *f*

district planning agency, district planning office · Bezirksplanungsstelle *f*

district planning commission · Bezirksplanungskommission *f*

district register, district registry · Bezirksregister *n*

district registry [*England*] · Gerichtsschreiberei *f* des Hohen Gerichtshofes in der Provinz, Provinz-Gerichtsschreiberei

District Social Court · Landessozialgericht *n* [*Bundesrepublik Deutschland*]

district superintendent · Polizeidistriktinspektor *m*

to disturb · stören

disturbance factor · Störfaktor *m*

disturbance of delivery · Lieferstörung *f*

disturbance of patronage · Patronatsstörung *f*

disturbance of performance · Leistungsstörung *f*

disturbance of (right-of-)way · Durchgangsrechtstörung *f*, Wegerechtstörung

disturbance of the landscape · Landschaftsstörung *f*

disturbance of work(s) · Arbeitsstörung *f*, Ausführungsstörung *f*

disuse, neglect to use, nonuse · Nichtgebrauch *m*, Nichtbenutzung *f*

disused, obsolete, antiquated, grown out of use · außer Gebrauch, nicht mehr verwendet

disutility · Nutzentgang *m*, negativer Nutzen *m*, Mißnutzen

ditch boundary · Grabengrenze *f*

diurnalis [*Latin*]; acre strip, day's work (at ploughing), daywere [*In old English law. A term applied to land, and signifying as much arable ground as could be ploughed up in one day's work*] · Tag(e)werk *n*; Tagwan *n*, Tagwen *n* [*In den Alpen*]

to diverge, to vary, to deviate [*from a norm*] · abweichen

divergence, deviation, variation [*from a norm*] · Abweichung *f*

diversification · Streuung *f* [*Fonds*]

diversified common stock fund · gestreuter Stammaktienfonds *m*

diversion · Umlegung *f* [*Straße; Weg; usw.*]

diversion, unlawful conversion · rechtswidrige Verwendung *f* (oder Verfügung) ohne bestimmten eigenen Vorteil, unrechtmäßige Verwendung (oder Verfügung) ohne bestimmten eigenen Vorteil [*einer einer Gesellschaft gehörenden Sache*]

diversion of purpose · Zweckentfremdung *f*

diversity of citizenship [*USA*] · verschiedene Staatsbürgerschaften *fpl*

to divert · umlegen [*Straße; Weg; usw.*]

divestiture · Entflechtung *f*, Kartellentflechtung

divided carrying · Eigenrisiko *n*, Eigenwagnis *n* [*kleines (Emissions)Übernahmesyndikat*]

divided farm, parted farm · Teilungshof *m*

divided forest → (sub)divided forest

divided (general) property → (sub)divided ownership (of property)

divided interest, divided right [*An interest in only a part of property*] · Teilrecht *n*

divided (into compartments) → (sub)divided (into compartments)

divided longitudinally into two equal halves · halbscheidig [*Kommunmauer*]

divided opinion · geteilte Meinung *f*

Divided Parishes Act [*England*] · Kirchspielgrenz(änderungs)gesetz *n*, (Pfarr-)Sprengelgrenz(änderungs)gesetz, kirchliches Sprengelgrenz(änderungs)gesetz, Parochialgrenz(änderungs)gesetz

divided property → (sub)divided (general) property)

divided right, divided interest [*An interest in only a part of property*] · Teilrecht *n*

(dividend) coupon, dividend warrant · Dividendenkupon *m*, Profitanteilschein *m*, Gewinnanteilschein, Dividendenschein, Profitkupon, Gewinnkupon

dividend of composition, composition dividend · Vergleichsquote *f*

dividends in arrears, accumulated dividend [*The amount of undeclared dividends accumulated on cumulative preferred stock*] · angesammelte Dividende *f*, angehäufte Dividende, aufgehäufte Dividende

dividend warrant, (dividend) coupon · Dividendenkupon *m*, Profitanteilschein *m*, Gewinnanteilschein, Dividendenschein, Profitkupon, Gewinnkupon

divider → (sub)divider

dividing (into compartments) → compartition

divine judg(e)ment; divinum judicium, judicium dei [*Latin*]; ordeal · Gottesurteil *n*

divine norm · Gottesnorm f

divine service, religious service · religiöse Dienstleistung f, religiöse Verrichtung [*Leh(e)n(s)mann*]

divisibility, divisibleness · Teilbarkeit f

divisible, severable · teilbar

divisible contract, severable contract, pro tanto contract, pro rata contract, proportionate contract · Vertrag m auf teilbare Leistung, teilbarer Vertrag

division, severance, separation [*The separation by defendants in their pleas; the adoption, by several defendants, of separate pleas, instead of joining in the same plea*] · (Ab)Trennung f

division [*In a specification. It is similar to a chapter in a book*] · Kapitel n

division · Spruchkörper m [*nicht verwechseln mit "Hauptabteilung" = division*]

division · Kammer f [*Landgericht*]

division · Hauptabteilung f [*Gericht. Nicht verwechseln mit Spruchkörper = division*]

division, district [*A specific portion of a larger area, such as of a city*] · Bezirk m

division, department, branch, sector, province [*public administration*] · Abteilung f, Referat n, Dezernat n, Ressort n

division · Hammelsprung m [*Parlament*]

division → (electoral) division

divisional unit, territorial division · Gebietsteil m

division into building (construction) lots · Teilung f in (Bau)Lose [*Hochbau*]

division into construction lots · Teilung f in (Bau)Lose [*Ingenieurbau*]

division of a land(ed) estate among the heirs [*The land is divided and no heirs are bought off*] · Naturalteilung f

division of common land within the area of one community · Spezialteilung f

division of common land within the area of several communities · Generalteilung f

division of cost(s), cost(s) splitting, splitting (up) of cost(s), cost(s) division · Kostenspaltung f, Kostentrennung

division of labour (Brit.); division of labor (US) · Arbeitsteilung f

division (of land) ordinance → (sub)division (of land) ordinance

division (of land) regulation → (sub)division (of land) regulation

division (of land(s)) → (sub)division into (estate) lots

division of law, department of law, law division, law department, legal department · Rechtsabteilung f

division of liability, liability division · Haftungsteilung f, Haftpflichtteilung, Haftbarkeitsteilung

division of opinion · Meinungsteilung f

division of rates · Teilung f der Lokalsteuerlast, Lokalsteuerüberwälzung [*Überwälzung eines Teiles der Lokalsteuerlast von den Mietern oder Pächtern auf die Grundeigentümer*]

division of the arable land according to the quality of the soil and lie of the land and surface area · Gewann-Flurteilung f

division ordinance → (sub)division (of land) ordinance

division plan → (sub)division plan

division stage → (sub)division stage

divorce → (absolute) divorce

divorce agreement · (Ehe)Scheidungsvertrag m

divorced woman · geschiedene Frau f

divorce from bed and board, (judicial) separation · Aufhebung f der ehelichen Gemeinschaft durch richterliche Anerkenntnis, gerichtliche Trennung f, richterliche Aufhebung f einer ehelichen Gemeinschaft, gerichtliche Aufhebung f einer ehelichen Gemeinschaft, Trennung f von Tisch und Bett

divortium [*Latin*]; (absolute) divorce · (Ehe)Scheidung f

D.M.V.R.G., Deserted Medi(a)eval Village Research Group · Forschungsgruppe f für mittelalterliche Wüstungen [*In England. Gegründet 1952*]

to do away with, to abate, to deprive of operation, to rescind, to nullify, to annul, to repeal, to overrule, to cancel, to abrogate, to abolish (by authority) · abschaffen, aufheben, rückgängig machen, annullieren, außer Kraft setzen, löschen, abbauen

dock receipt · Kaiempfangsschein m

dock warrant · Kailagerschein m

doctrine · Lehre f

doctrine in law general · rechtstheoretische Lehre f

doctrine of agrarian location(s), doctrine of agricultural location(s), doctrine of agricultural sites · landwirtschaftliche Standortlehre f, Agrarstandortlehre, Lehre von den landwirtschaftlichen Standorten

doctrine of distinctness, principle of distinctness, distinctness principle, distinctness doctrine · Bestimmtheitsgrundsatz m, Bestimmtheitsprinzip n, Spezialitätsgrundsatz, Spezialitätsprinzip [*Grundbuchrecht*]

doctrine of exhausting administrative remedies — doing away with 332

doctrine of exhausting administrative remedies · Lehre f der erschöpften Rechtsbehelfe innerhalb der Verwaltung

doctrine of free law, free law doctrine · Freirechtslehre f

doctrine of frustration, frustration doctrine · Nichtbindungslehre f

doctrine of housing → doctrine of (social) housing

doctrine of industrial locations, doctrine of industrial sites · Industriestandortlehre f, industrielle Standortlehre

doctrine of locations, doctrine of sites, location(al) doctrine, site doctrine · Standortlehre f, Lehre vom Standort

doctrine of national economy · Volkswirtschaftslehre f, Nationalökonomielehre

doctrine of primary administrative jurisdiction · Lehre f der vorausgehenden Verwaltungsentscheidung vor Anrufung eines Gerichtes

doctrine of sites, location(al) doctrine, site doctrine, doctrine of locations · Standortlehre f, Lehre vom Standort

doctrine of (social) housing, (social) housing doctrine · (soziale) Wohnungslehre f

doctrin of frustation · Doktrin f des Wegfalls der Geschäftsgrundlage

document · Urkunde f

document, writing · Dokument n, Unterlage f, Schriftstück n

documentary bill · Dokumententratte f, dokumentäre Tratte

documentary debt, debt secured by a document, bonded debt · Briefschuld f

documentary draft · Dokumententratte f, dokumentäre Tratte

documentary (land) charge, documentary (land) burden, documentary (land) encumbrance, documentary (land) incumbrance · Briefgrundschuld f [Neben einer Eintragung der Grundschuld in das Grundbuch besteht auch eine Brieferteilung an den Gläubiger]

documentary mortgage, bonded mortgage, indenture of mortgage, mortgage secured by a document · Briefhypothek f [Neben einer Eintragung der Hypothek in das Grundbuch besteht auch eine Brieferteilung an den Gläubiger]

documentary proof, documentary evidence · Urkundenbeweis m, dokumentarischer Beweis

document deposit, drawing deposit [Deposit that is required of a bidder to ensure prompt return of drawings and specifications in good condition] · Rückgabesicherheit f für Ausschreibungsunterlagen

document inspection, inspection of document(s) · Urkundeneinsicht f

document of (ad)measurement, (ad)measurement document · Aufmaßurkunde f

document of certification, certification document · Bestätigungsunterlage f

document of incorporation, instrument incorporation, incorporation document, incorporation instrument, constituting instrument, constituting document · Inkorporierungsurkunde f

document of residential possession · Wohnbesitzbrief m [Er ist kein Wertpapier sondern eine Beweisurkunde]

document of title, title document · (Rechts)Titeldokument n, Dispositionspapier n, Traditionspapier

document of title, title-deed, deed ot title, title certificate, evidence of title, title evidence, title document [A document establishing the title to property] · (gesiegelte) (Rechts)Titelurkunde f, (gesiegelte) Dispositionsurkunde, (gesiegelte) Besitzurkunde, Dispositionsurkunde

document of title to goods, title document to goods, document of title to commodities, title document to commodities · Warendispositionsurkunde f, Güterdispositionsurkunde, Dispositionsurkunde über Güter

document privileged from production · privilegierte Urkunde f

documents against acceptance, D/A · Dokumente n pl gegen Akzept

documents against cash, d/a, documents against cash, d/c · Aushändigung f der Dokumente gegen Annahme der Tratte durch den Importeur

documents against cash, d/c, documents against acceptance, d/a · Aushändigung f der Dokumente gegen Annahme der Tratte durch den Importeur

documents against payment, d/p, D/P · Aushändigung f der Dokumente gegen Zahlung des Rechnungsbetrages

document to be presented · Vorlage f

document under seal; charter [obsolete]; deed (under seal), sealed instrument · Siegelurkunde f, gesiegelte Urkunde, Urkunde unter Siegel

doing away with, nullifying, rescinding, making void, annulling, (a)voiding, repealing, abolishing, abrogating, cancelling, overruling, abating, rendering null and void · Aufheben n, Rückgängigmachen n, Annullieren n, Abschaffen n, Löschen n, Abbauen n

dolus eventualis [*Latin*] · Billigung f des als möglich vorausgesehenen Erfolges, bedingter Vorsatz m

doma [*Latin*] → curtis dominica

domain · Grundherrschaft f, Grundherrlichkeit f [*lm Mittelalter und danach vornehmlich im Westen Deutschlands*]

domain · Domäne f

domain of a baron; baronage [*obsolete*]; baron(r)y · Baronsgut n, Freiherrengut, Baronshof m, Freiherrenhof

domarie [*Norman French*] → (estate in) dower

Domesday (Book); liber judiciarius vel censualis Angliae [*Latin*] [*A record made in the time of William the Conqueror, and now kept at the Record Office, consisting of two volumes, a greater and lesser, the greater containing a survey of all the lands in England except the counties of Northumberland, Cumberland, Westmoreland, Durham, and part of Lancashire, which, it is said, were never surveyed, and excepting Essex, Suffolk, and Norfolk which three last are comprehended in the lesser volume*] · Katasteraufnahme f Wilhelms des Eroberers, Katasterbuch n Wilhelms des Eroberers

domestic · einheimisch [*von Sachen*]

domestic, fellow-countryman · Landsmann m

domestic air traffic, inland air traffic · Inlandsluftverkehr m

domestic(ated) animal · Haustier n

domestic bill (of exchange) [*USA*] · Wechsel m innerhalb eines Einzelstaates ausgestellt und zahlbar

domestic bill (of exchange), intraterritorial bill (of exchange), inland bill (of exchange) · inländischer Wechsel m, Inlandswechsel

domestic certificate of inheritance, domestic inheritance certificate · Eigenrechtserbschein m, Eigenrechtserbbescheinigung f, Eigenrechtserbattest n

domestic commission · innerstaatliche Kommission f

domestic fixture · haushalt(s)bezogener (Grundstücks)Bestandteil m

domestic garden; back garden (Brit.); dooryard (US); house garden · Hausgarten m

domestic industry, domestic system, home(-work) industry, cottage industry, financed work, sweated industry · Hausindustrie f, Verlagssystem n, Heim(arbeits)industrie, Verlag m

domestic inheritance certificate, domestic certificate of inheritance · Eigenrechtserbschein m, Eigenrechtserbbescheinigung f, Eigenrechtserbattest n

domestic investment · Inlandsinvestition f, Inlands(kapital)anlage f, Inlandsgeldanlage

domestic law · innerstaatliches Recht n, Inlandsrecht

domestic market · Inlandsmarkt m, Binnenmarkt

domestic product, home product · Inlandsprodukt n, IP, einheimisches Produkt

domestic relation(ship) · häusliche Beziehung f

domestic relief work, work to help households in distress · Haushalt(s)fürsorge f

domestic servants, menial servants · Hausgesinde n

domestic system, home(-work) industry, cottage industry, financed work, sweated industry, domestic industry · Hausindustrie f, Verlagssystem n, Heim(arbeits)industrie, Verlag m

domestic trade, inland trade, home trade · Binnenhandel m

domestic value, inland value · Inlandswert m

domestic violence · innere Gewalt f

domicil(e), place of habitation, habitation place, (place of) abode, (place of) residence, (permanent) residence, legal home, settlement · Aufenthaltsort m, gesetzlicher Aufenthaltsort, Wohnort m, Wohnsitz m

domicil(e) by operation of law; domicilium derivativum [*Latin*] · abgeleiteter Wohnsitz m, Wohnsitz kraft Rechtssatz

domiciled, residing, resident, living · wohnhaft

domiciled bill (of exchange) · Domizilwechsel m

domicil(e) of a dependent person · Wohnsitz m einer natürlichen abhängigen Person

domicil(e) of an independent person · Wohnsitz m einer natürlichen unabhängigen Person

domicil(e) of choice · Domizil n der Wahl, Wahlort m, Wahldomizil, gewählter Wohnsitz m, Wahlwohnsitz

domicil(e) of origin · Geburtswohnsitz m, Wohnsitz kraft Abstammung

domicilium derivativum [*Latin*]; domicil(e) by operation of law · abgeleiteter Wohnsitz m, Wohnsitz kraft Rechtssatz

dominant · berechtigt, herrschend, dominierend [*Grundstück*]

dominant central place — dominium plenum

dominant central place · dominierender zentraler Ort *m*, herrschender zentraler Ort, dominierender Zentralort, herrschender Zentralort

dominant factor · Dominante *f*, dominierender Faktor *m*

dominant factor theory · Dominationstheorie *f*

dominant leaseholder; dominant tacksman [*Scots law*]; dominant tenant, dominant (land) holder, dominant lessee, dominant occupier, dominant termor · herrschender Pächter *m*, berechtigter Pächter, dominierender Pächter

dominant possessor · herrschender Besitzer *m*, berechtigter Besitzer, dominierender Besitzer

dominant proprietor, dominant owner · berechtigter Eigentümer *m*, berechtigter Eigner, dominierender Eigner, dominierender Eigentümer, herrschender Eigner, herrschender Eigentümer, berechtigtes Eigentumssubjekt *n*, dominierendes Eigentumssubjekt, herrschendes Eigentumssubjekt

dominant (real) estate, dominant (real) property, dominant land, ruling (real) estate, ruling (real) property, dominant realty, ruling realty, ruling land; praedium dominans [*Latin*]; dominant tenement, ruling tenement · berechtigter Boden *m*, dominierender Boden, herrschender Boden, berechtigter Grund(besitz) *m*, dominierender Grund(besitz), herrschender Grund(besitz), berechtigter Besitz, dominierender Besitz, herrschender Besitz, herrschendes Grundstück *n*, dominierendes Grundstück, herrschendes Land, dominierendes Land, berechtigtes Land *n*, berechtigtes Grundstück *n*

dominant tacksman [*Scots law*]; dominant tenant, dominant (land) holder, dominant lessee, dominant occupier, dominant termor, dominant leaseholder · herrschender Pächter *m*, berechtigter Pächter, dominierender Pächter

dominant tenant, dominant (land) holder, dominant lessee, dominant occupier, dominant termor, dominant leaseholder; dominant tacksman [*Scots law*] · herrschender Pächter *m*, berechtigter Pächter, dominierender Pächter

dominant tenement, ruling tenement, dominant (real) estate, dominant (real) property, dominant land, ruling (real) estate, ruling (real) property, dominant realty, ruling realty, ruling land; praedium dominans [*Latin*] · berechtigter Boden *m*, dominierender Boden, herrschender Boden, berechtigter Grund(besitz) *m*, dominierender Grund(besitz), herrschender Grund(besitz), berechtigter Besitz, dominierender Besitz, herrschender Besitz, herrschendes Grundstück *n*, dominierendes Grundstück, herrschendes Land, dominierendes Land, berechtigtes Land *n*, berechtigtes Grundstück *n*

dominant termor, dominant leaseholder; dominant tacksman [*Scots law*]; dominant tenant, dominant (land) holder, dominant lessee, dominant occupier · herrschender Pächter *m*, berechtigter Pächter, dominierender Pächter

dominicum antiquum, antiquum dominicum, vetus patrimonium domini [*Latin*]; customary freehold, ancient demesne, copyhold tenure by custom of ancient demesne [*Such land(s) as were entered by William I., in Doomesday-book, under the title "De Terra Regis"; and which were held later by a species of copyhold tenure*] · altes Krongut(leh(e)n) *n*

dominion rate [*Great Britain*] · Steuersatz *m* der Besitzung

dominium [*Latin*]; ownership (of property), proprietorship, (general) property · Eigentum *n* [*Die uneingeschränkte Herrschaft einer Person über eine Sache, auch in rechtlicher Beziehung. „Eigentum" und „Besitz" sind nicht gleichbedeutend. Eigentum ist das dingliche Vollrecht, Besitz die tatsächliche, vom Rechtstitel unabhängige Innehabung einer Sache. Auch der Dieb ist Besitzer*]

dominium eminens [*Latin*]; (power of) eminent domain [*The right of a government to take private property for public purposes*] · Bodenenteignungsrecht *n*, (Land)Enteignungsrecht, Entscheidungsrecht für (Boden)Enteignungen, materielles Enteignungsrecht

dominium feudi [*Latin*]; ultimate ownership (of property), strict ownership (of property), direct dominion; nuda proprietas [*Latin*] [*The nominal or bare right of ownership remaining in an owner who has granted the exclusive right of enjoyment and of limited or unlimited disposition over the thing to another person*] · Obereigentum *n* (der Krone), Eigentumsrecht *n* des Leh(e)n(s)herrn, Leh(e)n(s)herrlichkeit *f* [*Das Eigentum an Land ruht in England in allen Fällen unbedingt und ausnahmslos beim Thron. Diese Tatsache ist eine der wichtigsten Unterschiede zwischen dem englischen Mobiliar- und Immobiliarsachenrecht und findet ihren Ausdruck in der Rechtsdoktrin: "Land is, and goods are not, the subject of tenure'*]

dominium plenum, dominium perpetuum [*Latin*], absolute ownership (of property), absolute interest, exclusive interest, sole interest, exclusive ownership (of property), sole ownership (of property), unlimited ownership (of property), sole property, sole proprietorship [*In English law absolute ownership can only exist in chattels, as all land is sub-*

ject theoretically to the obligations of tenure; but practically the fee simple in land gives absolute ownership] · absolutes Eigentum n, uneingeschränktes Eigentum, unbeschränktes Eigentum, unbegrenztes Eigentum, ausschließliches Eigentum, unbedingtes Eigentum, Alleineigentum

dominium supereminens [Latin] · Enteignungsgewalt f

dominium temporale [Latin]; limited ownership (of property), nonexclusive ownership (of property), limited proprietorship, nonexclusive proprietorship, limited (general) property, nonexclusive (general) property · beschränktes Eigentum n, begrenztes Eigentum, eingeschränktes Eigentum

dominium utile [Latin]; beneficial dominion, ownership in land(s) [In der englischen Umgangssprache und in einigen Parlamentsgesetzen werden vielfach die Benennungen "landowner" und "ownership in land(s)" an Stelle von "tenant or holder of land" und "estate in land(s)" gebraucht. In diesem Falle ist zu beachten, daß unter "ownership in land(s)" nur das "dominium utile" und nicht das "dominium directum" gemeint ist] · Nutzeigentum n, Untereigentum, leh(e)n(s)rechtliches Nutzungsrecht n

dominus, lord, master [These terms, prefixed to a man's name, in ancient times, usually denoted him a knight or clergyman, a gentleman or the lord of a manor. During medieval times these words (sometimes abbreviated to "don" or "dan") were commonly prefixed to the name of a clergyman or of a gentleman of position. It indicated no special dignity known to the law] · Herr m

dominus directus [Latin] → liege-lord

dominus terrae [Latin] · Landesherr m

donatarius, donatorius [Latin]; donee [One to whom a gift is made] · Beschenkte m, Schenkungsempfänger m, Geschenknehmer m

to donate · spenden

donating · Schenken n

donatio mortis causa, donatio post obitum [Latin]; gift causa mortis, gift in anticipation of death · Schenkung f auf den Todesfall, Schenkung von Todes wegen

donation · Hingabe f von Immobilien ohne Rücksicht auf den rechtlichen Charakter, Veräußerung f von Immobilien ohne Rücksicht auf den rechtlichen Charakter

donation, gift · Schenkung(svertrag) f, (m), unentgeltlicher dinglicher Vertrag [Durch ihn wird ein bestehendes dingliches Recht von der einen auf die andere Vertragspartei übertragen]

donation money, idle money, unemployment compensation, compensation of unemployment, relief of unemployment, out-of-work-pay, out-of-work-benefit, unemployment relief, unemployment benefit · Arbeitslosengeld n, Arbeitslosenunterstützung f, Erwerbslosengeld n, Erwerbslosenunterstützung

donatio sub modo facto [Latin]; gift sub modo · bedingte Schenkung f, eingeschränkte Schenkung, beschränkte Schenkung

donatio usufructaria [Latin] · Schenkung f mit Vorbehalt des Nießbrauchs, Schenkung mit Nießbrauchvorbehalt

donative advowson, (right of) patronage donative, advowson donative · Patronat(srecht) n bei dem der Patron ohne Inanspruchnahme eines Bischofs jemanden zum Inhaber einer geistlichen Pfründe ernennen konnte, Präsentation(srecht) bei dem der Patron ohne Inanspruchnahme eines Bischofs jemanden zum Inhaber einer geistlichen Pfründe ernennen konnte

donator [Latin]; donor · Schenk(end)e m, Schenkungsgeber, Geschenkgeber

done away with, deprived of operation, repealed, cancelled, abrogated, abated, annulled, nullified, abolished (by authority), rescinded, overruled · aufgehoben, annulliert, rückgängig gemacht, außer Kraft gesetzt, abgeschafft, gelöscht, abgebaut

donee [In old English law. He to whom lands were or land was given] · Landempfänger m

donee; donatarius, donatorius [Latin] [One to whom a gift is made] · Beschenkte m, Schenkungsempfänger m, Geschenknehmer m

donor; concessor [In old English law]; grantor [The person by whom a grant is made] · Überlassende m, Überlasser

donor; donator [Latin] · Schenk(end)e m, Schenkungsgeber, Geschenkgeber

donor, giver · Geber m

donor of a heritable building right, lease(hold) donor · Erbbaurechtgeber m

donor of an allowance, giver of an allowance · Zuschußgeber m

donor of an authority, grantor of an authority; mandator [Latin]; principal (constituent), employer · Vollmachtgeber m, Bevollmächtige, Vertretene [Jemand der ein Rechtsgeschäft zu eigenem Nutzen und auf eigene Rechnung selbständig vornehmen kann, aber zu dessen Vornahme eine andere Person verwendet]

donor of a power of attorney, grantor of a power of attorney · Geber *m* einer gesiegelten Vollmacht

donor of usufruct, usufruct donor · (Frucht)Genußbesteller *m*, Nießbrauchbesteller

doomsday [*In old English law*]; dies juridicus [*Latin*]; juridic(al) day, law day, court day; lage day, lagh day · Gerichtstag *m*

dooryard (US); house garden, domestic garden; back garden (Brit.) · Hausgarten *m*

dormant, unknown · unbekannt

dormant, abeyant, in abeyance · in der Schwebe (sein), schwebend, noch nicht entschieden, unentschieden

dormant, inactive · inaktiv

dormant account · unbeanspruchtes Konto *n*

dormant annuity upon one live, dormant value of the live · ruhende Annuität *f*

dormant partner, sleeping partner [*Is one who is both secret and inactive. His liabilities to third parties are the same as those of a general partner, if his connection with the firm is discovered. The fact that he is a dormant partner does not prevent him from asserting himself as an active partner and taking part in the firm's business, unless he is prevented from so doing by the partnership agreement*] · vertraglich untätiger mittelbarer Gesellschafter *m*, vertraglich untätiger mittelbarer Teilhaber, vertraglich untätiger verdeckter Gesellschafter, vertraglich untätiger verdeckter Teilhaber, vertraglich untätiger unerkannter Gesellschafter, vertraglich untätiger unerkannter Teilhaber, mittelbarer vertraglich untätiger Gesellschafter, mittelbarer vertraglich untätiger Teilhaber, verdeckter vertraglich untätiger Gesellschafter, verdeckter vertraglich untätiger Teilhaber, unerkannter vertraglich untätiger Gesellschafter, unerkannter vertraglich untätiger Teilhaber

dormant value of the live, dormant annuity (up)on one live · ruhende Annuität *f*

dormitory community, bedroom community · Schlafgemeinde *f*, Auspendlergemeinde, reine Wohngemeinde

dormitory settlement · Schlafsied(e)lung *f*

dormitory suburb(an place), bedroom suburb(an place) (Brit.) · Schlafvorort *m*, Auspendlervorort, reiner Wohnvorort

dormitory town, dormitory city · Schlafstadt *f*, Auspendlerstadt, reine Wohnstadt

dose metameter · Dosis-Metameter *n*, transformierter Dosiswert *m* [*Statistik*]

doss lodging-house (Brit.); common rooming house (US); common lodging-house · allgemeines Logierhaus *n*, öffentliches Logierhaus, Armenherberge *f*

dotard [*Dead tree not fit for use as timber*] · abgestorbener Baum *m*, Dürrständer *m*

dotatio [*Latin*]; endowment, indowment · Dotation *f*

dot map · Punkt(streuungs)karte *f*

double bond, conditional bond, bond with a condition · gesiegeltes Schuldversprechen *n* mit Strafklausel, gesiegelte Schuldurkunde *f* mit Strafklausel, beurkundete Schuldforderung *f* mit Strafklausel

double citizenship, twin nationality, twin citizenship, dual nationality, dual citizenship, double nationality · Doppelstaatsangehörigkeit *f*, Doppelnationalität *f*

double compensation, double indemnity, double damages, double indemnification · doppelte Entschädigung *f*, zweifache Entschädigung, doppelter Schadenersatz *m*, zweifacher Schadenersatz

double core, dual core, twin core · Doppelkern *m*

double damages, double indemnification, double compensation, double indemnity · doppelte Entschädigung *f*, zweifache Entschädigung, doppelter Schadenersatz *m*, zweifacher Schadenersatz

double declining-balance method of depreciation · geometrisch-degressive Abschreibungsmethode *f* mit Doppelrate

double effect, twin effect, dual effect · Doppelwirkung *f*

double entry, dual registration, dual recordation, dual recording, dual entry, double recordation, double registration, double recording · Doppelbuchung *f*, Doppelregistrierung, Doppeleintrag(ung) *m, (f)*

double-entry bookkeeping, dual-entry bookkeeping · doppelte Buchführung *f*

double farm, twin settlement, twin farm, double settlement · Doppel(an)sied(e)lung *f*, Doppelhof *m*, Zwiehof *m*

double farm by desertion, desertion double farm · Wüstungsdoppelhof *m*

double indemnification, double compensation, double indemnity, double damages · doppelte Entschädigung *f*, zweifache Entschädigung, doppelter Schadenersatz *m*, zweifacher Schadenersatz

double-level street, two-level street, dual-level street · Stadtstraße *f* mit zwei Ebenen

double logarithmic chart · doppelt logarithmisches Netz *n*

double nationality, double citizenship, twin nationality, twin citizenship, dual nationality, dual citizenship · Doppelstaatsangehörigkeit *f*, Doppelnationalität *f*

double promise, counter-promise, dependant promise, conditional promise, dependent promise, reciprocal promise, mutual promise · gegenseitiges Versprechen *n*

double ratio estimator · Doppelverhältnis-Schätzfunktion *f* [*Statistik*]

double recordation, double registration, double recording, double entry, dual registration, dual recordation, dual recording, dual entry · Doppelbuchung *f*, Doppelregistrierung, Doppeleintrag(ung) *m*, *(f)*

double rent · doppelter Pachtzins *m*

double right; jus duplicatum [*Latin*] [*The right of possession united with the right of property*] · Doppelrecht *n*

double-row village · Doppelreihendorf *n*

double settlement, double farm, twin settlement, twin farm · Doppel(an)sied(e)lung *f*, Doppelhof *m*, Zwiehof *m*

double sextile day, bissextile day, intercalary day · Schalttag *m* [*29. Februar*]

double taxation, dual taxation · Doppelbesteuerung *f*

double taxation agreement, dual taxation agreement · Doppelbesteuerungsabkommen *n*

double use · Doppelbenutzung *f*, Doppelgebrauch *m*

double will, counter will, common will, reciprocal will, mutual will · gegenseitiges Testament *n*

double working shift, dual working shift, twin working shift · Doppel(arbeits)schicht *f*

doubling up [*The practice of two or more families sharing a single dwelling unit, essentially to reduce the housing expenses of each family*] · Zusammenwohnen *n*

doubt, qualm · Bedenken *n*

doubtfulness of meaning, uncertainty of meaning, obscurity of meaning, uncertain meaning, doubtful meaning, ambiguity, obscure meaning · unklare Bedeutung *f*, Zweideutigkeit *f*

dower → (estate in) dower

dower and curtesy, curtesy and dower · eheliches Güterrecht *n*

doweyre [*Norman French*] → (estate in) dower

down-cross · Niveauschnitt *m* nach unten [*Statistik*]

down payment, first payment [*Of a sum of money paid by a purchaser to a seller in conjunction with a purchase, the full payment of which will be made over a period of time*] · Anzahlung *f*

downstream resident · Unterlieger *m* [*Vorflut*]

downstream riparian owner, downstream riparian proprietor, lower riparian owner, lower riparian proprietor · unterwasserseitiger Ufereigentümer, unterwasserseitiger Ufereigner *m*

downstream riparian possessor, lower riparian possessor · unterwasserseitiger Uferbesitzer *m*

downtown (area), urban center, town center, city center (US); urban centre, town centre, city centre (Brit.) · Stadtzentrum *n*, Innenstadt *f*, Stadtinnere *n* [*im funktionalen Sinne*]

down zoning · herabstufende bauliche Nutzung *f*, herabstufende Baunutzung, Herabzonung

dowry (marriage), portion, fortune, marriage goods; tocher [*in Scotland*]; maritagium [*Latin*] [*Not to be confounded with "dower". A portion given with a woman to her husband in marriage*] · Mitgift *f*, Heiratsgut *n*

d/p, D/P, documents against payment · Aushändigung *f* der Dokumente gegen Zahlung des Rechnungsbetrages

D/R, deposit receipt · Einzahlungsbeleg *m*

to draft, to construct, to draw up, to set up, to construe, to phrase , to word, to form [*To arrange or marshal words*] · abfassen, gestalten, entwerfen, ausarbeiten, formulieren

to draft, to construct, to construe, to draw up, to set up, to work out, to form · ausarbeiten, abfassen, gestalten, entwerfen [*Schriftstück*]

draft · Tratte *f*

draft at sight, sight draft, S/D · Sichttratte *f*

draft bill · Gesetz(es)entwurf *m*

draft contract · Vertragsentwurf *m*

draft contract stage · Vertragsentwurfstadium *n*

drafting, construction, drawing-up, setting up, construing, phrasing, wording, formulation, formation [*Arranging or marshalling words*] · Abfassung *f*, Entwurf *m*, Gestaltung, Ausarbeitung, Formulierung

drafting, construction, drawing up, setting up, formation · Entwurf *m*, Gestaltung *f*, Abfassung, Ausarbeitung [*Schriftstück*]

drafting of contract(s), drawing up of contract(s), setting up of contract(s), formation of contract(s), construction of

draft programme — drift of population

contract(s) · Vertragsgestaltung *f*, Vertragsausarbeitung, Vertragsabfassung, Vertragsentwurf *m*, Vertragsbildung

draft programme, draft scheme; draft program (US) · Programmentwurf *m*

drainage · Entwässerung *f*

drainage board · Kanalisationsamt *n*

drainage charge · Entwässerungsabgabe *f*

drainage code · Entwässerungsordnung *f*

drainage co-operative (society) · Entwässerungsgenossenschaft *f*

drainage facility · Entwässerungseinrichtung *f*

drainage plant · Entwässerungsanlage *f*

drainage rate · Entwässerungsabgabesatz *m*

drain of money, efflux of money · Geldabfluß *m*

draper · Tuchhändler *m*

to draw · trassieren

drawee · Bezogene *m*, Trassat *m*, Adressat *m* [*Wechsel*]

drawer · Aussteller *m*, Wechselaussteller, Trassant *m*

drawer, maker · Aussteller *m* [*Wechsel; Scheck*]

to draw for redemption · auslosen zur Tilgung

drawing [*A physical representation of something made by drawing*] · Plan *m*, Zeichnung *f*

drawing-board planning · Zeichenbrettplanung *f*

drawing clarification [*Graphic interpretation of the drawings issued by the owner or his agent as part of an addendum, change order, or field order*] · graphische Zeichendeutung *f*

drawing date, date of drawing · Ausstellungsdatum *n*, Wechselausstellungsdatum

drawing deposit, document deposit [*Deposit that is required of a bidder to ensure prompt return of drawings and specifications in good condition*] · Rückgabesicherheit *f* für Ausschreibungsunterlagen

drawing error · Zeichnungsfehler *m*

drawing for settlement (of account(s)) · Abrechnungszeichnung *f*

drawing legend, drawing reference · Zeichnungslegende *f*, Zeichnungszeichenerklärung *f*, Zeichnungszeichenschlüssel *m*

drawing of money, withdrawal of money · (Geld)Entnahme *f*

drawing power, attractiveness, attracting power, (force of) attraction · Anziehung(skraft) *f*, Attraktivität *f*

drawing reference, drawing legend · Zeichnungslegende *f*, Zeichnungszeichenerklärung *f*, Zeichnungszeichenschlüssel *m*

drawing right · Ziehungsrecht *n*

drawing submitted for approval, probationary drawing · Prüfungszeichnung *f*

drawing-up, setting up, construing, phrasing, wording, formulation, formation, drafting, construction [*Arranging or marshalling words*] · Abfassung *f*, Entwurf *m*, Gestaltung, Ausarbeitung, Formulierung

drawing up, setting up, formation, drafting, construction · Entwurf *m*, Gestaltung *f*, Abfassung, Ausarbeitung [*Schriftstück*]

drawing up of contract(s), setting up of contract(s), formation of contract(s), construction of contract(s), drafting of contract(s) · Vertragsgestaltung *f*, Vertragsausarbeitung, Vertragsabfassung, Vertragsentwurf *m*, Vertragsbildung

drawing (up)on, withdrawing · Abheben *n* [*Guthaben*]

draw out and embody · Mobilmachung *f*

to draw up, to set up, to construe, to phrase, to work out, to form, to draft, to construct [*To arrange or marshal words*] · abfassen, gestalten, entwerfen, ausarbeiten, formulieren

to draw up, to make up, to make out · ausfertigen

to draw up, to set up, to work out, to form, to draft, to construct, to construe · ausarbeiten, abfassen, gestalten, entwerfen [*Schriftstück*]

to draw (up)on, to withdraw · abheben [*Guthaben*]

drift, shift · Verschiebung *f*

drift, movement, flight, exodus · Flucht *f*, Wegziehen *n*

drift analysis, shift analysis · Verschiebungsanalyse *f*

to drift ashore, to wash ashore · anschwemmen, antreiben [*Teile eines untergegangenen Schiffes*]

drifting · Flößerei *f* mit unverbundenen Hölzern, Triften *n*

drifting ashore, washing ashore · Anschwemmen *n*, Antreiben *n* [*Teile eines untergegangenen Schiffes*]

drifting society · dahintreibende Gesellschaft *f*

drift of population, population shift, population drift, shift of population · Bevölkerungsverschiebung *f*

drift to the suburbs, exodus to the suburbs, movement to the suburbs (Brit.); flight to the suburbs · Vorortflucht *f*, Vorortexodus *m*, Flucht in die Vororte, Exodus in die Vororte

drift to the umland, movement to the umland, flight to the umland, exodus to the umland · Umlandflucht *f*, Umlandexodus *m*, Flucht ins Umland, Exodus ins Umland

drink industry · Getränkeindustrie *f*

drinking shop (US); pub(lic house) (Brit.) · Kneipe *f*, Schankwirtschaft *f*, Bierschenke *f*, Bierhaus *n*, Wirtshaus

drive; cursus [*Latin*]; running-ground · Trift *f*

drive-in restaurant · Autorestaurant *n*

drive-it-yourself car · Miet-PKW *m*, Mietpersonenkraftwagen *m*, Mietpersonenauto *n*

drive-it-yourself lorry (Brit.); drive-it-yourself truck (US) · Miet-Last(kraft)wagen *m*, Miet-LKW

driver-only bus · schaffnerloser (Auto)Bus *m*, schaffnerloser Omnibus

drive to site, vehicular access to site · Baustellenzufahrt *f*

driving for pleasure, pleasure driving · Autofahren *n* zum Vergnügen

driving right · Fahrrecht *n* [*Das Recht zum Fahren über ein fremdes Grundstück*]

droitural, relating to right · rechtsbezüglich

dropletter · Stadtbrief *m*

dropping to pieces, collapsing, breaking down, failing, crashing · Einstürzen *n*, Einfallen

drop shipper (US); desk jobber · Streckengeschäft-Großhändler *m*

drove [*The action of driving a number of beasts, as oxen, sheeps, etc., in a body*] · Trift *f*, Trieb *m*, Treiben *n*

drove right, feldage; actus, faldagium [*Latin*]; frank-fold, faldage, right of drove · Triftrecht *n*, Treibrecht

drove-road · Triftweg *m*, Viehtreibweg

drove stone, pastur(ag)e stone · Hutstein *m*, Triftstein; Tratstein [*oberdeutsch*] [*Er bezeichnet die Grenze der Hutgerechtigkeit*]

to drown [*"In some cases a right of freehold shall drown in a chattel"*] · aufgehen in

drowned, absorbed, extinguished, merged, sunk · untergegangen [*Wenn sich z. B. Eigentum und Pfandrecht in einer Hand vereinigen, geht das kleinere im größeren unter*]

drowning, sinking, absorption, extinguishment, merger [*Of one estate in another*] · Untergang *m* [*siehe Erklärung unter „untergegangen"*]

dry farming, dry tillage, dry husbandry · Ackerbau *m* bei dürftigen Niederschlägen, Ackerbau ohne Bewässerung, (Feld)Anbau bei dürftigen Niederschlägen, (Feld)Anbau ohne Bewässerung

dry field cultivation · Trockenfeldbau *m*

drying out · Austrocknen *n*

dry land · ausgetrocknetes Land *n*, Dürreland

dry point settlement · trockenliegende (An)Sied(e)lung *f*

dry refuse · Trockenabfall(stoff) *m*

dry rent, rent-seck; redditius siccus [*Latin*], barren rent [*A rent not supported by a right of distress. Ceased to exist after the Landlord and Tenant Act 1730*] · Rente *f* ohne Pfändungsrecht, trockene Rente

dry tillage → dry farming

dry timber line · Trockenbaumgrenze *f*

dry trust, naked trust, passive trust [*One which requires no action on the part of the trustee, beyond turning over money or property to the cestui que trust*] · passive Treuhand *f*

dry upland rice cultivation · Bergreisanbau *m*

DSGN, (structural) design · (baulicher) Entwurf *m*, Bauentwurf, zeichnerische Lösung *f*, (bauliche) Konstruktion *f*

D.S.M., dual simplex method · duale Simplexmethode *f*

D² statistic · D²-Abstands-Maßzahl *f*

DU, du, living unit, LU, lu, housing unit, apartment, unit of housing, dwelling unit (US); apartment (Brit.) [*archaic*]; tenement, residence, dwelling · Wohnung *f*

dual citizenship, double nationality, double citizenship, twin nationality, twin citizenship, dual nationality · Doppelstaatsangehörigkeit *f*, Doppelnationalität *f*

dual command · Befehlsgemeinschaft *f*

dual core, twin core, double core · Doppelkern *m*

dual effect, double effect, twin effect · Doppelwirkung *f*

dual entry, double recordation, double registration, double recording, double entry, dual registration, dual recordation, dual recording · Doppelbuchung *f*, Doppelregistrierung, Doppeleintrag(ung) *m*, *(f)*

dual-entry bookkeeping — during good behaviour

dual-entry bookkeeping, double-entry bookkeeping · doppelte Buchführung *f*

dualism · Dualismus *m*

dual-level street, double-level street, two-level street, twin-level street · Stadtstraße *f* mit zwei Ebenen

dual nationality, dual citizenship, double nationality, double citizenship, twin nationality, twin citizenship · Doppelstaatsangehörigkeit *f*, Doppelnationalität *f*

dual plan · Doppelführung *f* der Standardkosten

dual plan · Doppelverbuchung *f* von Plan- und Istkosten in einer Vierspaltenbuchführung, Übernahme *f* von Plankosten aus den Betriebsstatistiken zu den Istkosten in der Buchhaltung

dual recordation, dual recording, dual entry, double recordation, double registration, double recording, double entry, dual registration · Doppelbuchung *f*, Doppelregistrierung, Doppeleintrag(ung) *m*, *(f)*

dual simplex method, D.S.M. · duale Simplexmethode *f*

dual taxation, double taxation · Doppelbesteuerung *f*

dual working shift, twin working shift, double working shift · Doppel(arbeits)schicht *f*

ducal castle · Herzogschloß *n*, herzogliches Schloß

ducal librarian · herzoglicher Bibliothekar *m*

duchy · Herzogtum *n*

duchy chamber · herzogliche Kammer *f*, Herzogskammer

due · fällig

due and more than due, out of time, overdue · überfällig, längst fällig, lange fällig

due date, termination date, falling in date, running out date, accrual date, maturity date, expiry date, expiration date · Fälligkeitsdatum *n*, Fälligkeitstag *m*, Verfalldatum, Verfalltermin *m*, (First-)Ablauftermin, (Frist)Ablaufdatum, Fälligkeitstermin, Verfalltag, (Frist)Ablauftag

duke · Herzog *m*

duly, at the right time, on time, in due time · rechtzeitig

duly completed · vertragsgemäß fertiggestellt, vertragsmäßig fertiggestellt, vertraglich fertiggestellt

duly signed · vollzogen [*Vertrag*]

dummy, man of straw, lay-figure · „Strohmann" *m*

dummy activity · Scheintätigkeit *f*

dummy observation · fiktive Beobachtung *f*

dummy treatment · fiktive Behandlung *f*, vorgegebene Behandlung, fingierte Behandlung, vorgetäuschte Behandlung

dump · Schutt(ablade)platz *m*

dumping of refuse, dumping of waste · Müllabladen *n*, Müllabkippen, Abfallabladen, Abfallabkippen

duplicate, copy · Abschrift *f*, Ausfertigung *f*, Duplikat *n* [*Die Abschrift einer Urkunde ist dazu bestimmt die Originalurkunde im Verkehr zu vertreten*]

duplicate original, copy original [*e.g. if the authenticity of a carbon copy is fully conceded*] · Duplikatoriginal *n*

duplicating book-keeping system · Durchschreibebuchführung *f*

duplication · Vervielfältigung *f*

durante vita [*Latin*]; during life · zu Lebzeiten

duration · Dauer *f*

duration of discharge, period of redemption, term of redemption, duration of redemption, redemption period, redemption term, redemption duration, discharge period, discharge duration, discharge term, period of discharge, term of discharge · Auslösungsfrist *f*, Einlösungsfrist *f*, Ablösungsfrist *f*

duration of income, income duration · Einkommensdauer *f*

duration of life, life duration · Lebensdauer *f* [*Lebewesen*]

duration of redemption, redemption period, redemption term, redemption duration, discharge period, discharge duration, discharge term, period of discharge, term of discharge, duration of discharge, period of redemption, term of redemption · Auslösungsfrist *f*, Einlösungsfrist *f*, Ablösungsfrist *f*

duress · Nötigung *f*

duress by threats, duress per minas · Bedrohung *f* von Leib und Leben und Freiheit

duress of goods · Zwang *m* durch Wegnahme von Waren, Warenvorenthaltungszwang

duress of permission · Genehmigungszwang *m*, Erlaubniszwang

duressor [*One who compels another to do a thing, as by menace*] · Nötiger *m*

duress per minas, duress by threats · Bedrohung *f* von Leib und Leben und Freiheit

during good behaviour [*English law*] · auf Lebenszeit [*Richteramt*]

during life; durante vita [*Latin*] · zu Lebzeiten

during pleasure, revocable, at will, revokable, ambulatory, capable of being revoked, capable of revocation, able of being revoked, able of revocation, qualified of being revoked, qualified of revocation · auf Widerruf, widerruflich, widerrufbar, einvernehmlich geduldet

dust nuisance · Staubeinwirkung *f*

dust protection · Staubschutz *m*

dutiable, subject to duty · zollpflichtig

duties in common, joint duties, common duties · gemeinschaftliche Pflichten *fpl*, gemeinsame Pflichten

duty, (statutory) charge, legal charge · Finanzabgabe *f*, gesetzliche Abgabe [*Eine Pflichtleistung in Geld oder Sachgut, die kraft öffentlicher Finanzhoheit den Bürgern auferlegt wird. Man unterscheidet 1. Generelle Abgaben (Steuern und Zölle) und 2. Spezielle Abgaben (Beiträge und Gebühren)*]

duty, charge [*Charged in payment of services rendered by the state or public authority*] · Gebühr *f*

duty → (customs) duty

duty ad valorem → ad valorem (customs) duty

duty book, men's duty journal · Dienstbuch *n*

duty breach, breach of duty · Pflichtverstoß *m*, Pflichtverletzung *f*

duty for use, charge for use, use charge, use duty · Benutzungsgebühr *f*, Gebrauchsgebühr

duty free, free of duty · abgabe(n)frei

duty of (ab)alienation, duty of disposal, (ab)alienation duty, disposal duty · Veräußerungspflicht *f*

duty of acceptance, acceptance duty · Annahmepflicht *f*

duty of acceptance (of (the) work(s)), acceptance duty · Abnahmepflicht *f*, Bauabnahmepflicht

duty of acquisition, duty to acquire, acquisition duty · Beschaffungspflicht *f*, Erwerbspflicht

(duty of) anchorage · Ankergeld *n*, Ankerzoll *m*

duty of care, duty of diligence, duty to take care, duty to take diligence · Sorgfaltspflicht *f*

duty of care for safety · Sicherheitspflicht *f*

duty of compliance → duty of performance

duty of connection, duty to connect, connection duty · Anschlußpflicht *f*

duty of design · Konstruktionspflicht *f*

duty of disclosure, duty of clarification, disclosure duty, clarification duty · Aufklärungspflicht *f*, Offenbarungspflicht, (Beweis)Offenlegungspflicht, Auskunftspflicht, Vorlagepflicht

duty of discovery, duty of submission, duty of production, duty of presentation, duty of filing · Editionspflicht *f*, Enthüllungspflicht, Vorlagepflicht, Vorlegungspflicht, Abgabepflicht, Einreichungspflicht [*Pflicht zur Mitteilung von Tatsachen oder Vorlegung von Schriftstücken an den Prozeßgegner*]

duty of disposal, (ab)alienation duty, disposal duty, duty of (ab)alienation · Veräußerungspflicht *f*

duty of examination, examination duty, duty to examine · Prüfungspflicht *f*

duty of execution → duty of performance

duty of filing, duty of discovery, duty of submission, duty of production, duty of presentation · Editionspflicht *f*, Enthüllungspflicht, Vorlagepflicht, Vorlegungspflicht, Abgabepflicht, Einreichungspflicht [*Pflicht zur Mitteilung von Tatsachen oder Vorlegung von Schriftstücken an den Prozeßgegner*]

duty of fulfilment → duty of performance

duty of insurance → (statutory) duty of insurance

duty of nondisclosure · Geheimhaltungspflicht *f*

duty of payment, payment duty, duty to pay · Zahlungspflicht *f*

duty of performance, performance duty, fulfilment duty, execution duty, compliance duty, duty of fulfilment, duty of execution, duty of compliance · Erfüllungspflicht *f*, Vollziehungspflicht, Ausführungspflicht, Vollzugspflicht, Erbringungspflicht

duty of presentation, duty of filing, duty of discovery, duty of submission, duty of production · Editionspflicht *f*, Enthüllungspflicht, Vorlagepflicht, Vorlegungspflicht, Abgabepflicht, Einreichungspflicht [*Pflicht zur Mitteilung von Tatsachen oder Vorlegung von Schriftstücken an den Prozeßgegner*]

duty of preservation, duty of conservation, duty of conservancy, conservation duty, conservancy duty, preservation duty · Erhaltungspflicht *f*, Pflegepflicht [*Bauwerk*]

duty of recovery, duty of refunding, duty of reimbursement, duty of restitution, refunding duty, restitution duty, reimbursement duty, recovery duty · Abgeltungspflicht *f*, Ersetzungspflicht, Erstattungspflicht, Vergütungspflicht

duty of reporting, reporting duty · Anmeldepflicht *f*

duty of restitution — duty to register

duty of restitution → duty of refunding

duty of secrecy · Schweigepflicht f

duty of tonnage · Schiffszoll m

duty on letters of administration · Ermächtigungsabgabe f zur Verwaltung eines Intestatnachlasses

duty-paid price · Preis m einschließlich Zoll

duty rate, rate of duty, charge rate, rate of charge · Gebührensatz m

duty remission, remission of duty · Zollerlaß m

duty schedule, duty scale, scale of charges, schedule of charges, charge scale, charge schedule, scale of duties, schedule of duties · Gebührentabelle f, Gebührenrahmen

duty task, task of duty · Pflichtaufgabe f

duty to acquire, acquisition duty, duty of acquisition · Beschaffungspflicht f, Erwerbspflicht

duty to acquire substitute space · Ersatzraumbeschaffungspflicht f, Ersatzraumerwerbspflicht

duty to bear (the) cost(s) · Kostenpflicht f, Kostentragungspflicht

duty to build, duty to construct · Baupflicht f

duty to carry out work(s), duty to execute work(s), duty to perform work(s) · Arbeitsausführungspflicht f, (Bau)Ausführungspflicht f

duty to check, duty to control, duty to re-examine, checking duty, control duty, re-examination duty, check(ing) duty, duty to review, review(ing) duty · Nachprüfungspflicht f, Kontrollpflicht

duty to connect, connection duty, duty of connection · Anschlußpflicht f

duty to consult, consultative duty, advising duty, advisory duty, counsel(l)ing duty, consulting duty · Beratungspflicht f

duty to contribute, liability to contribute, contribution liability, contribution duty · Beitragspflicht f

duty to co-ordinate, duty of co-ordination, co-ordination duty, co-ordinative duty · Koordinationspflicht f, Koordinierungspflicht

duty to deliver → duty to hand over

duty to enquire, duty to make inquiries, duty to inquire · Erkundigungspflicht f

duty to examine, duty of examination, examination duty · Prüfungspflicht f

duty to execute work(s), duty to perform work(s), duty to carry out work(s) · Arbeitsausführungspflicht f, (Bau)Ausführungspflicht f

duty to give notice of extra work, duty to give notification of extra work · Ankündigungspflicht f [Siehe „Ankündigung"]

duty to hand over, duty to deliver, handing over duty, handover duty, (de)livery duty · Aushändigungspflicht f, Übergabepflicht f

duty to harmonize · Übereinstimmungspflicht f

duty to illuminate, illumination duty · Beleuchtungspflicht f

duty to indemnify, duty to pay damages · Entschädigungspflicht f, Schadenersatzpflicht

duty to inquire, duty to enquire, duty to make inquiries · Erkundigungspflicht f

duty to keep · Aufbewahrungspflicht f

duty to maintain, maintenance duty · Unterhaltungspflicht f, Instandhaltungspflicht

duty to maintain and educate infants, duty to maintain and educate minors · Aufsichtspflicht f über Minderjährige

duty to make good defects · Mängelbeseitigungspflicht f, Sachmängelbeseitigungspflicht, Baumängelbeseitigungspflicht, Nachbesserungspflicht

duty to make inquiries, duty to inquire, duty to enquire · Erkundigungspflicht f

duty to notify, duty to give notice, duty to give notification · Anzeigepflicht f, Mitteilungspflicht f, Benachrichtigungspflicht f [Pflicht ein Bauvorhaben bei der zuständigen Behörde anzuzeigen]

duty to participate · Beteiligungspflicht f, Mitsprachepflicht

duty to pay, duty of payment, payment duty · Zahlungspflicht f

duty to pay damages, duty to indemnify · Entschädigungspflicht f, Schadenersatzpflicht

duty to pay debt(s) · Schuldenzahlungspflicht f

duty to pay legal cost(s) in advance · Vorschußpflicht f

duty to pay tithe · Zehnt(en)pflicht f

duty to perform · Leistungspflicht f

duty to perform work(s), duty to carry out work(s), duty to execute work(s) · Arbeitsausführungspflicht f, (Bau)Ausführungspflicht f

duty to plan, planning duty · Planungspflicht f

duty to rebuild, rebuilding duty, reconstruction duty, duty to reconstruct · Aufbaupflicht f, Wiederaufbaupflicht f

duty to register, registering duty · Meldepflicht f

duty to review, review(ing) duty, duty to check, duty to control, duty to re-examine, checking duty, control duty, re-examination duty, check(ing) duty · Nachprüfungspflicht *f*, Kontrollpflicht

duty to suffer · Duldungspflicht *f*, stillschweigende Billigungspflicht

duty to supervise, duty of supervision, supervising duty · Aufsichtspflicht *f*, Überwachungspflicht *f*

duty to supply drawings · Zeichnungspflicht *f*

duty to surrender, surrendering duty · Rückgabepflicht *f*

duty to take care → duty of care

duty to take diligence → duty of care

duty to test building materials, duty to test construction materials · (Bau)Stoffprüfungspflicht *f*; Baumaterialprüfungspflicht [*Schweiz*]

duty to the employer, duty to the owner · Pflicht *f* gegenüber dem Bauherrn, Pflicht gegenüber dem Auftraggeber

duty toward(s) the public · Pflicht *f* gegen die Allgemeinheit

duty to warn, warning duty · Anzeigepflicht *f*, Mitteilungspflicht *f*, Benachrichtigungspflicht *f* [*Des Auftragnehmers bei Behinderung*]

duty to warn · Aufklärungspflicht *f*

dwarf brick wall · Zwergziegelmauer *f*

dwarf state · Zwergstaat *m*

to dwell, to live, to reside · ansässig sein, wohnen

dweller, resident, (house) occupier, (house) occupant, dwelling occupier, dwelling occupant, residential occupier, residential occupant · (Haus)Bewohner *m*, (Haus)Insasse *m*, Wohnungsinsasse, Beziecher

dwelling → dwelling unit

dwelling basic rent, dwelling fundamental rent, basic dwelling rent, fundamental dwelling rent · Wohnungskostenmiete *f*, Wohnungskosten(miet)zins *m*

dwelling contract, (residential) landlord/tenant lease, (residential) landlord/tenant contract, residential lease, dwelling lease, residential contract · Wohn(ungs)mietvertrag *m*

dwelling house, residential building, residence building, residential structure, residence structure, living house · Wohngebäude *n*, Wohnhaus *n*

dwelling house census, dwelling house count, residential building census, residential building count, residence building census, residence building count · Wohnhauszählung *f*, Wohngebäudezählung

dwelling landlord/tenant relation(ship) → dwelling tenancy

dwelling landlord/tenant relation(ship) at sufferance, residential tenancy at sufferance, residential tenure at sufferance, residential landlord/tenant relation(ship) at sufferance, dwelling tenancy at sufferance, dwelling tenure at sufferance · Wohn(ungs)mietverhältnis *n* auf Duldung, geduldetes Wohn(ungs)mietverhältnis [*Es liegt vor, wenn ein Wohnungsmieter sein ursprünglich rechtmäßiges Wohnungsmietverhältnis unrechtmäßig verlängert*]

dwelling lease, residential contract, dwelling contract, (residential) landlord/tenant lease, (residential) landlord/tenant contract, residential lease · Wohn(ungs)mietvertrag *m*

dwelling lease term, term of residential lease, term of dwelling lease, residential lease term · Wohnungsmietvertragsfrist *f*

dwelling lot, residential lot, residence lot · Wohn(ungs)parzelle *f*

dwelling parcel, residential plot, residential parcel, dwelling plot · Wohn(ungs)grundstück *n*

dwelling plot, dwelling parcel, residential plot, residential parcel · Wohn(ungs)grundstück *n*

dwelling purpose, residential purpose, residence purpose · Wohnzweck *m*

dwelling rent, residential rent · Wohnungsmiete *f*, Wohnungs(miet)zins *m*

dwelling rent act → residential rent (control) act

dwelling rent addition, addition of (residential) rent, addition of dwelling rent, (residential) rent addition · (Wohnungs)Mietzuschlag *m*

dwelling rent book, residential rent book · Wohnungsmiet(quittungs)buch *n*

dwelling rent (control) act → residential rent (control) act

dwelling rent (control) law → residential rent (control) act

dwelling rent (control) statute → residential rent (control) act

dwelling rent (court) action, (residential) rent (court) action, dwelling rent cause, (residential) rent cause, dwelling rent plea, (residential) rent plea, dwelling rent (law)suit, (residential) rent (law)suit · (Wohnungs)Mietklage *f*

dwelling rent debt, residential rent debt · Wohnungsmietschuld *f*

dwelling rent decrease, (residential) rent reduction, (residential) rent decrease, dwelling rent reduction · Mietherabset-

dwelling rent development — dwelling tenure at sufferance 344

zung f, Mietsenkung, Wohnungsmietherabsetzung, Wohnungsmietsenkung, (Wohnungs)Mietminderung

dwelling rent development, residential rent development · Wohnungsmietenentwick(e)lung f

dwelling rent fluctuation clause → residential rent (price) fluctuation clause

dwelling rent in arrear → residential rent in arrear

dwelling rent law, law of landlord and tenant, landlord/tenant law, (residential) rent law · Mietrecht n, Wohnungsmietrecht [*Sammelbegriff für alle für die Mietverhältnisse maßgebenden rechtlichen Vorschriften*]

dwelling rent law → residential rent (control) act

dwelling rent limit, (residential) rent limit · Mietgrenze f, Wohnungsmietgrenze

dwelling rent ordinance, residential rent ordinance · Wohnungsmietenverordnung f

dwelling rent pre-contract, residential rent pre-contract · Wohnungsmietvorvertrag m, Wohnungsmietabschließungsvertrag

dwelling rent price, residential rent price · Wohnungsmietpreis m, Wohnungs-(miet)zinspreis

dwelling rent (price) control, (residential) rent (price) control · (Wohnungs)-Miet(preis)überwachung f, (Wohnungs)-Mietgeldüberwachung, (Wohnungs)-Mietzinsüberwachung

dwelling rent (price) fluctuation clause → residential rent (price) fluctuation clause

dwelling rent (price) level, (residential) rent (price) level · (Wohnungs)Miet-(preis)höhe f, (Wohnungs)Mietgeldhöhe, (Wohnungs)Mietzinshöhe

dwelling rent (price) policy, (residential) rent (price) policy · Mietenpolitik f, Miet(preis)politik, Wohnungsmietenpolitik, Wohnungsmiet(preis)politik

dwelling rent rate, residential rent rate · Wohnungsmietsatz m

dwelling rent reduction, dwelling rent decrease, (residential) rent reduction, (residential) rent decrease · Mietherabsetzung f, Mietsenkung, Wohnungsmietherabsetzung, Wohnungsmietsenkung, (Wohnungs)Mietminderung

dwelling rent restriction, residential rent restriction · Wohnungsmiet(preis)-begrenzung f, Wohnungsmietzinsbegrenzung, Wohnungsmietgeldbegrenzung

dwelling rent room, residential rent room · Wohnungsmietraum m

dwelling rent stabilization policy, (residential) rent stabilization policy · Mietstabilisierungspolitik f, Wohnungsmietstabilisierungspolitik

dwelling rent statute → residential rent (control) act

dwelling rent table, residential rent table · Wohnungsmiettabelle f, Wohnungsmietspiegel m

dwelling rent tribunal, (residential) rent tribunal · Mietgericht n, Wohnungsmietgericht

dwelling rent with heating, residential rent with heating · Warmmiete f

dwelling room, residential room · Wohnraum m als bewohnbarer Einzelraum

dwelling servitude, housing servitude, residential servitude · Wohnungsdienstbarkeit f, Wohnungsgerechtigkeit, Wohnungsservitut n, f, (servitutisches) Wohn(ungs)recht n [*Das Recht ein Gebäude oder einen Teil eines Gebäudes unter Ausschluß des Eigentümers als Wohnung zu benutzen*]

dwelling tenancy, dwelling tenure, (residential) landlord/tenant relation(ship), dwelling landlord/tenant relation(ship), residential tenancy, residential tenure · Wohn(ungs)mietverhältnis n

dwelling tenancy at sufferance, dwelling tenure at sufferance, dwelling landlord/tenant relation(ship) at sufferance, residential tenancy at sufferance, residential landlord/tenant relation(ship) at sufferance · Wohn(ungs)mietverhältnis n auf Duldung, geduldetes Wohn(ungs)mietverhältnis [*Es liegt vor, wenn ein Wohnungsmieter sein ursprünglich rechtmäßiges Wohnungsmietverhältnis unrechtmäßig verlängert*]

dwelling tenant, residential tenant · Wohnungsmieter m

dwelling tenant at will, (residential) tenant at will · jederzeit kündbarer Wohnungsmieter m, all(e)zeit kündbarer Wohnungsmieter, willkürlich kündbarer Wohnungsmieter

dwelling tenant handbook, residential tenant handbook · Wohnungsmiet(er)buch n

dwelling tenants, residential tenants · Wohnungsmieter mpl, Wohnungsmietleute f

dwelling tenant's law, dwelling tenant's act, dwelling tenant's statute, residential tenant's law, residential tenant's act, residential tenant's statute · Wohnungsmietergesetz n

dwelling tenure → dwelling tenancy

dwelling tenure at sufferance, dwelling landlord/tenant relation(ship) at sufferance, residential tenancy at sufferance,

dwelling unit — earnest (money)

residential tenure at sufferance, residential landlord/tenant relation(ship) at sufferance, dwelling tenancy at sufferance · Wohn(ungs)mietverhältnis n auf Duldung, geduldetes Wohn(ungs)mietverhältnis [*Es liegt vor, wenn ein Wohnungsmieter sein ursprünglich rechtmäßiges Wohnungsmietverhältnis unrechtmäßig verlängert*]

dwelling unit, DU, du, living unit, LU, lu, housing unit, apartment, unit of housing (US); apartment (Brit.) [*archaic*]; tenement, residence, dwelling · Wohnung f

dwelling unit in the court-yard, living unit in the court-yard, housing unit in the court-yard (US); dwelling in the court-yard · Hofwohnung f

dwelling vacancy loss, residential vacancy loss [*Rent(al) not received because of housing being unrented*] · Wohnungsmietausfall m, Wohnungsmietverlust m

dwelling vacancy loss decline, residential vacancy loss decline · Wohnungsmietausfallrückgang m, Wohnungsmietverlustrückgang

dwelling vacancy loss risk, dwelling vacancy loss hazard, residential vacancy loss risk, residential vacancy loss hazard · Wohnungsmietausfallwagnis n, Wohnungsmietausfallrisiko n, Wohnungsmietverlustwagnis n, Wohnungsmietverlustrisiko

dwelling zone, residential zone · Wohn(ungs)zone f

dying declarations, deathbed declarations · Erklärungen fpl auf dem Sterbebett

dyke (general) property → dyke ownership (of property)

dyke law, dike law · Deichrecht n

dyke ownership (of property), dyke (general) property, dyke proprietorship, dike ownership (of property), dike (general) property, dike proprietorship · Deicheigentum n

dyke-reeve, dyke-reed, dike-reeve, dike-reed · Deichhauptmann m, Deichvogt m

dyke union, dike union · Deichverband m

dynamic economy · dynamische Wirtschaft f

dynamic location model, dynamic site model · dynamisches Standortmodell n

dynamic site model, dynamic location model · dynamisches Standortmodell n

dynamics of growth, growth dynamics · Wachstumsdynamik f

E

eagerness to buy, eagerness to purchase · Kaufbesessenheit f

earl · Graf m

earlier mortgage · frühere Hypothek f

Earl Marshal of England · Oberzeremonienmeister m des Königreiches und Chef des Heroldstandes

earl palatine · Pfalzgraf m

early · frühzeitig

early completion, acceleration (of work), acceleration of performance · Beschleunigung f [*Fertigstellung der Arbeit(en) vor der gesetzten Frist*]

early green village, old green village · Altangerdorf n

early retirement · vorzeitige Pensionierung f

early settled (agricultural) land, old settled (agricultural) land · Altsiedelland n

early settlement, old settlement · Alt(an)sied(e)lung n

early stage · Frühstadium n

early termination · frühzeitige Beend(ig)ung f

earmark · Eigentumskennzeichen n

earmarking · Eigentumskennzeichnung f

earned capital · erzielter Gewinn m, erzielter Profit m

earned income, earnings · Einkommen n aus Arbeit, verdientes Einkommen, Diensteinkommen, unfundiertes Einkommen, Arbeitseinkommen, Verdienst m

earned surplus, cash flow, retained earnings, retained income, available (earned) surplus [*The spendable income from an investment after paying all expenses, such as operating expenses and debt service*] · Gewinneinbehalt m, Profiteinbehalt, einbehaltener Gewinn, einbehaltener Profit

earner, breadwinner · Verdiener m

earnest (money), arles, erles, arrha(bo), handmoney, handsel [*A sum paid to bind a bargain*] · Angeld n, Kaufschilling m, Handgeld, D(a)rauf(gabe)geld, D(a)raufgabe f, Haftgeld, Mietstaler m [*Wenn Angeld gegeben wird, so gilt dies nach dem Gesetz als ein Zeichen, daß ein Vertrag abgeschlossen wurde*]

earning capital — eavesdropper

earning capital · werbendes Kapital *n*

earning plot (of land) · Ertragsgrundstück *n*

earning power · Ertragskraft *f*

earnings, earned income · Einkommen *n* aus Arbeit, verdientes Einkommen, Diensteinkommen, unfundiertes Einkommen, Arbeitseinkommen, Verdienst *m*

earnings allowance · allgemeiner Freibetrag *m*

earnings and profit and loss statement, statement of operations, results of operations, profit and loss account, income statement · Gewinn- und Verlustrechnung *f*

earnings from operation(s), cash profit, fund provided by profit, fund made available from operation(s), fund provided by operation(s); cash flow, cash earnings [*misnomers*]; fund (generated) from operation(s) · Geldgewinn *m* aus (Betriebs)Umsatz, Fondsbeitrag *m* aus (Betriebs)Umsatz, Fondszufluß *m* aus (Betriebs)Umsatz, Nettofondszugang *m* aus (Betriebs)Umsatz, Kapitalzufluß aus Betriebstätigkeit, Fondszuwachs *m* aus Betriebsleistungen, Zugang an flüssigen Mitteln aus Betriebstätigkeit, finanzwirtschaftlicher Überschuß *m*, Umsatzüberschuß, Fondszugang aus Betriebstätigkeit

earnings retention policy · Thesaurierungspolitik *f*

earnings statement · Verdienstrechnung *f*

earthly service, temporal service · weltliche Dienstleistung *f*, weltliche Verrichtung [*Leh(e)n(s)mann*]

earthmoving area · Fläche *f* für Erdbewegungen

(earth)quake map, seismic map · Erdbebenkarte *f*, Bebenkarte

earth resources technology satellite, ERTS · Erderkundungssatellit *m*

earth science · Geowissenschaft *f*

ear-witness · Ohrenzeuge *m*

easement; aisiamentum, aysiamentum [*Latin*]; aise(ment) [*Norman French*] · Grunddienstbarkeit *f* [*Ein Grundstück kann zugunsten des jeweiligen Eigentümers eines anderen Grundstücks in der Weise belastet werden, daß dieser das Grundstück in einzelnen Beziehungen benutzen darf oder daß auf dem Grundstück gewisse Handlungen nicht vorgenommen werden dürfen oder daß die Ausübung eines Rechtes ausgeschlossen ist, das sich aus dem Eigentum an dem belasteten Grundstück dem anderen Grundstück gegenüber ergibt*]

easement appurtenant · anhaftende Grunddienstbarkeit *f*, zugehörige Grunddienstbarkeit

easement area · Grunddienstbarkeitsfläche *f*

easement by necessity, easement of necessity · Grunddienstbarkeit *f* durch Notwendigkeit [*Der Ausdruck ,,Notwendigkeit" ist irreführend, denn es ist nicht die Notwendigkeit, die eine Grunddienstbarkeit schafft — wie etwa einige Naturrechte — sondern die stillschweigende Vereinbarung zwischen zwei Parteien*]

easement by prior use, prior-use easement · Quasigrunddienstbarkeit *f*

easement in fee simple · allodiale Grunddienstbarkeit *f*

easement in gross · Personalgrunddienstbarkeit *f*

easement law · Grunddienstbarkeitsrecht *n*

easement of (a right of) way, (right of) way easement · Wegegrunddienstbarkeit *f*, Durchgangsgrunddienstbarkeit

easement of light, light easement · Lichtgrunddienstbarkeit *f*

easement of necessity, easement by necessity · Grunddienstbarkeit *f* durch Notwendigkeit [*Der Ausdruck ,,Notwendigkeit" ist irreführend, denn es ist nicht die Notwendigkeit, die eine Grunddienstbarkeit schafft — wie etwa einige Naturrechte — sondern die stillschweigende Vereinbarung zwischen zwei Parteien*]

easement of tunnel(l)ing, tunnel(l)ing easement · Tunnelgrunddienstbarkeit *f*

easement of water, water easement · Wassergrunddienstbarkeit *f*

easement of watercourse, watercourse easement [*The right of receiving or discharging water through another person's land, the tenement for the benefit of which the watercourse exists being the dominant tenement*] · Wasserlauf-Grunddienstbarkeit *f*

easement of way → easement of (a right of) way

easement to air · Luftgrunddienstbarkeit *f*

easement to lay pipe(s), easement to lay pipelines · Rohrgrunddienstbarkeit *f*

easily realized capital · mobiles Kapital *n*, umlaufendes Kapital, Umlaufkapital

easily saleable · abgängig

Eastern frontier zone, Eastern frontier area, Eastern frontier territory · Zonenrandgebiet *n* [*Bundesrepublik Deutschland*]

eavesdropper · Haushorcher *m*

eavesdropping · Haushorchen n

to ebb · zurückweichen [Wasser beim Gezeitenwechsel]

ecclesia forensis [Latin]; market and church · Markt m und Kirche f

ecclesia forensis in civitate [Latin]; townsmen's church, market church · Marktkirche f

ecclesiastic(al) authority, spiritual authority · Kirchenbehörde f

ecclesiastic(al) authority → ecclesiastic(al) power

ecclesiastic(al) benefice, spiritual benefice · geistliche Pfründe f, kirchliche Pfründe, Kirchenpfründe

ecclesiastic(al) building, church-building (US) [A building for meetings, etc., adjoining a church] · Kirchengebäude n, kirchliches Gebäude

ecclesiastic(al) chapter · Kirchenkapitel n

ecclesiastic(al) community, spiritual community · Kirchengemeinde f

ecclesiastic(al) consolidation, ecclesiastic(al) fusion, spiritual consolidation, spiritual fusion · kirchliche Konsolidation f, kirchliche Verschmelzung, kirchliche Fusion, geistliche Konsolidation, geistliche Verschmelzung, geistliche Fusion

ecclesiastic(al) corporation, spiritual corporation, church corporation, religious house · geistliche Körperschaft f, geistliche Korporation, kirchliche Korporation, kirchliche Körperschaft

ecclesiastic(al) corporation sole, spiritual corporation sole · Pfarrei f, Pfarramt n, Pfarrbezirk m

ecclesiastic(al) court, consistorial court, church-court, court Christian, consistory court; commissary court [Scotland]; spiritual court · geistliches Gericht n, Kirchengericht, Konsistorialgericht, kirchliches Gericht [Die schottischen „ecclesiastical courts" haben nur eine Jurisdiktion über Fragen der Doktrin, des Gottesdienstes, der Sakramente und der Disziplin der Geistlichen]

ecclesiastic(al) dignitary · kirchlicher Würdenträger m, geistlicher Würdenträger

ecclesiastic(al) estate, church property, spiritual property, ecclesiastic(al) property, church estate, spiritual estate · Kirchenvermögen n, Kirchengut n, Kirchenhabe f

ecclesiastic(al) fee, ecclesiastic(al) feod, ecclesiastic(al) feud, ecclesiastic(al) fief, ecclesiastic(al) tenement, ecclesiastic(al) tenancy, ecclesiastic(al) (feodal) tenure (of land), tenure (of land) by divine service, tenure (of land) by religious service; feudum ecclesiasticum, feodum ecclesiasticum, feudum religiosum, feodum religiosum [Latin]; spiritual fee, spiritual feud, spiritual feod, spiritual fief, spiritual tenancy, spiritual tenement, spiritual (feodal) tenure (of land) · Gottesleh(e)n n, Kirchenleh(e)n, Klosterleh(e)n, geistliches Leh(e)n [Die geistlichen Verrichtungen waren genau definiert]

ecclesiastic(al) fee (tenure) (of land) → spiritual fee (tenure) (of land)

ecclesiastic(al) fusion, spiritual consolidation, spiritual fusion, ecclesiastic(al) consolidation · kirchliche Konsolidation f, kirchliche Verschmelzung, kirchliche Fusion, geistliche Konsolidation, geistliche Verschmelzung, geistliche Fusion

ecclesiastic(al) land, church-land, spiritual land · Kirchenland n, Kirchenboden m

ecclesiastic(al) (land(ed)) estate, spiritual (land(ed)) estate · kirchlicher Landbesitz m, kirchlicher Bodenbesitz, kirchlicher Grund(stücks)besitz

ecclesiastic(al) law, spiritual law; jus ecclesiasticum [Latin]; law Christian [Not to be confused with "jus canonicum"] · Kirchenrecht n, kirchliches Recht, geistliches Recht

ecclesiastic(al) parish · Kirchspiel n nur für kirchliche Zwecke, (Pfarr)Sprengel m nur für kirchliche Zwecke, kirchlicher Sprengel nur für kirchliche Zwecke, Parochie f nur für kirchliche Zwecke

ecclesiastic(al) power, ecclesiastic(al) authority, spiritual authority, spiritual power; jus majestaticum circa sacra, jus in sacra, potestas ecclesiastica [Latin] · Kirchengewalt f, Kirchenhoheit f, Kirchenmacht f, Kirchenkompetenz f, Kirchenregiment n

ecclesiastic(al) property, church estate, spiritual estate, ecclesiastic(al) estate, church property, spiritual property · Kirchenvermögen n, Kirchengut n, Kirchenhabe f

ecclesiastic(al) province, spiritual province, church province · Kirchenprovinz f

ecclesiastic(al) status; churchship [obsolete]; churchdom · Kirchenstatus m

ecclesiastic(al) tithe, parish tithe, spiritual tithe, parochial tithe · geistlicher Zehnt m, Pfarrerzehnt, kirchlicher Zehnt, Kirchenzehnt [altdeutsch: Pfarrerzehent, Pfarrerzehend]

ecclesiastic(al) writer, spiritual writer · Kirchenschriftsteller m

ECJ (US); European Court (Brit.) · EUGH m, Europäischer Gerichtshof

ecological approach · ökologischer Ansatz m

ecological equilibrium · ökologisches Gleichgewicht *n*

ecological equilibrium area · ökologischer Ausgleichsraum *m*

ecological planning basis, ecological basis of planning · ökologische Planungsgrundlage *f*

ecological research · Ökologieforschung *f*

ecological sociologist · Ökologiesoziologe *m*

ecological system · ökologisches System *n*

ecological theory of land use planning · ökologische Theorie *f* der Landnutzungsplanung

ecology · Ökologie *f* [*Von Ernst Haeckel 1866 in die wissenschaftliche Diskussion eingeführter Begriff. Ökologie ist die Lehre von der Standort- bzw. Umweltbedingtheit der Lebewesen*]

ecology of the city, urban ecology, town ecology, city ecology, ecology of the town · Stadtökologie *f*

econometrics · Ökonometrie *f* [*Quantitative Untersuchungsmethoden, welche die Volkswirtschaft mit Statistik und Mathematik kombinieren*]

economic affair · Wirtschaftsangelegenheit *f*

economical, profitable, lucrative · gewinnbringend, rentabel, wirtschaftlich, profitbringend

economic area, economic territory · Wirtschaftsgebiet *n*

economic assistance · Wirtschaftsförderung *f*

economic assistance measure · wirtschaftliche Förderungsmaßnahme *f*

economic atlas · Wirtschaftsatlas *m*

economic atlas of the world · Weltwirtschaftsatlas *m*

economic base · wirtschaftliche Grundlage *f*

economic base, primary occupations, basic employment, basic activity · Fernversorgungstätigkeit *f*, Erzeugung *f* von Ausfuhrgütern, Grundleistung, Originärbeschäftigung, Exportaktivität *f*, Ausfuhraktivität, primäre Aktivität [*Eine der Ausfuhr aus einer Region dienende Leistung*]

economic base theory · Außenhandelstheorie *f* [*funktionale Städteklassifikation*]

economic bill of rights · Erklärung *f* der wirtschaftlichen Grundrechte

economic boundary · wirtschaftliche Grenze *f*

economic capability, economic capacity · Wirtschaftsfähigkeit *f*

economic commission · Wirtschaftskommission *f*

economic cycle theory, theory of economic cycles · Konjunkturtheorie *f*

economic development · Wirtschaftsentwick(e)lung *f*

economic development plan · Wirtschaftsentwick(e)lungsplan *m*

economic dislocation · Wegfall *m* der Geschäftsgrundlage

economic dynamics · Wirtschaftsdynamik *f*

economic efficiency [*The degree to which maximum production with minimum effort is achieved*] · wirtschaftlicher Wirkungsgrad *m*

economic entity · Wirtschaftseinheit *f*

economic equality [*A principle to the effect that all individuals should have the opportunity to secure fair share of the comforts of life, and, conversely, that no one individual or group should receive special economic advantages at the expense of others*] · Wirtschaftsgleichheit *f*

economic equilibrium · Wirtschaftsgleichgewicht *n*

economic feudalism · wirtschaftlicher Feudalismus *m*

economic freedom, economic liberty · wirtschaftliche Freiheit *f*

economic function · Wirtschaftsfunktion *f*

economic geography · Wirtschaftsgeographie *f*, Wirtschaftserdkunde *f*

economic growth · wirtschaftliches Wachstum *n*, Wirtschaftswachstum

economic history · Wirtschaftsgeschichte *f*

economic incentive · wirtschaftlicher Anreiz *m*

economic integration, income mix · wirtschaftliche Eingliederung *f*, wirtschaftliche Einordnung, wirtschaftliche Integration

economic intensity · Wirtschaftsstärke *f*

economic law · Wirtschaftsrecht *n*

economic life [*The period during which a building produces a profit to its owner*] · Nutzungsdauer *f*

economic location(al) approach · wirtschaftlicher Standortansatz *m*

economic location(al) theory [*Such a theory tries to predict how people choose and change locations — locations to work, live, and play and locations from which to buy and to which to sell — by introducing distance into economic theory*] · wirtschaftliche Standorttheorie *f*

economic lot size, standard-run quantity · rationelle Stückzahl *f*

economic map · Wirtschaftskarte *f*

economic mapping · Wirtschaftskartierung *f*

economic metropolis · Wirtschaftsmetropole *f*

economic obsolescence, locational obsolescence · wirtschaftliche Überalterung *f*

economic order · Wirtschaftsordnung *f*

economic organization · Wirtschaftsorganisation *f*

economic plan, economic scheme [*A plan or scheme on which economic production or activity is based*] · Wirtschaftsplan *m*

economic planner · Wirtschaftsplaner *m*

economic planning board · Wirtschaftsplanungsamt *n* [*Bundesrepublik Deutschland*]

economic policy · Wirtschaftspolitik *f*

economic province · Wirtschaftsprovinz *f*

economic region, economy region · Wirtschaftsregion *f*, ökonomische Landschaft *f*

economic regionalism · Wirtschaftsregionalismus *m*

economic rent, market rent [*The amount of rent(al) a property would command if it were unencumbered by a lease or vacant and available for rent on the open market*] · Marktmiete *f*

economics, political economy, national economy, public economy · Volkswirtschaft *f*, politische Ökonomie *f*, Nationalökonomie

economic sabotage · Wirtschaftssabotage *f*

economic scheme, economic plan [*A plan or scheme on which economic production or activity is based*] · Wirtschaftsplan *m*

economic self-sufficiency · Wirtschaftsautarkie *f*

(economic) slowdown, recession, setback · Abschwung *m*, wirtschaftlicher Abschwung, Rezession *f*, Wirtschaftsabschwung

economics opportunity, economy opportunity · Wirtschaftsförderung *f*

economic space · Wirtschaftsraum *m*

economic stage · Wirtschaftsstufe *f*

economic structure · Wirtschaftsstruktur *f*

economic survey · Wirtschaftsenquête *f*

economic territory, economic area · Wirtschaftsgebiet *n*

economic value · wirtschaftlicher Wert *m*

economic value of goods · wirtschaftlicher Güterwert *m*

economic year · Wirtschaftsjahr *n*

economies of large scales · Ersparnisse *fpl* der Großbetriebe

economies of scale, scale economies · einsparende Massenproduktion *f*, Kostenersparnisse *fpl* durch optimale Betriebsgröße [*Sie führt zu internen Einsparungen*]

economist · Wirtschaftler *m*

economy · Wirtschaft *f*

economy control, control of economy · Wirtschaftslenkung *f*

economy of abundance · Überflußwirtschaft *f*

economy of large cities, economy of large towns, economy of big cities, economy of big towns · Großstadtwirtschaft *f*

economy of scale, scale economy, return to scale · Skalenertrag *m* [*Die Auswirkung der proportionalen Faktorerhöhung auf das Produktionsergebnis*]

economy of scale · Größenersparnis *f* [*Zentralorttheorie*]

economy region, economic region · Wirtschaftsregion *f*, ökonomische Landschaft *f*

ecosystem, balance of nature, natural balance · Naturhaushalt *m*

ecumene → ekumene

edict [*An official proclamation of a rule or law*] · Edikt *n*

EDR, environmental design research · Umweltentwurfsforschung *f*

education · Erziehung *f*

education · Bildung *f*

education(al) act, education(al) law, education(al) statute · Schulgesetz *n*, Bildungsgesetz

education(al) assistance · Bildungsförderung *f*

education(al) authority · Bildungsbehörde *f*, Schulbehörde

education(al) board, board of education · Bildungsamt *n*

education(al) committee · Schul(verwaltungs)ausschuß *m*

education(al) exchange · Bildungsaustausch *m*

education(al) facility · Bildungseinrichtung *f*

education(al) field, field of education · Bildungssektor *m*

educational institution — ekistics

educational institution · Bildungsanstalt f

education(al) law, education(al) statute, education(al) act · Schulgesetz n, Bildungsgesetz

education(al) level, level of education · Bildungsstand m

education(al) officer, education(al) official, school governor · Schulrat m

education(al) planner · Bildungsplaner m

education(al) planning · Bildungsplanung f

education(al) policy · Bildungspolitik f

education(al) practice · Bildungswesen n

education(al) research · Bildungsforschung f

education(al) reform · Bildungsreform f

(education(al)) scheme · Unterrichtsplan m

education(al) statute, education(al) act, education(al) law · Schulgesetz n, Bildungsgesetz

education(al) therapy · ausbildungsbezogene Strategie f [Stadtentwick(e)lungsplanung]

education-rate · (örtliche) Bildungssteuer f, lokale Bildungssteuer, kommunale Bildungssteuer, gemeindliche Bildungssteuer

to effect, to raise [mortgage] · aufnehmen [Hypothek]

effect, operation · (Aus)Wirkung f

effective citizenship, effective nationality · effektive Staatsangehörigkeit f [Bei einer mehrere Staatsangehörigkeiten besitzenden Person entscheidet die Angehörigkeit zu dem Staat, dem der Mehrstaater am engsten verbunden ist]

effective contribution margin · wirksamer Deckungsbeitrag m

effective conversion, effectual conversion · effektive Umsetzung f, effektive Umwandlung

effective date, appointed day, key day, cut-off-date · Stichtag m

effective date of appraisal, cut-off date of appraisal, appointed day of appraisal, key-day of appraisal, (e)valuation cut-off-date, (e)valuation key-day, appointed day of (e)valuation · Bewertungsstichtag m, Wertermitt(e)lungsstichtag, Taxierungsstichtag, (Ab)Schätzungsstichtag

effective demand, effectual demand · effektive Nachfrage f

effective interest yield(ing), effective interest bearing, effective interest return, effective yielding of interest, effective return(ing) of interest, effective bearing of interest · Effektivverzinsung f

effective nationality, effective citizenship · effektive Staatsangehörigkeit f [Bei einer mehrere Staatsangehörigkeiten besitzenden Person entscheidet die Angehörigkeit zu dem Staat, dem der Mehrstaater am engsten verbunden ist]

effectiveness · Tauglichkeit f

effectiveness of a plan, plan effectiveness · Planreife f

effective time · Gültigkeitsdauer f

effect of jet aircraft nuisance · Düsenflugzeugimmission f

effect (of law), legal effect, legal operation, operation (of law) · Gesetz(es)(aus)wirkung f, Rechts(aus)wirkung

effect of suspension, effect of postponement, suspensory effect · aufschiebende Wirkung f, verschiebende Wirkung f, hinausschiebende Wirkung f, Hemmungswirkung f, Hemmungseffekt m, Suspensivwirkung f, Suspensiveffekt m

effectual conversion, effective conversion · effektive Umsetzung f, effektive Umwandlung

effectual demand, effective demand · effektive Nachfrage f

efficiency · Leistungsstärke f

efficiency-wage, statement-wage, premium-wage, wage by results, piece-wage · Akkordlohn m, Leistungslohn

efficiency-wage contract, statement-wage contract, piece-wage contract, piecework contract, job(bing) work contract, premium-wage contract · Akkord(lohn)vertrag m

efficiency-wage rate, statement-wage rate, premium-wage rate, piece-wage rate · Akkord(lohn)satz m

efficient estimator · wirksame Schätzfunktion f, höchstleistungsfähige Schätzfunktion [Statistik]

efflux(ion) of time, running of time · Zeitablauf m, Zeitverlauf

efflux of money, drain of money · Geldabfluß m

eire, eyre · Sendrichtergericht n

eisnetia, enitia pars, dignitas primogeniti [Latin]; right of primogeniture, right of the eldest, right of the first born; easentia · (männliches) Erstgeburtsrecht n, Primogenitur f, Vorrecht des Erstgeborenen

to eject · exmittieren, entsetzen

ejectment · Exmittierung f, Entsetzung

ekistics · Ekistics f [Sie behandelt als Wissenschaft das Sied(e)lungswesen und

ekumene — elevation tint

die Erforschung und Lösung seiner Probleme. Sie ist 1941 in Athen erstmalig bekannt geworden]

ekumene, inhabited world, (o)ecumene [*That portion of the earth's surface which has been settled by man*] · Sied(e)lungsraum *m*, Ökumene *f*

elaboration · Aufstellung *f*, Ausarbeitung [*Plan*]

elaboration of (a) design · Durcharbeiten *n* eines Planungskonzepts, stufenweise Erarbeitung *f* einer zeichnerischen Lösung

elaboration of construction drawings, elaboration of building drawings · Anfertigung *f* von Bauzeichnungen

elaboration of (the) working documents · Ausführungsarbeit(en) *f (pl)* [*Die weitere Durcharbeitung eines Entwurfs mit allen Massen und Maßen und für die Ausführung des Bauwerkes erforderlichen Angaben und Anweisungen*]

elastic [*term*] · dehnbar [*Begriff*]

elder · Laienälteste *m*

elderly dwelling unit, elderly housing unit, elderly living unit, elderly apartment (US); elderly dwelling · Altenwohnung *f*

eldership, primogeniture(ship), seniority · (männliche) Erstgeburtserbfolge *f*, (männliche) Primogeniturerbfolge

elected body · gewähltes Organ *n*

elected committee · gewählter Ausschuß *m*

election · Wahl *f*

election assessor · Wahlbeisitzer *m*

election committee · Wahlvorstand *m*

election court · Wahlgericht *n*

election hours of poll act · Wahldauergesetz *n*

election-of-law, law choice, law election, choice-of-law · Rechtswahl *f*

election-of-law rule, law election norm, election-of-law norm, choice-of-law rule, choice-of-law norm, law choice rule, law choice norm, law election rule · Rechtswahlnorm *f*

election petition · Wahlprozeß *m* [*Anfechtung einer Wahl*]

election to the works council, election to the workers' council, election to the workmen's council · Betriebsratswahl *f*

elective franchise · öffentliches Wahlrecht *n*

elector, voter · Wähler *m*

electoral behavior (US); electoral behaviour (Brit.) · Wahlverhalten *n*

(electoral) division · Wahlkreis *m*

electoral role · Wählerliste *f*

elector apathy, voter apathy · Wahlmüdigkeit *f*

elector approval, voter approval · Wählerzustimmung *f*

electorate · Wählerschaft *f*

elector response, voter response · Wählerreaktion *f*

electrical work contractor · Elektroinstallationsunternehmer *m*

(electricity) power authority · Energiebehörde *f*

electricity price, power price · Elektrizitätspreis *m*, Strompreis, Energiepreis

electricity supply, energy supply, power supply · Elektrizitätsversorgung *f*, Stromversorgung, Energieversorgung

electricity supply act, electricity supply law, electricity supply statute · Stromversorgungsgesetz *n*, Energieversorgungsgesetz, Elektrizitätsversorgungsgesetz

electricity wayleave · Elektroleitung-Durchgangsrecht *n*

(electric) power economy · Energiewirtschaft *f*

electric sign · Lichtreklameeinrichtung *f*, Leuchtreklameeinrichtung, Lichtwerbungseinrichtung, Leuchtwerbungseinrichtung

electric signs, illuminated advertisement, illuminated advertising · Leuchtreklame *f*, Leuchtwerbung *f*, Lichtreklame, Lichtwerbung

eleemosinary corporation, charitable corporation · wohltätige Körperschaft *f*, wohltätige Korporation, karitative Körperschaft, karitative Korporation, Almosenkörperschaft, Almosenkorporation

elegit [*Writ of execution allowing a judgment creditor to enter into possession of the debtor's land and hold it until the debt is satisfied. Abolished under the A.J.A. 1956 and replaced by an order creating a charge over land or over an interest in the land*] · Exekutionsmandat *n* auf Grund des Statuts Westminster II (13 ED. I. c. 18)

elementary school, common school (US); day school, primary school, board school (Brit.) · Elementarschule, Grundschule, Volksschule *f*

element of contract, contract element · Vertragsbestandteil *m*

element of cost(s), cost(s) element · Kostenelement *n*

elevation tint · Höhenschichtenfarbe *f*

eligibility — emigration board

eligibility · Diskontfähigkeit f, Diskontierbarkeit [Wechsel]

eligibility · Wählbarkeit f

eligibility requirement · Bedingung f von einem Begünstigten zu erfüllen

eligible · diskontfähig [Wechsel]

eligible · antragsberechtigt

eligible · wählbar

eligible applicant [A person or entity that meets the criteria for applying for a particular form of assistance] · Antragsberechtigte m

eligible displacee, eligible displaced individual · unterstützungswürdiger Aussied(e)ler m, unterstützungswürdiger Ausgesiedelter, unterstützungswürdiger Umsied(e)ler, unterstützungswürdiger Umgesiedelter

elimination of smoke, smoke elimination, smoke abatement, smoke control · Rauchbekämpfung f, Rauchsanierung

eliminations ledger, consolidation ledger · Hilfsbuch n für Konzernbilanz

(e)locare [Latin]; to let · vermieten

elongated market · Längsmarkt m

embargo on (real) estate, embargo on (real) property, embargo on land, embargo on realty · Grund(stücks)sperre f, Bodensperre, Landsperre, Liegenschaftssperre

to embellish, to adorn, to beautify · verschönern

embezzlement [The fraudulent appropriation to one's own use of another's money or property entrusted to one's care. It is to be distinguished from theft in which the act of acquisition of the property is unlawful] · Unterschlagung f, Veruntreuung

emblements, industrial fruits, industrial products; fruits of labour, products of labour (Brit.); fruits of labor, products of labor (US); fructus industriales, fructus industriae [Latin]; fruits of industry [Those fruits of a thing, as of land, which are produced by the labo(u)r and industry of the occupant, as crops of grain; as distinguished from such as are produced solely by the powers of nature] · künstlicher Zuwachs m

embodied technical progress · kapitalgebundene technische Neuerung f, kapitalgebundener technischer Fortschritt m

to embody [A document is said to embody a provision if the provision is set out either in the document itself or in another document referred to in the document] · beinhalten

embracery · Geschworenenbestechung f

emergency → (state of) emergency

emergency act, emergency statute, emergency law · Notgesetz n, Ausnahmegesetz

emergency case · Eid(bedürftigkeits)fall m [Verwaltungsrecht]

emergency case, extraordinary occasion, case of emergency · Notfall m

emergency clause · Notklausel f

emergency dwelling unit (US); emergency tenement · Notwohnung f, Übergangswohnung, Schlichtwohnung

emergency hous(ebuild)ing scheme · Wohnungshilfswerk n

emergency housing · Notwohnungen f pl, Übergangswohnungen, Schlichtwohnungen

emergency law · Ausnahmerecht n, Notrecht

emergency law, emergency act, emergency statute · Notgesetz n, Ausnahmegesetz

emergency lawmaking, emergency legislation · Notgesetzgebung f

emergency note · Notstandsnote f

emergency power · Notstandsgewalt f

emergency power act, emergency power law, emergency power statute · Notstandsgesetz n

emergency purchase · Notkauf m

emergency requirement · Notausstattung f [Fläche]

emergency sale · Notverkauf m

emergency shelter, emergency lodging, emergency accommodation, emergency quarter · Notunterkunft f

emergency state, (state of) emergency · Notstand m

emergency statute, emergency law, emergency act · Notgesetz n, Ausnahmegesetz

emergency unemployment fund · Notstandsunterstützungsfonds m für Arbeitslose

emergency work(s), emergency operations · Notarbeit(en) f (pl), Notleistung(en) f (pl)

emigrant · Auswanderer m

emigrant's blocked account · Auswanderer-Sonderkonto n

emigration · Auswanderung f

emigration authority · Auswanderungsbehörde f

emigration board · Auswanderungsamt n

emigration contract · Auswanderungsvertrag *m*

emigration field, emigration sector · Auswanderungssektor *m*

emigration practice · Auswanderungswesen *n*

emigration sector, emigration field · Auswanderungssektor *m*

eminent domain → (power of) eminent domain

emission at a discount, issue at a discount · Unterpariemission *f*, Unterpariausgabe *f* [*Wertpapier*]

to emit, to issue · ausgeben [*Wertpapier*]

emotional bias · gefühlsmäßiges Vorurteil *n*

emphyteusis, emphyteosis, emphiteosis [*Latin*] · Erbzinsgut *n*, Emphyteuse *f*, Emphyteusis *f*

emphyteusis rent, emphyteutical rent · Erbzins(gut)rente *f*, Emphyteuserente

emphyteuta [*Latin*] [*The person to whom an emphyteusis is granted; the lessee or tenant under a contract of emphyteusis*] · Erbzinsguthalter *m*

emphyteutical rent → emphyteusis rent

empire law · Reichsrecht *n*

empirical regional research · empirische Regionalforschung *f*

employed · beschäftigt, erwerbstätig

employed person, working person, contributing person, working member (of the population), occupied person · erwerbstätige Person *f*, beschäftigte Person, arbeitende Person, berufstätige Person, Erwerbsperson, Erwerbstätige, Beschäftigte

employed population, working population, contributing population · erwerbstätige Bevölkerung *f*, beschäftigte Bevölkerung, arbeitende Bevölkerung, berufstätige Bevölkerung

employe(e), servant · Arbeitnehmer *m*

employe(e) morale, servant's morale · Arbeitsmoral *f*

employe(e)s' accounts, servants accounts · Lohn- und Gehaltskonten *n pl*

employe(e)s' benefit, servants' benefit · Arbeitnehmervergünstigung *f*

employ(e)e's household, servant's household · Arbeitnehmerhaushalt *m*

employ(e)e's liability, servant's liability · Arbeitnehmerhaftung *f*, Arbeitnehmerhaftpflicht *f*, Arbeitnehmerhaftbarkeit *f*

employe(e)s' parking space, servants' parking space · Arbeitnehmerparkraum *m*

employe(e)s' securities company, servants' security company · Arbeitnehmer-Investmentgesellschaft *f*

employ(e)e's vehicle, servant's vehicle · Arbeitnehmerfahrzeug *n*

employer, promoter, (building) owner, construction owner, project owner, client [*In Great Britain, the term "employer" is preferred since this is used in both the RIBA and ICE standard forms of contract*] · Bauherr(schaft) *m, (f)*, Auftraggeber *m*, BH *f*, AG *m* [*im Sinne der VOB*]; Besteller [*im Sinne des BGB*] [*Nach geläufiger Fachsprache ist „Bauherr" stets der „Letzt-Besteller" eines Bauwerkes (oder Bauwerk-Teils), also nicht der Unternehmer, der einen Subunternehmer bezieht. Dieser „Letzt-Besteller" ist Bauherr im engen (und eigentlichen) Sinne des Wortes. In einem übertragenen (nicht geläufigen) Sinne aber kann „Bauherr" auch ein Unternehmer sein, der übernommene Bauarbeiten durch Abschluß eines Bauvertrages an einen Subunternehmer weitervergibt. In diesem übertragenen Sinne muß das Wort dann verstanden werden, wenn die SIA-Norm 118 (Schweiz) auf den Bauvertrag zwischen Unternehmer und Subunternehmer zur Anwendung kommt. Im Verhältnis Unternehmer/Subunternehmer ist alsdann der erstere „Bauherr" im Sinne der Norm, der andere „Unternehmer"*]

employer, donor of an authority, grantor of an authority; mandator [*Latin*], principal (constituent) · Vollmachtgeber *m*, Bevollmächtiger, Vertretene [*Jemand der ein Rechtsgeschäft zu eigenem Nutzen und auf eigene Rechnung selbständig vornehmen kann, aber zu dessen Vornahme eine andere Person verwendet*]

employer, master · Arbeitgeber *m*

employer and employe(e), master and servant · Arbeitgeber *m* und Arbeitnehmer *m*

employer-designed project, promoter-designed project, owner-designed project, client-designed project · Bauherrenentwurfsprojekt *n*, Bauherrschaftsentwurfsprojekt

employer-employe(e) relation(ship), master-servant relation(ship) · Arbeitgeber-Arbeitnehmer-Verhältnis *n*

employers' association, employers' institution, employers' society · Arbeitgeberverein(igung) *m, (f)*

employer's delay, promoter's delay, owner's delay, client's delay · bauseitiger Verzug *m*

employer's design, promoter's design, owner's design, client's design · Ausschreibungsentwurf *m*, Bauherrenentwurf

employer's liability, owner's liability, promoter's liability, client's liability · Bauherrenhaftpflicht *f*, Bauherrenhaftung *f*, Bauherrenhaftbarkeit *f*

employer's liability, master's liability [*The employer's enforceable responsibility for accidents or injuries suffered by employees while they are engaged in the performance of their duties*] · Arbeitgeberhaftpflicht *f*, Arbeitgeberhaftung *f*

employer's liability act, employer's liability law, employer's liability statute · Arbeitgeberhaftpflichtgesetz *n*

employer's (liability) insurance, master's (liability) insurance · Arbeitgeberhaftpflichtversicherung *f*

employer's liability insurance, promoter's liability insurance, owner's liability insurance, client's liability insurance · Bauherrenhaftpflichtversicherung *f*, Bauherrschaftshaftpflichtversicherung

employer's (liability) insurance association · Berufsgenossenschaft *f*

employer's liability insurance association in the building and construction industry · Bauberufsgenossenschaft *f*

employer's loan, master's loan · Arbeitgeberdarleh(e)n *n*

employer's portion (of social security taxes), master's portion (of social security taxes) · Arbeitgeberanteil *m*

employer's risk, promoter's risk, owner's risk, client's risk · Bauherrenrisiko *n*, Bauherrenwagnis *n*, Bauherrschaftsrisiko, Bauherrschaftswagnis

employers' society, employers' association, employers' institution · Arbeitgeberverein(igung) *m*, *(f)*

employer's tax · Arbeitgebersteuer *f*

employer's union, master's union · Arbeitgeberverband *m*

employment, office, station · Posten *m*

employment, work, occupation · Arbeit *f*, Beschäftigung *f*

employment certificate, certificate of employment · Arbeitsnachweis *m*, Arbeitszeugnis *n*

employment contract, job contract, work contract, contract of service, contract of employment, contract of job, contract of work, service contract · Arbeitsvertrag *m*

employment creation, creation of work, creation of jobs, creation of employment, job creation, work creation · Arbeitsbeschaffung *f*

employment degree, degree of employment · Arbeitsgrad *m*, Beschäftigungsgrad *m*

employment density, density of employment, density of work, work density · Arbeitsdichte *f*, Beschäftigungsdichte *f*

employment growth · Beschäftigungswachstum *n*

employment in the building industry, employment in the construction industry, construction employment, building employment · Beschäftigung *f* in der Bauindustrie

employment location, employment site, location of employment, site of employment · Beschäftigungsstandort *m*

employment mobility, work mobility, occupational mobility · Arbeitsbeweglichkeit *f*, Arbeitsmobilität *f*, Beschäftigungsmobilität *f*, Beschäftigungsbeweglichkeit *f*

employment of space, utilization of space · Raumausnutzung *f*

employment pattern, work pattern, employment scheme, work scheme · Arbeitsmuster *n*, Arbeitsschema *n*, Beschäftigungsmuster *n*, Beschäftigungsschema *n*

employment percentage, employment rate · Beschäftigungsprozentsatz *m*

employment permission, permission of employment · Arbeitserlaubnis *f*, Arbeitsgenehmigung *f*

employment place, job place, place of employment, place of work(ing), work(ing) place · Arbeitsort *m*, Arbeitsplatz *m*, Beschäftigungsort *m*, Beschäftigungsplatz *m*

employment planning · Beschäftigungsplanung *f*

employment point, job point, point of employment, point of work(ing), work(ing) point · Arbeitsstätte *f*, Beschäftigungsstätte *f* [*Fehlbenennung: Arbeitsplatz m*]

employment policy · Beschäftigungspolitik *f*

employment rate, employment percentage · Beschäftigungsprozentsatz *m*

employment scheme, work scheme, employment pattern, work pattern · Arbeitsmuster *n*, Arbeitsschema *n*, Beschäftigungsmuster *n*, Beschäftigungsschema *n*

employment site, location of employment, site of employment, employment location · Beschäftigungsstandort *m*

employment volume [*The number of persons actually in employment at any time in any industry or region*] · Beschäftigtenzahl *f*

to empower, to enable, to give power to do something · ermächtigen, erteilen eines Rechtes, erteilen einer Befugnis

empty, vacant, unoccupied · frei, leer(stehend), unbesetzt, unbelegt, nicht belegt [*Raum*]

empty thread; brutum fulmen [*Latin*] · leere Drohung *f*

to enable, to give power to do something, to empower · ermächtigen, erteilen eines Rechtes, erteilen einer Befugnis

enabling act, law made by Parliament, act, statute; statutum, actus [*Latin*]; Act of Parliament · formelles Gesetz *n*, parlamentarisches Gesetz, (Parlaments)-Gesetz

enabling legislation, enabling lawmaking · Ermächtigungsgesetzgebung *f* [*Sie ermächtigt kommunale Gebietskörperschaften, sich auf dem Gebiet der Ortsplanung und des Städtebaues zu betätigen, ohne die Planung allerdings zu einer Pflicht zu machen*]

enabling statute, enabling act, enabling law · Ermächtigungsgesetz *n*

enacted · bewußt herbeigeführt

enacted law, statutory law, statutes; lex scripta, jus scriptum [*Latin*]; statute law, written law [*The body of law enacted by Parliament*] · geschriebenes Recht *n*, gesetztes Recht, geschriebenes Parlamentsrecht, gesetztes Parlamentsrecht, (Parlaments)Gesetz-(es)recht

to enact (into law), to establish by law · erheben zum Gesetz, (Gesetz) erlassen

enactment → (legislative) enactment

encampment · Wallburg *f*

encashment · Einlösung *f* von Versicherungsfondsanteilen

encirclement · Einkreisung *f*

enclave · Enklave *f*

to enclose, to inclose · abfrieden, einhegen, einfrieden, umfrieden, abschließen

enclosed, inclosed · abgefriedet, eingehegt, abgeschlossen, eingefriedet, umfriedet

enclosed chase, inclosed chase, park [*In English law. A tract of enclosed ground privileged for keeping wild beasts of the chase, particularly deer. Franchises of park were abolished in England by the Wild Creatures and Forest Laws Act 1971*] · Jagdgehege *n*, eingefriedetes Jagdrevier *n*, umfriedetes Jagdrevier

enclosed space, space enclosed, cube, cubic(al) capacity, (cubic(al)) content, structural volume, cubic extent, cubing, walled-in space, building volume, cubage [*Enclosed total volume measurements of a structure*] · Baumasse *f*, umbauter Raum *m*, Rauminhalt *m*

enclosing with shrubs and/or trees, inclosing with shrubs and/or trees · Eingrünung *f* [*Durch Gebüsche und/oder Bäume umgeben*]

enclosure · Anlage *f* [*Brief*]

enclosure, inclosure [*A hedge, structure, or partition, erected for the purpose of inclosing a piece of land, or to divide a piece of land into distinct portions, or to separate two continuous estates*] · Abfried(ig)ung *f*, Abschließung, Einfried(ig)ung, Einhegung, Umfried(ig)ung

enclosure commissioners, inclosure commissioners · Einhegungskommission *f*

enclosure (for the purpose of cultivation); approveamentum, appruvamentum [*Latin*]; approvement · Einfried(ig)ung *f* zum Kultivieren, Abfried(ig)ung zum Kultivieren, Einhegung zum Kultivieren, Abschließung zum Kultivieren, Umfried(ig)ung zum Kultivieren, Kultivierungseinhegung, Kultivierungsabfried(ig)ung, Kultivierungsabfried(ig)ung, Kultivierungsumfried(ig)ung, Kultivierungsabschließung

enclosure map, inclosure map [*A map prepared for the enclosure of open fields*] · Einfried(ig)ungskarte *f*, Einhegungskarte

enclosure plan, inclosure plan · Einfried(ig)ungsplan *m*

encounter group (US); face-to-face group (Brit.) · Intimgruppe *f*, Primärgruppe

to encroach, to intrude, to incroach, to trespass · beeinträchtigen, verletzen, stören, eindringen

to encroach by digging, to encroach by excavation, to incroach by digging, to incroach by excavation · abgraben, weggraben, entziehen durch graben

to encroach by fencing, to incroach by fencing · abhägen, abhagen [*Durch einen Hag Land wegnehmen*]

to encroach by water, to incroach by water · abschwemmen

to encroach furrows, to incroach furrows; to plough off, to plough away (Brit.); to plow off, to plow away (US) · abackern, abpflügen, abfurchen, wegackern [*Durch übergreifendes Pflügen ein Stück Land wegnehmen*]

encroaching, encroachment, adverse occupation, incroachment, incroaching, trespass, intrusion · Beeinträchtigung *f* (durch) Eindringen *n*, Verletzung durch Eindringen, Störung durch Eindringen, Besitzverletzung durch Eindringen, Besitzstörung durch Eindringen, Besitzbeeinträchtigung durch Eindringen

encroaching furrows, incroaching furrows, ploughing off, ploughing away (Brit.); plowing off, plowing away (US) · Abak-

encroachment — to endorse

kern n, Abpflügen, Abfurchen, Wegakkern

encroachment, incroachment [*Part of a building or an obstruction that intrudes on or invades a road, street, or sidewalk or trespasses on the property of another*] · Überbau m, Grenzüberbau

encroachment, encroaching, trespass, incroaching [*Invasion of private rights by persons or economic forces*] · Störung f, Beeinträchtigung

encroachment, incroachment [*An unlawful gaining upon the right or possession of another*] · Übergriff m

encroachment by balcony, incroachment by balcony · Balkonüberbau m

encroachment by digging, encroachment by excavation, incroachment by digging, incroachment by excavation · Abgrabung f, Weggrabung, Entziehung durch Graben

encroachment by water, incroachment by water · Abschwemmung f

encroachment revenue, incroachment revenue · (Grenz)Überbaurente f [*Rente zur Entschädigung für die Duldung eines Überbaues*]

to encroach (on to adjoining land) · überbauen [*Auf ein fremdes Grundstück baulich übergreifen*]

to encumber, to charge, to burden, to incumber, to load · belasten, dinglich belasten

encumbered, incumbered, loaded, burdened, charged, imperfect · belastet, dinglich belastet

encumbered by law, incumbered by law, charged by law, loaded by law, burdened by law · gesetzlich belastet

encumbered by mortgage(s), incumbered by mortgage(s), loaded by mortgage(s), burdened by mortgage(s), charged by mortgage(s) · hypothek(en)belastet

encumbered with lease(hold), incumbered with lease(hold), loaded with lease(hold), charged with lease(hold), burdened with lease(hold) · erbbaurechtbelastet, platzrechtbelastet

encumbering, loading, charging, burdening, incumbering · (dingliches) Belasten n

encumbrance, load, burden, incumbrance; incumbramentum [*Latin*]; charge [*A claim or lien attached to property as a mortgage*] · (dingliche) Belastung f, (dingliche) Last f

encumbrance of easement, incumbrance of easement, load of easement, burden of easement, charge of easement · Grunddienstbarkeitslast f

encumbrance of national debt, incumbrance of national debt, load of national debt, burden of national debt · Staatsschuldenlast f

encumbrance of the poor rates, incumbrance of the poor rates, charge of the poor rates, load of the poor rates, burden of the poor rates · Armenlast f

encumbrance on capital, incumbrance on capital, capital charge, capital burden, capital encumbrance, capital incumbrance, burden on capital, charge on capital · Kapitaldienst m, Kapitallast f

encumbrance on land(s), incumbrance on land(s), land charge, land(s) encumbrance, land(s) incumbrance [*Land charges are those rights and interests affecting land, e.g., estate contracts, restrictive covenants, general equitable charges and easements*] · Grund(stücks)belastung f, Grund(stücks)last f, Bodenlast, Landlast, Liegenschaftslast

encumbrance on personal property, incumbrance on personal property, load (up)on personal property, burden on personal property, charge on personal property · Fahrnislast f, Fahrhabelast, Mobiliarlast, Mobilienlast

encumbrance prohibition, incumbrance prohibition, burden prohibition, charge prohibition, load prohibition · Belastungsverbot n, Lastenverbot

encumbrancer, incumbrancer [*The holder of an incumbrance, e.g., a mortgage, on the estate of another*] · Belastende m

encumbrance rate, incumbrance rate, charge rate, load rate, burden rate · Belastungssatz m

encumbrances register → (land) encumbrances register

to end, to terminate, to lapse, to run out, to cease; to fall in (Brit.), to expire · ablaufen, verfristen

to end → to (come to an) end

end, head, front, butt(al), bout · Ende n, Grundstücksende

endangerment of building, endangerment of construction · Baugefährdung f

end building · Endgebäude n

end correction · Randbereinigung f, Extremwertkorrektur, Korrektur f eines Extremwertes [*Statistik*]

end-in-themself · absoluter Wert m, Ideal n

end-in-view · Mittelwert m [*Rechtsphilosophie*]

end of liability · Haftungsende n, Haftpflichtende, Haftbarkeitsende

to endorse, to indorse, to back · indossieren, girieren, begeben

to endorse, to indorse · angeben [*Anspruch in einer Klageladung*]

endorsee, indorsee; indossatarius [*Latin*] [*The party in whose favour a bill of exchange, promissory note or check is indorsed, the party, to whom it is transferred by the indorsement of the payee, or any previous holder*] · Indossat(ar) *m*, Giratar

endorsement, indorsement; indorsamentum, indossamentum [*The last term is used by continental writers*] [*Latin*] [*Something written on the back of a document, such as the claim indorsed on a writ*] · Rückseitenvermerk *m*

endorsement, indorsement; indorsamentum, indossamentum [*The last term is used by continental writers*] [*Latin*] [*A signature on the reverse side of a document*] · rückseitige Unterschrift *f*

endorsement; indorsamentum, indossamentum [*The last term is used by continental writers*] [*Latin*]; indorsement [*On a writ of summons*] · Aufschrift *f*

endorsement in blank, indorsement in blank, blank endorsement, blank indorsement · Blankoindossament *n*, Blankogiro *n*

endorsement of a bill (of exchange), indorsement of a bill (of exchange) · Wechselaufschrift *f*

endorsement of address, indorsement of address [*On a writ of summons*] · Adressenaufschrift *f*, Anschriftaufschrift

endorsement on service, indorsement on service [*Particulars of time, place and method of service endorsed on a writ within three days after personal or substituted service has been made*] · Zustellungsvermerk *m*, Vermerk des Zustellungstages

endorser, indorser · Indossant *m*, Indossent, Girant

endorsing, backing, indorsing · Indossieren *n*, Girieren, Begeben

to endow · stiften eines Dauerfonds

endowed estate, indowed estate, endowed property, indowed property · (Dauer)Stiftungsvermögen *n*, (Dauer)Stiftungsgut *n* [*Es steht einer bestimmten Institution dauernd zur Verfügung*]

endowed (incorporated collecting) charity · rechtsfähiges Sammelvermögen *n* [*Die Erträge des gesammelten Vermögens werden zur Erreichung des Stiftungszweckes verwendet*]

endowed school, foundation school · Stiftungsschule *f*

endowed with authority, placed in authority, authorized · bevollmächtigt

endowed with legal personality, legally capable, legally qualified, personable · gesetzlich fähig, gesetzlich geeignet, rechtsfähig

endowment [*The assignment or bestowment of dower to, or upon a woman*] · Witwenteilzuwendung *f*

endowment [*The act of settling a fund, or permanent pecuniary provision, for the maintenance of a public institution, charity, college, etc.*] · Stiften *n* eines Dauerfonds

endowment, indowment; dotatio [*Latin*] · Dotation *f*

endowment, indowment [*Property of any kind belonging in perpetuity to a charity, or property assured for the benefit of any person*] · (Dauer)Stiftung *f*

endowment fund · Dauerfonds *m* [*Er steht einer bestimmten Institution dauernd zur Verfügung*]

endowment (life) insurance [*A contract wherein the insurer agrees to pay a certain sum or annuity to the person whose life is insured if he lives a certain length of time, or to another person if the insured dies before this time*] · (Lebens)Versicherung *f* auf den Erlebensfall

endowment policy [*In life insurance. A policy which is payable when the insured reaches a given age, or upon his decease, if that occurs earlier*] · Rentenpolice *f*

enduring, continuing · fortsetzend

endware [*Lincolnshire*]; small hamlet · Kleinweiler *m*

enemy · Feind *m* [*Im Sinne des Wohnsitzkriteriums*]

enemy alien, alien enemi; hostile foreigner [*India*], alien enemy · Feindausländer *m*, feindlicher Ausländer

enemy estate, enemy property · Feindvermögen *n*, Feindgut *n*, Feindhabe *f*

enemy property, enemy estate · Feindvermögen *n*, Feindgut *n*, Feindhabe *f*

enemy subject · Feind *m* [*Im Sinne des Staatsangehörigkeitskriteriums*]

energy balance · Energiehaushalt *m*

energy conservation, conservation of energy · Energieeinsparung *f*

energy conservation act, energy conservation law, energy conservation statute · Energieeinsparungsgesetz *n*

energy conservation and control [*Powers exercised in regulating or prohibiting the production, supply, acquisition or use of crude liquid petroleum, natural gas, petroleum products, or other substances used for fuel, and electricity*] · Energieträgerbewirtschaftung *f*

energy conservation law, energy conservation statute, energy conservation act · Energieeinsparungsgesetz *n*

energy conserving equipment · energiesparende Ausstattung *f*, energiesparende Ausrüstung

energy-conserving measure · energiesparende Maßnahme *f*

energy industry · Energieindustrie *f*

energy resource · Energievorrat *m*

energy supply, power supply, electricity supply · Elektrizitätsversorgung *f*, Stromversorgung, Energieversorgung

to enfeoff, to bestow a fee, to bestow a fief, to bestow a feud; feoffare, infeodare, infeudare [*Latin*]; to invest [*old Scots law*]; to give possession of land(s), to give a seisin of land(s), to (give a) feud, to infeft, to infeoff · belehnen, feudal belehnen

enfeoffed to the use · eingewiesen für die (Be)Nutzung eines Dritten

(en)feoffment, infeftment; instrument of possession [*old Scots law*] [*The instrument or deed by which a person is invested with possession*] · Belehnungsurkunde *f*, Erbgutbelehnungsurkunde

(en)feoffment, infeftment, investiture, infeudation, infeodation; investitura, feof(f)amentum [*Latin*] · (feudale (Erbgut))Belehnung *f*, Verleihung (eines erblichen feudalen Leh(e)ns), Vergabe *f* (eines erblichen feudalen Leh(e)ns), Investitur *f*, Gewereübertragung, Übertragung der Gewere

(en)feoffment bill, infeftment bill, bill of (en)feoffment, bill of infeftment · Leh(e)n(s)brief *m*

(en)feoffment to the feoffer's will, infeftment to the feoffer's will · Übertragung *f* eigener Ländereien durch einen Leh(e)n(s)mann zu seinen Lebzeiten an einen Treuhänder

(en)feoffment to uses, infeftment to uses [*A feoffment of land(s) to one person to the use of another. In such case the feoffer was bound in conscience to hold the land(s) according to the use, and could himself derive no benefit. Sometime such feoffment was made to the use of the feoffer. The effect of such conveyance was entirely changed by the statute of uses*] · Belehnung *f* des wirksamen Eigentumanteils nach Parlamentsgesetz [*Spaltung des dinglichen Grund(stücks)rechts*]

to enforce · erzwingen, durchsetzen

enforceability · Durchsetzbarkeit *f*, Erzwingbarkeit

enforceable · durchsetzbar, erzwingbar

enforceable by (court) action, enforceable by (law)suit, enforceable by cause, enforceable by plea, actionable · einklagbar

(en)forced lease(hold), (en)forced tenancy, (en)forced demise, compulsory lease(hold), compulsory tenancy, compulsory demise · Zwangsnutzungsrecht *n*, Zwangspacht *f*

(en)forced letting (of rooms), compulsory letting (of rooms) · Zwangsvermietung *f* (von Räumen)

enforcement · Durchsetzung *f*, Erzwingung

enforcement judg(e)ment, judg(e)ment of enforcement · Durchsetzungsurteil *n*, Erzwingungsurteil, Exekutivurteil, Vollzugsurteil

enforcement of judg(e)ment(s) · Urteilsdurchsetzung *f*, Urteilserzwingung

enforcement of payment, collection, recovery [*amount*] · Beitreibung *f*, Eintreibung, Einziehung [*Betrag*]

enforcement procedure, procedure of enforcement · Durchsetzungsverfahren *n*, Erzwingungsverfahren

enforcement provision, provision of enforcement · Erzwingungsbestimmung *f*, Durchsetzungsbestimmung

enforcement punishment · Exekutivstrafe *f*, Vollzugsstrafe

to enforce payment, to collect, to obtain, to recover [*amount*] · beitreiben, eintreiben, einziehen [*Betrag*]

enforcing payment, collecting, obtaining, recovering · Beitreiben *n*, Eintreiben, Einziehen [*Betrag*]

enfranchise(ment) [*Conferring of the right to vote at an election*] · Wahlrechtverleihung *f*

to engage, to assure, to commit · zusagen

to engage · einstellen [*Arbeitnehmer*]

to engage in ligitation, to claim by action, to dispute by action, to litigate, to go to law, to carry on a (law)suit, to bring into ligitation [*Latin: litigare*] · prozessieren, einen Rechtsstreit austragen, einen Prozeß anhängig machen, rechtshängig werden lassen

engagement, assurance, commitment · Zusage *f* [*Bindende Verpflichtung für ein künftiges Verhalten*]

engagement · Einstellung *f* [*Arbeitnehmer*]

engagement conditions, conditions of engagement · Einstellungsbedingungen *fpl*

engagement to marry · Verlobung *f*

engineer → civil engineer

engineer · Ingenieur *m*, Ing.

engineer, Engineer · Bauleiter *m*, Bauleitung *f* [*des Bauherrn*]

engineer architect → architect engineer

engineer-architects, architect-engineers [*A firm offering professional services as architect and/or engineer*] · Architekt-Ingenieur-Gruppe *f*, Ingenieur-Architekt-Gruppe *f*

engineer contract → (civil) engineer contract

engineering → (civil) engineering

engineering activity → (civil) engineering activity

engineering administration → (civil) engineering administration

engineering agreement → (civil) engineering agreement

engineering approach · analytische Kostenplanung *f*

engineering board → (civil) engineering board

engineering claim → (civil) engineering claim

engineering code of practice → (civil) engineering code of practice

engineering condition → (civil) engineering condition

(engineering) construction, construction engineering, (civil) engineering construction [*It involves construction which is planned and designed by professional (civil) engineers. It is often divided into highway construction (= Straßenbau) and heavy construction (= Tiefbau)*] · Ingenieurbau *m*

(engineering) construction activity, construction engineering activity, (civil) engineering activity · Ingenieurbautätigkeit *f*

(engineering) construction administration, construction engineering administration, (civil) engineering administration · Ingenieurbauverwaltung *f*

(engineering) construction agreement, construction engineering agreement, (civil) engineering agreement [*It is a part of a construction contract*] · Ingenieurbauvertrag *m* [*Der Vertrag als Vertragsbestandteil; andere Vertragsbestandteile sind Zeichnungen, Angebot, Garantie usw.*]

(engineering) construction board, construction engineering board, (civil) engineering board · Ingenieurbauamt *n*

(engineering) construction code of practice, construction engineering code of practice, (civil) engineering code of practice · Ingenieurbaumerkblatt *n*

(engineering) construction condition, construction engineering condition, (civil) engineering condition · Ingenieurbaubedingung *f*

(engineering) construction contract, construction engineering contract, (civil) engineering contract · Ingenieurbauvertrag *m* [*Der Vertrag und alle Vertragsbestandteile zusammen*]

(engineering) construction contractor, construction engineering contractor, (civil) engineering contractor · Ingenieurbauunternehmer *m*

(engineering) construction cost(s), construction engineering cost(s), (civil) engineering cost(s) · Ingenieurbaukosten *f*

(engineering) construction cost(s) index, construction engineering cost(s) index, (civil) engineering cost(s) index · Ingenieurbau(kosten)index *m* [*Die Kennziffer für die Höhe der Ingenieurbaukosten, jeweils im Vergleich zu einer festgesetzten Basis auf Grund bestimmter Berechnungen aus der Praxis ermittelt*]

(engineering) construction department, construction engineering department, (civil) engineering department · Ingenieurbauabteilung *f*

(engineering) construction drawing, (engineering) construction plan, construction engineering drawing, construction engineering plan, (civil) engineering drawing, (civil) engineering plan · Ingenieurbauzeichnung *f*, Ingenieurbauplan *m*

(engineering) construction drawing, construction engineering drawing, (civil) engineering drawing · Ingenieurbauzeichnen *n*

(engineering) construction expert, construction engineering expert, (civil) engineering expert · Ingenieurbausachverständiger *m*

(engineering) construction expertise, construction engineering expertise, (civil) engineering expertise · Ingenieurbaugutachten *n*

(engineering) construction field, construction engineering sector, construction engineering field, (civil) engineering sector, (civil) engineering field, (engineering) construction sector · Ingenieurbausektor *m*

(engineering) construction financing, construction engineering financing, (civil) engineering financing · Ingenieurbaufinanzierung *f*

(engineering) construction geologist, construction engineering geologist, heavy construction geologist, (civil) engineering geologist · Tiefbaugeologe *m*, Bau(grund)geologe

(engineering) construction geology — engineering practice 360

(engineering) construction geology → (civil) engineering construction geology

(engineering) construction geology, construction engineering geology, (civil) engineering geology · Bau(grund)geologie *f*, Tiefbaugeologie

(engineering) construction industry, construction engineering industry, (civil) engineering industry · Ingenieurbauindustrie *f*

(engineering) construction legislation, (engineering) construction lawmaking, construction engineering legislation, construction engineering lawmaking, (civil) engineering legislation, (civil) engineering lawmaking · Ingenieurbaugesetzgebung *f*

(engineering) construction plan, construction engineering drawing, construction engineering plan, (civil) engineering drawing, (civil) engineering plan, (engineering) construction drawing · Ingenieurbauzeichnung *f*, Ingenieurbauplan *m*

(engineering) construction practice, construction engineering practice, (civil) engineering practice · Ingenieurbauwesen *n*

(engineering) construction price, construction engineering price, (civil) engineering price · Ingenieurbaupreis *m*

(engineering) construction provision, construction engineering provision, (civil) engineering provision · Ingenieurbaubestimmung *f*

(engineering) construction sector, (engineering) construction field, construction engineering sector, construction engineering field, (civil) engineering sector, (civil) engineering field · Ingenieurbausektor *m*

(engineering) construction sub-contract, construction engineering sub-contract, (civil) engineering sub-contract · Nachunternehmervertrag *m* im Ingenieurbau, Subunternehmervertrag im Ingenieurbau, Unterunternehmervertrag im Ingenieurbau; Unterakkordantenvertrag im Ingenieurbau [*Schweiz*]

(engineering) construction sub(contractor), construction engineering sub(contractor), (civil) engineering sub(contractor) · Ingenieurbaunachunternehmer *m*, Ingenieurbausubunternehmer, Ingenieurbauunterakkordant *m* [*Schweiz*]

(engineering) construction technique, construction engineering technique, (civil) engineering technique · Ingenieurbautechnik *f*, Ingenieurbaupraxis *f* [*als betriebstechnische Anwendung*]

(engineering) construction volume, construction engineering volume, (civil) engineering volume · Ingenieurbauvolumen *n*

(engineering) construction worker, construction engineering worker, (civil) engineering worker · Ingenieurbauarbeiter *m*

engineering contract → (civil) engineering contract

engineering contractor → (civil) engineering contractor

engineering cost(s) → (civil) engineering cost(s)

engineering cost(s) index → (civil) engineering cost(s) index

engineering department → (civil) engineering department

engineering document, technical document · technische Unterlage *f*

engineering drawing, technical drawing · technische Zeichnung *f*

engineering drawing → (civil) engineering drawing

engineering employe(e) · angestellter Ingenieur *m*

engineering expert → (civil) engineering expert

engineering expertise → (civil) engineering expertise

engineering field → (civil) engineering field

engineering financing → (civil) engineering financing

engineering force(s), technical personnel, technical staff, technical force(s), engineering personnel, engineering staff · technisches Personal *n*

engineering geologist → (civil) engineering geologist

engineering geology → (civil) engineering geology

engineering industry → (mechanical) engineering industry

engineering industry → (civil) engineering industry

engineering man hour · Technikerstunde *f*

engineering of consent, adjustment · Herbeiführung *f* von Übereinstimmungen

engineering operations → (civil) engineering operations

engineering personnel, engineering staff, engineering force(s), technical personnel, technical staff, technical force(s) · technisches Personal *n*

engineering practice → (civil) engineering practice

engineering press, technical press · technische Presse *f*

engineering price → (civil) engineering price

engineering provision → (civil) engineering provision

engineering sector → (civil) engineering sector

engineering staff, engineering force(s), technical personnel, technical staff, technical force(s), engineering personnel · technisches Personal *n*

engineering sub-contract → (civil) engineering sub-contract

engineering sub(contractor) → (civil) engineering sub(contractor)

engineering technique → (civil) engineering technique

engineering tender → (civil) engineering tender

engineering topography · Ingenieurtopographie *f*

engineering union, union of engineers · Ingenieurverband *m*

engineering volume → (civil) engineering volume

engineering worker → (civil) engineering worker

engineering work(s) → (civil) engineering operations

engineer in private practice → (civil) engineer in private practice

engineer's contract · Ingenieurverband *m*

engineer's geodesy · Ingenieurgeodäsie *f*, Ingenieurmessung *f*

English Law(s), Law(s) of England · englisches Recht *n*

to engross, to ingross · aufkaufen

to engross [*obsolete*]; to monopolize · monopolisieren

to engross [*To prepare the text of a document. An engrossment is a deed prior to its execution*] · ausarbeiten eines Dokument(en)textes

engrosser, ingrosser · Aufkäufer *m*

engrossing, ingrossing · Aufkaufen *n*

enheritance [*obsolete*]; haereditas [*Latin*]; inheritance [*"Inheritance" is also used in the old books in the sense of "hereditament"* = *Erbgut*] · Erbschaft *f*, Erbe *n*

enitia pars, dignitas primogeniti, aesnetia, eisnetia [*Latin*]; right of primogeniture, right of the eldest, right of the first born · (männliches) Erstgeburtsrecht *n*, Primogenitur *f*, Vorrecht des Erstgeborenen

to enjoy, to exercise a right · ausüben [*(subjektives) Recht*]

enjoying, exercising of a right · Ausüben *n* [*(subjektives) Recht*]

enjoying the usufruct; beneficient [*obsolete*]; beneficial [*Of or pertaining to the usufruct of property*] · nutznießend

enjoyment, exercise of a right [*Enjoyment is to a right what possession is to a corporeal thing, and it is therefore divisible, like possession, into simple, rightful, permissive, adverse, etc.*] · Ausübung *f* eines (subjektiven) Rechts, (subjektive) Rechtsausübung

enjoyment of air, exercise of the right to air · Ausübung *f* des (dinglichen) Rechtes am Luftraum

enjoyment of an easement · Ausübung *f* einer Grunddienstbarkeit

to enlarge · prolongieren, verlängern [*Frist*]

to enlarge, to extend · erweitern

to enlarge an estate · vergrößern eines (Besitz)Titels

enlarged, extended · erweitert

enlargement, addition, extension [*structure*] · Erweiterung *f* [*Bauwerk*]

enlargement area, extension area, enlargement territory, extension territory · Erweiterungsgebiet *n*

enlargement of (a) locality, extension of (a) locality · Ortserweiterung *f*

enlargement ordinance, extension ordinance · Erweiterungs(rechts)verordnung *f*

enlargement physical facility, extension physical facility, enlargement work, enlargement structure, extension work, extension structure · (bauliche) Erweiterungsanlage *f*, Erweiterungs(bau)werk *n*, Erweiterungsbau(anlage) *m, (f)*, Erweiterungsbaulichkeit *f*

enlargement plan, extension plan · Erweiterungsplan *m*

enlargement planner, extension planner · Erweiterungsplaner *m*

enlargement planning, extension planning · Erweiterungsplanung *f*

enlargement space, extension space · Erweiterungsraum *m*

enlargement structure, extension work, extension structure, enlargement physical facility, extension physical facility, enlargement work · (bauliche) Erweiterungsanlage *f*, Erweiterungs(bau)werk *n*, Erweiterungsbau(anlage) *m, (f)*, Erweiterungsbaulichkeit *f*

enlargement territory, extension territory, enlargement area, extension area · Erweiterungsgebiet *n*

enlargement work, enlargement structure, extension work, extension structure, enlargement physical facility, extension physical facility · (bauliche) Erweiterungsanlage *f*, Erweiterungs(bau)werk *n*, Erweiterungsbau(anlage) *m*, *(f)*, Erweiterungsbaulichkeit *f*

enlargement work(s), extension work(s) · Erweiterungsarbeit(en) *f (pl)*

enlarging, extending · Erweitern *n*

enlistment · Einberufung *f* [*zum Militärdienst*]

to ennoble · adeln

en parte application, application en parte · einseitiger Zwischenantrag *m*

to enquire, to make inquiries, to make enquiries, to inquire · erkundigen, sich erkundigen

enquiry, inquiry · Erkundigung *f*

enquiry, inquiry · Anfrage *f*

to enrich · bereichern

enrichment · Bereicherung *f*

enrichment law, law of enrichment · Bereicherungsrecht *n* [*BGB §§ 812 ff.*]

enrichment right, right to enrichment · Bereicherungsanspruch *m*, Bereicherungs(an)recht *n*

enrichment tax · Bereicherungssteuer *f*

enrolment [*Entering a copy of a document on an official record. Originally such records were kept in the shape of continuous rolls of parchment*] · Einfügen *n* einer Dokumentabschrift in ein amtliches Register

to enschedule, to list, to include in a list, to insert in a list · auflisten

ensuing year · Folgejahr *n*

to ensure, to follow after · nachfolgen

ensured risk, insured risk, insured hazard, ensured harzard · versichertes Risiko *n*, versichertes Wagnis *n*

to entail, to create an estate tail, to settle the succession to (real) property, to limit the succession to (real) property · beschränken, beschneiden [*Vererbung von Grundstücken*]

entail · gebundene (Land)Erbfolge(ordnung) *f*

entail; fidei-commissaria haereditas [*Latin*] [*A form of bequest requesting a transfer of property to be made by some one after the testator's death*] · Fideikommiß *n*, Majorat *n*, gebundene (Land)Erbfolge(ordnung), Erb(schafts)majorat, Erb(schafts)fideikommiß

entail deed, deed of entail · Fideikommißurkunde *f*, Majoratsurkunde

entailed, in tail · beschränkt, beschnitten [*Vererbung von Grundstücken*]

entailed estate, entailed interest, (estate in) tail, estate tail · gebundenes Gut *n* [*Gebundene Güter sind: Leh(e)n; (Familien)Stammgut; Familiengut des hohen Adels; Familienfideikommiß*]

entailed interest, (estate in) tail, estate tail, entailed estate · gebundenes Gut *n* [*Gebundene Güter sind: Leh(e)n; (Familien)Stammgut; Familiengut des hohen Adels; Familienfideikommiß*]

entailed (landed) property, fee tail estate, (landed) property in tail, (estate in) fee tail [*Estate limited to some particular class of heirs of the person to whom it is granted*] · beschränkter (Grund-)Besitz *m*, eingeschränkter (Grund-)Besitz, beschnittener (Grund)Besitz, begrenzter (Grund)Besitz, gebundener (Grund)Besitz, (Grund)Besitz(stand) *m* mit beschränkter Erbfolge(ordnung), (Grund)Besitz(stand) mit gebundener Erbfolge(ordnung)

entail law, law of entail · Erbrecht *n* für bestimmte Personen

entailment · Beschränkung *f* [*Vererbung von Grundstücken*]

to enter [*into a bond*] · ausstellen [*einer Schuldverschreibung*]

to enter [*inheritance; office*] · antreten [*Erbschaft; Amt*]

to (enter a) bid; to submit a (bid) proposal, to enter a (bid) proposal (US); to offer, to tender, to submit (a bid) · anbieten, submittieren, einreichen eines Angebots, abgeben eines Angebots

to enter a caveat, to lodge a caveat, to put in a caveat · Einspruch erheben

to enter an appearance · (sich auf einen Rechtsstreit) einlassen, protokollieren eines Rechtsstreites

entering, recording, registering · Eintragen *n*, Registrieren, Buchen

entering into a contract of mandate · Mandatseinholung *f*

entering into religion · Eintritt *m* in ein Kloster, Klostereintritt

to enter (on (the) land) · (Besitz) ergreifen, betreten [*Land*]

enterprise, undertaking · Betrieb *m*, Unternehmen *n*, Unternehmung *f*

enterprise contract, undertaking contract · Unternehmensvertrag *m*

enterprise financing, undertaking financing · Unternehmensfinanzierung *f*

enterprise value, undertaking value · Unternehmenswert *m*

enterprising, entrepreneurial · unternehmerisch

entertainment district · Vergnügungsviertel *n*

enticement advertising, advertising of enticement · Lockvogelwerbung *f*

entire, indivisible, unseverable, inseparable · ganz, unteilbar, untrennbar

entire aggregate of the community · Gesamtheit *f* der Bürger

entire contract, indivisible contract; lumpsum contract [*misnomer*] · Vertrag *m* auf unteilbare Leistung, Vertrag mit uneingeschränkter Vorleistungspflicht, unteilbarer (Leistungs)Vertrag, einheitlicher Vertrag

entire devotion · ungeteilte Interessenwahrnehmung *f* [*Pflicht des (Rechts)Anwaltes seinem Mandanten gegenüber*]

entirety · nichtteilbarer Besitz *m* ohne der Zustimmung aller Mitbesitzer

to entitle · berechtigen

entitled · berechtigt

entitled to a dwelling · wohnberechtigt

entitled to compensation · entschädigungsberechtigt

entitled to (court) action, entitled to (law)suit, entitled to plea, entitled to cause · klageberechtigt

entitled to performance, entitled to fulfilment, entitled to compliance, entitled to execution · ausführungsberechtigt, erfüllungsberechtigt, vollzugsberechtigt

entitled to reimbursement, entitled to payment, entitled to restitution, entitled to refunding, entitled to refundment, entitled to recovery · abgeltungsberechtigt, erstattungsberechtigt, ersetzungsberechtigt, vergütungsberechtigt

entitled to share · anteilberechtigt

entitled to take under the statute of descent and distribution, competent to inherit · erbberechtigt

entitled to usufruct · nießbrauchberechtigt, (frucht)genußberechtigt, nutzgewaltberechtigt, nutzungsberechtigt

entitlement to resid(enc)e, right to resid(enc)e · Aufenthaltsberechtigung *f*

entitling to compensation, compensable · entschädigungsfähig

entrance examination · Aufnahmeprüfung *f*

entrance fee, admission fee · Eintrittsgeld *n*

entrance (up)on an inheritance · Besitzergreifung *f* einer Erbschaft

entrepreneurial, enterprising · unternehmerisch

entrepreneurial hazard, entrepreneurial risk, contractor's risk, contractor's hazard · Unternehmerrisiko *n*, Unternehmerwagnis *n*

entrepreneurial skill · unternehmerische Fähigkeit *f*

entrepreneurship · Unternehmertum *n*

entrepreneur's rent, case of extra profit analogous to rent, rent of ability, profits partaking of the nature of rent, conjuncture-profit · Unternehmerpension *f*, Seltenheitsprämie *f*

entry · Grund(stücks)besitzergreifung *f*, Grund(stücks)(in)besitznahme

entry, registration, recordation, recording · Buchung *f*, (Buch)Eintrag(ung) *m*, *(f)*, Registrierung, Registereintrag(ung)

entry · Betreten *n*

entry, taking (in) possession · Besitzgreifen *n*, (In)Besitznehmen [*Grundstück*]

entry by interposition, abatement (of freehold); abatamentum [*Latin*] [*The unlawful entry and keeping possession of an estate by a stranger, after the death of the ancestor and before the heir or devisee takes possession*] · widerrechtliche Grund(stücks)(in)besitznahme *f*, widerrechtliche Grund(stücks)besitzergreifung *f*, widerrechtliche (Grund)Besitzergreifung, widerrechtliche (Grund)(In)Besitznahme

entry into possession [*The right of a legal mortgagee to enter into possession of the mortgaged property*] · Besitznahme *f*

entry made by a representative · (Grund(stücks))Besitzeinweisung *f*

entry of trial, trial entry · Eintrag(ung) *m*, *(f)* des Termins bei Gericht, Termineintrag(ung) bei Gericht, Eintrag(ung) des Verhandlungstermins

entry outwards · Zollausgangsdeklaration *f*

entry right, right of entry · Grund(stücks)besitzergreifungsanspruch *m*, Grund(stücks)besitzergreifungs(an)recht *n*, Grund(stücks)(in)besitznahme(an)recht, Grund(stücks)(in)besitznahmenanspruch, Recht der (In)Besitznahme, (In)Besitznahmerecht

enumerated · aufgezählt

enumerated population · erfaßte Bevölkerung *f*, gezählte Bevölkerung

enumeration principle · Enumerationsprinzip *n*, Enumerationsgrundsatz *m*

enumerator [*A person appointed to take a census*] · Zähler *m*

to enure, to operate, to come into existence, to come into operation, to come into being, to take effect, to become to have effect, to inure, to become operative · wirksam werden, in Kraft treten

environmental analysis, analysis of environment · Umweltanalyse *f*

environmental change · Umwelt(ver)änderung *f*

environmental choice · Umweltwahl *f*

environmental compatibility · Umweltverträglichkeit *f*

environmental condition · Umweltbedingung *f*

environmental constraint · Umweltzwang *m*

environmental control, pollution control, environmental protection · Umweltschutz *m*

environmental control agency, environmental protection agency · Umweltschutzdienststelle *f*

environmental control authority → environmental protection authority

environmental control board, environmental protection board, environmental prevention board, PCB, antipollution board, pollution control board, pollution prevention board · Umweltschutzamt *n*

environmental control law, environmental protection law · Umweltschutzrecht *n*

environmental control provision, environmental protection provision · Umweltschutzbestimmung *f*

environmental deficiency · Umweltschutzmangel *m*

environmental degradation · Umweltverschlechterung *f*

environmental design · Umweltentwurf *m*

environmental design research, EDR · Umweltentwurfsforschung *f*

environmental destruction · Umweltzerstörung *f*

environmental education act, environmental education law, environmental education statute · Umweltschutzerziehungsgesetz *n*

environmental education · Erziehung *f* im Umweltdenken

environmental engineering · Umwelttechnik *f*

environmental game · Umweltspiel *n*

environmental game simulation, environmental gaming simulation · Umwelt-(Plan)Spielsimulation *f*, Umwelt-Hybridspiel *n*

environmental geological atlas · geologisch-landeskundlicher Atlas *m*

environmental geometry, geometry of environment · Umweltgeometrie *f*

environmental hygiene · Umwelthygiene *f*

environmental impact · Umwelteinwirkung *f*

environmental improvement, improvement of environment · Umweltverbesserung *f*

environmental influence, influence of environment · Umwelteinfluß *m*

environmentalism · Umweltbewußtsein *n*

environmental issue · Umweltfrage *f*, Umweltproblem *n*

environmental law · Umweltrecht *n*

environmental lawmaking, environmental legislation · Umweltschutzgesetzgebung *f*

environmental loading · Umweltbelastung *f*

environmentally concerned citizen, environmentalist · Umweltschützer *m*

environmental perception · Umweltwahrnehmung *f*

environmental planning · Umweltplanung *f*

environmental planning research · Umweltplanungsforschung *f*

environmental policy, antipollution policy · Umweltpolitik *f*

(environmental) pollution · Verschmutzung *f*, Umweltverschmutzung

environmental prevention authority → environmental protection authority

environmental prevention board → environmental control board

environmental protection, environmental control, pollution control · Umweltschutz *m*

environmental protection agency, environmental control agency · Umweltschutzdienststelle *f*

environmental protection authority, environmental control authority, environmental prevention authority, pollution control authority, pollution prevention authority, antipollution authority · Umweltschutzbehörde *f*

environmental protection board → environmental control board

environmental protection law, environmental control law · Umweltschutzrecht *n*

environmental protection provision, environmental control provision · Umweltschutzbestimmung f

environmental psychology · Umweltpsychologie f

environmental quality · Umweltgüte f

environmental safety · Umweltsicherheit f

environmental setting · Umwelthintergrund m

environmental space · Umweltraum m

E. & O. E., errors and omissions excepted · Fehler m pl und Auslassungen f pl **ausgenommen**

epistola donationis, testamentum, carta donationis, cartula donationis [Latin] · (dispositive) Schenkungsurkunde f [Urkunde, in welcher ein Schenker erklärt die Schenkung vorzunehmen oder vorgenommen zu haben]

equal, of the same rank, co-ordinate · gleichgestellt, gleichrangig

equal education(al) opportunity · Bildungschancengleichheit f

equal housing opportunity, equal opportunity of housing · Wohnchancengleichheit f

equal importance · Gleichrang m [z. B. einer Hypothek]

equality · Gleichheit f

equality before law · Rechtsgleichheit f

equality law, law of equality · Gleichheitsrecht n

equality of sexes · Gleichberechtigung f von Mann und Frau, Gleichberechtigung der Geschlechter

equality of votes · Stimmengleichheit f

equality principle, principle of equal treatment, principle of equality, equal treatment principle · Gleichbehandlungsgrundsatz m, Gleichbehandlungsprinzip n, Gleichheits(grund)satz, Gleichheitsprinzip

equalization clause [Under such a clause a consideration may change in relation to the value of goods or services of a similar kind to those provided by the creditor] · Spannungsklausel f

Equalization of Burden Levies · LAG m, Lastenausgleich [Bundesrepublik Deutschland]

equal(ly), without preference; parie passu [French] · vorzugsfrei

equally divided court · Kollegialgericht n ohne Mehrheitsvotum

equal opportunity · Chancengleichheit f

equal opportunity of housing, equal housing opportunity · Wohnchancengleichheit f

equal protection of the laws · gleicher Rechtsschutz m, Gleichheit f vor dem Gesetz

equal size category · Gleichgrößenkategorie f

equal treatment · Gleichbehandlung f

equal treatment principle, equality principle, principle of equal treatment, principle of equality · Gleichbehandlungsgrundsatz m, Gleichbehandlungsprinzip n, Gleichheits(grund)satz, Gleichheitsprinzip

equated abstract of account · Staffelauszug m

equation form · Gleichungsform f

equation of growth, growth equation · Wachstumsgleichung f

equation of location, equation of site, site equation, location equation · Standortgleichung f

equation of site, site equation, location equation, equation of location · Standortgleichung f

equation of soil quality, soil quality equation · Bodengütegleichung f, Bonitätsgleichung, Bodenqualitätsgleichung

equation of value · Wertausgleich m

equestrian trail · Reitweg m

equidetectability curve, curve of equidetectability · Kurve f gleicher Schärfe [Statistik]

equilibrium of allocation, allocation equilibrium · Zuweisungsgleichgewicht n

equilibrium of site, equilibrium of location, location(al) equilibrium, site equilibrium · Standortgleichgewicht n

equilibrium of space, spatial equilibrium, space equilibrium · räumliches Gleichgewicht n, Raumgleichgewicht

equilibrium solution · Gleichgewichtslösung f

to equip, to furnish · ausrüsten, ausstatten

equipment [Fixed assets, such as furniture, that are not attached to real estate physically or legally] · Ausrüstung f, Ausstattung

equipment bond [USA. Bonds secured by equipment, which are issued by American airline, railroad and trucking companies] · Schuldverschreibung f durch Transportmittel des Anlagevermögens gesichert

equipment cost(s) report · Gerätekostenbericht m

equipment department → (construction) equipment department

**equipment hire, **equipment hiring, hire of equipment, hiring of equipment · (Bau)Gerätemieten *n*

equipment hire contract, contract for equipment hire · Baugerätemietvertrag *m*, (Geräte)Mietvertrag

equipment hiring, hire of equipment, hiring of equipment, equipment hire · (Bau)Gerätemieten *n*

equipment operating hour · Gerätelaufstunde *f*

equipment productivity · Geräteauslastung *f*

equipment rent · Gerätemiete *f*

equipment report · Gerätebericht *m*

equipping, furnishing · Ausstatten *n*, Ausrüsten

equitable, valid in equity [*In accordance with rules of equity*] · billigsrechtlich, billig, gültig nach Billigkeit(srecht)

equitable action → equitable cause

equitable assets · Billigkeitsvermögen *n*, Vermögen nach Billigkeit(srecht), Billigkeitsrechtvermögen

equitable assignment, equitable cession, equitable assignation · Abtretung *f* nach Billigkeit(srecht), Zession *f* nach Billigkeit(srecht), Billigkeitsabtretung, Billigkeitszession

equitable cause, (court) action of equity, cause of equity, (law)suit of equity, equitable plea, plea of equity, equitable (court) action, equitable (law)suit · Billigkeitsklage *f*, Billigkeitsrechtklage, Klage nach Billigkeit(srecht)

equitable cession, equitable assignation, equitable assignment · Abtretung *f* nach Billigkeit(srecht), Zession *f* nach Billigkeit(srecht), Billigkeitsabtretung, Billigkeitszession

equitable charge [*Die Benennung „equitable charge" ist nicht auf Grund(stücks)rechte beschränkt. Man versteht darunter auch alle Pfand- und Retentionsrechte des Billigkeitsrechts*] · Verpfändung *f* ohne Rechtstitelübertragung [*Grundstück*]

equitable charge by deposit of title deeds · Verpfändung *f* ohne Rechtstitelübertragung mit Grundstücksurkundenverwahrung durch den Gläubiger

equitable competition, fair competition, just competition · lauterer Wettbewerb *m*, uneigennütziger Wettbewerb

equitable condition, condition of equity · Billigkeits(recht)bedingung *f*

equitable construction, equitable interpretation · Auslegung *f* nach Billigkeit, Deutung *f* nach Billigkeit

equitable (court) action, equitable (law)suit, equitable cause, (court) action of equity, cause of equity, (law)suit of equity, equitable plea, plea of equity · 1Billigkeitsklage *f*, Billigkeitsrechtklage, Klage nach Billigkeit(srecht)

equitable debt · Billigkeitsschuld *f*

equitable decision, decision in equity, equity decision · Billigkeitsentscheid(ung) *m*, *(f)*

equitable discretion · billiges Ermessen *n*

equitable easement [*As opposed to a legal easement*] · Grunddienstbarkeit *f* nach Billigkeit(srecht)

equitable estate · bonitarischer Besitz *m*

equitable estate for life, equitable interest for life · benefiziarischer Eigentumsanteil *m* auf Lebenszeit, lebenslanger benefiziarischer Eigentumsanteil [*Grundstück*]

equitable estate tail, (estate in) equitable fee tail, equitable restricted fee · beschnittenes Leh(e)n *n* nach Billigkeit, beschränktes Leh(e)n nach Billigkeit, eingeschränktes Leh(e)n nach Billigkeit, begrenztes Leh(e)n nach Billigkeit, gebundenes Leh(e)n nach Billigkeit

equitable interest, equitable right [*A right originally recognized and enforced only in the courts of equity*] · (subjektives) Recht *n* nach Billigkeit, (subjektives) Billigkeitsrecht

equitable interest for life, equitable estate for life · benefiziarischer Eigentumsanteil *m* auf Lebenszeit, lebenslanger benefiziarischer Eigentumsanteil [*Grundstück*]

equitable interpretation, equitable construction · Auslegung *f* nach Billigkeit, Deutung *f* nach Billigkeit

equitable (law)suit, equitable cause, (court) action of equity, cause of equity, (law)suit of equity, equitable plea, plea of equity, equitable (court) action · Billigkeitsklage *f*, Billigkeitsrechtklage, Klage nach Billigkeit(srecht)

equitable liability · Billigkeitshaftung *f*, Billigkeitshaftpflicht *f*, Haftung nach Billigkeit(srecht), Haftpflicht nach Billigkeit(srecht), Billigkeitshaftbarkeit *f*, Haftbarkeit nach Billigkeit(srecht)

equitable lien · Billigkeits-Pfandrecht *n*, Billigkeits-Retentionsrecht, Billigkeits-(Zu)Rück(be)haltungsrecht, Billigkeits-Einbehaltungsrecht

equitable measure, measure of equity · Billigkeitsmaßnahme *f*, Maßnahme nach Billigkeit(srecht), Billigkeitsrechtmaßnahme

equitable mortgage [*A mortgage which transfers an equitable interest only, either because the mortgagor's interest is equitable, or because the conveyance or other mode of transfer is equitable*] ·

equitable mortgage creditor — equitable right of appointment

Verpfändung f die dem Gläubiger nur einen bonitarischen Besitz gibt, Verpfändung durch Deponierung der Urkunde über das Eigentum [*Grundstück*]

equitable mortgage creditor, equitable mortgagee · Hypothek(en)gläubiger m nach Billigkeit(srecht), Hypothekargläubiger nach Billigkeit(srecht), hypothekarischer Gläubiger nach Billigkeit(srecht)

equitable mortgagee, equitable mortgage creditor · Hypothek(en)gläubiger m nach Billigkeit(srecht), Hypothekargläubiger nach Billigkeit(srecht), hypothekarischer Gläubiger nach Billigkeit(srecht)

equitable obligation, obligation of equity · Billigkeitsverpflichtung f, Verpflichtung nach Billigkeit(srecht), Billigkeitsrechtverpflichtung

equitable owner, equitable proprietor, owner by equitable law, proprietor by equitable law [*As opposed to the "owner by (common) law" (also called "legal owner")*] · Eigentümer m im Innenverhältnis, Eigentümer nach Billigkeit(srecht), Eigentumssubjekt n im Innenverhältnis, Eigentumssubjekt nach Billigkeit(srecht), Eigner im Innenverhältnis, Eigner nach Billigkeit(srecht), wirtschaftlicher Eigner, wirtschaftlicher Eigentümer, wirtschaftliches Eigentumssubjekt, Billigkeitsrechteigentümer

equitable ownership (of property), equitable property, equitable proprietorship, ownership by equity law, property by equity law, proprietorship by equity law · Eigentum n nach Billigkeitsrecht

equitable personal property, personal equitable property, equitable personal estate, personal equitable estate, equitable personal chattel, personal equitable chattel · Fahrnis f nach Billigkeit(srecht), Fahrhabe f nach Billigkeit(srecht)

equitable plea, plea of equity, equitable (court) action, equitable (law)suit, equitable cause, (court) action of equity, cause of equity, (law)suit of equity · Billigkeitsklage f, Billigkeitsrechtklage, Klage nach Billigkeit(srecht)

equitable power, power given by equity · Billigkeitsermächtigung f, Ermächtigung nach Billigkeit(srecht)

equitable power of appointment, equitable right of appointment · Befugnis f an einem bestimmten Vermögen Treuhand zu erklären, Recht n an einem bestimmten Vermögen Treuhand zu erklären

equitable power of appointment, equitable right of appointment, equitable power of disposition, equitable right of disposition [*It allows the creation of an equitable interest only*] · billigkeitsrechtliche Verfügungsbefugnis f, billigkeitsrechtliche Bestimmungsbefugnis, billigkeitsrechtliches Verfügungsrecht n, billigkeitsrechtliches Bestimmungsrecht

equitable power of revocation, equitable right of revocation · Recht n an einem bestimmten Vermögen Treuhand zu widerrufen, Befugnis f an einem bestimmten Vermögen Treuhand zu widerrufen

equitable principle, equity principle, principle of equity · Billigkeitsgrundsatz m, Billigkeitsprinzip n, Grundsatz der Billigkeit, Prinzip der Billigkeit

equitable principle of separate estate, equitable principle of separate property · Billigkeitsgrundsatz m des freien Vermögens, Billigkeitsgrundsatz des getrennten Vermögens, Billigkeitsprinzip n des freien Vermögens, Billigkeitsprinzip des getrennten Vermögens, Billigkeitsgrundsatz des Sondervermögens, Billigkeitsgrundsatz des Vorbehaltgutes, Billigkeitsprinzip des Sondervermögens, Billigkeitsprinzip des Vorbehaltgutes

equitable property, equitable proprietorship, ownership by equity law, property by equity law, proprietorship by equity law, equitable ownership (of property) · Eigentum n nach Billigkeitsrecht

equitable proprietor, owner by equitable law, proprietor by equitable law, equitable owner [*As opposed to the "owner by (common) law" (also called "legal owner")*] · Eigentümer m im Innenverhältnis, Eigentümer nach Billigkeit(srecht), Eigentumssubjekt n im Innenverhältnis, Eigentumssubjekt nach Billigkeit(srecht), Eigner im Innenverhältnis, Eigner nach Billigkeit(srecht), wirtschaftlicher Eigner, wirtschaftlicher Eigentümer, wirtschaftliches Eigentumssubjekt, Billigkeitsrechteigentümer

equitable relation(ship), equity relation(ship) · Billigkeitsverhältnis n, Verhältnis nach Billigkeit(srecht)

equitable restricted fee, equitable estate tail, (estate in) equitable fee tail · beschnittenes Leh(e)n n nach Billigkeit, beschränktes Leh(e)n nach Billigkeit, eingeschränktes Leh(e)n nach Billigkeit, begrenztes Leh(e)n nach Billigkeit, gebundenes Leh(e)n nach Billigkeit

equitable right, equitable interest [*A right originally recognized and enforced only in the courts of equity*] · (subjektives) Recht n nach Billigkeit, (subjektives) Billigkeitsrecht

equitable right of appointment, equitable power of appointment · Befugnis f an einem bestimmten Vermögen Treuhand zu erklären, Recht n an einem bestimmten Vermögen Treuhand zu erklären

equitable right of appointment, equitable power of disposition, equitable right of disposition, equitable power of appointment [*It allows the creation of an equitable interest only*] · billigkeitsrechtliche Verfügungsbefugnis f, billigkeitsrecht-

equitable right of revocation — equivalency

liche Bestimmungsbefugnis, billigkeitsrechtliches Verfügungsrecht *n*, billigkeitsrechtliches Bestimmungsrecht

equitable right of revocation, equitable power of revocation · Recht *n* an einem bestimmten Vermögen Treuhand zu widerrufen, Befugnis *f* an einem bestimmten Vermögen Treuhand zu widerrufen

equitable right to possession of land(s) · Billigkeitsanspruch *m* auf Grund(stücks)besitz

equitable separate property, equitable separate estate · getrenntes Vermögen *n* nach Billigkeit(srecht), freies Vermögen nach Billigkeit(srecht), Sondervermögen nach Billigkeit(srecht), Vorbehaltgut *n* nach Billigkeit(srecht)

equitable suit → equitable (law)suit

equitable tenant for life · Leh(e)n(s)mann *m* auf Lebenszeit nach Billigkeit(srecht)

equitable waste [*Equitable waste is that which a prudent man would not do in the management of his own property. It is a peculiarly flagrant branch of voluntary waste, which the ordinary dispensation from waste will not excuse*] · unbillige Substanz(ver)änderung *f*

equitably [*In an equitable manner; according to the principles of equity*] · billigerweise

equity [*Value of real estate in excess of mortgaged indebtedness*] · hypothekarische Belastung *f* übersteigender Grundtückswert, Grundstückswert *m* minus Hypothekenverschuldung

equity · Kurswert *m* eines Unternehmens (Stückzahl der common shares × Kurs) unter Berücksichtigung der festen Kapitallasten [*amerikanische Bilanzkritik*]

equity · Billigkeit *f*

equity → law of equity

equity annuity (US) · (aktien)fondsgebundene Rentenversicherung *f*

equity (capital) · (gesamtes risikotragendes) Eigenkapital *n* [*Unternehmen*]

equity case, case in equity · Billigkeitsfall *m*

equity court, court of equity · Billigkeitsgericht *n*

equity decision, equitable decision, decision in equity · Billigkeitsentscheid(ung) *m, (f)*

equity dilution · Wertverschlechterung *f* durch Grund(stücks)belastung, Wertrückgang *m* durch Grund(stücks)belastung

equity draftsman · Anwalt *m* für Billigkeitsrecht, Rechtsanwalt für Billigkeitsrecht

equity estate → equitable (real) estate

equity financing · Beteiligungsfinanzierung *f*

equity fund (US) · Aktienfonds *m*

equity (general) jurisprudence, equity theoretical jurisprudence · allgemeine Billigkeitsrechttheorie *f*, Lehre *f* der allgemeinen Billigkeitsrechtfragen, rechtstheoretische Billigkeitsrechtwissenschaft *f*, Billigkeitsrechtlehre, Billigkeitsjurisprudenz *f*

equity is equality · Billigkeit *f* ist Gleichheit

equity jurisprudence [*misnomer*]; (law of) equity, equity law [*Law based upon discretion and conscience, derived from the old Court of Chancery*] · Billigkeitsrecht *n*, objektives Billigkeitsrecht

equity-linked assurance, equity-linked insurance · (aktien)fondsgebundene Versicherung *f*

equity of redemption, redemption equity · Rückkaufrecht *n* nach Billigkeit(srecht), Ablösungsrecht nach Billigkeit(srecht), Einlösungsrecht nach Billigkeit(srecht), Auslösungsrecht nach Billigkeit(srecht)

equity of redemption [*Mortgagor's right, after paying the debt and other cost(s), to redeem a mortgaged property if mortgage terms are not net*] · Hypothek(en)ablösungsrecht *n*

equity pleading, pleading in equity, proceeding equitable in nature · Billigkeitsverfahren *n*, Billigkeitsrechtverfahren

equity principle, principle of equity, equitable principle · Billigkeitsgrundsatz *m*, Billigkeitsprinzip *n*, Grundsatz der Billigkeit, Prinzip der Billigkeit

equity property → equitable (real) estate

equity receiver · gerichtlich bestellter Vermögensverwalter *m*

equity relation(ship), equitable relation(ship) · Billigkeitsverhältnis *n*, Verhältnis nach Billigkeit(srecht)

equity rule, rule of equity · Billigkeits(recht)regel *f*

equity saving, saving through investment in securities · Wertpapiersparen *n*

equity theoretical jurisprudence, equity (general) jurisprudence · allgemeine Billigkeitsrechttheorie *f*, Lehre *f* der allgemeinen Billigkeitsrechtfragen, rechtstheoretische Billigkeitsrechtwissenschaft *f*, Billigkeitsrechtlehre, Billigkeitsjurisprudenz *f*

equity versus efficiency · unerwünschte soziale Wirkungen *fpl* gegenüber gewünschten Produktionswirkungen

equivalency, equivalence · Gleichwertigkeit *f*, Gleichrangigkeit

equivalent reinstatement · gleichwertige Wiederherstellung *f*

equivalent scale · Vergleichsmaßstab *m*

equivalent value, countervalue · Gegenwert *m*

eradication of slums, demolition of slums, (slum) clearance, slum eradication, slum demolition, clearance of slums · Elendsviertelbeseitigung *f* [*1. Entkernung; 2. Totalsanierung*]

erection insurance · Montageversicherung *f*

erection of a structure, construction of a structure, building of a structure · Bauwerkerrichtung *f*, Bauwerkerstellung

erection of building(s), building erection · Gebäudeerrichtung *f*, Gebäudeerstellung

erection of dwelling units, production of housing units, erection of housing units, production of living units, erection of living units, production of dwelling units (US); production of tenements, erection of tenements, production of dwellings, erection of dwellings, production of housing, erection of housing, residential construction, residential building, hous(ebuild)ing, housing construction · Wohn(ungs)bau *m*, Wohnungserstellung *f*, Wohnungsproduktion *f*, Häuserbau, Hausbau, Mietwohn(ungs)bau, Mietwohnungserstellung, Mietwohnungsproduktion, Miethäuserbau, Miethausbau

erection of scaffold(ing)s · Gerüstaufbau *m*, Aufbau von Gerüsten

erf-land, alod, family land, heir land, ethel(-land) · Erbland *n*, erbliches Land

ergonomics, human factors engineering · Ergonomik *f*

erles, arrha(e), handmoney, handsel, earnest (money), arles [*A sum paid to bind a bargain*] · Angeld *n*, Kaufschilling *m*, Handgeld, D(a)rauf(gabe)geld, D(a)raufgabe *f*, Haftgeld, Mietstaler *m* [*Wenn Angeld gegeben wird, so gilt dies nach dem Gesetz als ein Zeichen, daß ein Vertrag abgeschlossen wurde*]

erosion control · Erosionsbekämpfung *f*

errant parking · Touristenparken *n*

erroneous estimation · Fehleinschätzung *f*

erroneous(ly), wrong, mistaken(ly), false(ly) · irrig(erweise), rechtsirrtümlich, irrtümlich(erweise), falsch

error · Fehler *m*

error band · Fehlerbereich *m* [*Statistik*]

error in description, descriptive error · Beschreibungsfehler *m*

error in law, legal error · Rechtsfehler *m*

error in quantity, quantity error · Mengenfehler *m*

error in statical analysis · Berechnungsfehler *m* [*Statik*]

error iuris [*Latin*]; mistake of law, mistake in law · Rechtsirrtum *m*

error of (ad)measurement, (ad)measurement error · Aufmaßfehler *m*

error of ascertainment, observation error, ascertainment error, error of observation · Beobachtungsfehler *m* [*Statistik*]

error of design, design error · Entwurfsfehler *m*

error of fact · Tatsachenfehler *m*

error of judg(e)ment, judg(e)ment error · Urteilsfehler *m*

error of judg(e)ment, judg(e)ment error · Beurteilungsfehler *m*

error of measurement → error of (ad)measurement

error of observation, error of ascertainment, observation error, ascertainment error · Beobachtungsfehler *m* [*Statistik*]

error of price, price error · Preisfehler *m*

errors and omissions excepted, E. & O. E. · Fehler *m pl* und Auslassungen *f pl* ausgenommen

error square · Fehlerquadrat *n*

error variance · Fehlervarianz *f*

ERTS, earth resources technology satellite · Erderkundungssatellit *m*

escalator clause · Indexklausel *f*

escape route, escape way · Rettungsweg, Fluchtweg *m* [*Treppe; Flur; Ausgang*]

to escheat · einziehen von Heimfallgut, heimfallen

escheat · Heimfall *m*

escheatable · heimfällig

escheat law, law of escheat · Heimfallrecht *n*, objektives Heimfallrecht

escheator · Verwalter *m* heimgefallener Güter, Verwalter heimgefallenen Gutes, Heimfallgutverwalter

escheator [*This obsolete office was terminated in England in 1887*] · Fiskal *m* für den Einzug heimgefallener Güter

escheat propter defectum sanguinis · Heimfall *m* wegen fehlender Erben

escheat right, right of escheat · Heimfallrecht *n*, Heimfallanrecht, Heimfallanspruch *m*

escheat title, title by escheat · Heimfall(rechts)titel *m*

escrow [*Deed delivered to a third person for the grantee, to be held by him until*

escrow account — estate act

the fulfilment or performance of some act or condition] · Urkunde *f* bei einem Dritten hinterlegt

escrow account, trust account, fiduciary account · Treuhandkonto *n*, Notar-Anderkonto

escrow deposit · Kundenzahlung *f* auf Anderkonto

escuage; scutagium [*Latin*]; scild-penig [*Saxon*]; scutage, shield-money · Schildgeld *n*, Ritterpferdsgeld

esplees · (Land)Pachtgelder *n pl*, Vollerträgnis *n* eines Landes

to essart; exartare [*Low Latin*]; to assart [*This, in the ancient forest laws of England, meant to stub up trees and bushes in a forest so that they could not grow again*] · ausholzen, ausreuten, roden

essartum [*Latin*] · Rodungstaxe *f*

essartum, assarting; disbocatio [*Latin*] [*Grubbing up trees and bushes from forest-land, so as to make it arable*] · Ausholzen *n*, Ausreuten *n*, Roden *n*

essayer · Goldschmied *m* für die Metallprobe [*(königliches) Schatzamt*]

essence of the contract · wesentlicher Vertragsbestandteil *m*

essential, material, substantial · wesentlich

essential ignorance, material ignorance · wesentliche Unkenntnis *f*

essentials · Dringliche *n*, Lebensnotwendige *n*

essential validity, intrinsic validity, essential validation, intrinsic validation · wesentliche Gültigkeit *f*

essential validity of contract, intrinsic validation of contract, essential validation of contract, intrinsic validity of contract · formeller Konsens *m*

to establish a foundation, to found · stiften einer Stiftung des öffentlichen Rechts

to establish by law, to enact (into law) · erheben zum Gesetz, (Gesetz) erlassen

established church, state church · Staatskirche *f*

established competition · verbürgter Wettbewerb *m*

established facts, ascertained facts, case facts, situation of facts, state of facts, actual situation · Sachlage *f*, Sachverhalt *m*, Tatbestand *m*

established investment · feststehende Investition *f*

established lines of judicial authority, rules established by the opinions of the courts, established opinions of the courts · ständige Rechtsprechung *f* der Gerichte

established opinions of the courts, established lines of judicial authority, rules established by the opinions of the courts · ständige Rechtsprechung *f* der Gerichte

establishing facts, ascertaining facts · Feststellung *f* des Lebenssachverhalts zum juristischen Sachverhalt, Fixierung des Lebenssachverhalts zum juristischen Sachverhalt [*In Deutschland im Urteil unter dem Titel ,,Tatbestand" zusammengefaßt*]

establishment · Betriebsstätte *f*

establishment of a trust, trust establishment · Treuhanderrichtung *f*

establishment right, right of establishment · Niederlassungsrecht *n*

estate [*Formerly, especially in feudal times, any of the three social classes having specific political powers: the first estate was the Lords Spiritual (clergy), the second estate the Lords Temporal (nobility), and the third estate the Commons (bourgeoisie)*] · Stand *m*

estate [*A condition or stage of life: as, he came to man's estate at the age of 21*] · Status *m*

estate [*The assets and liabilities of a dead person*] · Nachlaß *m*

estate, property [*The word "estate" is a word of the greatest extension, and comprehends every species of property, real and personal. It describes both the corpus and the extent of interest*] · Gut *n*, Vermögen *n*, Habe *f*

estate, landed property [*Piece of land containing a residence*] · Grundstück *n* mit Wohnhaus bebaut

estate · Besitzung *f*

estate, bankrupt's property, bankrupt's estate, active estate of a bankrupt, active property of a bankrupt [*The assets and liabilities of a bankrupt person*] · Konkursmasse *f*, Fallitmasse, Konkursvermögen *n*, Konkursgut *n*, Konkurshabe *f*

estate → (real) estate

estate, possession, possessing, enjoying of property, enjoyment of property; possessio [*Latin*] · Besitzen *n*, Besitz(stand) *m* [*Die tatsächliche, vom (Rechts)Titel unabhängige Innehabung einer Sache*]

estate acquisition → (real) property acquisition

estate acquisition right → land acquisition right

estate act → law of land (possession)

**estate administration, **asset administration, administration (of estate), administration of asset, administration of property, personal representation · erbrechtliche Verwaltung *f*, Nachlaßverwaltung, Erb(schafts)verwaltung

(estate) agent → ((real) estate) broker

estate appraisement → (real) property (e)valuation

estate appraiser → (real) property appraiser

estate barrister → conveyancing barrister

estate board → (real) estate board

(estate) broker → ((real) estate) broker

(estate) broking company → (land) broking company

estate builder → developer

estate builder's law → developer's law

estate business → (real) estate business

estate by elegit · Judikathypothek *f*

estate certifier → (real) property appraiser

estate company → (real) property company

estate compensation (court) action → (real) estate compensation (court) action

estate contract → (real) estate contract

estate contract → (real) property (purchase) contract

estate credit → (real) estate credit

estate credit bank → (real) estate credit bank

(estate) dealer → ((real) estate) broker

estate demise → (real) estate lease(hold)

estate depreciation fund → (real) estate depreciation fund

(estate) developer → developer

(estate) developer's law → developer's law

**estate duty, **death duty, inheritance duty [*England*]; inheritance tax, death tax [*USA*] [*The duty payable on the devolution of property at death. The one now commonly payable is estate duty. Legacy duty and succession duty were abolished in England by the Finance Act, 1949, ss. 27, 28*] · Erb(schafts)steuer *f*, Nachlaßsteuer, Vermächtnissteuer

estate (e)valuation → (real) property (e)valuation

estate exchange → (real) estate exchange

estate-farming · Landgutswirtschaft *f*

estate finance act → (real) estate finance act

estate financing → (real) estate financing

estate firm → (real) estate firm

estate for life → (real) estate for life

estate for the life of another → estate (in land) for the life of another

estate for years → term of years

estate fund → (real) estate fund

estate grant → land(s) grant

estate held by one person → (real) estate held by one person

estate held in trust → (real) estate held in trust

estate holder → (land) holder

**(estate in) base fee, **(estate in) qualified fee, (estate in) determinable fee, (estate in) fee simple defeasible, base estate [*An estate or fee which has a qualification subjoined thereto, and which must be determined wherever the qualification annexed to it is at an end*] · beschränkte (Grund)Besitzdauer *f*

**(estate in) (co)parcenary, **joint heirship, co-inheritance · Anteilerbschaft *f*, Anteilerbe *n*, (Bruch)Teilerbschaft, (Bruch)Teilerbe, Miterbschaft, Miterbe

**(estate in) determinable fee, **(estate in) fee simple defeasible, base estate, (estate in) base fee, (estate in) qualified fee [*An estate or fee which has a qualification subjoined thereto, and which must be determined wherever the qualification annexed to it is at an end*] · beschränkte (Grund)Besitzdauer *f*

**(estate in) dower, **estate of dower, tenancy in dower; doweyre, dowarie [*Norman French*] [*The life estate to which a married woman is entitled on death of her husband, intestate, or, in case she dissents from his will, one-third in value of all land(s) of which husband was beneficially seized in law or in fact, at any time during coverture*] · Witwengut *n*, Wittum(sgut) *n* der Ehefrau

**(estate in) equitable fee tail, **equitable restricted fee, equitable estate tail · beschnittenes Leh(e)n *n* nach Billigkeit, beschränktes Leh(e)n nach Billigkeit, eingeschränktes Leh(e)n nach Billigkeit, begrenztes Leh(e)n nach Billigkeit, gebundenes Leh(e)n nach Billigkeit

**estate in expectancy, **expectancy estate, expectant estate · (zu)künftige (Grund)Besitzdauer *f*, (zu)künftige Bodenbesitzdauer, (zu)künftige Landbesitzdauer

(estate in) fee simple → simple fee

(estate in) fee simple (absolute) (in possession) → ((freehold) estate in) fee simple (absolute in possession)

(estate in) fee simple defeasible — (estate in) tail female

(estate in) fee simple defeasible, base estate, (estate in) base fee, (estate in) qualified fee, (estate in) determinable fee [*An estate or fee which has a qualification subjoined thereto, and which must be determined wherever the qualification annexed to it is at an end*] · beschränkte (Grund)Besitzdauer *f*

(estate in) fee simple (de)terminable → ((real) estate in) fee simple determinable

(estate in) fee simple on condition subsequent → ((real) estate in) fee simple on condition subsequent

(estate in) fee tail [*A freehold estate in which there is a fixed line of inheritable issue of the body of the grantee or devisee, and in which the regular and general succession of heirs at law is cut off*] · beschränkt vererblicher Grundbesitz *m*, eingeschränkt vererblicher Grundbesitz, begrenzt vererblicher Grundbesitz

(estate in) fee tail → entailed (land(ed)) property

(estate in) fee tail, restricted fee, estate tail; feudum talliatum, feodum talliatum [*Latin*] · beschnittenes Leh(e)n *n*, eingeschränktes Leh(e)n, begrenztes Leh(e)n, beschränktes Leh(e)n, gebundenes Leh(e)n, Leh(e)n mit gebundener Erbfolge(ordnung), Leh(e)n mit beschränkter Erbfolge(ordnung), Stammgut *n*

estate (in land) for life, freehold, life (land(ed)) estate · lebenslanges Bodenbesitzrecht *n*, lebenslanges Landbesitzrecht, lebenslanges Grund(stücks)- besitzrecht

estate (in land) for life, possessory interest (in land) for life, life estate (in property), life estate in land · Landbesitzrecht *n* auf Lebenszeit des Verkäufers, Bodenbesitzrecht auf Lebenszeit des Verkäufers, Besitzrecht auf Lebenszeit des Landverkäufers, Besitzrecht auf Lebenszeit des Bodenverkäufers

estate (in land) for the life of another, estate (in land) pur auter vie [*More correctly, but less commonly, "pur autre vie"*] · (Land)Besitzrecht *n* auf Lebenszeit eines Dritten, (Land)Besitzrecht auf Lebenszeit einer dritten Person, (Land)Besitzrecht für die Dauer eines anderen Lebens

estate in land(s), immov(e)able estate, fixed estate, landholding, land(ed) property, tenancy of land(s)); immov(e)ables [*International Private Law*], (real) estate, (real) property, realty [*Estates in land(s) are divided into (a) freehold estates and (b) estates less than freehold*] · Bodenbesitz(stand) *m*, Grund(stücks)besitz(stand), Landbesitz(stand), Immobilienbesitz(stand), Immobiliarbesitz(stand), Liegenschaft (en) *f (pl)*, Immobilie(n) *f (pl)*, (unbeweglicher) Besitz(stand), liegendes Gut *n*, ungereides Gut

estate in land(s) for life → (real) estate for life

(estate in) legal fee tail, legal restricted fee, legal estate tail, common law fee tail, common law estate tail, common law restricted fee · beschnittenes Leh(e)n *n* nach gemeinem Recht, eingeschränktes Leh(e)n nach gemeinem Recht, begrenztes Leh(e)n nach gemeinem Recht, beschränktes Leh(e)n nach gemeinem Recht, gebundenes Leh(e)n nach gemeinem Recht

estate in parcenary → (estate in) (co)parcenary

estate in possession, possessory estate · dinglicher Besitz *m*

estate in property → (real) property

(estate in) qualified fee, (estate in) determinable fee, (estate in) fee simple defeasible, base estate, (estate in) base fee [*An estate or fee which has a qualification subjoined thereto, and which must be determined wherever the qualification annexed to it is at an end*] · beschränkte (Grund)Besitzdauer *f*

estate in (real) property → (real) property

estate in (real) property for life → (real) property for life

(estate in) realty → (real) property

(estate in) realty for life → (real) property for life

estate in remainder → remainder (land(ed)) estate

estate in reversion, reversionary estate, reversionary right, right of reversion, reversion of interest, right of reverter [*Residue of an estate left in the grantor, to commence in possession after the termination of some particular estate granted by him. In a lease the lessor has the estate in reversion after the lease is terminated*] · Rückfallrecht *n*

estate in severalty → (real) estate in severalty

estate insurance → (real) estate insurance

(estate in) tail, estate tail, entailed estate, entailed interest · gebundenes Gut *n* [*Gebundene Güter sind: Leh(e)n; (Familien)Stammgut; Familiengut des hohen Adels; Familienfideikommiß*]

(estate in) tail female · Besitzrecht *n* vererbbar auf weibliche eheliche Nachkommen, Grundbesitzrecht vererbbar auf weibliche eheliche Nachkommen, Bodenbesitzrecht vererbbar auf weibliche eheliche Nachkommen, Landbesitzrecht vererbbar auf weibliche eheliche Nachkommen

(estate in) tail general · Besitzrecht n vererbbar auf sämtliche eheliche Nachkommen, Grundbesitzrecht vererbbar auf sämtliche eheliche Nachkommen, Bodenbesitzrecht vererbbar auf sämtliche eheliche Nachkommen, Landbesitzrecht vererbbar auf sämtliche eheliche Nachkommen

(estate in) tail male · Erbmannleh(e)n n

(estate in) tail special · (Boden)Besitzrecht n vererbbar auf eheliche Nachkommen aus einer bestimmten Ehe des Leh(e)nsnehmers, Landbesitzrecht vererbbar auf eheliche Nachkommen aus einer bestimmten Ehe des Leh(e)n(s)nehmers, Grund(stücks)besitzrecht vererbbar auf eheliche Nachkommen aus einer bestimmten Ehe des Leh(e)n(s)nehmers

estate inventory → (real) estate inventory

estate investment → (real) estate investment

estate investment trust → land(s) investment trust

estate law → law of land (possession)

estate law → property law

estate lease (agreement) → (real) estate lease (agreement)

estate lease(hold) → (real) estate lease(hold)

estate leasing → (real) estate leasing

estate left, left estate · Hinterlassenschaft f

estate lessee → (land) holder

estate less than freehold, lease(hold), tenure, leasehold estate, demise, tenancy; demissio, dimissio [*Latin*]; assedation, tack [*Scots law*] [*Holding of real estate under a lease. Such an estate continues for a fixed or determinable period of time but not for a lifetime. It is a conveyance of land whereby the owner of landed property, called the lessor, grants the possession and use of his landed property to another party, called the lessee, in consideration of a sum of money, called the rent*] · Bodenpacht f, Landpacht, Bodennutzungsrechtvergabe f, Landnutzungsrechtvergabe, Bodenverpachtung f, Landverpachtung, (Boden)Nutzungsrecht

estate lien → (real) estate lien

estate limitation, limitation of an estate · Besitzrechtbegrenzung f

estate limitation act → (real) property limitation act

estate liquidated damages (court) action → (real) estate compensation (court) action

(estate) lot holder · Parzellant m

(estate) lot ownership (of property), (estate) lot proprietorship, (estate) lot (general) property · Parzelleneigentum n, Flurstückseigentum, Katastergrundstückseigentum, Katasterparzelleneigentum, Kartengrundstückseigentum

estate management → (real) estate management

estate management agent → (real) estate management agent

estate management plan → (real) estate management plan

estate manager → (real) estate manager

estate market → (real) estate market

estate mortgage → (real) estate mortgage

estate mortgage creditor → (real) estate mortgagee

estate mortgagee → (real) estate mortgagee

estate not of inheritance · nicht (ver)erbliches Leh(e)n n, unvererbliches Leh(e)n

estate occupier → (land) holder

estate of dower → (estate in) dower

estate of freehold → simple fee

estate of inheritance → fee of inheritance

estate of joint tenancy → (real) estate of joint tenancy

estate of noble kind → (feudal) estate of noble kind

estate owner → (real) property owner

estate policy → (real) estate policy

estate possessor → (real) estate possessor

estate practice → (real) estate practice

estate promoter → developer

estate promoter's law → developer's law

estate proprietor → (real) property owner

estate pur autre vie → estate (in land) for the life of mother

estate purchase → (real) estate purchase

estate (purchase) contract → (real) property (purchase) contract

estate sale → (real) estate sale

estate speculation → (real) estate speculation

estate speculator → (real) estate speculator

estate statute → law of land (possession)

estate surface → surface of (real) estate

estate syndicate → (real) estate syndicate

estate tail, entailed estate, entailed interest, (estate in) tail · gebundenes Gut *n* [*Gebundene Güter sind: Leh(e)n; (Familien)Stammgut; Familiengut des hohen Adels; Familienfideikommiß*]

estate tail → (estate in) fee tail

estate tax → (real) estate tax

estate taxation, taxation of estate · Nachlaßbesteuerung *f* [*unverteilte Erbmasse*]

estate tenancy → (real) estate lease(hold)

estate tenant → (land) holder

estate title → (real) estate title

estate transaction judg(e)ment → (real) estate transaction judg(e)ment

estate transfer cost(s) → (real) estate transfer cost(s)

estate transfer permission → land transfer permission

estate transfer tax → (real) estate transfer tax

estate usufruct, usufruct of estate, usufruct of property, property usufruct · Nießbrauch *m* an einem Vermögen, Nießbrauch an einem Gut, (Frucht)Genuß *m* an einem Vermögen, (Frucht)Genuß an einem Gut, Nutzgewalt *f* an einem Gut, Nutzgewalt an einem Vermögen

estate usufruct → (real) estate usufruct

estate valuation → (real) property (e)valuation

estate village [*A village developed by a landowner, often flanking the gates to his mansion house*] · Guts(herren)dorf *n*

esthetical disturbance → (a)esthetical disturbance

estimable · (ab)schätzbar, überschlagbar, (vor)anschlagbar

to estimate · (ab)schätzen, überschlagen

estimated (management) fee, (management) fee based on the estimated cost of the work · geschätzter Zuschlag *m*, überschlägiger Zuschlag [*Selbstkostenerstattungsvertrag*]

estimated price, appraisal, appraised price · (Ab)Schätzungspreis *m*

estimated quantity, provisional quantity · (ab)geschätzte Menge *f*, überschlägige Menge, Massenansatz *m*, Mengenansatz

estimated regression value · Regressionsschätzwert *m*

estimated sum · (ab)geschätzte Summe *f*, überschlägige Summe, Schätzungssumme

estimated value, appraisal value · (ab)geschätzter Wert *m*, überschlägiger Wert, (Ab)Schätzungswert

estimate method, estimating method · (Ab)Schätzungsmethode *f*

estimate of cost(s), cost(s) estimate · Kostenvoranschlag *m* [*Er ist die Vorstufe für einen Kostenanschlag*]

estimate proposal [*Determination of probable construction cost(s) prepared by the contractor as a basis for his proposal*] · Voranschlag *m*

estimating · (Ab)Schätzen *n*, Überschlagen

estimating (construction) cost(s), (construction) cost(s) estimating, pricing (construction work) · (Bau)Kostenkalkulation *f*

estimating equation · Schätzgleichung *f* [*Statistik*]

estimating method, estimate method · (Ab)Schätzungsmethode *f*

estimating sheet, calculation sheet, bidding sheet, tendering sheet · Angebotsbogen *m*, Kalkulationsbogen

estimation · (Ab)Schätzung *f*, (Vor)Anschlag *m*, Überschlag

estimation (of cost(s)), cost(s) estimation · (Ab)Schätzung *f*, Kosten(ab)schätzung, (Kosten)Überschlag *m* [*Überschlägige Ermitt(e)lung der Kosten*]

estimator, calculator, computer, reckoner [*A person who calculates*] · Kalkulator *m*

estimator · Schätzfunktion *f* [*Statistik*]

to estop · verhindern eine vorher behauptete Tatsache zu leugnen

to estop · klagehindernd einwenden

estoppel [*A rule of evidence whereby a party is precluded from denying the existance or non-existence of some state of facts which he has previously asserted*] · Leugnungsverhinderung *f* [*Eine Person, die eine andere absichtlich veranlaßt hat eine Tatsache als bestehend anzunehmen und danach zu handeln, kann in irgendeinem Rechtsstreit mit dieser anderen Person nicht das Vorhandensein oder Nichtvorhandensein der betreffenden Tatsache leugnen*]

estoppel by record · Einrede *f* der rechtskräftig entschiedenen Sache

estoppel certificate [*Certificate that shows the unpaid principal sum of a mortgage and the interest thereon, if the principal or interest notes are not produced or of the seller asserts that the amount due under the mortgage, that the purchaser is to assume, is less* than *shown on record*] · Valutabescheinigung f

estover, profit (à prendre) of estover, bot(e), boot, bota, estouvier [*The right to take wood from the land of another as hay-bote, house-bote or ploughbote*] · Holzzubuße, Holzentnahme f

estray, wandering cattle, cattle that has strayed away · herrenloses Rindvieh n, verlaufenes Rindvieh, eingeschüttetes Rindvieh

estray, animal that has strayed away, wandering beast [*Any beast, not wild, found within any lordship, and not owned by any man*] · herrenloses Tier n, verlaufenes Tier

to estrepe, to strip, to despoil, to lay waste, to devastate [*To commit waste upon a real estate, as by cutting down trees, removing buildings, etc. To injure the value of a reversionary interest by stripping the (real) estate*] · verschlechtern, verwüsten, mißbrauchen, über(be)nutzen, vernachlässigen

estrepement, devastation [*real estate*] · Vernachlässigung f (der Instandhaltung), Verschlechterung, Verwüstung, technische Wertminderung, Depravierung, Deteriorierung, Über(be)nutzung

estreping, despoiling, devastating, stripping, laying waste [*Committing waste upon a real estate*] · Verwüsten n, Mißbrauchen, Über(be)nutzen, Verschlechtern, Vernachlässigen (der Instandhaltung), Deteriorieren, Depravieren

ethel(-land), erf-land, alod, family land, heir land · Erbland n, erbliches Land

ethical jurisprudence · überpositivistische Rechtslehre f [*Sie beschränkt sich auf das Recht als solches*]

ethnic minority · Volksgruppe f

etiquette (Brit); canon of ethics, ethical rules, disciplinary rules (US) [*The forms established by convention or prescribed by social arbiters for behavio(u)r in polite society*] · Standesrecht n

European Court (Brit.); ECJ (US) · EUGH m, Europäischer Gerichtshof

Europeanization · Europäisierung f

European "snake" · europäische Währungsschlange f, europäischer Währungsverbund m

to evacuate, to vacate [*premises; dwelling; occupied country*] · freigeben, räumen, freimachen

evacuation · Räumung f

evacuation date · Räumungstermin m

evacuation judg(e)ment · Räumungsurteil n

evacuation of (a) dwelling unit (US); evacuation of (a) dwelling · Wohnungsräumung f

evacuation period, period of evacuation · Räumungsfrist f

evaluative council, evaluative panel, (e)valuation council, (e)valuation panel, appraisal council, appraisal panel, appraisement council, appraisement panel · (Ab)Schätzungsbeirat m, Bewertungsbeirat, Taxierungsbeirat, Wertermitt(e)lungsbeirat

to evaluate, to value, to appraise [*To estimate the value or amount of; to determine the worth of*] · (ab)schätzen, (be)werten, taxieren, ermitteln eines Wertes

(e)valuating, appraising [*The action of setting a price or value on*] · (Be)Werten n, (Ab)Schätzen, Taxieren, Ermitteln eines Wertes

(e)valuation [*The amount of estimated value*] · Bewertungsbetrag m, Taxierungsbetrag, Wertermitt(e)lungsbetrag

(e)valuation, val., appraisal (of value), appraisement (of value), assessment (of value) [*The determined or estimated value or price*] · (Ab)Schätzung f, Taxierung, Wertermitt(e)lung f, Bewertung

(e)valuation basis, appraisal basis, appraisement basis · Bewertungsgrundlage f, Wertermitt(e)lungsgrundlage

(e)valuation clause, appraisal clause, appraisement clause, evaluative clause, weighting clause · (Ab)Schätzungsklausel f, Bewertungsklausel, Taxierungsklausel, Wertermitt(e)lungsklausel

(e)valuation council, (e)valuation panel, appraisal council, appraisal panel, appraisement council, appraisement panel, evaluative council, evaluative panel · (Ab)Schätzungsbeirat m, Bewertungsbeirat, Taxierungsbeirat, Wertermitt(e)lungsbeirat

(e)valuation cut-off-date, (e)valuation key-day, appointed day of (e)valuation, effective date of appraisal, cut-off date of appraisal, appointed day of appraisal, key-day of appraisal · Bewertungsstichtag m, Wertermitt(e)lungsstichtag, Taxierungsstichtag, (Ab)Schätzungsstichtag

(e)valuation factor → factor of (e)valuation

(e)valuation for condemnation purposes (US); (e)valuation for expropriation purposes · Enteignungstaxe f [*Grund(stücks)wertfeststellung*]

(e)valuation for court purposes · gerichtliche Taxe f [*Grund(stücks)wertfeststellung*]

(e)valuation for expropriation purposes; (e)valuation for condemnation purposes (US) · Enteignungstaxe f [*Grund(stücks)wertfeststellung*]

(e)valuation for private purposes — event of nature

(e)valuation for private purposes · Privattaxe f [Grund(stücks)wertfeststellung]

(e)valuation guide lines, appraisal guide lines, appraisement guide lines, evaluative guide lines, weighting guide lines · (Ab)Schätzungsrichtlinien f pl, Wertermitt(e)lungsrichtlinien, Bewertungsrichtlinien, Taxierungsrichtlinien

(e)valuation key-day, appointed day of (e)valuation, effective date of appraisal, cut-off date of appraisal, appointed day of appraisal, key-day of appraisal, (e)valuation cut-off-date · Bewertungsstichtag m, Wertermitt(e)lungsstichtag, Taxierungsstichtag, (Ab)Schätzungsstichtag

(e)valuation method, appraisal method, appraisement method · Bewertungsverfahren n, (Ab)Schätzungsverfahren, Wertermitt(e)lungsverfahren, Taxierungsverfahren

(e)valuation of (building) (land) area, appraisement of (building) land, (e)valuation of (building) land, appraisal of (building) land, appraisal of (building) (land) area, appraisement of (building) (land) area · (Bau)Bodenbewertung f, (Bau)Landbewertung, (Bau)Flächenbewertung, (Bau)Flächen(ab)schätzung, (Bau)Bodenabschätzung, (Bau)Land(ab)schätzung

(e)valuation of estate → (real) property (e)valuation

(e)valuation officer, (e)valuation official, appraisal officer, appraisal official, appraisement officer, appraisement official · Schätzungsbeamte m

(e)valuation of land(s) → (real) property (e)valuation

(e)valuation of land(s) and houses and buildings · Grundstücks- und Gebäude(ab)schätzung f

(e)valuation of property → (real) property (e)valuation

(e)valuation of (real) estate → (real) property (e)valuation

(e)valuation of (real) property → (real) property (e)valuation

(e)valuation of tenders, (e)valuation of offers, (e)valuation of bids; (e)valuation of (bid) proposals (US) · Angebotsauswertung f, Auswertung von Angeboten

(e)valuation of urban land(s) and urban houses and urban buildings, appraisal of urban land(s) and urban houses and urban buildings · städtische Grundstücks- und Gebäude(ab)schätzung f

(e)valuation ordinance, appraisal ordinance, weighting ordinance, appraisement ordinance · Bewertungsverordnung f, (Ab)Schätzungsverordnung, Taxierungsverordnung, Wertermitt(e)lungsverordnung

(e)valuation panel → (e)valuation council

(e)valuation planning → evaluative planning

(e)valuation prescription, appraisal prescription, appraisement prescription, evaluative prescription, weighting prescription, weighting regulation, appraisal regulation, (e)valuation regulation, appraisement regulation, evaluative regulation · (Ab)Schätzungsvorschrift f, Bewertungsvorschrift, Wertermitt(e)lungsvorschrift, Taxierungsvorschrift

(e)valuation regulation, appraisement regulation, evaluative regulation, (e)valuation prescription, appraisal prescription, appraisement prescription, evaluative prescription, weighting prescription, weighting regulation, appraisal regulation · (Ab)Schätzungsvorschrift f, Bewertungsvorschrift, Wertermitt(e)lungsvorschrift, Taxierungsvorschrift

(e)valuation scheme, appraisal scheme, appraisement scheme · Schätzungsrahmen m, Abschätzungsrahmen, Bewertungsrahmen, Taxierungsrahmen, Wertermitt(e)lungsrahmen

(e)valuation theory, theory of appraisal, theory of appraisement, theory of (e)valuation, appraisal theory, appraisement theory · Bewertungstheorie f, Wertermitt(e)lungstheorie, Taxierungstheorie, (Ab)Schätzungstheorie

evaluative planning, appraisal planning, appraisement planning, (e)valuation planning · Bewertungsplanung f, Wertermitt(e)lungsplanung, Taxierungsplanung, (Ab)Schätzungsplanung

evaluative prescription, weighting prescription, weighting regulation, appraisal regulation, (e)valuation regulation, appraisement regulation, evaluative regulation, (e)valuation prescription, appraisal prescription, appraisement prescription · (Ab)Schätzungsvorschrift f, Bewertungsvorschrift, Wertermitt(e)lungsvorschrift, Taxierungsvorschrift

evasion [A subtle endeavo(u)ring to escape the law] · Umgehen n, Ausweichen

evasive answer [One which consists in refusing either to admit or deny a matter as to which the defendant is necessarily presumed to have knowledge] · ausweichende Klageverneinung f

evening institute, evening school, night school · Abendschule f

event, happening · Ereignis n [Es tritt unabhängig vom Willen ein]

event of nature, natural event · Naturereignis n

to evict — examinable

to evict, to dispossess by process of law, to dispossess by legal process, to legally oust from the land [*To recover (real) property through court judgment or superior claim*] · entziehen, entheben, aberkennen [*Grundbesitz*]

to evict, to dispossess, to oust · widerrechtlich entheben, widerrechtlich entziehen, widerrechtlich aberkennen [*Grundbesitz*]

to evict a tenant from his farm, to dispossess, to turn a tenant out of his farm · abmei(g)ern

evictee, expellee · Vertriebene *m*

evicting a tenant from his farm, dispossession, expulsion from a farm, distraint, turning a tenant out of his farm · Abmei(g)erung *f* [*In den Zeiten der feudalen Grund- und Gutsherrschaft das Recht des Grundherren, einem Bauern die Bauernstelle wegen Pflichtverletzung zu entziehen*]

eviction, dispossession, ouster · widerrechtliche Entziehung *f*, widerrechtliche Enthebung, widerrechtliche Aberkennung

eviction → dispossession by legal process

to evict lawfully · gesetzlich ausweisen [*Mieter aus einer Wohnung*]

evidence, proof [*Wills ,,Circumstantial Evidence", London, 1850 (3. Ausgabe), bezeichnet ,,evidence" und ,,proof" als ,,cause" und ,,effect". Beide Benennungen werden aber sehr häufig synonym verwendet und nur ein gerichtlich zugelassenes Beweisstück wird mit ,,evidence" bezeichnet*] · Beweis *m*

evidence [*Any species of proof, or probative matter, legally presented at the trial of an issue, by the act of the parties and through the medium of witnessess, records, documents, concrete objects, etc., for the purpose of including belief in the minds of the court or jury as to their contention*] · Beweismaterial *n*, (gerichtlich zugelassenes) Beweisstück *n*

evidence → legal evidence

evidence ab extrâ, proof ab extrâ · fremder Beweis *m*

evidence ab intrâ, proof ab intrâ · eigener Beweis *m*

evidence as to character, proof as to character · Charakterbeweis *m* [*Beweis nach dem Charakter einer Person, daß die ihr zugeschriebene Handlungsweise wahrscheinlich oder unwahrscheinlich ist*]

evidence law, proof law, law of evidence, law of proof [*The aggregate of rules and principles regulating the admissibility, relevancy, weight and sufficiency of evidence in legal proceedings*] · Beweisrecht *n*

evidence of claim, evidence of demand, proof of claim, proof of demand · Forderungsnachweis *m*, Verlangensnachweis

evidence of heirship, heirship proof, heirship evidence, proof of heirship · Erbnachweis *m*

evidence of succession, succession evidence · Rechtsnachfolgenachweis *m*

evidence of title, title proof, title evidence, proof of title · (Rechts)Titelbeweis *m*

evidence rules, rules of evidence · Beweisordnung *f*

evidence to the contrary, proof to the contrary, contradictory evidence, contradictory proof, rebutting testimony, disproof, counter-evidence, counter-proof · Gegenbeweis *m*, gegenteiliger Beweis

evidencing, constituting evidence, evidentiary · beweiskräftig, beweisrechtlich

evident, obvious, manifest, clear to the understanding · augenscheinlich, offensichtlich

evidentia rei vel facti [*Latin*]; real evidence, real proof · Augenscheinbeweis *m*, Realbeweis *m*

evidentiary, evidencing, constituting evidence · beweiskräftig, beweisrechtlich

evidentiary fact; factum probans [*Latin*] · Beweistatsache *f*

evil fame, ill repute, evil repute, ill fame · schlechter Ruf *m*

evil mind; mens vea, malitia (praecogitata) [*Latin*]; malice (prepense), aforethought · Dolus *m*, Vorsatz *m*, krimineller Wille *m*

evil repute, ill fame, evil fame, ill repute · schlechter Ruf *m*

evolutionary approach · Evolutionsansatz *m*

evolutionary sequence hypothesis, multilinear convergence hypothesis · Hypothese *f* der weltweiten standardisierten Stadtentwick(e)lung [*Durch zunehmende Teilhabe an gleichartigen Technologien und Märkten tritt in der Stadtentwick(e)lung weltweit eine Standardisierung und damit Annäherung ein*]

evolutionary sequence process, multilinear convergence process · weltweit gleichartiger Stadtentwick(e)lungsvorgang *m*

ewage; aquage, aquagium [*Latin*] [*In old English law. Toll paid for water passage*] · Wasserdurchleitungsgebühr *f*, Wasser(transport)zoll *m*

exactio [*Latin*] → petitio

examinable [*Capable of being examined*] · prüfbar

examinable capability — excess call

examinable capability, examinable capacity, capability of being examined, capacity of being examined · Prüfbarkeit *f*

examinant, examiner, examinator · Prüfer *m*

examination · Zeugenvernehme *f*

examination · Prüfung *f* [*Angebot; Verdingungsunterlagen*]

examination · Vernehmung *f*

examination code · Prüfungsordnung *f*

examination duty, duty to examine, duty of examination · Prüfungspflicht *f*

examination-in-chief, direct examination · erste Zeugenvernehme *f* durch die benennende Partei

examination in public · öffentliche Untersuchung *f*

examination of documents and site · Durchsicht *f* der Unterlagen und Begehung [*vor Angebotsabgabe*]

examination of site, visit of site, inspection of site, site inspection, site visit, site examination, construction site visit, construction site examination, construction site inspection, building site visit, building site inspection, building site examination · Baustellenbesichtigung *f*, (Baustellen)Begehung, Ortsbesichtigung [*Vor Abgabe eines Angebotes*]

examination of title (to land), investigation of title (to land), (land) title examination, (land) title investigation · (Land)(Rechts)Titelprüfung *f*, Prüfung des (Land)(Rechts)Titels

examinator, examinant, examiner · Prüfer *m*

examiner, examinator, examinant · Prüfer *m*

examiner (of the court) [*A person appointed by a court to take the examination of witnesses in an action, that is, to take down the result of their interrogation by the parties or their counsel either by written interrogatories or viva voce*] · Zeugenprüfer *m*

examiner of title, title man, title examiner · (Rechts)Titelprüfer *m*

example case · Beispielfall *m*

exartare [*Low Latin*] → to essart

excambiator [*obsolete*] → ((real) estate) broker

excambion, land exchange contract [*Scots law. A contract whereby one piece of land is exchanged for another*] · Landtauschvertrag *m*, Bodentauschvertrag, Flächentauschvertrag

excavated pit, worked-out pit · ausgebaggerte Grube *f*, erschöpfte Grube

to excavate sand, to dig sand · aussanden

excavation and foundation work contractor · Grundbauunternehmer *m*

excavator · Grubenausbeuter *m* [*Sand; Kies*]

excepted risk, excepted hazard · ausgenommenes Wagnis *n*, ausgenommenes Risiko, ausgeschlossenes Wagnis *n*, ausgeschlossenes Risiko *n*

except in time of war · Kriegszeit(en) ausgenommen

exception [*In legal descriptions, that portion of land(s) to be deleted or excluded*] · ausgenommenes Land *n*

exception · Ausnahme *f*

exception · Ausschluß *m* im engeren Sinne, Ausschließung *f* im engeren Sinne, Freizeichnung *f* im engeren Sinne, Haftungsausschluß *m* im engeren Sinne, Haftungsausschließung *f* im engeren Sinne, Haftungsfreizeichnung *f* im engeren Sinne [*Vereinbarung, durch die eine sonst bestehende Haftung ausgeschlossen wird*]

exceptional case, case of exception · Ausnahmefall *m*

exceptional grant of permission, exceptional permission, permission of exception · Ausnahmeerlaubnis *f*, Ausnahmegenehmigung *f*, Ausnahmebewilligung *f*, Ausnahmeerteilung *f* einer Genehmigung

exceptional permission, permission of exception, exceptional grant of permission · Ausnahmeerlaubnis *f*, Ausnahmegenehmigung *f*, Ausnahmebewilligung *f*, Ausnahmeerteilung *f* einer Genehmigung

exceptional power, power of exception · Ausnahmeermächtigung *f*

exceptional provision, provision of exception · Ausnahmebestimmung *f*

exceptions granted · stattgegeben [*Prozeßrüge*]

excerpt, abstract, extract · Auszug *m*

excess, overplus, surplus · Überschuß *m*

excess asset; excess paid-in capital (US); surplus asset [*In a balance sheet*] · überschießende Aktiva *f*, Überschußaktiva, Mehraktiva

excess birth rate, surplus birth rate, surplus of births over deaths · Geburtenüberschuß *m*

excess burden, excess charge, excess encumbrance, excess incumbrance · Zusatzbelastung *f*, Zusatzlast *f*

excess call, surplus demand, excess demand, surplus call · Mehrnachfrage *f*, Übernachfrage

excess capacity — exchange list

excess capacity, surplus capacity · Überkapazität *f*, überschießende Kapazität, Mehrkapazität

excess charge, excess encumbrance, excess incumbrance, excess burden · Zusatzbelastung *f*, Zusatzlast *f*

excess condemnation (US); excess expropriation (Brit.) · Überenteignung *f*

excess cost(s), surplus cost(s) · Mehrkosten *f*, Überkosten, überschießende Kosten

excess demand, surplus call, excess call, surplus demand · Mehrnachfrage *f*, Übernachfrage

excess dimension · Übermaß *n*

excess encumbrance, excess incumbrance, excess burden, excess charge · Zusatzbelastung *f*, Zusatzlast *f*

excess expropriation (Brit.); excess condemnation (US) · Überenteignung *f*

excess gain tax, surplus profit tax, surplus gain tax, excess profit tax · Übergewinnsteuer *f*, Überprofitsteuer

excess (general) property, surplus proprietorship, excess proprietorship, surplus ownership (of property), excess ownership (of property), surplus (general) property · Überschußeigentum *n*

excess hours controllable variance · Leistungsverbrauchsabweichung *f*

excess improvement, overimprovement · Übererschließung *f*

excess income, surplus income · Mehreinkommen *n*, Überschußeinkommen, überschießendes Einkommen

excess incumbrance, excess burden, excess charge, excess encumbrance · Zusatzbelastung *f*, Zusatzlast *f*

excess insurance, over-insurance · Überversicherung *f*

excessive (ad)measurement · Überaufmaß *n*

excessive appointment, excessive disposition, excessive exercise of a power of appointment · überzogene Verfügungsbefugnisausübung *f*

excessive distress, excessive distraint · übermäßige Selbstpfändung *f*, übermäßige eigenmächtige Pfändung, übermäßige Privatpfändung [*bewegliche Sache*]

excessive exercise of a power of appointment, excessive appointment, excessive disposition · überzogene Verfügungsbefugnisausübung *f*

excessive urbanization, hyperurbanization, over-urbanization · Überverstädterung *f*

excess (land) expropriation; excess (land) condemnation (US) · Überenteignung *f* von Land, Bodenüberenteignung

excess of liabilities over assets, overindebtedness · Überschuldung *f*

excess of men · Männerüberschuß *m*

excess of women · Frauenüberschuß *m*

excess ownership (of property), surplus (general) property, excess (general) property, surplus proprietorship, excess proprietorship, surplus ownership (of property) · Überschußeigentum *n*

excess paid-in capital (US); surplus asset, excess asset [*in a balance sheet*] · überschießende Aktiva *f*, Überschußaktiva, Mehraktiva

excess payment, overpayment · Über(be)zahlung *f*

excess population, surplus population · Überschußbevölkerung *f*

excess price, surplus price · Mehrpreis *m*, Überschußpreis, überschießender Preis

excess price clause, surplus price clause · Mehrpreisklausel *f*

excess production, surplus production · Überproduktion *f*

excess profit tax, surplus gain tax, surplus profit tax, surplus gain tax · Übergewinnsteuer *f*, Überprofitsteuer

excess proprietorship, surplus ownership (of property), excess ownership (of property), surplus (general) property, excess (general) property, surplus proprietorship · Überschußeigentum *n*

excess quantity, surplus quantity · Überschußmenge *f*, Mehrmenge

excess water, surplus water · Überschußwasser *n*, Mehrwasser

to exchange [*land*] · austauschen [*Land*]

exchange; change (Brit.) [*abbreviated*] · Börse *f*

exchangeable parcel, interchangeable piece of land, exchangeable piece of land, interchangeable plot, interchangeable parcel, exchangeable plot · Austauschgrundstück *n*

exchangeable plot, exchangeable parcel, interchangeable piece of land, exchangeable piece of land, interchangeable plot, interchangeable parcel · Austauschgrundstück *n*

exchange(able) value, value in exchange · Tauschwert *m*

exchange calculation · Wechselarbitrage *f*

exchange contract · Devisenvertrag *m*

exchange control · Devisenbewirtschaftung *f*

exchange hedging · Kurssicherung *f* [*Devisenhandel*]

exchange list · Kurszettel *m*

exchange (market) — exclusive heiress

exchange (market), foreign exchange market · Devisenmarkt *m*

exchange of land(s), exchange of (real) estate, exchange of (real) property, (real) estate exchange, (real) property exchange, land(s) exchange, barter of land for land, exchange of realty, realty exchange · Boden(aus)tausch *m*, Land(aus)tausch, Grund(stücks)(aus)tausch, Liegenschafts(aus)tausch, Immobiliar(aus)tausch, Immobilien(aus)tausch, Flächen(aus)tausch

exchange quotation · Börsenpreis *m*

exchange rate, rate of exchange · Devisenkurs *m*, Wechselkurs

Exchequer [*England*] · (königliches) Schatzamt *n*

Exchequer and Audit Act [*England*] · Gesetz *n* über die Staatskontrolle und den Obersten Rechnungshof [*England*]

Exchequer and Audit Department [*England*] · Oberster Rechnungshof *m*, Höchster Rechnungshof

Exchequer Chamber · Appellationsgericht *n* für gemeines Recht, Berufungsgericht *n* für gemeines Recht

Exchequer Contribution Account · Schatzkammerbeitragsfonds *m* [*England*]

Exchequer of Pleas, Court of Exchequer · Schatzkammergericht *n*, Schatzamtgericht [*England*]

excise(-duty), consumption tax, tax on articles of consumption · Verbrauchssteuer *f*

(excise) licence duty [*A tax payable to the state for the privilege of retailing intoxicating liquors both off and on the premises*] · Spirituosensteuer *f*

(excise) off-licence duty · Spirituosensteuer *f* für Verkauf außer Haus

(excise) on-licence duty · Schanksteuer *f*

to exclude, to shut out, to discriminate · ausschließen, nicht zulassen

to exclude from court, to expel from court, to banish from court · ausschließen vom Gericht

to exclude from inheriting, to disinherit; to exheredate [*In Scotch law*], to deprive of an inheritance, to debar from an inheritance, to put out of an inheritance · enterben

excluding from an inheritance; exheredating [*Scots law*]; disinheriting, depriving of an inheritance, putting out of an inheritance, debarring from an inheritance · Enterben *n*

exclusion, expulsion · Ausweisung *f*, Verweisung, Relegation *f*

exclusion · Ausschluß *m*, Nichtzulassung *f*, Ausschließung *f*

exclusionary land use practice, discriminatory land use practice, snob zoning, exclusionary zoning, discriminatory zoning, spot zoning [*A land use restraint which has the effect of barring prospective lower income or minority residents*] · diskriminierende (Bau)Nutzung *f*, diskriminierende (bauliche) Nutzung, Ausschluß(bau)nutzung

exclusionary state, state of exclusion · Ausschließlichkeit *f*

exclusionary zoning, discriminatory zoning, spot zoning, exclusionary land use practice, discriminatory land use practice, snob zoning [*A land use restraint which has the effect of barring prospective lower income or minority residents*] · diskriminierende (Bau)Nutzung *f*, diskriminierende (bauliche) Nutzung, Ausschluß(bau)nutzung

exclusion by citation (procedure) · Ausschluß *m* im Aufgebotsverfahren, Ausschließung *f* im Aufgebotsverfahren

exclusion by force of law, exclusion by strength of law, debarment by force of law, debarment by strength of law · Ausschließung *f* kraft Gesetzes, Ausschluß *m* kraft Gesetzes

exclusion clause, nonliability clause, exemption clause, saving clause [*A clause in a contract by which a purchaser repudiates liability in certain specified circumstances*] · Ausschließungsklausel *f*, Ausschlußklausel *f*, Freizeichnungsklausel *f*, Haftungsausschließungsklausel *f*, Haftungsausschlußklausel *f*, Haftungsfreizeichnungsklausel *f*

exclusion judg(e)ment → for(e)judg(e)ment

exclusion of limitation, limitation exclusion · Verjährungsausschluß *m*

exclusion of warranty, warranty exclusion · Garantieausschluß *m*

exclusion order, order of exclusion (US); expulsion order, order of expulsion [*In contradistinction to "deportation order"*] · Ausweisungsbefehl *m*, Verweisungsbefehl, Relegationsbefehl, Ausweisungsgebot *n*, Verweisungsgebot, Relegationsgebot, Ausweisungsanordnung *f*, Verweisungsanordnung, Relegationsanordnung, Ausweisungsverfügung, Verweisungsverfügung, Relegationsverfügung

exclusive, sole · alleinig, ausschließlich

exclusive agency → exclusive listing

exclusive authority, exclusive power · ausschließliche Gewalt *f*, ausschließliche Macht *f*, ausschließliche Hoheit *f*, ausschließliche Kompetenz *f*

exclusive heiress, sole heiress, absolute heir female, exclusive heir female, sole heir female, absolute heiress · absolute

Erbin *f,* unbegrenzte Erbin, unbedingte Erbin, uneingeschränkte Erbin, unbeschränkte Erbin, Alleinerbin

exclusive heir (male), absolute heir (male), sole heir (male) · absoluter Erbe *m,* unbeschränkter Erbe, uneingeschränkter Erbe, unbedingter Erbe, unbegrenzter Erbe, Alleinerbe, Vollerbe

exclusive interest, sole interest, exclusive ownership (of property), sole ownership (of property), unlimited ownership (of property); dominium plenum, dominium perpetuum [*Latin*]; absolute ownership (of property), absolute interest, sole property, sole proprietorship [*In English law absolute ownership can only exist in chattels, as all land is subject theoretically to the obligations of tenure; but practically the fee simple in land gives absolute ownership*] · absolutes Eigentum *n,* uneingeschränktes Eigentum, unbeschränktes Eigentum, unbegrenztes Eigentum, ausschließliches Eigentum, unbedingtes Eigentum, Alleineigentum

exclusive jurisdiction [*When a proceeding in respect of a certain subject-matter can only be brought in one court, that court is said to have exclusive jurisdiction*] · ausschließliche Zuständigkeit *f* [*Siehe Anmerkung unter „Zuständigkeit"*]

exclusive (land) owner, absolute proprietor, exclusive proprietor, al(l)odial proprietor, free man, holder of an allodium; liber homo, homo liber [*Latin*]; allodiary, allodialist, al(l)odial (land) owner, absolute (land) owner · absoluter Eigentümer *m,* unbeschränkter Eigentümer, Alleineigentümer, Freiguteigentümer, Allodialeigentümer, freier Mann *m,* Freie *m*

exclusive license, exclusive licence · Ausschließlichkeitslizenz *f*

exclusive licensee, exclusive licencee · Ausschließlichkeitslizenznehmer *m*

exclusive listing, exclusive agency [*Right given to a broker by a (real) property owner to sell the (real) property to the exclusion of any and all other brokers*] · (Land)Maklerausschließlichkeit *f,* Bodenmaklerausschließlichkeit, Grund(stücks)maklerausschließlichkeit

exclusive listing contract [*Contract to sell property as an agent, according to the terms of which the agent is given the sole right to sell the property or is made the sole agent for its sale*] · Allein-Landmaklervertrag *m,* Allein-Bodenmaklervertrag, Allein-(Grund(stücks))Maklervertrag

exclusive ownership (of property), sole ownership (of property), unlimited ownership (of property); dominium plenum, dominium perpetuum [*Latin*]; absolute ownership (of property), absolute interest, exclusive interest, sole interest, sole property, sole proprietorship [*In English law absolute ownership can only exist in chattels, as all land is subject theoretically to the obligations of tenure; but practically the fee simple in land gives absolute ownership*] · absolutes Eigentum *n,* uneingeschränktes Eigentum, unbeschränktes Eigentum, unbegrenztes Eigentum, ausschließliches Eigentum, unbedingtes Eigentum, Alleineigentum

exclusive possession, sole possession, absolute possession · absoluter Besitz *m,* unbegrenzter Besitz, uneingeschränkter Besitz, unbeschränkter Besitz, ausschließlicher Besitz, Alleinbesitz

exclusive possessor, absolute possessor, sole possessor · Alleinbesitzer *m*

exclusive power, exclusive authority · ausschließliche Gewalt *f,* ausschließliche Macht *f,* ausschließliche Hoheit *f,* ausschließliche Kompetenz *f*

exclusive proprietary right (of land), absolute proprietary right (of land), sole proprietary right (of land) · Alleinbesitzanspruch *m,* Alleinbesitz(an)recht *n* [*Grundstück*]

exclusive proprietor → allodiary

exclusive remedy, absolute remedy, sole remedy · ausschließlicher Rechtsbehelf *m,* alleiniger Rechtsbehelf *m*

exclusive right, sole right, absolute right [*A right which only the grantee thereof can exercise, and from which all others are prohibited or shut out*] · Alleinrecht *n,* Ausschließlichkeitsrecht, absolutes (subjektives) Recht

exclutory contract · unerfüllter Vertrag *m* [*Er ist vollkommen unerfüllt oder bei ihm ist noch etwas zu erfüllen*]

ex contractu [*Latin*]; arising out of a contract · vertragsbedingt

excursion traffic · Ausflugsverkehr *m*

excusability · Entschuldbarkeit *f*

excusable · entschuldbar

excuse, justification; justificatio [*Latin*]; just cause [*Just, lawful excuse for act*] · Rechtfertigung *f*

excuse in law · rechtliche Entschuldigung *f*

ex dock named port of importation · ab Kai benannter Einfuhrhafen

to execute, to carry out, to perform · ausführen, durchführen, erbringen [*Arbeit(en)*]

to execute a conveyance · siegeln und übergeben der eine dingliche Übertragung bewirkenden Urkunde

to execute a distress (upon), to distrain, to levy a distress (upon) · (privat)pfänden

executed, discharged, performed, fulfilled · erfüllt, ausgeführt, vollzogen, erbracht, nachgekommen

executed · ausgefertigt

executed and delivered · ausgefertigt und begeben

executed consideration, performed consideration, fulfilled consideration [*An act done or a value given before or at the time of making a contract*] · ausgeführte Gegenleistung *f*, erbrachte Gegenleistung *f*, erfüllte Gegenleistung *f*, vollzogene Gegenleistung *f*

executed contract, performed contract, fulfilled contract, contract complied with · ausgeführter Vertrag *m*, erfüllter Vertrag *m*, erbrachter Vertrag *m*, vollzogener Vertrag *m*

executed covenant, fulfilled covenant, performed covenant, covenant complied with · ausgeführter Formalvertrag *m*, erfüllter Formalvertrag *m*, vollzogener Formalvertrag *m*, erbrachter Formalvertrag

executed formal license, executed formal licence · förmliche Lizenzurkunde *f*

executed sale [*The completion of an agreement, whereby the seller transfers his property in the goods to the purchaser and receives from the purchaser the sales price of the goods, is said to be an executed sale*] · durchgeführter Verkauf *m*, ausgeführter Verkauf

to execute under seal · vollziehen unter Siegel

executing party, performing party, fulfilling party · ausführende Partei *f*, erbringende Partei *f*, vollziehende Partei *f*, erfüllende Partei *f*

executing person, performing person, fulfilling person · Ausführende *m*, Vollziehende *m*, Erbringende *m*, Erfüllende *m*

execution, performance, compliance, fulfilment, discharge [*The pursuance or carrying forth of the provisions of a plan or contract*] · Ausführung *f*, Vollzug *m*, Erbringung *f*, Vollziehung *f*, Erfüllung *f*, Leistung

execution [*Enforcing the rights of a judg(e)ment creditor by seizure of property*] · (Zwangs)Vollstreckung *f*

execution bond, compliance bond, discharge bond, performance bond, fulfilment bond · Erfüllungsgarantie *f*, Vollzugsgarantie, Vollziehungsgarantie, Erbringungsgarantie, Leistungsgarantie, Ausführungsgarantie

execution clause, clause of execution · Vollstreckungsklausel *f*

execution delay, delay in performance, performance delay, delay in execution · Ausführungsverzug *m*, Vollziehungsverzug *m*, Erbringungsverzug *m*, Erfüllungsverzug *m*

execution duty, compliance duty, duty of fulfilment, duty of execution, duty of compliance, duty of performance, performance duty, fulfilment duty · Erfüllungspflicht *f*, Vollziehungspflicht, Ausführungspflicht, Vollzugspflicht, Erbringungspflicht

execution instruction, instruction for execution · Ausführungsanweisung *f*

execution lien · Pfändungspfandrecht *n*

execution mortgage · Arresthypothek *f*

execution of a contract of mandate · Mandatsbearbeitung *f*

execution of a will, testatum execution, executorship · (Testaments)Vollstreckung *f*

execution of instrument [*Execution includes signing, sealing and delivering*] · Ausfertigung *f* und Zustellung *f* eines Schriftstückes

execution (of judg(e)ment), judg(e)ment execution · (Urteils)Vollstreckung *f*, gerichtliche Vollstreckung

execution of plan(s), performance of plan(s), planning execution, planning performance · Plan(ungs)vollzug *m*, Plan(ungs)durchführung *f*, Plan(ungs)ausführung

execution of punishment, punishment execution · Strafvollstreckung *f*

execution (of (the) work(s)), performance (of (the) work(s)), construction of (the) works · Arbeitsausführung *f*, Bau *m* (der Anlagen), Bauausführung *f*, Ausführung *f* (der (Bau)Arbeiten)

execution period, fulfilment period, performance period, compliance period · Ausführungsfrist *f*, Vollzugsfrist *f*, Erfüllungsfrist *f*, Vollziehungsfrist *f*, Erbringungsfrist *f*

execution planning, performance planning, planning of (the) execution, planning of (the) performance · Ausführungsplanung *f*

execution sale · Vollstreckungsverkauf *m*

executive · Geschäftsleiter *m*

executive [*That branch of the government which puts the laws into execution, as distinguished from the legislative and judicial branches*] · Exekutivgewalt *f*, Exekutive *f*, Vollzugsgewalt, vollziehende Gewalt

executive authority · Vollstreckungsvollmacht *f*

executive board → board of directors

executive board member → director

executive body — executory bequest

executive body · Vollzugsorgan n

executive committee, management committee, committee of management · geschäftsführender Auschuß m, Geschäftsführungsausschuß

executive director · Direktor m mit Vollziehungsfunktion

executive order, rule [*"Rule"* im amerikanischen Verwaltungsrecht und *"Verordnung"* im deutschen Verwaltungsrecht sind nicht ganz deckungsgleich] · Verwaltungsverordnung f

executive order making, rule making · Verwaltungsverordnungsgebung f

executive position f, managerial position · leitende Stellung f, leitende Position f, Spitzenstellung f, Spitzenposition f

executor → (testamentary) executor

executor ab episcopo constitutus [*Latin*]; executor appointed by a bishop · (Testaments)Vollstrecker m vom Bischof ernannt

executor ab testator constitutus [*Latin*]; executor appointed by a testator · (Testaments)Vollstrecker m vom Erblasser ernannt

executor according to the tenor → (testamentary) executor according to the tenor

executor appointed by a bishop; executor ab episcopo constitutus [*Latin*] · (Testaments)Vollstrecker m vom Bischof ernannt

executor appointed by a testator; executor ab testator constitutus [*Latin*] · (Testaments)Vollstrecker m vom Erblasser ernannt

executor by his own wrongful act; executor de son tort demesne [*Norman French*]; executor de son tort, executor of his (own) wrong · unberechtigter (Testaments)Vollstrecker m

executor dative [*Scotland*]; (probate) administrator · Nachlaßverwalter m, Erb(schafts)verwalter, erbrechtlicher Verwalter [*Er wird bestellt wenn der Erblasser entweder kein Testament hinterlassen oder in seinem Testament keinen Testamentsvollstrecker ernannt hat*]

executor dative cum testamento annexo [*Scotland*] → executor dative with the will annexed

executor dative de bonis non (administratis); executor dative of the unadministered estate [*Scotland*]; (probate) administrator de bonis non (administratis), (probate) administrator of the unadministered estate · Nachlaßverwalter m an Stelle eines verstorbenen Nachlaßverwalters, Erb(schafts)verwalter an Stelle eines verstorbenen erbrechtlichen Verwalters

executor dative durante minore aetate [*Scotland*]; (probate) administrator durante minore aetate · Nachlaßverwalter m während Minderjährigkeit, Erb(schafts)verwalter während Minderjährigkeit, erbrechtlicher Verwalter während Minderjährigkeit

executor dative of the unadministered estate [*Scotland*] → executor dative de bonis non (administratis)

executor dative pendente lite; executor dative during the litigation [*Scotland*]; (probate) administrator during the litigation, (probate) administrator pendente lite · Nachlaßverwalter m während eines Prozesses, Erb(schafts)verwalter während eines Prozesses, erbrechtlicher Verwalter während eines Prozesses

executor dative with the will annexed, executor dative cum testamento annexo [*Scotland*]; (probate) administrator with the will annexed, (probate) administrator cum testamento annexo · erbrechtlicher Verwalter m cum testamento annexo, Erb(schafts)verwalter cum testamento annexo, Nachlaßverwalter cum testamento annexo

executor de son tort, executor of his (own) wrong, executor by his own wrongful act; executor de son tort demesne [*Norman French*] · unberechtigter (Testaments)Vollstrecker m

executor of his (own) wrong, executor by his own wrongful act; executor de son tort demesne [*Norman French*]; executor de son tort · unberechtigter (Testaments)Vollstrecker m

executor's deed · (Testaments)Vollstreckerurkunde f

executorship, execution of a will, testatum execution · (Testaments)Vollstreckung f

executor's oath · (Testaments)Vollstreckereid m

executor testamentarius [*Latin*]; testamentary trustee, (testamentary) executor [*He is appointed by the will, either expressly or by necessary inference from the terms of the will (executor according to the tenor)*] · (Testaments)Vollstrecker m, Willensvollstrecker [*Die Benennung ,,Willensvollstrecker" ist treffender als die übliche ,,Testamentsvollstrecker", da eine Willensvollstreckung auch bei gesetzlicher Erbfolge eintreten kann, z. B. wenn ein Testament nur die Einsetzung eines Testamentsvollstreckers enthält*]

executory [*That which is yet to be executed or performed*] · vollziehbar

executory bequest, executory legacy · vollziehbares (Fahrnis)Legat n, vollziehbares (Fahrnis)Vermächtnis n

executory consideration [*A consideration which is to be performed after the making of the promise on which it is founded*] · vollziehbare Gegenleistung *f*

executory contract · vollziehbarer Vertrag *m*

executory covenant · vollziehbarer Formalvertrag *m*

executory devise [*It is a disposition of land(s) by will that thereby no estate vests at the death of the devisor, but only on some future contingency. Not to be confused with a "remainder"*] · vollziehbares (Land)Vermächtnis *n*

executory legacy, executory bequest · vollziehbares (Fahrnis)Legat *n*, vollziehbares (Fahrnis)Vermächtnis *n*

executory ordinance · Durchführungsverordnung *f*

executory provision · Durchführungsbestimmung *f*

executory remainder (land(ed)) estate, possibility of (a) future (land(ed)) estate; spes successionis [*Latin*]; contingent remainder (land(ed)) estate, conditional remainder (land(ed)) estate [*The remainder is contingent if the person who is to have the remainder is not yet living or if his identity is uncertain, or if the event which is to bring the remainder into existence is uncertain. The remainder becomes vested when such person is ascertained or upon the happening of the event*] · bedingter anwartschaftlicher Bodenbesitz(stand) *m*, möglicher anwartschaftlicher Bodenbesitz(stand), ungewisser anwartschaftlicher Bodenbesitz(stand)

executrix, female executor [*A woman who has been appointed by will to execute such will or testament*] · (Testaments)Vollstreckerin *f*

exemplary damages, exemplary compensation, exemplary indemnification, exemplary indemnity, punitive damages, punitive compensation, punitive indemnification, punitive indemnity, vindictive damages, vindictive compensation, vindictive indemnity, vindictive indemnification · Extraentschädigung(sleistung) *f*, Extraschadensersatz(leistung) *m*, *(f)*, exemplarische Entschädigung(sleistung), exemplarischer Schadenersatz, exemplarische Schadenersatzleistung

exemplificatio [*Latin*]; certified transcript, exemplification · rechtsgültige Abschrift *f*, rechtsgültige Kopie *f*

exemplification; exemplificatio [*Latin*]; certified transcript · rechtsgültige Abschrift *f*, rechtsgültige Kopie *f*

exemplification [*An official copy of a document made under the seal of a court or public functionary*] · gesiegeltes Duplikat *n*

exempt from duty · zollfrei

exemption, discharge, release, dispensation, immunity [*Relaxation of the law in a particular case by competent authority*] · Befreiung *f*, Freistellung, Entlastung, Freigabe *f*, Erlaß *m*, Dispens(ierung) *m*, *(f)*, Dispensation *f*, Ausnahmebewilligung

exemption application, discharge application, release application, dispensation application, immunity application · Befreiungsantrag *m*, Dispens(ier)ungsantrag, Freistellungsantrag, Entlastungsantrag, Freigabeantrag, Dispensationsantrag

exemption clause, saving clause, exclusion clause, nonliability clause [*A clause in a contract by which a purchaser repudiates liability in certain specified circumstances*] · Ausschließungsklausel *f*, Ausschlußklausel *f*, Freizeichnungsklausel *f*, Haftungsausschließungsklausel *f*, Haftungsausschlußklausel *f*, Haftungsfreizeichnungsklausel *f*

exemption from charges · Unentgeltlichkeit *f*

exemption from duties, freedom from duties, exemption from statutory charges, freedom from statutory charges, exemption from legal charges, freedom from legal charges · Abgabenbefreiung *f*, Abgabenfreiheit *f*

exemption (from liability), release (from liability), nonliability · (Haftungs)Ausschluß *m*, (Haftungs)Freizeichnung *f*, (Haftungs)Ausschließung, Haftpflichtausschluß, Haftbarkeitsausschluß, Haftbarkeitsausschließung

exemption from taxes, freedom from taxation, exemption from taxation, tax relief, taxation exemption, freedom from taxes · Steuerbefreiung *f*, Steuerfreiheit *f*, Besteuerungsausnahme *f*

exemption limit · Steuerfreigrenze *f*

exempt jurisdiction, peculiar [*In English ecclesiastic(al) law*] · autonome Zuständigkeit *f*

exequatur [*A permission by a government to the consul or commercial agent of another State to enter upon the discharge of his functions in the country of the government giving the exequatur. The government which issues it may at any time withdraw it; and its issue is entirely discretionary*] · Vollstreckbarkeitserklärung *f*

to exercise a right, to enjoy · ausüben [*(subjektives) Recht*]

exercise in the law, exercise of law, legal exercise · Rechtsausübung *f*, objektive Rechtsausübung

exercise of a right, enjoyment [*Enjoyment is to a right what possession is to a corporeal thing, and it is therefore divisible, like possession, into simple, rightful, permissive, adverse, etc.*] · Ausübung *f* eines (subjektiven) Rechts, (subjektive) Rechtsausübung

exercise of law, legal exercise, exercise in the law · Rechtsausübung *f*, objektive Rechtsausübung

exercise of the right to air, enjoyment of air · Ausübung *f* des (dinglichen) Rechtes am Luftraum

exercise of the will, act(ion) of the will, volition · Willensakt *m*, Willensausübung *f*, Willenshandlung, Wollen *n*

exercising of a right, enjoying · Ausüben *n* [*subjektives Recht*]

exertion of discretionary power · Ermessensausübung *f*

exertion of (the) will · Willensäußerung *f*

exhaeredatio [*Latin*]; disinheritance, dis(in)herison · Enterbung *f*

exhaeres [*Latin*]; disinherited person · enterbte Person *f*, Enterbte *m*

exhaustive rule · erschöpfende Regel *f*

to exheredate [*Scots law*]; to deprive of an inheritance, to debar from an inheritance, to put out of an inheritance, to exclude from inheriting, to disinherit · enterben

exheredating [*Scots law*]; disinheriting, depriving of an inheritance, putting out of an inheritance, debarring from an inheritance, excluding from an inheritance · Enterben *n*

exhibit [*A document used in evidence, especially when annexed to an affidavit*] · Beweisschrift *f*

exhibition · Ausstellung *f*

exhibition ground · Ausstellungsgelände *n*

exhibition of works of art, art exhibition · Kunstausstellung *f*

exhumation, disinterment, unburying · Exhumierung *f*

to exhume, to unbury, to disinter · exhumieren

existence · Bestehen *n*, Vorhandensein *n*

existence care, care of existence · Daseinsvorsorge *f*

existence form, form of existence · Daseinsform *f*

existence function, function of existence · Daseinsfunktion *f*

existence space, space of existence · Daseinsraum *m*

existing · bestehend, vorhanden

existing enjoyment · vorhandener Genuß *m*, bestehender Genuß

existing estate, existing property, present estate, present property · bestehendes Vermögen *n*, bestehendes Gut *n*, vorhandenes Vermögen, vorhandenes Gut, bestehende Habe *f*, vorhandene Habe

existing interest, present right, present interest, existing right · bestehendes Anrecht *n*, vorhandenes Anrecht, gegenwärtiges Anrecht, bestehendes (subjektives) Recht, vorhandenes (subjektives) Recht, gegenwärtiges (subjektives) Recht, bestehende Berechtigung *f*, gegenwärtige Berechtigung, vorhandene Berechtigung, bestehender Anspruch *m*, gegenwärtiger Anspruch, vorhandener Anspruch

existing population, real population, actual population · tatsächliche Bevölkerung *f*, wirkliche Bevölkerung, Istbevölkerung

existing possession · bestehender Besitz *m*, vorhandener Besitz

existing property, present estate, present property, existing estate · bestehendes Vermögen *n*, bestehendes Gut *n*, vorhandenes Vermögen, vorhandenes Gut, bestehende Habe *f*, vorhandene Habe

existing right, existing interest, present right, present interest · bestehendes Anrecht *n*, vorhandenes Anrecht, gegenwärtiges Anrecht, bestehendes (subjektives) Recht, vorhandenes (subjektives) Recht, gegenwärtiges (subjektives) Recht, bestehende Berechtigung *f*, gegenwärtige Berechtigung, vorhandene Berechtigung, bestehender Anspruch *m*, gegenwärtiger Anspruch, vorhandener Anspruch

existing together, concurrent · gleichzeitig bestehend, simultan bestehend

existing use value · bestehender Nutzungswert *m*, vorhandener Nutzungswert

exlex, utlagatus [*Latin*]; outlaw, lawless man · Geächtete *m*

exodus, drift, movement, flight · Flucht *f*, Wegziehen *n*

exodus of business firms, business exodus · Geschäftsflucht *f*

exodus of farm workers, exodus of agrarian workers, exodus of agricultural workers; exodus of labourers (Brit.) · Landarbeiterflucht *f*

exodus to the suburbs, movement to the suburbs (Brit.); flight to the suburbs, drift to the suburbs · Vorortflucht *f*, Vorortexodus *m*, Flucht in die Vororte, Exodus in die Vororte

exodus to the umland, drift to the umland, movement to the umland, flight to the umland · Umlandflucht *f*, Umlandexodus *m*, Flucht ins Umland, Exodus ins Umland

ex officio [*Latin*]; in the regular course, by virtue of the office · von Amts wegen

exorbitant contract, usurious contract [*A contract if interest contracted to be paid exceeds the rate established by statute*] · Wuchervertrag *m*

exorbitant price, usurious price · Wucherpreis *m*

exorbitant rent, usurious rent · Wuchermiete *f*

expanded town [*Town Development Act 1952. England*] · Förderungszentrum *n*

ex parte legal act(ion), ex parte lawful act(ion), ex parte proceeding · einseitiger Rechtsakt *m*, einseitiger rechtsetzender Akt, einseitige Rechtshandlung *f*, einseitige rechtsetzende Handlung

ex parte motion, motion ex parte · einseitiger Antrag *m* an ein Gericht

ex parte proceeding · abgetrenntes Verfahren *n* zur Entscheidung über Nebensachen

ex parte proceeding · einseitig rechtsetzendes Handeln *n*

to expatriate · ausbürgern

expatriated · ausgebürgert

expatriate differential · Auslandszuschlag *m* [*Gehalt oder Lohn*]

to expatriate (oneself) · selbstausbürgern, sich ausbürgern

expatriation [*The voluntary act of renouncing allegiance to one's own country so as to take up residence permanently in a foreign country*] · Sichausbürgern *n*, Sichausbürgerung *f*

expatriation [*The act of forcing a person to leave his native country*] · Ausbürgern *n*, Ausbürgerung *f*

expectable risk, possible risk [*Risk which is indefinite and uncertain*] · mögliches Risiko *n*, mögliches Wagnis *n*

expectancy, expectation · Erwartung *f*

expectancy (US) · Erwartung *f* einer Vermögens- oder Geldleistung

expectancy estate, expectant estate, estate in expectancy · (zu)künftige (Grund)Besitzdauer *f*, (zu)künftige Bodenbesitzdauer, (zu)künftige Landbesitzdauer

expectancy of law, contemplation of law; abeyantia [*Latin*]; abeyance, condition of abeyance, state of abeyance, state of suspension, abeyancy, temporary nonexistence [*In the law of real estate. Where there is no person in existence in whom an inheritance can vest, it is said to be in abeyance, that is, in expectation; the law considering is as always potentially existing, and ready to vest when ever a proper owner appears*] · Schwebe(zustand) *f*, *(m)*

expectant female heir, female heir expectant, heiress expectant, heir female expectant, expectant heiress, expectant heir female · Erbanwärterin *f*, Erbschaftsanwärterin

expectant heir (male), expectant male heir, male heir expectant, heir (male) expectant · Erbanwärter *m*, Erbschaftsanwärter

expectation, expectancy · Erwartung *f*

expected income · Erwartungseinkommen *n*

expedition doctrine → expedition theory

expedition theory, expedition doctrine, mail-box theory, mail-box doctrine · Absendetheorie *f* [*Vertragsabschluß*]

to expel from court, to banish from court, to exclude from court · ausschließen vom Gericht

expellee, evictee · Vertriebene *m*

expenditure, outgo(ing) · Ausgabe *f*

expenditure, outlay · Aufwand *m*, Verausgabung *f*

expenditure for preservation of housing · Erhaltungsaufwand *f*, Erhaltungsaufwendungen *f pl* [*Der Aufwand für die Instandhaltung und Instandsetzung von Wohngebäuden*]

(expense) budget (program) (US); (expense) budget (programme) · Kostenplan *m*, Budget *n*

expense(s), [*USA*]; expired cost(s) [*Those cost(s) which are directly or indirectly related to a given fiscal period of the flow of goods or services into the market and of related operations*] · Kosten *f* [*Die den erzeugten Gütern und Leistungen zuzurechnenden Aufwendungen*]

expenses of maintenance, maintenance expenses · (Lebens)Unterhaltsaufwendungen *f pl*

experimental design · Auslegung *f* eines Simulationsversuches

experimental research · Versuchsforschung *f*

expert · Gutachter *m*, Sachverständige

expert committee · Sachverständigenrat *m*

expert group · Sachverständigengruppe *f*

expertise, survey, advisory opinion · Gutachten *n*, Sachverständigenbericht *m*

expertise, special knowledge, expertness, professional knowledge · berufliches Wissen *n*, Fachwissen, Fachkenntnisse *f pl*, Fachkunde *f*, Sachkenntnis *f*,

Sachkunde, Sachwissen, Spezialkenntnis, Spezialwissen, Spezialkunde

expertise ordered by court (Brit.); expert witness of the court (US); survey ordered by court · Sachverständigengutachten *n*, unabhängiges Gutachten [*Es wird von einem neutralen, vom Gericht bestellten Sachverständigen angefertigt. §§ 402 ff. ZPO*]

expertly · fachmännisch

expert opinion · Sachverständigenmeinung *f*, Gutachtermeinung

expert ordered by court · Gerichtsgutachter *m*, Gerichtssachverständige

expert reimbursement · Sachverständigenvergütung *f*; Sachverständigenentschädigung [*Fehlbenennung*]

experts committee, committee of experts · Gutachterausschuß *m*, Sachverständigenausschuß

experts committee ordinance · Gutachterausschußverordnung *f*, Sachverständigenausschußverordnung

expert service · Sachverständigendienstleistung *f*

expert witness · sachverständiger Zeuge *m*

expert witness of the court (US); survey ordered by court, expertise ordered by court (Brit.) · Sachverständigengutachten *n*, unabhängiges Gutachten [*Es wird von einem neutralen, vom Gericht bestellten Sachverständigen angefertigt. §§ 402 ff. ZPO*]

expiration, expiry, running out, termination, falling in, lapse (of time) · Ablauf *m*, Fristablauf, Zeitablauf, Verfristung *f*

expiration date, due date, termination date, falling in date, running out date, accrual date, maturity date, expiry date · Fälligkeitsdatum *n*, Fälligkeitstag *m*, Verfalldatum, Verfalltermin *m*, (Frist)Ablauftermin, (Frist)Ablaufdatum, Fälligkeitstermin, Verfalltag, (Frist)Ablauftag

to expire, to end, to terminate, to lapse, to run out, to cease; to fall in (Brit.) · ablaufen, verfristen

expired cost(s), expense(s) [*USA*] [*Those cost(s) which are directly or indirectly related to a given fiscal period of the flow of goods or services into the market and of related operations*] · Kosten *f* [*Die den erzeugten Gütern und Leistungen zuzurechnenden Aufwendungen*]

expiry, running out, termination, falling in, lapse (of time), expiration · Ablauf *m*, Fristablauf, Zeitablauf, Verfristung *f*

expiry date, expiration date, due date, termination date, falling in date, running out date, accrual date, maturity date · Fälligkeitsdatum *n*, Fälligkeitstag *m*, Verfalldatum, Verfalltermin *m*, (Frist)Ablauftermin, (Frist)Ablaufdatum, Fälligkeitstermin, Verfalltag, (Frist)Ablauftag

explanation · Erläuterung *f*

explanation drawing, explanatory drawing · Erläuterungszeichnung *f*

explanation provision, explanatory provision · Erläuterungsbestimmung *f*

explanation report, explanatory report · Erläuterungsbericht *m*

explanation sheet, explanatory sheet · Erläuterungsblatt *n*

exploitation land(s), open-cut mining area, strip mining area, surface mining area, open-cast work(ing) area, surface mining land(s), strip mining land(s), open-cut mining land(s), open pit mining land(s), open work(ing) land(s), stripping land(s), open-cast work(ing) land(s) · Abbauland *n*, Tagebauland, Abbaufläche *f*, Tagebaufläche [*Grundstücke, die auf Grund ihrer Beschaffenheit die oberirdische Gewinnung von Bodenschätzen ermöglichen*]

exploitation right, mineral right, mineral interest, interest in minerals in land(s), right to take minerals, right to win minerals, right of exploitation, right to exploit minerals, right of taking minerals, right of winning, winning right · (Mineral(ien))Abbaurecht *n*, (Mineral(ien))Ausbeutungsrecht, (subjektives) Berg(bau)recht, (Mineral(ien))Abbaugerechtigkeit *f*

exploitation theory · Ausbeutungstheorie *f*

exploration of established facts, exploration of ascertained facts, exploration of case facts, exploration of the situation of facts, exploration of the state of facts, exploration of the actual situation · Erforschen *n* der Sachlage, Erforschen des Sachverhaltes, Erforschen des Tatbestandes

exploratory data analysis · erforschende Datenanalyse *f*, erforschende Datenstudie

exponential distribution · Exponentialverteilung *f*

export assistance, promotion of export, assistance of export, sponsoring of export, export promotion · Ausfuhrförderung *f*, Exportförderung

export bounty · Ausfuhrprämie *f*

export industry, carrier industry · Exportindustrie *f*

export prohibition, prohibition of export · Ausfuhrverbot *n*, Exportverbot *n*

exposition of law, law exposition · Rechtsdarlegung *f*

**ex post facto, **retroactive, retrospective · rückwirkend

exposure · Exposition *f*, Ausgesetztsein *n*

to express again in other words, to restate, to reword, to change the wording of, to state again in other words · umschreiben, neugestalten, neuschreiben, umgestalten [*Text*]

express authority · ausdrückliche Vollmacht *f*, ausdrückliche Vertretungsmacht

express bus service, rapid bus service · Schnellautobusbetrieb *m*, Schnell(omni)busbetrieb

express carriage, express vehicle [*One of the classifications of public service vehicles*] · Schnellfahrzeug *n*

express condition · ausdrückliche Bedingung *f*

express consideration [*A consideration distinctly declared by the terms of the contract itself, as where a man contracts to sell his land for a named sum of money*] · ausdrückliche Gegenleistung *f*

express declaration · ausdrückliche Erklärung *f*

expressing again in other words, changing the text, rewording, changing the wording, stating again in other words · Textumschreibung *f*, Textumgestaltung, Textneugestaltung, Textneuschreibung

expression of intent(ion) · Willensausdruck *m*

expression of opinion · Meinungsausdruck *m*

expressly, specially · ausdrücklicherweise

express malice, malice in fact · tatsächliche Böswilligkeit *f*

express permission · ausdrückliche Erlaubnis *f*, ausdrückliche Genehmigung *f*

express power, express right · ausdrückliche Befugnis *f*, ausdrückliches Recht *n*

express service [*Transit operation over long distances with minimum number of stops*] · Schnellverkehrsdienst *m*

express surrender · ausdrückliche Rückgabe *f*

express trust · ausdrückliche Treuhand *f*, Treuhand(verhältnis) durch Willenserklärung, ausdrückliches Treuhandverhältnis *n*, gewillkürtes Treuhandverhältnis, gewillkürte Treuhand

express vehicle, express carriage [*One of the classifications of public service vehicles*] · Schnellfahrzeug *n*

express warranty [*In conveyancing. A warranty in a deed expressed by particular words (such as "warrantizo", I warrant); as distinguished from that which was implied by law from other words (such as "dedi", I have given)*] · ausdrückliche Gewährleistung *f*, ausdrückliche Zusicherung *f*

to expropriate; to condemn (US) · enteignen

expropriated; condemned (US) · enteignet

expropriation; condemnation (US) · Enteignung *f*, enteignender Eingriff *m* [*Zugunsten der öffentlichen Hand*]

expropriation → (land) expropriation

expropriation act → (land) expropriation act

expropriation authority → (land) expropriation authority

expropriation by zone(s); condemnation by zone(s) (US) · Zonenenteignung *f*

expropriation for opening up → (land) expropriation for opening up

expropriation for substitute land; condemnation for substitute land (US) · Ersatzlandenteignung *f*, Ersatzbodenenteignung *f* [*Enteignung von Grundstücken zur Entschädigung in Land*]

expropriation for substitute right → (land) expropriation for substitute right

expropriation law → (land) expropriation act

expropriation legislation → (land) expropriation legislation

expropriation order → (land) expropriation order

expropriation plan → (land) expropriation plan

expropriation procedure → (land) expropriation procedure

expropriation statute → (land) expropriation act

expropriation theory → (land) expropriation theory

expulsion, exclusion · Ausweisung *f*, Verweisung, Relegation *f*

expulsion from a farm, distraint, turning a tenant out of his farm, evicting a tenant from his farm, dispossession · Abmei(g)erung *f* [*In den Zeiten der feudalen Grund- und Gutsherrschaft das Recht des Grundherrn, einem Bauern die Bauernstelle wegen Pflichtverletzung zu entziehen*]

expulsion order, order of expulsion; exclusion order, order of exclusion (US) [*In contradistinction to "deportation order"*] · Ausweisungsbefehl *m*, Verweisungsbefehl, Relegationsbefehl, Ausweisungsgebot *n*, Verweisungsgebot, Relegationsgebot, Ausweisungsanord-

ex ship — exterior advertisement facility

nung f, Verweisungsanordnung, Relegationsanordnung, Ausweisungsverfügung, Verweisungsverfügung, Relegationsverfügung

ex ship · ab Schiff

to extend [*To value the lands or tenements of a person bound by a statute or recognizance which has become forfeited, to their full extended value*] · (ab)schätzen zum vollen Wert, (be)werten zum vollen Wert, taxieren zum vollen Wert

to extend, to prolong, to lengthen · verlängern

to extend, to enlarge · erweitern

extended, prolonged, lengthened · verlängert

extended, enlarged · erweitert

extended family, large family [*A family which includes four or more minors*] · Großfamilie f

extended family single farm, large family single farm, single farm of an extended family, large farm of an extended family · Großfamilieneinzelhof m

extender clause, prolongation clause, extension clause · Verlängerungsklausel f

extending, enlarging · Erweitern n

extension, total price · Gesamtpreis m [*Preis pro Einheit × Menge*]

extension, enlargement, addition [*structure*] · Erweiterung f [*Bauwerk*]

extension, prolongation · Verlängerung f

extension → (building) extension

extension agreement, prolongation agreement · Verlängerungsabkommen n, Verlängerungsabmachung f, Verlängerungsvereinbarung

extension area, enlargement territory, extension territory, enlargement area · Erweiterungsgebiet n

extension clause, extender clause, prolongation clause · Verlängerungsklausel f

extension division · Außenstelle f [*Staatsuniversität in den USA*]

extension of (a) locality, enlargement of (a) locality · Ortserweiterung f

extension of limitation, prolongation of limitation · Verjährungsverlängerung f

extension of payment, prolongation of payment, payment extension, payment prolongation · Zahlungsfristverlängerung f

extension of period (for completion), extension of time (for completion), prolongation of period (for completion), prolongation of time (for completion), (performance) time extension · Nachfrist f, Fristverlängerung f

extension of time clause, extension of period clause, prolongation of time clause, prolongation of period clause · Frist(verlänger)ungsklausel f

extension ordinance, enlargement ordinance · Erweiterungs(rechts)verordnung f

extension physical facility, enlargement work, enlargement structure, extension work, extension structure, enlargement physical facility · (bauliche) Erweiterungsanlage f, Erweiterungs(bau)werk n, Erweiterungsbau(anlage) m, (f), Erweiterungsbaulichkeit f

extension plan, enlargement plan · Erweiterungsplan m

extension planner, enlargement planner · Erweiterungsplaner m

extension planning, enlargement planning · Erweiterungsplanung f

extension space, enlargement space · Erweiterungsraum m

extension structure, enlargement physical facility, extension physical facility, enlargement work, enlargement structure, extension work · (bauliche) Erweiterungsanlage f, Erweiterungs(bau)werk n, Erweiterungsbau(anlage) m, (f), Erweiterungsbaulichkeit f

extension territory, enlargement area, extension area, enlargement territory · Erweiterungsgebiet n

extension work, extension structure, enlargement physical facility, extension physical facility, enlargement work, enlargement structure · (bauliche) Erweiterungsanlage f, Erweiterungs(bau)werk n, Erweiterungsbau(anlage) m, (f), Erweiterungsbaulichkeit f

extension work(s), enlargement work(s) · Erweiterungsarbeit(en) f (pl)

extensive [*Widely extended in space, time, or scope*] · ausgedehnt

extent · Ausdehnung f

extenuating circumstance · mildernder Umstand m

exterior advertisement, display of advertisements, outdoor advertisement, open-air advertisement, external advertisement · Außenwerbung f, Außenreklame f

exterior advertisement facility, outdoor advertisement facility, open air advertisement facility, external advertisement facility · Außenwerbungseinrichtung f, Außenreklameeinrichtung

exterior facility — extra contract

exterior facility, outdoor facility, open air facility, external facility · Außenanlage f, Freianlage, Außeneinrichtung f, Freieinrichtung

exterior lot line [*Boundary line between a lot and a street, allay, public way, railway right of way, etc.*] · äußere Grundstücksgrenze f [*Eine vordere oder hintere Grundstücksgrenze*]

exterior relation(ship), third-party relation(ship), external relation(ship) · Außenverhältnis n

exterior (traffic) zone, external (traffic) zone · Außen(verkehrs)zone f

external account · Auslandskonto n

external advertisement, exterior advertisement, display of advertisements, outdoor advertisement, open-air advertisement · Außenwerbung f, Außenreklame f

external advertisement facility, exterior advertisement facility, outdoor advertisement facility, open air advertisement facility · Außenwerbungseinrichtung f, Außenreklameeinrichtung

external-external movements, through movements, through traffic, external-external traffic · Durchgangsverkehr m [*durch eine Ortschaft*]

external facility, exterior facility, outdoor facility, open air facility · Außenanlage f, Freianlage, Außeneinrichtung f, Freieinrichtung

external fund · Fremdmittel f, Fremdfonds m

external improvement · äußere Erschließung f [*Erschließung außerhalb eines neuen Baugebietes*]

external-internal traffic, external-internal movements · Einwärtsverkehr m

externality · externe Wirkung f

external land use, surrounding land use, service area use, umland use; suburban land use (US), peripheral land use · Umlandnutzung f

external recreation, out-(of-)door recreation · Freierholung f

external relation(ship), exterior relation(ship), third-party relation(ship) · Außenverhältnis n

external service area, umland; suburban land (US), peripheral land, surrounding land, surrounding area [*Sometimes, by local usage also called "landed estate" and "landed property" as distinguished from land in a city*] · äußeres Ergänzungsgebiet n, Vorortzone f, Umland n, Umgelände n

external (traffic) zone, exterior (traffic) zone · Außen(verkehrs)zone f

extinct · ausgerottet

extinct by limitation, extinguished by limitation · verjährt

extinction · Ausrottung f

to extinguish · löschen

to extinguish · erlöschen [*Recht*]

extinguished, merged, sunk, drowned, absorbed · untergegangen [*Wenn sich z. B. Eigentum und Pfandrecht in einer Hand vereinigen, geht das kleinere im größeren unter*]

extinguished · erloschen, gelöscht [*Recht*]

extinguished by limitation, extinct by limitation · verjährt

extinguishing · Löschen n

extinguishing · Erlöschen n [*Recht*]

extinguishment, merger, drowning, sinking, absorption [*Of one estate in another*] · Untergang m [*siehe Erklärung unter „untergegangen"*]

extinguishment [*The destruction or cancellation of a right, power, contract, estate, debt, legacy, rent, etc.*] · Löschung f

extinguishment of debt(s) · Schuldenlöschung f

extortion · Erpressung f

extortionate credit bargain · wucherischer Kreditvertrag m

extra, additional; additionary [*obsolete*]; accessory · zusätzlich

extra → extra (cost(s))

extra agreement, accessory agreement, additional agreement · Zusatzabkommen n, Zusatzabmachung f, Zusatzvereinbarung

extra bequest → extra legacy

extra capital, accessory capital, additional capital · Zusatzkapital n, zusätzliches Kapital

extra clause, accessory clause, additional clause · Zusatzklausel f

extra-community system · gemeindeübergreifendes System n

extra-community tie · gemeindeübergreifende Bindung f

extra condition, additional condition, accessory condition · Zusatzbedingung f

extra contract, accessory contract, additional contract [*Such a contract is made for assuring the performace of a prior contract, either by the same parties or by others; such as suretyship, mortgage, and pledge*] · Zusatzvertrag m

extra contract condition — extra value

extra contract condition, accessory contract condition, additional contract condition · zusätzliche Vertragsbedingung f

extracontractual, non-contractual, outside a contract · außervertraglich, nichtvertraglich

extra cost(s), accessory cost(s), additional cost(s) · zusätzliche Kosten f, Zusatzkosten

to extract, to get, to work, to win · abbauen [*Mineralien*]

extract, excerpt, abstract · Auszug m

extraction → extraction (of soil constituents)

extraction of minerals → extraction (of soil constituents)

extraction (of soil constituents), winning (of soil constituents), mineral working, mineral getting, working of minerals, getting of minerals, mineral winning, winning of minerals, extraction of minerals, mineral extraction, getting (of soil constituents), working (of soil constituents) · Abbau(en) m, (n) von Bodenbestandteilen, Abbau(en) von Mineralien, Mineralienabbau, Mineralienausbeuten, Ausbeuten von Mineralien), Ausbeutung f (von Mineralien), Ausbeutung von Bodenbestandteilen, Mineralienausbeutung, Mineraliengewinnung, Gewinnung (von Mineralien), Gewinnung von Bodenbestandteilen [*Die planmäßige Inangriffnahme einer Lagerstätte bei der Gewinnung von Lehm, Sand, Kies usw.*]

(extraction) trace, selection overlay, lift · transparenter Auszug m [*Kartographie*]

extractive industry [*Its chief function is to produce raw materials from which articles are manufactured*] · Rohstoffindustrie f

extradition [*Delivery by one nation or state to another, of fugitives from justice, in pursuance of a law or treaty*] · Auslieferung f

extra dividend, bonus on shares · Dividendenbonus m, Extradividende f, Superdividende

extra income, accessory income, additional income · Zusatzeinkommen n

extra item, additional item, accessory item · Zusatzposition f

extrajudicial, out of court; extra judicium [*Latin*]; extra-legal (US) · außergerichtlich

extrajudicial perpetuating testimony method, private perpetuating testimony method · außergerichtliches Beweissicherungsverfahren n, außergerichtliches (vorsorgliches) Beweisaufnahmeverfahren

extrajudicial (redressing) remedy, redressing extrajudicial remedy · außerrichterliches Abhilfemittel n

extra judicium [*Latin*]; extra-legal (US); extrajudicial, out of court · außergerichtlich

extra jus [*Latin*]; beyond the law, more than the law requires · übergesetzlich

extra legacy, extra bequest, accessory legacy, accessory bequest, additional legacy, aditional bequest · Zusatz(fahrnis)legat n, Zusatz(fahrnis)vermächtnis n

extra-legal (US); extrajudicial, out of court; extra judicium [*Latin*] · außergerichtlich

extra legem [*Latin*]; out of the (protection of the) law, outlawed · geächtet

extra loan, accessory loan, additional loan · Zusatzdarleh(e)n n

extra mortgage, additional mortgage, accessory mortgage · Zusatzhypothek f

extraordinary meeting · außerplanmäßige Versammlung f

extraordinary occasion, case of emergency, emergency case · Notfall m

extraordinary revenue · Extraordinarium n eines Staatshaushaltes

extraordinary traffic · außergewöhnlicher Verkehr m

extra over · zusätzlich [*Angebot*]

extraparochial · außerhalb eines Kirchspiels

extraparochial place, extraparochial locality · Ort m außerhalb eines Kirchspiels

extra pay, bonus, extra wage · Lohnzuschlag m, Bonus m

extra payment, accessory payment, additional payment · Nachzahlung f, zusätzliche Zahlung, Zusatzzahlung

extra reimbursement, accessory reimbursement, additional reimbursement · Vergütung f aus einem Zusatzauftrag, zusätzliche Vergütung

extra tax, surtax, additional tax, accessory tax · Zusatzsteuer f

extra (technical) spec(ification)(s), accessory (technical) spec(ification)(s), additional (technical) spec(ification)(s) · zusätzliche technische Vorschriften f pl

extraterritoriality · Außerstaatlichkeit f

extraterritorial (land) use zoning, extraterritorial zoning · (bauliche) Nutzung f außerhalb der Verwaltungsgrenze einer Stadt, Baunutzung außerhalb der Verwaltungsgrenze einer Stadt

extra value, accessory value, added value, additional value · Zusatzwert m, Mehrwert

extra wage, extra pay, bonus · Lohnzuschlag *m*, Bonus *m*

eye-draught (Brit.); thumb sketch (US) [*A drawing made by eye, without measurement*] · Zeichnung *f* nach Augenmaß

eye-witness · Augenzeuge *m*

eyre, eire · Sendrichtergericht *n*

F

fabric; shell [*Canada*], carcass · Rohbau *m*

fabric acceptance certificate; shell acceptance certificate [*Canada*]; carcass acceptance certificate · Rohbauschein *m*, Rohbauabnahmeschein, Rohbau(abnahme)bescheinigung *f*

fabricca ecclesiae [*Latin*] · Kirchenärar *n*, Kirchenfabrik *f* [*Das Kirchenvermögen welches zur Bestreitung der gottesdienstlichen Bedürfnisse und für die Unterhaltung der Kirchengebäude bestimmt ist*]

fabric contractor; shell contractor [*Canada*]; carcass contractor · Rohbauunternehmer *m*

fabric insurance; shell insurance [*Canada*]; carcass insurance · Rohbauversicherung *f*

fabric land(s) [*In English law: Land(s) given toward the maintenance, rebuilding and repairing of churches*] · Land *n* als Gegenleistung für Kirchenunterhaltung und -wiederaufbau

face [*document*] · Titelseite *f*, Vorderseite [*Dokument*]

face amount · Nennbetrag *m*, Nominalbetrag

face-amount certificate · Nennbetragszertifikat *n*, Nominalbetragszertifikat

face-amount certificate company, face-amount certificate fund · Investmentgesellschaft *f* mit Nennbetrag-Zertifikaten, Investmentfonds *m* mit Nennbetrag-Zertifikaten

facelessness [*architecture*] · Ausdrucksarmut *f* [*Architektur*]

face of the map, body of the map, face of the sheet, body of the sheet · Kartenfeld *n*

face-to-face group (Brit.); encounter group (US) · Intimgruppe *f*, Primärgruppe

face value, par value, denomination, nominal value [*The value mentioned on the face of a security as distinguished from the market value*] · Nennwert *m*, Nominalwert

facility · Einrichtung *f*

facility for common use, common use facility · Gemeingebrauchseinrichtung *f* [*Öffentliche Grünflächen, Spielplätze und öffentliche Verkehrseinrichtungen*]

facility to satisfy common needs · Gemeinbedarfseinrichtung *f*

fact · Tatsache *f*

fact finding · Beweisergebnis *n*

fact in issue · Streittatsache *f*

fact mistake, mistake of fact · Tatsachenirrtum *m*

fact not according to reality, false fact, unreal fact · falsche Tatsache *f*, unwirkliche Tatsache

fact not according to truth, untrue fact, fact not true · unwahre Tatsache *f*

factor, consignee, commission merchant [*He receives goods and sells them for a commission or on a percentage basis*] · (Verkaufs)Kommissionär *m*, Konsignatär

factor, trustee [*In a strict sense, a "trustee" is one who holds the legal title to property for the benefit of another, while, in a broad sense, the term is sometimes applied to anyone standing in a fiduciary or confidential relation to another, such as agent, attorney, bailee, etc.*] · Treuhänder *m*, Treuhandverwalter

factor · „Macher" *m* [*in der Politik*]

factor · Gegebenheit *f*

factor, garnishee [*When a judgment recovered by a creditor against a debtor remains unsatisfied and a debt is due to the debtor from a third party, the creditor can obtain an order from the court requiring the third party to show cause why he should not pay the debt to the creditor. The third party is called the "garnishee" and the order a "garnishee order"*] · Drittschuldner *m*

factor · Forderungskäufer *m*, Fakturenbeleiher *m*, Faktor *m*

factor [*Scots law*] → ((real) estate) broker

factorage [*The wages, allowances and commissions paid to a factor for his services*] · Kommissionsbezüge *m pl*, Verkaufskommissionsbezüge

factor allocation · Faktorzuweisung *f*

factorial cumulant · faktorielle Kumulante *f*

factorial ecology · faktorielle Ökologie *f*, Faktorialökologie

factoring · (offener) Debitorenverkauf *m*

factoring · Rediskontieren *n*, Forderungskauf *m*, Kauf von Forderungen, Fakturenbeleihung *f*, Faktoring *n*, Beleihung von Fakturen, Ankauf fälliger Forderungen

factoring client · Anschlußkunde *m* [*Forderungskauf*]

factor level · Faktorstufe *f*

factor loading · Faktorbewertung *f* [*Statistik*]

factor of conversion, conversion factor · Umrechnungsfaktor *m*

factor of (e)valuation, factor of appraisal, factor of appraisement, (e)valuation factor, appraisal factor, appraisement factor · Bewertungsfaktor *m*, (Ab)Schätzungsfaktor, Wertermitt(e)lungsfaktor, Taxierungsfaktor

factor of localization, localization factor · Lokalisierungsfaktor *m*

factor of the production, production factor · Produktionsfaktor *m*, Produktivfaktor

factor reversal test · Faktorumkehrprobe *f*, Faktorumkehrprüfung *f*, Faktorumkehrversuch *m*

factor reward · Faktorentlohnungssatz *m*; Faktorpreis *m* [*Fehlbenennung*]

factors' act, factors' law, factors' statute · Kommissionsgesetz *n*

factors' law, factors' statute, factors' act · Kommissionsgesetz *n*

factor's lien · Faktorsicherungsrecht *n* [*Am gesamten Lager in seinem jeweiligen Bestand*]

factors' statute, factors' act, factors' law · Kommissionsgesetz *n*

factory area, factory territory · Fabrikgebiet *n*, Fabrikterritorium *n*

factory employment · Fabrikbeschäftigung *f*

factory ground, factory terrain · Fabrikgelände *n*, Fabrikterrain *n*

factory industry · Fabrikindustrie *f*

factory price · Werkpreis *m*

factory quarter · Fabrikviertel *n*

factory site, factory location · Fabrikstandort *m*

factory territory, factory area · Fabrikgebiet *n*, Fabrikterritorium *n*

factory village · Fabrikdorf *n*

fact relevant to the issue · Tatsache *f* die zu Schlußfolgerung(en) über eine Streittatsache berechtigt

fact research · Tatsachenforschung *f*

facts of injustice · Unrechtstatbestand *m*

facts weighing, weighing the facts · Abwägen *n* der Tatsachen, Tatsachenabwägen

factual approach · systematische Herausarbeitung *f* der Rechtsfragen im abgesteckten Problembereich

factual judg(e)ment · Tatsachenurteil *n*

factum probandum [*Latin*]; principal fact, main fact · Haupttatsache *f*

factum probans [*Latin*]; evidentiary fact · Beweistatsache *f*

facultas alternativa [*Latin*] · Ersetzungsbefugnis *f*, Ersetzungsrecht *n*

faculty · Erlaubnis *f*, Ermächtigung *f* [*Kirchenrecht*]

faculty of law · Rechtsfakultät *f*

to fail, to lapse · hinfällig werden, in Verfall geraten, verfallen

to fail · pflichtwidrig versäumen

to fail · ausfallen

failed, lapsed · hinfällig, in Verfall geraten, verfallen

failed · ausgefallen [*Maschine*]

failing, crashing, dropping to pieces, collapsing, breaking down · Einstürzen *n*, Einfallen

failure, omission, omittance, forbearance, negligence, negative act(ion), default, neglect [*Omission of that which a person ought to do*] · (Ver)Säumnis *f*, *n*, *(f)*, Vernachlässigung *f*, Unterlassung(shandlung), Nichtleistung, Unterlassungsakt *m*, negativer Akt, negative Handlung

failure, insolvency · Zahlungsunfähigkeit *f*

failure, lapse · Hinfälligkeit *f* eines Vermächtnisses (wenn der Vermächtnisnehmer vor dem Erblasser stirbt), Verfall *m* eines Vermächtnisses (wenn der Vermächtnisnehmer vor dem Erblasser stirbt), Vermächtnisverfall *m*, Vermächtnishinfälligkeit

failure [*An unsuccessful attempt*] · Fehlschlag *m*, Versagen *n*, Nichtgelingen

failure → (business) failure

failure danger, collapse danger, crash danger · Einsturzgefahr *f*, Einfallgefahr

failure of consideration · Mangel *m* der Gegenleistung, Unmöglichwerden *n* einer Gegenleistung, Nichterhältlichkeit *f* einer Gegenleistung, mangelnde Gegenleistung

failure of evidence, failure of proof · Beweislosigkeit *f*

failure of issue · Nachkommenslosigkeit *f*

failure of the market — fair chart

failure of the market, market failure · Marktversagen *n*

failure of title, title failure · (Rechts)Titellosigkeit *f*

failure to commence · Beginnunterlassung *f*

failure to exercise care, negligence, negligent performance of the contract, failure to use ordinary care, breach of duty to exercise due care and skill, breach of duty to take care · Verletzung *f* der Sorgfaltspflicht, Verstoß *m* gegen die Sorgfaltspflicht, Sorgfalts(pflicht)verletzung, Sorgfalts(pflicht)verstoß *m*

failure to insure · Versicherungsunterlassung *f*

failure to make delivery, nondelivery, misdelivery · Nichtlieferung *f*

failure to meet obligations · Verpflichtungsunterlassung *f*

failure to pay · Zahlungsunterlassung *f*

failure to use ordinary care, breach of duty to exercise due care and skill, breach of duty to take care, failure to exercise care, negligence, negligent performance of the contract · Verletzung *f* der Sorgfaltspflicht, Verstoß *m* gegen die Sorgfaltspflicht, Sorgfalts(pflicht)verletzung, Sorgfalts(pflicht)verstoß *m*

faint, pretended, feigned, feint, fictitious · fiktiv, vorgegeben, vorgetäuscht, fingiert

faint bill, feigned bill, pretended bill; windmill, kite (Brit.); accommodation bill, fictitious bill, feint bill · Freundschaftswechsel *m*, Gefälligkeitswechsel, Kellerwechsel, Reitwechsel, Schornsteinwechsel, Scheinwechsel

faint business, pretended business, feint business, fictitious business, feigned business · fiktives Geschäft *n*, fingiertes Geschäft, vorgegebenes Geschäft, vorgetäuschtes Geschäft, Scheingeschäft

faint contract, fictitious contract, feigned contract, pretended contract · Scheinvertrag *m*

faint (court) action, fictitious (court) action, feint (court) action, pretended (court) action, feigned (court) action [*An action brought on a pretended right, when the plaintiff has no true cause of action, for some illegal purpose. In a feigned action the words of the writ are true. It differs from "false action", in which case the words of the writ are false*] · fiktive Klage *f*, vorgetäuschte Klage, vorgegebene Klage, fingierte Klage, Scheinklage

faint desertion, feint desertion, fictitious desertion, feigned desertion, pretended desertion · Scheinwüstung *f*, Trugwüstung

faint name, feint name, fictitious name, pretended name, feigned name · fiktiver Name *m*, vorgetäuschter Name, vorgegebener Name, fingierter Name, Scheinname

faint permission → feigned permission

faint plaintiff, feint plaintiff, fictitious plaintiff, feigned plaintiff, pretended plaintiff · fiktiver Kläger *m*, vorgegebener Kläger, vorgetäuschter Kläger, fingierter Kläger, Scheinkläger

faint promise, feint promise, fictitious promise, feigned promise, pretended promise · fiktives Versprechen *n*, vorgetäuschtes Versprechen, vorgegebenes Versprechen, fingiertes Versprechen, Scheinversprechen

faint purchase, pretended purchase, feint purchase, fictitious purchase, feigned purchase · fiktiver Kauf *m*, vorgetäuschter Kauf, fingierter Kauf, vorgegebener Kauf, Scheinkauf

fair · lauter, uneigennützig

fair and feasible · ausreichend und durchführbar

fair and full equivalent for loss, fair and full consideration · ausreichende und volle Gegenleistung *f* für Verlust *m*

fair and impartial jury · lautere und unparteiliche Geschworene *mpl*

fair and reasonable compensation, fair and reasonable damages, fair and reasonable indemnification, fair and reasonable indemnity · ausreichende und angemessene Entschädigung *f*, ausreichender und angemessener Schadenersatz *m*

fair and reasonable indemnity, fair and reasonable compensation, fair and reasonable damages, fair and reasonable indemnification · ausreichende und angemessene Entschädigung *f*, ausreichender und angemessener Schadenersatz *m*

fair and reasonable value · ausreichender und angemessener Wert *m*

fair (cash) value, capital value, true (cash) value [*The value of land imputed from the annual rent. Determined by dividing the annual rent specified in the lease agreement by the previously concurred-in current annual rate of rent. The capital value must be not less than the fair value of the land in fee at the time of the lease. The capital value of the annual rent determined in this way provides a valid basis for comparing the proposed lease with offers to purchase*] · Kapitalwert *m*

fair chart · Reinzeichnung *f* der Arbeitskarte [*Kartographie*]

fair competition, just competition, equitable competition · lauterer Wettbewerb *m*, uneigennütziger Wettbewerb

fair consideration, fair equivalent · ausreichende Gegenleistung *f*, angemessene Gegenleistung

fair draught (Brit.); fair drawing · Reinzeichnung *f* [*Kartographie*]

fair equivalent, fair consideration · ausreichende Gegenleistung *f*, angemessene Gegenleistung

fair ground · Messegelände *n*

fair knowledge · ausreichendes Wissen *n*

(fair) market value [*What a willing seller is willing to accept from a willing buyer neither being under any coercion and both having equal knowledge of all relevant facts*] · Handelswert *m*, Verkehrswert, Marktwert

fairness · Lauterkeit *f*, Uneigennützigkeit

fair price, paying price · auskömmlicher Preis *m*, rentierlicher Preis *m*

fair repair · Schönheitsreparatur *f*

fair sale · lauterer Verkauf *m*, uneigennütziger Verkauf

fair skill · ausreichende Fertigkeit *f*

fair wear and tear, normal wear and tear, regular wear and tear · normaler Verschleiß *m*, üblicher Verschleiß

faithful, trust(worth)y, credible · glaubwürdig, glaubhaft, vertrauenswürdig

faitour, idle person · Faulenzer *m*

faldae cursus [*Latin*]; fold course [*Land to which is appurtenant the sole right of folding the sheep of others*] · (Schaf)Pferchland *n*

faldage, right of drove, drove right, feldage; actus, faldagium [*Latin*]; frankfold · Triftrecht *n*, Treibrecht

falda libera, cursus faldae [*Latin*]; frank fold, free fold, course of fold, fold course, faldsoke; faldsoca [*Saxon law*] [*The privilege of setting up and moving about in a field a fold, for the purpose of manuring the ground, which several lords anciently reserved to themselves in any fields within their manors, not only with their own but their tenants sheep*] · (Schaf)Pferchrecht *n*

falk-land; terra popularis, ager publicus [*Latin*]; land of the people, folkland, folcland [*Anglo-Saxon land law. Folcland was held by customary law, without written title. Inheritance depended on custom. It could not be (ab)alienated without the consent of those who had some interest in it*] · Volksland *n*

to fall behind schedule · zurückbleiben hinter einer Frist

to fall due, to accrue, to become due, to mature [*As rent or interest*] · fällig werden, verfallen

to fall in (Brit.); to expire, to end, to terminate, to lapse, to run out, to cease · ablaufen, verfristen

falling in, lapse (of time), expiration, expiry, running out, termination · Ablauf *m*, Fristablauf, Zeitablauf, Verfristung *f*

falling in date, running out date, accrual date, maturity date, expiry date, expiration date, due date, termination date · Fälligkeitsdatum *n*, Fälligkeitstag *m*, Verfalldatum, Verfalltermin *m*, (Frist)Ablauftermin, (Frist)Ablaufdatum, Fälligkeitstermin, Verfalltag, (Frist)Ablauftag

falling off of (population) density, (population) density decay · (Bevölkerungs)Dichteschwund *m*, Volksdichteschwund

falling of fruit (up)on one's premises over a wall or hedge · Überfall *m* von Früchten, Früchteüberfall, Anries *m*

fallout · radioaktiver Niederschlag *m*

fallow · brach

fallow land, idle land, tract of fallow (land), waste, uncultivated land; novale, frusca terra [*Latin*] · Brachflur *f*, Brachland *n*, Brachacker *m*, Brachfeld *n*

fallow land afforestation, afforestation of fallow land · Brachlandaufforstung *f*

fallow pasture (ground), fallow pasture land · Brachhut *f*, Brach(vieh)weide *f*

fall population, autumn population · Herbstbevölkerung *f*

false, dishonest · unehrlich, falsch

false, not real, unreal, not according to realty · unwirklich, falsch

false, counterfeit, not genuine · gefälscht, imitiert, nachgemacht, falsch

false, not true, not truly, not according to truth, untrue · falsch, unwahr

false arrest · ungesetzliche Arretierung *f*

false fact, unreal fact, fact not according to reality · falsche Tatsache *f*, unwirkliche Tatsache

false front, false facade · Scheinfassade *f*

false(ly), erroneous(ly), wrong, mistaken(ly) · irrig(erweise), rechtsirrtümlich, irrtümlich(erweise), falsch

false oath; mainad [*In old English law*]; perjury (US); false swearing · Meineid *m*

false personation; impersonation (US) · Sichausgeben *n* als ein anderer

false recital, misrepresentation, misrecital, false representation · Falschdarstellung *f*, Falscherklärung

false recital of fact(s), misrepresentation of fact(s), misrecital of fact(s), false representation of fact(s) · Tatsachenfalschdarstellung *f*, Tatsachenfalscherklärung, Sachverhaltfalscherklärung, Sachverhaltfalschdarstellung, Falschdarstellung der Tatsachen, Falscherklärung der Tatsachen, Falschdarstellung des Sachverhalts, Falscherklärung des Sachverhalts

false representation, false recital, misrepresentation, misrecital · Falschdarstellung *f*, Falscherklärung, Falschinformation *f*

false representation of fact(s), false recital of fact(s), misrepresentation of fact(s), misrecital of fact(s) · Tatsachenfalschdarstellung *f*, Tatsachenfalscherklärung, Sachverhaltfalscherklärung, Sachverhaltfalschdarstellung, Falschdarstellung der Tatsachen, Falscherklärung der Tatsachen, Falschdarstellung des Sachverhalts, Falscherklärung des Sachverhalts

false representer, misrepresenter · Falschdarsteller *m*, Falscherklärer, Falschinformant

false statement, misstatement · Falschaussage *f*, Falschangabe *f*

false swearing, false oath; mainad [*In old English law*]; perjury (US) · Meineid *m*

falsification of account(s) · Kontenfälschung *f*

to falsify [*Where an account is being investigated in the Chancery Division, and the party at whose instance it is taken shows that an item of payment or discharge contained in it is false or erroneous, he is said to falsify it*] · widerlegen

to falsify, to disprove, to prove (to be) false, to prove (to be) erroneous, to prove (to be) untrue, to prove (to be) unfounded · widerlegen

to falsify · fälschen

falsity, knowledge of untruth · Kenntnis *f* der Unwahrheit

falsity [*Contrariety or want of conformity to truth or fact*] · Unrichtigkeit *f*

fame, repute · Ruf *m*

familia [*Latin*]; hide ((of) land), hyde (of land), higid, hiwise, virgate (land), verge of land, yardland, hydeland, husbandland, wista; hilda [*Scotland*]; terra hydata, virgate terrae, hida (terrae), hyda [*Latin*] [*A quantity of land not of any certain extent, but as much as a plough can by course of husbandry plough in a year. It meant in different places anything from sixty to 120 acres. A virgate is one fourth of a hide*] · Hufe(ngut) *f*, (*n*), Hufenschoß *n*, Hube *f*, Hufen(gut)land *n* [*Ältere Benennungen: Hof m, Hub m, Hu(o)ba f, und Hova f*] [*Unter gutsherrlich-bäuerlichen Verhältnissen hieß der gesamte Besitz eines Dorfgenossen ,,Hufe(ngut)". Diese Benennung war also keine Flächengröße, sondern eine Besitzeinheit, die zahlreiche, zerstreut liegende kleine Ackerteile im Besitz derselben Person umfaßte*]

family agricultural enterprise, family farm · Familiengehöft *n*, Familienhof *m*, landwirtschaftlicher Familienbetrieb *m*, Familien-Agrarbetrieb

family allowance, allowance for children, children allowance, family bonus · Kindergeld *n*, Kinderbeihilfe *f*

family bible · Stammbuchbibel *f*

family book · Stammbuch *n*

family break-up · Familienauflösung *f*

family budget · Familienhaushalt *m*, Familienbudget *n*

family composition · Familienzusammensetzung *f*

family council · Familienrat *m*

family endowment, family indowment · Familien(dauer)stiftung *f*

family enterprise, family undertaking · Familienbetrieb *m*, Familienunternehmen *n*, Familienunternehmung *f*

family farm, family agricultural enterprise · Familiengehöft *n*, Familienhof *m*, landwirtschaftlicher Familienbetrieb *m*, Familien-Agrarbetrieb

family formation · Familienbildung *f*

family garden · Familiengarten *m*

family (general) property, family ownership (of property), family proprietorship · Familieneigentum *n*

family home · Familienheim *n*

family home law · Familienheimrecht *n*

family home law, family home statute, family home act · Familienheimgesetz *n*

family household · Familienhaushalt *m*

family income supplement · Familienbeihilfe *f*, Familienunterstützung *f*, Familienzulage *f*

family indowment, family endowment · Familien(dauer)stiftung *f*

family land, heir land, ethel(-land), erfland, alod · Erbland *n*, erbliches Land

family law, law of domestic relations · Familienrecht *n*

family matter · Familienangelegenheit *f*

family name, last name, agnomination, surname · Nachname *m*, Familienname

family ownership (of property), family proprietorship, family (general) property · Familieneigentum *n*

family physician · Hausarzt *m*

family planning, birth control · Familienplanung *f*, Geburtenbegrenzung, Geburteneinschränkung, Geburtenbeschränkung

family proprietorship, family (general) property, family ownership (of property) · Familieneigentum *n*

family provision; family support (US) · Familienunterhalt *m*

family register, family registry · Familienregister *n*

family relationship, standing in the family, marital status, marital condition [*i.e. whether single, married, divorced or widowed*] · Familienstand *m*

family shelter · Familien-Schutzbunker *m*

family support (US); family provision · Familienunterhalt *m*

family undertaking, family enterprise · Familienbetrieb *m*, Familienunternehmen *n*, Familienunternehmung *f*

family with many children · kinderreiche Familie *f*

fancy value, sentimental value · Affektionswert *m*, Liebhaberwert

fan pattern, fan form, fan layout, fan scheme, radial pattern, radial form, radial layout, radial scheme · Fächermuster *n*, Fächerform *f*, Fächerschema *n*, Radialmuster, Radialform, Radialschema [*Stadtgrundriß*]

F.A.R., floor space index, F.S.I. (Brit.); basic floor area (US), floor area ratio [*The square-foot amount of total floor area (all stories) for each square foot of land area of a property*] · Geschoßflächenzahl *f*, GFZ, Geschoßflächendichte *f*, GFD; Ausnutzungsziffer *f* [*frühere Benennung*]

farm · Agrarbetrieb *m*, Hof *m*, Landschaftsbetrieb, landwirtschaftlicher Betrieb

to farm, to cultivate, to produce by tillage, to raise by tillage · kultivieren, anbauen

to farm [*To operate a farm*] · betreiben eines landwirtschaftlichen Betriebes

to farm, to rent land(s) · pachten von Land

to farm [*To collect taxes and other fees on a commission basis for a fixed amount*] · pachten von Steuereinnahmen

to farm [*To arrange for the care of children, paupers, etc.*] · übernehmen des Unterhaltes von Personen

to farm [*To let out the labour of a convict, etc. for a fixed amount*] · verpachten der Arbeitskraft von Menschen

to farm, to let land(s) · verpachten von Land

to farm [*To work on a farm*] · arbeiten in der Landwirtschaft

farm [*The letting out, for a fixed amount, of the collection of taxes, with the privilege of keeping all that is collected*] · Verpachtung *f* von Steuern, Steuerverpachtung

farm animal · Nutztier *n*

farm belt · landwirtschaftlicher Intensivnutzungsgürtel *m*, Gürtel landwirtschaftlicher Intensivnutzung

farm building · Hofgebäude *n*

farm code · Höfeordnung *f*

farm colony · ländliche Notstandsarbeits-(an)sied(e)lung *f*

farm condemnation (US); farm expropriation · Hofenteignung *f*

farm co-operative · landwirtschaftliche Genossenschaft *f*

farm demise, farm lease · Landwirtschaftsverpachtung *f*

farmed land, agriculturally zoned land, agriculturally used land, crop land, agricultural land, farming land, land agricultural in character, farmland, improved land [*Land may be assessable as "agricultural land" though it be covered by timber and underbrush, grass and weeds*] · landwirtschaftlicher Boden *m*, landwirtschaftlich genutzter Boden, landwirtschaftliches Land *n*, landwirtschaftlich genutztes Land, Kulturland, Kulturboden, Agrarland, landwirtschaftlich genutzte Fläche *f*, LN, landwirtschaftliche Nutzfläche, Fruchtland, Agrarnutzfläche

farm enlargement · Aufstockung *f* [*Vergrößerung der Fläche eines landwirtschaftlichen Betriebes*]

farmer · Landwirt *m*

farmer [*A person who contracts to collect taxes or revenues by paying a fixed sum to the government for the right to do so*] · Steuerpächter *m*

farmer → (tenant) farmer

farmer-city, agricultural town, agricultural city, agro-town, agro-city, peasant-city, peasant-town, rural agglomeration, farmer-town · Agrarstadt *f*, Agrostadt, Landwirtschaftsstadt [*Landwirtschaftliche Groß(an)sied(e)lung mit weiterverarbeitender Industrie und ausgebautem Dienstleistungsnetz*]

farmerette [*colloquial*]; female farm worker · Landarbeiterin *f*

farmers' union · Landbund *m*

farm expropriation; farm condemnation (US) · Hofenteignung *f*

farm house · landwirtschaftliches Wohnhaus *n*

farmhouse — farthing

farmhouse · Haus *n* eines landwirtschaftlichen Betriebes

farm housing sector, farm housing field, agricultural housing sector, agricultural housing field · landwirtschaftlicher Wohnungssektor *m*

farming, soil cultivation, agricultural use, cultivation (of land), cultivation of fields, cultivation of soil, land cultivation, field cultivation · Anbau *m*, Bodenkultivierung *f*, Landkultivierung, Bodenkultur *f*, Feldbau

farming area, agricultural territory, farming territory, cultivation area, cultivation territory, agrarian area, agrarian territory, agricultural area · Agrarfläche *f*, Agrargebiet *n*, landwirtschaftliche Fläche, landwirtschaftliches Gebiet, Anbaufläche, Anbaugebiet

farming land, land agricultural in character, farmland, improved land, farmed land, agriculturally zoned land, agriculturally used land, crop land, agricultural land [*Land may be assessable as "agricultural land" though it be covered by timber and underbrush, grass and weeds*] · landwirtschaftlicher Boden *m*, landwirtschaftlich genutzter Boden, landwirtschaftliches Land *n*, landwirtschaftlich genutztes Land, Kulturland, Kulturboden, Agrarland, landwirtschaftlich genutzte Fläche *f*, LN, landwirtschaftliche Nutzfläche, Fruchtland, Agrarnutzfläche

farming landowner, farmland owner, agrarian landowner, agricultural landowner · Agrarlandeigentümer *m*, Kulturlandeigentümer, Kulturbodeneigentümer, Agrarlandeigner, Kulturlandeigner, Kulturbodeneigner

farming region, agrarian region, agricultural region · Agrarregion *f*, Landwirtschaftsregion, Agrarraum *m*, Landwirtschaftsraum, landwirtschaftliche Region, landwirtschaftlicher Raum, Anbauraum, Anbauregion

farming territory, cultivation area, cultivation territory, agrarian area, agrarian territory, agricultural area, farming area, agricultural territory · Agrarfläche *f*, Agrargebiet *n*, landwirtschaftliche Fläche, landwirtschaftliches Gebiet, Anbaufläche, Anbaugebiet

farm labour hous(ebuild)ing (Brit.); farm labor hous(ebuild)ing (US) · Landarbeiterwohnungsbau *m*

farm labour housing (Brit.); farm labor housing (US) · Landarbeiterwohnungen *f pl*

farmland → agriculturally zoned land

farmland law, agricultural land law · Kulturlandrecht *n*

farmland owner, agrarian landowner, agricultural landowner, farming landowner · Agrarlandeigentümer *m*, Kulturlandeigentümer, Kulturbodeneigentümer, Agrarlandeigner, Kulturlandeigner, Kulturbodeneigner

farm lease, farm demise · Landwirtschaftsverpachtung *f*

farm livery contract · Hofübergabevertag *m*

farm-loan bank · Landeskulturrentenbank *f* [*Eine vom Staat oder einem höheren Kommunalverband gegründete Anstalt welche für Bodenmelioration den Grundbesitzern Darleh(e)n gegen feste, Zins- und Tilgungsbeitrag enthaltende, Jahresraten gewährt*]

farm lot · Hofparzelle *f*

farm machinery syndicate · Landmaschinenring *m*

farm office · Wirtschaftsgebäude *n*, Landwirtschaftsgebäude

farm of inheritance, inheritance farm · Erbhof *m*

farm-rent · Ackergeld *n*, Ackerzins *m*

farms relocation, relocation of farms · Abbau *m*, Ausbau *m*, Aussied(e)lung *f*, Vereinödung [*Die Versetzung der Hofstätten einzelner oder sämtlicher an der Vereinödung beteiligter Bauern aus dem Weiler oder Dorf hinaus auf die neu zugeteilten Flächen*]

farmstead · Hofstelle *f*, Gehöft *n*, Hof *m*

farmstead [*The land and buildings of a farm*] · Land *n* und Gebäude *f (pl)* eines landwirtschaftlichen Betriebes, Land und Gebäude eines landwirtschaftlichen Hofes

farm tenant, (tenant) farmer, leasehold farmer, tenant of a farm [*Die Benennung "farmer" bedeutet in England nicht nur Landwirt, sondern auch Pächter und nur wenn die Pächtereigenschaft hervorgehoben wird, heißt es tenant farmer*] · (landwirtschaftlicher) Pächter *m*, Landwirtschaftspächter, Agrarpächter

farm village · Höfedorf *n*; Eschdorf [*nach H. Riepenhauer, 1938*]

farm work, agrarian work, agricultural work · Landarbeit *f*, Agrararbeit

farm worker; labourer (Brit.); agricultural worker, agrarian worker · Landarbeiter *m*

farmyard [*The yard surrounding or enclosed by the farm buildings*] · Hof *m* eines landwirtschaftlichen Betriebes

far reaching regional centre (Brit.); far reaching regional center (US) · weitreichendes regionales Zentrum *n*

farthing · Heller *m*

fas, free alongside ship · frei Seeschiffseite f

fast boating, high-speed boating, rapid boating · motorisierter Bootssport m, motorischer Bootssport

fast transit → (public) rapid transit

fast transit line → (public) fast transit line

fast transit policy → (public) fast transit policy

fatal accident · tödlicher Unfall m, Unfall mit Todesfolge

fatal error · schwerwiegender Fehler m

fatigue allowance [*In working out the time standard for a job an allowance is made for some loss of speed and efficiency in the later hours of the day*] · Ermüdungszuschlag m

fatting cattle; feed-lot cattle (US) · Mastvieh n

fault · Verschulden n

fault · Mangel m [*in einem Antrag*]

faultiness, wrongness [*Want of correctness or exactness*] · Fehlerhaftigkeit f

faulty, defective · fehlerhaft

faulty (ad)measurement · Fehlaufmaß n, fehlerhaftes Aufmaß

faulty organization, defective organization · Organisationsmangel m

favo(u)rable [*balance of payment; balance of trade*] · positiv

favo(u)rable financial leverage, trading on the equity · positive Hebelwirkung f [*Der Grenzsachzins liegt über dem Grenzmarktzins*]

F.C.S., free of capture and seizure · frei von Beschlagnahmerisiko, frei von Beschlagnahmewagnis

F-distribution, variance ratio distribution · F-Verteilung f [*Statistik*]

fealty, fidelity, feodality, allegiance, feudality; fidelitas feudalis [*Latin*] [*It was due by feudal tenants to their lords*] · Leh(e)n(s)treue f

fealty oath, fidelity oath, oath of allegiance, oath of fealty, oath of fidelity [*It was sworn by feudal tenants to their lords*] · Leh(e)n(s)eid m, Leh(e)n(s)schwur m, Treu(e)eid, Treu(e)schwur

feasibility, workability, practicability · Ausführbarkeit f, Durchführbarkeit

feasibility analysis, feasibility study, workability analysis, workability study, practicability analysis, practicability study · Ausführbarkeitsstudie f, Durchführbarkeitsstudie f, Durchführbarkeitsanalyse f, Ausführbarkeitsanalyse f

feasibility survey, workability survey, practicability survey · Ausführbarkeitsenquête f, Durchführbarkeitsenquête f

feasible, practicable, workable · ausführbar, durchführbar

feather(edg)ing · Auflockerung f des Höhenlinienbildes [*bei dichter Scharung*] [*Kartographie*]

fecundity, child-woman ratio [*The ratio which the number of births per annum bears to the number of persons of reproductive age, or of women of reproductive age; or of married persons, or wives only, at that age*] · Fruchtbarkeitsziffer f, Fruchtbarkeitsrate f

federal act, federal law, federal statute · Bundesgesetz n

federal administration · Bundesverwaltung f, bundeseigene Verwaltung

Federal Administrative Court · Bundesverwaltungsgericht n, BVerwG [*Bundesrepublik Deutschland*]

federal administrative law · Bundesverwaltungsrecht n

federal agency, federal office · Bundesstelle f, Bundesdienststelle

federal aid · Bundeshilfe f

federal aid project · Bundeshilfeprojekt n

federal area, federal territory · Bundesgebiet n

federal assistance · Bundesförderung f

federal audit office, federal audit department · Bundesrechnungshof m

federal authority · Bundesbehörde f

federal authority, federal power · Bundesgewalt f, Bundesmacht f, Bundeshoheit f, Bundeskompetenz f

federal board · Bundesamt n

federal budget · Bundeshaushalt m

federal budgetary means · Bundeshaushaltsmittel f

federal building · Bundesgebäude n

federal building act, federal building law, federal building statute, federal construction act, federal construction statute, federal construction law · Bundesbaugesetz n

federal building law, federal construction law · Bundesbaurecht n

federal building law → federal building act

federal building project, federal construction project · Bundesbauprojekt n, Bundesbauvorhaben n

federal building statute → federal building act

Federal Cartel Office · Bundeskartellamt n [*Bundesrepublik Deutschland*]

federal citizen — Federal Law Gazette

federal citizen · Bundesbürger *m*

federal civil servant · Bundesbedienstete *m*

federal civil service official law · Bundesbeamtenrecht *n*

federal code · Bundesordnung *f*

federal compensation statute → federal tort claims act

federal constitution · Bundesverfassung *f*

Federal Constitution · Verfassung *f*, Grundgesetz *n* [*Bundesrepublik Deutschland*]

Federal Constitutional Court · Bundesverfassungsgericht *n*, BVerfG [*Bundesrepublik Deutschland*]

federal construction act, federal construction statute, federal construction law, federal building act, federal building law, federal building statute · Bundesbaugesetz *n*

federal construction administration · Bundesbauverwaltung *f*

federal construction directorate · Bundesbaudirektion *f*

federal construction law, federal building law · Bundesbaurecht *n*

federal construction law → federal construction act

federal construction project, federal building project · Bundesbauprojekt *n*, Bundesbauvorhaben *n*

federal construction statute → federal construction act

federal contribution · Bundesbeitrag *m*

federal court · Bundesgericht *n*

Federal Court of Justice, Federal Supreme Court · Bundesgerichtshof *m*, BGH [*Bundesrepublik Deutschland*]

federal credit aid · Bundeskredithilfe *f*

federal currency · Bundeswährung *f*

federal customs gazette · Bundeszollblatt *n*

federal damages statute → federal tort claims act

federal development plan · Bundesentwick(e)lungsplan *m*

federal estate, federal property · Bundesvermögen *n*, Bundesgut *n*

federal estate board, federal property board · Bundesvermögensamt *n*, Bundesgutamt

federal finance court · Bundesfinanzgericht *n*

Federal Finance Court, Federal Tax Court · Bundesfinanzhof *m*, BFH [*Bundesrepublik Deutschland*]

federal finance minister · Bundesfinanzminister *m*

federal forest law, federal forest act, federal forest statute · Bundesforstgesetz *n*, Bundeswaldgesetz

federal fund · Bundesfonds *m*, Bundesmittel *f*

federal gas(oline) tax, federal gasolene tax (US); federal petrol tax (Brit.) · Bundesbenzinsteuer *f*

Federal Gazette · Bundesanzeiger *m*, BAnz [*Bundesrepublik Deutschland*]

federal (general) property, federal ownership (of property), federal proprietorship · Bundeseigentum *n*

federal government · Bundesregierung *f*

federal grant-in-aid · Bundeszuschuß *m*

federal guarantee, federal guaranty, federal guarantie · Bundesbürgschaft *f*

federal guideline · Bundesrichtlinie *f*

federal highway, federal road · Bundesstraße *f*

federal highway administration, federal road administration, FHWA · Bundesstraßenverwaltung *f*

federal highway construction, federal road construction · Bundesstraßenbau *m*

Federal House and Home Finance Agency, FHA · oberste Bundesbehörde *f* für den Wohn(ungs)bau in den USA, höchste Bundesbehörde für den Wohn(ungs)bau in den USA

federal hous(ebuild)ing assistance · Bundeswohn(ungs)bauförderung *f*

federal housing ministry · Bundeswohnungsbauministerium *n*

federal housing policy · Bundeswohnungspolitik *f*

federal housing programme; federal housing program (US) · Bundeswohnungsbauprogramm *n*

federal indemnification law → federal tort claims act

federalism · Föderalismus *m*

Federal Labour Court (Brit.); Federal Labor Court (US) · Bundesarbeitsgericht *n*, BAG [*Bundesrepublik Deutschland*]

federal law, federal statute, federal act · Bundesgesetz *n*

federal law · Bundesrecht *n*

Federal Law Gazette · Bundesgesetzblatt *n*, BGBl. [*Bundesrepublik Deutschland*]

federal legislation, federal lawmaking · Bundesgesetzgebung *f*

federal level · Bundesebene *f*

federal loan · Bundesanleihe *f*

federally assisted · bundesgefördert

federally assisted housing · bundesgeförderte Wohnungen *fpl*

federally assisted urban renewal project · bundesgefördertes Stadterneuerungsprojekt *n*

federally financed · bundesfinanziert

federally owned · bundeseigen, im Eigentum des Bundes

federally subsidized · bundessubventioniert

federally subsidized urban renewal project · bundessubventioniertes Stadterneuerungsprojekt *n*

federal measure · Bundesmaßnahme *f*

Federal Mediation and Conciliation Service [*USA*] · Bundesschlichtungsstelle *f* für Arbeitsstreitigkeiten

federal minister of hous(ebuild)ing · Bundesminister *m* für Wohn(ungs)bau

federal ministry of health · Bundesgesundheitsministerium *n*

federal motorway · Bundesautobahn *f*

federal nature protection act, federal nature protection law, federal nature protection statute · Bundesnaturschutzgesetz *n*

federal office, federal agency · Bundesstelle *f*, Bundesdienststelle

federal ordinance · Bundes(rechts)verordung *f*

federal outlays · Bundesausgaben *fpl*

federal(-owned) land(s), land(s) in federal ownership · Bundesländerei(en) *f (pl)*, Bundesland *n*, bundeseigenes Land

federal ownership (of property), federal proprietorship, federal (general) property · Bundeseigentum *n*

federal participation · Bundesbeteiligung *f*, Bundesmitwirkung

federal past-president · Altbundespräsident *m*

federal petrol tax (Brit.); federal gas(oline) tax, federal gasolene tax (US) · Bundesbenzinsteuer *f*

federal physical planning, national spatial planning, national space planning, national physical planning, federal spatial planning, federal space planning · Bundesraumplanung *f*, BRP

federal planning · Bundesplanung *f*

federal power, federal authority · Bundesgewalt *f*, Bundesmacht *f*, Bundeshoheit *f*, Bundeskompetenz *f*

federal prescription, federal regulation, federal rule · Bundes(rechts)vorschrift *f*

federal president · Bundespräsident *m*

federal printing office · Bundesdruckerei *f*

federal programme; federal program (US) · Bundesprogramm *n*

federal project · Bundesprojekt *n*

federal property, federal estate · Bundesvermögen *n*, Bundesgut *n*

federal property board, federal estate board · Bundesvermögensamt *n*, Bundesgutamt

federal proprietorship, federal (general) property, federal ownership (of property) · Bundeseigentum *n*

federal railway law (Brit.); federal railraod law (US) · Bundesbahnrecht *n*

federal regional policy · Bundesraumordnung *f*, BRO

federal regional policy act, federal regional policy law, federal regional policy statute · Bundesraumordnungsgesetz *n*, BROG

federal regional policy programme; federal regional policy program (US) · Bundesraumordnungsprogramm *n*, BROP

federal register · Bundesverwaltungsblatt *n* [*in den USA*]

federal regulation, federal rule, federal prescription · Bundes(rechts)vorschrift *f*

federal rehabilitation area, federal rehabilitation territory · Bundesausbaugebiet *n*

federal rehabilitation plan · Bundesausbauplan *m*

federal rehabilitation site · Bundesausbauort *m*

federal rent (control) act, federal rent (control) law, federal rent (control) statute · Bundesmietengesetz *n*

federal road, federal highway · Bundesstraße *f*

federal road administration, FHWA, federal highway administration · Bundesstraßenverwaltung *f*

federal road construction, federal highway construction · Bundesstraßenbau *m*

federal rule, federal prescription, federal regulation · Bundes(rechts)vorschrift *f*

federal share · Bundesanteil *m*

Federal Social Court · Bundessozialgericht *n* [*Bundesrepublik Deutschland*]

(federal) state, constituent state [*USA*]; Land [*Federal Republic of Germany*] ·

federal statistics law — feedback

Staat m [USA]; (Bundes)Land n [Bundesrepublik Deutschland]

federal statistics law, federal statistics act, federal statistics statute · Bundesstatistikgesetz n

federal statute, federal act, federal law · Bundesgesetz n

federal subsidy, federal subvention · (Kapital)Zuwendung f durch den Bund, Bundessubvention f

federal superintendence, federal supervision · Bundesaufsicht f, Bundesüberwachung f

federal supervision, federal superintendence · Bundesaufsicht f, Bundesüberwachung f

Federal Supplement, F. Supp. [*In the USA*] · Sammlung f der Bundesgerichtsentscheidungen [*nicht der Staatsgerichte*]

Federal Supreme Court, Federal Court of Justice · Bundesgerichtshof m, BGH [*Bundesrepublik Deutschland*]

federal supreme court · oberstes Bundesgericht n, höchstes Bundesgericht

Federal Tax Court, Federal Finance Court · Bundesfinanzhof m, BFH [*Bundesrepublik Deutschland*]

federal territory, federal area · Bundesgebiet n

federal tort claims act, federal tort claims statute, federal tort claims law, federal indemnification statute, federal indemnification act, federal indemnification law, federal indemnity statute, federal indemnity act, federal indemnity law, federal compensation statute, federal compensation law, federal compensation act, federal damages statute, federal damages act, federal damages law · Bundesentschädigungsgesetz n, Bundesschadenersatzgesetz

Federal Tort Claims Act · Bundesschadenersatzgesetz n [*USA*]

federal traffic route plan · Bundesverkehrswegeplan m

federal trunk road act, federal trunk road law, federal trunk road statute · Bundesfernstraßengesetz n

federal trunk road, federal trunk highway · Bundesfernstraße f

federation · Spitzenorganisation f, Spitzenverband m, Dachverband, Dachorganisation, Bund m

federation · Bund m

federation of borrowers, society of borrowers, association of borrowers, institution of borrowers · landwirtschaftlicher Kreditverein m, Landschaft f, landwirtschaftliche Kreditvereinigung f

402

federation of building contractors, association of construction contractors, association of building contractors, society of construction contractors, society of building contractors, institution of construction contractors, institution of building contractors, federation of construction contractors · Bauunternehmerverein(igung) m, (f)

federation of construction contractors, federation of building contractors, association of construction contractors, association of building contractors, society of construction contractors, society of building contractors, institution of construction contractors, institution of building contractors · Bauunternehmerverein(igung) m, (f)

federation of engineering unions, association of engineering unions, institution of engineering unions, society of engineering unions · Verein(igung) m, (f) der Ingenieurverbände

federation of labour unions (Brit.); federation of labor unions (US); federation of trade unions · Gewerkschaftsbund m

federation of tenants · Mieterbund m

federative power, federative authority · föderative Gewalt, föderative Hoheit, föderative Kompetenz, föderative Macht

fee, inheritable estate (in land), inheritable land(ed) estate · erblicher (Grund)Besitz m

fee [*A payment for profit and indirect cost(s), such as management and office overheads, which cannot be allocated exclusively to a specific contract but have to be apportioned*] · Zuschlag m [*Selbstkostenerstattungsvertrag*]

fee · Gebühr f, Honorar n

fee → fee (tenure) (of land)

fee agreement → (collusive) fee agreement

fee based on the estimated cost of the work → (management) fee based on the estimated cost of the work

feeble minded · schwachsinnig

fee bracket · Honorarzone f, Gebührenzone

fee calculation, fee computation, calculation of fee(s), computation of fee(s) · Gebührenberechnung f, Honorarberechnung

fee contingent on success, contingent fee · Erfolgshonorar n, Erfolgsgebühr f

fee contract · Gebührenvertrag m, Honorarvertrag

to feed, to strengthen ex post facto, to lend additional support [*Example: "The interest when it accrues feeds the estoppel"*] · verstärken

feedback · Rückkopp(e)lung f

feedback loop · Rückkopp(e)lungsschleife *f*

feed back principle · Rückwirkungsprinzip *n*, Echoprinzip [*im Kommunikationsprozeß*]

feeder bus line · Zubringerbuslinie *f*

feeder industry · Zulieferindustrie *f*

feeder system · Zubringersystem *n*

feedlot · Futterplatz *m*, Futterstelle *f*

fee-farmer · Leh(e)n(s)bauer *m*

fee farm (rent); quieti reditus, reditus quieti [*Latin*]; forgavel [*In old English law*]; chief-rent, rent charge, quit-rent [*An annual or periodical sum issuing out of land, payable by holders of land in a manor to the lord. Some writers use "fee farm" to signify not only the estate itself, but the rent reserved on it, taking the word "farm" itself in the sense of rent. This practice should, however, be deprecated*] · Erbzins *m*, Befreiungszins, Leh(e)n(s)zins

fee farm (rent) law, chief-rent law, quit-rent law · Befreiungszinsrecht *n*, Erbzinsrecht, objektives Befreiungszinsrecht, objektives Erbzinsrecht

fee farm (rent) roll, chief-rent roll, quit-rent roll · Erbzinsbuch, Befreiungszinsbuch *n*

fee fixing → fee setting

fee fixing → (collusive) fee agreement

fee for gain, gain fee, profit fee, fee for profit [*A contractual arrangement whereby the contractor is paid the net prime cost plus a percentage to cover overheads and profit*] · aufzuschlagender Gewinnsatz *m*, Gewinnzuschlag *m*, Gewinnaufschlag *m*, Profitzuschlag *m*, Profitaufschlag *m*

fee for grinding, toll paid for grinding, multure; molitura, multura [*Latin*], grinding toll, suit and grist, grinding fee · Mahlgeld *n*, Mahlzins *m*, Mahlgebühr *f*

fee for life → fee (tenure) for life

fee framework · Honorarrahmen *m*, Gebührenrahmen

feeholder, holder of a fee, holder of a fief, fief-tenant, feoda(to)ry, feuda(to)ry; homo pertinens [*Latin*]; beneficiary, holder of a feudal benefice, land tenant, (feudal) tenant, manorial tenant, feudal bond(s)man, vassal, tenant of land [*A tenant or vassal who held his estate by feudal service*] · Leh(e)n(s)mann *m*, Leh(e)n(s)träger *m*, Gefolgsmann, Gutszinsmann, Vasall *m*

fee invoice · Honorarrechnung *f*, Gebührenrechnung

fee limited → fee (simple) limited

fee of acknowledg(e)ment, acknowledg(e)ment money, money of acknowledg(e)ment, acknowledg(e)ment fee [*A sum of money paid by copyhold tenants, in some parts of England, on the death of their landlords, as an acknowledg(e)ment of their new lords*] · Anerkennungsgeld *n*, Rekognitionsgeld, Anerkennungsgebühr *f*, Rekognitionsgebühr

fee of application, application fee, request fee, fee of request · Antragsgebühr *f*, Gesuchsgebühr

fee of clergy, clergy fee · Stolgebühr *f*

fee of inheritance, inheritance fee, estate of inheritance; feudum hereditarium, laudemium mortuarium, feodum hereditarium [*Latin*] · Erbleh(e)n *n*, erbliches Leh(e)n, Erbleh(e)n(s)gut *n*, vererbliches Leh(e)n

fee of request, fee of application, application fee, request fee · Antragsgebühr *f*, Gesuchsgebühr

fee of withdrawal, withdrawal fee · Rückforderungsgebühr *f* [*Bausparkasse*]

fee percentage, percentage of fee · Gebührenanteil *m*, Honoraranteil

fee range, range of fee(s) · Gebührenbereich *m*, Honorarbereich

fee rate, rate of fee · Gebührensatz *m*, Honorarsatz

fee rating, rating of fee(s) · Gebührenmessung *f*, Honorarbemessung

fee rating class · Bauklasse *f* [*Als Maßstab für das Architektenhonorar*]

fee scale, fee schedule, scale of fees, schedule of fees · Gebührentabelle *f*, Honorartabelle, Gebührentafel *f*, Honorartafel

fee schedule → (statutory) fee schedule

fee schedule for architects → (statutory) fee schedule for architects

fee schedule for architects and engineers → (statutory) fee schedule for architects and engineers

fee schedule for engineers → (statutory) fee schedule for engineers

fee setting, fee fixing, setting the fee, fixing the fee · Honorarfestsetzung *f*, Gebührenfestsetzung, Honorarbestimmung, Gebührenbestimmung

fee simple → simple fee

fee simple (absolute), absolute ownership of land [*Largest estate or ownership in real property; free from all manner of conditions or encumbrances*] · absolutes Grund(stücks)eigentum *n*

fee simple copyhold (tenure), fee simple copyhold tenure of land · frei vererb-

fee simple defeasible — feint (court) action

liches Schriftgut *n*, frei vererbbares Schriftgut

fee simple defeasible → (estate in) fee simple defeasible

fee simple determinable → ((real) estate in) fee simple determinable

fee (simple) limited, limited fee (simple) [*Estate giving the owner thereof fee rights as long as certain conditions obtain, termination being governed by the occurrence of some stated event*] · beschränkter (Grund)Besitz *m*, begrenzter (Grund)Besitz, eingeschränkter (Grund)Besitz

fee simple on condition subsequent → ((real) estate in) fee simple on condition subsequent

fee simple tenant, tenant in fee simple · freier Grundbesitzer *m*, uneingeschränkter Grundbesitzer, unbeschränkter Grundbesitzer, unbegrenzter Grundbesitzer

fee tail (estate) → entailed (landed) property

(fee) tail tenant, tenant in (fee) tail · Fideikommißbesitzer *m*, Majoratbesitzer

(fee) tail tenant → tenant in (fee) tail

fee (tenure) for life, fief for life, (feodal) tenure (of land) for life, tenancy for life, tenement for life · lebenslanges Leh(e)n *n*, Leh(e)n auf Lebenszeit

fee (tenure) (of land), fief, tenancy, land tenure, feud, feod, tenement, (feodal) tenure (of land), land held of a lord, land in fee; feodum, feudum, tenementum [*Latin*]; feu [*Scots law*] · Leh(e)n *n*, Leh(e)n(s)gut *n*, Leh(e)n(s)besitz *m*, leh(e)n(s)rechtlicher (Grund)Besitz(stand) *m*, Benefizium *n*

feigned, feint, fictitious, faint, pretended · fiktiv, vorgegeben, vorgetäuscht, fingiert

feigned bill, pretended bill; windmill, kite (Brit.); accommodation bill, fictitious bill, feint bill, faint bill · Freundschaftswechsel *m*, Gefälligkeitswechsel, Kellerwechsel, Reitwechsel, Schornsteinwechsel, Scheinwechsel

feigned business, faint business, pretended business, feint business, fictitious business · fiktives Geschäft *n*, fingiertes Geschäft, vorgegebenes Geschäft, vorgetäuschtes Geschäft, Scheingeschäft

feigned contract, pretended contract, faint contract, fictitious contract · Scheinvertrag *m*

feigned (court) action, faint (court) action, fictitious (court) action, feint (court) action, pretended (court) action [*An action brought on a pretended right, when the plaintiff has no true cause of action, for some illegal purpose. In a feigned action the words of the writ are true. It differs from "false action", in which case the words of the writ are false*] · fiktive Klage *f*, vorgetäuschte Klage, vorgegebene Klage, fingierte Klage, Scheinklage

feigned desertion, pretended desertion, faint desertion, feint desertion, fictitious desertion · Scheinwüstung *f*, Trugwüstung

feigned name, faint name, feint name, fictitious name, pretended name · fiktiver Name *m*, vorgetäuschter Name, vorgegebener Name, fingierter Name, Scheinname

feigned permission, fictitious permission, faint permission, pretended permission, collusive permission, feint permission · fingierte Genehmigung *f*, fingierte Erlaubnis, vorgetäuschte Genehmigung, fiktive Genehmigung, Scheingenehmigung, Scheinerlaubnis, Genehmigungsfiktion *f*, Erlaubnisfiktion

feigned plaintiff, pretended plaintiff, faint plaintiff, feint plaintiff, fictitious plaintiff · fiktiver Kläger *m*, vorgegebener Kläger, vorgetäuschter Kläger, fingierter Kläger, Scheinkläger

feigned promise, pretended promise, faint promise, feint promise, fictitious promise · fiktives Versprechen *n*, vorgetäuschtes Versprechen, vorgegebenes Versprechen, fingiertes Versprechen, Scheinversprechen

feigned purchase, faint purchase, pretended purchase, feint purchase, fictitious purchase · fiktiver Kauf *m*, vorgetäuschter Kauf, fingierter Kauf, vorgegebener Kauf, Scheinkauf

feint, fictitious, faint, pretended, feigned · fiktiv, vorgegeben, vorgetäuscht, fingiert

feint bill, faint bill, feigned bill, pretended bill; windmill, kite (Brit.); accommodation bill, fictitious bill · Freundschaftswechsel *m*, Gefälligkeitswechsel, Kellerwechsel, Reitwechsel, Schornsteinwechsel, Scheinwechsel

feint business, fictitious business, feigned business, faint business, pretended business · fiktives Geschäft *n*, fingiertes Geschäft, vorgegebenes Geschäft, vorgetäuschtes Geschäft, Scheingeschäft

feint (court) action, pretended (court) action, feigned (court) action, faint (court) action, fictitious (court) action [*An action brought on a pretended right, when the plaintiff has no true cause of action, for some illegal purpose. In a feigned action the words of the writ are true. It differs from "false action", in which case the words of the writ are false*] · fiktive Klage *f*, vorgetäuschte Klage, vorgegebene Klage, fingierte Klage, Scheinklage

feint desertion, fictitious desertion, feigned desertion, pretended desertion, faint desertion · Scheinwüstung *f*, Trugwüstung

feint name, fictitious name, pretended name, feigned name, faint name · fiktiver Name *m*, vorgetäuschter Name, vorgegebener Name, fingierter Name, Scheinname

feint permission → feigned permission

feint plaintiff, fictitious plaintiff, feigned plaintiff, pretended plaintiff, faint plaintiff · fiktiver Kläger *m*, vorgegebener Kläger, vorgetäuschter Kläger, fingierter Kläger, Scheinkläger

feint promise, fictitious promise, feigned promise, pretended promise, faint promise · fiktives Versprechen *n*, vorgetäuschtes Versprechen, vorgegebenes Versprechen, fingiertes Versprechen, Scheinversprechen

feint purchase, fictitious purchase, feigned purchase, faint purchase, pretended purchase · fiktiver Kauf *m*, vorgetäuschter Kauf, fingierter Kauf, vorgegebener Kauf, Scheinkauf

feldage; actus, faldagium [*Latin*]; frankfold, faldage, right of drove, drove right · Triftrecht *n*, Treibrecht

fellow-citizen · Mitbürger *m*

fellow-countryman, domestic · Landsmann *m*

fellow creditor, fellow promisee, fellow debtee, joint creditor, joint promisee, joint debtee, co-creditor, co-promisee, co-debtee · Mitgläubiger *m*, Mitversprechensempfänger, Gesamtgläubiger, Gesamtversprechensempfänger

fellow debtor, fellow obligor, joint debtor, joint obligor, co-debtor, co-obligor · Mitschuldner *m*, Gesamtschuldner

fellow-employe(e), fellow-servant [*One who serves and is controlled by the same master*] · Mitarbeitnehmer *m*

fellow-heir, joint-heir, co(in)heritor, joint inheritor, (co)parcener; coparticeps [*In old English law*]; co-heir · Anteilerbe, Miterbe *m*, Erbgenosse *m*, (Bruch-)Teilerbe

fellow-heiress, joint-heiress, co-heiress · Miterbin *f*, Erbgenossin *f*

fellow obligor → fellow debtor

fellow-owner, fellow-proprietor, co-owner, co-proprietor, part-owner, part-proprietor · Anteileigentümer *m*, Miteigentümer, (Bruch)Teileigentümer

fellow promisee, fellow debtee, joint creditor, joint promisee, joint debtee, co-creditor, co-promisee, co-debtee, fellow creditor · Mitgläubiger *m*, Mitversprechensempfänger, Gesamtgläubiger, Gesamtversprechensempfänger

fellow promisor → fellow debtor

fellow-proprietor, co-owner, co-proprietor, part-owner, part-proprietor, fellow-owner · Anteileigentümer *m*, Miteigentümer, (Bruch)Teileigentümer

fellow-servant, fellow-employe(e) [*One who serves and is controlled by the same master*] · Mitarbeitnehmer *m*

fellowship, (closed) scholarship · Stipendium *n*, Freistelle *f*

fellowship · Genossenschaft *f* [*Im Sinne von Otto Gierke*]

fellow villager · Dorfgenosse *m*

fellow (worker), co-worker, contributor · Mitarbeiter *m*

female absentee · Abwesende *f*

female administrator, (probate) administratrix, administratress; administratrice, administress [*obsolete*] [*A woman appointed to administer the estate of an intestate*] · erbrechtliche Verwalterin *f*, Erb(schafts)verwalterin, Nachlaßverwalterin

female adult, adult woman · Erwachsene *f*, erwachsene Frau *f*

female alien · Ausländerin *f*

female applicant · Antragstellerin *f*, Gesuchstellerin

female architect, architectress · Architektin *f*

female citizen, citizette, citizen(ess) · Bürgerin *f*

female commuter · Pendlerin *f*

female creditor, creditress, creditrix · Gläubigerin *f*

female curate; curatrix [*Latin*] · Kuratorin *f*, (Nachlaß)Pflegerin

female descendant, female issue, female offspring · weiblicher Nachkomme *m*, weiblicher Abkömmling, weiblicher Deszendent

female disseisor, disseisitrix, disseisoress · Gewereentsetzerin *f*

female executor, executrix [*A woman who has been appointed by will to execute such will or testament*] · (Testaments)Vollstreckerin *f*

female farm worker; farmerette [*colloquial*] · Landarbeiterin *f*

female fugitive from justice · Flüchtige *f*

female guardian · Vormünderin *f*, weiblicher Vormund *m*

female guardian by election · erwählter weiblicher Vormund *m*, weiblicher erwählter Vormund

female heir — feme covert 406

female heir; inheretrix [*deprecated*]; heiress, heir female · Erbin *f*

female heir apparent, heiress apparent, heir female apparent [*A woman whose right of inheritance is indefeasible, provided she outlives the ancestor*] · rechtmäßige Erbin *f*

female heir at law, female heir general, right female heir, heiress at law, heiress general, heir female at law, heir female general, right heiress, right heir female · Intestaterbin *f*, gesetzliche Erbin

female heir beneficiary, heiress beneficiary, heir female beneficiary · Erbin *f* mit Inventarerrichtung

female heir by adoption, heiress by adoption, heir female by adoption · Adoptiverbin *f*

female heir by custom, heiress by custom, heir female by custom · gewohnheitsrechtliche Erbin *f*

female heir conventional, heir female conventional, heiress conventional · Vertragserbin *f*

female heir expectant, heiress expectant, heir female expectant, expectant heiress, expectant heir female, expectant female heir · Erbanwärterin *f*, Erbschaftsanwärterin

female heir general → female heir at law

female heir in (fee) tail, female heir special, heiress in (fee) tail, heir female in (fee) tail, heiress special, heir female special · Anerbin *f*

female heir institute, heir female institute, heiress institute [*In Scots law a woman to whom the right of succession is ascertained by disposition or express deed of the deceased*] · eingesetzte Erbin *f*

female heir of inventory (in tail), fiduciary heiress, fiduciary heir female, fiduciary female heir, fiducial heiress, fiducial heir female, fiducial female heir, heiress of inventory (in tail), heir female of inventory (in tail) · Vorerbin *f*

female heir of line → female heir of the blood

female heir of the blood, female heir of the body, female heir of line, heiress of the blood, heiress of the body, heir female of the blood, heir female of the body, bodily heiress, bodily heir female, bodily female heir; heiress of line, heir female of line [*In Scotch law*] [*A woman who succeeds lineally by right of blood*] · Blutserbin *f*, Leibeserbin, natürliche Erbin, leibliche Erbin

female heir special, heiress in (fee) tail, heir female in (fee) tail, heiress special, heir female special, female heir in (fee) tail · Anerbin *f*

female heir testamentary, heiress testamentary, heir female testamentary · Testamentserbin *f*

female homeless person · Obdachlose *f*

female indemnitee · Entschädigungsberechtigte *f*, Schadenersatzberechtigte

female indemnitor · Entschädigungspflichtige *f*, Entschädigungsleistende, Entschädigende, Schadenersatzpflichtige, Schadenersatzleistende

female infant, female minor · Minderjährige *f*

female issue, female offspring, female descendant · weiblicher Nachkomme *m*, weiblicher Abkömmling, weiblicher Deszendent

female judge, judgess · Richterin *f*

female juror, jurywoman, woman juror · Geschworene *f*

female minor, female infant · Minderjährige *f*

female native (person), native woman · Altansässige *f*, Einheimische

female non-white · Farbige *f*

female oath-helper, compurgatrix · Eideshelferin *f* [*Einer Prozeßpartei im Mittelalter in England*]

female offspring, female descendant, female issue · weiblicher Nachkomme *m*, weiblicher Abkömmling, weiblicher Deszendent

female person capable of making a will · Testierfähige *f*

female person entitled · Berechtigte *f*, berechtigte weibliche Person *f*

female person of full age · Volljährige *f*

female person of unsound mind · Geisteskranke *f*, Geistesgestörte *f*

female petitioner · Bittstellerin *f*

female petitioner, oratress, oratrix [*A female plaintiff in a bill in Chancery was formerly so called*] · Bittstellerin *f*, Klägerin

female plaintiff, female plainant · (Zivilprozeß)Klägerin *f*

female relative, kinswoman · weibliche Verwandte *f*

female resident · Ansässige *f*, Gebietsansässige

female resident alien · ansässige Ausländerin *f*

female subject · Untertanin *f*

feme covert, married woman, wife · verheiratete Frau *f*, Ehefrau

feme discovert, single woman, sole woman, unmarried woman, feme sole · alleinstehende Frau f, unverheiratete Frau, ledige Frau

to fence [*In old Scots law, to defend or protect by formalities*] · formal sichern

fence · Zaun *m*

fence-bote · Beholzungsrecht *n* für Zäune, Holzbezugsrecht für Zäune, Zaunzubuße *f*

fence day · Hegungstag *m*

fence hamlet · Etterweiler *m*

fence hedge · Zaunhecke *f*

to fence in · einzäunen, umzäunen

fence month → (de)fence month

to fence off · abzäunen

fencing · Einzäunen *n*, Umzäunen

fencing around a site, site fencing · Baustellenumzäunung *f*, Baustelleneinzäunung

fencing right, right of fencing · Zaunrecht *n*

fencing works · Einzäunungsanlagen *fpl*, Umzäunungsanlagen

fen-colony · Fehnkolonie *f*

feneration; faeneratio [*Latin*]; usury · Wucher *m*, Schacher

feod → fief

feodal, feuda(to)ry, manorial, beneficiary, feudal [*Relating to feuds or feudal tenures. Held by feudal service*] · feudal, grundherr(schaft)lich, zu einer Grundherrschaft gehörig

feodal agriculture, feuda(to)ry agriculture, manorial agriculture, feudal agriculture · Feudallandwirtschaft *f*

feodal aid, manorial aid, feudal aid, feuda(to)ry aid · feudales Hilfsgeld *n*

feodal authority, feudal authority, feuda(to)ry authority, manorial power, feodal power, feudal power, feuda(to)ry power, manorial authority · Feudalgewalt *f*, Feudalmacht *f*, Feudalhoheit *f*, Feudalkompetenz *f*

feodal burden → feudal charge

feodal casualty, manorial casualty, feudal casualty, feuda(to)ry casualty [*The additional payment due to a superior on specified occasions such as the death of a vassal*] · Feudalsonderabgabe *f*

feodal chain, manorial chain, feudal chain, feuda(to)ry chain · Feudalkette *f*

feodal charge, feodal burden, feodal encumbrance, feodal incumbrance, feuda(to)ry charge, feuda(to)ry burden, feuda(to)ry incumbrance, feuda(to)ry encumbrance, manorial charge, manorial burden, manorial incumbrance, manorial encumbrance, feudal charge, feudal burden, feudal encumbrance, feudal incumbrance · Feudallast *f*, Leh(e)n(s)last, Feudalbelastung *f*

feodal charter, manorial charter, charter of (en)feoffment, charter of infeftment, feudal charter, feuda(to)ry charter · Belehnungs(frei)brief *m*, Leh(e)n(s)(frei)brief

feodal community, feuda(to)ry community, manorial community, feudal community [*It rested on the distinction between a number of persons holding land of the lord by free tenure and a number holding land of the lord by tenures of servile origin. Both classes were held together through a peculiar tribunal, the court of baron*] · Feudalgemeinschaft *f*, Feudalgemeinwesen *n*

feodal court, feuda(to)ry court, court of the baron, court of the lord, baron(-bailie) court, court-baron (proper), court of (the) manor, freeholders' court baron; curia legalis [*Latin*]; manor(ial) court, feudal court [*The court of justice held by a baron or his steward in the presence of the freehold tenants of the manor. In modern times lawyers have distinguished between court-baron which was the court of the freehold tenants, and the customary court-baron which was the court of the copyhold tenants. The early history of this distinction is obscure*] · Feudalgericht *n*, grundherrliches Gericht, Leh(e)n(s)herrengericht, Hofgericht, Patrimonialgericht, feudales Gutsgericht

feodal encumbrance → feudal charge

feodal estate of noble kind, feuda(to)ry estate of noble kind, (feudal) estate of noble kind · Edelgut *n*, Edelhof *m*, adeliges Gut, adeliger Hof

feodal hierarchy, feuda(to)ry hierarchy, manorial hierarchy, feudal hierarchy · Feudalhierarchie *f*, feudale Hierarchie, leh(e)n(s)rechtliche Hierarchie

feodal incumbrance → feudal charge

feodality, allegiance, feudality; fidelitas feudalis [*Latin*]; fealty, fidelity [*It was due by feudal tenants to their lords*] · Leh(e)n(s)treue *f*

feodal (landholding) system → feudal (landholding) system

feodal land(s), feudal land(s), feuda(to)ry land(s), tenemental land(s), land(s) of (a) manor, land(s) held of a lord, land(s) of tenure, outland(s), tenancy, tenure land(s) [*Land held of the lord by free tenure*] · Leh(e)n(s)land *n*, Feudalland, Außenland, Grenzland, verpachtetes Land

feodal language, feuda(to)ry language, manorial language, feudal language · Feudalsprache *f*

feodal law, feuda(to)ry law, manorial law; lex feudalis [*Latin*]; law of tenure(s) (of land), law of (the) manor, law of feuda(to)ry tenure, law of feudal tenure, law of feodal tenure, law of feuds, law of feudal estates, feudal law, tenure law · Leh(e)n(s)recht *n*, Feudalrecht

feodal limitation, feodal restriction, feuda(to)ry limitation, feuda(to)ry restriction, manorial limitation, manorial restriction, feudal limitation, feudal restriction · leh(e)n(s)rechtliche Beschränkung *f*, leh(e)n(s)rechtliche Einschränkung, leh(e)n(s)rechtliche Begrenzung, feudalrechtliche Beschränkung, feudalrechtliche Einschränkung, feudalrechtliche Begrenzung

feodal measure, feuda(to)ry measure, manorial measure, feudal measure · Feudalmaßnahme *f*, leh(e)n(s)rechtliche Maßnahme

feodal office, manorial office, feudal office, feuda(to)ry office · feudales Amt *n*, leh(e)n(s)rechtliches Amt

feodal organization → feudal (landholding) system

feodal plough service, feudal plough service, feuda(to)ry plough service, manorial plough service (Brit.) [*US = plow*] · (Acker)Fro(h)n(d)e *f*, Scharwerk *n*

feodal possession, feuda(to)ry possession, manorial possession, feudal possession · Besitz *m* nach feudalem Leh(e)n(s)recht, feudaler Leh(e)n(s)besitz, Feudalbesitz

feodal power, feudal power, feuda(to)ry power, manorial authority, feodal authority, feudal authority, feuda(to)ry authority, manorial power · Feudalgewalt *f*, Feudalmacht *f*, Feudalhoheit *f*, Feudalkompetenz *f*

feodal principality, feuda(to)ry principality, feudal principality · Leh(e)n(s)fürstentum *n*

feodal principle, feuda(to)ry principle, principle of (feudal) tenure, principle of feodal tenure, principle of feuda(to)ry tenure, feudal principle · Leh(e)n(s)grundsatz *m*, Leh(e)n(s)prinzip *n*, Feudalgrundsatz, Feudalprinzip

feodal realty law, feuda(to)ry realty law, manorial realty law, feudal (real) estate law, feodal (real) estate law, feuda(to)ry (real) estate law, manorial (real) estate law, feudal (real) property law, feodal (real) property law, feuda(to)ry (real) property law, manorial (real) property law, feudal realty law · feudales Liegenschaftsrecht *n*, feudales Bodenrecht, feudales Grundstücksrecht, feudales Landrecht

feodal restriction, feuda(to)ry limitation, feuda(to)ry restriction, manorial limitation, manorial restriction, feudal limitation, feodal restriction, feodal limitation · leh(e)n(s)rechtliche Beschränkung *f*, leh(e)n(s)rechtliche Einschränkung, leh(e)n(s)rechtliche Begrenzung, feudalrechtliche Beschränkung, feudalrechtliche Einschränkung, feudalrechtliche Begrenzung

feodal service, feuda(to)ry service, manorial service, feudal service · Feudaldienst *m*, Hörigkeitslast *f*, Leh(e)n(s)dienst, leh(e)n(s)rechtlicher Dienst, feudaler Dienst

feodal service by manual labo(u)r, feuda(to)ry service by manual labo(u)r, manorial service by manual labo(u)r, feudal service by manual labo(u)r · Handrobot *f*, Handdienst *m*

feodal system → feudal (landholding) system

feodal tailage, feuda(to)ry tailage, feudal tailage · Leh(e)n(s)abgabe *f*

(feodal) tenure (of land), land held of a lord, land in fee; feodum, feudum, tenementum [*Latin*]; feu [*Scots law*], fee (tenure) (of land), fief, tenancy, land tenure, feud, feod, tenement · Leh(e)n *n*, Leh(e)n(s)gut *n*, Leh(e)n(s)besitz *m*, leh(e)n(s)rechtlicher (Grund)Besitz(stand) *m*, Benefizium *n*

(feodal) tenure (of land) for life, tenancy for life, tenement for life, fee (tenure) for life, fief for life · lebenslanges Leh(e)n *n*, Leh(e)n auf Lebenszeit

(feodal) tenure (of land) in frankalmoign(e), frankalmoign(e), free alms, free spiritual tenure (of land), (free) alms tenure (of land) [*A tenure whereby religious corporations, aggregate or sole, held lands of the donor to them and their successors for ever. They were discharged of all other except religious services, and the trinoda necessitas. It differed from tenure by divine service, in that the latter required the performance of certain divine services, whereas the former, as its name imports, was free*] · (freies) Almosenleh(e)n *n*, Freialmosenleh(e)n, Gottesleh(e)n mit unbestimmten geistlichen Verrichtungen

feoda(to)ry, feuda(to)ry; homo pertinens [*Latin*]; beneficiary, holder of a feudal benefice, land tenant, (feudal) tenant, manorial tenant, feudal bond(s)man, vassal, tenant of land, feeholder, holder of a fee, holder of a fief, fief-tenant [*A tenant or vassal who held his estate by feudal service*] · Leh(e)n(s)mann *m*, Leh(e)n(s)träger *m*, Gefolgsmann, Gutszinsmann, Vasall *m*

feodum [*Latin*] → fee (tenure) (of land)

feof(f)amentum [*Latin*] → (en)feoffment

feoffare, infeodare, infeudare [*Latin*]; to invest [*old Scots law*]; to give possession of land(s), to give a seisin of land(s), to (give a) feud, to infeft, to infeoff, to enfeoff, to bestow a fee, to bestow a fief, to bestow a feud · belehnen, feudal belehnen

feoffator [*Latin*] → liege-lord

feoffee, grantee · Belehnte *m*, (feudaler) Leh(e)n(s)gutempfänger, Beliehene

feoffee to the use, feoffee to uses [*One to whom a feoffment was made to the use of another person*] · juristischer Eigentümer *m*

feoffment → (en)feoffment

feoffment to the feoffer's will → (en)feoffment to the feoffer's will

feoffment to uses → (en)feoffment to uses

feoffor → liege lord

ferial day · Feiertag *m*

ferlingus, ferlingum [*Low Latin*]; stadium, stade, quarentena terrae, furlongus [*Latin*]; furlong; furlang [*Anglo-Saxon*] [*A piece of land bounded or terminated by the length of a furrow*] · (Ge)Wende *(n)*, *f*, Gewann *n*, Wande *f*, Wanne *f*; Flagg *f* [*Ostfriesland*]

ferriage · Fährgeld *n*

ferry · Fähre *f*

ferry servitude · Fährgerechtigkeit *f*, Fährdienstbarkeit, Fährservitut *n*, *f*, (servitutisches) Fährrecht *n* [*Befugnis zum Halten von Fähren zum Übersetzen über eine Wasserfläche*]

fertility rate · Geburtenrate *f*

feu [*Scots law*] → feudum [*Latin*]

feu contract · Grundstücksverleihungsvertrag *m* auf ewige Zeit unter Auferlegung eines Zinses [*in Schottland*]

to feud → to give possession of land(s)

feud · Fehde *f*

feud → feudum [*Latin*]

feudal, feodal, feuda(to)ry, manorial, beneficiary [*Relating to feuds or feudal tenures. Held by feudal service*] · feudal, grundherr(schaft)lich, zu einer Grundherrschaft gehörig

feudal agriculture, feodal agriculture, feuda(to)ry agriculture, manorial agriculture · Feudallandwirtschaft *f*

feudal aid, feuda(to)ry aid, feodal aid, manorial aid · feudales Hilfsgeld *n*

feudal authority, feuda(to)ry authority, manorial power, feodal power, feudal power, feuda(to)ry power, manorial authority, feodal authority · Feudalgewalt *f*, Feudalmacht *f*, Feudalhoheit *f*, Feudalkompetenz *f*

feudal bond(s)man, vassal, tenant of land, feeholder, holder of a fee, holder of a fief, fief-tenant, feoda(to)ry, feuda(to)ry; homo pertinens [*Latin*]; beneficiary, holder of a feudal benefice, land tenant, (feudal) tenant, manorial tenant [*A tenant or vassal who held his estate by feudal service*] · Leh(e)n(s)mann *m*, Leh(e)n(s)träger *m*, Gefolgsmann, Gutszinsmann, Vasall *m*

feudal burden → feudal charge

feudal castle · Feudalburg *f*

feudal casualty, feuda(to)ry casualty, feodal casualty, manorial casualty [*The additional payment due to a superior on specified occasions such as the death of a vassal*] · Feudalsonderabgabe *f*

feudal chain, feuda(to)ry chain, feodal chain, manorial chain · Feudalkette *f*

feudal charge, feudal burden, feudal encumbrance, feudal incumbrance, feodal charge, feodal burden, feodal encumbrance, feodal incumbrance, feuda(to)ry charge, feuda(to)ry burden, feuda(to)ry incumbrance, feuda(to)ry encumbrance, manorial charge, manorial burden, manorial incumbrance, manorial encumbrance · Feudallast *f*, Leh(e)n(s)last, Feudalbelastung *f*

feudal charter, feuda(to)ry charter, feodal charter, manorial charter, charter of (en)feoffment, charter of infeftment · Belehnungs(frei)brief *m*, Leh(e)n(s)(frei)brief

feudal community, feodal community, feuda(to)ry community, manorial community [*It rested on the distinction between a number of persons holding land of the lord by free tenure and a number holding land of the lord by tenures of servile origin. Both classes were held together through a peculiar tribunal, the court of baron*] · Feudalgemeinschaft *f*, Feudalgemeinwesen *n*

feudal court, feodal court, feuda(to)ry court, court of the baron, court of the lord, baron(-bailie) court, court-baron (proper), court of (the) manor, freeholders' court baron; curia legalis [*Latin*]; manor(ial) court [*The court of justice held by a baron or his steward in the presence of the freehold tenants of the manor. In modern times lawyers have distinguished between court-baron which was the court of the freehold tenants, and the customary court-baron which was the court of the copyhold tenants. The early history of this distinction is obscure*] · Feudalgericht *n*, grundherrliches Gericht, Leh(e)n(s)herrengericht, Hofgericht, Patrimonialgericht, feudales Gutsgericht

feudal duty · Leh(e)n(s)pflicht *f*

feudal encumbrance → feudal charge

(feudal) estate of noble kind — feudal service

(feudal) estate of noble kind, feodal estate of noble kind, feuda(to)ry estate of noble kind · Edelgut *n*, Edelhof *m*, adeliges Gut, adeliger Hof

feudal hierarchy, feodal hierarchy, feuda(to)ry hierarchy, manorial hierarchy · Feudalhierarchie *f*, feudale Hierarchie, leh(e)n(s)rechtliche Hierarchie

feudal incident · Anfallung *f*, Leh(e)n(s)fall *m*, Leh(e)n(s)gefälle *f* [*Eine gelegentliche Einnahme die der Lehensherr unregelmäßig von seinen Vasallen erhob*]

feudal incumbrance → feudal charge

feudalistic · feudalistisch

feudalistic time · Feudalzeit *f*

feudality; fidelitas feudalis [*Latin*]; fealty, fidelity, feodality, allegiance [*It was due by feudal tenants to their lords*] · Leh(e)n(s)treue *f*

feudalization · Feudalisierung *f*

to feudalize · (be)lehnbar machen, feudalisieren

feudal (landholding) system, feodal (landholding) system, feuda(to)ry (landholding) system, manorial (landholding) system, feudal tenure system, manorial tenure system, feodal tenure system, feuda(to)ry tenure system, feudal organization, feodal organization, manorial organization, feuda(to)ry organization, system of (feudal) tenure, organization of tenure, feudalism, system of feuds, system of feods, system of fiefs, land tenure system, manorial land system · Feudalsystem *n*, Leh(e)n(s)system, Feudalordnung *f*, Leh(e)n(s)ordnung, Feudalismus *m*, Feudalwesen *n*, Leh(e)n(s)wesen

feudal land(s) → feodal land(s)

feudal language, feodal language, feuda(to)ry language, manorial language · Feudalsprache *f*

feudal law, tenure law, feodal law, feuda(to)ry law, manorial law; lex feudalis [*Latin*]; law of tenure(s) (of land), law of (the) manor, law of feuda(to)ry tenure, law of feudal tenure, law of feodal tenure, law of feuds, law of feudal estates · Leh(e)n(s)recht *n*, Feudalrecht

feudal limitation, feudal restriction, feodal limitation, feodal restriction, feuda(to)ry limitation, feuda(to)ry restriction, manorial limitation, manorial restriction · leh(e)n(s)rechtliche Beschränkung *f*, leh(e)n(s)rechtliche Einschränkung, leh(e)n(s)rechtliche Begrenzung, feudalrechtliche Beschränkung, feudalrechtliche Einschränkung, feudalrechtliche Begrenzung

(feudal) lord → liege-lord

feudal lord's privileges [*As to milling, baking, etc.*] · Bannrecht *n*

feudal measure, feodal measure, feuda(to)ry measure, manorial measure · Feudalmaßnahme *f*, leh(e)n(s)rechtliche Maßnahme

feudal office, feuda(to)ry office, feodal office, manorial office · feudales Amt *n*, leh(e)n(s)rechtliches Amt

feudal organization → feudal (landholding) system

feudal plough service, feuda(to)ry plough service, manorial plough service (Brit.), feodal plough service [*US = plow*] · (Acker)Fro(h)n(d)e *f*, Scharwerk *n*

feudal possession, feodal possession, feuda(to)ry possession, manorial possession · Besitz *m* nach feudalem Leh(e)n(s)recht, feudaler Leh(e)n(s)besitz, Feudalbesitz

feudal power, feuda(to)ry power, manorial authority, feodal authority, feudal authority, feuda(to)ry authority, manorial power, feodal power · Feudalgewalt *f*, Feudalmacht *f*, Feudalhoheit *f*, Feudalkompetenz *f*

feudal principality, feodal principality, feuda(to)ry principality · Leh(e)n(s)fürstentum *n*

feudal principle, feodal principle, feuda(to)ry principle, principle of (feudal) tenure, principle of feodal tenure, principle of feuda(to)ry tenure · Leh(e)n(s)grundsatz *m*, Leh(e)n(s)prinzip *n*, Feudalgrundsatz, Feudalprinzip

feudal (real) estate law, feodal (real) estate law, feuda(to)ry (real) estate law, manorial (real) estate law, feudal (real) property law, feodal (real) property law, feuda(to)ry (real) property law, manorial (real) property law, feudal realty law, feodal realty law, feuda(to)ry realty law, manorial realty law · feudales Liegenschaftsrecht *n*, feudales Bodenrecht, feudales Grundstücksrecht, feudales Landrecht

feudal realty law → feudal (real) estate law

feudal relation(ship) · Leh(e)n(s)verhältnis *n*, leh(e)n(s)rechtliches Verhältnis

feudal restriction, feodal limitation, feodal restriction, feuda(to)ry limitation, feuda(to)ry restriction, manorial limitation, manorial restriction, feudal limitation · leh(e)n(s)rechtliche Beschränkung *f*, leh(e)n(s)rechtliche Einschränkung, leh(e)n(s)rechtliche Begrenzung, feudalrechtliche Beschränkung, feudalrechtliche Einschränkung, feudalrechtliche Begrenzung

feudal service, feodal service, feuda(to)ry service, manorial service · Feudaldienst *m*, Hörigkeitslast *f*, Leh(e)n(s)dienst, leh(e)n(s)rechtlicher Dienst, feudaler Dienst

feudal service attached to landed property — feuda(to)ry law

feudal service attached to landed property · Reallast *f*

feudal service by manual labo(u)r, feodal service by manual labo(u)r, feuda(to)ry service by manual labo(u)r, manorial service by manual labo(u)r · Handrobot *f*, Handdienst *m*

feudal service in arrear · nicht geleisteter feudaler Dienst *m*

feudal system → feudal (landholding) system

feudal tailage, feodal tailage, feuda(to)ry tailage · Leh(e)n(s)abgabe *f*

(feudal) tenant, manorial tenant, feudal bond(s)man, vassal, tenant of land, feeholder, holder of a fee, holder of a fief, fief-tenant, feoda(to)ry, feuda(to)ry; homo pertinens [*Latin*]; beneficiary, holder of a feudal beneficie, land tenant [*A tenant or vassal who held his estate by feudal service*] · Leh(e)n(s)mann *m*, Leh(e)n(s)träger *m*, Gefolgsmann, Gutszinsmann, Vasall *m*

feudal tenure system → feudal (landholding) system

feuda(to)ry → (feudal) tenant

feuda(to)ry, manorial, beneficiary, feudal, feodal [*Relating to feuds or feudal tenures. Held by feudal service*] · feudal, grundherr(schaft)lich, zu einer Grundherrschaft gehörig

feuda(to)ry; homo pertinens [*Latin*], beneficiary, holder of a feudal beneficie, land tenant, (feudal) tenant, manorial tenant, feudal bond(s)man, vassal, tenant of land, feeholder, holder of a fee, holder of a fief, fief-tenant, feoda(to)ry [*A tenant or vassal who held his estate by feudal service*] · Leh(e)n(s)mann *m*, Leh(e)n(s)träger *m*, Gefolgsmann, Gutszinsmann, Vasall *m*

feuda(to)ry agriculture, manorial agriculture, feudal agriculture, feodal agriculture · Feudallandwirtschaft *f*

feuda(to)ry aid, feodal aid, manorial aid, feudal aid · feudales Hilfsgeld *n*

feuda(to)ry authority, manorial power, feodal power, feudal power, feuda(to)ry power, manorial authority, feodal authority, feudal authority · Feudalgewalt *f*, Feudalmacht *f*, Feudalhoheit *f*, Feudalkompetenz *f*

feuda(to)ry burden → feudal charge

feuda(to)ry charter, feodal charter, manorial charter, charter of (en)feoffment, charter of infeftment, feudal charter · Belehnungs(frei)brief *m*, Leh(e)n(s)(frei)brief

feuda(to)ry casualty, feodal casualty, manorial casualty, feudal casualty [*The additional payment due to a superior on specified occasions such as the death of a vassal*] · Feudalsonderabgabe *f*

feuda(to)ry chain, feodal chain, manorial chain, feudal chain, feuda(to)ry chain · Feudalkette *f*

feuda(to)ry charge, feuda(to)ry burden, feuda(to)ry incumbrance, feuda(to)ry encumbrance, manorial charge, manorial burden, manorial incumbrance, manorial encumbrance, feudal charge, feudal burden, feudal encumbrance, feudal incumbrance, feodal charge, feodal burden, feodal encumbrance, feodal incumbrance · Feudallast *f*, Leh(e)n(s)last, Feudalbelastung *f*

feuda(to)ry community, manorial community, feudal community, feodal community [*It rested on the distinction between a number of persons holding land of the lord by free tenure and a number holding land of the lord by tenures of servile origin. Both classes were held together through a peculiar tribunal, the court of baron*] · Feudalgemeinschaft *f*, Feudalgemeinwesen *n*

feuda(to)ry court, court of the baron, court of the lord, baron(-bailie) court, court-baron (proper), court of (the) manor, freeholders' court baron; curia legalis [*Latin*]; manor(ial) court, feudal court, feodal court [*The court of justice held by a baron or his steward in the presence of the freehold tenants of the manor. In modern times lawyers have distinguished between court-baron which was the court of the freehold tenants, and the customary court-baron which was the court of the copyhold tenants. The early history of this distinction is obscure*] · Feudalgericht *n*, grundherrliches Gericht, Leh(e)n(s)herrengericht, Hofgericht, Patrimonialgericht, feudales Gutsgericht

feuda(to)ry encumbrance → feudal charge

feuda(to)ry estate of noble kind, (feudal) estate of noble kind, feodal estate of noble kind · Edelgut *n*, Edelhof *m*, adeliges Gut, adeliger Hof

feuda(to)ry hierarchy, manorial hierarchy, feudal hierarchy, feodal hierarchy · Feudalhierarchie *f*, feudale Hierarchie, leh(e)n(s)rechtliche Hierarchie

feuda(to)ry incumbrance → feuda(to)ry charge

feuda(to)ry land(s) → feodal land(s)

feuda(to)ry language, manorial language, feudal language, feodal language · Feudalsprache *f*

feuda(to)ry law, manorial law; lex feudalis [*Latin*]; law of tenure(s) (of land), law of (the) manor, law of feuda(to)ry tenure, law of feudal tenure, law of feodal tenure, law of feuds, law of feudal estates, feudal law, tenure law, feodal law · Leh(e)n(s)recht *n*, Feudalrecht

feuda(to)ry limitation, feuda(to)ry restriction, manorial limitation, manorial restriction, feudal limitation, feudal restriction, feodal limitation, feodal restriction · leh(e)n(s)rechtliche Beschränkung *f*, leh(e)n(s)rechtliche Einschränkung, feudalrechtliche Beschränkung, feudalrechtliche Einschränkung, feudalrechtliche Begrenzung

feuda(to)ry measure, manorial measure, feudal measure, feodal measure · Feudalmaßnahme *f*, leh(e)n(s)rechtliche Maßnahme

feuda(to)ry office, feodal office, manorial office, feudal office · feudales Amt *n*, leh(e)n(s)rechtliches Amt

feuda(to)ry organization → feudal (landholding) system

feuda(to)ry plough service, manorial plough service (Brit.), feodal plough service, feudal plough service [*US = plow*] · (Acker)Fro(h)n(d)e *f*, Scharwerk *n*

feuda(to)ry possession, manorial possession, feudal possession, feodal possession · Besitz *m* nach feudalem Leh(e)n(s)recht, feudaler Leh(e)n(s)besitz, Feudalbesitz

feuda(to)ry power, manorial authority, feodal authority, feudal authority, feuda(to)ry authority, manorial power, feodal power, feudal power · Feudalgewalt *f*, Feudalmacht *f*, Feudalhoheit *f*, Feudalkompetenz *f*

feuda(to)ry principality, feudal principality, feodal principality · Leh(e)n(s)fürstentum *n*

feuda(to)ry principle, principle of (feudal) tenure, principle of feodal tenure, principle of feuda(to)ry tenure, feudal principle, feodal principle · Leh(e)n(s)grundsatz *m*, Leh(e)n(s)prinzip *n*, Feudalgrundsatz, Feudalprinzip

feuda(to)ry realty law, manorial realty law, feudal (real) estate law, feodal (real) estate law, feuda(to)ry (real) estate law, manorial (real) estate law, feudal (real) property law, feodal (real) property law, feuda(to)ry (real) property law, manorial (real) property law, feudal realty law, feodal realty law · feudales Liegenschaftsrecht *n*, feudales Bodenrecht, feudales Grundstücksrecht, feudales Landrecht

feuda(to)ry restriction, manorial limitation, manorial restriction, feudal limitation, feudal restriction, feodal limitation, feodal restriction, feuda(to)ry limitation · leh(e)n(s)rechtliche Beschränkung *f*, leh(e)n(s)rechtliche Einschränkung, leh(e)n(s)rechtliche Begrenzung, feudalrechtliche Beschränkung, feudalrechtliche Einschränkung, feudalrechtliche Begrenzung

feuda(to)ry service, manorial service, feudal service, feodal service · Feudaldienst *m*, Hörigkeitslast *f*, Leh(e)n(s)dienst, leh(e)n(s)rechtlicher Dienst, feudaler Dienst

feuda(to)ry service by manual labo(u)r, manorial service by manual labo(u)r, feudal service by manual labo(u)r, feodal service by manual labo(u)r · Handrobot *f*, Handdienst *m*

feuda(to)ry tailage, feudal tailage, feodal tailage · Leh(e)n(s)abgabe *f*

feuda(to)ry (tenure) system → feudal (landholding) system

feudum, feodum, tenementum [*Latin*]; feu [*Scots law*], fee (tenure) (of land), fief, tenancy, land tenure, feud, feod, tenement, (feodal) tenure (of land), land held of a lord, land in fee; feodum · Leh(e)n *n*, Leh(e)n(s)gut *n*, Leh(e)n(s)besitz *m*, leh(e)n(s)rechtlicher (Grund)Besitz(stand) *m*, Benefizium *n*

feudum ad antichresin datum, feodum ad antichresin datum, feudum pignoratitium, feodum pignoratitium [*Latin*] · Pfandleh(e)n *n*

feudum advocatiae, feodum advocatiae, feudum protectionis, feodum protectionis [*Latin*] · Vogteyleh(e)n *n*, Schirm(-Gerechtigkeits)leh(e)n

feudum aedificii, feodum aedificii [*Latin*] · Gebäudeleh(e)n *n*

feudum alienabile, feodum alienabile [*Latin*]; (ab)alienable fief, disposable fief · veräußerliches Leh(e)n, veräußerbares Leh(e)n *n*

feudum ambastee, feudum ministerialium, feudum officii, feudum preafecturae, feodum ambastee, feodum ministerialium, feodum officii, feodum praefecturae; feudum gastaldiae, feodum gastaldiae [*Longobardian law*] [*Latin*] · Ambachtsleh(e)n *n*, Amtsleh(e)n, Haushaltungsleh(e)n, Ökonomieleh(e)n, Wirtschaftsleh(e)n, wirtschaftliches Leh(e)n [*Es machte dem Lehensmann die Wahrnehmung der Rechte seines Herrn zur Aufgabe*]

feudum ambulatorium, feodum ambulatorium [*Latin*] · umgebendes Leh(e)n *n*

feudum annuae praestationis, feodum annuae praestationis [*Latin*] · Pfundleh(e)n *n*

feudum antiquum, feodum antiquum, feudum verus, feodum verus [*Latin*] · Altleh(e)n *n*, altes Leh(e)n, altväterliches Leh(e)n, Stammleh(e)n

feudum aperibile — feudum extra curtem

feudum aperibile, feodum aperibile, feudum apertum, feodum apertum [*Latin*] · (Er)Öffnungsleh(e)n *n*, eröffnetes Leh(e)n, heimgefallenes Leh(e)n, offenes Leh(e)n, Aperturleh(e)n

feudum aulicum, feodum palatinum, feodum aulicum, feodum palatinum [*Latin*] · Hof(raths)leh(e)n *n*

feudum burgense, feudum urbanum, feodum burgense, feodum urbanum, burgagium [*Latin*]; tenure of burgage, burgage (tenure), burgage tenancy, burgage-holding, tenure in burgage, tenancy in burgage, tenancy of burgage, burgage tenement, tenement in burgage [*A tenure whereby lands or houses in cities and towns were held of the king or queen or other lord, for a certain yearly rent*] · Bürgerleh(e)n *n*, Stadtleh(e)n, städtischer Freibesitz *m* (an Häusern und Land)

feudum burgimagistri, feodum burgimagistri [*Latin*] · Bürgermeisterleh(e)n *n*

feudum bursae, feudum bursale, feudum bursaticum, feudum nummorum, feudum pecuniarium, feodum bursae, feodum bursale, feodum bursaticum, feodum nummorum, feodum pecuniarium [*Latin*] · Beutelleh(e)n *n*, Geldleh(e)n, Bauernleh(e)n im engeren Sinne; Quadleh(e)n [*Im Mecklenburgischen*]

feudum caballinum, feodum caballinum [*Latin*] · Klepperleh(e)n *n*

feudum cambocae, feodum cambocae, feudum cambucal, feodum cambucal, feudum presbyteriale, feodum presbyteriale [*Latin*] · Krummstabsleh(e)n *n*, krummstäbisches Leh(e)n

feudum cambucal, feodum cambucal, feudum presbyteriale, feodum presbyteriale, feudum cambocae, feodum cambocae [*Latin*] · Krummstabsleh(e)n *n*, krummstäbisches Leh(e)n

feudum camerae, feodum camerae, feudum de camera, feodum de camera [*Latin*] · Kammerleh(e)n *n*

feudum caminatae, feodum caminatae, feudum keminatae, feodum keminatae [*Latin*] · Kem(me)nadenleh(e)n *n*

feudum caneva(e), feodum caneva(e) [*Latin*] · Kellerleh(e)n *n* [*Ein Leh(e)n, welches in einem Genusse aus dem herrschaftlichen Keller bestand*]

feudum castrense, peculium castrense, beneficium castrale [*Latin*] · Burgleh(e)n *n*, Burggut *n* [*Es wurde jemandem gegeben mit der Bedingung eine Burg zu schützen*]

feudum castri, feodum castri [*Latin*] · Burgleh(e)n *n* [*Es umfaßt die Burg und deren Besitz mit den ihr zugehörigen Gütern und Gerechtsamen*]

feudum censiticum [*Latin*] → copyhold

feudum censuale [*Latin*] → copyhold

feudum clypei, feudum clypeare, feodum clypei, feodum clypeare [*Latin*]; tenure by scutage · Schildleh(e)n *n*

feudum collaterale, feodum collaterale [*Latin*] · Seitenleh(e)n *n*, Collateralleh(e)n

feudum commissum, feodum commissum [*Latin*] · eingezogenes Leh(e)n *n*

feudum communal, feodum communal [*Latin*] · Gemeinleh(e)n *n*, gemeinschaftliches Leh(e)n

feudum conuentionale, feodum conuentionale [*Latin*] · gedingtes Leh(e)n *n*

feudum cuffodiae, feodum cuffodiae, feudum guardial, feodum guardial [*Latin*] · Bewahrungsleh(e)n *n*, Vormundschaftsleh(e)n, Guardeyleh(e)n

feudum culinare, feodum culinare [*Latin*] · Küchelleh(e)n *n*, Küchenleh(e)n

feudum dangerii, feodum dangerii [*Latin*] · Gefahrleh(e)n *n*

feudum datum, feodum datum [*Latin*] · gegebenes Leh(e)n *n*

feudum de camera, feodum de camera, feudum camerae, feodum camerae [*Latin*] · Kammerleh(e)n *n*

feudum decimanum, feodum decimanum [*Latin*] · Zehndleh(e)n *n*

feudum derivativum, feodum derivativum [*Latin*] · verwandeltes Leh(e)n *n*

feudum divisibile, feodum divisibile [*Latin*] · teilbares Leh(e)n *n*

feudum domesticum, feodum domesticum [*Latin*] · deutsches Leh(e)n *n*

feudum dotalitii, feodum dotalitii [*Latin*] · Leibgedingeleh(e)n *n*

feudum ecclesiasticum, feodum ecclesiasticum, feudum religiosum, feodum religiosum [*Latin*]; spiritual fee, spiritual feud, spiritual feod, spiritual fief, spiritual (feodal) tenure (of land), ecclesiastic(al) fee, ecclesiastic(al) feod, ecclesiastic(al) feud, ecclesiastic(al) fief, ecclesiastic(al) tenement, ecclesiastic(al) tenancy, ecclesiastic(al) (feodal) tenure (of land), tenure (of land) by divine service, tenure (of land) by religious service · Gottesleh(e)n *n*, Kirchenleh(e)n, Klosterleh(e)n, geistliches Leh(e)n [*Die geistlichen Verrichtungen waren genau definiert*]

feudum entitium, feodum entitium [*Latin*] · Kaufleh(e)n *n*

feudum equestre [*Latin*] → knight's fee (tenure)

feudum extra curtem, feodum nob landsassicum, feodum extra curtem, feu-

feudum femineum — feudum loricae

dum nob landsassicum [*Latin*] · Provinzialleh(e)n *n*, Landesleh(e)n, Außenleh(e)n, Butenleh(e)n

feudum femineum, feodum femineum [*Latin*] · Kunkelleh(e)n, Schleyerleh(e)n, Weiberleh(e)n [*Das Wort „Kunkelleh(e)n" ist hergeleitet von Kunkel, der Spinnrocken, oder die Spindel*]

feudum femineum promiscuum, feodum femineum promiscuum [*Latin*] · durchgehendes (Kunkel)Leh(e)n *n*, durchgehendes Schleyerleh(e)n, durchgehendes Weiberleh(e)n [*Bei diesem Leh(e)n hatten die Frauen das gleiche Erbrecht wie die Männer*]

feudum femineum successivum, feodum femineum successivum [*Latin*]; apronstring tenure [*Tenure of property in virtue of one's wife, or during her life-time only*] · Frauenleh(e)n *n*

feudum forestale, feodum forestale [*Latin*] · Forstleh(e)n *n*, Waldleh(e)n

feudum francum, feudum honorarium, feodum francum, feodum honorarium [*Latin*] · Ehrenleh(e)n *n*, Freileh(e)n, freies Leh(e)n

feudum fraternum, feodum fraternum [*Latin*] · brüderliches Leh(e)n *n*

feudum fuldense, feodum fuldense [*Latin*] · fuldisches Leh(e)n *n*

feudum furcale, feodum furcale, feudum furcae, feodum furcae [*Latin*] · Galgenleh(e)n *n*, Fehmleh(e)n, Vehmstalleh(e)n

feudum futurum, feodum futurum [*Latin*] · Expectanzleh(e)n *n*, Anerbschaftsleh(e)n

feudum galeatum, feodum galeatum [*Latin*] · Helmleh(e)n *n*

feudum gastaldiae [*Langobardian law*] → feudum ambastee

feudum gentilitium, feodum gentilitium [*Latin*] · Geschlechtsleh(e)n *n*

feudum gratiae, feodum gratiae [*Latin*] · Gnadenleh(e)n *n*

feudum guardial, feodum guardial, feudum cuffodiae, feodum cuffodiae [*Latin*] · Bewahrungsleh(e)n *n*, Vormundschaftsleh(e)n, Guardeyleh(e)n

feudum habitationis, feodum habitationis [*Latin*] · (Be)Wohnungsleh(e)n *n*

feudum halsbergae, feudum loricae, feudum hauberticum, feodum halsbergae, feodum loricae, feodum hauberticum [*Latin*] · Panzerleh(e)n *n*, Halsbergleh(e)n, Harnischleh(e)n

feudum hereditarium, laudemium mortuarium, feodum hereditarium [*Latin*]; fee of inheritance, inheritance fee · Erbleh(e)n *n*, erbliches Leh(e)n, Erbleh(e)n(s)gut *n*, vererbliches Leh(e)n

feudum honoratorum, feodum francum, feodum honoratorium, feodum francum [*Latin*] · Ehrenleh(e)n *n*, Freileh(e)n, freies Leh(e)n

feudum ignobile, feodum ignobile, feudum plebeium, feodum plebeium [*Latin*] · Schlechtleh(e)n *n*, unadeliges Leh(e)n

feudum ignobile rustico iure concessum, feodum ignobile rustico iure concessum, feudum rusticum, feodum rusticum [*Latin*] · Bauernleh(e)n *n*

feudum imperium, feodum imperium [*Latin*] · Reichsleh(e)n *n*

feudum imperium domesticum, feodum imperium domesticum [*Latin*] · einheimisches Reichsleh(e)n *n*

feudum imperium peregrinum, feodum imperium peregrinum [*Latin*] · auswärtiges Reichsleh(e)n *n*

feudum in curte [*Latin*] → feudum landsassicum

feudum informe, feodum informe [*Latin*] · unförmliches Leh(e)n *n*

feudum iniuratum, feodum iniuratum, feudum non iuratum, feodum non iuratum, feudum manuale, feodum manuale [*Latin*] · Handleh(e)n *n*, ungeschworenes Leh(e)n, Leh(e)n aus reinen Händen [*Bei der Belehnung wurde kein Leh(e)nseid abgelegt, sondern nur ein Handschlag getan*]

feudum insignium, feodum insignium [*Latin*] · Wappenleh(e)n *n*

feudum iuratum, feodum iuratum [*Latin*] · beschworenes Leh(e)n *n*

feudum juridictionis, feodum juridictionis [*Latin*] · Gerichts(barkeits)leh(e)n *n*

feudum keminatae, feodum keminatae, feudum caminatae, feodum caminatae [*Latin*] · Kem(me)nadenleh(e)n *n*

feudum laicum, feodum laicum [*Latin*]; lay feud, lay fief, lay feod, lay tenancy, lay tenement, lay fee, lay (feodal) tenure (of land); feudum seculare, feodum seculare · weltliches Leh(e)n *n*

feudum landsassicum, feudum in curte, feodum landsassicum, feodum in curte [*Latin*] · (B)Innenleh(e)n *n*, landsässiges Leh(e)n

feudum laudemiale, feodum laudemiale [*Latin*] · Laudemialleh(e)n *n*

feudum ligium, feodom ligium [*Latin*] · ligisches Leh(e)n *n*, lediges Leh(e)n, Letnigleh(e)n

feudum loricae, feudum hauberticum, feodum halsbergae, feodum loricae, feodum hauberticum, feudum halsbergae [*Latin*] · Panzerleh(e)n *n*, Halsbergleh(e)n, Harnischleh(e)n

feudum lusaticum, feodum lusaticum [*Latin*] · lausitzisches Leh(e)n *n*

feudum manuale, feodum manuale, feudum iniuratum, feodum iniuratum, feudum non iuratum, feodum non iuratum [*Latin*] · Handleh(e)n *n*, ungeschworenes Leh(e)n, Leh(e)n aus reinen Händen [*Bei der Belehnung wurde kein Leh(e)nseid abgelegt, sondern nur ein Handschlag getan*]

feudum maternum, feodum maternum [*Latin*] · (groß)mütterliches Leh(e)n *n*

feudum mere hereditarium, feodum mere hereditarium [*Latin*] · völliges Erbleh(e)n *n*

feudum militis, feodum militare, feudum militare, tenementum per servitium militare, feodum militis [*Latin*]; military fee (tenure), military fief, military tenancy, military feud, military feod, military tenement, military (feodal) tenure (of land(s)) · Kriegsleh(e)n *n*

feudum ministerialium → feudum ambastee

feudum mixte hereditarium, feodum mixte hereditarium [*Latin*] · gemischtes Erbleh(e)n *n*, vermischtes Erbleh(e)n, gemengtes Erbleh(e)n, Mischerbleh(e)n, Erbmischleh(e)n

feudum mixtum, feodum mixtum [*Latin*] · gemengtes Leh(e)n *n*, gemischtes Leh(e)n, vermischtes Leh(e)n, Mischleh(e)n

feudum mobile, feodum mobile [*Latin*] · Fall-Leh(e)n *n*, leibfälliges Leh(e)n, Schupfleh(e)n

feudum necessarium, feodum necessarium, feudum testamentarium, feodum testamentarium [*Latin*] · notwendiges Leh(e)n *n*

feudum nobile, feodum nobile [*Latin*] · Edelleh(e)n *n*, Adelsleh(e)n, ad(e)liges Leh(e)n

feudum nob landsassicum, feudum extra curtem, feodum nob landsassicum, feodum extra curtem [*Latin*] · Provinzialleh(e)n *n*, Landesleh(e)n, Außenleh(e)n, Butenleh(e)n

feudum non iuratum, feodum non iuratum, feudum manuale, feodum manuale, feudum iniuratum, feodum iniuratum [*Latin*] · Handleh(e)n *n*, ungeschworenes Leh(e)n, Leh(e)n aus reinen Händen [*Bei der Belehnung wurde kein Leh(e)nseid abgelegt, sondern nur ein Handschlag getan*]

feudum novum, feodum novum [*Latin*] · neues Leh(e)n *n*, neu erworbenes Leh(e)n

feudum novum datum, feodum novum datum [*Latin*] · neues gegebenes Leh(e)n *n*

feudum nummorum [*Latin*] → feudum bursae

feudum oblatum, feodum oblatum [*Latin*] · angebotenes Leh(e)n *n*, aufgetragenes Leh(e)n

feudum officii → feudum ambastee

feudum oppignoratum, feodum oppignoratum [*Latin*] · verpfändetes Leh(e)n *n*

feudum originarium, feodum originarium [*Latin*] · ursprüngliches Leh(e)n *n*

feudum palatinum, feodum aulicum, feodum palatinum, feudum aulicum [*Latin*] · Hof(raths)leh(e)n *n*

feudum paternum, feodum paternum [*Latin*] · (groß)väterliches Leh(e)n *n*

feudum patronalis, feodum patronalis [*Latin*] · Patronatsleh(e)n *n*

feudum peculiare, feodum peculiare [*Latin*] · Sonderleh(e)n *n*

feudum pecunarium [*Latin*] → feudum bursae

feudum peregrinum, feodum peregrinum [*Latin*] · fremdes Leh(e)n *n*, Fremdleh(e)n

feudum perfectum, feodum perfectum, feudum verum, feodum verum [*Latin*] · wahrhaftiges Leh(e)n *n*, vollkommenes Leh(e)n

feudum persionarium [*Latin*] → copyhold

feudum personae, feodum personae [*Latin*] · Personalleh(e)n *n*, persönliches Leh(e)n, Personenleh(e)n

feudum pignoratitium, feodum pignoratitium, feudum ad antichresin datum, feodum ad antichresin datum [*Latin*] · Pfandleh(e)n *n*

feudum plebeium, feodum plebeium, feudum ignobile, feodum ignobile [*Latin*] · Schlechtleh(e)n *n*, unadeliges Leh(e)n

feudum plegii, feodum plegii [*Latin*] · Bürgschaftsleh(e)n *n*, Geißelleh(e)n

feudum plenum, feodum plenum [*Latin*] · Volleh(e)n *n*

feudum postarum, feodum postarum [*Latin*] · Postleh(e)n *n*

feudum preafecturae → feudum ambastee

feudum presbyteriale, feodum presbyteriale, feudum cambocae, feodum cambocae, feudum cambucal, feodum cambucal [*Latin*] · Krummstabsleh(e)n *n*, krummstäbisches Leh(e)n

feudum privatum, feodum privatum [*Latin*] · Privatleh(e)n *n*

feudum promiscuum femineum, feodum promiscuum femineum [*Latin*] · Kunkelleh(e)n *n* mit gleichem Erbrecht der Frauen und der Männer, Schleyerleh(e)n

feudum proprietatis — FHA

mit gleichem Erbrecht der Frauen und der Männer, Weiberleh(e)n mit gleichem Erbrecht der Frauen und der Männer

feudum proprietatis, feodum proprietatis [*Latin*] · Eigentumsleh(e)n *n*

feudum protectionis, feodum protectionis, feudum advocatiae, feodum advocatiae [*Latin*] · Vogteyleh(e)n *n*, Schirm(-Gerechtigkeits)leh(e)n

feudum provincialium extraneum, feodum provincialium extraneum [*Latin*] · Leh(e)n *n* welches Teile eines anderen Landes ausmacht und darin landsässig ist

feudum provinciarum, feodum provinciarum, feudum territoriorum imperii, feodum territoriorum imperii [*Latin*] · Reichslandesleh(e)n *n*

feudum publicum, feodum publicum [*Latin*] · Staatsleh(e)n *n*, öffentliches Leh(e)n

feudum publicum extra territorium, feodum publicum extra territorium [*Latin*] · auswärtiges Staatsleh(e)n *n*, auswärtiges öffentliches Leh(e)n

feudum publicum in territorium, feodum publicum in territorium [*Latin*] · einheimisches Staatsleh(e)n *n*, einheimisches öffentliches Leh(e)n

feudum rectum, feodum rectum [*Latin*] · rechtes Leh(e)n *n*

feudum regale ecclesiasticum, feodum regale ecclesiasticum [*Latin*] · geistliches Regalleh(e)n *n*

feudum regale seculare, feodum regale seculare [*Latin*] · weltliches Regalleh(e)n *n*

feudum regalium, feodum regalium [*Latin*] · Fürstenleh(e)n *n*, Regalleh(e)n

feudum religiosum [*Latin*] → feudum ecclesiasticum

feudum rusticum, feodum rusticum, feudum ignobile rustico iure concessum, feodum ignobile rustico iure concessum [*Latin*] · Bauernleh(e)n *n*

feudum salinum, feodum salinum [*Latin*] · Thalleh(e)n *n*

feudum sceptri, feodum sceptri [*Latin*] · Zepterleh(e)n *n*, Scepterleh(e)n

feudum sculteti, feodum sculteti [*Latin*] · Schultheißleh(e)n *n*, Schulzenleh(e)n

feudum seculare, feodum seculare, feudum laicum, feodum laicum [*Latin*], lay feud, lay fief, lay feod, lay tenancy, lay tenement, lay fee, lay (feodal) tenure (of land) · weltliches Leh(e)n *n*

feudum silesiacum, feodum silesiacum [*Latin*] · schlesisches Leh(e)n *n*

feudum simplex [*Latin*] → simple fee

feudum simultaneum, feodum simultaneum [*Latin*] · (Ge)Samtleh(e)n *n*

feudum solare, feodum solis, feodum solare, feudum solis [*Latin*] · Sonnenleh(e)n *n*

feudum soldatae, feodum soldatae [*Latin*] · Soldleh(e)n *n*, Söldnerleh(e)n

feudum supplicium, feodum supplicium [*Latin*] · Henkerleh(e)n *n*

feudum talliatum [*Latin*] → (estate in) fee tail

feudum territoriorum imperii, feodum territoriorum imperii, feudum provinciarum, feodum provinciarum [*Latin*] · Reichslandesleh(e)n *n*

feudum testamentarium, feodum testamentarium, feudum necessarium, feodum necessarium [*Latin*] · notwendiges Leh(e)n *n*

feudum throni, feodum throni [*Latin*] · Thronleh(e)n *n*

feudum urbanum, feodum burgense, feodum urbanum, burgagium, feudum burgense [*Latin*]; tenure of burgage, burgage (tenure), burgage tenancy, burgage-holding, tenure in burgage, tenancy in burgage, tenancy of burgage, burgage tenement, tenement in burgage [*A tenure whereby lands or houses in cities and towns were held of the king or queen or other lord, for a certain yearly rent*] · Bürgerleh(e)n *n*, Stadtleh(e)n, städtischer Freibesitz *m* (an Häusern und Land)

feudum venationis, feodum venationis [*Latin*] · Jagdleh(e)n *n*

feudum verum, feodum verum, feudum perfectum, feodum perfectum [*Latin*] · wahrhaftiges Leh(e)n *n*, vollkommenes Leh(e)n

feudum verus [*Latin*] → feudum antiquum

feudum verus, feodum verus, feudum antiquum, feodum antiquum [*Latin*] · Altleh(e)n *n*, altes Leh(e)n, altväterliches Leh(e)n, Stammleh(e)n

feudum vexilli, feodum vexilli [*Latin*] · Fahn(en)leh(e)n *n*

feuduty [*Scotland*] · Landpachtzins *m*

feuing [*Scotland*] · Landpacht *f* [*Feudalwesen*]

feuing system, system of feuing [*Scotland*] · Landpachtsystem *n*

FHA, Federal House and Home Finance Agency · oberste Bundesbehörde *f* für den Wohn(ungs)bau in den USA, höchste Bundesbehörde für den Wohn(ungs)bau in den USA

FHWA, federal highway administration, federal road administration · Bundesstraßenverwaltung *f*

fiction of law, legal fiction, law(ful) fiction · Rechtsfiktion *f*

fictitious, faint, pretended, feigned, feint · fiktiv, vorgegeben, vorgetäuscht, fingiert

fictitious bill, feint bill, faint bill, feigned bill, pretended bill; windmill, kite (Brit.); accommodation bill · Freundschaftswechsel *m*, Gefälligkeitswechsel, Kellerwechsel, Reitwechsel, Schornsteinwechsel, Scheinwechsel

fictitious business, feigned business, faint business, pretended business, feint business · fiktives Geschäft *n*, fingiertes Geschäft, vorgegebenes Geschäft, vorgetäuschtes Geschäft, Scheingeschäft

fictitious contract, feigned contract, pretended contract, faint contract · Scheinvertrag *m*

fictitious (court) action, feint (court) action, pretended (court) action, feigned (court) action, faint (court) action [*An action brought on a pretended right, when the plaintiff has no true cause of action, for some illegal purpose. In a feigned action the words of the writ are true. It differs from "false action", in which case the words of the writ are false*] · fiktive Klage *f*, vorgetäuschte Klage, vorgegebene Klage, fingierte Klage, Scheinklage

fictitious desertion, feigned desertion, pretended desertion, faint desertion, feint desertion · Scheinwüstung *f*, Trugwüstung

fictitious name, pretended name, feigned name, faint name, feint name · fiktiver Name *m*, vorgetäuschter Name, vorgegebener Name, fingierter Name, Scheinname

fictitious permission → feigned permission

fictitious plaintiff, feigned plaintiff, pretended plaintiff, faint plaintiff, feint plaintiff · fiktiver Kläger *m*, vorgegebener Kläger, vorgetäuschter Kläger, fingierter Kläger, Scheinkläger

fictitious promise, feigned promise, pretended promise, faint promise, feint promise · fiktives Versprechen *n*, vorgetäuschtes Versprechen, vorgegebenes Versprechen, fingiertes Versprechen, Scheinversprechen

fictitious purchase, feigned purchase, faint purchase, pretended purchase, feint purchase · fiktiver Kauf *m*, vorgetäuschter Kauf, fingierter Kauf, vorgegebener Kauf, Scheinkauf

fide-commissary; fidei-commissarius [*Latin*]; object of the trust, fiduciary debtor · Berechtigte *m*, Benefiziar *m*, Bedachte *m*, Begünstigte *m*, Treuhandberechtigte *m*, Treuhandbenefiziar *m*, Treuhandbedachte *m*, Treuhandbegünstigte *m*, Treu(hand)nehmer *m*, Empfänger *m* der Treuhandeinkünfte

fidei-commissaria haereditas [*Latin*]; entail [*A form of bequest requesting a transfer of property to be made by some one after the testator's death*] · Fideikommiß *n*, gebundene (Land)Erbfolge(ordnung) *f*, Erb(schafts)majorat, Erb(schafts)fideikommiß

fidei-commission debt · Fideikommißschuld *f*, Majoratschuld

fidei-commission law, fidei-commissium law, fidei-commission statute · Fideikommißgesetz *n*, Majoratgesetz

fidei-commissium law · Fideikommißrecht *n*, Majoratrecht

fideicommissum inter vivos [*Latin*] · Fideikommiß *n* unter Lebenden

fidelitas domini [*Latin*] · Leh(e)n(s)herrntreue *f*

fidelitas feudalis [*Latin*]; fealty, fidelity, feodality, allegiance, feudality [*It was due by feudal tenants to their lords*] · Leh(e)n(s)treue *f*

fidelity, feodality, allegiance, feudality; fidelitas feudalis [*Latin*], fealty [*It was due by feudal tenants to their lords*] · Leh(e)n(s)treue *f*

fidelity bond · Veruntreuungskaution *f*

fidelity insurance [*If the contract of guaranty be against dishonesty or theft on the part of the principal debtor, the guarantor will be discharged if the person to whom the guaranty was made continues to keep the principal debtor in his service after he has been known to commit a dishonest act or theft*] · Bürgschaftsversicherung *f*, Vertrauensschadenversicherung

fidelity oath, oath of allegiance, oath of fealty, oath of fidelity, fealty oath [*It was sworn by feudal tenants to their lords*] · Leh(e)n(s)eid *m*, Leh(e)n(s)schwur *m*, Treu(e)eid, Treu(e)schwur

fiducial, under trusteeship, on trust, fiduciary, in trust · zur treuen Hand, treuhänderisch

fiducial capacity, fiduciary capacity · Treuhändereigenschaft *f*

fiducial contract, contract in trust, contract on trust, contract under trusteeship, trustee(ship) contract, fiduciary contract · Treuhandvertrag *m*, Treuhändervertrag

fiducial distribution · Fiduzialverteilung *f* [*Statistik*]

fiducial female heir, heiress of inventory (in tail), heir female of inventory (in tail), female heir of inventory (in tail), fiduciary heiress, fiduciary heir female, fiduciary female heir, fiducial heiress, fiducial heir female · Vorerbin f

fiducial heir (male), fiduciary heir (male), heir (male) of inventory (in tail), fiduciary; fiduciarius haeres [*Latin*]; provisional heir (male) · Vorerbe m

fiducial limit, confidence limit · Mutungsgrenze f [*Statistik*]

fiducial money, credit money · Kreditgeld n

fiduciary, in trust, fiducial, under trusteeship, on trust · zur treuen Hand, treuhänderisch

fiduciary [*A person or organization in a position of trust or confidence managing property and/or financial transactions on behalf of others*] · Betraute m, Vermögensverwalter

fiduciary account, escrow account, trust account · Treuhandkonto n, Notar-Anderkonto

fiduciary capacity, fiducial capacity · Treuhändereigenschaft f

fiduciary contract, fiducial contract, contract in trust, contract on trust, contract under trusteeship, trustee(ship) contract · Treuhandvertrag m, Treuhändervertrag

fiduciary debtor, fide-commissary; fideicommissarius [*Latin*]; object of the trust · Berechtigte m, Benefiziar m, Bedachte m, Begünstigte m, Treuhandberechtigte m, Treuhandbenefiziar m, Treuhandbedachte m, Treuhandbegünstigte m, Treu(hand)nehmer m, Empfänger m der Treuhandeinkünfte

fiduciary delegation · fiduziarische Übertragung f, fiduziarische Abtretung [*Vertragspflicht; Aufgabe*]

fiduciary heiress, fiduciary heir female, fiduciary female heir, fiducial heiress, fiducial heir female, fiducial female heir, heiress of inventory (in tail), heir female of inventory (in tail), female heir of inventory (in tail) · Vorerbin f

fiduciary issue · Vertrauensemission f, fiduziarische und nicht durch Gold gedeckte Emission von Kreditgeld

fiduciary legatee · Treuhänderlegatar m

fiduciary money · Vertrauensgeld n [*Sein Wert ruht auf dem Kredit*]

fiduciary ownership (of property), fiduciary proprietorship, fiduciary (general) property, trust ownership (of property), trust proprietorship, trust (general) property · fiduziarisches Eigentum n, Treuhandeigentum, Treuhändereigentum

fief, tenancy, land tenure, feud, feod, tenement, (feodal) tenure (of land), land held of a lord, land in fee; feodum, feudum, tenementum [*Latin*]; feu [*Scots law*], fee (tenure) (of land) · Leh(e)n n, Leh(e)n(s)gut n, Leh(e)n(s)besitz m, leh(e)n(s)rechtlicher (Grund)Besitz(stand) m, Benefizium n

fief for life, (feodal) tenure (of land) for life, tenancy for life, tenement for life, fee (tenure) for life · lebenslanges Leh(e)n n, Leh(e)n auf Lebenszeit

fief-tenant, feoda(to)ry, feuda(to)ry; homo pertinens [*Latin*]; beneficiary, holder of a feudal benefice, land tenant, (feudal) tenant, manorial tenant, feudal bond(s)man, vassal, tenant of land, feeholder, holder of a fee, holder of a fief [*A tenant or vassal who held his estate by feudal service*] · Leh(e)n(s)mann m, Leh(e)n(s)träger m, Gefolgsmann, Gutszinsmann, Vasall m

field [*Open land as opposed to woodland*] · Feld n

field administration, (job) site administration · Baustellenverwaltung f

field administrative staff, field administrative personnel, (job) site administrative staff, (job) site administrative personnel · Baustellenverwaltungspersonal n

field alternately used as arable land and pasture · Acker-Grünland n, AGr

field boundary, boundary of a field · Feldmarkung f, Feldgrenze f

field cultivation, farming, soil cultivation, agricultural use, cultivation (of land), cultivation of fields, cultivation of soil, land cultivation · Anbau m, Bodenkultivierung f, Landkultivierung, Bodenkultur f, Feldbau

field food, arable farming food · Ackernahrung f

field force(s) → field staff

field measure, measure of a field · Feldmaß n

field of commercial arbitration, commercial arbitration field · Handelsschieds(gerichts)wesen n

field of education, education(al) field · Bildungssektor m

field of forces · Kräftefeld n

field of March; campus martii [*Latin*] · Märzfeld n

field of May; campus maii [*Latin*] · Maifeld n

field of property, property field · Vermögenswesen n

field pattern of fragmental strips · Streifengemengeflur f

field pattern of groups of fragmented strips originating from blocks · Blockgewannflur f

field pattern with fragmented holdings ·
Gemenge(feld)flur *f*

field personnel, field staff · Außendienstpersonal *n*

field research · primäre Marktforschung *f*

fields · Flur *f* [*Eine parzellierte, gegebenenfalls auch nicht unterteilte, einem oder mehreren landwirtschaftlichen Betrieben besitzmäßig oder eigentumsmäßig zugeordnete landwirtschaftliche Nutzfläche eines Sied(e)lung, eines Sied(e)lungsverbandes oder eines Wirtschaftsverbandes*]

field sales engineer · Wirtschaftsingenieur *m*

fields form, fields scheme, fields pattern · Flurform *f*, Flurmuster *n*, Flurschema *n*

field sheet · Feldriß *m*

field staff, field personnel · Außendienstpersonal *n*

field staff, field force(s), field personnel, (job) site staff, (job) site forces, (job) site personnel · Bau(stellen)arbeitskräfte *f*

field vegetable cultivation, field vegetable farming · Feldgemüse(an)bau *m*

field windbreak · Flurwindschutz *m*

fifo, first in — first out · Ausgang *m* in der Reihenfolge des Eingangs, älteste Preise *m pl*

file · Akte *f*

to file · aktenkundig machen

to file → to discover

to file [*application*] · stellen [*Antrag*]

file · Datei *f*

to file a bill, to file a (law)suit, to file an action, to sue; actionare [*Latin*]; to bring an action (against) · einreichen (einer Klage), erheben (einer Klage), klagen

filed · aktenkundig

files of previous situation(s) · Einlagennachweis *m*, Einlagenverzeichnis *n*

filing, placing on file · Aktenaufnahme *f*, Aufnahme in Akten

filing, discovery, production, submission, presentation · Abgabe *f*, Einreichung *f*, Vorlage *f*, Vorlegung, Edition *f*, Enthüllung [*Mitteilung von Tatsachen oder Vorlegung von Schriftstücken an den Prozeßgegner*]

filing by interrogatories, discovery by interrogatories, submission by interrogatories, presentation by interrogatories, production by interrogatories · Abgabe *f* von Tatsachen, Einreichung *f* von Tatsachen, Vorlage *f* von Tatsachen, Vorlegung von Tatsachen, Edition *f* von Tatsachen, Enthüllung von Tatsachen [*An den Prozeßgegner*]

filing code · Aktenordnung *f*

filing date, application date, request date, date of filing, date of application, date of request · Antragsdatum *n*, Gesuchsdatum *n*

filing of an application, filing of a request · Antragstellung *f*, Gesuchstellung

filing of documents, production of documents, submission of documents, presentation of documents, discovery of documents · Abgabe *f* von Schriftstücken, Vorlage *f* von Schriftstücken, Einreichung *f* von Schriftstücken, Vorlegung von Schriftstücken, Enthüllung von Schriftstücken, Edition *f* von Schriftstücken [*An den Prozeßgegner*]

fill · Anschüttung *f*, Aufschüttung *f*

fill area · Aufschüttungsfläche *f*, Anschüttungsfläche *f*

filled up site · Auffüllplatz *m*

filling in function, pressure-relieving function, catching up function · Nachholfunktion *f* [*Funktion des Staates für die Infrastruktur*]

filling-in system · Restaurierungs- und Verdichtungs-System *n* [*Städtebau*]

to fill up [*form*] · ausfüllen [*Formular*]

filtering [*A change over time in the position of a given dwelling unit or group of dwelling units within the distribution of housing prices and rents than a community as a whole*] · dynamisches Element *n* des Wohn(ungs)marktes

filtering down, relative Veränderung *f* des Ertragswertes der Wohnung [*Die Miete jeder Wohnung sinkt im Laufe der Zeit relativ zur Durchschnittsmiete des gesamten Wohnungsbestandes*]

filtering up, percolation [*of the households*] · Veränderung *f* in der Bewohnerschaft [*Die Miete jeder Wohnung sinke im Laufe der Zeit, und infolgedessen würden die Bewohner für das gleiche Geld von Zeit zu Zeit eine relativ bessere Wohnung mieten*]

filthy house · schmutziges Haus *n*

final, determinate; perimere [*Latin*]; irrevocable, peremptory · bestimmt, endgültig, unwiderruflich

final acceptance · Endabnahme *f*, Schlußabnahme, Gebrauchsabnahme

final (ad)measurement · Endaufmaß *n*, Schlußaufmaß

final and conclusive · endgültig und verbindlich

final assembly — financial accountancy

final assembly [*An assembly to which no further parts need to be added*] · Endverbundprodukt *n*, Endverbunderzeugnis *n*, Verbundendprodukt, Verbundenderzeugnis

final attestation, completion certificate, completion attestation, certificate of completion, attestation of completion, final certificate · Endbescheinigung *f*, Endschein *m*, Endattest *n*, Schlußbescheinigung, Schlußschein, Schlußattest [*Über die Beendigung der Bauarbeiten*]

(final) award negotiation, (final) contract negotiation · Vergabeverhandlung *f*, Verdingungsverhandlung

final balance · Schlußsaldo *m*

final call, final demand · Endnachfrage *f*

final certificate, final attestation, completion certificate, completion attestation, certificate of completion, attestation of completion · Endbescheinigung *f*, Endschein *m*, Endattest *n*, Schlußbescheinigung, Schlußschein, Schlußattest [*Über die Beendigung der Bauarbeiten*]

final completion · endgültige Fertigstellung *f*, endgültige Vollendung

(final) contract negotiation, (final) award negotiation · Vergabeverhandlung *f*, Verdingungsverhandlung

final decision · Endentscheidung *f*, Endentscheid *m*

final decree (at law) → final judg(e)ment (at law)

(final degree of) utility, marginal utility, final utility, margin of profitableness · Nutzen *m* der letzten Einheit, Grenznutzen, Grenzwert *m*

final demand, final call · Endnachfrage *f*

final dividend · Schlußdividende *f*

final estimate [*It is made by the owner, or the architect/engineer representing the owner, at the completion of the project*] · Nachkalkulation *f*

final examination · Schlußprüfung *f*

final fee invoice · Honorarschlußrechnung *f*, Honorarendrechnung, Gebührenschlußrechnung, Gebührenendrechnung

final invoice · Endrechnung *f*, Schlußrechnung

finality, irrevocability · Endgültigkeit *f*, Unwiderruflichkeit

final judg(e)ment (at law), final decree (at law), final legal judg(e)ment, judg(e)ment (at law) absolute, legal judg(e)ment, decree absolute [*See remark under "gerichtliches Urteil"*] · Endurteil *n*, Schlußurteil

final payment, balance payment, payment of balance · Schlußzahlung *f*, Restzahlung, Abschlußzahlung

final price · Endpreis *m*, Schlußpreis

final project clean up, site clean(s)ing, rubbish removal · Bau(stellen)reinigung *f*, Bau(stellen)säuberung [*Reinigung einer Baustelle von Bauschutt und anderen Arbeitsrückständen*]

final provision · Schlußbestimmung *f*

final report · Schlußbericht *m*

final settlement (of accounts) · Endabrechnung *f*, Schlußabrechnung

final state · Endzustand *m*

final sum · Endsumme *f*, Schlußsumme

final utility, margin of profitableness, (final degree of) utility, marginal utility · Nutzen *m* der letzten Einheit, Grenznutzen, Grenzwert *m*

final value, terminal value · Endwert *m*

final winding-up meeting · Schlußversammlung *f*, Liquidations-Generalversammlung

to finance, to fund · finanzieren

finance · Finanzen *f*

finance bill · Finanzvorlage *f*

finance bill (of exchange), bank(er's) bill · Bankwechsel *m*, Finanzwechsel [*Wechsel, welchen eine Bank auf eine andere zieht*]

finance charge, credit charge · Finanzierungsaufschlag *m*

finance committee · Finanzausschuß *m*

finance company, financing company · Finanz(ierungs)gesellschaft *f*

finance controlling · Finanzplanung *f* und -kontrolle *f*

financed, funded · finanziert

financed mortgage → funded mortgage

financed with private means, privately financed · freifinanziert [*Wohnungsbau. Gegensatz: öffentlich gefördert*]

financed work, sweated industry, domestic industry, domestic system, home(-work) industry, cottage industry · Hausindustrie *f*, Verlagssystem *n*, Heim(arbeits)industrie, Verlag *m*

finance leasing · Finanzierungsleasing *n*

finance stock · Kreditaktie *f*

financial accommodation · finanzielles Entgegenkommen *n*

financial accountancy, financial accounting · Finanzrechnungswesen *n*

financial act — findings

financial act, financial statute, financial law · Finanzierungsgesetz n

financial administration · Finanzverwaltung f

financial aid, financial assistance, financial help, financial promotion, financial sponsoring, financing aid, financing assistance, financing help, financing promotion, financing sponsoring · finanzielle Hilfe f, finanzielle Förderung f, Finanzierungsförderung, Finanz(ierungs)hilfe

financial analyst · Finanzanalytiker m

financial bribe, bribe money; "palm oil" (Brit.); graft (US) · Bestechungsgeld n, Schmiergeld

financial centre (Brit.); financial center (US) · Finanzzentrum n

financial charge, financial encumbrance, financial incumbrance, financial burden · Finanzlast f, Finanzbelastung f

financial constitution · Finanzverfassung f

financial district · Bankenviertel n

financial equalization · Finanzausgleich m

financial help → financial aid

financial incumbrance, financial burden, financial charge, financial encumbrance · Finanzlast f, Finanzbelastung f

financial institution · Finanzinstitut n

financial law, financial act, financial statute · Finanzierungsgesetz n

financial law · Finanzrecht n

financial legislation, financial lawmaking · Finanzgesetzgebung f

(financial) leverage · Hebelwirkung f wachsender Verschuldung auf die Eigenkapitalrentabilität

financial liability, commitment · geldliche Verpflichtung f

financially able, sound, capable to pay, able to pay, trust(worth)y, solvent · zahlungsfähig, flüssig, kreditfähig, kreditwürdig

financially feasible · finanzierbar

financially strong, financially powerful · kapitalkräftig

financial promotion → financial aid

financial resources · wirtschaftliche Betriebsmittel n pl

financial science, science of finance · Finanzwissenschaft f

financial sponsoring → financial aid

financial statute, financial law, financial act · Finanzierungsgesetz n

financial year, budget year · Haushalt(s)jahr n

financing, funding · Fundieren n, Finanzieren, Mittelaufnahme f

financing ability, financing capacity, financing qualification, financing capability, ability to finance, capablility to finance, qualification to finance, capacity to finance · Finanzierungseignung f, Finanzierungsfähigkeit f

financing aid → financial aid

financing approach · Finanzierungsansatz m

financing assistance → financial aid

financing by outside help, outside financing · Fremdfinanzierung f

financing by own capital · Eigenkapitalfinanzierung f

financing capability, ability to finance, capablility to finance, qualification to finance, capacity to finance, financing ability, financing capacity, financing qualification · Finanzierungseignung f, Finanzierungsfähigkeit f

financing company, finance company · Finanz(ierungs)gesellschaft f

financing contribution · Finanzierungsbeitrag m

financing cost(s) · Finanzierungskosten f

financing gap · Finanzierungslücke f

financing of hous(ebuild)ing, hous(ebuild)ing financing · Wohn(ungs)baufinanzierung f

financing promotion → financial aid

financing qualification → financing ability

financing scheme · Finanzierungsplan m

financing sponsoring → financial aid

financing without recourse · Forfaitierung f, regreßloser Ankauf m von Forderungen

to find · erkennen, für Recht erklären

finder · Nachschlagesystem n

finder (of lost property) · Finder m

finder of treasure-trove [He is entitled thereto as against owner of land where treasure trove is found and all the world save the true owner, in absence of statute] · Schatzfinder m

finder's fee · Finderlohn m

finding of fact · Tatsachenfeststellungsergebnis n

finding (of the issue), verdict [From the Latin "vere dictum", a true declaration] · Wahrspruch m, Verdikt n

findings [The conclusions of an enquiry] · Befund m

findings and conclusions · Tatsachenfeststellungen *f pl* und rechtliche Gründe *m pl*

findings of (the) acceptance (of (the) work(s)) · Abnahmebefund *m*, Bauabnahmebefund

findings (up)on the facts · richterliche Feststellung *f* der strittigen Tatsachen

to fine · auferlegen von Bußgeld, auferlegen von Reugeld, auferlegen von Strafgeld

fine [*A money payment made by a feudal tenement to his lord. The most usual fine is that payable on the admittance of a new tenement, but there are also due in some manors fines upon alienation, on a license to demise the lands, or on the death of the lord, or other events*] · Leh(e)n(s)bußgeldzahlung *f*

fine · Bußgeld *n*, Reugeld, Strafgeld

fine · Geldbuße *f*, Geldstrafe *f*

fine bank bill · erstklassiger Bankwechsel *m*, Privatdiskont *m*

fine for (ab)alienation, fine for disposal · Veräußerungsbußgeld *n*, Veräußerungsstrafgeld, Veräußerungsreugeld

finem facere [*Latin*]; finire [*In old English law*]; to make a fine, to pay a fine · Bußgeld entrichten, Strafgeld entrichten, Reugeld entrichten, Bußgeld zahlen, Reugeld zahlen, Strafgeld zahlen

fine (of land(s)) [*An amicable composition of a (law) suit, either actual or fictitious, by leave of the court, by which the land(s) in question become, or are acknowledged to be, the right of one of the parties*] · Vergleich *m* in einem Grundstücksprozeß

fine rate, prime rate · Vorzugszinssatz *m*, Primarate *f*, Leitzinssatz für erste Adressen, Zinssatz für Kredite an erste Adressen

finger city, star(-shaped) town, finger town, star(-shaped) city · Radialstadt *f*, sternförmige Stadt

finger plan, radial corridors plan, star pattern plan · Plan *m* der linearen Anordnung einer Stadtregion

fingerprint · Fingerabdruck *m*

finire [*In old English law*]; to make a fine, to pay a fine; finem facere [*Latin*] · Bußgeld entrichten, Strafgeld entrichten, Reugeld entrichten, Bußgeld zahlen, Reugeld zahlen, Strafgeld zahlen

finis [*Latin*] · Leh(e)n(s)taxe *f*

to finish, to complete · fertigstellen

finished, completed · fertig(gestellt)

finished copy · Reinschrift *f*

finished product · Fertigerzeugnis *n*

finishing craft, finishing trade · (Innen)Ausbaugewerk *n*

finishing credit [*Credit allowed for finishing purposes*] · Veredelungskredit *m*

finishing industry, improvement industry · Veredelungsindustrie *f*

finishing trade, finishing craft · (Innen)Ausbaugewerk *n*

finishing trade, improvement trade · Veredelungsgewerbe *n*

finite multiplier · Endlichkeitsfaktor *m* [*Statistik*]

finite population · endliche Gesamtheit *f* [*Statistik*]

fire-bote, focage, focale; lignagium [*Latin*]; right to cut fuel in woods · Brennholzschlagrecht *n*, Feuerungszubuße *f*, Brennholzbezugsrecht

fire damage, damage by fire · Brandschaden *m*, Feuerschaden

fire(-fighting) code · Brandordnung *f*, Feuerlöschordnung

fire insurance · Brandversicherung *f*, Feuerversicherung

fire insurance fund · Brandkasse *f*

fire insurance value · Brandversicherungswert *m*, Feuerversicherungswert

fire prevention act, fire prevention law, fire prevention statute, fire protection act, fire protection statute, fire protection law · Brandschutzgesetz *n*, Feuerschutzgesetz

fire prevention board, fire protection board · Brandschutzamt *n*, Feuerschutzamt

fire prevention office, fire protection office · Brandschutzstelle *f*, Feuerschutzstelle

fire protection act, fire protection statute, fire prevention law, fire prevention act, fire prevention statute · Brandschutzgesetz *n*, Feuerschutzgesetz

fire protection board, fire prevention board · Brandschutzamt *n*, Feuerschutzamt

fire protection office, fire prevention office · Brandschutzstelle *f*, Feuerschutzstelle

fire safety · Brandsicherheit *f*, Feuersicherheit

fire wall · Brandwand *f* [*Wand, die bei einem Brand ihre Standsicherheit nicht verliert und die Ausbreitung von Feuer auf andere Gebäude oder Gebäudeabschnitte verhindert*]

firm (Brit.) [*Persons who have entered into partnership are collectively called a firm. There is no catch-all term for "Firma" in the USA. The term in the USA which is nearest to "Firma" is "company"*] · Firma *f*

firma alba — fiscal policy

firma alba [*Latin*] → blanch farm

firm commitment · feste Zusage *f*, verbindliche Zusage

firm (cost(s)) estimate, contractor's (cost(s)) estimate, detailed (cost(s)) estimate · detaillierter KV *m*, detaillierter (Bau)Kosten(vor)anschlag

firm name · Firmenname *m*

firm of brokers → ((real) estate) broking firm

firm of (land) brokers → ((real) estate) broking firm

firm of (land) jobbers → ((real) estate) broking firm

firm's health insurance scheme · Betriebskrankenkasse *f*

first, prior · älter, ranghöher, vorgehend

first acquirer, original acquirer · Ersterwerber *m*

first acquisition, original acquisition · Erstwerb *m*, Erstbeschaffung *f*, Ersterwerbung *f*

first afforestation, original afforestation · Erstaufforstung *f*

first branch of the government · erste Regierungsgewalt *f*, erste Regierungsmacht *f*, erste Regierungskompetenz *f*, erste Regierungshoheit *f*

first building loan, first construction loan · erst(stellig)es Baudarleh(e)n *n*

first buyer, original buyer, original purchaser, primary buyer, primary purchaser, first purchaser · Erstkäufer *m*

first-class location · Spitzenlage *f*

first construction loan, first building loan · erst(stellig)es Baudarleh(e)n *n*

first decision, initial decision · erste Entscheidung *f*, erster Entscheid *m*

first financing · erst(stellig)e Finanzierung *f*

first form · unterste Schulklasse *f*

first hazard, first risk · erstes Risiko *n*, erstes Wagnis

first in — first out, fifo · Ausgang *m* in der Reihenfolge des Eingangs, älteste Preise *m pl*

first instance, trial court · erste Instanz *f*, Tatsacheninstanz

first mortgage [*Mortgage that has precedence over all other mortgages*] · erst(stellig)e Hypothek *f*

first order centre, urban village [*750 to 1,000 inhabitants*], small town with between 1,000 and 2,000 inhabitants (Brit.); first order center, urban center (US); middle-order sub-central place, sub-town, market district, market town · Amtsort *m* [*nach W. Christaller*]

first order condition · Bedingung *f* erster Ordnung

first payment, down payment [*Of a sum of money paid by a purchaser to a seller in conjunction with a purchase, the full payment of which will be made over a period of time*] · Anzahlung *f*

first player, maximizing player · Maximalspieler *m*

first prospective occupier, first prospective occupant · Bewerber *m* [*Person, die sich um den Ersterwerb eines Kaufeigenheims, einer Trägerkleinsied(e)lung oder einer Kaufeigentumswohnung oder um die erstmalige mietweise Überlassung einer neugeschaffenen Miet- oder Genossenschaftswohnung bewirbt*]

first purchaser, first buyer, original buyer, original purchaser, primary buyer, primary purchaser · Erstkäufer *m*

first registration, first recording, first recordation · Erstbuchung *f*, Ersteintrag(ung) *m*, *(f)*, Erstregistrierung *f*

first risk, first hazard · erstes Risiko *n*, erstes Wagnis

first-run movie · Erstaufführungskino *n*

first-stage unit, primary unit · Einheit *f* der ersten Auswahlstufe [*Statistik*]

first tenant (of a new-built house) · Trokkenwohner *m*

first-to-file principle · Anmeldegrundsatz *m*, Anmeldeprinzip *n* [*Patent*]

first-to-invent principle · Erfinderprinzip *n*, Erfindergrundsatz *m* [*Patent*]

fisc · Fiskus *m*

fiscal approach · fiskalischer Ansatz *m*

fiscal burden, fiscal encumbrance, fiscal incumbrance, fiscal charge, tax burden, tax charge, tax incumbrance, tax encumbrance, tax load, fiscal load · Steuerlast *f*, Steuerbelastung *f*

fiscal duty · Finanzzoll *m*

fiscal (land) use zoning, fiscal zoning · (bauliche) Nutzung *f* nach steuerlichen Gesichtspunkten, Baunutzung nach steuerlichen Gesichtspunkten

fiscal law, taxing law · Steuerrecht *n*

fiscal load, fiscal burden, fiscal encumbrance, fiscal incumbrance, fiscal charge, tax burden, tax charge, tax incumbrance, tax encumbrance, tax load · Steuerlast *f*, Steuerbelastung *f*

fiscal policy · fiskalische Politik *f* [*Instrument zur quantitativen Lenkung der Kaufkraft der Haushalte und Betriebe*]

fiscal policy · Zolltarifpolitik *f*

fiscal system — five-arbitrator board

fiscal system · Steuersystem *n*

fiscal year · Etatjahr *n*

fiscal zoning, fiscal (land) use zoning · (bauliche) Nutzung *f* nach steuerlichen Gesichtspunkten, Baunutzung nach steuerlichen Gesichtspunkten

fiscus [*Latin*] · königlicher Ländereikomplex *m*

fish-breeding · Fischzucht *f*

fish destruction, destruction of fish · Fischsterben *n*

fisheries authority, fishery authority · Fischereibehörde *f*

fisheries board, fishery board · Fischereiamt *n*

fishermen's settlement · Fischer(an)sied(e)lung *f*

fishery authority, fisheries authority · Fischereibehörde *f*

fishery board, fisheries board · Fischereiamt *n*

fishery contract, fishing contract · Fischereivertrag *m*

fishery co-operative, fishing co-operative · Fischereigenossenschaft *f*

fishery franchise, fishery privilege, fishery liberty, franchise of fishery, privilege of fishery, liberty of fishery · Fischereigerechtsame *f*, Fischereiregalrecht *n*, Fischereiprivileg *n*

fishery law, fishing law · Fischereirecht *n*, objektives Fischereirecht

fishery law, fishery statute, fishery act · Fischereigesetz *n*

fishery legislation, fishing lawmaking, fishery lawmaking, fishing legislation · Fischereigesetzgebung *f*

fishery servitude, fishing servitude · Fischereiservitut *n*, *(f)*, servitutisches Fischereirecht *n*

fishery settlement, fishing settlement · Fischer(ei)(an)sied(e)lung *f*

fishery village, fishing village · Fischerdorf *n*

fish farm [*A tract of water for raising fish*] · Fischzuchtbetrieb *m*

fishing · Ausforschung *f* [*Parteibefragung*]

fishing · Fischen *n*

fishing bank · Fisch(fang)bank *f*

fishing contract, fishery contract · Fischereivertrag *m*

fishing co-operative, fishery co-operative · Fischereigenossenschaft *f*

fishing ground · Fisch(fang)gebiet *n*, Fischgrund *m*

fishing legislation, fishery legislation, fishing lawmaking, fishery lawmaking · Fischereigesetzgebung *f*

fishing right, right of fishing, piscary; libera piscaria [*Latin*]; free fishery [*The right or liberty of fishing in the waters of another person*] · Fischereirecht *n*, subjektives Fischereirecht

fishing servitude, fishery servitude · Fischereiservitut *n*, *(f)*, servitutisches Fischereirecht *n*

fishing settlement, fishery settlement · Fischer(ei)(an)sied(e)lung *f*

fishing village, fishery village · Fischerdorf *n*

fishing water(s) · Fischgewässer *n*

fish pond · Fischteich *m*

fish royal, royal fish, regal fish · Wale *mpl* und Störe *mpl* [*Sie sind in England königliches Eigentum wenn sie ans Ufer geworfen oder in Küstennähe gefangen werden*]

fist-right · Faustrecht *n*

fit · Anpassung *f* [*Statistik*]

fit (for a particular purpose), appropriate · geeignet

fit for habitation, (in)habitable, fit to live in, suitable for habitation · bewohnbar, belegbar

fit for tillage; capable of being ploughed (Brit.); capable of being plowed (US); arable · pflügbar, beackerbar

fit for work, able-bodied · arbeitsfähig

fitness, flexibility, adaptability, adaptableness, adaptiveness, adaptedness, suitableness, suitability · Anpassungsvermögen *n*, Anpassungsfähigkeit *f*

fitness (for a particular purpose), appropriateness · Eignung *f*

fitness for habitation, fitness for human occupation, habitability · Bewohnbarkeit *f*

fitness of materials · Materialeignung *f*, (Werk)Stoffeignung

fit(ted), adapted · angepaßt

fittest · Höchstbefähigste *m*, Höchstbegabte

fitting, adapting, suiting, rendering suitable · Anpassen *n*

fitting effect, suiting effect, adap(ta)tion effect, adapting effect · Anpassungswirkung *f*

fit to live in, suitable for habitation, fit for habitation, (in)habitable · bewohnbar, belegbar

five-arbitrator board · Fünferbesetzung *f* [*Schiedsgericht*]

five-field system — fixed-price contract with escalation

five-field system, five-field husbandry, five-field farming · Fünffelderwirtschaft f

to fix a term, to fix a period (of time) · festsetzen einer Frist, fristen

fixation of term, fixation of time period, fixation of time (allowed), fixation of period (of time) · Frist(fest)setzung f

fixed, in-place, built-in · eingebaut

fixed amount · Festbetrag m

fixed and regular date · regelmäßig wiederkehrender Zeitpunkt m

fixed burden, fixed encumbrance, fixed incumbrance, fixed charge · bestimmte Belastung f

fixed case · bestimmter Fall m

fixed cost(s); fixed expired cost(s), fixed expenses [USA]; period cost(s) [A cost which tends to be unaffected by variations in volume of output but to depend mainly on the passing of time, e.g. the cost of providing the facilities and organization to produce and market goods] · Festkosten f, Fixkosten, feste Kosten, fixe Kosten

fixed currency, bound currency [Currency fixed or bound to a special metal] · gebundene Währung f

fixed deposit, time deposit · zeitgebundene Einlage f, Festeinlage, Termineinlage, Zeitgeld n [Depositenbank]

fixed-deposit investment · Fest(geld)anlage f, Termin(geld)anlage, Festkapitalanlage, Festinvestition f, Terminkapitalanlage, Termininvestition

fixed encumbrance, fixed incumbrance, fixed charge, fixed burden · bestimmte Belastung f

fixed estate, landholding, land(ed) property, tenancy (of land(s)); immov(e)ables [International Private Law]; (real) estate, (real) property, realty, estate in land(s), immov(e)able estate [Estates in land(s) are divided into (a) freehold estates and (b) estates less than freehold] · Bodenbesitz(stand) m, Grund(stücks)besitz(stand), Landbesitz(stand), Immobilienbesitz(stand), Immobiliarbesitz(stand), Liegenschaft(en) f (pl), Immobilie(n) f (pl), (unbeweglicher) Besitz(stand), liegendes Gut n, ungereides Gut

fixed estate for life → (real) estate for life

fixed (expense) budget (program) (US) → forecast (type) budget (programme)

fixed expenses, fixed expired cost(s) [USA]; period cost(s), fixed cost(s) [A cost which tends to be unaffected by variations in volume of output but to depend mainly on the passing of time, e.g. the cost of providing the facilities and organization to produce and market goods] · Festkosten f, Fixkosten, feste Kosten, fixe Kosten

fixed fee/prime cost(s) contract, (prime) cost plus fixed fee contract [A contractual arrangement whereby a contractor is paid the prime cost(s) and a fixed fee calculated in relation to the estimated amount of the prime cost] · Selbstkostenerstattungsvertrag m mit begrenztem Zuschlag, Selbstkostenerstattungsvertrag mit begrenztem Aufschlag

fixed incumbrance, fixed charge, fixed burden, fixed encumbrance · bestimmte Belastung f

fixed-interest(-bearing) security, public issue; gilt(-edge) (Brit.) · Staatsschuldtitel m, börsennotierte festverzinsliche Schuldverschreibung f, festverzinsliches Wertpapier n, Rentenpapier

fixed limit of building cost(s), fixed limit of construction cost(s) [Established by the owner] · Baukostenobergrenze f

fixed overhead cost(s), fixed overhead(s) · fixe Gemeinkosten f, feste Gemeinkosten

(fixed) period (of time) → time (allowed)

(fixed) period (of time) for acceptance → acceptance time (allowed)

(fixed) period (of time) for appeal → time (allowed) for appeal

(fixed) period (of time) for complaint, time (allowed) for complaint, time period for complaint · Beschwerdefrist f, (bestimmter) Beschwerdezeitraum m

(fixed) period (of time) for prescription → prescription time (allowed)

fixed price · Festpreis m

fixed price clause · Festpreisklausel f, Fixpreisklausel

fixed-price contract, stipulated sum contract, lump-sum contract [Under such a contract the contractor agrees to perform the entire work specified in the contract at a price agreed to and fixed at the time the contract is entered into] · Pauschalvertrag m

fixed-price contract with billing price and price ceiling, lump-sum contract with billing price and price ceiling, stipulated sum contract with billing price and price ceiling · Pauschalvertrag m mit Kostenrechnung und Preishöchstgrenze [Der Pauschalvertragspreis wird erst während der Vertragsdurchführung festgelegt]

fixed-price contract with escalation, lump-sum contract with escalation, stipulated sum contract with escalation · Pauschalvertrag m mit Änderung [Ausnahmefall. Der Pauschalpreis kann gemäß einem vorher vereinbarten Verfahren geändert werden, wenn sich die wirtschaftliche Situation ändert]

fixed price (for a unit of specific work) — flexible trust

fixed price (for a unit of specific work), unit price, (unit) rate, rate per unit · Einheitspreis *m*, EP

(fixed) price freezing · Festpreisbindung *f*, Preisbindung

fixed price incentive contract · Vertrag *m* mit vereinbartem Kosten- und Gewinnziel und garantiertem Höchstpreis

fixed price (type) contract [*A contract of the fixed price type many be a lumpsum contract or a measurement contract*] · Leistungsvertrag *m*

fixed property → (real) property

fixed property for life → (real) property for life

fixed salary · Festgehalt *n*

fixed standard cost(s), basic standard cost(s), bogey standard cost(s), measure standard cost(s) · Maßstandardkosten *f*, Standardkosten 2. Art, Grundstandardkosten

fixed sum, standard sum · Einheitssumme *f*

fixed sum credit · Summenkredit *m*

fixed term of tenancy, fixed term of tenure, fixed tenancy term, fixed tenure term · Festmietzeit *f*

fixed time deposit · Festzeiteinlage *f*

fixed trust · bestimmter Investmentfonds *m* [*Die Anlagedichte ist art- und mengenmäßig schon bei der Gründung genau bestimmt*]

fixing letter · Schlußbrief *m* [*Chartergeschäft*]

fixing the fee, fee setting, fee fixing, setting the fee · Honorarfestsetzung *f*, Gebührenfestsetzung, Honorarbestimmung, Gebührenbestimmung

fixing the value date → (act of) fixing the value date

fixing up, recycling (US); improvement of houses, house improvement, renovation, refurbishing · Altbausanierung *f*, Altbaumodernisierung, Renovierung

fixity of tenure · fester (Land)Pachtvertrag *m*, fester Bodenpachtvertrag

fixture, component, object affixed to a structure, article · Bestandteil *m*, Grundstücksbestandteil, (grundstücks)verbundene Sache *f*, Sache mit einem Grundstück verbunden

fixture attached by the owner, component attached by the owner, article attached by the owner, fixture attached by the proprietor, component attached by the proprietor, article attached by the proprietor · Eigentümer-(Grundstücks)Bestandteil *m*

fixture attached by the tenant, component attached by the tenant, article attached by the tenant · Mieter-(Grundstücks)Bestandteil *m*

fixture depreciation, component depreciation [*Depreciation, for tax purposes, of the individual components of a structure*] · Bestandteilabschreibung *f*

to fix up → to redo (US)

flat · ohne Zinsvergütung *f*, zinsvergütungslos

flat · Kurs *m* einschließlich aufgelaufener Zinsen [*Gegensatz: Kurs mit gesondert vergüteten aufgelaufenen Zinsen*]

flat · Geschoßwohnung *f*, Etagenwohnung, Stockwerkwohnung

flat benefit · gleicher Pensionsbetrag *m* für jeden Arbeitnehmer

flat benefit service · fixer Pensionsbetrag *m* pro Jahr der Betriebszugehörigkeit

flat cost(s) [*The cost(s) of labo(u)r and material only*] · Lohn- und Materialkosten *f*, Lohn- und Stoffkosten

flat rate · Pauschalsatz *m*

flat-rate contribution · Pauschalbeitrag *m*

(flat-)sharer · Aufgenommene *m* [*Durch den Mieter einer Wohnung in diese aufgenommen*]

(flat-)sharing arrangement · Aufnahme *f* [*In eine Wohnung durch den Mieter derselben*]

flat tariff · Pauschaltarif *m*

flatted factory, standard factory [*A lowrise loft building*] · Gebäude *n* mit vielen kleinen Industriebetrieben, Mietfabrik *f*

flat (type) of coverage · Flachbauweise *f*, Flachbebauungsart *f* [*Höchstens zwei ausgebaute Geschosse*]

flaying fee · Abdeckereileh(e)n *n*

flaying right · Abdeckereirecht *n*

flexibility, adaptability, adaptableness, adaptiveness, adaptedness, suitableness, suitability, fitness · Anpassungsvermögen *n*, Anpassungsfähigkeit *f*

flexibility constraint · Flexibilitätsschranke *f*

flexible , adaptable [*Capable of being adapted or of adapting oneself*] · anpassungsfähig

flexible (expense) budget (program) (US); flexible budget (programme) · flexibler Kostenplan *m*, flexibles Budget *n*

flexible trust, general management trust · Investmentfonds *m* mit beweglicher Anlagepolitik

flight — floor-to-ceiling height

flight, exodus, drift, movement · Flucht *f*, Wegziehen *n*

flight across → flight over

flight from the land, movement of population from country to town, rural-to-urban movement, rural-urban drift, rural-urban migration, rural exodus · Land-Stadt-Wanderung *f*, Landflucht *f*

flight from the town, movement of population from town to country, urban-rural migration, urban-rural drift, urban-to-rural movement, urban exodus · Stadtflucht *f*, Stadtexodus *m*, Stadt-Land-Wanderung *f*

flight of capital, capital flight · Kapitalflucht *f*

flight over, flight across, flying over, flying across · Überflug *m*, Überfliegen *n*, Überfliegung *f*

flight photo(graph), aerial photo(graph), air photo(graph) · Luftbild *n*, Luftaufnahme *f*, Luftphoto *n*

flight to the suburbs, drift to the suburbs, exodus to the suburbs, movement to the suburbs (Brit.) · Vorortflucht *f*, Vorortexodus *m*, Flucht in die Vororte, Exodus in die Vororte

flight to the umland, exodus to the umland, drift to the umland, movement to the umland · Umlandflucht *f*, Umlandexodus *m*, Flucht ins Umland, Exodus ins Umland

flirt with bankruptcy · hohe effektive Verschuldung *f*

to float · freigeben [*Wechselkurs einer Währung*]

to float · auflegen [*Anleihe*]

to float, to issue · begeben [*Anleihe*]

floatable river, river for floating [*A river used for floating logs, rafts, etc.*] · Flößer(ei)strom *m*

floatable stream, stream for rafting [*A stream used for floating logs, rafts, etc.*] · Flößer(ei)fluß *m*

floater, floating voter · Wechselwähler *m*, Grenzwähler

floating, issue · Begebung *f* [*Anleihe*]

floating capital, circulating capital, working capital [*Capital available for the purpose of meeting current expenditure*] · Betriebskapital *n*

floating charge · besitzloses Pfandrecht *n* mit wechselndem Objekt

floating charge · Belastung *f* eines Unternehmens in seinem jeweiligen Wert

floating currency · frei schwankende Währung *f*

floating debt · schwebende Schuld *f*

floating policy · Abschreibepolice *f*

floating residential town, floating residential city · schwimmende Wohnstadt *f*

floating security · aufschiebende bedingte dingliche Sicherheit *f*, hinausschiebende bedingte dingliche Sicherheit *f*, verschiebende bedingte dingliche Sicherheit [*Sicherheit durch Zulässigkeit einer Verpfändung des gesamten gegenwärtigen und künftigen Gesellschaftsvermögens*]

floating vote · Grenzwählerstimme *f*, Wechselwählerstimme

floating voter, floater · Wechselwähler *m*, Grenzwähler

flockmaster · Schafzüchter *m*

flooded rice-land · Naßreisland *n*

flooding land [*Raising and setting back water on another's land, by a dam placed across a water course which is the natural drain and outlet for surplus water on such land*] · Überstauen *n* fremden Landes

flood plane, water surplus area, water surplus territory · Wasserüberschußgebiet *n*

flood protection structure, flood protection work(s) · Hochwasserschutzanlage *f*, Hochwasserschutzbau(werk) *m*, (*n*)

floor area, floor space · Etagenfläche *f*, Geschoßfläche, Stockwerkfläche

floor area ratio, F.A.R., floor space index, F.S.I. (Brit.); basic floor area (US) [*The square-foot amount of total floor area (all stories) for each square foot of land area of a property*] · Geschoßflächenzahl *f*, GFZ, Geschoßflächendichte *f*, GFD; Ausnutzungsziffer *f* [*frühere Benennung*]

floor area size, size of floor space, size of floor area, floor space size · Geschoßflächengröße *f*, Stockwerkflächengröße, Etagenflächengröße

flooring · Sockelbetrag *m*

floor space, floor area · Etagenfläche *f*, Geschoßfläche, Stockwerkfläche

floor space index, F.S.I. (Brit.); basic floor area (US); floor area ratio, F.A.R. [*The square-foot amount of total floor area (all stories) for each square foot of land area of a property*] · Geschoßflächenzahl *f*, GFZ, Geschoßflächendichte *f*, GFD; Ausnutzungsziffer *f* [*frühere Benennung*]

floor space size, floor area size, size of floor space, size of floor area · Geschoßflächengröße *f*, Stockwerkflächengröße, Etagenflächengröße

floor-to-ceiling height · Geschoßhöhe *f*, Etagenhöhe, Stockwerkhöhe

flower area — folkmoot

flower area · Blumenfläche f

flow map · Strömungskarte f

flow map, flow (physical) plan · Fließkarte f, Flußkarte

flow of a bill (of exchange) · Wechsellaufzeit f, Wechselverfallzeit

flow of fund, fund flow · Fondsfluß m, Mittelfluß

flow of fund statement · Geldstromrechnung f

flow of investment, investment flow · Investitionsstrom m, Geldanlagestrom, (Kapital)Anlagestrom

flow of (migration) movement, (migration) movement current, (migration) movement stream, (migration) movement flow, migration flow, migration stream, current of (migration) movement, stream of (migration) movement · Bewegungsstrom m, Wanderungsstrom

flow of population, population flow · Bevölkerungsstrom m

flow of population to a town, flow of population to a city · Bevölkerungszustrom m in eine Stadt

flow of private capital · Privatkapitalfluß m

flow of trips, flow of travels, flow of journeys · Fahrt(en)fluß m

flow rate · Flußrate f, Fließrate

fluctuating interest rate · schwankender Zinssatz m

fluctuation · Schwankung f

fluctuation clause · Gleitklausel

fluctuation factor · Gleitfaktor m

fluctuation in price rate, price fluctuation rate · Preisgleitsatz m

fluctuation margin · Bandbreite f, Schwankungsbreite

fluctuation of call, fluctuation of demand, demand fluctuation, call fluctuation · Nachfrageschwankung f

fluctuation of staff cost(s), fluctuation of personnel cost(s) · Personalkostengleitung f

fluctuation rate · Gleitsatz m

fluorescent map · Fluoreszenzkarte f, selbstleuchtende Karte

flusher of sewers, sewer flusher · Kanalarbeiter m, Kanalisationsarbeiter

flying across → flying over

flying over, flying across, flight over, flight across · Überflug m, Überfliegen n, Überfliegung f

flyposting · unerlaubter (Reklame)Anschlag m

flyspecking, construing against title · übervorsichtige (Rechts)Titelprüfung f, übervorsichtige (Rechts)Titelbegutachtung

focage, focale, hous(e)bote [*An allowance of wood made to a tenant, for repairing his house*] · Bauholzbezugsrecht n, Hauszubuße f, Bauholzberechtigung f

focage, focale; lignagium [*Latin*]; right to cut fuel in woods, fire-bote · Brennholzschlagrecht n, Feuerungszubuße f, Brennholzbezugsrecht

foedus [*Latin*]; treaty · völkerrechtlicher Vertrag m, Staatsvertrag

fold, pen for sheep, cot for sheep, sheepcot, sheep-pen · (Schaf)Pferch m

foldage [*A privilege possessed in some places by the lord of a manor, which consists in the right of having his tenant's sheep to feed on his fields, so as to manure the land*] · Einpferchen n von Schafen auf Gutsherrengrund

fold course; faldae cursus [*Latin*] [*Land to which is appurtenant the sole right of folding the sheep of others*] · (Schaf)Pferchland n

fold course, faldsoke; faldsoca [*Saxon law*]; falda libera, cursus faldae [*Latin*]; frank fold, free fold, course of fold [*The privilege of setting up and moving about in a field a fold, for the purpose of manuring the ground, which several lords anciently reserved to themselves in any fields within their manors, not only with their own but their tenants sheep*] · (Schaf)Pferchrecht n

fold hurdle; sheep-pen wattle, fold wattle, sheep-cot wattle (Brit.); sheep-cot hurdle, sheep-pen hurdle · (Schaf)Hürde f

folding money (US), paper money · Papiergeld n

fold-soke, suit of the fold, fold suit; seeta faldae [*Latin*] [*The duty of a tenant to set up and move about in the fields of a manor a fold for the purpose of manuring the ground*] · (Schaf)Pferchpflicht f

fold wattle, sheep-cot wattle (Brit.), sheep-pen wattle, sheep-pen hurdle, fold hurdle; sheep-pen wattle · (Schaf)Hürde f

folkland [*It was the surplus land which was not distributed to the free or dependent village communities when the English tribes conquered and settled in Britain*] · Stammesland n

folkland, folcland, falk-land; terra popularis, ager publicus [*Latin*]; land of the people [*Anglo-Saxon land law*]. Folcland was held by customary law, without written title. Inheritance depended on custom. It could not be (ab)alienated without the consent of those who had some interest in it] · Volksland n

folkmoot [*In old English law*] · Volksgericht n

folk society · ursprünglich-volkstümliche Gesellschaft f [Gegensatz: städtische Gesellschaft]

to follow · als bindend anerkennen

to follow after, to ensure · nachfolgen

following the trail · (Vieh)Spurfolge f

follow-on contract, continuity contract, continuation contract, subsequent contract · Anschlußvertrag m, Folgevertrag m

follow-on order, subsequent order, continuity order, continuation order · Anschlußauftrag m, Folgeauftrag m

follow-up report · Nachfolgebericht m

fond of litigation, prone to engage in (law)suits · prozeßsüchtig

food adulteration, adulteration of food · Nahrungsmittel(ver)fälschung f

food deficiency · Nahrungsmangel m

food production and trade · Ernährungswirtschaft f

food rent; (Welsh) gwestva · Lebensmittelrente f

food retail trade · Nahrungsmitteleinzelhandel m

foodstuff warehouse, warehouse for foodstuffs · Lebensmittellager n, Lebensmittelspeicher m

food supply · Lebensmittelversorgung f

footloose farm worker, migrant farm workman, migratory farm workman, migrating farm workman, footloose farm workman; migrant farm labourer, migrating farm labourer, footloose farm labourer (Brit.); migratory farm laborer, migrating farm laborer, migrant farm laborer, footloose farm laborer (US); migratory farm worker, migrant farm worker, migrating farm worker · Wander-Landarbeiter m, wandernder Landarbeiter

footloose industry · standortfaktorunabhängige Industrie f

footlooseness · Standortfaktorunabhängigkeit f

footloose population, migratory population, migrant population, migrating population · Wanderbevölkerung f

footloose worker, migratory workman, migrant workman, footloose workman; migratory labourer, migrating labourer, migrant labourer, footloose labourer (Brit.); migratory laborer, migrating laborer, migrant laborer, footloose laborer (US); migratory worker, migrating worker, migrant worker · Wanderarbeiter m, wandernder Arbeiter

footpath, walkway · Fußweg m

forbearance, negligence, negative act(ion), default, neglect, failure, omission, omittance [Omission of that which a person ought to do] · (Ver)Säumnis f, n, (f), Vernachlässigung f, Unterlassung(shandlung), Nichtleistung, Unterlassungsakt m, negativer Akt, negative Handlung

force(-)account (construction), force(-)account work; direct labour work (Brit.); direct labor work (US) [A public authority designs and builds] · Regiearbeit(en) f (pl), Regieleistung(en) f (pl)

forced, compulsory · zwangsweise

forced demise → (en)forced lease(hold)

forced dissolution, involuntary dissolution · unfreiwillige Auflösung f, Zwangsauflösung

forced heiress, forced heir female · Pflichtteil(s)erbin f

forced heir (male) · Pflichtteil(s)erbe m

forced heirship · Pflichtteilrecht n

forced lease(hold) → (en)forced lease(hold)

forced letting of rooms → (en)forced letting of rooms

forced lien → involuntary lien

forced loan · Zwangsdarleh(e)n n

forced sale [Sale of property under compulsion as to time and place; usually a sale made by virtue of a court order, ordinarily at public auction] · Zwangsverkauf m

forced sale at public auction · Zwangsversteigerung f

forced sale value · Zwangsverkaufswert m

forced saving, involuntary saving · Zwangssparen n, unfreiwilliges Sparen

forced tenancy → (en)forced lease(hold)

forced transfer → involuntary transfer

force majeure [French]; irresistible compulsion, coercion recognized as irresistible · höhere Gewalt f

force majeure clause · Klausel f über Höhere Gewalt

(force of) attraction, drawing power, attractiveness, attracting power · Anziehung(skraft) f, Attraktivität f

force of personality, strength of personality · Ausstrahlungskraft f

force of title, strength of title · (Rechts)Titelkraft

forcible · gewaltsam

forcible detainer [Exists where one upon a peacable or forcible entry refuses to surrender the land upon being called

forcible entry — foreign exchange market

to do so] · gewaltsame Grund(stücks)-retention *f*

forcible entry, trespass quare clausum fregit [*Entry by breaking open doors, windows, or other parts of a house, or by any kind of violence or circumstance of terror*] · Hausfriedensbruch *m*

forcible entry and detainer [*Legal action to recover possession of land(s) and tenement(s) that are unlawfully held*] · Wiedererlangung *f*

forcible entry and detainer [*Violently taking possession of lands and tenements with menaces, force, and arms, against the will of those entitled to the possession and without the authority of the law*] · gewaltsame Grund(stücks)besitznahme *f* und -retention *f*

forcible transfer → (mass) forcible transfer

forebalk → foreland

forecast [*It is judgmental and comprises the set of projections deemed most likely to occur*] · Vorhersage *f*

forecasting method · Vorhersageverfahren *n*

forecasting model · Vorhersagemodell *n*

forecasting system · Vorhersagesystem *n*

forecast year · Vorhersagejahr *n*

to foreclose [*To foreclose somebody of his or her equity of redemption*] · abschneiden, ausschließen der Einlösung [*Jemandem sein Einlösungsrecht nach Billigkeit abschneiden*]

foreclosed loan · notleidend gewordenes Darleh(e)n *n*

foreclosure absolute · Eigentumsübertragung *f* an den Pfandgläubiger

foreclosure (court) action, foreclosure (law)suit, foreclosure cause, foreclosure plea · (Pfand)Verfallklage *f*

foreclosure (right), right of foreclosure [*If the mortgagor does not pay the debt when due, the mortgagee has the right to have the property applied to the payment of the obligation for which the mortgage was given as security*] · (gerichtlicher) Ausschluß *m* der Einlösung, (gerichtliches) Ausschlußrecht der Einlösung, (Pfand)Verfall *m*, Verfallserklärungsrecht *n*

foreclosure sale [*A sale of mortgaged property to obtain satisfaction of the mortgage out of the proceeds, whether authorized by a decree of the court or by a power of sale contained in the mortgage*] · Verkauf *m* nach Aufhebung des Einlösungsrechtes

forehand rent · vorausgezahlte Miete *f*, Vorausmiete

foreign act, foreign statute, foreign law · Auslandsgesetz *n*

foreign aid, foreign help · Auslandshilfe *f*

foreign (arbitration) award, foreign arbitrator's award · ausländischer Schieds(gerichts)spruch *m*, ausländischer Spruch

foreign assignment, foreign cession, foreign assignation · ausländische Abtretung *f*, ausländische Zession *f*

foreign banker · ausländischer Bankier *m*

foreign bill (of exchange), long draft · ausländischer Wechsel *m*, Auslandswechsel

foreign-born female person · Fremdbürtige *f*

foreign-born male person · Fremdbürtige *m*

foreign-born person · fremdbürtige Person *f*

foreign-born white · fremdbürtiger Weißer *m*

foreign business · Auslandsgeschäft *n*

foreign capital · Auslandskapital *n*

foreign cession → foreign assignment

foreign coin · ausländische Münze *f*

foreign corporation · ausländische Körperschaft *f*, ausländische Korporation *f*

foreign countries · Ausland *n*

foreign court · ausländisches Gericht *n*

foreign court theory · Theorie *f* der doppelten Rückverweisung, doppelte Rückverweisungstheorie *f*

foreign credit · Auslandskredit *m*, ausländischer Kredit *m*

foreign currency · ausländische Währung *f*, Auslandswährung *f*

foreign currency mortgage · Valutahypothek *f* [*Sie lautet auf eine ausländische Währung*]

foreign exchange · Devisen *f*

foreign exchange act → foreign exchange law

foreign exchange broker · Devisenmakler *m*

foreign exchange law · Devisenrecht *n*

foreign exchange law, foreign exchange act, foreign exchange statute · Devisengesetz *n*

foreign exchange legislation, foreign exchange lawmaking · Devisengesetzgebung *f*

foreign exchange market, exchange (market) · Devisenmarkt *m*

foreign exchange restriction · Devisenbeschränkung f

foreign exchange statute → foreign exchange law

foreign help, foreign aid · Auslandshilfe f

foreign investment review act, foreign investment review law, foreign investment review statute · Gesetz n zur Überprüfung ausländischer Investitionen

foreign judg(e)ment · ausländisches Urteil n, Auslandsurteil

foreign law · ausländisches Recht n, Auslandsrecht n

foreign law, foreign act, foreign statute · Auslandsgesetz n

foreignness · Ausländersein n

foreign population · Ausländerbevölkerung f

foreign private ownership · ausländisches Privateigentum n

foreign private property · ausländischer Privatbesitz m

foreign profession [*English law does not recognize a foreign profession*] · ausländische Profeßleistung f [*von Mönchen und Nonnen*]

foreign securities fund · Fonds m für Auslandswerte

foreign statute, foreign law, foreign act · Auslandsgesetz n

foreign stock exchange · Börse f für fremde Papiere, Fremdpapierbörse

foreign tax law · Auslandssteuerrecht n

foreign trade and payments act, foreign trade and payments law, foreign trade and payments statute · Außenwirtschaftsgesetz n, AWG

foreign trade and payments order · Außenwirtschaftsordnung f, AWVO

foreign trade arbitrage · Außenhandelsarbitrage f, Differenzarbitrage f

foreign trade legislation, foreign trade lawmaking · Außenhandelsgesetzgebung f

foreign-trade zone (US) · Freihafen m

for(e)judg(e)ment, for(e)judger, judg(e)ment of exclusion, judg(e)ment of expulsion, judg(e)ment of banishment, exclusion judg(e)ment; forisjudicatio [*Latin*] [*A judg(e)ment by which somebody is deprived of a thing or a right by a judg(e)ment*] · Aberkennungsurteil n, Ausschließungsurteil, Ausschlußurteil

foreland · Gegenküste f

foreland, forebalk, foreherda, butt; headrig [*Scotch*]; pen tir [*Welsh*]; forera, terra capitalis, caput terrae, caputium, chevitia, forlandum, versura [*Latin*]; headland [*The slip of unploughed land left at the head or end of a ploughed field on which the plough is turned*] · Anwende f, Voracker m, Vorwart f, Anwänder m

foreman · Obmann m

forensic medicine, medical jurisprudence · Gerichtsmedizin f

forera [*Latin*] → foreland

foreseeability · Schulderwägung f

foreseeability, predictability · Vorsehbarkeit f

foreseeable, predictable · vorhersehbar

foresight [*Headful thought for the future*] · Voraussicht f

to forest · bewalden

forest act, forest statute, forest law · Waldgesetz n, Forstgesetz

forestage · Forstabgabe f

forestalling, forestalment [*The offence of raising the price of certain goods, by buying merchandise on its way to market, or dissuading persons from bringing their goods there*] · Vorwegkaufen n

forest area · Forstfläche f, Waldfläche

forest area, forest territory · Waldgebiet n, Forstgebiet, Waldterritorium n, Forstterritorium

forest authority · Forstbehörde f, Waldbehörde

forest board · Forstamt n

forest conservancy (Brit.); forest supervision commission (US) · Waldaufsicht(samt), Forstaufsicht(samt) f, (n)

forest conservation, forest retention, preservation of forests, retention of forests, conservation of forests, forest preservation · Walderhaltung f, Waldpflege f, Forsterhaltung, Forstpflege

forest convalescent home · Waldgenesungsheim n

forest court · Waldgericht n, Forstgericht

forest cover · Bewaldung f

forested · bewaldet

forest enterprise, forest undertaking · forstwirtschaftliche Unternehmung f, forstwirtschaftlicher Betrieb m, forstwirtschaftliches Unternehmen n

forest exploitation · Waldnutzung f

forest field · Hauberg m, Reuteland n, Reutfeld n, Reutberg m, Rottland, Rodeland, Hackwald m, Hackland, Schiftelland, Waldfeld

forest-field farming — forfeiting

forest-field farming, forest-field cultivation [*An agricultural system in which the forest is felled and the land thus gained is tilled until it is exhausted, it is then given up and another stretch of forest is felled*] · Waldfeldwirtschaft *f*, Reutfeldwirtschaft, Haubergwirtschaft, Hackwaldwirtschaft, Röderwaldwirtschaft

forest geography · Forstgeographie *f*, Waldgeographie

forest insurance · Waldversicherung *f*, Forstversicherung

forest inventory · Forstinventur *f*, Waldinventur, Inventur des Holzvorrats

forest law · (objektives) Forstrecht *n*, (objektives) Waldrecht

forest law, forest act, forest statute · Waldgesetz *n*, Forstgesetz

forest lot · Waldflurstück *n*, Forstflurstück, Wald(kataster)parzelle *f*, Forst(kataster)parzelle

forest management, management of forests · Waldbewirtschaftung *f*, Forstbewirtschaftung

forest map · Forstkarte *f*, Waldkarte

forest mapping · Forstkartierung *f*, Waldkartierung

forest mining, mining the forest · Waldraubbau *m*, Waldraubwirtschaft *f*

forest officer, forest official · Forstbeamte *m*

forest owner, forest proprietor · Waldeigentümer *m*, Forsteigentümer

forest parcel, forest plot · Waldgrundstück *n*, Forstgrundstück

forest park · Waldpark *m*, Forstpark

forest plot, forest parcel · Waldgrundstück *n*, Forstgrundstück

forest possessor · Waldbesitzer *m*, Forstbesitzer

forest preservation, forest conservation, forest retention, preservation of forests, retention of forests, conservation of forests · Walderhaltung *f*, Waldpflege *f*, Forsterhaltung, Forstpflege

forest product · Walderzeugnis *n*

forest proprietor, forest owner · Waldeigentümer *m*, Forsteigentümer

forest protection · Waldschutz *m*, Forstschutz

forest protection ordinance · Waldschutzverordnung *f*, Forstschutzverordnung

forest reserve · geschütztes Waldgebiet *n*

forest restaurant · Waldgaststätte *f*

forest retention, preservation of forests, retention of forests, conservation of forests, forest preservation, forest conservation · Walderhaltung *f*, Waldpflege *f*, Forsterhaltung, Forstpflege

forest right · (subjektives) Forstrecht *n*, (subjektives) Waldrecht

forestry · Forstwesen *n*, Forstkultur *f*

Forestry Act [*In England*]; afforestation act, afforestation law, afforestation statute · Aufforstungsgesetz *n*

forestry code · Forstordnung *f*, Waldordnung

forest(ry) development plan · Forstwirtschaftsplan, Waldwirtschaftsplan *m*

forestry land, woodland · Waldland *n*, Forstland

forestry science, science of forests · Forstwissenschaft *f*, Waldwissenschaft

forest shifting cultivation tribe, forest tribe utilizing shifting cultivation · Waldhackbauvolk *n*

forest statute, forest law, forest act · Waldgesetz *n*, Forstgesetz

forest supervision commission (US); forest conservancy (Brit.) · Waldaufsicht(samt), Forstaufsicht(samt) *f, (n)*

forest survey · Forstvermessung *f*, Waldvermessung, forstliche Vermessung

forest surveyor, regarder, surveyor of (the) forests · Forstinspektor *m*, Waldinspektor

forest territory, forest area · Waldgebiet *n*, Forstgebiet, Waldterritorium *n*, Forstterritorium

forest tribe utilizing shifting cultivation, forest shifting cultivation tribe · Waldhackbauvolk *n*

forest undertaking, forest enterprise · forstwirtschaftliche Unternehmung *f*, forstwirtschaftlicher Betrieb *m*, forstwirtschaftliches Unternehmen *n*

forest village · Waldhaufendorf *n*, Waldhufen *m*

forest waste · Waldverwüstung *f*, Forstverwüstung

forest worker · Forstarbeiter *m*, Waldarbeiter

forever → perpetual

forfaitiering · Ankauf *m* von Wechseln u. forfait, Ankauf von Wechseln in Bausch und Bogen

to forfeit; for(is)facere [*Latin*] · verwirken

forfeitable, liable to forfeiture · verwirkbar

forfeited; forisfactus [*Latin*] · verwirkt

forfeited, confiscated, adjudged · eingezogen, konfisziert

forfeiting · Verwirken *n*

forfeit money · Abstandgeld n

forfeit payment · Abstandzahlung f [*Eine vertraglich vereinbarte einmalige Geldleistung eines Mieters an einen Vermieter um diesen zum Abschluß oder zur Verlängerung eines Mietvertrages zu veranlassen*]

forfeit sum · Abstandsumme f

forfeiture; for(is)factura [*Latin*] [*A thing or sum of money forfeited*] · verwirktes Gut n

forfeiture; for(is)factura [*Latin*] · Verwirkung f

forfeiture clause · Verwirkungsklausel f

forfeiture of property · Vermögensverwirkung f

forfeiture principle, principle of forfeiture · Verwirkungsgrundsatz m, Verwirkungsprinzip n

forfeiture right, right of forfeiture · (subjektives) Verwirkungsrecht n

forgavel [*In old English law*]; chief-rent, rent charge, quit-rent, fee farm (rent); quieti reditus, reditus quieti [*Latin*] [*An annual or periodical sum issuing out of land, payable by holders of land in a manor to the lord. Some writers use "fee farm" to signify not only the estate itself, but the rent reserved on it, taking the word "farm" itself in the sense of rent. This practice should, however, be deprecated*] · Erbzins m, Befreiungszins, Leh(e)n(s)zins

to forge, to counterfeit, to make (something) false · (ver)fälschen, nachahmen, imitieren

forged instrument · unechte Urkunde f, gefälschte Urkunde, verfälschte Urkunde

forgery [*The false making or material alteration, with intent to defraud, of any writing which, if genuine, might apparently be of legal efficacy or the foundation of a legal liability*] · (Ver)Fälschung f

forgery of a will, forgery of wills · Testaments(ver)fälschung f

forherda → foreland

for(is)facere [*Latin*]; to forfeit · verwirken

for(is)factura [*Latin*]; forfeiture [*A thing or sum of money forfeited*] · verwirktes Gut n

for(is)factura [*Latin*]; forfeiture · Verwirkung f

forisfactus [*Latin*]; forfeited · verwirkt

to forisfamiliate; forisfamiliare [*Latin*] · einsetzen eines Sohnes in Ländereibesitz zu Lebzeiten des Vaters

forisjudicatio [*Latin*] → for(e)judg(e)ment

forlandum [*Latin*] → foreland

for law, in law, according to law, at law, by law · nach dem Gesetz, dem Gesetz nach

to form, to draft, to construct, to draw up, to set up, to construe, to phrase, to word [*To arrange or marshal words*] · abfassen, gestalten, entwerfen, ausarbeiten, formulieren

to form, to draft, to construct, to construe, to draw up, to set up, to work out · ausarbeiten, abfassen, gestalten, entwerfen [*Schriftstück*]

form; blank (form) (US) · Blankett n, Muster n, Formblatt n, Formular n, Vordruck m

form (Brit.); grade (US) · Schuljahrgang

formal · förmlich

formal acceptance (of (the) work(s)) · förmliche (Bau)Abnahme f [*Sie hat stattzufinden, wenn eine Vertragspartei es verlangt. Jede Partei kann auf ihre Kosten einen Sachverständigen zuziehen. Der Befund ist in gemeinsamer Verhandlung schriftlich niederzulegen*]

formal condemnation (US); formal expropriation · förmliche Enteignung f, formelle Enteignung

formal contract · Formalvertrag m, förmlicher Vertrag

formal crime · Tätigkeitsdelikt n

formal declaration of a testator, publication · Erklärung f des letzten Willens

formal defect, informality, irregularity in matter of form, defect of (legal) form, want of (legal) form · Formfehler m, Formmangel m

(formal) demand, prompt note, prompt notification, demand note, demand notification, reminder (of debt due), letter demanding payment [*Slang: dunning letter*] · Mahnbrief m, Mahnschreiben n, Mahnung f

formal document [*e.g. the standard form of building contract or, for civil engineering works, the I.C.E. conditions*] · Musterdokument n

formal expropriation; formal condemnation (US) · förmliche Enteignung f, formelle Enteignung

formal law · förmliches Recht n

(formal) livery of seisin; deliberatio seisinae [*Latin*] · (feierliche) Gewereübergabe f, (feierliche) Übergabe der Gewere, (formelle) leh(e)n(s)rechtliche Besitzeinweisung f, formelle Auflassung

formal logic · formale Logik f

formal pleading · formeller Schriftsatz m, förmlicher Schriftsatz

formal public planning · formelle öffentliche Planung f, förmliche öffentliche Planung

formal requirement · Formbedürftigkeit f

formal style · Formalstil m

to form a quorum · beschlußfähig sein

formation, drafting, construction, drawing-up, setting up, construeing, phrasing, wording, formulation [*Arranging or marshalling words*] · Abfassung f, Entwurf m, Gestaltung, Ausarbeitung, Formulierung

formation, drafting, construction, drawing up, setting up · Entwurf m, Gestaltung f, Abfassung, Ausarbeitung [*Schriftstück*]

formation auditor · Gründungsprüfer m [*AG*]

formation of belt(s), belt formation · Gürtelbildung f

formation of capital, accumulation of capital, capital accumulation, creation of capital, capital creation, capital formation · Kapitalschöpfung f, Kapitalbildung

formation of company, company formation · Gründung f einer Kapitalgesellschaft im engeren Sinne [*Sie ist mit der Erlangung der Rechtsfähigkeit beendet*]

formation of contract(s), construction of contract(s), drafting of contract(s), drawing up of contract(s), setting up of contract(s) · Vertragsgestaltung f, Vertragsausarbeitung, Vertragsabfassung, Vertragsentwurf m, Vertragsbildung

formation of (general) property, formation of proprietorship, formation of ownership (of property) · Eigentumsbildung f

formation of new capital, creation of new capital · Kapitalneubildung f

formation of sub(urb)s, suburban process, suburban urbanization, (urban) spread, (urban) sprawl, outward spread, outward sprawl, suburban spread, suburban sprawl, spread(ing) of cities, sprawl of cities, spread(ing) of towns, sprawl of towns, suburbanization, decentralization · Sied(e)lungsbrei m, Dezentralisation f, Ausufern n, Zersied(e)lung f, Überwucherung des städtischen Raumes, Dezentralisierung f

formative plan · Gestaltplan m, Gestaltungsplan

form-element · Einzelform f, Einzelgestalt f

to form (into) a corporation, to incorporate · inkorporieren [*Handelsrecht*]

form master (Brit.); home-room teacher (US) · Klassenlehrer m

form of agreement for final appraisal (US) · Vordruck m H-639 „Übereinkommen über abschließende Schätzung"

form of bid → form of tender

form of building coverage · Bauform f

form of citation; style (US); citation form · Zitierform f

form of contract, contract blank (form), blank (form) of contract · Vertragsmuster n, Vertragsformular n, Vertragsformblatt n, Vertragsblankett n, Vertragsvordruck m

form of (court) action, form of cause, form of (law)suit, form of plea · Klageform f

form of existence, existence form · Daseinsform f

form of ground, terrain form, form of terrain, ground form · Geländeform f, Terrainform

form of mortgage in the late Middle Ages in which a rent-charge on real estate was granted in return for the loan of a capital sum · Rentenkauf m, Gültkauf

form of offer → form of tender

form of pleading, litigious form · Prozeßform f

form of proposal (US) → form of tender

form of settlement, form of settling, settlement form, settling form · (An)Sied(e)lungsform f, Besied(e)lungsform f

form of tender, form of offer, form of bid, bid(ding) form; (bid) proposal form, form of (bid) proposal, (bid) proposal blank (form) (US); tender (blank) form, bid (blank) form, offer (blank) form · Angebotsblankett n, Angebotsformular n, Angebotsvordruck m

form of terrain, ground form, form of ground, terrain form · Geländeform f, Terrainform

formula [*In common law practice, a set form of words used in judicial proceedings*] · Formel f

formula fluctuation · Formelschwankung f

formula rule · Formelregel f

formulated rule · ausgesprochene Regel f

formulation, formation, drafting, construction, drawing-up, setting up, construing, phrasing, wording [*Arranging or marshalling words*] · Abfassung f, Entwurf m, Gestaltung, Ausarbeitung, Formulierung

formulation of theory, theory building, theory formulation, building of theory · Theoriegestaltung f, Theorieformulierung

form-value, coefficient of (value added by) manufacture [*Manufacturing in the process of giving "form" to coarse materials*] · Formkoeffizient m

for private benefit, for self-preference · eigennützig

to forsake, to let go, to abandon, to desert, to give up, to leave (to itself) [*place*] · aufgeben, preisgeben, verlassen

to forsake, to give up, to renounce, to disclaim, to abandon, to relinquish, to remise [*To relinquish with intent of never again resuming one's right or interest*] · aufgeben, preisgeben, Verzicht leisten, verzichten, ausschlagen, entsagen, derelinquieren

forsaken, cast off, derserted, cast away, thrown away, abandoned, derelict [*Personal property abandoned or thrown away by the owner in such manner as to indicate that he intends to make no further claim thereto*] · herrenlos, aufgegeben

forsaken, let gone, deserted, idle, abandoned, given up, left (to itself) [*place*] · aufgegeben, verlassen, preisgegeben

forsaken, given up, waived, disclaimed, abandoned, relinquished, renounced, remised · aufgegeben, preisgegeben, Verzicht geleistet, verzichtet, ausgeschlagen, entsagt, derelinquiert

forsaker, abandoner · Verzichtende *m*

forsaking, abandoning, giving up, renouncing, relinquishing · Aufgeben *n*, Preisgeben *n*, Verzichten *n*

forsaking, dereliction, abandonment, abandoning [*The act of abandoning a chattel or mov(e)able*] · Aufgabe *f*, Preisgabe *f*, Verzicht(leistung) *m*, *(f)*

for self-preference, for private benefit · eigennützig

to forswear, to renounce by oath, to renounce (up)on oath, to abjure · abschwören

for the benefit · im Interesse

for the life of another, pur autre vie, per autre vie [*An estate pur autre vie was a tenancy of land for the life of another who was called the cestui que vie; the lowest estate of freehold which the law allowed before 1925 the estate has become an equitable interest. Not in the USA — old rule still applies — cestui que estate = life estate pour autre vie; it is of course an equitable interest in land*] · für die Dauer eines anderen Lebens, für Lebenszeit eines Dritten, auf Lebenszeit eines Dritten, auf Dauer eines anderen Lebens, für das Leben eines anderen

for (the) separate use · zur freien Verfügung [*Vorbehaltgut*]

forthwith · unverzüglich

fortification · Befestigung *f*

fortification structure · Festungs(bau)werk *n*

fortified · befestigt

fortified belt · Festungsgürtel *m*

fortified camp; heribergum [*Latin*] · befestigtes Feldlager *n*

fortified place · befestigter Ort *m*

fortified settlement · Wehr(an)sied(e)lung *f*, befestigte (An)Sied(e)lung

fortified town, fortified city, walled town, walled city, fortress town, fortress city · Festungsstadt *f*, befestigte Stadt

fortified zone · Rayonbezirk *m*

to fortify · befestigen

fortress hill · Burgberg *m*

fortress town, fortress city, fortified town, fortified city, walled town, walled city · Festungsstadt *f*, befestigte Stadt

fortuitous, unforeseen, occasional, accidental, by chance · unvorhergesehen

fortune, marriage goods; tocher [*Scotland*]; maritagium [*Latin*]; dowry (marriage), portion [*Not to be confounded with "dower". A portion given with a woman to her husband in marriage*] · Mitgift *f*, Heiratsgut *n*

forum [*Latin*]; court · Gericht *n*

forum administrationis [*Latin*] · Vermögensverwaltungsort *m*, Ort der Vermögensverwaltung

for value · gegen Entgelt

to forward · expedieren

forward · auf Termin [*Käufe und Verkäufe in fremden Währungen*]

forward carrying of loss(es) · Verlustvortrag *m*

forward cover · Kurssicherung *f* durch Devisentermingeschäft

forwarding agent, freight forwarder, shipper · Spediteur *m*

forward integration · vertikaler Zusammenschluß *m* einer Unternehmung mit ihr nachgelagerten Unternehmungsstufen

forward linkage · Vorwärtsverflechtung *f*, Vorwärtskopplung [*Industriezweig*]

forward market · (Devisen)Terminmarkt *m*

forward planning, advance planning, planning from-the-top-down · Vorausplanung *f*, Planung von oben

forward rate · (Devisen)Terminkurs *m*

forward reference · Weiterverweisung *f*

forward transaction · (Devisen)Termingeschäft *n*

fosterage [*Care of a foster child, brother, sister, parent etc. — one considered as holding the relationship indicated in consequence of nursing and rearing, though not related by blood*] · Pflege *f*

fosterland — frankalmoign(e)

fosterland [*Land given, assigned, or allotted to the finding of food or victuals for any person or persons; as in monasteries for the monks, etc.*] · Nährland *n*

fosterlean [*The renumeration fixed for the nursing and rearing of a foster person*] · Pflegegeld *n*

foul bill of lading, foul B/L, dirty bill of lading, claused bill of lading · unreines Konnossement *n*

to found, to establish a foundation · stiften einer Stiftung des öffentlichen Rechts

foundation · öffentlich-rechtliche Stiftung *f*, Stiftung (des öffentlichen Rechts)

foundation of contract, contract foundation, basis of contract, contract basis · Vertragsgrundlage *f*, Vertragsbasis *f*

foundation school, endowed school · Stiftungsschule *f*

founder · Gründer *m*

founder member · Gründungsmitglied *n*

foundling · Findlingskind *n*, Findelkind

Founding Fathers · Väter *m pl* der Verfassung

foundor; fundator [*Latin*] · Stifter *m* einer öffentlich-rechtlichen Stiftung

fountain of jurisdiction, jurisdiction fountain, law source, law fountain, source of law, fountain of law · Rechtsquelle *f*

four-family row house · Vierfamilienreihenhaus *n*

four-field system, four-field husbandry · Vierfelderwirtschaft *f*

fourfold table · Vierfeldertafel *f*

fourth estate, journalism · Journalismus *m*

fowls of warren, birds of game · Jagdgeflügel *n*, Jagdvögel *m pl*

fractional scale, numerical scale · Maßstabverhältnis *n*, Zahlenmaßstab *m*

fraction defective · Ausschußanteil *m* [*Statistik*]

frame, fringe · Kernsaum *m*, Übergangssaum [*Stadt*]

frame · Erhebungsgrundlage *f* [*Statistik*]

frame area, fringe territory, frame territory, fringe area · Übergangssaumgebiet *n*, Kernsaumgebiet

frame of reference, reference frame · Bezugsrahmen *m*

frame population, fringe population · Kernsaumbevölkerung *f*, Übergangssaumbevölkerung

framework for decision, decision(al) framework · Entscheidungsrahmen *m*

framework plan, skeleton plan · Rahmenplan *m*

framework planning, skeleton planning · Rahmenplanung *f*

framework provision, skeleton provision · Rahmenbestimmung *f*

framus bancus, free-bench; sedes libera, libera sedes, liber bancus [*Latin*] · Freisitz *m* [*Der Anteil der Witwe eines Hintersassen an dessen Immobiliarbesitz*]

franc-al(l)eu [*French law*]; al(l)odial estate, al(l)odial property, al(l)odial chattel, absolute estate, absolute property, absolute chattel, allodial ownership, absolute ownership, al(l)odium [*An estate held without service or acknowledg(e)ment of any superior, as among the early Teutonic peoples, opposed to feud(um)*] · Allodialgut *n*, allodiales Eigentum *n*, allodiales Erbgut, allodiales Eigengut, leh(e)n(s)freies Eigentum, leh(e)n(s)freies Erbgut, leh(e)n(s)freies Eigengut, absolutes Eigentum, absolutes Erbgut, absolutes Eigengut, erbeigenes Eigentum, erbeigenes Eigengut, erbeigenes Erbgut, unbeschränktes Erbgut, unbeschränktes Eigentum, unbeschränktes Eigengut, (zins)freies Erbgut, (zins)freies Eigentum, (zins)freies Eigengut, uneingeschränktes Erbgut, uneingeschränktes Eigentum, uneingeschränktes Eigengut, unbegrenztes Erbgut, unbegrenztes Eigentum, unbegrenztes Eigengut, Allodialeigentum, Allodialvermögen *n*, Al(l)odium *n*, Alodis *n*, Alode *f*, Alodus *m*, Alaudium *n*, Vollgut, echtes Eigen(gut) *n*, lediges Eigen(gut), Ludeigen(gut)

franchise, liberty, privilege; franchesia, francisia [*Latin*] [*A privilege conferred by government on individuals or corporations, and which does not belong to citizens of country generally of common right*] · Gerechtsame *f*, Privileg *n*, Regalrecht *n*

franchise → (royal) franchise

franchise of fishery → fishery franchise

franchise tax · (kommunale) Konzessionssteuer *f*

franchising · Konzessionsvergabe *f* im Einzelhandel

francus plegius, francum plegium, franciplegium [*Latin*]; frank pledge, free pledge [*In old English law, a pledge or surety for freeman, that is, the pledge, or corporate responsibility, of all the inhabitants of a tithing for the general good behaviour of each free-born citizen above the age of fourteen, and for his being forthcoming to answer any infraction of the law*] · Freienbürgschaft *f*, Zwangsbürgschaft

frankalmoign(e); libera eleemosyna [*Latin*]; free alms · (freies) Almosen *n*

frankalmoign(e), free alms, free spiritual tenure (of land), (free) alms tenure (of land), (feodal) tenure (of land) in frankalmoign(e) [*A tenure whereby religious corporations, aggregate or sole, held lands of the donor to them and their successors for ever. They were discharged of all other except religious services, and the trinoda necessitas. It differed from tenure by divine service, in that the latter required the performance of certain divine services, whereas the former, as its name imports, was free*] · (freies) Almosenleh(e)n *n*, Freialmosenleh(e)n, Gottesleh(e)n mit unbestimmten geistlichen Verrichtungen

frank chase; libera chasea, libera fugacia [*Latin*]; free chase · freies Jagdrecht *n*, Recht auf freie Jagd

frank fee → simple fee

frank (feudal) tenant, frank land tenant, frank manorial tenant, frank fief-tenant, frank feuda(to)ry, frank feodatory, frank feeholder, frank tenant of land, franklyn, free-man, freeholder, possessor of a freehold estate · freier Leh(e)n(s)mann *m*, freier Grundzinsmann, freier Leh(e)n(s)träger, freier Gefolgsmann, freier Vasall, Freisasse *m*, Landsasse, Freimann

frank (feodal) tenure (of land) → simple fee

frank-fold, faldage, right of drove, drove right, feldage; actus, faldagium [*Latin*] · Triftrecht *n*, Treibrecht

frank fold → fold course

Frankish colonization settlement · fränkische Kolonisations(an)sied(e)lung *f*

frank law, free law; libera lex [*Latin*] · Recht *n* der Freien, Recht eines Freien, Freienrecht [*Englisches mittelalterliches Recht*]

franklyn → freeholder

frank pledge, free pledge; francus plegius, francum plegium, franciplegium [*Latin*] [*In old English law, a pledge or surety for freeman, that is, the pledge, or corporate responsibility, of all the inhabitants of a tithing for the general good behaviour of each free-born citizen above the age of fourteen, and for his being forthcoming to answer any infraction of the law*] · Freienbürgschaft *f*, Zwangsbürgschaft

frank tenancy → simple fee

frank tenure (of land) → simple fee

fraternity aspect · geistliches Element *n* [*einer Zunftgenossenschaft*]

fraud, deceit · Arglist *f*, Betrug *m*

fraud defence (Brit.); fraud objection; fraud defense (US) · Arglisteinwand *m*, Betrugseinwand *m*, Einwand *m* der Arglist, Einwand *m* des Betruges

fraud law, law of fraud · Betrugsrecht *n*

fraud objection; fraud defense (US); fraud defence (Brit.) · Arglisteinwand *m*, Betrugseinwand *m*, Einwand *m* der Arglist, Einwand *m* des Betruges

fraud of the law; fraus legis [*Latin*] · Gesetz(es)umgehung *f*

fraud on a power, fraud on a right · rechtswidriger Gebrauch *m* einer Befugnis, rechtswidriger Gebrauch eines Rechtes

fraudulent · arglistig, betrügerisch

fraudulent (ab)alienation, fraudulent disposal · arglistige Veräußerung *f*, betrügerische Veräußerung *f*

fraudulent act(ion) · arglistige Handlung *f*, betrügerische Handlung *f*, arglistiger Akt *m*, betrügerischer Akt *m*

fraudulent appointment → fraudulent (exercise of a power of) appointment

fraudulent bankruptcy, act of fraudulent bankruptcy [*An act done or suffered by a trader, tending to defraud his creditors, by which he becomes a bankrupt, within the meaning of the bankrupt laws, and liable to be proceeded against as such*] · betrügerischer Bank(e)rott *m*, Konkursbetrug *m*, böswilliger Bank(e)rott

fraudulent concealment, concealed fraud [*Designed fraud by which a party knowing to whom the right belongs, conceals the cirumstances giving that right, and, by means of such concealment, enables himself to enter and hold the land*] · arglistiges Verschweigen *n*, betrügerisches Verschweigen *n*

fraudulent deception · arglistige Täuschung *f*, betrügerische Täuschung

fraudulent disposal, fraudulent (ab)alienation · arglistige Veräußerung *f*, betrügerische Veräußerung *f*

fraudulent (exercise of a power of) appointment, fraudulent (exercise of a power of) disposition · betrügerische Ausübung *f* einer Verfügungsbefugnis

fraudulent intent(ion), inten(tion) to defraud · Betrugsabsicht *f*, betrügerische Absicht, arglistige Absicht

fraudulent issue of stocks and bonds · Ausgabe *f* falscher aktienrechtlicher Urkunden

fraudulently concealed land [*Land privily held from the Crown by a person or persons having no title thereto; used especially of land that had been monastic property before the Reformation*] · arglistig verschwiegenes Land *n*, betrügerisch verschwiegenes Land *n*

fraudulent (mis)representation, fraudulent (mis)recital, fraudulent (false) representation, fraudulent (false) recital [*A false representation made knowingly*] · betrügerische (Falsch)Darstellung *f*, betrüge-

fraudulent preference — freedom of the air

rische (Falsch)Erklärung, arglistige (Falsch)Darstellung, arglistige (Falsch)Erklärung

fraudulent preference · Gläubigerbevorzugung f, Gläubigerbegünstigung

fraudulent preference · betrügerischer Vorzug m

fraus legis [Latin]; fraud of the law · Gesetz(es)umgehung f

free (ab)alienable · freiveräußerlich

free accrued liability, other accrued liability, free (liability) reserve, other (liability) reserve · freie Rückstellung f, andere Rückstellung

free alms, frankalmoign(e); libera eleemosyna [Latin] · (freies) Almosen n

(free) alms tenure (of land), (feodal) tenure (of land) in frankalmoign(e), frankalmoign(e), free alms, free spiritual tenure (of land) [A tenure whereby religious corporations, aggregate or sole, held lands of the donor to them and their successors for ever. They were discharged of all other except religious services, and the trinoda necessitas. It differed from tenure by divine service, in that the latter required the performance of certain divine services, whereas the former, as its name imports, was free] · (freies) Almosenleh(e)n n, Freialmosenleh(e)n, Gottesleh(e)n mit unbestimmten geistlichen Verrichtungen

free alongside ship, fas · frei Seeschiffseite

free and lawful man [In old English law]; judex, liber et legalis homo [Latin]; juror, jury member, jurator, member of a jury · Geschworene m

free-bench; sedes libera, libera sedes, liber bancus, framus bancus [Latin] · Freisitz m [Der Anteil der Witwe eines Hintersassen an dessen Immobiliarbesitz]

free board and room · freie Verpflegung f und Unterkunft f

free chase, frank chase; libera chasea, libera fugacia [Latin] · freies Jagdrecht n, Recht auf freie Jagd

free church · Freikirche f

free city, free town · freie Stadt f

free competition, open competition · freier Wettbewerb m

free contract [A contract in which the parties are free to act as they choose] · freier Vertrag m

free division (of land(s)) among the heirs · Freiteilung f

freedom; libertas [Latin]; liberty · Freiheit f

freedom from arrest · Freiheit f von Verhaftung

freedom from charges, freedom from duties · Gebührenbefreiung f

freedom from contribution(s) · Beitragsfreiheit f

freedom from duties, exemption from statutory charges, freedom from statutory charges, exemption from legal charges, freedom from legal charges, exemption from duties · Abgabenbefreiung f, Abgabenfreiheit f

freedom from incumbrances, freedom from encumbrances, freedom from loads, freedom from burdens · Lastenfreiheit f, Belastungsfreiheit

freedom from legal charges, exemption from duties, freedom from duties, exemption from statutory charges, freedom from statutory charges, exemption from legal charges · Abgabenbefreiung f, Abgabenfreiheit f

freedom from taxes, exemption from taxes, freedom from taxation, exemption from taxation, tax relief, taxation exemption · Steuerbefreiung f, Steuerfreiheit f, Besteuerungsausnahme f

freedom of (ab)alienation, freedom of disposal · Veräußerungsfreiheit f

freedom of act(ion), freedom to act · Handlungsfreiheit f

freedom of assembly, assembly freedom · Versammlungsfreiheit f

freedom of charges · Gebührenfreiheit f

(freedom of) choice, option · Option f, Entscheidungsrecht n, Wahl(möglichkeit) f

freedom of construction, freedom to build, freedom to construct, freedom of building · Baufreiheit f [Die Befugnis eines Grundstückeigentümers auf seinem Grundstück nach Belieben zu bauen]

freedom of cropping, cultivation freedom, cropping freedom, freedom of cultivation · (Boden)Kultivierungsfreiheit f, Anbaufreiheit

freedom of discretion, discretionary freedom · Ermessensfreiheit f

freedom of disposal, freedom of (ab)alienation · Veräußerungsfreiheit f

freedom of (general) property, freedom of ownership (of property), freedom of proprietorship · Eigentumsfreiheit f

freedom of movement, freedom of settlement, freedom of settling, freedom to move about, freedom to settle anywhere · Freizügigkeit f

freedom of permission to build, freedom of permission to construct · (Bau)Erlaubnisfreiheit f, (Bau)Genehmigungsfreiheit

freedom of speech · Redefreiheit f

freedom of the air, air freedom · Luftfreiheit f, Freiheit des Luftraumes, Freiheit des Luftgebietes

freedom of the city — freehold estate

freedom of the city · Stadtbürgerrecht n

freedom of the (high) seas · Meeresfreiheit f

freedom to act, freedom of act(ion) · Handlungsfreiheit f

freedom to build → freedom of construction

freedom to move · Wanderungsfreiheit f

freedom to move about, freedom to settle anywhere, freedom of movement, freedom of settlement, freedom of settling · Freizügigkeit f

freedom to settle anywhere, freedom of movement, freedom of settlement, freedom of settling, freedom to move about · Freizügigkeit f

free drinking shop (US); free pub(lic house), free house (Brit.) · freie Kneipe f, freie Schankwirtschaft f

free enterprise economy, free enterprise system · freie Marktwirtschaft f

free enterprise farming settlement · individualwirtschaftliche (An)Sied(e)lung f

free entry · nicht zollpflichtige Ware f

free estate of inheritance → free (real) estate of inheritance

free evaluation of evidence by (the) judge, free evalution of proof by (the) judge · freie richterliche Beweiswürdigung f, richterliche freie Beweiswürdigung

free exchange of ideas, free trade in ideas · freier Gedankenaustausch m

free farm → free(hold) farm

free fee → simple fee

free (feodal) tenure (of land) → simple fee

free fishery, fishing right, right of fishing, piscaria; libera piscaria [Latin] [The right or liberty of fishing in the waters of another person] · Fischereirecht n, subjektives Fischereirecht

free fold, course of fold, fold course, faldsoke; faldsoca [Saxon law]; falda libera, cursus faldae [Latin]; frank fold [The privilege of setting up and moving about in a field a fold, for the purpose of manuring the ground, which several lords anciently reserved to themselves in any fields within their manors, not only with their own but their tenants sheep] · (Schaf)Pferchrecht n

free from accountableness, irresponsible, accountless · nicht verantwortlich, nicht rechenschaftspflichtig

free from encumbrance(s), free from charge(s), free from incumbrance(s), free from burden(s), uncharged, unburdened, unencumbered, unincumbered, clear, perfect, free from load(s), unloaded, not imperfect, without a burden, without a load, burdenless · entschuldet, lastenfrei, (dinglich) unbelastet, (dinglich) nicht belastet

free from permission, not requiring permission · genehmigungsfrei, erlaubnisfrei

to free from secrecy, to free from ignorance, to lay bare, to disclose, to reveal, to knowledge, to make known, to clarify · aufklären, enthüllen, offenbaren, offenlegen, offen darlegen, preisgeben, kundtun

freehand method · geographische Ausgleichung f nach Augenmaß [Statistik]

freehold, life (land(ed)) estate, estate (in land) for life · lebenslanges Bodenbesitzrecht n, lebenslanges Landbesitzrecht, lebenslanges Grund(stücks)besitzrecht

freehold · (Land)Eigentumsrecht n, Bodeneigentumsrecht, Grund(stücks)eigentumsrecht, Liegenschaftseigentumsrecht, Immobiliareigentumsrecht, Immobilieneigentumsrecht

freehold · freier (Grund)Besitz m, freier Grundstücksbesitz

freehold → seisin

freehold → simple fee

freeholder, possessor of a freehold estate, frank (feudal) tenant, frank land tenant, frank manorial tenant, frank fief-tenant, frank feuda(to)ry, frank feoda(to)ry, frank feeholder, frank tenant of land, franklyn, free-man · freier Leh(e)n(s)mann m, freier Grundzinsmann, freier Leh(e)n(s)träger, freier Gefolgsmann, freier Vasall, Freisasse m, Landsasse, Freimann

freeholder → (real) property owner

freeholders' court baron; curia legalis [Latin]; manor(ial) court, feudal court, feodal court, feuda(to)ry court, court of the baron, court of the lord, baron(-bailie) court, court-baron (proper), court of (the) manor [The court of justice held by a baron or his steward in the presence of the freehold tenants of the manor. In modern times lawyers have distinguished between court-baron which was the court of the freehold tenants, and the customary court-baron which was the court of the copyhold tenants. The early history of this distinction is obscure] · Feudalgericht n, grundherrliches Gericht, Leh(e)n(s)herrengericht, Hofgericht, Patrimonialgericht, feudales Gutsgericht

freeholder's right, right of a freeholder · Landsässigkeit f

freehold estate → simple fee

freehold estate, (estate of) freehold, freehold land(s), ownership of land(s), ownership in land(s), land(ed) owner-

((freehold) estate in) — freely and voluntary 440

ship [*An estate in land(s) which lasts for life or forever and which can be owned as fully as possible under the law. A freehold estate which lasts forever is known as an "(estate in) fee simple (absolute) (in possession)". A freehold estate which lasts only during the lifetime of its owner or for the life of some other person is known as a "life estate (in property)" or an "estate (in land) pur autre vie". It is called a freehold estate because it is an estate such as was held by freemen under the feudal system in England*] · Bodeneigentum *n*, Landeigentum, Grund(stücks)eigentum, Immobiliareigentum, Immobilieneigentum, Liegenschaftseigentum

((freehold) estate in) equitable fee simple (absolute) (in possession) · absolutes Bodenbesitzrecht *n* nach Billigkeit, absolutes Landbesitzrecht nach Billigkeit, immerwährendes Bodenbesitzrecht nach Billigkeit, immerwährendes Landbesitzrecht nach Billigkeit

((freehold) estate in) legal fee simple (absolute) (in possession), common law fee simple (absolute) (in possession) · absolutes Bodenbesitzrecht *n* nach gemeinem Recht, absolutes Landbesitzrecht nach gemeinem Recht, immerwährendes Landbesitzrecht nach gemeinem Recht, immerwährendes Bodenbesitzrecht nach gemeinem Recht, gemeinrechtliches absolutes Bodenbesitzrecht, gemeinrechtliches absolutes Landbesitzrecht, gemeinrechtliches immerwährendes Bodenbesitzrecht, gemeinrechtliches immerwährendes Landbesitzrecht

free(hold) farm · Freihof *m*

freehold land (held of the manor) → simple fee

freehold land tenure · Privatlandbesitz *m*

freehold of inheritance (absolute) → simple fee

freehold (possession) in law; saisine in law, infeoffment in law, seisin in law [*Scotland*] · Erbganggewere *f*, ideelle Gewere

freehold (possession), seizin, possession as of freehold, possession of an estate of freehold; infeoffment [*Scotland*]; seisina, saisine, seysina [*Latin*]; seisin · Gewere *f* [*Eine historische Untersuchung über das Wesen der Gewere muß ihren Ausgang von der „investitura" des alten Rechts nehmen. Denn mit diesem Ausdruck geben die lateinischen Quellen der karolingischen Periode das Wort Gewere wieder, wie das aus der altdeutschen Übersetzung von C. 6 der Capitularia leg. add. v. 817 bei Pertz, l. S. 261 und aus den zwei parallel laufenden Stellen der traditiones Fuldenses in zwei Urkunden von 824 „testes qui vestitionem viderunt" und „testes qui viderunt giweridam" unwidersprechlich hervorgeht*]

freehold property · Besitz *m* von Grund (und Boden) mit Haus (oder Häusern)

freehold rent · Feudalrente *f*, Freisassenrente, leh(e)n(s)rechtliche Rente

free(hold) tenement → simple fee

freehold (tenure) → simple fee

freehold title · freier (Grund)Besitztitel *m*

free house (Brit.); free drinking shop (US); free pub(lic house) · freie Kneipe *f*, freie Schankwirtschaft *f*

free hous(ebuild)ing enterprise, free hous(ebuild)ing undertaking · freies Wohn(ungs)unternehmen *n*

free-lance activity, activity in private practice · freiberufliche Tätigkeit *f*, freischaffende Tätigkeit

free-lance contributor · freier Mitarbeiter *m*, freischaffender Mitarbeiter

free land, land held in absolute ownership, absolute ownership land, alody, inheritable land, al(l)odial land · allodiales Land *n*, erbeigenes Land, leh(e)n(s)freies Land, absolutes Land, unbeschränktes Land, uneingeschränktes Land, unbegrenztes Land, zinsfreies Land, Allodialland

free land of inheritance → free (real) estate of inheritance

free law; libera lex [*Latin*]; frank law · Recht *n* der Freien, Recht eines Freien, Freienrecht [*Englisches mittelalterliches Recht*]

free law doctrine, doctrine of free law · Freirechtslehre *f*

free lay fief, free lay feud, free lay feod, free lay tenancy, free lay tenement, free lay fee, free lay (feodal) tenure (of land), tenure in (socage), socage tenure; socagium [*Latin*] · freies weltliches Leh(e)n *n*, weltliches Freileh(e)n

free lay tenure (of land) → free fief

free (liability) reserve, other (liability) reserve, free accrued liability, other accrued liability · freie Rückstellung *f*, andere Rückstellung

free library, public library · Volksbücherei *f*, Volksbibliothek *f*

free licensee, free licencee · freier Schankwirt *m* [*an keinen Lieferanten gebunden*]

free list · Liste *f* zollfreier Güter

freely (ab)alienable, freely disposable · frei veräußerlich, frei veräußerbar

freely and voluntary · ungezwungen und freiwillig

free man, holder of an allodium; liber homo, homo liber [*Latin*]; allodiary, allodialist, al(l)odial (land) owner, absolute (land) owner, exclusive (land) owner, absolute proprietor, exclusive proprietor, al(l)odial proprietor · absoluter Eigentümer *m*, unbeschränkter Eigentümer, Alleineigentümer, Freiguteigentümer, Allodialeigentümer, freier Mann *m*, Freie *m*

free-man, freeholder, possessor of a freehold estate, frank (feudal) tenant, frank land tenant, frank manorial tenant, frank fief-tenant, frank feuda(to)ry, frank feodatory, frank feeholder, frank tenant of land, franklyn · freier Leh(e)n(s)mann *m*, freier Grundzinsmann, freier Leh(e)n(s)träger, freier Gefolgsmann, freier Vasall, Freisasse *m*, Landsasse, Freimann

freeman · wahlberechtigter Stadtbürger *m*

freeman borough · Stadt *f* in der die Zunftmitglieder das aktive Wahlrecht hatten [*England*]

freeman of a borough, townman; cityman [*obsolete*]; urban resident, town resident, city resident, urban inhabitant, town inhabitant, city inhabitant, urban dweller, town dweller, city dweller, urbanite, citizen, burgess · Stadtbewohner *m*, Stadteinwohner, Städter, Stadtbürger

freemen householders · erbgesessene Bürgerschaft *f* [*in London*]

free mortgage · freie Hypothek *f* [*Nicht zu einer Deckung bestimmt*]

free of capture and seizure, F.C.S. · frei von Beschlagnahmerisiko, frei von Beschlagnahmewagnis

free of carriage, freight free, freight paid, free of freight, carriage paid, carriage free · frachtfrei, Fracht bezahlt

free of charge, non-priced · gratis, kostenfrei, kostenlos, ohne Entgelt, unentgeltlich

free of claim(s), free of demand(s) · forderungslos

free of damage · unbeschädigt

free of duty, duty free · abgabe(n)frei

to free of encumbrance(s), to disencumber, to disburden, to free of incumbrance(s) · entlasten, entschulden, lastenfrei machen, schuldenfrei machen [*Grundstück*]

free of freight, carriage paid, carriage free, free of carriage, freight free, freight paid · frachtfrei, Fracht bezahlt

free on quay · frei Quai, frei Kai

free on rail, free on track · frei Bahnhof

free on track, free on rail · frei Bahnhof

free on truck · frei Waggon

free pledge; francus plegius, francum plegium, franciplegium [*Latin*]; frank pledge [*In old English law, a pledge or surety for freeman, that is, the pledge, or corporate responsibility, of all the inhabitants of a tithing for the general good behaviour of each free-born citizen above the age of fourteen, and for his being forthcoming to answer any infraction of the law*] · Freienbürgschaft *f*, Zwangsbürgschaft

free pub(lic house), free house (Brit.); free drinking shop (US) · freie Kneipe *f*, freie Schankwirtschaft *f*

free (real) estate of inheritance, free (real) property of inheritance, free land of inheritance, free realty of inheritance · freier Erb(grund)besitz(stand) *m*, freier erblicher (Grund)Besitz(stand)

free reserve → free (liability) reserve

free share · freier Anteil *m*, nicht verpfändeter Anteil, Anteil eines sparenden Mitgliedes, Mitglied-Sparanteil [*Bausparkasse*]

free spiritual tenure (of land), (free) alms tenure (of land), (feodal) tenure (of land) in frankalmoign(e), frankalmoign(e), free alms [*A tenure whereby religious corporations, aggregate or sole, held lands of the donor to them and their successors for ever. They were discharged of all other except religious services, and the trinoda necessitas. It differed from tenure by divine service, in that the latter required the performance of certain divine services, whereas the former, as its name imports, was free*] · (freies) Almosenleh(e)n *n*, Freialmosenleh(e)n, Gottesleh(e)n mit unbestimmten geistlichen Verrichtungen

free-standing single-family house, isolated single-family house, detached single-family house · freistehendes Einfamilienhaus *n*

free state · Freistaat *m*

free tenancy → simple fee

free tenure by socage, sokemanry [*The tenure of land(s) by a sokeman*] · freier weltlicher Leh(e)n(s)besitz *m*, (weltlicher) Freigutbesitz

free tenure (of land) → simple fee

free time, spare time, nonwork time, leisure time · Freizeit *f*

free to move about, free to settle anywhere · freizügig

free to settle anywhere, free to move about · freizügig

free town, free city · freie Stadt *f*

free trade area, free trade territory · Freihandelsgebiet *n*

free trade in ideas, free exchange of ideas · freier Gedankenaustausch *m*

free trade in land(s) — front

free trade in land(s), land(s) free trade · Landfreihandel *m*, Bodenfreihandel

free trade movement · Freihandelsbewegung *f*

free trade zone · Freihandelszone *f*

free warren → (liberty of) free warren

free wharfage · frei von Kaigebühren

to freeze, to block · sperren [*Guthaben*]

freeze · Sperre *f* [*1. Bausperre; 2. Veränderungssperre*]

freeze → (development) freeze

freeze ordinance → (development) freeze ordinance

freezing of assets, blocking of assets · Guthabensperre *f*, Sperren *n* von Guthaben

freezing of property, property freezing, property blocking, blocking of property · Vermögenssperre *f*, Sperren *n* von Vermögen

freight bracket · Frachtspanne *f*

freight cost(s), carrying cost(s) · Frachtkosten *f*

freight cost(s) in the finished product · Fabrikfrachtkosten *f*

freight cost(s) on raw material(s) · Rohstoff-Frachtkosten *f*

freight forwarder, shipper, forwarding agent · Spediteur *m*

freight free, freight paid, free of freight, carriage paid, carriage free, free of carriage · frachtfrei, Fracht bezahlt

freight paid, free of freight, carriage paid, carriage free, free of carriage, freight free · frachtfrei, Fracht bezahlt

freight rate · Frachtsatz *m*

frequency distribution · Häufigkeitsverteilung *f*

freshening up · Auffrischung *f* [*z. B. Werbeschild*]

fresh land, fresh ground; terra frusca, terra frisca [*Latin*] · Frischland *n*, Frischboden *m*

fresh (legal) evidence · neues Beweismittel *n*

fresh step · neue Prozeßhandlung *f*

freshwater fishing, freshwater fishery · Binnenfischerei *f*

frictional unemployment, temporary unemployment · vorübergehende Arbeitslosigkeit *f*, vorläufige Arbeitslosigkeit, zeitweilige Arbeitslosigkeit

friendly fire [*Fire burning in place where it was intended to burn, although damages may result*] · nützliches Feuer *n*

Friendly Societies Registry · Aufsichtsbehörde *f* für genossenschaftliche Unterstützungs-, Krankheits- und Sterbekassen [*in England*]

friendly society, benefit club, benefit society [*A society whose members, by the regular payment of small sums, are entitled to pecuniary help in time of age or sickness*] · Hilfskasse *f*, Selbsthilfeorganisation *f*, Unterstützungsverein *m*, Förderungsverein(igung) *m*, *(f)*, Unterstützungskasse

friendship league, league of friendship · Freundschaftsbündnis *n*

fringe, frame · Kernsaum *m*, Übergangssaum [*Stadt*]

fringe area, frame area, fringe territory, frame territory · Übergangssaumgebiet *n*, Kernsaumgebiet

fringe benefit · zusätzliche Arbeitgeberleistung *f*

fringe population, frame population · Kernsaumbevölkerung *f*, Übergangssaumbevölkerung

frithgild(a), guildhall [*A company or fraternity for the maintenance of peace and security*] · Schutzgilde *f*

frithman · Schutzgildengenosse *m*

from an intestate, ab intestato [*Succession ab intestato refers to succession to property of a person who has not disposed of it by will*] · nichttestamentarisch, ohne Testament

from day to day; de die in diem [*Latin*] · von Tag zu Tag

from home trip, from home travel, from home journey · Hinfahrt *f*

from inadvertence, from oversight, by inadvertence, by oversight, inadvertently · versehentlich

from old times; ab antiquo [*Latin*] · seit alter Zeit

from outside, ab extra · von außen

from oversight, by inadvertence, by oversight, inadvertently, from inadvertence · versehentlich

from the beginning, ab initio [*Latin*] · von Anfang an

from-to type of interindustry model · Von-Zu-Modell *n* [*Zur Quantifizierung wirtschaftlicher Wirkungen regionaler Investitionsentscheidungen*]

from year to year, yearly, annual · auf unbestimmte Zeit, von Jahr zu Jahr [*Land(besitz)recht*]

front, butt(al), bout, end, head · Ende *n*, Grundstücksende

frontage highway, frontage road · Straße *f* parallel zur Schnellstraße

frontage line, building line, BL · (Bau)Fluchtlinie *f* [*Die amtlich festgesetzte Linie, allgemein parallel zur Straße, über die nicht hinaus gebaut werden darf und die die vordere Gebäudekante festlegt*]

frontager · Anlieger *m*, Anwohner, Anrainer, Adjazent *m* [*An Bahnstrecken, Straßen usw.*]

frontage road, frontage highway · Straße *f* parallel zur Schnellstraße

frontager-owner, frontager-proprietor · Anliegereigentümer *m*

frontager ownership (of property), frontager (general) property, frontager proprietorship · Anliegereigentum *n*

frontager-possessor · Anliegerbesitzer *m*

frontager's automobile traffic, frontager's motor traffic · Anliegerautoverkehr *m*

frontager's contribution · (echter) Anliegerbeitrag *m* [*Der Unterschied zwischen Anliegerbeitrag und Anliegerkosten besteht darin, daß es sich beim Anliegerbeitrag um einen Zuschuß eines Anliegers zu den Aufwendungen der Herstellung und Unterhaltung von Gemeindeanlagen handelt, während die Anliegerkosten allein von den Anliegern — also ohne Gemeindebeteiligung — getragen werden*]

frontager's cost(s) · Anliegerkosten *f,* unechter Anliegerbeitrag *m*

frontager's law · Anliegerrecht *n* [*Gesamtheit aller Gesetze und Vorschriften, durch die dem Besitzer oder Eigentümer eines an eine öffentliche Straße angrenzenden Grundstücks bestimmte Rechte zugebilligt und entsprechende Pflichten auferlegt werden*]

frontager's motor traffic, frontager's automobile traffic · Anliegerautoverkehr *m*

frontager's proportion, frontager's share, frontager's rate, frontager's part · Anliegeranteil *m*

frontgager's right, frontgager's interest · Anliegerrecht *n*, subjektives Anliegerrecht

frontager's service · Anliegerleistung *f*

frontager's street · Anliegerstraße *f,* Wohnstraße

frontager's traffic · Anliegerverkehr *m*

front building · Frontgebäude *n*, Vordergebäude

front-end load plan, contractual plan · Nennwert-Gebühren-Vorabzugs-Plan *m*, Vertragsplan, Anlageplan, Anlageprogramm *n*, Sparplan, Sparprogramm [*Investmentfonds*]

front garden; front yard (US) · Vorgarten *m*

front garden area · Vorgartenfläche *f*

front garden ground · Vorgartengelände *n,* Vorgartenterrain *n*

frontier, border · Grenze *f*

frontier · Grenzsaum *m*

frontier area, frontier territory, border area, border territory · Grenzgebiet *n*

frontier fortress · Grenzfestung *f*

frontier land, borderland · Grenzland *n*

frontier man · Grenzbewohner *m*

frontier region, border region · Grenzregion *f*

frontier settlement · Grenz(an)sied(e)lung *f*

frontier territory, border area, border territory, frontier area · Grenzgebiet *n*

front street · Frontstraße *f*

(front) street line · Straßenfluchtlinie *f*

front yard (US); front garden · Vorgarten *m*

frozen account, blocked balance, frozen balance, blocked account · Sperrkonto *n*

frozen assets · eingefrorene Aktiva *f,* eingefrorenes Guthaben *n*

frozen balance, blocked account, frozen account, blocked balance · Sperrkonto *n*

frozen standard, basic standard · Plankostenverrechnungssatz *m* nicht an Tagespreisen orientiert

fructus industriales, fructus industriae [*Latin*]; fruits of industry, emblements, industrial fruits, industrial products; fruits of labour, products of labour (Brit.); fruits of labor, products of labor (US) [*Those fruits of a thing, as of land, which are produced by the labo(u)r and industry of the occupant, as crops of grain; as distinguished from such as are produced solely by the powers of nature*] · künstlicher Zuwachs *m*

fructus naturales [*Latin*]; natural fruits, fruits of nature [*The produce of the soil, or of fruit-trees, bushes, vines, etc., which are edible or otherwise useful or serve for the reproduction of their species*] · Naturfrüchte *fpl*

fruit farm · Obsthof *m*, Obstgut *n*

fruit farming, fruit growing, fruit cultivation · Obst(an)bau *m*

fruit plantation · Obstplantage *f*

fruits of industry, emblements, industrial fruits, industrial products; fruits of labour, products of labour (Brit.); fruits of labor, products of labor (US); fructus industriales, fructus industriae [*Latin*] [*Those fruits of a thing, as of land, which are produced by the labo(u)r and industry of the occupant, as crops of grain; as distinguished from such as are produced solely by the powers of nature*] · künstlicher Zuwachs *m*

fruits of nature; fructus naturales [*Latin*]; natural fruits [*The produce of the soil, or of fruit-trees, bushes, vines, etc., which are edible or otherwise useful or serve for the reproduction of their species*] · Naturfrüchte *f pl*

fruits of nature; fructus naturales [*Latin*]; natural products, natural fruits [*Those products which are produced by the powers of nature alone; as wool, metals, milk, young animals, etc.*] · natürlicher Zuwachs *m*

fruit tree · Obstbaum *m*

frusca terra [*Latin*]; fallow land, idle land, tract of fallow (land), waste, uncultivated land; novale · Brachflur *f*, Brachland *n*, Brachacker *m*, Brachfeld *n*

to frustrate · nicht binden

frustrated contract · nichtbindender Vertrag *m*

frustrating event · nichtbindendes Ereignis *n*

frustration [*The legal term for a doctrine whereby in certain circumstances a contract is held no longer binding on the parties without default of either party. Not to be confused with "impossibility"*] · Nichtbindung *f*

frustration · Wegfall *m* der Geschäftsgrundlage

frustration by fire · Nichtbindung *f* durch Brand

frustration doctrine, doctrine of frustration · Nichtbindungslehre *f*

frustration principle, principle of frustration · Nichtbindungsprinzip *n*, Nichtbindungsgrundsatz *m*

F.S.I. (Brit.); basic floor area (US); floor area ratio, F.A.R., floor space index [*The square-foot amount of total floor area (all stories) for each square foot of land area of a property*] · Geschoßflächenzahl *f*, GFZ, Geschoßflächendichte *f*, GFD; Ausnutzungsziffer *f* [*frühere Benennung*]

F. Supp., Federal Supplement [*In the USA*] · Sammlung *f* der Bundesgerichtsentscheidungen [*nicht der Staatsgerichte*]

F-test, variance-ratio test · F-Prüfung *f* [*Statistik*]

fugare [*Latin*]; to chase, to hunt · jagen

fugitive from justice · flüchtige Person *f*

to fulfill, to discharge, to comply with [*contract*] · erfüllen, vollziehen, nachkommen [*Vertrag*]

fulfilled, executed, discharged, performed · erfüllt, ausgeführt, vollzogen, erbracht, nachgekommen

fulfilled consideration, executed consideration, performed consideration [*An act done or a value given before or at the time of making a contract*] · ausgeführte Gegenleistung *f*, erbrachte Gegenleistung *f*, erfüllte Gegenleistung *f*, vollzogene Gegenleistung *f*

fulfilled contract, contract complied with, executed contract, performed contract · ausgeführter Vertrag *m*, erfüllter Vertrag *m*, erbrachter Vertrag *m*, vollzogener Vertrag *m*

fulfilled covenant, performed covenant, covenant complied with, executed covenant · ausgeführter Formalvertrag *m*, erfüllter Formalvertrag *m*, vollzogener Formalvertrag *m*, erbrachter Formalvertrag

fulfilling party, executing party, performing party · ausführende Partei *f*, erbringende Partei *f*, vollziehende Partei *f*, erfüllende Partei *f*

fulfilling person, executing person, performing person · Ausführende *m*, Vollziehende *m*, Erbringende *m*, Erfüllende *m*

fulfilment, discharge, execution, performance, compliance [*The pursuance or carrying forth of the provisions of a plan or contract*] · Ausführung *f*, Vollzug *m*, Erbringung *f*, Vollziehung *f*, Erfüllung *f*, Leistung

fulfilment bond, execution bond, compliance bond, discharge bond, performance bond · Erfüllungsgarantie *f*, Vollzugsgarantie, Vollziehungsgarantie, Erbringungsgarantie, Leistungsgarantie, Ausführungsgarantie

fulfilment duty, execution duty, compliance duty, duty of fulfilment, duty of execution, duty of compliance, duty of performance, performance duty · Erfüllungspflicht *f*, Vollziehungspflicht, Ausführungspflicht, Vollzugspflicht, Erbringungspflicht

fulfilment period, performance period, compliance period, execution period · Ausführungsfrist *f*, Vollzugsfrist *f*, Erfüllungsfrist *f*, Vollziehungsfrist *f*, Erbringungsfrist *f*

full accounting → full (cost(s)) accounting

full age, (age of (legal)) majority, age of consent, mature years, statutory age, legal age [*The age fixed by law at which a person's consent to certain acts is valid in law*] · Majorennität *f*, Volljährigkeit(salter) *f*, *(n)*

full and complete right, real right; jus in re [*Latin*]; complete and full right [*A right existing or subject of property, inherent in his relation to it, implying complete ownership with possession*] · (dingliches) Recht *n* auf Beherrschung einer Sache im ganzen, volles Recht zu einer Sache, volles Recht zur Sache

full approach · Vollansatz *m*

full compensation, full damages, full indemnification, full indemnity · Vollentschädigung *f*, Vollschadenersatz *m*

full costing, absorption (cost(s)) accounting, full (cost(s)) accounting, actual cost(s) system, absorption costing [*The practice of charging all cost(s), both variable and fixed, to products, processes or services*] · Vollkostenkalkulation *f*, Voll(kosten)rechnung *f*, Vollkostenermitt(e)lung, Vollkostenberechnung

full cost(s), absorbed cost(s) · Vollkosten *f*

full (cost(s)) accounting, actual cost(s) system, absorption costing, full costing, absorption (cost(s)) accounting [*The practice of charging all cost(s), both variable and fixed, to products, processes or services*] · Vollkostenkalkulation *f*, Voll(kosten)rechnung *f*, Vollkostenermitt(e)lung, Vollkostenberechnung

full damage, total damage · Vollschaden *m*, Totalschaden

full damages, full indemnification, full indemnity, full compensation · Vollentschädigung *f*, Vollschadenersatz *m*

full employment · Vollbeschäftigung *f*

full endorsement, special indorsement, full indorsement, special endorsement · Wechselaufschrift *f* mit Bezeichnung des Indossators

full faith and credit clause [*This is a very basic principle of the U.S. Constitution which allows unforcement of judg(e)ments of one state in all other states of the Union*] · Treu- und Glauben-Klausel *f*

full indorsement → full endorsement

full life of contract, length of contract, contract length, contract time, time of contract · Vertrags(lauf)zeit *f*, Vertragsdauer *f*

full (on-)licence [*It covers the sale of beers, wines and spirits*] · volle Schankerlaubnis *f*, volle Schankkonzession *f*, volle Schankgerechtigkeit *f*, volles Schankrecht *n*

full participating membership share · Rentenanteil *m*, Anteil mit voller Gewinnbeteiligung [*gemischte Bürgschaftsbausparkasse*]

full power of representation · Prokura *f*

full price · Vollpreis *m*

full-service leasing · echte Sachmiete *f*

full-time employe(e) · Ganztagsarbeitnehmer *m*

full title · volles Eigentumsrecht *n*

full vesting · volle Verfügung *f* über erworbene Pensionsansprüche, volle Anrechnung

full warranty deed; statutory warranty deed (US) [*It contains five warranties: 1. that the grantor is the owner of the lands and has the right to convey them; 2. that the lands are unincumbered by mortgage or other burden (unless otherwise stated); 3. that the grantee shall have quiet enjoyment, that is, shall not be put out of possession by anyone having superior title; 4. that the grantor will warrant and defend the grantee in these rights and 5. that the grantor will execute any further instrument necessary to make perfect the grantee's title to the property*] · volle Gewährleistungsurkunde *f*

fully developed · vollständig bebaut; vollständig überbaut [*Schweiz*]

fully fledged town, fully fledged city (Brit.); full-fledged town, full-fledged city (US) · Stadt *f* mit vollen wirtschaftlichen und sozialen Diensten

fully flexible budgeting · vollflexible Kostenplanung *f*, vollflexible Budgetierung

fully funded plan, fully financed plan · voll finanzierter Plan *m*

fully packaged (industrial) estate · Groß-Industriepark *m*

full(y) paid, paid-up · volleingezahlt

full(y) paid share, paid-up share · volleingezahlter Anteil *m*

fully qualified lawyer, fully trained lawyer, member of the bar [*Lawyers reporting to major law directory in the USA and those qualified by 2nd state examination in the Federal Republic of Germany*] · Volljurist *m* [*In den USA in die maßgebenden Juristenverzeichnisse aufgenommene und in der Bundesrepublik Deutschland mit dem 2. Staatsexamen qualifizierte Juristen*]

function · Funktion *f* [*Eine wirtschaftlich bewertete Tätigkeit einer Sied(e)lungseinheit, die von dem Umfang und der Raumstruktur der Nachfrage abhängig ist*]

function · Funktion *f*, Zweckbestimmung *f*

functional approach · Funktionsansatz *m*

functional area(l) unit · funktionsräumliche Einheit *f*, funktionale Raumeinheit

functional change · Funktionswandel *m*

**functional citizenship, **functional nationality · funktionelle Staatsangehörigkeit f [Gesetze und Staatsverträge gehen für bestimmte Zwecke von einer bestimmten Staatsangehörigkeit aus]

functional classification, classification of functions · Funktions(auf)gliederung f

functional composition, functional structure · Funktionsaufbau m, Funktionsgefüge n, Funktionsstruktur f, Funktionszusammensetzung f

functional deconcentration, deconcentration of functions · Funktionsentflechtung f

functional description of (the) work(s) · funktionale Leistungsbeschreibung f

functional development · funktionelle Entwick(e)lung f

functional game · Funktionsspiel n, spezielles Unternehmungsspiel

functional index · Funktionsindex m

functional industrial estate · Gewerbepark m mit aufeinander abgestimmten Produktionsvorgängen

functional interaction research · funktionale Verflechtungsforschung f

functional nationality, functional citizenship · funktionelle Staatsangehörigkeit f [Gesetze und Staatsverträge gehen für bestimmte Zwecke von einer bestimmten Staatsangehörigkeit aus]

functional obsolescene · funktionelle Überalterung f

functional obsolete · funktionell veraltet

functional order · Funktionsordnung f

functional organization [It was developed around 1900 by Frederick W. Taylor] · Funktions(meister)system n, Funktions(meister)organisation f, funktionelles System

functional plan · Funktionsplan m

functional planner · Funktionsplaner m

functional planning · Funktionsplanung f

functional reform · Funktionalreform f

functional region · funktionale Region f

functional relation(ship) · funktionale Beziehung f, funktionales Verhältnis n

functional society · Funktionsgesellschaft f [Die Phase der gesellschaftlichen Entwicklung nach der Industriegesellschaft]

functional space system, functional spatial system · funktionelles Raumsystem n, funktionelles räumliches System, räumliches funktionelles System

functional structure, functional composition · Funktionsaufbau m, Funktionsgefüge n, Funktionsstruktur f, Funktionszusammensetzung f

functional unit · funktionale Einheit f, Funktionseinheit

functional zone · Funktionszone f

function of existence, existence function · Daseinsfunktion f

to fund → to finance

fund · Fonds m, Mittel(gesamtheit) f

fund allocation, allocation of fund · Mittelzuweisung f, Geldzuweisung, Finanzzuweisung, Fondszuweisung

fundamental, basic · grundlegend

fundamental amount, basic amount · Grundbetrag m

fundamental breach (of contract), repudiatory breach (of contract), fundamental contract breach, repudiatory contract breach · fundamentaler (Vertrags)Bruch m, schwerwiegender (Vertrags)Bruch

fundamental central community, basic central community · Grundzentrum n

fundamental composition, basic structure, fundamental structure, basic composition · Grundgefüge n, Grundaufbau m, Grundstruktur f, Grundzusammensetzung f

fundamental contract breach, repudiatory contract breach, fundamental breach (of contract), repudiatory breach (of contract) · fundamentaler (Vertrags)Bruch m, schwerwiegender (Vertrags)Bruch

fundamental (contract) term · fundamentaler Vertragsbestandteil m

fundamental cost(s), basic cost(s) · Grundkosten f

fundamental data, basic data · Ausgangsdaten f, Basisdaten f, grundlegende Daten f, Grunddaten f

fundamental design, basic design · Ausgangsentwurf m, Grundentwurf m

fundamental duality theorem · Fundamentaltheorem n der Dualität

fundamental dwelling rent, dwelling basic rent, dwelling fundamental rent, basic dwelling rent · Wohnungskostenmiete f, Wohnungskosten(miet)zins m

fundamental error, basic error · Grundfehler m

fundamental fact, basic fact · Grundtatsache f

fundamental fee, basic fee · Grundgebühr f, Grundhonorar n

fundamental fee rate, basic fee rate · Grundgebührensatz m, Grundhonorarsatz

fundamental form — fungible goods

fundamental form, fundamental shape, basic form, basic shape · Grundgestalt *f*, Grundform *f*

fundamental function, basic function · Grundfunktion *f*

fundamental industry, basic industry, primary industry · Grundindustrie *f*

fundamental law, organic law of a state, basic law, constitutional law [*The law which determines the constitution of government in a state, and prescribes and regulates the manner of its exercise*] · Grundgesetz *n*

fundamental map, base map, basic map · Grund(land)karte *f*

fundamental measure, basic measure · Grundmaßnahme *f*

fundamental mistake, basic mistake · Grundirrtum *m*

fundamental norm, basic norm · Grundnorm *f*

fundamental obligation, basic obligation · Grundverpflichtung *f*, Kardinalverpflichtung

fundamental order, basic order · Grundauftrag *m*

fundamental plan, basic plan · Grundplan *m*

fundamental price, basic price · Grundpreis *m*

fundamental rate, basic rate, · Grundtarif *m*

fundamental rent, basic rent [*Rent on which calculations for other rents are based*] · Grundrente *f*, Basisrente

fundamental research, basic research · Grundlagenforschung *f*

fundamental rule, basic rule · Ausgangsregel *f*, Grundregel *f*

fundamental salary, base salary, basic salary · Grundgehalt *n*

fundamental shape, basic form, basic shape, fundamental form · Grundgestalt *f*, Grundform *f*

fundamental solution, basic solution, b.s. · Grundlösung *f*

fundamental spatial pattern, fundamental spatial scheme, fundamental space pattern, fundamental space scheme · raumrelevantes Grundmuster *n*, raumrelevantes Grundschema *n*

fundamental structure, basic composition, fundamental composition, basic structure · Grundgefüge *n*, Grundaufbau *m*, Grundstruktur *f*, Grundzusammensetzung *f*

fundamental term → fundamental (contract) term

fundamental value, basic value · Ausgangswert *m*, Grundwert *m*

fundamental variable, basic variable · Grundvariable *f*

fundamental wage, basic wage · Ausgangslohn *m*, Grundlohn *m*, Ecklohn *m*

fundator [*Latin*]; foundor · Stifter *m* einer öffentlich-rechtlichen Stiftung

funded → financed

funded mortgage, financed mortgage [*The mortgage has made the money available so that it can be paid out*] · finanzierte Hypothek *f*

fund flow, flow of fund · Fondsfluß *m*, Mittelfluß

fund (generated) from operation(s), earnings from operation(s), cash profit, fund provided by profit, fund made available from operation(s), fund provided by operation(s); cash flow, cash earnings [*misnomers*] · Geldgewinn *m* aus (Betriebs)Umsatz, Fondsbeitrag *m* aus (Betriebs)Umsatz, Fondszufluß *m* aus (Betriebs)Umsatz, Nettofondszugang *m* aus (Betriebs)Umsatz, Kapitalzufluß aus Betriebstätigkeit, Fondszuwachs *m* aus Betriebsleistungen, Zugang an flüssigen Mitteln aus Betriebstätigkeit, finanzwirtschaftlicher Überschuß *m*, Umsatzüberschuß, Fondszugang aus Betriebstätigkeit

funding, financing · Fundieren *n*, Finanzieren, Mittelaufnahme *f*

fund in the treasury; cash on hand, cash in bank (US); cash in vaults · Bankbarbestand *m*, Bankkassenbestand

fund of a Land, Land fund · Landesmittel *f*, Landesfonds *m* [*Bundesrepublik Deutschland*]

funds for expenditures · Mittel *f* für Ausgaben

funds statement, summary of financial operations; capital-reconciliation statement (Brit.); accounting for the flow of funds, statement of (sources and applications of) funds · Kapital(zu)flußrechnung *f*, Finanzierungsrechnung, Finanz(zu)flußrechnung, Bewegungsbilanz *f*, Mittelherkunft- und -verwendungsrechnung

fund theory of accounting · Kapitalzuflußrechnungstheorie *f*

fungible, marketable, sal(e)able, merchantable, mercable · absetzbar, verkaufbar, marktgängig, verkäuflich

fungible goods, interchangeable goods (US) [*For instance, a ton of wheat of certain kind is the same as another ton of the same kind*] · austauschbare Güter *n pl*, ersetzbare Güter, vertretbare Güter

funnel city, funnel town, intrapolis · Trichterstadt *f*, Intrapolis *f* [*Eine Vision der Stadt von morgen nach dem Schweizer Architekten Walter Jonas. Trichterförmige Gebilde, die eine nach innen gekehrte Stadt bilden. Die Garagen sollen in Gegentrichtern unterirdisch liegen*]

furlong; furlang [*Anglo-Saxon*]; furlongus, stadium, stade, quarentena terrae [*Latin*]; ferlingus, ferlingum [*Low Latin*] [*A piece of land bounded or terminated by the length of a furrow*] · (Ge)Wende *(n)*, *f*, Gewann *n*, Wande *f*, Wanne *f*; Flagge *f* [*Ostfriesland*]

to furnish, to provide [*construction materials*] · liefern [*Baustoffe*]

to furnish, to provide [*construction machinery and equipment*] · vorhalten [*Baumaschinen und -geräte*]

to furnish, to provide [*labo(u)r*] · stellen [*Arbeitskräfte*]

to furnish, to supply · beistellen [*Baustoff(e)*]

to furnish, to equip · ausrüsten, ausstatten

furnished · möbliert

furnished living space, furnished residential space · möblierter Wohnraum *m*

furnished residential space, furnished living space · möblierter Wohnraum *m*

furnishing, supply · Beistellung *f* [*Baustoff(e)*]

furnishing, equipping · Ausstatten *n*, Ausrüsten

furnishing by client → supply by owner

to furnish reasons · begründen

furniture storage, storage of furniture · Möbellagerung *f*

further consideration · nochmalige Verhandlung *f* [*im Zivilprozeß*]

further education · Weiterbildung *f*

fur-trading station · Pelzstation *f*

fusion, merger, consolidation [*In the civil law, the uniting of possession, occupancy, profits, etc., of land(s) with property, and vice versa*] · Konsolidation *f*, Verschmelzung *f*, Fusion *f*

fusioning, uniting, consolidating · Konsolidieren *n*, Fusionieren, Verschmelzen

fusion of capitals, merger of capitals, consolidation of capitals, capital consolidation, capital merger, capital fusion · Kapitalverschmelzung *f*, Kapitalkonsolidation *f*, Kapitalfusion

fusion of urban and rural land, rurbanization · Verschmelzung *f* von Stadt und Land mit Hilfe des Verkehrs

future interest (in land(s)), future right (in land(s)) · dingliches Recht *n* auf (zu)künftigen Grundstücksgenuß, Grundstücksbindung *f* durch Fideikommiß, (zu)künftiges Landbesitzrecht, (zu)künftiges Bodenbesitzrecht

future interest (in land(s)) at common law, interest in expectancy at common law · gemeinrechtlicher zukünftig wirkender Eigentumsanteil *m*

future interest (in land(s)) under statute, future right (in land(s)) under statute · dingliches Recht *n* auf (zu)künftigen Grundstücksgenuß gemäß Gesetzgebung, Grundstücksbindung durch Fideikommiß gemäß Gesetzgebung, (zu)künftiges Landbesitzrecht gemäß Gesetzgebung, (zu)künftiges Bodenbesitzrecht gemäß Gesetzgebung

future right · (zu)künftiger Anspruch *m*, (zu)künftiges (An)Recht *n*

future use, dead use · (zu)künftige Benutzung *f*, (zu)künftiger Gebrauch *m*

G

gabella emigrationis, detractus personalis [*Latin*] · Abfahrtsgeld *n*, Abzugsgeld, Auswanderungsgebühr *f*, Emigrationsgebühr [*Eine Abgabe welche früher von einem Auswanderer an den Staat oder die Gemeinde, welcher derselbe angehörte, zu entrichten war*]

gabella hereditaria, quindena, detractus realis, census hereditarius [*Latin*] · Abschoß *m*, Erb(schafts)geld *n*

gable masonry wall · Giebelmauer *f*

gable wall · Giebelwand *f*

gable (wall) advertisement · Giebel(wand)werbung *f*, Giebel(wand)reklame *f*

gage and pledge · Pfand *n* und Bürgschaft *f* [*Beim Retentionsrecht des englischen Mobiliarpfandrechts im Mittelalter*]

gage having the right to use the article pledged → (mort)gage having the right to use the article pledged

gain, profit · Gewinn *m*, Profit *m*

gain fee, profit fee, fee for profit, fee for gain [*A contractual arrangement whereby the contractor is paid the net prime cost plus a percentage to cover overheads and profit*] · aufzuschlagender Gewinnsatz *m*, Gewinnzuschlag *m*, Gewinnaufschlag *m*, Profitzuschlag *m*, Profitaufschlag *m*

gain forecast, profit forecast · Gewinnvorhersage f, Profitvorhersage

gain loss, loss of profit(s), loss of gain(s), profit loss · Gewinnentgang m, Gewinnverlust m, Profitentgang, Profitverlust

gain-maker, profit-maker · Gewinnbringer m, Profitbringer

gain margin, margin of profit, margin of gain, profit margin · Gewinnspanne f, Profitspanne

gain matrix, profit matrix · Gewinnmatrix f, Profitmatrix

gain of sale, sale's profit, sale's gain, profit of sale · Verkaufsprofit m, Verkaufsgewinn m

gain of stock, profit of stock · Gewinn m aus Kapitalanlage

gainor, sok(e)man, socman, socheman, socager, tenant by socage, tenant in socage, tenant in ancient demesne, colibert, tenant of socage-land, socage-land tenant, socage tenant · freier weltlicher Leh(e)n(s)besitzer m, (weltlicher) Freigutbesitzer

gain percentage, profit percentage · Gewinnprozentsatz m, Profitprozentsatz

gain pool, profit pool · Gewinngemeinschaft f, Profitgemeinschaft

gain rate, profit rate · Gewinnsatz m, Profitsatz

gain-sharing, profit-sharing, participation in the profit, participation in the gain · Gewinnbeteiligung f, Profitbeteiligung

gain-sharing contract, profit-sharing contract · Gewinnbeteiligungsvertrag m, Profitbeteiligungsvertrag

gain-sharing plan, profit-sharing plan · Gewinnbeteiligungsplan m, Profitbeteiligungsplan

gain split, profit split · Gewinnteilung f, Profitteilung

gain tax, profit tax · Gewinnsteuer f, Profitsteuer

gain transfer, profit transfer · Gewinnabführung f, Profitabführung

galloping inflation, hyperinflation, runaway inflation · galoppierende Inflation f

Galton's individual difference problem · Galton'sches Rangordnungsproblem n

GAM, goals achievement matrix · Zielerfüllungsmatrix f

gambler, speculator, adventurer · Spekulant m

game, wild animals, (wild) beasts of the chase, chase beasts · (Jagd)Wild n, jagdbare Tiere npl

game → (planning) game

game act, game statute, game law [Laws passed for the preservation of game, usually forbidding the killing of specified game during certain seasons, or by certain described means] · Jagdgesetz n, Wildgesetz

game area, wildlife area · Wildgebiet n

game certificate · Jagdschein m

gamekeeper · Wildheger m, Wildpfleger

gamekeeping · Wildhaltung f, Wildpflege f

game law, game act, game statute [Laws passed for the preservation of game, usually forbidding the killing of specified game during certain seasons, or by certain described means] · Jagdgesetz n, Wildgesetz

game law · Jagdrecht n, objektives Jagdrecht, Wildrecht

game licence, game license [formerly: game certificate] · Jagdschein m

game licence, game license · Jagdlizenz f

game of chance for winnings in money · Glücksspiel n

game preserve, wildlife refuge, game refuge, wildlife preserve · Wildreservat n, Wildschutzgebiet n, Wildschongebiet

game protection law · Wildschutzrecht n

game simulation, gaming simulation, planning game simulation · (Plan)Spielsimulation f, Hybridspiel n

game statute, game law, game act [Laws passed for the preservation of game, usually forbidding the killing of specified game during certain seasons, or by certain described means] · Jagdgesetz n, Wildgesetz

game theoretic(al) approach · spieltheoretischer Ansatz m

game theoretic(al) concept · theoretischer Spielbegriff m

game theory, theory of games, gaming theory · Theorie f der Spiele, Spieltheorie

game with saddle point, strictly determined game · streng bestimmtes Spiel n, Spiel mit Sattelpunkt, Sattelpunktspiel

gaming · Spielen n

gaming · Glücksspielerei f

gaming approach · Spielansatz m

gaming simulation, planning game simulation, game simulation · (Plan)Spielsimulation f, Hybridspiel n

gaming simulation model, (planning) game simulation model · (Plan)Spielsimulationsmodell n, Hybridspielmodell

gaming theory — to gather

gaming theory, game theory, theory of games · Theorie *f* der Spiele, Spieltheorie

gaol (Brit.); jail, prison · Gefängnis *n*

gaol delivery (Brit.); jail delivery, prison delivery · Gefängnisbereinigung *f* [*Im englischen Ständestaat*]

gaol delivery (Brit.); jail delivery, prison delivery · Einlieferung *f* ins Gefängnis

gaoler (Brit.); master of a prison, keeper of a prison · Gefängnisvorsteher *m*

gaol money (Brit.); prison money, jail money [*In old English law*] · Steuer *f* für Unterhaltung von Gefangenen

gap financing · Überbrückungsfinanzierung *f*

gap (land) parcel, vacant parcel of land, gap parcel of land, vacant site, gap site, vacant plot, gap plot, vacant (land) parcel · Baulücke *f*, Bebauungslücke, unbebautes Grundstück *n* in einem bebauten Gebiet, nichtbebautes Grundstück in einem bebauten Gebiet, freies Grundstück in einem bebauten Gebiet

gap site, vacant plot, gap plot, vacant (land) parcel, gap (land) parcel, vacant parcel of land, gap parcel of land, vacant site · Baulücke *f*, Bebauungslücke, unbebautes Grundstück *n* in einem bebauten Gebiet, nichtbebautes Grundstück in einem bebauten Gebiet, freies Grundstück in einem bebauten Gebiet

gap undertaking, gap enterprise · Lückenbetrieb *m*, Lückenunternehmen *n*, Lückenunternehmung *f*

garage building law · Garagenbaurecht *n*

garage law · Garagenrecht *n*

garage ordinance · Garagenverordnung *f*

to garble [*In old English statutes*]; to sort out, to cull out [*The good from the bad*] · aussortieren

garden architect · Gartenarchitekt *m*

garden board · Gartenamt *n*

garden city, garden town, town-county · Gartenstadt *f*

gardening · Gartenbau *m*

garden(ing) land (area), garden(ing) area, land (zoned) for gardening · Gartenboden *m*, Gartenfläche *f*, Gartenland *n*, gärtnerisch genutzter Boden, gärtnerisch genutztes Land, gärtnerisch genutzte Fläche

garden on lease, garden on tenancy, garden on demise · Pachtgarten *m*

garden suburb(an place) · Gartenvorort *m*

garden swimming pool · Gartenschwimmbecken *n*

garden town, town-county, garden city · Gartenstadt *f*

garden village · Gartendorf *n*

to garnish [*In the process of attachment*] · vorladen, zitieren

garnishee, factor [*When a judgment recovered by a creditor against a debtor remains unsatisfied and a debt is due to the debtor from a third party, the creditor can obtain an order from the court requiring the third party to show cause why he should not pay the debt to the creditor. The third party is called the "garnishee" and the order a "garnishee order"*] · Drittschuldner *m*

garnishee order · (gerichtlicher) Drittschuldnerbefehl *m*

garnishee proceeding, garnishment [*A statutory proceeding whereby person's property, money, or credits in possession or under control of, or owing by, another are applied to payment of former's debt to third person by proper statutory process against debtor and garnishee*] · Drittschuldnerverfahren *n*, Arrestverfahren

garnisher · Drittschuldnergläubiger *m*

garnishment, garnishee proceeding [*A statutory proceeding whereby person's property, money, or credits in possession or under control of, or owing by, another are applied to payment of former's debt to third person by proper statutory process against debtor and garnishee*] · Drittschuldnerverfahren *n*, Arrestverfahren

garnishment [*In the process of attachment. A warning to a person not to pay money or deliver property to another, but to appear and answer a plaintiff creditor's suit*] · Vorladung *f*, Zahlungswarnung an den Drittschuldner

gas and water works · Gas- und Wasserwerk *n*

gas company · Gasgesellschaft *f*

gas connection · Gasanschluß *m*

gas discharge, discharge of gas · Gasaustritt *m*

gas nuisance · Gasemission *f*

gas nuisance effect · Gasimmission *f*

gas price · Gaspreis *m*

gas supply, supply of gas · Gasversorgung *f*

gas supply code · Gasversorgungsordnung *f*

gateway city, gateway town · Schlüsselstadt *f*

to gather, to procure, to raise, to collect [*money, etc.*] · erheben

gathering, procuring, raising, collecting · Erheben *n*

Gauss distribution, normal distribution · Normalverteilung *f* [*Statistik*]

gazette → (official) gazette

gazetteer · Ortsverzeichnis *n*

gazumping · nachträgliche Preiserhöhung *f* [*Grundstückkauf*]

GC/Works/1 [*Great Britain*]; CCC/Works/1 [*deprecated*]; general conditions of government contracts for building and civil engineering works · Vertragsbedingungen *fpl* für staatliche Bauten

gearing, leverage · Hebelwirkung *f* des Fremdkapitals, Multiplikatorwirkung *f* des Fremdkapitals (auf die Ertragslage des Eigenkapitals), Verhältnis *n* Eigenkapital-Fremdkapital

gearing factor, leverage factor · Hebelwirkungsfaktor *m*

geldable, liable to pay; g(u)ildable [*In old English law*] · zahlungspflichtig

geneat · Hörige *mpl* aller Art

general · abstrakt, generell, allgemein

general · unbefristet [*(Land)Pacht*]

general acceptability criterion, general acceptance criterion · allgemeiner Abnahmebewertungsmaßstab *m*, allgemeines Abnahmemerkmal *n*

general acceptance of a bill (of exchange), absolute acceptance of a bill (of exchange) · allgemeine Wechselannahme *f*

general acceptance provisions · allgemeine (Bau)Abnahmebestimmungen *fpl*

General Accounting Office [*USA*] · Bundesrechnungsbehörde *f*

(general) accounting office (US); audit office, audit department, commissioners of audit (Brit.) [*It is entrusted with the audit and control of public accounts*] · (Rechnungs)Prüfungsbehörde *f*, (Rechnungs)Revisionsbehörde, Rechnungshof *m*, Oberrechnungskammer *f*

general act, general law, general statute, legislative act, legislative law, legislative statute, session act, session statute, resolve act; slip law, session law [*USA*]; public act, public law, public statute · allgemeines Gesetz *n* [*In den Gliedstaaten der USA erscheinen die Gesetze nach ihrer Verabschiedung zunächst als „slip laws", die am Ende einer Sitzungsperiode der Legislative chronologisch zu den „session laws" zusammengefaßt werden*]

general administration cost(s) [*The sum of those costs of general management, and of secretarial, accounting and administrative services, which cannot be directly related to the production, marketing research or development functions of the enterprise*] · allgemeine Verwaltungskosten *f*

general administration of estate(s), unlimited administration of estate(s) · allgemeine Nachlaßverwaltung *f*, unbeschränkte Nachlaßverwaltung, allgemeine erbrechtliche Verwaltung, unbeschränkte erbrechtliche Verwaltung, allgemeine Erb(schafts)verwaltung, unbeschränkte Erb(schafts)verwaltung

general administrative law, general administration law · allgemeines Verwaltungsrecht *n*

general administrative prescription(s) · allgemeine Verwaltungsvorschrift(en) *f (pl)*

general administrator → general (probate) administrator

general advantage, general benefit · allgemeiner Nutzen *m*, allgemeiner Vorteil, Nutzen der Allgemeinheit, Vorteil der Allgemeinheit

general age group · Hauptaltersgruppe *f*

general agent · Bevollmächtigte *m* für bestimmte Geschäfte

general agricultural labourer (Brit.); ordinary agricultural laborer, general agricultural laborer (US); orraman [*Scotland*]; spade hind [*In den Grenzgrafschaften Südschottlands*], ordinary agricultural labourer · gewöhnlicher Landarbeiter *m*

general allocation · Schlüsselzuweisung *f*

general appropriation · generelle (Mittel)Bewilligung *f*

general assignment, general cession · Globalabtretung *f*, Globalzession *f*

general assistance [*USA*] · allgemeine Wohlfahrt *f*

general assumpsit, common assumpsit, indebted assumpsit; indebitatus assumpsit [*Latin*] · ausdrückliches Schuldtilgungsversprechen *n*

general average · große Havarie *f*

general bad debt allowance, general reserve for bad debts · Pauschalwertberichtigung *f* auf Forderungen

general bank manager, chief bank officer; cashier (US) · Bankdirektor *m*

general benefit, general advantage · allgemeiner Nutzen *m*, allgemeiner Vorteil, Nutzen der Allgemeinheit, Vorteil der Allgemeinheit

general bequest, general legacy [*A pecuniary legacy, payable out of the general assets of a testator*] · General(fahrnis)vermächtnis *n*, General(fahrnis)legat *n*

general board of health · Zentralgesundheitsamt n

general body of architects · Architektenstand m

general boundaries · ungefährer (Grundstücks)Grenzverlauf m

general boundary · allgemeine Grundstücksgrenze f

general building scheme · allgemeiner Bebauungsplan m, allgemeiner verbindlicher Bauleitplan; allgemeiner Überbauungsplan [Schweiz]; allgemeiner Bauplan [Fehlbenennung]

general cession, general assignment · Globalabtretung f, Globalzession f

general change of population, general demographic change, general population change · (allgemeine) Bewegung f der Bevölkerung, (allgemeine) (Ver)Änderung der Bevölkerung, (allgemeine) Bevölkerungsbewegung, (allgemeine) Bevölkerungs(ver)änderung [In der Demographie ist das Wort „Bewegung" häufig synonym mit Änderung, ganz gleich ob es sich um eine (Ver)Änderung im Raum (= Wanderungsbewegung) oder um eine Größen(ver)änderung in der Zeit handelt. Im letzteren Sinne ist hier die „Bewegung" der Geburten, der Sterbefälle und der Außenwanderung gemeint]

general chart, survey chart · Übersichtskarte f [Seegebiete]

general charter plan [USA] · einheitliches Gemeindegesetz n

general clause · allgemeine Klausel f, Generalklausel

general company period cost(s) · Unternehmensfixkosten f, Unternehmensfestkosten

general compensation, general indemnification, general indemnity, general damages · nichtspezifizierter Schadenersatz m, nichtspezifizierte Entschädigung f

general concept · Allgemeinbegriff m

general conditions · allgemeine Bedingungen f pl

general conditions of business · AGB, allgemeine Geschäftsbedingungen f pl

general conditions of contract for the execution of construction work · allgemeine Vertragsbedingungen f (pl) für die Ausführung von Bauleistungen

general conditions of government contracts for building and civil engineering works, GC/Works/1 [Great Britain]; CCC/Works/1 [deprecated] · Vertragsbedingungen f pl für staatliche Bauten

general contract → (prime) general contract

general contract condition(s), principal contract condition(s), main contract condition(s) · allgemeine Vertragsbedingung(en) f (pl)

general contractor → (prime) general contractor

general contractor's liability in respect of subcontractor · Baustellenabsicherung f [Haftung des Generalunternehmers gegenüber Nachunternehmer]

general contract provisions, standard form contract provisions, adhesion contract provisions · allgemeine Geschäftsbestimmungen f pl

general counsel [administrative tribunal] · Rechtsabteilung f [Verwaltungstribunal]

general covenant · allgemeiner Formalvertrag m

general creditor, ordinary creditor · unbevorrechtigter Gläubiger m

general customs, customary law, (common) custom, universal custom of the realm, custom which runs through the whole land (Brit.); jus commune [Latin]; common (law) · gemeines Recht n, objektives gemeines Recht, (objektives) Gemeinrecht, Präjudizienrecht, (gemeines) Gewohnheitsrecht [England. Das gemeine Recht, das von reisenden Richtern ("itinerant justices" oder "justices in eyre") des königlichen Gerichts zu Westminster gebildet wurde. Neben der Gegenüberstellung "common law" (oder "law") — "equity" (= „strenges Recht — Billigkeitsrecht") wird "common law" noch stellvertretend für das gesamte case law und das anglo-amerikanische Rechtssystem verwandt: "common law — statute law" (= „Richterrecht — Gesetzesrecht"), bzw. "common law — civil law" (anglo-amerikanisches Recht im Gegensatz zum kontinentaleuropäischen Recht)]

general customs liability, customary law liability, common law liability · gemeinrechtliche Haftung f, gemeinrechtliche Haftpflicht f, gemeinrechtliche Haftbarkeit f

general damages, general compensation, general indemnification, general indemnity · nichtspezifizierter Schadenersatz m, nichtspezifizierte Entschädigung f

general demographic change, general population change, general change of population · (allgemeine) Bewegung f der Bevölkerung, (allgemeine) (Ver)Änderung der Bevölkerung, (allgemeine) Bevölkerungsbewegung, (allgemeine) Bevölkerungs(ver)änderung [In der Demographie ist das Wort „Bewegung" häufig synonym mit Änderung, ganz gleich ob es sich um eine (Ver)Änderung im Raum (= Wanderungsbewegung) oder um eine Größen-

(ver)änderung in der Zeit handelt. Im letzteren Sinne ist hier die „Bewegung" der Geburten, der Sterbefälle und der Außenwanderung gemeint]

general (development) analysis, comprehensive (development) analysis · Generalbebauungsanalyse *f*, Generalbebauungsuntersuchung *f*

general (development) plan, master (development) plan, comprehensive (development) plan, structure (development) plan, three-dimensional master (development) plan [*A long-range plan officially recognized as a guide for the physical growth and development of a community, together with the basic regulatory and administrative controls needed to attain the physical objectives*] · General(bebauungs)plan *m*

general (development) planning, master (development) planning, comprehensive (development) planning, three-dimensional master planning, structure planning · General(bebauungs)planung *f*

general devise [*It passes land(s) of the testator without a particular enumeration or description of them. For example: "I devise all my lands"*] · allgemeines (Land)Vermächtnis *n*, allgemeines Liegenschaftsvermächtnis, allgemeines Bodenvermächtnis, allgemeines Grund(stücks)vermächtnis, allgemeines Immobiliarlegat, allgemeines Immobilienlegat, allgemeines Grundbesitzvermächtnis, allgemeines Bodenlegat, allgemeines (Land)Legat, allgemeines Grundstückslegat, allgemeines Immobiliarvermächtnis, allgemeines Immobilienvermächtnis, allgemeines Grundbesitzlegat, allgemeines Liegenschaftslegat

general distribution expense · allgemeine Verteilungskosten *f*

general endorsement of claim, general indorsement of claim [*On a writ of summons*] · gewöhnliche Aufschrift *f* [*Sie enthält die Natur des Anspruchs oder den Inhalt des Klageantrages*]

general equation of location, general location(al) equation, general equation of site, general site equation · allgemeine Standortgleichung *f*, allgemeine Lagegleichung

general equitable burden, general equitable charge, general equitable load, general equitable encumbrance, general equitable incumbrance · allgemeine Billigkeitslast *f*, allgemeine Billigkeitsbelastung *f*

general equitable power of appointment, general equitable right of appointment · allgemeine Befugnis *f* an einem bestimmten Vermögen Treuhand zu erklären, allgemeines Recht *n* an einem bestimmten Vermögen Treuhand zu erklären

general farm · gemischter (landwirtschaftlicher) Betrieb *m*

general field theory of spatial behaviour, general field theory of spatial behaviour (Brit.); general field theory of space behavior, general field theory of spatial behavior (US) · allgemeine Feldtheorie *f* des räumlichen Verhaltens

general good, prosperity of the community, public welfare, public weal, public good, public necessity, public convenience, common welfare, common weal, common good, common necessity, common convenience, good of the community, public interests, common well-being · Gemeinwohl *n*, öffentliches Wohl, öffentliches Interesse *n*, allgemeines Wohl, allgemeines Interesse *n*, Allgemeinwohl, öffentliche Belange *mpl*

general government · Gesamtregierung *f*

general guarantee, general guaranty, general guarantie [*The guarantor does not address his written promise to any particular individual or firm, but directs it in such a way that it may be accepted by anyone to whom it is presented by the principal debtor. However, a general guaranty may be limited as to the time within which it must be accepted, or limited as to the amount beyond which the guarantor will not be responsible*] · allgemeine Bürgschaft *f*

general heir (male), heir (male) whatsoever, statutory heir (male), heir (male) at law, right heir (male), legal heir (male), lawful heir (male), nearest kin, heir (male) general [*One who takes the succession by relationship to the decedent and by force of law*] · Intestaterbe *m*, gesetzlicher Erbe

general (house) improvement area · Altbausanierungsgebiet *n*, Altbaumodernisierungsgebiet

general housing territory → general residential area

general indemnification, general indemnity, general damages, general compensation · nichtspezifizierter Schadenersatz *m*, nichtspezifizierte Entschädigung *f*

general indorsement of claim, general endorsement of claim [*On a writ of summons*] · gewöhnliche Aufschrift *f* [*Sie enthält die Natur des Anspruchs oder den Inhalt des Klageantrages*]

general issue [*The general answer "not guilty"*] · Schuldlosbekenntnis *n*, Bestreitung *f* der Klägerbehauptung(en)

generalization · Verallgemeinerung *f*

to generalize · verallgemeinern

general jurisdiction · allgemeine Zuständigkeit *f* [*Siehe Anmerkung unter „Zuständigkeit"*]

general land(s) — general offer 454

general land(s), public land(s) · öffentliche Länderei(en) *f (pl)*

general law · allgemeines Recht *n*, Allgemeinrecht

general law, general statute, legislative act, legislative law, legislative statute, session act, session statute, resolve act; slip law, session law [*USA*]; public act, public law, public statute, general act · allgemeines Gesetz *n* [*In den Gliedstaaten der USA erscheinen die Gesetze nach ihrer Verabschiedung zunächst als „slip laws", die am Ende einer Sitzungsperiode der Legislative chronologisch zu den „session laws" zusammengefaßt werden*]

general legacy, general bequest [*A pecuniary legacy, payable out of the general assets of a testator*] · General(fahrnis)vermächtnis *n*, General(fahrnis)legat *n*

general legal power of appointment, general legal right of appointment, general power of appointment under the statute of uses, general right of appointment under the statute of uses · allgemeine Befugnis *f* an einem bestimmten Vermögen Nutzung zu erklären, allgemeines Recht *n* an einem bestimmten Vermögen Nutzung zu erklären

general legal provisions · allgemeine gesetzliche Bestimmungen *f pl*

general legal right of appointment, general power of appointment under the statute of uses, general right of appointment under the statute of uses, general legal power of appointment · allgemeine Befugnis *f* an einem bestimmten Vermögen Nutzung zu erklären, allgemeines Recht *n* an einem bestimmten Vermögen Nutzung zu erklären

general level of economic activity · (Gesamt)Konjunktur *f*, allgemeine konjunkturelle Lage *f*

general location(al) equation, general equation of site, general site equation, general equation of location · allgemeine Standortgleichung *f*, allgemeine Lagegleichung

general location(al) theory, general site theory, general theory of locations, general theory of sites · allgemeine Standorttheorie *f*, allgemeine Lagetheorie

generally accepted auditing standard · Grundsatz *m* ordnungsmäßiger Abschlußprüfung, Prinzip *n* ordnungsmäßiger Abschlußprüfung

(generally accepted) rules of building and construction, universally accepted rules of building and construction · (allgemein) anerkannte Regeln *f pl* der Baukunst, (allgemein) anerkannte Regeln der Bautechnik

(generally accepted) rules of engineering, universally accepted rules of engineering · (allgemein) anerkannte Regeln *f pl* der Technik

generally crossed · allgemein gekreuzt [*Scheck*]

general management game, general managerial game, general managing game · allgemeines Unternehmungsspiel *n*

general management trust, flexible trust · Investmentfonds *m* mit beweglicher Anlagepolitik

general map, survey map · Übersichts(land)karte *f*

general map (Brit.) → cadastral map

general meeting → (annual) general meeting

general meeting of shareholders · Aktionärshauptversammlung *f*

general moratorium · Generalmoratorium *n*, Generalindult *m*, Generalanstandsbrief *m* [*Eine obrigkeitliche Anordnung die einer Gruppe von Schuldnern die fälligen Schulden stundet*]

general mortgage · Generalhypothek *f*

general mortgage-bond [*Written instrument representing an obligation secured by a mortgage but preceded by senior issues*] · Generalgrundpfandbrief *m*

general norm · abstrakte (Rechts)Norm *f*, generelle (Rechts)Norm, allgemeine (Rechts)Norm

general notice, general notification · allgemeine Anzeige *f*, allgemeine Mitteilung *f*, allgemeine Benachrichtigung

general occupancy · allgemeine Besitzhaltung *f* auf Lebenszeit eines Dritten, allgemeine Besitzhaltung für die Dauer eines anderen Lebens

general occupant, common occupant [*At common law where a man was tenant pur autre vie, or had an estate granted to himself only (without mentioning his heirs) for the life of another man, and died without alienation during the life of cestuy que vie, or him by whose life it was holden, he that could first enter on the land(s) might lawfully retain the possession, so long as cestuy que vie lived, by right of occupancy, and was hence termed a general or common occupant*] · Besitzergreifende *m* von nicht erblichem Leh(e)n beim Tode des Vasallen

general offer · Offerte *f* an die Allgemeinheit [*Z. B. einer Schiffahrtsgesellschaft nach ihren Beförderungsbedingungen die Beförderung von Personen und Gütern durchzuführen*]

general offer, offer of a public reward · Auslobung *f*, öffentliches Angebot *n*

general order — (general) property presumption

[*Das öffentliche Versprechen einer Belohnung für den Fall der Vornahme einer bestimmten Handlung, insbesondere der Herbeiführung eines Erfolges*]

general order · allgemeine Anordnung *f*, allgemeine Verfügung, allgemeiner Befehl *m*, allgemeines Gebot, Allgemeinanordnung, Allgemeinverfügung, Allgemeinbefehl, Allgemeingebot *n*

general overhead cost(s), plant overhead cost(s), plant overhead(s), general overhead(s) · Geschäftsgemeinkosten *f*, Geschäftsgeneralkosten

general partner · persönlich haftender Gesellschafter *m*, Vollhafter, Komplementär

general planning → general (development) planning

general planning legislation, general planning lawmaking, master planning legislation, master planning lawmaking, comprehensive planning legislation, comprehensive planning lawmaking, threedimensional master legislation, threedimensional master lawmaking, structure planning legislation, structure planning lawmaking · Generalplanungsgesetzgebung *f*

general population change, general change of population, general demographic change · (allgemeine) Bewegung *f* der Bevölkerung, (allgemeine) (Ver)Änderung der Bevölkerung, (allgemeine) Bevölkerungsbewegung, (allgemeine) Bevölkerungs(ver)änderung [*In der Demographie ist das Wort „Bewegung" häufig synonym mit Änderung, ganz gleich ob es sich um eine (Ver)Änderung im Raum (= Wanderungsbewegung) oder um eine Größen(ver)änderung in der Zeit handelt. Im letzteren Sinne ist hier die „Bewegung" der Geburten, der Sterbefälle und der Außenwanderung gemeint*]

general power · allgemeine Ermächtigung *f*

general power, general right · allgemeine Befugnis *f*, allgemeines Recht *n*

general power of appointment, general right of appointment, general power of disposition, general right of disposition [*It enables the appointor to make an appointment in favour of any person, including himself*] · allgemeine Verfügungsbefugnis *f*, allgemeine Bestimmungsbefugnis, allgemeines Verfügungsrecht *n*, allgemeines Bestimmungsrecht, Verfügungsbefugnis zugunsten jedes Beliebigen, Verfügungsrecht zugunsten jedes Beliebigen, Bestimmungsbefugnis zugunsten jedes Beliebigen, Bestimmungsrecht zugunsten jedes Beliebigen [*Vermögen*]

general power of appointment under the statute of uses, general right of appointment under the statute of uses, general legal power of appointment, general legal right of appointment · allgemeine Befugnis *f* an einem bestimmten Vermögen Nutzung zu erklären, allgemeines Recht *n* an einem bestimmten Vermögen Nutzung zu erklären

general (probate) administrator · allgemeiner Nachlaßverwalter *m*, allgemeiner Erb(schafts)verwalter, allgemeiner erbrechtlicher Verwalter [*Er steht an sachlichem Umfang und Zeitraum seines Amtes dem Testamentsvollstrecker gleich*]

(general) property composition, proprietorship structure, proprietorship composition, ownership structure, ownership composition, (general) property structure · Eigentumsaufbau *m*, Eigentumsgefüge *n*, Eigentumsstruktur *f*, Eigentumszusammensetzung *f*

(general) property; dominium [*Latin*]; ownership (of property), proprietorship · Eigentum *n* [*Die uneingeschränkte Herrschaft einer Person über eine Sache, auch in rechtlicher Beziehung. „Eigentum" und „Besitz" sind nicht gleichbedeutend. Eigentum ist das dingliche Vollrecht, Besitz die tatsächliche, vom Rechtstitel unabhängige Innehabung einer Sache. Auch der Dieb ist Besitzer*]

(general) property certificate, proprietorship certificate, ownership (of property) certificate · Eigentumsbescheinigung *f*, Eigentumsschein *m*, Eigentumsattest *n*

(general) property contract, ownership (of property) contract, proprietorship contract · Eigentumsvertrag *m*

(general) property dispute, proprietorship dispute, ownership (of property) dispute · Eigentumsauseinandersetzung *f*, Eigentumsstreit(igkeit) *m*, *(f)*

(general) property law, proprietorship law, law of (general) property, law of proprietorship, law of ownership (of property), ownership (of property) law · Eigentumsrecht *n*, objektives Eigentumsrecht

(general) property of soil under highways, ownership of soil under highways, proprietorship of soil under highways · Erdreicheigentum *n* unter Straßen

(general) property of space, ownership of space, proprietorship of space · Raumeigentum *n*

(general) property policy, ownership (of property) policy, proprietorship policy · Eigentumspolitik *f*

(general) property presumption, proprietorship presumption, ownership (of property) presumption, presumption of property, presumption of proprietorship, presumption of ownership (of property) · Eigentumsvermutung *f*

(general) property protection — general statute

(general) property protection, ownership (of property) protection, proprietorship protection · Eigentumsschutz *m*

(general) property restriction, proprietorship restriction, ownership restriction, proprietorship limitation, property limitation, ownership limitation, ownership restraint, proprietorship restraint, property restraint · Eigentumsbegrenzung *f*, Eigentumsbeschränkung, Eigentumseinschränkung

(general) property tax, proprietorship tax, ownership (of property) tax · Eigentumssteuer *f*

(general) property theory, proprietorship theory, ownership (of property) theory · Eigentumstheorie *f*

general provision · allgemeine Bestimmung *f*

general provisions for awards of construction work · allgemeine Bestimmungen *f pl* für die Vergabe von Bauleistungen

general purpose committee · allgemeiner (Gemeinde)Exekutivausschuß *m*

general purpose government [*USA*] · kommunale Einheit *f* mit allgemeiner Zuständigkeit und Zwecksetzung

general rate · Gemeindesteuer *f* die auf dem jährlich geschätzten Wert des unbeweglichen Eigentums der Gemeindebewohner aufbaut

general rate · Distriktratsteuer *f* [*in England*]

general region, generic region · regionaler Raumtyp *m*

general register office, central statistical office · statistisches Zentralbüro *n*

general requirements [*General conditions, amendments, and supplements to general conditions, special conditions, and alternates are grouped together under this title*] · allgemeine Auflagen *f pl*

general reserve for bad debts, general bad debt allowance · Pauschalwertberichtigung *f* auf Forderungen

general residential area, general residential territory, general housing area, general housing territory, general residence area, general residence territory · allgemeines Wohn(ungs)gebiet *n*, WA [*Ein vorwiegend zum Wohnen bestimmtes Gebiet*]

general residuary devisee · Hauptrestvermächtnisnehmer *m* von Land

general restraint of trade · allgemeine Beschränkung *f* der Gewerbefreiheit, allgemeine Einschränkung der Gewerbefreiheit

general right, general power · allgemeine Befugnis *f*, allgemeines Recht *n*

general right of appointment, general power of disposition, general right of disposition, general power of appointment [*It enables the appointor to make an appointment in favour of any person, including himself*] · allgemeine Verfügungsbefugnis *f*, allgemeine Bestimmungsbefugnis, allgemeines Verfügungsrecht *n*, allgemeines Bestimmungsrecht, Verfügungsbefugnis zugunsten jedes Beliebigen, Verfügungsrecht zugunsten jedes Beliebigen, Bestimmungsbefugnis zugunsten jedes Beliebigen, Bestimmungsrecht zugunsten jedes Beliebigen [*Vermögen*]

general right of appointment under the statute of uses, general legal power of appointment, general legal right of appointment, general power of appointment under the statute of uses · allgemeine Befugnis *f* an einem bestimmten Vermögen Nutzung zu erklären, allgemeines Recht *n* an einem bestimmten Vermögen Nutzung zu erklären

general right of disposition → general right of appointment

general right of ownership (of property), general title (of right) · allgemeines (subjektives) Eigentumsrecht *n*, allgemeiner (Rechts)Titel *m*

general (right of) pre-emption · allgemeines Vorkaufsrecht *n*

general rule · Regulativgewalt *f*

general rule · Allgemeinregel *f*

general rules · Rechtsprechungsregeln *f pl*

general serviceability, public utility, public usefulness, public serviceability, general utility, general usefulness · Gemeinnützigkeit *f*

general site equation → general equation of location

general site theory, general theory of locations, general theory of sites, general location(al) theory · allgemeine Standorttheorie *f*, allgemeine Lagetheorie

(general) (standing) rules of court, court (practice) rules, procedural code, code of (court) procedure, (court) procedure code, rules of (court) practice, rules of (court) procedure · Prozeßregeln *f pl*, Prozeßordnung *f*, Gerichtsverfahrensregeln, Gerichtsverfahrensordnung, (gerichtliche) Verfahrensregeln, (gerichtliche) Verfahrensordnung

general statute, legislative act, legislative law, legislative statute, session act, session statute, resolve act; slip law, session law [*USA*]; public act, public law, public statute, general act, general law · allgemeines Gesetz *n* [*In den Gliedstaaten der USA erscheinen die Gesetze nach ihrer Verabschiedung zunächst als „slip laws", die am Ende einer Sitzungs-*

general steward — geographic(al) region

periode der Legislative chronologisch zu den "session laws" zusammengefaßt werden]

general steward · Meier *m* [*Verwalter einer Grundherrschaft*]

general steward of a (Roman) villa, vilicus [*Latin*]; Roman manorial officer · römischer Herrengutverwalter *m*, römischer Frongutverwalter

general sub(-contractor) · Generalnachunternehmer *m*, Generalsubunternehmer, Generalunterunternehmer; Generalunterakkordant *m* [*Schweiz*]

(general) summons for directions, omnibus summons · (Prozeß)Ladung *f* für mehrere Zwischenanträge

general surveyor · Generalinspektor *m*

general systems theory · allgemeine Systemtheorie *f*

general (technical) spec(ification)(s) · allgemeine technische Vorschrift(en) *f (pl)*, ATV

general (technical) spec(ification)(s) for construction work · allgemeine technische Vorschrift(en) *f (pl)* für Bauleistungen

general theory · allgemeine Theorie *f*

general theory of Keynes · keynesianische Theorie *f*

general theory of locations, general theory of sites, general location(al) theory, general site theory · allgemeine Standorttheorie *f*

general theory of sites, general location(al) theory, general site theory, general theory of locations · allgemeine Standorttheorie *f*

general theory of (the) state · allgemeine Staatslehre *f*

general title (of right), general right of ownership (of property) · allgemeines (subjektives) Eigentumsrecht *n*, allgemeiner (Rechts)Titel *m*

general underwriter · Generalübernehmer *m*, Gesamtübernehmer

general utility, general usefulness, general serviceability, public utility, public usefulness, public serviceability · Gemeinnützigkeit *f*

general verdict · gewöhnliches Verdikt *n*, gewöhnlicher Geschworenenspruch *m*, gewöhnlicher Spruch der Geschworenen

general works council · Gesamtbetriebsrat *m*

general youth representation · Gesamtjugendvertretung *f*

generating globe · Hilfskugel *f* [*Zur Verdeutlichung kartographischer Abbildungen*]

generation game · Erzeugungsspiel *n*

generative growth · gesamtwirtschaftliches Wachstum *n*

generator of movement, traffic generator · Verkehrserzeuger *m*

generic region · Gattungsraum *m*

generic region, general region · regionaler Raumtyp *m*

genetic mapping · genetische Kartierung *f*

genime wed; capiat vadium [*Latin*] · Viehpfändungsakt *m*

gentleman farm · Rittergut *n*

gentleman farmer · Rittergutbesitzer *m*

gentlemen of the law, leisured people · grundbesitzender Herrenstand *m*

gentlemen('s) agreement · Frühstückskartell *n*, bindende Absprache *f* [*ohne Schriftform*]

gentry · niederer Adel *m*

genuine decision · Entscheid(ung) *m*,(f) von Grund auf

genuine link · sinnvoller Anknüpfungspunkt *m*

geochorological location · Lagebeziehung *f*, geochorologische Lage *f*

geoeconomy · Geoökonomie *f*

geographers' meeting · Geographentag *m*

geographic(al) area, geographic(al) territory · geographisches Gebiet *n*

geographic(al) basic map · geographische Grundkarte *f*

geographic(al) cluster · geographische gedrängte Mittelpunkte *mpl*

geographic(al) constraint [*river; flood plain; quarry, etc.*] · geographischer Zwang *m*

geographic(al) entity · Individium *n* [*nach Ritter*]

geographic(al) ethnography · geographische Völkerkunde *f*

(geographic(al)) location · (geographische) Lage *f*

geographic(al) mobility · geographische Mobilität *f*, geographische Beweglichkeit

geographic(al) physical conditions of the earth's surface in their coherent interrelation, natural coherent interrelation · Naturzusammenhang *m* [*nach Ritter*]

geographic(al) price discrimination · geographische Preisabstufung *f*

geographic(al) region, landscape · Landschaft *f*

geographic(al) space · geographischer Raum *m*

geographic(al) territory, geographic(al) area · geographisches Gebiet *n*

geographic(al) theory · Geographietheorie *f*

geographic(al) work area [*of a firm*] · Auftragseinzugsgebiet *n*

geography of cities, town geography, city geography, urban geography, geography of towns · Stadtgeographie *f*, Städtegeographie

geography of country settlements, rural settlement geography, country settlement geography, geography of rural settlements · ländliche (An)Sied(e)lungsgeographie *f*

geography of enterprise, geography of undertaking · Unternehmensgeographie *f*

geography of rural settlements, geography of country settlements, rural settlement geography, country settlement geography · ländliche (An)Sied(e)lungsgeographie *f*

geography of settlement(s), geography of settling, settlement geography · (An)Sied(e)lungsgeographie *f*, Besied(e)lungsgeographie *f*

geography of settling, settlement geography, geography of settlement(s) · (An)Sied(e)lungsgeographie *f*, Besied(e)lungsgeographie *f*

geography of towns, geography of cities, town geography, city geography, urban geography · Stadtgeographie *f*, Städtegeographie

geography of transport(ation), transport(ation) geography · Verkehrsgeographie *f*

geography of urban land use · städtische Landnutzungsgeographie *f*

geological basic map · geologische Grundkarte *f*

geological map · geologische Karte *f*

geological mapping · geologisches Kartieren *n*

geological map series · geologisches Kartenwerk *n*

geometrical shape · geometrische Form *f*, geometrische Gestalt *f*

geometry of environment, environmental geometry · Umweltgeometrie *f*

geometry of graphs · Diagrammgeometrie *f*, Schaubildgeometrie

geomorphology · Morphologie *f* der Erdoberfläche

geonomic space · geonomischer Raum *m*

geonomie · Geonomie *f* [*Exakte Naturwissenschaft von der Erde und ihren kosmischen Beziehungen*]

geonomist · Geonom *m* [*Ein in Forschung und Praxis der Raumplanung qualifizierter Fachmann*]

geotopological location · geotopologische Lage *f*

geriatric clinic · Altenpflegeheim *n*

(German) Award Rules for Building and Construction Work, (German) Federal Contract Procedure in the Building and Construction Industry · Verdingungsordnung *f* für Bauleistungen, VOB *f*

German Civil Code, German Code of Civil Law · Bürgerliches Gesetzbuch *n*, BGB [*Bundesrepublik Deutschland*]

German Civil Procedure · deutsches Zivilprozeßrecht *n*

German conversion (of the Reichsmark obligations into DM on the basis 10:1) · Währungsreform *f* [*Bundesrepublik Deutschland 1948*]

German Federal Building Law, German Federal Construction Law, German Federal Building Act, German Federal Construction Act, German Federal Building Statute, German Federal Construction Statute · Bundesbaugesetz *n*, BBauG [*Bundesrepublik Deutschland*]

German Federal Central Bank · Deutsche Bundesbank *f*

(German) Federal Contract Procedure in the Building and Construction Industry, (German) Award Rules for Building and Construction Work · Verdingungsordnung *f* für Bauleistungen, VOB

German federal motorway · Bundesautobahn *f* [*Bundesrepublik Deutschland*]

German Federal Motorway Administration · Bundesautobahnverwaltung *f* [*Bundesrepublik Deutschland*]

German Federal Railway Law (Brit.); German Federal Railroad Law (US) · Bundesbahngesetz *n* [*Bundesrepublik Deutschland*]

German Federation of Tenants · Deutscher Mieterbund *m*

Germanic law · germanisches Recht *n*

German indemnification · Wiedergutmachung *f* [*an den Staat Israel*]

German Integrated Bar Association [*It is set up by statute*] · Bundesrechtsanwaltkammer *f* [*Bundesrepublik Deutschland*]

German Lawyers Bar Association · Deutscher Anwaltverein *m*

German Patent Office · Deutsches Patentamt *n*

to get, to work, to win, to extract · abbauen [*Mineralien*]

to get again, to obtain again, to recover, to win back, to regain, to collect, to get renewed possession of · zurückerhalten, wiedererlangen, wiedererhalten, zurückgewinnen, zurückbekommen

to get renewed possession of, to get again, to obtain again, to recover, to win back, to regain, to collect · zurückerhalten, wiedererlangen, wiedererhalten, zurückgewinnen, zurückbekommen

getting → getting (of soil constituents)

getting in · Einbringen *n* [*z. B. ausstehendes Treugut*]

getting (of soil constituents), working (of soil constituents), extraction (of soil constituents), winning (of soil constituents), mineral working, mineral getting, working of minerals, getting of minerals, mineral winning, winning of minerals, extraction of minerals, mineral extraction · Abbau(en) *m*, *(n)* von Bodenbestandteilen, Abbau(en) von Mineralien, Mineralienabbau, Mineralienausbeuten, Ausbeuten (von Mineralien), Ausbeuten von Bodenbestandteilen, Ausbeutung *f* (von Mineralien), Ausbeutung von Bodenbestandteilen, Mineralienausbeutung, Mineraliengewinnung, Gewinnung von Bodenbestandteilen, Gewinnung von Mineralien [*Die planmäßige Inangriffnahme einer Lagerstätte bei der Gewinnung von Lehm, Sand, Kies usw.*]

ghetto core · G(h)ettokern *m*

ghetto fringe · G(h)ettorand(gebiet) *m*, *(n)*

ghetto resident · Gettobewohner *m*, Ghettobewohner

ghost town, ghost city · Geisterstadt *f*

ghost village · Geisterdorf *n*

gift, donation · Schenkung(svertrag) *f*, *(m)*, unentgeltlicher dinglicher Vertrag [*Durch ihn wird ein bestehendes dingliches Recht von der einen auf die andere Vertragspartei übertragen*]

gifta aquae [*Latin*] [*The stream of water to a mill*] · Mühl(en)wasser *n*

gift by will, testamentary gift · testamentarische Schenkung *f*

gift causa mortis, gift in anticipation of death; donatio mortis causa, donatio post obitum [*Latin*] · Schenkung *f* auf den Todesfall, Schenkung von Todes wegen

gift inter vivos, absolute gift, irrevocable gift [*A gift made by one living person to another, as opposed to a gift by will*] · Schenkung *f* unter Lebenden

gift of land(s), land(s) gift · Landschenkung *f*

gift sub modo; donatio sub modo facto [*Latin*] · bedingte Schenkung *f*, eingeschränkte Schenkung, beschränkte Schenkung

gift tax · Schenkungssteuer *f*

gift taxation · Schenkungsbesteuerung *f*

gilda [*Latin*]; g(u)ild, company · Verband *m*, Gilde *f*

gilt-edged market [*Great Britain*] · Markt *m* für Staatsanleihen

gilt(-edged security) [*In Great Britain*] · mündelsicheres Kapitalmarktpapier *n*, mündelsicheres Wertpapier

gipsy caravan site, caravan site for gipsies · Zigeunerlager *n*

gist [*e. g. of an action*] · Kernpunkt *m* [*z. B. einer Klage*]

to (give a) bonus, to pay a bonus · sondervergüten, zulegen, zuschlagen

to give a certificate, to attest; certificare [*Latin*]; to certify, to testify in writing · bescheinigen

to give advice, to counsel, to advise, to consult · beraten

to (give a) feud → to give possession of land(s)

to give a seisin of land(s) → to give possession of land(s)

to give bail · stellen [*Kaution*]

to give by will, to dispose by will, to leave by will, to bestow by will · (testamentarisch) vermachen, letztwillig verfügen, testamentarisch verfügen, letztwillig vermachen

to give effect (to), to carry into effect · wirksam machen

to give evidence · Zeugnis ablegen

given · gesetzt [*Pfand*]

given by will, disposed by will, left by will, bestowed by will · letztwillig verfügt, letztwillig vermacht, (testamentarisch) vermacht, testamentarisch verfügt

to give notice · kündigen

to give notice, to advise, to inform, to notify · anzeigen, benachrichtigen, mitteilen, informieren

to give notice of (end of) tenancy, to give notice of termination of tenancy, to give (tenant) notice (to quit) · kündigen [*Wohnung*]

to give notification of withdrawal, to give notice of withdrawal · abmelden

given up, left (to itself), forsaken, let gone, deserted, idle, abandoned [*place*] · aufgegeben, verlassen, preisgegeben

given up, waived, disclaimed, abandoned, relinquished, renounced, remised, for-

to give oder — good discharge

saken · aufgegeben, preisgegeben, Verzicht geleistet, verzichtet, ausgeschlagen, entsagt, derelinquiert

to give oder, to part with · abgeben

to give possession of land(s), to give a seisin of land(s), to (give a) feud, to infeft, to infeoff, to enfeoff, to bestow a fee, to bestow a fief, to bestow a feud; feoffare, infeodare, infeudare [*Latin*]; to invest [*old Scots law*] · belehnen, feudal belehnen

to give power to do something, to empower, to enable · ermächtigen, erteilen eines Rechtes, erteilen einer Befugnis

giver, donor · Geber *m*

giver of an allowance, donor of an allowance · Zuschußgeber *m*

to give (tenant) notice (to quit), to give notice of (end of) tenancy, to give notice of termination of tenancy · kündigen [*Wohnung*]

to give up, to leave (to itself), to forsake, to let go, to abandon, to desert [*place*] · aufgeben, preisgeben, verlassen

to give up, to renounce, to disclaim, to abandon, to relinquish, to remise, to forsake [*To relinquish with intent of never again resuming one's right or interest*] · aufgeben, preisgeben, Verzicht leisten, verzichten, ausschlagen, entsagen, derelinquieren

giving a certificate, attesting, attestation, certifying, testifying in writing · Bescheinigen *n*

giving (contractor) possession of (the) site · Baustellenübergabe *f*

giving of possession of the site · Übergeben *n* der Baustelle

giving of security, giving of surety · Sicherheitsleistung *f*

giving over the official guardianship, parting with the official guardianship · Abgabe *f* der Amtsvormundschaft

giving up, renouncing, relinquishing, forsaking, abandoning · Aufgeben *n*, Preisgeben *n*, Verzichten *n*

giving up, leaving (a thing) (to itself), abandoning, letting go, abandoning, deserting · Aufgeben *n*, Verlassen *n* [*Gebäude; Betrieb; Flußbett usw.*]

Glanvillian gage · Glanvill'sches Pfand *n*

glass insurance · Glasversicherung *f*

glebne adscriptus [*Latin*]; pr(a)edial slave · Grundhörige *m* [*Im Mittelalter zwischen Freien und Leibeigenen stehend*]

global control · Globallenkung *f*

global growth · Globalwachstum *n*

global level · Globalebene *f*

global planning · Globalplanung *f*

glossator · Glossator *m*

goal-conscious · normzielbewußt, oberzielbewußt

goal (of policy), target goal, policy goal · Zielnorm *f*, Oberziel *n*, übergeordnetes Ziel

goal (of policy) conflict, target goal conflict, policy goal conflict · Ziel(norm)konflikt *m*, Oberzielkonflikt, Konflikt übergeordneter Ziele

goal (of policy) formation, target goal formation, policy goal formation · Ziel(norm)bildung *f*, Oberzielbildung

goal (of policy) research, policy goal research, target goal research · Ziel(norm)forschung *f*, Oberzielforschung

goals achievement matrix, GAM · Zielerfüllungsmatrix *f*

goals research · Zielforschung *f*

to go to court · vor Gericht gehen

go-go fund · Fonds *m* mit dem Ziel überdurchschnittlichen Wachstums, Mittel *f* mit dem Ziel überdurchschnittlichen Wachstums

going concern · bestehendes Handelsgeschäft *n*

going value · Betriebswert *m*

gold clause [*Condition that payment is to be made in gold*] · Gold(münz)klausel *f*

gold coast · Wohlstandsquartier *n*

gold exchange standard · Devisenkernwährung *f*

gold mortgage · Goldhypothek *f* [*mit Goldmünzklausel*]

golf-link · Golfplatz *m*

good, valid in law · rechtsgültig

good, marketable, clear, sal(e)able, perfect · frei, vollgültig [*(Rechts)Titel*]

good against all the world · lückenlos [*Nachweis eines Klägertitels*]

good balance · Saldo *m* zu eigenen Gunsten

good conduct · Wohnverhalten *n*

good-conduct certificate · Leumundszeugnis *n*

good conscience · Redlichkeit *f*

good consideration · nicht vermögenswertes Interesse *n* an einem Vertragsabschluß

good discharge · wirksame Entlastung *f*

good equitable title · gültiger (Rechts)Titel *m* nach Billigkeit(srecht)

good faith, loyalty and faith, honesty, sincerity; bona fides [*Latin*] · Aufrichtigkeit *f*, Ehrlichkeit *f*, guter Glaube *m*, Treu' *f* und Glauben *m*

good holding title · (Rechts)Titel *m* wie er unter den üblichen Einschränkungen nachgewiesen werden kann

(good) lease(hold) title → term of years

good manners · gute Sitten *fpl*

good of the community, public interests, common well-being, general good, prosperity of the community, public welfare, public weal, public good, public necessity, public convenience, common welfare, common weal, common good, common necessity, common convenience · Gemeinwohl *n*, öffentliches Wohl, öffentliches Interesse *n*, allgemeines Wohl, allgemeines Interesse, Allgemeinwohl, öffentliche Belange *mpl*

good root of title, good title root · gute (Rechts)Titelwurzel *f*

goods, commodities · Güter *npl*, Waren *fpl*

(goods and) chattels, chattels personal, mov(e)able properties · bewegliche Güter *npl*, Mobilien *fpl*, Mobiliar *n*, bewegliche Sachen *fpl*, bewegliche Gegenstände *mpl*

goods distribution · Güterverteilung *f*

goods enabling one to overcome time · Zeitüberwindungsgüter *n pl*

good sense · gesunder Menschenverstand *m*

goods handling, handling of commodities, commodities handling, handling of goods · Güterumschlag *m*, Warenumschlag

goods market, commodity market · Gütermarkt *m*, Warenmarkt

goods market equilibrium, commodities market equilibrium · Gütermarktgleichgewicht *n*

goods of the first order, consumers' goods, consumption goods [*These goods satisfy wants directly*] · Verkaufsgüter *npl*

good title · guter (Rechts)Titel *m*

good title root, good root of title · gute (Rechts)Titelwurzel *f*

good-until-cancelled order, G.T.C. order, open order · Auftrag *m* auf Widerruf gültig [*Börse*]

goodwill · Wohlwollen *n*

goodwill · Kundschaftswert *m*, Firmenwert, Geschäftswert, Organisationswert [*Die Summe der Eigenschaften eines* — *Unternehmens, deren Wert von den persönlichen Einschätzungen eines jeden von diesem Unternehmen abhängt*]

goodwill sale, sale of goodwill · Verkauf *m* der Kundschaft (eines Geschäftes)

to go out to tender, to obtain tenders, to invite tenders, to tender out, to invite offers, to invite bids; to invite (bid) proposals (US), to put out to tender · ausschreiben, (Angebote) einholen, auffordern zur Angebotsabgabe

go-slow, working to rule [*A form of industrial action by workers taking the form of working more slowly than usual, i.e., reducing output by paying exaggerated attention to rules relating to working conditions*] · Dienst *m* nach Vorschrift

Gothic law, law of the Goths; lex gothica [*Latin*] [*First promulgated in writing A. D. 466*] · gotisches Recht *n*

to go to law, to carry on a (law)suit, to bring into ligitation, to engage in litigation, to claim by action, to dispute by action, to litigate [*Latin: litigare*] · prozessieren, einen Rechtsstreit austragen, einen Prozeß anhängig machen, rechtshängig werden lassen

governing body, government(al) body · Regierungsorgan *n*

governing branch · regierender Zweigverein *m* [*Gewerkverein in England*]

governing law · anwendbares Recht *n*

governing mayor · regierender Bürgermeister *m*

governing power, government · regierende Gewalt *f* in einem Staat

government (Brit.); administration (US) · Regierung *f*

government (US) · Staatsapparat *m*, Staat *m* (im Sinne von Staatswesen)

governmental · hoheitlich

government(al) act(ion) · Regierungsakt *m*, Regierungshandlung *f*

government(al) agency · Regierungsstelle *f*

government(al) annuity · Regierungsannuität *f*

government(al) body, governing body · Regierungsorgan *n*

government(al) boundary · Regierungsgrenze *f*

government(al) character · hoheitlicher Charakter *m*

government(al) contract, contract of government · Herrschaftsvertrag *m*

government(al) corporation (US) · öffentliche Gesellschaft *f*

government(al) design — grantee

government(al) design · Regierungsentwurf *m*

government(al) gazette · Regierungsamtsblatt *n*

governmental interest, national interest · Staatsinteresse *n*

government(al) jurist, government(al) lawyer · Regierungsjurist *m*

government(al) land · Regierungsland *n*

government(al) official, government(al) officer · Regierungsbeamte *m*

government(al) power · Regierungsgewalt *f*

government(al) quarter · Regierungsviertel *n*

government(al) superintendence, government(al) supervision · Regierungsaufsicht *f,* Regierungsüberwachung *f*

government by rule of law, law state · Rechtsstaat *m*

government contract, contract of adhesion, contract by regulation, adhesion contract [*As opposed to a private contract*] · (Beschaffungs)Vertrag *m* mit einer Regierung, Vertrag durch Beitritt

government district · Regierungsbezirk *m*

government in business · staatseigener Betrieb *m*

government-in-exile · Exilregierung *f*

government mortgage bank · Landeskreditkasse *f*

Government Operations Committee [*USA*] · Senatsausschuß *m* für Verwaltungsfragen

government proprietorship, government (general) ownership, government ownership (of property) · Regierungseigentum *n*

government security · Staatspapier *n*

government stock · Staatsobligation *f,* Staatsschuldverschreibung *f*

Government stock, British fund [*There are short-dated stocks (up to five years until maturity), medium-dated stocks (between five and ten years until maturity) and long-dated stocks (over ten years until maturity)*] · Staatsschuldverschreibung *f,* Staatsobligation *f* [*Ein festverzinsliches Wertpapier der britischen Regierung oder der verstaatlichten Industrien*]

government stock holder, holder of government stock · Gläubiger *m* einer staatlichen Darleh(e)n(s)schuld

governor · Gouverneur *m*

governor · Chef *m* in der Exekutive

governor-general · Generalgouverneur *m*

governors · Verwaltungsrat *m*

gown · Talar *m*

grace day, day of grace · Respekttag *m*

grace year · tilgungsfreies Jahr *n*

grade (US); form (Brit.) · Schuljahrgang *m*

graded pension · abgestufte Pension *f*

gradient of density, density gradient · Dichtegradient *m*

graduated freight rate · Staffel(fracht)tarif *m*

graduated house-tax · Hausklassensteuer *f*

Gr(a)eco-Roman private law in Egypt · griechisch-römisches Privatrecht *n* in Ägypten

graft (US); financial bribe, bribe money; "palm oil" (Brit.) · Bestechungsgeld *n,* Schmiergeld

grain farming, grain husbandry, grain tillage · Felderwirtschaft *f,* Körnerwirtschaft [*Das dem Ackerbau dienende Land wird nur zum Anbau von Getreide und sonstigen Körnerfrüchten verwendet*]

grain tithe, tithe of grain, corn tithe, tithe of corn (Brit.) · Getreidezehnt *m,* Kornzehnt [*altdeutsch: Kornzehent, Kornzehend*]

grammatical construction, literal interpretation, literal construction, grammatical interpretation · Literalauslegung *f,* Literaldeutung

granary rent, rent for granary · Bodengeld *n,* Bodenmiete *f,* Trockenbodengeld, Trockenbodenmiete, Kornbodengeld, Kornbodenmiete

grand duke · Großherzog *m*

grand jury · Anklagejury *f*

grand serjeanty → (honorary service of) grand serjeanty

grand sum, (sum) total · Gesamtsumme *f*

grand theft · schwerer Diebstahl *m*

to grant · überlassen

to grant [*permission*] · erteilen [*Genehmigung*]

to grant · einräumen [*Kredit*]

grant deed, deed of grant · Überlassungsurkunde *f*

grant deed, deed of grant · Bewilligungsurkunde *f* [*Grundstückskaufvertrag*]

granted land · überlassener Boden *m,* überlassenes Land *n*

grantee [*One to whom a grant is made*] · Überlassungsempfänger *m*

grantee, feoffee · Belehnte m, (feudaler) Leh(e)n(s)gutempfänger, Beliehene

grantee of a (right-of-)way · Wegerechtempfänger m, Durchgangsrechtempfänger

grant(-in-aid) · verlorener Zuschuß m

granting · (dingliches) Überlassen n

granting act(ion), act(ion) of granting · Überlassungsakt m, Überlassungshandlung f

granting (free) legal aid, counselling a legally-aided party · Armenvertretung f [(Rechts)Anwalt]

to grant (land) out in tenancy · verleihen [Land]

grant of a privilege · Privilegierung f

grant of estate → grant of (real) estate

grant of judicature · Justizhoheit f

grant of land(s), grant of (real) estate, grant of (real) property, grant of realty, (real) estate grant, (real) property grant, realty grant, land(s) grant · Landverleihung f, Landvergabe f, Landüberlassung, Bodenverleihung, Bodenvergabe, Bodenüberlassung, Flächenvergabe, Flächenüberlassung, Flächenverleihung, Landschenkung, Bodenschenkung, Flächenschenkung

grant of license, grant of licence · Lizenzverteilung

grant of permission · (Genehmigungs)Erteilung f, Erlaubniserteilung

grantor; cedent [Scots law]; assignor, assigner [A person who assigns a claim, right, property, etc.] · Abtreter m, Geber, Zedent m

grantor, (ab)alienor [He who makes a grant, transfer of title, conveyance, or (ab)alienation] · Veräußerer m

grantor, donor; concessor [In old English law] [The person by whom a grant is made] · Überlassende m, Überlasser

grantor → liege-lord

grantor [easement] · Besteller m

grantor of an authority; mandator [Latin]; principal (constituent), employer, donor of an authority · Vollmachtgeber m, Bevollmächtiger, Vertretene [Jemand der im Rechtsgeschäft zu eigenem Nutzen und auf eigene Rechnung selbständig vornehmen kann, aber zu dessen Vornahme eine andere Person verwendet]

grantor of a power of attorney, donor of a power of attorney · Geber m einer gesiegelten Vollmacht

grantor of a (right-of-)way · Wegerechtgeber m, Durchgangsrechtgeber

to grant respite for a payment, to attermin, to respite a payment [To allow time for the payment of a debt] · stunden, Zahlungsaufschub bewilligen, Zahlungsfrist gewähren, Zahlungsfrist bewilligen, Zahlungsaufschub gewähren

grant to uses [The common grant with uses superadded, which has become the favorite mode of transferring realty in England] · Überlassung f mit Nutzung

grant under seal · (dingliche) Überlassung f unter Siegel

graph · Graph m

Graphical Evaluation and Review Technique · GERT n [Ein stochastisches Netzwerkverfahren]

graphic(al) extrapolation method · graphisches Extrapolationsverfahren n

graphic(al) method · graphisches Verfahren n

graphic scale, bar scale · Linearmaßstab m, Maßstableiste f

graph theoretic(al) analysis · graphentheoretische Analyse f

graph theory, theory of graphs · Graphentheorie f

grass-cutting right, right of grass-cutting · Grasnutzungsrecht n

grassed · begrast

grass farm, grazing farm · Weidebetrieb m, Grasbetrieb

grass farming, pastoral economy, business of grazing, grazing business · Graswirtschaft f, (Vieh)Weidewirtschaft

grass field → grass land

grass ground → grass land

grass land, grass ground, grass field, pasturage, herdwick; lea [In old English law]; pastitium [Low Latin]; pasture (ground), pasture land, pasture field, pastoral ground, pastoral land, pastoral field, grazing land, grazing ground, grazing field · Weideland n, (Vieh)Weide f, Hut f, Viehweideland [Der Ort wohin das Vieh zur Weide getrieben wird]

graticule intersection · Netz(schnitt)kreuz n [Kartographie]

graticule line · geographische Netzlinie f

graticule tick · Netzmarke f

gratification, gratuity · Gratifikation f

gratuitous bailment · unentgeltliche Verwahrung f durch eine Bank

gratuitous contract, nude contract, one-sided contract, unilateral contract, contract of benevolence, deed poll, contract without consideration · einseitiger Vertrag m, Vertrag ohne Gegenleistung

gratuitous gift · Gabe *f* ohne Gegenleistung

gratuitous goods, natural goods · natürliche Güter *n pl*, Naturgüter, freie Güter [*z. B. Sonnenwärme, Wasserkraft usw.*]

gratuitous promise, promise of benevolence, promise without consideration, one-sided promise, nude promise, unilateral promise · einseitiges (Leistungs)Versprechen *n*, einseitiges Naturalversprechen, (Leistungs)Versprechen ohne Gegenleistung, Naturalversprechen ohne Gegenleistung

gratuity, gratification · Gratifikation *f*

gravel digging, gravel excavation · Auskiesung *f*

gravelly ground, gravelly land · kiesiges Gelände *n*, kiesiges Land *n*, kiesiges Terrain *n*

gravel pit · Kiesausbeute *f*, Kiesgrube *f*

gravel winning right, gravel exploitation right, gravel digging right, right to win gravel, right to dig gravel, right to take gravel, right to exploit gravel · Kiesausbeutungsrecht *n*, Kiesgewinnungsrecht

grave-yard, cemetery, burying ground, burial-ground, burial-yard · Friedhof *m*

gravity approach · Gravitationsansatz *m*

gravity model · Gravitationsmodell *n*

gray area, gray territory, grey area, grey territory · Graugebiet *n*, Zwischengebiet

gray level, grey level [*mapping*] · Graustufe *f*

gray-level mapping, grey-level mapping · Kartierung *f* mittels Graustufen, Graustufenkartierung

to graze · grasen, hüten [*Vieh*]

grazing → grazing (of cattle)

grazing act, grazing law, grazing statute · Weidegesetz *n*

grazing business, grass farming, pastoral economy, business of grazing · Graswirtschaft *f*, (Vieh)Weidewirtschaft

grazing demise → pastoral tenancy

grazing district, pastur(ag)e district, pastoral district · (Vieh)Weidebezirk *m*

grazing farm, grass farm · Weidebetrieb *m*, Grasbetrieb

grazing holding, pastur(ag)e holding, pastoral holding · (Vieh)Weidegrundstück *n*

grazing land, grazing ground, grazing field, grass land, grass ground, grass field, pasturage, herdwick; lea [*In old English law*]; pastitium [*Low Latin*]; pasture (ground), pasture land, pasture field, pastoral ground, pastoral land, pastoral field · Weideland *n*, (Vieh)Weide *f*, Hut *f*, Viehweideland [*Der Ort wohin das Vieh zur Weide getrieben wird*]

grazing lease(hold) → pastoral tenancy

grazing management · Weidebewirtschaftung *f*

grazing (of cattle), pastur(ag)e, pasturing (of cattle); pascuagium, pascuage [*Low Latin*] [*The action or occupation of pasturing*] · Grasung *f*, Hütung, Hut(ung) *f*, Weidegang *m*, (Vieh)Weide *f*, Hutweide

grazing right, shack, common pastur(ag)e, commonage, common right; jus pascendi, communis pasturae, herbagium [*Latin*]; (right of) pastur(ag)e, (right of) grazing, pastoral right, herbage · Angerrecht *n*, Hütungsrecht, Atzung *f*, Ätzung, (Vieh)Weiderecht, (Vieh)Weideberechtigung

grazing tenancy → pastoral tenancy

grazing tenure → pastoral tenancy

great baron(r)y, great baronage; great baronady [*obsolete*] [*The body of great barons collectively*] · Großbaronie *f*, Großfreiherrentum *n*

Great Chamberlain · Großkämmerer *m*

great city dweller, big city dweller, great city inhabitant, big city inhabitant · Großstadteinwohner *m*, Großstadtbewohner

great city life, big city life · Großstadtleben *n*

great city population, big city population · Großstadtbevölkerung *f*, großstädtische Bevölkerung

Greater Berlin, Outer Berlin, metropolitan Berlin · Großberlin *n*

Greater Breslau, Outer Breslau, metropolitan Breslau · Groß-Breslau *n*

Greater London, Metropolitan London, Outer London · Außenlondon *n*, Großlondon *n*

great fee (tenure), great (feodal) tenure, great fief, great tenure of demesne, (tenure of) serjeanty · Kronleh(e)n *n*, Leh(e)n unmittelbar unter dem König (oder der Königin)

great (land)owner, large (land) proprietor, great (land) proprietor, large (land)owner · Großgrundeigentümer *m*, Großgrundeigner

great (land) possessor, large (land) possessor · Großgrundbesitzer *m*

great tithe, large tithe, coarse tithe [*A chief predial tithe, as corn, hay, wood and fruit*] · großer Zehnt *m*

great village, big village · Großdorf *n*

greed for land, land-hunger · Landhunger *m*

to green — gross density

to green · begrünen

green → (village) green

green area, landscape area, green land · Grünfläche f, begrünte Fläche

green area, landscape territory, green territory, landscape area · Grüngebiet n

green area network, network of green areas · Grünnetz n

green areas and green facilities conducive to public health · sanitäres Grün n [*Alle Grünflächen und Grünanlagen, die auf die Gesundheit des Menschen fördernden Einfluß haben*]

green areas and green facilities for decorative purposes · dekoratives Grün n

green balk of unploughed turf, untilled green strip of land, unploughed (turf) balk, ridge · Rainbalken m

green belt, belt of green · Grüngürtel m [*Von Eugen Faßbender 1898 als „Volksring" und ab 1905 als „Wald- und Wiesen-Gürtel" bezeichnet. Jetzt wird die Benennung „Grüngürtel" allgemein verwendet*]

greenbelt area, greenbelt territory · Grüngürtelgebiet n

green hamlet, plaza hamlet · Angerweiler m, Platzweiler

green land, green area, landscape area · Grünfläche f, begrünte Fläche

green land board, green area board, landscape area board · Grünflächenamt n

green land committee, green area committee, landscape area committee · Grünflächenausschuß m

green land conservation, green area conservation, landscape area conservation · Grünflächenerhaltung f, Grünflächenpflege f

green land development, green area development, landscape area development · Grünflächenbau m

green (land) planning · Grünplanung f, Grünflächenplanung

green (open) space · Grünraum m, grünbestimmter Freiraum

green planner · Grünplaner m

green strip · Grünstreifen m

green territory, landscape area, green area, landscape territory · Grüngebiet n

green village, plaza village · Angerdorf n, Platzdorf

green wedge · Grünkeil m

green zone · Grünzone f

grey area, grey territory, gray area, gray territory · Graugebiet n, Zwischengebiet

grey level, gray level [*mapping*] · Graustufe f

grey-level mapping, gray-level mapping · Kartierung f mittels Graustufen, Graustufenkartierung

grey territory, gray area, gray territory, grey area · Graugebiet n, Zwischengebiet

griblet · Grundkartengraudruck m

grid (iron) pattern, grid (iron) scheme, grid (iron) plan, grid (iron) layout, chessboard pattern, chessboard scheme, chessboard plan, chessboard layout, checkerboard pattern, checkerboard plan, checkerboard scheme, checkerboard layout · Gitternetzmuster n, Schachbrettmuster, Gitternetzschema n, Schachbrettschema, Gitternetzgrundriß m, Schachbrettgrundriß

grid of streets · Stadtstraßengitter n

grid reference · Gittermeldung f [*Kartographie*]

grid sampling · Gitter-Stichprobenverfahren n [*Statistik*]

grid square · Rasterquadrat n

grievous bodily harm · schwere Körperverletzung f

grinding toll, suit and grist, grinding fee, fee for grinding, toll paid for grinding, multure; molitura, multura [*Latin*] · Mahlgeld n, Mahlzins m, Mahlgebühr f

gritting duty · Streupflicht f

grocer · Spezereihändler m

gross annual income, gross yearly income, annual gross income, yearly gross income · Bruttojahreseinkommen n, Jahresbruttoeinkommen

gross annual salary, gross yearly salary · Bruttojahresgehalt n, Jahresbruttogehalt

gross annual value, gross yearly value, annual gross value, yearly gross value · Bruttoertragswert m [*Liegenschaft*]

gross base area, gross (ground(-))plan area · Brutto-Grundrißfläche f

gross (building) (land) area, gross (building) land · Brutto(bau)boden m, Brutto(bau)land n, Brutto(bau)fläche f [*Fläche, die im Flächennutzungsplan zur Bebauung ausgewiesen ist. Das Brutto(bau)land umfaßt das Nettobauland und die Flächen für die Gemeingebrauchs- und Gemeinbedarfseinrichtungen*]

gross cash proceeds · Brutto-Barertrag m

gross delay · langer Verzug m

gross density · Bruttodichte f

gross density gradient · Bruttodichtegefälle *n*

gross density of housing, gross residential density, gross housing density · Bruttowohndichte *f*, Bruttoarealdichte

gross density of population, gross population density · Bruttobevölkerungsdichte *f*, Brutto(be)sied(e)lungsdichte, Bruttovolksdichte, Bruttoansied(e)lungsdichte, Bruttomenschenausstattung *f* einer Fläche [*Anzahl der Einwohner/ha Bruttobauland*]

gross domestic product · Bruttoinlandsprodukt *n*, BIP

gross figures principle [*All figures entered in the budget must be gross figures*] · Bruttoprinzip *n*, Bruttogrundsatz *m*

gross floor area, gross floor space, total floor area, total floor space · Bruttogeschoßfläche *f*, Bruttoetagenfläche, Bruttostockwerkfläche [*Summe aller Geschoßflächen ohne Boden und Keller. Wände, Flure und nichtbewohnbare Nebenräume der Vollgeschosse sind mit einbegriffen*]

gross gain, gross profit · Bruttoprofit *m*, Bruttogewinn *m*

gross (ground(-))plan area, gross base area · Brutto-Grundrißfläche *f*

gross housing density, gross density of housing, gross residential density · Bruttowohndichte *f*, Bruttoarealdichte

gross housing land (area), gross area, gross residential land (area) · Brutto-Wohn(ungs)boden *m*, Brutto-Wohn(ungs)(bau)fläche *f*, Brutto-Wohn(ungs)(bau)land *n* [*Summe aller Baugrundstücksflächen, die mit Wohnhäusern bebaut sind oder bebaut werden dürfen, zuzüglich der anteiligen Flächen für Folgeeinrichtungen der Wohnbebauung*]

gross income · Bruttoeinkommen *n*, Roheinkommen

gross income multiplier · Bruttoeinkommenvervielfältiger *m*, Roheinkommenvervielfältiger

gross in-migration · Bruttozuwanderung *f*

gross interest · Bruttozinsen *f*

gross migration · Bruttowanderung *f*

gross monthly rent · Bruttomonatsmiete *f*, Monatsbruttomiete

gross negligence, gross carelessness, gross negligent conduct, gross careless conduct, gross reckless conduct, gross recklessness [*The intentional failure to perform a manifest duty in reckless disregard of the consequences as affecting the life or property of another*] · grobe Fahrlässigkeit *f*, grobe Nachlässigkeit, grobe Leichtsinnigkeit, grobe Leichtfertigkeit

gross plan area → gross (ground(-))plan area

gross population density, gross density of population · Bruttobevölkerungsdichte *f*, Brutto(be)sied(e)lungsdichte, Bruttovolksdichte, Bruttoansied(e)lungsdichte, Bruttomenschenausstattung *f* einer Fläche [*Anzahl der Einwohner/ha Bruttobauland*]

gross possible income [*The total rent or income obtainable from a property if all units and space are occupied and all rents paid*] · maximale Bruttoeinnahme *f*, maximale Roheinnahme

gross price, long price · Bruttopreis *m*

gross proceeds · Bruttoerlös *m*

gross profit, gross gain · Bruttoprofit *m*, Bruttogewinn *m*

gross recklessness, gross negligence, gross carelessness, gross negligent conduct, gross careless conduct, gross reckless conduct [*The intentional failure to perform a manifest duty in reckless disregard of the consequences as affecting the life or property of another*] · grobe Fahrlässigkeit *f*, grobe Nachlässigkeit, grobe Leichtsinnigkeit, grobe Leichtfertigkeit

gross rent → gross (residential) rent

gross rent less heating and hot water cost(s) → gross (residential) rent less heating and hot water cost(s)

gross rent multiplier · Bruttomietenvervielfältiger *m*, Rohmietenvervielfältiger

gross residential density, gross housing density, gross density of housing · Bruttowohndichte *f*, Bruttoarealdichte

gross residential land (area) → gross housing land (area)

gross (residential) rent · Brutto(wohnungs)miete *f*, Gesamt(wohnungs)miete

gross (residential) rent less heating and hot water cost(s) · Kalt(wohnungs)miete *f*

gross return, gross yield · Rohrendite *f*, Bruttorendite

gross return multiplier, gross yield multiplier · Rohrenditevervielfältiger, Bruttorenditevervielfältiger

gross value · Bruttowert *m*

gross value added · Bruttowertschöpfung *f* [*zu Marktpreisen*]

gross variance · Bruttoabweichung *f*, ganze Schwankung [*Kostenelement*]

(gross) working capital, (total) current assets, total quick assets [*The term "working capital" has two meanings. It* may refer to the total current assets or to the difference between current assets and current liabilities] · Umlaufvermögen n, Umlaufmittel f

gross yearly income, annual gross income, yearly gross income, gross annual income · Bruttojahreseinkommen n, Jahresbruttoeinkommen

gross yearly salary, gross annual salary · Bruttojahresgehalt n, Jahresbruttogehalt

gross yearly value, annual gross value, yearly gross value, gross annual value · Bruttoertragswert m [Liegenschaft]

gross yield, gross return · Rohrendite f, Bruttorendite

gross yield multiplier, gross return multiplier · Rohrenditevervielfältiger, Bruttorenditevervielfältiger

ground, terrain · Gelände n, Terrain n

ground, reason, cause · Grund m

ground area, area of ground, terrain area, area of terrain · Geländefläche f, Terrainfläche

groundbook → land register

groundcheck · Feldvergleich m [Luftphotogrammetrie. Arbeitsvorgang vom Objekt zum Bild und vom Bild zum Objekt]

ground conditions · Baugrundverhältnisse f

ground cover · Bodenbedeckung f

ground fill(ing) · Boden(auf)füllung f, Gelände(auf)füllung, Boden(auf)schüttung, Gelände(auf)schüttung

ground form, form of ground, terrain form, form of terrain · Geländeform f, Terrainform

ground game · Bodenwild n

ground game law, ground game act, ground game statute · Bodenwildgesetz n

ground landlord [The absolute property in or fee-simple of the land belongs to him] · absoluter Landbesitzer m, uneingeschränkter Landbesitzer, unbeschränkter Landbesitzer, unbedingter Landbesitzer, unbegrenzter Landbesitzer

ground level street, surface street · ebenerdige Stadtstraße f

ground monument · Bodendenkmal n [Eine von Menschen geschaffene und zum festen Bestandteil des Bodens gewordene nicht bauliche Anlage von kulturgeschichtlicher Bedeutung]

(ground-)plan [Two-dimensional graphic representation of the design, location, and dimensions of the project, or parts thereof, seen in a horizontal plane viewed from above] · Grundriß m

ground reinstatement, reinstatement of ground on completion (of work(s)) · Wiederherstellung f des früheren Geländezustandes, Wiederherstellung des vorherigen Geländezustandes [Nach Beendigung der Bauarbeiten]

ground rent, (true) rent of land(s), (true) rent of ground, land(s) rent [It issues out of the land, as a compensation for the possession during the term] · Bodenrente f, Landrente, Grund(stücks)rente

ground rent, land(s) rent, rent of ground, rent of land(s) [It is an acknowledgment made by the tenant to the lord] · Bodenzins m, Landzins, Grund(stücks)zins

grounds of complaint and defence · Gründe m pl und Gegengründe

ground strip, strip of terrain, terrain strip, strip of ground · Geländestreifen m, Terrainstreifen

ground value portion, land value share, ground value share, land value portion · Bodenwertanteil m, Landwertanteil, Grund(stücks)wertanteil

ground-water law, law of ground-water · Grundwasserrecht n [objektiv]

ground-water map · Grundwasserkarte f

ground-water mapping · Grundwasserkartierung f

ground-water right, right to ground-water · Grundwasserrecht n [subjektiv]

ground-water supply · Grundwasserversorgung f

ground-water withdrawal, withdrawal of ground-water · Grundwasserentzug m

to group · zusammenlegen, zusammensetzen, gruppieren

group → (working) team

group account · Gruppenjahresabschluß m [Holdinggesellschaft]

group banking · Bankenverflechtung f

group city, group town · Gruppenstadt f

grouping · Einteilung f, Gruppierung [Statistik]

grouping correction, correction for grouping · Gruppierungskorrektur f [Statistik]

grouping lattice · Einteilungsgitter n, Gruppierungsgitter [Statistik]

grouping of parishes · Vereinigung f von Kirchspielen, Vereinigung von (Pfarr)Sprengeln, Vereinigung von kirchlichen Sprengeln

grouping of scattered farm(stead)s to form a village · Verdorfung f

group insurance — guarantee

group insurance · Gruppenversicherung f

group interview · Gruppenbefragung f

group of buildings, building group · Gebäudegruppe f

group of co-existing individuals · Gruppe f gleichzeitig vorhandener Individuen

group of houses, house group · Hausgruppe f, Häusergruppe

group of parishes · Kirchspielgruppe f, (Pfarr)Sprengelgruppe, kirchliche Sprengelgruppe, Parochialgruppe

group of premises · Hausstättenverband m, Anwesenverband

group of tenants, tenant group · Mieterinitiative f

group-person(ality) · Gesamtpersönlichkeit f

group practice facility · Gruppenpraxiseinrichtung f

group settlement, nucleated settlement · Gruppen(an)sied(e)lung f

to group together, to consolidate · zusammenfassen, verbinden [Klagen; Sicherheiten]

group town, group city · Gruppenstadt f

groupwork, teamwork · Gruppenarbeit f

group worker [social welfare] · Gruppenarbeiter m

to grow, to accrue · (an)wachsen, zuwachsen

grower · Pflanzer m

growing crop · Ernte f auf dem Halm, wachsende Feldfrucht f

growing of seed, seed growing · Saatzucht f

growing to, accrual, accruing, accruement, accruer, running up · Auflaufen n [Betrag]

grown out of use, disused, obsolete, antiquated · außer Gebrauch, nicht mehr verwendet

grown to · gewachsen

grown to, accumulated, accrued, run up · angewachsen, angehäuft, zugewachsen, aufgehäuft, aufgelaufen

grown to maturity, matured; adulted [obsolete] · erwachsen

growth (allocation) model, model of economic growth · Wachstumsmodell n, wirtschaftliches Wachstumsmodell

growth allotment, growth apportionment · Wachstumszuteilung f

growth apportionment, growth allotment · Wachstumszuteilung f

growth area, growth territory · Wachstumsgebiet n

growth bond · Wachstumsrentenversicherungssparbrief m [Keine Ausschüttung, mit garantiertem Kapitalwachstum]

growth by assimilation [obsolete]; concretion, growing together, uniting in one mass, concrescence · Zusammenwachsen n

growth by size · Größenwachstum n

growth cycle · Wachstumszyklus m

growth dynamics, dynamics of growth · Wachstumsdynamik f

growth equation, equation of growth · Wachstumsgleichung f

growth fund · Wachstumsfonds m

growth industry · Wachstumsindustrie f

growth island · Wachstumsinsel f

growth model → (economic) growth model

growth of population, population increase, population growth, increase of population · Bevölkerungszunahme f, Bevölkerungswachstum n, Wachstum der Bevölkerung

growth-orien(ta)ted, growth-related · wachstumsbezogen, wachstumsorientiert

growth path · Wachstumspfad m

growth planning · Wachstumsplanung f

growth pole, pole of growth · Wachstumspol m

growth pole theory · Wachstumspoltheorie f

growth rate, rate of growth · Wachstumsrate f

growth rate of zero, no-growth rate, zero growth rate · Nullwachstumsrate f

growth ring · Wachstumsring m

growth territory, growth area · Wachstumsgebiet n

growth theory · Wachstumstheorie f

growth town · künftiger zentraler Ort m höherer Ordnung

to grow to, to accumulate, to accrue, to run up · auflaufen, anwachsen, zuwachsen, aufhäufen, anhäufen [Betrag]

g-statistics · g-Maßzahl f [Statistik]

G.T.C. order, open order, good-until-cancelled order · Auftrag m auf Widerruf gültig [Börse]

guarantee, guarantie, guaranty, warranty [Contractor's or manufacturer's guarantee of the quality, workmanship, and *performance of his work or equipment or product*] · Gewähr(leistung) *f*, Garantie *f*

guarantee bond → guaranty bond

guarantee capital, guaranty capital, guarantie capital · Bürgschaftskapital *n*

guarantee capital stock, guaranty capital stock, guarantie capital stock · Bürgschaftskapitalanteile *m pl*

guaranteed bond, money-back annuity, annuity bond, annuity certificate, annuity contract, annuity agreement · Renten(versicherungsspar)brief *m*, Renten(versicherungsspar)schein *m*

guaranteed debenture [*Great Britain*]; guaranteed corporate bond [*USA*] · Schuldverschreibung *f* durch Bürgschaft einer anderen Gesellschaft gesichert, Obligation *f* durch Bürgschaft einer anderen Gesellschaft gesichert [*einer privaten Kapitalgesellschaft*]

guarantee debt, guarantie debt, guaranty debt · Bürgschaftsschuld *f*

guaranteed property bond (fund) · Immobilienversicherungsfonds *m* mit garantiertem Mindestrückkaufkurs

guaranteeing company, title insurance company · Versicherungsgesellschaft *f* für Schuldner-Eigentumsrecht

guarantee of collection, guarantie of collection, guaranty of collection [*The guarantor agrees that he will pay the obligation if it is impossible to collect it from the principal debtor*] · Ausfallbürgschaft *f*, Schad(los)bürgschaft *f*, Rückbürgschaft *f*

guarantee of payment, payment guaranty, guaranty of payment, payment guarantee [*The guarantor actually is in the same position as a principal because the guarantor is primarily liable on the obligation*] · selbstschuldnerische Bürgschaft *f*

guarantee stock, guarantie stock, guaranty stock [*Of a building and loan association. A fixed non-withdrawal investment which guarantees to all other investors in the association a fixed rate of dividend or interest*] · (Garantie)Einlage *f*, Garantieanteil *m* [*Bausparkasse*]

guarantee stock plan, guarantie stock plan, guaranty stock plan · (Einlagen)Garantieplan *m*, (Garantie)Einlagenplan [*Bausparkasse*]

guarantie → guarantee

guarantie bond → guaranty bond

guarantie capital stock, guarantee capital stock, guaranty capital stock · Bürgschaftskapitalanteile *m pl*

guarantie contract → guaranty contract

guarantie debt, guaranty debt, guarantee debt · Bürgschaftsschuld *f*

guarantie of collection, guaranty of collection, guarantee of collection [*The guarantor agrees that he will pay the obligation if it is impossible to collect it from the principal debtor*] · Ausfallbürgschaft *f*, Schad(los)bürgschaft *f*, Rückbürgschaft *f*

guarantie stock, guaranty stock, guarantee stock [*Of a building and loan association. A fixed non-withdrawal investment which guarantees to all other investors in the association a fixed rate of dividend or interest*] · (Garantie)Einlage *f*, Garantieanteil *m* [*Bausparkasse*]

guarantie stock plan, guaranty stock plan, guarantee stock plan · (Einlagen)Garantieplan *m*, (Garantie)Einlagenplan [*Bausparkasse*]

guarantor, cautioner, pledge, surety, insurer of a debt [*The party who expresses his willingness to answer for the debt, default, or obligation of another. The word "surety" is sometimes used interchangeably for the word "guarantor"; but, strictly speaking, a "surety" is one who is bound with the principal debtor upon the original contract, the same as if he had made the contract himself, while a "guarantor" is bound upon a separate contract to make good in case the principal debtor fails. The guarantor is therefore an insurer of the solvency of the debtor. A surety is held primarily liable on an instrument while a guarantor is held secondarily liable on it; that is, the surety agrees that he will pay the obligation in any event, while the guarantor merely agrees that he will pay the obligation if the principal debtor fails to pay*] · Bürge *m*

guarantor of collection, surety of collection, cautioner of collection, collection surety, collection cautioner, collection guarantor · Ausfallbürge *m*, Rückbürge, Schad(los)bürge

guarantor right, cautioner right, right of the surety, right of the guarantor, right of the cautioner, right of the insurer of a debt, surety right · Bürgenrecht *n*, subjektives Bürgenrecht

guarantorship · Bürgschaftswesen *n*

guaranty, guarantee, guarantie [*A collateral promise to be answerable for another's debt, default, obligation, or miscarriage*] · Bürgschaft *f*

guaranty bond, guarantee bond, guarantie bond, surety bond [*Guarantee by a surety company that the contractor will either complete the work or pay all obligations or both, depending on how the bond is worded. If the bond guarantees payment of financial obligation, it is*

guaranty building society (Brit.) — **guardianship (of the property)** 470

called a "payment bond". If the bond guarantees the completion of the work, it is called a "performance bond" or a "completion bond"] · Kautionsversicherung f

guaranty building society (Brit.); guaranty stock association, permanent stock association, capital stock association; guaranty building (and loan) association (US) · Bausparkasse f mit Eigenkapital, kapitalistische Bausparkasse

guaranty capital, guarantie capital, guarantee capital · Bürgschaftskapital n

guaranty capital stock, guarantie capital stock, guarantee capital stock · Bürgschaftskapitalanteile m pl

guaranty contract, guarantee contract, contract of guarantie, guarantie contract, contract of guaranty, contract of guarantee · Bürgschaftsvertrag m

guaranty debt, guarantee debt, guarantie debt · Bürgschaftsschuld f

guaranty declaration, guarantee declaration, declaration of guaranty, declaration of guarantee, garantie declaration, declaration of guarantie · Bürgschaftserklärung f

guaranty fund, guarantie fund, guarantee fund · Stützungsfonds m

guaranty of bill of exchange, guarantee of bill of exchange, guarantie of bill of exchange · Wechselbürgschaft f

guaranty of collection, guarantee of collection, guarantie of collection [*The guarantor agrees that he will pay the obligation if it is impossible to collect it from the principal debtor*] · Ausfallbürgschaft f, Schad(los)bürgschaft f, Rückbürgschaft f

guaranty of payment, payment guarantee, guarantee of payment, payment guaranty [*The guarantor actually is in the same position as a principal because the guarantor is primarily liable on the obligation*] · selbstschuldnerische Bürgschaft f

guaranty share · Anteil m zur Beschaffung von Eigenkapital [*kapitalistische Bausparkasse*]

guaranty stock, guarantee stock, guarantie stock [*Of a building and loan association. A fixed non-withdrawal investment which guarantees to all other investors in the association a fixed rate of dividend or interest*] · (Garantie)Einlage f, Garantieanteil m [*Bausparkasse*]

guaranty stock association, permanent stock association, capital stock association, guaranty building (and loan) association (US); guaranty building society (Brit.) · Bausparkasse f mit Eigenkapital, kapitalistische Bausparkasse

guaranty stock plan, guarantee stock plan, guarantie stock plan · (Einlagen)Garantieplan m, (Garantie)Einlagenplan [*Bausparkasse*]

guardian · Vormund m

guardian ad litem · Prozeßvormund m

guardian by appointment (of court), (court-)appointed guardian, guardian by judicial appointment · gerichtlich ernannter Vormund m, gerichtlicher Vormund

guardian by common law · gemeinrechtlicher Vormund m

guardian by custom, common guardian, customary guardian · gewohnheitsrechtlicher Vormund m

guardian by election · erwählter Vormund m

guardian by estoppel, guardian de son tort, quasi-guardian [*One who assumes to act as guardian without valid authority*] · Quasi-Vormund m

guardian by judicial appointment, guardian by appointment (of court), (court-)appointed guardian · gerichtlich ernannter Vormund m, gerichtlicher Vormund

guardian de son tort, quasi-guardian, guardian by estoppel [*One who assumes to act as guardian without valid authority*] · Quasi-Vormund m

guardian (of the poor), almoner, poor law overseer, poor law guardian, parish officer, overseer (of the poor) · Armenvater m, Armenaufseher m, Armenpfleger m

guardianship · Vormundschaft f

guardianship by appointment (of court), guardianship by judicial appointment, (court-)appointed guardianship · gerichtlich ernannte Vormundschaft f, gerichtliche Vormundschaft

guardianship by custom, common guardianship, customary guardianship · gewohnheitsrechtliche Vormundschaft f

guardianship by election · erwählte Vormundschaft f

guardianship by nature · natürliche Vormundschaft f, leibliche Vormundschaft

guardianship by statute, testamentary guardianship · gesetzliche Vormundschaft f

guardianship court · Vormundschaftsgericht n

guardianship of the father · väterliche Vormundschaft f

guardianship of the mother · mütterliche Vormundschaft f

guardianship (of the property) · Vermögenssorge f

guardians of public morals · Sittenpolizei f

guide line · Richtlinie f

guiding private value · Bodenrichtwert m

g(u)ild, company; gilda [*Latin*] · Verband m, Gilde f

g(u)ildable, geldable, liable to pay [*In old English law*] · zahlungspflichtig

guildhalda teutonicorum [*Latin*]; steel yard, stilyard [*A place or house in London, where the fraternity of the "Easterling merchants", otherwise called "The merchants of the Hanse and Almaine", had their abode*] · Stahlhof m in London

g(u)ild merchant, company merchant, merchant g(u)ild, merchant company · Kaufmannsgilde f, Kaufmannsverband m

guilty knowledge · schuldhafte Kenntnis f

guilty mind → mens-rea

gustator cerevisiae [*Latin*]; ale-taster, ale-conner, ale-founder, ale-kenner [*This was the title of an officer formerly appointed under the Assize of Bread and Ale (1267) to inspect the quality and regulate the sale of those commodities in every borough and manor*] · Bierkoster m, Bieraufseher, Bierprober

H

habit, mode, custom, usage [*Uniform course of dealing in a particular trade*] · Brauch m, Üblichkeit f, Gepflogenheit f, Gewohnheit

habitability, fitness for habitation, fitness for human occupation · Bewohnbarkeit f

habitable → (in)habitable

habitableness · Wohnlichkeit f

habitable space, shelter, housing, habitable room [*The word "housing", which is used in combinations, includes, however, all of the immediate physical environment, both within and outside of residential buildings*] · Wohnraum m [*Sammelbezeichnung für Wohnungen und einzelne Wohnräume*]

habitancy → (in)habitancy

habitation [*A place in which to live*] · Behausung f

habitation place, (place of) abode, (place of) residence, (permanent) residence, legal home, settlement, domicil(e), place of habitation · Aufenthaltsort m, gesetzlicher Aufenthaltsort m, Wohnort m, Wohnsitz m

habit persistence effect · sozialpsychologisches Verhaltensmuster n

habitual drunkenness · gewohnheitsmäßige Trunkenheit f, Trunksucht f

hachure · Schraffe f

hackney coach · (Miet)Droschke f

haereditas [*Latin*]; inheritance; enheritance [*obsolete*] [*"Inheritance" is also used in the old books in the sense of "hereditament"* = *Erbgut*] · Erbschaft f, Erbe n

haeres [*Latin*]; heir (male), real representative, heres · Erbe m

haggling, higgling, bargaining [*Bargaining over prices as an alternative to fixed prices for commodities*] · Aushandeln n von Preisen, Feilschen

Hague Tribunal, Tribunal of The Hague · Haager Gerichtshof m

haiebote [*French and Saxon*] → haybote

hail damage · Hagelschaden m

hailing distance · Rufweite f

hail insurance · Hagelversicherung f

half-invariant, cumulant · Kumulante f [*Statistik*]

half-holder of yardland, half-holder of verge of land, half-yardling, half-tenant by the verge · Halbhüf(e)ner m, Halbhufenbauer, Halbhuf(e)ner, Kleinhüf(e)ner, Kleinhufenbauer, Kleinhuf(e)ner

half-rural, semi-rural · halbländlich

half standard cost(s) · Ist-Soll-Kosten f

half-tenant by the verge, half-holder of yardland, half-holder of verge of land, half-yardling · Halbhüf(e)ner m, Halbhufenbauer, Halbhuf(e)ner, Kleinhüf(e)ner, Kleinhufenbauer, Kleinhuf(e)ner

half-villein, half-villain · Halbhörige m

half-virgate, half-yardland · Halbhufenland n

half-yardling, half-tenant by the verge, half-holder of yardland, half-holder of verge of land · Halbhüf(e)ner m, Halbhufenbauer, Halbhuf(e)ner, Kleinhüf(e)ner, Kleinhufenbauer, Kleinhuf(e)ner

half-yearly, semi-annual · halbjährlich, semestral

halimôt [*In old English law*] · Hallengericht n

hall, country seat · Schloß n, Herrensitz m

hallmark · Feingehaltstempel m [*auf Gold oder Silber*]

hallmoot · Zunftversammlung f

halted payment, default of payment, non-payment · Nicht(be)zahlung f

hamlet — hardship equalization

hamlet, nucleated village; ham(e)leta, hameletta [*Latin*] · Weiler *m*, ländliche Gruppensied(e)lung *f*

hamlet and isolated farms, hamlet and single farms · Einzelhof-Weiler-(An)Sied(e)lung *f*

hamlet and isolated farms union, hamlet and single farms union · Einzelhof-Weiler-Verband *m*

hamlet area, hamlet territory · Weilergebiet *n*

handbill · Flugblatt *n*

handbook of building law, handbook of construction law · Baurechthandbuch *n*

(hand) craft · Handwerk *n*

(hand) craft code · Handwerksordnung *f*

(hand) craft line, line of (hand) craft · Handwerkszweig *m*

(hand) craftsman, artisan · Handwerker *m*

handed over, delivered (up), surrendered · ausgehändigt, übergeben

handicap, aggravating circumstance, aggravation · erschwerender Umstand *m*, Erschwerung *f*, Erschwernis *f*

handicapped · (körperlich) behindert, versehrt

handicapped female person · Behinderte *f*

handicapped male person · Behinderte *m*

handicapped person · behinderte Person *f*

handing over, handover, (de)livery, tradition; traditio [*Latin*] · Aushändigung *f*, Übergabe *f*, Aushändigen *n*, Übergeben, Tradition *f*

handing over date, surrender date, handover date, (de)livery date, date of handing over, date of handover, date of (de)livery, date of surrender · Aushändigungstermin *m*, Übergabetermin *m*, Aushändigungsdatum *n*, Übergabedatum *n*

handing over duty, handover duty, (de)livery duty, duty to hand over, duty to deliver · Aushändigungspflicht *f*, Übergabepflicht *f*

to handle, to wind up · abwickeln [*Geschäft*]

handling (of business), winding(-)up (of business) · Abwick(e)lung *f*, Geschäftsabwick(e)lung

handling of commodities, commodities handling, handling of goods, goods handling · Güterumschlag *m*, Warenumschlag

handmoney, handsel, earnest (money), arles, erles, arrha(bo) [*A sum paid to bind a bargain*] · Angeld *n*, Kaufschilling *m*, Handgeld, D(a)rauf(gabe)geld, D(a)raufgabe *f*, Haftgeld, Mietstaler *m* [*Wenn Angeld gegeben wird, so gilt dies nach dem Gesetz als ein Zeichen, daß ein Vertrag abgeschlossen wurde*]

to hand over, to surrender, to deliver (up) · aushändigen, übergeben

handover, (de)livery, tradition; traditio [*Latin*]; handing over · Aushändigung *f*, Übergabe *f*, Aushändigen *n*, Übergeben, Tradition *f*

handover date → handing over date

handover duty → handing over duty

handsale [*A sale of chattels concluded by a shaking of hands*] · Handkauf *m*

handsel, earnest (money), arles, erles, arrha(bo), handmoney [*A sum paid to bind a bargain*] · Angeld *n*, Kaufschilling *m*, Handgeld, D(a)rauf(gabe)geld, D(a)raufgabe *f*, Haftgeld, Mietstaler *m* [*Wenn Angeld gegeben wird, so gilt dies nach dem Gesetz als ein Zeichen, daß ein Vertrag abgeschlossen wurde*]

handwriting · Handschrift *f*

hanging fruits · hängende Früchte *fpl*

Hanseatic Laws of the Sea · hanseatisches Seerecht *n*

Hanseatic League · Hanse *f*

Hanse town, Hanse city · Hansestadt *f*

haphazard building, haphazard construction · wildes Bauen *n*, regelloses Bauen

happening, event · Ereignis *n* [*Es tritt unabhängig vom Willen ein*]

harbour quarter (Brit.); harbor quarter (US) · Hafenviertel *n*

harbour town, harbour city (Brit.); harbor town, harbor city (US) · Hafenstadt *f*

hard copy · Bildschirmkopie *f*

hard core, crystal of the core, core crystal · harter Kern *m*, Kern im Kern [*Stadt*]

hard core of a contract · Leistungskern *m*

hard currency · harte Währung *f*

hard labour (Brit.); hard labor (US) · Zwangsarbeit *f*

hard money (US); coins, base-metal money · Metallgeld *n*, Hartgeld, Münzen *fpl*

hardship · Härte *f*

hardship aid · Härtehilfe *f*

hardship case, case of hardship · Härtefall *m*

hardship clause, clause of hardship · Härteklausel *f*

hardship equalization · Härteausgleich *m*

hardship fund · Härtefonds *m*

to harm, to prejudice, to derogate, to hurt · beeinträchtigen, schmälern

harm, derogation, hurt · Abbruch *m*, Beeinträchtigung *f*, Schmälerung, Schädigung

harmful dust · Schadstaub *m*

harmful to the landscape · landschaftsschädlich

harmless to the landscape · landschaftsunschädlich

harmonization · Übereinstimmung *f* [*Übereinstimmung bestehender und neuer Pläne und Programme fachlicher, städtebaulicher oder raumordnerischer Art mit verbindlichen Raumordnungsplänen und -programmen*]

harmonization claim, claim of harmonization, harmonization demand, demand of harmonization · Übereinstimmungsforderung *f*, Übereinstimmungsverlangen *n*

harmonization demand, demand of harmonization, harmonization claim, claim of harmonization · Übereinstimmungsforderung *f*, Übereinstimmungsverlangen *n*

har(r)iot [*Latin*] → heriot

harvested cropland · effektiv genutztes Ackerland

harvest wage · Erntelohn *m*

to have and to hold · zu unbeschränktem Eigentum [*Grundstücksübertragungsurkunde*]

to have control of · verfügen über

having effect in law, legally binding, binding in law, having the force of law · rechtsverbindlich

having no legal effect · schwebend unwirksam

having no means · mittellos

having standing under public law, quasi-public, semi-governmental · öffentlich-rechtlich

having the force of law, having effect in law, legally binding, binding in law · rechtsverbindlich

hawker · Trödler *m*

hawthorn hedge, quick-set hedge · Weißdornhecke *f*, Hagedornhecke

haybote, heybote; haiebote [*French and Saxon*]; hedge-bote · Beholzungsrecht *n* für Hecken, Holzbezugsrecht für Hecken, Heckenzubuße *f*

hayment, hedge fence; heimenium [*Latin*] · Heckenzaun *m*

hay tithe; hay teind [*Scots law*] · Heuzehnt *m* [*altdeutsch: Heuzehent, Heuzehend*]

hazard, risk · Risiko *n*, Wagnis *n*

hazard area, risk area · Risikobereich *m*, Wagnisbereich

hazard aversion, adventure aversion, risk aversion · Risikoabneigung *f*, Wagnisabneigung

hazard bonus, risk bonus · Risikozuschlag *m*, Wagniszuschlag

hazard clause, risk clause · Risikoklausel *f*, Wagnisklausel

hazard concept, risk concept, concept of risk, concept of hazard · Interessenabwägung *f*

hazard distribution, risk distribution, risk sharing, hazard sharing, distribution of risk(s), distribution of hazard(s), sharing of risk(s), sharing of hazard(s), splitting (up) of risk(s), splitting (up) of hazard(s) · Verteilung *f* des Risikos, Verteilung des Wagnisses, Risikoverteilung, Wagnisverteilung

hazard insurance, risk insurance · Risikoversicherung *f*

hazard involved in costing, risk involved in costing · kalkulatorisches Risiko *n*, kalkulatorisches Wagnis *n*

hazard management, risk management · Handhabung *f* von Entscheidungswagnissen, Handhabung von Entscheidungsrisiken

hazard of an enterprise, hazard of an undertaking, risk of an enterprise, risk of an undertaking · Betriebsrisiko *n*, Betriebswagnis *n*

hazard of loss, loss risk, loss hazard, risk of loss · Verlustrisiko *n*, Verlustwagnis *n*

hazardous negligence, hazardous carelessness, hazardous careless conduct, hazardous negligent conduct · gefährliche Fahrlässigkeit *f*, gefährliche Nachlässigkeit

hazard principle, risk principle · Risikogrundsatz *m*, Wagnisgrundsatz

hazard sharing, distribution of risk(s), distribution of hazard(s), sharing of risk(s), sharing of hazard(s), splitting (up) of risk(s), splitting (up) of hazard(s), hazard distribution, risk distribution, risk sharing · Verteilung *f* des Risikos, Verteilung des Wagnisses, Risikoverteilung, Wagnisverteilung

hazard-taking, risk-taking · Risikoübernahme *f*, Wagnisübernahme

hazard threshold, risk threshold · Wagnisschwelle *f*, Risikoschwelle

HBA, homebuyers association · Eigenheimkäufergesellschaft *f*, Eigenhauskäufergesellschaft

head, front, butt(al), bout, end · Ende *n*, Grundstücksende

head-borough, tithing-man, borough's ealder, borough's ealdor, parochial constable, borsholder · Polizeischulze *m*

head commissary → commissary general

head demise, head lease(hold), main tenancy, main demise, main lease(hold), principal tenancy, principal lease(hold), principal demise, head tenancy · Hauptpacht *f*, Hauptnutzungsrecht *n*

heading, title, headline, caption · Überschrift *f*

headland, foreland, forebalk, foreherda, butt; head-rig [*Scotch*]; pen tir [*Welsh*]; forera, terra capitalis, caput terrae, caputium, chevitia, forlandum, versura [*Latin*] [*The slip of unploughed land left at the head or end of a ploughed field on which the plough is turned*] · Anwende *f*, Voracker *m*, Vorwart *f*, Anwänder *m*

headland right; pen tir right [*Welsh*]; head-rig right [*Scotch*] · Anwenderecht *n*, Pflugrecht *n*, Kehrrecht *n*, Tretrecht *n* [*Das Recht beim Pflügen auf dem Boden des Nachbarn den Pflug wenden zu dürfen*]

head lease(hold), main tenancy, main demise, main lease(hold), principal tenancy, principal lease(hold), principal demise, head tenancy, head demise · Hauptpacht *f*, Hauptnutzungsrecht *n*

headline, caption, heading, title · Überschrift *f*

headmaster · Schulleiter *m*

headmistress · Schulleiterin *f*

headnote, syllabus · Leitsatz *m*, Zusammenfassung *f* am Anfang eines Urteilsberichtes, Rechtsauszug *m* [*Er wird der veröffentlichten Entscheidung eines Gerichtes vorangestellt*]

head of a village, village head, re(e)ve · Schultheiß *m*, Schulze *m*

head of cattle [*In old records, a stock of cattle. A term of common occurrence in the accounts of monastic establishments*]; staurum [*Latin*] · Rinderbestand *m*, Rindviehbestand

head of (consular) post · Leiter *m* [*Konsularposten*]

head of state, state head, state chief, chief of state · Staatsoberhaupt *n*

head of strip, strip head · Vorhaupt *n*

head of (the) household, householder, household head · Haushalt(ungs)vorstand *m*

headquarters · Hauptquartier *n*

headquarters → (corporation) headquarters

head-rig [*Scotch*] → headland

head-rig right [*Scotch*]; headland right; pen tir right [*Welsh*] · Anwenderecht *n*, Pflugrecht *n*, Kehrrecht *n*, Tretrecht *n* [*Das Recht beim Pflügen auf dem Boden des Nachbarn den Pflug wenden zu dürfen*]

headship rate, incidence of households, household incidence [*The proportion of people in any given age category who are heads of households*] · Haushaltvorstandsziffer *f*

head tax, capitation tax, poll-tax [*A tax on each person in consideration of his labour, office, rank, etc.*] · Kopfsteuer *f*

head tenancy, principal tenancy, main tenancy, master tenancy · Hauptmietverhältnis *n*

head tenancy, head demise, head lease(hold), main tenancy, main demise, main lease(hold), principal tenancy, principal lease(hold), principal demise · Hauptpacht *f*, Hauptnutzungsrecht *n*

head tenant, principal tenant, master tenant, main tenant · Hauptmieter *m*

health authority, sanitary authority; (medical) officer of health [*England*] · Gesundheitsbehörde *f*

health bill, bill of health · Gesundheitspaß *m*

health commitee · Gesundheitsausschuß *m*

health control · Gesundheitssicherung *f*

health insurance · Krankenversicherung *f*

health legislation → public health legislation

health officer, health official · Medizinalbeamte *m*

health practice · Gesundheitswesen *n*

health resort · Kurort *m*

health resort park · Kurpark *m*

health service · Gesundheitsdienst *m*

heap of debris, debris heap · Schutthalde *f*

hearing · Anhörung *f*

hearing date, date of hearing, · Anhörungstermin *m*, Anhörungsdatum *n*

hearing method, method of hearing · Anhörungsverfahren *n*

hearing of citizens, public hearing, citizen hearing · Bürgeranhörung *f*, öffentliche Anhörung

hearing officer · Anhörungsbeamte *m*

hearing on desired lot(s) before reallotment · (Plan)Wunschentgegennahme *f*

hearsay [*Testimony by a witness as to a matter not within his personal knowledge*] · Hörensagen *n*

hearsay evidence · Zeugnis *n* vom Hörensagen

hearsay statement · Angabe *f* vom Hörensagen, Aussage *f* vom Hörensagen

heath ground; bruarium, bruyrium [*Latin*] · Heideland *n*

heating contractor · Heizungsunternehmer *m*

heating (cost(s)) subsidy · Heizkostenbeihilfe *f*

heat nuisance · Wärmeemission *f*

heat nuisance effect · Wärmeimmission *f*

heat protection ordinance · Wärmeschutzverordnung *f*

heat supply · Wärmeversorgung *f*

heat supply contract · Wärmeversorgungsvertrag *m*

heavy construction · Tiefbau *m*

heavy construction act, heavy construction law, heavy construction statute · Tiefbaugesetz *n*

heavy construction activity · Tiefbautätigkeit *f*

heavy construction administration · Tiefbauverwaltung *f*

heavy construction agreement [*It is a part of a construction contract*] · Tiefbauvertrag *m* [*Der Vertrag als Vertragsbestandteil; andere Vertragsbestandteile sind Zeichnungen, Angebot, Garantie usw.*]

heavy construction authority · Tiefbaubehörde *f*

heavy construction board · Tiefbauamt *n*

heavy construction condition · Tiefbaubedingung *f*

heavy construction contracting practice · Tiefbauvergabewesen *n*

heavy construction contractor · Tiefbauunternehmer *m*

heavy construction cost(s) · Tiefbaukosten *f*

heavy construction cost(s) index · Tiefbau(kosten)index *m*

heavy construction department · Tiefbauabteilung *f*

heavy construction drawing · Tiefbauzeichnen *n*

heavy construction drawing · Tiefbauzeichnung *f*

heavy construction engineer · Tiefbauingenieur *m*

heavy construction engineer contract · Tiefbauingenieurvertrag *m*

heavy (construction) engineering · Tiefbautechnik *f* [*als Wissenschaft*]

heavy construction engineer in private practice · beratender Tiefbauingenieur *m*, Beratungstiefbauingenieur

heavy construction expert · Tiefbausachverständige *m*, Tiefbaugutachter

heavy construction expertise · Tiefbaugutachten *n*

heavy construction field, heavy construction sector · Tiefbausektor *m*

heavy construction firm, heavy construction enterprise, heavy construction undertaking · Tiefbaufirma *f*, Tiefbaubetrieb *m*, Tiefbauunternehmen *n*, Tiefbauunternehmung *f*

heavy construction geologist, (civil) engineering geologist, (engineering) construction geologist, construction engineering geologist · Tiefbaugeologe *m*, Bau(grund)geologe

heavy construction geology → (civil) engineering geology

heavy construction industry · Tiefbauindustrie *f*

heavy construction law · Tiefbaurecht *n*

heavy construction law → heavy construction act

heavy construction lawmaking, heavy construction legislation · Tiefbaugesetzgebung *f*

heavy construction (law)suit · Tiefbauprozeß *m*

heavy construction measure · Tiefbaumaßnahme *f*

heavy construction operation(s), heavy construction work(s) · Tiefbauarbeit(en) *f (pl)*, Tiefbauleistung(en) *f (pl)*

heavy construction order · Tiefbauauftrag *m*

heavy construction planner · Tiefbauplaner *m*

heavy construction planning · Tiefbauplanung *f*

heavy construction practice · Tiefbauwesen *n*

heavy construction price · Tiefbaupreis *m*

heavy construction project · Tiefbauprojekt *n*, Tiefbauvorhaben *n*

heavy construction provision · Tiefbaubestimmung *f*

heavy construction sector, heavy construction field · Tiefbausektor *m*

heavy construction statute → heavy construction act

heavy construction sub-contract — heiress apparent 476

heavy construction sub-contract · Nachunternehmervertrag *m* im Tiefbau, Subunternehmervertrag im Tiefbau, Unterunternehmervertrag im Tiefbau; Unterakkordantenvertrag im Tiefbau [*Schweiz*]

heavy construction sub(contractor) · Tiefbaunachunternehmer *m*, Tiefbausubunternehmer; Tiefbauunterakkordant *m* [*Schweiz*]

heavy construction sum, sum of heavy construction · Herstellungssumme *f*, Bausumme [*Tiefbau*]

heavy construction surveyor · Tiefbaubeamte *m*

heavy construction technique · Tiefbautechnik *f* [*als betriebstechnische Anwendung*]

heavy construction tender, heavy construction offer, heavy construction bid; heavy construction (bid) proposal (US) · Tiefbauangebot *n*

heavy construction volume · Tiefbauvolumen *n*

heavy construction worker · Tiefbauarbeiter *m*

heavy construction work(s), heavy construction operation(s) · Tiefbauarbeit(en) *f (pl)*, Tiefbauleistung(en) *f (pl)*

heavy engineering → heavy (construction) engineering

heavy engineering general contractor → heavy engineering (prime) general contractor

heavy engineering single contractor, heavy engineering (prime) general contractor · Tiefbaugeneralunternehmer *m*, Tiefbaugesamtunternehmer

hedge · Hecke *f*

hedge-bote, haybote, heybote; haiebote [*French and Saxon*] · Beholzungsrecht *n* für Hecken, Holzbezugsrecht für Hecken, Heckenzubuße *f*

hedge boundary · Heckengrenze *f*

hedge-bound field system, open-bound field system · Zelgensystem *n*

hedge enclosure, hedge inclosure · Hekkenland *n*

hedge fence; heimenium [*Latin*]; hayment · Heckenzaun *m*

hedge landscape · Heckenlandschaft *f*

hedge planting · Heckenbepflanzung *f*

hedge-row · Heckenreihe *f*

hedge-timber · Heckenholz *n*

hedging · Heckeneinfried(ig)ung *f*, Heckenumzäunung

hedging · Sicherung *f* [*Preis; Kurs*]

heightening (of a building) · Aufstockung *f*, Aufsetzung *f* neuer Geschosse [*Erhöhung der Geschoßzahl eines Gebäudes durch Hinzufügung eines oder mehrerer Geschosse*]

height index · Höhenindex *m*

height of (a) building, building height · Gebäudehöhe *f*

height of coverage, coverage height · Bebauungshöhe *f*; Überbauungshöhe [*Schweiz*]

height of structure, height of work, height of physical facility · Bauhöhe *f*, Bauwerkhöhe

height restriction, restriction of height · Höhenbeschränkung *f*

height zoning [*Zoning regulations that limit the height of buildings in certain areas*] · Höhenregelung *f*

heimenium [*Latin*]; hayment, hedge fence · Heckenzaun *m*

heinous trespass · Frevel *m*

heinous trespasser · Frevler *m*

heir apparent → heir (male) apparent

heir apparent to the Crown · Thronfolger *m*

heir conventional → heir (male) conventional

heirdom, succession by inheritance, (hereditary) succession, (hereditary) descent [*Succession to the ownership of an estate by inheritance*] · Erbgang *m*, Erbfolge *f*, erbrechtliche Nachfolge

heirdom according to foreign law, (hereditary) descent according to foreign law, (hereditary) succession according to foreign law, succession by inheritance according to foreign law · Erbfolge *f* nach ausländischem Recht, Erbfolge nach fremdem Recht, Erbgang *m* nach ausländischem Recht, Erbgang nach fremdem Recht, erbrechtliche Nachfolge nach ausländischem Recht, erbrechtliche Nachfolge nach fremdem Recht

heirdom per capita, succession by inheritance per capita, (hereditary) succession per capita, (hereditary) descent per capita · Erbgang *m* nach Köpfen, Erbfolge *f* nach Köpfen, erbrechtliche Nachfolge nach Köpfen

heiress, heir female, female heir; inheretrix [*deprecated*] · Erbin *f*

heiress apparent, heir female apparent, female heir apparent [*A woman whose right of inheritance is indefeasible, provided she outlives the ancestor*] · rechtmäßige Erbin *f*

heiress at law, heiress general, heir female at law, heir female general, right heiress, right heir female, female heir at law, female heir general, right female heir · Intestaterbin *f*, gesetzliche Erbin

heiress beneficiary, heir female beneficiary, female heir beneficiary · Erbin *f* mit Inventarerrichtung

heiress by adoption, heir female by adoption, female heir by adoption · Adoptiverbin *f*

heiress by custom, heir female by custom, female heir by custom · gewohnheitsrechtliche Erbin *f*

heiress collateral, heir female collateral, collateral heiress, collateral heir female · Seitenlinienerbin *f*

heiress conventional, female heir conventional, heir female conventional · Vertragserbin *f*

heiress expectant, heir female expectant, expectant heiress, expectant heir female, expectant female heir, female heir expectant · Erbanwärterin *f*, Erbschaftsanwärterin

heiress general → heiress at law

heiress in (fee) tail, heir female in (fee) tail, heiress special, heir female special, female heir in (fee) tail, female heir special · Anerbin *f*

heiress institute, female heir institute, heir female institute [*In Scots law a woman to whom the right of succession is ascertained by disposition or express deed of the deceased*] · eingesetzte Erbin *f*

heiress of inventory (in tail), heir female of inventory (in tail), female heir of inventory (in tail), fiduciary heiress, fiduciary heir female, fiduciary female heir, fiducial heiress, fiducial heir female, fiducial female heir · Vorerbin *f*

heiress of line, heir female of line [*Scots law*], female heir of the blood, female heir of the body, female heir of line, heiress of the blood, heiress of the body, heir female of the blood, heir female of the body, bodily heiress, bodily heir female, bodily female heir [*A woman who succeeds lineally by right of blood*] · Blutserbin *f*, Leibeserbin, natürliche Erbin, leibliche Erbin

heiress special, heir female special, female heir in (fee) tail, female heir special, heiress in (fee) tail, heir female in (fee) tail · Anerbin *f*

heiress testamentary, heir female testamentary, female heir testamentary · Testamentserbin *f*

heir expectant → heir (male) expectant

heir female, female heir; inheretrix [*deprecated*], heiress · Erbin *f*

heir female apparent, female heir apparent, heiress apparent [*A woman whose right of inheritance is indefeasible, provided she outlives the ancestor*] · rechtmäßige Erbin *f*

heir female at law → heiress at law

heir female beneficiary, female heir beneficiary, heiress beneficiary · Erbin *f* mit Inventarerrichtung

heir female by adoption, female heir by adoption, heiress by adoption · Adoptiverbin *f*

heir female by custom, female heir by custom, heiress by custom · gewohnheitsrechtliche Erbin *f*

heir female collateral, collateral heiress, collateral heir female, heiress collateral · Seitenlinienerbin *f*

heir female conventional, heiress conventional, female heir conventional · Vertragserbin *f*

heir female expectant, expectant heiress, expectant heir female, expectant female heir, female heir expectant, heiress expectant · Erbanwärterin *f*, Erbschaftsanwärterin

heir female general → heiress at law

heir female in (fee) tail, heiress special, heir female special, female heir in (fee) tail, female heir special, heiress in (fee) tail · Anerbin *f*

heir female institute, heiress institute, female heir institute [*In Scots law a woman to whom the right of succession is ascertained by disposition or express deed of the deceased*] · eingesetzte Erbin *f*

heir female of inventory (in tail) → heiress of inventory (in tail)

heir female of line, heiress of line, female heir of line [*Scots law*], female heir of the blood, female heir of the body, heiress of the blood, heiress of the body, heir female of the blood, heir female of the body, bodily heiress, bodily heir female, bodily female heir [*A woman who succeeds lineally by right of blood*] · Blutserbin *f*, Leibeserbin, natürliche Erbin, leibliche Erbin

heir female special, female heir in (fee) tail, female heir special, heiress in (fee) tail, heir female in (fee) tail, heiress special · Anerbin *f*

heir female testamentary, female heir testamentary, heiress testamentary · Testamentserbin *f*

heir land, ethel(-land), erf-land, alod, family land · Erbland *n*, erbliches Land

heirless, without heir(s) · erbenlos, ohne Erben

heirloom — heirship right

heirloom [*A personal chattel which by the custom of a particular place is attached to an estate of inheritance in land. It is not bequeathable but always descends with the estate*] · Fahrnis *f* untrennbar vom Erbe, Fahrhabe *f* untrennbar vom Erbe, immobilisierte Fahrnis, immobilisierte Fahrhabe

heir (male), real representative; heres, haeres [*Latin*] · Erbe *m*

heir (male) apparent [*A man whose right of inheritance is indefeasible, provided he outlives the ancestor*] · rechtmäßiger Erbe *m*

heir (male) at law, right heir (male), legal heir (male), lawful heir (male), nearest kin, heir (male) general, general heir (male), heir (male) whatsoever, statutory heir (male) [*One who takes the succession by relationship to the decedent and by force of law*] · Intestaterbe *m*, gesetzlicher Erbe

heir (male) beneficiary [*A man who has accepted the succession under the benefit of an inventory regularly made*] · Erbe *m* mit Inventarerrichtung

heir (male) by adoption, male heir by adoption · Adoptiverbe *m*

heir (male) by custom, customary heir (male), common heir (male) [*A man whose right of inheritance depends upon a particular and local custom, such as gavelkind, or borough English*] · gewohnheitsrechtlicher Erbe *m*

heir (male) collateral, collateral heir (male) · Seitenlinienerbe *m*

heir (male) conventional · Vertragserbe *m*

heir (male) expectant, expectant heir (male), expectant male heir, male heir expectant · Erbanwärter *m*, Erbschaftsanwärter

heir (male) general, general heir (male), heir (male) whatsoever, statutory heir (male), heir (male) at law, right heir (male), legal heir (male), lawful heir (male), nearest kin [*One who takes the succession by relationship to the decedent and by force of law*] · Intestaterbe *m*, gesetzlicher Erbe

heir (male) in (fee) tail, heir (male) special · Anerbe *m* [*Der Erbe eines Erbhofes, auf den der Hof ungeteilt übergeht*]

heir (male) institute [*In Scotch law a man to whom the right of succession is ascertained by disposition or express deed of the deceased*] · eingesetzter Erbe *m*

heir (male) of inventory (in tail), fiduciary; fiduciarius haeres [*Latin*]; provisional heir (male), fiducial heir (male), fiduciary heir (male) · Vorerbe *m*

heir (male) of the body, heir (male) of the blood, bodily heir (male), natural heir (male); heir (male) of line [*Scots law*] [*An heir (male) begotten or borne by the person referred to, or a child of such heir; any lineal descendant, excluding a surviving husband or wife, adopted children, and collateral relations*] · Leibeserbe *m*, leiblicher Erbe, Blutserbe, natürlicher Erbe

heir (male) of usufruct, usufruct heir (male) · Nießbraucherbe *m*, (Frucht)Genußerbe, Nutzgewalterbe

heir (male) presumptive, presumptive heir (male) [*A man who, if the ancestor should die immediately, would, in the present circumstances of things, be his heir, but whose right of inheritance may be defeated by the contingency of some nearer heir being born, as a brother or nephew, whose presumptive succession may be destroyed by the birth of a child*] · angeblicher Erbe *m*, scheinbarer Erbe, vermeintlicher Erbe, vermutlicher Erbe, anscheinender Erbe

heir (male) special, heir (male) in (fee) tail · Anerbe *m* [*Der Erbe eines Erbhofes, auf den der Hof ungeteilt übergeht*]

heir (male) testamentary · Testamentserbe *m*

heir (male) unconditional [*A man who inherits without reservation, or without making an inventory, whether his acceptance be express or tacit. Distinguished from "heir beneficiary"*] · Erbe *m* ohne Inventarerrichtung

heir (male) whatsoever, statutory heir (male), heir (male) at law, right heir (male), legal heir (male), lawful heir (male), nearest kin, heir (male) general, general heir (male) [*One who takes the succession by relationship to the decedent and by force of law*] · Intestaterbe *m*, gesetzlicher Erbe

heir presumptive → heir (male) presumptive

heirship [*The relation between the heir and his ancestor*] · Erb(schafts)verhältnis *n*

heirship [*The quality or condition of being heir*] · Erbenstand *m*, Erbenstellung *f*

heirship dispute, dispute of heirship, dispute of inheritance, inheritance dispute · Erbauseinandersetzung *f*, Erbstreit(igkeit) *m*, (*f*)

heirship evidence, proof of heirship, evidence of heirship, heirship proof · Erbnachweis *m*

heirship in (fee) tail, special heirship · Anerbschaft *f*, Anerbenschaft

heirship proof, heirship evidence, proof of heirship, evidence of heirship · Erbnachweis *m*

heirship right, hereditary right, heritable right, right of inheritance, right of

heirship, inheritance right · Erb(schafts)anspruch *m*, Erb(schafts)(an)recht *n*

heir's liability; heirs' liability · Erbenhaftung *f*, Erbenhaftpflicht *f*, Erbenhaftbarkeit *f*

heir testamentary → heir (male) testamentary

held in mortmain, (ab)alienated in mortmain, conveyed to mortmain, amortized, amortised · veräußert an die tote Hand

help, aid · Hilfe *f*

henceforth [*A word of futurity, which, as employed in legal documents, statutes, and the like always imports a continuity of action or condition from the present time forward, but excludes all the past*] · von jetzt an

hengen [*A prison for persons condemned to hard labour*] · Zwangsarbeitsgefängnis *n*

herbage, grazing right, shack, common pastur(ag)e, commonage, common right; jus pascendi, communis pasturae, herbagium [*Latin*]; (right of) pastur(ag)e, (right of) grazing, pastoral right · Angerrecht *n*, Hütungsrecht, Atzung *f*, Ätzung, (Vieh)Weiderecht, (Vieh)Weideberechtigung

her(d)ship [*Scots law*]; brigancy [*The crime of driving away cattle by force*] · Rindviehraub *m*

herdwick, sheep walk, sheep run · Schaftrift *f*

herdwick → pasture (ground)

hereafter [*A word of futurity, always used in statutes and legal documents as indicative of future time, excluding both the present and the past*] · in Zukunft

her(ed)itable · erbfähig

hereditament, inheritable property, inheritable estate, hereditary property, hereditary estate · Erb(schafts)gut *n*, Erb(schafts)vermögen *n*, Erb(schafts)habe *f*

hereditament (purely) incorporeal appendant, (purely) incorporeal hereditament appendant [*Also spelled "appendent"*] · ununterbrochenes unkörperliches Erbgut *n*

hereditament (purely) incorporeal appurtenant, (purely) incorporeal hereditament appurtenant · nichtkörperliches anhaftendes Erbgut *n*, nichtkörperliches zugehöriges Erbgut, unkörperliches anhaftendes Erbgut, unkörperliches zugehöriges Erbgut, immaterielles anhaftendes Erbgut, immaterielles zugehöriges Erbgut

hereditary · Erb . . .

hereditary acceptance · Erbannahme *f*, Erbschaftsannahme

hereditary bondage (on an estate) → hereditary villanage

hereditary conveyance, hereditary transfer · Anerfälltnis *n*, Anfallung *f*, Anfall *m* einer Erbschaft, Übergang *m* einer Erbschaft auf einen Erben, Erb(schafts)anfall, Erb(schafts)übergang

hereditary demise → long-term lease(hold)

(hereditary) descent, heirdom, succession by inheritance, (hereditary) succession [*Succession to the ownership of an estate by inheritance*] · Erbgang *m*, Erbfolge *f*, erbrechtliche Nachfolge

(hereditary) descent according to foreign law, (hereditary) succession according to foreign law, succession by inheritance according to foreign law, heirdom according to foreign law · Erbfolge *f* nach ausländischem Recht, Erbfolge nach fremdem Recht, Erbgang *m* nach ausländischem Recht, Erbgang nach fremdem Recht, erbrechtliche Nachfolge nach ausländischem Recht, erbrechtliche Nachfolge nach fremdem Recht

(hereditary) descent per capita, heirdom per capita, succession by inheritance per capita, (hereditary) succession per capita · Erbgang *m* nach Köpfen, Erbfolge *f* nach Köpfen, erbrechtliche Nachfolge nach Köpfen

(hereditary) descent which tolls entry · Erbgang *m* welcher die Besitzergreifung aufhebt, Erbfolge *f* welche die Besitzergreifung aufhebt, erbrechtliche Nachfolge welche die Besitzergreifung aufhebt

hereditary duty · Erbanfallsteuer *f*, Erbschaftsanfallsteuer

hereditary estate, hereditament, inheritable property, inheritable estate, hereditary property · Erb(schafts)gut *n*, Erb(schafts)vermögen *n*, Erb(schafts)habe *f*

hereditary excise · unveränderliche Accise *f*

hereditary infeoffment [*Scotland*] → hereditary seisin

hereditary law, law of (hereditary) succession (and distribution), law of descent (and distribution), law of inheritance, inheritance law · Erb(folge)recht *n*, Erbgangrecht, Erbschaftsrecht, Nachkommensrecht, Vermögensnachfolgerecht

hereditary lease(hold) → hereditary tenancy

hereditary monarchy · Erbmonarchie *f*

hereditary peerage — hexagonal lattice

hereditary peerage · erbliche Pairswürde f

hereditary (pra(e)dial) bondage → hereditary villanage

hereditary property, hereditary estate, hereditament, inheritable property, inheritable estate · Erb(schafts)gut n, Erb(schafts)vermögen n, Erb(schafts)habe f

hereditary right, heritable right, right of inheritance, right of heirship, inheritance right, heirship right · Erb(schafts)anspruch m, Erb(schafts)(an)recht n

hereditary right in (fee) tail, right of heirship in (fee) tail, right of inheritance in (fee) tail, heritable right in (fee) tail · Anerbenrecht n [Das Recht eines einzelnen Erben eines bäuerlichen Besitzers in die ungeteilte Nachfolge des bäuerlichen Besitzes unter Ausschluß der Miterben]

hereditary servile status → hereditary villanage

hereditary status of a serf → hereditary villanage

(hereditary) succession according to foreign law, succession by inheritance according to foreign law, heirdom according to foreign law, (hereditary) descent according to foreign law · Erbfolge f nach ausländischem Recht, Erbfolge nach fremdem Recht, Erbgang m nach ausländischem Recht, Erbgang nach fremdem Recht, erbrechtliche Nachfolge nach ausländischem Recht, erbrechtliche Nachfolge nach fremdem Recht

(hereditary) succession, (hereditary) descent, heirdom, succession by inheritance [Succession to the ownership of an estate by inheritance] · Erbgang m, Erbfolge f, erbrechtliche Nachfolge

(hereditary) succession per capita, (hereditary) descent per capita, heirdom per capita, succession by inheritance per capita · Erbgang m nach Köpfen, Erbfolge f nach Köpfen, erbrechtliche Nachfolge nach Köpfen

hereditary tenancy, hereditary tenure, hereditary lease(hold) · Erbpacht(gut) f, (n) [Der Unterschied zwischen Erbpachtgut und Erbzinsgut besteht darin, daß beim Erbzinsgut eine niedrigere Abgabe gegeben wird, die nur zur Anerkennung des Obereigentums des Erbzinsherrn dient, bei dem Erbpachtgut die Abgabe höher und dem Ertrag entsprechend verschieden hoch ist]

hereditary tenure → hereditary tenancy

hereditary tenure of an office · erbliche Amtshaltung f

hereditary transfer, hereditary conveyance · Anerfälltnis n, Anfallung f, Anfall m einer Erbschaft, Übergang m einer Erbschaft auf einen Erben, Erb(schafts)anfall

hereditary village-magistrate · Leh(e)n(s)schulze m

hereditary villain status → hereditary villanage

hereditary villanage, hereditary bondage on an estate, hereditary (pra(e)dial) bondage, hereditary status of a serf, hereditary villain status, hereditary villein status, hereditary servile status, hereditary serfdom (on an estate), hereditary ville(i)nage · Erb(grund)hörigkeit f, Erbleibeigenschaft f, Erbhörigenstatus m, Erb-Bauerndienst m

hereditas jacens [Latin] · ruhende Erbschaft f

heregeat [Norman French] → heriot

heres, haeres [Latin]; heir (male), real representative · Erbe m

hergeative [Anglo-Saxon] → heriot

heribergum, fortified camp [Latin] · befestigtes Feldlager n

heriot, heriotum, har(r)iot [Latin]; heriet [Norman French]; heregeat, hergeative [Anglo-Saxon]; herezeld [Scotch term] [The right of the lord of a manor to the best beast of the deceased tenant of a manor, which beast might be seized by the lord, although it had never been within the manor; but if a customary freehold tenement was mortgaged, and the mortgagor being in possession died, the heriot was not due because he had no legal seisin at the time of his death] · Besthaupt n, Heergewätte n, Kumede f, Recht n auf den Fall, Sterbhaupt, Mortuarium f

heritable building right, lease(hold) · Erbbaurecht n [Das Recht auf fremdem Boden ein Bauwerk zu errichten]

heritable right, right of inheritance, right of heirship, inheritance right, heirship right, heritage right · Erb(schafts)anspruch m, Erb(schafts)(an)recht n

heritable right in (fee) tail, hereditary right in (fee) tail, right of heirship in (fee) tail, right of inheritance in (fee) tail · Anerbenrecht n [Das Recht eines einzelnen Erben eines bäuerlichen Besitzers in die ungeteilte Nachfolge des bäuerlichen Besitzes unter Ausschluß der Miterben]

hexagonal distribution → hexagonal lattice

hexagonal hierarchy · Hexagonalhierarchie f, Sechseckhierarchie, Sechskanthierarchie

hexagonal lattice, hexagonal system, hexagonal distribution, hexagonal pattern ·

Hexagonalgitter n, Sechseckgitter, Sechskantgitter

hexagonal market area · Hexagonal-Marktgebiet n, Sechseck-Marktgebiet, Sechskant-Marktgebiet

hexagonal pattern → hexagonal lattice

hexagonal system → hexagonal lattice

heybote → hedge-bote

hidage, hidegild, hydage, tax on hide (of land); hidagium [*Latin*] [*In old English law. An extraordinary tax payable to the king of every hide of land*] · Hufengeld n, Hufengroschen m, Hufensteuer f

hidare [*Latin*] [*To tax or assess land(s) by hides*] · veranlagen nach Hufe(ngut), veranlagen nach Hufenschoß

hida (terrae), hyda, familia, terra hydata, virgate terrae [*Latin*]; hide ((of) land), hyde (of land), higid, hiwise, virgate (land), verge of land, yardland, hydeland, husbandland, wista; hilda [*Scotland*] [*A quantity of land not of any certain extent, but as much as a plough can by course of husbandry plough in a year. It meant in different places anything from sixty to 120 acres. A virgate is one fourth of a hide*] · Hufe(ngut) f, (n), Hufenschoß n, Hube f, Hufen(gut)land n [*Ältere Benennungen: Hof m, Hub m, Hu(o)ba f, und Hova f*] [*Unter gutsherrlich-bäuerlichen Verhältnissen hieß der gesamte Besitz eines Dorfgenossen „Hufe(ngut)". Diese Benennung war also keine Flächengröße, sondern eine Besitzeinheit, die zahlreiche, zerstreut liegende kleine Ackerteile im Besitz derselben Person umfaßte*]

hidden, concealed · verborgen

hidden cost(s) · versteckte Kosten f

hidden defect, concealed defect, latent defect · verborgener (Sach)Mangel m, verborgener Baumangel, verdeckter (Sach)Mangel, verdeckter Baumangel

hidden household, potential household, concealed household [*It consists of a family living with relatives or other people because they are unable to obtain a separate dwelling*] · statistisch nicht erfaßbarer Haushalt m

hidden household, potential household, concealed household · Gemeinschaftshaushalt m

hidden unemployment, concealed unemployment · verdeckte Arbeitslosigkeit f

to hide, to secrete, to conceal · verbergen

hide and gain [*In ancient English law*] → arable land

to hide away, to abscond [*To depart secretly or to hide oneself from the jurisdiction of the court so as to avoid legal process. It may amount to an act of bankruptcy*] · flüchtig sein

hide ((of) land), hyde (of land), higid, hiwise, virgate (land), verge of land, yardland, hydeland, husbandland, wista; hilda [*Scotland*]; terra hydata, virgate terrae, hida (terrae), hyda, familia [*Latin*] [*A quantity of land not of any certain extent, but as much as a plough can by course of husbandry plough in a year. It meant in different places anything from sixty to 120 acres. A virgate is one fourth of a hide*] · Hufe(ngut) f, (n), Hufenschoß n, Hube f, Hufen(gut)land n [*Ältere Benennungen: Hof m, Hub m, Hu(o)ba f, und Hova f*] [*Unter gutsherrlich-bäuerlichen Verhältnissen hieß der gesamte Besitz eines Dorfgenossen „Hufe(ngut)". Diese Benennung war also keine Flächengröße, sondern eine Besitzeinheit, die zahlreiche, zerstreut liegende kleine Ackerteile im Besitz derselben Person umfaßte*]

hiding, abscondence · Flüchtigsein n

hiding debtor, absconding debtor · flüchtiger Schuldner m, flüchtig gewordener Schuldner

hierarchic(al) structure, hierarchy structure · hierarchische Stufung f

hierarchy of central places, nodality, central place hierarchy, centrality · Zentralität f, Hierarchie f zentraler Orte, Bedeutungsüberschuß m, Zentralorthierarchie, zentralörtliche Bedeutung f, Knotenpunktlage f, Zentralitätsgrad m [*Ein Ort versorgt sich und seine ländliche Umgebung mit Gütern und Dienstleistungen. Die Zentralität ist gleich seinem Bedeutungsüberschuß, d. h. gleich der relativen Bedeutung in bezug auf ein ihm zugehöriges Gebiet definiert*]

hierarchy structure, hierarchic(al) structure · hierarchische Stufung f

higgling, bargaining, haggling [*Bargaining over prices as an alternative to fixed prices for commodities*] · Aushandeln n von Preisen, Feilschen

high bid, high offer, high tender; high (bid) proposal (US) · Höchstangebot n, Meistangebot, Maximalangebot

high bidder, high tenderer, high offerer · Höchst(an)bieter m, Höchstfordernde, Meistfordernde, Meist(an)bieter

high (bid) proposal (US) → high bid

high capitalistic stage · hochkapitalistische Stufe f

high constable → high (parochial) constable

high contact · Berührung f höchster Ordnung [*Statistik*]

High Court of Chancery → Chancery Division

High Court of Delegates — highway construction authority

High Court of Delegates · Appellationsgericht *n* für geistliche und Admiralitätssachen [*Es wurde durch 2 und 3 Wilhelm IV. c. 92 ersetzt durch Judicial Committee of the Privy Council*]

High Court (of Justice) · Hoher Justizhof *m*, Obergerichtshof [*In England. Er hat drei Abteilungen: 1. für Erbschafts- und Vormundschaftssachen (Kanzleigericht(shof) = Chancery Division); 2. für Testaments-, Ehescheidungs- und Schiffahrtssachen (Probate, Divorce, Admiralty Division); 3. Schwurgericht für große Zivil- und schwere Kriminalsachen (Kings Bench Division)*]

high crime · schweres Verbrechen *n*

higher administrative court · Oberverwaltungsgericht *n*

higher education · höhere Bildung *f*

higher instance · höhere Instanz *f*

higher level · vorgesetzte Stelle *f*

higher level planning, planning on a higher than local level · überörtliche Planung *f*

higher than local level · überörtlich

higher unit, major world region, world's great regional belt, major natural region · Landschaftsgürtel *m*

highest-order fully-central place; super metropolis (US) · Reichs-Hauptort *m* [*nach W. Christaller*]

highest-order semi-central place · Reichs-Teilort *m* [*nach W. Christaller*]

highest tenure; alta tenura [*Latin*] · höchstes Leh(e)n *n*

high flyer · Wertpapier *n* mit hohem Kursanstieg

high-grade · hochwertig

high level analysis · Kosten-Wirksamkeits-Analyse *f* in der erweiterten Definition, KWA in der erweiterten Definition

high-low graph · Saisonkorridor *m* [*Statistik*]

highly developed cultural landscape, highly developed mand-made landscape · Vollkulturlandschaft, Hochkulturlandschaft *f* [*Völlig vom Menschen veränderter Naturraum*]

high offer, high tender; high (bid) proposal (US); high bid · Höchstangebot *n*, Meistangebot, Maximalangebot

high offerer, high bidder, high tenderer · Höchst(an)bieter *m*, Höchstfordernde, Meistfordernde, Meist(an)bieter

high-order fully central place → metropolitan city

high-order semi-central place · Gauort *m* [*nach W. Christaller*]

high (parochial) constable, chief (parochial) constable · Oberpolizeischulze *m*

high proposal (US) → high bid

high-rise development · Hochhausbebauung *f*; Hochhausüberbauung [*Schweiz*]

high-rise housing · Hochhauswohnungen *fpl*

high school · Oberschule *f*

high sea [*By this term, in the United States, is understood all of the uninclosed waters of the ocean beyond low-water mark*] · offene See *f*

high sea; altum mare [*Latin*] · hohe See *f*

high-speed boating, rapid boating, fast boating · motorisierter Bootssport *m*, motorischer Bootssport

high speed transit line → (public) high speed transit line

high speed transit policy → (public) high speed transit policy

high steward · Schutzherr *m* [*Ein von einer Stadt formell anerkannter und geehrter Großgrundbesitzer*]

high tender; high (bid) proposal (US); high bid, high offer · Höchstangebot *n*, Meistangebot, Maximalangebot

high tenderer, high offerer, high bidder · Höchst(an)bieter *m*, Höchstfordernde, Meistfordernde, Meist(an)bieter

high-wage, wage intensive · lohnstark, lohnintensiv

highway, road · Straße *f*

highway appearance, road appearance · Straßenbild *n*

highway authority, road authority · Straßenbehörde *f*

highway building, highway construction, road construction, roadbuilding · Straßenbau *m*

highway clean(s)ing, road clean(s)ing · Straßenreinigung *f*

highway clean(s)ing department, highway clean(s)ing division, road clean(s)ing department, road clean(s)ing division · Straßenreinigungsabteilung *f*

highway clean(s)ing division → highway clean(s)ing department

highway code, road code · Straßenverkehrsordnung *f*

highway construction, road construction, roadbuilding, highway building · Straßenbau *m*

highway construction administration, road construction administration · Straßenbauverwaltung *f*

highway construction authority, road construction authority · Straßenbaubehörde *f*

highway (construction) land, land for road construction, land for highway construction, land for road works, land for highway works, road (construction) land · Straßenbauboden *m*, Straßenbaufläche *f*, Straßen(bau)land *n*

highway construction of a Land, road construction of a Land, Land highway construction, Land road construction · Landesstraßenbau *m* [*Bundesrepublik Deutschland*]

highway construction office, road construction office · Straßenbauamt *n*

highway cost(s), road cost(s) · Straßenherstellungskosten *f*, Straßenbaukosten

highway cost(s) law, road cost(s) law · Straßenbaukostenrecht *n*

highway financing, road financing · Straßenbaufinanzierung *f*

highway ground, highway land, road ground, road land · Straßengelände *n*, Straßenland *n*, Straßenterrain *n*

highway land → highway (construction) land

highway law, road law · Straßenrecht *n*

highway lawmaking, highway legislation, road legislation, road lawmaking · Straßenbaugesetzgebung *f*

highway level, road level · Straßenhöhe *f*

highway maintenance cost(s), road maintenance cost(s) · Straßenunterhaltungskosten *f*

highway map, road map · Straßenkarte *f*

highway map series, road map series · Straßenkartenwerk *n*

highway noise, road noise · Straßenlärm *m*

highway nuisance, road nuisance · Straßenverkehrsgefährdung *f*

highway-orien(ta)ted, highway-related, road-related, road-orien(ta)ted · straßenbezogen, straßenorientiert

highway owner, road owner, highway proprietor, road proprietor · Straßeneigentümer *m*, Straßeneigner

highway planner, road planner · Straßenplaner *m*

highway planning, road planning · Straßenplanung *f*

highway pricing, road pricing · Anwendung *f* des Preismechanismus im Straßenverkehr

highway proprietor, road proprietor, highway owner, road owner · Straßeneigentümer *m*, Straßeneigner

highway relocation, road relocation · Straßenverlegung *f*

highway surveyor, road surveyor, surveyor of highways, surveyor of roads · Straßenaufseher *m*, Wegeaufseher

highway toll, road toll · Straßengeld *n*, Straßenzoll *m*, Straßen(benutzungs)gebühr *f*, Wegegeld *n*; Straßenmaut *f* [*Österreich*]

highway traffic authority, road traffic authority · Straßenverkehrsbehörde *f*

highway traffic law, road traffic law · Straßenverkehrsrecht *n*

highway user tax, road user tax · Straßenverkehrssteuer *f*

highway widening, road widening · Straßenerweiterung *f*, Straßenverbreiterung

higid, hiwise, virgate (land), verge of land, yardland, hydeland, husbandland, wista; hilda [*Scotland*]; terra hydata, virgate terrae, hida (terrae), hyda, familia [*Latin*]; hide ((of) land), hyde (of land) [*A quantity of land not of any certain extent, but as much as a plough can by course of husbandry plough in a year. It meant in different places anything from sixty to 120 acres. A virgate is one fourth of a hide*] · Hufe(ngut) *f*, (*n*), Hufenschoß *m*, Hube *f*, Hufen(gut)land *n* [*Ältere Benennungen: Hof m, Hub m, Hu(o)ba f, und Hova f*] [*Unter gutsherrlich-bäuerlichen Verhältnissen hieß der gesamte Besitz eines Dorfgenossen ,,Hufe(ngut)". Diese Benennung war also keine Flächengröße, sondern eine Besitzeinheit, die zahlreiche, zerstreut liegende kleine Ackerteile im Besitz derselben Person umfaßte*]

hiking trail · Wanderweg *m*

hilda [*Scotland*] → higid

hill city, hill town · Hügelstadt *f*

hill of debris · Trümmerberg *m*, Trümmerhügel *m*

hill of meeting, moot-hill, parl(ing)e hill [*In old records. A hill where courts were anciently held*] · Gerichtshügel *m*

hill-shading · Schräglichtschattierung *f*

hillside location, slope location · Hanglage *f*

hillside terraced coverage, slope-terraced coverage · Hang-Terrassenbebauung *f*; Hang-Terrassenüberbauung [*Schweiz*]

hill-top agro-town, hill-top agro-city · Hügelagrostadt *f*

hilltop settlement · Hügel(an)sied(e)lung *f*

hill town, hill city · Hügelstadt *f*

hilly ground, hilly terrain · Hügelgelände *n*, Hügelterrain *n*

hill(y) pasture · Hügelweide *f*

hilly terrain, hilly ground · Hügelgelände *n*, Hügelterrain *n*

**hinterland, ** catchment land, catchment area, catchment territory, tributary area, tributary territory, tributary land, outlay territory · Hinterland *n*, Einzugsgebiet *n*, Einzugsbereich *m*

hinterland population · Hinterlandbevölkerung *f*

hinterland town, hinterland city, subdominant · Hinterlandstadt *f*

to hire · mieten [*bewegliche Sache*]

to hire · dingen, einstellen [*Arbeiter*]

hire · (Sach)Miete *f* [*bewegliche Sache*]

hire, wage [*Compensation for labo(u)r and services*] · (Arbeits)Lohn *m*

hire burden, hire encumbrance, lease charge, lease incumbrance, lease burden, hire charge, hire incumbrance · Mietlast *f*, Mietbelastung *f*

hire-buyer, lease-purchaser, lease-buyer, hire-purchaser · Mietkäufer *m*

to hire by the day [*workman*] · dingen im Tagelohn, einstellen im Tagelohn [*Arbeiter*]

hire charge, hire incumbrance, hire burden, hire encumbrance, lease charge, lease incumbrance, lease burden · Mietlast *f*, Mietbelastung *f*

hire contract, hiring contract, contract of hire [*A contract by which one person grants to another either the enjoyment of a thing or the use of the labour and industry, either of himself, or his servant, during a certain time, for a stipulated compensation, or by which one contracts for the labour or services of another about a thing bailed to him for a specific purpose*] · Mietvertrag *m*

hire contract, contract of hiring, hiring contract [*A contract by which one person grants to another the use of the labour and industry, either of himself or his servant*] · Verdingungsvertrag *m*

hire contract, hiring contract, (contract of) hiring [*A contract by which one person grants to another the enjoyment of a thing*] · Sachmietvertrag *m*

hired equipment, hired plant · Fremdgerät(e) *n (pl)*, Mietgerät(e)

hired garden · Mietgarten *m*

hired labour (Brit.); hired labor (US) · eingestellte Arbeitskräfte *f pl*, gedingte Arbeitskräfte

hired plant, hired equipment · Fremdgerät(e) *n (pl)*, Mietgerät(e)

hired thing, thing hired · gemietete Sache *f*, gemieteter Gegenstand *m*, gemietetes Ding *n*

hire encumbrance, lease charge, lease incumbrance, lease burden, hire charge, hire incumbrance, hire burden · Mietlast *f*, Mietbelastung *f*

hire of custody, bailment for reward · Deponieren *n* gegen Entgelt durch eine Bank, entgeltliche Deponierung *f* durch eine Bank

hire of equipment, hiring of equipment, equipment hire, equipment hiring · (Bau)Gerätemieten *n*

hire-purchase, lease-purchase, lease with purchase option · Mietkauf *m*

hire-purchase act, hire-purchase law, lease-purchase act, lease-purchase statute, lease-purchase law, hire-purchase statute · Mietkaufgesetz *n*

hire-purchase agreement, lease-purchase agreement · Mietkaufabkommen *n*, Mietkaufabmachung *f*, Mietkaufvereinbarung

hire-purchase construction, lease-purchase construction · Mietkaufbau *m*

hire-purchase contract, lease-purchase contract, contract for hire-purchase, contract for lease-purchase · Mietkaufvertrag *m*

hire-purchase equipment, lease-purchase equipment · Mietkaufgerät *n*

hire-purchase finance house · Teilzahlungsbank *f*

hire-purchase law, lease-purchase law · Mietkaufrecht *n*

hire-purchase legislation, lease-purchase lawmaking, hire-purchase lawmaking, lease-purchase legislation · Mietkaufgesetzgebung *f*

hire-purchase project, lease-purchase project · Mietkaufprojekt *n*

hire-purchaser, hire-buyer, lease-purchaser, lease-buyer · Mietkäufer *m*

hirer, conductor · (Sach)Mieter *m* [*bewegliche Sache*]

hiring · Mieten *n* [*bewegliche Sache*]

hiring contract, contract of hire, hire contract [*A contract by which one person grants to another either the enjoyment of a thing or the use of the labour and industry, either of himself, or his servant, during a certain time, for a stipulated compensation, or by which one contracts for the labour or services of another about a thing bailed to him for a specific purpose*] · Mietvertrag *m*

hiring contract, hire contract, contract of hiring [*A contract by which one person grants to another the use of the labour and industry, either of himself or his servant*] · Verdingungsvertrag *m*

hiring contract, (contract of) hiring, hire contract [*A contract by which one person grants to another the enjoyment of a thing*] · Sachmietvertrag *m*

hiring of equipment, equipment hire, equipment hiring, hire of equipment · (Bau)Gerätemieten *n*

(his) clergy, benefit of (his) clergy [*Old Law. Originally the privilege of exemption from trial by a secular court, allowed to or claimed by clergymen arraigned for felony; in later times the privilege of exemption from the sentence, which in the case of certain offences might be pleaded on his first conviction by every one who could read. Abolished in England, after various earlier modifications, in 1827*] · Besserstellung *f* der Geistlichkeit, Kirchenasyl *n*

histogramm · Histogramm *n*, Staffelbild *n*, Treppenbild, Treppendiagramm, Staffeldiagramm

historian of law, law historian · Rechtshistoriker *m*

historic(al) city, historic(al) town · historische Stadt *f*, geschichtliche Stadt

historic(al) cityscape, historic(al) townscape, historic(al) urban landscape · geschichtliche Stadtlandshaft *f*, geschichtliche Städtelandschaft, historische Städtelandschaft, historische Stadtlandschaft

historic(al) consciousness · Geschichtsbewußtsein *n*

historic(al) core, kernel · Altstadt *f*

historic(al) costing, actual cost(s) accounting, historic(al) cost(s) accounting, actual costing [*The ascertainment of cost(s) after they have been incurred*] · Istkostenrechnung *f*

historic(al) cost(s), actual cost(s) · tatsächliche Kosten *f*, wirkliche Kosten, historische Kosten, Istkosten, wirklicher Anschaffungswert, tatsächlicher Anschaffungswert, historischer Anschaffungswert, Istanschaffungswert *m*

historic(al) jurisprudence · geschichtliche Rechtslehre *f*, historische Rechtslehre [*Sie ist von der Rechtsgeschichte zu unterscheiden, denn sie sucht aus der Rechtsgeschichte allgemeine Erkenntnisse in bezug auf die Rechtsentwick(e)lung und ihrer Erscheinungen zu gewinnen*]

historic(al) monument [*A structure surviving from a former period*] · historisches Denkmal *n*, geschichtliches Denkmal

historic(al) pictorial map · geschichtliche Bildkarte *f*, historische Bildkarte

historical province · historische Landschaft *f*, geschichtliche Landschaft

historic(al) site · geschichtliche Stätte *f*, historische Stätte, geschichtlicher Ort *m*, historischer Ort

historic(al) space research, historic(al) spatial research · historische Raumforschung *f*, geschichtliche Raumforschung

historic(al) street · geschichtliche (Stadt)Straße *f*, historische (Stadt)Straße

historic(al) structure [*A structure or group of structures constructed by man, connected to the earth and judged to have historical significance*] · Baudenkmal *n*, historisches Bauwerk *n*, geschichtliches Bauwerk

historic(al) town, historic(al) city · historische Stadt *f*, geschichtliche Stadt

historic(al) townscape, historic(al) urban landscape, historic(al) cityscape · geschichtliche Stadtlandshaft *f*, geschichtliche Städtelandschaft, historische Städtelandschaft, historische Stadtlandschaft

historic(al) urban landscape, historic(al) cityscape, historic(al) townscape · geschichtliche Stadtlandshaft *f*, geschichtliche Städtelandschaft, historische Städtelandschaft, historische Stadtlandschaft

historic preservation, historic conservation, conservation of monuments, preservation of monuments · Denkmalerhaltung *f*, Denkmalpflege *f*, Denkmalschutz *m*

history atlas · Geschichtsatlas *m*

history of law, legal history · Rechtsgeschichte *f*

history of prices, price history · Geschichte *f* der Preise, Preisgeschichte

history of private law, private law history · Privatrechtsgeschichte *f*

history of settlement · Sied(e)lungsgeschichte *f*

history of the common law, common law history · Gemeinrechtsgeschichte *f*

hiwise, virgate (land), verge of land, yardland, hydeland, husbandland, wista; hilda [*Scotland*]; terra hydata, virgate terrae, hida (terrae), hyda, familia [*Latin*]; hide ((of) land), hyde (of land), higid [*A quantity of land not of any certain extent, but as much as a plough can by course of husbandry plough in a year. It meant in different places anything from sixty to 120 acres. A virgate is one fourth of a hide*] · Hufe(ngut) *f*, *(n)*, Hufenschoß *n*, Hube *f*, Hufen(gut)land *n* [*Ältere Benennungen: Hof m, Hub m, Hu(o)ba f, und Hova f*] [*Unter gutsherrlich-bäuerlichen Verhältnissen hieß der gesamte Besitz eines Dorfgenossen „Hufe(ngut)". Diese Benennung war also keine Flächengröße, sondern eine Besitzeinheit, die zahlreiche, zerstreut liegende kleine Ackerteile im Besitz derselben Person umfaßte*]

to hoard [*To accumulate and hide or keep in reserve*] · hamstern

hoarding · Holzbauzaun *m*

hoarding [*something hoarded*] · Hamstergut *n*

hoarding · Hamstern *n*

hoarding → (advertisement) hoarding

to hold [*office*] · innehaben [*Amt*]

to hold [*To have an estate on condition of paying rent, or performing service*] · gepachtet (haben)

to hold accountable, to call to account, to make responsible · verantwortlich machen, rechenschaftspflichtig machen

to hold and to enjoy · behaupten [*Grundeigentum*]

holder, bearer [*The possessor of any personal endowment or quality; the holder of rank or office*] · Träger *m*, Inhaber

holder → (land) holder

holder at will → (land) holder at will

holder by law · Rechtsinhaber *m*

holder for life → life (land) lessee

holder for value, cheque bearer, cheque holder (Brit.); check bearer, check holder (US) · Scheckinhaber *m*, Scheckträger

holder from year to year → (land) holder from year to year

holder in fact, bearer in fact · tatsächlicher Inhaber *m*, tatsächlicher Träger, wirklicher Inhaber, wirklicher Träger

holder in good faith, bona fide holder · gutgläubiger Inhaber *m*

holder of a feudal benefice, land tenant, (feudal) tenant, manorial tenant, feudal bond(s)man, vassal, tenant of land, feeholder, holder of a fee, holder of a fief, fief-tenant, feoda(to)ry, feuda(to)ry; homo pertinens [*Latin*]; beneficiary [*A tenant or vassal who held his estate by feudal service*] · Leh(e)n(s)mann *m*, Leh(e)n(s)träger *m*, Gefolgsmann, Gutszinsmann, Vasall

holder of an allodium; liber homo, homo liber [*Latin*]; allodiary, allodialist, al(l)odial (land) owner, absolute (land) owner, exclusive (land) owner, absolute proprietor, exclusive proprietor, al(l)odial proprietor, free man · absoluter Eigentümer *m*, unbeschränkter Eigentümer, Alleineigentümer, Freiguteigentümer, Allodialeigentümer, freier Mann, Freie

holder of a pawn, pawn holder, pledgee, holder of a pledge, mortgagee, pledge holder, pawnee [*The person who receives the security and lends the money to the pledgor*] · Pfandgläubiger *m*, Pfandnehmer, Pfandbesitzer, Pfandhalter, Pfandinhaber, Sicherungsnehmer

holder of estate → (land) holder

holder of government stock, government stock holder · Gläubiger *m* einer staatlichen Darleh(e)n(s)schuld

holder of land, land tenant, (real) estate possessor, (real) property possessor, realty possessor, landed estate possessor, land possessor, land(ed) property possessor, landholder, possessor of land, possessor of (real) estate, possessor of (real) property, tenant of land · Grund(stücks)besitzer *m*, Landbesitzer, Bodenbesitzer, Immobilienbesitzer, Immobiliarbesitzer, Liegenschaftsbesitzer

holder of land at will → (land) holder at will

holder of land from year to year → (land) holder from year to year

holder of property → (land) holder

holder of (real) estate → (land) holder

holder of (real) property → (land) holder

holder of virgate, holder of verge of land, yardling; virgarius [*Latin*]; tenant by the verge, holder of yardland [*Tenant who held copyhold after a symbolic surrender and delivery of a small rod (= verge)*] · Hüf(e)ner *m*, Hufenbauer, Huf(e)ner

holder paying in products of the soil → (land) holder paying in products of the soil

holder policy, bearer policy · Inhaberpolice *f*, Trägerpolice

holder's association → (land) holder's association

holder's lien → (land)holder's lien

to hold harmless, to indemnify, to save harmless [*To secure against loss or damage*] · decken, schadlos halten

hold-harmless clause · Schadloshaltungsklausel *f*, Haftungsübernahmeklausel, Haftpflichtübernahmeklausel

hold-harmless contract [*A collateral contract by which one person engages to secure another against an anticipated loss or to prevent him from being damnified by the legal consequences of an act or forbearance on the part of one of the parties or of some third person*] · Haftpflichtübernahmevertrag *m*, Haftungsübernahmevertrag, Schadloshaltungsvertrag

holding · Inbesitzhaben *n*

holding capacity (of an area), physical capacity (of an area) · Aufnahmefähigkeit *f*, Sied(e)lungskapazität *f*, Trag-

holding (company) — **home farm (of the lord of the manor)**

fähigkeit, tragbare Bevölkerung f, Aufnahmevermögen n, potentielle Einwohnerzahl f [*Die Einwohnerzahl, die aus dem gegebenen Sachpotential eines Gebietes bei Zugrundelegung eines bestimmten Standards unter rationalen Verhältnissen auf längere Sicht eine Existenz finden kann*]

holding (company); shell company [*colloquial term*] · Holdinggesellschaft f, Dachgesellschaft, Kontrollgesellschaft, Effektenhaltegesellschaft

holding harmless [*Protection against any loss, damage, or injury which has occurred or may occur in the future*] · Haftungsübernahme f, Haftpflichtübernahme, Schadloshaltung f, Haftbarkeitsübernahme

holding out, holdout [*A person "holds out" another as having authority to act as his agent when he so acts as to induce third persons to believe in the existence of such authority, which he is estopped from denying if they act on that belief. On the principle of estoppel, any representation made by words or conduct or knowingly suffered to be made by others that a person is a partner in a firm, on the faith of which representation credit has been given to the firm, makes the person so representing himself liable as a partner to that creditor, to the extent of the loss which the creditor has thereby suffered (Partnership Act, 1890, s. 3)*] · Haftung f von Nichtpartnern, Haftpflicht f von Nichtpartnern, Haftbarkeit f von Nichtpartnern

holding over [*Retaining possession as tenant of property leased, after the end of the term*] · Pachtverlängerung f, Verharren n

holding over · Auszugsverweigerung f [*Verweigerung aus einer Wohnung auszuziehen*]

to hold land for estate · nutznießen [*Land*]

to hold over [*To retain possession as tenant of property leased, after the end of the term*] · verharren

to hold over after expiration of lease · unrechtmäßig verlängern [*Mietverhältnis*]

hold period · Bindungszeit f des Bieters an sein Angebot

holiday letting (of premis(s)es) · Ferienvermietung f

holiday pay · Feiertagsgeld n

holiday period (camping) site → (summer) holiday period (camping) site

holiday-period caravan site · Ferien-Wohnwagenplatz m

holiday resort · Ferienort m

holidays with pay · bezahlter Urlaub m

(h)olographic will [*It is written entirely in the handwriting of the testator*] · eigenhändiges Testament n

homage, manhood; homagium, hominiscum, hominium, hominatus, hominatio, hominiscatus [*Latin*] [*In feudal law. A service (or the ceremony of rendering it) which a tenant was bound to perform to his lord on receiving investiture of a fee, or succeeding to it as heir, in acknowledgment of the tenure. Not to be confused with "fealty"*] · Huldigung f

home, dwelling place [*The present intention of a person to reside permanently or for an indefinite period within the limits of a country*] · Niederlassung f [*Die Niederlassung wird „facto et amino" erworben, der Aufenthalt nur „facto"*]

home(-based) trip, home(-based) travel, home(-based) journey · Heimfahrt f

homebuilder, homemaker · Eigenhausbauer m, Eigenheimbauer

homebuilding, homemaking · Eigenhausbau m, Eigenheimbau

homebuilding activity, homemaking activity · Eigenhausbautätigkeit f, Eigenheimbautätigkeit

homebuilding industry, homemaking industry · Eigenhausbauindustrie f, Eigenheimbauindustrie

homebuilding loan · Bauspardarleh(e)n n

homebuilding market, homemaking market · Eigenhausbaumarkt m, Eigenheimbaumarkt

home buyer · Eigenhauskäufer m, Eigenheimkäufer

home buyers association, HBA · Eigenheimkäufergesellschaft f, Eigenhauskäufergesellschaft

home buying · Eigenhauskauf m, Eigenheimkauf

home care · Eigenhauspflege f, Eigenheimpflege

home city, home town · Heimatstadt f

home colonization, home settlement, colonization within a State's own territory, settlement within a State's own territory · (B)Innenkolonisation f, innere Kolonisation

home development · Eigenhausbebauung f, Eigenheimbebauung

home economics · Eigenhaus-Hauswirtschaft f, Eigenheim-Hauswirtschaft

home farm (of the lord of the manor), demesnial settlement; terra indominicata, terra dominica [*Latin*]; demain (land), demeyne (land), demeine (land), demesne (land), inland, land in (the lord's) demesne, bordland, table

home for the elderly — homestead estate

demesne [*Those lands of a manor not granted out in tenancy, but reserved by the lord for his own use and occupation. The opposite of "tenemental lands"*] · Hoffeld *n*, Salland *n*, grundherrliches Eigenland, Hofländerei *f*, Hofland, grundherrschaftliches Eigenland

home for the elderly, (residential) home for the elderly people, hostel for the elderly people, hostel for the elderly · (Alten)Wohnheim *n*, Seniorenwohnheim

home freight, back freight, return freight · Rückfracht *f*

home furnishing · Eigenheimausstattung *f*, Eigenhausausstattung

home improvement · Eigenhausmodernisierung *f*, Eigenheimmodernisierung

homeless · wohnungslos, obdachlos

homelessness · Obdachlosigkeit *f*

homeless person · obdachlose Person *f*

home loan · Eigenheimdarleh(e)n *n*, Eigenhausdarleh(e)n

home maintenance · Eigenhausunterhaltung *f*, Eigenheimunterhaltung

homemaker, homebuilder · Eigenhausbauer *m*, Eigenheimbauer

homemaking, homebuilding · Eigenhausbau *m*, Eigenheimbau

homemaking activity, homebuilding activity · Eigenhausbautätigkeit *f*, Eigenheimbautätigkeit

homemaking industry, homebuilding industry · Eigenhausbauindustrie *f*, Eigenheimbauindustrie

homemaking market, homebuilding market · Eigenhausbaumarkt *m*, Eigenheimbaumarkt

home manufacturer, home prefabricator · Fertigeigenheimhersteller *m*

home market · Eigenhausmarkt *m*, Eigenheimmarkt

home mortgage · Eigenhaushypothek *f*, Eigenheimhypothek

home mortgage debt · Eigenheimhypothekenschuld *f*

Home Office [*England*] · Innenministerium *n*

homeowner · Eigenhauseigentümer *m*, Eigenheimeigentümer, Eigenheimer

home(owner's estate) · Eigenheim *n*, Eigenhaus *n*

home ownership · Heimeigentum *n*

home planner · Eigenhausgestalter *m*, Eigenheimgestalter

home possessor · Eigenhausbesitzer *m*, Eigenheimbesitzer

home prefabricator, home manufacturer · Fertigeigenheimhersteller *m*

home product, domestic product · Inlandsprodukt *n*, IP, einheimisches Produkt

home-room teacher (US); form master (Brit.) · Klassenlehrer *m*

home rule, municipal ordinances and rules and regulations · Selbstverwaltungsrecht *n*

home rule all round · allgemeine Autonomie *f*

Home Secretary · Innenminister *m* [*Großbritannien*]

home seeker · Eigenhausreflektant *m*, Eigenheimreflektant

home settlement, colonization within a State's own territory, settlement within a State's own territory, home colonization · (B)Innenkolonisation *f*, innere Kolonisation

home shelter · Eigenhaus-Schutzbunker *m*, Eigenheim-Schutzbunker

homesite · Eigenhausgrundstück *n*, Eigenheimgrundstück

homestead [*The dwelling place of a family, including house, accessory buildings, and land*] · Heimstätte *f*

homestead → (right of) homestead

homestead accessories · Heimstättenzubehör *n*

homestead act, homestead statute, homestead law; homestead exemption act, homestead exemption statute, homestead exemption law [*USA*] · Heimstättengesetz *n*

homestead area, homestead territory · Heimstättenfläche *f*, Heimstättengebiet *n*

homestead association, homestead institution, homestead society · Heimstättenverein(igung) *m*, (*f*)

homestead authority · Heimstättenbehörde *f*

homestead board · Heimstättenamt *n*

homestead company · Heimstätte *f*, Wohnungsfürsorgegesellschaft *f*, WoG.

homestead contract · Heimstättenvertrag *m*

homestead corporation · Heimstättengesellschaft *f*

homestead declaration, declaration of homestead · Heimstättenerklärung *f*

homesteader, homestead owner · Heimstätter *m*, Heimstätteneigentümer

homestead estate, homestead right, (right of) homestead [*It is created by statute, and consists in the right to enjoy, free from liability for debts, a certain speci-*

homestead exemption — hopeless

fied amount of land which is being occupied as a residence] · Heimstätte f

homestead exemption · Heimstätte f einer gerichtlichen Pfändung entzogen

homestead garden · Heimstättengarten m

homestead heiress, homestead female heir · Heimstättenerbin f

homestead heir (male) · Heimstättenerbe m

homesteading · Heimstättenbildung f

homestead inheritance · Heimstättenerbe n, Heimstättenerbschaft f

homestead inheritance act, homestead inheritance law, homestead inheritance statute · Heimstättenerbgesetz n

homestead inheritance law · Heimstättenerbrecht n

homestead land · Heimstättenland n, Heimstättenboden m

homestead law · Heimstättenrecht n

homestead legislation, homestead lawmaking · Heimstättengesetzgebung f

homestead owner, homesteader · Heimstätter m, Heimstätteneigentümer

homestead ownership (of property), homestead proprietorship, homestead (general) property · Heimstätteneigentum n

homestead property → homestead ownership (of property)

homestead right, (right of) homestead, homestead estate [*It is created by statute, and consists in the right to enjoy, free from liability for debts, a certain specified amount of land which is being occupied as a residence*] · Heimstätte f

homestead settlement · Heimstättensied(e)lung f, Heimstättenansied(e)lung

homestead succession · Heimstättenfolge f

homestead successor · Heimstättennachfolger m

homestead territory, homestead area · Heimstättenfläche f, Heimstättengebiet n

home town, home city · Heimatstadt f

home trade, domestic trade, inland trade · Binnenhandel m

homeworker · Heimarbeiter m

home(-work) industry, cottage industry, financed work, sweated industry, domestic industry, domestic system · Hausindustrie f, Verlagssystem n, Heim(arbeits)industrie, Verlag m

homo ecclesiasticus [*Latin*]; church vassal · Kirchenvasall m

homogeneity degree, degree of homogeneity · Homogenitätsgrad m, Einheitlichkeitsgrad

homogeneous area · homogene Fläche f [*Theorie der zentralen Orte*]

homo liber, liber homo [*Latin*]; allodiary, allodialist, al(l)odial (land) owner, absolute (land) owner, exclusive (land) owner, absolute proprietor, exclusive proprietor, al(l)odial proprietor, free man, holder of an allodium · absoluter Eigentümer m, unbeschränkter Eigentümer, Alleineigentümer, Freiguteigentümer, Allodialeigentümer, freier Mann m, Freie m

homo pertinens [*Latin*]; beneficiary, holder of a feudal benefice, land tenant, (feudal) tenant, manorial tenant, feudal bondman, vassal, tenant of land, feeholder, holder of a fee, holder of a fief, fief-tenant, feoda(to)ry, feuda(to)ry [*A tenant or vassal who held his estate by feudal service*] · Leh(e)n(s)mann m, Leh(e)n(s)träger m, Gefolgsmann, Gutszinsmann, Vasall m

honestly, without fraud; bona fide [*Latin*]; in good faith, of good faith, innocent · aufrichtig, in gutem Glauben, ehrlich, gutgläubig

honesty, sincerity; bona fides [*Latin*]; good faith, loyalty and faith · Aufrichtigkeit f, Ehrlichkeit f, guter Glaube m, Treu' f und Glauben m

honorable service (US); honourable service (Brit.) · Ehrendienst m

honorarium [*A payment made for services for which custom or professional ethics precludes the setting of a price or the presentation of a bill. It is sometimes considered a token payment for free services*] · Ehrensold m

honorary freedom · Ehrenbürgerrecht n

honorary freedom act, honorary freedom law, honorary freedom statute · Ehrenbürgergesetz n

honorary law; jus honorarium [*Latin*] · Ehrenrecht n

honorary magistrate, justice of the peace · ehrenamtlicher Friedensrichter m

(honorary service of) grand serjeanty; magna serjeantia, magna serjanteria, magnum servitium [*Latin*] · persönlicher Leh(e)n(s)dienst m [*gegenüber dem Souverän*]

honour(able) degree · Ehren(universitäts)grad m [*England*]

honourable service (Brit.); honorable service (US) · Ehrendienst m

hop-district · Hopfenbezirk m

hopeless, non collectable, noncollectible, nonrecoverable, nonobtainable, uncollectable, unrecoverable, uncollectible, bad, irrecoverable, unobtainable, desperate · nicht beitreibbar, nicht einziehbar, nicht eintreibbar, uneinziehbar, uneintreibbar, uneinbringlich, unbeitreibbar [*Schuld*]

hope of success (in achievement), hope of achieving success · Erfolgshoffnung *f*

horizon light, sky light · Himmelslicht *n*

horizontal mobility, internal migration · Binnenwanderung *f*

horizontal pattern, horizontal scheme · waag(e)rechtes Muster *n*, waag(e)rechtes Schema

horizontal privity · Beziehung *f* zwischen Verkäufer und Letztabnehmer

horizontal scale · Linienmaßstab *m*, Längenmaßstab, Horizontalmaßstab

horizontal tie · waag(e)rechte Bindung *f*

horizontal utilization of (a) plot · horizontale (Grundstücks)Ausnutzung *f*, waag(e)rechte (Grundstücks)Ausnutzung

horned beasts, horned cattle · Hornvieh *n*

horseshoe-shaped row village · hufeisenförmiges Reihendorf *n*

horseback riding stable · Reitstall *m*

"horse deal" · ,,Pferdekauf" *m*

horse-drawn vehicle · (Pferde)Fuhrwerk *n*

horse ranch · Pferdezuchtgut *n*

horseway · Reitweg *m*

horticultural settlement · gärtnerische (An)Sied(e)lung *f*

hospital-rate · (örtliche) Krankenhaussteuer *f*, lokale Krankenhaussteuer, gemeindliche Krankenhaussteuer, kommunale Krankenhaussteuer

hospital uses [*Those uses related to the functions of a hospital in providing care and treatment of the ill or injured, including the housing, feeding, and care of resident interns, physicians, and nurses*] · Krankenhausfürsorge *f*

hostel for the elderly, hostel for elderly people, (residential) home for elderly people, (residential) home for the elderly · Wohnheim *n*, Altenwohnheim, Seniorenwohnheim

hostel for the homeless · Obdachlosenheim *n*

hostile capture · Beuterecht *n*

hostile foreigner [*India*]; alien enemy, enemy alien, alien enemi · Feindausländer *m*, feindlicher Ausländer

hostilities · Feindseligkeiten *fpl*

hotchpot(ch), collation; collatio bonorum [*Latin*] [*In Roman and Scots law. The throwing together of the possessions of several persons, in order to an equal division of the whole stock*] · Besitzzusammenlegung *f* zwecks gleichmäßiger Verteilung, Gemengsel *n*, Farrago *n*

hot house vegatable cultivation · Treibhaus-Gemüseanbau *m*, Treibhaus-Gemüsekultur *f*

hot money, bad money · heißes Geld *n*, Fluchtgeld [*Devisenbörse*]

hour benefit plan → hour(ly) (pension) plan

hour earning → hour(ly) earning

hour fee → hour(ly) fee

hour(ly) benefit plan → hour(ly) (pension) plan

hour(ly) earning · Stundenverdienst *m*

hourly earning · Stundenverdienst *m*

hour(ly) (pension) plan, hour(ly) benefit plan, hour(ly) retirement plan · Pensionsplan *m* für Lohnempfänger, (Alters)Versorgungsplan für Lohnempfänger

hour(ly) rate · Stundensatz *m*

hour(ly) retirement plan → hour(ly) (pension) plan

hour(ly) wage · Stundenlohn *m*

hour(ly) wage contract · Stundenlohnvertrag *m*

hour(ly) wage rate · Stundenlohnsatz *m*

hour(ly) wage sheet · Stundenlohnzettel *m*

hour of supervision, supervising hour · Aufsichtsstunde *f*, Überwachungsstunde *f*

hour of work, work(ing) hour · Arbeitsstunde *f*

to house, to accommodate · unterbringen

house, residential structure [*In Schottland bedeuten ,,house" eine Wohnung, auch wenn sie aus nur einem Raum besteht, und ,,tenement" ein Haus. In England ist es umgekehrt*] · Haus *n*

house acquisition · Häuserwerb(ung) *m*, *(f)*

house-agent · Gebäudemakler *m*, Häusermakler

house alteration, house conversion · Hausumbau *m*

house-boat · Hausboot *n*

hous(e)bote, focage, focale [*An allowance of wood made to a tenant, for repairing his house*] · Bauholzbezugsrecht *n*, Hauszubuße *f*, Bauholzberechtigung *f*

(house)breaker · Einbrecher *m*

(house)breaking · Einbruch *m*

hous(ebuild)ing, housing construction, production of dwelling units, erection of dwelling units, production of housing units, erection of housing units, production of living units, erection of living units (US); production of tenements, erection of tenements, production of dwellings, erection of dwellings, production of housing, erection of housing, residential construction, residential building · Wohn(ungs)bau *m*, Wohnungserstellung *f*, Wohnungsproduktion *f*, Häuserbau, Hausbau, Mietwohn(ungs)bau, Mietwohnungserstellung, Mietwohnungsproduktion, Miethäuserbau, Miethausbau

hous(ebuild)ing act, hous(ebuild)ing law, hous(ebuild)ing statute · WBauG *n*, WoBauG, Wohn(ungs)baugesetz

hous(ebuild)ing action area · Wohn(ungs)baugebiet *n*

hous(ebuild)ing activity · Wohn(ungs)bautätigkeit *f*, Wohnungsfürsorge *f* [*Im weitesten Sinne jede zielbewußte auf die geregelte Befriedigung des Wohnungsbedürfnisses namentlich anderer Personen gerichtete Tätigkeit*]

hous(ebuild)ing amendment act · Wohn(ungs)bauzusatzgesetz *n*

hous(ebuild)ing and urban development law · Recht *n* über Wohn(ungs)bau und Stadtentwick(e)lung

hous(ebuild)ing assistor, hous(ebuild)ing sponsor, hous(ebuild)ing promoter, hous(ebuild)ing assistant, hous(ebuild)ing assister · Wohn(ungs)baufördernde *m*, Wohn(ungs)bauförderer

hous(ebuild)ing by extension, residential building by extension, residential construction by extension, production of dwelling units by extension, production of housing units by extension, production of living units by extension (US); production of tenements by extension, production of dwellings by extension, production of housing by extension · Wohn(ungs)bau *m* durch Erweiterung, Wohnungserstellung *f* durch Erweiterung, Wohnungsproduktion *f* durch Erweiterung [*Schaffung von Wohnraum durch Aufstockung oder Anbau*]

hous(ebuild)ing code of practice · Wohn(ungs)baumerkblatt *n*

hous(ebuild)ing committee · Wohn(ungs)bauausschuß *m*

hous(ebuild)ing contract · Wohn(ungs)bauvertrag *m*

hous(ebuild)ing cooperative, benefit housing society, cooperative housing society, benefit housing association, cooperative housing association · Wohnungsgenossenschaft *f* [*Fehlbenennungen: (Wohnungs)Baugenossenschaft*] [*Wohnungsunternehmen in der Rechtsform der eingetragenen Genossenschaft, deren Zweck der Bau, die Bewirtschaftung und/oder die Verwaltung von Wohnungen und deren Überlassung zur Nutzung oder zu Eigentum an die Mitglieder ist. Die häufig verwendeten Benennungen „(Wohnungs)Baugenossenschaft" sind begrifflich insofern irreführend, als die deutschen Wohnungsgenossenschaften keine Produktivgenossenschaften (Bauunternehmen) sind; zutreffender ist daher die Benennung „Wohnungsgenossenschaft"*]

hous(ebuild)ing credit · Wohn(ungs)baukredit *m*

hous(ebuild)ing enterprise, hous(ebuild)ing undertaking · Wohn(ungs)unternehmen *n*

hous(ebuild)ing enterprise of public usefulness, hous(ebuild)ing enterprise of public utility, hous(ebuild)ing enterprise useful to the public · gemeinnütziges Wohn(ungs)unternehmen *n*, gemeinnötiges Wohn(ungs)unternehmen

hous(ebuild)ing field, hous(ebuild)ing sector · Wohn(ungs)bausektor *m*

hous(ebuild)ing financing, financing of hous(ebuild)ing · Wohn(ungs)baufinanzierung *f*

hous(ebuild)ing financing act, hous(ebuild)ing financing law, hous(ebuild)ing financing statute · Wohn(ungs)baufinanzierungsgesetz *n*

hous(ebuild)ing financing provision · Wohn(ungs)baufinanzierungsbestimmung *f*

hous(ebuild)ing for officers, hous(ebuild)ing for officials · Beamtenwohn(ungs)bau *m*

hous(ebuild)ing for the elderly · Altenwohn(ungs)bau *m*

hous(ebuild)-ing for the working classes · Arbeiterwohn(ungs)bau *m*

hous(ebuild)ing fund · Wohn(ungs)baumittel *f*, Wohn(ungs)baufonds *m*

hous(ebuild)ing industry · Wohn(ungs)bauindustrie *f*

hous(ebuild)ing law · Wohn(ungs)baurecht *n*

hous(ebuild)ing law, hous(ebuild)ing statute, hous(ebuild)ing act · WBauG *n*, WoBauG, Wohn(ungs)baugesetz

hous(ebuild)ing lawmaking, hous(ebuild)ing legislation · Wohn(ungs)baugesetzgebung *f*

hous(ebuild)ing loan · Wohn(ungs)baudarleh(e)n *n*, Wohnungsfürsorgedarleh(e)n

hous(ebuild)ing loan bank · Wohn(ungs)baukreditbank *f*

hous(ebuild)ing market · Wohn(ungs)baumarkt *m*

hous(ebuild)ing mortgage, residential mortgage · Wohn(ungs)bauhypothek *f*, Wohn(ungs)hypothek

hous(ebuild)ing mortgage interest rate, residential mortgage interest rate · Wohn(ungs)bauhypothekenzinssatz *m*

hous(ebuild)ing order · Wohn(ungs)bauauftrag *m*

hous(ebuild)ing ordinance · Wohn(ungs)bauverordnung *f*

hous(ebuild)ing planner · Wohn(ungs)bauplaner *m*

hous(ebuild)ing planning · Wohn(ungs)bauplanung *f*

hous(ebuild)ing practice · Wohn(ungs)bauwesen *n*

hous(ebuild)ing premium · Wohn(ungs)bauprämie *f*

hous(ebuild)ing premium law, hous(ebuild)ing premium act, hous(ebuild)ing premium statute · Wohnbauprämiengesetz *n*, Wohnungsbauprämiengesetz, WoPG, Wohn(ungs)bauaufgeldgesetz

hous(ebuild)ing project · Wohn(ungs)bauprojekt *n*, Wohn(ungs)bauvorhaben *n*

hous(ebuild)ing promoter, hous(ebuild)ing assistant, hous(ebuild)ing assister, hous(ebuild)ing assistor, hous(ebuild)ing sponsor · Wohn(ungs)baufördernde *m*, Wohn(ungs)bauförderer

hous(ebuild)ing research · Wohn(ungs)bauforschung *f*

hous(ebuild)ing scheme; hous(ebuild)ing programme; hous(ebuild)ing program (US) · Wohn(ungs)bauprogramm *n*

hous(ebuild)ing sector, hous(ebuild)ing field · Wohn(ungs)bausektor *m*

hous(ebuild)ing site · Wohn(ungs)baustelle *f*

hous(ebuild)ing sponsor, hous(ebuild)ing promoter, hous(ebuild)ing assistant, hous(ebuild)ing assister, hous(ebuild)ing assistor · Wohn(ungs)baufördernde *m*, Wohn(ungs)bauförderer

hous(ebuild)ing standard · Wohn(ungs)baunorm *f*

hous(ebuild)ing statistics · Wohn(ungs)baustatistik *f*

hous(ebuild)ing statute, hous(ebuild)ing act, hous(ebuild)ing law · WBauG *n*, WoBauG, Wohn(ungs)baugesetz

hous(ebuild)ing trust · Wohn(ungs)bautrust *m*

hous(ebuild)ing undertaking, hous(ebuild)ing enterprise · Wohn(ungs)unternehmen *n*

house-burner · Hausbrandstifter *m*

house buying, house purchase · Hauskauf *m*

house conversion, house alteration · Hausumbau *m*

house counsel, staff counsel · Haus(rechts)anwalt *m*, Firmen(rechts)anwalt, Unternehmens(rechts)anwalt

house depth, depth of a house · Haustiefe *f*

house estate, house property · Hausvermögen *n*

house-famine, housing shortage, housing deficiency, housing stringency, housing scarcity, shortage of housing, stringency of housing, scarcity of housing, deficiency of housing · Wohnungsbedarf *m*, Wohnungsfehlbestand *m*, Wohnraumfehlbestand, Wohnungsmangel *m*, Wohnraummangel, Wohnungsknappheit *f*, Wohnraumknappheit, Wohnungsdefizit *n*, Wohnraumdefizit, Wohnungsnot *f*, Wohnungsverknappung *f*, Wohnraumverknappung, Wohnraumklemme *f*, Wohnraumnot, Wohnungsklemme, Wohnraumbedarf [*Die sich aus der zahlenmäßigen Gegenüberstellung von Haushalten und Normalwohnungen in abgegrenzten Gebieten oder Bereichen ergebende Zahl fehlender Wohnungen*]

housefarmer, intermediary, middleman · Mittelsmann *m* [*Er mietet ein Gebäude nicht zum Selbstbewohnen, sondern um die Räume weiter zu vermieten*]

house garden, domestic garden; back garden (Brit.); dooryard (US) · Hausgarten *m*

house group, group of houses · Hausgruppe *f*, Häusergruppe

household · Haushalt *m*

householder · Mieter *m* zu 10 Pfund Miete und darüber [*Verfassung der Londoner City*]

householder · Hausherr *m* [*Jeder der ein Haus allein oder mit seiner Familie bewohnt gleichviel ob als Mieter oder Eigentümer*]

householder, household head, head of (the) household · Haushalt(ungs)vorstand *m*

household garden, kitchen-garden · Gemüsegarten *m*, Küchengarten, Nutzgarten

household head, head of (the) household, householder · Haushalt(ungs)vorstand *m*

household incidence, headship rate, incidence of households [*The proportion of people in any given age category who are heads of households*] · Haushaltvorstandsziffer *f*

household management, housekeeping, management of a household · Haushaltung *f*

household size · Haushalt(s)größe *f*

household suffrage · Hausherrenstimmrecht n [in England]

household water, water for domestic purposes · Haushalt(s)wasser n

house improvement, renovation, refurbishing (Brit.); fixing up recycling (US); improvement of houses · Altbausanierung f, Altbaumodernisierung, Renovierung

house inspection · Hausaufsicht f

house jobber · Vermitt(e)ler m für Untervermietungen

house jurist → house lawyer

housekeeping, management of a household, household management · Haushaltung f

housekeeping money · Haushalt(s)geld n, Wirtschaftsgeld

house-knacker · mittellose Person f die ein Haus völlig vernachlässigt

house lawyer, staff lawyer, house jurist, staff jurist, lawyer employed in business, jurist employed in business · Hausjurist, Firmenjurist m, Unternehmensjurist

house let in lodging · möbliertes Kleinhaus n

house-lot · Hausanteil m, Anteil am Haus

house lot · Hausflurstück n, Hausparzelle f, Hausgrundstück (im katastertechnischen Sinne)

house management · Hausbewirtschaftung f

house numbering · Hausnumerierung f

(house) occupier, (house) occupant, dwelling occupier, dwelling occupant, residential occupier, residential occupant, dweller, resident · (Haus)Bewohner m, (Haus)Insasse m, Wohnungsinsasse, Bezieher

house of a wealthy citizen · Bürgerhaus n

house of correction, reformatory (school), reform school, workhouse · Arbeitshaus n, Besserungsanstalt f, Erziehungsanstalt f, Besserungshaus n [Für jugendliche Straftäter]

house of deputies · Deputiertenkammer f

house of husbandry · Bauern(hof)haus n

house of issue, issuing house, issuing bank, issuing firm, issue house, issue firm, issue bank, bank of issue · Notenbank f, Emissionsbank, Zettelbank, Emissionshaus n

house owner, house proprietor · Hauseigentümer m, Hauseigner; Hausbesitzer [Fehlbenennung]

house ownership (of property), house proprietorship, house (general) property · Hauseigentum n; Hausbesitz m [Fehlbenennung]

house parcel (of land), house plot (of land) · Hausgrundstück n (im tatsächlichen Sinne)

house plot (of land), house parcel (of land) · Hausgrundstück n (im tatsächlichen Sinne)

house project promoter, house project producer, house project developer, residential (project) developer, residential (project) promoter, residential (project) producer, housing (project) promoter, housing (project) producer, housing (project) developer · Wohn(ungs)bauträger m

house property, house estate · Hausvermögen n

house proprietor, house owner · Hauseigentümer m, Hauseigner; Hausbesitzer [Fehlbenennung]

house proprietorship → house ownership (of property)

house purchase, house buying · Hauskauf m

house registry, housing registry · Wohnungsnachweis m

house rent · Hausrente f

house rent · Haus(miet)zins m, Hausmiete f

house rent tax composition · Hauszinssteuerablösung f

(house) rent(s) tax · Gebäudeentwertungsausgleich m bei bebauten Grundstücken, Hausmietsteuer f, Mietertragsteuer, Aufwertungssteuer [frühere Benennungen: Mietzinssteuer, Hauszinssteuer]

house reserved by an old person for himself after the bulk has passed to the heir(s) · Altenteilerhaus n, Austragshaus

house row, row of houses · Wohnzeile f

house sale · Hausverkauf m

house speculation · Hausspekulation f, Häuserspekulation

house squatter · Hausbesetzer m

house squatting · Hausbesetzung f

house tax · Haussteuer f

house to house collection · Haussammlung f

housewife · Hausfrau f

housing · Wohnungen fpl

housing, habitable room, habitable space, shelter [The word "housing", which is used in combinations, includes, however, all of the immediate physical environment, both within and outside of residential buildings] · Wohnraum m

housing — housing deficiency relief act

[*Sammelbezeichnung für Wohnungen und einzelne Wohnräume*]

housing, accommodating · Unterbringen *n*

housing · Wohnungswesen *n*

housing affair · Wohnungsangelegenheit *f*

housing aid, housing help · Wohn(raum)hilfe *f*

Housing and Development Act [*USA*] · Gesetz *n* über Wohnungswesen und Städtebau

housing and home finance, housing and home financing · Wohn(ungs)- und Eigenheimbaufinanzierung *f*

Housing and Home Finance Agency [*USA*] · Bundesamt *n* für Wohnungswesen und Eigenheimfinanzierung

housing and urban development act, housing and urban development law, housing and urban development statute · Gesetz *n* über Wohnungsbau und Stadtentwick(e)lung

housing appeals board (US) board of appeal · Appellationsamt *n*, Berufungsamt *n* [*Es behandelt Einsprüche von Eigentümern, denen eine Bauerlaubnis versagt wurde*]

housing area, housing territory, residential area, residential territory, residence area, residence territory · Wohngebiet *n*, Wohnungsgebiet

housing authority · Wohnungsbehörde *f*

housing board · Wohnungsamt *n* [*Kommunale Dienststelle für die Wohnraumbewirtschaftung*]

housing building authority, housing production authority · Wohn(ungs)baubehörde *f*

housing business · Wohnungswirtschaft *f*

housing call, demand for housing, call for housing, housing demand · Wohnungsnachfrage *f*

housing care · Wohnungspflege *f* [*Pflege der Wohnungen als Gegenstand von Vorschriften*]

housing census, housing count · Wohnungszählung *f*

housing code [*Official regulations establishing minimum standards of occupancy which housing units must meet to be occupied legally*] · Wohn(ungs)ordnung *f*

housing colony, residential colony · Wohn(an)sied(e)lung *f*, Wohnkolonie *f*

housing company, housing corporation · Wohn(ungs)baugesellschaft *f*

housing conditions · Wohn(ungs)verhältnisse *f*

housing conditions · Wohn(ungs)bedingungen *fpl*

housing congress · Wohnungskongreß *m*

housing conservation, housing retention · Wohnungserhaltung *f*, Wohnungspflege *f*

housing construction, production of dwelling units, erection of dwelling units, production of housing units, erection of housing units, production of living units, erection of living units (US); production of tenements, erection of tenements, production of dwellings, erection of dwellings, production of housing, erection of housing, residential construction, residential building, hous(ebuild)ing · Wohn(ungs)bau *m*, Wohnungserstellung *f*, Wohnungsproduktion *f*, Häuserbau, Hausbau, Mietwohn(ungs)bau, Mietwohnungserstellung, Mietwohnungsproduktion, Miethäuserbau, Miethausbau

housing control, control of housing · Wohn(ungs)zwangswirtschaft *f*, Wohnraumbewirtschaftung *f*

housing corporation, housing company · Wohn(ungs)baugesellschaft *f*

housing count, housing census · Wohnungszählung *f*

housing court · Wohnungsgericht *n*

housing credit · Wohnungskredit *m*

housing decrease · Abgang *m* an Wohnungen, Wohnungsabgang

housing defect · Wohnungsmangel *m*

housing defect law · Wohnungsmangelgesetz *n*

housing defect ordinance · Wohnungsmangelverordnung *f*

housing deficiency, housing stringency, housing scarcity, shortage of housing, stringency of housing, scarcity of housing, deficiency of housing, housefamine, housing shortage · Wohnungsbedarf *m*, Wohnungsfehlbestand *m*, Wohnraumfehlbestand, Wohnungsmangel *m*, Wohnraummangel, Wohnungsknappheit *f*, Wohnraumknappheit, Wohnungsdefizit *n*, Wohnraumdefizit, Wohnungsnot *f*, Wohnungsverknappung *f*, Wohnraumverknappung, Wohnraumklemme *f*, Wohnraumnot, Wohnungsklemme, Wohnraumbedarf [*Die sich aus der zahlenmäßigen Gegenüberstellung von Haushalten und Normalwohnungen in abgegrenzten Gebieten oder Bereichen ergebende Zahl fehlender Wohnungen*]

housing deficiency relief act, housing deficiency relief law, housing deficiency relief statute, housing shortage relief act, housing shortage relief law, housing shortage relief statute · Wohnungsmangelgesetz *n*

housing demand — housing mobility

housing demand, housing call, demand for housing, call for housing · Wohnungsnachfrage f

housing design · Wohnungsentwurf m

housing development, residential development · Wohngebäudebebauung f, Wohn(ungs)bebauung, Wohnhausbebauung; Wohngebäudeüberbauung, Wohnhausüberbauung [Schweiz]

housing discrimination, discrimination in housing · Wohn(ungs)benachteiligung f

housing district, residential district · Wohnbezirk m, Wohnungsbezirk

housing doctrine → (social) housing doctrine

housing economy · Wohnungswirtschaft f

housing enterprise → hous(ebuild)ing enterprise

housing enterprise of public usefulness → hous(ebuild)ing enterprise of public usefulness

housing enterprise rent, housing undertaking rent · (Wohnungs)Unternehmensmiete f [Die Kosten aller Wohn(ungs)bestände eines Wohnungsunternehmens werden unter Berücksichtigung des Wohnwertes auf die Wohnungen verteilt]

housing environment, residential environment · Wohnumwelt f, Wohnumfeld n, Nahumwelt, Nahumfeld [Umfaßt die Umgebung eines Wohnhauses und die Lebensbedingungen eines Wohngebietes]

housing exhibition · Wohnungsausstellung f

housing expenditure · Wohn(ungs)aufwand m

housing expert · Wohnungsfachmann m

housing field, housing sector · Wohnungssektor m

housing field → hous(ebuild)ing field

housing for displaced families · Wohnungen fpl für Familien aus einem Sanierungsgebiet

housing for the aged · Altenwohnungen fpl

housing for the handicapped · Behindertenwohnungen fpl

housing help, housing aid · Wohn(raum)hilfe f

(housing) improvement act, (housing) improvement law, (housing) improvement statute, (housing) modernization act, (housing) modernization law, (housing) rehabilitation act, (housing) rehabilitation statute, (housing) rehabilitation law · (Wohnungs)Modernisierungsgesetz n, WoModG, (bauliches) Verbesserungsgesetz

housing increase · Zugang m an Wohnungen

housing inspection, inspection of housing · Wohnungsaufsicht f, Wohnungsüberwachung f, Wohnungsinspektion f

housing inspection authority · Wohnungsaufsichtsbehörde f, Wohnungsüberwachungsbehörde, Wohnungsinspektionsbehörde

housing inspection law, housing inspection act, housing inspection statute · Wohnungsaufsichtsgesetz n, Wohnungsüberwachungsgesetz, Wohnungsinspektionsgesetz

housing inventory, housing stock · Wohn(ungs)vorrat m, Wohn(ungs)bestand m [Die Zahl aller in einem Gebiet oder Bereich an einem Stichtag vorhandener Wohnungen]

housing land, residential land · Wohn(ungs)(bau)boden m, Wohn(ungs)(bau)land n, Wohn(ungs)(bau)fläche f [Im Flächennutzungsplan für den Wohn(ungs)bau bestimmte Baufläche, die nach ihrer baulichen Nutzung in Kleinsied(e)lungsgebiete, reine Wohngebiete und allgemeine Wohngebiete gegliedert werden kann]

(housing) landlord/tenant contract, housing lease · Wohnraummietvertrag m

housing landscape, residential landscape · Wohn(ungs)landschaft f

housing (land) use zoning, housing zoning, residential (land) use zoning, residential zoning · (bauliche) Nutzung f für Wohnzwecke, Baunutzung für Wohnzwecke, Wohn-(ungs)baunutzung, Bauzonenfestlegung für Wohnzwecke, Wohn(ungs)bauzonenfestlegung

housing law · (objektives) Wohn(ungs)recht n

housing lease, (housing) landlord/tenant contract · Wohnraummietvertrag m

housing location, residential site, housing site, residential location · Wohn(ungs)standort m

housing location model, housing site model, residential site model, residential location model · Wohn(ungs)standortmodell n

housing luxury · Wohnluxus m

housing maintenance · Wohnungsunterhaltung f

housing market · Wohn(ungs)markt m

housing market economy · Wohnungsmarktwirtschaft f

housing medicine, residential medicine · Wohn(ungs)medizin f

housing mobility · Wohnmobilität f, Wohnbeweglichkeit f

housing need · Wohnungsbedürfnis n

housing obsolescence · Überalterung f der Wohnungen

housing of homeless persons, accommodation of homeless persons · Obdachlosenunterbringung f, Unterbringung von Obdachlosen

housing of public usefulness, housing useful to the public, housing of public utility · gemeinnütziges Wohnungswesen n, gemeinnötiges Wohnungswesen

housing of the working classes act, housing of the working classes law, housing of the working classes statute · Arbeiterwohn(ungs)(bau)gesetz n

housing of the working classes committee · Arbeiterwohnungsausschuß m

housing ordinance · Wohn(ungs)verordnung f

housing ordinance → hous(ebuild)ing ordinance

housing pattern, housing scheme, residential pattern, residential scheme · Wohnmuster n, Wohnschema n

housing planning · Wohnungsplanung f

housing policy · Wohnungspolitik f

housing policy by the state · staatliche Wohnungspolitik f

housing practice → hous(ebuild)ing practice

housing preference, residential preference · Wohn(ungs)standortvorzug m

housing price · Wohnungspreis m

housing price · Wohn(ungs)baupreis m

housing problem, housing question · Wohnungsfrage f, Wohnungsproblem n

housing production · Wohnungsbauleistung f

housing production authority, housing building authority · Wohn(ungs)baubehörde f

housing (project) promoter, housing (project) producer, housing (project) developer, house project promoter, house project producer, house project developer, residential (project) developer, residential (project) promoter, residential (project) producer · Wohn(ungs)-bauträger m

housing question, housing problem · Wohnungsfrage f, Wohnungsproblem n

housing rate (Brit.); local tax for housing · kommunale Wohn(ungs)steuer f, gemeindliche Wohn(ungs)steuer f

housing reform · Wohnungsreform f

housing reform movement · Wohn(ungs)reformbewegung f

housing reform policy · Wohnungsreformpolitik f

housing registry, house registry · Wohnungsnachweis m

housing repairs and rents act, housing repairs and rents law, housing repairs and rents statute · Wohnungsreparatur- und -mietgesetz n

housing research · Wohnungsforschung f

housing reserves policy, housing stock policy · Wohnungsbestandspolitik f, Wohnungsvorratspolitik

housing retention, housing conservation, housing conservancy · Wohnungserhaltung f, Wohnungspflege f

housing scarcity, shortage of housing, stringency of housing, scarcity of housing, deficiency of housing, housefamine, housing shortage, housing stringency · Wohnungsbedarf m, Wohnungsfehlbestand m, Wohnraumfehlbestand, Wohnungsmangel m, Wohnraummangel, Wohnungsknappheit f, Wohnraumknappheit, Wohnungsdefizit n, Wohnraumdefizit, Wohnungsnot f, Wohnungsverknappung f, Wohnraumverknappung, Wohnraumklemme f, Wohnraumnot, Wohnungsklemme, Wohnraumbedarf [*Die sich aus der zahlenmäßigen Gegenüberstellung von Haushalten und Normalwohnungen in abgegrenzten Gebieten oder Bereichen ergebende Zahl fehlender Wohnungen*]

housing scheme, residential pattern, residential scheme, housing pattern · Wohnmuster n, Wohnschema n

housing sector, housing field · Wohnungssektor m

housing sector → hous(ebuild)ing sector

housing servitude, residential servitude, dwelling servitude · Wohnungsdienstbarkeit f, Wohnungsgerechtigkeit, Wohnungsservitut n, f, (servitutisches) Wohn(ungs)recht n [*Das Recht ein Gebäude oder einen Teil eines Gebäudes unter Ausschluß des Eigentümers als Wohnung zu benutzen*]

housing settlement act, residential settlement act, housing settlement law, residential settlement law, housing settlement statute, residential settlement statute · Wohnsied(e)lungsgesetz n

housing settlement area, housing settlement territory, residential settlement area, residential settlement territory · Wohn(an)sied(e)lungsgebiet n

housing shortage, housing deficiency, housing stringency, housing scarcity, shortage of housing, stringency of housing, scarcity of housing, deficiency of housing, house-famine · Wohnungsbedarf m, Wohnungsfehlbestand m, Wohnraumfehlbestand, Wohnungsmangel m, Wohnraummangel, Wohnungsknappheit f, Wohnraumknappheit, Wohnungsdefizit n, Wohnraumdefizit, Wohnungsnot f, Wohnungsverknappung f, Wohnraumverknappung, Wohnraumklemme f, Wohnraumnot, Wohnungsklemme, Wohnraumbedarf [*Die sich aus der zahlenmäßigen Gegenüberstellung von Haushalten und Normalwohnungen in abgegrenzten Gebieten oder Bereichen ergebende Zahl fehlender Wohnungen*]

housing shortage relief act, housing shortage relief law, housing shortage relief statute, housing deficiency relief act, housing deficiency relief law, housing deficiency relief statute · Wohnungsmangelgesetz n

housing site, residential location, housing location, residential site · Wohn(ungs)standort m

housing site model, residential site model, residential location model, housing location model · Wohn(ungs)standortmodell n

housing standard · Wohnungsausstattungsnorm f

housing standard · normale Wohnweise f

housing statistics · Wohnungsstatistik f

housing stock, housing inventory · Wohn(ungs)vorrat m, Wohn(ungs)bestand m [*Die Zahl aller in einem Gebiet oder Bereich an einem Stichtag vorhandener Wohnungen*]

housing stock policy, housing reserves policy · Wohnungsbestandspolitik f, Wohnungsvorratspolitik

housing stringency, housing scarcity, shortage of housing, stringency of housing, scarcity of housing, deficiency of housing, house-famine, housing shortage, housing deficiency · Wohnungsbedarf m, Wohnungsfehlbestand m, Wohnraumfehlbestand, Wohnungsmangel m, Wohnraummangel, Wohnungsknappheit f, Wohnraumknappheit, Wohnungsdefizit n, Wohnraumdefizit, Wohnungsnot f, Wohnungsverknappung f, Wohnraumverknappung, Wohnraumklemme f, Wohnraumnot, Wohnungsklemme, Wohnraumbedarf [*Die sich aus der zahlenmäßigen Gegenüberstellung von Haushalten und Normalwohnungen in abgegrenzten Gebieten oder Bereichen ergebende Zahl fehlender Wohnungen*]

housing subsidies act, housing subsidies law, housing subsidies statute, housing subvention(s) statute, housing subvention(s) law, housing subvention(s) act, housing subsidy act, housing subsidy law, housing subsidy statute · Wohn(ungs)bausubventionsgesetz n

housing supply, supply of housing · Wohnraumangebot n, Wohnungsangebot, Wohnraumbereitstellung f, Wohnungsbereitstellung, Wohnraumversorgung, Wohnungsversorgung

housing survey · Wohnungsenquête f

housing territory, residential area, residential territory, residence area, residence territory, housing area · Wohngebiet n, Wohnungsgebiet

housing trust · Wohnungstrust m

housing-type trailer, (travel) trailer, mobile home, caravan · Wohnwagen m, Wagenheim n

housing undertaking → hous(eubild)ing undertaking

housing undertaking rent, housing enterprise rent · (Wohnungs)Unternehmensmiete f [*Die Kosten aller Wohn(ungs)bestände eines Wohnungsunternehmens werden unter Berücksichtigung des Wohnwertes auf die Wohnungen verteilt*]

housing unit, apartment, unit of housing (US); apartment (Brit.) [*archaic*]; tenement, residence, dwelling; dwelling unit, DU, du, living unit, LU, lu (US) · Wohnung f

housing unit in the court-yard (US); dwelling in the court-yard; dwelling unit in the court-yard, living unit in the court-yard (US) · Hofwohnung f

housing useful to the public, housing of public utility, housing of public usefulness · gemeinnütziges Wohnungswesen n, gemeinnötiges Wohnungswesen

housing zoning, residential (land) use zoning, residential zoning, housing (land) use zoning · (bauliche) Nutzung f für Wohnzwecke, Baunutzung für Wohnzwecke, Wohn-(ungs)baunutzung, Bauzonenfestlegung für Wohnzwecke, Wohn(ungs)bauzonenfestlegung

hue and cry · Aufruf m [*Um Verbrechern auf die Spur zu kommen*]

human basic function, basic human function · Daseinsgrundfunktion f

human being, natural person · natürliche Person f, Mensch m

human capital · Fähigkeitskapital n, Humankapital, personelle Infrastruktur f

human capital approach · Ansatz m der personellen Infrastruktur, Fähigkeitskapitalansatz m, Humankapitalansatz m

(human) community, [*A group of people living or working close to one another and sharing common interests*] · Gemeinschaft f, Gemeinwesen n, Gemeinde f

(human) community formation · Gemeinschaftsbildung f, Gemeinwesenbildung

(human) community organization · Gemeinschaftsorganisation f, Gemeinwesenorganisation

human ecology — hydage

human ecology, social ecology · Menschenökologie *f*, Humanökologie, Sozialökologie

human environment · menschliche Umwelt *f*

human factors engineering, ergonomics · Ergonomik *f*

human geography, social geography · Anthropogeographie *f*, Sozialgeographie *f*

human group · soziale Gruppe *f*

human occupancy, sequent occupancy · Besied(e)lung *f* durch den Menschen, Landnahme *f*

human-orien(ta)ted, human-related · menschenorientiert, menschenbezogen

human population · menschliche Bevölkerung *f*

human resources · personelle Betriebsmittel *n pl*

(human) rural community, (human) village community · Dorfgemeinschaft *f*, Dorfgemeinwesen *n*, ländliche Gemeinschaft, ländliches Gemeinwesen, Dorfgemeinde, ländliche Gemeinde *f* [*Aus Menschen bestehend*]

human settlement · menschliche (An)Sied(e)lung *f*

human spatial decision-making · räumliche Entscheidung *f* des Menschen

(human) village community, (human) rural community · Dorfgemeinschaft *f*, Dorfgemeinwesen *n*, ländliche Gemeinschaft, ländliches Gemeinwesen, Dorfgemeinde, ländliche Gemeinde *f* [*Aus Menschen bestehend*]

hundred court; curia hundredi [*Latin*] [*In old English law. A larger court baron, being held for all the inhabitants of a particular hundred, instead of a manor. This is not to be confounded with the hundred court of the Saxon times, called hundred gemote*] · Hundertgericht *n*

hundred percent location, hundred percent site [*Location or site that is best adapted to carrying on a given type of activity*] · bestmöglicher Standort *m*

hundred rate · Hundertgerichtssteuer *f*

hunger bedripe, hunger biderepe, hunger bederepe · befohlener Erntearbeitstag *m* an welchem keine Nahrung verabreicht wurde [*Fronhofarbeit*]

to hunt; fugare [*Latin*]; to chase · jagen

hunting, chasing · Jagen *n*

hunting castle · Jagdschloß *n*

hunting ground, chase [*District of land privileged for wild beasts of chase, with the exclusive right of hunting therein*] · Jagdrevier *n*

hunting lodge · Jagdhaus *n*

hunting right, chase [*The right of hunting over a tract of country; also, that of keeping beasts of the chase therein*] · Jagdrecht *n*, subjektives Jagdrecht

to hurt, to harm, to prejudice, to derogate · beeinträchtigen, schmälern

hurt, harm, derogation · Abbruch *m*, Beeinträchtigung *f*, Schmälerung, Schädigung

to husband · landwirtschaftlich bewirtschaften

husband and wife · Eheleute *f*, Ehepaar *n*

husbandland, wista; hilda [*Scotland*]; terra hydata, virgate terrae, hida (terrae), hyda, familia [*Latin*]; hide ((of) land), hyde (of land), higid, hiwise, virgate (land), verge of land, yardland, hydeland [*A quantity of land not of any certain extent, but as much as a plough can by course of husbandry plough in a year. It meant in different places anything from sixty to 120 acres. A virgate is one fourth of a hide*] · Hufe(ngut) *f*, *(n)*, Hufenschoß *n*, Hube *f*, Hufen(gut)land *n* [*Ältere Benennungen: Hof m, Hub m, Hu(o)ba f, und Hova f*] [*Unter gutsherrlich-bäuerlichen Verhältnissen hieß der gesamte Besitz eines Dorfgenossen ,,Hufe(ngut)". Diese Benennung war also keine Flächengröße, sondern eine Besitzeinheit, die zahlreiche, zerstreut liegende kleine Ackerteile im Besitz derselben Person umfaßte*]

husbandman, peasant (cultivator) · Bauer *m*

husbandry works · bäuerliche Dienste *m pl*

hush-money · Schweigegeld *n*

hybrid guarantee (building and loan) association, hybrid guaranty (building and loan) association (US) · gemischte Bürgschaftsbausparkasse *f*

hybrid power of appointment, hybrid power of disposition, hybrid right of appointment, hybrid right of disposition [*It is one which is neither special nor general, e.g. as where A and B are given a general power which may be exercised jointly, or as where C is given a general power which may be exercised only with D's content, or as where E is given a power to appoint to anyone except F*] · gemischte Verfügungbefugnis *f*, gemischte Bestimmungsbefugnis, gemischtes Bestimmungsrecht *n*, gemischtes Verfügungsrecht

hyda, [*Latin*] → husbandland

hydage, tax on hide (of land); hidagium [*Latin*], hidage, hidegild [*In old English law. An extraordinary tax payable to the king of every hide of land*] · Hufengeld *n*, Hufengroschen *m*, Hufensteuer *f*

hyde and gain [*In ancient English law*] → arable land

hydeland → husbandland

hydraulic structure, hydraulic work, hydraulic physical facility · wasserbauliche Anlage *f*, Wasserbauwerk *n*

hydroelectric development · Wasserkraftausbau *m*

hyperemployment, over-full employment · Überbeschäftigung *f*

hyperinflation, runaway inflation, galloping inflation · galoppierende Inflation *f*

hypermarket · Großeinkaufzentrum *n*, Verbrauchergroßmarkt *m*

hyperocha · Erlösüberschuß *m* [*Pfandkauf*]

hyperurbanization, over-urbanization, excessive urbanization · Überverstädterung *f*

to hypothecate, to pledge (property as security) · verpfänden

to hypothecate (US); to complete, to mortgage (Brit.) · bestellen, hypothekieren, hypothekarisch belasten

hypothetical, conditional; conditionary [*obsolete*] · hypothetisch

hypsometric tint · Höhenstufenfarbton *m*

I

IAMS, International Association of Municipal Statisticians · Städtestatistischer Ausschuß *m* des Internationalen Statistischen Instituts

I.D.C., industrial development certificate · Grundsatzattest *n* für Industrieplanung, Grundsatzbescheinigung *f* für Industrieplanung, Grundsatzschein *m* für Industrieplanung

ideal city, ideal town · Idealstadt *f*

ideal community [*A theoretical projection of utopian concepts*] · Idealgemeinde *f*, Idealkommune *f*

ideal standard cost(s), current standard cost(s) · Soll(standard)kosten *f*, Standardkosten 1. Art

ideal town, ideal city · Idealstadt *f*

idea of sectors, sector idea · Sektoridee *f*

ideas competition · Leistungsbeschreibung *f* mit Leistungsprogramm, Ideenwettbewerb *m* [*Sie entspricht nur einem Teil der vom Auftraggeber geforderten Beschreibung der Bauleistung. Es wird nur das Programm (= Rahmen) der gewünschten Bauleistung angegeben und die Bieter füllen bei der Angebotsbearbeitung den Rahmen (= Programm) aus, indem sie die erforderlichen Leistungseinzelheiten nach ihrer Vorstellung erarbeiten und ihrem Angebot zugrunde legen*]

identifiability · Identifizierbarkeit *f*

identifying prefix [*construction drawing*] · Kennzeichen *n* [*Bauzeichnung*]

identity mistake, mistake as to identity · Identitätsirrtum *m*

idle, abandoned, given up, left (to itself), forsaken, let gone, deserted [*place*] · aufgegeben, verlassen, preisgegeben

idle and disorderly · müßig und unordentlich, faul und unordentlich

idle land, tract of fallow (land), waste, uncultivated land; novale, frusca terra [*Latin*]; fallow land · Brachflur *f*, Brachland *n*, Brachacker *m*, Brachfeld *n*

idle money, unemployment compensation, compensation of unemployment, relief of unemployment, out-of-work-pay, out-of-work-benefit, unemployment relief, unemployment benefit, donation money · Arbeitslosengeld *n*, Arbeitslosenunterstützung *f*, Erwerbslosengeld *n*, Erwerbslosenunterstützung

idleness cost(s), cost(s) of idleness, cost(s) of unused capacity · Leerkosten *f*, ungedeckte Fixkosten, ungedeckte Festkosten, nicht ausgenutzter Teil *m* der Fixkosten, Kosten der ungenutzten Kapazität [*Die anteiligen Fixkosten der nicht genutzten Kapazität einer Kostenstelle. Nach Plaut sind „Leerkosten" in der Grenzplankostenrechnung nicht nur die ungedeckten Fixkosten, sondern der gesamte Block der Fixkosten*]

idle person, faitour · Faulenzer *m*

ignorance, want of knowledge; ignorantia [*Latin*] · Unkenntnis *f*

ignorant of, unacquainted with, miscognizant · nichtwissend, unwissend

ill-constructed · schlecht gebaut

ille cujus usui [*Latin*] → cestui (à) que use

illegal → nonlegal

illegality → violation (of law)

illegal practice · leichtes Wahldelikt *n* [*Munizipalstadt*]

illegitimate infant, illegitimate minor · unehelicher Minderjähriger *m*

illegitimate natural child [*A child by concubinage, in contradistinction to a child by marriage*] · uneheliches Kind *n*

ill fame, evil fame, ill repute, evil repute · schlechter Ruf *m*

illicit, prohibited, not allowed, not permitted · unerlaubt, verboten

illicit purchase · Schwarzkauf *m*

illicit sale [*When in order to pay less increment-tax, the seller and purchaser of a house understate the selling price to the revenue authorities*] · Schwarzverkauf *m*

illicit trade · Schwarzhandel *m*

illicit work · Schwarzarbeit *f*

illicit work contract · Schwarzarbeitsvertrag *m*

illicit worker · Schwarzarbeiter *m*

illicit work law · Schwarzarbeitsgesetz *n*

illiquidity · Illiquidität *f*

illiteracy · Analphabetentum *n*, Analphabetismus *m*

illiterate (person) · Analphabet *m*

illiterate vote · Stimmabgabe *f* eines Analphabeten

ill repute, evil repute, ill fame, evil fame · schlechter Ruf *m*

illuminated advertisement, illuminated advertising, electric signs · Leuchtreklame *f*, Leuchtwerbung *f*, Lichtreklame, Lichtwerbung

illuminated advertisement lettering · Leuchtwerbeschrift *f*, Leuchtreklameschrift

illuminated relief, shadow relief representation · Schattenplastik *f* [*Kartographie*]

illumination duty, duty to illuminate · Beleuchtungspflicht *f*

illusory association · Scheinverbundenheit *f* [*Statistik*]

illustration · zum Sachverhalt

imposed by law · auf zwingendem Recht beruhend

image · erkennbares Bild *n*, Profil *n*, subjektives Bild

imageability · Bildfähigkeit *f*

image processing · Bildverarbeitung *f*

imaginable, supposable, conceivable · denkbar, vorstellbar

I.M.F., International Monetary Fund · Internationaler Währungsfonds *m*

immaterial · unwesentlich

Immediate Aid · Soforthilfe *f*, SH [*Bundesrepublik Deutschland*]

Immediate Aid Authority · Soforthilfebehörde *f* [*Bundesrepublik Deutschland*]

Immediate Aid Fund · Soforthilfemittel *f* [*Bundesrepublik Deutschland*]

Immediate Aid Law, Immediate Aid Act, Immediate Aid Statute · Soforthilfegesetz *n* [*Bundesrepublik Deutschland*]

Immediate Aid Tax · Soforthilfeabgabe *f* [*Bundesrepublik Deutschland*]

immediate annuity · gleich fällige Annuität *f*, sofort auszahlbare Annuität

immediate cause · unmittelbare Ursache *f*

immediate enjoyment · unmittelbarer Genuß *m*

immediate execution · Unterwerfung *f*, sofortige (Zwangs)Vollstreckung

immediate full vesting · sofortige volle Verfügung *f* über erworbene Pensionsansprüche, sofortige volle Anrechnung

immediate partial vesting · sofortige teilweise Verfügung *f* über erworbene Pensionsansprüche, sofortige teilweise Anrechnung

immediate payment gain-sharing plan, immediate payment profit-sharing plan · Gewinnbeteiligungsplan *m* mit sofortiger Barausschüttung, Profitbeteiligungsplan mit sofortiger Barausschüttung

immemorial custom · unvordenklicher Brauch *m*

immemorial existence · unvordenkliches Bestehen *n*

immemorial limitation (period), limitation by time immemorial · unvordenkliche Verjährung(sfrist) *f*, Immemorialverjährung(sfrist)

immigrant absorption, immigrant assimilation, immigrant integration, absorption of immigrants, assimilation of immigrants, integration of immigrants · Einwanderereingliederung *f*, Einwandererintegration *f*

immigrant population, immigration population · Einwanderungsbevölkerung *f*, Einwandererbevölkerung

immigrant wave · Einwandererwelle *f*, Einwanderungswelle

to immigrate · einwandern

immigration · Einwanderung *f*

immigration inspector · Einwanderungsinspektor *m*

immigration population, immigrant population · Einwanderungsbevölkerung *f*, Einwandererbevölkerung

imminent collapse, threatening collapse, imminent crash, threatening crash · drohender Einsturz *m* [*Bauwerk*]

imminent death · früher Tod *m*

immobile · lagerfest

immoral · sittenwidrig, unsittlich

immorality — Imperial Federation

immorality · Sittenwidrigkeit *f*, Unsittlichkeit

immov(e)able [*International Private Law*], immov(e)able thing, real thing, thing immov(e)able, thing real, chose local, local chose · Immobilie *f*, unbeweglicher Gegenstand *m*, unbewegliche (Einzel)Sache *f*, unbewegliches Ding *n*, unbewegliches Rechtsobjekt *n*

immov(e)able · unbeweglich [*Gegenstand*]

immov(e)able [*Right over an immov(e)able thing*] · Recht *n* über eine unbewegliche Sache, Recht über eine Immobilie

immov(e)able estate, fixed estate, landholding, land(ed) property, tenancy (of land(s)); immov(e)ables [*International Private Law*], (real) estate, (real) property, realty, estate in land(s) [*Estates in land(s) are divided into (a) freehold estates and (b) estates less than freehold*] · Bodenbesitz(stand) *m*, Grund(stücks)besitz(stand), Landbesitz(stand), Immobilienbesitz(stand), Immobiliarbesitz(stand), Liegenschaft(en) *f(pl)*, Immobilien *f(pl)*, (unbeweglicher) Besitz(stand), liegendes Gut *n*, ungereides Gut

immov(e)able (estate) for life → (real) estate for life

immov(e)able property → (real) property

immov(e)able property for life → (real) property for life

immov(e)ables [*International Private Law*]; (real) estate, (real) property, realty, estate in land(s), immov(e)able estate, fixed estate, landholding, land(ed) property, tenancy (of land(s)) [*Estates in land(s) are divided into (a) freehold estates and (b) estates less than freehold*] · Bodenbesitz(stand) *m*, Grund(stücks)besitz(stand), Landbesitz(stand), Immobilienbesitz(stand), Immobiliarbesitz(stand), Liegenschaft(en) *f(pl)*, Immobilien *f(pl)*, (unbeweglicher) Besitz(stand), liegendes Gut *n*, ungereides Gut

immov(e)able thing, real thing, thing immov(e)able, thing real, chose local, local chose; immov(e)able [*International Private Law*] · Immobilie *f*, unbeweglicher Gegenstand *m*, unbewegliche (Einzel)Sache *f*, unbewegliches Ding *n*, unbewegliches Rechtsobjekt *n*

immunity, exemption, discharge, release, dispensation [*Relaxation of the law in a particular case by competent authority*] · Befreiung *f*, Freistellung, Entlastung, Freigabe *f*, Erlaß *m*, Dispens(ierung) *m*, *(f)*, Dispensation *f*, Ausnahmebewilligung

immunity application, exemption application, discharge application, release application, dispensation application · Befreiungsantrag *m*, Dispens(ier)ungsantrag, Freistellungsantrag, Entlastungsantrag, Freigabeantrag, Dispensationsantrag

impact, penetration · Tiefe *f* [*Werbung*]

impact · Induktion *f*, Einwirkung *f* [*Die belebende Wirkung, die unmittelbar von den Aufträgen der ansässigen Fernbedarfstätigen an die nahbedarfstätige Wirtschaft ausgeht*]

impact of space, spatial impact, space impact · Raumbedeutung *f*

impairment of capital · Kapitalverringerung *f*

impartial · unparteiisch, unparteilich, überparteiisch, überparteilich

impartiality, impartialness · Unparteilichkeit *f*

impassable, impracticable · unwegsam, unbefahrbar [*Straße*]

impassableness, impracticable condition · Unwegsamkeit *f*, Unbefahrbarkeit [*Straße*]

to impeach, to accuse by public authority · öffentlich anklagen, amtlich anklagen

impeachment · öffentliche Anklage *f*, Amtsanklage

impeachment of waste, waste impeachment; impetitio vasti [*Latin*] [*Liability to be proceeded against or sued for committing waste upon land(s) or tenement(s)*] · Grund(stücks)veränderungshaftung *f*, Veränderungshaftung am Grundstück, Haftung für Substanzveränderung

impecunious · unvermögend

imperative, peremptory, obligatory; perimere [*Latin*]; mandatory, preceptive [*As opposed to "permissive"*] · pflichtbedingt, zwingend [*in Gesetzen*]

imperator [*Latin*]; presiding arbiter [*This term is rarely used*]; presiding arbitrator, presiding referee, impier, umpire; oversman [*Scots law*] · dritter Schiedsrichter *m*, Obmann *m* [*Bei einer Dreierbesetzung des Schiedsgerichts*]

imperfect · unvollkommen

imperfect, encumbered, incumbered, loaded, burdened, charged · belastet, dinglich belastet

imperfect negative prescription, limitation of action · Klageverjährung *f*

imperfect stability · unvollkommene Stabilität *f*

imperfect trust · unvollständiges Treuhandverhältnis *n*, unvollständige Treuhand *f*

Imperial Council · Reichsrat *m*

Imperial Federation · Reichsstaatenbund *m*

Imperial Free City · freie Reichsstadt *f* [*z. B. Köln*]

impersonal account, real account · Sachkonto *n*

impersonal investor (of capital) · anonymer (Geld)Anleger *m*

impersonalization · Entpersönlichung *f*

impersonation (US); false personation · Sichausgeben *n* als ein anderer

impertinence · Unnötige *n*, Irrelevante [*in Schriftsätzen*]

impetitio vasti [*Latin*]; impeachment of waste, waste impeachment [*Liability to be proceeded against or sued for committing waste upon land(s) or tenement(s)*] · Grund(stücks)veränderungshaftung *f*, Veränderungshaftung am Grundstück, Haftung für Substanzveränderung

impier, umpire; oversman [*Scots law*]; imperator [*Latin*]; presiding arbiter [*This term is rarely used*]; presiding arbitrator, presiding referee · dritter Schiedsrichter *m*, Obmann *m* [*Bei einer Dreierbesetzung des Schiedsgerichts*]

to implead, to sue, to prosecute by due course of law; implacitare [*Latin*] · (privatrechtlich) verklagen, gerichtlich belangen

implementation, realization · Verwirklichung *f*

implementation of (a) plan, realization of (a) plan, plan implementation, plan realization · Planverwirklichung *f*, Plandurchführung

implementing regulation · Durchführungsregelung *f*

implication · Rechtsvermutung *f*

implied, tacit, by implication · stillschweigend

implied antichresis; antichresis tacita [*Latin*]; antichresis by implication, tacit antichresis · stillschweigende Antichrese *f*

implied appointment, tacit appointment, appointment by implication · stillschweigende Benennung *f*, stillschweigende Ernennung, stillschweigende Namhaftmachung, stillschweigende Nominierung, gefolgerte Benennung, gefolgerte Ernennung, gefolgerte Namhaftmachung, gefolgerte Nominierung, konkludente Benennung, konkludente Ernennung, konkludente Namhaftmachung, konkludente Nominierung

implied authority, tacit authority, authority implied, authority in law · gefolgerte Vollmacht *f*, gefolgerte Vertretungsmacht, konkludente Vollmacht, konkludente Vertretungsmacht, stillschweigende Vollmacht, stillschweigende Vertretungsmacht

implied condition, tacit condition, condition implied · konkludente Bedingung *f*, gefolgerte Bedingung, stillschweigende Bedingung

implied construction, tacit construction, implied interpretation, tacit interpretation, construction by implication, interpretation by implication · stillschweigende Deutung *f*, stillschweigende Auslegung

implied contract, tacit contract, contract by implication · stillschweigender Vertrag *m*

implied covenant, tacit covenant, covenant in law, covenant by implication · stillschweigender Formalvertrag *m*

implied intention (of party), tacit intention (of party) · stillschweigender Parteiwille *m*

implied interpretation, tacit interpretation, construction by implication, interpretation by implication, implied construction, tacit construction · stillschweigende Deutung *f*, stillschweigende Auslegung

implied license, implied licence · Konsumtion [*Patentrecht*]

implied license based on estoppel, implied licence based on estoppel, license by estoppel, licence by estoppel · Lizenz *f* kraft Verwirkung

impliedly · stillschweigenderweise

implied malice, malice in law · juristisch konstruierter Dolus *m*

implied power, implied authority · implizierte Kompetenz *f*, implizierte Macht, implizierte Gewalt, implizierte Hoheit

implied promise, tacit promise, promise implied · gefolgertes Versprechen *n*, konkludentes Versprechen, stillschweigendes Versprechen

implied re-letting [*Of premises, where the tenant continues in possession after the expiration of his term*], tacit relocation [*in Scotch law*] · stillschweigende Wiedervermietung *f*

implied renunciation, tacit renunciation, implied repudiation, tacit repudiation · stillschweigende Vertragsaufsage *f*, stillschweigende Leistungsverweigerung *f*

implied repeal · konkludente Aufhebung *f* früherer Gesetze

implied repudiation, tacit repudiation, implied renunciation, tacit renunciation · stillschweigende Vertragsaufsage *f*, stillschweigende Leistungsverweigerung *f*

implied trust, tacit trust, trust by implication [*A trust raised or created by implication of law; a trust implied or presumed from circumstances*] · stillschweigende Treuhand *f*

implied undertaking as to title, tacit undertaking as to title · Rechtsgewährleistungspflicht *f*

implied warranty · stillschweigende Gewähr *f*, stillschweigende Garantie *f*, gesetzlich unterstellte Haftung *f*, stillschweigendes Gewährleistungsversprechen, stillschweigendes Haftungsversprechen *n*

import, negative export [*The negative expression is used because a sale of goods or services to another nation (an actual export) is a credit item in the balance of trade and a purchase from another nation has a negative effect on balance of trade. Net exports are equal to actual exports minus imports*] · Einfuhr *f*, Import *m*

importance · Rang *m*, Wichtigkeit *f* [*z. B. einer Hypothek*]

importance of space, spatial importance · Raumbedeutsamkeit *f*

importation of water · Wasserüberleitung *f* [*Von einem Einzugsgebiet ins andere*]

import duty · Einfuhrzoll *m*

import prohibition · Einfuhrverbot *n*

importunity; importunitas [*Latin*] · Drängen *n*

to impose, to surcharge · auferlegen

imposition · Auferlegung *f*

imposition of the rate · Steuerausschreibung *f*

impossibility [*Not to be confused with "frustration"*] · Unmöglichkeit *f*

impossible condition [*It is contrary to the course of nature or human limitations that it should even be performed*] · unmögliche Bedingung *f*

impost on land(s) · Grundabgabe *f*

impotent poor · arbeitsunfähiger Armer *m*

to impound, to secure for (safe) custody [*To put goods in the custody of the law*] · (gerichtlich) verwahren, in gerichtliche Verwahrung nehmen

to impound · einpferchen [*gepfändetes oder verirrtes Vieh*]

impounding, securing for (safe) custody · Verwahren *n*

to impoverish · verarmen

impracticability · Undurchführbarkeit *f*

impracticable, infeasible · undurchführbar, nicht durchführbar

impracticable, impassable · unwegsam, unbefahrbar [*Straße*]

impracticable condition, impassableness · Unwegsamkeit *f*, Unbefahrbarkeit [*Straße*]

imprescriptible, non prescribable · unersitzbar

improper · vertragswidrig [*(Bau)Stoff; Bauteile; Leistung*]

improper, defective · mangelhaft, nachbesserungsbedürftig

improper performance, defective work, improper work, defective performance · mangelhafte Leistung *f*, nachbesserungsbedürftige Leistung, nachbesserungsbedürftige Arbeit *f*, mangelhafte Arbeit

to improve · verbessern

to improve → to redo

improved · baureif, erschlossen, bebaubar, fertig; überbaubar [*Schweiz*]

improved area → improved (land) area

improved ground rent · Meliorationsrente *f*

improved land, farmed land, agriculturally zoned land, agriculturally used land, crop land, agricultural land, farming land, land agricultural in character, farmland [*Land may be assessable as "agricultural land" though it be covered by timber and underbrush, grass and weeds*] · landwirtschaftlicher Boden *m*, landwirtschaftlich genutzter Boden, landwirtschaftliches Land *n*, landwirtschaftlich genutztes Land, Kulturland, Kulturboden, Agrarland, landwirtschaftlich genutzte Fläche *f*, LN, landwirtschaftliche Nutzfläche, Fruchtland, Agrarnutzfläche

improved land, improved (land) area [*A land (area) that has been prepared for construction upon it, as by the installation of utility connections or services, streets, sidewalks, etc.*] · baureifes Land *n*, bebaubares Land, fertiges Land, baureife Fläche *f*, bebaubare Fläche, baureifes Bauland, fertige Fläche; überbaubares Land, überbaubare Fläche [*Schweiz*]

improved piece (of land), improved plot (of land), improved plot of ground, improved parcel (of land) · baureifes Grundstück *n*, fertiges Grundstück, bebaubares Grundstück; überbaubares Grundstück [*Schweiz*]

improved state · Baureife *f*, Bebauungsreife, Bebaubarkeit *f*

improved value · wachsender Nutzertrag *m* [*Land*]

to improve (land); impruiare [*Latin*] · baureif machen, bebaubar machen, erschließen; überbaubar machen [*Schweiz*]

improvement → (physical) improvement

improvement → (land) improvement

improvement act → (housing) improvement act

improvement act — improvement project

improvement act, improvement law, improvement statute [*A law that authorizes installation of improvements, which may then be assessed directly to the properties involved*] · Erschließungsgesetz *n*

improvement advantage → (land) improvement advantage

improvement application → (land) improvement request

improvement area · Erschließungsfläche *f*

improvement area, improvement territory · Erschließungsgebiet *n*, Erschließungsterritorium *n*

improvement bond [*A bond issued by any government or public authority for the installation of improvements such as highways or streets, and which is then sold to investors to finance the projects covered*] · Erschließungsobligation *f*, Erschließungsschuldverschreibung *f*

improvement burden → (land) improvement burden

improvement charge → (land) improvement burden

improvement company → (land) improvement company

improvement contract → (land) improvement contract

improvement contract law → (land) improvement contract law

improvement contribution by(e)-law → (land) improvement contribution by(e)-law

improvement corporation → (land) improvement corporation

improvement cost(s) → (physical) improvement cost(s)

improvement cost(s) → (land) improvement cost(s)

improvement credit → (land) improvement credit

improvement district · Erschließungsbezirk *m*

improvement duty → (land) improvement duty

improvement encumbrance → (land) improvement burden

improvement expenditure → (land) improvement expenditure

improvement expense → (land) improvement expense

improvement gain → (land) improvement gain

improvement green area · Erschließungsgrünfläche *f*

improvement guide line → (physical) improvement guide line

improvement highway → (land) improvement highway

improvement incumbrance → (land) improvement burden

improvement indicator → (land) improvement indicator

improvement industry, finishing industry · Veredelungsindustrie *f*

improvement law → improvement act

improvement law → (physical) improvement statute

improvement loan → (physical) improvement loan

improvement measure → (physical) improvement measure

improvement measure → (land) improvement measure

improvement of (a) building, improvement of buildings · Gebäudeverbesserung *f*

improvement of (building) area → improvement of (building) (land) area

improvement of environment, environmental improvement · Umweltverbesserung *f*

improvement of houses, house improvement, renovation; fixing up, recycling (US); returbishment · Altbausanierung *f*, Altbaumodernisierung, Renovierung

improvement of (land) area → improvement of (building) (land) area

improvement of residential environment, improvement of housing environment · Wohnumfeldverbesserung *f*, Wohnumweltverbesserung, Nahumfeldverbesserung, Nahumweltverbesserung

improvement on land [*Structures, of whatever nature, erected on a site, for example, buildings, fences, driveways, and retaining walls*] · Grund(stücks)bebauung *f*; Grund(stücks)überbauung [*Schweiz*]

improvement ordinance → (physical) improvement ordinance

improvement pattern → (land) improvement pattern

improvement permission → (land) improvement permission

improvement physical facility → (land) improvement work

improvement plan → (physical) improvement plan

improvement plan → (land) improvement plan

improvement profit → (land) improvement gain

improvement project → (land) improvement project

improvement request → (land) improvement request

improvement road → (land) improvement road

improvement scheme → (land) improvement scheme

improvement statute → improvement act

improvement structure → (land) improvement structure

improvement system → (land) improvement system

improvement territory, improvement area · Erschließungsgebiet *n*, Erschließungsterritorium *n*

improvement to land, installation of improvements, (land) improvement, building land improvement [*Facilities, usually public utilities, such as sidewalks or sewers, added to land which increase its usefulness*] · Erschließung, (Bau)Landerschließung, (Bau)Bodenerschließung, (Bau)Flächenerschließung, (Bau)Geländeerschließung, (Bau)-Terrainerschließung, Baureifmachung, Zuwegung

improvement trade, finishing trade · Veredelungsgewerbe *n*

improvement unit → (land) improvement unit

improvement work, work of improvement · Verbesserungsarbeit(en) *f (pl)*

improvement work → (land) improvement work

improvement work(s) → (physical) improvement work(s)

improvement zone → (physical) improvement zone

impruiare [*Latin*]; to improve (land) · baureif machen, bebaubar machen, erschließen; überbaubar machen [*Schweiz*]

imputation · Zurechnung *f*, Anrechnung

to impute · zurechnen, anrechnen

imputed · zugerechnet, angerechnet

imputed cost(s) · kalkulatorische Kosten *f*

imputed interest, calculatory interest, calculable interest · kalkulatorische Zinsen *f*

in abeyance · herrenlos [*Der Grundbesitz einer Pfarrei ist nach dem Tode des Inhabers herrenlos, bis ein Nachfolger ernannt ist, desgleichen der Titel eines Pairs, der nur Töchter hinterläßt. Herrenlose Objekte sind mit „hereditas jacens" des römischen Rechtes vergleichbar*]

in abeyance, dormant, abeyant · in der Schwebe (sein), schwebend, noch nicht entschieden, unentschieden

inability, incapacity, incapability, disability · Unvermögen *n*, Unfähigkeit *f*

inability, incapacity, disability, incapability [*The want of legal capability to perform an act*] · (Geschäfts)Unvermögen *n*, (Geschäfts)Unfähigkeit *f*

inability of infancy, disability of infancy, incapacity of infancy, incapability of infancy · (Geschäfts)Unvermögen *n* als Minderjähriger, (Geschäfts)Unfähigkeit *f* als Minderjähriger

inability supervening, incapacity supervening, incapability supervening, disability supervening · (Geschäfts)Unvermögen *n* nach Beginn der Verjährungsfrist, (Geschäfts)Unfähigkeit *f* nach Beginn der Verjährungsfrist

inaccessible, without access, accessless · ohne Zugang, unzugänglich, zuganglos

in accordance with (the) term(s), in accordance with (the) condition(s) · bedingungsgemäß

in a comparable manner, comparatively, comparingly, in the way of comparison, comparably · vergleichsweise

inactive, dormant · inaktiv

inactivity (court) action, inactivity cause, inactivity (law)suit, inactivity plea · Untätigkeitsklage *f*

inadequacy · Unzulänglichkeit *f*

inadmissible · unzulässig

inadmitted asset, nonadmitted asset [*insurance accounting*] · ungeeignetes Deckungsmittel *n*, geringwertiges Deckungsmittel

inadvertence, oversight · Versehen *n*

inadvertently, from inadvertence, from oversight, by inadvertence, by oversight · versehentlich

inalienability · Unveräußerlichkeit *f*, Nichtveräußerlichkeit

inalienable · unveräußerlich, nichtveräußerlich

inapplicable wording · Nichtzutreffende *n*

in a state (to do a thing), prepared (to do a thing), in condition (to do a thing) · in der Lage (etwas zu tun), vorbereitet (etwas zu tun)

in balance · ausgeglichen [*Konten*]

inbound traffic · Stadteinwärtsverkehr *m*

in camera · unter Ausschluß der Öffentlichkeit

incapability, disability, inability, incapacity · Unvermögen *n*, Unfähigkeit *f*

incapability, inability, incapacity, disability [*The want of legal capability to perform an act*] · (Geschäfts)Unvermögen *n*, (Geschäfts)Unfähigkeit *f*

incapability of infancy, inability of infancy, disability of infancy, incapacity of infancy · (Geschäfts)Unvermögen *n* als Minderjähriger, (Geschäfts)Unfähigkeit *f* als Minderjähriger

incapability to perform official duties, disability to perform official duties, incapacity to perform official duties · Amtsunfähigkeit *f*, Amtsunvermögen *n*

incapability supervening, disability supervening, inability supervening, incapacity supervening · (Geschäfts)Unvermögen *n* nach Beginn der Verjährungsfrist, (Geschäfts)Unfähigkeit *f* nach Beginn der Verjährungsfrist

incapable, uncapable, unable · unfähig, nicht fähig

incapable of acting, unable of acting, uncapable of acting · handlungsunfähig, nicht handlungsfähig

incapable of being fairly estimated · unschätzbar

incapable of being terminated by notice · unkündbar

incapable of working, unfit for work, disable (for work) · arbeitsunfähig

incapable person · Geschäftsunfähige *m*

incapacity, incapability, disability, inability · Unvermögen *n*, Unfähigkeit *f*

incapacity, disability, incapability, inability [*The want of legal capability to perform an act*] · (Geschäfts)Unvermögen *n*, (Geschäfts)Unfähigkeit *f*

incapacity of infancy, incapability of infancy, inability of infancy, disability of infancy · (Geschäfts)Unvermögen *n* als Minderjähriger, (Geschäfts)Unfähigkeit *f* als Minderjähriger

incapacity supervening, incapability supervening, disability supervening, inability supervening · (Geschäfts)Unvermögen *n* nach Beginn der Verjährungsfrist, (Geschäfts)Unfähigkeit *f* nach Beginn der Verjährungsfrist

incapacity to perform official duties, incapability to perform official duties, disability to perform official duties · Amtsunfähigkeit *f*, Amtsunvermögen *n*

incendiary · Brandstifter *m*

incentive, inducement [*Anything that induces*] · Anreizmittel *n*, Motiv *n*

incentive contract · Vertrag *m* mit vereinbartem Kosten- und Gewinnziel [*Der Gewinn steigt, wenn die tatsächlichen Kosten unter dem Kostenziel bleiben und er mindert sich, wenn das Kostenziel überschritten wird*]

inception stage · Anlaufstadium *n*, Entstehungsphase *f*

inchoate [*Not yet vested or completed. The right to dower is inchoate until the husband dies*] · anwartschaftlich

inchoate curtesy [*The imperfective interest which the law gives a husband in the land(s) of his wife; the interest which, upon the death of the wife, may ripen into possession and use*] · Anwartschaft *f* auf das Witwerpflichtteil

inchoate development, incipient development · beginnende Entwick(e)lung *f*

inchoate instrument [*An instrument which the law requires to be registered or recorded is said to be "inchoate" prior to registration, in that it is then good only between the parties and privies and as to persons having notice*] · unvollständiges Rechtsinstitut *n*, unvollständiges rechtliches Institut

inchoate interest, inchoate right [*An interest in (real) estate which is not a present interest, but which may ripen into a vested estate, if not barred, extinguished, or divested*] · anwartschaftliches Recht *n*, Anwartschaftsrecht *n*

inchoate right, inchoate interest [*In patent law. The right of an inventor to his invention while his application is pending which matures as "property" when the patent issues*] · anwartschaftliches Recht *n*, Anwartschaftsrecht *n*

inchocate dower [*The imperfective interest which the law gives a wife in the land(s) of her husband; the interest which, upon the death of the husband, may ripen into possession and use*] · Anwartschaft *f* auf das Witwenpflichtteil

incidence of households, household incidence, headship rate [*The proportion of people in any given age category who are heads of households*] · Haushaltvorstandsziffer *f*

incident, accompanying condition · Begleitbedingung *f*, unentziehbare Eigenschaft *f*, Attribut *n*

incidental cost(s), incidentals · Nebenkosten *f*

incidental reader · Zufallsleser *m* [*Ein Leser der die Veröffentlichung nicht gekauft hat*]

incidental variance, composite variance · Abweichung *f* 2. Grades [*Sie errechnet sich theoretisch aus dem Produkt der Mengenabweichung der Preisabweichung, d. h. die Abweichung 2. Grades ist die mit der Preisabweichung bewertete Mengenabweichung*]

incinerating, cremation, burning to ashes [*The act of reducing a corpse by means of fire*] · Einäschern *n*

incipient development, inchoate development · beginnende Entwick(e)lung *f*

incitement of perjury, perjury incitement · Verleitung *f* zum Meineid

to inclose, to enclose · abfrieden, einhegen, einfrieden, umfrieden, abschließen

inclosed, enclosed · abgefriedet, eingehegt, abgeschlossen, eingefriedet, umfriedet

inclosed chase, park, enclosed chase [*In English law. A tract of enclosed ground privileged for keeping wild beasts of the chase, particularly deer. Franchises of park were abolished in England by the Wild Creatures and Forest Laws Act 1971*] · Jagdgehege *n*, eingefriedetes Jagdrevier *n*, umfriedetes Jagdrevier

inclosing with shrubs and/or trees, enclosing with shrubs and/or trees · Eingrünung *f* [*Durch Gebüsche und/oder Bäume umgeben*]

inclosure commissioners, enclosure commissioners · Einhegungskommission *f*

inclosure map, enclosure map [*A map prepared for the enclosure of open fields*] · Einfried(ig)ungskarte *f*, Einhegungskarte

inclosure plan, enclosure plan · Einfried(ig)ungsplan *m*

to include · einschließen

to include in a list, to insert in a list, to enschedule, to list · auflisten

inclusive · einschließlich

inclusive amount · Globalbetrag *m*

inclusive award · Gesamtzuschlag *m*, Gesamtvergabe *f*, Gesamtauftragserteilung *f* [*Zuschlag an einen Generalunternehmer*]

inclusive cost(s) · Globalkosten *f*

inclusive (e)valuation, inclusive val., inclusive appraisal, inclusive appraisement, inclusive assessment of value · Globalbewertung *f*, Global(ab)schätzung, Globalwertermitt(e)lung, Globaltaxierung

inclusive loan · Globaldarleh(e)n *n*

inclusive price · Globalpreis *m*

inclusive sum · Globalsumme *f*

income · Einkommen *n*

income account · Einkommensrechnung *f*

income (admission) limit, ceiling · Einkommensgrenze *f* (für Sozialwohnungsmieter)

income and growth bond · kombinierter Rentenversicherungssparbrief *m*

income approach · Einkommensansatz *m*

income bond · Renten(versicherungs-)brief *m* mit laufender Ausschüttung [*Rückzahlung des Nomialwertes am Ende der Laufzeit*]

income corporate bond [*USA*]; income debenture [*Great Britain*] [*These debentures receive no interest unless there is a profit*] · Schuldverschreibung *f* aus Gewinn verzinst, Obligation *f* aus Gewinn verzinst [*private Kapitalgesellschaft*]

income deduction, nonoperating expense · Erlösschmälerung *f*

income determination model · Einkommensermitt(e)lungsmodell *n*

income distribution, distribution of income · Einkommensverteilung *f*

income duration, duration of income · Einkommensdauer *f*

income earned from basic work(s) · fernbedarfstätiges Einkommen *n*

income flow · Einkommensstrom *m*

income formation · Einkommensbildung *f*

income from an appliance for production made by man, quasi-rent · Quasirente *f* [*Ein der Bodenrente ähnliches und nicht aus Naturquellen fließendes Einkommen*]

income from possession, investment income, unearned income, unearned increment · Besitzrente *f*, Besitzeinkommen *n*, nichterarbeitete Wertsteigerung *f*, Zuwachsrente, fundiertes Einkommen

income from rent(s) · Renteneinkommen *n*

income from work(ing), work(ing) income · Arbeiteinkommen *n*

income fund · Einkommensfonds *m*

income group · Einkommensgruppe *f*

income incentive, income inducement · Einkommensanreiz *m*

income inequality · Einkommensungleichheit *f*

income line · Bilanzg(e)rade *f*

income mix, economic integration · wirtschaftliche Eingliederung *f*, wirtschaftliche Einordnung, wirtschaftliche Integration

income multiplier · Einkommensvervielfältiger *m*

income-orien(ta)ted, income-related · einkommensorientiert, einkommensbezogen

income policy · Einkommenspolitik *f*

income-price ratio [*Ratio established by dividing the net income from a property by the selling price*] · Einkommen-Preis-Verhältnis *n*

income property, capital property, capital estate [*Property that is expected to produce an income to its owner from rents or leases*] · Kapitalvermögen *n*

income redistribution · Einkommensumverteilung *f*

income-rent relation(ship) — incorporated municipality

income-rent relation(ship) · Einkommen-Miete-Verhältnis *n*

income share · Rentenanteil *m* [*Bausparkasse*]

income-splitting · Einkommenstrennung *f*

income statement, earnings and profit and loss statement, statement of operations, results of operations, profit and loss account · Gewinn- und Verlustrechnung *f*

income stream, stream of income · Einkommensstrom *m*

income tax · Einkommenssteuer *f*

income taxation, taxation of income(s) · Einkommensbesteuerung *f*

income tax declaration · Einkommenssteuererklärung *f*

income theory, theory of income · Einkommenstheorie *f*

income value, capitalized value · Ertragswert *m*

income value appraisal → capitalized value appraisal

income value of a building, capitalized value of a building · Gebäudeertragswert *m*

in commission [*Of persons: In the exercise of delegated duty*] · bestellt, beauftragt

(in) common, together, joint(ly), unitedly · gemeinsam, gemeinschaftlich, miteinander, gemeinheitlich, verbunden, solidarisch, zusammen

in-commuter · Einpendler *m*, Zupendler

in-commuting · Einpendeln *n*, Zupendeln

incomparable, without comparison; compareless [*obsolete*] · unvergleichbar

incompatibility · Unvereinbarkeit *f*, Unverträglichkeit

incompatibility clause · Unverträglichkeitsklausel *f*

incompetent · geschäftsunfähig

incompetent female person · Entmündigte *f*

incompetent male person · Entmündigte *m*

incompetent person · entmündigte Person *f*

incomplete Latin square · unvollständiges lateinisches Quadrat *n*

incompleteness, diminution [*It signifies that the record sent up from an inferior to a superior court for review is incomplete, or not fully certified. In such case the party may suggest a "diminution of the record", which may be rectified by a certiorari*] · Unvollständigkeit *f*, Abbrüchigkeit

in condition (to do a thing), in a state (to do a thing), prepared (to do a thing) · in der Lage (etwas zu tun), vorbereitet (etwas zu tun)

inconsistency · Widerspruch *m* [*Er kann sich aus dem grammatischen Wortlaut eines Gesetzes ergeben*]

inconsistent with possessory right, adverse, wrongful · entgegenstehend, fehlerhaft, entgegen dem Recht, rechtswidrig [*(subjektives) Besitzrecht*]

to incorporate, to form (into) a corporation · inkorporieren [*Handelsrecht*]

to incorporate · eingliedern, einverleiben

to incorporate, to annex, to municipalize, to communalize · eingemeinden, einbezirken, vereinigen, verschmelzen, ausbezirken, umbezirken, inkorporieren, angemeinden

incorporated · inkorporiert

incorporated area, incorporated territory, local area, local territory, communal area, communal territory, community area, community territory · Gemeindegebiet *n*, gemeindliches Gebiet, Kommunalgebiet, kommunales Gebiet, Ortsgebiet

incorporated building society (Brit.); incorporated (building and loan) association (US) · eingetragene Bausparkasse *f*, inkorporierte Bausparkasse

incorporated charity · rechtsfähige Stiftung *f*

incorporated collecting charity · sammelnde Stiftung *f*

incorporated community, incorporated place · inkorporierte Gemeinde *f* [*Gemeinde mit dem Status einer Gebietskörperschaft*]

incorporated community, city, incorporated municipality, incorporated city [*USA*] · Stadt(gemeinde) *f* erster Ordnung [*In den USA ist eine corporate oder legal city eine verhältnismäßig große Stadt mit höherem gebietskörperschaftlichem Status als eine "town"*]

incorporated co-operative · eingetragene Genossenschaft *f*

incorporated group · inkorporierte Gruppe *f*

incorporated institution · rechtsfähige Anstalt *f*, selbständige Anstalt [*Eine durch die Rechtsordnung mit Rechtspersönlichkeit ausgestattete Anstalt*]

incorporated municipality, incorporated city, incorporated community, city [*USA*] · Stadt(gemeinde) *f* erster Ordnung [*In den USA ist eine corporate oder legal city eine verhältnismäßig große Stadt mit höherem gebietskörperschaftlichem Status als eine "town"*]

incorporated person · inkorporierte Person *f*

incorporated place, incorporated community · inkorporierte Gemeinde *f* [*Gemeinde mit dem Status einer Gebietskörperschaft*]

incorporated public company; stock company (US), joint-stock company · Aktiengesellschaft *f*, AG

incorporated territory, local area, local territory, communal area, communal territory, community area, community territory, incorporated area · Gemeindegebiet *n*, gemeindliches Gebiet, Kommunalgebiet, kommunales Gebiet, Ortsgebiet

incorporatio [*Latin*]; incorporation · (Sach)Verbindung *f*, (Sach)Zufügung, Subjektverbindung, Subjektzufügung [*Ein fester Körper wird mit einem anderen derart vereinigt, daß sie voneinander nicht getrennt werden können, ohne daß der eine oder der andere zerstört oder verändert wird*]

incorporation · Verselbständigung *f*, Verleihung körperschaftlicher Rechte, Inkorporierung, Gründung

incorporation; incorporatio [*Latin*] · (Sach)Verbindung *f*, (Sach)Zufügung, Subjektverbindung, Subjektzufügung [*Ein fester Körper wird mit einem anderen derart vereinigt, daß sie voneinander nicht getrennt werden können, ohne daß der eine oder der andere zerstört oder verändert wird*]

incorporation · gebietskörperschaftliche Eigenständigkeit *f*

incorporation · Einbeziehung *f*

incorporation, annexation, communalization, municipalization, suburbanization · Einbezirkung *f*, Vereinigung, Eingemeindung, Fusion(ierung) *f*, Verschmelzung, Ausbezirkung, Umbezirkung, Einverleibung, Inkorporation *f*, Inkommunalisation *f*, Inkommunalisierung, Angemeindung, Ausgemeindung, Umgemeindung [*Der rechtliche Vorgang einer organischen Verbindung mehrerer Gemeinden oder Gemeindeteile*]

incorporation contract, suburbanization contract, annexation contract, communalization contract, municipalization contract · Angemeindungsvertrag *m*, Eingemeindungsvertrag, Einbezirkungsvertrag, Vereinigungsvertrag, Verschmelzungsvertrag, Fusion(ierung)svertrag, Ausbezirkungsvertrag, Umbezirkungsvertrag, Einverleibungsvertrag, Inkorporationsvertrag, Inkommunalisationsvertrag, Inkommunalisierungsvertrag, Ausgemeindungsvertrag, Umgemeindungsvertrag

incorporation document, incorporation instrument, constituting instrument, constituting document, document of incorporation, instrument incorporation · Inkorporierungsurkunde *f*

incorporation instrument, constituting instrument, constituting document, document of incorporation, instrument incorporation, incorporation document · Inkorporierungsurkunde *f*

incorporation in the works · Einbau *m* [*Baustoff*]

incorporation of land(s), land(s) incorporation · (Grund(stücks))Zuschreibung *f*, Grund(stücks)verbindung [*Einem Grundstück als Hauptstück wird ein anderes als unwesentlicher Bestandteil hinzugefügt*]

incorporator · Gründungsaktionär *m*

incorporeal, intangible [*Not admitting of physical possession*] · immateriell, unkörperlich, nichtkörperlich

incorporeal chattel (personal), intangible chattel (personal), thing incorporeal; res incorporales [*Latin*]; incorporeal thing, intangible thing · unkörperliches Ding *n*, immaterielles Ding, nichtkörperliches Ding, unkörperliches Rechtsobjekt *n*, nichtkörperliches Rechtsobjekt, immaterielles Rechtsobjekt, immaterieller Gegenstand *m*, unkörperlicher Gegenstand, nichtkörperlicher Gegenstand

incorporeal chattel (personal) → incorporeal personal property

incorporeal freehold possession, intangible freehold possession, incorporeal seisin, intangible seisin · nichtkörperliche Gewere *f*, unkörperliche Gewere, immaterielle Gewere

incorporeal hereditament; incorporeale haereditamentum [*Latin*] [*In a large sense — any possession or subject of property, whether real or personal, capable of being transmitted to heirs, and not the object of bodily sense. In a strict sense — a right annexed to, or issuing out of, or exercisable within a corporeal hereditament, or land*] · nichtkörperliches Erbgut *n*, unkörperliches Erbgut, immaterielles Erbgut

incorporeal hereditament appendant → (purely) incorporeal hereditament appendant

incorporeal hereditament appurtenant → (purely) incorporeal hereditament appurtenant

incorporeal interest, incorporeal right · nichtdingliches Grundstücksrecht *n*

incorporeal ownership (of property), intangible ownership (of property), incorporeal proprietorship, intangible proprietorship, incorporeal property, intangible property · unkörperliches Eigentum *n*, nichtkörperliches Eigentum, immaterielles Eigentum

incorporeal personal property, incorporeal personal estate, incorporeal personal

incorporeal right — incroaching

chattel, incorporeal chattel (personal), incorporal personalty, intangible personal property · nichtkörperliche Fahrnis f, nichtkörperliche Fahrhabe, nichtkörperliche Mobilie, unkörperliche Fahrhabe, unkörperliche Fahrnis, unkörperliche Mobilie, immaterielle Fahrnis, immaterielle Fahrhabe, immaterielle Mobilie

incorporeal right, incorporeal interest · nichtdingliches Grundstücksrecht n

incorporeal seisin, intangible seisin, incorporeal freehold possession, intangible freehold possession · nichtkörperliche Gewere f, unkörperliche Gewere, immaterielle Gewere

incorporeal thing, intangible thing, incorporeal chattel (personal), intangible chattel (personal), thing incorporeal; res incorporales [*Latin*] · unkörperliches Ding n, immaterielles Ding, nichtkörperliches Ding, unkörperliches Rechtsobjekt n, nichtkörperliches Rechtsobjekt, immaterielles Rechtsobjekt, immaterieller Gegenstand m, unkörperlicher Gegenstand, nichtkörperlicher Gegenstand

incorrigible rogues · unverbesserliches Gesindel n

incorruptibility · Unbestechlichkeit f

incorruptible · unbestechlich

to increase, to accrue · zunehmen

to increase · zunehmen, anwachsen [*Kapital*]

increase, augmentation · Steigerung f, Zunahme f, Erhöhung

increased depletion for wear (and tear) · erhöhte Absetzung f für Abnutzung, erhöhte AfA [*Höhere AfA als die gewöhnlich zulässige*]

increase of buildings · Zugang m an Gebäuden

increase of capital, capital increase · Aufstockung f, Kapitalaufstockung f

increase of population, growth of population, population increase, population growth · Bevölkerungszunahme f, Bevölkerungswachstum n, Wachstum der Bevölkerung

increase of property, accession of property, addition of property, augmentation of property · Besitzzunahme f, Besitzzuwachs m, Besitzerhöhung f, Besitzsteigerung

increase of value, value increase, (prospective) development value, betterment, (capital) appreciation [*An improvement which adds to the cost(s) of a property. Distinguished from a repair or replacement*] · Wertverbesserung f, Wertzuwachs m, Wertsteigerung, Wertzunahme f, Werterhöhung

increase of value clause, (capital) appreciation clause, betterment clause, value increase clause, (prospective) development value clause · Werterhöhungsklausel f, Wertsteigerungsklausel, Wertzuwachsklausel, Wertzunahmeklausel, Wertverbesserungsklausel

increase rate, augmentation rate, rate of increase, rate of augmentation · Steigerungssatz m, Erhöhungssatz, Steigerungsrate, Erhöhungsrate

increasing annuity · steigende Annuität f, wachsende Annuität, zunehmende Annuität

increasing city, increasing town · Stadt f mit zunehmender Bevölkerung

increasing income bond · Renten(versicherungsspar)brief m mit steigender Ausschüttung

increasing town, increasing city · Stadt f mit zunehmender Bevölkerung

incremental cost(s) · Zuwachskosten f

incrementalism, piecemeal (social) engineering, social piecemeal engineering · Inkrementalismus m, pragmatisches Ideal n, problemorientiertes Vorgehen n, problembezogenes Vorgehen [*Planung als pragmatisches, quasirationales, allein am Kriterium des Möglichen ausgerichtetes, zusammenhangloses und schrittweises Vorgehen*]

incroaching furrows; ploughing off, ploughing away (Brit.); plowing off, plowing away (US); encroaching furrows · Abackern n, Abpflügen, Abfurchen, Wegackern

to incroach, to trespass, to encroach, to intrude · beeinträchtigen, verletzen, stören, eindringen

to incroach by digging, to incroach by excavation, to encroach by digging, to encroach by excavation · abgraben, weggraben, entziehen durch graben

to incroach by excavation, to encroach by digging, to encroach by excavation, to incroach by digging · abgraben, weggraben, entziehen durch graben

to incroach by fencing, to encroach by fencing · abhägen, abhagen [*Durch einen Hag Land wegnehmen*]

to incroach by water, to encroach by water · abschwemmen

to incroach furrows, to plough off, to plough away (Brit.); to plow off, to plow away (US); to encroach furrows · abakkern, abpflügen, abfurchen, wegackern [*Durch übergreifendes Pflügen ein Stück Land wegnehmen*]

incroaching, encroachment, encroaching, trespass [*Invasion of private rights by persons or economic forces*] · Störung f, Beeinträchtigung

incroachment, encroachment [*Part of a building or an obstruction that intrudes on or invades a road, street, or sidewalk or trespasses on the property of another*] · Überbau *m*, Grenzüberbau

incroachment, incroaching, trespass, intrusion, encroaching, encroachment, adverse occupation · (Beeinträchtigung *f* durch) Eindringen *n*, Verletzung durch Eindringen, Störung durch Eindringen, Besitzverletzung durch Eindringen, Besitzstörung durch Eindringen, Besitzbeeinträchtigung durch Eindringen

incroachment, encroachment [*An unlawful gaining upon the right or possession of another*] · Übergriff *m*

incroachment by balcony, encroachment by balcony · Balkonüberbau *m*

incroachment by digging, incroachment by excavation, encroachment by digging, encroachment by excavation · Abgrabung *f*, Weggrabung, Entziehung durch Graben

incroachment by water, encroachment by water · Abschwemmung *f*

incroachment revenue, encroachment revenue · (Grenz)Überbaurente *f* [*Rente zur Entschädigung für die Duldung eines Überbaues*]

incumbent (of (an) office), office-bearer, office-holder [*A person who is in possession of an office*] · Amtsträger *m*, Amtsinhaber

to incumber, to load, to encumber, to charge, to burden · belasten, dinglich belasten

incumbered, loaded, burdened, charged, imperfect, encumbered · belastet, dinglich belastet

incumbered by law, charged by law, loaded by law, burdened by law, encumbered by law · gesetzlich belastet

incumbered by mortgage(s), loaded by mortgage(s), burdened by mortgage(s), charged by mortgage(s), encumbered by mortgage(s) · hypothek(en)belastet

incumbered with lease(hold), loaded with lease(hold), charged with lease(hold), burdened with lease(hold), encumbered with lease(hold) · erbbaurechtbelastet, platzrechtbelastet

incumbering, encumbering, loading, charging, burdening · (dingliches) Belasten *n*

incumbramentum [*Latin*]; charge, encumbrance, load, burden, incumbrance [*A claim or lien attached to property as a mortgage*] · (dingliche) Belastung *f*, (dingliche) Last *f*

incumbrance of easement, load of easement, burden of easement, charge of easement, encumbrance of easement · Grunddienstbarkeitslast *f*

incumbrance of national debt, load of national debt, burden of national debt, encumbrance of national debt · Staatsschuldenlast *f*

incumbrance of the poor rates, charge of the poor rates, load of the poor rates, burden of the poor rates, encumbrance of the poor rates · Armenlast *f*

incumbrance on capital, capital charge, capital burden, capital encumbrance, capital incumbrance, burden on capital, charge on capital, encumbrance on capital · Kapitaldienst *m*, Kapitallast *f*

incumbrance on land(s), land charge, land(s) encumbrance, land(s) incumbrance, encumbrance on land(s) [*Land charges are those rights and interests affecting land, e.g., estate contracts, restrictive covenants, general equitable charges and easements*] · Grund(stücks)belastung *f*, Grund(stücks)last *f*, Bodenlast, Landlast, Liegenschaftslast

incumbrance on personal property, load (up)on personal property, burden on personal property, charge on personal property, encumbrance on personal property · Fahrnislast *f*, Fahrhabelast, Mobiliarlast, Mobilienlast

incumbrance prohibition, burden prohibition, charge prohibition, load prohibition, encumbrance prohibition · Belastungsverbot *n*, Lastenverbot

incumbrancer, encumbrancer [*The holder of an incumbrance, e.g., a mortgage, on the estate of another*] · Belastende *m*

incumbrance rate, charge rate, load rate, burden rate, encumbrance rate · Belastungssatz *m*

incumbrances register → (land) incumbrances register

to incur, to sustain · erleiden [*Schaden; Verlust*]

incurred, sustained · erlitten [*Schaden; Verlust*]

in custodia legis [*Latin*]; in the custody of the law · in Rechtsgewahrsam, in gesetzlichem Gewahrsam, im Gewahrsam des Gesetzes, gesetzlich verwahrt

indebitatus assumpsit [*Latin*]; general assumpsit, common assumpsit, indebted assumpsit · ausdrückliches Schuldtilgungsversprechen *n*

indebted, debt-laden · verschuldet

indebted assumpsit; indebitatus assumpsit [*Latin*]; general assumpsit, common assumpsit · ausdrückliches Schuldtilgungsversprechen *n*

indebtedness · Verschuldung *f*

indebtedness — indemnifying

indebtedness · Schuldnerschaft *f*

indebtedness of land(s) · Bodenverschuldung *f*, Landverschuldung

indebtedness sum, debt sum · Schuldensumme, Verschuldungssumme *f*

indecimable; indecimabilis [*Latin*]; not titheable, tithe-free [*Exempted from the payment of tithes*] · zehnt(en)frei

in deed · effektiv [*Besitzübertragung*]

indefeasibility · Unanfechtbarkeit *f*

indefeasibility of title · (Rechts)Titelunanfechtbarkeit *f*

indefeasible [*That which cannot be defeated, undone, or made void*] · unanfechtbar

indefeasible title · unanfechtbarer (Rechts)Titel *m*

indefinite legacy, indefinite bequest · unbeschränktes Legat *n*, unbeschränktes Vermächtnis *n*, unbeschränktes Fahrnisvermächtnis, unbeschränktes Fahrnislegat

indelible substance · urkundenechter Schreibstoff *m*

indemnification, compensation, damages, indemnity [*"Compensation" is distinguishable from "damages" inasmuch as the former may mean the sum which will remunerate an owner for land actually taken, while the latter signifies an allowance made for injury to the residue; but such destinction is not ordinarily observed*] · Entschädigung *f*, Schadenersatz *m*, *(f)*

indemnification claim, damages claim, claim for indemnification, claim for indemnity, claim for compensation, claim for damages, compensation claim, indemnity claim · Entschädigungsforderung *f*, Schadenersatzforderung, Entschädigungsverlangen *n*, Schadenersatzverlangen

indemnification clause, damages clause, compensation clause, indemnity clause · Entschädigungsklausel *f*, Schadenersatzklausel

indemnification for breach of contract, indemnity for breach of contract, damages for breach of contract, compensation for breach of contract · Entschädigung(sleistung) *f* wegen Vertragsbruch, Schadensersatz(leistung) *m*, *(f)* wegen Vertragsbruch

indemnification for delay, compensation for delay, damages for delay, indemnity for delay · Schadenersatz *m* bei Verzug, Entschädigung *f* bei Verzug

indemnification for (land) condemnation (US) → compensation for (land) expropriation

indemnification for (land) expropriation → compensation for (land) expropriation

indemnification for negligence, indemnity for negligence, damages for negligence, compensation for negligence · Entschädigung *f* für Fahrlässigkeit, Schadenersatz *m* für Fahrlässigkeit

indemnification for nonperformance, indemnity for nonperformance, damages for nonperformance, compensation for nonperformance · Schadenersatz *m* wegen Nichterfüllung, Entschädigung *f* wegen Nichterfüllung

indemnification in land, damages in land, compensation in land, indemnity in land · Entschädigung *f* in Land, Schadenersatz *m* in Land, Landentschädigung, Landschadenersatz, Landabfindung

indemnification in lieu of injunction, indemnity in lieu of injunction, damages in lieu of injunction, compensation in lieu of injunction · Entschädigung *f* für richterlich privilegierten Eingriff, Schadenersatz *m* für richterlich privilegierten Eingriff

indemnification law, damages law, compensation law, indemnity law · (objektives) Entschädigungsrecht *n*, (objektives) Schadenersatzrecht,

indemnification measure, indemnity measure, compensation measure, measure of damages, measure of compensation, measure of indemnification, measure of indemnity, indemnifying measure, damages measure · Entschädigungsmaßnahme *f*, Schadenersatzmaßnahme

indemnification (paid) in kind, indemnity (paid) in kind, in-kind compensation, in-kind indemnification, in-kind damages, in-kind indemnity, compensation (paid) in kind, damages (paid) in kind · Entschädigung *f* in Natur, Natural(schaden)ersatz, Naturalentschädigung

indemnification (paid) in money, damages (paid) in money, compensation (paid) in money, indemnity (paid) in money, money indemnity, payment of damages, money damages, pecuniary damages, pecuniary compensation, pecuniary indemnification, money compensation, money indemnification · Entschädigung *f* in Geld, Schadenersatz *m* in Geld, Geldentschädigung, Geld(schaden)ersatz, Schadenersatzzahlung, Entschädigungszahlung

indemnification under public law, indemnity under public law, damages under public law, compensation under public law · öffentlich-rechtliche Entschädigung *f*, öffentlich-rechtlicher Schadenersatz *m*

to indemnify, to save harmless, to hold harmless [*To secure against loss or damage*] · decken, schadlos halten

to indemnify, to compensate · entschädigen

indemnifying, compensating · Entschädigen *n*

indemnifying measure, damages measure, indemnification measure, indemnity measure, compensation measure, measure of damages, measure of compensation, measure of indemnification, measure of indemnity · Entschädigungsmaßnahme *f*, Schadenersatzmaßnahme

indemnitee · entschädigungsberechtigte Person *f*, schadenersatzberechtigte Person

indemnitor · entschädigungspflichtige Person *f*, entschädigungsleistende Person, schadenersatzpflichtige Person, schadenersatzleistende Person

indemnity, indemnification, compensation, damages [*"Compensation" is distinguishable from "damages" inasmuch as the former may mean the sum which will remunerate an owner for land actually taken, while the latter signifies an allowance made for injury to the residue; but such destinction is not ordinarily observed*] · Entschädigung *f*, Schadenersatz *m*, *(f)*

indemnity claim, indemnification claim, damages claim, claim for indemnification, claim for indemnity, claim for compensation, claim for damages, compensation claim · Entschädigungsforderung *f*, Schadenersatzforderung, Entschädigungsverlangen *n*, Schadenersatzverlangen

indemnity clause, indemnification clause, damages clause, compensation clause · Entschädigungsklausel *f*, Schadenersatzklausel

indemnity for breach of contract, damages for breach of contract, compensation for breach of contract, indemnification for breach of contract · Entschädigung(sleistung) *f* wegen Vertragsbruch, Schadenersatz(leistung) *m*, *(f)* wegen Vertragsbruch

indemnity for delay, indemnification for delay, compensation for delay, damages for delay · Schadenersatz *m* bei Verzug, Entschädigung *f* bei Verzug

indemnity for (land) condemnation (US) → compensation for (land) expropriation

indemnity for (land) expropriation → compensation for (land) expropriation

indemnity for negligence, damages for negligence, compensation for negligence, indemnification for negligence · Entschädigung *f* für Fahrlässigkeit, Schadenersatz *m* für Fahrlässigkeit

indemnity for nonperformance, damages for nonperformance, compensation for nonperformance, indemnification for nonperformance · Schadenersatz *m* wegen Nichterfüllung, Entschädigung *f* wegen Nichterfüllung

indemnity in land, indemnification in land, damages in land, compensation in land · Entschädigung *f* in Land, Schadenersatz *m* in Land, Landentschädigung, Landschadenersatz, Landabfindung

indemnity in lieu of injunction, damages in lieu of injunction, compensation in lieu of injunction, indemnification in lieu of injunction · Entschädigung *f* für richterlich privilegierten Eingriff, Schadenersatz *m* für richterlich privilegierten Eingriff

indemnity insurance, liability insurance · Haftpflichtversicherung *f*

indemnity law, indemnification law, damages law, compensation law · (objektives) Entschädigungsrecht *n*, (objektives) Schadenersatzrecht,

indemnity letter, letter of indemnity · Konnossementgarantie *f*, Konnossementrevers *m*

indemnity measure, compensation measure, measure of damages, measure of compensation, measure of indemnification, measure of indemnity, indemnifying measure, damages measure, indemnification measure · Entschädigungsmaßnahme *f*, Schadenersatzmaßnahme

indemnity (paid) in kind, in-kind compensation, in-kind indemnification, in-kind damages, in-kind indemnity, compensation (paid) in kind, damages (paid) in kind, indemnification (paid) in kind · Entschädigung *f* in Natur, Schadenersatz *m* in Natur, Natural(schaden)ersatz, Naturalentschädigung

indemnity (paid) in money, money indemnity, payment of damages, money damages, pecuniary damages, pecuniary compensation, pecuniary indemnification, money compensation, money indemnification, indemnification (paid) in money, damages (paid) in money, compensation (paid) in money · Entschädigung *f* in Geld, Schadenersatz *m* in Geld, Geldentschädigung, Geld(schaden)ersatz, Schadenersatzzahlung, Entschädigungszahlung

indemnity risk, third-party risk, liability risk · Haftpflichtwagnis *n*, Haftpflichtrisiko *n*, Haftungsrisiko, Haftungswagnis

indemnity under public law, damages under public law, compensation under public law, indemnification under public law · öffentlich-rechtliche Entschädigung *f*, öffentlich-rechtlicher Schadenersatz *m*

indenture, deed of apprenticeship · Lehrbrief *m*

indenture, deed indented; scriptum indentatum [*Latin*] [*A deed to which two or more persons are parties, and in which these enter into reciprocal and corresponding grants or obligations towards each other*] · gesiegelte mehrseitige Urkunde *f*, mehrseitige gesiegelte Urkunde, zahnförmig ausgeschnittene

indenture of mortgage — indictment

gesiegelte mehrseitige Urkunde, zahnförmig ausgeschnittene mehrseitige gesiegelte Urkunde

indenture of mortgage, mortgage secured by a document, documentary mortgage, bonded mortgage · Briefhypothek *f* [*Neben einer Eintragung der Hypothek in das Grundbuch besteht auch eine Brieferteilung an den Gläubiger*]

independence axiom, axiom of independence · Axiom *n* der Unabhängigkeit, Unabhängigkeitsaxiom

independent · selbständig

independent agreement · Abmachung *f* mit selbständiger Verpflichtung, Abkommen *n* mit selbständiger Verpflichtung, Vereinbarung *m* mit selbständiger Verpflichtung [*Die eine Partei kann die ihr gebührende Leistung verlangen ohne die Gegenleistung anzubieten*]

independent condition · unabhängige Bedingung *f*

independent contract [*The mutual acts or promises have no relation to each other, neither as equivalents nor as consideration*] · Vertrag *m* mit selbständiger Verpflichtung, selbständiger Vertrag

independent contractor · selbständiger Unternehmer *m*

independent economic existence · wirtschaftliche Selbständigkeit *f*

independent homeworker · Hausgewerbetreibende *m*

independent lawmaking, autonomous legislation, autonomous lawmaking, independent legislation · autonome Gesetzgebung *f*, unabhängige Gesetzgebung

independent person; person sui juris [*Latin*] · unabhängige Person *f* [*Eine Person, die rechtlich fähig ist einen Wohnsitzwechsel selbständig vorzunehmen*]

independent person · natürliche unabhängige Person *f*

independent power, autocracy, self-sustained power · Selbstherrlichkeit *f*

(independent) professional man · Freiberufliche *m*, Freischaffende, Freiberufler

(independent) professional woman · Freiberufliche *f*, Freischaffende, Freiberuflerin

independent regulatory commission, I.R.C. [*Any commission which lies outside the regular executive departments and which has restrictive or disciplinary control over private conduct or private property*] · unabhängige (wirtschafts)regelnde Kommission *f* [*USA*]

in deposit · zur Verwahrung

indeterminate · unbestimmt

index, registry, register, bill, list, schedule, tabulation · Verzeichnis *n*, Liste *f*, Aufstellung *f*, Register *n*

index · Index *m*

index contour · Zählhöhenlinie *f*, Zählkurve *f*

index figure · Indexziffer *f*

index formulae method · System *n* der Preisfluktuation für Bauverträge

index map · Übersichtskarte *f* [*Flurbereinigung*]

index map · Grundstücksverzeichnis *n* [*im englischen Grundbuch*]

index number · Indexzahl *f*

index of abnormality, abnormality index · Anormalitätsindex *m*

index of accessibility, accessibility index · Wegsamkeitsindex *m*, Zugänglichkeitsindex

index of architects, tabulation of architects, register of architects, registry of architects, list of architects, schedule of architects · Architektenaufstellung *f*, Architektenliste *f*, Architektenregister *n*, Architektenverzeichnis *n*

index of case-notes, list of case-notes · Register *n* der Entscheidungsanmerkungen, Verzeichnis *n* der Entscheidungsanmerkungen, Liste *f* der Entscheidungsanmerkungen

index of centrality · Zentralitätsindex *m*

index of cost(s), cost(s) index · Kostenindex *m*

index of place names, list of place names · Ortsnamenverzeichnis *n*, Ortsnamenliste *f*, Ortsnamenregister *n*

index of private values · Bodenpreisindex *m*, Landpreisindex, Index der Bodenpreise, Index der Landpreise

index of residence · Wohnindex *m*

$$\left[= \frac{Nachtbevölkerung}{Tagesbevölkerung} \cdot 100 \right]$$

index of the taxable value of land, register of the taxable value of land · Generalhufenschoß *n*

index of utility, utility index · Nutzenindex *m*

index to book reviews · Buchbesprechungsregister *n*, Buchbesprechungsverzeichnis *n*

indicative · hinleitend

to indict · aburteilen

indictable · aburteilbar

indictable offence · schweres Vergehen *n*

indictment [*A written accusation against one or more persons of a crime for-*

merly preferred to and presented upon oath by a grand jury] · (Straf)Anklagebeschluß m, Strafanklage f

indictment at common law · (Straf)Anklagebeschluß m nach gemeinem Recht, Strafanklage nach gemeinem Recht

indifference · Gleichgültigkeit f

indifference curve · Indifferenzkurve f

indigenous, native · einheimisch, altansässig [*von Personen*]

indigenous culture, native culture · ursprüngliche Kultur f der Einheimischen [*Kolonialstadt*]

indigenous person, native (person) · einheimische Person f, altansässige Person

indigenous population, native population, nonmobile population [*People enumerated in their places of birth*] · altansässige Bevölkerung f, einheimische Bevölkerung, autochthone Bevölkerung

indignity to inherit · Erbunwürdigkeit f, Erbuntüchtigkeit

indirect control · mittelbare Lenkung f

indirect cost(s), overhead(s), overhead cost(s) [*The total cost(s) of indirect materials, wages and expenses. NOTE "oncost" and "burden" are synonymous terms which are not recommended*] · Gemeinkosten f, Generalkosten, indirekte Kosten, mittelbare Kosten

indirect cost(s) markup, overhead cost(s) markup, overhead(s) markup · Gemeinkostenzuschlag m, Generalkostenzuschlag

indirect evidence, indirect proof · mittelbarer Beweis m

indirect possession; constitutum possessorium [*Latin*]; constructive possession · (Besitz)Konstitut n, Besitzauftragung f, mittelbarer Besitz m, verdeckter Besitz, indirekter Besitz, vergeistigte Sachherrschaft f [*Der unmittelbare Besitzer macht einen anderen zum mittelbaren und behält selbst unmittelbaren Besitz*]

indirect possessor, constructive possessor · indirekter Besitzer m, mittelbarer Besitzer, verdeckter Besitzer

indirect proof, indirect evidence · mittelbarer Beweis m

indirect real evidence, indirect real proof · berichteter Realbeweis m

indirect tax credit · Anrechnung f der von einer ausländischen Untergesellschaft gezahlten Körperschaftssteuern

indispensable · unerläßlich

indisputable · unbestreitbar

in distress, in distraint · notleidend [*Wechsel*]

individual, single person [*A person who is not a member of a family*] · alleinstehende Person f

individual calculation, individual computation · Einzelberechnung f, Einzelkalkulation f

individual call, individual demand · Einzelnachfrage f

individual demand, individual call · Einzelnachfrage f

individual land area, area of distribution of the individual groups of elements, area of the earth's surface [*Climate; water; land; plants and cultural phenomena*] · Erdraum m

individual liberty · persönliche Freiheit f

individually, several(ly) [*As opposed to „joint(ly)"*] · einzeln, jeder für sich [*im Gegensatz zu gemeinschaftlich*]

individual performance · Einzelleistung f

individual promotion(al) system, individual sponsoring system, individual assistance system, promotion(al) individual system, sponsoring individual system, assisting individual system · Individualförderungssystem n

individual recreation · individuelle Erholung f

individual region · Einzelregion f

individual right, indivisible right, right incapable of division, nondivisible right; jus individuum [*Latin*] · unteilbares Recht n

individual space · Einzelraum m

individual traffic, private car transport(ation), private car transit · Individualverkehr m

individual trustee · Treuhänder m für Privatpersonen

individual understanding · Individualabrede f [*Im einzelnen ausgehandelte Abrede*]

indivisibility, non-divisibility · Unteilbarkeit f

indivisible, unseverable, inseparable, entire · ganz, unteilbar, untrennbar

indivisible contract; lump-sum contract [*misnomer*]; entire contract · Vertrag m auf unteilbare Leistung, Vertrag mit uneingeschränkter Vorleistungspflicht, unteilbarer (Leistungs)Vertrag, einheitlicher Vertrag

indivisible right, right incapable of division, nondivisible right; jus individuum [*Latin*]; individual right · unteilbares Recht n

in-door recreation, internal recreation · Innenerholung f [*Erholung in einem*

indoor-relief — industrial court 516

geschlossenen Raum, z. B. Hallenschwimmbad]

indoor-relief · geschlossene Armenfürsorge f, geschlossene Armenpflege f

to indorse, to endorse · angeben [Anspruch in einer Klageladung]

to indorse, to back, to endorse · indossieren, girieren, begeben

indorsee; indossatarius [Latin]; endorsee [The party in whose favour a bill of exchange, promissory note or check is indorsed, the party, to whom it is transferred by the indorsement of the payee, or any previous holder] · Indossat(ar) m, Giratar

indorsement, endorsement; indorsamentum, indossamentum [The last term is used by continental writers] [Latin] [On a writ of summons] · Aufschrift f

indorsement; indorsamentum, indossamentum [The last term is used by continental writers] [Latin]; endorsement [Something written on the back of a document, such as the claim indorsed on a writ] · Rückseitenvermerk m

indorsement; indorsamentum, indossamentum [The last term is used by continental writers] [Latin]; endorsement [A signature on the reverse side of a document] · rückseitige Unterschrift f

indorsement in blank, blank endorsement, blank indorsement, endorsement in blank · Blankoindossament n, Blankogiro n

indorsement of a bill (of exchange), endorsement of a bill (of exchange) · Wechselaufschrift f

indorsement of address, endorsement of address [On a writ of summons] · Adressenaufschrift f, Anschriftaufschrift

indorsement on service, endorsement on service [Particulars of time, place and method of service endorsed on a writ within three days after personal or substituted service has been made] · Zustellungsvermerk m, Vermerk des Zustellungstages

indorser, endorser · Indossant m, Indossent, Girant

indorsing, endorsing, backing · Indossieren n, Girieren, Begeben

indossatarius [Latin]; endorsee, indorsee [The party in whose favour a bill of exchange, promissory note or check is indorsed, the party, to whom it is transferred by the indorsement of the payee, or any previous holder] · Indossat(ar) m, Giratar

indowed estate, endowed property, indowed property, endowed estate · (Dauer)Stiftungsvermögen n, (Dauer)Stiftungsgut n [Es steht einer bestimmten Institution dauernd zur Verfügung]

indowment; dotatio [Latin]; endowment · Dotation f

indowment, endowment [Property of any kind belonging in perpetuity to a charity, or property assured for the benefit of any person] · (Dauer)Stiftung f

indubitable · unzweifelhaft, zweifelsfrei

inducement f zum Klagegrund, Klagegrundeinleitung

inducement [An inducing or being induced] · Anreiz m

inducement, incentive [Anything that induces] · Anreizmittel n, Motiv n

inducing breach of contract, procuring breach of contract · Verleiten n zum Vertragsbruch

in due form, as prescribed · vorschriftsmäßig, wie vorgeschrieben

in due time, duly, at the right time, on time · rechtzeitig

industrial agglomeration, industrial massing · Industrie(zusammen)ballung f, Industriemassierung, Industriezentralisation f, Industriezentralisierung

industrial archeology · Industriearchäologie f

industrial area, industrial territory · Gl n, Industriegebiet n

industrial assurance, industrial insurance · Lebensversicherung f der arbeitenden Klassen

industrial belt, industry belt, belt of industry · Industriegürtel m

industrial branch, branch of industry · Industriezweig m

industrial building · Industriegebäude n

industrial category · Industriebaukategorie f [Baunutzungsverordnung]

industrial city, industrial town, paleotechnic city, paleotechnic town · Industriestadt f

industrial colony → industrial (housing) colony

industrial community; industrial commune [obsolete] · Industriegemeinde f, Industriekommune f

industrial complex, industry complex · Industriekomplex m

industrial construction · Industriebau m

industrial consumption · Industrieverbrauch m

industrial court [Established in England in 1919]; industrial disputes tribunal [Established in England in 1951 as an alternative to the industrial court] [A court to consider industrial disputes when both the employers' association

industrial democracy — industrial location planning

and the trade union concerned agree to submit the case to arbitration] · Schlichtungskommission f

industrial democracy, codetermination [*An economic system in which the workers have a share in the management of industry*] · Mitbestimmung f

industrial density [*The number of manufacturing employe(e)s per gross industrially used acre*] · Industriedichte f

industrial development · industrielle Entwick(e)lung f

industrial development certificate, I.D.C. · Grundsatzattest n für Industrieplanung, Grundsatzbescheinigung f für Industrieplanung, Grundsatzschein m für Industrieplanung

industrial dispersion, dispersion of industries · Industriestreuung f

industrial dispute · Tarifkonflikt m

industrial disputes tribunal [*Established in England in 1951 as an alternative to the industrial court*], industrial court [*Established in England in 1919*] [*A court to consider industrial disputes when both the employers' association and the trade union concerned agree to submit the case to arbitration*] · Schlichtungskommission f

industrial district → industrial park

industrial drift, industrial movement, industrial exodus, industrial flight · Industrieflucht f

industrial dust · Industriestaub m

industrial enterprise, industrial undertaking · Industrieunternehmen n, Industrieunternehmung f, Industriebetrieb m

industrial estate · Gewerbepark m

industrial estate, industrial property [*Property used in industry*] · Industrievermögen n

industrial exodus, industrial flight, industrial drift, industrial movement · Industrieflucht f

(industrial) explosives act, (industrial) explosives law, (industrial) explosives statute · Sprengstoffgesetz n

(industrial) explosives law · Sprengstoffrecht n

industrial flight, industrial drift, industrial movement, industrial exodus · Industrieflucht f

industrial fruits, industrial products; fruits of labour, products of labour (Brit.); fruits of labor, products of labor (US); fructus industriales, fructus industriae [*Latin*]; fruits of industry, emblements [*Those fruits of a thing, as of land, which are produced by the labo(u)r and industry of the occupant, as crops of grain; as distinguished from such as are produced solely by the powers of nature*] · künstlicher Zuwachs m

industrial garden town, industrial garden city · Industriegartenstadt f

industrial (housing) colony, industrial residential colony, workers' (housing) colony, workers' residential colony, workmen's (housing) colony, workmen's residential colony, industrial housing estate, workers' housing estate, workmen's housing estate, industrial residential estate, workers' residential estate, workmen's residential estate, industrial settlement, workers' settlement, workmen's settlement, working class settlement · Arbeiter(wohn)kolonie f, Arbeiter(wohn)(an)sied(e)lung f, Industrie(wohn)(an)sied(e)lung, Industrie(wohn)kolonie

industrial housing estate → industrial (housing) colony

industrial hygiene · Industriehygiene f

industrial improvement area, industrial improvement territory · industrielles Verbesserungsgebiet n

industrial injuries insurance · Betriebsunfallversicherung f

industrial inspection · Fabrikaufsicht f, Fabrikinspektion f

industrial inspector · Fabrikinspektor m

industrialist · Industrielle m

industrialization · Industrialisierung f

industrial labourer (Brit.); industrial laborer (US); industrial worker, industrial workman · Industriearbeiter m

industrial land · Industrieland n

industrial land need, industrial land requirement · Industrielandbedarf m

industrial landscape · Industrielandschaft f

industrial land(s) use · industrielle Flächenbenutzung f, industrieller Flächengebrauch m

industrial linkage · Industrieverflechtung f

industrial localization · Industriestandortbestimmung f

industrial localization, localization of industry · Industrieansied(e)lung f [*als Vorgang*]

industrial location, industrial site · Industriestandort m

industrial location model, industrial site model · Industriestandortmodell n

industrial location plan, industrial site plan · Industriestandortplan m

industrial location planning, industrial site planning · Industriestandortplanung f

industrially zoned land · industriell genutztes Land *n*

industrial massing, industrial agglomeration · Industrie(zusammen)ballung *f*, Industriemassierung, Industriezentralisation *f*, Industriezentralisierung

industrial migration · Industriewanderung *f*

industrial-mix · Standortkomponente *f* [*Beschäftigungswachstum*]

industrial mobility · Industriemobilität *f*, Industriebeweglichkeit *f*

industrial monument · Industriedenkmal *n*

industrial movement, industrial exodus, industrial flight, industrial drift · Industrieflucht *f*

industrial nuisance · Industrieemission *f*

industrial nuisance effect · Industrieimmission *f*

industrial out-migration · Industrieabwanderung *f*

industrial park (US); organized industrial district, planned industrial district [*Beide unterscheiden sich dadurch, daß bei der Auswahl der in einem „industrial park" aufzunehmenden Betriebe Gesichtspunkte wie z. B. ästhetische oder solche der Verträglichkeit mit Nachbarbezirken berücksichtigt werden*] · Gewerbeplansiedlung *f*

industrial (physical) development certificate · Industriebebauungsschein *m*, Industriebebauungsattest *n*, Industriebebauungsbescheinigung *f*

industrial physical facility, industrial structure, industrial work · Industriebau(werk) *m, (n)*

industrial planner · Industrieplaner *m*

industrial plant · Industrieanlage *f*

industrial plant building, industrial plant construction · Industrieanlagenbau *m*

industrial population · Industriebevölkerung *f*

industrial premises · Industrieanwesen *n*

industrial problem area, industrial problem territory · industrielles Problemgebiet *n*

industrial products → industrial fruits

industrial property [*In real estate the land and buildings used in manufacturing, processing and fabricating products*] · Produktionsvermögen *n*

industrial property, industrial estate [*Property used in industry*] · Industrievermögen *n*

industrial psychology [*The study of man or woman in relation to his or her works*] · Arbeitspsychologie *f*

industrial real estate investment project · Industrieobjekt *n*

industrial relocation, industrial shifting, resettlement of industry, displacement of industry, transfer of industry, relocation of industry, industrial resettlement · Industrieaussied(e)lung *f*, Industriumsied(e)lung, Industrieumsetzung, Industrieverlegung, industrielle Standortveränderung, Industrieverlagerung

industrial research park · Forschungsindustriepark *m*

industrial resettlement, industrial relocation, industrial shifting, resettlement of industry, displacement of industry, transfer of industry, relocation of industry · Industrieaussied(e)lung *f*, Industriumsied(e)lung, Industrieumsetzung, Industrieverlegung, industrielle Standortveränderung, Industrieverlagerung

industrial residential estate → industrial (housing) estate

industrial residential slum, residential industrial slum · Industrie-Wohn-Elendsviertel *n*, Wohn-Industrie-Elendsviertel

industrial school · Fürsorgeerziehungsanstalt, Zwangserziehungsanstalt *f* [*Für jugendliche Straftäter*]

industrial settlement · Industrie(an)sied(e)lung *f*

industrial settlement → industrial (housing) colony

industrial shifting, resettlement of industry, displacement of industry, transfer of industry, relocation of industry, industrial resettlement, industrial relocation · Industrieaussied(e)lung *f*, Industriumsied(e)lung, Industrieumsetzung, Industrieverlegung, industrielle Standortveränderung, Industrieverlagerung

industrial site, industrial location · Industriestandort *m*

industrial site model, industrial location model · Industriestandortmodell *n*

industrial site plan, industrial location plan · Industriestandortplan *m*

industrial site planning, industrial location planning · Industriestandortplanung *f*

industrial slum · Industrieelendsviertel *n*

industrial society · Industriegesellschaft *f*

industrial structure, industrial work, industrial physical facility · Industriebau(werk) *m, (n)*

industrial subdivision [*An improved tract of land with industrial buildings, designed for a small group or cluster of enterprises. No special services, or facilities are provided*] · Industriegelände *n* ohne Sondereinrichtungen

industrial suburb(an place) · Industrievorort *m*

industrial syndicate · Gewerbegenossenschaft f

industrial territory, industrial area · GI n, Industriegebiet n

industrial town, paleotechnic city, paleotechnic town, industrial city · Industriestadt f

industrial tract [*An improved tract of land including provisions for roads, and installation of utilities. No buildings are provided*] · Industriegelände n ohne Gebäude

industrial (trade) union · Industriegewerkschaft f

industrial undertaking, industrial enterprise · Industrieunternehmen n, Industrieunternehmung f, Industriebetrieb m

industrial unit [*shift-share analysis*] · Standortkomponente f

industrial urbanization · industrielle Verstädterung f

industrial village · Industriedorf n

industrial wage · Industrielohn m

industrial water supply · industrielle Wasserversorgung f

industrial work, industrial physical facility, industrial structure · Industriebau(werk) m, (n)

industrial worker, industrial workman; industrial labourer (Brit.); industrial laborer (US) · Industriearbeiter m

industrial work(ing) place · Industriearbeitsplatz m

industrial zoning · industrielle bauliche Nutzung f, industrielle Zonung

industrious concealment · geflissentliche Verschweigung f

industry belt, belt of industry, industrial belt · Industriegürtel m

industry complex, industrial complex · Industriekomplex m

industry conducive to the environment, industry without noxious effects · umweltfreundliche Industrie f

industry planning, planning for industry · Industrieplanung f

industry with noxious effects [*smoke; noise; congestion*] · umweltschädliche Industrie f

industry without noxious effects, industry conducive to the environment · umweltfreundliche Industrie f

ineffectual → nugatory

inefficient estimator · nichtwirksame Schätzfunktion f [*Statistik*]

inelastic demand [*A demand where a considerable rise or fall in the price of a commodity has little effect on the quantity demanded*] · starre Nachfrage f

inequality, disparity · Disparität f, Ungleichheit f

inequitable, unjust, unfair, undue · unbillig, ungerecht(fertigt), unlauter

inequity · Unbilligkeit f

in expectancy · (zu)künftig [*Besitz(stand)*]

infamous character · ehrlose Gesinnung f

infancy plea, plea of infancy · Einrede f der Minderjährigkeit

infant, minor · minderjährig

infant, minor · minderjährige Person f

infant → (male) infant

infant acting as (a) guardian, minor acting as (a) guardian · minderjähriger Vormund m

infant acting as an agent, minor acting as an agent · minderjähriger Vertreter m

infant debtor, minor debtor, infant obligor, minor obligor · minderjähriger Schuldner m

infant life protection act, infant life protection law, infant life protection statute · Kinderschutzgesetz n

infant renter, minor renter · minderjähriger Mieter m

infant's school, kindergarten · Kindergarten m

infant widow, minor widow · minderjährige Witwe f

infant widower, minor widower · minderjähriger Witwer m

infant witness, minor witness · minderjähriger Zeuge m

infant worker, minor worker · minderjähriger Arbeiter m

infeasible, impracticable · undurchführbar, nicht durchführbar

to infeft, to infeoff, to enfeoff, to bestow a fee, to bestow a fief, to bestow a feud; feoffare, infeodare, infeudare [*Latin*]; to invest [*old Scots law*], to give possession of land(s), to give a seisin of land(s), to (give a) feud · belehnen, feudal belehnen

infeftment; instrument of possession [*old Scots law*], (en)feoffment [*The instrument or deed by which a person is invested with possession*] · Belehnungsurkunde f, Erbgutbelehnungsurkunde

infeftment bill, bill of (en)feoffment, bill of infeftment, (en)feoffment bill · Leh(e)n(s)brief m

infeftment to the feoffer's will, (en)feoffment to the feoffer's will · Übertragung f eigener Ländereien durch einen

infeftment to uses — informality 520

Leh(e)n(s)mann zu seinen Lebzeiten an einen Treuhänder

infeftment to uses → (en)feoffment to uses

infeodare [*Latin*] → to infeft

infeodation → (en)feoffment

to infeoff → to infeft

infeoffment [*Scotland*]; seisina seysina [*Latin*]; seisin, freehold (possession), seizin, possession as of freehold, possession of an estate of freehold; saisine [*Latin*] · Gewere *f* [*Eine historische Untersuchung über das Wesen der Gewere muß ihren Ausgang von der „investitura" des alten Rechts nehmen. Denn mit diesem Ausdruck geben die lateinischen Quellen der karolingischen Periode das Wort Gewere wieder, wie das aus der altdeutschen Übersetzung von C. 6 der Capitularia leg. add. v. 817 bei Pertz, I. S. 261 und aus den zwei parallel laufenden Stellen der traditiones Fuldenses in zwei Urkunden von 824 „testes qui vestitionem viderunt" und „testes qui viderunt giweridam" unwidersprechlich hervorgeht*]

infeoffment in law, seisin in law, freehold (possession) in law; saisine in law [*Scotland*] · Erbganggewere *f*, ideelle Gewere

to infer, to come to a conclusion, to conclude, to prove · folgern, ableiten, schließen (von etwas auf etwas)

inferential, inferred · abgeleitet, gefolgert, konkludent, schlüssig

inferential act(ion), inferred act(ion) · schlüssiger Akt *m*, konkludenter Akt, abgeleiteter Akt, gefolgerter Akt, schlüssige Handlung *f*, abgeleitete Handlung, gefolgerte Handlung, konkludente Handlung

inferior · minderwertig

inferior, subordinate · Untergebene *m*

inferior, ancillary, paravail, subordinate · nachgeordnet, untergeordnet

inferior commercial value, decreased commercial value · merkantiler Minderwert *m* [*Die Minderung des Verkaufswertes einer Sache, die trotz völliger und ordnungsmäßiger Instandsetzung deshalb verbleibt, weil vor allem wegen des Verdachts verborgen gebliebener Schäden, eine den Preis beeinflussende Abneigung gegen den Erwerb besteht*]

inferior commissary court · Diözesangericht *n* [*In Schottland*]

inferior court · unteres Gericht *n*, niederes Gericht, nachgeordnetes Gericht

inferiority · Untergeordnetsein *n*

inferiority gradient · Leistungsabnahmerate *f*

inferior Land authority · untere Landesbehörde *f* [*Bundesrepublik Deutschland*]

inferior value, decreased value · Minderwert *m*

inferred, inferential · abgeleitet, gefolgert, konkludent, schlüssig

inferred act(ion), inferential act(ion) · schlüssiger Akt *m*, konkludenter Akt, abgeleiteter Akt, gefolgerter Akt, schlüssige Handlung *f*, abgeleitete Handlung, gefolgerte Handlung, konkludente Handlung

inferred election of law, inferred choice of law · schlüssige Rechtswahl *f*

infeudare [*Latin*] → to infeft

infeudation → (en)feoffment

in-fill housing (units) [*Housing (units) built on vacant lots in built-up areas*] · Wohnungen *fpl* in Baulücken, Wohnungen in Bebauungslücken

infilling [*The filling-in of a gap, ripe for development, within an established group of buildings, whether clustered or in linear form, by building(s) of a similar kind at similar density and standard, which by so doing will complete the development of the group*] · Baulückenausfüllung *f*, Bebauungslückenausfüllung

infiltration [*The replacement, over a period of time, of one social group by another*] · Infiltration *f*, Durchsetzung *f*

infinite population · unendliche Grundgesamtheit *f* [*Statistik*]

infirmary · Armenkrankenhaus *n*

inflation · Geldentwertung *f*, Inflation *f*

inflation (of rate) of interest, interest inflation · Zinsinflation *f*

inflation rate, rate of inflation · Inflationsrate *f*

inflexibility · Schwerfälligkeit *f*

inflow, influx · Mittelherkunft *f*, Zufluß *m*

inflow of population, population inflow · Bevölkerungszustrom *m*

influence land · Einflußbereich *m*

influence of environment, environmental influence · Umwelteinfluß *m*

influence of noise · Lärmeinwirkung *f*

influx, inflow · Mittelherkunft *f*, Zufluß *m*

to inform, to notify, to give notice, to advise · anzeigen, benachrichtigen, mitteilen, informieren

informal · formlos, nichtförmlich, nichtformell

informality, irregularity in matter of form, defect of (legal) form, want of (legal) form, formal defect · Formfehler *m*, Formmangel *m*

informality — inheritance case

informality · Formlosigkeit, Nichtförmlichkeit *f*

informant [*Somebody who answers questions*] · Auskunftsgeber *m*, Befragte

information, advice · Information *f*, Ankündigung *f*

information; declaration [*obsolete*] [*It is in the nature of pleading. It is the step by which several civil and criminal proceedings are commenced*] · Klageschrift *f*, Klagebegründung(sschrift) *f*

information board · Informationsamt *n*

information bulletin · Mitteilungsblatt *n*

information feedback · Informationsrückkopp(e)lung *f*

information (in Chancery) · Klageschrift *f* bei Angelegenheiten der Krone [*Chancery Court*]

infrablock sub-group · Binnenblock-Untergruppe *f* [*Statistik*]

infrastructure · Grundausstattung *f*, Infrastruktur *f*, Folgeeinrichtungen *fpl*

infringement → violation (of law)

infringement (court) action, infringement (law)suit, infringement cause, infringement plea · (Patent)Verletzungsklage *f*

infringement of contract, default of contract, contract violation, contract default, contract infringement, contract contravention, contravention of contract · Vertragswidrigkeit *f*, Vertragsverletzung *f*

infringement of law, law infringement · Gesetz(es)verstoß *m*

in good faith, of good faith, innocent, honestly, without fraud; bona fide [*Latin*] · aufrichtig, in gutem Glauben, ehrlich, gutgläubig

ingress, access, right to enter and leave over the land(s) of another, way right, right-of-way, wayleave · Durchgangsrecht *n*, Wegerecht

ingress for vehicles, access for vehicles, way right for vehicles, right-of-way for vehicles, wayleave for vehicles · Fahrzeugwegerecht *n*

to ingross, to engross · aufkaufen

in gross [*Common in gross is such as is neither appendant nor appurtenant to land, but is annexed to a man's person*] · subjektiv persönlich

ingrosser, engrosser · Aufkäufer *m*

ingrossing, engrossing · Aufkaufen *n*

(in)habitable, fit to live in, suitable for habitation, fit for habitation · bewohnbar, belegbar

(in)habitancy, residing · Wohnen *n*

inhabitant · Einwohner *m*

inhabitants · Einwohner(schaft) *mpl, (f)*

inhabited house duty · Wohngebäudesteuer *f*

inhabited houses tax · Steuer *f* auf bewohnte Häuser

inhabited world, (o)ecumene, ekumene [*That portion of the earth's surface which has been settled by man*] · Sied(e)lungsraum *m*, Ökumene *f*

inherent condition, condition inherent [*One attaching to the tenure of property, and descending therewith to the inheritor*] · anhaftende Bedingung *f*, inbegriffene Bedingung

inherent force of law · innere Rechtskraft *f*

inherent right · unentziehbares Recht *n*

to inhere together, to co-inhere · miterben

inheretrix [*deprecated*]; heiress, heir female, female heir · Erbin *f*

to inherit · erben

inheritable estate, hereditary property, hereditary estate, hereditament, inheritable property · Erb(schafts)gut *n*, Erb(schafts)vermögen *n*, Erb(schafts)habe *f*

inheritable estate (in land), inheritable land(ed) estate, fee · erblicher (Grund)Besitz *m*

inheritable land, al(l)odial land, free land, land held in absolute ownership, absolute ownership land, alody · allodiales Land *n*, erbeigenes Land, leh(e)n(s)freies Land, absolutes Land, unbeschränktes Land, uneingeschränktes Land, unbegrenztes Land, zinsfreies Land, Allodialland

inheritable property, inheritable estate, hereditary property, hereditary estate, hereditament · Erb(schafts)gut *n*, Erb(schafts)vermögen *n*, Erb(schafts)habe *f*

inheritance; enheritance [*obsolete*]; haereditas [*Latin*] [*"Inheritance" is also used in the old books in the sense of "hereditament"* = *Erbgut*] · Erbschaft *f*, Erbe *n*

inheritance accrual, inheritance accruer, accrual by inheritance, accruer by inheritance · Erbzuwachs *m*

inheritance act, inheritance law, inheritance statute, law of inheritance, act of inheritance, statute of inheritance · Erb(schafts)gesetz *n*

inheritance brotherhood, inheritance confraternity · Erbverbrüderung *f*, Erbeinung

inheritance by adoption, adoption inheritance · Adoptiverbe *n*, Adoptiverbschaft *f*

inheritance case, case of inheritance · Erbfall *m*

inheritance certificate, certificate of inheritance · Erbschein *m,* Erbzeugnis *n,* Erbbescheinigung *f,* Erbattest *n*

inheritance certificate confined to definite assets, certificate of inheritance confined to definite assets · gegenständlich beschränkter Erbschein *m,* gegenständlich beschränkte Erbbescheinigung *f,* gegenständlich beschränktes Erbattest *n,* gegenständlich beschränktes Erbzeugnis *n*

inheritance claim, demand to inheritance, inheritance demand, claim to inheritance · Erb(schafts)forderung *f,* Erb(schafts)verlangen *n*

inheritance clause · Erb(schafts)klausel *f*

inheritance confraternity, inheritance brotherhood · Erbverbrüderung *f,* Erbeinung

inheritance contract, contract of inheritance · Erb(schafts)vertrag *m,* Erbeinsetzungsvertrag, Vermächtnisvertrag

inheritance demand, claim to inheritance, inheritance claim, demand to inheritance · Erb(schafts)forderung *f,* Erb(schafts)verlangen *n*

inheritance dispute, heirship dispute, dispute of heirship, dispute of inheritance · Erbauseinandersetzung *f,* Erbstreit(igkeit) *m, (f)*

inheritance duty [*England*]; inheritance tax, death tax [*USA*]; estate duty, death duty [*The duty payable on the devolution of property at death. The one now commonly payable is estate duty. Legacy duty and succession duty were abolished in England by the Finance Act, 1949, ss. 27, 28*] · Erb(schafts)steuer *f,* Nachlaßsteuer, Vermächtnissteuer

inheritance farm, farm of inheritance · Erbhof *m*

inheritance farm land · Erbhofland *n*

inheritance farm mortgage · Erbhofhypothek *f*

inheritance fee; feudum hereditarium, laudemium mortuarium, feodum hereditarium [*Latin*]; fee of inheritance · Erbleh(e)n *n,* erbliches Leh(e)n, Erbleh(e)n(s)gut *n,* vererbliches Leh(e)n

inheritance in abeyance · schwebende Erbschaft *f,* schwebendes Erbe *n*

inheritance law, hereditary law, law of (hereditary) succession (and distribution), law of descent (and distribution), law of inheritance · Erb(folge)recht *n,* Erbgangrecht, Erbschaftsrecht, Nachkommensrecht, Vermögensnachfolgerecht

inheritance law → inheritance act

inheritance of usufruct, usufruct inheritance · Nießbraucherbschaft *f,* Nießbraucherbe *n,* (Frucht)Genußerbschaft, (Frucht)Genußerbe, Nutzgewalterbschaft, Nutzgewalterbe

inheritance possession, possession of inheritance · Erb(en)besitz *m*

inheritance possessor, possessor of (an) inheritance · Erb(schafts)besitzer *m*

inheritance right, heirship right, hereditary right, heritable right, right of inheritance, right of heirship · Erb(schafts)anspruch *m,* Erb(schafts)(an)recht *n*

inheritance share, share of an inheritance · Erb(schafts)(an)teil *m,* Anteil an einer Erbschaft

inheritance snatcher, inheritance sneaker · Erbschleicher *m*

inheritance snatching, inheritance sneaking · Erbschleicherei *f*

inheritance statute → inheritance act

inheritance tax death tax [*USA*]; estate duty, death duty, inheritance duty [*England*] [*The duty payable on the devolution of property at death. The one now commonly payable is estate duty. Legacy duty and succession duty were abolished in England by the Finance Act, 1949, ss. 27, 28*] · Erb(schafts)steuer *f,* Nachlaßsteuer, Vermächtnissteuer

inheritance taxation, taxation of inheritance · Erb(schafts)besteuerung *f*

inherited possession · ererbter Besitz *m*

inherited property, inherited proprietorship, inherited ownership (of property) · Erbtum *n,* ererbtes Eigentum

to inhibit · untersagen

inhibition · Untersagung *f*

inintelligible condition · unverständliche Bedingung *f*

to initial · abzeichnen

initial allowance · Sonderabschreibung *f*

initial decision, first decision · erste Entscheidung *f,* erster Entscheid *m*

initial (local) development plan, initial local plan · ursprünglicher Bebauungsplan *m*

initial local plan, initial (local) development plan · ursprünglicher Bebauungsplan *m*

initial operating deficit [*The deficit incurred by a project before it becomes self-supporting*] · Anlaufbetriebsdefizit *n*

to initiate, to commence · einleiten [*Verfahren*]

initiating function, pressure-creating function · Zündungsfunktion *f* [*Funktion des Staates für die Infrastruktur*]

initiating party, commencing party · einleitende Partei *f*

initiation — (in)land city

initiation · Inaussichtnahme *f*

initiation, commencement, institution [*The commencement of an action or prosecution; as, A. has instituted an action against B. to recover damages for trespass*] · Einleitung *f*

initiation fee, membership fee [*The sum paid on joining an organization for privileges of membership*] · Aufnahmegebühr *f*, Aufnahmegeld *n*, Eintrittsgebühr *f*, Eintrittsgeld *n*

injunction · Gerichtsverbot *n*

injunctive · interdizierend

injured feeling · verletztes Gefühl *n*

injured party, party injured · rechtsverletzte Partei *f*

injuria sine damno, injuria absque [*Latin*] · Rechtsverletzung *f* ohne Schadenzufügung

injurious affection · Nachteilzufügung *f*

injurious affection held with land taken · Nachteilzufügung *f* mit Grundbesitzverlust, Nachteilzufügung mit Landverlust, Nachteilzufügung mit Bodenverlust [*Entschädigungsrecht*]

injurious affection not held with land taken · Nachteilzufügung *f* ohne Grundbesitzverlust, Nachteilzufügung ohne Landverlust, Nachteilzufügung ohne Bodenverlust [*Entschädigungsrecht*]

injurious enterprise, injurious undertaking, obnoxious enterprise, obnoxious undertaking · störender Betrieb *m*, störendes Unternehmen *n*, störende Unternehmung *f*

injurious falsehood · Verunglimpfung *f*

injurious industry, obnoxious industry · störende Industrie *f*

injuriously affected, damaged [*Made less valuable, less useful, or less desirable*] · beschädigt

injurious project, obnoxious project · störendes Vorhaben *n*

injurious undertaking → injurious enterprise

injury, offense · Belästigung *f*, Störung, Beeinträchtigung [*Gewerbe; Industrie*]

injury damage to person(s), physical damage to person(s) · körperlicher Schaden *m*, Personenschaden

injury not immediate but consequential · indirekte Schädigung *f*

injury to health · Gesundheitsverletzung *f* [*Die Störung der inneren Lebensvorgänge*]

injustice · Ungerechtigkeit *f*, Unrecht *n*

in(-)kind · Natural . . . [*In Zusammensetzungen mit Rente, Wert, Steuer, Pächter usw. gebraucht, um Leistungen in Arbeit oder in Gütern zu bezeichnen. Gegensatz: Leistungen in der Geldwirtschaft*]

in-kind compensation, in-kind indemnification, in-kind damages, in-kind indemnity, compensation (paid) in kind, damages (paid) in kind, indemnification (paid) in kind, indemnity (paid) in kind · Entschädigung *f* in Natur, Schadenersatz *m* in Natur, Natural(schaden)ersatz, Naturalentschädigung

in-kind lease(hold), lease(hold) paid in kind · Naturalpacht *f*

in-kind lessee, in-kind leaseholder, in-kind (land) holder, leaseholder paying in products of the soil, lessee paying in products of the soil, leaseholder paying in kind, lessee paying in kind, (land) holder paying in products of the soil, (land) holder paying in kind · Natural(ien)pächter *m*

in-kind payment, payment in kind · Natural(be)zahlung *f*

in-kind relief, relief in kind · Natural(ien)unterstützung *f*

in-kind rent, rent (paid) in kind · Naturalwertrente *f*, Naturalzins *m*

in-kind tax, tax paid in kind · Naturalsteuer *f*, Naturalabgabe *f*

in-kind tithe, tithe (paid) in kind · Naturalzehnte *m*

in-kind value, value in kind · Naturalwert *m*

in-kind wage, wage in products of the soil, wage in kind · Deputat *n*, Naturallohn *m*

ink jet · Tintenstrahl *m*

ink jet plotter, colour jet plotter (Brit.); color jet plotter (US) · Farbbildschreiber *m*, Tintenstrahlplotter, Tintenstrahlzeichenautomat *m*

inland, land in (the lord's) demesne, bordland, table demesne, home farm (of the lord of the manor), demesnial settlement; terra indominicata, terra dominica [*Latin*]; demain (land), demeyne (land), demeine (land), demesne (land) [*Those lands of a manor not granted out in tenancy, but reserved by the lord for his own use and occupation. The opposite of "tenemental lands"*] · Hoffeld *n*, Salland *n*, grundherrliches Eigenland, Hofländerei *f*, Hofland, grundherrschaftliches Eigenland, Großgrundherrenland

inland · Domanialland *n* des Ritterleh(e)ns

inland air traffic, domestic air traffic · Inlandsluftverkehr *m*

inland bill (of exchange), domestic bill (of exchange), intraterritorial bill (of exchange) · inländischer Wechsel *m*, Inlandswechsel

(in)land city → in(land) town

inland fishery — inquiry office

inland fishery → inland fishing

inland navigable watercourse · Binnenwasserstraße f

inland navigation · Binnenschiffahrt f

inland navigation vessel · Binnenschiff n

inland revenue · Binnensteuereinnahmen fpl

(in)land town, (in)land city · Binnenstadt f, Landstadt

inland trade, home trade, domestic trade · Binnenhandel m

inland value, domestic value · Inlandswert m

inland water transportation · Binnenschiffsverkehr m

in law, according to law, at law, by law, for law · nach dem Gesetz, dem Gesetz nach

in litigation, pending (at law) · rechtshängig

in-migrant · Zuwanderer m

in-migration, inward migration, migration to an area · Zuwanderung f

innate value, objective value, intrinsic value [*The popular idea that a commodity as, for example, a precious metal has an innate value apart from its price. Economists regard value as subjective, depending on the demand of consumers in relation to the available supply. According to this view, therefore, there is no such thing as intrinsic value*] · innerer Wert m

innavigable, nonnavigable · unschiffbar, nicht schiffbar

in need of repair, needing repair(s) · reparaturbedürftig

inner area of protection, inner protective area · Innenschutzgebiet n

inner belt · Innengürtel m

inner belt line · Innengürtellinie f

inner border, neat line · Blattschnittlinie f, Blattbegrenzungslinie [*Kartographie*]

inner protective area, inner area of protection · Innenschutzgebiet n

inner urban ring, inner town ring, inner city ring · innerstädtischer Ring m

inn-keeper, inn-holder [*Also called "tavern-keeper" in the USA*] · Gastwirt m

innocent, honestly, without fraud; bona fide [*Latin*]; in good faith, of good faith · aufrichtig, in gutem Glauben, ehrlich, gutgläubig

inn of court [*A private unincorporated association in the nature of a collegiate house, having the exclusive privilege of calling to the bar, that is, conferring the rank or degree of barrister*] · Juristeninnung f, Rechtsinnung, Advokateninnung, Rechtsschule f

innovation · Innovation f, Neuerung f

innovation diffusion · Innovationsausbreitung f, Neuerungsausbreitung

innovation wave, wave of innovation · Innovationswelle f

inobservance, nonobservance · Nichtbeachtung f

inofficial market, over-the-counter market · außerbörslicher Wertpapiermarkt m

inoperative, ineffectual · unwirksam, wirkungslos

in own cause · in eigener Sache

in particular, detailed · ausführlich

in-place, built-in, fixed · eingebaut

in-place unit cost(s) estimate [*A forecast of project construction cost(s) based on the cost(s) of units of construction installed*] · Kostenschätzung f für eingebauten Zustand

in proportion to value; ad valorem [*Latin*]; proportional to value · wertverhältnismäßig

input · Zugang m [*Zugang in Form von Sachgütern, Dienstleistungen und Informationen die eine Unternehmung aus der Umwelt erhält*]

input · Einsatz m

input expansion path · Faktorexpansionsweg m [*Einprodukt-Unternehmung*]

input-output analysis · Einsatz-Ausstoß-Analyse f

inquest · Beweiserhebung f, Untersuchung

to inquire, to enquire, to make inquiries, to make enquiries · erkundigen, sich erkundigen

inquiring writ, enquiring writ, writ of inquiry, writ of enquiry · Ermitt(e)lungsverfügung f

inquiry, enquiry · Erkundigung f

inquiry, enquiry · Anfrage f

inquiry by a jury, inquisition · schwurgerichtliche Untersuchung f, Untersuchung durch ein Geschworenengericht

inquiry commission, commission of inquiry · Untersuchungskommission f

inquiry committee, committee of inquiry · Untersuchungsausschuß m

inquiry contract · Auskunftsvertrag m

inquiry in lunacy, inquisition · (schwurgerichtliches) Entmündigungsverfahren n

inquiry office · Auskunftsbüro n

inquisition, inquiry by a jury · schwurgerichtliche Untersuchung *f*, Untersuchung durch ein Geschworenengericht

inquisition, inquiry in lunacy · (schwurgerichtliches) Entmündigungsverfahren *n*

inquisition [*In lunacy, the formal statement and finding, under the hands and seals, of the master and jury (if there was one) before whom the inquiry was held*] · (schwurgerichtliches) Untersuchungsprotokoll *n* beim Entmündigungsverfahren

in re [*Latin*]; in the matter of · in Sachen

in rem, real · dinglich

insane, deranged; insanus [*Latin*]; unsound in mind, disordered in mind, diseased in mind, of unsound mind, non-sane · geistesgestört, geisteskrank

insane person → person of unsound mind

insanitary, unhealthy · ungesund [*z. B. Wohnung*]

insanitary dwelling unit, unfit dwelling unit, insanitary living unit, unfit living unit, insanitary housing unit, unfit housing unit (US); insanitary dwelling, unfit dwelling · Verfallswohnung *f*

insanitary house, unfit house · Verfallshaus *n*

insanity, unsoundness of mind, madness, derangement of intellect, mental unsoundness, mental alienation, mental disorder, mental derangement [*Lunacy is properly a species of insanity, although the terms are frequently used as synonyms*] · Geisteskrankheit *f*, Geistesgestörtheit

insanus [*Latin*]; unsound in mind, disordered in mind, diseased in mind, of unsound mind, non-sane, insane, deranged · geistesgestört, geisteskrank

inscribed stock, registered stock · Namensaktie *f*

inseparable, entire, indivisible, unseverable · ganz, unteilbar, untrennbar

to insert in a list, to enschedule, to list, to include in a list · auflisten

in-service loan · Kriegsteilnehmerdarleh(e)n *n*

inset · Nebenkarte *f* [*auf Seekarten*]

in severalty · allein [*keine Besitzteilung*]

insinuation · Unterstellung *f*

insolvency, failure · Zahlungsunfähigkeit *f*

insolvency decree, decree of insolvency [*In Sotch law. One entered in a probate court, declaring the estate in question to be insolvent, that is, that the assets are not sufficient to pay the debts in full*] · Vergleichsverfahrensurteil *n*

insolvency presumption, presumption of insolvency · Vermutung *f* der Zahlungsunfähigkeit

insolvent · zahlungsunfähig

insolvent · Zahlungsunfähige *m*

to inspect · Einsicht nehmen, einsehen

to inspect a site, to visit a site · besichtigen [*Baustelle vor Angebotsabgabe*]

to inspect a site by car · befahren [*Baustelle vor Angebotsabgabe*]

to inspect a site from the air · überfliegen [*Baustelle vor Angebotsabgabe*]

to inspect a site on foot · begehen [*Baustelle vor Angebotsabgabe*]

inspection [*Examination of work completed or in progress to determine its compliance with contract requirements*] · Augenschein *m*, Einsicht *f*, Einsehen *n*

inspection · Ortstermin *m*

inspection, visit · Besichtigung *f* [*Baustelle vor Angebotsabgabe*]

inspection by attributes · Abnahmeprüfung *f* mittels qualitativer Merkmale [*Statistik*]

inspection by mining authorities · berg(bau)behördliche Aufsicht *f*, berg(bau)behördliche Überwachung *f*

inspection by the public, public inspection, public notice, publicity · Auslegung *f*, öffentliche Auslegung *f*, öffentliche Einsicht(nahme) *f*, öffentliche Auslage *f*, (öffentliche) Offenlegung *f* [*Bauzeitplan; Umlegungskarte; usw.*]

inspection committee, comittee of inspection · Gläubigerausschuß *m*

inspection lot · Prüflos *n*, Prüfposten *m* [*Statistik*]

inspection of books · Büchereinsicht *f*

inspection of document(s), document inspection · Urkundeneinsicht *f*

inspection of files · Akteneinsicht *f*

inspection of housing, housing inspection · Wohnungsaufsicht *f*, Wohnungsüberwachung *f*, Wohnungsinspektion *f*

inspection of places for sale of butchers meat · Beaufsichtigung *f* des Fleischverkaufs

inspection of site, site inspection, site visit, site examination, construction site visit, construction site examination, construction site inspection, building site visit, building site inspection, building site examination, examination of site, visit of site · Baustellenbesichtigung *f*, (Baustellen)Begehung, Ortsbesichtigung [*Vor Abgabe eines Angebotes*]

inspection punch list — institutional discipline 526

inspection punch list [*List of items of work to be completed or corrected by the contractor by a given date*] · Terminliste *f*, Fertigstellungsliste

inspector, checkman · Kontrolleur *m*

inspector of nuisances, sanitary inspector · Gesundheitsinspektor *m*, Sanitätsinspektor, Sanitärinspektor, Gesundheitskontrolleur, Sanitätskontrolleur, Sanitärkontrolleur

inspector (of weights and measures (Brit.); sealer (of weights and measures) (US) · Eichmeister *m*

instability of employment · Beschäftigungslabilität *f*

to instal, to admit, to vest, to order, to commission · einsetzen, bestallen

installation, vesting, admission, commission, order · (Amts)Einsetzung *f*, (Amts)Bestallung

installation of improvements, (land) improvement, building land improvement, improvement to land [*Facilities, usually public utilities, such as sidewalks or sewers, added to land which increase its usefulness*] · Erschließung, (Bau)Landerschließung, (Bau)Bodenerschließung, (Bau)Flächenerschließung, (Bau)Geländeerschließung, (Bau)Terrainerschließung, Baureifmachung, Zuwegung

instal(l)ment · Rate *f*, Abschlag *m* [*Zahlung*]

instal(l)ment business · Abzahlungsgeschäft *n*, Raten(zahlungs)geschäft, Teilzahlungsgeschäft

instal(l)ment certificate → instal(l)ment (payment) certificate

instal(l)ment contract · Abzahlungsvertrag *m*, Raten(zahlungs)vertrag, Teilzahlungsvertrag

instal(l)ment credit · Abzahlungskredit *m*, Raten(zahlungs)kredit, Teilzahlungskredit

instal(l)ment investment certificate · Abzahlungseinlageschein *m*, Einlageschein auf Abzahlung, Einlageschein auf Ratenzahlung, Einlageschein auf Teilzahlung, Teilzahlungseinlageschein, Ratenzahlungseinlageschein

instal(l)ment invoice · Abschlagsrechnung *f*

instal(l)ment loan · Abzahlungsdarleh(e)n *n*, Raten(zahlungs)darleh(e)n, Teilzahlungsdarleh(e)n

instal(l)ment mortgage · Abzahlungshypothek *f*, Raten(zahlungs)hypothek, Teilzahlungshypothek [*Zum Unterschied von der Amortisationshypothek, bei der der Schuldner gleichbleibende sich aus Zins- und Tilgungsleistungen zusammengesetzte Jahresleistungen erbringt, wobei die durch die fortschreitende Tilgung eintretenden Zinsersparnisse verwendet werden, wird bei der Abzahlungshypothek die Zinsersparnis nicht zur verstärkten Tilgung verwendet*]

instal(l)ment of redemption · Tilgungsrate *f*, Tilgungsquote *f*, Amortisatonsrate, Amortisationsquote

instal(l)ment payment, payment on account, interim payment, progress payment · Abschlagszahlung *f*, Akontozahlung [*für geleistete Arbeit(en)*]

instal(l)ment payment · Ratenzahlung *f*, Abzahlung, Teilzahlung

instal(l)ment (payment) certificate, progress (payment) certificate, interim (payment) certificate, payment on account certificate · Abschlags(zahlungs)schein *m*, Abschlags(zahlungs)bescheinigung *f*, Abschlags(zahlungs)attest *n*, Akonto(zahlungs)schein, Akonto(zahlungs)bescheinigung, Akonto(zahlungs)attest

instal(l)ment plan · Abzahlungsplan *m*

instal(l)ment share, partly paid share, membership share, subscription share, share of stock · Raten(geschäfts)anteil *m* [*aufhörende Bausparkasse*]

instant rehabilitation, instant modernization, instant (physical) improvement, instant upgrading · Modernisierung *f* mit kurzer Durchführungsdauer, (bauliche) Verbesserung mit kurzer Durchführungsdauer

to instigate · anstiften

instigation · Anstiften *n*

instinct of right · Rechtstrieb *m*

to institute [*(court) action*] · anstrengen [*Klage*]

institute of architects · Architektenkammer *f*

Institute of World Economics · Weltwirtschaftsinstitut *n*

institution, association, society [*An establishment, specially one of public character or one affecting a community*] · (Personen)Verein(igung) *m*, (*f*)

institution, initiation, commencement [*The commencement of an action or prosecution; as, A. has instituted an action against B. to recover damages for trespass*] · Einleitung *f*

institution · Anstalt *f* [*Eine juristische Person mit ungeteiltem oder in Anteile zerlegtem Kapital, die wirtschaftliche oder andere, also auch gemeinnützige Zwecke, verfolgen kann*]

institution, appointment of an heir · Erbenernennung *f*

institutional code · Anstaltsordnung *f*

institutional discipline · Anstaltsdisziplin *f*

institutional household — insurance bond

institutional household [*It consists of a large number of people living together in an institution such as a prison, boarding school, military barracks, etc.*] · Anstaltshaushalt *m*

institutional investor, investing institution, accumulation trust · Kapitalsammelstelle *f* [*Ein Institut, welches nach Gesetz oder Satzung langfristig ausleihbares Kapital ansammelt. §§ 103 und 104 des II. WoBauG*]

institutional police · Anstaltspolizei *f*

institutional population · Bevölkerung *f* in Anstalten, Bevölkerung in Gemeinschaftsunterkünften

institution of architects, association of architects, society of architects · Architektenverein(igung) *m, (f)*

Institution of Architects of the Federal Republic of Germany, Association of Architects of the Federal Republic of Germany, Society of Architects of the Federal Republic of Germany · Bundesarchitektenkammer *f*

institution of borrowers, federation of borrowers, society of borrowers, association of borrowers · landwirtschaftlicher Kreditverein *m*, Landschaft *f*, landwirtschaftliche Kreditvereinigung *f*

institution of civil engineers, association of civil engineers, society of civil engineers · Bauingenieurverein(igung) *m, (f)*

institution of construction contractors, institution of building contractors, federation of construction contractors, federation of building contractors, association of construction contractors, association of building contractors, society of construction contractors, society of building contractors · Bauunternehmerverein(igung) *m, (f)*

institution of contractors, contractors' association, contractors' institution, contractors' society, society of contractors, association of contractors · Unternehmerverein(igung) *m, (f)*

institution of engineering unions, society of engineering unions, federation of engineering unions, association of engineering unions · Verein(igung) *m, (f)* der Ingenieurverbände

instruction · (An)Weisung *f*

instructional simulation system · Lehrsimulationssystem *n*

instruction for execution, execution instruction · Ausführungsanweisung *f*

instructions to bidders, instructions to tenderers · (An)Weisungen *fpl* an die Bieter

instrument → (legal) instrument

instrumental industry, capital producing industry [*The capital is instrumental to the production of goods*] · Ertragsgüterindustrie *f*

instrumentality of government · Regierungsinstrument *n*

instrumental trust, ministerial trust [*A trust which demands no further exercise of reason or understanding than every intelligent agent must necessarily employ; as to convey an estate*] · verwaltungslose Treuhand *f*

instrument incorporation, incorporation document, incorporation instrument, constituting instrument, constituting document, document of incorporation · Inkorporierungsurkunde *f*

instrument in writing, written instrument; writ [*Scots law*] · schriftliches Rechtsinstitut *n*, schriftliches rechtliches Institut

instrument of appeal, appeal instrument · Berufungsinstitut *n*, Appellationsinstitut

instrument of dissolution, dissolution instrument · Auflösungsinstitut *n* [*Gesellschaft*]

instrument of possession [*In old Scots law*]; (en)feoffment, infeftment [*The instrument or deed by which a person is invested with possession*] · Belehnungsurkunde *f*, Erbgutbelehnungsurkunde

instrument of writing for the payment of money · geldwerte Urkunde *f*

insufficiency, legal invalidity · Rechtsungültigkeit *f*

insufficiency in progress, insufficient progress · Rückstand *m* [*(Bau)Arbeit(en)*]

insufficient, legally invalid · rechtsungültig

insurable; assurable [*deprecated*] · versicherungsfähig, versicherbar

insurance; assurance [*deprecated*] · Versicherung *f*, Assekuranz *f*

insurance against accidents to workmen, insurance against accidents to workers · Arbeiterunfallversicherung *f*

insurance against injury · Personenschadenversicherung *f*

insurance against injury to workmen, insurance against injury to workers · Arbeiterschadenversicherung *f*

insurance against liability for water damage · Wasserschadenversicherung *f*

insurance against loss of property, insurance against property loss · Vermögensschaden-Versicherung *f*, Vermögensverlust-Versicherung

insurance at value as new · Neuwertversicherung *f*

insurance benefit · Versicherungssumme *f*

insurance bond · Versicherungssparbrief *m*

insurance broker — intangible ownership (of property)

insurance broker · Versicherungsmakler m

insurance business · Versicherungsgeschäft n

insurance carrier · Versicherungsträger m

insurance clause, clause stipulating insurance · Versicherungsklausel f

insurance contract, contract of insurance · Versicherungsvertrag m

insurance contract law, insurance contract act, insurance contract statute · Versicherungsvertragsgesetz n

insurance contract law · Versicherungsvertragrecht n

insurance covenant, covenant to insure · gesiegeltes Versicherungsversprechen n

insurance for the benefit of surviving dependents · Hinterbliebenenversicherung f

insurance law, law of insurance · Versicherungsrecht n

insurance mathematics · Versicherungsmathematik f

insurance of capital, capital insurance · Kapitalversicherung f

insurance of (construction) equipment, (construction) equipment insurance · (Bau)Geräteversicherung

insurance of (the) work(s), work(s) insurance · (Bau)Leistungsversicherung f

insurance of title (to land), (land) title insurance · (Rechts)Titelversicherung f, Grund(stücks)titelversicherung, Bodentitelversicherung, Landtitelversicherung

insurance parlance · Versicherungssprache f

insurance policy, policy of insurance · Versicherungspolice f

insurance practice · Versicherungswesen n

insurance protection · Versicherungsschutz m

insurance provision · Versicherungsbestimmung f

insurance scheme for salaried employe(e)s · Angestelltenversicherung f

insurance value · Versicherungswert m

to insure, to assure · versichern

insured fund · Fonds m von Versicherung(en) verwaltet

insured hazard → insured risk

insured mortgage · versicherte Hypothek f

insured (party), assured (party), insuree · Versicherte m, Assekurat m, Versicherungsnehmer

insured person · versicherte Person f

insured risk, insured hazard, ensured harzard, ensured risk · versichertes Risiko n, versichertes Wagnis n

insurer; assurer (Brit.) · Versicherer m, Assekurant m

insurer of a debt, guarantor, cautioner, pledge, surety [*The party who expresses his willingness to answer for the debt, default, or obligation of another. The word "surety" is sometimes used interchangeably for the word "guarantor"; but, strictly speaking, a "surety" is one who is bound with the principal debtor upon the original contract, the same as if he had made the contract himself, while a "guarantor" is bound upon a separate contract to make good in case the principal debtor fails. The guarantor is therefore an insurer of the solvency of the debtor. A surety is held primarily liable on an instrument while a guarantor is held secondarily liable on it; that is, the surety agrees that he will pay the obligation in any event, while the guarantor merely agrees that he will pay the obligation if the principal debtor fails to pay*] · Bürge m

in tail, entailed · beschränkt, beschnitten [*Vererbung von Grundstücken*]

intake, close, paddock · (Tier)Gehege n

intangible · Zielertrag m der nicht in Geld bewertet werden kann, nicht vom Markt bewerteter Infrastrukturertrag

intangible, incorporeal [*Not admitting of physical possession*] · immateriell, unkörperlich, nichtkörperlich

intangible asset [*An asset that has no negotiable substance, e.g. goodwill*] · nicht (sofort) greifbarer Aktivposten m, ideeller Wert m

intangible chattel (personal), thing incorporeal; res incorporales [*Latin*]; incorporeal thing, intangible thing, incorporeal chattel (personal) · unkörperliches Ding n, immaterielles Ding, nichtkörperliches Ding, unkörperliches Rechtsobjekt n, nichtkörperliches Rechtsobjekt, immaterielles Rechtsobjekt, immaterieller Gegenstand m, unkörperlicher Gegenstand, nichtkörperlicher Gegenstand

intangible freehold possession, incorporeal seisin, intangible seisin, incorporeal freehold possession · nichtkörperliche Gewere f, unkörperliche Gewere, immaterielle Gewere

intangible ownership (of property), incorporeal proprietorship, intangible proprietorship, incorporeal property, intangible property, incorporeal ownership (of property) · unkörperliches Eigentum n, nichtkörperliches Eigentum, immaterielles Eigentum

intangible personal property, incorporeal personal property, incorporeal personal estate, incorporeal personal chattel, incorporeal chattel (personal), incorporal personalty · nichtkörperliche Fahrnis f, nichtkörperliche Fahrhabe, nichtkörperliche Mobilie, unkörperliche Fahrhabe, unkörperliche Fahrnis, unkörperliche Mobilie, immaterielle Fahrnis, immaterielle Fahrhabe, immaterielle Mobilie

intangible proprietorship, incorporeal property, intangible property, incorporeal ownership (of property), intangible ownership (of property), incorporeal proprietorship · unkörperliches Eigentum n, nichtkörperliches Eigentum, immaterielles Eigentum

intangible seisin, incorporeal freehold possession, intangible freehold possession, incorporeal seisin · nichtkörperliche Gewere f, unkörperliche Gewere, immaterielle Gewere

intangible thing, incorporeal chattel (personal), intangible chattel (personal), thing incorporeal; res incorporales [Latin], incorporeal thing · unkörperliches Ding n, immaterielles Ding, nichtkörperliches Ding, unkörperliches Rechtsobjekt n, nichtkörperliches Rechtsobjekt, immaterielles Rechtsobjekt, immaterieller Gegenstand m, unkörperlicher Gegenstand, nichtkörperlicher Gegenstand

integral part · integraler Bestandteil m

integrated planning, integration planning · Einordnungsplanung f, Integrationsplanung, Eingliederungsplanung, integrierte Planung

integrated traffic system · Verkehrsverbund m

integrated traffic system with unit taxes · Tarifverbund m [öffentlicher Massenverkehr]

Integration · Eingliederung f, Einordnung, f, Integration f

integration of immigrants, immigrant absorption, immigrant assimilation, immigrant integration, absorption of immigrants, assimilation of immigrants · Einwanderereingliederung f, Einwandererintegration f

integration theory, theory of integration · Integrationslehre f

intellectual property, literary property · geistiges Eigentum n

intendment of law; intellectus legis [Latin] · Rechtssinn m, Gesetz(es)sinn

intensity index [Central business space divided by total floor space multiplied by 100] · Intensitätsindex m

intensive gardening, spade cultivation · Spatenkultur f, Spatenanbau m

intent, will [A somewhat formal term connecting more deliberation than intent(ion)] · feste Absicht f, Wille m

intent(ion) [It implies a having somewhat in mind as a plan or design or referring to the plan had in mind] · Absicht f

intent(ion) to abscond; meditatio fugae [Latin], contemplation of flight · Verdunkelungsgefahr f

intentional · absichtlich, vorsätzlich

intentionally false, knowingly not true, deliberately not true, designedly not true, intentionally not true, knowingly untrue, deliberately untrue, designedly untrue, intentionally untrue, knowingly false, deliberately false, designedly false · absichtlich unwahr, wissentlich unwahr, bewußt unwahr, absichtlich falsch, bewußt falsch, wissentlich falsch

intentionally mischievous, intentionally harmful, malicious, spiteful · schikanös

intentional negative act(ion) [A determination of will, producing a negative effect in the sensible world] · Abstandnahme f, Enthaltungshandlung f, beabsichtigte negative Handlung

intention mistake, mistake of intention · Willensirrtum m [Der Irrtum einer Partei über den Willen der anderen Partei]

intention of party · Parteiabsicht f

intention of possession, possessory intention; animus possidendi [Latin] · Besitzabsicht f

intention of remaining → intention to establish a permanent residence

intention of revoking; animus revocandi [Latin] · Widerrufabsicht f

intent(ion) to contract · Vertrags(ab)schlußabsicht f

inten(tion) to defraud, fraudulent intent(ion) · Betrugsabsicht f, betrügerische Absicht, arglistige Absicht

intent(ion) to establish a permanent residence, intent(ion) of remaining; animus manendi [Latin] · Absicht f sich dauernd in einem Rechtsgebiet niederzulassen und dort einen Wohnsitz zu erlangen, Absicht zum Bleiben

interaction land · Verflechtungsbereich m

interaction model · Verflechtungsmodell n

interaction of effects · Wirkungszusammenhang m

interaction research · Verflechtungsforschung f

intercalary day, double sextile day, bissextile day · Schalttag m [29. Februar]

intercensal period · Zeit(raum) f, (m) zwischen Zählungen

interchange — interest in (real) estate

interchange · Autobahnkreuz n

interchangeability, substitutability · Auswechselbarkeit f

interchangeable, reciprocal, common to both parties, mutual · gegenseitig, wechselseitig

interchangeable goods (US) → fungible goods

interchangeable parcel, exchangeable plot, exchangeable parcel, interchangeable piece of land, exchangeable piece of land, interchangeable plot · Austauschgrundstück n

intercity movement of persons · innerstädtische Personenwanderung f

intercity passenger transport(ation), intercity passenger transit · Personenfernverkehr m

intercommunal · zwischengemeindlich

intercommunity variation · Unterschiede mpl zwischen den klassifizierten Gemeinwesen

intercultivation · Stockwerkanbau m, Stockwerkkultur f

interdependency coefficient · Matrixmultiplikator m

interdictum ne quid in flumine publico [Latin] · prohibitorisches Wasserrechtsinterdikt n

interdictum quod in flumine publico [Latin] · restitutorisches Wasserrechtsinterdikt n

interest · Belang m, Interesse n

interest arrear(age), arrear(age) of interest · Zinsrückstand m

interest at will, right at will, revocable interest, revocable right · Anrecht n auf Widerruf, Anspruch m auf Widerruf, Berechtigung f auf Widerruf, (subjektives) Recht auf Widerruf, widerrufliches (subjektives) Recht

interest balance, balance of interest · Zins(en)saldo m

interest-bearing · zinsbringend

interest bearing, interest return, returning of interests, yielding of interests, bearing of interests, interest yield(ing) · Verzinsung f

interest bracket · Zinsspanne f

interest burden, interest encumbrance, interest charge, interest incumbrance, interest load · Zinslast f, Zinsbelastung f

interest ceiling · Zinsobergrenze f

interest charged on leasehold · Pachtzinsen f

interest cost(s) · Zinskosten f

interest-coupon · Zinsabschnitt m, Zinsschein m

interest degression · Zinsdegression f [Abnahme der Zinsbelastung bei gleichbleibendem Zinssatz innerhalb einer gleichbleibenden Annuität]

interest-due date · Zinstermin m

interested party, participator, participant · Beteiligte m, Teilnehmer

interest equalization tax · Zinsausgleichsteuer f

interest fluctuation clause · Zinsgleitklausel f

interest-free · zinslos, ohne Zinsen

interest group impact theory · Theorie f des Einflusses von Interessengruppen

interest in a business, business share, business interest, share in a business · Geschäftsanteil m

interest in estate → interest in (real) estate

interest in expectancy at common law, future interest in land at common law · gemeinrechtlicher zukünftig wirkender Eigentumsanteil m

interest inflation, inflation (of rate) of interest · Zinsinflation f

interest in land(s) → interest in (real) estate

interest in land(s) by elegit, tenancy by elegit · Boden(besitz)recht n durch Einweisung, (Land)Besitzrecht durch Einweisung

interest in minerals in land(s), right to take minerals, right to win minerals, right of exploitation, right to exploit minerals, right of taking minerals, right of winning, winning right, exploitation right, mineral right, mineral interest · (Mineral(ien))Abbaurecht n, (Mineral(ien))Ausbeutungsrecht, (subjektives) Berg(bau)recht, (Mineral(ien))Abbaugerechtigkeit f

interest in personalty, personalty right, personalty interest, right of personalty · (subjektives) Fahrnisrecht n [Die Rechtsstellung, die einer bestimmten Person an einem bestimmten Fahrnisgut zusteht]

interest in possession, interest of present possession, present enjoyment, present interest in land · Besitzanteil m der dem Berechtigten der gegenwärtigen Grund(stücks)genuß gewährt

interest in possession → possessory interest

interest in (real) estate, right in (real) estate, interest in land(s), right in land(s), right of realty, interest in realty, realty right, realty interest, possessory right of land(s), right of possession of

interest in realty — interim certificate

land(s), interest in possession of land(s), tenure, chattel real, chattel interest in land(s), right over land(s), right over (real) estate, right over realty, right over land(s), tenancy · Besitzrecht n, Grund(stücks)besitzrecht, Immobiliar(besitz)recht, Immobilien(besitz)recht, subjektives Grund(stücks)besitzrecht, (subjektives) Land(besitz)recht, (subjektives) Bodenbesitzrecht, subjektives Immobiliarbesitzrecht, subjektives Immobilien(besitz)recht, subjektives Grund(stücks)recht, subjektives Liegenschaftsrecht, nichtleh(e)n(s)rechtliches Recht an einem Grundstück, (subjektives) Recht über ein Grundstück, gemeinrechtliches Grundstücksrecht, gemeinrechtliches Recht an einem Grundstück [*Die Rechtsstellung, die einer bestimmten Person an einer bestimmten Immobilie zusteht*]

interest in realty → interest in (real) estate

interest in rem → real right

interest loan, loan on interest · Zinsendarleh(e)n n

interest loss, loss of interest · Zinsverlust m

interest of present possession, present enjoyment, present interest in land, interest in possession · Besitzanteil m der dem Berechtigten den gegenwärtigen Grund(stücks)genuß gewährt

interest of use, right to use, interest to use, use right, use interest, right of use · Gebrauchsrecht n, Benutzungsrecht, subjektives Gebrauchsrecht, subjektives Benutzungsrecht

interest on building loan(s), interest on construction loan(s), construction interest, building interest · Bauzinsen f

interest on debt, debt-interest · Schuldzins m

interest on deferment of payment, interest on respite of payment · Stundungszinsen f

interest on intermediate credit(s) · Baugeldzinsen f, Zwischenkreditzinsen

interest on loan (capital), loan (capital) interest, cost(s) of money · Darleh(e)nszinsen f

interest on owned capital, rent earned by own capital · Eigenkapitalzins m

interest other than in land(s) → personal estate

interest payable · Zinsverbindlichkeit f

interest rate, rate of interest · Zinssatz m, Zinsfuß m

interest receivable · Zinsforderung f

interest reduction, reduction of interest · Zinsherabsetzung f, Zinssenkung

interest return, returning of interests, yielding of interests, bearing of interests, interest yield(ing), interest bearing · Verzinsung f

interest schedule, interest table · Zins(en)tabelle f

interest to use, use right, use interest, right of use, interest of use, right to use · Gebrauchsrecht n, Benutzungsrecht, subjektives Gebrauchsrecht, subjektives Benutzungsrecht

interest upon interest, compound interest · Zinseszinsen f

interest yield(ing), interest bearing, interest return, returning of interests, yielding of interests, bearing of interests · Verzinsung f

interest yield of the ground · Bodenverzinsung f, Landverzinsung, Grund(stücks)verzinsung

to interfere, to intervene · eingreifen

interference, lappage, conflict, interlock, (over)lap · Überschneidung f, Überlagerung

interference, intervention · Eingriff m

interference with advantageous relations · Geschäftsstörung f [*vorsätzliches Delikt*]

interference with contractual relations · Einmischung f in fremde Vertragsverhältnisse

interfering with discretionary powers · Einschreiten n bei Ermessensmißbrauch

intergovernmental fiscal relations, intergovernmental fiscal equity · interkommunaler Finanzausgleich m, zwischengemeindlicher Finanzausgleich

intergovernment(al) relations · Regierungsbehördenverkehr m

intergroup relation · Gruppenbeziehung f

interim, intermediate, temporary, interlocutory, provisional · einstweilig, zwischenzeitlich, vorübergehend, inzidentiell

interim agreement · Kaufvorvertrag m

interim attestation, intermediate certificate, progress certificate, intermediate attestation, progress attestation, interim certificate · Zwischenbescheinigung f, Zwischenschein m, Zwischenattest n [*Über den Fortschritt der Bauarbeiten*]

interim balance · Zwischenbilanz f

interim certificate, interim attestation, intermediate certificate, progress certificate, intermediate attestation, progress attestation · Zwischenbescheinigung f, Zwischenschein m, Zwischenattest n [*Über den Fortschritt der Bauarbeiten*]

interim certificate · Zwischenbescheinigung f, Zwischenschein m, Zwischenattest n

interim certificate → interim (payment) certificate

interim custody · Sequestration f bis zum Erlaß der Bankerotterklärung

interim injunction · provisorische Verfügung f

interim invoice · Zwischenrechnung f

interim lawmaking, intermediate legislation, intermediate lawmaking, interim legislation · Zwischengesetzgebung f, zwischenzeitliche Gesetzgebung

interim loan, short-term loan · Zwischendarleh(en) n

interim payment, progress payment, instal(l)ment payment, payment on account · Abschlagszahlung f, Akontozahlung [für geleistete Arbeit(en)]

interim (payment) certificate, payment on account certificate, instal(l)ment (payment) certificate, progress (payment) certificate · Abschlags(zahlungs)schein m, Abschlags(zahlungs)bescheinigung f, Abschlags(zahlungs)attest n, Akonto(zahlungs)schein, Akonto(zahlungs)bescheinigung, Akonto(zahlungs)attest

interim period (of time), interim time period, interim term · Zwischenfrist f

interim stage, intermediate stage · Zwischenstadium n, zwischenzeitliches Stadium

interior court · Innenhof m

interior lot [A lot whose side lines do not abutt upon a street] · Innenflurstück n, Innenparzelle f

interior lot line, side lot line [This line does not abut on a street, allay, public way, railway right of way, etc.] · seitliche Grundstücksgrenze f

interlacing · Ineinandergreifen n

interlinkage → (spatial) interlinkage

interlock, (over)lap, interference, lappage, conflict · Überschneidung f, Überlagerung

interlocking enterprise, interlocking undertaking · wechselseitig beteiligtes Unternehmen n, gegenseitig beteiligtes Unternehmen

interlocutory, provisional, interim, intermediate, temporary · einstweilig, zwischenzeitlich, vorübergehend, inzidentiell

interlocutory application · Zwischenantrag m, Zwischengesuch n

interlocutory injunction · einstweilige Verfügung f [Sicherungsmaßregel während eines Rechtsstreits]

interlocutory judg(e)ment · Zwischenurteil n, einstweiliges Urteil

interlocutory order · Zwischenentscheid m [Ablehnung eines Vorlageantrages]

interlocutory proceeding, pre-trial proceeding · Widerspruchsverfahren n, Vorverfahren [Vor der Erhebung der Anfechtungsklage sind Rechtmäßigkeit und Zweckmäßigkeit eines Verwaltungsaktes in einem Vorverfahren zu prüfen]

to intermeddle with · sich einmischen in

(inter)meddling · Einmischung f

intermediary, middleman, housefarmer · Mittelsmann m [Er mietet ein Gebäude nicht zum Selbstbewohnen, sondern um die Räume weiter zu vermieten]

intermediary, middle-man [A distributor from producer to consumer] · Zwischenhändler m

intermediate, temporary, interlocutory, provisional, interim · einstweilig, zwischenzeitlich, vorübergehend, inzidentiell

intermediate appellate court · erstes Berufungsgericht n, erstes Appellationsgericht

intermediate area, intermediate territory · Zwischengebiet n, Zwischenterritorium n

intermediate attestation, progress attestation, interim certificate, interim attestation, intermediate certificate, progress certificate · Zwischenbescheinigung f, Zwischenschein m, Zwischenattest n [Über den Fortschritt der Bauarbeiten]

intermediate credit · Baugeld n, Zwischenkredit m [Die als Bevorschussung der endgültigen Finanzierung kurzfristig aufgenommenen Mittel]

intermediate credit book · Baubuch n [Zur Führung eines Baubuches ist ein Bauherr verpflichtet der eine Hypothek aufnimmt]

intermediate credit law, intermediate credit act, intermediate credit statute · Baugeldsicherungsgesetz n

intermediate credit lender · Baugeldgeber m, Zwischenkreditgeber

intermediate fief, intermediate fee, intermediate tenure, arriere fief, arriere fee, arriere tenure, mesne fief, mesne fee, mesne tenure, mean fief, mean fee, mean tenure, middle fief, middle fee, middle tenure [A fief dependent on a superior one; an inferior fief granted by a vassal of the king, out of the fief held by him] · Afterleh(e)n n

intermediate goods, partly-finished goods · Teilfertigerzeugnisse npl

intermediate government · staatliche Fachbehörde f

intermediate heir · Zwischenerbe *m*

intermediate lawmaking, interim legislation, interim lawmaking, intermediate legislation · Zwischengesetzgebung *f*, zwischenzeitliche Gesetzgebung

intermediate lord, arriere lord, mesne lord, mean lord, middle lord; tenente in capite [*Latin*] · (feudaler) Belehner *m* von Aftervasallen, Feudalherr von Aftervasallen, Leh(e)n(s)herr von Aftervasallen, Leh(e)n(s)gutgeber von Aftervasallen, mittlerer Leh(e)n(s)herr, mittlerer Feudalherr, Vasall *m* der Krone, Kronvasall, Afterleh(e)nsherr

intermediate process, mesne process [*A process intervening between the beginning and end of a (law)suit*] · Nebenprozeß *m*

intermediate ring · Zwischenring *m*

intermediate stage, interim stage · Zwischenstadium *n*, zwischenzeitliches Stadium

intermediate tenant, mesne tenant, arriere tenant, mean tenant, middle tenant · Afterleh(e)n(s)mann *m*

intermediate tenure → intermediate fief

intermediate territory, intermediate area · Zwischengebiet *n*, Zwischenterritorium *n*

intermittent rent · aussetzende Rente *f*, intermittierende Rente

to (inter)mix · vermischen

(inter)mixed · vermischt

(inter)mixed fields, open fields, pattern of intermingled fragmented holdings · Gemengelage *f* [*Die Grundstücke verschiedener Eigentümer liegen in der Flur durcheinander gemengt ohne Zu- und Abfahrtswege*]

intermixed fields owned by different peasants · Flur *f*

(inter)mixed-fields system, open-fields system · landwirtschaftliche Betriebsweise *f* auf Grundlage der Gemenglage der Äcker und der gemeinsamen Nutzung von Wald und Weide

internal colonialism → Binnenkolonisation *f*

internal colony, · Binnenkolonie *f*

internal debt [*That part of a country's national debt owned by the State to its own people or institutions within its own borders*] · Binnenschuld *f*

internal decorative repair · Innenschmuckreparatur *f*

(internal) economies of scale · interne Ersparnisse *f pl* [*Sie entstehen, wenn bei Auswertung des Produktionsvolumens und entsprechend wachsenden Betriebsgrößen die Durchschnittskosten pro Produktionseinheit sinken*]

internal-external traffic, internal-external movements · Auswärtsverkehr *m*

internal improvement · innere Erschließung *f* [*Erschließung innerhalb eines neuen Baugebietes*]

internal migrant · Binnenwandernde *m*, Binnenwanderer

internal migration, horizontal mobility · Binnenwanderung *f*

internal recreation, in-door recreation · Innenerholung *f* [*Erholung in einem geschlossenen Raum, z. B. Hallenschwimmbad*]

internal relationship · Innenverhältnis *n*

internal traffic · Binnenverkehr *m*

internal (traffic) zone · Innen(verkehrs)zone *f*

International Association of Municipal Statisticians, IAMS · Städtestatistischer Ausschuß *m* des Internationalen Statistischen Instituts

International Bank for Reconstruction and Development, World Bank · Weltbank *f*

International Court of Justice · Internationaler Gerichtshof *m*

international customary law, customary international law · Völkergewohnheitsrecht *n*, VGR

international encyclopedia of comparative law · rechtsvergleichendes Handwörterbuch *n*, rechtsvergleichende Enzyklopädie *f*

International Federation for Housing and Town Planning · Internationaler Verband *m* für Wohnungswesen und Städtebau

international fiscal law · I St R *n*, internationales Steuerrecht

international intercompany pricing for tax purposes · steuerliche Verrechnungspreise *m pl* in internationalen Konzernen

**International Labour Office (Brit.); **International Labor Office (US) · Internationales Arbeitsamt *n*

international law → (public) international law

international monetary conference · Internationale Währungskonferenz *f*

International Monetary Fund, I.M.F. · Internationaler Währungsfonds *m*

International Postal Union, Universal Postal Union [*Established in 1875*] · Weltpostverein *m*

International Private Law, IPL, conflict of laws, law of conflicts, Private International Law, conflicts law · Außenprivatrecht *n*, Kollisionsrecht, zwischenstaatliches (Privat)Recht n, Internationales Privatrecht n, IPR n, Zwischenprivatrecht n, Grenzrecht n

International Real Estate Federation · FIABCI, Internationaler Verband m der Immobilienberufe

international regional policy · internationale Raumordnung f

international trade theory · Außenhandelstheorie f

International Union of Local Authorities, IULA · Internationaler Gemeindeverband m, IGV

interpleader · Interventionsklage f

to interpose · einschieben, einschalten

interposition · Einschiebung f, Einschaltung

to interpret, to construct, to construe [*To ascertain the meaning of language by a process of arrangement and interference*] · auslegen, deuten [*Text*]

interpretability · Auswertbarkeit f [*Erd- und Luftbildmessung*]

interpretation · Auswertung f [*Erd- und Luftbildmessung*]

interpretation, construction [*wording*] · Auslegung f, Deutung [*Text*]

interpretation by implication, implied construction, tacit construction, implied interpretation, tacit interpretation, construction by implication · stillschweigende Deutung f, stillschweigende Auslegung

interpretation clause, construction clause, clause of interpretation, clause of construction · Auslegungsklausel f, Deutungsklausel f

interpretation ex visceribus actus, interpretation on all parts together, construction ex visceribus actus · Auslegung f aus dem Zusammenhang des Ganzen heraus, Deutung f aus dem Zusammenhang des Ganzen heraus

interpretation of act(s), interpretation of law(s), interpretation of statute(s), construction of act(s), construction of law(s), construction of statute(s) · Gesetz(es)auslegung f, Gesetz(es)deutung

interpretation of aerial photography, air-photo interpretation, aerial photograph(ic) interpretation · Luftbildauswertung f, Luftaufnahmeauswertung, Luftphotoauswertung

interpretation of contract, construction of contract · Vertragsauslegung f, Vertragsdeutung

interpretation on all parts together, construction ex visceribus actus, interpretation ex visceribus actus · Auslegung f aus dem Zusammenhang des Ganzen heraus, Deutung f aus dem Zusammenhang des Ganzen heraus

interpretation (up)on the equity of the statute, construction upon the equity of the statute · Gesetz(es)auslegung f auf Grund der ratio legis, Gesetz(es)deutung auf Grund der ratio legis

interpretative executive order, interpretative rule · interpretierende Verwaltungsverordnung f [*amerikanisches Verwaltungsrecht*]

interpreted, construed · ausgelegt, gedeutet [*Text*]

interpreting, construing [*wording*] · Auslegen n, Deuten n [*Text*]

interregional · zwischenregional

interregional compatibility · zwischenregionale Verträglichkeit f

interregional economy, multi(ple)-region economy · multiregionale Wirtschaft f

interregional exchange · zwischenregionaler Austausch m

interregional linear programming · zwischenregionale Linearplanung f

interregional migration · zwischenregionale Wanderung f

interregional model, multi(ple)-region model · multiregionales Modell n, mehrregionales Modell, vielregionales Modell

interrelated working · Durcheinanderwirken n

interrogatories [*Written questions addressed on behalf of one party to a cause, before the trial thereof, to the other party, who is bound to answer them in writing upon oath*] · schriftliche Beweisfragen f pl

to interrupt, to discontinue · unterbrechen [*Arbeit(en)*]

interrupted, discontinued · unterbrochen [*Arbeit(en)*]

interrupted prescription, discontinued prescription · unterbrochene Ersitzung f

interruption of limitation · Verjährungsunterbrechung f, Unterbrechung der Verjährung

intersection of building lines · Fluchtlinienschneidung f, Baufluchtlinienschneidung

inter-suburban travel to work, inter-suburban journey to work, inter-suburban trip to work [*The movement from a home in one suburb to a place of employment in another suburb*] · Berufsfahrt f von Vorort zu Vorort

interurban migration · Stadt-Stadt-Wanderung f

interurbia; suburbia [*obsolete*] · Auffüllung *f* der Räume zwischen zwei Städten, aufgefüllter Raum *m* zwischen zwei Städten

to intervene, to interfere · eingreifen

intervening opportunity · dazwischenliegende Chance *f* [*Wanderung*]

intervention, interference · Eingriff *m*

intervention amounting to expropriation (Brit.); intervention amounting to condemnation (US) · enteignungsgleicher Eingriff *m*

interviewer bias · Ergebnisbeeinflussung *f* durch (die) Befrager

interview technique · Umfragetechnik *f*, Befragungstechnik

interview unit · Befragungseinheit *f*

inter vivos [*Latin*]; between parties who are alive, between persons who are alive, between living people, between living persons · unter Lebenden

intestable; intestabilis [*Latin*] [*Incompetent to make a will*] · nicht testierfähig, nicht testamentsfähig

intestacy, state of an intestate [*The condition of a party who dies without having made a will*] · Intestatzustand *m*

intestate, without a will; intestato [*Latin*] · testamentlos

intestate; intestate; intestatus [*Latin*] [*A person who dies without making a (valid) will*] · Person *f* ohne Testament, testamentlose Person

intestate inheritance · Intestaterbschaft *f*, Intestaterbe *n*

intestate succession, succession ab intestato [*The succession of an heir at law to the property and estate of his ancestor when the latter has died intestate, or leaving a will which has been annulled or set aside*] · gesetzliche Erbfolge *f*, Intestaterbfolge

in testimony whereof → in witness whereof

in the custody of the law; in custodia legis [*Latin*] · in Rechtsgewahrsam, in gesetzlichem Gewahrsam, im Gewahrsam des Gesetzes, gesetzlich verwahrt

in the matter of; in re [*Latin*] · in Sachen

in the regular course, by virtue of the office; ex officio [*Latin*] · von Amts wegen

in the way of comparison, comparably, in a comparable manner, comparatively, comparingly · vergleichsweise

intimidation · Einschüchterung *f*

intolerable · untragbar

intoxicating liquor · geistiges Getränk, alkoholisches Getränk *n*

intra-class variance · Binnenklassenvarianz *f* [*Statistik*]

intracommunal · innergemeindlich

intraregional · innergebietlich

intrastate, municipal [*Of or relating to the internal affairs as distinguished from the foreign relations of a nation*] · innerstaatlich

intraterritorial bill (of exchange), inland bill (of exchange), domestic bill (of exchange) · inländischer Wechsel *m*, Inlandswechsel

intraurban · innerstädtisch

intraurban location(al) theory, intraurban theory of location · innerstädtische Standorttheorie *f*

intraurban migration · innerstädtische Wanderung *f*

intraurban recreation · innerstädtische Erholung *f*

intraurban traffic · innerstädtischer Verkehr *m*

intra vires · innerhalb der Machtbefugnis

intrinsic validity, essential validation, intrinsic validation, essential validity · wesentliche Gültigkeit *f*

intrinsic validity of contract, essential validity of contract, intrinsic validation of contract, essential validation of contract · formeller Konsens *m*

intrinsic value, innate value, objective value [*The popular idea that a commodity as, for example, a precious metal has an innate value apart from its price. Economists regard value as subjective, depending on the demand of consumers in relation to the available supply. According to this view, therefore, there is no such thing as intrinsic value*] · innerer Wert *m*

intrinsic value of coins · stofflicher Münzwert *m*

introduction · Einführung *f*

introduction letter, letter of introduction · Einführungsschreiben *n*

introductory recital · einleitender (Rechts)Titelbericht *m* [*Auflassung. Im Gegensatz zum berichtenden (Rechts)Titelbericht*]

introductory sentence · Vorschaltsatz *m*

introvert-type shopping centre, plaza-type shopping centre (Brit.); introvert-type shopping center, plaza-type shopping center (US) · Kern-Einkaufszentrum *n*

to intrude, to incroach, to trespass, to encroach · beeinträchtigen, verletzen, stören, eindringen

intruder, invader, trespasser · Beeinträchtigende *m*, Störer, Verletzer, Eindring-

intruder ab initio — investing contract for home building

ling *m*, Besitzbeeinträchtigende, Besitzstörer, Besitzverletzer, Besitzeindringling, unbefugter Betreter

intruder ab initio, intruder from the beginning, intruder from the first act(ion), trespasser from the beginning, trespasser from the first act(ion), trespasser ab initio [*A person who, after lawfully entering on another's premises, commits some wrongful act, which in law is construed to affect and have relation back to his first entry so as to make the whole a trespass*] · rückwirkender Eindringling *m*, rückwirkender (Besitz)- Störer, rückwirkender (Besitz)Beeinträchtigender, rückwirkender (Besitz)- Verletzer, (Besitz)Verletzer von Anfang an, (Besitz)Störer von Anfang an, (Besitz)Beeinträchtigender von Anfang an, Eindringling von Anfang an

intrusion, encroaching, encroachment, adverse occupation, incroachment, incroaching, trespass · (Beeinträchtigung *f* durch) Eindringen *n*, Verletzung durch Eindringen, Störung durch Eindringen, Besitzverletzung durch Eindringen, Besitzstörung durch Eindringen, Besitzbeeinträchtigung durch Eindringen

in trust, fiducial, under trusteeship, on trust, fiduciary · zur treuen Hand, treuhänderisch

to inure · nutzen, dienen [*einer Person*]

to inure, to become operative, to enure, to operate, to come into existence, to come into operation, to come into being, to take effect, to become to have effect · wirksam werden, in Kraft treten

invader, trespasser, intruder · Beeinträchtigende *m*, Störer, Verletzer, Eindringling *m*, Besitzbeeinträchtigende, Besitzstörer, Besitzverletzer, Besitzeindringling, unbefugter Betreter

invalid, void, null [*"Void" in the strict sense means that an instrument or transaction is negatory and ineffectual so that nothing can cure it. But frequently "void" is used and construed as having the meaning of "voidable"*] · ungültig, nichtig, unwirksam

to invalidate, to make void, to annul, to avoid · ungültig machen, für ungültig erklären

invalidated, annulled, made void, avoided, cancelled · ungültig gemacht, für ungültig erklärt

invalid care allowance · Invalidenfürsorge *f*

invalidity, avoidance, nullity · Nichtigkeit *f*, Ungültigkeit

invalidity declaration, declaration of invalidity · Kraftloserklärung *f*, Mortifikation *f*; Amortisation [*Fehlbenennung*]

invasion of right, breach of right · Störung *f* eines subjektiven Rechts, Behinderung eines subjektiven Rechts

inventors' law · Erfinderrecht *n*

inventory · Bestandsverzeichnis *n*

inventory (US); balance(-sheet), statement of financial position, statement of financial condition, position of the company, statement of assets and liabilities · Bilanz *f*

inventory heir · Inventarerbe *m*

inventorying · Inventarisieren *n*

inventory map · Bestandkarte *f* [*Die kartographische Darstellung eines bestehenden Zustandes*]

inverse condemnation · Planungsschaden *m*

inverse correlation · negative Korrelation *f* [*Statistik*]

inverse-function rule · Differentiation *f* der Umkehrfunktion, Regel *f* der Differentiation der Umkehrfunktion

inverse probability · Rückschlußwahrscheinlichkeit *f* [*Statistik*]

to invest [*old Scots law*]; to give possession of land(s), to give a seisin of land(s), to (give a) feud, to infeft, to infeoff, to enfeoff, to bestow a fee, to bestow a fief, to bestow a feud; feoffare, infeodare, infeudare [*Latin*] · belehnen, feudal belehnen

investigation area, study territory, investigation territory, study area · Untersuchungsgebiet *n*

investigation of title · (Rechts)Titeluntersuchung *f*, (Rechts)Titelprüfung

investigation of title (to land), (land) title examination, (land) title investigation, examination of title (to land) · (Land)(Rechts)Titelprüfung *f*, Prüfung des (Land)(Rechts)Titels

investigation principle, principle of investigation · formeller Legalitätsgrundsatz *m*, formelles Legalitätsprinzip *n*, formeller Prüfungsgrundsatz, formelles Prüfungsprinzip [*formell(rechtlich)es Grundbuchrecht*]

investigation sheet, survey sheet · Erhebungsbogen *m*, Untersuchungsbogen

investigation territory, study area, investigation area, study territory · Untersuchungsgebiet *n*

investigative technique · Untersuchungstechnik *f*

investing contract for home building · Bausparvertrag *m* [*Vertrag zwischen Bausparer und Bausparkasse, in dem sich der Bausparer zur Leistung von Sparzahlungen in bestimmter Höhe, die Bausparkasse zur Gewährung eines Bau-*

investing for home building — investment (e)valuation

spardarlehens nach Zuteilung des Bausparvertrages verpflichtet]

investing for home building · (Bau)Sparen n

investing institution, accumulation trust, institutional investor · Kapitalsammelstelle f [Ein Institut, welches nach Gesetz oder Satzung langfristig ausleihbares Kapital ansammelt. §§ 103 und 104 des II. WoBauG]

investing member, (share) investor, unadvanced member [A member having not obtained advances from the building society but simply participating in the profits arising from the interest paid by the borrower] · nichtborgendes Mitglied n [Bausparkasse]

investing (of capital) · Anlegen n, Geldanlegen

investitura [Latin]; investiture · Nießbraucherrichtung f, (Frucht)Genußerrichtung, Nutzgewalterrichtung

investitura [Latin]; investiture · Libellbestellung f

(in)vestitura [Latin] → (en)feoffment

investitura simultanea [Latin] · (Ge)Samtbelehnung f, Mitbelehnung, Mitbeleh(e)nschaft f, gesamte Hand f, Geding n, Insatz m

investitura simultanea germanica communis [Latin] · deutsche gemeine gesamte Hand f [Belehnung]

investitura simultanea specialis [Latin] · eigentliche gesamte Hand f [Belehnung]

investiture; investitura [Latin] [In feudal law investiture was the delivery of corporeal possession of land granted by a lord to his tenant. It answered to the more modern livery of seisin] · Grundbesitzübergabe f, Grundbesitzeinweisung f

investiture → (en)feoffment

investment advisor, investment adviser, investment counsel(l)or, investment consultant [A person or firm who, for a fee, undertakes to manage an individual's investments] · Anlageberater m, Kapitalanlageberater, Investitionsberater, Geldanlageberater

investment advisory service · Beratungsdienst m für Wertpapiere

investment allocation · Investitionszuweisung f, (Kapital)Anlagezuweisung, Geldanlagezuweisung

investment appraisal, investment appraisement, investment (e)valuation, investment analysis [A means of assessing whether expenditure of capital on a project would show a satisfactory rate of return to an undertaking, either absolutely or when compared with expenditure on alternative projects; and of indicating the optimum time to commit expenditure] · Investitionsbewertung f, Investitionstaxierung, Investitions(ab)schätzung, Investitionswertermitt(e)lung, Geldanlagebewertung, Geldanlage(ab)schätzung, Geldanlagewertermitt(e)lung, Geldanlagetaxierung, (Kapital)Anlage(ab)schätzung, (Kapital)Anlagewertermitt(e)lung, (Kapital)Anlagetaxierung, (Kapital)Anlagebewertung

investment bank · Investitionsbank f, (Kapital)Anlagebank, Geldanlagebank

investment banking · Anlagegeschäft n, bankmäßige Vermögensanlage f, Kapitalanlagegeschäft, Geldanlagegeschäft

investment certificate · Einlageschein m

investment company, investment fund, investment trust; investment corporation (US) · Anlagegesellschaft f, Kapitalanlagegesellschaft, Investmentgesellschaft, Geldanlagegesellschaft, Kapitalfonds m, Investmentfonds, Geldanlagefonds, Kapital(anlage)fonds, Anlagefonds

investment contribution · Investitionszulage f

investment control; investment channelling (Brit.); investment channeling (US) · Investitionslenkung f, Geldanlagelenkung, (Kapital)Anlagelenkung,

investment corporation (US); investment company, investment fund, investment trust · Anlagegesellschaft f, Kapitalanlagegesellschaft, Investmentgesellschaft, Geldanlagegesellschaft, Kapitalfonds m, Investmentfonds, Geldanlagefonds, Kapital(anlage)fonds, Anlagefonds

investment counsel(l)or, investment consultant, investment advisor, investment adviser [A person or firm who, for a fee, undertakes to manage an individual's investments] · Anlageberater m, Kapitalanlageberater, Investitionsberater, Geldanlageberater

investment credit · Investitionskredit m, Geldanlagekredit, (Kapital)Anlagekredit

investment decision · Investitionsentscheid(ung) m, (f)

investment duration · Anlagedauer f, Investitionsdauer, Geldanlagedauer, Kapitalanlagedauer

investment (e)valuation, investment analysis, investment appraisal, investment appraisement [A means of assessing whether expenditure of capital on a project would show a satisfactory rate of return to an undertaking, either absolutely or when compared with expenditure on alternative projects; and of indicating the optimum time to commit expenditure] · Investitionsbewertung f, Investitionstaxierung, Investi-

investment feasibility — investor (of capital)

tions(ab)schätzung, Investitionswertermitt(e)lung, Geldanlagebewertung, Geldanlage(ab)schätzung, Geldanlagewertermitt(e)lung, Geldanlagetaxierung, (Kapital)Anlage(ab)schätzung, (Kapital)Anlagewertermitt(e)lung, (Kapital)Anlagetaxierung, (Kapital)Anlagebewertung

investment feasibility · Rentabilität *f* von Immobilienvermögen

investment flow, flow of investment · Investitionsstrom *m*, Geldanlagestrom, (Kapital)Anlagestrom

investment fund, investment trust; investment corporation (US); investment company · Anlagegesellschaft *f*, Kapitalanlagegesellschaft, Investmentgesellschaft, Geldanlagegesellschaft, Kapitalfonds *m*, Investmentfonds, Geldanlagefonds, Kapital(anlage)fonds, Anlagefonds

investment fund saving · Anlagesparen *n*, Investmentsparen

investment grant · Anlagezuschuß *m*, Kapitalanlagezuschuß, Geldanlagezuschuß, Investitionszuschuß, Investitionszulage *f*

investment in a company · Gesellschaftsbeteiligung *f*

investment incentive, investment inducement · Investitionsanreiz *m*, (Kapital)Anlageanreiz, Geldanlageanreiz

investment income, unearned income, unearned increment, income from possession · Besitzrente *f*, Besitzeinkommen *n*, nichterarbeitete Wertsteigerung *f*, Zuwachsrente, fundiertes Einkommen

investment inducement, investment incentive · Investitionsanreiz *m*, (Kapital)Anlageanreiz, Geldanlageanreiz

investment in fixed assets, investment in material assets, investment in physical assets · Sachanlage *f*, Sachinvestition *f*

investment loan · Investitionsdarleh(e)n *n*, (Kapital)Anlagedarleh(e)n, Geldanlagedarleh(e)n

investment location, investment site · Anlagestandort *m*, Kapitalanlagestandort, Geldanlagestandort, Investitionsstandort

investment market · Investitionsmarkt *m*, (Kapital)Anlagemarkt, Geldanlagemarkt

investment method [*(E)Valuation of (real) estate*] · Anlageverfahren *n*, Kapitalanlageverfahren, Geldanlageverfahren, Investitionsverfahren

investment mortgage · Anlagehypothek *f*, Kapitalanlagehypothek, Geldanlagehypothek, Investmenthypothek

investment plan · Anlageplan *m*, Investitionsplan, Geldanlageplan, Kapitalanlageplan

investment planning · Anlageplanung *f*, Investitionsplanung, Geldanlageplanung, Kapitalanlageplanung

investment policy · Anlagepolitik *f*, Investitionspolitik, Geldanlagepolitik, Kapitalanlagepolitik

investment project · (Anlage)Objekt *n*

investment property [*Property purchased for investment rather than for speculative possibilities. Such a purchase connotes permanency of the capital investment as opposed to quick turnover*] · Investitionsvermögen *n*

investment restriction · Anlagebeschränkung *f*, Anlageeinschränkung, Anlagebegrenzung, Geldanlagebeschränkung, Geldanlageeinschränkung, Geldanlagebegrenzung, Kapitalanlagebeschränkung, Kapitalanlageeinschränkung, Kapitalanlagebegrenzung, Investitionsbeschränkung, Investitionseinschränkung, Investitionsbegrenzung

investment return → investment yield

investments [*balance sheet*] · Finanzanlagen *fpl*

investment-seeking capital · anlagesuchendes Kapital *n*

investment share · Einlageanteil *m*

investment site, investment location · Anlagestandort *m*, Kapitalanlagestandort, Geldanlagestandort, Investitionsstandort

investment surplus → (capital) investment surplus

investment survey · Investitionserhebung *f*, (Kapital)Anlageerhebung, Geldanlageerhebung

investment theory, theory of investment · Investitionstheorie *f*

investment trust; investment corporation (US); investment company, investment fund · Anlagegesellschaft *f*, Kapitalanlagegesellschaft, Investmentgesellschaft, Geldanlagegesellschaft, Kapitalfonds *m*, Investmentfonds, Geldanlagefonds, Kapital(anlage)fonds, Anlagefonds

investment trust → land(s) investment trust

investment valuation → investment appraisal

investment yield, investment return, ROI, return on investment, yield on investment, return on capital, yield on capital, capital yield, capital return · Kapitalrendite *f* [*Verhältnis von erzielten Gewinn zum eingesetzten Kapital*]

investor → (share) investor

investor (of capital), capital investor · Anleger *m*, Geldanleger, Kapitalanleger, Investitionsträger, Anlagesuchende

to invigorate · ankurbeln [*Wirtschaft*]

inviolability · Immunität *f*

invitation letter · (Angebots)Aufforderungsschreiben *n*

invitation to tender, invitation to bid, bidding invitation, invitation to (submit a) bid, request for tender, request for offer, request for bid, call for tender, call for offer, call for bid; request for (bid) proposal, call for (bid) proposal (US); tendering invitation · (Angebots)Aufforderung *f*, Aufforderung zur Angebotsabgabe

invitation to treat · Geschäftsanbahnung *f*

invited bidder, invited tenderer [*He is selected from an approved list*] · ausgesuchter Bieter *m*

to invite tenders, to tender out, to invite offers, to invite bids; to invite (bid) proposals (US); to put out to tender, to go out to tender, to obtain tenders · ausschreiben, (Angebote) einholen, auffordern zur Angebotsabgabe

to invite to selective tendering · beschränkt ausschreiben

invoice, bill · Rechnung *f*

involuntary dissolution, forced dissolution · unfreiwillige Auflösung *f*, Zwangsauflösung

involuntary saving, forced saving · Zwangssparen *n*, unfreiwilliges Sparen

involuntary transfer, forced transfer · Übertragung *f* kraft Gesetzes

involutary lien, forced lien [*Lien on real property imposed without the owner's authorization such as taxes*] · Zwangsforderung *f* auf einem Grundstück

involvement of citizens, citizen participation, citizen control, public participation, participation of citizens, citizen involvement · Bürgerbeteiligung *f*, Bürgermitwirkung *f*, Bürgerteilnahme *f*, bürgerschaftliche Beteiligung, bürgerschaftliche Mitwirkung, bürgerschaftliche Teilnahme [*z. B. an der Bauleitplanung*]

inward migration, migration to an area, inmigration · Zuwanderung *f*

inward processing · aktive Veredelung *f*

in witness whereof, in testimony whereof · urkundlich dessen, zu urkund dessen

in writing, written · schriftlich

IPL, conflict of laws, law of conflicts, Private International Law, conflicts law, International Private Law · Außenprivatrecht *n*, Kollisionsrecht, zwischenstaatliches (Privat)Recht *n*, Internationales Privatrecht *n*, IPR *n*, Zwischenprivatrecht *n*, Grenzrecht *n*

I.R.C., independent regulatory commission [*Any commission which lies outside the regular executive departments and which has restrictive or disciplinary control over private conduct or private property*] · unabhängige (wirtschafts)-regelnde Kommission *f* [*USA*]

iron-ore digging right · Eisenerzgraberecht *n*

irrational, contrary to reason · verstandeswidrig, vernunftwidrig, vernunftlos

irrationality · Vernunftlosigkeit *f*

irrebuttable, unconditional, absolute, total, unrestricted, unlimited · absolut, unbeschränkt, uneingeschränkt, unbedingt, unbegrenzt, bedingungslos

irrebuttable · unwiderlegbar, unwiderleglich

irrebuttable binding authority of precedents, absolute binding authority of precedents, total binding authority of precedents, unrestricted binding authority of precedents, unlimited binding authority of precedents · absolute Bindungswirkung *f*, unbeschränkte Bindungswirkung, unbegrenzte Bindungswirkung, uneingeschränkte Bindungswirkung, unbedingte Bindungswirkung

irrebuttable estate → irrebuttable (real) property

irrebuttable failure to perform, total failure to perform, absolute failure to perform, unrestricted failure to perform, unlimited failure to perform · absolute Nichterfüllung *f*, uneingeschränkte Nichterfüllung, unbeschränkte Nichterfüllung, unbedingte Nichterfüllung, unbegrenzte Nichterfüllung

irrebuttable jurisdiction, total jurisdiction, unlimited jurisdiction, absolute jurisdiction, unrestricted jurisdiction · absolute Gerichtsbarkeit *f*, uneingeschränkte Gerichtsbarkeit, unbeschränkte Gerichtsbarkeit, unbedingte Gerichtsbarkeit, unbegrenzte Gerichtsbarkeit, absolute Rechtspflege(funktion) *f*, uneingeschränkte Rechtspflege(funktion), unbeschränkte Rechtspflege(funktion), unbedingte Rechtspflege(funktion), unbegrenzte Rechtspflege(funktion)

irrebuttable necessity, total necessity, absolute necessity, natural necessity, unlimited necessity, unrestricted necessity · absolute Notwendigkeit *f*, unbedingte Notwendigkeit, unbegrenzte Notwendigkeit, uneingeschränkte Notwendigkeit, unbeschränkte Notwendigkeit

irrebuttable presumption, absolute presumption, unrestricted presumption, total presumption, unlimited presumption · absolute Rechtsvermutung *f*, unbeschränkte Rechtsvermutung, unbegrenzte Rechtsvermutung, uneingeschränkte Rechtsvermutung, unbedingte Rechtsvermutung

irreconcilable — isolated settlement

irreconcilable · unvereinbar

irrecoverability · Uneinbringlichkeit f

irrecoverable, unobtainable, desperate, hopeless, non collectable, noncollectible, nonrecoverable, nonobtainable, uncollectable, unrecoverable, uncollectible, bad · nicht beitreibbar, nicht einziehbar, nicht eintreibbar, uneinziehbar, uneintreibbar, uneinbringlich, unbeitreibbar [*Schuld*]

irredeemable corporate bond [*USA*]; irredeemable debenture [*Great Britain*] · Obligation f ohne Tilgungsverpflichtung, Schuldverschreibung f ohne Tilgungsverpflichtung [*private Kapitalgesellschaft*]

irredeemable debenture [*Great Britain*]; irredeemable corporate bond [*USA*] · Obligation f ohne Tilgungsverpflichtung, Schuldverschreibung f ohne Tilgungsverpflichtung [*private Kapitalgesellschaft*]

irregular, without regularity · unregelmäßig

irregular heiress, irregular heir female [*A heiress who is neither testamentary nor legal, and who has been established by law to take the succession*] · Erbscheinerbin f, Erbattesterbin, Erbzeugniserbin, Erbbescheinigungserbin

irregular heir (male) [*A heir (male) who is neither testamentary nor legal, and who has been established by law to take the succession*] · Erbscheinerbe m, Erbbescheinigungserbe, Erbzeugniserbe, Erbattesterbe

irregularity → violation (of law)

irregularity in matter of form, defect of (legal) form, want of (legal) form, formal defect, informality · Formfehler m, Formmangel m

irregular nucleated road village, cluster road village · (Haufen)Wegedorf n, (Haufen)Straßendorf

irregular nucleated village, cluster village · Haufendorf n

irregular row village · unregelmäßiges Reihendorf n

irremovability · Unausweisbarkeit f

irremov(e)able · unentfernbar

irrespective of percentage · ohne Franchise f

irresponsible, accountless, free from accountableness · nicht verantwortlich, nicht rechenschaftspflichtig

irretrievably lost thing · unwiederbringlich verlorene Sache f

irrevocability, finality · Endgültigkeit f, Unwiderruflichkeit

irrevocable, peremptory, final, determinate; perimere [*Latin*] · bestimmt, endgültig, unwiderruflich

irrevocable gift, gift inter vivos, absolute gift [*A gift made by one living person to another, as opposed to a gift by will*] · Schenkung f unter Lebenden

irrevocable (letter of) credit, confirmed (letter of) credit · unwiderrufliches Akkreditiv n

irrigated border cultivation, irrigated border gardening · Beetanbau m mit Bewässerung, Beetkultur f mit Bewässerung

irrigated rice cultivation, wet rice cultivation · Naßreisanbau m

irrigation agriculture · Bewässerungslandwirtschaft f

irrigation cooperative (society), irrigation cooperative association · Bewässerungsgenossenschaft f

irrigation district · Bewässerungsbezirk m

irrigation facility · Bewässerungseinrichtung f

irrigation law · Bewässerungsrecht n

irrigation law, irrigation statute, irrigation act · Bewässerungsgesetz n

irrigation plant · Bewässerungsanlage f

irrigation system · Bewässerungssystem n

island country · Insenland n

island of poverty, poverty island · Armutsinsel f

isocost (line), price curve, iso-outlay curve, isocost curve, iso-outlay line, price line · Kostenisoquante f, Isokostenlinie f, Isokostenkurve f

isodapane · Isodapane f [*Linie gleicher Gesamtfracht für die Produkteinheit*]

isogram map; isoline map [*deprecated*] · Isolinienkarte f, Isogrammkarte, Karte mit Isolinien

isolate · Sektor m der unverbunden neben den anderen Zwischenproduktbereichen besteht [*Graphentheorie*]

isolated building, detached building [*Building surrounded by open space*] · freistehendes Gebäude n

isolated business cluster · isolierte Geschäftsanhäufung f

isolated farm, single farm · Einzelhof m

isolated farm area, single farm area · Einzelhofgebiet n

isolated farm row, single farm row · Einzelhofreihe f

isolated settlement, solitary settlement, single settlement · Einzel(an)sied(e)lung f

isolated single-family house — (issue) syndicate

isolated single-family house, detached single-family house, free-standing single-family house · freistehendes Einfamilienhaus n

isoline · Liniengleiche f, Isolinie f [1. Verbindungslinie vermessener Geländepunkte, früher „Isoline" genannt. 2. Interpolierte Skalenwertlinie, früher „Isorithme" genannt]

isoline map [deprecated] → isogram map

isometric map · isometrische Karte f

iso-outlay line, price line, isocost (line), price curve, iso-outlay curve, isocost curve · Kostenisoquante f, Isokostenlinie f, Isokostenkurve f

isopleth [A line showing density of population] · Volksdichtekurve f, Bevölkerungsdichtekurve

isopleth [A line connecting points assumed to have equal values] · Isowertlinie f, Isoplethe f

isopleth (diagram), isopleth-graph · Isoplethendiagramm n; Isoplethe f [In der deutschen Fachsprache]

isopleth map · Isoplethenkarte f

iso-product curve, isoquant (line) (of equal output) · (Ertrags)Isoquante f, Isophore f

isoquant plane · Isoquantenebene f

iso-revenue-less-outlay line · Linie f gleicher Nettowarenpreise

iso-revenue line · Linie f zwischen Orten gleicher Warenpreise

to issue [order] · erlassen [Anordnung]

to issue [certificate] · ausstellen [Bescheinigung]

to issue, to emit · ausgeben [Wertpapier]

to issue, to float · begeben [Anleihe]

issue · Einkünfte fpl

issue, offspring, descendant · Abkömmling m, Nachkomme m, Deszendent m

issue; defence (Brit.); defense (US) · Verteidigung f

issue, floating · Begebung f [Anleihe]

issue · Problembereich m

issue · Prozeßinhalt m

issue · Ausstellung f [Bescheinigung]

issue · Ausgang m [einer Angelegenheit]

issue · Gewinn m aus Landeigentum

issue · Gewinn m aus Landbesitz

issue [Die Benennung „issue" bedeutet sowohl den Prozeßinhalt als auch die Verteidigung, vermutlich, weil erst diese den Streitinhalt zur vollen Feststellung bringt, daher sie denn den Ausgang der Verhandlungen darüber, welches Recht Prozeßgegenstand sein soll, bildet], plea [The defendant's answer of fact to the plaintiff's declaration] · Verteidigung f

issue at a discount, emission at a discount · Unterpariemission f, Unterpariausgabe f [Wertpapier]

issue audience · Leserschaft f einer einzelnen Nummer

issue bank → issue house

issue book · Ausgabebuch n [z. B. über Schriftstücke]

issue business, business of issue · Emissionsgeschäft n

issue date, date of issue · Ausfertigungsdatum n, Ausstellungsdatum n [Bescheinigung]

issue department · Emissionsabteilung f, Notenemissionsabteilung [Bank von England]

issued in spite of law, issued contrary to law, issued against law, issued illegally · gesetzwidrig erteilt, gesetzeswidrig erteilt, rechtswidrig erteilt

issue house, issue firm, issue bank, bank of issue, house of issue, issuing house, issuing bank, issuing firm · Notenbank f, Emissionsbank, Zettelbank, Emissionshaus n

issue in tail, offspring in tail, descendant in tail · sukzessionsberechtigter Nachkomme m, sukzessionsberechtigter Abkömmling m, sukzessionsberechtigter Deszendent m

issueless, childless, without issue, without child(ren) · kinderlos, ohne Nachkommen(schaft)

issue of drawings · Zeichnungsausgabe f

issue (of fact), point in dispute, contention, contentious issue · Streitfrage f, Streitpunkt m

issue of shares at a premium · Überpariemission f

issue price, rate of issue, price of issue, issue rate · Emissionskurs m, Ausgabekurs, Emissionspreis m, Ausgabepreis

issue prohibition · Emissionsverbot n

issue rate, issue price, rate of issue, price of issue · Emissionskurs m, Ausgabekurs, Emissionspreis m, Ausgabepreis

issuer (of securities) · (Wertpapier)Emittent m, (Wertpapier)Ausgeber m

(issue) sub-syndicate · (Emissions)Unterkonsortium n, (Emissions)Untersyndikat n

(issue) syndicate, underwriting syndicate · (Emissions)Konsortium n, (Emissions)Syndikat n

(issue) syndicate loan, underwriting syndicate loan · (Emissions)Konsortialanleihe f, (Emissions)Syndikatanleihe

issue system · Emissionssystem n

issuing · Ausstellen n [Bescheinigung]

issuing bank · Käuferbank f, eröffnende Bank

issuing house, issuing bank, issuing firm, issue house, issue firm, issue bank, bank of issue, house of issue · Notenbank f, Emissionsbank, Zettelbank, Emissionshaus n

issuing institution · emittierende Anstalt f

item · Position f, Pos.

itemization · Positionierung f

to itemize · positionieren

itemized price, bill price · L.V.-Preis m, Leistungsverzeichnispreis

itemized quotation, bill of quantities · Leistungsbeschreibung f mit Mengenansätzen, Leistungsverzeichnis n, LV

item number · Positionsnummer f

item of work · Teil(bau)leistung f [Ein einheitliches Leistungselement der Bauleistung]

item of work, item of a contract bill, item of a bill of quantities · L.V.-Position f

iterative method · Iterationsverfahren n

itinerant judge, justice in eyre, justice in eire, justice itinerant, circuit justice, itinerant justice, circuit judge · Sendrichter m, Umgangsrichter, reisender Richter

itinerant trade · Wandergewerbe n

itinerant trade card · Reisegewerbekarte f

itinerant trade tax · Wandergewerbesteuer f

it seems; semble [French] [Terms used to suggest that a particular point may be doubtful] · fraglich

IULA, International Union of Local Authorities · Internationaler Gemeindeverband m, IGV

iura in re [Latin] · Sachenrecht n

ius gentium [Latin] · Handels- und Verkehrsrecht n [römisches Recht]

ius honorarium [Latin] · Amtsrecht n [römisches Recht]

J

jactitation · Prahlerei f

jactitation of marriage · Ehevorspiegelung f

jail, prison; gaol (Brit.) · Gefängnis n

jail delivery, prison delivery; gaol delivery (Brit.) · Gefängnisbereinigung f [Im englischen Ständestaat]

jail delivery, prison delivery; gaol delivery (Brit.) · Einlieferung f ins Gefängnis

jailer · Gefängniswärter m

jail money; gaol money (Brit.); prison money [In old English law] · Steuer f für Unterhaltung von Gefangenen

jail-rate · (örtliche) Gefängnissteuer f, lokale Gefängnissteuer, kommunale Gefängnissteuer, gemeindliche Gefängnissteuer

jerry-builder · Bauspekulant m

jet aircraft nuisance · Düsenflugzeugemission f

jetsam [The goods which float upon the sea when cast overboard for the safety of the ship, or when a ship is sunk or sinks]; flotsam [Goods floating in the water for whatever reason] · Strandgut n, Strandungsgut, angeschwemmtes Gut, angeschwemmte Gegenstände m pl [Alles was in Seenot über Bord geworfen wird]

Jewish gage · jüdisches Mobiliarpfand n

job accounting → (order) costing

jobber · Akkordarbeiter m

jobber → (securities) jobber

jobbery · Mißwirtschaft f im öffentlichen Dienst

jobbing contract, daywork(s) contract · Tagelohnvertrag m

jobbing-in-bills, cross-drawing, cross-acceptance · Wechselreiterei f

jobbing interim payment, daywork(s) interim payment · Tagelohnabschlagszahlung f

jobbing rate, daywork(s) rate, day wage rate, daily wage rate · Tagelohnsatz m

jobbing schedule, jobbing scheme, daywork(s) schedule, daywork(s) scheme · Tagelohnplan m

jobbing scheme — (job) site administration

jobbing scheme, daywork(s) schedule, daywork(s) scheme, jobbing schedule · Tagelohnplan *m*

jobbing wage → daily wage

job(bing) work, piece-work · Akkordarbeit *f*

job(bing) work contract, premium-wage contract, efficiency-wage contract, statement-wage contract, piece-wage contract, piece-work contract · Akkord(lohn)vertrag *m*

job card, work ticket, operation card [*A document which authorizes an operation and is fed back after its operation to record any relevant information — time, quantity, operator, etc. — for such purposes as monitoring progress, wage payments, etc*] · Arbeitskarte *f*

job change · Arbeitsstellenwechsel *m*

job contract, work contract, contract of service, contract of employment, contract of job, contract of work, service contract, employment contract · Arbeitsvertrag *m*

job costing → job (order) costing

job cost(s) → job (order) cost(s)

job creation, work creation, employment creation, creation of work, creation of jobs, creation of employment · Arbeitsbeschaffung *f*

job (daily) record, job diary, construction site diary, building site diary, construction site daily record, building site daily record, (job) site diary, (job) site daily record · Bau(stellen)tagebuch *n*, Bau(stellen)buch

job description · Stellenbeschreibung *f*

job ladder · Laufbahnvorschrift *f*

jobless, unemployed · arbeitslos, erwerbslos

jobless female person, unemployed female person · Erwerbslose *f*, Arbeitslose

jobless male person, unemployed male person · Erwerbslose *m*, Arbeitslose

jobless person, unemployed person · erwerbslose Person *f*, arbeitslose Person

job meeting → job (progress) meeting

job operations, (job) site operations, building site operations, construction site operations · Bau(stellen)betrieb *m*

job opportunity · Arbeitsgelegenheit *f*

job (order) costing, job (order) (cost(s)) accounting · Zuschlags(kosten)rechnung *f*, Zuschlagskostenkalkulation *f*, Zuschlagskostenberechnung, Zuschlagskostenermitt(e)lung, spezifische Einzelkostenrechnung

job overhead(s), job overhead cost(s), (on-)site overhead(s), (on-)site overhead cost(s) · Baustellen-Gemein(un)kosten *f*, Baustellen-General(un)kosten

job place, place of employment, place of work(ing), work(ing) place, employment place · Arbeitsort *m*, Arbeitsplatz *m*, Beschäftigungsort *m*, Beschäftigungsplatz *m*

job point, point of employment, point of work(ing), work(ing) point, employment point · Beschäftigungsstätte *f* [*Fehlbenennung: Arbeitsplatz m*]

job policy · Arbeitsplatzpolitik *f*

job profit, job gain · (Bau)Leistungsprofit *m*, (Bau)Leistungsgewinn *m*

(job) progress, building progress, progress of the work(s), construction progress · Baufortschritt *m*, Arbeitsfortschritt

(job) progress chart, (job) progress schedule, working progress chart, working progress schedule, progress of the work(s) chart, progress of the work(s) schedule · Arbeitsfortschrittplan *m*, (Bau)Fortschrittplan *m*, Bauzeit(en)plan *m* [*vom Auftraggeber aufgestellt*]

(job) progress meeting, (construction) site meeting, building site meeting, job site meeting · Bau(stellen)besprechung *f*

(job) progress report, progress of the work(s) report · Arbeitsfortschrittbericht *m*, (Bau)Fortschrittbericht *m*

(job) progress schedule → (job) progress chart

job ratio · Beschäftigungsquotient *m*
$$\left[= \frac{\text{Tagesbevölkerung}}{\text{Nachtbevölkerung}} \cdot 100 \right]$$

job report, construction report, work(s) report, site report · Arbeitsbericht *m*, Bau(stellen)bericht *m*

job safety · Arbeitssicherheit *f*

job safety lawmaking, job safety legislation · Arbeitssicherheitsgesetzgebung *f*

job security · Arbeitsplatzsicherheit *f*, Sicherheit *f* des Arbeitsplatzes

job sharing · Arbeits(platz)teilung *f*

(job) site → (construction) (job) site

(job) site accident, construction site accident, building site accident · Bau(stellen)unfall *m*

(job) site accident damage, building site accident damage, construction site accident damage · Bauunfallschaden *m*

(job) site administration, field administration · Baustellenverwaltung *f*

(job) site administrative staff — to join

(job) site administrative staff, (job) site administrative personnel, field administrative staff, field administrative personnel · Baustellenverwaltungspersonal *n*

(job) site administrative personnel → (job) site administrative staff

(job) site architect · Baustellenarchitekt *m*

(job) site bookkeeping, construction site bookkeeping, building site bookkeeping, site bookkeeping · Baustellenbuchführung *f*

(job) site clearance cost(s), construction site clearance cost(s), building site clearance cost(s) · Baustellenräumungskosten *f*

(job) site conditions, construction site conditions, building site conditions · Bau(stellen)verhältnisse *f,* Verhältnisse (auf) der Baustelle

(job) site control, site checking, construction site checking, construction site control, building site checking, building site control, job site checking · Baustellenkontrolle *f* [*Aufsuchen der Baustelle in Zeitabständen zur Prüfung der Arbeiten des Bauunternehmers*]

(job) site cost(s) · Baustellenkosten *f*

(job) site diary, (job) site daily record, job (daily) record, job diary, construction site diary, building site diary, construction site daily record, building site daily record · Bau(stellen)tagebuch *n,* Bau(stellen)buch

(job) site facilities, construction site facilities, building site facilities · Bau(stellen)einrichtung *f* [*Alle Maschinen und Geräte einer Baustelle*]

(job) site facilities cost(s), building site facilities cost(s), construction site facilities cost(s) · Bau(stellen)einrichtungskosten *f*

(job) (site) facilities plan, building site facilities plan, construction site facilities plan · Bau(stellen)ordnungsplan *m* [*Fehlbenennungen: Bau(stellen)einrichtungsplan*]

(job) site fence, construction site fence, building site fence · Bau(stellen)zaun *m*

(job) site illumination, site lighting, building site lighting, building site illumination, construction site illumination, job site lighting · Bau(stellen)beleuchtung *f*

(job) site land → (construction) (job) site land

(job) site limit, building site limit, construction site limit · Baustellengrenze *f*

(job) site management, construction site management, building site management · Bau(stellen)führung *f,* örtliche Bauaufsicht *f*

(job) site manager, manager on site, construction site manager, building site manager · Baustellenführer *m,* örtlicher Bauführer [*des Unternehmers*]

(job) site meeting, job (progress) meeting, construction site meeting, building site meeting · Bau(stellen)besprechung *f*

(job) site meeting minutes, construction site meeting minutes, building site meeting minutes · Bau(stellen)besprechungsprotokoll *n*

(job) site operations, building site operations, construction site operations, job operations · Bau(stellen)betrieb *m*

(job) site organization, construction site organization, building site organization · Bau(stellen)organisation *f*

(job) site planning, building site planning, construction site planning · Baustellenplanung *f*

(job) site preparation, building site preparation, construction site preparation · Baustellenherrichtung *f*

(job) site relocation, relocation of job sites · Standortveränderung *f* von Arbeitsplätzen

(job) site safety, safety of (construction) site, safety of building site, construction site safety, building site safety, safety of job site · Baustellensicherheit *f*

(job) site salary, construction site salary, building site salary · Bau(stellen)gehalt *n*

(job) site sign → site sign

(job) site staff, (job) site forces, (job) site personnel, field staff, field force(s), field personnel · Bau(stellen)arbeitskräfte *f*

(job) site storage · Baustellenlagerung *f*

(job) site supervision, job site superintendence, building site superintendence, building site supervision, supervision of site(s), superintendence of site(s), site supervision, construction site supervision, construction site superintendence · Bau(stellen)aufsicht *f,* Bau(stellen)überwachung *f,* Objektaufsicht, Objektüberwachung

(job) site turnover, construction site turnover, building site turnover · Bau(stellen)umsatz *m*

(job) site wage; construction labour wage (Brit.); construction labor wage (US); construction (site) wage, building (site) wage · Bau(stellen)lohn *m*

(job) site water supply, construction site water supply, building site water supply · Bau(stellen)wasserversorgung *f*

to join · vereinigen

to join · häufen, kumulieren

to join as party defendant — joint committee

to join as party defendant · (eine Klage auf ...) ausdehnen

joinder [*Joint action with one or more persons*] · Gemeinschaftshandlung *f*

joinder, joining · Verbinden *n*

joinder of causes, joinder of (court) actions, joinder of (law)suits, joinder of pleas · Klagenhäufung *f*, Klagenkumulation *f*, Klagenverbindung

joinder of issue · Bestreiten *n* des gegnerischen Schriftsatzes, Bestreiten des Inhalts der Verteidigungsschrift

joinder of parties [*The uniting of two or more persons as co-plaintiffs or as co-defendants in one suit*] · Parteienhäufung *f*, Parteienkumulation *f*

joinder of possessions · Besitzzurechnung *f*, Besitzzuzählung, Besitzverbindung [*Die Zeit eines Vorbesitzers wird zur eigenen Besitzzeit hinzugezählt*]

joinder of times · Zeitverbindung *f*, Zusammenrechnung von Zeiträumen, Zusammenzählung von Zeiträumen

joining, joinder · Verbinden *n*

to join in signing · mitzeichnen

joint account → joint (bank) account

joint action → joint (court) action

joint (ad)measurement · gemeinsames Aufmaß *n*, gemeinschaftliches Aufmaß [*Es wird vom Auftraggeber und Auftragnehmer gemeinsam durchgeführt*]

joint administration, co-administration · Mit(nachlaß)verwaltung *f*, erbrechtliche Mitverwaltung, Erb(schafts)mitverwaltung, gerichtliche (Nachlaß)Mitverwaltung

joint administrator → (probate) co-administrator

joint advisory committee · gemeinsamer Beratungsausschuß *m*, gemeinsamer beratender Ausschuß, gemeinschaftlicher Beratungsausschuß, gemeinschaftlicher beratender Ausschuß

joint aid, co-help, joint help, co-aid · Mithilfe *f*

joint and several debtor, joint and several oblig(at)or, joint and several promisor · Mit- und Einzelschuldner *m*, Gesamt- und Einzelschuldner, Mit- und Einzelversprechender, Gesamt- und Einzelversprechender, Mit- und Einzelverpflichteter, Gesamt- und Einzelverpflichteter, Mit- und Einzelversprechensgeber, Gesamt- und Einzelversprechensgeber

joint and several liability · Solidarhaftung *f*, Solidarhaftpflicht *f*, Solidarhaftbarkeit *f* [*Die Schuldner haften sowohl einzeln als auch gemeinschaftlich*]

joint and several note [*Same as a joint note, except that makers may be sued together or individually if action is necessary*] · Zahlungsversprechen *n* zur gesamten Hand und jeder für sich

joint and several promisor · gemeinschaftlich und einzeln haftender Versprechensgeber *m*, gemeinsam und einzeln haftender Versprechensgeber

joint and several promisors · gemeinsame Versprechensgeber *mpl* für dasselbe Versprechen wobei sich jeder zur Bewirkung derselben Leistung verpflichtet

joint annuitants · gemeinsame Annuitätenempfänger *mpl*, gemeinschaftliche Annuitätenempfänger

joint assign(ee), joint cessionary, co-assign(ee), co-cessionary · Mitzessionar *m*, Mitzessionär

joint (bank) account, community account [*A bank account of separate and community funds commingled in such manner that neither can be distinguished from the other*] · gemeinsames Konto *n*, Gemeinschafts(bank)konto, gemeinschaftliches Konto

joint beneficial owner · benefiziarischer Miteigentümer *m* zur gesamten Hand mit jus accrescendi

joint beneficial ownership · benefiziarisches Miteigentum *n* zur gesamten Hand mit jus accrescendi

joint benefit, (common) advantage, common benefit · gemeinsamer Nutzen *m*, gemeinsamer Vorteil, gemeinschaftlicher Nutzen, gemeinschaftlicher Vorteil

joint bidders · gemeinsame Bieter *mpl*, gemeinschaftliche Bieter

joint burden, joint encumbrance, joint charge, joint incumbrance, joint load · Mitbelastung *f*, Mitlast *f*

joint buyer, co-purchaser, co-buyer, joint purchaser · Mitkäufer *m*

joint cause, joint (court) action, joint (law)suit, joint plea · Gemeinschaftsklage *f*

joint cessionary, co-assign(ee), co-cessionary, joint assign(ee) · Mitzessionar *m*, Mitzessionär

joint charge, joint incumbrance, joint load, joint burden, joint encumbrance · Mitbelastung *f*, Mitlast *f*

joint committee · Gemeinschaftsausschuß *m*, gemeinsamer Ausschuß, gemeinschaftlicher Ausschuß

joint committee [*According to E.S.Cowdrick in "Manpower in Industry", 1924, page 138*], joint workers' council, joint workmen's council · paritätischer Betriebsrat *m*

joint community (development) plan →
joint general (development) plan

joint comprehensive (development) plan
→ joint general (development) plan

joint concurrent tortfeasors · Mehrtäter *mpl* die zusammen auf ein gemeinsames Ziel hinwirken

joint contract · gemeinschaftlicher Vertrag *m*, gemeinsamer Vertrag, Gemeinschaftsvertrag

joint contractor, co-contractor · Mitunternehmer *m*

joint control committee · gemeinsamer Lenkungsausschuß *m*, gemeinschaftlicher Lenkungsausschuß

joint (court) action, joint (law)suit, joint plea, joint cause · Gemeinschaftsklage *f*

joint covenant (in deed) · gemeinsamer Formalvertrag *m*, gemeinschaftlicher Formalvertrag

joint creditor, joint promisee, joint debtee, co-creditor, co-promisee, co-debtee, fellow creditor, fellow promisee, fellow debtee · Mitgläubiger *m*, Mitversprechensempfänger, Gesamtgläubiger, Gesamtversprechensempfänger

joint debt · gemeinsame Schuld *f*, gemeinschaftliche Schuld

joint debtee, co-creditor, co-promisee, co-debtee, fellow creditor, fellow promisee, fellow debtee, joint creditor, joint promisee · Mitgläubiger *m*, Mitversprechensempfänger, Gesamtgläubiger, Gesamtversprechensempfänger

joint debtor, joint obligor, co-debtor, co-obligor, fellow debtor, fellow obligor · Mitschuldner *m*, Gesamtschuldner

joint duties, common duties, duties in common · gemeinschaftliche Pflichten *fpl*, gemeinsame Pflichten

joint effect table · Gesamtwirkungstabelle *f*

joint encumbrance, joint charge, joint incumbrance, joint load, joint burden · Mitbelastung *f*, Mitlast *f*

joint estate · Gesamtgut *n*

joint executor dative [*Scotland*] → (probate) co-administrator

joint facility · gemeinsame Einrichtung *f*, gemeinschaftliche Einrichtung, Gemeinschaftseinrichtung

joint general (development) plan, joint master (development) plan, joint comprehensive (development) plan, joint community (development) plan, joint structure plan, joint three-dimensional master plan [*Two or more local planning authorities may, with the consent of the secretary of state, prepare and submit a joint structure plan covering their combined areas or any part of their combined areas*] · Gebietsplan *m*, überörtlicher General(bebauungs)plan

joint-heir, co(in)heritor, joint inheritor, (co)parcener; coparticeps [*In old English law*]; co-heir, fellow-heir · Anteilerbe, Miterbe *m*, Erbgenosse *m*, (Bruch)Teilerbe

joint-heiress, co-heiress, fellow-heiress · Miterbin *f*, Erbgenossin *f*

joint heirship, co-inheritance, (estate in) (co)parcenary · Anteilserbschaft *f*, Anteilerbe *n*, (Bruch)Teilerbschaft, (Bruch)Teilerbe, Miterbschaft, Miterbe

joint help, co-aid, joint aid, co-help · Mithilfe *f*

joint holding → (real) estate of joint tenancy

joint incumbrance, joint load, joint burden, joint encumbrance, joint charge · Mitbelastung *f*, Mitlast *f*

joint inheritor → joint heir

joint interest, joint right · gemeinsamer Anspruch *m*, gemeinschaftlicher Anspruch, gemeinsame Berechtigung *f*, gemeinschaftliche Berechtigung

joint judge, co-judge · Mitrichter *m*

joint land tenancy, joint tenancy of land [*Real property held by two or more persons together with the distinct character of survivorship*] · solidarisches Landvermögen *n*, Landvermögen zur gesamten Hand

joint (law)suit, joint plea, joint cause, joint (court) action · Gemeinschaftsklage *f*

joint lease(hold), collective lease(hold), concurrent lease(hold) · Teilerbbaurecht *n*, gemeinsames Erbbaurecht, gemeinschaftliches Erbbaurecht, Gemeinerbbaurecht, Bruchteilerbbaurecht, Mehrheitserbbaurecht, Miterbbaurecht, Anteilerbbaurecht [*Bruchteil eines mehreren Personen gemeinschaftlich zustehenden Erbbaurechts, welcher in der Weise beschränkt ist, daß jedem der Mitberechtigten das Sondereigentum an nicht zu Wohnzwecken dienenden bestimmten Räumen in einem aufgrund des Erbbaurechts errichteten oder zu errichtenden Gebäuden eingeräumt wird. (§ 30 Abs. 1 WoEigG)*]

joint legatary, co-legatary · Mitvermächtnisnehmer *m*

joint lessee, co-lessee · Mitpächter *m*

joint lessor, co-lessor · Mitverpächter *m*, Mitpachtherr

joint liability · Solidarhaftung *f*, Solidarhaftbarkeit *f*, Solidarhaftpflicht *f* [*Die Forderung kann nur gegen die Schuldner zusammen geltend gemacht werden und mit dem Tode eines Mitschuldners*

joint load — joint right

geht die Haft(ung) auf die Überlebenden über]

joint load, joint burden, joint encumbrance, joint charge, joint incumbrance · Mitbelastung *f*, Mitlast *f*

joint loan (of money) · gemeinsames Darleh(e)n *n*, gemeinschaftliches Darleh(e)n

joint local planning authorities, standing conference of local planning authorities · Planungsverband *m* [*In der Bauleitplanung. Zusammenschluß von Gemeinden und sonstigen Trägern öffentlich-rechtlicher Planungen mit dem Ziel, durch gemeinsame Bauleitplanung den Ausgleich der verschiedenen Belange zu erreichen. (§ 4 BBauG)*]

joint(ly), unitedly, (in) common, together · gemeinsam, gemeinschaftlich, miteinander, gemeinheitlich, verbunden, solidarisch, zusammen

jointly acquired property · gemeinsam erworbenes Vermögen *n*, gemeinschaftlich erworbenes Vermögen

joint(ly) and several(ly), together and individually · gemeinsam und einzeln, gemeinsam und allein, gemeinschaftlich und einzeln, gemeinschaftlich und allein, solidarisch und jeder für sich, gemeinsam und jeder für sich, zur gesamten Hand und jeder für sich

jointly and severally liable · mit- und einzeln haftbar, mit- und einzeln haftpflichtig

jointly liable · gemeinsam haftbar, gemeinsam haftpflichtig, gemeinschaftlich haftbar, gemeinschaftlich haftpflichtig

joint master (development) plan → joint general (development) plan

joint measurement → joint (ad)measurement

joint membership · verbundene Mitgliedschaft *f*

joint note [*Note signed by more than one person, each with equal responsibility for payment, who must be sued together if action is necessary*] · solidarisches Zahlungsversprechen *n*

joint oblig(at)or → joint debtor

joint perception, co-perception · Mitwahrnehmung *f*

joint plaintiff, co-plaintiff · Mitkläger *m*

joint planning board, standing conference of planning boards · Planungsgemeinschaft *f* [*Vereinigung von Trägern öffentlich-rechtlicher Planungen zwecks gemeinsamer Raumplanung*]

joint planning corporation · Planungsverband *m* [*Allgemein. Aus Trägern öffentlich-rechtlicher Planungen als Mitgliedern gebildete Körperschaft, auf welche die Mitglieder bestimmte Planungsbefugnisse übertragen haben*]

joint planning of ministries · Ressortplanung *f* [*Gemeinsame Planung von Ministerien des Bundes oder Ministerien eines Landes in der Bundesrepublik Deutschland, also Planung auf gleicher Ebene*]

joint plea, joint cause, joint (court) action, joint (law)suit · Gemeinschaftsklage *f*

joint possession, co-possession · Mitbesitz(stand) *m*

joint possessors · Gesamtbesitzer *m pl*

joint power, joint right · gemeinsame Befugnis *f*, gemeinsames Recht *n*, gemeinschaftliche Befugnis, gemeinschaftliches Recht

joint product · Verbundprodukt *n*, Verbunderzeugnis *n* [*Ein aus demselben Vorgang entstehendes Erzeugnis, z. B. Gas und Koks aus Kohle*]

joint product · Kuppelprodukt *n*, Kuppelerzeugnis *n*

joint promise · gemeinsames (Leistungs)Versprechen *n*, gemeinschaftliches (Leistungs)Versprechen

joint promisee, joint debtee, co-creditor, co-promisee, co-debtee, fellow creditor, fellow promisee, fellow debtee, joint creditor · Mitgläubiger *m*, Mitversprechensempfänger, Gesamtgläubiger, Gesamtversprechensempfänger

joint promisor → joint debtor

joint promisors · gemeinsame Versprechensgeber *m pl* für dasselbe Versprechen

joint proprietor · Mitinhaber *m*

joint purchaser, joint buyer, co-purchaser, co-buyer · Mitkäufer *m*

joint regional planning authorities, standing conference of regional planning authorities, standing conference on regional planning · regionaler Planungsverband *m*, Regionalplanungsverband [*Bundesrepublik Deutschland*]; Landesplanungsverband

joint rent-charge · Gesamtgrundschuld *f* [*Es haften mehrere Grundstücke zur Sicherung einer Forderung*]

joint resolution · gemeinsamer Entschluß, gemeinsame Entschließung *f*, gemeinsamer Beschluß *m*, gemeinschaftliche Entschließung, gemeinschaftlicher Beschluß

joint right, joint power · gemeinsame Befugnis *f*, gemeinsames Recht *n*, gemeinschaftliche Befugnis, gemeinschaftliches Recht

joint right, joint interest · gemeinsamer Anspruch *m*, gemeinschaftlicher Anspruch, gemeinsame Berechtigung *f*, gemeinschaftliche Berechtigung

joint rule, condominium (Brit.); joint sovereignty · gemeinsame hoheitliche Befugnis *f*, gemeinschaftliche hoheitliche Befugnis, gemeinschaftliche Hoheitsbefugnis, gemeinsame Hoheitsbefugnis, gemeinsames hoheitliches Recht *n*, gemeinschaftliches hoheitliches Recht, gemeinsames Hoheitsrecht, gemeinschaftliches Hoheitsrecht

joint share · Gesamthandanteil *m*

joint-stock, stocks · Aktien *fpl*

(joint-)stock bank, limited company bank · Aktiengesellschaftsbank *f*

joint-stock company, incorporated public company; stock company (US) · Aktiengesellschaft *f*, AG

(joint stock) company limited by guarantee, (joint stock) company limited by guaranty, (joint stock) company limited by guarantie · (Kapital)Gesellschaft *f* bei der die Gesellschafter bis zur Höhe einer im Falle der Liquidation übernommenen Garantiesumme haften, (Kapital)Gesellschaft mit beschränkter Nachschußpflicht im Falle einer Liquidation

(joint stock) company limited by shares · (Kapital)Gesellschaft *f* mit auf den Aktienbetrag beschränkter Haftung

joint structure plan → joint general (development) plan

joint suit → joint (law)suit

joint tenancy · solidarisches Miteigentum *n*, quotenloses Miteigentum, Miteigentum zur gesamten Hand, Miteigentum ohne Quoten [*Nach Billigkeitsrecht (equity law) kann allerdings „joint tenancy" als „tenancy in common" gewertet werden*]

joint tenancy of land, joint land tenancy [*Real property held by two or more persons together with the distinct character of survivorship*] · solidarisches Landvermögen *n*, Landvermögen zur gesamten Hand

joint tenure → joint tenancy

joint three-dimensional master plan → general (development) plan

joint tort · gemeinsames Delikt *n*, gemeinschaftliches Delikt

joint tortfeasors · gemeinsame Delikttäter *mpl*, gemeinschaftliche Delikttäter

joint trustee, co-trustee · Mittreuhänder *m*, Mittreuhandverwalter

joint undertaking, joint venture · Partizipationsgeschäft *n*

jointure · Wittum *n*

joint use, co-use · Mitbenutzung *f*, Mitgebrauch *m*

joint use, use of the whole jointly · Gesamtgebrauch *m*, Gesamtbenutzung *f*

joint venture, joint undertaking · Partizipationsgeschäft *n*

joint venture construction, joint venture building · Argebau *m*, Arbeitsgemeinschaftsbau *m*

joint venture contract · Arbeitsgemeinschaftsvertrag *m*, Arge-Vertrag

joint venture (firm), contracting combine, partnership, contractor combination, contracting group · Arbeitsgemeinschaft *f* [*Ein Zusammenschluß von Unternehmern auf vertraglicher Grundlage mit dem Zweck, meist große Bauaufträge der gleichen oder verschiedenen Fachrichtungen gemeinsam durchzuführen*]

joint-venture of architects, architects' joint venture · Architekten(arbeits)gemeinschaft *f*, Architektenarge *f* [*Zwei oder mehrere Architekten schließen sich zur Planung und/oder Leitung eines Bauvorhabens zusammen*]

joint venture of engineers · Ingenieurarbeitsgemeinschaft *f*, Ingenieurarge *f*

joint venturer, joint venture partner · Arbeitsgemeinschaftsgesellschafter *m*, Arbeitsgemeinschaftspartner *m*, Arbeitsgemeinschaftsmitglied *n*, Arge-Gesellschafter *m*, Arge-Partner *m*, Arge-Mitglied *n*

joint will; testamentum mutuum [*Latin*] · gemeinschaftliches Testament *n*, gemeinsames Testament

joint workers' council, joint workmen's council; joint committee [*According to E.S.Cowdrick in "Manpower in Industry", 1924, page 138*] · paritätischer Betriebsrat *m*

joint working group, joint working party, joint working team · gemeinsame Arbeitsgruppe *f*, gemeinschaftliche Arbeitsgruppe

journal entry · Journalbuchung *f*, Journaleintrag(ung) *m*, *(f)*

journalism, fourth estate · Journalismus *m*

journey, trip, travel · Fahrt *f*

journey assignation, trip assignation, travel assignation · Fahrtzuweisung *f* (auf Verkehrsnetze)

journey attraction, travel attraction, trip atraction [*That which gives motivation, specific direction, and destination of a trip, e.g. going downtown*] · Fahrtanziehungskraft *f*

journey destination-end, (trip) destination-end, travel destination-end · (Fahrt)Endpunkt *m*

journey distribution, trip distribution, travel distribution · Fahrt(en)verteilung *f*

journey distribution model, trip distribution model, travel distribution model · Fahrt(en)verteilungsmodell *n*

journey from work, travel from work, trip from work · Fahrt *f* vom Arbeitsplatz

journey generation, trip generation, travel generation · Fahrt(en)erzeugung *f*

journey-maker, trip-maker, travel-maker · Fahrtteilnehmer *m*

journeyman, y(e)oman · Geselle *m*

journey matrix, trip matrix, travel matrix · Fahrt(en)matrix *f*

journey origin-end, (trip) origin-end, travel origin-end · (Fahrt)Startpunkt *m*

journey pattern, journey scheme, trip pattern, trip scheme, travel pattern, travel scheme · Fahrt(en)muster *n*, Fahrt(en)schema *n*

journey production, travel production, trip production [*The motivation to make a trip, e.g. going to work*] · Fahrterzeugung *f*

journey-time survey, travel-time survey, trip-time survey · Fahrzeitenenquête *f*

journey to work, travel to work, trip to work · Fahrt *f* zum Arbeitsplatz

judex, liber et legalis homo [*Latin*]; juror, jury member, jurator, member of a jury; free and lawful man [*In old English law*] · Geschworener *m*

judex ad quem [*Latin*]; justice of appeal, judge of appeal, appellate judge, appellate justice [*A judge to whom an appeal is made*] · Appellationsrichter *m*, Berufungsrichter *m*

judex [*Latin*]; judge · Richter *m*

judex [*Latin*]; (official) referee, arbitrator appointed by court · gerichtlich ernannter Schiedsrichter *m*

to judge [*To hear and determine, as in cause of trial*] · urteilen, Recht sprechen

to judge [*To form an authoritative opinion about*] · beurteilen, erachten

judge; judex [*Latin*] · Richter *m*

(judge) chamber [*In England*] · Richterbüro *n*

judge-made law, case law, judicial law · richterliches Recht *n*, gerichtliches Recht, Richterrecht, Fallrecht, Spruchrecht, Präzedenzienrecht

judg(e)ment · Beurteilung *f*

judg(e)ment absolute → final judg(e)ment (at law)

judg(e)ment after trial, judg(e)ment agreed (up)on, agreed judg(e)ment, contradictory judg(e)ment · kontradiktorisches Urteil *n*, vereinbartes Urteil

judg(e)ment (at law), decree (at law), judg(e)ment of a court, adjudication, (legal) judg(e)ment [*abbreviated: judgt.*] [*The words "judg(e)ment" and "decree" are often used synonymously; especially now that the codes have abolished the distinction between "law" and "equity". But of the two terms "judg(e)ment" (Urteil) is the more comprehensive, and includes "decree" (Erlaß)*] · gerichtliches Urteil *n*, (Gerichts)Urteil, Rechtsspruch *m*, Erkenntnis *f* eines Gerichts(hofes)

judg(e)ment (at law) absolute → final judg(e)ment (at law)

judg(e)ment book, plea list, plea book, cause list, cause book, register of pleading actions, judg(e)ment docket · Klagenverzeichnis *n*, Klagenregister *n*, Prozeßverzeichnis, Prozeßregister

judg(e)ment by default, default judg(e)ment [*It is obtained when one party neglects to take a certain step in the action within the proper time*] · (Ver)Säumnisurteil *n*

judg(e)ment creditor · Judikatgläubiger *m*, Prozeßgläubiger, Urteilsgläubiger

judg(e)ment day, day of judg(e)ment [*The day fixed by statute, rule, or custom of a court on which judg(e)ments are pronounced or entered upon the court records*] · Urteilstag *m*

judg(e)ment debt, debt of record · Prozeßschuld *f*, Judikatschuld, Urteilsschuld

judg(e)ment debtor, judg(e)ment obligor · Judikatschuldner *m*, Prozeßschuldner, Urteilsschuldner

judg(e)ment debtor summons, judg(e)ment obligor summons · Vollstreckungsverfahren *n*

judg(e)ment docket, judg(e)ment book, plea list, plea book, cause list, cause book, register of pleading actions · Klagenverzeichnis *n*, Klagenregister *n*, Prozeßverzeichnis, Prozeßregister

judg(e)ment error, error of judg(e)ment · Urteilsfehler *m*

judg(e)ment error, error of judg(e)ment · Beurteilungsfehler *m*

judg(e)ment execution, execution of judg(e)ment · Urteilsvollstreckung *f*

judg(e)ment extension · Urteilserstreckung *f*

judg(e)ment for possession, possession judg(e)ment · Besitzeinräumungsurteil *n*

judg(e)ment in default of appearance · Kontumazurteil *n*

judg(e)ment in personam, personal judg(e)ment · Leistungsurteil *n*, schuldrechtliches Urteil, Verurteilungsurteil, Urteil auf Grund schuldrechtlicher Haftung

**judg(e)ment in rem, **judg(e)ment on the merit · Bewirkungsurteil *n*, Sachurteil, (Rechts-)Gestaltungsurteil

judg(e)ment latitude, latitude of judg(e)ment · Urteilsspielraum *m*

judg(e)ment mistake, mistake of judg(e)ment · Urteilsirrtum *m*

judg(e)ment mistake, mistake of judg(e)ment · Beurteilungsirrtum *m*

judg(e)ment motion, motion for judg(e)ment · Antrag *m* auf Fällung eines Urteils, Gesuch *n* auf Fällung eines Urteils, Antrag *m* auf sofortiges Urteil, Gesuch *n* auf sofortiges Urteil, Urteilsfällungsantrag *m*, Urteilsfällungsgesuch *n*

judg(e)ment note (US) [*A promissory note of a kind illegal in some states of the USA upon which the holder is enabled to enter judg(e)ment and take out execution ex parte in case of default in payment*] · Schuld(en)anerkenntnisschein *m*, Eigenwechsel *m* mit Unterwerfungsklausel

judg(e)ment obligor, judg(e)ment debtor · Judikatschuldner *m*, Prozeßschuldner, Urteilsschuldner

judg(e)ment obligor summons, judg(e)ment debtor summons · Vollstreckungsverfahren *n*

judg(e)ment of a court, adjudication, (legal) judg(e)ment [*abbreviated: judgt.*], judg(e)ment (at law), decree (at law) [*The words "judg(e)ment" and "decree" are often used synonymously; especially now that the codes have abolished the distinction between "law" and "equity". But of the two terms "judg(e)ment" (Urteil) is the more comprehensive, and includes "decree" (Erlaß)*] · gerichtliches Urteil *n*, (Gerichts)Urteil, Rechtsspruch *m*, Erkenntnis *f* eines Gerichts(hofes)

judg(e)ment of a court of equity, decree (in equity); decretum [*Latin*] [*The judg(e)ment of a court of equity, answering for most purposes to the judg(e)ment of a court of common law*] · Billigkeits(recht)urteil *n*, Urteil nach Billigkeit(srecht), Billigkeitsgerichtsurteil

judg(e)ment of a court of record · protokolliertes Urteil *n*

judg(e)ment of appeal, appeal judg(e)ment · Berufungsurteil *n*, Appellationsurteil

judg(e)ment of banishment → for(e)judgment

judg(e)ment of enforcement, enforcement judg(e)ment · Durchsetzungsurteil *n*, Erzwingungsurteil

judg(e)ment of exclusion → for(e)judgment

judg(e)ment of injunction · Unterlassungsurteil *n*

judg(e)ment of outlawry · Achtserklärung *f*, Achtsurteil *n*

judg(e)ment of revocation · gerichtlicher Widerruf *m*

judg(e)ment on the merit, judg(e)ment in rem · Bewirkungsurteil *n*, Sachurteil, (Rechts-) Gestaltungsurteil

judg(e)ment range, range of judg(e)ment · Beurteilungsspielraum *m*

judg(e)ment sample · willkürliche Stichprobe *f* [*Umfragetechnik*]

judg(e)ment summons [*A summons issued in an English county court requiring a judg(e)ment debtor to appear and show cause why he should not be imprisoned*] · gerichtliche Vorladung *f* wegen Nichtzahlung der Urteilsschuld

judge of appeal, appellate judge, appellate justice; judex ad quem [*Latin*]; justice of appeal [*A judge to whom an appeal is made*] · Appellationsrichter *m*, Berufungsrichter *m*

judgeship, office of a judge, judicial office · Richteramt *n*

judge's order · Richterbescheid *m*

judgess, female judge · Richterin *f*

judicable [*Capable of being or liable to be judged*] · verhandlungsfähig [*Gericht*]

judicature act · Gesetz *n* über das Zivilgerichtsverfahren, Gerichtsverfassungsgesetz

judicature acts · Gesetze *n pl* über das Zivilgerichtsverfahren

judicial · richterlich

judicial · gerichtlich

judicial act, judicial statute, judicial law · Gerichtsverfassungsgesetz *n*, Gerichtswesengesetz [*Es regelt die Organisation der ordentlichen Gerichte*]

judicial act(ion) · gerichtliche Handlung *f*, gerichtlicher Akt *m*

judicial activism · richterliche Entscheidungsfreudigkeit *f*

judicial administration · Justizverwaltung *f*

judicial affairs, judiciary affairs · Gerichtswesen *n*

judicial assembly · Richtergremium *n*

judicial authority, judicial power · richterliche Gewalt *f*, richterliche Macht *f*, richterliche Hoheit, richterliche Kompetenz *f*, judizielle Kompetenz, judizielle Gewalt, judizielle Macht, judizielle Hoheit

judicial capacity · richterliche Eigenschaft *f*

Judicial Committee of the Privy Council · Justizausschuß m des Staatsrats, Rechtsausschuß des Staatsrats [*Großbritannien*]

judicial composition · gerichtlicher Vergleich m, Gerichtsvergleich

judicial construction, judiciary interpretation, judiciary construction, judicial interpretation · Auslegung f auf Grund gerichtlicher Entscheidung, Deutung f auf Grund gerichtlicher Entscheidung, richterliche Auslegung, richterliche Deutung

judicial contest, judicial controversy, (contentious) litigation, process (in law) [*Contest in a court of justice for the purpose of enforcing a right*] · Prozeß m

judicial control, judicial review · Gerichtskontrolle f, gerichtliche Kontrolle, gerichtliche Nachprüfung f, Gerichtsnachprüfung, richterliche Nachprüfung, richterliche Kontrolle, Richternachprüfung, Richterkontrolle, Normenkontrolle

judicial council · Justizrat m

judicial creation · Rechtsschöpfung f durch (die) Gerichte

judicial decision, judiciary decision · richterliche Entscheidung f, richterlicher Entscheid m

judicial discretion · richterliches Ermessen n

judicial discretion [*The power, residing in the court, of deciding a question where latitude of judg(e)ment is allowed*] · gerichtliches Ermessen n

judicial disfavour (Brit.); judicial disfavor (US) · richterliche Ungnade f

judicial document · Gerichtsunterlage f, Gerichtsdokument n

judicial evidence, judicial proof · gerichtsbekannte Tatsachen f pl

judicial examination · richterliche Überprüfung f

judicial function · richterliche Funktion f, rechtsprechende Funktion, Richterfunktion

judicial inquest, assise, assize · richterliche Untersuchung f

judicial interpretation, judicial construction, judiciary interpretation, judiciary construction · Auslegung f auf Grund gerichtlicher Entscheidung, Deutung f auf Grund gerichtlicher Entscheidung, richterliche Auslegung, richterliche Deutung

judicial investigation, judiciary investigation · richterliche Prüfung f

judicial knowledge · Gerichtskundigkeit f

judicial law, judge-made law, case law · richterliches Recht n, gerichtliches Recht, Richterrecht, Fallrecht, Spruchrecht, Präzedenzienrecht

judicial law, judicial act, judicial statute · Gerichtsverfassungsgesetz n, Gerichtswesengesetz [*Es regelt die Organisation der ordentlichen Gerichte*]

judicial legislation, judicial lawmaking [*Development of the law by judicial decision*] · richterliche Gesetz(es)formung f, Rechtsetzung durch Rechtsprechung

judicial mortgage · Urteilshypothek f, gerichtliche Hypothek

judicial notice · gerichtliche Berücksichtigung f gewisser Tatsachen

judicial notice of foreign law · richterliche Kenntnisnahme f fremden Rechts

judicial oath · Richtereid m

judicial office, judgeship, office of a judge · Richteramt n

judicial organ · richterliches Organ n

judicial organization · Gerichtsverfassung f

judicial possession · juristischer Besitz m

judicial power, judicial authority · richterliche Gewalt f, richterliche Macht f, richterliche Hoheit, richterliche Kompetenz f, judizielle Kompetenz, judizielle Gewalt, judizielle Macht, judizielle Hoheit

judicial process · Rechtsfindungsprozeß m

judicial proof, judicial evidence · gerichtsbekannte Tatsachen f pl

judicial redress, judicial remedy · richterliche Abhilfe f, richterlicher Behelf m

judicial restraint · richterliche Rechtsbindung f

judicial review, judicial control · Gerichtskontrolle f, gerichtliche Kontrolle, gerichtliche Nachprüfung f, Gerichtsnachprüfung, richterliche Nachprüfung, richterliche Kontrolle, Richternachprüfung, Richterkontrolle, Normenkontrolle

judicial review of administration action · richterliche Verwaltungskontrolle f

judicial sale (of real estate) · Grund(stücks)verkauf m durch (ein) Gericht, Landverkauf durch (ein) Gericht, Bodenverkauf durch (ein) Gericht

judicial self-restraint · richterliche Zurückhaltung f, richterliche Selbstbeschränkung

judicial sentence · Richterspruch m

(judicial) separation, divorce from bed and board · Aufhebung f der ehelichen Gemeinschaft durch richterliche Anerkenntnis, gerichtliche Trennung f, richterliche Aufhebung f einer ehelichen Gemeinschaft, gerichtliche Aufhebung f einer ehelichen Gemeinschaft, Trennung f von Tisch und Bett

judicial statute, judicial law, judicial act · Gerichtsverfassungsgesetz n, Gerichtswesengesetz [Es regelt die Organisation der ordentlichen Gerichte]

judicial supremacy · Gerichtsoberhoheit f, Oberhoheit der Gerichte, gerichtliche Oberhoheit

judicial task · Richteraufgabe f

judicial trustee · gerichtlich bestellter Treuhänder m, gerichtlicher Treuhänder [Er wird vom Gericht ernannt und beaufsichtigt]

judicial writ · Gerichtsdekret n

judiciary · Richterschaft f

judiciary, lawyer in judicial office · Justizjurist m, Jurist im Justizwesen

judiciary affairs, judicial affairs · Gerichtswesen n

judiciary construction, judicial interpretation, judicial construction, judiciary interpretation · Auslegung f auf Grund gerichtlicher Entscheidung, Deutung f auf Grund gerichtlicher Entscheidung, richterliche Auslegung, richterliche Deutung

judiciary decision, judicial decision · richterliche Entscheidung f, richterlicher Entscheid m

judiciary investigation, judicial investigation · richterliche Prüfung f

judicium dei [Latin]; ordeal, divine judg(e)ment; divinum judicium · Gottesurteil n

jumble of clauses · Klauseldickicht n

junior financing, later financing · nachstellige Finanzierung f, nachstehende Finanzierung

junior lien [A lien recorded on a property subsequent to the recording of a prior lien] · jüngeres Retentionsrecht n, nachstehendes Retentionsrecht, nachstehendes Zurück(be)haltungsrecht, jüngeres Zurück(be)haltungsrecht

junior mortgage, later (legal) mortage · nachstehende Hypothek f, nachstellige Hypothek, rangschlechtere Hypothek

junk value, scrap value · Schrottwert m

jural relation(ship) · Rechtsverhältnis n durch ein Versprechen begründet

juramentum, jus jurandum [Latin]; sacramentum [Latin]; ath [Saxon], oath; othe [old English] · Eid m

jura singulorum [Latin] · Privatrechtstitel m

jurat · eidliche Bekräftigung f

jurator, member of a jury; free and lawful man [In old English law]; judex liber et legalis homo [Latin]; juror, jury member · Geschworener m

juratory · eidlich

juratory cautionary [Scots law. Inadequate cautionry allowed in some cases where the party swears he cannot find other or better cautionary] · eidliche Bürgschaft f, Eidesbürgschaft

juridic(al), juristic [Acting in the distribution of justice] · juristisch; juridisch [Österreich]

juridic(al) act(ion), juristic act(ion) · juristischer Akt m, juristische Handlung f, Rechtsgeschäft n

juridic(al) day, law day, court day; lage day, lagh day [Latin]; doomsday [old English law]; dies juridicus [Latin] · Gerichtstag m

juridic(al) error, juristic error · Justizfehler m

jurisdiction, use of (the) law, adjudication of disputes, declaration of the law; jurisdictio [Latin]; administration of justice · Rechtsprechung f, Entscheidung von Einzelfällen, Justizausübung, Rechtspflege f

jurisdiction, administrative legal authority, administrative legal power · Verwaltungsgerichtsbarkeit f

jurisdiction → (territorial) jurisdiction

jurisdiction; jurisdictio [Latin]; power to make law, authority to make law, power to legislate, authority to legislate, legislative authority, legislative power, legislature · gesetzgebende Gewalt f, gesetzgebende Hoheit, gesetzgebende Macht, gesetzgebende Kompetenz, Gesetzgebungsgewalt, Gesetzgebungskompetenz, Gesetzgebungsmacht, Gesetzgebungshoheit

jurisdiction; jurisdictio [Latin]; legal authority, legal power · Gerichtsbarkeit f [Die Machtvollkommenheit des Staates zur gerichtlichen Entscheidung]

jurisdictional amount (US); amount in controversy, amount in dispute, value in dispute, disputed value · Streitwert m

jurisdiction fountain, law source, law fountain, source of law, fountain of law, fountain of jurisdiction · Rechtsquelle f

jurisdiction of a court · Gerichtszuständigkeit f

jurisdiction of a judge · Richterzuständigkeit f [Siehe Anmerkung unter „Zuständigkeit"]

jurisdiction over the subject matter · Zuständigkeit f einen Rechtsfall an sich zu ziehen

jurisprudence — jus civile

jurisprudence, body of law, law body · Rechtskomplex *m*

jurisprudence, legal science; jurisprudentia [*Latin*]; law science, science of law · Jurisprudenz *f*, Rechtswissenschaft *f*, Lehre *f* der allgemeinen Rechtsfragen, Rechtslehre

jurisprudence [*misnomer*]; law, objective right; lex [*Latin*] [*A system of law existing objectively as an external norm for persons*] · (objektives) Recht *n*

jurisprudence of conceptions · Begriffsjurisprudenz *f*

jurisprudence of interests · Interessenjurisprudenz *f*

jurisprudence of natural law, natural law jurisprudence, natural law science, science of natural law · Lehre *f* der allgemeinen Naturrechtsfragen, Lehre des Naturrechts, Naturrechtswissenschaft *f*, Wissenschaft des Naturrechts, Naturrechtslehre, Naturjurisprudenz *f*

jurisprudence province, province of jurisprudence · Bereich *m* der Jurisprudenz

jurisprudentia [*Latin*]; law learning · Rechtsstudium *n*, Studium der Rechte

jurist [*A person learned in law*] · Rechtsgelehrte *m*

jurist employed in business, house lawyer, staff lawyer, house jurist, staff jurist, lawyer employed in business · Hausjurist, Firmenjurist *m*, Unternehmensjurist

juristic, juridic(al) [*Acting in the distribution of justice*] · juristisch; juridisch [*Österreich*]

juristic act(ion), juridic(al) act(ion) · juristischer Akt *m*, juristische Handlung *f*, Rechtsgeschäft *n*

juristic act(ion) violating public policy · unsittliche juristische Handlung *f*, unsittlicher juristischer Akt *m*, unsittliches Rechtsgeschäft *n*

juristic error, juridic(al) error · Justizfehler *m*

juristic law, law of the forum; lex non scripta [*Latin*]; unwritten law [*It comprises both, judge-made law and juristmade law*] · Gerichtsrecht *n*; ungeschriebenes Recht [*Fehlbenennung, weil Gerichtsentscheide wegen ihrer bindenden Kraft für die Zukunft geschrieben sind*]

juristic papyrology · juristische Papyruskunde *f*

jurist in administration, lawyer in administration · Verwaltungsjurist *m*

jurist-made law, lawyer's law · Juristenrecht *n*, Recht der Wissenschaft, wissenschaftliches Recht

juror, jury member, jurator, member of a jury; free and lawful man [*old English law*]; judex liber et legalis homo [*Latin*] · Geschworener *m*

juror's book, juror's list, pan(n)el of jurors, juror's pan(n)el, jury pan(n)el [*A list of persons qualified to serve on juries*] · Geschworenenliste *f*, Geschworenenverzeichnis *n* [*Für eine Sitzungsperiode*]

juror's pan(n)el, jury pan(n)el, juror's book, juror's list, pan(n)el of jurors [*A list of persons qualified to serve on juries*] · Geschworenenliste *f*, Geschworenenverzeichnis *n* [*Für eine Sitzungsperiode*]

jury · Prüfungsausschuß *m*

jury box · Geschworenenbank *f*

jury foreman · Geschworenenobmann *m*

jury member, jurator, member of a jury; free and lawful man [*old English law*]; judex liber et legalis homo [*Latin*], juror · Geschworener *m*

jury(men), lay people · Jury *f*, Geschworene *m pl*

jury of matrons, jury-women · Frauenjury *f*

jury pan(n)el, juror's book, juror's list, pan(n)el of jurors, juror's pan(n)el [*A list of persons qualified to serve on juries*] · Geschworenenliste *f*, Geschworenenverzeichnis *n* [*Für eine Sitzungsperiode*]

jury system · Geschworenensystem *n*, Jurysystem

jury trial, trial by jury, assize [*A trial in which sworn assessors or jurymen decide questions of fact*] · Gerichtsverhandlung *f* vor Geschworenen, (Haupt)Verhandlung vor Geschworenen, Geschworenen(haupt)verhandlung, Geschworenengerichtsverhandlung, Schwurgerichtsverfahren *n*, Geschworenenverfahren, Schwurgerichtsverhandlung

jurywoman, woman juror, female juror · Geschworene *f*

jury-women, jury of matrons · Frauenjury *f*

jus accrescendi [*Latin*]; right of survivorship · Recht *n* des Überlebenden, Überlebensrecht, Anwachsungsrecht

jus belli [*Latin*]; law of war, martial law · Kriegsrecht *n*

jus canonicum [*Latin. Formerly: law canon. It is laid down in decrees of the pope and statutes of councils. Not to be confused with "jus ecclesiasticum"*], canons collectively, canon law, the canons, canonry · kanonisches Recht *n*, geistliches Recht

jus civile corpus juris civilis [*Latin*]; civil law · (objektives) Zivilrecht *n*, bürgerliches Recht

jus civile Romanum — justice

jus civile Romanum [*Latin*]; (civil) law of Rome, Roman (civil) law [*As distinguished from the English law*] · römisches Recht *n* [*„Civil law" ist die englische Sammelbezeichnung für die im römischen Recht wurzelnden Rechtsordnungen*]

jus commune [*Latin*] → common (law)

jus compascendi [*Latin*] · Mithut *f*

jus coronae [*Latin*]; right of the Crown · Kronrecht *n*

jus ecclesiasticum [*Latin*]; law Christian, ecclesiastic(al) law, spiritual law [*Not to be confused with "jus canonicum"*] · Kirchenrecht *n*, kirchliches Recht, geistliches Recht

jus falcandi [*Latin*]; right of cutting wood · Holzfällrecht *n*, Holzschlagrecht

jus grutiae [*Latin*]; rafting right, right of rafting · Flößer(ei)recht *n*, Floßrecht

jus honorarium [*Latin*]; honorary law · Ehrenrecht *n*

jus individuum [*Latin*]; individual right, indivisible right, right incapable of division, nondivisible right · unteilbares Recht *n*

jus in re [*Latin*]; complete and full right, full and complete right, real right [*A right existing or subject of property, inherent in his relation to it, implying complete ownership with possession*] · (dingliches) Recht *n* auf Beherrschung einer Sache im ganzen, volles Recht zu einer Sache, volles Recht zur Sache

jus jurandum, sacramentum [*Latin*]; ath [*Saxon*], oath; othe [*old English*]; juramentum · Eid *m*

jus legitimum [*Latin*]; (subjective) right, (legal) interest, legal right, statutory interest, statutory right [*A system of rights enjoyed by persons, as "subjects" or owner of rights, and by virtue of law*] · (subjektives) Recht *n*, Berechtigung *f*, Anrecht, (Rechts)Anspruch *m*, gesetzliches (subjektives) Recht, subjektives (gesetzliches) Recht, dingliches Recht [*im B.G.B. auch als „Gegenstand" bezeichnet*]

jus majestaticum circa sacra, jus in sacra potestas ecclesiastica [*Latin*]; ecclesiastic(al) power, ecclesiastic(al) authority, spiritual authority, spiritual power · Kirchengewalt *f*, Kirchenhoheit *f*, Kirchenmacht *f*, Kirchenkompetenz *f*, Kirchenregiment *n*

jus naturale [*Latin*]; law of nature · Naturrecht *n*, natürliches Recht, nichtpositives Recht

jus pascendi, communis pasturae, herbagium [*Latin*]; (right of) pastur(ag)e, (right of) grazing, pastoral right, herbage, grazing right, shack, common pastur(ag)e, commonage, common right · Angerrecht *n*, Hütungsrecht, Atzung *f*, Ätzung, (Vieh)Weiderecht, (Vieh)Weideberechtigung

jus patronatus [*Latin*]; (right of) patronage, advowson [*The right of presentation, i.e. the right of appointing a parson to a rectory, vicarage or other ecclesiastical benefice*] · Patronat(srecht) *n*, Präsentation(srecht) *f*, *(n)* [*Ein dauerndes Präsentationsrecht zu einer geistlichen Pfründe*]

jus privatum [*Latin*]; private law · (objektives) Privatrecht *n*, objektives privates Recht, privates (objektives) Recht

jus proprietatis [*Latin*] → interest of ownership

jus publicum [*Latin*]; public law, constitutional law, law of constitution [*The law concerned with the rights and duties of the state. It is contrasted with private law, which deals with the rights and duties of subjects inter se*] · öffentliches Recht

jus retractus [*Latin*] · Näherecht *n*, Retraktrecht, Zugrecht [*Erblosung*]

jus scriptum [*Latin*]; statute law, written law, enacted law, statutory law, statutes; lex scripta [*The body of law enacted by Parliament*] · geschriebenes Recht *n*, gesetztes Recht, geschriebenes Parlamentsrecht, gesetztes Parlamentsrecht, (Parlaments)Gesetz(es)recht

jus singulare [*Latin*]; several interest, several right, single interest, single right · Einzelanspruch *m*, Einzel(an)recht *n*, Einzelberechtigung *f*, getrennter Anspruch, getrenntes (An)Recht, getrennte Berechtigung

jus stapulae [*Latin*]; right of staple [*old European law. The right or privilege of certain towns of stopping imported merchandise, and compelling it to be offered for sale in their own markets*] · Stapelrecht *n*

just, conforming to truth · wahrheits(ge)treu

just cause, excuse, justification; justificatio [*Latin*] [*Just, lawful excuse for act*] · Rechtfertigung *f*

just competition, equitable competition, fair competition · lauterer Wettbewerb *m*, uneigennütziger Wettbewerb

jus tertii [*Latin*]; right of (a) third party, third party right · Drittenrecht *n*

justice [*The title given in England to the judges of the King's bench and the common pleas, and in the USA to the judges of the supreme court of the United States and of the appellate courts of many of the states. It was called "justicier" in old English law*] · Richter *m*

justice [*In jurisprudence. The constant and perpetual disposition to render every man his due*] · Gerechtigkeit *f*

justice in eyre, justice in eire, justice itinerant, circuit justice, itinerant justice, circuit judge, itinerant judge · Sendrichter *m*, Umgangsrichter, reisender Richter

justice nisi prius, justice of assise, justice of assize [*A judge of a superior English court, who goes on circuit into the various counties of England and Wales for the purpose of disposing of such causes as are ready for trial at the assizes*] · Assisenrichter *m*

justice of appeal, judge of appeal, appellate judge, appellate justice; judex ad quem [*Latin*] [*A judge to whom an appeal is made*] · Appellationsrichter *m*, Berufungsrichter *m*

justice of assize, justice nisi prius, justice of assise [*A judge of a superior English court, who goes on circuit into the various counties of England and Wales for the purpose of disposing of such causes as are ready for trial at the assizes*] · Assisenrichter *m*

justice of the peace, honorary magistrate · ehrenamtlicher Friedensrichter *m*

justiciable [*Proper to be examined in courts of justice*] · gerichtsfähig

justifiable self-preference · berechtigter Eigennutz *m*

justification; justificatio [*Latin*]; just cause, excuse [*Just, lawful excuse for act*] · Rechtfertigung *f*

to justify; justificare [*Latin*] · rechtfertigen

jus tigni immittendi [*Latin*] [*In Roman law. A servitude which gave the right of inserting a beam into the wall of another*] · Balkendienstbarkeit *f*, Balkengerechtigkeit, Balkenservitut *n, f*, (servitutisches) Balkenrecht *n*

Justinian law · justinianisches Recht *n*

Justinian's legislation, Justinian's lawmaking · justinianische Gesetzgebung *f*

justitium, non terminus [*Latin*]; vacation time of (a) court, non term · Gerichtsferien *f*

justness, conformity to truth · Wahrheitstreue *f*

jus utendi [*Latin*]; demise of property without destroying its substance, tenancy of property without destroying its substance, lease(hold) of property without destroying its substance · Pacht *f* ohne Zerstörung, Nutzungsrecht *n* ohne Zerstörung

jus venandi et piscandi [*Latin*]; right of hunting and fishing · (subjektives) Jagd- und Fisch(erei)recht *n*

juvenile adult · jugendlicher Erwachsener *m*

juvenile court · Jugendgericht *n*

juvenile delinquency · Jugendkriminalität *f*, Jugendstraffälligkeit *f*

juvenile offender · jugendlicher Gesetz(es)übertreter *m*

juvenile unemployment · Jugendarbeitslosigkeit *f*

juvenile welfare · Jugendwohlfahrt *f*

K

Kantian philosophy of law · kantische Rechtsphilosophie *f*

keener competition · verschärfter Wettbewerb *m*

to keep · aufbewahren

to keep alive, to sustain · aufrechterhalten, beibehalten

keeper · Halter *m*

keeper · Bewahrer *m*

keeper → protector

keeper of a prison; gaoler (Brit.); master of a prison · Gefängnisvorsteher *m*

keeper of the forests, chief warden of the forests, master of the woods, master of the forests, chief warden of the woods, keeper of the woods [*In old English law. An officer who had the principal government of all things relating to the forest, and the control of all officers belonging to the same*] · Waldbewahrer *m*, Forstbewahrer, Oberforstmeister

Keeper of the Great Seal · Großsiegelbewahrer *m*, Lordkanzler

keeper of the rolls; custos rotulorum [*Latin*] · Rollenbewahrer *m*, Rollenarchivar, aktenbewahrender Friedensrichter

Keeper of the Signet · Siegelbewahrer *m*

keeping · Aufbewahrung *f*

keeping clean · Reinhalten *n*

keeping land free · Freihaltung *f* von Land, Landfreihaltung

keeping (of) documents · Aufbewahrung *f* von Urkunden

keeping possession · Besitzhaltung *f*, Inbesitzhaltung

keeping safe, custody · Gewahrsam *m*, Verwahrung *f*

keeping small domestic animals — knowingly untrue

keeping small domestic animals · Kleintierhaltung f

keeping up to schedule · Fristeinhaltung f

to keep in repair, to maintain · unterhalten

to keep safely · sicher aufbewahren

Kendall's tau (τ) · Rangkorrelationskoeffizient m [Statistik]

kennel [Any lot or premise on which animals are boarded] · Koppel f

ker [Brittanic]; clachan [Galic]; bally [Irish]; balley [Manx]; tref [Welsh] · Drubbel m; Eschdorf n [nach Rothert 1924]; Eschweiler m [nach Helbok 1938]

kerb(stone) parking (Brit.); curb parking (US) · Bordsteinparken n

kernel, historic(al) core · Altstadt f

key currency, leading currency · Leitwährung f

key data · Schlüsseldaten f

key day, cut-off-date, effective date, appointed day · Stichtag m

key-day of appraisal, (e)valuation cut-off-date, (e)valuation key-day, appointed day of (e)valuation, effective date of appraisal, cut-off date of appraisal, appointed day of appraisal · Bewertungsstichtag m, Wertermitt(e)lungsstichtag, Taxierungsstichtag, (Ab)Schätzungsstichtag

key factor, key determinant · wesentlicher (Bestimmungs)Faktor m, Schlüsselfaktor

key flat, layout guide · Anhaltekopie f [Kartographie]

key industry · Schlüsselindustrie f

key money; tea money, pugree, salaami [In the Far East] [An undercover rent payment] · Schlüsselgeld n

Keynesian growth model · keynesianisches Wachstumsmodell n

Keynesian two-region model · keynesianisches Zweiregionenmodell n

key number · Schlüsselnummer f

key sector · Schlüsselsektor m

key sector approach · Schlüsselsektoransatz m

key variable · Schlüsselveränderliche f

kindergarten, infant's school · Kindergarten m

kind of economic system · Wirtschaftsart f

King's advocate, advocate-general, Queen's advocate [England] · Kronjurist m für See- und Kriegsrecht

king's baron, baron by tenure [One who held by military or other honourable service, directly from the king, and at length mostly applied to the grantor of these (the Great Barons) who personally attended the Great Council, or, from the time of Henry III, were summoned by writ to Parliament (barons by writ)] · Baron m mit Leh(e)n(s)pflicht dem König zugetan, Freiherr m mit Leh(e)n(s)pflicht dem König zugetan, Leh(e)n(s)baron, Leh(e)n(s)freiherr

Kings Bench Division → High Court of Justice

King's Court; Curia Regis [Latin] · Königsgericht n, königliches Gericht

kinswoman, female relative · weibliche Verwandte f

kitchen-garden, household garden · Gemüsegarten m, Küchengarten, Nutzgarten

kite (Brit.); accommodation bill, fictitious bill, feint bill, faint bill, feigned bill, pretended bill; windmill · Freundschaftswechsel m, Gefälligkeitswechsel, Kellerwechsel, Reitwechsel, Schornsteinwechsel, Scheinwechsel

knacker's yard, knackery (Brit.); rendering establishment (US) · Abdeckerei f, Tierkörperbeseitigungsanstalt f, Wasenmeisterei f, Kleemeisterei, Kleemeierei, Kavillerie f

knight · Ritter m

knight banneret · Bannerherr m

knighthood, chivalry [The position and character of a knight] · Ritterschaft f

knight service; servitium militare, servitium militis [Latin]; military service on horseback · Ritterdienst m

knight's fee (tenure), knight's fief, knight's feud, knight's feod, knight's tenancy, knight's tenement, knight's (feodal) tenure (of land(s)), knight's estate (of land) tenure by knight service, capital fee (tenure); feudum equestre, feodum equestre, feodum equi [Latin] · Ritterleh(e)n n

to knock down [auction] · zuschlagen [Versteigerung]

know-how · praktisches Wissen n, Anwendung f der Kenntnisse

knowingly, designedly, scienter · bewußt, wissentlich

knowingly untrue, deliberately untrue, designedly untrue, intentionally untrue, knowingly false, deliberately false, designedly false, intentionally false, knowingly not true, deliberately not true, designedly not true, intentionally not true · absichtlich unwahr, wissentlich unwahr, bewußt unwahr, absichtlich falsch, bewußt falsch, wissentlich falsch

to knowledge, to make known, to clarify, to free from secrecy, to free from ignorance, to lay bare, to disclose, to reveal · aufklären, enthüllen, offenbaren, offenlegen, offen darlegen, preisgeben, kundtun

knowledge of untruth, falsity · Kenntnis *f* der Unwahrheit

known circulation · bekannte Verbreitung *f*, bekannte Streuung [*Umfragetechnik*]

know-probability sample · Stichprobe *f* nach Wahrscheinlichkeitsauswahl [*Umfragetechnik*]

to know the untruth · Unwahrheit kennen

L

Löschian approach · Löschansatz *m*, Ansatz nach Lösch

Löschian system, network of hexagons, network of hexagonal market areas · Netz *n* sechseckiger Marktgebiete, Netz sechskantiger Marktgebiete, Marktnetz, Wirtschaftslandschaft *f* (nach Lösch), Raumbild *n* einer Wirtschaftslandschaft nach Lösch, Wabenmuster *n* einer Wirtschaftslandschaft nach Lösch, Marktnetzkonstruktion *f* einer Wirtschaftslandschaft nach Lösch

label · Etikett *n*

label(l)ing method · Kennzeichnungsverfahren *n* [*Zur Bestimmung des maximalen Flusses durch ein Netzwerk*]

labor (US); manpower; labour (Brit.) [*The amount of labour, both male and female, available at a particular time*] · Arbeitskräfte *f pl*

labor bank (US); worker's bank; labour bank (Brit.) · Arbeitnehmerbank *f* [*Fehlbenennung: Arbeiterbank*]

labor housing (US); workers' housing, workmen's housing, labour housing (Brit.) · Arbeiterwohnungen *f pl*, Arbeiterwohnstätten *f pl*

labor inspection (US); labour inspection (Brit.) · Arbeitsaufsicht *f*, Arbeitsinspektion *f*

laborious, diligent, steadily applied, active · aktiv, unermüdlich, fleißig

labor law (US); labour law (Brit.) · Arbeitsrecht *n*

labor legislation, labor lawmaking (US); labour legislation, labour lawmaking (Brit.) · Arbeiterschutzgesetzgebung *f*

labor market (US); labour market (Brit.) · Arbeitsmarkt *m*

labor rent (US) → labour rent

labor skate (US); (trade) unionist · Gewerkschaftler *m*

labour (Brit.); labor (US); manpower [*The amount of labour, both male and female, available at a particular time*] · Arbeitskräfte *f pl*

labour and material payment bond (Brit.); labor and material payment bond (US) [*Bond guaranteeing to the owner that the contractor will satisfy all obligations incurred by him on the project*] · Arbeits- und Baustoffzahlungsgarantie *f*

labour bank (Brit.); labor bank (US); worker's bank · Arbeitnehmerbank *f* [*Fehlbenennung: Arbeiterbank*]

labour-class suburb(an place) (Brit.); labor-class suburb(an place) (US); working-class suburb(an place) · Arbeitervorort *m*

labourer (Brit.), agricultural worker, agrarian worker, farm worker · Landarbeiter *m*

labourer (Brit.); blue collar worker, laborer (US), worker, workman, operative [*A wage-earning worker, skilled or semi-skilled, whose work is characterized largely by physical exertion*] · Arbeiter *m*

labourer-farmer village (Brit.); laborer-farmer village (US); worker peasant village · Arbeiter-Bauern-Dorf *n*

labour exchange (Brit.); labor exchange (US) · Arbeitsnachweis *m*, Arbeitsvermitt(e)lung *f*

labour housing (Brit.); labor housing (US); workers' housing, workmen's housing · Arbeiterwohnungen *f pl*, Arbeiterwohnstätten *f pl*

labouring classes lodging (Brit.); laboring classes lodging (US); workers' lodging, workmen's lodging · Arbeiterlogierhaus *n*

labour inspection (Brit.); labor inspection (US) · Arbeitsaufsicht *f*, Arbeitsinspektion *f*

labour intensive (Brit.); labor intensive (US) · arbeitsintensiv

labour law (Brit.); labor law (US) · Arbeitsrecht *n*

labour legislation, labour lawmaking (Brit.); labor legislation, labor lawmaking (US) · Arbeiterschutzgesetzgebung *f*

Labo(u)r Management Relations Act · Betriebsverfassungsgesetz *n*, Betr.VG [*Bundesrepublik Deutschland*]

labour market (Brit.); labor market (US) · Arbeitsmarkt *m*

labour only sub(-contractor) (Brit.); labor only sub(-contractor) (US) [*He supplies workmen to the contractor to work under the contractor's direction and does not undertake responsibility for any particular part of the works*] · Nachunternehmer *m* der nur Arbeitskräfte stellt, Subunternehmer der nur Arbeitskräfte stellt, Unterunternehmer der nur Arbeitskräfte stellt; Unterakkordant der nur Arbeitskräfte stellt [*Schweiz*]

labour protection (Brit.); labor protection (US) · Arbeitsschutz *m*

labour rent (Brit.); labor rent (US); serf rent, villein rent, villain rent · Arbeitsrente *f*, Hörigenrente *f*, Leibeigenrente *f* [*Sie bestand aus Diensten und Leistungen der Leibeigenen auf dem Herrenakker*]

labour share (Brit.); labor share (US) · Dienstleistungsaktie *f*

labo(u)r standard, output rate per man hour · Mannstundenleistung *f*

labour struggle (Brit.); labor struggle (US) · Arbeitskampf *m*

labour supply (Brit.); labor supply (US); manpower supply · Arbeitskräfteangebot *n*

labour union (Brit.); labor union (US); trade union · Gewerkschaft *f*

laches · Vernachlässigung *f*, Säumigkeit *f* [*In der Nichtgeltendmachung eines Anfechtungsrechts während eines unangemessen langen Zeitraumes in Kenntnis des Rechts*]

lack of authority · mangelnde Vollmacht *f*, mangelnde Vertretungsmacht

lack of care, lack of diligence · Sorgfaltsmangel *m*

lack of educational opportunities · Bildungsnotstand *m*

lack of knowledge · Unwissenheit *f*

lack of quorum, absence of quorum · Beschlußunfähigkeit *f* [*Wenn über einen Beschluß abgestimmt werden muß*]

lack of responsibility · Verantwortungsmangel *m*, Rechenschaftspflichtmangel

lack of standing to sue · mangelnde Aktivlegitimation *f*

ladder right · Leiterrecht *n*, Hammerschlagsrecht [*Das Recht auf dem Nachbargrundstück oder über ihm ein Gerüst aufzustellen*]

lady of independent means, woman of private means, woman of independent means, lady of private means · Rentnerin *f*

lady paramount, liege lady · Leh(e)n(s)herrin *f*

lag covariance · Kovarianz *f* zwischen Zeitreihen mit Verschiebung

lage day, lagh day [*Latin*]; **doomsday** [*In old English law*]; **dies juridicus** [*Latin*]; **juridic(al) day, law day, court day** · Gerichtstag *m*

lagged supply adjustment · verzögerte Angebotsanpassung *f*

lagging · rückständig

Lagrangean method · Lagrangesches Verfahren *n*

lag regression · Regression *f* zwischen Zeitreihen mit Verschiebung

lag time · Verzögerungszeit *f*

laic community · Laiengemeinschaft *f*

laity · Laienschaft *f*

lake · Binnensee *m*, Landsee

lake bank · Seeufer *n*

lake for boating, boating lake · Bootsteich *m*

land · Land *n*, (Grund *m* und) Boden *m*

land · Bereich *m* [*Im planerischen Sinn*]

land → (building) land

land (ab)alienation → (ab)alienation of (real) estate

land accretion, alluvion, alluvium, accretion (of land) · (Land)Anschwemmung *f*, (Land)Anschutt *m*, (Land)Akkreszenz *f*, (Land)Gewinnung durch Anschwemmung, Alluvion *n*, Alluvium *n*, Zulandung

land accretion right, right of alluvion, right of alluvium, right of accretion (of land) · (Land)Anschwemmungsrecht *n*, (Land) Anwachs(ungs)recht, (Land)Akkreszenzrecht, Alluvionsrecht, (Land)Zuwachsrecht, (Land)Anschuttrecht, Alluviumsrecht, Recht auf (Land)Gewinnung durch Anschwemmung

land accumulation → land(s) accumulation

land acquired by gift · geschenktes Land *n*

land acquisition → (building) land acquisition

land acquisition → (real) property acquisition

land acquisition act → (building) land acquisition act

land acquisition act, land acquisition law, land acquisition statute · Bodenbeschaffungsgesetz *n*, Landbeschaffungsgesetz *f*, Flächenbeschaffungsgesetz, Bodenerwerbsgesetz, Landerwerbsgesetz, Flächenerwerbsgesetz

land acquisition law, law of land acquisition · Bodenerwerbsrecht *n*, Landerwerbsrecht, Bodenbeschaffungsrecht, Landbeschaffungsrecht, Grund(stücks)-erwerbsrecht, Grund(stücks)beschaffungsrecht [*objektiv*]

land acquisition law → land acquisition act

land acquisition law → (building) land acquisition law

land acquisition right, (real) estate acquisition right, (real) property acquisition right, right to acquire land, right to acquire (real) estate, right to acquire (real) property, realty acquisition right, right to acquire realty · Bodenerwerbsrecht n, Bodenbeschaffungsrecht, Landerwerbsrecht, Landbeschaffungsrecht, Grund(stücks)beschaffungsrecht, Grund(stücks)erwerbsrecht [*subjektiv*]

land acquisition statute → land acquisition act

land acquisition statute → (building) land acquisition statute

land acquisition tax → (building) land acquisition tax

Land act, Land law, Land statute · Landesgesetz n [*Bundesrepublik Deutschland*]

land act → (building) land act

land addition, land swell, acreage swell, swell of acreage, swell of land, addition of acreage, acreage addition, addition of land [*of a real estate*] · Landzuwachs m, Flächenzuwachs, Bodenzuwachs, Landzunahme f, Bodenzunahme, Flächenzunahme

Land administration, Land government · Landesregierung f [*Bundesrepublik Deutschland*]

land affair → (building) land affair

land agent → ((real) estate) broker

land agricultural in character, farmland, improved land, farmed land, agriculturally zoned land, agriculturally used land, crop land, agricultural land, farming land [*Land may be assessable as "agricultural land" though it be covered by timber and underbrush, grass and weeds*] · landwirtschaftlicher Boden m, landwirtschaftlich genutzter Boden, landwirtschaftliches Land n, landwirtschaftlich genutztes Land, Kulturland, Kulturboden, Agrarland, landwirtschaftlich genutzte Fläche f, LN, landwirtschaftliche Nutzfläche, Fruchtland, Agrarnutzfläche

land alienation → (ab)alienation of (real) estate

land alienation → land (ab)alienation

land alienation contract → land(s) (ab)alienation contract

land allowance → land(s) allowance

land analysis, (land) area analysis · Bodenanalyse f, Landanalyse, Flächenanalyse

land appraisal → (real) property (e)valuation

land appraiser → (real) property appraiser

land area, land territory · Landgebiet n

land area, area of land · Landfläche f [*Im Gegensatz zur Meeresfläche*]

Land area, Land territory · Landesgebiet n [*Bundesrepublik Deutschland*]

(land) area → (building) (land) area

(land) area acquisition → (building) (land) area acquisition

(land) area analysis → land analysis

(land) area demise → (building) (land) area tenancy

(land) area improvement loan → (building) (land) area improvement loan

(land) area lease(hold) → (building) (land) area tenancy

(land) area market → (building) (land) area market

(land) area monopoly → (building) (land) area monopoly

(land) area need → (building) (land) area need

(land) area owner → (building) (land) area owner

land area per capita · Pro-Kopf-Landfläche f, Pro-Kopf-Bodenfläche

(land) area proprietor → (building) (land) area proprietor

(land) area quality → (building) (land) area quality

(land) area relocation → (building) (land) area relocation

(land) area speculation → (building) (land) area speculation

(land) area supply → (building) (land) area supply

(land) area tax → (building) (land) area tax

(land) area use, land use, use of land, use of (land) area · Bodennutzung f, Flächennutzung, Landnutzung [*Die Inanspruchnahme einer Fläche durch den Menschen für bestimmte Zwecke*]

(land) area use regulation, land use regulation · Bodenbenutzungsregelung f, Landbenutzungsregelung, Flächenbenutzungsregelung

land assignation, assignment of land, cession of land, land assignment, land cession, assignation of land · Bodenabtretung f, Landabtretung, Grund(stücks)abtretung, Grund(stücks)zession f, Bodenzession, Landzession

land at rent · zinspflichtiges Land n

Land authority · Landesbehörde f [*Bundesrepublik Deutschland*]

land availability — land clearance

land availability · Landdargebot *n*, Bodendargebot, Flächendargebot

land bank, agricultural bank, agrarian bank · Landwirtschaftsbank *f*

land bank → mortgage bank

land banking [*Acquiring land for future use by a public body*] · Landerwerb *m* durch die öffentliche Hand, Bodenerwerb durch die öffentliche Hand, Landbeschaffung *f* durch die öffentliche Hand, Bodenbeschaffung durch die öffentliche Hand, Grund(stücks)erwerb durch die öffentliche Hand, Grund(stücks)beschaffung durch die öffentliche Hand

land barrister, conveyancing barrister, (real) property barrister, (real) estate barrister, realty barrister, conveyancer · Grundstücksspezialist *m*, Grundstücksadvokat *m*

land betterment tax (Brit.); land value tax · Bodenwertzuwachssteuer *f*, Landwertzuwachssteuer, Grund(stücks)wertzuwachssteuer

land birds, land fowl · Erdgeflügel *n*, Erdvögel *m pl*

land boundary, land frontier · Landgrenze *f*

land broker → ((real) estate) broker

(land) brokerage → (real) estate broking

land brokerage company, land-broker agency, land(-jobber) agency, ((real) estate) brokerage company, (real) property brokerage company · (Boden)Maklerfirma *f*, Landmaklerfirma, Grund(stücks)maklerfirma, Bodenmakelei *f*, Grund(stücks)makelei, Landmakelei, Grund(stücks)maklerbüro *n*, Grund(stücks)maklerbüro

(land) broker agency → ((real) estate) broking firm

(land) broking → (real) estate broking

(land) broking firm → ((real) estate) broking firm

Land building authority, Land construction authority · Landesbaubehörde *f* [*Bundesrepublik Deutschland*]

Land building code, Land construction code · Landesbauordnung *f*, LandesbauO, LBO [*Bundesrepublik Deutschland*]

Land building law, Land construction law · Landesbaurecht *n* [*Bundesrepublik Deutschland*]

Land building law, Land building act, Land building statute, Land construction law, Land construction act, Land construction statute · Landesbaugesetz *n* [*Bundesrepublik Deutschland*]

Land building project, Land construction project · Landbauvorhaben *n*, Landbauprojekt *n* [*Bundesrepublik Deutschland*]

land burdens law, land encumbrances law, land charges law, land incumbrances law · Grund(stücks)belastungsrecht *n*, Grund(stücks)lastrecht, Bodenlastrecht, Landlastrecht, Liegenschaftslastrecht, Immobilienlastrecht, Immobiliarlastrecht

land business → (real) estate business

land buyer, land purchaser, purchaser of (real) estate, purchaser of (real) property, buyer of (real) estate, buyer of (real) property, vendee of (real) estate, vendee of (real) property, purchaser of realty, vendee of realty, buyer of realty · Grund(stücks)käufer *m*, Bodenkäufer *m*, Liegenschaftskäufer, Landkäufer, Immobilienkäufer, Immobiliarkäufer

land capacity → land(s) capacity

Land capital [*In the Federal Republic of Germany*]; state capital · Landeshauptstadt *f*

Land central bank, central Land bank [*The Deutsche Bundesbank delegates its function of "lender of last resort" to the branches of the Landeszentralbanken, with which it is essential to maintain a balance if a German bank wishes to borrow from the central bank*] · Landeszentralbank *f*

land certifier → (real) property appraiser

land cession, assignation of land, land assignation, assignment of land, cession of land, land assignment · Bodenabtretung *f*, Landabtretung, Grund(stücks)abtretung, Grund(stücks)zession *f*, Bodenzession, Landzession

land charge, land(s) encumbrance, land(s) incumbrance, encumbrance on land(s), incumbrance on land(s) [*Land charges are those rights and interests affecting land, e.g., estate contracts, restrictive covenants, general equitable charges and easements*] · Grund(stücks)belastung *f*, Grund(stücks)last *f*, Bodenlast, Landlast, Liegenschaftslast, Immobilienlast, Immobiliarlast

land charges act, LCA · Grund(stücks)lastgesetz *n*

land charges law, land incumbrances law, land burdens law, land encumbrances law · Grund(stücks)belastungsrecht *n*, Grund(stücks)lastrecht, Bodenlastrecht, Landlastrecht, Liegenschaftslastrecht, Immobilienlastrecht, Immobiliarlastrecht

(land) charges register → (land) encumbrances register

land city → (in)land town

land clearance → (building) land clearance

land clearance cost(s) → (building) land clearance cost(s)

land code → (building) land code

land code law → (building) land code law

Land Commission Act 1967 [*England*] · Gesetz *n* zur Errichtung einer staatlichen Bodenanstalt

land commissioners for England, copyhold inclosure and tithe commission, copyhold inclosure and tithe commission · Zehnt- und Einfriedungskommission *f*

land company → (real) estate company

land compensation act, land compensation statute, land compensation law, land indemnification act, land indemnification statute, land indemnification law, land damages act, land damages statute, land damages law, land indemnity act, land indemnity statute, land indemnity law · Bodenentschädigungsgesetz *n*, Landentschädigungsgesetz, Grund(stücks)entschädigungsgesetz, Grund(stücks)schadenersatzgesetz, Bodenschadenersatzgesetz, Landschadenersatzgesetz

land compensation action → (real) estate compensation (court) action

land compensation (court) action → (real) estate compensation (court) action

land compensation practice, land indemnification practice, land indemnity practice, land damages practice · Grund(stücks)schadenersatzwesen *n*, Grund(stücks)entschädigungswesen, Bodenschadenersatzwesen, Bodenentschädigungswesen, Landschadenersatzwesen, Landentschädigungswesen

(land) condemnation (US); (land) expropriation · Bodenenteignung *f*, (Land)Enteignung, enteignender Eingriff *m*

(land) condemnation act (US) → (land) expropriation act

(land) condemnation authority (US); (land) expropriation authority · Bodenenteignungsbehörde *f*, (Land)Enteignungsbehörde

(land) condemnation for opening up (US); (land) expropriation for opening up · Aufschließungsenteignung *f*

(land) condemnation for substitute interest (US); (land) expropriation for substitute right, (land) expropriation for substitute interest; (land) condemnation for substitute right (US) · Ersatzrecht(land)enteignung *f*, Ersatzrechtbodenenteignung [*Diese Enteignung ersetzt entzogene Rechte durch neue*]

(land) condemnation law (US) → (land) expropriation act

(land) condemnation legislation, (land) condemnation lawmaking (US); (land) expropriation legislation, (land) expropriation lawmaking · Enteignungsgesetzgebung *f*, Landenteignungsgesetzgebung, Bodenenteignungsgesetzgebung

(land) condemnation order (US); compulsory (land) purchase order, (land) expropriation order, declaratory order · Bodenenteignungsanordnung *f*, Bodenenteignungsverfügung, Bodenenteignungsbefehl *m*, Bodenenteignungsgebot *n*, (Land)Enteignungsanordnung, (Land)Enteignungsverfügung, (Land)-Enteignungsbefehl, (Land)Enteignungsgebot

(land) condemnation plan (US); (land) expropriation plan · (Boden)Enteignungsplan *m*, Landenteignungsplan

(land) condemnation procedure (US); (land) expropriation procedure · (Land)Enteignungsverfahren *n*, Bodenenteignungsverfahren

(land) condemnation statute (US) → (land) expropriation act

(land) condemnation theory (US); (land) expropriation theory · Enteignungstheorie *f*, Landenteignungstheorie, Bodenenteignungstheorie

land conservation, preservation of land, conservation of land, land preservation · Landeserhaltung *f*, Landespflege *f*

(land) consolidation, (land) merger · Landverschmelzung *f*, Bodenverschmelzung, Bodenzusammenlegung, (Land)Zusammenlegung, (Flur)Verschmelzung, Flurzusammenlegung, Konsolidation *f*, Verkoppelung, Grund(stücks)zusammenlegung, Grund(stücks)verschmelzung, Feldzusammenlegung, Feldverschmelzung

(land) consolidation legislation, (land) consolidation lawmaking, (land) merger legislation, (land) merger lawmaking · Landverschmelzungsgesetzgebung *f*, Bodenverschmelzungsgesetzgebung, Flurzusammenlegungsgesetzgebung, Feldzusammenlegungsgesetzgebung

land consortium → (real) estate syndicate

Land constitution · Landesverfassung *f* [*Bundesrepublik Deutschland*]

Land construction authority, Land building authority · Landesbaubehörde *f* [*Bundesrepublik Deutschland*]

Land construction code, Land building code · Landesbauordnung *f*, LandesbauO, LBO [*Bundesrepublik Deutschland*]

Land construction law, Land building law · Landesbaurecht *n* [*Bundesrepublik Deutschland*]

Land construction law, Land construction act, Land construction statute, Land building law, Land building act, Land building statute · Landesbaugesetz *n* [*Bundesrepublik Deutschland*]

Land construction project, Land building project · Landbauvorhaben *n*, Landbauprojekt *n* [*Bundesrepublik Deutschland*]

land-consuming · landfressend

land consumption, area consumption, consumption of land, consumption of area · Bodenbeanspruchung *f*, Landbeanspruchung, Flächenbeanspruchung, Flächenverbrauch *m*, Bodenverbrauch, Landverbrauch

land contract, realty contract, (real) estate contract, (real) property contract · Grundstücksvertrag *m*, Landvertrag, Bodenvertrag

land contract → (real) estate (purchase) contract

land contract (US) · Hauskaufvertrag *m* mit Eigentumsvorbehalt [*In den USA ein Vertrag zum Hauskauf ohne Übertragung von Eigentumsrechten auf den Käufer. Der Kauflustige wohnt vorläufig zur Miete, aber mit Anrecht auf Kauf, nachdem die im Vertrag vorgesehenen Zahlungen geleistet wurden*]

land control, (real) estate control, (real) property control, realty control · Grundstückslenkung *f*, Bodenlenkung, Landlenkung

land conveyance, conveyance (of land), (voluntary) transfer (of land), (voluntary) land transfer · freiwillige Übertragung (von Land), freiwillige Landübertragung, freiwillige Bodenübertragung

land conveyance law, law of conveyances (of land), law of land conveyances, law of voluntary transfer, voluntary transfer law, conveyance law · Auflassungsrecht *n*, freiwilliges Übertragungsrecht

land country [*As distinguished from a maritime country*] · Landstaat *m*

land court → (building) land court

land coverage [*The area of a lot covered by structures as compared to the total lot area*] · bebaute Grund(stücks)fläche *f*; überbaute Gund(stücks)fläche [*Schweiz*]

land credit → (real) estate credit

land credit bank → land(s) credit bank

land cultivation, field cultivation, farming, soil cultivation, agricultural use, cultivation (of land), cultivation of fields, cultivation of soil · Anbau *m*, Bodenkultivierung *f*, Landkultivierung, Bodenkultur *f*, Feldbau

land damages act → land compensation act

land damages law → land compensation act

land damages statute → land compensation act

land dealer → ((real) estate) broker

land dearth → land(s) dearth

land decoration · Landesverschönerung *f*

land demise → (building) (land) area tenancy

land depreciation fund → (real) estate depreciation fund

land dereliction, (accretion by) dereliction (of land) · (Land)Anwachs(ung) *m*, (f) durch Meeresspiegelsenkung, (Land)Zuwachs durch Meeresspiegelsenkung, (Land)Anwachs(ung) durch zurückweichendes Wasser, (Land)Zuwachs durch zurückweichendes Wasser, (Land)Gewinnung durch zurückweichendes Wasser

land desertion, desertion of land · Flurwüstung *f*

land designated for expropriation; land designated for condemnation (US); designated land · enteignungsbestimmter Boden *m*, enteignungsbestimmtes Land *n*

land developer · (Land)Erschließungsträger *m*

land disposal → (ab)alienation of (real) estate

land drainage · Landentwässerung *f*

land drainage act, land drainage law, land drainage statute · Landentwässerungsgesetz *n*

land drainage law · Landentwässerungsrecht *n*

land drainage scheme · Landentwässerungsplan *m*

landed aristocracy · Landadel *m*, Grundadel

land(ed) estate for life → (real) estate for life

(land(ed)) estate in remainder → remainder (land(ed)) estate

landed estate law → (real) estate law

landed estate possessor → (real) estate possessor

landed estate that cannot be broken up on inheritance · Landgut *n*

landed estate title → (real) estate title

landed interest · Grundeigentümer(klasse) *m pl, (f)*

landed owner, (building) land proprietor, (building) (land) area owner, (building) (land) (area) proprietor, (building) land owner, proprietor of (the) (building) land, owner of (the) (building) land, landed proprietor · (Bau)Bodeneigentümer m, (Bau)Flächeneigentümer, (Bau)Landeigentümer, (Bau)Landherr, (Bau)Bodeneigner, (Bau)Flächeneigner, (Bau)Landeigner

land(ed) ownership → freehold estate

landed property, estate [*Piece of land containing a residence*] · Grundstück n mit Wohnhaus bebaut

land(ed) property, tenancy (of land(s)); immov(e)ables [*International Private Law*]; (real) estate, (real) property, realty, estate in land(s), immov(e)able estate, fixed estate, landholding [*Estates in land(s) are divided into (a) freehold estates and (b) estates less than freehold*] · Bodenbesitz(stand) m, Grund(stücks)besitz(stand), Landbesitz(stand), Immobilienbesitz(stand), Immobiliarbesitz(stand), Liegenschaft(en) f (pl), Immobilie(n) f (pl), (unbeweglicher) Besitz(stand), liegendes Gut n, ungereides Gut

land(ed) property for life → (real) property for life

land(ed) property possessor → (real) estate possessor

landed property register → land register

land(ed) property tax · Grundvermögenssteuer f

land(ed) property title → (real) estate title

landed proprietor, landed owner, (building) land proprietor, (building) (land) area owner, (building) (land) (area) proprietor, (building) land owner, proprietor of (the) (building) land, owner of (the) (building) land · (Bau)Bodeneigentümer m, (Bau)Flächeneigentümer, (Bau)Landeigentümer, (Bau)Landherr, (Bau)Bodeneigner, (Bau)Flächeneigner, (Bau)Landeigner

landed servitude, pr(a)edial servitude; servitus praediorum [*Latin*]; real servitude [*A servitude affecting land*] · Realservitut n, f, Prädialservitut

landed terms · Preis m einschließlich Fracht- und Löschkosten

land encumbrance → land(s) encumbrance

land encumbrances law, land charges law, land incumbrances law, land burdens law · Grund(stücks)belastungsrecht n, Grund(stücks)lastrecht, Bodenlastrecht, Landlastrecht, Liegenschaftslastrecht, Immobilienlastrecht

land estate → land(s) estate

land estate for life → (real) estate for life

(land) estate in remainder → remainder (land(ed)) estate

land (e)valuation → (real) property (e)valuation

land exchange contract, excambion [*Scot law. A contract whereby one piece of land is exchanged for another*] · Landtauschvertrag m, Bodentauschvertrag, Flächentauschvertrag

(land) expropriation; (land) condemnation (US) · Bodenenteignung f, (Land)Enteignung, enteignender Eingriff m

(land) expropriation act, (land) expropriation law, (land) expropriation statute; (land) condemnation statute, (land) condemnation act, (land) condemnation law (US) · Enteignungsgesetz n, Landenteignungsgesetz, Bodenenteignungsgesetz

(land) expropriation authority; (land) condemnation authority (US) · Bodenenteignungsbehörde f, (Land)Enteignungsbehörde

(land) expropriation for substitute right, (land) expropriation for substitute interest; (land) condemnation for substitute right, (land) condemnation for substitute interest (US) · Ersatzrecht(land)enteigung f, Ersatzrechtbodenenteignung [*Diese Enteignung ersetzt entzogene Rechte durch neue*]

(land) expropriation for opening up; (land) condemnation for opening up (US) · Aufschließungsenteignung f

(land) expropriation law → (land) expropriation act

(land) expropriation legislation, (land) expropriation lawmaking; (land) condemnation legislation, (land) condemnation lawmaking (US) · Enteignungsgesetzgebung f, Landenteignungsgesetzgebung, Bodenenteignungsgesetzgebung

(land) expropriation order, declaratory order; (land) condemnation order (US); compulsory (land) purchase order · Bodenenteignungsanordnung f, Bodenenteignungsverfügung, Bodenenteignungsbefehl m, Bodenenteignungsgebot n, (Land)Enteignungsanordnung, (Land)Enteignungsverfügung, (Land)-Enteignungsbefehl, (Land)-Enteignungsgebot

(land) expropriation plan; (land) condemnation plan (US) · (Boden)Enteignungsplan m, Landenteignungsplan

(land) expropriation procedure; (land) condemnation procedure (US) · (Land)Enteignungsverfahren n, Bodenenteignungsverfahren

(land) expropriation statute → (land) expropriation act

(land) expropriation theory; (land) condemnation theory (US) · Enteignungstheorie f, Landenteignungstheorie, Bodenenteignungstheorie

Land — (land) holder

Land [*Federal Republic of Germany*], (federal) state, constituent state [*USA*] · Staat *m* [*USA*]; (Bundes)Land *n* [*Bundesrepublik Deutschland*]

land field → field of (real) estate

land finance act → (real) estate finance act

land financing → (real) estate financing

land firm → (real) estate firm

land for afforestation, afforestation land · Aufforstungsland *n*, Aufforstungsboden *m*, Aufforstungsfläche *f*

land for car parking · Parkplatzland *n*

land for digging · Grabeland *n*

Land forest law · Landeswaldrecht *n*, Landesforstrecht [*Bundesrepublik Deutschland*]

land for ferries · Fährland *n*

land for long-distance routes · Fernstreckenland *n*

land for mixed development → (building) land for mixed development

land for pipelines · Rohrfernleitungsland *n*

land for potential industrial development, potential industrial land · Industrieerwartungsland *n*

land for road construction, land for highway construction, land for road works, land for highway works, road (construction) land, highway (construction) land · Straßenbauboden *m*, Straßenbaufläche *f*, Straßen(bau)land *n*

land for short-distance routes · Nahstreckenland *n*

land for traffic purposes · Boden *m* für Verkehrszwecke, Grund *m* für Verkehrszwecke, Land *n* für Verkehrszwecke

land fowl, land birds · Erdgeflügel *n*, Erdvögel *mpl*

land freight · Landfracht *f*

land frontier, land boundary · Landgrenze *f*

Land fund, fund of a Land · Landesmittel *f*, Landesfonds *m* [*Bundesrepublik Deutschland*]

land fund → (real) estate fund

Land government, Land administration · Landesregierung *f* [*Bundesrepublik Deutschland*]

land-grabbing · Erwerb *m* von Grund und Boden, Erwerbung *f* von Grund und Boden [*Im England des 14., 15. und 16. Jahrhunderts*]

land grant → land(s) grant

landgrave · Landgraf *m*

Land groundwater service · Landesgrundwasserdienst *m* [*Bundesrepublik Deutschland*]

Land growth · Landesentwick(e)lung *f* [*Bundesrepublik Deutschland*]

Land growth plan · Landesentwick(e)lungsplan *m* [*Bundesrepublik Deutschland*]

Land growth planning · Landesentwick(e)lungsplanung *f* [*Bundesrepublik Deutschland*]

Land growth programme; Land growth program (US) · Landesentwick(e)lungsprogramm *n* [*Bundesrepublik Deutschland*]

Land growth programme law; Land growth program law (US) · Landesentwick(e)lungsprogrammrecht *n* [*Bundesrepublik Deutschland*]

land held by copy of court roll, land held by copi of court roll, copyhold land, copihold land · Hintersassenland *n*, Regalland, Schriftsassenland, Schriftgutland

land held in absolute ownership, absolute ownership land, alody, inheritable land, al(l)odial land, free land · allodiales Land *n*, erbeigenes Land, leh(e)n(s)freies Land, absolutes Land, unbeschränktes Land, uneingeschränktes Land, unbegrenztes Land, zinsfreies Land, Allodialland

land held of a lord → land(s) of (a) manor

land held of a lord, land in fee; feodum, feudum, tenementum [*Latin*]; feu [*Scots law*]; fee (tenure) (of land), fief, tenancy, land tenure, feud, feod, tenement, (feodal) tenure (of land) · Leh(e)n *n*, Leh(e)n(s)gut *n*, Leh(e)n(s)besitz *m*, leh(e)n(s)rechtlicher (Grund)Besitz(stand) *m*, Benefizium *n*

land held on trust for sale · Land *n* für treuhänderischen Verkauf

Land highway construction, Land road construction, highway construction of a Land, road construction of a Land · Landesstraßenbau *m* [*Bundesrepublik Deutschland*]

land holder → (real) estate possessor

(land) holder, (land) lessee, (land) tenant, (land) occupier, (real) estate holder, (real) estate lessee, (real) estate tenant, (real) estate occupier, (real) property holder, (real) property lessee, (real) property tenant, (real) property occupier, realty tenant, realty holder, realty lessee, realty occupier, tenant of land, holder of land, tenant of (real) estate, holder of (real) estate, tenant of (real) property, holder of (real) property, leaseholder; tacksman [*Scots law*]; terretenant, tertenant [*Norman French*] [*Das Wort "tenant" bezeichnet im englischen Recht jede Person, welche die Nutzung eines Grundstücks, aber nicht das vollständige Eigentum hat, also den*

Vasallen, den Nießbraucher und den Pächter. Da das vollständige Eigentum in England außer der Krone niemandem zusteht, sind alle Inhaber genau genommen nur "tenants". Im gewöhnlichen Sprachgebrauch wird indessen die Benennung "owner" für Vasallen und beschränkte Eigentümer gebraucht: nur die Pächter werden stets als "tenants" bezeichnet] · Pächter *m*, Landpächter, Bodenpächter, Grund(stücks)pächter

(land) holder at will, (land) lessee at will, (land) tenant at will, (land) occupier at will, tenant of land at will, holder of land at will, lessee (of land) at will, leaseholder (of land) at will, occupier (of land) at will, land leaseholder at will · jederzeit kündbarer (Land)Pächter *m*, jederzeit kündbarer Bodenpächter, jederzeit kündbarer Grund(stücks)pächter, willkürlich kündbarer (Land)Pächter, willkürlich kündbarer Bodenpächter, willkürlich kündbarer Grund(stücks)pächter, all(e)zeit kündbarer (Land)Pächter, all(e)zeit kündbarer Bodenpächter, all(e)zeit kündbarer Grund(stücks)pächter, Prekarist *m*

(land) holder for life → life (land) lessee

(land) holder from year to year, (land) lessee from year to year, (land) tenant from year to year, (land) occupier from year to year, tenant of land from year to year, holder of land from year to year, lessee (of land) from year to year, occupier (of land) from year to year, yearly (land) holder, yearly lessee, yearly tenant, yearly occupier · (Land)Pächter *m* von Jahr zu Jahr, Bodenpächter von Jahr zu Jahr, Grund(stücks)pächter von Jahr zu Jahr

(land) holder paying in products of the soil, (land) holder paying in kind, in-kind lessee, in-kind leaseholder, in-kind (land) holder, leaseholder paying in products of the soil, lessee paying in products of the soil, leaseholder paying in kind, lessee paying in kind · Natural(ien)pächter *m*

(land) holder's association, leaseholder's association, tenant's association, lessee's association · Pächtergenossenschaft *f*, Pachtgenossenschaft

(land)holder's lien · Pächterpfandrecht *n*

landholding, land(ed) property, tenancy (of land(s)); immov(e)ables [*International Private Law*]; (real) estate, (real) property, realty, estate in land(s), immov(e)able estate, fixed estate [*Estates in land(s) are divided into (a) freehold estates and (b) estates less than freehold*] · Bodenbesitz(stand) *m*, Grund(stücks)besitz(stand), Landbesitz(stand), Immobilienbesitz(stand), Immobiliarbesitz(stand), Liegenschaft(en) *f (pl)*, Immobilie(n) *f (pl)*, (unbeweglicher) Besitz(stand), liegendes Gut *n*, ungereites Gut

land(holding) title → (real) estate title

land-hunger, greed for land · Landhunger *m*

landimer [*old Scots law*], (land) surveyor · (Land)Vermesser *m*

(land) improvement, building land improvement, improvement to land, installation of improvements [*Facilities, usually public utilities, such as sidewalks or sewers, added to land which increase its usefulness*] · Erschließung, (Bau)Landerschließung, (Bau)Bodenerschließung, (Bau)Flächenerschließung, (Bau)Geländeerschließung, (Bau)Terrainerschließung, Baureifmachung, Zuwegung

land improvement, agricultural melioration, agricultural improvement, soil improvement, land melioration · (Boden)Melioration *f*, landwirtschaftliche Verbesserung *f*, Landmelioration [*Maßnahmen zur Verbesserung der Standortbedingungen für die Kulturpflanzen*]

(land) improvement advantage · (Land)Erschließungsvorteil *m*

(land) improvement application, (land) improvement request · Erschließungsgesuch *n*, Erschließungsantrag *m*, Landerschließungsgesuch, Landerschließungsantrag

(land) improvement burden, (land) improvement encumbrance, (land) improvement incumbrance, (land) improvement charge · Erschließungslast *f*, Erschließungsabgabe *f*, Landerschließungslast, Landerschließungsabgabe

(land) improvement charge, (land) improvement burden, (land) improvement encumbrance, (land) improvement incumbrance · Erschließungslast *f*, Erschließungsabgabe *f*, Landerschließungslast, Landerschließungsabgabe

(land) improvement contract · Erschließungsvertrag *m*, Landerschließungsvertrag

(land) improvement contract law · Erschließungsvertragsrecht *n*, Landerschließungsvertragsrecht

(land) improvement contribution · Erschließungsbeitrag *m*

(land) improvement contribution by(e)-law, (land) improvement contribution statute · Erschließungsbeitragssatzung *f*

(land) improvement corporation · Erschließungskörperschaft *f*, Erschließungskorporation *f*, Landerschließungskörperschaft, Landerschließungskorporation

(land) improvement cost(s), cost(s) of (land) improvement · (Land)Erschließungskosten *f*

(land) improvement credit — landing account

(land) improvement credit · (Land)Erschließungskredit *m*

(land) improvement duty · Erschließungspflicht *f*, Landerschließungspflicht

(land) improvement encumbrance, (land) improvement incumbrance, (land) improvement charge, (land) improvement burden · Erschließungslast *f*, Erschließungsabgabe *f*, Landerschließungslast, Landerschließungsabgabe

(land) improvement expenditure · Erschließungsaufwand *m*

(land) improvement gain, (land) improvement profit · Erschließungsgewinn *m*, Erschließungsprofit *m*, Landerschließungsgewinn, Landerschließungsprofit

(land) improvement highway, (land) improvement road · (Land)Erschließungsstraße *f*

(land) improvement incumbrance, (land) improvement charge, (land) improvement burden, (land) improvement encumbrance · Erschließungslast *f*, Erschließungsabgabe *f*, Landerschließungslast, Landerschließungsabgabe

(land) improvement indicator · Erschließungsindikator *m*, Landerschließungsindikator

(land) improvement law · (objektives) (Land)Erschließungsrecht *n*

land improvement loan → (building) land improvement loan

(land) improvement measure · (Land)Erschließungsmaßnahme *f*

(land) improvement pattern, (land) improvement scheme · Erschließungsmuster *n*, Erschließungsschema *n*, Landerschließungsmuster, Landerschließungsschema

(land) improvement permission · Erschließungsgenehmigung *f*, Erschließungserlaubnis *f*, Landerschließungsgenehmigung, Landerschließungserlaubnis

(land) improvement plan · Erschließungsplan *m*, Landerschließungsplan

(land) improvement planning · Erschließungsplanung *f*, Landerschließungsplanung

(land) improvement profit, (land) improvement gain · Erschließungsgewinn *m*, Erschließungsprofit *m*, Landerschließungsgewinn, Landerschließungsprofit

(land) improvement programme; (land) improvement program (US) · Erschließungsprogramm *n*, Landerschließungsprogramm

(land) improvement project · Erschließungsprojekt *n*, Landerschließungsprojekt

land improvement provision → (building) land improvement provision

(land) improvement request, (land) improvement application · Erschließungsgesuch *n*, Erschließungsantrag *m*, Landerschließungsgesuch, Landerschließungsantrag

(land) improvement road, (land) improvement highway · (Land)Erschließungsstraße *f*

(land) improvement scheme, (land) improvement pattern · Erschließungsmuster *n*, Erschließungsschema *n*, Landerschließungsmuster, Landerschließungsschema

(land) improvement structure, (land) improvement physical facility, (land) improvement work · Erschließungswerk *n*, Erschließungsbauwerk, Erschließungsbaulichkeit *f*, Erschließungs(bau)anlage *f*, Erschließungsbau *m*; Erschließungsbaute *f* [*Schweiz*]

(land) improvement system · (Land)Erschließungssystem *n*

(land) improvement unit · (Land)Erschließungseinheit *f*

(land) improvement zone · Erschließungszone *f*, Landerschließungszone

land increase · Flächenvermehrung *f*, Landvermehrung, Bodenvermehrung [*durch Abdeichen, Roden, Meliorationen*]

land incumbrance → land(s) incumbrance

land incumbrances law, land burdens law, land encumbrances law, land charges law · Grund(stücks)belastungsrecht *n*, Grund(stücks)lastrecht, Bodenlastrecht, Landlastrecht, Liegenschaftslastrecht, Immobilienlastrecht

land indemnification act → land compensation act

land indemnification (court) action → (real) estate compensation (court) action

land indemnification law → land compensation act

land indemnification statute → land compensation act

land indemnity act → land compensation act

land indemnity (court) action → (real) estate compensation (court) action

land indemnity law → land compensation act

land indemnity statute → land compensation act

land in fee → land held of a lord

landing account · Bescheinigung *f* über gelöschtes Gut

landing (place); bunder [*Anglo-Indian*] [*A place on a navigable water for loading and unloading goods, or for the reception and delivery of passengers*] · Landestelle *f*, Schiff(s)anlegestelle

land in its natural state, virgin land · jungfräuliches Land *n*

land inquiry committee · Untersuchungsausschuß *m* für innere Kolonisation

(land in) run-rig, (land in) run-dale [*Scotland*] · Innenfeld *n* [*Landwirtschaft*]

land insurance → land(s) insurance

land in (the lord's) demesne, bordland, table demesne, home farm (of the lord of the manor), demesnial settlement; terra indominicata terra dominica [*Latin*]; demain (land), demeyne (land), demeine (land), demesne (land), inland [*Those lands of a manor not granted out in tenancy, but reserved by the lord for his own use and occupation. The opposite of "tenemental lands"*] · Hoffeld *n*, Salland *n*, grundherrliches Eigenland, Hofländerei *f*, Hofland, grundherrschaftliches Eigenland

land investment → (real) estate investment

land investment trust → land(s) investment trust

land in villanage, villanage land, land in ville(i)nage, ville(i)nage land [*It was in the occupation of tenants, but held in villanage, at the will of the lord, and at customary services*] · Hörigenland *n*, Leibeigenschaftsland, höriges Land

Land joint planning board, Land standing conference of planning boards · Landesplanungsgemeinschaft *f* [*Bundesrepublik Deutschland. Eine unmittelbar kraft Gesetzes bestehende Planungsgemeinschaft*]

landlady · Hauswirtin *f*

Land law, Land statute, Land act · Landesgesetz *n* [*Bundesrepublik Deutschland*]

Land law, law of the Land · Landesrecht *n* [*Bundesrepublik Deutschland*]

land law → building land law

land law → (real) estate law

Land lawmaker, Land legislator · Landesgesetzgeber *m* [*Bundesrepublik Deutschland*]

Land lawmaking, Land legislation · Landesgesetzgebung *f* [*Bundesrepublik Deutschland*]

land lawmaking → (building) land legislation

land lease → (building) (land) area tenancy

(land) lease (agreement) → (real) estate lease (agreement)

land lease(hold) → (real) estate lease(hold)

land lease(hold) → (building) (land) area tenancy

(land) leaseholder at will → (land) holder at will

land lease law, land lease act, land lease statute, land tenancy law, land tenancy act, land tenancy statute · Bodenpachtgesetz *n*, (Land)Pachtgesetz

land lease rent, land tenancy rent, rent for land on lease, rent for land tenancy · Bodenpachtabgabe *f*, (Land)Pachtabgabe

land lease statute → land lease law

land leasing → (real) estate leasing

Land legislation, Land lawmaking · Landesgesetzgebung *f* [*Bundesrepublik Deutschland*]

land legislation → (building) land legislation

Land legislator, Land lawmaker · Landesgesetzgeber *m* [*Bundesrepublik Deutschland*]

landless · landlos, landbesitzlos

(land) lessee → (land) holder

(land) lessee at will → (land) holder at will

(land) lessee from year to year → (land) holder from year to year

landlessness · Landlosigkeit *f*

land lessor, lessor (of land), landlord [*He of whom land is held*] · Landpachtherr *m*, (Boden)Pachtherr, Landverpächter, (Boden)Verpächter, Grund(stücks)verpächter, Grund(stücks)pachtherr

landless person · landlose Person *f*

land let to a farm; terra affirmata [*Latin*] · landwirtschaftliches Pachtland *n*

Land Lieutenant; capitalis justitiarius [*Latin*] [*In the British Empire*] · Statthalter *m*

land limitation act → (real) property limitation act

land liquidated damages (court) action → (real) estate compensation (court) action

landlocked [*An expression sometimes applied to a piece of land belonging to one person and surrounded by land belonging to another person or other persons, so that it cannot be approached except over his or their land*] · eingeschlossen

land-locked sea · Binnenmeer *n*

land-locked state · Binnenstaat *m*

landlord — land not built upon

landlord [*He of whom tenements are held*] · (Wohnungs)Vermieter *m*, Hauswirt, Mietherr

landlord, grantor, feoffor, feoffer, manor lord, langeman, bestower of a fee, feudal chief; dominus directus, feoffator [*Latin*]; (feudal) lord, chief lord, possessory lord, liege-lord, over lord, lord of (the) manor, supreme owner, superior lord · Leh(e)n(s)herr *m*, Feudalherr, (feudaler) Belehner, Leh(e)n(s)gutgeber, Obereigentümer, Landübertragende, Übertragende von Land

landlord, land lessor, lessor (of land) [*He of whom land is held*] · Landpachtherr *m*, (Boden)Pachtherr, Landverpächter, (Boden)Verpächter, Grund(stücks)verpächter, Grund(stücks)pachtherr

landlord and tenant, lessor and lessee [*(real) estate*] · Verpächter *m* und Pächter, Pachtherr und Pächter

landlord and tenant · Hauswirt *m* und Mieter *m*

landlord and tenant act (Brit.); tenants' protection law, tenants' protection act, tenants' protection statute · Mieterschutzgesetz *n*

landlord and tenant system · zweifaches Eigentumssystem *n*, doppeltes Eigentumssystem

landlord/tenant contract → dwelling contract

landlord/tenant law, (residential) rent law, dwelling rent law, law of landlord and tenant · Mietrecht *n*, Wohnungsmietrecht [*Sammelbegriff für alle für die Mietverhältnisse maßgebenden rechtlichen Vorschriften*]

landlord/tenant lease → (residential) landlord/tenant lease

landlord/tenant relation(ship) → (residential) landlord/tenant relation(ship)

landlord/tenant relation(ship) at sufferance, tenancy at sufferance, tenure at sufferance · Mietverhältnis *n* auf Duldung, geduldetes Mietverhältnis [*Es liegt vor, wenn ein Mieter sein ursprünglich rechtmäßiges Mietverhältnis unrechtmäßig verlängert*]

landlord/tenant relation(ship) at will, tenancy at will, tenure at will [*It is created by any letting for a time not limited. Such a tenancy is determinable at the will of either landlord or tenant, even though it be expressed to be determinable at the will of the landlord only*] · jederzeit kündbares Mietverhältnis *n*, all(e)zeit kündbares Mietverhältnis, willkürlich kündbares Mietverhältnis, einvernehmlich geduldetes Mietverhältnis

landlordism · Vermietertum *n*

landlordism · Verpächtertum *n*

landlord-slanted · vermieterfreundlich

landlord's lien · (Wohnungs)Vermieterpfandrecht *n*

landlord title, lessor title · Pachtherrentitel *m*, Verpächtertitel

land management → land(s) management

land management code → land(s) management code

land manager → land(s) manager

landmark, monument · festes Seezeichen *n*, Landmarke *f*

land market → (building) land market

land (market) submodel · Bodenmarkt-Untermodell *n*, Untermodell über den Bodenmarkt

land mass [*It is given in square kilometres or square miles*] · Bodenfläche *f*, Landfläche

land matter → (building) land matter

land measure, measure of land · Landmaß *n*

land melioration, land improvement, agricultural melioration, agricultural improvement, soil improvement · (Boden)Melioration *f*, landwirtschaftliche Verbesserung *f*, Landmelioration [*Maßnahmen zur Verbesserung der Standortbedingungen für die Kulturpflanzen*]

(land) merger, (land) consolidation · Landverschmelzung *f*, Bodenverschmelzung, Bodenzusammenlegung, (Land)Zusammenlegung, (Flur)Verschmelzung, Flurzusammenlegung, Konsolidation *f*, Verkoppelung, Grund(stücks)zusammenlegung, Grund(stücks)verschmelzung, Feldzusammenlegung, Feldverschmelzung

(land) merger lawmaking, (land) consolidation legislation, (land) consolidation lawmaking, (land) merger legislation · Landverschmelzungsgesetzgebung *f*, Bodenverschmelzungsgesetzgebung, Flurzusammenlegungsgesetzgebung, Feldzusammenlegungsgesetzgebung

land mobility → land(s) mobility

land monopoly → (building) land monopoly

land nationalization → land(s) nationalization

Land nature reserve · Landesnaturschutzgebiet *n* [*Bundesrepublik Deutschland*]

land need → (building) (land) area need

land not built upon, unbuilt land, open land, uncovered land · freier Boden *m*, freier Grund, unbebauter Boden, nichtbebauter Boden, unbebautes Land *n*, freies Land, nichtbebautes Land, unbebauter Grund, nichtbebauter Grund

land occupancy · Landbelegung *f*

(land) occupier → (land) holder

(land) occupier at will → (land) holder at will

(land) occupier from year to year → (land) holder from year to year

land of (a) manor → land(s) of (a) manor

land of tenure → land(s) of (a) manor

land of the people, folkland, folcland, falkland; terra popularis [*Latin*]; ager publicus [*Latin*] [*Anglo-Saxon land law. Folcland was held by customary law, without written title. Inheritance depended on custom. It could not be (ab)alienated without the consent of those who had some interest in it*] · Volksland *n*

land of the public, public land · Land *n* der öffentlichen Hand, öffentliches Land

Land-owned · landeseigen [*Bundesrepublik Deutschland*]

landowner, squire · Gutsbesitzer *m*, Gutsherr

land owner → (real) property owner

land owner → (building) land owner

land owner operator, land owner specificator, owner farmer · Eigentumslandwirt *m*, selbstbewirtschaftender Landeigentümer

landowners' association, association of landowners · Grundeigentümergenossenschaft *f*, Genossenschaft von Grundeigentümern

land ownership → freehold estate

(land) ownership rule [*The owner of the surface of land owns everything beneath the land as well*] · Eigentumsregel *f*, Landeigentumsregel, Bodeneigentumsregel

landowner's mining · Grundeigentümerbergbau *m*

(land) parcel area, plot area · Grundstücksfläche *f*

(land) parcel for exchange → plot (of land) for exchange

(land) parcel not built upon, parcel of land not built upon, uncovered plot, unbuilt plot, open plot, uncovered (land) parcel, uncovered parcel of land · nichtbebautes Grundstück *n*, unbebautes Grundstück, freies Grundstück, nichtbenutztes Grundstück, Feldgrundstück

land pattern → area(l) pattern

land piece, piece of land, portion of land, land portion · Landstück *n*

land planning · Landplanung *f*, Bodenplanung, Flächenplanung

Land planning · Landesplanung *f* [*Bundesrepublik Deutschland. Die auf das Gebiet eines Bundeslandes unter Berücksichtigung der nachbarschaftlichen Räume bezogene Planung. Mitunter wird darunter auch derjenige Teil der Planung verstanden, der mit den Mitteln übergeordneter und zusammenfassender Raumordnungspläne und -programme arbeitet*]

Land planning advisory council, Land planning advisory panel, advisory council for Land planning, advisory panel for Land planning, advisory Land planning council, advisory Land planning panel · Landesplanungbeirat *m* [*Bundesrepublik Deutschland*]

Land planning law, Land planning act, Land planning statute · Landesplanungsgesetz *n* [*Bundesrepublik Deutschland*]

Land planning office · Landesplanungsstelle *f* [*Bundesrepublik Deutschland*]

Land planning work(s) · Landesplanungsarbeit(en) *f (pl)* [*Bundesrepublik Deutschland*]

land plenty · Landfülle *f*

land plot for barter → plot (of land) for exchange

land policy → building land policy

land policy → land(s) policy

land portion, land piece, piece of land, portion of land · Landstück *n*

land possession for life → (real) estate for life

land possessor → (real) estate possessor

land power · Landmacht *f*

land practice → real estate practice

land preservation, land conservation, preservation of land, conservation of land · Landeserhaltung *f*, Landespflege *f*

land pressure · Übervölkerungsdruck *m*

land price, price of land · Bodenpreis *m*, Baubodenpreis, (Bau)Landpreis, Liegenschaftspreis, Grund(stücks)preis

land price peak · Bodenpreisspitze *f*, Bodenpreiskulmination *f*

land problem · Bodenfrage *f*, Landfrage

land profiteering, land price-kiting · Bodenpreistreiberei *f*, Bodenpreiswucher *m*

land property → land(ed) property

land property for life → (real) property for life

land property possessor → (real) estate possessor

land property tax → land(ed) property tax

land property title — land register law

land property title → (real) estate title

land proprietor → (building) land proprietor

land proprietor → (real) property owner

land protection · Landesschutz *m*

land purchase → (building) land purchase

land (purchase) contract → (real) property (purchase) contract

land purchaser → land buyer

land quality → (building) land quality

(land) reclamation district → (land(s)) reclamation district

land record, land register, land registry, register of deeds, registry of deeds · Landregister *n* [*Abgesehen vom Torrenssystem gibt es in den USA keine Grundbücher, sondern Landregister*]

land recordation → land registration

land recording → land registration

land recording act, land registration act, LRA, land recordation act · Grundbuchgesetz *n*

land recording rules, land registration rules, land recordation rules · formell(rechtlich)es Grundbuchrecht *n* [*Es betrifft das Eintragungsverfahren*]

(land) redistribution · Landbereinigung *f*, Landregulierung, (Flur)Bereinigung, Flurregulierung, Feldbereinigung, Feldregulierung, Bodenbereinigung, Bodenseparation *f*, Bodenregulierung, Arrondierung, Bodenaufteilung, (Land)Neuaufteilung, Vereinödung, (Land)Separation; Kommasation, Commasation [*Österreich*]

(land) redistribution area, (land) redistribution territory · Flurbereinigungsgebiet *n*

(land) redistribution authority · (Flur)Bereinigungsbehörde *f*, Bodenbereinigungsbehörde, Feldbereinigungsbehörde, (Land)Neuaufteilungsbehörde, Feldregulierungsbehörde, Arrondierungsbehörde

(land) redistribution community · Flurbereinigungsgemeinde *f*

(land) redistribution court · Flurbereinigungsgericht *n*, Senat *m* für Flurbereinigung [*In jedem Land der Bundesrepublik Deutschland ist beim obersten Verwaltungsgericht ein Senat für Flurbereinigung (= Flurbereinigungsgericht) eingerichtet*]

(land) redistribution law · Flurbereinigungsrecht *n*

(land) redistribution plan · Flurbereinigungsplan *m*

(land) redistribution procedure · Flurbereinigungsverfahren *n*

land-reeve [*A person whose business it is to overlook certain parts of a farm or estate and to report to the land steward*] · Landaufseher *m*

land reform → land(s) reform

land reform district · Landreformbezirk *m*, Bodenreformbezirk

land reformer · Bodenreformer *m*

land reform law → land(s) reform law

land reform legislation → land(s) reform legislation

land reform movement → land(s) reform movement

land reform plan → land(s) reform plan

land reform statute → land(s) reform statute

Land regional policy · Landesraumordnung *f*, LRO [*Bundesrepublik Deutschland*]

Land regional policy plan · Landesraumordnungsplan *m* [*Bundesrepublik Deutschland*]

Land regional policy programme; Land regional policy program (US) · Landesraumordnungsprogramm *n* [*Bundesrepublik Deutschland*]

land register → land record

land register, land registry, register of land(s), registry of land(s), groundbook, landed property register, landed property registry · Grundbuch *n*, GBuch, GB

land register act, LRA, land register law, land register statute, land registry act, land registry statute, land registry law · Grundbuchgesetz *n*

land register certificate, land registry certificate · Grundbuchabschrift *f*

land register code, land registry code · Grundbuchordnung *f*

land register content, land registry content · Grundbuchinhalt *m*

land register department, land registry department · Grundbuchamt *n*

land register district, land registry district · Grundbuchbezirk *m*

land register fee, land registry fee · Grundbuchgebühr *f*

land register files, land registry files · Grundbuchakten *fpl*

land register keeping, land registry keeping · Grundbuchführung *f*

land register law → land register act

land register legislation, land register lawmaking, land registry legislation, land registry lawmaking · Grundbuchgesetzgebung f

land register part, land registry part · (Grundbuch)Abteilung f

land register sheet, land registry sheet · Grundbuchblatt n

land register sheet for partial (real) estate, land registry sheet for partial (real) estate · Teileigentumsgrundbuchblatt n

land register statute → land register act

land register volume, land registry volume · Grundbuchband m

land registrar · Grundbuchführer m, Grundbuchverwalter, Grundbuchbeamte

land registration, registration of immov(e)able property · Landeintragung f, Bodeneintragung

land registration, land recordation, land recording, registration of land, recordation of land, recording of land · Grundbucheintrag(ung) m, (f)

land registration act, LRA, land recordation act, land recording act · Grundbuchgesetz n

land registration law, land registry law, law of land registration, law of land registry · Grundbuchrecht n, GB-Recht

land registration rules, land recordation rules, land recording rules · formell(rechtlich)es Grundbuchrecht n [Es betrifft das Eintragungsverfahren]

land registry → land record

land registry → land register

land registry act → land register act

land registry certificate, land register certificate · Grundbuchabschrift f

land registry code, land register code · Grundbuchordnung f

land registry content, land register content · Grundbuchinhalt m

land registry department, land register department · Grundbuchamt n

land registry district, land register district · Grundbuchbezirk m

land registry fee, land register fee · Grundbuchgebühr f

land registry files, land register files · Grundbuchakten fpl

land registry keeping, land register keeping · Grundbuchführung f

land registry law → land registration law

land registry law → land register act

land registry lawmaking → land register legislation

land registry legislation → land register legislation

land registry part, land register part · (Grundbuch)Abteilung f

land registry sheet → land register sheet

land registry statute → land register act

land registry volume, land register volume · Grundbuchband m

(land) regrouping authority · (Landes)Kulturbehörde f

(land) regrouping board · (Landes)Kulturamt n [frühere Benennung: Generalkommission f]

land relocation → (building) land relocation

land rent → land(s) rent

land rent → (agricultural) land rent

land replotting, replotting of land · Landumlegung f, Bodenumlegung, Flächenumlegung

land reserve, land resource, resource of land, reserve of land, stock of land(s) · Bodenreserve f, Bodenvorrat m, Flächenreserve, Flächenvorrat, Landreserve, Landvorrat

land reserve policy, resource-of-land(s) policy, policy of resources of land(s) · Landreservepolitik f, Bodenreservepolitik, Flächenreservepolitik, Bodenvorratspolitik, Landvorratspolitik, Flächenvorratspolitik

land residual technique · Bodenrestwertverfahren n, Landrestwertverfahren

land residual value, residual land value · Bodenrestwert m, Landrestwert

land resource, resource of land, reserve of land, stock of land(s), land reserve · Bodenreserve f, Bodenvorrat m, Flächenreserve, Flächenvorrat, Landreserve, Landvorrat

land resource region · agrarwirtschaftliche Region f, landwirtschaftliche Region

land return, land yield · Bodenertrag m, Landertrag, Bodenrendite f, Landrendite

land return multiplier, land yield multiplier · Bodenrenditevervielfältiger m, Landrenditevervielfältiger

Land road construction, highway construction of a Land, road construction of a Land, Land highway construction · Landesstraßenbau m [Bundesrepublik Deutschland]

land(s) · Ländereien) f (pl), Gut n, Land n, Boden m

land(s) accumulation, accumulation of land(s) · Bodenhortung f, Landhortung

land(s) acquisition — landscape preservation land

land(s) acquisition → (real) property acquisition

land sale → land(s) sale

land sale by auction, sale of land by auction · Landversteigerung *f*, Landauktion *f*, Bodenversteigerung, Bodenauktion

land salesman (US) → (real) estate vendor

land(s) alienation contract → land(s) (ab)alienation contract

land(s) appraisement → (real) property (e)valuation

land(s) appraiser → (real) property appraiser

(land(s)) brokerage → (real) estate broking

(land(s)) broking → (real) estate broking

land(s) business → (real) estate business

landscape, geographical region · Landschaft *f*

landscape appearance, scenery of the landscape · Landschaftsbild *n*

landscape architect · Landschaftsgestalter *m*

landscape architect's fee · Landschaftsgestaltergebühr *f*, Landschaftsgestalterhonorar *n*

landscape area, green land, green area · Grünfläche *f*, begrünte Fläche

landscape area, green area, landscape territory, green territory · Grüngebiet *n*

landscape as an areal composition of the individual groups of elements [*Climate; water; land; plants and cultural phenomena*] · Landschaftsraum *m*

landscape balance · Landschaftshaushalt *m* [*Wirkungsgefüge der die Landschaft bestimmenden Faktoren, wie Boden, Wasser, Klima, Grundgestein, Pflanzen- und Tierwelt*]

landscape change · Landschaftswechsel *m*

landscape compatibility · Landschaftsverträglichkeit *f*

landscape conservation, landscape retention, landscape preservation · Landschaftspflege *f*, Landschaftserhaltung *f*

landscape conservation act, landscape preservation act, landscape conservation law, landscape preservation law, landscape preservation statute, landscape conservation statute · Landschaftspflegegesetz *n*, Landschaftserhaltungsgesetz

landscape conservation land, landscape preservation land · Landschaftserhaltungsbereich *m*, Landschaftspflegebereich

landscape conservation map, landscape preservation map, map for retention of (the) landscape · Landschaftserhaltungskarte *f*, Landschaftspflegekarte

landscape damage · Landschaftsschaden *m*

landscape damage map · Landschaftsschädenkarte *f*

landscaped walkway · landschaftlich gestalteter Fußweg *m*

landscape ecology · Landschaftsökologie *f*

landscape entity · Landschaftseinheit *f*

landscape facility · gestaltete Grünfläche *f*, Grünanlage *f*

landscape fertility · Fruchtbarkeit *f* der Landschaft

landscape formations; sequent occupancies [*According to Whittlesley 1929*] · zeitliche Schichtung *f* der Landschaftselemente und Landschaftseinheiten

landscape framework plan, landscape skeleton plan · Landschaftsrahmenplan *m*

landscape framework plan, landscape skeleton plan · Landschaftsrahmenplan *m* [*Darstellung der überörtlichen Ziele der Landschaftspflege und des Naturschutzes*]

landscape garden · Landschaftsgarten *m*

landscape gardener · Landschaftsgärtner *m*

landscape gardening · Landschaftsgärtnerei *f*

landscape image · Landschaftsbild *n*

landscape nature, nature of the landscape · Eigenart *f* der Landschaft, Landschaftseigenart

landscape pattern · Landschaftsmosaik *n*

landscape plan · Landschaftsplan *m*

landscape planning · Landschaftsplanung *f*

landscape planting · Landschaftsbepflanzung *f*

landscape preservation, landscape conservation · Landschaftspflege *f*, Landschaftserhaltung *f*

landscape preservation act, landscape conservation law, landscape preservation law, landscape preservation statute, landscape conservation statute, landscape conservation act · Landschaftspflegegesetz *n*, Landschaftserhaltungsgesetz

landscape preservation land, landscape conservation land · Landschaftserhaltungsbereich *m*, Landschaftspflegebereich

landscape preservation map — land(s) free trade

landscape preservation map, landscape conservation map · Landschaftserhaltungskarte *f*, Landschaftspflegekarte

landscape preserve, landscape refuge · Landschaftsschutzgebiet *n*, Landschaftsschongebiet

landscape project · Landschaftsprojekt *n*

landscape protection · Landschaftsschutz *m* [*Die Abwehr menschlicher Eingriffe in die Landschaft*]

landscape protection authority · Landschaftsschutzbehörde *f*

landscape protection law · Landschaftsschutzrecht *n*

landscape protection law, landscape protection act, landscape protection statute · Landschaftsschutzgesetz *n*

landscape protection map · Landschaftsschutzkarte *f*

landscape protection ordinance · Landschaftsschutzverordnung *f*

landscape refuge, landscape preserve · Landschaftsschutzgebiet *n*, Landschaftsschongebiet

landscape region, unit of landscape, landscape unit · Landschaftsindividuum *n*

landscape skeleton plan, landscape framework plan · Landschaftsrahmenplan *m* [*Darstellung der überörtlichen Ziele der Landschaftspflege und des Naturschutzes*]

landscape source analysis · Landschaftswertanalyse *f*

landscape spoiling · Landschaftszerstörung *f*

landscape territory, green territory, landscape area, green area · Grüngebiet *n*

landscape treatment · Landschaftsgestaltung *f*

landscape unit, landscape region, unit of landscape · Landschaftsindividuum *n*

land scarcity → land(s) scarcity

land(s) certifier → (real) property appraiser

land scheme → area(l) pattern

land(s) communization, communization of land(s) · Landkommunalisierung *f*, Bodenkommunalisierung, Kommunalisierung des Bodens, Kommunalisierung des Landes

land(s) company → (real) estate company

land(s) consortium → (real) estate syndicate

land(s) contract → (real) estate (purchase) contract

land(s) credit → (real) estate credit

land(s) credit bank, (real) estate credit bank, (real) property credit bank, realty credit bank · Grundkreditbank *f*, Landkreditbank, Bodenkreditbank, Grundstückskreditbank

land(s) dearth, dearth of land(s), land(s) shortage, land(s) scarcity, shortage of land(s), scarcity of land(s) · Bodenknappheit *f*, Landknappheit, Bodenverknappung *f*, Landverknappung, Bodenmangel *m*, Landmangel

land(s) deepening, deepening of land(s) · Grund(stücks)vertiefung *f*

land(s) depreciation fund → (real) estate depreciation fund

(land(s)) developer · (Land)Entwick(e)lungsträger *m*, Bodenentwick(e)lungsträger

(land(s)) development, (land(s)) growth · (Land)Entwick(e)lung *f*, Bodenentwick(e)lung

(land(s)) development plan, (land(s)) growth plan · (Land)Entwick(e)lungsplan *m*, Bodenentwick(e)lungsplan

land(s) distribution, distribution of land(s) · Bodenverteilung *f*, Landverteilung

land(s) encumbrance, land(s) incumbrance, encumbrance on land(s), incumbrance on land(s), land charge [*Land charges are those rights and interests affecting land, e.g., estate contracts, restrictive covenants, general equitable charges and easements*] · Grund(stücks)belastung *f*, Grund(stücks)last *f*, Bodenlast, Landlast, Liegenschaftslast, Immobilienlast, Immobiliarlast

land settlement association, association for providing settlers with land · Landlieferungsverband *m*

land settlement facilities act, land settlement facilities law, land settlement facilities statute · Ansied(e)lungsgesetz *n*, Besied(e)lungsgesetz

land(s) (e)valuation → (real) property (e)valuation

land(s) exchange, barter of land for land, exchange of realty, realty exchange, exchange of land(s), exchange of (real) estate, exchange of (real) property, (real) estate exchange, (real) property exchange · Boden(aus)tausch *m*, Land(aus)tausch, Grund(stücks)(aus)tausch, Liegenschafts(aus)tausch, Immobiliar(aus)-tausch, Immobilien(aus)tausch, Flächen(aus)tausch

land(s) finance act → (real) estate finance act

land(s) financing → (real) estate financing

land(s) firm → (real) estate firm

land(s) free trade, free trade in land(s) · Landfreihandel *m*, Bodenfreihandel

land(s) fund — land(s) of a manor

land(s) fund → (real) estate fund

land(s) gift, gift of land(s) · Landschenkung *f*, Bodenschenkung

land(s) grant, grant of land(s), grant of (real) estate, grant of (real) property, grant of realty, (real) estate grant, (real) property grant, realty grant · Landverleihung *f*, Landvergabe *f*, Landüberlassung, Bodenverleihung, Bodenvergabe, Bodenüberlassung, Flächenvergabe, Flächenüberlassung, Flächenverleihung, Landschenkung, Bodenschenkung, Flächenschenkung

(land(s)) growth, (land(s)) development · (Land)Entwick(e)lung *f*, Bodenentwick(e)lung

(land(s)) growth plan, (land(s)) development plan · (Land)Entwick(e)lungsplan *m*, Bodenentwick(e)lungsplan

land(s) held by tenure of knight service · Ritterleh(e)n(s)land *n*

land(s) held in trust, trust (real) estate, trust (real) property, trust land(s), (real) estate held in trust, (real) property held in trust · Treuhandgrund(stück) *m, (n)*, Treuhandboden *m*, Treuhandland *n*, Treuhandimmobilie *f*

land(s) held of a lord → land(s) of (a) manor

land shortage → land(s) shortage

land(s) incorporation, incorporation of land(s) · (Grund(stücks))Zuschreibung *f*, Grund(stücks)verbindung [*Einem Grundstück als Hauptstück wird ein anderes als unwesentlicher Bestandteil hinzugefügt*]

land(s) incumbrance, encumbrance on land(s), incumbrance on land(s), land charge, land(s) encumbrance [*Land charges are those rights and interests affecting land, e.g., estate contracts, restrictive covenants, general equitable charges and easements*] · Grund(stücks)belastung *f*, Grund(stücks)last *f*, Bodenlast, Landlast, Liegenschaftslast, Immobilienlast, Immobiliarlast

land(s) in federal ownership, federal(-owned) land(s) · Bundesländerei(en) *f (pl)*, Bundesland *n*, bundeseigenes Land, Bundesboden *m*, bundeseigener Boden

land(s) insurance, realty insurance, (real) estate insurance, (real) property insurance · Immobilienversicherung *f*, Immobiliarversicherung, Liegenschaftsversicherung

land(s) inventory, realty inventory, (real) estate inventory, (real) property inventory · Bodennachlaßverzeichnis *n*, Liegenschaftsnachlaßverzeichnis, Grund(stücks)nachlaßverzeichnis, Immobiliennachlaßverzeichnis, Landnachlaßverzeichnis, Immobiliarnachlaßverzeichnis, Liegenschaftsnachlaßverzeichnis

land(s) investment → (real) estate investment

land(s) investment trust, (real) estate investment trust, (real) property investment trust, realty investment trust · Immobilien(investment)trust *m*, Immobiliar(investment)trust, Liegenschafts(investment)trust, Land(investment)trust, Grund(stücks)(investment)trust, Boden(investment)trust

land(s) lease(hold) → (real) estate lease(hold)

land(s) leasing → (real) estate leasing

land(s) ledger → (real) estate ledger

land(s) limitation act → (real) property limitation act

land(s) management, realty management, (real) property management, (real) estate management · Grund(stücks)verwaltung *f*, Landverwaltung, Bodenverwaltung, Liegenschaftsverwaltung, Immobilienverwaltung, Immobiliarverwaltung

land(s) management, management of land(s) · Landbewirtschaftung *f*, Bodenbewirtschaftung

land(s) management, management of (real) property, management of (real) estate, management of land(s), realty management, management of realty, (real) estate management, (real) property management · Grundbesitzbetreuung *f*, Verwaltungsbetreuung, Landbetreuung, Bodenbetreuung, Immobilienbetreuung, Immobiliarbetreuung

land(s) management code, code of land(s) management · Bodenbewirtschaftungsordnung *f*, Landbewirtschaftungsordnung

land(s) manager, realty manager, (real) estate manager, (real) property manager · Grund(stücks)verwalter *m*, Bodenverwalter, Liegenschaftsverwalter, Landverwalter, Immobilienverwalter, Immobiliarverwalter

land(s) mobility, mobility of land(s) [*The ability to shift the uses of land by means of irrigation or other capital investment*] · Bodennutzungsfähigkeit *f*, Landnutzungsfähigkeit, Flächennutzungsfähigkeit

land(s) nationalization, nationalization of land(s) · Landverstaatlichung *f*, Bodenverstaatlichung

land(s) of a manor, manorial land(s), bordland [*Land held by a bordar in bordage tenure*] · Herr(e)ngutland *n*, Fron(dienst)land, Frongutland, Fronbauernland, Herr(e)nhofland

land(s) of (a) manor, land(s) held of a lord, land(s) of tenure, outland(s), tenancy, tenure land(s), feodal land(s), feudal land(s), feuda(to)ry land(s), tenemental land(s) [*Land held of the lord by free tenure*] · Leh(e)n(s)land *n*, Feudalland, Außenland, Grenzland, verpachtetes Land

land(s) of tenure → land(s) of (a) manor

land(s) owner → (real) property owner

land speculation → (bulding) land speculation

land speculation → land(s) speculation

land speculator → land(s) speculator

land(s) policy, (real) estate policy, (real) property policy · Grund(stücks)politik *f*, Bodenpolitik, Landpolitik, Liegenschaftspolitik, Immobiliarpolitik, Immobilienpolitik

land(s) possession for life → (real) estate for life

land(s) practice → real estate practice

land(s) profit, vesture, profit of land(s) [*In old English law. The value of the vesture of the land(s)*] · Wert *m* der Grundstücksbewachsung außer Bäumen

land(s) proprietor → (real) property owner

land(s) (purchase) contract → (real) property (purchase) contract

land(s) quantity, quantity of land(s) · Landmenge *f*, Bodenmenge, Flächenmenge

land(s) reclamation, reclamation (of land(s)) · (Land)Gewinnung *f*, Neulandgewinnung

(land(s)) reclamation district · (Land)Gewinnungsbezirk *m*, Neulandgewinnungsbezirk

land(s) reform authority, agrarian reform authority · Bodenreformbehörde *f*, Landreformbehörde

land(s) reformer, agrarian (reformer) [*One in favour of a redistribution of landed property*] · Bodenreformer *m*, Landreformer

land(s) reform law, agrarian reform law, law of land(s) reform, law of agrarian reform · Bodenreformrecht *n*, Landreformrecht

land(s) reform legislation, agrarian reform legislation, land(s) reform lawmaking, agrarian reform lawmaking · Bodenreformgesetzgebung *f*, Landreformgesetzgebung

land(s) reform plan, agrarian reform plan · Bodenreformplan *m*, Landreformplan

land(s) reform statute, land(s) reform act, land(s) reform law, agrarian reform law, agrarian reform act, agrarian reform statute · Bodenreformgesetz *n*, Landreformgesetz

land(s) regrouping, regrouping (of land(s)) · Gemeinheitsteilung *f* [*Oberbegriff für (Land)Zusammenlegung ((land) consolidation) und (Land)Neuaufteilung ((land) redistribution)*]

land(s) rent, ground rent, (true) rent of land(s), (true) rent of ground [*It issues out of the land, as a compensation for the possession during the term*] · Bodenrente *f*, Landrente, Grund(stücks)rente

land(s) rent, rent of ground, rent of land(s), ground rent [*It is an acknowledg(e)ment made by the tenant to the lord*] · Bodenzins *m*, Landzins, Grund(stücks)zins

land(s) reserve policy, resource-of-land(s) policy, policy of resources of land(s) · Bodenreservepolitik *f*, Bodenvorratpolitik, Flächenreservepolitik, Flächenvorratpolitik, Landreservepolitik, Landvorratpolitik

land(s) sale, sale of realty, sale of (real) property, sale of (real) estate, sale of land(s), (real) property sale, (real) estate sale, realty sale · Grund(stücks)verkauf *m*, Immobilienverkauf, Immobiliarverkauf, Landverkauf, Bodenverkauf, Liegenschaftsverkauf

land(s) sale contract, contract for sale of land(s) · Bodenverkaufsvertrag *m*, Landverkaufsvertrag

land(s) scarcity, shortage of land(s), scarcity of land(s), land(s) dearth, dearth of land(s), land(s) shortage · Bodenknappheit *f*, Landknappheit, Bodenverknappung *f*, Landverknappung, Bodenmangel *m*, Landmangel

land(s) scarcity factor, area scarcity factor · Bodenknappheitsgrad *m*, Landknappheitsgrad, Flächenknappheitsgrad

land(s) shortage, land(s) scarcity, shortage of land(s), scarcity of land(s), land(s) dearth, dearth of land(s) · Bodenknappheit *f*, Landknappheit, Bodenverknappung *f*, Landverknappung, Bodenmangel *m*, Landmangel

land(s) speculation, speculation in land(s), realty speculation, speculation in realty, (real) estate speculation, (real) property speculation, speculation in (real) estate, speculation in (real) property · Grund(stücks)spekulation *f*, Bodenspekulation, Landspekulation, Liegenschaftsspekulation, Immobiliarspekulation, Immobilienspekulation

land(s) speculator, realty speculator, (real) estate speculator, (real) property speculator · Bodenspekulant *m*, Landspekulant, Grund(stücks)spekulant, Liegenschaftsspekulant, Immobiliarspekulant, Immobilienspekulant

(land(s)) (sub)division, (sub)division into (estate) lots, (sub)division (of land(s)),

land(s) supply — land syndicate

lotting · Parzelli(si)erung f, Landparzelli(si)erung, Bodenparzelli(si)erung

land(s) supply, supply of land(s) · Bodenangebot n, Landangebot, Bodenbereitstellung f, Landbereitstellung

land(s) surveyor, surveyor of land(s) · Domäneninspektor m

land(s) syndicate → (real) estate syndicate

Land standing conference of planning boards, Land joint planning board · Landesplanungsgemeinschaft f [*Bundesrepublik Deutschland. Eine unmittelbar kraft Gesetzes bestehende Planungsgemeinschaft*]

Land statute, Land act, Land law · Landesgesetz n [*Bundesrepublik Deutschland*]

land statute → building land statute

land(s) tax; capitatio terrena [*Latin*]; realty tax, tax on realty, tax on (real) estate, tax on land(s), tax on (real) property, (real) estate tax, (real) property tax · Grund(besitz)steuer f, Grundstückssteuer

land(s) tax → building land(s) tax

land(s) taxation, taxation of land(s) · Landbesteuerung f, Bodenbesteuerung

land(s) tax authority · Grund(besitz)steuerbehörde f

land(s) tax book · Grund(besitz)steuerbuch n

(land) steward, steward of manor, bailiff [*A person that has administration and charge of lands, goods and chattels to make the best benefit for the owner*] · Amtmann m, (Guts)Verwalter, Gutsschulze, Vogt, Rentenmeister, Haushofmeister

land steward and surveyor · Chefgeometer m

land(s) transaction judg(e)ment, realty transaction judg(e)ment, (real) estate transaction judg(e)ment, (real) property transaction judg(e)ment · Bodenverkehrsurteil n, Grundstücksverkehrsurteil, Immobiliarverkehrsurteil, Immobilienverkehrsurteil, Liegenschaftsverkehrsurteil

land(s) transaction law, law for dealing with land(s), (real) property transaction law, (real) estate transaction law · Bodenrecht n, Grundstücksverkehrsrecht, Liegenschaftsrecht, Immobiliarrecht, Immobilienrecht

land(s) transactions, dealing with land(s), realty transactions, (real) estate transactions, (real) property transactions [*Acquiring, holding and disposing of land*] · Bodenverkehr m, Grundstücksverkehr, Liegenschaftsverkehr, Immobiliarverkehr, Immobilienverkehr

land strip → (building) land strip

land succession · Bodennachfolge f, Landnachfolge

land(s) underwriting group → (real) estate syndicate

land supply → (building) (land) area supply

land surface, realty surface, surface of realty, surface of (real) estate, surface of (real) property, surface of land, (real) estate surface, (real) property surface · Grund(stücks)oberfläche f, Bodenoberfläche, Landoberfläche

land survey(ing) [*The measuring of land and the making of maps and plans for the purpose of recording land*] · Landaufnahme f, Landvermessung f

land survey law · Landaufnahmerecht n

(land) surveyor; landimer [*old Scots law*] · (Land)Vermesser m

land surveyor and valuer · Katasterbeamte m

land(s) use legislation, land(s) use lawmaking · Landnutzungsgesetzgebung f, Bodennutzungsgesetzgebung, Flächennutzungsgesetzgebung

land(s) use ordinance · Flächennutzungsverordnung f, Bodennutzungsverordnung, Landnutzungsverordnung

land(s) use system, system of land(s) use · Bodennutzungssystem n, Landnutzungssystem, Flächennutzungssystem

land(s) usufruct, realty usufruct, (real) property usufruct, (real) estate usufruct · Grund(stücks)(frucht)genuß m, Grund(stücks)nießbrauch m, Land(frucht)genuß, Landnießbrauch, Boden(frucht)genuß, Bodennießbrauch, Liegenschafts(frucht)genuß, Liegenschaftsnießbrauch, Immobilien(frucht)genuß, Immobiliennießbrauch

land(s) usury · Landwucher m, Bodenwucher, Landschacher, Bodenschacher

land(s) utilization, utilization of land(s), utilization of land area(s) · Bodenverwertung f, Landverwertung, Flächenverwertung

land(s) valuation → (real) property (e)valuation

land(s) valuer → (real) property appraiser

land swell, acreage swell, swell of acreage, swell of land, addition of acreage, acreage addition, addition of land, land addition [*of a real estate*] · Landzuwachs m, Flächenzuwachs, Bodenzuwachs, Landzunahme f, Bodenzunahme, Flächenzunahme

land syndicate → (real) estate syndicate

land taken up in street(s) — land use allotment

land taken up in street(s) · Stadtstraßenfläche *f*

land tax → (building) land(s) tax

land tax → land(s) tax

land taxation → land(s) taxation

land tenancy → (building) (land) area tenancy

land tenancy act → land lease law

(land) tenancy agreement → (real) estate lease (agreement)

land tenancy law → land lease law

land tenancy rent, rent for land on lease, rent for land tenancy, land lease rent · Bodenpachtabgabe *f*, (Land)Pachtabgabe

land tenancy statute → land lease law

land tenant, (real) estate possessor, (real) property possessor, realty possessor, landed estate possessor, land possessor, land(ed) property possessor, landholder, possessor of land, possessor of (real) estate, possessor of (real) property, tenant of land, holder of land · Grund(stücks)besitzer *m*, Landbesitzer, Bodenbesitzer, Immobilienbesitzer, Immobiliarbesitzer, Liegenschaftsbesitzer

land tenant, (feudal) tenant, manorial tenant, feudal bond(s)man, vassal, tenant of land, feeholder, holder of a fee, holder of a fief, fief-tenant, feoda(to)ry, feuda(to)ry; homo pertinens [*Latin*]; beneficiary, holder of a feudal benefice [*A tenant or vassal who held his estate by feudal service*] · Leh(e)n(s)mann *m*, Leh(e)n(s)träger, Gefolgsmann, Gutszinsmann, Vasall

(land) tenant → (land) holder

(land) tenant at sufferance, (land) tenant by sufferance [*One who comes into possession of land by lawful title and keeps it after expiration of lease without any title at all*] · geduldeter (Land)Pächter *m*

(land) tenant from year to year → (land) holder from year to year

land tenure → fee (tenure) (of land)

land tenure system → feudal (landholding) system

land territory, land area · Landgebiet *n*

Land territory, Land area · Landesgebiet *n* [*Bundesrepublik Deutschland*]

land title → (real) estate title

(land) title company → (land) title (insurance) company

(land) title examination, (land) title investigation, examination of title (to land), investigation of title (to land) · (Land)(Rechts)Titelprüfung *f*, Prüfung des (Land)(Rechts)Titels

(land) title insurance, insurance of title (to land) · (Rechts)Titelversicherung *f*, Grund(stücks)titelversicherung, Bodentitelversicherung, Landtitelversicherung

(land) title (insurance) company [*Such a company investigates titles to land and also issues for an additional payment a policy of title insurance on the property. This protects a purchaser against any flaws which may later develop in the title*] · (Rechts)Titelversicherungsgesellschaft *f*, Grund(stücks)titelversicherungsgesellschaft, Bodentitelversicherungsgesellschaft, Landtitelversicherungsgesellschaft

land title law firm · Grundstücksanwaltfirma *f*, Liegenschaftsanwaltfirma, Immobilienanwaltfirma, Immobiliaranwaltfirma

land town → (in)land town

land tract, country tract, tract of country, countryside, tract of land [*It has a kind of natural unity*] · Landtrakt *m*, Landstrich *m*

land transaction judg(e)ment → land(s) transaction judg(e)ment

land transfer → (voluntary) land transfer

land transfer permission, (real) estate transfer permission, (real) property transfer permission, permission for (real) estate transactions, permission for (real) property transactions, permission for land transactions, permission to deal with land(s), permission for realty transactions, realty transfer permission · Bodenverkehrserlaubnis *f*, Bodenverkehrsgenehmigung *f*, Grundstücksverkehrserlaubnis, Grundstücksverkehrsgenehmigung, Immobiliarverkehrserlaubnis, Immobiliarverkehrsgenehmigung, Immobilienverkehrserlaubnis, Immobilienverkehrsgenehmigung, Liegenschaftsverkehrserlaubnis, Liegenschaftsverkehrsgenehmigung

land underwriting group → (real) estate syndicate

land unit · Bodeneinheit *f*, Landeinheit, Flächeneinheit

land use, use of land, use of (land) area, (land) area use · Bodennutzung *f*, Flächennutzung, Landnutzung [*Die Inanspruchnahme einer Fläche durch den Menschen für bestimmte Zwecke*]

land use act, land use statute, land use law · Bodennutzungsgesetz *n*, Flächennutzungsgesetz, Landnutzungsgesetz

land use allotment, allotment of land use, land use apportionment, apportionment of land use · Flächenzuteilung *f*, Bodenzuteilung, Landzuteilung

**land use change, **change of use of land ·
Landnutzungswechsel *m*

land use characteristic · Bodennutzungsmerkmal *n*, Flächennutzungsmerkmal, Landnutzungsmerkmal

land use class · Bodennutzungsklasse *f*, Flächennutzungsklasse, Landnutzungsklasse

**land use classification, **classification of land use · Bodennutzungseinteilung *f*, Flächennutzungseinteilung, Landnutzungseinteilung

**land use classification system, **system of land use classification · Bodennutzungsklassifizierungssystem *n*, Flächennutzungsklassifizierungssystem, Landnutzungsklassifizierungssystem

**land use control, **planning and zoning, control of land use · Flächennutzungslenkung *f*, Bodennutzungslenkung, Landnutzungslenkung

**land use density, **density of land use · Bodennutzungsdichte *f*, Landnutzungsdichte, Flächennutzungsdichte

land use game · Bodennutzungsspiel *n*, Landnutzungsspiel, Flächennutzungsspiel

land use geometry · Bodennutzungsgeometrie *f*, Flächennutzungsgeometrie, Landnutzungsgeometrie

**land use intensity, **LUI [*The overall relationships of structural mass and open space of a developed property or a development plan*] · (bauliches) Nutzungsmaß *n*, Baunutzungsmaß, Maß der (baulichen) Nutzung

**land use intensity rating, **LIR · (bauliches) Mindestnutzungsmaß *n*, Mindestbaunutzungsmaß, Mindestmaß der (baulichen) Nutzung

**land use law, **land use act, land use statute · Bodennutzungsgesetz *n*, Flächennutzungsgesetz, Landnutzungsgesetz

**land use law, **law of land use · (Boden)Nutzungsrecht *n*, Flächennutzungsrecht, Landnutzungsrecht [*Es regelt die Inanspruchnahme von Flächen durch den Menschen für bestimmte Zwecke*]

land use legislation → land(s) use legislation

land use lot · Nutzungsparzelle *f*

land use map · Bodennutzungskarte *f*, Flächennutzungskarte, Landnutzungskarte

land use mapping · Bodennutzungskartierung *f*, Flächennutzungskartierung, Landnutzungskartierung

**land use pattern, **land use scheme · Bodennutzungsmuster *n*, Flächennutzungsmuster, Landnutzungsmuster

**land use plan, **plan of land use, outline development plan · Aufbauplan *m* [*veraltete Benennung*]; Flächenwidmungsplan *m* [*Österreich*]; vorbereitender Bauleitplan *m*, Flächennutzungsplan *m*, Landnutzungsplan *m*, Bodennutzungsplan *m*, FNP *m*

land use planner · Bodennutzungsplaner *m*, Landnutzungsplaner, Flächennutzungsplaner; Aufbauplaner [*veraltete Benennung*]

**land use planning, **planning of land use · Bodennutzungsplanung *f*, Landnutzungsplanung, Flächennutzungsplanung, FNP, vorbereitende Bauleitplanung; Flächenwidmungsplanung [*Österreich*]; Aufbauplanung [*veraltete Benennung*]

**land use regulation, **(land) area use regulation · Bodenbenutzungsregelung *f*, Landbenutzungsregelung, Flächenbenutzungsregelung

land use restraint · Bodennutzungseinschränkung *f*, Landnutzungseinschränkung, Flächennutzungseinschränkung, Flächennutzungsbeschränkung, Bodennutzungsbeschränkung, Landnutzungsbeschränkung

**land use scheme, **land use pattern · Bodennutzungsmuster *n*, Flächennutzungsmuster, Landnutzungsmuster

land use segregation · Flächennutzungsentmischung *f*, Bodennutzungsentmischung, Landnutzungsentmischung

land use sketch · Bodennutzungsskizze *f*, Flächennutzungsskizze, Landnutzungsskizze

**land use statute, **land use law, land use act · Bodennutzungsgesetz *n*, Flächennutzungsgesetz, Landnutzungsgesetz

land use survey · Bodennutzungsenquête *f*, Flächennutzungsenquête, Landnutzungsenquête

**land use theory, **theory of land use · Bodennutzungstheorie *f*, Flächennutzungstheorie, Landnutzungstheorie

**(land) use zoning, **zoning · (bauliche) Nutzung *f*, Baunutzung, Bauzonenfestlegung

**(land) use zoning mix(ture), **zoning mix(ture) · (bauliche) Nutzungsmischung *f*, Baunutzungsmischung

**(land) use zoning order, **zoning order · (bauliche) Nutzungsanordnung *f*, (bauliche) Nutzungsverfügung, Baunutzungsanordnung, Baunutzungsverfügung, (bauliches) Nutzungsgebot *n*, Baunutzungsgebot, (baulicher) Nutzungsbefehl *m*, Baunutzungsbefehl

**(land) use zoning prohibition, **zoning prohibition · (bauliches) Nutzungsverbot *n*, Baunutzungsverbot

(land) use zoning separation, zoning separation · (bauliche) Nutzungstrennung f, Baunutzungstrennung

land-using · bodenbeanspruchend, landbeanspruchend

land usufruct → land(s) usufruct

land val. → (real) property (e)valuation

land valuation → (real) property (e)valuation

land value duty, land value tax · Steuer f auf dem gemeinen Wert des Landes

land value portion, ground value portion, land value share, ground value share · Bodenwertanteil m, Landwertanteil, Grund(stücks)wertanteil

land valuer → (real) property appraiser

land value tax; land betterment tax (Brit.) · Bodenwertzuwachssteuer f, Landwertzuwachssteuer, Grund(stücks)wertzuwachssteuer

landward [*Scots law*]; rural · ländlich

land waste for the worse · Bodenverödung f, Landverödung

Land water law · Landeswasserrecht n [*Bundesrepublik Deutschland*]

land-weariness, weariness of life on the land · Landmüdigkeit f

land yield, land return · Bodenertrag m, Landertrag, Bodenrendite f, Landrendite

land yield multiplier, land return multiplier · Bodenrenditevervielfältiger m, Landrenditevervielfältiger

land (zoned) for gardening, garden(ing) land (area), garden(ing) area · Gartenboden m, Gartenfläche f, Gartenland n, gärtnerisch genutzter Boden, gärtnerisch genutztes Land, gärtnerisch genutzte Fläche

land zoned for residential purposes · wohnmäßig genutztes Land n, wohnmäßig genutzter Boden m

lane village · Gassendorf n

langeman → liege-lord

language community · Sprachgemeinschaft f

language map · Sprachenkarte f

language used in acts, language used in laws, language used in statutes · Gesetz(es)sprache f

language used in Acts of Parliament · Parlamentsgesetz(es)sprache f

lap → lappage

lappage, conflict, interlock, (over)lap, interference · Überschneidung f, Überlagerung

to lapse, to run out, to cease; to fall in (Brit.), to expire, to end, to terminate · ablaufen, verfristen

to lapse, to fail · hinfällig werden, in Verfall geraten, verfallen

to lapse · erlöschen [*Legat*]

lapse, failure · Hinfälligkeit f eines Vermächtnisses (wenn der Vermächtnisnehmer vor dem Erblasser stirbt), Verfall m eines Vermächtnisses (wenn der Vermächtnisnehmer vor dem Erblasser stirbt), Vermächtnisverfall m, Vermächtnishinfälligkeit

lapsed · abgelaufen, verfristet

lapsed, failed · hinfällig, in Verfall geraten, verfallen

lapsed · erloschen, gelöscht [*Legat*]

lapse (of time), expiration, expiry, running out, termination, falling in · Ablauf m, Fristablauf, Zeitablauf, Verfristung f

lapsing · Erlöschen n [*Legat*]

larceny, latrociny; latrocinium [*Latin*] · Diebstahl m [*Der englische Begriff umfaßt nach deutschem Recht auch noch Besitzentziehung, Unterschlagung und Betrug*]

larceny from the person · Taschendiebstahl m

larceny of cattle, cattle-stealing, cattle larceny, stealing of cattle · Rindviehdiebstahl m

large area, large territory · Großgebiet n

large cluster village with a fragmented strip field pattern · großes Haufendorf n mit Gewannflur und Geschlossenheit der Ackerfläche

large construction company · Großbaufirma f, Großbauunternehmen n, Großbauunternehmung f

large estate; latifundium [*Latin*] · großes Gut n, großes Landgut, Latifundium n, Großgrundbesitz m

large family, extended family [*A family which includes four or more minors*] · Großfamilie f

large family single farm, extended family single farm, single farm of an extended family, large farm of an extended family · Großfamilieneinzelhof m

large farmer · Großlandwirt m

large freehold estate; barony [*In Scotland*]; manor [*It is called so even though the proprietor is a simple commoner*] · Herr(e)ngut n, Herr(e)nhof m

large group city, large group town, big group city, big group town · Gruppengroßstadt f

large hamlet · Großweiler m

large industrial city — lavatory

large industrial city; coke-town [*in England*]; large industrial town · Industriegroßstadt *f*, industrielle Großstadt

large (land)owner, great (land)owner, large (land) proprietor, great (land) proprietor · Großgrundeigentümer *m*, Großgrundeigner

large (land) possessor, great (land) possessor · Großgrundbesitzer *m*

largelot (land) use zoning, large-lot zoning · Großparzellennutzung *f*

large mortgage · Großhypothek *f*

large-scale census, large-scale count · Großzählung *f*

large-scale condemnation (US); large-scale expropriation · Großenteignung *f*

large-scale (construction(al)) project, large-scale building project · Groß(bau)projekt *n*, Groß(bau)vorhaben *n*

large-scale contract · Großvertrag *m*

large-scale detail [*On working drawings to clarify the intent*] · großmaßstäbliche Einzelheit *f*

large-scale development · Großentwick(e)lung *f*

large-scale expropriation; large-scale condemnation (US) · Großenteignung *f*

large-scale hous(ebuild)ing · Wohn(ungs)bau *m* in großem Maßstab

large-scale industry · Großindustrie *f*

large-scale migration · Massenwanderung *f*

large-scale work(s) · Großbauleistung(en) *f (pl)*, Großbauarbeit(en) *f (pl)*

large settlement · Groß(an)sied(e)lung *f*

large space planning · Großraumplanung *f*

large space territory of preference, large-space area of preference, large-space perference area, large-space preference territory · großräumiges Vorranggebiet *n*

large space town, large space city · Großraumstadt *f*

large supermarket · Großsupermarkt *m*

large territory, large area · Großgebiet *n*

large tithe, coarse tithe, great tithe [*A chief predial tithe, as corn, hay, wood and fruit*] · großer Zehnt *m*

large trade area, large trade territory · Großgewerbegebiet *n*

large village, church village · Kirchdorf *n*

laser (beam) plotter · Laser(strahl)zeichenautomat *m*

last day for giving notice · Kündigungstermin *m*

last in — first out, lifo · zuerst Abgang *m* des letzten Zugangs, jüngste Preise *m pl*

last name, agnomination, surname, family name · Nachname *m*, Familienname

last resort, ultimate court of appeal · höchste Instanz *f*, letzte Instanz

late, defunct · verstorben

late letter · Spätlingsbrief *m*

latent defect, hidden defect, concealed defect · verborgener (Sach)Mangel *m*, verborgener Baumangel, verdeckter (Sach)Mangel, verdeckter Baumangel

lateral boundary distance · seitlicher Grenzabstand *m*

later endorsement, subsequent indorsement, subsequent endorsement, later indorsement · Nachindossament *n*

later financing, junior financing · nachstellige Finanzierung *f*, nachstehende Finanzierung

later (legal) mortage, junior mortgage · nachstehende Hypothek *f*, nachstellige Hypothek, rangschlechtere Hypothek

late settled (agricultural) land, young settled (agricultural) land · Jungsiedelland *n*

late settlement, young settlement · Jung(an)sied(e)lung *f*

late snow melt · Spätschneeschmelze *f*

latifundium [*Latin*]; large estate · großes Gut *n*, großes Landgut, Latifundium *n*, Großgrundbesitz *m*

Latin Monetary Union · Lateinische Münzunion *f*

latitude of judg(e)ment, judg(e)ment latitude · Urteilsspielraum *m*

latrociny; latrocinium [*Latin*]; larceny · Diebstahl *m* [*Der englische Begriff umfaßt nach deutschem Recht auch noch Besitzentziehung, Unterschlagung und Betrug*]

lattice; quincunx [*Latin*] · Wabenstreuung *f*

laudemium, relief, relevium · Laudemium *n*, Mannfall *m*, [*Es wurde beim Tod des letzten Leh(e)n(s)mannes fällig, wenn der Nachkomme Leh(e)n(s)mann werden wollte*]

laudemium mortuarium, feodum hereditarium [*Latin*]; fee of inheritance, inheritance fee; feudum hereditarium · Erbleh(e)n *n*, erbliches Leh(e)n, Erbleh(e)n(s)gut *n*, vererbliches Leh(e)n

launching date · erster Fondszeichnungstag *m*

lavatory · Bedürfnisanstalt *f*

law, objective right; lex [*Latin*]; jurisprudence [*misnomer*] [*A system of law existing objectively as an external norm for persons*] · (objektives) Recht *n*

law against luxury, sumptuary law · Antiluxusgesetz *n*

law against perpetuities · Gesetz *n* gegen immerwährende Verfügungen

law agent [*In Scotland*]; solicitor [*In England and North Ireland*] · Anwalt *m* mit beratender Funktion, Rechtsanwalt *m* mit beratender Funktion, Büro(rechts)anwalt *m*, Rechtsagent *m*, Geschäftsanwalt *m*

law agent of choice [*In Scotland*]; solicitor of choice · Vertrauensgeschäftsanwalt *m*

law alteration, change of law, variation of law, alteration of law, law change, law variation · Rechts(ab)änderung *f*, Rechtsumänderung, Rechtsveränderung

law applied to aliens, law of aliens, law on aliens, alien law · Ausländerrecht *n*, Fremdenrecht *n* [*Rechtssätze, die einen Ausländer anders behandeln als einen Inländer*]

lawbinding, legal binding, statutory binding · gesetzliche Bindung *f*, gesetzliche Gebundenheit *f*

law body, jurisprudence, body of law · Rechtskomplex *m*

lawbreaker · Rechtsbrecher *m*, Rechtsübertreter

law change, law variation, law alteration, change of law, variation of law, alteration of law · Rechts(ab)änderung *f*, Rechtsumänderung, Rechtsveränderung

law choice, law election, choice-of-law, election-of-law · Rechtswahl *f*

law choice rule, law choice norm, law election rule, election-of-law rule, law election norm, election-of-law norm, choice-of-law rule, choice-of-law norm · Rechtswahlnorm *f*

law Christian, ecclesiastic(al) law, spiritual law; jus ecclesiasticum [*Latin*] [*Not to be confused with "jus canonicum"*] · Kirchenrecht *n*, kirchliches Recht, geistliches Recht

law comment(ary) · Gesetz(es)kommentar *m*

law committee, committee on the judiciary · Rechtsausschuß *m*

law comparison, comparison of law · Rechtsvergleichung *f*

law concerning unfair competition, act concerning unfair competition, statute concerning unfair competition · Gesetz *n* gegen unlauteren Wettbewerb

law course, course of law · Rechtsweg *m*

law court, court of law, court of justice [*As opposed to a "court of equity"*] · rechtsprechendes Gericht *n*

law day, court day; lage day, lagh day, doomsday [*In old English law*]; dies juridicus [*Latin*]; juridic(al) day · Gerichtstag *m*

law defined as norm · Recht *n* als Norm

law department, legal department, division of law, department of law, law division · Rechtsabteilung *f*

law dictionary · Rechtswörterbuch *n*

law division, law department, legal department, division of law, department of law · Rechtsabteilung *f*

law election, choice-of-law, election-of-law, law choice · Rechtswahl *f*

law election rule, election-of-law rule, law election norm, election-of-law norm, choice-of-law rule, choice-of-law norm, law choice rule, law choice norm · Rechtswahlnorm *f*

law encyclopedia · Rechtsenzyklopädie *f*, Rechtshandwörterbuch *n*

law exposition, exposition of law · Rechtsdarlegung *f*

law fiction → law(ful) fiction

law finder · Rechtsnachschlagesystem *n*

law firm · (Rechts)Anwaltsfirma *f*

law for dealing with land(s), (real) property transaction law, (real) estate transaction law, land(s) transaction law · Bodenrecht *n*, Grundstücksverkehrsrecht, Liegenschaftsrecht, Immobiliarrecht, Immobilienrecht

law for execution, act for execution, statute for execution · Ausführungsgesetz *n*

law for public utility housing, act for public utility housing, statute for public utility housing · Wohnungsgemeinnützigkeitsgesetz *n*

law for the conservation of monuments, statute for the conservation of monuments, act for the conservancy of monuments, law for the conservancy of monuments, statute for the conservancy of monuments, act for the preservation of monuments, law for the preservation of monuments, statute for the preservation of monuments, act for the conservation of monuments · Denkmalpflegegesetz *n*, Denkmalerhaltungsgesetz, Denkmalschutzgesetz

law for the protection of monuments · Denkmalschutzrecht *n*

law fountain, source of law, fountain of law, fountain of jurisdiction, jurisdiction fountain, law source · Rechtsquelle *f*

law-French · altfranzösische Juristensprache *f*

lawful [*This is a more general term as "legal", and may suggest conformity to the principle rather than to the letter of the law or may broadly refer to that which is not contrary to the law*]; legal · rechtserheblich (anerkannt), rechtlich, rechtmäßig

lawful ability, lawful capability, lawful capacity, lawful qualification, lawful condition, lawful status, legal ability, legal capability, legal capacity, legal qualification, legal condition, legal status, civil status, personal condition · Eignung *f* zu rechtswirksamem Verhalten, Fähigkeit *f* zu rechtswirksamem Verhalten, Geschäftsfähigkeit, Rechtsfähigkeit, rechtliche Fähigkeit

lawful ability to sue, lawful qualification to sue, lawful condition to sue, legal status to sue, legal capacity to sue, legal capability to sue, legal qualification to sue, legal condition to sue, legal ability to sue, lawful capacity to sue, lawful status to sue, lawful capability to sue · Klagefähigkeit *f*

lawful act(ion), proceeding, legal act(ion) · Rechtsakt *m*, Rechtshandlung *f*, rechtsetzender Akt, rechtsetzende Handlung [*Akt eines Gesetzgebers oder Richters, durch welchen Recht erst „geschaffen" wird*]

lawful affair, cause, matter of law, legal affair · Rechtsangelegenheit *f*, Rechtssache *f*

lawful argument, lawful ground, legal argument, legal ground · Rechtsgrund *m*

lawful base, lawful basis, legal base, legal basis, base in law, basis in law · rechtliche Grundlage *f*, rechtliche Basis *f*

lawful capability → lawful ability

lawful capability to sue, lawful ability to sue, lawful qualification to sue, lawful condition to sue, legal status to sue, legal capacity to sue, legal capability to sue, legal qualification to sue, legal condition to sue, legal ability to sue, lawful capacity to sue, lawful status to sue · Klagefähigkeit *f*, Klagevermögen *n*

lawful complaint, legal complaint · Rechtsbeschwerde *f*

lawful compulsion, legal compulsion · Rechtszwang *m*

law(ful) concept, legal concept, concept of law, concept of (legal) validity · Rechtsbegriff *m*, (Rechts)Geltungsbegriff, Legalbegriff

lawful condition, legal condition, status, lawful position, legal position · rechtliche Stellung *f*, Status *m*, Rechtsstellung

lawful condition → lawful ability

lawful condition to sue, legal status to sue, legal capacity to sue, legal capability to sue, legal qualification to sue, legal condition to sue, legal ability to sue, lawful capacity to sue, lawful status to sue, lawful capability to sue, lawful ability to sue, lawful qualification to sue · Klagefähigkeit *f*, Klagevermögen *n*

lawful contract conditions, legal terms of contract, legal contract terms, legal conditions of contract, legal contract conditions, lawful terms of contract, lawful contract terms, lawful conditions of contract · rechtliche Vertragsbedingungen *f pl*

lawful decision, legal decision · Rechtsentscheid(ung) *m, (f)*

lawful disability, legal incapacity, lawful incapacity, lawful inability, non ability, legal disability, legal incapability, legal incapacity, legal inability, legal inability [*Want of ability to do an act in law*] · rechtliche Unfähigkeit *f*, rechtliches Unvermögen *n*, Rechtsunfähigkeit, Rechtsunvermögen

lawful discretion, legal discretion [*It is the exercise of discretion where there are two alternative provisions of law applicable under either of which court could proceed*] · Verfahrensermessen *n*

lawful entity, legal entity · rechtliche Einheit *f* einer juristischen Person, Rechtsträger *m*

lawful ethics, legal ethics · Rechtsethik *f*

lawful excuse · rechtliche Entschuldigung *f*

law(ful) fiction, fiction of law, legal fiction · Rechtsfiktion *f*

lawful form, legal form · Rechtsform *f*

lawful ground, legal argument, legal ground, lawful argument · Rechtsgrund *m*

lawful heir (male), nearest kin, heir (male) general, general heir (male), heir (male) whatsoever, statutory heir (male), heir (male) at law, right heir (male), legal heir (male) [*One who takes the succession by relationship to the decedent and by force of law*] · Intestaterbe *m*, gesetzlicher Erbe

lawful hours · gesetzliche Arbeitszeit *f*

lawful impossibility, legal impossibility · rechtliche Unmöglichkeit *f*

lawful incapability, lawful inability, non ability, legal disability, legal incapability, legal incapacity, legal inability, lawful disability, lawful incapacity [*Want of ability to do an act in law*] · rechtliche Unfähigkeit *f*, rechtliches Unvermögen *n*, Rechtsunfähigkeit, Rechtsunvermögen

lawful information, legal information · Rechtsauskunft *f*

lawful instrument, (legal) instrument · Institut *n*, rechtliches Institut, Rechtsinstitut

lawfully passed · formell rechtlich beschlossen [*Gesetz*]

lawful memory, legal memory · Rechtsgedächtnis *n*

lawful natural child, legitimate natural child · eheliches Kind

lawful obedience, legal obedience, allegiance · gesetzmäßiger Gehorsam *m*

lawful obligation, (legal) obligation [*The relation between two persons, one of whom can take judicial proceedings or other legal steps to compel the other to do or abstain from doing a certain act. Although it includes both the right of the one and the duty of the other, the term is more frequently used to denote the latter*] · Schuldverhältnis *n*, Rechtsbindung *f*, Rechtsverbindlichkeit *f*, rechtliche Bindung, rechtliche Verbindlichkeit, Verpflichtung (zur Leistung), Leistungsverpflichtung

lawful position, legal position, lawful condition, legal condition, status · rechtliche Stellung *f*, Status *m*, Rechtsstellung

lawful qualification → lawful ability

lawful qualification to sue, lawful condition to sue, legal status to sue, legal capacity to sue, legal capability to sue, legal qualification to sue, legal condition to sue, legal ability to sue, lawful capacity to sue, lawful status to sue, lawful capability to sue, lawful ability to sue · Klagefähigkeit *f*, Klagevermögen *n*

lawful reasoning, opinion (of the court), legal reasoning · Rechtsfindung *f*

lawful residence · ordnungsmäßiger Aufenthalt *m*

lawful right according to common law, legal right according to common law · (subjektives) Recht *n* nach gemeinem Recht

lawful signification, legal signification · rechtliche Bedeutung *f*

lawful state order · rechtsstaatliche Ordnung *f*

lawful status → lawful ability

lawful status to sue, lawful capability to sue, lawful ability to sue, lawful qualification to sue, lawful condition to sue, legal status to sue, legal capacity to sue, legal capability to sue, legal qualification to sue, legal condition to sue, legal ability to sue, lawful capacity to sue, lawful ability to sue · Klagefähigkeit *f*, Klagevermögen *n*

lawful terms of contract, lawful contract terms, lawful conditions of contract, lawful contract conditions, legal terms of contract, legal contract terms, legal conditions of contract, legal contract conditions · rechtliche Vertragsbedingungen *fpl*

lawful thing, legal thing · Rechtsgegenstand *m*

lawful trust instrument, (legal) trust instrument · Treuhandrechtsinstitut *n*, (rechtliches) Treuhandinstitut

lawgiver, nomotheta [*Such as Solon and Lycurgus among the Greeks, and Caesar, Pompey, and Sylla among the Romans*] · Rechtsgeber *m*

law historian, historian of law · Rechtshistoriker *m*

law in action, legal realism · lebendiges Recht *n*, lebendes Recht

law in force, valid law · gültiges Gesetz *n*

law infringement, infringement of law · Gesetz(es)verstoß *m*

law in the books · abstraktes Recht *n*, Paragraphenrecht, totes Recht

law in the making · entstehendes Recht *n*

law journal, legal periodical, legal journal, law periodical · Rechtszeitschrift *f*

law learning; jurisprudentia [*Latin*] · Rechtsstudium *n*, Studium der Rechte

lawless · gesetz(es)los

lawlessness · Gesetzlosigkeit *f*

law literature, literature of the law · Rechtsliteratur *f*

law lord · rechtsgelehrtes Mitglied *n* des Oberhauses [*England*]

law made by Parliament, act, statute; statutum, actus [*Latin*]; Act of Parliament, enabling act · formelles Gesetz *n*, parlamentarisches Gesetz, (Parlaments)Gesetz

lawmaker, legislator · Gesetzgeber *m*

lawmaking, (legislative) enactment, making of law, legislation · Gesetzgebung *f*, Erlassen *n* von Gesetzen

lawmaking as required by federal interest(s), legislation as required by federal interest(s) · Bedarfsgesetzgebung *f* [*Bundesrepublik Deutschland. Die konkurrierende Gesetzgebung des Bundes ist nach Artikel 72 Absatz 2 Grundgesetz (GG) stets eine Bedarfsgesetzgebung. Sie kommt nur zur Anwendung wenn ein Bedürfnis nach bundesgesetzlicher Regelung besteht*]

lawmaking assembly, legislative assembly · gesetzgebende Versammlung *f*

lawmaking body, legislative body · gesetzgebendes Organ *n*

lawmaking committee, legislative committee · gesetzgeberischer Ausschuß *m*, gesetzgebender Auschuß

lawmaking council, legislative council · gesetzgebender Rat *m*, gesetzgeberischer Rat

lawmaking for the protection of ancient monuments and buildings of historic interest, legislation for the protection of ancient monuments and buildings of historic interest · Denkmalschutzgesetzgebung *f*

lawmaking local authority, local legislative authority, legislative local authority · gesetzgebende örtliche Behörde *f*, örtliche gesetzgebende Beörde

lawmaking of arbitration, arbitration lawmaking, legislation of arbitration, arbitration legislation · Schieds(gerichts)gesetzgebung *f*

lawmaking of planning, planning legislation, legislation of planning, planning lawmaking · Planungsgesetzgebung *f*

lawmaking procedure, procedure of legislation, legislation procedure, procedure of lawmaking · Gesetzgebungsverfahren *n*

lawmaking treaty · Staatsvertrag *m* mit vereinbarten Rechtssätzen

law memorandum · schriftliche Stellungnahme *f* zu den Rechtsgrundlagen des geltend gemachten Anspruchs

law merchant; lex mercatoria [*Latin*]; merchant law, mercantile law, commercial law, business law · Handelsrecht *n*

lawn area, turf area · Rasenfläche *f*

law norm, rule (of law), norm of law, legal rule, (legal) norm, law rule [*It is a rule of general application, sanctioned by the recognition of authorities, and usually expressed in the form of maxim or logical proposition. Called a "rule", because in doubtful or unforeseen cases it is a guide or norm for their decision*] · Gesetz(es)norm *f*, Sachnorm *f*, normative Festlegung *f*, (Rechts)Norm

law number, act number, statute number · Gesetz(es)nummer *f*

law observer · Rechtsbefolger *m*

law of administrative process, law of administrative procedure, administrative procedure law, administrative process law · Verwaltungsverfahrensrecht *n*

law of adoption, adoption law · Adoptionsrecht *n*

law of agrarian reform, land(s) reform law, agrarian reform law, law of land(s) reform · Bodenreformrecht *n*, Landreformrecht

law of aliens, law on aliens, alien law, law applied to aliens · Ausländerrecht *n*, Fremdenrecht [*Rechtssätze, die einen Ausländer anders behandeln als einen Inländer*]

law of arbitration, arbitration law · Schiedsrecht *n*, Schiedsgerichtsrecht

law of area replotting → act of (building) (land) area replotting

law of assignation, assignation law, law of cession, law of assignment, assignment law, cession law · Abtretungsrecht *n*, Zessionsrecht

law of authorities · Behördenrecht *n*

law of banking, statute of banking, act of banking, bank(ing) law, bank(ing) statute, bank(ing) act · Kreditwesengesetz *n*

law of banking, bank(ing) law · Kreditwesenrecht *n*

law of bankruptcy, bankruptcy law · Konkursrecht *n*

law of bills of exchange · Wechselrecht *n*

law of budget(s), budget(ary) law · Haushalt(s)recht *n*

law of building (and loan) associations (US); building society law (Brit.); building (and loan) association law · Bauspar(kassen)recht *n*

law of (building) (land) area replotting → act of (building) (land) area replotting

law of building lines, act of building lines, statute of building lines, building line act, building line law, building line statute · Fluchtliniengesetz *n*, Baufluchtlinien)gesetz

law of building lines, building line law, BL law · (Bau)Fluchtlinienrecht *n* [*Es betrifft die Anlegung und Veränderung von Straßen und Plätzen in Gemeinden aller Art*]

law of cession, law of assignment, assignment law, cession law, law of assignation, assignation law · Abtretungsrecht *n*, Zessionsrecht

law of cheques, law of checks · Scheckrecht *n*

law of claims, law of demands · Forderungsrecht *n*, Verlangensrecht, objektives Forderungsrecht, objektives Verlangensrecht, objektives Beanspruchungsrecht

law of common villanage, law of common ville(i)nage · lassitisches Recht *n*

law of competition, competition law · Wettbewerbsrecht *n*

law of components → law relating to fixtures

law of conflicts, Private International Law, conflicts law, International Private Law, IPL, conflict of laws · Außenprivatrecht *n*, Kollisionsrecht, zwischenstaatliches (Privat)Recht *n*, Internationales Privatrecht *n*, IPR *n*, Zwischenprivatrecht *n*, Grenzrecht *n*

law of constitution — law officer of the Crown

law of constitution; jus publicum [*Latin*]; public law, constitutional law [*The law concerned with the rights and duties of the state. It is contrasted with private law, which deals with the rights and duties of subjects inter se*] · öffentliches Recht

law of contract; lex loci (contractus) [*Latin*]; contract law, conventionary law [*The law of the place of a contract; the law of the place where a contract is made, or is to be performed*] · Vertragsrecht *n*, Recht des Vertragsschlusses

law of contract award, law of contract letting · Auftragsrecht *n*

law of contract letting, law of contract award · Auftragsrecht *n*

law of conveyances (of land), law of land conveyances, law of voluntary transfer, voluntary transfer law, conveyance law, land conveyance law · Auflassungsrecht *n*, freiwilliges Übertragungsrecht *n*

law of corporations, corporation law · (objektives) Körperschaftsrecht *n*, (objektives) Korporationsrecht

law of (court) procedure (and practice), adjective law, remedial law, procedural law, procedure law [*Law consisting of rules of conduct prescribed by substantive law, and enforced by adjective law. In other words, substantive law is administered by the courts and deals with right and duties, whereas adjective law relates to practice and procedure and deals with remedies. "Substantive law" and "adjective law" were first used by Bentham (2 works, 6) and are now generally adopted, notwithstanding Austin's criticism of them (2 Jurisprudence, 788—789)*] · Formalrecht *n*, formelles Recht, Verfahrensrecht, Prozeßrecht

law of debtor and creditor · Schuldner- und Gläubigerrecht *n*

law of deeds · Urkundenrecht *n*

law of demands, law of claims · Forderungsrecht *n*, Verlangensrecht, objektives Forderungsrecht, objektives Verlangensrecht, objektives Beanspruchungsrecht

law of descent (and distribution), law of inheritance, inheritance law, hereditary law, law of (hereditary) succession (and distribution) · Erb(folge)recht *n*, Erbgangrecht, Erbschaftsrecht, Nachkommensrecht, Vermögensnachfolgerecht

law of development · Entwick(e)lungsgesetz *n* [*Wirtschaftslehre*]

law of diminishing return, law of diminishing increment, law of less proportional return · Bodengesetz *n*, Gesetz des abnehmenden Ertragszuwachses, Gesetz des fallenden Ertragszuwachses; Gesetz vom abnehmenden Bodenertrag, Gesetz vom fallenden Bodenertrag [*Fehlbenennungen*] [*Unter sonst gleichen Umständen vermögen in der Landwirtschaft steigende Aufwendungen von einem gewissen Punkte an keine in demselben Verhältnis mehr steigende Erträge hervorzubringen, oder mit anderen Worten: Eine zur Pflanzenproduktion benutzte Fläche liefert von einer bestimmten Grenze an einen pro Aufwandseinheit abfallenden Ertrag*]

law of disappeared persons, act of disappeared persons, law of missing persons, act of missing persons, statute of missing persons, statute of disappeared persons · Verschollenheitsgesetz *n*

law of domestic relations, family law · Familienrecht *n*

law of duties, law of statutory charges, law of legal charges · Abgabenrecht *n*

law of enrichment, enrichment law · Bereicherungsrecht *n* [*BGB §§ 812 ff.*]

law of entail, entail law · Erbrecht *n* für bestimmte Personen

(law of) equity, equity law; equity jurisprudence [*misnomer*] [*Law based upon discretion and conscience, derived from the old Court of Chancery*] · Billigkeitsrecht *n*, objektives Billigkeitsrecht

law of error · Fehlergesetz *n*

law of escheat, escheat law · Heimfallrecht *n*, objektives Heimfallrecht

law of estate → (real) estate law

law of estate brokers → law of (real) estate brokers

law of estates less than freehold, lease(hold) law, leasehold estate law, demise law, tenancy law; tack law, assedation law [*Scots law*] · (Boden)Pachtrecht *n*, (Boden)Nutzungsrecht, Landpachtrecht, Landnutzungsrecht, Flächenpachtrecht, Flächennutzungsrecht [*objektiv*]

law of evidence, law of proof, evidence law, proof law [*The aggregate of rules and principles regulating the admissibility, relevancy, weight and sufficiency of evidence in legal proceedings*] · Beweisrecht *n*

law of excavation, law of unearthing, excavation law, unearthing law · Ausgrabungsrecht *n* [*Zur Erhaltung völkischen Geschichts- und Überlieferungsgutes*]

law of exploiting minerals → law of taking minerals

law of feodal tenure → law of tenure(s) (of land)

law of feudal estates → law of tenure(s) (of land)

law officer of the Crown, Crown law officer · Kronjurist *m*

law of finders (of lost property) · Fundrecht *n*

law of fitness and flavo(u)r · Gesetz *n* des Gesamtzusammenhangs [*Es verlangt vom Richter, seine Entscheidung in Übereinstimmung mit dem Sinn des Gesetzes zu bringen*]

law of fixtures → law relating to fixtures

law of fraud, statute of fraud, act of fraud · Betrugsgesetz *n*

law of fraud, fraud law · Betrugsrecht *n*

law of future interest (in land), law of future right (in land) · Recht *n* des zukünftig wirksamen Eigentumsanteils

law of (general) property, law of proprietorship, law of ownership (of property), ownership (of property) law, (general) property law, proprietorship law · Eigentumsrecht *n*, objektives Eigentumsrecht

law of ground-water, ground-water law · Grundwasserrecht *n* [*objektiv*]

law of (hereditary) succession (and distribution), law of descent (and distribution), law of inheritance, inheritance law, hereditary law · Erb(folge)recht *n*, Erbgangrecht, Erbschaftsrecht, Nachkommensrecht, Vermögensnachfolgerecht

law of increasing return on land, law of increasing yield of land · Gesetz *n* vom zunehmenden Bodenertrag

law of indifference · Marktspaltungsgesetz *n* [*Aufspaltung der Marktpreise nach Jevons*]

law of inheritance, act of inheritance, statute of inheritance, inheritance act, inheritance law, inheritance statute · Erb(schafts)gesetz *n*

law of inheritance, inheritance law, hereditary law, law of (hereditary) succession (and distribution), law of descent (and distribution) · Erb(folge)recht *n*, Erbgangrecht, Erbschaftsrecht, Nachkommensrecht, Vermögensnachfolgerecht

law of institutions · Anstaltsrecht *n*, objektives Anstaltsrecht

law of insurance, insurance law · Versicherungsrecht *n*

law of intestate inheritance, law of intestate succession, law of succession ad intestato, law of intestacy · Erbrecht *n* der Erstgeburt beim Fehlen eines Testaments, Intestaterbrecht

Law of King, Act of King, Statute of King · Königsgesetz *n*

law of land → law of land (possession)

law of land acquisition, land acquisition law · Bodenerwerbsrecht *n*, Landerwerbsrecht, Bodenbeschaffungsrecht, Landbeschaffungsrecht, Grund(stücks)-erwerbsrecht, Grund(stücks)beschaffungsrecht [*objektiv*]

law of land conveyances, law of voluntary transfer, voluntary transfer law, conveyance law, land conveyance law, law of conveyances (of land) · Auflassungsrecht *n*, freiwilliges Übertragungsrecht *n*

law of landed estate → (real) estate law

law of landlord and tenant, landlord/tenant law, (residential) rent law, dwelling rent law · Mietrecht *n*, Wohnungsmietrecht [*Sammelbegriff für alle für die Mietverhältnisse maßgebenden rechtlichen Vorschriften*]

law of land (possession), act of land (possession), statute of land (possession), possessory land law, possessory land act, possessory land statute, (real) estate law, (real) estate act, (real) estate statute, realty law, realty act, realty statute · Bodenbesitzgesetz *n*, Grund(stücks)besitzgesetz, Immobiliarbesitzgesetz, Immobilienbesitzgesetz, Liegenschaftsbesitzgesetz, Landbesitzgesetz

law of land registration, law of land registry, land registration law, land registry law · Grundbuchrecht *n*, GB-Recht

law of land(s) reform, law of agrarian reform, land(s) reform law, agrarian reform law · Bodenreformrecht *n*, Landreformrecht

law of lawful discretion, law of legal discretion · Gesetz *n* des rechtlichen Ermessensspielraums

law of leeways · Gesetz *n* des Spielraumes

law of legal charges → law of duties

law of legal discretion, law of lawful discretion · Gesetz *n* des rechtlichen Ermessensspielraums

law of legal discretion, law of statutory discretion · Gesetz *n* des gesetzlichen Ermessensspielraums

law of less proportional return, law of diminishing return, law of diminishing increment · Bodengesetz *n*, Gesetz des abnehmenden Ertragszuwachses, Gesetz des fallenden Ertragszuwachses; Gesetz vom abnehmenden Bodenertrag, Gesetz vom fallenden Bodenertrag [*Fehlbenennungen*] [*Unter sonst gleichen Umständen vermögen in der Landwirtschaft steigende Aufwendungen von einem gewissen Punkte an keine in demselben Verhältnis mehr steigende Erträge hervorzubringen, oder mit anderen Worten: Eine zur Pflanzenproduktion benutzte Fläche liefert von einer bestimmten Grenze an einen pro Aufwandseinheit abfallenden Ertrag*]

law of limitation, act of limitation, limitation statute, limitation law, limitation act, statute of limitation · Verjährungsgesetz *n*

law of manor → law of tenure(s) (of land)

law of marine insurance · Seeversicherungsrecht n

law of master and servant, master and servant law · individuelles Arbeits(vertrags)recht n

law of merchant shipping, merchant shipping law · Handelsschiffahrtsrecht n

law of migration, migration law · Wanderungsgesetz n

law of mining minerals → law of taking minerals

law of missing persons, act of missing persons, statute of missing persons, statute of disappeared persons, law of disappeared persons, act of disappeared persons · Verschollenheitsgesetz n

law of nations, (public) international law · Völkerrecht n, (öffentliches) internationales Recht

law of nature, scientific law · Naturgesetz n

law of nature; jus naturale [*Latin*] · Naturrecht n, natürliches Recht, nichtpositives Recht

law of obligations · Schuldrecht n

law of organization, organizational law · Organisationsgesetz n

law of ownership (of property), ownership (of property) law, (general) property law, proprietorship law, law of (general) property, law of proprietorship · Eigentumsrecht n, objektives Eigentumsrecht

law of percolating water, law of seepage water, seepage water law, percolating water law · (objektives) Sickerwasserrecht n

law of personality and status and capacity, law of persons · Personenrecht n

law of prescription, prescription law · Ersitzungsrecht n, objektives Ersitzungsrecht

law of private land (possession), (possessory) private land law · Privatboden(besitz)recht n, Privatland(besitz)recht

law of proof, evidence law, proof law, law of evidence [*The aggregate of rules and principles regulating the admissibility, relevancy, weight and sufficiency of evidence in legal proceedings*] · Beweisrecht n

law of property → (real) estate law

law of property act · sogenanntes Grundstücksverkehrsrecht n, Grundstücksverkehrsgesetz n, Normen fpl des Grundstücksverkehrsgesetzes, Boden(verkehrs)gesetz, Liegenschafts(verkehrs)gesetz, Immobiliar(verkehrs)gesetz, Immobilien(verkehrs)gesetz

law of proprietorship, law of ownership (of property), ownership (of property) law, (general) property law, proprietorship law, law of (general) property · Eigentumsrecht n, objektives Eigentumsrecht

law of public health, public health law · öffentliches Gesundheitsrecht n, Volksgesundheitsrecht

law of (real) estate → (real) estate law

law of (real) estate brokers, law of (real) property brokers, law of land property, law of realty property · Bodenhändlerrecht n, Landhändlerrecht, Grund(stücks)händlerrecht, Grund(stücks)maklerrecht, (Boden)Maklerrecht, Landmaklerrecht

law of realty → (real) estate law

law of registry → law of (land) registration

law of (residential) rent prices · (Wohnungs)Mietpreisrecht n

law of retail (trade) gravitation · Gravitationsgesetz n, Kleinhandelsgravitationsgesetz [*Zur Bestimmung der Marktbereiche von Zentren*]

law of return, law of yield, return law, yield law · Renditegesetz n, Ertragsgesetz

law of Rome → (civil) law of Rome

law of sales · Kaufrecht n

law of sanctions, sanction law · Sanktionsrecht n

law of seepage water, seepage water law, percolating water law, law of percolating water · (objektives) Sickerwasserrecht n

law of settlement, act of settlement, statute of settlement · Ortsangehörigkeitsgesetz n [*In England. Die Arbeiter mußten an dem Ort wo sie heimatberechtigt waren bleiben, um zu verhüten, daß eine Gemeinde die Armen einer anderen unterstützen müßte*]

law of statutory charges → law of duties

law of succession → law of (hereditary) succession

law of succession ad intestato, law of intestacy, law of intestate inheritance, law of intestate succession · Erbrecht n der Erstgeburt beim Fehlen eines Testaments, Intestaterbrecht

law of supply and demand · Gesetz n von Angebot und Nachfrage

law of taking minerals, law of mining minerals, law of exploiting minerals, mining law, mineral law · (Mineral(ien))Abbaurecht n, (Mineral(ien)-)Ausbeutungsrecht, (Mineral(ien))Gewinnungsrecht, (objektives) Berg(bau)recht

law of taxation, taxation law · Besteuerungsrecht n

law of taxes on objects yielding rent or profit or income · Ertragssteuerrecht n

law of tenure(s) (of land), law of (the) manor, law of feuda(to)ry tenure, law of feudal tenure, law of feodal tenure, law of feuds, law of feudal estates, feudal law, tenure law, feodal law, feuda(to)ry law, manorial law; lex feudalis [*Latin*] · Leh(e)n(s)recht *n*, Feudalrecht

law of testate inheritance · Testaterbrecht *n*

law of (the) constitution, constitutional law · Verfassungsrecht *n*

law of the country, national law, municipal law, state law [*The law of a particular country as distinguished from international law*] · Nationalrecht *n*, Staatsrecht, Landesrecht

law of the country, statute of the country, national act, national law, national statute, act of the country · Landesgesetz *n*, Nationalgesetz, Staatsgesetz

law of the forum; lex non scripta [*Latin*]; unwritten law, juristic law [*It comprises both, judge-made law and jurist-made law*] · Gerichtsrecht *n*; ungeschriebenes Recht [*Fehlbenennung, weil Gerichtsentscheide wegen ihrer bindenden Kraft für die Zukunft geschrieben sind*]

law of the Goths; lex gothica [*Latin*]; Gothic law [*First promulgated in writing A. D. 466*] · gotisches Recht *n*

law of the Land, Land law · Landesrecht *n* [*Bundesrepublik Deutschland*]

law of the land → (real) estate law

law of (the) manor → law of tenure(s) (of land)

law of the place of solutions; lex loci solutionis [*Latin*] [*The law of the place where payment or performance of a contract is to be made*] · Erfüllungsortrecht *n*, Recht des Erfüllungsortes

law of the place where a contract is made; lex loci celebrationis [*Latin*] · Vertragsortrecht *n*, Recht des Vertragsortes

law of the single variable · Gesetz *n* der Isolierung von Situationen und Standardisierung aller Faktoren mit Ausnahme eines freigelassenen Faktors

law of (the) staple, staple law · Stapelgesetz *n*

law of the welfare state, law of the social service state · Sozialstaatrecht *n*

law of tithes, tithe law · Zehnt(en)recht *n*

law of tort(s) · Deliktrecht *n*, Recht der unerlaubten Handlung(en)

law of trade-marks · Schutzmarkengesetz *n*

law of treaties · völkerrechtliches Vertragsrecht *n*

law of unearthing, act of unearthing, unearthing law, unearthing statute, unearthing act, statute of unearthing · Ausgrabungsgesetz *n*

law of unearthing, unearthing law · Ausgrabungsrecht *n* [*Zur Erhaltung völkischen Geschichts- und Überlieferungsgutes*]

law of unsplit farm inheritance [*Law of inheritance by which a farm of moderate size is not split up but is inherited as a whole*] · Höferecht *n*

law of voluntary transfer, voluntary transfer law, conveyance law, land conveyance law, law of conveyances (of land), law of land conveyances · Auflassungsrecht *n*, freiwilliges Übertragungsrecht

law of wage(s), wage(s) law · Lohnrecht *n*

law of Wales; lex Wallensica [*Latin*]; Welsh law · walisisches Recht *n*

law of war, martial law; jus belli [*Latin*] · Kriegsrecht *n*

law of water (rights), water (rights) law · (objektives) Wasserrecht *n*

law of water use · Wassernutzungsrecht *n*

law of wills, wills act, wills statute, wills law, statute of wills, act of wills · Testamentsgesetz *n*

law of wills, testamentary law, wills law · Testamentsrecht *n*

law of yield, return law, yield law, law of return · Renditegesetz *n*, Ertragsgesetz

law of zoning, zoning law · Baunutzungsrecht *n*

law on inspection of insurance, act on inspection of insurance, statute on inspection of insurance · Versicherungsaufsichtsgesetz *n*

law on rights in registered ships, act on rights in registered ships, statute on rights in registered ships · Schiffsrechtegesetz *n*

Law on Utility Models · Gebrauchsmustergesetz *n*, GebrMG [*Bundesrepublik Deutschland*]

law passed by parliament, political law [*As distinguished from a scientific law*] · Rechtsgesetz *n*

law philosopher, legal philosopher, philosopher of law · Rechtsphilosoph *m*

law philosophy, legal philosophy, philosophy of law · Rechtsphilosophie *f*

law point, question of law, point of law, law question · Rechtsfrage *f*

law practice · Rechtswesen *n*

law principle, principle of law · Rechtsgrundsatz *m*, Rechtsprinzip *n*

law procedure, procedure of law · Rechtsverfolgung *f*

law professor · Rechtsprofessor *m*

law proposition, rule, proposition of law · Rechtssatz *m*

law provision, legal provision, provision of law · Gesetz(es)bestimmung *f*, gesetzliche Bestimmung

law question, law point, question of law, point of law · Rechtsfrage *f*

law reform, reform of law · Rechtsreform *f*

law reform committee · Rechtsreformausschuß *m*

law reformer · Rechtsreformer *m*

law regulating the relation(ship) between state and churches · Staatskirchenrecht *n*

law relating to fixtures, law relating to components, law of fixtures, law of components [*This law involves the distinction between realty and personalty*] · Bestandteilrecht *n*, Grundstücksbestandteilrecht, Recht über die mit einem Grundstück verbundenen körperlichen Gegenstände

law relating to protection against notice to terminate, statute relating to protection against notice to terminate, act relating to protection against notice to terminate · Kündigungsschutzgesetz *n*

law relating to protection against notice to terminate residential leases, statute relating to protection against notice to terminate residential leases, act relating to protection against notice to terminate residential leases · Mieterkündigungsschutzgesetz *n*

(law) reports, (law) report(er) [*Authenticated reports of decided cases in the superior courts*] · Entscheidungssammlung *f*, Urteilssammlung

law rule, law norm, rule (of law), norm of law, legal rule, (legal) norm [*It is a rule of general application, sanctioned by the recognition of authorities, and usually expressed in the form of maxim or logical proposition. Called a "rule", because in doubtful or unforeseen cases it is a guide or norm for their decision*] · Gesetz(es)norm *f*, Sachnorm, normative Festlegung *f*, (Rechts)Norm

law science, science of law, jurisprudence, legal science; jurisprudentia [*Latin*] · Jurisprudenz *f*, Rechtswissenschaft *f*, Lehre *f* der allgemeinen Rechtsfragen, Rechtslehre

law sociology, sociology of law · Rechtssoziologie *f*, Soziologie des Rechts

Law(s) of England, English Law(s) · englisches Recht *n*

law source, law fountain, source of law, fountain of law, fountain of jurisdiction, jurisdiction fountain · Rechtsquelle *f*

law state, government by rule of law · Rechtsstaat *m*

law state, state of law · Rechtszustand *m*

law student, student of law · Jurastudent *m*

(law) suit, plea, cause; writ, (court) action [*In old English law, "writ" is used as equivalent to "action", hence writs are sometimes divided into real, personal, and mixed. It is not uncommon to call a proceeding in a common law court an action(-at-law), and one in an equity court a (law-)suit, but this is not a necessary distinction*] · (Gerichts)Klage *f*

(law)suit at common law, plea at common law, common law (court) action, common law (law)suit, common law cause, common law plea, (court) action at common law, case at common law · Klage *f* nach gemeinem Recht, gemeinrechtliche Klage

(law)suit de bonis asportatis, cause de bonis asportatis, plea de bonis asportatis, (court) action de bonis asportatis · Klage *f* wegen rechtswidriger (Besitz)Entziehung einer beweglichen Sache

(law)suit for an account, cause for an account, plea for an account, (court) action for an account · Abrechnungsklage *f*, Klage auf Abrechnung [*Billigkeitsrecht*]

(law)suit for breach of contract, cause for breach of contract, plea for breach of contract, (court) action for breach of contract · Vertragsbruchklage *f*

(law)suit for delivery, cause for delivery, plea for delivery, (court) action for delivery · Nichtlieferungsklage *f*, Klage wegen Nichtlieferung

(law)suit for dissolution, (court) action for dissolution, cause for dissolution, plea for dissolution · Auflösungsklage *f*

(law)suit for exemption from liability, cause for exemption from liability, plea for exemption from liability, (court) action for exemption from liability · negative Feststellungsklage *f*

(law)suit for intrusion → (law)suit for trespass

(law) suit for money had and received, cause for money had and received, plea for money had and received, (court) action for money had and received · Geldrückerstattungsklage *f*

(law)suit for payment, cause for payment, plea for payment, (court) action for payment · Zahlungsklage *f*

(law)suit for recovery, cause for reimbursement, cause for restitution, cause for refunding, plea for reimbursement,

(law)suit for redemption — (law)suit of advowson

plea for refunding, plea for restitution, (law)suit for reimbursement, (law)suit for refunding, (law)suit for restitution, (court) action for reimbursement, (court) action for restitution, (court) action for refunding, (court) action for recovery, cause for recovery, plea for recovery · Abgeltungsklage f, Ersetzungsklage, Erstattungsklage, Vergütungsklage

(law)suit for redemption, plea for redemption, (court) action for redemption, cause for redemption · Klage f auf Freigabe von Sicherheiten, Sicherheit(en)freigabeklage

(law)suit for reimbursement, (law)suit for refunding, (law)suit for restitution, (court) action for reimbursement, (court) action for restitution, (court) action for refunding, (court) action for recovery, cause for recovery, plea for recovery, (law)suit for recovery, cause for reimbursement, cause for restitution, cause for refunding, plea for reimbursement, plea for refunding, plea for restitution · Abgeltungsklage f, Ersetzungsklage, Erstattungsklage, Vergütungsklage

(law)suit for removal, cause for removal, plea for removal, (court) action for removal · Beseitigungsklage f

(law)suit for specific performance, (court) action for completion of contract, (law)suit for completion of contract, cause for completion of contract, plea for completion of contract, cause for specific performance, plea for specific performance, (court) action for specific performance · (Vertrags)Erfüllungsklage f, Naturalerfüllungsklage

(law)suit for the recovery of land, cause for the recovery of land, plea for the recovery of land, (court) action for the recovery of land [*The mixed action at common law to recover the possession of land (which is real), and damages and cost(s) for the wrongful withholding of the land (which are personal)*] · (Immobilien)Besitzklage f, Liegenschaftsbesitzklage, Immobiliarbesitzklage, Grund(stücks)besitzklage, eigentliche Besitzklage, Klage aus (widerrechtlicher) Besitzentziehung, (D)Ejektionsklage, possessorische Klage in bezug auf Immobilien, Delogierungsklage [*Als uneigentliche Besitzklage kann diese Klage auch als Räumungsklage des Vermieters gegen den Mieter angewendet werden*]

(law)suit for (the tort of) deceit, cause for (the tort of) deceit, plea for (the tort of) deceit, (court) action for (the tort of) deceit · Betrugsklage f

(law)suit for tort, (law)suit in tort, cause for tort, cause in tort, plea for tort, plea in tort, (court) action for tort, (court) action in tort · Deliktklage f

(law)suit for trespass, (law)suit for intrusion, plea for trespass, plea for intrusion, (court) action for trespass, (court) action for intrusion, cause for trespass, cause for intrusion · (Besitz)Verletzungsklage f wegen Eindringen, (Besitz)Störungsklage wegen Eindringen, (Besitz)Beeinträchtigungsklage wegen Eindringen

(law)suit for unjust detention, (law)suit for unjust retention, (law)suit for unjust detainment, (law)suit for unjust detainer, (court) action of detinue, plea of detinue, (law)suit of detinue, cause of detinue, (court) action for unjust detention, (court) action for unjust retention, (court) action for unjust detainment, (court) action for unjust detainer, plea for unjust detention, plea for unjust retention, plea for unjust detainment, plea for unjust detainer, cause for unjust detention, cause for unjust retention, cause for unjust detainment, cause for unjust detainer · Klage f wegen ungerechtfertigter Vorenthaltung, Klage wegen ungerechtfertigter Zurück(be)haltung, Klage wegen ungerechtfertigter Einbehaltung, Klage wegen ungerechtfertigter Retention, Klage wegen ungerechtfertigtem Einbehalt, Klage wegen ungerechtfertigtem Vorenthalt

(law)suit founded on contract, cause founded on contract, plea founded on contract, (court) action founded on contract · Entschädigungsklage f ex contractu vel quasi, Schadenersatzklage ex contractu vel quasi, Forderungsklage ex contractu vel quasi, Personenklage ex contractu vel quasi, Personalklage ex contractu vel quasi [*Fehlbenennung*]

(law)suit founded on tort, cause founded on tort, plea founded on tort, (court) action founded on tort · Entschädigungsklage f im engeren Sinne, Schadenersatzklage im engeren Sinne, Forderungsklage im engeren Sinne, Personenklage im engeren Sinne; Personalklage im engeren Sinne [*Fehlbenennung*]

(law)suit in error, cause in error, plea in error, (court) action in error · Nichtigkeitsklage f, Revisionsklage

(law)suit in personam → personal (court) action

(law)suit in tort, cause for tort, cause in tort, plea for tort, plea in tort, (court) action for tort, (court) action in tort, (law)suit for tort · Deliktklage f

(law)suit of account, plea of account, (court) action of account, cause of account · Klage f auf Rechnungslegung, Rechnungslegungsklage

(law)suit of advowson, cause of patronage, cause of advowson, plea of patronage, plea of advowson, (court) action of patronage, (court) action of advowson, (law)suit of patronage · Patronats(recht)klage *f*

(law)suit of assumpsit, cause of assumpsit, (plea of) assumpsit, (court) action of assumpsit · Nichteinhaltungsklage *f*, Nichterfüllungsklage [*Schadenersatzklage wegen schuldhafter Nichterfüllung eines formlosen mündlich oder schriftlich gegebenem Versprechen*]

(law)suit of debt, plea of debt, (court) action of debt, cause of debt · Schuld(en)klage *f* [*Zur Einklagung einer Schuld*]

(law)suit of deceit, cause of deceit, plea of deceit, (court) action of deceit · Klage *f* wegen Täuschung, Täuschungsklage

(law)suit of detinue, (court) action of detinue, cause of detinue, plea of detinue [*An action by a plaintiff who seeks to recover goods in specie, or on failure thereof the value, and also damages for the detention*] · Klage *f* auf Wiedererlangung einer beweglichen Sache und Schadenersatz, Klage auf Herausgabe einer beweglichen Sache und Schadenersatz

(law)suit of detinue → (law)suit for unjust detention

(law)suit of devastation, cause of estrepement, cause of devastation, plea of estrepement, plea of devastation, (court) action of estrepement, (court) action of devastation, (law)suit of estrepement · Verwüstungsklage *f*

(law)suit of equity, equitable plea, plea of equity, equitable (court) action, equitable (law)suit, equitable cause, (court) action of equity, cause of equity · Billigkeitsklage *f*, Billigkeitsrechtklage, Klage nach Billigkeit(srecht)

(law)suit of estrepement, (law)suit of devastation, cause of estrepement, cause of devastation, plea of estrepement, plea of devastation, (court) action of estrepement, (court) action of devastation · Verwüstungsklage *f*

(law)suit of eviction, cause of eviction, plea of eviction, (court) action of eviction · Grund(stücks)besitzklage *f* wegen Grund(stücks)besitzentziehung

(law)suit of injunction, cause of injunction, plea of injunction, (court) action of injunction · Verfügungsklage *f*

(law)suit of mistake, cause of mistake, plea of mistake, (court) action of mistake · Irrtumsklage *f*

(law)suit of patronage, (law)suit of advowson, cause of patronage, cause of advowson, plea of patronage, plea of advowson, (court) action of patronage, (court) action of advowson · Patronats(recht)klage *f*

(law)suit of possessory right, cause of possessory right, plea of possessory right, (court) action of possessory right · Besitzrechtklage *f*

(law)suit of replevin, cause of replevin, plea of replevin, (court) action of replevin · Klage *f* auf Wiedererlangung einer beweglichen Sache und Schadenersatz bei unzulässiger Selbstpfändung, Klage auf Rückgabe einer selbstgepfändeten Sache

(law)suit of transumpt, transumpt, (court) action of transumpt, plea of transumpt, cause of transumpt [*Scots law. An action brought for the purpose of obtaining transumpt(s)*] · Klage *f* auf Schriftstückabschrift

(law)suit of trover (and conversion), plea of trover (and conversion), (court) action of trover (and conversion), cause of trover (and conversion) · Bereicherungsklage *f*, Schatzfundklage, Deliktsklage wegen Unterschlagung, Unterschlagungsklage [*Klage auf Schadenersatz für die Besitzentziehung von beweglichen Sachen (= goods)*]

(law)suit on the case, (court) action on the case, cause on the case, plea on the case · tatsächlich angestellte Klage *f*

(law)suit on trespass, plea on trespass, cause on trespass, (court) action on trespass · Rechtsverletzungsklage *f*, Klage wegen Rechtsverletzung

(law)suit per se, plea per se, (court) action per se, cause per se · Klage *f* die nicht von einem Schadensnachweis abhängt

(law)suit personal, cause personal, plea personal, personal (court) action, personal plea, personal (law)suit, personal cause; personal writ [*In old English law*]; (court) action personal · Entschädigungsklage *f*, Schadenersatzklage, Forderungsklage, Personenklage [*Fehlbenennung: Personalklage*]

(law)suit to gain an injunction, plea to gain an injunction, action to gain an injunction, cause to gain an injunction · Unterlassungsklage *f*

(law)suit to quiet title, cause to quiet title, plea to quiet title, (court) action to quiet title · Klage *f* nach § 256 ZPO, Feststellungsklage

law system, system of law · Rechtssystem *n*

law teacher, teacher of law · Rechtslehrer *m*

law term, law word, legal term, legal word, term of law, word of law · Rechtswort *n*, Rechtsbenennung *f*

law that the capacity of land(s) increases with the population [*As population increases, the extent of land(s) necessary to support one member of it decreases*] · Bodenkapazitätsgesetz *n*,

law theory — to lay waste

Landkapazitätsgesetz, Flächenkapazitätsgesetz

law theory, theory of law · Rechtstheorie *f*

law unification, unification of law(s) · Rechtsvereinheitlichung *f*

law variation, law alteration, change of law, variation of law, alteration of law, law change · Rechts(ab)änderung *f*, Rechtsumänderung, Rechtsveränderung

law wager, Beweisabnahme *f* durch Eideshelfer, · Beweisabnahme *f* durch Eideshelfer · wager of law · Prozeßaustrag *m* durch Eideshelfer, Reinigungseid *m*, Beweisabnahme *f* durch Eideshelfer

law with reference to which the parties contracted; locus contractus [*Latin*]; seat of the obligation, seat of the contract, proper law of the contract · Sitz *m* der Obligation [*nach Savigny*]; Sitz des Vertrages

law word, legal term, legal word, term of law, word of law, law term · Rechtswort *n*, Rechtsbenennung *f*

law work · juristische Arbeit *f*

lawyer [*A person licensed to practice law*] · zugelassener Jurist *m*, praktizierender Jurist

lawyer employed in business, jurist employed in business, house lawyer, staff lawyer, house jurist, staff jurist · Hausjurist, Firmenjurist *m*, Unternehmensjurist

lawyer in administration, jurist in administration · Verwaltungsjurist *m*

lawyer in government service · Staatsjurist *m*

lawyer in judicial office, judiciary · Justizjurist *m*, Jurist im Justizwesen

lawyer in permanent private employment · privat angestellter Jurist *m*

lawyer in private employment, privately employed lawyer · selbständig praktizierender Jurist *m*, privat bestellter Jurist

lawyer's law, jurist-made law · Juristenrecht *n*, Recht der Wissenschaft, wissenschaftliches Recht

lay, not clerical · weltlich

to lay bare, to disclose, to reveal, to knowledge, to make known, to clarify, to free from secrecy, to free from ignorance · aufklären, enthüllen, offenbaren, offenlegen, offen darlegen, preisgeben, kundtun

lay-by; waiting-bay [*deprecated*] · Ausbuchtung *f*, Straßenausbuchtung

to lay claim to, to defend a right, to maintain a right, to assert · beanspruchen, geltend machen [*Forderung; Recht*]

lay corporation; temporal corporation [*obsolete*] · Laienkörperschaft *f*, Laienkorporation *f*

lay court, temporal court · weltliches Gericht *n*

to lay damages, to lay a compensation, to lay an indemnification, to lay an indemnity [*To state at the conclusion of the declaration the amount of damages which the plaintiff claims*] · festsetzen einer Entschädigung

lay day · Liegetag *m* [*Schiff im Hafen; Güter auf der Eisenbahn*]

lay feud, lay fief, lay feod, lay tenancy, lay tenement, lay fee, lay (feodal) tenure (of land); feudum seculare, feodum seculare, feudum laicum, feodum laicum [*Latin*] · weltliches Leh(e)n *n*

lay-figure, dummy, man of straw · „Strohmann" *m*

to lay from arable (land) to grass · niederlegen zu Gras

lay impropriator · Laienpfründner *m*

lay in grant · Grund(stücks)übertragung *f* mittels gesiegelter Urkunde

laying waste, estreping, despoiling, devastating, stripping [*Committing waste upon a real estate*] · Verwüsten *n*, Mißbrauchen, Über(be)nutzen, Verschlechtern, Vernachlässigen (der Instandhaltung), Deteriorieren, Depravieren

lay judge · Laienrichter *m*

layman · Laienbruder *m*

layout guide, key flat · Anhaltekopie *f* [*Kartographie*]

layout plan · innerbetrieblicher Standortplan *m*

layout plan · Lageplan *m*

layout planning · innerbetriebliche Standortplanung *f*

lay people, jury(men) · Jury *f*, Geschworene *m pl*

lay person · Laie *m*

lay press · Nicht-Fachpresse *f*

lay tenancy → lay feud

lay tenement → lay feud

lay tenure (of land) → lay feud

lay tithe, tithe impropriate · Laienzehnt *m*

to lay waste, to devastate, to estrepe, to strip, to despoil [*To commit waste upon a real estate, as by cutting down trees, removing buildings, etc. To injure the value of a reversionary interest by stripping the (real) estate*] · verschlechtern, verwüsten, mißbrauchen, über(be)nutzen, vernachlässigen

LCA, land charges act · Grund(stücks)lastgesetz *n*

L.C.C., London County Council · Grafschaftsrat *m* London

lea [*In old English law*] → pasture (ground)

(leaching) cesspool emptying service, pervious cesspool emptying service, cesspit emptying service, cesspool emptying service · Senkgrubenentleerungsdienst *m*

"lead" firm, pilot firm, management sponsor; sponsor(ing firm) (US) · federführende Firma *f*

leading currency, key currency · Leitwährung *f*

leading office, principal office, main office, chief office · Hauptbüro *n*

leading opinion, current opinion · Verkehrsauffassung *f*, Verkehrsmeinung, herrschende Meinung, herrschende Auffassung

leading question [*A question put or framed in such a form as to suggest the answer sought to be obtained by the person interrogating*] · Fangfrage *f*, Suggestivfrage

lead time · Anlaufzeit *f*

leaflet data · Prospektangaben *fpl*

league · Bund *m*, Liga *f*

league of friendship, friendship league · Freundschaftsbündnis *n*

leakage · versickernder Betrag *m*

leakage · Abflußwirkung *f* [*Regionalwirtschaft*]

leap frog development, leap frogging · fleckenhafte Ausdehnung *f* der nichtagrarischen Nutzungsform mit landwirtschaftlicher Nutzfläche oder zumindest vorübergehend ungenutzter Fläche dazwischen eingestreut

leapfrogging, leapfrog procedure, direct appeal · Sprungappellation *f*, Sprungberufung *f*

leap-frogging · Lohnwellen *f (pl)*

leap year · Schaltjahr *n*

learned in the law, skilled in the law, versed in the law · rechtsbeflissen, rechtsgelehrt, rechtsbeschlagen

learning · Gelehrsamkeit *f*

learning certificate [*In Scotland*] · Abschlußschulzeugnis *n*

learning curve · Anlernkurve *f*

leasability, demisability · Verpachtbarkeit *f*

leasable, demisable · verpachtbar

to lease, to demise, to let; demittere, dimittere [*Latin*] · verpachten

lease, (real) estate lease (agreement), (real) property lease (agreement), (land) lease (agreement), (land) tenancy agreement, realty lease (agreement) [*The document used to bring into existence a term of years*] · (Land)Pachtvertrag *m*, (Land)Pachtbrief, Bodenpachtvertrag, Bodenpachtbrief, Grund(stücks)pachtvertrag, Grund(stücks)pachtbrief, Immobilienpachtvertrag, Immobilienpachtbrief, Immobiliarpachtvertrag, Immobiliarpachtbrief *m*, Liegenschaftspachtvertrag, Liegenschaftspachtbrief

lease → term of years

lease → estate less than freehold

lease → lease(hold)

lease agreement → agreement of tenancy

lease and release · Verpachtung *f* und Rechtsverzicht *m* [*Besitzübertragungsart*]

lease-back [*A transaction in which an owner sells a property and then leases it back from the buyer*] · Rückpacht *f*

lease-back [*Selling a building coupled with a renting arrangement by the vendor*] · Verkauf *m* auf Rentenbasis

lease-back transaction · Rückpachtgeschäft *n*

lease brokerage, tenancy brokerage · Pachtvermitt(e)lung *f*

lease burden, hire charge, hire incumbrance, hire burden, hire encumbrance, lease charge, lease incumbrance · Mietlast *f*, Mietbelastung *f*

lease-buyer, hire-purchaser, hire-buyer, lease-purchaser · Mietkäufer *m*

lease condition, tenancy condition, condition of lease, condition of tenancy · Pachtbedingung *f*

lease covenant · urkundliche Pachtvertragsklausel *f*

leased, demised · verpachtet

leased housing, demise(d) housing · Pachtwohnungen *fpl*

leased housing without rehabilitation, demise(d) housing without rehabilitation · Pachtwohnungen *fpl* ohne Instandsetzung

leased housing with rehabilitation, demise(d) housing with rehabilitation · Pachtwohnungen *fpl* mit Instandsetzung

leased lot, demise(d) lot, leasing lot, tenancy lot, lease(hold) lot · Pachtflurstück *n*, Pachtparzelle *f*

lease donor → lease(hold) donor

leased plot (of land), leased plot of ground, leased piece of land, leased piece of ground, leased parcel (of land), leased parcel of ground, demise(d) plot (of land), demise(d) plot of ground, demise(d) piece of land, demise(d) piece of ground, demise(d) parcel (of land), demise(d) parcel of ground, lease(hold) plot (of land), lease(hold) plot of ground, lease(hold) piece of land, lease(hold) piece of ground, lease(hold) parcel (of land), lease(hold) parcel of ground, leasing plot (of land), leasing piece of ground, leasing piece of ground, leasing parcel (of land), leasing parcel of ground, tenancy plot (of land), tenancy plot of ground, tenancy piece of land, tenancy piece of ground, tenancy parcel (of land), tenancy parcel of ground · Pachtgrundstück *n* (im tatsächlichen Sinne)

leased value, lease(hold) value, tenancy value, demise(d) value · Pachtwert *m*

lease for life → tenancy for life

lease for 3,000 years → tenancy for 3,000 years

lease from year to year → tenancy from year to year

leasehold [*Right held by virtue of a lease*] · (subjektives) Pachtrecht *n*

lease(hold), heritable building right · Erbbaurecht *n* [*Das Recht auf fremdem Boden ein Bauwerk zu errichten*]

leasehold, leasehold land [*Estate in realty held under a lease. The person owning the estate gives exclusive use of the land to another for a payment of rent, the term of lease being fixed. The parties are known as landlord and tenant*] · Pachtboden *m*, Pachtland *n*

lease(hold), tenure, leasehold estate, demise, tenancy; demissio, dimissio [*Latin*]; assedation, tack [*Scots law*], estate less than freehold [*Holding of real estate under a lease. Such an estate continues for a fixed or determinable period of time but not for a lifetime. It is a conveyance of land whereby the owner of landed property, called the lessor, grants the possession and use of his landed property to another party, called the lessee, in consideration of a sum of money, called the rent*] · Bodenpacht *f*, Landpacht, Bodennutzungsrechtvergabe *f*, Landnutzungsrechtvergabe, Bodenverpachtung *f*, Landverpachtung, (Boden)Nutzungsrecht *n*

lease(hold), tenure; demissio, dimissio [*Latin*]; tenancy, demise · Pacht *f*, Nutzungsrechtvergabe *f*, Verpachtung *f*

lease(hold) → estate less than freehold

lease(hold) → term of years

lease(hold) agreement → agreement of tenancy

lease(hold) cession, lease(hold) assignment, demise cession, demise assignment, tenancy cession, tenancy assignment, cession of lease(hold), cession of demise, cession of tenancy, assignment of lease(hold), assignment of demise, assignment of tenancy · Pachtabtretung *f*, Pachtzession *f*

lease(hold) contract, demise contract, contract of tenancy, contract of demise, contract of lease(hold), contract of tenure, tenancy contract, tenure contract · Pachtvertrag *m*, Nutzungsrechtvertrag, Verpachtungsvertrag

lease(hold) contract · Erbbauvertrag *m*

lease(hold) donor, donor of a heritable building right · Erbbaurechtgeber *m*

leaseholder; superficiar(ius) [*Latin*] [*A builder (up)on another's land under a contract*] · Erbbauherr *m*, Superfiziar *m*, Erbbaurechtnehmer

leaseholder → (land) holder

(lease)holder for life → life (land) lessee

leaseholder (of land) at will → (land) holder at will

leaseholder paying in products of the soil, lessee paying in products of the soil, leaseholder paying in kind, lessee paying in kind, (land) holder paying in products of the soil, (land) holder paying in kind, in-kind lessee, in-kind leaseholder, in-kind (land) holder · Natural(ien)pächter *m*

leaseholder's association, tenant's association, lessee's association, (land) holder's association · Pächtergenossenschaft *f*, Pachtgenossenschaft

leasehold estate, lessee's interest [*Right in property terminating at a date specified by a contract, usually a lease*] · Pächterrecht *n*

leasehold estate, demise, tenancy; demissio, dimissio [*Latin*]; assedation, tack [*Scots law*], estate less than freehold, lease(hold), tenure [*Holding of real estate under a lease. Such an estate continues for a fixed or determinable period of time but not for a lifetime. It is a conveyance of land whereby the owner of landed property, called the lessor, grants the possession and use of his landed property to another party, called the lessee, in consideration of a sum of money, called the rent*] · Bodenpacht *f*, Landpacht, Bodennutzungsrechtvergabe *f*, Landnutzungsrechtvergabe, Bodenverpachtung *f*, Landverpachtung, (Boden)Nutzungsrecht *n*

leasehold estate → estate less than freehold

leasehold estate interest → lease(hold) right

leasehold estate law → law of estates less than freehold

leasehold farmer, tenant of a farm, farm tenant, (tenant) farmer [*Die Benennung "farmer" bedeutet in England nicht nur Landwirt, sondern auch Pächter und nur wenn die Pächtereigenschaft hervorgehoben wird, heißt es tenant farmer*] · (landwirtschaftlicher) Pächter *m*, Landwirtschaftspächter, Agrarpächter

lease(hold) for life → tenancy for life

lease(hold) for 3,000 years → tenancy for 3,000 years

lease(hold) from year to year → tenancy from year to year

lease(hold) homestead · Erbbauheimstätte *f*

leaseholding · Nutzungsrecht *n*

lease(hold) interest → term of years

leasehold land, leasehold [*Estate in realty held under a lease. The person owning the estate gives exclusive use of the land to another for a payment of rent, the term of lease being fixed. The parties are known as landlord and tenant*] · Pachtboden *m*, Pachtland *n*

lease(hold) law → law of estates less than freehold

lease(hold) legislation, lease(hold) lawmaking · Erbbaurechtgesetzgebung *f*

lease(hold) lot, leased lot, demise(d) lot, leasing lot, tenancy lot · Pachtflurstück *n*, Pachtparzelle *f*

lease(hold) matters (in general), tenancy matters (in general), demise matters (in general), lease(hold) practice, tenancy practice, demise practice · Pachtwesen *n*

lease(hold) of (building) (land) area → (building) (land) area tenancy

lease(hold) of estate → (real) estate lease(hold)

lease(hold) of (land) area → (building) (land) area tenancy

lease(hold) of land(s) → (real) estate lease(hold)

lease(hold) of land(s) at will → tenancy of land(s) at will

lease(hold) of property → (real) estate lease(hold)

lease(hold) of property without destroying its substance; jus utendi [*Latin*]; demise of property without destroying its substance, tenancy of property without destroying its substance · Pacht *f* ohne Zerstörung, Nutzungsrecht *n* ohne Zerstörung

lease(hold) of (real) estate → (real) estate lease(hold)

lease(hold) of (real) property → (real) estate lease(hold)

lease(hold) option, demise option, tenancy option · Pachtoption *f*

lease(hold) paid in kind, in-kind lease(hold) · Naturalpacht *f*

lease(hold) plot (of land), lease(hold) plot of ground, lease(hold) piece of land, lease(hold) piece of ground, lease(hold) parcel (of land), lease(hold) parcel of ground, leasing plot (of land), leasing plot of ground, leasing piece of land, leasing piece of ground, leasing parcel (of land), leasing parcel of ground, tenancy plot (of land), tenancy plot of ground, tenancy piece of land, tenancy piece of ground, tenancy parcel (of land), tenancy parcel of ground, leased plot (of land), leased plot of ground, leased piece of land, leased piece of ground, leased parcel (of land), leased parcel of ground, demise(d) plot (of land), demise(d) plot of ground, demise(d) piece of land, demise(d) piece of ground, demise(d) parcel (of land), demise(d) parcel of ground · Pachtgrundstück *n* (im tatsächlichen Sinne)

lease(hold) practice, tenancy practice, demise practice, lease(hold) matters (in general), tenancy matters (in general), demise matters (in general) · Pachtwesen *n*

lease(hold) protection code, tenancy protection code, demise protection code · Pachtschutzordnung *f*

lease(hold) rent · Erbbauzins *m* [*Das Entgelt des Grundstückseigentümers für die Einräumung des Erbbaurechts am Grundstück*]

lease(hold) rentcharge · Pachtschuld *f*

lease(hold) right → term of years

lease(hold) (tenure) → term of years

lease(hold) title → term of years

lease(hold) to a third party, demise to a third party, tenancy to a third party, third party lease(hold), third party tenancy, third party demise · Zwischenpacht *f*

lease(hold) value, tenancy value, demise(d) value, leased value · Pachtwert *m*

lease(hold) with an option to purchase, lease(hold) with an option to buy, tenancy with an option to purchase, tenancy with an option to buy, demise with an option to purchase, demise with an option to buy · Kaufoptionspacht *f*, Pacht mit Kaufoption

lease incumbrance, lease burden, hire charge, hire incumbrance, hire burden, hire encumbrance, lease charge · Mietlast *f*, Mietbelastung *f*

lease interest → term of years

lease law → law of estates less than freehold

lease of (building) (land) area → (building) (land) area tenancy

lease of estate → (real) estate lease(hold)

lease of land(s) → (real) estate lease(hold)

lease of land(s) at will → tenancy of land(s) at will

lease of property → (real) estate lease(hold)

lease of (real) estate → (real) estate lease(hold)

lease of (real) property → (real) estate lease(hold)

lease option → lease(hold) option

lease-purchase, lease with purchase option, hire-purchase · Mietkauf *m*

lease-purchase act, lease-purchase statute, lease-purchase law, hire-purchase statute, hire-purchase act, hire-purchase law · Mietkaufgesetz *n*

lease-purchase agreement, hire-purchase agreement · Mietkaufabkommen *n*, Mietkaufabmachung *f*, Mietkaufvereinbarung

lease-purchase construction, hire-purchase construction · Mietkaufbau *m*

lease-purchase contract, contract for hire-purchase, contract for lease-purchase, hire-purchase contract · Mietkaufvertrag *m*

lease-purchase equipment, hire-purchase equipment · Mietkaufgerät *n*

lease-purchase law, hire-purchase law · Mietkaufrecht *n*

lease-purchase legislation, hire-purchase legislation, lease-purchase lawmaking, hire-purchase lawmaking · Mietkaufgesetzgebung *f*

lease-purchase project, hire-purchase project · Mietkaufprojekt *n*

lease-purchaser, lease-buyer, hire-purchaser, hire-buyer · Mietkäufer *m*

(lease) rent; reditus [*Latin*] [*"Rent" may be regarded as of a twofold nature — first, as something issuing out of the land or other corporeal hereditament as a compensation for the possession during the term; and secondly, as an acknowledg(e)ment made by the tenant to the lord*] · Rente *f*, Pacht(zins) *f, (m)*

(lease) rent charge, (lease) rent paid · Pacht(zins)last *f*, Rentenlast

(lease) rent paid [*An amount paid as rent(al)*] · Rentenbetrag *m*, Pachtlastbetrag

(lease) rent received [*An amount received as rent*] · Rentenbetrag *m*, Pachtertragbetrag

lease right → term of years

lease (tenure) → term of years

lease term, term of lease · Mietvertragsfrist *f*

lease title → term of years

lease with purchase option, hire-purchase, lease-purchase, leasing · Mietkauf *m*

leasing, letting (out on lease), demising · Vergeben *n* von Nutzungsrecht(en), Verpachten

leasing · Mitfinanzierung *f*

leasing lot, tenancy lot, lease(hold) lot, leased lot, demise(d) lot · Pachtflurstück *n*, Pachtparzelle *f*

leasing of space, leasing of land, demising of space, demising of land · Pachten *n* von Land, Pachten von Boden

leasing plot (of land), leasing plot of ground, leasing piece of land, leasing piece of ground, leasing parcel (of land), leasing parcel of ground, tenancy plot (of land), tenancy plot of ground, tenancy piece of land, tenancy piece of ground, tenancy parcel (of land), tenancy parcel of ground, leased plot (of land), leased plot of ground, leased piece of land, leased piece of ground, leased parcel (of land), leased parcel of ground, demise(d) plot (of land), demise(d) plot of ground, demise(d) piece of land, demise(d) piece of ground, demise(d) parcel (of land), demise(d) parcel of ground, lease(hold) plot (of land), lease(hold) plot of ground, lease(hold) piece of land, lease(hold) piece of ground, lease(hold) parcel (of land), lease(hold) parcel of ground · Pachtgrundstück *n* (im tatsächlichen Sinne)

least-cost(s) location, least-cost(s) site · kostengünstigster Standort *m*

least-effort principle, principle of least effort · Grundsatz *m* der geringsten Anstrengung, Prinzip *n* der geringsten Anstrengung [*Ableitung von Standortentscheidungen des Einzelhandels*]

least-squares method · Methode *f* der kleinsten Quadrate, Kleinstquadratmethode, Verfahren *n* der kleinsten Quadrate, Kleinstquadratverfahren [*Statistik*]

least-squares regression · Regression *f* der kleinsten Quadrate, Kleinstquadratregression

to leave by will, to bestow by will, to give by will, to dispose by will · (testamentarisch) vermachen, letztwillig verfügen, testamentarisch verfügen, letztwillig vermachen

leave of absence — legal ability to sue

leave of absence [*Temporary absence from duty with intention to return during which time remuneration is suspended*] · Beurlaubung *f*

leave of court [*Permission obtained from a court to take some action which, without such permission, would not be allowable; as, to sue a receiver, to file an amended pleading, to plead several pleas*] · gerichtliche Erlaubnis *f*, gerichtliche Genehmigung

leave on full salary, leave on full pay · vollbezahlter Urlaub *m*

leave to appeal · Zulässigkeit *f* der Berufung

leave to institute legal proceedings · Zulässigkeit *f* des Rechtsweges

to leave (to itself), to forsake, to let go, to abandon, to desert, to give up [*place*] · aufgeben, preisgeben, verlassen

leaving (a thing) (to itself), abandoning, letting go, abandoning, deserting, giving up · Aufgeben *n*, Verlassen *n* [*Gebäude; Betrieb; Flußbett usw.*]

leaving land unplanted, leaving land uncultivated · Brachlegen *n*

leaving of employe(e)s to third party, leaving of servants to third party · Arbeitnehmerüberlassung *f* [*Unerlaubte Überlassung von Arbeitnehmern an Dritte zur Arbeitsleistung*]

to lecture · lehren [*An einer Universität oder technischen Hochschule*]

lecturer, assistant professor · (Privat)Dozent *m*

lecturer in law, assistant professor in law · Rechtsdozent *m*

ledger · Hauptbuch *n* [*Buchführung*]

ledger account · Hauptbuchkonto *n*

ledgerless accounting · kontoblattloses Rechnungswesen *n*

Leeman's Act, Borough Funds Act [*In England. 1872 and 1903*] · Munizipalstadtkassengesetz *n*

leet jury · Ausschuß *m* [*Seit Heinrich VI. begann die Krone in England den Städten zur Verbesserung ihrer zivilrechtlichen Stellung vor den Gerichten "Charters of incorporation" zu verleihen, d. h. sie durch einen Akt zur juristischen Person zu erheben und zwar in der Gestalt, daß der zur Verwaltung des Vermögens und Ausübung der Gerechtsame der Städte bestehende, von der Bürgerschaft gewählte Ausschuß förmlich zu einem "Body Corporate" erhoben wurde*]

left by will, bestowed by will, given by will, disposed by will · letztwillig verfügt, letztwillig vermacht, (testamentarisch) vermacht, testamentarisch verfügt

left estate, estate left · Hinterlassenschaft *f*

left (to itself), forsaken, let gone, deserted, idle, abandoned, given up [*place*] · aufgegeben, verlassen, preisgegeben

legacy, bequest [*A gift made by will of money or mov(e)able things*] · Legat *n*, Vermächtnis *n*, Fahrnisvermächtnis, Fahrnislegat, Fahrhabevermächtnis, Fahrhabelegat

legacy ademption, bequest ademption, legacy revocation, bequest revocation; ademptio legati [*Latin*]; ademption of legacy, revocation of legacy, ademption of bequest, revocation of bequest [*It occurs where a legacy does not take effect owing to some act on the part of a testator not affecting the validity of the will*] · (Fahrnis)Legatrücknahme *f*, (Fahrnis)Legatentziehung *f*, (Fahrnis)Vermächtnisrücknahme, (Fahrnis)Vermächtnisentziehung, Fahrhabelegatrücknahme, Fahrhabelegatentziehung, Fahrhabevermächtnisrücknahme, Fahrhabevermächtnisentziehung

legacy by particular title, bequest by particular title · Einzelvermächtnis *n* einer beweglichen Sache, Einzellegat *n* einer beweglichen Sache, Einzel(fahrnis)vermächtnis, Einzel(fahrnis)legat

legacy duty, legacy tax, bequest tax, bequest duty · (Fahrnis)Legatsteuer *f*, (Fahrnis)Erb(schafts)steuer, Fahrhabelegatsteuer, Fahrhabeerb(schafts)steuer, Fahrhabevermächtnissteuer

legacy revocation, bequest revocation; ademptio legati [*Latin*]; ademption of legacy, revocation of legacy, ademption of bequest, revocation of bequest, legacy ademption, bequest ademption [*It occurs where a legacy does not take effect owing to some act on the part of a testator not affecting the validity of the will*] · (Fahrnis)Legatrücknahme *f*, (Fahrnis)Legatentziehung *f*, (Fahrnis)Vermächtnisrücknahme, (Fahrnis)Vermächtnisentziehung, Fahrhabelegatrücknahme, Fahrhabelegatentziehung, Fahrhabevermächtnisrücknahme, Fahrhabevermächtnisentziehung

legal, statutory [*These two terms imply literal connection or conformity with statute law or its administration*] · gesetzlich

legal ability → lawful ability

legal ability to sue, lawful capacity to sue, lawful status to sue, lawful capability to sue, lawful ability to sue, lawful qualification to sue, lawful condition to sue, legal status to sue, legal capacity to sue, legal capability to sue, legal qualification to sue, legal condition to sue · Klagefähigkeit *f*, Klagevermögen *n*

legal acknowledg(e)ment — legal city 598

legal acknowledg(e)ment, legal recognition, legal recognizance, statutory acknowledg(e)ment, statutory recognizance, statutory recognition · gesetzliche Anerkenntnis f, gesetzliche Anerkennung

legal act(ion), lawful act(ion), proceeding · Rechtsakt m, Rechtshandlung f, rechtsetzender Akt, rechtsetzende Handlung [*Akt eines Gesetzgebers oder Richters, durch welchen Recht erst „geschaffen" wird*]

legal advice · Rechtsrat m

legal affair, lawful affair, cause, matter of law · Rechtsangelegenheit f, Rechtssache f

legal age, full age, (age of (legal)) majority, age of consent, mature years, statutory age [*The age fixed by law at which a person's consent to certain acts is valid in law*] · Majorennität f, Volljährigkeit(salter) f, (n)

legal agent, legal attorney, (authorized) agent by statute, attorney by statute, representative by statute, legal representative · gesetzlicher Verteter m

legal aid, poor's privilege (in (law)suits), pauper's right, legal help [*A system for providing free or assisted legal advice or representation, for persons of slender means*] · Armenrecht n

legal alien, statutory alien · Ausländer m durch Gesetz(es)kraft

legal announcement, statutory announcement · gesetzliche öffentliche Bekanntmachung f, öffentliche gesetzliche Bekanntmachung, gesetzliche öffentliche Bekanntgabe f, öffentliche gesetzliche Bekanntgabe

legal antiquity · Rechtsaltertum n

legal argument, legal ground, lawful argument, lawful ground · Rechtsgrund m

legal assets, statutory assets [*That portion of the assets of a deceased party which by law are directly liable, in the hands of his executor or administrator, to the payment of debts and legacies. Such assets as can be reached in the hands of an executor or administrator, by a suit at law against him*] · gesetzliche Einlage f

legal assignation, legal assignment, legal cession · Abtretung f nach gemeinem Recht, Zession f nach gemeinem Recht

legal assistance · Rechtsbeistand m

legal attestation, acknowledg(e)ment · (amtliche) Beurkundung f

legal attestation fee · Beurkundungsgebühr f, Beurkundungshonorar n

legal attestation law, legal attestation act, legal attestation statute · Beurkundungsgesetz n

legal attestation under seal, acknowledg(e)ment under seal · Beurkundung f unter Siegel, gesiegelte Beurkundung

legal attorney, (authorized) agent by statute, attorney by statute, representative by statute, legal representative, legal agent · gesetzlicher Verteter m

legal authority, legal power, jurisdiction; jurisdictio [*Latin*] · Gerichtsbarkeit f [*Die Machtvollkommenheit des Staates zur gerichtlichen Entscheidung*]

legal authority, legal power, statutory authority, statutory power, public authority, public power · gesetzliche Gewalt f, gesetzliche Macht f, gesetzliche Hoheit f, gesetzliche Kompetenz f

legal authority · Justizbehörde f

legal basis, base in law, basis in law, lawful base, lawful basis, legal base · rechtliche Grundlage f

legal bibliography · Rechtsbibliographie f

legal binding, statutory binding, lawbinding · gesetzliche Bindung f, gesetzliche Gebundenheit f

legal bond, statutory bond [*A bond given to comply with the terms of a statute. Such a bond must cover whatever liability the statute imposes on the principal and the surety*] · gesetzliche Garantie f

legal capability → lawful ability

legal capability to sue, legal qualification to sue, legal condition to sue, legal ability to sue, lawful capacity to sue, lawful status to sue, lawful capability to sue, lawful ability to sue, lawful qualification to sue, lawful condition to sue, legal status to sue, legal capacity to sue · Klagefähigkeit f, Klagevermögen n

legal capacity → lawful ability

(legal) case, case in law · Fall m, Rechtsfall

(legal) case at bar · vorliegender (Rechts)Fall m

legal cession, legal assignation, legal assignment · Abtretung f nach gemeinem Recht, Zession f nach gemeinem Recht

legal charge, duty, (statutory) charge · Finanzabgabe f, gesetzliche Abgabe [*Eine Pflichtleistung in Geld oder Sachgut, die kraft öffentlicher Finanzhoheit den Bürgern auferlegt wird. Man unterscheidet 1. Generelle Abgaben (Steuern und Zölle) und 2. Spezielle Abgaben (Beiträge und Gebühren)*]

legal city, corporat(iv)e city · korporierte Stadt f [*USA. Eine Stadt die nach Erreichen einer Mindesteinwohnerzahl, im Staate Pennsylvania etwa 10 000 Menschen, im Staate Kansas dagegen bereits ab 1000 Menschen, auf Antrag und durch Beschluß der einzelstaatlichen Regierung eine City Charter verliehen bekommen hat*]

legal coin · gesetzliche Münze *f*

legal committee, statutory committee · gesetzlich vorgeschriebener Ausschuß *m*

legal complaint, lawful complaint · Rechtsbeschwerde *f*

legal compulsion, lawful compulsion · Rechtszwang *m*

legal compulsion, statutory compulsion · Gesetz(es)zwang *m*

legal concept, concept of law, concept of (legal) validity, law(ful) concept · Rechtsbegriff *m*, (Rechts)Geltungsbegriff, Legalbegriff

legal concept, statutory concept · Gesetz(es)begriff *m*

legal condition, status, lawful position, legal position, lawful condition · rechtliche Stellung *f*, Status *m*, Rechtsstellung

legal condition, condition in law [*In a legal instrument, e.g. a will, or contract, a provision on which its legal force or effect is made to depend*] · Rechtsbedingung *f*

legal condition, statutory condition · gesetzliche Bedingung *f*

legal condition → lawful ability

legal conditions of contract, legal contract conditions, lawful terms of contract, lawful contract terms, lawful conditions of contract, lawful contract conditions, legal terms of contract, legal contract terms · rechtliche Vertragsbedingungen *fpl*

legal condition to sue, legal ability to sue, lawful capacity to sue, lawful status to sue, lawful capability to sue, lawful ability to sue, lawful qualification to sue, lawful condition to sue, legal status to sue, legal capacity to sue, legal capability to sue, legal qualification to sue · Klagefähigkeit *f*, Klagevermögen *n*

legal consciousness · Rechtsbewußtsein *n*

legal consequence · Rechtsfolge *f*

legal construction, legal interpretation · authentische Auslegung *f*, authentische Deutung, Legalauslegung, Legaldeutung [*Auslegung durch den Normgeber*]

legal contract conditions, lawful terms of contract, lawful contract terms, lawful conditions of contract, lawful contract conditions, legal terms of contract, legal contract terms, legal conditions of contract · rechtliche Vertragsbedingungen *fpl*

legal contribution, statutory contribution · gesetzlicher Beitrag *m*

legal corporation, statutory corporation · gesetzliche Körperschaft *f*, gesetzliche Korporation

legal counsel, counsel(l)or-at-law, legal counsel(l)or · Rechtsberater *m*, Rechtskonsulent

legal currency · Landeswährung *f*

legal debt, common law debt · gemeinrechtliche Schuld *f*

legal decision, lawful decision · Rechtsentscheid(ung) *m, (f)*

legal definition · gesetzliche Definition *f*, Legaldefinition, gesetzliche Begriffsbestimmung *f*, Legalbegriffsbestimmung

legal department, division of law, department of law, law division, law department · Rechtsabteilung *f*

legal development · Rechtsentwick(e)lung *f*

legal device · Rechtsfigur *f*

legal disability, legal incapability, legal incapacity, statutory disability, statutory incapacity, statutory incapability, non ability [*Want of ability to do an act in law*] · gesetzliche Unfähigkeit *f*, gesetzliches Unvermögen *n*

legal disability, legal incapability, legal incapacity, legal inability, lawful disability, lawful incapacity, lawful incapability, lawful inability, non ability [*Want of ability to do an act in law*] · rechtliche Unfähigkeit *f*, rechtliches Unvermögen *n*, Rechtsunfähigkeit, Rechtsunvermögen

legal discharge, statutory discharge, legal release, statutory release, legal exoneration, statutory exoneration, legal dispensation, statutory dispensation, legal exemption, statutory exemption · gesetzlicher Dispens *m*, gesetzliche Freistellung *f*, gesetzliche Freigabe, gesetzliche Entlastung, gesetzliche Dispensierung, gesetzliche Befreiung

legal discretion, lawful discretion [*It is the exercise of discretion where there are two alternative provisions of law applicable under either of which court could proceed*] · Verfahrensermessen *n*

legal dispute · Rechtsauseinandersetzung *f*, Rechtsstreit(igkeit) *m, (f)*

legal document · Rechtsdokument *n*

legal draftsman · Gesetz(es)entwurfsverfasser *m*, Gesetz(es)gestalter

legal duty · Rechtspflicht *f*

legal duty, statutory duty · gesetzliche Pflicht *f*

legal duty of insurance, (statutory) duty of insurance · Versicherungspflicht *f*

legal duty to register, legal duty to record, statutory duty to register, statutory duty to record · gesetzliche Eintragungspflicht *f*

legal (dwelling) rent, statutory residential rent, legal residential rent, statutory (dwelling) rent · gesetzliche (Wohnungs)Miete *f*, gesetzlicher (Wohnungs)(Miet)Zins *m*

legal easement, common law easement [*As opposed to an equitable easement*] · Grunddienstbarkeit *f* nach gemeinem Recht, gemeinrechtliche Grunddienstbarkeit

legal education · Juristenausbildung *f*

legal effect, legal operation, operation (of law), effect (of law) · Gesetz(es)(aus)wirkung *f*, Rechts(aus)wirkung

legal entity, lawful entity · rechtliche Einheit *f* einer juristischen Person, Rechtsträger *m*

legal error, error in law · Rechtsfehler *m*

legalese · Juristensprache *f*

legal estate · echtes Grundstücksrecht *n* [*Es kann nur durch gesiegelte Urkunde (deed) erworben werden*]

legal estate for life, legal life estate · gemeinrechtliches lebenslanges Grundstücksrecht *n*, gemeinrechtliches lebenslanges Recht an einem Grundstück

legal estate tail, common law fee tail, common law estate tail, common law restricted fee, (estate in) legal fee tail, legal restricted fee · beschnittenes Leh(e)n *n* nach gemeinem Recht, eingeschränktes Leh(e)n nach gemeinem Recht, begrenztes Leh(e)n nach gemeinem Recht, beschränktes Leh(e)n nach gemeinem Recht, gebundenes Leh(e)n nach gemeinem Recht

legal ethics, lawful ethics · Rechtsethik *f*

(legal) evidence · Beweismittel *n*

legal evidence of a will, probate · gerichtliche Feststellung *f* einer letztwilligen Verfügung, richterliche Testamentsanerkennung

legal exception, statutory exception · gesetz(esrecht)liche Ausnahme *f*

legal exemption, statutory exemption, legal discharge, statutory discharge, legal release, statutory release, legal exoneration, statutory exoneration, legal dispensation, statutory dispensation · gesetzlicher Dispens *m*, gesetzliche Freistellung *f*, gesetzliche Freigabe, gesetzliche Entlastung, gesetzliche Dispensierung, gesetzliche Befreiung

legal exercise, exercise in the law, exercise of law · Rechtsausübung *f*, objektive Rechtsausübung

legal existence, statutory existence · gesetzliches Dasein *n*

legal exoneration, statutory exoneration, legal dispensation, statutory dispensation, legal exemption, statutory exemption, legal discharge, statutory discharge, legal release, statutory release · gesetzlicher Dispens *m*, gesetzliche Freistellung *f*, gesetzliche Freigabe, gesetzliche Entlastung, gesetzliche Dispensierung, gesetzliche Befreiung

legal expert · Rechtsspezialist *m*

legal expertise · juristisches Fachwissen *n*

legal fee, statutory fee · gesetzliche Gebühr *f*, gesetzliches Honorar *n*

legal fee tail → (estate in) legal fee tail

legal fiction, law(ful) fiction, fiction of law · Rechtsfiktion *f*

legal field, legal sphere · Rechtssphäre *f*, Rechtsgebiet *n*

legal force, legal strength, legal validity, statutory force, statutory strength, statutory validity · Gesetz(es)kraft *f*

legal form, lawful form · Rechtsform *f*

legal form, statutory form · gesetzlich vorgeschriebene Form *f*

legal framework, statutory framework · Gesetz(es)rahmen *m*

legal ground, lawful argument, lawful ground, legal argument · Rechtsgrund *m*

legal guide · Rechtsführer *m* [*im Titel eines Buches*]

legal heir (male), lawful heir (male), nearest kin, heir (male) general, general heir (male), heir (male) whatsoever, statutory heir (male), heir (male) at law, right heir (male) [*One who takes the succession by relationship to the decedent and by force of law*] · Intestaterbe *m*, gesetzlicher Erbe

legal help, legal aid, poor's privilege (in (law)suits), pauper's right [*A system for providing free or assisted legal advice or representation, for persons of slender means*] · Armenrecht *n*

legal history, history of law · Rechtsgeschichte *f*

legal history research · Rechtsgeschichtsforschung *f*

legal holiday, public holiday, statutory holiday · gesetzlicher Feiertag *m*

legal home, settlement, domicil(e), place of habitation, habitation place, (place of) abode, (place of) residence, (permanent) residence · Aufenthaltsort *m*, gesetzlicher Aufenthaltsort, Wohnort, Wohnsitz *m*

legal impossibility, lawful impossibility · rechtliche Unmöglichkeit *f*

legal inability, lawful disability, lawful incapacity, lawful incapability, lawful inability, non ability, legal disability, legal

legal information — to legally oust from the land

incapability, legal incapacity [*Want of ability to do an act in law*] · rechtliche Unfähigkeit *f*, rechtliches Unvermögen *n*, Rechtsunfähigkeit, Rechtsunvermögen

legal information, lawful information · Rechtsauskunft *f*

legal information office · Rechtsberatungsbüro *n*

(legal) instrument, lawful instrument · Institut *n*, rechtliches Institut, Rechtsinstitut

(legal) interest, legal right, statutory interest, statutory right; jus legitimum [*Latin*]; (subjective) right [*A system of rights enjoyed by persons, as "subjects" or owner of rights, and by virtue of law*] · (subjektives) Recht *n*, Berechtigung *f*, Anrecht, (Rechts)Anspruch *m*, gesetzliches (subjektives) Recht, subjektives (gesetzliches) Recht, dingliches Recht [*im B.G.B. auch als „Gegenstand" bezeichnet*]

legal interpretation, legal construction · authentische Auslegung *f*, authentische Deutung, Legalauslegung, Legaldeutung [*Auslegung durch den Normgeber*]

legal invalidity, insufficiency · Rechtsungültigkeit *f*

(legal) irregularity → violation (of law)

legality, sufficiency in law · Legalität *f*, Rechtsstaatlichkeit *f*

legality certificate, certificate of legality · Rechtskraftattest *n*, Rechtskraftbescheinigung *f*, Rechtskraftschein *m*, Legalitätsattest, Legalitätsbescheinigung, Legalitätsschein

legalization · Legalisierung *f*, Rechtskrafterklärung, Legalisation *f*

to legalize · legalisieren, rechtskräftig machen, für rechtskräftig erklären

legalized · rechtskräftig, legalisiert

Legal journal → legal periodical

(legal) judg(e)ment [*abbreviated: judgt.*], judg(e)ment (at law), decree (at law), judg(e)ment of a court, adjudication [*The words "judg(e)ment" and "decree" are often used synonymously; especially now that the codes have abolished the distinction between "law" and "equity". But of the two terms "judg(e)ment" (Urteil) is the more comprehensive, and includes "decree" (Erlaß)*] · gerichtliches Urteil *n*, (Gerichts)Urteil, Rechtsspruch *m*, Erkenntnis *f* eines Gerichts(hofes)

legal judg(e)ment absolute → final judg(e)ment (at law)

legal landlord/tenant relation(ship), statutory tenancy, statutory tenure, legal tenancy, legal tenure, statutory landlord/tenant relation(ship) · gesetzliches Mietverhältnis *n* [*Wohnungen; Geschäftsräume*]

legal life estate, legal estate for life · gemeinrechtliches lebenslanges Grundstücksrecht *n*, gemeinrechtliches lebenslanges Recht an einem Grundstück

legal limit, statutory limit · gesetzliche Grenze *f*

legal limitation (period), statutory limitation (period), legal period of limitation, statutory period of limitation · gesetzliche Verjährungsfrist *f*

legal (local) venue, statutory (local) venue · gesetzlicher Gerichtsstand *m*, gesetzlicher Gerichtsort

legal logic · juristische Logik *f*

legally binding, binding in law, having the force of law, having effect in law · rechtsverbindlich

legally binding agreement, contract, legally binding promise [*It is that form of agreement which directly contemplates and creates an obligation and is enforceable at law*] · (obligatorischer) Vertrag *m*, Legalversprechen *n*, Schuldvertrag [*Ein zweiseitiges Rechtsgeschäft, welches auf Begründung eines Schuldverhältnisses gerichtet ist*]

legally binding plan · Rechtsplan *m*, rechtsverbindlicher Plan

legally binding planning, planning having effect in law, planning binding in law, planning having the force of law · rechtsverbindliche Planung *f*, Planfeststellung

legally binding promise, legally binding agreement, contract [*It is that form of agreement which directly contemplates and creates an obligation and is enforceable at law*] · (obligatorischer) Vertrag *m*, Legalversprechen *n*, Schuldvertrag [*Ein zweiseitiges Rechtsgeschäft, welches auf Begründung eines Schuldverhältnisses gerichtet ist*]

legally bound · gesetzlich gebunden, gesetzlich verpflichtet

legally capable, legally qualified, personable, endowed with legal personality · gesetzlich fähig, gesetzlich geeignet

legally invalid, insufficient · rechtsungültig

legally irregular · ordnungswidrig

to legally oust from the land, to evict, to dispossess by process of law, to dispossess by legal process [*To recover (real) property through court judg(e)ment or superior claim*] · entziehen, entheben, aberkennen [*Grundbesitz*]

legally qualified — legal power

legally qualified, personable, endowed with legal personality, legally capable · gesetzlich fähig, gesetzlich geeignet

legally required window · notwendiges Fenster n [*Ein Fenster, das zur Belichtung und Belüftung eines Aufenthaltsraumes gesetzlich gefordert wird. Z. B. § 8 Abs. 3, § 59 BauO NW*]

legally settled · gesetzmäßigerweise niedergelassen

legal material · Rechtsstoff m

legal maxim, maxim of (the) law · Rechtsmaxime f

legal means, means of law · Rechtsinstrumentarium n

legal measure · Rechtsmaßnahme f

legal memory, lawful memory · Rechtsgedächtnis n

legal method · Fallanalyse f

legal mortgage, conventional mortgage, common law mortgage [*In the USA, "conventional mortgage" means a mortgage that is not insured by the Federal Housing Administration or guaranteed by the Veterans Administration*] · Verkehrshypothek f, gewöhnliche Hypothek [*Der Gläubiger erteilt über sein Pfandrecht als Urkunde einen vom Grundbuchamt ausgestellten Hypothekenbrief*]

(legal) norm, law rule, law norm, rule (of law), norm of law, legal rule [*It is a rule of general application, sanctioned by the recognition of authorities, and usually expressed in the form of maxim or logical proposition. Called a "rule", because in doubtful or unforeseen cases it is a guide or norm for their decision*] · Gesetz(es)norm f, Sachnorm, normative Festlegung f, (Rechts)Norm

legal obedience, allegiance, lawful obedience · gesetzmäßiger Gehorsam m

(legal) obligation, lawful obligation [*The relation between two persons, one of whom can take judicial proceedings or other legal steps to compel the other to do or abstain from doing a certain act. Although it includes both the right of the one and the duty of the other, the term is more frequently used to denote the latter*] · Schuldverhältnis n, Rechtsbindung f, Rechtsverbindlichkeit f, rechtliche Bindung, rechtliche Verbindlichkeit, Verpflichtung (zur Leistung), Leistungsverpflichtung

legal operation, operation (of law), effect (of law), legal effect · Gesetz(es)(aus)wirkung f, Rechts(aus)wirkung

legal opinion · Rechtsauffassung f, Rechtsmeinung

legal order · Rechtsordnung f

legal ousting from the land → dispossession by legal process

legal owner, statutory owner, statutory proprietor, legal proprietor, owner by (common) law, proprietor by (common) law, owner in (common) law, proprietor in (common) law [*As opposed to the "equitable owner"*] · Eigentümer m nach Gemeinrecht, gesetzlicher Eigentümer [*Die Eigentumsaufspaltung nach Gemeinrecht und Billigkeitsrecht ist die Folge dieser dualistischen Entwicklung in England bis 1873/75*]

legal ownership (of property) → legal title

legal pecuniary charge, statutory pecuniary charge · gesetzliche Geldlast f, gesetzliche Geldbelastung f

legal periodical, law journal, legal journal, law periodical · Rechtszeitschrift f

legal period of commencement of title · rechtlich vorgeschriebener Beginn m eines (Rechts)Titels

legal period of limitation, statutory period of limitation, legal limitation (period), statutory limitation (period) · gesetzliche Verjährungsfrist f

legal person, artificial person · juristische Person f, Rechtsperson, J. P.

legal personality · Rechtspersönlichkeit f

legal personal representative · gesetzlicher persönlicher Vertreter m, persönlicher gesetzlicher Vertreter

legal philosopher, philosopher of law, law philosopher · Rechtsphilosoph m

legal philosophy, philosophy of law, law philosophy · Rechtsphilosophie f

legal phraseology, phraseology of law · Rechtssprache f

legal pitfall · Rechtsfalle f

legal plan, statutory plan · gesetzlicher Plan m

legal planning, statutory planning · gesetzliche Planung f

legal policy, policy of law · Rechtspolitik f

legal position, lawful condition, legal condition, status, lawful position · rechtliche Stellung f, Status m, Rechtsstellung

legal position, statutory position · gesetzliche Stellung f

legal possession, statutory possession · gesetzlicher Besitz m

legal possessor, statutory possessor · gesetzlicher Besitzer m

legal power, jurisdiction; jurisdictio [*Latin*]; legal authority · Gerichtsbarkeit f [*Die Machtvollkommenheit des Staates zur gerichtlichen Entscheidung*]

legal power, statutory authority, statutory power, public authority, public power, legal authority · gesetzliche Gewalt *f*, gesetzliche Macht *f*, gesetzliche Hoheit *f*, gesetzliche Kompetenz *f*

legal power, statutory power · gesetzliche Ermächtigung *f*

legal power of appointment, legal right of appointment, power of appointment under the statute of uses, right of appointment under the statute of uses · Befugnis *f* an einem bestimmten Vermögen Nutzung zu erklären, Recht *n* an einem bestimmten Vermögen Nutzung zu erklären

legal power of appointment, legal power of disposition, legal right of appointment, legal right of disposition, statutory power of appointment, statutory power of disposition, statutory right of appointment, statutory right of disposition, public power of appointment, public power of disposition, public right of appointment, public right of disposition [*It is conferred by statute upon persons exercising the duties of a particular office, e.g. as trustee, or as tenant for life*] · gesetzliche Verfügungsbefugnis *f*, gesetzliche Bestimmungsbefugnis, gesetzliches Verfügungsrecht *n*, gesetzliches Bestimmungsrecht

legal power of disposition → legal power of appointment

legal practice · Rechtsgang *m*

legal practice · Rechtspraxis *f*

legal prescription, legal regulation, statutory rule, legal rule, statutory prescription, statutory regulation · gesetzliche Vorschrift *f*, Gesetz(es)vorschrift

legal prevention, statutory prevention · gesetzliche Verhütung *f*

legal proceeding · Zivilprozeßverhandlung *f*

legal profession · Rechtsberuf *m*

legal proprietor, owner by (common) law, proprietor by (common) law, owner in (common) law, proprietor in (common) law, legal owner, statutory owner, statutory proprietor [*As opposed to the "equitable owner"*] · Eigentümer *m* nach Gemeinrecht, gesetzlicher Eigentümer [*Die Eigentumsaufspaltung nach Gemeinrecht und Billigkeitsrecht ist die Folge dieser dualistischen Entwicklung in England bis 1873/75*]

legal protection, relief, statutory protection · Gesetz(es)schutz *m*

legal provision, provision of law, law provision · Gesetz(es)bestimmung *f*, gesetzliche Bestimmung

legal purpose, statutory purpose · gesetzlicher Zweck *m*

legal qualification → lawful ability

legal qualification to sue, legal condition to sue, legal ability to sue, lawful capacity to sue, lawful status to sue, lawful capability to sue, lawful ability to sue, lawful qualification to sue, lawful condition to sue, legal status to sue, legal capacity to sue, legal capability to sue · Klagefähigkeit *f*, Klagevermögen *n*

legal realism, law in action · lebendiges Recht *n*, lebendes Recht

legal reasoning, lawful reasoning, opinion (of the court) · Rechtsfindung *f*

legal reasoning · gesetz(es)prüfende Vernunft *f*

legal recognizance, statutory acknowledg(e)ment, statutory recognizance, statutory recognition, legal acknowledg(e)ment, legal recognition · gesetzliche Anerkenntnis *f*, gesetzliche Anerkennung

legal redemption right, statutory right of redemption, legal right of redemption, statutory right to redeem, legal right to redeem, statutory redemption right · gesetzliches Ablösungsrecht *n*, gesetzliches Einlösungsrecht, gesetzliches Auslösungsrecht

legal redress, legal remedy, redress by operation of law, (redressing) remedy by operation of law, redressing legal remedy · Rechtsabhilfe(mittel) *f, (n)*, Rechtsbehelf *m*

legal regulation, statutory regulation · gesetzliche Regelung *f*

legal regulation, statutory rule, legal rule, statutory prescription, statutory regulation, legal prescription · gesetzliche Vorschrift *f*, Gesetz(es)vorschrift

legal relation(ship), statutory relation(ship) · gesetzliche Beziehung *f*, gesetzliches Verhältnis *n*

legal release, statutory release, legal exoneration, statutory exoneration, legal dispensation, statutory dispensation, legal exemption, statutory exemption, legal discharge, statutory discharge · gesetzlicher Dispens *m*, gesetzliche Freistellung *f*, gesetzliche Freigabe, gesetzliche Entlastung, gesetzliche Dispensierung, gesetzliche Befreiung

legal remedy, redress by operation of law, (redressing) remedy by operation of law, redressing legal remedy, legal redress · Rechtsabhilfe(mittel) *f, (n)*, Rechtsbehelf *m*

legal representative, legal agent, legal attorney, (authorized) agent by statute, attorney by statute, representative by statute · gesetzlicher Verteter *m*

legal research · Rechtsforschung *f*, (Rechts)Quellenstudium *n*

legal reserve → legal (surplus) reserve

legal residential rent, statutory (dwelling) rent, legal (dwelling) rent, statutory residential rent(al) · gesetzliche (Wohnungs)Miete f, gesetzlicher (Wohnungs)(Miet)Zins m

legal restricted fee, legal estate tail, common law fee tail, common law estate tail, common law restricted fee, (estate in) legal fee tail · beschnittenes Leh(e)n n nach gemeinem Recht, eingeschränktes Leh(e)n nach gemeinem Recht, begrenztes Leh(e)n nach gemeinem Recht, beschränktes Leh(e)n nach gemeinem Recht, gebundenes Leh(e)n nach gemeinem Recht

legal review, statutory review · Gesetzmäßigkeitskontrolle f

legal right, statutory interest, statutory right; jus legitimum [*Latin*]; (subjective) right, (legal) interest [*A system of rights enjoyed by persons, as "subjects" or owner of rights, and by virtue of law*] · (subjektives) Recht n, Berechtigung f, Anrecht, (Rechts)Anspruch m, gesetzliches (subjektives) Recht, subjektives (gesetzliches) Recht, dingliches Recht [*im B.G.B. auch als „Gegenstand" bezeichnet*]

legal right according to common law, lawful right according to common law · (subjektives) Recht n nach gemeinem Recht

legal right of appointment, power of appointment under the statute of uses, right of appointment under the statute of uses, legal power of appointment · Befugnis f an einem bestimmten Vermögen Nutzung zu erklären, Recht n an einem bestimmten Vermögen Nutzung zu erklären

legal right of appointment, legal right of disposition, statutory power of appointment, statutory power of disposition, statutory right of appointment, statutory right of disposition, public power of appointment, public power of disposition, public right of appointment, public right of disposition, legal power of appointment, legal power of disposition [*It is conferred by statute upon persons exercising the duties of a particular office, e.g. as trustee, or as tenant for life*] · gesetzliche Verfügungsbefugnis f, gesetzliches Bestimmungsbefugnis, gesetzliches Verfügungsrecht n, gesetzliches Bestimmungsrecht

legal right of disposition → legal right of appointment

legal right of redemption, statutory right to redeem, legal right to redeem, statutory redemption right, legal redemption right, statutory right of redemption · gesetzliches Ablösungsrecht n, gesetzliches Einlösungsrecht, gesetzliches Auslösungsrecht

legal role · Rechtsbedeutung f [*Stellung im rechtlichen Sinn*]

legal rule, statutory prescription, statutory regulation, legal prescription, legal regulation, statutory rule · gesetzliche Vorschrift f, Gesetz(es)vorschrift

legal rule, (legal) norm, law rule, law norm, rule (of law), norm of law [*It is a rule of general application, sanctioned by the recognition of authorities, and usually expressed in the form of maxim or logical proposition. Called a "rule", because in doubtful or unforeseen cases it is a guide or norm for their decision*] · Gesetz(es)norm f, Sachnorm, normative Festlegung f, (Rechts)Norm

legal science; jurisprudentia [*Latin*]; law science, science of law, jurisprudence · Jurisprudenz f, Rechtswissenschaft f, Lehre f der allgemeinen Rechtsfragen, Rechtslehre

legal seisin, statutory seisin · gesetzliche Gewere f

legal separate property, legal separate estate, statutory separate property, statutory separate estate · Vorbehaltgut n nach Gesetz(es)recht, Sondervermögen n nach Gesetz(es)recht, freies Vermögen nach Gesetz(es)recht, getrenntes Vermögen nach Gesetz(es)recht

legal signification, lawful signification · rechtliche Bedeutung f

legal signification, statutory signification · gesetzliche Bedeutung f

legal society · Rechtsgesellschaft f [*Einheit von Menschen, die durch die Geltung eines Rechtssystems oder einer Rechtsordnung gebildet ist*]

legal sphere, legal field · Rechtssphäre f, Rechtsgebiet n

legal status → lawful ability

legal status to sue, legal capacity to sue, legal capability to sue, legal qualification to sue, legal condition to sue, legal ability to sue, lawful capacity to sue, lawful status to sue, lawful capability to sue, lawful ability to sue, lawful qualification to sue, lawful condition to sue · Klagefähigkeit f, Klagevermögen n

legal strength, legal validity, statutory force, statutory strength, statutory validity, legal force · Gesetz(es)kraft f

legal structure · Rechtsstruktur f

(legal) succession, succession in title, title sucession; communio incidens [*Latin*], privity, participation in interest [*A successive relationship to or mutual interest in the same property, etc., established by law or legalized by contract, as between a testator and legatee, lessor and lessee, etc.*] · Rechtsgemein-

(legal) succession after death — legislation of arbitration

schaft *f*, rechtliche Beteiligung *f*, Rechtsbez«ehung, Rechtsverhältnis *n*, Rechtsnachfolge *f*

(legal) succession after death, privity after death, succession in title after death · Rechtsnachfolge *f* von Todes wegen

(legal) succession inter vivos, privity inter vivos, succession in title inter vivos · Rechtsnachfolge *f* unter Lebenden

legal successor, successor in right, representative, privy successor · Rechtsnachfolger *m*

legal (surplus) reserve, statutory (surplus) reserve · gesetzliche Rücklage *f*

legal tenancy, legal tenure, statutory landlord/tenant relation(ship), legal landlord/tenant relation(ship), statutory tenancy, statutory tenure · gesetzliches Mietverhältnis *n* [*Wohnungen; Geschäftsräume*]

legal tender · Legalkurs *m* [*Eigenschaft des Geldes gesetzliches Zahlungsmittel zu sein*]

legal tenure, statutory tenure · gesetzliche Dienstzeit *f* [*Beamte*]

legal tenure, statutory landlord/tenant relation(ship), legal landlord/tenant relation(ship), statutory tenancy, statutory tenure, legal tenancy · gesetzliches Mietverhältnis *n* [*Wohnungen; Geschäftsräume*]

legal term, legal word, term of law, word of law, law term, law word · Rechtswort *n*, Rechtsbenennung *f*

legal terminology · Rechtsterminologie *f*

legal terminology, statutory terminology · Gesetz(es)terminologie *f*

legal terms of contract, legal contract terms, legal conditions of contract, legal contract conditions, lawful terms of contract, lawful contract terms, lawful conditions of contract, lawful contract conditions · rechtliche Vertragsbedingungen *f pl*

legal theory · Gesetz(es)theorie *f*

legal thing, lawful thing · Rechtsgegenstand *m*

legal thinking · Rechtsdenken *n*

legal thought · Rechtsgedanke *m*

legal title · Vollrecht *n*

legal title, legal proprietorship, legal ownership (of property), legal property, statutory ownership (of property), statutory property, statutory proprietorship, ownership (of property) by common law, proprietorship by common law, property by common law, ownership (of property) in law, proprietorship in law, property in law · Eigentum *n* nach Gemeinrecht, Eigentum nach gemeinem Recht, gesetzliches Eigentum, gemeinrechtliches Eigentum, gesetzlich anerkanntes Eigentum

(legal) title root, root of (legal) title · (Rechts)Titelursprung *m*, (Rechts)Titelwurzel *f*

legal trust, statutory trust [*Part of the property is held by a personal representative to be divided equally among issue and other classes of relatives of an intestate who are alive at the death of the intestate as soon as they attain 18, or marry*] · Nachlaß(vermögen) *m*, (*n*) in den Händen des Erbschaftsverwalters als Treuhänder

(legal) trust instrument, lawful trust instrument · Treuhandrechtsinstitut *n*, (rechtliches) Treuhandinstitut

legal unity · Rechtseinheit *f*

legal validity, statutory force, statutory strength, statutory validity, legal force, legal strength · Gesetz(es)kraft *f*

legal word, term of law, word of law, law term, law word, legal term · Rechtswort *n*, Rechtsbenennung *f*

legal writer · juristischer Autor *m*, juristischer Schriftsteller, Rechtsautor, Rechtsschriftsteller

legate · Legat *m*

legatee by general title, universal legatee · Gesamtlegatnehmer *m*, Universallegatnehmer

legator, bequeather [*One who makes a will, and leaves legacies*] · (Fahrnis)Legatgeber *m*, (Fahrnis)Vermächtnisgeber

legatum per damnationem [*Latin*] · Damnationslegat *n*

legend, reference · Legende *f*, (Zeichen)Erklärung *f*, (Zeichen)Schlüssel *m*, (Zeichen)Erläuterung

legislation, lawmaking, (legislative) enactment, making of law · Gesetzgebung *f*, Erlassen *n* von Gesetzen

legislation as required by federal interest(s), lawmaking as required by federal interest(s) · Bedarfsgesetzgebung *f* [*Bundesrepublik Deutschland. Die konkurrierende Gesetzgebung des Bundes ist nach Artikel 72 Absatz 2 Grundgesetz (GG) stets eine Bedarfsgesetzgebung. Sie kommt nur zur Anwendung wenn ein Bedürfnis nach bundesgesetzlicher Regelung besteht*]

legislation for the protection of ancient monuments and buildings of historic interest, lawmaking for the protection of ancient monuments and buildings of historic interest · Denkmalschutzgesetzgebung *f*

legislation of arbitration, arbitration legislation, lawmaking of arbitration, arbitration lawmaking · Schieds(gerichts)gesetzgebung *f*

legislation of planning, planning lawmaking, lawmaking of planning, planning legislation · Planungsgesetzgebung *f*

legislation procedure, procedure of lawmaking, lawmaking procedure, procedure of legislation · Gesetzgebungsverfahren *n*

legislative · gesetzgebend, gesetzgeberisch

legislative act, legislative law, legislative statute, session act, session statute, resolve act; slip law, session law [*USA*]; public act, public law, public statute, general act, general law, general statute · allgemeines Gesetz *n* [*In den Gliedstaaten der USA erscheinen die Gesetze nach ihrer Verabschiedung zunächst als "slip laws", die am Ende einer Sitzungsperiode der Legislative chronologisch zu den "session laws" zusammengefaßt werden*]

legislative assembly, lawmaking assembly · gesetzgebende Versammlung *f*

legislative authority, legislative power, legislature, jurisdiction; jurisdictio [*Latin*], power to make law, authority to make law, power to legislate, authority to legislate · gesetzgebende Gewalt *f*, gesetzgebende Hoheit, gesetzgebende Macht, gesetzgebende Kompetenz, Gesetzgebungsgewalt, Gesetzgebungskompetenz, Gesetzgebungsmacht, Gesetzgebungshoheit

legislative body, lawmaking body · gesetzgebendes Organ *n*

legislative budget · Haushalt(s)gesetz *n*

legislative committee, lawmaking committee · gesetzgeberischer Ausschuß *m*, gesetzgebender Auschuß

legislative council, lawmaking council · gesetzgebender Rat *m*

legislative court [*USA*] · Gericht *n* auf Kongreßakt beruhend

legislative court · Gericht *n* mit begrenzter örtlicher oder sachlicher Zuständigkeit

(legislative) enactment, making of law, legislation, lawmaking · Gesetzgebung *f*, Erlassen *n* von Gesetzen

legislative executive order, legislative rule · gesetz(es)ausfüllende Verwaltungsverordnung *f*, gesetz(es)ergänzende Verwaltungsverordnung [*amerikanisches Verwaltungsrecht*]

legislative (land) use zoning change, legislative zoning change · gesetzgeberischer Baunutzungswechsel *m*, gesetzgeberischer baulicher Nutzungswechsel

legislative law, legislative statute, session act, session statute, resolve act; slip law, session law [*USA*]; public act, public law, public statute, general act, general law, general statute, legislative act · allgemeines Gesetz *n* [*In den Gliedstaaten der USA erscheinen die Gesetze nach ihrer Verabschiedung zunächst als "slip laws", die am Ende einer Sitzungsperiode der Legislative chronologisch zu den "session laws" zusammengefaßt werden*]

legislative local authority, lawmaking local authority, local legislative authority · gesetzgebende Behörde *f*, örtliche gesetzgebende Behörde

legislative measure · gesetzgeberische Maßnahme *f*

legislative power, legislature, jurisdiction; jurisdictio [*Latin*]; power to make law, authority to make law, power to legislate, authority to legislate, legislative authority · gesetzgebende Gewalt *f*, gesetzgebende Hoheit, gesetzgebende Macht, gesetzgebende Kompetenz, Gesetzgebungsgewalt, Gesetzgebungskompetenz, Gesetzgebungsmacht, Gesetzgebungshoheit

legislative proposal · Gesetzgebungsvorschlag *m*

legislative protection of labour (Brit.); legislative protection of labor (US) · Arbeiterschutz *m*

legislative reorganization act, legislative reorganization law, legislative reorganization statute · Gesetzgebungsreformgesetz *n*

legislative rule, legislative executive order · gesetz(es)ausfüllende Verwaltungsverordnung *f*, gesetz(es)ergänzende Verwaltungsverordnung [*amerikanisches Verwaltungsrecht*]

legislative standard · Generalklausel *f* [*Umreißen von Verwaltungsaufgaben*]

legislative statute, session act, session statute, resolve act; slip law, session law [*USA*]; public act, public law, public statute, general act, general law, general statute, legislative act, legislative law · allgemeines Gesetz *n* [*In den Gliedstaaten der USA erscheinen die Gesetze nach ihrer Verabschiedung zunächst als "slip laws", die am Ende einer Sitzungsperiode der Legislative chronologisch zu den "session laws" zusammengefaßt werden*]

legislative zoning change, legislative (land) use zoning change · gesetzgeberischer Baunutzungswechsel *m*, gesetzgeberischer baulicher Nutzungswechsel

legislator, lawmaker · Gesetzgeber *m*

legislature, jurisdiction; jurisdictio [*Latin*]; power to make law, authority to make law, power to legislate, authority to legislate, legislative authority, legislative power · gesetzgebende Gewalt *f*, gesetzgebende Hoheit, gesetzgebende

Macht, gesetzgebende Kompetenz, Gesetzgebungsgewalt, Gesetzgebungskompetenz, Gesetzgebungsmacht, Gesetzgebungshoheit

legitimacy · Legitimität *f*, Rechtmäßigkeit *f*

legitimate · legitim

legitimate descent, legitimate lineage, legitimate ancestry · eheliche Abstammung *f*, legitim(iert)e Abstammung

legitimate infant, legitimate minor · ehelicher Minderjähriger *m*, legitim(iert)er Minderjähriger

legitimate minor, legitimate infant · ehelicher Minderjähriger *m*, legitim(iert)er Minderjähriger

legitimate natural child, lawful natural child · eheliches Kind

legitimate social change · legitimer sozialer Wandel *m*

legitimation, marking legitimate · Legitimation *f*

leisure activity, nonwork activity · Freizeitbetätigung *f*

leisure area, leisure territory, nonwork area, nonwork territory · Freizeitgebiet *n*

leisure domicil(e), nonwork domicil(e) · Freizeitwohnsitz *m*

leisured people, gentlemen of the law · grundbesitzender Herrenstand *m*

leisure facility, nonwork facility · Freizeiteinrichtung *f*

leisure field, nonwork field · Freizeitwesen *n*

leisure function, nonwork function · Freizeitfunktion *f*

leisure grounds, nonwork grounds · Freizeitgelände *n*

leisure infrastructure, nonwork infrastructure · Freizeitinfrastruktur *f*

leisure landscape, nonwork landscape · Freizeitlandschaft *f*

leisurely seller · nicht genötigter Verkäufer *m*

leisure passenger, nonwork passenger · Freizeitfahrgast *m*

leisure planning, nonwork planning, planning for leisure · Freizeitplanung *f*

leisure pursuit, nonwork pursuit · Freizeitinteresse *n*

leisure region, nonwork region · Freizeitregion *f*

leisure research, nonwork research · Freizeitforschung *f*

leisure territory, nonwork area, nonwork territory, leisure area · Freizeitgebiet *n*

leisure time, free time, spare time, nonwork time · Freizeit *f*

leisure-time orien(ta)ted, leisure-time related · freizeitbezogen, freizeitorientiert

leisure travel, leisure trip, leisure journey, nonwork travel, nonwork trip, nonwork journey · Freizeitfahrt *f*, Nicht-Berufsfahrt

leisure value, nonwork value · Freizeitwert *m*

leisure zone, nonwork zone · Freizeitzone *f*

to lend · beleihen

to lend additional support → to feed

lender · Verleiher *m* [*bewegliche Sache*]

lender → (loan) lender

lender of money, moneylender, loaner, (loan) lender · Geld(ver)leiher *m*, Geldgeber, Darleh(e)nsgeber, Kreditgeber

lending · Beleihung *f*

lending prescription, lending regulation, lending rule · Beleihungsvorschrift *f*

lending restriction, lending limitation, lending restraint · Beleihungseinschränkung *f*, Beleihungsbeschränkung, Beleihungsbegrenzung, Beleihungsgrenze *f*

lending value · Beleihungswert *m* [*Nachhaltiger aufgrund gesetzlicher und einschlägiger Vorschriften der Kreditinstitute ermittelter Objektwert*]

to lengthen, to extend, to prolong · verlängern

lengthened, extended, prolonged · verlängert

length of contract, contract length, contract time, time of contract, full life of contract · Vertrags(lauf)zeit *f*, Vertragsdauer *f*

less developed cultural landscape, less developed man-made landscape · Primitiv-Kulturlandschaft *f* [*Nur wenig vom Menschen veränderter Naturraum*]

lessee → (land) holder

lessee for life → life (land) lessee

lessee from year to year → (land) holder from year to year

lessee (of land) at will → (land) holder at will

lessee (of land) from year to year → (land) holder from year to year

lessee paying in products of the soil, leaseholder paying in kind, lessee paying in kind, (land) holder paying in products of the soil, (land) holder paying in kind, in-kind lessee, in-kind leaseholder, in-kind

lessee's association — letter of affirmation

(land) holder, leaseholder paying in products of the soil · Natural(ien)pächter m

lessee's association, (land) holder's association, leaseholder's association, tenant's association · Pächtergenossenschaft f, Pachtgenossenschaft

lessee's interest, leasehold estate [*Right in property terminating at a date specified by a contract, usually a lease*] · Pächterrecht n

to lessen, to reduce, to abate · reduzieren, mindern, herabsetzen, verringern

lessening, reducing, abating · Verringern n, Herabsetzen, Mindern, Reduzieren

less interest · abzüglich Zinsen

lessor and lessee, landlord and tenant [*(real) estate*] · Verpächter m und Pächter, Pachtherr und Pächter

lessor (of land), landlord, land lessor [*He of whom land is held*] · Landpachtherr m, (Boden)Pachtherr, Landverpächter, (Boden)Verpächter, Grund(stücks)verpächter, Grund(stücks)pachtherr

lessor title, landlord title · Pachtherrentitel m, Verpächtertitel

less prosperous agricultural area, special agricultural area, depressed agricultural area, distressed agricultral area · landwirtschaftliches Notstandsgebiet n, landwirtschaftliches Passivgebiet

less prosperous area, depressed territory, special territory, distressed territory, les prosperous territory, depressed area, distressed area, special area · Notstandsgebiet n, Passivgebiet, Sondergebiet, SO

less prosperous community, depressed community, distressed community, special community · Notstandsgemeinde f, Passivgemeinde, Notstandskommune f, Passivkommune

less prosperous rural area, less prosperous rural region, rural depressed area, rural depressed region · ländlicher Passivraum m, ländliches Notstandsgebiet n, ländliches Passivgebiet, ländliches Sondergebiet

less-than-average, below average, substandard · unterdurchschnittlich

less-than-carload lot · Stückgutsendung f

to let; (e)locare [*Latin*] · vermieten

to let; demittere, dimittere, [*Latin*]; to lease, to demise · verpachten

to let a contract, to contract, to award (a contract), to let (out), to commission a project, to appoint a contractor · zuschlagen, erteilen eines (Bau)Auftrages

to let go, to abandon, to desert, to give up, to leave (to itself), to forsake [*place*] · aufgeben, preisgeben, verlassen

let gone, deserted, idle, abandoned, given up, left (to itself), forsaken [*place*] · aufgegeben, verlassen, preisgegeben

let home · nichteigengenutztes Eigenheim n, vermietetes Eigenheim, nichteigengenutztes Eigenhaus, vermietetes Eigenhaus n

to let land(s), to farm · verpachten von Land

to let land(s) yearly; arrendare [*Latin*] · verpachten von Land jährlich

to let (out), to commission a project, to appoint a contractor, to let a contract, to contract, to award (a contract) · zuschlagen, erteilen eines Auftrages

let private flat (Brit.); let condo(minium) (US) · nichteigengenutzte Eigen(tums)wohnung f, nichteigengenutzte EW, vermietete Eigen(tums)wohnung, vermietete EW

lettable, tenantable · vermietbar [*Wohnungen; Geschäftsräume*]

lettable repair, tenantable repair [*The quality of repair in a house rendering it fit for occupation by tenants*] · Vermietungsreparatur f

letter, locator · (Sach)Vermieter m [*bewegliche Sache*]

letter and spirit of a contract · Buchstabe m und Geist m eines Vertrages

letter-carrier, postman · Briefträger m, Briefbote m, Postbote

letter demanding payment, (formal) demand, prompt note, prompt notification, demand note, demand notification, reminder (of debt due) [*Slang: dunning letter*] · Mahnbrief m, Mahnschreiben n, Mahnung f

lettergram (US); letter telegramm, L.T. (Brit.) · Brieftelegramm n

lettering · Aufschrift f, Beschriftung f [*Schild*]

letter of acceptance, notice of acceptance, letter of award of contract, letter of letting of contract, notice of award of contract, notice of letting of contract, letter of award, notice of award, acceptance letter · Auftragsschreiben n, Zuschlag(s)schreiben n

letter of administration · Nachlaßverwalterernennungsschreiben n

letter of advice · Avisbrief m

letter of affirmation, confirmatory letter, affirmatory letter, letter of confirmation · Bestätigungsschreiben n

letter of allotment, scrip (certificate), allotment letter · Interimsschein *m* [*Für neuausgegebene Wertpapiere*]

letter of attorney, proxy form · Vollmachturkunde *f*

letter of award of contract, letter of letting of contract, notice of award of contract, notice of letting of contract, letter of award, notice of award, acceptance letter, letter of acceptance, notice of acceptance · Auftragsschreiben *n*, Zuschlag(s)schreiben

letter of confirmation, letter of affirmation, confirmatory letter, affirmatory letter · Bestätigungsschreiben *n*

letter of credit, credit letter · Akkreditiv *n*, Kreditbrief *m*

letter of credit at will, unconfirmed letter of credit, revocable letter of credit, revokable letter of credit · Akkreditiv *n* auf Widerruf, Kreditbrief *m* auf Widerruf, widerruflicher Kreditbrief, widerrufliches Akkreditiv

letter of executorship, certificate of executorship · (Testaments)Vollstreckerzeugnis *n*

letter of hypothecation, mortgage-bond, mortgage-debenture · Grundpfandbrief *m*, Bodenpfandbrief, Hypothekenpfandbrief, hypothekarisch gesicherter Pfandbrief, Obligation *f* mit hypothekarischer Sicherheit, hypothekarisch gesicherte Schuldverschreibung

letter of indemnity, indemnity letter · Konnossementgarantie *f*, Konnossementrevers *m*

letter of indication [*When a bank issues to a customer a circular letter of credit it also provides him with a letter of indication bearing a copy of his signature as a safeguard for the paying bank*] · Ausweisschreiben *n*

letter of inquiry, letter of enquiry · Erkundigungsschreiben *n*

letter of intent(ion) [*A letter signifying intent(ion) to enter into a formal contract and setting forth the general terms*] · Absichtsschreiben *n*

letter of introduction, letter of recommendation · Empfehlungsschreiben *n*, Einführungsschreiben

letter of law; litera [*Latin*] [*To be distinguished from the spirit of law*] · Buchstabe *m* des Gesetzes

letter of letting of contract → letter of acceptance

letter of marque, letter of reprisal · Kaperbrief *m*

letter of recommendation → letter of introduction

letter ruling, determinations letter · verbindliche Auskunft *f* [*Steuerfestsetzung in den USA*]

letters of administration, administration letters [*A document issued to a probate administrator granting his authority*] · Bestellungsdekret *n*, Bestellungserlaß *m*, Erbschaftsverwalterdekret, Erbschaftsverwaltererlaß, Nachlaßverwalterdekret, Nachlaßverwaltererlaß

letters of administration cum testamento annexo · Nachlaßverwaltererlaß *m* mit beigefügtem Testament, Erbschaftsverwaltererlaß mit beigefügtem Testament

letters of request (addressed to a foreign court) (Brit.); rogatory letters [*International law*] · Rechtshilfeersuchen *n*

letter telegramm, L.T. (Brit.); lettergram (US) · Brieftelegramm *n*

letter telegram sent at night, L.T. sent at night (Brit.); night lettergram (US) · Nacht-Brieftelegramm *n*

letter telegram sent during the day, , L.T. sent during the day (Brit.); day lettergram (US) · Tag-Brieftelegramm *n*

let the buyer beware, let the buyer take care; caveat emptor [*Latin*] · ohne Gewähr für die Mängelfreiheit, Risiko *n* trägt der Käufer, Wagnis *n* trägt der Käufer, Käufer *m* trägt die Mängelgefahr

let thing, thing let · vermietete Sache *f*, vermieteter Gegenstand *m*, vermietetes Ding *n*

letting · Vermieten *n*

letting, ablocation; locatio [*Latin*] · Vermietung *f*

letting → (contract) letting

letting date, date of award, date of letting, award date · Auftragsdatum *n*, Zuschlag(s)datum *n*, Auftragstermin *m*, Zuschlag(s)termin *m*

letting go, abandoning, deserting, giving up, leaving (a thing) (to itself), abandoning · Aufgeben *n*, Verlassen *n* [*Gebäude; Betrieb; Flußbett usw.*]

letting notice, letting notification, notice of letting, notification of letting · Vergabevermerk *m* [*in Ausschreibungsunterlagen*]

letting of a contract, letting out, (contract) award, (contract) letting, contracting, award(ing) of a contract · Zuschlag *m*, Auftragserteilung *f*

letting of (real) estate → (real) estate leasing

letting out negotiations, contract letting negotiations, contract award negotiations, contracting negotiations · Auftragsverhandlungen *fpl*

**letting (out on lease), ** demising, leasing · Vergeben *n* von Nutzungsrecht(en), Verpachten

level · Grundsystembereich *m* [*Stadtentwick(e)lungsmodell*]

level · Ebene *f*, Stufe *f* [*Hierarchie*]

level crossing act, level crossing law, level crossing statute · Kreuzungsgesetz *n* [*Eisenbahn/Straße*]

to level down · herabdrücken [*auf ein niedrigeres Niveau*]

level of administration, administration level · Verwaltungsstufe *f*, Verwaltungsebene *f*

level of attainment, target, attainment level · Programmziel *n*

level of call, demand level, call level, level of demand · Nachfragestand *m*

level of collection losses, level of (vacancy) losses · Mietausfallhöhe *f*, Mietverlusthöhe

level of demand, level of call, demand level, call level · Nachfragestand *m*

level of dwelling (vacancy) losses, level of residential (vacancy) losses · Wohnungsmietausfallhöhe *f*, Wohnungsmietverlusthöhe

level of education, education(al) level · Bildungsstand *m*

level of government · Regierungsebene *f*

level of living, living level (US); standard of living, standard of comfort, living standard, comfort standard · Lebensstandard *m*, Lebensniveau *n*, Lebenshaltung *f*

level of living survey · Lebensstandardübersicht *f*

level of planning, planning stage, planning level, stage of planning · Planungsebene *f*; Planungsstufe *f* [*Fehlbenennung*]

level of population, population level, demographic level · Bevölkerungsstand *m*

level of residential (vacancy) losses, level of dwelling (vacancy) losses · Wohnungsmietausfallhöhe *f*, Wohnungsmietverlusthöhe

level of satisfaction, satisfaction level · Befriedigungsniveau *n*

level of significance, significance level · Irrtumswahrscheinlichkeit *f* [*Statistik*]

level of training, training level · Ausbildungsstand *m*, Schulungsstand

level of utility, utility level · Nutzenniveau *n*

level of vacancy losses, level of collection losses · Mietausfallhöhe *f*, Mietverlusthöhe

level of well-being, level of prosperity, well-being level, prosperity level · Wohlstandsniveau *n*

level variable · Zustandsvariable *f*

leverage, gearing · Hebelwirkung *f* des Fremdkapitals, Multiplikatorwirkung *f* des Fremdkapitals (auf die Ertragslage des Eigenkapitals), Verhältnis *n* Eigenkapital-Fremdkapital

leverage · Leihkapital *n*, Fremdmittel *f*

leveraged [*Property is said to be leveraged when the owner's cash equity is small in relation to the total value of the property*] · fremdmittelbelastet, leihkapitalbelastet

leverage factor, gearing factor · Hebelwirkungsfaktor *m*

leverage fund · Fremdmittel-Investmentfonds *m*, Leihkapital-Investmentfonds

levis culpa [*Latin*]; ordinary fault, ordinary neglect · gewöhnliches Verschulden *n*

levissima culpa [*Latin*]; slight culpable neglect, slight culpable negligence · leichtes Verschulden *n*, gering(fügig)es Verschulden

to levy [*execution*] · vornehmen [*Zwangsvollstreckung*]

levy · Umlage *f*

to levy a distress (upon), to execute a distress (upon), to distrain · (privat)pfänden

levy rate, rate of levy · Umlagesatz *m*

to levy war · bekriegen

lex [*Latin*]; jurisprudence [*misnomer*]; law, objective right [*A system of law existing objectively as an external norm for persons*] · (objektives) Recht *n*

lex Alamannorum [*Latin*] · Recht *n* der Alemannen

lex burgundiorum [*Latin*]; Burgundian law [*The law of the Burgundians, first compiled and published by Gundebald, one of the last of their kings, about A.D. 500*] · Burgundisches Recht *n*

lex causae [*Latin*] · Geschäftsstatut *n*, Wirkungsstatut [*Das für das Rechtsverhältnis im ganzen maßgebliche Recht*]

lex commissaria [*Latin*] · Verwirkungsvorbehalt *m*

lex domicili [*Latin*] · Domizilrecht *n*, Wohnsitzrecht [*Das Recht des Ortes an dem die Person ihr Domizil hat*]

lex feudalis [*Latin*]; law of tenure(s) (of land), law of (the) manor, law of feudary tenure, law of feudal tenure, law of feodal tenure, law of feuds, law of feudal estates, feudal law, tenure law, feodal law, feuda(to)ry law, manorial law · Leh(e)n(s)recht *n*, Feudalrecht

lex fori [*Latin*] [*The law of the place of action. The forms of remedies, modes of proceeding, rules of evidence and execution of judgments are regulated by the law of the place where the action is instituted*] · Recht *n* am Ort des angegangenen Gerichts, heimisches Recht des Gerichts

lex Francorum Chamavorum [*Latin*] · Recht *n* der chamarischen Franken

lex gothica [*Latin*]; Gothic law, law of the Goths [*First promulgated in writing A. D. 466*] · gotisches Recht *n*

lex loci celebrationis [*Latin*]; law of the place where a contract is made · Vertragsortrecht *n*

lex loci (contractus) [*Latin*]; contract law, conventionary law, law of contract [*The law of the place of a contract; the law of the place where a contract is made, or is to be performed*] · Vertragsrecht *n*, Recht des Vertragsschlusses

lex loci solutionis [*Latin*]; law of the place of solutions [*The law of the place where payment or performance of a contract is to be made*] · Erfüllungsortrecht *n*, Recht des Erfüllungsortes

lex loquens [*Latin*] · sprechendes Gesetz *n*

lex mercatoria [*Latin*]; merchant law, mercantile law, commercial law, business law, law merchant · Handelsrecht *n*

lex non scripta [*Latin*]; unwritten law, juristic law, law of the forum [*It comprises both, judge-made law and juristmade law*] · Gerichtsrecht *n*; ungeschriebenes Recht [*Fehlbenennung, weil Gerichtsentscheide wegen ihrer bindenden Kraft für die Zukunft geschrieben sind*]

lex rei sitae [*Latin*] · Gebietsrecht *n*, Gebietsstatut *n*, Rechtsordnung *f* mittels einer Sache gewonnen, Realstatut, Recht der belegten Sache, Realrecht, Statut der belegten Sache, Belegenheitsortrecht

lex Ripuaria [*Latin*] · Recht *n* der ripuarischen Franken

lex Salica [*Latin*] · Recht *n* der salischen Franken

lex scripta, jus scriptum [*Latin*]; statute law, written law, enacted law, statutory law, statutes [*The body of law enacted by Parliament*] · geschriebenes Recht *n*, gesetztes Recht, geschriebenes Parlamentsrecht, gesetztes Parlamentsrecht, (Parlaments)Gesetz(esrecht

lex terrae [*Latin*] → (real) estate law

lex Wallensica [*Latin*]; Welsh law, law of Wales · walisisches Recht *n*

lex Wisigothorum [*Latin*] · Recht *n* der Westgoten, westgotisches Recht

ley-farming · Rotationsgraswirtschaft *f*

LHA, local housing building authority, local housing production authority · Gemeindewohn(ungs)baubehörde *f*, Kommunalwohn(ungs)baubehörde, Ortswohn(ungs)baubehörde

liabilities · Bilanzpassiva *f*

liabilities expected to rank · Schuldenmasse *f*

liability; obligatio [*Latin*] · Haftung *f*, Haftpflicht *f*, Haftbarkeit *f*

liability → liability (for defects)

liability act, liability law, liability statute · Haftpflichtgesetz *n*, Haftungsgesetz, Haftbarkeitsgesetz

liability bond · Haftungserklärung *f*, Haftpflichterklärung, Haftbarkeitserklärung

liability chain, chain of liability · Haftpflichtkette *f*, Haftungskette, Haftbarkeitskette

liability clause · Haftungsklausel *f*, Haftpflichtklausel, Haftbarkeitsklausel

liability division, division of liability · Haftungsteilung *f*, Haftpflichtteilung, Haftbarkeitsteilung

liability (for defects) · Gewährleistung *f* [*Bauvertrag*]

liability for delay · Verzugshaftung *f*, Verzugshaftpflicht *f*, Verzugshaftbarkeit *f*

liability for mistake(s), mistake liability · Irrtumshaftung *f*, Irrtumshaftpflicht *f*, Irrtumshaftbarkeit *f*

liability for negligence, liability for carelessness · Fahrlässigkeitshaftung *f*, Fahrlässigkeitshaftpflicht *f*, Fahrlässigkeitshaftbarkeit *f*, Nachlässigkeitshaftung, Nachlässigkeitshaftpflicht, Nachlässigkeitshaftbarkeit

liability for unlawful act(s), liability for tort(s) · deliktische Haftung *f*, deliktische Haftpflicht *f*, Haftung aus unerlaubter Handlung, Haftpflicht aus unerlaubter Handlung, deliktische Haftbarkeit

liability insurance, indemnity insurance · Haftpflichtversicherung *f*

liability law, liability statute, liability act · Haftpflichtgesetz *n*, Haftungsgesetz, Haftbarkeitsgesetz

liability law · Haftpflichtrecht *n*, Haftungsrecht, Haftbarkeitsrecht

liability limitation, liability restriction, restriction of liability, limitation of liability · Haftungsbegrenzung *f*, Haftpflichtgrenzung, Haftpflichtbeschränkung, Haftungsbeschränkung, Haftpflichteinschränkung, Haftungseinschränkung, Haftbarkeitsbegrenzung, Haftbarkeitsbeschränkung, Haftbarkeitseinschränkung

liability limitation contract, limitation of liability contract · Haftungsbeschränkungsvertrag *m*, Haftungseinschränkungsvertrag, Haftungsbegrenzungsvertrag, Haftpflichteinschränkungsvertrag, Haftpflichtbegrenzungsvertrag, Haftpflichtbeschränkungsvertrag, Haftbarkeitsbeschränkungsvertrag, Haftbarkeitsbegrenzungsvertrag

liability loss, loss of liability · Haftpflichtschaden *m*, Haftungsschaden, Haftbarkeitsschaden

liability of inactive co-trustee · Haftung *f* für Treubrüche des Mittreuhänders, Haftpflicht *f* für Treubrüche des Mittreuhänders, Haftbarkeit *f* für Treubrüche des Mittreuhänders

liability period (for defects), period of liability (for defects) · Gewährleistungsfrist *f* [*Bauvertrag*]

liability prescription, liability regulation, liability rule · Haftungsvorschrift *f*, Haftpflichtvorschrift, Haftbarkeitsvorschrift

liability privilege, privilege of liability · Haftungsprivileg *n*, Haftpflichtprivileg, Haftbarkeitsprivileg

liability regulation, liability rule, liability prescription · Haftungsvorschrift *f*, Haftpflichtvorschrift, Haftbarkeitsvorschrift

(liability) reserve, accrued liability · Rückstellung *f*

liability restriction, restriction of liability, limitation of liability, liability limitation · Haftungsbegrenzung *f*, Haftpflichtbegrenzung, Haftpflichtbeschränkung, Haftungsbeschränkung, Haftpflichteinschränkung, Haftungseinschränkung, Haftbarkeitsbegrenzung, Haftbarkeitsbeschränkung, Haftbarkeitseinschränkung

liability risk, indemnity risk, third-party risk · Haftpflichtwagnis *n*, Haftpflichtrisiko *n*, Haftungsrisiko, Haftungswagnis, Haftbarkeitswagnis, Haftbarkeitsrisiko

liability rule, liability prescription, liability regulation · Haftungsvorschrift *f*, Haftpflichtvorschrift, Haftbarkeitsvorschrift

liability statute, liability act, liability law · Haftpflichtgesetz *n*, Haftungsgesetz, Haftbarkeitsgesetz

liability sum, sum of liability · Haftsumme *f*, Haftpflichtsumme, Haftbarkeitssumme

liability to answer to law, amenableness, amenability [*The quality of being amenable*] · Verantwortlichkeit *f* vor dem Gesetz, Rechenschaftspflicht *f* vor dem Gesetz

liability to contribute, contribution liability, contribution duty, duty to contribute · Beitragspflicht *f*

liable · verpflichtet

liable · haftpflichtig, haftbar

liable funds · haftendes Eigenkapital *n*

liable to answer to law, responsible to law, answerable to law, liable to be brought before any jurisdiction, amenable, subject to answer to law · verantwortlich vor dem Gesetz, rechenschaftspflichtig vor dem Gesetz

liable to be brought before any jurisdiction, amenable, subject to answer to law, liable to answer to law, responsible to law, answerable to law · verantwortlich vor dem Gesetz, rechenschaftspflichtig vor dem Gesetz

liable to be registered · registrierpflichtig

liable to be registered, liable to be recorded · buchungspflichtig, eintrag(ungs)pflichtig, registrier(ungs)pflichtig [*Grund(stück)*]

liable to contribution(s), subject to contribution(s), contributory · beitragspflichtig

liable to evacuate, liable to quit · räumungspflichtig

liable to forfeiture, forfeitable · verwirkbar

liable to pay; g(u)ildable, geldable [*In old English law*] · zahlungspflichtig

liable to pay duties, liable to pay charges · gebührenpflichtig

liable to pay improvement contribution(s) · erschließungsbeitragspflichtig

liable to pay tithe, tith(e)able, tithed · zehnt(en)pflichtig

liable to permission, subject to permission, requiring permission · erlaubnisbedürftig, erlaubnispflichtig, genehmigungsbedürftig, genehmigungspflichtig

liable to prosecution, subject to prosecution, punishable · strafbar

liable to provide a way of necessity · notwegpflichtig [*Grundstück*]

liable to quit, liable to evacuate · räumungspflichtig

libel, written defamation, defamation by writing; libellus [*Latin*] · schriftliche Ehrenkränkung *f*, Schmähschrift *f*

libera chasea, libera fugacia [*Latin*], free chase, frank chase · freies Jagdrecht *n*, Recht auf freie Jagd

libera eleemosyna [*Latin*]; free alms, frankalmoign(e) · freies Almosen *n*

libera fugacia [*Latin*]; free chase, frank chase; libera chasea · freies Jagdrecht *n*, Recht auf freie Jagd

liberal education · Allgemeinbildung *f*

libera lex [*Latin*]; frank law, free law · Recht *n* der Freien, Recht eines Freien,

libera piscaria — licensed premise

Freienrecht [*Englisches mittelalterliches Recht*]

libera piscaria [*Latin*]; free fishery, fishing right, right of fishing, piscary [*The right or liberty of fishing in the waters of another person*] · Fischereirecht *n*, subjektives Fischereirecht

libera sedes, liber bancus, framus bancus, sedes libera [*Latin*]; free-bench · Freisitz *m* [*Der Anteil der Witwe eines Hintersassen an dessen Immobiliarbesitz*]

liberation of land(s) from feudal service · Bodenentlastung *f*, Landentlastung, Grundentlastung

libera warrena [*Latin*]; (liberty of) free warren · freies königliches Jagdrecht *n*, königliches freies Jagdrecht

liber et legalis homo [*Latin*]; juror, jury member, jurator, member of a jury; free and lawful man [*In old English law*]; judex · Geschworene *m*

liber homo, homo liber [*Latin*]; allodiary, allodialist, al(l)odial (land) owner, absolute (land) owner, exclusive (land) owner, absolute proprietor, exclusive proprietor, al(l)odial proprietor, free man, holder of an allodium · absoluter Eigentümer *m*, unbeschränkter Eigentümer, Alleineigentümer, Freiguteigentümer, Allodialeigentümer, freier Mann *m*, Freie *m*

liber judiciarius vel censualis Angliae [*Latin*] → Domesday (Book)

liberty · eximierter Gutsbezirk *m* [*im mittelalterlichen England*]

liberty, supremacy, authority, majesty, pre-eminence; majestas [*Latin*]; sovereign power, sovereign right, sovereign dominion, sovereignty · Hoheitsrecht *n*, Hoheitsbefugnis *f*, hoheitliches Recht, hoheitliche Befugnis, Souveränität *f*, Oberhoheit *f*, Hoheitsmacht *f*, vollziehende Gewalt *f*

liberty, privilege; franchesia, francisia [*Latin*]; franchise [*A privilege conferred by government on individuals or corporations, and which does not belong to citizens of country generally of common right*] · Gerechtsame *f*, Privileg *n*, Regalrecht *n*

liberty, freedom; libertas [*Latin*] · Freiheit *f*

liberty · Freibezirk *m* mit eigenem Beamten (bailiff) mit den Kompetenzen eines Sheriff [*England*]

liberty, prerogative right, privilege · Vorrecht *n*

liberty loan [*USA*]; war loan [*Great Britain*] · Kriegsanleihe *f*

liberty of fishery → fishery franchise

(liberty of) free warren; libera warrena [*Latin*] · freies königliches Jagdrecht *n*, königliches freies Jagdrecht

liberty of jurisdiction, jurisdiction liberty · Vorrecht *n* auf Jurisdiktion, Jurisdiktionsvorrecht

liberum tenementum [*Latin*] → simple fee

to licence, to license · konzessionieren

licence, license · Lizenz *f*

licence, license · Konzession *f*

licence application, application for licence, license application, application for license · Lizenzgesuch *n*, Lizenzantrag *m*, Lizenzersuchen *n*

licence bond, license bond [*This bond is required in jurisdictions where contractor's licenses are required. It indemnifies the obligee against damage caused him by the non-compliance of a contractor with the license law*] · Lizenzgarantie *f* [*Bauwesen*]

licence charge, license charge · Konzessionsgebühr *f*

licenced public house, licensed public house · Haus *n* mit (allgemeiner) Schankgerechtigkeit

licence duty → (excise) licence duty

licence fee, license fee, royalty · Patentabgabe *f*, Lizenzgebühr *f*

licence fee, license fee · Konzessionsgebühr *f*, Konzessionshonorar *n*

licence to pollute, license to pollute · Verschmutzungsfreiheit *f*

licence transfer(ence), license transfer(ence), transfer(ence) of licence, transfer(ence) of license, turning over of licence, turning over of license · Lizenzübertragung *f*

to license, to licence · konzessionieren

license, licence · Lizenz *f*

license, licence, registration [*Privilege or right granted by the state to operate as a real estate broker*] · staatliche Genehmigung *f*, staatliche Erlaubnis *f* [*Grundstücksmakler*]

license, licence, registration [*Authority to go upon or use another person's land(s) without possessing any estate therein*] · (Land)Benutzungsvollmacht *f*, Bodenbenutzungsvollmacht, Landgebrauchsvollmacht, Bodengebrauchsvollmacht

license → (on-)licence

license by estoppel, licence by estoppel, implied license based on estoppel, implied licence based on estoppel · Lizenz *f* kraft Verwirkung

license charge, licence charge · Konzessionsgebühr *f*

licensed premise, licensed property, licenced premise, licenced property [*The term "licensed premises" is a very*

licensed price — life estate in land 614

wide one and includes all those premises which are licensed for the sale of intoxicating liquors, such as hotels, public-houses, beer-houses, refreshment rooms, restaurants and "off-licences"] · Schankbetrieb m, Schankstätte f

licensed price, licenced price, statutory price, official price, price fixed by authority · Taxe f [Ein aufgrund eines Rechtes behördlich festgesetzter Preis]

licensed public house, licenced public house · Haus n mit (allgemeiner) Schankgerechtigkeit

licensed trade · Schankgewerbe n

licensee, licencee · Lizenznehmer m

licensee, licencee, licensed victualler, licenced victualler · Konzessionsinhaber m, Schankwirt m, konzessionierter Gastwirt

license fee, royalty, licence fee · Patentabgabe f, Lizenzgebühr f

license fee, licence fee · Konzessionsgebühr f, Konzessionshonorar n

license repudiation, licence repudiation · Lizenzpreisgabe f

license to mine, licence to mine · Bergbaulizenz f

licensing act, licensing statute, licensing law, licencing act, licencing statute, lincencing law · Schankgesetz n

licensing area, licensing territory, licencing area, licencing territory · Schankgebiet n

licensing committee, licencing committee [England] · Friedensrichterausschuß m für (Aus-) Schankkonzession

licensing judge, licencing judge · Schankrichter m

licensing law, licensing act, licensing statute · Schankgesetz n

licensing law, licencing law · Schankrecht n

licensing statute → licensing act

licensing territory → licensing area

licensor, licenser, licencer, licencor · Lizenzgeber m

licitation; licitatio [Latin] · Versteigerungsangebot n, Auktionsangebot

licitator [Latin]; bidder at a sale · Versteigerungsbieter m, Auktionsbieter

to lie, to be applicable, to be proper to be used [An action is said to lie in a case in which it may properly be brought] · anwendbar sein

to lie fallow · brachliegen [Land]

liege lady, lady paramount · Leh(e)n(s)herrin f

liege-lord, over lord, lord of (the) manor, supreme owner, landlord, grantor, feoffor, feoffer, manor lord, langeman, bestower of a fee, feudal chief; dominus directus, feoffator [Latin]; (feudal) lord, chief lord, possessory lord, superior lord · Leh(e)n(s)herr m, Feudalherr, (feudaler) Belehner, Leh(e)n(s)gutgeber, Obereigentümer, Landübertragende, Übertragende von Land

liege poustie [Scots law. A state of health which gives a person lawful power of disposition by will. The term appears to be a corruption or accommodation of ligia potestas] · testierfähige Gesundheit f

lien; ligamen [Latin] [A right which a person is entitled to obtain satisfaction of a debt by means of property belonging to the person indebted to him] · Einbehaltungsrecht n, Retentionsrecht, (Zu)Rück(be)haltungsrecht, Pfandrecht

lie of the ground, lie of the terrain · Geländezustand m, Geländebeschaffenheit f, Terrainzustand, Terrainbeschaffenheit, Landbeschaffenheit, Landzustand

to lie over [To stay and wait until some future time] · abwarten

to lie scattered · verstreut liegen, gestreut liegen

lieu land(s) [Public lands within the indemnity limits granted in lieu of those lost within place limits] · Tauschland n

to lie (up)on, to border (up)on, to be co(n)terminous with, to adjoin · angrenzen

lieu tax · Ersatzsteuer f

life · Leben n

life, term, currency · Dauer f, (Lauf)Zeit f [z. B. eines Vertrages]

life annuity, annuity for life [The payments cease at the death of the investor] · lebenslange Annuität f, lebenslängliche Annuität, Annuität auf Lebensdauer

life assurance [A species of insurance by which the insurer, in consideration of a sum in gross, or of periodical payments, undertakes to pay a certain sum, or an annuity, depending upon the death of a person whose life is insured] · Lebensversicherung f

life demise → tenancy for life

life duration, duration of life · Lebensdauer f [Lebewesen]

life economy · lebensorientierte Wirtschaft f, lebensbezogene Wirtschaft

life estate in land, estate (in land) for life, possessory interest (in land) for life, life estate (in property) · Landbesitzrecht n auf Lebenszeit des Verkäufers, Bodenbesitzrecht auf Lebenszeit des Verkäu-

life estate in land — likelihood model

fers, Besitzrecht auf Lebenszeit des Landverkäufers, Besitzrecht auf Lebenszeit des Bodenverkäufers

life estate in land → (real) estate for life

life estate (in property), life estate in land, estate (in land) for life, possessory interest (in land) for life · Landbesitzrecht *n* auf Lebenszeit des Verkäufers, Bodenbesitzrecht auf Lebenszeit des Verkäufers, Besitzrecht auf Lebenszeit des Landverkäufers, Besitzrecht auf Lebenszeit des Bodenverkäufers

life estate in (real) property → (real) property for life

life (estate in) realty → (real) property for life

life fixed property → (real) property for life

life holder → life (land) lessee

life immov(e)able property → (real) property for life

life immov(e)ables [*International Private Law*] → (real) property for life

life in realty → (real) property for life

life interest, life right · lebenslängliches (subjektives) Recht *n*

life (land(ed)) estate, estate (in land) for life, freehold · lebenslanges Bodenbesitzrecht *n*, lebenslanges Landbesitzrecht, lebenslanges Grund(stücks)besitzrecht

life land(ed) property → (real) property for life

life (land) lessee, life (land) (lease)holder, life tenant (of land), (land) holder for life, (land) lessee for life, (land) (lease)holder for life, tenant (of land) for life · (Land)Pächter *m* auf Lebenszeit, lebenslanger (Land)Pächter

life lease(hold) → tenancy for life

life limitation presumption, presumption of life limitation · Verschollenheitsvermutung *f*

life-linked investment · versicherungsgebundene Kapitalanlage *f*, Kapitalanlage mit Versicherungsschutz

life-owner, life-proprietor · Eigentümer *m* auf Lebenszeit, Eigentumssubjekt *n* auf Lebenszeit, Eigner auf Lebenszeit

life-peer · Pair *m* auf Lebenszeit

life policy · Lebensversicherungspolice *f*

life presumption, presumption of life · Lebensvermutung *f*

life property (of land(s)) → (real) property for life

life-proprietor, life-owner · Eigentümer *m* auf Lebenszeit, Eigentumssubjekt *n* auf Lebenszeit, Eigner auf Lebenszeit

life (real) property → (real) property for life

life rent · Lebensrente *f*

life right · lebenslänglicher Anspruch *m*, lebenslängliches (An)Recht *n*

life right, life interest · lebenslängliches (subjektives) Recht *n*

life style, style of life · Lebensstil *m*

life tenancy → tenancy for life

life tenure · Lebenszeit *f* [*Angestellten- und Beamtenverhältnis*]

life tenure → tenancy for life

life usufruct, usufruct for life · lebenslänglicher Nießbrauch *m*, lebenslänglicher (Frucht)Genuß *m*, lebenslängliche Nutzgewalt *f*

lifo, last in — first out · zuerst Abgang *m* des letzten Zugangs, jüngste Preise *mpl*

lift, (extraction) trace, selection overlay · transparenter Auszug *m* [*Kartographie*]

ligamen [*Latin*] → lien

light amount, quantum of light, quantity of light, amount of light, light quantity, light quantum · Lichtmenge *f*

light bill · Lichtrechnung *f*

light easement, easement of light · Lichtgrunddienstbarkeit *f*

light obstruction · Lichtentziehung *f*

light quantity, light quantum, light amount, quantum of light, quantity of light, amount of light · Lichtmenge *f*

light right, ancient light(s), ancient windows, servitude not to hinder lights; servitus ne luminibus officiatur [*Latin*]; right of light, right to light · Lichtrecht *n*, Abwehrrecht des Fenstereigentümers gegen den Nachbarn [*Schutz gegen Verbauung des Lichteinfalls durch den Grundstücksnachbarn*]

lignagium [*Latin*]; right to cut fuel in woods, fire-bote, focage, focale · Brennholzschlagrecht *n*, Feuerungszubuße *f*, Brennholzbezugsrecht

likelihood axiom, probabilistic axiom, probability axiom · Wahrscheinlichkeitsaxiom *n*

likelihood estimate, probabilistic estimate, probability estimate · Wahrscheinlichkeitsschätzung *f*

likelihood method, probability method, probabilistic method · Wahrscheinlichkeitsverfahren *n*

likelihood model, probability model, probabilistic model · Wahrscheinlichkeitsmodell *n*

likelihood network, probabilistic network, probability network · Wahrscheinlichkeitsnetz n

likelihood theory, probabilistic theory, probability theory · Wahrscheinlichkeitstheorie f

likelihood value, probabilistic value, probability value · Wahrscheinlichkeitswert m

lime(stone) (winning) right, lime(stone) exploitation right, right to win lime(stone), right to take lime(stone), right to exploit lime(stone) · Kalkabbaurecht n, Kalkausbeutungsrecht, Kalkabbaugerechtigkeit f

to limit, to restrain, to constrain, to restrict · begrenzen, beschränken, einschränken

to limit [*To mark out the extreme period during which an estate or interest is to continue*] · Verjährungsfrist festsetzen

limit · Preisgrenze f, äußerster Preis m [*Börse*]

limit · Grenze f

limitation, restriction, restraint, constraint · Begrenzung f, Einschränkung, Beschränkung

limitation; limitatio [*Latin*] · Verjährung f

limitation act, statute of limitation, law of limitation, act of limitation, limitation statute, limitation law · Verjährungsgesetz n

limitation by time immemorial, immemorial limitation (period) · unvordenkliche Verjährung(sfrist) f, Immemorialverjährung(sfrist)

limitation exclusion, exclusion of limitation · Verjährungsausschluß m

limitation law, limitation act, statute of limitation, law of limitation, act of limitation, limitation statute · Verjährungsgesetz n

limitation of action, imperfect negative prescription · Klageverjährung f

limitation of an estate, estate limitation · Besitzrechtbegrenzung f

limitation of appeal, restraint of appeal, restriction of appeal · Berufungsbeschränkung f, Appellationsbeschränkung

limitation of claim(s), limitation of demand(s) · Forderungsverjährung(sfrist) f

limitation of inheritance, restriction of inheritance [*land*] · Gebundenheit f [*Boden*]

limitation of liability, liability limitation, liability restriction, restriction of liability · Haftungsbegrenzung f, Haftpflichtbegrenzung, Haftpflichtbeschränkung, Haftungsbeschränkung, Haftpflichteinschränkung, Haftungseinschränkung, Haftbarkeitsbegrenzung, Haftbarkeitsbeschränkung, Haftbarkeitseinschränkung

limitation of liability contract, liability limitation contract · Haftungsbeschränkungsvertrag m, Haftungseinschränkungsvertrag, Haftungsbegrenzungsvertrag, Haftpflichteinschränkungsvertrag, Haftpflichtbegrenzungsvertrag, Haftpflichtbeschränkungsvertrag, Haftbarkeitsbeschränkungsvertrag, Haftbarkeitsbegrenzungsvertrag

limitation of (plot) utilization · Ausnutzungsbeschränkung f, Ausnutzungsbegrenzung, Ausnutzungseinschränkung

limitation of time, time limitation · Befristung f

limitation of use · Nutzungsbeschränkung f, Nutzungseinschränkung, Nutzungsbegrenzung

limitation of utilization → limitation of (plot) utilization

limitation period, period of limitation · Verjährungsfrist f

limitation period for defective work(s) · Baumangelbeseitigungsfrist f, Nachbesserungsfrist, (Sach)Mangelbeseitigungsfrist

limitation statute, limitation law, limitation act, statute of limitation, law of limitation, act of limitation · Verjährungsgesetz n

limited administration (of estate(s)), restricted administration (of estate(s)), restrained administration (of estate(s)), special administration (of estate(s)) · besondere Nachlaßverwaltung f, eingeschränkte Nachlaßverwaltung, beschränkte Nachlaßverwaltung, begrenzte Nachlaßverwaltung

limited choice of law by the parties · materiell(rechtlich)e Verweisung f

limited company bank, (joint-)stock bank · Aktiengesellschaftsbank f

limited competition → limited (competitive) tendering

limited (competitive) tendering, limited competition, selective competition, selective (competitive) tendering · beschränkte Ausschreibung f, beschränkter Wettbewerb m [*Bauleistungen werden im vorgeschriebenen Verfahren nach Aufforderung einer beschränkten Zahl von Unternehmern zur Einreichung von Angeboten vergeben*]

limited fee (simple), fee (simple) limited [*Estate giving the owner thereof fee rights as long as certain conditions obtain, termination being governed by the occurrence of some stated event*] · beschränkter (Grund)Besitz m, begrenzter (Grund)Besitz, eingeschränkter (Grund)Besitz

limited (general) property, nonexclusive (general) h‹operty; dominium temporale [*Latin*], limited ownership (of property), nonexclusive ownership (of property), limited proprietorship, nonexclusive proprietorship · beschränktes Eigentum *n*, begrenztes Eigentum, eingeschränktes Eigentum

limited guaranty, limited guarantee, limited guarantie [*A general guaranty limited as to the amount beyond which the guarantor will not be responsible*] · Betragsbürgschaft *f*

limited guaranty, limited guarantee, limited guarantie [*A general guaranty limited as to the time within which it must be accepted*] · Bürgschaft *f* auf Zeit, Zeitbürgschaft

limited information method · Methode *f* der eingeschränkten Informationsverwendung, Verfahren *n* der eingeschränkten Informationsverwendung [*Statistik*]

limited interest, restricted right, restricted interest, limited right · begrenztes (subjektives) Recht *n*, eingeschränktes (subjektives) Recht, beschränktes (subjektives) Recht, subjektives begrenztes Recht, subjektives eingeschränktes Recht, subjektives beschränktes Recht

limited interest in (real) estate, limited right in (real) estate, limited interest in (real) property, limited right in (real) property, restrained interest in (real) estate, restrained interest in (real) property, restrained right in (real) property, restricted interest in (real) estate, restricted right in (real) estate, restricted interest in (real) property, restricted right in (real) property, limited interest in realty, limited right in realty, restrained right in realty, restrained interest in realty, restricted right in realty, restricted interest in realty · begrenztes (dingliches) Recht *n* an einem Grund(stück), beschränktes (dingliches) Recht an einem Grund(stück), eingeschränktes (dingliches) Recht an einem Grund(stück), begrenztes (Boden)Besitzrecht, begrenztes Landbesitzrecht, begrenztes Grund(stücks)besitzrecht, beschränktes (Boden)Besitzrecht, beschränktes Landbesitzrecht, beschränktes Grund(stücks)besitzrecht, eingeschränktes Grund-(stücks)besitzrecht, eingeschränktes (Boden)Besitzrecht, eingeschränktes Landbesitzrecht

limited in time, restricted in time, restrained in time · befristet, zeitbegrenzt, zeitbeschränkt

limited jurisdiction [*Where the jurisdiction of a court is limited either by the amount or value of the property in litigation, or with reference to the question where the cause of action arose, it is called a court of limited jurisdiction, as opposed to a court of general jurisdiction*] · beschränkte Zuständigkeit *f*, eingeschränkte Zuständigkeit, begrenzte Zuständigkeit [*Siehe Anmerkung unter „Zuständigkeit"*]

limited liability, restricted liability, restrained liability · begrenzte Haftung *f*, begrenzte Haftpflicht *f*, begrenzte Haftbarkeit *f*, beschränkte Haftung, beschränkte Haftpflicht, beschränkte Haftbarkeit, eingeschränkte Haftung, eingeschränkte Haftpflicht, eingeschränkte Haftbarkeit

limited monarchy, constitutional monarchy · konstitutionelle Monarchie *f*

limited number · beschränkte Anzahl *f*, begrenzte Anzahl, eingeschränkte Anzahl

limited owner's charge, limited poprietor's charge · Eigentümerhypothek *f*, Eignerhypothek

limited ownership (of property), nonexclusive ownership (of property), limited proprietorship, nonexclusive proprietorship, limited (general) property, nonexclusive (general) property; dominium temporale [*Latin*] · beschränktes Eigentum *n*, begrenztes Eigentum, eingeschränktes Eigentum

limited partner, special partner · Kommanditist *m*, beschränkt haftender Partner *m*, beschränkt haftender Gesellschafter; Kommanditär *m* [*Schweiz*]

limited period (of time), limited (time) period · befristeter Zeitraum *m*

limited personal servitude, restricted personal servitude · beschränkte persönliche Dienstbarkeit *f*, eingeschränkte persönliche Dienstbarkeit, begrenzte persönliche Dienstbarkeit

limited poprietor's charge, limited owner's charge · Eigentümerhypothek *f*, Eignerhypothek

limited (private) partnership, commandite partnership, (private) partnership with limited liability · Kommanditgesellschaft *f*, KG [*Sie besteht aus Gesellschaftern, von denen mindestens einer, der Komplementär, den Gläubigern unbeschränkt haftet, und auch mindestens einer, der Kommanditist, nur mit dem Betrag seiner Einlage*]

limited probate, restricted probate, special probate · begrenzte Nachlaßbestätigung *f*, eingeschränkte Nachlaßbestätigung, beschränkte Nachlaßbestätigung, besondere Nachlaßbestätigung

limited (probate) administrator, limited trustee for sale · interimistischer erbrechtlicher Verwalter *m*, interimistischer gerichtlicher Verwalter, interimistischer Erb(schafts)verwalter, interimistischer (Nachlaß)Verwalter

limited proprietorship, nonexclusive proprietorship, limited (general) property, nonexclusive (general) property; dominium temporale [*Latin*]; limited ownership (of property), nonexclusive ownership (of property) · beschränktes Eigentum *n*, begrenztes Eigentum, eingeschränktes Eigentum

limited right, limited interest, restricted right, restricted interest · begrenztes (subjektives) Recht *n*, eingeschränktes (subjektives) Recht, beschränktes (subjektives) Recht, subjektives begrenztes Recht, subjektives eingeschränktes Recht, subjektives beschränktes Recht

limited right in estate → limited interest in (real) estate

limited right in property → limited interest in (real) estate

limited right in (real) estate → limited interest in (real) estate

limited right in (real) property → limited interest in (real) estate

limited right in realty → limited interest in (real) estate

limited stockholder · Kommanditaktionär *m*

limited tendering → limited (competitive) tendering

limited (time) period, limited period (of time) · befristeter Zeitraum *m*

limited trustee for sale, limited (probate) administrator · interimistischer erbrechtlicher Verwalter *m*, interimistischer gerichtlicher Verwalter, interimistischer Erb(schafts)verwalter, interimistischer (Nachlaß)Verwalter

limiting right of pre-emption, limiting option of purchase, limiting right of preemption · limitierendes Ankaufsrecht *n*, limitierendes Vorkaufsrecht

limit of burdens, limit of encumbrances, limit of charges, limit of incumbrances, limit of loads · Belastungsgrenze *f* [*Grundstück*]

limit of indebtedness, debt-limit [*Legally fixed limit on the amount of money a governmental entity may borrow*] · Verschuldungsgrenze *f*

limit of range of validity, limit of scope, scope limit · Geltungsgrenze *f*

limit of settlement, settlement limit · (An)Sied(e)lungsgrenze *f*

limit of waste, waste limit · Wertminderungsgrenze *f*, Depravierungsgrenze, Verwüstungsgrenze, Schwundgrenze, Übernutzungsgrenze, Verschlechterungsgrenze, Vernachlässigungsgrenze, Mißbrauchgrenze, Deteriorierungsgrenze

limit on planning · Planungsgrenze *f*

limits to growth · Grenzen *fpl* des Wachstums

limit theorem · Grenzwertsatz *m* [*Statistik*]

to limit the succession to (real) property, to entail, to create an estate tail, to settle the succession to (real) property · beschränken, beschneiden [*Vererbung von Grundstücken*]

limping (gold) standard [*A term applied to the gold standard during the period 1925—1931 when it did not work as effectively as before 1914 because many countries did not keep to the "rules", namely, to inflate when gold was coming in and to deflate when gold was being exported*] · hinkende Goldwährung *f*

line · Fluchtlinie *f* [*Es gibt Straßen- und Baufluchtlinien*]

line · Leitung *f*

line [*Route followed by a scheduled transit system vehicle*] · Linie *f*

linea (di)recta [*Latin*]; direct line, right line [*The direct line of ascendants and descendants*] · direkte (Abstammungs)Linie *f*, direkte Folge *f*

lineage, descent, ancestry · Abstammung *f*

lineal · in direkter Linie [*Erbfolge*]

lineal ancestor, lineal testator · linearer Bescheider *m*, linearer Erblasser, linearer Testator

lineal consanguinity, lineal descent, descent in direct line · lineare Blutsverwandschaft *f*

lineal descendant, lineal issue, lineal offspring · linearer Abkömmling *m*, linearer Nachkomme, linearer Deszendent

lineal descent, descent in direct line, lineal consanguinity · lineare Blutsverwandschaft *f*

lineal heirdom, lineal succession by inheritance · direkte Erb(schafts)nachfolge *f*

lineal heiress, lineal heir female; lineal inheretrix [*obsolete*] · Erbin *f* in direkter Folge, Erbin in direkter Linie, Linienerbin

lineal heir (male) · Erbe *m* in direkter Folge, Erbe in direkter Linie, Linienerbe

lineal inheritance; lineal enheritance [*obsolete*] · Erbschaft *f* in direkter Folge, Erbe *n* in direkter Folge, Linienerbschaft

lineal issue, lineal offspring, lineal descendant · linearer Abkömmling *m*, linearer Nachkomme, linearer Deszendent

lineal succession by inheritance, lineal heirdom · direkte Erb(schafts)nachfolge *f*

lineal testator, lineal ancestor · linearer Bescheider *m*, linearer Erblasser, linearer Testator

lineal warranty · Rechtsmängelgarantie *f* durch den Aszendenten

line-and-staff organization · Stabliniensystem *n*, Stablinienorganisation *f* [*Einheit der Auftragserteilung nach Fayol und Arbeitsspezialisierung auch in Bereiche*]

linear centre (Brit.); linear center (US) · lineares Zentrum *n*

linear cities, ribbon cities, corridor (of cities), strip cities, semicontinuous cities · Städteband *n*

linear city, ribbon town, linear town, ribbon city · Bandstadt *f*

linear composition, ribbon structure, linear structure, ribbon composition · Bandaufbau *m*, Bandzusammensetzung *f*, Bandstruktur *f*, Bandgefüge *n*

linear constraint · lineare Nebenbedingung *f* [*Statistik*]

linear dependence · lineare Abhängigkeit *f*

linear depletion for wear (and tear) · lineare Absetzung *f* für Abnutzung, lineare AfA [*Der Wert des abnutzbaren Wirtschaftsguts wird auf die Gesamtdauer seiner Verwendung oder Nutzung in gleichen Jahresbeiträgen verteilt*]

linear development, row development, ribbon development · Bandentwick(e)lung *f*, Reihenentwick(e)lung

linear discriminant function · lineare Trennfunktion *f* [*Statistik*]

linear industrial agglomeration · Industriegasse *f*

linear infrastructure, ribbon infrastructure · Bandinfrastruktur *f*, bandartige Infrastruktur [*Die Infrastruktur im Bereich des Verkehrs, des Transports und der Kommunikation*]

linear model · lineares Modell *n*

linear optimization model · lineares Optimierungsmodell *n*

linear regression · lineare Regression *f*

linear settlement · lineare (An)Sied(e)lung *f*

linear settlement of crofters with compact strips · Einödstreifen *m*

linear site, ribbon site · Bandort *m*

linear structure, ribbon composition, linear composition, ribbon structure · Bandaufbau *m*, Bandzusammensetzung *f*, Bandstruktur *f*, Bandgefüge *n*

linear town, ribbon city, linear city, ribbon town · Bandstadt *f*

linear village, row village, ribbon village · Banddorf *n*, Reihendorf

line data · Liniendaten *f*, Streckendaten

line diagram map · Liniendiagrammkarte *f*

line fence [*Fence placed on a boundary line*] · Grenzzaun *m*

line hamlet · Zeilenweiler *m*

line-haul rate, transport(ation) rate · Verkehrstarif *m*, Fahrtarif

line location · Leitungsführung *f*

line map · Strichkarte *f*

line of amity · Freundschaftslinie *f* [*Sie wurde im 16. und in der ersten Hälfte des 17. Jahrhunderts von den Kolonialmächten vereinbart*]

line of ancestry, line of descent · Abstammungslinie *f*

line of best fit · Gerade *f* die sich den Punkten am besten angleicht [*graphische Kostenzerlegung*]

line of (hand) craft, (hand) craft line · Handwerkszweig *m*

line of thought, thoughtway, consecutive thought · Gedankenfolge *f*, Gedankengang *m*

line organization, scalar organization · Liniensystem *n*, Linienorganisation *f* [*Nur eine Instanz darf von anderen Anweisungen geben*]

line position, supervisor [*Organization of business enterprises*] · Linienstelle *f*, Linieninstanz *f*, Chef *m*

line position map · Linienpositionskarte *f*

liner · Linienschiff *n*

line settlement · Zeilen(an)sied(e)lung *f*

line symbol map · Linienkartenzeichenkarte *f*, Liniensignaturenkarte

line village · Zeilendorf *n*

linguistic minority · Sprachminderheit *f*

linguistic usage · Sprachgebrauch *m*

link · Anknüpfungspunkt *m*

linkage · Leistungsverflechtung *f*

linkage advantage · räumlicher Fühlungsvorteil *m*

linkage coefficient, coefficient of geographical association, coefficient of linkage · Koeffizient *m* der räumlichen Verflechtung

linkage tree · Matrixreduzierungsdiagramm *n* [*Die (n · n) = Matrix der Entfernungen wird schrittweise durch Verknüpfung der jeweils am engsten benachbarten Einheiten auf eine (n−1) · (n−1) = Matrix, (n−2) · (n−2) = Matrix ... (2 · 2) = Matrix reduziert*]

linked blocks · gekoppelte Blöcke *mpl* [*Statistik*]

linked contract · fondsgebundener Versicherungsvertrag *m*

to liquidate, to wind up · abwickeln, liquidieren [*Konkurs*]

to liquidate, to settle, to redeem, to pay off, to discharge [*indebtedness*] · tilgen, begleichen, abbezahlen, rückzahlen

liquidated claim [*Claim, amount of which has been agreed on by parties to action or is fixed by operation of law*] · festgesetzte Forderung *f*

liquidated claim [*Claim, amount of which has been determined by a judg(e)ment in a legal action*] · festgestellte Forderung *f*

liquidated damages, liquidated compensation, liquidated indemnification, liquidated indemnity [*A sum of money agreed upon in advance by the parties to a contract under which either party may obtain compensation for a breach of the contract by the other*] · festgesetzte Entschädigung *f*, festgesetzter Schadenersatz *m*

liquidated damages, liquidated compensation, liquidated indemnification, liquidated indemnity [*The amount of damages determined by a judg(e)ment in a legal action*] · festgestellte Entschädigung *f*, festgestellter Schadenersatz *m*

liquidation, winding(-)up · Abwick(e)lung *f*, Liquidation *f* [*Konkurs*]

liquidation by court, winding(-)up by court · Abwick(e)lung *f* durch ein Gericht, Liquidation *f* durch ein Gericht, gerichtliche Liquidation, gerichtliche Abwick(e)lung [*Konkurs*]

liquidation law, winding(-)up law · Liquidationsrecht *n*, Abwick(e)lungsrecht

liquidation of a debt, discharge of a debt, settlement of a debt, redemption of a debt · Tilgung *f*, Schuldrückzahlung

liquidation of arrangement, winding(-)up of arrangement · außergerichtliche Abwick(e)lung *f*, außergerichtliche Liquidation *f*

liquidation order, order for winding(-)up, order for liquidation, winding(-)up order · Liquidationsbefehl *m*, Abwick(e)lungsbefehl

liquidation petition, petition for winding(-)up, petition for liquidation, winding(-)up petition · Liquidationsantrag *m*, Abwick(e)lungsantrag

liquidation proceeds, proceeds of liquidation · Liquidationserlös *m*, Abwick(e)lungserlös

liquidator · Abwickler *m*, Liquidator

liquid capital, money(ed) capital [*Capital in the form of money as distinct from real capital*] · Geldkapital *n*, freies Kapital

liquid credit · Geldkredit *m*

liquid debt [*One which is immediately and unconditionally due*] · Sofortschuld *f*

liquidity · Liquidität *f*, Zahlungsbereitschaft *f*

liquid waste · flüssiger Abfall(stoff) *m*

liquor dealer · Spirituosenhändler *m*

liquor-shop · Spirituosenladen *m*

LIR, landuse intensity rating · (bauliches) Mindestnutzungsmaß *n*, Mindestbaunutzungsmaß, Mindestmaß der (baulichen) Nutzung

to list · aufführen [*von Punkten*]

to list, to include in a list, to insert in a list, to enschedule · auflisten

list, schedule, tabulation, index, registry, register, bill · Verzeichnis *n*, Liste *f*, Aufstellung *f*, Register *n*

listed building, building to be preserved, building to be conserved · erhaltungswürdiges Gebäude *n*, erhaltenswertes Gebäude

listed security · börsennotiertes Wertpapier *n*

listing [*Record of real property for sale by a broker who has been authorized by the owner to sell*] · Grundstücksverkaufsverzeichnis *n*, Grundstücksverkaufsliste *f*

listing, authorization to sell · Verkaufsauftrag *m* [*Grundstücksmakler*]

listing [*Real property listed for sale by a broker who has been authorized by the owner to sell*] · Verkaufsgrundstück *n*

listing [*An agreement, not necessarily in writing, under the terms of which a real estate broker agrees to sell a property for a seller, who agrees to allow the broker to do so, for which the broker will be paid a fee*] · (Grund(stücks))Maklervereinbarung *f*, Landmaklervereinbarung, Bodenmaklervereinbarung, Liegenschaftsmaklervereinbarung

listing contract [*A contract documenting the terms of a listing*] · Bodenmaklervertrag *m*, Landmaklervertrag, (Grund(stücks))Maklervertrag

listing-fee · Einführungsgebühr *f* [*Börse*]

listing of buildings · Gebäudeauflistung *f*

list of abbreviations, schedule of abbreviations · Abkürzungsverzeichnis *n*

list of addresses · Anschriftenliste *f*, Anschriftenverzeichnis *n*

list of architects, schedule of architects, index of architects, tabulation of architects, register of architects, registry of architects · Architektenaufstellung f, Architektenliste f, Architektenregister n, Architektenverzeichnis n

list of case-notes, index of case-notes · Register n der Entscheidungsanmerkungen, Verzeichnis n der Entscheidungsanmerkungen, Liste f der Entscheidungsanmerkungen

list of contributories · Liste f der haftbaren Teilhaber, Liste der haftenden Teilhaber

list of deserted localities, list of lost localities · Wüstungsliste f, Wüstungsverzeichnis n

list of desired new lots · Planwunschliste f [früher: Planwunschbogen m]

list of green lands, list of green areas, list of landscape areas · Grünflächenverzeichnis n, Grünflächenliste f

list of lot surfaces · Bodennachweis m, Bodenverzeichnis n, Flächennachweis, Flächenverzeichnis, Landnachweis, Landverzeichnis

list of monuments · Denkmalliste f, Denkmalverzeichnis n

list of place names, index of place names · Ortsnamenverzeichnis n, Ortsnamenliste f, Ortsnamenregister n

list of prices, price schedule, price list, schedule of prices · Preisverzeichnis n, Preisliste f

list of tenderers → list of bidders

list price · Listenpreis m

list rotation, list seniority, rotation of the list, seniority of the list · Reihenfolge f der Anträge [Zuteilungsverfahren einer Bausparkasse]

list seniority, rotation of the list, seniority of the list, list rotation · Reihenfolge f der Anträge [Zuteilungsverfahren einer Bausparkasse]

list to be ticked, check list · Abhakliste f

litera [Latin]; letter of law [To be distinguished from the spirit of a law] · Buchstabe m des Gesetzes

literacy · Lesekundigkeit f

literal interpretation, literal construction, grammatical interpretation, grammatical construction · Literalauslegung f, Literaldeutung

literary property, intellectual property · geistiges Eigentum n

literature of the law, law literature · Rechtsliteratur f

litigans [Latin] → litigator

litigant (party) → litigator

to litigate, to go to law, to carry on a (law)suit, to bring into litigation, to engage in ligitation, to claim by action, to dispute by action [Latin: litigare] · prozessieren, einen Rechtsstreit austragen, einen Prozeß anhängig machen, rechtshängig werden lassen

litigating, contesting in a court of justice · Prozessieren n

litigation → (contentious) litigation

litigation fact · Tatsache f die erst im Prozeß bekannt wird

litigator, suitor, litigant (party), party to a (law)suit; sectator, litigans [Latin] · Prozessierende m, Prozeßpartei f

litigious [That which is the subject of a (law)suit; that which is contested in a court of justice] · prozeßhängig

litigious form, form of pleading · Prozeßform f

litigious right [A right which can not be exercised without undergoing a (law)suit] · strittiges Recht n, streitiges Recht

little tithe, small tithe, petty tithe, privy tithe · kleiner Zehnt m, Schmalzehnt

lit(t)oral, belonging to shore · litoral

lit(t)oral right, riparian right [The legal right regarding a water area which belongs to one who owns or possesses land bordering upon it] · (subjektives) Ufer(anlieger)recht n

to live, to reside, to dwell · ansässig sein, wohnen

to live beyond another, to survive, to outlive, to over-live · überleben

to live in, to occupy · bewohnen

livelihood area, livelihood territory · Gebiet n gleicher Art der Gewinnung des Lebensunterhaltes

liver · lebende Person f

livery · Meistergildentracht f, Herrengildentracht

livery · Leh(e)n(s)investitur f

livery → (de)livery

livery company [Any of the London city companies that grew out of earlier trade guilds, characterized by a distinctive dress] · Meistergilde f, Herrengilde

liveryman · Meistergildenmitglied n, Herrengildenmitglied

liveryman · Gildenmitglied n

livery of seisin(a) → (formal) livery of seisin(a)

(live)stock · Viehbestand m

**(live)stock breeder, **breeder of (live)stock · Viehzüchter *m*

(live)stock breeding, (live)stock raising, breeding of (live)stock, raising of (live)stock · Vieh(auf)zucht *f*

(live)stock dealer · Viehhändler *m*

(live)stock farm · Viehbetrieb *m*

(live)stock farmer, (live)stock holder, (live)stock man · Viehhalter *m*

(live)stock farming, (live)stock husbandry · Viehhaltung *f*

(live)stock holder → (live)stock farmer

(live)stock husbandry → (live)stock farming

(live)stock insurance · Viehversicherung *f*

(live)stock man → (live)stock farmer

(live)stock market · Viehmarkt *m*

(live)stock raising → (live)stock breeding

(live)stock size · Viehbesatz *m*

(live)stock yard · Viehhof *m*

living, domiciled, residing, resident · wohnhaft

living accommodation, residential accommodation · Wohnunterkunft *f*

living allowance (US); separating allowance, separation allowance; cost of living allowance (Brit.); subsistence allowance (Brit.); subsistence · Auslösung *f*, Trennungsgeld *n*, Trennungsentschädigung [*Ein Arbeitnehmer, der auf einer Baustelle außerhalb des Betriebssitzes arbeitet, erhält eine Auslösung, wenn die tägliche Rückkehr zum Wohnort nicht zumutbar ist*]

living climate [*The physical living conditions inside a dwelling*] · Wohnklima *n*

living condition · Lebensbedingung *f*

living cost(s), cost(s) of living · Lebenshaltungskosten *f*

living environment · Lebensumwelt *f*, Lebensumfeld *n*

living floor space, total area of habitable rooms · Wohnfläche *f*

living house, dwelling house, residential building, residence building, residential structure, residence structure · Wohngebäude *n*, Wohnhaus *n*

living in serfdom on an estate, bound to the soil · grunduntertänig

living level, level of living (US); standard of living, standard of comfort, living standard, comfort standard · Lebensstandard *m*, Lebensniveau *n*, Lebenshaltung *f*

living memory · Erinnerungsvermögen *n*

living pledge, vadium vivum, vivum vadium; vifgage [*In France*] [*When a person borrowed money of another, and granted to him an estate to hold till the rents and profits repaid the sum borrowed with interest. The estate was conditioned to be void as soon as the sum was realized*] · Totsatzung *f*, Todsatzung

living space, space of living · Lebensraum *m*

living unit, LU, lu, housing unit, apartment, unit of housing (US); apartment (Brit.) [*archaic*]; tenement, residence, dwelling; dwelling unit, DU, du (US) · Wohnung *f*

living unit in the court-yard, housing unit in the court-yard (US); dwelling in the court-yard; dwelling unit in the courtyard (US) · Hofwohnung *f*

to load, to encumber, to charge, to burden, to incumber · belasten, dinglich belasten

load, burden, incumbrance; incumbramentum [*Latin*], charge, encumbrance [*A claim or lien attached to property as a mortgage*] · (dingliche) Belastung *f*, (dingliche) Last *f*

load bias, weight error, load error, weight bias · Gewichtungsfehler *m*, Bewertungsfehler [*Statistik*]

loaded, burdened, charged, imperfect, encumbered, incumbered · belastet, dinglich belastet

loaded by law, burdened by law, encumbered by law, incumbered by law, charged by law · gesetzlich belastet

loaded by mortgage(s), burdened by mortgage(s), charged by mortgage(s), encumbered by mortgage(s), incumbered by mortgage(s) · hypothek(en)belastet

loaded with lease(hold), charged with lease(hold), burdened with lease(hold), encumbered with lease(hold), incumbered with lease(hold) · erbbaurechtbelastet, platzrechtbelastet

load error, weight bias, load bias, weight error · Gewichtungsfehler *m*, Bewertungsfehler [*Statistik*]

load hour · Belastungsstunde *f*

loading, weighting · Gewichtung *f*, Bewertung [*Statistik*]

loading, charging, burdening, incumbering, encumbering · (dingliches) Belasten *n*

load mistake, weight mistake · Bewertungsirrtum *m*, Gewichtungsirrtum [*Statistik*]

load of contribution(s), charge of contribution(s), contribution(s) charge, contribution(s) load · Beitragslast *f*

load of easement, burden of easement, charge of easement, encumbrance of easement, incumbrance of easement · Grunddienstbarkeitslast *f*

load of national debt, burden of national debt, encumbrance of national debt, incumbrance of national debt · Staatsschuldenlast *f*

load of the poor rates, burden of the poor rates, encumbrance of the poor rates, incumbrance of the poor rates, charge of the poor rates · Armenlast *f*

load prohibition, encumbrance prohibition, incumbrance prohibition, burden prohibition, charge prohibition · Belastungsverbot *n*, Last(en)verbot

load rate, burden rate, encumbrance rate, incumbrance rate, charge rate · Belastungssatz *m*, Last(en)satz

load (up)on personal property, burden on personal property, charge on personal property, encumbrance on personal property, incumbrance on personal property · Fahrnislast *f*, Fahrhabelast, Mobiliarlast, Mobilienlast

loafing · Müßiggang *m*

loan → loan (of money)

loanable · verleihbar

loan against deposit, security loan, deposit loan, loan against security · Sicherungsdarleh(e)n *n*, Sicherheitsdarleh(e)n

loan allowance · Darleh(e)nsbewilligung *f*

loan association → (mutual) loan association

loan assumption, assumption of loan · Darleh(e)nsübernahme *f*

loan bank · Darleh(e)nsbank *f*, Darleh(e)nskasse *f*

loan banknote · Darleh(e)nskassenschein *m*, Darleh(e)nsbankschein

loan capital · Darleh(e)nskapital *n*

loan (capital) interest, cost(s) of money, interest on loan (capital) · Darleh(e)nszinsen *f*

loan certificate, certificate of loan · Darleh(e)nsschein *m*

loan contract · Leihvertrag *m* [*bewegliche Sache*]

loan contract, contract of loan (of money) · Darleh(e)nsvertrag *m*

loan creditor · Darleh(e)nsgläubiger *m*

loan debt, borrowings · Darleh(e)nsschuld *f*

loanee, loan subscriber · Darleh(e)nsnehmer *m*, Darleh(e)nszeichner

loaner, (loan) lender, lender of money, moneylender · Geld(ver)leiher *m*, Geldgeber, Darleh(e)nsgeber, Kreditgeber

loan market · Darleh(e)nsmarkt *m*

loan maturation, loan maturity [*The end of the term of a loan*] · Darleh(e)nsfälligkeit *f*, Darleh(e)nsverfall *m*

loan mortgage · Darleh(e)nshypothek *f* [*für Darleh(e)n bestellt*]

loan obligation · Darleh(e)nsverpflichtung *f*

loan of a thing · Kommodation *f*

loan (of money) · Darleh(e)n *n*

loan on interest, interest loan · Zinsendarleh(e)n *n*

loan package [*Interim, standby, and permanent financing arrangements*] · Gesamtdarleh(e)n *n*

loan policy · Darleh(e)nspolitik *f*

loan premium · Darleh(e)nsagio *n*

loan repayable in a lump sum · Kündigungsdarleh(e)n *n*

loan repayment · Darleh(e)nsrückzahlung *f*

loan service, loan servicing · Darleh(e)nsverzinsung *f*

loan shark · Darleh(e)nswucherer *m*

loan stock, debentures, debenture stock · Schuldverschreibungen *fpl*

loan subscriber, loanee · Darleh(e)nsnehmer *m*, Darleh(e)nszeichner

loan to shareholder · Darleh(e)n *n* an Anteilseigner

loan value · Darleh(e)nswert *m* [*Ein um bestimmte Sicherheitsabschläge gekürzter Verkehrswert*]

loan with equal annuities · Tilgungsdarleh(e)n *n* [*Verzinsliches (Geld)Darleh(e)n mit gleichbleibenden Annuitäten, innerhalb deren die jeweils gegenüber der ersten Annuität überzahlten Zinsanteile den Tilgungsanteilen zugerechnet werden*]

local, communal [*Belonging to a place having the right of local government; belonging to, or affecting a particular state or separate community*] · gemeindlich, kommunal, örtlich

local accessibility · Ortszugänglichkeit *f*

local action → local (court) action

local administrative union [*A union of branches of local administration (towns, local councils, etc.) for some common purpose such as, for instance, street construction*] · Zweckverband *m*

local administrative union formed by law · Pflichtverband *m*

local administrative union for the umland · Umlandverband *m*

local administrative union law, local administrative union act, local administrative union statute · Zweckverbandsgesetz *n*

local administrative union law · Zweckverbandsrecht *n*

local advantage · Lagevorteil *m*, Standortvorteil

local advisory council, communal advisory council, local advisory panel, communal advisory panel · Ortsbeirat *m*, Gemeindebeirat, Kommunalbeirat

local affair, community affair, communal affair · Gemeindeangelegenheit *f*, Kommunalangelegenheit, Ortsangelegenheit

local agency, local office, community agency, community office, communal agency, communal office · kommunale Dienststelle *f*, Kommunaldienststelle, Gemeindedienststelle, gemeindliche Dienststelle, Ortsdienststelle

local allegiance, local liegance, local legal obedience, local statutory obedience · gesetzmäßiger Gehorsam *m* eines Ausländers dem Gaststaat gegenüber

local and customary tenure · gewohnheitsrechtliches Sonderleh(e)n *n*

local announcement, local publication, local promulgation · ortsübliche Bekanntmachung *f*, ortsübliche Bekanntgabe *f*, ortsübliche Kundmachung, ortsübliche Veröffentlichung

local area, local territory, communal area, communal territory, community area, community territory, incorporated area, incorporated territory · Gemeindegebiet *n*, gemeindliches Gebiet, Kommunalgebiet, kommunales Gebiet, Ortsgebiet

local authority, communal authority, community authority · Gemeindebehörde *f*, Ortsbehörde, Kommunalbehörde, kommunale Behörde, örtliche Behörde

local authority area, local authority land (area) · Gemeindebehördenland *n*, Kommunalbehördenland, Ortsbehördenland

local authority bond [*Great Britain*]; shortdated municipal bond [*USA*]; corporation bond · kurzfristige Kommunalschuldverschreibung *f*, kurzfristige Kommunalobligation *f*

local authority dwelling, local authority tenement, local authority residence · Gemeindewohnung *f*, Kommunalwohnung

local authority land (area) → local authority area

local authority stock [*Great Britain*]; municipal bond [*USA*]; corporation stock · Kommunalschuldverschreibung *f*, Kommunalobligation *f*

local banker · Lokalbankier *m*, Platzbankier, Ortsbankier

local bill · Platzwechsel *m*

local board, community board · Gemeindeamt *n*, Kommunalamt, Ortsamt

local body, community body, communal body · Gemeindeorgan *n*, Ortsorgan, Kommunalorgan

local border map, communal boundary map, community boundary map, local boundary map, community border map, communal border map · Gemeindegrenzenkarte *f*, Ortsgrenzenkarte, Kommunalgrenzenkarte

local branch of the central government bureaucracy · örtliche Zentralinstanzbehörde *f*

local budget, communal budget, community budget · Gemeindehaushalt *m*, Kommunalhaushalt

local budget law, communal budget law, community budget law · Gemeindehaushaltsrecht *n*, Kommunalhaushaltsrecht

local budget ordinance, community budget ordinance, communal budget ordinance, · Gemeindehaushaltsordnung *f*, Kommunalhaushaltsordnung

local building, local construction, communal building, communal construction, community building, community construction · Gemeindebau *m*, Kommunalbau

local (building and) construction law, local construction and building law · Gemeindebaurecht *n*, Kommunalbaurecht, Ortsbaurecht, örtliches Baurecht, kommunales Baurecht, gemeindliches Baurecht

(local) building by(e)-law, (local) construction by(e)-law, (local) construction code, (local) building code · Gemeindebauordnung *f*, Kommunalbauordnung

local building (construction), communal building (construction), community building (construction) · Gemeinde(hoch)bau *m*, gemeindlicher (Hoch)Bau, örtlicher (Hoch)Bau, kommunaler (Hoch)Bau

local building prescriptions, local construction prescriptions · örtliche Bauvorschriften *fpl*, gemeindliche Bauvorschriften, kommunale Bauvorschriften

(local) by(e)-law, local ordinance, local statute, communal by(e)-law, communal ordinance, communal statute, community by(e)-law, community ordinance, community statute · Gemeindegesetz *n*, Ortsgesetz, Ortsstatut *n*, Ortssatzung *f*, kommunales Gesetz, örtliches Gesetz, gemeindliches Gesetz, Kommunalgesetz, Kommunalsatzung, Kommunalstatut, Gemeindestatut, Gemeindesat-

local call — local government

zung, gemeindliche Satzung, gemeindliches Statut, kommunale Satzung, kommunales Statut, örtliche Satzung, örtliches Statut

local call, local demand · örtliche Nachfrage *f*

local cause, local (law)suit, local (court) action, local plea · Klage *f* wenn die Rechtsverletzung nur an einem bestimmten Platz möglich war [*z. B. widerrechtliches Eindringen in ein Grundstück, Veränderung eines Flußbettes usw.*]

local chapter · Ortsverein *m* [*Deutscher Anwaltverein*]

local chose; immov(e)able [*International Private Law*]; immov(e)able thing, real thing, thing immov(e)able, thing real, chose local · Immobilie *f*, unbeweglicher Gegenstand *m*, unbewegliche (Einzel)Sache *f*, unbewegliches Ding *n*, unbewegliches Rechtsobjekt *n*

local choses; immov(e)ables [*International Private Law*]; things immov(e)able, things real, real things, immov(e)able things, choses local · Immobilien *fpl*, unbewegliche (Einzel)Sachen *fpl*, unbewegliche Dinge *npl*, unbewegliche Gegenstände *mpl*, unbewegliche Rechtsobjekte *npl*

local code, community code, communal code · Gemeindeordnung *f*, Kommunalordnung

local community, urban quarter, town quarter, city quarter · Stadtviertel *n*, Stadtteil *m, n*, Stadtquartier *n*

local construction, communal building, communal construction, community building, community construction, local building · Gemeindebau *m*, Kommunalbau

local construction and building law, local (building and) construction law · Gemeindebaurecht *n*, Kommunalbaurecht, Ortsbaurecht, örtliches Baurecht, kommunales Baurecht, gemeindliches Baurecht

(local) construction by(e)-law, (local) construction code, (local) building code, (local) building by(e)-law · Gemeindebauordnung *f*, Kommunalbauordnung

(local) construction code, (local) building code, (local) building by(e)-law, (local) construction by(e)-law · Gemeindebauordnung *f*, Kommunalbauordnung

local construction law → local (building and) construction law

local construction prescriptions, local building prescriptions · örtliche Bauvorschriften *fpl*, gemeindliche Bauvorschriften, kommunale Bauvorschriften

local council, (community) council, (court of) common council · Kommunalrat *m*, Ortsrat, (Gemeinde)Rat, (Gemeinde)Vertretung *f*, Kommunalvertretung, Ortsvertretung, Vertretungskörperschaft *f*

local court [*In England*] · Amtsgericht *n*, AG, Registrargericht, lokales Gericht, Ortsgericht

local (court) action, local plea, local cause, local (law)suit · Klage *f* wenn die Rechtsverletzung nur an einem bestimmten Platz möglich war [*z. B. widerrechtliches Eindringen in ein Grundstück, Veränderung eines Flußbettes usw.*]

local custom, special custom, local usage, local habit, special usage, special habit · örtliche Gewohnheit *f*, örtliche Gepflogenheit, örtlicher Brauch *m*, Ortsüblichkeit, Ortsgewohnheit, Ortsgepflogenheit, Ortsbrauch

local demand, local call · örtliche Nachfrage *f*

local development, community development, communal development · Gemeindeentwick(e)lung *f*, Kommunalentwick(e)lung, Ortsentwick(e)lung, kommunale Entwick(e)lung

local development planning, communal development planning, community developement planning · Gemeindeentwick(e)lungsplanung *f*, Ortsentwick(e)lungsplanung, kommunale Entwick(e)lungsplanung, Kommunalentwick(e)lungsplanung

local district, community district, communal district · Gemeindebezirk *m*, Ortsbezirk, Kommunalbezirk

local dwelling rent, local (residential) rent · ortsübliche (Wohnungs)Miete *f*

local eduction(al) authority, communal education(al) authority, community education(al) authority · Gemeindeschulbehörde *f*, Kommunalschulbehörde

local facility, communal facility, community facility · Gemeindeeinrichtung *f*, Kommunaleinrichtung, gemeindliche Einrichtung, kommunale Einrichtung, öffentlicher Standort *m*

local finance reform, communal finance reform, community finance reform · Gemeindefinanzreform *f*, Kommunalfinanzreform, Ortsfinanzreform, gemeindliche Finanzreform, kommunale Finanzreform

local forest · Ortswald *m*

local government; local self-government [*deprecated*] · Gemeindeverwaltung *f*, Lokalverwaltung, Kommunalverwaltung, innere Verwaltung, staatliche Verwaltung des Innerern, Ortsverwaltung [*Alle Ausdrücke (ausgenommen „innere Verwaltung") sind der deutschen Staatsrechtswissenschaft nicht geläufig, sondern werden in der deutschen Rechts-*

local government bill — local land reform

sprache höchstens ganz allgemein als Bezeichnungen der örtlich tätigen, öffentlichen Verwaltung gebraucht, ohne daß damit über die Organisation, staatsrechtliche Stellung oder Funktion dieser Verwaltung schon etwas gesagt wäre. Hier werden diese Ausdrücke jedoch als technische Ausdrücke gebraucht, nämlich als die Übersetzung von „local government". Das richtige deutsche Wort ist „innere Verwaltung". Die Lokalverwaltung in England wird von den natürlich gegebenen örtlichen Verbänden der Staatsbürger geführt]

local government bill · Gesetz(es)entwurf *m* über Selbstverwaltung

local government board · Zentralstelle *f* für Ortsverwaltung, Selbstverwaltungsamt *n*

Local Government Board [*called Ministry of Health since 1909*] · Armenaufsichtsbehörde *f* und Gesundheitsbehörde [*In England. Beide Behörden wurden durch ein Gesetz von 1871 zusammengelegt*]

local (government) election, communal (government) election · Gemeindewahl *f,* Kommunalwahl

local government unit [*USA*] · kommunale Gebietskörperschaft *f*

local habit, special usage, special habit, local custom, special custom, local usage · örtliche Gewohnheit *f,* örtliche Gepflogenheit, örtlicher Brauch *m,* Ortsüblichkeit, Ortsgewohnheit, Ortsgepflogenheit, Ortsbrauch

local health authority, local sanitary authority, communal health authority, communal sanitary authority, community health authority, community sanitary authority · örtliche Gesundheitsbehörde *f,* kommunale Gesundheitsbehörde, gemeindliche Gesundheitsbehörde, Ortsgesundheitsbehörde, Gemeindegesundheitsbehörde, Kommunalgesundheitsbehörde

local health board, local sanitary board; local (medical) officer of health [*England*] · Gemeindegesundheitsamt *n,* Ortsgesundheitsamt, Kommunalgesundheitsamt, kommunales Gesundheitsamt, gemeindliches Gesundheitsamt, örtliches Gesundheitsamt

Local Health Insurance Fund · Allgemeine Ortskrankenkasse *f*

local housing authority, communal housing authority, community housing authority · Ortswohn(ungs)behörde *f,* Gemeindewohn(ungs)behörde, Kommunalwohn(ungs)behörde

local housing building authority, local housing production authority, LHA · Gemeindewohn(ungs)baubehörde *f,* Kommunalwohn(ungs)baubehörde, Ortswohn(ungs)baubehörde

local housing code, communal housing code · Gemeindewohn(ungs)ordnung *f,* Kommunalwohn(ungs)ordnung

local improvement [*A public improvement made in a particular locality, by which the real property adjoining or near such locality is specially benefited*] · örtliche Verbesserung *f*

local industrial tax rate · örtlicher Gewerbesteuersatz *m*

localism · örtliche Verhältnisse *f*

locality, place [*A definite region in any part of space*] · Ort(schaft) *m, (f)*

locality desertion, place desertion · Ortswüstung *f*

localization coefficient, coefficient of localization · Lokalisierungskoeffizient *m*

localization curve, curve of localization · Lokalisierungskurve *f*

localization economies · Branchenagglomerationsvorteile *mpl,* brancheninterne Agglomerationsvorteile, Vorteile der räumlichen Branchenkonzentration, Produktionsstätten-Nachbarschaft *f,* Vorhandensein *n* mehrerer Betriebe derselben Branche am selben Ort, Konzentration *f* gleicher Branchen

localization factor, factor of localization · Lokalisierungsfaktor *m*

localization of industry, industrial localization · Industrieansied(e)lung *f* [*als Vorgang*]

local land charge [*Any land charge acquired by a local authority which is binding on successive owners of the land affected*] · kommunale Grund(stücks)belastung *f,* kommunale Grund(stücks)last *f,* gemeindliche Grund(stücks)belastung, gemeindliche Grund(stücks)last

local land charges act, local land charges statute, local land charges law · kommunales Grund(stücks)belastungsgesetz *n,* kommunales Grund(stücks)lastgesetz, gemeindliches Grund(stücks)belastungsgesetz, gemeindliches Grund(stücks)lastgesetz

local land law, communal land law, community land law · Gemeindelandrecht *n,* Kommunallandrecht, Gemeindebodenrecht, Kommunalbodenrecht

local land policy, community land policy, communal land policy · kommunale Bodenpolitik *f,* gemeindliche Bodenpolitik, Kommunallandpolitik, Gemeindelandpolitik, Kommunalbodenpolitik, Gemeindebodenpolitik

local land reform, community land reform, communal land reform · gemeindliche Bodenreform *f,* kommunale Bodenreform, gemeindliche Landreform, kommunale Landreform

local land(s) use planning · örtliche Flächennutzungsplanung f, örtliche Landnutzungsplanung, örtliche Bodennutzungsplanung

local (land(s)) use zoning → local zoning

local law, communal law, community law · Gemeinderecht n, Kommunalrecht, Ortsrecht, Lokalrecht

local lawmaker, local legislator, communal lawmaker, communal legislator, community lawmaker, community legislator · Ortsgesetzgeber m, Gemeindegesetzgeber, Kommunalgesetzgeber

local (law)suit, local (court) action, local plea, local cause · Klage f wenn die Rechtsverletzung nur an einem bestimmten Platz möglich war [z. B. widerrechtliches Eindringen in ein Grundstück, Veränderung eines Flußbettes usw.]

local law theory · Theorie f der Ausbildung eigenen Rechts nach dem Muster des fremden

local legal obedience, local statutory obedience, local allegiance, local liegance · gesetzmäßiger Gehorsam m eines Ausländers dem Gaststaat gegenüber

local legislative authority, legislative local authority, lawmaking local authority · gesetzgebende örtliche Behörde f, örtliche gesetzgebende Behörde

local legislator, communal lawmaker, communal legislator, community lawmaker, community legislator, local lawmaker · Ortsgesetzgeber m, Gemeindegesetzgeber, Kommunalgesetzgeber

local level, community level, communal level · Gemeindeebene f, lokale Ebene, örtliche Ebene, Kommunalebene

local liegance, local legal obedience, local statutory obedience, local allegiance · gesetzmäßiger Gehorsam m eines Ausländers dem Gaststaat gegenüber

local loan · Kommunaldarleh(e)n n, Gemeindedarleh(e)n

local location · örtliche Lage f [Die Lagebeziehung einer (An)Sied(e)lung zu ihrem unmittelbaren, funktionell mit ihr verbundenem Umland]

local mass transit vehicle, local mass transport(ation) vehicle, local (public) transport(ation) vehicle, local (public) transit vehicle · örtliches Massenverkehrsfahrzeug n, örtliches Massenbeförderungsfahrzeug

local mass transport(ation), local (public) transit, local (public) transport(ation), local mass transit · örtlicher Massenverkehr m, örtliche Massenbeförderung f

local (medical) officer of health [*England*]; local health board, local sanitary board · Gemeindegesundheitsamt n, Ortsgesundheitsamt, Kommunalgesundheitsamt, kommunales Gesundheitsamt, gemeindliches Gesundheitsamt, örtliches Gesundheitsamt

local multiplier · ortsüblicher Vervielfältiger m

local network · Ortsnetz n

local office, community agency, community office, communal agency, communal office, local agency · kommunale Dienststelle f, Kommunaldienststelle, Gemeindedienststelle, gemeindliche Dienststelle, Ortsdienststelle

local option · Ortsentscheid(ung) m, (f) über Schankgerechtigkeit

local option, communal option, community option · Gemeindebestimmungsrecht n, Kommunalbestimmungsrecht

(local) ordinance → (local) by(e)-law

local organization, communal organization, community organization · Gemeindeorganisation f

local outline scheme, local outline programme; local outline program (US) · örtliches Rahmenprogramm n

local park, communal park, community park · Gemeindepark m, Kommunalpark

local partial planning · örtliche Teilplanung f

local (passenger) (transport(ation)) service, local (passenger) transit service · örtlicher (Personen)Massenverkehrsbetrieb m, örtlicher Personenverkehrsbetrieb

local pasture, communal pasture, community pasture · Gemeindeweide f, Kommunalweide, Ortsweide

local plan → (detailed) local plan

local planning, communal planning, community planning · gemeindliche Planung f, örtliche Planung, kommunale Planung, lokale Planung, Gemeindeplanung, Ortsplanung, Kommunalplanung, Lokalplanung

local planning authority, community planning authority, communal planning authority · Gemeindeplanungsbehörde f, Ortsplanungsbehörde, gemeindliche Planungsbehörde, örtliche Planungsbehörde, kommunale Planungsbehörde, Kommunalplanungsbehörde

local planning law, community planning law, communal planning law · Ortsplanungsgesetz n, Gemeindeplanungsgesetz, Kommunalplanungsgesetz, örtliches Planungsgesetz, gemeindliches Planungsgesetz, kommunales Planungsgesetz

local planning office, communal planning office, community planning office · Ortsplanungsstelle f, Gemeindeplanungsstelle, Kommunalplanungsstelle

local planning policy, community planning policy, communal planning policy · Gemeindeplanungspolitik f, Kommunalplanungspolitik, Ortsplanungspolitik

local plea, local cause, local (law)suit, local (court) action · Klage f wenn die Rechtsverletzung nur an einem bestimmten Platz möglich war [z. B. *widerrechtliches Eindringen in ein Grundstück, Veränderung eines Flußbettes usw.*]

local police (authority), community police (authority), communal police (authority) · Ortspolizei(behörde) f, Kommunalpolizei(behörde), Gemeindepolizei(behörde)

local population · ortsansässige Bevölkerung f

local prescription, local regulation, communal prescription, communal regulation, community prescription, community regulation · gemeindliche Vorschrift f, kommunale Vorschrift, Ortsvorschrift, Gemeindevorschrift, örtliche Vorschrift, Kommunalvorschrift

local promulgation, local announcement, local publication · ortsübliche Bekanntmachung f, ortsübliche Bekanntgabe f, ortsübliche Kundmachung, ortsübliche Veröffentlichung

local property tax · gemeindliche Vermögenssteuer f, kommunale Vermögenssteuer

local public · lokale Öffentlichkeit f, örtliche Öffentlichkeit

local publication, local promulgation, local announcement · ortsübliche Bekanntmachung f, ortsübliche Bekanntgabe f, ortsübliche Kundmachung, ortsübliche Veröffentlichung

local public body · örtliche öffentliche Körperschaft f, örtliche öffentliche Korporation f, lokale öffentliche Körperschaft, lokale öffentliche Korporation

local (public) transport(ation), local mass transit, local mass transport(ation), local (public) transit · örtlicher Massenverkehr m, örtliche Massenbeförderung f

local (public) transport(ation) vehicle, local (public) transit vehicle, local mass transit vehicle, local mass transport(ation) vehicle · örtliches Massenverkehrsfahrzeug n, örtliches Massenbeförderungsfahrzeug

(local) rate · Kommunalsteuer f, Gemeindesteuer

(local) rate law · Gemeindesteuerrecht n, Ortssteuerrecht, Kommunalsteuerrecht, Lokalsteuerrecht

(local) ratepayer (Brit.); local tax payer (US) · Kommunalsteuerzahler m, Gemeindesteuerzahler, Kommunalsteuerpflichtige, Gemeindesteuerpflichtige

local reapportionment → local reorganization

local reform, community reform, communal reform · Gemeindereform f, Kommunalreform, Ortsreform

local region · örtliche Region f

local regulation, communal prescription, communal regulation, community prescription, community regulation, local prescription · gemeindliche Vorschrift f, kommunale Vorschrift, Ortsvorschrift, Gemeindevorschrift, örtliche Vorschrift, Kommunalvorschrift

local rent → local (residential) rent

local reorganization, local reapportionment, communal reorganization, communal reapportionment, community reorganization, community reapportionment · gemeindliche Neugliederung f, kommunale Neugliederung, gemeindliche Neuordnung, kommunale Neuordnung, gemeindliche Gebietsreform, kommunale Gebietsreform

local (residential) rent, local dwelling rent · ortsübliche (Wohnungs)Miete f

local resistance (to planning) · Bürgerwiderstand m (gegen Planung)

local sanitary authority, communal health authority, communal sanitary authority, community health authority, community sanitary authority, local health authority · örtliche Gesundheitsbehörde f, kommunale Gesundheitsbehörde, gemeindliche Gesundheitsbehörde, Ortsgesundheitsbehörde, Gemeindegesundheitsbehörde, Kommunalgesundheitsbehörde

local sanitary board; local (medical) officer of health [*England*], local health board · Gemeindegesundheitsamt n, Ortsgesundheitsamt, Kommunalgesundheitsamt, kommunales Gesundheitsamt, gemeindliches Gesundheitsamt, örtliches Gesundheitsamt

local self-administration, communal self-administration, community self-administration · kommunale Selbstverwaltung f, gemeindliche Selbstverwaltung, Gemeindeselbstverwaltung, Ortsselbstverwaltung, Kommunalselbstverwaltung

local self-government [*deprecated*], local government · Gemeindeverwaltung f, Lokalverwaltung, Kommunalverwaltung, innere Verwaltung, staatliche Verwaltung des Inneren, Ortsverwaltung [*Alle Ausdrücke (ausgenommen „innere Verwaltung") sind der deutschen Staatsrechtswissenschaft nicht geläufig, sondern werden in der deutschen Rechts-*

sprache höchstens ganz allgemein als Bezeichnungen der örtlich tätigen, öffentlichen Verwaltung gebraucht, ohne daß damit über die Organisation, staatsrechtliche Stellung oder Funktion dieser Verwaltung schon etwas gesagt wäre. Hier werden diese Ausdrücke jedoch als technische Ausdrücke gebraucht, nämlich als die Übersetzung von „local government". Das richtige deutsche Wort ist „innere Verwaltung". Die Lokalverwaltung in England wird von den natürlich gegebenen örtlichen Verbänden der Staatsbürger geführt]

local sentiment · Heimatbewußtsein *n*

local sociologist, communal sociologist, community sociologist · Gemeindesoziologe *m*, Kommunalsoziologe

local sociology, community sociology, communal sociology · Gemeindesoziologie *f*, Kommunalsoziologie

local statistics, communal statistics, community statistics · Gemeindestatistik *f*, Kommunalstatistik, Ortsstatistik

(local) statute → (local) by(e)-law

local statutory obedience, local allegiance, local liegance, local legal obedience · gesetzmäßiger Gehorsam *m* eines Ausländers dem Gaststaat gegenüber

local suit → local (law)suit

local taxation, communal taxation, community taxation · Gemeindebesteuerung *f*, Kommunalbesteuerung

local tax for housing, housing rate (Brit.) · kommunale Wohn(ungs)steuer *f*, gemeindliche Wohn(ungs)steuer

local tax payer (US); (local) ratepayer (Brit.) · Kommunalsteuerzahler *m*, Gemeindesteuerzahler, Kommunalsteuerpflichtige, Gemeindesteuerpflichtige

local (territorial) reorganization, local (territorial) reapportionment, community (territorial) reorganization, community (territory) reapportionment, communal (territory) reorganization · Gemeindeneugliederung *f*, kommunale Neugliederung, Gemeindegebietsreform *f*, (territoriale) Gemeindeneuordnung

local territory, communal area, communal territory, community area, community territory, incorporated area, incorporated territory, local area · Gemeindegebiet *n*, gemeindliches Gebiet, Kommunalgebiet, kommunales Gebiet, Ortsgebiet

local traffic area · örtliche Verkehrsfläche *f*

local traffic planner · Kommunalverkehrsplaner *m*, Gemeindeverkehrsplaner

local transit → local (public) transit

local transit service → local (passenger) (transport(ation)) service

local transport(ation) location · Gemarkungslage *f*, Bannverkehrslage

local unit, communal unit, CU, community unit · lokale Einheit *f*, örtliche Einheit, gem- eindliche Einheit, Gemeindeeinheit, Ortseinheit

local usage, local habit, special usage, special habit, local custom, special custom · örtliche Gewohnheit *f*, örtliche Gepflogenheit, örtlicher Brauch *m*, Ortsüblichkeit, Ortsgewohnheit, Ortsgepflogenheit, Ortsbrauch

local zoning, communal zoning, community zoning, local (land(s)) use zoning, communal (land(s)) use zoning, community (land(s)) use zoning · gemeindliche Baunutzung, kommunale Baunutzung, örtliche Baunutzung, gemeindliche bauliche Nutzung, kommunale bauliche Nutzung, örtliche bauliche Nutzung, lokale Baunutzung, lokale bauliche Nutzung *f*

locare [*Latin*] → to let

to locate · festlegen [*Grundstücksgrenze*]

to locate, to discover by survey · auffinden

locatio [*Latin*]; letting, ablocation · Vermietung *f*

location, pegging (out) · Absteckung *f* des Feldes, Besitzergreifung [*Erwerb von Bergbauland*]

location, site [*Position in space; place where a factory, house, etc. is*] · Standort *m*, Lage *f*

location, siting, site location [*A locating or being located*] · Standortbestimmung *f*, Lagebestimmung

location → (mining) location

location → location (of land)

location(al) activity, location(al) activeness, activity at location, activeness at location · standortmäßige Aktivität *f*, lagemäßige Aktivität

location(al) analysis, location(al) study, analysis of site, study of site, site analysis, site study, analysis of location, study of location [*The evaluation of the qualities of a site by comparison with those of other comparable sites*] · Standortanalyse *f*, Standortuntersuchung, Lageanalyse, Lageuntersuchung

locational behaviour (Brit.); locational behavior (US) · Standortverhalten *n*

location(al) choice, site choice · Standortwahl *f*, Lagewahl

location(al) composition, location(al) structure, site composition, site structure · Standortaufbau *m*, Standortgefüge n, Standortstruktur f, Standortzusammensetzung f

location(al) decision, site decision · Standortentscheidung f

location(al) determinant, site determinant · Standortdeterminante f

locational distribution · Standortverteilung f, Lageverteilung

location(al) doctrine, site doctrine, doctrine of locations, doctrine of sites · Standortlehre f, Lehre vom Standort

location(al) equilibrium, site equilibrium, equilibrium of site, equilibrium of location · Standortgleichgewicht n, Lagegleichgewicht

location(al) factor, site factor, demand factor of location, demand factor of site · Standortfaktor m, Lagefaktor

location(al) game, site game · Standortspiel n, Lagespiel

location(al) influence, site influence · Standorteinfluß m, Lageeinfluß

location(al) model · Standortmodell n, Lagemodell

location(al) movement, site movement · Standortveränderung f, Lageveränderung

locational obsolescence, economic obsolescence · wirtschaftliche Überalterung f

location along a spring water table · Quellhorizontlage f

location(al) orientation, site orientation · Standortorientierung f, Lageorientierung

location(al) planning, site planning, planning of locations, planning of sites · Standortplanung f, Lageplanung

location(al) quotient, site quotient · Standortquotient m, Lagequotient

location(al) scheme, site pattern, site scheme, location(al) pattern · Standortmuster n, Standortschema n, Lagemuster, Lageschema

location(al) solution, site solution · Standortlösung f, Lagelösung

location(al) structure, site composition, site structure, location(al) composition · Standortaufbau m, Standortgefüge n, Standortstruktur f, Standortzusammensetzung f

location(al) study, analysis of site, study of site, site analysis, site study, analysis of location, study of location, location(al) analysis [*The evaluation of the qualities of a site by comparison with those of other comparable sites*] · Standortanalyse f, Standortuntersuchung

location(al) theory, site theory, theory of location, theory of sites · Standorttheorie f, Lagetheorie

location(al) triangle, site triangle · Standortdreieck n, Lagedreieck

location at a center of gravity (US); location at a centre of gravity (Brit.) · Schwerpunktlage f

location control, site control · Standortlenkung f, Lagelenkung

location equation, equation of location, equation of site, site equation · Standortgleichung f, Lagegleichung

location for enlargement, location for extension, site for extension, site for enlargement · Erweiterungsstandort m, Erweiterungslage

location limitation, location restriction, location restraint, site limitation, site restriction, site restraint · Standorteinschränkung f, Standortbeschränkung, Standortbegrenzung

location of employment, site of employment, employment location, employment site · Beschäftigungsstandort m

location (of land) [*American land law. The designation of the boundaries of a particular piece of land, either upon record or on the land itself*] · Landfestsetzung f

location of physical facility → location of structure

location of settlement, settlement location · (An)Sied(e)lungsstandort m, (An)Sied(e)lungslage f

location of structure, location of work, location of physical facility, site of structure, site of work, site of physical facility · Bau(werk)standort m, Bauanlagestandort; Bautestandort [*Schweiz*]

location of the most favourable market, site of the most favourable market · Standort m des besten Absatzes

location of winning, winning site, winning location, site of winning · Gewinnungsstelle f, Gewinnungsstandort m

location of work → location of structure

location-orien(ta)ted, location-related, site-orien(ta)ted, site-related · lagebezogen, lageorientiert, standortbezogen, standortorientiert

location policy, site policy · Standortpolitik f

location preference, site preference · Standortbevorzugung f

location problem, site problem, problem of location, problem of site · Standortfrage f

location protected from wind · Windschutzlage f

location quality, site quality · Standortgüte f, Lagegüte

location quotient · Verhältnis *n* des regionalen Branchenanteils zum nationalen Branchenanteil

location rank, rank of location, site rank, rank of site · Standortrang *m*

location rank size, size of location rank, site rank size, size of site rank · Standortranggröße *f*, Lagerungsgröße

location-related, site-orien(ta)ted, site-related, location-orien(ta)ted · lagebezogen, lageorientiert, standortbezogen, standortorientiert

location rent, site rent · Standortrente *f*, Lagerente

location search · Standortsuche *f*, Lagesuche

location separation, site separation, separation of locations, separation of sites · Auseinanderfallen *n* von Standorten

location theorist, site theorist · Standorttheoretiker *m*, Lagetheoretiker

location value, site value · Grund(stücks)wert *m*

locatio operis faciendi [*Latin*] · Frachtführung, Vercharterung

locative call [*In a deed, patent, or other instrument containing a description of land, locative calls are specific calls, descriptions, or marks of location referring to landmarks, physical objects, or other points by which the land can be exactly located and identified*] · Landfestsetzungszeichen *n*

locator [*American land law. One who locates land, or intends or is entitled to locate*] · Landfestsetzer *m*

locator, letter · (Sach)Vermieter *m* [*bewegliche Sache*]

to lock, to tie up, to sink · festlegen [*Kapital*]

to lock in · einschließen

lockout · Aussperrung *f*

to lock up · verschließen

lock-up · Obligation *f* mit höheren Erträgen nach einiger Zeit

lock-up house · Detentionshaus *n*

locus castrense [*Latin*] · Burgsitz *m*

locus contractus [*Latin*]; seat of the obligation, seat of the contract, proper law of the contract, law with reference to which the parties contracted · Sitz *m* der Obligation [*nach Savigny*]; Sitz des Vertrages

locus regit actum [*Latin*]; the place governs the act [*The act is governed by the law of the place where it is done*] · Ortsrecht *n* das ein Rechtsgeschäft beherrscht, Ortsrecht ein Rechtsgeschäft beherrschend

locus sigilli, L.S. [*Latin*]; place of the seal · Siegelort *m*

to lodge a caveat, to put in a caveat, to enter a caveat · Einspruch erheben

to lodge an appeal, to appeal (against) · einlegen [*Berufung*]

lodg(e)ment of an appeal · Berufungseinlegung *f*, Appellationseinlegung

lodger · Pensionsgast *m*

lodging, shelter, quarter, accommodation · Unterkunft *f*

lodging a complaint · Einlegen *n* einer Beschwerde

lodging-house (Brit); rooming house (US) [*Building that contains sleeping rooms and which is regularly used or available for permanent occupancy*] · Logierhaus *n*, Herberge *f* zur Heimat

lodging tax · Beherbergungssteuer *f*

lodging trade · Beherbergungsgewerbe *n*

loglog transformation · doppelt logarithmische Transformation *f*

log-rolling · politisches Schachergeschäft *n*

Lombard Street, bill market, discount market · Diskontmarkt *m*

London County Council, L.C.C. · Grafschaftsrat *m* London

London Fire Engine Establishment · Londoner Feuerspritzdepot *n*

London proper · eigentliches London *n*

long-dated → long-period

long-dated stock [*Over ten years until maturity*] · langfristige Staatsschuldverschreibung *f*, langfristige Staatsobligation *f* [*in Großbritannien*]

long-distance footpath, long-distance walkway · Fernfußweg *m*

long-distance migration · Fernwanderung *f*, Langwanderung

long-distance road, long-distance highway; trunk road, trunk highway (Brit.) · Fernstraße *f*

long-distance route · Fernstrecke *f*

long-distance traffic · Fernverkehr *m*

long-distance transit vehicle, long-distance transport(ation) vehicle · Fernverkehrsmittel *n*, Fernverkehrsfahrzeug *n*

long draft, foreign bill (of exchange) · ausländischer Wechsel *m*

long end of the market [*Great Britain*] · Teilmarkt *m* für Staatsanleihen mit mittlerer und langer Laufzeit

longer liver, survivor, surviving person, longest liver · Überlebende *m*

long-period, long-dated, long-range, long-term, long-run · langfristig, Langzeit . . . . .

long-period contract, long-term contract, long-range contract, long-run contract · langfristiger Vertrag *m*, Langzeitvertrag

long-period effect, long-run effect, long-term effect, long-range effect · Langzeitwirkung *f*, langfristige Wirkung

long-period equilibrium, long-run equilibrium, long-term equilibrium, long-range equilibrium · langfristiges Gleichgewicht *n*, Langzeitgleichgewicht

long-period finance, long-term finance, long-range finance, long-run finance · langfristige Finanzierung *f*, Langzeitfinanzierung

long-period lower price limit, long-term lower price limit, long-range lower price limit, long-run lower price limit · langfristige Preisuntergrenze *f*

long-period planning, long-run planning, long-range planning, long-term planning · langfristige Planung *f*, Langzeitplanung

long-period recreation, long-term recreation, long-range recreation, long-run recreation · Langzeiterholung *f*, langfristige Erholung

long price, gross price · Bruttopreis *m*

long-range → long-period

long-range aggregate supply function, long-run aggregate supply function, long-term aggregate supply function, long-period aggregate supply function, long-range total supply function, long-run total supply function, long-term total supply function, long-period total supply function · langfristige Gesamtangebotsfunktion *f*, Langzeit-Gesamtangebotsfunktion

long-range contract, long-run contract, long-period contract, long-term contract · langfristiger Vertrag *m*, Langzeitvertrag

long-range effect, long-period effect, long-run effect, long-term effect · Langzeitwirkung *f*, langfristige Wirkung

long-range finance, long-run finance, long-period finance, long-term finance · langfristige Finanzierung *f*, Langzeitfinanzierung

long-range lower price limit, long-run lower price limit, long-period lower price limit, long-term lower price limit · langfristige Preisuntergrenze *f*

long-range planning, long-term planning, long-period planning, long-run planning · langfristige Planung *f*, Langzeitplanung

long-range recreation, long-run recreation, long-period recreation, long-term recreation · Langzeiterholung *f*, langfristige Erholung

long-run → long-period

long-run average cost(s), LRAC, average cost(s) in the long run · langfristige Durchschnittskosten *f*

long-run contract, long-period contract, long-term contract, long-range contract · langfristiger Vertrag *m*, Langzeitvertrag

long-run-cost(s) curve · Kostenkurve *f* bei langfristiger Anpassung

long-run effect, long-term effect, long-range effect, long-period effect · Langzeitwirkung *f*, langfristige Wirkung

long-run finance, long-period finance, long-term finance, long-range finance · langfristige Finanzierung *f*, Langzeitfinanzierung

long-run lower price limit, long-period lower price limit, long-term lower price limit, long-range lower price limit · langfristige Preisuntergrenze *f*, Langzeit-Preisuntergrenze

long-run planning, long-range planning, long-term planning, long-period planning · langfristige Planung *f*, Langzeitplanung

long-run recreation, long-period recreation, long-term recreation, long-range recreation · Langzeiterholung *f*, langfristige Erholung

long-run total cost(s), LRTC, total cost(s) in the long run · langfristige Gesamtkosten *f*

long-standing decision · alte unbestrittene Entscheidung *f*, alter unbestrittener Entscheid *m*

long strip lot · Langstreifenparzelle *f*

long-term → long-period

long-term contract, long-range contract, long-run contract, long-period contract · langfristiger Vertrag *m*, Langzeitvertrag

long-term effect, long-range effect, long-period effect, long-run effect · Langzeitwirkung *f*, langfristige Wirkung

long-term executor · Dauertestamentsvollstrecker *m*

long-term finance, long-range finance, long-run finance, long-period finance · langfristige Finanzierung *f*, Langzeitfinanzierung

long-term lower price limit, long-range lower price limit, long-run lower price limit, long-period lower price limit · langfristige Preisuntergrenze *f*

long-term parker, all-day parker · Dauerparker *m*

long-term planning, long-period planning, long-run planning, long-range planning · langfristige Planung *f*, Langzeitplanung

long-term recreation, long-range recreation, long-run recreation, long-period recreation · Langzeiterholung *f*, langfristige Erholung

long village · Langdorf *n*, Liniendorf

loop · Innenstadt *f* von Chicago [*Der gewerblich genutzte Kern der Stadt und die ihn ringförmig umgebende Hochbahn*]

loophole market · Lückenmarkt *m*

loose leaf atlas · Loseblattatlas *m*

looseleaf (land) register, looseleaf register of land · Loseblattgrundbuch *n*

looseleaf series, looseleaf collection · Loseblattsammlung *f*

loosing operation → (money-)loosing operation

lord → lord of (the) manor

lord, master, dominus [*These terms, prefixed to a man's name, in ancient times, usually denoted him a knight or clergyman, a gentleman or the lord of a manor. During medi(a)eval times these words (sometimes abbreviated to "don" or "dan") were commonly prefixed to the name of a clergyman or of a gentleman of position. It indicated no special dignity known to the law*] · Herr *m*

Lord Commissioner of Justiciary · Strafrichter *m* des höchsten Strafgerichts in Schottland

Lord high treasurer · Lordschatzmeister *m*

Lord Justice of Appeal in Chancery · Appellationsrichter *m* des Kanzleramtes [*England*]

lord of (the) manor, supreme owner, landlord, grantor, feoffor, feoffer, manor lord, langeman, bestower of a fee, feudal chief; dominus directus, feoffator [*Latin*], (feudal) lord, chief lord, possessory lord, liege-lord, over lord, superior lord · Leh(e)n(s)herr *m*, Feudalherr, (feudaler) Belehner, Leh(e)n(s)gutgeber, Obereigentümer, Landübertragende, Übertragende von Land

lord paramount (of a fee), supreme lord (of a fee), paramount lord (of a fee), sovereign lord (of a fee) [*The Queen or the King are lords paramount of all the lands in the Kingdom*] · oberster Leh(e)n(s)herr *m*, höchster Leh(e)n(s)herr, oberster Feudalherr, höchster Feudalherr

Lord Privy Seal · Geheimsiegelbewahrer *m*

lord's house on the villa, lord's seat on the villa · römisches Herrschaftshaus *n*, römisches Gutshaus, römischer Herrensitz *m*

lord spiritual · geistlicher Pair *m*

lord's woods, lord's forest · Fronwald *m*

Lord Tenderden's Act, Prescription Act 1832 · Ersitzungsgesetz *n* von 1832 [*in England*]

lorry owner (Brit.); truck owner (US) · LKW-Halter *m*

lorry survey (Brit.); truck survey (US) · LKW-Enquête *f*, Last(kraft)wagenenquête

loser · Verlierer *m*

loss [*It may mean act of losing, or the thing lost*] · Verlust *m*

loss carried forward · vorgetragener Verlust *m*

loss hazard, risk of loss, hazard of loss, loss risk · Verlustrisiko *n*, Verlustwagnis *n*

loss of amenity, loss of faculty, loss of enjoyment of life [*Result of injury or injuries depriving a natural person of some enjoyment*] · Körperschaden *m*

loss of credit, credit loss · Kreditverlust *m*

loss of earnings · Verdienstausfall *m*

loss of enjoyment of life, loss of amenity, loss of faculty [*Result of injury or injuries depriving a natural person of some enjoyment*] · Körperschaden *m*

loss of faculty, loss of enjoyment of life, loss of amenity [*Result of injury or injuries depriving a natural person of some enjoyment*] · Körperschaden *m*

loss of future earnings · Verlust *m* der Verdienstmöglichkeit

loss of (general) property, loss of ownership (of property), loss of proprietorship · Eigentumsverlust *m*

loss of interest, interest loss · Zinsverlust *m*

loss of liability, liability loss · Haftpflichtschaden *m*, Haftungsschaden

loss of possession, possession loss · Besitzverlust *m*

loss of profit(s), loss of gain(s), profit loss, gain loss · Gewinnentgang *m*, Gewinnverlust *m*, Profitentgang, Profitverlust

loss of property, property loss · Vermögensverlust *m*, Vermögensschaden *m* [*Jede in Geld bewertbare Vermögenseinbuße*]

loss of useful value · Entwertung *f*

loss risk, loss hazard, risk of loss, hazard of loss · Verlustrisiko *n*, Verlustwagnis *n*

lost, mislaid · unauffindbar, verlegt

lost · verloren

lost city, deserted town, deserted city, lost town · wüste Stadt *f*

lost community — lower class

lost community, deserted community · wüste Gemeinde f, wüste Kommune f

lost gain; lucrum cessans [*Latin*]; prevented profit, lost profit, prevented gain · verlorener Gewinn m, entgangener Gewinn, verlorener Profit, entgangener Profit

lost grant · nachträglich verlorener Erwerbstitel m

lost land, deserted land · wüste Flur f, wüstes Land n, wüster Boden m, Wüstland, Wüstflur, Wüstboden

lost locality, deserted locality · wüste Ortschaft f, wüster Ort m

lost locality research, desertion research, deserted locality research · Wüstungsforschung f

lost profit, prevented gain, lost gain; lucrum cessans [*Latin*]; prevented profit · verlorener Gewinn m, entgangener Gewinn, verlorener Profit, entgangener Profit

lost town, lost city, deserted town, deserted city · wüste Stadt f

lost village, deserted village · wüstes Dorf n

to lot, to (sub)divide into lots · parzell(is)ieren

lot · Flurstück n, (Kataster)Parzelle f, Kartengrundstück, Katastergrundstück, Grundstück (im katastertechnischen Sinn) [*Die buchungstechnische Grundstückseinheit eines Katasters*]

lot [*Any group of goods or services, making up a single transaction*] · Los n

lot → (estate) lot

lot area [*Total horizontal area within the lot lines of the lot*] · Parzellenfläche f, Flurstückfläche, Grundstückfläche

lot bundle, bundle of lots · Parzellenverband m

lot complex · Parzellenkomplex m

lot depth [*The mean horizontal distance of a lot from the front street line to its rear line*] · Flurstückstiefe f, Parzellentiefe, Grundstückstiefe

lot (general) property → (estate) lot ownership (of property)

lot holder → (estate) lot holder

lot lease(hold) → (estate) lot tenancy

lot line; bonda, bunda, bonna [*In old English law*]; boundary (line), abuttal [*A legally defined line dividing one lot of property from another*] · Grund(stücks)grenze f

lot ownership (of property) → (estate) lot ownership (of property)

lot property → (estate) lot ownership (of property)

lot proprietorship → (estate) lot ownership (of property)

lot size, lot quantity · Losgröße f, Losmenge f

lotted forest, (sub)divided forest · parzell(is)ierter Wald m

lot tenancy → (estate) lot tenancy

lotting, (land(s)) (sub)division, (sub)division into (estate) lots, (sub)division (of land(s)) · Parzelli(si)erung f, Landparzelli(si)erung, Bodenparzelli(si)erung

lotting plan, plan of estate lots, (sub)division plan, plan of (division into) lots, plan of (sub)division (of land(s)), plan of lotting · Parzelli(si)erungsplan m

lotting practice · Parzelli(si)erungswesen n, Bodenparzelli(si)erungswesen, Landparzelli(si)erungswesen

lotting proposal · Parzelli(si)erungsvorschlag m

lot tolerance per cent. defective · Ablehn(ungs)grenze f [*Statistik*]

lot width, width of lot · Parzellenbreite f, Flurstücksbreite, Grundstücksbreite

low bid, low offer, low tender; low (bid) proposal (US) [*Bid stating the bid price, including selected alternates, and complying with all bidding requirements, which is determined by review of all bids to be the low bid*] · Mindestangebot n, Niedrigstangebot

low bidder, low tenderer [*Bidder who submits the lowest bid price after alternates have been considered but who does not become the lowest responsible bidder until so qualified*] · Mindestbieter m, Niedrigstbieter

low bid price, low offer price, low tender price; low (bid) proposal price (US) · Mindestangebotspreis m, Niedrigstangebotspreis

low coast(al) land, coast(al) low land · Küstentiefland n, Küstentiefebene f

low-cost(s) housing, publicly(-)assisted housing, publicly(-)provided housing, subsidized housing, low-rent housing, social housing, low-income housing · Zuschußwohnungen fpl, Sozialwohnungen, öffentlich geförderte Wohnungen, Wohnungen des sozialen Wohn(ungs)baues, Wohnungen der öffentlichen Hand

low density continuous development · allseitige und dünne und geschlossene Ausdehnung f

to lower, to bring down, to cut (down) · ermäßigen

lower class · Unterschicht f

lower court · nächstniedrigere Instanz f

Lower House of Legislature · Bürgerschaft f, Senat m [Bremen; Hamburg; Berlin]

lower-income apartment → publicly-assisted dwelling unit

lower-income dwelling → publicly-assisted dwelling unit

lower-income family [A family in need of subsidization] · sozialschwache Familie f, hilfsbedürftige Familie, minderbemittelte Familie

lower-income house, publicly-assisted house, subsidized house, social house · Sozialhaus n, öffentlich gefördertes Haus, Haus der öffentlichen Hand, Haus des sozialen Wohn(ungs)baues, Zuschußhaus

lower-income hous(ebuild)ing, social hous(ebuild)ing, production of public housing, public(ly-assisted) hous(ebuild)ing, subsidized hous(ebuild)ing · Zuschußwohn(ungs)bau m, Sozialwohn(ungs)bau, öffentlich geförderter Wohn(ungs)bau, geförderter öffentlicher Wohn(ungs)bau, sozialer Wohn(ungs)bau, Wohn(ungs)bau der öffentlichen Hand

lower-income residence → publicly-assisted dwelling unit

lower-income tenement → publicly-assisted dwelling unit

lowering, bringing down, cutting (down) · Ermäßigen n, Ermäßigung f

lower instance · niedrigere Instanz f, untere Instanz, vorherige Instanz, Vorinstanz

lower limit · Untergrenze f

lower-lower class · untere Unterschicht f

lower middle class · untere Mittelschicht f

lower price limit · Preisuntergrenze f

lower riparian owner, lower riparian proprietor, downstream riparian owner, downstream riparian proprietor · unterwasserseitiger Ufereigentümer, unterwasserseitiger Ufereigner m

lower riparian possessor, downstream riparian possessor · unterwasserseitiger Uferbesitzer m

lower-than-average rate · Unterdurchschnittssatz m

lowest · unterst

lowest level · absoluter Tiefstand m [Währung]

lowest level ever · bisher tiefster Stand m, bisheriger Tiefststand [Währung]

lowest-order fully-central place · Marktort m [nach W. Christaller]

lowest tenant (of a fee), tenant paravail [A tenant who held land(s) in fee of another and had no tenant who held of him, as opposed to a mesne lord and a lord paramount] · niedrigster Leh(e)n(s)mann m

low-income family · Familie f mit geringem Einkommen, schwachbemittelte Familie

low-income housing, low-cost(s) housing, publicly(-)assisted housing, publicly(-)provided housing, subsidized housing, low-rent(al) housing, social housing · Zuschußwohnungen fpl, Sozialwohnungen, öffentlich geförderte Wohnungen, Wohnungen des sozialen Wohn(ungs)baues, Wohnungen der öffentlichen Hand

low land · Niederung f

lowland embayment · Tieflandbucht f

lowland site · Tiefenlage f [Ortschaft]

low level analysis · Kosten-Wirksamkeitsanalyse f in der engeren Definition, KWA in der engeren Definition

low offer → low bid

low-order semi-central place · hilfszentraler Ort m [nach Christaller]

low proposal (US) → low bid

low-rent housing, social housing, low-income housing, low-cost(s) housing, publicly(-)assisted housing, publicly(-)provided housing, subsidized housing · Zuschußwohnungen fpl, Sozialwohnungen, öffentlich geförderte Wohnungen, Wohnungen des sozialen Wohn(ungs)baues, Wohnungen der öffentlichen Hand

low-rent housing unit (US) → public housing unit

low responsible bidder, successful bidder, approved tenderer, low responsible tenderer, successful tenderer, successful contractor, approved bidder [He is not necessarily the bidder whose bid is the lowest. "Responsible" means that the bid is taken together with the bidders financial ability, reputation and past performance] · Auftragnehmer m, AN

low tender → low bid

low tenderer → low bidder

low-tide line · Ebbelinie f

low-wage · lohnschwach

low-wage country · Niedriglohnland n

loyalty to contract · Vertragstreue f

LRA, land recordation act, land recording act, land registration act · Grundbuchgesetz n

LRAC — lying fallow

LRAC, average cost(s) in the long run, long-run average cost(s) · langfristige Durchschnittskosten *f*

LRTC, total cost(s) in the long run, long-run total cost(s) · langfristige Gesamtkosten *f*

L.S. [*Latin*]; place of the seal; locus sigilli · Siegelort *m*

L.T. (Brit.); lettergram (US); letter telegramm · Brieftelegramm *n*

LU, lu, housing unit, apartment, unit of housing (US); apartment (Brit.) [*archaic*]; tenement, residence, dwelling; dwelling unit, DU, du, living unit (US) · Wohnung *f*

lucid interval; lucidum intervallum [*Latin*] [*An interval of reason by an insane person, or lunatic*] · lichter Augenblick *m* [*Geisteskranke*]

lucrative, economical, profitable · gewinnbringend, rentabel, wirtschaftlich, profitbringend

lucrative cost(s), remunerative cost(s), "pay" cost(s) · rentierliche Kosten *f*

lucrum cessans [*Latin*]; prevented profit, lost profit, prevented gain, lost gain · verlorener Gewinn *m*, entgangener Gewinn, verlorener Profit, entgangener Profit

LUI, land-use intensity [*The overall relationships of structural mass and open space of a developed property or a development plan*] · (baulicher) Nutzungsmaß *n*, Baunutzungsmaß, Maß der (baulichen) Nutzung

lumping sale, sale in mass [*Several parcels of real estate, or several articles of personal property, are sold together for a lump or single gross sum*] · Pauschalverkauf *m*

lump-sum [*A fixed price, but in a single sum for the total contract work and not intended to be adjusted by variation or remeasurement*] · Pauschal(summ)e *f*, Pauschalpreis *m*

lump-sum agreement, stipulated sum agreement · Pauschalabkommen *n*, Pauschalabmachung *f*, Pauschalvereinbarung

lump-sum allocation · Pauschalzuweisung *f*

lump-sum building (construction) contract · Pauschalhochbauvertrag *m*

lump-sum charge, lump-sum duty · Gebührenpauschale *f*, Pauschalgebühr *f*

lump-sum (civil) engineering contract, lump-sum construction contract · Pauschaltiefbauvertrag *m*

lump-sum contract, fixed-price contract, stipulated sum contract [*Under such a contract the contractor agrees to perform the entire work specified in the contract at a price agreed to and fixed at the time the contract is entered into*] · Pauschalvertrag *m*

lump-sum contract [*misnomer*]; entire contract, indivisible contract · Vertrag *m* auf unteilbare Leistung, Vertrag mit uneingeschränkter Vorleistungspflicht, unteilbarer (Leistungs)Vertrag, einheitlicher Vertrag

lump-sum contract with escalation, stipulated sum contract with escalation, fixed-price contract with escalation · Pauschalvertrag *m* mit Änderung [*Ausnahmefall. Der Pauschalpreis kann gemäß einem vorher vereinbarten Verfahren geändert werden, wenn sich die wirtschaftliche Situation ändert*]

lump-sum cost(s) · Pauschalkosten *f*

lump-sum cost(s) figure · Pauschalkostensumme *f*

lump-sum fee · Gebührenpauschale *f*, Honorarpauschale, Pauschalgebühr *f*, Pauschalhonorar *n*

lump-sum payment [*Within compensation act is a payment before it becomes due under monthly payment*] · Pauschalzahlung *f*

lump-sum price · Pauschalpreis *m*

lump-sum price fixing between client and contractor · Pauschalpreisabrede *f*, Pauschalpreisabsprache *f*

lump-sum purchase, basket purchase · Pauschalkauf *m*

lump-sum reimbursement · Pauschalvergütung *f*

lump-sum rent · Pauschalmiete *f*

lump-sum settlement [*Within compensation act, means that the entire amount of compensation due the employee is paid at one and the same time*] · Pauschalabfindung *f*

lunacy · Geistesgestörtsein *n*

lunar month, twenty-eight days · Mondmonat *m*

lunatic → person of unsound mind

lunatic asylum · Irrenhaus *n*, Irrenanstalt *f*

lunaticus [*Latin*] → person of unsound mind

luxury hous(ebuild)ing [*Housing units intended for renters or purchasers of substantial income, characterized by more and/or better amenities, services, and facilities available to the occupants, and larger living areas*] · Luxuswohnungsbau *m*

luxury tax · Luxussteuer *f*

lying fallow · Brachliegen *n* [*Land*]

lying (up)on, bordering (up)on, adjoining, co(n)terminous with [*The term "adjoining" also sometimes means "near" or "neighbo(u)ring"*] · angrenzend [*(Grundstücks)Seiten*]

lynchet · Ackerterrasse *f*

M

mace · Zepter *n*

macebearer · Stabträger *m*

machination · Machenschaft *f*

machine(-aided) cartography, machine-assisted cartography, computer-assisted cartography, computer(-aided) cartography · Rechnerkartographie *f*, rechnergestützte Kartographie

machine(-aided) digitization of boundary networks, computer-assisted digitization of boundary networks, machine-assisted digitization of boundary networks, computer(-aided) digitization of boundary networks · Digitalisierung *f* flächenbezogener Netzwerke, Übertragung von Flächengrenzen in maschinenlesbare Form

machine allocation, routing · Verfahrenswahl *f* [*Fertigungstechnisches Verfahren*]

machine bookkeeping · Maschinenbuchhaltung *f*

machine hour · Maschinenstunde *f*

machinery (and equipment) department → (construction) equipment department

machinery of planning, planning mechanism · Planungsmechanismus *m*

machine simulation · maschinelle Simulation *f*

macro-economic theory · Makrowirtschaftstheorie *f*, Wirtschaftsmakrotheorie, wirtschaftliche Makrotheorie

macro-geography · Makrogeographie *f*, Makroerdkunde *f*

macro level · Makroebene *f*

macro-location, macro-site · Makrostandort *m*, Makrolage *f*

macro(scale) approach · Makroansatz *m*

macro-theory · Makrotheorie *f*

made by a notary (public) · notariell ausgefertigt

made void, avoided, cancelled, invalidated, annulled · ungültig gemacht, für ungültig erklärt

madness, derangement of intellect, mental unsoundness, mental alienation, mental disorder, mental derangement, insanity, unsoundness of mind [*Lunacy is properly a species of insanity, although the terms are frequently used as synonyms*] · Geisteskrankheit *f*, Geistesgestörtheit

magical meaning · geheimnisvoller Sinn *m*

magistrate [*Magistrates are of two kinds, honorary and stipendiary*] · Friedensrichter *m*

magistrates' court · Friedensgericht *n*

magna serjeantia, magna serjanteria, magnum servitium [*Latin*]; (honorary service of) grand serjeanty · persönlicher Leh(e)n(s)dienst *m* [*gegenüber dem Souverän*]

magnum servitium, magna serjeantia, magna serjanteria [*Latin*]; (honorary service of) grand serjeanty · persönlicher Leh(e)n(s)dienst *m* [*gegenüber dem Souverän*]

mailable · postversendbar

mail-box theory, mail-box doctrine, expedition theory, expedition doctrine · Absendetheorie *f* [*Vertragsabschluß*]

mailing charges · Postausgaben *f pl*

mail matter [*This term includes letters, packets, etc., received for transmission, and to be transmitted by post to the person to whom such matter is directed*] · Postsendung *f*

mail order business · Versandhandel *m*

mail order house · Versandhaus *n*

mainad [*In old English law*], perjury (US); false swearing, false oath · Meineid *m*

main administration (of estate(s)), principal administration (of estate(s)) · Erb(schafts)verwaltung *f* am Wohnsitz des Verstorbenen, Nachlaßverwaltung am Wohnsitz des Verstorbenen

main building, principal building · Hauptgebäude *n*

main claim, principal demand, main demand, principal claim · Hauptforderung *f*, Hauptverlangen *n*

main committee, principal committee · Hauptausschuß *m*

main contour, principal contour · Haupthöhenlinie *f*

main contract condition(s), general contract condition(s), principal contract condition(s) · allgemeine Vertragsbedingung(en) *f (pl)*

main contractor, principal contractor · Hauptunternehmer *m*

main creditor, principal creditor · Hauptgläubiger *m*

main debtor, principal debtor [*The party who owes the obligation and for whose*

main defendant — major artery

debt the guarantor agrees to answer] · Hauptschuldner *m*

main defendant, principal defendant · Hauptbeklagte *m*

main demand, principal claim, main claim, principal demand · Hauptforderung *f*, Hauptverlangen *n*

main demise, main lease(hold), principal tenancy, principal lease(hold), principal demise, head tenancy, head demise, head lease(hold), main tenancy · Hauptpacht *f*, Hauptnutzungsrecht *n*

main fact; factum probandum [*Latin*]; principal fact · Haupttatsache *f*

mainland · Festland *n*

main (land) condemnation principal (land) condemnation (US); main (land) expropriation, principal (land) expropriation · Haupt(land)enteignung *f*, Hauptbodenenteignung

main landlord, principal landlord · Hauptvermieter *m*

main lease(hold), principal tenancy, principal lease(hold), principal demise, head tenancy, head demise, head lease(hold), main tenancy, main demise · Hauptpacht *f*, Hauptnutzungsrecht *n*

main obligation, principal obligation · Hauptverpflichtung *f*

main office, chief office, leading office, principal office · Hauptbüro *n*

main participator, principal participator · Hauptbeteiligte *m*

main place of business, principal place of business · Hauptverwaltungssitz *m*

main principle, principal principle · Hauptgrundsatz *m*, Hauptprinzip *n*

main reinstatement, principal reinstatement · Hauptinstandsetzung *f*

main repair, principal repair · Hauptreparatur *f*

main security, principal security · Hauptdeckung *f*, Hauptsicherheit *f*, Hauptsicherung, Hauptunterlage *f*

main sewer, principal sewer · Hauptsammler *m*, Haupt(abwasser)kanal *m*

main supply line, principal supply line · Hauptversorgungsleitung *f*

to maintain, to keep in repair · unterhalten, instandhalten

to maintain a right, to assert, to lay claim to, to defend a right · beanspruchen, geltend machen [*Forderung; Recht*]

to maintain former adjudications; stare decisis [*Latin*]; to stand by decided cases, to uphold precedents · bindend wirken [*Entscheid*]

maintenance, support · Unterhalt *m* [*Person*]

maintenance · Unterhaltung *f*, Instandhaltung

maintenance bond · Unterhaltungsgarantie *f*, Instandhaltungsgarantie

maintenance certificate, certificate of maintenance · Unterhaltungsschein *m*, Unterhaltungsbescheinigung *f*, Unterhaltungsattest *n*, Instandhaltungsschein, Instandhaltungsbescheinigung, Instandhaltungsattest

maintenance clause · Unterhaltungsklausel *f*, Instandhaltungsklausel

maintenance duty, duty to maintain · Unterhaltungspflicht *f*, Instandhaltungspflicht

maintenance expenses, expenses of maintenance · (Lebens)Unterhaltsaufwendungen *f pl*

maintenance management · Unterhaltungsbetrieb *m*, Instandhaltungsbetrieb

maintenance of a minimum width in the streets of a medi(a)eval town to permit their use by traffic · Stangenrecht *n*

maintenance of structure, maintenance of work, maintenance of physical facility · Bauanlageunterhaltung *f*, Bau(werk)unterhaltung; Bauteunterhaltung [*Schweiz*]

maintenance reserve [*Amount reserved to cover cost(s) of maintenance*] · Unterhaltungsrücklage *f*, Instandhaltungsrücklage

maintenance work(s) · Unterhaltungsarbeit(en) *f (pl)*, Instandhaltungsarbeit(en)

main tenancy, master tenancy, head tenancy, principal tenancy · Hauptmietverhältnis *n*

main tenancy, main demise, main lease(hold), principal tenancy, principal lease(hold), principal demise, head tenancy, head demise, head lease(hold) · Hauptpacht *f*, Hauptnutzungsrecht *n*

main tenant, head tenant, principal tenant, master tenant · Hauptmieter *m*

main variable, principal variable · Hauptvariable *f*

main work(s), principal work(s), permanent work(s) · (bauliche) Hauptarbeit(en) *f (pl)*, (bauliche) Hauptleistung(en) *f (pl)*

majesty, preëminence, pre-eminence; majestas [*Latin*]; sovereign power, sovereign right, sovereign dominion, sovereignty, liberty, supremacy, authority · Hoheitsrecht *n*, Hoheitsbefugnis *f*, hoheitliches Recht, hoheitliche Befugnis, Souveränität *f*, Oberhoheit *f*, Hoheitsmacht *f*, vollziehende Gewalt *f*

major artery, thoroughfare · Durchgangsstraße *f*

major conurbation (Brit.); major urban agglomeration · große Städteschar *f*, große städtebauliche Einheit *f* mit kompakter Bebauung und hoher Bevölkerungsdichte

major disaster · Großkatastrophe *f*

major item · Hauptposition *f*

majority · Mehrheit *f*, absolutes Mehr *n*

majority → statutory age

majority decision · Mehrheitsentscheid(ung) *m, (f)*

majority declaration, declaration of majority · Volljährigkeitserklärung *f*

majority interest · Mehrheitsbeteiligung *f*

majority-owned enterprise, majority-owned undertaking · Unternehmen *n* im Mehrheitsbesitz

majority-owned subsidiary · Tochtergesellschaft *f* im Mehrheitsbesitz stehend

majority verdict · Mehrheitsspruch *m* [*Geschworenenverfahren*]

majority vote · absolute Stimmenmehrheit *f*

majority-will · Mehrheitswille *m*

major natural region, higher unit, major world region, world's great regional belt · Landschaftsgürtel *m*

major, person of age · großjährige Person *f*, volljährige Person

major street [*Street identified by the street plan as having large volumes of traffic*] · Hauptstraße *f*

major street plan · Hauptstraßenplan *m* einer Stadt

major underwriter, principal underwriter · Hauptübernehmer *m*

major urban agglomeration, major conurbation (Brit.) · große Städteschar *f*, große städtebauliche Einheit *f* mit kompakter Bebauung und hoher Bevölkerungsdichte

major world region, world's great regional belt, major natural region, higher unit · Landschaftsgürtel *m*

to make [*a ruling by a court*] · treffen [*Entscheidung durch ein Gericht*]

to make [*will*] · errichten [*Testament*]

to make a confession, to admit, to confess, to avow [*To admit the truth of what is charged*] · (ein)gestehen, bekennen, zugeben, geständig sein [*Schuld*]

to make a contract, to contract, to settle a contract, to conclude a contract, to adopt a contract · abschließen eines Vertrages, vertraglich vereinbaren

to make active, to develop · aktivieren

to make a declaration on one's oath of allegiance · amtseidlich versichern

to make a fine, to pay a fine; finem facere [*Latin*]; finire [*In old English law*] · Bußgeld entrichten, Strafgeld entrichten, Reugeld entrichten, Bußgeld zahlen, Reugeld zahlen, Strafgeld zahlen

to make a good title · belegen eines (Rechts)Titels

to make an abatement from, to abate, to deduct, to strike off a part, to subtract · abstreichen, abziehen

to make an entry · Grundstück *n* in Besitz nehmen

to make an understanding · abreden, verabreden, absprechen

to make authentic by document(s), to prove (authentic) by document(s), to authenticate by document(s) · belegen

to make a will · testieren, Testament errichten

to make a will of land(s), to devise; devisare [*Latin*] · vermachen, testamentarisch vermachen, letztwillig verfügen, testamentarisch verfügen [*Liegenschaft(en)*]

to make default · nicht erfüllen

to make default · in (Ver)Säumnis geraten

to make enquiries, to inquire, to enquire, to make inquiries · erkundigen, sich erkundigen

to make faith [*old Scots law*], to make oath, to swear · schwören, beeiden

to make false → to make (something) false

to make firm, to confirm; affirmare [*Latin*]; to affirm · bestätigen

to make inquiries, to make enquiries, to inquire, to enquire · erkundigen, sich erkundigen

to make known, to clarify, to free from secrecy, to free from ignorance, to lay bare, to disclose, to reveal, to knowledge · aufklären, enthüllen, offenbaren, offenlegen, offen darlegen, preisgeben, kundtun

to make liable, to hold liable · haftbar machen

to make oath, to swear; to make faith [*old Scots law*] · schwören, beeiden

to make out · ausstellen [*Scheck; Wechsel*]

to make out, to draw up, to make up · ausfertigen

to make out to be true; verificare [*Latin*]; to verify, to prove · beweisen

maker, drawer · Aussteller *m* [*Wechsel; Scheck*]

makeready time [*The time spent on the preparation of machines and other facilities before starting production*] · Arbeitsvorbereitungszeit *f*

to make responsible, to hold accountable, to call to account · verantwortlich machen, rechenschaftspflichtig machen

maker (of promissory note) [*Sometimes he is spoken of as the "drawer", but he must be distinguished from the drawer of a bill of exchange*] · Solawechselaussteller *m*

to make (something) false, to forge, to counterfeit · (ver)fälschen, nachahmen, imitieren

to make suitable, to adapt, to suit [*To fit a person or thing to another, to or for a purpose*] · anpassen

to make up, to make out, to draw up · ausfertigen

make-up, (sub)division, breakdown · (Auf)Gliederung *f*, Aufschlüsselung *f*

to make up (accounts), to settle (accounts) · abrechnen

make-up of cost(s), subdivision of cost(s), cost(s) breakdown, cost(s) make-up, cost(s) subdivision, breakdown of cost(s) · Kosten(auf)gliederung *f*, Kostenaufschlüsselung *f*

to make urban, to urbanize, to civicize · verstädtern

to make void, to annul, to avoid, to invalidate · ungültig machen, für ungültig erklären

making a contract, adopting a contract, contracting, settling a contract, concluding a contract · Abschließen *n* eines Vertrages

making-good of defect · Baumangelbeseitigung *f*, (Sach)Mangelbeseitigung, Beseitigung eines (Sach)Mangels, Nachbesserung, Beseitigung eines Baumangels

making-good of defects · (Sach)Mängelbeseitigung *f*, Baumängelbeseitigung, Beseitigung von (Sach)Mängeln, Beseitigung von Baumängeln, Nachbesserung

making of an affidavit · Glaubhaftmachung *f*

making of law, legislation, lawmaking, (legislative) enactment · Gesetzgebung *f*, Erlassen *n* von Gesetzen

making up (of accounts), settling (of accounts) · Abrechnen *n*, Abrechnung *f*

making void, annulling, (a)voiding, repealing, abolishing, abrogating, cancelling, overruling, abating, rendering null and void, doing away with, nullifying, rescinding · Aufheben *n*, Rückgängigmachen *n*, Annullieren *n*, Abschaffen *n*, Löschen *n*, Abbauen *n*

mala fides [*Latin*]; bad faith · böser Glaube *m*

maldevelopment · Fehlentwick(e)lung *f*

male absentee · Abwesende *m*

male adult, adult man · Erwachsene *m*, erwachsener Mann *m*

male commuter · Pendler *m*

male descendant, male issue, male offspring · männlicher Nachkomme *m*, männlicher Abkömmling, männlicher Deszendent

malefactor [*Latin*]; wrong-doer · Übeltäter *m*

maleficium [*Latin*]; mischief, wrong-doing · Übeltat *f*

male fugitive from justice · Flüchtige *m*

male guardian by election · erwählter männlicher Vormund *m*, männlicher erwählter Vormund

male heir by adoption, heir (male) by adoption · Adoptiverbe *m*

male heir expectant, heir (male) expectant, expectant heir (male), expectant male heir · Erbanwärter *m*, Erbschaftsanwärter

male homeless person · Obdachlose *m*

male indemnitee · Entschädigungsberechtigte *m*, Schadenersatzberechtigte

male indemnitor, compensatory; compenser [*obsolete*] [*The male person who is bound, by an indemnity contract, to indemnify or protect the other*] · Entschädigende *m*, Entschädigungsleistende, Schadenersatzleistende, Schadenersatzpflichtige, Entschädigungspflichtige

(male) infant, (male) minor · Minderjährige *m*

male issue, male offspring, male descendant · männlicher Nachkomme *m*, männlicher Abkömmling, männlicher Deszendent

(male) minor, (male) infant · Minderjährige *m*

male non-white · Farbige *m*

male person capable of making a will · Testierfähige *m*

male person entitled · Berechtigte *m*, berechtigte männliche Person *f*

male person of full age · Volljährige *m*

male person of unsound mind · Geisteskranke *m*, Geistesgestörte

male person of unsound mind so found by inquisition · entmündigte Geisteskranke *m*

male resident alien · ansässiger Ausländer *m*

(male) subject · Untertan *m*

malfeasance · mangelhafte Ausführung *f*, mangelhafte Erfüllung, mangelhafte Befolgung, mangelhafte Einhaltung

malice · böswilliger Rechtsmißbrauch *m*, Schikane *f*, Böswilligkeit *f*, Boshaftigkeit

malice in fact, express malice · tatsächliche Böswilligkeit *f*,tatsächlicher Dolus

malice in law, implied malice · juristisch konstruierter Dolus *m*, juristisch konstruierte Böswilligkeit

malice (prepense), aforethought, evil mind; mens vea, malitia (praecogitata) [*Latin*] · Dolus *m*, Vorsatz *m*, krimineller Wille *m*

malicious, spiteful, intentionally mischievous, intentionally harmful · schikanös

malicious prosecution · arglistige gerichtliche Verfolgung *f*

Malthusian check [*famine; pestilence; war*] · malthusischer Faktor *m* [*Hungersnot; Seuche; Krieg*]

malt tax [*An excise (duty) (up)on malt in England*] · Malzsteuer *f*

to manage, to adminster, to operate · durchführen, handhaben, verwalten [*Vertrag*]

to manage · bewirtschaften

to manage · betreuen

managed currency · Planwährung *f*, manipulierte Währung, staatsgeregelte Währung

managed fund, mixed bond, selective bond, three-way fund, balanced bond, umbrella fund · gemischter Versicherungsfonds *m*

managed fund certificate, mixed bond certificate, umbrella fund certificate, balanced bond certificate, three-way fund certificate · gemischtes Versicherungsfondszertifikat *n*

management · Geschäftsführung *f*, Geschäftsleitung, Unternehmensführung, Unternehmensleitung

management, sponsoring, sponsorship · Federführung *f* [*Arge*]

management · Bewirtschaftung *f* [*z. B. eines landwirtschaftlichen Betriebes*]

management · Betreuung *f*

management · Betriebsführung *f*

management · Führung *f*

management accounting → management costing

management adviser, managing consultant, managing adviser, management consultant · Betriebsberater *m*

management agent, managing agent [*A person or entity, such as a company, that manages and/or operates a property on behalf of its owner in accordance with a pre-established management plan*] · Betreuer *m*

management agreement, agreement of management · Betreuungsabkommen *n*, Betreuungsabmachung *f*, Betreuungsvereinbarung

management by decision rules · Führung *f* nach Verfahrensvorschriften

management by delegation · Führung *f* durch Delegation

management by exception [*An arrangement under which only exceptional cases are referred to management, other cases being dealt with according to precise instructions or general principles in accordance with the objectives of the undertaking*] · auftraggebundenes Kennziffernwesen *n*, auftraggebundenes Kennzahlenwesen, zielorientierte Führung *f*, zielbezogene Führung

management by objectives [*A technique under which targets are fixed as a basis for achieving greater effectiveness throughout the whole of an organization or part of an organization*] · Koordination *f* aller Teilentscheidungen auf das Oberziel, Führung *f* durch Ziele, Führung durch Zielvereinbarung

management-by-objective system · Mbo-System *n* [*Ein dynamisches, leistungs- und zufriedenheitsorientiertes Führungsmodell*]

management by systems · Führung *f* nach Regelkreisen, Regelkreisführung

management committee, committee of management, executive committee · geschäftsführender Ausschuß *m*, Geschäftsführungsausschuß

management consultant, management adviser, managing consultant, managing adviser, management advisor, managing advisor · Betriebsberater *m*

management contract, managing contract · Betreuungsvertrag *m*

management control system · Unternehmensentscheid(ungs)system *n*

management costing, management (cost(s)) accounting, managerial (cost(s)) accounting, managerial costing · Kostenrechnung *f* zur Informationsgewinnung, Kostenkalkulation *f* zur Informationsgewinnung, (Kostenbe)Rechnung zur Informationsgewinnung, Kostenermitt(e)lung zur Informationsgewinnung

management cost(s), cost(s) of management · Bewirtschaftungskosten *f*

management decision · unternehmerische Entscheidung *f*, unternehmerischer Entscheid *m*

management decision, managerial decision, managing decision · Führungsentscheid(ung) *m, (f)*

(management) decision simulation, managerial decision simulation, managing decision simulation · (Unternehmens)Führungsentscheid(ungs)simulation *f*

(management) fee based on the estimated cost of the work, estimated (management) fee · geschätzter Zuschlag *m*, überschlägiger Zuschlag [*Selbstkostenerstattungsvertrag*]

(management) fee based on the actual cost of the work, actual (management) fee · festgesetzter Zuschlag *m* [*Selbstkostenerstattungsvertrag*]

management firm, managing firm · Betreuungsfirma *f*

management game, managing game, managerial game, business game · Unternehmungs(plan)spiel *n*

management gaming, managerial gaming, managing gaming [*Not to be confused with "operational gaming"*] · Unternehmungsspielen *n*

management information · Führungsinformation *f*

management (investment) company, management (investment) fund · Management-Investment-Gesellschaft *f*, Management-Investment-Fonds *m*

management of (a) contract, operation of (a) contract, administration of (a) contract, contract management, contract operation, contract administration · Durchführung *f* eines Vertrages, Handhabung eines Vertrages, Verwaltung eines Vertrages, Vertragsdurchführung, Vertragshandhabung, Vertragsverwaltung

management of a household, household management, housekeeping · Haushaltung *f*

management of construction, management of project, management of building, construction management, project management, building management · (Bau)Betreuung *f*, Betreuung von Bauvorhaben [*Die technische und wirtschaftliche Vorbereitung und Überwachung eines Bauvorhabens in fremdem Namen und für fremde Rechnung*]

management of construction, management of project, management of building, building management, construction management, project management · Bau(betriebs)führung *f* [*Die technische und wirtschaftliche Vorbereitung und Überwachung eines Bauvorhabens in eigenem Namen*]

management of forests, forest management · Waldbewirtschaftung *f*, Forstbewirtschaftung

management of land(s), land(s) management · Landbewirtschaftung *f*, Bodenbewirtschaftung

management of project, project management · Objektbetreuung *f*, Projektbetreuung

management of (real) property, management of (real) estate, management of land(s), realty management, management of realty, (real) estate management, (real) property management, land(s) management · Grundbesitzbetreuung *f*, Verwaltungsbetreuung

management of traffic, traffic management · Verkehrsabwick(e)lung *f*, Verkehrsführung

management plan, managing plan · Betreuungsplan *m*

management planning, managing planning · Betreuungsplanung *f*

management reimbursement · Betreuungsvergütung *f*

management research, operations research · Unternehmensforschung *f*

management science, operations science · Unternehmungswissenschaft *f*

management sponsor; sponsor(ing firm) (US); "lead" firm, pilot firm · federführende Firma *f*

management technique · Führungstechnik *f*

manager · Bauführer *m* [*des Unternehmers*]

manager · Leiter *m*

manager [*Low Latin*] → protector

managerial (cost(s)) accounting, managerial costing, management costing, management (cost(s)) accounting · Kostenrechnung *f* zur Informationsgewinnung, Kostenkalkulation *f* zur Informationsgewinnung, (Kostenbe)Rechnung zur Informationsgewinnung, Kostenermitt(e)lung zur Informationsgewinnung

managerial decision, managing decision, management decision · Führungsentscheid(ung) *m, (f)*

managerial decision simulation, managing decision simulation, (management) decision simulation · (Unternehmens)Führungsentscheid(ungs)simulation *f*

managerial game, business game, management game, managing game · Unternehmungs(plan)spiel *n*

managerial gaming, managing gaming, management gaming [*Not to be con-*

fused with "operational gaming"] · Unternehmungsspielen *n*

managerial position, executive position *f* · leitende Stellung *f*, leitende Position *f*, Spitzenstellung *f*, Spitzenposition *f*

managerial salaried employe(e), person employed in a managerial position · leitender Angestellter *m*

manager on site, site manager, construction site manager, building site manager, job site manager · Baustellenführer *m*, örtlicher Bauführer [*des Unternehmers*]

managing, operating, administering · Durchführen *n*, Verwalten, Handhaben [*Vertrag*]

managing adviser, management consultant, management adviser, managing consultant · Betriebsberater *m*

managing agent, management agent [*A person or entity, such as a company, that manages and/or operates a property on behalf of its owner in accordance with a pre-established management plan*] · Betreuer *m*

managing board → board of directors

managing board member, director · Vorstandsmitglied *n*, Direktor *m*, Verwaltungsratmitglied

managing consultant, managing adviser, management consultant, management adviser · Betriebsberater *m*

managing contract, management contract · Betreuungsvertrag *m*

managing decision, management decision, managerial decision · Führungsentscheid(ung) *m, (f)*

managing decision simulation, (management) decision simulation, managerial decision simulation · (Unternehmens)Führungsentscheid(ungs)simulation *f*

managing director · geschäftsführendes Aufsichtsratmitglied *n*

managing firm, management firm · Betreuungsfirma *f*

managing game, managerial game, business game, management game · Unternehmungs(plan)spiel *n*

managing gaming, management gaming, managerial gaming [*Not to be confused with "operational gaming"*] · Unternehmungsspielen *n*

managing owner · Korrespondenzreeder *m*

managing partner · geschäftsführender Teilhaber *m*

managing plan, management plan · Betreuungsplan *m*

managing planning, management planning · Betreuungsplanung *f*

managing trustee · geschäftsführender Treuhänder *m*

man-capital ratio · Kapitalausstattung *f* je Arbeitskraft

Manchester School · Manchestertum *n*

mandamus → (writ of) mandamus

mandatary → mandatory

mandate [*A direction or request. Thus, a cheque is a mandate by the drawer to his banker to pay the amount to the holder of the cheque*] · Mandat *n*

mandate contract, contract of mandate · Mandatsvertrag *m*

mandated territory, mandated area · Treuhandgebiet *n*, Mandatsgebiet

mandator, director · Mandatsgeber *m*

mandatory, preceptive, imperative, peremptory, obligatory; perimere [*Latin*] [*As opposed to "permissive"*] · pflichtbedingt, zwingend [*in Gesetzen*]

mandatory; mandatarius [*Latin*]; mandatary [*He to whom a mandate, charge, or commandment is given*] · Mandatsträger *m*, Mandatsempfänger

mandatory injunction, positive injunction · positiver Befehl *m*, Verfügung *f* zur Vornahme einer Handlung, gerichtliches (Handlungs)Gebot *n* [*Eine ,,mandatory injunction" befiehlt nicht eine Unterlassung, sondern positives Handeln*]

mandatory power · Mandatsmacht *f*

mandatory provision · zwingende Bestimmung *f*, Mußbestimmung

mandatum qualificatum [*Latin*]; continuing guaranty, continuing guarantee, continuing guarantie [*It is an agreement to be responsible for money, goods, or services to be furnished by the creditor to the principal debtor from time to time in the future*] · Kreditbürgschaft *f*, Kreditauftrag *m*, Dauerbürgschaft

man-day · Arbeitstag *m* [*Arbeiter*]

manhood; homagium, hominiscum, hominium, hominatus, hominatio, hominiscatus [*Latin*]; homage [*In feudal law. A service (or the ceremony of rendering it) which a tenant was bound to perform to his lord on receiving investiture of a fee, or succeeding to it as heir, in acknowledgment of the tenure. Not to be confused with "fealty"*] · Huldigung *f*

man hour · Mannstunde *f*

manifest, clear to the understanding, evident, obvious · augenscheinlich, offensichtlich

manifest absurdity · offenbarer Unsinn *m*

manifest act(ion) — manorial language

manifest act(ion), overt act(ion), open act(ion) · objektiver Tatbestand *m*, offenkundige Handlung *f*

manifestation · Kundbarmachung *f*, Erkennbarmachung

manipulating [*price*] · Normierung *f* [*Preis*]

man-land-ratio · Verhältnis *n* von landwirtschaftlichen Erwerbstätigen zur verfügbaren landwirtschaftlichen Fläche bei gegebenem Produktivitätsstand

manless · menschenleer

man-made environment, artificial environment · künstliche Umwelt *f*

man-made land mark, man-made monument, artificial landmark, artificial monument · künstliche Landmarke *f*, künstliches festes Seezeichen *n*

man-made landscape, cultural landscape · Kulturlandschaft *f*, Sied(e)lungslandschaft

man-made (land) surface form, artificial (land) surface form · anthropogene (Land)Oberflächenform *f*, künstliche (Land)Oberflächenform *f*

man-made monument, artificial landmark, artificial monument, man-made land mark · künstliche Landmarke *f*, künstliches festes Seezeichen *n*

man-made river · ausgebauter Strom *m*

manner of payment · Zahlungsweise *f*

manner of performing the duty, mode of performance · Erfüllungsart *f*

man of straw, lay-figure, dummy · „Strohmann" *m*

manor, large freehold estate; barony [*Scotland*] [*It is called so even though the proprietor is a simple commoner*] · Herr(e)ngut *n*, Herr(e)nhof *m*

manorial, beneficiary, feudal, feodal, feuda(to)ry [*Relating to feuds or feudal tenures. Held by feudal service*] · feudal, grundherr(schaft)lich, zu einer Grundherrschaft gehörig

manorial agriculture, feudal agriculture, feodal agriculture, feuda(to)ry agriculture · Feudallandwirtschaft *f*

manorial aid, feudal aid, feuda(to)ry aid, feodal aid · feudales Hilfsgeld *n*

manorial authority, feodal authority, feudal authority, feuda(to)ry authority, manorial power, feodal power, feudal power, feuda(to)ry power · Feudalgewalt *f*, Feudalmacht *f*, Feudalhoheit *f*, Feudalkompetenz *f*

manorial borough · Mediatflecken *m*

manorial burden → feudal charge

manorial casualty, feudal casualty, feuda(to)ry casualty, feodal casualty [*The additional payment due to a superior on specified occasions such as the death of a vassal*] · Feudalsonderabgabe *f*

manorial chain, feudal chain, feuda(to)ry chain, feodal chain · Feudalkette *f*

manorial charge → feudal charge

manorial charge, manorial burden, manorial incumbrance, manorial encumbrance, feudal charge, feudal burden, feudal encumbrance, feudal incumbrance, feodal charge, feodal burden, feodal encumbrance, feodal incumbrance, feuda(to)ry charge, feuda(to)ry burden, feuda(to)ry incumbrance, feuda(to)ry encumbrance · Feudallast *f*, Leh(e)n(s)last, Feudalbelastung *f*

manorial community, feudal community, feodal community, feuda(to)ry community [*It rested on the distinction between a number of persons holding land of the lord by free tenure and a number holding land of the lord by tenures of servile origin. Both classes were held together through a peculiar tribunal, the court of baron*] · Feudalgemeinschaft *f*, Feudalgemeinwesen *n*

manor(ial) court, feudal court, feodal court, feuda(to)ry court, court of the baron, court of the lord, baron(-bailie) court, court-baron (proper), court of (the) manor, freeholders' court baron; curia legalis [*Latin*] [*The court of justice held by a baron or his steward in the presence of the freehold tenants of the manor. In modern times lawyers have distinguished between court-baron which was the court of the freehold tenants, and the customary court-baron which was the court of the copyhold tenants. The early history of this distinction is obscure*] · Feudalgericht *n*, grundherrliches Gericht, Leh(e)n(s)herrengericht, Hofgericht, Patrimonialgericht, feudales Gutsgericht

manorial encumbrance → feudal charge

manorial hierarchy, feudal hierarchy, feodal hierarchy, feuda(to)ry hierarchy · Feudalhierarchie *f*, feudale Hierarchie, leh(e)n(s)rechtliche Hierarchie

manorial incumbrance → feudal charge

manorial (landholding) system → feudal (landholding) system

manorial land(s), bordland, land(s) of a manor [*Land held by a bordar in bordage tenure*] · Herr(e)ngutland *n*, Fron(dienst)land, Frongutland, Fronbauernland, Herr(e)nhofland

manorial land system → feudal (landholding) system

manorial language, feudal language, feodal language, feuda(to)ry language · Feudalsprache *f*

manorial law — manslaughter

manorial law; lex feudalis [*Latin*]; law of tenure(s) (of land), law of (the) manor, law of feuda(to)ry tenure, law of feudal tenure, law of feodal tenure, law of feuds, law of feudal estates, feudal law, tenure law, feodal law, feuda(to)ry law · Leh(e)n(s)recht *n*, Feudalrecht

manorial limitation, manorial restriction, feudal limitation, feudal restriction, feodal limitation, feodal restriction, feuda(to)ry limitation, feuda(to)ry restriction · leh(e)n(s)rechtliche Beschränkung *f*, leh(e)n(s)rechtliche Einschränkung, leh(e)n(s)rechtliche Begrenzung, feudalrechtliche Beschränkung, feudalrechtliche Einschränkung, feudalrechtliche Begrenzung

manorial measure, feudal measure, feodal measure, feuda(to)ry measure · Feudalmaßnahme *f*, leh(e)n(s)rechtliche Maßnahme

manorial office, feudal office, feuda(to)ry office, feodal office · feudales Amt *n*, leh(e)n(s)rechtliches Amt

manorial organization → feudal (landholding) system

manorial plough service (Brit.); feodal plough service, feudal plough service, feuda(to)ry plough service [*US = plow*] · (Acker)Fro(h)n(d)e *f*, Scharwerk *n*

manorial possession, feudal possession, feodal possession, feuda(to)ry possession · Besitz *m* nach feudalem Leh(e)n(s)recht, feudaler Leh(e)n(s)besitz, Feudalbesitz

manorial power, feodal power, feudal power, feuda(to)ry power, manorial authority, feodal authority, feudal authority, feuda(to)ry authority · Feudalgewalt *f*, Feudalmacht *f*, Feudalhoheit *f*, Feudalkompetenz *f*

manorial realty law, feudal (real) estate law, feodal (real) estate law, feuda(to)ry (real) estate law, manorial (real) estate law, feodal (real) property law, feudal (real) property law, feuda(to)ry (real) property law, manorial (real) property law, feudal realty law, feodal realty law, feuda(to)ry realty law · feudales Liegenschaftsrecht *n*, feudales Bodenrecht, feudales Grundstücksrecht, feudales Landrecht

manorial restriction, feudal limitation, feudal restriction, feodal limitation, feodal restriction, feuda(to)ry limitation, feuda(to)ry restriction, manorial limitation · leh(e)n(s)rechtliche Beschränkung *f*, leh(e)n(s)rechtliche Einschränkung, leh(e)n(s)rechtliche Begrenzung, feudalrechtliche Beschränkung, feudalrechtliche Einschränkung, feudalrechtliche Begrenzung

manorial service, feudal service, feodal service, feuda(to)ry service · Feudaldienst *m*, Hörigkeitslast *f*, Leh(e)n(s)dienst, leh(e)n(s)rechtlicher Dienst, feudaler Dienst

manorial service by manual labo(u)r, feudal service by manual labo(u)r, feodal service by manual labo(u)r, feuda(to)ry service by manual labo(u)r · Handrobot *f*, Handdienst *m*

manorial system → feudal (landholding) system

manorial tenant, feudal bondman, vassal, tenant of land, feeholder, holder of a fee, holder of a fief, fief-tenant, feoda(to)ry, feuda(to)ry; homo pertinens [*Latin*]; beneficiary, holder of a feudal benefice, land tenant, (feudal) tenant [*A tenant or vassal who held his estate by feudal service*] · Leh(e)n(s)mann *m*, Leh(e)n(s)träger *m*, Gefolgsmann, Gutszinsmann, Vasall *m*

manorial tenure system → feudal (landholding) system

(manorial) waste [*obsolete*]; common (land), corporate land, allmend, common field, commonable land, commonable field, public land, community land, communal land, mark; county (US); waste of the manor · Al(l)mend(e) *f*, Allmeind *f*, Allmid *f*, Allmein(i) *f*, Allmen *f*, Allmig *f*, Allmand(e) *f*, Allmat *f*, All(ge)meinde *f*, Allmandgut *n*, Allmente *f*, (Feld)Mark *f*, Gemarkung *f*, Kommunalboden *m*, Gemeindeboden *m*, Bürgerland *n*, bürgerliches Nutzungsland *n*, Gemeindeland *n*, Gemeinheit(sland) *f*, *(n)*, Kommunalland *n*, unverteilter Gemeindegrund *m*, ländliches Gemeingut, Gemein(de)anger *m*, Gemeindeimmobilien *f pl*; Korporationsland *n* [*Schweiz*]

manor in gross · Patrimonialjurisdiktion *f*

manor lord, langeman, bestower of a fee, feudal chief; dominus directus, feoffator [*Latin*]; (feudal) lord, chief lord, possessory lord, liege-lord, over lord, lord of (the) manor, supreme owner, landlord, grantor, feoffor, feoffer, superior lord · Leh(e)n(s)herr *m*, Feudalherr, (feudaler) Belehner, Leh(e)n(s)gutgeber, Obereigentümer, Landübertragende, Übertragende von Land

manor pound · Pfandstall *m* der Gutsherrschaft

manpower; labour (Brit.); labor (US) [*The amount of labour, both male and female, available at a particular time*] · Arbeitskräfte *f pl*

manpower planning; labour planning (Brit.); labor planning (US) · Arbeitskräfteplanung *f*

manpower supply, labour supply (Brit.); labor supply (US) · Arbeitskräfteangebot *n*

manslaughter · fahrlässige Tötung *f*

manual — marginal balance

manual · Handbuch *n*

manual labour (Brit.); manual labor (US); opus manificum [*Latin*] · Handarbeit *f*

manufactured home, prefab(ricated) home · Fertig(bau)eigenheim *n*

manufactured housing, prefab(ricated) housing · Fertig(bau)wohnungen *fpl*

manufacturer, processor · Fabrikant *m*, Hersteller *m*

manufacturer, prefabricator · Fertigbauer *m*

manufacturing industry, producing industry · erzeugende Industrie *f*, herstellende Industrie, produzierende Industrie, Herstellungsindustrie, Produkt(ions)industrie, Fertigungsindustrie, fertigende Industrie

manufacturing jobs · Sekundärsektor *m*

manufacturing position · Produktionsarbeitsplatz *m*

manufacturing trade, producing trade · herstellendes Gewerbe *n*, produzierendes Gewerbe, erzeugendes Gewerbe

manufacturing under licence, manufacturing under license · Lizenzfertigung *f*

manuscript map · Kartenentwurf *m*

manus mortua [*Latin*]; mortification [*Scots law*]; dead hand; mortmain [*French*] [*A condition of property in which it is held without the power of change or (ab)alienation*] · tote Hand *f*

to map · kartieren

map · (Land)Karte *f*

map accuracy · Kartengenauigkeit *f*

map by means of proportional area(l) symbols · Karte *f* mit gestuften Gebietskartenzeichen

map by means of proportional line symbols · Karte *f* mit gestuften Linienkartenzeichen

map by means of proportional symbols · Karte *f* mit gestuften Positionskartenzeichen

map by means of proportional vectors · gestufte Vektorkarte *f*

(map) characteristic · Kartenzeichen *n* [*Verallgemeinerndes Zeichen (Symbol, Signatur) auf Karten zur Darstellung der verschiedenen Objekte der Erdoberfläche*]

map chart · kombinierte Land- und Seekarte *f*

map co-ordinate · Kartenkoordinate *f*

map design · Kartengestaltung *f*

map face · Kartenbild *n*

map frame · (Land)Kartenrahmen *m*

map legend, map reference · (Karten)Legende *f*, Karten(zeichen)erklärung *f*, Karten(zeichen)erläuterung, Karten(zeichen)schlüssel *m*

map lettering · Kartenbeschriftung *f*

map-making · Kartenherstellung *f*

map margin · (Land)Kartenrand *m*

map of previous situation(s) · Einlagenkarte *f*

map of standard form, standard form map · Musterblattkarte *f*

map of the world, world map · Weltkarte *f*

mapping · Kartierung *f*

mapping act, mapping statute, mapping law · Kartierungsgesetz *n*

mapping law · Kartierungsrecht *n*

map point · Kartenpunkt *m*

map presentation · Kartendarstellung *f*

map reading · Kartenlesen *n*

(map) recompilation · (Karten)Neubearbeitung *f*

map reference, map legend · (Karten)Legende *f*, Karten(zeichen)erklärung *f*, Karten(zeichen)erläuterung, Karten(zeichen)schlüssel *m*

map revision · Kartenfortführung *f*

maps, map series · Kartenwerk *n*

map scale · Kartenmaßstab *m*

map series, maps · Kartenwerk *n*

map series, series of maps · Kartenreihe *f*

map sheet · Kartenblatt *n*

map unit · Flächensignatur *f* [*Kartenzeichen zur Wiedergabe flächenhaft verbreiteter Erscheinungen (Wald, landwirtschaftliche Sonderkulturen, usw.)*]

to mar, to disfigure, to deface · beeinträchtigen, verschandeln, entstellen, verunstalten, verunzieren [*Ortsbild*]

margin [*In monetary transactions. On a security the difference between the amount advanced against goods or securities and their market value*] · Preisunterschied *m*

margin [*In economics. A limit fixing the position of economic equilibrium*] · Grenze *f*

marginal balance, marginal income, variable gross margin, profit contribution, contribution margin, marginal revenue · Deckungsbeitrag *m*, Beitragsüberschuß *m*, Überschußsaldo *m*, Erfolgsbeitrag, variabler Bruttoüberschuß, Grenzerfolg *m*, (Kosten)Deckungszuschlag *m*

marginal caption — maritagium

marginal caption, marginal headline, marginal heading · Randüberschrift *f*

marginal category · Randklasse *f* [*Statistik*]

marginal costing, marginal cost(s) accounting [*The assignment of marginal or variable cost(s) to an activity, department, or product, as contrasted with absorption costing and direct costing*] · Grenzkostenrechnung *f* [*Deckungsbeitragsrechnung auf der Grundlage von Grenzkosten*]

marginal cost(s) [*The amount at any given volume of output by which aggregate cost(s) are changed if the volume of output is increased or decreased by one unit*] · Grenzkosten *f*

marginal (cost(s)) accounting → marginal accouting

marginal coverage · Randbebauung *f*; Randüberbauung [*Schweiz*] [*Die Bebauung von Baublockrändern längs der blockbildenden Straßen*]

marginal data, marginal information, border data, border information · Blattrandangaben *f pl*, Randausstattung *f*, Randangaben, Blattrandausstattung [*Alle Angaben im Kartenrand und im Kartenrahmen*]

marginal heading, marginal caption, marginal headline · Randüberschrift *f*

marginal income, variable gross margin, profit contribution, contribution margin, marginal revenue, marginal balance · Deckungsbeitrag *m*, Beitragsüberschuß *m*, Überschußsaldo *m*, Erfolgsbeitrag, variabler Bruttoüberschuß, Grenzerfolg *m*, (Kosten)Deckungszuschlag *m*

marginal income per the scarce factor, marginal profit opportunity by machine hour · Bruttogewinn *m* pro Einheit der Engpaßbelastung

marginal information, border data, border information, marginal data · Blattrandangaben *f pl*, Randausstattung *f*, Randangaben, Blattrandausstattung [*Alle Angaben im Kartenrand und im Kartenrahmen*]

marginalism, theory of marginal utility · Grenznutzentheorie *f*, Grenzwerttheorie

marginal land [*Land that barely repays the cost(s) of working or using it; land whereon the cost(s) of operating approximately equal the gross income*] · Grenzertragsboden *m*, Grenzertragsland *n*

marginal net product · Nettogrenzerzeugnis *n*

marginal note · Randbemerkung *f*

marginal population · Randbevölkerung *f*

marginal principle · Grenzprinzip *n*, Grenzgrundsatz *m*

marginal product, marginal return [*The extra output resulting from the employment of one or more unit of land, labo(u)r, or capital*] · Grenzertrag *m*

marginal product · Grenzprodukt *n*

marginal productivity · Grenzproduktivität *f*

marginal profit opportunity by machine hour, marginal income per the scarce factor · Bruttogewinn *m* pro Einheit der Engpaßbelastung

marginal return, marginal product [*The extra output resulting from the employment of one or more unit of land, labo(u)r, or capital*] · Grenzertrag *m*

marginal revenue, marginal balance, marginal income, variable gross margin, profit contribution, contribution margin · Deckungsbeitrag *m*, Beitragsüberschuß *m*, Überschußsaldo *m*, Erfolgsbeitrag, variabler Bruttoüberschuß, Grenzerfolg *m*, (Kosten)Deckungszuschlag *m*

marginal utility, final utility, margin of profitableness, (final degree of) utility · Nutzen *m* der letzten Einheit, Grenznutzen, Grenzwert *m*

marginal-value product · Wertgrenzprodukt *n*

margin buying [*USA*] · Wertpapierkäufe *m pl* auf Kreditbasis

margin of border, border margin · Bauabstand *m*, (Bau)Wich *m*, Reihe *f*, Schupf *m*, Grenzabstand *m* [*Bei der Errichtung von Gebäuden sind in voller Tiefe des Grundstücks von den seitlichen Grundstücksgrenzen Bauwiche von baulichen Anlagen freizuhalten, soweit nicht an die Grundstücksgrenze gebaut werden darf (geschlossene Bauweise). Von der hinteren Grundstücksgrenze ist ein Abstand freizuhalten, der der Breite des Bauwichs entspricht (hinterer Grenzabstand)*]

margin of profit, margin of gain, profit margin, gain margin · Gewinnspanne *f*, Profitspanne

margin of profitableness, (final degree of) utility, marginal utility, final utility · Nutzen *m* der letzten Einheit, Grenznutzen, Grenzwert *m*

marina [*A place for docking or storage of pleasure boats*] · Vergnügungsbootshafen *m*

marine hazard, marine risk · Seewagnis *n*, Seerisiko *n*

marine insurance, sea insurance · Seeversicherung *f*

marine underwriter · Seeversicherer *m*

maritagium [*Latin*]; dowry (marriage), portion, fortune, marriage goods; tocher [*in*

(marital) community property — market gardener

Scotland] [*Not to be confounded with "dowe·ù". E portion given with a woman to her husband in marriage*] · Mitgift *f*, Heiratsgut *n*

(marital) community property · (eheliche) Gütergemeinschaft *f*, eheliches Gesamtgut *n*

marital condition, family relationship, standing in the family, marital status [*i.e. whether single, married, divorced or widowed*] · Familienstand *m*

marital domicil(e), matrimonial domicil(e) · ehelicher Wohnsitz *m*

marital property, matrimonial property · Ehegut *n*, Ehevermögen *n*

marital status, marital condition, family relationship, standing in the family [*i.e. whether single, married, divorced or widowed*] · Familienstand *m*

marital union, matrimonial union · eheliche Verbindung *f*

maritime belt, belt of sea, sea belt [*In political sense*]; coast(al) waters [*In geographic and nautical sense*], territorial waters, territorial sea · Küstengewässer *n*, Küstenmeer *n*, Territorialgewässer, Hoheitsgewässer, Meeresstreifen *m*, Hoheitsmeer, Territorialmeer

maritime claim, maritime demand · seerechtliches Verlangen *n*, seerechtliche Forderung *f*

maritime demand, maritime claim · seerechtliches Verlangen *n*, seerechtliche Forderung *f*

maritime law; Admiralty law [*Great Britain*] · Seerecht *n*

maritime legislation, maritime lawmaking · Seegesetzgebung *f*

maritime power, naval power, sea power · Seemacht *f*

maritime state, coast(al) state · Küstenstaat *m*

mark; county (US); waste of the manor, (manorial) waste [*obsolete*]; common (land), corporate land, allmend, common field, commonable land, commonable field, public land, community land, communal land · Al(l)mend(e) *f*, Allmeind *f*, Allmid *f*, Allmein(i) *f*, Allmen *f*, Allmig *f*, Allmand(e) *f*, Allmat *f*, All(ge)meinde *f*, Allmandgut *n*, Allmente *f*, (Feld)Mark *f*, Gemarkung *f*, Kommunalboden *m*, Gemeindeboden *m*, Bürgerland *n*, bürgerliches Nutzungsland *n*, Gemeindeland *n*, Gemeinheit(sland) *f*, *(n)*, Kommunalland *n*, unverteilter Gemeindegrund *m*, ländliches Gemeingut, Gemein(de)anger *m*, Gemeindeimmobilien *fpl*; Korporationsland *n* [*Schweiz*]

mark → (corner) mark

marketability, sal(e)ability, salableness · Absetzbarkeit *f*, Verkaufbarkeit, Marktgängigkeit

marketability · Umlauffähigkeit *f* [*(Rechts)Titel*]

marketable, sal(e)able, merchantable, mercable, fungible · absetzbar, verkaufbar, marktgängig, verkäuflich

marketable, clear, sal(e)able, perfect, good · frei, vollgültig [*(Rechts)Titel*]

market-access(-sensitive) activity · marktabhängiger Produktionszweig *m*

market and church; ecclesia forensis [*Latin*] · Markt *m* und Kirche *f*

market church; ecclesia forensis in civitate [*Latin*]; townsmen's church · Marktkirche *f*

market clerk, clerk of the market · Marktschreiber *m*

market data approach · Marktdatenansatz *m*

market demand · Marktnachfrage *f*

market distortion, distortion of the market · Marktverzerrung *f*

market district, market town; first order centre, urban village [*750 to 1,000 inhabitants*], small town with between 1,000 and 2,000 inhabitants (Brit.); first order center, urban center (US); middle-order sub-central place, subtown · Amtsort *m* [*nach W. Christaller*]

market economy · Marktwirtschaft *f*

market entry · Markterschließung *f*

market equilibrium · Marktgleichgewicht *n*

market exchange · Markthandel *m*

market failure, failure of the market · Marktversagen *n*

market forces, demand and supply, call and supply, supply and demand, supply and call · Angebot *n* und Nachfrage *f*, Nachfrage und Angebot

market fruit-culture, market fruit-growing, commercial fruit-culture, commercial fruit-growing · Erwerbsobst(an)bau *m*, Handelsobst(an)bau

market garden, commercial garden (Brit.); truck garden, truck farm (US) · Garten(bau)betrieb *m*, Handelsgärtnerei *f*, (Erwerbs)Gärtnerei, gärtnerischer Betrieb, Erwerbsgarten *m*, Handelsgarten

market garden area, commercial garden area (Brit.); truck garden area, truck farm area (US) · gartenbaulich genutzte Fläche *f*, Gartenbaufläche

market gardener, commercial gardener (Brit.); truck farmer (US) · Erwerbsgärtner *m*, Handelsgärtner

648

market gardening, commercial gardening (Brit.); truck farming (US) · Erwerbsgartenbau *m*, Handelsgartenbau

market garden produce, commercial garden produce (Brit.); truck garden produce (US) · Garten(bau)erzeugnisse *n pl*

market gradient · Marktgefälle *n*

market in (building) land, (building) (land) area market, (building) land market, (real) estate market, (real) property market · (Bau)Bodenmarkt *m*, (Bau)Landmarkt, (Bau)Grundstücksmarkt

marketing [*The business of distributing a product to the people who want it*] · Absatz *m*

market(ing) area, market(ing) territory, sales area, sales territory · Absatzgebiet *n*, Marktgebiet, Verkaufsgebiet

marketing control(ling) · Absatzüberwachung *f*

marketing geography · Marktgeographie *f*

marketing mix · Kombination *f* absatzpolitischer Mittel

marketing planning · Absatzplanung *f*

marketing research, sales research · Absatzforschung *f*, Verkaufsforschung

marketing territory → marketing area

market in land → market in (building) land

market in urban (building) land(s), urban (real) estate market, urban (real) property market, urban (building) land market · städtischer (Bau)Bodenmarkt *m*, städtischer (Bau)Landmarkt, städtischer (Bau)Grund(stücks)markt

market of country estate → rural (real) estate market

market of country land → rural (real) estate market

market of country property → rural (real) estate market

market of country (real) estate → rural (real) estate market

market of country (real) property → rural (real) estate market

market of country realty → rural (real) estate market

market of rural estate → rural (real) estate market

market of rural land → rural (real) estate market

market of rural (real) estate → rural (real) estate market

market of rural (real) property → rural (real) estate market

market of rural realty → rural (real) estate market

market order [*USA*] · unlimitierter Börsenauftrag *m*

market-orien(ta)ted, market-related · marktorientiert, marktbezogen

market overt, open market · freier Markt *m*

market place · Marktort *m*

market price [*The amount of money actually paid or asked for a property; it may be more or less than market value*] · Handelspreis *m*, Verkehrspreis, Marktpreis

market quarter · Marktviertel *n*

market rent, economic rent [*The amount of rent(al) a property would command if it were unencumbered by a lease or vacant and available for rent on the open market*] · Marktmiete *f*

market research · Marktforschung *f*

Markets and Fair Clauses Act [*England*] · Marktpolizeigesetz *n*

market stability · Marktstabilität *f*

market supply · Marktangebot *n*

market system · Marktsystem *n*

market town; first order centre (Brit.); urban village [*750 to 1,000 inhabitants*] (Brit.); small town with between 1,000 and 2,000 inhabitants (Brit.); first order center, urban center (US); middle-order sub-central place, sub-town, market district · Amtsort *m* [*nach W. Christaller*]

market town · Flecken *m*

market value → (fair) market value

marking legitimate, legitimation · Legitimation *f*

marking out with boundary stones, separating by boundary stones · Absteinen *n*, Versteinen

marking out with green strips (of land), separating by green strips (of land) · Abrainen *n*, Verrainen

mark of location (of land) · Landfestsetzungsmarkierung *f*

to mark out with boundary stones, to separate by boundary stones · absteinen, versteinen

marksman · Analphabet *m* der statt der Unterschrift ein Kreuz macht

markup, surcharge, addition [*That which is added to price(s) or cost(s)*] · Zuschlag *m*, Aufschlag [*Preis; Kosten*]

markup [*for decrease in contract price*] · Abschlag *m* [*Bau(kosten)kalkulation*]

markup factor · prozentualer Bruttogewinnzuschlag *m*

markup factor on material · prozentualer Materialfaktor *m*

markup for alteration → markup for conversion

markup for conversion, markup for alteration, conversion markup, alteration markup · Umbauzuschlag *m*

markup for resumption of work, surcharge for resumption of work, addition for resumption of work · Wiederaufnahmezuschlag *m*, Wiederaufnahmeaufschlag

markup rate, surcharge rate, addition rate · Aufschlag(s)rate *f*, Zuschlag(s)rate

marriage; matrimonium [*Latin*]; matrimony · Ehe *f*

marriageable · heiratsfähig

marriage articles · Ehepunktation *f*

marriage dissolution, dissolution of marriage · Eheauflösung *f*

marriage goods; tocher [*in Scotland*]; maritagium [*Latin*]; dowry (marriage), portion, fortune [*Not to be confounded with "dower". A portion given with a woman to her husband in marriage*] · Mitgift *f*, Heiratsgut *n*

marriage law, marriage act, marriage statute · Ehegesetz *n*

marriage promise, promise of marriage · Eheversprechen *n*, Heiratsversprechen

marriage settlement, ante-nuptial contract, ante-nuptial settlement, contract before marriage, settlement before marriage [*A contract or agreement between a man and a woman before marriage, but in contemplation and generally in consideration of marriage, whereby the property rights and interests of either the prospective husband or wife, or both of them, are determined, or where property is secured to either or both of them, or to their children*] · Ehevertrag *m*, Ehestiftung *f*

marriage statute, marriage law, marriage act · Ehegesetz *n*

married woman, feme covert, wife · verheiratete Frau *f*, Ehefrau

marring, disfiguring, defacing · Beeinträchtigen *n*, Verschandeln, Verunstalten, Entstellen, Verunzieren [*Ortsbild*]

marshal · Bundesgerichtsvollzieher *m* [*USA*]

marshalling · Haftungsregulierung *f*, Regulierung der Haftung, Haftpflichtregulierung, Regulierung der Haftpflicht, Regulierung der Haftbarkeit, Haftbarkeitsregulierung

marshalling (of) assets · Regulierung *f* der Nachlaßhaftung, Vertretung der Aktiva im Konkurs

marsh village · Marschhufen *m*

marsh(y) ground, marsh(y) land; croy, mere [*In old English law*] · Marschland *n*

martial law; jus belli [*Latin*]; law of war · Kriegsrecht *n*

masonry (work) contractor · Mauerbauunternehmer *m*

mass, aggregate [*A collection of individuals, units, or things, in order to form a whole*] · Masse *f*

Massachusetts trust, business trust, common law trust [*A business organization wherein property is conveyed to trustees and managed for benefit of holders of certificates like corporate stock certificates*] · treuhänderisch geleitetes Unternehmen *n*, treuhänderisch geleitete Unternehmung *f*

mass buying power, mass purchasing power · Massenkaufkraft *f*

mass destruction · Massenvernichtung *f*

mass emigration · Massenauswanderung *f*

(mass) forcible transfer · (Massen)Vertreibung *f*, (Massen)Austreibung

mass homebuilder · industrieller Eigenheimbauer *m*, industrieller Eigenhausbauer

mass hous(ebuild)ing · Massenwohn(ungs)bau *m*

mass hous(ebuild)ing developer, mass hous(ebuild)ing builder · Massenwohn(ungs)bauträger *m*

mass inmigration · Masseneinwanderung *f*

mass medium · Massenmedium *n*

mass (migration) movement · Massenbewegung *f*, Massenwanderungsbewegung

mass poverty, pauperism · Massenarmut *f*

mass-produced suburb(an place) (Brit.) · Vorort *m* mit Fertigteilhäusern

mass production · Massenfertigung *f*

mass purchasing power, mass buying power · Massenkaufkraft *f*

mass rapid transit → (public) rapid transit

mass recreational transit, recreational (public) transit, recreational (public) transport(ation), recreational mass transit, recreational mass transport(ation), public recreational transit, public recreational transport(ation), mass recreational transport(ation) · (öffentlicher) Erholungsmassenverkehr *m*, (öffentliche) Erholungsmassenbeförderung *f*

mass society · Massengesellschaft *f*

mass strike · Generalstreik *m*

mass transit, collective transport(ation), passenger transport(ation), mass transport(ation), (public) transit, (public) transport(ation), collective transit, passenger transit · Massenverkehr *m*, Personen(massen)verkehr, (öffentlicher) Massentransport *m*, öffentlicher Massenverkehr, (öffentliche) Massenbeförderung *f*, öffentliche Beförderung, Personen(massen)transport, Personen(massen)beförderung, Kollektiv(personen)transport, Kollektiv(personen)verkehr, Kollektiv(personen)beförderung

mass transit business → mass transport(ation) business

mass transit company, (public) transport(ation) company, mass transport(ation) company, (public) transit company · (öffentliche) (Massen)Verkehrsgesellschaft *f*, (öffentliche) (Massen)Beförderungsgesellschaft

mass transit enterprise, mass transit line, mass transport(ation) enterprise, mass transport(ation) line, (public) transit enterprise, (public) transit line, (public) transport(ation) enterprise, (public) transport(ation) line · (öffentlicher) (Massen)Verkehrsbetrieb *m*, (öffentlicher) (Massen)Beförderungsbetrieb, (öffentliches) (Massen)Verkehrsunternehmen *n*, (öffentliches) (Massen)Beförderungsunternehmen

mass transit fare, (public) transport(ation) fare, mass transport(ation) fare, passenger fare, (public) transit fare · Massenverkehrsfahrpreis *m*, Massenbeförderungsfahrpreis

mass transit line → mass transit enterprise

mass transit operator, mass transport(ation) operator, (public) transit operator, (public) transport(ation) operator · (öffentlicher) (Massen)Verkehrsbetreiber *m*, (öffentlicher) (Massen)Beförderungsbetreiber

mass transit rider, mass transport(ation) rider, (public) transit rider, (public) transport(ation) rider · (öffentlicher) Massenverkehrsteilnehmer *m*

mass transit system, (public) transport(ation) system, mass transport(ation) system, (public) transit system · (öffentliches) (Massen)Verkehrssystem *n*, (öffentliches) (Massen)Beförderungssystem

mass (transit) vehicle, (public) transport(ation) vehicle, mass (transport(ation)) vehicle, public vehicle, (public) transit vehicle · (öffentliches) Massenverkehrsfahrzeug *n*, (öffentliches) Massenbeförderungsfahrzeug

mass transport(ation), (public) transit, (public) transport(ation), collective transit, passenger transit, mass transit, collective transport(ation), passenger transport(ation) · Massenverkehr *m*, Personen(massen)verkehr, (öffentlicher) Massentransport *m*, öffentlicher Massenverkehr, (öffentliche) Massenbeförderung *f*, öffentliche Beförderung, Personen(massen)transport, Personen(massen)beförderung, Kollektiv(personen)transport, Kollektiv(personen)verkehr, Kollektiv(personen)beförderung

mass transport(ation) business, mass transit business, (public) transit business, public transport(ation) business · (öffentliches) (Massen)Verkehrsgeschäft *n*, (öffentliches) (Massen)Beförderungsgeschäft

mass transport(ation) company → mass transit company

mass transport(ation) enterprise, mass transport(ation) line, (public) transit enterprise, (public) transit line, (public) transport(ation) enterprise, (public) transport(ation) line, mass transit enterprise, mass transit line · (öffentlicher) (Massen)Verkehrsbetrieb *m*, (öffentlicher) (Massen)Beförderungsbetrieb, (öffentliches) (Massen)Verkehrsunternehmen *n*, (öffentliches) (Massen)Beförderungsunternehmen

mass transport(ation) fare, passenger fare, (public) transit fare, mass transit fare, (public) transport(ation) fare · Massenverkehrsfahrpreis *m*, Massenbeförderungsfahrpreis

mass transport(ation) line → mass transport(ation) enterprise

mass transport(ation) operator → mass transit operator

mass transport(ation) system → mass transit system

mass (transport(ation)) vehicle, public vehicle, (public) transit vehicle, mass (transit) vehicle, (public) transport(ation) vehicle · (öffentliches) Massenverkehrsfahrzeug *n*, (öffentliches) Massenbeförderungsfahrzeug

mass unemployment · Massenarbeitslosigkeit *f*

mass vehicle → mass (transit) vehicle

mast; boscagium [*Latin*]; boscage, browse-wood [*In English law. The food which wood and trees yield to cattle*] · Viehfutter *n* von Bäumen und Sträuchern

master, dominus, lord [*These terms, prefixed to a man's name, in ancient times, usually denoted him a knight or clergyman, a gentleman or the lord of a manor. During medi(a)eval times these words (sometimes abbreviated to "don" or "dan") were commonly prefixed to the name of a clergyman or a gentleman of position. It indicated no special dignity known to the law*] · Herr *m*

master, principal · Geschäftsherr *m*

master — material

master · Dienstherr *m*

master, employer · Arbeitgeber *m*

master · Vorverfahrensrichter *m*

master and servant, employer and employe(e) · Arbeitgeber *m* und Arbeitnehmer *m*

master-and-servant contract, contract for personal service, contract of (personal) service, contract of master and servant, personal service contract · Dienst(leistungs)vertrag *m*

master and servant law, law of master and servant · individuelles Arbeits(vertrags)recht *n*

master (development) plan, comprehensive (development) plan, structure (development) plan, three-dimensional master (development) plan, general (development) plan [*A long-range plan officially recognized as a guide for the physical growth and development of a community, together with the basic regulatory and administrative controls needed to attain the physical objectives*] · General(bebauungs)plan *m*

master (development) planning, comprehensive (development) planning, three-dimensional master planning, structure planning, general (development) planning · General(bebauungs)planung *f*

master general of the ordnance · General-Feldzeugmeister *m*

master of a prison, keeper of a prison, gaoler (Brit.) · Gefängnisvorsteher *m*

master of the forests, chief warden of the woods, keeper of the woods, chief warden of the forests, master of the woods [*In old English law. An officer who had the principal government of all things relating to the forest, and the control of all officers belonging to the same*] · Waldbewahrer *m*, Forstbewahrer, Oberforstmeister

Master of the Horse · Oberstallmeister *m* [*England*]

Master of the Mint · Münzmeister *m* [*England*]

master of the supreme court; associate [*obsolete*] [*England*] · richterlicher Hilfsbeamter *m* eines gemeinrechtlichen Gerichtes

master of the woods, master of the forests, chief warden of the woods, keeper of the woods, keeper of the forests, chief warden of the forests [*In old English law. An officer who had the principal government of all things relating to the forest, and the control of all officers belonging to the same*] · Waldbewahrer *m*, Forstbewahrer, Oberforstmeister

master of the workhouse, workhouse master · Arbeitshausinspektor *m*

to master plan · ausarbeiten eines General(bebauungs)planes

master planner · Generalplaner *m*

master planning legislation, master planning lawmaking, comprehensive planning legislation, comprehensive planning lawmaking, three-dimensional master legislation, three-dimensional master lawmaking, structure planning legislation, structure planning lawmaking, general planning legislation, general planning lawmaking · Generalplanungsgesetzgebung *f*

master policy · Rahmenpolice *f* [*Exportkreditversicherung*]

master processor · Hauptrechner *m* [*LIS-Hardware*]

master's certificate; associate certificate [*obsolete*] · Zeugnis *n* des richterlichen Hilfsbeamten über das vom Richter bei der Assisenverhandlung gefällte Urteil zur Registrierung beim Hohen Justizhof [*An Stelle des ehemaligen „postea"*]

master-servant relation(ship), employeremploye(e) relation(ship) · Arbeitgeber-Arbeitnehmer-Verhältnis *n*

master's liability, principal's liability · Geschäftsherrenhaftung *f*, Geschäftsherrnhaftpflicht *f*, Geschäftsherrenhaftbarkeit *f*

master's liability, employer's liability [*The employer's enforceable responsibility for accidents or injuries suffered by employees while they are engaged in the performance of their duties*] · Arbeitgeberhaftpflicht *f*, Arbeitgeberhaftung *f*

master's (liability) insurance, employer's (liability) insurance · Arbeitgeberhaftpflichtversicherung *f*

master's loan, employer's loan · Arbeitgeberdarleh(e)n *n*

master's portion (of social security taxes), employer's portion (of social security taxes) · Arbeitgeberanteil *m*

master's union, employer's union · Arbeitgeberverband *m*

master tenancy, head tenancy, principal tenancy, main tenancy · Hauptmietverhältnis *n*

master tenant, main tenant, head tenant, principal tenant · Hauptmieter *m*

master transport(ation) plan · Generalverkehrsplan *m*

mastery of the will · Willensherrschaft *f*

matching of cost(s) and revenues · Verrechnung *f* zusammengehöriger Kosten und Erträge

material, substantial, essential · wesentlich

material agent — matured value

material agent · Sachproduktionskraft f

material contract · Vertrag m für die Wertschätzung der angebotenen Aktien

material damage; damnum corpori datum [Latin] · Sachschaden m, Sachbeschädigung f

material density, population concentration · Bevölkerungskonzentration f

material detail, material particular · wesentliche Einzelheit f

material ignorance, essential ignorance · wesentliche Unkenntnis f

materiality · materieller Gehalt m

materialman · (Bau)Stoffhändler m; Baumaterialhändler [Schweiz]

material mistake, mistake of intrinsic fact · wesentlicher Irrtum m

material object · greifbarer Gegenstand m

material particular, material detail · wesentliche Einzelheit f

materials cost(s) [The cost(s) of commodities, other than fixed assets, introduced into products or consumed in the operation of an organization] · Stoffkosten f, Materialkosten

materials cost(s) increase · Materialkostenerhöhung f, Materialkostensteigerung, Stoffkostenerhöhung, Stoffkostensteigerung

material(s) overhead(s) · Materialgemeinkosten f, Materialgeneralkosten, Stoffgemeinkosten, Stoffgeneralkosten

material(s) price · Materialpreis m, Stoffpreis

material(s) (price) fluctuation clause · Material(preis)gleitklausel f, Stoff(preis)gleitklausel

material(s) price variance · (Werk)Stoffpreisabweichung f, Materialpreisabweichung

material(s) supplied by owner → (construction) material(s) supplied by owner

material(s) supply by owner → (construction) material(s) supply by owner

material testing standard → (building) material testing standard

material variance · (Werk)Stoffabweichung f, Materialabweichung

maternal line · mütterliche (Abstammungs)Linie f

mathematical approach · mathematische Kostenauflösung f

mathematical decision research · mathematische Entscheidungsforschung f

mathematization · Mathematisierung f

matrimonial cause, matrimonial plea, matrimonial (court) action, matrimonial (law)suit [It is any action for divorce, nullity of marriage, judicial separation, jactitation of marriage or restitution of conjugal rights] · Eheklage f

matrimonial causes act, matrimonial causes law, matrimonial causes statute · Eheklagegesetz n

matrimonial domicil(e), marital domicil(e) · ehelicher Wohnsitz m

matrimonial law · Eherecht n

matrimonial property, marital property · Ehegut n, Ehevermögen n

matrimonial right, conjugal right · eheliches Recht n

matrimonial rights, conjugal rights [The privilege which husband and wife have of each other's society, comfort, and affection (Wharton)] · eheliche Rechte npl, Eherechte

matrimonial union, marital union · eheliche Verbindung f

matrimony, marriage; matrimonium [Latin] · Ehe f

matter, affair · Angelegenheit f, Sache f

matter in dispute, matter in issue, matter in litigation, subject of issue, subject of dispute, subject of litigation, disputed matter, disputed subject · (Rechts)Streitsache f

matter in fait · Rechtsgeschäft n welches kein vor einem Court of Record abgegebenes Schuldanerkenntnis ist

matter in issue → matter in dispute

matter in litigation → matter in dispute

matter of law, legal affair, lawful affair, cause · Rechtsangelegenheit f, Rechtssache f

matter of remedy · prozeßrechtliche Frage f

matter of substance · materiellrechtliche Frage f

matter of trifling importance · geringfügige Angelegenheit f, geringfügige Sache f

maturation, becoming due, maturity · Fälligkeit f, Verfall m

to mature, to fall due, to accrue, to become due [As rent or interest] · fällig werden, verfallen

matured · gereift, reif geworden

matured; adulted [obsolete]; grown to maturity · erwachsen

matured share · fälliger Anteil m, reifer Anteil

matured value · Nennwertbetrag m [Bausparkasse]

mature years, statutory age, legal age, full age, (age of (legal)) majority, age of consent [*The age fixed by law at which a person's consent to certain acts is valid in law*] · Majorennität *f*, Volljährigkeit(salter) *f, (n)*

maturity, maturation, becoming due · Fälligkeit *f*, Verfall *m*

maturity date, expiry date, expiration date, due date, termination date, falling in date, running out date, accrual date · Fälligkeitsdatum *n*, Fälligkeitstag *m*, Verfalldatum, Verfalltermin *m*, (Frist)Ablauftermin, (Frist)Ablaufdatum, Fälligkeitstermin, Verfalltag, (Frist)Ablauftag

maturity of performance, maturity of execution · Ausführungsreife *f*

maverick, outlier · Ausreißer *m*, herausfallende Beobachtung *f* [*Statistik*]

max-flow min-cut theorem · Satz *m* von Ford-Faulkerson [*Zur Bestimmung des maximalen Flusses durch ein Netzwerk*]

maxim · Maxime *f*, Grundprinzip *n*

maxima and minima without constraints · Maxima *npl* und Minima *npl* ohne Nebenbedingungen

maximal-size constraint · Maximalgrößenzwang *m*

maximization · Maximierung *f*

maximization criterion · Maximierungskriterium *n*

maximization of gain, maximization of profit · Gewinnmaximierung *f*, Profitmaximierung

maximization of proceeds, proceeds maximization · Erlösmaximierung *f*

maximization of utility, utility maximization · Nutzenmaximierung *f*

maximization of yield, return maximization, yield maximization, maximization of return · Renditemaximierung *f*

to maximize · maximieren

maximizing player, first player · Maximalspieler *m*

maxim of (the) law, legal maxim · Rechtsmaxime *f*

maximum amount · Höchstbetrag *m*, Meistbetrag, Maximalbetrag

maximum average dwelling rent(al), maximum average (residential) rent(al), maximum mean dwelling rent(al), maximum mean residential rent(al) · Höchstdurchschnitts(wohnungs)miete *f*

maximum charge rate, maximum rate of charge · Gebührenhöchstsatz *m*

maximum fee rate, maximum rate of fee · Gebührenhöchstsatz *m*, Honorarhöchstsatz

maximum F-ratio · maximaler Varianzquotient *m* [*Statistik*]

maximum income, peak income · Höchsteinkommen *n*, Maximaleinkommen, Meisteinkommen

maximum level, peak level · Höchststand *m*, Maximalstand, Spitzenstand

maximum likelihood, maximum probability, MP · Höchstwahrscheinlichkeit *f*, Maximalwahrscheinlichkeit

maximum limit, upper limit, ceiling · Höchstgrenze *f*, Obergrenze

maximum load point [*Point on a mass transit route where the greatest number of passengers has been noted*] · Beförderungsspitze *f*

maximum mean dwelling rent, maximum mean residential rent, maximum average dwelling rent, maximum average (residential) rent · Höchstdurchschnitts(wohnungs)miete *f*

maximum mortgage, peak mortgage [*A mortgage in which the maximum amount for which the object mortgaged can be made liable is entered in the land register, the amount really given on mortgage is determined by circumstances*] · Höchst(betrags)hypothek *f*, Maximalhypothek, Meist(betrags)hypothek, Ultimathypothek

maximum occupancy rate, maximum rate of occupancy · Höchstbelegungszahl *f*

maximum price limit, peak price limit · Höchstpreisgrenze *f*, Maximalpreisgrenze, Meistpreisgrenze

maximum probability, MP, maximum likelihood · Höchstwahrscheinlichkeit *f*, Maximalwahrscheinlichkeit

maximum rate, peak rate · Höchstsatz *m*, Maximalsatz, Meistsatz, Spitzensatz

maximum rate of charge, maximum charge rate · Gebührenhöchstsatz *m*

maximum rate of fee, maximum fee rate · Gebührenhöchstsatz *m*, Honorarhöchstsatz

maximum rate of occupancy, maximum occupancy rate · Höchstbelegungszahl *f*

maximum rate overrun, overrun of peak rate, peak rate overrun, overrun of maximum rate · Höchstsatzüberschreitung *f*, Maximalsatzüberschreitung, Meistsatzüberschreitung

maximum rent, peak rent · Höchstmiete *f*, Maximalmiete, Meistmiete, Spitzenmiete

maximum requirements technique · Maximumbedarfsberechnung *f*

maximum sum, peak sum · Höchstsumme f, Maximalsumme, Meistsumme, Spitzensumme

mayor; provost [*Scotland*] · Bürgermeister m

mayor-council system · Bürgermeisterverfassung f

mayor's auditor · Buchprüfer m vom Bürgermeister ernannt, (Bücher)Revisor vom Bürgermeister ernannt

meadow cultivation · Wiesenanbau m

meadow ground · Wiesengrund m

meadow land · Wiesenland n

meal-rent [*A rent formerly paid in meal*] · Mehlzins m

mean, average · Durchschnitt m

mean construction site wage → mean site wage

mean crowding, average crowding · wahrscheinlichkeitstheoretische Häufung f [*Besied(e)lung*]

mean deviation, average deviation [*A measure of the variation of a group of numerical data from a designated point*] · durchschnittliche Abweichung f, mittlere Abweichung

mean duration of life · mittlere Lebensdauer f, durchschnittliche Lebensdauer

mean dwelling rent, average (residential) rent, mean (residential) rent, average dwelling rent · Durchschnittswohnungsmiete f, Durchschnittswohnungs(miet)zins m, mittlere Wohnungsmiete, mittlerer Wohnungs(miet)zins

mean earner, average earner · Durchschnittsverdiener m, mittlerer Verdiener

mean earning, average earning · Durchschnittsverdienst m, mittlerer Verdienst

mean expectation of life, average expectation of life · durchschnittliche voraussichtliche Lebensdauer f, voraussichtliche durchschnittliche Lebensdauer

mean fief, mean fee, mean tenure, middle fief, middle fee, middle tenure, intermediate fief, intermediate fee, intermediate tenure, arriere fief, arriere fee, arriere tenure, mesne fief, mesne fee, mesne tenure [*A fief dependent on a superior one; an inferior fief granted by a vassal of the king, out of the fief held by him*] · Afterleh(e)n n

mean gain → mesne gain

mean income, average income · Durchschnittseinkommen n, mittleres Einkommen

meaningless word · inhaltsloses Wort n

mean length of life, average length of life · durchschnittliches Lebensalter n, Lebensalterdurchschnitt m

mean life, average life [*The estimated useful-life expectancy of a group of assets subject to depreciation*] · durchschnittliche Nutzungsdauer f, durchschnittliche Lebensdauer

mean lord, middle lord; tenente in capite [*Latin*]; intermediate lord, arriere lord, mesne lord · (feudaler) Belehner m von Aftervasallen, Feudalherr von Aftervasallen, Leh(e)n(s)herr von Aftervasallen, Leh(e)n(s)gutgeber von Aftervasallen, mittlerer Leh(e)n(s)herr, mittlerer Feudalherr, Vasall m der Krone, Kronvasall, Afterleh(e)nsherr

mean number, average number · Durchschnittszahl f, mittlere Zahl

mean price, average price · Durchschnittspreis m, mittlerer Preis

mean profit → mesne gain

mean quality, average standard, average quality, mean standard · Durchschnittsgüte f, mittlere Güte

mean rate, average rate · Durchschnittssatz m, mittlerer Satz

mean rent, average rent · Durchschnittsmiete f, mittlere Miete

mean (residential) rent, average dwelling rent, mean dwelling rent, average (residential) rent · Durchschnittswohnungsmiete f, Durchschnittswohnungs(miet)zins m, mittlere Wohnungsmiete, mittlerer Wohnungs(miet)zins

mean site wage, average construction site wage, mean construction site wage, average building site wage, mean building site wage, average job (site) wage, mean job (site) wage, average site wage · Bau(stellen)-Mittellohn m

(means of) access, approach, means of approaching · Zugang m

means of access to site · Baustellenzugang m

means of coercion, compulsory means · Zwangsmittel n

means of control · Lenkungsmittel n

means of escape · Fluchtmöglichkeit f

means of information, means of advice · Ankündigungsmittel n, Informationsmittel [*z. B. Reklameschild; Leuchtschrift usw.*]

means of law, legal means · Rechtsinstrumentarium n

means of permanent finance · Dauerfinanzierungsmittel n

means of planning, planning means · Planungsinstrumentarium n

means of remedy, means of redress · Abhilfemittel n, Behelfsmittel

means of subsistence — measuring recall 656

means of subsistence · Subsistenzmittel n, Unterhaltsmittel [malthusische Bevölkerungstheorie]

mean square error · mittlerer quadratischer Fehler m

mean standard, mean quality, average standard, average quality · Durchschnittsgüte f, mittlere Güte

mean tenant, middle tenant, intermediate tenant, mesne tenant, arriere tenant · Afterleh(e)n(s)mann m

mean tenure → mean fief

mean value, average value · Durchschnittswert m, Mittelwert, mittlerer Wert

measure · Maßnahme f

measure-and-value contract, bill contract, contract for measure and value, unit-price contract, measurement contract, measured contract · Einheits(preis)vertrag m [Ein Vertrag zu Einheitspreisen für technisch und wirtschaftlich einheitliche Teilleistungen, deren Menge nach Maß, Gewicht oder Stückzahl vom Auftraggeber in den Verdingungsunterlagen angegeben ist]

measured price → (ad)measured price

measurement book → (ad)measurement book

measurement document → (ad)measurement document

measurement engineer → (ad)measurement engineer

measurement error, measuring error · Meßfehler m

measurement error → (ad)measurement error

measurement method → (ad)measurement method

measurement mistake → (ad)measurement mistake

measurement of association · Assoziationsmessung f

measurement of consumption · Verbrauchsmessung f

measurement (of (the) work(s)) → (ad)measurement (of (the) works)

measurement prescription → (ad)measurement prescription

measurement provision → (ad)measurement provision

measurement unit, unit of measurement · Maßeinheit f

measure of a field, field measure · Feldmaß n

measure of attractiveness, attractiveness measure · Anziehungsmaß n, Attraktivitätsmaß n

measure of coercion, coerci(ti)ve measure · Zwangsmaßnahme f

measure of development, development measure · Entwick(e)lungsmaßnahme f

measure of equity, equitable measure · Billigkeitsmaßnahme f, Maßnahme nach Billigkeit(srecht), Billigkeitsrechtmaßnahme

measure of freedom (of contract) · (Vertrags)Spielraum m

measure of indemnification, measure of indemnity, indemnifying measure, damages measure, indemnification measure, indemnity measure, compensation measure, measure of damages, measure of compensation · Entschädigungsmaßnahme f, Schadensersatzmaßnahme

measure of land, land measure · Landmaß n

measure of police power · Ordnungsmaßnahme f

measure of productivity, productivity measure · Leistungsindikator m [Sozialprodukt]

measure of protection, protective measure, protection measure · Schutzmaßnahme f, Schutzvorkehrung f

measure of skewness, skewness measure · Schiefemaß n [Statistik]

measure of urbanization · Verstädterungsmaßnahme f

measure of utility, utility measure · Nutzenmaß n

measure of value · Wertmaßstab m

measure of welfare, welfare measure · Wohlstandsindikator m [Sozialprodukt]

to measure out by steps, to pace, to step off (a distance) · abschreiten [Behördlich messend abgehen]

measurer · Aufmesser m

measure standard cost(s), fixed standard cost(s), basic standard cost(s), bogey standard cost(s) · Maßstandardkosten f, Standardkosten 2. Art, Grundstandardkosten

to measure together → to (ad)measure together

to measure (up) → to (ad)measure (up)

measuring · Messen n

measuring attitudes · Verhaltensmessung f [Umfragetechnik]

measuring awareness · Bewußtheitsmessung f [Umfragetechnik]

measuring error, measurement error · Meßfehler m

measuring recall · Erinnerungsmessung f [Umfragetechnik]

measuring (up) → (ad)measuring (up)

mechanic → building mechanic

mechanical budget · unabhängiger Kostenplan *m*, unabhängiges Budget *n*

mechanical department → (construction) equipment department

(mechanical) engineering industry · Maschinenindustrie *f*

mechanical excavation, mechanical digging · Abgrabung *f* großen Umfangs, Baggerung

mechanical solidarity · Gemeinschaft *f*

mechanical sub(contractor) · Nachunternehmer *m* für mechanische Arbeit(en) Subunternehmer für mechanische Arbeit(en), Unterunternehmer für mechanische Arbeit(en); Unterakkordant *m* für mechanische Arbeit(en) [*Schweiz*]

mechanical traffic · technisierter Verkehr *m*

mechanic's lien → (building) mechanic's lien

mechanism of exchange · Geldverkehr *m*

meddling → (inter)meddling

medi(a)eval desertion · mittelalterliche Wüstung *f*

medi(a)eval-German law · mittelalterlich-deutsches Recht *n*

medi(a)eval land law · mittelalterliches Bodenrecht *n*, mittelalterliches Landrecht

mediation, conciliation · Schlichtung *f*, Vermitt(e)lung bei Streitigkeiten

mediation board → board of conciliation

mediation code, conciliation code · Schlichtungsordnung *f*

mediator · Schlichter *m*

medical care · ärztliche Pflege *f*

medical care station · Pflegeabteilung *f* [*Teil eines Wohnheims*]

medical cartography · medizinische Kartographie *f*

medical certificate · ärztliches Zeugnis *n*, ärztliche Bescheinigung *f*, ärztliches Attest *n*

medical geography · medizinische Geographie *f*, medizinische Erdkunde

medical jurisprudence, forensic medicine · Gerichtsmedizin *f*

medical officer for the poor, medical official for the poor · Armenarzt *m*

(medical) officer of health [*England*]; health authority, sanitary authority · Gesundheitsbehörde *f*

medical officer of health, medical official of health · Leiter *m* eines Gesundheitsamtes

medical official for the poor, medical officer for the poor · Armenarzt *m*

medical practitioner · (praktischer) Arzt *m*

medical relief of paupers, medical relief of poors · Armenkrankenpflege *f*

medico-legal [*Relating to the law concerning medical questions*] · gerichtsmedizinisch, rechtsmedizinisch

meditatio fugae [*Latin*]; contemplation of flight, intent(ion) to abscond · Verdunkelungsgefahr *f*

medium-dated, medium-term, medium-period, medium-run, medium-range · mittelfristig

medium-dated stock, bond [*Between five and ten years until maturity*] · mittelfristige Staatsschuldverschreibung *f*, mittelfristige Staatsobligation *f* [*in Großbritannien*]

medium-income family, medium-earnings family · Familie *f* mit mittlerem Einkommen

medium-period, medium-run, medium-range, medium-dated, medium-term · mittelfristig

medium-range, medium-dated, medium-term, medium-period, medium-run · mittelfristig

medium-run, medium-range, medium-dated, medium-term, medium-period · mittelfristig

medium-sized region · mittelgroße Region *f*

medium-sized town, middle town, medium-sized city, middle city · mittelgroße Stadt *f*, Mittelstadt

medium-term, medium-period, medium-run, medium-range, medium-dated · mittelfristig

meeting · Zusammenkunft *f*

meetinghouse · Gottes- und Gemeindehaus *n* [*der Puritaner in den USA*]

meeting minutes · Tagungsprotokoll *n*

meeting place · Treffpunkt *m*

meeting places order · Versammlungsstättenverordnung *f*

megacity, megatown · Megastadt *f*

megalopolis · Megalopole *f*, Riesenstadt, multizentrische Regionalstadt *f*

member, associate · Mitglied *n*

member of a jury; free and lawful man [*In old English law*]; judex, liber et legalis homo [*Latin*]; juror, jury member, jurator · Geschworener *m*

**member of the bar, **fully qualified lawyer, fully trained lawyer [*Lawyers reporting to major law directory in the USA and those qualified by 2nd state examination in the Federal Republic of Germany*] · Volljurist *m* [*In den USA in die maßgebenden Juristenverzeichnisse aufgenommene und in der Bundesrepublik Deutschland mit dem 2. Staatsexamen qualifizierte Juristen*]

membership association, association unincorporate · Verein *m* ohne Korporationsrecht, nicht eingetragener Verein, nicht rechtsfähiger Verein

membership corporation, non-stock corporation · (Kapital)Gesellschaft *f* mit nicht in übertragbare selbständige Anteile zerfallendem Grundkapital an deren Eigentum eine Mitgliedschaft gebunden ist

membership corporation, association corporate · rechtsfähiger Verein *m*, Verein mit Korporationsrecht, eingetragener Verein, e.V.

membership fee, initiation fee [*The sum paid on joining an organization for privileges of membership*] · Aufnahmegebühr *f*, Aufnahmegeld *n*, Eintrittsgebühr *f*, Eintrittsgeld *n*

membership qualification · Mitgliedschaftsvoraussetzung *f*

membership register, membership registry, register of members, registry of members · Mitgliederverzeichnis *n*

membership registry, membership register, registry of members, register of members · Gesellschaftsregister *n*, Mitgliederverzeichnis *n*

membership right, right of membership · Mitgliedschaftsrecht *n*

membership share, subscription share, share of stock, instal(l)ment share, partly paid share · Raten(geschäfts)anteil *m* [*aufhörende Bausparkasse*]

member state · Gliedstaat *m*, Einzelstaat

member state court · Gliedstaatengericht *n*, Einzelstaatengericht

member union · Mitgliedsverband *m*

memorandum decision · Entscheid(ung) *m, (f)* ohne eingehende Begründung

memorandum for file, memorandum to file · Aktenvermerk *m*

memorandum (of association), deed of partnership, partnership deed; deed of settlement [*obsolete*]; articles of incorporation (US); social contract, partnership contract [*Business corporations are now usually created under a general statute which permits a specified number of persons to form a corporation by preparing and filing with the proper public official, usually the secretary of state, a document known as the articles of incorporation*] · Gründungsurkunde *f*, Gründungssatzung *f*, Gesellschaftsvertrag *m*, Gründungsvertrag, Gesellschaftsurkunde [*1.) Körperschaft, Korporation; 2.) (Kapital)Gesellschaft; 3.) vereinsähnliche Gemeinschaft*]

memorandum of law [*An abbreviated statement of the pleadings, proofs, and affidavits in any legal proceeding*] · Schriftsatz *m* brief

memorandum to file, memorandum for file · Aktenvermerk *m*

memorial [*It is an abstract of the material parts of an instrument, with the parcels at full length, and concludes with a statement that the party desires the deed to be registered*] · Urkundenauszug *m* zum Registrieren

memorial of deed, deed memorial · Auszug *m* einer gesiegelten Urkunde zum Registrieren

memorial of endorsed deed, memorial of indorsed deed · Auszug *m* einer indossierten gesiegelten Urkunde zum Registrieren

memorial of will, will memorial · Testamentsauszug *m* zum Registrieren

memorial park · Ahnenpark *m*

menials · Gesinde *n*

menials contract · Gesindevertrag *m*

menial servants, domestic servants · Hausgesinde *n*

men's duty journal, duty book · Dienstbuch *n*

men-space relation(ship) · Mensch-Raum-Beziehung *f*

mens rea [*Latin*]; guilty mind · schuldhafter Geisteszustand *m*

mens vea, malitia (praecogitata) [*Latin*]; malice (prepense), aforethought, evil mind · Dolus *m*, Vorsatz *m*, krimineller Wille *m*

mental alienation, mental disorder, mental derangement, insanity, unsoundness of mind, madness, derangement of intellect, mental unsoundness [*Lunacy is properly a species of insanity, although the terms are frequently used as synonyms*] · Geisteskrankheit *f*, Geistesgestörtheit

mental attitude · innere Haltung *f*

mental disability, mental incompetency, mental incapacity · geistiges Unvermögen *n*, geistige Unfähigkeit *f*

mental hospital · Heil(- und Pflege)anstalt *f*

mental incapacity — merger

mental incapacity, mental disability, mental incompetency · geistiges Unvermögen *n*, geistige Unfähigkeit *f*

mentally capable by law, mentally qualified by law, mentally competent by law, of sound mind; compos mentis [*Latin*] · zurechnungsfähig

mentally incompetent person → person of unsound mind

mentally qualified, mentally capable · geistig geeignet, geistig fähig, geistig befähigt

mentally uncapable by law, mentally unqualified by law, mentally uncompetent by law · unzurechnungsfähig

mental map · psychisches Raumbild *n*

mental patient → person of unsound mind

mental reservation [*A silent exception to the general words of a promise or agreement not expressed, on account of a general understanding on the subject*] · stillschweigender Vorbehalt *m*

mental state · innere Tatseite *f*, subjektive Hinsicht *f*, Geisteszustand *m*

mental unsoundness, mental alienation, mental disorder, mental derangement, insanity, unsoundness of mind, madness, derangement of intellect [*Lunacy is properly a species of insanity, although the terms are frequently used as synonyms*] · Geisteskrankheit *f*, Geistesgestörtheit

mental vigour · Verstandsreife *f*

mercable → merchantable

mercantile agency, credit enquiry agency, commercial agency · Handelsauskunftei *f*

mercantile agent, commercial agent · Handelsagent *m*

mercantile broker, commercial broker · Handelsmakler *m*

mercantile contract, commercial contract · Handelsvertrag *m*

mercantile law, commercial law, business law, law merchant; lex mercatoria [*Latin*]; merchant law · Handelsrecht *n*

mercantile port · Handelshafen *m*

mercantile treaty, commercial treaty · Handelsvertrag *m* [*zwischen Nationen*]

mercer · Schnittwarenhändler *m*

merchandise · Handelsware *f*

merchandise mark · Schutzmarke *f*

Merchandise Marks Act [*1887. Great Britain*] · Schutzmarkengesetz *n*

merchantable, mercable, fungible, marketable, sal(e)able · absetzbar, verkaufbar, marktgängig, verkäuflich

merchant bank (Brit.); commercial bank (US) [*Sometimes known as "accepting house", such a bank owes its name to the fact that in most cases the banking and financial sides of its business originally developed as a sideline to its trading activities*] · Handelsbank *f*, Geschäftsbank

merchant company, g(u)ild merchant, company merchant, merchant g(u)ild · Kaufmannsgilde *f*, Kaufmannsverband *m*

merchant g(u)ild, merchant company, g(u)ild merchant, company merchant · Kaufmannsgilde *f*, Kaufmannsverband *m*

merchant law, mercantile law, commercial law, business law, law merchant; lex mercatoria [*Latin*] · Handelsrecht *n*

merchant navy · Handelsmarine *f*

merchant shipping · Handelsschiffahrt *f*

merchant shipping law, law of merchant shipping · Handelsschiffahrtsrecht *n*

mere, croy [*In old English law*]; marsh(y) ground, marsh(y) land · Marschland *n*

mere lordship appendant, seigniory appendant, signory appendant · unterbrochene Kronvasallenherrschaft *f*

mere lordship appurtenant, seigniory appurtenant, signory appurtenant · zugehörige Kronvasallenherrschaft *f*, zugehörige Herrschaft eines Kronvasallen

mere lordship in gross, seigniory in gross, signory in gross · persönliche Kronvasallenherrschaft *f*, persönliche Herrschaft eines Kronvasallen

mere residence, simple residence · einfacher Aufenthalt *m*

mere right; merum jus [*Latin*]; abstract right of property [*The mere right of property in land, without either possession or even the right of possession*] · Besitzrecht *n* ohne Nießbrauch

mere-stone [*In old English law, a stone for bounding or dividing land(s)*] · Grenzstein *m*

mere urban tract [*According to Wooldridge and East*]; town-village, city-village, urban village [*According to Dickinson*] · Pseudostadt *f*, unechte Stadt, Stadtdorf *n*

merged · zusammengeschlossen, verschmolzen

merged, sunk, drowned, absorbed, extinguished · untergegangen [*Wenn sich z. B. Eigentum und Pfandrecht in einer Hand vereinigen, geht das kleinere im größeren unter*]

merger, drowning, sinking, absorption, extinguishment [*Of one estate in*

merger — method of citation

another] · Untergang *m* [*siehe Erklärung unter „untergegangen"*]

merger, consolidation, fusion [*In the civil law, the uniting of possession, occupancy, profits, etc., of land(s) with property, and vice versa*] · Konsolidation *f,* Verschmelzung *f,* Fusion *f*

merger, merging · (Subjekt)Vereinigung *f,* Sachvereinigung [*1.) (Sach)Verbindung; 2.) Vermischung; 3.) Vermengung*]

merger of capitals, consolidation of capitals, capital consolidation, capital merger, capital fusion, fusion of capitals · Kapitalverschmelzung *f,* Kapitalkonsolidation *f,* Kapitalfusion

merger of incorporated places, municipal consolidation · Verschmelzung *f* inkorporierter Gemeinden

merger of parcels, merger of plots · Vereinigung *f* von Grundstücken

merit certificate · Schlußschulzeugnis *n*

meritocracy · Regime *n* der Besten

merit review · Zweckmäßigkeitskontrolle *f*

merit system promotion · Beförderung *f* nach Leistung

merum jus [*Latin*]; abstract right of property, mere right [*The mere right of property in land, without either possession or even the right of possession*] · Besitzrecht *n* ohne Nießbrauch

mesnal(i)ty [*In old English law. The estate or right of a mesne*] · Afterleh(e)n(s)herrlichkeit *f*

mesne fief, mesne fee, mesne tenure, mean fief, mean fee, mean tenure, middle fief, middle fee, middle tenure, intermediate fief, intermediate fee, intermediate tenure, arriere fief, arriere fee, arriere tenure [*A fief dependent on a superior one; an inferior fief granted by a vassal of the king, out of the fief held by him*] · Afterleh(e)n *n*

mesne lord, mean lord, middle lord; tenente in capite [*Latin*]; intermediate lord, arriere lord · (feudaler) Belehner *m* von Aftervasallen, Feudalherr von Aftervasallen, Leh(e)n(s)herr von Aftervasallen, Leh(e)n(s)gutgeber von Aftervasallen, mittlerer Leh(e)n(s)herr, mittlerer Feudalherr, Vasall der Krone, Kronvasall, Afterleh(e)nsherr

mesne process, intermediate process [*A process intervening between the beginning and end of a (law)suit*] · Nebenprozeß *m*

mesne profit [*Profit derived from land, whilst the possession of it has been improperly withheld*] · geldwerter Vorteil *m* gezogen aus einem Grundstück während der Dauer einer unbefugten Besitzentziehung

mesne tenant, arriere tenant, mean tenant, middle tenant, intermediate tenant · Afterleh(e)n(s)mann *m*

mesne tenure → mesne fief

messenger; misstaicus [*Latin*] [*One who carries an errand*] · Bote *m*

metachronism [*An error in computation of time*] · Zeitrechnungsfehler *m*

metage [*The corporation of the City of London had under charter and by prescription been in receipt of a large income arising from their right of compulsory metage, at first of all merchandise, and finally only of grain, brought into the Port of London*] · Messen *n*

metayage, metayer system, colonat partiaire, share-tenancy, share-tenure [*Under this system land is divided in small farms, among single families, the landlord generally supplying the stock and receiving, in lieu of rent a fixed proportion of the produce. This proportion, which is generally paid in kind, is usually one-half*] · Halbscheidwirtschaft *f,* Halbpacht *f*

metayer, share-tenant · Halbmeier *m,* Halbmeyer, Halbpächter

met-bedrip, met-bidrip(e), met-bed(e)repe, met-bedrape, met-bidrepe · befohlene Erntearbeit *f* bei der Fleisch verabreicht wurde [*Fronhofarbeit*]

meter [*An instrument of measurement, as a gas meter or an electricity meter*] · Zähler *m,* Messer

metered cab · Taxi *n* mit Zähler, Zählertaxi

meter rent · Zählermiete *f,* Messermiete

metes and bounds, meths and marches [*In old Scots law*]; metae et bundae [*Latin*] [*The boundary lines of land(s), with their terminating points or angles; terminal lines, with their distinctive objects; end lines and side lines*] · Grund(stücks)grenzlinien *fpl*

metewand, meteyard [*A staff of a certain length wherewith measures are taken*] · Meßstab *m*

method · Methode *f,* Verfahren *n*

method for deriving multi-factor uniform regions · Methode *f* zur Bildung homogener Regionen mehrdimensionaler Definitionen, Verfahren *n* zur Bildung homogener Regionen mehrdimensionaler Definitionen

method-mindedness · Methodenbewußtsein *n*

method of (ad)measurement, (ad)measurement method · Aufmaßmethode *f,* Aufmaßverfahren *n*

method of citation, citation method · Zitierweise *f*

method of discharge — metropolitan growth

method of discharge, redemption method, method of redemption, discharge method · Ablösungsverfahren n, Auslösungsmethode f, Ablösungsmethode, Einlösungsmethode, Auslösungsverfahren, Einlösungsverfahren

method of hearing, hearing method · Anhörungsverfahren n

method of measurement → method of (ad)measurement

method of overlapping maps · koordinierte Doppelauswahl f [Statistik]

method of planning, planning method · Planmethode f, Planungsmethode, Plan(ungs)verfahren n

method of redemption, discharge method, method of discharge, redemption method · Ablösungsverfahren n, Auslösungsmethode f, Ablösungsmethode, Einlösungsmethode, Auslösungsverfahren, Einlösungsverfahren

method of semi-averages · Methode f der Halbreihenmittelwerte, Regressions-(ab)schätzung f mit den Halbreihendurchschnitten, Verfahren n der Halbreihenmittelwerte [Statistik]

method of working, working method · Arbeitsweise f, Ausführungsweise

method-related bill (of quantities), m-r bill (of quantities) · verfahrensbezogenes Leistungsverzeichnis n, verfahrensbezogenes L.V.

method to obtain a building permit · (Bau)Genehmigungsverfahren n, (Bau)-Erlaubnisverfahren

meths and marches [In old Scots law]; metae et bundae [Latin]; metes and bounds [The boundary lines of land(s), with their terminating points or angles; terminal lines, with their distinctive objects; end lines and side lines] · Grund(stücks)grenzlinien fpl

metrication, metric system · metrisches (Maß)System n, Metersystem

metric change · Umstellung f auf metrische Maße

metric city, metric town · metrisch(-plantreu)e Stadt f

metric dimension · Meterabmessung f

metric size · Metergröße f

metric system, metrication · metrisches (Maß)System n, Metersystem

metric town, metric city · metrisch(-plantreu)e Stadt f

metropolis → metropolitan city

Metropolis Management Act [1855] · Gesetz n für die Verwaltung Londons

metropolitan [One of the titles of an archbishop. Derived from the circumstance that archbishops were consecrated at first in the metropolis of a province] · Metropolit m

metropolitan approach · Metropolenansatz m

metropolitan area; city settlement area [According to Dickinson "the urban tract" (verstädtertes Gebiet) and the rural urban fringe (ländlicher Gürtel)]; metropolitan region [Metropolis together with a surrounding area which is strongly influenced by and dependent on the metropolis, as evidenced by activities which would not be there but for the proximity of the metropolis] · Metropolenregion f, Stadt f und (ihr) Hinterland

metropolitan Berlin, Greater Berlin, Outer Berlin · Großberlin n

metropolitan biology · Metropolenbiologie f

metropolitan borough · Einzelstadt f, Bezirksstadt [Durch das London Government Act von 1899 wurden alle Einzelgemeinden zu 29 Einzelstädten, auch Bezirksstädte genannt, zusammengefaßt]

metropolitan borough council · Einzelstadtrat m, Bezirksstadtrat [Rat eines Teiles von London]

metropolitan Breslau, Greater Breslau, Outer Breslau · Groß-Breslau n

metropolitan centre (Brit.) → metropolitan city

metropolitan city, central city, core city, core town, central town, high-order fully central place, metropolis; metropolitan centre (Brit.); metropolitan center (US) [The hypothetically dominant aggregate at the center of a metropolitan community] · Provinz-Hauptort m, Oberzentrum n, Landeszentrale f, Metropolis f, Metropole f, Zentralstadt f, Kernstadt [nach W. Christaller]

metropolitan-clearing · Abrechnung f von Schecks auf die Filialen der Clearingbanken außerhalb der Londoner City

metropolitan council of government · Stadtunion f

metropolitan county (Brit.) · Metropolengrafschaft f

metropolitan culture · ursprüngliche Kultur f der fremden Elite [Kolonialstadt]

metropolitan development · Metropolenentwick(e)lung f

metropolitan ecology · Metropolenökologie f

metropolitan fringe · Metropolensaum m

metropolitan green belt · Metropolengrüngürtel m

metropolitan growth · Metropolenwachstum n

metropolitan influence · Metropoleneinfluß *m*

metropolitanism · Metropolenwesen *n*

to metropolitanize · metropolisieren

Metropolitan London, Outer London, Greater London · Außenlondon *n*, Großlondon *n*

Metropolitan Police District · Londoner Polizeibezirk *m*

metropolitan population · Metropolenbevölkerung *f*

metropolitan region, metropolitan area; city settlement area [*According to Dickinson "the urban tract" (verstädtertes Gebiet) und the rural urban fringe (ländlicher Gürtel)*] [*Metropolis together with a surrounding area which is strongly influenced by and dependent on the metropolis, as evidenced by activities which would not be there but for the proximity of the metropolis*] · Metropolenregion *f*, Stadt *f* und (ihr) Hinterland

metropolitan research · Metropolenforschung *f*

metropolitan ring · Metropolenring *m*

metropolitan science · Metropolenwissenschaft *f*

metropolitan suburb(an place) (Brit.) · Metropolenvorort *m*

metropolitan village [*A village within commuting distance of an urban centre which is socially and economically no longer rural*] · Metropolendorf *n*

metropolization · Metropolenbildung *f*

micro climate · (örtliches) Kleinklima *n*, Mikroklima

microeconomics, microeconomy · Mikrowirtschaft *f*

microfilm plotter · Mikrofilmplotter *m*

micro level · Mikroebene *f*

micro(scale) approach · Mikroansatz *m*

micro(scale) approach provided by economic theory · mikroökonomischer Theorienansatz *m*

micro(scale) theory · Mikrotheorie *f*

micro-state · Kleinstaat *m*

middle city, medium-sized town, middle town, medium-sized city · mittelgroße Stadt *f*, Mittelstadt

middle class · Mittelschicht *f*

middle-class commuter · Mittelschichtpendler *m*

middle-earnings housing, middle-income housing · Wohnungen *f pl* für Wohnungssuchende mit mittlerem Einkommen

middle fief, middle fee, middle tenure, intermediate fief, intermediate fee, intermediate tenure, arriere fief, arriere fee, arriere tenure, mesne fief, mesne fee, mesne tenure, mean fief, mean fee, mean tenure [*A fief dependent on a superior one; an inferior fief granted by a vassal of the king, out of the fief held by him*] · Afterleh(e)n *n*

middle lord; tenente in capite [*Latin*]; intermediate lord, arriere lord, mesne lord, mean lord · (feudaler) Belehner *m* von Aftervasallen, Feudalherr von Aftervasallen, Leh(e)n(s)herr von Aftervasallen, Leh(e)n(s)gutgeber von Aftervasallen, mittlerer Leh(e)n(s)herr, mittlerer Feudalherr, Vasall der Krone, Kronvasall, Afterleh(e)nsherr

middleman, housefarmer, intermediary · Mittelsmann *m* [*Er mietet ein Gebäude nicht zum Selbstbewohnen, sondern um die Räume weiter zu vermieten*]

middle-man, intermediary [*A distributor from producer to consumer*] · Zwischenhändler *m*

middle middle class · mittlere Mittelschicht *f*

middle-order fully-central place · Bezirks(haupt)ort *m*, zentraler Ort der mittleren Stufe; Stadt *f* [*Schweiz*] [*nach W. Christaller*]

middle-order semi-central place · Kreisort *m* [*nach W. Christaller*]

middle-order sub-central place, sub-town, market district, market town; first order centre, urban village [*750 to 1,000 inhabitants*], small town with between 1,000 and 2,000 inhabitants (Brit.); first order center, urban center (US) · Amtsort *m* [*nach W. Christaller*]

middle state policy · Mittelstandspolitik *f*

middle tenant, intermediate tenant, mesne tenant, arriere tenant, mean tenant · Afterleh(e)n(s)mann *m*

middle tenure → middle fief

middle term · Mittelbegriff *m*

middle town, medium-sized city, middle city, medium-sized town · mittelgroße Stadt *f*, Mittelstadt

middle town life · Mittelstadtleben *n*

mid-rank method · Methode *f* der durchschnittlichen Rangzahlen, Verfahren *n* der durchschnittlichen Rangzahlen

migrant, mover · Wandernde *m*, Wanderer

migrant force, migrating force, migratory force · Wanderungstriebkraft *f*

migrant population, migrating population, footloose population, migratory population · Wanderbevölkerung *f*

to migrate, to move · wandern

migrating, moving · Wandern *n*

migrating force, migratory force, migrant force · Wanderungstriebkraft *f*

migrating population, footloose population, migratory population, migrant population · Wanderbevölkerung *f*

migration, residential mobility · räumliche Bevölkerungsbewegung *f*, horizontale Bevölkerungsbewegung, waag(e)rechte Bevölkerungsbewegung, Wanderung [*Verlegung des Wohnsitzes*]

migrational component · Wanderungsbestandteil *m*, Wanderungskomponente *f*

migration analysis, migration study, analysis of migration, study of migration · Wanderungsuntersuchung *f*, Wanderungsanalyse *f*

migration area, migration territory · Wanderungsgebiet *n*

migration balance · Wanderungssaldo *m*

migration border · Wanderungsgrenze *f*

migration distance, distance of move · Wanderungsentfernung *f*

migration distribution, distribution of migration(s) · Wanderungsverteilung *f*

migration field · Einzugsbereich *m* [*Wanderung*]

migration flow → (migration) movement current

migration frequency · Wanderungshäufigkeit *f*

migration from an area, migration outwards, out-migration, outward migration · Abwanderung *f*

migration from an urban area, urban outward migration, urban out-migration · Stadtabwanderung *f*

migration gain · Wanderungsgewinn *m*

migration in stages, migration in steps, stage-by-stage migration, step-by-step migration, stagewise migration, stepwise migration · stufenweise Wanderung *f*, Stufenwanderung

migration law, law of migration · Wanderungsgesetz *n*

migration loss · Wanderungsverlust *m*

migration matrix · Wanderungsmatrix *f*

(migration) movement · Bewegung *f*, Wanderungsbewegung

(migration) movement current, (migration) movement stream, (migration) movement flow, migration flow, migration stream, current of (migration) movement, stream of (migration) movement, flow of (migration) movement · Bewegungsstrom *m*, Wanderungsstrom

(migration) movement flow → (migration) movement current

(migration) movement stream → (migration) movement current

migration of capital, capital migration · Kapitalwanderung *f*

migration outwards, out-migration, outward migration, migration from an area · Abwanderung *f*

migration pattern, migration scheme · Wanderungsschema *n*, Wanderungsmuster *n*

migration probability · Wanderungswahrscheinlichkeit *f*

migration region · Wanderungsregion *f*

migration research · Wanderungsforschung *f*

migration scheme, migration pattern · Wanderungsschema *n*, Wanderungsmuster *n*

migration stream → (migration) movement current

migration study, analysis of migration, study of migration, migration analysis · Wanderungsuntersuchung *f*, Wanderungsanalyse *f*

migration territory, migration area · Wanderungsgebiet *n*

migration to an area, in-migration, inward migration · Zuwanderung *f*

migratory farm worker, migrant farm worker, migrating farm worker, footloose farm worker, migrant farm workman, migratory farm workman, migrating farm workman, footloose farm workman; migrant farm labourer, migratory farm labourer, migrating farm labourer, footloose farm labourer (Brit.); migratory farm laborer, migrating farm laborer, migrant farm laborer, footloose farm laborer (US) · Wander-Landarbeiter *m*, wandernder Landarbeiter

migratory force, migrant force, migrating force · Wanderungstriebkraft *f*

migratory population, migrant population, migrating population, footloose population · Wanderbevölkerung *f*

migratory settlement · bodenvage (An)Sied(e)lung *f*, nomadische (An)Sied(e)lung

migratory worker, migrating worker, migrant worker, footloose worker, migratory workman, migrating workman, migrant workman, footloose workman; migratory labourer, migrating labourer, migrant labourer, footloose labourer (Brit.); migratory laborer, migrating laborer, migrant laborer, footloose laborer (US) · Wanderarbeiter *m*, wandernder Arbeiter

mileage tariff · Entfernungstarif *m*

**military cemetery, **military graveyard · Kriegerfriedhof m, Militärfriedhof, Soldatenfriedhof, Heldenfriedhof

**military fee (tenure), **military fief, military tenancy, military feud, military feod, military tenement, military (feodal) tenure (of land(s)); feodum militare, feudum militare, tenementum per servitium militare, feodum militis, feudum militis [*Latin*] · Kriegsleh(e)n n

military forces · Streitkräfte f

military law · Militärrecht n

military pay · Sold m

military reserve · militärischer Sperrbezirk m

**military road, **military highway · Militärstraße f

**military service on horseback, **knight service; servitium militare, servitium militis [*Latin*] · Ritterdienst m

**military testament, **military will · Militärtestament n

militia · Miliz f

**mil-leat, **milleate [*A trench to convey water to or from a mill*] · Mühl(en)graben m

**milled money, **coined money · Münzgeld n

mille map · Tausendpunktkarte f

**million millions, **billion [*Great Britain*] · (eine) Million Millionen

mill vilage · Mühldorf n

minable · abbauwürdig, gewinnungswürdig, abbaubar, gewinnbar, ausbeutungswürdig, ausbeutbar [*Mineralien*]

minator [*Latin*]; mine worker, miner, mine workman · Bergmann m, Berg(bau)arbeiter, Bergwerkarbeiter, Grubenarbeiter

minator carucae [*Latin*]; ploughman (Brit.); plowman (US) · Pflüger m

mine · Bergwerk n

**mine (general) property, **mine proprietorship, mine ownership (of property) · Bergwerkeigentum n

**mine operator, **adventurer · Bergwerkbetreibende m, Bergwerkbetreiber, Bergbaubetreibende, Bergbaubetreiber

mine possession · Bergwerkbesitz m

mine possessor · Bergwerkbesitzer m

**miner, **mine workman; minator [*Latin*]; mine worker · Bergmann m, Berg(bau)arbeiter, Bergwerkarbeiter, Grubenarbeiter

**mineral, **soil constituent · Bodenbestandteil m, Mineral n [*Z. B. Lehm, Sand, Kies usw.*]

mineral deposits law · Lagerstättenrecht n

**mineral deposits law, **mineral deposits act, mineral deposits statute · Lagerstättengesetz n

mineral extraction → mineral working

mineral getting → mineral working

mineral interest → mineral right

mineral land(s) · Mineralienland n

**mineral law, **law of taking minerals, law of mining minerals, law of exploiting minerals, mining law · (Mineral(ien))Abbaurecht n, (Mineral(ien))Ausbeutungsrecht, (Mineral(ien))Gewinnungsrecht, (objektives) Berg(bau)recht

mineral resource · mineralisches Rohstoffvorkommen n

**mineral right, **mineral interest, interest in minerals in land(s), right to take minerals, right to win minerals, right of exploitation, right to exploit minerals, right of taking minerals, right of winning, winning right, exploitation right · (Mineral(ien))Abbaurecht n, (Mineral(ien))-Ausbeutungsrecht, (subjektives) Berg(bau)recht, (Mineral(ien))Abbaugerechtigkeit f

mineral rights duty · Bergwerkabgabe f

mineral spring · Mineralquelle f

**mineral(s workings) act, **mineral(s workings) law, mineral(s workings) statute, mining act, mining law, mining statute · (Mineral(ien))Abbaugesetz n, (Mineral(ien))Ausbeutungsgesetz, (Mineral(ien))Gewinnungsgesetz, Berg(bau)gesetz

**mineral treasure, **treasure of the earth · Bodenschatz m, Bodenreichtum m

mineral winning → mineral working

**mineral working, **mineral getting, working of minerals, getting of minerals, mineral winning, winning of minerals, extraction of minerals, mineral extraction, getting (of soil constituents), working (of soil constituents), extraction (of soil constituents), winning (of soil constituents) · Abbau(en) m, (n) von Bodenbestandteilen, Abbau(en) von Mineralien, Mineralienabbau, Mineralienausbeuten, Ausbeuten (von Mineralien), Ausbeuten von Bodenbestandteilen, Ausbeutung f (von Mineralien), Ausbeutung von Bodenbestandteilen, Mineralienausbeutung, Mineraliengewinnung, Gewinnung (von Mineralien), Gewinnung von Bodenbestandteilen [*Die planmäßige Inangriffnahme einer Lagerstätte bei der Gewinnung von Lehm, Sand, Kies usw.*]

**miner's dwelling (Brit.); **mine worker's dwelling unit, miner's dwelling unit, mine workman's dwelling unit (US); mine worker's dwelling, mine workman's dwelling (Brit.) · Bergmannswohnung f,

Berg(bau)arbeiterwohnung, Bergwerkarbeiterwohnung, Grubenarbeiterwohnung

miners' row, pit row · Bergarbeiterreihensied(e)lung *f*

mine's own consumption, mine's self-consumption · Zechenselbstverbrauch *m*

mines' register, mines' registry, mining register, mining registry, register of mines, registry of mines · Berg(werk)grundbuch *n*

mine worker, miner, mine workman; minator [*Latin*] · Bergmann *m*, Berg(bau)arbeiter, Bergwerkarbeiter, Grubenarbeiter

mine worker's dwelling, mine workman's dwelling, miner's dwelling (Brit.), mine worker's dwelling unit, miner's dwelling unit, mine workman's dwelling unit (US) · Bergmannswohnung *f*, Berg(bau)arbeiterwohnung, Bergwerkarbeiterwohnung, Grubenarbeiterwohnung

mine workers' hous(ebuild)ing, mine workmens' hous(ebuild)ing, miners' hous(ebuild)ing · Bergarbeiterwohn(ungs)bau *m*, Bergmannswohn(ungs)bau, Bergwerkarbeiterwohn(ungs)bau, Grubenarbeiterwohn(ungs)bau, Bergbauarbeiterwohn(ungs)bau

mine workers' law, mine workmen's law, miners' law · Berg(bau)arbeiterrecht, Bergmannsrecht, Grubenarbeiterrecht, Bergwerkarbeiterrecht *n*

mine workers' settlement, mine workmen's settlement, miners' settlement · Bergmannssied(e)lung *f*, Berg(werk)arbeitersied(e)lung, Bergbauarbeitersied(e)lung, Grubenarbeitersied(e)lung

mine workers' village, mine workmen's village, miners' village, mining village · Berg(bau)arbeiterdorf *n*, Grubenarbeiterdorf, Bergbaudorf, Bergmannsdorf, Bergwerkarbeiterdorf

minidistrict · Kleinbezirk *m*

minima determination, determination of minima · Minimafestsetzung, Minimafeststellung, Minimabestimmung *f*

minimal protection · Minimalschutz *m*

minimization · Minimierung *f*

to minimize · minimieren

minimum amount · Mindestbetrag *m*

minimum (bank-)balance · Mindestguthaben *n*

minimum capital · Mindestkapital *n*

minimum Chi square method · Chi-Quadrat-Mindest-Verfahren *n*

minimum compensation against damage, minimum indemnity against damage, minimum indemnification against damage, minimum damages · Mindestentschädigung *f*, Mindestschadenersatz *m*

minimum hire rate, minimum rate of wage, minimum rate of hire, minimum wage rate · Mindestlohnsatz *m*, Mindestarbeitslohnsatz

minimum hourly rate · Mindeststundensatz *m*

minimum insurance sum · Mindestversicherungssumme *f*

minimum lending rate, MLR · Mindestausleihsatz *m*

minimum limit · Mindestgrenze *f*

minimum living floor space, minimum total area of habitable rooms · Mindestwohnfläche *f*

minimum occupancy rate, minimum rate of occupancy · Mindestbelegungszahl *f*

minimum of subsistence, poverty line, subsistence level · Existenzminimum *n*

minimum period · Mindestfrist *f*

minimum property standard, MPS [*Any overall minimum technical standard of housebuilding*] · (bauliche) Wohnungsmindestnorm *f*

minimum rate · Mindestsatz *m*

minimum-rate clause · Mindestsatzklausel *f*

minimum rate of hire, minimum wage rate, minimum hire rate, minimum rate of wage · Mindestlohnsatz *m*, Mindestarbeitslohnsatz

minimum rate of occupancy, minimum occupancy rate · Mindestbelegungszahl *f*

minimum rate of wage, minimum rate of hire, minimum wage rate, minimum hire rate · Mindestlohnsatz *m*, Mindestarbeitslohnsatz

minimum requirement · Mindestausstattung *f* [*einer Fläche*]

minimum (residential) rent · Kostenmiete *f* [*Beim preisgebundenen Wohnraum, vor allem bei Sozialwohnungen und Wohnungen der gemeinnützigen Wohnungsunternehmen ist die Miete gesetzlich begrenzt. Sie deckt nur die Unkosten die für Kapitaldienst und Bewirtschaftung eines Objektes entstehen*]

minimum size · Mindestgröße *f*

minimum-size constraint · Mindestgrößenzwang *m*

minimum standard of occupancy [*Legal or socially accepted standard applied to the condition of housing units*] · Wohnmindestnorm *f*

minimum subscription · Mindestzeichnung *f*

minimum sum — minister of labour

minimum sum · Mindestsumme f

minimum tariff · Minimaltarif m, Minimumtarif

minimum (technical) standard · Mindestnorm f, technische Mindestnorm

minimum value · Mindestwert m

minimum wage · Mindestlohn m

minimum wage lawmaking, minimum wage legislation · Mindestlohngesetzgebung f

minimum wage rate, minimum hire rate, minimum rate of wage, minimum rate of hire · Mindestlohnsatz m, Mindestarbeitslohnsatz

mining · unterirdischer Abbau m [*Mineralien*]

mining act, mining law, mining statute, mineral(s workings) act, mineral(s workings) law, mineral(s workings) statute · (Mineral(ien))Abbaugesetz n, (Mineral(ien))Ausbeutungsgesetz, (Mineral(ien))Gewinnungsgesetz, Berg(bau)gesetz

mining activity, mining operation · Bergbautätigkeit f

mining-and-agricultural village · (Berg)Arbeiter-Bauern-Gemeinde f

mining authority · Berg(bau)behörde f

mining board · Bergamt n

mining city, mining town · Bergbaustadt f, Bergarbeiterstadt, Grubenarbeiterstadt

(mining) claim, (mining) location · Mutung f

mining code · Bergbauordnung f

mining community [*obsolete*]; mining commune · Bergbaugemeinde f, Bergbaukommune f

mining company · bergrechtliche Gewerkschaft f

mining damage, damage due to mining · Bergschaden m

mining district · Bergbaubezirk m

mining field, mining sector · Berg(bau)sektor m

mining geology · Bergbaugeologie f

mining land(s) · Bergbauland n

mining landscape · Bergbaulandschaft f

mining law, mineral law, law of taking minerals, law of mining minerals, law of exploiting minerals · (Mineral(ien))Abbaurecht n, (Mineral(ien)-)Ausbeutungsrecht, (Mineral(ien))Gewinnungsrecht, (objektives) Berg(bau)recht

mining law → mining act

(mining) location, (mining) claim · Mutung f

mining operation, mining activity · Bergbautätigkeit f

mining plot, mining parcel · Bergwerkgrundstück n

mining policy · Bergbaupolitik f

mining population · Bergbaubevölkerung f

mining practice · Berg(bau)wesen n

mining prohibition · Abbauverbot n, Gewinnungsverbot, Ausbeutungsverbot, Bergbauverbot [*Verbot des Abbauens von Mineralien in einem Landschaftsschutzgebiet*]

mining region · Bergbauregion f

mining register, mining registry, register of mines, registry of mines, mines' register, mines' registry · Berg(werk)grundbuch n

mining rent · Bergwerkrente f

mining sector, mining field · Berg(bau)sektor m

mining settlement · Bergbau(an)sied(e)lung f

mining statute → mining act

mining subsidence · Bergsenkung f

mining the forest, forest mining · Waldraubbau m, Waldraubwirtschaft f

mining tithe · Bergbauzehnt m

mining town, mining city · Bergbaustadt f, Bergarbeiterstadt, Grubenarbeiterstadt

mining village, mine workers' village, mine workmen's village, miners' village · Berg(bau)arbeiterdorf n, Grubenarbeiterdorf, Bergbaudorf, Bergmannsdorf, Bergwerkarbeiterdorf

mining year, year of mining · Nutzungsjahr n [*Abbau einer Lagerstätte*]

mini sports field · Kleinstsportplatz m

minister (Brit.); secretary (US) · Minister m

ministerial circular (letter) · ministerielles Rundschreiben n, Ministerrundschreiben

ministerial trust, instrumental trust [*A trust which demands no further exercise of reason or understanding than every intelligent agent must necessarily employ; as to convey an estate*] · verwaltungslose Treuhand f

minister of agriculture · Landwirtschaftsminister m

minister of hous(ebuild)ing · Wohn(ungs)bauminister m

minister of labour · Arbeitsminister m

ministry; department [*USA*] · Ministerium *n*

ministry of building and public works · Bauministerium *n*, Ministerium für öffentliche (Bau)Arbeiten

ministry of health · Gesundheitsministerium *n*

ministry of hous(ebuild)ing (Brit.); department of hous(ebuild)ing (US) · Wohn(ungs)bauministerium *n*

ministry of hous(ebuild)ing and local government · Ministerium *n* für Wohn(ungs)bau und Kommunalangelegenheiten

ministry of housing and urban development · Ministerium *n* für Wohnungs- und Städtebau

ministry of justice (Brit.); state department of justice (US) · Justizministerium *n*

ministry of labour (Brit.); department of labor (US) · Arbeitsministerium *n*

ministry of labour exchange area (Brit.) · Arbeitsamtsbezirk *m*

ministry of reconstruction (Brit.); department of reconstruction (US) · Aufbauministerium *n*, Wiederaufbauministerium *n*

ministry of the interior · Innenministerium

mini supermarket · Kleinsupermarkt *m*

minor, infant · minderjährig

minor, infant · minderjährige Person *f*

minor → (male) minor

minor acting as (a) guardian, infant acting as (a) guardian · minderjähriger Vormund *m*

minor acting as an agent, infant acting as an agent · minderjähriger Vertreter *m*

minor canon · niederer Kanoniker *m*

minor clause · Bagatellklausel *f*

minor (construction) site, minor building site, minor job site · Kleinbaustelle *f*

minor debtor, infant obligor, minor obligor, infant debtor · minderjähriger Schuldner *m*

minor interests · untergeordnete Interessen *fpl*

minority · Minderheit *f*

minority → (age of (legal)) minority

minority group · Minderheitsgruppe *f*

minority group law · Minderheitsrecht *n*, objektives Minderheitenrecht

minority group right · Minderheitenrecht *n*, subjektives Minderheitenrecht

minor obligor, infant debtor, minor debtor, infant obligor · minderjähriger Schuldner *m*

minor of a determinant · Unterdeterminante *f*

minor order · Kleinauftrag *m*

minor renter, infant renter · minderjähriger Mieter *m*

minor upholding · kleine Instandhaltung *f*

minor widow, infant widow · minderjährige Witwe *f*

minor widower, infant widower · minderjähriger Witwer *m*

minor witness, infant witness · minderjähriger Zeuge *m*

minor worker, infant worker · minderjähriger Arbeiter *m*

mint [*The place where money is coined*] · Münzerei *f*

mintcharge, brassage [*A charge made by a mint for the minting of coins*] · Prägegebühr *f*

mint price, mint rate, mint value, commercial value · Münzwert *m*

mint rate, mint value, commercial value, mint price · Münzwert *m*

mint ratio [*The ratio between the value of the two metals where a bi-metallic currency system is in operation*] · Verhältnis *n* zwischen dem Nennwert von Gold- und Silbermünzen

mint value, commercial value, mint price, mint rate · Münzwert *m*

minutes · Protokoll *n*, Niederschrift *f*

minutes of acceptance (of (the) work(s)), acceptance minutes · Abnahmeniederschrift *f*, Abnahmeprotokoll *n*, Bauabnahmeniederschrift, Bauabnahmeprotokoll

minutes of delivery, minutes of handover, minutes of handing over · Übergabeniederschrift *f*, Übergabeprotokoll *n*

minutes of evidence · Beweisprotokoll *n*, Beweisniederschrift *f*

minutes of negotiation(s) · Verhandlungsniederschrift *f*, Verhandlungsprotokoll *n*

mirror reversed · seitenverkehrt [*Luftbildauswertung*]

misallocation · Fehlzuweisung *f*

misapprehension · Mißverständnis *n*

misappropriation · rechtswidrige Aneignung *f*

misbehaviour (Brit.); misbehavior (US); misconduct · fehlerhaftes Verhalten *n*, Fehlverhalten

Misc., Miscellaneous · Sammlung *f* erstinstanzlicher Entscheidungen der New Yorker Gerichte

miscarriage · schadenersatzpflichtige rechtswidrige Handlung f

miscegenation, mixture of races, mixed racial composition · Rassenmischung f

Miscellaneous, Misc. · Sammlung f erstinstanzlicher Entscheidungen der New Yorker Gerichte

mischief [*This word is often used as referring to the object or purpose of a statute, as where it is said that the office of the judge is to make such construction as will suppress the mischief and advance the remedy, and to suppress all evasions for the continuation of the mischief*] · Mißstand m

mischief, wrong-doing; maleficium [*Latin*] · Übeltat f

mischievous damage done to growing crops · Feldfrevel m, Flurschaden m

miscognizant, ignorant of, unacquainted with · nichtwissend, unwissend

misconduct; misbehaviour (Brit.); misbehavior (US) · fehlerhaftes Verhalten n, Fehlverhalten

misconstruction, misinterpretation · Fehlauslegung f, Fehldeutung, Falschauslegung, Falschdeutung

to misdate, to date wrongly · falsch datieren, unrichtig datieren

misdeed → misfeasance · Unrecht n

misdelivery, failure to make delivery, nondelivery · Nichtlieferung f

misdemeano(u)r · Vergehen n

misdemeano(u)r committed in public office · Amtsvergehen n, Vergehen im Amt

to misdescribe, to describe wrongly · falsch beschreiben, unrichtig beschreiben

misdescription · Fehlbeschreibung f

to misdirect · fehlleiten

misdirection · Falschbelehrung f der Geschworenen durch den Richter, falsche Rechtsbelehrung der Geschworenen durch den Richter, unrichtige Rechtsbelehrung der Geschworenen durch den Richter

misdirection · Fehlleitung f

misfeasance, misdeed, active misconduct [*The doing of an act which is unlawful*] · schuldhaftes Tun n, Unrecht n, gesetz(es)widrige Handlung f, rechtswidrige Handlung, widerrechtliche Handlung

misinformation · Fehlinformation f, Falschinformation

misinterpretation, misconstruction · Fehlauslegung f, Fehldeutung, Falschauslegung, Falschdeutung

mislaid, lost · unauffindbar, verlegt

mislaid thing · verlegte Sache f

misleading · irreführend

misnaming · Fehlbenennen n

misnomer, mistake in name · Fehlbenennung f

misplaced improvement [*Improvement to land that does not conform to its best utilization*] · Fehlerschließung f

misrecital, false representation, false recital, misrepresentation · Falschdarstellung f, Falscherklärung

misrecital of fact(s), false representation of fact(s), false recital of fact(s), misrepresentation of fact(s) · Tatsachenfalschdarstellung f, Tatsachenfalscherklärung, Sachverhaltfalscherklärung, Sachverhaltfalschdarstellung, Falschdarstellung der Tatsachen, Falscherklärung der Tatsachen, Falschdarstellung des Sachverhalts, Falscherklärung des Sachverhalts

to misrepresent, to represent falsely · falsch darstellen, falsch erklären

misrepresentation, misrecital, false representation, false recital · Falschdarstellung f, Falscherklärung

misrepresentation act, misrepresentation law, misrepresentation statute · Gesetz n über Falscherklärungen, Gesetz über Falschdarstellungen

misrepresentation of fact(s), misrecital of fact(s), false representation of fact(s), false recital of fact(s) · Tatsachenfalschdarstellung f, Tatsachenfalscherklärung, Sachverhaltfalscherklärung, Sachverhaltfalschdarstellung, Falschdarstellung der Tatsachen, Falscherklärung der Tatsachen, Falschdarstellung des Sachverhalts, Falscherklärung des Sachverhalts

misrepresenter, false representer · Falschdarsteller m, Falscherklärer, Falschinformant

missae presbyter [*Latin*]; priest in orders · Ordenspriester m

missing person, disappeared person · Verschollene m

missing persons' service, disappeared persons' service · Suchdienst m

misstaicus [*Latin*]; messenger [*One who carries an errand*] · Bote m

to misstate, to state falsely · falsch aussagen, falsch angeben

misstatement, false statement · Falschaussage f, Falschangabe f

mistake · Irrtum m [*„Mistake" bedeutet in weitgehendem Maße „Dissens", aber „Irrtum" hat sich in der deutschen Literatur eingebürgert*]

mistake as to identity, identity mistake · Identitätsirrtum *m*

mistake as to the nature of the subject matter · Beweggrundirrtum *m*, Irrtum im Beweggrund

mistake in description, descriptive mistake · Beschreibungsirrtum *m*

mistake in law; error iuris [*Latin*]; mistake of law · Rechtsirrtum *m*

mistake in name, misnomer · Fehlbenennung *f*

mistake in statical analysis · Berechnungsirrtum *m* [*Statik*]

mistake liability, liability for mistake(s) · Irrtumshaftung *f*, Irrtumshaftpflicht *f*, Irrtumshaftbarkeit *f*

mistaken(ly), false(ly), erroneous(ly), wrong · irrig(erweise), rechtsirrtümlich, irrtümlich(erweise), falsch

mistake of (ad)measurement, (ad)measurement mistake · Aufmaßirrtum *m*

mistake of fact, fact mistake · Tatsachenirrtum *m*

mistake of intent(ion), intent(ion) mistake · Willensirrtum *m* [*Der Irrtum einer Partei über den Willen der anderen Partei*]

mistake of intrinsic fact, material mistake · wesentlicher Irrtum *m*

mistake of judg(e)ment, judg(e)ment mistake · Urteilsirrtum *m*

mistake of judg(e)ment, judg(e)ment mistake · Beurteilungsirrtum *m*

mistake of law, mistake in law, error iuris · Rechtsirrtum *m*

mistake of measurement → mistake of (ad)measurement

mistakes (and omissions) excepted · Irrtum vorbehalten

misuser [*In law, abuse of some privilege, liberty, benefit, etc.*] · Mißbrauch *m*, Überschreitung *f*

misuser of an office · Amtsüberschreitung *f*, Amtsmißbrauch *m*

misuser of contract, abuse of contract · Vertragsmißbrauch *m*, Vertragsüberschreitung *f*

misuser of discretion, abuse of discretion · Ermessensmißbrauch *m*, Ermessensüberschreitung *f*

misuser of process, abuse of process · Mißbrauch *m* der prozessualen Formen, Überschreitung *f* der prozessualen Formen, prozessualer Formenmißbrauch, prozessuale Formenüberschreitung [*Um einen Vorteil über einen Gegner zu erlangen*]

misuser of right(s) → abuse of right(s)

to mitigate [*To abate loss or damage*] · abschwächen, mildern

mitigation [*Abatement of loss or damage*] · Abschwächung *f*, Milderung *f*

mittimus [*It was a precept or command in writing directed to the gaoler or keeper of some prison for the receiving and safe keeping of an offender charged with any crime, until he should be delivered by due course of law*] · Haftbefehl *m*

mittimus book, warrant book · Buch *n* der Haftbefehle

to mix → to (inter)mix

mixed → (inter)mixed

mixed action → mixed (court) action

mixed administration · Mischverwaltung *f*, gemischte Verwaltung

mixed bond, selective bond, three-way fund, balanced bond, umbrella fund, managed fund · gemischter Versicherungsfonds *m*

mixed bond certificate, umbrella fund certificate, balanced bond certificate, three-way fund certificate, managed fund certificate · gemischtes Versicherungsfondszertifikat *n*

mixed building land (area), (building) land for mixed development, (building) (land) area for mixed development · gemischte (Bau)Fläche, *f*, gemischter (Bau)-Boden *m*, gemischtes (Bau)Land *n*, Misch(bau)boden, Misch(bau)fläche, Misch(bau)land, M

mixed business and residential premises, mixed residential and business premises · Wohn(ungs)-Geschäftsanwesen *n*, Geschäfts-Wohn(ungs)anwesen

mixed case · Mischfall *m*

mixed claims · kombinierte Klageansprüche *mpl*

mixed condition [*It depends at the same time on the will of one of the parties and on the will of a third person, or on the will of one of the parties and also on a casual event*] · Mischbedingung *f*, gemischte Bedingung

mixed (court) action, mixed cause, mixed (law)suit, mixed plea; actio mixta, actio mista [*Latin*] [*An action partaking of the nature of real and personal actions, by which some property is demanded and also damages for a wrong sustained*] · gemischte Klage *f*, Mischklage

mixed cultivation · Mischanbau *m*, Mischkultur *f*

mixed-data-problem · Problem *n* der Verwendung metrischer und nicht-metrischer Attribute

mixed development region · Mischregion *f*, gemischte Region

mixed development zone · Mischzone f, gemischte Zone

mixed duty · Mischzoll m

mixed economy · kombinierte Plan- und Privatwirtschaft f

mixed enterprise → multi(ple)-purpose enterprise

mixed estate, mixed property [*A compound of realty and personalty*] · Mischvermögen n, Mischgut n, Mischhabe f, gemischtes Vermögen, gemischtes Gut, gemischte Habe

mixed farming; mixte farming [*Canada*] · Ackerbau m und Viehzucht f

mixed fields → (inter)mixed fields

mixed-fields system → open-fields system

mixed function · Mischfunktion f

mixed gardening · Mischgartenbau m

mixed hexagonal hierarchies of central places · gemischtes System n, Mischsystem [*Zur Entwick(e)lung eines allgemeinen probabilistischen Modells für Energieflüsse im Raum und räumliche Strukturen*]

mixed (incorporated collecting) charity · rechtsfähiges Sammelvermögen n [*Die Erträge des gesammelten Vermögens und laufendes gesammeltes Vermögen bzw. dessen Erträge werden ausgeschüttet*]

mixed (law)suit, mixed plea; actio mixta, actio mista [*Latin*]; mixed (court) action, mixed cause [*An action partaking of the nature of real and personal actions, by which some property is demanded and also damages for a wrong sustained*] · gemischte Klage f, Mischklage

mixed occupancy · Mischbelegung f, gemischte Belegung

mixed ownership · einheitliches Eigentum n [*Vermengung; Vermischung*]

mixed package deal [*The warranty by the contractor also extends to the employer's work, subject to safeguards enabling the contractor to object at the time to the design or suitability for the employer's work*] · (Bau)Planung f und (Bau)Ausführung aus gemeinsamer Hand, (Bau)Projektierung und (Bau)Ausführung aus gemeinsamer Hand

mixed plea; actio mixta, actio mista [*Latin*]; mixed (court) action, mixed cause, mixed (law)suit [*An action partaking of the nature of real and personal actions, by which some property is demanded and also damages for a wrong sustained*] · gemischte Klage f, Mischklage

mixed property, mixed estate [*A compound of realty and personalty*] · Mischvermögen n, Mischgut n, Mischhabe f, gemischtes Vermögen, gemischtes Gut, gemischte Habe

mixed question of law and fact · gemischte Frage f, Rechts- und Tatsachenfrage, Tatsachen- und Rechtsfrage

mixed questions of fact and law · vermischte Tat- und Rechtsfragen fpl

mixed racial composition, miscegenation, mixture of races · Rassenmischung f

mixed residential and business premises, mixed business and residential premises · Wohn(ungs)-Geschäftsanwesen n, Geschäfts-Wohn(ungs)anwesen

mixed (residential and industrial) land(s) use · gemischte Bodennutzung f, gemischte Flächennutzung, gemischte Landnutzung

mixed scanning · Wechselspiel n von kurzfristigen und langfristigen Überlegungen, konzeptorientierter Inkrementalismus m [*Planung*]

mixed suit → mixed (law)suit

mixed tenancy · Wohn(ungs)-Geschäfts-Mietverhältnis n, Geschäfts-Wohn(ungs)-Mietverhältnis

mixed tithe [*In English law. That species of tithes which consists of natural products, but natured and preserved in part by the care of man; as of wool, milk, etc.*] · gemischter Zehnt m, Mischzehnt

mixed traffic [*All forms of vehicular traffic*] · Mischverkehr m, gemischter Verkehr

mixed-use building, multi(ple)-use building · Mischgebäude n, gemischt genutztes Gebäude

mixed-use (land) parcel, mixed-use (land) plot, multi(ple)-use (land) parcel, multi(ple)-use (land) plot, mixed-use parcel of land, multi(ple)-use parcel of land, mixed-use plot of land, multi(ple)-use plot of land · gemischt genutztes Grundstück n, gemischt genutzter Grund m

mixed-use space, multi(ple)-use space, multi(ple)-functional space · gemischt genutzter Raum m [*Raum in einem Gebäude, der teils zu Wohnzwecken und teils zu anderen Zwecken genutzt wird*]

mixte farming [*Canada*]; mixed farming · Ackerbau m und Viehzucht f

mix(ture) of functions · Funktionsmischung f

mix(ture) sub-variance · Einzelmaterialmischungsabweichung f, Rezepturabweichung

MLR, minimum lending rate · Mindestausleihsatz m

mob, populace · Pöbel *m*

mobbing, unlawful assembly [*Combination against peace and good order for an illegal purpose of an assemblage of people*] · Zusammenrottung *f*

mobile · lagerlöslich

mobile · beweglich, mobil, wanderungsfähig

mobile home, caravan, housing-type trailer, (travel) trailer · Wohnwagen *m*, Wagenheim *n*

mobile home court → (housing-type) trailer development

mobile home development → (housing-type) trailer development

mobile population [*People enumerated in a place different from place of birth*] · zugewanderte Bevölkerung *f*

mobile population · mobile Bevölkerung *f*

mobile raw material · lagerlöslicher Rohstoff *m*

mobile shop [*A motor van arranged as a shop which customers can enter*] · Wanderladen *m*

mobility · Beweglichkeit *f*, Mobilität *f*

mobility · (räumliche) Mobilität *f*, (räumliche) Beweglichkeit [*Verkehr von Menschen zwischen verschiedenen Orten*]

mobility characteristic, characteristic of mobility · Beweglichkeitsmerkmal *n*, Mobilitätsmerkmal

mobility of land(s), land(s) mobility [*The ability to shift the uses of land by means of irrigation or other capital investment*] · Bodennutzungsfähigkeit *f*, Landnutzungsfähigkeit, Flächennutzungsfähigkeit

mobility radius, radius of mobility · Beweglichkeitshalbmesser *m*, Mobilitätshalbmesser

mob rule, populace rule, ochlocracy · Pöbelherrschaft *f*

mock auction · Scheinauktion *f*

mock bidder, mock tenderer, by-bidder, by-tenderer [*One employed by the seller or his agent to bid on property with no purpose to become a purchaser, so that bidding thereon may be stimulated in others who are bidding in good faith*] · Scheinbieter *m*

modal bequest, modal legacy · Auflagenvermächtnis *n*, Auflagenfahrnisvermächtnis, Auflagen(fahrnis)legat *n*

modal choice · Verkehrsmittelwahl *f*

modal choice model · Verkehrsmittelwahlmodell *n*

modal split · Verkehrsaufteilung *f*, Verhältnis *n* vom Individualverkehr zu öffentlichem Verkehr

mode · Maximumstelle *f*, dichtester Wert *m* [*Statistik*]

mode, custom, usage, habit [*Uniform course of dealing in a particular trade*] · Brauch *m*, Üblichkeit *f*, Gepflogenheit *f*, Gewohnheit

mode · Besetzung *f* [*Hauptverhandlung*]

mode · dichtester Wert *m*, häufigster Wert, Maximumstelle *f* [*Der innerhalb einer bestimmten Vielheit von Werten am häufigsten vorkommende Wert*]

mode cons, amenities, modern conveniences · Wohnkomfort *m*

model, overall concept · Leitbild *n*

model building code, model construction code · Musterbauordnung *f*, MBO

model by(e)-law, model statute, model ordinance · Mustersatzung *f*, Musterstatut *n*

model city, model town · Modellstadt *f*

model clause · Formularklausel *f*, Musterklausel

model community · Modellgemeinde *f*, Modellkommune *f*

model condition · Formularbedingung *f*, Musterbedingung

model construction code, model building code · Musterbauordnung *f*, MBO

model contract · Formularvertrag *m*, Mustervertrag

model contract condition · Mustervertragsbedingung *f*, Formularvertragsbedingung

model landlord/tenant contract, model lease · Mustermietvertrag *m*, Formularmietvertrag [*Wohnungen; Geschäftsräume*]

model lease, model landlord/tenant contract · Mustermietvertrag *m*, Formularmietvertrag [*Wohnungen; Geschäftsräume*]

model neighbourhood (Brit.); model neighborhood (US) · Modellnachbarschaft *f*

model of binary choice, binary choice model · Modell *n* der dualen Entscheidung, Verkehrsmodell der dualen Entscheidung, duales Entscheidungs(verkehrs)modell

model of economic growth, growth (allocation) model · Wachstumsmodell *n*, wirtschaftliches Wachstumsmodell

model ordinance, model by(e)-law, model statute · Mustersatzung *f*, Musterstatut *n*

model planting, planting of (a) model · Aufstellen *n* eines Modells

model program (US); model scheme, model programme · Modellprogramm *n*

model project · Modellvorhaben *n*

model statute, model ordinance, model by(e)-law · Mustersatzung *f*, Musterstatut *n*

model tenancy contract · Formularmietvertrag *m*, Formularwohnungsmietvertrag, Muster(wohnungs)mietvertrag

model text, model wording · Formulartext *m*, Mustertext

model town, model city · Modellstadt *f*

model validity, model validation · Modellgültigkeit *f*

model wording, model text · Formulartext *m*, Mustertext

model zoning ordinance · Musterbaunutzungsverordnung *f*, Musterverordnung über die bauliche Nutzung, Muster-BauNVO, Muster-BNutzVO

mode of (ab)alienation, mode of disposal, (ab)alienation mode, disposal mode · Veräußerungsweise *f*

mode of being, condition, nature, state, position · Beschaffenheit *f*

mode of disposal, (ab)alienation mode, disposal mode, mode of (ab)alienation · Veräußerungsweise *f*

mode of performance, manner of performing the duty · Erfüllungsart *f*

moderate income · mäßiges Einkommen *n*

moderate-income family, moderate-earnings family · Familie *f* mit mäßigem Einkommen

modern conveniences, mode cons, amenities · Wohnkomfort *m*

modernization act, modernization law, (physical) improvement statute, (physical) improvement act, (physical) improvement law, rehabilitation statute, rehabilitation act, rehabilitation law, modernization statute · (bauliches) Verbesserungsgesetz *n*, (Wohnungs)- Modernisierungsgesetz, WoModG

modernization guide line, rehabilitation guide line, upgrading guide-line, (physical) improvement guide line · (bauliche) Verbesserungsrichtlinie *f*, Modernisierungsrichtlinie

modernization loan, upgrading loan, rehabilitation loan, (physical) improvement loan · (bauliche) Verbesserungsanleihe *f*, Modernisierungsanleihe

modernization order, upgrading order, order to improve, order to modernize, order to rehabilitate, (physical) improvement order, rehabilitation order · Modernisierungsverfügung *f*, Modernisierungsanordnung, Modernisierungsgebot *n*, Modernisierungsbefehl *m*, (baulicher) Verbesserungsbefehl

modernization ordinance, upgrading ordinance, rehabilitation ordinance, (physical) improvement ordinance · Modernisierungsverordnung *f*, (bauliche) Verbesserungsverordnung

modernization plan, rehabilitation plan, upgrading plan, (physical) improvement plan · Modernisierungsplan *m*, (baulicher) Verbesserungsplan

modernization work(s), rehabilitation work(s), upgrading work(s), (physical) improvement work(s) · (bauliche) Verbesserungsarbeit(en) *f (pl)*, Modernisierungsarbeit(en)

modernization zone, upgrading zone, (physical) improvement zone, rehabilitation zone · Modernisierungsschwerpunkt *m*, (baulicher) Verbesserungsschwerpunkt [*früher: Modernisierungszone f*]

modern ruval settlement · ländliche Mittelpunktgemeinde *f*

modifiable unit · Grundeinheit *f* mit veränderbarer Größe

modified absorption costing, modified full costing · Voll(kosten)rechnung *f* mit fixen und proportionalen Kosten

modified full costing, modified absorption costing · Voll(kosten)rechnung *f* mit fixen und proportionalen Kosten

to modify, to alter slightly, to change slightly, to vary slightly · geringfügig (ab)ändern, geringfügig umändern, geringfügig verändern

modus (decimandi) [*Latin*] [*In English ecclesiastic(al) law. A particular manner of tithing growing out of custom, different from the general law of taking tithes in kind*] · Zehnt(en)ablösung *f*

molitura, multura [*Latin*]; grinding toll, suit and grist, grinding fee, fee for grinding, toll paid for grinding, multure · Mahlgeld *n*, Mahlzins *m*, Mahlgebühr *f*

mom(ma)-and-pop(pa) store (US); old neighbourhood store (Brit.); old neighborhood store (US) · Tante-Emma-Laden *m*

monastery land(s), monastic land(s) · Klosterland *n*, Klosterboden *m*, Klosterländerei(en) *f (pl)*

monastery possession, monastic possession · Klosterbesitz *m*

monastery settlement, monastic settlement · Klostersied(e)lung *f*

monastery tithe, monastic tithe · Klosterzehnt *m*

monastic farm, monastery farm · Klostergut *n*

monastic (general) property → monastic ownership (of property)

monastic land(s), monastery land(s) · Klosterland *n*, Klosterboden *m*, Klosterländerei(en) *f (pl)*

monastic ownership (of property), monastic (general) property, monastic proprietorship · Klostereigentum *n*

monastic possession, monastery possession · Klosterbesitz *m*

monastic settlement, monastery settlement · Klostersied(e)lung *f*

monastic society · Klostergemeinschaft *f*

monastic tithe, monastery tithe · Klosterzehnt *m*

monetary act, monetary statute, monetary law · Währungsgesetz *n*

monetary authority · Währungsbehörde *f*

monetary compensation, compensation in cash · Geldabfindung *f*

monetary consideration, consideration in money, money consideration · Gegenleistung *f* in Geld, geldliche Gegenleistung

monetary control instruments · kreditpolitisches Instrumentarium *n*

monetary fine proceeding · Bußgeldverfahren *n*

monetary loss, pecuniary loss · Geldverlust *m*

monetary policy · Geldpolitik *f*

monetary reform, currency reform · Währungsreform *f*

mone(tar)y rent · Geldrente *f*

monetary stability · Geldwertstabilität *f*

monetary statute, monetary law, monetary act · Währungsgesetz *n*

monetary union [*An arrangement between a number of countries to maintain an agreed exchange rate between their currencies*] · Zahlungsunion *f*

monetary unit · Geldeinheit *f*, Währungseinheit

monetary value · Geldwert *m*

money advance(ment), cash advance(ment), advance(ment) (of money) · Vorschuß *m*

money amount, amount of money · Geldbetrag *m*

money at call and short notice, call money, demand money · tägliches Geld *n*, Tagesgeld, sofort abrufbares Geld

money-back annuity, annuity bond, annuity certificate, annuity contract, annuity agreement, guaranteed bond · Renten(versicherungsspar)brief *m*, Renten(versicherungsspar)schein *m*

money bargain · Bargeschäft *n*

money bill · Gesetz(es)vorlage *f* zur Bewilligung von Geld an eine Regierung

money bond · Geldgarantie *f*

money-borrower, borrower (of money) · Kreditnehmer *m*, Geld(auf)nehmer

money changer · Geldwechsler *m*

money charged on land · (Geld)Schuld *f* auf Land

money claim, claim to money, demand to money, money demand, pecuniary demand, pecuniary claim · Geldforderung *f*, Geldverlangen *n*

money compensation, money indemnification, indemnification (paid) in money, damages (paid) in money, compensation (paid) in money, indemnity (paid) in money, money indemnity, payment of damages, money damages, pecuniary damages, pecuniary compensation, pecuniary indemnification · Entschädigung *f* in Geld, Schadenersatz *m* in Geld, Geldentschädigung, Geld(schaden)ersatz, Schadenersatzzahlung, Entschädigungszahlung

money consideration, monetary consideration, consideration in money · Gegenleistung *f* in Geld, geldliche Gegenleistung

money cost(s) · Geld(beschaffungs)kosten *f*

money debt, debt (of money) [*A sum of money due by certain and express agreement*] · (Geld)Schuld *f*

money deficiency → shortage of money

money demand, pecuniary demand, pecuniary claim, money claim, claim to money, demand to money · Geldforderung *f*, Geldverlangen *n*

money devaluation → devaluation (of money)

money economy · Geldwirtschaft *f*

money(ed) capital, liquid capital [*Capital in the form of money as distinct from real capital*] · Geldkapital *n*, freies Kapital

moneyed corporation · (Kapital)Gesellschaft *f* mit quotenmäßigem Grundkapital als Bank- oder Finanzinstitut

moneyed interest · Finanzwelt *f*

money gift · Geldschenkung

money had and received · empfangenes Geld *n*

money held in trust for a ward, pupil money, ward money, ward trust money · Mündelgeld *n*

moneylender, loaner, (loan) lender, lender of money · Geld(ver)leiher *m*, Geldgeber, Darleh(en)sgeber, Kreditgeber

moneyless economy · geldlose Wirtschaft *f*

(money-)loosing operation · Verlustgeschäft *n*

money market, capital market · Geldmarkt *m*, Kapitalmarkt, Markt für kurzfristige Kredite

**money of account, ** account money · Rechengeld *n*, Schuldwährung *f*

**money of acknowledg(e)ment, ** acknowledg(e)ment fee, fee of acknowledg(e)ment, acknowledg(e)ment money [*A sum of money paid by copyhold tenants, in some parts of England, on the death of their landlords, as an acknowledg(e)ment of their new lords*] · Anerkennungsgeld *n*, Rekognitionsgeld, Anerkennungsgebühr *f*, Rekognitionsgebühr

money of payment · Zahlungswährung *f*

**money order, ** post office order, postal order · Postanweisung *f*

**money paid into a co-operative society as shares, ** money paid into a co-operative association as shares · Geschäftsguthaben *n* [*Betrag, den die Kapitalkonti bei einer Genossenschaft jeweilig aufweisen*]

money payment · Geldleistung *f*, Geldzahlung

money power · Finanzgewalt *f*

money receipts · Gelderlös *m*

**money rent, ** pecuniary rent · Geldmiete *f*, Geld(miet)zins *m*

money scarcity → shortage of money

money shortage → shortage of money

money squeeze → shortage of money

money stringency → shortage of money

money supply increase rate · Geldzuwachsrate *f*

money's worth · geldwerte Leistung *f*

money transaction · Geldgeschäft *n*

money wage · Geldlohn *m*

**monitory teacher, ** pupil teacher · Schüler *m* als Anfangslehrer [*Ein älterer Schüler als Lehrer der jüngeren*]

monocentric · monozentrisch

monofunctional · monofunktional

monometallic system of currency · Einzelwährungssystem *n*

monometallism · Einzelwährung *f*

mononuclear [*Deriving identity from a single centre*] · einkernig

monopolistic company · Monopolgesellschaft *f*

monopolistic competition · Monopolwettbewerb *m*

**monopolistic enterprise, ** monopolistic undertaking · Monopolunternehmen *n*, Monopolunternehmung *f*, Monopolbetrieb *m*

to monopolize; to engross [*obsolete*] · monopolisieren

monopoly revenue · Monopolrente *f*

monopoly value · Monopolwert *m*

monorail (system) · Einschienenbahn *f*

**monthly claim, ** monthly demand · monatliche Forderung *f*, monatliches Verlangen *n*

**monthly demand, ** monthly claim · monatliche Forderung *f*, monatliches Verlangen *n*

monthly income certificate · monatlicher Rentenschein *m* [*kapitalistische Bausparkasse*]

monthly payment · monatliche Zahlung *f*, Monatszahlung

monthly rent [*Payment received monthly for the use of property*] · Monatsmiete *f*, Monats(miet)zins *m*

monument [*Fixed object such as a stone or concrete marker, used to establish real estate boundaries*] · Grund(stücks)grenzzeichen *n*

**monument, ** landmark · festes Seezeichen *n*, Landmarke *f*

monument [*Anything connected to the earth and which commemorates a person, action, period or event*] · Denkmal *n*

monument board · Denkmalamt *n*

moor game · Moorwild *n*

**moot, ** adversary, contested, undecided, contentious, unsettled, controversial [*Litigated between adverse parties*] · streitig, strittig

to moot · erörtern, disputieren

**moot case, ** moot point · strittiger Fall *m*, streitiger Fall, Streitfall

**moot-hill, ** parl(ing)e hill, hill of meeting [*In old records. A hill where courts were anciently held*] · Gerichtshügel *m*

**moot-house, ** moot-hall, city-hall, town-hall · Stadthaus *n*, Rathaus

mooting · Disputierübung *f*, Erörtern *n*, Erörterung [*Rechtsfrage*]

mooting date · Erörterungstermin *m* [*Eine Gemeinde hat Eigentümer, Mieter, Pächter und Erwerbstätige vor der Ausübung von Grunderwerbsrechten zu einem Erörterungstermin zu laden*]

moral blameworthiness · moralischer Unwert *m*

moral duty · moralische Pflicht *f*

moral insanity · moralisches Irresein *n*

moral(ity) · Sittlichkeit *f*, Moral *f*

moral law · moralisches Recht *n*

moral obligation — mortgage corporate bond

moral obligation · moralische Verpflichtung f

moral person; persona moralis [*Latin*] [*This word simply means a nonphysical person — a person such as exists in the world of men's thoughts (and particularly in the world of their legal thought), but not in the world of physical nature. No ethical connotation is involved, but it is the danger of the term that an ethical connotation may be imported. Rousseau's theory, that the general will of the moral person of the community is always right, does not escape this danger*] · moralische Person f (der Naturrechtslehre)

moral suasion · Seelenmassage f

moral tutor · persönlicher Tutor m

moratorium · Moratorium n, Indult m, Anstandsbrief m [*Eine obrigkeitlich angeordnete Stundung fälliger Schulden*]

more-than-average, above-average · überdurchschnittlich

more than the law requires; extra jus [*Latin*]; beyond the law · übergesetzlich

morganatic marriage · morganatische Ehe f

mors civilis [*Latin*]; civil death [*That change of a person's civil condition which is produced by certain acts or offences on his part; and which extinguishes his civil rights and capacities, just as natural death extinguishes his bodily existence*] · bürgerlicher Tod m

mortality · Sterbefall m

mortality · Sterblichkeit f

mortality table · Sterblichkeitstabelle f, Sterblichkeitstafel f

to mortgage, to hypothecate · hypothekisieren

to mortgage · verpfänden, Sicherung geben, Sicherheit geben

to mortgage (Brit.); to hypothecate (US); to complete · bestellen, hypothekieren, hypothekarisch belasten

mortgage [*in France*] → mortuum radium

mortgage, dead pledge [*A thing put into the hands of a creditor*] · totes Pfand n

mortgage · Pfandverschreibung f

mortgage [*A pledge of land(s) of which the mortgage did not necessarily receive the possession or have the rents and profits in reduction of the demand. In the time of Glanville this form of security was looked upon with much disfavour as a species of usury*]; vadium mortuum, mortuum vadium; mort gage [*in France*] · Lebendsatzung f, Zinssatzung, ewige Satzung, Ewigsatzung [*Immobiliarpfandrecht. Die Nutzung diente als Zins der Forderung*]

mortgage against loss, deficiency mortgage · Ausfallsicherungshypothek f

mortgage allotment, mortgage apportionment · Hypothekenzuteilung f

mortgage apportionment, mortgage allotment · Hypothekenzuteilung f

mortgage as security · Hypothek(en)sicherung f

mortgage-backed · hypothekengesichert, hypothekengetragen, hypothekenunterstützt, hypothekengestützt

mortgage bank, Hypothekenbank f

mortgage bank (US) → building society

mortgage bank act, mortgage bank law, mortgage bank statute · Hypothekenbankgesetz n

mortgage based on entry in the land charges register · Buchhypothek f

mortgage-bond, mortgage-debenture, letter of hypothecation · Grundpfandbrief m, Bodenpfandbrief, Hypothekenpfandbrief, hypothekarisch gesicherter Pfandbrief, Obligation f mit hypothekarischer Sicherheit, hypothekarisch gesicherte Schuldverschreibung

mortgage bond act, mortgage bond law, mortgage bond statute · Pfandbriefgesetz n

mortgage business · Hypothekengeschäft n

mortgage by conditional sale · Hypothek f die in dem Verkauf unter der auflösenden Bedingung des Rückerwerbs oder dem Wiederkaufsrecht des Eigentümers besteht

to mortgage by giving possession · belasten mit Grundpfand, belasten mit Faustpfand, belasten mit Besitzpfand

mortgage by sub-lease, mortgage by underlease, mortgage by under-tenancy, mortgage by sub-tenancy · Hypothek f durch Unterpacht, Hypothek durch Afterpacht, Hypothek durch Afterbestand, Unterpachthypothek, Afterpachthypothek, Afterbestandhypothek

mortgage capital · Hypothekenkapital n

mortgage certificate · Hypothek(en)anteilschein m

mortgage code · Hypothekenordnung f

mortgage coefficient · Hypothekenkoeffizient m

mortgage company → mortgage (lending) company

mortgage corporate bond [*USA*]; mortgage debenture [*Great Britain*] · hypothekarisch gesicherte Schuldverschreibung f, hypothekarisch gesicherte Obligation f [*private Kapitalgesellschaft*]

mortgage creditor in possession — mortgage on land(ed property) 676

mortgage creditor in possession, mortgagee in possession [*A mortgagee of real property who is in possession of it with the agreement or absent of the mortgagor, express or implied, and in recognition of his mortgage and because of it, and under such circumstances as to make the satisfaction of his lien an equitable prerequisite to his being dispossessed*] · Hypothek(en)gläubiger *m* mit Pfandbesitz, Besitzpfandnehmer, Hypothekargläubiger mit Pfandbesitz, hypothekarischer Gläubiger mit Pfandbesitz, Pfandgläubiger im Besitz des Grundstücks, Grundpfandgläubiger

mortgage debenture [*Great Britain*]; mortgage corporate bond [*USA*] · hypothekarisch gesicherte Schuldverschreibung *f*, hypothekarisch gesicherte Obligation *f* [*private Kapitalgesellschaft*]

mortgage debt · Hypothekenschuld *f*, Hypothekarschuld, hypothekarische Schuld

mortgage debtor, pawner, pledger, mortgager, mortgagor · Pfandschuldner *m*

mortgage debtor, mortgager, mortgagor · Hypothekenschuldner *m*, hypothekarischer Schuldner, Hypothekarschuldner

mortgage deed (Brit.); mortgage note (US) · Hypothekenbrief *m*, (Hypotheken)Bestellungsurkunde *f*

mortgaged indebtedness · Hypothekenverschuldung *f*

mortgagee, pledge holder, pawnee, holder of a pawn, pawn holder, pledgee, holder of a pledge [*The person who receives the security and lends the money to the pledgor*] · Pfandgläubiger *m*, Pfandnehmer, Pfandbesitzer, Pfandhalter, Pfandinhaber, Sicherungsnehmer

(mort)gagee having the right to use the article pledged, pledgee having the right to use the article pledged, pawnee having the right to use the article pledged · nutzungsberechtigter Pfandgläubiger *m*, nutzungsberechtigter Pfandnehmer

mortgagee in possession, mortgage creditor in possession [*A mortgagee of real property who is in possession of it with the agreement or absent of the mortgagor, express or implied, and in recognition of his mortgage and because of it, and under such circumstances as to make the satisfaction of his lien an equitable prerequisite to his being dispossessed*] · Hypothek(en)gläubiger *m* mit Pfandbesitz, Besitzpfandnehmer, Hypothekargläubiger mit Pfandbesitz, hypothekarischer Gläubiger mit Pfandbesitz, Pfandgläubiger im Besitz des Grundstücks, Grundpfandgläubiger

mortgage financing · Hypothekenfinanzierung *f*

mortgage for recovery of damages · Regreßhypothek *f* [*Sie dient zur Deckung eines Ersatzanspruches*]

mortgage for unpaid part of purchase-money · Restkaufgeldhypothek *f* [*Der Käufer des Grundstückes läßt für den nicht bar gezahlten Teil der Kaufsumme eine Hypothek eintragen*]

mortgage fund · Hypothekenfonds *m*, Hypothekenmittel *f*

mortgage guarantee insurance · Hypothek(en)-Bonitätsversicherung *f*

mortgage guaranteeing company, mortgage insurance company, company for guaranteering mortgages · Hypothekenversicherungsgesellschaft *f*

mortgage indebtedness · Hypothekenverschuldung *f*

mortgage in possession; pignus [*Latin*] · Besitzpfand *n*, Faustpfand, Grundpfand [*Der Eigentümer übergibt die Sache dem Gläubiger*]

mortgage insurance · verbürgter Pfandbrief *m*

mortgage insurance company, company for guaranteering mortgages, mortgage guaranteing company · Hypothekenversicherungsgesellschaft *f*

mortgage interest · Hypothekenzins *m*

mortgage interest rate · Hypothekenzinssatz *m*

mortgage investor · Hypothekenanleger *m*

mortgage law · Hypothekenrecht *n*

mortgage lender · Hypothekengeber *m*, Hypothekenverleiher

mortgage (lending) company · Hypothekengesellschaft *f*

mortgage (lending) institution · Hypothekenanstalt *f*

mortgage liability · Hypothekenhaftung *f*, Hypothekenhaftpflicht *f*, Hypothekenhaftbarkeit *f*

mortgage market · Hypothekenmarkt *m*

mortgage money · Hypothekengeld *n*

mortgage note (US); mortgage deed (Brit.) · Hypothekenbrief *m*, (Hypotheken)Bestellungsurkunde *f*

mortgage on land(ed property), (real) estate mortgage, (real) property mortgage, realty mortgage [*A conveyance of the title to land(s) to secure the performance of some act(ion) or obligation, with a clause stating that in case the act(ion) or obligation is performed as agreed, the conveyance shall be of no effect*] · Grund(stücks)hypothek *f*, Landhypothek, Bodenhypothek, Realhypothek, Liegenschaftshypothek, Immobilienhypothek, Immobiliarhypothek

mortgage on yield, yield mortgage [*Not on real estate*] · Revenü(en)hypothek *f*, Revenu(en)hypothek [*Nur die Grundstückserträge haften*]

mortgage payment · Hypothekenzahlung *f*

mortgage pay-office · Hypothekenkasse *f*

(mortgage) percentage · Auszahlungskurs *m* [*Hypothek*]

mortgage processing charge · Hypothekenbearbeitungsgebühr *f*

mortgage purchase · Hypothekenkauf *m*

mortgager, pledg(e)or, pledger, pledging party, mortgagor · Verpfänder *m*, Pfandgeber

mortgage rate · Hypothekensatz *m*

mortgage receivable, receivable mortgage · Hypothekenforderung *f*

mortgage redemption · Hypothekentilgung *f*, Hypothekenablösung

mortgage redemption insurance · Bausparer-Lebensversicherung *f*, Rückzahlungslebensversicherung bei Grundstücksverpfändung

mortgage registry, mortgage register, register of mortgages, registry of mortgages · Hypothekenregister *n*, Hypothekenbuch *n*

mortgage relief · Hypothekenbefreiung *f*

mortgager, mortgagor, mortgage debtor, pawner, pledger · Pfandschuldner *m*

mortgager, mortgagor, mortgage debtor · Hypothekenschuldner *m*, hypothekarischer Schuldner, Hypothekarschuldner

mortgage repayable in a lump sum · Kündigungshypothek *f*

mortgage secured by a document, documentary mortgage, bonded mortgage, indenture of mortgage · Briefhypothek *f* [*Neben einer Eintragung der Hypothek in das Grundbuch besteht auch eine Brieferteilung an den Gläubiger*]

mortgage share · Hypothek(en)anteil *m*

mortgage sold at a loss · Damnohypothek *f* [*Vorweggenommener Zins wird als ,,Damnum" alsbald am dargeliehenen Betrag gekürzt oder später bei Verlängerung vom Schuldner bar gezahlt*]

mortgage speculation · Hypothekenspekulation *f*

mortgage speculator · Hypothekenspekulant *m*

mortgage tax, tax on mortgages · Hypothekensteuer *f*

mortgage term · Hypothekenlaufzeit *f*

mortgage transferred by endorsement, mortgage transferred by indorsement, mortgage transferred by backing · Inhaberhypothek *f*, Orderhypothek

mortgagor, mortgager, pledg(e)or, pledger, pledging party · Verpfänder *m*, Pfandgeber

mortification [*Scots law*]; dead hand; mortmain [*French*]; manus mortua [*Latin*] [*A condition of property in which it is held without the power of change or (ab)alienation*] · tote Hand *f*

mortmain [*French*]; manus mortua [*Latin*]; mortification [*Scots law*]; dead hand [*A condition of property in which it is held without the power of change or (ab)alienation*] · tote Hand *f*

mortuarium [*Latin*]; soul-scot [*So called in the laws of King Canute*]; mortuary, corsepresent · Vermächtnis *n* an eine Kirche

mortuum vadium, vadium mortium; mort gage [*in France*]; mortgage [*A pledge of land(s) of which the mortgage did not necessarily receive the possession or have the rents and profits in reduction of the demand. In the time of Glanville this form of security was looked upon with much disfavour as a species of usury*] · Lebensatzung *f*, Zinssatzung, ewige Satzung, Ewigsatzung [*Immobiliarpfandrecht. Die Nutzung diente als Zins der Forderung*]

most acceptable offer, most acceptable bid, most acceptable tender; most acceptable (bid) proposal (US) · annehmbarstes Angebot *n*

most-efficient estimator · höchstwirksame Schätzfunktion *f* [*Statistik*]

most-favored principle (US); most-favoured principle (Brit) · Meistbegünstigungsgrundsatz *m*, Meistbegünstigungsprinzip *n*

most-favoured(-nation) clause (Brit.); most-favored(-nation) clause (US) · Meistbegünstigungsklausel *f*

most powerful critical region · trennschärfster kritischer Bereich *m* [*Statistik*]

most significant relation(ship) · Schwerpunktanknüpfung *f*

most-significant-relation(ship) test; centre-of-gravity-approach (Brit.); center-of-gravity-approach (US) · Schwerpunkt-Anknüpfungsregel *f* [*Bestimmung des maßgeblichen Rechts durch Feststellung des Schwerpunktes im Wege einer objektiven, individualisierenden Methode*]

motel, motor court · Kfz-Hotel *n*, Motel

mother country, motherland · Mutterland *n*

motio [*Latin*]; motion · Antrag *m* bei Gericht

motion · mündlicher Zwischenantrag *m* [*Über ihn wird in öffentlicher Sitzung verhandelt*]

motion ex parte — mov(e)able property

motion ex parte · schriftlicher Zwischenantrag *m* über den ohne Parteienvorladung verhandelt wird

motion ex parte, ex parte motion · einseitiger Antrag *m* an ein Gericht

motion for a repleader · Gesuch *n* um Plädoyerwiederholung

motion for judg(e)ment, judg(e)ment motion · Antrag *m* auf Fällung eines Urteils, Gesuch *n* auf Fällung eines Urteils, Antrag *m* auf sofortiges Urteil, Gesuch *n* auf sofortiges Urteil, Urteilsfällungsantrag *m*, Urteilsfällungsgesuch *n*

motion for judg(e)ment non obstante veredicto · Gesuch *n* daß ungeachtet des Geschworenenspruches das Urteil zugunsten der beim Beweisverfahren unterlegenen Partei gefällt werden möge

motion for summary judg(e)ment · Antrag *m* auf Urteil (nach Aktenlage) ohne strittige Verhandlung

motion in arrest of judg(e)ment, writ of error; breve de errore [*Latin*] [*In criminal cases the accused may at any time between conviction and sentence move an arrest of judg(e)ment — that is to say, move that judg(e)ment be not pronounced — because of some defect in the indictment which is more than a mere formal defect and which has not been amended or used by verdict*] · Formfehlergesuch *n*, Gesuch daß ein Urteil nicht auf einen Geschworenenspruch gegründet wird

motion of appeal, appeal motion · Berufungsantrag *m*, Appellationsantrag

motion practice · Manövrieren *n* der Parteien [*Anträge an das Gericht zur Vorbereitung der Hauptverhandlung. Im deutschen Prozeßrecht unbekannt*]

motion to correct award · Antrag *m* auf Schiedsspruchberichtigung

motion to dismiss · (Klage)Abweisungsantrag *f*

motion to modify award · Antrag *m* auf Schiedsspruch(ab)änderung

motion to reverse (a judg(e)ment), request to reverse (a judg(e)ment), application to reverse (a judg(e)ment), application to set aside (a judg(e)ment, motion to set aside (a judg(e)ment), request to set aside (a judg(e)ment) · Aussetzungsantrag *m*, Aussetzungsgesuch *n* [*Urteil*]

motion to set aside the service of the writ, plea to the jursidiction · Verteidigung *f* auf Unzuständigkeit

motion to vacate award · Antrag *m* auf Schiedsspruchaufhebung

motion to vary the minutes · Antrag *m* auf Abänderung der Abfassung des Urteils

motorable · kfz-befahrbar

motor age town, motor age city · autogerechte Stadt *f*

motor court, motel · Kfz-Hotel *n*, Motel

motor cycle density · Krafträderdichte *f*, Motorräderdichte

motor dealer · Autohändler *m*

motoring atlas · Autoatlas *m*

motoring map · Autokarte *f*

motoring map series · Autokartenwerk *n*

motorist · Kraftfahrer *m*

to motorize · motorisieren

motor pool · Kraftwagenpark *m*

motor traffic, automobile traffic · Autoverkehr *m*

motor vehicle code · Kraftfahrzeugordnung *f*

motor vehicle inventory · Kraftfahrzeugbestand *m*, Kfz-Bestand

motor vehicle law, automobile law · Kfz.-Recht *n*, Kraftfahrzeugrecht

motorway toll (Brit.); turnpike toll (US) · Autobahngebühr *f*

to mould into a legal form, to mould into a statutory form (Brit.); to mold into a legal form, to mold into a statutory form (US) · gesetzlich gestalten

mountain barrier · Gebirgsschranke *f*

mountain health resort · Luftkurort *m*

mountain lake · Gebirgssee *m*

mountain pass · Gebirgspaß *m*

mountain rescue organization · Bergwacht *f*

mountain shifting cultivation tribe, mountain tribe utilizing shifting cultivation · Berghackbauvolk *n*

movant, moving party, moveat [*An applicant for an order by way of motion before a court*] · Antragsteller *m* an ein Gericht, Gesuchsteller an ein Gericht

to move, to migrate · wandern

mov(e)able · beweglich [*Gegenstand*]

mov(e)able → mov(e)able thing

mov(e)able estate → personal estate

mov(e)able possession → personal estate

mov(e)able properties, (goods and) chattels, chattels personal · bewegliche Güter *npl*, Mobilien *fpl*, Mobiliar *n*, bewegliche Sachen *fpl*, bewegliche Gegenstände *mpl*

mov(e)able property → personal estate

mov(e)able(s) → personal estate

mov(e)able structure · fliegendes Bauwerk n, Zeitbauwerk [Ein nur zu einem vorübergehenden Zweck mit dem Boden verbundenes Bauwerk, z. B. Hilfsbahnhof, Schaubude, Zelt]

mov(e)able thing(s) → personal estate

moveat, movant, moving party [An applicant for an order by way of motion before a court] · Antragsteller m an ein Gericht, Gesuchsteller an ein Gericht

move chance · Zugzufall m

move from the country to the town · Zuzug m vom Lande

move from the town to the country, move from the city to the country · Zuzug m von der Stadt

movement, flight, exodus, drift · Flucht f, Wegziehen n

movement → (migration) movement

movement certificate · Warenverkehrsbescheinigung f

movement current → (migration) movement current

movement flow → (migration) movement current

movement of population from country to town, rural-to-urban movement, rural-urban drift, rural-urban migration, rural exodus, flight from the land · Land-Stadt-Wanderung f, Landflucht f

movement of population from town to country, urban-rural migration, urban-rural drift, urban-to-rural movement, urban exodus, flight from the town · Stadtflucht f, Stadtexodus m, Stadt-Land-Wanderung f

movements in legal thought · Rechtsverkehr m

movement stream → (migration) movement current

movement to the suburbs (Brit.); flight to the suburbs, drift to the suburbs, exodus to the suburbs · Vorortflucht f, Vorortexodus m, Flucht in die Vororte, Exodus in die Vororte

movement to the umland, flight to the umland, exodus to the umland, drift to the umland · Umlandflucht f, Umlandexodus m, Flucht ins Umland, Exodus ins Umland

move out · Auszug m aus einer Wohnung

mover, migrant · Wandernde m, Wanderer

to move up, to rise · steigen [Kosten]

moving · Umziehen n, Umzug m

moving, migrating · Wandern n

moving annual total, moving yearly total · gleitende Jahressumme f [Statistik]

moving average, moving mean · gleitender Durchschnitt m

moving-average method · Methode f der gleitenden Mittel, Verfahren n der gleitenden Mittel [Statistik]

moving company · Umzugsunternehmen n, Möbelspeditionsfirma f

moving day · Umzugstag m

moving mean, moving average · gleitender Durchschnitt m

moving party, moveat, movant [An applicant for an order by way of motion before a court] · Antragsteller m an ein Gericht, Gesuchsteller m an ein Gericht

MP, maximum likelihood, maximum probability · Höchstwahrscheinlichkeit f, Maximalwahrscheinlichkeit

MPS, minimum property standard [Any overall minimum technical standard of housebuilding] · (bauliche) Wohnungsmindestnorm f

m-r bill (of quantities), method-related bill (of quantities) · verfahrensbezogenes Leistungsverzeichnis n, verfahrensbezogenes L.V.

"muddling through" · ,,Durchwursteln'' n, ,,Herumbasteln''

multi-axis street village → multi(ple)-axis street village

multi-car pileup · Autoschlange f, (Auto)Stau m

multicentre framework (Brit.); multicenter framework (US) · mehrkerniges Ortssystem n, mehrkerniges System von Orten, vielkerniges Ortssystem, vielkerniges System von Orten, Mehrkernsystem, Vielkernsystem

multi-cities plan, multi-towns plan · Plan m für die Entwick(e)lung städtischer Zentren innerhalb einer Stadtregion [Mehr, aber kleinere städtische Zentren als beim multiple centers plan]

multi-commodity space system · Mehrgüter-Raumsystem n

multidimensional grouping · Distanzgruppierung f [Raumordnung]

multi-employer pension plan · Gemeinschaftspensionsplan m

multi-family hous(ebuild)ing · Mehrfamilienhausbau m, Mehrfamilienhäuserbau, Mehrwohnungshausbau, Mehrwohnungshäuserbau

multifamily mortgage · Mehrfamilienhypothek f

multifarious; multifarius [Latin] [In equity pleading. Composed of a variety of distinct and independent matters] · mannigfaltig, vielfaltig

multifunctional · multifunktional, mehrfunktional, vielfunktional

multi-legged holding → multi(ple)-legged holding

multilinear convergence hypothesis, evolutionary sequence hypothesis · Hypothese *f* der weltweiten standardisierten Stadtentwick(e)lung [*Durch zunehmende Teilhabe an gleichartigen Technologien und Märkten tritt in der Stadtentwick(e)lung weltweit eine Standardisierung und damit Annäherung ein*]

multilinear convergence process, evolutionary sequence process · weltweit gleichartiger Stadtentwick(e)lungsvorgang *m*

multinational enterprise, multinational undertaking · multinationales Unternehmen *n*, multinationale Unternehmung *f*

multipartite · mehrteilig, vielteilig

multi-part street village → multi(ple)-part street village

multi(ple)-arbitrator board · Mehrfachbesetzung *f* [*Schiedsgericht*]

multi(ple)-axis street village · mehrachsiges Straßendorf *n*, vielachsiges Straßendorf

multi(ple)-centered pattern, multi(ple)-centered scheme (US); arrangement by multiple nuclei · Mehrkernschema *n*, Vielkernschema, Mehrkernmuster *n*, Vielkernmuster

multiple centers plan, satellite cities greenbelt plan, core-satellite regional plan · Plan *m* der neben der zentral in der Stadtregion gelegenen Kernstadt die Herausbildung mehrerer Großstädte zwischen 500 000 und 1 Mio. Einwohnern innerhalb derselben im Abstand von etwa 50 km oder mehr vom Zentrum der Kernstadt anstrebt

multi(ple)-factor analysis · Faktorenanalyse *f*, Faktorenuntersuchung *f*

multi(ple)-factor uniform region · homogene Region *f* mehrdimensionaler Definition

multi(ple)-functional space, mixed-use space, multi(ple)-use space · gemischt genutzter Raum *m* [*Raum in einem Gebäude, der teils zu Wohnzwecken und teils zu anderen Zwecken genutzt wird*]

multi(ple)-legged holding · Entscheidung *f* die auf mehreren Gründen oder Rechtsregeln aufbaut, Entscheid *m* der auf mehreren Gründen oder Rechtsregeln aufbaut

multi(ple)-level street · Vielebenen(stadt)straße, Stadtstraße *f* mit mehreren Ebenen, Mehrebenen(stadt)straße

multi(ple)-market stability · Stabilität *f* auf mehreren Märkten

multi(ple)-nuclei region · Mehrkernregion *f*, Vielkernregion, Mehr-Kerne-Region, Viel-Kerne-Region

multi(ple)-nuclei theory · Mehr-Kerne-Theorie *f*, Viel-Kerne-Theorie, Mehrkerntheorie, Vielkerntheorie

multiple occupation · Mehrfachbelegung *f*, Vielfachbelegung [*Haus*]

multi(ple)-part street village · mehrteiliges Straßendorf *n*, vielteiliges Straßendorf

multi(ple)-period total supply function, multi(ple)-period aggregate supply function · mehrperiodische Gesamtangebotsfunktion *f*, vielperiodische Gesamtangebotsfunktion

multi(ple)-purpose enterprise, mixed enterprise, mixed undertaking, multi(ple)-purpose undertaking · gemischter Betrieb *m*, gemischtes Unternehmen *n*, gemischte Unternehmung, Mischbetrieb, Mischunternehmen, Mischunternehmung *f*

multi(ple)-purpose hall · Vielzweckhalle *f*, Mehrzweckhalle

multi(ple)-purpose local administration union · Mehrzweckverband *m*

multi(ple)-purpose planning · Planung *f* von Projekten mit mehreren Entwick(e)lungszielen

multi(ple)-purpose project · Mehrzweckprojekt *n*, Vielzweckprojekt

multi(ple)-purpose trip, multi(ple)-purpose travel, multi(ple)-purpose journey · Vielzweckfahrt *f*, Mehrzweckfahrt

multi(ple)-region economy, interregional economy · multiregionale Wirtschaft *f*

multi(ple)-region model, interregional model · multiregionales Modell *n*, mehrregionales Modell, vielregionales Modell

multiple regression · Mehrfachregression *f*, Vielfachregression [*Statistik*]

multi(ple)-room dwelling, multi(ple)-room tenement, multi(ple)-room residence, multiroomed dwelling, multiroomed tenement, multiroomed residence · Mehrraumwohnung *f*, Vielraumwohnung, Mehrzimmerwohnung, Vielzimmerwohnung, mehrräumige Wohnung, vielräumige Wohnung

multi(ple)-row village · Mehrreihendorf *n*, Vielreihendorf

multiple sale · Doppelverkauf *m* [*Fehlbenennung*]; Mehrfachverkauf [*Der Eigentümer eines Grundstücks kann dasselbe an mehrere Käufer gleichzeitig verkaufen. Außerdem vermag er das Grundstück einem Käufer zu übergeben, während ein anderer Käufer als Eigentümer desselben Grundstücks im Grundbuch eingetragen wird*]

multiple shops, chain stores · Kettenläden *m pl*

multi(ple)-stage interview · Mehrstufenbefragung *f*, Vielstufenbefragung

multi(ple)-street village · Mehrstraßendorf *n*, Vielstraßendorf

multi(ple)-use building → mixed-use building

multi(ple)-use (land) parcel, multi(ple)-use (land) plot, mixed-use parcel of land, multi(ple)-use parcel of land, mixed-use plot of land, multi(ple)-use plot of land, mixed-use (land) parcel, mixed-use (land) plot · gemischt genutztes Grundstück *n*, gemischt genutzter Grund *m*

multi(ple)-use space, multi(ple)-functional space, mixed-use space · gemischt genutzter Raum *m* [*Raum in einem Gebäude, der teils zu Wohnzwecken und teils zu anderen Zwecken genutzt wird*]

multiplicity · Mannigfaltigkeit *f*, Vielfalt *f*, Vielfältigkeit

multiplier · Multiplikator *m*, Vervielfältiger *m*

multiplier effect · Mantelfaktor *m* [*für das produzierende Gewerbe*]

multi-roomed dwelling, multiroomed tenement, multiroomed residence, multi(ple)-room dwelling, multi(ple)-room tenement, multi(ple)-room residence · Mehrraumwohnung *f*, Vielraumwohnung, Mehrzimmerwohnung, Vielzimmerwohnung, mehrräumige Wohnung, vielräumige Wohnung

multi-row village → multi(ple)-row village

multi-street village → multi(ple)-street village

multi-towns plan, multi-cities plan · Plan *m* für die Entwick(e)lung städtischer Zentren innerhalb einer Stadtregion [*Mehr, aber kleinere städtische Zentren als beim multiple centers plan*]

multivariate · mehrdimensional, vieldimensional [*Statistik*]

multivariate normal distribution · mehrdimensionale Normalverteilung *f*, vieldimensionale Normalverteilung [*Statistik*]

multure; molitura, multura [*Latin*]; grinding toll, suit and grist, grinding fee, fee for grinding, toll paid for grinding · Mahlgeld *n*, Mahlsus *m*, Mahlgebühr *f*

municipal, intrastate [*Of or relating to the internal affairs as distinguished from the foreign relations of a nation*] · innerstaatlich

municipal area · Weichbild *n*

municipal bank → municipal (savings) bank

municipal bond [*USA*]; corporation stock, local authority stock [*Great Britain*] · Kommunalschuldverschreibung *f*, Kommunalobligation *f*

(municipal) borough, non-county borough, quarter session (municipal) borough [*Created 1835 in England by the Municipal Corporations Act*] · Munizipalstadt *f*, grafschaftsfreie Stadt, Stadt im rechtlichen Sinne, Stadt mit korporativer Verfassung, selbständige Stadt [*Gegensatz: Reichsstadt. „(Municipal) borough" ist der offizielle Name einer Stadt in England; in Schottland „burgh". „Town" gehört der Umgangssprache an. „City" ist in England ein auszeichnender Titel, den altberühmte Städte, meistens Bischofssitze, tragen. In der Verwaltung besteht zwischen „city" und „borough" kein Unterschied*]

(municipal) borough (civil) court [*It means an inferior court of record for the trial of civil actions which by charter, custom or otherwise, is, or ought to be, holden in a borough, but does not include a county court*] · Munizipalstadtgericht *n*

(municipal) borough council, municipality [*The mayor, aldermen and councillors of a (municipal) borough*] · Munizipalstadtrat *m*

(municipal) borough election · Munizipalstadtwahl *f*

(municipal) borough fund · Munizipalstadtkasse *f*

(municipal) borough police · Munizipalstadtpolizei *f*

(municipal) borough rate · Munizipalstadtsteuer *f*

(municipal) borough surveyor · Munizipalstadtbaumeister *m*

municipal by(e)-law, municipal statute, municipal ordinance · Munizipalstadtsatzung *f*, Munizipalstadtstatut *n*

municipal by(e)-law → (local) by(e)-law

municipal charter (US); council system · Gemeindeverfassung *f*, (Gemeinde)Hauptsatzung, Ortsverfassung, Ortshauptsatzung, Kommunalverfassung, Kommunalhauptsatzung

municipal code · Munizipalstädteordnung *f*

municipal community [*obsolete*]; municipal commune · Munizipalgemeinde *f*, Munizipalkommune *f*

municipal consolidation, merger of incorporated places · Verschmelzung *f* inkorporierter Gemeinden

municipal corporation [*A body of persons (mayor, aldermen, councillors, and burgesses) in a town or city having the powers of acting as one person, of holding and transmitting property, and of*

municipal corporation — murenger

regulating the government of such town or city. Such corporations existed, for instance, in the chief towns of England (as of other countries from very early times), deriving their authority from incorporating charters granted by the Crown] · Selbstregierungskorporation *f*, Munizipalkörperschaft *f*, Munizipalkorporation, Selbstregierungskörperschaft, echte kommunale Gebietskörperschaft

municipal corporation [*The body corporate constituted by the incorporation of the inhabitants of a borough*] · Einwohnerstadtgemeinde *f*

Municipal Corporations Act · Munizipalkörperschaftsgesetz *n*, Munizipalkorporationsgesetz, Munizipalstädteordnungsgesetz, Selbstregierungsgesetz [*in England. 1835, 1882 und 1883*]

municipal council · Munizipalrat *m*

municipal enterprise, urban enterprise [*An enterprise which is essentially a business organization, but is owned by a city government. Utilities such as electric companies are often this type of enterprise*] · städtisches Unternehmen *n*, städtischer Betrieb *m*

municipal exchequer · Munizipalstadtkämmerei *f*

(municipal) executive board, municipality council, municipal government [*The body of officers taken collectively, belonging to a community, who are appointed to manage its affairs and defend its interests*] · Magistrat *m*

municipality, (municipal) borough council [*The mayor, aldermen and councillors of a (municipal) borough*] · Munizipalstadtrat *m*

municipality [*A city or town chartered to govern itself*] · Gemeinde *f* mit Verfassung

municipality council, municipal government, (municipal) executive board [*The body of officers taken collectively, belonging to a community, who are appointed to manage its affairs and defend its interests*] · Magistrat *m*

municipalization, suburbanization, incorporation, annexation, communalization · Einbezirkung *f*, Vereinigung, Eingemeindung, Fusion(ierung) *f*, Verschmelzung, Ausbezirkung, Umbezirkung, Einverleibung, Inkorporation *f*, Inkommunalisation *f*, Inkommunalisierung, Angemeindung, Ausgemeindung, Umgemeindung [*Der rechtliche Vorgang einer organischen Verbindung mehrerer Gemeinden oder Gemeindeteile*]

municipalization contract, incorporation contract, suburbanization contract, annexation contract, communalization contract · Angemeindungsvertrag *m*, Eingemeindungsvertrag, Einbezirkungsvertrag, Vereinigungsvertrag, Verschmelzungsvertrag, Fusion(ierung)svertrag, Ausbezirkungsvertrag, Umbezirkungsvertrag, Einverleibungsvertrag, Inkorporationsvertrag, Inkommunalisationsvertrag, Inkommunalisierungsvertrag, Ausgemeindungsvertrag, Umgemeindungsvertrag

to municipalize, to communalize, to incorporate, to annex · eingemeinden, einbezirken, vereinigen, verschmelzen, ausbezirken, umbezirken, inkorporieren, angemeinden

municipal law, state law, law of the country, national law [*The law of a particular country as distinguished from international law*] · Nationalrecht *n*, Staatsrecht, Landesrecht

municipal ordinance, municipal by(e)-law, municipal statute · Munizipalstadtsatzung *f*, Munizipalstadtstatut *n*

municipal ordinance → (local) by(e)-law

municipal ordinances and rules and regulations, home rule · Selbstverwaltungsrecht *n*

municipal (savings) bank · städtische Sparkasse *f*, Stadtsparkasse

municipal socialism · Munizipalsozialismus *m*

municipal statute, municipal ordinance, municipal by(e)-law · Munizipalstadtsatzung *f*, Munizipalstadtstatut *n*

municipal statute → (local) by(e)-law

(municipal) trading enterprise, (municipal) trading undertaking · Gemeindebetrieb *m*, Kommunalbetrieb, werbender Betrieb, gemeindlicher Betrieb, kommunaler Betrieb, werbendes Unternehmen *n*, Kommunalunternehmen, Gemeindeunternehmen, Kommunalunternehmung, Gemeindeunternehmung, werbende Unternehmung, gemeindliches Unternehmen, gemeindliche Unternehmung [*Wasser-, Gas- und Elektrizitätswerk und Straßenbahn einer Stadt*]

municipal treasury, city treasury, town treasury · Stadtkasse *f*

muniment (of title) [*The evidence or writing whereby somebody is enabled to defend the title of his estate*] · urkundlicher (Rechts)Titelbeleg *m*

muot-scara · Idealteilung, Nutzungsteilung, Mutschierung *f* [*Erbengemeinschaft*]

murage; muragium [*Latin*] [*A toll formerly levied in England for building and repairing public walls*] · Mauerzoll *m*, Mauergeld *n*

murenger [*In England, formerly one in charge of building and repairing public walls*] · Mauerbaumeister *m*

murorum opertio [Latin]; wall-work [The service of work and labour done by inhabitants and adjoining tenants, in building or repairing the walls of a town or castle] · Mauerbaudienst m

mushrooming · unkontrolliertes Stadtwachstum n, wildes Stadtwachstum

music hall · Tonhalle f

mutatio nominis [Latin]; change of name · Namenswechsel m

Mutiny Act · Militärverwaltungsgesetz n [England]

mutual, co-operative · genossenschaftlich, kooperativ

mutual, interchangeable, reciprocal, common to both parties · gegenseitig, wechselseitig

mutual agreement, accord, amicable composition (of differences), (amicable) arrangement, mutuality, (pacific) settlement, accommodation · Einigung f, Willenseinigung, gütliche Regelung, Einvernehmen n, gütliche Einigung, Vergleich m, Konsensus m, Übereinstimmung, Einverständnis n

mutual agreement, dependant agreement, conditional agreement, dependent agreement, reciprocal agreement · gegenseitiges Abkommen n, gegenseitige Abmachung f, gegenseitige Vereinbarung

mutual aid, mutual help · gegenseitige Selbsthilfe f, Gemeinschafts(selbst)hilfe, Gruppen(selbst)hilfe

mutual building and loan association, cooperative building and loan association (US); mutual building society, cooperative building society (Brit.) · genossenschaftliche Bausparkasse f, Genossenschaftsbausparkasse

mutual building society, cooperative building society (Brit.), mutual building and loan association, cooperative building and loan association (US) · genossenschaftliche Bausparkasse f, Genossenschaftsbausparkasse

mutual conditions, reciprocal conditions, common conditions, concurrent conditions · gegenseitige Bedingungen fpl, Zug-um-Zug-Bedingungen [Bedingungen, daß die Parteien die Leistungen Zug um Zug erfüllen]

mutual contract, common contract, reciprocal contract · gegenseitiger Vertrag m [Ein beide Teile verpflichtender Vertrag, bei dem wenigstens einige der beiderseitigen Leistungspflichten dadurch miteinander verbunden sind, daß die Leistungen des einen nach dem Willen beider Parteien die Gegenleistung, das Entgelt, für die des anderen darstellt]

mutual credits, reciprocal credits, common credits [In bankruptcy law. Credits which must, from their nature, terminate in debts; as where a debt is due from one party, and credit given by him on the other for a sum of money payable at a future day, and which will then become a debt; or where there is a debt on one side; and a delivery of property with directions to turn it into money on the other] · gegenseitige Guthaben npl, gegenseitige Gutschriften fpl,

mutual debt, reciprocal debt, common debt · Gegenschuld f

mutual geese pasture, common geese pasture · Gänseanger m, Gänseweide f

mutual help, mutual aid · gegenseitige Selbsthilfe f, Gemeinschafts(selbst)hilfe, Gruppen(selbst)hilfe

mutual (housing) cooperative (US) · Wohnungs(bau)genossenschaft f [Sie übernimmt Häuser, die von der Bundesregierung der USA als Kriegsbauten oder der Regierung von Puerto Rico errichtet wurden]

mutual inheritance contract, reciprocal inheritance contract, common inheritance contract · gegenseitiger Erb(schafts)vertrag m, gemeinsamer Erb(schafts)vertrag

mutual insurance · Gegenseitigkeitsversicherung f, Versicherung auf Gegenseitigkeit

mutual (insurance) company [One in which the members are both the insurers and the insured] · Versicherungsgesellschaft f auf Gegenseitigkeit

mutuality, co-operation · genossenschaftliches Prinzip n

mutuality · Gegenseitigkeit f

mutuality, (pacific) settlement, accommodation, mutual agreement, accord, amicable composition (of differences), (amicable) arrangement · Einigung f, Willenseinigung, gütliche Regelung, Einvernehmen n, gütliche Einigung, Vergleich m, Konsensus m, Übereinstimmung, Einverständnis n

mutuality of obligation · Verpflichtungsgegenseitigkeit f, Verpflichtungswechselseitigkeit

(mutual) loan association, (mutual) loan society · Darleh(e)ns(kassen)verein m, Darleh(e)nsbankverein

mutually explanatory · gegenseitig erklärend

mutual mistake, common mistake, reciprocal mistake · gegenseitiger Irrtum m, gemeinsamer Irrtum

mutual pasture, common pasture · Gemeinweide f, Koppelweide, Gemeinanger m

mutual promise, double promise, counter-promise, dependant promise, conditional promise, dependent promise, reciprocal promise · gegenseitiges Versprechen *n*

mutual relation(ship) · gemeinsames Verhältnis *n*, gemeinschaftliches Verhältnis, Gemeinschaftsverhältnis

mutual savings bank, cooperative savings bank [*A bank organized by depositors, whose interest is shown by certificates of deposit, for the purpose of furnishing a safe depository for money of members. It need not be incorporated or under supervision unless state law so requires*] · genossenschaftliche Sparkasse *f*, kooperative Sparkasse, Sparkasse auf Gegenseitigkeit

mutual will, double will, counter will, common will, reciprocal will · gegenseitiges Testament *n*

mystic testament [*In the law of Louisiana, a closed or sealed will, required by statute to be executed in a particular manner and to be signed (on the outside of the paper or of the envelope containing it) by a notary and seven witnesses as well as the testator*] · versiegeltes Notariatstestament *n*

N

naked debenture, simple debenture, unsecured debenture [*Great Britain*]; unsecured corporate bond, debenture (corporate) bond, plain corporate bond [*USA*] · ungesicherte Schuldverschreibung *f*, ungesicherte Obligation *f* [*einer privaten Kapitalgesellschaft*]

naked trust, passive trust, dry trust [*One which requires no action on the part of the trustee, beyond turning over money or property to the cestui que trust*] · passive Treuhand *f*

name-day, ticket-day [*A stock exchange term, it is the day when the names of buyers are transmitted to the sellers of securities*] · Skontierungstag *m*

name desertion · Namenswüstung *f*

name recording, name recordation, name registration · Namensbuchung *f*, Namensregistrierung, Namenseintragung

names list, register of names, names registry, registry of names, names register · Namensliste *f*, Namensregister *n*, Namensverzeichnis *n*

naming · Namensgebung *f*

narrative (recital) · berichtender (Rechts)Titelbericht *m*, beschreibender (Rechts)Titelbericht [*Auflassung. Im Gegensatz zum einleitenden (Rechts)Titelbericht*]

narrow-land, selion of land [*A ridge of ground rising between two furrows, containing no certain quantity*] · Furchenrücken *m*

narrow (sea), straits [*A sea which runs between two coasts not far apart. This term is sometimes applied to the English Channel*] · Meer(es)enge *f*, Kanal *m*

narrow strip lot · Schmalstreifenparzelle *f*

nation, body politic · Nation *f*

national act, national law, national statute, act of the country, law of the country, statute of the country · Landesgesetz *n*, Nationalgesetz, Staatsgesetz

national atlas · Nationalatlas *m*

national border, national frontier · Landesgrenze *f*, Staatsgrenze

national building and loan association (US) · nationale Bausparkasse *f*

national capital · Reichshauptstadt *f*

national capital · Nationalhauptstadt *f*

national consciousness, national sentiment · Nationalbewußtsein *n*

national debt · Staatsschuld *f*

national disposition · Volksanlage *f*

national dividend, national product, national income, national earnings · Volkseinkommen *n*, Nationaleinkommen

national earnings, national dividend, national product, national income · Volkseinkommen *n*, Nationaleinkommen

national economic accounting · volkswirtschaftliche Gesamtrechnung *f*

national economy, public economy, economics, political economy · Volkswirtschaft *f*, politische Ökonomie *f*, Nationalökonomie

national emergency · nationaler Notstand *m*, Staatsnotstand

national forest · Nationalwald *m*

national foundation · Nationalstiftung *f*

national frontier, national border · Landesgrenze *f*, Staatsgrenze

National Goals Research Staff [*USA*] · Präsidialer Forschungsstab *m* für nationale Ziele

national health service · Staatsgesundheitsdienst *m*

national income, national earnings, national dividend, national product · Volkseinkommen *n*, Nationaleinkommen

national insurance, social insurance · Sozialversicherung f

national insurance act, national insurance law, national insurance stutute, social insurance act, social insurance law, social insurance statute · Sozialversicherungsgesetz n

national insurance law, social insurance law · Sozialversicherungsrecht n

national insurance legislation, national insurance lawmaking, social insurance legislation, social insurance lawmaking · Sozialversicherungsgesetzgebung f

national interest, governmental interest · Staatsinteresse n

nationality, citizenship [*human being*] · Staatsangehörigkeit f

nationality act, nationality law, nationality statute, citizenship act, citizenship law, citizenship statute · Staatsangehörigkeitsgesetz n

nationality certificate, certificate of citizenship, citizenship certificate, certificate of nationality · Staatsangehörigkeitsausweis m

nationality law, citizenship law · Staatsangehörigkeitsrecht n

nationality law, nationality act, nationality statute · Nationalitätengesetz n

nationality law · Nationalitätenrecht n

nationality lawmaking → nationality legislation

nationality legislation, nationality lawmaking, citizenship legislation, citizenship lawmaking · Staatsangehörigkeitsgesetzgebung f

nationalization · Verstaatlichung f

nationalization of land(s), land(s) nationalization · Landverstaatlichung f, Bodenverstaatlichung

to nationalize · verstaatlichen

nationalized · verstaatlicht

nationalized industry · verstaatlichte Industrie f

national law, municipal law, state law, law of the country [*The law of a particular country as distinguished from international law*] · Nationalrecht n, Staatsrecht, Landesrecht

national law, national statute, act of the country, law of the country, statute of the country, national act · Landesgesetz n, Nationalgesetz, Staatsgesetz

national map series · nationales Kartenwerk n

national monument · Nationaldenkmal n

national origin · nationale Herkunft f

national park, reservation · Nationalpark m

national park act, national park law, national park statute · Nationalparkgesetz n

national physical planning, federal spatial planning, federal space planning, federal physical planning, national spatial planning, national space planning · Bundesraumplanung f, BRP

national planning, state planning, planning at national level · staatliche Planung f, Nationalplanung

national planning · Staatsplanung f

national planning · Landesplanung f [*Schweiz*]

National Planning Board · Reichsstelle f für Raumordnung [*Deutschland*]

national planning policy · nationale Planungspolitik f

national population · Staatsbevölkerung f

national product, national income, national earnings, national dividend · Volkseinkommen n, Nationaleinkommen

national property · Volksvermögen n

national savings certificate · Staatssparschein m

national security · Staatssicherheit f

national sentiment, national consciousness · Nationalbewußtsein n

national spatial planning, national space planning, national physical planning, federal spatial planning, federal space planning, federal physical planning · Bundesraumplanung f, BRP

national statute, act of the country, law of the country, statute of the country, national act, national law · Landesgesetz n, Nationalgesetz, Staatsgesetz

national treatment · Inländerbehandlung f

national wealth, wealth of nations · Volksreichtum m, Nationalreichtum

nation-state · Nationalstaat m

native, indigenous · einheimisch, altansässig [*von Personen*]

native (born) citizen · gebürtiger Staatsbürger m

native culture, indigenous culture · ursprüngliche Kultur f der Einheimischen [*Kolonialstadt*]

native (person), indigenous person · einheimische Person f, altansässige Person

native population, nonmobile population, indigenous population [*People enumerated in their places of birth*] · altansässige Bevölkerung f, einheimische Bevölkerung, autochthone Bevölkerung

native woman — natural increase of property 686

native woman, female native (person) · Altansässige f, Einheimische

nativitas [*Latin*]; servile status, villein status, villain status, status of a serf, (pr(a)edial) bondage, bondage (on an estate), serfdom (on an estate), villanage, ville(i)nage [*Called by Britton "naifte"*] · Hörigenstatus m, Leibeigenschaft f, Grundhörigkeit f, (Grund)Untertänigkeit, Bauerndienst m

natural accession of property, natural addition of property, natural augmentation of property, natural increase of property · natürliche Besitzzunahme f, natürlicher Besitzzuwachs m, natürliche Besitzerhöhung, natürliche Besitzsteigerung f

natural addition of property, natural augmentation of property, natural increase of property, natural accession of property · natürliche Besitzzunahme f, natürlicher Besitzzuwachs m, natürliche Besitzerhöhung, natürliche Besitzsteigerung f

natural allegiance, natural liegance, natural lawful obedience · geburtsbedingter rechtmäßiger Gehorsam m, geburtsbedingter gesetzmäßiger Gehorsam

natural area, unit defined on the basis of physical criteria · Naturraum m

natural area · großes Teilgebiet n einer Gemeinde, großes Gemeindeteilgebiet [*Im Gegensatz zur „Nachbarschaft"*]

natural augmentation of property, natural increase of property, natural accession of property, natural addition of property · natürliche Besitzzunahme f, natürlicher Besitzzuwachs m, natürliche Besitzerhöhung, natürliche Besitzsteigerung f

natural balance, ecosystem, balance of nature · Naturhaushalt m

natural beauty · Naturschönheit f

natural-born subject · Staatsangehörige m kraft Geburt

natural change of population, natural demographic change, natural population change · natürliche Bevölkerungsbewegung f [*Geburten und Sterbefälle*]

natural child, child by birth [*A child distinguished from a child by adoption*] · leibliches Kind n

natural city, natural town, brick-and-mortar unit · Städteregion f, Städtezusammenschluß m, Städtezone f, Stadtverband m, Regionalstadt f

natural coherent interrelation, geographic physical conditions of the earth's surface in their coherent interrelation · Naturzusammenhang m [*nach Ritter*]

natural demographic change, natural population change, natural change of population · natürliche Bevölkerungsbewegung f [*Geburten und Sterbefälle*]

natural economy, barter economy, nonmonetary economy [*Goods are exchanged for goods*] · Tauschwirtschaft f

natural entity · natürliche Einheit f

natural environment · natürliche Umwelt f, Naturumwelt

natural event, event of nature · Naturereignis n

natural factor · Naturfaktor m

natural family of nations · Völkerfamilie f

natural flood channel · natürliche Hochwasser(abfluß)rinne f

natural forest · Naturwald m, natürlicher Wald

natural forest mapping · Naturwaldkartierung f

natural fruits, fruits of nature; fructus naturales [*Latin*] [*The produce of the soil, or of fruit-trees, bushes, vines, etc., which are edible or otherwise useful or serve for the reproduction of their species*] · Naturfrüchte fpl

natural fruits, fruits of nature; fructus naturales [*Latin*]; natural products [*Those products which are produced by the powers of nature alone; as wool, metals, milk, young animals, etc.*] · natürlicher Zuwachs m

natural goods, gratuitous goods · natürliche Güter npl, Naturgüter, freie Güter [*z. B. Sonnenwärme, Wasserkraft usw.*]

natural grade [*The elevation of the original or undisturbed natural surface of the ground*] · natürliche Geländehöhe f

natural growth, unplanned growth · natürliches Wachstum n

natural heir (male); heir (male) of line [*Scots law*], heir (male) of the body, heir (male) of the blood, bodily heir (male) [*An heir (male) begotten or borne by the person referred to, or a child of such heir; any lineal descendant, excluding a surviving husband or wife, adopted children, and collateral relations*] · Leibeserbe m, leiblicher Erbe, Blutserbe, natürlicher Erbe

natural increase → natural (population) increase

natural increase of population, natural growth of population, natural (population) growth, natural (population) increase [*Excess of births over deaths*] · natürliche Bevölkerungszunahme f, natürliches Bevölkerungswachstum n, natürliches Wachstum der Bevölkerung, Bevölkerungsvermehrung f

natural increase of property, natural accession of property, natural addition of property, natural augmentation of

naturalis possessio — nature recreation(al) area

property · natürliche Besitzzunahme f, natürlicher Besitzzuwachs m, natürliche Besitzerhöhung, natürliche Besitzsteigerung f

naturalis possessio [*Latin*] · Leh(e)n(s)gewere f

naturalization [*Passing from the condition of alien to that of natural-born subject*] · Naturalisierung f

to naturalize · naturalisieren

naturalized · naturalisiert

natural justice · natürliche Gerechtigkeit f

natural landmark, natural monument · natürliche Landmarke f, natürliches festes Seezeichen n

natural landscape · Naturlandschaft f, natürliche Landschaft [*Die von Menschen nicht oder nur wenig beeinflußte Landschaft*]

natural lawful obedience, natural allegiance, natural liegance, natural legal obedience · geburtsbedingter rechtmäßiger Gehorsam m, geburtsbedingter gesetzmäßiger Gehorsam, geburtsmäßiger gesetzmäßiger Gehorsam m

natural law jurisprudence, natural law science, science of natural law, jurisprudence of natural law · Lehre f der allgemeinen Naturrechtsfragen, Lehre des Naturrechts, Naturrechtswissenschaft f, Wissenschaft des Naturrechts, Naturrechtslehre, Naturjurisprudenz f

natural law theorist, natural law thinker · Naturrechtslehrer m

natural law theory of society · naturrechtliche Gesellschaftslehre f

natural liegance, natural lawful obedience, natural allegiance · geburtsbedingter rechtmäßiger Gehorsam m, geburtsbedingter gesetzmäßiger Gehorsam

natural life [*The period of a person's existence considered as continuing until terminated by physical death; used in contradistinction to that juristic conception of life as an aggregate of legal rights or the possession of a legal personalty which could be terminated by "civil death" by which a person loses all his civil rights, and as to them, is considered as dead*] · natürliches Leben n

natural money, commodity money · Naturalgeld n, Nutzgeld

natural monument, natural landmark · natürliche Landmarke f, natürliches festes Seezeichen n

natural monument [*An object permanent in character which is found on the land as it was placed by nature, such as streams, rivers, lakes, shores, beaches, trees, hedges, springs, rocks, and the like*] · Naturdenkmal n

natural monument register, natural monument registry · Naturdenkmalbuch n

natural necessity, unlimited necessity, unrestricted necessity, irrebuttable necessity, total necessity, absolute necessity · absolute Notwendigkeit f, unbedingte Notwendigkeit, unbegrenzte Notwendigkeit, uneingeschränkte Notwendigkeit, unbeschränkte Notwendigkeit

natural object [*In interpretation of boundaries, this term includes mountains, lakes, rivers, etc.*] · natürliches Hindernis n

natural person, human being · natürliche Person f, Mensch m

natural population change, natural change of population, natural demographic change · natürliche Bevölkerungsbewegung f [*Geburten und Sterbefälle*]

natural (population) growth, natural (population) increase, natural increase of population, natural growth of population [*Excess of births over deaths*] · natürliche Bevölkerungszunahme f, natürliches Bevölkerungswachstum n, natürliches Wachstum der Bevölkerung, Bevölkerungsvermehrung f

natural products, natural fruits, fruits of nature; fructus naturales [*Latin*] [*Those products which are produced by the powers of nature alone; as wool, metals, milk, young animals, etc.*] · natürlicher Zuwachs m

natural resource · natürliche Hilfsquelle f

natural right · natürliches subjektives Recht n, subjektives natürliches Recht, (subjektives) Naturrecht

natural state · natürlicher Zustand m [*Land*]

natural town, brick-and-mortar unit, natural city · Städteregion f, Städtezusammenschluß m, Stadtzone f, Stadtverband m, Regionalstadt f

natural unit · Land n im geographischen Sinn

natural watercourse · natürlicher Wasserlauf m

natural wealth · Sachfrucht f

nature, state, position, mode of being, condition · Beschaffenheit f

nature · Charakter m [*im Rechtssinn*]

nature-given, physical · naturgegeben

nature of law · Natur f des Rechts, Rechtsnatur

nature of the landscape, landscape nature · Eigenart f der Landschaft, Landschaftseigenart

nature recreation(al) area · Natur(schutz)park m

nature reserve · Naturschutzgebiet n

nature-rightly [*A term invented by Maitland*] · naturrechtlich

nautical chart, Admiralty chart [*Great Britain*] · See(navigations)karte f [*Mit nautischen Angaben versehene Karte der Küstengebiete und Meere*]

naval base · Marinestützpunkt m

naval law · Marinerecht n

naval power, sea power, maritime power · Seemacht f

navigability · Schiffbarkeit f

navigable · schiffbar

navigable water course · Wasserstraße f, Wasserweg m, Schiffahrtsstraße, Schiffahrtsweg, schiffbarer Wasserlauf m

to navigate · schiffen

navigation authority · Schiffahrtsbehörde f

navigation law · Schiffahrtsrecht n

navigation right, aerial navigation right [*Right to use the air above the land for aerial navigation*] · Überflugrecht n

near, neighbouring (Brit.); neighboring (US); adjacent · benachbart

nearest kin, heir (male) general, general heir (male), heir (male) whatsoever, statutory heir (male), heir (male) at law, right heir (male), legal heir (male), lawful heir (male) [*One who takes the succession by relationship to the decedent and by force of law*] · Intestaterbe m, gesetzlicher Erbe

nearest-neighbour method, nearest-neighbour technique (Brit.); nearest-neighbor method, nearest-neighbor technique (US) · Verfahren n des nächsten Nachbars, Methode f des nächsten Nachbars, Nächst-Nachbar-Verfahren n, Nächst-Nachbar-Methode f

nearness · Nähe f, nahe Entfernung f

nearness to nature · Naturnähe f

near vicinity · nahe Umgebung f

neat line, inner border · Blattschnittlinie f, Blattbegrenzungslinie [*Kartographie*]

necessaries · Schlüsselgewalt f der Frau

necessaries · notwendiger Unterhalt m

necessary, needful · notwendig

necessary · Bedarfsgegenstand m

necessary parties · Streitgenossenschaft f

necessitas [*Latin*]; necessity [*A force, power, or influence which compels one to act against his will*] · Aggressivnotstand m

necessitas culpabilis [*Latin*]; culpable necessity, unfortunate necessity [*A necessity which, while it excuses the act done under its compulsion, does not leave the doer entirely free from blame*] · schuldhafter Aggressivnotstand m

necessity; necessitas [*Latin*] [*A force, power, or influence which compels one to act against his will*] · Aggressivnotstand m

necessity [*The quality or state of being necessary*] · Erforderlichkeit f, Notwendigkeit

necessity · Gebot n

necessity of facts weighing, necessity of weighing the facts · Abwägungsgebot n

necessity of permission · Erlaubnisbedürftigkeit f, Genehmigungsbedürftigkeit

necessity principle, principle of necessity · Erforderlichkeitsprinzip n, Erforderlichkeitsgrundsatz m, Notwendigkeitsprinzip, Notwendigkeitsgrundsatz

necropolis [*A city whose "life" is considered to be dying*] · absterbende Stadt f

necropolis [*A city whose "life" is considered to be dead*] · tote Stadt f

N.E.D., normal equivalent deviate · Normalfraktil n [*Statistik*]

need · Bedarf m

needful, necessary · notwendig

needing repair(s), in need of repair · reparaturbedürftig

need of success (in achievement) · Erfolgszwang m

negative · Verneinung f

negative · negative Bestimmung f

negative act(ion), default, neglect, failure, omission, omittance, forbearance, negligence [*Omission of that which a person ought to do*] · (Ver)Säumnis f, n, (f), Vernachlässigung f, Unterlassung(shandlung), Nichtleistung, Unterlassungsakt m, negativer Akt, negative Handlung

negative binominal distribution, Pascal distribution · Pascalverteilung f

negative certificate, certificate of nonobjection, nonobjection certificate · Unbedenklichkeitsattest n, Unbedenklichkeitsbescheinigung f, Unbedenklichkeitsschein m, Bodenverkehrszeugnis n, Negativattest, Negativbescheinigung, Negativschein

negative condition [*One by which it is stipulated that a given thing shall not happen*] · Negativbedingung f

negative contract · Negativvertrag m, Unterlassungsvertrag

negative duty · Negativpflicht f, Unterlassungspflicht, negative Pflicht

negative easement [*The servient owner is compelled by the dominant owner not to perform a certain act or certain acts upon the servient tenement*] · negative Grunddienstbarkeit *f*

negative evidence, negative proof [*Testimony that an alleged fact did not exist*] · Negativbeweis *m*

negative export, import [*The negative expression is used because a sale of goods or services to another nation (an actual export) is a credit item in the balance of trade and a purchase from another nation has a negative effect on balance of trade. Net exports are equal to actual exports minus imports*] · Einfuhr *f*

negative function · Negativfunktion *f*, Unterlassungsfunktion

negative incentive · Abschreckungsmittel *n*, negatives Anreizmittel

negative injunction, restrictive injunction, restraining injunction, preventive injunction · gerichtliches Verbot *n*, gerichtliche Verbotsverfügung *f*

negative planning · Negativplanung *f*, negative Planung [*Verbot der Niederlassung in Agglomerationsgebieten*]

negative prescription [*The divesting of a right by reason of lapse of time*] · Versitzung *f*

negative proof, negative evidence [*Testimony that an alleged fact did not exist*] · Negativbeweis *m*

negative right · Negativrecht *n* [*Dingliches Recht — im Vergleich zum dinglichen Recht auf Beherrschung einer Sache im ganzen (complete right) — als beschränktes Recht weil es die Sache nur in einzelnen Beziehungen ergreift*]

negative skewness · negative Schiefe *f* [*Statistik*]

neglect, failure, omission, omittance, forbearance, negligence, negative act(ion), default [*Omission of that which a person ought to do*] · (Ver)Säumnis *f, n, (f)*, Vernachlässigung *f*, Unterlassung(shandlung), Nichtleistung, Unterlassungsakt *m*, negativer Akt, negative Handlung

neglectable · vernachlässigbar

neglectful of duty, derelict, remiss · pflichtvergessen, pflichtuntreu

neglect to use, nonuse, disuse · Nichtgebrauch *m*, Nichtbenutzung *f*

negligence, carelessness, recklessness, careless conduct, negligent conduct, reckless conduct · Fahrlässigkeit *f*, Nachlässigkeit, Leichtfertigkeit, Leichtsinnigkeit

negligence, negative act(ion), default, neglect, failure, omission, omittance, forbearance [*Omission of that which a person ought to do*] · (Ver)Säumnis *f, n, (f)*, Vernachlässigung *f*, Unterlassung(shandlung), Nichtleistung, Unterlassungsakt *m*, negativer Akt, negative Handlung

negligence, negligent performance of the contract, failure to use ordinary care, breach of duty to exercise due care and skill, breach of duty to take care, failure to exercise care · Verletzung *f* der Sorgfaltspflicht, Verstoß *m* gegen die Sorgfaltspflicht, Sorgfalts(pflicht)verletzung, Sorgfalts(pflicht)verstoß *m*

negligence without fault · technische Fahrlässigkeit *f*

negligent, without care, careless, reckless [*With an indifference whether anything is true or false*] · leichtsinnig, fahrlässig, nachlässig, leichtfertig

negligent conduct, reckless conduct, negligence, carelessness, recklessness, careless conduct · Fahrlässigkeit *f*, Nachlässigkeit, Leichtfertigkeit, Leichtsinnigkeit

negligent damage · Bagatellschaden *m*

negligently · schuldhaft fahrlässig

negligently false, negligently untrue, negligently not true, recklessly untrue, recklessly false, recklessly not true, carelessly untrue, carelessly false, carelessly not true · leichtsinning unwahr, leichtsinnig falsch, leichtfertig unwahr, leichtfertig falsch, fahrlässig unwahr, fahrlässig falsch, nachlässig unwahr, nachlässig falsch

negligently fraudulent (mis)representation, carelessly fraudulent (mis)representation, recklessly fraudulent (false) representation, negligently fraudulent (false) representation, carelessly fraudulent (false) representation, recklessly fraudulent (false) recital, negligently fraudulent (false) recital, carelessly fraudulent (false) recital, recklessly fraudulent (mis)representation · fahrlässige betrügerische (Falsch)Darstellung *f*, fahrlässige betrügerische (Falsch)Erklärung, fahrlässige arglistige (Falsch)Darstellung, fahrlässige arglistige (Falsch)Erklärung

negligently untrue, negligently false, negligently not true, carelessly untrue, carelessly false, carelessly not true · fahrlässig unwahr, fahrlässig falsch, nachlässig unwahr, nachlässig falsch

negligent performance of the contract, failure to use ordinary care, breach of duty to exercise due care and skill, breach of duty to take care, failure to exercise care, negligence · Verletzung *f* der Sorgfaltspflicht, Verstoß *m* gegen die Sorgfaltspflicht, Sorgfalts(pflicht)verletzung, Sorgfalts(pflicht)verstoß *m*

negligent repair · Bagatellreparatur *f*

negligible part of a building · untergeordneter (Gebäude)Bauteil *m*, untergeordneter Gebäudeteil [*Ein Gebäudeteil der, ohne in den umbauten Raum einbezogen zu sein, von der Baumasse her unbedeutend ist und von der Art, dem Umfang und den Auswirkungen auf das Gebäude gegenüber diesem nur unerheblich ins Gewicht fällt*]

negotiability (of instrument), transferable quality · Begebbarkeit *f*, Umlauffähigkeit, Umlaufbarkeit [*handelsrechtliches Wertpapier*]

negotiable, transferable by endorsement, transferable by indorsement · begebbar, umlaufbar, umlauffähig, indossabel

negotiable instrument (payable to bearer), negotiable instrument payable to order, bearer(-)security · begebbares Papier *n*, umlauffähiges Papier, indossables Papier, Handelspapier, Orderpapier, umlaufbares Papier

negotiable instruments act, negotiable instruments law, negotiable instruments statute, securities act, securities statute, securities law · Wertpapiergesetz *n*

negotiable instruments dealer → (securities) dealer

negotiable instruments exchange act, negotiable instruments exchange law, negotiable instruments exchange statute, securities exchange act, securities exchange law, securities exchange statute · Wertpapier-Börsen-Gesetz *n*

negotiable instruments law, securities law · Wertpapierrecht *n*

negotiable instruments law, negotiable instruments act, negotiable instruments statute · Gesetz *n* über begebbare Urkunden

negotiable warehouse receipt · Orderlagerschein *m*

negotiable words [*Words necessary to render a bill of exchange, promissory note or check negotiable; words which give a bill, note or check a negotiable quality. The usual word for this purpose, in a bill or note is "order", and in a check, "bearer"; as "to A.B. or order", or, "to the order of A.B."; "to A.B. or bearer", or "to bearer"*] · Begebbarkeitsklausel *f*, Orderklausel, Umlauffähigkeitsklausel, Umlaufbarkeitsklausel

to negotiate · begeben [*durch Verkauf, Zession usw.*]

to negotiate [*To negotiate a bill or note, is to indorse and deliver it to another*] · begeben

negotiated(-price) contract · Vertrag *m* aus freihändiger Vergabe, freihändiger Vertrag [*Nicht in einer Ausschreibung erhalten*]

negotiating stage · Verhandlungsstadium *n*

negotiation · Begebung *f* [*Wechsel*]

negotiation · Begebung *f* [*Durch Verkauf, Zession usw.*]

negotiation · Verhandlung *f*

negotiator, party in negotiation(s) · Verhandlungspartner *m*, Verhandlungspartei *f*

negotiorum gestio [*Latin*]; conduct of another's affairs · Geschäftsführung *f* ohne Auftrag

negro migration, black migration · Negerwanderung *f*

negro population, black population · Negerbevölkerung *f*

neighbouring (real) estate, neighbouring (real) property, neighbouring realty (Brit.); neighboring (real) estate, neighboring (real) property, neighboring realty (US) · benachbarter (Grund)Besitz *m*

neighborhood guild (US); settlement (Brit.) · Nachbarschaftsgilde *f* [*Die seit 1887 in den USA und seit 1889 in England sich bildenden Vereinigungen von Arbeiterfamilien einer oder mehrerer benachbarter Straßen (etwa je 100 Familien), mit dem Ziel eine Hebung der unteren Klassen durch Reformen im Haus-, Erziehungs-, Gewerbe- und Erholungswesen sowie durch Zukunftsfürsorge herbeizuführen*]

neighboring (US) → neighbouring

neighboring community (US); adjacent community; neighbouring community (Brit.) · Nachbargemeinde *f*, Nachbarkommune *f*

neighboring (real) estate, neighboring (real) property, neighbouring realty (US); neighbouring (real) estate, neighbouring (real) property, neighbouring realty (Brit.) · benachbarter (Grund)Besitz *m*

neighboring (real) property, neighboring realty (US); neighboring (real) estate, neighbouring (real) property, neighbouring realty (Brit.); neighbouring (real) estate · benachbarter (Grund)Besitz *m*

neighboring realty, neighboring (real) estate, neighboring (real) property (US); neighbouring (real) estate, neighbouring (real) property, neighbouring realty (Brit.) · benachbarter (Grund)Besitz *m*

neighbor's aid, neighbor's help (US); neighbour's help, neighbour's aid (Brit.) · Gruppen(selbst)hilfe *f* unter Nachbarn, Nachbarschaftshilfe

neighbourhood (Brit.); neighborhood (US) · Nachbarschaft *f*

neighbourhood business street (Brit.); neighborhood business street (US) · Nachbarschaftsgeschäftsstraße f

neighbourhood centre (Brit.); neighborhood center (US) · Nachbarschaftszentrum n

neighbourhood club (Brit.); neighborhood club (US) · Nachbarverein m

neighbourhood council (Brit.); neighborhood council (US); citizen group, civic enterprise [*The citizens of a city cooperate to promote the common good and general welfare of the people of the city*] · Bürgerinitiative f, Interessengruppe f, Einwohnerinitiative, Bürgergruppe f

neighbourhood cult association (Brit.); neighborhood cult association (US) · nachbarschaftliche Kultgemeinschaft f [*chinesische Stadt*]

neighbourhood density (Brit.); neighborhood density (US) [*Dwelling units per acre of land area in use or proposed for development as a neighbo(u)rhood area including residential land, areas for local shopping, school, public open spaces, and land taken up in streets*] · Nachbarschaftsdichte f

neighbourhood playground (Brit.); neighborhood playground (US) · Nachbarschaftsspielplatz m

neighbourhood shop (Brit.); neighborhood shop (US) · neutrales (Laden)Geschäft n, ubiquitäres (Laden)Geschäft

neighbourhood (unit) (Brit.); neighborhood (unit) (US) · Nachbarschaft(seinheit) f, Wohneinheit, Stadtzelle f [*Ein Ortsteil, der alle für ein nachbarliches Zusammenleben seiner Bewohner nötigen Gemeinschafts- und Versorgungseinrichtungen enthält*]

neighbourhood unit movement (Brit.); neighborhood unit movement (US) · Nachbarschaftsbewegung f

neighbouring (Brit.); neighboring (US); adjacent, near · benachbart

neighbouring area, neighbouring territory (Brit.); neighboring area, neighboring territory (US); adjacent area, adjacent territory · Nachbargebiet n

neighbouring area (Brit.); neighboring area (US); vicinage, adjacent area · Nachbarfläche f, benachbarte Fläche

neighbouring boundary (Brit.); neighboring boundary (US) · Nachbargrenze f

neighbouring community (Brit.); neighboring community (US); adjacent community · Nachbargemeinde f, Nachbarkommune f

neighbouring estate → neighbouring (real) estate

neighbouring owner → neighbouring (property) owner

neighbouring plot, neighbouring parcel (Brit.); neighboring plot, neighboring parcel (US); adjacent plot, adjacent parcel · Nachbargrundstück n

neighbouring (property) owner (Brit.); neighboring (property) owner (US); adjacent (property) owner · Nachbar(eigentümer) m

neighbouring (real) property, neighbouring realty, neighbouring (real) estate (Brit.); neighboring (real) estate, neighboring (real) property, neighboring realty (US) · benachbarter (Grund)Besitz m

neighbouring territory (Brit.); neighboring area, neighboring territory (US); adjacent area, adjacent territory; neighbouring area · Nachbargebiet n

neighbouring town, neighbouring city (Brit.); neighboring town, neighboring city (US) · Nachbarstadt f [*Sie hat selbständige Struktur und nur lockere Bindungen an die Kernstadt*]

neighbour in the sense of law (Brit.); neighbor in the sense of law (US) · Angrenzer m [*Nachbar im rechtlichen Sinne*]

neighbourliness (Brit.); neighborliness (US) · nachbarschaftliches Verhältnis n, Nachbarschaftlichkeit f

neighbourly mutual relation(ship) (Brit.); neighborly mutual relation(ship) (US) · nachbarliches Gemeinschaftsverhältnis n

neighbour-protecting (Brit.); neighbor-protecting (US) · nachbarschützend

neighbour's aid (Brit.); neighbor's help, neighbor's aid (US); neighbour's help · Gruppen(selbst)hilfe f unter Nachbarn, Nachbarschaftshilfe

neighbour's help, neighbour's aid (Brit.); neighbor's help, neighbor's aid (US) · Gruppen(selbst)hilfe f unter Nachbarn, Nachbarschaftshilfe

neighbour's law (Brit.); neighbor's law (US) · Nachbarrecht n, objektives Nachbarrecht

neighbour's protection (Brit.); neighbor's protection (US) · Nachbarschutz m

neighbour's protection according to civil law (Brit.); neighbor's protection according to civil law (US) · zivilrechtlicher Nachbarschutz m

neighbour's right (Brit.); neighbor's right (US) · Nachbarrecht n, subjektives Nachbarrecht

neo-city, neo-town · Neustadt f

neoclassical economic theory · neoklassische Wirtschaftstheorie f

neoclassical theory of production · neoklassische Produktionstheorie f

neotechnic city, neotechnic town, planned city, planned town [*See remark under "Stadt"*] · geplante Stadt f, Planstadt

neo-town, neo-city · Neustadt f

nepotism · Günstlingswirtschaft f, Vetternwirtschaft

network technique · Netzwerktechnik f [*als Anwendung*]

net annual income, net yearly income, annual net income, yearly net income · Jahresnettoeinkommen n, Nettojahreseinkommen

net annual value, rat(e)able value · Nettoertragswert m, Veranlagungswert, Steuerwert [*Liegenschaft*]

net area → net residential land (area)

net asset value · Fonds-Nettoinventarwert m

net (building) (land) area, net (building) land · Netto(bau)boden m, Netto(bau)land n, Netto(bau)fläche f [*Summe der bebauten und/oder zur Bebauung freigegebenen Grundstücksflächen, ausgenommen öffentliche Freiflächen*]

net currency inflow · Nettodevisenzufluß m

net currency outflow · Nettodevisenabfluß m

net current assets, net quick assets, (net) working capital, current assets minus current liabilities [*The term "working capital" has two meanings. It may refer to the total current assets or to the difference between current assets and current liabilities*] · Nettoumlaufvermögen n, Nettoumlaufmittel f, Reinumlaufvermögen, Reinumlaufmittel

net density [*Density relating to a net area*] · Nettodichte f

net density (Brit.); block density (US) [*Density relating to a block area*] · Blockdichte f

net density gradient · Nettodichtegefälle n

net density of population, net population density · Nettobevölkerungsdichte f, Netto(be)sied(e)lungsdichte, Netto(volks)dichte, Nettomenschenausstattung f einer Fläche, Nettoansied(e)lungsdichte

net deposits · Bankdepositen f pl nach Zinsabzug

net disinvestment · negative Nettoinvestition f, negative Netto(kapital)anlage f, negative Nettogeldanlage

net dwelling rent, net (residential) rent · Netto(wohnungs)miete f, Netto(wohnungs)(miet)zins m

net excess, net surplus · Reinüberschuß m

net floor area, net floor space · Nettogeschoßfläche f, Nettoetagenfläche, Nettostockwerkfläche

net gain, net profit, pure gain, pure profit, clear gain, clear profit · Reingewinn m, Reinprofit m, Nettogewinn, Nettoprofit

net gain from trading, trading net profit, trading net gain, net profit from trading · Handelsnettogewinn m, Handelsnettoprofit m

net holding capacity, net physical capacity of an area · Nettotragfähigkeit f, Nettoaufnahmefähigkeit, Nettosied(e)lungskapazität f

net income, actual income · Reineinkommen n, Nettoeinkommen

net in-migration · Nettozuwanderung f

net interest · Reinzinsen f

net (land) area → net (building) (land) area

net loss · Nettoverlust m

net migration · Nettowanderung f

net operating profit, operating income · Betriebseinkommen n

net out-migration · Nettoabwanderung f

net payment · Nettozahlung f

net physical capacity of an area, net holding capacity · Nettotragfähigkeit f, Nettoaufnahmefähigkeit, Nettosied(e)lungskapazität f

net population density, net density of population · Nettobevölkerungsdichte f, Netto(be)sied(e)lungsdichte, Netto(volks)dichte, Nettomenschenausstattung f einer Fläche, Nettoansied(e)lungsdichte

net proceeds · Reinerlös m, Nettoerlös

net produce [*The portion of produce, which finds the way to market, and supports the part of the population of a country not immediately concerned in its cultivation*] · Nettoprodukt n

net produce of a building, net yield of a building · Gebäudereinertrag m

net profit from trading, net gain from trading, trading net profit, trading net gain · Handelsnettogewinn m, Handelsnettoprofit m

net project cost(s) · Netto-Projektkosten f

net proportionality shift, proportionality net shift [*shift analysis*] · Proportionalitätseffekt m, Proportionalitätswirkung f

net quick assets, (net) working capital, current assets minus current liabilities, net current assets [*The term "working capital" has two meanings. It may refer to the total current assets or to the dif-

net rent — new(ly-erected) house

ference between *current assets and current liabilities*] · Nettoumlaufvermögen *n*, Nettoumlaufmittel *f*, Reinumlaufvermögen, Reinumlaufmittel

net rent · Nettorente *f*

net rent · Nettomiete *f*

net residential land (area), net area, net housing land (area) · Netto-Wohn(ungs)(bau)boden *m*, Netto-Wohn(ungs)(bau)land *n*, Netto-Wohn(ungs)(bau)fläche *f* [*Mit Wohngebäuden bebaute und/oder zur Bebauung freigegebene Grundstücke*]

net (residential) rent, net dwelling rent · Netto(wohnungs)miete *f*, Netto(wohnungs)(miet)zins *m*

net return, net yield · Reinrendite, Nettorendite, effektive Rendite

net return mutiplier, net yield multiplier · Reinrenditevervielfältiger, Nettorenditevervielfältiger *m*

net room area · Nettoraumfläche *f*

net social dividend, net social product · Nettosozialprodukt *n*

net social product, net social dividend · Nettosozialprodukt *n*

net surplus, net excess · Reinüberschuß *m*

net-to-gross ratio · Netto-Brutto-Verhältnis *n*

net value added · Nettowertschöpfung *f* [*zu Faktorkosten*]

net value added by manufacture · Wertzuwachs *m* durch Verarbeitung, Wertverbesserung *f* durch Verarbeitung, Wertzunahme *f* durch Verarbeitung, Werterhöhung durch Verarbeitung

network · Netzwerk *n*

network city, network town · verflochtene Stadt *f*

network construction · Netzwerkbildung *f*

network engineering · Netzwerktechnik *f* [*als Wissenschaft*]

network flow · Netzfluß *m*

(net) working capital, current assets minus current liabilities, net current assets, net quick assets [*The term "working capital" has two meanings. It may refer to the total current assets or to the difference between current assets and current liabilities*] · Nettoumlaufvermögen *n*, Nettoumlaufmittel *f*, Reinumlaufvermögen, Reinumlaufmittel

network of green areas, green area network · Grünnetz *n*

network of hexagonal market areas, Löschian system, network of hexagons · Netz *n* sechseckiger Marktgebiete, Netz sechskantiger Marktgebiete, Marktnetz, Wirtschaftslandschaft *f* (nach Lösch), Raumbild *n* einer Wirtschaftslandschaft nach Lösch, Wabenmuster *n* einer Wirtschaftslandschaft nach Lösch, Marktnetzkonstruktion *f* einer Wirtschaftslandschaft nach Lösch

network town, network city · verflochtene Stadt *f*

net worth, stockholder's equity, owner's equity (US); total equity (Brit.) · Eigenkapital *n*

net yearly income, annual net income, yearly net income, net annual income · Jahresnettoeinkommen *n*, Nettojahreseinkommen

net yield, net return · Nettorendite *f*, effektive Rendite, Reinrendite

net yield multiplier, net return mutiplier · Reinrenditevervielfältiger, Nettorenditevervielfältiger *m*

net yield of a building, net produce of a building · Gebäudereinertrag *m*

neutrality law · Neutralitätsrecht *n*

neutrality of policy goals, neutrality of target goals · Zielneutralität *f*

neutrality proclamation · Neutralitätsverkündung *f*

new acquisition [*An estate derived from any source other than descent, devise, or gift from father or mother or any relative in the paternal or maternal line*] · Neuerwerb(ung) *m*, (*f*), Neubeschaffung *f*

new building, new construction · Neubau *m*

new development · Entwick(e)lung *f* die nicht unter die 3. Ausführungsverordnung des T.C.P.A. 1962 fällt [*England*]

new dwelling, new residence, new tenement · Neubauwohnung *f*

new habitable space, new(ly-erected) housing · Neubauwohnung *fpl*, neugeschaffener Wohnraum *m*

new home · Neueigenheim *n*, Neueigenhaus *n*

new house · Neuhaus *n*

new house rent ordinance · Neubaumietenverordnung *f*

new lot [*As opposed to an original lot*] · Bruchflurstück *n*, Bruchparzelle *f*, Bruchgrundstück (im katastertechnischen Sinne)

new(ly-erected) building · Neubaugebäude *n*

new(ly-erected) home · Neubaueigenheim *n*, Neubaueigenhaus *n*

new(ly-erected) house · Neubauhaus *n*

new(ly-erected) housing — noise generation

new(ly-erected) housing, new habitable space · Neubauwohnungen *fpl*, neugeschaffener Wohnraum *m*

new residence, new tenement, new dwelling · Neubauwohnung *f*

newspaper ad(vertisement) · Zeitungsanzeige *f*

new structure, new work, new physical facility · Neubau(anlage) *m, (f)*, Neubauwerk *n*, Neubaulichkeit *f*, neue (bauliche) Anlage; Neubaute *f* [*Schweiz*]

new tenement, new dwelling, new residence · Neubauwohnung *f*

New Town Act 1965 [*England*] · Gesetz *n* zur Errichtung und Entwick(e)lung neuer Städte

new town in town, NTIT · neue Stadt *f* in der Stadt

new trial · Wiederaufnahme *f* des Verfahrens

new work, new physical facility, new structure · Neubau(anlage) *m, (f)*, Neubauwerk *n*, Neubaulichkeit *f*, neue (bauliche) Anlage; Neubaute *f* [*Schweiz*]

next and most lawful friend, relative, next of blood, next of kin · Verwandte *m*

next-best-rule · NB-Regel *f* [*für Standortentscheidungen*]

next friend, (prochein) amy, (prochein) ami; proximus amicus [*Latin*] [*He sues on behalf of an infant. Infants sue by a next friend and defend by a guardian ad litem*] · Beistand *m*, prozessualer Stellvertreter *m* auf der Klägerseite

next of blood, next of kin, next and most lawful friend, relative · Verwandte *m*

next presentation · Präsentationsrecht *n* für die nächste aber noch nicht eingetretene Vakanz

next-year operating advantage · Betriebsgewinn *m* des nächsten Jahres, nächstjähriger Betriebsgewinn

Neyman allocation · Neyman'sche Stichprobenaufteilung *f* [*Statistik*]

nigh dwelling · räumliches Zusammensiedeln *n*

night lettergram (US); letter telegram sent at night · Nacht-Brieftelegramm *n*

night lodger · Schlafgänger *m*, Einlogierer, Schlafbursche *m*, Schlafsteller, Schlafgast *m*, Schläfer

night-lodging (system) · Schlafgängertum *n*

night poaching, poaching in nighttime · Nachtwilddieberei *f*, Nachtwildfrevel *m*

night school, evening institute, evening school · Abendschule *f*

night work · Nachtarbeit *f*

ninety-nine years lease, building-lease · (Bau)Pacht(vertrag) *f, (m)* für 99 Jahre

ninety-nine years lease law → building lease law

nisi [*Latin*]; unless · falls nicht

nobility · höherer Adel *m*

noble estate → manor

nobles, aristocracy · Hochadel *m*

no-claim bonus · Schadensfreiheitsrabatt *m* [*Versicherungswesen*]

nocturnal (house)breaker, burglar; burglator [*Latin*] · Einbrecher *m* in der Nacht, Einbrecher zur Nacht, Nachteinbrecher

nocturnal (house)breaking, burglary · Einbrechen *n* zur Nachtzeit, Einbruch *m* zur Nachtzeit, Einbruch in der Nacht, Nachteinbruch, Einbrechen in der Nacht

nocturnal (house)breaking insurance, burglary insurance · Nachteinbruchversicherung *f*

nodal · zentralörtlich

nodality, central place hierarchy, centrality, hierarchy of central places · Zentralität *f*, Hierarchie *f* zentraler Orte, Bedeutungsüberschuß *m*, Zentralorthierarchie, zentralörtliche Bedeutung *f*, Kotenpunktlage *f*, Zentralitätsgrad *m* [*Ein Ort versorgt sich und seine ländliche Umgebung mit Gütern und Dienstleistungen. Die Zentralität ist gleich seinem Bedeutungsüberschuß, d. h. gleich der relativen Bedeutung in bezug auf ein ihm zugehöriges Gebiet definiert*]

nodal region · Kernregion *f*, Nodalregion, polarisierende Region

nodal region · regionaler Teilmarkt *m* [*zentralörtlich orientiert*]

nodal structure · Knotenaufbau *m*, Knotenstruktur *f*, Knotengefüge *n*, Knotenzusammensetzung *f*

node · Knoten *m*

node of migration · Wanderungsknoten(punkt) *m*

no-growth, zero growth · Nullwachstum *n*

no-growth rate, zero growth rate, growth rate of zero · Nullwachstumsrate *f*

noise · Lärm *m*

noise abatement · Lärmminderung *f*

noise control · Lärmbekämpfung *f*

noise control act, noise control law, noise control statute · Lärmbekämpfungsgesetz *n*

noise control law · Lärmbekämpfungsrecht *n*

noise generation · Lärmerzeugung *f*, Lärmverursachung

noise level · Lärmpegel *m*

noise nuisance · Geräuschemission *f*, Lärmemission

noise nuisance effect · Lärmimmission *f*, Geräuschimmission

noise protection · Lärmschutz *m*

noise protection area, noise protection territory · Lärmschutzgebiet *n*

noise protection embankment, noise protection bank · Lärmschutzwall *m*

noise protection facility · Lärmschutzeinrichtung *f*

noise protection range · Lärmschutzbereich *m*

noise protection wall · Lärmschutzwand *f*

noise source · Lärmquelle *f*

noisy · geräuschvoll

nolle prosequi [*Latin*]; discontinuance of an action · Klagezurücknahme *f* vor Abgabe des Wahrspruches [*Zivilprozeß. Nicht verwechseln mit „nonsuit" in der Hauptverhandlung*]

nomadic herdsman · Hirtennomade *m*

nomadism · Nomadentum *n*

no man's-land · Niemandsland *n*

nominal, titular [*Existing in name only; not real or substantial; connected with the transaction or proceeding in name only; not in interest; not real or actual; merely named, stated, or given; without reference to actual conditions*] · nominell, nur dem Namen nach

nominal capital, original capital, authorized capital, registered capital [*When a company is formed its application for registration is accompanied by a statement indicating the amount of capital with which it purposes to be registered*] · Grundkapital *n* [*Nicht verwechseln mit der deutschen Benennung „genehmigtes (Aktien)Kapital"; denn dieses ist ein durch Beschluß der Hauptversammlung festgesetzter Betrag, um den der Vorstand während einer bestimmten Zeit das Grundkapital erhöhen kann*]

nominal compensation, nominal indemnification, nominal indemnity, nominal damages · Strafentschädigung *f*

nominal consideration [*In the very old Lombard laws, the giver of a gift always received some valueless trifle in return, which just served to make his gift not a gift but an exchange. This is the Lombard "launichild".*] · Lohngeld *n*

nominal damages, nominal compensation, nominal indemnification, nominal indemnity · Strafentschädigung *f*

nominal gain, nominal profit · Nominalprofit *m*, Nominalgewinn *m*

nominal indemnification, nominal indemnity, nominal damages, nominal compensation · Strafentschädigung *f*

nominal interest · Nominalzinsen *f*

nominal interest yield · Nominalverzinsung *f*

nominal owner, nominal proprietor · nomineller Eigentümer *m*, nominelles Eigentumssubjekt *n*, nomineller Eigner

nominal partner [*One who appears, or is held out to the world as a partner, but who has no real interest in the firm or business*] · Scheingesellschafter *m*

nominal prescription, nominal rule, nominal regulation · Sollvorschrift *f*, Sollrechtsvorschrift

nominal production quantity · Sollproduktionsmenge *f*

nominal profit, nominal gain · Nominalprofit *m*, Nominalgewinn *m*

nominal proprietor, nominal owner · nomineller Eigentümer *m*, nominelles Eigentumssubjekt *n*, nomineller Eigner

nominal regulation, nominal prescription, nominal rule · Sollvorschrift *f*, Sollrechtsvorschrift

nominal rent, peppercorn rent [*Where only a nominal sum has to be paid for a period*] · nominelle Grundrente *f*, Pfefferkornrente

nominal rule, nominal regulation, nominal prescription · Sollvorschrift *f*, Sollrechtsvorschrift

nominal value, face value, par value, denomination [*The value mentioned on the face of a security as distinguished from the market value*] · Nennwert *m*, Nominalwert

nominal wage · Nominallohn *m*

to nominate, to appoint · benennen, nominieren, namhaft machen, ernennen

nominated bill (of quantities) [*A priced bill of quantities for another project recently won in competition, on the understanding that the rates shall form the basis of pricing for the new contract*] · Vorschlagsleistungsverzeichnis *n*

nominated sub(contractor), appointed sub(contractor) · ernannter Nachunternehmer *m*, ernannter Subunternehmer, bauseitiger Nachunternehmer, bauseitiger Subunternehmer, benannter Subunternehmer, benannter Subunternehmer, nominierter Nachunternehmer, nominierter Subunternehmer

nominated supplier, appointed supplier · bauseitiger Lieferant *m*, ernannter Lieferant, benannter Lieferant, nominierter Lieferant [*Von der Bauherrschaft ernannter Lieferant*]

nominating, appointing · Benennen *n*, Ernennen, Nominieren, Namhaftmachen

nominating party, appointing party · benennende Partei *f*, nominierende Partei *f*, ernennende Partei *f*

nomination, appointment · Benennung *f*, Nominierung, Namhaftmachung, Ernennung

nomination · Wahlvorschlag *m*

nomination certificate, declaration of candidacy, nomination petition, certificate of nomination, paper of nomination, nomination paper [*USA*] · Vorwahlvorschlag *m*

nomination committee, appointment committee · Benennungsausschuß *m*, Ernennungsausschuß, Nominierungsausschuß

nomination contract, appointment contract, contract to nominate, contract to appoint · Benennungsvertrag *m*, Ernennungsvertrag

nomination paper, nomination certificate, declaration of candidacy, nomination petition, certificate of nomination, paper of nomination [*USA*] · Vorwahlvorschlag *m*

nominee, appointee · Benannte *m*, Ernannte

nomography [*A treatise or description of law(s)*] · Rechtsabhandlung *f*

nomotheta, lawgiver [*Such as Solon and Lycurgus among the Greeks, and Caesar, Pompey, and Sylla among the Romans*] · Rechtsgeber *m*

non ability, legal disability, legal incapability, legal incapacity, lawful disability, lawful inability, lawful incapability, lawful inability [*Want of ability to do an act in law*] · rechtliche Unfähigkeit *f*, rechtliches Unvermögen *n*, Rechtsunfähigkeit, Rechtsunvermögen

non ability, legal disability, legal incapability, legal incapacity, statutory disability, statutory incapacity, statutory incapability [*Want of ability to do an act in law*] · gesetzliche Unfähigkeit *f*, gesetzliches Unvermögen *n*

nonacceptance, rejection · Nichtannahme *f*

nonadmitted asset, inadmitted asset [*insurance accounting*] · ungeeignetes Deckungsmittel *n*, geringwertiges Deckungsmittel

nonadversary, noncontentious · nicht streitig, nicht strittig, unbestritten

non-adverse, non-wrongful, consistent with · nicht entgegenstehend, nicht entgegen dem Recht [*(subjektives) Besitzrecht*]

non-age, (age of (legal)) minority · Minderjährigkeit *f*

non-agrarian village · nicht-agrarisches Dorf *n*

nonagreed performance · nicht vereinbarte Leistung *f*, unvereinbarte Leistung

nonagression pact · Nichtangriffspakt *m*

nonagricultural, nonfarm · landwirtschaftsfremd, nichtlandwirtschaftlich

nonagricultural population, nonfarm population · landwirtschaftsfremde Bevölkerung *f*, nichtlandwirtschaftliche Bevölkerung

nonappearance, default of appearance · Kontumaz *f* [*Nichterscheinen einer Prozeßpartei bei einer gerichtlichen Verhandlung*]

nonappearance, default of appearance · Nichterscheinen *n*, Fernbleiben, Wegbleiben

nonapplication · Nichtanwendung *f*

nonassignable · nicht abtretbar, nicht zedierbar

non-assisted → non-subsidized

non-assumpsit [*Latin*] · formloses Versprechen *n*

nonauthoritative, nonbinding, nonobligatory, not binding, without prejudice · nicht bindend, nicht verpflichtend, nicht verbindlich, unverbindlich

nonauthorized female person, unauthorized female person · Unbefugte *f*

nonauthorized male person, unauthorized male person · Unbefugte *m*

nonauthorized person, unauthorized person · unbefugte Person *f*

nonbasic · nahbedarfstätig

nonbasic activity, nonbasic employment, auxiliary occupations, service activity · Nahversorgungstätigkeit *f*, Folgeleistung, Befriedigung *f* der örtlichen Nachfrage, Versorgung der Bevölkerung der eigenen Stadt, sekundäre Aktivität *f* [*Eine innerhalb der Region abgesetzte wirtschaftliche Leistung*]

nonbasic employment, auxiliary occupations, service activity, nonbasic activity · Nahversorgungstätigkeit *f*, Folgeleistung, Befriedigung *f* der örtlichen Nachfrage, Versorgung der Bevölkerung der eigenen Stadt, sekundäre Aktivität *f* [*Eine innerhalb der Region abgesetzte wirtschaftliche Leistung*]

nonbasic sector · nahbedarfstätiger Sektor *m*

nonbasic trade · Nahbedarfsgewerbe *n*

nonbasic work(s) · besondere Leistung(en) *f (pl)*, besondere Arbeit(en) *f (pl)* [*Im Gegensatz zu „Grundleistung(en)" eines Architekten*]

non-bidder, nontenderer · Nicht(an)bieter *m*

nonbinding, nonobligatory, not binding, without prejudice, nonauthoritative · nicht bindend, nicht verpflichtend, nicht verbindlich, unverbindlich

non-building cost(s), non-construction cost(s) · nichtbauliche Kosten *f*

non built-up, open, uncovered, unbuilt, not built (up)on · frei, nichtbebaut, unbebaut; unüberbaut [*Schweiz*]

nonbureaucratic · unbürokratisch

non-business corporation, non-profit corporation [*USA*] · Körperschaft *f* mit ideeller Zweckrichtung, Korporation *f* mit ideeler Zweckrichtung

noncentral function, dispersed function, scattered function · disperse Funktion *f*, nichtzentrale Funktion, Streufunktion

noncentral population, scattered population, dispersed population · nichtzentrale Bevölkerung *f*, disperse Bevölkerung, Streubevölkerung

noncentral x^2 distribution · nicht zentrale Chi-Quadrat-Verteilung *f*

non-city, non-town · formlose Stadt *f*

non-city resident, non-town resident · Nichtstädter *m*

non-codified law · unkodifiziertes Recht *n*

non collectable, noncollectible, nonrecoverable, nonobtainable, uncollectable, unrecoverable, uncollectible, bad, irrecoverable, unobtainable, desperate, hopeless · nicht beitreibbar, nicht einziehbar, nicht eintreibbar, uneinziehbar, uneintreibbar, uneinbringlich, unbeitreibbar [*Schuld*]

noncollegiate man, unattached man [*College*] · Nichtangeschlossene *m*

(non-)collusion affidavit · eidesstattliche Erklärung *f* über Nichtabsprache (unter Bietern), eidesstattliche Versicherung über Nichtabsprache (unter Bietern), Erklärung an Eidesstatt über Nichtabsprache (unter Bietern), Versicherung an Eidesstatt über Nichtabsprache (unter Bietern)

noncollusive · nicht abgesprochen [*Angebot*]

non-combatants [*French*]; civilian population · Zivilbevölkerung *f*

noncommercial corporation · Laienkörperschaft *f* ohne (halb)wirtschaftlichen Geschäftsbetrieb, Laienkorporation *f* ohne (halb)wirtschaftlichen Geschäftsbetrieb

non-commital price · Vorbehaltpreis *m*

non-compact development, sporadic development, scattered development, dispersed development [*Developments occurring here and there without any co-ordinating feature to lick them or give them identity*] · Splitterbebauung *f*, Streubebauung, wilde Bebauung; Splitterüberbauung, Streuüberbauung, wilde Überbauung [*Schweiz*]

non-compact land(ed) estate, scattered land(ed) estate, dispersed land(ed) estate · Streu(land)besitz *m*, disperser (Land)Besitz, Streubodenbesitz, disperser Bodenbesitz

non-compact landscape, dispersed landscape, scattered landscape · Streulandschaft *f*, disperse Landschaft

non-compact location, dispersed location, scattered location · Streulage *f*, disperse Lage

non-compact pattern, dispersed scheme, scattered scheme, non-compact scheme, dispersed pattern, scattered pattern · Streumuster *n*, Streuschema *n*, disperses Muster, disperses Schema

non-compact settlement, non-compact settling, dispersed settlement, dispersed settling, scattered settlement, scattered settling · Streubesied(e)lung, Splitter(be)sied(e)lung, Streu(an)sied(e)lung, Splitteransied(e)lung, Streusiedeln, Splittersiedeln, Streubesiedeln, Splitterbesiedeln *n* [*Tätigkeit, die zum Entstehen einer Streuansied(e)lung führt*]

non-compact site housing [*Housing units dispersed, usually by a local housing authority, in small numbers on numerous, noncontiguous sites throughout a community*], scattered-site housing, dispersed-site housing · Streuwohnungen *f pl*

non-compact territorial domain, dispersed territorial domain, scattered territorial domain · Streugrundherrschaft *f* disperse Grundherrschaft

noncompany personnel, noncompany staff · firmenfremdes Personal *n*

non-competitive · wettbewerbslos, ohne Konkurrenz

noncompletion · Nichtvollendung *f*, Nichtfertigstellung

noncompliance, default, nonconformity, nonfeasance, nonperformance [*An omission of that which ought to be done. Specifically, the omission or failure to perform a legal duty*] · Nichtbefolgung *f*, Nichteinhaltung, Nichterfüllung, technisches Versäumnis *n*, Nichtausführung

non-compulsory area · Nicht-Zwangsbuchungsgebiet *n*

nonconforming use, pre-existing use [*A use of land which lawfully existed prior to the enactment of a zoning ordinance and which is maintained after the ordinance, although it not longer complies with the use restrictions applicable to the area*] · nicht übereinstimmende

Benutzung f, nicht übereinstimmender Gebrauch m

nonconforming work [*Work that does not meet the contract requirements*] · nicht vertragsgetreue Arbeit f

nonconformity, nonfeasance, nonperformance, noncompliance, default [*An omission of that which ought to be done. Specifically, the omission or failure to perform a legal duty*] · Nichtbefolgung f, Nichteinhaltung, Nichterfüllung, technisches Versäumnis n, Nichtausführung

non constat [*Latin*]; not clear · unklar

non-construction cost(s), non-building cost(s) · nichtbauliche Kosten f

noncontentious, nonadversary · nicht streitig, nicht strittig, unbestritten

noncontentious proceedings, noncontentious jurisdiction · freiwillige Gerichtsbarkeit f

non-contract-breaking party, nondefaulting party · vertragstreue Partei f, nichtsäumige Partei

non-contractual, outside a contract, extracontractual · außervertraglich, nichtvertraglich

noncontributing, non-employed, nonworking · nicht berufstätig, nicht erwerbstätig, nicht beschäftigt, nicht arbeitend

noncontributing population · nichtarbeitende Bevölkerung f, Nicht-Erwerbsbevölkerung

non-cooperative game · nichtkooperatives Spiel n

non-county borough, quarter session (municipal) borough, (municipal) borough [*Created 1835 in England by the Municipal Corporations Act*] · Munizipalstadt f, grafschaftsfreie Stadt, Stadt im rechtlichen Sinne, Stadt mit korporativer Verfassung, selbständige Stadt [*Gegensatz: Reichsstadt. ,,(Municipal) borough" ist der offizielle Name einer Stadt in England; in Schottland ,,burgh". ,,Town" gehört der Umgangssprache an. ,,City" ist in England ein auszeichnender Titel, den altberühmte Städte, meistens Bischofssitze, tragen. In der Verwaltung besteht zwischen ,,city" und ,,borough" kein Unterschied*]

nondefaulting party, non-contract-breaking party · vertragstreue Partei f, nichtsäumige Partei

non-defective, proper · baumangelfrei, (sach)mangelfrei, nachbesserungsfrei

non-defective, proper · baumangelfrei, (sach)mängelfrei, nachbesserungsfrei

nondelegable · nicht delegierbar

nondelivery, misdelivery, failure to make delivery · Nichtlieferung f

nondevelopment · Nichtentwick(e)lung f

non-disclosure, concealment [*The intentional suppression of truth or fact known, to the injury or prejudice of another*] · Verschweigung f, Verheimlichung, Unterdrückung der Wahrheit

non-disclosure, confidential treatment · vertrauliche Behand(e)lung f, Unterlassung einer Mitteilung

non-disclosure letter · vertrauliches Schreiben n

nondisposable possession, possession held in mortmain, un(ab)alienable possession · Tothandbesitz m, unveräußerlicher Besitz, unveräußerbarer Besitz

non-diversified fund · ungestreuter Fonds m

non-diversion · Zweckbindung f

non-divisibility, indivisibility · Unteilbarkeit f

nondivisible right; jus individuum [*Latin*]; individual right, indivisible right, right incapable of division · unteilbares Recht n

nondutiable · zollfrei

non-eligible · nicht antragsberechtigt

non-employed, non-working, non-contributing · nicht berufstätig, nicht erwerbstätig, nicht beschäftigt, nicht arbeitend

nonessential · Nicht-Dringliche n, Nicht-Lebensnotwendige

nonessential ignorance, accidental ignorance · unwesentliche Unkenntnis f

nonexclusive (general) property; dominium temporale [*Latin*]; limited ownership (of property), nonexclusive ownership (of property), limited proprietorship, nonexclusive proprietorship, limited (general) property · beschränktes Eigentum n, begrenztes Eigentum, eingeschränktes Eigentum

nonexecution, nonimplementation · Nichtdurchführung f, Durchführungsunterlassung

nonexecutive director · Direktor m ohne Vollziehungsfunktion

nonexistence · Nichtbestehen n

nonfarm, nonagricultural · landwirtschaftsfremd, nichtlandwirtschaftlich

nonfarm economy · Nichtlandwirtschaft f

nonfarm mortgage · landwirtschaftsfremde Hypothek f

nonfarm population, nonagricultural population · landwirtschaftsfremde Bevölkerung f, nichtlandwirtschaftliche Bevölkerung

nonfeasance, nonperformance, noncompliance, default, nonconformity

[*An omission of that which ought to be done. Specifically, the omission or failure to perform a legal duty*] · Nichtbefolgung f, Nichteinhaltung, Nichterfüllung, technisches Versäumnis n, Nichtausführung

non-food retail trade · Nicht-Lebensmittel-Einzelhandel m

nonforested, unforested · unbewaldet, waldlos

nonforfeiture · Unverfallbarkeit f

non-fortified · unbefestigt, festungslos

non-free, unfree, customary, at (the) will (of the lord) · unfrei, nichtfrei, zugestanden, prekarisch, auf Ruf und Widerruf, willkürlich aufkündbar [*Leh(e)n*]

non-free (feodal) tenement → copyhold

non-free fief → copyhold

non-free tenancy → copyhold

non-free tenement → copyhold

non-free tenure → copyhold

non-fulfilled contract · nicht erfüllter Vertrag m

non-full-pay-out- leasing · Teilamortisation f

nongrowth · Nichtwachstum n

nonimplementation, nonexecution · Nichtdurchführung f, Durchführungsunterlassung

non-incorporated building society, benefit building society (Brit.); non-incorporated (building and loan) association, benefit (building and loan) association (US) · nichteingetragene Bausparkasse f

non-inflationary investment financing · geldwertneutrale Investitionsfinanzierung f, nichtinflationäre Investitionsfinanzierung

non-interest bearing · unverzinslich

noninterference · Nichteinmischung f

nonjoinder [*The omission to join some person as party to a suit, whether as plaintiff or defendant, who ought to have been so joined, according to the rules of pleading and practice*] · Nichthäufung f

non-key sector of building (construction) · Nichtwohn(ungs)bau m

nonlegal, nonstatutory, contrary to law, illegal, against law, wrongful, unlawful; wrongous [*Scotland*] · gesetz(es)widrig, ungesetzlich, rechtsunerheblich, nicht rechtserheblich, widerrechtlich, unrechtmäßig, rechtswidrig

nonliability, exemption (from liability), release (from liability) · (Haftungs)Ausschluß m, (Haftungs)Freizeichnung f, (Haftungs)Ausschließung, Haftpflichtausschluß, Haftbarkeitsausschluß, Haftbarkeitsausschließung

nonliability clause, exemption clause, saving clause, exclusion clause [*A clause in a contract by which a purchaser repudiates liability in certain specified circumstances*] · Ausschließungsklausel f, Ausschlußklausel f, Freizeichnungsklausel f, Haftungsausschließungsklausel f, Haftungsausschlußklausel f, Haftungsfreizeichnungsklausel f

non-linearity · Nichtlinearität f

nonlinear regression, skew regression, curvilinear regression · nichtlineare Regression f

non-living environment · unbelebte Umwelt f

nonlocal · nicht ortsansässig, ortsfremd

nonlocal traffic · überörtlicher Verkehr m

non-manufacturing jobs, tertiary sector [*administration; service*] · Tertiärwirtschaft f, Teritärsektor, tertiärer Wirtschaftssektor m, tertiär(wirtschaftlich)er Sektor [*Er ist fernbezugstätig und nahbedarfstätig*]

nonmap · Nichtkarte f

nonmarket interdependency, direct interdependency · Wirkung f die nicht über den Marktmechanismus gelenkt wird

non-mediate territory · Immediatgebiet n

non-mediate town · Immediatstadt f [*Die Obrigkeiten werden selbst gewählt*]

nonmember · Nichtmitglied n

nonmembership · Nichtmitgliedschaft f

non-metered zone cab · Zonentaxi n ohne Zähler, zählerloses Taxi

nonmigrant, nonmover · nichtwandernde Person f, seßhafte Person

nonmigrating female person, nonmigratory female person · Nichtwanderin f, Nichtwandernde f, seßhafte weibliche Person f, weibliche seßhafte Person

nonmigrating male person, nonmigratory male person · Nichtwandernde m, seßhafte männliche Person f, männliche seßhafte Person

nonmilitary person, civilian · Zivilist m, Zivilperson f

nonmobile population, indigenous population, native population [*People enumerated in their places of birth*] · altansässige Bevölkerung f, einheimische Bevölkerung, autochthone Bevölkerung

nonmobility · verhinderte Mobilität f [*Den Wünschen der Bevölkerung nach Mobilität stehen mangelnde Verkehrsmöglichkeiten, vor allem im öffentlichen Verkehr, entgegen*]

non-monetary · nichtgeldlich

non-monetary advantage · nichtgeldlicher Vorteil *m*

non-monetary consideration · nichtgeldliche Gegenleistung *f*

non-monetary economy, natural economy, barter economy [*Goods are exchanged for goods*] · Tauschwirtschaft *f*

nonmoney income · geldloses Einkommen *n*

nonmover, nonmigrant · nichtwandernde Person *f*, seßhafte Person

nonmunicipal community · nichtmunizipale Gemeinde *f*, nichtmunizipale Kommune *f*

nonnatural state, unnatural state · veränderter Zustand *m* [*Land*]

nonnavigable, innavigable · unschiffbar, nicht schiffbar

nonnegotiability · Nichtbegebbarkeit *f*

nonnegotiable, not negotiable, nontransferable by endorsement, unnegotiable · nicht umlaufbar, nicht begebbar, nicht umlauffähig

nonnegotiable warehouse receipt, unnegotiable warehouse receipt, not negotiable warehouse receipt, warehouse receipt nontransferable by endorsement · Lagerempfangsschein *m*

non-notifiable construction project, non-notifiable building project · anzeigefreies Bauvorhaben *n*

non-null hypothesis, alternative hypothesis · Gegenhypothese *f* [*Statistik*]

nonobjection · Unbedenklichkeit *f*

nonobjection certificate, negative certificate, certificate of nonobjection · Unbedenklichkeitsattest *n*, Unbedenklichkeitsbescheinigung *f*, Unbedenklichkeitsschein *m*, Bodenverkehrszeugnis *n*, Negativattest, Negativbescheinigung, Negativschein

nonobligatory, not binding, without prejudice, nonauthoritative, nonbinding · nicht bindend, nicht verpflichtend, nicht verbindlich, unverbindlich

nonobservance, inobservance · Nichtbeachtung *f*

nonobtainable, uncollectable, unrecoverable, uncollectible, bad, irrecoverable, unobtainable, desperate, hopeless, non collectable, noncollectible, nonrecoverable · nicht beitreibbar, nicht einziehbar, nicht eintreibbar, uneinziehbar, uneintreibbar, uneinbringlich, unbeitreibbar [*Schuld*]

nonoccupational [*Not of or pertaining to an occupation, trade, or work*] · nicht berufsbezogen

non-opened-up (building) (land) area, non-opened-up (building) land · unaufgeschlossenes (Bau)Land *n*

nonoperating expense, income deduction · Erlösschmälerung *f*

nonoperating revenue, other revenue · betriebsfremder Ertrag *m*, sonstiger Ertrag

non-original property, non-original dominion · Nebensache *f* [*Vermengung; Vermischung*]

nonowner, nonproprietor · Nichteigentümer *m*, Nichteigner

non-parametric · nicht parametrisch

nonparametric method · verteilungsunabhängige Methode *f*, nichtparametrische Methode [*Statistik*]

nonparticipation · Nichtteilnahme *f*, Nichtbeteiligung *f*

nonpayment, halted payment, default of payment · Nicht(be)zahlung *f*

nonperformance, noncompliance, default, nonconformity, nonfeasance [*An omission of that which ought to be done. Specifically, the omission or failure to perform a legal duty*] · Nichtbefolgung *f*, Nichteinhaltung, Nichterfüllung, technisches Versäumnis *n*, Nichtausführung

nonperishable · unverderblich

non-plan · formloser Plan *m*

non prescribable, imprescriptible · unersitzbar

non-price-bound · nicht preisgebunden, preisfrei

non-priced, free of charge · gratis, kostenfrei, kostenlos, ohne Entgelt, unentgeltlich

non-privileged, unprivileged · nichtprivilegiert, unprivilegiert

non-privileged commercial lay corporation, unprivileged commercial lay corporation · nichtprivilegierte wirtschaftliche Laienkörperschaft *f*, unprivilegierte wirtschaftliche Laienkörperschaft, unprivilegierte wirtschaftliche Laienkorporation *f*

nonprofit, useful to the public, of public utility, of public usefulness · gemeinnützig, gemeinnötig

non-profit corporation, non-business corporation [*USA*] · Körperschaft *f* mit ideeller Zweckrichtung, Korporation *f* mit ideeller Zweckrichtung

nonproprietor, nonowner · Nichteigentümer *m*, Nichteigner

non-public · nichtöffentlich

non-publicly-assisted hous(ebuild)ing · nicht öffentlich geförderter Wohnungsbau *m*

non-receipt · Nichterhalt *m*

non-recording, non-recordation, nonregistration · Nichteintragung *f*, Nichtbuchung, Nichtregistrierung

nonrecoverable, nonobtainable, uncollectable, unrecoverable, uncollectible, bad, irrecoverable, unobtainable, desperate, hopeless, non collectable, noncollectible · nicht beitreibbar, nicht einziehbar, nicht eintreibbar, uneinziehbar, uneintreibbar, uneinbringlich, unbeitreibbar [*Schuld*]

nonrecurrent cost(s) · einmalige Kosten *f*

nonrefundable · nichtrückerstattbar

nonregistrability · Buchungsfreiheit *f*, Eintragungsfreiheit, Registrierungsfreiheit [*Grund(stück)*]

nonregistrable · buchungsfrei, eintragungsfrei, registrierungsfrei [*Grund(stück)*]

non-registration, non-recording, nonrecordation · Nichteintragung *f*, Nichtbuchung, Nichtregistrierung

nonremunerative cost(s) · unrentierliche Kosten *f*

non-renunciation, non-waiver · Nichtverzicht *m*, Rechtsnichtaufgabe *f*, Vorbehalt *m* aller Rechte, Rechtsvorbehalt

nonrepayable · nicht rückzahlbar, unrückzahlbar

nonresident [*One who is not a dweller within jurisdiction in question*] · Nichtansässige *m*, Gebietsfremde

nonresidential building · Nichtwohn(ungs)gebäude *n*

nonresidential development · nichtwohngebietliche Entwick(e)lung *f*

nonresidential floor area, nonresidential floor space · Nichtwohn(ungs)-Geschoßfläche *f*, Nichtwohn(ungs)-Etagenfläche, Nichtwohn(ungs)-Stockwerkfläche

nonresidential function · Nichtwohnfunktion *f*

nonresidential land · Nichtwohn(ungs)land *n*

nonresidential land use · wohnungsfremde Landnutzung *f*

nonresidential structure, nonresidential work, nonresidential physical facility · Nichtwohn(ungs)-Bauwerk *n*

nonrural space · nichtländlicher Raum *m*

non-sane, insane, deranged; insanus [*Latin*]; unsound in mind, disordered in mind, diseased in mind, of unsound mind · geistesgestört, geisteskrank

nonscientific · geisteswissenschaftlich

nonseasonal worker, nonseasonal workman; nonseasonal labourer (Brit.); nonseasonal laborer (US) · Nichtsaisonarbeiter *m*

nonselective, unselective · ausleseindifferent

non-self-executing treaty · nicht unmittelbar anwendungsfähiger völkerrechtlicher Vertrag *m*

nonsense correlation · sinnlose Korrelation *f*

non-separate property · unfreies Frauenvermögen *n*

non-serial (building and loan) association (US) · Nicht-Serien(plan-Bauspar)kasse *f*

non-service, basic · fest [*Von der Bevölkerungsverteilung unabhängiger Standort*]

nonspeculator · Nichtspekulant *m*, Bauinteressent *m*

nonstandard operation variance · Arbeitsablaufabweichung *f*

nonstatutory → nonlegal

non-stock corporation, membership corporation · (Kapital)Gesellschaft *f* mit nicht in übertragbare selbständige Anteile zerfallendem Grundkapital an deren Eigentum eine Mitgliedschaft gebunden ist

non-suable claim · Naturalobligation *f*

nonsubsidized, unassisted · nichtgefördert, frei [*Wohn(ungs)bau*]

to nonsuit, to strike out, to dismiss · abweisen [*Klage*]

nonsuit, dismissal of (court) action, dismissal of plea, dismissal of (law)suit, dismissal of cause [*An order or judg(e)ment finally disposing of an action, suit, motion, etc., by sending it out of court, though without a trial of the issues involved*] · Abweisung *f*, Klageabweisung

non-tenderer, non-bidder · Nicht(an)bieter *m*

non tenure [*In pleading. A plea by a tenant in a real action, where he is not in fact the tenant of the freehold, denying that he was tenant of the freehold of the land or rent demanded. It is usually called a plea in abatement, but is not strictly so*] · Bestreiten *n* der Pächtereigenschaft

non term; justitium, non terminus [*Latin*]; vacation time of (a) court · Gerichtsferien *f*

non-tidal river, stream · Fluß *m*

non-town, non-city · formlose Stadt *f*

non-town resident, non-city resident · Nichtstädter *m*

**nontrade corporation, **nontrading corporation · Körperschaft f ohne Handelsgewerbe, Korporation f ohne Handelsgewerbe

nontrading partnership · Sozietät f

nontransferable, untransferable · unübertragbar, nicht übertragbar

nontransferable by endorsement, unnegotiable, nonnegotiable, not negotiable · nicht umlaufbar, nicht begebbar, nicht umlauffähig

nonurban · nichtstädtisch

nonurban land · nichtstädtisches Land n, nichtstädtischer Boden m

nonurban settlement · nichtstädtische (An)Sied(e)lung f

nonuse, disuse, neglect to use · Nichtgebrauch m, Nichtbenutzung f

non-voidable pricing mistake · interner Kalkulationsirrtum m, interner Preisgestaltungsirrtum [*Ein Irrtum, der dem Bieter bei der Kalkulation unterläuft. Da der Preis keine „Eigenschaft" der Leistung ist, scheidet eine Anfechtung wegen eines Eigenschaftsirrtums nach § 119 Abs. 2 BGB aus*]

nonvoting age · Nichtwahlalter n

nonvoting preferred stock, nonvoting preference stock, nonvoting preferential stock · Vorzugsaktie f ohne Stimmrecht

nonvoting stock · Aktie f ohne Stimmrecht, stimmrechtlose Aktie

nonwage cost(s) · nicht lohngebundene Kosten f, lohnungebundene Kosten

non-waiver, non-renunciation · Nichtverzicht m, Rechtsnichtaufgabe f, Vorbehalt m aller Rechte, Rechtsvorbehalt

non-white area, non-white territory · Gebiet n mit farbiger Bevölkerung

non-white person · farbige Person f

non-white population · farbige Bevölkerung f

non-white territory, non-white area · Gebiet n mit farbiger Bevölkerung

nonwork activity, leisure activity · Freizeitbetätigung f

nonwork area, nonwork territory, leisure area, leisure territory · Freizeitgebiet n

nonwork domicil(e), leisure domicil(e) · Freizeitwohnsitz m

nonwork facility, leisure facility · Freizeiteinrichtung f

nonwork function, leisure function · Freizeitfunktion f

nonwork grounds, leisure grounds · Freizeitgelände n

nonwork infrastructure, leisure infrastructure · Freizeitinfrastruktur f

nonworking, non-contributing, nonemployed · nicht berufstätig, nicht erwerbstätig, nicht beschäftigt, nicht arbeitend

nonwork landscape, leisure landscape · Freizeitlandschaft f

nonwork passenger, leisure passenger · Freizeitfahrgast m

nonwork planning, planning for leisure, leisure planning · Freizeitplanung f

nonwork pursuit, leisure pursuit · Freizeitinteresse n

nonwork region, leisure region · Freizeitregion f

nonwork research, leisure research · Freizeitforschung f

nonwork territory, leisure area, leisure territory, nonwork area · Freizeitgebiet n

nonwork time, leisure time, free time, spare time · Freizeit f

nonwork travel, nonwork trip, nonwork journey, leisure travel, leisure trip, leisure journey · Freizeitfahrt f, Nicht-Berufsfahrt

non-wrongful, consistent with, non-adverse · nicht entgegenstehend, nicht entgegen dem Recht [*(subjektives) Besitzrecht*]

non-zero sum game · Spiel n dessen Summe nicht Null ist

no par (value) share, share of no par value · nennwertloser Anteil m, Anteil ohne Nennwert

no punishment without previous legal authority; nulla poena sine lege poenali [*Latin*] · keine Strafe f ohne Strafgesetz

no-rent land, rentless land · pachtzinsfreies Land n

normal distribution, Gauss distribution · Normalverteilung f [*Statistik*]

normal equivalent deviate, N.E.D. · Normalfraktil n [*Statistik*]

normal person · Person f mit voller Geschäftsfähigkeit

normal return, regular yield, standard yield, regular return, standard return, normal yield · Normalrendite f

normal use, ordinary use · gewöhnliche Benutzung f, gewöhnlicher Gebrauch m

normal wear and tear, regular wear and tear, fair wear and tear · normaler Verschleiß m, üblicher Verschleiß

normal (working) day · Normal(arbeits)tag m

normal yield, normal return, regular yield, standard yield, regular return, standard return · Normalrendite f

Norman French · Normannisch-Französisch n [*Die Gerichtssprache bis auf 36 Ed. III*]

normative · normativ

norm effectiveness · Normwirkung f

norm-execution · Normausübung f

normmaking · Normengebung f

norm of law, legal rule, (legal) norm, law rule, law norm, rule (of law) [*It is a rule of general application, sanctioned by the recognition of authorities, and usually expressed in the form of maxim or logical proposition. Called a "rule", because in doubtful or unforeseen cases it is a guide or norm for their decision*] · Gesetz(es)norm f, Sachnorm, normative Festlegung f, (Rechts)Norm

norm system · Normensystem n

not absolute, contingent ((up)on), depending (up)on, conditional [*Operative only (up)on an uncertain event*] · bedingt durch, abhängig von, abhängend von

not according to realty, false, not real, unreal · unwirklich, falsch

not according to truth, untrue, false, not true, not truly · falsch, unwahr

not acquirable · unerwerbbar, unbeschaffbar, nicht erwerbbar, nicht beschaffbar

not allowed, not permitted, illicit, prohibited · unerlaubt, verboten

notarial; notoriol [*Scots law*] · notariell

notarial acknowledg(e)ment, notarial attestation · Beurkundung f, notarielle Beurkundung

notarial agreement · notarielle Abmachung f, notarielle Vereinbarung, notarielles Abkommen n

notarial attestation → notarial acknowledg(e)ment

notarial contract · notarieller Vertrag m

notarial deed · notarielle Urkunde f

notarial seal · Notariatssiegel n

notary (public), actuarius · Notar m

notation symbol · Planzeichen n

notation symbol ordinance · Planzeichenverordnung f

not binding, without prejudice, nonauthoritative, nonbinding, nonobligatory · nicht bindend, nicht verpflichtend, nicht verbindlich, unverbindlich

not built (up)on, non built-up, open, uncovered, unbuilt · frei, nichtbebaut, unbebaut; unüberbaut, nichtüberbaut [*Schweiz*]

not (capable) of inheritance · nicht(ver)erblich, un(ver)erblich

not capable of registration, unregistrable · nicht eintragungsfähig, nicht eintragungsreif, nicht buchungsfähig, nicht buchungsreif, nicht registrierfähig, nicht registrierreif, unregistrierbar

not capable of repair, beyond repair · nicht reparaturfähig, reparaturunfähig

not clear; non constat [*Latin*] · unklar

not clerical, lay · weltlich

not contradictory, concurrent, agreeing with, according to, consonant, conformable, accordant, consistent [*Having agreement with itself or something else*] · gemäß, nicht gegenteilig, konform mit, übereinstimmend, gerecht mit

not covered pound, pound-overt, open pound, uncovered pound · nicht eingefriedetes Grundstück n, uneingefriedetes Grundstück [*Es wird der Vollstreckung unterworfen*]

note [*Instrument given to attest a debt*] · Schuldpapier n, Schuldschein m, Schuldbescheinigung f

note, remark · Bemerkung f

note → (bank) note

note circulation · Notenumlauf m

note issue → (bank) note issue

not entitled to a dwelling · nichtwohnberechtigt

note (of hand), single bill, sole bill, only bill, promissory note · Eigenwechsel m, (eigener) Wechsel, Solawechsel, Verpflichtungsschein m [*Ein unbedingtes, von einer Person an eine andere gerichtetes, vom Aussteller unterschriebenes schriftliches Versprechen, auf Verlangen oder zu einer festgesetzten oder zu einer bestimmbar zukünftigen Zeit an eine bestimmte Person oder deren Order oder an den Inhaber eine bestimmte Summe in Geld zu zahlen*]

note of portion of land removed from the title · Abschreibung f [*Die im Grundbuch anzugebende Trennung des Teiles eines Grundstückes von einem eingetragenen Grundstück bei einer Belastung dieses Teils mit einem Recht*]

not free of charge · entgeltlich, mit Entgelt

not genuine, false, counterfeit · gefälscht, imitiert, nachgemacht, falsch

to notice · Kenntnis nehmen

notice · Kenntnis f

notice · Kenntnisnahme f

notice · Einladung f [*Eines Liquidators an die Mitglieder einer Gesellschaft*]

notice, notification · Anzeige f, Mitteilung f, Benachrichtigung f

notice [*The result of observation, whether by the senses or the mind*] · Wahrnehmung *f*

notice, notification · Vermerk *m*

notice-board, bulletin board · Anschlagbrett *n*, schwarzes Brett *n*, Aushangbrett

notice in writing, notification in writing, written notice, written notification · schriftliche Anzeige *f*, schriftliche Benachrichtigung *f*, schriftliche Mitteilung

notice of acceptance, letter of award of contract, letter of letting of contract, notice of award of contract, notice of letting of contract, letter of award, notice of award, acceptance letter, letter of acceptance · Auftragsschreiben *n*, Zuschlag(s)schreiben *n*

notice of affirmation → notice of confirmation

notice of appeal, appellate notice · Appellationsanmeldung *f*, Berufungsanmeldung

notice of appearance, appearance notice, notification of appearance, appearance notification [*A notice given by defendant for a plaintiff that he appears in the action in person or by attorney*] · Einlassungsmitteilung *f*, Einlassungsanzeige *f*, Einlassungsbenachrichtigung

notice of arbitration, notification of arbitration · Schiedsanzeige *f*, Schiedsmitteilung *f*, Schiedsbenachrichtigung

notice of assignment, notice of cession, notification of assignment, notification of cession, assignment notice, assignment notification, cession notice, cession notification · Zessionsanzeige *f*, Zessionsmitteilung *f*, Abtretungsanzeige, Abtretungsmitteilung

notice of award of contract, notice of letting of contract, letter of award, notice of award, acceptance letter, letter of acceptance, notice of acceptance, letter of award of contract, letter of letting of contract · Auftragsschreiben *n*, Zuschlag(s)schreiben *n*

notice of confirmation, notice of affirmation, notification of confirmation, notification of affirmation, confirmation notice, confirmation notification, affirmation notice, affirmation notification · Bestätigungsmitteilung *f*, Bestätigungsanzeige *f*, Bestätigungsbenachrichtigung

notice of damage, notification of damage · Schadensanzeige *f*, Schadensmitteilung *f*, Schadensbenachrichtigung

notice of default, notification of default, default notice, default notification · Anzeige *f* der Vertragsverletzung, Mitteilung *f* der Vertragsverletzung, Benachrichtigung *f* der Vertragsverletzung, Vertragsverletzungsanzeige *f*, Vertragsverletzungsmitteilung *f*, Vertragsverletzungsbenachrichtigung *f*

notice of defect, notification of defect, customer's complaint · Baumangelbenachrichtigung *f*, Baumangelmitteilung, Baumangelanzeige *f*, (Sach)Mangelanzeige, (Sach)Mangelmitteilung, Nachbesserungsanzeige, Nachbesserungsmitteilung, Nachbesserungsbenachrichtigung, (Sach)Mangelbenachrichtigung, (Sach)Mangelrüge *f*, Baumangelrüge

notice of defects, notification of defects, customer's complaints · Baumängelanzeige *f*, Baumängelmitteilung *f*, (Sach)Mängelanzeige, Nachbesserungsanzeige, Baumängelbenachrichtigung, (Sach)Mängelbenachrichtigung, (Sach)Mängelmitteilung, Nachbesserungsmitteilung, Nachbesserungsbenachrichtigung, (Sach)Mängelrüge *f*, Baumängelrüge

notice of demolition, notice of wrecking, notification of demolition, notification of wrecking, notice of pulling down, notification of pulling down, notification of razing, notice of razing · Abbruchanzeige *f*, Abbruchmitteilung *f*, Abbruchbenachrichtigung, Abrißanzeige, Abrißmitteilung, Abrißbenachrichtigung, Abreißanzeige, Abreißmitteilung, Abreißbenachrichtigung, Einreißanzeige, Einreißmitteilung, Einreißbenachrichtigung [*Sie ist der betreffenden Behörde zur Erteilung einer Abbruchgenehmigung zu erstatten*]

notice of determination, notification of determination · Auftragskündigungsschreiben *n*

notice of dishonour, notification of dishonour (Brit.); notice of dishonor, notification of dishonor (US) · Nichtzahlungsanzeige *f*, Nichtzahlungsmitteilung *f*, Nichtzahlungsbenachrichtigung

notice of dishonour, notification of dishonour (Brit.); notice of dishonor, notification of dishonor (US) · Notifikation *f* eines notleidenden Wechsels

notice of dissolution, notification of dissolution · Auflösungsbenachrichtigung *f*, Auflösungsmitteilung, Auflösungsanzeige *f*

notice of extra work, notification of extra work · Ankündigung *f* [*Wird eine Bauleistung vom BU gefordert, zu der er nach dem Vertrag nicht verpflichtet ist, so hat er bei Ausführung dieser Leistung einen Anspruch auf besondere Vergütung. Dieser Vergütungsanspruch setzt allerdings beim VOB-Vertrag voraus, daß der BU den Anspruch dem BH ankündigt bevor er mit der Ausführung der Leistung beginnt*]

notice of intent(ion), notification of intent(ion) · Absichtsmitteilung *f*,

notice of letting — notification of appearance

Absichtsbenachrichtigung, Absichtsanzeige f

notice of letting, notification of letting, letting notice, letting notification · Vergabevermerk m [in Ausschreibungsunterlagen]

notice of letting of contract → notice of acceptance

notice of motion · Terminnachricht f

notice of motion, notification of motion [A notice in writing entitled in a cause, dated and signed by the attorney of the party in whose behalf it is given, and addressed to the opposite party or his attorney; stating that on a certain day designated, a motion will be made to the court for the purpose or object stated] · Benachrichtigung f über einen Antrag an das Gericht

notice of priority, notification of priority, priority notice, priority notification · Auflassungsvormerkung f

notice of pulling down → notice of demolition

notice of razing, notice of demolition, notice of wrecking, notification of demolition, notification of wrecking, notice of pulling down, notification of pulling down, notification of razing · Abbruchanzeige f, Abbruchmitteilung f, Abbruchbenachrichtigung, Abrißanzeige, Abrißmitteilung f, Abrißbenachrichtigung, Abreißanzeige, Abreißmitteilung, Abreißbenachrichtigung, Einreißanzeige, Einreißmitteilung, Einreißbenachrichtigung [Sie ist der betreffenden Behörde zur Erteilung einer Abbruchgenehmigung zu erstatten]

notice of removal, notification of removal, removal notification, removal notice · Beseitigungsanzeige f, Beseitigungsbenachrichtigung f, Beseitigungsmitteilung

notice of revocation, notification of revocation, revocation notice, revocation notification · Widerrufsmitteilung f, Widerrufsanzeige f, Widerrufsbenachrichtigung

notice of termination, notification of termination, notice to terminate, notification to terminate · Kündigungsschreiben n, Beend(ig)ungsanzeige f, Beend(ig)ungsmitteilung f, Beend(ig)ungsbenachrichtigung

notice of time for completion, notification of time for completion · Fertigstellungsfristanzeige f, Fertigstellungsfristbenachrichtigung, Fertigstellungsfristmitteilung

notice of trial, trial notice · Terminanzeige f an die Gegenpartei, Anzeige des Termins an die Gegenpartei

notice of withdrawal, notification of withdrawal · Abmeldung f

notice of wrecking → notice of demolition

notice principle, principle of notice · Schutz m des gutgläubigen Erwerbers

notice server · Zustellungsbeamte m

notice to determine a contract, notification to determine a contract, notice to terminale a contract, notification to terminale a contract · Vertragskündigung f

notice to evacuate, notice to quit · Räumungskündigung f

notice to leave, notice to quit · Mietvertragskündigung f [Wohnung; Geschäftsräume]

notice to plead [This is a notice which is prerequisite to the taking judgement by default. It proceeds from the plaintiff, and warns the defendant that he must plead to the declaration or complaint within a prescribed time] · Einlassungsfrist f

notice to proceed, notification to proceed [Written communication issued by the owner to the contractor authorizing him to proceed with the work and establishing the date of commencement of the work] · Arbeitsaufnahmemitteilung f

notice to produce, notification to produce [A notice in writing, given in an action at law, requiring the opposite party to produce a certain described paper or document at the trial] · Aufforderung f zur Urkundenvorlage, Vorlagemitteilung, Vorlagebenachrichtigung, Vorlageanzeige f

notice to produce for inspection · Aufforderung f zum Vorzeigen zur Besichtigung [Schriftstück]

notice to quit, notice to leave · Mietvertragskündigung f [Wohnung; Geschäftsräume]

notice to quit, notice to evacuate · Räumungskündigung f

notifiable · anzeigepflichtig, mitteilungspflichtig, benachrichtigungspflichtig

notification, notice · Anzeige f, Mitteilung f, Benachrichtigung f

notification, notice · Vermerk m

notification address, notify address · Notadresse f, Notanschrift f

notification of affirmation, confirmation notice, confirmation notification, affirmation notice, affirmation notification, notice of confirmation, notice of affirmation, notification of confirmation · Bestätigungsmitteilung f, Bestätigungsanzeige f, Bestätigungsbenachrichtigung

notification of appearance, appearance notification, notice of appearance, appearance notice [A notice given by defendant for a plaintiff that he appears in the action in person or by attorney] · Einlassungsmitteilung f, Einlassungsanzeige f, Einlassungsbenachrichtigung

notification of arbitration, notice of arbitration · Schiedsanzeige f, Schiedsmitteilung f, Schiedsbenachrichtigung

notification of assignment, notification of cession, assignment notice, assignment notification, cession notice, cession notification, notice of assignment, notice of cession · Zessionsanzeige f, Zessionsmitteilung f, Abtretungsanzeige, Abtretungsmitteilung

notification of cession → notification of assignment

notification of confirmation → notification of affirmation

notification of damage, notice of damage · Schadensanzeige f, Schadensmitteilung f, Schadensbenachrichtigung

notification of default, default notice, default notification, notice of default · Anzeige f der Vertragsverletzung, Mitteilung f der Vertragsverletzung, Benachrichtigung f der Vertragsverletzung, Vertragsverletzungsanzeige f, Vertragsverletzungsmitteilung f, Vertragsverletzungsbenachrichtigung f

notification of defect, customer's complaint, notice of defect · Baumangelbenachrichtigung f, Baumangelmitteilung f, Baumangelanzeige f, (Sach)Mangelanzeige, (Sach)Mangelmitteilung, Nachbesserungsanzeige f, Nachbesserungsmitteilung, Nachbesserungsbenachrichtigung, (Sach)Mangelbenachrichtigung, (Sach)Mangelrüge f, Baumangelrüge

notification of defects, customer's complaints, notice of defects · Baumängelanzeige f, Baumängelmitteilung f, (Sach)Mängelanzeige, Nachbesserungsanzeige, Baumängelbenachrichtigung, (Sach)Mängelbenachrichtigung, (Sach)Mängelmitteilung, Nachbesserungsmitteilung, Nachbesserungsbenachrichtigung, (Sach)Mängelrüge f, Baumängelrüge

notification of demolition → notification of wrecking

notification of determination, notice of determination · Auftragskündigungsschreiben n

notification of dishonour, notice of dishonour (Brit.); notice of dishonor, notification of dishonor (US) · Nichtzahlungsanzeige f, Nichtzahlungsmitteilung f, Nichtzahlungsbenachrichtigung

notification of dishonour, notice of dishonour (Brit.); notice of dishonor, notification of dishonor (US); · Notifikation f eines notleidenden Wechsels

notification of extra work, notice of extra work · Ankündigung f [Wird eine Baulei-

stung vom BU gefordert, zu der er nach dem Vertrag nicht verpflichtet ist, so hat er bei Ausführung dieser Leistung einen Anspruch auf besondere Vergütung. Dieser Vergütungsanspruch setzt allerdings beim VOB-Vertrag voraus, daß der BU den Anspruch dem BH ankündigt bevor er mit der Ausführung der Leistung beginnt]

notification of letting, letting notice, letting notification, notice of letting · Vergabevermerk m [in Ausschreibungsunterlagen]

notification of motion, notice of motion [A notice in writing entitled in a cause, dated and signed by the attorney of the party in whose behalf it is given, and addressed to the opposite party or his attorney; stating that on a certain day designated, a motion will be made to the court for the purpose or object stated] · Benachrichtigung f über einen Antrag an das Gericht

notification of pulling down → notification of wrecking

notification of razing, notice of razing, notice of demolition, notice of wrecking, notification of demolition, notification of wrecking, notice of pulling down, notification of pulling down · Abbruchanzeige f, Abbruchmitteilung f, Abbruchbenachrichtigung, Abrißanzeige, Abrißmitteilung, Abrißbenachrichtigung, Abreißanzeige, Abreißmitteilung, Abreißbenachrichtigung, Einreißanzeige, Einreißmitteilung, Einreißbenachrichtigung [Sie ist der betreffenden Behörde zur Erteilung einer Abbruchgenehmigung zu erstatten]

notification of removal, removal notification, removal notice, notice of removal · Beseitigungsanzeige f, Beseitigungsbenachrichtigung f, Beseitigungsmitteilung

notification of residence, notice of residence · Aufenthaltsmitteilung f, Aufenthaltsanzeige f, Aufenthaltsbenachrichtigung f

notification of revocation, revocation notice, revocation notification, notice of revocation · Widerrufsmitteilung f, Widerrufsanzeige f, Widerrufsbenachrichtigung

notification of termination, notice to terminate, notification to terminate, notice of termination · Kündigungsschreiben n, Beend(ig)ungsanzeige f, Beend(ig)ungsmitteilung f, Beend(ig)ungsbenachrichtigung

notification of time for completion, notice of time for completion · Fertigstellungsfristanzeige f, Fertigstellungsfristbenachrichtigung, Fertigstellungsfristmitteilung f

notification of withdrawal, notice of withdrawal · Abmeldung f

notification of wrecking, notice of pulling down, notification of pulling down, notification of razing, notice of razing, notice of demolition, notice of wrecking, notification of demolition · Abbruchanzeige f, Abbruchmitteilung f, Abbruchbenachrichtigung, Abrißanzeige, Abrißmitteilung, Abrißbenachrichtigung, Abreißanzeige, Abreißmitteilung, Abreißbenachrichtigung, Einreißanzeige, Einreißmitteilung, Einreißbenachrichtigung [*Sie ist der betreffenden Behörde zur Erteilung einer Abbruchgenehmigung zu erstatten*]

notification to determine a contract, notice to terminale a contract, notification to terminale a contract, notice to determine a contract · Vertragskündigung f

notification to proceed → notice to proceed

notification to produce, notice to produce [*A notice in writing, given in an action at law, requiring the opposite party to produce a certain described paper or document at the trial*] · Aufforderung f zur Urkundenvorlage, Vorlagemitteilung, Vorlagebenachrichtigung, Vorlageanzeige f

to notify, to give notice, to advise, to inform · anzeigen, benachrichtigen, mitteilen, informieren

notify address, notification address · Notadresse f, Notanschrift f

notilia donationis, breve donationis [*Latin*]; commemoratorium · (schlichte) Schenkungsurkunde f [*Urkunde, in welcher die stattgehabte Schenkung als eine geschehene Tatsache beurkundet wird*]

not imperfect, without a burden, without a load, burdenless, free from encumbrance(s), free from charge(s), free from incumbrance(s), free from burden(s), uncharged, unburdened, unencumbered, unincumbered, clear, perfect, free from load(s), unloaded · entschuldet, lastenfrei, (dinglich) unbelastet, (dinglich) nicht belastet

not improved, raw, unimproved · unfertig, (bau)unreif, unerschlossen, roh, unverbessert, nicht baureif

noting a bill (of exchange) · Vormerken n zum Protest [*Wechsel*]

not (in)habitable, unfit to live in, unfit for (human) habitation, unfit for (human) occupation, unsuitable for (human) habitation, unsuitable for (human) occupation, un(in)habitable · unbewohnbar, unbelegbar

notional · imaginär, gedanklich

notional existence · gedankliches Dasein n, imaginäres Dasein

not married, alone, sole, single · ledig

not negotiable, nontransferable by endorsement, unnegotiable, nonnegotiable · nicht umlaufbar, nicht begebbar, nicht umlauffähig

not negotiable bill of lading, straight bill of lading · nicht begebbares Konnossement n

not negotiable warehouse receipt, warehouse receipt nontransferable by endorsement, nonnegotiable warehouse receipt, unnegotiable warehouse receipt · Lagerempfangsschein m

not operative → nugatory

notoriol [*Scots law*], notarial · notariell

notorious, undisguised, open · offenkundig

not paid, unliquidated, unpaid · nichtbezahlt, offenstehend, unbezahlt

not permitted, illicit, prohibited, not allowed · unerlaubt, verboten

not provable · unbeweisbar

not real, unreal, not according to realty, false · unwirklich, falsch

not recognized school · Schule f ohne Regierungsinspektion [*In England und Wales*]

not requiring permission, free from permission · genehmigungsfrei, erlaubnisfrei

not severable · einheitlich [*Kaufvertrag*]

not subject to dispute, unopposed · unwidersprochen

not titheable, tithe-free, indecimable; indecimabilis [*Latin*] [*Exempted from the payment of tithes*] · zehnt(en)frei

not to follow · nicht als bindend anerkennen

not true, not truly, not according to truth, untrue, false · falsch, unwahr

not under seal, unsealed, simple · nicht gesiegelt, ungesiegelt, ohne Siegel, siegellos

novale, frusca terra [*Latin*]; fallow land, idle land, tract of fallow (land), waste, uncultivated land · Brachflur f, Brachland n, Brachacker m, Brachfeld n

novale [*Latin*] [*Land newly plowed (US)/ ploughed (Brit.) and converted into tillage, and which has not been tilled before within the memory of man*] · erstmals (um)gepflügtes Land n

novation · Schuldübernahme f, Schuldumschaftung f, Schuldersetzung f

NTIT, new town in town · neue Stadt f in der Stadt

nuclear law, atomic law · Atomrecht n, Kernrecht n

nuclear plant, atomic plant, nuclear station, atomic station · Atomanlage *f,* Kernanlage *f*

nuclear station, atomic station, nuclear plant, atomic plant · Atomanlage *f,* Kernanlage *f*

nucleated expansion, nucleated pattern of growth, nucleated growth pattern [*A metropolitan growth alternative*] · kernförmige Erweiterung *f*

nucleated pattern, nucleated scheme · Kernschema *n,* Kernmuster *n*

nucleated settlement, group settlement · Gruppen(an)sied(e)lung *f*

nucleated settlement with an irregular street-plan, agglomerated settlement, cluster settlement · Haufen(an)sied(e)lung *f,* unregelmäßig zusammengewachsene (An)Sied(e)lung, Gruppen(an)sied(e)lung mit unregelmäßigem Grundriß

nucleated village; ham(e)leta, hameletta [*Latin*]; hamlet · Weiler *m,* ländliche Gruppensied(e)lung *f*

nuda proprietas, dominium feudi [*Latin*]; ultimate ownership (of property), strict ownership (of property), direct dominion [*The nominal or bare right of ownership remaining in an owner who has granted the exclusive right of enjoyment and of limited or unlimited disposition over the thing to another person*] · Obereigentum *n* (der Krone), Eigentumsrecht *n* des Leh(e)n(s)herrn, Leh(e)n(s)herrlichkeit *f* [*Das Eigentum an Land ruht in England in allen Fällen unbedingt und ausnahmslos beim Thron. Diese Tatsache ist eine der wichtigsten Unterschiede zwischen dem englischen Mobiliar- und Immobiliarsachenrecht und findet ihren Ausdruck in der Rechtsdoktrin: "Land is, and goods are not, the subject of tenure"*]

nude contract, one-sided contract, unilateral contract, contract of benevolence, deed poll, contract without consideration, gratuitous contract · einseitiger Vertrag *m,* Vertrag ohne Gegenleistung

nude promise, unilateral promise, gratuitous promise, promise of benevolence, promise without consideration, one-sided promise · einseitiges (Leistungs)Versprechen *n,* einseitiges Naturalversprechen, (Leistungs)Versprechen ohne Gegenleistung, Naturalversprechen ohne Gegenleistung

nudo consensus [*Latin*] · formlose Willensübereinstimmung *f*

nugatory, not operative, ineffectual [*For example, judicial proceedings in a court that lacks jurisdiction are sometimes nugatory*] · unwirksam

nuisance · Emission *f,* Zuführung *f* unwägbarer Stoffe [*Von einem Grundstück auf ein Nachbargrundstück ausgehende Einwirkung. § 906 BGB. Immission ist die Einwirkung einer Emission auf Menschen, Tiere und/oder Pflanzen beurteilt aus der Sicht der Betroffenen. Emissionen sind auf den Verursacher bezogen*]

nuisance effect · Immission *f* [*Siehe Anmerkung unter "Emission"*]

nuisance group · Dramatisierungsgruppe *f* [*Bürgerinitiative*]

null, invalid, void [*"Void" in the strict sense means that an instrument or transaction is negatory and ineffectual so that nothing can cure it. But frequently "void" is used and construed as having the meaning of "voidable"*] · ungültig, nichtig, unwirksam

null and void → (rendered) null and void

nulla poena sine lege poenali [*Latin*]; no punishment without previous legal authority · keine Strafe *f* ohne Strafgesetz

nullification, rescission, avoidance, repeal, abrogation, cancellation, abolition, abatement, abolishment (by authority), annulment · Annullierung *f,* Rückgängigmachung, Aufhebung, Abschaffung, Abbau *m,* Löschung

nullification ordinance · Nichtigkeitsverordnung *f*

nullified, abolished (by authority), rescinded, overruled, done away with, deprived of operation, repealed, cancelled, abrogated, abated, annulled · aufgehoben, annulliert, rückgängig gemacht, außer Kraft gesetzt, abgeschafft, gelöscht, abgebaut

to nullify, to annul, to repeal, to overrule, to cancel, to abrogate, to abolish (by authority), to do away with, to abate, to deprive of operation, to rescind · abschaffen, aufheben, rückgängig machen, annullieren, außer Kraft setzen, löschen, abbauen

nullifying, rescinding, making void, annulling, (a)voiding, repealing, abolishing, abrogating, cancelling, overruling, abating, rendering null and void, doing away with · Aufheben *n,* Rückgängigmachen *n,* Annullieren *n,* Abschaffen *n,* Löschen *n,* Abbauen *n*

nullity, invalidity, avoidance · Nichtigkeit *f,* Ungültigkeit

nullity of form · Formnichtigkeit *f*

nullity of marriage · Nichtigkeit *f* einer Ehe, Ehenichtigkeit

nul waste · Bestreiten *n* des Substanzschadens, Bestreiten der Wertminderung, Bestreiten der Verschlechterung, Bestreiten der Substanzschädigung [*Pachtland*]

to number · numerieren

to number consecutively — objection proceeding

to number consecutively · laufend numerieren

numbering · Numerieren *n*

number of acceptance, acceptance number · Annahmezahl *f* [*Statistik*]

number of floors · Geschoßzahl *f*, Etagenzahl, Stockwerkzahl

number of inhabitants · Einwohnerzahl *f*

number of visitors, admission · Besucher(an)zahl *f*

numerical approach · Zahlenansatz *m*

numerically controlled draughting · numerisch gesteuertes Zeichnen *n*

numerical scale, fractional scale · Maßstabverhältnis *n*, Zahlenmaßstab *m*

nuncupation [*Latin*] · mündliche Testamenterrichtung *f*

nuncupative will, verbal will, oral will · mündliches Testament *n*

nursery class · Kleinkinderklasse *f*

O

oasis agriculture, oasis farming, oasis husbandry · Oasenlandwirtschaft *f*

oasis cultivation · Oasenanbau *m*

oath; othe [*old English*]; juramentum, jus jurandum, sacramentum [*Latin*]; ath [*Saxon*] · Eid *m*

oathable · eidesfähig, eideswürdig

(oath) administration, administering of oath, administration of oath · Eidabnahme *f*, Eidesleistung *f*, Beeidigung, Abnahme, Schwören *n*

oath-helper, compurgator · Eideshelfer *m* [*Einer Prozeßpartei im Mittelalter in England*]

oath of abjuration, abjuration oath · Abschwörungseid *m* der Leh(e)n(s)treue

oath of abnegation, abnegation oath · Ableugnungseid *m*

oath of allegiance, oath of fealty, oath of fidelity, fealty oath, fidelity oath [*It was sworn by feudal tenants to their lords*] · Leh(e)n(s)eid *m*, Leh(e)n(s)schwur *m*, Treu(e)eid, Treu(e)schwur

oath of allegiance · Amtseid *m*, Diensteid, Treu(e)eid

oath of a witness, witness oath · Zeugeneid *m*

oath of disclosure, oath of manifestation · Offenbarungseid *m*

oath of executor → oath of (testamentary) executor

oath of fealty, oath of fidelity, fealty oath, fidelity oath, oath of allegiance [*It was sworn by feudal tenants to their lords*] · Leh(e)n(s)eid *m*, Leh(e)n(s)schwur *m*, Treu(e)eid, Treu(e)schwur

oath of manifestation, oath of disclosure · Offenbarungseid *m*

oath of office, oath of (testamentary) executor [*The executor swears by this oath that the will annexed to the affidavit is the true and original last will and testament of the testator and that he will faithfully administer the estate, and an affidavit for inland revenue*] · (Testaments)Vollstreckereid *m*

oath of qualification · Vermögenseid *m*

oath of supremacy, supremacy oath · Supremat(s)eid *m*, Kirchentreu(e)eid [*1534—1829. Eid der englischen Beamten, den König oder die Königin als obersten geistlichen Herren oder oberste geistliche Herrn anzuerkennen*]

oath of (testamentary) executor, oath of office [*The executor swears by this oath that the will annexed to the affidavit is the true and original last will and testament of the testator and that he will faithfully administer the estate, and an affidavit for inland revenue*] · (Testaments)Vollstreckereid *m*

oath-rite · Eidesform *f*

obedience · Gehorsam *m*

obfuscation · Verwischung *f*

obiter dictum [*Latin*] [*An opinion of a judge delivered or expressed by the way, and not (up)on the point in question before him*] · (Richter)Äußerung *f* welche eine Urteilsentscheidung nicht trägt, beiläufige (Rechts)Bemerkung

object affixed to a structure, article, fixture, component · Bestandteil *m*, Grundstücksbestandteil, (grundstücks)verbundene Sache *f*, Sache mit einem Grundstück verbunden

objection · Einwand *m*, Einwendung *f*, Einspruch *m*, Gegenrecht *n*

objection · Widerspruch *m*

objection in point of law, demurrer (to a lawsuit) [*A kind of pause or stop put to an action, and usually in the pleadings, upon a point of difficulty which must be determined by the court before any further proceeding can be had*] · Rechtseinrede *f*, Prozeßeinrede, Bestreiten *n* der Schlüssigkeit der Klage

objection proceeding · Widerspruchsverfahren *n*

**objection right, **right of objection · Einspruchsrecht *n*

**objective of research, **research objective · Forschungsgegenstand *m*

**objective right; **lex [*Latin*]; jurisprudence [*misnomer*]; law [*A system of law existing objectively as an external norm for persons*] · (objektives) Recht *n*

**objective value, **intrinsic value, innate value [*The popular idea that a commodity as, for example, a precious metal has an innate value apart from its price. Economists regard value as subjective, depending on the demand of consumers in relation to the available supply. According to this view, therefore, there is no such thing as intrinsic value*] · innerer Wert *m*

**object of property, **object of proprietorship, object of ownership (of property), object of a right of ownership · Eigentumsobjekt *n*, Eigentumsgegenstand *m*

**object of purchase, **purchase object · Kaufgegenstand *m*, Kaufobjekt *n*

object of relief sought · Ziel *n* des Klagebegehrens

**object of the trust, **fiduciary debtor, fidecommissary; fidei-commissarius [*Latin*] · Berechtigte *m*, Benefiziar *m*, Bedachte *m*, Begünstigte *m*, Treuhandberechtigte *m*, Treuhandbenefiziar *m*, Treuhandbedachte *m*, Treuhandbegünstigte *m*, Treu(hand)nehmer *m*, Empfänger *m* der Treuhandeinkünfte

**object pawned, **object pledged, pawn, vadium, pledged article, pledged object, pawned article, pawned object, article pawned, article pledged · Pfand *n*, Pfandstück *n*, verpfändeter Gegenstand *m*, gegebenes (Mobiliar)Pfand, Pfandsache *f*

object permanent in character which is found on the land as it was placed by nature · Einzelgebilde *n* der Natur, Natureinzelgebilde

object pledged → object pawned

obligatio [*Latin*]; liability · Haftung *f*, Haftpflicht *f*, Haftbarkeit *f*

obligation to furnish reasons · Begründungsverpflichtung *f*

obligation to inform · Unterrichtungspflicht *f*

**obligation of (ab)alienation, **obligation of disposal, (ab)alienation obligation, disposal obligation · Veräußerungsbindung *f*, Veräußerungsgebundenheit *f*, Veräußerungsverpflichtung, Veräußerungsverbindlichkeit *f*

**obligation of disposal, **(ab)alienation obligation, disposal obligation, obligation of (ab)alienation · Veräußerungsbindung *f*, Veräußerungsgebundenheit *f*, Veräußerungsverpflichtung, Veräußerungsverbindlichkeit *f*

**obligation of equity, **equitable obligation · Billigkeitsverpflichtung *f*, Verpflichtung nach Billigkeit(srecht), Billigkeitsrechtverpflichtung

obligation of peaceful conduct · Friedenspflicht *f*

**obligation of social service, **obligation of welfare-work · Fürsorgeverpflichtung *f* [*Fürsorgepflicht des BU gegenüber seinen Arbeitnehmern aus dem Arbeitsvertrage*]

obligation to pay · Zahlungsverpflichtung *f*

**obligation to perform, **obligation to execute, obligation to complete, obligation to fulfil · Erfüllungsverpflichtung *f*, Vollzugsverpflichtung, Vollziehungsverpflichtung, Ausführungsverpflichtung, Erbringungsverpflichtung

**obligation to plan, **planning obligation · Planungsverpflichtung *f*

**obligation to repair, **repair obligation · Reparaturverpflichtung *f*

obligatory · verpflichtend

**obligatory; **perimere [*Latin*]; mandatory, preceptive, imperative, peremptory [*As opposed to "permissive"*] · pflichtbedingt, zwingend [*in Gesetzen*]

obligatory declaration · Verpflichtungserklärung *f*

**obligee, **promisee [*Person, firm, or corporation protected by the surety bond. The obligee under a bond is similar to the insured under an insurance policy*] · Versprechensempfänger *m*

**obligee, **person entitled · berechtigte Person *f*

obligee entitled to Immediate Aid · Soforthilfeberechtigte *m* [*Bundesrepublik Deutschland*]

**obligor, **promisor, principal, covenantor [*One bound by an obligation. Under a bond both the "principal" and "surety" are "obligors"*] · Versprechensgeber *m*, Versprechende, Verpflichtete

**obligor-executor, **debtor-executor · Schuldner *m* vom Gläubiger als (Testaments)Vollstrecker bestellt

**obligor's default, **debtor's default · Schuldner(ver)säumnis *f, n, (f)* [*Es liegt vor, wenn die vertraglich vereinbarte Leistung nach Eintritt der Fälligkeit trotz Mahnung nicht erbracht wird*]

**obligor's delay, **debtor's delay · Schuldnerverzug *m*

**obligor's land, **debtor's land · Schuldnerland *n*, Schuldnerboden *m*

**obligor's summons, **debtor's summons · Zahlungsaufforderung *f* [*Aufforderung an einen Schuldner durch ein Konkurs-*

oblique (aerial) photograph — occupancy problem

gericht die im Schriftstück genannte Summe an den darin genannten Gläubiger zu zahlen oder Einspruch zu erheben, andernfalls über ihn das Konkursverfahren verhängt wird]

oblique (aerial) photograph · Schräg(luft)aufnahme f, Schräg(luft)bild n

oblique factor · nichtorthogonaler Faktor m

obnoxious enterprise, obnoxious undertaking, injurious enterprise, injurious undertaking · störender Betrieb m, störendes Unternehmen n, störende Unternehmung f

obnoxious industry, injurious industry · störende Industrie f

obnoxious project, injurious project · störendes Vorhaben n

obscurity of meaning, uncertain meaning, doubtful meaning, ambiguity, obscure meaning, doubtfulness of meaning, uncertainty of meaning · unklare Bedeutung f, Zweideutigkeit f

observation [Professional examination of the contractor's work to determine in general if it is proceeding in accordance with the contract requirements] · Arbeitsüberprüfung f

observation error, ascertainment error, error of observation, error of ascertainment · Beobachtungsfehler m [Statistik]

observation of aggregate, observation of mass · Massenbeobachtung f

obsolescence · Überalterung f

obsolescence rate, rate of obsolescence · Überalterungsgeschwindigkeit f, Überalterungstempo n

obsolete, antiquated, grown out of use, disused · außer Gebrauch, nicht mehr verwendet

obstruction · Behinderung f, hindernder Umstand m, hinderlicher Umstand

obstructive building · behinderndes Gebäude n, hinderliches Gebäude

to obtain, to recover, to enforce payment, to collect [amount] · beitreiben, eintreiben, einziehen [Betrag]

obtainable, recoverable, collectible, collectable · beitreibbar, eintreibbar, einziehbar

to obtain again, to recover, to win back, to regain, to collect, to get renewed possession of, to get again · zurückerhalten, wiedererlangen, wiedererhalten, zurückgewinnen, zurückbekommen

to obtain a judg(e)ment against · obsiegen, gewinnen

obtaining, recovering, enforcing payment, collecting · Beitreiben n, Eintreiben, Einziehen [Betrag]

obtainment · Verschaffung f

obtainment of ownership (of property), obtainment of (general) property, obtainment of proprietorship · Eigentumsverschaffung f

to obtain tenders, to invite tenders, to tender out, to invite offers, to invite bids; to invite (bid) proposals (US); to put out to tender, to go out to tender · ausschreiben, (Angebote) einholen, auffordern zur Angebotsabgabe

obvious, manifest, clear to the understanding, evident · augenscheinlich, offensichtlich

to occasion [e.g. a loss] · verursachen

occasional, accidental, by chance, fortuitous, unforeseen · unvorhergesehen

occupancy; occupatio [Latin]; appropriation [The taking of the first possession by any one, of a thing of which there is no owner] · tatsächliche Besitznahme f, Besitzergreifung f, (In)Besitznahme, Aneignung, Besitznehmung

occupancy [Occupation of land(s) held pur autre vie, after the death of the tenant, and during the life of the cestuy que vie] · Besitzergreifung f auf Lebenszeit eines Dritten, Besitzergreifung für die Dauer eines anderen Lebens

occupancy, occupation · Belegung f

occupancy → (beneficial) occupancy

occupancy agreement · Besitzergreifungsabkommen, (In)Besitznahmeabkommen n

occupancy certificate, certificate of occupancy [Certificate issued by governmental authority certifying that all or a designated portion of a building complies with the provisions of applicable statutes and regulations] · Gebäudeabnahmezeugnis n

occupancy certificate, certificate of occupancy [Certificate issued by the governing authority granting permission to occupy a project for a specific use. It is procured by the prime contractor] · Übergabezeugnis n

occupancy certificate, certificate of occupancy · Beziehbarkeitsbescheinigung f [Wohnraum]

occupancy density, density of occupancy · (Wohnungs)Belegungsdichte f [qm Bruttogeschoßfläche je Bewohner]

occupancy ordinance · Belegungsverordnung f [Gebäude]

occupancy problem, occupation problem · Belegungsproblem n, Besetzungsproblem [Statistik]

occupancy rate, rate of occupancy · (Wohnungs)Belegungsziffer f [*Sie gibt an wieviel Personen durchschnittlich auf die Wohnung oder einen Wohnraum entfallen*]

occupancy right, right of occupancy [*Privilege to use and occupy a property for a certain period under some contractual guarantee, such as a lease or other formal agreement*] · Belegungsrecht n

occupancy (up)on an occupancy → (beneficial) occupation (up)on an occupation

occupancy without transmutation of possession at common law → (beneficial) occupation without transmutation of possession at common law

occupant [*One who takes possession of land(s) held pur autre vie, after the death of the tenant, and during the life of the cestuy que vie*] · Besitzergreifer m auf Lebenszeit eines Dritten, Besitzergreifer für die Dauer eines anderen Lebens

occupant → beneficial occupant

occupant → (house) occupier

occupant at will · prekarischer Besitzergreifer m

occupatio [*Latin*]; appropriation, occupancy [*The taking of the first possession by any one, of a thing of which there is no owner*] · tatsächliche Besitznahme f, Besitzergreifung f, (In)Besitznahme, Aneignung, Besitznehmung

occupation, employment, work · Arbeit f, Beschäftigung f

occupation, occupancy · Belegung f

occupation · Beruf m

occupation → (beneficial) occupancy

occupational advisory service, vocational (guidance) service, vocational guidance, occupational guidance, careers guidance, occupational consulting service, vocational consulting service, occupational (guidance) service · Berufsberatung f

occupational benefit plan → occupational pension plan

occupational concept · Lebensunterhaltsicherung f durch Erwerbstätigkeit oder Unterhaltsansprüchen aus derselben

occupational education, vocational education, vocational training, occupational training · Berufsausbildung f

occupation(al) forces · Besatzungsstreitkräfte f (pl)

occupation(al forces') law · Besatzungsrecht n

occupation(al forces') law, occupation(al forces') act, occupation(al forces') statute · Besatzungsgesetz n

occupational (guidance) service, occupational advisory service, vocational (guidance) service, vocational guidance, occupational guidance, careers guidance, occupational consulting service, vocational consulting service · Berufsberatung f

occupational hazard, occupational risk · Berufsrisiko n, Berufswagnis n

occupational mobility, employment mobility, work mobility · Arbeitsbeweglichkeit f, Arbeitsmobilität f, Beschäftigungsmobilität f, Beschäftigungsbeweglichkeit f

occupational pension plan, company benefit plan, occupational benefit plan, company retirement plan, occupational retirement plan, company pension plan · betrieblicher Pensionsplan m, betrieblicher (Alters)Versorgungsplan

occupation(al) power · Besatzungsmacht f

occupational practice · Berufswesen n

occupational prestige · Berufsprestige n

occupational risk, occupational hazard · Berufsrisiko n, Berufswagnis n

occupational standards · Berufskodex m

occupational training, occupational education, vocational education, vocational training · Berufsausbildung f

occupational training facility, vocational education facility, occupational education facility, vocational training facility · Berufsausbildungseinrichtung f

occupation(al) zone, zone of occupation · Besatzungszone f

occupation corporate, craft company corporat(iv)e, craft (g(u)ild) corporate · korporierte (Handwerker)Zunft f, korporiertes Gewerk n

occupation in self-employment, self-employed occupation · freier Beruf m

occupation problem → occupancy problem

occupation rent · Miete f, Mietzins m [*für Räume*]

occupation (up)on an occupation → (beneficial) occupation (up)on an occupation

occupation without transmutation of possession at common law → (beneficial) occupation without transmutation of possession at common law

occupied · belegt [*Gebäude*]

occupied · bewohnt

occupier → house occupier

occupier → (beneficial) occupant

occupier → (land) holder

occupier at will → (land) holder at will

occupier from year to year → (land) holder from year to year

occupier of a small portion of land, allotment holder [*A cultivator who, while he has some spare time and money to cultivate land, is partially employed in some other occupation or business*] · (landwirtschaftlicher) Parzellenbesitzer *m*

occupier of land at will → (land) holder at will

occupier of land from year to year → (land) holder from year to year

to occupy · belegen [*Gebäude*]

to occupy, to live in · bewohnen

occupying ownership (of property), occupying (general) property, occupying proprietorship · bewirtschaftetes Landeigentum *n*

occurring but once · einmalig [*Ereignis*]

ocean chart, sailing chart, track chart · Segelkarte *f*, Übersegler *m*

oceanography · Meereskunde *f*

ochlocracy, mob rule, populace rule · Pöbelherrschaft *f*

oddman, catchman, dayman · (landwirtschaftlicher) Gelegenheitsarbeiter *m*, Gelegenheitslandarbeiter

odhal [*In old English law*] → al(l)odial

odour nuisance (Brit.); odor nuisance (US) · Geruchemission *f*

odour nuisance effect (Brit.); odor nuisance effect (US) · Geruchimmission *f*

(o)ecumene, ekumene, inhabited world [*That portion of the earth's surface which has been settled by man*] · Sied(e)lungsraum *m*, Ökumene *f*

of a freeholder, relating to a freeholder · landsässig

offence → violation (of law)

offence committed in public office; offense committed in public office (US) · Amtsdelikt *n*, Delikt im Amt

offender, violator · Gesetz(es)übertreter *m*, Zuwiderhandelnde

offense, injury · Belästigung *f*, Störung, Beeinträchtigung [*Gewerbe; Industrie*]

offense (US) → violation (of law)

offensive, unsanitary, prejudicial to health, detrimental to health · gesundheitsschädlich, gesundheitsgefährdend

offensive smell · Gestank *m*

to offer, to tender, to submit (a bid), to (enter a) bid; to submit a (bid) proposal, to enter a (bid) proposal (US) · anbieten, submittieren, einreichen eines Angebots, abgeben eines Angebots

offer, prospective agreement · (Vertrags)Antrag *m*, Offerte *f*, Vertragsangebot *n* [*Das einem anderen mitgeteilte Angebot, mit ihm einen Vertrag abzuschließen*]

offer · Anerbieten *n*

offer, bid; (bid) proposal (US); tender · Angebot *n*

offer analysis, bid analysis; (bid) proposal analysis (US); tender analysis · Angebotsanalyse *f*, Angebotsuntersuchung *f*

offer and acceptance · Antrag *m* und Annahme *f* [*Vertrag*]

offer (blank) form, form of tender, form of offer, form of bid, bid(ding) form; (bid) proposal form, form of (bid) proposal, (bid) proposal blank (form) (US); tender (blank) form, bid (blank) form · Angebotsblankett *n*, Angebotsformular *n*, Angebotsvordruck *m*

offer bond, bid bond, tender bond; (bid) proposal bond (US) [*A bid guarantee by bond. The function of a bid bond is to guarantee the good faith of the bidder, so that if awarded the contract within the time stipulated, he will enter into the contract and furnish the prescribed performance and payment bonds*] · Bietungsgarantie *f* [*Eine Bietungssicherheit durch beurkundete Schuldforderung*]

to offer competitively, to tender competitively, to submit a competitive bid, to bid competitively · abgeben eines Wettbewerbsangebotes, einreichen eines Wettbewerbsangebotes, anbieten im Wettbewerb, submittieren im Wettbewerb

offer conditions, tender conditions; conditions of the (bid) proposal, (bid) proposal conditions (US); conditions of the bid, conditions of the offer, conditions of the tender, bid conditions · Angebotsbedingungen *f pl*

offer covering letter; (bid) proposal covering letter (US); tender covering letter, bid covering letter · Angebots(an)schreiben *n*, Angebotsbegleitschreiben

offer curve · Tauschfunktionskurve *f* [*Außenhandel*]

offer document; (bid) proposal document (US); tendering document, bid(ding) document · Ausschreibungsunterlage *f*, Ausschreibungsdokument *n* [*Fehlbenennungen: Angebotsunterlage, Angebotsdokument*]

offer drawing → tender drawing

offer(ed) price, bid price · Ausgabepreis *m*, Rücknahmepreis, Rückkaufpreis [*Investmentanteil*]

offeree · Annehmende *m*, Angebotsannehmende

offer estimate — office-holder

offer estimate, bid estimate; (bid) proposal estimate; tender estimate · Angebotsvoranschlag *m*

offer figure → offer sum

offer form → offer (blank) form

offer function · Tauschfunktion *f* [*Außenhandel*]

offer guarantee, offer guarantie, offer guaranty, offer security; (bid) proposal guarantee, (bid) proposal guarantie, (bid) proposal guaranty, (bid) proposal security (US); bid guarantee, bid guarantie, bid guaranty, bid security, tender guarantie, tender guarantee, tender guaranty, tender security [*Deposit for cash, check, money order, or bid bond when the bid is submitted by the bidder to guarantee that he will sign the contract and furnish the required surety if awarded*] · Bietungsbürgschaft *f*, Bietungssicherheit *f*

offer item; (bid) proposal item (US); bid item, tender item · Angebotsposition *f*

offer of a public reward, general offer · Auslobung *f,* öffentliches Angebot *n* [*Das öffentliche Versprechen einer Belohnung für den Fall der Vornahme einer bestimmten Handlung, insbesondere der Herbeiführung eines Erfolges*]

offer of evidence, offer of proof · Beweisantrag *m*

offer opening; (bid) proposal opening, opening of (bid) proposal (US); opening of tenders, opening of offers, opening of bids, bid opening, tender opening · Angebotseröffnung *f,* Submission *f*

offeror, competitor, tendering contractor, competing contractor, bidder, tenderer · (an)bietende Firma *f,* (An)Bieter *m,* Angebotsabgeber

offer prescriptions, offer regulations, bid prescriptions, bid regulations; (bid) proposal prescriptions, (bid) proposal regulations (US); tender prescriptions, tender regulations · Angebotsvorschriften *fpl*

offer price → offer sum

offer rate → tender rate

offer regulations → offer prescriptions

offer request, bid request; (bid) proposal request (US); tender request · Angebotsanforderung *f*

offer request form; (bid) proposal request form (US); bid request form, tender request form · Angebotsanforderungsformular *n*

offer security → offer guarantee

offer sum, bid sum, tender(ed) figure, offer figure, bid figure; (bid) proposal sum, (bid) proposal figure, (bid) proposal price (US); tender(ed) price, offer price, bid price, tender(ed) sum [*Amount stated in the bid as the sum for which the bidder offers to perform the work*] · Angebotspreis *m*, Angebotssumme *f*

offer to purchase, purchase offer · Kaufangebot *n*

offer to sell (real) estate, offer to sell (real) property, offer to sell (real) property, offer to sell land(s), offer to sell realty · Grund(stücks)verkaufsangebot *n*, Bodenverkaufsangebot, Landverkaufsangebot

offer total; (bid) proposal total (US); tender total, bid total [*The total of the priced bill of quantities at the date of acceptance of the contractor's tender for the works*] · Angebotsendsumme *f,* Angebotsendpreis *m*

office, station, employment · Posten *m*

office · (Firmen)Niederlassung *f,* Geschäftslokal *n*

office · Büro *n*

office [*A function or duty assigned to someone*] · Amt *n*

office → (public) office

office-bearer, office-holder, incumbent (of (an) office) [*A person who is in possession of an office*] · Amtsträger *m*, Amtsinhaber

office building · Bürogebäude *n*

office building investment project · Büroobjekt *n*

office centre (Brit.); office center (US) · Büro(haus)zentrum *n*, Bürogebäudezentrum

office complex · Bürokomplex *m*

office coverage · Bebauung *f* mit Bürogebäuden, Bürogebäudebebauung; Überbauung mit Bürogebäuden, Bürogebäudeüberbauung [*Schweiz*] [*Das Ergebnis des Bebauens einer Fläche mit Bürogebäuden*]

office employment · Bürobeschäftigung *f*

office estate → (real) office estate

office for Federal plots (of land) · Liegenschaftsstelle [*Bundesrepublik Deutschland. Bei einer Finanzverwaltung für die Liegenschaften des Bundes*]

office for plots (of land) of a (Federal) Land · Liegenschaftsstelle *f* [*Bundesrepublik Deutschland. Bei einer Finanzverwaltung für die Liegenschaften eines Landes*]

office for the preservation of monuments · Baupflegeamt *n*, Baudenkmalpflegeamt

office-holder, incumbent (of (an) office), office-bearer [*A person who is in possession of an office*] · Amtsträger *m,* Amtsinhaber

office industry — official offer

office industry · Büroindustrie f

office labour, clerical labour (Brit.); office labor, clerical labor (US) · Büroarbeitskräfte fpl

office location, office site · Bürostandort m, Bürolage f

office manager · Büroleiter m

office of a judge, judicial office, judgeship · Richteramt n

office of a judgess, office of a female judge · Richterinamt n

office of municipal finances, town exchequer, city exchequer · Stadtkämmerei f

office of the president · Präsidialkanzlei f

office of the secretary [*USA*] · Büro n des Behördenleiters, Behördenleiterbüro

office of trustee, trusteeship · Treuhänderamt n, Treuhänderstellung f, Treuhänderschaft f

office overhead(s), office overhead cost(s) · Bürogemeinkosten f, Bürogeneralkosten

office personnel, clerical personnel, clerical staff, office staff · Büropersonal n

officer, official; officialis [*Latin*] · Beamte m

officer · Subalternbeamte m, Unterbeamte [*Oberster Gerichtshof und Revisionsgerichtshöfe in England*]

officer · Direktor m [*Einer AG in den USA. Er ist nicht notwendigerweise Vorstandsmitglied*]

office (real) estate, office (real) property, office realty · Bürogrundstück n

office re-location · Büroumsied(e)lung f

officer (in civil services), official (in civil services) · Beamte m (im öffentlichen Dienst)

office site, office location · Bürostandort m

office space · Büroraum m

office staff, office personnel, clerical personnel, clerical staff · Büropersonal n

office tenable for life · lebenslanges Amt n

office tenure, tenure of an office · Amtshaltung f

office term → term of office

office(-type) activity · Bürotätigkeit f

office worker · Büroangestellte m, kaufmännischer Angestellter

official · Offizial m [*Kirchenrecht*]

official → officer

official act(ion) · Amtsakt m, Amtshandlung f

(official) agency, public agency, (public) office · Dienststelle f, öffentliche Dienststelle, (amtliche) Stelle

official announcement, official promulgation, official publication · amtliche Verlautbarung f, öffentliche Bekanntmachung, öffentliche Bekanntgabe f, öffentliche Kundmachung, öffentliche Veröffentlichung, amtliche Bekanntmachung, amtliche Veröffentlichung, öffentliche Verlautbarung, amtliche Bekanntgabe, amtliche Kundmachung

official architect · Behördenarchitekt m

official authority, official power · behördliche Macht f, behördliche Gewalt f, behördliche Kompetenz f, behördliche Hoheit f, Amtsgewalt, Amtshoheit, Amtskompetenz, Amtsmacht, amtliche Macht, amtliche Gewalt, amtliche Kompetenz, amtliche Hoheit

official bid → official offer

official building scheme · amtlicher Bebauungsplan m, amtlicher verbindlicher Bauleitplan; amtlicher Überbauungsplan [*Schweiz*]; amtlicher Bauplan [*Fehlbenennung*]

official certificate · Amtszeugnis n

official channels · Dienstweg m

official condition, condition imposed by an authority · behördliche Bedingung f, amtliche Bedingung

official conduct · amtliches Verhalten n, Disziplinarverhalten

official dress · Amtstracht f

official duty · Amtspflicht f, Dienstpflicht

official engineer · Behördeningenieur m

official function · amtliche Funktion f

(official) gazette · Amtsblatt n, Gesetz(es)blatt, Gesetz(es)- und Verordnungsblatt

official guardianship · Amtsvormundschaft f

official interference, official intervention · Amtseingriff m

officialism · Beamtenapparat m

official language · Amtssprache f

official liability · Amtshaftung f, Amtshaftpflicht f, Amtshaftbarkeit f

official(ly) · amtlich, amtsgemäß, amtsmäßig

official map · amtliche (Land)Karte f

official maps, official map series · amtliches (Land)Kartenwerk n

official offer, public offer, official tender, public tender, official bid, public bid; official (bid) proposal, public (bid) proposal (US) · Angebot n für die öffentliche Hand

official permission · behördliche Erlaubnis f, behördliche Genehmigung f

official personnel, official staff · Amtspersonal n

official power, official authority · behördliche Macht f, behördliche Gewalt f, behördliche Kompetenz f, behördliche Hoheit f, Amtsgewalt, Amtshoheit, Amtskompetenz, Amtsmacht, amtliche Macht, amtliche Gewalt, amtliche Kompetenz, amtliche Hoheit

official practice · Behördenpraxis f

official price, price fixed by authority, licensed price, licenced price, statutory price · Taxe f [Ein aufgrund eines Rechtes behördlich festgesetzter Preis]

official promulgation → official announcement

official proposal (US) → official offer

official provision · amtliche Bestimmung f

official publication → official announcement

official receiver; collector (US) · gerichtlicher Zwangsverwalter m, gerichtlicher Empfänger, gerichtlicher Masse(n)verwalter, gerichtlicher Kurator [Er nimmt das Eigentum des Schuldners bis zur Ernennung eines Treuhänders in Empfang]

(official) referee, arbitrator appointed by court; judex [Latin] · gerichtlich ernannter Schiedsrichter m

official referee · gerichtlicher Sachverständiger m

official referee, recorder, single judge · Einzelrichter m, beauftragter Richter

official register, official registry · amtlicher Nachweis m, amtliches Verzeichnis n, Amtsbuch n

official secret · Amtsgeheimnis n, Amtsverschwiegenheit f

official self-help, official self-aid · amtliche Selbsthilfe f

official staff, official personnel · Amtspersonal n

official tender → official offer

official topographical map series · amtliches topographisches Kartenwerk n

official trustee · amtlicher Treuhänder m, amtlicher Treuhandverwalter, staatlicher Treuhänder, staatlicher Treuhandverwalter

official value, conventional value, declared value · Wert m für Zollzwecke deklariert

official value · amtlicher Wert m

off (job) site, off-site, off the site · außerhalb der Baustelle (befindlich)

off-licence [It permits the sale of intoxicating liquors for consumption off the premises only] · Spirituosenverkaufserlaubnis f außer Haus

off-licence duty → (excise) off-licence duty

off-peak travel, off-peak trip, off-peak journey · Fahrt f außerhalb der Spitzenzeit

offset (US); deduction, setting off; setoff (Brit.) · Anrechnung f, Kompensation f, Saldierung f, Abziehung f, Aufrechnung f, Abrechnung f, Abzug m; Verrechnung f [Schweiz] [Gegenforderung]

offset credit · Verrechnungskredit m

off-site, off the site, off (job) site · außerhalb der Baustelle (befindlich)

off site → off (job) site

offspring, descendant, issue · Abkömmling m, Nachkomme m, Deszendent m

offspring in tail, descendant in tail, issue in tail · sukzessionsberechtigter Nachkomme m, sukzessionsberechtigter Abkömmling m, sukzessionsberechtigter Deszendent m

off street parking area [Space provided for vehicular parking outside the dedicated street right-of-way] · Grundstücksparkraum m

off the site, off (job) site, off-site · außerhalb der Baustelle (befindlich)

of full age · volljährig

of further education · weiterführend [Schule]

off-year election · Zwischenwahl f

of good faith, innocent, honestly, without fraud; bona fide [Latin]; in good faith · aufrichtig, in gutem Glauben, ehrlich, gutgläubig

of goods not yet administered, relating to assets which have not been administered; de bonis non (administratis) [Latin] [A grant "de bonis non administratis", or more shortly "de bonis non", is made where an executor dies intestate or an administrator dies, in either case without having fully administered] · von nicht verwalteten Nachlaßgegenständen

of mixed racial composition · gemischtrassig

of no effect in law · rechtsunwirksam

of original jurisdiction · erstinstanzlich, in erster Instanz

of public usefulness, nonprofit, useful to the public, of public utility · gemeinnützig, gemeinnötig

of sound mind; compos mentis [Latin]; mentally capable by law, mentally qualified by law, mentally competent by law · zurechnungsfähig

of the same rank, co-ordinate, equal · gleichgestellt, gleichrangig

of three parts; tripartitus [*Latin*]; tripartite · dreiteilig

of three places · dreistellig [*Zahl*]

of trifling importance · geringfügig

of two parts, bipartite · zweiteilig

of unsound mind, non-sane, insane, deranged; insanus [*Latin*]; unsound in mind, disordered in mind, diseased in mind · geistesgestört, geisteskrank

Ohio plan, Dayton permanent plan, optional payment plan · individueller unregelmäßiger Plan *m* [*Eine dauernde Form einer amerikanischen Bausparkasse*]

oil accident committee · Ölunfallausschuß *m*

oil pollution · Ölverschmutzung *f*, Ölverunreinigung

oil search, search for oil · (Erd)Ölsuche *f*

old age insurance, social security insurance · Altersversicherung *f*

old age pensions act, old age pensions law, old age pensions statute · Altersrentengesetz *n*

old age pensions law · Altersrentenrecht *n*

old age security · Altersversorgung *f*

old and new situation of the consolidation area · Feldeinteilung *f*

old (construction) material, old building material · Altbaustoff *m*

old dwelling, old residence, old tenement · Alt(bau)wohnung *f*

old green village, early green village · Altangerdorf *n*

old hamlet · Altweiler *m*

old housing stock, old residential stock, old residence stock · Alt(bau)wohn(ungs)bestand *m*

old housing territory, old residential territory, old residence area, old residential area, old residence territory, old housing area · Altbau(wohn)gebiet *n*, Altbauwohnungsgebiet

old neighbourhood store (Brit.); old neighborhood store, mom(ma)-and-pop(pa) store (US) · Tante-Emma-Laden *m*

old peoples' home, old person's home, aged person's home · Altenheim *n*, Altersheim

old peoples' welfare, welfare of old people · Altersfürsorge *f*

old residence, old tenement, old dwelling · Alt(bau)wohnung *f*

old residence area, old residential area, old residence territory, old housing area, old housing territory, old residential territory · Altbau(wohn)gebiet *n*, Altbauwohnungsgebiet

old residence stock, old housing stock, old residential stock · Alt(bau)wohn(ungs)bestand *m*

old settled (agricultural) land, early settled (agricultural) land · Altsiedelland *n*

old settlement, early settlement · Alt(an)sied(e)lung *f*

old settlement area, old settlement land · Alt(an)sied(e)lungsland *n*

old tenement, old dwelling, old residence · Alt(bau)wohnung *f*

old tenement act, old tenement law, old tenement statute · Altmiethausgesetz *n*

omission, omittance, forbearance, negligence, negative act(ion), default, neglect, failure [*Omission of that which a person ought to do*] · (Ver)Säumnis *f, n, (f)*, Vernachlässigung *f*, Unterlassung(shandlung), Nichtleistung, Unterlassungsakt *m*, negativer Akt, negative Handlung

omnibus item, collective item · Gesamtposition *f*, Sammelposition

omnibus summons, (general) summons for directions · (Prozeß)Ladung *f* für mehrere Zwischenanträge

on account · auf Abschlag

on account of whom it may concern, to whom it may concern · wen es angeht

on allotment · bei Zuteilung in Abschnitten

oncost [*obsolete*] → indirect cost(s)

on demise, on lease, on tenancy, by way of lease, by way of tenancy, by way of demise · pachtweise

one-class hospital · klassenloses Krankenhaus *n*

one-coloured map, single-coloured map (Brit.); one-colored map, single-colored map (US) · einfarbige Karte *f*

one-dimensional spatial market, one-dimensional space market · eindimensionaler räumlicher Markt *m*, räumlicher eindimensionaler Markt

one-dwelling family hous(ebuild)ing, one-family hous(ebuild)ing, single-family hous(ebuild)ing, single-dwelling family hous(ebuild)ing · Einwohnungshausbau *m*, Einwohnungshäuserbau, Einfamilienhausbau, Einfamilienhäuserbau

one-dwelling family row house, single-dwelling family row house, one-family row house, single-family row house ·

Einfamilienreihenhaus n, Einwohnungsreihenhaus

one-dwelling house, single-dwelling house; cottage (Brit.); one-family house, single-family house · Einfamilienhaus n, Einwohnungshaus

one-family house garden, cottage garden (Brit.); single-family house garden · Einfamilienhausgarten m

one-field system, one-field husbandry, single-field system, single-field husbandry · Einfeldwirtschaft f

one-generation family · Eingenerationsfamilie f

one-man business, sole proprietor, owner-manager [*A type of business unit where one person is solely responsible for providing the capital, for bearing the risk of the enterprise and for the management of the business*] · Einmannbetrieb m

one-room school, single-room school · Ein-Klassen-Schule f

onerous [*A contract, lease, share, property or other right is said to be onerous when the obligations attaching to it counterbalance or exceed the advantage(s) be to derived from it, either absolutely or with reference to the particular possessor*] · fraglich

onerous goods, acquired goods · erworbene Güter n pl, beschaffte Güter, erstandene Güter

onerous property [*It may be disclaimed by a trustee in bankruptcy*] · fragliches Vermögen n

one-sided contract, unilateral contract, contract of benevolence, deed poll, contract without consideration, gratuitous contract, nude contract · einseitiger Vertrag m, Vertrag ohne Gegenleistung

one-sided obligation, requirement, unilateral obligation · Auflage f, einseitige Verpflichtung f

one-sided promise, nude promise, unilateral promise, gratuitous promise, promise of benevolence, promise without consideration · einseitiges (Leistungs)Versprechen n, einseitiges Naturalversprechen, (Leistungs)Versprechen ohne Gegenleistung, Naturalversprechen ohne Gegenleistung

one-side orientation, one-way orientation · einseitige Orientierung f, einseitiger Bezug m

(one's) own fund(s) · Eigenfonds m, Eigenmittel f

one-way, unilateral · einseitig

one-way classification · Klassifizierung f nach einem Merkmal

one-way error, unilateral error · einseitiger Fehler m

one-way exchange, unilateral exchange [*A gives something exchangeable to B, but B gives nothing exchangeable to A*] · einseitige Übertragung f

one-way mistake, unilateral mistake · einseitiger Irrtum m

one-way orientation, one-side orientation · einseitige Orientierung f, einseitiger Bezug m

ongoing programme; ongoing program (US) · laufendes Programm n

(on-)licence, (on-)license [*It permits the sale of intoxicating liquors for consumption on and off the premises*] · Schankkonzession f

only bill, promissory note, note (of hand), single bill, sole bill · Eigenwechsel m, (eigener) Wechsel, Solawechsel, Verpflichtungsschein m [*Ein unbedingtes, von einer Person an eine andere gerichtetes, vom Aussteller unterschriebenes schriftliches Versprechen, auf Verlangen oder zu einer festgesetzten oder zu einer bestimmbar zukünftigen Zeit an eine bestimmte Person oder deren Order oder an den Inhaber eine bestimmte Summe in Geld zu zahlen*]

on or about [*A phrase used in conveyancing, in reciting the date of an instrument referred to. To avoid the injurious consequences of error in the recital of dates, etc., the safe and correct practice in conveyancing (a practice inadmissible in pleading) is to recite deeds as bearing date "on or about", etc., thus allowing the deed to be produceable in evidence in support of the title, though the date be mistaken*] · etwa am [*Datum*]

on schedule, timely · fristgerecht, fristgemäß

on-site clerk, clerk of the works · Baustellenverwaltungsangestellte m

(on-)site overhead(s), (on-)site overhead cost(s), job overhead(s), job overhead cost(s) · Baustellen-Gemein(un)kosten f, Baustellen-General(un)kosten

on the case · nach Lage des Falles

on the commission [*Having the office of Justice of the Peace*] · bekleiden eines Friedensrichteramtes

(on-the-)site engineer, resident engineer, resident project administrator [*On-the-site administrator of the project for the owner*] · Baustellenleiter m, örtlicher Bauleiter, örtliche Bauleitung f, Baustellenleitung

on time, in due time, duly, at the right time · rechtzeitig

on trust — open-country neighbourhood (Brit.)

on trust, fiduciary, in trust, fiducial, under trusteeship · zur treuen Hand, treuhänderisch

onus of justifying one's action · Rechtfertigungslast *f*

onus of proof, burden of evidence, onus of evidence, burden of proving, onus of proving; onus probandi [*Latin*]; burden of proof · Beweislast *f*

to open [*To undo a proceeding, or recall an act, for the purpose of restoring a party to the position he was in before such proceeding or act was done; to relieve a party who has merits, against a proceeding by which he has been formally and regularly barred*] · rückgängig machen

to open, to commence, to begin [*trial of a cause*] · eröffnen, anfangen, beginnen

open, notorious, undisguised · offenkundig

open, uncovered, unbuilt, not built (up)on, non built-up · frei, nichtbebaut, unbebaut; unüberbaut [*Schweiz*]

open account, account current, demand account, continuing account, running account · laufendes Konto *n*, Kontokorrent *n*

open act(ion), manifest act(ion), overt act(ion) · objektiver Tatbestand *m*, offenkundige Handlung *f*

to open a default [*To allow a party a new opportunity of doing the act, for not doing which the default was entered*] · ermöglichen ein Versäumnis zu erfüllen

open air advertisement, external advertisement, exterior advertisement, display of advertisements, outdoor advertisement · Außenwerbung *f*, Außenreklame *f*

open air advertisement facility, external advertisement facility, exterior advertisement facility, outdoor advertisement facility · Außenwerbungseinrichtung *f*, Außenreklameeinrichtung

open air advertisement law → outdoor advertisement law

open air facility, external facility, exterior facility, outdoor facility · Außenanlage *f*, Freianlage, Außeneinrichtung *f*, Freieinrichtung

open air recreation, outdoor recreation, external recreation · Außenerholung *f*, Freilanderholung

open-air recreational facility, outdoor recreational facility, external recreational facility · Freilufterholungseinrichtung *f*

open-air resort · Freilufterholungsort *m*

open area, open space, open land · Freifläche *f*, Freiraum *m*, Freiland *n* [*Von Bebauung freie Fläche, und zwar Verkehrs-, Erholungs-, Grün- und sonstige von Bebauung freie Flächen*]

open area policy · Freiflächenpolitik *f*

open bidding, open competition, advertisement of a project, project advertisement, public tendering (out), public tender(ing) action, public bidding (action), public invitation to tender, open tendering · öffentliche Ausschreibung *f*, öffentliche Aufforderung (zur Angebotsabgabe), offenes Verfahren *n*, offener Wettbewerb *m*, Ausschreibung der öffentlichen Hand [*Bauleistungen werden im vorgeschriebenen Verfahren nach öffentlicher Aufforderung einer unbeschränkten Zahl von Unternehmern zur Einreichung von Angeboten vergeben*]

to open biddings [*In equity, is to allow a re-sale of property which has once been sold under a decree. The expression is a figurative one, like that of "letting in", which imports nearly the same idea*] · ermöglichen eines Wiederverkaufs nach einem Billigkeitsurteil

open book credit, credit on open account · offenes Ziel *n*

open-bound field system, hedge-bound field system · Zelgensystem *n*

opencast coal working · Kohlentagebau *m*

open cheque, uncrossed cheque (Brit.); open check, uncrossed check (US) · Barscheck *m*, Inhaberscheck, offener Scheck

open competition, advertisement of a project, project advertisement, public tendering (out), public tender(ing) action, public bidding (action), public invitation to tender, open tendering, open bidding · öffentliche Ausschreibung *f*, öffentliche Aufforderung (zur Angebotsabgabe), offenes Verfahren *n*, offener Wettbewerb *m*, Ausschreibung der öffentlichen Hand [*Bauleistungen werden im vorgeschriebenen Verfahren nach öffentlicher Aufforderung einer unbeschränkten Zahl von Unternehmern zur Einreichung von Angeboten vergeben*]

open competition, free competition · freier Wettbewerb *m*

open contract · einfacher Vertrag *m* des Grundstücksrechts [*Er basiert auf einer privaten Abmachung zwischen Käufer und Verkäufer und seine wesentlichen Kennzeichen sind Angebot und Annahme und die Gegenleistung in Geld oder Geldeswert*]

open contract of sale · Verkaufvertrag *m* ohne näher bestimmte Bedingung [*Die Parteien haben nur vereinbart zu kaufen und zu verkaufen*]

open-country neighbourhood (Brit.); open-country neighborhood (US) · Nachbar-

open countryside — to open publicly (in front of all the bidders) 720

schaft *f* bei gestreutem Siedeln, Nachbarschaft auf dem Lande

open countryside · flaches Land *n*

open court · öffentliche (Gerichts)Sitzung *f*

open credit · laufender Kredit *m*, offener Kredit

open-cut mining land(s), open pit mining land(s), open work(ing) land(s), stripping land(s), exploitation land(s), opencut mining area, strip mining area, surface mining area, surface mining land(s), strip mining land(s) · Abbauland *n*, Tagebauland, Abbaufläche *f*, Tagebaufläche [*Grundstücke, die auf Grund ihrer Beschaffenheit die oberirdische Gewinnung von Bodenschätzen ermöglichen*]

open decisional pattern, open decisional scheme · offenes Entscheidungsmuster *n*, offenes Entscheidungsschema *n*, Programmverschachtelung *f*

open development, open system · offene Bauweise *f*

open field · Offenland *n*, Offenfeld *n*, offenes Land, offenes Feld

open fields, pattern of intermingled fragmented holdings, (inter)mixed fields · Gemengelage *f* [*Die Grundstücke verschiedener Eigentümer liegen in der Flur durcheinander gemengt ohne Zu- und Abfahrtswege*]

open-fields system, (inter)mixed-fields system · landwirtschaftliche Betriebsweise *f* auf Grundlage der Gemengelage der Äcker und der gemeinsamen Nutzung von Wald und Weide

open force · Brachialgewalt *f*

opening [*tender*] · Eröffnung *f* [*Angebot*]

opening balance(-sheet); opening inventory (US) · Anfangsbilanz *f*

opening ceremony · Eröffnungsfeier *f*

opening date → (bid) opening date

opening of tenders, opening of offers, opening of bids, bid opening, tender opening, offer opening; (bid) proposal opening, opening of (bid) proposal (US) · Angebotseröffnung *f*, Submission *f*

opening statement · Eröffnungsplädoyer *n*

opening time → (bid) opening time

opening up · Aufschließung *f*, Geländeaufschließung *f* [*Gesamtheit der Maßnahmen um in nicht genügend entwickelten Räumen eine angemessene Grundausstattung als Voraussetzung für eine bestmögliche Nutzung planmäßig zu schaffen*]

opening-up cost(s), cost(s) of opening up · Aufschließungskosten *f*

opening up for traffic purposes · verkehrsmäßige Aufschließung *f*

opening up for utilities · versorgungswirtschaftliche Aufschließung *f*

opening up (of work(s)) · Freilegen *n*

opening-up time · Aufschließungsdauer *f*

open item system · Offene-Posten-Buchhaltung *f*

open land, uncovered land, land not built upon, unbuilt land · freier Boden *m*, freier Grund, unbebauter Boden, nichtbebauter Boden, unbebautes Land *n*, freies Land, nichtbebautes Land, unbebauter Grund, nichtbebauter Grund *m*

open land, open area, open space · Freifläche *f*, Freiraum *m*, Freiland *n* [*Von Bebauung freie Fläche, und zwar Verkehrs-, Erholungs-, Grün- und sonstige von Bebauung freie Flächen*]

open landscape · freie Landschaft *f*

open market, market overt · freier Markt *m*

open market policy · Offenmarktpolitik *f* [*Mittel der Notenbanken zur Beeinflussung des Geldmarktes*]

open mining, strip mining, surface mining · Tage(ab)bau *m*, oberirdischer Abbau

open order, good-until-cancelled order, G.T.C. order · Auftrag *m* auf Widerruf gültig [*Börse*]

open parking (area), surface parking (area) [*As distinguished from a parking garage*] · Freiparkfläche *f*

open pit mining land(s) → open-cut mining land(s)

open plot, uncovered (land) parcel, unbuilt (land) parcel, open (land) parcel, uncovered parcel of land, unbuilt parcel of land, open parcel of land, (land) parcel not built upon, parcel of land not built upon, uncovered plot, unbuilt plot · Feldgrundstück *n*, freies Grundstück, nichtbenutztes Grundstück, unbebautes Grundstück

open police · Generalpolice *f*

open pound, uncovered pound, not covered pound, pound-overt · nicht eingefriedetes Grundstück, uneingefriedetes Grundstück [*Es wird der Vollstreckung unterworfen*]

open pound, overt pound · offener Pfandstall *m*

open primary (election) [*USA*] · offene Vorwahl *f*, offene Urwahl, offene Erstwahl [*Der Vorwahlteilnehmer braucht seine Parteizugehörigkeit nicht aufdecken*]

to open publicly (in front of all the bidders) · öffentlich öffnen [*verschlossene (Brief)Umschläge am Submissionstermin*]

open public space, public open space · öffentlicher Freiraum *m*

open range · freie Weidenutzung *f*

open shed [*Any structure that has no enclosing walls*] · Unterstand *m*

open shop [*England*] · Betrieb *m* mit Gewerkschaftsmitgliedern und gewerkschaftslosen Arbeitnehmern, Unternehmen *n* mit Gewerkschaftsmitgliedern und gewerkschaftslosen Arbeitnehmern

open society · offene Gesellschaft *f*

open space, open land, open area · Freifläche *f*, Freiraum *m*, Freiland *n* [*Von Bebauung freie Fläche, und zwar Verkehrs-, Erholungs-, Grün- und sonstige von Bebauung freie Flächen*]

open system, open development · offene Bauweise *f*

open tendering, open bidding, open competition, advertisement of a project, project advertisement, public tendering (out), public tender(ing) action, public bidding (action), public invitation to tender · öffentliche Ausschreibung *f*, öffentliche Aufforderung (zur Angebotsabgabe), offenes Verfahren *n*, offener Wettbewerb *m*, Ausschreibung der öffentlichen Hand [*Bauleistungen werden im vorgeschriebenen Verfahren nach öffentlicher Aufforderung einer unbeschränkten Zahl von Unternehmern zur Einreichung von Angeboten vergeben*]

open to prospecting · schürffrei

to open up (for inspection) [*works covered up*] · bloßlegen, freimachen, freilegen

open work(ing) land(s) → open-cut mining land(s)

open writ, writ not sealed up, writ not closed, patent writ · unverschlossenes Dekret *n*, offenes Dekret, unversiegeltes Dekret

to operate, to come into existence, to come into operation, to come into being, to take effect, to become to have effect, to inure, to become operative, to enure · wirksam werden, in Kraft treten

to operate · rechtswirksam wirken

to operate, to manage, to administer · durchführen, handhaben, verwalten [*Vertrag*]

operating, administering, managing · Durchführen *n*, Verwalten, Handhaben [*Vertrag*]

operating area · Betriebsfläche *f*

operating area, operating territory · Betriebsgebiet *n*

operating capacity, working capacity · Betriebskapazität *f*

operating company [*A company actively engaged in business with outsiders*] · Betriebs(kapital)gesellschaft *f*

operating costing, variable cost(s) accounting, operating cost(s) accounting, variable costing · variable Kostenrechnung *f*

operating cost(s), variable cost(s) [*A cost(s) which tends to vary directly with volume of output, e.g. the additional cost(s) incurred in producing and marketing goods once the organization has been set up*] · variable Kosten *f*

operating deficit · Betriebsdefizit *n*

operating directions, operating instructions · Betriebsanweisungen *fpl*, Betra

operating ground, operating terrain · Betriebsgelände *n*, Betriebsterrain *n*

operating income, net operating profit · Betriebseinkommen *n*

operating instructions, operating directions · Betriebsanweisungen *fpl*, Betra

operating on the same subject, concurrent, co-operating · zusammenarbeitend

operating revenue · Betriebseinnahme *f*

operating terrain, operating ground · Betriebsgelände *n*, Betriebsterrain *n*

operating territory, operating area · Betriebsgebiet *n*

operating year · Betriebsjahr *n*

operation · Betrieb *m*, Betreiben *n*

operation, effect · (Aus)Wirkung *f*

operation(al) cost(s) · Betriebskosten *f*

operational gaming [*Not to be confused with "management gaming"*] · Durchspielen *n* und Bewerten echt geplanter Strategien an einem ökonomischen Modell

operationality [*The extent to which it is possible to observe and test how well goals are being achieved*] · Operationalität *f*

operational land · Betriebsland *n*

operational readiness · Betriebsbereitschaft *f*

operational research (Brit.); operations research (US) [*The application of science to the practical end of assisting decision-makers*] · Anwendung *f* von System- und Methodenanalysen für Entscheidungen, Systemforschung *f*

operation card, job card, work ticket [*A document which authorizes an operation and is fed back after its completion to record any relevant information — time, quantity, operator, etc. — for such purposes as monitoring progress, wage payments, etc*] · Arbeitskarte *f*

operation cost(s) → operation(al) cost(s)

operation of (a) contract, administration of (a) contract, contract management, contract operation, contract administration, management of (a) contract · Durchführung f eines Vertrages, Handhabung eines Vertrages, Verwaltung eines Vertrages, Vertragsdurchführung, Vertragshandhabung, Vertragsverwaltung

operation (of law), effect (of law), legal effect, legal operation · Gesetz(es)(aus)wirkung f, Rechts(aus)wirkung

operations research, management research · Unternehmensforschung f

operations research (US) → operational research

operations science, management science · Unternehmungswissenschaft f

operative; labourer (Brit.); blue collar worker, laborer (US); worker, workman [*A wage-earning worker, skilled or semi-skilled, whose work is characterized largely by physical exertion*] · Arbeiter m

operative clause · rechtsbegründende Klausel f

operative date · Datum n des Inkrafttretens, Termin m des Inkrafttretens

operative part [*deed*] · rechtsbegründender Teil m, rechtsbegründendes Teil n [*Urkunde*]

operative technological theory · ad hoc-Hypothese f [*Für die Konstruktion technologischer Modelle*]

operative words [*deed*] · rechtsbegründende Worte npl [*Urkunde*]

operative words of transfer · sakramentale Übertragungsformel f

operator · Betreibende m, Betreiber

opinion leader · Meinungsmacher m

opinion (of the court), legal reasoning, lawful reasoning · Rechtsfindung f

opinion per curiam · Kurzbegründung f

opinion poll, straw poll · Meinungsumfrage f

opinion research · Meinungsforschung f

opinion survey · Meinungsbefragung f

opinion testimony, statement of opinion · Meinungsaussage f, Meinungsangabe f

opportunity · Lokalisierungschance f [*Wanderung*]

opportunity costing [*It is a forecasting technique used to predict cost(s) if a specific change in production is implemented*] · Opportunitätskostenrechnung f

opportunity cost(s), alternative cost(s) · Schattenkosten f, Alternativkosten, Opportunitätskosten [*Kosten die nicht oder nicht sofort als solche entstehen, sondern ihren Ausdruck in der verpaßten Gelegenheit einer noch vorteilhafteren Gestaltung finden*]

opposed to sound reason, absurd, unreasonable · sinnwidrig, unvernünftig

opposing counsel · Justitiar m der Gegenpartei

opposing party, adverse party, opposite party, opponent (party), adversary · Prozeßgegner m

opposing version (of a case) · Gegendarstellung f

oppression [*The common law misdemeanour committed by a public officer who, under colour of his office, wrongfully inflicts upon any person any bodily harm, imprisonment or other injury*] · Amtsmißbrauch m gegenüber einer natürlichen Person, Amtsüberschreitung f gegenüber einer natürlichen Person

optimization model · Optimierungsmodell n

optimization theory · Optimierungstheorie f

to optimize · optimieren

optimum planning · Optimalplanung f

optimum population · Maximalbevölkerung f

optimum transport point · Transportoptimalpunkt m

option, (freedom of) choice · Option f, Entscheidungsrecht n, Wahl(möglichkeit) f

option, call · Bezugsoption f, Empfangsoption, Prämiengeschäft n auf Nehmen [*Börse*]

optional · fakultativ, wahlweise

option(al) clause · Optionsklausel f, Wahlklausel

optional payment plan, Ohio plan, Dayton permanent plan · individueller unregelmäßiger Plan m [*Eine dauernde Form einer amerikanischen Bausparkasse*]

optional payment plan (building (and loan)) association (US) · Bausparkasse f mit einer Mindestzahlung und keinen regelmäßigen Zahlungen in bestimmten Beträgen und in bestimmten Zeitabständen

optional primary (election) [*USA*] · wahlfreie Vorwahl f

option(al) procedure · wahlweises Verfahren n, Optionsverfahren(sweise) n, (f)

option bar · Auswahlsperre f

optionee · Wahlrechtbegünstigte m

option graph · Auswahldiagramm n

optionor · Wahlrechtverpflichtete m

option right — order of course

option right, right of option, option to buy, option to purchase · Option(srecht) *f, (n)*, Vorhand *f*

option to buy, option to purchase, option right, right of option · Option(srecht) *f, (n)*, Vorhand *f*

opus manificum [*Latin*]; manual labour (Brit.); manual labor (US) · Handarbeit *f*

oral, parol, by word of mouth, verbal [*In early times few persons could write, and therefore when a document was required to record a transaction the parties put their seals to it and made it a deed. Transactions of less importance were testified by word of mouth or by parol, and this use of "parol", to signify the absence of a deed, remained after simple writing without sealing had come into use*] · mündlich

oral agreement, agreement by word of mouth, agreement by parol, parol agreement, verbal agreement · mündliches Abkommen *n*, mündliche Vereinbarung *f*, mündliche Abmachung

oral deposition, verbal deposition · mündliche Vernehmung *f*

oral evidence, oral proof, verbal evidence, verbal proof [*That which is given by word of mouth; the ordinary kind of evidence, given by witness in court*] · mündlicher Beweis *m*

oral evidence rule, verbal evidence rule · Ausschließung *f* mündlicher Beweise wenn schriftliche vorliegen, Ausschluß *m* mündlicher Beweise wenn schriftliche vorliegen

oral instruction, verbal instruction, parol instruction · mündliche Anweisung *f*

orality principle, principle of orality · Grundsatz *m* der Mündlichkeit, Prinzip *n* der Mündlichkeit, Mündlichkeitsgrundsatz, Mündlichkeitsprinzip

(oral) pleading, verbal pleading, pleading by word of mouth, statement · Plädoyer *n*

oral promise, verbal promise · mündliches Versprechen *n*

oral proof, verbal evidence, verbal proof, oral evidence [*That which is given by word of mouth; the ordinary kind of evidence, given by witness in court*] · mündlicher Beweis *m*

oral testimony, verbal testimony · mündliche Zeugenaussage *f* unter Eid

oral tradition, verbal tradition · mündliche Überlieferung *f*

oral will, nuncupative will, verbal will · mündliches Testament *n*

orator, petitioner [*A plaintiff in a bill, or information, in Chancery was so called before the statute 1852, 15 & 16 Vict. c. 86*] · Bittsteller *m*, Kläger

oratress, oratrix, female petitioner [*A female plaintiff in a bill in Chancery was formerly so called*] · Bittstellerin *f*, Klägerin

orbital remote sensing (of environment), orbital remote sensory perception · Fernerkundung *f* aus dem Weltraum

ordeal, judg(e)ment of God, divine judg(e)ment; divinum judicium, judicium dei [*Latin*] · Gottesurteil *n*

to order · anordnen, verfügen, befehlen, gebieten

to order → to instal

order · Rangfolge *f*, Rangordnung *f*, Rangverhältnis *n*

order [*A fixed or definite plan, system, law or arrangement*] · Ordnung *f*

order · Auftrag *m*, Bestellung *f*

order, installation, vesting, admission, commission · (Amts)Einsetzung *f*, (Amts)Bestallung

order · Anordnung *f*, Verfügung, Befehl *m*, Gebot *n*

order amount · Auftragsbetrag *m*

order and disposition clause, reputed ownership clause · Klausel *f* des englischen Konkursrechts nach der in gewissem Umfange auch Vermögen Dritter zur Masse gehört

order bill of lading · Orderkonnossement *n*

order blank (form), order form · Auftragsformular *n*, Auftragsvordruck *m*

order council · Verordnung *f* der Krone

ordered indicator matrix · Distanzindikatormatrix *f*, Entfernungsindikatormatrix

order for foreclosure absolute · endgültiges Ausschlußurteil *n* [*Pfandverwertung des Gläubigers*]

order for foreclosure nisi · nisi-Urteil *n* [*Pfandverwertung des Gläubigers*]

order for payment, payment order · Zahlungsbefehl *m*, Zahlungsanordnung, Zahlungsverfügung *f*, Zahlungsgebot *n*

order for winding(-)up, order for liquidation, winding(-)up order, liquidation order · Liquidationsbefehl *m*, Liquidationsgebot *n*, Liquidationsverfügung *f*, Liquidationsanordnung

order in council · Gerichtsbeschluß *m*

order of attachment, attachment order · Arrestbefehl *m*, Personalarrestbefehl

order of citation, citation order · Zitierfolge *f*

order of course · Verfügung *f* als Folge eines (formellen) Antrages [*Verhandlung in öffentlicher Gerichtssitzung*]

**order of delivery, **delivery bill, bill of delivery, delivery order · Lieferschein m

**order of descent and distribution, **order of succession and distribution · Erbfolgeordnung f, Erbgangordnung

**order of discharge, **discharge order · Entlastungsverfügung f, Entlastungsanordnung, Entlastungsbefehl m, Entlastungsgebot n

**order of distringas **[obsolete]; charging order · Befehl m zur Pfändung von Anteilsrechten

**order of exclusion, **exclusion order (US); expulsion order, order of expulsion [in contradistinction to "deportation order"] · Ausweisungsbefehl m, Verweisungsbefehl, Relegationsbefehl, Ausweisungsgebot n, Verweisungsgebot, Relegationsgebot, Ausweisungsanordnung f, Verweisungsanordnung, Relegationsanordnung, Ausweisungsverfügung, Verweisungsverfügung, Relegationsverfügung

**order of knighthood **· Ritterorden m

**order of magnitude **· Größenordnung f

**order of magnitude estimate (US); **ratio estimate · grobe Schätzung f der Baukosten, grobe Baukostenschätzung

**order-of-merit-rating **· Verdienst-Rangskala f, Bedeutungs-Rangskala [Umfragetechnik]

**order of protection, **protection order · Schutzbefehl m, Schutzanordnung f, Schutzverfügung, Schutzgebot n

**order of registration, **order of recordation, order of recording · Eintragungsverfügung f, Eintragungsanordnung, Eintragungsbefehl m, Eintragungsgebot n

**order of service, **service order · Beantwortungsbefehl m, Beantwortungsanordnung, Beantwortungsverfügung f, Beantwortungsgebot n [Durch ihn wird ein Revisionsbeklagter aufgefordert seine Beantwortung einzureichen]

**order of stationarity **· Stationaritätsordnung f

**order of succession and distribution, **order of descent and distribution · Erbfolgeordnung f, Erbgangordnung

**order of (the) court, **court order, writ [A mandatory precept issuing from court of justice] · Gerichtsverfügung f, Gerichtsgebot n, Gerichtsanordnung, Gerichtsbefehl m, (gerichtliche) Verfügung, gerichtliche Anordnung, gerichtliches Gebot, gerichtlicher Befehl, Mandat n

**order-preserving function **· ordnungserhaltende Funktion f

**order public, **peace, public security and good order, public policy, public safety, public order · öffentliche (Sicherheit f und) Ordnung f, öffentliche (Ordnung und) Sicherheit

**orders in council **· Anordnungen fpl der Krone, Gebote npl der Krone, Verfügungen fpl der Krone, Befehle mpl der Krone

**order-statistic **· Anordnungsmaßzahl f [Statistik]

**order statistics **· Anordnungsstatistik f

**order sum **· Auftragssumme f

**order to construct, **order to build · Baubefehl m, Bauanordnung f, Baugebot n, Bauverfügung [Verwaltungsakt das Grundstück zu bebauen]

**order to improve, **order to modernize, order to rehabilitate, (physical) improvement order, rehabilitation order, modernization order, upgrading order · Modernisierungsverfügung f, Modernisierungsanordnung, Modernisierungsgebot n, Modernisierungsbefehl m, (baulicher) Verbesserungsbefehl

**order to maintain, **order to support [person] · Unterhaltsverfügung f, Unterhaltsanordnung, Unterhaltsbefehl m, Unterhaltsgebot n

**order to modernize, **order to rehabilitate, (physical) improvement order, rehabilitation order, modernization order, upgrading order, order to improve · Modernisierungsverfügung f, Modernisierungsanordnung, Modernisierungsgebot n, Modernisierungsbefehl m, (baulicher) Verbesserungsbefehl

**order to negotiate **· Negotiationskredit m

**order to one of the tellers **[England] · Kassenanweisung f [(königliches) Schatzamt]

**order to pay **· (Zahlungs)Anweisung f

**order to plant **· Pflanzgebot n, Pflanzbefehl m

**order to rehabilitate, **(physical) improvement order, rehabilitation order, modernization order, upgrading order, order to improve, order to modernize · Modernisierungsverfügung f, Modernisierungsanordnung, Modernisierungsgebot n, Modernisierungsbefehl m, (baulicher) Verbesserungsbefehl

**order to reinstate, **reinstatement order · Instandsetzungsbefehl m, Instandsetzungsverfügung f, Instandsetzungsanordnung, Instandsetzungsgebot n

**order to support, **order to maintain [person] · Unterhaltsverfügung f, Unterhaltsanordnung, Unterhaltsbefehl m, Unterhaltsgebot n

**order to use **· Nutzungsgebot n, Nutzungsbefehl m, Nutzungsverfügung f, Nutzungsverordnung

**ordinance **· (Rechts)Verordnung f

**ordinance **→ (local) by(e)-law

**ordinance board, **board of ordinance · Arsenalamt n

ordinance for construction documents, ordinance for building documents · Bauvorlagenverordnung *f*

ordinance to control building height(s) · Gebäudehöhenverordnung *f*

ordinary, common, usual, customary · herkömmlich, üblich

ordinary · geistlicher ordentlicher Richter *m*, ordentlicher geistlicher Richter

ordinary agricultural labourer, general agricultural labourer (Brit.); ordinary agricultural laborer, general agricultural laborer (US); orraman [*Scotland*]; spade hind [*In den Grenzgrafschaften Südschottlands*] · gewöhnlicher Landarbeiter *m*

ordinary annuity [*An annuity payable at the end of each period; the opposite of "annuity due"*] · nachschüssige Rente *f*

ordinary common law remedy · gewöhnlicher Rechtsbehelf *m* des gemeinen Rechts

ordinary creditor, general creditor · unbevorrechtigter Gläubiger *m*

ordinary damages, ordinary compensation, ordinary indemnification, ordinary indemnity · gewöhnliche Entschädigung(sleistung) *f*, gewöhnliche Schadenersatzleistung, gewöhnlicher Schadenersatz *m*

ordinary damages, unliquidated compensation, ordinary compensation, unliquidated indemnification, ordinary indemnification, unliquidated indemnity, ordinary indemnity, unliquidated damages · nicht festgestellte Entschädigung *f*, nicht festgestellter Schadenersatz *m*

ordinary fault, ordinary neglect; levis culpa [*Latin*] · gewöhnliches Verschulden *n*

ordinary large society [*England*] · Landesverein *m*

ordinary maintenance, current maintenance, permanent maintenance · planmäßige Unterhaltung *f*, Routineunterhaltung

ordinary neglect; levis culpa [*Latin*]; ordinary fault · gewöhnliches Verschulden *n*

ordinary point [*A sector which is not a transmitter, a receiver, a carrier and an isolate*] · gewöhnlicher Sektor *m* [*Graphentheorie*]

ordinary residence · gewöhnlicher Aufenthalt *m*

ordinary resolution · ordentlicher Beschluß *m*, ordentliche Entschließung *f*

ordinary service (of the writ) · normale Zustellung *f* (der Klag(e)schrift)

ordinary share, common share · Stammanteil *m*

ordinary stock, common stock · Stammaktie *f*

ordinary-stock fund, common-stock fund · Stammaktienfonds *m*, Fonds für Stammaktienwerte

ordinary trustee · gewöhnlicher Treuhänder *m*

ordinary use, normal use · gewöhnliche Benutzung *f*, gewöhnlicher Gebrauch *m*

ordnance · Feldzeugamt *n*

ordnance · Feldzeugwesen *n* [*Artillerie- und Ingenieurwesen*]

or equal [*Phrase used in a specification after a brand or trade name to indicate that a substitution will be considered when required by the contractor*] · oder gleichwertig

organic solidarity · Gesellschaft *f*

organization [*A body of persons organized for some specific purpose*] · Organisation *f*

organization · Aufbau *m* und Gliederung *f* [*Behörden*]

organizational goal · Organisationzielnorm *f*, Organisationsoberziel *n*

organizational law, law of organization · Organisationsgesetz *n*

organizational relation(ship) · organisatorisches Verhältnis *n*

organizational work(s), work(s) of management · organisatorische Arbeit(en) *f (pl)*

organization of an enterprise, organization of an undertaking · Betriebsorganisation *f*, Unternehmensorganisation

organization of society · Gesellschaftsordnung *f*

organization of tenure → feudal (landholding) system

organized entity · organisierte Einheit *f*

organized industrial district, planned industrial district; industrial park (US) [*Beide unterscheiden sich dadurch, daß bei der Auswahl der in einem "industrial park" aufzunehmenden Betriebe Gesichtspunkte wie z. B. ästhetische oder solche der Verträglichkeit mit Nachbarbezirken berücksichtigt werden*] · Gewerbeplansiedlung *f*

oriental cluster village, oriental irregular nucleated village · orientalisches Haufendorf *n*

orient(at)ed to raw materials(s) · rohstoffbezogen, rohstofforientiert

orien(ta)ted to the turnover, orien(ta)ted to the stockturn, related to the turnover, related to the stockturn · umsatzbezogen, umsatzorientiert

orien(ta)ted toward passers-by — originator

orien(ta)ted toward passers-by · passantenorientiert, passantenbezogen

orientation according to total cost(s), orientation according to whole cost(s), orientation according to aggregate cost(s) · Orientierung f an den Gesamtkosten

orientation by gain, orientation by profit · Gewinnorientierung f, Profitorientierung, Orientierung auf Gewinn, Orientierung auf Profit

orientation by production · Erzeugungsorientierung f, Produktionsorientierung, Herstellungsorientierung, Fertigungsorientierung

orientation by quantity, quantity orientation · Mengenorientierung f

orientation data · Orientierungsdaten f

orientation period · Einarbeitungszeit f, Probezeit

orient(ta)ted, related · bezogen, orientiert

original acquirer, first acquirer · Ersterwerber m

original acquisition, first acquisition · Ersterwerb m, Erstbeschaffung f, Ersterwerbung f

original afforestation, first afforestation · Erstaufforstung f

original amount, principal, capital sum [*The total amount of capital of an estate, fund, mortgage, bond, note, or other form of financial investment, together with accretions not yet recognized as income*] · Kapitalsumme f, Hauptsumme

original bill [*In old practice. The ancient mode of commencing actions in the English Court of King's Bench*] · erste Klag(e)schrift f

original buyer, original purchaser, primary buyer, primary purchaser, first purchaser, first buyer · Erstkäufer m

original capital, authorized capital, registered capital, nominal capital [*When a company is formed its application for registration is accompanied by a statement indicating the amount of capital with which it purposes to be registered*] · Grundkapital n [*Nicht verwechseln mit der deutschen Benennung „genehmigtes (Aktien)Kapital"; denn dieses ist ein durch Beschluß der Hauptversammlung festgesetzter Betrag, um den der Vorstand während einer bestimmten Zeit das Grundkapital erhöhen kann*]

original (contracting) party · Erstpartei f, Erstvertragspartei, Erst(vertrags)partner m

original copy, archetype · Originalausfertigung f, Urausfertigung

original debtor, original obligor · Erstschuldner m

original dominion, original property · Hauptsache f [*Vermengung; Vermischung*]

original impossibility · ursprüngliche Unmöglichkeit f

original interest, original right · Urrecht n

original (issue) syndicate · (Emissions)Übernahmekonsortium n, (Emissions)Übernahmesyndikat n

original jurisdiction [*A court is said to have original jurisdiction in a particular matter when that matter can be initiated before it*] · erstinstanzliche Zuständigkeit f [*Siehe Anmerkung unter „Zuständigkeit"*]

original lot · Stammflurstück n, Stammparzelle f, Urflurstück, Urparzelle

original obligor, original debtor · Erstschuldner m

original party → (contracting) party

original possession · Urbesitz m, Stammbesitz

original possessor · Urbesitzer m, Stammbesitzer

original property, original dominion · Hauptsache f [*Vermengung; Vermischung*]

original purchaser, primary buyer, primary purchaser, first purchaser, first buyer, original buyer · Erstkäufer m

original right, original interest · Urrecht n

original settlement · Ur(an)sied(e)lung f

original surface and value of property · Einlage(grundstück) f,(n)

original syndicate → original (issue) syndicate

original weight, base weight · Ausgangsgewicht n, Originalgewicht, Ursprungsgewicht

original (writ); breve originale [*Latin*] [*In English practice. A writ issuing out of chancery, and so called because it anciently gave origin and commencement to an action at common law. In modern practice, the use of an original (writ) is confined to real actions exclusively. In American practice, original writs have been employed to some extent, but are now in general superseded by other forms of process*] · prozeßeinleitende Kabinettorder f [*Hofgericht*]

originating petition · Verfahrenseröffnungsantrag m [*Verhandlung in öffentlicher Gerichtssitzung*]

originating process · Klageerhebung f

originating summons · (Prozeß)Ladung f zur Verfahrenseröffnung

originator · Veranlasser m

origin community, community of origin · Ausgangsgemeinde *f*

origion of traffic, traffic origin · Verkehrsausgang *m*, Verkehrsursprung *m*

ornamental fixture, decorative fixture, ornamental object fixed to a building, decorative object fixed to a building · Dekor(ations)einrichtung *f*, Schmuckeinrichtung, Ziereinrichtung, dekorativer (Grundstücks)Bestandteil *m*

ornamental garden, pleasure garden · Ziergarten *m*, Schmuckgarten

ornamental ground · Zierfläche *f*, Schmuckfläche

ornamental timber, timber planted for ornament · Schmuckgehölz *n*, Ziergehölz, Zierholz, Schmuckholz

orphan's court, surrogate's court (US); probate court, court of probate [*A court in which wills are probated, or proved. Called "orphans" court in a few states of the USA*] · Nachlaßgericht *n*, Erb(schafts)gericht

orraman [*Scotland*]; spade hind [*In den Grenzgrafschaften Südschottlands*]; ordinary agricultural labourer, general agricultural labourer (Brit.); ordinary agricultural laborer, general agricultural laborer (US) · gewöhnlicher Landarbeiter *m*

osken (of land) → oxgang (of land)

ostensible · plausibel

ostensible · offen, solidarisch, verbindlich [*Teilhaber*]

ostensible, apparent, presumptive, presumed, reputed · angeblich, anscheinend, scheinbar, mutmaßlich, vermutlich, vermeintlich

ostensible · (vor)zeigbar

ostensible authority, authority by estoppel, apparent authority · Scheinvollmacht *f*, Scheinvertretungsmacht, Anscheinvollmacht, allgemeine Vollmacht, allgemeine Vertretungsmacht, Vollmacht kraft Rechtsschein, Vertretungsmacht kraft Rechtsschein, Vollmacht kraft Partnerstellung, Vertretungsmacht kraft Partnerstellung

ostensible partner, apparent partner [*If a man holds himself out to the world as a partner, or permits others to hold him out as a partner, when in fact he is not, he is called an ostensible partner or apparent partner*] · Scheinpartner *m*, Partner kraft Rechtsschein, Anscheinpartner

othe [*old English*]; juramentum, jus jurandum, sacramentum [*Latin*]; ath [*Saxon*]; oath · Eid *m*

other accrued liability, free (liability) reserve, other (liability) reserve, free accrued liability · freie Rückstellung *f*, andere Rückstellung

other revenue, nonoperating revenue · betriebsfremder Ertrag *m*, sonstiger Ertrag

other right · sonstiges Recht *n*

other than floating debt · nicht schwebende Schuld *f* [*Die tilgungspflichtigen lang- und mittelfristigen Kredite*]

to oust, to evict, to dispossess · widerrechtlich entheben, widerrechtlich entziehen, widerrechtlich aberkennen [*Grundbesitz*]

ouster, eviction, dispossession · widerrechtliche Entziehung *f*, widerrechtliche Enthebung, widerrechtliche Aberkennung

outbound traffic · Stadtauswärtsverkehr *m*

outbreak of hostilities · Ausbruch *m* von Feindseligkeiten

outbreak of war · Kriegsausbruch *m*

out-commuter · Auspendler *m*, Wegpendler *m*

out-commuting · Auspendeln *n*, Wegpendeln

outcounty estate · Außen(an)sied(e)lung *f* [*Eine (An)Sied(e)lung außerhalb der Grafschaft London*]

outdoor advertisement, open air advertisement, external advertisement, exterior advertisement, display of advertisements · Außenwerbung *f*, Außenreklame *f*

outdoor advertisement facility, open air advertisement facility, external advertisement facility, exterior advertisement facility · Außenwerbungseinrichtung *f*, Außenreklameeinrichtung

outdoor facility, open air facility, external facility, exterior facility · Außenanlage *f*, Freianlage, Außeneinrichtung *f*, Freieinrichtung

outdoor recreation, open air recreation · Außenerholung *f*, Freilanderholung

outdoor relief · Hausarmenpflege *f*, Hausunterstützung *f*, offene Armenfürsorge *f*

outer area of protection, outer protective area · Außenschutzgebiet *n*

outer belt line · Außengürtellinie *f*

Outer Berlin, metropolitan Berlin, Greater Berlin · Großberlin *n*

Outer Breslau, metropolitan Breslau, Greater Breslau · Groß-Breslau *n*

Outer London, Greater London, Metropolitan London · Außenlondon *n*, Großlondon *n*

outer protective area, outer area of protection · Außenschutzgebiet *n*

outer ring — out-of-town bank 728

outer ring · Außenring *m*

outer town (US); suburban city, suburban town (Brit.); outer city · Außenstadt *f*, Vorstadt

outer zone, rural urban fringe, rural town fringe, rural city fringe, rurban fringe, outskirt · ,,eingebauter" Gürtel *m*, ländlich-städtischer Gürtel [*Die Benennungen ,,rural urban fringe" usw. können heute nicht mehr mit ,,Stadtrandzone" übersetzt werden, weil es sich heute um nur noch durch ihre aus der einstigen Randlage resultierenden besonderen Funktionen gekennzeichnete und den geschlossenen Stadtkörper ,,eingebaute" Gürtel handelt*]

outgo(ing), expenditure · Ausgabe *f*

outland(s), tenancy, tenure land(s), feodal land(s), feudal land(s), feuda(to)ry land(s), tenemental land(s), land(s) of (a) manor, land(s) held of a lord, land(s) of tenure [*Land held of the lord by free tenure*] · Leh(e)n(s)land *n*, Feudalland, Außenland, Grenzland, verpachtetes Land

outlaw, lawless man; exlex, utlagatus [*Latin*] · Geächtete *m*

outlawry; utla(w)ry [*old forms*]; utlagaria [*Latin*] · Acht *f*, Geächtetsein *n*, Außergesetzlichkeit *f*

outlay, expenditure · Aufwand *m*, Verausgabung *f*

outlay territory, hinterland, catchment land, catchment area, catchment territory, tributary area, tributary territory, tributary land · Hinterland *n*, Einzugsgebiet *n*, Einzugsbereich *m*

outlet · Absatzmarkt *m*

outlier, maverick · Ausreißer *m*, herausfallende Beobachtung *f* [*Statistik*]

outline description · Rahmenbeschreibung *f*

outline development plan, land use plan, plan of land use · Aufbauplan *m* [*veraltete Benennung*]; Flächenwidmungsplan *m* [*Österreich*]; vorbereitender Bauleitplan *m*, Flächennutzungsplan *m*, Landnutzungsplan *m*, Bodennutzungsplan *m*, FNP *m*

outline map · Leerkarte *f*, Umrißkarte

outline of construction procedure, (contractor's) completion schedule, working chart, working schedule, building chart, building schedule, construction chart, construction schedule [*Written or graphically explained, the procedure of construction prepared by the contractor, usually by a bar chart of scheduled dates by trades or a critical path chart*] · (Ausführungs)Fristenplan *m*, Baufristenplan

outline permission · Vorbescheid *m*

outline plan [*A governmental entity's official statement of its plans and policies for its long-term development. Usually related to the capital improvement program(me)*] · Gesamtplan *m*

outline planner · Gesamtplaner *m*

outline planning law · Gesamtplanungsrecht *n*

outline planning permission · Gesamtplanungserlaubnis *f*, Gesamtplanungsgenehmigung *f*

outline scheme, outline programme; outline program (US) · Gesamtprogramm *n*

outline spec(ification)s [*Specifications containing adequate technical information but written in an abbreviated manner*] · technische Kurzbeschreibung *f*

to outlive, to over-live, to live beyond another, to survive · überleben

outlying farm, relocated farm, consolidated farm · Einödhof *m*, Einöde *f*, Aussiedlerhof

outlying location, outlying site · Außenstandort *m*, Außenlage *f*

outlying (parish) portion · isolierter Kirchspielteil *m*, nicht zusammenhängender Kirchspielteil

outlying space [*A space not forming part of an urban settlement*] · Außenraum *m*

out-migration, outward migration, migration from an area, migration outwards · Abwanderung *f*

out-migration area, out-migration territory, outward migration area, outward migration territory · Abwanderungsgebiet *n*

out-migration of young people, outward migration of young people · Jugendabwanderung *f*

out-migrator, outward migrator · Abwanderer *m*, Abwandernde *m*

out of balance · unausgeglichen [*Konten*]

out of court; extra judicium [*Latin*]; extralegal (US); extrajudicial · außergerichtlich

out-of-court settlement, composition by deed of arrangement · außergerichtlicher (Gläubiger)Vergleich *m*

out-(of-)door recreation, external recreation · Freierholung *f*

out-of-term period · Semesterferien *f*

out of the (protection of the) law, outlawed; extra legem [*Latin*] · geächtet

out of time, overdue, due and more than due · überfällig, längst fällig, lange fällig

out-of-town bank · inländische auswärtige Bank *f*

out-of-town location, out-of-town site · außerstädtischer Standort *m*

out-of-work-benefit, unemployment relief, unemployment benefit, donation money, idle money, unemployment compensation, compensation of unemployment, relief of unemployment, out-of-work-pay · Arbeitslosengeld *n*, Arbeitslosenunterstützung *f*, Erwerbslosengeld *n*, Erwerbslosenunterstützung

output · Ausbringung *f*, Ausstoß *m* [*Abgang in Form von Sachgütern, Dienstleistungen und Informationen, die eine Unternehmung an die Umwelt abgibt*]

output expansion path · Erzeugungsexpansionsweg *m*, Produktionsexpansionsweg, Herstellungsexpansionsweg, Fertigungsexpansionsweg [*Der geometrische Ort aller Berührungsprodukte bei der Erlösmaximierung unter Nebenbedingungen*]

output rate [*per man or machine hour*] · Leistungssatz *m*

output rate per machine hour, plant standard · Maschinenstundenleistung *f*

output rate per man hour, labo(u)r standard · Mannstundenleistung *f*

output-restriction cartel · Produktionskartell *n*

outside a contract, extracontractual, noncontractual · außervertraglich, nichtvertraglich

outside area, outside territory · Außengebiet *n*

outside capital, debt capital, borrowed capital · Fremdkapital *n*, Schuldenkapital

outside financing, financing by outside help · Fremdfinanzierung *f*

outside repair · Fremdreparatur *f*

outside security · Freiverkehrswert *m*

outside territory, outside area · Außengebiet *n*

outskirt, outer zone, rural urban fringe, rural town fringe, rural city fringe, rurban fringe · „eingebauter" Gürtel *m*, ländlich-städtischer Gürtel [*Die Benennungen „rural urban fringe" usw. können heute nicht mehr mit „Stadtrandzone" übersetzt werden, weil es sich heute um nur noch durch ihre aus der einstigen Randlage resultierenden besonderen Funktionen gekennzeichnete und in den geschlossenen Stadtkörper „eingebaute" Gürtel handelt*]

outstanding money, outstanding debt, bookdebt, contract money · Außenstand *m*, (Geschäfts)Forderung *f*

outward migration, migration from an area, migration outwards, out-migration · Abwanderung *f*

outward migration area, outward migration territory, out-migration area, outmigration territory · Abwanderungsgebiet *n*

outward migration of young people, out-migration of young people · Jugendabwanderung *f*

outward migrator, out-migrator · Abwanderer *m*, Abwandernde *m*

outward spread, outward sprawl, suburban spread, suburban sprawl, spread(ing) of cities, sprawl of cities, spread(ing) of towns, sprawl of towns, suburbanization, decentralization, formation of sub(urb)s, suburban process, suburban urbanization, (urban) spread, (urban) sprawl · Sied(e)lungsbrei *m*, Dezentralisation *f*, Ausufern *n*, Zersied(e)lung *f*, Überwucherung des städtischen Raumes, Dezentralisierung *f*

ovelty of land exchange, owelty of land exchange · Wertausgleich *m* bei Grundstückstausch

overabsorbed burden · Fixkostenüberdeckung *f*, Festkostenüberdeckung

overall area, overall territory, total area, total territory · Gesamtgebiet *n*

overall concept, model · Leitbild *n*

overall density, total density, aggregate density · Gesamtdichte *f*

(overall) design and construction time · Entwurfs- und Bauzeit *f*

overall environment · Gesamtumwelt *f*

overall floor space; overall storey space (Brit.); overall story space (US) · Außenmaßfläche *f*, Geschoßaußenmaßfläche *f*, Etagenaußenmaßfläche *f*, Stockwerkaußenmaßfläche *f* [*Sie ergibt sich aus den äußeren Begrenzungen eines Geschosses in Fußbodenhöhe*]

overall form, overall shape [*The relation of developed areas to open land*] · Gesamtform *f*, Gesamtgestalt *f* [*Großstadt*]

overall profitability · Gesamtrentabilität *f*

overall shape, overall form [*The relation of developed areas to open land*] · Gesamtform *f*, Gesamtgestalt *f* [*Großstadt*]

overall territory, total area, total territory, overall area · Gesamtgebiet *n*

overall time (allowed), overall term, overall time period, overall (fixed) period (of time) · Gesamtfrist *f*, Gesamtzeit(raum) *f*, *(m)*, (bestimmte) Gesamtzeit

overbilling · Überfakturieren *n*

overburdened with traffic · verkehrsüberlastet

overcapitalization · Überkapitalisierung *f*

overcaution — overriding interests

overcaution · Übervorsicht f

over-certifying, over-certification [*Of an amount due to a contractor by the architect or engineer*] · Überbescheinigen n

to overcommit [*time*] · überbeanspruchen [*Zeit*]

to overcrowd, to overuse [*To crowd to many people in or on*] · übervoll belegen, überlasten

overcrowded, overused · überbelegt, übervoll, überlastet

overcrowding, overusing · Überbelegen n, Überfüllen, Überbelasten

to overdraw · überziehen [*Bankkonto*]

overdue · verfallen [*Wechsel*]

overdue, due and more than due, out of time · überfällig, längst fällig, lange fällig

overdue order [*An order which is not complete when the finish date is past*] · unvollständig erfüllter Auftrag m

to overestimate · überschätzen

overexpansion · Überausdehnung f

overfinancing · Überfinanzierung f

to overfuel [*economy*] · überhitzen [*Wirtschaft*]

over-full employment, hyperemployment · Überbeschäftigung f

overgrowth · Überwachstum n

overhanging of branches · Überhang m von Zweigen, Zweig(e)überhang

overhead cost(s) → overhead(s)

overhead cost(s) markup, overhead(s) markup, indirect cost(s) markup · Gemeinkostenzuschlag m, Generalkostenzuschlag

overhead rate · Gemeinkostenverrechnungssatz m, Zuschlagsatz

overhead(s), overhead cost(s), indirect cost(s) [*The total cost(s) of indirect materials, wages and expenses. NOTE "oncost" and "burden" are synonymous terms which are not recommended*] · Gemeinkosten f, Generalkosten, indirekte Kosten, mittelbare Kosten

overimprove · übererschließen

overimprovement, excess improvement · Übererschließung f

overincome tenant · unberechtigter Sozialmieter m

over-indebtedness, excess of liabilities over assets · Überschuldung f

over-insurance, excess insurance · Überversicherung f

(over)lap, interference, lappage, conflict, interlock · Überschneidung f, Überlagerung

overlapping of areas → area(l) overlapping

to over-live, to live beyond another, to survive, to outlive · überleben

overloading · Überbelastung f

over lord, lord of (the) manor, supreme owner, landlord, grantor, feoffor, feoffer, manor lord, langeman, bestower of a fee, feudal chief; dominus directus, feoffator [*Latin*]; (feudal) lord, chief lord, possessory lord, liege-lord, superior lord · Leh(e)n(s)herr m, Feudalherr, (feudaler) Belehner, Leh(e)n(s)gutgeber, Obereigentümer, Landübertragende, Übertragende von Land

overlying right [*Right of owner of land(s) to take water from ground underneath for use on his land within basin or watershed. Right is based on ownership of land(s) and is appurtenant thereto*] · Grundwasserentnahmerecht n

overmanaged society · überkontrollierte Gesellschaft f

overmodernization, overrehabilitation, (physical) overimprovement · Übermodernisierung f, (bauliche) Überverbesserung

overnight population · Nachtbevölkerung f

overnight population density, density of overnight population · Nachtbevölkerungsdichte f

to overpay · überzahlen, überbezahlen

overpayment, excess payment · Über(be)zahlung f

overplus, surplus · Mehrerlös m

overplus, surplus, excess · Überschuß m

overplus clause, surplus clause · Mehrerlösklausel f [*Maklervertrag*]

overpopulated · überbevölkert

overpopulation · Überbevölkerung f

to overreach · überholen [*Auflassung*]

overreaching · Überholung f [*Auflassung*]

overreaching principle, principle of overreaching · Überholungsgrundsatz m, Überholungsprinzip n [*Auflassung*]

overrehabilitation, (physical) overimprovement, overmodernization · Übermodernisierung f, (bauliche) Überverbesserung

to override · Priorität genießen, Priorität haben, Vorrang genießen, Vorrang haben

overriding clause, repealing clause, determinative clause · Aufhebungsklausel f

overriding interests · übergeordnete Interessen npl

to overrule — over-urbanization

to overrule, to refuse to follow · abweichen, außer Kraft setzen [*Durch ein höheres Gericht oder eine höhere Behörde*]

to overrule, to cancel, to abrogate, to abolish (by authority), to do away with, to abate, to deprive of operation, to rescind, to nullify, to annul, to repeal · abschaffen, aufheben, rückgängig machen, annullieren, außer Kraft setzen, löschen, abbauen

over-ruled · abgewichen [*Ein Gerichtshof höheren Ranges kann von einer Entscheidung abweichen*]

overruled, done away with, deprived of operation, repealed, cancelled, abrogated, abated, annulled, nullified, abolished (by authority), rescinded · aufgehoben, annulliert, rückgängig gemacht, außer Kraft gesetzt, abgeschafft, gelöscht, abgebaut

overruling, abating, rendering null and void, doing away with, nullifying, rescinding, making void, annulling, (a)voiding, repealing, abolishing, abrogating, cancelling · Aufheben *n*, Rückgängigmachen *n*, Annullieren *n*, Abschaffen *n*, Löschen *n*, Abbauen *n*

overruling, refusal to follow · Außerkraftsetzung *f*, Abweichung [*Durch ein höheres Gericht oder eine höhere Behörde*]

overruling wording, overruling text, authentic wording, authentic text · maßgebender Text *m*, maßgebender Wortlaut *m*

to overrun · überschreiten

overrun · Überschreitung *f*

overrunning · Überschreiten *n*

overrun of construction sum, overrun of building sum, overrun of production sum · Bausummenüberschreitung *f*, Herstellungssummenüberschreitung

overrun of cost(s), cost(s) overrun · Kostenüberschreitung *f*

overrun of maximum rate, maximum rate overrun, overrun of peak rate, peak rate overrun · Höchstsatzüberschreitung *f*, Maximalsatzüberschreitung, Meistsatzüberschreitung

overrun of minimum rate · Mindestsatzüberschreitung *f*

overrun of quantities · Massenüberschreitung *f*, Mengenüberschreitung

overrun of sum, sum overrun · Summenüberschreitung *f*

overrun of target date, overrun of deadline (date) · (End)Datumüberschreitung *f*, (End)Terminüberschreitung

to oversee, to supervise, to superintend · beaufsichtigen, überwachen

overseeing, supervising, superintending · Beaufsichtigen *n*, Überwachen

overseeing activity, supervising activity, superintending activity · beaufsichtigende Tätigkeit *f*, überwachende Tätigkeit

overseer of highways, overseer of roads · Wegemeister *m*, Straßenmeister

overseer (of the poor), guardian (of the poor), almoner, poor law overseer, poor law guardian, parish officer · Armenvater *m*, Armenaufseher *m*, Armenpfleger *m*

oversight, inadvertence · Versehen *n*

oversman [*Scots law*]; imperator [*Latin*]; presiding arbiter [*This term is rarely used*]; presiding arbitrator, presiding referee, impier, umpire · dritter Schiedsrichter *m*, Obmann *m* [*Bei einer Dreierbesetzung des Schiedsgerichts*]

overspill [*The quantity involved in the process of decentralization*] · Überhang *m*, Überschuß *m*

overspill, deconcentration, decongestion [*misnomer*] · Auflockerung *f*, Deglomeration *f*, Auslagerung *f*, Entballung *f*, Entflechtung *f*

overspill of labour (Brit.); overspill of labor (US); workers' overspill, overspill of workers · Arbeiterüberschuß *m*, Arbeiterüberhang *m*

overspill of population, population overspill · Bevölkerungsüberhang *m*, Bevölkerungsüberschuß *m*

overspill planning · Überhangplanung *f*, Überschußplanung

over-stretched · überbeansprucht

over-subscribed [*A situation in which purchase subscriptions are in excess of the amount of securities offered for sale*] · überzeichnet

overt act · objektives Verbrechensmerkmal *n*

overt act(ion), open act(ion), manifest act(ion) · objektiver Tatbestand *m*, offenkundige Handlung *f*

over-the-counter market, inofficial market · außerbörslicher Wertpapiermarkt *m*, Freiverkehrswertpapiermarkt

over-the-counter security · Freiverkehrswertpapier *n*, außerbörsliches Wertpapier

overtime wage · Überstundenlohn *m*

overtime work · Überstundenarbeit *f*

overt pound, open pound · offener Pfandstall *m*

overt word [*A word the meaning of which is clear and beyond doubt*] · eindeutiges Wort *n*, klares Wort

over-urbanization, excessive urbanization, hyperurbanization · Überverstädterung *f*

to overuse — owner of small property 732

to overuse, to overcrowd [*To crowd to many people in or on*] · übervoll belegen, überlasten

overused, overcrowded · überbelegt, übervoll, überlastet

overusing, overcrowding · Überbelegen *n*, Überfüllen, Überlasten

overview · Überblick *m*, Übersicht *f*

to overzone · (baulich) übernutzen

overzoned · übergenutzt, baulich übergenutzt

overzoning · (bauliche) Übernutzung *f*

owelty of land exchange, ovelty of land exchange · Wertausgleich *m* bei Grundstückstausch

to own · Eigentum haben

owned capital interest rate, owned capital rate of interest · Eigenkapitalzinsfuß *m*

owner, proprietor · Eigentümer *m*, Eigentumssubjekt *n*, Eigner *m*

owner → client

owner by (common) law, proprietor by (common) law, owner in (common) law, proprietor in (common) law, legal owner, statutory owner, statutory proprietor, legal proprietor [*As opposed to the "equitable owner"*] · Eigentümer *m* nach Gemeinrecht, gesetzlicher Eigentümer [*Die Eigentumsaufspaltung nach Gemeinrecht und Billigkeitsrecht ist die Folge dieser dualistischen Entwicklung in England bis 1873/75*]

owner by equitable law, proprietor by equitable law, equitable owner, equitable proprietor [*As opposed to the "owner by (common) law" (also called "legal owner")*] · Eigentümer *m* im Innenverhältnis, Eigentümer nach Billigkeit(srecht), Eigentumssubjekt *n* im Innenverhältnis, Eigentumssubjekt nach Billigkeit(srecht), Eigner im Innenverhältnis, Eigner nach Billigkeit(srecht), wirtschaftlicher Eigner, wirtschaftlicher Eigentümer, wirtschaftliches Eigentumssubjekt, Billigkeitsrechteigentümer

owner by prescription, proprietor by prescription, prescription owner, prescription proprietor · Ersitzungseigentümer *m*, Ersitzungseigner, Ersitzungseigentumssubjekt *n*

owner-contractor contract, construction (industry) contract · Bauvertrag *m*, Unternehmervertrag [*Auf Bauleistungen gerichteter Werkvertrag*]

owner-contractor-subcontractor relation · Bauherr-Auftragnehmer-Nachunternehmer-Verhältnis *n*

owner-designed project, client-designed project, employer-designed project, promoter-designed project · Bauherrenentwurfsprojekt *n*, Bauherrschaftsentwurfsprojekt

owner-employe(e) · Arbeitgeber *m* im Unternehmen tätig

owner farmer, land owner operator, land owner specificator · Eigentumslandwirt *m*, selbstbewirtschaftender Landeigentümer *m*

owner-furnished · bauseits gestellt

owner-furnished (construction) materials, owner-furnished building materials, (construction) materials supplied by owner, building materials supplied by owner · (Bau)Stoffe *mpl* vom Bauherrn, (Bau)Materialien *npl* vom Bauherrn, bauseits gestellte (Bau)Stoffe, bauseits gestellte (Bau)Materialien *npl*

owner in (common) law, proprietor in (common) law, legal owner, statutory owner, statutory proprietor, legal proprietor, owner by (common) law, proprietor by (common) law [*As opposed to the "equitable owner"*] · Eigentümer *m* nach Gemeinrecht, gesetzlicher Eigentümer [*Die Eigentumsaufspaltung nach Gemeinrecht und Billigkeitsrecht ist die Folge dieser dualistischen Entwicklung in England bis 1873/75*]

owner in fee simple → (real) property owner

ownerless, proprietorless · eigentümerlos, ohne Eigentümer

owner-manager, one-man business, sole proprietor [*A type of business unit where one person is solely responsible for providing the capital, for bearing the risk of the enterprise and for the management of the business*] · Einmannbetrieb *m*

owner-occupation · Eigennutzung *f* [*Eigentumswohnung; Grundstück*]

owner-occupied · eigengenutzt [*Eigentumswohnung; Eigenheim; Grundstück*]

owner-occupier, proprietor-occupier, owner-occupant, proprietor-occupant · Selbstnießer, Eigennießer *m* [*Eigentumswohnung; Grundstück*]

owner of a share in (real) property, owner of a share in (real) estate, owner of a share in realty · Landanteileigner *m*

owner of freehold land(s) → (real) property owner

owner of land → owner of (the) (building) land

owner of share(s), share owner · Anteileigner *m*

owner of small property, proprietor of small property, small property proprietor, small property owner · Kleineigentümer *m*

owner of (the) (building) land, landed proprietor, landed owner, (building) land proprietor, (building) (land) area owner, (building) (land) (area) proprietor, (building) land owner, proprietor of (the) (building) land · (Bau)Bodeneigentümer *m*, (Bau)Flächeneigentümer, (Bau)Landeigentümer, (Bau)Landherr, (Bau)Bodeneigner, (Bau)Flächeneigner, (Bau)Landeigner

owner-possessor relation(ship), proprietor-possessor relation(ship) · Eigentümer-Besitzer-Verhältnis *n*

owner's delay, client's delay, employer's delay, promoter's delay · bauseitiger Verzug *m*

owner's design, client's design, employer's design, promoter's design · Ausschreibungsentwurf *m*, Bauherrenentwurf *m*

owner's easement, proprietor's easement · Eigentümergrunddienstbarkeit *f*

owner's equity, net worth, stockholder's equity (US); total equity (Brit.) · Eigenkapital *n*

ownership → ownership (of property)

ownership by common law → legal title

ownership by equity law, property by equity law, proprietorship by equity law, equitable ownership (of property), equitable property, equitable proprietorship · Eigentum *n* nach Billigkeitsrecht

ownership certificate, certificate (of ownership) · Einlageschein *m* [*gemischte Bürgschaftsbausparkasse*]

ownership composition, (general) property structure, (general) property composition, proprietorship structure, proprietorship composition, ownership structure · Eigentumsaufbau *m*, Eigentumsgefüge *n*, Eigentumsstruktur *f*, Eigentumszusammensetzung *f*

ownership in equity → property in equity

ownership in land(s); dominium utile [*Latin*]; beneficial dominion [*In der englischen Umgangssprache und in einigen Parlamentsgesetzen werden vielfach die Benennungen "landowner" und "ownership in land(s)" an Stelle von "tenant or holder of land" und "estate in land(s)" gebraucht. In diesem Falle ist zu beachten, daß unter "ownership in land(s)" nur das "dominium utile" und nicht das "dominium directum" gemeint ist*] · Nutzeigentum *n*, Untereigentum, leh(e)n(s)rechtliches Nutzungsrecht *n*

ownership in law → legal title

ownership interest → ownership right

ownership limitation, ownership restraint, proprietorship restraint, property restraint, (general) property restriction, proprietorship restriction, ownership restriction, proprietorship limitation, property limitation · Eigentumsbegrenzung *f*, Eigentumsbeschränkung, Eigentumseinschränkung

ownership of bed of river, proprietorship of bed of river, property of bed of river · Strombetteigentum *n*

ownership of land(s) → freehold estate

ownership of materials, proprietorship of materials, property of materials · (Werk)Stoffeigentum *n*, Materialeigentum

ownership (of property), proprietorship, (general) property; dominium [*Latin*] · Eigentum *n* [*Die uneingeschränkte Herrschaft einer Person über eine Sache, auch in rechtlicher Beziehung. "Eigentum" und "Besitz" sind nicht gleichbedeutend. Eigentum ist das dingliche Vollrecht, Besitz die tatsächliche, vom Rechtstitel unabhängige Innehabung einer Sache. Auch der Dieb ist Besitzer*]

ownership (of property) according to civil law, property according to civil law, proprietorship according to civil law · zivilrechtliches Eigentum *n*

ownership (of property) by common law → legal title

ownership (of property) certificate, (general) property certificate, proprietorship certificate · Eigentumsbescheinigung *f*, Eigentumsschein *m*, Eigentumsattest *n*

ownership (of property) contract, proprietorship contract, (general) property contract · Eigentumsvertrag *m*

ownership (of property) in equity, property in equity, proprietorship in equity · Billigkeitseigentum *n*

ownership (of property) in law → legal title

ownership (of property) in water, water property, water proprietorship, water ownership (of property), property in water, proprietorship in water · Wassereigentum *n*

ownership (of property) law, (general) property law, proprietorship law, law of (general) property, law of proprietorship, law of ownership (of property) · Eigentumsrecht *n*, objektives Eigentumsrecht

ownership (of property) policy, proprietorship policy, (general) property policy · Eigentumspolitik *f*

ownership (of property) presumption, presumption of property, presumption of proprietorship, presumption of ownership (of property), (general) property presumption, proprietorship presumption · Eigentumsvermutung *f*

ownership (of property) protection — package deal

ownership (of property) protection, proprietorship protection, (general) property protection · Eigentumsschutz *m*

ownership (of property) register, proprietorship register, register of ownership (of property), register of proprietorship · Abteilung I *f*, Eigentümerregister *n*, erste (Grundbuch)Abteilung, Grundbuchabteilung I

ownership (of property) tax, (general) property tax, proprietorship tax · Eigentumssteuer *f*

ownership (of property) theory, (general) property theory, proprietorship theory · Eigentumstheorie *f*

ownership of rural land(s), rural land(s) ownership · ländliches Bodeneigentum *n*, ländliches Grund(stücks)eigentum, ländliches Landeigentum, Landbodeneigentum, Landgrund(stücks)eigentum

ownership of soil under highways, proprietorship of soil under highways, (general) property of soil under highways · Erdreicheigentum *n* unter Straßen

ownership of space, proprietorship of space, (general) property of space · Raumeigentum *n*

ownership of urban land, ownership of town land, ownership of city land · städtisches Grund(stücks)eigentum *n*, städtisches Landeigentum, städtisches Bodeneigentum, Stadtgrund(stücks)eigentum, Stadtbodeneigentum, Stadtlandeigentum

ownership register → ownership (of property) register

ownership restriction, proprietorship limitation, property limitation, ownership limitation, ownership restraint, proprietorship restraint, property restraint, (general) property restriction, proprietorship restriction · Eigentumsbegrenzung *f*, Eigentumsbeschränkung, Eigentumseinschränkung

ownership rule → (land) ownership rule

ownership structure, ownership composition, (general) property structure, (general) property composition, proprietorship structure, proprietorship composition · Eigentumsaufbau *m*, Eigentumsgefüge *n*, Eigentumsstruktur *f*, Eigentumszusammensetzung *f*

owner's interest, proprietor's interest · Eigentümerbelang *m*, Eigentümerinteresse *n*

owner's land charge, proprietor's land charge · Eigentümergrundschuld *f*

owner's liability, promoter's liability, client's liability, employer's liability · Bauherrenhaftpflicht *f*, Bauherrenhaftung *f*, Bauherrenhaftbarkeit *f*

owner's liability insurance, client's liability insurance, employer's liability insurance, promoter's liability insurance · Bauherrenhaftpflichtversicherung *f*, Bauherrschaftshaftpflichtversicherung

owner's lien · Eigentümerpfandrecht *n*, Eigentümerzugriffsrecht

owner's risk, client's risk, employer's risk, promoter's risk · Bauherrenrisiko *n*, Bauherrenwagnis *n*, Bauherrschaftsrisiko, Bauherrschaftswagnis

owner's servitude, proprietor's servitude · Eigentümerdienstbarkeit *f*, Eigentümergerechtigkeit, Eigentümerservitut *n*, *f*, (servitutisches) Eigentümerrecht *n*

owning interests in land · Rechte *npl* an Grundstücken im Eigentum

own use, self-use · Eigenbenutzung *f*, Eigengebrauch *m*, Selbstbenutzung, Selbstgebrauch

oxgang (of land), oxgate (of land), osken (of land); bovata terrae [*Latin*]; bovate [*An oxgang, or as much land as one ox could plough in a year; one-eighth of a carucate or plough-land; varying in amount from 10 to 18 acres according to the system of tillage*] · Flächeneinheit *f* des Domesday (Book) zwischen 10 und 18 acres

P

P., petty court, summary court, registrar's court, court of summary jurisdiction, court of request, registrary's court, court of conscience, police court · Bagatellgericht *n*, Friedensgericht für kleine Straf- und Zivilsachen, Polizeigericht, Ortsgericht für gering(fügig)e Schuldklagen [*in England*]

to pace, to step off (a distance), to measure out by steps · abschreiten [*Behördlich messend abgehen*]

(pacific) settlement, accommodation, mutual agreement, accord, amicable composition (of differences), (amicable) arrangement, mutuality · Einigung *f*, Willenseinigung, gütliche Regelung, Einvernehmen *n*, gütliche Einigung, Vergleich *m*, Konsensus *m*, Übereinstimmung, Einverständnis *n*

package deal · (Bau)Planung *f* und (Bau)Ausführung aus einer Hand, (Bau)Projektierung und (Bau)Ausführung aus einer Hand

package (deal), design and construct contract, design and build contract [*The contractor carries out, in addition to* *building the works, some or all of the duties of architect, engineer or even surveyor*] · Entwurfs- und Bauauftrag *m*

package dealer [*Person or company assuming a single contract for total responsibility for the delivery of a complete project, including all services, such as architectural, engineering, construction, furnishings, and financing, if required*] · planender Generalunternehmer *m*, planender Gesamtunternehmer, projektierender Generalunternehmer, projektierender Gesamtunternehmer, Totalunternehmer

packed parcels · Sammelgüter *n pl*

packing cost(s) · Verpackungskosten *f*

pactum de cedendo [*Latin*] · Verkauf *m* der Hypothekenforderung

pactum de non cedendo [*Latin*]; prohibition of assignment, prohibition of cession, prohibition of assignation · Abtretungsverbot *n*, Zessionsverbot

pactum de oppignerando [*Latin*] · (obligatorischer) Vertrag *m* zur Verpflichtung einer Rechtspfandbestellung

pactum protimiseos [*Latin*] · Vorkaufsvertrag *m*

pactum reservati dominii [*Latin*]; reservation of proprietorship, reservation of (general) property, reservation of ownership (of property) · Eigentumsvorbehalt *m*

paddock, intake, close · (Tier)Gehege *n*

pagus, comitatus · Gau *m* [*Im fränkischen Reich*]

paid-in surplus, paid-up surplus, capital surplus · eingezahlte Rücklage(n) *f (pl)*, einbezahlte Rücklage(n)

paid-up, full(y) paid · volleingezahlt, volleinbezahlt

paid-up capital, paid-in capital, capital paid in, capital paid up · einbezahltes Kapital *n*, eingezahltes Kapital

paid-up share, full(y) paid share · volleingezahlter Anteil *m*, volleinbezahlter Anteil

pain cost(s) · Arbeitsleidkosten *f*

painting contractor · Anstreichunternehmer *m*

pair farm · Paarhof *m*

pair of variables · Veränderlichenpaar *n*

pair-page audience per exposure day · Leserschaft *f* von zwei gegenüberstehenden Seiten einer Zeitschriften-Nummer

palatinate · Pfalz *f*

palatin(at)e county, county palatin(at)e · Pfalzgrafschaft *f*

paleotechnic city, paleotechnic town, industrial city, industrial town · Industriestadt *f*

"palm oil" (Brit.); graft (US); financial bribe, bribe money · Bestechungsgeld *n*, Schmiergeld

Pandects; Pandectae [*Latin*] [*A compilation of Roman law in fifty books, published A.D. 533, consisting of selections from the writings of old jurists, made by Tribonian and sixteen associates, under the direction of Justinian, and constituting one of the four principal divisions of the Corpus juris Civilis*] · Pandektenrecht *n*

panel, (court) department · Senat *m*, Gerichtsabteilung *f*

panel, council · Rat *m*

panel of judges, council of judges · Richterkollegium *n*

pannage, pawnage, pawnes; pannagium, pascuage, pascuagium [*Low Latin*]; pathnage, pasnage [*The money paid for agisting swine*] · Geld *n* für Waldfrüchte als Schweinefutter

pannage, pawnage, pawnes; pannagium, pascuage, pascuagium [*Low Latin*]; pathnage, pasnage [*Food that swine feed on in the woods*] · Waldfrüchte *f (pl)* als Schweinefutter

pan(n)el of arbitrators · Schiedsrichterliste *f*

pan(n)el of jurors, juror's pan(n)el, jury pan(n)el, juror's book, juror's list [*A list of persons qualified to serve on juries*] · Geschworenenliste *f*, Geschworenenverzeichnis *n* [*Für eine Sitzungsperiode*]

panoramic view · Panorama(aus)blick *m*

pant · genommenes Pfand *n*

paper, treatise · Abhandlung *f* [*Thema*]

paper currency, paper standard · Papierwährung *f*

paper money; folding money (US) · Papiergeld *n*

paper of nomination, nomination paper, nomination certificate, declaration of candidacy, nomination petition, certificate of nomination [*USA*] · Vorwahlvorschlag *m*

paper standard, paper currency · Papierwährung *f*

papyrology [*The science concerned with those ancient documents written in Greek and Latin on papyri which were found in Egypt. These papyri cover a period of approximately one thousand years (332 B.C. — 640 A.D.) from the establishment of the Ptolemaic dynasty in Egypt through the period of Roman rule up to the beginning of the Arab invasion*] · Papyruskunde *f*

par — parish apprentice

par [*Latin*] · Standesgenosse *m*

particulars, details · Angaben *fpl*, Einzelheiten *fpl*

parabolic regression · parabolische Regression *f*

paragraph · Abschnitt *m* [*Gesetz*]

paramount, supreme · oberst, höchst

paramount lord (of a fee), sovereign lord (of a fee), lord paramount (of a fee), supreme lord (of a fee) [*The Queen or the King are lords paramount of all the lands in the Kingdom*] · oberster Leh(e)n(s)herr *m*, höchster Leh(e)n(s)herr, oberster Feudalherr, höchster Feudalherr

paramount title, title paramount · besserer (Rechts)Titel *m*, überwiegender (Rechts)Titel

parasitic settlement · Burgflecken *m*

parasitic town, parasitic city · Parasitenstadt *f*

paravail, subordinate, inferior, ancillary · nachgeordnet, untergeordnet

parcel · (Waren)Partie *f*

parcel area → (land) parcel area

parcel bound to a certain architect, plot bound to a certain architect [*for (physical) development*] · architektengebundenes Grundstück *n*

parcelling out, sorting out · Aussonderung *f* im Konkurs

parcel neighbor, plot neighbor (US); plot neighbour (Brit.); parcel neighbour · Grundstücksnachbar *m*

parcel of arable land, plot of arable land; cultura [*Latin*] · Ackerstück *n*

parcel of (construction(al)) work(s) · Teil(bau)arbeit(en) *f (pl)*, Teil(bau)leistung(en) *f (pl)*

parcel (of land) accessible by public right of way, plot (of land) accessible by public right of way · anliegendes Grundstück *n*, Anliegergrundstück [*Grundstück an einer Verkehrsfläche, die Zugang und/oder Zufahrt zu dem Grundstück ermöglicht*]

parcel (of land) for compensation, plot (of land) for compensation · Abfindungsgrundstück *n* [*Flurbereinigung*]

parcel (of land) for exchange → plot (of land) for exchange

parcel of land not built upon, uncovered plot, unbuilt plot, open plot, uncovered (land) parcel, uncovered parcel of land, (land) parcel not built upon · nichtbebautes Grundstück *n*, unbebautes Grundstück, freies Grundstück, nichtbenutztes Grundstück, Feldgrundstück

parcel (of land) with building(s), plot (of land) with building(s), piece of land with building(s) · Gebäudegrundstück *n*

parcel of usufruct, piece of usufruct, plot of usufruct · (Frucht)Genußgrundstück *n*, Nießbrauchgrundstück

parcel-owner → (real) property owner

parcel-proprietor → (real) property owner

parcels [*The technical term for the description of the property dealt with by a conveyance, mortgage or other assurance*] · Beschreibung *f*

parcel scheme, plot pattern, parcel pattern, plot scheme · Grundstücksschema *n*, Grundstücksmuster *n*

parcel side, side (of plot), plot side, side of parcel · (Grundstücks)Seite *f*

parcels of conveyance, conveyance parcels [*The technical term for the description of the property dealt with by a conveyance*] · Grund(stücks)beschreibung *f*

parcenary → (estate in) (co)parcenary

parcener → co-heir

parchment roll, roll of parchment · Pergamentrolle *f*

parci fractio [*Latin*]; pundbreach [*Saxon*]; breach of pound, pound breach [*The offence of breaking a pound, for the purpose of taking out the cattle and/or goods impounded*] · Einbruch *m* in einen Pfandstall, Pfandstalleinbruch

parcus [*Latin*]; pound [*A place where goods which have been seized as distress are placed by the distrainor, and in which the goods are in the custody of the law. A pound is either overt (open overhead) or covert (closed in)*] · Pfandstall *m*

parental right · Elternrecht *n*

parent; parens [*Latin*] · Elternteil *m*, *n*

parent company · Muttergesellschaft *f*

(parent) population, universe · Ausgangsgesamtheit *f*, Grundgesamtheit [*Statistik*]

parents · Eltern *f*

parents-teachers association, PTA · Eltern-Lehrer-Vereinigung *f*

parie passu [*French*]; equal(ly), without preference · vorzugsfrei

parish; parochia [*Low Latin*] · Kirchspiel *n*, (Pfarr)Sprengel *m*, kirchlicher Sprengel, Parochie *f*, Kirchenbezirk *m*

parish administration, parochial administration · Kirchspielverwaltung *f*, (Pfarr)Sprengelverwaltung, Parochialverwaltung, kirchliche Sprengelverwaltung

parish apprentice · Kirchspiellehrling *m*

parish boundary · Kirchspielgrenze *f*, (Pfarr)Sprengelgrenze, kirchliche Sprengelgrenze, Parochialgrenze

parish church · Pfarrkirche *f*

parish clerk · Küster *m*

parish committee, parochial committee · Kirchspielausschuß *m*, (Pfarr)Sprengelausschuß, kirchlicher Sprengelausschuß, Parochialausschuß

parish community; parish commune [*obsolete*] · Kirchspielgemeinde *f*

parish constable, beadle, bedell; bedellus [*Latin*]; beodan, bydel [*Anglo-Saxon*] [*A common law parish officer whose office dates from time immemorial. He is chosen by, and holds office at the pleasure of, the vestry; he gives notice to parishioners of the meetings of the vestry and attends the meetings; and he sometimes summons jurors for coroners' inquests*] · Ratsdiener *m*, Pedell *m*

parish constable · Ortsschulze *m*

Parish Constables Act 1872 [*In England. In this Act provision was made for the abolition of parish constables*] · Ortsschulzengesetz *n*

parish constitution, parochial constitution · Kirchspielverfassung *f*, (Pfarr)Sprengelverfassung, kirchliche Sprengelverfassung, Parochialverfassung

parish council, parochial council [*This was established in England by the Local Government Act, 1894 (later the Local Government Act, 1933), for every rural parish. A parish council consists of a chairman and parish councillors*] · Kirchspielrat *m*, (Pfarr)Sprengelrat, kirchlicher Sprengelrat, Parochialrat

parish councillor · (Pfarr)Sprengelrat(smitglied) *m*, *(n)*, Kirchspielrat(smitglied), kirchliches Sprengelratsmitglied, kirchlicher Sprengelrat, Parochialrat(smitglied)

parish land, parochial land, parish realty, parochial realty, parish (real) estate, parochial (real) estate, parish (real) property, parochial (real) property · Kirchspielland *n*, Kirchspielboden *m*, (Pfarr)Sprengelland, (Pfarr)Sprengelboden

parish meeting, parochial meeting · Kirchspielversammlung *f*, kirchliche Sprengelversammlung, (Pfarr)Sprengelversammlung, Parochialversammlung

parish officer, overseer (of the poor), guardian (of the poor), almoner, poor law overseer, poor law guardian · Armenvater *m*, Armenaufseher *m*, Armenpfleger *m*

parish priest, parson; persone [*obsolete*] [*A minister who holds a parish as a benefice, called, if the predial tithes were unappropriated, rector, and if appropriated, vicar*] · Kirchspielgeistliche *m*, (Pfarr)Sprengelgeistliche, kirchlicher Sprengelgeistlicher

parish (real) estate, parochial (real) estate, parish (real) property, parochial (real) property, parish land, parochial land, parish realty, parochial realty · Kirchspielland *n*, Kirchspielboden *m*, (Pfarr)Sprengelland, (Pfarr)Sprengelboden

parish register [*The register of marriages, baptisms and burials*] · Kirchspielregister *n*, (Pfarr)Sprengelregister, kirchliches Sprengelregister, Parochialregister

parish tithe, spiritual tithe, parochial tithe, ecclesiastic(al) tithe · geistlicher Zehnt *m*, Pfarrerzehnt, kirchlicher Zehnt, Kirchenzehnt [*altdeutsch:* Pfarrerzehent, Pfarrerzehend]

parish trustee [*In a parish not having a separate council, the chairman of the parish meeting and the proper officer of the district council are a body corporate by the name of "The Parish Trustees of . . ."*] · Kirchspieltreuhänder *m*, (Pfarr)Sprengeltreuhänder, kirchlicher Sprengeltreuhänder, Parochialtreuhänder

(parish) union, parochial union · Kirchspielverband *m*, (Pfarr)Sprengelverband, kirchlicher Sprengelverband, Parochialverband

parish vestry, parochial vestry · weltliche Gemeindeversammlung *f* unter Leitung des Ortsgeistlichen

parity of value, value parity · Wertparität *f*

park, enclosed chase, inclosed chase [*In English law. A tract of enclosed ground privileged for keeping wild beasts of the chase, particularly deer. Franchises of park were abolished in England by the Wild Creatures and Forest Laws Act 1971*] · Jagdgehege *n*, eingefriedetes Jagdrevier *n*, umfriedetes Jagdrevier

parker → park(-keep)er

parking · Parken *n*

parking area [*Lot or part thereof used for storage or parking of motor vehicles, on impervious, open hard-surface area*] · Parkfläche *f*, Parkplatz *m*

parking ground · Abstellfläche *f*

parking space [*Stall or berth that is arranged and intended for the parking of one motor vehicle in a parking area or a garage*] · Einstellplatz *m*

park(-keep)er · Parkwächter *m*

parkland · Parkland *n*

park(land) belt · Parkgürtel *m*

parkland town, parkland city [*In South Australia and New Zealand*] · Parkgeländestadt *f*, Grüngürtelstadt

park location, park site · Parkstandort *m*, Parklage *f*

park meadow · Parkwiese f

parkway → beltway

parlamentary borough [*England*] · Parlamentswahlkreis m

parliamentary borough [*England*] · Stadt f im Parlament vertreten

parliamentary election · Parlamentswahl f

parl(ing)e hill, hill of meeting, moot-hill [*In old records. A hill where courts were anciently held*] · Gerichtshügel m

parochia [*Low Latin*]; parish · Kirchspiel n, (Pfarr)Sprengel m, kirchlicher Sprengel, Parochie f, Kirchenbezirk m

parochial administration, parish administration · Kirchspielverwaltung f, (Pfarr)-Sprengelverwaltung, Parochialverwaltung, kirchliche Sprengelverwaltung

parochial committee, parish committee · Kirchspielausschuß m, (Pfarr)Sprengelausschuß, kirchlicher Sprengelausschuß, Parochialausschuß

parochial constable, borsholder, headborough, tithing-man, borough's ealder, borough's ealdor · Polizeischulze m

parochial constitution, parish constitution · Kirchspielverfassung f, (Pfarr)Sprengelverfassung, kirchliche Sprengelverfassung, Parochialverfassung

parochial council, parish council [*This was established in England by the Local Government Act, 1894 (later the Local Government Act, 1933), for every rural parish. A parish council consists of a chairman and parish councillors*] · Kirchspielrat m, (Pfarr)Sprengelrat, kirchlicher Sprengelrat, Parochialrat

parochial elector, parochial voter · Kirchspielwähler m

parochial farm · Kirchspielgut n, (Pfarr)Sprengelgut, Parochialgut

parochial land, parish realty, parochial realty, parish (real) estate, parochial (real) estate, parish (real) property, parochial (real) property, parish land · Kirchspielland n, Kirchspielboden m, (Pfarr)Sprengelland, (Pfarr)Sprengelboden

parochial meeting, parish meeting · Kirchspielversammlung f, kirchliche Sprengelversammlung, (Pfarr)Sprengelversammlung, Parochialversammlung

parochial mind · Kirchengemeindesinn m

parochial (real) estate, parish (real) property, parochial (real) property, parish land, parochial land, parish realty, parochial realty, parish (real) estate · Kirchspielland n, Kirchspielboden m, (Pfarr)-Sprengelland, (Pfarr)Sprengelboden

parochial tithe, ecclesiastic(al) tithe, parish tithe, spiritual tithe · geistlicher Zehnt m, Pfarrerzehnt, kirchlicher Zehnt, Kirchenzehnt [*altdeutsch: Pfarrerzehent, Pfarrerzehend*]

parochial union, (parish) union · Kirchspielverband m, (Pfarr)Sprengelverband, kirchlicher Sprengelverband, Parochialverband

parochial vestry, parish vestry · weltliche Gemeindeversammlung f unter Leitung des Ortsgeistlichen

parochial voter, parochial elector · Kirchspielwähler m

parol, by word of mouth, verbal, oral [*In early times few persons could write, and therefore when a document was required to record a transaction the parties put their seals to it and made it a deed. Transactions of less importance were testified by word of mouth or by parol, and this use of "parol", to signify the absence of a deed, remained after simple writing without sealing had come into use*] · mündlich

parol agreement, verbal agreement, oral agreement, agreement by word of mouth, agreement by parol · mündliches Abkommen n, mündliche Vereinbarung f, mündliche Abmachung

parol contract [*Any contract not of record, nor under seal, whether it be written or verbal*] · nichturkundlicher Vertrag m [*In amtlichen oder gerichtlichen Urkunden nicht enthaltener Vertrag*]

parol contract, (written) contract not under seal, (written) contract without seal, contract by unsealed writing, simple contract, unsealed contract [*A simple contract made by writing without seal. By a strange misuse of language, both kinds of simple contract (1. The simple contract made by word of mouth and 2. The simple contract made by writing without seal) are frequently spoken of in English law as parol contracts notwithstanding that the term "parol", both etymologically and in general parlance, means "by word of mouth"*] · nicht gesiegelter (schriftlicher) Vertrag m, ungesiegelter (schriftlicher) Vertrag, nicht formeller Vertrag, nicht notarieller Vertrag, (schriftlicher) Vertrag ohne Siegel, schriftlicher ungesiegelter Vertrag

parol evidence, parol proof [*Testimony by the mouth of a witness*] · mündliche Zeugenaussage f

parol instruction, oral instruction, verbal instruction · mündliche Anweisung f

parson; persone [*obsolete*]; parish priest [*A minister who holds a parish as a benefice, called, if the predial tithes were unappropriated, rector, and if appropriated, vicar*] · Kirchspielgeistliche m, (Pfarr)Sprengelgeistliche, kirchlicher Sprengelgeistlicher

part — partially funded (pension) plan

part, component [*An uniquely identifiable product that is considered indivisible for a particular planning or control purpose. NOTE. A part for one organizational group may be the final assembly of another group, e.g. an electric motor*] · (Bestand)Teil *m*

part, rate, proportion, share [*A charge, valuation, payment or price fixed according to ratio, scale or standard. A fixed relation of quantity, amount or degree. A comparative price or amount of demands*] · Anteil *m*

part → land register part

part collapse → partial collapse

part compliance, part execution, part performance, part fulfilment · Teilausführung *f,* Teilvollzug *m,* Teilerbringung, Teilerfüllung, Teilvollziehung

part crash → partial collapse

parted farm, divided farm · Teilungshof *m*

part execution, part performance, part fulfilment, part compliance · Teilausführung *f,* Teilvollzug *m,* Teilerbringung, Teilerfüllung, Teilvollziehung

part fulfilment, part compliance, part execution, part performance · Teilausführung *f,* Teilvollzug *m,* Teilerbringung, Teilerfüllung, Teilvollziehung

partial acceptance (of (the) work(s)), acceptance of part of (the) works · Teilabnahme *f,* Teilbauabnahme

partial amount · Teilbetrag *m*

partial approach · Teilansatz *m*

partial area · Teilfläche *f*

partial arrangement, partial composition · Teileinigung *f*

partial assign(ee) · Teilzessionar *m*

partial assignment, partial cession · Teilabtretung *f,* Teilzession *f*

partial breach of contract, partial contract breach · teilweiser Vertragsbruch *m*

partial (building) permission [*building (construction)*]; partial (construction) permission [*(civil) engineering construction*] · Teil(bau)genehmigung *f,* Teil(bau)erlaubnis *f*

partial certificate of inheritance · Teilerbschein *m*

partial cession, partial assignment · Teilabtretung *f,* Teilzession *f*

part(ial) collapse, part(ial) crash · Teileinsturz *m,* Teileinfall *m*

partial composition, partial arrangement · Teileinigung *f*

partial condemnation (US) → partial (land) expropriation

partial (construction) permission [*(civil) engineering construction*]; partial (building) permission [*building (construction)*] · Teil(bau)genehmigung *f,* Teil(bau)erlaubnis *f*

partial contract breach, partial breach of contract · teilweiser Vertragsbruch *m*

part(ial) crash, part(ial) collapse · Teileinsturz *m,* Teileinfall *m*

partial damage · Teilschaden *m*

partial (de)livery, partial surrender, partial handing over, partial handover · Teilaushändigung *f,* Teilübergabe *f*

partial demolition · Teilabbruch *m*

partial desertion · Teilwüstung *f*

partial disability · teilweise Arbeitsunfähigkeit *f*

partial discharge, partial redemption · Teileinlösung *f,* Teilablösung, Teilauslösung

partial discharge, partial dispensation, partial exoneration, partial exemption, partial release · Teilfreigabe *f,* Teilbefreiung *f,* Teildispens(ierung) *m, (f),* Teilfreistellung, Teilentlastung

partial equilibrium approach · partieller Gleichgewichtsansatz *m*

partial equilibrium theory · partielle Gleichgewichtstheorie *f*

partial exemption, partial release, partial discharge, partial dispensation, partial exoneration · Teilfreigabe *f,* Teilbefreiung *f,* Teildispens(ierung) *m, (f),* Teilfreistellung, Teilentlastung

partial exoneration, partial exemption, partial release, partial discharge, partial dispensation · Teilfreigabe *f,* Teilbefreiung *f,* Teildispens(ierung) *m, (f),* Teilfreistellung, Teilentlastung

partial expropriation → partial (land) expropriation

partial final invoice · Teilschlußrechnung *f*

partial final payment · Teilschlußzahlung *f,* Teilabschlußzahlung

partial handover, partial (de)livery, partial surrender, partial handing over · Teilaushändigung *f,* Teilübergabe *f*

partial invalidity, partial voidness, partial nullity · Teilungültigkeit *f,* Teilnichtigkeit

partial (land) expropriation; partial (land) condemnation (US) · Teil-Bodenenteignung *f,* Teil(-Land)enteignung, teilweise enteignender Eingriff *m*

partial loan · Teildarleh(e)n *n*

partially developed · teilweise überbaut [*Schweiz*]; teilweise bebaut

partially funded (pension) plan · teilfinanzierter (Pensions)Plan *m*

partial mortgage · Teilhypothek f

partial notice · Teilkündigung f

partial nullity, partial invalidity, partial voidness · Teilungültigkeit f, Teilnichtigkeit

part(ial) ownership (of property), part(ial) proprietorship, part(ial) property · Teileigentum n

part(ial) performance · Teilleistung f

partial period · Teilzeit f, Teilfrist f

partial permission → partial (construction) permission

partial plan · Übernahme f der Plankosten bei der Verbuchung der Halb- und Fertigerzeugnisbestände

partial plan · Teilführung f der Standardkosten

partial plan · Teilplan m

partial planning · Teilplanung f

partial possession · Teilbesitz m

partial possessor · Teilbesitzer m

part(ial) proprietorship, part(ial) property, part(ial) ownership (of property) · Teileigentum n

partial receipt, receipt in part · Teilquittung f

partial redemption, partial discharge · Teileinlösung f, Teilablösung, Teilauslösung

partial regression · Teilregression f

partial release, partial discharge, partial dispensation, partial exoneration, partial exemption · Teilfreigabe f, Teilbefreiung f, Teildispens(ierung) m, (f), Teilfreistellung, Teilentlastung

partial renewal · Teilerneuerung f

partial repayment · Teilrückzahlung f

partial structure · Teil(bau)werk n

partial surrender, partial handing over, partial handover, partial (de)livery · Teilaushändigung f, Teilübergabe f

partial theory · Teiltheorie f

partial vesting · teilweise Verfügung f über erworbene Pensionsansprüche, teilweise Anrechnung

partial voidance · Teilanfechtung f

partial voidness, partial nullity, partial invalidity · Teilungültigkeit f, Teilnichtigkeit

partial withdrawal · Teilentziehung f, Teilrücknahme f

partibility [*Term applied to the divisibility of inheritance among children*] · Teilbarkeit f eines Erbes unter die Kinder

participant, interested party, participator · Beteiligte m, Teilnehmer

participant in a succession · Nachlaßbeteiligte m

participating authority · beteiligte Behörde f

participating bond · Anleihe f mit Zusatzverzinsung

participating debenture [*Great Britain*]; participating corporate bond [*USA*] [*The debentures share in the net profit of the issuing company, in addition to receiving a fixed rate of interest*] · Gewinnschuldverschreibung f, Gewinnobligation f [*private Kapitalgesellschaft*]

participation · Beteiligung f, Teilnahme f, Mitwirkung

participation aid, participation help · Beteiligungshilfe f, Mitsprachehilfe

participation bond [*USA*] · festverzinsliches Wertpapier n mit Gewinnbeteiligung

participation clause · Beteiligungsklausel f

participation deed, deed of participation · Beteiligungsurkunde f

participation help, participation aid · Beteiligungshilfe f, Mitsprachehilfe

participation in interest, (legal) succession, succession in title, title sucession; communio incidens [*Latin*]; privity [*A successive relationship to or mutual interest in the same property, etc., established by law or legalized by contract, as between a testator and legatee, lessor and lessee, etc.*] · Rechtsgemeinschaft f, rechtliche Beteiligung f, Rechtsbeziehung f, Rechtsverhältnis n, Rechtsnachfolge f

participation in planning, planning participation · Planungsbeteiligung f, Planungsmitwirkung, Planungsteilnahme f

participation in the profit, participation in the gain, gain-sharing, profit-sharing · Gewinnbeteiligung f, Profitbeteiligung

participation of citizens, citizen involvement, involvement of citizens, citizen participation, citizen control, public participation · Bürgerbeteiligung f, Bürgermitwirkung, Bürgerteilnahme f, bürgerschaftliche Beteiligung, bürgerschaftliche Mitwirkung, bürgerschaftliche Teilnahme [*z. B. an der Bauleitplanung*]

participation procedure · Beteiligungsverfahren n, Mitspracheverfahren

participator, commoner, sharer [*One who shares or takes part in anything*] · Gemeinberechtigte m, Gemeinheitsgenosse m

particular, detail · Einzelheit f

particular · Einzelangabe f

particular coverture, particular marriage · bestimmte Ehe f

particular custom, special custom, particular usage, special usage, particular habit, special habit [*A particular custom is nearly the same as a local custom, being such as affects only the inhabitants of some particular district*] · spezielle Gewohnheit *f*, spezielle Gepflogenheit, spezieller Brauch *m*

particular estate [*A limited interest in land(s) or tenement(s), an interest less than the simple estate, which is the largest interest that a subject can have in land(s). An estate for life is an example of a particular estate*] · Landbesitz(stand) *m* ohne vollkommenes Eigentumsrecht, (Boden)Besitz(stand) ohne vollkommenes Eigentumsrecht, Grund(stücks)besitz(stand) ohne vollkommenes Eigentumsrecht

particular habit → particular custom

particular legal relation(ship) · Sonderrechtsverhältnis *n*

particular marriage, particular coverture · bestimmte Ehe *f*

particular norm · judizielle (Rechts)Norm *f*

particular provision · bestimmte Vorschrift *f*

particular scale; relative scale (Brit.) · Partikularmaßstab *m* [*Kartographie*]

particular usage → particular custom

parting with the official guardianship, giving over the official guardianship · Abgabe *f* der Amtsvormundschaft

partisan advice · parteiischer Rat *m*

partisan counsel(l)ing to clients · parteiische Beratung *f* von Mandanten

partisanship, taking sides · Parteinahme *f*

partly-finished goods, intermediate goods · Teilfertigerzeugnisse *npl*

partly paid share, membership share, subscription share, share of stock, instal(l)ment share · Raten(geschäfts)-anteil *m* [*aufhörende Bausparkasse*]

partner · Gesellschafter *m*

partners as to profits, partners as to gains · Gesellschafter *mpl* hinsichtlich der Gewinne, Gesellschafter hinsichtlich der Profite

partnership · Gesellschaft *f* [*kleiner Personenkreis*]

partnership, contractor combination, contracting group, joint venture (firm), contracting combine · Arbeitsgemeinschaft *f*, Arge, Baufirmengruppe *f*, Partnerschaftsfirma *f* [*Ein Zusammenschluß von Unternehmern auf vertraglicher Grundlage mit dem Zweck, meist große Bauaufträge der gleichen oder verschiedenen Fachrichtungen gemeinsam durchzuführen*]

partnership → (private) partnership

partnership → (co)partnership

partnership at will · Gesellschaft *f* auf unbestimmte Zeit

partnership by estoppel · Gesellschaft *f* kraft Rechtsschein

partnership contract, memorandum (of association), deed of partnership, partnership deed; deed of settlement [*obsolete*]; articles of incorporation (US); social contract [*Business corporations are now usually created under a general statute which permits a specified number of persons to form a corporation by preparing and filing with the proper public official, usually the secretary of state, a document known as the articles of incorporation*] · Gründungsurkunde *f*, Gründungssatzung *f*, Gesellschaftsvertrag *m*, Gründungsvertrag, Gesellschaftsurkunde [*1.) Körperschaft, Korporation; 2.) (Kapital)Gesellschaft; 3.) vereinsähnliche Gemeinschaft*]

partnership debts · Gesellschaftsschulden *fpl*

partnership estate, partnership property · Gesellschaftsvermögen *n*, Gesellschaftsgut *n*, Gesellschaftshabe *f*

partnership for a fixed term · Gesellschaft *f* auf bestimmte Zeit

partnership limited by stocks → (private) partnership limited by stocks

partnership property, partnership estate · Gesellschaftsvermögen *n*, Gesellschaftsgut *n*, Gesellschaftshabe *f*

partnership stock, common stock · (Gesellschafts)Stammvermögen *n*, gemeinsames Betriebskapital *n*

partnership with capital-contributing partner(s) according to German law · stille Gesellschaft *f* [*§§ 335—342 HGB*]

partnership with limited liability → (private) partnership with limited liability

part of a locality · Ortsteil *m, n*

part of an area, part of a territory · Gebietsausschnitt *m*, Territorialausschnitt

part of a practice · Verfahrensabschnitt *m* [*Teil eines Verfahrensganges*]

part of parcel (of land), part of plot (of land), part of land parcel, part of land plot · Grund(stücks)teil *m, n*

part of (the) population, section of (the) population, segment of (the) population · Bevölkerungsteil *m, n*

part of (the) population contributing to growth · Bevölkerungszuwachs *m*, Zuwachs der Bevölkerung [*Der Bevölkerungsteil, der das Wachstum verursacht hat*]

part-owner, part-proprietor, fellow-owner, fellow-proprietor, co-owner, co-proprietor · Anteileigentümer *m*, Miteigentümer, (Bruch)Teileigentümer

part ownership (of property) → part(ial) ownership (of property)

part payment (of a debt) · teilweise Schuldenzahlung *f*

part performance, part fulfilment, part compliance, part execution · Teilausführung *f*, Teilvollzug *m*, Teilerbringung, Teilerfüllung, Teilvollziehung

part property → part(ial) property

part proprietorship → part(ial) proprietorship

particriate · Bürgeradel *m*

part-time employment · Teilzeitbeschäftigung *f*

part-time farming, part-time husbandry · Nebenerwerbslandwirtschaft *f*

part-time holding, part-time farm · (landwirtschaftliche) Nebenerwerbstelle *f*, (landwirtschaftlicher) Nebenerwerbsbetrieb *m*

part-time judge · Richter *m* auf Zeit

part-timer · Teilzeit(arbeits)kraft *f*

to part with, to give oder · abgeben

party [*A person concerned, or having or taking part in any affair, matter, transaction or proceeding, considered individually*] · Partei *f*

party → (working) team

party act(ion), act(ion) of (a) party · Parteihandlung *f*, Parteiakt *m*

party-appointed arbitrator, party-appointed referee; party-appointed arbiter [*This term is rarely used*] [*He may usefully act as consultant to the neutral arbitrator*] · Parteienschiedsrichter *m*

party autonomy · Parteiautonomie *f*

party entitled · berechtigte Partei *f*

party in breach · vertragsuntreue Partei *f*

party injured, injured party · rechtsverletzte Partei *f*

party in negotiation(s), negotiator · Verhandlungspartner *m*, Verhandlungspartei *f*

party masonry wall · Brandmauer *f*, Kommunmauer, gemeinschaftliche Giebelmauer, gemeinsame Giebelmauer

party to a dispute · Streitpartei *f*

party to a (law)suit; sectator, litigans [*Latin*], litigator, suitor, litigant (party) · Prozessierende *m*, Prozeßpartei *f*

party to an arbitration, arbitration party, arbitral party · Schiedspartei *f*

party to a procedure · Verfahrensbeteiligter *m*

party to sale · Verkaufspartei *f*

party wall · Brandwand *f*, Kommunwand, gemeinschaftliche Giebelwand, gemeinsame Giebelwand

par value, denomination, nominal value, face value [*The value mentioned on the face of a security as distinguished from the market value*] · Nennwert *m*, Nominalwert

Pascal distribution, negative binominal distribution · Pascalverteilung *f*

pascuage [*Low Latin*] → pannage

pascuage [*Low Latin*] → grazing (of cattle)

pasnage → pannage

to pass [*judg(e)ment*] · abgeben [*Urteil*]

to pass [*act*] · verabschieden [*Gesetz*]

passage · Durchleitung *f*

passage right, right of passage · (Durch)Leitungsrecht *n*

passage right contract, right-of-passage contract · (Durch)Leitungsrechtvertrag *m*

passage zone, zone of passage · Übergangszone *f*

pass book · Bankbuch *n*, Sparkassenbuch [*gemischte Bürgschaftsbausparkasse*]

pass-book, banker's book, bank-book [*A book furnished by a banker to a customer, containing a transcript of his account in the bank ledger*] · Bankeinlagebuch *n*

pass book account · kurzfristiges Sparkonto *n* [*kapitalistische Bausparkasse*]

to pass by succession, to descent (to) · anheimfallen, übergehen (auf), zufallen [*Erbschaft*]

pass degree · gewöhnlicher (Universitäts)Grad *m* [*England*]

to pass down from generation to generation, to descend · abstammen

passenger fare, (public) transit fare, mass transit fare, (public) transport(ation) fare, mass transport(ation) fare · Massenverkehrsfahrpreis *m*, Massenbeförderungsfahrpreis

passenger liner · Fahrgastlinienschiff *n*, Passagierlinienschiff

passenger's transport(ation) act, passenger's transport(ation) law, passenger's transport(ation) statute · PBefG *n*, Personenbeförderungsgesetz

passenger transit, mass transit, collective transport(ation), passenger trans-

(passenger) transport(ation) law — pasture field

port(ation), mass transport(ation), (public) transit, (public) transport(ation), collective transit · Massenverkehr m, Personen(massen)verkehr, (öffentlicher) Massentransport m, öffentlicher Massenverkehr, (öffentliche) Massenbeförderung f, öffentliche Beförderung, Personen(massen)transport, Personen(massen)beförderung, Kollektiv(personen)transport, Kollektiv(personen)verkehr, Kollektiv(personen)beförderung

(passenger) transport(ation) law, public transport(ation) law, collective transport(ation) law, mass transport(ation) law, passenger transit law, public transit law, mass transit law, collective transit law · Personenbeförderungsrecht n, (Personen)Massenbeförderungsrecht

passer-by · Vorübergehende m

passing into law · Inkrafttreten n [*Gesetz; Verordnung*]

passing off, unfair dealing, unfair competition, unlawful dealing, unlawful competition · unlauterer Wettbewerb m

passing of risk, passing of hazard · Risikoübergang m, Risikoabwälzung f, Wagnisübergang, Wagnisabwälzung

passing of the cost(s) on to the tenant · Überwälzen n der Kosten auf den Mieter

passing on, shifting on · Abwälzen n

passive industry, residentiary industry · Industrie f für innerräumlichen Austausch

passive legitimation · Passivlegitimation f [*Besitzklage*]

passive trust, dry trust, naked trust [*One which requires no action on the part of the trustee, beyond turning over money or property to the cestui que trust*] · passive Treuhand f

passive trustee, custodian trustee [*The custodian trustee holds the trust property as if it were sole trustee, but, except as regards that matter, the appointment of a custodian trustee does not effect the powers and duties of the ordinary trustees*] · passiver Treuhänder m

past consideration · vergangene Gegenleistung f

pastitium [*Low Latin*] → pasture (ground)

pastoral demise → pastoral tenancy

pastoral district, grazing district, pastur(ag)e district · (Vieh)Weidebezirk m

pastoral economy, business of grazing, grazing business, grass farming · Graswirtschaft f, (Vieh)Weidewirtschaft

pastoral ground, pastoral land, pastoral field, grazing land, grazing ground, grazing field, grass land, grass ground, grass field, pasturage, herdwick; lea [*In old English law*]; pastitium [*Low Latin*]; pasture (ground), pasture land, pasture field · Weideland n, (Vieh)Weide f, Hut f, Viehweideland [*Der Ort wohin das Vieh zur Weide getrieben wird*]

pastoral holding, grazing holding, pastur(ag)e holding · (Vieh)Weidegrundstück n

pastoral land → pastoral ground

pastoral lease(hold) → pastoral tenancy

pastoral right, herbage, grazing right, shack, common pastur(ag)e, commonage, common right; jus pascendi, communis pasturae, herbagium [*Latin*]; (right of) pastur(ag)e, (right of) grazing · Angerrecht n, Hütungsrecht, Atzung f, Ätzung, (Vieh)Weiderecht, (Vieh)Weideberechtigung

pastoral tenancy, pastoral demise, pastoral lease(hold), pastoral tenure, pastur(ag)e tenancy, pastur(ag)e demise, pastur(ag)e lease(hold), pastur(ag)e tenure, grazing tenancy, grazing demise, grazing lease(hold), grazing tenure · (Vieh)Weidepacht f, (Vieh)Weideverpachtung f, (Vieh)Weidenutzungsrechtvergabe f

past-president · Altpräsident m

past service funding · Finanzierung f von Dienstjahrleistungen vor Wirksamwerden eines (Pensions)Planes

past the time of payment · zahlungsüberfällig

pastur(ag)e → (right of) pastur(ag)e

pastur(ag)e → grazing (of cattle)

pasturage → pasture (ground)

pastur(ag)e and drove · Hut f und Trift f; Trieb m und Trat m [*oberdeutsch*]

pastur(ag)e demise → pastoral tenancy

pastur(ag)e district, pastoral district, grazing district · (Vieh)Weidebezirk m

pastur(ag)e holding, pastoral holding, grazing holding · (Vieh)Weidegrundstück n

pastur(ag)e lease(hold) → pastoral tenancy

pastur(ag)e map · Weidekarte f

pastur(ag)e stone, drove stone · Hutstein m, Triftstein; Tratstein [*oberdeutsch*] [*Er bezeichnet die Grenze der Hutgerechtigkeit*]

pastur(ag)e tenancy → pastoral tenancy

to pasture · weiden

pasture beast · Weidetier n

pasture demise → pastoral tenancy

pasture field → pasture (ground)

pasture (ground), pasture land, pasture field, pastoral ground, pastoral land, pastoral field, grazing land, grazing ground, grazing field, grass land, grass ground, grass field, pasturage, herdwick; lea [*In old English law*]; pastitium [*Low Latin*] · Weideland *n*, (Vieh)Weide *f*, Hut *f*, Viehweideland [*Der Ort wohin das Vieh zur Weide getrieben wird*]

pasture lease(hold) → pastoral tenancy

pasture mapping · Weidekartierung *f*

pasture tenure → pastoral tenancy

pasturing (of cattle); pascuagium, pascuage [*Low Latin*]; grazing (of cattle), pastur(ag)e [*The action or occupation of pasturing*] · Grasung *f*, Hütung, Hut(ung) *f*, Weidegang *m*, (Vieh)Weide *f*, Hutweide

patchiness · Ungleichmäßigkeit *f* [*Besied(e)lung*]

patent defect · offensichtlicher (Sach)-Mangel *m*, offensichtlicher Baumangel

patent (US) [*Conveyance of title to government land*] · Zuweisung *f* von Regierungsland

patent writ, open writ, writ not sealed up, writ not closed · unverschlossenes Dekret *n*, offenes Dekret, unversiegeltes Dekret

paternal line · väterliche (Abstammungs)Linie *f*

pathbreaking · bahnbrechend

pathless, trackless, untrodden · unwegsam [*Gelände*]

pathlessness, tracklessness · Unwegsamkeit *f* [*Gelände*]

pathnage, pasnage, pannage, pawnage, pawns; pannagium, pascuage, pascuagium [*Low Latin*] [*The money paid for agisting swine*] · Geld *n* für Waldfrüchte als Schweinefutter

pathnage → pannage

patientia [*Latin*]; sufferance, toleration; sufferentia · Duldung *f*, stillschweigende Billigung

patrimonial monarchy · Patrimonialmonarchie *f*

patrol · Kriminalschutzmann *m*

patronage · Anstellungswesen *n* [*Staatsverwaltung*]

patronage → (right of) patronage

patronage appendant, patronage incident, advowson appendant, advowson incident [*An advowson annexed to a manor, and passing with it, as incident or appendant to it, by a grant of the manor only, without adding any other words*] · Grundbesitzpatronat(srecht) *n*, ununterbrochene Präsentation *f*, ununterbrochenes Präsentationsrecht *n*, ununterbrochenes Patronat(srecht), Grundbesitzpräsentationsrecht, Patronat(srecht) mit Grundbesitz, Präsentationsrecht mit Grundbesitz

patronage collative → (right of) patronage collative

patronage donative → (right of) patronage donative

patronage in gross, patronage at large, advowson in gross, advowson at large · losgelöste Präsentation *f*, persönliche Präsentation, losgelöstes Präsentationsrecht *n*, persönliches Präsentationsrecht, losgelöstes Patronat(srecht) *n*, persönliches Patronat(srecht)

patronage presentative → (right of) patronage presentative

to patronize · vorzugsweise benutzen

pattern, scheme · Muster *n*, Schema *n*

patterned transaction · nachgeformtes Rechtsgeschäft *n*

pattern of activities, scheme of activities, activity pattern, activity scheme · Tätigkeitsmuster *n*, Tätigkeitsschema *n*, Tätigkeitenmuster, Tätigkeitenschema

pattern of argumentation → pattern of reasoning

pattern of commuting, scheme of commuting, commuting pattern, commuting scheme · Pendler(verkehrs)muster *n*, Pendler(verkehrs)schema *n*

pattern of compact holdings · Einödlage *f*

pattern of density, scheme of density, density pattern, density scheme · Dichteschema *n*, Dichtemuster *n*

pattern of intermingled fragmented holdings, (inter)mixed fields, open fields · Gemengelage *f* [*Die Grundstücke verschiedener Eigentümer liegen in der Flur durcheinander gemengt ohne Zu- und Abfahrtswege*]

pattern of reasoning, pattern of arguing, pattern of argumentation, scheme of reasoning, scheme of argumentation, scheme of arguing · Argumentationsmuster *n*, Argumentationsschema *n*

pattern of rural settlement, scheme of rural settlement, rural settlement pattern, rural settlement scheme · Land(an)sied(e)lungsmuster *n*, Land(an)sied(e)lungsschema *n*, ländliches (An)Sied(e)lungsmuster, ländliches (An)Sied(e)lungsschema

pattern plan · tarifvertraglicher Standardplan *m*

pauper [*A person suing or defending an action in forma pauperis*] · Armenrechtnehmer *m*

pauper, poor person [*A person in receipt of relief under, formerly, the poor laws*] · Arme *m*

pauper act, pauper statute, pauper law, poor act, poor law, poor statute · Armengesetz *n*

pauper asylum · Armenirrenhaus *n*

pauper existence · Armutsdasein *n*

pauperism, mass poverty · Massenarmut *f*

pauperism [*The sum of paupers*] · Armen(an)zahl *f*

pauperizing effect · Verarmungswirkung *f*

pauper law, poor act, poor law, poor statute, pauper act, pauper statute · Armengesetz *n*

pauper law, poor law · Armenrecht *n*

pauper law reform, pauper act reform, pauper statute reform, poor law reform, poor act reform, poor statute reform · Armengesetzreform *f*

pauper legislation, poor legislation, pauper lawmaking, poor lawmaking · Armengesetzgebung *f*

pauper lunatic, poor lunatic · armer Geisteskranker *m*

pauper relief, poor relief, welfare work for the poor · Armenpflege *f*, Armenwohlfahrt *f*, Armenfürsorge *f*, Armenversorgung *f*

pauper's right, legal help, legal aid, poor's privilege (in (law)suits) [*A system for providing free or assisted legal advice or representation, for persons of slender means*] · Armenrecht *n*

pauper statistics, poor statistics · Armenstatistik *f*

pavilion court · Zeltgericht *n* [*Im mittelalterlichen England*]

pawn, pledge(d article), pledged object, pawned article, pawned object, article pawned, article pledged, object pawned, object pledged; vadium · Pfandstück *n*, verpfändeter Gegenstand *m*, gegebenes (Mobiliar)Pfand *n*, Pfandsache *f*

pawnage → pannage

pawnbroker · Pfandleiher *m*

pawn (broker's-)shop · Pfandleihanstalt *f*, Pfandleihe *f*, Pfandleihgeschäft *n*, Pfandhaus *n*

pawnbroking [*The professional lending of small sums on the security of a pledge*] · Pfandleihen *n*

pawnbroking · Pfandleihgeschäft *n*, Pfandleihgewerbe *n*

pawn contract, contract of pawn, contract of pledge, pledge contract · Pfandvertrag *m*

pawned article, pawned object, article pawned, article pledged, object pawned, object pledged, pawn; vadium [*Latin*]; pledged article, pledge(d object) · Pfand *n*, Pfandstück *n*, verpfändeter Gegenstand *m*, gegebenes (Mobiliar)Pfand, Pfandsache *f*

pawnee, holder of a pawn, pawn holder, pledgee, holder of a pledge, mortgagee, pledge holder [*The person who receives the security and lends the money to the pledgor*] · Pfandgläubiger *m*, Pfandnehmer, Pfandbesitzer, Pfandhalter, Pfandinhaber, Sicherungsnehmer

pawnee having the right to use the article pledged, (mort)gagee having the right to use the article pledged, pledgee having the right to use the article pledged · nutzungsberechtigter Pfandgläubiger *m*, nutzungsberechtigter Pfandnehmer

pawner, pledger, mortgager, mortgagor, mortgage debtor · Pfandschuldner *m*

pawnes → pannage

pawn holder, pledgee, holder of a pledge, mortgagee, pledge holder, pawnee, holder of a pawn [*The person who receives the security and lends the money to the piedgor*] · Pfandgläubiger *m*, Pfandnehmer, Pfandbesitzer, Pfandhalter, Pfandinhaber, Sicherungsnehmer

pawn of chattels, pledge of chattels · Fahrnispfand *n*, Fahrhabepfand, Mobiliarpfand, Mobilienpfand

pawn of personal property, pledge of personal property · Verpfändung *f* von Mobilien, Mobiliarverpfändung

pawn taken in distress, pawn taken in distraint, pledge taken in distress, pledge taken in distraint · außergerichtlich gepfändete Sache *f*, Selbstpfand *n*

pawn-ticket · Pfandschein *m*, Pfandzettel *m*

payable · zahlbar

to pay a bonus, to (give a) bonus · sondervergüten, zulegen, zuschlagen

to pay a fine; finem facere [*Latin*]; finire [*In old English law*]; to make a fine · Bußgeld entrichten, Strafgeld entrichten, Reugeld entrichten, Bußgeld zahlen, Reugeld zahlen, Strafgeld zahlen

pay-back, pay-out · Rückgewinnung *f* investierten Kapitals

pay-back period, pay-out period, pay-off period · Amortisationsdauer *f*, Erwirtschaftungsdauer

"pay" cost(s), lucrative cost(s), remunerative cost(s) · rentierliche Kosten *f*

pay day — payment of damages

pay day · Zahltag *m*

to pay down, to disburse, to pay out · auszahlen

paying deposit, workable deposit, profitable deposit · Fundstätte *f*, Vorkommen *n*, Lager(stätte) *n*, *(f)* [*Fehlbenennung: Vorkommnis n*]

paying guest · zahlender Gast *m*

paying off · Abbezahlen *n*

paying off by (one's) services · Abdienung *f*

paying price, fair price · auskömmlicher Preis *m*, rentierlicher Preis *m*

pay item, work item, performance item · (kosten)vergütete Position *f*, Leistungsposition, Arbeitsposition

Paymaster General [*The officer who makes the payments out of public money required for the Government Departments, by issuing drafts on the Bank of England*] · Generalzahlmeister *m*

Paymaster General('s Office) · Generalzahlkasse *f*, Zentralkasse [*England*]

payment, submission, deposit(ing) · Erstattung *f* [*Für den Erhalt von Ausschreibungsunterlagen*]

payment acceptance, acceptance of payment · Zahlungsannahme *f*

payment against documents · Dokumentenakkreditiv *m*, Warenakkreditiv, Barzahlung *f* gegen Dokumente

payment amount, deposit(ing) amount, submission amount · Erstattungsbetrag *m* [*Betrag für den Erhalt von Ausschreibungsunterlagen*]

payment application, payment request, application for payment [*Statement of amounts on proper acceptables or forms claimed by the contractor as payment due on account of work performed or materials stored*] · Zahlungsantrag *m*, Zahlungsgesuch *n*

payment bond [*It is given by a contractor to an owner to guarantee prompt payment to persons supplying labo(u)r and materials on the work*] · Zahlungsgarantie *f*

payment by results → (grant-in-aid) payment by results

payment certificate, certificate for payment · Zahlungsbescheinigung *f*, Zahlungsattest *n*, Zahlungsschein *m*

payment claim, demand for payment, claim for payment, payment demand · Zahlungsverlangen *n*, Zahlungsforderung *f*

payment condition, condition of payment · Zahlungsbedingung *f*

payment date, date of payment · Zahlungstermin *m*, Zahlungsdatum *n*

payment delay, delay of payment · Zahlungsverzug *m*

payment demand, payment claim, demand for payment, claim for payment · Zahlungsverlangen *n*, Zahlungsforderung *f*

(payment) discount, prompt payment discount · Skonto *n*, Rabatt *m*, (Preis)Nachlaß *m*

payment duty, duty to pay, duty of payment · Zahlungspflicht *f*

payment estimate · Zahlungs(vor)anschlag *m*

payment extension, payment prolongation, extension of payment, prolongation of payment · Zahlungsfristverlängerung *f*

payment for extra work(s) · Bezahlung *f* für Zusatzleistung(en), Bezahlung für Zusatzarbeit(en), Bezahlung für zusätzliche Arbeit(en), Bezahlung für zusätzliche Leistung(en)

payment guarantee, guarantee of payment, payment guaranty, guaranty of payment [*The guarantor actually is in the same position as a principal because the guarantor is primarily liable on the obligation*] · selbstschuldnerische Bürgschaft *f*

payment in advance, prepayment · Voraus(be)zahlung *f*

payment in cash, cash (down), ready-money payment, cash payment · Bar(be)zahlung *f*

payment in kind, in-kind payment · Natural(be)zahlung *f*

payment in satisfaction · Befriedigungszahlung *f*

payment into court · Einzahlung *f* in die Gerichtskasse, Hinterlegung (bei Gericht)

payment made in lieu of providing sufficient garaging · Garagenablösung *f*

payment of charge(s), payment of duties · Gebührenzahlung *f*

payment of commission, commission payment · Kommissionszahlung *f*

payment of contribution, contributing payment, contribution payment, contributory payment · Beitragszahlung *f*

payment of damages, money damages, pecuniary damages, pecuniary compensation, pecuniary indemnification, money compensation, money indemnification, indemnification (paid) in money, damages (paid) in money, compensation (paid) in money, indemnity (paid) in money, money indemnity · Entschädigung *f* in Geld, Schadenersatz *m* in

payment of duties — peacemeal (physical) development

Geld, Geldentschädigung, Geld(schaden)ersatz, Schadenersatzzahlung, Entschädigungszahlung

payment of duties, payment of charge(s) · Gebührenzahlung *f*

payment of dwelling rent, payment of residential rent · Wohnungsmietzahlung *f*

payment of fee(s) · Gebührenzahlung *f*, Honorierung, Honorarzahlung

payment of lease rent from year to year · jährliche Pachtgeldzahlung *f*, jährliche Pachtzinszahlung

payment of residential rent, payment of dwelling rent · Wohnungsmietzahlung *f*

payment of retention (money) · Rückbehaltzahlung *f*

payment of tithes, tithe payment, tithe-giving, tithe-paying, tithing · Zehnt(en)zahlung *f*, Zehntenleistung

payment on account, interim payment, progress payment, instal(l)ment payment · Abschlagszahlung *f*, Akontozahlung [*für geleistete Arbeit(en)*]

payment on account certificate, instal(l)ment (payment) certificate, progress (payment) certificate, interim (payment) certificate · Abschlags(zahlungs)schein *m*, Abschlags(zahlungs)bescheinigung *f*, Abschlags(zahlungs)attest *n*, Akonto(zahlungs)schein, Akonto(zahlungs)bescheinigung, Akonto(zahlungs)attest

payment order, order for payment · Zahlungsbefehl *m*

payment period · Zahlungsfrist *f*

payment plan, payment schedule · Zahlungsplan *m*

payment plan certificate → (periodic) payment certificate

payment prolongation, extension of payment, prolongation of payment, payment extension · Zahlungsfristverlängerung *f*

payment request, application for payment, payment application [*Statement of amounts on proper acceptables or forms claimed by the contractor as payment due on account of work performed or materials stored*] · Zahlungsantrag *m*, Zahlungsgesuch *n*

payment schedule, schedule of payments · Fälligkeitstabelle *f*

payment schedule, payment plan · Zahlungsplan *m*

payment supra protest · Ehrenzahlung *f*

payment (surety) bond · Zahlungsbürgschaft *f*

to pay off, to discharge, to liquidate, to settle, to redeem [*indebtedness*] · tilgen, begleichen, abbezahlen, rückzahlen

to pay off · entlohnen

to pay off by (one's) services · abdienen

pay-off period, pay-back period, pay-out period · Amortisationsdauer *f*, Erwirtschaftungsdauer

pay-off table · Auszahlungstabelle *f* [*Eine Tabelle, welche den Spielausgang in Abhängigkeit von den Entscheidungen beider Spieler wiedergibt*]

payor · Zahlende *m*, Zahler

to pay out, to pay down, to disburse · auszahlen

pay-out, pay-back · Rückgewinnung *f* investierten Kapitals

pay roll, wage(s) roll · Lohnliste *f*

pay roll account · Lohnkonto *n*

pay roll clerk · Lohnbuchhalter *m*

pay roll cost(s), wage(s) cost(s) · Lohnkosten *f*

pay station [*In the Eastern states of the USA*]; phone booth [*In the Western states of the USA*] · Fernsprechzelle *f*, Telefonzelle

PBSA, planning balance sheet analysis · Planungsbilanzanalyse *f*

PCB → pollution control board

P.D., port due · Hafengebühr *f*

peace, public security and good order, public policy, public safety, public order, order public · öffentliche (Sicherheit *f* und) Ordnung *f*, öffentliche (Ordnung und) Sicherheit

peaceable · friedlich

peaceable entry · friedliche Grund(stücks)besitznahme *f*

peace conclusion, conclusion of peace · Friedensschluß *m*

peace conservation, conservation of the peace, police power [*The power that enables the legislature to pass laws for the protection of the public health, morals, and safety, or laws which are otherwise very clearly for the general welfare*] · Ordnungsrecht *n*, Friedensbewahrung *f* [*Mit dem deutschen „Polizeigewalt", auch der älteren Zeit, läßt sich dieses Institut „police power" kaum vergleichen. Es dient viel zu einseitig nur der Rechtfertigung der gesetzgeberischen Maßnahmen der Staatsgewalt*]

peacemeal (physical) development, piecemeal binding (physical) development, piecemeal physical binding development · Einzelbebauung *f*; Einzelüberbauung [*Schweiz*]

peak call, peak demand · Nachfragespitze *f,* Spitzennachfrage *f*

peak growth · Spitzenwachstum *n*

peak (hour) traffic, rush (hour) traffic · Spitzen(stunden)verkehr *m*

peak income, maximum income · Höchsteinkommen *n,* Maximaleinkommen, Meisteinkommen

peak journey, peak trip, peak travel · Spitzenzeitfahrt *f*

peak land value intersection · Stadtbereich *m* mit höchstem Grund(stücks)wert

peak level, maximum level · Höchststand *m,* Maximalstand, Spitzenstand

peak mortgage, maximum mortgage [*A mortgage in which the maximum amount for which the object mortgaged can be made liable is entered in the land register, the amount really given on mortgage is determined by circumstances*] · Höchst(betrags)hypothek *f,* Maximalhypothek, Meist(betrags)hypothek, Ultimathypothek

peak movement of (public) transit, peak movement of (public) transport(ation), peak movement of mass transport(ation), peak movement of mass transit · Spitzenmassenverkehr *m,* Spitzenmassenbeförderung *f,* Massenspitzenverkehr, Massenspitzenbeförderung

peak period, rush period · Spitzen(verkehrs)zeit *f,* Verkehrsspitzenzeit

peak price limit, maximum price limit · Höchstpreisgrenze *f,* Maximalpreisgrenze, Meistpreisgrenze

peak rate, maximum rate · Höchstsatz *m,* Maximalsatz, Meistsatz, Spitzensatz

peak rate overrun, overrun of maximum rate, maximum rate overrun, overrun of peak rate · Höchstsatzüberschreitung *f,* Maximalsatzüberschreitung, Meistsatzüberschreitung

peak rent, maximum rent · Höchstmiete *f,* Maximalmiete, Meistmiete, Spitzenmiete

peak sum, maximum sum · Höchstsumme *f,* Maximalsumme, Meistsumme, Spitzensumme

peak traffic · Spitzenverkehr *m,* Stoßverkehr

peak trip, peak travel, peak journey · Spitzenzeitfahrt *f*

peasant agriculture · Bauernlandwirtschaft *f*

peasant-city, peasant-town, rural agglomeration, farmer-town, farmer-city, agricultural town, agricultural city, agrotown, agro-city · Agrarstadt *f,* Agrostadt, Landwirtschaftsstadt [*Landwirtschaftliche Groß(an)sied(e)lung mit wei-*

terverarbeitender Industrie und ausgebautem Dienstleistungsnetz]

peasant (cultivator), husbandman · Bauer *m*

peasant farm · Bauernhof *m*

peasant farming · bäuerliche Bodenkultivierung *f*

peasant holding · Bauernstelle *f*

peasant of Crown land, Crown tenant · Kronbauer *m*

peasant owner, peasant proprietor · Bauerneigentümer *m*

peasant proprietor, peasant owner · Bauerneigentümer *m*

peasant proprietorship, peasant ownership (of property), peasant property · Bauerneigentum *n*

peasantry · Bauernschaft *f*

peasant-tenant [*Ireland*]; cotset(h)us [*Latin*]; cotman, cottager, cotter, cosset, cot dweller; cottier · (freier) Tagelöhner *m,* besitzloser Tagelöhner, (Leer)Häusler, Kotter, Kätner, Kossat

peasant village, agrarian village, agricultural village, agro-village · Agrardorf *n,* Bauerndorf, Landwirtschaftsdorf, landwirtschaftliches Dorf

peat-cutting, peat-digging, cutting of peat, digging of peat · Torfgraben *n,* Torfstechen

peat digger, peat cutter · Torfgräber *m,* Torfstecher

peculiar, exempt jurisdiction [*In English ecclesiastic(al) law*] · autonome Zuständigkeit *f*

peculiar [*In English ecclesiastical law. A parish which is exempt from the jurisdiction of the ordinary of the diocese, and is subject to the metropolitan only*] · autonomes Kirchspiel *n*

peculium castrense, beneficium castrale, feudum castrense [*Latin*] · Burgleh(e)n *n,* Burggut *n* [*Es wurde jemandem gegeben mit der Bedingung eine Burg zu schützen*]

pecuniary ability to perform, pecuniary capability to perform, pecuniary capacity to perform, pecuniary qualification to perform · finanzielles Leistungsvermögen *n,* finanzielle Leistungsfähigkeit *f*

pecuniary advange, benefit · Geldvorteil *m*

pecuniary bequest, pecuniary legacy · Geldlegat *n,* Geldvermächtnis *n*

pecuniary charge · Geldlast *f,* Geldbelastung *f*

pecuniary claim, money claim, claim to money, demand to money, money demand, pecuniary demand · Geldforderung f, Geldverlangen n

pecuniary damages, pecuniary compensation, pecuniary indemnification, money compensation, money indemnification, indemnification (paid) in money, damages (paid) in money, compensation (paid) in money, indemnity (paid) in money, money indemnity, payment of damages, money damages · Entschädigung f in Geld, Schadenersatz m in Geld, Geldentschädigung, Geld(schaden)ersatz, Schadenersatzzahlung, Entschädigungszahlung

pecuniary demand, pecuniary claim, money claim, claim to money, demand to money, money demand · Geldforderung f, Geldverlangen n

pecuniary fidei-commissum · Geldmajorat n, Geldfideikommiß n

pecuniary incentive, pecuniary inducement · geldlicher Anreiz m

pecuniary legacy, pecuniary bequest · Geldlegat n, Geldvermächtnis n

pecuniary loss, monetary loss · Geldverlust m

pecuniary rent, money rent · Geldmiete f, Geld(miet)zins m

pedage, toll-traverse [Toll paid for passing through a place] · Wegegeld n, Wegezoll m

pedage-paying traffic, toll-paying traffic · Wegegeldverkehr m, Wegezollverkehr

pedagium, chiminage [Toll due by custom for having a way through a forest] · Waldgebühr f, Waldzoll m

pedestrian count, pedestrian census · Fußgängerzählung f

pedestrian precinct · Fußgängerzone f, Fußgängerbezirk m, Fußgängerbereich m

pedestrian(-prone) town, walking city, walking town, pedestrian(-prone) city · Fußgängerstadt f, fußgängergerechte Stadt

pedestrian shopping street · fußläufige Ladenstraße f

pedestrian street · Fußgängerstraße f

pedestrian through-block connection · Fußgängerpassage f

pedestrian traffic · Fußgängerverkehr m

pedlar, tallyman · Hausierer m

pedlar trade, tally trade · Hausieren n

peerage · Pairswürde f

peeress in her own rights · alleinige Erbin f eines Adelstitels, alleinige Adelstitelerbin

pegged parity · feste Parität f, starre Parität

pegging (out), location · Absteckung f des Feldes, Besitzergreifung [Erwerb von Bergbauland]

penal · strafrechtlich

penal bond · Vertragsstrafeversprechen n

penal law, criminal law [That portion of the law which relates to the definition of crimes and to their punishment] · Strafrecht n

penal norm, penal rule · Strafnorm f

penal settlement · Strafkolonie f

penal(ty) clause · Strafklausel f

penalty for breach of contract, penalty for non-performance of contract, (conventional) penalty, contract penalty · Konventionalstrafe f, Vertragsstrafe

penalty provision · Vertragsstrafenbestimmung f, Konventionalstrafenbestimmung

penal(ty) sum · Vertragsstrafensumme f, Konventionalstrafensumme

pendency, state of being pendent · Anhängigkeit f

pendente lite [Latin]; while litigation is pending · schwebend [Verfahren]

pending · anhängig

pending (at law), in litigation · rechtshängig

pending matter · schwebendes Verfahren n

to penetrate · durchdringen

penetration, impact · Tiefe f [einer Werbung]

penetration · Durchdringung f

pen for sheep, cot for sheep, sheep-cot, sheep-pen, fold · (Schaf)Pferch m

penitentiary(-house), convict prison · Zuchthaus n

penny arcade (US); amusement arcade (Brit.) · Spielhalle f

penny pinching · Pfennigfuchserei f

penny stocks · spekulative Aktien f pl mit weniger als 1 $ angeboten

pension, annuity [A periodic payment to a retired employe(e)] · Pension f, Rente f

pensionable age · Pensionsalter n, Rentenalter

pensioner · Pensionär m, Rentner

pension plan, benefit plan, retirement plan · (Alters)Versorgungsplan m, Pensionsplan

pen tir [Welsh] → terra capitalis [Latin]

pen tir right — percolation

pen tir right [*Welsh*]; head-rig right [*Scotch*]; headland right · Anwenderecht *n*, Pflugrecht, Kehrrecht, Tretrecht [*Das Recht beim Pflügen auf dem Boden des Nachbarn den Pflug wenden zu dürfen*]

pent-up demand, pent-up call · angestaute Nachfrage *f*, Nachfragestau *m*

to people, to populate · bevölkern

peopled, populated · bevölkert

people's bank · Volksbank *f*

people's capitalism · Aktionärsdemokratie *f*, Jedermann-Kapitalismus *m*

people's dwelling, people's tenement, people's residence · Volkswohnung *f*

people seeking accommodation, prospective tenants · Wohnungssuchende *mpl*

people's park · Volkspark *m*

people without space · Volk *n* ohne Raum

peopling, populating · Bevölkern *n*

peppercorn rent, nominal rent [*Where only a nominal sum has to be paid for a period*] · nominelle Grundrente *f*, Pfefferkornrente

PER, price-earnings ratio · Kurs-Gewinn-Verhältnis *n* von Aktien

per account · laut Rechnung

per autre vie, for the life of another, pur autre vie [*An estate pur autre vie was a tenancy of land for the life of another who was called the cestui que vie; the lowest estate of freehold which the law allowed before 1925 the estate has become an equitable interest. Not in the USA — old rule still applies — cestui que estate = life estate pour autre vie; it is of course an equitable interest in land*] · für die Dauer eines anderen Lebens, für Lebenszeit eines Dritten, auf Lebenszeit eines Dritten, auf die Dauer eines anderen Lebens, für das Leben eines anderen

per capita floor space, per capita floor area · Pro-Kopf-Geschoßfläche *f*, Pro-Kopf-Etagenfläche, Pro-Kopf-Stockwerkfläche

per capita income · Pro-Kopf-Einkommen *n*

percentage addition · Prozentzuschlag *m*

percentage clause · Prozentklausel *f*

percentage connectivity · prozentualer direkter Verknüpfungsgrad *m* [*Graphentheorie*]

percentage demise → percentage lease(hold)

percentage depletion · Absetzung *f* in festen Prozentsätzen vom Bruttoeinkommen

percentage for adap(ta)tion, percentage for adjustment · Anpassungsprozentsatz *m*

percentage lease(hold), percentage demise, percentage tenancy [*Lease (-hold) arrangement under which the tenant's rent is based on a percentage of the tenant's gross or net income*] · Anteilnutzungsrecht *n*, Anteilpacht *f*

percentage (management) fee · prozentualer Zuschlag *m* [*Selbstkostenerstattungsvertrag*]

percentage of (building) land, percentage of (building) (land) area · (Bau)Flächenanteil *m*, (Bau)Bodenanteil, (Bau)Landanteil

percentage of fee, fee percentage · Gebührenanteil *m*, Honoraranteil

percentage of green area · Grünflächenanteil *m*

percentage of open space, percentage of open land, percentage of open area, vacant land percentage, vacant space percentage, vacant area percentage · Freiflächenanteil *m*, Freiraumanteil, Freilandanteil

percentage of population in each size of household · prozentuale Bevölkerungsverteilung *f* auf die Haushaltsgrößen

percentage (rate), rate per cent · Anteil(verhältnis) *m*, *(f)*, (Vom)Hundertsatz *m*, Prozentsatz

percentage standard deduction · Freibetrag *m* für Sonderausgaben

percentage sum(mation) frequency · prozentuale Summenhäufigkeit *f*

percentage tenancy → percentage lease(hold)

percentile · Hundertstelwert *m*

perceptible source, reasoning source, source of reasoning · Erkenntnisquelle *f*

perceptual feature · Wahrnehmungsmerkmal *n*

perceptual form · Wahrnehmungsform *f*

percolating water, seepage water · Sickerwasser *n*

percolating water law, law of percolating water, law of seepage water, seepage water law · (objektives) Sickerwasserrecht *n*

percolating water right, right to percolating water, right to seepage water, seepage water right · Sickerwasser(an)recht *n*, Sickerwasseranspruch *m*

percolation, filtering up [*of the households*] · Veränderung *f* in der Bewohnerschaft [*Die Miete jeder Wohnung sinke im Laufe der Zeit, und infolgedessen würden die Bewohner für das gleiche*

per curiam — performance period

Geld von Zeit zu Zeit eine relativ bessere Wohnung mieten]

per curiam, per cur. [*Latin*]; by the court · durch das Gericht

peregrine law · Volksrecht *n*

peremptory, obligatory; perimere [*Latin*]; mandatory, preceptive, imperative [*As opposed to "permissive"*] · pflichtbedingt, zwingend [*in Gesetzen*]

peremptory, final, determinate; perimere [*Latin*]; irrevocable · bestimmt, endgültig, unwiderruflich

peremptory plea → plea in bar

peremptory (writ of) mandamus, absolute (writ of) mandamus [*A (writ of) mandamus which absolutely requires an act to be done, without any alternative of showing cause against it. Usually granted on the return of an alternative mandamus, where such return is found insufficient in law or false in fact*] · absolutes gerichtliches Mandat *n*, zwingendes gerichtliches Mandat, gerichtliches absolutes Mandat, gerichtliches zwingendes Mandat

perfect, good, marketable, clear, sal(e)able · frei, vollgültig [*(Rechts)Titel*]

perfect, free from load(s), unloaded, not imperfect, without a burden, without a load, burdenless, free from encumbrance(s), free from charge(s), free from incumbrance(s), free from burden(s), uncharged, unburdened, unencumbered, unincumbered, clear · entschuldet, lastenfrei, (dinglich) unbelastet, (dinglich) nicht belastet

perfect segmentation · perfekte Anpassung *f* [*Alle Produktionsfaktoren können bis zur Erreichung der Kapazitätsgrenze zur Verwirklichung beliebiger Produktionshöhen optimal kombiniert werden*]

perfect stability · vollkommene Stabilität *f*

to perform, to complete an act · leisten

to perform, to execute, to carry out · ausführen, durchführen, erbringen [*Arbeit(en)*]

to perform, to complete [*contract*] · ausführen, durchführen, erfüllen [*Vertrag*]

performance, compliance, fulfilment, discharge, execution [*The pursuance or carrying forth of the provisions of a plan or contract*] · Ausführung *f*, Vollzug *m*, Erbringung, Vollziehung, Erfüllung, Leistung

performance and fee code for engineers · Leistungs- und Honorarordnung *f* für Ingenieure, LHO

performance bond, bond of completion, bond of performance, completion bond [*Bond given by the contractor to the owner and lending institution guaranteeing that the work will be completed and that funds will be provided for that purpose*] · Fertigstellungsgarantie *f*, Ausführungsgarantie

performance bond, fulfilment bond, execution bond, compliance bond, discharge bond · Erfüllungsgarantie *f*, Vollzugsgarantie, Vollziehungsgarantie, Erbringungsgarantie, Leistungsgarantie, Ausführungsgarantie

performance bond, contract surety, performance surety, contract bond [*It is a guarantee of contractor performance and is the instrument by which a corporate surety company (the guarantor) guarantees the owner of a construction project (the obligee) that the contractor to whom a construction contract has been awarded (the principal) will fulfil the contract in accordance with the plans and specifications and with all attendant financial obligations having been paid in full. The bond is not a contract of insurance and, unless specially conditioned and certainly in its standard forms most frequently encountered, will not cover all the contingencies which can occur on a construction project.*] · Ausführungsbürgschaft *f*

performance delay, delay of performance · Leistungsverzug *m*

performance delay, delay in execution, execution delay, delay in performance · Ausführungsverzug *m*, Vollziehungsverzug *m*, Erbringungsverzug *m*, Erfüllungsverzug *m*

performance duty, fulfilment duty, execution duty, compliance duty, duty of fulfilment, duty of execution, duty of compliance, duty of performance · Erfüllungspflicht *f*, Vollziehungspflicht, Ausführungspflicht, Vollzugspflicht, Erbringungspflicht

performance item, pay item, work item · (kosten)vergütete Position *f*, Leistungsposition, Arbeitsposition

performance of function · Funktionserfüllung *f*

performance of plan(s), planning execution, planning performance, execution of plan(s) · Plan(ungs)vollzug *m*, Plan(ungs)durchführung *f*, Plan(ungs)ausführung

performance (of (the) work(s)), construction of (the) works, execution (of (the) work(s)) · Arbeitsausführung *f*, Bau *m* (der Anlagen), Bauausführung, Ausführung (der (Bau)Arbeiten)

performance orientation · Leistungsorientierung *f* [*Gegensatz: Zuschreibung*]

performance period, compliance period, execution period, fulfilment period · Ausführungsfrist *f*, Vollzugsfrist,

performance phase — periodic tenancy

Erfüllungsfrist, Vollziehungsfrist, Erbringungsfrist *f*

performance phase, phase of performance · Leistungsstadium *n*, Leistungsphase *f*

performance place, place of performance · Leistungsort *m*

performance planning, planning of (the) execution, planning of (the) performance, execution planning · Ausführungsplanung *f*

performance programme; performance program (US) · (Bau)Leistungsprogramm *n*

performance refusal, refusal of performance, breach · Bruch *m*, Erfüllungs(ver)weigerung *f*

performance reservation, reservation of performance · Leistungsvorbehalt *m*

performance subject, subject of performance · Leistungsgegenstand *m*

performance surety, contract bond, performance bond, contract surety [*It is a guarantee of contractor performance and is the instrument by which a corporate surety company (the guarantor) guarantees the owner of a construction project (the obligee) that the contractor to whom a construction contract has been awarded (the principal) will fulfil the contract in accordance with the plans and specifications and with all attendant financial obligations having been paid in full. The bond ist not a contract of insurance and, unless specially conditioned and certainly in its standard forms most frequently encountered, will not cover all the contingencies which can occur on a construction project.*] · Ausführungsbürgschaft *f*

(performance) time extension, extension of period (for completion), extension of time (for completion), prolongation of period (for completion), prolongation of time (for completion) · Nachfrist *f*, Fristverlängerung *f*

performance warranty · Leistungsgewährleistung *f* [*Maschine*]

performed, fulfilled, executed, discharged · erfüllt, ausgeführt, vollzogen, erbracht, nachgekommen

performed but once · einmalig [*Leistung*]

performed consideration, fulfilled consideration, executed consideration [*An act done or a value given before or at the time of making a contract*] · ausgeführte Gegenleistung *f*, erbrachte Gegenleistung *f*, erfüllte Gegenleistung *f*, vollzogene Gegenleistung *f*

performed contract, fulfilled contract, contract complied with, executed contract · ausgeführter Vertrag *m*, erfüllter Vertrag *m*, erbrachter Vertrag *m*, vollzogener Vertrag *m*

performed covenant, covenant complied with, executed covenant, fulfilled covenant · ausgeführter Formalvertrag *m*, erfüllter Formalvertrag *m*, vollzogener Formalvertrag *m*, erbrachter Formalvertrag

performing party, fulfilling party, executing party · ausführende Partei *f*, erbringende Partei *f*, vollziehende Partei *f*, erfüllende Partei *f*

performing person, fulfilling person, executing person · Ausführende *m*, Vollziehende *m*, Erbringende *m*, Erfüllende *m*

perimere [*Latin*]; mandatory, preceptive, imperative, peremptory, obligatory [*As opposed to "permissive"*] · pflichtbedingt, zwingend [*in Gesetzen*]

perimere [*Latin*]; irrevocable, peremptory, final, determinate · bestimmt, endgültig, unwiderruflich

period → time (allowed)

period cost(s) · Periodenkosten *f*, zeitproportionale Kosten [*nach Rummel*]; Zeitkosten [*nach Schmalenbach*]

period cost(s), fixed cost(s); fixed expired cost(s), fixed expenses [*USA*] [*A cost which tends to be unaffected by variations in volume of output but to depend mainly on the passing of time, e.g. the cost of providing the facilities and organization to produce and market goods*] · Festkosten *f*, Fixkosten, feste Kosten, fixe Kosten

period for acceptance → acceptance time (allowed)

period for appeal → time (allowed) for appeal

period for complaint → (fixed) period (of time) for complaint

period for execution of (the) work(s), period for performance of (the) work(s), period for construction of (the) works, time for execution of (the) work(s), time for performance of (the) work(s), time for construction of (the) works · (Arbeits)Ausführungsfrist *f*, Arbeitsausführungszeit *f*, (Bau)Ausführungszeit *f*, Bauausführungsfrist *f*

period for prescription → prescription time (allowed)

periodical ticket, commutation ticket · Abonnementsbillet *n*, Zeit(fahr)karte *f*

periodic intervals · gleichmäßiger zeitlicher Abstand *m*

periodic payment · regelmäßige Zahlung *f*

(periodic) payment plan certificate · Zahlungsplanzertifikat *n*

periodic tenancy, periodic lease(hold) right, periodic lease(hold) tenure, periodic lease(hold) interest [Lease(hold) for short terms, e.g. weeks or months] · kurzfristiges (Besitz)Recht n, kurzfristiges Grund(stücks)besitzrecht, kurzfristiges Landbesitzrecht, kurzfristiges Bodenbesitzrecht, kurzfristiges (subjektives) (Land)Pachtrecht, kurzfristiges (subjektives) Bodenpachtrecht

period of (ab)alienation, period of disposal, (ab)alienation period, disposal period · Veräußerungsfrist f

period of a week, term of a week · Wochenfrist f

period of bidding, time of bidding, tendering period, tendering time, bidding period, bidding time, period of tendering, time of tendering · Angebotsfrist f, Angebotszeitraum m, Ausschreibungsfrist, Ausschreibungszeitraum

period of binding, time of binding, binding period, binding time · Bindungsfrist f, Bindefrist [Die Zeit, in welcher der Bieter an sein Angebot gegenüber dem Auftraggeber gebunden ist]

period of claim, period of demand, claim period, demand period · Forderungsfrist f

period of delay, delay period · Verzugsfrist f

period of depression, depression period, depression time, time of depression · (wirtschaftliche) Notzeit f

period of discharge, term of discharge, duration of discharge, period of redemption, term of redemption, duration of redemption, redemption period, redemption term, redemption duration, discharge period, discharge duration, discharge term · Auslösungsfrist f, Einlösungsfrist, Ablösungsfrist f

period of disposal, (ab)alienation period, disposal period, period of (ab)alienation · Veräußerungsfrist f

period of evacuation, evacuation period · Räumungsfrist f

period of exclusion, term of exclusion, time of exclusion, exclusion period, exclusion time, exclusion term · Ausschlußfrist f, Ausschließungsfrist f

period of hearing after reallotment · Anhörungsfrist f [Flurbereinigung]

period of liability (for defects), liability period (for defects) · Gewährleistungsfrist f [Bauvertrag]

period of life limitation · Verschollenheitsfrist f

period of limitation, limitation period · Verjährungsfrist f

period of notice of stockholders' meeting · Einberufungsfrist f [zur Hauptversammlung]

period of office → period of tenure

period of redemption, term of redemption, duration of redemption, redemption period, redemption term, redemption duration, discharge period, discharge duration, discharge term, period of discharge, term of discharge, duration of discharge · Auslösungsfrist f, Einlösungsfrist, Ablösungsfrist

period of respite, time of respite · Stundungsfrist f

period of settlement, settlement period · Abrechnungsfrist f

period of tendering, time of tendering, period of bidding, time of bidding, tendering period, tendering time, bidding period, bidding time · Angebotsfrist f, Angebotszeitraum m, Ausschreibungsfrist, Ausschreibungszeitraum

period of tenure, period of office, term of office, office term, office period, tenure period · Amtszeit f

period (of time) → time (allowed)

period (of time) for acceptance → acceptance time (allowed)

period (of time) for appeal → time (allowed) for appeal

period (of time) for complaint → (fixed) period (of time) for complaint

period (of time) for prescription → prescription time (allowed)

period of validity · Geltungsdauer f

period of warranty, warranty term, warranty time, warranty period, term of warranty, time of warranty · Garantiefrist f, Garantiezeitraum m

period required for examination and evaluation of tenders, time required for examination and evaluation of tenders · Zuschlag(s)frist f [Der Zeitraum, den der Auftraggeber braucht um festzustellen, welches der eingereichten Angebote für ihn das günstigste ist]

peripheral accretion · Umlandzuwachs m

peripheral area, peripheral territory, umland territory, umland area; suburban territory, suburban area (US) · Umlandgebiet n

peripheral city, umland town, umland city, peripheral town · Umlandstadt f

peripheral community, umland community; suburb(an place) (US) · Umlandgemeinde f

peripheral community development, umland community development; suburban development (US) · Umlandgemeindeentwick(e)lung f

peripheral community district, umland community district; suburban district (US) · Umlandgemeindebezirk m

peripheral community expansion, umland community expansion; suburban expansion (US) · Umlandgemeindeerweiterung *f*

peripheral community group, umland community group; suburban group (US) · Umlandgemeindegruppe *f*

peripheral community growth, umland community growth; suburban growth (US) · Umlandgemeindewachstum *n*

peripheral community house, umland community house; suburban house (US) · Umlandgemeindehaus *n*

peripheral community inhabitant, umland community inhabitant; suburban inhabitant (US) · Umlandgemeindeeinwohner *m*

peripheral community migration, umland community migration; suburban migration (US) · Umlandwanderung *f*

peripheral community pattern, umland community pattern, peripheral community scheme, umland community scheme; suburban pattern, suburban scheme (US) · Umlandgemeindemuster *n*, Umlandgemeindeschema *n*

peripheral community population, umland community population; suburban population (US) · Umlandgemeindebevölkerung *f*

peripheral community residential area, umland community residential area, peripheral community residential territory, umland community residential territory; suburban residential area, suburban residential territory (US) · Umlandgemeindewohn(ungs)gebiet *n*

peripheral community ring, umland community ring; suburban ring (US) · Umlandgemeindering *m*

peripheral community scheme, umland community scheme; suburban pattern, suburban scheme (US); peripheral community pattern, umland community pattern · Umlandgemeindemuster *n*, Umlandgemeindeschema *n*

peripheral community school, umland community school; suburban school (US) · Umlandgemeindeschule *f*

peripheral community society, umland community society; suburban society (US) · Umlandgemeindegesellschaft *f*

peripheral community traffic, umland community traffic; suburban traffic (US) · Umlandgemeindeverkehr *m*

peripheral land, surrounding land, surrounding area, external service area, umland; suburban land (US) [*Sometimes, by local usage also called "landed estate" and "landed property" as distinguished from land in a city*] · äußeres Ergänzungsgebiet *n*, Vorortzone *f*, Umland *n*, Umgelände *n*

peripheral land use, external land use, surrounding land use, service area use, umland use; suburban land use (US) · Umlandnutzung *f*

peripheral settlement · Umland(an)sied(e)lung *f*

peripheral territory, umland territory, umland area; suburban territory, suburban area (US), peripheral area · Umlandgebiet *n*

peripheral town, peripheral city, umland town, umland city · Umlandstadt *f*

perishable · verderbliches Gut *n*, verderbliche Ware *f*

perjury · falsches Zeugnis *n*

perjury incitement, incitement of perjury · Verleitung *f* zum Meineid

perjury (US); false swearing, false oath; mainad [*In old English law*] · Meineid *m*

permanent advantage · Dauervorteil *m*

permanent alimony · lebenslängliche Alimente *f*

permanent building financing, permanent construction financing · Baudauerfinanzierung *f*

permanent building society (Brit.); Dayton permanent (building and loan) association (US) · Realkreditinstitut *n* für langfristige Baudarleh(e)n, Realkreditverein *m* für langfristige Baudarleh(e)n [*Fehlbenennungen: dauernde Bausparkasse, permanente Bausparkasse. Diese Institute bauen nicht selbst und geben ihre Darleh(e)n nicht nur an ihren Sparerkreis*]

permanent camping site, permanent caravan site, all-the-year-round camping site, all-the-year-round caravan site · Dauercampingplatz *m*

permanent council · ständiger Rat *m*

permanent credit · Dauerkredit *m*

permanent demise → long-term lease(hold)

permanent dwelling right · Dauerwohnrecht *n*

permanent file, carryover file [*Auditing. Papers and schedules kept in a separate file for use in succeeding audits*] · Buchprüfungsunterlagen *fpl*

permanent finance · Dauerfinanzierung *f*

permanent grass land, permanent pasture land · Dauerweideland *n*

permanent green area · Dauergrünfläche *f*

permanent improvement · dauernde Verbesserung *f*

permanent investment · Daueranlage *f*

permanent lease(hold) → long-term lease(hold)

permanent loan · Dauerdarleh(e)n *n*

permanent loan contract · Dauerdarleh(e)nsvertrag *m*

permanent maintenance, ordinary maintenance, current maintenance · planmäßige Unterhaltung *f*, Routineunterhaltung

permanent pasture land, permanent grass land · Dauerweideland *n*

permanent personnel, direct staff, direct personnel, permanent staff · Stammbelegschaft *f*, Stammpersonal *n*

permanent population, de-jure population, resident(ial) population · Wohnbevölkerung *f*, De-jure-Bevölkerung, wohnberechtigte Bevölkerung

permanent regular plan, regular permanent plan · individueller regelmäßiger Plan *m* [*Eine dauernde Form einer amerikanischen Bausparkasse*]

(permanent) residence, legal home, settlement, domicil(e), place of habitation, habitation place, (place of) abode, (place of) residence · Aufenthaltsort *m*, gesetzlicher Aufenthaltsort, Wohnort *m*, Wohnsitz *m*

permanent residence for tax purposes · steuerlicher Wohnsitz *m*

permanent settlement, sedentary settlement · Dauer(an)sied(e)lung *f*

permanent staff, permanent personnel, direct staff, direct personnel · Stammbelegschaft *f*, Stammpersonal *n*

permanent stock association, capital stock association, guaranty building (and loan) association (US); guaranty building society (Brit.), guaranty stock association · Bausparkasse *f* mit Eigenkapital, kapitalistische Bausparkasse

permanent structure, permanent work, permanent physical facility [*Despite important distinctions which are made between permanent work and temporary work, a definition of universal application is impossible, what is left permanently in place may be more than the permanent work (e.g. sheet piles, coffer dams, etc.); and the obligation to maintain by no means clearly excludes the temporary work. Where included in the bill of quantities, "temporary work" should, however, be defined. But there must always be items incapable of precise labelling, e.g. ground treatment which is partly to facilitate construction (and therefore of a "temporary" nature) but which is relied upon in the design of the "permanent" work*] · (bauliche) Hauptanlage *f*, Haupt(bau)werk *n*, Hauptbau *m*, Dauer(bau)werk, Dauerbau, Dauerbau(anlage) *m*, (*f*), Dauerbaulichkeit *f*; Dauerbaute *f*, Hauptbaute [*Schweiz*]

permanent structures, permanent works, permanent physical facilities [*The works to be constructed, completed and maintained in accordance with the contract*] · (bauliche) Hauptanlagen *f pl*, Hauptbauten *f*, Haupt(bau)werke *n pl*, Dauer(bau)werke, Dauerbauten, Hauptbaulichkeiten *f pl*, Dauerbaulichkeiten, Dauerbauanlagen, (bauliche) Daueranlagen, Hauptbauanlagen

permanent tenancy → long-term lease(hold)

permanent tenancy right, right of permanent tenancy · Dauerwohnrecht *n*

permanent tenure → long-term lease(hold)

permanent use · Dauerbenutzung *f*, Dauergebrauch *m*

permanent user · Dauerbenutzer *m*

permanent work(s), main work(s), principal work(s) · (bauliche) Hauptarbeit(en) *f (pl)*, (bauliche) Hauptleistung(en) *f (pl)*

permissible building area, admissible building area · zulässige Grundfläche *f*

permission · Bewilligung *f*, Erlaubnis *f*, Genehmigung

permission charge, permission duty · Bewilligungsgebühr *f*, Genehmigungsgebühr, Erlaubnisgebühr

permission duty, permission charge · Bewilligungsgebühr *f*, Genehmigungsgebühr, Erlaubnisgebühr

permission for (common) assurance (on conveyance of land) · Auflassungserlaubnis *f*, Auflassungsgenehmigung *f*

permission for land transactions, permission to deal with land(s), permission for realty transactions, realty transfer permission, land transfer permission, (real) estate transfer permission, (real) property transfer permission, permission for (real) estate transactions, permission for (real) property transactions · Bodenverkehrserlaubnis *f*, Bodenverkehrsgenehmigung *f*, Grundstücksverkehrserlaubnis, Grundstücksverkehrsgenehmigung, Immobiliarverkehrserlaubnis, Immobiliarverkehrsgenehmigung, Immobilienverkehrserlaubnis, Immobilienverkehrsgenehmigung, Liegenschaftsverkehrserlaubnis, Liegenschaftsverkehrsgenehmigung

permission of (ab)alienation, permission of disposal, (ab)alienation permission, disposal permission · Veräußerungsgenehmigung *f*, Veräußerungserlaubnis *f*

permission of employment, employment permission · Arbeitserlaubnis *f*, Arbeitsgenehmigung *f*

permission of exception, exceptional grant of permission, exceptional permission · Ausnahmeerlaubnis *f*, Ausnahmegenehmigung f, Ausnahmebewilligung f, Ausnahmeerteilung f einer Genehmigung

permission of settlement, settlement permission · (An)Sied(e)lungsgenehmigung f, (An)Sied(e)lungserlaubnis f, Besied(e)lungsgenehmigung, Besied(e)lungserlaubnis

permission of use, permission to use, use permission · Gebrauchsgenehmigung f, Benutzungsgenehmigung, Benutzungserlaubnis f, Gebrauchserlaubnis

permission to build, building permission, construction permission, permission to construct · (Bau)Genehmigung f, (Bau)Erlaubnis f, Ausführungsgenehmigung, Ausführungserlaubnis [*Entscheidung einer Baugenehmigungsbehörde über die Zulässigkeit eines Vorhabens auf einem bestimmten Grundstück (§ 36 BBauG)*]

permission to deal with land(s), permission for realty transactions, realty transfer permission, land transfer permission, (real) estate transfer permission, (real) property transfer permission, permission for (real) estate transactions, permission for (real) property transactions, permission for land transactions · Bodenverkehrserlaubnis f, Bodenverkehrsgenehmigung f, Grundstücksverkehrserlaubnis, Grundstücksverkehrsgenehmigung, Immobiliarverkehrserlaubnis, Immobiliarverkehrsgenehmigung, Immobilienverkehrserlaubnis, Immobilienverkehrsgenehmigung, Liegenschaftsverkehrserlaubnis, Liegenschaftsverkehrsgenehmigung

permission to develop, development permission · Entwick(e)lungserlaubnis f, Entwick(e)lungsgenehmigung f

permission to erect a facility · Anlageerlaubnis f, Anlagegenehmigung f

permission to reside, residence permission · Aufenthaltserlaubnis f, Aufenthaltsgenehmigung f

permissive law · dispositives Recht n

permit → building permit

permit fee → (building) permit fee

(permitted) development [*The carrying out of building, engineering, mining, or other operations in, on, over or under land, or the making of any material change in the use of any buildings or the land. Definition from the T.C.P.A. 1971. Development requires a planning permission*] · Entwick(e)lung f mit Planungserlaubnis, (genehmigte) Entwick(e)lung

permit to appropriate · Aneignungsbescheinigung f

pernor (of profits), taker of profits, receiver of profits · Berechtigte m, Nutzungsberechtigte

perpetual, forever · ewig, immerwährend, dauernd [*Pacht; Familienfideikommiß; usw.*]

perpetual annuity, annuity in perpetuity [*The payments cease only on repayment of the principal*] · immerwährende Annuität f, Dauerannuität, dauernde Annuität, ewige Annuität, Ewigannuität

perpetual demise → long-term lease(hold)

perpetual easement · Dauergrunddienstbarkeit f

perpetual lease(hold) → long-term lease(hold)

perpetual tenancy → long-term lease(hold)

perpetual tenure → long-term lease(hold)

perpetuating testimony [*The taking of testimony in order to preserve it for future use, as where it is in danger of being lost before the matter to which it relates can be made the subject of judicial investigation*] · Beweissicherung f, (vorsorgliche) Beweisaufnahme f

perpetuating testimony method · Beweissicherungsverfahren n, (vorsorgliches) Beweisaufnahmeverfahren

perpetuities · Familienfideikommiß n [*Ein durch private Willenserklärung für eine bestimmte Familie gestiftes unveräußerliches Vermögen, das innerhalb der Familie einer Sondererbfolge unterliegt, und an dem dem jeweiligen Besitzer nur ein durch die Rechte der zur Nachfolge berufenen Familienmitglieder beschränktes Verfügungsrecht zusteht*]

perpetuities possessor, possessor of perpetuities · Familienfideikommißbesitzer m

perpetuity [*A disposition of property by which its absolute vesting is postponed for ever*] · Dauerzustand m, Fortdauer f

persistency · Erhaltensneigung f

persistent inflation, creeping inflation · schleichende Inflation f

persistent unemployment, chronic unemployment · Dauerarbeitslosigkeit f, Dauererwerbslosigkeit

person [*In jurisprudence, a person is the object of rights and duties, that is, capable of having rights and of being liable to duties, while a thing is the subject of rights and duties. Persons are of two kinds, natural and artificial*] · Person f, Rechtssubjekt n

personable, endowed with legal personality, legally capable, legally qualified · gesetzlich fähig, gesetzlich geeignet

person affected, person concerned · Betroffene m

personal action → personal cause

personal act(ion) → personal lawful act(ion)

personal and substantial — (personal) representative

personal and substantial · persönlich und dinglich

personal assets · beweglicher Nachlaß *m*

(personal behavior (US); (personal) behaviour (Brit.); conduct · Führung *f*, (persönliches) Verhalten *n*

personal cause; personal writ [*In old English law*]; (court) action personal, (law)suit personal, cause personal, plea personal, personal (court) action, personal plea, personal (law)suit · Entschädigungsklage *f*, Schadenersatzklage, Forderungsklage, Personenklage [*Fehlbenennung: Personalklage*]

personal chattel → personal estate

personal condition → lawful ability

personal corporation · Einmannvermögensverwaltungsgesellschaft *f*

personal (court) action, personal plea, personal (law)suit, personal cause; personal writ [*In old English law*]; (court) action personal, (law)suit personal, cause personal, plea personal · Entschädigungsklage *f*, Schadenersatzklage, Forderungsklage, Personenklage [*Fehlbenennung: Personalklage*]

personal credit · Personalkredit *m*

personal earnings · Einkünfte *f* aus eigener Arbeit

personal equitable estate → equitable personal property

personal equitable property → equitable personal property

personal estate, personal property, personal chattel, thing(s) personal, thing(s) mov(e)able, personalty, mov(e)able property, mov(e)able thing(s), chattel (personal), mov(e)able(s), mov(e)able estate, interest other than in land(s), mov(e)able possession; res mobilis [*Latin*] · Fahrnis *f*, Fahrhabe *f*, Mobilie *f*, bewegliches Gut *n*, bewegliche Sache *f*, bewegliche Habe, fahrendes Gut, loses Gut, greifbares Gut, Mobiliargut, fahrende Sache, bewegliches Vermögen *n*, greifbares Vermögen, fahrendes Vermögen, Mobiliarvermögen, fahrende Habe, greifbare Habe, greifbare Sache, lose Sache, lose Habe, loses Vermögen

personal estate law, personalty law, personal property law · Fahrnisrecht *n*, Fahrhaberecht, Mobiliarrecht, Mobilienrecht

personal estate of a bankrupt, personalty of a bankrupt, personal property of a bankrupt · Mobilienmasse *f*, Mobiliarmasse, Fahrnismasse, Fahrhabemasse

personal estate of a deceased person, personalty of a deceased person, personal property of a deceased person · Mobiliennachlaß *m*, Mobiliarnachlaß, Fahrnisnachlaß, Fahrhabenachlaß

personal harm, personal injury, trespass to the person, bodily injury, bodily harm · Körperverletzung *f* [*Jeder äußere Eingriff in die körperliche Unversehrtheit*]

personal injustice · persönliches Unrecht *n*

personal interest, right in personam, personal right · persönliches Recht *n*

personal judg(e)ment, judg(e)ment in personam · Leistungsurteil *n*, schuldrechtliches Urteil, Verurteilungsurteil, Urteil auf Grund schuldrechtlicher Haftung

personal lawful act(ion), personal (legal) act(ion) · persönlicher Rechtsakt *m*, persönliche Rechtshandlung *f*, persönliches Rechtsgeschäft *n*

personal (law)suit, personal cause; personal writ [*In old English law*]; (court) action personal, (law)suit personal, cause personal, plea personal, personal (court) action, personal plea · Entschädigungsklage *f*, Schadenersatzklage, Forderungsklage, Personenklage [*Fehlbenennung: Personalklage*]

personally chargeable · persönlich haftbar

personal property → personal estate

personal property community · Fahrnisgemeinschaft *f*, Fahrhabegemeinschaft

personal property law, personal estate law, personalty law · Fahrnisrecht *n*, Fahrhaberecht, Mobiliarrecht, Mobilienrecht

personal property of a bankrupt, personal estate of a bankrupt, personalty of a bankrupt · Mobilienmasse *f*, Mobiliarmasse, Fahrnismasse, Fahrhabemasse

personal property of a deceased person, personal estate of a deceased person, personalty of a deceased person · Mobiliennachlaß *m*, Mobiliarnachlaß, Fahrnisnachlaß, Fahrhabenachlaß

personal property tax, tax on personal property · Mobilien(vermögens)steuer *f*, Mobiliar(vermögens)steuer

personal rent · Vorzugsrente *f* (bei) der Arbeit

(personal) representation · Nachlaßvertretung *f* [*1. Nachlaßverwaltung; 2. Testamentsvollstreckung*]

personal representation, estate administration, asset administration, administration (of estate), administration of asset, administration of property · erbrechtliche Verwaltung *f*, Nachlaßverwaltung, Erb(schafts)verwaltung

(personal) representative [*The executor, original or by representation, or administrator for the time being of a deceased person. The "real representative" is the heir of the deceased person*] · Person *f* die die Persönlichkeit des Erblassers fortsetzt, Nachlaßvertreter m [Oberbegriffe für „Nachlaßverwalter" und „Testamentsvollstrecker"]

personal right, personal interest, right in personam · persönliches Recht n

personal security, registered security · Namenpapier n, Rectapapier [Auf den Namen eines bestimmten Gläubigers ohne weiteren Zusatz ausgestelltes Wertpapier]

personal service contract, master-and-servant contract, contract for personal service, contract of (personal) service, contract of master and servant · Dienst(leistungs)vertrag m

personal service (of the writ) · persönliche Zustellung f (der Klag(e)schrift)

personal suit → personal (law-)suit

personal tax · Personensteuer f

personal tithe [Tithe of the produce of labo(u)r or occupation] · Personalzehnt m, persönlicher Zehnt

personalty → personal estate

personalty interest, right of personalty, interest in personalty, personalty right · (subjektives) Fahrnisrecht n [Die Rechtsstellung, die einer bestimmten Person an einem bestimmten Fahrnisgut zusteht]

personalty law, personal property law, personal estate law · Fahrnisrecht n, Fahrhaberecht, Mobiliarrecht, Mobilienrecht

personalty of a bankrupt, personal property of a bankrupt, personal estate of a bankrupt · Mobilienmasse f, Mobiliarmasse, Fahrnismasse, Fahrhabemasse

personalty of a deceased person, personal property of a deceased person, personal estate of a deceased person · Mobiliennachlaß m, Mobiliarnachlaß, Fahrnisnachlaß, Fahrhabenachlaß

personalty right, personalty interest, right of personalty, interest in personalty · (subjektives) Fahrnisrecht n [Die Rechtsstellung, die einer bestimmten Person an einem bestimmten Fahrnisgut zusteht]

personalty trust, trust of personalty · Fahrnistreuhand f, Fahrhabetreuhand

personal writ [In old English law]; (court) action personal, (law)suit personal, cause personal, plea personal, personal (court) action, personal plea, personal (law)suit, personal cause · Entschädigungsklage f, Schadenersatzklage, Forderungsklage, Personenklage [Fehlbenennung: Personalklage]

persona moralis [Latin]; moral person [This word simply means a nonphysical person — a person such as exists in the world of men's thoughts (and particularly in the world of their legal thought), but not in the world of physical nature. No ethical connotation is involved, but it is the danger of the term that an ethical connotation may be imported. Rousseau's theory, that the general will of the moral person of the community is always right, does not escape this danger] · moralische Person f (der Naturrechtslehre)

person capable of earning a living · Erwerbsperson f, erwerbsfähige Person, erwerbsgeeignete Person

person capable of making a will · testierfähige Person f

person concerned, person affected · Betroffene m

person employed in a managerial position, managerial salaried employe(e) · leitender Angestellter m

person entitled, obligee · berechtigte Person f

person entitled to Immediate Aid · sofortberechtigte Person f [Bundesrepublik Deutschland]

person entitled to mineral right(s) · Gewinnungsberechtigte m, Ausbeutungsberechtigte

persone [obsolete]; parish priest, parson [A minister who holds a parish as a benefice, called, if the predial tithes were unappropriated, rector, and if appropriated, vicar] · Kirchspielgeistliche m, (Pfarr)Sprengelgeistliche, kirchlicher Sprengelgeistlicher

person in charge of something · (Sach)Bearbeiter m

person-indexing system · Personenindex m, Personenfolium n

person invited to tender, prospective bidder, prospective tenderer, prospective offeror, prospective competitor, prospective tendering contractor, prospective competing contractor, applicant · Bewerber m [Ein Bauunternehmer, der sich um eine Bauleistung bewirbt, aber noch kein Angebot auf diese Bauleistung abgegeben hat]

personnel, staff · Belegschaft f, Personal n

personnel administration, staff administration · Personalverwaltung f

personnel cost(s), staff cost(s) · Personalkosten f

personnel department, staff department · Personalabteilung f

personnel management → staff management

personnel officer · Personalchef m

personnel shortage — petroleum products company

personnel shortage, staff shortage · Personalknappheit f, Personalmangel m, Personalverknappung f

personnel structure, personnel composition, staff composition, staff structure · Personalstruktur f, Personalgefüge n, Personalzusammensetzung f

personnel supplement, staff supplement · Personalausbau m

person non compotes mentis → person of unsound mind

person not capable of earning a living · Nichterwerbsperson f

person not sui juris [*Latin*]; dependent person [*The English law has two types of dependent persons, viz. minors and married women*] · abhängige Person f [*Eine Person, die rechtlich unfähig ist einen Wohnsitzwechsel selbständig vorzunehmen*]

person of dual nationality, person of dual citizenship, person of double nationality, person of double citizenship, person of twin nationality, person of twin citizenship · Doppelstaatler m

person of slender means · Minderbemittelte m

person of sound mind · geistig gesunde Person f

person of unsound mind, person suffering from mental disorder, person non compotes mentis, lunatic, mental patient, mentally incompetent person, insane person; lunaticus [*Latin*] · geisteskranke Person f, geistesgestörte Person

person of unsound mind so found by inquisition · entmündigte geisteskranke Person f

person responsible for building maintenance · Gebäudeunterhalt(ung)spflichtige m

persons employed in industry per 1,000 inhabitants · Industriebesatz m

persons missing register · Vermißtenliste f

person subject to law · Rechtsunterworfene m

person sui juris [*Latin*]; independent person · unabhängige Person f [*Eine Person, die rechtlich fähig ist einen Wohnsitzwechsel selbständig vorzunehmen*]

perspective drawing · Perspektivzeichnung f

persuant to contract, subject to contract, contractual · vertragsgemäß, vertragsmäßig, vertraglich

persuasion · Überredung f

persuasive authority · Autorität f

pertinent, to the point, relevant · erheblich, wesentlich

pertinent, pertinance [*Scots law*]; appenditia [*Latin*]; thing of an accessory character, appurtenant, appendage, appurtenance; appertainance [*obsolete*] [*A thing belonging to another thing. Things appendant can be claimed only by prescription, while things appurtenant can be claimed either by prescription or by express grant*] · Zubehör n, Dazugehörige n, Pertinenz f; Zugehör n [*Schweiz*]

per totam curiam [*Latin*] · durch das gesamte Gericht

pervious cesspool emptying service, cesspit emptying service, (leaching) cesspool emptying service · Senkgrubenentleerungsdienst m

pessimum distance · schlechteste Entfernung f

pest control · Schädlingsbekämpfung f

petens [*Latin*]; demandant, actor in a real action · Grundstücksprozeßkläger m

Peter-pence, Romescot, Romefee, Romepenny · Peterspfennig m

petitio, precaria, precatura, exactio, collecta, demanda, talia, stiura [*Latin*] · Bede f, Stiure f, Schatz m, Schoß m [*Seit dem 10. Jahrhundert in den deutschen Gebieten eine öffentlich-rechtliche direkte Abgabe an bestimmte Autoritäten, wie Vogt, Graf, Bischof, Landesherr oder König. Ihre Form war vorwiegend Grund- und Gebäudesteuer*]

to petition · nachsuchen [*Ein Bittgesuch einreichen*]

petition · Eingabe f, Bittgesuch n, Antrag m

petition · schriftlicher Zwischenantrag m [*Über ihn wird in öffentlicher Sitzung verhandelt*]

petition · Klageschrift f [*Ehescheidungsprozeß*]

petitioner · Bittsteller m

petitioner, orator [*A plaintiff in a bill, or information, in Chancery was so called before the statute 1852, 15 & 16 Vict. c. 86*] · Bittsteller m, Kläger

petition for winding(-)up, petition for liquidation, winding(-)up petition, liquidation petition · Liquidationsantrag m

petition of course · (formeller) Antrag m auf welchen die betreffende Verfügung ohne weiteres erfolgen muß [*Verhandlung in öffentlicher Gerichtssitzung*]

petitory · eingabefähig, eingabebereit

petrified forest · versteinerter Wald m

petrographic map · petrographische Karte f, Karte der Gesteinsarten

petroleum products company · Petrogesellschaft f

pettifogger — phraseology of law

pettifogger; shyster (US) · Winkeladvokat *m*

petty assise, petty assize [*This was a proceeding introduced by Henry II before justices in eyre to obtain a remedy for loss of seisin or possession*] · possessorische Assise *f*

(petty) assise of darrein presentment, (petty) assize of darrein presentment, (petty) assize of last presentation, (petty) assize of last presentation [*This was a real action which lay where a man (or his ancestor under whom he claimed) had presented a clerk to a benefice, who was instituted, and afterwards, upon the next avoidance, a stranger presented a clerk, and thereby disturbed the real patron. It was abolished by the Real Property Limitation Act, 1833, s. 36, having been previously superseded in practice by the action of quare impedit (3 Bl. Comm. 245)*] · possessorische Assise *f* wegen eines vom Gegner in Anspruch genommenen Kirchenpatronats

(petty) assise of mort d'ancestor, (petty) assize of mort d'ancestor [*This was a real action which lay to recover land of which a person had been deprived on the death of his ancestor by the abatement or intrusion of a stranger. It was abolished by the Real Property Limitation Act, 1833, s. 36 (3 Bl. Comm. 185; Co. Litt. 159 a)*] · possessorische Assise *f* des Erben gegen den Nichtberechtigten [*Vorzugsweise gegen den Leh(e)n(s)herrn der nach dem Tode des Erblassers widerrechtlich Besitz vom Land ergriff*]

petty cash · Portokasse *f*

petty cash voucher · Portokassenausgangsformular *n*

petty court, summary court, registrar's court, court of summary jurisdiction, court of request, registrar's court, court of conscience, police court, P. · Bagatellgericht *n*, Friedensgericht für kleine Straf- und Zivilsachen, Polizeigericht, Ortsgericht für gering(füg)ige Schuldklagen [*in England*]

petty seal · königliches Privatsiegel *n*

petty session · kleine Sitzung *f* der Friedensrichter, regelmäßige Sitzung der Friedensrichter

petty sessional court house · Polizeigerichtsgebäude *n* [*In einem Bezirk einer Grafschaft in England*]

petty sessional division · Bezirk *m* einer Grafschaft zum Zwecke der Polizeigerichtsbarkeit, friedensrichterlicher Bezirk

petty sessional divisional court · kleiner Gerichtshof *m* für kleine Strafsachen [*In England*]

petty sessions book · Friedensrichterbuch *n* [*Es enthält die vor die Friedensrichter gebrachten Fälle und deren Entscheidungen*]

petty theft · leichter Diebstahl *m*

petty tithe, privy tithe, little tithe, small tithe · kleiner Zehnt *m*, Schmalzehnt

phased completion · gestaffelte Fertigstellung *f*

phased programme; phased program (US) · gestaffeltes Programm *n*

phase of performance, performance phase · Leistungsstadium *n*, Leistungsphase *f*

phasing · Staffeln *n* [*Eine Zahlung über einen gewissen Zeitraum hinweg*]

phasing of the work(s) by the contractor, work(s) phasing by the contractor · (Ausführungs)Fristenplanung *f*, Baufristenplanung *f*

phasing of work(s) by the owner, phasing of work(s) by the client, work(s) phasing by the owner, work(s) phasing by the client · Arbeitsfortschrittplanung *f*, Bauzeit(en)planung *f*, (Bau)Fortschrittplanung *f*

pheasantry · Fasanerie *f*

philosopher of law, law philosopher, legal philosopher · Rechtsphilosoph *m*

philosophy of law, law philosophy, legal philosophy · Rechtsphilosophie *f*

phone booth [*In the Western states of the USA*]; pay station [*In the Eastern states of the USA*] · Fernsprechzelle *f*, Telefonzelle

phoney corporation · Schwindelgesellschaft *f*

photogeology · Bildgeologie *f*, Aufnahmegeologie, Photogeologie

photo(graph) · photographische Aufnahme *f*

photographic album · Photoalbum *n*

photo(graphic) interpreter · Bildauswerter *m*, Photoauswerter, Aufnahmeauswerter

photo(graphic) interpretability · Photoauswertbarkeit *f*

photo(graphic) interpretation key, PI key · Bildauswertungsschlüssel *m*, Aufnahmeauswertungsschlüssel

photo (type) setter · Photosetzgerät *n*

to phrase , to word, to form, to draft, to construct, to draw up, to set up, to construe [*To arrange or marshal words*] · abfassen, gestalten, entwerfen, ausarbeiten, formulieren

phraseology of law, legal phraseology · Rechtssprache *f*

phrasing, wording, formulation, formation, drafting, construction, drawing-up, setting up, construing [*Arranging or marshalling words*] · Abfassung *f*, Entwurf *m*, Gestaltung, Ausarbeitung, Formulierung

PHS, public health service, public hygiene · öffentliche Gesundheitspflege *f*, öffentlicher Gesundheitsdienst *m*

physical community development, physical communal development · bauliche Gemeindeentwick(e)lung *f*

physical, nature-given · naturgegeben

physical → corporeal

physical alteration, physical conversion · bauliche (Ver)Änderung *f*, Umbau *m*

physical asset, tangible asset, corporeal asset [*Asset for which a value can be established, e.g. real estate, equipment, furniture, inventories*] · stoffliche Aktiva *f*, körperliche Aktiva

physical capacity (of an area), holding capacity (of an area) · Aufnahmefähigkeit *f*, Sied(e)lungskapazität *f*, Tragfähigkeit, tragbare Bevölkerung *f*, Aufnahmevermögen *n*, potentielle Einwohnerzahl *f* [*Die Einwohnerzahl, die aus dem gegebenen Sachpotential eines Gebietes bei Zugrundelegung eines bestimmten Standards unter rationalen Verhältnissen auf längere Sicht eine Existenz finden kann*]

physical condition, physical state · baulicher Zustand *m*

physical condition · materielle Bedingung *f*

(physical) control (over a thing) · Sachherrschaft *f*, (rechtliche) Beherrschung *f* einer Sache

physical conversion, physical alteration · bauliche (Ver)Änderung *f*, Umbau *m*

physical damage · baulicher Schaden *m*

physical damage to person(s), injury damage to person(s) · körperlicher Schaden *m*, Personenschaden

(physical) decay, dilapidation, (physical) deterioration [*A state of disrepair, relating to structures where legal liability is imposed on those responsible*] · Baufälligkeit *f*, (baulicher) Verfall *m*

physical detail, physical particular · bauliche Einzelheit *f*

physical development · bauliche Entwick(e)lung *f*

(physical) development law → law of (physical) development

(physical) development of unallocated land(s), binding (physical) development of unallocated land(s), physical binding development of unallocated land(s), (physical) development of white land(s) · Außen(bereich)bebauung *f*, Bebauen *n* einer Außen(bereich)fläche; Außen(bereich)überbauung *f*, Überbauen *n* einer Außen(bereich)fläche [*Schweiz*]

(physical) development ordinance · Bauregelungsverordnung *f* [*Verordnung über die Regelung der Bebauung in Deutschland vom 15. Februar 1936*]

(physical) development plan, plan for (physical) development, area development plan, town and country plan · Bauleitplan *m* [*Förmlicher Plan einer Gemeinde zur Ordnung ihrer gemeindlichen Entwick(e)lung (§ 1 Abs. 1 BBauG). Bauleitpläne unterscheiden sich mit unterschiedlicher Genauigkeit und Verbindlichkeit in: 1.) Flächennutzungsplan = vorbereitender Bauleitplan und 2.) Bebauungsplan = verbindlicher Bauleitplan*]

(physical) development planning, planning for (physical) development, town and country planning, area development planning · Bauleitplanung *f*

physical disability, crippling · Versehrtheit *f*

physical disfigurement · bauliche Verunstaltung *f*, bauliche Verschandelung

physical environment · bauliche Umwelt *f*, gebaute Umwelt

physical environmentalism · bauliches Umweltbewußtsein *n*

physical environmental setting · bauliche Umweltgestaltung *f*, baulicher Umwelthintergrund *m*, gebaute Umweltgestaltung, gebauter Umwelthintergrund

physical facility, structure, work · (Bau)Werk *n*, (bauliche) Anlage *f*, Baulichkeit *f*, Bau(anlage) *m*, *(f)*; Baute *f* [*Schweiz*] [*Hierunter ist nach der höchstrichterlichen Rechtsprechung zu § 638 BGB „eine unbewegliche, durch Verwendung von Arbeit und Material in Verbindung mit dem Baugrund hergestellte Sache" zu verstehen, die sich auf oder unter Geländeoberkante befinden kann*]

physical facility for common need, structure for common need, work for common need · (bauliche) Anlage *f* für Gemeinbedarf, (Bau)Werk *n* für Gemeinbedarf, Baulichkeit *f* für Gemeinbedarf, Bau(anlage) *m*, *(f)* für Gemeinbedarf; Baute *f* für Gemeinbedarf [*Schweiz*]

physical facility to be demolished, structure to be demolished, work to be demolished · Abrißbauwerk *n*, Abreißbauwerk, Einreißbauwerk

physical geography · physische Geographie *f*, physische Erdkunde *f*, Physiogeographie *f*, (städtebaulich-)technische Geographie, (städtebaulich-)technische Erdkunde, Physioerdkunde

(physical) improvement guide line — physical thing

(physical) improvement guide line, modernization guide line, rehabilitation guide line, upgrading guide-line · (bauliche) Verbesserungsrichtlinie *f*, Modernisierungsrichtlinie

(physical) improvement law, rehabilitation statute, rehabilitation act, rehabilitation law, modernization statute, modernization act, modernization law, (physical) improvement statute, (physical) improvement act · (bauliches) Verbesserungsgesetz *n*, (Wohnungs)Modernisierungsgesetz, WoModG

(physical) improvement loan, modernization loan, upgrading loan, rehabilitation loan · (bauliche) Verbesserungsanleihe *f*, Modernisierungsanleihe

(physical) improvement order, rehabilitation order, modernization order, upgrading order, order to improve, order to modernize, order to rehabilitate · Modernisierungsverfügung *f*, Modernisierungsanordnung, Modernisierungsgebot *n*, Modernisierungsbefehl *m*, (baulicher) Verbesserungsbefehl

(physical) improvement ordinance, modernization ordinance, upgrading ordinance, rehabilitation ordinance · Modernisierungsverordnung *f*, (bauliche) Verbesserungsverordnung

(physical) improvement plan, modernization plan, rehabilitation plan, upgrading plan · Modernisierungsplan *m*, (baulicher) Verbesserungsplan

(physical) improvement statute, (physical) improvement act, (physical) improvement law, rehabilitation statute, rehabilitation act, rehabilitation law, modernization statute, modernization act, modernization law · (bauliches) Verbesserungsgesetz *n*, (Wohnungs)Modernisierungsgesetz, WoModG

(physical) improvement work(s), modernization work(s), rehabilitation work(s), upgrading work(s) · (bauliche) Verbesserungsarbeit(en) *f(pl)*, Modernisierungsarbeit(en)

(physical) improvement zone, rehabilitation zone, modernization zone, upgrading zone · Modernisierungsschwerpunkt *m*, (baulicher) Verbesserungsschwerpunkt [*früher: Modernisierungszone f*]

physical injury caused by negligence, physical injury caused by carelessness, physical injury resulting from negligence, physical injury resulting from carelessness · fahrlässige Körperverletzung *f*

physical invasion · körperlicher Eingriff *m* in einen Gegenstand, Zugriff auf einen Gegenstand

(physical) meander development · Mäanderbebauung *f*; Mäanderüberbauung [*Schweiz*] [*Als begleitende Struktur eines Hanggeländes*]

physical obsolescence · bauliche Überalterung *f*

(physical) overimprovement, overmodernisation, overrehabilitation · Übermodernisierung *f*, (bauliche) Überverbesserung

physical particular, physical detail · bauliche Einzelheit *f*

physical planner · (städtebaulich-)technischer Planer *m*, physischer Planer *m*

physical planning · physische Planung *f*, (städtebaulich-)technische Planung *f*

physical possession, de facto possession, actual physical control (over a thing), potential physical control (over a thing), actual possession · tatsächliche Sachherrschaft *f*, tatsächliche Beherrschung *f* einer Sache, unmittelbarer Besitz *m*, wirklicher Besitz, tatsächlicher Besitz, wirkliche Sachherrschaft, wirkliche Beherrschung einer Sache, unmittelbare Sachherrschaft, unmittelbare Beherrschung einer Sache

physical relation to an object · körperliche Besitzmacht *f* über einen Gegenstand

physical renewal, physical revival · bauliche Erneuerung *f*

physical repair · Baureparatur *f*

physical return, physical yield · Naturalrendite *f*, physische Rendite

physical revival, physical renewal · bauliche Erneuerung *f*

physical security [*The land and all improvements within the boundaries of a lot*] · stoffliche Sicherheit *f*

physical state, physical condition · baulicher Zustand *m*

physical symbol [*e.g. a high-rise building of a city*] · bauliches Symbol *n*

(physical) taking (away), seizing · Ergreifung *f*, Wegnahme *f*, körperliche Ergreifung, körperliche Wegnahme

physical taking over · Abnahme *f* [*Körperliche Übernahme einer gekauften Sache durch den Käufer, so daß der Verkäufer vom Besitz einer Sache befreit wird*]

physical thing, thing corporeal, corporeal chattel (personal); res corporales, res singula [*Latin*]; corporeal thing, tangible thing, chose [*A thing that affects the senses and may be seen and handled*] · (Einzel)Sache *f*, körperliches Rechtsobjekt *n*, materielles Rechtsobjekt, körperliches Ding *n*, materielles Ding, körperlicher (Rechts)Gegenstand *m*, materieller (Rechts)Gegenstand [*Ausgenommen lebender menschlicher Körper. Unter den Sachbegriff fallen nicht die Rechte, die Sachgesamtheiten, d. h.*

Mehrheiten von Sachen, die eine besondere Benennung haben, z. B. Bücherei, Warenlager usw. und die Inbegriffe von Sachen und Rechten, z. B. Erbschaftsvermögen usw. Im Preußischen Allgemeinen Landrecht von 1794 (A.L.R.) ist (Einzel)Sache allerdings alles, was Gegenstand eines Rechtes oder einer Verbindlichkeit sein kann (§ 1. I. 2)]

physical training · Leibesübungen f pl

physical yield, physical return · Naturalrendite f, physische Rendite

picket · Streikposten m

picketing · Streikpostenstehen n

pictogram · Bildstatistik f

pictorial form · Bildform f

pictorial guide · Bildführer m

pictorial map · Bildkarte f

piecemeal (social) engineering, social piecemeal engineering, incrementalism · Inkrementalismus m, pragmatisches Ideal n, problemorientiertes Vorgehen n, problembezogenes Vorgehen [Planung als pragmatisches, quasirationales, allein am Kriterium des Möglichen ausgerichtetes, zusammenhangloses und schrittweises Vorgehen]

piece of forest · Waldstück n, Forststück

piece of land, portion of land, land portion, land piece · Landstück n

piece of land for exchange → plot (of land) for exchange

piece of land with building(s), parcel (of land) with building(s), plot (of land) with building(s) · Gebäudegrundstück n

piece of usufruct, plot of usufruct, parcel of usufruct · (Frucht)Genußgrundstück n, Nießbrauchgrundstück

piece-wage, efficiency-wage, statement-wage, premium-wage, wage by results · Akkordlohn m, Leistungslohn

piece-wage contract, piece-work contract, job(bing) work contract, premium-wage contract, efficiency-wage contract, statement-wage contract · Akkord(lohn)vertrag m, Leistungslohnvertrag

piece-wage rate, efficiency-wage rate, statement-wage rate, premium-wage rate · Akkord(lohn)satz m

piece-work, job(bing) work · Akkordarbeit f

pie chart · Tortendiagramm n, Kreisdiagramm

pie graph · Kreissektoren(karto)diagramm n [Darstellung eines Mengenverhältnisses durch entsprechende Aufteilung einer Kreisfläche in Sektoren]

piepowder court, court of pie-powder [So genannt wegen der staubigen Füße der Rechtsuchenden] · Messegericht n, Gastgericht [Im mittelalterlichen England]

pignus [Latin]; mortgage in possession · Besitzpfand n, Faustpfand, Grundpfand [Der Eigentümer übergibt die Sache dem Gläubiger]

PI key, photo(graphic) interpretation key · Bildauswertungsschlüssel m, Aufnahmeauswertungsschlüssel

pilgrimage place · Wallfahrtsort m

pilot (building) project, pilot construction project · Demonstrations(bau)vorhaben n, Demonstrativ(bau)vorhaben

pilot chart · (nautische) Monatskarte f

pilot firm, management sponsor; sponsor(ing firm) (US); "lead" firm · federführende Firma f

pin-money [Money allowed to, or settled upon a wife for the purpose of supplying her with dress and the means of defraying her other personal expenses] · Nadelgeld n

pioneer colonization · Pionierkolonisation f

pioneer settlement · Pionier(an)sied(e)lung f

piped water, tap water · Leitungswasser n

piped water damage, tap water damage · Leitungswasserschaden m

piped water damage insurance, tap water damage insurance · Leitungswasserschadenversicherung f

piped water supply · (Rohr)Leitungswasserversorgung f

pipelines act, pipelines law, pipelines statute · Rohrfernleitungsgesetz n

pipelines law · Rohrfernleitungsrecht n

pipe roll · Steuerrolle f [In der Normannenzeit in England]

piscary; libera piscaria [Latin]; free fishery, fishing right, right of fishing [The right or liberty of fishing in the waters of another person] · Fischereirecht n, subjektives Fischereirecht

pit row, miners' row · Bergarbeiterreihensied(e)lung f

pit village · Löß-Schachtdorf n

pit-(work)shop · Höhlenwerkstatt f

placard, bill, poster, placart · Plakat n

placard-posting, bill sticking, placard sticking, poster sticking, (bill-)posting, placart-posting, placart sticking · Plakatankleben, Plakatanschlagen

place · Stellenwert m

place, locality [A definite region in any part of space] · Ort(schaft) m, (f)

place-bound — plainant in error

place-bound · ortsgebunden

place-bound enterprise, place-bound undertaking · ortsgebundenes Unternehmen n, ortsgebundener Betrieb m, ortsgebundene Unternehmung f

place desertion, locality desertion · Ortswüstung f

placed in authority, authorized, endowed with authority · bevollmächtigt

place for sale of butchers meat · Fleischmarkt m

place image · Ortsbild n

placeman · Sinekurenträger m

place-name · Ortsname m

place not built upon · Freiplatz m

(place of) abode, (place of) residence, (permanent) residence, legal home, settlement, domicil(e), place of habitation, habitation place · Aufenthaltsort m, gesetzlicher Aufenthaltsort, Wohnort m, Wohnsitz m

place of arbitration, arbitration place · Schiedsort m, Schiedsgerichtsort

place of assembly · Versammlungsstätte f

place of birth, birth place · Geburtsort m

place of business, business place · Geschäftsort m

place of contract, contract place · Vertragsort m

place of destination, destination place · Bestimmungsort m

place of employment, place of work(ing), work(ing) place, employment place, job place · Arbeitsort m, Arbeitsplatz m, Beschäftigungsort m, Beschäftigungsplatz m

place of entertainment · Vergnügungsort m

place of execution of (the) work(s), place of performance of the work(s), place of construction of (the) works · Arbeitsausführungsort m, (Bau)Ausführungsort m

place of fulfilment, place of execution, place of performance, place of compliance · Erfüllungsort m

place of habitation, habitation place, (place of) abode, (place of) residence, (permanent) residence, legal home, settlement, domicil(e) · Aufenthaltsort m, gesetzlicher Aufenthaltsort, Wohnort m, Wohnsitz m

place of insurance · Versicherungsort m

place of origin, source · Ursprungsort m

place of payment · Zahlungsort m

place of performance, performance place · Leistungsort m

place of public resort · öffentlicher Vergnügungsort m

(place of) residence, (permanent) residence, legal home, settlement, domicil(e), place of habitation, habitation place, (place of) abode · Aufenthaltsort m, gesetzlicher Aufenthaltsort, Wohnort, Wohnsitz m

place of sale · Verkaufsort m

place of the execution of the contract [*Die englische Benennung bedeutet nicht immer nur Entstehungs- oder Abschlußort, sondern kann auch "Ausführungs- oder Erfüllungsort" bezeichnen. In manchen Entscheidungen und Schriften amerikanischer Rechtsgelehrter ist nicht ohne weiteres ersichtlich, ob dem Wort "execution" diese oder jene Bedeutung beizulegen ist*] · Entstehungsort m, Abschlußort [*Vertrag*]

place of the seal; locus sigilli, L.S. [*Latin*] · Siegelort m

place of voting, voting place · Wahlsprengel m

place of work(ing) → place of employment

to place to account, to put to account, to charge · anrechnen, in Anrechnung bringen

place utility · Ortsnutzen m

place with monument(s) · Denkmalort m

placing to account, putting to account, charging · Anrechnung f

placing on file, filing · Aktenaufnahme f, Aufnahme in Akten

placita [*Latin*]; pleadings · beid(er)seitige schriftsätzliche Vorbereitungen f pl einer mündlichen Verhandlung, zweiseitige schriftsätzliche Vorbereitungen einer mündlichen Verhandlung

placitans advocatus [*Latin*]; (special) pleader [*Formerly when pleading at common law was a highly technical and difficult art, there was a class of men known as (special) pleaders not at the bar, who held a position intermediate between counsel and attorneys. The class is now extinct*] · Schriftsatzausarbeiter m

placitare [*Latin*], to plead · plädieren

placitator → (special) pleader

placitum, pl. [*Latin*] · Gerichtsgefälle f

plainant; actor [*Latin*]; plaintiff · Kläger m, Zivilprozeßkläger

plainant in error, plaintiff in error [*The party who sues out a writ of error to review a judg(e)ment or other proceeding at law*] · Nichtigkeitskläger m, Revisionskläger

plain charity → (incorporated collecting) charity

plain corporate bond [*USA*]; naked debenture, simple debenture, unsecured debenture [*Great Britain*]; unsecured corporate bond, debenture (corporate) bond [*USA*] · ungesicherte Schuldverschreibung *f*, ungesicherte Obligation *f* [*private Kapitalgesellschaft*]

plain (incorporated collecting) charity · rechtsfähiges Sammelvermögen *n* [*Das gesammelte Vermögen wird ausgeschüttet*]

plain meaning of the text · einfacher Wortlaut *m*

plaintiff, plainant; actor [*Latin*] · Kläger *m*, Zivilprozeßkläger

plaintiff in appeal; appelator [*Latin*]; appealer, appellant, appealing party · Appellant *m*, Appellationskläger *m*, Berufungskläger *m*

plaintiff in error, plainant in error [*The party who sues out a writ of error to review a judg(e)ment or other proceeding at law*] · Nichtigkeitskläger *m*, Revisionskläger

to plan · planen

plan [*An orderly arrangement of parts of an objective*] · Plan *m*

plan [*A method for doing something*] · Plan *m*

plan → (ground)plan

plan area · Planbereich *m*

plan content, content of plan · Planinhalt *m*

plan coordinate → (physical) plan coordinate

plan-design model · Planungsmodell *n*

plan effectiveness, effectiveness of a plan · Planreife *f*

plane table map · Meßtischblatt *n*

plan for application to construct · (Bau)Antragsplan *m*

plan for graphic determination of original surface · Rechnungskarte *f* [*Einlagenberechnung*]

plan for (physical) development, area development plan, town and country plan, (physical) development plan · Bauleitplan *m* [*Förmlicher Plan einer Gemeinde zur Ordnung ihrer gemeindlichen Entwick(e)lung (§ 1 Abs. 1 BBauG). Bauleitpläne unterscheiden sich mit unterschiedlicher Genauigkeit und Verbindlichkeit in: 1.) Flächennutzungsplan = vorbereitender Bauleitplan und 2.) Bebauungsplan = verbindlicher Bauleitplan*]

plan for treatment of open areas · Freiflächengestaltungsplan *m*

planimetric map · Situationszeichnung *f*, Grundrißkarte *f*, Lageplan *m*, Situationskarte, Grundrißzeichnung [*Kartographie. Umfaßt unabhängig vom Relief auf die Ebene projizierte linien- und flächenhafte Erscheinungen, wie Küsten- und Länderumrisse, Grenzen, Gewässernetz, Verkehrsnetz, Siedlungen, häufigste Arten der Bodenbedeckung usw. Wichtige, aus Maßstabsgründen im Grundriß nicht darstellbare Objekte werden durch Kartenzeichen (Signaturen, Symbole) wiedergegeben*]

plan implementation, plan realization, implementation of (a) plan, realization of (a) plan · Planverwirklichung *f*, Plandurchführung *f*

plan-implementing, plan-realizing · planverwirklichend

to plan in advance · vorausplanen

planlessness · Planlosigkeit *f*

planless town, planless city · planlose Stadt *f*

planned city, planned town, neotechnic city, neotechnic town [*See remark under "Stadt"*] · geplante Stadt *f*, Planstadt

planned (construction) period (of time), programme (construction) time period, planned (construction) time period, programme (construction) period (of time) · geplante Baufrist *f*, geplante Zeit des Bauablaufes

planned economy, controlled economy, directed economy · Planwirtschaft *f*

planned environment · geplante Umwelt *f*

planned growth, unnatural growth · geplantes Wachstum *n*

planned (growth) pole · geplanter (Wachstums)Pol *m*, Planpol

planned industrial district; industrial park (US); organized industrial district [*Beide unterscheiden sich dadurch, daß bei der Auswahl der in einem „industrial park" aufzunehmenden Betriebe Gesichtspunkte wie z. B. ästhetische oder solche der Verträglichkeit mit Nachbarbezirken berücksichtigt werden*] · Gewerbeplansiedlung *f*

planned overspill · geplanter Überschuß *m*, geplanter Überhang *m*

planned population · geplante Bevölkerung *f*

planned regional adjustment theory · Theorie *f* der geplanten regionalen Anpassung

planned regional adjustment · geplante regionale Ausgleichung *f*

planned settlement of modern times · neuzeitliche Plan(an)sied(e)lung *f*

**planned town, ** neotechnic city, neotechnic town, planned city [*See remark under "Stadt'*] · geplante Stadt *f,* Planstadt

planned village · geplantes Dorf *n,* Plandorf

planner · Planer *m,* Planverfasser

planning · Planen *n,* Planung *f* [*als Tätigkeit*]

planning · Planung *f* [*als Ergebnis der Tätigkeit*]

planning act → planning (enabling) act

planning activity · planende Tätigkeit *f*

planning administration, administration of planning · Planungshandhabung *f*

planning advance · Planungsvorschuß *m*

planning advisory council, planning advisory panel, advisory planning council, advisory planning panel · Planungsbeirat *m*

planning advisory group · Planungsberatungsgruppe *f*

planning aid center (US); planning aid centre (Brit.) · Planungshilfezentrum *n*

planning analysis · Plan(ungs)analyse *f*

planning and zoning, control of land use, land use control · Flächennutzungslenkung *f,* Bodennutzungslenkung, Landnutzungslenkung

planning appeal · Planungsberufung *f,* Berufung gegen eine Planung

planning approach, approach in planning · Planungsansatz *m*

planning approbation, planning consensus, planning consent, planning approval, planning assent · Planungsbilligung *f,* Planungseinwilligung, Planungszustimmung, Planungskonsens *m*

planning area, planning territory · Planungsgebiet *n*

planning assistance · Planungsförderung *f*

planning atlas · Planungsatlas *m*

planning at national level, national planning, state planning · staatliche Planung *f,* Nationalplanung

planning authority · Planungsbehörde *f*

planning authority, planning power · Planungskompetenz *f,* Planungsmacht *f,* Planungsgewalt *f,* Planungshoheit *f*

planning balance sheet analysis, PBSA · Planungsbilanzanalyse *f*

planning base · Planungsgrundlage *f*

planning binding in law, planning having the force of law, legally binding planning, planning having effect in law · rechtsverbindliche Planung *f,* Planfeststellung

planning blight · Planungsschaden *m* im engeren Sinne [*Die Beseitigung oder Minderung eines vorhandenen Entwick(e)lungswerkes durch Planung*]

planning board · Planungsamt *n*

planning boundary · (räumliche) Planungsgrenze *f*

planning by stages · Stufenplanung *f*

planning case · Planungsfall *m*

planning charge · Planungsbelastung *f,* Planungslast *f*

planning checking · Planungskontrolle *f*

planning code · Planungsordnung *f*

planning commission · Planungskommission *f*

planning committee · Planungsausschuß *m*

planning condition · Planungsbedingung *f*

planning consciousness · Planungsbewußtsein *n*

planning consent, planning approval, planning assent, planning approbation, planning consensus · Planungsbilligung *f,* Planungseinwilligung, Planungszustimmung, Planungskonsens *m*

planning constraint, planning restriction, planning restraint, planning limitation · Planungsbeschränkung *f,* Planungsbegrenzung, Planungseinschränkung, Planungszwang *m*

planning consultant · freiberuflicher Planer *m,* frei(schaffend)er Planer, freiberuflicher Planungsberater, frei(schaffend)er Planungsberater

planning consultation, planning advice, planning counsel, planning consultancy · Planungsberatung *f*

planning control · Planungslenkung *f*

planning coordination, coordination of planning · Planungskoordination *f*

planning core · Planergrundausbildung *f*

planning cost(s) · Planungskosten *f*

planning counsel → planning consultation

planning data · Planungsgrundlagen *fpl*

planning data bank · Planungsdatenbank *f*

planning decision · Planungsentscheid(ung) *m, (f)*

planning design, tentative planning · Plan(ungs)entwurf *m*

planning dispute · Planungsauseinandersetzung *f,* Planungsstreit(igkeit) *m, (f)*

planning district · Planungsbezirk *m*

planning document, planning instrument · Planungsunterlage *f,* Planungsdokument *n*

planning duty, duty to plan · Planungspflicht f

planning education, training of planners · Planerausbildung f, Planverfasserausbildung

planning efficiency · Planungswirksamkeit f

planning element · Planungselement n

planning (enabling) act, planning (enabling) statute, planning (enabling) law · Planungsgesetz n

planning engineering · Planungstechnik f [als Wissenschaft]

planning environment · Planungsklima n

planning error · Planungsfehler m

planning execution, planning performance, execution of plan(s), performance of plan(s) · Plan(ungs)vollzug m, Plan(ungs)durchführung f, Plan(ungs)ausführung

planning expert · Planungssachverständige m

planning expertise · Planungsgutachten n

planning field, planning sector · Planungssektor m

planning for advertisements, advertisement planning, advertizement planning · Werbungsplanung f, Reklameplanung

planning for development → (physical) development planning

planning forecast · Planungsvorhersage f

planning for industry, industry planning · Industrieplanung f

planning for leisure, leisure planning, non-work planning · Freizeitplanung f

planning for permission to construct, planning for permission to build · (Bau)Genehmigungsplanung f, (Bau)-Erlaubnisplanung [Architektenleistung. Erarbeiten und Einreichen der Vorlagen für die erforderlichen Genehmigungen]

planning for (physical) development, town and country planning, area development planning, (physical) development planning · Bauleitplanung f

planning for schools, school planning · Schulplanung f

planning for young people · Jugendplanung f

planning framework · Planungsrahmen m

planning from-the-bottom-up, planning from below, backward planning · Planung f von unten

planning from-the-top-down, forward planning, advance planning · Vorausplanung f, Planung von oben

planning function · Planungsfunktion f

planning gain, planning profit · Planungsgewinn m, Planungsprofit m

(planning) game · (Plan)Spiel n

planning game simulation, game simulation, gaming simulation · (Plan)Spielsimulation f, Hybridspiel n

(planning) game simulation model, gaming simulation model · (Plan)Spielsimulationsmodell n, Hybridspielmodell

planning goal · Planungsoberziel n, Planungszielnorm f

planning group, planning team · Planungsgruppe f

planning guide-line · Planungsrichtlinie f

planning having effect in law, planning binding in law, planning having the force of law, legally binding planning · rechtsverbindliche Planung f, Planfeststellung

planning hearing · Planungsanhörung f

planning inquiry commission · Planungsuntersuchungskommission f

planning instrument, planning document · Planungsunterlage f, Planungsdokument n

planning intent(ion) · Planungsabsicht f

planning law · Planungsrecht n

planning law → planning (enabling) act

planning law committee · Planungsrechtsausschuß m

planning (legal) norm, planning law rule, planning law norm, planning rule (of law), planning norm of law, planning legal rule · Planungs(rechts)norm f

planning legislation, legislation of planning, planning lawmaking, lawmaking of planning · Planungsgesetzgebung f

planning level, stage of planning, level of planning, planning stage · Planungsebene f, Planungsstufe f [Fehlbenennung]

planning limitation, planning constraint, planning restriction, planning restraint · Planungsbeschränkung f, Planungsbegrenzung, Planungseinschränkung, Planungszwang m

planning literature · Planungsliteratur f, Planungsschrifttum n

planning map · Arbeitskarte f [Für Eintragung bestimmter Inhalte hergestellte Umriß-, Gemeindegrenzen-, Flur-, Höhenlinien- oder Gewässernetzkarte, auch farbschwache Graudrucke]

planning measure · planerische Maßnahme f

planning mechanism, machinery of planning · Planungsmechanismus m

planning method — planning stage

planning method, method of planning · Planmethode *f*, Planungsmethode, Plan(ungs)verfahren *n*

planning mistake · Planungsirrtum *m*

planning norm → planning (legal) norm

planning obligation, obligation to plan · Planungsverpflichtung *f*

planning office · Planungsstelle *f*

planning official, planning officer · Planungsbeamte *m*

planning of land use, land use planning · Bodennutzungsplanung *f*, Landnutzungsplanung, Flächennutzungsplanung, FNP, vorbereitende Bauleitplanung; Flächenwidmungsplanung [*Österreich*]; Aufbauplanung [*veraltete Benennung*]

planning of lines · Leitungsplanung *f*

planning of locations, planning of sites, location(al) planning, site planning · Standortplanung *f*

planning of sites, location(al) planning, site planning, planning of locations · Standortplanung *f*, Lageplanung *f*

planning of spending, spending planning · Ausgabenplanung *f*

planning of structure, planning of work, planning of physical facility · Bauwerkplanung *f*, Planung eines Bauwerkes, Planung einer Baulichkeit, Planung einer (baulichen) Anlage; Bauteplanung [*Schweiz*]

planning of the structure (of a building) · Tragwerkplanung *f* [*Unter ,,Tragwerk" ist hier der lasttragende Teil eines Gebäudes zu verstehen*]

planning of (the) execution, planning of (the) performance, execution planning, performance planning · Ausführungsplanung *f*

planning of work → planning of structure

planning on a higher than local level, higher level planning · überörtliche Planung *f*

planning optimization · Planungsoptimierung *f*

planning organization · (öffentlicher) Planungsträger *m* [*Bundesbaugesetz § 4, Abs. 5; § 7. Laut Bundesbaugesetz sind es nicht Gemeinden, Planungsverbände, Gebietskörperschaften oder Verbände mit gemeindlicher Willensbildung, sondern eine Behörde oder Stelle, die Träger öffentlicher Belange ist*]

planning-orien(ta)ted, planning-related · planungsbezogen, planungsorientiert

planning participation, participation in planning · Planungsbeteiligung *f*, Planungsmitwirkung, Planungsteilnahme *f*

planning participator · Planungsbeteiligte *m*

planning permission application, planning permission request, application for planning permission, request for planning permission · Planungserlaubnisantrag *m*, Planungserlaubnisgesuch *n*, Planungsgenehmigungsantrag, Planungsgenehmigungsgesuch

planning phase · Planungsphase *f*

planning power, planning authority · Planungskompetenz *f*, Planungsmacht *f*, Planungsgewalt *f*, Planungshoheit *f*

planning practice · Planungswesen *n*

planning prescription, planning regulation · Planungsvorschrift *f*

planning principle, principle of planning · Planungsgrundsatz *m*, Planungsprinzip *n*

planning procedure · Planungsverfahren *n*

planning process, process of planning · Planungsvorgang *m*

planning profession · Planerberuf *m*

planning profit, planning gain · Planungsgewinn *m*, Planungsprofit *m*

planning proposal · Planungsvorschlag *m*

planning region · Planungsregion *f*, Planungsraum *m*

planning regulation, planning prescription · Planungsvorschrift *f*

planning-related, planning-orien(ta)ted · planungsbezogen, planungsorientiert

planning requirement · Planungsanforderung *f*

planning research · Planungsforschung *f*

planning responsibility · Planungsverantwortung *f*

planning restriction, planning restraint, planning limitation, planning constraint · Planungsbeschränkung *f*, Planungsbegrenzung, Planungseinschränkung, Planungszwang *m*

planning rule (of law), planning norm of law, planning legal rule, planning (legal) norm, planning law rule, planning law norm · Planungs(rechts)norm *f*

planning scheme, scheme of planning · Planaufstellung *f*

planning school · Planerschule *f*

planning science, science of planning · Planungswissenschaft *f*

planning sector, planning field · Planungssektor *m*

planning sequence · Planungsfolge *f*

planning staff · Planungspersonal *n*

planning stage, planning level, stage of planning, level of planning · Planungsebene *f*; Planungsstufe *f* [*Fehlbenennung*]

planning status — plant standard

planning status, status of planning · Planungsstatus *m*

planning statute → planning (enabling) act

planning strategy, strategy of planning · Planungsstrategie *f*

planning structure · Planungsstruktur *f*, Planungsaufbau *m*, Planungsgefüge *n*, Planungszusammensetzung *f*

planning subcommission · Planungsunterkommission *f*

planning sub-committee · Planungsunterausschuß *m*

planning supervision, planning superintendence, supervision of planning, superintendence of planning · Planungsaufsicht *f*, Planungsüberwachung *f*

planning survey · Planungsübersicht *f*

planning system · Planungssystem *n*

planning team, planning group · Planungsgruppe *f*

planning technician · Planungstechniker *m*

planning technologist · Planungstechnologe *m*

planning technology, technology of planning · Planungstechnologie *f*

planning territory, planning area · Planungsgebiet *n*

planning theory, theory of planning · Planungstheorie *f*

planning thought · Planungsgedanke *m*

planning to keep land free · Freihalteplanung *f*

planning trend · Planungsrichtung *f*

planning unit · Planungseinheit *f*

planning value equalization · Planungswertausgleich *m*

planning work(s) · Planarbeit(en) *f (pl)*, Planungsarbeit(en)

plan of accumulation, accumulation plan · Ansammlungsplan *m*, Anhäufungsplan, Aufhäufungsplan

plan of building lines, building line plan · Fluchtlinienplan *m*, Baufluchtlinienplan

plan of (division into) lots, plan of (sub)division (of land(s)), plan of lotting, lotting plan, plan of estate lots, (sub)division plan · Parzell(is)ierungsplan *m*

plan of income and expenditure, budget(ary) plan · Wirtschaftsplan *m*, Haushalt(s)plan *m*, Budget *n*

plan of land use, outline development plan, land use plan · Aufbauplan *m* [*veraltete Benennung*]; Flächenwidmungsplan *m* [*Österreich*]; vorbereitender Bauleitplan *m*, Flächennutzungsplan *m*, Landnutzungsplan *m*, Bodennutzungsplan *m*, FNP *m*

plan of previous situations → (physical) plan of previous situations

plan pattern, plan scheme · Planmuster *n*, Planschema *n*

plan period · Planzeitraum *m*

plan publicity, publicity of a plan · Planauslegung *f*, Auslegung eines Planes, Planoffenlage *f*, Offenlage eines Planes

plan realization, implementation of (a) plan, realization of (a) plan, plan implementation · Planverwirklichung *f*, Plandurchführung

plan-realizing, plan-implementing · planverwirklichend

plan review · Planfortschreibung *f*

plant [*By plant = Betrieb is not meant an enterprise, since an enterprise does not need to be confined to a local unit*] · Anlage *f*, Werk *n*, Betrieb *m*

plant and machinery · Anlagegüter *n pl*

plantation agriculture, plantation system [*crops for sale*] · Landwirtschaft *f* für Fremdverbrauch

plant cover, plant vegetation · Pflanzenbewuchs *m*, Pflanzenkleid *n*, Pflanzendecke *f*

plant ecology · Pflanzenökologie *f*

planted area · bewachsene Fläche *f*

plant geography · Pflanzengeographie *f*, Pflanzenerdkunde *f*

plant growing on debris · Schuttpflanze *f* [*z. B. Brennessel, Kamille, Schierling, Stechapfel oder Vogelmiere*]

plant industry · Pflanzenbau *m*

planting · Bepflanzung *f*

planting · Anpflanzen *n*

planting of (a) model, model planting · Aufstellen *n* eines Modells

plant location, plant site · Anlagenstandort *m*

plant-orien(ta)ted, plant-related · werkbezogen, werkorientiert, anlagenbezogen, anlagenorientiert

plant overhead cost(s), plant overhead(s), general overhead(s), general overhead cost(s) · Geschäftsgemeinkosten *f*, Geschäftsgeneralkosten

plant-related, plant-orien(ta)ted · werkbezogen, werkorientiert, anlagenbezogen, anlagenorientiert

plant sale · Pflanzenverkauf *m*

plant site, plant location · Anlagenstandort *m*

plant standard, output rate per machine hour · Maschinenstundenleistung *f*

plant vegetation, plant cover · Pflanzenbewuchs *m*, Pflanzenkleid *n*, Pflanzendecke *f*

plastering and lathing contractor · Putzunternehmer *m*

platform of policy · Ausgangsbasis *f* [*Öffentlichkeitsarbeit*]

play-debt · Spielschuld *f*

playground · Spielplatz *m*

plaza, square · Gartenplatz *m*, Schmuckplatz

plaza → (village) plaza

plaza hamlet, green hamlet · Angerweiler *m*, Platzweiler

plaza settlement · Platz(an)sied(e)lung *f*

plaza-type shopping centre, introvert-type shopping centre (Brit.); introvert-type shopping center, plaza-type shopping center (US) · Kern-Einkaufszentrum *n*

plaza village, green village · Angerdorf *n*, Platzdorf

plea [*The defendant's answer of fact to the plaintiff's declaration*]; issue [*Die Benennung ,,issue" bedeutet sowohl den Prozeßinhalt als auch die Verteidigung, vermutlich, weil erst diese den Streitinhalt zur vollen Feststellung bringt, daher sie denn den Ausgang der Verhandlungen darüber, welches Recht Prozeßgegenstand sein soll, bildet*] · Verteidigung *f*

plea [*Before the Judicature Acts 1873*] · Verteidigungsschrift *f* [*Gegen die vorgebrachten Tatsachen*]

plea, cause, (court) action, (law)suit; writ [*In old English law, "writ" is used as equivalent to "action", hence writs are sometimes divided into real, personal, and mixed. It is not uncommon to call a proceeding in a common law court an action(-at-law), and one in an equity court a (law)suit, but this is not a necessary distinction*] · (Gerichts)Klage *f*

plea at common law, common law (court) action, common law (law)suit, common law cause, common law plea, (court) action at common law, cause at common law, (law)suit at common law · Klage *f* nach gemeinem Recht, gemeinrechtliche Klage

plea book, cause list, cause book, register of pleading actions, judg(e)ment docket, judgment book, plea list · Klagenverzeichnis *n*, Klagenregister *n*, Prozeßverzeichnis, Prozeßregister

to plead; placitare [*Latin*] · plädieren

plea de bonis asportatis, (court) action de bonis asportatis, (law)suit de bonis asportatis, cause de bonis asportatis · Klage *f* wegen rechtswidriger (Besitz)Entziehung einer beweglichen Sache

pleader → (special) pleader

to plead guilty · sich für schuldig erklären

to plead in bar · sich zur Anschuldigung äußern [*Strafprozeß*]

pleading · Plädieren *n*

pleading [*Pleadings are written statements delivered alternately by the parties to one another until the questions of facts and law to be decided in the action have been ascertained*] · Parteischrift(satz) *f*, *(m)*, vorbereitender Schriftsatz, vorbereitende Schrift

pleading by word of mouth, statement, (oral) pleading, verbal pleading · Plädoyer *n*

pleading default, default of pleading · Säumnis *f*, *n* wegen unterlassener Klagebegründung, Versäumnis *f* wegen unterlassener Klagebegründung, (Ver)Säumnis wegen Nichtablieferung einer Klagebegründung

pleading in equity, proceeding equitable in nature, equity pleading · Billigkeitsverfahren *n*, Billigkeitsrechtverfahren

pleadings; placita [*Latin*] · beid(er)seitige schriftsätzliche Vorbereitungen *fpl* einer mündlichen Verhandlung, zweiseitige schriftsätzliche Vorbereitungen einer mündlichen Verhandlung

plea for an account, (court) action for an account, (law)suit for an account, cause for an account · Abrechnungsklage *f*, Klage auf Abrechnung [*Billigkeitsrecht*]

plea for breach of contract, (court) action for breach of contract, (law)suit for breach of contract, cause for breach of contract · Vertragsbruchklage *f*

plea for delivery, (court) action for delivery, (law)suit for delivery, cause for delivery · Nichtlieferungsklage *f*, Klage wegen Nichtlieferung

plea for dissolution, (law)suit for dissolution, (court) action for dissolution, cause for dissolution · Auflösungsklage *f*

plea for exemption from liability, (court) action for exemption from liability, (law)suit for exemption from liability, cause for exemption from liability · negative Feststellungsklage *f*

plea for intrusion → plea for trespass

plea for money had and received, (court) action for money had and received, (law)suit for money had and received, cause for money had and received · Geldrückerstattungsklage *f*

plea for payment, (court) action for payment, (law)suit for payment, cause for payment · Zahlungsklage *f*

plea for recovery, (law)suit for recovery, cause for reimbursement, cause for restitution, cause for refunding, plea for reimbursement, plea for refunding, plea for restitution, (law)suit for reimbursement, (law)suit for refunding, (law)suit for restitution, (court) action for reimbursement, (court) action for restitution, (court) action for refunding, (court) action for recovery, cause for recovery · Abgeltungsklage *f*, Ersetzungsklage, Erstattungsklage, Vergütungsklage

plea for redemption, (court) action for redemption, cause for redemption, (law)suit for redemption · Klage *f* auf Freigabe von Sicherheiten, Sicherheit(en)freigabeklage

plea for reimbursement, plea for refunding, plea for restitution, (law)suit for reimbursement, (law)suit for refunding, (law)suit for restitution, (court) action for reimbursement, (court) action for refunding, (court) action for recovery, cause for recovery, plea for recovery, (law)suit for recovery, cause for reimbursement, cause for restitution, cause for refunding · Abgeltungsklage *f*, Ersetzungsklage, Erstattungsklage, Vergütungsklage

plea for removal, (court) action for removal, (law)suit for removal, cause for removal · Beseitigungsklage *f*

plea for specific performance, (court) action for specific performance, (law)suit for specific performance, (court) action for completion of contract, (law)suit for completion of contract, cause for completion of contract, plea for completion of contract, cause for specific performance · (Vertrags)Erfüllungsklage *f*, Naturalerfüllungsklage

plea for the recovery of land, (court) action for the recovery of land, (law)suit for the recorvery of land, cause for the recovery of land [*The mixed action at common law to recover the possession of land (which is real), and damages and cost(s) for the wrongful withholding of the land (which are personal)*] · (Immobilien)Besitzklage *f*, Liegenschaftsbesitzklage, Immobiliarbesitzklage, Grund(stücks)besitzklage, eigentliche Besitzklage, Klage aus (widerrechtlicher) Besitzentziehung, (D)Ejektionsklage, possessorische Klage in bezug auf Immobilien, Delogierungsklage [*Als uneigentliche Besitzklage kann diese Klage auch als Räumungsklage des Vermieters gegen den Mieter angewendet werden*]

plea for (the tort of) deceit, (court) action for (the tort of) deceit, (law)suit for (the tort of) deceit, cause for (the tort of) deceit · Betrugsklage *f*

plea for tort, plea in tort, (court) action for tort, (court) action in tort, (law)suit for tort, (law)suit in tort, cause for tort, cause in tort · Deliktklage *f*

plea for trespass, plea for intrusion, (court) action for trespass, (court) action for intrusion, cause for trespass, cause for intrusion, (law)suit for trespass, (law)suit for intrusion · (Besitz)Verletzungsklage *f* wegen Eindringen, (Besitz)Störungsklage wegen Eindringen, (Besitz)Beeinträchtigungsklage wegen Eindringen

plea for unjust retention, plea for unjust detainment, plea for unjust detainer, cause for unjust detention, cause for unjust retention, cause for unjust detainment, cause for unjust detainer, (law)suit for unjust detention, (law)suit for unjust retention, (law)suit for unjust detainment, (law)suit for unjust detainer, (court) action of detinue, plea of detinue, (law)suit of detinue, cause of detinue, (court) action for unjust detention, (court) action for unjust retention, (court) action for unjust detainment, (court) action for unjust detainer, plea for unjust detention · Klage *f* wegen ungerechtfertigter Vorenthaltung, Klage wegen ungerechtfertigter Zurück(be)haltung, Klage wegen ungerechtfertigter Einbehaltung, Klage wegen ungerechtfertigter Retention, Klage wegen ungerechtfertigtem Einbehalt, Klage wegen ungerechtfertigtem Vorenthalt

plea founded on contract, (court) action founded on contract, (law)suit founded on contract, cause founded on contract · Entschädigungsklage *f* ex contractu vel quasi, Schadenersatzklage ex contractu vel quasi, Forderungsklage ex contractu vel quasi, Personenklage ex contractu vel quasi; Personalklage ex contractu vel quasi [*Fehlbenennung*]

plea founded on tort, (court) action founded on tort, (law)suit founded on tort, cause founded on tort · Entschädigungsklage *f* im engeren Sinne, Schadenersatzklage im engeren Sinne, Forderungsklage im engeren Sinne, Personenklage im engeren Sinne; Personalklage im engeren Sinne [*Fehlbenennung*]

plea in abatement · Parteieinrede *f* [*Einrede in bezug auf Parteifähigkeit des Gegners oder unrichtige Zuziehung oder Weglassung einer Partei*]

plea in bar, peremptory plea [*A plea founded on some matter tending to impeach the right of action*] · perem(p)torische Einrede *f*, vernichtende Einrede, aufhebende Einrede, zwingende Einrede

plea in error, (court) action in error, (law)suit in error, cause in error · Nichtigkeitsklage *f*, Revisionsklage

plea in personam → personal (court) action

plea in suspension of the action — plea personal

plea in suspension of the action, summons to stay proceeding · Verteidigung *f* auf zeitweise Abweisung der Klage

plea in tort, (court) action for tort, (court) action in tort, (law)suit for tort, (law)suit in tort, cause for tort, cause in tort, plea for tort · Deliktklage *f*

plea list, plea book, cause list, cause book, register of pleading actions, judg(e)ment docket, judgment book · Klagenverzeichnis *n*, Klagenregister *n*, Prozeßverzeichnis, Prozeßregister

plea of abatement, abatement plea · Antrag *m* auf Niederschlagung

plea of account, (court) action of account, cause of account, (law)suit of account · Klage *f* auf Rechnungslegung, Rechnungslegungsklage

plea of advowson, (court) action of patronage, (court) action of advowson, (law)suit of patronage, (law)suit of advowson, cause of patronage, cause of advowson, plea of patronage · Patronats(recht)klage *f*

(plea of) assumpsit, (court) action of assumpsit, (law)suit of assumpsit, cause of assumpsit · Nichteinhaltungsklage *f*, Nichterfüllungsklage [*Schadenersatzklage wegen schuldhafter Nichterfüllung eines formlosen mündlich oder schriftlich gegebenem Versprechen*]

plea of debt, (court) action of debt, cause of debt, (law)suit of debt · Schuld(en)klage *f* [*Zur Einklagung einer Schuld*]

plea of deceit, (court) action of deceit, (law)suit of deceit, cause of deceit · Klage *f* wegen Täuschung, Täuschungsklage

plea of detinue, (law)suit of detinue, (court) action of detinue, cause of detinue [*An action by a plaintiff who seeks to recover goods in specie, or on failure thereof the value, and also damages for the detention*] · Klage *f* auf Wiedererlangung einer beweglichen Sache und Schadenersatz, Klage auf Herausgabe einer beweglichen Sache und Schadenersatz

plea of devastation, (court) action of estrepement, (court) action of devastation, (law)suit of estrepement, (law)suit of devastation, cause of estrepement, cause of devastation, plea of estrepement · Verwüstungsklage *f*

plea of equity, equitable (court) action, equitable (law)suit, equitable cause, (court) action of equity, cause of equity, (law)suit of equity, equitable plea · Billigkeitsklage *f*, Billigkeitsrechtklage, Klage nach Billigkeit(srecht)

plea of estrepement, plea of devastation, (court) action of estrepement, (court) action of devastation, (law)suit of estrepement, cause of estrepement, cause of devastation · Verwüstungsklage *f*

plea of eviction, (court) action of eviction, (law)suit of eviction, cause of eviction · Grund(stücks)besitzklage *f* wegen Grund(stücks)besitzentziehung

plea of infancy, infancy plea · Einrede *f* der Minderjährigkeit

plea of injunction, (court) action of injunction, (law)suit of injunction, cause of injunction · Verfügungsklage *f*

plea of mistake, (court) action of mistake, (law)suit of mistake, cause of mistake · Irrtumsklage *f*

plea of patronage, plea of advowson, (court) action of patronage, (court) action of advowson, (law)suit of patronage, (law)suit of advowson, cause of patronage, cause of advowson · Patronats(recht)klage *f*

plea of possessory right, (court) action of possessory right, (law)suit of possessory right, cause of possessory right · Besitzrechtklage *f*

plea of replevin, (court) action of replevin, (law)suit of replevin, cause of replevin · Klage *f* auf Wiedererlangung einer beweglichen Sache und Schadenersatz bei unzulässiger Selbstpfändung, Klage auf Rückgabe einer selbstgepfändeten Sache

plea of the Crown [*England*] · Strafverfahren *n*

plea of transumpt, cause of transumpt, (law)suit of transumpt, transumpt, (court) action of transumpt [*Scots law. An action brought for the purpose of obtaining transumpt(s)*] · Klage *f* auf Schriftstückabschrift

plea of trover (and conversion), (court) action of trover (and conversion), cause of trover (and conversion), (law)suit of trover (and conversion) · Bereicherungsklage *f*, Schatzfundklage, Deliktsklage wegen Unterschlagung, Unterschlagungsklage [*Klage auf Schadenersatz für die Besitzentziehung von beweglichen Sachen (= goods)*]

plea on the case, (law)suit on the case, (court) action on the case, cause on the case · tatsächlich angestellte Klage *f*

plea on trespass, cause on trespass, (court) action on trespass, (law)suit on trespass · Rechtsverletzungsklage *f*, Klage wegen Rechtsverletzung

plea per se, (court) action per se, cause per se, (law)suit per se · Klage *f* die nicht von einem Schadensnachweis abhängt

plea personal, personal (court) action, personal plea, personal (law)suit, personal cause; personal writ [*In old Eng-*

lish law]; (court) action personal, (law)suit personal, cause personal · Entschädigungsklage, Forderungsklage, Personenklage [*Fehlbenennung: Personalklage*]

pleasure area, pleasure territory · Vergnügungsgebiet *n*

pleasure boat · Vergnügungsboot *n*

pleasure driving, driving for pleasure · Autofahren *n* zum Vergnügen

pleasure garden, ornamental garden · Ziergarten *m*, Schmuckgarten

pleasure ground · Vergnügungsgelände *n*

pleasure navigation · Vergnügungsschiffahrt *f*

pleasure territory, pleasure area · Vergnügungsgebiet *n*

plea to gain an injunction, action to gain an injunction, cause to gain an injunction, (law)suit to gain an injunction · Unterlassungsklage *f*

plea to quiet title, (court) action to quiet title, (law)suit to quiet title, cause to quiet title · Klage *f* nach § 256 ZPO, Feststellungsklage

plea to the jursidiction, motion to set aside the service of the writ · Verteidigung *f* auf Unzuständigkeit

pledge, surety, insurer of a debt, guarantor, cautioner [*The party who expresses his willingness to answer for the debt, default, or obligation of another. The word "surety" is sometimes used interchangeably for the word "guarantor"; but, strictly speaking, a "surety" is one who is bound with the principal debtor upon the original contract, the same as if he had made the contract himself, while a "guarantor" is bound upon a separate contract to make good in case the principal debtor fails. The guarantor is therefore an insurer of the solvency of the debtor. A surety is held primarily liable on an instrument while a guarantor is held secondarily liable on it; that is, the surety agrees that he will pay the obligation in any event, while the guarantor merely agrees that he will pay the obligation if the principal debtor fails to pay*] · Bürge *m*

pledge [*Pawnee's rights over an article taken in pawn*] · Pfandrecht, subjektives Pfandrecht *n*

pledge, promise, commitment · Versprechen *n*, Verpflichtung *f*

pledge contract, pawn contract, contract of pawn, contract of pledge · Pfandvertrag *m*

pledged article, pledge(d object), pawned article, pawned object, article pawned, article pledged, object pawned, object pledged, pawn, vadium · Pfand *n*, Pfandstück *n*, verpfändeter Gegenstand *m*, gegebenes (Mobiliar)Pfand, Pfandsache *f*

pledged share · gebundener Anteil *m*, verpfändeter Anteil, Anteil eines borgenden Mitgliedes, Borganteil, Verpfändungsanteil [*Bausparkasse*]

pledgee, holder of a pledge, mortgagee, pledge holder, pawnee, holder of a pawn, pawn holder [*The person who receives the security and lends the money to the pledg(e)or*] · Pfandgläubiger *m*, Pfandnehmer, Pfandbesitzer, Pfandhalter, Pfandinhaber, Sicherungsnehmer

pledgee having the right to use the article pledged, pawnee having the right to use the article pledged, (mort)gagee having the right to use the article pledged · nutzungsberechtigter Pfandgläubiger *m*, nutzungsberechtigter Pfandnehmer

pledge of chattels, pawn of chattels · Fahrnispfand *n*, Fahrhabepfand, Mobiliarpfand, Mobilienpfand

pledge of personal property, pawn of personal property · Verpfändung *f* von Mobilien, Mobiliarverpfändung

pledg(e)or, pledger, pledging party, mortgagor, mortgager · Verpfänder *m*, Pfandgeber

to pledge (property as security), to hypothecate · verpfänden

pledger, mortgager, mortgagor, mortgage debtor, pawner · Pfandschuldner *m*

pledge taken in distress, pledge taken in distraint, pawn taken in distress, pawn taken in distraint · außergerichtlich gepfändete Sache *f*, selbstgepfändete Sache *f*, Selbstpfand *n*

plot access, access to a plot · Grundstückszufahrt *f*

plot area, (land) parcel area · Grundstücksfläche *f*

plot bound to a certain architect, parcel bound to a certain architect [*for (physical) development*] · architektengebundenes Grundstück *n*

plot neighbour (Brit.); parcel neighbour, parcel neighbor, plot neighbor (US) · Grundstücksnachbar *m*

plot of arable land; cultura [*Latin*], parcel of arable land · Ackerstück *n*

plot of building land → building (estate) parcel

plot (of land), plot of ground, piece of land, piece of ground, parcel (of land), parcel of ground, land plot, land parcel, estate, (real) estate parcel, (real) estate plot, real property parcel, real property plot, realty parcel, realty plot [*A parcel of land consisting of one or more lots*] ·

Grundstück n (im tatsächlichen Sinn) [*Diesem steht das Grundstück im katastertechnischen Sinn und im Rechtssinn gegenüber. Ein Grundstück muß mindestens ein Flurstück umfassen. Es kann daher nicht aus nur einem Teil eines Flurstückes bestehen*]

plot (of land) accessible by public right of way, parcel (of land) accessible by public right of way · anliegendes Grundstück n, Anliegergrundstück [*Grundstück an einer Verkehrsfläche, die Zugang und/oder Zufahrt zu dem Grundstück ermöglicht*]

plot (of land) for compensation, parcel (of land) for compensation · Abfindungsgrundstück n [*Flurbereinigung*]

plot (of land) for exchange, plot (of land) for barter, parcel (of land) for exchange, parcel (of land) for barter, piece of land for exchange, piece of land for barter, (land) parcel for exchange, land parcel for barter, land plot for exchange, land plot for barter · Tauschgrundstück n

plot (of land) with building(s), piece of land with building(s), parcel (of land) with building(s) · Gebäudegrundstück n

plot of usufruct, parcel of usufruct, piece of usufruct · (Frucht)Genußgrundstück n, Nießbrauchgrundstück

plot-owner → (real) property owner

plot pattern, parcel pattern, plot scheme, parcel scheme · Grundstücksschema n, Grundstücksmuster n

plot-proprietor → (real) property owner

plot ratio · Dichtequotient m [*Bei Geschäfts- und Bürobauten, analog GFZ. Verhältnis von Bruttogeschoßfläche zu Bruttobauland, d. h. Bauland einschließlich der halben Breite angrenzender Straßen, aber ohne örtlichen Erschließungsstraßen*]

plot scheme, parcel scheme, plot pattern, parcel pattern · Grundstücksschema n, Grundstücksmuster n

plot side, side of parcel, parcel side, side (of plot) · (Grundstücks)Seite f

plottage, assembling real properties, assembling (real) estates, assembling lands, assembling realties, assemblage · Grund(stücks)zusammenschreibung f, Bodenzusammenschreibung, (Land)Zusammenschreibung

plotter · automatisches Zeichengerät n, Plotter m, Zeichenautomat m

plotter cartography · Plotterkartographie f, Zeichenautomatkartographie, Kartographie mit automatischem Zeichengerät

plotting increment [*Appreciation in unit value created by joining smaller ownerships into one ownership*] · Wertzuwachs m durch (Land)Zusammenschreibung

plotting scale, compilation scale · Zeichenmaßstab m, Arbeitsmaßstab [*Kartographie*]

plotting to scale, scale plotting · maßstabsgerechtes Auftragen n

(plot) utilization · Ausnutzung f, bauliche Ausnutzung, (bauliche) Grundstücksausnutzung [*Sie wird durch Geschoßflächenzahl, Grundflächenzahl und Vollgeschoßzahl bestimmt*]

plough-back · Reinvestierung f von Kapitalerträgen

plough-bote [*A tenant's right to take wood for the making and repair of ploughs, carts, harrows, forks, etc.*] · Beholzungsrecht n für landwirtschaftliche Geräte, Holzbezugsrecht für landwirtschaftliche Geräte, Pflugzubuße f

ploughed off furrow (Brit.); plowed off furrow (US) · Abfurche f

plough-gate [*Scotland*]; car(r)ucate, plough-land, caruk [*A measure of land, varying with the nature of the soil etc., being as much as could be tilled with one plough with its team of 8 oxen in a year*] · Pflugland n

ploughing lot (Brit); plowing lot (US) · Pflugparzelle f

ploughing off, ploughing away (Brit.); plowing off, plowing away (US); encroaching furrows, incroaching furrows · Abackern n, Abpflügen, Abfurchen, Wegackern

ploughman (Brit.); plowman (US); minator carucae [*Latin*] · Pflüger m

to plough off, to plough away (Brit.); to plow off, to plow away (US); to encroach furrows, to incroach furrows · abackern, abpflügen, abfurchen, wegackern [*Durch übergreifendes Pflügen ein Stück Land wegnehmen*]

plowed off furrow (US) → ploughed off furrow

plowing lot (US); ploughing lot (Brit) · Pflugparzelle f

plowman (US); minator carucae [*Latin*]; ploughman (Brit.) · Pflüger m

to plow off, to plow away (US); to encroach furrows, to incroach furrows; to plough off, to plough away (Brit.) · abackern, abpflügen, abfurchen, wegackern [*Durch übergreifendes Pflügen ein Stück Land wegnehmen*]

pluck-in city, pluck-in town · Stadt f mit versetzbaren Wohneinheiten

plumbing contractor · Klempnerunternehmer m

pluralistic society · pluralistische Gesellschaft f

plurality · relatives Mehr n

plurality of creditors — police notice

plurality of creditors · Gesamtgläubigerschaft *f*

plurality of heirs, community of heirs · Erbengemeinschaft *f*

plurality vote · relative Stimmenmehrheit *f*

plutocracy [*A state in which government is in the hands of the wealthy*] · Plutokratie *f*, Plutokratenherrschaft *f*

pluvious policy, rain insurance policy · Regenversicherungspolice *f*

P.O., purchase order · Einkaufsauftrag *m*, Kaufauftrag

poaching · Wilddieberei *f*, Wildfrevel *m*

poaching in daytime, daytime poaching · Tagwilddieberei *f*, Tagwildfrevel *m*

poaching in nighttime, night poaching · Nachtwilddieberei *f*, Nachtwildfrevel *m*

poaching prevention act, poaching prevention law, poaching prevention statute · Wildfrevelgesetz *n*

poaching prevention lawmaking, poaching prevention legislation · Wildfrevelgesetzgebung *f*

to pocket [*(payment) discount*] · einstekken [*Skonto*]

pocket-sheriff · Sheriff *m* durch Kabinettsorder

point → (position) point

point diagram map · Punktdiagrammkarte *f*, Positionsdiagrammkarte

point in dispute, contention, contentious issue, issue (of fact) · Streitfrage *f*, Streitpunkt *m*

point of employment, point of work(ing), work(ing) point, employment point, job point · Arbeitsstätte *f*, Beschäftigungsstätte [*Fehlbenennung: Arbeitsplatz m*]

point of law, law question, law point, question of law · Rechtsfrage *f*

point of minimum cost(s) · Kostenminimalpunkt *m*

point of minimum transport cost(s) · Transportminimalpunkt *m* [*Der Ort kleinster Gesamtfracht je Stück*]

point of saturation, saturation point · Sättigungspunkt *m*

point of time · Zeitpunkt *n*

point of work(ing) → point of employment

point output · einmaliger Ausstoß *m*

point pattern, point scheme · Punktmuster *n*, Punktschema *n*

point position map · Punktpositionskarte *f*

point sampling · Punktstichprobe *f* [*Statistik*]

point scheme, point pattern · Punktmuster *n*, Punktschema *n*

point set, set of points · Punktmenge *f*, Punktwolke *f*

point symbol map · Ortskartenzeichenkarte *f*, Ortssignaturenkarte

polarization, backwash effect · Entzugswirkung *f*, Konterwirkung [*räumliches Entwick(e)lungsgefälle*]

polarized region · Polregion *f*

pole environment · Polumland *n*

pole of growth, growth pole · Wachstumspol *m*

police act, police law, police statute · Polizeigesetz *n*

police administration · Polizeiverwaltung *f*

police administration act, police administration law, police administration statute · Polizeiverwaltungsgesetz *n*

police administration law · Polizeiverwaltungsrecht *n*

police agency, police office · Polizei(dienst)stelle *f*

police authority · Polizeibehörde *f*

police court, P., petty court, summary court, registrar's court, court of summary jurisdiction, court of request, registrary's court, court of conscience · Bagatellgericht *n*, Friedensgericht für kleine Straf- und Zivilsachen, Polizeigericht, Ortsgericht für gering(fügig)e Schuldklagen [*in England*]

police court [*obsolete; stipendiary magistrate's court* [*A petty sessional court, held in London and in other cities by a magistrate*] · Polizeigericht *n*, Friedensgericht unter Vorsitz eines berufsmäßigen Friedensrichters

police department · Polizeiabteilung *f*

police discretion · polizeiliches Ermessen *n*

police division (Brit.); precinct (US) · Polizeirevier *n*

police duty · Polizeidienst *m*

police force · Polizeimacht *f*

police general clause · polizeirechtliche Generalklausel *f*

police grant(-in-aid) · Polizeizuschuß *m*

police law, police statute, police act · Polizeigesetz *n*

police law · Polizeirecht *n*

policeman, constable · Polizist *m*, Polizeibeamte *m*; Schutzmann *m* [*volkstümlich*]

police notice [*In the system of police registration of arrivals and departures*] · polizeiliche Anmeldung *f*

police office, police agency · Polizei(dienst)stelle *f*

police order · Polizeibefehl *m*, Polizeiverfügung *f*, Polizeigebot *n*, Polizeianordnung *f*

police power, peace conservation, conservation of the peace [*The power that enables the legislature to pass laws for the protection of the public health, morals, and safety, or laws which are otherwise very clearly for the general welfare*] · Ordnungsrecht *n*, Friedensbewahrung *f* [*Mit dem deutschen Wort „Polizeigewalt", auch der älteren Zeit, läßt sich dieses Institut „police power" kaum vergleichen. Es dient viel zu einseitig nur der Rechtfertigung der gesetzgeberischen Maßnahmen der Staatsgewalt*]

police-rate, watch rate · (örtliche) Polizeisteuer *f*, lokale Polizeisteuer, gemeindliche Polizeisteuer, kommunale Polizeisteuer

police registration · polizeiliche Registrierung *f*

police statute, police act, police law · Polizeigesetz *n*

police supervision · Polizeiaufsicht *f*

policitor, proctor, procurator, attorney [*A manager of another person's affair*] · Prokurator *m*

policy goal, goal (of policy), target goal · Zielnorm *f*, Oberziel *n*, übergeordnetes Ziel

policy goal conflict, goal (of policy) conflict, target goal conflict · Ziel(norm)konflikt *m*, Oberzielkonflikt, Konflikt übergeordneter Ziele

policy goal formation, goal (of policy) formation, target goal formation · Ziel(norm)bildung *f*, Oberzielbildung

policy goal research, target goal research, goal (of policy) research · Ziel(norm)forschung *f*, Oberzielforschung

policy goal system, target goal system · Zielsystem *n*

policyholder · Policeninhaber *m*

(policy) objective · (strukturpolitisches) Entwick(e)lungsziel *n*

(policy) objective function [*Linear programming relates to problems where the objective is to maximise or minimise some linear function, called the objective function, subject to certain linear inequalities (the constraints)*] · (strukturpolitische) Entwick(e)lungszielfunktion *f*

policy of insurance, insurance policy · Versicherungspolice *f*

policy of law, legal policy · Rechtspolitik *f*

policy of marine insurance, policy of sea insurance · Seeversicherungspolice *f*

policy of resources of land(s), land(s) reserve policy, resource-of-land(s) policy · Bodenreservepolitik *f*, Bodenvorratpolitik, Flächenreservepolitik, Flächenvorratpolitik, Landreservepolitik, Landvorratpolitik

policy of sea insurance, policy of marine insurance · Seeversicherungspolice *f*

policy research · Grundsatzfragenforschung *f*

policy statement · Grundsatzerklärung *f*

political arithmetics · politische Arithmetik *f*

political class · Stand *m*

political control over a territory, political control over an area · Gebietshoheit *f*, Territorialhoheit

political corporation, body politic · politische Körperschaft *f*

political economic area, political economic territory · politisches Wirtschaftsgebiet *n* [*Ein Gebiet das besteht, weil es einen Staat gibt und sich mit diesem in der Regel deckt*]

political economic space · politisch-wirtschaftlicher Raum *m*

political economy, national economy, public economy, economics · Volkswirtschaft *f*, politische Ökonomie *f*, Nationalökonomie

political equality · politische Gleichstellung *f*

political feudalism · politischer Feudalismus *m*

political law, law passed by parliament [*As distinguished from a scientific law*] · Rechtsgesetz *n*

political regionalism · politische Neugliederung *f*

political science · politische Wissenschaft *f*

political status · politischer Status *m*, Untertanenstatus

politicization · Politisierung *f*

politico-geographic reorganization, politico-geographic reapportionment · politisch-geographische Neuordnung *f*, politisch-geographische Neugestaltung

to poll, to cast a vote · abstimmen

poll · Abstimmung *f*

poll · Umfrage *f*

polling, casting (of) votes · Abstimmen *n*

poll(ing) method · Abstimmungsverfahren *n*

poll(ing) place · Stimmbezirk *m*

poll-tax, head tax, capitation tax [*A tax on each person in consideration of his labour, office, rank, etc.*] · Kopfsteuer *f*

polluter (US) — population analyst

polluter (US); pollutor (Brit.) · (Umwelt)Verschmutzer *m*, Verursacher

polluting substance, polluting matter · Verschmutzungsstoff *m*, Verunreinigungsstoff

pollution control, environmental protection, environmental control · Umweltschutz *m*

pollution control authority, pollution prevention authority, antipollution authority, environmental protection authority, environmental control authority, environmental prevention authority · Umweltschutzbehörde *f*

pollution control board, pollution prevention board, environmental control board, environmental protection board, environmental prevention board, PCB, antipollution board · Umweltschutzamt *n*

pollutor (Brit.); polluter (US) · (Umwelt)Verschmutzer *m*, Verursacher

polycentric · polyzentrisch

pond bank · Teichufer *n*

pooling · Gewinnzusammenlegung *f*, Profitzusammenlegung

poor act, poor law, poor statute, pauper act, pauper statute, pauper law · Armengesetz *n*

poor board, board of guardians, poor law guardians · (Orts)Armenamt *n*

poor fund · Armenfonds *m*

poorhouse, almshouse, almonry [*It is supported by private endowment*] · Armenhaus, privates Armenhaus *n*, Armenspital *n*, Spital für Arme

poor law, poor statute, pauper act, pauper statute, pauper law, poor act · Armengesetz *n*

poor law, pauper law · Armenrecht *n*

poor law amendment act · Armengesetznovelle *f*

poor law guardians, poor board, board of guardians · (Orts)Armenamt *n*

poor law overseer, poor law guardian, parish officer, overseer (of the poor), guardian (of the poor), almoner · Armenvater *m*, Armenaufseher *m*, Armenpfleger *m*

poor law parish · Kirchspiel *n* der Armenverwaltung, (Pfarr)Sprengel *m* der Armenverwaltung, kirchlicher Sprengel der Armenverwaltung, Parochie *f* der Armenverwaltung

poor law reform, poor act reform, poor statute reform, pauper law reform, pauper act reform, pauper statute reform · Armengesetzreform *f*

(poor law) union [*In England*] · Armen(pflege)verband *m*

(poor law) union assessment committee · Armensteuerveranlagungsausschuß *m*

(poor law) union clerk, clerk of the (poor law) union [*In England*] · Armen(pflege)verbandvorsteher *m*

poor legislation, pauper lawmaking, poor lawmaking, pauper legislation · Armengesetzgebung *f*

poor lunatic, pauper lunatic · armer Geisteskranker *m*

poormaster (US); relieving officer, relieving official (Brit.) · Armenunterstützungsbeamte *m*, Armenvorsteher *m*, Armenrat *m*

poor person, pauper [*A person in receipt of relief under, formerly, the poor laws*] · Arme *m*

poor-rate · (örtliche) Armensteuer *f*, gemeindliche Armensteuer, lokale Armensteuer, kommunale Armensteuer

(poor) rate book · Armensteuerbuch *n*

poor relief, welfare work for the poor, pauper relief · Armenpflege *f*, Armenwohlfahrt *f*, Armenfürsorge *f*, Armenversorgung *f*

poor relief system, system of poor relief · Armenwesen *n*

poor's privilege (in (law)suits), pauper's right, legal help, legal aid [*A system for providing free or assisted legal advice or representation, for persons of slender means*] · Armenrecht *n*

poor statistics, pauper statistics · Armenstatistik *f*

poor statute, pauper act, pauper statute, pauper law, poor act, poor law · Armengesetz *n*

poort-reve [*In old English law*] · Stadtrichter *m*

populace, mob · Pöbel *m*

populace rule, ochlocracy, mob rule · Pöbelherrschaft *f*

popular bank, credit association, association of credit · Vorschußverein *m*

popular enthusiasm · Volksbegeisterung *f*

popular name, short title · Kurztitel *m*

to populate, to people · bevölkern

populated, peopled · bevölkert

populating, peopling · Bevölkern *n*

population [*statistics*] → (parent) population

population agglomeration · Bevölkerungsagglomeration *f*

population analyst · Bevölkerungsanalytiker *m*

population atlas · Bevölkerungsatlas *m*

population at the destination of movement [*migration*] · Zielbevölkerung *f*

population at the origin of movement [*migration*] · Quellbevölkerung *f*

population balance · Bevölkerungsausgleich *m*

population biology · Bevölkerungsbiologie *f*

population boom, demographic boom · Bevölkerungsaufschwung *m*

population capable of earning a living · Erwerbsbevölkerung *f*, erwerbsfähige Bevölkerung, erwerbsgeeignete Bevölkerung

population census, population count, census of population, count of population · Bevölkerungszählung *f*, Volkszählung

population change, change of population · Bevölkerungszahlwechsel *m*, Bevölkerungsstandwechsel

population characteristic, demographic characteristic · Bevölkerungsmerkmal *n*

population c(h)artography, demographic c(h)artography · Bevölkerungskartographie *f*

population class, class of population · Bevölkerungsklasse *f*

population composition, population factors, population structure · Bevölkerungsstruktur *f*, Bevölkerungsaufbau *m*, Bevölkerungszusammensetzung *f*, Bevölkerungsgefüge *n*

population concentration, material density · Bevölkerungskonzentration *f*

population count, census of population, count of population, population census · Bevölkerungszählung *f*, Volkszählung

population decrease · Bevölkerungsabnahme *f*, Bevölkerungsschwund *m*, Bevölkerungsrückgang *m*, Bevölkerungsminderung *f*

population density, density of population · (Be)Sied(e)lungsdichte *f*, Volksdichte, Bevölkerungsdichte, Menschenausstattung *f* einer Fläche, Ansied(e)lungsdichte

(population) density decay, falling off of (population) density · (Bevölkerungs)Dichteschwund *m*, Volksdichteschwund

(population) density gradient · (Bevölkerungs)Dichtegefälle *n*, Volksdichtegefälle

(population) density map, map of (population) density · (Bevölkerungs)Dichtekarte *f*, Volksdichtekarte

(population) density shift, shift of (population) density · (Bevölkerungs)Dichteverschiebung *f*, Volksdichteverschiebung *f*

population development, demographic development · Bevölkerungsentwick(e)lung *f*

population dispersion, population scatter, dispersion of population, scatter of population · Bevölkerungsstreuung *f*

population distribution, distribution of population · Bevölkerungsverteilung *f*

population drift, shift of population, drift of population, population shift · Bevölkerungsverschiebung *f*

population dynamics, demographic dynamics · Bevölkerungsdynamik *f*

population equilibrium, demographic equilibrium · Bevölkerungsgleichgewicht *n*

population explosion, demographic explosion · Bevölkerungsexplosion *f*, schneller Bevölkerungszuwachs *m*, demographischer Drang *m*, Bevölkerungsdrang, demographische Explosion

population factors, population structure, population composition · Bevölkerungsstruktur *f*, Bevölkerungsaufbau *m*, Bevölkerungszusammensetzung *f*, Bevölkerungsgefüge *n*

population flow, flow of population · Bevölkerungsstrom *m*

population geography, demographic geography · Bevölkerungsgeographie *f*

population group · Bevölkerungsgruppe *f*

population growth, increase of population, growth of population, population increase · Bevölkerungszunahme *f*, Bevölkerungswachstum *n*, Wachstum der Bevölkerung

population growth rate, population increase rate, demographic growth rate, demographic increase rate, rate of population growth, rate of population increase · Bevölkerungswachstumsrate *f*, Bevölkerungszunahmerate

population history, demographic history · Bevölkerungsgeschichte *f*

population increase, population growth, increase of population, growth of population · Bevölkerungszunahme *f*, Bevölkerungswachstum *n*, Wachstum der Bevölkerung

population increase rate, demographic growth rate, demographic increase rate, rate of population growth, rate of population increase, population growth rate · Bevölkerungswachstumsrate *f*, Bevölkerungszunahmerate

population inflow, inflow of population · Bevölkerungszustrom *m*

population level, demographic level, level of population · Bevölkerungsstand *m*

population mapping · Bevölkerungskartierung *f*

population migration — position map

population migration · Bevölkerungswanderung f

population mobility · Bevölkerungsbeweglichkeit f, Bevölkerungsmobilität f

population not capable of earning a living · Nichterwerbsbevölkerung f

population number · Bevölkerungszahl f

population out-migration · Bevölkerungsabwanderung f

population overspill, overspill of population · Bevölkerungsüberhang m, Bevölkerungsüberschuß m

population policy, demographic policy · Bevölkerungspolitik f

population potential · Bevölkerungspotential n

population pressure, demographic pressure · Bevölkerungsdruck m [*Er entsteht, wenn die einer Bevölkerung zur Verfügung stehenden Unterhaltsmittel im Verhältnis zur Bevölkerungszahl zu klein werden*]

population principle, demographic principle · Bevölkerungsprinzip n, Bevölkerungsgrundsatz m

population pyramid, demographic pyramid · Bevölkerungspyramide f

population redistribution · Bevölkerungsumverteilung f

population redistribution, redistribution of population · Bevölkerungsumverteilung f

population relocation, population resettlement, relocation of population, resettlement of population · Bevölkerungsumsied(e)lung f, Bevölkerungsverlegung f, Bevölkerungsaussied(e)lung, Bevölkerungsumsetzung

population scatter, dispersion of population, scatter of population, population dispersion · Bevölkerungsstreuung f

population science, science of population · Bevölkerungswissenschaft f

population shift, population drift, shift of population, drift of population · Bevölkerungsverschiebung f

population size · Bevölkerungsgröße f

population stagnation, demographic stagnation, stagnation of population · Bevölkerungsstagnation f, Bevölkerungsstillstand m, Bevölkerungsstockung f

population structure, population composition, population factors · Bevölkerungsstruktur f, Bevölkerungsaufbau m, Bevölkerungszusammensetzung f, Bevölkerungsgefüge n

population subregion, demographic subregion · Bevölkerungsteilregion f, Bevölkerungsteilraum m

population succession, demographic succession · Bevölkerungsfolge f

population target · Bevölkerungszielgröße f

population target rate · Bevölkerungszielzahl f

population theory, theory of population · Bevölkerungstheorie f

population trait · Bevölkerungsgrundlage f

population variable, demographic variable · Bevölkerungsvariable f

populous · bevölkerungsreich, volkreich

populousness · Bevölkerungsreichtum m, Volksreichtum

port conservancy (Brit.); port supervision commission (US) · Verkehrshafenaufsicht(samt) f, (n)

port due, P.D. · Hafengebühr f

porter → protector

portfolio [*investment company*] · Sondervermögen n, Wertpapierbestand m [*(Kapital)Anlagegesellschaft*]

portfolio management · Geschäftsfeldplanung f

portion, fortune, marriage goods; tocher [*in Scotland*]; maritagium [*Latin*]; dowry (marriage) [*Not to be confounded with "dower". A portion given with a woman to her husband in marriage*] · Mitgift f, Heiratsgut n

portioned off, portioned out, bought off · ausgezahlt [*Erb(schafts)anteil*]

portion of land, land portion, land piece, piece of land · Landstück n

to portion out, to allot, to apportion [*To divide and distribute proportionally or according to a plan*] · zuteilen

to portion out, to portion off, to buy off · auszahlen [*Erb(schafts)anteil*]

Port of London Authority · Londoner Hafenbehörde f

portolan chart · Windstrahlenkarte f, Portulankarte, Portolankarte, Rumbenkarte; Kompaßkarte [*Fehlbenennung*] [*Mittelalterliche Seekarte ohne Gradnetz mit Eintragung der Windstrahlen (= Rumben) im Kartenbild*]

port supervision commission (US); port conservancy (Brit.) · Verkehrshafenaufsicht(samt) f, (n)

position, mode of being, condition, nature, state · Beschaffenheit f

position in law · Rechtslage f, Rechtsposition f

position map · Standortkarte f, Lagekarte, Positionskarte

position map of an area — possession of (a) right

position map of an area, area(l) position map · Gebietslagekarte f, Lagekarte eines Gebietes; Mosaikkarte [nach Imhof]

position of the company, statement of assets and liabilities; inventory (US); balance(-sheet), statement of financial position, statement of financial condition · Bilanz f

position of trust, trust position · Vertrauensstellung f

(position) point · Positionspunkt m; miniaturhaftes Tüpflein n [nach Imhof] [Kartographie]

positive duty · Positivpflicht f

positive easement, affirmative easement [The servient owner allows the dominant owner to perform a certain act or certain acts upon the servient tenement] · positive Grunddienstbarkeit f

positive injunction, mandatory injunction · positiver Befehl m, Verfügung f zur Vornahme einer Handlung, gerichtliches (Handlungs)Gebot n [Eine „mandatory injunction" befiehlt nicht eine Unterlassung, sondern positives Handeln]

positive law [Law specifically ordained and adopted for the government of society, as distinguished from natural law] · geltendes Recht n, positives Recht, Satzungsrecht

positive morality · Konventionalnorm f

positive planning · positive Planung f, Positivplanung f [Förderung des Wachstums in noch ungenügend entwickelten Gebieten]

positive prescription, prescription of incorporeal hereditament(s), prescription of not tangible hereditament(s), acquisitive prescription [Acquisition of a right. See remark under "incorporeal hereditament". In international law "aquisitive" or "positive" prescription means title to territory based on uninterrupted and uncontested occupation over a reasonably long period] · Ersitzung f nichtkörperlichen Erbgutes, Ersitzung unkörperlichen Erbgutes, Ersitzung immateriellen Erbgutes

positive skewness · positive Schiefe f, positive Asymmetrie f, Linksschiefe, Linksasymmetrie [Statistik]

to possess · besitzen

possessing, possession · Besitzen n, Besitz(stand) m [Die tatsächliche, vom (Rechts)Titel unabhängige Innehabung einer Sache]

possession acquisition, acquisition of possession · Besitzerwerb m, Besitzbeschaffung f

possession as of freehold, possession of an estate of freehold; saisine, seisina, seysina [Latin]; infeoffment [Scotland]; seisin, freehold (possession), seizin · Gewere f [Eine historische Untersuchung über das Wesen der Gewere muß ihren Ausgang von der „investitura" des alten Rechts nehmen. Denn mit diesem Ausdruck geben die lateinischen Quellen der karolingischen Periode das Wort Gewere wieder, wie das aus der altdeutschen Übersetzung von C. 6 der Capitularia leg. add. v. 817 bei Pertz, I. S. 261 und aus den zwei parallel laufenden Stellen der traditiones Fuldenses in zwei Urkunden von 824 „testes qui vestitionem viderunt" und „testes qui viderunt giweridam" unwidersprechlich hervorgeht]

possession assignation, assignment of possession, cession of possession, possession assignment, possession cession, assignation of possession · Besitzabtretung f, Besitzzession f

possession at common law · Besitz m nach Gemeinrecht, gemeinrechtlicher Besitz

possession by prescription, prescription possession · Ersitzungsbesitz m, ersessener Besitz

possession by virtue of an agency · Besitzdienerschaft f

possession certificate, certificate of possession · Besitzzeugnis n

possession clause · Besitzklausel f

possession held in mortmain, un(ab)alienable possession, nondisposable possession · Tothandbesitz m, unveräußerlicher Besitz, unveräußerbarer Besitz

possession in bad faith · bösgläubiger Besitz m

possession judg(e)ment, judg(e)ment for possession · Besitzeinräumungsurteil n

possession loss, loss of possession · Besitzverlust m

possession of an estate of freehold; saisine, seisina, seysina [Latin]; infeoffment [Scotland]; seisin, freehold (possession), seizin, possession as of freehold · Gewere f [Eine historische Untersuchung über das Wesen der Gewere muß ihren Ausgang von der „investitura" des alten Rechts nehmen. Denn mit diesem Ausdruck geben die lateinischen Quellen der karolingischen Periode das Wort Gewere wieder, wie das aus der altdeutschen Übersetzung von C. 6 der Capitularia leg. add. v. 817 bei Pertz, I. S. 261 und aus den zwei parallel laufenden Stellen der traditiones Fuldenses in zwei Urkunden von 824 „testes qui vestitionem viderunt" und „testes qui viderunt giweridam" unwidersprechlich hervorgeht]

possession of (a) right · Rechtsbesitz m, Besitz eines Rechts

possession of forest(s) — possessory right

possession of forest(s) · Forstbesitz m, Waldbesitz

possession of inheritance, inheritance possession · Erb(en)besitz m

possession of land(s) for life → (real) estate for life

possession of land title → (real) estate title

possession of rights · Rechtsbesitz m, Besitz von Rechten

possession of (the) site · Baustellenübernahme f

possession order [*It is made by a court in order that a landlord can obtain possession of his premises once a notice to quit expires*] · Besitznahmebefehl m, Besitznahmegebot n

possession presumption, presumption of possession · Besitzvermutung f

possession proceeds, proceeds of possession · Besitzerlös m

possession tax, tax on possession · Besitzsteuer f

possession tax law · Besitzsteuerrecht n

possession tax law, possession tax act, possession tax statute · Besitzsteuergesetz n

possession writ, writ of possession · Besitzergreifungsdekret n, gerichtliche Besitzeinweisungsverfügung f, gerichtliches Besitzeinweisungsmandat n, gerichtlicher Besitzeinweisungsbefehl m [*Einweisung in ein Grundstück*]

possessor · Besitzer m

possessor by prescription, prescription possessor · Ersitzungsbesitzer m

possessor in bad faith · bösgläubiger Besitzer m

possessor non vitiosus [*Latin*]; bona fide possessor · gutgläubiger Besitzer m

possessor of a freehold estate, frank (feudal) tenant, frank land tenant, frank manorial tenant, frank fief-tenant, frank feuda(to)ry, frank feodatory, frank feeholder, frank tenant of land, franklyn, free-man, freeholder · freier Leh(e)n(s)mann m, freier Grundzinsmann, freier Leh(e)n(s)träger, freier Gefolgsmann, freier Vasall, Freisasse, Landsasse, Freimann

possessor of (an) inheritance, inheritance possessor · Erb(schafts)besitzer m

possessor of land → (real) estate possessor

possessor of perpetuities, perpetuities possessor · Familienfideikommißbesitzer m

possessor of (real) property → (real) estate possessor

possessor's agent · Besitzdiener m

possessory · besitzrechtlich

possessory act → law of possession

possessory (common law) lien · (gemeinrechtliches) Besitzsicherungsrecht n, gemeinrechtliches Besitz-Sicherheitsrecht [*Das Recht gewisser Personen, eine bewegliche Sache bis zur Erfüllung einer Verbindlichkeit in Gewahrsam zu halten*]

possessory community, community of possession · Besitzgemeinschaft f

possessory estate, estate in possession · dinglicher Besitz m

possessory estate title → (real) estate title

possessory freehold → simple fee

possessory intention; animus possidendi [*Latin*]; intention of possession · Besitzabsicht f

possessory interest, possessory right, interest in possession, right of possession, estate · Besitzrecht n, subjektives Besitzrecht, (subjektives) Recht zum Besitz

possessory interest for life → estate (in land) for life

possessory interest (in land) for life, life estate (in property), life estate in land, estate (in land) for life · Landbesitzrecht n auf Lebenszeit des Verkäufers, Bodenbesitzrecht auf Lebenszeit des Verkäufers, Besitzrecht auf Lebenszeit des Landverkäufers, Besitzrecht auf Lebenszeit des Bodenverkäufers

possessory land act → law of land (possession)

possessory land(ed) estate for life → (real) estate for life

possessory land law → law of land (possession)

possessory land statute → law of land (possession)

possessory lien → possessory (common-law) lien

possessory lord, liege-lord, over lord, lord of (the) manor, supreme owner, landlord, grantor, feoffor, feoffer, manor lord, langeman, bestower of a fee, feudal chief; dominus directus, feoffator [*Latin*]; (feudal) lord, chief lord, superior lord · Leh(e)n(s)herr m, Feudalherr, (feudaler) Belehner, Leh(e)n(s)gutgeber, Obereigentümer, Landübertragende, Übertragende von Land

(possessory) private land law, law of private land (possession) · Privatboden(besitz)recht n, Privatland(besitz)recht

possessory right → possessory interest

possessory right of land(s) → interest in (real) estate

possessory statute → law of possession

possessory successor, successor in possession, (ab)alienee · Besitznachfolger *m*, Veräußerungsbegünstigte

possessory title of land(s) → interest in (real) estate

possessory value, value of possession · Besitzwert *m*

possibility of (a) future (land(ed)) estate; spes successionis [*Latin*]; contingent remainder (land(ed)) estate, conditional remainder (land(ed)) estate, executory remainder (land(ed)) estate [*The remainder is contingent if the person who is to have the remainder is not yet living or if his identity is uncertain, or if the event which is to bring the remainder into existence is uncertain. The remainder becomes vested when such person is ascertained or upon the happening of the event*] · bedingter anwartschaftlicher Bodenbesitz(stand) *m*, möglicher anwartschaftlicher Bodenbesitz(stand), ungewisser anwartschaftlicher Bodenbesitz(stand)

possibility of connection · Anschlußmöglichkeit *f* [*Leitung*]

possibility of extinct issue · Möglichkeit *f* der erloschenen Nachkommenschaft

possibility of future estate [*misnomer*] → contingent remainder

possibility of future purchase · Kaufanwartschaft *f*

possibility of termination · (Besitz)Beend(ig)ungsmöglichkeit *f*, (Besitz)Auflösungsmöglichkeit, (Besitz)Auflösbarkeit

possible condition [*It admits of performance in the ordinary course of events*] · mögliche Bedingung *f*

possible risk, expectable risk [*Risk which is indefinite and uncertain*] · mögliches Risiko *n*, mögliches Wagnis *n*

postage-paid envelope · Freiumschlag *m*

postal order, money order, post office order · Postanweisung *f*

postal voting, voting by post, voting by mail · Briefwahl *f*

post-bidding negotiation, post-tendering negotiation · Nachverhandlung *f* [*Verhandlung einer ausschreibenden Dienststelle mit den Bietern nach Öffnung der Angebote*]

postcensal population · Bevölkerung *f* nach einer Zählung

poster, placard, bill, placart · Plakat *n*

poste restante · postlagernd

posteriority; posterioritas [*Latin*] · Nachrangigkeit *f*

posterity, descendants, succeeding generation(s) · Nachkommenschaft *f*, Nachkommen *mpl*

poster sticking, (bill-)posting, placard-posting, bill sticking, placard sticking, placart sticking, placart-posting · Plakatankleben, Plakatanschlagen

post-formation · Nachgründung *f*

post glossators [*An Italian law school in the fourteenth and fifteenth centuries*] · Postglossatoren *mpl*

postgraduate · Senior *m* [*Collegemitglied*]

post-graduate trainee in law practice · Referendar *m*

post-graduate traineeship in law practice · Referendariat *n*

post-industrial · nachindustriell

post-industrial society · nachindustrielle Gesellschaft *f*

posting · Anschlagen *n* [*Reklame; Bekanntmachung(en)*]

posting, accounting entry, accountancy entry [*Entering a business transaction in the books of account*] · Buchung *f*, (Buch)Eintrag(ung) *m, (f)*

posting date, date of posting · Aufgabedatum *n* [*Postsendung*]

postman, letter-carrier · Briefträger *m*, Briefbote *m*, Postbote

post-manufacture duty to warn · Produktbeobachtungs- und Aufklärungspflicht *f*

post-mortem examination · Obduktion *f*

post-nuptial settlement, voluntary settlement [*A settlement made after marriage upon a wife or children*] · erbvertragliche Regelung *f* nach der Eheschließung

post office order, postal order, money order · Postanweisung *f*

to postpone · aufschieben, hinausschieben, verschieben

postponed annuity, reversionary annuity, annuity put off, deferred annuity · aufgeschobene Annuität *f*, Zukunftsannuität, Anwartschaftsannuität

postponement, suspension, deferment, putting off · Aufschub *m*, Aufschiebung *f*, Hinausschiebung *f*, Verschiebung *f*

post-primary (election) convention [*USA*] · Nachvorwahlkonvent *m*

postremo-geniture [*Latin*] → borow English

post-tendering negotiation, post-bidding negotiation · Nachverhandlung *f* [*Verhandlung einer ausschreibenden Dienst-*

post-termination provisions — powerlessness

stelle mit den Bietern nach Öffnung der Angebote]

post-termination provisions · Bestimmungen *f pl* nach der (Vertrags)Aufhebung, Bestimmungen nach der (Vertrags)Beendigung

postwar growth · Nachkriegswachstum *n*

postwar private value · Nachkriegsbaulandpreis *m*, Nachkriegsgrundstückspreis, Nachkriegs(bau)bodenpreis, Nachkriegsliegenschaftspreis

postwar rent · Nachkriegsmiete *f*

postwar urbanization · Nachkriegsverstädterung *f*

potato cultivation · Kartoffelanbau *m*

potential household, concealed household, hidden household [*It consists of a family living with relatives or other people because they are unable to obtain a separate dwelling*] · statistisch nicht erfaßbarer Haushalt *m*

potential household, concealed household, hidden household · Gemeinschaftshaushalt *m*

potential industrial land, land for potential industrial development · Industrieerwartungsland *n*

potential model · Potentialmodell *n*

potential physical control (over a thing), actual possession, physical possession, de facto possession, actual physical control (over a thing) · tatsächliche Sachherrschaft *f*, tatsächliche Beherrschung *f* einer Sache, unmittelbarer Besitz *m*, wirklicher Besitz, tatsächlicher Besitz, wirkliche Sachherrschaft, wirkliche Beherrschung einer Sache, unmittelbare Sachherrschaft, unmittelbare Beherrschung einer Sache

potential value [*Value that would or will exist if and when future probabilities would become actualities*] · Erwartungswert *m*

potestas ecclesiastica [*Latin*]; ecclesiastic(al) power, ecclesiastic(al) authority, spiritual authority, spiritual power; jus majestaticum circa sacra, jus in sacra · Kirchengewalt *f*, Kirchenhoheit *f*, Kirchenmacht *f*, Kirchenkompetenz *f*, Kirchenregiment *n*

potestative condition [*It makes the execution of the agreement depend on an event which it is in the power of the one or the other of the contracting parties to bring about or to hinder*] · Potestativbedingung *f*

poultry breeding, poultry raising · Geflügelzucht *f*

poultry farm · Geflügel(haltungs)betrieb *m*

poultry farming, poultry keeping · Geflügelhaltung *f*

pound; parcus [*Latin*] [*A place where goods which have been seized as distress are placed by the distrainor, and in which the goods are in the custody of the law. A pound is either overt (open overhead) or covert (closed in)*] · Pfandstall *m*

poundage · Warenausfuhrzoll *m*

pound breach; parci fractio [*Latin*]; pundbreach [*Saxon*]; breach of pound [*The offence of breaking a pound, for the purpose of taking out the cattle and/or goods impounded*] · Einbruch *m* in einen Pfandstall

pound-overt, open pound, uncovered pound, not covered pound · nicht eingefriedetes Grundstück *n*, uneingefriedetes Grundstück [*Es wird der Vollstreckung unterworfen*]

poverty · Armut *f*

poverty alleviation, alleviation of poverty · Linderung *f* der Armut

poverty area, poverty territory, area of poverty, territory of poverty · Armutsgebiet *n*

poverty island, island of poverty · Armutsinsel *f*

poverty line, subsistence level, minimum of subsistence · Existenzminimum *n*

poverty-reducing · armutbekämpfend

poverty threshold · Armutsschwelle *f*

power · Macht *f* [*Im politischen Sinn*]

power · Ermächtigung *f*

power, right · Befugnis *f*, Recht *n*

power, authority · Gewalt *f*, Hoheit *f*, Macht *f*, Kompetenz *f*

power balance, balance of power · Machtgleichgewicht *n*

power delegation, delegation of power · Ermächtigungsübertragung *f*

power distribution, power separation, separation of powers, distribution of powers · (Staats)Gewaltentrennung *f*, (Staats)Gewaltenteilung

power exercisable with consent, right exercisable with consent · Befugnis *f* mit Zustimmung eines Dritten, Recht *n* mit Zustimmung eines Dritten

power force · Tarifpartner *m* [*Gewerkschaft; Arbeitgeber*]

power function · Gütefunktion *f* [*Statistik*]

power given by equity, equitable power · Billigkeitsermächtigung *f*, Ermächtigung nach Billigkeit(srecht)

power holder · Machthaber *m*

powerless · Machtlose *m*

powerlessness · Machtlosigkeit *f*

**power of (ab)alienation, ** right of disposal, power of disposal, (ab)alienation right, (ab)alienation power, disposal power, right of (ab)alienation · Veräußerungsbefugnis *f*, Veräußerungsrecht *n*

**power of access, ** access right, access power, admittance, right of access · Betretungsbefugnis *f*, Betretungsrecht *n*, Zutrittsbefugnis, Zutrittsrecht, Zugangsbefugnis, Zugangsrecht

**power of amotion, ** right of amotion [*from membership or office*] · Ausschlußbefugnis *f*, Ausschlußrecht *n*

**power of appointment, ** right of appointment, power of nomination, right of nomination · Benennungsbefugnis *f*, Benennungsrecht *n*, Ernennungsbefugnis, Ernennungsrecht

**power of appointment, ** power of disposition, right of appointment, right of disposition [*A power given to a person which enables him to dispose of an interest in property, real or personal, which is not his. Such a power is usually conferred under a trust or settlement by which a person is enabled to make an eppointment of the trust or settlement property*] · Bestimmungsbefugnis *f*, Bestimmungsrecht *n*, Verfügungsbefugnis, Verfügungsrecht [*Vermögen*]

**power of appointment appendant, ** power of appointment appurtenant, power of disposition appendant, power of disposition appurtenent, right of appointment appendant, right of appointment appurtenant, right of disposition appendant, right of disposition appurtenant [*It is a power exercised by a person who has an interest in the property, and that interest will be affected by the exercise of the power*] · Pertinenz-Verfügungsbefugnis *f*, Pertinenz-Bestimmungsbefugnis, Pertinenz-Verfügungsrecht *n*, Pertinenz-Bestimmungsrecht

**power of appointment by deed, ** right of appointment by deed, power of disposition by deed, right of disposition by deed · urkundliche Verfügungsbefugnis *f*, urkundliche Bestimmungsbefugnis, urkundliches Verfügungsrecht *n*, urkundliches Bestimmungsrecht

**power of appointment in gross, ** right of appointment in gross, power of disposition in gross, right of disposition in gross [*It is a power given to a person who has an interest in the property, but that interest will not be affected by the exercise of the power*] · subjektiv persönliche Verfügungsbefugnis *f*, subjektiv persönliche Bestimmungsbefugnis, subjektiv persönliches Verfügungsrecht *n*, subjektiv persönliches Bestimmungsrecht

**power of appointment of land, ** right of appointment of land, power of disposition of land, right of dispositon of land · Bodenverfügungsbefugnis *f*, Landverfügungsbefugnis, Bodenbestimmungsbefugnis, Landbestimmungsbefugnis, Bodenverfügungsrecht, Landverfügungsrecht, Bodenbestimmungsrecht, Landbestimmungsrecht

**power of appointment under the statute of uses, ** right of appointment under the statute of uses, legal power of appointment, legal right of appointment · Befugnis *f* an einem bestimmten Vermögen Nutzung zu erklären, Recht *n* an einem bestimmten Vermögen Nutzung zu erklären

**power of attorney, ** authority under seal [*Where the authority is given formally by deed, it is called a power of attorney*] · gesiegelte Vollmacht *f*, unter Siegel erteilte Vollmacht, unter Siegel verliehene Vollmacht

**power of collection of contribution(s), ** right of collection of contribution(s) · Beitragserhebungsbefugnis *f*, Beitragserhebungsrecht *n*

**power of contract(ing), ** right of contract(ing), contracting power, contracting right, contractual power, contractual right · Vertragsbefugnis *f*, Vertragsrecht *n*

**power of decision, ** right of decision · Entscheidungsbefugnis *f*, Entscheidungsrecht *n*

**power of direction, ** direction power · Leitungsmacht *f*

**power of discretion, ** discretionary power · Ermessensermächtigung *f*

**power of disposal, ** (ab)alienation right, (ab)alienation power, disposal power, right of (ab)alienation, power of (ab)alienation, right of disposal · Veräußerungsbefugnis *f*, Veräußerungsrecht *n*

**power of disposition, ** right of appointment, right of disposition, power of appointment [*A power given to a person which enables him to dispose of an interest in property, real or personal, which is not his. Such a power is usually conferred under a trust or settlement by which a person is enabled to make an eppointment of the trust or settlement property*] · Bestimmungsbefugnis *f*, Bestimmungsrecht *n*, Verfügungsbefugnis, Verfügungsrecht [*Vermögen*]

**power of disposition, ** disposition power · Verfügungsermächtigung *f*

**power of disposition appendant, ** power of disposition appurtenent, right of appointment appendant, right of appointment appurtenant, right of disposition appendant, right of disposition appurtenant, power of appointment appendant, power of appointment appurtenant [*It is a power exercised by a person who has an interest in the property, and that interest will be affected by the exercise of the power*] · Pertinenz-Verfügungsbefugnis f, Pertinenz-Bestimmungsbefugnis, Pertinenz-Verfügungsrecht n, Pertinenz-Bestimmungsrecht

power of disposition by deed, right of disposition by deed, power of appointment by deed, right of appointment by deed · urkundliche Verfügungsbefugnis f, urkundliche Bestimmungsbefugnis, urkundliches Verfügungsrecht n, urkundliches Bestimmungsrecht

power of disposition in gross, right of disposition in gross, power of appointment in gross, right of appointment in gross [*It is a power given to a person who has an interest in the property, but that interest will not be affected by the exercise of the power*] · subjektiv persönliche Verfügungsbefugnis f, subjektiv persönliche Bestimmungsbefugnis, subjektiv persönliches Verfügungsrecht n, subjektiv persönliches Bestimmungsrecht

power of disposition of land, right of dispositon of land, power of appointment of land, right of appointment of land · Bodenverfügungsbefugnis f, Landverfügungsbefugnis, Bodenbestimmungsbefugnis, Landbestimmungsbefugnis, Bodenverfügungsrecht, Landverfügungsrecht, Bodenbestimmungsrecht, Landbestimmungsrecht n

(power of) eminent domain; dominium eminens [*Latin*] [*The right of a government to take private property for public purposes*] · Bodenenteignungsrecht n, (Land)Enteignungsrecht, Entscheidungsrecht für (Boden)Enteignungen, materielles Enteignungsrecht

power of exception, exceptional power · Ausnahmeermächtigung f

power of exchange, power to exchange, right to exchange, right of exchange · Tauschbefugnis f, Tauschrecht n

power of incorporation, authority of incorporation · Inkorporierungsmacht f, Inkorporierungshoheit f, Inkorporierungsgewalt f, Inkorporierungskompetenz f

power of nomination, right of nomination, power of appointment, right of appointment · Benennungsbefugnis f, Benennungsrecht n, Ernennungsbefugnis, Ernennungsrecht

power of possession as to third persons · Besitzgewalt f gegen Dritte

power of production, production power, productive power · Produktionskraft f, Herstellungskraft, Erzeugungskraft

power of renewal, power of revival, right of renewal, right of revival · Erneuerungsbefugnis f, Erneuerungsrecht n

power of resumption, right of resumption · Zwangsrückkaufbefugnis f, Zwangsrückkaufrecht n

power of revival, right of renewal, right of revival, power of renewal · Erneuerungsbefugnis f, Erneuerungsrecht n

power of revocation, right of revocation, revocation power, revocation right · Befugnis f an einem bestimmten Vermögen Nutzung zu widerrufen, Recht n an einem bestimmten Vermögen Nutzung zu widerrufen

power of sale, right of sale, power to sell, right to sell · Verkaufsbefugnis f, Verkaufsrecht n

power of sale · Verkaufsermächtigung f

power of supervision, supervising power, supervising right, power of superintendence, right to supervise, right to superintend, power to supervise, power to superintend, superintending power, superintending right, right of supervision, right of superintendence · Aufsichtsbefugnis f, Aufsichtsrecht n, Überwachungsbefugnis, Überwachungsrecht

power of termination, right of termination, power to terminate, right to terminate · Beend(ig)ungsbefugnis f, Beend(ig)ungsrecht n

power plant location, power plant site, power station site, power station location · Energiestandort m, Kraftwerkstandort

power politics · Machtpolitik f

power price, electricity price · Elektrizitätspreis m, Strompreis, Energiepreis

power separation, separation of powers, distribution of powers, power distribution · (Staats)Gewaltentrennung f, (Staats)Gewaltenteilung

power station site, power station location, power plant location, power plant site · Energiestandort m, Kraftwerkstandort

power structure · Machtstruktur f, Machtgefüge n, Machtaufbau m, Machtzusammensetzung f

power sum · Potenzsumme f

power supply, electricity supply, energy supply · Elektrizitätsversorgung f, Stromversorgung, Energieversorgung

power to exchange, right to exchange, right of exchange, power of exchange · Tauschbefugnis f, Tauschrecht n

power to give ordinances, authority to give ordinances · Verordnungsgewalt f, Verordnungskompetenz f, Verordnungshoheit f, Verordnungsmacht f

power to legislate, authority to legislate, legislative authority, legislative power, legislature, jurisdiction; jurisdictio [*Latin*], power to make law, authority to make law · gesetzgebende Gewalt f, gesetzgebende Hoheit f, gesetzgebende Macht, gesetzgebende Kompetenz, Gesetzgebungsgewalt, Gesetzgebungs-

power to order alterations — precaria

kompetenz, Gesetzgebungsmacht, Gesetzgebungshoheit

power to order alterations → power to order changes

power to sell, right to sell, power of sale, right of sale · Verkaufsbefugnis *f*, Verkaufsrecht *n*

power to supervise, power to superintend, superintending power, superintending right, right of supervision, right of superintendence, power of supervision, supervising power, supervising right, power of superintendence, right to supervise, right to superintend · Aufsichtsbefugnis *f*, Aufsichtsrecht *n*, Überwachungsbefugnis *f*, Überwachungsrecht *n*

power to terminate, right to terminate, power of termination, right of termination · Beend(ig)ungsbefugnis *f*, Beend(ig)ungsrecht *n*

power to transfer · Übertragungsermächtigung *f*

power to view, right to view · Besichtigungsrecht *n*, Besichtigungsbefugnis *f* [*künftiger Mieter*]

practicability, feasibility, workability · Ausführbarkeit *f*, Durchführbarkeit

practicability analysis, practicability study, feasibility analysis, feasibility study, workability analysis, workability study · Ausführbarkeitsstudie *f*, Durchführbarkeitsstudie *f*, Durchführbarkeitsanalyse *f*, Ausführbarkeitsanalyse *f*

practicability survey, feasibility survey, workability survey · Ausführbarkeitsenquête *f*, Durchführbarkeitsenquête *f*

practicable, workable, feasible · ausführbar, durchführbar

practical approximate term · praktischer (An)Näherungsbegriff *m*

practical completion · Ende *n* der Ausführungsphase

practice · Verfahrensgang *m*

practice book · Handbuch *n* für die Praxis

practice court · selbständiges Nebengericht *n*

(practice) directions · richterliche Verfahrensrichtlinien *fpl*, Verfahrensrichtlinien (für die Prozeßpraxis)

practice long continued, usage · Sitte *f*

practice of banking, banking practice · Bankwesen *n*

practice of entailing · Beschränkungswesen *n* [*Vererbung von Grundstücken*]

practice of the courts, court practice · Prozeßwesen *n*, Gerichtswesen

practitioner · Praktiker *m*

pr(a)edial [*That which arises or comes from the ground*] · prädial

(pr(a)edial) bondage, bondage (on an estate), serfdom (on an estate), villanage, ville(i)nage; nativitas [*Latin*]; servile status, villein status, villain status, status of a serf [*Called by Britton "naifte"*] · Hörigenstatus *m*, Leibeigenschaft *f*, Grundhörigkeit *f*, (Grund)Untertänigkeit, Bauerndienst *m*

pr(a)edial servitude; servitus praediorum [*Latin*]; real servitude, landed servitude [*A servitude affecting land*] · Realservitut *n, f*, Prädialservitut

pr(a)edial slave; glebne adscriptus [*Latin*] · Grundhörige *m* [*Im Mittelalter zwischen Freien und Leibeigenen stehend*]

pr(a)edial tithe, tithe arising immediately from the ground · Grundzehnt *m*, Prädialzehnt, Realzehnt, Feldzehnt

praedium dominans [*Latin*]; dominant tenement, ruling tenement, dominant (real) estate, dominant (real) property, dominant land, ruling (real) estate, ruling (real) property, dominant realty, ruling realty · berechtigter Boden *m*, dominierender Boden, herrschender Boden, berechtigter Grund(besitz) *m*, dominierender Grund(besitz), herrschender Grund(besitz), berechtigter Besitz, dominierender Besitz, herrschender Besitz, herrschendes Grundstück *n*, dominierendes Grundstück, herrschendes Land *n*, dominierendes Land, berechtigtes Land, berichtigtes Grundstück

pratum bovis; carucae [*Latin*] [*A meadow for oxen employed in tillage*] · Ochsenwiese *f*

preamble [*That part of an Act of Parliament which contains the recitals showing the necessity for it*] · Eingang *m*, Präambel *f*

preappointed evidence, preappointed proof, pre-constituted evidence, pre-constituted proof · vorbereiteter Beweis *m*

pre-audience [*The right of being heard before another. A privilege belonging to the English bar, the members of which are entitled to be heard in their order, according to rank, beginning with the Queen's or King's attorney general and ending with barristers at large*] · Recht *n* von einem anderen gehört zu werden, Advokatenrangfolge *f* vor Gericht

prebend [*In English ecclesiastic(al) law. A stipend or revenue; that portion which every member or canon of a cathedral church receives in the right of his place, for his maintenance*] · Präbende *f*

prebendary · Präbendar *m*

precaria, bind day, boon-day, reaping day [*The day (up)on which a tenant was required to perform the service of bedrip*] · befohlener Erntearbeitstag *m*, Frontag auf besonderes Begehr

precaria [*Latin*] → petitio

precarium — pre-existing use

precarium [*Latin*] · Leihe *f* auf jederzeitigen Widerruf

precatory words [*Expressions in a will praying or recommending that a thing be done*] · letztwillige Bitte *f*

precatura [*Latin*] → petitio

precedent condition, condition precedent, condition suspensive, suspensive condition · Anfangsbedingung *f*, Suspensivbedingung, suspensive Bedingung, aufschiebende Bedingung, hinausschiebende Bedingung, verschiebende Bedingung

precedent contract, contract precedent · früherer Vertrag *m*

precedent discharge, suspensive discharge · Anfangsentlastung *f*, Suspensiventlastung, aufschiebbare Entlastung, aufschiebende Entlastung, hinausschiebende Entlastung, suspensive Entlastung [*Sie tritt nach Ablauf einer in der gerichtlichen Entlastungsverfügung festgesetzten Frist in Wirksamkeit*]

precedent interest, precedent right · vorausgehendes dingliches Grund(stücks)recht *n*, vorangehendes dingliches Grund(stücks)recht

precedent right, precedent interest · vorausgehendes dingliches Grund(stücks)recht *n*, vorangehendes dingliches Grund(stücks)recht

preceding · vorhergehend

precept [*A command in writing*] · schriftliche Weisung *f*, Vorschreibung

preceptive, imperative, peremptory, obligatory; perimere [*Latin*]; mandatory [*As opposed to "permissive"*] · pflichtbedingt, zwingend [*in Gesetzen*]

precinct (US); police division (Brit.) · Polizeirevier *n*

precinct of a jurisdiction, territory of a jurisdiction · Bann(meile) *m, (f)* [*Rechtsprechung*]

precise plan · Ergänzungsplan *m* zum Bauleitplan

precondition, condition previously necessary, preliminary condition, prerequisite · Voraussetzung *f*, Vorbedingung

pre-constituted evidence, pre-constituted proof, preappointed evidence, preappointed proof · vorbereiteter Beweis *m*

pre-contract · Vorvertrag *m*, Abschließungsvertrag [*Ein Vertrag, durch den beide Teile, oder nur ein Teil, sich dazu verpflichten bzw. verpflichtet, später einen Hauptvertrag abzuschließen*]

pre-contract planning · Vorvertragplanung *f*

pre-contractual · vorvertraglich

pre-costing · (Kosten)Vorkalkulation *f*

pre-costing pattern · (Kosten)Vorkalkulationsschema *n*

predatory cultivation, robber economy, ruthless exploitation · Raubbau *m*, Raubwirtschaft *f*

predecessor [*Not to be confused with "ancestor"* = *Vorfahre*] · Vorgänger *m*

predecessor in business · Geschäftsvorgänger *m*

predecessor in law · Rechtsvorgänger *m*

predecessor in office · Amtsvorgänger *m*

predecessor in title · (Rechts)Titelvorgänger *m*

predesign, sketch plan, preliminary design · vorläufige (Bebauungs)Planfassung *f*, Vorentwurf *m*

predesign · Vorentwurf *m*

predesign drawing · Vorentwurfzeichnung *f*

predetermined price · festgesetzter Preis *m*

predeveloped · vorentwickelt

predicated variable, regressor · Regressor *m*

predictability, foreseeability · Vorhersehbarkeit *f*

predictable, foreseeable · vorhersehbar

predictive model · Voraussagemodell *n*, explikatives Modell

predominantly residential area, predominantly residential territory, predominantly residence area, predominantly residence territory, predominantly housing area, predominantly housing territory · vorwiegendes Wohn(ungs)gebiet *n*

pre-eminence; majestas [*Latin*]; sovereign power, sovereign right, sovereign dominion, sovereignty, liberty, supremacy, authority, majesty · Hoheitsrecht *n*, Hoheitsbefugnis *f*, hoheitliches Recht, hoheitliche Befugnis, Souveränität *f*, Oberhoheit *f*, Hoheitsmacht *f*, vollziehende Gewalt *f*

pre-eminence · Vormachtstellung *f*

pre-emption, preëmption · Vorkauf *m*

pre-emption right, preëmption right, right of pre-emption, right of preëmption · Vorkaufsrecht *n*

pre-emptive right, preëmptive right · Bezugsrecht *n* [*Aktionär*]

pre-existing use, nonconforming use [*A use of land which lawfully existed prior to the enactment of a zoning ordinance and which is maintained after the ordinance, although it not longer complies with the use restrictions applicable to the area*] · nicht übereinstimmende Benutzung *f*, nicht übereinstimmender Gebrauch *m*

prefab(ricated) home — premap 788

prefab(ricated) home, manufactured home · Fertig(bau)eigenheim *n*

prefab(ricated) housing, manufactured housing · Fertig(bau)wohnungen *fpl*

prefabricator, manufacturer · Fertigbauer *m*

preface · Vorwort *n*

pre-feasibility analysis, pre-practicability analysis · Voranalyse *f*, Voruntersuchung *f*

prefect of a district, president of a district · Landrat *m*

preference · Begünstigung *f* [*Konkursverfahren*]

preference area, territory of preference, area of preference, preference territory · Vorranggebiet *n*

preference bondholder, preferred bondholder, preferential bondholder · Vorzugsobligationär *m*, Vorzugsobligationeninhaber *m*

preference principle, principle of preference · Günstigkeitsgrundsatz *m*, Günstigkeitsprinzip *n*

preference share, preferred share, preferential share · Vorzugsanteil *m*

preference stock, preferred stock, preferential stock · Vorzugsaktie *f*

preference system, preferential system, preferred system · Vorzugssystem *n*

preference territory, preference area, territory of preference, area of preference · Vorranggebiet *n*

preferential, preferred · bevorrechtigt

preferential creditor, preferred creditor · bevorrechtigter Gläubiger *m*, Vorzugsgläubiger

preferential debt, preferred debt, preference debt · Vorzugsschuld *f*

preferential payment, preference payment, preferred payment · Vorzugszahlung *f*

preferential system, preferred system, preference system · Vorzugssystem *n*

preferred, preferential · bevorrechtigt

preferred creditor, preferential creditor · bevorrechtigter Gläubiger *m*, Vorzugsgläubiger

preferred payment, preferential payment, preference payment · Vorzugszahlung *f*

prefinancing, preliminary financing, advance financing · Vorfinanzierung *f*

pre-industrial · vorindustriell

pre-industrial age · vorindustrielles Zeitalter *n*

pre-industrial village · vorindustrielles Dorf *n*

prejudg(e)ment · Vorausurteil *n*

to prejudice, to derogate, to hurt, to harm · beeinträchtigen, schmälern

prejudice · Vorurteil *n*

prejudicial to health, detrimental to health, offensive, unsanitary · gesundheitsschädlich, gesundheitsgefährdend

prejudicial to safety · sicherheitsgefährdend

preliminaries (for site facilities) · Vorhaltekosten *f* (für Baustelleneinrichtung(en))

preliminary · vorrangig

preliminary acceptance · Vorabnahme *f*

preliminary act · Schiffsklageschrift *f* [*Bei der Schadenersatzklage eines Schiffes gegen ein anderes wegen Zusammenstoß*]

preliminary building scheme design · Bebauungsvorentwurf; Überbauungsvorentwurf *m* [*Schweiz*]

preliminary condition, prerequisite, precondition, condition previously necessary · Voraussetzung *f*, Vorbedingung

preliminary design, predesign, sketch plan · vorläufige (Bebauungs)Planfassung *f*, Vorentwurf *m*

preliminary discussion · Vorgespräch *n*

preliminary examination · Vorprüfung *f*

preliminary financing, advance financing, prefinancing · Vorfinanzierung *f*

preliminary measure, preparatory measure · Vorbereitungsmaßnahme *f*, vorbereitende Maßnahme

preliminary negotiation · Vorverhandlung *f*

preliminary notice · Vormerkung *f* [*Grundbuch*]

preliminary oath; antejuramentum, praejuramentum, juramentum calumniae [*Latin*] · Klageeid *m*, Voreid

preliminary operation, preparatory operation · Vorbereitungshandlung *f* [*z. B. das Einrichten einer Baustelle*]

preliminary planning, preparatory planning, preplanning · vorbereitende Planung *f*, Planung im engeren Sinne, Vorplanung

preliminary remark · Vorbemerkung *f*

preliminary site work(s) · Baustellenvorbereitungsarbeit(en) *f(pl)*

preliminary stage, preparatory stage · Vorbereitungsstadium *n*, Vorbereitungsphase *f*

preliminary work(s), preparatory work(s) · Vor(bereitungs)arbeit(en) *f (pl)*

premap · Vorkarte *f*

premature escheat — prerequisite

premature escheat · vorzeitiger Heimfall *m*

premature termination [*contract*] · vorzeitige Beendigung *f* [*Vertrag*]

premises [*Matter previously stated or set forth*] · Vorangehende *n*, Vorstehende

premises [*A piece of land with house(s) and/or building(s)*] · Anwesen *n*, Hausstätte *f*

premises → (business) premises

premises (of deed) [*The premises of a deed contain the names of the parties, sometimes the date (though this may be at the end), and a statement of the consideration to be paid and of its payment. The description of the property is also included in the premises of the deed. An accurate description is necessary so that the property may be readily identified*] · Obenerwähnte *n*, Einleitung *f* [*in Urkunden*]

premium, agio [*A charge made for exchanging the currency of one country for that of another*] · Agio *n*, Aufgeld *n*, Übersatz *m*

premium on capital stocks · Aktienausgabe *f* mit Agio

premium on shares [*Difference between issue-price and market-price of shares or stock*] · Aufgeld *n*, Prämie *f*

premium plan of paying for labour (Brit.); premium plan of paying for labor (US); premium-wage system, reward system · Prämienlohnsystem *n*

premium resource · Kapazitätsreserve *f*

premium-wage, wage by results, piece-wage, efficiency-wage, statement-wage · Akkordlohn *m*, Leistungslohn

premium-wage contract, efficiency-wage contract, statement-wage contract, piece-wage contract, piece-work contract, job(bing) work contract · Akkord(lohn)vertrag *m*

premium-wage rate, piece-wage rate, efficiency-wage rate, statement-wage rate · Akkord(lohn)satz *m*

premium-wage system, reward system; premium plan of paying for labour (Brit.); premium plan of paying for labor (US) · Prämienlohnsystem *n*

prepaid · vorbezahlt

prepaid share (of stock) · vorbezahlter (Ratengeschäfts)Anteil *m* [*Bausparkasse*]

preparation of construction, preparation of building, construction preparation, building preparation · Bauvorbereitung *f*

preparatory measure, preliminary measure · Vorbereitungsmaßnahme *f*, vorbereitende Maßnahme

preparatory operation, preliminary operation · Vorbereitungshandlung *f* [*z. B. das Einrichten einer Baustelle*]

preparatory planning, preplanning, preliminary planning · vorbereitende Planung *f*, Planung im engeren Sinne, Vorplanung

preparatory school (US); private secondary school, public school (Brit.) · höhere Privatschule *f*

preparatory stage, preliminary stage · Vorbereitungsstadium *n*

preparatory work(s), preliminary work(s) · Vor(bereitungs)arbeit(en) *f (pl)*

prepared (to do a thing), in condition (to do a thing), in a state (to do a thing) · in der Lage (etwas zu tun), vorbereitet (etwas zu tun)

prepayment, payment in advance · Voraus(be)zahlung *f*

prepayment damages · Vorfälligkeitsentschädigung *f* [*Ist mit einem Kreditinstitut für eine Hypothek eine feste Laufzeit vereinbart, so ist der Hypothekengeber meistens nur bei Zahlung einer Vorfälligkeitsentschädigung bereit den Vertrag aufzulösen*]

prepayment invoice, advance payment invoice · Vorauszahlungsrechnung *f*

to preplan · vorplanen

preplanning, preliminary planning, preparatory planning · vorbereitende Planung *f*, Planung im engeren Sinne, Vorplanung

preplanning contract · Vorplanungsvertrag *m*

prepossession · Vorbesitz *m*

prepossessor · Vorbesitzer *m*

pre-primary (election) · förmliche Vorwahl *f*, förmliche Erstwahl, förmliche Urwahl

pre-project financing · Vorprojektfinanzierung *f*

prequalification of bidders, prequalification of tenderers [*Process of investigating and qualifying bidders as acceptable contractors, prior to the award of contracts, on the basis of their skills, integrity, and responsibility relative to the project contemplated*] · (An)Bieter(aus)wahl *f*

pre-renter · Vormieter *m*

to prerequire, to require beforehand · vorbedingen, voraussetzen

prerequired, required beforehand, prerequisite · vorbedingt, vorausgesetzt

prerequisite, precondition, condition previously necessary, preliminary condition · Voraussetzung *f*, Vorbedingung

prerequisite for application, application prerequisite · Anwendungsvoraussetzung f

prerequisite for operative effect, prerequisite for operation · Wirksamkeitsvorbedingung f, Wirksamkeitsvoraussetzung

prerogative court [*England*] · geistliches Testamentsgericht n [*Alle auf Testamente bezüglichen Prozesse wurden hier vorgebracht, wenn der Verstorbene bona notabilia, d. h. Gegenstände im Wert von mehr als fünf Pfund Sterling in zwei verschiedenen Diözesen hinterlassen hatte*]

prerogative of a sovereign, sovereign right, royal right of a sovereign, royal prerogative · Reg(al)ie f, königliches Recht n

prerogative order of mandamus, (writ of) mandamus [*It is issued from a court of superior jurisdiction and directed to a private or municipal corporation, or any of its officers, or to an executive, administrative or judicial officer, or to an inferior court, commanding the performance of a particular act therein specified, and belonging to his or their public, official, or ministerial duty, or directing the restoration of the complainant to rights or privileges of which he has been illegally deprived*] · Erfüllungsdekret n, Erfüllungsbefehl m, Vornahmedekret, Vornahmebefehl

prerogative right, privilege, liberty · Vorrecht n

prescribability · Ersitzbarkeit f

prescribable · ersitzbar

to prescribe [*To claim a right or title through long use or possession*] · ersitzen

to prescribe [*To lay down authoritatively*] · vorschreiben

prescribed · ersessen

(prescribed) (land) improvement standard · (Land)Erschließungsrichtlinie f, legislative (Land)Erschließungsrichtlinie

prescribed thing · ersessene Sache f

prescribing · Ersitzen n

prescribing female person · Ersitzende f

prescribing male person · männliche Ersitzende m, Ersitzende

prescribing person · ersitzende Person f

prescription, regulation, rule · (Rechts)Vorschrift f

prescription · Ersitzung f [*Erwerb eines Rechtes durch ungestörte Ausübung während eines gesetzlich bestimmten Zeitraumes*]

prescription absolute, rule absolute, regulation absolute · unbedingte (Rechts)Vorschrift f, absolute (Rechts)Vorschrift

prescription act, prescription law, prescription statute · Ersitzungsgesetz n

Prescription Act 1832, Lord Tenderden's Act · Ersitzungsgesetz n von 1832 [*in England*]

prescription by factual error in the land register · Buchersitzung f, Tabularersitzung

prescription corporation, corporation by prescription · Körperschaft f durch Vermutung, Korporation f durch Vermutung [*Inkorporierung auf Grund einer vermuteten Vollmacht*]

prescription for organization, rule for organization, regulation for organization · Organisationsvorschrift f

prescription law, prescription statute, prescription act · Ersitzungsgesetz n

prescription law, law of prescription · Ersitzungsrecht n, objektives Ersitzungsrecht

prescription of (ad)measurement, (ad)measurement prescription, · Aufmaßvorschrift f

prescription of incorporeal hereditament(s), prescription of not tangible hereditament(s), acquisitive prescription, positive prescription [*Acquisition of a right. See remark under "incorporeal hereditament". In international law "aquisitive" or "positive" prescription means title to territory based on uninterrupted and uncontested occupation over a reasonably long period*] · Ersitzung f nichtkörperlichen Erbgutes, Ersitzung unkörperlichen Erbgutes, Ersitzung immateriellen Erbgutes

prescription of not tangible hereditament(s), acquisitive prescription, positive prescription, prescription of incorporeal hereditament(s) [*Acquisition of a right. See remark under "incorporeal hereditament". In international law "aquisitive" or "positive" prescription means title to territory based on uninterrupted and uncontested occupation over a reasonably long period*] · Ersitzung f nichtkörperlichen Erbgutes, Ersitzung unkörperlichen Erbgutes, Ersitzung immateriellen Erbgutes

prescription of usufruct, usufruct prescription · Ersitzung f des Nießbrauchs, Nießbrauchersitzung

prescription of zoning, zoning regulation, zoning rule, rule of zoning, regulation of zoning, zoning prescription · (bauliche) Nutzungsvorschrift f, Baunutzungsvorschrift

prescription owner, prescription proprietor, owner by prescription, proprietor by prescription · Ersitzungseigentümer m, Ersitzungseigner, Ersitzungseigentumssubjekt n

prescription period → prescription time (allowed)

prescription possession, possession by prescription · Ersitzungsbesitz *m,* ersessener Besitz

prescription possessor, possessor by prescription · Ersitzungsbesitzer *m*

prescriptions for topsoil protection, rules for topsoil protection, regulations for topsoil protection · Mutterbodenschutz *m* [*Schutz des Mutterbodens durch (Rechts)Vorschriften*]

prescription statute, prescription act, prescription law · Ersitzungsgesetz *n*

prescription term → prescription time (allowed)

prescription time (allowed), prescription period, prescription term, (fixed) period (of time) for prescription · Ersitzungsfrist *f,* (bestimmte) Ersitzungszeit *f,* (bestimmter) Ersitzungszeitraum *m*

prescription title, prescriptive title, title by prescription · Ersitzungs(rechts)titel *m,* ersessener (Rechts)Titel, (Rechts)Titel kraft Ersitzung

prescriptive interest, prescriptive right · (subjektives) Ersitzungsrecht *n*

prescriptive ratio · Norm *f* die aus dem Präzedenzfall für künftige Entscheidungen zu entnehmen ist [*Doppelnatur des tragenden Urteilsgrundes*]

prescriptive right, prescriptive interest · (subjektives) Ersitzungsrecht *n*

presence · Anwesenheit *f*

to present, to discover, to produce, to fille, to submit · abgeben, einreichen, vorlegen, enthüllen [*Mitteilen von Tatsachen oder Vorlegen von Schriftstücken an den Prozeßgegner*]

present · gegenwärtig, anwesend

presentation, filing, discovery, production, submission · Abgabe *f,* Einreichung *f,* Vorlage *f,* Vorlegung, Edition *f,* Enthüllung [*Mitteilung von Tatsachen oder Vorlegung von Schriftstücken an den Prozeßgegner*]

presentation [*In ecclesiastic(al) law. The act of a patron or proprietor of a living, in offering a clerk to the ordinary for institution*] · Vorstellung *f* [*Kirchenrecht*]

presentation by interrogatories, production by interrogatories, filing by interrogatories, discovery by interrogatories, submission by interrogatories · Abgabe *f* von Tatsachen, Einreichung *f* von Tatsachen, Vorlage *f* von Tatsachen, Vorlegung von Tatsachen, Edition *f* von Tatsachen, Enthüllung von Tatsachen [*An den Prozeßgegner*]

presentation of documents, discovery of documents, filing of documents, production of documents, submission of documents · Abgabe *f* von Schriftstücken, Vorlage *f* von Schriftstücken, Einreichung *f* von Schriftstücken, Vorlegung von Schriftstücken, Enthüllung von Schriftstücken [*An den Prozeßgegner*]

presentation of merchandise, unregistered trademark · Ausstattung *f*

present enjoyment, present interest in land, interest in possession, interest of present possession · Besitzanteil *m* der dem Berechtigten den gegenwärtigen Grund(stücks)genuß gewährt

present estate, present property, existing estate, existing property · bestehendes Vermögen *n,* bestehendes Gut *n,* vorhandenes Vermögen, vorhandenes Gut, bestehende Habe *f,* vorhandene Habe

present-in-area · ortsanwesend

present-in-area population, de facto population · ortsanwesende Bevölkerung *f*

presenting, submitting · Einreichen *n,* Vorlegen

present interest, existing right, existing interest, present right · bestehendes Anrecht *n,* vorhandenes Anrecht, gegenwärtiges Anrecht, bestehendes (subjektives) Recht, vorhandenes (subjektives) Recht, bestehende Berechtigung *f,* gegenwärtige Berechtigung, vorhandene Berechtigung, bestehender Anspruch *m,* gegenwärtiger Anspruch, vorhandener Anspruch

present interest in land, interest in possession, interest of present possession, present enjoyment · Besitzanteil *m* der dem Berechtigten den gegenwärtigen Grund(stücks)genuß gewährt

presentment · amtliche Anzeige *f* [*Bei den Sessionen der Friedensrichter*]

presentment of a promissory note · Präsentation *f* eines eigenen Wechsels

present price, current price · gegenwärtiger Preis *m*

present property, existing estate, existing property, present estate · bestehendes Vermögen *n,* bestehendes Gut *n,* vorhandenes Vermögen, vorhandenes Gut, bestehende Habe *f,* vorhandene Habe

present right, present interest, existing right, existing interest · bestehendes Anrecht *n,* vorhandenes Anrecht, gegenwärtiges Anrecht, bestehendes (subjektives) Recht, gegenwärtiges (subjektives) Recht, bestehende Berechtigung *f,* gegenwärtige Berechtigung, vorhandene Berechtigung, bestehender Anspruch *m,* gegenwärtiger Anspruch, vorhandener Anspruch

present state of space · räumliche Ordnung *f* [*Der jeweilige tatsächliche Zustand des Raumes eines bestimmten Gemeinwesens (Staat, Verwaltungsbe-*

present value — presumed owner 792

zirk, Gemeinde) ohne Rücksicht darauf, inwieweit dieser Zustand einem Ordnungsbild entspricht. Es wird der gegenwärtige Zustand ohne jede Wertung beschrieben]

present value · abgezinster Wert m, Gegenwartswert, Barwert mit Bezugszeitpunkt t_0, gegenwärtiger Wert [Wert auf den Bezugszeitpunkt t_0 abgezinst]

present-value factor, discount factor · Abzinsungsfaktor m, AbF [Er zinst einen nach soundsoviel Jahren fälligen Geldbetrag unter Berücksichtigung von Zins und Zinseszins auf einen jetzt fälligen Geldbetrag ab]

present value of the incumbrance, present value of the encumbrance, cast value of the incumbrance, cast value of the encumbrance · Barwert m der Belastung [z. B. durch Wegerecht]

present-value table · Gegenwerttabelle f

preservable, conservable · erhaltbar, pflegbar

preservation, conservation · Erhaltung f, Pflege f, Substanzerhaltung, Substanzpflege

preservation area, preservation territory, conservation area, conservation territory [An area of special architectural or historic interest the character or appearance of which it is desirable to preserve or enhance] · Denkmalpflegegebiet n, Denkmalerhaltungsgebiet

preservation duty, duty of preservation, duty of conservation, conservation duty · Erhaltungspflicht f, Pflegepflicht [Bauwerk]

preservation of art, conservation of art · Kunstpflege f, Kunsterhaltung f

preservation of buildings, building preservation, building conservation, conservation of buildings · Gebäudeerhaltung f, Gebäudepflege f

preservation of forests, conservation of forests, forest preservation, forest conservation, forest retention · Walderhaltung f, Waldpflege f, Forsterhaltung, Forstpflege

preservation of housing act, preservation of housing law, preservation of housing statute · Wohnungsbindungsgesetz n

preservation of land, conservation of land, land preservation, land conservation · Landeserhaltung f, Landespflege f

preservation of monuments, historic preservation, historic conservation, conservation of monuments · Denkmalerhaltung f, Denkmalpflege f, Denkmalschutz m

preservation of soil, soil conservation, soil preservation, conservation of soil · Bodenerhaltung f, Bodenpflege f

preservation of structures, conservation of structures, retention of structures · Bau(werk)erhaltung f, Bau(werk)pflege f

preservation of the historic(al) core, conservation of the historic(al) core · Altstadterhaltung f, Altstadtpflege f

preservation of trees, conservation of trees, tree conservation, tree preservation · Baumerhaltung f, Baumpflege f

preservation territory, conservation area, conservation territory, preservation area [An area of special architectural or historic interest the character or appearance of which it is desirable to preserve or enhance] · Denkmalpflegegebiet n, Denkmalerhaltungsgebiet

preserve, refuge [for animals] · Schutzgebiet n, Schongebiet [für Tiere]

presidential constitution · Präsidialverfassung f

president of a district, prefect of a district · Landrat m

president of police · Polizeipräsident m

presiding arbiter [This term is rarely used]; presiding arbitrator, presiding referee, impier, umpire; oversman [Scots law]; imperator [Latin] · dritter Schiedsrichter m, Obmann m [Bei einer Dreierbesetzung des Schiedsgerichts]

presiding judge (Brit.) · präsidierender Oberrichter m

pressing necessity · drückende Notwendigkeit f

pressure-creating function, initiating function · Zündungsfunktion f [Funktion des Staates für die Infrastruktur]

pressure group · Interessengruppe f, Interessenverband m

pressure of schedule(s) · Zeitdruck m

pressure politics · Politik f des organisierten Drucks

pressure-relieving function, catching up function, filling in function · Nachholfunktion f [Funktion des Staates für die Infrastruktur]

presumed, reputed, ostensible, apparent, presumptive · angeblich, anscheinend, scheinbar, mutmaßlich, vermutlich, vermeintlich

presumed intention (of party) · mutmaßlicher Parteiwille m, hypothetischer Parteiwille

presumed owner, apparent proprietor, presumptive proprietor, presumed proprietor, reputed owner, reputed proprietor, apparent owner, presumptive owner · angeblicher Eigentümer m, vermutlicher Eigentümer, anscheinender Eigentümer, mutmaßlicher Eigentümer, scheinbarer Eigentümer, vermeintlicher Eigentümer

presumed ownership, presumed proprietorship, presumed property, apparent ownership, apparent proprietorship, apparent property, presumptive ownership, presumptive proprietorship, presumptive property, reputed ownership, reputed property, reputed proprietorship · angebliches Eigentum n, mutmaßliches Eigentum, scheinbares Eigentum, vermutliches Eigentum, anscheinendes Eigentum, vermeintliches Eigentum, Vermögen n Dritter in einer Konkursmasse

presumed property → presumed ownership

presumed proprietor → presumed owner

presumed proprietorship → presumed ownership

presumptio juris et de jure [*Latin*]; conclusive presumption, conclusory presumption · schlüssige Vermutung f, gefolgerte Vermutung, abgeleitete Vermutung

presumption · Vermutung f

presumption of abandonment, abandonment presumption · Aufgabevermutung f, Preisgabevermutung f, Verzichtsvermutung f

presumption of advancement, advancement presumption [*It means that a gift was intended and arises where a voluntary conveyance has been made to the wife or child of the donor or to a person to whom he stands in loco parentis*] · Schenkungsvermutung f

presumption of death, death presumption · Todesvermutung f

presumption of fact · Tatsachenvermutung f

presumption of insolvency, insolvency presumption · Vermutung f der Zahlungsunfähigkeit

presumption of life, life presumption · Lebensvermutung f

presumption of life limitation, life limitation presumption · Verschollenheitsvermutung f

presumption of possession, possession presumption · Besitzvermutung f

presumption of property, property presumption · Vermögensvermutung f

presumption of property, presumption of proprietorship, presumption of ownership (of property), (general) property presumption, proprietorship presumption, ownership (of property) presumption · Eigentumsvermutung f

presumptive, presumed, reputed, ostensible, apparent · angeblich, anscheinend, scheinbar, mutmaßlich, vermutlich, vermeintlich

presumptive evidence, presumptive proof, circumstantial evidence, circumstantial proof [*"Circumstantial evidence" and "circumstantial proof" haben auch einen besonderen juristischen Sinn und bezeichnen denjenigen indirekten Beweis, welcher nach dem positiven Recht eines Landes ausreicht, um zur Grundlage gerichtlicher Entscheidungen zu dienen. Beide Benennungen werden aber auch ganz allgemein als Gegensatz zu Zeugen und Urkunden gebraucht. Wo eine philosophische oder historische Wahrheit durch Schlußfolgerungen aus entfernt liegenden Momenten oder durch Analogie dargetan wird kann man wohl nicht von circ. ev. und circ. proof reden. Im Deutschen würde "Anzeigebeweis" dafür gewiß nicht gebraucht werden*] · Anzeigebeweis m, indirekter Beweis m, Beweis m durch Nebenumstände, Indizienbeweis m

presumptive heiress, presumptive heir female · angebliche Erbin f, anscheinende Erbin, scheinbare Erbin, vermeintliche Erbin, mutmaßliche Erbin, vermutliche Erbin

presumptive heir (male), heir (male) presumptive [*A man who, if the ancestor should die immediately, would, in the present circumstances of things, be his heir, but whose right of inheritance may be defeated by the contingency of some nearer heir being born, as a brother or nephew, whose presumptive succession may be destroyed by the birth of a child*] · angeblicher Erbe m, scheinbarer Erbe, vermeintlicher Erbe, vermutlicher Erbe, anscheinender Erbe

presumptive owner, presumed owner, apparent owner, presumptive proprietor, presumed proprietor, reputed owner, reputed proprietor, apparent owner · angeblicher Eigentümer m, vermutlicher Eigentümer, anscheinender Eigentümer, mutmaßlicher Eigentümer, scheinbarer Eigentümer, vermeintlicher Eigentümer

presumptive ownership, presumptive proprietorship, presumptive property, reputed ownership, reputed property, reputed proprietorship, presumed ownership, presumed proprietorship, presumed property, apparent ownership, apparent proprietorship, apparent property · angebliches Eigentum n, mutmaßliches Eigentum, scheinbares Eigentum, vermutliches Eigentum, anscheinendes Eigentum, vermeintliches Eigentum, Vermögen n Dritter in einer Konkursmasse

presumptive proof → presumptive evidence

presumptive property → presumptive ownership

presumptive proprietor → presumptive owner

presumptive proprietorship → presumptive ownership

presumptive title · vermutlicher (Rechts)Titel *m*

pretence; colour (Brit.); color (US); appearance, pretext [*A fictitious allegation of a right. A person is said to have no colour of title when he has not even a prima facie title*] · Deckmantel *m*, Vorwand *m*, Anschein *m*

pretended, feigned, feint, fictitious, faint · fiktiv, vorgegeben, vorgetäuscht, fingiert

pretended bill; windmill, kite (Brit.); accommodation bill, fictitious bill, feint bill, faint bill, feigned bill · Freundschaftswechsel *m*, Gefälligkeitswechsel, Kellerwechsel, Reitwechsel, Schornsteinwechsel, Scheinwechsel

pretended business, feint business, fictitious business, feigned business, faint business · fiktives Geschäft *n*, fingiertes Geschäft, vorgegebenes Geschäft, vorgetäuschtes Geschäft, Scheingeschäft

pretended contract, faint contract, fictitious contract, feigned contract · Scheinvertrag *m*

pretended (court) action, feigned (court) action, faint (court) action, fictitious (court) action, feint (court) action [*An action brought on a pretended right, when the plaintiff has no true cause of action, for some illegal purpose. In a feigned action the words of the writ are true. It differs from "false action", in which case the words of the writ are false*] · fiktive Klage *f*, vorgetäuschte Klage, vorgegebene Klage, fingierte Klage, Scheinklage

pretended desertion, faint desertion, feint desertion, fictitious desertion, feigned desertion · Scheinwüstung *f*, Trugwüstung

pretended name, feigned name, faint name, feint name, fictitious name · fiktiver Name *m*, vorgetäuschter Name, vorgegebener Name, fingierter Name, Scheinname

pretended permission → feigned permission

pretended plaintiff, faint plaintiff, feint plaintiff, fictitious plaintiff, feigned plaintiff · fiktiver Kläger *m*, vorgegebener Kläger, vorgetäuschter Kläger, fingierter Kläger, Scheinkläger

pretended promise, faint promise, feint promise, fictitious promise, feigned promise · fiktives Versprechen *n*, vorgetäuschtes Versprechen, vorgegebenes Versprechen, fingiertes Versprechen, Scheinversprechen

pretended purchase, feint purchase, fictitious purchase, feigned purchase, faint purchase · fiktiver Kauf *m*, vorgetäuschter Kauf, fingierter Kauf, vorgegebener Kauf, Scheinkauf

pre-tender investigation · Untersuchung *f* vor Angebotsabgabe

pretext, pretence; colour (Brit.); color (US); appearance [*A fictitious allegation of a right. A person is said to have no colour of title when he has not even a prima facie title*] · Deckmantel *m*, Vorwand *m*, Anschein *m*

pre-trial conference · Gerichtskonferenz *f* vor der Hauptverhandlung

pre-trial confinement, pre-trial commitment, pre-trial committal · Untersuchungshaft *f*

pre-trial proceeding, interlocutory proceeding · Widerspruchsverfahren *n*, Vorverfahren [*Vor der Erhebung der Anfechtungsklage sind Rechtmäßigkeit und Zweckmäßigkeit eines Verwaltungsaktes in einem Vorverfahren zu prüfen*]

prevarication [*Any (secret) abuse committed in a public office or private commission*] · Amtspflichtverletzung *f*, Amtspflichtverstoß *m*, Dienstpflichtverletzung, Dienstpflichtverstoß

to prevent · verhüten

preventability, preventibility · Verhütbarkeit *f*

preventable, preventible · verhütbar

preven(ta)tive maintenance · vorbeugende Unterhaltung *f*

prevented profit, lost profit, prevented gain, loss of prospective profit, lost gain; lucrum cessans [*Latin*] · verlorener Gewinn *m*, entgangener Gewinn, verlorener Profit, entgangener Profit

preventibility, preventability · Verhütbarkeit *f*

preventing remedy · Vorbeugungsmittel *n* gegen Rechtsverletzung

prevention · Verhütung *f*

prevention of a danger · Abwendung *f* einer Gefahr, Gefahr(en)abwendung

preventive detention · Vorbeugungshaft *f*

preventive injunction, negative injunction, restrictive injunction, restraining injunction · gerichtliches Verbot *n*, gerichtliche Verbotsverfügung *f*

preventive law · Vorbeugungsrecht *n*

previous owner · Voreigner *m*, Voreigentümer

prewar contract · Vorkriegsvertrag *m*

prewar growth · Vorkriegswachstum *n*

prewar level · Vorkriegsstand *m*

prewar private value · Vorkriegsbaulandpreis *m*, Vorkriegs(bau)bodenpreis, Vorkriegsgrundstückspreis, Vorkriegsliegenschaftspreis

price advance, price dip, price reduction · Preisherabsetzung f

price approach · Preisansatz m

price association, price ring [*A group of firms in an industry loosely associated together to operate a common price policy*] · Preisring m

price authority · Preisbehörde f

price basis, basis of prices · Preisgrundlage f

price below cost price, ruinous price, cut(throat) price, slaughtered price · Schleuderpreis m

price-booster · Preistreiber m

price-bound · preisgebunden

price bracket, price range · Preisspanne f, Preisbereich m

price calculation, price computation, pricing · Preisberechnung f, Preiskalkulation f

price calculation errror, price computation error, pricing error · Preisberechnungsfehler m, Preiskalkulationsfehler

price calculation ordinance, price computation ordinance, pricing ordinance · Preisberechnungsverordnung f, Preiskalkulationsverordnung

price ceiling, upper price limit · Preishöchstgrenze f, Preisobergrenze

price change, price variation · Preis(ab)änderung f

price check(ing) · Preiskontrolle f, Preis(über)prüfung f, Preisnachprüfung

price code · Preisordnung f

price column · Preisspalte f

price control · Preislenkung f

price control board · Preisamt n, Preisprüfungsamt, Preisüberwachungsamt

price control committee · Preisausschuß m

price control office · Preis(prüfungs)stelle f, Preisüberwachungsstelle

price curve, iso-outlay curve, isocost curve, iso-outlay line, price line, isocost (line) · Kostenisoquante f, Isokostenlinie f, Isokostenkurve f

price cutting · Preisschnitt m

price determination, price fixing · Preisbestimmung f

price dip, price reduction, price advance · Preisherabsetzung f

price-earnings ratio, PER · Kurs-Gewinn-Verhältnis n von Aktien

price error, error of price · Preisfehler m

price fixed by authority, licensed price, licenced price, statutory price, official price · Taxe f [*Ein aufgrund eines Rechtes behördlich festgesetzter Preis*]

price fixing, price determination · Preisbestimmung f

price fixing → collusion among bidders

price fixing trust · Preiskartell n

price fluctuation · Preisschwankung f

price fluctuation clause · Preisgleitklausel f

price fluctuation factor · Preisgleitfaktor m

price fluctuation rate, fluctuation in price rate · Preisgleitsatz m

price for settling daywork(s) · Tagelohnabrechnungspreis m

price freeze · Preisstopp m

price freezing → (fixed) price freezing

price gradient · Preisgefälle n

price hazard, price risk · Preisrisiko n, Preiswagnis n

price hedging · Preissicherung f

price history, history of prices · Geschichte f der Preise, Preisgeschichte

price-kiting, profiteering · Preiswucher m, Preistreiberei f

price law · Preisrecht n, PR

price leadership · Preisführerschaft f

price level · Preisniveau n, Preisstand m

price limit · Preisgrenze f

price line, isocost (line), price curve, iso-outlay curve, isocost curve, iso-outlay line · Kostenisoquante f, Isokostenlinie f, Isokostenkurve f

price list, schedule of prices, list of prices, price schedule · Preisverzeichnis n, Preisliste f

price mechanism · Preismechanismus m

price negotiation · Preisverhandlung f

price of discharge, redemption price, discharge price, price of redemption · Ablösungspreis m, Einlösungspreis, Auslösungspreis

price of issue, issue rate, issue price, rate of issue · Emissionskurs m, Ausgabekurs, Emissionspreis m, Ausgabepreis

price of land, land price · Bodenpreis m, Baubodenpreis, (Bau)Landpreis, Liegenschaftspreis, Grund(stücks)preis

price of redemption, price of discharge, redemption price, discharge price · Ablösungspreis m, Einlösungspreis, Auslösungspreis

price policy · Preisgestaltung f

price policy · Preispolitik f

price prescription — primary input 796

price prescription, price regulation · Preisvorschrift *f*

price-quality function · Preis-Güte-Funktion *f*

price-quantity function · Preis-Mengen-Funktion *f*

price range, price bracket · Preisspanne *f*, Preisbereich *m*

price reduction, price advance, price dip · Preisherabsetzung *f*

price regulation, price prescription · Preisvorschrift *f*

price reservation, price reserving, price proviso · Preisvorbehalt *m*

price reservation clause, price reserving clause, price proviso clause · Preisvorbehaltsklausel *f*

price ring → price association

price risk, price hazard · Preisrisiko *n*, Preiswagnis *n*

price schedule, price list, schedule of prices, list of prices · Preisverzeichnis *n*, Preisliste *f*

price sheet · Preisblatt *n*, Preisbogen *m* [*Teil eines Angebots*]

price(s) index · Preisindex *m*

price supervision · Preisüberwachung *f*

price support · Subvention *f*, Preissubvention

price system · Preissystem *n*

price taking, collusive agreement, combining to eliminate competition, restrictive covenant, restrictive tendering agreement, taking a price, collusive tendering, collusive bidding, (collusive) price fixing, bid-rigging, bid collusion, rigging bids, collusion among(st) bidders, collusion among(st) offerers, collusion among(st) tenderers [*The frequently heavy cost of tendering sometimes leads contractors to put forward tenders which are not genuine, in the sense that, rather than refuse to make a tender when invited to do so, the contractor tenders a price higher than that "taken" from another contractor who does desire to obtain the contract, thus avoiding expense and leading the employer to believe that he has had genuine competitive tenders for the work*] · Abrede *f* unter Bietern, Absprache *f* unter Bietern, Preisabrede, Preisabsprache, Submissionsabrede, Submissionsabsprache, Konkurrenzvereinbarung *f*, Verständigung unter Bietern, Angebotsabsprache

price target · Preisvorgabe *f*

price variance · Preisabweichung *f*

price variation, price change · Preis(ab)änderung *f*

price winner · Preisträger *m*

pricing, price calculation, price computation · Preisberechnung *f*, Preiskalkulation *f*

pricing (construction work), estimating (construction) cost(s), (construction) cost(s) estimating · (Bau)Kostenkalkulation *f*

pricing error, price calculation errror, price computation error · Preisberechnungsfehler *m*, Preiskalkulationsfehler

pricing for return on investment, pricing for yield on investment · renditebestimmte Preiskalkulation *f*

pricing ordinance, price calculation ordinance, price computation ordinance · Preisberechnungsverordnung *f*, Preiskalkulationsverordnung

priest in orders; missae presbyter [*Latin*] · Ordenspriester *m*

prima facie case · widerlegbarer Beweisfall *m*, Anscheinsbeweisfall

prima facie evidence, prima facie proof, apparent evidence, apparent proof · Anscheinsbeweis *m*, widerlegbarer Beweis, Beweis des ersten Anscheins

primage · Frachtzuschlag *m*, Primgeld *n*

primary · Nominierungswahl *f*

primary activity · motorischer Leistungsbereich *m*

primary assembly, caucus · Vorversammlung *f*, Urversammlung, Erstversammlung [*Vorwahlen in den USA*]

primary buyer, primary purchaser, first purchaser, first buyer, original buyer, original purchaser · Erstkäufer *m*

primary communal equiqment, primary community equipment, (communal) primary equipment · Erstausstattung *f*, kommunale Erstausstattung, gemeindliche Erstausstattung

primary contractor · Erstunternehmer *m*

primary conveyance [*A conveyance by means of which an estate is created or first arises*] · rechtsbegründende Eigentumsverschaffung *f*

primary evidence · Vorzeigung *f* einer Urkunde als Beweis

primary express authority · Grundvollmacht *f*, Grundvertretungsmacht

primary function · primäre Funktion *f*, städtebildende Funktion

primary goal (of policy) · Primäroberziel *n*, Primärzielnorm *f*

primary industry, fundamental industry, basic industry · Grundindustrie *f*

primary input · Primärzugang *m*

primary occupations, basic employment, basic activity, economic base · Fernversorgungstätigkeit *f*, Erzeugung *f* von Ausfuhrgütern, Grundleistung, Originärbeschäftigung, Exportaktivität *f*, Ausfuhraktivität, primäre Aktivität [*Eine der Ausfuhr aus einer Region dienende Leistung*]

primary population · Erstbevölkerung *f*, Primärbevölkerung

primary purchaser, first purchaser, first buyer, original buyer, original purchaser, primary buyer · Erstkäufer *m*

primary school, board school (Brit.); elementary school, common school (US); day school · Elementarschule, Grundschule, Volksschule *f*

primary sector [*raw materials; agriculture; mining; fishing*] · Primärwirtschaft *f*, primärer Wirtschaftssektor *m*, primär(wirtschaftlich)er Sektor, Primärsektor, erster Sektor

primary unit, first-stage unit · Einheit *f* der ersten Auswahlstufe [*Statistik*]

prime · Differenz *f* zwischen Übernahmekurs und Abnehmerkurs [*Emissionsgeschäft*]

prime accounting → prime costing

prime bidder, prime tenderer [*One who submits a bid directly to the owner*] · Direkt(an)bieter *m*

prime contract, direct contract · Direktvertrag *m*, direkter Vertrag

prime contractor, direct contractor [*A contractor having a contract with the owner*] · Direktunternehmer *m*

prime costing, prime (cost(s)) accounting · Teilkostenrechnung *f* mit variablen Einzelkosten, Teilkostenkalkulation *f* mit variablen Einzelkosten, Teilkostenermitt(e)lung mit variablen Einzelkosten, Teilkostenberechnung mit variablen Einzelkosten

(prime) cost plus fixed fee contract, fixed fee/prime cost(s) contract [*A contractual arrangement whereby a contractor is paid the prime cost(s) and a fixed fee calculated in relation to the estimated amount of the prime cost*] · Selbstkostenerstattungsvertrag *m* mit begrenztem Zuschlag, Selbstkostenerstattungsvertrag mit begrenztem Aufschlag

(prime) cost plus percentage contract [*The management is calculated as a percentage of the prime cost(s)*] · Selbstkostenerstattungsvertrag *m* mit prozentualem Zuschlag, Selbstkostenerstattungsvertrag mit prozentualem Aufschlag

prime (cost(s)) accounting, prime costing · Teilkostenrechnung *f* mit variablen Einzelkosten, Teilkostenkalkulation *f* mit variablen Einzelkosten, Teilkostenermitt(e)lung mit variablen Einzelkosten, Teilkostenberechnung mit variablen Einzelkosten

prime cost(s) item · Selbstkostenposition *f*

(prime) general contract, single contract [*A construction contract where all work is contracted under the responsibility of a single or (prime) general contractor*] · Generalvertrag *m*, Gesamtvertrag

(prime) general contractor, single contractor · Generalunternehmer *m*, Gesamtunternehmer [*Er wird vom Bauherrn mit sämtlichen Leistungen beauftragt*]

prime rate, fine rate · Vorzugszinssatz *m*, Primarate *f*, Leitzinssatz für erste Adressen, Zinssatz für Kredite an erste Adressen

primer seisin [*It was the right of the Kings of England after the Norman Conquest to exact, on the death of a tenant-in-chief from the heir, if of full age, one year's profits of the land in addition to the ordinary relief. Abolished by the statute 1660, 12 Car. 2, c. 24*] · Kronleh(e)nerträgnis *n* eines Jahres

prime tenderer → prime bidder

"priming the pump" [*A popular term for state investment undertaken for the purpose of stimulating demand in order to reduce unemployment*] · Wirtschaftsankurbelung *f*

primogeniture(ship), seniority, eldership · (männliche) Erstgeburtserbfolge *f*, (männliche) Primogeniturerbfolge

primogeniture(ship) → (right of) primogeniture(ship)

Prince Consort · Prinzgemahl *m*

principal, covenantor, obligor, promisor [*One bound by an obligation. Under a bond both the "principal" and "surety" are "obligors"*] · Versprechensgeber *m*, Versprechende, Verpflichtete

principal, capital sum, original amount [*The total amount of capital of an estate, fund, mortgage, bond, note, or other form of financial investment, together with accretions not yet recognized as income*] · Kapitalsumme *f*, Hauptsumme

principal · Machtgeber *m*

principal, master · Geschäftsherr *m*

principal · Auftraggeber *m* eines Kommissionsgeschäftes, Kommittent *m*

principal · Hauptangeklagte *m*

principal administration (of estate(s)), main administration (of estate(s)) · Erb(schafts)verwaltung *f* am Wohnsitz des Verstorbenen, Nachlaßverwaltung am Wohnsitz des Verstorbenen

principal architect, architect-in-charge, supervising architect · ausführender Architekt *m*, (bau)leitender Architekt *m*

principal building, main building · Hauptgebäude *n*

principal business thoroughfare · verkehrsorientiertes Einzelhandelsband *n*, verkehrsbezogenes Einzelhandelsband

principal challenge · Ablehnung *f* von Geschworenen auf Grund objektiver Tatsachen

principal claim, main claim, principal demand, main demand · Hauptforderung *f*, Hauptverlangen *n*

principal committee, main committee · Hauptausschuß *m*

principal (constituent), employer, donor of an authority, grantor of an authority; mandator [*Latin*] · Vollmachtgeber *m*, Bevollmächtiger, Vertretene [*Jemand der ein Rechtsgeschäft zu eigenem Nutzen und auf eigene Rechnung selbständig vornehmen kann, aber zu dessen Vornahme eine andere Person verwendet*]

principal contour, main contour · Haupthöhenlinie *f*

principal contract condition(s), main contract condition(s), general contract condition(s) · allgemeine Vertragsbedingung(en) *f (pl)*

principal contractor, main contractor · Hauptunternehmer *m*

principal creditor, main creditor · Hauptgläubiger *m*

principal debtor, main debtor [*The party who owes the obligation and for whose debt the guarantor agrees to answer*] · Hauptschuldner *m*

principal defendant, main defendant · Hauptbeklagte *m*

principal demand, main demand, principal claim, main claim · Hauptforderung *f*, Hauptverlangen *n*

principal demise, head tenancy, head demise, head lease(hold), main tenancy, main demise, main lease(hold), principal tenancy, principal lease(hold) · Hauptpacht *f*, Hauptnutzungsrecht *n*

principal duty, main duty · Hauptpflicht *f*

principal estimator · Hauptkalkulator *m*

principal fact, main fact; factum probandum [*Latin*] · Haupttatsache *f*

principal (land) condemnation, main (land) condemnation (US); main (land) expropriation, principal (land) expropriation · Haupt(land)enteignung *f*, Hauptbodenenteignung

principal landlord, main landlord · Hauptvermieter *m*

principal lease(hold), principal demise, head tenancy, head demise, head lease(hold), main tenancy, main demise, main lease(hold), principal tenancy · Hauptpacht *f*, Hauptnutzungsrecht *n*

principal mansion (house), chief mansion (house), capital messuage [*The only one mansion (house) on settled land*] · alleiniges Gutshaus *n*, alleiniges Herrschaftshaus, alleiniger Herrensitz *m*

principal note [*Promissary note that is secured by mortgage*] · hypothekarisch gesicherter Schuldschein *m*, hypothekarisch gesichertes Schuldpapier *n*

principal obligation, main obligation · Hauptverpflichtung *f*

principal office, main office, chief office, leading office · Hauptbüro *n*

principal participator, main participator · Hauptbeteiligte *m*

principal place of business, main place of business · Hauptverwaltungssitz *m*

principal principle, main principle · Hauptgrundsatz *m*, Hauptprinzip *n*

principal reinstatement, main reinstatement · Hauptinstandsetzung *f*

principal repair, main repair · Hauptreparatur *f*

principal security, main security · Hauptdeckung *f*, Hauptsicherheit *f*, Hauptsicherung, Hauptunterlage *f*

principal sewer, main sewer · Hauptsammler *m*, Haupt(abwasser)kanal *m*

principal's liability, master's liability · Geschäftsherrenhaftung *f*, Geschäftsherrenhaftpflicht *f*, Geschäftsherrenhaftbarkeit *f*

principal supply line, main supply line · Hauptversorgungsleitung *f*

principal tenancy, main tenancy, master tenancy, head tenancy · Hauptmietverhältnis *n*

principal tenancy, principal lease(hold), principal demise, head tenancy, head demise, head lease(hold), main tenancy, main demise, main lease(hold) · Hauptpacht *f*, Hauptnutzungsrecht *n*

principal tenant, master tenant, main tenant, head tenant · Hauptmieter *m*

principal underwriter, major underwriter · Hauptübernehmer *m*

principal variable, main variable · Hauptvariable *f*

principal work(s), permanent work(s), main work(s) · (bauliche) Hauptarbeit(en) *f (pl)*, (bauliche) Hauptleistung(en) *f (pl)*

principle · Grundsatz *m*, Prinzip *n*

principle of accession, accession principle · Grundsatz *m* vom wesentlichen

principle of advantage — principle of preference

Bestandteil, Prinzip n vom wesentlichen Bestandteil

principle of advantage, advantage principle · Vorteilsgrundsatz m, Vorteilsprinzip n

principle of application, application principle · Anwendungsgrundsatz m, Anwendungsprinzip n

principle of betterment · Wertsteigerungsprinzip n, Wertsteigerungsgrundsatz m

principle of citizenhood → citizenism

principle of citizenship → citizenism

principle of coincidence of intent(ion), principle of consent, consent principle · Bewilligungsprinzip n, Bewilligungsgrundsatz m, Einigungsprinzip, Einigungsgrundsatz, Konsensprinzip, Konsensgrundsatz [*Grundbuchrecht*]

principle of consent, consent principle, principle of coincidence of intent(ion) · Bewilligungsprinzip n, Bewilligungsgrundsatz m, Einigungsprinzip, Einigungsgrundsatz, Konsensprinzip, Konsensgrundsatz [*Grundbuchrecht*]

principle of consideration, consideration principle · Gegenleistungsgrundsatz m, Gegenleistungsprinzip n

principle of construction, principle of interpretation · Auslegungsgrundsatz m, Deutungsgrundsatz m, Auslegungsprinzip n, Deutungsprinzip n

principle of control, control principle · Lenkungsgrundsatz m, Lenkungsprinzip n

principle of directness, directness principle · Grundsatz m der Unmittelbarkeit, Prinzip n der Unmittelbarkeit, Unmittelbarkeitsprinzip, Unmittelbarkeitsgrundsatz

principle of distinctness, distinctness principle, distinctness doctrine, doctrine of distinctness · Bestimmtheitsgrundsatz m, Bestimmtheitsprinzip n, Spezialitätsgrundsatz, Spezialitätsprinzip [*Grundbuchrecht*]

principle of equal treatment, principle of equality, equal treatment principle, equality principle · Gleichbehandlungsgrundsatz m, Gleichbehandlungsprinzip n, Gleichheits(grund)satz m, Gleichheitsprinzip

principle of equity, equitable principle, equity principle · Billigkeitsgrundsatz m, Billigkeitsprinzip n, Grundsatz der Billigkeit, Prinzip der Billigkeit

principle of equivalent reinstatement · Grundsatz m der gleichwertigen Wiederherstellung, Prinzip n der gleichwertigen Wiederherstellung

principle of exclusion, exclusion principle · Ausschlußgrundsatz m, Ausschlußprinzip n

principle of (feudal) tenure, principle of feodal tenure, principle of feuda(to)ry tenure, feudal principle, feodal principle, feuda(to)ry principle · Leh(e)n(s)grundsatz m, Leh(e)n(s)prinzip n, Feudalgrundsatz, Feudalprinzip

principle of forfeiture, forfeiture principle · Verwirkungsgrundsatz m, Verwirkungsprinzip n

principle of frustration, frustration principle · Nichtbindungsprinzip n, Nichtbindungsgrundsatz m

principle of interpretation → principle of construction

principle of intrinsic validity of contract · formelles Konsensprinzip n, formeller Konsensgrundsatz m

principle of investigation, investigation principle · formeller Legalitätsgrundsatz m, formelles Legalitätsprinzip n, formeller Prüfungsgrundsatz, formelles Prüfungsprinzip [*formell(rechtlich)es Grundbuchrecht*]

principle of law, law principle · Rechtsgrundsatz m, Rechtsprinzip n

principle of least effort, least-effort principle · Grundsatz m der geringsten Anstrengung, Prinzip n der geringsten Anstrengung [*Ableitung von Standortentscheidungen des Einzelhandels*]

principle of necessity, necessity principle · Erforderlichkeitsprinzip n, Erforderlichkeitsgrundsatz m, Notwendigkeitsprinzip, Notwendigkeitsgrundsatz

principle of notice, notice principle · Schutz m des gutgläubigen Erwerbers

principle of opportune cases · Grundsatz m der Zweckmäßigkeit, Grundsatz der Interessenabwägung, Prinzip n der Zweckmäßigkeit, Prinzip der Interessenabwägung, Opportunitätsprinzip, Opportunitätsgrundsatz [*Es stellt die Verfolgung in das Ermessen der Staatsanwaltschaft. Gegensatz: Legalitätsprinzip*]

principle of orality, orality principle · Grundsatz m der Mündlichkeit, Prinzip n der Mündlichkeit, Mündlichkeitsgrundsatz, Mündlichkeitsprinzip

principle of overreaching, overreaching principle · Überholungsgrundsatz m, Überholungsprinzip n [*Auflassung*]

principle of party presentation · Verhandlungsgrundsatz m Verhandlungsprinzip n

principle of planning, planning principle · Planungsgrundsatz m, Planungsprinzip n

principle of preference, preference principle · Günstigkeitsgrundsatz m, Günstigkeitsprinzip n

principle of priority, priority principle · Prioritätsgrundsatz *m*, Prioritätsprinzip *n*, Vorranggrundsatz, Vorrangprinzip

principle of priority rules, rules of principle of priority · formell(rechtlich)er Vorranggrundsatz *m*, formell(rechtlich)er Prioritätsgrundsatz, formell(rechtlich)es Vorrangprinzip *n*, formell(rechtlich)es Prioritätsprinzip [*Grundbuchrecht*]

principle of publicity, publicity principle · Publizitätsgrundsatz *m*, Publizitätsprinzip *n*, Öffentlichkeitsgrundsatz, Öffentlichkeitsprinzip

principle of registration, principle of recordation, principle of recording, registration principle, recordation principle, recording principle · Eintragungsgrundsatz *m*, Eintragungsprinzip *n*, Buchungsgrundsatz, Buchungsprinzip, Registrierungsgrundsatz, Registrierungsprinzip

principle of self-interest [*General right of a landowner to do what he wants with his land(s)*] · Grundsatz *m* der Freizügigkeit, Prinzip *n* der Freizügigkeit

principle of stare decisis, binding effect, binding force (of decided cases), authoritative force (of decided cases), binding authority (of precedents) · bindende Kraft *f* (der Präjudizien), verbindliche Kraft (der Präjudizien), Bindekraft (der Präjudizien), Bindungswirkung *f* (der Präjudizien), Prinzip *n* der bindenden Kraft gerichtlicher Entscheidungen, Beharren *n* auf der gefällten Entscheidung, Grundsatz *m* der bindenden Kraft gerichtlicher Entscheidungen

principle of surrogating, surrogating principle · Ersatzgrundsatz *m*, Ersatzprinzip *n*, Surrogationsgrundsatz, Surrogationsprinzip, Grundsatz der Ersatzhaftung, Prinzip der Ersatzhaftung

principle of the case, case principle · Fallgrundsatz *m*

principle of ultra vires, ultra-vires principle · Ultravires-Grundsatz *m*, Ultravires-Prinzip *n*

principle of universal law, universal law principle · allgemeingültiger Grundsatz *m*, allgemeingültiges Prinzip *n*

principle that liability on a mortgage is confined to the object mortgaged · Grundsatz *m* der Spezialität, Prinzip *n* der Spezialität, Spezialitätsgrundsatz, Spezialitätsprinzip

printed case · Revisionsschriftsatz *m* [*Enthält die Argumentation und Gegenargumentation der Parteien in bezug auf den Revisionsgegenstand*]

printed copy · Abdruck *m*

(printed) standard form contract · Standardformularvertrag *m*, Verbandsformularvertrag

printer · Schnelldrucker *m* [*Ausgabegerät einer Datenverarbeitungsanlage*]

printer map · Schnelldruckerkarte *f*

prior, first · älter, ranghöher, vorgehend

priority · Priorität *f*, Vorrang *m*

priority application, priority request, application for priority, request for priority · Dringlichkeitsantrag *m*, Dringlichkeitsgesuch *n*

priority clause · Prioritätsklausel *f*, Vorrangklausel

priority debt, debt of priority · Vorrangschuld *f*, Vorrechtschuld

priority notice, priority notification, notice of priority, notification of priority · Auflassungsvormerkung *f*

priority of clauses · Klauselvorrang *m*

priority of policy goals, priority of target goals · Zielpriorität *f*

priority order, urgent order, rush order [*An order which is identified as taking precedence over other orders to ensure its completion in the minimum time*] · Vorzugsauftrag *m*, Dringlichkeitsauftrag

priority plan · Vordringlichkeitsplan *m*

priority principle, principle of priority · Prioritätsgrundsatz *m*, Prioritätsprinzip *n*, Vorranggrundsatz, Vorrangprinzip

priority request, application for priority, request for priority, priority application · Dringlichkeitsantrag *m*, Dringlichkeitsgesuch *n*

priority system, system of priorities · Prioritätensystem *n*

prior iure [*Latin*]; prior loco · Lokussystem *n* [*materielles Grundbuchrecht*]

prior right of entry · Besitzergreifungsvorrecht *n*, Vorrecht zur Besitzergreifung [*Grundstück*]

prior-use easement, easement by prior use · Quasigrunddienstbarkeit *f*

prison, jail; gaol (Brit.) · Gefängnis *n*

prison authority, jail authority; gaol authority (Brit.) · Gefängnisaufsichtsbehörde *f*

prison-breach, breach of prison [*An escape by a prisoner lawfully in prison*] · Strafanstaltsflucht *f*, Ausbruch *m*

prison delivery, jail delivery; gaol delivery (Brit.) · Gefängnisbereinigung *f* [*Im englischen Ständestaat*]

prison delivery, jail delivery; gaol delivery (Brit.) · Einlieferung *f* ins Gefängnis

prison money, jail money; gaol money (Brit.) [*In old English law*] · Steuer *f* für Unterhaltung von Gefangenen

privacy, secludedness · Abgeschlossenheit *f*, Privatheit [*z. B. durch Gebüsch als Sichtblende*]

private · nicht generell [*Gesetz*]

private · unregistriert [*(Grundstücks)Auflassung*]

private access · Privatzugang *m*

private act, private statute, private law · Einzelfallgesetz *n,* Spezialgesetz

private Act of Parliament [*England*] · Privat-Parlamentsgesetz *n,* spezielles Parlamentsgesetz

private advisory opinion, private survey, private expertise · Parteigutachten *n,* Privatgutachten, Parteisachverständigenbericht, Privatsachverständigenbericht *m* [*außergerichtliche Beweissicherung.* Gegensatz: *Sachverständigengutachten*]

private assistance, private promotion, private sponsoring · private Förderung *f*

private assisting, private promoting, private sponsoring · privates Fördern *n*

private banker · Privatbankier *m*

private benefit, self-preference · Eigennutz *m*

private bidding (action), private tendering (out), private tender(ing) action · private Ausschreibung *f*

private bill legislation, private bill lawmaking · verfassungsmäßig normale Form *f* der staatlichen Zentralverwaltungstätigkeit

private body · privates Organ *n*

private brewer · Privatbrauer *m*

private budget · privates Budget *n,* privater Haushalt *m,* Privatbudget, Privathaushalt

private building, private construction · Privatbau *m*

private building activity, private construction activity · private Bautätigkeit *f*

private (building and) construction law, private (construction and) building law · privates Baurecht *n,* privates objektives Baurecht

private building (construction) contracting practice · privates Hochbauvergabewesen *n*

private building contracting practice, private construction contracting practice · privates Bauvergabewesen *n*

private building law → private (building and) construction law

private burden, private charge · private Last *f*

private carrier → (traffic) carrier

private carrier (of goods) [*It is one who carries goods under special contract without being engaged in the business as a public employment*] · privater Frachtführer *m*

private car transport(ation), private car transit, individual traffic · Individualverkehr *m*

private charge, private burden · private Last *f*

private charity · private Wohltätigkeit *f*

private client, private promoter, private owner, private employer · private Bauherrschaft *f,* privater Auftraggeber *m,* privater Bauherr, privater Besteller

private company, company with limited liability · Gesellschaft *f* mit beschränkter Haftung, GmbH

private construction, private building · Privatbau *m*

private construction activity, private building activity · private Bautätigkeit *f*

private (construction and) building law, private (building and) construction law · privates Baurecht *n,* privates objektives Baurecht

private construction contracting practice, private building contracting practice · privates Bauvergabewesen *n*

private contract [*As opposed to a government contract*] · Privatvertrag *m*

private control · Privatlenkung *f*

private conveyancing, secret conveyancing · anonymes (freiwilliges) Übertragen *n,* unregistriertes (freiwilliges) Übertragen

private corporation [*USA*] · privatrechtliche Gesellschaft *f*

private corporation · privat(rechtlich)e Körperschaft *f,* privat(rechtlich)e Korporation *f,* Privatkorporation, Privatkörperschaft

(private) corporation aggregate; corpus corporatum [*Latin*]; body corporate, corporat(iv)e body [*An incorporated group of coexisting persons*] · Körperschaft *f* mit Personenmehrheit, Korporation *f* mit Personenmehrheit, inkorporierte Körperschaft

private developer → private (property) developer

private division → private (land(s)) (sub)division

private document · Privatdokument *n*

private employer, private client, private promoter, private owner · private Bauherrschaft *f,* privater Auftraggeber *m,* privater Bauherr, privater Besteller

private endowment, private indowment · Privat(dauer)stiftung *f*

private estate, private property · Privatvermögen *n,* Privatgut *n,* Privathabe *f*

private expert · Parteigutachter *m*, Parteisachverständige, Privatgutachter, Privatsachverständige

private expertise, private advisory opinion, private survey · Parteigutachten *n*, Privatgutachten, Parteisachverständigenbericht, Privatsachverständigenbericht *m* [*außergerichtliche Beweissicherung. Gegensatz: Sachverständigengutachten*]

private field, private sector [*That part of the economy which is left to private enterprise*] · private Hand *f*, Privatsektor *m*

private flat (Brit.) [*Form of complete ownership by which the buyer has the entire undivided interest in an apartment or dwelling as opposed to ownership of the land on which the apartment or dwelling sits*]; condo(minium) (US) · Wohnungseigentum *n*, WE, Stockwerkeigentum, Geschoßeigentum, Etageneigentum, EW, Eigen(tums)wohnung *f* [*Das Sondereigentum an einer Wohnung in Verbindung mit dem Miteigentumsanteil am zugehörigen gemeinschaftlichen Eigentum*]

private flat fee (Brit.); condo(minium) fee (US) · Hausgeld *n* [*Bewirtschaftung und Verwaltung von Eigentumswohnungen*]

private flat law, private flat act, private flat statute (Brit.); condo(minium) law, condo(minium) act, condo(minium) statute (US) · Wohnungseigentumsgesetz *n*, WEG

private flat owner (Brit.); condo(minium) owner (US) · Wohnungseigentümer *m*, WEer, Wohnungseigner

private garage · Privatgarage *f*

private garden · Privatgarten *m*

private (general) property, private ownership (of property), private proprietorship · Privateigentum *n*

private (general) property of land(s) → private ownership of land(s)

private green land · private Grünfläche *f*, Privatgrünfläche

private hearing · Privatanhörung *f*

private heavy construction contracting practice · privates Tiefbauvergabewesen *n*

private highway, private road · Privatstraße *f*

private household · privater Haushalt *m*, Privathaushalt

private house ownership (of property), private house (general) property, private house proprietorship · privates Hauseigentum *n*; privater Hausbesitz *m* [*Fehlbenennung*]

private house property → private house (general) property

private indemnity insurance, private liability insurance, private third-party insurance · Privathaftpflichtversicherung *f*

private indowment, private endowment · Privat(dauer)stiftung *f*

private insurance, commercial insurance · Privatversicherung *f*

private insurance law, commercial insurance law · Privatversicherungsrecht *n*

private interests · private Belange *mpl*, privates Interesse *n*, private Interessen *npl*

Private International Law, conflicts law, International Private Law, IPL, conflict of laws, law of conflicts · Außenprivatrecht *n*, Kollisionsrecht, zwischenstaatliches (Privat)Recht *n*, Internationales Privatrecht *n*, IPR *n*, Zwischenprivatrecht *n*, Grenzrecht *n*

private (land) division → private (land(s)) (sub)division

private land grant [*A grant by a public authority vesting title to public land in a private person*] · öffentliche Landüberlassung *f* an Privatperson, öffentliche Landverleihung an Privatperson

private land law → (possessory) private land law

private landlord · Privathausherr *m*, Privathauswirt *m*

private land market · Privatlandmarkt *m*, Privatbodenmarkt, Privatgrundstücksmarkt

private land owner, private land proprietor · Privatbodeneigentümer *m*, Privatlandeigentümer, Privatgrundeigentümer, Privatbodeneigner, Privatlandeigner, Privatgrundeigner

private land(s), privately owned land(s) · Privatland *n*, Privatboden *m*

private (land(s)) (sub)division, private lotting · private Parzelli(si)erung *f*, Privatparzelli(si)erung

private law; jus privatum [*Latin*] · (objektives) Privatrecht *n*, objektives privates Recht, privates (objektives) Recht

private law, private act, private statute · Einzelfallgesetz *n*, Spezialgesetz

private law history, history of private law · Privatrechtsgeschichte *f*

private legal practice · juristische Privatpraxis *f*, private Rechtspraxis

private lender → private (money-)lender

private liability insurance, private third-party insurance, private indemnity insurance · Privathaftpflichtversicherung *f*

private lordship, private signory, private seigniory · privates Kronvasallenrecht *n*

private lordship appendant, private signory appendant, private seigniory appendant · privates ununterbrochenes Kronvasallenrecht *n*

private lordship over lands in fee simple, sub-infeudation, sub-(en)feoffment *f,* sub-infeftment, sub-infeodation, sub-investiture · Afterbelehnung *f,* Unterbelehnung, Afterleihe, Unterleihe *f*

private lotting, private (land(s)) (sub)division · private Parzelli(si)erung *f,* Privatparzelli(si)erung

privately employed lawyer, lawyer in private employment · selbständig praktizierender Jurist *m,* privat bestellter Jurist

privately financed, financed with private means · freifinanziert [*Wohnungsbau. Gegensatz: öffentlich gefördert*]

privately owned building · Privatgebäude *n*

privately owned land(s), private land(s) · Privatland *n,* Privatboden *m*

private mass hous(ebuild)ing · privater Massenwohn(ungs)bau *m*

private mobility (in the automobile) · private räumliche Mobilität *f,* private räumliche Beweglichkeit

private (money-)lender · privater Geldgeber *m*

private neighbour's law (Brit.); private neighbor's law (US) · privates Nachbarrecht *n,* objektives privates Nachbarrecht

private neighbour's protection (Brit.); private neighbor's protection (US) · privatrechtlicher Nachbarschutz *m*

private neighbour's right (Brit.); private neighbor's right (US) · privates Nachbarrecht *n,* subjektives privates Nachbarrecht

private nuisance [*It affects only one or a few persons*] · Privatschädlichkeit *f* [*Emission*]

private office building · privates Bürogebäude *n*

private operator · Privatbetreiber *m*

private owner, private employer, private client, private promoter · private Bauherrschaft *f,* privater Auftraggeber *m,* privater Bauherr, privater Besteller

private owner, private proprietor · Privateigentümer *m,* Privateigner

private ownership of land(s), private proprietorship of land(s), private (general) property of land(s) · Landprivateigentum *n,* Bodenprivateigentum, Privatlandeigentum, Privatbodeneigentum, Privatgrund(stücks)eigentum

private ownership (of property), private proprietorship, private (general) property · Privateigentum *n*

private parcel (of land), private parcel of ground, private plot (of land), private plot of ground · Privatgrundstück *n*

private park · Privatpark *m*

(private) partnership · Personalgesellschaft *f*

(private) partnership limited by stocks · Kommanditgesellschaft *f* auf Aktien

(private) partnership with limited liability, limited (private) partnership, commandite partnership · Kommanditgesellschaft *f,* KG [*Sie besteht aus Gesellschaftern, von denen mindestens einer, der Komplementär, den Gläubigern unbeschränkt haftet, und auch mindestens einer, der Kommanditist, nur mit dem Betrag seiner Einlage*]

private perpetuating testimony method, extrajudicial perpetuating testimony method · außergerichtliches Beweissicherungsverfahren *n,* außergerichtliches (vorsorgliches) Beweisaufnahmeverfahren

private physician · Privatarzt *m*

private placement · Schuldscheindarleh(e)n *n*

private placement fund · Fonds *m* für Schuldscheindarleh(e)n

private planning control · private Planungslenkung *f*

private plot (of land), private plot of ground, private parcel (of land), private parcel of ground · Privatgrundstück *n*

private power of appointment, private right of appointment, private power of disposition, private right of disposition · private Verfügungsbefugnis *f,* private Bestimmungsbefugnis, privates Verfügungsrecht, privates Bestimmungsrecht *n*

private practice · Privatpraxis *f,* freie Berufstätigkeit *f*

private promoter, private owner, private employer, private client · private Bauherrschaft *f,* privater Auftraggeber *m,* privater Bauherr, privater Besteller

private promoting → private assisting

private promotion → private assistance

private property, private estate · Privatvermögen *n,* Privatgut *n,* Privathabe *f*

private property → private ownership (of property)

private (property) builder, private (property) developer · Privat(bau)träger *m*

private (property) developer · privater Erschließungsträger *m*

private proprietor, private owner · Privateigentümer *m,* Privateigner

private proprietorship, private (general) property, private ownership (of property) · Privateigentum *n*

private proprietorship of land(s) → private ownership of land(s)

private (real) estate law, private (real) property law, private realty law · private Bodenordnung *f,* privates Bodenrecht *n,* private Grundeigentumsverfassung

private register, private registry · Privatregister *n*

private registered piece of land, private registered plot (of land), registered private plot (of land), private recorded plot (of land), recorded private plot (of land), private registered plot of ground, registered private plot of ground, private recorded plot of ground, private recorded plot of land, private registered parcel (of land), registered private parcel (of land), private recorded parcel (of land), recorded private parcel (of land), private registered parcel of ground, registered private parcel of ground, private recorded parcel of ground, recorded private parcel of ground, registered private piece of land, private recorded piece of land, recorded private piece of land, private registered piece of gro · Privatgrundstück *n* im Rechtssinn, Privatgrundstück im Sinne des Grundbuchrechts, Privatgrundbuchland, Privatgrundbuchgrund(stück) *m, (n),* Privatgrundbuchboden *m,* privater gebuchter Boden, privater gebuchter Grund, privater eingetragener Boden, privater eingetragener Grund, privates eingetragenes Land *n,* privates eingetragenes Grundstück, privates gebuchtes Land, privates gebuchtes Grundstück, gebuchter privater Boden, gebuchter privater Grund, eingetragener privater Boden, eingetragener privater Grund, eingetragenes privates Land, eingetragenes privates Grundstück, gebuchtes privates Land, gebuchtes privates Grundstück

private residence · Privatwohnung *f*

private right · privater Anspruch *m,* privates (An)Recht *n*

private right of appointment, private power of disposition, private right of disposition, private power of appointment · private Verfügungsbefugnis *f,* private Bestimmungsbefugnis, privates Verfügungsrecht, privates Bestimmungsrecht *n*

private road, private highway · Privatstraße *f*

private sale · freihändiger Verkauf *m*

private sale · Privatverkauf *m*

private secondary school, public school (Brit.); preparatory school (US) · höhere Privatschule *f*

private sector, private field [*That part of the economy which is left to private enterprise*] · private Hand *f,* Privatsektor *m*

private sector planning, private specialized planning, private subject planning · private Fachplanung *f,* private Sektorplanung, private sektorale Planung

private seigniory appendant, private lordship appendant, private signory appendant · privates ununterbrochenes Kronvasallenrecht *n*

private signory, private lordship, private seigniory · privates Kronvasallenrecht *n*

private specialized planning, private subject planning, private sector planning · private Fachplanung *f,* private Sektorplanung, private sektorale Planung

private sponsoring → private assisting

private statute, private law, private act · Einzelfallgesetz *n,* Spezialgesetz

private stream · privater Fluß *m,* nicht regaler Fluß, Privatfluß

private stream law, private stream act, private stream statute · Privatflußgesetz *n*

private street · Privatstadtstraße *f*

private (sub)division → private (land(s)) (sub)division

private subject planning, private sector planning, private specialized planning · private Fachplanung *f,* private Sektorplanung, private sektorale Planung

private (surety) bond · Privatbürgschaft *f*

private survey, private expertise, private advisory opinion · Parteigutachten *n,* Privatgutachten, Parteisachverständigenbericht, Privatsachverständigenbericht *m* [*außergerichtliche Beweissicherung. Gegensatz: Sachverständigengutachten*]

private tender(ing) action, private bidding (action), private tendering (out) · private Ausschreibung *f*

private third-party insurance, private indemnity insurance, private liability insurance · Privathaftpflichtversicherung *f*

private timber, private wood · privater Holzbestand *m*

private traffic, private transport(ation) · Privattransport *m,* Privatbeförderung *f,* Privatverkehr *m*

private traffic area · private Verkehrsfläche *f*

private (traffic) carrier · privater Verkehrsträger *m*

private transport(ation), private traffic · Privattransport *m,* Privatbeförderung *f,* Privatverkehr *m*

private trust — privy successor

private trust · private Treuhand f

private trust which has failed, private trust which has lapsed · hinfälliges privates Treuhandverhältnis n

private use · Privatbenutzung f, Privatgebrauch m

private utility enterprise, private utility undertaking · privater Versorgungsbetrieb m, privater Träger der Versorgung, privates Versorgungsunternehmen n, private Versorgungsunternehmung f

private value · Liegenschaftswert m, Landwert, Bodenwert, Grund(stücks)wert

private value abatement, private value reduction · Grund(stücks)wertminderung f, Grund(stücks)wertherabsetzung, Grund(stücks)wertreduzierung, Grund(stücks)wertverringerung

private value compensation, private value damages, private value indemnity, private value indemnification · Grund(stücks)wertentschädigung f, Grund(stücks)wertschadenersatz m, Grund(stücks)wertrestitution f

private vehicular access · Privatzufahrt f

private way · Privatweg m

private welfare body · privates Wohlfahrtsorgan n

private wood, private timber · privater Holzbestand m

priveleged against distress, privileged against distraint, undistrainable · unpfändbar

privies in title, successors in title · Rechtsnachfolger m pl die sich auf denselben Titel stützen

privilege, liberty, prerogative right · Vorrecht n

privilege; franchesia, francisia [Latin]; franchise, liberty [A privilege conferred by government on individuals or corporations, and which does not belong to citizens of country generally of common right] · Gerechtsame f, Privileg n, Regalrecht n

privilege case · Privilegfall m

privileged · privilegiert

privileged against distraint → privileged against distress

privileged from distress · privat unpfändbar [bewegliche Sachen]

privileged occasion · berechtigter Anlaß m

privileged undertaking · privilegiertes Vorhaben n [z. B. der Abbau von Mineralien]

privileged ville(i)nage · privilegierter Bauernbesitz m

privilege of fishery → fishery franchise

privilege of liability, liability privilege · Haftungsprivileg n, Haftpflichtprivileg, Haftbarkeitsprivileg

privilege of witness · Zeugnisverweigerungsrecht n

privilegium germanicum [Latin] · Begünstigung f eines deutschen Erben nach Artikel 14 S. 2 EGBGB

privity · Fehlen n vertraglicher Beziehungen

privity, participation in interest, (legal) succession, succession in title, title sucession; communio incidens [Latin] [A successive relationship to or mutual interest in the same property, etc., established by law or legalized by contract, as between a testator and legatee, lessor and lessee, etc.] · Rechtsgemeinschaft f, rechtliche Beteiligung f, Rechtsbeziehung, Rechtsverhältnis n, Rechtsnachfolge f

privity after death, succession in title after death, (legal) succession after death · Rechtsnachfolge f von Todes wegen

privity inter vivos, succession in title inter vivos, (legal) succession inter vivos · Rechtsnachfolge f unter Lebenden

privity of contract · Beschränkung f des Schuldverhältnisses auf die Vertragsparteien, mittelbare vertragliche Beziehung

privity of contract between two parties · Zwei-Partner-Vinkulation f

privity of lease, privity of tenancy · Pachtverhältnis n

privity of (real) estate, privity of (real) property, privity of realty · Nachfolge f in ein Grundstücksrecht

privity of tenancy, privity of lease · Pachtverhältnis n

Privy Council · Kronrat m

Privy Councillor · Kronratmitglied n

privy in (real) estate, privy in (real) property, privy in realty, successor in realty, successor in (real) property, successor in (real) estate · Rechtsnachfolger m in ein Grundstücksrecht

privy in (real) estate with the original covenantee, privy in (real) property with the original covenantee, successor in (real) estate with the original covenantee, successor in (real) property with the original covenantee, privy in realty with the original covenantee, successor in realty with the original covenantee · Rechtsnachfolger m in das Grundstücksrecht der ursprünglichen Vertragspartei

privy seal; secretum sigillum [Latin] · Geheimsiegel n

privy successor, legal successor, successor in right, representative · Rechtsnachfolger m

privy tithe, little tithe, small tithe, petty tithe · kleiner Zehnt *m*, Schmalzehnt

prize competition, prize contest, competition for prizes, contest for prizes · Preiswettbewerb *m*

probability axiom, likelihood axiom, probabilistic axiom · Wahrscheinlichkeitsaxiom *n*

probability-density function · Wahrscheinlichkeitsverteilung *f*, Dichtefunktion *f*

probability estimate, likelihood estimate, probabilistic estimate · Wahrscheinlichkeitsschätzung *f*

probability method, probabilistic method, likelihood method · Wahrscheinlichkeitsverfahren *n*

probability model, probabilistic model, likelihood model · Wahrscheinlichkeitsmodell *n*

probability network, likelihood network, probabilistic network · Wahrscheinlichkeitsnetz *n*

probability theory, likelihood theory, probabilistic theory · Wahrscheinlichkeitstheorie *f*

probability value, likelihood value, probabilistic value · Wahrscheinlichkeitswert *m*

probable cause, reason of suspicion · Verdachtsgrund *m*

to probate [*will*] · gerichtlich feststellen [*letztwillige Verfügung*]

to probate, to prove [e. g. to probate, or prove, a will. A probate court is one in which wills are proved] · bestätigen

probate, legal evidence of a will · gerichtliche Feststellung *f* einer letztwilligen Verfügung, richterliche Testamentsanerkennung

(probate) administrator; executor dative [*Scotland*] · Nachlaßverwalter *m*, Erb(schafts)verwalter, erbrechtlicher Verwalter [*Er wird bestellt wenn der Erblasser entweder kein Testament hinterlassen oder in seinem Testament keinen Testamentsvollstrecker ernannt hat*]

(probate) administrator de bonis non (administratis), (probate) administrator of the unadministered estate; executor dative of the unadministered estate [*Scotland*] · Nachlaßverwalter *m* an Stelle eines verstorbenen Nachlaßverwalters, Erb(schafts)verwalter an Stelle eines verstorbenen Erb(schafts)verwalters, erbrechtlicher Verwalter an Stelle eines verstorbenen erbrechtlichen Verwalters

(probate) administrator durante minore aetate; executor dative durante minore aetate [*Scotland*] · Nachlaßverwalter *m* während Minderjährigkeit, Erb(schafts)verwalter während Minderjährigkeit, erbrechtlicher Verwalter während Minderjährigkeit

(probate) administrator during the litigation, (probate) administrator pendente lite; executor dative pendente lite, executor dative during the litigation [*Scotland*] · Nachlaßverwalter *m* während eines Prozesses, Erb(schafts)verwalter während eines Prozesses, erbrechtlicher Verwalter während eines Prozesses

(probate) administrator of the unadministered estate → (probate) administrator de bonis non (administratis)

(probate) administrator with the will annexed, (probate) administrator cum testamento annexo; executor dative with the will annexed, executor dative cum testamento annexo [*Scotland*] · erbrechtlicher Verwalter *m* cum testamento annexo, Erb(schafts)verwalter cum testamento annexo, Nachlaßverwalter cum testamento annexo

(probate) administratrix, administratress; administratrice, administress [*obsolete*]; female administrator [*A woman appointed to administer the estate of an intestate*] · erbrechtliche Verwalterin *f*, Erb(schafts)verwalterin, Nachlaßverwalterin

probate (and administration) duty [*A tax (now merged in estate duty) on the gross value of the personal property of the deceased testator, first introduced in 1694. It was payable under the Stamp Act, 1815, the Customs and Inland Revenue Act, 1880, and the Customs and Inland Revenue Act 1881. By the Stamp Act, 1815, s. 37, a penalty of £ 100 and 10 per cent additional duty is payable by a person acting as executor and not obtaining probate within six months. The Finance Act, 1894, substitutes estate duty, to which both real property and personal property are liable, for probate duty*] · Steuer *f* für die Prüfungsverhandlung eines Nachlaßgerichts über die Rechtsgültigkeit der Testamente und der den Testamentsvollstreckern ausgestellten Vollmachten

(probate) co-administrator, (probate) joint administrator; co-executor dative, joint executor dative [*Scotland*] · Mitnachlaßverwalter *m*, Miterb(schafts)verwalter, erbrechtlicher Mitverwalter

probate (copy) · amtliche Testamentsabschrift *f*, richterliche Testamentsabschrift, Testamentsabschrift mit Gerichtssiegel

probate court, court of probate; surrogate's court, orphan's court (US) [*A court in which wills are probated, or proved. Called "orphans" court in a few states of the USA*] · Nachlaßgericht *n*, Erb(schafts)gericht

Probate Division see under High Court of Justice

probate duty → probate (and administration) duty

probate in common form · einfache Testamentsbestätigung f

probate in solemn form · formelle Testamentsbestätigung f, förmliche Testamentsbestätigung

(probate) joint administrator → (probate) co-administrator

probate judge · Nachlaßrichter m

probate law · Nachlaßrecht n

probate (of (the) will) in solemn form · feierliche Nachlaßbestätigung f, feierliche Testamentsbestätigung

probate practice · Nachlaßwesen n, Erb(schafts)wesen

probatio diabolica [Latin] · Beweis m beim Eigentum

probation · Bewährung f

probationary drawing, drawing submitted for approval · Prüfungszeichnung f

probation officer · Bewährungshelfer m

to probe · ausloten, sondieren

probing · Auslotung f, Sondierung

probing discussion · auslotende Diskussion f, auslotendes Gespräch n, Sondierungsgespräch n, Sondierungsdiskussion f

problem area, problem territory, area of problems, territory of problems · Problemgebiet n

problem group · Problemgruppe f, Randgruppe

problem of site, location problem, site problem, problem of location · Standortfrage f, Lagefrage

problem-orien(ta)ted, problem-related · problemorientiert, problembezogen

problem territory, area of problems, territory of problems, problem area · Problemgebiet n

processing error · Aufbereitungsfehler m [Statistik]

process planning · anpassungsfähige Planung f, Anpassungsplanung, Auffangplanung

procedural · verfahrensrechtlich

procedural act(ion) · Verfahrensakt m, Verfahrenshandlung f

procedural arrangement · Verfahrensvorkehrung f

procedural code, code of (court) procedure, (court) procedure code, rules of (court) practice, rules of (court) procedure, (general) (standing) rules of court, court (practice) rules · Prozeßregeln fpl, Prozeßordnung f, Gerichtsverfahrensregeln, Gerichtsverfahrensordnung, (gerichtliche) Verfahrensregeln, (gerichtliche) Verfahrensordnung

procedural committee · Verfahrensausschuß m

procedural due process of law · prozessuales gehöriges Rechtsverfahren n, gehöriges prozessuales Rechtsverfahren

procedural error · Verfahrensfehler m

procedural law, procedure law, law of (court) procedure (and practice), adjective law, remedial law [Law consisting of rules of conduct prescribed by substantive law, and enforced by adjective law. In other words, substantive law is administered by the courts and deals with right and duties, whereas adjective law relates to practice and procedure and deals with remedies. "Substantive law" and "adjective law" were first used by Bentham (2 works, 6) and are now generally adopted, notwithstanding Austin's criticism of them (2 Jurisprudence, 788—789)] · Formalrecht n, formelles Recht, Verfahrensrecht, Prozeßrecht

procedural law of (land) condemnation (US); procedural law of (land) expropriation · (Land)Enteignungsverfahrensrecht n, Bodenenteignungsverfahrensrecht, (Land)Enteignungsformalrecht, Bodenenteignungsformalrecht

procedural matter · Verfahrensangelegenheit f, Verfahrenssache f

procedural mistake · Verfahrensirrtum m

procedural planning · Verfahrensplanung f

procedural question · Verfahrensfrage f

procedural rule, procedural regulation, procedural prescription · Verfahrensvorschrift f

procedural safeguard · verfahrensrechtliche Garantie f

procedural sequence · Verfahrensfolge f

procedural step · Verfahrensschritt m, Verfahrensstufe f

procedure [The mode in which the successive steps in litigation are taken] · Verfahrensweise f

procedure code → rules of (court) practice

procedure for allowance of public grants(-in-aid) and public loans · Bewilligungsverfahren n [Verwaltungsverfahren zur Bewilligung von Zuschüssen und Darleh(e)n aus öffentlichen Mitteln]

procedure law → procedural law

procedure of certiorari · Abberufungsverfahren *n*

procedure of enforcement, enforcement procedure · Durchsetzungsverfahren *n*, Erzwingungsverfahren

procedure of law, law procedure · Rechtsverfolgung *f*

procedure of legislation, legislation procedure, procedure of lawmaking, lawmaking procedure · Gesetzgebungsverfahren *n*

procedure of recall, recall procedure [*political science*] · Abberufungsverfahren *n*

procedure rules, rules of procedure · Geschäftsordnung *f* [*z. B. eines Planungsrates*]

to proceed [*To adopt a course of action*] · (gerichtlich) vorgehen

proceeding, legal act(ion), lawful act(ion) · Rechtsakt *m*, Rechtshandlung *f*, rechtsetzender Akt, rechtsetzende Handlung [*Akt eines Gesetzgebers oder Richters, durch welchen Recht erst „geschaffen" wird*]

proceeding [*The taking of legal action(s)*] · rechtsetzendes Handeln *n*

proceeding equitable in nature, equity pleading, pleading in equity · Billigkeitsverfahren *n*, Billigkeitsrechtverfahren

proceeding in error · Revision *f*, Revisionsverfahren *n*

proceeds · Erlös *m*

proceeds maximization, maximization of proceeds · Erlösmaximierung *f*

proceeds of liquidation, liquidation proceeds · Liquidationserlös *m*

proceeds of possession, possession proceeds · Besitzerlös *m*

proceeds of sale, sale proceeds · Verkaufserlös *m*, Absatzerlös

to process, to treat [*application*] · bearbeiten [*Antrag*]

process · Vorgang *m*

process costing, process (cost(s)) accounting · mehrstufige Divisionskalkulation *f*, vielstufige Divisionskalkulation

processing, treatment · Bearbeitung *f*, Behandlung [*Bauantrag; Angebot*]

process (in law), judicial contest, judicial controversy, (contentious) litigation [*Contest in a court of justice for the purpose of enforcing a right*] · Prozeß *m*

process of planning, planning process · Planungsvorgang *m*

process of rezoning, rezoning process · Umzonungsvorgang *m*

processor, manufacturer · Fabrikant *m*, Hersteller *m*

process server · Klageurkundenzusteller *m*, Ladungszusteller, Zusteller (einer gerichtlichen Vorladung)

(prochein) amy, (prochein) ami; proximus amicus [*Latin*]; next friend [*He sues on behalf of an infant. Infants sue by a next friend and defend by a guardian ad litem*] · Beistand *m*, prozessualer Stellvertreter *m* auf der Klägerseite

proclamation of a state of emergency · Ausrufung *f* des Notstandes

proctor, procurator, attorney, policitor [*A manager of another person's affair*] · Prokurator *m*

procuration, collection, raise, procurement · Erhebung *f*

to procure, to raise, to collect, to gather [*money, etc.*] · erheben

procurement, procuration, collection, raise · Erhebung *f*

procurement manager, procurement representative, purchasing manager, purchasing representative · Einkäufer *m*

procuring, raising, collecting, gathering · Erheben *n*

procuring breach of contract, inducing breach of contract · Verleiten *n* zum Vertragsbruch

procuring contracting officer, procuring contracting official · Vergabebeamte *m*

to produce [*document(s)*] · beibringen

to produce, to fille, to submit, to present, to discover · abgeben, einreichen, vorlegen, enthüllen [*Mitteilen von Tatsachen oder Vorlegen von Schriftstücken an den Prozeßgegner*]

to produce [*witness*] · vorführen [*Zeuge*]

to produce · vorzeigen [*Urkunde; Schriftstück*]

to produce by tillage, to raise by tillage, to farm, to cultivate · kultivieren, anbauen

produced · vorgezeigt [*Urkunde; Schriftstück*]

to produce for inspection · vorzeigen zur Besichtigung [*Schriftstück*]

producer [*Manufacturer, processor, or assembler of materials or equipment*] · Produzent *m*

producer location, producer site, production location, production site · Produktionsstandort *m*, Herstellungsstandort, Erzeugungsstandort

producers' capital, capital goods, producers' goods [*Capital used to further production. These terms may also refer to the material forms of producers' goods, such as machines, equipment, etc., in*

producer site — production (of the works)

contact with capital values, the monetary measures of such goods] · Produktionsmittel *f pl*

producer site, production location, production site, producer location · Produktionsstandort *m*, Herstellungsstandort, Erzeugungsstandort

producer's liability · Produzentenhaftung *f*, Produzentenhaftpflicht *f*, Produzentenhaftbarkeit *f*

producing industry, manufacturing industry · erzeugende Industrie *f*, herstellende Industrie, produzierende Industrie, Herstellungsindustrie, Produkt(ions)industrie, Fertigungsindustrie, fertigende Industrie

producing trade, manufacturing trade · herstellendes Gewerbe *n*, produzierendes Gewerbe, erzeugendes Gewerbe, fertigendes Gewerbe

product · Erzeugnis *n*, Produkt *n*

production [*document(s)*] · Beibringung *f*

production · Erzeugung *f*, Produktion *f*, Herstellung, Fertigung

production, submission, presentation, filing, discovery · Abgabe *f*, Einreichung *f*, Vorlage *f*, Vorlegung, Edition *f*, Enthüllung [*Mitteilung von Tatsachen oder Vorlegung von Schriftstücken an den Prozeßgegner*]

production · Vorzeigung *f* [*Urkunde; Schriftstück*]

production area, production territory · Erzeugungsgebiet *n*, Herstellungsgebiet, Produktionsgebiet, Fertigungsgebiet

production by interrogatories, filing by interrogatories, discovery by interrogatories, submission by interrogatories, presentation by interrogatories · Abgabe *f* von Tatsachen, Einreichung *f* von Tatsachen, Vorlage *f* von Tatsachen, Vorlegung von Tatsachen, Edition *f* von Tatsachen, Enthüllung von Tatsachen [*An den Prozeßgegner*]

production by order · Vorzeigung *f* auf Aufforderung [*Urkunde; Schriftstück*]

production capacity, productive capacity · Produktionskapazität *f*, Herstellungskapazität, Erzeugungskapazität

production capital → production goods

production clause · Erzeugungsklausel *f*, Produktionsklausel, Herstellungsklausel, Fertigungsklausel

production control · Produktionsüberwachung *f*

production cost(s), cost(s) of production · Erzeugungskosten *f*, Herstellungskosten, Produktionskosten, Fertigungskosten

production error · Herstellungsfehler *m* (der Bauleistung) [*Er liegt vor, wenn eine von vornherein mit Mängeln behaftete Sache hergestellt wird*]

production factor, factor of the production · Produktionsfaktor *m*, Produktivfaktor

production location, production site, producer location, producer site · Produktionsstandort *m*, Herstellungsstandort, Erzeugungsstandort

production method of depreciation · leistungsproportionale Abschreibungsmethode *f*

production of documents, submission of documents, presentation of documents, discovery of documents, filing of documents · Abgabe *f* von Schriftstücken, Vorlage *f* von Schriftstücken, Einreichung *f* von Schriftstücken, Vorlegung von Schriftstücken, Enthüllung von Schriftstücken, Edition *f* von Schriftstücken [*An den Prozeßgegner*]

production of dwelling units, erection of dwelling units, production of housing units, erection of housing units, production of living units, erection of living units (US); production of tenements, erection of tenements, production of dwellings, erection of dwellings, production of housing, erection of housing, residential construction, residential building, hous(ebuild)ing, housing construction · Wohn(ungs)bau *m*, Wohnungserstellung *f*, Wohnungsproduktion *f*, Häuserbau, Hausbau, Mietwohn(ungs)bau, Mietwohnungserstellung, Mietwohnungsproduktion, Miethäuserbau, Miethausbau

production of dwelling units by extension, production of housing units by extension, production of living units by extension (US); production of tenements by extension, production of dwellings by extension, production of housing by extension, hous(ebuild)ing by extension, residential building by extension, residential construction by extension · Wohn(ungs)bau *m* durch Erweiterung, Wohnungserstellung *f* durch Erweiterung, Wohnungsproduktion *f* durch Erweiterung [*Schaffung von Wohnraum durch Aufstockung oder Anbau*]

production of joint products · Kuppelerzeugung *f*, Kuppelproduktion *f*

production of public housing, public(ly-)assisted) hous(ebuild)ing, subsidized hous(ebuild)ing, lower-income hous(ebuild)ing, social hous(ebuild)ing · Zuschußwohn(ungs)bau *m*, Sozialwohn(ungs)bau, öffentlich geförderter Wohn(ungs)bau, geförderter öffentlicher Wohn(ungs)bau, sozialer Wohn(ungs)bau, Wohn(ungs)bau der öffentlichen Hand

production (of the works) · Herstellung *f* (der Bauleistung)

production overhead(s) · Fertigungsgemeinkosten *f*, Fertigungsgeneralkosten, Herstellungsgemeinkosten, Herstellungsgeneralkosten, Produktionsgemeinkosten, Produktionsgeneralkosten, Erzeugungsgemeinkosten, Erzeugungsgeneralkosten

production planning · Produktionsplanung *f*

production power, productive power, power of production · Produktionskraft *f*, Herstellungskraft, Erzeugungskraft

production produce · Produktionsgut *n*

production site, producer location, producer site, production location · Produktionsstandort *m*, Herstellungsstandort, Erzeugungsstandort

production sum, sum of construction, sum of building, sum of production, construction sum, building sum · Bausumme *f*, Herstellungssumme

production territory, production area · Erzeugungsgebiet *n*, Herstellungsgebiet, Produktionsgebiet, Fertigungsgebiet

production theory, theory of production · Erzeugungstheorie *f*, Produktionstheorie, Herstellungstheorie, Fertigungstheorie

production value, value of production · Erzeugungswert *m*, Herstellungswert, Produktionswert, Fertigungswert

production wage, wage of production · Fertigungslohn *m*, Produktionslohn, Herstellungslohn, Erzeugungslohn

productive capacity, production capacity · Produktionskapazität *f*, Herstellungskapazität, Erzeugungskapazität

productive function · Nutz(ungs)funktion *f*, produktive Funktion

productive power, power of production, production power · Produktionskraft *f*, Herstellungskraft, Erzeugungskraft

productivity measure, measure of productivity · Leistungsindikator *m* [*Sozialprodukt*]

product liability · Produkthaftung *f*, Produkthaftpflicht *f*, Produkthaftbarkeit *f*

product mix · Produktemischung *f*

product of event(s), product of happening(s) · Ereignisprodukt *n*

product of work(s) · Arbeitsprodukt *n*

products liability · Warenherstellerhaftung *f*, Warenherstellerhaftbarkeit *f*, Warenherstellerhaftpflicht *f* [*gegenüber dem Verbraucher*]

products of labour (Brit.); fruits of labor, products of labor (US); fructus industriales, fructus industriae [*Latin*]; fruits of industry, emblements, industrial fruits, industrial products; fruits of labour [*Those fruits of a thing, as of land, which are produced by the labo(u)r and industry of the occupant, as crops of grain; as distinguished from such as are produced solely by the powers of nature*] · künstlicher Zuwachs *m*

professed persons · Mönche *mpl* und Nonnen *fpl*

professional charge, professional fee · geregelte Gebühr *f*, geregeltes Honorar *n*

professional fee, professional charge · geregelte Gebühr *f*, geregeltes Honorar *n*

professional institution · Berufsverband *m*

professional knowledge, expertise, expertness, special knowledge · Fachwissen *n*, Fachkenntnisse *fpl*, Fachkunde *f*, berufliches Wissen, Spezialwissen, Spezialkenntnis, Spezialkunde, Sachkenntnis, Sachkunde, Sachwissen

professional man → (independent) professional man

professional planner · Berufsplaner *m*

professional woman → (independent) professional woman

profile scanning · profilweises Abtasten *n* [*Kartographie*]

profit · Nutzung *f* [§ *100 des BGB*]

profit, gain · Gewinn *m*, Profit *m*

profitability, profitableness · Wirtschaftlichkeit *f*, Rentabilität *f*

profitability calculation, profitableness calculation · Wirtschaftlichkeitsberechnung *f*, Rentabilitätsberechnung

profitability index, profitableness index · Erfolgssatz *m*

profitability limit, profitableness limit · Wirtschaftlichkeitsgrenze, Rentabilitätsgrenze *f*

profitable, lucrative, economical · gewinnbringend, rentabel, wirtschaftlich, profitbringend

profitable deposit, paying deposit, workable deposit · Fundstätte *f*, Vorkommen *n*, Lager(stätte) *n*, (f) [*Fehlbenennung: Vorkommnis n*]

profitableness, profitability · Wirtschaftlichkeit *f*, Rentabilität *f*

profitableness calculation, profitability calculation · Wirtschaftlichkeitsberechnung *f*, Rentabilitätsberechnung

profitableness limit, profitability limit · Wirtschaftlichkeitsgrenze, Rentabilitätsgrenze *f*

profit and loss account, income statement, earnings and profit and loss

statement, statement of operations, results of operations · Gewinn- und Verlustrechnung f

profit à prendre [A profit (à prendre) differs from an easement in the fact that it imports the taking of some thing which is capable of ownership from the servient land] · Frucht(ent)ziehung f, Substanzentnahme f

profit (à prendre) in alieno solo, several profits (à prendre) · alleinige Frucht(ent)ziehung f, ausschließliche Frucht(ent)ziehung, selbständige Frucht(ent)ziehung, alleinige Substanzentnahme f, ausschließliche Substanzentnahme, selbständige Substanzentnahme

profit (à prendre) in common [A right exercised in common with others to take something from another's land] · gemeinsame Substanzentnahme f, gemeinsame Frucht(ent)ziehung f, gemeinschaftliche Substanzentnahme, gemeinschaftliche Frucht(ent)ziehung

profit (à prendre) in the soil [The right to enter the servient tenement and take sand, stone, gravel, brick-earth, coal, and the like. It may exist as appurtenant or in gross] · Mineral(ien)entnahme f, Mineral(ien)(ent)ziehung f

profit (à prendre) of estover, bot(e), boot, bota, estouvier, estover [The right to take wood from the land of another as hay-bote, house-bote or plough-bote] · Holzzubuße, Holzentnahme f, Holzentziehung f

profit (à prendre) of piscary · Fischentnahme f, Fisch(ent)ziehung f

profit (à prendre) of turbary · Torfentnahme f, Torfentziehung f

profit centre (Brit.); profit center (US) · Verantwortungsbereich m für Leistung und Erfolg

profit contribution, contribution margin, marginal revenue, marginal balance, marginal income, variable gross margin · Deckungsbeitrag m, Beitragsüberschuß m, Überschußsaldo m, Erfolgsbeitrag, variabler Bruttoüberschuß, Grenzerfolg m, (Kosten)Deckungszuschlag m

profiteering, price-kiting · Preiswucher m, Preistreiberei f

profiteering ordinance · Preistreibereiverordnung f, Preiswucherverordnung

profit fee, fee for profit, fee for gain, gain fee [A contractual arrangement whereby the contractor is paid the net prime cost plus a percentage to cover overheads and profit] · aufzuschlagender Gewinnsatz m, Gewinnzuschlag m, Gewinnaufschlag m, Profitzuschlag m, Profitaufschlag m

profit forecast, gain forecast · Gewinnvorhersage f, Profitvorhersage

profit in alieno solo → profit (à prendre) in alieno solo

profit in common → profit (à prendre) in common

profit in the soil → profit (à prendre) in the soil

profit loss, gain loss, loss of profit(s), loss of gain(s) · Gewinnentgang m, Gewinnverlust m, Profitentgang, Profitverlust

profit-maker, gain-maker · Gewinnbringer m, Profitbringer

profit margin, gain margin, margin of profit, margin of gain · Gewinnspanne f, Profitspanne

profit matrix, gain matrix · Gewinnmatrix f, Profitmatrix

profit of land(s), land(s) profit, vesture [In old English law. The value of the vesture of the land(s)] · Wert m der Grundstücksbewachung außer Bäumen

profit of sale, gain of sale, sale's profit, sale's gain · Verkaufsprofit m, Verkaufsgewinn m

profit of stock, gain of stock · Gewinn m aus Kapitalanlage

profit percentage, gain percentage · Gewinnprozentsatz m, Profitprozentsatz

profit pool, gain pool · Gewinngemeinschaft f, Profitgemeinschaft

profit rate, gain rate · Gewinnsatz m, Profitsatz

profit-sharing, participation in the profit, participation in the gain, gain-sharing · Gewinnbeteiligung f, Profitbeteiligung

profit-sharing contract, gain-sharing contract · Gewinnbeteiligungsvertrag m, Profitbeteiligungsvertrag

profit-sharing plan, gain-sharing plan · Gewinnbeteiligungsplan m, Profitbeteiligungsplan

profits partaking of the nature of rent, conjuncture-profit, entrepreneur's rent, case of extra profit analogous to rent, rent of ability · Unternehmerpension f, Seltenheitsprämie f

profit split, gain split · Gewinnteilung f, Profitteilung

profit tax, gain tax · Gewinnsteuer f, Profitsteuer

profit transfer, gain transfer · Gewinnabführung f, Profitabführung

pro-forma invoice · Proformarechnung f

progenitor, ascendant, ancestor [Not to be confused with "predecessor" = Vorgänger] · Vorfahre m, Ahn m

programme (construction) period (of time), planned (construction) period (of time),

programme — prohibition of disposition

programme (construction) time period, planned (construction) time period · geplante Baufrist *f*, geplante Zeit des Bauablaufes

programme; program (US); scheme · Programm *n*

programme scheduling; program scheduling (US) · Programmterminplanung *f*

progress → (job) progress

progress attestation, interim certificate, interim attestation, intermediate certificate, progress certificate, intermediate attestation · Zwischenbescheinigung *f*, Zwischenschein *m*, Zwischenattest *n* [*Über den Fortschritt der Bauarbeiten*]

progress certificate, intermediate attestation, progress attestation, interim certificate, interim attestation, intermediate certificate · Zwischenbescheinigung *f*, Zwischenschein *m*, Zwischenattest *n* [*Über den Fortschritt der Bauarbeiten*]

progress certificate → progress (payment) certificate

progress chart → progress of the work(s) chart

progress estimate [*It is made by the owner, or the architect/engineer representing the owner, after the project has been awarded to the contractor*] · Ausführungsvoranschlag *m*

progressing · Fortschreiten *n* [*Bauleistung*]

progressive agglomeration of industry · Stufenagglomeration *f* der Industrie

progressive proof; progressive pull (Brit.) · Skalenandruck *m* [*Kartographie*]

progressive taxation · progressive Besteuerung *f*, Progressivbesteuerung

progressive tax system · progressives Steuersystem *n*

progress of the work(s), construction progress, (job) progress, building progress · Baufortschritt *m*, Arbeitsfortschritt

progress of the work(s) chart, progress of the work(s) schedule, (job) progress chart, (job) progress schedule, working progress chart, working progress schedule · Arbeitsfortschrittplan *m*, (Bau)Fortschrittplan, Bauzeit(en)plan [*vom Auftraggeber aufgestellt*]

progress of the work(s) report, (job) progress report · Arbeitsfortschrittbericht *m*, (Bau)Fortschrittbericht *m*

progress payment, instal(l)ment payment, payment on account, interim payment · Abschlagszahlung *f*, Akontozahlung [*für geleistete Arbeit(en)*]

progress (payment) certificate, interim (payment) certificate, payment on account certificate, instal(l)ment (payment) certificate · Abschlags(zahlungs)schein *m*, Abschlags(zahlungs)bescheinigung *f*, Abschlags(zahlungs)attest *n*, Akonto(zahlungs)schein, Akonto(zahlungs)bescheinigung, Akonto(zahlungs)attest

progress rate, speed of progress, progress speed, construction speed, speed rate, speed of construction, rate of construction, rate of progress, construction rate · Baugeschwindigkeit *f*, Bautempo *n*, (Bau)Fortschrittempo, (Bau)Fortschrittgeschwindigkeit

progress speed, construction speed, speed rate, speed of construction, rate of construction, rate of progress, construction rate, progress rate, speed of progress · Baugeschwindigkeit *f*, Bautempo *n*, (Bau)Fortschrittempo, (Bau)Fortschrittgeschwindigkeit

to prohibit · entziehen [*Zuständigkeit*]

prohibited, not allowed, not permitted, illicit · unerlaubt, verboten

prohibited air space, prohibited air domain · Luftsperrgebiet *n*

prohibited area, prohibited territory, closed area, closed territory · Sperrgebiet *n*

prohibited month; (de)fence month (Brit.); **defense month** (US) [*A period of thirty-one days in the year, during which time it is unlaw-ful for anybody to hunt in the forest*], close season · Schonzeit *f*, Hegezeit, Setzzeit

prohibition · Verbot *n*

prohibition against assigning a share of the cost(s) · Umlageverbot *n*

prohibition by law · gesetzliches Verbot *n*, Rechtsverbot

prohibition clause · Verbotsklausel *f*

prohibition of acquisition, acquisition prohibition · Beschaffungsverbot *n*, Erwerbsverbot

prohibition of advertisement, advertizement prohibition, advertisement prohibition, prohibition of advertizement · Werbeverbot *n*, Reklameverbot

prohibition of arbitrary action(s) · Willkürverbot *n*

prohibition of assignment, prohibition of cession, prohibition of assignation; pactum de non cedendo [*Latin*] · Abtretungsverbot *n*, Zessionsverbot

prohibition of demolition, prohibition of wrecking, prohibition of pulling down, demolition stop, wrecking stop, pulling down stop, razing stop · Abbruchverbot *n*, Abrißverbot, Einreißverbot

prohibition of disposition · Verfügungsverbot *n* [*§ 135 des Bürgerlichen Gesetzbuches*]

prohibition of export — project management law

prohibition of export, export prohibition · Ausfuhrverbot *n*, Exportverbot *n*

prohibition of (freedom of) assembly · Versammlungsverbot *n*

prohibition of pulling down, demolition stop, wrecking stop, pulling down stop, razing stop, prohibition of demolition, prohibition of wrecking · Abbruchverbot *n*, Abrißverbot, Einreißverbot

prohibition of use, prohibition to use · Benutzungsverbot *n*, Gebrauchsverbot

prohibition of vehicular access · Zufahrtverbot *n*

prohibition of vehicular exit · Ausfahrtverbot *n*

prohibition of wrecking, prohibition of pulling down, demolition stop, wrecking stop, pulling down stop, razing stop, prohibition of demolition · Abbruchverbot *n*, Abrißverbot, Einreißverbot

prohibition on all development, development freeze · Veränderungssperre *f* [*Wenn für ein Gebiet ein Bebauungsplan aufgestellt werden soll, können Neu- und Umbauten und Nutzungsanlagen auf den dort gelegenen Grundstücken nach dem BBauG §§ 14—18 befristet verboten werden, höchstens für 2 bis 4 Jahre*]

prohibition to build, prohibition to construct · Bauverbot *n*, Baueinstellungsverfügung *f*

prohibition to build along a street, prohibition to build along a road, prohibition to build along a highway · (straßenrechtliches) Anbauverbot *n*

prohibition to use, prohibition of use · Benutzungsverbot *n*, Gebrauchsverbot

prohibitive tariff · Sperrzoll *m*

prohibitory · verbietend

project · Vorhaben *n*, Projekt *n*

project administration · Projektverwaltung *f*

project advertisement, public tendering (out), public tender(ing) action, public bidding (action), public invitation to tender, open tendering, open bidding, open competition, advertisement of a project · öffentliche Ausschreibung *f*, öffentliche Aufforderung (zur Angebotsabgabe), offenes Verfahren *n*, offener Wettbewerb *m*, Ausschreibung der öffentlichen Hand [*Bauleistungen werden im vorgeschriebenen Verfahren nach öffentlicher Aufforderung einer unbeschränkten Zahl von Unternehmern zur Einreichung von Angeboten vergeben*]

project area, project territory · Projektgebiet *n*

project area committee, project territory committee · Projektgebietsausschuß *m*

project boundary · Projektgrenze *f*

project central (cost(s)) estimate, definite (cost(s)) estimate (US) · genereller KV *m*, genereller (Bau)Kosten(vor)anschlag

project consultant · Projektberater *m*

project contractor · Projektunternehmer *m*

project coordination · Projektkoordinierung *f*

project description · Projektbeschreibung *f*

project duration, project life · Projektdauer *f*

project execution, project realisation · Projektdurchführung *f*, Projektausführung

(project) inspection after handover · Baubegehung *f* nach Übergabe

projection · Projektion *f* [*Modellfunktion. Abschätzung der Zukunft eines Gegenstandsbereiches*]

project life, project duration · Projektdauer *f*

project list with fee brackets · Objektliste *f*, Projektliste [*§§ 12 und 14 HOAI enthalten jeweils eine Objektliste für Gebäude und Freianlagen. In diesen Objektlisten sind die Honorarzonen I bis V angegeben, in die die jeweiligen Objekte einzuordnen sind*]

project management, management of project · Objektbetreuung *f*, Projektbetreuung

project management, building management, management of construction, management of project, management of building, construction management · (Bau)Betreuung *f*, Betreuung von Bauvorhaben [*Die technische und wirtschaftliche Vorbereitung und Überwachung eines Bauvorhabens in fremdem Namen und für fremde Rechnung*]

project management, management of construction, management of project, management of building, building management, construction management · Bau(betriebs)führung *f* [*Die technische und wirtschaftliche Vorbereitung und Überwachung eines Bauvorhabens in eigenem Namen*]

project management agent, construction management agent, building management agent [*Er bereitet ein Bauvorhaben im Namen und für Rechnung des Betreuten (= Bauherrn) vor und/oder führt es durch. Der Umfang der Betreuung und der Vollmacht wird in einem Betreuungsvertrag vereinbart*] · (Bau)Betreuer *m*

project management law, construction management law, building management law · (Bau)Betreuungsrecht *n*

project management law, building management law, construction management law · Baubetriebsrecht *n*

project observation · Projektbeobachtung *f* [*Zum Sammeln von Erfahrungswerten*]

project overhead(s), project overhead cost(s) · Projektgemeinkosten *f*, Projektgeneralkosten

project owner, client, employer, promoter, (building) owner, construction owner [*In Great Britain, the term "employer" is preferred since this is used in both the RIBA and ICE standard forms of contract*] · Bauherr(schaft) *m*, (*f*), Auftraggeber *m*, BH *f*, AG *m* [*im Sinne der VOB*]; Besteller [*im Sinne des BGB*] [*Nach geläufiger Fachsprache ist „Bauherr" stets der „Letzt-Besteller" eines Bauwerkes (oder Bauwerk-Teils), also nicht der Unternehmer, der einen Subunternehmer bezieht. Dieser „Letzt-Besteller" ist Bauherr im engen (und eigentlichen) Sinne des Wortes. In einem übertragenen (nicht geläufigen) Sinne aber kann „Bauherr" auch ein Unternehmer sein, der übernommene Bauarbeiten durch Abschluß eines Bauvertrages an einen Subunternehmer weitervergibt. In diesem übertragenen Sinne muß das Wort dann verstanden werden, wenn die SIA-Norm 118 (Schweiz) auf den Bauvertrag zwischen Unternehmer und Subunternehmer zur Anwendung kommt. Im Verhältnis Unternehmer/Subunternehmer ist alsdann der erstere „Bauherr" im Sinne der Norm, der andere „Unternehmer"*]

project planning · Projektplanung *f*

project procurement manager · Projekteinkäufer *m*

project realisation, project execution · Projektdurchführung *f*, Projektausführung

project territory, project area · Projektgebiet *n*

project territory committee, project area committee · Projektgebietsausschuß *m*

(project) work quantity · Baumenge *f*

to prolong, to lengthen, to extend · verlängern

prolongation, extension · Verlängerung *f*

prolongation agreement, extension agreement · Verlängerungsabkommen *n*, Verlängerungsabmachung *f*, Verlängerungsvereinbarung

prolongation clause, extension clause, extender clause · Verlängerungsklausel *f*

prolongation of a term, (additional) respite · Nachfrist *f*

prolongation of limitation, extension of limitation · Verjährungsverlängerung *f*

prolongation of payment, payment extension, payment prolongation, extension of payment · Zahlungsfristverlängerung *f*

prolongation of time clause, prolongation of period clause, extension of time clause, extension of period clause · Frist(verlänger)ungsklausel *f*

prolonged, lengthened, extended · verlängert

to promise, to undertake · versprechen

promise, undertaking; assumpsit [*Latin*] [*obsolete*] · (Leistungs)Versprechen *n*, Naturalversprechen

promise · Hauptleistung *f* [*Vertrag*]

promise, commitment, pledge · Versprechen *n*, Verpflichtung *f*

promisee, covenantee · Vertragsgläubiger *m*, Vertragsempfänger, Versprechensgläubiger, Versprechensempfänger [*Durch Vertrag berechtigte Person*]

promisee, obligee [*Person, firm, or corporation protected by the surety bond. The obligee under a bond is similar to the insured under an insurance policy*] · Versprechensempfänger *m*

promise implied, implied promise, tacit promise · gefolgertes Versprechen *n*, konkludentes Versprechen, stillschweigendes Versprechen

promise of benevolence, promise without consideration, one-sided promise, nude promise, unilateral promise, gratuitous promise · einseitiges (Leistungs)Versprechen *n*, einseitiges Naturalversprechen, (Leistungs)Versprechen ohne Gegenleistung, Naturalversprechen ohne Gegenleistung

promise of marriage, marriage promise · Eheversprechen *n*, Heiratsversprechen

promise of performance in favo(u)r of a third party · Erfüllungsübernahme *f*

promise to pay · Zahlungsversprechen *n*

promise without consideration, one-sided promise, nude promise, unilateral promise, gratuitous promise, promise of benevolence · einseitiges (Leistungs)Versprechen *n*, einseitiges Naturalversprechen, (Leistungs)Versprechen ohne Gegenleistung, Naturalversprechen ohne Gegenleistung

promisor, principal, covenantor, obligor [*One bound by an obligation. Under a bond both the "principal" and "surety" are "obligors"*] · Versprechensgeber *m*, Versprechende, Verpflichtete

promissory note, note (of hand), single bill, sole bill, only bill · Eigenwechsel *m*, (eigener) Wechsel, Solawechsel, Verpflichtungsschein *m* [*Ein unbedingtes, von einer Person an eine andere gerichtetes, vom Aussteller unterschriebenes* schriftliches Versprechen, auf Verlangen oder zu einer festgesetzten oder zu einer bestimmbar zukünftigen Zeit an eine bestimmte Person oder deren Order oder an den Inhaber eine bestimmte Summe in Geld zu zahlen]

to promote, to sponsor · fördern

promoter, sponsor · Fördernde m, Förderer

promoter, (building) owner, construction owner, project owner, client, employer [*In Great Britain, the term "employer" is preferred since this is used in both the RIBA and ICE standard forms of contract*] · Bauherr(schaft) m, (f), Auftraggeber m, BH f, AG m [*im Sinne der VOB*]; Besteller [*im Sinne des BGB*] [*Nach geläufiger Fachsprache ist „Bauherr" stets der „Letzt-Besteller" eines Bauwerkes (oder Bauwerk-Teils), also nicht der Unternehmer, der einen Subunternehmer bezieht. Dieser „Letzt-Besteller" ist Bauherr im engen (und eigentlichen) Sinne des Wortes. In einem übertragenen (nicht geläufigen) Sinne aber kann „Bauherr" auch ein Unternehmer sein, der übernommene Bauarbeiten durch Abschluß eines Bauvertrages an einen Subunternehmer weitervergibt. In diesem übertragenen Sinne muß das Wort dann verstanden werden, wenn die SIA-Norm 118 (Schweiz) auf den Bauvertrag zwischen Unternehmer und Subunternehmer zur Anwendung kommt. Im Verhältnis Unternehmer/Subunternehmer ist alsdann der erstere „Bauherr" im Sinne der Norm, der andere „Unternehmer"*]

promoter · Gründungsorganisator m [*AG*]

promoter → developer

promoter-designed project, owner-designed project, client-designed project, employer-designed project · Bauherrenentwurfsprojekt n, Bauherrschaftsentwurfsprojekt

promoterism · Gründungsschwindel m

promoter's delay, owner's delay, client's delay, employer's delay · bauseitiger Verzug m

promoter's design, owner's design, client's design, employer's design · Ausschreibungsentwurf m, Bauherrenentwurf

promoter's law → developer's law

promoter's liability, client's liability, employer's liability, owner's liability · Bauherrenhaftpflicht f, Bauherrenhaftung f, Bauherrenhaftbarkeit f

promoter's liability insurance, owner's liability insurance, client's liability insurance, employer's liability insurance · Bauherrenhaftpflichtversicherung f, Bauherrschaftshaftpflichtversicherung

promoter's risk, owner's risk, client's risk, employer's risk · Bauherrenrisiko n, Bauherrenwagnis n, Bauherrschaftsrisiko, Bauherrschaftswagnis

promoter's share · Gründeranteil m

promoter's stock · Gründeraktie f

promoting, sponsoring · Fördern n

promotion, sponsoring · Förderung f

promotion, advancement · Beförderung f [*In eine höhere Stellung oder ein höheres Amt*]

promotional [*For a promotion*] · förderungsfähig

promotion(al) area, sponsoring area, sponsoring territory, promotion(al) territory · Förderungsgebiet n, gefördertes Gebiet

promotion(al) committee, sponsoring committee · Förderungsausschuß m

promotion(al) contract, sponsoring contract · Förderungsvertrag m

promotion(al) fund, promotion(al) money, sponsoring fund, sponsoring money · Förderungsfonds m, Förderungsmittel f, Förderungsgeld n

promotion(al) hous(ebuild)ing, sponsoring hous(ebuild)ing, assisted hous(ebuild)ing · geförderter Wohn(ungs)bau m, Wohn(ungs)bauförderung f

promotion(al) hous(ebuild)ing for students · Studentenwohnraumförderung f, Studentenwohn(ungs)bauförderung

promotion(al) hous(ebuild)ing institution, assistance hous(ebuild)ing institution, sponsoring hous(ebuild)ing institution · Wohn(ungs)bauförderungsanstalt f

promotion(al) individual system, sponsoring individual system, assisting individual system, individual promotion(al) system, individual sponsoring system, individual assistance system · Individualförderungssystem n

promotion(al) measure, sponsoring measure · Förderungsmaßnahme f

promotion(al) money, sponsoring fund, sponsoring money, promotion(al) fund · Förderungsfonds m, Förderungsmittel f, Förderungsgeld n

promotion(al) plan, sponsoring plan · Förderungsplan m

promotion(al) planner, sponsoring planner · Förderungsplaner m

promotion(al) planning, sponsoring planning · Förderungsplanung f

promotion(al) rate, sponsoring rate · Förderungssatz m

promotion(al) subject, sponsoring subject · Förderungsgegenstand m

promotion(al) system — propensity to save

promotion(al) system, sponsoring system · Förderungssystem *n*

promotion(al) territory, promotion(al) area, sponsoring area, sponsoring territory · Förderungsgebiet *n*, gefördertes Gebiet

promotion of construction, promotion of building, construction promotion, building promotion · Bauförderung *f*

promotion of export, assistance of export, sponsoring of export, export promotion, export assistance · Ausfuhrförderung *f*, Exportförderung

promotion of winter construction, promotion of winter building · Winterbauförderung *f*

prompt note, prompt notification, demand note, demand notification, reminder (of debt due), letter demanding payment, (formal) demand [*Slang: dunning letter*] · Mahnbrief *m*, Mahnschreiben *n*, Mahnung *f*

prompt payment discount, (payment) discount · Skonto *n*, Rabatt *m*, (Preis)Nachlaß *m*

to promulgate, to publicize, to publish, to announce · veröffentlichen, verbreiten, (öffentlich) bekanntgeben, (öffentlich) bekanntmachen

promulgating, announcing, publicizing · Bekanntgeben *n*, Bekanntmachen, Veröffentlichen, Kundmachen, Verbreiten

promulgating by ringing a bell, announcing by ringing a bell, publicizing by ringing a bell · Ausklingeln *n*, Ausschellen

promulgation, announcement, publication · Bekanntmachung *f*, Bekanntgabe *f*, Veröffentlichung, Kundmachung, Verlautbarung, Verbreitung

promulgation by (the) bulletin board, publication by (the) bulletin board, publicity by (the) bulletin board, announcement by (the) bulletin board · Aushängung *f*, Bekanntgabe *f* durch Aushang, Bekanntmachung durch Aushang, Veröffentlichung durch Aushang, Kundmachung durch Aushang, Verbreitung durch Aushang

promulgation posting, publicity posting, public notice by poster, announcement posting, publication posting · Anschlagung *f*, Bekanntmachung durch Anschlag, Veröffentlichung durch Anschlag, Bekanntgabe durch Anschlag, Kundmachung durch Anschlag, Verbreitung durch Anschlag

prone to engage in (law)suits, fond of litigation · prozeßsüchtig

proneness to accidents · Unfallträchtigkeit *f*

to pronounce · verkünden [*Urteil*]

to pronounce not guilty, to discharge, to absolve from, to acquit · freisprechen

proof · Nachweis *m*

proof, evidence [*Wills „Circumstantial Evidence", London, 1850 (3. Ausgabe), bezeichnet „evidence" und „proof" als „cause" und „effect". Beide Benennungen werden aber sehr häufig synonym verwendet und nur ein gerichtlich zugelassenes Beweisstück wird mit „evidence" bezeichnet*] · Beweis *m*

proof ab extrâ, evidence ab extrâ · fremder Beweis *m*

proof ab intrâ, evidence ab intrâ · eigener Beweis *m*

proof as to character, evidence as to character · Charakterbeweis *m* [*Beweis nach dem Charakter einer Person, daß die ihr zugeschriebene Handlungsweise wahrscheinlich oder unwahrscheinlich ist*]

proof law, law of evidence, law of proof, evidence law [*The aggregate of rules and principles regulating the admissibility, relevancy, weight and sufficiency of evidence in legal proceedings*] · Beweisrecht *n*

proof of age · Altersnachweis *m*

proof (of a will) in common form, proof of wills in common form · Testamentsprüfung *f* ohne bestrittene Rechtsgültigkeit

proof (of a will) in solemn form per testes, proof (of a will) by action · Testamentsprüfung *f* bei Widerspruch

proof of claim, proof of demand, evidence of claim, evidence of demand · Forderungsnachweis *m*, Verlangensnachweis

proof of heirship, evidence of heirship, heirship proof, heirship evidence · Erbnachweis *m*

proof of ownership (of property), proof of proprietorship, proof of (general) property · Eigentumsbeweis *m*

proof of quality, quality proof · Gütenachweis *m*

proof of title, evidence of title, title proof, title evidence · (Rechts)Titelbeweis *m*

proof of wills, proof of a will · Testamentsprüfung *f*

proof to the contrary, contradictory evidence, contradictory proof, rebutting testimony, disproof, counter-evidence, counter-proof, evidence to the contrary · Gegenbeweis *m*, gegenteiliger Beweis

propensity to consume · Verbraucheigung *f*

propensity to consume · Hang *m* zum Verbrauch

propensity to migrate · Wanderungsneigung *f*

propensity to save · Sparneigung *f*

proper, non-defective · baumangelfrei, (sach)mangelfrei, nachbesserungsfrei

proper, non-defective · baumängelfrei, (sach)mängelfrei, nachbesserungsfrei

proper law of the contract, law with reference to which the parties contracted; locus contractus [*Latin*]; seat of the obligation, seat of the contract · Sitz *m* der Obligation [*nach Savigny*]; Sitz *m* des Vertrages

proper law of the contract · rechtes Vertragsstatut *n*, vereinbartes Vertragsrecht *n* [*Das Recht welches auf Grund freier Würdigung der Umstände des Einzelfalles für einen Vertrag als maßgebend zu erachten ist*]

propertied class · besitzende Klasse *f*

property, aggregate of rights, total of rights · Masse *f* von (subjektiven) Rechten, Menge *f* von (subjektiven) Rechten

property, asset, valuable thing · geldwerter Gegenstand *m*, Vermögensgegenstand, Vermögenssache *f*, geldwerte Sache, Vermögensding *n*, geldwertes Ding, Vermögensrechtsobjekt *n*, geldwertes Rechtsobjekt

property, estate [*The word "estate" is a word of the greatest extension, and comprehends every species of property, real and personal. It describes both the corpus and the extent of interest*] · Gut *n*, Vermögen *n*, Habe *f*

property → (real) property

property → ownership (of property)

property (ab)alienation contract → (real) property (ab)alienation contract

property according to civil law, proprietorship according to civil law, ownership (of property) according to civil law · zivilrechtliches Eigentum *n*

property acquisition, acquisition of property · Vermögenserwerb *m*, Vermögensbeschaffung *f*

property acquisition → (real) property acquisition

property acquisition right → land acquisition right

property agent → ((real) estate) broker

property appraisal → (real) property (e)valuation

property appraiser → (real) property appraiser

property arm · Immobilienportefeuille *f* eines gemischten Versicherungsfonds

property barrister → conveyancing barrister

property blocking, blocking of property, freezing of property, property freezing · Vermögenssperre *f*, Sperren *n* von Vermögen

property board → (real) property board

property bond (fund) · Immobilienversicherungsfonds *m*, Liegenschaftsversicherungsfonds, Grund(stücks)versicherungsfonds

property broker → ((real) estate) broker

property builder → developer

(property) builder's contract, (property) developer's contract · (Bau)Trägervertrag *m*

property builder's law → developer's law

(property) builder's ordinance, (property) developer's ordinance · (Bau)Trägerverordnung *f*

property business → (real) estate business

property by common law → legal title

property by equity law, proprietorship by equity law, equitable ownership (of property), equitable property, equitable proprietorship, ownership by equity law · Eigentum *n* nach Billigkeitsrecht

property by prescription → (general) property by prescription

property certificate → (general) property certificate

property certifier → (real) property appraiser

property change, change in property · Vermögenswechsel *m*

property class, class of property · Vermögensklasse *f*

property collection, collection of property · Zusammenfassung *f* von Besitzen, Besitzzusammenfassung

property community · Vermögensgemeinschaft *f*

property company → (real) property company

property compensation (court) action → (real) estate compensation (court) action

property composition → (general) property composition

property confusion, confusion of property · Güterzusammenschluß *m*

property consortium → (real) estate syndicate

property constituted for a particular purpose, property deeded for a particular purpose [*e.g. a charitable trust*] · Zweckvermögen *n*

property contract → (general) property contract

property contract → (real) property (purchase) contract

property control — property limitation 818

property control → land control

property corporation → (real) property corporation

property credit → (real) estate credit

property credit bank → (real) property credit bank

property (damage liability) insurance · Sachversicherung *f*

property dealer → ((real) estate) broker

property demise → (real) estate lease(hold)

property depreciation fund → (real) estate depreciation fund

(property) developer → developer

(property) developer's contract, (property) builder's contract · (Bau)Trägervertrag *m*

(property) developer's law → developer's law

(property) developer's ordinance, (property) builder's ordinance · (Bau)Trägerverordnung *f*

property disposal contract → (real) property disposal contract

property dispute · Vermögensauseinandersetzung *f*, Vermögensstreit(igkeit) *m*, *(f)*

property (e)valuation → (real) property (e)valuation

property exchange → exchange of land(s)

property field, field of property · Vermögenswesen *n*

property finance act → (real) estate finance act

property financing → (real) estate financing

property firm → (real) estate firm

property for life → (real) property for life

property for sale · verkäufliches Vermögen *n*

property freezing, property blocking, blocking of property, freezing of property · Vermögenssperre *f*, Sperren *n* von Vermögen

property fund → (real) estate fund

property-gage · Substanzpfand *n* [*Die Benennungen „Proprietätspfand" und „Eigentumspfand" sollten gemäß Harold Dexter Hazeltine nicht als Synonyma für das Substanzpfand verwendet, sondern den Verpfändungsformen mit Übereignung vorbehalten werden*]

property grant → land(s) grant

property hazard, property risk · Sachwagnis *n*, Sachrisiko *n*

property held by one person → (real) property held by one person

property held in trust → (real) property held in trust

property held jointly → (real) property held jointly

property holder → (land) holder

property improvement loan · Grundstücksverbesserungsdarleh(e)n *n*

property increase · Vermögenszuwachs *m*, Vermögenszunahme *f*

property increase tax · Vermögenszuwachssteuer *f*

property indemnification (court) action → (real) estate compensation (court) action

property in equity, proprietorship in equity, ownership (of property) in equity · Billigkeitseigentum *n*

(property in) fee simple (de)terminable → ((real) estate in) fee simple (de)terminable

property in kind · Sachvermögen *n*

property in law → legal title

property in possession · Eigentum *n* mit Besitz verbunden

property in severalty → (real) property in severalty

property insurance → property (damage liability) insurance

property insurance → (real) property insurance

property inventory → (real) property inventory

property investment trust → land(s) investment trust

property in water, proprietorship in water, ownership (of property) in water, water property, water proprietorship, water ownership (of property) · Wassereigentum *n*

property law → (general) property law

property law → (real) estate law

property lease (agreement) → (real) estate lease (agreement)

property lease(hold) → (real) estate lease(hold)

property leasing → (real) estate leasing

property legislation, property lawmaking · Vermögensgesetzgebung *f*

property lessee → (land) holder

property limitation, property restraint, property restriction · Vermögensbeschränkung *f*, Vermögenseinschränkung, Vermögensbegrenzung

property limitation — property speculation

property limitation, ownership limitation, ownership restraint, proprietorship restraint, property restraint, (general) property restriction, proprietorship restriction, ownership restriction, proprietorship limitation · Eigentumsbegrenzung f, Eigentumsbeschränkung, Eigentumseinschränkung

property limitation act → (real) property limitation act

property liquidated damages (court) action → (real) estate compensation (court) action

property loss, loss of property · Vermögensverlust m, Vermögensschaden m [*Jede in Geld bewertbare Vermögenseinbuße*]

property management → (real) property management

property management agent → (real) property management agent

property management plan → (real) property management plan

property manager → (real) property manager

property mortgage → (real) property mortgage

property mortgage creditor → (real) estate mortgagee

property occupier → (land) holder

property of bed of river, ownership of bed of river, proprietorship of bed of river · Strombetteigentum n

property of joint tenancy → (real) property of joint tenancy

property of land(s) → (real) property

property of land(s) for life → (real) property for life

property of materials, ownership of materials, proprietorship of materials · (Werk)Stoffeigentum n, Materialeigentum

property of soil under highways → (general) property of soil under highways

property of space → (general) property of space

property owner → (real) property owner

property plan · Vermögensplan m

property planner · Vermögensplaner m

property planning · Vermögensplanung f

property policy → (general) property policy

property policy → (real) property policy

property practice → (real) estate practice

property presumption, presumption of property · Vermögensvermutung f

property presumption → (general) property presumption

property promoter → developer

property promoter's law → developer's law

property proprietor → (real) property owner

property protection → (general) property protection

property purchase → real property purchase

property (purchase) contract → (real) property (purchase) contract

property register, property registry · (Grundbuch)Abteilung II f

property residual technique [*In those cases where neither the land value nor the building value can be estimated independently, the property is valued as a single unit*] · Grundstücksrestwertverfahren n

property restraint, property restriction, property limitation · Vermögensbeschränkung f, Vermögenseinschränkung, Vermögensbegrenzung

property restraint, (general) property restriction, proprietorship restriction, ownership restriction, proprietorship limitation, property limitation, ownership limitation, ownership restraint, proprietorship restraint · Eigentumsbegrenzung f, Eigentumsbeschränkung, Eigentumseinschränkung

property restriction, property limitation, property restraint · Vermögensbeschränkung f, Vermögenseinschränkung, Vermögensbegrenzung

property restriction → (general) property restriction

property right, valuable right, valuable interest, proprietary right, right in property, right of property · (subjektives) Vermögensrecht n, vermögenswertes Recht

property risk, property hazard · Sachwagnis n, Sachrisiko n

property sale → (real) property sale

property separation, separation of property · Gütertrennung f

property settlement, settlement of property · Bindung f von Vermögen, Vermögensbindung, Gebundenheit f von Vermögen, Vermögensgebundenheit

property settlement for value, settlement (of property) for value · Vermögensbindung f mit geldwerter Gegenleistung

property speculation → (real) property speculation

property speculator → proprietary chapel 820

property speculator → (real) property speculator

property structure → (general) property structure

property subject, subject of property · Besitzobjekt *n*

property surface → surface of (real) estate

property syndicate → (real) estate syndicate

property tax, wealth tax [*In English law, this is understood to be an income tax payable in respect to landed property. In America, it is a tax imposed on property, whether real or personal, as distinguished from poll taxes, and taxes on successions, transfers, and occupations, and from license taxes*] · Vermögenssteuer *f*

property tax → (general) property tax

property tax → (real) property tax

property taxation, taxation of property, estate taxation, taxation of estate · Vermögensbesteuerung *f*

property tenancy → (real) estate lease(hold)

property tenant → (land) holder

property theory → (general) property theory

property title → (real) estate title

property transaction judg(e)ment → (real) property transaction jud(e)gment

property transfer cost(s) → (real) property transfer cost(s)

property transfer permission → land transfer permission

property transfer tax → (real) property transfer tax

property trespass, trespass (up)on property · Eigentumsfrevel *m*, Eigentumsrechtsverletzung *f*

property underwriting group → (real) estate syndicate

property usufruct, estate usufruct, usufruct of estate, usufruct of property · Nießbrauch *m* an einem Vermögen, Nießbrauch an einem Gut, (Frucht)Genuß *m* an einem Vermögen, (Frucht)Genuß an einem Gut, Nutzgewalt *f* an einem Gut, Nutzgewalt an einem Vermögen

property usufruct → (real) property usufruct

property valuation → (real) property (e)valuation

property value, value of property · Vermögenswert *m*

property valuer → (real) property appraiser

proper value · Eigenwert *m*, Selbstwert

proponent, supporter · Befürworter *m*

proportion, share, part, rate [*A charge, valuation, payment or price fixed according to ratio, scale or standard. A fixed relation of quantity, amount or degree. A comparative price or amount of demands*] · Anteil *m*

proportional arrow (symbol) map · gestufte Pfeillinienkarte *f*

proportionality, proportionateness · Verhältnismäßigkeit *f*

proportionality net shift, net proportionality shift [*shift analysis*] · Proportionalitätseffekt *m*, Proportionalitätswirkung *f*

proportional net shift [*shift analysis*] · PS *f*, Strukturkomponente *f*, Strukturfaktor *m*

proportional to value, in proportion to value; ad valorem [*Latin*] · wertverhältnismäßig

proportionate, pro tanto, pro rata · anteilig, anteilmäßig

to proportionate, to pro-rate · anteil(mäß)ig zuteilen

proportionate basis, pro-rata basis, pro-tanto basis · anteil(mäß)ige Grundlage *f*

proportionate contract, divisible contract, severable contract, pro tanto contract, pro rata contract · Vertrag *m* auf teilbare Leistung, teilbarer Vertrag

proportionateness, proportionality · Verhältnismäßigkeit *f*

proportionate sharing, pro-rata sharing, pro-tanto sharing · Anteiligkeit *f*

proportion (of values) · Wertverhältnis *n*

proportion of working men · männliche Erwerbsquote *f*

proportion of working women · weibliche Erwerbsquote *f*

proposal · Vorschlag *m*

proposal (US) → bid

to propose, to support, to set forth, to propound [*To put forward for consideration*] · befürworten, vorschlagen

proposer · Versicherungsantragsteller *m*

proposition of exterior angles · Außenwinkelsatz *m*

proposition of law, law proposition, rule · Rechtssatz *m*

to propound, to propose, to support, to set forth [*To put forward for consideration*] · befürworten, vorschlagen

proprietary act → law of possession

proprietary chapel · Privatkapelle *f*

proprietary function — proprietorship limitation

proprietary function · fiskalische Funktion *f*

proprietary government · Feudalregierung *f*

proprietary office · Versicherungs-Aktiengesellschaft *f*

proprietary possession · Eigenbesitz *m*

proprietary possessor · Eigenbesitzer *m*

proprietary right, right in property, right of property, property right, valuable right, valuable interest · (subjektives) Vermögensrecht *n*, vermögenswertes Recht

proprietary school · Eigentümerschule *f* [*Eine bürgerliche Schule von Interessenten als Kapitalgesellschaft betrieben*]

proprietary statute → law of possession

proprietor, owner · Eigentümer *m*, Eigentumssubjekt *n*, Eigner *m*

proprietor by (common) law, owner in (common) law, proprietor in (common) law, legal owner, statutory owner, statutory proprietor, legal proprietor, owner by (common) law [*As opposed to the "equitable owner"*] · Eigentümer *m* nach Gemeinrecht, gesetzlicher Eigentümer [*Die Eigentumsaufspaltung nach Gemeinrecht und Billigkeitsrecht ist die Folge dieser dualistischen Entwicklung in England bis 1873/75*]

proprietor by equitable law, equitable owner, equitable proprietor, owner by equitable law [*As opposed to the "owner by (common) law" (also called "legal owner")*] · Eigentümer *m* im Innenverhältnis, Eigentümer nach Billigkeit(srecht), Eigentumssubjekt *n* im Innenverhältnis, Eigentumssubjekt nach Billigkeit(srecht), Eigner im Innenverhältnis, Eigner nach Billigkeit(srecht), wirtschaftlicher Eigner, wirtschaftlicher Eigentümer, wirtschaftliches Eigentumssubjekt, Billigkeitsrechteigentümer

proprietor by prescription → prescription owner

proprietorless, ownerless · eigentümerlos, ohne Eigentümer

proprietor-occupier, owner-occupant, proprietor-occupant, owner-occupier · Selbstnießer, Eigennießer *m* [*Eigentumswohnung; Grundstück*]

proprietor of small property, small property proprietor, small property owner, owner of small property · Kleineigentümer *m*, Kleineigner

proprietor of (the) (building) land, owner of (the) (building) land, landed proprietor, landed owner, (building) land proprietor, (building) (land) area owner, (building) (land) (area) proprietor, (building) land owner · (Bau)Bodeneigentümer *m*, (Bau)Flächeneigentümer, (Bau)Landeigentümer, (Bau)Landherr, (Bau)Bodeneigner, (Bau)Flächeneigner, (Bau)Landeigner

proprietor-possessor relation(ship), owner-possessor relation(ship) · Eigentümer-Besitzer-Verhältnis *n*

proprietor's easement, owner's easement · Eigentümergrunddienstbarkeit *f*

proprietorship, (general) property; dominium [*Latin*]; ownership (of property) · Eigentum *n* [*Die uneingeschränkte Herrschaft einer Person über eine Sache, auch in rechtlicher Beziehung. „Eigentum" und „Besitz" sind nicht gleichbedeutend. Eigentum ist das dingliche Vollrecht, Besitz die tatsächliche, vom Rechtstitel unabhängige Innehabung einer Sache. Auch der Dieb ist Besitzer*]

proprietorship according to civil law, ownership (of property) according to civil law, property according to civil law · zivilrechtliches Eigentum *n*

proprietorship by common law → legal title

proprietorship by equity law, equitable ownership (of property), equitable property, equitable proprietorship, ownership by equity law, property by equity law · Eigentum *n* nach Billigkeitsrecht

proprietorship certificate, ownership (of property) certificate, (general) property certificate · Eigentumsbescheinigung *f*, Eigentumsschein *m*, Eigentumsattest *n*

proprietorship composition, ownership structure, ownership composition, (general) property structure, (general) property composition, proprietorship structure · Eigentumsaufbau *m*, Eigentumsgefüge *n*, Eigentumsstruktur *f*, Eigentumszusammensetzung *f*

proprietorship contract, (general) property contract, ownership (of property) contract · Eigentumsvertrag *m*

proprietorship equities and liabilities · langfristig bereitgestelltes Kreditkapital *n*

proprietorship in equity, ownership (of property) in equity, property in equity · Billigkeitseigentum *n*

proprietorship in law → legal title

proprietorship law, law of (general) property, law of proprietorship, law of ownership (of property), ownership (of property) law, (general) property law · Eigentumsrecht *n*, objektives Eigentumsrecht

proprietorship limitation, property limitation, ownership limitation, ownership restraint, proprietorship restraint, property restraint, (general) property restriction, proprietorship restriction, ownership restriction · Eigentumsbegrenzung *f*, Eigentumsbeschränkung *f*, Eigentumseinschränkung

proprietorship of bed of river, property of bed of river, ownership of bed of river · Strombetteigentum *n*

proprietorship of materials, property of materials, ownership of materials · (Werk)Stoffeigentum *n*, Materialeigentum

proprietorship of soil under highways, (general) property of soil under highways, ownership of soil under highways · Erdreicheigentum *n* unter Straßen

proprietorship of space, (general) property of space, ownership of space · Raumeigentum *n*

proprietorship policy, (general) property policy, ownership (of property) policy · Eigentumspolitik *f*

proprietorship presumption, ownership (of property) presumption, presumption of property, presumption of proprietorship, presumption of ownership (of property), (general) property presumption · Eigentumsvermutung *f*

proprietorship protection, (general) property protection, ownership (of property) protection · Eigentumsschutz *m*

proprietorship register, register of ownership (of property), register of proprietorship, ownership (of property) register · Abteilung I *f*, Eigentümerregister *n*, erste (Grundbuch)Abteilung, Grundbuchabteilung I

proprietorship restriction, ownership restriction, proprietorship limitation, property limitation, ownership limitation, ownership restraint, proprietorship restraint, property restraint, (general) property restriction · Eigentumsbegrenzung *f*, Eigentumsbeschränkung, Eigentumseinschränkung

proprietorship structure, proprietorship composition, ownership structure, ownership composition, (general) property structure, (general) property composition · Eigentumsaufbau *m*, Eigentumsgefüge *n*, Eigentumsstruktur *f*, Eigentumszusammensetzung *f*

proprietorship tax, ownership (of property) tax, (general) property tax · Eigentumssteuer *f*

proprietorship theory, ownership (of property) theory, (general) property theory · Eigentumstheorie *f*

proprietor's interest, owner's interest · Eigentümerbelang *m*, Eigentümerinteresse *n*

proprietor's land charge, owner's land charge · Eigentümergrundschuld *f*

proprietor's servitude, owner's servitude · Eigentümerdienstbarkeit *f*, Eigentümergerechtigkeit, Eigentümerservitut *n, f*, (servitutisches) Eigentümerrecht *n*

proprietress · Eigentümerin *f*, Eignerin

pro-rata basis, pro-tanto basis, proportionate basis · anteil(mäß)ige Grundlage *f*

pro-rata sharing, pro-tanto sharing, proportionate sharing · Anteiligkeit *f*

to pro-rate, to proportionate · anteil(mäß)ig zuteilen

to prosecute · (strafrechtlich) verklagen

to prosecute by due course of law; implacitare [*Latin*]; to implead, to sue · (privatrechtlich) verklagen, gerichtlich belangen

prosecuting attorney · Staatsanwalt *m*

prosecution · Strafanzeige *f*

prosecution cost(s) · Strafverfolgungskosten *f*

prosecutor · Klägeranwalt *m* [*Strafsache*]

prospect (US) [*Potential customer for real estate purchase or lease*] · potentieller Grund(stücks)erwerber *m*

prospecting area · Schürfgebiet *n*

prospecting license, prospecting licence · Schürfgenehmigung *f*, Schürferlaubnis *f* [*für Edelsteine*]

prospecting permit · Schürfgenehmigung *f*, Schürferlaubnis *f* [*für Edelmetalle*]

prospecting right · Schürfrecht *n* [*für Edelmetalle und Edelsteine*]

prospective agreement, offer · (Vertrags)Antrag *m*, Offerte *f*, Vertragsangebot *n* [*Das einem anderen mitgeteilte Angebot, mit ihm einen Vertrag abzuschließen*]

prospective bidder, prospective tenderer, prospective offeror, prospective competitor, prospective tendering contractor, prospective competing contractor, applicant, person invited to tender · Bewerber *m* [*Ein Bauunternehmer, der sich um eine Bauleistung bewirbt, aber noch kein Angebot auf diese Bauleistung abgegeben hat*]

prospective buyer, prospective purchaser · Bewerber *m*, Kaufanwärter *m*

prospective buyer's contract, prospective purchaser's contract · Bewerbervertrag *m*, Kaufanwärtervertrag

prospective competing contractor → prospective bidder

prospective competitor → prospective bidder

prospective cost(s) · Zukunftskosten *f*

prospective customer · Kaufinteressent *m*, möglicher Käufer *m*

(prospective) development value, betterment, (capital) appreciation, increase of value, value increase [*An improvement which adds to the cost(s) of a property. Distinguished from a repair or replacement*] · Wertverbesserung *f*, Wertzuwachs *m*, Wertsteigerung, Wertzunahme *f*, Werterhöhung

(prospective) development value clause, increase of value clause, (capital) appreciation clause, betterment clause, value increase clause · Werterhöhungsklausel *f*, Wertsteigerungsklausel, Wertzuwachsklausel, Wertzunahmeklausel, Wertverbesserungsklausel

prospective home buyer, prospective home purchaser · Eigenhausbewerber *m*, Eigenhauskaufanwärter, Eigenheimbewerber, Eigenheimkaufanwärter

prospective home purchaser's contract, prospective home buyer's contract · Eigenhausbewerbervertrag *m*, Eigenheimbewerbervertrag, Eigenhauskaufanwärtervertrag, Eigenheimkaufanwärtervertrag

prospective offeror → prospective bidder

prospective purchaser, prospective buyer · Bewerber *m*, Kaufanwärter *m*

prospective purchaser's contract, prospective buyer's contract · Bewerbervertrag *m*, Kaufanwärtervertrag

prospective tenant · Wohnungssuchende *m*

prospective tenants, people seeking accommodation · Wohnungssuchende *mpl*

prospective tenderer → prospective bidder

prospective tendering contractor → prospective bidder

prosperity, well-being · Wohlstand *m*

prosperity area, prosperity territory · Wohlstandsgebiet *n*

prosperity level, level of well-being, level of prosperity, well-being level · Wohlstandsniveau *n*

prosperity of the community, public welfare, public weal, public good, public necessity, public convenience, common welfare, common weal, common good, common necessity, common convenience, good of the community, public interests, common well-being, general good · Gemeinwohl *n*, öffentliches Wohl, öffentliches Interesse *n*, allgemeines Wohl, allgemeines Interesse, Allgemeinwohl, öffentliche Belange *mpl*

prosperity territory, prosperity area · Wohlstandsgebiet *n*

prosperous time · Blütezeit *f*, Wohlstandszeit

pro tanto, pro rata, proportionate · anteilig, anteilmäßig

pro tanto basis, proportionate basis, prorata basis · anteil(mäß)ige Grundlage *f*

pro tanto contract, pro rata contract, proportionate contract, divisible contract, severable contract · Vertrag *m* auf teilbare Leistung, teilbarer Vertrag

pro tanto sharing, proportionate sharing, pro rata sharing · Anteiligkeit *f*

to protect, to safeguard · wahrnehmen [*Interessen*]

protected forest · Schutzwald(ung) *m*, *(f)* [*Wald(ung) durch die Staatsgewalt im öffentlichen Interesse geschützt*]

protected tenancy · geschütztes Mietverhältnis *n*

protection · Schutz *m*

protection against disfigurement(s) · Verunstaltungsschutz *m*, Verschandelungsschutz

protection against evacuation · Räumungsschutz *m*

protection against oscillation(s), protection against vibration(s) · Erschütterungsschutz *m*

protection against termination of tenancy · Kündigungsschutz *m* [*Wohnung*]

protection against theft · Schutz *m* vor Diebstahl

protection against unjust dismissal · Kündigungsschutz *m* [*Arbeitnehmer*]

protection against vibration(s), protection against oscillation(s) · Erschütterungsschutz *m*

protection belt · Schutzgürtel *m*

protection by rule (of law), protection by norm (of law), protection by legal rule, protection by (legal) norm, protection by law rule, protection by law norm · normativer Schutz *m*

protection facility, protective facility · Schutzeinrichtung *f*

protection for the tenant, security of tenants; rent control (Brit.), tenants' protection, protection of tenants · Mieterschutz *m*

protection measure, measure of protection, protective measure · Schutzmaßnahme *f*, Schutzvorkehrung *f*

protection money · Schutzgeld *n*

protection of animals act, protection of animals statute, protection of animals law · Tierschutzgesetz *n*

protection of area, protection of territory, area protection, territory protection · Gebietsschutz *m*

protection of birds act, protection of birds law, protection of birds statute · Vogelschutzgesetz *n*

protection of birds law · Vogelschutzrecht *n*

protection of buildings, building protection · Gebäudeschutz *m*

protection of construction labour, protection of building labour (Brit.); protection of construction labor, protection of building labor (US) · Bauarbeiterschutz *m*

protection of creditors, protection of debtees · Gläubigerschutz *m*

protection of housing stock · Bestandsschutz *m* von Wohnraum

protection of leaseholders, protection of lessees, protection of (land) holders · Pachtschutz *m*, Pächterschutz

protection of minority groups · Minderheitenschutz *m*

protection of possession · Besitzschutz *m*

protection of purchaser(s), protection of buyer(s), protection of vendee(s) · Käuferschutz *m*

protection of (real) estate, protection of (real) property, protection of realty · (Boden)Besitzschutz *m*, Landbesitzschutz, Grund(stücks)besitzschutz, Bodenschutz

protection of tenants, protection for the tenant, security of tenants; rent control (Brit.), tenants' protection · Mieterschutz *m*

protection of territory, area protection, territory protection, protection of area · Gebietsschutz *m*

protection of the territory of a state from disfigurement and litter and other vulgarity · Heimatschutz *m*

protection of third party · Drittschutz *m*

protection of trees, tree protection · Baumschutz *m*

protection of vendee(s), protection of purchaser(s), protection of buyer(s) · Käuferschutz *m*

protection order, order of protection · Schutzbefehl *m*, Schutzanordnung *f*, Schutzverfügung, Schutzgebot *n*

protection rule (of law), protection legal rule, protection (legal) norm, protection law rule, protection law norm · Schutz(rechts)norm *f*, Schutzsachnorm, Schutzgesetz(es)norm, normative Schutzfestlegung *f*

protective act, protective law, protective statute · Schutzgesetz *n*

protective building, protective construction · Schutzbau *m*

protective construction, protective building · Schutzbau *m*

protective custody · Schutzgewahrsam *m*, Schutzhaft *f* [*bei Gefährdung des Lebens*]

protective duty · Schutzzoll *m*

protective effect · Schutzwirkung *f*

protective facility, protection facility · Schutzeinrichtung *f*

protective function · Schutzfunktion *f*

protective law, protective statute, protective act · Schutzgesetz *n*

protective law · Schutzrecht *n*

protective lawmaking, protective legislation · Schutzgesetzgebung *f*

protective measure, protection measure, measure of protection · Schutzmaßnahme *f*, Schutzvorkehrung *f*

protective regulation, protective prescription · Schutzvorschrift *f*

protective statute, protective act, protective law · Schutzgesetz *n*

protector · Reichsverweser *m*

protector, porter, keeper, bailee; bajulus [*Latin*]; manager, bailiff [*Low Latin*] [*A person to whom goods are entrusted for a specific purpose without any intention of transferring the ownership to him*] · Beschützer *m*, Bewahrer, Empfänger anvertrauten Gutes, Empfänger anvertrauter Sachen, Hinterlegungsempfänger, Verwahrer

protest-referendum, referendum by petition · Protest-Volksentscheid *m*

protest waiver · Protesterlaß *m* [*Scheck*]

pro-urban policy · stadtfreundliche Politik *f*

provable · anmeldbar [*Schuldforderungen und Ansprüche gegen einen Gemeinschuldner*]

provable debts, debts provable · Konkursforderung *f*

to prove, to infer, to come to a conclusion, to conclude · folgern, ableiten, schließen (von etwas auf etwas)

to prove, to make out to be true; verificare [*Latin*]; to verify · beweisen

to prove · anmelden [*Konkursforderung*]

to prove, to probate [*e. g. to probate, or prove, a will. A probate court is one in which wills are proved*] · bestätigen

to prove (authentic) by document(s), to authenticate by document(s), to make authentic by document(s) · belegen

to prove (to be) false, to prove (to be) erroneous, to prove (to be) untrue, to prove (to be) unfounded, to falsify, to disprove · widerlegen

to provide, to furnish [*construction materials*] · liefern [*Baustoffe*]

to provide, to furnish [*construction machinery and equipment*] · vorhalten [*Baumaschinen und -geräte*]

to provide, to furnish [*labo(u)r*] · stellen [*Arbeitskräfte*]

provided school, council elementary school · Gemeindeschule *f*

provident co-operative (society), provident society, consumers' co-operative (society), retail co-operative (society) · Konsumverein *m*, Konsumgenossenschaft *f*, Verbrauchergenossenschaft

to provide the requirement(s) · ausstatten [*Fläche*]

province, division, department, branch, sector [*public administration*] · Abteilung *f*, Referat *n*, Dezernat *n*, Ressort *n*

province of jurisprudence, jurisprudence province · Bereich *m* der Jurisprudenz

provincial capital · Provinzhauptstadt *f*

provincial city, provincial town · Provinzstadt *f*

provincial court, archiepiscopal court [*In English law. The courts in the two ecclesiastic(al) provinces of England*] · erzbischöfliches Gericht *n*

provincial diet, "states" of a province · Landstände *m (pl)*

provincial government · Provinzialregierung *f*

provincial town, provincial city · Provinzstadt *f*

provision · Bestimmung *f*

provision [*Of a sum or sums for a special purpose or special purposes*] · Bereitstellung *f*

provisional, interim, intermediate, temporary, interlocutory · einstweilig, zwischenzeitlich, vorübergehend, inzidentiell

provisional area, reserve area · Reservefläche *f*, Vorbehaltfläche

provisional heir (male), fiducial heir (male), fiduciary heir (male), heir (male) of inventory (in tail), fiduciary; fiduciarius haeres [*Latin*] · Vorerbe *m*

provisional orders [*Sie werden nicht vom Parlament, sondern von den einzelnen Ministerien, soweit sie als Zentralbehörden für bestimmte Gemeindeverwaltungen fungieren, erlassen und haben den Zweck, die Gemeinden zu bestimmten Verwaltungsmaßnahmen zu ermächtigen. Die endgültige Genehmigung der provisional orders bleibt zwar dem Parlament vorbehalten, ist jedoch in den meisten Fällen nur eine Formsache*] · sekundäre Form *f* der englischen Zentralverwaltung

provisional quantity, estimated quantity · (ab)geschätzte Menge *f*, überschlägige Menge, Massenansatz *m*, Mengenansatz

provisional sum · angesetzte Summe *f*

provision for (building) land improvement, (building) land improvement provision · (Bau)Landerschließungsbestimmung *f*, (Bau)Bodenerschließungsbestimmung, (Bau)Flächenerschließungsbestimmung

provision of acceptance, acceptance provision · (Bau)Abnahmebestimmung *f*

provision of (ad)measurement, (ad)measurement provision · Aufmaßbestimmung *f*

provision of an authority · behördliche Bestimmung *f*

provision of coverage, coverage provision · Bebauungsbestimmung *f*; Überbauungsbestimmung [*Schweiz*]

provision of enforcement, enforcement provision · Erzwingungsbestimmung *f*, Durchsetzungsbestimmung

provision of exception, exceptional provision · Ausnahmebestimmung *f*

provision of labour (Brit.); provision of labor (US) · Gestellung *f* von Arbeitskräften

provision of law, law provision, legal provision · Gesetz(es)bestimmung *f*, gesetzliche Bestimmung

provision of measurement → provision of (ad)measurement

proviso for cesser · Aufhebungsklausel *f* für eine Familienstiftung

proviso of (building) permission, reservation of (building) permission · Erlaubnisvorbehalt *m*, Genehmigungsvorbehalt

provocation, challenge · Herausforderung *f*

provost [*In Scotland*]; mayor · Bürgermeister *m*

proximately · adäquat

proximus amicus [*Latin*]; next friend, (prochein) amy, (prochein) ami [*He sues on behalf of an infant. Infants sue by a next friend and defend by a guardian ad litem*] · Beistand *m*, prozessualer Stellvertreter *m* auf der Klägerseite

proxy, (authorized) agent, attorney (in fact), representative, delegate [*A person either actually or by law held to be authorized and employed by one person to bring him into contractual or other legal relations with a third party*] · Beauftragte *m*, Bevollmächtigte, Sachwalter, (Stell)Vertreter, Agent

proxy form, letter of attorney · Vollmachturkunde *f*

proxy-voting, accumulative voting · Logenabstimmung *f* [*z. B. bei den Bergarbeitern in Northumberland*]

prudence, vigilant activity, diligence · Wachsamkeit *f*

pseudo area map — public bidding (action) 826

pseudo area map, distribution area map · Arealkarte *f*, Pseudogebietskarte, Verbreitungskarte

pseudo component · Scheinbestandteil *m, n*

pseudo isoline · Pseudoisolinie *f*, Pseudoliniengleiche *f*

pseudo-isoline map · Pseudoisolinienkarte *f*

pseudonym · Deckname *m*, Pseudonym *n*

psychological testing centre (Brit.); psychological testing center (US) · Personalprüfstelle *f*

PTA, parents-teachers association · Eltern-Lehrer-Vereinigung *f*

Ptolemaic legislation, Ptolemaic lawmaking · ptolemäische Gesetzgebung *f*

public acceptance (of (the) work(s)) · behördliche (Bau)Abnahme *f* [*Sie richtet sich nach den Vorschriften des öffentlichen Rechts, so daß eine zivilrechtliche Anerkennung der Bauleistung des Bauunternehmers oder Architekten damit in keiner Weise verbunden ist*]

public access land · öffentlich zugängliches Land *n*

public accountant · öffentlicher Wirtschaftsprüfer *m*

Public Accounts Committee · Parlamentsausschuß *m* für öffentliche Rechnungsprüfung [*England*]

public acquisition · Erwerb *m* durch die öffentliche Hand, Beschaffung *f* durch die öffentliche Hand

public acquisition contract · öffentlicher Beschaffungsvertrag, öffentlicher Erwerbsvertrag *m*

public act, public law, public statute, general act, general law, general statute, legislative act, legislative law, legislative statute, session act, session statute, resolve act; slip law, session law [*USA*] · allgemeines Gesetz *n* [*In den Gliedstaaten der USA erscheinen die Gesetze nach ihrer Verabschiedung zunächst als „slip laws", die am Ende einer Sitzungsperiode der Legislative chronologisch zu den „session laws" zusammengefaßt werden*]

public activity · öffentliche Tätigkeit *f*

public Act of Parliament [*England*] · öffentliches Parlamentsgesetz *n*

public administration · öffentliche Verwaltung *f*

public advantage, public benefit · öffentlicher Nutzen *m*, öffentlicher Vorteil

public agency, (public) office, (official) agency · (amtliche) Stelle *f*, (öffentliche) Dienststelle

publican · Kleinhändler *m*

public annoyance · öffentliches Ärgernis *n*

public area, public land(s) · Gemeingebrauchsfläche *f*, öffentliche Fläche, öffentliches Land *n*, Gemeingebrauchsland

public area use → public land(s) use

public assistance, public relief [*The last term is a literal translation of the French "assistance publique" which roughly corresponds to the English poor law*] · öffentliche Fürsorge *f*, Wohlfahrtsunterstützung *f*

public assistance [*USA*] · gehobene Fürsorge *f*

publication, formal declaration of a testator · Erklärung *f* des letzten Willens

publication, promulgation, announcement · Bekanntmachung *f*, Bekanntgabe *f*, Veröffentlichung *f*, Kundmachung, Verlautbarung, Verbreitung

publication by (the) bulletin board, publicity by (the) bulletin board, announcement by (the) bulletin board, promulgation by (the) bulletin board · Aushängung *f*, Bekanntgabe *f* durch Aushang, Bekanntmachung durch Aushang, Veröffentlichung durch Aushang, Kundmachung durch Aushang, Verbreitung durch Aushang

publication by way of excerpt, publication in part(s), publication in abridged form · auszugsweise Veröffentlichung *f*

publication in abridged form, publication by way of excerpt, publication in part(s) · auszugsweise Veröffentlichung *f*

publication in part(s), publication in abridged form, publication by way of excerpt · auszugsweise Veröffentlichung *f*

publication posting, promulgation posting, publicity posting, public notice by poster, announcement posting · Anschlagung *f*, Bekanntmachung *f* durch Anschlag, Veröffentlichung *f* durch Anschlag, Bekanntgabe *f* durch Anschlag, Kundmachung *f* durch Anschlag, Verbreitung durch Anschlag

public auction, (sale by) auction · Versteigerung *f*, Auktion *f*

public authority, public power, legal authority, legal power, statutory authority, statutory power · gesetzliche Gewalt *f*, gesetzliche Macht *f*, gesetzliche Hoheit *f*, gesetzliche Kompetenz *f*

public benefit, public advantage · öffentlicher Nutzen *m*, öffentlicher Vorteil

public bidding (action), public invitation to tender, open tendering, open bidding, open competition, advertisement of a project, project advertisement, public tendering (out), public tender(ing) action · öffentliche Ausschreibung *f*, öffentliche Aufforderung (zur Angebotsabgabe), offenes Verfahren *n*, offener Wettbewerb *m*, Ausschreibung der öffentlichen Hand [*Bauleistungen werden im vorgeschriebenen Verfahren nach öffentlicher Aufforderung einer unbeschränkten Zahl von Unternehmern zur Einreichung von Angeboten vergeben*]

public (bid) proposal (US) → official offer

public bond [*USA*]; public stock [*Great Britain*] · öffentliche Schuldverschreibung *f*, öffentliche Obligation *f*, Schuldverschreibung der öffentlichen Hand, Obligation der öffentlichen Hand

public builder → public developer

public (building and) construction, public (construction and) building · öffentliches Bauen *n*

(public) building board, (public) construction board · Bauamt *n*

public building (construction) contracting practice · öffentliches Hochbauvergabewesen *n*

public building (construction) order · öffentlicher Hochbauauftrag *m*

public building (construction) practice · öffentliches Hochbauwesen *n*

public building (construction) sector, public building (construction) field · öffentlicher Hochbausektor *m*, Hochbausektor der öffentlichen Hand

public building contracting practice, public construction contracting practice · öffentliches Bauvergabewesen *n*

public building contracting practice → public building (construction) contracting practice

public building field, public building sector, public construction sector, public construction field · öffentlicher Bausektor *m*, Bausektor der öffentlichen Hand

public building field → public building (construction) sector

public building law, public construction law · öffentliches Baurecht *n*

public building law, public building statute, public building act, public construction law, public construction statute, public construction act · allgemeines Baugesetz *n*

public building loan, public construction loan · öffentliches Baudarleh(e)n *n* [*Darleh(e)n aus öffentlichen Mitteln zur Deckung der für den Bau einer Wohnung entstehenden Gesamtkosten (§ 42 Abs. 1 des II. WoBauG)*]

public building order, public construction order · öffentlicher Bauauftrag *m*

public building practice → public building (construction) practice

public building sector, public construction sector, public construction field, public building field · öffentlicher Bausektor *m*, Bausektor der öffentlichen Hand

public building sector → public building (construction) sector

public call, public demand · Nachfrage *f* der öffentlichen Hand, öffentliche Nachfrage

public calling of the defendant · öffentlicher Beruf *m* des Beklagten

(public) carrier, common carrier, public traffic carrier, common traffic carrier · (öffentlicher) (Massen)Verkehrsträger *m*, (öffentlicher) (Massen)Beförderungsträger

public charge · öffentliche Last *f*

public construction → public (building and) construction

public (construction and) building, public (building and) construction · öffentliches Bauen *n*

(public) construction board, (public) building board · Bauamt *n*

public construction contracting practice, public building contracting practice · öffentliches Bauvergabewesen *n*

public construction field, public building field, public building sector, public construction sector · öffentlicher Bausektor *m*, Bausektor der öffentlichen Hand

public construction law, public building law · öffentliches Baurecht *n*

public construction loan, public building loan · öffentliches Baudarleh(e)n *n* [*Darleh(e)n aus öffentlichen Mitteln zur Deckung der für den Bau einer Wohnung entstehenden Gesamtkosten (§ 42 Abs. 1 des II. WoBauG)*]

public construction order, public building order · öffentlicher Bauauftrag *m*

public construction sector, public construction field, public building field, public building sector · öffentlicher Bausektor *m*, Bausektor der öffentlichen Hand

public convenience, common welfare, common weal, common good, common necessity, common convenience, good of the community, public interests, common well-being, general good, prosperity of the community, public welfare, public weal, public good, public necessity · Gemeinwohl *n*, öffentliches Wohl, öffentliches Interesse *n*, allgemeines Wohl, allgemeines Interesse, Allgemeinwohl, öffentliche Belange *mpl*

public corporation · Körperschaft *f* des öffentlichen Rechts, Korporation *f* des öffentlichen Rechts, öffentlich-rechtliche Körperschaft, öffentlich-rechtliche Korporation

public debts · öffentliche Schulden *fpl*, Schulden der öffentlichen Hand

public deposits · Regierungskassenbestände *mpl*, Staatsdepositen *f*

public developer, public builder, public promoter, public (real) property developer, public (real) property builder, public (real) property promoter, public (real) estate developer, public (real) estate promoter, public (real) estate builder, public realty developer, public realty promoter, public realty builder · öffentlicher (Bau)Träger *m*

public development work, public development structure, public development physical facility · öffentliche Erschließungsanlage *f*, öffentliche Erschließungseinrichtung *f*

public document · öffentliches Dokument *n*

public duty, public legal charge, public statutory charge · öffentliche Abgabe *f*

public easement · öffentliche Grunddienstbarkeit *f*

public economy, economics, political economy, national economy · Volkswirtschaft *f*, politische Ökonomie *f*, Nationalökonomie

public education · öffentliche Bildung *f*, Volksbildung

public employe(e), public servant · Arbeitnehmer *m* im öffentlichen Dienst

public enterprise, public undertaking, (public) service company · (öffentlicher) Dienstleistungsbetrieb *m*, (öffentliches) Dienstleistungsunternehmen *n*

public estate, public property · öffentliches Vermögen *n*, öffentliches Gut *n*, öffentliche Habe *f*

public estate builder → public developer

public estate developer → public developer

public estate promoter → public developer

public examination · öffentliche Vernehmung *f*

public examination of the debtor · öffentliche Gemeinschuldnersitzung *f* [*Konkursverfahren*]

public facilities, common facilities · Gemeinbedarf *m* [*Die der Allgemeinheit dienenden baulichen Anlagen und Einrichtungen (§ 5 Abs. 2 Nr. 2, § 9, Abs. 1 Nr. 1 Buchst. f BBauG)*]

public facilities plan, common facilities plan · Plan *m* der öffentlichen Standorte, Plan der Gemeineinrichtungen

public faith in (land) register entries, public faith in (land) registry entries · materiell(rechtlich)er Öffentlichkeitsgrundsatz *m*, materiell(rechtlich)er Publizitätsgrundsatz, materiell(rechtlich)er öffentlicher Glaube *m* des Grundbuches, materiell(rechtlich)es Öffentlichkeitsprinzip *n*, materiell(rechtlich)es Publizitätsprinzip

(public) fast transit line, (public) rapid transit line, (public) high speed transit line · (öffentliche) Schnellverkehrslinie *f*

(public) fast transit policy, (public) rapid transit policy, (public) high speed transit policy · Schnellverkehrspolitik *f*, öffentliche Schnellverkehrspolitik

public fee · öffentliche Gebühr *f*

public field, public sector [*That part of the economy in which the state acts as entrepreneur*] · öffentliche Hand *f*

public finance · öffentliche Finanzen *f*

public financial aid · öffentliche Finanzierungshilfe *f*

public forest · öffentlicher Wald *m*, Gemein(schafts)wald

public fund · öffentliche Mittel *f*, Mittel aus öffentlichen Haushalten

public garden · öffentlicher Garten *m*

public gathering · öffentliche Zusammenkunft *f*

public (general) property, public ownership (of property), public proprietorship · öffentliches Eigentum *n*

public good, public necessity, public convenience, common welfare, common weal, common good, common necessity, common convenience, good of the community, public interests, common well-being, general good, prosperity of the community, public welfare, public weal · Gemeinwohl *n*, öffentliches Wohl, öffentliches Interesse *n*, allgemeines Wohl, allgemeines Interesse, Allgemeinwohl, öffentliche Belange *mpl*

public goods · Kollektivgüter *npl*, öffentliche Güter

public green area → public green land

public green area, public green territory, public landscape area, public landscape territory · öffentliches Grüngebiet *n*

public green land, public green area · öffentliche Grünfläche *f*

public ground, public terrain · Gelände *n* für öffentliche Zwecke, Terrain *n* für öffentliche Zwecke, öffentliches Gelände, öffentliches Terrain

public health · öffentliche Gesundheit *f*, Volksgesundheit

public health act, public health law, public health statute · Volksgesundheitsgesetz *n*

public health administration · öffentliche Gesundheitsverwaltung *f*

public health board → (local) public health board

public health committee · Ausschuß *m* für öffentliche Gesundheitspflege

public health law, law of public health · öffentliches Gesundheitsrecht *n*, Volksgesundheitsrecht

(public) health lawmaking, (public) health legislation · Gesundheitsgesetzgebung *f*

public health service, public hygiene, PHS · öffentliche Gesundheitspflege *f*, öffentlicher Gesundheitsdienst *m*

public hearing, citizen hearing, hearing of citizens · Bürgeranhörung *f*, öffentliche Anhörung

public heavy construction contracting practice · öffentliches Tiefbauvergabewesen *n*

public heavy construction practice · öffentliches Tiefbauwesen *n*

public heavy construction sector, public heavy construction field · öffentlicher Tiefbausektor *m*, Tiefbausektor der öffentlichen Hand

(public) high speed transit line, (public) fast transit line, (public) rapid transit line · (öffentliche) Schnellverkehrslinie *f*

(public) high speed transit policy, (public) fast transit policy, (public) rapid transit policy · Schnellverkehrspolitik *f*, öffentliche Schnellverkehrspolitik

public highway, public road · öffentliche Straße *f*

public holiday, statutory holiday, legal holiday · gesetzlicher Feiertag *m*

pub(lic house) (Brit.); drinking shop (US) · Kneipe *f*, Schankwirtschaft *f*, Bierschenke *f*, Bierhaus *n*, Wirtshaus

public hous(ebuild)ing → public(ly-assisted) hous(ebuild)ing

public housing agency, public housing office · Dienststelle *f* für öffentlich geförderte Wohnungen

public housing office, public housing agency · Dienststelle *f* für öffentlich geförderte Wohnungen

public housing project · öffentliches Wohn(ungs)projekt *n*

public housing (real) estate, public housing (real) property, public housing realty · öffentlicher Wohn(ungs)baugrundbesitz *m*

public housing rent, social residential rent, social housing rent · Sozialmiete *f*

public housing tenant, social housing tenant · Sozialmieter *m*

public hygiene, PHS, public health service · öffentliche Gesundheitspflege *f*, öffentlicher Gesundheitsdienst *m*

public indebtedness · öffentliche Verschuldung *f*

public inspection, public notice, publicity, inspection by the public · Auslegung *f*, öffentliche Auslegung *f*, öffentliche Einsicht(nahme) *f*, öffentliche Auslage *f*, (öffentliche) Offenlegung *f* [*Bauzeitplan; Umlegungskarte; usw.*]

public institution → public (law) institution

public interest, public right · öffentliches Recht *n*, subjektives öffentliches Recht, rechtlich geschütztes Interesse

public interests, common well-being, general good, prosperity of the community, public welfare, public weal, public good, public necessity, public convenience, common welfare, common weal, common good, common necessity, common convenience, good of the community · Gemeinwohl *n*, öffentliches Wohl, öffentliches Interesse *n*, allgemeines Wohl, allgemeines Interesse, Allgemeinwohl, öffentliche Belange *mpl*

(public) international law, law of nations · Völkerrecht *n*, (öffentliches) internationales Recht

public invitation to tender, open tendering, open bidding, open competition, advertisement of a project, project advertisement, public tendering (out), public tender(ing) action, public bidding (action) · öffentliche Ausschreibung *f*, öffentliche Aufforderung (zur Angebotsabgabe), offenes Verfahren *n*, offener Wettbewerb *m*, Ausschreibung der öffentlichen Hand [*Bauleistungen werden im vorgeschriebenen Verfahren nach öffentlicher Aufforderung einer unbeschränkten Zahl von Unternehmern zur Einreichung von Angeboten vergeben*]

public issue; gilt(-edge) (Brit.); fixed-interest(-bearing) security · Staatsschuldtitel *m*, börsennotierte festverzinsliche Schuldverschreibung *f*, festverzinsliches Wertpapier *n*, Rentenpapier

publicity · Erkennbarkeit *f*, Publizität *f*, Offenkundigkeit

publicity, inspection by the public, public inspection, public notice · Auslegung *f*, öffentliche Auslegung *f*, öffentliche Einsicht(nahme) *f*, öffentliche Auslage *f*, (öffentliche) Offenlegung *f* [*Bauzeitplan; Umlegungskarte; usw.*]

publicity by (the) bulletin board, announcement by (the) bulletin board, promulgation by (the) bulletin board, publication by (the) bulletin board · Aushängung *f*, Bekanntgabe *f* durch Aushang, Bekanntmachung *f* durch Aushang, Veröffentlichung *f* durch Aushang, Kundmachung *f* durch Aushang, Verbreitung durch Aushang

publicity of a plan, plan publicity · Planauslegung f, Auslegung eines Planes, Planoffenlage f, Offenlage eines Planes

publicity planning procedure · offenes Planungsverfahren n [*Die Gemeinde informiert rechtzeitig die Bürger über die Planungsziele*]

publicity posting → publication posting

publicity principle, principle of publicity · Publizitätsgrundsatz m, Publizitätsprinzip n, Öffentlichkeitsgrundsatz, Öffentlichkeitsprinzip

to publicize, to publish, to announce, to promulgate · bekanntgeben, veröffentlichen, verbreiten, öffentlich bekanntgeben, (öffentlich) bekanntmachen

publicizing, promulgating, announcing · Bekanntgeben n, Bekanntmachen, Veröffentlichen, Kundmachen, Verbreiten

publicizing by ringing a bell, promulgating by ringing a bell, announcing by ringing a bell · Ausklingeln n, Ausschellen

public land, land of the public · Land n der öffentlichen Hand, öffentliches Land

public land, allmend, community land, communal land, mark; county (US); waste of the manor, (manorial) waste [*obsolete*]; common (land), corporate land, common field, commonable land, commonable field · Al(l)mend(e) f, Allmeind f, Allmid f, Allmein(i) f, Allmen f, Allmig f, Allmand(e) f, Allmat f, All(ge)meinde f, Allmandgut n, Allmente f, (Feld)Mark f, Gemarkung f, Kommunalboden m, Gemeindeboden m, Bürgerland n, bürgerliches Nutzungsland n, Gemeindeland n, Gemeinheit(sland) f, (n), Kommunalland n, unverteilter Gemeindegrund m, ländliches Gemeingut, Gemein(de)anger m, Gemeindeimmobilien fpl; Korporationsland n [*Schweiz*]

public land charge [*Any prohibition or restriction on the use of land imposed by a local authority or minister or government department which is binding on successive owners of the land affected*] · öffentliche Grund(stücks)belastung f, öffentliche Grund(stücks)last f

public landing (place) · öffentliche Landestelle f

public land in possession → public land(s) in possession

public land ownership, public land property, public land proprietorship · öffentliches Landeigentum n, öffentliches Bodeneigentum, öffentliches Grund(stück)eigentum

public land(s), general land(s) · öffentliche Ländereien f (pl)

public land(s), public area · Gemeingebrauchsfläche f, öffentliche Fläche, öffentliches Land n, Gemeingebrauchsland

public land states · Staatsgebiet n der USA und der größte Teil des Staatsgebietes Kanadas mit Ausnahme der 13 US-Gründerstaaten an der atlantischen Küste und eines großen Teiles von Texas [*Vermessen nach einem in den USA 1785 gesetzlich festgelegten Vermessungssystem in quadratmeilengroßen "sections"*]

public land(s) use, public area use · öffentliche Flächennutzung f, öffentliche Landnutzung, öffentliche Bodennutzung

public law, constitutional law, law of constitution; jus publicum [*Latin*] [*The law concerned with the rights and duties of the state. It is contrasted with private law, which deals with the rights and duties of subjects inter se*] · öffentliches Recht n

public law, public statute, general act, general law, general statute, legislative act, legislative law, legislative statute, session act, session statute, resolve act; slip law, session law [*USA*]; public act · allgemeines Gesetz n [*In den Gliedstaaten der USA erscheinen die Gesetze nach ihrer Verabschiedung zunächst als "slip laws", die am Ende einer Sitzungsperiode der Legislative chronologisch zu den "session laws" zusammengefaßt werden*]

Public Law [*USA*] · Bundesgesetz n

public (law) institution · Anstalt f des öffentlichen Rechts, öffentlich-rechtliche Anstalt

public lawmaking, public legislation · öffentliche Gesetzgebung f

public legal charge, public statutory charge, public duty · öffentliche Abgabe f

public library, free library · Volksbücherei f, Volksbibliothek f

public local inquiry · öffentliche örtliche Untersuchung f [*Bei Einwendungen gegen eine Planung*]

public long-distance traffic · öffentlicher Fernverkehr m

public long-distance transit vehicle, public long-distance transport(ation) vehicle · öffentliches Fernverkehrsmittel n, öffentliches Fernverkehrsfahrzeug

publicly-assisted dwelling unit, social dwelling unit, subsidized dwelling unit, lower-income dwelling unit, lower-income apartment, publicly-assisted apartment, subsidized apartment, social apartment (US); publicly-assisted dwelling, social dwelling, subsidized dwelling, lower-income dwelling, publicly-assisted tenement, subsidized tenement, lower-income tenement, social tenement, publicly-assisted residence, subsidized residence, lower-income residence, social residence · Sozialwohnung f, öffentlich geförderte

Wohnung, Wohnung der öffentlichen Hand, Wohnung des sozialen Wohnungsbaues, Zuschußwohnung

public(ly-assisted) hous(ebuild)ing, subsidized hous(ebuild)ing, lower-income hous(ebuild)ing, social hous(ebuild)ing, production of public housing · Zuschußwohn(ungs)bau m, Sozialwohn(ungs)bau, öffentlich geförderter Wohn(ungs)bau, geförderter öffentlicher Wohn(ungs)bau, sozialer Wohn(ungs)bau, Wohn(ungs)bau der öffentlichen Hand

publicly-assisted house, subsidized house, social house, lower-income house · Sozialhaus n, öffentlich gefördertes Haus, Haus der öffentlichen Hand, Haus des sozialen Wohn(ungs)baues, Zuschußhaus

publicly(-)assisted housing, publicly(-)provided housing, subsidized housing, low-rent housing, social housing, low-income housing, low-cost(s) housing · Zuschußwohnungen f pl, Sozialwohnungen, öffentlich geförderte Wohnungen, Wohnungen des sozialen Wohn(ungs)baues, Wohnungen der öffentlichen Hand

public management, public trading · Gemeinwirtschaft f

public mass hous(ebuild)ing · öffentlicher Massenwohn(ungs)bau m

public mortgage · öffentliche Hypothek f

public necessity, public convenience, common welfare, common weal, common good, common necessity, common convenience, good of the community, public interests, common well-being, general good, prosperity of the community, public welfare, public weal, public good · Gemeinwohl n, öffentliches Wohl, öffentliches Interesse n, allgemeines Wohl, allgemeines Interesse, Allgemeinwohl, öffentliche Belange m pl

public need, common need · öffentlicher Bedarf m

public notice, publicity, inspection by the public, public inspection · Auslegung f, öffentliche Auslegung f, öffentliche Einsicht(nahme) f, öffentliche Auslage f, (öffentliche) Offenlegung f [*Bauzeitplan; Umlegungskarte; usw.*]

public nuisance [*It affects the community*] · Gemeinschädlichkeit f [*Emission*]

public obligation · Baulast f [*Öffentlich-rechtliche Verpflichtung eines Grundstückseigentümers zu einem sein Grundstück betreffenden Tun, Dulden und/oder Unterlassen*]

public offence · öffentliches Vergehen n

public offer, official tender, public tender, official bid, public bid; official (bid) proposal, public (bid) proposal (US); official offer · Angebot n für die öffentliche Hand

(public) office, (official) agency, public agency · Dienststelle f, öffentliche Dienststelle, (amtliche) Stelle

public office building · öffentliches Bürogebäude n

public open space, open public space · öffentlicher Freiraum m

public opinion survey · Bürgerbefragung f, Bürgergespräch n

public order, order public, peace, public security and good order, public policy, public safety · öffentliche (Sicherheit f und) Ordnung f, öffentliche (Ordnung und) Sicherheit

public order · öffentlicher Auftrag m

public-orient(at)ed · gemeinwohlorientiert, gemeinwohlbezogen

public ownership (of property), public proprietorship, public (general) property · öffentliches Eigentum n

public parking area · öffentliche Parkfläche f, öffentlicher Parkplatz m

public participation, participation of citizens, citizen involvement, involvement of citizens, citizen participation, citizen control · Bürgerbeteiligung f, Bürgermitwirkung, Bürgerteilnahme f, bürgerschaftliche Beteiligung, bürgerschaftliche Mitwirkung, bürgerschaftliche Teilnahme [*z. B. an der Bauleitplanung*]

public participation in planning, citizen participation in planning · Bürgerbeteiligung f an der Planung, Partizipation f an der Planung

public path, public way · öffentlicher Weg m

public peace · öffentliche Ruhe f und Ordnung f

public person · Berufspolitiker m

public physical facilites, public works, public structures · Bauten f der öffentlichen Hand, öffentliche (bauliche) Anlagen f pl, öffentliche (Bau)Werke n pl, öffentliche Bauanlagen, öffentliche Bauten f, öffentliche Baulichkeiten f pl

public physician · öffentlich bestellter Arzt m

public planning · öffentliche Planung f, Planung der öffentlichen Hand

public planning law · öffentliches Planungsrecht n

public policies, public policy · rechtspolitische Erwägungen f pl

public policy · unantastbarer Teil m der eigenen Rechtsordnung, Prohibitionsgesetze n pl [*Fremdes Recht, das diesem Teil widerspricht, darf nicht angewendet werden*]

public policy, public policies · rechtspolitische Erwägungen f pl

public policy — public relief

public policy, public safety, public order, order public, peace, public security and good order · öffentliche (Sicherheit *f* und) Ordnung *f*, öffentliche (Ordnung und) Sicherheit

public policy · Gemeinwohlpolitik *f*

public policy act, public policy statute, public policy law · Gesetz *n* zum Schutz der öffentlichen Sicherheit und Ordnung, Gesetz über die öffentliche Sicherheit und Ordnung, SOG, Ordnungsgesetz

public policy authority · Ordnungsbehörde *f*

public policy office · Ordnungsamt *n*

public power, legal authority, legal power, statutory authority, statutory power, public authority · gesetzliche Gewalt *f*, gesetzliche Macht *f*, gesetzliche Hoheit *f*, gesetzliche Kompetenz *f*

public power of appointment, public power of disposition, public right of appointment, public right of disposition, legal power of appointment, legal power of disposition, legal right of appointment, legal right of disposition, statutory power of appointment, statutory power of disposition, statutory right of appointment, statutory right of disposition [*It is conferred by statute upon persons exercising the duties of a particular office, e.g. as trustee, or as tenant for life*] · gesetzliche Verfügungsbefugnis *f*, gesetzliche Bestimmungsbefugnis, gesetzliches Verfügungsrecht *n*, gesetzliches Bestimmungsrecht

public power of disposition → public power of appointment

public programme; public program (US); public scheme · Programm *n* der öffentlichen Hand

public promoter → public developer

public property, public estate · öffentliches Vermögen *n*, öffentliches Gut *n*, öffentliche Habe *f*

public property builder → public developer

public property developer → public developer

public property promoter → public developer

public proposal (US) → official offer

public proprietorship, public (general) property, public ownership (of property) · öffentliches Eigentum *n*

public publication → public announcement

public purpose · öffentlicher Zweck *m*

(public) rapid transit, (public) rapid transport(ation), public high-speed transit, (public) high-speed transport(ation), (public) fast transit, (public) fast transport(ation), mass rapid transport(ation), mass rapid transit, rapid mass transit, rapid mass transport(ation) · (öffentlicher) Schnell(bahnmassen)verkehr *m*, (öffentliche) Schnell(bahnmassen)beförderung *f*

(public) rapid transit line, (public) high speed transit line, (public) fast transit line · (öffentliche) Schnellverkehrslinie *f*

(public) rapid transit policy, (public) high speed transit policy, (public) fast transit policy · Schnellverkehrspolitik *f*, öffentliche Schnellverkehrspolitik

public (real) estate builder → public developer

public (real) estate developer → public developer

public (real) estate promoter → public developer

public (real) property builder → public developer

public (real) property developer → public developer

public (real) property promoter → public developer

public realty builder → public developer

public realty developer → public developer

public realty promoter → public developer

public record office · Staatsarchiv *n*

public recreation · Volkserholung *f*, öffentliche Erholung

public recreation(al) facility · öffentliche Erholungseinrichtung *f*

public recreation(al) transit, public recreation(al) transport(ation), mass recreation(al) transport(ation), mass recreation(al) transit, recreation(al) (public) transit, recreation(al) (public) transport(ation), recreation(al) mass transit, recreation(al) mass transport(ation) · (öffentlicher) Erholungsmassenverkehr *m*, (öffentliche) Erholungsmassenbeförderung *f*

(public) register, (public) registry · Buch *n*, Register *n*, öffentliches Buch, öffentliches Register [*Die Unterscheidung zwischen (öffentlichem) Register und (öffentlichem) Buch ist nicht rechtssystematisch durchgeführt. Grundbuch, Schiffsregister und Kabelbuch haben viel Gemeinsames, obwohl einmal von Buch, das andere mal von Register gesprochen wird*]

public relations · Öffentlichkeitsarbeit *f*

public release · Veröffentlichungsfreigabe *f*

public relief, public assistance [*The last term is a literal translation of the French* "assistance publique" which roughly corresponds to the English poor law] · öffentliche Fürsorge f, Wohlfahrtsunterstützung f

public relief for jobless persons, public relief for unemployed persons · Arbeitslosenfürsorge f, Erwerbslosenfürsorge f

public riding · Benutzung f von (öffentlichen) Massenverkehrsmitteln, Benutzung von öffentlichen Massenbeförderungsmitteln

public right, public interest · öffentliches Recht n, subjektives öffentliches Recht, rechtlich geschütztes Interesse

public right of appointment, public right of disposition, legal power of appointment, legal power of disposition, legal right of appointment, legal right of disposition, statutory power of appointment, statutory power of disposition, statutory right of appointment, statutory right of disposition, public power of appointment, public power of disposition [*It is conferred by statute upon persons exercising the duties of a particular office, e.g. as trustee, or as tenant for life*] · gesetzliche Verfügungsbefugnis f, gesetzliche Bestimmungsbefugnis, gesetzliches Verfügungsrecht n, gesetzliches Bestimmungsrecht

public right of disposition → public right of appointment

public river · öffentlicher Strom m, regaler Strom

public road, public highway · öffentliche Straße f

public room · öffentlicher Raum m

public safety, public order, order public, peace, public security and good order, public policy · öffentliche (Sicherheit f und) Ordnung f, öffentliche (Ordnung und) Sicherheit

public scheme, public programme; public program (US) · Programm n der öffentlichen Hand

public school (Brit.); preparatory school (US); private secondary school · höhere Privatschule f

public sector, public field [*That part of the economy in which the state acts as entrepreneur*] · öffentliche Hand f

public sector planning, public subject planning, public specialized planning · öffentliche Fachplanung f, öffentliche Sektorplanung, öffentliche sektorale Planung

public security and good order, public policy, public safety, public order, order public, peace · öffentliche (Sicherheit f und) Ordnung f, öffentliche (Ordnung und) Sicherheit

public servant, public employe(e) · Arbeitnehmer m im öffentlichen Dienst

public service · öffentliche Dienstleistung f

public serviceability, general utility, general usefulness, general serviceability, public utility, public usefulness · Gemeinnützigkeit f

(public) service company, public enterprise, public undertaking · (öffentlicher) Dienstleistungsbetrieb m, (öffentliches) Dienstleistungsunternehmen n

(public) short-distance transit, (public) short-distance transport(ation), collective short-distance transit, collective short-distance transport(ation), short-distance passenger transit, short-distance mass transit, short-distance passenger transport(ation), short-distance mass transport(ation), short-distance collective transit, short-distance collective transport(ation) · (öffentlicher) (Personen)Nahverkehr m, ÖPNV

public specialized planning, public sector planning, public subject planning · öffentliche Fachplanung f, öffentliche Sektorplanung, öffentliche sektorale Planung

public spending policy · öffentliche Ausgabenpolitik f

public spirit, sense of citizenship, civic spirit · Bürgersinn m

public statute, general act, general law, general statute, legislative act, legislative law, legislative statute, session act, session statute, resolve act; slip law, session law [*USA*]; public act, public law · allgemeines Gesetz n [*In den Gliedstaaten der USA erscheinen die Gesetze nach ihrer Verabschiedung zunächst als „slip laws", die am Ende einer Sitzungsperiode der Legislative chronologisch zu den „session laws" zusammengefaßt werden*]

public statutory charge, public duty, public legal charge · öffentliche Abgabe f

public stock [*Great Britain*]; public bond [*USA*] · öffentliche Schuldverschreibung f, öffentliche Obligation f, Schuldverschreibung der öffentlichen Hand, Obligation der öffentlichen Hand

public stock of the county, county treasure · Grafschaftskasse f

public stream · öffentlicher Fluß m, regaler Fluß

public structures, public physical facilites, public works · Bauten f der öffentlichen Hand, öffentliche (bauliche) Anlagen fpl, öffentliche (Bau)Werke npl, öffentliche Bauanlagen, öffentliche Bauten f, öffentliche Baulichkeiten fpl

public subject planning, public specialized planning, public sector planning · öffentliche Fachplanung f, öffentliche Sektorplanung, öffentliche sektorale Planung

public supply · öffentliche Versorgung f

(public) surface utility — (public) transit vehicle 834

(public) surface utility · oberirdische (öffentliche) Versorgungsanlage *f*, oberirdische (öffentliche)Versorgungseinrichtung *f*

public task · öffentliche Aufgabe *f*

public tender → official offer

public tender(ing) action, public bidding (action), public invitation to tender, open tendering, open bidding, open competition, advertisement of a project, project advertisement, public tendering (out) · öffentliche Ausschreibung *f*, öffentliche Aufforderung (zur Angebotsabgabe), offenes Verfahren *n*, offener Wettbewerb *m*, Ausschreibung der öffentlichen Hand [*Bauleistungen werden im vorgeschriebenen Verfahren nach öffentlicher Aufforderung einer unbeschränkten Zahl von Unternehmern zur Einreichung von Angeboten vergeben*]

public tendering and contract procedure · öffentliches Vergabeverfahren *n*

public tendering (out), public tender(ing) action, public bidding (action), public invitation to tender, open tendering, open bidding, open competition, advertisement of a project, project advertisement · öffentliche Ausschreibung *f*, öffentliche Aufforderung (zur Angebotsabgabe), offenes Verfahren *n*, offener Wettbewerb *m*, Ausschreibung der öffentlichen Hand [*Bauleistungen werden im vorgeschriebenen Verfahren nach öffentlicher Aufforderung einer unbeschränkten Zahl von Unternehmern zur Einreichung von Angeboten vergeben*]

public terrain, public ground · Gelände *n* für öffentliche Zwecke, Terrain *n* für öffentliche Zwecke, öffentliches Gelände, öffentliches Terrain

public timber, public wood · Holzbestand *m* der öffentlichen Hand, öffentlicher Holzbestand

public tort · unerlaubte Handlung *f* des öffentlichen Rechts

public trading, public management · Gemeinwirtschaft *f*

public traffic, public transport(ation) · öffentlicher Verkehr *m*

public traffic area · öffentliche Verkehrsfläche *f*

public traffic carrier, common traffic carrier, (public) carrier, common carrier · (öffentlicher) (Massen)Verkehrsträger *m*, (öffentlicher) (Massen)Beförderungsträger

(public) transit, (public) transport(ation), collective transit, passenger transit, mass transit, collective transport(ation), passenger transport(ation), mass transport(ation) · Massenverkehr *m*, Personen(massen)verkehr, (öffentlicher) Massentransport *m*, öffentlicher Massenverkehr, (öffentliche) Massenbeförderung *f*, öffentliche Beförderung, Personen(massen)transport, Personen(massen)beförderung, Kollektiv(personen)transport, Kollektiv(personen)verkehr, Kollektiv(personen)beförderung

(public) transit business, public transport(ation) business, mass transport(ation) business, mass transit business · (öffentliches) (Massen)Verkehrsgeschäft *n*, (öffentliches) (Massen)Beförderungsgeschäft

(public) transit company, mass transit company, (public) transport(ation) company, mass transport(ation) company · (öffentliche) (Massen)Verkehrsgesellschaft *f*, (öffentliche) (Massen)Beförderungsgesellschaft

(public) transit enterprise, (public) transit line, (public) transport(ation) enterprise, (public) transport(ation) line, mass transit enterprise, mass transit line, mass transport(ation) enterprise, mass transport(ation) line · (öffentlicher) (Massen)Verkehrsbetrieb *m*, (öffentlicher) (Massen)Beförderungsbetrieb, (öffentliches) (Massen)Verkehrsunternehmen *n*, (öffentliches) (Massen)Beförderungsunternehmen

(public) transit fare, mass transit fare, (public) transport(ation) fare, mass transport(ation) fare, passenger fare · Massenverkehrsfahrpreis *m*, Massenbeförderungsfahrpreis

(public) transit line, (public) transport(ation) enterprise, (public) transport(ation) line, mass transit enterprise, mass transit line, mass transport(ation) enterprise, mass transport(ation) line, (public) transit enterprise · (öffentlicher) (Massen)Verkehrsbetrieb *m*, (öffentlicher) (Massen)Beförderungsbetrieb, (öffentliches) (Massen)Verkehrsunternehmen *n*, (öffentliches) (Massen)Beförderungsunternehmen

(public) transit operator, (public) transport(ation) operator, mass transit operator, mass transport(ation) operator · (öffentlicher) (Massen)Verkehrsbetreiber *m*, (öffentlicher) (Massen)Beförderungsbetreiber

(public) transit rider, (public) transport(ation) rider, mass transit rider, mass transport(ation) rider · (öffentlicher) Massenverkehrsteilnehmer *m*

(public) transit system, mass transit system, (public) transport(ation) system, mass transport(ation) system · (öffentliches) (Massen)Verkehrssystem *n*, (öffentliches) (Massen)-Beförderungssystem

(public) transit vehicle, mass (transit) vehicle, (public) transport(ation) vehicle, mass (transport(ation)) vehicle, public vehicle · (öffentliches) Massenverkehrsfahrzeug *n*, (öffentliches) Massenbeförderungsfahrzeug

public transport(ation) — puisne mortgage

public transport(ation), public traffic · öffentlicher Verkehr *m*

(public) transport(ation) fare, mass transport(ation) fare, passenger fare, (public) transit fare, mass transit fare · Massenverkehrsfahrpreis *m*, Massenbeförderungsfahrpreis

(public) transport(ation) business → (public) transit business

(public) transport(ation) company → (public) transit company

(public) transport(ation) enterprise → (public) transit enterprise

(public) transport(ation) line → (public) transit enterprise

(public) transport(ation) operator → (public) transit operator

(public) transport(ation) system → (public) transit system

(public) transport(ation) vehicle, mass (transport(ation)) vehicle, public vehicle, (public) transit vehicle, mass (transit) vehicle · (öffentliches) Massenverkehrsfahrzeug *n*, (öffentliches) Massenbeförderungsfahrzeug

public trust area, public trust land (area) · öffentliches Treuhandland *n*, öffentliches Stiftungsland

public undertaking, (public) service company, public enterprise · (öffentlicher) Dienstleistungsbetrieb *m*, (öffentliches) Dienstleistungsunternehmen *n*

public use [*Use of any land, water, or buildings by a public body for a public service or purpose*] · öffentliche Benutzung *f*, öffentlicher Gebrauch *m*

public utility, public usefulness, public serviceability, general utility, general usefulness, general serviceability · Gemeinnützigkeit *f*

(public) utility (US); statutory undertaker (Brit.) · (öffentlicher) Versorgungsbetrieb *m*, (öffentliches) Versorgungsunternehmen *n*, (öffentliche) Versorgungsunternehmung *f*

public utility corporation [*USA*] · privater halböffentlich organisierter Versorgungsbetrieb *m*, privates halböffentlich organisiertes Versorgungsunternehmen *n*, private halböffentlich organisierte Versorgungsunternehmung *f*

(public) utility law (US); statutory undertaker law (Brit.) · Versorgungsbetriebsrecht *n*, Versorgungsunternehmensrecht

(public) vaccinator · (Gemeinde)Impfarzt *m*

public water law · öffentliches Wasserrecht *n*

public water supply · öffentliche Wasserversorgung *f*

public way, public path · öffentlicher Weg *m*

public weal, public good, public necessity, public convenience, public welfare, common weal, common good, common necessity, common convenience, good of the community, public interests, common well-being, general good, prosperity of the community, public welfare · Gemeinwohl *n*, öffentliches Wohl, öffentliches Interesse *n*, allgemeines Wohl, allgemeines Interesse, Allgemeinwohl, öffentliche Belange *m pl*

public will · öffentliches Testament *n*

public wood, public timber · Holzbestand *m* der öffentlichen Hand, öffentlicher Holzbestand

public works, public structures, public physical facilites · Bauten *f* der öffentlichen Hand, öffentliche (bauliche) Anlagen *f pl*, öffentliche (Bau)Werke *n pl*, öffentliche Bauanlagen, öffentliche Bauten *f*, öffentliche Baulichkeiten *f pl*

public work(s) · Arbeit(en) *f (pl)* der öffentlichen Hand, öffentliche Arbeit(en) *f (pl)*

public (works) client, public (works) owner, public (works) employer, public (works) promoter · öffentliche Bauherrschaft *f*, öffentlicher Bauherr *m*, öffentlicher Auftraggeber (für Bauarbeiten), öffentlicher Besteller (für Bauarbeiten)

(public) works department · Abteilung *f* für öffentliche Arbeiten

Public Works Loan Commission · Körperschaft *f* zur Prüfung von Anleihen aus öffentlichen Mitteln [*1875 in England durch Gesetz geschaffen*]

public works programme; public works program (US) · Bauprogramm *n* der öffentlichen Hand

to publish, to announce, to promulgate, to publicize · bekanntgeben, veröffentlichen, verbreiten, öffentlich bekanntgeben, (öffentlich) bekanntmachen

publisher · Verleger *m*

to publish the banns · (öffentlich) aufbieten [*Ehe*]

puffer [*One who attends a sale by auction, to bid on the part of the owner, for the purpose of raising the price and exciting the eagerness of the bidders*] · bietende Mittelsperson *f* [*Versteigerung*]

pugree, salaami, tea money [*In the Far East*]; key money [*An undercover rent payment*] · Schlüsselgeld *n*

puisne judge · einfacher Richter *m* [*Mitglied eines Gerichtes im Gegensatz zum Vorsitzenden*]

puisne mortgage [*A legal mortgage not being a mortgage protected by a deposition of documents relating to the legal estate affected. This mortgage,* although a legal interest, does not therefore bind a purchaser for value unless registered] · Nachhypothek f [Zweite Hypothek die nicht durch Übergabe der Auflassungsurkunde begründet und gesichert werden kann]

to pull down, to raze, to demolish, to wreck · abbrechen, abreißen, einreißen, niederreißen [Bauwerk]

pull factor · anziehender Faktor m [im Wanderungszielgebiet]

pulling down, razing, demolishing, wrecking · Abbrechen n, Abreißen, Einreißen, Niederreißen

pulling down, razing, demolition, wrecking · Abbruch m, Abriß m, Bauabbruch, Bauabriß

pulling down area, pulling down territory, razing territory, demolition area, demolition territory, wrecking area, wrecking territory · Abbruchgebiet n, Einreißgebiet, Abrißgebiet

pulling down certificate, razing certificate, demolition certificate, wrecking certificate · Abbruchbescheinigung f, Abbruchschein m, Einreißschein, Abreißschein, Abrißschein, Einreißbescheinigung, Abreißbescheinigung, Abrißbescheinigung

pulling down contract, razing contract, demolition contract, wrecking contract · Abbruchvertrag m, Abrißvertrag, Einreißvertrag

pulling down contractor, razing contractor, demolition contractor, wrecking contractor · Abbruchunternehmer m

pulling down cost(s), razing cost(s), demolition cost(s), wrecking cost(s) · Abbruchkosten f, Abreißkosten, Einreißkosten, Abrißkosten

pulling down operation, razing operation, demolition operation, wrecking operation · Abbruchvorgang m, Abrißvorgang, Einreißvorgang

pulling down operations → pulling down work(s)

pulling down order, demolition order, wrecking order · (Bau)Abbruchanordnung f, (Bau)Abbruchverfügung, (Bau)Abbruchgebot n, (Bau)Abbruchbefehl m, (Bau)Einreißverfügung, (Bau)Einreißanordnung, (Bau)Einreißbefehl, (Bau)Einreißgebot, (Bau)Abrißanordnung, (Bau)Abrißverfügung, (Bau)Abrißbefehl, (Bau)Abrißgebot [In den Landesbauordnungen einiger Länder der Bundesrepublik Deutschland und in § 19 des Städtebauförderungsgesetzes]

pulling down ordinance, demolition ordinance, wrecking ordinance · (Bau)Abbruchverordnung f, (Bau)Einreißverordnung, (Bau)Abrißverordnung

pulling down parcel → pulling down plot

pulling down permission, razing permission, demolition permission, wrecking permission · Abbrucherlaubnis f, Abbruchgenehmigung f, Einreißerlaubnis, Einreißgenehmigung, Abrißerlaubnis, Abrißgenehmigung

pulling down plot, demolition parcel, pulling down parcel, wrecking parcel, razing parcel, demolition plot, wrecking plot · Abbruchgrundstück n, Einreißgrundstück, Abreißgrundstück, Abrißgrundstück

pulling down stop, razing stop, prohibition of demolition, prohibition of wrecking, prohibition of pulling down, demolition stop, wrecking stop · Abbruchverbot n, Abrißverbot, Einreißverbot

pulling down territory, razing territory, demolition area, demolition territory, wrecking area, wrecking territory, pulling down area · Abbruchgebiet n, Einreißgebiet, Abrißgebiet

pulling down work(s), pulling down operations, razing operations, razing work(s), demolition work(s), demolition operations, wrecking work(s), wrecking operations · Abbrucharbeit(en) f (pl), Abrißarbeit(en), Einreißarbeit(en)

pull policy [In Great Britain] · Politik f zur Umsied(e)lung von Arbeitern in die Großstädte

punch list [A list prepared by inspection of the contractor's uncompleted and/or uncorrected work] · Liste f der ausstehenden Arbeiten

punctiform · punktförmig

pundbreach [Saxon]; breach of pound, pound breach; parci fractio [Latin] [The offence of breaking a pound, for the purpose of taking out the cattle and/or goods impounded] · Einbruch m in einen Pfandstall

punishable, liable to prosecution, subject to prosecution · strafbar

punishment execution, execution of punishment · Strafvollstreckung f

punitive damages, punitive compensation, punitive indemnification, punitive indemnity, vindictive damages, vindictive compensation · Abbruchgenehmigung f, vindictive indemnification, exemplary damages, exemplary compensation, exemplary indemnification, exemplary indemnity · Extraentschädigung(sleistung) f, Extraschadenersatz(leistung)

pupil, ward · Mündel m

pupilage, state of being a pupil, pupil state, ward state, state of being a ward · Mündelstand m

pupil money, ward money, ward trust money, money held in trust for a ward · Mündelgeld n

pupil mortgage — purchasing of landed estate

pupil mortgage, ward mortgage · Mündelhypothek *f*

pupil population · Schülerbevölkerung *f*

pupil state, ward state, state of being a ward, pupilage, state of being a pupil · Mündelstand *m*

pupil teacher, monitory teacher · Schüler *m* als Anfangslehrer [*Ein älterer Schüler als Lehrer der jüngeren*]

pupil transportation · Schülerbeförderung *f*

pur autre vie, per autre vie, for the life of another [*An estate pur autre vie was a tenancy of land for the life of another who was called the cestui que vie; the lowest estate of freehold which the law allowed before 1925 the estate has become an equitable interest. Not in the USA — old rule still applies — cestui que estate = life estate pour autre vie; it is of course an equitable interest in land*] · für die Dauer eines anderen Lebens, für Lebenszeit eines Dritten, auf Lebenszeit eines Dritten, auf die Dauer eines anderen Lebens, für das Leben eines anderen

purchase by sample · Probekauf *m*, Musterkauf, Kauf nach Probe, Kauf nach Muster

purchase condition · Einkaufsbedingung *f*, Kaufbedingung

purchase deed · Abkaufbrief *m*, Kaufurkunde *f*

purchase for value · entgeltliches Kaufgeschäft *n*

purchase (land) parcel, purchase plot, purchase parcel of land · Kaufgrundstück *n*

purchase-money mortgage · Kaufgeldhypothek *f*, Kaufschillingshypothek [*Der Käufer des Grundstückes läßt für die Kaufsumme eine Hypothek eintragen*]

purchase notice, purchase notification · Kaufanzeige *f*, Kaufmitteilung *f*

purchase object, object of purchase · Kaufgegenstand *m*, Kaufobjekt *n*

purchase of ascertained goods, purchase of specific goods · Spezieskauf *m*

purchase of (building) land, (real) estate purchase, (real) property purchase, (building) land purchase, purchase of (real) estate, purchase of (real) property · Grund(stücks)kauf *m*, (Bau)Landkauf, (Bau)Bodenkauf, Liegenschaftskauf [*Österreich: Grundeinlösung f*]

purchase of building(s) · Gebäudekauf *m*

purchase offer, offer to purchase · Kaufangebot *n*

purchase (of land) by compulsion, compulsory purchase (of land), compulsory acquisition (of land), acquisition (of land) by compulsion · Landzwangsbeschaffung *f*, (Boden)Zwangsbeschaffung, (Boden)Zwangserwerb *m*, (Boden)Zwangskauf *m*, Landzwangserwerb, Landzwangskauf, (Boden)Enteignung gegen Entschädigung, Landenteignung gegen Entschädigung

purchase of (real) estate, purchase of (real) property, purchase of (building) land, (real) estate purchase, (real) property purchase, (building) land purchase · Grund(stücks)kauf *m*, (Bau)Landkauf, (Bau)Bodenkauf, Liegenschaftskauf [*Österreich: Grundeinlösung f*]

purchase of specific goods, purchase of ascertained goods · Spezieskauf *m*

purchase of unascertained goods · Gattungskauf *m*, Genuskauf

purchase on annuity basis · Kauf *m* auf Rentenbasis, Rentenbasiskauf

purchase order, P.O. · Einkaufsauftrag *m*, Kaufauftrag

purchase order revision · Einkaufsauftragänderung *f*, Kaufauftragänderung

purchase parcel of land, purchase (land) parcel, purchase plot · Kaufgrundstück *n*

purchase plot, purchase parcel of land, purchase (land) parcel · Kaufgrundstück *n*

purchase price fixing · Kaufpreisbindung *f*

purchaser, vendee, buyer · Käufer *m*

purchaser for value, buyer for value · entgeltlicher Käufer *m*

purchaser of (real) estate, purchaser of (real) property, buyer of (real) estate, buyer of (real) property, vendee of (real) estate, vendee of (real) property, purchaser of realty, vendee of realty, buyer of realty, land buyer, land purchaser · Grund(stücks)käufer *m*, Bodenkäufer, Liegenschaftskäufer, Landkäufer, Immobilienkäufer, Immobiliarkäufer

purchaser's market, vendee's market, buyer's market · Käufermarkt *m*

purchase tax · Kaufsteuer *f*

purchasing ability, buying ability, purchasing power, buying power · Kaufkraft *f*

purchasing behaviour, buying behaviour (Brit.); purchasing behavior, buying behavior (US) · Kaufverhalten *n*

purchasing habit, buying habit · Kaufgewohnheit *f*

purchasing manager, purchasing representative, procurement manager, procurement representative · Einkäufer *m*

purchasing of landed estate on time bargains, buying of landed estate on time bargains · Protokollhandel *m*

purchasing policy, buying policy · Kaufpolitik *f*

purchasing power, buying power, purchasing ability, buying ability · Kaufkraft *f*

purchasing power flow, buying power flow, buying power stream, purchasing power stream · Kaufkraftstrom *m*

purchasing trap, buying trap · Kauffalle *f*

pure · rein

pure and perpetual alms · reines und dauerndes Almosen *n*

pure-blooded · reinblütig

(pure) estate of freehold → simple fee

pure fee → simple fee

pure (feodal) tenure (of land) → simple fee

(pure) freehold estate → simple fee

pure gain, pure profit, clear gain, clear profit, net gain, net profit · Reingewinn *m*, Reinprofit *m*, Nettogewinn, Nettoprofit

pure geography · reine Geographie *f*

pure gold · Feingold *n*

pure gold clause · Feingoldklausel *f*

pure gold mortgage [*In the inflation-time in Germany, mortgage of property for an amount of pure gold*] · Feingoldhypothek *f*

pure guarantee (building and loan) association, pure guaranty (building and loan) association (US) · reine Bürgschaftsbausparkasse *f*

pure interest · reine Zinsen *f*

pure law of Reason · Gesetz *n* der reinen Vernunft

purely arbitrary · rein willkürlich

(purely) incorporeal hereditament appurtenant, hereditament (purely) incorporeal appurtenant · nichtkörperliches anhaftendes Erbgut *n*, nichtkörperliches zugehöriges Erbgut, unkörperliches anhaftendes Erbgut, unkörperliches zugehöriges Erbgut, immaterielles anhaftendes Erbgut, immaterielles zugehöriges Erbgut

(purely) incorporeal hereditament appendant, hereditament (purely) incorporeal appendant [*Also spelled "appendent"*] · ununterbrochenes unkörperliches Erbgut *n*

pure profit → pure gain

pure residential zone, pure residence zone, pure housing zone · reines Wohn(ungs)gebiet *n*, WR

pure simulation model · reines Simulationsmodell *n*

pure strategy · reine Strategie *f*

pure tenancy → simple fee

pure tenure (of land) → simple fee

purpose-built · zweckgebaut

purpose-built factory · bestellte Fabrik *f* [*In einem britischen Gewerbepark*]

purposiveness · Zweckrichtung *f*

purprestura [*Latin*] · Aneignung *f* von Forstteilen

pursuance · Verfolg *m*

pursuit of happiness · Streben *n* nach Wohlergehen

pursuit of hue and cry · Nachsuchung *f* [*Einem Verbrecher auf die Spur kommen*]

purveyance, Crown's prerogative right · königliches Vorkaufsrecht *n*, Vorkaufsrecht der Krone

push factor · abstoßender Faktor *m* [*im Wanderungsherkunftsgebiet*]

push policy [*In Great Britain*] · Politik *f* zum Verlassen von Ballungsgebieten und Ansied(e)lung in Fördergebieten [*Industriebetriebe*]

put · Rückprämie *f* [*Amerikanischer Wertpapierhandel*]

put and call · Rück- und Vorprämiengeschäft *n* [*Amerikanischer Wertpapierhandel*]

putative title, supposed title, reputed title · Putativ(rechts)titel *m*

to put in a caveat, to enter a caveat, to lodge a caveat · Einspruch erheben

to (put into) commission, to put into operation · in Betrieb setzen, in Betrieb nehmen

to put out of an inheritance, to exclude from inheriting, to disinherit; to exheredate [*Scots law*]; to deprive of an inheritance, to debar from an inheritance · enterben

to put out to tender, to go out to tender, to obtain tenders, to invite tenders, to tender out, to invite offers, to invite bids; to invite (bid) proposals (US) · ausschreiben, (Angebote) einholen, auffordern zur Angebotsabgabe

to put right, to rectify, to correct · verbessern, richtigstellen, korrigieren, berichtigen, (ab)ändern [*Z. B. Fehler oder Irrtum in einer Rechnung*]

putting into operation, commissioning, putting into service · Inbetriebnahme *f*, Ingebrauchnahme

putting off, postponement, suspension, deferment · Aufschub *m*, Aufschiebung *f*, Hinausschiebung *f*, Verschiebung *f*

putting out of an inheritance — qualified of being revoked

putting out of an inheritance, debarring from an inheritance, excluding from an inheritance; exheredating [*Scots law*]; disinheriting, depriving of an inheritance · Enterben *n*

putting to account, charging, placing to account · Anrechnung *f*

to put to account → to place to account

Q

quad · quadratische Flächeneinheit *f*

quadratic estimator · quadratische Schätzfunktion *f* [*Statistik*]

qualification, capability, capacity, ability · (Leistungs)Fähigkeit *f*, (Leistungs)Vermögen *n*

qualification for being cultivated, ability for being cultivated, capacity for being cultivated, capability for being cultivated · Anbaufähigkeit *f*, Anbaubarkeit, Anbaueignung *f*, Kultivierbarkeit

qualification for office · Amtseignung *f*

qualification for performing legal acts, capability for performing legal acts, capacity for performing legal acts, ability for performing legal acts · Handlungsfähigkeit *f*, Handlungseignung *f*

qualification of being re-examined, qualification of being checked, qualification of being controlled, ability of being controlled, ability of being re-examined, ability of being checked, capability of being checked, capability of being controlled, capability of being re-examined, capacity of being checked, capacity of being re-examined, capacity of being controlled · Nachprüfbarkeit, Kontrollierbarkeit

qualification of the testator, testamentary capacity, disposing capacity, disposing capability, testamentary capability, testamentary qualification, disposing qualification, capacity of the testator, capability of the testator · Testierfähigkeit *f*, Testiereignung *f*, Testamentsfähigkeit, Testamentseignung

qualification order · Approbationsverordnung *f*

qualification share · Qualifikationsaktie *f*

qualification stock · Pflichtaktie *f*

qualification to be a party, ability to be a party, capacity to be a party, capability to be a party · Parteifähigkeit *f*

qualification to commit crime, ability to commit crime, capacity to commit crime, capability to commit crime · (kriminelle) Schuldfähigkeit *f*, (kriminelle) Schuldeignung *f*

qualification to deal with land, capability to deal with land, ability to deal with land, capacity to deal with land · Bodenverkehrsfähigkeit *f*, Bodenverkehrseignung *f*, Grundstücksverkehrsfähigkeit, Grundstücksverkehrseignung, Immobiliarverkehrsfähigkeit, Immobiliarverkehrseignung, Immobilienverkehrsfähigkeit, Immobilienverkehrseignung, Liegenschaftsverkehrsfähigkeit, Liegenschaftsverkehrseignung

qualification to earn profits, ability to earn profits, capacity to earn profits, capability to earn profits · Gewinneignung *f*, Gewinnfähigkeit *f*, Profiteignung, Profitfähigkeit

qualification to finance, capacity to finance, financing ability, financing capacity, financing qualification, financing capability, ability to finance, capability to finance · Finanzierungseignung *f*, Finanzierungsfähigkeit *f*

qualification to inherit, capability to inherit, ability to inherit, capacity to inherit · (aktive) Erbfähigkeit *f*, (aktive) Erbeignung *f*

qualification to purchase, qualification to buy, ability to buy, ability to purchase, capacity to buy, capacity to purchase, capability to buy, capability to purchase · Kauffähigkeit *f*, Kaufeignung *f*

qualification to sue, standing to sue, active legitimation, capacity to sue, capability to sue · Aktivlegitimation *f* [*Zur gerichtlichen Geltendmachung von Ansprüchen*]

qualified [*title*] · vollberechtigt

qualified, able, capable · (leistungs)fähig

qualified acceptance of a bill (of exchange), conditional acceptance of a bill (of exchange) · bedingte Wechselannahme *f*

qualified fee → (estate in) qualified fee

qualified for protection, qualified to be protected · schutzwürdig

qualified medical practitioner · approbierter Arzt *m*

qualified of being checked, qualified of being controlled, qualified of being re-examined, capable of being checked, capable of being controlled, capable of being re-examined, able of being checked, able of being controlled, able of being re-examined · kontrollierbar, nachprüfbar

qualified of being revoked, qualified of revocation, during pleasure, revocable, at will, revokable, ambulatory, capable of being revoked, capable of revocation, able of being revoked, able of revocation · auf Widerruf, widerruflich, widerrufbar, einvernehmlich geduldet

qualified of being tested — quantity mechanism 840

qualified of being tested, capable of being tested, able of being tested · prüfungsfähig, prüfungsreif, prüfungsgeeignet

qualified of contracting, capable to contract, able to contract, qualified to contract, competent to contract, capable of contracting, able of contracting · vertragsfähig, vertragsgeeignet

qualified of earning, capable of earning, able to earn, capable to earn, qualified to earn, able of earning · erwerbsgeeignet, erwerbsfähig

qualified of revocation, during pleasure, revocable, at will, revokable, ambulatory, capable of being revoked, capable of revocation, able of being revoked, able of revocation, qualified of being revoked · auf Widerruf, widerruflich, widerrufbar, einvernehmlich geduldet

qualified property, special property · besitzmäßiges Eigentum, eigenartiges Eigentum *n*, eigenartiges Interesse *n* an einer Sache

qualified title [*Under the Land Registration Act 1925 land may be registered with a qualified title*] · bedingter (Rechts)Titel *m*, bedingtes Recht *n*

qualified to be protected, qualified for protection · schutzwürdig

qualified to buy, qualified to purchase, able to buy, able to purchase, capable to buy, capable to purchase · kauffähig, kaufgeeignet

qualified to contract, competent to contract, capable of contracting, able of contracting, qualified of contracting, capable to contract, able to contract · vertragsfähig, vertragsgeeignet

qualified to earn, able of earning, qualified of earning, capable of earning, able to earn, capable to earn · erwerbsgeeignet, erwerbsfähig

qualified to make a will, able of making a will, qualified of making a will, capable of making a will, able to make a will, capable to make a will · testierfähig, testiergeeignet, testamentsfähig, testamentsgeeignet

qualified to purchase, able to buy, able to purchase, capable to buy, capable to purchase, qualified to buy · kauffähig, kaufgeeignet

qualifying standard · Auflagenorm *f*

qualitas [*Latin*] · Leh(e)n(s)besitz *m* in eigenem Namen

quality assurance [*B.S.4778 and B.S.4891. All activities and functions concerned with the attainment of quality*] · Gütesicherung *f*

quality certificate, certificate of quality · Gütezeugnis *n*

quality certification mark ordinance · (Güte)Prüfzeichenverordnung *f*

quality control [*A system for programming and co-ordinating the efforts of the various groups in an organization to maintain or improve quality, at an economical level which allows for customer satisfaction*] · Güteüberwachung *f*

quality control certificate · Güteüberwachungsschein *m*, Güteüberwachungsbescheinigung *f*, Güteüberwachungsattest *n*

quality control contract · Güteüberwachungsvertrag *m*

quality control representative · Güteüberwachungsbeauftragte *m*

quality guide lines · Güterichtlinien *fpl*

quality of being approbative, approvableness, worthiness of approval, ability to be approved, approvable quality, approbativeness · Zulassungswürdigkeit *f*, Zustimm(ungs)würdigkeit, Zulassungsfähigkeit, Zustimm(ungs)fähigkeit

quality of workmanship, workmanship quality · Güte *f* der Arbeitsausführung

quality proof, proof of quality · Gütenachweis *m*

quality provision · Gütebestimmung *f*

quality test · Güteprüfung *f*

qualm, doubt · Bedenken *n*

quantal response · Reaktion *f* nach dem Alles-oder-Nichts-Gesetz, Alles-oder-Nichts-Reaktion, Ja-Nein-Reaktion [*Statistik*]

quantification · mengenmäßige Bestimmung *f*

to quantify · mengenmäßig bestimmen, mengenmäßig festlegen, mengenmäßig festsetzen

quantile · Häufigkeitsstufe *f* [*Statistik*]

quantitative method · Mengenverfahren *n*

quantity · Masse *f*, Menge *f*

quantity alteration, quantity change, quantity variation · Massenänderung *f*, Massenabänderung, Mengen(ab)änderung, Mengenumänderung, Massenumänderung

quantity and cost(s) estimate · Mengen- und Kosten(ab)schätzung *f*

quantity change, quantity variation, quantity alteration · Massenänderung *f*, Massenabänderung, Mengen(ab)änderung, Mengenumänderung, Massenumänderung

quantity deviation · Massenabweichung *f*, Mengenabweichung

quantity error, error in quantity · Mengenfehler *m*

quantity mechanism · Mengenmechanismus *m*

quantity of interest · Dauer *f* von Rechten, Dauer der Rechte [*Sie ist das Unterscheidungsmerkmal zwischen Hauptrechten und Realrechten niederer Bedeutung*]

quantity of land(s), land(s) quantity · Landmenge *f*, Bodenmenge, Flächenmenge

quantity of light, amount of light, light quantity, light quantum, light amount, quantum of light · Lichtmenge *f*

quantity orientation, orientation by quantity · Mengenorientierung *f*

quantity-proportional · massenanteilig, mengenanteilig

quantity rebate · Mengenrabatt *m*

quantity rebate variance · Mengenrabattabweichung *f*

quantity-relative · Mengenmeßziffer *f* [*Statistik*]

quantity surveying · Massenberechnung *f*

quantity surveyor · Massenkalkulator *m*

quantity theory of money · Geldquantentheorie *f*

quantity variation, quantity alteration, quantity change · Massenänderung *f*, Massenabänderung, Mengen(ab)änderung, Mengenumänderung, Massenumänderung

quantum meruit [*Latin*]; right to restitution, right to reimbursement, right to recovery, right to refunding [*It is a right to be paid a reasonable remuneration for work done*] · Abgeltungs(an)recht *n*, Abgeltungsanspruch *m*, Erstattungsanspruch, Vergütungsanspruch, Ersetzungsanspruch, Erstattungs(an)recht, Vergütungs(an)recht, Ersetzungs(an)recht

quantum of light, quantity of light, amount of light, light quantity, light quantum, light amount · Lichtmenge *f*

quarantine, quarent(a)ine · Quarantäne *f*

quarentena terrae, furlongus, stadium stade [*Latin*]; furlong; furlang [*Anglo-Saxon*]; ferlingus, ferlingum [*Low Latin*] [*A piece of land bounded or terminated by the length of a furrow*] · (Ge)Wende *(n), f*, Gewann *n*, Wande *f*, Wanne *f*; Flagge [*Ostfriesland*]

quarrying · Steinbruchabbau *m*

quarter · Viertel *n*; Quartier *n* [*Schweiz*]

quarter, accommodation, lodging, shelter · Unterkunft *f*

quarterage · Vierteljahresgeld *n*, Quartalgeld

quarter day · Quartaltag *m*, Vierteljahrestag

quarterly payment · Vierteljahreszahlung *f*

quarterly tenant [*premises*] · Mieter *m* mit vierteljährlicher Kündigung

quarternary activity · quartärer Wirtschaftszweig *m*

quarter session, county session · Vierteljahresversammlung *f* der Grafschaftsrichter, Quartalversammlung der Grafschaftsrichter, (Grafschafts)Quartalsitzung

quarter session (municipal) borough, (municipal) borough, non-county borough [*Created 1835 in England by the Municipal Corporations Act*] · Munizipalstadt *f*, grafschaftsfreie Stadt, Stadt im rechtlichen Sinne, Stadt mit korporativer Verfassung, selbständige Stadt [*Gegensatz: Reichsstadt. „(Municipal) borough" ist der offizielle Name einer Stadt in England; in Schottland „burgh". „Town" gehört der Umgangssprache an. „City" ist in England ein auszeichnender Titel, den altberühmte Städte, meistens Bischofssitze, tragen. In der Verwaltung besteht zwischen „city" und „borough" kein Unterschied*]

quarter session(s) court, county session(s) court, court of (quarter) session(s), court of county session(s) · Vierteljahresgericht *n*, Quartalgericht

quartile deviation, semi-interquartile range · halber Quartilabstand *m* [*Statistik*]

quartile measure of skewness · Quartilschiefmaß *n*

quasi · gleichsam

quasi-arbitral · quasi-schiedsrichterlich, schiedsähnlich

quasi-arbitrator → valuer

quasi-compact cluster · Klumpen *m* in weiterer Nachbarschaft liegender Einheiten [*Statistik*]

quasi-contract · vertragsähnliches (Rechts)Verhältnis *n*

quasi-dominant (real) estate, quasi-dominant (real) property, quasi-dominant land, quasi-dominant realty · quasiherrschendes Land *n*, quasiherrschendes Grundstück, quasiherrschender Grund *m*, quasiherrschender Boden

quasi-guardian, guardian by estoppel, guardian de son tort [*One who assumes to act as guardian without valid authority*] · Quasi-Vormund *m*

quasi-interest in (real) estate, quasi-interest in (real) property, quasi-interest in realty · Quasibodenbesitzrecht *n*, Quasilandbesitzrecht, Quasi(grund)besitzrecht

quasi-judge · Quasi-Richter *m*

quasi-judicial · gleichsam richterlich, richterähnlich

quasi-judicial duty · richterähnliche Pflicht *f*, gleichsam richterliche Pflicht

quasi-municipal corporation — quit-rent law 842

quasi-municipal corporation [*USA*] · quasikommunale Gebietskörperschaft *f*

quasi-possession · Quasibesitz *m*

quasi-possessor · Quasibesitzer *m*

quasi-public, semi-governmental, having standing under public law · öffentlich-rechtlich

quasi-public load, semi-governmental load · öffentlich-rechtliche Last *f*

quasi-public neighbour's protection, semi-governmental neighbour's protection (Brit.); quasi-public neighbor's protection, semi-governmental neighbor's protection (US) · öffentlich-rechtlicher Nachbarschutz *m*

quasi-public use, semi-governmental use [*Use serving a community or public purpose, and operated by a noncommercial entity, or by a public agency*] · öffentlich-rechtlicher Gebrauch *m*, öffentlich-rechtliche Benutzung *f*

quasi-rent, income from an appliance for production made by man · Quasirente *f* [*Ein der Bodenrente ähnliches und nicht aus Naturquellen fließendes Einkommen*]

quasi usufruct, quasiususfructus [*Latin*] · Quasinießbrauch *m*, Quasi(frucht)genuß *m*, uneigentlicher Nießbrauch, uneigentlicher (Frucht)Genuß

Queen's advocate, King's advocate, advocate-general [*England*] · Kronjurist *m* für See- und Kriegsrecht

querens [*Latin*]; complainant · Beschwerdeführer *m*

question · Anfrage *f* [*im Parlament*]

questionnaire · Fragebogen *m*

questionnaire data · Fragebogenmaterial *n*

questionnaire survey · Fragebogenerhebung *f*, Fragebogenaktion *f*

question of fact, konkreter Umstand *m* eines Rechtsstreites, Tat(sachen)frage *f*

question of law, point of law, law question, law point · Rechtsfrage *f*

question period · Fragestunde *f* [*im Parlament*]

question suggesting the answer · Suggestivfrage *f*

questman, sidesman, synodsman · Synodalzeuge *m*

quick asset, current asset [*An asset that can be converted readily into cash, e.g. stocks, notes, inventory*] · kurzfristiger Aktivposten *m*, kurzfristig realisierbarer Vermögensteil *m*

quick asset ratio [*The ratio of the total of cash, trade receivables, and marketable securities of a business concern to its current liabilities. The term is used by credit analysts. If the ratio is 2 or more, a minimum risk is presumably indicated*] · Liquiditätsverhältnis *n*

quick-set hedge, hawthorn hedge · Weißdornhecke *f*, Hagedornhecke

quiet · ungestört

quiet and peaceful possession · ungestörter und friedlicher Besitz *m*

quiet enjoyment, quiet exercise of a right · ungestörte (subjektive) Rechtsausübung *f*, ungestörte Ausübung eines (subjektiven) Rechts

quiet enjoyment of real property · ungestörter Grundbesitz *m*

quieti reditus, reditus quieti [*Latin*]; forgavel [*In old English law*]; chief-rent, rent charge, quit-rent, fee farm (rent) [*An annual or periodical sum issuing out of land, payable by holders of land in a manor to the lord. Some writers use "fee farm" to signify not only the estate itself, but the rent reserved on it, taking the word "farm" itself in the sense of rent. This practice should, however, be deprecated*] · Erbzins *m*, Befreiungszins, Leh(e)n(s)zins

quiet title · rechtsbeständiger Titel *m*

quincunx [*Latin*]; lattice · Wabenstreuung *f*

quindena, detractus realis, census hereditarius, gabella hereditaria [*Latin*] · Abschoß *m*, Erb(schafts)geld *n*

quitclaim · freiwillige Übertragung *f* ohne Zusicherung des Nichtbestehens von Rechtsmängeln

quitclaim deed, release deed [*A deed of conveyance operating by way of release; that is, intended to pass any title which the grantor may have in the premises, but not professing that such title is valid, or containing any warranty or convenants for title*] · Übertragungsurkunde *f* ohne Zusicherung des Nichtbestehens von Rechtsmängeln, freiwillige Übertragungsurkunde *f* ohne Zusicherung des Nichtbestehens von Rechtsmängeln

quit notice [*Notice to a tenant to vacate rental real property*] · Kündigungsschreiben *n*

quit-rent, fee farm (rent); quieti reditus, reditus quieti [*Latin*]; forgavel [*In old English law*]; chief-rent, rent charge [*An annual or periodical sum issuing out of land, payable by holders of land in a manor to the lord. Some writers use "fee farm" to signify not only the estate itself, but the rent reserved on it, taking the word "farm" itself in the sense of rent. This practice should, however, be deprecated*] · Erbzins *m*, Befreiungszins, Leh(e)n(s)zins

quit-rent law, fee farm (rent) law, chief-rent law · Befreiungszinsrecht *n*, Erbzinsrecht, objektives Befreiungszinsrecht, objektives Erbzinsrecht

quit-rent roll, fee farm (rent) roll, chiefrent roll · Erbzinsbuch, Befreiungszinsbuch *n*

quomodo [*Latin*] · Fehlerfreiheit *f* [*Gewere*]

quorum [*The specified number of members of a body, in the absence of which it cannot formally meet or act legally*] · beschlußfähige Mehrheit *f*

quota · Quotient *m*

quotation · unverbindliche Preiszusage *f*

quotation [*On the stock exchange, or in commercial markets generally, the price of the day as quoted in the official list of any particular security or commodity*] · Notierung *f*

R

race issue, racial issue, race problem, racial problem · Rassenfrage *f*, Rassenproblem *n*

race problem, racial problem, race issue, racial issue · Rassenfrage *f*, Rassenproblem *n*

race tension, racial tension · Rassenspannung *f*

racial balance, race balance · Rassenausgewogenheit *f*, Rassengleichgewicht *n*

racial composition, racial structure · Rassenzusammensetzung *f*, Rassenaufbau *m*, Rassengefüge *n*, Rassenstruktur *f*

racial discrimination, race discrimination · Rassismus *m*

racial factor, race factor · Rassengegebenheit *f*

racial issue, race problem, racial problem, race issue · Rassenfrage *f*, Rassenproblem *n*

racially discriminatory · rassistisch

racially integrated hous(ebuild)ing project · gemischtrassiges Wohn(ungs)bauvorhaben *n*, gemischtrassiges Wohn(ungs)bauprojekt *n*

racial problem, race issue, racial issue, race problem · Rassenfrage *f*, Rassenproblem *n*

racial separation, race separation · Rassentrennung *f*

racial structure, racial composition · Rassenzusammensetzung *f*, Rassenaufbau *m*, Rassengefüge *n*, Rassenstruktur *f*

racial tension, race tension · Rassenspannung *f*

radar geology · Funkmeßgeologie *f*

radial corridors plan, star pattern plan, finger plan · Plan *m* der linearen Anordnung einer Stadtregion

radial pattern, radial form, radial layout, radial scheme, fan pattern, fan form, fan layout, fan scheme · Fächermuster *n*, Fächerform *f*, Fächerschema *n*, Radialmuster, Radialform, Radialschema [*Stadtgrundriß*]

radial street · Zugstraße *f*, Radialstraße, Ausstrahlstraße, Ausstrahler *m*, Ausfallstraße [*In manchen deutschen Städten wird eine Ausfallstraße auch Heerstraße nach einem bestimmten Ort, z. B. Celler Heerstraße in Hannover, nach der Stadt Celle benannt*]

radial-street cluster settlement, radial-street irregular nucleated settlement · strahlwegige Haufen(an)sied(e)lung *f*

radial-street irregular nucleated settlement, radial-street cluster settlement · strahlwegige Haufen(an)sied(e)lung *f*

radial street system [*A street layout in which streets radiate from a centre point or area, as opposed to a gridiron system*] · Ausstrahlstraßensystem *n*, Ausstrahlersystem, Ausfallstraßensystem, Radialstraßensystem, Zugstraßensystem

radioactive waste · radioaktiver Abfall *m*

radius of mobility, mobility radius · Beweglichkeitshalbmesser *m*, Mobilitätshalbmesser

rafting · Flößerei *f* mit verbundenen Hölzern, Floßfahrt *f*

rafting right, right of rafting; jus grutiae [*Latin*] · Flößer(ei)recht *n*, Floßrecht

raiding [*USA*] · Vorwahlunterwanderung *f*

rail carrier · Schienenverkehrsträger *m*

railroad-bill-of-lading (US); railway-bill-of-lading (Brit.) · (Eisen)Bahnfrachtbrief *m*

railroad commuter (US); railway commuter (Brit.) · (Eisen)Bahnpendler *m*

railroad commuting (US); railway commuting (Brit.) · (Eisen)Bahnpendeln *n*

railroad ground (US); railway ground (Brit.) · (Eisen)Bahnterrain *n*, (Eisen)Bahngelände *n*

rail transport(ation), rail transit · Schienentransport *m*, Schienenverkehr *m*, Schienenbeförderung *f*

railway premises and other property (Brit.); railroad premises and other property (US) · Bahneinheit *f* [*Alle einem Eisenbahnunternehmen gewidmeten Grundstücke und andere Vermögensgegenstände, die rechtlich als Einheit gelten*]

railway security (Brit.); railroad security (US) · Eisenbahnwert *m*

rain insurance policy, pluvious policy · Regenversicherungspolice *f*

rain-wash · Abspülung *f* [*Grundstück*]

rainwater collection facility · Regenwasserauffanganlage *f*

rainwater retention basin · Regenwasserrückhaltebecken *n*

to raise, to effect [*mortgage*] · aufnehmen [*Hypothek*]

to raise, to collect, to gather, to procure [*money, etc.*] · erheben

to raise [*objection*] · erheben [*Einspruch*]

raise, procurement, procuration, collection · Erhebung *f*

to raise by tillage, to farm, to cultivate, to produce by tillage · kultivieren, anbauen

raising, collecting, gathering, procuring · Erheben *n*

raising · Hochrechnen *n*

raising factor · Hochrechnungsfaktor *m*

raising of cattle, cattle breeding, cattle raising, breeding of cattle · Rindvieh(auf)zucht *f*

raising of ground level · Bodenerhöhung *f*

raising of interest on loan conversion · Arrosierung *f*

raising of (live)stock, (live)stock breeding, (live)stock raising, breeding of (live)stock · Vieh(auf)zucht *f*

raising of the ground · Erhöhen *n* des Bodens

ramp · Auffahrt *f*, Rampe *f*

ranch · Viehzuchtgut *n*

random error · Zufallfehler *m*

random number generator · Zufallzahlengenerator *m*

(random) sample · Stichprobe *f*

(random) sample frequency distribution · Stichprobenhäufigkeitsverteilung *f*

(random) sample frequency function · Stichprobenhäufigkeitsfunktion *f*

(random) sample mean · Stichprobenmittelwert *m*

(random) sample size · Stichprobengröße *f*

(random) sample space · Stichprobenraum *m*

(random) sample statistic · Stichprobenmaßzahl *f*

random sample survey · Stichprobenerhebung *f*

(random) sampling · Stichprobennahme *f*

random variable, stochastic variable, variate, aleatory variable · stochastische Variable *f*, Zufallvariable

random walk · Irrfahrt *f* [*Statistik*]

random-walk theory · Zufallpfadtheorie *f* [*Anlageplanung*]

range of judg(e)ment, judg(e)ment range · Beurteilungsspielraum *m*

range of fee(s), fee range · Gebührenbereich *m*, Honorarbereich

range of validity, scope of validity, validity range · Geltungsbereich *m*

range of validity as to place, scope of validity as to place · örtlicher Geltungsbereich *m*

range of validity as to time, scope of validity as to time · zeitlicher Geltungsbereich *m*

range of work(s), work(s) range · (Bau)Arbeitsbereich *m*, (Bau)Leistungsbereich

ranger of forest(s) → **(sworn) ranger of forest(s)**

rangership of forests · Waldaufseheramt *n* unter Eid

rank, condition, social position [*A position with reference to the grades of society*] · Stellung *f*, Rang *m*

rank correlation · Rangkorrelation *f* [*Statistik*]

rank in life, social rank, social state, social condition, state in life, condition in life · soziale Stellung *f*, sozialer Rang *m*

rank of a citizen, status of a citizen, condition of a citizen · Bürgerstand *m*, Bürgerstatus *m*

rank of being gilt-edged, condition of being gilt-edged · Mündelsicherheit *f*

rank of location, site rank, rank of site, location rank · Standortrang *m*

rank order degree · Rangordnungsgrad *m* [*Statistik*]

rank order number · Rangordnungsnummer *f* [*Statistik*]

rank order statistic · Rangordnungsmaßzahl *f* [*Statistik*]

rank-size relation(ship) · Rang-Größen-Verhältnis *n*

rank-size rule · Rang-Größen-Regel *f*

rape · Bezirk *m* [*In England zur Zeit der normannischen Eroberung*]

rapid boating, fast boating, high-speed boating · motorisierter Bootssport *m*, motorischer Bootssport

rapid bus service, express bus service · Schnellautobusbetrieb *m*, Schnell(omni)busbetrieb

rapidity of circulation · Umlaufgeschwindigkeit *f* [*Geld*]

rapid mass transit, rapid mass transport(ation), (public) rapid transit, (public) rapid transport(ation), public high-speed transit, (public) high-speed transport(ation), (public) fast transit, (public) fast transport(ation), mass rapid transport(ation), mass rapid transit · (öffentlicher) Schnell(bahnmassen)verkehr *m*, (öffentliche) Schnell(bahnmassen)beförderung *f*

(rapid) transit by rail, (rapid) rail transit · Schienenschnellverkehr *m*, Schnellschienenverkehr

rapid transit line → (public) rapid transit line

rapid transit policy → (public) rapid transit policy

(rapid) transit station · Schnellverkehrsbahnhof *m*

rapid transit (system), rapid transport(ation) (system) · Schnellbahn(system) *f, (n)*

ratchet effect · Sperrklinkenwirkung *f* [*Dem Einkommensrückgang wird ein nur unterproportionaler Konsumrückgang zugerechnet*]

rat control, deratting · Entrattung *f,* Rattenbekämpfung

to rate, to assess (for rating purposes) · veranlagen, steuerlich einstufen

to rate, to assess · anteil(mäß)ig festsetzen, bemessen, einstufen, einschätzen, festsetzen eines Satzes [*z. B. ein Bauwerk für Versicherungszwecke; Steuern*]

rate [*In connection with public utilities, a charge to the public for a service open to all and upon the same terms*] · Tarif *m*

rate [*Proportional or relative value, measure, or degree; the proportion or standard by which quantity or value is adjusted*] · Satz *m*

rate · Ansatz *m* [*Rechnung; Leistungsverzeichnis*]

rate, proportion, share, part [*A charge, valuation, payment or price fixed according to ratio, scale or standard. A fixed relation of quantity, amount or degree. A comparative price or amount of demands*] · Anteil *m*

rate · Gemeindesteuer *f,* Kommunalsteuer

rate → (unit) rate

rat(e)able, assessable for tax(ation) (purposes), assessible for tax(ation) (purposes), taxable, subject to tax(ation) · veranlagbar, steuerlich einstufbar, besteuerbar, versteuerbar

rat(e)able value; assessable value [*deprecated*]; reduced net annual value, reduced rat(e)able value · reduzierter Nettoertragswert *m* [*Die landwirtschaftlich genutzten Grundstücke werden mit einem herabgesetzten Nettoertragswert zur Steuer eingeschätzt*]

rat(e)able value, net annual value · Nettoertragswert *m,* Veranlagungswert, Steuerwert [*Liegenschaft*]

rate book · Gemeindesteuerliste *f,* Kommunalsteuerliste

rate book → (poor) rate book

rate collection, collection of rates · Gemeindesteuereinziehung *f,* Gemeindesteuererhebung, Gemeindesteuereintreibung

rate collector, collector of rates · Gemeindesteuererheber *m,* Gemeindesteuereintreiber, Gemeindesteuereinzieher

rated property value, rated value of property · Mietertragswert *m* [*Grundstück*]

rated tax, apportioned tax · Umlegesteuer *f,* Repartitionssteuer, Repartierungssteuer, Kontigentierungssteuer, Verteilungssteuer

rated value, taxable value, assessed value [*The value of property as appraised for taxation*] · bemessener Wert *m,* eingestufter Wert, festgesetzter Wert, veranlagter Wert

rated value of property, rated property value · Mietertragswert *m* [*Grundstück*]

rate equation · Ratengleichung *f*

rate law → (local) rate law

rate of accession, rate of addition, rate of accretion, addition rate, accession rate, accretion rate · Zunahmerate *f,* Zuwachsrate, Zunahmesatz, Zuwachssatz *m*

rate of amortization of debt(s), debt(s) amortization rate · Schuldentilgungsrate *f*

rate of assessment, assessment rate · Bemessungssatz *m,* Festsetzungssatz

rate of augmentation, increase rate, augmentation rate, rate of increase · Steigerungssatz *m,* Erhöhungssatz, Steigerungsrate, Erhöhungsrate

rate of birth, birth rate · Geborenenziffer *f,* Geburtenziffer

rate of charge, duty rate, rate of duty, charge rate · Gebührensatz *m,* Gebührenrate *f*

rate of charge, charge rate · Abgabensatz *m*

rate of commodity substitution, commodity substitution rate · (marginale) Substitutionsrate *f*

rate of construction — rating (and valuation) act

rate of construction, rate of progress, construction rate, progress rate, speed of progress, progress speed, construction speed, speed rate, speed of construction · Baugeschwindigkeit *f*, Bautempo *n*, (Bau)Fortschrittempo, (Bau)Fortschrittgeschwindigkeit

rate of contract, contract(ed) rate [*for services*] · Vertragssatz *m*

rate of contribution, contributory rate, contributing rate, contribution rate · Beitragssatz *m*, Beitragsrate *f*

rate of death, death rate · Sterbeziffer *f*, Sterberate *f*

rate of deposit, deposit rate · Lombardsatz *m*, Lombardrate *f*

rate of depreciation, depreciation rate · Abschreibungssatz *m*, Abschreibungsrate *f*

rate of discount, discount rate · Diskontsatz *m*, Diskontrate *f*

rate of duty, charge rate, rate of charge, duty rate · Gebührensatz *m*

rate of exchange, exchange rate · Devisenkurs *m*, Wechselkurs

rate of fee, fee rate · Gebührensatz *m*, Honorarsatz, Gebührenrate *f*, Honorarrate

rate of growth, growth rate · Wachstumsrate *f*, Wachstumssatz *m*

rate of increase, rate of augmentation, increase rate, augmentation rate · Steigerungssatz *m*, Erhöhungssatz, Steigerungsrate, Erhöhungsrate

rate of inflation, inflation rate · Inflationsrate *f*

rate of interest, interest rate · Zinssatz *m*, Zinsfuß *m*

rate of issue, price of issue, issue rate, issue price · Emissionskurs *m*, Ausgabekurs, Emissionspreis *m*, Ausgabepreis

rate of levy, levy rate · Umlagesatz *m*

rate of obsolescence, obsolescence rate · Überalterungsgeschwindigkeit *f*, Überalterungstempo *n*

rate of occupancy, occupancy rate · (Wohnungs)Belegungsziffer *f* [*Sie gibt an wieviel Personen durchschnittlich auf die Wohnung oder einen Wohnraum entfallen*]

rate of population growth, rate of population increase, population growth rate, population increase rate, demographic growth rate, demographic increase rate · Bevölkerungswachstumsrate *f*, Bevölkerungszunahmerate

rate of progress, construction rate, progress rate, speed of progress, progress speed, construction speed, speed rate, speed of construction · Baugeschwindigkeit *f*, Bautempo *n*, (Bau)Fortschrittempo, (Bau)Fortschrittgeschwindigkeit

rate of redemption, redemption rate · Tilgungssatz *m*, Amortisationssatz

rate of return over cost(s) · Differenzgewinnrate *f*, Differenzprofitrate

rate of tax, tax rate · Steuersatz *m*

rate of unemployment, unemployment rate · Arbeitslosenzahl *f*, Erwerbslosenzahl *f* [*Fehlbenennungen: Arbeitslosenziffer f, Erwerbslosenziffer*]

rate of value added tax, rate of VAT · Mehrwertsteuersatz *m*

rate of wage(s), wage(s) rate · Lohnsatz *m*

rate of waste, waste rate · Wertminderungssatz *m*, Verwüstungssatz, Übernutzungssatz, Verschlechterungssatz, Vernachlässigungssatz, Mißbrauchsatz, Deteriorierungssatz, Depravierungssatz, Schwundsatz

rate of working, working speed, working rate, speed of working · Arbeitsgeschwindigkeit *f*, Ausführungsgeschwindigkeit *f*, Arbeitstempo *n*, Ausführungstempo *n*

rate per cent, percentage (rate) · Anteil(verhältnis) *m*, *(f)*, (Vom)Hundertsatz *m*, Prozentsatz

rate per unit, fixed price (for a unit of specific work), unit price, (unit) rate · Einheitspreis *m*, EP

rate per unit, standard rate, fixed rate, unit rate · Einheitssatz *m*

rate poundage · Hebesatz *m* [*britische Kommunalsteuer*]

rate rebate · Gemeindesteuernachlaß *m*, Kommunalsteuernachlaß

rate rebate · Satznachlaß *m*

rate schedule, schedule of rates · Satztabelle *f*

rate-tithe [*In English law. When any sheep, or cattle, are kept in a parish for less time than a year, the owner must pay tithe for them pro rata, according to the custom of the place*] · Zehnt(en)satz *m*

rate variable · Veränderungsvariable *f*

rate war, cut(-throat) competition · ruinöser Wettbewerb *m*

ratification · Genehmigung *f*, Ratifizierung, staatliche Bestätigung

rating, assessment · (anteilige) Festsetzung *f*, anteilmäßige Festsetzung *f*, Bemessung *f*, Einstufung *f*, Einschätzung *f*, Festsetzung *f* eines Satzes, Satzfestsetzung

rating (and valuation) act, rating (and valuation) statute, rating (and valuation) law

· Veranlagungsgesetz n, Steuerveranlagungsgesetz

rating area · Steuer(einschätzungs)gebiet n [Stadtgrafschaft]

rating area · Gemeindesteuergebiet n, Kommunalsteuergebiet

rating of fee(s), fee rating · Gebührenbemessung f, Honorarbemessung

rating officer, rating official, assessor [A public official who evaluates property for the purposes of taxation] · Veranlagungsbeamte m, Steuerveranlagungsbeamte

ratio analysis · Bilanzanalyse f

ratio estimate, order of magnitude estimate (US) · grobe Schätzung f der Baukosten, grobe Baukostenschätzung

rationalistic conceptual grid, structuralism · Strukturalismus m

ratio technique · Verhältnistechnik f

ravage of game, damage by game · Wildschaden m

raw, unimproved, not improved · unfertig, (bau)unreif, unerschlossen, roh, unverbessert, nicht baureif

raw land → undeveloped land

to raze, to demolish, to wreck, to pull down · abbrechen, abreißen, einreißen [Bauwerk]

razing, demolishing, wrecking, pulling down · Abbrechen n, Abreißen, Einreißen, Niederreißen

razing, demolition, wrecking, pulling down · Abbruch m, Abriß m, Bauabbruch, Bauabriß

razing and rebuilding territory, demolition and rebuilding area, demolition and rebuilding territory, wrecking and rebuilding area, area of demolition and rebuilding, area of wrecking and rebuilding, territory of demolition and rebuilding, territory of wrecking and rebuilding, wrecking and rebuilding territory · Abbruch- und Wiederaufbaugebiet n, Abriß- und Wiederaufbaugebiet, Abreiß- und Wiederaufbaugebiet

razing certificate, demolition certificate, wrecking certificate, pulling down certificate · Abbruchbescheinigung f, Abbruchschein m, Einreißschein, Abreißschein, Abrißschein, Einreißbescheinigung, Abreißbescheinigung, Abrißbescheinigung

razing contract, demolition contract, wrecking contract, pulling down contract · Abbruchvertrag m, Abrißvertrag, Einreißvertrag

razing contractor, demolition contractor, wrecking contractor, pulling down contractor · Abbruchunternehmer m

razing cost(s), demolition cost(s), wrecking cost(s), pulling down cost(s) · Abbruchkosten f, Abreißkosten, Einreißkosten, Abrißkosten

razing operation, demolition operation, wrecking operation, pulling down operation · Abbruchvorgang m, Abrißvorgang, Einreißvorgang

razing operations, razing work(s), demolition work(s), demolition operations, wrecking work(s), wrecking operations, pulling down work(s), pulling down operations · Abbrucharbeit(en) f (pl), Abrißarbeit(en), Einreißarbeit(en)

razing parcel, demolition plot, wrecking plot, pulling down plot, demolition parcel, pulling down parcel, wrecking parcel · Abbruchgrundstück n, Einreißgrundstück, Abreißgrundstück, Abrißgrundstück

razing permission, demolition permission, wrecking permission, pulling down permission · Abbrucherlaubnis f, Abbruchgenehmigung f, Einreißerlaubnis, Einreißgenehmigung, Abrißerlaubnis, Abrißgenehmigung

razing stop, prohibition of demolition, prohibition of wrecking, prohibition of pulling down, demolition stop, wrecking stop, pulling down stop · Abbruchverbot n, Abrißverbot, Einreißverbot

razing territory, demolition area, demolition territory, wrecking area, wrecking territory, pulling down area, pulling down territory · Abbruchgebiet n, Einreißgebiet, Abrißgebiet

razing work(s), demolition work(s), demolition operations, wrecking work(s), wrecking operations, pulling down work(s), pulling down operations, razing operations · Abbrucharbeit(en) f (pl), Abrißarbeit(en), Einreißarbeit(en)

R & D, research and development · Forschung f und Entwick(e)lung

re-acceptance · Nachabnahme f [Zweite und jede weitere Abnahme eines fliegenden Baues nach der Gebrauchsabnahme auf demselben Aufstellungsplatz]

to reach, to touch; abuttare [Latin]; to abut · angrenzen [(Grundstücks)Enden]

reaching, contiguous, touching, abutting · angrenzend [(Grundstücks)Enden]

to readvertise a project · öffentlich wiederausschreiben

reader comment · Leserzuschrift f

readiness for acceptance, acceptability · Abnahmefähigkeit f, Abnahmereife f, Bauabnahmefähigkeit, Bauabnahmereife

readiness for examination · Prüfungsbereitschaft f

readiness for occupation — (real) estate acquisition

readiness for occupation · Bezugsfertigkeit f, Beziehbarkeit [Raum]

readiness statement, statement of readiness · Ankündigung f der Hauptverhandlungsbereitschaft

readiness to (ab)alienate, readiness to dispose · Veräußerungsbereitschaft f

readiness to invest · Investitionsbereitschaft f, (Kapital)Anlagebereitschaft, Geldanlagebereitschaft

reading in chambers · Praxis f bei einem Rechtsanwalt [Zur Erlernung der Rechtspraxis]

readjustment to society · Resozialisierung f

to readjust to society · resozialisieren

re-(ad)measurement · Nachaufmaß n, nachträgliches Aufmaß

readvertisement of a project · öffentliche Wiederausschreibung f

readvertising a project · öffentliches Wiederausschreiben n

ready for acceptance, acceptable · abnahmefähig, abnahmereif, bauabnahmefähig, bauabnahmereif

ready for occupation, ready to be occupied · bezugsfertig, beziehbar, belegungsfertig

ready money, cash · Bargeld n, Barschaft f, bares Geld

ready-money discount, cash discount · Barzahlungsrabatt m, Kassaskonto n, Kassarabatt, Bargeldskonto, Barbezahlungsrabatt

ready-money payment, cash payment, payment in cash, cash (down) · Bar(be)zahlung f

ready-money purchase, cash purchase · Barkauf m

ready-money reimbursement, cash reimbursement · Barvergütung f

ready-money value, cash value · Barwert m

ready to be occupied, ready for occupation · bezugsfertig, beziehbar, belegungsfertig

to re-afforest · wiederaufforsten

re-afforestation · Wiederaufforstung f

real, in rem · dinglich

real account, impersonal account · Sachkonto n

real action (of the civil law) [It includes personal as well as real property] · dingliche Klage f nach bürgerlichem Recht

real claim, demand in rem, real demand, claim in rem · dingliche Forderung f, dingliches Verlangen n

(real) composition [In English ecclesiastical law. An agreement, made between the owner of land(s), and a parson or vicar, with the consent of the ordinary and the patron, that such land(s) shall, for the future, be discharged from payment of tithes by reason of some · land(s), or other real recompense given to the parson or vicar, in lieu and satisfaction thereof] · Zehntenvergleich m

real debt, debt in rem · dingliche Schuld f

real demand, claim in rem, real claim, demand in rem · dingliche Forderung f, dingliches Verlangen n

real direct evidence, real direct proof, direct real evidence, direct real proof · unmittelbarer Realbeweis m

(real) estate, (real) property, property of land(s), land(ed) property, estate in (real) property, (estate in) realty, immov(e)able property, fixed property; immov(e)ables [International Private Law] [The degree, nature, extent, and quality of interest or property that one has in land. Abbreviated "est.". Many real estate terms with undefined or ambiguous meanings are widely used. Thus, in law, "real property" is used as an antithesis to "personal property," and both are used to signify either rights or physical objects. Sometimes, "realty" and "personalty" are used to apply to things, the term "property" being reserved for rights; but, in common language, "property" is frequently used to signify a parcel of land and its improvements. The term "real estate" is no more precise, for in common parlance it may mean land and improvements, or rights in land and improvements, whether technically real or personal property. In the expression, "real estate market," reference is usually to the sale or transfer of any of the rights, principally fees and leaseholds, and the pledge of these interests by execution of mortgages or their equivalent] · Bodenvermögen n, Landvermögen, Grund(stücks)vermögen, Bodengut, Grund(stücks)gut, Immobiliarvermögen, Immobiliargut n, Immobilienvermögen, Immobiliengut, unbewegliches Vermögen, unbewegliches Gut, Liegenschaft f

(real) estate, (real) property, realty, estate in land(s), immov(e)able estate, fixed estate, landholding, land(ed) property, tenancy (of land(s)); immov(e)ables [International Private Law] [Estates in land(s) are divided into (a) freehold estates and (b) estates less than freehold] · Bodenbesitz(stand) m, Grund(stücks)besitz(stand), Landbesitz(stand), Immobilienbesitz(stand), Immobiliarbesitz(stand), Liegenschaft(en) f (pl), Immobilie(n) f (pl), (unbeweglicher) Besitz(stand), liegendes Gut n, ungereides Gut

(real) estate acquisition → (real) property acquisition

(real) estate acquisition right → land acquisition right

(real) estate act → law of land (possession)

((real) estate) agent → ((real) estate) broker

(real) estate appraisal → (real) property (e)valuation

(real) estate appraiser → (real) property appraiser

(real) estate area market, (real) property market, market in (building) land, (building) (land) area market, (building) land market · Grundstücksmarkt *m*, (Bau)Landmarkt, (Bau)Bodenmarkt

(real) estate barrister, realty barrister, conveyancer, land barrister, conveyancing barrister, (real) property barrister · Grundstücksspezialist *m*, Grundstücksadvokat *m*

(real) estate board, (real) property board, realty board · Grundstücksamt *n*, Liegenschaftsamt

((real) estate) broker, ((real) estate) dealer, ((real) estate) agent, (real) property agent, land agent; realtor (US); excambiator [*obsolete*]; factor [*Scots law*]; broc(c)arius, broccator, abrocator, correctarius [*Latin*] · Grund(stücks)makler *m*, Landmakler, (Boden)Makler, Grund(stücks)händler, Landhändler, Bodenhändler, Liegenschaftsmakler, Liegenschaftshändler

((real) estate) brokerage company, (real) property brokerage company, land brokerage company, land-broker agency, land(-jobber) agency · (Boden)Maklerfirma *f*, Landmaklerfirma, Grund(stücks)maklerfirma, Bodenmakelei *f*, Grund(stücks)makelei, Landmakelei, Grund(stücks)maklerbüro *n*, Grund(stücks)mäklerbüro

(real) estate builder → developer

(real) estate builders' law → developer's law

(real) estate business, (real) property business, land(s) business, transaction in (real) estate, transaction in (real) property, transaction in land(s), realty business, transaction in realties · Bodengeschäft *n*, Bodenhandel *m*, Grund(stücks)geschäft, Grund(stücks)handel, Liegenschaftsgeschäft, Liegenschaftshandel, Landgeschäft, Landhandel, Immobiliengeschäft, Immobilienhandel, Immobiliargeschäft, Immobiliarhandel

(real) estate certifier → (real) property appraiser

(real) estate company → (real) property company

(real) estate compensation (court) action, (real) property compensation (court) action, (real) estate indemnity (court) action, (real) property indemnity (court) action, (real) estate indemnification (court) action, (real) property indemnification (court) action, (real) estate liquidated damages (court) action, (real) property liquidated damages (court) action, land compensation (court) action, land indemnity (court) action, land indemnification (court) action, land liquidated damages (court) action, realty compensation (court) action, realty indemnification (court) action, realty indemnity (court) action, realty liquidated damages (court) action · Grund(stücks)schadensersatzklage *f*, Grund(stücks)entschädigungsklage, Landschadensersatzklage, Landentschädigungsklage, Bodenschadensersatzklage, Bodenentschädigungsklage

(real) estate consortium → (real) estate syndicate

(real) estate contract, (real) property contract, land contract, realty contract · Grundstücksvertrag *m*, Landvertrag, Bodenvertrag

(real) estate contract → (real) property (purchase) contract

(real) estate control → land control

(real) estate credit, (real) property credit, land(s) credit, realty credit · Grund(stücks)kredit *m*, Landkredit, Bodenkredit, Hypothekenkredit, Liegenschaftskredit, Immobiliarkredit, Immobilienkredit [*Durch Eintragung einer Hypothek auf ein Grundstück gewährter Kredit*]

(real) estate credit bank, (real) property credit bank, realty credit bank, land(s) credit bank · Grundkreditbank *f*, Landkreditbank, Bodenkreditbank

((real) estate) dealer → ((real) estate) broker

(real) estate demise → (real) estate lease(hold)

(real) estate depreciation fund, (real) property depreciation fund, land(s) depreciation fund, realty depreciation fund · Grund(stücks)entwertungsfonds *m*, Landentwertungsfonds, Bodenentwertungsfonds, Liegenschaftsentwertungsfonds, Immobiliarentwertungsfonds, Immobilienentwertungsfonds

(real) estate developer → developer

(real) estate developer's law → developer's law

(real) estate (e)valuation → (real) property (e)valuation

(real) estate exchange, (real) property exchange, land(s) exchange, barter of land for land, exchange of realty, realty exchange, exchange of land(s), exchange of (real) estate, exchange of (real) property · Boden(aus)tausch *m*, Land(aus)tausch, Grund(stücks)(aus)-tausch, Liegenschafts(aus)tausch, Immobiliar(aus)tausch, Immobilien-(aus)tausch, Flächen(aus)tausch

(real) estate exchange plan, realty exchange plan, barter-of-land-for-land plan, (real) property exchange plan · Grund(stücks)tauschplan *m*, (Boden)Tauschplan, Landtauschplan

(real) estate finance act, (real) property finance act, land(s) finance act, land(s) finance law, realty finance act, realty finance law, realty finance statute, land(s) finance statute, (real) estate finance law, (real) estate finance statute, (real) property finance statute, (real) property finance law · Grund(stücks)finanzierungsgesetz *n*, Bodenfinanzierungsgesetz, Landfinanzierungsgesetz, Liegenschaftsfinanzierungsgesetz, Immobiliarfinanzierungsgesetz, Immobilienfinanzierungsgesetz

(real) estate financing, (real) property financing, land(s) financing, realty financing · Grund(stücks)finanzierung *f*, Bodenfinanzierung, Landfinanzierung, Liegenschaftsfinanzierung, Immobilienfinanzierung, Immobiliarfinanzierung

(real) estate firm, (real) property firm, realty firm, land(s) firm · Liegenschaftsfirma *f*, Bodenfirma, Terrainfirma, Landfirma, Immobilienfirma, Grundstücksfirma, Immobiliarfirma

(real) estate for life, estate in land(s) for life, land(ed) estate for life, immov(e)able estate for life, fixed estate for life, life estate; immov(e)able for life [*International Private Law*] [*The holder of a life estate can use and enjoy if only during his life. Life estates are of two classes: (a) those created by deed or will and (b) those created by law. Life estates created by law are: (1) dower; (2) curtesy, and (3) homestead*] · Bodenbesitz(stand) *m* auf Lebenszeit, Grund(stücks)besitz(stand) auf Lebenszeit, Landbesitz(stand) auf Lebenszeit, lebenslanger Bodenbesitz(stand), lebenslanger Grund(stücks)besitz-(stand), lebenslanger Landbesitz(stand)

(real) estate fund, (real) property fund, land(s) fund, realty fund · Grund(stücks)(investment)fonds *m*, Land(investment)fonds, Boden(investment)fonds, Immobilienfonds, Liegenschaftsfonds, Immobiliarfonds

(real) estate grant → land(s) grant

(real) estate held by one person, (real) property held by one person, (real) estate in severalty, (real) property in severalty, severalty, realty held by one person, realty in severalty · einzelner Grund(stücks)besitz(stand) *m*, einzelner (Land)Besitz(stand), einzelner Bodenbesitz(stand), einzelner Immaterialgüterbesitz(stand), einzelner Immobiliarbesitz(stand), einzelner Immobilienbesitz(stand), einzelnes Gut *n*

(real) estate held in trust, (real) property held in trust, land(s) held in trust, trust (real) estate, trust (real) property, trust land(s) · Treuhandgrund(stück) *m*, *(n)*, Treuhandboden *m*, Treuhandland *n*, Treuhandimmobilie *f*

(real) estate held jointly → (real) estate of joint tenancy

(real) estate holder → (land) holder

(real) estate indemnification (court) action → (real) estate compensation (court) action

((real) estate in) fee simple on condition subsequent · (Land)Besitz(stand) *m* der bei Eintritt der Bedingung erst nach einer Erklärung des Veräußerers an ihn zurückfiel, Bodenbesitz(stand) der bei Eintritt der Bedingung erst nach einer Erklärung des Veräußerers an ihn zurückfiel, Grund(stücks)besitz(stand) der bei Eintritt der Bedingung erst nach einer Erklärung des Veräußerers an ihn zurückfiel, Liegenschaftsbesitz(stand) der bei Eintritt der Bedingung erst nach einer Erklärung des Veräußerers an ihn zurückfiel, Immobilienbesitz(stand) der bei Eintritt der Bedingung erst nach einer Erklärung des Veräußerers an ihn zurückfiel, Immobiliarbesitz(stand) der bei Eintritt der Bedingung erst nach einer Erklärung des Veräußerers an ihn zurückfiel

(real) estate in fee simple determinable, fee simple determinable, (real) property in fee simple determinable, realty in fee simple determinable · Besitz(stand) *m* der bei Eintritt einer Bedingung ipso iure auf den Veräußerer zurückfiel, Landbesitz(stand) der bei Eintritt einer Bedingung ipso iure auf den Veräußerer zurückfiel, Bodenbesitz(stand) der bei Eintritt einer Bedingung ipso iure auf den Veräußerer zurückfiel

(real) estate in severalty, (real) property in severalty, severalty, realty held by one person, realty in severalty, (real) estate held by one person, (real) property held by one person · einzelner Grund(stücks)besitz(stand) *m*, einzelner (Land)Besitz(stand), einzelner Bodenbesitz(stand), einzelner Immaterialgüterbesitz(stand), einzelner Immobiliarbesitz(stand), einzelner Immobilienbesitz(stand), einzelnes Gut *n*

(real) estate insurance, (real) property insurance, land(s) insurance, realty insurance · Immobilienversicherung *f*, Immobiliarversicherung, Liegenschaftsversicherung

(real) estate inventory, (real) property inventory, land(s) inventory, realty inventory · Bodennachlaßverzeichnis *n*, Liegenschaftsnachlaßverzeichnis, Grund(stücks)nachlaßverzeichnis,

(real) estate investment — (real) estate of joint tenancy

Immobiliennachlaßverzeichnis, Landnachlaßverzeichnis, Immobiliarnachlaßverzeichnis

(real) estate investment, (real) property investment, realty investment, land(s) investment · Liegenschaftsinvestition f, Landinvestition, Bodeninvestition, Terraininvestition, Grundstückinvestition, Immobiliarinvestition, Immobilieninvestition

(real) estate investment project, (real) property investment project, realty investment project · (Liegenschafts)-Objekt n

(real) estate investment trust → land(s) investment trust

(real) estate law, realty law, land law, possessory land law, law of land (possession), land(ed) estate law, law of (real) estate, law of realty, law of land(ed) estate, law of the land; lex terrae [Latin] · Besitzrecht n, Grund(stücks)besitzrecht, Immobiliar(besitz)recht, Immobilien(besitz)recht, Liegenschaftsrecht, objektives Besitzrecht, (objektives) Boden(besitz)recht, objektives Immobiliarbesitzrecht, objektives Immobilienbesitzrecht, (objektives) Landbesitzrecht, (objektives) Grund(stücks)recht, Grundeigentumsverfassung f

(real) estate lease (agreement), (real) property lease (agreement), (land) lease (agreement), (land) tenancy agreement, realty lease (agreement), lease [*The document used to bring into existence a term of years*] · (Land)Pachtvertrag m, (Land)Pachtbrief, Bodenpachtvertrag, Bodenpachtbrief, Grund(stücks)pachtvertrag, Grund(stücks)pachtbrief, Immobilienpachtvertrag, Immobilienpachtbrief, Immobiliarpachtvertrag, Immobiliarpachtbrief m, Liegenschaftspachtvertrag, Liegenschaftspachtbrief

(real) estate lease(hold), (real) property lease(hold), (real) estate tenancy, (real) property tenancy, (real) estate demise, (real) property demise, demise of (real) estate, demise of (real) property, tenancy of (real) estate, tenancy of (real) property, lease(hold) of (real) estate, lease(hold) of (real) property, land(s) lease(hold), lease(hold) of land(s) · Grund(stücks)pacht f, Pacht, Liegenschaftspacht, Landpacht, Bodenpacht, Immobilienpacht, Immobiliarpacht

(real) estate leasing, (real) estate demising, (real) property leasing, (real) property demising, realty leasing, realty demising, land(s) leasing, land(s) demising, letting (out on lease) of (real) estate · Immobilienverpachten n, Vergeben von Nutzungsrecht(en) an Immobilien

(real) estate lessee → (land) holder

(real) estate limitation act → (real) property limitation act

(real) estate liquidated damages (court) action → (real) estate compensation (court) action

(real) estate management, land(s) management, realty management, (real) property management · Grund(stücks)-verwaltung f, Landverwaltung, Bodenverwaltung, Liegenschaftsverwaltung, Immobilienverwaltung, Immobiliarverwaltung

(real) estate management, (real) property management, land(s) management, management of (real) property, management of (real) estate, management of land(s), realty management, management of realty · Grundbesitzbetreuung f, Verwaltungsbetreuung

(real) estate management agent, (real) property management agent, realty management agent · Grundbesitzbetreuer m, Verwaltungsbetreuer

(real) estate management plan, (real) property management plan, realty management plan · Grundbesitzbetreuungsplan m, Verwaltungsbetreuungsplan

(real) estate manager, (real) property manager, land(s) manager, realty manager · Grund(stücks)verwalter m, Bodenverwalter, Liegenschaftsverwalter, Landverwalter, Immobiliarverwalter, Immobilienverwalter

(real) estate market, (real) property market, market in (building) land, (building) (land) area market, (building) land market · (Bau)Bodenmarkt m, (Bau)Landmarkt, (Bau)Grundstücksmarkt

(real) estate mortgage, (real) property mortgage, realty mortgage, mortgage on land(ed property) [*A conveyance of the title to land(s) to secure the performance of some act(ion) or obligation, with a clause stating that in case the act(ion) or obligation is performed as agreed, the conveyance shall be of no effect*] · Grund(stücks)hypothek f, Landhypothek, Bodenhypothek, Realhypothek, Liegenschaftshypothek, Immobilienhypothek, Immobiliarhypothek

(real) estate mortgagee, (real) property mortgagee, (real) estate mortgage creditor, (real) property mortgage creditor · Immobiliarhypothek(en)gläubiger m, Immobilienhypothek(en)gläubiger, Immobilienhypothekargläubiger, Immobiliarhypothekargläubiger, Immobiliarhypothek(en)empfänger, Immobilienhypothek(en)empfänger

(real) estate occupier → (land) holder

(real) estate of joint tenancy, (real) property of joint tenancy, realty of joint tenancy, joint tenancy, joint holding, (real) estate held jointly, (real) property held jointly, realty held jointly [*The principal feature of this estate is that if one of the joint tenants dies, the survivor(s)*

(real) estate owner — (real) estate transaction judg(e)ment 852

take(s) the whole estate and nothing passes to the heirs or devisees of the deceased joint tenant. Joint tenancy has been abolished except in the case of trustees and executors] · Grund(stücks)besitz(stand) *m* zur gesamten Hand, (Land)Besitz(stand) zur gesamten Hand, Bodenbesitz(stand) zur gesamten Hand, Immaterialgüterbesitz(stand) zur gesamten Hand, Immobilienbesitz(stand) zur gesamten Hand, Gut *n* zur gesamten Hand, Immobiliarbesitz(stand) zur gesamten Hand

(real) estate owner → (real) property owner

(real) estate policy, (real) property policy, land(s) policy · Grund(stücks)politik *f*, Bodenpolitik, Landpolitik, Liegenschaftspolitik, Immobiliarpolitik, Immobilienpolitik

(real) estate possessor, (real) property possessor, realty possessor, landed estate possessor, land possessor, land(ed) property possessor, land holder, possessor of land, possessor of (real) estate, possessor of (real) property, tenant of land, holder of land, land tenant · Grund(stücks)besitzer *m*, Landbesitzer, Bodenbesitzer, Immobilienbesitzer, Immobiliarbesitzer, Liegenschaftsbesitzer

(real) estate practice, (real) property practice, realty practice, land(s) practice · Grundstückswesen *n*, Liegenschaftswesen, Immobiliarwesen, Immobilienwesen

(real) estate promoter → developer

(real) estate promoter's law → developer's law

(real) estate proprietor → (real) property owner

(real) estate purchase, (real) property purchase, (building) land purchase, purchase of (real) estate, purchase of (real) property, purchase of (building) land · Grund(stücks)kauf *m*, (Bau)Landkauf, (Bau)Bodenkauf, Liegenschaftskauf [*Österreich: Grundeinlösung f*]

(real) estate (purchase) contract → (real) property (purchase) contract

(real) estate sale, realty sale, land(s) sale, sale of realty, sale of (real) property, sale of (real) estate, sale of land(s), (real) property sale · Grund(stücks)verkauf *m*, Immobilienverkauf, Immobiliarverkauf, Landverkauf, Bodenverkauf, Liegenschaftsverkauf

(real) estate solicitor, (real) property solicitor, realty solicitor, conveyancer, conveyancor, conveyancing solicitor · Grundstücksanwalt *m*, Liegenschaftsanwalt

(real) estate speculation, (real) property speculation, speculation in (real) estate, speculation in (real) property, land(s) speculation, speculation in land(s), realty speculation, speculation in realty · Grund(stücks)spekulation *f*, Bodenspekulation, Landspekulation, Liegenschaftsspekulation, Immobiliarspekulation, Immobilienspekulation

(real) estate speculator, (real) property speculator, land(s) speculator, realty speculator · Bodenspekulant *m*, Landspekulant, Grund(stücks)spekulant, Liegenschaftsspekulant, Immobiliarspekulant, Immobilienspekulant

(real) estate statute → law of land (possession)

(real) estate surface, (real) property surface, land surface, realty surface, surface of realty, surface of (real) estate, surface of (real) property, surface of land · Grund(stücks)oberfläche *f*, Bodenoberfläche, Landoberfläche

(real) estate syndicate, (real) property syndicate, (real) estate consortium, (real) property consortium, land(s) syndicate, land(s) consortium, (real) estate underwriting group, (real) property underwriting group, land(s) underwriting group, realty syndicate, realty consortium, realty underwriting group · Grund(stücks)konsortium *n*, Bodenkonsortium, Landkonsortium, Liegenschaftskonsortium, Immobiliarkonsortium, Immobilienkonsortium

(real) estate tax, (real) property tax, land(s) tax; capitatio terrena [*Latin*]; realty tax, tax on realty, tax on (real) estate, tax on land(s), tax on (real) property · Grund(besitz)steuer *f*, Grundstückssteuer

(real) estate tax reduction, (real) property tax reduction, realty tax reduction · Grund(stücks)steuerherabsetzung *f*

(real) estate tenancy → (real) estate lease(hold)

(real) estate tenant → (land) holder

(real) estate title, (real) property title, realty title, landed estate title, possession of land title, land (holding) title, land(ed) property title, possessory estate title, title to (real) estate, title to (real) property, title to realty, title to landed estate, title to possession of land, title to land(holding), title to landed property, title to possessory estate · Grund(stücks)besitz(rechts)titel *m*, Landbesitz(rechts)titel, Bodenbesitz(rechts)titel, Immobiliarbesitz(rechts)titel, Immobilienbesitz(rechts)titel, Liegenschaftsbesitz(rechts)titel

(real) estate transaction judg(e)ment, (real) property transaction judg(e)ment, land(s) transaction judg(e)ment, realty transaction judg(e)ment · Bodenverkehrsurteil *n*, Grundstücksverkehrsurteil, Immobiliarverkehrsurteil, Immobilienverkehrsurteil, Liegenschaftsverkehrsurteil

(real) estate transaction law, land(s) transaction law, law for dealing with land(s), (real) property transaction law · Bodenrecht *n,* Grundstücksverkehrsrecht, Liegenschaftsrecht, Immobiliarrecht, Immobilienrecht

(real) estate transactions, (real) property transactions, land(s) transactions, dealing with land(s), realty transactions [*Acquiring, holding and disposing of land*] · Bodenverkehr *m,* Grundstücksverkehr, Liegenschaftsverkehr, Immobiliarverkehr, Immobilienverkehr

(real) estate transfer cost(s), (real) property transfer cost(s), realty transfer cost(s) · Grund(stücks)erwerbskosten *f*

(real) estate transfer permission, (real) property transfer permission, permission for (real) estate transactions, permission for (real) property transactions, permission to deal with land(s), permission for realty transactions, realty transfer permission, land transfer permission · Bodenverkehrserlaubnis *f,* Bodenverkehrsgenehmigung *f,* Grundstücksverkehrserlaubnis, Grundstücksverkehrsgenehmigung, Immobiliarverkehrserlaubnis, Immobiliarverkehrsgenehmigung, Immobilienverkehrserlaubnis, Immobilienverkehrsgenehmigung, Liegenschaftsverkehrserlaubnis, Liegenschaftsverkehrsgenehmigung

(real) estate transfer tax, (real) property transfer tax, realty transfer tax · Grunderwerbssteuer *f,* Grundstückserwerbssteuer

(real) estate underwriting group → (real) estate syndicate

(real) estate usufruct, land(s) usufruct, realty usufruct, (real) property usufruct · Grund(stücks)(frucht)genuß *m,* Grund(stücks)nießbrauch *m,* Landgenuß, Landnießbrauch, Bodengenuß, Bodennießbrauch, Liegenschaftsgenuß, Liegenschaftsnießbrauch, Immobiliengenuß, Immobiliennießbrauch

(real) estate valuation → (real) property (e)valuation

real evidence, real proof; evidentia rei vel facti [*Latin*] · Augenscheinbeweis *m,* Realbeweis *m*

real income · Realeinkommen *n*

real interest → real right

realistic jurisprudence · Rechtspragmatismus *m*

reality of power politics · Realpolitik *f*

reality science, science of reality · Wirklichkeitswissenschaft *f*

realization, implementation · Verwirklichung *f*

realization of (a) plan, plan implementation, plan realization, implementation of (a) plan · Planverwirklichung *f,* Plandurchführung

to realize [*To convert any kind of property into money*] · zu Geld machen

to realize [*To receive the return(s) from an investment*] · einnehmen [*Ertrag*]

realized quantity · ausgeführte Menge *f* [*Bauarbeit(en)*]

realized work(s) · ausgeführte Arbeit(en) *f (pl)*

reallotment files · Abfindungsnachweis *m,* Abfindungsverzeichnis *n* [*Flurbereinigung*]

real mistake · tatsächlicher Irrtum *m,* wirklicher Irrtum

real money · wahres Geld *n*

real population, actual population, existing population · tatsächliche Bevölkerung *f,* wirkliche Bevölkerung, Istbevölkerung

real proof; evidentia rei vel facti [*Latin*]; real evidence · Augenscheinbeweis *m,* Realbeweis

(real) property, property of land(s), land(ed) property, estate in (real) property, (estate in) realty, immov(e)able property, fixed property; immov(e)ables [*International Private Law*], (real) estate [*The degree, nature, extent, and quality of interest or property that one has in land. Abbreviated "est.". Many real estate terms with undefined or ambiguous meanings are widely used. Thus, in law, "real property" is used as an antithesis to "personal property," and both are used to signify either rights or physical objects. Sometimes, "realty" and "personalty" are used to apply to things, the term "property" being reserved for rights; but, in common language, "property" is frequently used to signify a parcel of land and its improvements. The term "real estate" is no more precise, for in common parlance it may mean land and improvements, or rights in land and improvements, whether technically real or personal property. In the expression, "real estate market," reference is usually to the sale or transfer of any the rights, principally fees and leaseholds, and the pledge of these interests by execution of mortgages or their equivalent*] · Bodenvermögen *n,* Landvermögen, Grund(stücks)vermögen, Bodengut, Grund(stücks)gut, Immobiliarvermögen, Immobiliargut, Immobilienvermögen, Immobiliengut, unbewegliches Vermögen, unbewegliches Gut, Liegenschaft *f*

(real) property, realty, estate in land(s), immov(e)able estate, fixed estate, landholding, land(ed) property, tenancy (of land(s)); immov(e)ables [*International Private Law*]; (real) estate [*Estates in land(s) are divided into (a) freehold estates and (b) estates less than*

(real) property (ab)alienation contract — (real) property (e)valuation

freehold] · Bodenbesitz(stand) *m*, Grund(stücks)besitz(stand), Landbesitz(stand), Immobilienbesitz(stand), Immobiliarbesitz(stand), Liegenschaft(en) *f (pl)*, Immobilie(n) *f (pl)*, (unbeweglicher) Besitz(stand), liegendes Gut *n*, ungereides Gut

(real) property (ab)alienation contract, (real) property disposal contract, (real) estate (ab)alienation contract, (real) estate disposal contract, (real) (ab)alienation contract, land(s) disposal contract, realty (ab)alienation contract, realty disposal contract · Landveräußerungsvertrag *m*, Bodenveräußerungsvertrag, Immobilienveräußerungsvertrag, Liegenschaftsveräußerungsvertrag, Grund(stücks)veräußerungsvertrag, Immobiliarveräußerungsvertrag

(real) property acquisition, (real) estate acquisition, land(s) acquisition, acquisition of (real) property, acquisition of land(s), acquisition of (real) estate, acquisition of realty, realty acquisition · Grund(stücks)beschaffung *f*, Bodenbeschaffung, Landbeschaffung, Liegenschaftsbeschaffung, Immobiliarbeschaffung, Immobilienbeschaffung, Bodenerwerb, Grund(stücks)erwerb, Landerwerb, Liegenschaftserwerb, Immobiliarerwerb, Immobilienerwerb, Erwerb(ung) von Grund und Boden, Bodenerwerb(ung) *m,(f)*, Landerwerbung, Grund(stücks)erwerb(ung), Liegenschaftserwerb(ung), Immobiliarerwerb(ung), Immobilienerwerb(ung)

(real) property acquisition right → land acquisition right

(real) property act → law of land (possession)

(real) property agent → ((real) estate) broker

(real) property alienation contract → (real) property (ab)alienation contract

(real) property appraisal → (real) property (e)valuation

(real) property appraiser, (real) estate appraiser, (real) property certifier, (real) estate certifier, (real) property valuer, (real) estate valuer, land(s) appraiser, land(s) certifier, land(s) valuer, realty appraiser, realty certifier, realty valuer · Grund(stücks)(ab)schätzer *m*, Land(ab)schätzer, Boden(ab)schätzer, Liegenschafts(ab)schätzer, Immobiliar(ab)schätzer, Immobilien(ab)schätzer, Liegenschaftstaxator, Grund(stücks)taxator, Landtaxator, Bodentaxator, Immobilientaxator, Immobiliartaxator

(real) property barrister, (real) estate barrister, realty barrister, conveyancer, land barrister, conveyancing barrister · Grundstücksspezialist *m*, Grundstücksadvokat *m*

(real) property board, realty board, (real) estate board · Grundstücksamt *n*, Liegenschaftsamt

((real) property) broker → ((real) estate) broker

((real) property) brokerage → ((real) estate) broking

((real) property) broking → ((real) estate) broking

((real) property) broking company → ((real) estate) broking firm

((real) property) broking firm → ((real) estate) broking firm

(real) property builder → developer

(real) property builder's law → developer's law

(real) property business → (real) estate business

(real) property certifier → (real) property appraiser

(real) property company, realty company, (real) estate company, land(s) company · Grund(stücks)gesellschaft *f*, Bodengesellschaft, Landgesellschaft, Liegenschaftsgesellschaft, Immobiliargesellschaft, Immobiliengesellschaft, Terraingesellschaft

(real) property compensation (court) action → (real) estate compensation (court) action

(real) property consortium → (real) estate syndicate

(real) property contract, land contract, realty contract, (real) estate contract · Grundstücksvertrag *m*, Landvertrag, Bodenvertrag

(real) property contract → (real) property (purchase) contract

(real) property control → land control

(real) property credit → (real) estate credit

(real) property credit bank, realty credit bank, land(s) credit bank, (real) estate credit bank · Grundkreditbank *f*, Landkreditbank, Bodenkreditbank

(real) property dealer → ((real) estate) broker

(real) property demise → (real) estate lease(hold)

(real) property depreciation fund → (real) estate depreciation fund

(real) property developer → developer

(real) property developer's law → developer's law

(real) property (e)valuation, (real) property val., (real) property appraisal, (real) property appraisement, (real) estate (e)valuation, (real) estate val., (real) estate appraisal, (real) estate appraisement, land(s) (e)valuation, land(s) val., land(s) appraisal, land(s) appraisement, (e)valuation of (real) property, val. of (real) property, (e)valuation of (real) estate, val. of (real) estate, val. of land(s), (e)valuation of land(s), appraisal of (real) property, appraisal of (real) estate, appraisal of land(s), appraisement of (real) property, appraisement of (real) estate, appraisement of land(s) · Land(ab)schätzung f, Landbewertung, Grund(stücks)(ab)schätzung, Grund(stücks)bewertung, Boden(ab)schätzung, Bodenbewertung, Liegenschafts(ab)schätzung, Liegenschaftsbewertung, Immobilien(ab)schätzung, Immobilienbewertung, Immobiliar(ab)schätzung, Immobiliarbewertung, Landtaxierung, Bodentaxierung, Immobiliartaxierung, Immobilientaxierung, Grund(stücks)taxierung, Liegenschaftstaxierung

real property exchange → (real) estate exchange

(real) property exchange plan, (real) estate exchange plan, realty exchange plan, barter-of-land-for-land plan · Grund(stücks)tauschplan m, (Boden)Tauschplan, Landtauschplan

(real) property finance act → (real) estate finance act

(real) property financing → (real) estate financing

(real) property firm → (real) estate firm

(real) property for life, property of land(s) for life, land(ed) property for life, estate in (real) property for life, (estate in) realty for life, immov(e)able property for life, fixed property for life, life (real) property, life (estate in) realty, life property of land(s), life land[ed] property, life estate in (real) property, life fixed property, life immov(e)able property; life immov(e)ables, immov(e)eables for life [*International Private Law*] · Bodenvermögen n auf Lebenszeit, Landvermögen auf Lebenszeit, Grund(stücks)vermögen auf Lebenszeit, Bodengut n auf Lebenszeit, Grund(stücks)gut auf Lebenszeit, Liegenschaft f auf Lebenszeit, Immobiliarvermögen auf Lebenszeit, Immobiliargut auf Lebenszeit, Immobilienvermögen auf Lebenszeit, Immobiliengut auf Lebenszeit

(real) property fund → (real) estate fund

(real) property grant → land(s) grant

(real) property held by one person, (real) estate in severalty, (real) property in severalty, severalty, realty held by one person, realty in severalty, (real) estate held by one person · einzelner Grund(stücks)besitz(stand) m, einzelner (Land)Besitz(stand), einzelner Bodenbesitz(stand), einzelner Immaterialgüterbesitz(stand), einzelner Immobiliarbesitz(stand), einzelner Immobilienbesitz(stand), einzelnes Gut n

(real) property held in trust, land(s) held in trust, trust (real) estate, trust (real) property, trust land(s), (real) estate held in trust · Treuhandgrund(stück) m, (n), Treuhandboden m, Treuhandland n, Treuhandimmobilie f

(real) property held jointly → (real) estate of joint tenancy

(real) property holder → (land) property holder

(real) property indemnification (court) action → (real) estate compensation (court) action

((real) property in) fee simple (de)terminable → ((real) estate in) fee simple (de)terminable

(real) property in severalty, severalty, realty held by one person, realty in severalty, (real) estate held by one person, (real) property held by one person, (real) estate in severalty · einzelner Grund(stücks)besitz(stand) m, einzelner (Land)Besitz(stand), einzelner Bodenbesitz(stand), einzelner Immaterialgüterbesitz(stand), einzelner Immobiliarbesitz(stand), einzelner Immobilienbesitz(stand), einzelnes Gut n

(real) property insurance, land(s) insurance, realty insurance, (real) estate insurance · Immobiliarversicherung f, Immobiliarversicherung, Liegenschaftsversicherung

(real) property inventory, land(s) inventory, realty inventory, (real) estate inventory · Bodennachlaßverzeichnis n, Liegenschaftsnachlaßverzeichnis, Grund(stücks)nachlaßverzeichnis, Immobiliennachlaßverzeichnis, Landnachlaßverzeichnis, Immobiliarnachlaßverzeichnis

(real) property investment → (real) estate investment

(real) property investment project, realty investment project, (real) estate investment project · (Liegenschafts)Objekt n

(real) property investment trust → land(s) property investment trust

(real) property lease (agreement) → (real) estate lease (agreement)

(real) property lease(hold) → (real) estate lease(hold)

(real) property lessee → (land) holder

(real) property limitation act, (real) property limitation statute, (real) property limitation law, (real) estate limitation act, (real) estate limitation act, (real) estate limitation statute, (real) estate limitation law, land(s)limitation act, land(s) limitation law, land(s) limitation statute · Grund(stücks)verjährungsgesetz n, Landverjährungsgesetz, Bodenverjährungsgesetz, Liegenschaftsverjährungsgesetz, Immobiliarverjährungsgesetz, Immobilienverjährungsgesetz

(real) property liquidated damages — (real) property surface 856

(real) property liquidated damages (court) action → (real) estate compensation (court) action

(real) property management, (real) estate management, land(s) management realty management · Grund(stücks)verwaltung f, Landverwaltung, Bodenverwaltung, Liegenschaftsverwaltung, Immobilienverwaltung, Immobiliarverwaltung

(real) property management, land(s) management, management of (real) property, management of (real) estate, management of land(s), realty management, management of realty, (real) estate management · Grundbesitzbetreuung f, Verwaltungsbetreuung

(real) property management agent, realty management agent, (real) estate management agent · Grundbesitzbetreuer m, Verwaltungsbetreuer

(real) property management plan, realty management plan, (real) estate management plan · Grundbesitzbetreuungsplan m, Verwaltungsbetreuungsplan

(real) property manager, land(s) manager, realty manager, (real) estate manager · Grund(stücks)verwalter m, Bodenverwalter, Liegenschaftsverwalter, Landverwalter, Immobiliarverwalter, Immobilienverwalter

(real) property market, market in (building) land, (building) (land) area market, (building) land market, (real) estate market · (Bau)Bodenmarkt m, (Bau)Landmarkt, (Bau)Grundstücksmarkt

(real) property mortgage, realty mortgage, mortgage on land(ed property), (real) estate mortgage [*A conveyance of the title to land(s) to secure the performance of some act(ion) or obligation, with a clause stating that in case the act(ion) or obligation is performed as agreed, the conveyance shall be of no effect*] · Grund(stücks)hypothek f, Landhypothek, Bodenhypothek, Realhypothek, Liegenschaftshypothek, Immobilienhypothek, Immobiliarhypothek

(real) property mortgage creditor → (real) estate mortgagee

(real) property mortgagee → (real) estate mortgagee

(real) property occupier → (land) holder

(real) property of joint tenancy → (real) estate of joint tenancy

(real) property owner, (real) property proprietor, (real) estate owner, (real) estate proprietor, land(s) owner, land(s) proprietor, owner in fee simple, owner of freehold land(s), proprietor of freehold land(s), freeholder, parcel-owner, plot-owner, parcel-proprietor, plot-proprietor; terrarius [*Latin*] · Grund(stücks)eigentümer m, Landeigentümer, Bodeneigentümer, Liegenschaftseigentümer, Immobiliareigentümer, Immobilieneigentümer

(real) property policy, land(s) policy, (real) estate policy · Grund(stücks)politik f, Bodenpolitik, Landpolitik, Liegenschaftspolitik, Immobiliarpolitik, Immobilienpolitik

(real) property possessor → (real) estate possessor

(real) property promoter → developer

(real) property promoter's law → developer's law

(real) property proprietor → (real) property owner

(real) property purchase, (building) land purchase, purchase of (real) estate, purchase of (real) property, purchase of (building) land, (real) estate purchase · Grund(stücks)kauf m, (Bau)Landkauf, (Bau)Bodenkauf, Liegenschaftskauf [*Österreich: Grundeinlösung f*]

(real) property (purchase) contract, (real) estate (purchase) contract, land(s) (purchase) contract, realty (purchase) contract, contract for purchase of (real) property, contract for purchase of (real) estate, contract for purchase of realty, contract for purchase of land(s) · Grund(stücks)kaufvertrag m, Bodenkaufvertrag, Landkaufvertrag, Liegenschaftskaufvertrag, Immobiliarkaufvertrag, Immobilienkaufvertrag

real property right · unbewegliches Sachenrecht n

(real) property sale, (real) estate sale, realty sale, land(s) sale, sale of realty, sale of (real) property, sale of (real) estate, sale of land(s) · Grund(stücks)verkauf m, Immobilienverkauf, Immobiliarverkauf, Landverkauf, Bodenverkauf, Liegenschaftsverkauf

(real) property speculation, speculation in (real) estate, speculation in (real) property, land(s) speculation, speculation in land(s), realty speculation, speculation in realty, (real) estate speculation · Grund(stücks)spekulation f, Bodenspekulation, Landspekulation, Liegenschaftsspekulation, Immobiliarspekulation, Immobilienspekulation

(real) property speculator, land(s) speculator, realty speculator, (real) estate speculator · Bodenspekulant m, Landspekulant, Grund(stücks)spekulant, Liegenschaftsspekulant, Immobiliarspekulant, Immobilienspekulant

(real) property statute → law of land (possession)

(real) property surface, land surface, realty surface, surface of realty, surface of (real) estate, surface of (real) property, surface of land, (real) estate surface · Grund(stücks)oberfläche f, Bodenoberfläche, Landoberfläche

(real) property syndicate → (real) estate syndicate

(real) property tax, land(s) tax; capitatio terrena [*Latin*]; realty tax, tax on realty, tax on (real) estate, tax on land(s), tax on (real) property, (real) estate tax · Grund(besitz)steuer f, Grundstückssteuer

(real) property tax reduction, realty tax reduction, (real) estate tax reduction · Grund(stücks)steuerherabsetzung f

(real) property tenancy → (real) estate lease(hold)

(real) property tenant → (land) holder

(real) property title → (real) estate title

(real) property transaction judg(e)ment, land(s) transaction judg(e)ment, realty transaction judg(e)ment, (real) estate transaction judg(e)ment · Bodenverkehrsurteil n, Grundstücksverkehrsurteil, Immobiliarverkehrsurteil, Immobilienverkehrsurteil, Liegenschaftsverkehrsurteil

(real) property transaction law, (real) estate transaction law, land(s) transaction law, law for dealing with land(s) · Bodenrecht n, Grundstücksverkehrsrecht, Liegenschaftsrecht, Immobiliarrecht, Immobilienrecht

(real) property transactions, land(s) transactions, dealing with land(s), realty transactions, (real) estate transactions [*Acquiring, holding and disposing of land*] · Bodenverkehr m, Grundstücksverkehr, Liegenschaftsverkehr, Immobiliarverkehr, Immobilienverkehr

(real) property transfer cost(s), realty transfer cost(s), (real) estate transfer cost(s) · Grund(stücks)erwerbskosten f

(real) property transfer permission, permission for (real) estate transactions, permission for (real) property transactions, permission for land transactions, permission to deal with land(s), permission for realty transactions, realty transfer permission, land transfer permission, (real) estate transfer permission · Bodenverkehrserlaubnis f, Bodenverkehrsgenehmigung f, Grundstücksverkehrserlaubnis, Grundstücksverkehrsgenehmigung, Immobiliarverkehrserlaubnis, Immobiliarverkehrsgenehmigung, Immobilienverkehrserlaubnis, Immobilienverkehrsgenehmigung, Liegenschaftsverkehrserlaubnis, Liegenschaftsverkehrsgenehmigung

(real) property transfer tax, realty transfer tax, (real) estate transfer tax · Grunderwerbssteuer f, Grundstückserwerbssteuer

(real) property underwriting group → (real) estate syndicate

(real) property usufruct, (real) estate usufruct, land(s) usufruct, realty usufruct · Grund(stücks)(frucht)genuß m, Grund(stücks)nießbrauch m, Landgenuß, Landnießbrauch, Bodengenuß, Bodennießbrauch, Liegenschaftsgenuß, Liegenschaftsnießbrauch, Immobiliengenuß, Immobiliennießbrauch

(real) property valuation → (real) property (e)valuation

(real) property valuer → (real) property appraiser

real representative; heres, haeres [*Latin*]; heir (male) · Erbe m

real right; jus in re [*Latin*]; complete and full right, full and complete right [*A right existing or subject of property, inherent in his relation to it, implying complete ownership with possession*] · (dingliches) Recht n auf Beherrschung einer Sache im ganzen, volles Recht zu einer Sache, volles Recht zur Sache

real right, real interest, absolute right, absolute interest, right in rem, interest in rem · uneingeschränktes (subjektives) Recht n, unbeschränktes (subjektives) Recht, unbedingtes (subjektives) Recht, absolutes (subjektives) Recht, subjektives uneingeschränktes Recht, subjektives unbeschränktes Recht, subjektives unbedingtes Recht, subjektives absolutes Recht

real right according to the German Civil Code · Recht n an der Sache [*Laut B.G.B. sind „dingliches Recht" und „Recht an der Sache" nicht synonym. „Recht an der Sache" ist nach B.G.B. ein dingliches Recht, aber es gibt auch dingliche Rechte die im Sinne des B.G.B. nicht Rechte an der Sache sind*]

real security · Hypothek f auf Grundeigentum, Grundeigentumshypothek

real servitude, landed servitude, pr(a)edial servitude; servitus praediorum [*Latin*] [*A servitude affecting land*] · Realservitut n, f, Prädialservitut

real tax · Realsteuer f

real tax reform · Realsteuerreform f

real thing, thing immov(e)able, thing real, chose local, local chose; immov(e)able [*International Private Law*]; immov(e)able thing · Immobilie f, unbeweglicher Gegenstand m, unbewegliche (Einzel)Sache f, unbewegliches Ding n, unbewegliches Rechtsobjekt n

real things, immov(e)able things, choses local, local choses; immov(e)ables [*International Private Law*]; things immov(e)able, things real · Immobilien f pl, unbewegliche (Einzel)Sachen f pl, unbewegliche Dinge n pl, unbewegliche Gegenstände *mpl*, unbewegliche Rechtsobjekte *npl*

real time · Echtzeit *f*

realtor (US) → ((real) estate) broker

realty, estate in land(s), immov(e)able estate, fixed estate, landholding, land(ed) property, tenancy (of land(s)); immov(e)ables [*International Private Law*]; (real) estate, (real) property [*Estates in land(s) are divided into (a) freehold estates and (b) estates less than freehold*] · Bodenbesitz(stand) *m*, Grund(stücks)besitz(stand), Landbesitz(stand), Immobilienbesitz(stand), Immobiliarbesitz(stand), Liegenschaft(en) *f (pl)*, Immobilie(n) *f (pl)*, (unbeweglicher) Besitz(stand), liegendes Gut *n*, ungereides Gut

realty acquisition → (real) property acquisition

realty act → law of land (possession)

realty appraiser → (real) property appraiser

realty barrister, conveyancer, land barrister, conveyancing barrister, (real) property barrister, (real) estate barrister · Grundstücksspezialist *m*, Grundstücksadvokat *m*

realty board, (real) estate board, (real) property board · Grundstücksamt *n*, Liegenschaftsamt

realty builder → developer

realty builder's law → developer's law

realty business → (real) estate business

realty certifier → (real) property appraiser

realty company → (real) property company

realty compensation (court) action, realty indemnification (court) action, realty indemnity (court) action, realty liquidated damages (court) action, (real) estate compensation (court) action, (real) property compensation (court) action, (real) estate indemnity (court) action, (real) property indemnity (court) action, (real) estate indemnification (court) action, (real) property indemnification (court) action, (real) estate liquidated damages (court) action, (real) property liquidated damages (court) action, land compensation (court) action, land indemnity (court) action, land indemnification (court) action, land liquidated damages (court) action · Grund(stücks)schadenersatzklage *f*, Grund(stücks)entschädigungsklage, Landschadenersatzklage, Landentschädigungsklage, Bodenschadenersatzklage, Bodenentschädigungsklage

realty consortium → (real) estate syndicate

realty contract, (real) estate contract, (real) property contract, land contract · Grundstücksvertrag *m*, Landvertrag, Bodenvertrag

realty contract → (real) property (purchase) contract

realty control, land control, (real) estate control, (real) property control · Grundstückslenkung *f*, Bodenlenkung, Landlenkung

realty credit bank, land(s) credit bank, (real) estate credit bank, (real) property credit bank · Grundkreditbank *f*, Landkreditbank, Bodenkreditbank

realty demising → (real) estate leasing

realty depreciation fund → (real) estate depreciation fund

(realty) developer → developer

(realty) developer's law → developer's law

realty exchange, exchange of land(s), exchange of (real) estate, exchange of (real) property, (real) estate exchange, (real) property exchange, land(s) exchange, barter of land for land, exchange of realty · Boden(aus)tausch *m*, Land(aus)tausch, Grund(stücks)(aus)tausch, Liegenschafts(aus)tausch, Immobiliar(aus)tausch, Immobilien(aus)tausch, Flächen(aus)tausch

realty exchange plan, barter-of-land-for-land plan, (real) property exchange plan, (real) estate exchange plan · Grund(stücks)tauschplan *m*, (Boden)Tauschplan, Landtauschplan

realty finance act → (real) estate finance act

realty financing → (real) estate financing

realty firm → (real) estate firm

realty for life → (real) property for life

realty fund → (real) estate fund

realty grant → land(s) grant

realty held by one person, realty in severalty, (real) estate held by one person, (real) property held by one person, (real) estate in severalty, (real) property in severalty, severalty · einzelner Grund(stücks)besitz(stand) *m*, einzelner (Land)Besitz(stand), einzelner Bodenbesitz(stand), einzelner Immaterialgüterbesitz(stand), einzelner Immobiliarbesitz(stand), einzelner Immobilienbesitz(stand), einzelnes Gut *n*

realty held jointly → (real) estate of joint tenancy

realty holder → (land) holder

(realty in) fee simple (de)terminable → ((real) estate in) fee simple (de)terminable

realty in severalty, (real) estate held by one person, (real) property held by one person, (real) estate in severalty, (real) property in severalty, severalty, realty held by one person · einzelner Grund(stücks)besitz(stand) *m*, einzelner (Land)Besitz(stand), einzelner Bodenbesitz(stand), einzelner Immaterialgüterbesitz(stand), einzelner Immobiliarbesitz(stand), einzelner Immobilienbesitz(stand), einzelnes Gut *n*

realty insurance, (real) estate insurance, (real) property insurance, land(s) insurance · Immobilienversicherung *f*, Immobiliarversicherung, Liegenschaftsversicherung

realty interest → interest in (real) estate

realty inventory, (real) estate inventory, (real) property inventory, land(s) inventory · Bodennachlaßverzeichnis *n*, Liegenschaftsnachlaßverzeichnis, Grund(stücks)nachlaßverzeichnis, Immobiliennachlaßverzeichnis, Landnachlaßverzeichnis, Immobiliarnachlaßverzeichnis

realty investment → (real) estate investment

realty investment trust → land(s) investment trust

realty law → (real) estate law

realty lease (agreement), lease, (real) estate lease (agreement), (real) property lease (agreement), (land) lease (agreement), (land) tenancy agreement [*The document used to bring into existence a term of years*] · (Land)Pachtvertrag *m*, (Land)Pachtbrief, Bodenpachtvertrag, Bodenpachtbrief, Grund(stücks)pachtvertrag, Grund(stücks)pachtbrief, Immobilienpachtvertrag, Immobilienpachtbrief, Immobiliarpachtvertrag, Immobiliarpachtbrief *m*, Liegenschaftspachtvertrag, Liegenschaftspachtbrief

realty leasing → (real) estate leasing

realty lessee → (land) holder

realty management, (real) property management, (real) estate management, land(s) management · Grund(stücks)verwaltung *f*, Landverwaltung, Bodenverwaltung, Liegenschaftsverwaltung, Immobilienverwaltung, Immobiliarverwaltung

realty management, management of realty, (real) estate management, (real) property management, land(s) management, management of (real) property, management of (real) estate, management of land(s) · Grundbesitzbetreuung *f*, Verwaltungsbetreuung

realty management agent, (real) estate management agent, (real) property management agent · Grundbesitzbetreuer *m*, Verwaltungsbetreuer

realty management plan, (real) estate management plan, (real) property management plan · Grundbesitzbetreuungsplan *m*, Verwaltungsbetreuungsplan

realty manager, (real) estate manager, (real) property manager, land(s) manager · Grund(stücks)verwalter *m*, Bodenverwalter, Liegenschaftsverwalter, Landverwalter, Immobiliarverwalter, Immobilienverwalter

realty mortgage, mortgage on land(ed property), (real) estate mortgage, (real) property mortgage [*A conveyance of the title to land(s) to secure the performance of some act(ion) or obligation, with a clause stating that in case the act(ion) or obligation is performed as agreed, the conveyance shall be of no effect*] · Grund(stücks)hypothek *f*, Landhypothek, Bodenhypothek, Realhypothek, Liegenschaftshypothek, Immobilienhypothek, Immobiliarhypothek

realty occupier → (land) holder

realty of joint tenancy → (real) estate of joint tenancy

realty possessor → (real) estate possessor

realty practice → (real) estate practice

realty promoter → developer

realty promoter's law → developer's law

realty (purchase) contract → (real) property (purchase) contract

realty right → interest in (real) estate

realty sale, land(s) sale, sale of realty, sale of (real) property, sale of (real) estate, sale of land(s), (real) property sale, (real) estate sale · Grund(stücks)verkauf *m*, Immobilienverkauf, Immobiliarverkauf, Landverkauf, Bodenverkauf, Liegenschaftsverkauf

realty speculation, speculation in realty, (real) estate speculation, (real) property speculation, speculation in (real) estate, speculation in (real) property, land(s) speculation, speculation in land(s) · Grund(stücks)spekulation *f*, Bodenspekulation, Landspekulation, Liegenschaftsspekulation, Immobiliarspekulation, Immobilienspekulation

realty speculator, (real) estate speculator, (real) property speculator, land(s) speculator · Bodenspekulant *m*, Landspekulant, Grund(stücks)spekulant, Liegenschaftsspekulant, Immobiliarspekulant, Immobilienspekulant

realty statute → law of land (possession)

realty surface, surface of realty, surface of (real) estate, surface of (real) property, surface of land, (real) estate surface, (real) property surface, land surface · Grund(stücks)oberfläche *f*, Bodenoberfläche, Landoberfläche

realty syndicate → (real) estate syndicate

realty tax, tax on realty, tax on (real) estate, tax on land(s), tax on (real) property, (real) estate tax, (real) property tax, land(s) tax; capitatio terrena [*Latin*] · Grund(besitz)steuer *f*, Grundstückssteuer

realty tax reduction, (real) estate tax reduction, (real) property tax reduction · Grund(stücks)steuerherabsetzung *f*

realty tenant → (land) holder

realty transactions, (real) estate transactions, (real) property transactions, land(s) transactions, dealing with land(s) [*Acquiring, holding and disposing of land*] · Bodenverkehr *m*, Grundstücksverkehr, Liegenschaftsverkehr, Immobiliarverkehr, Immobilienverkehr

realty transfer cost(s), (real) estate transfer cost(s), (real) property transfer cost(s) · Grund(stücks)erwerbskosten *f*

realty transfer tax, (real) estate transfer tax, (real) property transfer tax · Grunderwerbssteuer *f*, Grundstückserwerbssteuer

realty underwriting group → (real) estate syndicate

realty usufruct, (real) property usufruct, (real) estate usufruct, land(s) usufruct · Grund(stücks)(frucht)genuß *m*, Grund(stücks)nießbrauch *m*, Landgenuß, Landnießbrauch, Bodengenuß, Bodennießbrauch, Liegenschaftsgenuß, Liegenschaftsnießbrauch, Immobiliengenuß, Immobiliennießbrauch

real value · Realwert *m*, Sachwert, Substanzwert [*Er setzt sich zusammen aus dem Wert des Grund(stück)es wenn es unbebaut wäre (= Bodenwert) und dem Wert der baulichen Anlage (= Bauwert)*]

reaping day, precaria, bind day, boon-day [*The day (up)on which a tenant was required to perform the service of bedrip*] · befohlener Erntearbeitstag *m*, Frontag auf besonderes Begehr

reapportionment → (territorial) reorganization

reapportionment act [*USA*] · Wahlkreiseinteilungsgesetz *n*

reappraisal, reappraisement, revaluation · Neu(ab)schätzung *f*, Neubewertung, Neutaxierung

reappraisal lease(hold), revaluation lease(hold) · Pacht *f* mit nach periodischen Schätzungen festgesetzter Rente

rear building · Hintergebäude *n*

rear (building) extension · rückwärtiger (Gebäude)Anbau *m*

rear extension → rear (building) extension

rear garden · Hintergarten *m*

rear-lot line · hintere Grundstücksgrenze *f*

rear yard · Hinterhof *m*

reason · Vernunft *f*

reason, cause, ground · Grund *m*

reasonable · vertretbar

reasonable [*This word has in law the prima facie meaning of reasonable in regard to those circumstances of which the actor, called on to act reasonably, knows or ought to know*] · sachgemäß

reasonable care · gehörige Bewachung *f* [*gemietete Sache*]

reasonable cause, reasonable ground · triftiger Grund *m*, vertretbarer Grund

reasonable diligence, reasonable care · zumutbare Sorgfalt *f*

reasonableness · Vertretbarkeit *f*

reasonable part [*In old English law. That share of a man's goods which the law gave to his wife and children after his decease*] · Pflichtterbteil *n*

reasonable person · denkender Mensch *m*

reasonable person standard · normale (rechts)verkehrstüchtige Person *f*

reasonable price · angemessener Preis *m*

reasonable-use rule · Angemessenheitsregel *f*

reasonably · vernünftigerweise

reasonably practicable · tunlich(st)

reasoned justification · Begründetheit *f*, Begründung *f*

reasoning, arguing [*The drawing of inferences or conclusions from known or assumed facts*] · Argumentieren *n*

reasoning mind · überlegender Verstand *m*

reasoning source, source of reasoning, perceptible source · Erkenntnisquelle *f*

reason of disaffirmance, reason of refusal, reason of rejection, reason of repudiation, reason of disaffirmation · Ablehnungsgrund *m*, (Ver)Weigerungsgrund, Zurückweisungsgrund, Versagungsgrund, Aufsagegrund

reason of suspicion, probable cause · Verdachtsgrund *m*

reason of termination · Beendigungsgrund *m*

reassessment, revaluation, revalorization · Aufwertung *f* [*Die Wiedergutmachung eines Teiles des durch eine Inflation an privaten Vermögen angerichteten Schadens*]

reassessment mortgage, revaluation mortgage, revalorized mortgage · Aufwertungshypothek *f*

reassurance, reinsurance · Rückversicherung *f*

rebate, abatement [*A proportionate reduction of a payment allowed for special reasons, e.g. for prompt payment*] · Abzug *m*, Rabatt *m*

rebate variance · Rabattabweichung *f*

rebooking · Umbuchung *f*

rebuilding, reconstruction · Aufbau *m*, Wiederaufbau [*Das Schaffen von Wohnraum oder von anderem auf die Dauer benutzbaren Raum durch Aufbau eines zerstörten Gebäudes oder durch Bebauung von Trümmerflächen. § 16 Abs. 1 Satz 1 des II.WobauG*]

rebuilding · (Wieder)Aufbau *m* im Hochbau

rebuilding activity, rebuilding operations · (Wieder)Aufbautätigkeit *f* im Hochbau

rebuilding area, rebuilding territory, reconstruction area, reconstruction territory · Aufbaugebiet *n*, Wiederaufbaugebiet *n*

rebuilding assistance, reconstruction assistance · (Wieder)Aufbauförderung *f*

rebuilding clause, reconstruction clause [*A clause in an insurance contract that the premium must be used to re-erect the building(s) insured*] · Aufbauklausel *f*, Wiederaufbauklausel *f*

rebuilding contract, reconstruction contract · Aufbauvertrag *m*, Wiederaufbauvertrag *m*

rebuilding duty, reconstruction duty, duty to reconstruct, duty to rebuild · Aufbaupflicht *f*, Wiederaufbaupflicht *f*

rebuilding fund, reconstruction fund · Aufbaufonds *m*, Wiederaufbaufonds *m*

rebuilding law, reconstruction law · Aufbaurecht *n*, Wiederaufbaurecht *n*

rebuilding law, reconstruction act, rebuilding act, reconstruction statute, rebuilding statute, reconstruction law · (Wieder)Aufbaugesetz *n*

rebuilding legislation, rebuilding lawmaking, reconstruction legislation, reconstruction lawmaking · (Wieder)Aufbaugesetzgebung *f*

rebuilding loan, reconstruction loan · Aufbaudarleh(e)n *n*, Wiederaufbaudarleh(e)n *n*

rebuilding operations, rebuilding activity · (Wieder)Aufbautätigkeit *f* im Hochbau

rebuilding plan, reconstruction plan · Aufbauplan *m*, Wiederaufbauplan *m*

rebuilding planning, reconstruction planning · Aufbauplanung *f*, Wiederaufbauplanung

rebuilding site, reconstruction site · (Wieder)Aufbauort *m*

rebuilding territory, reconstruction area, reconstruction territory, rebuilding area · Aufbaugebiet *n*, Wiederaufbaugebiet *n*

rebuttable, conditional · widerlegbar, widerleglich

rebuttable presumption, conditional presumption · widerlegliche Vermutung *f*, widerlegbare Vermutung

rebutter [*In pleading. A defendants's answer of fact to a plaintiff's resurrejoinder; the third pleading in the series on the part of the defendant. In old books, "rebutter" had also the general sense of bar or estoppel*] · vierte Gegenschrift *f*, Quadruplik *f*

rebutting testimony, disproof, counter-evidence, counter-proof, evidence to the contrary, proof to the contrary, contradictory evidence, contradictory proof · Gegenbeweis *m*, gegenteiliger Beweis

recadastration, cadastral resurvey(ing) · Katasternachvermessung *f*, Katasternachaufnahme *f*

to recall [*In political science, to remove an official from office by popular vote*] · abberufen

to recall, to call back; to revocate [*obsolete*]; to revoke · widerrufen, rückgängig machen

recall [*In political science, the process of removing an official from office by popular vote*] · Abberufung *f*

recall election · Abberufungsabstimmung *f*

recall procedure, procedure of recall [*political science*] · Abberufungsverfahren *n*

recall right, right of recall [*political science*] · Abberufungsrecht *n*

receipt, acquittal, discharge, acquittance · Quittung *f*, Empfangsbestätigung

receipt in part, partial receipt · Teilquittung *f*

receipt of payment · Zahlungsquittung *f*

receipt tick · Eingangsvermerk *m*

receivable mortgage, mortgage receivable · Hypothekenforderung *f*

received for shipment bill of lading · Übernahmekonnossement *n*

receiver · Mündung *f*, Senke *f* [*Graphentheorie*]

receiver, treasurer · Rendant *m*

receiver, recipient · Empfänger *m* [*Mitteilung; Brief usw.*]

receiver · Zwangsverwalter *m*, Kommissar, Empfänger [*Er nimmt des Eigentum des Schuldners in Empfang*]

receiver of an allowance, recipient of an allowance · Zuschußempfänger *m*

receiver of profits — reckless

receiver of profits, pernor (of profits), taker of profits · Berechtigte *m*, Nutzungsberechtigte

receiver of rent(s), rent-receiver · Rentenempfänger *m*

receiver (of stolen goods); resetter [*Scots law*] · Hehler *m*

receiver of wrecks, wreck-master · Strandhauptmann *m*, Strandvogt *m*

receivership [*USA*] · Geschäftsaufsicht *f*

receiving district · Aufnahmebezirk *m*

receiving order · Gerichtsverfügung *f* zur Einsetzung eines Zwangsverwalters, vorläufige Konkurseröffnungsverfügung

receiving stolen property · Hehlerei *f*

recently settled area · Neu(an)sied(e)lungsland *n*, Neubesied(e)lungsland

reception · Empfangnahme *f*

recession, setback, (economic) slowdown · Abschwung *m*, wirtschaftlicher Abschwung, Rezession *f*, Wirtschaftsabschwung

recession year, setback year · (wirtschaftliches) Abschwungjahr *n*, Rezessionsjahr

recipient, receiver · Empfänger *m* [*Mitteilung; Brief usw.*]

recipient of an allowance, receiver of an allowance · Zuschußempfänger *m*

reciprocal, common to both parties, mutual, interchangeable · gegenseitig, wechselseitig

reciprocal agreement, mutual agreement, dependant agreement, conditional agreement, dependent agreement · gegenseitiges Abkommen *n*, gegenseitige Abmachung *f*, gegenseitige Vereinbarung

reciprocal conditions, common conditions, concurrent conditions, mutual conditions · gegenseitige Bedingungen *fpl*, Zug-um-Zug-Bedingungen [*Bedingungen, daß die Parteien die Leistungen Zug um Zug erfüllen*]

reciprocal contract, mutual contract, common contract · gegenseitiger Vertrag *m* [*Ein beide Teile verpflichtender Vertrag, bei dem wenigstens einige der beiderseitigen Leistungspflichten dadurch miteinander verbunden sind, daß die Leistungen des einen nach dem Willen beider Parteien die Gegenleistung, das Entgelt, für die des anderen darstellt*]

reciprocal credits, common credits, mutual credits [*In bankruptcy law. Credits which must, from their nature, terminate in debts; as where a debt is due from one party, and credit given by him on the other for a sum of money payable at a future day, and which will then become a debt; or where there is a debt on one side; and a delivery of property with directions to turn it into money on the other*] · gegenseitige Guthaben *npl*, gegenseitige Gutschriften *fpl*,

reciprocal debt, common debt, mutual debt · Gegenschuld *f*

reciprocal enforcement · grundsätzliche Gewährung *f* der Gegenseitigkeit

reciprocal inheritance contract, common inheritance contract, mutual inheritance contract · gegenseitiger Erb(schafts)vertrag *m*, gemeinsamer Erb(schafts)vertrag

reciprocal mistake, mutual mistake, common mistake · gegenseitiger Irrtum *m*, gemeinsamer Irrtum

reciprocal promise, mutual promise, double promise, counter-promise, dependant promise, conditional promise, dependent promise · gegenseitiges Versprechen *n*

reciprocal will, mutual will, double will, counter will, common will · gegenseitiges Testament *n*

reciprocity agreement · Gegenseitigkeitsvereinbarung *f*, Gegenseitigkeitsabkommen *n*, Gegenseitigkeitsabmachung *f*

recital, representation · Darstellung *f*, Erklärung

recital (of contract) [*A recital is the part of a contract, usually beginning "whereas", which indicates what the parties are desirous of effecting by their contract*] · grundlegende Erklärungen *fpl*

recital of debts · Schuldenverzeichnis *n*

recital of fact(s), representation of fact(s) · Darstellung *f* des Sachverhalts, Darstellung der Tatsache(n), Erklärung des Sachverhalts, Erklärung der Tatsache(n), Sachverhaltserklärung, Tatsachenerklärung, Sachverhaltsdarstellung, Tatsachendarstellung

recital (of title), title recital · Titelbericht *m* [*Auflassung*]

recital of title, title recital · Berufung *f* auf eine Rechtsgrundlage, (Rechts)Titelberufung

recitals · einleitender Teil *m*, einleitendes Teil *n*, Präambel *f* [*Dieser Teil einer Urkunde führt zum rechtsbegründenden Teil*]

to recite, to state a case, to count, to declare [*To narrate the facts constituting a plaintiff's cause of action*] · vorbringen einer Klage

to recite · berufen [*(Rechts)Titel*]

reckless · rücksichtslos

reckless, negligent, without care, careless [*With an indifference whether anything is true or false*] · leichtsinnig, fahrlässig, nachlässig, leichtfertig

reckless conduct, negligence, carelessness, recklessness, careless conduct, negligent conduct · Fahrlässigkeit *f,* Nachlässigkeit, Leichtfertigkeit, Leichtsinnigkeit

recklessly fraudulent (mis)representation, negligently fraudulent (mis)representation, carelessly fraudulent (mis)representation, recklessly fraudulent (false) representation, negligently fraudulent (false) representation, carelessly fraudulent (false) representation, recklessly fraudulent (false) recital, negligently fraudulent (false) recital, carelessly fraudulent (false) recital · fahrlässige betrügerische (Falsch)Darstellung *f,* fahrlässige betrügerische (Falsch)Erklärung, fahrlässige arglistige (Falsch)Darstellung, fahrlässige arglistige (Falsch)Erklärung

recklessly untrue, recklessly false, recklessly not true, carelessly untrue, carelessly false, carelessly not true, negligently false, negligently untrue, negligently not true · leichtsinnig unwahr, leichtsinnig falsch, leichtfertig unwahr, leichtfertig falsch, fahrlässig unwahr, fahrlässig falsch, nachlässig unwahr, nachlässig falsch

recklessness, careless conduct, negligent conduct, reckless conduct, negligence, carelessness · Fahrlässigkeit *f,* Nachlässigkeit, Leichtfertigkeit, Leichtsinnigkeit

recklessness · Rücksichtslosigkeit *f*

reckoner, estimator, calculator, computer [*A person who calculates*] · Kalkulator *m*

to reclaim, to claim back, to demand back · zurückfordern, zurückverlangen

reclaimed land · neugewonnenes Land *n*

reclaiming days → time (allowed) for appeal

reclamation · Zurückforderung *f*

reclamation [*The process of converting waste natural resources (such as land) into productive use*] · Nutzbarmachung *f*

reclamation district → (land(s)) reclamation district

reclamation (of land(s)), land(s) reclamation · (Land)Gewinnung *f,* Neulandgewinnung

reclamation of tidal land(s) · Gezeitenlandgewinn *m,* Tidelandgewinn

reclassification · Umklassifizierung *f*

reclassification → (zoning) reclassification

recognition → acknowledg(e)ment ((up)on record)

recognizable · anerkennbar

recognizance · Bewährungsfrist *f*

recognizance · (gerichtliche) Kaution *f*

to recognize, to acknowledge ((up)on record); recognoscere [*Latin*] [*The authority or claim of*] · anerkennen

recognized school · Schule *f* mit Regierungsinspektion [*In England und Wales*]

recognoscere [*Latin*]; to recognize, to acknowledge ((up)on record) [*The authority or claim of*] · anerkennen

recoinage · Nachprägung *f*

recommendation · Empfehlung *f*

recommended decision · empfohlene Entscheidung *f,* empfohlener Entscheid *m*

reconstruction, rebuilding · Aufbau *m,* Wiederaufbau *m* [*Das Schaffen von Wohnraum oder von anderem auf die Dauer benutzbaren Raum durch Aufbau eines zerstörten Gebäudes oder durch Bebauung von Trümmerflächen. § 16 Abs. 1 Satz 1 des II.WobauG*]

reconstruction area, reconstruction territory, rebuilding area, rebuilding territory · Aufbaugebiet *n,* Wiederaufbaugebiet *n*

reconstruction assistance, rebuilding assistance · (Wieder)Aufbauförderung *f*

reconstruction clause, rebuilding clause [*A clause in an insurance contract that the premium must be used to re-erect the building(s) insured*] · Aufbauklausel *f,* Wiederaufbauklausel *f*

reconstruction contract, rebuilding contract · Aufbauvertrag *m,* Wiederaufbauvertrag *m*

reconstruction duty, duty to reconstruct, duty to rebuild, rebuilding duty · Aufbaupflicht *f,* Wiederaufbaupflicht *f*

reconstruction fund, rebuilding fund · Aufbaufonds *m,* Wiederaufbaufonds *m*

reconstruction law, rebuilding law, reconstruction act, rebuilding act, reconstruction statute, rebuilding statute · (Wieder)Aufbaugesetz *n*

reconstruction law, rebuilding law · Aufbaurecht *n,* Wiederaufbaurecht *n*

reconstruction legislation, reconstruction lawmaking, rebuilding legislation, rebuilding lawmaking · (Wieder)Aufbaugesetzgebung *f*

reconstruction loan, rebuilding loan · Aufbaudarleh(e)n *n,* Wiederaufbaudarleh(e)n *n*

reconstruction plan, rebuilding plan · Aufbauplan *m,* Wiederaufbauplan *m*

reconstruction planning, rebuilding planning · Aufbauplanung *f,* Wiederaufbauplanung *f*

reconstruction site, rebuilding site · (Wieder)Aufbauort *m*

reconstruction territory, rebuilding area, rebuilding territory, reconstruction area · Aufbaugebiet *n*, Wiederaufbaugebiet *n*

reconstruction utopia, utopia of reconstruction · konstruktive Utopie *f* [*Nach Lewis Mumford die Vision einer wiederhergestellten Umwelt, die der Natur und den Zielen des Menschen besser als die derzeitige angepaßt ist*]

reconversion [*Notional process whereby property which has been subject to notional conversion is treated as having been restored to its original state*] · Rückumwand(e)lung *f* [*Vermögen*]

to record · protokollieren

to record · aufzeichnen, niederschreiben, schriftlich festhalten

record · Gerichtsakte *f* der Tatsacheninstanz

record · Aufzeichnung *f*, Niederschrift *f*

recordable, capable of being recorded, capable of being registered, capable of registration, capable of recordation, capable of recording, registrable · eintragungsfähig, registrierfähig, buchungsfähig, registrierbar, eintragungsreif, buchungsreif, registrierreif

recordation, recording, entry, registration · Buchung *f*, (Buch)Eintrag(ung) *m*, *(f)*, Registrierung, Registereintrag(ung)

recordation allowance, recording allowance, registering allowance, registration allowance · Buchungsbewilligung *f*, Eintragungsbewilligung, Registrierungsbewilligung

recordation fee, registration fee, recording fee · Buchungsgebühr *f*, Registrierungsgebühr, Eintragungsgebühr

recordation formula, registering formula, registration formula, recording formula · Eintragungsformel *f*, Buchungsformel, Registrierungsformel

recordation machinery, recording machinery, registering machinery, registration machinery · Eintragungsmechanismus *m*, Registrierungsmechanismus, Buchungsmechanismus

recordation of companies, recording of companies, registration of companies · Gesellschaftenregistrierung *f*

recordation of deeds, recording of deeds, deed recording, deed recordation, deed registration, registration of deeds · Urkundeneintrag(ung) *m*, *(f)*, Urkundenregistrierung

recordation of electors, recordation of voters, recording of electors, recording of voters, registration of electors, registration of voters · Wählerregistrierung *f*, Wählereintrag(ung) *m*, *(f)*

recordation of land → land registration

recordation of title (to land), recording of title (to land), title registration, title recordation, title recording, registration of title (to land) · (Rechts)Titelbuchung *f*, (Rechts)Titeleintrag(ung) *m*, *(f)*

recordation principle → principle of registration

recordation statement, registering statement, recording statement, registration statement · Eintragungserklärung *f*, Registrierungserklärung, Buchungserklärung

recordation system, recording system, registration system · Buchungssystem *n*, Eintragungssystem, Registrierungssystem

record debt, debt of record · gerichtlich festgestellte Schuld *f*, titulierte Schuld

record drawing [*A drawing made at the site*] · Baustellenzeichnung *f*

recorded delivery · Einschreiben *n* [*Postsendung*]

recorded delivery slip · Einschreibzettel *m* [*Postsendung*]

recorded house plot (of land), registered house parcel (of land), recorded house parcel (of land), registered house plot (of land) · Hausgrundstück *n* im Rechtssinn, Hausgrundstück im Sinne des Grundbuchrechts, Grundbuch-Hausgrundstück, gebuchtes Hausgrundstück, eingetragenes Hausgrundstück

recorded interest, registered interest, registered right, recorded right · eingetragenes (subjektives) Recht *n*, registriertes (subjektives) Recht, gebuchtes (subjektives) Recht

recorded in writing · schriftlich festgelegt

recorded (land(ed)) estate, registered real estate, registered (real) property, recorded real estate, recorded (real) property, registered realty, recorded realty, registered (land(ed)) estate · Grundbuchbesitz *m*

recorded land parcel, registered plot (of land), recorded plot (of land), registered parcel (of land), recorded parcel (of land), registered piece of land, recorded piece of land, registered land (piece), recorded land (piece), registered land parcel · eingetragenes Grundstück *n*, eingetragenes Land *n*, eingetragener Grund *m*, eingetragener Boden *m*, Grundbuchboden, (Grund)Buchgrund(stück) *m*, *(n)*, Grundbuchland, gebuchter Boden, gebuchter Grund, Grundstück im Rechtssinn, Grundstück im Sinne des Grundbuchrechts, gebuchtes Grundstück, gebuchtes Land [*Die buchungstechnische Bodeneinheit des Grundbuchs. Grundbuchgrundstück und Katasterparzelle sind nicht notwendigerweise identisch. Ein Grundbuchgrundstück kann aus mehre-*

ren Katasterparzellen bestehen, aber eine Katasterparzelle kann nicht mehrere Grundbuchgrundstücke umfassen]

recorded private (real) estate → private registered plot (of land)

recorded right, recorded interest, registered interest, registered right · eingetragenes (subjektives) Recht *n*, registriertes (subjektives) Recht, gebuchtes (subjektives) Recht

recorded title, registered title · eingetragener (Rechts)Titel *m*, registrierter (Rechts)Titel, gebuchter (Rechts)Titel

recorded urban land parcel, registered urban land plot (of land), recorded urban plot (of land), registered urban piece of land, recorded urban piece of land, registered urban land parcel · Stadtgrundstück *n* im Rechtssinn, eingetragenes Stadtgrundstück, gebuchtes Stadtgrundstück, eingetragener städtischer Boden *m*, gebuchter städtischer Boden, städtischer gebuchter Boden, städtisches Grundbuchland *n*

recorder [*England*] · königlicher Stadtrichter *m*

recorder, single judge, official referee · Einzelrichter *m*, beauftragter Richter

recorder → town recorder

recorder of London [*One of the justices of oyer and terminer, and a justice of the peace of the quorum for putting the laws in execution for the preservation of the peace and government of the City of London*] · Stadtrichter *m* von London

recording, registering, entering · Eintragen *n*, Registrieren, Buchen

recording, entry, registration, recordation · Buchung *f*, (Buch)Eintrag(ung) *m*, *(f)*, Registrierung, Registereintrag(ung)

recording allowance, registering allowance, registration allowance, recordation allowance · Buchungsbewilligung *f*, Eintragungsbewilligung, Registrierungsbewilligung

recording documents, registration documents · Eintragungsunterlagen *f pl*

recording fee, recordation fee, registration fee · Buchungsgebühr *f*, Registrierungsgebühr, Eintragungsgebühr

recording formula, recordation formula, registering formula, registration formula · Eintragungsformel *f*, Buchungsformel, Registrierungsformel

recording machinery, registering machinery, registration machinery, recordation machinery · Eintragungsmechanismus *m*, Registrierungsmechanismus, Buchungsmechanismus

recording of companies, registration of companies, recordation of companies · Gesellschaftenregistrierung *f*

recording of deeds, deed recording, deed recordation, deed registration, registration of deeds, recordation of deeds · Urkundeneintrag(ung) *m*, *(f)*, Urkundenregistrierung

recording of electors, recording of voters, registration of electors, registration of voters, recordation of electors, recordation of voters · Wählerregistrierung *f*, Wählereintrag(ung) *m*, *(f)*

recording of land → land registration

recording of title (to land), title registration, title recordation, title recording, registration of title (to land), recordation of title (to land) · (Rechts)Titelbuchung *f*, (Rechts)Titeleintrag(ung) *m*, *(f)*

recording principle → principle of registration

recording statement, registration statement, recordation statement, registering statement · Eintragungserklärung *f*, Registrierungserklärung, Buchungserklärung

recording system, registration system, recordation system · Buchungssystem *n*, Eintragungssystem, Registrierungssystem

record of (ad)measurement, (ad)measurement record · Aufmaßaufzeichnung *f*

record of completion, completion record · Fertigstellungsniederschrift *f*

record of earnings · Ertragslage *f*

recount · Nachprüfung *f* der Stimmenauszählung

to recoup [*To reduce or diminish a claim for damages by defalcating or keeping back a part*] · mindern einer Entschädigung, mindern einer Schadloshaltung

recoupment [*Reduction or diminution of damages in an action on a contract, from breach of warranty or defects in the performance*] · Minderung *f* der Entschädigung, Minderung der Schadloshaltung

recoupment · Zonenenteignung *f* zur Sicherung und Abschöpfung des Mehrwertes

recourse · Regreß *m*, Rückgriff *m*

to recover, to reimburse, to refund, to restitute · abgelten, ersetzen, erstatten, vergüten

to recover · erlangen einer Vergütung

to recover, to win back, to regain, to collect, to get renewed possession of, to get again, to obtain again · zurückerhalten, wiedererlangen, wiedererhalten, zurückgewinnen, zurückbekommen

to recover, to enforce payment, to collect, to obtain [*amount*] · beitreiben, eintreiben, einziehen [*Betrag*]

recoverable — recreation(al) (public) transit

recoverable, collectible, collectable, obtainable · beitreibbar, eintreibbar, einziehbar

recoverableness [*amount*] · Beitreibbarkeit *f*, Eintreibbarkeit, Einziehbarkeit [*Betrag*]

re-coverage · Wiederbebauung *f*; Wiederüberbauung [*Schweiz*] [*Das Ergebnis des Wiederbebauens einer Fläche*]

recovered, reimbursed, refunded, restituted · abgegolten, ersetzt, erstattet, vergütet

recoveree · Regreßpflichtige *m*

recoveree [*In old conveyancing. The party who suffered a common recovery; the tenant of a freehold, against whom land(s) were recovered by the process of a common recovery, and by that means conveyed to the party recovering*] · Grundstückspflichtige *m*

recovering, enforcing payment, collecting, obtaining · Beitreiben *n*, Eintreiben, Einziehen [*Betrag*]

recoveror [*In old conveyancing. The party recovering land(s) by the process of a common recovery; the party to whom the land(s) were, by this process, conveyed*] · Grund(stücks)erwerber *m*

recovery, restitution, refunding, reimbursement · Abgeltung *f*, Ersetzung, Vergütung, Erstattung, Entgelt *n*, Restitution *f*

recovery · Rückerhalt *m*, Wiedererlangung *f*

recovery [*The amount finally collected*] · beigetriebener Betrag *m*, eingetriebener Betrag

recovery, enforcement of payment, collection [*amount*] · Beitreibung *f*, Eintreibung, Einziehung [*Betrag*]

recovery [*The amount of judg(e)ment*] · eingeklagter Betrag *m*

recovery → (true) recovery

recovery claim, reimbursement claim, refunding claim, restitution claim · Abgeltungsforderung *f*, Erstattungsforderung, Ersetzungsforderung, Vergütungsforderung

recovery duty, duty of recovery, duty of refunding, duty of reimbursement, duty of restitution, refunding duty, restitution duty, reimbursement duty · Abgeltungspflicht *f*, Ersetzungspflicht, Erstattungspflicht, Vergütungspflicht

recovery for supervision, recovery for superintendence, restitution for supervision, restitution for superintendence, reimbursement for supervision, refunding for supervision, refunding for superintendence, reimbursement for superintendence · Aufsichtsvergütung *f*, Überwachungsvergütung

recovery mortgage, restitution mortgage, reimbursement mortgage, refunding mortgage · Abgeltungshypothek *f*, Vergütungshypothek, Ersetzungshypothek, Erstattungshypothek

recovery of wits · Wiedererlangung *f*, der geistigen Gesundheit

recovery rate, reimbursement rate, refunding rate, restitution rate · Abgeltungssatz *m*, Erstattungssatz, Ersetzungssatz, Vergütungssatz

recovery sum, refunding sum, restitution sum, reimbursement sum · Abgeltungssumme *f*, Erstattungssumme, Vergütungssumme, Ersetzungssumme

recreation · Erholung *f*

recreation(al) activity · Erholungstätigkeit *f*

recreation(al) area · Erholungsfläche *f*

recreation(al) area, recreation(al) territory · Erholungsgebiet *n*

recreation(al) benefit · Erholungsnutzen *m*, Nutzen eines Erholungsprojektes

recreation(al) centre (Brit.); recreation(al) center (US) · Erholungszentrum *n*

recreation(al) coverage · Erholungsbebauung *f*; Erholungsüberbauung [*Schweiz*]

recreation(al) facility · Erholungseinrichtung *f*

recreation(al) field · Erholungswesen *n*

recreation(al) forest · Erholungswald *m*

recreation(al) ground · Erholungsgelände *n*

recreation(al) hinterland → (urban) recreation(al) hinterland

recreation(al) journey, recreation(al) trip, recreation(al) travel · Erholungsfahrt *f*

recreation(al) lake · Erholungssee *m*

recreation(al) landscape · Erholungslandschaft *f*

recreation(al) location, recreation(al) site, recreation(al) place · Erholungsort *m*

recreation(al) parkway · Erholungs-Schnellstraßenring *m*

recreation(al) planner · Erholungsplan(verfass)er *m*

recreation(al) planning · Erholungs(gebiets)planung *f*

recreation(al) plant · Erholungsanlage *f*

recreation(al) (public) transit, recreation(al) (public) transport(ation), recreation(al) mass transit, recreation(al) mass transport(ation), public recreation(al) transit, public recreation(al) transport(ation), mass recreation(al)

transport(ation), mass recreation(al) transit · (öffentlicher) Erholungsmassenverkehr *m*, (öffentliche) Erholungsmassenbeförderung *f*

recreation(al) research · Erholungsforschung *f*

recreation(al) service system · Erholungsdienstleistungssystem *n*

recreation(al) site, recreation(al) place, recreation(al) location · Erholungsort *m*

recreation(al) space · Erholungsraum *m*

recreation(al) territory, recreation(al) area · Erholungsgebiet *n*

recreational transit → recreational (public) transit

recreation(al) trip, recreation(al) travel, recreation(al) journey · Erholungsfahrt *f*

recreation(al) use · Erholungsnutzung *f*, Erholungsbenutzung, Erholungsgebrauch *m*

recreation(al) value · Erholungswert *m*

recreation(al) village · Erholungsdorf *n*

recreation(al) water(s) [*Often plural. A large body of water, as river, stream, lake, etc., for recration(al) purposes*] · Erholungsgewässer *n*

recreation (e)valuation, recreation appraisal, recreation appraisement, recreation assessment, recreation val. · Erholungsbewertung *f*, Erholungs(ab)schätzung, Erholungstaxierung

recreation succession · negative Beeinflussung *f* [*Vorgang bei dem eine neu auftretende Gruppe von Erholungssuchenden die Bedürfnisbefriedigung der bereits vorhandenen Nutzer von Erholungseinrichtungen negativ beeinflußt*]

recross examination · Zeugenvernahme *f* durch den Anwalt des Beklagten

rectangular distribution, uniform distribution · Rechteckverteilung *f*, gleichförmige Verteilung, Gleichverteilung [*Statistik*]

rectangular pattern, rectangular scheme · Rechteckmuster *n*, Rechteckschema *n*

rectification, correction · (Ab)Änderung *f*, Richtigstellung, Korrektur *f*, Berichtigung, Verbesserung [*z. B. Fehler oder Irrtum in einer Rechnung*]

rectification note, rework note [*A document which authorizes additional operations to bring a substandard product up to specification*] · Nacharbeitungszettel *m*, Nacharbeitungsanzeige *f*

rectification of arithmetical error · Irrtumsanfechtung *f* bei Rechenfehler

rectification of error(s), correction of error(s) · Fehlerberichtigung *f*, Fehlerkorrektur *f*, Fehlerverbesserung, Fehlerrichtigstellung

rectification register, registry of rectification, rectification registry, register of rectification · Berichtigungsregister *n*, Korrekturregister, Verbesserungsregister, Richtigstellungsregister

rectification sheet, correction sheet · Berichtigungsblatt *n*, Korrekturblatt, Verbesserungsblatt, Richtigstellungsblatt

to rectify, to rework [*To perform additional operations to bring a substandard product up to specification*] · nacharbeiten

to rectify, to correct, to put right · verbessern, richtigstellen, korrigieren, berichtigen, (ab)ändern [*Z. B. Fehler oder Irrtum in einer Rechnung*]

recultivation · Rekultivierung *f*

recurrent cost(s), taxes and mortgage interest on (real) estate, carrying charges · wiederkehrende Grundstückskosten *f*, Grundstücksspesen *f*

recurrent cost(s), carrying charges [*A recurring cost incident to the possession or ownership of property, usually regarded as a current expense but occasionally added to the cost of an asset held for ultimate disposition where the market or likely disposal proceeds are judged to be sufficient to absorb the cost thus enhanced*] · wiederkehrende Kosten *f*, Spesen *f*

recurrent cost(s) for storage and insurance on merchandise, carrying charges · wiederkehrende Lagerkosten *f*, Lagerspesen *f*

recusation [*An appeal grounded on the judge's relationship or personal enmity to one of the parties*] · Ablehnung *f*

recycling (US); improvement of houses, house improvement, renovation (Brit.); fixing up, refurbishing · Altbausanierung *f*, Altbaumodernisierung, Renovierung

reddition [*In old practice. A judicial confession and acknowledg(e)ment that the land(s) or thing in demand belonged to the demandant, or at least, not to the person so surrendering*] · Eigentumsanerkennung *f*, Eigentumsanerkenntnis *f* [*in der Rechtswissenschaft: n*]

redditius siccus [*Latin*]; barren rent, dry rent, rent-seck [*A rent not supported by a right of distress. Ceased to exist after the Landlord and Tenant Act 1730*] · Rente *f* ohne Pfändungsrecht, trockene Rente

redditus ad mensam [*Latin*]; table rent [*In old English law. A rent paid to a bishop or religious prelate, reserved or appropriated to his table or housekeeping*] · Tafelgeld *n*

rededication · Umwidmung *f*, Umzueignung

to redeem, to discharge · ablösen, einlösen, auslösen [*Einen Gegenstand durch Zahlung der Gläubigerforderung*]

to redeem, to pay off, to discharge, to liquidate, to settle [*indebtedness*] · tilgen, begleichen, abbezahlen, rückzahlen

redeemable, dischargeable · ablösbar, auslösbar, einlösbar [*Einen Gegenstand durch Zahlung der Gläubigerforderung*]

redeemable debenture [*Great Britain*]; redeemable corporate bond, callable corporate bond [*USA*]; callable debenture · (vorzeitig) kündbare Schuldverschreibung, (vorzeitig) kündbare Obligation *f*, Obligation mit Tilgungsverpflichtung, Schuldverschreibung mit Tilgungsverpflichtung [*einer privaten Kapitalgesellschaft*]

redeemableness · Auslösbarkeit *f*, Einlösbarkeit, Ablösbarkeit

redeemable right, dischargeable right [*A right which returns to the conveyor or disposer of land, etc., upon payment of the sum for which such right was granted*] · einlösbares Recht *n*, auslösbares Recht, ablösbares Recht

to re-deliver, to surrender · freiwillig zurückgeben

re-delivered, surrendered · freiwillig zurückgegeben

re-delivery, surrender · freiwillige (Zu)Rückgabe *f*

redemption, discharge · Ablösung *f*, Auslösung, Einlösung [*Einen Gegenstand durch Zahlung der Gläubigerforderung*]

redemption (court) action, redemption (law-)suit, redemption cause, redemption plea · Einlösungsklage *f*, Ablösungsklage, Auslösungsklage

redemption duration → redemption period

redemption equity, equity of redemption · Rückkaufrecht *n* nach Billigkeit(srecht), Ablösungsrecht nach Billigkeit(srecht), Einlösungsrecht nach Billigkeit(srecht), Auslösungsrecht nach Billigkeit(srecht)

redemption fee, discharge fee · Ablösungsgebühr *f*, Auslösungsgebühr, Einlösungsgebühr

redemption fund, sinking fund · Tilgungsfonds *m*, Amortisationsfonds, Tilgungsstock, Amortisationsstock *m*, Tilgungskasse *f*, Amortisationskasse

redemption loan, discharge loan · Ablösungsdarleh(e)n *n*, Einlösungsdarleh(e)n, Auslösungsdarleh(e)n

redemption method, method of redemption, discharge method, method of discharge · Ablösungsverfahren *n*, Auslösungsmethode *f*, Ablösungsmethode, Einlösungsmethode, Auslösungsverfahren, Einlösungsverfahren

redemption notice, redemption notification · Einlösungsanzeige *f*, Auslösungsanzeige, Ablösungsanzeige, Einlösungsmitteilung *f*, Auslösungsmitteilung, Ablösungsmitteilung, Einlösungsbenachrichtigung, Auslösungsbenachrichtigung, Ablösungsbenachrichtigung

redemption of a debt, liquidation of a debt, discharge of a debt, settlement of a debt · Tilgung *f*, Schuldrückzahlung

redemption of shares, share redemption · Ablösung *f* von Anteilen, Auslösung von Anteilen, Einlösung von Anteilen, Anteilablösung, Anteilauslösung, Anteileinlösung [*Bausparkasse*]

redemption period, redemption term, redemption duration, discharge period, discharge term, discharge term, period of discharge, term of discharge, duration of discharge, period of redemption, term of redemption, duration of redemption · Auslösungsfrist *f*, Einlösungsfrist, Ablösungsfrist

redemption price, discharge price, price of redemption, price of discharge · Ablösungspreis *m*, Einlösungspreis, Auslösungspreis

redemption rate, rate of redemption · Tilgungssatz *m*, Amortisationssatz

redemption rent, rent of redemption · Ablösungsrente *f*

redemption right, right of redemption, right to redeem, right to regain property, right to reclaim property, discharge right, right of discharge, right to discharge · Ablösungsrecht *n*, Einlösungsrecht, Auslösungsrecht

redemption sum, sum of redemption, discharge sum, sum of discharge · Ablösungssumme *f*, Auslösungssumme, Einlösungssumme

redemption term → redemption period

redeveloper → (slum) redeveloper

redevelopment (US); comprehensive redevelopment (Brit.) · Wiederbebauung *f*, Wiederbebauen *n* (einer Fläche); Wiederüberbauen (einer Fläche), Wiederüberbauung (einer Fläche) [*Schweiz*]

redevelopment → (slum) redevelopment

redevelopment area, area of redevelopment (US); comprehensive redevelopment area, area of comprehensive redevelopment (Brit.) · Wiederbebauungsgebiet *n*; Wiederüberbauungsgebiet [*Schweiz*]

redevelopment area map (US); comprehensive redevelopment area map (Brit.) · Wiederbebauungsgebietskarte *f*; Wiederüberbauungsgebietskarte [*Schweiz*]

redevelopment companies law (US) · Gesetz *n* zur Verbesserung minderwertiger Stadtviertel und dem Wohnungsbau für Minderbemittelte

redirect examination · Zeugenvernahme *f* durch den Anwalt des Klägers

rediscount · Rediskont *m* [*Weiterdiskontierung eines angekauften Wechsels*]

redisseisin, redisseizin · wiederholte Entwerung *f*

to redistribute · umverteilen

redistributing · Umverteilen *n*

redistribution · Umverteilung *f*

redistribution → (land) redistribution

redistribution authority → (land) redistribution authority

redistribution community → (land) redistribution community

redistribution law → (land) redistribution law

redistribution of parcels by replotting of building land, redistribution of lots by replotting of building land · Boden(neu)ordnung *f*, Grund(stücks)bereinigung durch Bodenumlegung, (Neu)Ordnung und Bereinigung der Grundstücke

redistribution of plots, redistribution of parcels · Grund(stücks)bereinigung *f*, Bereinigung

redistribution of population, population redistribution · Bevölkerungsumverteilung *f*

redistribution procedure → (land) redistribution procedure

redistriction · Sitzverteilung *f*

reditus [*Latin*]; (lease) rent [*"Rent" may be regarded as of a twofold nature — first, as something issuing out of the land or other corporeal hereditament as a compensation for the possession during the term; and secondly, as an acknowledg(e)ment made by the tenant to the lord*] · Rente *f*, Pacht(zins) *f*, *(m)*

reditus albus [*Latin*] → blanch farm

reditus quieti, quieti reditus [*Latin*]; forgavel [*In old English law*]; chief-rent, rent charge, quit-rent, fee farm (rent) [*An annual or periodical sum issuing out of land, payable by holders of land in a manor to the lord. Some writers use "fee farm" to signify not only the estate itself, but the rent reserved on it, taking the word "farm" itself in the sense of rent. This practice should, however, be deprecated*] · Erbzins *m*, Befreiungszins, Leh(e)n(s)zins

to redo, to fix up (US); to improve, to renovate, to refurbish, to upgrade · sanieren, modernisieren, renovieren [*Altbauten*]

redress, remedy · Abhilfe *f*, Behelf *m*

redress by operation of law, (redressing) remedy by operation of law, redressing legal remedy, legal redress, legal remedy · Rechtsabhilfe(mittel) *f*, *(n)*, Rechtsbehelf *m*

redressing extrajudicial remedy, extrajudicial (redressing) remedy · außerrichterliches Abhilfemittel *n*

redressing legal remedy, legal redress, legal remedy, redress by operation of law, (redressing) remedy by operation of law · Rechtsabhilfe(mittel) *f*, *(n)*, Rechtsbehelf *m*

(redressing) remedy by act of the party injured · Selbstabhilfemittel *n*

to reduce, to abate, to lessen · reduzieren, mindern, herabsetzen, verringern

reduced cost(s) · Minderkosten *f*

reduced net annual value, reduced rat(e)able value, rat(e)able value; assessable value [*deprecated*] · reduzierter Nettoertragswert *m* [*Die landwirtschaftlich genutzten Grundstücke werden mit einem herabgesetzten Nettoertragswert zur Steuer eingeschätzt*]

reduced rat(e)able value, rat(e)able value; assessable value [*deprecated*]; reduced net annual value · reduzierter Nettoertragswert *m* [*Die landwirtschaftlich genutzten Grundstücke werden mit einem herabgesetzten Nettoertragswert zur Steuer eingeschätzt*]

reduced rate relief · Degressionsabzug *m* [*Besteuerung von Reineinkommen*]

to reduce (in)to writing · schriftlich abfassen

to reduce (laws) to a code, to codify, to digest · kodifizieren

reducing, abating, lessening · Verringern *n*, Herabsetzen, Mindern, Reduzieren

reductio ad absurdum [*Latin*] · Beweis *m* der Unsinnigkeit einer Behauptung

reduction, ábatement · Verringerung *f*, Minderung, Reduzierung, Herabsetzung

reduction by matured shares · Tilgung *f* durch Reifen der Anteile [*Bausparhypothek*]

reduction of contribution, contribution reduction · Beitragsermäßigung *f*

reduction of debts and legacies, abatement of debts and legacies · Herabsetzung *f* der Schuldforderungen und Vermächtnisse nach Maßgabe des Mankos am hinterlassenen Vermögen, Reduzierung der Schuldforderungen und Vermächtnisse nach Maßgabe des Mankos am hinterlassenen Vermögen, Minderung der Schuldforderungen und Vermächtnisse nach Maßgabe des Mankos am hinterlassenen Vermögen, Verringerung der Schuldforderungen und Vermächtnisse nach Maßgabe des Mankos am hinterlassenen Vermögen

reduction of interest, interest reduction · Zinsherabsetzung f, Zinssenkung

reduction of value, depreciation, diminution of value · Wertminderung f, Wertherabsetzung, Wertverringerung, Wertreduzierung

reduction to practice · Niederlegung f einer Erfindung

redundancy pay(ment), severance pay(ment) [*A compensation paid by a firm to an employe(e) whose services are no longer required by that firm on account of the introduction of automation or labour saving machinery or because of a change of demand*] · Abfindung f

re-election · Wiederwahl f

re-eligible · wiederwählbar

re-entry clause, clause of re-entry · (Besitz)Wiederübernahmeklausel f, Wiederinbesitznahmeklausel, Wiedereintrittklausel

to re-enact, to re-establish by law · wieder zum Gesetz erheben, wieder (zum Gesetz) erlassen

re-enactment · Wiedererhebung f zum Gesetz

to re-enter · wiedereintreten [*In einen (Grund)Besitz*]

re-entry · (Besitz)Wiederübernahme f, Wiederinbesitznahme, Wiedereintritt m [*Grundstück nach widerrechtlicher Besitzentziehung*]

re-entry right, right of re-entry · Wiedereintrittsrecht n [*In einen (Grund)Besitz*]

re-erection · Wiedererstellung f, Wiedererrichtung

to re-establish by law, to re-enact · wieder zum Gesetz erheben, wieder (zum Gesetz) erlassen

re(e)ve, head of a village, village head · Schultheiß m, Schulze m

re-examinating, checking, controlling · Kontrollieren n, Nachprüfen

re-examination [*When a witness is again examined by the party calling him in order to give him an opportunity of explaining or contradicting any false impression produced by the cross-examination, this is called re-examination*] · Rückverhör n [*Verhör wiederum durch die Partei, die den Zeugen benannt hat*]

re-examination, review, check, control · Kontrolle f, Nachprüfung f

re-examination authority, authority of control, authority of checking, control authority, check(ing) authority, review(ing) authority · Kontrollvollmacht f, Nachprüf(ungs)vollmacht

re-examination duty, check(ing) duty, duty to review, review(ing) duty, duty to check, duty to control, duty to re-examine, checking duty, control duty · Nachprüfungspflicht f, Kontrollpflicht

re-examination measure, check(ing) measure, control measure · Nachprüfungsmaßnahme, Kontrollmaßnahme f

to re-examine, to review, to check, to control · kontrollieren, nachprüfen

re-exchange · Rückwechselbetrag m

to re-execute (defective work) · wiederausführen

to re-export · wiederausführen

re-exportation · Wiederausfuhr f

re-export of plant, re-export of equipment · Wiederausfuhr f von Geräten, Gerätewiederausfuhr

re-expropriation (of land(s)); re-condemnation (of land(s)) (US) · Rückenteignung f (von Land)

to refer · verweisen

referee → (official) referee

referee in bankruptcy, trustee in bankruptcy, commissioner in bankruptcy, accountant in bankruptcy, assignee in bankruptcy · (Konkurs)Masse(n)kurator m, Konkursverwalter m, Kurator m

reference, legend · Legende f, (Zeichen)Erklärung f, (Zeichen)Schlüssel m, (Zeichen)Erläuterung

reference · Verweisung f

reference to a court, appeal at law · Anruf(ung) m, (f) eines Gerichtes

reference basis · Bezugsgrundlage f

reference book, reference manual · Nachschlagebuch n, Nachschlagewerk n

reference frame, frame of reference · Bezugsrahmen m

reference map · Bezugs(land)karte f

reference mode · Bezugslauf m

reference value · Bezugsgröße f, Bezugswert m

referendum by petition, protest-referendum · Protest-Volksentscheid m

referral pattern, referral scheme · Verweisungsmuster n, Verweisungsschema n

refiling · Erneuerung f einer Aktenaufnahme

reform act, reform statute, reform law · Reformgesetz n

reformation [*Action to correct a mistake in a deed or other instrument*] · Richtigstellung f

reformatory (school), reform school, workhouse, house of correction · Arbeits-

reform in stages — refusal of specific performance

haus n, Besserungsanstalt f, Erziehungsanstalt f, Besserungshaus n [Für jugendliche Straftäter]

reform in stages, step-by-step reform · stufenweise Reform f, Stufenreform

reform law · Reformrecht n

reform of administrative functions · funktionale Verwaltungsreform f

reform of law, law reform · Rechtsreform f

reform of taxation, tax(ation) reform · Steuerreform f

reform school → reformatory (school)

reform zeal · Reformeifer m

re-forwarding · Weiterversand m

refractoriness · Widersetzlichkeit f

refractory · widersetzlich

refraining [from collection of contribution(s)] · Absehen n [von Beitragserhebung]

refresher [for a barrister] · Zusatzhonorar n

refreshment room · Erfrischungsstube f

refuge, preserve [for animals] · Schutzgebiet n, Schongebiet [für Tiere]

refuge camp, camp of refuge · Fluchtburg f

refugee · Flüchtling m

refugee relocation, relocation of refugees · Flüchtlingsumsied(e)lung f, Flüchtlingsumsetzung

refugee settlement, settlement of refugees · Flüchtlings(an)sied(e)lung f

to refund, to restitute, to recover, to reimburse · abgelten, ersetzen, erstatten, vergüten

refunding, reimbursement, recovery, restitution · Abgeltung f, Ersetzung, Vergütung, Erstattung, Entgelt n, Restitution f

refundable, compensable, reimbursable · (kosten)abgeltbar, (kosten)vergütbar, (kosten)ersetzbar, (kosten)erstattbar, (kosten)entgeltbar

refunded, restituted, recovered, reimbursed · abgegolten, ersetzt, erstattet, vergütet

refunding assessment, recovery assessment, reimbursement assessment, restitution assessment · Bemessung f der Vergütung, Bemessung f der Abgeltung, Bemessung f der Erstattung, Bemessung f der Ersetzung, Vergütungsbemessung, Erstattungsbemessung, Abgeltungsbemessung, Ersetzungsbemessung

refunding bond [A bond which replaces or pays off outstanding bond which holder surrenders in exchange for new security] · Ablösungsschuldverschreibung f, Einlösungsschuldverschreibung, Auslösungsschuldverschreibung

refunding claim, restitution claim, recovery claim, reimbursement claim · Abgeltungsforderung f, Erstattungsforderung, Ersetzungsforderung, Vergütungsforderung

refunding duty, restitution duty, reimbursement duty, recovery duty, duty of recovery, duty of refunding, duty of reimbursement, duty of restitution · Abgeltungspflicht f, Ersetzungspflicht, Erstattungspflicht, Vergütungspflicht

refunding for supervision, refunding for superintendence, reimbursement for superintendence, recovery for supervision, recovery for superintendence, restitution for supervision, restitution for superintendence, reimbursement for supervision · Aufsichtsvergütung f, Überwachungsvergütung f

refunding mortgage, recovery mortgage, restitution mortgage, reimbursement mortgage · Erstattungshypothek f, Abgeltungshypothek, Ersetzungshypothek, Vergütungshypothek

refunding rate, restitution rate, recovery rate, reimbursement rate · Ersetzungssatz m, Erstattungssatz, Abgeltungssatz, Vergütungssatz

refunding sum, restitution sum, reimbursement sum, recovery sum · Abgeltungssumme f, Erstattungssumme, Vergütungssumme, Ersetzungssumme

to refurbish → to redo

refurbishing, fixing up, recycling (US); improvement of houses, house improvement, renovation · Altbausanierung f, Altbaumodernisierung, Renovierung

refusal, rejection, repudiation, disaffirmation, disaffirmance · Ablehnung f, Zurückweisung, (Ver)Weigerung, Versagung, Aufsage f

refusal of acceptance (of (the) work(s)) · Abnahmeverweigerung f, Bauabnahmeverweigerung

refusal of justice · Rechts(ver)weigerung f, Rechtsversagung

refusal of performance, breach, performance refusal · Bruch m, Erfüllungs(ver)weigerung f, Erfüllungsversagung

refusal of permission · Erlaubnisablehnung f, Genehmigungsablehnung, Erlaubnis(ver)weigerung, Genehmigungs(ver)weigerung, Genehmigungsversagung, Erlaubnisversagung, Genehmigungszurückweisung, Erlaubniszurückweisung

refusal of specific performance · (Ver)Weigerung f der Naturalerfüllung

refusal to accept · Annahme(ver)weigerung f

refusal to act, unwillingness to act · Handlungs(ver)weigerung f

refusal to follow, overruling · Außerkraftsetzung f [Durch ein höheres Gericht oder eine höhere Behörde]

refusal to issue (a) building permit, refusal to issue (a) construction permit · Bauversagung f, Bau(ver)weigerung f

refusal to pay · Zahlungs(ver)weigerung f

refusal value · Grund(stücks)wert m ohne Planungsgenehmigung

to refuse, to repudiate, to reject, to decline, to disaffirm · ablehnen, versagen, verweigern, zurückweisen

refuse collection, waste collection · Abfallabfuhr f, Müllabfuhr

refused, repudiated, rejected, declined, disaffirmed · abgelehnt, versagt, verweigert, zurückgewiesen

refused charge book · Buch n derjenigen Fälle in denen der diensttuende Inspektor die erhobene Anklage als unbegründet oder ungerechtfertigt ansieht

refuse disposal, waste disposal · Abfallbeseitigung f, Müllbeseitigung

refuse disposal act, refuse disposal statute, refuse disposal law · Abfallbeseitigungsgesetz n, Müllbeseitigungsgesetz

refuse disposal area, waste disposal area, refuse tip, waste tip · Abfallhalde f, Abfalldeponie f, Abfallkippe f, Müllhalde, Mülldeponie, Müllkippe

refuse disposal law, waste disposal law · Abfallbeseitigungsrecht n, Müllbeseitigungsrecht

to refuse to follow, to overrule · abweichen, außer Kraft setzen [Durch ein höheres Gericht oder eine höhere Behörde]

refuse removal facility, waste removal facility · Abfallbeseitigungseinrichtung f, Müllbeseitigungseinrichtung

refuse tip, waste tip, refuse disposal area, waste disposal area · Abfallhalde f, Abfalldeponie f, Abfallkippe f, Müllhalde, Mülldeponie, Müllkippe

refuse utilization plant, waste utilization plant · Müllverwertungsanlage f, Abfallverwertungsanlage

to regain, to collect, to get renewed possession of, to get again, to obtain again, to recover, to win back · zurückerhalten, wiedererlangen, wiedererhalten, zurückgewinnen, zurückbekommen

regal fish, fish royal, royal fish · Wale m pl und Störe m pl [Sie sind in England königliches Eigentum wenn sie ans Ufer geworfen oder in Küstennähe gefangen werden]

regard; visitatio hemorum [Latin] · Waldbereinigung f [Zur Feststellung von Forstfrevlern]

regardant (to the manor), bond tenant, villain (tenant), villein (tenant), bondager, bond(s)man, culvert, serf; villarus [Latin] [Strictly a man of servile condition holding usually one virgate of land, this is the fourth part of a hide, in the common fields of a manor by base services; but the term is sometimes applied to one of free status who holds land by servile tenure] · Leibeigene, unfreier Bauer, Dienstbauer m, Hörige, Unfreie, Knechtsleh(e)n(s)mann

regarder, surveyor of (the) forests, forest surveyor · Forstinspektor m

regency · Regentschaft f

region, specific region · Region f

regional adjustment · regionale Anpassung f

regional approach · Regionalansatz m

regional capital · Regionalhauptstadt f

regional centre (Brit.); regional center (US) · Regionalzentrum n

regional city, regional town · Regionalstadt f

regional classification · Regionsklassifizierung f

regional competition [The market process by which economic activities or employed factors of production are allocated through time among the regions of a nation] · regionaler Wettbewerb m

regional competitiveness · regionale Wettbewerbsfähigkeit f

regional comprehensive (development) plan, regional structure plan, regional three-dimensional master plan, regional general (development) plan, regional master (development) plan · regionaler General(bebauungs)plan m

regional concept · Regionalbegriff m

regional consciousness · Regionalbewußtsein n

regional control · regionale Lenkung f

regional core · Regionalkern m

regional delineation, delineation of regions · Abgrenzung f von Regionen

regional development · regionale Entwick(e)lung f, Regionalentwick(e)lung

regional development planning · regionale Entwick(e)lungsplanung f

regional development policy · Regionalentwick(e)lungspolitik f

regional division · Regionalteilung f

regional ecology · Regionalökologie f

regional economical development · regionale Wirtschaftsentwick(e)lung *f*

regional economic(al) policy · regionale Wirtschaftspolitik *f*, Regionalwirtschaftspolitik

regional economics planning, regional economy planning · Regionalwirtschaftsplanung *f*, regionale Wirtschaftsplanung

regional education(al) planning · regionale Bildungsplanung *f*

regional employment premium · regionale Arbeitsplatzprämie *f*

regional environmental policy · Regionalumweltpolitik *f*

regional factor · Regionalfaktor *m*

regional general (development) plan, regional master (development) plan, regional comprehensive (development) plan, regional structure plan, regional three-dimensional master plan · regionaler General(bebauungs)plan *m*

regional geographic(al) analysis, regional geographic(al) study · Analyse *f* der geographischen Raumausstattung einer Region, Studie *f* der geographischen Raumausstattung einer Region

regional geography · Länderkunde *f*

regional growth · Regionalwachstum *n*, regionales Wachstum

regional growth policy · Regionalwachstumspolitik *f*, regionale Wachstumspolitik

regional growth theory, theory of regional growth · Regionalwachstumstheorie *f*, regionale Wachstumstheorie

(regional) guide series · Führerserie *f*

regional hierarchy · Regionalhierarchie *f*

regional human geography · regionale Sozialgeographie *f*

regional importance · regionale Bedeutung *f*

regional improvement · Regionalerschließung, regionale Erschließung *f* [*Bundesrepublik Deutschland*]

regional index · Regionalregister *n*

regional industrial park · regionaler Industriepark *m*

regional inequality · regionale Ungleichheit *f*

regionalization, region-building · Region(alis)ierung *f*

regionalization of national policies, region-building of national policies · Region(alis)ierung *f* der nationalen Politiken

regional labour market (Brit.); regional labor market (US) · regionaler Arbeitsmarkt *m*

regional level · Regionalebene *f*

regional location · regionale Lage *f*, regionaler Standort *m* [*Die Lagebeziehung einer (An)Sied(e)lung im näheren und weitern Umkreis*]

regional master (development) plan, regional comprehensive (development) plan, regional structure plan, regional three-dimensional master plan, regional general (development) plan · regionaler General(bebauungs)plan *m*

regional metropolis · Regionalmetropole *f*

regional migration · regionale Wanderung *f*

regional (migration) movement · Regionalbewegung *f*, Regionalwanderungsbewegung

regional model · Regionalmodell *n*

regional multiplier · regionaler Multiplikator *m*

regional name · Regionalname *m*

regional network · Regionalnetz *n*

regional office · Regionalbüro *n*

regional open space · regionaler Freiraum *m*

regional passenger transportation · Personenregionalverkehr *m*

regional pattern · Regionsform *f*

regional planner · Regionalplaner *m*

regional planning · Regionalplanung *f*, regionale Planung, sektorale Planung mit regionalem Bezug

regional planning authority · Regionalplanungsbehörde *f*

regional planning board · Regionalplanungsamt *n*

regional planning commission · Regionalplanungskommission *f*

regional planning council · Regionalplanungsrat *m*

regional planning district · Regionalplanungsbezirk *m*

regional planning legislation, regional planning lawmaking · Regionalplanungsgesetzgebung *f*

regional planning office · Regionalplanungsstelle *f*

regional planning policy · Regionalplanungspolitik *f*, regionale Planungspolitik

regional policy; regional planning [*obsolete*] · Raumordnung *f* [*Derjenige Teil der raumwirksamen Tätigkeit des Staates und seiner Gebietskörperschaften, der auf die Herstellung und Erhaltung einer dem jeweiligen gesellschaftspolitischen Leitbild entsprechenden Ordnung des Raumes gerichtet ist. Es muß*

regional policy act — registered capital 874

zwischen der praktischen Raumordnung als Aufgabe des Staates und seiner Gebietskörperschaften und der Raumordnungstheorie unterschieden werden]

regional policy act, regional policy law, regional policy statute · Raumordnungsgesetz *n*

regional policy law · Raumordnungsrecht *n*, Recht der Raumordnung

regional policy planning legislation, regional policy planning lawmaking · Raumordnungsplanungsgesetzgebung *f*

regional policy programme; regional policy program (US) · Raumordnungsprogramm *n*

regional programme; regional program (US) · Regionalprogramm *n*

regional reconstruction · regionaler (Wieder)Aufbau *m*

regional recreation(al) area planning, regional recreation(al) territory planning · regionale Erholungsgebietsplanung *f*

regional research · Regionalforschung *f*

regional science · Regionalwissenschaft *f*

regional scientist · Regionalwissenschaftler *m*

regional segregation · regionale Ungleichverteilung *f*

regional share [*shift-share analysis*] · Strukturkomponente *f*

regional space plan, regional spatial plan · Regionalraumplan *m*, regionaler Raumplan

regional space system, regional spatial system, regional system of space · regionales Raumsystem *n*

regional spatial planning, regional space planning · Regionalraumplanung *f*, RRP

regional special planning, special regional planning · regionale Spezialplanung *f*, spezielle Regionalplanung

regional statistics · Regionalstatistik *f*

regional structural policy · Raum(ordnungs)politik *f* als Strukturpolitik, regionale Strukturpolitik, Regionalstrukturpolitik

regional structure · Regionalgefüge *n*, Regionalaufbau *m*, Regionalstruktur *f*, Regionalzusammensetzung *f*

regional structure plan, regional three-dimensional master plan, regional general (development) plan, regional master (development) plan, regional comprehensive (development) plan · regionaler General(bebauungs)plan *m*

regional survey · Regionalenquête *f*

regional system · Regionalsystem *n*

regional system of space, regional space system, regional spatial system · regionales Raumsystem *n*

regional three-dimensional master plan, regional general (development) plan, regional master (development) plan, regional comprehensive (development) plan, regional structure plan · regionaler General(bebauungs)plan *m*

regional town, regional city · Regionalstadt *f*

regional unbalance · regionales Ungleichgewicht *n*

regional union · Regionalverband *m*

regional unit · Regionaleinheit *f*

region-building, regionalization · Region(alis)ierung *f*

region-building of national policies, regionalization of national policies · Region(alis)ierung *f* der nationalen Politiken

region concept, concept of region · Regionsbegriff *m*

region of competition · konkurrierende Region *f*

region of social geography · sozialgeographische Region *f*

region's spatial structure, region's space structure · Regionalraumstruktur *f*

to register · buchen, registrieren, eintragen

to register, to create · bestellen [*Grundschuld*]

register, bill, list, schedule, tabulation, index, registry · Verzeichnis *n*, Liste *f*, Aufstellung *f*, Register *n*

register → (public) register

registered · eingetragen

registered agricultural land parcel, registered agrarian land parcel · landwirtschaftliches Grundstück *n* im Rechtssinn, eingetragenes landwirtschaftliches Grundstück, landwirtschaftliches eingetragenes Grundstück, gebuchtes landwirtschaftliches Grundstück, landwirtschaftliches gebuchtes Grundstück, landwirtschaftliches Grundbuchland *n*, gebuchter landwirtschaftlicher Boden *m*, landwirtschaftlicher gebuchter Boden

registered capital, nominal capital, original capital, authorized capital [*When a company is formed its application for registration is accompanied by a statement indicating the amount of capital with which it purposes to be registered*] · Grundkapital *n* [*Nicht verwechseln mit der deutschen Benennung „genehmigtes (Aktien)Kapital"; denn dieses ist ein durch Beschluß der Hauptversammlung* *festgesetzter Betrag, um den der Vorstand während einer bestimmten Zeit das Grundkapital erhöhen kann]*

registered company · eingetragene Gesellschaft *f*

registered corporate bond [*USA*]; registered debenture [*Great Britain*] · Namensschuldverschreibung *f*, Namensobligation *f* [*private Kapitalgesellschaft*]

registered coupon corporate bond [*USA. A registered bond with interest coupons payable to bearer*] · Namensschuldverschreibung *f* mit Zinsscheinen, Namensobligation *f* mit Zinsscheinen [*einer privaten Kapitalgesellschaft*]

registered debenture [*Great Britain*]; registered corporate bond [*USA*] · Namensschuldverschreibung *f*, Namensobligation *f* [*private Kapitalgesellschaft*]

registered design, utility model · Gebrauchsmuster *n*

registered disposition · eingetragene Disposition *f*, eingetragene freie Verfügung *f*

registered female person · Eingetragene *f*

registered house plot (of land), recorded house plot (of land), registered house parcel (of land), recorded house parcel (of land) · Hausgrundstück *n* im Rechtssinn, Hausgrundstück im Sinne des Grundbuchrechts, Grundbuch-Hausgrundstück, gebuchtes Hausgrundstück, eingetragenes Hausgrundstück

registered interest, registered right, recorded right, recorded interest · eingetragenes (subjektives) Recht *n*, registriertes (subjektives) Recht, gebuchtes (subjektives) Recht

registered (land(ed)) estate, recorded (land(ed)) estate, registered real estate, registered (real) property, recorded real estate, recorded (real) property, registered realty, recorded realty · Grundbuchbesitz *m*

registered (land) owner → registered (land) proprietor

registered land parcel, recorded land parcel, registered plot (of land), recorded plot (of land), registered parcel (of land), recorded parcel (of land), registered piece of land, recorded piece of land, registered land (piece), recorded land (piece) · eingetragenes Grundstück *n*, eingetragenes Land, eingetragener Grund *m*, eingetragener Boden *m*, Grundbuchboden, (Grund)Buchgrund(stück) *m, (n)*, Grundbuchland, gebuchter Boden, gebuchter Grund, Grundstück im Rechtssinn, Grundstück im Sinne des Grundbuchrechts, gebuchtes Grundstück, gebuchtes Land [*Die buchungstechnische Bodeneinheit des Grundbuchs. Grundbuchgrundstück und Katasterparzelle sind nicht notwendigerweise identisch. Ein Grundbuchgrundstück kann aus mehreren Katasterparzellen bestehen, aber eine Katasterparzelle kann nicht mehrere Grundbuchgrundstücke umfassen*]

registered (land) proprietor, registered (land) owner · Grundbuchlandeigentümer *m*, Grundbuchbodeneigentümer, Grundbuchlandeigner, Grundbuchbodeneigner

registered male person · Eingetragene *m*

registered office · eingetragene (Firmen)Niederlassung *f*, eingetragenes Geschäftslokal *n*

registered owner → registered (land) proprietor

registered person · eingetragene Person *f*

registered private plot (of land) → private registered plot (of land)

registered rent-charge · Buchrentenschuld *f* [*Es wird nur eine Eintragung in das Grundbuch vorgenommen ohne eine Brieferteilung an den Gläubiger*]

registered right, recorded right, recorded interest, registered interest · eingetragenes (subjektives) Recht *n*, registriertes (subjektives) Recht, gebuchtes (subjektives) Recht

registered rural land parcel · Landgrundstück *n* im Rechtssinn, eingetragenes Landgrundstück, gebuchtes Landgrundstück, eingetragener ländlicher Boden *m*, gebuchter ländlicher Boden, ländlicher gebuchter Boden, ländliches Grundbuchland *n*

registered security, personal security · Namenpapier *n*, Rectapapier [*Auf den Namen eines bestimmten Gläubigers ohne weiteren Zusatz ausgestelltes Wertpapier*]

registered share · Namensanteil *m*

registered small plot (of land), registered small parcel (of land), recorded small plot (of land), recorded small parcel (of land), small recorded plot (of land), small registered plot (of land), small registered parcel (of land), small recorded parcel (of land) · Klein(grund)stück *n* (im Rechtssinn)

registered stock, inscribed stock · Namensaktie *f*

registered title, recorded title · eingetragener (Rechts)Titel *m*, registrierter (Rechts)Titel, gebuchter (Rechts)Titel

registered urban land parcel, recorded urban land parcel, registered urban plot (of land), recorded urban plot (of land), registered urban piece of land, recorded urban piece of land · Stadtgrundstück *n* im Rechtssinn, eingetragenes Stadtgrundstück, gebuchtes

to register for (land-)tax — register of requests

Stadtgrundstück, eingetragener städtischer Boden m, gebuchter städtischer Boden, städtischer gebuchter Boden, städtisches Grundbuchland n

to register for (land-)tax, to assess for (land-)tax · katastrieren

registering, entering, recording · Eintragen n, Registrieren, Buchen

registering, creating · Bestellen n [*Grundschuld*]

registering allowance, registration allowance, recordation allowance, recording allowance · Buchungsbewilligung f, Eintragungsbewilligung, Registrierungsbewilligung

registering duty, duty to register · Meldepflicht f

registering formula, registration formula, recording formula, recordation formula · Eintragungsformel f, Buchungsformel, Registrierungsformel

registering machinery, registration machinery, recordation machinery, recording machinery · Eintragungsmechanismus m, Registrierungsmechanismus, Buchungsmechanismus

registering statement, recording statement, registration statement, recordation statement · Eintragungserklärung f, Registrierungserklärung, Buchungserklärung

register mark, register tick, registration mark, registration tick, (corner) mark, (corner) tick · Passermarke f [*Kartographie*]

register of annuities, registry of annuities, annuity register, annuity registry · Annuitätenregister n, Annuitätenverzeichnis n, Annuitätenliste f

register of applications, register of requests, registry of applications, registry of requests · Antragsliste f, Gesuchsliste f, Gesuchsverzeichnis n, Antragsverzeichnis n

register of architects, registry of architects, list of architects, schedule of architects, index of architects, tabulation of architects · Architektenaufstellung f, Architektenliste f, Architektenregister n, Architektenverzeichnis n

register of charges → (land) encumbrances register

register of cooperative societies, register of cooperative associations · Genossenschaftsregister n

register of deeds, registry of deeds, land record, land register, land registry · Landregister n [*Abgesehen vom Torrensystem gibt es in den USA keine Grundbücher, sondern Landregister*]

register of deeds of arrangement affecting land(s), registry of deeds of arrangement affecting land(s) · Register n über

Grundstücks(konkurs)vergleiche, Verzeichnis n über Grundstücks(konkurs)vergleiche, Grundstücksvergleichsregister, Grundstücksvergleichsverzeichnis

register of farms inherited as a whole, registry of farms inherited as a whole, register of landed estates that cannot be broken up on inheritance · Höferolle f, Landgüterrolle

register of land(s) → land register

register of land(s) charges, registry of land(s) charges · Grund(stücks)lastenregister n, Register der Grund(stücks)lasten

register of licences, register of licenses, registry of licences, registry of licenses · Lizenzregister n

register of members, membership registry, membership register, registry of members · Gesellschaftsregister n, Mitgliederverzeichnis n

register of members, registry of members, membership register, membership registry · Mitgliederverzeichnis n

register of mines, registry of mines, mines' register, mines' registry, mining register, mining registry · Berg(werk)grundbuch n

register of mortgages, registry of mortgages, mortgage registry, mortgage register · Hypothekenregister n, Hypothekenbuch n

register of names, names registry, registry of names, names register, names list · Namensliste f, Namensregister n, Namensverzeichnis n

register of ownership (of property), register of proprietorship, ownership (of property) register, proprietorship register · Abteilung I f, Eigentümerregister n, erste (Grundbuch)Abteilung, Grundbuchabteilung I

register of pending actions, registry of pending actions · Verzeichnis n schwebender Klagen

register of pleading actions, judg(e)ment docket, judg(e)ment book, plea list, plea book, cause list, cause book · Klagenverzeichnis n, Klagenregister n, Prozeßverzeichnis, Prozeßregister

register of public obligations, registry of public obligations · Baulastenbuch n, Baulastenverzeichnis n [*Das öffentliche Buch mit den eingetragenen Baulasten*]

register of rectification, rectification register, registry of rectification, rectification registry · Berichtigungsregister n, Korrekturregister n, Verbesserungsregister, Richtigstellungsregister

register of requests, registry of applications, registry of requests, register of

register of Sasines — registration of companies

applications · Antragsliste f, Gesuchsliste f, Gesuchsverzeichnis n, Antragsverzeichnis n

register of Sasines, Sasines Register [*The national land register for the whole of Scotland*]; Register of Title at the Land Registry [*England*] · Land(rechts)titelregister n

register of summons, registry of summons · Ladungsverzeichnis n

register of the taxable value of land, index of the taxable value of land · Generalhufenschoß n

register of the yield from land, schedule of the yield from land, register of the yield from (real) estate, register of the yield from (real) property, schedule of the yield from (real) estate, schedule from the yield of (real) property · Ertragskataster n, m

Register of Title at the Land Registry [*England*]; register of Sasines, Sasines Register [*The national land register for the whole of Scotland*] · Land(rechts)titelregister n

register (of writs), registry (of writs); registrum brevium [*Latin*] [*A celebrated collection, in Latin, of writs original and judicial, generally called, by way of eminence, "The Register", and one of the most ancient books of the common law*] · Formelsammlung f

register tick, registration mark, registration tick, (corner) mark, (corner) tick, register mark · Passermarke f [*Kartographie*]

registrability · Buchungsfähigkeit f, Eintragungsfähigkeit, Registrierfähigkeit, Registrierbarkeit

registrable, recordable, capable of being recorded, capable of being registered, capable of registration, capable of recordation, capable of recording · eintragungsfähig, registrierfähig, buchungsfähig, registrierbar, eintragungsreif, buchungsreif, registrierreif

registrar → (land) registrar

registrar (of births and marriages and deaths), civil registrar · Zivilstandsbeamte m, Standesbeamte

registrar's court, court of summary jurisdiction, court of request, registrary's court, court of conscience, police court, P., petty court, summary court · Bagatellgericht n, Friedensgericht für kleine Straf- und Zivilsachen, Polizeigericht, Ortsgericht für gering(fügig)e Schuldklagen [*in England*]

registrar(y) · Registerführer m, Registrar

registrar(y) central office · Meldebehörde f

registrar(y) of deeds [*USA*] · Landregisterführer m

registrar(y) of the county court [*England*]; sheriff clerk of the county [*Scotland*] · Protokollführer m eines Grafschaftsgerichts

registrary's court, court of conscience, police court, registrar's court, court of summary jurisdiction, court of request · Bagatellgericht n, Friedensgericht für kleine Straf- und Zivilsachen, Polizeigericht, Ortsgericht für gering(fügig)e Schuldklagen [*in England*]

registration, license, licence [*Privilege or right granted by the state to operate as a real estate broker*] · staatliche Genehmigung f, staatliche Erlaubnis f [*Grundstücksmakler*]

registration, license, licence [*Authority to go upon or use another person's land(s) without possessing any estate therein*] · (Land)Benutzungsvollmacht f, Bodenbenutzungsvollmacht, Landgebrauchsvollmacht, Bodengebrauchsvollmacht

registration, recordation, recording, entry · Buchung f, (Buch)Eintrag(ung) m, (f), Registrierung, Registereintrag(ung)

registration allowance, recordation allowance, recording allowance, registering allowance · Buchungsbewilligung f, Eintragungsbewilligung, Registrierungsbewilligung

registration certificate, certificate of registration · Beurkundung f über Grund(stücks)rechte [*Torrens-System*]

registration documents, recording documents · Eintragungsunterlagen f pl

registration fee, recording fee, recordation fee · Buchungsgebühr f, Registrierungsgebühr, Eintragungsgebühr

registration formula, recording formula, recordation formula, registering formula · Eintragungsformel f, Buchungsformel, Registrierungsformel

registration law → (land) registration law

registration machinery, recordation machinery, recording machinery, registering machinery · Eintragungsmechanismus m, Registrierungsmechanismus, Buchungsmechanismus

registration mark, registration tick, (corner) mark, (corner) tick, register mark, register tick · Passermarke f [*Kartographie*]

registration of births · Geburtenregistrierung f

registration of burials · Begräbnisregistrierung f

registration of business names · Geschäftsnamenregistrierung f

registration of companies, recordation of companies, recording of companies · Gesellschaftenregistrierung f

registration of deaths — registry of summons

registration of deaths · Todesfallregistrierung *f*, Totenregistrierung, Sterbefallregistrierung

registration of deeds, recordation of deeds, recording of deeds, deed recording, deed recordation, deed registration · Urkundeneintrag(ung) *m*, *(f)*, Urkundenregistrierung

registration of electors, registration of voters, recordation of electors, recordation of voters, recording of electors, recording of voters · Wählerregistrierung *f*, Wählereintrag(ung) *m*, *(f)*

registration of immov(e)able property, land registration · Landeintragung *f*, Bodeneintragung

registration of judg(e)ments · Urteilsregistrierung *f*

registration of land → land registration

registration of marriages · Eheschließungsregistrierung *f*

registration of road vehicles · Straßenfahrzeugregistrierung *f*

registration of title (to land), recordation of title (to land), recording of title (to land), title registration, title recordation, title recording · (Rechts)Titelbuchung *f*, (Rechts)Titeleintrag(ung) *m*, *(f)*

registration of title to settled land · (Rechts)Titeleintrag(ung) *m*, *(f)* auf festgelegtes Land, (Rechts)Titelbuchung auf festgelegtes Land

registration principle → principle of registration

registration statement, recordation statement, registering statement, recording statement · Eintragungserklärung *f*, Registrierungserklärung, Buchungserklärung

registration system, recordation system, recording system · Buchungssystem *n*, Eintragungssystem, Registrierungssystem

registration tick, (corner) mark, (corner) tick, register mark, register tick, registration mark · Passermarke *f* [*Kartographie*]

registrum brevium [*Latin*]; register (of writs), registry (of writs) [*A celebrated collection, in Latin, of writs original and judicial, generally called, by way of eminence, "The Register", and one of the most ancient books of the common law*] · Formelsammlung *f*

registry, register, bill, list, schedule, tabulation, index · Verzeichnis *n*, Liste *f*, Aufstellung *f*, Register *n*

registry · Registeramt *n*

registry → (public) registry

registry act, registry law, registry statute · Registergesetz *n*

registry law, registry statute, registry act · Registergesetz *n*

registry law · Registerrecht *n*

registry law → (land) registration law

registry of annuities, annuity register, annuity registry, register of annuities · Annuitätenregister *n*, Annuitätenverzeichnis *n*, Annuitätenliste *f*

registry of applications, registry of requests, register of applications, register of requests · Antragsliste *f*, Gesuchsliste *f*, Gesuchsverzeichnis *n*, Antragsverzeichnis *n*

registry of architects, list of architects, schedule of architects, index of architects, tabulation of architects, register of architects · Architektenaufstellung *f*, Architektenliste *f*, Architektenregister *n*, Architektenverzeichnis *n*

registry of deeds → register of deeds

registry of deeds of arrangement affecting land(s), register of deeds of arrangement affecting land(s) · Register *n* über Grundstücks(konkurs)vergleiche, Verzeichnis *n* über Grundstücks(konkurs)vergleiche, Grundstücksvergleichsregister, Grundstücksvergleichsverzeichnis

registry of land(s) → land register

registry of land(s) charges, register of land(s) charges · Grund(stücks)lastenregister *n*, Register der Grund(stücks)lasten

registry of members, register of members, membership registry, membership register · Gesellschaftsregister *n*, Mitgliederverzeichnis *n*

registry of members, membership register, membership registry, register of members · Mitgliederverzeichnis *n*

registry of mines → register of mines

registry of pending actions, register of pending actions · Verzeichnis *n* schwebender Klagen

registry of public obligations, register of public obligations · Baulastenbuch *n*, Baulastenverzeichnis *n* [*Das öffentliche Buch mit den eingetragenen Baulasten*]

registry of rectification, rectification registry, register of rectification, rectification register · Berichtigungsregister *n*, Korrekturregister, Verbesserungsregister, Richtigstellungsregister

registry of requests, register of applications, register of requests, registry of applications · Antragsliste *f*, Gesuchsliste *f*, Gesuchsverzeichnis *n*, Antragsverzeichnis *n*

registry of summons, register of summons · Ladungsverzeichnis *n*

registry (of writs) — to rehabilitate

registry (of writs); registrum brevium [*Latin*]; register (of writs) [*A celebrated collection, in Latin, of writs original and judicial, generally called, by way of eminence, "The Register", and one of the most ancient books of the common law*] · Formelsammlung *f*

registry statute, registry act, registry law · Registergesetz *n*

regnal year [*The year as calculated from the sovereign's accession to the throne*] · Herrscherjahr *n*, (monarchisches) Regierungsjahr

to regreen · wieder begrünen

regress; regressus [*Latin*] [*Going back upon land(s)*] · Wiederinbesitznahme *f* von Land

regressand · Regressand *m* [*Statistik*]

regression analysis, analysis of regression · Regressionsanalyse *f*

regression approach · Regressionsansatz *m*

regression area, regression surface · Regressionsfläche *f*

regression constant, constant of regression · Regressionskonstante *f*

regression curve · Regressionskurve *f*

regression equation · Regressionsgleichung *f*

regression line · Regressionslinie *f*

regression surface, regression area · Regressionsfläche *f*

regression (up)on condition, conditional regression · bedingte Regression *f*, Regression mit Vorbedingung, Regression unter Vorbehalt

regressor, predicated variable · Regressor *m*

regrouping authority → (land) regrouping authority

regrouping board → (land) regrouping board

regrouping (of land(s)), land(s) regrouping · Gemeinheitsteilung *f* [*Oberbegriff für (Land)Zusammenlegung ((land) consolidation) und (Land)Neuaufteilung ((land) redistribution)*]

regrouping of lots → regrouping of parcels

regular canon, Augustinian canon · regulierter Kanoniker *m*, Augustiner

regular checking account [*USA*] · laufendes Konto *n* mit Minimumsaldo

regular court · ordentliches Gericht *n*

regular meeting · Pflichtversammlung *f*

regular permanent (building (and loan)) association (US) · Bausparkasse *f* mit individuellem regelmäßigen Plan

regular permanent plan, permanent regular plan · individueller regelmäßiger Plan *m* [*Eine dauernde Form einer amerikanischen Bausparkasse*]

regular premium scheme · Versicherungsfonds-Sparprogramm *n*

regular return, standard return, normal yield, normal return, regular yield, standard yield · Normalrendite *f*

regular street village · regelmäßiges Straßendorf *n*, regelmäßiges Wegedorf

regular wear and tear, fair wear and tear, normal wear and tear · normaler Verschleiß *m*, üblicher Verschleiß

regular yield, standard yield, regular return, standard return, normal yield, normal return · Normalrendite *f*

regulated investment company, regulated investment fund · steuerbegünstigte Investmentgesellschaft *f*, steuerbegünstigter Investmentfonds *m*

regulation · Regelung *f*

regulation, rule, prescription · (Rechts)Vorschrift *f*

regulation absolute, prescription absolute, rule absolute · unbedingte (Rechts)Vorschrift *f*, absolute (Rechts)Vorschrift

regulation for organization, prescription for organization, rule for organization · Organisationsvorschrift *f*

regulation of traffic, traffic regulation · Verkehrsregelung *f*

regulation of zoning, zoning prescription, prescription of zoning, zoning regulation, zoning rule, rule of zoning · (bauliche) Nutzungsvorschrift *f*, Baunutzungsvorschrift

regulation(s) · Regelung(en) *f (pl)*

regulations as to carts and carriages [*In medi(a)eval England*] · Fahrordnung *f*

regulations for topsoil protection, prescriptions for topsoil protection, rules for topsoil protection · Mutterbodenschutz *m* [*Schutz des Mutterbodens durch (Rechts)Vorschriften*]

regulator, canon, rule · Regel *f*, Regulativ *n*

regulatory · regelnd

regulatory commission · regulative Kommission *f*

regulatory power · regelnde Gewalt *f*

to rehabilitate [*company*] · sanieren [*Gesellschaft*]

to rehabilitate [*To restore a delinquent to former rank, privilege, or right*] · rehabilitieren

rehabilitation [*company*] · Sanierung *f* [*Gesellschaft*]

rehabilitation · Ausbau *m*

rehabilitation act → (housing) improvement act

rehabilitation area, rehabilitation territory · Ausbaugebiet *n*

rehabilitation certificate · Freigabeattest *n*, Freigabeschein *m*, Freigabebescheinigung *f* [*Konkurswesen*]

rehabilitation characteristic · Ausbaumerkmal *n*

rehabilitation guide line, upgrading guideline, (physical) improvement guide line, modernization guide line · (bauliche) Verbesserungsrichtlinie *f*, Modernisierungsrichtlinie

rehabilitation law, modernization statute, modernization act, modernization law, (physical) improvement statute, (physical) improvement act, (physical) improvement law, rehabilitation statute, rehabilitation act · (bauliches) Verbesserungsgesetz *n*, (Wohnungs-) Modernisierungsgesetz, WoModG

rehabilitation loan, (physical) improvement loan, modernization loan, upgrading loan · (bauliche) Verbesserungsanleihe *f*, Modernisierungsanleihe

rehabilitation order, modernization order, upgrading order, order to improve, order to modernize, order to rehabilitate, (physical) improvement order · Modernisierungsverfügung *f*, Modernisierungsanordnung, Modernisierungsgebot *n*, Modernisierungsbefehl *m*, (baulicher) Verbesserungsbefehl

rehabilitation ordinance, (physical) improvement ordinance, modernization ordinance, upgrading ordinance · Modernisierungsverordnung *f*, (bauliche) Verbesserungsverordnung

rehabilitation plan, upgrading plan, (physical) improvement plan, modernization plan · Modernisierungsplan *m*, (baulicher) Verbesserungsplan

rehabilitation plan · Ausbauplan *m*

rehabilitation planner · Ausbauplaner *m*

rehabilitation planning · Ausbauplanung *f*

rehabilitation programme; rehabilitation program (US) · Ausbauprogramm *n*

rehabilitation site · Ausbauort *m*

rehabilitation statute, rehabilitation act, rehabilitation law, modernization statute, modernization act, modernization law, (physical) improvement statute, (physical) improvement act, (physical) improvement law · (bauliches) Verbesserungsgesetz *n*, (Wohnungs-) Modernisierungsgesetz, WoModG

rehabilitation territory → (federal) rehabilitation area

rehabilitation work(s), upgrading work(s), (physical) improvement work(s), modernization work(s) · (bauliche) Verbesserungsarbeit(en) *f(pl)*, Modernisierungsarbeit(en)

rehabilitation zone, modernization zone, upgrading zone, (physical) improvement zone · Modernisierungsschwerpunkt *m*, (baulicher) Verbesserungsschwerpunkt [*früher: Modernisierungszone f*]

to rehouse [*people*] · wieder unterbringen, umsiedeln

rehousing, resettlement, transfer from congested areas, (tenant) relocation, displacement [*Of persons from land acquired or appropriated for planning purposes*] · Aussied(e)lung *f*, Umsied(e)lung, Standortveränderung, Verlegung, Umsetzung, Wiederunterbringung

reimbursable, refundable, compensable · (kosten)abgeltbar, (kosten)vergütbar, (kosten)ersetzbar, (kosten)erstattbar, (kosten)entgeltbar

to reimburse, to refund, to restitute, to recover · abgelten, ersetzen, erstatten, vergüten

reimbursed, refunded, restituted · abgegolten, ersetzt, erstattet, vergütet

reimbursement, recovery, restitution, refunding · Abgeltung *f*, Ersetzung, Vergütung, Erstattung, Entgelt *n*, Restitution *f*

reimbursement assessment, restitution assessment, refunding assessment · Bemessung *f* der Vergütung, Bemessung *f* der Abgeltung, Bemessung *f* der Erstattung, Bemessung *f* der Ersetzung, Vergütungsbemessung, Erstattungsbemessung, Abgeltungsbemessung, Ersetzungsbemessung

reimbursement claim, refunding claim, restitution claim, recovery claim · Abgeltungsforderung *f*, Erstattungsforderung, Ersetzungsforderung, Vergütungsforderung

reimbursement duty → refunding duty

reimbursement for supervision, refunding for supervision, refunding for superintendence, reimbursement for superintendence, recovery for supervision, recovery for superintendence, restitution for supervision, restitution for superintendence · Aufsichtsvergütung *f*, Überwachungsvergütung *f*

reimbursement mortgage, refunding mortgage, recovery mortgage, restitution mortgage · Erstattungshypothek *f*, Abgeltungshypothek, Ersetzungshypothek, Vergütungshypothek

reimbursement rate, refunding rate, restitution rate, recovery rate · Abgeltungssatz *m*, Erstattungssatz, Ersetzungssatz, Vergütungssatz

reimbursement sum, recovery sum, refunding sum, restitution sum · Abgeltungssumme *f*, Erstattungssumme, Vergütungssumme, Ersetzungssumme

reinsurance, reassurance · Rückversicherung *f*

to reinstate · instandsetzen, wiederherstellen

to reinstate · wiedereinsetzen

reinstatement · Instandsetzung *f*, Wiederherstellung

reinstatement · Wiedereinsetzung *f*

reinstatement after termination · Instandsetzung *f* nach Beend(ig)ung, Wiederherstellung nach Beend(ig)ung

reinstatement cost(s) · Instandsetzungskosten *f*, Wiederherstellungskosten

reinstatement loan · Instandsetzungsdarleh(e)n *n*, Wiederherstellungsdarleh(e)n

reinstatement of ground on completion (of work(s)), ground reinstatement · Wiederherstellung *f* des früheren Geländezustandes, Wiederherstellung des vorherigen Geländezustandes [*Nach Beendigung der Bauarbeiten*]

reinstatement order, order to reinstate · Instandsetzungsbefehl *m*, Instandsetzungsverfügung *f*, Instandsetzungsanordnung, Instandsetzungsgebot *n*

reinstatement work(s) · Instandsetzungsarbeit(en) *f (pl)*, Wiederherstellungsarbeit(en)

reinsuree · Rückversicherte *m*

reinsurer · Rückversicherer *m*

to reinvigorate · wiederbeleben [*Wirtschaft*]

rei obligatio [*Latin*] · Sachhaftung *f*

reissue patent · Wiederholungspatent *n*

rei vindicatio [*Latin*] · (Eigentums)Herausgabeanspruch *m*, (Eigentums)Rückgabeanspruch, (Eigentums)Wiedererlangungsanspruch, Anspruch auf (Eigentums)Herausgabe, Anspruch auf (Eigentums)Rückgabe, Anspruch auf (Eigentums)Wiedererlangung

to reject, to decline, to disaffirm, to refuse, to repudiate · ablehnen, versagen, verweigern, zurückweisen

rejected, declined, disaffirmed, refused, repudiated · abgelehnt, versagt, verweigert, zurückgewiesen

rejected · nicht berücksichtigt [*Angebot*]

rejection, repudiation, disaffirmation, disaffirmance, refusal · Ablehnung *f*, Zurückweisung, (Ver)Weigerung, Versagung, Aufsage *f*

rejection, nonacceptance · Nichtannahme *f*

rejection line · Ablehn(ungs)linie *f* [*Statistik*]

rejection number · Ablehn(ungs)zahl *f* [*Statistik*]

rejection region · Ablehnungsbereich *m* [*Statistik*]

reject note [*A document which records that an item or batch does not conform to specification*] · Nichtabnahmeanzeige *f*, Nichtabnahmezettel *m*

to rejoin; rejungere [*Latin*] [*In pleading. To answer a plaintiff's replication in an action at law, by some matter of fact*] · duplizieren

rejoining gratis [*Rejoining voluntarily, or without being required to do so by a rule to rejoin*] · unnötige Duplik *f*, freiwillige Duplik

rejunctio [*Latin*]; (defendant's) rejoinder [*In pleading. A defendant's answer of fact to a plaintiff's replication. Corresponding to the duplicatio of the civil law, and the triplicatio of Bracton*] · Duplik *f*, zweite Gegenschrift *f*, Gegenerwiderung *f*

rejungere [*Latin*]; to rejoin [*In pleading. To answer a plaintiff's replication in an action at law, by some matter of fact*] · duplizieren

re-landscaping · Landschaftsumbildung *f*

related, orient(ta)ted · bezogen, orientiert

related enterprises, related undertakings · verbundene Unternehmen *n pl*, verbundene Unternehmungen *f pl*

related to land use, orien(ta)ted to land use, land use related, land use orien(ta)ted · bodennutzungsbezogen, bodennutzungsorientiert, flächennutzungsbezogen, flächennutzungsorientiert, landnutzungsbezogen, landnutzungsorientiert

related to the turnover, related to the stockturn, orien(ta)ted to the turnover, orien(ta)ted to the stockturn · umsatzbezogen, umsatzorientiert

related undertakings → related enterprises

relating to a freeholder, of a freeholder · landsässig

relating to assets which have not been administered; de bonis non (administratis) [*Latin*], of goods not yet administered [*A grant "de bonis non administratis", or more shortly "de bonis non", is made where an executor dies intestate or an administrator dies, in either case without having fully administered*] · von nicht verwalteten Nachlaßgegenständen

relating to (building) land policy · (bau)bodenpolitisch, (bau)landpolitisch

relating to legal form — relief

relating to legal form · formalrechtlich

relating to right, droitural · rechtsbezüglich

relation · Rückbeziehung f

relation of fact · tatsächliche Beziehung f

relation(ship) between employer and employe(e) · Arbeitsverhältnis n

relation(ship) by blood, blood relation(ship), consanguinity · Blutsbande f, Blutsverwandtschaft f, Verwandtschaft durch gleiche Abstammung

relation to space, spatial orientation, space orientation · Raumbezug m, Raumorientierung f

relative · Meßziffer f [Statistik]

relative, next of blood, next of kin, next and most lawful friend · Verwandte m

relative by marriage · Verschwägerte m

relative lot value · Wertverhältniszahl f

relative quantitiy of labo(u)r · verhältnismäßige Arbeitsmenge f

relative right · relatives (subjektives) Recht n

relative rule of precedent · beschränkte Selbstbindung f, eingeschränkte Selbstbindung, begrenzte Selbstbindung [Gericht]

relative scale (Brit.); particular scale · Partikularmaßstab m [Kartographie]

relative space · Relativraum m

relative space map, relative spatial map · Relativraumkarte f

to release [equity of redemption] · verkaufen [Einlösungsrecht]

to release, to acquit, to discharge, to set free [Required to be under seal] · freistellen, entlasten, befreien, freigeben, dispensieren

release [Relinquishment of a right or claim for a stated consideration] · Freigabe f

release · Rechtsverzicht m [Verpachtung. Er befreit den Besitzer auf Zeit von seiner Verpflichtung der Räumung nach Ablauf der Zeit]

release, dispensation, immunity, exemption, discharge [Relaxation of the law in a particular case by competent authority] · Befreiung f, Freistellung, Entlastung, Freigabe f, Erlaß m, Dispens(ierung) m, (f), Dispensation f, Ausnahmebewilligung

release application, dispensation application, immunity application, exemption application, discharge application · Befreiungsantrag m, Dispens(ier)ungsantrag, Freistellungsantrag, Entlastungsantrag, Freigabeantrag, Dispensationsantrag

release deed, deed of release · formelle Freigabeerklärung f, förmliche Freigabeerklärung, Rückauflassung an den Schuldner

release deed, quitclaim deed [A deed of conveyance operating by way of release; that is, intended to pass any title which the grantor may have in the premises, but not professing that such title is valid, or containing any warranty or convenants for title] · Übertragungsurkunde f ohne Zusicherung des Nichtbestehens von Rechtsmängeln, freiwillige Übertragungsurkunde f ohne Zusicherung des Nichtbestehens von Rechtsmängeln

released [Required to be under seal], acquitted, discharged, set free [From debt, obligation, duty, etc.] · befreit, entlastet, freigestellt, freigegeben, dispensiert

release (from liability), nonliability, exemption (from liability) · (Haftungs)Ausschluß m, (Haftungs)Freizeichnung f, (Haftungs)Ausschließung, Haftpflichtausschluß, Haftbarkeitsausschluß, Haftbarkeitsausschließung

release from liability · Gewährleistungsbefreiung f

release of (building) (land) area, release of (building) land · (Bau)Bodenfreigabe f, (Bau)Flächenfreigabe, (Bau)Landfreigabe

release of cautioner, discharge of insurer of a debt, release of insurer of a debt, discharge of guarantor, release of guarantor, discharge of surety, release of surety, discharge of cautioner · Bürgenbefreiung f, Bürgenfreistellung

releasing [Required to be under seal], acquittance, acquitting, setting free, discharging [The act by which a discharge in writing is effected] · Befreien n, Freistellen, Freigeben, Entlasten, Dispensieren

relevant, pertinent, to the point · erheblich

relevant cost(s) · relevante Kosten f

relevium, laudemium, relief · Laudemium n, Mannfall m [Es wurde beim Tod des letzten Leh(e)n(s)mannes fällig, wenn der Nachkomme Leh(e)n(s)mann werden wollte]

reliability · Verläßlichkeit f

reliable · verläßlich

relief · Fürsorge f, Pflege f [z. B. Armenfürsorge]

relief, accommodation [Pecuniary aid in an emergency] · Unterstützung f

relief · Relief n [Kartographie. Dritte Dimension, durch geeignete graphische Ausdrucksmittel in der Kartenebene ausdrücklich und meßbar wiedergegeben]

relief, relevium, laudemium · Laudemium *n*, Mannfall *m* [*Es wurde beim Tod des letzten Leh(e)n(s)mannes fällig, wenn der Nachkomme Leh(e)n(s)mann werden wollte*]

relief, statutory protection, legal protection · Gesetz(es)schutz *m*

relief · Entlastung *f*

relief · Anfallsgeld *n* [*Zur Erinnerung und Anerkennung, daß der Leh(e)n(s)nehmer dem Leh(e)n(s)herrn seine Ausrüstung verdankt, wurde bei Veränderung in der dienenden Hand eine Menge von Waffen und Kleidungsstücken, in deren Ermangelung eine Geldsumme gezahlt*]

relief · Klagebegehren *n*

relief against forfeitures · Schutz *m* gegen Verfall von Rechten, Rechtsverfallschutz, Schutz gegen Rechtsverfall

relief community · Entlastungsgemeinde *f*, Entlastungskommune *f*

relief from obligation to supply · Versorgungsbefreiung *f*

relief fund · Unterstützungsfonds *m*

relief in kind, in-kind relief · Natural(ien)unterstützung *f*

relief in money · Geldunterstützung *f*

relief locality · Entlastungsort *m*

relief location · Relieflage *f*

relief map · Reliefkarte *f*, (ebene) Hochbildkarte [*Durch Photographieren eines Präzisionsreliefs (Wenschow-Verfahren) hergestellte Karte mit schattenplastischer Geländedarstellung*]

relief of the poor · Armenunterstützung *f*

relief of unemployment, out-of-work-pay, out-of-work-benefit, unemployment relief, unemployment benefit, donation money, idle money, unemployment compensation, compensation of unemployment · Arbeitslosengeld *n*, Arbeitslosenunterstützung *f*, Erwerbslosengeld, Erwerbslosenunterstützung

relief order · Unterstützungsbefehl *m*

relief presentation · Reliefdarstellung *f*

relief station · (Armen)Verpflegungsstation *f*

relieving officer, relieving official (Brit.); poormaster (US) · Armenunterstützungsbeamte *m*, Armenvorsteher, Armenrat

relieving road, relieving highway · Entlastungsstraße *f*

religious community · Religionsgemeinschaft *f*

religious house, ecclesiastic(al) corporation, spiritual corporation, church corporation · geistliche Körperschaft *f*, geistliche Korporation, kirchliche Korporation, kirchliche Körperschaft

religious liberty, right of religious belief · Religionsfreiheit *f*, Glaubensrecht *n*

religious order of men · Männerorden *m*

religious order of women · Frauenorden *m*

religious service, divine service · religiöse Dienstleistung *f*, religiöse Verrichtung [*Leh(e)n(s)mann*]

religious settlement · Kult(an)sied(e)lung *f*

to relinquish, to remise, to forsake, to give up, to renounce, to disclaim, to abandon [*To relinquish with intent of never again resuming one's right or interest*] · aufgeben, preisgeben, Verzicht leisten, verzichten, ausschlagen, entsagen, derelinquieren

relinquished, renounced, remised, forsaken, given up, waived, disclaimed, abandoned · aufgegeben, preisgegeben, Verzicht geleistet, verzichtet, ausgeschlagen, entsagt, derelinquiert

relinquishing, forsaking, abandoning, giving up, renouncing · Aufgeben *n*, Preisgeben, Verzichten

relinquishment, renunciation, renouncement, disclaimer, waiver, abandonment [*It includes the intention, and also the external act(ion) by which it is carried into effect*] · Aufgabe *f*, Preisgabe, Verzicht(leistung) *m*, (*f*), Entsagung, Ausschlagung

relinquishment of inheritance, relinquishment of heirship, renunciation of heirship, renunciation of inheritance, renouncement of heirship, renouncement of inheritance, abandonment of inheritance, abandonment of heirship · Erbaufgabe *f*, Erbentsagung *f*, Erbpreisgabe, Erbverzicht(leistung) *m*, (*f*), Erbausschlagung

relinquishment of light, renunciation of light, renouncement of light, abandonment of light · Lichtrechtaufgabe *f*, Lichtrechtverzicht *m*, Lichtrechtpreisgabe

to relocate, to resettle, to displace, to transfer from congested areas, to decentralize, to disperse, to resite · aussiedeln, umsiedeln, verlegen, verändern des Standortes, umsetzen

relocated, resited, displaced, resettled · ausgesiedelt, planungsverdrängt, umgesetzt, verlegt, umgesiedelt

relocated family, resettled family, resited family, displaced family · Aussied(e)lerfamilie *f*, Umsied(e)lerfamilie, umgesiedelte Familie, ausgesiedelte Familie, verlegte Familie, umgesetzte Familie, planungsverdrängte Familie

relocated farm, consolidated farm, outlying farm · Einödhof m, Einöde f, Aussiedlerhof

relocated individual, resettled person, resettled individual, resited person, resited individual, displacee, displaced individual, displaced person, relocated person · Aussied(e)ler m, Aussied(e)lerperson f, Umsied(e)lerperson f, Umsied(e)ler, Umgesiedelte, Ausgesiedelte

relocation · Verlegung f [z. B. eine Straße]

relocation area, resettlement area · Aussied(e)lungsgebiet n, Verlegungsgebiet, Umsied(e)lungsgebiet, Umsetzungsgebiet

relocation assistance, resettlement assistance · Aussied(e)lungsförderung f, Umsied(e)lungsförderung, Verlegungsförderung, Umsetzungsförderung

relocation authority, resettlement authority · Aussied(e)lungsbehörde f, Umsied(e)lungsbehörde, Verlegungsbehörde, Umsetzungsbehörde

relocation map, resettlement map · Aussied(e)lungskarte f, Verlegungskarte, Umsied(e)lungskarte, Umsetzungskarte

relocation of farms, farms relocation · Abbau m, Ausbau m, Aussied(e)lung f, Vereinödung [Die Versetzung der Hofstätten einzelner oder sämtlicher an der Vereinödung beteiligter Bauern aus dem Weiler oder Dorf hinaus auf die neu zugeteilten Flächen]

relocation of industry, industrial resettlement, industrial relocation, industrial shifting, resettlement of industry, displacement of industry, transfer of industry · Industrieaussied(e)lung f, Industrieumsied(e)lung, Industrieumsetzung, Industrieverlegung, industrielle Standortveränderung, Industrieverlagerung

relocation of job sites, job site relocation · Standortveränderung f von Arbeitsplätzen

relocation of persons · Standortveränderung f von Personen

relocation of population, resettlement of population, population relocation, population resettlement · Bevölkerungsumsied(e)lung f, Bevölkerungsverlegung, Bevölkerungsaussied(e)lung, Bevölkerungsumsetzung

relocation of refugees, refugee relocation · Flüchtlingsumsied(e)lung f, Flüchtlingsumsetzung

relocation plan, resettlement plan · Aussied(e)lungsplan m, Verlegungsplan, Umsied(e)lungsplan, Umsetzungsplan

relocation planning, resettlement planning · Aussied(e)lungsplanung f, Umsied(e)lungsplanung, Umsetzungsplanung, Verlegungsplanung

relocation survey, resettlement survey · Aussied(e)lungsenquête f, Umsied(e)lungsenquête, Verlegungsenquête, Umsetzungsenquête

relocation zone, resettlement zone · Aussied(e)lungszone f, Umsied(e)lungszone, Verlegungszone, Umsetzungszone

remaining useful life · Restnutzungsdauer f

remark, note · Bemerkung f

remarks column, column for remarks · Bemerkungsspalte f

re-marriage · Wiederheirat f

remedial action → remedial (court) action

remedial law, procedural law, procedure law, law of (court) procedure (and practice), adjective law [Law consisting of rules of conduct prescribed by substantive law, and enforced by adjective law. In other words, substantive law is administered by the courts and deals with right and duties, whereas adjective law relates to practice and procedure and deals with remedies. "Substantive law" and "adjective law" were first used by Bentham (2 works, 6) and are now generally adopted, notwithstanding Austin's criticism of them (2 Jurisprudence, 788—789)] · Formalrecht n, formelles Recht, Verfahrensrecht, Prozeßrecht

remedial liability · Entschädigungsrecht n, Schadenersatzrecht, Recht auf Schadenersatz, Recht auf Entschädigung [subjektiv]

remedial work(s) · Baumängelbeseitigungsarbeit(en) f (pl), (Sach)Mängelbeseitigungsarbeit(en), Nachbesserungsarbeit(en)

remedy, redress · Abhilfe f, Behelf m

remedy by act of the party injured → (redressing) remedy by act of the party injured

remedy by agreement between the parties · rechtsgeschäftliches Abhilfemittel n

remedy by operation of law → redress by operation of law

reminder (of debt due), letter demanding payment, (formal) demand, prompt note, prompt notification, demand note, demand notification [Slang: dunning letter] · Mahnbrief m, Mahnschreiben n, Mahnung f

to remise, to forsake, to give up, to renounce, to disclaim, to abandon, to relinquish [To relinquish with intent of never again resuming one's right or interest] · aufgeben, preisgeben, Verzicht leisten, verzichten, ausschlagen, entsagen, derelinquieren

remised, forsaken, given up, waived, disclaimed, abandoned, relinquished, renounced, · aufgegeben, preisgegeben, Verzicht geleistet, verzichtet, ausgeschlagen, entsagt, derelinquiert

remiss, neglectful of duty, derelict · pflichtvergessen, pflichtuntreu

remission of duty, duty remission · Zollerlaß *m*

remittance of debt(s) · Schuldennachlaß *m*

remnant of a building, building remnant · Gebäuderest *m*

remote · abgelegen

remote cause · entfernte Ursache *f*

remoteness · Abgelegenheit *f*

remoteness · Mangel *m* eines unmittelbaren Zusammenhangs

remote sensing (of environment), remote sensory perception · Fernerkundung *f* [*Luftbildtechnik*]

removal, disposal · Beseitigung *f*, Wegschaffung [*z. B. Abfall*]

removal, abatement [*nuisance*] · Aufhebung *f*, Beseitigung, Entfernung, Abstellung [*Immission*]

removal · Aufhebung *f*, Beseitigung, Entfernung

removal; amotio [*Latin*]; amotion · Absetzung *f*, Entsetzung, Enthebung, Untersagung, Entziehung, Ausschluß *m*

removal from (a) membership, amotion from (a) membership · Mitgliedschaftsausschluß *m*, Mitgliedschaftsentziehung *f*

removal from (an) office, amotion from (an) office, deprivation of office · Amtsabsetzung *f*, Amtsenthebung, Amtsentsetzung, Amtsentziehung, Amtsausschluß *m*, Amtsuntersagung

removal of possession of (real) property → dispossession by legal process

removal (from the site) of improper materials · Beseitigung *f* vertragswidriger (Bau)Stoffe, Wegschaffung vertragswidriger (Bau)Stoffe

removal notification, removal notice, notice of removal, notification of removal · Beseitigungsanzeige *f*, Beseitigungsbenachrichtigung *f*, Beseitigungsmitteilung

removal of (a) name from (a) register · (Namens)Streichung *f*

removal of debris · Schuttbeseitigung *f*

removal of physical facilities, removal of structures, removal of works · Bau(werk)beseitigung *f*, Beseitigung baulicher Anlagen, Beseitigung von Bauwerken, Beseitigung von Bauten, Beseitigung von Baulichkeiten

removal of rent and occupancy control act · Gesetz *n* über den Abbau der Wohnungszwangswirtschaft

removal of restraint on anticipation · Beseitigung *f* des Verbots einer Verfügung im voraus, Beseitigung der Beschränkung der Ehefrau in der Verfügungsfreiheit über ihr Vorbehaltgut

removal of structures, removal of works, removal of physical facilities · Bau(werk)beseitigung *f*, Beseitigung baulicher Anlagen, Beseitigung von Bauwerken, Beseitigung von Bauten, Beseitigung von Baulichkeiten

removal of war damages · Kriegsschädenbeseitigung *f*

removal of works, removal of physical facilities, removal of structures · Bau(werk)beseitigung *f*, Beseitigung baulicher Anlagen, Beseitigung von Bauwerken, Beseitigung von Bauten, Beseitigung von Baulichkeiten

removal order · Beseitigungsgebot *n*, Beseitigungsbefehl *m*, Beseitigungsverfügung *f*, Beseitigungsverordnung

removal power, removal right · Entlassungsrecht *n*, Entlassungsbefugnis *f*

removal right → removal power

removal work(s) · Beseitigungsarbeit(en) *f (pl)*

to remove; amovere [*Latin*]; to depose, to amove [*From membership or office*] · absetzen, entsetzen, entheben, untersagen, entziehen, ausschließen

to remove, to abate, to break down, to destroy [*To abate a structure is to beat it down*] · zerstören

to remove from (a) membership; amovere [*Latin*], to amove · ausschließen [*von einer Mitgliedschaft*]

remunerative cost(s), "pay" cost(s), lucrative cost(s) · rentierliche Kosten *f*

(rendered) null and void · absolut nichtig (gemacht), null und nichtig (gemacht)

to render ineffectual, to render inoperative · unwirksam machen

rendering establishment (US); knacker's yard, knackery (Brit.) · Abdeckerei *f*, Tierkörperbeseitigungsanstalt *f*, Wasenmeisterei *f*, Kleemeisterei, Kleemeierei, Kavillerie *f*

rendering null and void, doing away with, nullifying, rescinding, making void, annulling, (a)voiding, repealing, abolishing, abrogating, cancelling, overruling, abating · Aufheben *n*, Rückgängigmachen *n*, Annullieren *n*, Abschaffen *n*, Löschen *n*, Abbauen *n*

rendering of no effect, avoidance, rendering void · Ungültigmachen *n*, Nichtigmachen

rendering suitable — rent ceiling 886

rendering suitable, fitting, adapting, suiting · Anpassen *n*

to render inoperative, to render ineffectual · unwirksam machen

to render null and void · absolut nichtig machen, null und nichtig machen

renegotiation · Nachverhandlung *f*

to renew, to revive, to revivify · erneuern

renewability · Erneuerbarkeit *f,* Erneuerungsfähigkeit, Erneuerungsvermögen *n*

renewable, revivable · erneuerungsfähig, erneuerbar

renewal, revival · Erneuerung *f*

renewal area, renewal territory, revival area, revival territory · Erneuerungsgebiet *n*

renewal contract, revival contract, contract of renewal, contract of revival · Erneuerungsvertrag *m*

renewal date, revival date · Erneuerungstermin *m,* Erneuerungsdatum *n*

renewal measure, revival measure · Erneuerungsmaßnahme *f*

renewal of lease, revival of lease, renewal of tenancy, revival of tenancy · Pachterneuerung *f*

renewal of tenancy, revival of tenancy, renewal of lease, revival of lease · Pachterneuerung *f*

renewal programming, revival programming · Erneuerungsprogrammierung *f*

renewal territory, revival area, revival territory, renewal area · Erneuerungsgebiet *n*

renewal warrant, talon · Erneuerungsschein *m,* Talon *m* [*Depotgesetz*]

renewing, reviving · Erneuern *n*

to renounce, to disclaim, to abandon, to relinquish, to remise, to forsake, to give up [*To relinquish with intent of never again resuming one's right or interest*] · aufgeben, preisgeben, Verzicht leisten, verzichten, ausschlagen, entsagen, derelinquieren

to renounce by oath, to renounce (up)on oath, to abjure, to forswear · abschwören

renounced, remised, forsaken, given up, waived, disclaimed, abandoned, relinquished · aufgegeben, preisgegeben, Verzicht geleistet, verzichtet, ausgeschlagen, entsagt, derelinquiert

renouncement of heirship, renouncement of inheritance, abandonment of inheritance, abandonment of heirship, relinquishment of inheritance, relinquishment of heirship, renunciation of heirship, renunciation of inheritance · Erbaufgabe *f,* Erbentsagung *f,* Erbpreisgabe, Erbverzicht(leistung) *m, (f),* Erbausschlagung

renouncement of light, abandonment of light, relinquishment of light, renunciation of light · Lichtrechtaufgabe *f,* Lichtrechtverzicht *m,* Lichtrechtpreisgabe

to renounce probate · verweigern der Übernahme einer (Testaments)Vollstreckung

renouncing, relinquishing, forsaking, abandoning, giving up · Aufgeben *n,* Preisgeben *n,* Verzichten *n*

to renovate → to redo

renovation, refurbishing; fixing up, recycling (US); improvement of houses, house improvement · Altbausanierung *f,* Altbaumodernisierung, Renovierung

to rent · mieten

rent → (land) rent

rent [*Payment received or made periodically for the use of property*] · Miete *f,* (Miet)Zins *m*

rent → (lease) rent

rent → (residential) rent

rentable · mietbar

rent act → rent (control) act

rent action → (residential) rent (court) action

rent addition → (residential) rent addition

rent advance · Mietvorauszahlung *f,* Mietvorausleistung

rent advance payment · Mietvorauszahlung *f*

rent allowance · Mietzuschuß *m*

rent amendment law → (residential) rent amendment law

rent apartment, dwelling unit, housing unit, living unit (US); dwelling Brit.) · Mietwohnung *f*

rent arrear · Abgift *f*

rent assistance · Mietförderung

rent bond on landed estate → rent(-charge) bond on landed estate

rent book · Miet(quittungs)buch *n*

rent capitalism · Rentenkapitalismus *m* [*Eine eigenständige Entwick(e)lungsstufe zwischen der Stufe der herrschaftlich organisierten Agrargesellschaft und der des produktiven Kapitalismus*]

rent cause → (residential) rent(court) action

rent ceiling, rent upper limit · Mietobergrenze *f*

rent charge — rent increase

rent charge, quit-rent, fee farm (rent); quieti reditus [*Latin*]; reditus quieti [*Latin*]; forgavel [*In old English law*], chief-rent [*An annual or periodical sum issuing out of land, payable by holders of land in a manor to the lord. Some writers use "fee farm" to signify not only the estate itself, but the rent reserved on it, taking the word "farm" itself in the sense of rent. This practice should, however, be deprecated*] · Erbzins *m*, Befreiungszins, Leh(e)n(s)zins

rent-charge · Grundschuld *f*

rent charge → (lease) rent charge

rent charge → chief rent

rent(-charge) bond on landed estate · Rentenschuldbrief *m*

rent(-charge) creditor on landed estate · Rentenschuldgläubiger *m*

rent(-charge) debt on landed estate · Rentenschuld *f*

rent-charger, creditor under a rent charge · Rentengläubiger *m*

rent collector · Mieteinnehmer *m*

rent conciliation board → (residential) rent conciliation board

rent contract · Mietvertrag *m*

rent contract settlement · Mietvertragsabschluß *m*

rent control · Miet(en)überwachung *f*

rent control (Brit.), tenants' protection, protection of tenants, protection for the tenant, security of tenants · Mieterschutz *m*

rent (control) act, rent (control) law, rent (control) statute · Mietengesetz *n*

rent-controlled flat (Brit.); tenant-protected flat · Mieterschutzwohnung *f*

rent debt · Mietschuld *f*

rent decrease → (residential) rent decrease

rent development → (residential) rent development

rent development · Mietenentwick(e)lung *f*

rent dwelling unit, rent housing unit, rent living unit, rent apartment (US); rent dwelling, rent tenement, rent residence · Mietwohnung *f*

rent earned by capital, capital earning, capital rent · Kapitalrente *f*

rent earned by own capital, interest on owned capital · Eigenkapitalzins *m*

rented garage · Mietgarage *f*

rented (residential) accommodation, rental · Mietunterkunft

renter · Mieter *m* [*allgemein*]

renter household · Mieterhaushalt *m*

renter-occupied, tenant-occupied · mieterbelegt

rent farm · Rentengut *n* [*Ein landwirtschaftliches Grundstück welches nicht gegen Zahlung eines in einem Kapitalbetrage bestehenden Kaufpreises, sondern gegen fortlaufende Rente als Eigentum erworben wird*]

rent field → rent sector

rent fixing · Verrentung *f*

rent fluctuation clause → (residential) rent (price) fluctuation clause

rent for granary, granary rent · Bodengeld *n*, Bodenmiete *f*, Trockenbodengeld, Trockenbodenmiete, Kornbodengeld, Kornbodenmiete

rent for land tenancy, land lease rent, land tenancy rent, rent for land on lease · Bodenpachtabgabe *f*, (Land)Pachtabgabe

rent garden · Mietgarten *m*

rent-gatherer · Renteneintreiber *m*

rent guarantee · Mietgarantie *f*

rent housing [*Housing, the occupancy of which is permitted by the owner thereof in consideration of the payment of agreed charges*] · Mietwohnungen *fpl*

rent housing field, rent housing sector · Mietwohn(ungs)sektor *m*, Wohn(ungs)mietsektor

rent housing loan · Mietwohn(ungs)baudarlehen *n*

rent housing practice · Mietwohn(ungs)wesen *n*, Wohn(ungs)mietwesen

rent housing sector, rent housing field · Mietwohn(ungs)sektor *m*, Wohn(ungs)mietsektor

rent housing unit, rent living unit, rent dwelling unit, rent apartment (US); rent dwelling (Brit.) · Mietwohnung *f*

rent in arrear, arrearage of rent · Mietrückstand *m*

rent in arrear(age) → (residential) rent in arrear(age)

rent income · Mieteinkommen *n*

rent-income ratio, shelter-to-income ratio · Miet(zins)-Einkommens-Verhältnis *n*

rent increase → (residential) rent increase

rent in kind — rent statute

rent in kind, rent paid in kind, rent (paid) in farm-produce · Natural(ien)rente *f*, Natural(ien)zins *m*

to rent land(s), to farm · pachten von Land

rent law → (residential) rent (control) act

rent law → rent (control) act

rentless land, no-rent land · pachtzinsfreies Land *n*

rent level → (residential) rent (price)

rent limit, residential rent limit, dwelling rent limit · (Wohnungs)Mietgrenze *f*

rent living unit, rent housing unit, rent dwelling unit, rent apartment (US); rent dwelling (Brit.) · Mietwohnung *f*

rent of ability → entrepreneur's rent

rent of ability, profits partaking of the nature of rent, conjuncture-profit, entrepreneur's rent, case of extra profit analogous to rent · Unternehmerpension *f*, Seltenheitsprämie *f*

rent of assize → quit rent

rent-offer function, rent-bid function · Bietrentenfunktion *f*

rent of ground, rent of land(s), ground rent, land(s) rent [*It is an acknowledgment made by the tenant to the lord*] · Bodenzins *m*, Landzins, Grund(stücks)zins

rent of land → (agricultural) rent of land

rent of land(s), ground rent, land(s) rent, rent of ground [*It is an acknowledgment made by the tenant to the lord*] · Bodenzins *m*, Landzins, Grund(stücks)zins

rent of land(s) → (true) rent of land(s)

rent of redemption, redemption rent · Ablösungsrente *f*

rent on lease → paid for lease

rent ordinance · Mietenverordnung

rent paid → (lease) rent paid

rent paid in kind, in-kind rent · Naturalwertrente *f*, Naturalzins *m*

rent payment · Rentenzahlung *f*

rent period [*premises*] · Mietzahlungszeitraum *m*

rent period · Mietzeit *f*

rent plea → (residential) rent (court) action

rent policy, (residential) rent (price) policy, dwelling rent (price) policy · (Wohnungs)Miet(preis)politik *f*, (Wohnungs)Mietenpolitik

rent practice · Mietwesen *n*

rent pre-contract · Mietvorvertrag *m*, Mietabschließungsvertrag

rent premises and dwellings, rent premises and apartments (US) · Mischräume *mpl* [*Vermietete Räume, die nicht für nur einen Zweck, sondern für den Wohn- und Geschäftsgebrauch bestimmt sind*]

rent price · Rentenpreis *m*

rent price · Mietpreis *m*

rent (price) control → (residential) rent (price) control

rent (price) fluctuation clause → (residential) rent (price) fluctuation clause

rent (price) level → (residential) rent (price) level

rent rate · Mietsatz *m*

rent rate → (residential) rent rate

rent received · Rente *f*, Pachtertrag *m*, Rentenertrag, Pachtrente

rent-receiver, receiver of rent(s) · Rentenempfänger *m*

rent reduction, rent remission · Mietherabsetzung *f*, Mietermäßigung

rent reduction → (residential) rent reduction

rent relief · Mieterleichterung *f*, (Miet)Zinserleichterung, (Miet)zinsbefreiung *f*, Mietenbefreiung *f*

rent remission, rent reduction · Mietherabsetzung *f*, Mietermäßigung

rent residence → rent dwelling unit

rent (residential) accommodation · Mietunterkunft *f*

rent restriction · Miet(preis)begrenzung *f*

rent restriction act, rent restriction law, rent restriction statute · Gesetz *n* zur Begrenzung des Mietanstiegs [*Wohnungen; Geschäftsräume*]

rent review · Mietenneufestsetzung *f*

rent room · Mietraum *m*

rent-seck; redditius siccus [*Latin*]; barren rent, dry rent [*A rent not supported by a right of distress. Ceased to exist after the Landlord and Tenant Act 1730*] · Rente *f* ohne Pfändungsrecht, trockene Rente

rent sector, rent field · Mietsektor *m*

rent security · Mietsicherheit *f*, Mietdeckung *f*, Mietsicherung, Mietkaution *f*

rent stabilization policy → (residential) rent stabilization policy

rent statute, rent act, rent law · Mietgesetz *n*

rent(s) tax → house rent(s) tax

rent subsidy, rent subvention · Mietsubvention *f*

rent supplement · Mietergänzung *f*

rent-supplemented · mietsubventioniert, mietbezuschußt

rent table · Mietspiegel *m*, Miettabelle [*Wohnungen; Geschäftsräume*]

rent tax · Rentensteuer *f*

rent tenement → rent dwelling unit

rent theory, theory of rents · Rententheorie *f*

rent tribunal · Mieteinigungsamt *n*

rent tribunal → (residential) rent tribunal

rent upper limit → rent upper ceiling

rent usury · Mietwucher *m*, Mietschacher

rent value [*Amount of money for which a real property does or would rent. It is sometimes used as a base for determining a supposed capital value*] · Mietwert *m*

rent value → (residential) rent value

rent value chart → (residential) rent value chart

rent without heating → (dwelling) rent without heating

renumeration for selling of mortgage letters · Bonifikation *f* [*Vergütung der Realkreditinstitute an die Banken für die Verbreitung ihrer Pfandbriefe*]

renumerative rate, beneficial rate [*Terms used by Alfred Marshall for local rates where the money is spent on lighting, drainage, etc., the services so provided being regarded as a net benefit to the people paying the rates, in contrast to onerous rates which yield no compensating benefit to the ratepayer*] · nutzbringende Kommunalabgabe *f*, nutzbringende Gemeindeabgabe

renunciation, renouncement, disclaimer, waiver, abandonment, relinquishment [*It includes the intention, and also the external act(ion) by which it is carried into effect*] · Aufgabe *f*, Preisgabe *f*, Verzicht(leistung) *m*, *(f)*, Entsagung, Ausschlagung

renunciation of (a) contract of mandate · Mandatsniederlegung *f*

renunciation of heirship, renunciation of inheritance, renouncement of heirship, renouncement of inheritance, abandonment of inheritance, abandonment of heirship, relinquishment of inheritance, relinquishment of heirship · Erbaufgabe *f*, Erbentsagung *f*, Erbpreisgabe, Erbverzicht(leistung) *m*, *(f)*, Erbausschlagung

renunciation of light, renouncement of light, abandonment of light, relinquishment of light · Lichtrechtaufgabe *f*, Lichtrechtverzicht *m*, Lichtrechtpreisgabe

renunciation of probate · Verweigerung *f* der Übernahme einer (Testaments)Vollstreckung

reorder · Nachbestellung *f*

reorganization · Umorganisation *f*, Umstellung *f*

reorganization → (territorial) reorganization

to reorganize · umorganisieren, umstellen

reorientation · Neuorientierung *f*, Umorientierung

repair · Reparatur *f*

repairable, capable of repair · reparierbar

repair-backlog · Reparatur(an)stau *m*, vernachlässigter Bauunterhalt *m*

repair clause · Reparaturklausel *f*

repairing covenant, covenant to repair · gesiegeltes Reparaturversprechen *n*

repair lien · Reparatursicherungsrecht *n*, Reparatursicherheitsrecht

repair lump-sum · Reparaturpauschale *f*

repair obligation, obligation to repair · Reparaturverpflichtung *f*

repair service · Reparaturdienst *m*

repair(s) notice, repair(s) notification · Reparaturanzeige *f*, Reparaturbenachrichtigung *f*, Reparaturmitteilung

repair work(s), work(s) of repair · Reparaturarbeit(en) *f (pl)*

reparations plan · Reparationsplan *m*

to repay · (zu)rückzahlen

repayable · rückzahlbar

repayment · Rückerstattung *f*, Rückzahlung

repayment of capital · Rückgewähr *f*

to repeal, to overrule, to cancel, to abrogate, to abolish (by authority), to do away with, to abate, to deprive of operation, to rescind, to nullify, to annul · abschaffen, aufheben, rückgängig machen, annullieren, außer Kraft setzen, löschen, abbauen

repeal, abrogation, cancellation, abolition, abatement, abolishment (by authority), annulment, nullification, rescission, avoidance · Annullierung *f*, Rückgängigmachung, Aufhebung, Abschaffung, Abbau *m*, Löschung

repealed, cancelled, abrogated, abated, annulled, nullified, abolished (by authority), rescinded, overruled, done away with, deprived of operation · aufgehoben, annulliert, rückgängig gemacht, außer Kraft gesetzt, abgeschafft, gelöscht, abgebaut

repealing, abolishing, abrogating, can(cell)ing, overruling, abating, rendering null and void, doing away with, nullifying, rescinding, making void, annulling, (a)voiding · Aufheben n, Rückgängigmachen, Annullieren, Abschaffen, Löschen, Abbauen

repealing clause, determinative clause, overriding clause · Aufhebungsklausel f

to re-people · wiederbevölkern

repercussion · Wiederabwälzung f

replacement, substitution · Ersetzung f, Substitution f

replacement cost(s), reproduction cost(s) [*Appraisers sometimes use the terms "reproduction cost" and "replacement cost" interchangeably, but the terms are not synonymous. Reproduction cost refers to the current cost of constructing a building which would be physically identical to the building being appraised, using the same or very similar materials. Replacement cost refers to the current cost of replacing a building with one having the same functional utility, but which might be composed of different materials or which might be somewhat different in size, floor plan, architecture, etc.*] · Wiederbeschaffungskosten f

replacement housing · Ersatzwohnungen fpl

replacement worker, replacement workman · Ersatzarbeiter m

to replan · umplanen, nachplanen

replanning · Umplanung f, Nachplanung

replanting · Umpflanzen n, Verpflanzen

repleader · Plädoyerwiederholung f

replenishment · Auffüllen n [*Lagerbestand*]

replenishment quantity · Auffüllmenge f [*Lagerbestand*]

replication [*obsolete*]; reply · Replik f

replotting act → replotting law

replotting agency, replotting office · Umlegungsstelle f

replotting area, replotting territory · Umlegungsgebiet n

replotting authority · Umlegungsbehörde f

replotting board · Umlegungsamt n

replotting commission · Umlegungskommission f

replotting committee · Umlegungsausschuß m

replotting law · Umlegungsrecht n

replotting law, replotting act, replotting statute · Umlegungsgesetz n

replotting list · Umlegungsverzeichnis n, Umlegungsliste f

replotting lot, replotting parcel · Umlegungsgrund(stück) m, (n)

replotting map · Umlegungskarte f

replotting mass · Umlegungsmasse f

replotting notice, replotting notification · Umlegungsvermerk m [*Eintragung im Grundbuch über die Einleitung eines Umlegungsverfahrens*]

replotting office, replotting agency · Umlegungsstelle f

replotting of land, land replotting · Landumlegung f, Bodenumlegung, Flächenumlegung

replotting of plots, replotting of parcels · Grund(stücks)umlegung f in Baugebieten, Umlegung der Grundstücke in Baugebieten [*Die Ersetzung des bestehenden Netzes von Grundstücksgrenzen im Umlegungsgebiet durch ein Netz bebauungsmäßig zweckvoll gezogener Grundstücksgrenzen*]

replotting order · Umlegungsanordnung f, Umlegungsbefehl m, Umlegungsgebot n, Umlegungsverfügung f

replotting parcel, replotting lot · Umlegungsgrund(stück) m, (n)

replotting participant · Umlegungsteilnehmer m

replotting plan · Umlegungsplan m

replotting procedure · Umlegungsverfahren n

replotting resolution · Umlegungsbeschluß m, Umlegungsentschließung f

replotting statute → replotting law

replotting territory, replotting area · Umlegungsgebiet n

reply; replication [*obsolete*] · Replik f

reply by return of post · postwendende Rückantwort f

reply of necessaries · Replik f der in rem versio

reply paid, R.P. · Antwort bezahlt

reply to counterclaim · Erwiderung f auf einen geltend gemachten Anspruch

to report · anmelden

report · Anmeldung f

report · Bericht m

report(er) → (law) report(er)

report form — to repurchase

report form, vertical form · Staffelform *f* [*Bilanz*]

reporting · Berichterstattung *f*

reporting · Anmelden *n*

reporting duty, duty of reporting · Anmeldepflicht *f*

to repossess · wieder in Besitz nehmen

representation, recital · Darstellung *f*, Erklärung

representation [*In a plan*] · Darstellung *f*

representation · Ausweisung *f* [*Dieser Begriff hat keine juristische Bedeutung. Er wird aber im allgemeinen für Festlegungen in Plänen verwendet. „Ausweisung" wird im Regionalplan und im Flächennutzungsplan „Darstellung" und im Bebauungsplan „Festsetzung" genannt*]

representation → (personal) representation

representation chain, chain of representation · Kette *f* der Rechtsnachfolge, Rechtsnachfolgekette

representation of fact(s), recital of fact(s) · Darstellung *f* des Sachverhalts, Darstellung der Tatsache(n), Erklärung des Sachverhalts, Erklärung der Tatsache(n), Sachverhaltserklärung, Tatsachenerklärung, Sachverhaltsdarstellung, Tatsachendarstellung

representative · Vertrauensmann *m*

representative, privy successor, legal successor, successor in right · Rechtsnachfolger *m*

representative, delegate, proxy, (authorized) agent, attorney (in fact) [*A person either actually or by law held to be authorized and employed by one person to bring him into contractual or other legal relations with a third party*] · Beauftragte *m*, Bevollmächtigte, Sachwalter, (Stell)Vertreter, Agent *m*

representative by statute, legal representative, legal agent, legal attorney, (authorized) agent by statute, attorney by statute · gesetzlicher Verteter *m*

representative government · parlamentarische Regierung *f*

representative party · Repräsentativpartei *f* [*Zur Führung eines Rechtsstreites im Gegensatz zur Streitgenossenschaft*]

representative's year · Nachlaßverteilungsjahr *n* [*Das Jahr vom Erbfall an gerechnet*]

representee · Erklärungsempfänger *m*

to represent falsely, to misrepresent · falsch darstellen, falsch erklären

representor · Darsteller *m*, Erklärer *m*

reprisal → withernam

reproducible · Reproduktionsfolie *f* [*Kartographie*]

reproduction [*Exact duplication of a structure as of a certain date*] · Ersatznachbildung *f*

reproduction cost(s), replacement cost(s) [*Appraisers sometimes use the terms "reproduction cost" and "replacement cost" interchangeably, but the terms are not synonymous. Reproduction cost refers to the current cost of constructing a building which would be physically identical to the building being appraised, using the same or very similar materials. Replacement cost refers to the current cost of replacing a building with one having the same functional utility, but which might be composed of different materials or which might be somewhat different in size, floor plan, architecture, etc.*] · Wiederbeschaffungskosten *f*

reproduction value less depreciation, cost(s) of reproduction less depreciation · Bauwert *m* [*Beim Sachwertverfahren setzt sich der Bauwert zusammen aus dem Gebäudeherstellungswert, dem Wert der Außenanlagen und sonstiger baulicher Anlagen und Betriebseinrichtungen und berücksichtigt die technische und wirtschaftliche Wertminderung*]

reproductive age · zeugungsfähiges Alter *n*

republication · Wiederveröffentlichung *f*

to repudiate, to reject, to decline, to disaffirm, to refuse · ablehnen, versagen, verweigern, zurückweisen

repudiated, rejected, declined, disaffirmed, refused · abgelehnt, versagt, verweigert, zurückgewiesen

to repudiate liability for, to contract (oneself) out of · freizeichnen, sich freizeichnen

repudiation, disaffirmation, disaffirmance, refusal, rejection · Ablehnung *f*, Zurückweisung, (Ver)Weigerung, Versagung, Aufsage *f*

repudiation right, right of repudiation · Leistungsverweigerungsrecht *n* [§ 320 BGB]

repudiator (of a contract) · Leistungsverweigerer *m*, vertragsaufsagende Partei *f*

repudiatory contract breach, fundamental breach (of contract), repudiatory breach (of contract), fundamental contract breach · fundamentaler (Vertrags)Bruch *m*, schwerwiegender (Vertrags)Bruch

repugnant · widerstreitend

repugnant condition · widersinnige Bedingung *f*

to repurchase, to buy back · zurückkaufen

repurchase · Rückkauf *m*

repurchase agreement, buy back agreement · Rückkaufabkommen *n*, Rückkaufabmachung *f*, Rückkaufvereinbarung

repurchase value, buy back value · Rückkaufwert *m*

repurchasing, buying back · Rückkaufen *n*

repute, fame · Ruf *m*

reputed, ostensible, apparent, presumptive, presumed · angeblich, anscheinend, scheinbar, mutmaßlich, vermutlich, vermeintlich

reputed to appertain to, reputed to belong to · angeblich zugehören, vermeintlich zugehören, anscheinend zugehören, vermutlich zugehören, mutmaßlich zugehören, scheinbar zugehören

reputed owner, reputed proprietor, apparent owner, presumptive owner, presumed owner, apparent proprietor, presumptive proprietor, presumed proprietor · angeblicher Eigentümer *m*, vermutlicher Eigentümer, anscheinender Eigentümer, mutmaßlicher Eigentümer, scheinbarer Eigentümer, vermeintlicher Eigentümer

reputed ownership, reputed property, reputed proprietorship, presumed ownership, presumed proprietorship, presumed property, apparent ownership, apparent proprietorship, apparent property, presumptive ownership, presumptive proprietorship, presumptive property · angebliches Eigentum *n*, mutmaßliches Eigentum, scheinbares Eigentum, vermutliches Eigentum, anscheinendes Eigentum, vermeintliches Eigentum, Vermögen *n* Dritter in einer Konkursmasse

reputed ownership clause, order and disposition clause · Klausel *f* des englischen Konkursrechts nach der in gewissem Umfange auch Vermögen Dritter zur Masse gehört

reputed property → reputed ownership

reputed proprietor → reputed owner

reputed proprietorship → reputed ownership

reputed title, putative title, supposed title · Putativ(rechts)titel *m*

to request · auffordern

request · Aufforderung *f*

request [*A direction or command in law of wills*] · Gebot *n*

request, application · Antrag *m*, Gesuch *n*, Ersuchen *n*

request blank (form), blank (form) of request, blank (form) of application, application blank (form) · Gesuchsformular *n*, Gesuchsmuster *n*, Antragsformular, Antragsmuster, Antragsformblatt *n*, Antragsblankett, Antragsvordruck *m*, Gesuchsformblatt, Gesuchsblankett *n*, Gesuchsvordruck

request date, date of filing, date of application, date of request, filing date, application date · Antragsdatum *n*, Gesuchsdatum

request fee, fee of request, fee of application, application fee · Antragsgebühr *f*, Gesuchsgebühr

request for admission · Ersuchen *n* Tatsachen anzuerkennen

request for cancelling, application for ruling through, request for ruling through, application for cancelling · Löschungsantrag *m*, Löschungsgesuch *n* [*Löschung im Grundbuch*]

request for demolition, request for wrecking, application for demolition, application for wrecking, request for pulling down, application for pulling down, application for razing, request for razing · Abbruchantrag *m*, Abbruchgesuch *n*, Abrißantrag, Abrißgesuch, Einreißantrag, Einreißgesuch

request for further information on offer · angebotsbezogene Rückfrage *f*

request for planning permission, planning permission application, planning permission request, application for planning permission · Planungserlaubnisantrag *m*, Planungserlaubnisgesuch *n*, Planungsgenehmigungsantrag, Planungsgenehmigungsgesuch

request for priority, priority application, priority request, application for priority · Dringlichkeitsantrag *m*, Dringlichkeitsgesuch *n*

request for pulling down → request for demolition

request for razing → request for demolition

request for registration, application for recording, request for recording, application for recordation, request for recordation, application for registration · Buchungsgesuch *n*, Buchungsantrag *m*, Eintragungsantrag, Eintragungsgesuch, Registrierungsantrag, Registrierungsgesuch, Eintragungsersuchen *n*, Registrierungsersuchen, Buchungsersuchen

request for ruling through, application for cancelling, request for cancelling, application for ruling through · Löschungsantrag *m*, Löschungsgesuch *n* [*Löschung im Grundbuch*]

request for tender, request for offer, request for bid, call for tender, call for offer, call for bid; request for (bid) proposal, call for (bid) proposal (US); ten-

request for the summons — rescission (court) action

dering invitation, invitation to tender, invitation to bid, bidding invitation, invitation to (submit a) bid · (Angebots)Aufforderung f, Aufforderung zur Angebotsabgabe

request for the summons, application for the summons · Ladungsantrag m, Ladungsgesuch n

request for wrecking → request for demolition

request of motion, application of motion · Initiativantrag m

request procedure, application procedure · Antragsverfahren n, Gesuchsverfahren

request to reverse (a judg(e)ment), application to reverse (a judg(e)ment), application to set aside (a judg(e)ment, motion to set aside (a judg(e)ment), request to set aside (a judg(e)ment), motion to reverse (a judg(e)ment) · Aussetzungsantrag m, Aussetzungsgesuch n [Urteil]

to require beforehand, to prerequire · vorbedingen, voraussetzen

required beforehand, prerequisite, prerequired · vorbedingt, vorausgesetzt

required setback line · Baugrenze f [Die in einem Bebauungsplan festgesetzte Grenzlinie einer überbaubaren Grundstücksfläche bis zu der gebaut werden darf, aber nicht gebaut werden muß]

requirement · Ausstattung f [einer Fläche]

requirement · Anforderung f, Erfordernis n, Auflage f

requirement, unilateral obligation, one-sided obligation · Auflage f, einseitige Verpflichtung f

requirements society · landwirtschaftliche Bezugsgenossenschaft f

requiring a (registered) certification (trade)mark · (güte)prüfzeichenbedürftig [Baustoff]

requiring a way of necessity · notwegbedürftig [Grundstück]

requiring maintenance · unterhaltungsbedürftig, instandhaltungsbedürftig

requiring permission, liable to permission, subject to permission · erlaubnisbedürftig, erlaubnispflichtig, genehmigungsbedürftig, genehmigungspflichtig

requiring recognition · anerkennungsbedürftig, anerkennungspflichtig

requisition [Compulsory taking of property] · Requisition f

requisitioned land · requiriertes Land n, requirierter Boden m

requisitioning · Requirieren n

requisition on title, title requisition · (Rechts)Titelnachforschung f, Nachforschung über einen (Rechts)Titel

rerouting · Flugumbuchung f

res [Latin]; thing [(subjektives) Recht is in English (subjective) right or interest] · Gegenstand m, Rechtsobjekt n, Ding n, Sache f [Im B.G.B. werden Sachen und (subjektive) Rechte als Gegenstände bezeichnet. §§ 260, 434, 581]

resale · Wiederverkauf m

resale · Deckungsverkauf m

resale value · Wiederverkaufswert m

rescheduling · Terminumplanung f

to rescind, to nullify, to annul, to repeal, to overrule, to cancel, to abrogate, to abolish (by authority), to do away with, to abate, to deprive of operation · abschaffen, aufheben, rückgängig machen, annullieren, außer Kraft setzen, löschen, abbauen

rescindable, annullable, defeasible, abrogatable · annullierbar, aufhebbar, löschbar, abschaffbar, abbaubar

rescinded, overruled, done away with, deprived of operation, repealed, cancelled, abrogated, abated, annulled, nullified, abolished (by authority) · aufgehoben, annulliert, rückgängig gemacht, außer Kraft gesetzt, abgeschafft, gelöscht, abgebaut

rescinding, making void, annulling, (a)voiding, repealing, abolishing, abrogating, cancelling, overruling, abating, rendering null and void, doing away with, nullifying · Aufheben n, Rückgängigmachen n, Annullieren n, Abschaffen n, Löschen n, Abbauen n

rescission, withdrawal · Rücktritt m

rescission, avoidance, repeal, abrogation, cancellation, abolition, abatement, abolishment (by authority), annulment, nullification · Annullierung f, Rückgängigmachung, Aufhebung f, Abschaffung f, Abbau m, Löschung

rescission by agreement · vertraglich vereinbarter Rücktritt m

rescission cause → rescission (court) action

rescission clause, withdrawal clause · Rücktrittsklausel f

rescission contract; contractus consensus [Latin] · Aufhebungsvertrag m

rescission (court) action, rescissory (court) action, rescission (law)suit, rescissory (law)suit, rescission cause, rescissory cause, rescission plea, rescissory plea [An action to rescind or annul a deed or contract] · Aufhebungsklage f, Aussetzungsklage f

rescission from a case — reserved land

rescission from a case, withdrawal from a case · Rücktritt m von einem (Rechts)Fall

rescission (law)suit → rescission (court) action

rescission of contract, withdrawal from contract · Vertragsrücktritt m

rescission plea → rescission (court) action

rescission suit → rescission (court) action

rescissory action → rescissory (court) action

rescissory cause → rescissory (court) action

rescissory (court) action, rescission (law)suit, rescissory (law)suit, rescission cause, rescissory cause, rescission plea, rescissory plea, rescission (court) action [*An action to rescind or annul a deed or contract*] · Aufhebungsklage f, Aussetzungsklage f

rescissory (law)suit → rescissory (court) action

rescissory plea → rescissory (court) action

res composita [*Latin*] · zusammengesetzte Sache f

res comunis, res publica [*Latin*] · gemeine Sache f

res corporales, res singula [*Latin*]; corporeal thing, tangible thing, chose, physical thing, thing corporeal, corporeal chattel (personal) [*A thing that affects the senses and may be seen and handled*] · (Einzel)Sache f, körperliches Rechtsobjekt n, materielles Rechtsobjekt, körperliches Ding n, materielles Ding, körperlicher (Rechts)Gegenstand m, materieller (Rechts)Gegenstand [*Ausgenommen lebender menschlicher Körper. Unter den Sachbegriff fallen nicht die Rechte, die Sachgesamtheiten, d. h. Mehrheiten von Sachen, die eine besondere Benennung haben, z. B. Bücherei, Warenlager usw. und die Inbegriffe von Sachen und Rechten, z. B. Erbschaftsvermögen usw. Im Preußischen Allgemeinen Landrecht von 1794 (A.L.R.) ist (Einzel)Sache allerdings alles, was Gegenstand eines Rechtes oder einer Verbindlichkeit sein kann (§ 1. I. 2)*]

to rescue · sanieren durch Fusion, fusionssanieren

rescue (merger) · Sanierungsfusion f, Fusionssanierung

rescue take over · Übernahmesanierung f

research and development, R & D · Forschung f und Entwick(e)lung

research approach · Forschungsansatz m

research cost(s) · Forschungskosten f

research council · Forschungsbeirat m

research discipline · Forschungsdisziplin f

research finding · Forschungsergebnis n

research method, research technique · Forschungsverfahren n, Forschungstechnik f

research objective, objective of research · Forschungsgegenstand m

research of central places, central place research · Forschung f der zentralen Orte, Forschung zentraler Orte, zentralörtliche Forschung

research-orien(ta)ted, research-related · forschungsorientiert, forschungsbezogen

research scholar · Forschungsgelehrte m

research topic · Forschungsthema n

research training · Forschungsausbildung f

research work · Forschungsarbeit f

reservation, reserve · Vorbehalt m

reservation, reserved land [*Public land that has been withheld or kept back from sale or disposition*] · Reservat(land) n

reservation, national park · Nationalpark m

reservation of (building) permission, proviso of (building) permission · Erlaubnisvorbehalt m, Genehmigungsvorbehalt

reservation of performance, performance reservation · Leistungsvorbehalt m

reservation of proprietorship, reservation of (general) property, reservation of ownership (of property), pactum reservati dominii [*Latin*] · Eigentumsvorbehalt m

reservation of title, title reservation · (Rechts)Titelvorbehalt m

reserve · langfristige Rückstellung f

reserve, reservation · Vorbehalt m

reserve · Sperrbezirk m

reserve · Reserve f

reserve → (surplus) reserve

reserve → (liability) reserve

reserve → (valuation) reserve

reserve area, provisional area · Reservefläche f, Vorbehaltfläche

reserved judg(e)ment, considered judg(e)ment · Urteil n nach vertagter Verkündung

reserved land, reservation [*Public land that has been withheld or kept back*

reserved price — residence area

from sale or disposition] · Reservat(land) *n*

reserved price · Versteigerungsmindestpreis *m*, Mindestversteigerungspreis, Auktionsmindestpreis, Mindestauktionspreis

reserve for depreciation · Wertberichtigung *f* auf Anlagevermögen

reserve fund · Rücklage *f*

reserve ground · Vorratsgelände *n*

reserve liability · Nachschußpflicht *f*

reserve of exemption, reserve of discharge, reserve of dispensation, reserve of release · Befreiungsvorbehalt *m*, Entlastungsvorbehalt, Dispens(ierungs)vorbehalt, Freistellungsvorbehalt, Freigabevorbehalt, Erlaßvorbehalt

reserve of land, stock of land(s), land reserve, land resource, resource of land · Bodenreserve *f*, Bodenvorrat *m*, Flächenreserve, Flächenvorrat, Landreserve, Landvorrat

reserve price · Minimalverkaufspreis *m*

resetter [*Scots law*]; receiver (of stolen goods) · Hehler *m*

to resettle, to displace, to transfer from congested areas, to decentralize, to disperse, to resite, to relocate · aussiedeln, umsiedeln, verlegen, verändern des Standortes, umsetzen

resettled, relocated, resited, displaced · ausgesiedelt, planungsverdrängt, umgesetzt, verlegt, umgesiedelt

resettled family, resited family, displaced family, relocated family · Aussied(e)lerfamilie *f*, Umsied(e)lerfamilie, umgesiedelte Familie, ausgesiedelte Familie, verlegte Familie, umgesetzte Familie, planungsverdrängte Familie

resettled individual, resited person, resited individual, displacee, displaced individual, displaced person, relocated person, relocated individual, resettled person · Aussied(e)ler *m*, Aussied(e)lerperson *f*, Umsied(e)lerperson, Umsied(e)ler, Umgesiedelte, Ausgesiedelte

resettlement · Neuerrichtung *f* einer Familienstiftung, Neufestlegung einer Fideikommißnachfolge, Wiederstiftung

resettlement, transfer from congested areas, (tenant) relocation, displacement, rehousing [*Of persons from land acquired or appropriated for planning purposes*] · Aussied(e)lung *f*, Umsied(e)lung, Standortveränderung, Verlegung, Umsetzung, Wiederunterbringung

resettlement · Wiederansied(e)lung *f*

resettlement area, relocation area · Aussied(e)lungsgebiet *n*, Verlegungsgebiet, Umsied(e)lungsgebiet, Umsetzungsgebiet

resettlement assistance, relocation assistance · Aussied(e)lungsförderung *f*, Umsied(e)lungsförderung, Verlegungsförderung, Umsetzungsförderung

resettlement authority, relocation authority · Aussied(e)lungsbehörde *f*, Umsied(e)lungsbehörde, Verlegungsbehörde, Umsetzungsbehörde

resettlement map, relocation map · Aussied(e)lungskarte *f*, Verlegungskarte, Umsied(e)lungskarte, Umsetzungskarte

resettlement of industry, displacement of industry, transfer of industry, relocation of industry, industrial resettlement, industrial relocation, industrial shifting · Industrieaussied(e)lung *f*, Industrieumsied(e)lung, Industrieumsetzung, Industrieverlegung, industrielle Standortveränderung, Industrieverlagerung

resettlement of population, population relocation, population resettlement, relocation of population · Bevölkerungsumsied(e)lung *f*, Bevölkerungsverlegung, Bevölkerungsaussied(e)lung, Bevölkerungsumsetzung

resettlement place · Nachfolgeort *m*

resettlement plan, relocation plan · Aussied(e)lungsplan *m*, Verlegungsplan, Umsied(e)lungsplan, Umsetzungsplan

resettlement planning, relocation planning · Aussied(e)lungsplanung *f*, Umsied(e)lungsplanung, Umsetzungsplanung, Verlegungsplanung

resettlement survey, relocation survey · Aussied(e)lungsenquête *f*, Umsied(e)lungsenquête, Verlegungsenquête, Umsetzungsenquête

resettlement zone, relocation zone · Aussied(e)lungszone *f*, Umsied(e)lungszone, Verlegungszone, Umsetzungszone

res gestae [*Latin*]; accompanying facts, incident facts [*The facts surrounding or accompanying a transaction which is the subject of legal proceedings*] · Begleittatsachen *f pl*

res habilis [*Latin*] · Sacheigenschaft *f*

to reside, to dwell, to live · ansässig sein, wohnen

residence [*The habitual physical presence within the limits of a country*] · Aufenthalt *m* [*Die Tatsache, daß sich jemand innerhalb eines Landes gewöhnlich aufhält. Der Aufenthalt wird „facto" erworben, die Niederlassung „facto et animo"*]

residence → (place of) abode

residence, dwelling; dwelling unit, DU, du, living unit, LU, lu, housing unit, apartment, unit of housing (US); apartment (Brit.) [*archaic*]; tenement · Wohnung *f*

residence area, residence territory, housing area, housing territory, residential

residence building — residential community

area, residential territory · Wohngebiet *n*, Wohnungsgebiet

residence building, residential structure, residence structure, living house, dwelling house, residential building · Wohngebäude *n*, Wohnhaus *n*

residence building census, residence building count, dwelling house census, dwelling house count, residential building census, residential building count · Wohnhauszählung *f*, Wohngebäudezählung

residence certificate, certificate of residence · Heimatbescheinigung *f*, Heimatschein *m*, Heimatattest *n*

residence lot, dwelling lot, residential lot · Wohn(ungs)parzelle *f*

residence permission, permission to reside · Aufenthaltserlaubnis *f*, Aufenthaltsgenehmigung *f*

residence purpose, dwelling purpose, residential purpose · Wohnzweck *m*

residence structure, living house, dwelling house, residential building, residence structure · Wohngebäude *n*, Wohnhaus *n*

residence territory, housing area, housing territory, residential area, residential territory, residence area · Wohngebiet *n*, Wohnungsgebiet

residence town, residence city · Residenzstadt *f*

resident · (Gebiets)Ansässige *m*

resident, living, domiciled, residing · wohnhaft

resident, (house) occupier, (house) occupant, dwelling occupier, dwelling occupant, residential occupier, residential occupant, dweller · (Haus)Bewohner *m*, (Haus)Insasse, Wohnungsinsasse, Beziehrer

resident · ansässig

resident · Anlieger *m* [*als Verkehrsteilnehmer*]

resident engineer, resident project administrator, (on-the-)site engineer [*On-the-site administrator of the project for the owner*] · Baustellenleiter *m*, örtlicher Bauleiter, örtliche Bauleitung *f*, Baustellenleitung

residential accommodation, living accommodation · Wohnunterkunft *f*

residential advice, residential consultation, residential counsel, residential consultancy · Wohnberatung *f*

residential amenity, residential desirability · Wohnwert *m*

residential and restaurant (on-)licence · Hotel- und Restaurationsschankerlaubnis *f*

residential area, residential territory, residence area, residence territory, housing area, housing territory · Wohngebiet *n*, Wohnungsgebiet

residential (beneficial) occupation, residential use · Wohn(ungs)nutz(nieß)ung *f*

residential building, hous(ebuild)ing, housing construction, production of dwelling units, erection of dwelling units, production of housing units, erection of housing units, production of living units, erection of living units (US); production of tenements, erection of tenements, production of dwellings, erection of dwellings, production of housing, erection of housing, residential construction · Wohn(ungs)bau *m*, Wohnungserstellung *f*, Wohnungsproduktion *f*, Häuserbau, Hausbau, Mietwohn(ungs)bau, Mietwohnungserstellung, Mietwohnungsproduktion, Miethäuserbau, Miethausbau

residential building, residence building, residential structure, residence structure, living house, dwelling house · Wohngebäude *n*, Wohnhaus *n*

residential building by extension, residential construction by extension, production of dwelling units by extension, production of housing units by extension, production of living units by extension (US); production of tenements by extension, production of dwellings by extension, production of housing by extension, hous(ebuild)ing by extension · Wohn(ungs)bau *m* durch Erweiterung, Wohnungserstellung *f* durch Erweiterung, Wohnungsproduktion *f* durch Erweiterung [*Schaffung von Wohnraum durch Aufstockung oder Anbau*]

residential building census, residential building count, residence building census, residence building count, dwelling house census, dwelling house count · Wohnhauszählung *f*, Wohngebäudezählung

residential building insurance · Wohngebäudeversicherung *f*

residential building zone · Wohn(ungs)bauzone *f*

residential category · Wohn(ungs)baukategorie *f* [*Baunutzungsverordnung*]

residential choice · Wohnwahl *f*

residential city, residential town · Wohnstadt *f*

residential clearance · Wohnsanierung *f*, Wohnungssanierung

residential collecting street · (Wohn)Sammelstraße *f*

residential colony, housing colony · Wohn(an)sied(e)lung *f*, Wohnkolonie *f*

residential community · Wohngemeinde *f* [*Ein Ort in dem jemand wohnt, der an*

residential contract — residential (on-)licence

einem anderen Ort, der Betriebsgemeinde, arbeitet]

residential contract, dwelling contract, (residential) landlord/tenant lease, (residential) landlord/tenant contract, residential lease, dwelling lease · Wohn(ungs)mietvertrag *m*

residential desirability, residential amenity · Wohnwert *m*

residential development, housing development · Wohngebäudebebauung *f*, Wohn(ungs)bebauung, Wohnhausbebauung; Wohngebäudeüberbauung, Wohnhausüberbauung [*Schweiz*]

residential district, housing district · Wohnbezirk *m*, Wohnungsbezirk

residential environment, housing environment · Wohnumwelt *f*, Wohnumfeld *n*, Nahumwelt, Nahumfeld [*Umfaßt die Umgebung eines Wohnhauses und die Lebensbedingungen eines Wohngebietes*]

residential floor · Wohngeschoß *n*, Wohnetage *f*, Wohnstockwerk *n*

residential floor space · Wohngeschoßfläche *f*

residential fluctuation clause → residential rent(al) (price) fluctuation clause

residential hire-purchase, residential lease-purchase · Wohnungskauf *m* [*Eine Mischung aus Miete und Kauf auf Kredit*]

(residential) home for (the) elderly people, hostel for (the) elderly people, hostel for (the) elderly, home for (the) elderly · (Alten)Wohnheim *n*, Seniorenwohnheim

residential homestead · Wohnheimstätte *f* [*Grundstück mit Einfamilienhaus und Nutzgarten*]

residential hotel · Hotelpension *f*

residential hunting lodge · Wohn- und Jagdhaus *n*

residential industrial slum, industrial residential slum · Industrie-Wohn-Elendsviertel *n*, Wohn-Industrie-Elendsviertel

residential land, housing land · Wohn(ungs)(bau)boden *m*, Wohn(ungs)(bau)land *n*, Wohn(ungs)(bau)fläche *f* [*Im Flächennutzungsplan für den Wohn(ungs)bau bestimmte Baufläche, die nach ihrer baulichen Nutzung in Kleinsied(e)lungsgebiete, reine Wohngebiete und allgemeine Wohngebiete gegliedert werden kann*]

(residential) landlord/tenant lease, (residential) landlord/tenant contract, residential lease, dwelling lease, residential contract, dwelling contract · Wohn(ungs)mietvertrag *m*

(residential) landlord/tenant relation(ship), dwelling landlord/tenant relation(ship), residential tenancy, residential tenure, dwelling tenancy, dwelling tenure · Wohn(ungs)mietverhältnis *n*

residential landlord/tenant relation(ship) at sufferance → residential tenancy at sufferance

residential landscape, housing landscape · Wohn(ungs)landschaft *f*

residential land use, residential (land) area use · Bodenbenutzung *f* für Wohn(ungs)zwecke

residential (land) use zoning, residential zoning, housing (land) use zoning, housing zoning · (bauliche) Nutzung *f* für Wohnzwecke, Baunutzung für Wohnzwecke, Wohn-(ungs)baunutzung, Bauzonenfestlegung für Wohnzwecke, Wohn(ungs)bauzonenfestlegung

residential lease, dwelling lease, residential contract, dwelling contract, (residential) landlord/tenant lease, (residential) landlord/tenant contract · Wohn(ungs)mietvertrag *m*

residential lease-purchase, residential hire-purchase · Wohnungskauf *m* [*Eine Mischung aus Miete und Kauf auf Kredit*]

residential lease term, dwelling lease term, term of residential lease, term of dwelling lease · Wohnungsmietvertragsfrist *f*

residential locality · Wohnortschaft *f* [*Sie hat wenig oder gar keine Industrie*]

residential location, housing location, residential site, housing site · Wohn(ungs)standort *m*

residential location model, housing location model, housing site model, residential site model · Wohn(ungs)standortmodell *n*

residential lot, residence lot, dwelling lot · Wohn(ungs)parzelle *f*

residential medicine, housing medicine · Wohn(ungs)medizin *f*

residential mortgage, hous(ebuild)ing mortgage · Wohn(ungs)bauhypothek *f*, Wohn(ungs)hypothek

residential mortgage interest rate, hous(ebuild)ing mortgage interest rate · Wohn(ungs)bauhypothekenzinssatz *m*

residential occupancy, residential occupation · Wohnungsbelegung *f*

residential occupier, residential occupant, dweller, resident, (house) occupier, (house) occupant, dwelling occupier, dwelling occupant · (Haus)Bewohner *m*, (Haus)Insasse, Wohnungsinsasse, Bezieher

residential (on-)licence, residential (on-)license · Hotelschankerlaubnis *f*

residential overcrowding — residential rent ordinance

residential overcrowding · Wohnungsüberbelegung f, Wohnungsüberfüllung

residential parcel, dwelling plot, dwelling parcel, residential plot · Wohn(ungs)grundstück n

residential path · Wohnweg m

residential pattern, residential scheme, housing pattern, housing scheme · Wohnmuster n, Wohnschema n

residential place · Wohnplatz m

residential plot, residential parcel, dwelling plot, dwelling parcel · Wohn(ungs)grundstück n

resident(ial) population, permanent population, de-jure population · Wohnbevölkerung f, De-jure-Bevölkerung, wohnberechtigte Bevölkerung

residential possession · Wohnbesitz m [*Ein mit einer Beteiligung an einem zweckgebundenen Vermögen verbundenes schuldrechtliches Dauerwohnrecht*]

residential possessor · Wohnbesitzer m [*Nicht verwechseln mit „Wohneigentümer"*]

residential preference, housing preference · Wohn(ungs)standortvorzug m

residential premises · Wohnungsanwesen n

residential (project) developer, residential (project) promoter, residential (project) producer, housing (project) promoter, housing (project) producer, housing (project) developer, house project promoter, house project producer, house project developer · Wohn(ungs)bauträger m

residential purpose, residence purpose, dwelling purpose · Wohnzweck m

residential quarter · Wohn(ungs)viertel n

residential (real) estate, residential (real) property, residential realty · Wohn(ungs)-Grund(stücks)besitz m

residential reconstruction loan, residential rebuilding loan · Aufbaudarleh(e)n n für den Wohn(ungs)bau, Wiederaufbaudarleh(e)n n für den Wohn(ungs)bau

residential renewal, residential revival · Wohnungserneuerung f

residential rent, dwelling rent · Wohnungsmiete f, Wohnungs(miet)zins m

residential rent act → residential rent (control) act

(residential) rent addition, dwelling rent addition, addition of (residential) rent, addition of dwelling rent(al) · (Wohnungs)Mietzuschlag m

(residential) rent amendment law, (residential) rent amendment act, (residential) rent amendment statute · (Wohnungs)Mietrechtänderungsgesetz n

residential rent assistance payment · Wohn(ungs)geld n [*Zuschuß zur Wohn(ungs)miete*]

residential rent book, dwelling rent book · Wohnungsmiet(quittungs)buch n

(residential) rent conciliation board · MEA n, (Wohnungs)Mieteinigungsamt

residential rent (control) act, residential rent (control) law, residential rent (control) statute, dwelling rent (control) act, dwelling rent (control) law, dwelling rent (control) statute · Wohnungsmietengesetz n

residential rent (control) law → residential rent (control) act

residential rent (control) statute → residential rent (control) act

(residential) rent (court) action, dwelling rent cause, (residential) rent cause, dwelling rent plea, (residential) rent plea, dwelling rent (law)suit, (residential) rent (law)suit, dwelling rent (court) action · (Wohnungs)Mietklage f

(residential) rent decrease, dwelling rent reduction, dwelling rent decrease, (residential) rent reduction · Mietherabsetzung f, Mietsenkung, Wohnungsmietherabsetzung, Wohnungsmietsenkung, (Wohnungs)Mietminderung

residential rent debt, dwelling rent debt · Wohnungsmietschuld f

residential rent development, dwelling rent development · Wohnungsmietenentwick(e)lung f

residential rent in arrear(age), dwelling rent in arrear(age), arrear(age) of residential rent, arrear(age) of dwelling rent · Wohnungsmietrückstand m

(residential) rent increase, dwelling rent increase, increase of (residential) rent, increase of dwelling rent · Mieterhöhung f, Mietsteigerung, Wohnungsmieterhöhung, Wohnungsmietsteigerung

(residential) rent law, dwelling rent law, law of landlord and tenant, landlord/tenant law · Mietrecht n, Wohnungsmietrecht [*Sammelbegriff für alle für die Mietverhältnisse maßgebenden rechtlichen Vorschriften*]

residential rent law → residential rent (control) act

(residential) rent limit, dwelling rent limit · Mietgrenze f, Wohnungsmietgrenze

residential rent ordinance, dwelling rent ordinance · Wohnungsmietenverordnung f

**residential rent price, **dwelling rentprice ·
Wohnungsmietpreis *m,* Wohnungs(miet)zinspreis

**(residential) rent (price) control, **dwelling rent (price) control · (Wohnungs)Miet(preis)überwachung *f* (Wohnungs)Mietgeldüberwachung, (Wohnungs)Mietzinsüberwachung

**residential rent (price) fluctuation clause, **dwelling rent (price) fluctuation clause · Wohnungsmiet(preis)gleitklausel *f,* Wohnungsmietzinsgleitklausel

**(residential) rent (price) level, **dwelling rent (price) level · (Wohnungs)Miet(preis)höhe *f,* (Wohnungs)Mietgeldhöhe, (Wohnungs)Mietzinshöhe

**(residential) rent (price) policy, **dwelling rent (price) policy · Mietenpolitik *f,* Miet(preis)politik, Wohnungsmietenpolitik, Wohnungsmiet(preis)politik

**residential rent rate, **dwelling rent rate · Wohnungsmietsatz *m*

**(residential) rent reduction, **(residential) rent decrease, dwelling rent reduction, dwelling rent decrease · Mieterabsetzung *f,* Mietsenkung, Wohnungsmietherabsetzung, Wohnungsmietsenkung, (Wohnungs)Mietminderung

**residential rent restriction, **dwelling rent restriction · Wohnungsmiet(preis)begrenzung *f,* Wohnungsmietzinsbegrenzung, Wohnungsmietgeldbegrenzung

**residential rent room, **dwelling rent room · Wohnungsmietraum *m*

**(residential) rent stabilization policy, **dwelling rent stabilization policy · Mietstabilisierungspolitik *f,* Wohnungsmietstabilisierungspolitik

**residential rent statute ** → residential rent (control) act

**residential rent subvention, **residential rent subsidy, dwelling rent subsidy, dwelling rent subvention · Wohnungsmietsubvention *f*

**residential rent table, **dwelling rent table · Wohnungsmiettabelle *f,* Wohnungsmietspiegel *m*

**(residential) rent tribunal, **dwelling rent tribunal · Mietgericht *n,* Wohnungsmietgericht

**residential rent usury ** · Wohnungsmietwucher *m,* Wohnungsmietschacher

**(residential) rent value ** · (Wohnungs)Mietwert *m*

**(residential) rent value chart ** · (Wohnungs)Mietspiegel *m,* (Wohnungs)Mietwerttabelle *f*

**residential rent with heating, **dwelling rent(al) with heating · Warmmiete *f*

**residential revival, **residential renewal · Wohnungserneuerung *f*

**residential room, **dwelling room · Wohnraum *m* als bewohnbarer Einzelraum

**residential scheme, **housing pattern, housing scheme, residential pattern · Wohnmuster *n,* Wohnschema *n*

**residential servitude, **dwelling servitude, housing servitude · Wohnungsdienstbarkeit *f,* Wohnungsgerechtigkeit, Wohnungsservitut *n, f,* (servitutisches) Wohn(ungs)recht *n* [*Das Recht ein Gebäude oder einen Teil eines Gebäudes unter Ausschluß des Eigentümers als Wohnung zu benutzen*]

**residential settlement act, **housing settlement law, residential settlement law, housing settlement statute, residential settlement statute, housing settlement act · Wohnsied(e)lungsgesetz *n*

**residential settlement area, **residential settlement territory, housing settlement area, housing settlement territory · Wohn(an)sied(e)lungsgebiet *n*

**residential ship ** · Wohnschiff *n*

**residential site, **housing site, residential location, housing location · Wohn(ungs)standort *m*

**residential site model, **residential location model, housing location model, housing site model · Wohn(ungs)standortmodell *n*

**residential speculation ** · Wohnungsspekulation *f*

**residential street ** · bewohnte Straße *f,* Wohnstraße

**residential structure, **residence structure, living house, dwelling house, residential building, residence building · Wohngebäude *n,* Wohnhaus *n*

**residential structure, **house [*In Schottland bedeuten „house" eine Wohnung, auch wenn sie aus nur einem Raum besteht, und „tenement" ein Haus. In England ist es umgekehrt*] · Haus *n*

**residential structures ** · Wohn(ungs)bauten *f*

**residential suburb(an place) (Brit.) **[*See remark under "suburb(an place"*)] · Wohnvorort *m*

**residential tenancy, **residential tenure, dwelling tenancy, dwelling tenure, (residential) landlord/tenant relation(ship), dwelling landlord/tenant relation(ship) · Wohn(ungs)mietverhältnis *n*

**residential tenancy at sufferance, **residential tenure at sufferance, residential landlord/tenant relation(ship) at suffer-

residential tenant — residuary legatee

ance, dwelling tenancy at sufferance, dwelling tenure at sufferance, dwelling landlord/tenant relation(ship) at sufferance · Wohn(ungs)mietverhältnis n auf Duldung, geduldetes Wohn(ungs)mietverhältnis [*Es liegt vor, wenn ein Wohnungsmieter sein ursprünglich rechtmäßiges Wohnungsmietverhältnis unrechtmäßig verlängert*]

residential tenant, dwelling tenant · Wohnungsmieter m

(residential) tenant at will, dwelling tenant at will · jederzeit kündbarer Wohnungsmieter m, all(e)zeit kündbarer Wohnungsmieter, willkürlich kündbarer Wohnungsmieter

residential tenant handbook, dwelling tenant handbook · Wohnungsmiet(er)buch n

residential tenants, dwelling tenants · Wohnungsmieter mpl, Wohnungsmietleute f

residential tenant's law, residential tenant's act, residential tenant's statute, dwelling tenant's law, dwelling tenant's act, dwelling tenant's statute · Wohnungsmietergesetz n

residential tenure → residential tenancy

residential territory, residence area, residence territory, housing area, housing territory, residential area · Wohngebiet n, Wohnungsgebiet

residential tower building · Wohnhochhaus n, „Wohnsilo" m

residential town, residential city · Wohnstadt f

residential traffic · Wohnverkehr m

residential use, residential (beneficial) occupation · Wohn(ungs)nutz(nieß)ung f

residential (vacancy) loss, dwelling (vacancy) loss [*Rent(al) not received because of housing being unrented*] · Wohnungsmietausfall m, Wohnungsmietverlust m

residential (vacancy) loss decline, dwelling (vacancy) loss decline · Wohnungsmietausfallrückgang m, Wohnungsmietverlustrückgang

residential (vacancy) loss risk, residential (vacancy) loss hazard, dwelling (vacancy) loss risk, dwelling (vacancy) loss hazard · Wohnungsmietausfallwagnis n, Wohnungsmietausfallrisiko n, Wohnungsmietverlustwagnis, Wohnungsmietverlustrisiko

residential village · Wohndorf n

residential working settlement, working/residential settlement · Arbeitsstätten-Wohn-(An)Sied(e)lung f, Wohn-Arbeitsstätten-(An)Siedelung

residential yard · Wohnhof m

residential zone, dwelling zone · Wohn(ungs)zone f

residential zoning, housing (land) use zoning, housing zoning, residential (land) use zoning · (bauliche) Nutzung f für Wohnzwecke, Baunutzung für Wohnzwecke, Wohn-(ungs)baunutzung, Bauzonenfestlegung für Wohnzwecke, Wohn(ungs)bauzonenfestlegung

residentiary industry, passive industry · Industrie f für innerräumlichen Austausch

resident of a small town, small town resident (Brit.); small-towner (US) · Kleinstädter m

resident project administrator → resident engineer

residents' and visitors' traffic · Anlieger- und Besucherverkehr m

"residents only" · „Anliegerverkehr" m [*Verkehrsschild*]

residents registration board · Einwohnermeldeamt n

residing, (in)habitancy · Wohnen n

residing, resident, living, domiciled · wohnhaft

residual claim, residual demand, residuary claim, residuary demand · Restforderung f, Restverlangen n

residual cost(s), residuary cost(s) · Restkosten f

residual income · Residualeinkommen n

residual land value, land residual value · Bodenrestwert m, Landrestwert

residual sum of squares, residuary sum of squares · Restquadratsumme f

residual value, residuary value · Restwert m

residual value method, residuary value method · Restwertverfahren n

residuary devise · Universal(land)vermächtnis n, Universalbodenvermächtnis

residuary devisee [*The person named in a will who is to take all the real property remaining over and above the other devises*] · Universal(boden)vermächtnisnehmer m, Universallandvermächtnisnehmer

residuary legacy, residuary bequest · Universal(fahrnis)vermächtnis n, Universal(fahrnis)legat n, Universalfahrhabevermächtnis, Universalfahrhabelegat

residuary legatee [*The person to whom the surplus of the personal estate, after the discharge of all debts and particular legacies, is left by the testator's will*] · Universal-(Fahrnis)Vermächtnisnehmer m

900

residuary loan, residual loan · Restdarleh(e)n n

residuary power, residuary authority · übriggebliebene Kompetenz f, übriggebliebene Gewalt, übriggebliebene Macht, übriggebliebene Hoheit

res incorporales [*Latin*]; incorporeal thing, intangible thing, incorporeal chattel (personal), intangible chattel (personal), thing incorporeal · unkörperliches Ding n, immaterielles Ding, nichtkörperliches Ding, unkörperliches Rechtsobjekt n, nichtkörperliches Rechtsobjekt, immaterielles Rechtsobjekt, immaterieller Gegenstand m, unkörperlicher Gegenstand, nichtkörperlicher Gegenstand

res inter alias actae [*Latin*] · Tatsachen fpl analog den nachzuweisenden aber ohne Kausalzusammenhang mit ihnen

to resite, to relocate, to resettle, to displace, to transfer from congested areas, to decentralize, to disperse · aussiedeln, umsiedeln, verlegen, verändern des Standortes, umsetzen

resited, displaced, resettled, relocated · ausgesiedelt, planungsverdrängt, umgesetzt, verlegt, umgesiedelt

resited family, displaced family, relocated family, resettled family · Aussied(e)lerfamilie f, Umsied(e)lerfamilie, umgesiedelte Familie, ausgesiedelte Familie, verlegte Familie, umgesetzte Familie, planungsverdrängte Familie

resited person, resited individual, displacee, displaced individual, displaced person, relocated person, relocated individual, resettled person, resettled individual · Aussied(e)ler m, Aussied(e)lerperson f, Umsied(e)lerperson f, Umsied(e)ler, Umgesiedelte, Ausgesiedelte

res judicata [*Latin*] [*A final judg(e)ment already decided between the same parties or their privies on the same question by a legally constituted court having jurisdiction is conclusive between the parties, and the issue cannot be raised again*] · Vorhandensein n eines rechtskräftigen Urteils, bereits entschiedene Rechtsfrage

res mobilis [*Latin*] → personal estate

res nova [*Latin*] [*A matter not yet decided*] · bisher unentschiedene Rechtsfrage f, noch nicht entschiedene Rechtsfrage

res nullius [*Latin*] [*A thing which has no owner*] · eigentümerlose Sache f

resolution · Beschluß m, Entschließung f

resolution authority · Beschlußbehörde f, Entschließungsbehörde

resolution committee · Beschlußausschuß m, Entschließungsausschuß

resolution giving directions · Vorverhandlungsbeschluß m, Vorverhandlungsentschließung f

resolution of (bankruptcy) discharge, (bankrupty) discharge resolution · Entlassungsbeschluß m, Entlassungsentschließung f, Entlastungsbeschluß, Entlastungsentschließung, Konkursentlassungsbeschluß, Konkursentlassungsentschließung, Konkursentlassungsbeschluß, Konkursentlassungsentschließung, Konkursentlastungsentschließung

resolution to stay (a proceeding), resolution to stop (a proceeding) · Einstellungsbeschluß m, Aussetzungsbeschluß, Einstellungsentschließung f, Aussetzungsentschließung [*Verfahren*]

resolutory condition, condition subsequent, condition resolutive · auflösende Bedingung f, resolutive Bedingung f, Endbedingung f, Resolutivbedingung f [*Die Wirkung des Geschäftes tritt sofort ein und endigt mit dem Eintritt des künftigen ungewissen Umstandes*]

resolutory provision · Resolutivbestimmung f

to resolve · beschließen

resolve act; slip law, session law [*USA*]; public act, public law, public statute, general act, general law, general statute, legislative act, legislative law, legislative statute, session act, session statute · allgemeines Gesetz n [*In den Gliedstaaten der USA erscheinen die Gesetze nach ihrer Verabschiedung zunächst als ,,slip laws", die am Ende einer Sitzungsperiode der Legislative chronologisch zu den ,,session laws" zusammengefaßt werden*]

resort town, resort city · Erholungsstadt f, Kurstadt

resource · Rohstoffvorkommen n, Bodenschatz m

resource commitment · Mitteleinsatz m

resourcefulness · Findigkeit f

resource of land, reserve of land, stock of land(s), land reserve, land resource · Bodenreserve f, Bodenvorrat m, Flächenreserve, Flächenvorrat, Landreserve, Landvorrat

resource-of-land(s) policy, policy of resources of land(s), land(s) reserve policy · Bodenreservepolitik f, Bodenvorratpolitik, Flächenreservepolitik, Flächenvorratpolitik, Landreservepolitik, Landvorratpolitik

respect · Ansehen n

respite → (additional) respite

to respite a payment, to grant respite for a payment, to attermin [*To allow time for the payment of a debt*] · stunden, Zahlungsaufschub bewilligen, Zahlungsfrist

respite of payment — restitution

gewähren, Zahlungsfrist bewilligen, Zahlungsaufschub gewähren

respite of payment, attermination, atterminement [*Adjournment of the payment of a debt to a fixed future date*] · Zahlungsaufschub *m*, Stundung *f* [*Schuld*]

response · Reaktion *f*

responsibility, accountability · Verantwortung *f*, Rechenschaftspflicht *f*, Verantwortlichkeit *f*, Verpflichtung

responsibility accounting system [*It is a system of accounting which is tailored to an organization so that cost(s) are accumulated and reported by levels or responsibility within the organization. Each supervisory area in the organization is charged only with the cost(s) for which it is responsible and over which it has control*] · Kostenstellenrechnung *f* der Organisationsstruktur angepaßt [*Eine der Organisationsstruktur angepaßte Kostenstellenrechnung, nach der jeder Kostenstellenleiter ausschließlich für die von ihm und seinen Unterstellten innerhalb einer bestimmten Rechnungsperiode beeinflußbaren Kosten verantwortlich gemacht wird*]

responsibility (cost(s)) accounting, responsibility costing · (Kosten)Verantwortungsrechnung *f*, Verantwortungskostenrechnung

responsible, accountable, answerable [*responsible applies to one who has been delegated some duty or responsibility by one in authority and who is subject to penalty in case of default (he is responsible for making out the reports); answerable implies a legal or moral obligation for which one must answer to someone sitting in judg(e)ment (he is not answerable for the crimes of his parents; accountable implies liability for something of value, or responsibility for one's own actions, for which one may be called to account (he will be held accountable for anything he may say)*] · verantwortlich, rechenschaftspflichtig

responsible agency, responsible office, competent agency, competent office · zuständige Stelle *f*

responsible authority, competent authority · zuständige Behörde *f*

responsible condition, accountable condition, answerable condition [*A condition giving rise to a transaction, and requiring recognition*] · rechenschaftspflichtige Bedingung *f*, verantwortliche Bedingung

responsible court, competent court · zuständiges Gericht *n*

responsible event, accountable event, answerable event [*An event giving rise to a transaction, and requiring recognition*] · rechenschaftspflichtiges Ereignis *n*, verantwortliches Ereignis

responsible office, competent agency, competent office, responsible agency · zuständige Stelle *f*

responsible person, accountable person, answerable person · verantwortliche Person *f*, rechenschaftspflichtige Person

responsible to law, answerable to law, liable to be brought before any jurisdiction, amenable, subject to answer to law, liable to answer to law · verantwortlich vor dem Gesetz, rechenschaftspflichtig vor dem Gesetz

res prestita [*Latin*] · Leihe *f*

res publica, res comunis [*Latin*] · gemeine Sache *f*

res publicae [*Latin*] [*Things belonging to the state, as navigable rivers and highways*] · Staatseigentum *n*

res singula [*Latin*]; corporeal thing, tangible thing, chose, physical thing, thing corporeal, corporeal chattel, thing (personal); res corporales [*Latin*] [*A thing that affects the senses and may be seen and handled*] · (Einzel)Sache *f*, körperliches Rechtsobjekt *n*, materielles Rechtsobjekt, körperliches Ding *n*, materielles Ding, körperlicher (Rechts)Gegenstand *m*, materieller (Rechts)Gegenstand [*Ausgenommen lebender menschlicher Körper. Unter den Sachbegriff fallen nicht die Rechte, die Sachgesamtheiten, d. h. Mehrheiten von Sachen, die eine besondere Benennung haben, z. B. Bücherei, Warenlager usw. und die Inbegriffe von Sachen und Rechten, z. B. Erbschaftsvermögen usw. Im Preußischen Allgemeinen Landrecht von 1794 (A.L.R.) ist (Einzel)Sache allerdings alles, was Gegenstand eines Rechtes oder einer Verbindlichkeit sein kann (§ 1. l. 2)*]

to restate, to reword, to change the wording of, to state again in other words, to express again in other words · umschreiben, neugestalten, neuschreiben, umgestalten [*Text*]

Restatement [*In the USA*] · Sammlung *f* von Präzedenzentscheidungen des gemeinen Rechts

restaurant (on-)licence · Restaurantschankerlaubnis *f*

resting place, street refuge, saving place · Bürgersteiginsel *f*

to restitute, to recover, to reimburse, to refund · abgelten, ersetzen, erstatten, vergüten

restituted, recovered, reimbursed, refunded · abgegolten, ersetzt, erstattet, vergütet

restitution, refunding, reimbursement, recovery · Abgeltung *f*, Ersetzung, Vergütung, Erstattung, Entgelt *n*, Restitution *f*

restitution assessment, refunding assessment, recovery assessment, reimbursement assessment · Bemessung *f* der Vergütung, Bemessung *f* der Abgeltung, Bemessung *f* der Erstattung, Bemessung *f* der Ersetzung, Vergütungsbemessung, Erstattungsbemessung, Abgeltungsbemessung, Ersetzungsbemessung

restitution claim, recovery claim, reimbursement claim, refunding claim · Abgeltungsforderung *f*, Erstattungsforderung, Ersetzungsforderung, Vergütungsforderung

restitution duty → refunding duty

restitution for supervision, restitution for superintendence, reimbursement for supervision, refunding for supervision, refunding for superintendence, reimbursement for superintendence, recovery for supervision, recovery for superintendence · Aufsichtsvergütung *f*, Überwachungsvergütung *f*

restitution mortgage, reimbursement mortgage, refunding mortgage, recovery mortgage · Erstattungshypothek *f*, Abgeltungshypothek, Ersetzungshypothek, Vergütungshypothek

restitution of conjugal rights · Wiederherstellung *f* des ehelichen Lebens

restitution rate, recovery rate, reimbursement rate, refunding rate · Abgeltungssatz *m*, Erstattungssatz, Ersetzungssatz, Vergütungssatz

restitution sum, reimbursement sum, recovery sum, refunding sum · Abgeltungssumme *f*, Erstattungssumme, Vergütungssumme, Ersetzungssumme

to restrain, to constrain, to restrict, to limit · begrenzen, beschränken, einschränken

restrained administration (of estate(s)), special administration (of estate(s)), limited administration (of estate(s)), restricted administration (of estate(s)) · besondere Nachlaßverwaltung *f*, eingeschränkte Nachlaßverwaltung, beschränkte Nachlaßverwaltung, begrenzte Nachlaßverwaltung

restrained interest in (real) estate, restrained right in (real) estate, restrained interest in (real) property, restrained right in (real) property, restricted interest in (real) estate, restricted right in (real) estate, restricted interest in (real) property, restricted right in (real) property, limited interest in realty, limited right in realty, restrained right in realty, restrained interest in realty, restricted right in realty, restricted interest in realty, limited interest in (real) estate, limited right in (real) estate, limited interest in (real) property, limited right in (real) property · begrenztes (dingliches) Recht *n* an einem Grund(stück), beschränktes (dingliches) Recht an einem Grund(stück), eingeschränktes (dingliches) Recht an einem Grund(stück), begrenztes (Boden)Besitzrecht, begrenztes Landbesitzrecht, begrenztes Grund(stücks)besitzrecht, beschränktes (Boden)Besitzrecht, beschränktes Landbesitzrecht, beschränktes Grund(stücks)besitzrecht, eingeschränktes Grund-(stücks)besitzrecht, eingeschränktes (Boden)Besitzrecht, eingeschränktes Landbesitzrecht

restrained in time, limited in time, restricted in time · befristet, zeitbegrenzt, zeitbeschränkt

restrained liability, limited liability, restricted liability · begrenzte Haftung *f*, begrenzte Haftpflicht *f*, beschränkte Haftung, beschränkte Haftpflicht, eingeschränkte Haftung, eingeschränkte Haftpflicht

restrained probate, special probate, limited probate, restricted probate · begrenzte Nachlaßbestätigung *f*, eingeschränkte Nachlaßbestätigung, beschränkte Nachlaßbestätigung, besondere Nachlaßbestätigung

restrained right in realty → restrained interest in (real) estate

restraining injunction, preventive injunction, negative injunction, restrictive injunction · gerichtliches Verbot *n*, gerichtliche Verbotsverfügung *f*

restraining notice · Veräußerungsverbotanzeige *f*

restraint, constraint, limitation, restriction · Begrenzung *f*, Einschränkung, Beschränkung

restraint of appeal, restriction of appeal, limitation of appeal · Berufungsbeschränkung *f*, Appellationsbeschränkung

restraint of appointment, restraint of disposition, restriction of disposition, restriction of appointment, limitation of disposition, limitation of appointment · Verfügungsbegrenzung *f*, Verfügungsbeschränkung, Verfügungseinschränkung

restraint of disposition, restriction of disposition, restriction of appointment, limitation of disposition, restraint of appointment · Verfügungsbegrenzung *f*, Verfügungsbeschränkung, Verfügungseinschränkung

restraint of limitation · Hemmung *f* der Verjährung, Verjährungshemmung

restraint of trade · Konkurrenzverbot *n*, Wettbewerbsverbot

restraint on (ab)alienation, restraint on disposal, (ab)alienation against anticipation, disposal of anticipation, (ab)alienation restraint, disposal restraint · Veräußerungsverbot *n*

restraint on anticipation, anticipatory restraint · Beschränkung *f* der Ehefrau in der Verfügungsfreiheit über ihr Vorbehaltgut, Verbot *n* einer Verfügung im voraus

restraint on imports · Einfuhrbeschränkung *f*

restraint (up)on (ab)alienation · Veräußerungsbeschränkung *f*

to restrict, to limit, to restrain, to constrain · begrenzen, beschränken, einschränken

restricted administration (of estate(s)), restrained administration (of estate(s)), special administration (of estate(s)), limited administration (of estate(s)) · besondere Nachlaßverwaltung *f*, eingeschränkte Nachlaßverwaltung, beschränkte Nachlaßverwaltung, begrenzte Nachlaßverwaltung

restricted agglomeration of locations, restricted agglomeration of sites · gebundene Häufung *f* von Standorten, gebundene Standorthäufung

restricted concept [*immunity*] · Differenzierungstheorie *f*, Unterscheidungstheorie

restricted fee → (estate in) fee tail

restricted interest, limited right, limited interest, restricted right · begrenztes (subjektives) Recht *n*, eingeschränktes (subjektives) Recht, beschränktes (subjektives) Recht, subjektives begrenztes Recht, subjektives eingeschränktes Recht, subjektives beschränktes Recht

restricted interest in (real) estate, restricted right in (real) estate, restricted interest in (real) property, restricted right in (real) property, limited interest in realty, limited right in realty, restrained right in realty, restrained interest in realty, restricted right in realty, restricted interest in realty, limited interest in (real) estate, limited right in (real) estate, limited interest in (real) property, limited right in (real) property, restrained interest in (real) estate, restrained right in (real) estate, restrained interest in (real) property, restrained right in (real) property · begrenztes (dingliches) Recht *n* an einem Grund(stück), beschränktes (dingliches) Recht an einem Grund(stück), eingeschränktes (dingliches) Recht an einem Grund(stück), begrenztes (Boden)Besitzrecht, begrenztes Landbesitzrecht, begrenztes Grund(stücks)besitzrecht, beschränktes (Boden)Besitzrecht, beschränktes Landbesitzrecht, beschränktes Grund(stücks)besitzrecht, eingeschränktes (Boden)Besitzrecht, eingeschränktes Landbesitzrecht

restricted in time, restrained in time, limited in time · befristet, zeitbegrenzt, zeitbeschränkt

restricted letter of credit, special letter of credit · Spezialkreditbrief *m*

restricted liability, restrained liability, limited liability · begrenzte Haftung *f*, begrenzte Haftpflicht *f*, beschränkte Haftung, beschränkte Haftpflicht, eingeschränkte Haftung, eingeschränkte Haftpflicht

restricted list of bidders, restricted list of tenderers, select list of bidders, select list of tenderers · beschränkte (An)Bieterliste *f*

restricted personal servitude, limited personal servitude · beschränkte persönliche Dienstbarkeit *f*, eingeschränkte persönliche Dienstbarkeit, begrenzte persönliche Dienstbarkeit

restricted probate, restrained probate, special probate, limited probate · begrenzte Nachlaßbestätigung *f*, eingeschränkte Nachlaßbestätigung, beschränkte Nachlaßbestätigung, besondere Nachlaßbestätigung

restricted right, restricted interest, limited right, limited interest · begrenztes (subjektives) Recht *n*, eingeschränktes (subjektives) Recht, beschränktes (subjektives) Recht, subjektives begrenztes Recht, subjektives eingeschränktes Recht, subjektives beschränktes Recht

restricted right in (real) estate → restricted interest in (real) estate

restricted value · Grund(stücks)wert *m* ohne Änderung der gegenwärtigen Nutzung

restriction, restraint, constraint, limitation · Begrenzung *f*, Einschränkung, Beschränkung

restriction covenant [*Clause in a deed limiting the use of the real property conveyed for a certain period of time*] · Fristklausel *f*, Zeitklausel

restriction of appeal, limitation of appeal, restraint of appeal · Berufungsbeschränkung *f*, Appellationsbeschränkung

restriction of height, height restriction · Höhenbeschränkung *f*

restriction of inheritance, limitation of inheritance [*land*] · Gebundenheit *f* [*Boden*]

restriction of liability, limitation of liability, liability limitation, liability restriction · Haftungsbegrenzung *f*, Haftpflichtbegrenzung, Haftpflichtbeschränkung, Haftungsbeschränkung, Haftpflichteinschränkung, Haftungseinschränkung, Haftbarkeitsbegrenzung, Haftbarkeitsbeschränkung, Haftbarkeitseinschränkung

restriction of purchaser(s), restriction of buyer(s), restriction of vendee(s) · Käuferbeschränkung *f,* Käufereinschränkung

restriction of vendee(s), restriction of purchaser(s), restriction of buyer(s) · Käuferbeschränkung *f,* Käufereinschränkung

restrictive covenant · einschränkende (urkundliche) (Vertrags)Klausel *f*

restrictive covenant, restrictive tendering agreement, taking a price, collusive tendering, collusive bidding, (collusive) price fixing, bid-rigging, bid collusion, rigging bids, collusion among(st) bidders, collusion among(st) offerers, collusion among(st) tenderers, price taking, collusive agreement, combining to eliminate competition [*The frequently heavy cost of tendering sometimes leads contractors to put forward tenders which are not genuine, in the sense that, rather than refuse to make a tender when invited to do so, the contractor tenders a price higher than that "taken" from another contractor who does desire to obtain the contract, thus avoiding expense and leading the employer to believe that he has had genuine competitive tenders for the work*] · Abrede *f* unter Bietern, Absprache *f* unter Bietern, Preisabrede, Preisabsprache, Submissionsabrede, Submissionsabsprache, Konkurrenzvereinbarung *f,* Verständigung *f* unter Bietern, Angebotsabsprache, Angebotsabrede

restrictive injunction, restraining injunction, preventive injunction, negative injunction · gerichtliches Verbot *n,* gerichtliche Verbotsverfügung *f*

restrictive tendering agreement, taking a price, collusive tendering, collusive bidding, (collusive) price fixing, bid-rigging, bid collusion, rigging bids, collusion among(st) bidders, collusion among(st) offerers, collusion among(st) tenderers, price taking, collusive agreement, combining to eliminate competition, restrictive covenant [*The frequently heavy cost of tendering sometimes leads contractors to put forward tenders which are not genuine, in the sense that, rather than refuse to make a tender when invited to do so, the contractor tenders a price higher than that "taken" from another contractor who does desire to obtain the contract, thus avoiding expense and leading the employer to believe that he has had genuine competitive tenders for the work*] · Abrede *f* unter Bietern, Absprache *f* unter Bietern, Preisabrede, Preisabsprache, Submissionsabrede, Submissionsabsprache, Konkurrenzvereinbarung *f,* Verständigung *f* unter Bietern, Angebotsabsprache, Angebotsabrede

to restructure · umstrukturieren

restructuring · Umstrukturierung *f*

resubdivision [*The dividing of a lot of land without creating a new street or road*] · Nachparzell(is)ierung *f*

resubmission · Wiedereinrichtung *f*

to resubmit · wieder einreichen

resulting · resultierend

resulting trust · vermutete Treuhand *f*

results of operations, profit and loss account, income statement, earnings and profit and loss statement, statement of operations · Gewinn- und Verlustrechnung *f*

to resume · zwangsweise zurückkaufen

resumption · Zwangsrückkauf *m*

res unita [*Latin*] · Einheitssache *f*

resurvey · Nachenquête *f*

retail closing → retail (trade) closing

retail co-operative (society), provident co-operative (society), provident society, consumers' co-operative (society) · Konsumverein *m,* Konsumgenossenschaft *f,* Verbrauchergenossenschaft

retail (cost(s)) accounting, retail costing · Einzelhandelskostenrechnung *f*

retailer · Einzelhändler *m*

retailing, retail trade · Einzelhandel *m*

retail purchase [*Purchase of energy and water by tenants from supplying public utility companies and billed to tenants by the utility, as distinguished from a wholesale purchase*] · Einzelbezug *m*

retail trade, retailing · Einzelhandel *m*

retail (trade) activity · Einzelhandelstätigkeit *f*

retail (trade) area, retail (trade) space · Einzelhandelsfläche *f*

retail (trade) area, retail (trade) territory · Einzelhandelsgebiet *n*

retail (trade) axis · Einzelhandelsachse *f*

retail (trade) building · Einzelhandelsgebäude *n*

retail (trade) centre (Brit.); retail (trade) center (US) · Einzelhandelszentrum *n*

retail (trade) closing · Ladenschluß *m*

retail (trade) component · Einzelhandelskomponente *f*

retail (trade) composition, retail (trade) structure · Einzelhandelsstruktur *f,* Einzelhandelsaufbau *m,* Einzelhandelszusammensetzung *f,* Einzelhandelsgefüge *n*

retail (trade) district · Einzelhandelsbezirk *m*

retail (trade) field, retail (trade) sector · Einzelhandelssektor *m*

retail (trade) firm, retail (trade) store · Einzelhandelsbetrieb *m*, Einzelhandelsgeschäft *n*, Einzelhandelsfirma *f*

retail (trade) floor space · Einzelhandelsverkaufsfläche *f*

retail (trade) industry · Einzelhandelsgewerbe *n*

retail (trade) location, retail (trade) site · Einzelhandelsstandort *m*

retail (trade) market · Einzelhandelsmarkt *m*

retail (trade) quarter · Einzelhandelsviertel *n*

retail (trade) sale, sale by retail (trade) · Einzel(handels)verkauf *m*, Detailverkauf

retail (trade) sector, retail (trade) field · Einzelhandelssektor *m*

retail (trade) site, retail (trade) location · Einzelhandelsstandort *m*

retail (trade) space, retail (trade) area · Einzelhandelsfläche *f*

retail (trade) store, retail (trade) firm · Einzelhandelsbetrieb *m*, Einzelhandelsgeschäft *n*, Einzelhandelsfirma *f*

retail (trade) structure, retail (trade) composition · Einzelhandelsstruktur *f*, Einzelhandelsaufbau *m*, Einzelhandelszusammensetzung *f*, Einzelhandelsgefüge *n*

retail (trade) territory, retail (trade) area · Einzelhandelsgebiet *n*

retail (trade) turnover · Einzelhandelsumsatz *m*

to retain, to withhold, to detain · einbehalten, zurück(be)halten, vorenthalten

retainage, retained percentage [*Sum withheld from each payment to the contractor in accordance with the terms of the owner-contractor agreement*] · (Sicherheits)Einbehalt *m*

retainage bond, retained percentage bond [*Under some statutes retained percentages may not be released until contract has been completed and accepted, unless a contractor gives bond to indemnify the owner against loss by reason of the premature release*] · Einbehaltsgarantie *f*

retained earnings, retained income, available (earned) surplus, earned surplus, cash flow [*The spendable income from an investment after paying all expenses, such as operating expenses and debt service*] · Gewinneinbehalt *m*, Profiteinbehalt, einbehaltener Gewinn, einbehaltener Profit

retained earnings, consolidated surplus [*The combined surplus accounts of all companies whose accounts are consolidated, after deducting minority stockholders' interests therein, the interest acquired by the parent company in the subsidiary companies' surpluses existing at the date of their acquisition, and intercompany eliminations*] · Konzernüberschuß *m*

retaining, withholding, detaining · Einbehalten *n*, Zurück(be)halten, Vorenthalten

retaining fee · Präsenzgeld *n*

to retake, to take back · zurücknehmen

retaking, taking back · Zurücknehmen *n*

retaliatory duty · Kampfzoll *m*, Retorsionszoll [*Zollzuschlag vom Inland gegen einen fremden Staat zum gewöhnlichen Zoll errichtet*]

retardation · Verzögerung *f* [*Im Gegensatz zum Verzug setzt die Verzögerung kein Verschulden voraus*]

retardation of construction, retardation of building, construction retardation, building retardation · Bauverzögerung *f*

retarded execution of (the) work(s) · verzögerte Bauausführung *f*

retention, detention, detainment, detainer; retentio [*Latin*] [*The act of keeping back or withholding, either accidentally or by design, a person or thing*] · Rückbehalt *m*, Retention *f*, Zurück(be)haltung *f*, Einbehalt(ung), Vorenthalt(ung)

retention · Einbehalt *m*

retention money, detention money, detainer money, detainment money · Einbehaltungsgeld *n*, (Zu)Rück(be)haltungsgeld, Retentionsgeld

retired · zurückgezogen [*Bausparkassenanteil*]

retired partner · ausgetretener Partner *m*

retirement migration · Ruhestandswanderung *f*

retirement of shares · Anteilzurückziehung *f*, Zurückziehung *f* von Anteilen [*Bausparkasse*]

retirement plan, pension plan, benefit plan · (Alters)Versorgungsplan *m*, Pensionsplan

retraining · Umschulung *f*

retrenchment in administration · Abbau *m* der Verwaltung, Verwaltungsabbau

retroactive, retrospective, ex post facto · rückwirkend

retroactive clause, retrospective clause · Rückwirkungsklausel *f*

retroactive effect, retrospective effect · rückwirkende Kraft *f*, Rückwirkung *f*

retroactive law — revaluation mortgage

retroactive law, retrospective law [*A law which looks backward or contemplates the past; one which is made to affect acts or facts occuring, or rights accruing, before it came into force*] · rückwirkendes Recht *n*

retroactive legislation, retrospective legislation, retrospective lawmaking, retroactive lawmaking · rückwirkende Gesetzgebung *f*

retroactively effective, retrospectively effective · rückwirkend wirksam

retroactive permission, retrospective permission · rückwirkende Genehmigung *f*, rückwirkende Erlaubnis *f*

retroactive planning permission, retrospective planning permission · rückwirkende Planungserlaubnis *f*, rückwirkende Planungsgenehmigung *f*

retrospective, ex post facto, retroactive · rückwirkend

retrospective clause, retroactive clause · Rückwirkungsklausel *f*

retrospective effect, retroactive effect · rückwirkende Kraft *f*, Rückwirkung *f*

retrospective law, retroactive law [*A law which looks backward or contemplates the past; one which is made to affect acts or facts occuring, or rights accruing, before it came into force*] · rückwirkendes Recht *n*

retrospective permission, retroactive permission · rückwirkende Genehmigung *f*, rückwirkende Erlaubnis *f*

retrospective planning permission, retroactive planning permission · rückwirkende Planungserlaubnis *f*, rückwirkende Planungsgenehmigung *f*

retrotransfer · Rückübertragung *f*

return, yield · Ertrag *m*, Rendite *f*

return · einzureichender Bericht *m*

return envelope · Rück(sende)umschlag *m*

return freight, home freight, back freight · Rückfracht *f*

return from housing property, yield from housing property · Hausrendite *f*

returning officer [*For a ward of a (municipal) borough*] · Wahlleiter *m*, Wahlkommissar *m* [*Für einen Stadtbezirk einer Minizipalstadt*]

returning of interests, yielding of interests, bearing of interests, interest yield(ing), interest bearing, interest return · Verzinsung *f*

return law, yield law, law of return, law of yield · Renditegesetz *n*, Ertragsgesetz

return mass (migration) movement · Rückmassenbewegung *f*, Rückmassenwanderungsbewegung

return maximization, yield maximization, maximization of return, maximization of yield · Renditemaximierung *f*

return (migration) movement · Rückbewegung *f*, Rückwanderungsbewegung

return move · Rückwanderung *f*, Rückeinzelwanderung

return of writ, writ return · Wiedereinlieferung *f* eines Dekrets

return on capital → yield in investment

return on investment, yield on investment, return on capital, yield on capital, capital yield, capital return, investment yield, investment return, ROI · Kapitalrendite *f* [*Verhältnis von erzielten Gewinn zum eingesetzten Kapital*]

return on investment analysis, ROI analysis · DuPont-Formula *f*

return ticket · Rückfahrkarte *f*

to return to, to revert, to turn back [*With respect to property to go back to and lodge in former owner, who parted with it by creating estate in another which has expired, or to his heirs*] · rückfallen, zurückkehren

return to scale, economy of scale, scale economy · Skalenertrag *m* [*Die Auswirkung der proportionalen Faktorerhöhung auf das Produktionsergebnis*]

re-use · Wiederbenutzung *f*, Wiedergebrauch *m*

re-use appraisal, re-use (e)valuation, re-use appraisement, disposition re-use [*An appraisal of re-use value*] · Wiedernutzungs(ab)schätzung *f*, Wiedernutzungsbewertung

re-use value, disposition price [*The price a local public agency places on land, cleared through the urban renewal process, to be sold to a redeveloper, based upon a re-use appraisal*] · Wiedernutzungswert *m*

revalorization, reassessment, revaluation · Aufwertung *f* [*Die Wiedergutmachung eines Teiles des durch eine Inflation an privaten Vermögen angerichteten Schadens*]

revalorized mortgage, reassessment mortgage, revaluation mortgage · Aufwertungshypothek *f*

revaluation, reappraisal, reappraisement · Neu(ab)schätzung *f*, Neubewertung, Neutaxierung

revaluation lease(hold), reappraisal lease(hold) · Pacht *f* mit nach periodischen Schätzungen festgesetzter Rente

revaluation mortgage, revalorized mortgage, reassessment mortgage · Aufwertungshypothek *f*

to reveal — revival

to reveal, to knowledge, to make known, to clarify, to free from secrecy, to free from ignorance, to lay bare, to disclose · aufklären, enthüllen, offenbaren, offenlegen, offen darlegen, preisgeben, kundtun

revealed preference · faktischer Vorzug *m*

revenue board · Finanzamt *n*

reversal of judg(e)ment · Urteilsaufhebung *f*, Urteilsaussetzung

to reverse (a judg(e)ment), to set aside (a judg(e)ment) · aufheben, aussetzen [*Urteil wegen Rechtsfehler*]

reversed, set aside · aufgehoben, ausgesetzt [*Urteil wegen Rechtsfehler*]

reversed and new trial, set aside and new trial · aufgehoben und neues Verfahren angeordnet

reversed and remanded, set aside and remanded · aufgehoben und an die untere Instanz zurückverwiesen, aufgehoben und (zur abermaligen Verhandlung) zurückverwiesen [*Urteil*]

reverse (direction) travel (to work), reverse (direction) journey (to work), reverse (direction) trip (to work) [*It involves the journey to work from a home in the city to a suburban place of employment*] · Stadtauswärtsberufsfahrt *f*

reversion [*Return of real estate to the original owner or his heirs after the termination of some temporary grant*] · Rückfall *m*

reversionary annuity, annuity put off, deferred annuity, postponed annuity · aufgeschobene Annuität *f*, Zukunftsannuität, Anwartschaftsannuität

reversionary demise → reversionary lease(hold)

reversionary estate, reversionary right, right of reversion, reversion of interest, right of reverter, estate in reversion [*Residue of an estate left in the grantor, to commence in possession after the termination of some particular estate granted by him. In a lease the lessor has the estate in reversion after the lease is terminated*] · Rückfallrecht *n*

reversionary lease(hold), reversionary tenancy, reversionary demise · Anschlußnutzungsrecht *n*, Anschlußpacht *f*

reversionary right, right of reversion, reversion of interest, right of reverter, estate in reversion, reversionary estate [*Residue of an estate left in the grantor, to commence in possession after the termination of some particular estate granted by him. In a lease the lessor has the estate in reversion after the lease is terminated*] · Rückfallrecht *n*

reversionary tenancy → reversionary lease(hold)

reversioner · Rückfallberechtigte *m* [*Derjenige, dem ein Recht an einem Grundstück kraft Gesetzes zufällt, nachdem alle Berechtigten weggefallen sind*]

reversion of interest, right of reverter, estate in reversion, reversionary estate, reversionary right, right of reversion [*Residue of an estate left in the grantor, to commence in possession after the termination of some particular estate granted by him. In a lease the lessor has the estate in reversion after the lease is terminated*] · Rückfallrecht *n*

to revert, to turn back, to return to [*With respect to property to go back to and lodge in former owner, who parted with it by creating estate in another which has expired, or to his heirs*] · rückfallen, zurückkehren

to review · revidieren

to review, to check, to control, to re-examine · kontrollieren, nachprüfen

review, check, control, re-examination · Kontrolle *f*, Nachprüfung *f*

review(ing) authority, re-examination authority, authority of control, authority of checking, control authority, check(ing) authority · Kontrollvollmacht *f*, Nachprüf(ungs)vollmacht

review(ing) duty, duty to check, duty to control, duty to re-examine, checking duty, control duty, re-examination duty, check(ing) duty, duty to review · Nachprüfungspflicht *f*, Kontrollpflicht

revised statutes, statutes revised · Gesetz(es)sammlung *f* nach Sachsystem geordnet

revised statutes annotated, statutes revised and annotated · annotierte Gesetzessammlung *f* nach Sachsystemen geordnet

revising barrister · Wahlrichter *m*, Revisionsrichter [*Munizipalstadt*]

revision · Fortführung *f* [*Kartographie*]

revisional court · Gerichtshof *m* für die Wählerlistenprüfung

revisionary heir (male), substitute, after heir (male), second heir (male) · Aftererbe *m*, Nacherbe *m*, Substitut *m*, Ersatzerbe [*Derjenige, der nach einem ernannten Erben als Erbe in einem Testament ernannt ist, wenn der erste Erbe die Erbschaft nicht erwerben würde*]

revisions variance · Verrechnungsabweichung *f*, Revisionsabweichung

revivable, renewable · erneuerungsfähig, erneuerbar

revival · Wiederaufleben *n* [*Wiedererrichtung einer letztwilligen früher widerrufenen Verfügung*]

revival — reward system

revival, renewal · Erneuerung f

revival area, revival territory, renewal area, renewal territory · Erneuerungsgebiet n

revival contract, contract of renewal, contract of revival, renewal contract · Erneuerungsvertrag m

revival date, renewal date · Erneuerungstermin m, Erneuerungsdatum n

revival measure, renewal measure · Erneuerungsmaßnahme f

revival of lease, renewal of tenancy, revival of tenancy, renewal of lease · Pachterneuerung f

revival programming, renewal programming · Erneuerungsprogrammierung f

revival territory, renewal area, renewal territory, revival area · Erneuerungsgebiet n

to revivify, to renew, to revive · erneuern

reviving, renewing · Erneuern n

revocability · Widerrufbarkeit f, Widerruflichkeit

revocable, at will, revokable, ambulatory, capable of being revoked, capable of revocation, able of being revoked, able of revocation, qualified of being revoked, qualified of revocation, during pleasure · auf Widerruf, widerruflich, widerrufbar, einvernehmlich geduldet

revocable interest, revocable right, interest at will, right at will · Anrecht n auf Widerruf, Anspruch m auf Widerruf, Berechtigung f auf Widerruf, (subjektives) Recht auf Widerruf, widerrufliches (subjektives) Recht

revocable letter of credit, revokable letter of credit, letter of credit at will, unconfirmed letter of credit · Akkreditiv n auf Widerruf, Kreditbrief m auf Widerruf, widerruflicher Kreditbrief, widerrufliches Akkreditiv

revocable right, interest at will, right at will, revocable interest · Anrecht n auf Widerruf, Anspruch m auf Widerruf, Berechtigung f auf Widerruf, (subjektives) Recht auf Widerruf, widerrufliches (subjektives) Recht

to revocate [*obsolete*]; to revoke, to recall, to call back · widerrufen, rückgängig machen

revocation · Widerruf m

revocation by operation of law · Widerruf m von Gesetzes wegen

revocation notice, revocation notification, notice of revocation, notification of revocation · Widerrufsmitteilung f, Widerrufsanzeige f, Widerrufsbenachrichtigung

revocation of legacy, ademption of bequest, revocation of bequest, legacy ademption, bequest ademption, legacy revocation, bequest revocation; ademptio legati [*Latin*]; ademption of legacy [*It occurs where a legacy does not take effect owing to some act on the part of a testator not affecting the validity of the will*] · (Fahrnis)Legatrücknahme f, (Fahrnis)Legatentziehung f, (Fahrnis)Vermächtnisrücknahme, (Fahrnis)Vermächtnisentziehung, Fahrhabelegatrücknahme, Fahrhabelegatentziehung, Fahrhabevermächtnisrücknahme, Fahrhabevermächtnisentziehung

revocation of permission · Erlaubnisrücknahme f, Genehmigungsrücknahme

revocation of will, revoking of will · Testamentswiderruf m

revocation power, revocation right, power of revocation, right of revocation · Befugnis f an einem bestimmten Vermögen Nutzung zu widerrufen, Recht n an einem bestimmten Vermögen Nutzung zu widerrufen

revocation right, power of revocation, right of revocation, revocation power · Befugnis f an einem bestimmten Vermögen Nutzung zu widerrufen, Recht n an einem bestimmten Vermögen Nutzung zu widerrufen

revokable, ambulatory, capable of being revoked, capable of revocation, able of being revoked, able of revocation, qualified of being revoked, qualified of revocation, during pleasure, revocable, at will · auf Widerruf, widerruflich, widerrufbar, einvernehmlich geduldet

revokable letter of credit, letter of credit at will, unconfirmed letter of credit, revocable letter of credit · Akkreditiv n auf Widerruf, Kreditbrief m auf Widerruf, widerruflicher Kreditbrief, widerrufliches Akkreditiv

to revoke, to recall, to call back; to revocate [*obsolete*] · widerrufen, rückgängig machen

revoking of will, revocation of will · Testamentswiderruf m

revolving credit · rotierendes Akkreditiv n, roulierendes Akkreditiv [*Kredit der sich bei Ablauf automatisch erneuert*]

revolving system · revolvierendes System n [*Schuldscheindarleh(e)n mehrerer Kreditgeber zeitlich so aneinanderreihen, daß die gewünschte langfristige Finanzierung zustandekommt*]

reward · Belohnung f

reward of merit · Verdienstbelohnung f

reward system; premium plan of paying for labour (Brit.); premium plan of paying for labor (US); premium wage system · Prämienlohnsystem n

**to reword, ** to change the wording of, to state again in other words, to express again in other words, to restate · umschreiben, neugestalten, neuschreiben, umgestalten [*Text*]

rewording, changing the wording, stating again in other words, expressing again in other words, changing the text · Textumschreibung f, Textumgestaltung, Textneugestaltung, Textneuschreibung

to rework, to rectify [*To perform additional operations to bring a substandard product up to specification*] · nacharbeiten

rework note, rectification note [*A document which authorizes additional operations to bring a substandard product up to specification*] · Nacharbeitungszettel m, Nacharbeitungsanzeige f

to rezone · verändert (baulich) nutzen, umzonen

rezoning, change in zoning [*Action by a governing body changing the zoning classification of a land area to another classification*] · Baunutzungswechsel m, veränderte (bauliche) Nutzung f, veränderte Baunutzung, Umzonung

rezoning process, process of rezoning · Umzonungsvorgang m

rezoning (up)on condition, change in zoning (up)on condition, conditional rezoning, conditional change in zoning · bedingter Baunutzungswechsel m, Baunutzungswechsel mit Vorbedingung, Baunutzungswechsel unter Vorbehalt

ribbon cities, corridor (of cities), strip cities, semicontinuous cities, linear cities · Städteband n

ribbon city, linear city, ribbon town, linear town · Bandstadt f

ribbon composition, linear composition, ribbon structure, linear structure · Bandaufbau m, Bandzusammensetzung f, Bandstruktur f, Bandgefüge n

ribbon development, string street development · Bandbebauung f, Straßenrandbebauung, Reihenbebauung, Perlschnurbebauung; Bandüberbauung, Straßenrandüberbauung, Reihenüberbauung, Perlschnurüberbauung [*Schweiz*]

ribbon development, linear development, row development · Bandentwick(e)lung f, Reihenentwick(e)lung

ribbon infrastructure, linear infrastructure · Bandinfrastruktur f, bandartige Infrastruktur [*Die Infrastruktur im Bereich des Verkehrs, des Transports und der Kommunikation*]

ribbon site, linear site · Bandort m

ribbon structure, linear structure, ribbon composition, linear composition · Bandaufbau m, Bandzusammensetzung f, Bandstruktur f, Bandgefüge n

ribbon town, linear town, ribbon city, linear city · Bandstadt f

ribbon village, linear village, row village · Banddorf n, Reihendorf

ridge, untilled green strip of land; unploughed (turf) balk, green balk of unploughed turf (Brit.) · Rainbalken m

ridge · Hochackerrücken m

ridge and furrow field · Hochacker m

ridge location · Kammlage f

ridge-stone · Rainstein m

ridge-tree · Rainbaum m

riding public · (öffentliche) Massenverkehrsteilnehmer mpl, (öffentliche) Massenbeförderungsteilnehmer

riding-school · Reitschule f

to rid of debt(s) · schuldenfrei machen

rig · Besitzstreifenfurche f

rigging bids, collusion among(st) bidders, collusion among(st) offerers, collusion among(st) tenderers, price taking, collusive agreement, combining to eliminate competition, restrictive covenant, restrictive tendering agreement, taking a price, collusive tendering, collusive bidding, (collusive) price fixing, bid-rigging, bid collusion [*The frequently heavy cost of tendering sometimes leads contractors to put forward tenders which are not genuine, in the sense that, rather than refuse to make a tender when invited to do so, the contractor tenders a price higher than that "taken" from another contractor who does desire to obtain the contract, thus avoiding expense and leading the employer to believe that he has had genuine competitive tenders for the work*] · Abrede f unter Bietern, Absprache f unter Bietern, Preisabrede, Preisabsprache, Submissionsabrede, Submissionsabsprache, Konkurrenzvereinbarung f, Verständigung unter Bietern, Angebotsabsprache, Angebotsabrede

right · seitenrichtig [*Luftbildauswertung*]

right, power · Befugnis f, Recht n

right at will, revocable interest, revocable right, interest at will · Anrecht n auf Widerruf, Anspruch m auf Widerruf, Berechtigung f auf Widerruf, (subjektives) Recht auf Widerruf, widerrufliches (subjektives) Recht

right exercisable with consent, power exercisable with consent · Befugnis f mit Zustimmung eines Dritten, Recht n mit Zustimmung eines Dritten

right female heir → right heiress

rightful owner, rightful proprietor · berechtigter Eigentümer m, Eigentümer zum Eigentum berechtigt, rechtmäßiger

Eigentümer, rechtmäßiger Eigner, berechtigter Eigner, Eigner zum Eigentum berechtigt, Eigentumssubjekt *n* zum Eigentum berechtigt, rechtmäßiges Eigentumssubjekt, berechtigtes Eigentumssubjekt

rightful possession · berechtigter Besitz *m*, Besitz mit Recht zum Besitz

rightful possessor · berechtigter Besitzer *m*, rechtmäßiger Besitzer, Besitzer zum Besitz berechtigt

rightful proprietor, rightful owner · berechtigter Eigentümer *m*, Eigentümer zum Eigentum berechtigt, rechtmäßiger Eigentümer, rechtmäßiger Eigner *m*, berechtigter Eigner, Eigner zum Eigentum berechtigt, Eigentumssubjekt *n* zum Eigentum berechtigt, rechtmäßiges Eigentumssubjekt, berechtigtes Eigentumssubjekt

right heiress, right heir female, female heir at law, female heir general, right female heir, heiress at law, heiress general, heir female at law, heir female general · Intestaterbin *f*, gesetzliche Erbin

right heir (male), legal heir (male), lawful heir (male), nearest kin, heir (male) general, general heir (male), heir (male) whatsoever, statutory heir (male), heir (male) at law [*One who takes the succession by relationship to the decedent and by force of law*] · Intestaterbe *m*, gesetzlicher Erbe

right incapable of division, nondivisible right; jus individuum [*Latin*], individual right, indivisible right · unteilbares Recht *n*

right in estate → interest in (real) estate

right in land(s) → interest in (real) estate

right in personam, personal right, personal interest · persönliches Recht *n*

right in property, right of property, property right, valuable right, valuable interest, proprietary right · (subjektives) Vermögensrecht *n*, vermögenswertes Recht

right in (real) estate → interest in (real) estate

right in rem → real right

right line; linea (di)recta [*Latin*]; direct line [*The direct line of ascendants and descendants*] · direkte (Abstammungs)Linie *f*, direkte Folge *f*

rightness · Richtigkeit *f*

right of (ab)alienation, power of (ab)alienation, right of disposal, power of disposal, (ab)alienation right, (ab)alienation power, disposal power · Veräußerungsbefugnis *f*, Veräußerungsrecht *n*

right of access, power of access, access right, access power, admittance · Betretungsbefugnis *f*, Betretungsrecht *n*, Zutrittsbefugnis, Zutrittsrecht, Zugangsbefugnis, Zugangsrecht

right of accretion (of land), land accretion right, right of alluvion, right of alluvium · (Land)Anschwemmungsrecht *n*, (Land-)Anwachs(ungs)recht, (Land)Akkreszenzrecht, Alluvionsrecht, (Land)Zuwachsrecht, (Land)Anschuttrecht, Alluviumsrecht, Recht auf (Land)Gewinnung durch Anschwemmung

right of a freeholder, freeholder's right · Landsässigkeit *f*

right of air → right (to flow) of air

right of allotment, right of apportionment · Zuteilungsanspruch *m*, Zuteilungs(an)recht *n*

right of alluvion, right of alluvium, right of accretion (of land), land accretion right · (Land)Anschwemmungsrecht *n*, (Land-)Anwachs(ungs)recht, (Land)Akkreszenzrecht, Alluvionsrecht, (Land)Zuwachsrecht, (Land)Anschuttrecht, Alluviumsrecht, Recht auf (Land)Gewinnung durch Anschwemmung

right of amotion, power of amotion [*from membership or office*] · Ausschlußbefugnis *f*, Ausschlußrecht *n*

right of appeal, appeal right · Appellationsrecht *n*, Berufungsrecht, subjektives Appellationsrecht, subjektives Berufungsrecht

right of appointment, power of nomination, right of nomination, power of appointment · Benennungsbefugnis *f*, Benennungsrecht *n*, Ernennungsbefugnis, Ernennungsrecht

right of appointment, right of disposition, power of appointment, power of disposition [*A power given to a person which enables him to dispose of an interest in property, real or personal, which is not his. Such a power is usually conferred under a trust or settlement by which a person is enabled to make an eppointment of the trust or settlement property*] · Bestimmungsbefugnis *f*, Bestimmungsrecht *n*, Verfügungsbefugnis, Verfügungsrecht [*Vermögen*]

right of appointment appendant, right of appointment appurtenant, right of disposition appendant, right of disposition appurtenant, power of appointment appendant, power of appointment appurtenant, power of disposition appurtenant [*It is a power exercised by a person who has an interest in the property, and that interest will be affected by the exercise of the power*] · Pertinenz-Verfügungsbefugnis *f*, Pertinenz-Bestimmungsbefugnis, Pertinenz-Verfügungsrecht *n*, Pertinenz-Bestimmungsrecht

right of appointment by deed — right of disposition

right of appointment by deed, power of disposition by deed, right of disposition by deed, power of appointment by deed · urkundliche Verfügungsbefugnis *f*, urkundliche Bestimmungsbefugnis, urkundliches Verfügungsrecht *n*, urkundliches Bestimmungsrecht

right of appointment in gross, power of disposition in gross, right of disposition in gross, power of appointment in gross [*It is a power given to a person who has an interest in the property, but that interest will not be affected by the exercise of the power*] · subjektiv persönliche Verfügungsbefugnis *f*, subjektiv persönliche Bestimmungsbefugnis, subjektiv persönliches Verfügungsrecht *n*, subjektiv persönliches Bestimmungsrecht

right of appointment of land, power of disposition of land, right of dispositon of land, power of appointment of land · Bodenverfügungsbefugnis *f*, Landverfügungsbefugnis, Bodenbestimmungsbefugnis, Landbestimmungsbefugnis, Bodenverfügungsrecht, Landverfügungsrecht, Bodenbestimmungsrecht, Landbestimmungsrecht

right of appointment under the statute of uses, legal power of appointment, legal right of appointment, power of appointment under the statute of uses · Befugnis *f* an einem bestimmten Vermögen Nutzung zu erklären, Recht *n* an einem bestimmten Vermögen Nutzung zu erklären

right of apportionment, right of allotment · Zuteilungsanspruch *m*, Zuteilungs(an)recht *n*

right of (a) third party, third party right; jus tertii [*Latin*] · Drittenrecht *n*

right of audience, Postulationsfähigkeit *f*, Recht *n* auf gerichtliches Gehör

right of building, right of surface · (dingliches) Baurecht *n*

right of certiorari · Abberufungsrecht *n*

right of citizenship · Bürgerrecht *n*

right of coinage, coinage right · Münzrecht *n*

right of collection of contribution(s), power of collection of contribution(s) · Beitragserhebungsbefugnis *f*, Beitragserhebungsrecht *n*

right of commonage, commonage right, commonable right to land · Al(l)mend(e)recht *n*, Markrecht, subjektives Al(l)mend(e)recht, subjektives Markrecht

right of complaint · Beschwerderecht *n*, subjektives Beschwerderecht

right of compliance, right of execution, right of performance, right of discharge, right of fulfilment · Erfüllungsanspruch *m*, Erfüllungs(an)recht *n*, Vollzugs(an)recht, Vollzugsanspruch, Vollziehungs(an)recht, Vollziehungsanspruch, Ausführungs(an)recht, Ausführungsanspruch, Erbringungs(an)recht, Erbringungsanspruch

right of consolidation, right to consolidate, consolidation right · (subjektives) Verbindungsrecht *n*

right of contract(ing), contracting power, contracting right, contractual power, contractual right, power of contract(ing) · Vertragsbefugnis *f*, Vertragsrecht *n*

right of contribution, contribution right · Beitrags(an)recht *n*, Beitragsanspruch *m*

right of counterclaim · Gegenforderungsrecht *n*

right of (court) action, right of plea, right of (law)suit, right of cause · Klagerecht *n*, Recht auf Klage

right of coverage, coverage right · Bebauungsanspruch *m*, Bebauungs(an)recht *n*; Überbauungsanspruch, Überbauungs(an)recht [*Schweiz*]

right of cutting wood; jus falcandi [*Latin*] · Holzfällrecht *n*, Holzschlagrecht

right of decision, power of decision · Entscheidungsbefugnis *f*, Entscheidungsrecht *n*

right of development, development right · Entwick(e)lungs(an)recht *n*, Entwick(e)lungsanspruch *m*

right of digging (on another's land); jus fodiendi [*Latin*] · (Aus)Schachtrecht *n*, Graberecht *n*

right of discharge, right to discharge, redemption right, right of redemption, right to redeem, right to regain property, right to reclaim property, discharge right · Ablösungsrecht *n*, Einlösungsrecht, Auslösungsrecht

right of discharge, right of fulfilment, right of compliance, right of execution, right of performance · Erfüllungsanspruch *m*, Erfüllungs(an)recht *n*, Vollzugs(an)recht, Vollzugsanspruch, Vollziehungs(an)recht, Vollziehungsanspruch, Ausführungs(an)recht, Ausführungsanspruch, Erbringungs(an)recht, Erbringungsanspruch

right of disposal, power of disposal, (ab)alienation right, (ab)alienation power, disposal power, right of (ab)alienation, power of (ab)alienation · Veräußerungsbefugnis *f*, Veräußerungsrecht *n*

right of disposition, power of appointment, power of disposition, right of appointment [*A power given to a person which enables him to dispose of an interest in property, real or personal, which is not*

right of disposition appendant — right of hunting and fishing

his. Such a power is usually conferred under a trust or settlement by which a person is enabled to make an eppointment of the trust or settlement property] · Bestimmungsbefugnis f, Bestimmungsrecht n, Verfügungsbefugnis, Verfügungsrecht [*Vermögen*]

right of disposition appendant, right of disposition appurtenant, power of appointment appendant, power of appointment appurtenant, power of disposition appendant, power of disposition appurtenent, right of appointment appendant, right of appointment appurtenant [*It is a power exercised by a person who has an interest in the property, and that interest will be affected by the exercise of the power*] · Pertinenz-Verfügungsbefugnis f, Pertinenz-Bestimmungsbefugnis, Pertinenz-Verfügungsrecht n, Pertinenz-Bestimmungsrecht

right of disposition by deed, power of appointment by deed, right of appointment by deed, power of disposition by deed · urkundliche Verfügungsbefugnis f, urkundliche Bestimmungsbefugnis, urkundliches Verfügungsrecht n, urkundliches Bestimmungsrecht

right of dispositon of land, power of appointment of land, right of appointment of land, power of disposition of land · Bodenverfügungsbefugnis f, Landverfügungsbefugnis, Bodenbestimmungsbefugnis, Landbestimmungsbefugnis, Bodenverfügungsrecht, Landverfügungsrecht, Bodenbestimmungsrecht, Landbestimmungsrecht

right of dower · Wittumsrecht n der Ehefrau, Leibzuchtrecht der Ehefrau

right of drove, drove right, feldage; actus, faldagium [*Latin*], frank-fold, faldage · Triftrecht n, Treibrecht

right of entry, entry right · Grund(stücks)-besitzergreifungsanspruch m, Grund(stücks)besitzergreifungs(an)recht n, Grund(stücks)(in)besitznahme-(an)recht, Grund(stücks)(in)besitznahmeanspruch, Recht der (In)Besitznahme, (In)Besitznahmerecht

right of escheat, escheat right · Heimfallrecht n, Heimfallanrecht, Heimfallanspruch m

right of establishment, establishment right · Niederlassungsrecht n

right of exchange, power of exchange, power to exchange, right to exchange · Tauschbefugnis f, Tauschrecht n

right of execution, right of performance, right of discharge, right of fulfilment, right of compliance · Erfüllungsanspruch m, Erfüllungs(an)recht n, Vollzugs(an)recht, Vollzugsanspruch, Vollziehungs(an)recht, Vollziehungsanspruch, Ausführungs(an)recht, Ausführungsanspruch, Erbringungs(an)recht, Erbringungsanspruch

right of exploitation, right to exploit minerals, right of taking minerals, right of winning, winning right, exploitation right, mineral right, mineral interest, interest in minerals in land(s), right to take minerals · (Mineral(ien))Abbaurecht n, (Mineral(ien))-Ausbeutungsrecht, (subjektives) Berg(bau)recht, (Mineral(ien))Abbaugerechtigkeit f

right of fencing, fencing right · Zaunrecht n

right of fishing, piscary; libera piscaria [*Latin*]; free fishery, fishing right [*The right or liberty of fishing in the waters of another person*] · Fischereirecht n, subjektives Fischereirecht

right of foreclosure, foreclosure (right) [*If the mortgagor does not pay the debt when due, the mortgagee has the right to have the property applied to the payment of the obligation for which the mortgage was given as security*] · (gerichtlicher) Ausschluß m der Einlösung, (gerichtliches) Ausschlußrecht der Einlösung, (Pfand)Verfall m, Verfallserklärungsrecht n

right of forfeiture, forfeiture right · (subjektives) Verwirkungsrecht n

right of fulfilment, right of compliance, right of execution, right of performance, right of discharge · Erfüllungsanspruch m, Erfüllungs(an)recht n, Vollzugs(an)recht, Vollzugsanspruch, Vollziehungs(an)recht, Vollziehungsanspruch, Ausführungs(an)recht, Ausführungsanspruch, Erbringungs(an)recht, Erbringungsanspruch

right of full dominion · volles Herrschaftsrecht n

right of grass-cutting, grass-cutting right · Grasnutzungsrecht n

right of heirship, inheritance right, heirship right, hereditary right, heritable right, right of inheritance · Erb(schafts)anspruch m, Erb(schafts)(an)recht n

right of heirship in (fee) tail, right of inheritance in (fee) tail, heritable right in (fee) tail, hereditary right in (fee) tail · Anerbenrecht n [*Das Recht eines einzelnen Erben eines bäuerlichen Besitzers in die ungeteilte Nachfolge des bäuerlichen Besitzes unter Ausschluß der Miterben*]

(right of) homestead, homestead estate, homestead right [*It is created by statute, and consists in the right to enjoy, free from liability for debts, a certain specified amount of land which is being occupied as a residence*] · Heimstätte f

right of hunting and fishing; jus venandi et piscandi [*Latin*] · (subjektives) Jagd- und Fisch(erei)recht n

right of immediate entry into actual possession · Recht *n* sofort in den tatsächlichen Besitz einzutreten

right of immunity, cathedral immunity · Domfreiheit *f*

right of inheritance, right of heirship, inheritance right, heirship right, hereditary right, heritable right · Erb(schafts)anspruch *m*, Erb(schafts)(an)recht *n*

right of inheritance in (fee) tail, heritable right in (fee) tail, hereditary right in (fee) tail, right of heirship in (fee) tail · Anerbenrecht *n* [*Das Recht eines einzelnen Erben eines bäuerlichen Besitzers in die ungeteilte Nachfolge des bäuerlichen Besitzes unter Ausschluß der Miterben*]

right of jurisdiction · Recht *n* auf Jurisdiktion

right of light, right to light, light right, ancient light(s), ancient windows, servitude not to hinder lights; servitus ne luminibus officiatur [*Latin*] · Lichtrecht *n*, Abwehrrecht des Fenstereigentümers gegen den Nachbarn [*Schutz gegen Verbauung des Lichteinfalls durch den Grundstücksnachbarn*]

right of lop and top, right of lopping, right of top and lop, right of lop(wood); right of lop (US) · Reisigrecht *n*, Reis(er)holzrecht

right of membership, membership right · Mitgliedschaftsrecht *n*

right of nomination, power of appointment, right of appointment, power of nomination · Benennungsbefugnis *f*, Benennungsrecht *n*, Ernennungsbefugnis, Ernennungsrecht

right of objection, objection right · Einspruchsrecht *n*

right of occupancy, occupancy right [*Privilege to use and occupy a property for a certain period under some contractual guarantee, such as a lease or other formal agreement*] · Belegungsrecht *n*

right of omission, right to omit · Auslassungsrecht *n*

right of option, option to buy, option to purchase, option right · Option(srecht) *f, (n)*, Vorhand *f*

right of ownership (of property), title (of right) · (Rechts)Titel *m*, (subjektives) Eigentumsrecht *n*

right of participation, right to participate · Beteiligungsrecht *n*, Mitspracherecht

right of passage, passage right · (Durch)Leitungsrecht *n*

right-of-passage contract, passage right contract · (Durch)Leitungsrechtvertrag *m*

(right of) pastur(ag)e, (right of) grazing, pastoral right, herbage, grazing right, shack, common pastur(ag)e, commonage, common right; jus pascendi communis pasturae, herbagium [*Latin*] · Angerrecht *n*, Hütungsrecht, Atzung *f*, Ätzung, (Vieh)Weiderecht, (Vieh)Weideberechtigung

(right of) patronage, advowson; jus patronatus [*Latin*] [*The right of presentation, i.e. the right of appointing a parson to a rectory, vicarage or other ecclesiastic(al) benefice*] · Patronat(srecht) *n*, Präsentation(srecht) *f, (n)* [*Ein dauerndes Präsentationsrecht zu einer geistlichen Pfründe*]

(right of) patronage donative, advowson donative, donative advowson · Patronat(srecht) *n* bei dem der Patron ohne Inanspruchnahme eines Bischofs jemanden zum Inhaber einer geistlichen Pfründe ernennen konnte, Präsentation(srecht) bei dem der Patron ohne Inanspruchnahme eines Bischofs jemanden zum Inhaber einer geistlichen Pfründe ernennen konnte

(right of) patronage presentative, advowson presentative · Patronat(srecht) *n* wenn der Patron das Recht hat eine geeignete Person für die erledigte Pfründe dem Bischof zu präsentieren, und der letztere verpflichtet ist, die Investitur sowohl mit den Spiritualien als auch mit den Temporalien vorzunehmen

right of pawn · Pfandrecht *n*

right of performance, right of discharge, right of fulfilment, right of compliance, right of execution · Erfüllungsanspruch *m*, Erfüllungs(an)recht *n*, Vollzugs(an)recht, Vollziehungsanspruch, Vollziehungs(an)recht, Vollziehungsanspruch, Ausführungs(an)recht, Ausführungsanspruch, Erbringungs(an)recht, Erbringungsanspruch

right of permanent tenancy, permanent tenancy right · Dauerwohnrecht *n*

right of personalty, interest in personalty, personalty right, personalty interest · (subjektives) Fahrnisrecht *n* [*Die Rechtsstellung, die einer bestimmten Person an einem bestimmten Fahrnisgut zusteht*]

right of (physical) taking (away) · Wegnahmerecht *n*, Ergreifungsrecht, körperliches Wegnahmerecht, körperliches Ergreifungsrecht

right of possession → possessory interest

right of possession of land(s) → interest in (real) estate

right of postponement, right of suspension, suspensory right · Aufschiebungsrecht *n*, Aufschubsrecht, Hinausschiebungsrecht

right of pre-emption, right of preëmption, pre-emption right, preëmption right · Vorkaufsrecht *n*

right of primogeniture, right of the eldest, right of the first born; aesnetia eisnetia enitia pars dignitas primogeniti [*Latin*] · (männliches) Erstgeburtsrecht *n*, Primogenitur *f*, Vorrecht des Erstgeborenen

right of property, property right, valuable right, valuable interest, proprietary right, right in property · (subjektives) Vermögensrecht *n*, vermögenswertes Recht

right of protection · Schutzrecht *n*

right of protection of (real) estate, right of protection of (real) property, right of protection of realty · Besitzschutz(an)recht *n*, Besitzschutzanspruch *m*, Grund(stücks)besitzschutzanspruch, Grund(stücks)besitzschutz(an)recht

right of rafting; jus grutiae [*Latin*]; rafting right · Flößer(ei)recht *n*, Floßrecht

right of realty → interest in (real) estate

right of recall, recall right [*political science*] · Abberufungsrecht *n*

right of redemption, right to redeem, right to regain property, right to reclaim property, discharge right, right of discharge, right to discharge, redemption right · Ablösungsrecht *n*, Einlösungsrecht, Auslösungsrecht

right of reduction · Minderungs(an)recht *n*, Minderungsanspruch *m*

right of re-entry, re-entry right · Wiedereintrittsrecht *n* [*In einen (Grund)Besitz*]

right of refusal to pay · Zahlungsverweigerungs(an)recht *n*, Zahlungsverweigerungsanspruch *m*

right of religious belief, religious liberty · Religionsfreiheit *f*, Glaubensrecht *n*

right of removal (of structures) · (Bau)Beseitigungs(an)recht *n*, (Bau)Beseitigungsanspruch *m*

right of renewal, right of revival, power of renewal, power of revival · Erneuerungsbefugnis *f*, Erneuerungsrecht *n*

right of repudiation, repudiation right · Leistungsverweigerungsrecht *n* [*§ 320 BGB*]

right of rescinding, right of withdrawal · Rücktrittsrecht *n*

right of resumption, power of resumption · Zwangsrückkaufbefugnis *f*, Zwangsrückkaufrecht *n*

right of reversion, reversion of interest, right of reverter, estate in reversion, reversionary estate, reversionary right [*Residue of an estate left in the grantor, to commence in possession after the termination of some particular estate granted by him. In a lease the lessor has the estate in reversion after the lease is terminated*] · Rückfallrecht *n*

right of reverter, estate in reversion, reversionary estate, reversionary right, right of reversion, reversion of interest [*Residue of an estate left in the grantor, to commence in possession after the termination of some particular estate granted by him. In a lease the lessor has the estate in reversion after the lease is terminated*] · Rückfallrecht *n*

right of revival, power of renewal, power of revival, right of renewal · Erneuerungsbefugnis *f*, Erneuerungsrecht *n*

right of revocation, revocation power, revocation right, power of revocation · Befugnis *f* an einem bestimmten Vermögen Nutzung zu widerrufen, Recht *n* an einem bestimmten Vermögen Nutzung zu widerrufen

right of sale, power to sell, right to sell, power of sale · Verkaufsbefugnis *f*, Verkaufsrecht *n*

right of selection · Auswahlrecht *n*, Ausleserecht

right of separate treatment of a creditor, right of separation of claims · Absonderungs(an)recht *n*, Absonderungsanspruch *m* [*Konkursverfahren*]

right of separation of claims, right of separate treatment of a creditor · Absonderungs(an)recht *n*, Absonderungsanspruch *m* [*Konkursverfahren*]

right of severance, severance right · (Ab)Trennungsrecht *n*

right of staple; jus stapulae [*Latin*] [*In old European law. The right or privilege of certain towns of stopping imported merchandise, and compelling it to be offered for sale in their own markets*] · Stapelrecht *n*

right of stoppage in transit, stoppage in transitu, stoppage in transit right [*The right which a vendor, when he sells goods on credit to another, has of resuming the possession of the goods, while they are in the hands of a carrier or middle man, in their transit to the consignee or vendee, and before they arrive into his actual possession, or to the destination which he has appointed for them, on his becoming bankrupt or insolvent*] · Anhalterecht *n*, Rückkaufrecht, Verfolgungsrecht, Hemmungsrecht

right of supervision, right of superintendence, power of supervision, supervising power, supervising right, power of superintendence, right to supervise, right to superintend, power to supervise, power to superintend, superintending power, superintending right · Aufsichtsbefugnis *f*, Aufsichtsrecht *n*, Überwachungsbefugnis, Überwachungsrecht

right of support, right to support of building(s), right to lateral support [*A land-*

right of surface — right to acquisition

owner has a so-called natural right of support for his land. A right to support of building(s) cannot exist as an easement] · Stütz(ungs)recht n

right of surface, right of building · (dinglisches) Baurecht n

right of survivorship; jus accrescendi [*Latin*] · Recht n des Überlebenden, Überlebensrecht, Anwachsungsrecht

right of suspension, suspensory right, right of postponement · Aufschiebungsrecht n, Aufschubsrecht n, Hinausschiebungsrecht n

right of taking (in) possession, right to take (in) possession · Besitzergreifungsanspruch m, Besitzergreifungs(an)recht n, (In)Besitznahme(an)recht, (In)Besitznahmeanspruch

right of taking minerals → right to take minerals

right of tenancy, tenancy right · (subjektives) Wohn(ungs)recht n

right of tenant with the permission of his landlord to mortgage up to 35% of his land · Registerpfandrecht n

right of the cautioner, right of the insurer of a debt, surety right, guarantor right, cautioner right, right of the surety, right of the guarantor · Bürgenrecht n, subjektives Bürgenrecht

right of the Crown; jus coronae [*Latin*] · Kronrecht n

right of the eldest → right of primogeniture

right of the first born → right of primogeniture

right of the guarantor, right of the cautioner, right of the insurer of a debt, surety right, guarantor right, cautioner right, right of the surety · Bürgenrecht n, subjektives Bürgenrecht

right of the insurer of a debt, surety right, guarantor right, cautioner right, right of the surety, right of the guarantor, right of the cautioner · Bürgenrecht n, subjektives Bürgenrecht

right of the public · Recht n der Öffentlichkeit

right of the surety, right of the guarantor, right of the cautioner, right of the insurer of a debt, surety right, guarantor right, cautioner right · Bürgenrecht n, subjektives Bürgenrecht

right of top and lop, right of lop(wood); right of lop (US); right of lop and top, right of lopping · Reisigrecht n, Reis(er)holzrecht

right of trade connected with the possession of a piece of real property · Realgewerberecht n

right of transit, transit right · Durchfuhrrecht n, Durchgangsrecht

right of trustee · Treuhänderrecht n

right of use, interest of use, right to use, interest to use, use right, use interest · Gebrauchsrecht n, Benutzungsrecht, subjektives Gebrauchsrecht, subjektives Benutzungsrecht

right of (vehicular) access [*An owner of land adjoining a road has a right of access to it for any kind of traffic required for the reasonable enjoyment of his property*] · Zufahrtrecht n

right of vote, right to vote, voting right · Wahlrecht n, Wahlberechtigung f

right of water, aquatic right, water right [*Right to the use of sea, rivers, streams, lakes, ponds and canals, for the purpose of fishing and navigation, and also to the soil of them*] · (subjektives) Wasserrecht n

right-of-way, wayleave, ingress, access, right to enter and leave over the land(s) of another, way right · Durchgangsrecht n, Wegerecht

(right of) way easement, easement of (a right of) way · Wegegrunddienstbarkeit f, Durchgangsgrunddienstbarkeit

right-of-way for vehicles, wayleave for vehicles, ingress for vehicles, access for vehicles, way right for vehicles · Fahrzeugwegerecht n

right of winning, winning right, exploitation right, mineral right, mineral interest, interest in minerals in land(s), right to take minerals, right to win minerals, right of exploitation, right to exploit minerals, right of taking minerals · (Mineral(ien))Abbaurecht n, (Mineral(ien))Ausbeutungsrecht, (subjektives) Berg(bau)recht, (Mineral(ien))Abbaugerechtigkeit f

right of withdrawal, right of rescinding · Rücktrittsrecht n

right over a thing · Recht n über eine Sache

right over estate → interest in (real) estate

right over land(s) → interest in (real) estate

right over (real) estate → interest in (real) estate

right over realty → interest in (real) estate

right pour cause de vicinage, common pour cause de vicinage · Vizinitätsrecht n

rights in respect of other rights, rights to rights · Rechte npl an Rechten, (subjektive) Rechte an subjektiven Rechten

right to acquisition, acquisition right · Beschaffungsrecht n, Erwerbsrecht

right to action in the courts · Recht n gerichtliche Schritte zu unternehmen

right to advance · Vorschußanspruch m, Vorschuß(an)recht n

right to a hearing · Recht n auf rechtliches Gehör

right to air · (dingliches) Recht n am Luftraum

right to appear in person · postulationsfähig

right to appoint (somebody) to office connected with land(s) · (subjektives) Recht n auf die Ernennung einer Person zu einem als Immobiliarrecht geltenden Amt

right to a thing; jus ad rem [Latin] A right exercisable by one person over a particular article of property in virtue of a contract or obligation incurred by another person in respect to it, and which is enforceable only against or through such other person. It is thus distinguished from "jus in re", which is a complete and absolute dominion over a thing available against all persons · Recht n zu einer Sache, Recht n zur Sache

right to attach, right to seize · Beschlagnahmerecht n

right to a way of necessity · Notweg(e)recht n

right to build along a highway, right to build along a street; right to build along a road · Anbaurecht n

right to compensation, right to damages, right to indemnification, right to indemnity · Schadenersatzanspruch m, Schadenersatz(an)recht n, Entschädigungsanspruch, Entschädigungs(an)recht

right to contract, right of contract, power to contract, contractual right · Vertragsbefugnis f, Vertragsrecht n

right to cut fuel in woods, fire-bote, focage, focale; lignagium [Latin] · Brennholzschlagrecht n, Feuerungszubuße f, Brennholzbezugsrecht

right to cut turf, right to dig turf · Torfstichrecht n

right to damages → right to compensation

right to determine → power to terminate

right to dig gravel → right to exploit gravel

right to discharge → right of redemption

right to discuss · Erörterungsrecht n

right to emblements · Ernterecht n

right to enrichment, enrichment right · Bereicherungsanspruch m, Bereicherungs(an)recht n

right to enter and leave over the land(s) of another, way right, right-of-way, wayleave, ingress, access · Durchgangsrecht n, Wegerecht

right to exchange, right of exchange, power of exchange, right to exchange · Tauschbefugnis f, Tauschrecht n

right to exploit → right to win

right to exploit gravel, right to win gravel, right to take gravel, right to dig gravel, gravel winning right, gravel exploitation right, gravel digging right · Kiesgewinnungsrecht n, Kiesausbeutungsrecht

right to exploit lime(stone) → right to win lime(stone)

right to exploit minerals → right to take minerals

right to exploit sand, right to take sand, right to win sand, sand winning right, sand exploitation right · Sandabbaurecht n, Sandgewinnungsrecht, Sandausbeutungsrecht

right (to flow) of air [The right can subsist as an easement if claimed in respect of some defined channel, e.g., a fan] · Luftrecht n

right to follow · Folgerecht n

right to give notice (of termination) · subjektives Kündigungsrecht n

right to give orders · Anordnungsrecht n [Bauausführung]

right to groundwater → groundwater right

right to halt · Halterecht n [z. B. zum Be- und Entladen von Fahrzeugen]

right to housing · Recht n auf Wohnung

right to impound water · Staurecht n

right to indemnification → right to compensation

right to indemnity → right to compensation

right to information · Auskunftsrecht n

right to inquiry, right to enquiry · Auskunftsanspruch m, Auskunfts(an)recht n

right to insist on arbitration · Schiedsanspruch m, Schieds(an)recht n

right to labour (Brit.); right to labor (US) · Recht n auf Arbeit

right to lateral support → right of support

right to light → right of light

right to live · Versorgungsnutznießung f, Versorgungsnießbrauch m [Ein Elternteil überträgt z. B. einem Kind ein Grundstück, läßt sich aber für die Dauer seines Lebens den Nießbrauch an dem Grundstück einräumen]

right to make changes — right to win

right to make changes, right to make variations · (Ab)Änderungsrecht *n*

right to making-good of defect · Mangelbeseitigungsanspruch *m*, Mangelbeseitigungs(an)recht *n*, Sachbeseitigungs(an)recht, Baubeseitigungs(an)recht, Nachbesserungs(an)recht, Nachbesserungsanspruch

right to obtain · Verschaffungsanspruch *m*, Verschaffungs(an)recht *n*

right to obtain property, right to obtain proprietorship, right to obtain ownership (of property) · Eigentumsverschaffungsanspruch *m*, Eigentumsverschaffungs(an)recht *n*

right to office connected with land(s) · subjektives Recht *n* auf ein als Immobiliarrecht geltendes Amt

right to omit · Auslassungsrecht *n*

right to order alterations → right to order changes

right to order changes, right to order alterations, right to order variations, power to order changes · (Ab)Änderungsbefugnis *f*, (Ab)Änderungsrecht *n*

right to order variations → right to order changes

right to participate, right of participation · Mitspracherecht *n*, Beteiligungsrecht

right to pasture geese · Gänseweiderecht *n*

right to pasture goats · Ziegenweiderecht *n*

right to pasture sheep · Schafweiderecht *n*

right to pasture swines, right to pasture hogs · Schweineweiderecht *n*

right to percolating water → seepage water right

right to possess → possessory interest

right to reclaim property → redemption right

right to reconstruction of defective work(s) · Neuherstellungsanspruch *m*, Neuherstellungs(an)recht *n*

right to redeem, redemption right

right to refuse acceptance · Abnahmeverweigerungsrecht *n*, Bauabnahmeverweigerungsrecht

right to regain property → redemption right

right to reimbursement → right to restitution

right to resid(enc)e → entitlement to resid(enc)e

right to seepage water → right to percolating water

right ro seize, right to attach · Beschlagnahmerecht *n*

right to sell, power of sale, right of sale, power to sell · Verkaufsbefugnis *f*, Verkaufsrecht *n*

right to supervise → power of supervision

right to support of building(s) → right of support

right to take (in) possession → right of taking (in) possession

right to take lime(stone) → right to take win lime(stone)

right to take minerals, right to win minerals, right of exploitation, right to exploit minerals, right of taking minerals, right of winning, winning right, exploitation right, mineral right, mineral interest, interest in minerals in land(s) · (Mineral(ien))Abbaurecht *n*, (Mineral(ien))-Ausbeutungsrecht, Gewinnungsrecht, (subjektives) Berg(bau)recht, (Mineral(ien))

right to take minerals granted by the State · (Mineral(ien))Gewinnungsrecht *n* [*vom Staat übertragen*]

right to take part of land's profit · (subjektives) Recht *n* auf Anteilnahme an den Erträgnissen eines fremden Grundstücks

right to take salt · Salzabbaurecht *n*, Salzabbaugerechtigkeit *f*

right to take sand, right to win sand, sand winning right, sand exploitation right, right to exploit sand · Sandabbaurecht *n*, Sandgewinnungsrecht, Sandausbeutungsrecht

right to take the benefit of the poor laws · Anspruch *m* auf Armenunterstützung

right to terminate → power to terminate

right to the flow of water · Recht *n* auf Benutzung von Fließwasser

right to the possession of property owned by some other person · Recht *n* auf den Besitz eines im Eigentum eines Anderen befindlichen Vermögensgegenstandes

right to trade-marks · Markenrecht *n*

right to transfer · Übertragungsrecht *n*

right to treasure-trove, treasure-trove right · Schatzfundrecht *n*, Recht auf Schatzfund(e)

right to use → right of use

right to use land in a definite way · subjektives Recht *n* auf Benutzung eines fremden Grundstücks in bestimmter Weise

right to view · (Wohnungs)Besichtigungsrecht *n*

right to vote, right of vote, voting right · Wahlrecht *n*, Wahlberechtigung *f*

right to water cattle · Tränkrecht *n*

right ro win → right to take minerals

right to win gravel, right to dig gravel, to take gravel, right to exploit gravel, gravel winning right, gravel exploitation right, gravel digging right · Kiesausbeutungsrecht *n*, Kiesgewinnungsrecht

right to win lime(stone), right to take lime(stone), right to exploit lime(stone), lime(stone) (winning) right, lime(stone) exploitation right · Kalkabbaurecht *n*, Kalkausbeutungsrecht, Kalkabbaugerechtigkeit *f*

right to win minerals → right to take minerals

right to win sand, sand winning right, sand exploitation right, right to exploit sand, right to take sand · Sandabbaurecht *n*, Sandgewinnungsrecht, Sandausbeutungsrecht

right to withdraw (a contract), right of withdrawal (of a contract) · (Vertrags)Rücktrittsrecht *n*

right to withdraw a bid, right to withdraw an offer, right to withdraw a tender; right to withdraw a (bid) proposal (US) · Angebotsrücknahmerecht *n*

right to wrecks · Recht *n* auf Seeauswurf und strandtriftige Güter

ring-fence village, round village, circular village · Rundling *m*

riparian [*Pertaining to the banks of a body of water*] · uferzugehörig, Ufer...

riparian [*One who dwells on the bank of a water area*] · Uferanlieger *m*

riparian grant [*Conveyance of riparian rights*] · Übertragung *f* subjektiver Uferanliegerrechte

riparian land · Uferland *n*

riparian law · Ufer(anlieger)recht *n*

riparian lease [*Written instrument setting forth the terms, conditions, and date of expiration of the rights to use lands lying between the high-water mark and the low-water mark*] · Gezeitenzonenpachtvertrag *m*

riparian lot · Uferparzelle *f*

riparian owner · Ufereigentümer *m*, Ufereigentumssubjekt *n*, Ufereigner [*Im Wasserrecht: Eigentümer der an oberirdische Gewässer angrenzenden Grundstücke und die zur Nutzung dieser Grundstücke Berechtigten. § 24. Abs. 2 WasHG*]

riparian plot (of land) · Ufergrundstück *n*

riparian right, lit(t)oral right [*The legal right regarding a water area which belongs to one who owns or possesses land bordering upon it*] · (subjektives) Ufer(anlieger)recht *n*

riparian state · Ufer(anlieger)staat *m*

ripe for improvement · erschließungsreif

to rise, to move up · steigen [*Kosten*]

rising [*court*] · Vertagung *f* [*Gericht*]

risk, hazard · Risiko *n*, Wagnis *n*

risk area, hazard area · Risikobereich *m*, Wagnisbereich

risk aversion, hazard aversion, adventure aversion · Risikoabneigung *f*, Wagnisabneigung

risk bonus, hazard bonus · Risikozuschlag *m*, Wagniszuschlag

risk clause, hazard clause · Risikoklausel *f*, Wagnisklausel

risk concept, concept of risk, concept of hazard, hazard concept · Interessenabwägung *f*

risk distribution, risk sharing, hazard sharing, distribution of risk(s), distribution of hazard(s), sharing of risk(s), sharing of hazard(s), splitting (up) of risk(s), splitting (up) of hazard(s), hazard distribution · Verteilung *f* des Risikos, Verteilung des Wagnisses, Risikoverteilung, Wagnisverteilung

risk insurance, hazard insurance · Risikoversicherung *f*

risk involved in costing, hazard involved in costing · kalkulatorisches Risiko *n*, kalkulatorisches Wagnis *n*

risk management, hazard management · Handhabung *f* von Entscheidungswagnissen, Handhabung von Entscheidungsrisiken

risk of an enterprise, risk of an undertaking, hazard of an enterprise, hazard of an undertaking · Betriebsrisiko *n*, Betriebswagnis *n*

risk of loss, hazard of loss, loss risk, loss hazard · Verlustrisiko *n*, Verlustwagnis *n*

risk principle, hazard principle · Risikogrundsatz *m*, Wagnisgrundsatz

risk sharing, hazard sharing, distribution of risk(s), distribution of hazard(s), sharing of risk(s), sharing of hazard(s), splitting (up) of risk(s), splitting (up) of hazard(s), hazard distribution, risk distribution · Verteilung *f* des Risikos, Verteilung des Wagnisses, Risikoverteilung, Wagnisverteilung

risk-taking, hazard-taking · Risikoübernahme *f*, Wagnisübernahme

risk threshold, hazard threshold · Wagnisschwelle *f*, Risikoschwelle

risky contract, uncertain contract, aleatory contract · zufallabhängiger Vertrag *m*, ungewisser Vertrag, riskanter Vertrag

risky shift · Neigung *f* zu riskanter Entscheidung

rivage · Stromzoll *m*

rival firm — road planning

rival firm · Konkurrenzfirma *f*

river authority · Strombehörde *f*

river bank · Stromufer *n*

river (bank) town, river (bank) city · Strom(ufer)stadt *f*

river basin · Stromsystem *n*

river border, river frontier · Stromgrenze *f*

river city → river (bank) town

river conservancy (Brit.); river supervision commission (US) · Stromaufsicht(samt) *f, (n)*

river construction department · Strombauabteilung *f*

river development · Stromausbau *m*

river for floating, floatable river [*A river used for floating logs, rafts, etc.*] · Flößer(ei)strom *m*

river frontier → river border

riverfront park · Stromuferpark *m*

riverlot · Stromhufe *f*

river (resources) board, water (resources) board · Wasserwirtschaftsamt *n*

riverside premises · Lagerhäuser *n pl* mit Schiffahrtsanschluß

rivers (prevention of pollution) act, rivers (prevention of pollution) law, rivers (prevention of pollution) statute · Stromreinhaltungsgesetz *n*

river supervision commission (US); river conservancy (Brit.) · Stromaufsicht(samt) *f, (n)*

river town → river (bank) town

road · lange Stadtstraße *f*

road, highway · Straße *f*

road appearance, highway appearance · Straßenbild *n*

road authority, highway authority · Straßenbehörde *f*

roadbuilding, highway building, highway construction, road construction · Straßenbau *m*

road clean(s)ing, highway clean(s)ing · Straßenreinigung *f*

road clean(s)ing department, road clean(s)ing division, highway clean(s)ing department, highway clean(s)ing division · Straßenreinigungsabteilung *f*

road clean(s)ing division → road clean(s)ing department

road code, highway code · Straßenverkehrsordnung *f*

road construction, roadbuilding, highway building, highway construction · Straßenbau *m*

road construction administration, highway construction administration · Straßenbauverwaltung *f*

road construction authority, highway construction authority · Straßenbaubehörde *f*

road (construction) land, highway (construction) land, land for road construction, land for highway construction, land for road works, land for highway works · Straßenbauboden *m*, Straßenbaufläche *f*, Straßen(bau)land *n*

road construction of a Land, Land highway construction, Land road construction, highway construction of a Land · Landesstraßenbau *m* [*Bundesrepublik Deutschland*]

road construction office, highway construction office · Straßenbauamt *n*

road cost(s), highway cost(s) · Straßenherstellungskosten *f*, Straßenbaukosten

road cost(s) law, highway cost(s) law · Straßenbaukostenrecht *n*

road financing, highway financing · Straßenbaufinanzierung *f*

road ground, road land, highway ground, highway land · Straßengelände *n*, Straßenland *n*, Straßenterrain *n*

road land, highway ground, highway land, road ground · Straßengelände *n*, Straßenland *n*, Straßenterrain *n*

road land → road (construction) land

road law, highway law · Straßenrecht *n*

road lawmaking, highway lawmaking, highway legislation, road legislation · Straßenbaugesetzgebung *f*

road level, highway level · Straßenhöhe *f*

road maintenance cost(s), highway maintenance cost(s) · Straßenunterhaltungskosten *f*

road map, highway map · Straßenkarte *f*

road map series, highway map series · Straßenkartenwerk *n*

road noise, highway noise · Straßenlärm *m*

road nuisance, highway nuisance · Straßenverkehrsgefährdung *f*

road-orien(ta)ted, highway-orien(ta)ted, highway-related, road-related · straßenbezogen, straßenorientiert

road owner, highway proprietor, road proprietor, highway owner · Straßeneigentümer *m*, Straßeneigner

road planner, highway planner · Straßenplaner *m*

road planning, highway planning · Straßenplanung *f*

road pricing, highway pricing · Anwendung f des Preismechanismus im Straßenverkehr

road proprietor, highway owner, road owner, highway proprietor · Straßeneigentümer m, Straßeneigner

road relocation, highway relocation · Straßenverlegung f

road surveyor, surveyor of highways, surveyor of roads, highway surveyor · Straßenaufseher m, Wegeaufseher

road toll, highway toll · Straßengeld n, Straßenzoll m, Straßen(benutzungs)gebühr f, Wegegeld n; Straßenmaut f [Österreich]

road traffic authority, highway traffic authority · Straßenverkehrsbehörde f

road traffic law, highway traffic law · Straßenverkehrsrecht n

road user tax, highway user tax · Straßenverkehrssteuer f

road widening, highway widening · Straßenerweiterung f, Straßenverbreiterung

robber economy, ruthless exploitation, predatory cultivation · Raubbau m, Raubwirtschaft f

robotigation · Robotertum n

rockery house, block building · Miet(s)kaserne f, Wohnkaserne, Massenmiet(s)haus n

rodent control · Nagetierbekämpfung f

rogatory letters [International law]; letters of request (addressed to a foreign court) (Brit.) · Rechtshilfeersuchen n

rogue · gewerbsmäßiger Bettler m

rogues · Gesindel n

ROI, return on investment, yield on investment, return on capital, yield on capital, capital yield, capital return, investment yield, investment return · Kapitalrendite f [Verhältnis von erzielten Gewinn zum eingesetzten Kapital]

ROI analysis, return on investment analysis · DuPont-Formula f

rolling plan · gleitender Plan m [Er ermöglicht die notwendige Anpassung der Planung]

roll of a manorial court, court roll [A book in which an account of all the proceedings and transactions of the customary court of a manor was entered by a person duly authorized] · Hofesrolle f, Gutsherrenregister n, Leh(e)n(s)herrenregister, Stammrolle des Herrenhofs

roll of fees, roll of fiefs · Leh(e)n(s)buch n

roll of parchment, parchment roll · Pergamentrolle f

Roman city, Roman town · Römerstadt f

Roman (civil) law; jus civile Romanum [Latin], (civil) law of Rome [As distinguished from the English law] · römisches Recht n [„Civil law" ist die englische Sammelbezeichnung für die im römischen Recht wurzelnden Rechtsordnungen]

Roman Dutch law · römisch-holländisches Recht n

Roman-Germanic law · römisch-germanisches Recht n

Roman law → (civil) law

Roman private law · römisches Privatrecht n

Roman reckoning · römische Zeitrechnung f

Roman town, Roman city · Römerstadt f

(Roman) villa [It was not a mere residence, but, like the villa of the present day in Italy, a territory or an estate in land under a villicus, worked by slaves. It was, in fact, exceedingly like a manor] · römisches Herrengut n, römisches Frongut

Romescot, Peter-pence, Romeke, Romepenny · Peterspfennig m

roof advertisement · Dachwerbung f, Dachreklame

room arrangement · Zimmeranordnung f, Raumanordnung

roomer (US); subtenant · Untermieter m

rooming house (US); lodging-house (Brit.) [Building that contains sleeping rooms and which is regularly used or available for permanent occupancy] · Logierhaus n, Herberge f zur Heimat

rootless, uprooted · entwurzelt, wurzellos

root-mean-square divergence, root-mean-square deviation · mittlere quadratische Abweichung f vom Bezugspunkt

root of (legal) title, (legal) title root · (Rechts)Titelursprung m, (Rechts)Titelwurzel f

ro replace, to substitute, to surrogate · ersetzen

rotating crops, rotation of crops, crop rotation · Fruchtwechsel m, Fruchtfolge f

rotation of crops, crop rotation, rotating crops · Fruchtwechsel m, Fruchtfolge f

rotation of the list, seniority of the list, list rotation, list seniority · Reihenfolge f der Anträge [Zuteilungsverfahren einer Bausparkasse]

rough (design) drawing · Rohzeichnung f, Rohentwurfszeichnung

rough grazing — royal privilege

rough grazing · Bergweide f

round green village, round plaza village · Rundangerdorf n, Rundplatzdorf

round hamlet · Rundweiler m

rounding-off [*The completion of an incomplete grouping of buildings, on land ripe for development, in such a way that will either complete the local road pattern, or finally define and complete the boundaries of the group, or both, without exceeding or distorting the original conception of the group, or infringing any of the restrictions that may govern the unbuilt-on land concerned*] · Abrundung f, Aufrundung

round journey, round trip, round travel · Rundfahrt f

round plaza settlement · Rundplatz(an)sied(e)lung f

round plaza village, round green village · Rundangerdorf n, Rundplatzdorf

round settlement · Rund(an)sied(e)lung f

round travel, round journey, round trip · Rundfahrt f

round trip, round travel, round journey · Rundfahrt f

round village, circular village, ring-fence village · Rundling m

roup [*scots law*] → (sale by) auction

Rousseau's contrat social, social contract, social compact · Sozialvertrag m

route position · Verkehrslage f [*einer Ortschaft*]

route research · Routensuche f

routing, machine allocation · Verfahrenswahl f [*fertigungstechnisches Verfahren*]

row development, ribbon development, linear development · Bandentwick(e)lung f, Reihenentwick(e)lung

row dwelling [*Dwelling of which the walls on two sides are party or lot line walls*] · Reihenwohnung f

row hamlet · Reihenweiler m

row house · eingebautes Haus n, Reihenhaus

row of farmstead groups · Gehöftgruppenreihe f

row of houses, house row · Wohnzeile f

row of trees, tree row · Baumreihe f

row village, ribbon village, linear village · Banddorf n, Reihendorf

row village with strip parcels with farmstead access · Streifengutsdorf n

royal assent · königliche Zustimmung f

(royal) borough, (royal) burgh [*Scots law. A corporate body erected by the charter of the sovereign, consisting of the inhabitants of the territory erected into the borough. The four boroughs are Edinburgh, Stirling, Linlithgow and Lanark*] · (königlicher) Burgflecken m

royal burgh [*In Scotland. The charter is derived from the king*] · Stadt f mit königlichem Stadtrecht

royal charter · königlicher Freibrief m, königliche Verleihungsurkunde f, königliche Privilegierungsurkunde

Royal Commission · Immediatkommission f [*in England*]

royal commission of inquiry, royal inquiry commission · königliche Untersuchungskommission f

royal demeine (lands), royal demain (lands), demesne (lands) of the Crown, Crown demesne land(s) held in socage, Crown lands, royal demesne (lands) · Kronländer(eien) fl, Krongüter, Länder(eien) der Krone, Domänen f der Krone, Güter der Krone, königliche Domänen, königliche Länder(eien), königliche Güter, Krondomänen, Land der Krone, Kronland n

royal demesne revenues, (Crown) land(s) revenues [*Income derived from Crown land(s) in Great Britain*] · Kronguteinkünfte fpl, Kronlandeinkünfte, Kronländerei(en)einkünfte

royal fish, regal fish, fish royal · Wale mpl und Störe mpl [*Sie sind in England königliches Eigentum wenn sie ans Ufer geworfen oder in Küstennähe gefangen werden*]

(royal) franchise, royal privilege [*At common law, a franchise is a royal privilege or branch of the Crown's prerogative subsisting in the hands of a subject, either by grant or by prescription*] · Kron(en)recht n, Kron(en)privileg n, königliches Privileg

royal inquiry commission, royal commission of inquiry · königliche Untersuchungskommission f

royal manor · königliches Landgut n

Royal mines [*England*] · Gold- und Silberminen fpl

Royal Mint · Münzamt n [*Großbritannien*]

Royal Ordinance factory [*Great Britain*] · staatliche Rüstungsfabrik f

royal park · königlicher Park m

royal prerogative, prerogative of a sovereign, sovereign right, royal right of a sovereign · Reg(al)ie f, königliches Recht n

royal privilege, (royal) franchise [*At common law, a franchise is a royal privilege or branch of the Crown's prerogative*

royal right of a sovereign — rule of interpretation

subsisting in the hands of a subject, either by grant or by prescription] · Kron(en)recht n, Kron(en)privileg n, königliches Privileg, königliches Recht

royal right of a sovereign, royal prerogative, prerogative of a sovereign, sovereign right · Reg(al)ie f, königliches Recht n

royal stables · Marstall m

royalty, licence fee, license fee · Patentabgabe f, Lizenzgebühr f

royalty · Nutzungsabgabe f, Regal n

royalty → mineral royalty

R.P., reply paid · Antwort bezahlt

rubber-tyred rapid-transit system (Brit.); rubber-tired rapid-transit system (US) · gummibereiftes Schnellbahnsystem n, gummibereifte Schnellbahn f

rubbish removal, final project clean up, site clean(s)ing · Bau(stellen)reinigung f, Bau(stellen)säuberung [*Reinigung einer Baustelle von Bauschutt und anderen Arbeitsrückständen*]

Ruhr Coalfield Settlement Association · Siedlungsverband m Ruhrkohlenbezirk

to ruin · abhausen, abwirtschaften [*Grundherr*]

ruinous price, cut(-throat) price, slaughtered price, price below cost price · Schleuderpreis m

ruins plot (of land) · Ruinengrundstück n

ruins town, ruins city · Ruinenstadt f

to rule, to decide, to try [*To settle by authoritative sentence*] · entscheiden [*Rechtsstreit*]

rule, executive order [*"Rule" im amerikanischen Verwaltungsrecht und "Verordnung" im deutschen Verwaltungsrecht sind nicht ganz deckungsgleich*] · Verwaltungsverordnung f

rule, regulator, canon · Regel f, Regulativ n

rule, proposition of law, law proposition · Rechtssatz m

rule, prescription, regulation · (Rechts)-Vorschrift f

rule absolute, regulation absolute, prescription absolute · unbedingte (Rechts)Vorschrift f, absolute (Rechts)-Vorschrift

rule against perpetuities · Verbot n dauernder Vermögensbindung, Fideikommißverbot

rule as to citation, citation rule, rule of citation · Zitierregel f

rule committee [*Die "rules" sind Rechtsverordnungen (statutory instruments) des englischen Rechts, zu deren Erlaß mit Richtern — teilweise auch Unterrichtern — und Anwälten beider Anwaltsstände besetzte Juristenausschüsse ermächtigt sind, die vom Lord Chancellor eingesetzt werden. Die Ermächtigung bezieht sich ausschließlich auf das Verfahrensrecht*] · Juristenausschuß m

ruled → adjudicated

rule day · erster Montag m im Monat [*An diesem Tag muß die Gerichtsschreiberei geöffnet sein*]

rule for organization, regulation for organization, prescription for organization · Organisationsvorschrift f

rule making, executive order making · Verwaltungsverordnungsgebung f

rule of absolute (general) ownership, rule of absolute ownership (of property), rule of absolute proprietorship · absolute Eigentumsregel f

rule of citation, rule as to citation, citation rule · Zitierregel f

rule of competition · Wettbewerbsregel f

rule of conduct, conduct rule · Verhaltensnorm f

rule of conflict of laws, conflict rule · Kollisionsregel f

rule of construction, canon of construction, canon of interpretation, rule of interpretation [*Canons of construction are the system of fundamental rules and maxims which are recognized as governing the construction or interpretation of written instruments*] · Auslegungsregel f, Deutungsregel

rule of construction, rule of drawing up, rule of setting up, canon of formation, canon of drafting, canon of construing, canon of phrasing, canon of wording, canon of construction, canon of drawing up, canon of setting up, rule of formation, rule of construing, rule of drafting, rule of phrasing, rule of wording [*Canon of arranging or marshalling words*] · Entwurfsregel f, Gestaltungsregel, Abfassungsregel, Ausarbeitungsregel

rule of court, court rule · Gerichtsentscheid(ung) m, (f) [*z. B. einen Schiedsvertrag vor einem Gericht zu Protokoll geben um ihn zum Gerichtsentscheid erheben zu lassen*]

rule of distance, distance rule · Abstandregel f

rule of equity, equity rule · Billigkeits(recht)regel f

rule of evidence, rule of proof · Beweisregel f

rule of interpretation, rule of construction, canon of construction, canon of interpretation [*Canons of construction are*

rule (of law) — rules of principle of priority

the system of fundamental rules and maxims which are recognized as governing the construction or interpretation of written instruments] · Auslegungsregel *f*, Deutungsregel *f*

rule (of law), norm of law, legal rule, (legal) norm, law rule, law norm [*It is a rule of general application, sanctioned by the recognition of authorities, and usually expressed in the form of maxim or logical proposition. Called a "rule", because in doubtful or unforeseen cases it is a guide or norm for their decision*] · Gesetz(es)norm *f*, Sachnorm, normative Festlegung *f*, (Rechts)Norm

rule of phrasing, rule of wording, rule of construction, rule of drawing up, rule of setting up, canon of formation, canon of drafting, canon of construing, canon of phrasing, canon of wording, canon of construction, canon of drawing up, canon of setting up, rule of formation, rule of construing, rule of drafting [*Canon of arranging or marshalling words*] · Entwurfsregel *f*, Gestaltungsregel, Abfassungsregel, Ausarbeitungsregel

rule of planning (enabling) law, rule of planning (enabling) act, rule of planning (enabling) statute · Planungsgesetzregel *f*

rule of precedent · Selbstbindung *f* [*Gericht*]

rule of proof, rule of evidence · Beweisregel *f*

rule of reason · Vernunftregel *f*, Regel der Vernunft

rule of setting up, canon of formation, canon of drafting, canon of construing, canon of phrasing, canon of wording, canon of construction, canon of drawing up, canon of setting up, rule of formation, rule of construing, rule of drafting, rule of phrasing, rule of wording, rule of construction, rule of drawing up [*Canon of arranging or marshalling words*] · Entwurfsregel *f*, Gestaltungsregel, Abfassungsregel, Ausarbeitungsregel

rule of survivorship, survivorship rule · Überlebensregel *f*

rule of thumb, thumb rule, tentative working rule · Faustregel *f*

rule of wording, rule of construction, rule of drawing up, rule of setting up, canon of formation, canon of drafting, canon of construing, canon of phrasing, canon of wording, canon of drawing up, canon of setting up, rule of formation, rule of construing, rule of drafting, rule of phrasing [*Canon of arranging or marshalling words*] · Entwurfsregel *f*, Gestaltungsregel, Abfassungsregel, Ausarbeitungsregel

rule of zoning, regulation of zoning, zoning prescription, prescription of zoning, zoning regulation, zoning rule · (bauliche) Nutzungsvorschrift *f*, Baunutzungsvorschrift

ruler, Sovereign · Herrscher *m*

rules established by the opinions of the courts, established opinions of the courts, established lines of judicial authority · ständige Rechtsprechung *f* der Gerichte

rules for topsoil protection, regulations for topsoil protection, prescriptions for topsoil protection · Mutterbodenschutz *m* [*Schutz des Mutterbodens durch (Rechts)Vorschriften*]

rules of building and construction → (generally accepted) rules of building and construction

rules of civil procedure, civil procedure rules, Code of Civil Procedure · ZPO *f*, Zivilprozeßordnung

rules of (court) practice, rules of (court) procedure, (general) (standing) rules of court, court (practice) rules, procedural code, code of (court) procedure, (court) procedure code · Prozeßregeln *f pl*, Prozeßordnung *f*, Gerichtsverfahrensregeln, Gerichtsverfahrensordnung, (gerichtliche) Verfahrensregeln, (gerichtliche) Verfahrensordnung

rules of descent, canons of inheritance, canons of descent, rules of inheritance [*The legal rules by which inheritances are regulated, and according to which estates are transmitted by descent from the ancestor to the heir*] · Erbordnung *f*, Erbschaftsordnung, Regeln *f pl* der Abstammungserbfolge

rules of engineering → universally accepted rules of engineering

rules of evidence, evidence rules · Beweisordnung *f*

rules of federal civil procedure · Bundeszivilprozeßordnung *f*

rules of inheritance, rules of descent, canons of inheritance, canons of descent [*The legal rules by which inheritances are regulated, and according to which estates are transmitted by descent from the ancestor to the heir*] · Erbordnung *f*, Erbschaftsordnung, Regeln *f pl* der Abstammungserbfolge

rules of principle of distinctness, distinctness principle rules · formell(rechtlich)er Bestimmtheitsgrundsatz *m*, formell(rechtlich)er Spezialitätsgrundsatz, formell(rechtlich)es Bestimmtheitsprinzip *n*, formell(rechtlich)es Spezialitätsprinzip [*Grundbuchrecht*]

rules of principle of priority, principle of priority rules · formell(rechtlich)er Vorranggrundsatz *m*, formell(rechtlich)er

Prioritätsgrundsatz, formell(rechtlich)es Vorrangprinzip *n*, formell(rechtlich)es Prioritätsprinzip [*Grundbuchrecht*]

rules of procedure, procedure rules · Geschäftsordnung *f* [*z. B. eines Planungsrates*]

to rule through, to cancel · löschen [*im Grundbuch*]

to rule through, to strike out, to cancel · ausstreichen, durchstreichen

ruling · Entscheid(ung) *m*, *(f)* [*Gericht*]

ruling class · herrschende Klasse *f*

ruling councillor · Präsidialrat *m*

ruling doctrine · herrschende Lehre *f*

ruling language · geltende Sprache *f*

ruling of the court · richterliche Stellungnahme *f* zu strittigen Rechtsfragen

ruling power · herrschende Gewalt *f*

ruling (real) estate, ruling (real) property, dominant realty, ruling realty; praedium dominans [*Latin*], dominant tenement, ruling tenement, dominant (real) estate, dominant (real) property, dominant land, ruling land · berechtigter Boden *m*, dominierender Boden, herrschender Boden, berechtigter Grund(besitz) *m*, dominierender Grund(besitz), herrschender Grund(besitz), berechtigter Besitz, dominierender Besitz, herrschender Besitz, herrschendes Grundstück *n*, dominierendes Grundstück, herrschendes Land, dominierendes Land, berechtigtes Land, berechtigtes Grundstück *n*

ruling through, cancelling, cancellation · (Amts)Löschung *f* [*im Grundbuch*]

ruling through, cancelling, striking out · Durchstreichen *n*, Ausstreichen

ruling through declaration, cancelling declaration · Löschungsbewilligung *f* [*Erklärung eines Berechtigten zur Löschung eines in einem Grundbuch eingetragenen Rechts*]

run · (Merkmal)Iteration *f* [*Statistik*]

runaway from justice, absconder · Flüchtige *m*

runaway inflation, galloping inflation, hyperinflation · galoppierende Inflation *f*

run-down · verwohnt

run item [*The quantity of the item is expressed as a linear measurement*] · Längenposition *f*

running account, open account, account current, demand account, continuing account · laufendes Konto *n*, Kontokorrent *n*

running account credit, (bank) overdraft · Überziehung(skredit) *f*, *(m)*, Kontokredit

running (bill) broker · Vermitt(e)lungs-Wechselhändler *m*, Vermitt(e)lungs-Wechselmakler [*Er kauft keine Wechsel und indossiert sie auch nicht*]

running-ground, drive; cursus [*Latin*] · Trift *f*

running of a business, working of a business · Geschäftsbetrieb *m*

running of time, efflux(ion) of time · Zeitablauf *m*, Zeitverlauf

running out, termination, falling in, lapse (of time), expiration, expiry · Ablauf *m*, Fristablauf, Zeitablauf, Verfristung *f*

running out date, accrual date, maturity date, expiry date, expiration date, due date, termination date, falling in date · Fälligkeitsdatum *n*, Fälligkeitstag *m*, Verfalldatum, Verfalltermin *m*, (Frist)-Ablauftermin, (Frist)Ablaufdatum, Fälligkeitstermin, Verfalltag, (Frist)Ablauftag

running share · laufender Anteil *m*

running together, concurrent · gleichlaufend

running up, growing to, accrual, accruing, accruement, accruer · Auflaufen *n* [*Betrag*]

runoff management · Abflußbewirtschaftung *f*

run-off primary (election), second primary (election) [*USA*] · zweite Vorwahl *f*, zweite Urwahl, zweite Erstwahl, Entscheidungsvorwahl, Entscheidungsurwahl, Entscheidungserstwahl

to run out, to cease; to fall in (Brit.); to expire, to end, to terminate, to lapse · ablaufen, verfristen

to run over time · zeitlich überschreiten

to run up, to grow to, to accumulate, to accrue · auflaufen, anwachsen, zuwachsen, aufhäufen, anhäufen [*Betrag*]

run up, grown to, accumulated, accrued · angewachsen, angehäuft, zugewachsen, aufgehäuft, aufgelaufen

run up interest, accumulated interest, undistributed interest, accrued interest · aufgelaufene Zinsen *f*, Stückzinsen *f*, angehäufte Zinsen, angewachsene Zinsen, aufgehäufte Zinsen, zugewachsene Zinsen, Vorzugszinsen

rural; landward [*Scots law*] · ländlich

rural agglomeration, farmer-town, farmer-city, agricultural town, agricultural city, agro-town, agro-city, peasant-city, peasant-town · Agrarstadt *f*, Agrostadt, Landwirtschaftsstadt [*Landwirtschaftliche Groß(an)sied(e)lung mit weiterverarbeitender Industrie und ausgebautem Dienstleistungsnetz*]

rural area, rural territory, country area, country territory · ländliches Gebiet *n*,

rural authority — rural house possessor

rural Landgebiet [*Phänomenologisch in der Regel ein Gebiet in welchem Bodennutzung und (An)Sied(e)lung vorherrschend von der Land- und Forstwirtschaft bestimmt werden. Eine genaue Begriffsabgrenzung ist aber besonders bei dem in den Randgebieten der Verdichtungsräume vorhandenen Kontinuum kaum möglich; ebenso ist wegen der verschiedenen sied(e)lungsgeschichtlichen und natürlichen Gegebenheiten eine innergebietliche Unterscheidung sehr schwierig*]

rural authority, country authority · ländliche Behörde *f*, Landbehörde

rural belt, country belt · ländlicher Gürtel *m*

rural board · Landamt *n* [*Gegensatz: Stadtamt*]

rural building zone · Dorf(bau)gebiet *n*, Dorfbebauungsgebiet, MD [*Es dient vorwiegend der Unterbringung der Wirtschaftsstellen land- und forstwirtschaftlicher Betriebe und dem Wohnen*]

rural city, country town, country city, rural town · Landstadt *f*

rural city fringe, rurban fringe, outskirt, outer zone, rural urban fringe, rural town fringe · „eingebauter" Gürtel *m*, ländlich-städtischer Gürtel [*Die Benennungen „rural urban fringe" usw. können heute nicht mehr mit „Stadtrandzone" übersetzt werden, weil es sich heute um nur noch durch ihre aus der einstigen Randlage resultierenden besonderen Funktionen gekennzeichnete und in den geschlossenen Stadtkörper „eingebaute" Gürtel handelt*]

rural community, Landgemeinde *f*, Landkommune *f*, ländliche Gemeinde, ländliche Kommune [*Als Organisationsform*]

rural community → (human) rural community

rural community code · Landgemeindeordnung *f*, Landkommuneordnung

rural community constitution · Landgemeindeverfassung *f*, Landkommuneverfassung

rural community law, rural commune law · Landgemeinderecht *n*, Landkommunalrecht

rural community organization (for social welfare), rural community welfare organization · ländliche Wohlfahrtsarbeit *f*

rural composition, country structure, country composition, rural structure · ländliches Gefüge *n*, ländlicher Aufbau *m*, ländliche Struktur *f*, ländliche Zusammensetzung *f*

rural condemnation → rural (land) condemnation

rural cultural life, country cultural life · ländliches Kulturleben *n*

rural dean · Landdekan *m*

rural depressed area, rural depressed region, less prosperous rural area, less prosperous rural region · ländlicher Passivraum *m*, ländliches Notstandsgebiet *n*

rural development, country development · ländlicher Entwick(e)lung *f*

rural district [*A place not urban, usually in incorporated areas, but in some cases within city limits where sparse population density permits*] · Landbezirk *m*, ländlicher Bezirk

rural district council, rural sanitary authority · ländliche Sanitätsbehörde *f*

rural economy · Landeswirtschaft *f*, ländliche Wirtschaft [*Sie umfaßt Landwirtschaft, Forstwirtschaft und landschaftsgebundenes Ingenieurwesen*]

rural engineering · landschaftsgebundenes Ingenieurwesen *n*

rural estate in possession → rural land in possession

rural estate market → rural (real) estate market

rural exodus, flight from the land, movement of population from country to town, rural-to-urban movement, rural-urban drift, rural-urban migration · Land-Stadt-Wanderung *f*, Landflucht *f*

rural expropriation → rural (land) expropriation

rural family, country family · Landfamilie *f*

rural form of settlement, country form of settlement, country settlement form, rural settlement form · ländliche (An)Sied(e)lungsform *f*, Land(an)sied(e)lungsform

rural geography, country geography · ländliche Geographie *f*

rural highway, rural road · Landstraße *f*

rural highway authority, rural road authority · Landstraßenbehörde *f*

rural highway construction, rural road construction · Landstraßenbau *m*

rural highway map, rural road map · Landstraßenkarte *f*

rural home, country(side) home · Landeigenheim *n*, Landeigenhaus *n*

rural homestead, country homestead · ländliche Heimstätte *f*

rural hous(ebuild)ing · Landwohn(ungs)bau *m*, ländlicher Wohn(ungs)bau

rural house possession, country house possession · ländlicher Hausbesitz *m*

rural house possessor, country house possessor · ländlicher Hausbesitzer *m*

rural housing · Landwohnungen *fpl*, ländliche Wohnungen

rural housing practice · Landwohn(ungs)wesen *n*, ländliches Wohn(ungs)wesen

rural (immov(e)able) property, country (immov(e)able) property · ländliches Immobiliarvermögen *n*, ländliches Immobilienvermögen, ländliches Grund(stücks)vermögen, ländliches Liegenschaftsvermögen, ländliches Bodenvermögen

rural improvement, country improvement · ländliche Erschließung *f*

rural improvement planning, country improvement planning · ländliche Erschließungsplanung *f*

rurality · ländlicher Charakter *m*

rural land, country land · ländlicher Bereich *m* [*Im planerischen Sinne*]

rural land, country land [*Sometimes, by local usage also called "landed estate" and "landed property" as distinguished from (real) estate situated in a city*] · ländlicher Grund *m*, ländlicher Boden *m*, ländliches Land *n*, Landgrund, Landboden

rural (land) condemnation (US); rural (land) expropriation · ländliche Enteignung *f*

rural land in possession, country land in possession, rural (real) estate in possession, country (real) estate in possession, rural (real) property in possession, rural realty in possession, country (real) property in possession, country realty in possession · ländlicher Grund(stücks)besitz *m*, ländlicher Bodenbesitz, ländlicher Landbesitz

rural land law, country land law · ländliches Landrecht *n*, ländliches Bodenrecht

rural land market → rural (real) estate market

rural land ownership, ownership of rural land · ländliches Bodeneigentum *n*, ländliches Grund(stücks)eigentum, ländliches Landeigentum, Landbodeneigentum, Landgrund(stücks)eigentum

rural land possessor, possessor of rural land, country land possessor, possessor of country land · ländlicher Grund(stücks)besitzer *m*

rural land price, rural realty price, country (real) estate price, country (real) property price, country land price, country realty price, rural (real) estate price, rural (real) property price · ländlicher Grundstückspreis *m*, ländlicher Bodenpreis, ländlicher Landpreis

rural land reform, country land reform · ländliche Bodenreform *f*, ländliche Landreform

rural landscape, country landscape · ländliche Landschaft *f* [*im Gegensatz zur "Stadtlandschaft"*]

rural land use, country land use, use of rural land, use of country land · ländliche Landnutzung *f*, ländliche Bodennutzung, ländliche Flächennutzung

rural land use density, country land use density · ländliche Landnutzungsdichte *f*, ländliche Bodennutzungsdichte, ländliche Flächennutzungsdichte

rural land use plan, country land use plan · Landflächennutzungsplan *m*

rural land use planning, country land use planning · Landflächennutzungsplanung *f*

rural land use studies · Bestandsaufnahme *f* der ländlichen Flächennutzung, Bestandsaufnahme der ländlichen Bodennutzung, Bestandsaufnahme der ländlichen Landnutzung

rural (land) use zoning, country (land) use zoning, rural zoning, country zoning · ländliche Baunutzung *f*, ländliche bauliche Nutzung

rural life, country life · Landleben *n*, ländliches Leben

rural local government, country local government · ländliche Gemeindeverwaltung *f*

rural locality, country locality · ländlicher Ort *m*

rural location, country site, country location, rural site · ländlicher Standort *m*

rural-nonfarm · ländlich-nichtagrar(isch), ländlich-nicht-landwirtschaftlich

rural-nonfarm population · ländliche nichtlandwirtschaftliche Bevölkerung *f*

rural officer, rural official, country officer, country official · Landbeamte *m*

rural outdoor recreation, country outdoor recreation · ländliche Außenerholung *f*

rural parish, country parish · ländliches Kirchspiel *n*

rural parish community, country parish community · Kirchspiellandgemeinde *f*

rural pattern, rural scheme · ländliches Muster *n*, ländliches Schema *n*

rural place of work, rural place of employment, country place of work, country place of employment · ländlicher Arbeitsort *m*

rural planner, country planner · Landplaner *m* [*Im Gegensatz zum Stadtplaner, die Benennung "Landesplaner" sollte hier nicht verwendet werden um Verwechselungen mit dem Landesplaner eines Landes der Bundesrepublik Deutschland zu vermeiden*]

rural planning (advisory) panel, rural planning (advisory) council, country planning (advisory) panel, country planning (advisory) council · Landplanungsbeirat *m*, ländlicher Planungsbeirat

rural planning assistance, rural planning sponsoring, rural planning promotion, country planning assistance, country planning sponsoring, country planning promotion · ländliche Planungsförderung *f*

rural planning committee, country planning committee · Landplanungsausschuß *m*, ländlicher Planungsausschuß

rural planning, country planning · Landplanung *f*, ländliche Planung; Landesplanung [*Fehlbenennung*] [*Jede über das Gebiet einer Gemeinde hinausgehende Planung. Sie ist nicht an Verwaltungsgrenzen gebunden*]

rural planning law, country planning law · Landplanungsrecht *n*, ländliches Planungsrecht

rural planning law, rural planning act, rural planning statute, country planning law, country planning act, country planning statute · Landplanungsgesetz *n*, ländliches Planungsgesetz

rural planning office, country planning office · Landplanungsstelle *f*, ländliche Planungsstelle

rural planning organization, country planning organization · Landplanungsorganisation *f*, ländliche Planungsorganisation

rural planning practice, country planning practice · Landplanungswesen *n*, ländliches Planungswesen

rural planning promotion → rural planning assistance

rural planning science, country planning science · Landplanungswissenschaft *f*, ländliche Planungswissenschaft

rural planning sponsoring → rural planning assistance

rural plot, country plot · ländliches Katastergrundstück *n*, ländliches Grundstück (im katastertechnischen Sinne), ländliches Kartengrundstück, ländliches Flurstück, ländliche (Kataster)Parzelle *f*, Landgrundstück (im katastertechnischen Sinne), Landkatastergrundstück, Land-Kartengrundstück, Land(kataster)parzelle, Landflurstück

rural population, country population · ländliche Bevölkerung *f*, Landbevölkerung *f*, Landvolk *n*

rural poverty, country poverty · Armut *f* auf dem Lande, Landarmut *f*

rural property → rural (immov(e)able) property

rural property in possession → rural land in possession

rural property market → rural (real) estate market

rural property transactions → rural (real) property transactions

rural rate, country rate · ländliche Steuer *f*

rural (real) estate in possession → rural land in possession

rural (real) estate market, rural (real) property market, rural realty market, rural land market, market of rural land, market of rural realty, market of rural (real) estate, market of rural (real) property, country land market, country (real) estate market, country (real) property market, country realty market, market of country land, market of country (real) estate, market of country (real) property, market of country realty · ländlicher Grundstücksmarkt *m*, ländlicher Bodenmarkt, ländlicher Landmarkt

rural (real) estate price, rural (real) property price, rural land price, rural realty price, country (real) estate price, country (real) property price, country land price, country realty price · ländlicher Grundstückspreis *m*, ländlicher Bodenpreis, ländlicher Landpreis

rural (real) property in possession → rural land in possession

rural (real) property market → rural (real) estate market

rural (real) property price, rural land price, rural realty price, country (real) estate price, country (real) property price, country land price, country realty price, rural (real) estate price · ländlicher Grundstückspreis *m*, ländlicher Bodenpreis, ländlicher Landpreis

rural (real) property transactions, rural (real) estate transactions, rural land(s) transactions, dealing with rural land(s), rural realty transactions · ländlicher Grundstücksverkehr *m*, ländlicher Bodenverkehr, ländlicher Immobiliarverkehr, ländlicher Immobilienverkehr, ländlicher Liegenschaftsverkehr

rural realty in possession → rural land in possession

rural realty market → rural (real) estate market

rural realty price, country (real) estate price, country (real) property price, country land price, country realty price, rural (real) estate price, rural (real) property price, rural land price · ländlicher Bodenpreis *m*, ländlicher Landpreis

rural realty transactions → rural (real) property transactions

rural region, country region · ländlicher Raum *m*, Landraum, ländliche Region *f*, Landregion

rural regional planning — rural (use) zoning

rural regional planning, country regional planning · ländliche Regionalplanung *f*

rural relocation, rural resettlement · Aussied(e)lung *f* landwirtschaftlicher Bevölkerung, Umsied(e)lung landwirtschaftlicher Bevölkerung, Verlegung landwirtschaftlicher Bevölkerung, Umsetzung landwirtschaftlicher Bevölkerung

rural resettlement, rural relocation · Aussied(e)lung *f* landwirtschaftlicher Bevölkerung, Umsied(e)lung landwirtschaftlicher Bevölkerung, Verlegung landwirtschaftlicher Bevölkerung, Umsetzung landwirtschaftlicher Bevölkerung

rural resettlement, rural relocation · Aussied(e)lung *f* ländlicher Bevölkerung, Umsied(e)lung ländlicher Bevölkerung, Umsetzung ländlicher Bevölkerung, Verlegung ländlicher Bevölkerung

rural residential place, country residential place · ländlicher Wohnplatz *m*

rural road, rural highway · Landstraße *f*

rural road authority, rural highway authority · Landstraßenbehörde *f*

rural road construction, rural highway construction · Landstraßenbau *m*

rural road map, rural highway map · Landstraßenkarte *f*

rural sanitary authority, rural district council · ländliche Sanitätsbehörde *f*

rural (sanitary) district · Verwaltungsbereich *m* einer ländlichen Sanitätsbehörde [*England*]

rural scheme, rural pattern · ländliches Muster *n*, ländliches Schema *n*

rural school, village school · Dorfschule *f*, Landschule

rural servitude · ländliche Dienstbarkeit *f*, ländliche Gerechtigkeit, ländliche Servitut *f*, ländliches Servitut *n*, ländliches (servitutisches) Recht *n*

rural setting, country surrounding, country setting, rural surrounding · ländliche Umgebung *f*

rural settlement, country settlement · ländliche (An)Sied(e)lung *f*, Land(an)sied(e)lung

rural settlement form, rural form of settlement, country form of settlement, country settlement form · ländliche (An)Sied(e)lungsform *f*, Land(an)sied(e)lungsform

rural settlement geography, country settlement geography, geography of rural settlements, geography of country settlements · ländliche (An)Sied(e)lungsgeographie *f*

rural settlement pattern, rural settlement scheme, pattern of rural settlement, scheme of rural settlement · Land(an)sied(e)lungsmuster *n*, Land(an)sied(e)lungsschema *n*, ländliches (An)Sied(e)lungsmuster, ländliches (An)Sied(e)lungsschema

rural site, rural location, country site, country location · ländlicher Standort *m*

rural social system, country social system · ländliches Sozialsystem *n*

rural sociology, country sociology · ländliche Soziologie *f*

rural structure, rural composition, country structure, country composition · ländliches Gefüge *n*, ländlicher Aufbau *m*, ländliche Struktur *f*, ländliche Zusammensetzung *f*

rural surrounding, rural setting, country surrounding, country setting · ländliche Umgebung *f*

rural territory, country area, country territory, rural area · ländliches Gebiet *n*, Landgebiet [*Phänomenologisch in der Regel ein Gebiet in welchem Bodennutzung und (An)Sied(e)lung vorherrschend von der Land- und Forstwirtschaft bestimmt werden. Eine genaue Begriffsabgrenzung ist aber besonders bei dem in den Randgebieten der Verdichtungsräume vorhandenen Kontinuum kaum möglich; ebenso ist wegen der verschiedenen sied(e)lungsgeschichtlichen und natürlichen Gegebenheiten eine innergebietliche Unterscheidung sehr schwierig*]

rural-to-urban movement, rural-urban drift, rural-urban migration, rural exodus, flight from the land, movement of population from country to town · Land-Stadt-Wanderung *f*, Landflucht *f*

rural town, rural city, country town, country city · Landstadt *f*

rural town · Ackerbürgerstadt *f*

rural trade, country trade · Landgewerbe *n*, ländliches Gewerbe

rural-urban drift, rural-urban migration, rural exodus, flight from the land, movement of population from country to town, rural-to-urban movement · Land-Stadt-Wanderung *f*, Landflucht *f*

rural urban fringe, rural town fringe, rural city fringe, rurban fringe, outskirt, outer zone · „eingebauter" Gürtel *m*, ländlich-städtischer Gürtel [*Die Benennungen „rural urban fringe" usw. können heute nicht mehr mit „Stadtrandzone" übersetzt werden, weil es sich heute um nur noch durch ihre aus der einstigen Randlage resultierenden besonderen Funktionen gekennzeichneten und in den geschlossenen Stadtkörper „eingebaute" Gürtel handelt*]

rural-urban sociology · Stadt-Land-Soziologie *f*

rural (use) zoning → rural zoning

rural zone, country zone · ländliche Zone f

rural zoning, country zoning, rural (land) use zoning, country (land) use zoning · ländliche Baunutzung f, ländliche bauliche Nutzung

rurban fringe, outskirt, outer zone, rural urban fringe, rural town fringe, rural city fringe · „eingebauter" Gürtel m, ländlich-städtischer Gürtel [*Die Benennungen „rural urban fringe" usw. können heute nicht mehr mit „Stadtrandzone" übersetzt werden, weil es sich heute um nur noch durch ihre aus der einstigen Randlage resultierenden besonderen Funktionen gekennzeichnete und in den geschlossenen Stadtkörper „eingebaute" Gürtel handelt*]

rurbanization, fusion of urban and rural land · Verschmelzung f von Stadt und Land mit Hilfe des Verkehrs

rush (hour) traffic, peak (hour) traffic · Spitzen(stunden)verkehr m

rush order, priority order, urgent order [*An order which is identified as taking precedence over other orders to ensure its completion in the minimum time*] · Vorzugsauftrag m, Dringlichkeitsauftrag

rush period, peak period · Spitzen(verkehrs)zeit f, Verkehrsspitzenzeit

rush to sub(urb)s, centripetal migration · Randwanderung f

ruthless exploitation, predatory cultivation, robber economy · Raubbau m, Raubwirtschaft f

S

S/D, draft at sight, sight draft · Sichttratte f

sacramentum [*Latin*]; ath [*Saxon*]; oath; othe [*old English*]; juramentum, jus jurandum [*Latin*] · Eid m

sacrifice value [*Value of goods calculated according to the sacrifice necessary to acquire them*] · Opferwert m

saddle point · Sattelpunkt m

saddlers' company · Sattlerinnung f

safe condition · sicherer Zustand m

safe-conduct · freies Geleit n

safe custody company, safe deposit company · Schrankfachgesellschaft f [*Nur der Kunde besitzt den Schlüssel und nur er kann das Fach öffnen*]

safe-deposit box · Bankfach n

safe deposit contract, safe custody contract · Schrankfachvertrag m

to safeguard, to protect · wahrnehmen [*Interessen*]

safe guardel land tenant · unkündbarer Landpächter m

safeguarding of data, data protection, computer security · Datenschutz m

safeguarding the election · Wahlschutz m

safety · Sicherheit f

safety expert · Sicherheitsfachmann m

safety legislation, safety lawmaking · Sicherheitsgesetzgebung f

safety measure · Sicherheitsvorkehrung f, Sicherheitsmaßnahme f

safety of commodities, safety of goods · Warensicherheit f, Gütersicherheit

safety of (construction) site, safety of building site, (construction) site safety, building site safety, safety of job site, job site safety · Baustellensicherheit f

safety of goods, safety of commodities · Warensicherheit f, Gütersicherheit

safety provisions · Sicherheitsbestimmungen f pl

safety regulations · Sicherheitsvorschriften f pl

sag in call, sag in demand · Nachfragerückgang m

sag in demand, sag in call · Nachfragerückgang m

sailing chart, track chart, ocean chart · Segelkarte f, Übersegler m

saisine [*Latin*]; infeoffment [*Scotland*]; seisina seysina [*Latin*]; seisin, freehold (possession), seizin, possession as of freehold, possession of an estate of freehold · Gewere f [*Eine historische Untersuchung über das Wesen der Gewere muß ihren Ausgang von der „investitura" des alten Rechts nehmen. Denn mit diesem Ausdruck geben die lateinischen Quellen der karolingischen Periode das Wort Gewere wieder, wie das aus der altdeutschen Übersetzung von C. 6 der Capitularia leg. add. v. 817 bei Pertz, l. S. 261 und aus den zwei parallel laufenden Stellen der traditiones Fuldenses in zwei Urkunden von 824 „testes qui vestitionem viderunt" und „testes qui viderunt giweridam" unwidersprechlich hervorgeht*]

saisine in law, infeoffment in law, seisin in law, freehold (possession) in law [*Scotland*] · Erbganggewere f, ideelle Gewere

sala, traditio [*Latin*] · dingliche Einigung f [*nach deutschem Recht*]

salaami, pugree, tea money [*In the Far East*]; key money [*An undercover rent payment*] · Schlüsselgeld *n*

salableness → sal(e)ability

sala regis [*Latin*] · königlicher Saalhof *m*

salaried · besoldet

salaried architect · angestellter Architekt *m*

salaried employe(e) · Angestellte *m*, Gehaltsempfänger

salaried employe(e) in civil service · Angestellte *m* im öffentlichen Dienst

salaried employment · Beschäftigung *f* als Gehaltsempfänger

salaried personnel · Gehaltsempfänger *m pl*, Angestellte *m pl*

salaried programme; salaried program (US) · Pensionsplan *m* für Angestellte, (Alters)Versorgungsplan für Angestellte

salary · Gehalt *n*

salary expected · Gehaltsvorstellung *f*

salary roll · Gehaltsliste *f*

salary to start, starting salary · Anfangsgehalt *n*

sale · Verkauf *m*, Übertragung *f* des Eigentums an der Kaufsache

sale [*A transfer of property or of a right from one person to another, in consideration of a sum of money, as opposed to barters, exchanges and gifts*] · dinglicher Vertrag *m*

sal(e)ability, salableness, marketability · Absetzbarkeit *f*, Verkaufbarkeit, Marktgängigkeit

sal(e)able, merchantable, mercable, fungible, marketable · absetzbar, verkaufbar, marktgängig, verkäuflich

sal(e)able, perfect, good, marketable, clear · frei, vollgültig [*(Rechts)Titel*]

(sale by) auction, public auction; roup [*Scots law*] · Versteigerung *f*, Auktion *f*

sale by description · Verkauf *m* nach Angabe, Verkauf nach Beschreibung

sale by retail (trade), retail (trade) sale · Einzel(handels)verkauf *m*, Detailverkauf

sale by sample · Musterverkauf *m*, Probeverkauf, Verkauf nach Muster, Verkauf nach Probe

sale by the court · gerichtlicher Verkauf *m*

sale contract, contract of sale · Verpflichtungsvertrag *m* [*Übertragung von Grundstücksrechten*]

sale contract, contract to sell, contract of sale · Verkaufsvertrag *m*

sale deed, deed of sale · Verkaufsurkunde *f*

sale in mass, lumping sale [*Several parcels of real estate, or several articles of personal property, are sold together for a lump or single gross sum*] · Pauschalverkauf *m*

sale-lease-back · Finanzierungsleasing *n* mit Verkauf und Rückmietung

sale of a pawn, sale of a pledge · Pfandverkauf *m*

sale of ascertained goods, sale of specific goods · Speziesverkauf *m*

sale of building(s) · Gebäudeverkauf *m*

sale of discretion, discretionary sale · Ermessensverkauf *m*

sale of estate → (real) property sale

sale of goods · Verkauf *m* beweglicher Sachen, Warenverkauf

sale of goods by description, descriptive sale of goods · Verkauf *m* beweglicher Sachen nach Angabe, Verkauf beweglicher Sachen nach Beschreibung, Warenverkauf nach Angabe, Warenverkauf nach Beschreibung

sale of goodwill, goodwill sale · Verkauf *m* der Kundschaft (eines Geschäftes)

sale of land by auction, land sale by auction · Landversteigerung *f*, Landauktion *f*, Bodenversteigerung, Bodenauktion

sale of land(s) → (real) property sale

sale of public land(s) · Landverkauf *m* der öffentlichen Hand

sale of (real) estate → (real) property sale

sale of (real) property → (real) property sale

sale of realty → (real) property sale

sale of specific goods, sale of ascertained goods · Speziesverkauf *m*

sale of unascertained goods · Gattungsverkauf *m*, Genusverkauf

sale of uncollected goods, disposal of uncollected goods · Verkauf *m* nicht eingelöster Pfandgüter

sale price, selling price · Verkaufspreis *m*

sale proceeds, proceeds of sale · Verkaufserlös *m*, Absatzerlös

sales area, sales territory, marketing area, marketing territory · Absatzgebiet *n*, Marktgebiet, Verkaufsgebiet

sales company · Vertriebsgesellschaft *f*, Verkaufsgesellschaft

sales contract memorandum · Verkaufsschlußzettel *m*

sale's gain, profit of sale, gain of sale, sale's profit · Verkaufsprofit *m*, Verkaufsgewinn *m*

sales letter — sanitary authority

sales letter · Werbebrief *m*

sales load · Verkaufsspesen *f*

salesman · (gewerbsmäßiger) Verkäufer *m*

sales manager · Vertriebsleiter *m*, Verkaufsleiter

sale's profit, sale's gain, profit of sale, gain of sale · Verkaufsprofit *m*, Verkaufsgewinn *m*

sales promotion · Verkaufsförderung *f*, Absatzförderung

sales research, marketing research · Absatzforschung *f*, Verkaufsforschung

sales territory, marketing area, marketing territory, sales area · Absatzgebiet *n*, Marktgebiet, Verkaufsgebiet

sales volume · Verkaufsvolumen *n*, Absatzvolumen

sale value, selling value · Verkaufswert *m*

Salic Law · salisches Recht *n*

salina [*A house or place were salt is made*] · Saline *f*

salmon and freshwater fisheries act, salmon and freshwater fisheries law, salmon and freshwater fisheries statute · Gesetz *n* über den Fang von Lachs und Süßwasserfischen

to salvage [*To use for some purpose products which cannot be used for the purpose for which they were originally intended*] · verwerten

salvage · Bergung *f*

salvageable · noch brauchbar [*Gebäude, das nicht abgerissen, sondern verbessert wird*]

salvage note [*A document which authorizes the use of a product for a purpose for which it was not originally intended*] · Verwertungsanzeige *f*, Verwertungszettel *m*

sameness · Schematismus *m*, Schablone *f*

sample [*Material or assembly submitted by the contractor to the owner or his representative*] · Probe(stück) *f*, (*n*)

sample → (random) sample

sample drawing · Probezeichnung *f*

sample frequency distribution → (random) sample frequency distribution

sample frequency function → (random) sample frequency function

sample mean → (random) sample mean

sample of time · Stichprobe *f* nach Zeit(einheiten) [*Umfragetechnik*]

sample of words · Wortstichprobe *f* [*Umfragetechnik*]

sample size → (random) sample size

sample space → (random) sample space

sample statistic → (random) sample statistic

sampling → (random) sampling

to sanction → to approbate

sanction, admission, approval · Zulassung *f*

sanctioning, approbating, approving, consenting, assenting, action of giving assent · Billigen *n*, Einwilligen, Zustimmen

sanctioning authority, approving authority · Zulassungsbehörde *f*

sanction in writing, approval in writing, written assent, written approval, written consent, written sanction, consent in writing, assent in writing · schriftliche Billigung *f*, schriftliche Einwilligung, schriftliche Zustimmung

sanction law, law of sanctions · Sanktionsrecht *n*

sanction to assignment, sanction to cession, approval to assignment, approval to cession, assent to assignment, assent to cession, consent to assignment, consent to cession · Abtretungseinwilligung *f*, Abtretungszustimmung, Abtretungsbilligung, Zessionseinwilligung, Zessionszustimmung, Zessionsbilligung

sand excavation, sand digging · Aussandung *f*

sand exploitation right, right to exploit sand, right to take sand, right to win sand, sand winning right · Sandabbaurecht *n*, Sandgewinnungsrecht, Sandausbeutungsrecht

sand pit · Sandgrube *f*

sand winning right, sand exploitation right, right to exploit sand, right to take sand, right to win sand · Sandabbaurecht *n*, Sandgewinnungsrecht, Sandausbeutungsrecht

sandy ground, sandy land; terra sabulosa [*Latin*] · sandiges Gelände *n*, sandiges Land *n*, sandiges Terrain *n*

sanitary authority, district council [*In den inkorporierten Städten Englands übt die Stadtverwaltung zugleich die Funktionen einer „sanitary authority" aus und somit bildet eine solche Stadt zugleich einen „county district" (= Verwaltungsbereich einer Sanitätsbehörde) und die Stadtverwaltung ist ein „district council" doch mit dem Unterschied von anderen „district councils", daß ihr Name und ihre Verfassung ihr gewahrt bleiben*] · Sanitätsbehörde *f*

sanitary authority; (medical) officer of health [*England*]; health authority · Gesundheitsbehörde *f*

sanitary board — scalar organization

sanitary board, district board [*England*]. A board constituted under the Metropolis Management Act, 1855, for the management of the sanitary affairs of groups of parishes as were formed into districts] · Sanitätsamt *n*

sanitary councillor, district councillor · Rat *m* des Verwaltungsbereiches einer Sanitätsbehörde

sanitary inspector, inspector of nuisances · Gesundheitsinspektor *m*, Sanitätsinspektor, Sanitärinspektor, Gesundheitskontrolleur, Sanitätskontrolleur, Sanitärkontrolleur

sanitary nuisance · Gesundheitsübelstand *m*

sartare [*Latin*] → assartare

Sasines Register, Register of Sasines [*The national land register for the whole of Scotland*]; Register of Title at the Land Registry [*England*] · Land(rechts)titelregister *n*

satellite cities greenbelt plan, core-satellite regional plan, multiple centers plan · Plan *m* der neben der zentral in der Stadtregion gelegenen Kernstadt die Herausbildung mehrerer Großstädte zwischen 500 000 und 1 Mio. Einwohnern innerhalb derselben im Abstand von etwa 50 km oder mehr vom Zentrum der Kernstadt anstrebt

satellite geodesy · Satellitengeodäsie *f*, Satellitenmessung *f*

satellite place · Satellitenort(schaft) *m, (f)* [*Er liegt in der Regel innerhalb einer Stadtregion, ist weniger selbständig und besitzt eine stärkere Bindung an die Kernstadt*]

satellite town, satellite city · Satellitenstadt *f*

satisfaction · Befriedigung *f*

satisfaction agreement, agreement of satisfaction · Befriedigungsabkommen *n*, Befriedigungsabmachung *f*, Befriedigungsvereinbarung

satisfaction certificate, certificate of satisfaction · Befriedigungsattest *n*, Befriedigungsschein *m*, Befriedigungsbescheinigung *f*, Befriedigungsnachweis *m*

satisfaction level, level of satisfaction → Befriedigungsniveau *n*

satisfaction of debt(s) · Befriedigung *f* von Schulden, Schuld(en)befriedigung

satisfaction of wants, satisfaction of needs · Befriedigung *f* der Bedürfnisse, Bedürfnisbefriedigung

satisfaction piece [*Instrument for recording and acknowledging payment of an indebtedness secured by a mortgage*] · löschungsfähige Quittung *f*

satisfied · gerechtfertigt

to satisfy · befriedigen

saturation (level) · Sättigung *f*

saturation point, point of saturation · Sättigungspunkt *m*

savanna village · Savannendorf *n*

"save as you earn" [*In Great Britain*] · Vertragssparen *n*

to save harmless, to hold harmless, to indemnify [*To secure against loss or damage*] · decken, schadlos halten

saving · Sparen *n*

saving account [*Saving banks in the USA*]; compound interest account [*National City Bank*]; thrift account [*Chase National Bank*]; deposit account (Brit.) · Sparkonto *n* [*In den USA dürfen die Sparkonten nur von den „saving banks" als „saving accounts" bezeichnet werden*]

saving clause, exclusion clause, nonliability clause, exemption clause [*A clause in a contract by which a purchaser repudiates liability in certain specified circumstances*] · Ausschließungsklausel *f*, Ausschlußklausel, Freizeichnungsklausel, Haftungsausschließungsklausel *f*, Haftungsausschlußklausel, Haftungsfreizeichnungsklausel

saving place, resting place, street refuge · Bürgersteiginsel *f*, Fußgängerinsel

savings · Ersparnisse *fpl*

savings and loan company (US) → building society

savings bank · Sparkasse *f*

savings bank trust, Totten bank trust · Treuhand *f* zugunsten eines Dritten, Dritten-Treuhand

savings share · Sparanteil *m*

saving through investment in securities, equity saving · Wertpapiersparen *n*

Saxon (farming) system · Zelgensystem *n* mit Gewannflur

Saxon field · Langstreifenflur *f*

Saxon Mirror [*It is one of the most important of all medi(a)eval law books and a statement or digest of territorial and feudal law in use in certain districts of the territory occupied by the Saxons*] · Das Sächsische Landrecht *n*, Sachsenspiegel *m*

scab (US); strike-breaker; blackleg (Brit.) · Streikbrecher *m*

scaffold(ing) code · (Bau)Gerüstordnung *f*

scaffold(ing) fee · (Bau)Gerüstgebühr *f*, Platzzins *m*

scalar organization, line organization · Liniensystem *n*, Linienorganisation *f* [*Nur eine Instanz darf einer anderen Anweisungen geben*]

scale — scattered settlement

scale · Maßstab *m*

scale economies, economies of scale · einsparende Massenproduktion *f*, Kostenersparnisse *fpl* durch optimale Betriebsgröße [*Sie führt zu internen Einsparungen*]

scale economy, return to scale, economy of scale · Skalenertrag *m* [*Die Auswirkung der proportionalen Faktorerhöhung auf das Produktionsergebnis*]

scale error · Maßstabverzerrung *f* [*Durch Verzerrung des Papiers hervorgerufene Änderung(en) des Kartenmaßstabes*]

scale of charges, schedule of charges, charge scale, charge schedule, scale of duties, schedule of duties, duty schedule, duty scale · Gebührentabelle *f*, Gebührentafel

scale of distribution, distribution scale · Verteilungsmaßstab *m*, Maßstab *m* der Verteilung

scale of duties, schedule of duties, duty schedule, duty scale, scale of charges, schedule of charges, charge scale, charge schedule · Gebührentabelle *f*, Gebührentafel

scale of fees, schedule of fees, fee scale, fee schedule · Gebührentabelle *f*, Honorartabelle, Gebührentafel *f*, Honorartafel

scale plotting, plotting to scale · maßstabsgerechtes Auftragen *n*

scale rate · Tabellensatz *m*, Tabellenrate *f*

scarcity, shortage, stringency, deficiency · Knappheit *f*, Verknappung *f*, Mangel *m*, Klemme *f*, Not *f*

scarcity degree, degree of shortage, degree of scarcity, shortage degree · Verknappungsgrad *m*, Mangelgrad, Knappheitsgrad

scarcity of credit, stringency of credit, credit scarcity, credit stringency, credit shortage, credit deficiency, deficiency of credit, shortage of credit · Kreditknappheit *f*, Kreditklemme *f*, Kreditnot *f*, Kreditmangel *m*, Kreditverknappung *f*, Kreditdefizit *n*

scarcity of housing, deficiency of housing, house-famine, housing shortage, housing deficiency, housing stringency, housing scarcity, shortage of housing, stringency of housing · Wohnungsbedarf *m*, Wohnungsfehlbestand *m*, Wohnraumfehlbestand, Wohnungsmangel *m*, Wohnraummangel, Wohnungsknappheit *f*, Wohnraumknappheit, Wohnungsdefizit *n*, Wohnraumdefizit, Wohnungsnot *f*, Wohnungsverknappung *f*, Wohnraumverknappung, Wohnraumklemme *f*, Wohnraumnot, Wohnungsklemme, Wohnraumbedarf [*Die sich aus der zahlenmäßigen Gegenüberstellung von Haushalten und Normalwohnungen in abgegrenzten Gebieten oder Bereichen ergebende Zahl fehlender Wohnungen*]

scarcity of land(s), land(s) dearth, dearth of land(s), land(s) shortage, land(s) scarcity, shortage of land(s) · Bodenknappheit *f*, Landknappheit, Bodenverknappung *f*, Landverknappung, Bodenmangel *m*, Landmangel

scarcity of money → shortage of money

scarcity rent · Knappheitsrente *f*

scarcity value · Knappheitswert *m*

scatter, dispersion · Dekonzentration *f*, (Ver)Streuung *f* [*Raumordnung*]

scatter diagram · Korrelationsbild *n*

scattered, dispersed · gestreut, dekonzentriert, verstreut [*Raumordnung*]

scattered country location → scattered rural location · ländliche Streulage *f*

scattered development, dispersed development, non-compact development, sporadic development [*Developments occurring here and there without any co-ordinating feature to lick them or give them identity*] · Splitterbebauung *f*, Streubebauung, wilde Bebauung; Splitterüberbauung, Streuüberbauung, wilde Überbauung [*Schweiz*]

scattered function, noncentral function, dispersed function · disperse Funktion *f*, nichtzentrale Funktion, Streufunktion

scattered land(ed) estate, dispersed land(ed) estate, non-compact land(ed) estate · Streu(land)besitz *m*, disperser (Land)Besitz, Streubodenbesitz, disperser Bodenbesitz

scattered landscape, non-compact landscape, dispersed landscape · Streulandschaft *f*, disperse Landschaft

scattered location, non-compact location, dispersed location · Streulage *f*, disperse Lage

scattered pattern, non-compact pattern, dispersed scheme, scattered scheme, non-compact scheme, dispersed pattern · Streumuster *n*, Streuschema *n*, disperses Muster, disperses Schema

scattered population, dispersed population, noncentral population · nichtzentrale Bevölkerung *f*, disperse Bevölkerung, Streubevölkerung

scattered rural location, scattered country location · ländliche Streulage *f*

scattered settlement, scattered settling, non-compact settlement, non-compact settling, dispersed settlement, dispersed settling · Streubesied(e)lung *f*, Splitter(be)sied(e)lung, Streu(an)sied(e)lung, Splitteransied(e)lung, Streusiedeln, Splittersiedeln, Streubesiedeln, Splittersiedeln *n* [*Tätigkeit, die zum Entstehen einer Streuansied(e)lung führt*]

scattered-site housing — scheme of planning

scattered-site housing, dispersed-site housing; non-compact site housing [*Housing units dispersed, usually by a local housing authority, in small numbers on numerous, noncontiguous sites throughout a community*] · Streuwohnungen *f pl*

scattered territorial domain, non-compact territorial domain, dispersed territorial domain · Streugrundherrschaft *f* disperse Grundherrschaft

scatter-graph · Streupunktdiagramm *n*

scatter of population, population dispersion, population scatter, dispersion of population · Bevölkerungsstreuung *f*

scenery of the landscape, landscape appearance · Landschaftsbild *n*

scenery of the locality, community appearance · Gemeindebild *n*, Ortsbild

scenic highway, scenic road · Panoramastraße *f*

scenic site · Panoramaort *m*

schedule, sch. · Ausführungsanordnung *f* [*Im Anschluß an ein Gesetz erlassen*]

schedule, sch. · Ausführungsbestimmung *f* [*Im Anschluß an ein Gesetz erlassen*]

schedule, tabulation, index, registry, register, bill, list · Verzeichnis *n*, Liste *f*, Aufstellung *f*, Register *n*

schedule · Terminplan *m*

schedule of abbreviations, list of abbreviations · Abkürzungsverzeichnis *n*

schedule of accumulation, accumulation table, accumulation schedule, table of accumulation · Ansammlungstabelle *f*, Anhäufungstabelle, Aufhäufungstabelle

schedule of architects, index of architects, tabulation of architects, register of architects, registry of architects, list of architects · Architektenaufstellung *f*, Architektenliste *f*, Architektenregister *n*, Architektenverzeichnis *n*

schedule of bids, schedule of tenders, schedule of offers; summary of (bid) proposals, schedule of (bid) proposals (US), summary of bids, summary of tenders, summary of offers · Angebotsgegenüberstellung *f*

schedule of charges, charge scale, charge schedule, scale of duties, schedule of duties, duty schedule, duty scale, scale of charges · Gebührentabelle *f*, Gebührentafel

schedule of defects · (Bau)Mängelaufstellung *f*, Sachmängelaufstellung, Nachbesserungsaufstellung

schedule of duties, duty schedule, duty scale, scale of charges, schedule of charges, charge scale, charge schedule, scale of duties · Gebührentabelle *f*, Gebührentafel *f*

schedule of fees, fee scale, fee schedule, scale of fees · Gebührentabelle *f*, Honorartabelle, Gebührentafel *f*, Honorartafel

schedule of payments, payment schedule · Fälligkeitstabelle *f*

schedule of prices, list of prices, price schedule, price list · Preisverzeichnis *n*, Preisliste *f*

schedule of rates, rate schedule · Satztabelle *f*

schedule of the yield from land, register of the yield from (real) estate, register of the yield from (real) property, schedule of the yield from (real) estate, schedule from the yield of (real) property, register of the yield from land · Ertragskataster *n, m*

schedules [*company act*] · Ausführungsbestimmungen *f pl* [*Kapitalgesellschaftsgesetz*]

schedules service · Liniendienst *m*, fahrplanmäßiger Dienst

scheduling · Terminplanung *f*

scheme, programme; program (US) · Programm *n*

scheme, pattern · Muster *n*, Schema *n*

scheme · Vorlage *f*

scheme · Kasse *f* [*Im Sinne von z. B. einer Pensionskasse*]

scheme of activities, activity pattern, activity scheme, pattern of activities · Tätigkeitsmuster *n*, Tätigkeitsschema *n*, Tätigkeitenmuster, Tätigkeitenschema

scheme of argumentation → scheme of reasoning

scheme of arrangement, arrangement scheme · Nachlaßvertrag *m* mit Vermögensabtretung, Akkord *m* mit Vermögensabtretung

scheme of arrangement, composition scheme, arrangement scheme, scheme of composition · (Gläubiger)Vergleichsvorschlag *m*, Konkursakkordvorschlag

scheme of commuting, commuting pattern, commuting scheme, pattern of commuting · Pendler(verkehrs)muster *n*, Pendler(verkehrs)schema *n*

scheme of composition, scheme of arrangement, composition scheme, arrangement scheme · (Gläubiger)Vergleichsvorschlag *m*, Konkursakkordvorschlag

scheme of density, density pattern, density scheme, pattern of density · Dichteschema *n*, Dichtemuster *n*

scheme of planning, planning scheme · Planaufstellung *f*

scheme of reasoning — score

scheme of reasoning, scheme of argumentation, scheme of arguing, pattern of reasoning, pattern of arguing, pattern of argumentation · Argumentationsmuster *n*, Argumentationsschema *n*

scheme of regional policy · raumplanerisches Verfahren *n*, Raumordnungsverfahren [*Es dient der Abstimmung der den Raum beeinflussenden Planungen einzelner Planungsträger (z. B. Fachbehörden) mit den Belangen der Landesplanung. Nicht verwechseln mit dem Planfeststellungsverfahren*]

scheme of rural settlement, rural settlement pattern, rural settlement scheme, pattern of rural settlement · Land(an)sied(e)lungsmuster *n*, Land(an)sied(e)lungsschema *n*, ländliches (An)Sied(e)lungsmuster, ländliches (An)Sied(e)lungsschema

scholar · Gelehrte *m*

scholarly writing · wissenschaftliche Schrift *f*

scholarship → (closed) scholarship

scholastic agency · Schulagentur *f* [*in England*]

scholastic appointment · Lehrerstelle *f*

school attendance committee · Schulüberwachungsausschuß *m*

school board · Schulamt *n*

school code · Schulordnung *f*

school crossing · Schulübergang *m*, Schulüberweg *m*

school district [*USA*] · Schulgemeinde *f*

school examination · Schulprüfung *f*

school governor, education(al) officer, education(al) official · Schulrat *m*

schooling · Schulwesen *n*

school leaver · Schulabgänger *m*

school map · Schul(land)karte *f*

school of study · Studienabteilung *f*

school planning, planning for schools · Schulplanung *f*

school playing field · Schulspielplatz *m*

school rate · Schulsteuer *f*

school village · Schuldorf *n*

science of administration, administration science · Verwaltungswissenschaft *f*

science of comparative law · Rechtsvergleichungswissenschaft *f*, vergleichende Rechtswissenschaft

science of finance, financial science · Finanzwissenschaft *f*

science of forests, forestry science · Forstwissenschaft *f*, Waldwissenschaft

science of history of law · Rechtsgeschichtswissenschaft *f*

science of human settlement · Sied(e)lungswissenschaft *f*

science of law, jurisprudence, legal science; jurisprudentia [*Latin*]; law science · Jurisprudenz *f*, Rechtswissenschaft *f*, Lehre *f* der allgemeinen Rechtsfragen, Rechtslehre

science of natural law, jurisprudence of natural law, natural law jurisprudence, natural law science · Lehre *f* der allgemeinen Naturrechtsfragen, Lehre des Naturrechts, Naturrechtswissenschaft *f*, Wissenschaft des Naturrechts, Naturrechtslehre, Naturjurisprudenz *f*

science of objective meaning · Sinneswissenschaft *f*

science of planning, planning science · Planungswissenschaft *f*

science of population, population science · Bevölkerungswissenschaft *f*

science of reality, reality science · Wirklichkeitswissenschaft *f*

science of sociology · Soziowissenschaft *f*

science of soils → soil science

science of the earth's surface · Erdoberflächenkunde *f*, Erdoberflächenwissenschaft *f*

science of values · Wertwissenschaft *f*

scienter, knowingly, designedly · bewußt, wissentlich

scientific field · Wissenschaftsbereich *m*

scientific law, law of nature · Naturgesetz *n*

scientific management · wissenschaftliche Betriebsweise *f*, wissenschaftliche Betriebsführung *f*

scild-penig [*Saxon*]; scutage, shield-money, escuage; scutagium [*Latin*] · Schildgeld *n*, Ritterpferdsgeld

scope · Umfang *m*

scope limit, limit of range of validity, limit of scope · Geltungsgrenze *f*

scope of contract, contract scope · Vertragsumfang *m*

scope of liability, amount of liability · Haftungsumfang *m*

scope of space, spatial scope, space scope · räumlicher Geltungsbereich *m*

scope of space, space scope, spatial scope · räumlicher Umfang *m*

scope of validity as to place, range of validity as to place · örtlicher Geltungsbereich *m*

score · Maßgröße *f* [*Umfragetechnik*]

score · Punktwert m, Punktziffer f [Statistik]

score · Punktwert m, Punktzahl f [Statistik]

to scrap [To discard products or materials as economically incapable of being rectified or salvaged] · ausmustern

scrap value, junk value · Schrottwert m

scrapyard · Schrottplatz m

screening (off) · Schutz m vor Einsicht, Verhinderung f der Einsicht

scrip (certificate), allotment letter, letter of allotment · Interimsschein m [Für neuausgegebene Wertpapiere]

scrip holder · Interimsscheininhaber m

scriptum indentatum [Latin]; indenture, deed indented [A deed to which two or more persons are parties, and in which these enter into reciprocal and corresponding grants or obligations towards each other] · gesiegelte mehrseitige Urkunde f, mehrseitige gesiegelte Urkunde, zahnförmig ausgeschnittene gesiegelte mehrseitige Urkunde, zahnförmig ausgeschnittene mehrseitige gesiegelte Urkunde

scroll · Siegelersatz m

to scrutinize · durchlesen

scutage, shield-money, escuage; scutagium [Latin]; scild-penig [Saxon] · Schildgeld n, Ritterpferdsgeld

scutage tenant, tenant by scutage · Schildgeldleh(e)n(s)mann m

scutagium [Latin]; scild-penig [Saxon]; scutage, shield-money, escuage · Schildgeld n, Ritterpferdsgeld

scyran [Saxon]; county, shire · Grafschaft f

seabed subsoil, subsoil of the seabed · Meeresuntergrund m

sea belt [In political sense]; coast(al) waters [In geographic and nautical sense]; territorial waters, territorial sea, maritime belt, belt of sea · Küstengewässer n, Küstenmeer n, Territorialgewässer, Hoheitsgewässer, Meeresstreifen m, Hoheitsmeer, Territorialmeer

seaborne commerce · Überseehandel m

sea insurance, marine insurance · Seeversicherung f

to seal · siegeln

seal · Siegel n

sealed · verschlossen [Angebot]

sealed · versiegelt

sealed and delivered [In conveyancing. The common formula of attestation of deeds and other instruments, written immediately over the witness' name] · gesiegelt und begeben

sealed competitive bidding, sealed competitive tendering · Ausschreibung f mit verschlossenen Angeboten

sealed contract, (contract by) specialty, contract under seal, contract by seal, contract by deed, covenant in deed, covenant in fact, special(ty) contract, contract in sealed writing [Contracts under seal, such as deeds and bonds, are instruments which are not rarely in writing, but which are sealed by the party bound thereby, and delivered by him to, or for the benefit of, the person to whom the liability is thereby incurred] · (schriftlicher) gesiegelter Vertrag m, gesiegelter schriftlicher Vertrag, Formalvertrag unter Siegel, Vertrag mit Siegel, förmlicher Vertrag unter Siegel

sealed envelope · verschlossener (Brief)Umschlag m

sealed instrument, document under seal; charter [obsolete], deed (under seal) · Siegelurkunde f, gesiegelte Urkunde, Urkunde unter Siegel

sealer (of weights and measures) (US); inspector (of weights and measures (Brit.) · Eichmeister m

sealing · Siegelung f

sea pollution · Meeresverunreinigung f, Meeresverschmutzung

seaport town, seaport city · Seehafenstadt f

sea power, maritime power, naval power · Seemacht f

search for coal · Kohlensuche f

search for (natural) gas · Erdgassuche f, (Natur)Gassuche

search for oil, oil search · (Erd)Ölsuche f

search of job(s), search for job(s), search of work, search for work · Arbeitssuche f

search warrant · Hausdurchsuchungsbefehl m

sea resort, coast(al) resort · Seebad(eort) n, (m)

seasonal population · Saisonbevölkerung f

seasonal sale · Schlußverkauf m

seasonal settlement, temporary settlement · jahreszeitliche Sied(e)lung f, Saisonsied(e)lung, temporäre Sied(e)lung

seasonal unemployment · jahreszeitlich bedingte Arbeitslosigkeit f, Saisonarbeitslosigkeit, jahreszeitlich bedingte Erwerbslosigkeit, Saisonerwerbslosigkeit

seasonal worker, seasonal workman · Saisonarbeiter m

seat — secret agency

seat · Sitz *m* [*Einer juristischen Person oder Handelsgesellschaft*]

seated, used [*plot*] · genutzt [*Grundstück*]

seat of a bishopric · Bischofssitz *m*

seat of commerce, commercial seat · Handelssitz *m*

seat of government · Regierungssitz *m*

seat of the contract, proper law of the contract, law with reference to which the parties contracted; locus contractus [*Latin*]; seat of the obligation · Sitz *m* der Obligation [*nach Savigny*]; Sitz des Vertrages

SEC, security exchange commission · Börsenaufsichtsbehörde *f*

secession · Widerstand *m* gegen die Staatsgewalt

secludedness, privacy · Abgeschlossenheit *f*, Privatheit [*z. B. durch Gebüsch als Sichtblende*]

secondary audience · Mitleserschaft *f*, Zweitleserschaft

secondary building · Nebengebäude *n*

secondary business centre, subcentre (Brit.); secondary business center, subcenter (US) · Satellit-Geschäftszentrum, Stadtteilzentrum, Subzentrum, C-Zentrum, sekundäres Geschäftszentrum, Unterzentrum

secondary circulation · Mitverbreitung *f*, Mitstreuung, Zweitverbreitung, Zweitstreuung [*Umfragetechnik*]

secondary clause · Nebenklausel *f*

secondary contractor · Nebenunternehmer *m*, Zweitunternehmer [*Ein Unternehmer, der unter der Leitung des Hauptunternehmers Teile der Bauleitung erstellt und — im Gegensatz zum Nachunternehmer — zum Auftraggeber in einem unmittelbaren Vertragsverhältnis steht*]

secondary core · Nebenkern *m*, Zweitkern

secondary enterprise, secondary undertaking · Nebenunternehmen *n*, Nebenbetrieb *m*, Nebenunternehmung *f*

secondary evidence · Nachweis *m* über Vorhandensein und Inhalt einer Urkunde

secondary facility · Nebeneinrichtung *f*

secondary function · Lokalfunktion *f*, sekundäre Funktion

secondary metropolis · Nebenmetropole *f*

secondary offer, secondary tender, secondary bid; secondary (bid) proposal (US) · Nebenangebot *n*

secondary physical facility, secondary structure, secondary work · Nebenanlage *f*, Nebenbauwerk *n*, Nebenbaulichkeit *f*; Nebenbaute *f* [*Schweiz*] [*Bau-*

technisch selbständige, ihrem Zweck und ihrer Nutzung nach aber unselbständige bauliche Anlage]

secondary possession · Nebenbesitz *m*

secondary profession · Nebenberuf *m*

secondary school · höhere Schule *f*

secondary sector [*manufacturing; construction*] · Sekundärwirtschaft *f*, sekundärer Wirtschaftssektor *m*, sekundär(wirtschaftlich)er Sektor, Sekundär(wirtschafts)sektor

secondary structure, secondary work, secondary physical facility · Nebenanlage *f*, Nebenbauwerk *n*, Nebenbaulichkeit *f*; Nebenbaute *f* [*Schweiz*] [*Bautechnisch selbständige, ihrem Zweck und ihrer Nutzung nach aber unselbständige bauliche Anlage*]

secondary undertaking, secondary enterprise · Nebenunternehmen *n*, Nebenbetrieb *m*, Nebenunternehmung *f*

secondary work, secondary physical facility, secondary structure · Nebenanlage *f*, Nebenbauwerk *n*, Nebenbaulichkeit *f*; Nebenbaute *f* [*Schweiz*] [*Bautechnisch selbständige, ihrem Zweck und ihrer Nutzung nach aber unselbständige bauliche Anlage*]

second branch of the government · zweite Regierungsgewalt *f*

secondhand bookseller [*misnomer*]; dealer in secondhand books · Antiquar *m*

secondhand home · Gebrauchteigenheim *n*, Gebrauchteigenhaus *n*

secondhand house · Gebrauchthaus *n*

second heir (male), revisionary heir (male), substitute, after heir (male) · Aftererbe *m*, Nacherbe, Substitut, Ersatzerbe [*Derjenige, der nach einem ernannten Erben als Erbe in einem Testament ernannt ist, wenn der erste Erbe die Erbschaft nicht erwerben würde*]

second inheritance · Nacherbschaft *f*

second limit theorem · zweiter Grenzwertsatz *m* [*Statistik*]

second mortgage [*A mortgage on real estate already encumbered with a first mortgage*] · zweite Hypothek *f*

second-order condition · Bedingung *f* zweiter Ordnung

second primary (election), run-off primary (election) [*USA*] · zweite Vorwahl *f*, zweite Urwahl, zweite Erstwahl, Entscheidungsvorwahl, Entscheidungsurwahl, Entscheidungserstwahl

secrecy · Geheimhaltung *f*

secret agency, undisclosed agency · mittelbare Vertretung *f*, verdeckte Vertretung, unerkannte Vertretung

secret agent, undisclosed agent · mittelbarer Vertreter, verdeckter Vertreter, unerkannter Vertreter [*Er ist im eigenen Namen tätig ohne daß ihm die Rechte des Vertretenen fiduziarisch übertragen sind*]

secretary (US); minister (Brit.) · Minister *m*

Secretary of Agriculture [*USA*] · Landwirtschaftsminister *m*

secret conveyancing, private conveyancing · anonymes freiwilliges Übertragen *n*, unregistriertes freiwilliges Übertragen

to secrete, to conceal, to hide · verbergen

secret gain, secret profit · geheime Gewinnbeteiligung *f* [*Architekt*]

secret partner, undisclosed partner [*Is one whose connection with the firm is not disclosed. He may be active in the conduct of the business, and if his connection with the firm becomes disclosed, third parties may hold him liable, like and any other general partner*] · mittelbarer Gesellschafter *m*, verdeckter Gesellschafter, mittelbarer Teilhaber, verdeckter Teilhaber, unerkannter Gesellschafter, unerkannter Teilhaber

secret profit, secret gain · geheime Gewinnbeteiligung *f* [*Architekt*]

secretum sigillum [*Latin*]; privy seal · Geheimsiegel *n*

secret voting, ballot · geheime Abstimmung *f*

secta, suit · Prozeßgefolge *n*

sectator [*Latin*]; credible witness, suitor · glaubwürdiger Zeuge *m*

sectator, litigants [*Latin*]; litigator, suitor, litigant (party), party to a (law)suit · Prozessierende *m*, Prozeßpartei *f*

section [*A part of the work(s)*] · Abschnitt *m*, Bauabschnitt, Arbeitsabschnitt

section · Quadratmeile *f* [*Stadt in den USA*]

section · Unterabteilung *f*

section, s. [*English law*] · Gesetz(es)artikel *m*, Artikel, Gesetz(es)paragraph *m*, Paragraph

sectional capital · Reichsteilhauptstadt *f*

sectional completion, stage completion, completion in stages, completion in sections, completion by stages, stagewise completion, completion by sections, sectionwise completion · abschnittsweise Fertigstellung *f*, etappenweise Fertigstellung, stufenweise Fertigstellung

section of an area · Flächenabschnitt *m*

section of (the) population, segment of (the) population, part of (the) population · Bevölkerungsteil *m, n*

section value · Abschnittswert *m*, Bauabschnittswert, Arbeitsabschnittswert

sector, subject (field) · Fachbereich *m*, Sachbereich, Sachgebiet *n*, Fach(gebiet) *n*, Sektor *m*, Sachkomplex *m*

sector, province, division, department, branch [*public administration*] · Abteilung *f*, Referat *n*, Dezernat *n*, Ressort *n*

sector authority · Fachbehörde *f*, Sachbehörde

sector committee · Fachausschuß *m*, Sachausschuß

sector(ial) cluster [*It is constituted by an industry which buys and sells mainly from and to a subset of industries and through that subset*] · gedrängte Marktmittelpunkte *mpl*

sector(ial) equilibrium · sektorales Gleichgewicht *n*, Sektor(al)-Gleichgewicht

sector(ial) growth · Sektor(al)wachstum *n*, sektorales Wachstum

sector(ial) pattern, sector(ial) scheme · Sektorenmuster *n*, Sektorenschema *n*

sector(ial) structure · Sektor(al)struktur *f*, Sektor(al)gefüge *n*, Sektor(al)zusammensetzung *f*, sektorale Struktur, sektorale Zusammensetzung, sektorales Gefüge

sector(ial) theory, axial development theory, theory of axial development · Grundsatz *m* der sektoralen Differenzierung einer Stadt, Prinzip *n* der sektoralen Differenzierung einer Stadt, Sektortheorie *f*, Sektorentheorie

sector idea, idea of sectors · Sektor(en)idee *f*

sector plan, subject plan · fachlicher Entwick(e)lungsplan *m*, sektoraler Plan, Fachplan, Sektorplan

sector planning, specialized planning, subject planning [*Planning based on consideration of a particular type or types of development*] · fachliche Entwick(e)lungsplanung *f*, Sektorplanung, Fachplanung, sektorale Planung

sector planning act, sector planning law, sector planning statute, subject planning act, subject planning law, subject planning statute, specialized planning act, specialized planning law, specialized planning statute · Fachplanungsgesetz *n*, Sektorplanungsgesetz, sektorales Planungsgesetz, fachliches Entwick(e)lungsplanungsgesetz

sector planning law, subject planning law, specialized planning law · Fachplanungsrecht *n*, Sektorplanungsrecht, sektorales Planungsrecht, fachliches Planungsrecht

sector planning practice, subject planning practice, specialized planning practice · Fachplanungswesen n, Sektorplanungswesen, sektorales Planungswesen, fachliches Planungswesen

sector policy · Fachpolitik f, Sachpolitik

secular canon · weltlicher Kanoniker m

secular tithe · weltlicher Zehnt m

to secure [*payment*] · sicherstellen [*Zahlung*]

secured by (a) lien · gesichert durch Sicherungsrecht, gesichert durch Sicherheitsrecht

secured corporate bond [*USA*]; secured debenture [*Great Britain*] · gesicherte Schuldverschreibung f, gesicherte Obligation f [*einer privaten Kapitalgesellschaft*]

secured creditor · absonderungsberechtigter Gläubiger m, gesicherter Gläubiger

secured debenture [*Great Britain*]; secured corporate bond [*USA*] · gesicherte Schuldverschreibung f, gesicherte Obligation f [*private Kapitalgesellschaft*]

to secure for (safe) custody, to impound [*To put goods in the custody of the law*] · (gerichtlich) verwahren, in gerichtliche Verwahrung nehmen

securing for (safe) custody, impounding · Verwahren n, gerichtlich verwahren

securities act, securities statute, securities law, negotiable instruments act, negotiable instruments law, negotiable instruments statute · Wertpapiergesetz n

(securities) dealer, (securities) jobber, negotiable instruments dealer, negotiable instruments jobber · Börsenhändler m, Effektenhändler, Wertpapierhändler [*Er nimmt keine Aufträge von börsenfremden Kunden an, sondern nur von den „brokers"*]

securities deposit examination · Depotprüfung f

securities exchange act, securities exchange law, securities exchange statute, negotiable instruments exchange act, negotiable instruments exchange law, negotiable instruments exchange statute · Wertpapier-Börsen-Gesetz n

(securities) jobber, negotiable instruments dealer, negotiable instruments jobber, (securities) dealer · Börsenhändler m, Effektenhändler, Wertpapierhändler [*Er nimmt keine Aufträge von börsenfremden Kunden an, sondern nur von den „brokers"*]

securities law, negotiable instruments law · Wertpapierrecht n

securities market · Wertpapiermarkt m

security · Wertpapier n

security · Sicherheit f, Sicherung f, Pfandwert m

security, deposit; caution [*In Scotland*] · Deckung f, (Bar)Sicherheit f, Unterlage f, Sicherung, Kaution f

security against risks in granting credit(s), credit (risk(s)) security [*e.g. by means of an inquiry office*] · Kreditsicherung f, Kreditdeckung

security analyst · Effektenanalytiker m

security assignment, security cession, security assignation · Sicherungsabtretung f, Sicherungszession f, Vollabtretung einer Forderung

security bill of sale · Fahrnisverschreibung f, Fahrhabeverschreibung

security exchange commission, SEC · Börsenaufsichtsbehörde f

security index · Wertpapierindex m

security loan, deposit loan, loan against security, loan against deposit · Sicherungsdarleh(e)n n, Sicherheitsdarleh(e)n

security measure · Sicherungsmaßnahme f

security mortgage [*Mortgage as pledge for credit*] · Deckungshypothek f, Unterlagehypothek, Sicherungshypothek, Sicherheitshypothek, Kautionshypothek

security of employment · Sicherung f des Arbeitsplatzes, Arbeitsplatzsicherung

security of tenants; rent control (Brit.); tenants' protection, protection of tenants, protection for the tenant(s) · Mieterschutz m

security of tenure · Sicherheit f der Beziehungen zwischen Landwirt und dem von ihm bewirtschafteten Boden

security sum · Deckungssumme f, Sicherheitssumme, Sicherungssumme, Unterlagesumme

security value · Sicherheitswert m, Sicherungswert

security zone · Sicherheitszone f

sedentary · seßhaft

sedentary settlement, permanent settlement · Dauer(an)sied(e)lung f

sedes libera, libera sedes, liber bancus, framus bancus [*Latin*]; free-bench · Freisitz m [*Der Anteil der Witwe eines Hintersassen an dessen Immobiliarbesitz*]

sedition · Anstiftung f zum Aufruhr

sedition act, sedition law, sedition statute · Aufruhrgesetz n

seditious libel [*Sedition in the form of printed words*] · Anstiftung *f* zum Aufruhr durch Schriften

seed growing, growing of seed · Saatzucht *f*

seeker · Reflektant *m*, Suchende *m*

seepage water, percolating water · Sickerwasser *n*

seepage water law, percolating water law, law of percolating water, law of seepage water · (objektives) Sickerwasserrecht *n*

seepage water right, percolating water right, right to percolating water, right to seepage water · Sickerwasser(an)recht *n*, Sickerwasseranspruch *m*

seeta faldae [*Latin*]; fold-soke, suit of the fold, fold suit [*The duty of a tenant to set up and move about in the fields of a manor a fold for the purpose of manuring the ground*] · (Schaf)Pferchpflicht *f*

segmentation · Anpassung *f* [*Bei der Aussagefähigkeit empirischer Kostenfunktionen*]

segment of (the) population, part of (the) population, section of (the) population · Bevölkerungsteil *m, n*

segregation · Ungleichverteilung *f*

segregation index · Ungleichverteilungsindex *m*

segregation of pedestrian and vehicular traffic · Trennung *f* von Fußgänger- und Fahrzeugverkehr

seigniorage · Prägeschatz *m* [*A charge made by a mint for turning bullion brought to it into coins*]

seignorial, seignorial, seigneurial · herrschaftlich, leh(e)n(s)herrlich

seignorial right, seignoral right, seigneurial right · herrschaftliches Recht *n*, leh(e)n(s)herrliches Recht

seign(i)ory in gross, mere lordship in gross · persönliche Kronvasallenherrschaft *f*, persönliche Herrschaft eines Kronvasallen

seigniory appendant, mere lordship appendant, signory appendant · unterbrochene Kronvasallenherrschaft *f*

seigniory appurtenant, mere lordship appurtenant, signory appurtenant · zugehörige Kronvasallenherrschaft *f*, zugehörige Herrschaft eines Kronvasallen

seisin, freehold (possession), seizin, possession as of freehold, possession of an estate of freehold; saisine [*Latin*]; infeoffment [*Scotland*]; seisina seysina [*Latin*] · Gewere *f* [*Eine historische Untersuchung über das Wesen der Gewere muß ihren Ausgang von der „investitura" des alten Rechts nehmen. Denn mit diesem Ausdruck geben die lateinischen Quellen der karolingischen Periode das Wort Gewere wieder, wie das aus der altdeutschen Übersetzung von C. 6 der Capitularia leg. add. v. 817 bei Pertz, I. S. 261 und aus den zwei parallel laufenden Stellen der traditiones Fuldenses in zwei Urkunden von 824 „testes qui vestitionem viderunt" und „testes qui viderunt giweridam" unwidersprechlich hervorgeht*]

seisin in deed, actual seisin [*Seisin acquired by purchase*] · Kaufgewere *f*

seisin in law, freehold (possession) in law; saisine in law, infeoffment in law [*Scotland*] · Erbganggewere *f*, ideelle Gewere

seisin in law [*That seisin which an heir had when his ancestor died intestate seised of land and neither the heir nor any other person had taken actual possession of the land*] · Erbengewere *f*, Gewere des Erben

seismic map, (earth)quake map · Erdbebenkarte *f*, Bebenkarte

to seize the cattle of a stranger damage feasants · schütten, pfänden [*Vieh*]

seizure of (real) estate, seizure of (real) property, seizure of land(s) · Grund(stücks)beschlagnahme *f*, Landbeschlagnahme, Bodenbeschlagnahme

select body, committee · Ausschuß *m*

select committee · engerer Ausschuß *m*

selected bidder, selected tenderer, selected contractor [*Bidder selected by the owner for discussions relative to the possible award of a contract*] · potentieller Auftragnehmer *m*, potentieller AN

selecting the facts from the amorphous mass of data of experience · Konstituierung *f* des Sachverhalts

selection · Auslese *f*, Auswahl *f*

selection method ·Ausleseverfahren *n*, Auswahlverfahren *n*

selection overlay, lift, (extraction) trace · transparenter Auszug *m* [*Kartographie*]

selective bond, three-way fund, balanced bond, umbrella fund, managed fund, mixed bond · gemischter Versicherungsfonds *m*

selective (competitive) tendering, limited (competitive) tendering, limited competition, selective competition · beschränkte Ausschreibung *f*, beschränkter Wettbewerb *m* [*Bauleistungen werden im vorgeschriebenen Verfahren nach Aufforderung einer beschränkten Zahl von Unternehmern zur Einreichung von Angeboten vergeben*]

selective compulsion · Grundbuchzwang *m* für einzelne Grafschaften oder Städte [*England. Er kann durch den Kronrat angeordnet werden*]

selective employment tax [*Great Britain*] · selektive Beschäftigungssteuer *f*

selective migration · Auslesewanderung *f*

select list of bidders, select list of tenderers, restricted list of bidders, restricted list of tenderers · beschränkte (An)Bieterliste *f*

self-aid, self-help · Selbsthilfe *f*

self-aid hous(ebuild)ing, self-help hous(ebuild)ing · bauliche Selbsthilfe *f*, Selbsthilfe im Wohn(ungs)bau, Bauselbsthilfe

self-aid performance, self-help performance · Selbsthilfeleistung *f*

self-challenge · Selbstablehnung *f*

self-contained · selbständig [*Wohnung. Sie hat alle Reinigungs- und Gesundheitseinrichtungen*]

self-contained commercial state · geschlossener Handelsstaat *m*

self-contained unity · ausgewogene (An)Sied(e)lungseinheit *f*

self-defence (Brit.); self-defense (US) · Notwehr *f*

self-disserving evidence, self-disserving proof · Beweis *m* gegen eigenes Interesse

self-employed female person · Selbständige *f*

self-employed individuals tax relievement act · Steuer-Pensionierungsgesetz *n* für Freiberufliche

self-employed male person · Selbständige *m*

self-employed occupation, occupation in self-employment · freier Beruf *m*

self-executing · unmittelbar anwendungsfähig [*Vertragsnorm*]

self-executing treaty · rechtsgeschäftlicher Staatsvertrag *m*, unmittelbar anwendungsfähiger völkerrechtlicher Vertrag [*Er wirkt ohne Transformation oder Vollzugsbefehl*]

self-execution · Selbstausführung *f*

self-finance · Eigenfinanzierung *f*

self-government · Selbstregierung *f* [*Staatsverwaltung. Die Ursache hierfür liegt in der geschichtlichen Entwicklung der inneren Verwaltung Englands, die sich gänzlich anders als in Deutschland vollzog. Schon in frühester Zeit übten die Kirchspiele, Stadtschaften, Grafschaften und Städte gewisse innerstaatliche Verwaltungsbefugnisse aus. Heute sind die Gemeinden und Gemeindeverbände in England verfassungsmäßig mit der gesamten inneren Landesverwaltung betraut. Im Gegensatz zu den Großstaaten des Kontinents, deren innere Organisation regelmäßig mittlere staatliche Verwaltungsbehörden erster und zweiter Instanz kennt, gibt es in England keine mittleren und unteren Behörden der staatlichen Verwaltung, welche den Verwaltungsbefehlen einer zentralen Staatsregierung unterstehen.*]

self-help, self-aid · Selbsthilfe *f*

self-help hous(ebuild)ing, self-aid hous(ebuild)ing · bauliche Selbsthilfe *f*, Selbsthilfe im Wohn(ungs)bau, Bauselbsthilfe

self-help performance, self-aid performance · Selbsthilfeleistung *f*

self-incriminating · selbstanklagend

self-incrimination · Selbstbezichtigung *f*

self-induced frustration · Selbstvereitelung *f*

self-insured · selbstversichert

self(ish) interest · Selbstsüchtigkeit *f*

self-limitation · Selbstbeschränkung *f*

self-making-good of defects · Selbstbeseitigung *f* von (Sach)Mängeln, Selbstnachbesserung

self-performance · Selbstleistung *f*

self-potential · Eigenpotential *n*

self-preference, private benefit · Eigennutz *m*

self-production · Eigenproduktion *f*

self-regarding evidence, self-regarding proof · Beteiligtenbeweis *m*, Beweis der Beteiligten

self-regulating contract · lückenloser Vertrag *m*

self-reliant · selbstsicher

self-service shop · Selbstbedienungsgeschäft *n*, SB-Geschäft

self-sufficiency · Selbstgenügsamkeit *f*

self-sufficient · selbstgenügsam

self-supply · Selbstversorgung *f*

self-supporter · Selbstversorger *m*

self-supporting · autark, selbstversorgend

self-sustained growth · eigenständiges Wachstum *n*

self-sustained power, independent power, autocracy · Selbstherrlichkeit *f*

self-use, own use · Eigenbenutzung *f*, Eigengebrauch *m*, Selbstbenutzung, Selbstgebrauch

self-used [*Used for one's own purpose*] · eigengenutzt, selbst gebraucht

selion of land, narrow-land [*A ridge of ground rising between two furrows, containing no certain quantity*] · Furchenrücken *m*

to sell · begeben, verkaufen

sell-and-lease of (real) estate, sell-and-lease of (real) property, sell-and-lease of land, sell-and-lease of realty · Grund(stücks)verkauf *m* mit langjährigem Pachtvertrag, Landverkauf mit langjährigem Pachtvertrag, Bodenverkauf mit langjährigem Pachtvertrag

to sell at public auction; subhastare [*Latin*]; to auction(eer) · versteigern, meistbietend verkaufen

to sell back · zurückverkaufen

seller's liability for defects of title · Haftung *f* des Verkäufers wegen Mangels im Recht, Haftpflicht *f* des Verkäufers wegen Mangels im Recht, Haftbarkeit *f* des Verkäufers wegen Mangels im Recht

selling commission · Verkaufsprovision *f*

selling group · Verkaufsgruppe *f*

selling of vote · Stimmenverkauf *m*

selling price, sale price · Verkaufspreis *m*

selling value, sale value · Verkaufswert *m*

semble [*French*]; it seems [*Terms used to suggest that a particular point may be doubtful*], fraglich

semi-annual, half-yearly · halbjährlich, semestral

semi-commercial corporation · Laienkörperschaft *f* mit halbwirtschaftlichem Geschäftsbetrieb, Laienkorporation *f* mit halbwirtschaftlichem Geschäftsbetrieb

semicontinuous cities, linear cities, ribbon cities, corridor (of cities), strip cities · Städteband *n*

semicontinuous city, semicontinuous town · Städtebandstadt *f*, Stadt eines Städtebandes

semidetached foundation · Stiftung *f* (des öffentlichen Rechts) mit Fonds aus eigenen Mitteln angesammelt, öffentlich-rechtliche Stiftung mit Fonds aus eigenen Mitteln angesammelt

semi-feudal · halbfeudal

semi-governmental, having standing under public law, quasi-public · öffentlich-rechtlich

semi-governmental load, quasi-public load · öffentlich-rechtliche Last *f*

semi-governmental neighbor's protection (US), quasi-public neighbour's protection, semi-governmental neighbour's protection (Brit.); quasi-public neighbor's protection · öffentlich-rechtlicher Nachbarschutz *m*

semi-governmental use, quasi-public use [*Use serving a community or public purpose, and operated by a noncommercial entity, or by a public agency*] · öffentlich-rechtlicher Gebrauch *m*, öffentlich-rechtliche Benutzung *f*

semi-interquartile range, quartile deviation · halber Quartilabstand *m* [*Statistik*]

semi-logarithmic chart · einfachlogarithmisches Netz *n*

semi-official · halbamtlich

semi-open primary (election), technically-closed primary (election) [*USA*] · technisch-geschlossene Vorwahl *f*, technisch-geschlossene Urwahl, halb-offene Vorwahl, halb-offene Erstwahl, halb-offene Urwahl [*Der Vorwahlteilnehmer muß seine Parteizugehörigkeit angeben*]

semi-permanent settlement · halbfeste (An)Sied(e)lung *f*, Halbdauer(an)sied(e)lung

semipublic · halböffentlich

semi-rural, half-rural · halbländlich

semi-urban · halbstädtisch

semi-variable cost(s); semi-variable expired cost(s), semi-variable expense(s) [*USA*] [*These cost(s) may increase in a discontinuous manner. For example, two foremen may be required for normal production, but if another five labo(u)rers are hired, another foreman is required. Thus the need for foremen may be related to direct labo(u)r, but it may not be directly proportional to the number of workers*] · Mischkosten *f* [*nach Schmalenbach und Rummel*]

seniority, eldership, primogeniture(ship) · (männliche) Erstgeburtserbfolge *f*, (männliche) Primogeniturerbfolge

seniority of the list, list rotation, list seniority, rotation of the list · Reihenfolge *f* der Anträge [*Zuteilungsverfahren einer Bausparkasse*]

senior judge · dienstältester Richter *m*

senior manager · Prokurist *m*

senior mortgage · rangbessere Hypothek *f*

senior officer · leitender Beamter *m*

sensed environment · empfundene Umwelt *f*

sense of citizenship, civic spirit, public spirit · Bürgersinn *m*

sense of community, community sense, togetherness · Zusammengehörigkeitsbewußtsein *n*, Gemeinschaftssinn *m*

sense of contractual obligation — separating allowance

sense of contractual obligation · vertraglicher Verpflichtungswille *m*

sense of inferiority · Minderwertigkeitsgefühl *n*

sentence · Strafprozeßurteil *n*

to sentence judicially, to condemn, to adjudge [*Any one to a penalty, or to do or suffer something*] · verurteilen

sentimental value, fancy value · Affektionswert *m*, Liebhaberwert

separable · ablöslich [*Teil von einem Ganzen*]

to separate · ablösen [*Eines Teiles von seinem Ganzen, z. B. bei einem Gebäude (vgl. § 836 BGB)*]

to separate [*To see the differences between; to distinguish or discriminate between*] · aussondern [*z. B. ein Angebot als ungeeignet aussondern*]

separate absolute (general) property, separate absolute ownership (of property), separate absolute proprietorship [*Of a self-contained unit in a building*] · Sondereigentum *n*

separate account · Sonderkonto *n*

separate approach, single approach · Einzelansatz *m*

to separate by boundary stones, to mark out with boundary stones · absteinen, versteinen

to separate by boundary marks, to delimit by boundary marks · abmark(ier)en

to separate by green strips of land, to separate by green land strips · abrainen, verrainen

to separate claims · absondern [*Konkursverfahren*]

separate clearance, separate redevelopment · Einzelsanierung *f*

separate commission of the peace · besonderes Friedensgericht *n* [*in England*]

separate (construction) time period, separate (construction) period (of time) · Einzelfrist *f* [*Für einen in sich abgeschlossenen Teil einer Bauleistung*]

separate contract · Einzelvertrag *m*, getrennter Vertrag [*Zum Unterschied von einem Generalvertrag. Es können einzelne Verträge mit dem Generalunternehmer und Nachunternehmerverträge sein*]

separate contract (for extra work(s)) · Zusatzvertrag *m*

separate contractor (for a portion of the work), sub(contractor) · Nachunternehmer *m*, Subunternehmer, Unterunternehmer; Unterakkordant *m* [*Schweiz*] [*Er führt auf Grund eines Werkvertrages mit dem Unternehmer einzelne oder alle der von diesem übernommenen Arbeiten aus*]

separate covenant, several(ty) covenant, sole covenant [*It binds the several covenantors each for himself, but not jointly*] · Einzelformalvertrag *m*

separate creditor, separate debtee, separate promisee, sole creditor, sole debtee, sole promisee, several(ty) creditor, several(ty) debtee, several(ty) promisee · Einzelgläubiger *m*, Einzelversprechensempfänger

separated (real) estate, separated (real) property, separated parcel (of land), separated parcel of ground, separated plot (of land), separated plot of ground, separated piece of land, separated land piece, separated land (parcel), separated land plot · abgetrennter Boden *m*, abgetrennter Grund, abgetrenntes Land *n*, abgetrenntes Grundstück *n* (im Rechtssinn), Abspließ *m*

separate estate, separate property [*Property owned by a married person in his or her own right during marriage*] · getrenntes Vermögen *n*, Sondervermögen, Vorbehaltgut *n*, freies Vermögen

separate gain, separate profit · Einzelprofit *m*, Einzelgewinn *m*

separate legal identity · eigene Rechtspersönlichkeit *f*

separate profit, separate gain · Einzelprofit *m*, Einzelgewinn *m*

separate promisee → separate creditor

separate property, separate estate [*Property owned by a married person in his or her own right during marriage*] · getrenntes Vermögen *n*, Sondervermögen, Vorbehaltgut *n*, freies Vermögen

separate property at law, separate estate at law · legales freies Vermögen *n*, legales getrenntes Vermögen, legales Sondervermögen, legales Vorbehaltgut *n*

separate redevelopment, separate clearance · Einzelsanierung *f*

separate reimbursement, separate refunding, separate restitution · Einzelabgeltung *f*, Einzelvergütung [*für eine Teilleistung*]

separate treatment of a creditor, separation of claims · Absonderung *f* [*Konkursverfahren*]

separate use · freie Verfügung *f* [*Vorbehaltgut*]

separate value · Einzelwert *m*

separating · Ablösen *n*

separating · Trennen *n*, Abtrennen

separating · Aussondern *n*

separating allowance, separation allowance; cost of living allowance subsistence allowance (Brit.); subsistence, living allowance (US) · Auslösung f, Trennungsgeld n, Trennungsentschädigung [*Ein Arbeitnehmer, der auf einer Baustelle außerhalb des Betriebssitzes arbeitet, erhält eine Auslösung, wenn die tägliche Rückkehr zum Wohnort nicht zumutbar ist*]

separating by boundary marks, delimiting by boundary marks · Abmark(ier)en n

separating by boundary stones, marking out with boundary stones · Absteinen n, Versteinen

separating by green strips (of land), marking out with green strips (of land) · Abrainen n, Verrainen

separatio bonorum [*Latin*] · Massentrennung f, Ausschluß der Eigengläubiger vom Nachlaß m

separation, division, severance [*The separation by defendants in their pleas; the adoption, by several defendants, of separate pleas, instead of joining in the same plea*] · (Ab)Trennung f

separation · Ablösung f [*Lösung eines Teiles von seinem Ganzen, z. B. Ablösung von Teilen eines Gebäudes (vgl. § 836 BGB)*]

separation · Aussonderung f

separation → judicial separation

separation allowance; cost of living allowance, subsistence allowance (Brit.); subsistence, living allowance (US); separating allowance · Auslösung f, Trennungsgeld n, Trennungsentschädigung [*Ein Arbeitnehmer, der auf einer Baustelle außerhalb des Betriebssitzes arbeitet, erhält eine Auslösung, wenn die tägliche Rückkehr zum Wohnort nicht zumutbar ist*]

separation by boundary marks, boundary delimitation, delimitation by boundary marks · Abmark(ier)ung f [*§ 919. BGB. Kenntlichmachung von Grundstücksgrenzen durch Grenzzeichen*]

separation by boundary stones · Absteinung f, Versteinung

separation by green strips (of land) · Abrainung f, Verrainung

separation of claims, separate treatment of a creditor · Absonderung f [*Konkursverfahren*]

separation of functions, split in functions · Funktionstrennung f, Funktionsteilung

separation of locations, separation of sites, location separation, site separation · Auseinanderfallen n von Standorten

separation of powers, distribution of powers, power distribution, power separation · (Staats)Gewaltentrennung f, (Staats)Gewaltenteilung

separation of property, property separation · Gütertrennung f

separation of sites, location separation, site separation, separation of locations · Auseinanderfallen n von Standorten

sequence · Reihenfolge f

sequence of data, data sequence · Datenfolge f

sequence of priorities · Dringlichkeitsfolge f

sequence of spaces · Raumfolge f

sequential estimation · Folgeschätzung f

sequent occupancies [*According to Whittlesley 1929*], landscape formations · zeitliche Schichtung f der Landschaftselemente und Landschaftseinheiten

sequent occupancy, human occupancy · Besied(e)lung f durch den Menschen, Landnahme f

sequester [*A receiver appointed by court*] · Sequester m

sequestration [*A means of enforcing property to be temporarily placed in the hands of persons called sequestrators, who manage it and receive the rents and profits*] · Sequestration f

serf; villarus [*Latin*]; regardant (to the manor), bond tenant, villain (tenant), villein (tenant), bondager, bond(s)man, culvert [*Strictly a man of servile condition holding usually one virgate of land, this is the fourth part of a hide, in the common fields of a manor by base services; but the term is sometimes applied to one of free status who holds land by servile tenure*] · Leibeigene, unfreier Bauer, Dienstbauer m, Hörige, Unfreie, Knechtsleh(e)n(s)mann

serfdom (on an estate), villanage, ville(i)nage; nativitas [*Latin*]; servile status, villein status, villain status, status of a serf, (pr(a)edial) bondage, bondage (on an estate) [*Called by Britton "naifte"*] · Hörigenstatus m, Leibeigenschaft f, Grundhörigkeit f, (Grund)Untertänigkeit, Bauerndienst m

serf rent → labour rent

serf tenement → copyhold

serf tenure → copyhold

serf; villarus [*Latin*], bond(s)man, bondager, regardant (to the manor), bond tenant, villain (tenant), villein (tenant), culvert [*Strictly a man of servile condition holding usually one virgate of land, this is the fourth part of a hide, in the common fields of a manor by base services; but the term is sometimes applied to one of free status who holds land by servile tenure*] · Dienstbauer m, Hörige, Unfreie m, Knechtsleh(e)n(s)mann, Leibeigene, unfreier Bauer

sergeant-at-mace · Zepterträger *m*

serial bond · Serienobligation *f*

serial contract · Reihenvertrag *m*

serial correlation coefficient · Reihenkorrelationskoeffizient *m*

serial plan (building and loan) association (US) · Serien(plan-Bauspar)kasse *f* [*Sparen und Darleh(e)nszuteilung vollziehen sich nach einem Zahlungsplan*]

series · Serie *f* [*Bausparkasse*]

series · Sammelwerk *n*

series in force · laufende Serie *f* [*Bausparkasse*]

series of maps, map series · Kartenreihe *f*

serjeant · Reisige *m*

serjeanty → (tenure of) serjeanty

servant, employe(e) · Arbeitnehmer *m*

servant → colibert

servant morale, employe(e) morale · Arbeitsmoral *f*

servants' accounts, employe(e)s' accounts · Lohn- und Gehaltskonten *n pl*

servants' benefit, employe(e)s' benefit · Arbeitnehmervergünstigung *f*

servants' household, employe(e)s' household · Arbeitnehmerhaushalt *m*

servants in husbandry · Landwirtschaftsgesinde *n*

servants' liability, employe(e)s' liability · Arbeitnehmerhaftung *f*, Arbeitnehmerhaftpflicht *f*, Arbeitnehmerhaftbarkeit *f*

servants' parking space, employe(e)s' parking space · Arbeitnehmerparkraum *m*

servants' security company, employe(e)s' securities company · Arbeitnehmer-Investmentgesellschaft *f*

servants' vehicle, employe(e)s' vehicle · Arbeitnehmerfahrzeug *n*

to serve gratuitously · ehrenamtlich dienen

to serve (on) · zustellen [*Schriftstück*]

service · Zustellung *f* [*Schriftstück*]

service · Kundendienst *m*

service · Dienstleistung *f*

service · bevölkerungsorientiert [*Standort*]

serviceability acceptance · Betriebsabnahme *f* [*Für fliegende Bauten*]

service activity, nonbasic activity, nonbasic employment, auxiliary occupations · Nahversorgungstätigkeit *f*, Folgeleistung, Befriedigung *f* der örtlichen Nachfrage, Versorgung der Bevölkerung der eigenen Stadt, sekundäre Aktivität *f* [*Eine innerhalb der Region abgesetzte wirtschaftliche Leistung*]

service area, service territory · Ergänzungsgebiet *n* [*Es ist die Ergänzung der Kernstadt und bildet mit ihr das Kerngebiet*]

service area use, umland use; suburban land use (US); peripheral land use, external land use, surrounding land use · Umlandnutzung *f*

service burden, service encumbrance, service incumbrance, service load, service charge · Dienstleistungslast *f*

service centre, serving centre (Brit.); serving center, service center (US) · Dienstleistungszentrum *n*, Versorgungszentrum

service charge, service burden, service encumbrance, service incumbrance, service load · Dienstleistungslast *f*

service community · Dienstleistungsgemeinde *f*, Dienstleistungskommune *f*

service company → (public) service company

service contract, employment contract, job contract, work contract, contract of service, contract of employment, contract of job, contract of work · Arbeitsvertrag *m*

service curtailment, curtailment of service · Absperren *n* [*Gas, Wasser oder Strom bei Nichtzahlung der Gebühren*]

service date, date of service · Zustellungstermin *m*, Zustellungsdatum *n*

service employment · Dienstleistungsbeschäftigung *f*

service encumbrance, service incumbrance, service load, service charge, service burden · Dienstleistungslast *f*

service establishment · Groß-Dienstleistungszentrum *n*

service facility · Dienstleistungseinrichtung *f*

service field, service sector · Dienstleistungssektor *m*

service flats (Brit.); apartment hotel (US) · Wohnhotel *n*, Wohnhaus *n* mit Bedienung

service function · Dienstleistungsfunktion *f*

service group (of buildings) · Betriebsgebäudegruppe *f*

service incumbrance, service load, service charge, service burden, service encumbrance · Dienstleistungslast *f*

service industry · Dienstleistungsindustrie *f*

service institution · Dienstleistungsanstalt f

service instruction · Dienstanweisung f

service life of buildings · Gebäudelebensdauer f, Lebensdauer von Gebäuden

service load, service charge, service burden, service encumbrance, service incumbrance · Dienstleistungslast f

service (of process), service (of the writ) · Zustellung f (der Klag(e)schrift)

service (of the writ), service (of process) · Zustellung f (der Klag(e)schrift)

service of warranty, warranty service · Garantieleistung f

service order, order of service · Beantwortungsbefehl m [*Durch ihn wird ein Revisionsbeklagter aufgefordert seine Beantwortung einzureichen*]

service place · Dienstleistungsort m

service-rent [*It consists of an annual return, made by the tenant in labour, money, or provisions, in retribution for the land that passes, and this is the rent which is due whenever a tenant holds his lands of a reversioner*] · Dienstrente f, Freibesitz m auf Geldzins, Geldzinsfreibesitz

service (residential) tenancy, service (residential) tenure [*A tenancy existing between an employer and his employe(e)e*] · Betriebsmietverhältnis n

service road · Andienungsstraße f

service sector, service field · Dienstleistungssektor m

service system · Dienstleistungssystem n

service tenant [*A tenant to whom accommodation is let by his employer*] · Betriebsmieter m

service territory, service area · Ergänzungsgebiet n [*Es ist die Ergänzung der Kernstadt und bildet mit ihr das Kerngebiet*]

service to the lord of the manor · Grunddienst m

service(-type) activity · Dienstleistungstätigkeit f

service(-type) transit, service(-type) transport(ation) · (öffentlicher) Dienstleistungsverkehr m

service unit · Leistungseinheit f

servient · dienend, dienstbar, belastet [*Grundstück*]

servient (land) holder, servient tenant, servient lessee, servient occupier, servient termor, servient leaseholder; servient tacksman [*Scots law*] · dienender Pächter m, dienstbarer Pächter, belasteter Pächter

servient owner, servient proprietor · dienender Eigentümer m, dienstbarer Eigentümer, belasteter Eigentümer, dienender Eigner, belasteter Eigner

servilely; bondly [*obsolete*] · knechtisch, unterwürfig

servile status, villein status, villain status, status of a serf, (pr(a)edial) bondage, bondage (on an estate), serfdom (on an estate), villanage, ville(i)nage; nativitas [*Latin*] [*Called by Britton "naifte"*] · Hörigenstatus m, Leibeigenschaft f, Grundhörigkeit f, (Grund)Untertänigkeit, Bauerndienst m

servile tenement → copyhold

servile tenure → copyhold

serving centre (Brit.); serving center, service center (US); service centre · Dienstleistungszentrum n, Versorgungszentrum

serving-man · Knecht m

serving to compensate, compensatory, affording compensation, compensative, compensating · entschädigend

servitium militare, servitium militis [*Latin*]; military service on horseback, knight service · Ritterdienst m

servitude · Dienstbarkeit f, Gerechtigkeit, (servitutisches) Recht n, dingliches Nutzungsrecht

servitude book, book of servitudes · Dienstbarkeitsbuch n, Gerechtigkeitsbuch, Servitutenbuch

servitude law · Dienstbarkeitsrecht n

servitude not to hinder lights; servitus ne luminibus officiatur [*Latin*]; right of light, right to light, light right, ancient light(s), ancient windows · Lichtrecht n, Abwehrrecht des Fenstereigentümers gegen den Nachbarn [*Schutz gegen Verbauung des Lichteinfalls durch den Grundstücksnachbarn*]

servitude of bearing weight; servitus oneris ferendi [*Latin*] · Lastdienstbarkeit f, Lastgerechtigkeit, Lastrecht n, Lastservitut n, f [*Das Recht, auf einer baulichen Anlage des belasteten Grundstückes eine bauliche Anlage zu halten*]

servitude of draining water from another's spring or well; servitus aquae haurienlae, servitus aquae haustus [*Latin*] · Wasserschöpfservitut n, f, Wasserschöpfgerechtigkeit f, Wasserschöpfrecht n, Wasserschöpfdienstbarkeit

servitude of having a sewer through the ground of one's neighbour; servitus cloacae (mittendae) [*Latin*] · Ausgußgerechtigkeit f, Ausgußservitut n, f, Ausgußdienstbarkeit f, (servitutisches) Ausgußrecht n [*Der Berechtigte darf nur Spül- und Waschwasser durch den Kanal abführen und keine übelriechenden Flüssigkeiten*]

servitude of leading water; servitus aquaeductus, servitus aquae ducendae [*Latin*] · Wasserleitungsservitut *n*, *f*, Wasserleitungsdienstbarkeit *f*, Wasserleitungsgerechtigkeit, Wasserleitungsrecht *n*

servitude of letting in a beam; servitus tigni immittendi [*Latin*] · Tramdienstbarkeit *f*, Tramgerechtigkeit, (servitutisches) Tramrecht *n*, Tramservitut *n*, *f*

servitude of not building higher; servitus altius non tollendi [*Latin*] · Servitut *n*, *f* nicht höher bauen zu dürfen

servitude of projecting; servitus projiciendi [*Latin*] · Erkergerechtigkeit *f*, Erkerdienstbarkeit, Erkerservitut *n*, *f*, Erkerrecht *n*

servitus altius non tollendi [*Latin*]; servitude of not building higher · Servitut *n*, *f* nicht höher bauen zu dürfen

servitus aquaeductus, servitus aquae ducendae [*Latin*]; servitude of leading water · Wasserleitungsservitut *n*, *f*, Wasserleitungsdienstbarkeit *f*, Wasserleitungsgerechtigkeit, Wasserleitungsrecht *n*

servitus aquae haurienlae, servitus aquae haustus [*Latin*]; servitude of draining water from another's spring or well · Wasserschöpfservitut *n*, *f*, Wasserschöpfgerechtigkeit *f*, Wasserschöpfrecht *n*, Wasserschöpfdienstbarkeit

servitus cloacae (mittendae) [*Latin*]; servitude of having a sewer through the ground of one's neighbour · Ausgußgerechtigkeit *f*, Ausgußservitut *n*, *f*, Ausgußdienstbarkeit *f*, (servitutisches) Ausgußrecht *n* [*Der Berechtigte darf nur Spül- und Waschwasser durch den Kanal abführen und keine übelriechenden Flüssigkeiten*]

servitus fluminis [*Latin*] · Strahlgußrecht *n*

servitus fluminis immittendi [*Latin*] · Rinnendienstbarkeit *f*, Rinnengerechtigkeit, (servitutisches) Rinnenrecht *n*, Rinnenservitut *n*, *f* [*Der Nachbar muß das in einer Rinne gesammelte Regenwasser aufnehmen*]

servitus fluminis immittendi [*Latin*] · Röhrendienstbarkeit *f*, Röhrengerechtigkeit, Röhrenrecht *n*, Röhrenservitut *n*, *f* [*Der Nachbar muß das in einer Röhre gesammelte Regenwasser aufnehmen*]

servitus fluminis non recipiendi [*Latin*] · Regenwasserservitut *n*, *f*, Regenwassergerechtigkeit *f*, (servitutisches) Regenwasserrecht *n*, Regenwasserdienstbarkeit *f* [*Ein Nachbar darf sein Regenwasser nicht für sich behalten sondern muß es geschehen lassen, daß der andere Nachbar es in Röhren oder Rinnen auf sein Grundstück überleitet*]

servitus ne luminibus officiatur [*Latin*]; right of light, right to light, light right, ancient light(s), ancient windows, servitude not to hinder lights · Lichtrecht *n*, Abwehrrecht des Fenstereigentümers gegen den Nachbarn [*Schutz gegen Verbauung des Lichteinfalls durch den Grundstücksnachbarn*]

servitus ne propectui officiatur sive prospiciendi, servitus prospectus [*Latin*] · Aussichtsdienstbarkeit *f*, Aussichtsgerechtigkeit, (servitutisches) Aussichtsrecht *n*, Aussichtsservitut *n*, *f*

servitus ne veatus excludatur [*Latin*] · Mahlwindrecht *n* [*Einer Windmühle darf der Mahlwind nicht entzogen werden*]

servitus oneris ferendi [*Latin*]; servitude of bearing weight · Lastdienstbarkeit *f*, Lastgerechtigkeit, Lastrecht *n*, Lastservitut *n*, *f* [*Das Recht, auf einer baulichen Anlage des belasteten Grundstückes eine bauliche Anlage zu halten*]

servitus praediorum [*Latin*]; real servitude, landed servitude, pr(a)edial servitude [*A servitude affecting land*] · Realservitut *n*, *f*, Prädialservitut

servitus praediorum rusticorum [*Latin*] · Felddienstbarkeit *f*

servitus praediorum urbanorum [*Latin*]; urban servitude · städtisches Realservitut *n*, städtisches Prädialservitut, städtisches (servitutisches) Realrecht *n*, städtisches (servitutisches) Prädialrecht, städtische Prädialdienstbarkeit *f*, städtische Prädialdienstbarkeit, städtische Realgerechtigkeit, städtische Realdienstbarkeit, städtische Realservitut *f*, städtische Prädialservitut *f*

servitus projiciendi [*Latin*]; servitude of projecting · Erkergerechtigkeit *f*, Erkerdienstbarkeit, Erkerservitut *n*, *f*, Erkerrecht *n*

servitus prospectus, servitus ne propectui officiatur sive prospiciendi [*Latin*] · Aussichtsdienstbarkeit *f*, Aussichtsgerechtigkeit, (servitutisches) Aussichtsrecht *n*, Aussichtsservitut *n*, *f*

servitus protegendi [*Latin*] · Wetterdachservitut *n*, *f*, Wetterdachgerechtigkeit *f*, Wetterdachrecht *n*, Wetterdachdienstbarkeit *f* [*Die Servitut ein Wetterdach am Nachbargebäude anbringen zu dürfen*]

servitus stillicidii [*Latin*] · Regenwassertropfendienstbarkeit *f*, Regenwassertropfengerechtigkeit *f*, Regenwassertropfenservitut *n*, *f*, (servitutisches) Regenwassertropfenrecht *n* [*Das Regenwasser läuft tropfenweise vom Dach herunter*]

servitus stillicidii recipiendi [*Latin*] · Regenwassergerechtigkeit *f*, Regenwasserservitut *n*, *f*, Regenwasserdienstbarkeit, (servitutisches) Regenwasserrecht *n* [*Das Regenwasser gelangt tropfenweise vom Dach auf das Nachbargrundstück*]

servitus tigni immittendi [*Latin*]; servitude of letting in a beam · Tramdienstbar-

servitus usus — to settle a contract

keit f, Tramgerechtigkeit, (servitutisches) Tramrecht n, Tramservitut n, f

servitus usus [Latin] · Dienstbarkeit f des Gebrauchs

session act, session statute, resolve act; slip law, session law [USA]; public act, public law, public statute, general act, general law, general statute, legislative act, legislative law, legislative statute · allgemeines Gesetz n [In den Gliedstaaten der USA erscheinen die Gesetze nach ihrer Verabschiedung zunächst als „slip laws", die am Ende einer Sitzungsperiode der Legislative chronologisch zu den „session laws" zusammengefaßt werden]

settling pattern, settling scheme, settlement pattern, settlement scheme · (An)Sied(e)lungsschema n, (An)Sied(e)lungsmuster n, Besied(e)lungsschema n, Besied(e)lungsmuster n

to set aside · für ungültig erklären [Urkunden]

to set aside · aussetzen [Maßnahme]

set aside, reversed · aufgehoben, ausgesetzt [Urteil wegen Rechtsfehler]

to set aside (a) judg(e)ment, to reverse (a judg(e)ment) · aufheben, aussetzen [Urteil wegen Rechtsfehler]

set aside and new trial, reversed and new trial · aufgehoben und neues Verfahren angeordnet

set aside and remanded, reversed and remanded · aufgehoben und an die untere Instanz zurückverwiesen, aufgehoben und (zur abermaligen Verhandlung) zurückverwiesen [Urteil]

setback, (economic) slowdown, recession · Abschwung m, wirtschaftlicher Abschwung, Rezession f, Wirtschaftsabschwung

setback year, recession year · (wirtschaftliches) Abschwungjahr n, Rezessionsjahr

to set down for trial · anberaumen, ansetzen [Hauptverhandlung]

to set forth, to propound, to propose, to support [To put forward for consideration] · befürworten, vorschlagen

to set free; to release, to acquit, to discharge [Required to be under seal] · freistellen, entlasten, befreien, freigeben, dispensieren

to set free, to discharge, to absolve from · entbinden von (Verpflichtungen)

set free, discharged, absolved from · entbunden von (Verpflichtungen)

set free; released [Required to be under seal], acquitted, discharged [From debt, obligation, duty, etc.] · befreit, entlastet, freigestellt, freigegeben, dispensiert

set of actions, action set · Aktionsfolge f, Handlungsfolge

set of chambers [barristers in England] · Bürogemeinschaft f

to set off, to deduct · aufrechnen, abziehen, abrechnen, kompensieren; verrechnen [Schweiz] [Gegenforderung]

setoff (Brit.) → setting off

set of points, point set · Punktmenge f, Punktwolke f

set of values · Wertsystem n

setting aside awards · Kassation f schiedsrichterlicher Sprüche

setting free, discharging; releasing [Required to be under seal], acquittance, acquitting [The act by which a discharge in writing is effected] · Befreien n, Freistellen, Freigeben, Entlasten, Dispensieren

setting off; setoff (Brit.); offset (US), deduction · Anrechnung f, Kompensation f, Saldierung f, Abziehung f, Aufrechnung f, Abrechnung f, Abzug m; Verrechnung f [Schweiz] [Gegenforderung]

setting-off prohibition · Aufrechnungsverbot n

setting out (of the) work(s) · Absteckung f der Arbeit(en)

setting out plan · Absteckungsriß m

setting the fee, fixing the fee, fee setting, fee fixing · Honorarfestsetzung f, Gebührenfestsetzung, Honorarbestimmung, Gebührenbestimmung

setting up, construing, phrasing, wording, formulation, formation, drafting, construction, drawing-up [Arranging or marshalling words] · Abfassung f, Entwurf m, Gestaltung, Ausarbeitung, Formulierung

setting up, formation, drafting, construction, drawing up · Entwurf m, Gestaltung f, Abfassung f, Ausarbeitung [Schriftstück]

setting up of contract(s), formation of contract(s), construction of contract(s), drafting of contract(s), drawing up of contract(s) · Vertragsgestaltung f, Vertragsausarbeitung, Vertragsabfassung, Vertragsentwurf m, Vertragsbildung

to settle, to adjust, to compromise [difference; conflicting claims; etc.] · beilegen

to settle, to redeem, to pay off, to discharge, to liquidate [indebtedness] · tilgen, begleichen, abbezahlen, rückzahlen

to settle (accounts), to make up (accounts) · abrechnen

to settle a contract, to conclude a contract, to adopt a contract, to make a

to settle an account — settlement consolidation

contract, to contract · abschließen eines Vertrages, vertraglich vereinbaren

to settle an account, to close an account, to state an account · abschließen [*Konto*]

to settle by arbitration · schiedsgerichtlich beilegen, schiedsrichterlich beilegen

to settle by mutual concession, to come to terms about, to come to terms by mutual concession · einigwerden

settled, closed, stated · abgeschlossen [*Konto*]

settled · gebunden [*Grund(stücks)besitz(stand)*]

settled account [*A statement of accounts between parties, in writing, agreed and accepted by them as correct. A defence to a claim for an account*] · Begleichungserklärung *f*

settled estate, settled property · Nießbrauchvermögen *n*, (Frucht)Genußvermögen, Nutzgewaltvermögen

settled land act, settled land law, settled land statute · Gesetz *n* für festgelegtes Land

settled land restriction · Einschränkung *f* für festgelegtes Land, Begrenzung für festgelegtes Land, Beschränkung für festgelegtes Land

settled land(s) · festgelegtes Land *n*

settled law · feststehendes Recht *n*

settled pauper · Arme *m* im Kirchspiel heimatberechtigt

settled property, settled estate · Nießbrauchvermögen *n*, (Frucht)Genußvermögen, Nutzgewaltvermögen

to settle in an examinable way · prüfbar abrechnen

to settle in the lump · pauschalieren

settlement · Vermögensstiftung *f*

settlement · Überweisung *f* von Kapital oder Kapitalnutzung wobei das Kapital vom Bedachten nicht aufgebracht wird

settlement · Festlegung *f* [*Land*]

settlement (Brit.); neighborhood guild (US) · Nachbarschaftsgilde *f* [*Die seit 1887 in den USA und seit 1889 in England sich bildenden Vereinigungen von Arbeiterfamilien einer oder mehrerer benachbarter Straßen (etwa je 100 Familien), mit dem Ziel eine Hebung der unteren Klassen durch Reformen im Haus-, Erziehungs-, Gewerbe- und Erholungswesen sowie durch Zukunftsfürsorge herbeizuführen*]

settlement, domicil(e), place of habitation, habitation place, (place of) abode, (place of) residence, (permanent) residence, legal home · Aufenthaltsort *m*, gesetzlicher Aufenthaltsort, Wohnort *m*, Wohnsitz *m*

settlement, settling · (An)Sied(e)lung *f*, Besied(e)lung *f*, (An)Siedeln *n*, Besiedeln *n* [*Tätigkeit, die zum Entstehen einer (An)Sied(e)lung führt*]

settlement · (An)Sied(e)lung *f* [*Das Ergebnis des (An)Siedelns*]

settlement → (agreed) settlement

settlement account, account of settlement · Saldierungsrechnung *f*

settlement amount · Abrechnungsbetrag *m*

settlement and land use stage, stage of settlement and land use · Sied(e)lungsstaffel *f*

settlement area, settlement territory, settling area, settling territory · (An)Sied(e)lungsgebiet *n*, Besied(e)lungsgebiet *n*

settlement association · Sied(e)lungsverband *m*

settlement authority · (An)Sied(e)lungsbehörde *f*, Besied(e)lungsbehörde *f*

settlement before marriage, marriage settlement, ante-nuptial contract, ante-nuptial settlement, contract before marriage [*A contract or agreement between a man and a woman before marriage, but in contemplation and generally in consideration of marriage, whereby the property rights and interests of either the prospective husband or wife, or both of them, are determined, or where property is secured to either or both of them, or to their children*] · Ehevertrag *m*, Ehestiftung *f*

settlement by individuals · Einsied(e)lung *f*

settlement commission · (An)Sied(e)lungskommission *f*, Besied(e)lungskommission *f*

settlement committee · (An)Sied(e)lungsausschuß *m*, Besied(e)lungsausschuß *m*

settlement complex · Sied(e)lungskomplex *m*

settlement composition, settling composition, settlement structure, settling structure · (An)Sied(e)lungsaufbau *m*, (An)Sied(e)-lungsstruktur *f*, (An)Sied(e)-lungszusammensetzung *f*, (An)Sied(e)-lungsgefüge *n*, Besied(e)lungsaufbau *m*, Besied(e)lungsstruktur *f*, Besied(e)-lungsgefüge *n*, Besied(e)lungszusammensetzung *f* [*Das eine Fläche bedeckende Netz von Gemeinden*]

settlement consisting of consolidated farms · Einöd(an)sied(e)lung *f*

settlement consisting of separated parts · zusammengesetzte (An)Sied(e)lung *f*

settlement consolidation, settlement expansion · Sied(e)lungsausbau *m*, Sied(e)lungserweiterung *f*

settlement continuity, continuity of settlement · (An)Sied(e)lungskontinuität *f*

settlement contract · Sied(e)lungsvertrag *m*, (An)Sied(e)lungsvertrag

settlement contractor · Sied(e)lungsunternehmer *m*

settlement control, settling control · (An)Sied(e)lungslenkung *f*, (An)Sied(e)lungssteuerung *f*, Besied(e)lungslenkung *f*, Besied(e)lungssteuerung *f*

settlement cooperative · Sied(e)lungsgenossenschaft *f*

settlement credit · Sied(e)lungskredit *m*

settlement enterprise, settlement undertaking · Sied(e)lungsunternehmen *n*, Sied(e)lungsunternehmung *f*

settlement expansion, settlement consolidation · Sied(e)lungsausbau *m*, Sied(e)lungserweiterung *f*

settlement for homeless persons · Obdachlosen(an)sied(e)lung *f*

settlement form, settling form, form of settlement, form of settling · (An)Sied(e)lungsform *f*, Besied(e)lungsform *f*

settlement formula · Abrechnungsschlüssel *m*, Abrechnungsformel *f*

settlement founded during the rule of Frederic the Great · friderizianische (An)Sied(e)lung *f*

settlement geography, geography of settlement(s), geography of settling · (An)Sied(e)lungsgeographie *f*, Besied(e)lungsgeographie *f*

settlement ground, settlement land, settling ground, settling land · (An)Sied(e)lungsland *n*, Besied(e)lungsland

settlement hierarchy · (An)Sied(e)lungshierarchie *f*

settlement land, settling ground, settling land, settlement ground · (An)Sied(e)lungsland *n*, Besied(e)lungsland

settlement law · Sied(e)lungsrecht *n*, (An)Sied(e)lungsrecht [*objektiv*]

settlement legislation, settlement lawmaking · Sied(e)lungsgesetzgebung *f*, Ansied(e)lungsgesetzgebung

settlement limit, limit of settlement · (An)Sied(e)lungsgrenze *f*

settlement location, location of settlement · (An)Sied(e)lungsstandort *m*, (An)Sied(e)lungslage *f*

settlement negotiation · Beilegungsverhandlung *f*

settlement of a contract, contract settlement, contract conclusion, conclusion of a contract · Vertragsabschluß *m*, Abschluß eines Vertrages

settlement of a debt, redemption of a debt, liquidation of a debt, discharge of a debt · Tilgung *f*, Schuldrückzahlung

settlement of (an) account, statement of (an) account · (Konto)Abschluß *m*, (Konto)Abrechnung *f*, Saldierung

settlement of contract, settling of contract · Auftragsabwick(e)lung *f*

settlement of part-time holdings, settlement of part-time farms · Nebenerwerbs(an)sied(e)lung *f*

settlement of property, property settlement · Bindung *f* von Vermögen, Vermögensbindung, Gebundenheit *f* von Vermögen, Vermögensgebundenheit

settlement (of property) for value, property settlement for value · Vermögensbindung *f* mit geldwerter Gegenleistung

settlement of refugees, refugee settlement · Flüchtlings(an)sied(e)lung *f*

settlement on a flood endangered area · Wurt(an)sied(e)lung *f*

settlement pattern, settlement scheme, settling pattern, settling scheme · (An)Sied(e)lungsschema *n*, (An)Sied(e)lungsmuster *n*, Besied(e)lungsschema *n*, Besied(e)lungsmuster *n*

settlement period, period of settlement · Abrechnungsfrist *f*

settlement permission, permission of settlement · (An)Sied(e)lungsgenehmigung *f*, (An)Sied(e)lungserlaubnis *f*, Besied(e)lungsgenehmigung, Besied(e)lungserlaubnis

settlement policy, settling policy · (An)Sied(e)lungspolitik *f*, Besied(e)lungspolitik

settlement price · Abrechnungspreis *m*

settlement procedure · Sied(e)lungsverfahren *n*, (An)Sied(e)lungsverfahren

settlement provision · Abrechnungsbestimmung *f*

settlement restriction, settling restriction · (An)Sied(e)lungsbeschränkung *f*, Besied(e)lungsbeschränkung *f*

settlement right, settling right · (An)Sied(e)lungsrecht *n*, (An)Sied(e)lungsanrecht *n*, (An)Sied(e)lungsanspruch *m*, Besied(e)lungsanspruch *m*, Besied(e)lungs(an)recht *n*

settlement scheme, settling pattern, settling scheme, settlement pattern · (An)Sied(e)lungsschema *n*, (An)Sied(e)lungsmuster *n*, Besied(e)lungsschema *n*, Besied(e)lungsmuster *n*

settlement sector · (An)Sied(e)lungswesen *n*, Besied(e)-lungswesen *n*

settlement statistics, settling statistics · (An)Sied(e)lungsstatistik f, Besied(e)lungsstatistik f

settlement stratification, vertical stratification of different settlement types · Sied(e)lungsschichtung f

settlement stratum · Sied(e)lungsschicht f, Sied(e)lungsstockwerk n

settlement structure, settling structure, settlement composition, settling composition · (An)Sied(e)lungsaufbau m, (An)Sied(e)lungsstruktur f, (An)Sied(e)lungszusammensetzung f, (An)Sied(e)lungsgefüge n, Besied(e)lungsaufbau m, Besied(e)lungsstruktur f, Besied(e)lungsgefüge n, Besied(e)lungszusammensetzung f [*Das eine Fläche bedeckende Netz von Gemeinden*]

settlement style region · Sied(e)lungsstilregion f

settlement sum · Abrechnungssumme f

settlement termination, termination of settlement · Festlegungsbeendigung f [*Land*]

settlement territory, settling area, settling territory, settlement area · (An)Sied(e)lungsgebiet n, Besied(e)lungsgebiet

settlement undertaking, settlement enterprise · Sied(e)lungsunternehmen n, Sied(e)lungsunternehmung f

settlement unit, unit of settlement · (An)Sied(e)lungseinheit f, (An)Sied(e)lungszelle f

settlement with agricultural population · (An)Sied(e)lung f mit landwirtschaftlicher Bevölkerung

settlement with a planned street network · regelmäßige Straßennetz(an)sied(e)lung f

settlement with a population not active in agriculture · (An)Sied(e)lung f mit landbewohnender Bevölkerung

settlement within a State's own territory, home colonization, home settlement, colonization within a State's own territory · (B)Innenkolonisation f, innere Kolonisation

settlement with land-related population · (An)Sied(e)lung f mit landgebundener Bevölkerung

settlement with large farms · Großbetriebs(an)sied(e)lung f

settlement with miniature agricultural enterprises · Kleinstbetriebs(an)sied(e)lung f

settlement with more than one exit · Durchgangs(an)sied(e)lung f, Durchgangsort m [*nach M. Sidaritsch, 1925*]

settlement without central functions · azentrale (An)Sied(e)lung f

settlement year, year of settlement · Abrechnungsjahr n

settler · (An)Siedler m

settler's holding · (An)Siedlerstelle f

to settle the succession to (real) property, to limit the succession to (real) property, to entail, to create an estate tail · beschränken, beschneiden [*Vererbung von Grundstücken*]

settling, settlement · (An)Sied(e)lung f, Besied(e)lung f, (An)Siedeln n, Besiedeln n [*Tätigkeit, die zum Entstehen einer (An)Sied(e)lung führt*]

settling a contract, concluding a contract, making a contract, adopting a contract, contracting · Abschließen n eines Vertrages

settling area, settling territory, settlement area, settlement territory · (An)Sied(e)lungsgebiet n, Besied(e)lungsgebiet n

settling composition, settlement structure, settling structure, settlement composition · (An)Sied(e)lungsaufbau m, (An)Sied(e)lungsstruktur f, (An)Sied(e)lungszusammensetzung f, (An)Sied(e)lungsgefüge n, Besied(e)lungsaufbau, Besied(e)lungsstruktur, Besied(e)lungsgefüge, Besied(e)lungszusammensetzung f [*Das eine Fläche bedeckende Netz von Gemeinden*]

settling control, settlement control · (An)Sied(e)lungslenkung f, Besied(e)lungslenkung

settling form, form of settlement, form of settling, settlement form · (An)Sied(e)lungsform f, Besied(e)lungsform f

settling ground, settling land, settlement ground, settlement land · (An)Sied(e)lungsland n, Besied(e)lungsland

settling in the lump · Pauschalieren n

settling land, settlement ground, settlement land, settling ground · (An)Sied(e)lungsland n, Besied(e)lungsland

settling (of accounts), making up (of accounts) · Abrechnen n, Abrechnung f

settling of contract, settlement of contract · Auftragsabwick(e)lung f

settling policy, settlement policy · (An)Sied(e)lungspolitik f, Besied(e)lungspolitik f

settling restriction, settlement restriction · (An)Sied(e)lungsbeschränkung f, Besied(e)lungsbeschränkung f

settling right, settlement right · (An)Sied(e)lungsrecht n, (An)Sied(e)lungsanrecht n, (An)Sied(e)lungsanspruch m, Besied(e)lungsanspruch m, Besied(e)lungs(an)recht n

settling scheme — several(ty) creditor

settling scheme, settlement pattern, settlement scheme, settling pattern · (An)Sied(e)lungsschema n, (An)Sied(e)lungsmuster n, Besied(e)lungsschema n, Besied(e)lungsmuster n

settling statistics, settlement statistics · (An)Sied(e)lungsstatistik f, Besied(e)lungsstatistik f

settling structure, settlement composition, settling composition, settlement structure · (An)Sied(e)lungsaufbau m, (An)Sied(e)lungsstruktur f, (An)Sied(e)lungszusammensetzung f, (An)Sied(e)lungsgefüge n, Besied(e)lungsaufbau, Besied(e)lungsstruktur, Besied(e)lungsgefüge n, Besied(e)lungszusammensetzung [*Das eine Fläche bedeckende Netz von Gemeinden*]

settling territory, settlement area, settlement territory, settling area · (An)Sied(e)lungsgebiet n, Besied(e)lungsgebiet n

settlor → (trust) settlor

to set up, to construe, to phrase, to word, to form, to draft, to construct, to draw up [*To arrange or marshal words*] · abfassen, gestalten, entwerfen, ausarbeiten, formulieren

to set up, to work out, to form, to draft, to construct, to construe, to draw up · ausarbeiten, abfassen, gestalten, entwerfen [*Schriftstück*]

severance · Abtrennung f [*Grundbuchordnung*]

severable, divisible · teilbar

severable contract, pro tanto contract, pro rata contract, proportionate contract, divisible contract · Vertrag m auf teilbare Leistung, teilbarer Vertrag

severable interest · abtrennbare Beteiligung f [*An den Vermögensgegenständen einer Gesellschaft*]

several → several(ly)

several concurrent tortfeasors · Mehrtäter mpl die getrennt einen einheitlichen Schaden verursachen

several creditor → several(ty) creditor

several debtee → several(ty) creditor

several fishery → several (right of) fishery

several fishery right, several piscary, several (right of) fishery · ausschließliches Fischereirecht n, alleiniges Fischereirecht n

several interest, several right, single interest, single right; jus singulare [*Latin*] · Einzelanspruch m, Einzel(an)recht n, Einzelberechtigung f, getrennter Anspruch, getrenntes (An)Recht, getrennte Berechtigung

several liability · Solidarhaftung f, Solidarhaftpflicht f, Solidarhaftbarkeit f, Einzelhaftung, Einzelhaftpflicht, Einzelhaftbarkeit f, korreale Haftung, korreale Haftbarkeit, korreale Haftpflicht [*Jeder aus demselben Rechtsgeschäft verpflichtete haftet einzeln für die ganze Schuld*]

several(ly), individually [*As opposed to "joint(ly)"*] · einzeln, jeder für sich [*im Gegensatz zu gemeinschaftlich*]

severally liable · einzeln haftbar, einzeln haftpflichtig

several pastur(ag)e → several (right of) pastur(ag)e

several piscary, several (right of) fishery, several fishery right · ausschließliches Fischereirecht n, alleiniges Fischereirecht n

several profits (à prendre), profit (à prendre) in alieno solo · alleinige Frucht(ent)ziehung f, ausschließliche Frucht(ent)ziehung, selbständige Frucht(ent)ziehung, alleinige Substanzentnahme f, ausschließliche Substanzentnahme, selbständige Substanzentnahme

several promisee → several(ty) creditor

several promisors · Versprechensgeber mpl zu derselben Leistung unabhängig voneinander

several right, single interest, single right; jus singulare [*Latin*] · Einzelanspruch m, Einzel(an)recht n, Einzelberechtigung f, getrennter Anspruch, getrenntes (An)Recht, getrennte Berechtigung

several (right of) fishery, several fishery right, several piscary · ausschließliches Fischereirecht n, alleiniges Fischereirecht n

several (right of) pastur(ag)e · alleiniges (Vieh)Weiderecht n, ausschließliches (Vieh)Weiderecht

several rights · verschiedene Rechte npl mehrerer Personen

severalty, state of separation · Trennungszustand m

severalty, realty held by one person, realty in severalty, (real) estate held by one person, (real) property held by one person, (real) estate in severalty, (real) property in severalty · einzelner Grund(stücks)besitz(stand) m, einzelner (Land)Besitz(stand), einzelner Bodenbesitz(stand), einzelner Immaterialgüterbesitz(stand), einzelner Immobiliarbesitz(stand), einzelner Immobilienbesitz(stand), einzelnes Gut n

several(ty) covenant, sole covenant, separate covenant [*It binds the several covenantors each for himself, but not jointly*] · Einzelformalvertrag m

several(ty) creditor, several(ty) debtee, several(ty) promisee, separate creditor, separate debtee, separate promisee,

several(ty) obligor — share

sole creditor, sole debtee, sole promisee · Einzelgläubiger m, Einzelversprechensempfänger

several(ty) obligor, sole obligor · einzelne Verpflichtete m

severance, separation, division [*The separation by defendants in their pleas; the adoption, by several defendants, of separate pleas, instead of joining in the same plea*] · (Ab)Trennung f

severance · teilweise Inanspruchnahme f eines Grundbesitzes

severance damage, damage of severance · (Ab)Trennungsschaden m

severance pay(ment), redundancy pay(ment) [*A compensation paid by a firm to an employe(e) whose services are no longer required by that firm on account of the introduction of automation or labour saving machinery or because of a change of demand*] · Abfindung f

severance right, right of severance · (Ab)Trennungsrecht n

sewage · Abwasser n

sewage act, sewage statute, sewage law · Abwassergesetz n

sewage land, disposal area · Rieselfeld n

sewage law · Abwasserrecht n

sewage law → sewage act

sewage legislation, sewage lawmaking · Abwassergesetzgebung f

sewage practice · Abwasserwesen n

sewage (removal) plant, sewage (removal) installation · Abwasser(beseitigungs)anlage f

sewage statistics · Abwasserstatistik f

sewage statute → sewage act

sewage utilization, utilization of sewage · Abwasserverwertung f

sewer · (Abwasser)Kanal m

sewer authority · Kanal(isations)behörde f

sewer charge · Kanal(isations)gebühr f, Kanalbenutzungsgebühr

sewer clean(s)ing, clean(s)ing of sewers · (Abwasser)Kanalreinigung f

sewer duct contribution · Kanalbaubeitrag m

sewer flusher, flusher of sewers · Kanalarbeiter m, Kanalisationsarbeiter

sewer outlet · (Abwasser)Kanalauslaß m

sewer rate · Kanal(isations)steuer f, Kanalbenutzungssteuer

sex composition · Geschlechterzusammensetzung f, Geschlechteraufbau m, Geschlechterstruktur f, Geschlechtergefüge n [*Bevölkerung*]

sex ratio · Entmischungsfaktor m der Geschlechter

sex segregation · Entmischung f der Geschlechter

sex selection · Geschlechterauslese f

sex-specific · geschlechterspezifisch

sexton · Sakristan m

seysina [*Latin*]; seisin, freehold (possession), seizin, possession as of freehold, possession of an estate of freehold; saisine [*Latin*]; infeoffment [*Scotland*]; seisina · Gewere f [*Eine historische Untersuchung über das Wesen der Gewere muß ihren Ausgang von der „investitura" des alten Rechts nehmen. Denn mit diesem Ausdruck geben die lateinischen Quellen der karolingischen Periode das Wort Gewere wieder, wie das aus der altdeutschen Übersetzung von C. 6 der Capitularia leg. add. v. 817 bei Pertz, I. S. 261 und aus den zwei parallel laufenden Stellen der traditiones Fuldenses in zwei Urkunden von 824 „testes qui vestitionem viderunt" und „testes qui viderunt giweridam" unwidersprechlich hervorgeht*]

shack, common pastur(ag)e, commonage, common right; jus pascendi, communis pasturae, herbagium [*Latin*]; (right of) pastur(ag)e, (right of) grazing, pastoral right, herbage, grazing right · Angerrecht n, Hütungsrecht, Atzung f, Ätzung, (Vieh)Weiderecht, (Vieh)Weideberechtigung

shadow price · Schattenpreis m

shadow relief representation, illuminated relief · Schattenplastik f [*Kartographie*]

shadow site · schattenwerfendes Denkmal n

shallow level railway (Brit.); shallow level railroad (US) · Unterpflasterbahn f [*Sie liegt in geringer Tiefe unter der Straßenpflaster*]

sham marriage · Scheinehe f

shanty town, (suburban) squatting colony, (suburban) squatting community, squatter settlement, witch town · Blechhüttenvorort m [*Fehlbenennung: Blechhüttenstadt f*]

shape · Form f, Gestalt f

shape component · Formkomponente f

shaping the future · Zukunftsgestaltung f

share [*It is not divisible as is a stock*] · Anteil m

share, part, rate, proportion [*A charge, valuation, payment or price fixed according to ratio, scale or standard. A fixed relation of quantity, amount or degree. A comparative price or amount of demands*] · Anteil m

share accumulation plan · Anteilansammlungsplan m [*Bausparkasse*]

share bonus (Brit.); splitup (US) · Gewinnprämie f

share capital · Anteilkapital n

share certificate · Anteilschein m

share creditor, share debtee · Teilgläubiger m

share-cropping, share-farming · Teilbau m [*Landwirtschaft*]

share debtee, share creditor · Teilgläubiger m

share-farming, share-cropping · Teilbau m [*Landwirtschaft*]

shareholder · Anteilinhaber m

share in a business, interest in a business, business share, business interest · Geschäftsanteil m

share in (real) estate, share in (real) property, share in realty · Grund(stücks)anteil m

(share) investor, unadvanced member, investing member [*A member having not obtained advances from the building society but simply participating in the profits arising from the interest paid by the borrower*] · nichtborgendes Mitglied n [*Bausparkasse*]

share loan · Anteildarleh(e)n n [*Bausparkasse*]

share of an inheritance, inheritance share · Erb(schafts)(an)teil m, Anteil m an einer Erbschaft

share of no par value, no par (value) share · nennwertloser Anteil m, Anteil ohne Nennwert

share of stock, instal(l)ment share, partly paid share, membership share, subscription share · Raten(geschäfts)anteil m [*aufhörende Bausparkasse*]

share owner, owner of share(s) · Anteileigner m

share premium account · Überpari(kapital)konto n

sharer, participator, commoner [*One who shares or takes part in anything*] · Gemeinberechtigte m, Gemeinheitsgenosse m

share redemption, redemption of shares · Ablösung f von Anteilen, Auslösung von Anteilen, Einlösung von Anteilen, Anteilablösung, Anteilauslösung, Anteileinlösung [*Bausparkasse*]

share-tenancy, share-tenure, metayage, metayer system, colonat partiaire [*Under this system land is divided in small farms, among single families, the landlord generally supplying the stock and receiving, in lieu of rent a fixed portion of the produce. This proportion, which is generally paid in kind, is usually one-half*] · Halbscheidwirtschaft f, Halbpacht f

share-tenant, metayer · Halbmeier m, Halbmeyer, Halbpächter

share warrant · Inhaberanteil m

share warrant to bearer, bearer stock · Inhaberaktie f

sharing arrangement → (flat-)sharing arrangement

sharing of cost(s), cost(s) sharing · Kostenbeteiligung f

sharing of risk(s), sharing of hazard(s), splitting (up) of risk(s), splitting (up) of hazard(s), hazard distribution, risk distribution, risk sharing, hazard sharing, distribution of risk(s), distribution of hazard(s) · Verteilung f des Risikos, Verteilung des Wagnisses, Risikoverteilung, Wagnisverteilung

shark [*in England*] · Wucherer m

sheaf tithe, tithe of the sheaf · Garbenzehnt m

shed · Bude f [*Untergeordneter fliegender Bau einfacher Art*]

sheep-cot, sheep-pen, fold, pen for sheep, cot for sheep · (Schaf)Pferch m

sheep-cot hurdle, sheep-pen hurdle, fold hurdle; sheep-pen wattle, fold wattle, sheep-cot wattle (Brit.) · (Schaf)Hürde f

sheep farming · Schafhaltung f

sheep pasture · Schafweide f

sheep-pen, fold, pen for sheep, cot for sheep, sheep-cot · (Schaf)Pferch m

sheep ranch · Schafzuchtgut n

sheep run, herdwick, sheep walk · Schaftrift f

sheep-skin · gesiegelte Pergamenturkunde f

sheep walk, sheep run, herdwick · Schaftrift f

shell [*Canada*]; carcass, fabric · Rohbau m

shell acceptance certificate [*Canada*]; carcass acceptance certificate, fabric acceptance certificate · Rohbauschein m, Rohbauabnahmeschein, Rohbau(abnahme)bescheinigung f

shell company [*colloquial term*]; holding (company) · Holdinggesellschaft f, Dachgesellschaft, Kontrollgesellschaft, Effektenhaltegesellschaft

shell contractor [*Canada*]; carcass contractor, fabric contractor · Rohbauunternehmer m

shelter, housing, habitable room, habitable space [*The word "housing", which is used in combinations, includes, how-*

ever, all of the immediate physical environment, both within and outside of residential buildings] · Wohnraum *m* [*Sammelbezeichnung für Wohnungen und einzelne Wohnräume*]

shelter, quarter, accommodation, lodging · Unterkunft *f*

shelter belt · Windschutzanlage *f*

shelterbelt forest · Schutzwald(ung) *m*, *(f)* [*Wald(ung) zum Schutz gegen gewisse nachteilige Einflüsse*]

shelter-to-income ratio, rent-income ratio · Miet(zins)-Einkommens-Verhältnis *n*

sheriff [*USA*] · Staatsgerichtsvollzieher *m*, Vollziehungsbeamter

sheriff clerk of the county [*Scotland*]; registrar(y) of the county court [*England*] · Protokollführer *m* eines Grafschaftsgerichts

shield-money, escuage; scutagium [*Latin*]; scild-penig [*Saxon*]; scutage · Schildgeld *n*, Ritterpferdsgeld

shift, drift · Verschiebung *f*

shift → (working) shift

shift analysis, drift analysis · Verschiebungsanalyse *f*

shifting · Verlagerung *f*

shifting cultivation · wandernder Feldbau *m*, Wanderfeldbau

shifting devise · zerstörendes vollziehbares (Land)Vermächtnis *n*

shifting of priority · Rangverschiebung *f*, Dringlichkeitsverschiebung

shifting on, passing on · Abwälzen *n*

shifting trust [*An express trust which is so settled that it may operate in favour of beneficiaries additional to, or substituted for, those first named, upon specified contingencies*] · Treuhand *f* mit festgelegtem Ersatzberechtigten

shifting use · zerstörendes vollziehbares dingliches Grund(stücks)recht *n* [*Ein künftig wirksames dingliches Recht, welches mit seinem Wirksamwerden ein vorausgehendes dingliches Recht an dem fraglichen Grundstück zerstört*]

shift of population, drift of population, population shift, population drift · Bevölkerungsverschiebung *f*

shift of (population) density, (population) density shift · (Bevölkerungs)Dichteverschiebung *f*, Volksdichteverschiebung *f*

shift working · Schichtarbeit *f*

ship canal [*A canal capable of taking ocean-going ships*] · Seekanal *m*

ship deserted at sea, unclaimed wreck, derelict · herrenloses Wrack *n*

shipment to (the) site · Anlieferung *f* zur Baustelle

shipped bill of lading · An-Bord-Frachtbrief *m*, Bordkonossement *n*

shipper, forwarding agent, freight forwarder · Spediteur *m*

shipping · Versand *m*

shipping clearance · Versandfreigabe *f*

shire; scyran [*Saxon*]; county · Grafschaft *f*

shire hall rate, county hall rate · Steuer *f* zur baulichen Verbesserung und den Bau von Grafschaftsgerichtsgebäuden

shooting preserve, shooting refuge · Jagdreservat *n*

shooting refuge, shooting preserve · Jagdreservat *n*

shooting right [*hunting*] · Abschußrecht *n*

shop, store · Ladengeschäft *n*, (Verkaufs)Laden *m*

shop demise, store lease, store demise, shop lease · Ladenpacht *f*

shopkeeper, storekeeper · Ladenkrämer *m*

shop lease, shop demise, store lease, store demise · Ladenpacht *f*

shop lessee, store lessee · Ladenpächter *m*

shop location, store location, shop site, store site · (Verkaufs)Ladenstandort *m*, Ladengeschäftsstandort

shop ownership (of property), shop proprietorship, shop property, store ownership (of property), store proprietorship, store property · Ladeneigentum *n*

shop parcel, store plot, store parcel, shop plot · Ladengrundstück *n*

shop(ping) centre (Brit.); shop(ping) center (US); block of grouped shops, shopping district · D-Zentrum *n*, Ladengruppe *f*, Wohnbezirkszentrum, Ladenzentrum, (Ein)Kaufzentrum

shopping commodities, shopping goods [*Those consumers' goods which the customer in the process of selection and purchase characteristically compares on such bases as suitable, quality, price and style*] · Güter *npl* des periodischen Bedarfs, Waren *fpl* des periodischen Bedarfs

shopping demand · Einkaufsnachfrage *f*

shopping floor space, shopping floor area · Einkaufsgeschoßfläche *f*, Einkaufsetagenfläche, Einkaufsstockwerkfläche

shopping front(age), store front(age) · Ladenfront *f*

shopping goods, shopping commodities [*Those consumers' goods which the*

shopping in-commuter — short-dated interest rate

customer in the process of selection and purchase characteristically compares on such bases as suitable, quality, price and style] · Güter n pl des periodischen Bedarfs, Waren f pl des periodischen Bedarfs

shopping in-commuter · Einkaufseinpendler m, Einkaufszupendler

shopping location, shopping site · Einkaufsplatz m, Einkaufsstandort m

shopping on foot · Einkaufen n zu Fuß

shopping out-commuter · Einkaufsauspendler m, Einkaufswegpendler

shopping site, shopping location · Einkaufsplatz m, Einkaufsstandort m

shopping street · Ladenstraße, (Ein)Kaufstraße

shopping traffic · Einkaufsverkehr m

shopping trip, shopping journey, shopping travel · Einkaufsfahrt f

shop plot, shop parcel, store plot, store parcel · Ladengrundstück n

shop quarter, store quarter · Ladenquartier n, Ladengeschäftsquartier, Laden(geschäfts)viertel n

shop rent, store rent · Ladenmiete f

shop right · Arbeitgeberlizenz f an Arbeitnehmererfindung

shop site, store site, shop location, store location · (Verkaufs)Ladenstandort m, Ladengeschäftsstandort m

shop steward [A representative of the trade union, elected by members, in a department or section of a firm] · Gewerkschaftsvertreter m

shop underdemise, shop underlease, store underlease, store underdemise · Ladenunterpacht f

shop wage → (work)shop wage

shortening [term] · Abkürzung f, Verkürzung [Frist]

shortening of period (for completion), shortening of time (for completion) · (Ausführungs)Frist(ver)kürzung f, (Ver-)Kürzung f der Ausführungsfrist

shortage, stringency, deficiency, scarcity · Knappheit f, Verknappung f, Mangel m, Klemme f, Not f, Defizit n

shortage degree, scarcity degree, degree of shortage, degree of scarcity · Verknappungsgrad m, Mangelgrad, Knappheitsgrad

shortage of credit, scarcity of credit, stringency of credit, credit scarcity, credit stringency, credit shortage, credit deficiency, deficiency of credit · Kreditknappheit f, Kreditklemme f, Kreditnot f, Kreditmangel m, Kreditverknappung f, Kreditdefizit n

shortage of housing, stringency of housing, scarcity of housing, deficiency of housing, house-famine, housing shortage, housing deficiency, housing stringency, housing scarcity · Wohnungsbedarf m, Wohnungsfehlbestand m, Wohnraumfehlbestand, Wohnungsmangel m, Wohnraummangel m, Wohnungsknappheit f, Wohnraumknappheit, Wohnungsdefizit n, Wohnraumdefizit, Wohnungsnot f, Wohnungsverknappung f, Wohnraumverknappung, Wohnraumklemme f, Wohnraumnot f, Wohnungsklemme, Wohnraumbedarf [Die sich aus der zahlenmäßigen Gegenüberstellung von Haushalten und Normalwohnungen in abgegrenzten Gebieten oder Bereichen ergebende Zahl fehlender Wohnungen]

shortage of land(s), scarcity of land(s), land(s) dearth, dearth of land(s), land(s) shortage, land(s) scarcity · Bodenknappheit f, Landknappheit, Bodenverknappung f, Landverknappung, Bodenmangel m, Landmangel

shortage of money, scarcity of money, stringency of money, deficiency of money, squeeze of money, money squeeze, money scarcity, money shortage, money stringency, money deficiency · Geldmangel m, Geldknappheit f, Geldnot f, Geldverknappung f, Geldklemme f, Gelddefizit n

shortage of water, water shortage · Wassermangel m, Wasserknappheit f, Wasserverknappung f, Wasserklemme f, Wassernot f, Wasserdefizit n

shortcut estimate, approximate estimate [The owner's or his architect/engineer's project estimate, made prior to awarding the project contract, is approximate, since it is not based on a detailed costing of the project work quantities] · Preisvorstellung f

short-dated, short-term, short-range, short-period, short-run · kurzfristig

short-dated aggregate supply function, short-dated total supply function, short-run aggregate supply function, short-run total supply function, short-term aggregate supply function, short-term total supply function, short-range aggregate supply function, short-range total supply function, short-period aggregate supply function, short-period total supply function · kurzfristige Gesamtangebotsfunktion f

short-dated equilibrium, short-period equilibrium, short-run equilibrium, short-term equilibrium, short-range equilibrium · kurzfristiges Gleichgewicht n

short-dated interest rate, short period interest rate, short-term interest rate, short-run interest rate, short-range interest rate · Zinssatz m für kurzfristigen Kredit, Zinsfuß m für kurzfristigen Kredit

short-dated municipal bond [*USA*]; corporation bond, local authority bond [*Great Britain*] · kurzfristige Kommunalschuldverschreibung *f*, kurzfristige Kommunalobligation *f*

short-dated recreation, short-term recreation, short-period recreation, short-range recreation, short-run recreation · Kurzzeiterholung *f*

short-dated stock, bond [*Up to five years until maturity*] · kurzfristige Staatsschuldverschreibung *f*, kurzfristige Staatsobligation [*in Großbritannien*]

short-dated total supply function → short-run aggregate supply function

short-distance migration · Kurzwanderung *f*

short-distance movement · Nahverlagerung *f*

short-distance passenger transit, short-distance mass transit, short-distance passenger transport(ation), short-distance mass transport(ation), short-distance collective transit, short-distance collective transport(ation), (public) short-distance transit, (public) short-distance transport(ation), collective short-distance transit, collective short-distance transport(ation) · (öffentlicher) (Personen)Nahverkehr *m*, ÖPNV

short-distance route · Nahstrecke *f*

short-distance traffic, short-distance transport(ation) · Nahverkehr *m*

short-distance transport(ation), short-distance traffic · Nahverkehr *m*

short end of the market [*Great Britain*] · Teilmarkt *m* für Staatsanleihen mit einer Laufzeit bis zu fünf Jahren

shortening of period (for completion), shortening of time (for completion) · (Ver)Kürzung *f* der Ausführungsfrist, (Ausführungs)Frist(ver)kürzung

short-period, short-run, short-dated, short-term, short-range · kurzfristig

short-period aggregate supply function, short-period total supply function, short-dated aggregate supply function, short-dated total supply function, short-run aggregate supply function, short-run total supply function, short-term aggregate supply function, short-term total supply function, short-range aggregate supply function, short-range total supply function · kurzfristige Gesamtangebotsfunktion *f*

short-period equilibrium, short-run equilibrium, short-term equilibrium, short-range equilibrium, short-dated equilibrium · kurzfristiges Gleichgewicht *n*

short-period interest rate, short-term interest rate, short-run interest rate, short-range interest rate, short-dated interest rate · Zinssatz *m* für kurzfristigen Kredit, Zinsfuß *m* für kurzfristigen Kredit

short-period recreation, short-range recreation, short-run recreation, short-dated recreation, short-term recreation · Kurzzeiterholung *f*

short-period total supply function → short-run aggregate supply function

short-range, short-period, short-run, short-dated, short-term · kurzfristig

short-range aggregate supply function, short-range total supply function, short-period aggregate supply function, short-period total supply function, short-dated aggregate supply function, short-dated total supply function, short-run aggregate supply function, short-run total supply function, short-term aggregate supply function, short-term total supply function · kurzfristige Gesamtangebotsfunktion *f*

short-range equilibrium, short-dated equilibrium, short-period equilibrium, short-run equilibrium, short-term equilibrium · kurzfristiges Gleichgewicht *n*

short-range interest rate, short-dated interest rate, short period interest rate, short-term interest rate, short-run interest rate · Zinssatz *m* für kurzfristigen Kredit, Zinsfuß *m* für kurzfristigen Kredit

short-range recreation, short-run recreation, short-dated recreation, short-period recreation · Kurzzeiterholung *f*

short-range total supply function → short-run aggregate supply function

short-run, short-dated, short-term, short-range, short-period · kurzfristig

short-run aggregate supply function, short-run total supply function, short-term aggregate supply function, short-term total supply function, short-range aggregate supply function, short-range total supply function, short-period aggregate supply function, short-period total supply function, short-dated aggregate supply function, short-dated total supply function · kurzfristige Gesamtangebotsfunktion *f*

short-run average cost(s), SRAC, average cost(s) in the short run · kurzfristige Durchschnittskosten *f*

short-run-cost(s) curve · Kostenkurve *f* bei kurzfristiger Anpassung

short-run equilibrium, short-term equilibrium, short-range equilibrium, short-dated equilibrium, short-period equilibrium · kurzfristiges Gleichgewicht *n*

short-run graphic method of multiple correlations · graphisches Verfahren *n* zur Ermitt(e)lung multipler Korrelationen

short-run interest rate, short-range interest rate, short-dated interest rate, short period interest rate, short-term interest rate · Zinssatz *m* für kurzfristigen Kredit, Zinsfuß *m* für kurzfristigen Kredit

short-run recreation, short-dated recreation, short-term recreation, short-period recreation, short-range recreation · Kurzzeiterholung *f*

short-run total supply function → short-run aggregate supply function

short selling [*USA*] · Leerverkauf *m*, Baisseengagement *n*, Blankoverkauf von Wertpapieren

short strip lot · Kurzstreifenparzelle *f*

short-term, short-range, short-period, short-run, short-dated · kurzfristig

short-term aggregate supply function, short-term total supply function, short-range aggregate supply function, short-range total supply function, short-period aggregate supply function, short-period total supply function, short-dated aggregate supply function, short-dated total supply function, short-run aggregate supply function, short-run total supply function · kurzfristige Gesamtangebotsfunktion *f*

short-term equilibrium, short-range equilibrium, short-dated equilibrium, short-period equilibrium, short-run equilibrium · kurzfristiges Gleichgewicht *n*

short-term interest rate, short-run interest rate, short-range interest rate, short-dated interest rate, short period interest rate · Zinssatz *m* für kurzfristigen Kredit, Zinsfuß *m* für kurzfristigen Kredit

short-term loan, interim loan · Zwischendarleh(en) *n*

short-term parker · Kurz(zeit)parker *m*

short-term recreation, short-period recreation, short-range recreation, short-run recreation, short-dated recreation · Kurzzeiterholung *f*

short-term total supply function → short-run aggregate supply function

short-time worker, short-time workman; short-time labourer (Brit.); short-time laborer (US) · Kurzarbeiter *m*

short-time working · Kurzarbeit *f*

short title, popular name · Kurztitel *m*

short use · Nutzungsausfall *m*, entgangener Gebrauchsvorteil *m*

to show a cause · angeben eines Grundes

to show a gain, to yield, to show a profit · abwerfen, Gewinn abwerfen

to show a good title · gemeines Recht *n* zur Veräußerung eines (Rechts)Titels nachweisen

to show a profit, to show a gain, to yield · abwerfen, Gewinn abwerfen

to show causes · angeben von Gründen

shutdown · Stillegung *f*

shutdown of work(s), suspension of work(s) · Einstellung *f* der Arbeit(en), Aussetzung der Arbeit(en), Arbeitseinstellung, Arbeitsaussetzung [*Einstellung der Arbeiten mit der Absicht der Wiederaufnahme derselben seitens Bauherr und Bauunternehmer*]

shutdown time · Stilliegezeit *f*

to shut out, to discriminate, to exclude · ausschließen, nicht zulassen

shuttle bus service · Buspendlerdienst *m*

shyster (US); pettifogger · Winkeladvokat *m*

S.I., statutory instrument · Verwaltungserlaß *m*

sickness leave · Krankenurlaub *m*

side effect, spillover effect · mittelbare Wirkung *f*, indirekte Wirkung, Nebenwirkung [*Stadtentwick(e)lungsplanung. Eine Wirkung die nicht in den Zielen der Wirtschaftsakteure enthalten ist*]

side lot line, interior lot line [*This line does not abut on a street, allay, public way, railway right of way, etc.*] · seitliche Grundstücksgrenze *f*

side (of plot), plot side, side of parcel, parcel side · (Grundstücks)Seite *f*

side school [*Scotland*] · Notschule *f*

sidesman, synodsman, questman · Synodalzeuge *m*

sidewalk café · Straßencafé *n*

side yard [*Yard between the building and the side line of the lot and extending from the street line of the lot to the rear yard*] · Seitenhof *m*

sight draft, S/D, draft at sight · Sichttratte *f*

sightseeing map · Rundfahrtkarte *f*

sightseeing trip, sightseeing journey, sightseeing travel · Rundfahrt *f*, Besichtigungsrundfahrt

to sign [*To write the name at any place of a document, not necessarily underneath*] · zeichnen

to sign · eintragen [*Urteil*]

signatory · Unterzeichnete *m*

signature [*Name written at any place of a document not necessarily underneath*] · Zeichnung *f*

signature card · Unterschriftskarte *f*

signature specimen · Unterschriftsprobe *f*, Probeunterschrift *f*

signature underneath, subscription · Unterschrift f

signed binder · Vorverkaufsvertrag m [*Landkauf*]

signed contract · unterschriebener Vertrag m, unterzeichneter Vertrag

signet · Kleinsiegel n

significance · statistische Sicherung f

significance level, level of significance · Irrtumswahrscheinlichkeit f [*Statistik*]

significance of distance for an enterprise, significance of distance for an undertaking · einzelwirtschaftliche Bedeutung f der Entfernung

signification · Bedeutung f

signing · Unterschriftsleistung f

signing of contract · Vertragsunterzeichnung f

signory . . . . . → seigniory . . . . .

silenced majority · schweigende Mehrheit f

silent partner [*Is one who has no voice in the management. Unless he is also a special partner, his liability to the firm's obligations is the same as that of any other partner*] · Gesellschafter m ohne Führungsbefugnis, Teilhaber ohne Führungsbefugnis

simple, not under seal, unsealed · nicht gesiegelt, ungesiegelt, ohne Siegel, siegellos

simple accumulation · Ansammlung f der Zinsen aus einem bestimmten Kapital, Zinsenansammlung aus einem bestimmten Kapital

simple bailee · einfacher Empfänger m anvertrauten Gutes

simple building scheme · einfacher Bebauungsplan m, schlichter Bebauungsplan, einfacher verbindlicher Bauleitplan, nicht qualifizierter Bebauungsplan, nicht qualifizierter verbindlicher Bauleitplan, schlichter verbindlicher Bauleitplan; einfacher Überbauungsplan, schlichter Überbauungsplan, nicht qualifizierter Überbauungsplan [*Schweiz*]

simple complaint · einfache Beschwerde f

simple contract, unsealed contract, parol contract, (written) contract not under seal, (written) contract without seal, contract by unsealed writing [*A simple contract made by writing without seal. By a strange misuse of language, both kinds of simple contract (1. The simple contract made by word of mouth and 2. The simple contract made by writing without seal) are frequently spoken of in English law as parol contracts notwithstanding that the term "parol", both etymologically and in general parlance, means "by word of mouth"*] · nicht gesiegelter (schriftlicher) Vertrag m, ungesiegelter (schriftlicher) Vertrag, nicht formeller Vertrag, nicht notarieller Vertrag, (schriftlicher) Vertrag ohne Siegel, schriftlicher ungesiegelter Vertrag

simple correlation and regression analysis · einfache Korrelationsrechnung f

simple debenture, unsecured debenture [*Great Britain*]; unsecured corporate bond, debenture (corporate) bond, plain corporate bond [*USA*]; naked debenture [*Great Britain*] · ungesicherte Schuldverschreibung f, ungesicherte Obligation f [*einer privaten Kapitalgesellschaft*]

simple discount, bank discount [*The charge by a bank for discounting a note or bill of exchange*] · Bankdiskont m

simple discount rate, bank discount rate · Bankdiskontsatz m

simple fee, simple (feodal) tenure (of land), pure (feodal) tenure (of land), simple feud, pure feud, simple feod, pure feod, simple fief, pure fief, simple tenancy, pure tenancy, simple tenement, pure tenement, free tenancy, frank tenancy, free fief, frank fief, free fee, frank fee, free (feodal) tenure (of land), frank (feodal) tenure (of land), frank tenement, common law tenure, freehold (tenure), freehold land (held of the manor), possessory freehold, free feud, free feod, frank feud, frank feod, pure tenure (of land), pure fee, (pure) freehold tenure, (estate in) fee simple, (pure) estate of freehold, free(hold) tenement, freehold of inheritance (absolute), absolute fee; fee simple (US); feudum simplex, feodum simplex, liberum tenementum [*Latin*] · Freileh(e)n n, Stammleh(e)n n, freies Leh(e)n, Leh(e)n mit freier Erbfolge, unbeschränkt vererbliches Freigut n, Eigenleh(e)n [*Beim Ableben des Leh(e)n(s)mannes ohne Hinterlassung eines Testaments ging das Recht am Land unbeschränkt auf einen nach gesetzlichen Regeln zur Erbfolge berufenen Blutsverwandten des Verstorbenen über. Im Falle eines erbenlosen Ablebens fiel das Leh(e)n an den Leh(e)n(s)herrn zurück*]

simple (feodal) tenure (of land) → simple fee

simple form · einfache Form f

simple living unit, simple dwelling unit, simple housing unit (US); simple dwelling, simple tenement · Aufbauwohnung f, Schlichtwohnung f, Einfachwohnung f

simple mortgage · Hypothek f die dem Gläubiger nur ein Recht auf Grundstücksverkauf einräumt

simple residence, mere residence · einfacher Aufenthalt m

simple tenancy → simple fee

simple tenement, simple living unit, simple dwelling unit, simple housing unit (US); simple dwelling · Aufbauwohnung f, Schlichtwohnung f, Einfachwohnung f

simple tenure (of land) → simple fee

simple trust · einfache Treuhand f, Treuhand mit bloßer Sorgfaltspflicht

simple warranty deed [*It contains two warranties: (1) that the grantor warrants that the grantee will have the quiet enjoyment of the property and (2) that the grantor warrants that he has title to the property*] · einfache Gewährleistungsurkunde f [*Landübertragung*]

simplification of administration, administrative simplification · Verwaltungsvereinfachung f

simplified change, simplified variation · vereinfachte (Ab)Änderung f

simplified procedure for allowance of public grants(-in-aid) and public loans · vereinfachtes Bewilligungsverfahren n [*Z. B. § 49 des II. WoBauG*]

simplified variation, simplified change · vereinfachte (Ab)Änderung f

simplifying · vereinfachend

simulation approach · Simulationsansatz m

simulation game · Simulationsspiel n

simulation model · Simulationsmodell n

simulator · physikalisches Analogiemodell n [*Statistik*]

sincerity; bona fides [*Latin*]; good faith, loyalty and faith, honesty · Aufrichtigkeit f, Ehrlichkeit f, guter Glaube m, Treu f und Glauben m

single, not married, alone, sole · ledig

single [*premium*] · einmalig [*Prämie*]

single approach, separate approach · Einzelansatz m

single arbitrator board · Einerbesetzung f [*Schiedsgericht*]

single bill, sole bill, only bill, promissory note, note (of hand) · Eigenwechsel m, (eigener) Wechsel, Solawechsel, Verpflichtungsschein m [*Ein unbedingtes, von einer Person an eine andere gerichtetes, vom Aussteller unterschriebenes schriftliches Versprechen, auf Verlangen oder zu einer festgesetzten oder zu einer bestimmbar zukünftigen Zeit an eine bestimmte Person oder deren Order oder an den Inhaber eine bestimmte Summe in Geld zu zahlen*]

single bond, bedingungslose einfache Verpflichtungsurkunde f, unbedingter Schuldschein m

single-colored map (US); one-coloured map, single-coloured map (Brit.); one-colored map · einfarbige Karte f

single contract, (prime) general contract [*A construction contract where all work is contracted under the responsibility of a single or (prime) general contractor*] · Generalvertrag m, Gesamtvertrag

single contractor, (prime) general contractor · Generalunternehmer m, Gesamtunternehmer [*Er wird vom Bauherrn mit sämtlichen Leistungen beauftragt*]

single crop cultivation, cultivation of a single crop · Monokultur f

single-dwelling family hous(ebuild)ing, one-dwelling family hous(ebuild)ing, one-family hous(ebuild)ing, single-family hous(ebuild)ing · Einwohnungshausbau m, Einwohnungshäuserbau, Einfamilienhausbau, Einfamilienhäuserbau

single-dwelling house; cottage (Brit.); one-family house, single-family house, one-dwelling house · Einfamilienhaus n, Einwohnungshaus

single-employer pension plan · Einzelpensionsplan m

single expropriation · Einzelenteignung f [*Gegensatz: Flächenenteignung*]

single factor theory · Einfaktortheorie f [*Statistik*]

single-family hous(ebuild)ing, single-dwelling family hous(ebuild)ing, one-dwelling family hous(ebuild)ing, one-family hous(ebuild)ing · Einwohnungshausbau m, Einwohnungshäuserbau, Einfamilienhausbau, Einfamilienhäuserbau

single-family house garden, one-family house garden, cottage garden (Brit.) · Einfamilienhausgarten m

single-family row house, one-dwelling family row house, single-dwelling family row house, one-family row house · Einfamilienreihenhaus n, Einwohnungsreihenhaus

single farm, isolated farm · Einzelhof m

single farm area, isolated farm area · Einzelhofgebiet n

single farm of an extended family, extended family single farm, large family single farm, single farm of a large family · Großfamilieneinzelhof m

single farm row, isolated farm row · Einzelhofreihe f

single-field system, single-field husbandry, one-field system, one-field husbandry · Einfeldwirtschaft f

single interest, single right; jus singulare [*Latin*]; several interest, several right · Einzelanspruch m, Einzel(an)recht n, Einzelberechtigung f, getrennter Anspruch, getrenntes (An)Recht, getrennte Berechtigung

single judge, official referee, recorder · Einzelrichter m, beauftragter Richter

single line settlement · einzeilige (An)Sied(e)lung f

single-line store · Branchengeschäft n

single-market stability · Einzelmarktstabilität f

single-membered constituency · Stadtwahlkreis m [*Das Redistribution Act von 1885 in England verfügte, daß Städte, die mehr als einen Abgeordneten wählen, in einzelne Wahlkreise einzuteilen sind*]

single mortgage · Einzelhypothek f

single permission · Einzelgenehmigung f, Einzelerlaubnis f

single person, individual [*A person who is not a member of a family*] · alleinstehende Person f

single plan · Übernahme f der Plankosten bei der Verbuchung der Herstellkosten der in Arbeit befindlichen Erzeugnisse

single plan · Einzelführung f der Standardkosten

single price · Einzelpreis m

single purpose movement · Einzweckbewegung f

single right; jus singulare [*Latin*]; several interest, several right, single interest · Einzelanspruch m, Einzel(an)recht n, Einzelberechtigung f, getrennter Anspruch, getrenntes (An)Recht, getrennte Berechtigung

single-room school, one-room school · Einklassenschule f

single row village · Einreihendorf n

single settlement, isolated settlement, solitary settlement · Einzel(an)sied(e)lung f

single-street cluster settlement, single-street irregular nucleated settlement · einwegige Haufen(an)sied(e)lung f

single-street village · Einstraßendorf n, Einwegedorf

single-tax movement · Bodenreformbewegung f von Henry George, Landreformbewegung von Henry George

single tenant · Einzelmieter m

single trader · Einzelkaufmann m

single woman, sole woman, unmarried woman, feme sole, feme discovert · alleinstehende Frau f, unverheiratete Frau, ledige Frau

singling out facts by law, defining facts by law · Tatbestandsetzung f

singular privity, singular succession · Einzel(rechts)nachfolge f

singular privy, singular successor · Einzel(rechts)nachfolger m

singular succession, singular privity · Einzel(rechts)nachfolge f

singular successor, singular privy · Einzel(rechts)nachfolger m

to sink, to lock, to tie up · festlegen [*Kapital*]

to sink capital in land(s) · anlegen [*Kapital in Grund und Boden*]

sinking, absorption, extinguishment, merger, drowning [*Of one estate in another*] · Untergang m [*siehe Erklärung unter „untergegangen"*]

sinking fund, redemption fund · Tilgungsfonds m, Amortisationsfonds, Tilgungsstock, Amortisationsstock m, Tilgungskasse f, Amortisationskasse

sinking fund bond · Amortisationsobligation f, Tilgungsobligation

sinking fund debt, debt redeemable in instal(l)ments, amortization debt · Tilgungsschuld f, Amortisationsschuld

sit-down strike · Sitzstreik m

site, location [*Position in space; place where a factory, house, etc. is*] · Standort m, Lage f

site · Örtlichkeit f

site · Ortslage f [*Die topographische, kleinräumliche Lage*]

site → (construction) site

site accident damage, building site accident damage, construction site accident damage, job site accident damage · Bauunfallschaden m

site administration → (job) site administration

site administrative personnel → (job) site administrative staff

site administrative staff → (job) site administrative staff

site agent, site supervisor, agent (on site), supervisor (on site) · Bauleiter m, Bauleitung f, Baustellenleiter, Baustellenleitung, örtlicher Bauleiter, örtliche Bauleitung [*des Unternehmers*]

site analysis, site study, analysis of location, study of location, location(al) analysis, location(al) study, analysis of site, study of site [*The evaluation of the qualities of a site by comparison with those of other comparable sites*] · Standortanalyse f, Standortstudie f

site architect → (job) site architect

site bookkeeping, job site bookkeeping, construction site bookkeeping, building site bookkeeping · Baustellenbuchführung f

site checking, site control, construction site checking, construction site control, building site checking, building site control, job site checking, job site control · Baustellenkontrolle f [*Aufsuchen der*

site choice — site movement

Baustelle in Zeitabständen zur Prüfung der Arbeiten des Bauunternehmers

site choice, location(al) choice · Standortwahl *f*

site clean(s)ing, rubbish removal, final project clean up · Bau(stellen)reinigung *f*, Bau(stellen)säuberung [*Reinigung einer Baustelle von Bauschutt und anderen Arbeitsrückständen*]

site clearance cost(s), building site clearance cost(s), job site clearance cost(s), construction site clearance cost(s) · Baustellenräumungskosten *f*

site clearance (on completion), clearance of site (on completion) · Baustellenräumung *f*

site composition, site structure, location(al) composition, location(al) structure · Standortaufbau *m*, Standortgefüge *n*, Standortstruktur *f*, Standortzusammensetzung *f*

site control, location control · Standortlenkung *f*

site cost(s) → (job) site cost(s)

site daily record → (job) site diary

site decision, location(al) decision · Standortentscheidung *f*

site determinant, location(al) determinant · Standortdeterminante *f*, Lagedeterminante

site diary → (job) site diary

sited in isolation · einzeln gelegen, isoliert

site doctrine, doctrine of locations, doctrine of sites, location(al) doctrine · Standortlehre *f*, Lehre vom Standort

site engineer → (on-the-)site engineer

site equation, location equation, equation of location, equation of site · Standortgleichung *f*

site equilibrium, equilibrium of site, equilibrium of location, location(al) equilibrium · Standortgleichgewicht *n*

site examination, construction site visit, construction site examination, construction site inspection, building site visit, building site inspection, building site examination, examination of site, visit of site, inspection of site, site inspection, site visit · Baustellenbesichtigung *f*, (Baustellen)Begehung, Ortsbesichtigung [*Vor Abgabe eines Angebotes*]

site facilities, construction site facilities, building site facilities, job site facilities · Bau(stellen)einrichtung *f* [*Alle Maschinen und Geräte einer Baustelle*]

site facilities cost(s), building site facilities cost(s), construction site facilities cost(s), job site facilities cost(s) · Bau(stellen)einrichtungskosten *f*

site factor, demand factor of location, demand factor of site, location(al) factor · Standortfaktor *m*

site fence, job site fence, construction site fence, building site fence · Bau(stellen)zaun *m*

site fencing, fencing around a site · Baustellenumzäunung *f*, Baustelleneinzäunung

site forces → field staff

site for enlargement, location for enlargement, location for extension, site for extension · Erweiterungsstandort *m*

site game, location(al) game · Standortspiel *n*

site improvements and supporting facilities · Verbesserung *f* der Infrastruktur und Gebietsneuerschließung

site influence, location(al) influence · Standorteinfluß *m*

site inspection, site visit, site examination, construction site visit, construction site examination, construction site inspection, building site visit, building site inspection, building site examination, examination of site, visit of site, inspection of site · Baustellenbesichtigung *f*, (Baustellen)Begehung, Ortsbesichtigung [*Vor Abgabe eines Angebotes*]

site land → construction site land

site lighting, site illumination, building site lighting, building site illumination, construction site lighting, construction site illumination, job site lighting, job site illumination · Bau(stellen)beleuchtung *f*

site limit, building site limit, construction site limit, job site limit · Baustellengrenze *f*

site limitation, site restriction, site restraint, location limitation, location restriction, location restraint · Standorteinschränkung *f*, Standortbeschränkung, Standortbegrenzung

site location, location, siting [*A locating or being located*] · Standortbestimmung *f*

site management, job site management, construction site management, building site management · Bau(stellen)führung *f*, örtliche Bauaufsicht *f*

site manager, construction site manager, building site manager, job site manager, manager on site · Baustellenführer *m*, örtlicher Bauführer [*des Unternehmers*]

site meeting → construction site meeting

site meeting minutes, construction site meeting minutes, building site meeting minutes, job site meeting minutes · Bau(stellen)besprechungsprotokoll *n*

site movement, location(al) movement · Standortveränderung *f*

site occupancy index · Grundflächenzahl f, GRZ, Bebauungsgrad m [Anteil der überbauten oder überbaubaren Fläche an der Grundstücksfläche]

site of employment, employment location, employment site, location of employment · Beschäftigungsstandort m

site of physical facility → location of structure

site of structure → location of structure

site of the most favourable market, location of the most favourable market · Standort m des besten Absatzes

site of winning, location of winning, winning site, winning location · Gewinnungsstelle f, Gewinnungsstandort m

site of work → location of structure

site organization, construction site organization, building site organization, job site organization · Bau(stellen)organisation f

site-orien(ta)ted, site-related, location-related, location-orien(ta)ted · standortorientiert, standortbezogen, lagebezogen

site orientation, location(al) orientation · Standortorientierung f

site overhead(s) → (on-)site overhead(s)

site pattern, site scheme, location(al) pattern, location(al) scheme · Standortmuster n, Standortschema n

site personnel → field staff

site planning, building site planning, construction site planning, job site planning · Baustellenplanung f

site planning, planning of locations, planning of sites, location(al) planning · Standortplanung f

site policy, location policy · Standortpolitik f

site preference, location preference · Standortbevorzugung f

site preparation → (job) site preparation

site problem, problem of location, problem of site, location problem · Standortfrage f

site protection · Bodenschutz m, Landschutz, Flächenschutz [Schutz von Naturdenkmälern und wertvollen Flächen]

site protection map · Bodenschutzkarte f, Landschutzkarte, Flächenschutzkarte

site quality, location quality · Standortgüte f

site quotient, location(al) quotient · Standortquotient m

site rank, rank of site, location rank, rank of location · Standortrang m

site rank size, size of site rank, location rank size, size of location rank · Standortranggröße f

site rent, location rent · Standortrente f

site report, job report, construction report, work(s) report · Arbeitsbericht m, Bau(stellen)bericht m

site restraint, location limitation, location restriction, location restraint, site limitation, site restriction · Standorteinschränkung f, Standortbeschränkung, Standortbegrenzung

site safety → (construction) site safety

site safety code, construction safety code, building safety code · Bau(stellen)sicherheitsordnung f

site salary, job site salary, construction site salary, building site salary · Bau(stellen)gehalt n

site scheme, location(al) pattern, location(al) scheme, site pattern · Standortmuster n, Standortschema n

site separation, separation of locations, separation of sites, location separation · Auseinanderfallen n von Standorten

site sign, building site sign, job site sign, construction site sign · Bau(stellen)schild n, Bau(stellen)tafel f

site solution, location(al) solution · Standortlösung f

site staff → field staff

site state, state of (the) site · Baustellenzustand m

site structure, location(al) composition, location(al) structure, site composition · Standortaufbau m, Standortgefüge n, Standortstruktur f, Standortzusammensetzung f

site study, analysis of location, study of location, location(al) analysis, location(al) study, analysis of site, study of site, site analysis [The evaluation of the qualities of a site by comparison with those of other comparable sites] · Standortanalyse f, Standortstudie f

site sub-agent, site sub-supervisor, sub-agent (on site), sub-supervisor (on site) · Unterbauleiter m, Unterbauleitung f, örtlicher Unterbauleiter, örtliche Unterbauleitung, Unterbaustellenleiter [des Unternehmers]

site sub-supervisor, sub-agent (on site), sub-supervisor (on site), site sub-agent · Unterbauleiter m, Unterbauleitung f, örtlicher Unterbauleiter, örtliche Unterbauleitung, Unterbaustellenleiter [des Unternehmers]

site superintendence → site supervision

site supervision, site superintendence, construction site supervision, construc-

site supervisor — sleeping partner

tion site superintendence, job site supervision, job site superintendence, building site superintendence, building site supervision, supervision of site(s), superintendence of site(s) · Bau(stellen)aufsicht f, Bau(stellen)überwachung f, Objektaufsicht, Objektüberwachung

site supervisor, agent (on site), supervisor (on site), site agent · Bauleiter m, Bauleitung f, Baustellenleiter, Baustellenleitung, örtlicher Bauleiter, örtliche Bauleitung [des Unternehmers]

site theorist, location theorist · Standorttheoretiker m

site theory, theory of location, theory of sites, location(al) theory · Standorttheorie f

site triangle, location(al) triangle · Standortdreieck n

site value, location value · Grund(stücks)wert m

site visit, site examination, construction site visit, construction site examination, construction site inspection, building site visit, building site inspection, building site examination, examination of site, visit of site, inspection of site, site inspection · Baustellenbesichtigung f, (Baustellen)Begehung, Ortsbesichtigung [Vor Abgabe eines Angebotes]

site wage, construction (site) wage, building (site) wage, job (site) wage; construction labour wage (Brit.); construction labor wage (US) · Bau(stellen)lohn m

site water supply → job (site) water supply

site without notation, white land(s), unallocated land(s) [Land in agricultural or other mainly open use on which, for the period of the plan, the present uses are to remain for the most part undisturbed] · Außenbereich m

siting, site location, location [A locating or being located] · Standortbestimmung f

sittings in banc, court in banc [England] · Gerichtssitzung f von mindestens zwei Mitgliedern des Hohen Justizhofes, gesessenes Gericht n [Im Gegensatz zum Einzelrichter bei den Assisen]

situation, space position, spatial position · Raumlage f [Die geographische, großräumliche Lage]

situation of facts, state of facts, actual situation, established facts, ascertained facts, case facts · Sachlage f, Sachverhalt m, Tatbestand m

situation of sources of supply · Lage f zu lagern

situs [Latin] · Belegenheit f

sixth form · sechste Schulklasse f

size, dimensions · Abmessungen f pl, Größe f

size category · Größenkategorie f

size class · Größenklasse f

size component · Größenkomponente f

size distribution · Größenverteilung f

size group · Größengruppe f

size of area, area size · Flächengröße f

size of floor space, size of floor area, floor space size, floor area size · Geschoßflächengröße f, Stockwerkflächengröße, Etagenflächengröße

size of location rank, site rank size, size of site rank, location rank size · Standortranggröße f

size of zone, zone size · Zonengröße f

skeleton line · Gerippelinie f

skeleton plan, framework plan · Rahmenplan m

skeleton planning, framework planning · Rahmenplanung f

skeleton provision, framework provision · Rahmenbestimmung f

sketch map · Kartenskizze f

sketch plan, preliminary design, predesign · vorläufige (Bebauungs)Planfassung f, Vorentwurf m

skew correlation · schiefe Korrelation f

skewness measure, measure of skewness · Schiefemaß n [Statistik]

skew regression, curvilinear regression, nonlinear regression · nichtlineare Regression f

skilled in the law, versed in the law, learned in the law · rechtsbeflissen, rechtsgelehrt, rechtsbeschlagen

skilled work · gelernte Arbeit f

skilled work · Stand m der gelernten Arbeiter

sky light, horizon light · Himmelslicht n

skyline · Silhouette f, Stadtsilhouette, Stadtkrone f

slander · mündliche Ehrenkränkung f

slander of title [Tort resulting from attacking a person's title to property] · (Rechts)Titelverunglimpfung f, (Rechts)-Titelschmähung, Schmähung des (Rechts)Titels, Verunglimpfung des (Rechts)Titels

slaughtered price, price below cost price, ruinous price, cut(-throat) price · Schleuderpreis m

sleeping partner, dormant partner [Is one who is both secret and inactive. His liabilities to third parties are the same as *those of a general partner, if his connection with the firm is discovered. The fact that he is a dormant partner does not prevent him from asserting himself as an active partner and taking part in the firm's business, unless he is prevented from so doing by the partnership agreement]* · vertraglich untätiger mittelbarer Gesellschafter *m*, vertraglich untätiger mittelbarer Teilhaber, vertraglich untätiger verdeckter Gesellschafter, vertraglich untätiger verdeckter Teilhaber, vertraglich untätiger unerkannter Gesellschafter, vertraglich untätiger unerkannter Teilhaber, mittelbarer vertraglich untätiger Gesellschafter, mittelbarer vertraglich untätiger Teilhaber, verdeckter vertraglich untätiger Gesellschafter, verdeckter vertraglich untätiger Teilhaber, unerkannter vertraglich untätiger Gesellschafter, unerkannter vertraglich untätiger Teilhaber

sliding interest rate, sliding rate of interest · gleitender Zinssatz *m*, Gleitzinssatz, Gleitzinsfuß *m*, gleitender Zinsfuß

sliding scale · Gleitskala *f*

slight culpable neglect, slight culpable negligence; levissima culpa [*Latin*] · leichtes Verschulden *n*, gering(fügig)es Verschulden

slight negligence, slight carelessness, slight careless conduct, slight negligent conduct · gering(fügig)e Fahrlässigkeit *f*, gering(fügig)e Nachlässigkeit, leichte Fahrlässigkeit, leichte Nachlässigkeit

slip law, session law [*USA*]; public act, public law, public statute, general act, general law, general statute, legislative act, legislative law, legislative statute, session act, session statute, resolve act · allgemeines Gesetz *n* [*In den Gliedstaaten der USA erscheinen die Gesetze nach ihrer Verabschiedung zunächst als „slip laws", die am Ende einer Sitzungsperiode der Legislative chronologisch zu den „session laws" zusammengefaßt werden*]

slippage of schedule · Zurückbleiben *n* hinter einem Fristenplan, Frist(en)verzug *m*

slope hachure · Böschungsschraffe *f*

slope location, hillside location · Hanglage *f*

slow boating · nichtmotorisierter Bootssport *m*

slowdown → (economic) slowdown

slum · verwahrlostes Wohnviertel, Elendsviertel *n*, Elendsquartierviertel, (groß)städtisches Notstandsgebiet *n*, Verwahrlosungsbezirk *m*, verwahrlostes Wohnviertel

(slum) clearance, slum eradication, slum demolition, clearance of slums, eradication of slums, demolition of slums · Elendsviertelbeseitigung *f* [*1. Entkernung; 2. Totalsanierung*]

(slum) clearance area, slum eradication area, slum demolition area · Elendsviertelbeseitigungsfläche *f*

(slum) clearance order, (slum) eradication order, (slum) demolition order · Elendsviertelbeseitigungsbefehl *m*, Elendsviertelbeseitigungsgebot *n*, Elendsviertelbeseitigungsanordnung *f*, Elendsviertelbeseitigungsverfügung

slum demolition, clearance of slums, eradication of slums, demolition of slums, (slum) clearance, slum eradication · Elendsviertelbeseitigung *f* [*1. Entkernung; 2. Totalsanierung*]

slum demolition area, (slum) clearance area, slum eradication area · Elendsviertelbeseitigungsfläche *f*

(slum) demolition order, (slum) clearance order, (slum) eradication order · Elendsviertelbeseitigungsbefehl *m*, Elendsviertelbeseitigungsgebot *n*, Elendsviertelbeseitigungsanordnung *f*, Elendsviertelbeseitigungsverfügung

slum dweller, slum inhabitant · Elendsviertelbewohner *m*

slum eradication, slum demolition, clearance of slums, eradication of slums, demolition of slums, (slum) clearance · Elendsviertelbeseitigung *f* [*1. Entkernung; 2. Totalsanierung*]

slum eradication area, slum demolition area, (slum) clearance area · Elendsviertelbeseitigungsfläche *f*

(slum) eradication order, (slum) demolition order, (slum) clearance order · Elendsviertelbeseitigungsbefehl *m*, Elendsviertelbeseitigungsgebot *n*, Elendsviertelbeseitigungsanordnung *f*, Elendsviertelbeseitigungsverfügung

slum flats, slum housing · Elendsviertelwohnungen *fpl*

slum formation · Elendsviertelbildung *f*, (Wohnungs)Verwahrlosung *f*

slum housing, slum flats · Elendsviertelwohnungen *fpl*

slum inhabitant, slum dweller · Elendsviertelbewohner *m*

slump · Wirtschaftsverfall *m*

slump · Baisse *f*, Preissturz *m*

slum population · Elendsviertelbevölkerung *f*

(slum) redeveloper, (slum) redevelopment builder · (Elendsviertel)Sanierungsträger *m*

(slum) redevelopment · (Elendsviertel)Sanierung *f*

(slum) redevelopment area · (Elendsviertel)Sanierungsfläche *f*

(slum) redevelopment area, (slum) redevelopment territory · (Elendsviertel)Sanierungsgebiet *n*

(slum) redevelopment authority · (Elendsviertel)Sanierungsbehörde *f*

(slum) redeveloper, (slum) redeveloper · (Elendsviertel)Sanierungsträger *m*

(slum) redevelopment committee · (Elendsviertel)Sanierungsausschuß *m*

(slum) redevelopment conditions · (Elendsviertel)Sanierungsverhältnisse *f*

(slum) redevelopment corporation · (Elendsviertel)Sanierungsgemeinschaft *f*

(slum) redevelopment cost(s) · (Elendsviertel)Sanierungskosten *f*

(slum) redevelopment gain, (slum) redevelopment profit · (Elendsviertel)Sanierungsprofit *m*, (Elendsviertel)Sanierungsgewinn *m*

(slum) redevelopment law · (Elendsviertel)Sanierungsrecht *n*

(slum) redevelopment loss · (Elendsviertel)Sanierungsverlust *m*

(slum) redevelopment measure · (Elendsviertel)Sanierungsmaßnahme *f*

(slum) redevelopment order · (Elendsviertel)Sanierungsanordnung *f*, (Elendsviertel)Sanierungsbefehl *m*, (Elendsviertel)Sanierungsgebot *n*, (Elendsviertel)Sanierungsverfügung

(slum) redevelopment parcel, (slum) redevelopment plot · (Elendsviertel)Sanierungsgrundstück *n*

(slum) redevelopment plan · (Elendsviertel)Sanierungsplan *m*

(slum) redevelopment plot → (slum) redevelopment parcel

(slum) redevelopment procedure · (Elendsviertel)Sanierungsverfahren *n*

(slum) redevelopment profit, (slum) redevelopment gain · (Elendsviertel)Sanierungsprofit *m*, (Elendsviertel)Sanierungsgewinn *m*

(slum) redevelopment resolution · (Elendsviertel)Sanierungsbeschluß *m*, (Elendsviertel)Sanierungsentschließung *f*

(slum) redevelopment sale · (Elendsviertel)Sanierungsverkauf *m*

(slum) redevelopment site · (Elendsviertel)Sanierungsbauplatz *m*

(slum) redevelopment territory, (slum) redevelopment area · (Elendsviertel)Sanierungsgebiet *n*

slum school · Elendsviertelschule *f*

slurb (Brit.) [*Combined from slum and suburb*] · Vorortelendsviertel *n*, Elendsviertel in einem Vorort, qualitativ minderes Vorortwohngebiet *n*

slurb (US) [*Combined from slum and suburb*] · Elendsviertel *n* in einer Umlandgemeinde, Umlandgemeindeelendsviertel, qualitativ minderes Umlandgemeindewohngebiet *n*

small (agricultural) holding · Familienwirtschaft *f*, (landwirtschaftlicher) Kleinbesitz *m*, (landwirtschaftliches) Kleingut *n*, große (landwirtschaftliche) Parzelle *f*, kleines (landwirtschaftliches) Gut, kleine Wirtschaft [*In England versteht man unter „small (agricultural) holding": 1. Kleingut, welches die Familie des Landwirtes völlig erhält und 2. kleine landwirtschaftliche Parzelle, die eine Ergänzung zum Einkommen aus einer anderen Quelle oder anderen Quellen gibt*]

small area, small territory · Kleingebiet *n*

small blocks with a pattern of fragmented holdings · Weilerflur *f*, Blockgemengeflur

small bomb shelter · Luftschutzraum *m*

small central community · Kleinzentrum *n*

small change · Kleingeld *n*

small claim court · Gericht *n* für Klagen mit einem Streitwert bis zu 100 $

small country town, small rural town · Landstädtchen *n*

small dwelling, small tenement, small residence · Kleinwohnung *f*

small farm · Kleinbetrieb *m*, kleiner landwirtschaftlicher Betrieb

small farmer, small holder [*A cultivator who gets his living from the land by raising produce for sale*] · Kleinlandwirt

small garden, allotment garden · Kleingarten *m*, Schrebergarten

small garden ground · Kleingartengelände *n*, Kleingartenterrain *n*, Schrebergartengelände, Schrebergartenterrain

small garden law · Kleingartenrecht *n*, Schrebergartenrecht

small hamlet · Kleinweiler *m*

small holder, small farmer [*A cultivator who gets his living from the land by raising produce for sale*] · Kleinlandwirt *m*

small holding · kleine (landwirtschaftliche) Parzelle *f*, Kleinparzelle, Arbeiterstelle *f*, Klein(siedler)stelle, (landwirtschaftlicher) Parzellenbetrieb *m*, Kleinsied(e)lung *f*

small holdings account · Kleinbetriebsfonds *m*

Small Holdings Act · Kleingutgesetz *n* [*England*]

Small Holdings and Allotments Act — snob zoning

Small Holdings and Allotments Act · Kleingut- und Kleinparzellengesetz n [England]

small holdings system · Kleingutsystem n

small house building · Kleinhausbau m

small industry · Kleinindustrie f

small (land) owner, small (land) proprietor · Kleingrundeigentümer m

small (land) possession · Kleingrundbesitz m

small loan company · Kleinkreditgesellschaft f

small lot · Klein(grund)stück n im katastertechnischen Sinne

small mortgage · Kleinhypothek f

small piece of land, small portion of land · kleines Landstück n

small plot (of land), small parcel (of land), small piece of land · Klein(grund)stück n (im tatsächlichen Sinne)

small portion of land, small piece of land · kleines Landstück n

small possession → small (land) possession

small print · Kleingedruckte n

small property owner, owner of small property, proprietor of small property, small property proprietor · Kleineigentümer m

small recorded plot (of land), small registered plot (of land), small registered parcel (of land), small recorded parcel (of land), registered small plot (of land), registered small parcel (of land), recorded small plot (of land), recorded small parcel (of land) · Klein(grund)stück n (im Rechtssinn)

small repair · Kleinreparatur f, Bagatellreparatur

small residence, small dwelling, small tenement · Kleinwohnung f

small rural town, small country town · Landstädtchen n

small-scale hous(ebuild)ing · Wohn(ungs)bau m in kleinem Maßstab

small-space · kleinräumig

small-space territory of preference, small-space area of preference, small-space preference area, small-space preference territory · kleinräumiges Vorranggebiet n

small sports field · Kleinsportplatz m

small suburban settlement · vorstädtische Klein(an)sied(e)lung f

small tenement, small residence, small dwelling · Kleinwohnung f

small territory, small area · Kleingebiet n

small tithe, petty tithe, privy tithe, little tithe · kleiner Zehnt m, Schmalzehnt

small town · Kleinstadt f

small-towner (US); resident of a small town, small town resident (Brit.) · Kleinstädter m

small town with between 1,000 and 2,000 inhabitants (Brit.); first order center, urban center (US); middle-order subcentral place, sub-town, market district, market town; first order centre (Brit.), urban village [750 to 1,000 inhabitants] · Amtsort m [nach W. Christaller]

small trade · Kleingewerbe n

small tradesman · Kleingewerbetreibende n

small trades people and shopkeepers · kleines Bürgertum n

SMED, spatial macroeconomic development · räumliche makroökonomische Entwick(e)lung f

Smithsonian Agreement · Washingtoner Währungsabkommen n [Dezember 1971]

smog layer · Dunstglocke f, Dunstschirm m

smoke abatement, smoke control, elimination of smoke, smoke elimination · Rauchbekämpfung f, Rauchsanierung

smoke damage · Rauchschaden m

smoke damage control · Rauchschädenbekämpfung f

smoke elimination, smoke abatement, smoke control, elimination of smoke · Rauchbekämpfung f, Rauchsanierung

smoke inspector · Rauchinspektor m

smoke nuisance · Rauchemission f

smoke nuisance effect · Rauchimmission f

smoke prevention · Rauchverhütung f

smooth test · Neyman'scher Anpassungsversuch m [Statistik]

SM(S)A, standard metropolitan (statistical) area [Formerly called: metropolitan area. Standard metropolitan (statistical) areas with 100,000 inhabitants and more are termed "principal standard metropolitan (statistical) areas"] · (statistische) städtische Raumeinheit f, städtische statistische Raumeinheit

snob zoning, exclusionary zoning, discriminatory zoning, spot zoning, exclusionary land use practice, discriminatory land use practice [A land use restraint which has the effect of barring prospective lower income or minority residents] · diskriminierende (Bau)Nutzung f, diskriminierende (bauliche) Nutzung, Ausschluß(bau)nutzung

968

snowball technique — social-economic order

snowball technique · Schneeballverfahren *n*

snow-forest landscape · Schnee-Wald-Landschaft *f*

snow removal · Schneebeseitigung *f*

SOC, social overhead capital · Infrastrukturkapital *n*, materielle Infrastruktur *f*

soca [*A seigniory or lordship, enfranchised by the king with liberty of holding a court of his soc-men or socagers, i.e., his tenants*] · grundherr(schaft)liche Gerichtsbarkeit *f*, feudale Gerichtsbarkeit

socage → tenure in socage

socage tenant, gainor, sok(e)man, socman, socheman, socager, tenant by socage, tenant in socage, tenant in ancient demesne, colibert, tenant of socage-land, socage-land tenant · freier weltlicher Leh(e)n(s)besitzer *m*, (weltlicher) Freigutbesitzer

socage tenure; socagium [*Latin*]; free lay fief, free lay feud, free lay feod, free lay tenancy, free lay tenement, free lay fee, free lay (feodal) tenure (of land), tenure in (socage) · freies weltliches Leh(e)n *n*, weltliches Freileh(e)n

socage tenure subject to the custom of gavelkind, tenure of gavelkind · weltliches Freileh(e)n *n* mit Erschaft aller Söhne zu gleichen Teilen, freies weltliches Leh(e)n mit Erbschaft aller Söhne zu gleichen Teilen

socheman → socage tenant

social accounting · Einbeziehung *f* gesellschaftsbezogener Zielsetzungen in das einzelbetriebliche Rechnungswesen

social administration · Verwaltung *f* sozialer Einrichtungen

social aid, social help · Sozialhilfe *f*

social apartment → publicly-assisted dwelling unit

social ascendancy, social ascendency · gesellschaftliche Herkunft *f*, soziale Herkunft

social benefit · sozialer Ertrag *m* [*z. B. Parknutzung*]

social building, building for social needs · Sozialbau *m*

social burdens, social charges, social encumbrances, social loads, social incumbrances · soziale Lasten *fpl*, soziale Leistungen *fpl*, Soziallasten, Sozialleistungen

social capital, social wealth · Sozialvermögen *n*, Sozialkapital *n*

social change · sozialer Wandel *m*

social characteristic · Sozialmerkmal *n*

social charges, social encumbrances, social loads, social incumbrances,

social burdens · soziale Lasten *fpl*, soziale Leistungen *fpl*, Soziallasten, Sozialleistungen

social city, social town · Stadt *f* geeignet für die Entfaltung sozialen Lebens

social clause · Sozialklausel *f*

social code · Sitte *f*

social compact, Rousseau's contrat social, social contract · Sozialvertrag *m*

social composition, social structure · Sozialgefüge *n*, Sozialaufbau *m*, Sozialstruktur *f*, Sozialzusammensetzung *f*

social condition, state in life, condition in life, rank in life, social rank, social state · soziale Stellung *f*

social constitution · Sozialverfassung *f*

social contract, social compact, Rousseau's contrat social · Sozialvertrag *m*

social contract, partnership contract, memorandum (of association), deed of partnership, partnership deed; deed of settlement [*obsolete*]; articles of incorporation (US) [*Business corporations are now usually created under a general statute which permits a specified number of persons to form a corporation by preparing and filing with the proper public official, usually the secretary of state, a document known as the articles of incorporation*] · Gründungsurkunde *f*, Gründungssatzung *f*, Gesellschaftsvertrag *m*, Gründungsvertrag, Gesellschaftsurkunde [*1.) Körperschaft, Korporation; 2.) (Kapital)Gesellschaft; 3.) vereinsähnliche Gemeinschaft*]

social control · soziale Lenkung *f*

social cost(s) · gemeindliche Ausgaben *fpl*, kommunale Ausgaben, Infrakosten *f*, Industriefolgelasten *fpl*

social court · Sozialgericht *n*

social court law · Sozialgerichtsrecht *n*

social court law, social court act, social court statute · Sozialgerichtsgesetz *n*

social degradation · gesellschaftliche Abwertung *f*, soziale Abwertung

social demand approach · Nachfrageansatz *m* [*Bildungsplanung*]

social dividend, social product · Sozialprodukt *n*

social dwelling → publicly-assisted dwelling unit

social ecology, human ecology · Menschenökologie *f*, Humanökologie, Sozialökologie

social-economic group, socioeconomic group · sozialwirtschaftliche Gruppe *f*, soziowirtschaftliche Gruppe

social-economic order, socioeconomic order · sozialwirtschaftliche Ordnung *f*, soziowirtschaftliche Ordnung

**social-economic planning, ** socioeconomic planning · soziowirtschaftliche Planung f, sozialwirtschaftliche Planung

social-economic structure, socioeconomic structure · sozialwirtschaftlicher Aufbau m, sozio-wirtschaftlicher Aufbau; sozialwirtschaftliches Gefüge n, soziowirtschaftliches Gefüge, sozialwirtschaftliche Struktur f, soziowirtschaftliche Struktur

social encumbrances, social loads, social incumbrances, social burdens, social charges · soziale Lasten f pl, soziale Leistungen f pl, Soziallasten, Sozialleistungen

social engineer · sozialer Gestalter m

social environment · soziale Umwelt f, Sozialumwelt, Sozioumwelt

social fallow · Sozialbrache f

social geography, human geography · Anthropogeographie f, Sozialgeographie f

social gradient · soziales Gefälle n, Sozialgefälle

social group · Sozialgruppe f

social groupwork, social teamwork · Gruppenpädagogik f, sozial(pädagogisch)e Gruppenarbeit f

social help, social aid · Sozialhilfe f

social hierarchy · Sozialhierarchie f

social house, lower-income house, publicly-assisted house, subsidized house · Sozialhaus n, öffentlich gefördertes Haus, Haus der öffentlichen Hand, Haus des sozialen Wohn(ungs)baues, Zuschußhaus

social hous(ebuild)ing, production of public housing, public(ly-assisted) hous(ebuild)ing, subsidized hous(ebuild)ing, lower-income hous(ebuild)ing · Zuschußwohn(ungs)bau m, Sozialwohn(ungs)bau, öffentlich geförderter Wohn(ungs)bau, geförderter öffentlicher Wohn(ungs)bau, sozialer Wohn(ungs)bau, Wohn(ungs)bau der öffentlichen Hand

social hous(ebuild)ing law, social hous(ebuild)ing act, social hous(ebuild)ing statute · Sozialwohn(ungs)baugesetz n, soziales Wohn(ungs)baugesetz

social hous(ebuild)ing legislation, social hous(ebuild)ing lawmaking · Sozialwohn(ungs)baugesetzgebung f, Zuschußwohn(ungs)baugesetzgebung

social housing, low-income housing, low-cost(s) housing, publicly(-)assisted housing, publicly(-)provided housing, subsidized housing, low-rent housing · Zuschußwohnungen f pl, Sozialwohnungen, öffentlich geförderte Wohnungen, Wohnungen des sozialen Wohn(ungs)baues, Wohnungen der öffentlichen Hand

(social) housing doctrine, doctrine of (social) housing · (soziale) Wohnungslehre f

social housing law · Sozialwohn(ungs)baurecht n, soziales Wohn(ungs)baurecht

social housing rent, public housing rent, social residential rent · Sozialmiete f

social housing stock, social housing inventory · Sozialwohn(ungs)bestand m, Sozialmietwohn(ungs)vorrat m

social housing tenant, public housing tenant · Sozialmieter m

social incumbrances, social burdens, social charges, social encumbrances, social loads · soziale Lasten f pl, soziale Leistungen f pl, Soziallasten, Sozialleistungen

social indicator · Sozialindikator m

social insurance, national insurance · Sozialversicherung f

social insurance act, social insurance law, social insurance statute, national insurance act, national insurance law, national insurance statute · Sozialversicherungsgesetz n

social insurance law, national insurance law · Sozialversicherungsrecht n

social insurance legislation, social insurance lawmaking, national insurance legislation, national insurance lawmaking · Sozialversicherungsgesetzgebung f

socialization of loss · Überwälzung f von Ansprüchen durch Schäden der öffentlichen Hand auf die Allgemeinheit

socialized agriculture · sozialisierte Landwirtschaft f

social jurisdiction · Sozialgerichtsbarkeit f

social (land) use zoning, social zoning · (bauliche) Nutzung f nach sozialen Gesichtspunkten, Baunutzung nach sozialen Gesichtspunkten

social law · Sozialrecht n

social leader · Honoratiorenpolitiker m

social level · soziale Ebene f

social loads, social incumbrances, social burdens, social charges, social encumbrances · soziale Lasten f pl, soziale Leistungen f pl, Soziallasten, Sozialleistungen

socially binding · sozial bindend

social map · Sozialkarte f

social mapping · Sozialkartierung f

social market economy · soziale Marktwirtschaft f

social migration · soziale Wanderung *f*

social mix(ture) · soziale Mischung *f*, soziales Gemisch *n*

social morphology · soziale Morphologie *f*

social obligation · soziale Verpflichtung *f*

social order · Sozialordnung *f* [*frühere Benennung: gesellige Ordnung*]

social overhead capital, SOC · Infrastrukturkapital *n*, materielle Infrastruktur *f*

social pattern, social scheme · Sozialmuster *n*, Sozialschema *n*

social peace · sozialer Frieden *m*

social philosopher · Sozialphilosoph *m*

social piecemeal engineering, incrementalism, piecemeal (social) engineering · Inkrementalismus *m*, pragmatisches Ideal *n*, problemorientiertes Vorgehen *n*, problembezogenes Vorgehen [*Planung als pragmatisches, quasirationales, allein am Kriterium des Möglichen ausgerichtetes, zusammenhangloses und schrittweises Vorgehen*]

social plan · Sozialplan *m*

social planner · Sozialplaner *m*

social planning · Sozialplanung *f*

social political, sociopolitical · sozialpolitisch

social position, rank, condition [*A position with reference to the grades of society*] · Stellung *f*, Rang *m*

social problem, social question · soziale Frage *f*, soziales Problem *n*

social product, social dividend · Sozialprodukt *n*

social promotion · sozialer Aufstieg *m*

social question, social problem · soziale Frage *f*, soziales Problem *n*

social rank, social state, social condition, state in life, condition in life, rank in life · soziale Stellung *f*

social research · Sozialforschung *f*

social research in rural area(s), social research in country area(s) · Land-Sozialforschung *f*

social research in urban area(s) · Stadt-Sozialforschung *f*

social residence → publicly-assisted dwelling unit

social residential rent, social housing rent, public housing rent · Sozialmiete *f*

social rise and fall, vertical mobility · senkrechte Mobilität *f*, sozialer Aufstieg *m* und Niedergang *m*

social saving · kollektives Sparen *n*

social scheme, social pattern · Sozialmuster *n*, Sozialschema *n*

social science, sociology · Soziologie *f*, Sozialwissenschaft *f*

social scientific planning basis · sozialwissenschaftliche Planungsgrundlage *f*

social scientist, sociologist · Soziologe *m*, Sozialwissenschaftler

social security · soziale Sicherheit *f*

social security insurance, old age insurance · Altersversicherung *f*

social segregation · soziale Ungleichverteilung *f*

social service · soziale Dienstleistung *f*, Sozialdienstleistung

social service state, welfare state · Sozialstaat *m*, Wohlfahrtsstaat

social space · Sozialraum *m*

social spatial, sociospatial · sozialräumlich

social spatial division, sociospatial division · sozialräumliche Gliederung *f*, Sozialraumgliederung

social state, social condition, state in life, condition in life, rank in life, social rank · soziale Stellung *f*

social stratification, socioeconomic stratification · Sozialschichtung *f*, soziale Schichtung

social stratum, socioeconomic stratum · soziale Schicht *f*, Sozialschicht

social structure, social composition · Sozialgefüge *n*, Sozialaufbau *m*, Sozialstruktur *f*, Sozialzusammensetzung *f*

social survey · Sozialenquête *f*

social teamwork, social groupwork · Gruppenpädagogik *f*, sozial(pädagogisch)e Gruppenarbeit *f*

social tenement → publicly-assisted dwelling unit

social town, social city · Stadt *f* geeignet für die Entfaltung sozialen Lebens

social unbalance · soziales Ungleichgewicht *n*

social unit · Sozialuntersuchungseinheit *f*

social variable · soziale Veränderliche *f*

social wealth, social capital · Sozialvermögen *n*, Sozialkapital *n*

social welfare · Wohlfahrt(spflege) *f*

social work, casework · Sozialarbeit *f*, Sozialfürsorge *f*

social worker, community worker, communal worker, caseworker · Sozialarbeiter *m*, Sozialfürsorger

social zoning, social (land) use zoning · (bauliche) Nutzung *f* nach sozialen Gesichtspunkten, Baunutzung nach sozialen Gesichtspunkten

societal action — soil cultivation

societal action · gesellschaftliches Handeln *n*

societas erecto non cieto [*Latin*] · ungeteilte Erbengemeinschaft *f* [*römisches Recht*]

society, institution, association [*An establishment, specially one of public character or one affecting a community*] · (Personen)Verein(igung) *m*, (*f*)

society of architects, institution of architects, association of architects · Architektenverein(igung) *m*, (*f*)

Society of Architects of the Federal Republic of Germany, Institution of Architects of the Federal Republic of Germany, Association of Architects of the Federal Republic of Germany · Bundesarchitektenkammer *f*

society of borrowers, association of borrowers, institution of borrowers, federation of borrowers · landwirtschaftlicher Kreditverein *m*, Landschaft *f*, landwirtschaftliche Kreditvereinigung *f*

society of building contractors, institution of construction contractors, institution of building contractors, federation of construction contractors, federation of building contractors, association of construction contractors, association of building contractors, society of construction contractors · Bauunternehmerverein(igung) *m*, (*f*)

society of civil engineers, institution of civil engineers, association of civil engineers · Bauingenieurverein(igung) *m*, (*f*)

society of construction contractors, society of building contractors, institution of construction contractors, institution of building contractors, federation of construction contractors, federation of building contractors, association of construction contractors, association of building contractors · Bauunternehmerverein(igung) *m*, (*f*)

society of contractors, association of contractors, institution of contractors, contractors' association, contractors' institution, contractors' society · Unternehmerverein(igung) *m*, (*f*)

society of engineering unions, federation of engineering unions, association of engineering unions, institution of engineering unions · Verein(igung) *m*, (*f*) der Ingenieurverbände

society of landlords, association of landlords · Haus- und Grundeigentümerverein *m*

society of tenants, association of tenants · Mieterverein *m*

socioeconomic group, social-economic group · sozialwirtschaftliche Gruppe *f*, soziowirtschaftliche Gruppe

socioeconomic order, social-economic order · sozialwirtschaftliche Ordnung *f*, soziowirtschaftliche Ordnung

socioeconomic planning, social-economic planning · soziowirtschaftliche Planung *f*, sozialwirtschaftliche Planung

socioeconomic stratification, social stratification · Sozialschichtung *f*, soziale Schichtung

socioeconomic stratum, social stratum · soziale Schicht *f*, Sozialschicht

socioeconomic structure, social-economic structure · sozialwirtschaftlicher Aufbau *m*, sozio-wirtschaftlicher Aufbau; sozialwirtschaftliches Gefüge *n*, soziowirtschaftliches Gefüge, sozialwirtschaftliche Struktur *f*, soziowirtschaftliche Struktur

sociologist, social scientist · Soziologe *m*, Sozialwissenschaftler

sociology, social science · Soziologie *f*, Sozialwissenschaft *f*

sociology of law, law sociology · Rechtssoziologie *f*, Soziologie des Rechts

sociopolitical, social political · sozialpolitisch

sociospatial, social spatial · sozialräumlich

sociospatial division, social spatial division · sozialräumliche Gliederung *f*, Sozialraumgliederung

socman → socage tenant

sodded lawn · Sodenrasen *m*

soft currency · weiche Währung *f*

soil appraisal, soil appraisement, soil (e)valuation · Bodenbewertung *f*, Boden(ab)schätzung, Bodentaxierung, Bodenwertermitt(e)lung [*Die Kennzeichnung des Bodens nach seiner Beschaffenheit in Ackerland, Gartenland und Grünland und die Feststellung der Ertragsfähigkeit*]

soil appraisal law, soil appraisement law, soil appraisement act, soil appraisement statute, soil appraisal act, soil appraisal statute, soil (e)valuation statute, soil (e)valuation act, soil (e)valuation law · Boden(ab)schätzungsgesetz *n*, Bodenbewertungsgesetz, BodSchätzG

soil category · Bodenkategorie *f*

soil conditions · Bodenverhältnisse *f*

soil conservation, soil preservation, conservation of soil, preservation of soil · Bodenerhaltung *f*, Bodenpflege *f*

soil constituent, mineral · Bodenbestandteil *m*, Mineral *n* [*Z. B. Lehm, Sand, Kies usw.*]

soil cultivation, agricultural use, cultivation (of land), cultivation of fields, cultivation of soil, land cultivation, field cultivation, farming · Anbau *m*, Bodenkultivierung *f*,

Landkultivierung, Bodenkultur f, Feldbau

soil erosion · Bodenerosion f, Bodenabtrag m, Bodenverwüstung f, Bodenverheerung, anthropogene Bodenzerstörung

soil erosion map · Bodenerosionskarte f

soil (e)valuation, soil appraisal, soil appraisement · Bodenbewertung f, Boden(ab)schätzung, Bodentaxierung, Bodenwertermitt(e)lung [*Die Kennzeichnung des Bodens nach seiner Beschaffenheit in Ackerland, Gartenland und Grünland und die Feststellung der Ertragsfähigkeit*]

soil (e)valuation law, soil appraisal law, soil appraisement law, soil appraisement act, soil appraisement statute, soil appraisal act, soil appraisal statute, soil (e)valuation statute, soil (e)valuation act · Boden(ab)schätzungsgesetz n, Bodenbewertungsgesetz, BodSchätzG

soil exhaustion [*Diminution of the fertility of the soil*] · Bodenerschöpfung f

soil fertility · Bodenfruchtbarkeit f

(soil) fertility differential rent · (Boden)-Fruchtbarkeitsdifferentialrente f

soil geography · Bodengeographie f

soil improvement, land melioration, land improvement, agricultural melioration, agricultural improvement · (Boden)Melioration f, landwirtschaftliche Verbesserung f, Landmelioration [*Maßnahmen zur Verbesserung der Standortbedingungen für die Kulturpflanzen*]

soil improvement credit · Meliorationskredit m

soil improvement loan (of money) · Meliorationsdarleh(e)n n

soil improvement mortgage · Meliorationshypothek f

soil in its natural state, virgin soil · jungfräulicher Boden m

soil mark · Bodenverfärbung f

soil preservation, conservation of soil, preservation of soil, soil conservation · Bodenerhaltung f, Bodenpflege f

soil quality · Bonität f, Bodengüte f, Bodenqualität f

soil quality equation, equation of soil quality · Bodengütegleichung f, Bonitätsgleichung, Bodenqualitätsgleichung

soil valuation → soil (e)valuation

soil valuation law → soil (e)valuation law

sojourn · Aufenthalt m [*von Menschen in Räumen*]

soke-land [*It was copyhold which descended to the eldest son*] · (weltliches) Freigutland n

sok(e)man → socage tenant

sokemanry · freie weltliche Leh(e)n(s)-besitzer m pl, (weltliche) Freigutbesitzer

sokemanry, free tenure by socage [*The tenure of land(s) by a sokeman*] · freier weltlicher Leh(e)n(s)besitz m, (weltlicher) Freigutbesitz

soke-reeve [*The lord's rent-gatherer in the soca*] · Renteneintreiber m beim weltlichen Freigutbesitz

solace, solatium · Schmerzensgeld n

solar month, calendar month · Kalendermonat m

sold and delivered · verkauft und übergeben

sold by description · verkauft nach Angabe, verkauft nach Beschreibung

sold note [*It is delivered to the seller*] · Verkaufszettel m, Verkaufsnota f

sole, exclusive · alleinig, ausschließlich

sole, single, not married, alone · ledig

sole arbitrator · Einzelschiedsrichter m

sole bill, only bill, promissory note, note (of hand), single bill · Eigenwechsel m, (eigener) Wechsel, Solawechsel, Verpflichtungsschein m [*Ein unbedingtes, von einer Person an eine andere gerichtetes, vom Aussteller unterschriebenes schriftliches Versprechen, auf Verlangen oder zu einer festgesetzten oder zu einer bestimmbar zukünftigen Zeit an eine bestimmte Person oder deren Order oder an den Inhaber eine bestimmte Summe in Geld zu zahlen*]

sole chattel → sole property

sole contractor · Alleinunternehmer m [*Gegensatz: Arbeitsgemeinschaft f*]

sole covenant, separate covenant, several(ty) covenant [*It binds the several covenantors each for himself, but not jointly*] · Einzelformalvertrag m

sole creditor, sole debtee, sole promisee, several(ty) creditor, several(ty) debtee, several(ty) promisee, separate creditor, separate debtee, separate promisee · Einzelgläubiger m, Einzelversprechensempfänger

sole debtee → sole creditor

sole estate → sole property

sole (general) property → sole ownership (of property)

sole heiress, absolute heir female, exclusive heir female, sole heir female, absolute heiress, exclusive heiress · absolute Erbin f, unbegrenzte Erbin, unbedingte Erbin, uneingeschränkte Erbin, unbeschränkte Erbin, Alleinerbin

sole heir female → sole heiress

sole heir (male), exclusive heir (male), absolute heir (male) · absoluter Erbe *m*, unbeschränkter Erbe, uneingeschränkter Erbe, unbedingter Erbe, unbegrenzter Erbe, Alleinerbe, Vollerbe

sole interest, exclusive ownership (of property), sole ownership (of property), unlimited ownership (of property); dominium plenum, dominium perpetuum [*Latin*]; absolute ownership (of property), absolute interest, exclusive interest [*In English law absolute ownership can only exist in chattels, as all land is subject theoretically to the obligations of tenure; but practically the fee simple in land gives absolute ownership*] · absolutes Eigentum *n*, uneingeschränktes Eigentum, unbeschränktes Eigentum, unbegrenztes Eigentum, ausschließliches Eigentum, unbedingtes Eigentum, Alleineigentum

sole (land) owner → allodiary

solemn declaration without oath, affirmation · Gelöbnis *n*, feierliche Erklärung *f*

sole obligor, several(ty) obligor · einzelne Verpflichtete *m*

sole ownership (of property), unlimited ownership (of property); dominium plenum, dominium perpetuum [*Latin*]; absolute ownership (of property), absolute interest, exclusive interest, sole interest, exclusive ownership (of property), sole property, sole proprietorship [*In English law absolute ownership can only exist in chattels, as all land is subject theoretically to the obligations of tenure; but practically the fee simple in land gives absolute ownership*] · absolutes Eigentum *n*, uneingeschränktes Eigentum, unbeschränktes Eigentum, unbegrenztes Eigentum, ausschließliches Eigentum, unbedingtes Eigentum, Alleineigentum

sole possession, absolute possession, exclusive possession · absoluter Besitz *m*, unbegrenzter Besitz, uneingeschränkter Besitz, unbeschränkter Besitz, ausschließlicher Besitz, Alleinbesitz

sole possessor, exclusive possessor, absolute possessor · Alleinbesitzer *m*

sole promisee → sole creditor

sole property → sole ownership (of property)

sole proprietary right (of land), exclusive proprietary right (of land), absolute proprietary right (of land) · Alleinbesitzanspruch *m*, Alleinbesitz(an)recht *n* [*Grundstück*]

sole proprietor, owner-manager, one-man business [*A type of business unit where one person is solely responsible for providing the capital, for bearing the risk of the enterprise and for the management of the business*] · Einmannbetrieb *m*

sole proprietorship → sole ownership (of property)

sole remedy, exclusive remedy, absolute remedy · ausschließlicher Rechtsbehelf *m*, alleiniger Rechtsbehelf *m*

sole right, absolute right, exclusive right [*A right which only the grantee thereof can exercise, and from which all others are prohibited or shut out*] · Alleinrecht *n*, Ausschließlichkeitsrecht, absolutes (subjektives) Recht

sole right of negotiation · Ausschließlichkeitserklärung *f*

sole trustee · Alleintreuhandverwalter *m*, Alleintreuhänder

sole woman, unmarried woman, feme sole, feme discovert, single woman · alleinstehende Frau *f*, unverheiratete Frau, ledige Frau

solicitation of orders · Akquisition *f*

solicitor [*A person who solicits orders*] · Akquisiteur *m*

solicitor [*In England and North Ireland*]; law agent [*In Scotland*] · Anwalt *m* mit beratender Funktion, Rechtsanwalt *m* mit beratender Funktion, Büro(rechts)anwalt *m*, Rechtsagent *m*, Geschäftsanwalt *m*

solicitor-client privilege · Anwaltgeheimnis *n*, Büro(rechts)anwaltgeheimnis *n*, Rechtsanwaltgeheimnis *n*

to solicit orders · akquirieren

Solicitor-General (of England) [*The second of the Law officers. His functions are political as well as legal, for he is almost invariably a member of the House of Commons. He acts as the deputy or assistant of the Attorney-General*] · stellvertretender Kronanwalt *m*

solicitor of choice; law agent of choice [*Scotland*] · Vertrauensgeschäftsanwalt *m*

solicitor to the treasury, treasury solicitor · Generalfiskalat *n*

solid waste · fester Abfall(stoff) *m*

solitary confinement · Einzelhaft *f*

solitary settlement, single settlement, isolated settlement · Einzel(an)sied(e)lung *f*

solum superficies cedit [*Latin*] · Grund *m* und Boden *m* folgen dem Gebäude, Land folgt dem Gebäude, Boden folgt dem Gebäude

solution approach · Lösungsansatz *m*

solution process · Lösungsvorgang *m*

solvency → capacity to pay

solvent — space development

solvent, financially able, sound, capable to pay, able to pay, trust(worth)y · zahlungsfähig, flüssig, kreditfähig, kreditwürdig

sonic environment · Schallumwelt f

soot nuisance · Rußemission f

soot nuisance effect · Rußimmission f

sorting out, parcelling out · Aussonderung f im Konkurs

to sort out, to cull out; to garble [*In old English statutes*] [*The good from the bad*] · aussortieren

soul-scot [*So called in the laws of King Canute*]; mortuary, corsepresent; mortuarium [*Latin*] · Vermächtnis n an eine Kirche

sound, capable to pay, able to pay, trust(worth)y, solvent, financially able · zahlungsfähig, flüssig, kreditfähig, kreditwürdig

sounding · Lotung f

soundness → capacity to pay

sound (public) sentiment of (the) people · gesundes Volksempfinden n

source, place of origin · Ursprungsort m

source of law, fountain of law, fountain of jurisdiction, jurisdiction fountain, law source, law fountain · Rechtsquelle f

source of reasoning, perceptible source, reasoning source · Erkenntnisquelle f

source of revenue · Einkommensquelle f

source of supply · Bezugsquelle f

Sovereign, ruler · Herrscher m

sovereign authority · Staatsakt m

sovereign capacity · Hoheitsfähigkeit f

sovereign dominion → sovereign power

sovereign lord (of a fee), lord paramount (of a fee), supreme lord (of a fee), paramount lord (of a fee) [*The Queen or the King are lords paramount of all the lands in the Kingdom*] · oberster Leh(e)n(s)herr m, höchster Leh(e)n(s)herr, oberster Feudalherr, höchster Feudalherr

sovereign plenitude of power · souveräne Machtvollkommenheit f

sovereign power, temporal authority · weltliche Obrigkeit f

sovereign power, sovereign right, sovereign dominion, sovereignty, liberty, supremacy, authority, majesty, pre-eminence; majestas [*Latin*] · Hoheitsrecht n, Hoheitsbefugnis f, hoheitliches Recht, hoheitliche Befugnis, Souveränität f, Oberhoheit f, Hoheitsmacht f, vollziehende Gewalt f

sovereign right, royal right of a sovereign, royal prerogative, prerogative of a sovereign · Reg(al)ie f, königliches Recht n

sovereign right → sovereign power

sovereign state · souveräner Staat m

sovereignty → sovereign power

space · Raum m

space → (building) space

space acquisition → building space acquisition

space allocation, allocation of space · Raumzuweisung f

space allotment, allotment of space, apportionment of space, space apportionment · Raumzuteilung f

space analysis, spatial analysis · Raumanalyse f

space apportionment, space allotment, allotment of space, apportionment of space · Raumzuteilung f

space arrangement, spatial arrangement · Raumanordnung f

space association, spatial association · räumliche Assoziation f

space call, spatial demand, space demand, spatial call · räumliche Nachfrage f, Raumnachfrage

space characteristic, spatial characteristic · Raummerkmal n

space city, spatial town, spatial city, space town · Raumstadt f, räumliche Stadt

space city development, spatial urban development, space urban development, spatial town development, space town development, spatial city development · räumliche Stadtentwick(e)lung f

space classification · Raumtypisierung f

space component, spatial component · Raumkomponente f

space concept, spatial concept, concept of space · Raumbegriff m

space-consuming planning · raumbeanspruchende Planung f, raumbedeutsame Planung, raumbeeinflussende Planung, raumrelevante Planung

space coordination, spatial coordination · Raumkoordination f

space cost(s) · Raumkosten f

space demand, spatial call, space call, spatial demand · räumliche Nachfrage f, Raumnachfrage

space description, spatial description · Raumbeschreibung f

space development, spatial development · Raumentwick(e)lung f

space diagram — space program

space diagram, spatial diagram · Raumdiagramm *n*

space diffusion, spatial diffusion · räumliche Ausbreitung *f*

space dimension, spatial dimension · Raumabmessung *f*

space dispersion, space scatter, spatial dispersion, spatial scatter · Raumstreuung *f*, räumliche Streuung

space division, spatial division · Raumaufteilung *f*, Raumgliederung

space ecology, spatial ecology · Raumökologie *f*

space economy, spatial economics, space economics, spatial economy · Raumwirtschaft *f*, räumliche Wirtschaft

space-effective · raumwirksam, raumrelevant

space-effective measure · raumwirksame Maßnahme *f*

space effectiveness of public means · Raumwirksamkeit *f* öffentlicher Mittel

space effectiveness of traffic system · Raumwirksamkeit *f* des Verkehrssystems

space enclosed, cube, cubic(al) capacity, (cubic(al)) content, structural volume, cubic extent, cubing, walled-in space, building volume, cubage, enclosed space [*Enclosed total volume measurements of a structure*] · Baumasse *f*, umbauter Raum *m*, Rauminhalt *m*

space entity, spatial unit, spatial entity, space unit · Raumeinheit *f*, Raumganze *n* [*nicht als Maßeinheit*]

space environment, spatial environment · Raumumwelt *f*, räumliche Umwelt

space equilibrium, equilibrium of space, spatial equilibrium · räumliches Gleichgewicht *n*, Raumgleichgewicht

space for construction purposes · Bauraum *m*

space form, spatial form · Raumform *f*

space free of dense development · ballungsfreier Raum *m*

space growth, spatial growth · Raumwachstum *n*, räumliches Wachstum

space impact, impact of space, spatial impact · Raumbedeutung *f*

space improvement planning, spatial improvement planning · Raumerschließungsplanung *f*

space individual, spatial individual · Raumindividuum *n*

space interlinkage, (spatial) interlinkage · (Raum)Verflechtung *f*

space law, spatial law · (Welt)Raumrecht *n*

space law, spatial law · Raumrecht *n*

space legislation, space lawmaking, spatial legislation, spatial lawmaking · Raumgesetzgebung *f*

space market, spatial market · Markt *m* einer räumlichen Wirtschaft

space model, spatial model · Raummodell *n*

space module, spatial module · Raummodul *m*

space need · Raumbedarf *m*

space of existence, existence space · Daseinsraum *m*

space of living, living space · Lebensraum *m*

space organization, spatial organization · Raumorganisation *f*

space-orien(ta)ted, space-related · raumorientiert, raumbezogen

space orientation, relation to space, spatial orientation · Raumbezug *m*, Raumorientierung *f*

space pattern, spatial scheme, space scheme, spatial pattern · Raummuster *n*, Raumschema *n*

space-people-framework · Raum-Mensch-Modell *n* [*Korrelation von Bevölkerungsgrad und Umwelt*]

space planner, spatial planner · Raumplaner *m*

space planning, spatial planning · Raumplanung *f* [*Mit unterschiedlichen Inhalten verwendeter Begriff für Planungen, die sich auf die gegenständliche Umwelt, die strukturräumliche Ordnung beziehen; der Begriff ist sowohl auf Raumordnung und Bauleitplanung als auch auf sektorale Planungen, soweit sie einen regionalen Bezug haben, anwendbar*]

space planning education, spatial planning education · Raumplanerausbildung *f*

space planning law, spatial planning law · Raumplanungsrecht *n*

space policy, spatial policy · Raum(ordnungs)politik *f*

space policy science, spatial policy science · Raum(ordnungs)politik *f* als Wissenschaft, wissenschaftliche Raum(ordnungs)politik [*Die Lehre von den Spannungen und Lösungen zwischen Strukturen und Normen*]

space position, spatial position, situation · Raumlage *f* [*Die geographische, großräumliche Lage*]

space preference · Raumbevorzugung *f*

space program spatial program (US); spatial programme, space programme · Raumprogramm *n* [*Aufstellung der*

Räume nach Größe und Zweckbestimmung für ein Bauvorhaben]

space-related, space-orien(ta)ted · raumorientiert, raumbezogen

space research, spatial research · Raumforschung f [Zielorientierte normative Raum(ordnungs)wissenschaft]

space reserve, reserve of space, stock of space, space stock · Raumvorrat m, Raumreserve f

space scatter, spatial dispersion, spatial scatter, space dispersion · Raumstreuung f, räumliche Streuung

space scheme, spatial pattern, space pattern, spatial scheme · Raummuster n, Raumschema n

space science, spatial science · Raumwissenschaft f

space scope, scope of space, spatial scope · räumlicher Geltungsbereich m

space scope, spatial scope, scope of space · räumlicher Umfang m

space sensation, spatial sensation · Raumempfinden n

space separation, spatial separation · räumliche Trennung f, Raumtrennung

space sociology, spatial sociology · Raumsoziologie f

space stock, space reserve, reserve of space, stock of space · Raumvorrat m, Raumreserve f

space structure, spatial structure · Raumstruktur f, räumliche Struktur

space structuring, spatial structuring · Raumstrukturierung f

space system, spatial system · Raumsystem n, räumliches System

space system(s) theory, spatial system(s) theory · Raumsystemtheorie f

space theory, spatial theory · Raumtheorie f

space time autoregressive integrated moving average regression · STARIMAR

space-time budget · Raum-Zeit-Haushalt m

space-time model, spatio-temporal model · Raum-Zeit-Modell n

space town, space city, spatial town, spatial city · Raumstadt f, räumliche Stadt

space town development, spatial city development, space city development, spatial urban development, space urban development, spatial town development · räumliche Stadtentwick(e)lung f

space uniformity, spatial uniformity · Raumgleichförmigkeit f

space unit, space entity, spatial unit, spatial entity · Raumeinheit f, Raumganze n [nicht als Maßeinheit]

space urban development, spatial town development, space town development, spatial city development, space city development, spatial urban development · räumliche Stadtentwick(e)lung f

space use · Raumnutzung f

space use analysis · Raumnutzungsuntersuchung f, Raumnutzungsanalyse f

space-using · raumnutzend

spacious · geräumig

spaciousness · Geräumigkeit f

spade cultivation, intensive gardening · Spatenkultur f, Spatenanbau m

spade hind [In den Grenzgrafschaften Südschottlands]; ordinary agricultural labourer, general agricultural labourer (Brit.); ordinary agricultural laborer, general agricultural laborer (US); orraman [Scotland] · gewöhnlicher Landarbeiter m

spare time, nonwork time, leisure time, free time · Freizeit f

sparsely-peopled, sparsely-populated · dünnbesiedelt, dünnbevölkert

spatial abstraction in transportation planning · räumliche Abstraktion f [Die Formen der Abstraktion (Aggregation, Reduktion) vom räumlichen Aspekt der verschiedenen Komponenten des Verkehrsgeschehens]

spatial adjustment · räumliche Anpassung f

spatial analysis, space analysis · Raumanalyse f, Raumuntersuchung f

spatial arrangement, space arrangement · Raumanordnung f

spatial association, space association · räumliche Assoziation f

spatial autocorrelation, space autocorrelation · Raumautokorrelation f

spatial awareness, awareness of space · Raumbewußtsein n

spatial behaviour (Brit.); spatial behavior (US) · Raumverhalten n, räumliches Verhalten

spatial call, space call, spatial demand, space demand · räumliche Nachfrage f, Raumnachfrage

spatial characteristic, space characteristic · Raummerkmal n

spatial choice, choice of space · Raumwahl f

spatial city, space town, space city, spatial town · Raumstadt f, räumliche Stadt

spatial city development, space city development, spatial urban development,

spatial component — spatial organization

space urban development, spatial town development, space town development · räumliche Stadtentwick(e)lung f

spatial component, space component · Raumkomponente f

spatial concentration · räumliche Konzentration f

spatial concept, concept of space, space concept · Raumbegriff m

spatial coordination, space coordination · Raumkoordination f

spatial demand, space demand, spatial call, space call · räumliche Nachfrage f, Raumnachfrage

spatial description, space description · Raumbeschreibung f

spatial development, space development · Raumentwick(e)lung f

spatial diagram, space diagram · Raumdiagramm n

spatial difference · räumlicher Unterschied m

spatial diffusion, space diffusion · räumliche Ausbreitung f, Raumausbreitung

spatial dimension, space dimension · Raumabmessung f

spatial dispersion, spatial scatter, space dispersion, space scatter · Raumstreuung f, räumliche Streuung

spatial distribution · räumliche Verteilung f, Raumverteilung

spatial distribution of city functions · räumliche Verteilung f der Stadtfunktionen

spatial distribution of income, spatial income distribution · räumliche Einkommensverteilung f

spatial distribution of population · räumliche Bevölkerungsverteilung f

spatial division, space division · Raumaufteilung f, Raumgliederung

spatial ecology, space ecology · Raumökologie f

spatial economic structure · räumliche Wirtschaftsstruktur f

spatial economy, space economy, spatial economics, space economics · Raumwirtschaft f, räumliche Wirtschaft

spatial entity, space unit, space entity, spatial unit · Raumeinheit f, Raumganze n [nicht als Maßeinheit]

spatial environment, space environment · Raumumwelt f, räumliche Umwelt

spatial equilibrium, space equilibrium, equilibrium of space · räumliches Gleichgewicht n, Raumgleichgewicht

spatial equilibrium analysis · Raumgleichgewichtsanalyse f

spatial expansion · räumliche Erweiterung f, Raumerweiterung

spatial form, space form · Raumform f

spatial geography, space geography · Raumgeographie f

spatial growth, space growth · Raumwachstum n, räumliches Wachstum

spatial identity · räumliche Verwurzelung f

spatial impact, space impact, impact of space · Raumbedeutung f

spatial importance, importance of space · Raumbedeutsamkeit f

spatial improvement planning, space improvement planning · Raumerschließungsplanung f

spatial income distribution, spatial distribution of income · räumliche Einkommensverteilung f

spatial individual, space individual · Raumindividuum n

spatial interaction · räumliche Verflechtung f

(spatial) interlinkage, space interlinkage · (Raum)Verflechtung f

spatial-juxtaposition economies · Vorteile m pl der räumlichen Nähe, Vorteile der räumlichen Konzentration, Fühlungsvorteile

spatial law, space law · (Welt)Raumrecht n

spatial law, space law · Raumrecht n

spatial legislation, spatial lawmaking, space legislation, space lawmaking · Raumgesetzgebung f

spatial(ly) · räumlich

spatially delineated · räumlich skizziert

spatially free-standing town, spatially free-standing city · räumlich freistehende Stadt f

spatially neutral · raumneutral

spatially separated · räumlich getrennt

spatial macroeconomic development, SMED · räumliche makroökonomische Entwick(e)lung f

spatial market, space market, spacial market · Markt m einer räumlichen Wirtschaft

spatial model, space model · Raummodell n

spatial module, space module · Raummodul m

spatial movement · veränderliche Bewegung f

spatial organization, space organization · Raumorganisation f

spatial orientation, space orientation, relation to space · Raumbezug *m*, Raumorientierung *f*

spatial pattern, space pattern, spatial scheme, space scheme · Raummuster *n*, Raumschema *n*

spatial picture of wages · räumliches Bild *n* der Löhne

spatial planner, space planner · Raumplaner *m*

spatial planning, space planning · Raumplanung *f* [*Mit unterschiedlichen Inhalten verwendeter Begriff für Planungen, die sich auf die gegenständliche Umwelt, die strukturräumliche Ordnung beziehen; der Begriff ist sowohl auf Raumordnung und Bauleitplanung als auch auf sektorale Planungen, soweit sie einen regionalen Bezug haben, anwendbar*]

spatial planning education, space planning education · Raumplanerausbildung *f*

spatial planning law, space planning law · Raumplanungsrecht *n*

spatial policy, space policy · Raum(ordnungs)politik *f*

spatial policy science, space policy science · Raum(ordnungs)politik *f* als Wissenschaft, wissenschaftliche Raum(ordnungs)politik [*Die Lehre von den Spannungen und Lösungen zwischen Strukturen und Normen*]

spatial position, situation, space position · Raumlage *f* [*Die geographische, großräumliche Lage*]

spatial price system · räumliches Preissystem *n*

spatial programme, space programme; space program, spatial program (US) · Raumprogramm *n* [*Aufstellung der Räume nach Größe und Zweckbestimmung für ein Bauvorhaben*]

spatial research, space research · Raumforschung *f* [*Zielorientierte normative Raum(ordnungs)wissenschaft*]

spatial scatter, space dispersion, space scatter, spatial dispersion · Raumstreuung *f*, räumliche Streuung

spatial scheme, space scheme, spatial pattern, space pattern · Raummuster *n*, Raumschema *n*

spatial science, space science · Raumwissenschaft *f*

spatial scope, space scope, scope of space · räumlicher Geltungsbereich *m*

spatial scope, scope of space, space scope · räumlicher Umfang *m*

spatial sensation, space sensation · Raumempfinden *n*

spatial separation, space separation · räumliche Trennung *f*, Raumtrennung

spatial sociology, space sociology · Raumsoziologie *f*

spatial structure, space structure · Raumstruktur *f*, räumliche Struktur

spatial structuring, space structuring · Raumstrukturierung *f*

spatial system, space system · Raumsystem *n*, räumliches System

spatial system(s) theory, space system(s) theory · Raumsystemtheorie *f*

spatial theory, space theory · Raumtheorie *f*

spatial town, spatial city, space town, space city · Raumstadt *f*, räumliche Stadt

spatial town development, space town development, spatial city development, space city development, spatial urban development, space urban development · räumliche Stadtentwick(e)lung *f*

spatial uniformity, space uniformity · Raumgleichförmigkeit *f*

spatial unit, spatial entity, space unit, space entity · Raumeinheit *f*, Raumganze *n* [*nicht als Maßeinheit*]

spatial urban development, space urban development, spatial town development, space town development, spatial city development, space city development · räumliche Stadtentwick(e)lung *f*

spatio-temporal model, space-time model · Raum-Zeit-Modell *n*

special act, special statute, special law · Sondergesetz *n*

special administration (of estate(s)), limited administration (of estate(s)), restricted administration (of estate(s)), restrained administration (of estate(s)) · besondere Nachlaßverwaltung *f*, eingeschränkte Nachlaßverwaltung, beschränkte Nachlaßverwaltung, begrenzte Nachlaßverwaltung

special administrative law · besonderes Verwaltungsrecht *n*

special administrator → special (probate) administrator

special agent · Bevollmächtigte *m* für einzelne Handlungen

special agricultural area, depressed agricultural area, distressed agricultural area, less prosperous agricultural area · landwirtschaftliches Notstandsgebiet *n*, landwirtschaftliches Passivgebiet

special area, less prosperous area, depressed territory, special territory, distressed territory, less prosperous territory, depressed area, distressed area · Notstandsgebiet *n*, Passivgebiet, Sondergebiet, SO

special area → special (building) (land) area

special assumpsit · schriftvertragliches Versprechen *n*

special auditor · Sonderprüfer *m*

special averment · Bekräftigung *f* durch Aufzeichnung, Behauptung durch Aufzeichnung [*Vor einem Geschworenengericht*]

special bequest → specified bequest

special building board, special construction board · Sonderbauamt *n*

special (building) (land) area, special (building) land · Sonder(bau)fläche *f*, Sonder(bau)boden *m*, Sonder(bau)land *n*

special (building) (land) zone · Sondergebiet *n*, SO [*Teil einer Sonder(bau)fläche*]

special burden, special charge, special encumbrance, special load, special incumbrance · Sonderbelastung *f*, Sonderlast *f*

special case · Formulierung *f* der Rechtsfragen

special case (arbitration) procedure · Schieds(gerichts)verfahren *n* bei dem alle Schiedsrichter einer vollen vorgezogenen Rechtsanwendungskontrolle unterliegen

special charge · Sonderabgabe *f*

special charge, special encumbrance, special load, special incumbrance, special burden · Sonderbelastung *f*, Sonderlast *f*

special checking account [*USA*] · laufendes Konto *n* ohne Minimumsaldo

special committee · Spezialausschuß *m*, Sonderausschuß

special (common) custom → special customary law

special community, less prosperous community, depressed community, distressed community · Notstandsgemeinde *f*, Passivgemeinde, Notstandskommune *f*, Passivkommune

special compensation, special indemnity, special indemnification, special damages · spezifizierte Entschädigung *f*, spezifizierter Schadenersatz *m*

special condition · Sonderbedingung *f*, besondere Bedingung

special condition of contract, special contract condition · besondere Vertragsbedingung *f*, Sondervertragsbedingung

special construction board, special building board · Sonderbauamt *n*

special contract → specialty contract

special contract condition, special condition of contract · besondere Vertragsbedingung *f*, Sondervertragsbedingung

special cost(s) · Sonderkosten *f*

special custom, local usage, local habit, special usage, special habit, local custom · örtliche Gewohnheit *f*, örtliche Gepflogenheit, örtlicher Brauch *m*, Ortsüblichkeit, Ortsgewohnheit, Ortsgepflogenheit, Ortsbrauch

special custom, particular usage, special usage, particular habit, special habit, particular custom [*A particular custom is nearly the same as a local custom, being such as affects only the inhabitants of some particular district*] · spezielle Gewohnheit *f*, spezielle Gepflogenheit, spezieller Brauch *m*

special customary law; special universal custom of the realm, special (common) custom, special custom which runs through the whole land, special general customs (Brit.) · besonderes Gewohnheitsrecht *n*

special custom which runs through the whole land → special customary law

special damages, special compensation, special indemnity, special indemnification · spezifizierte Entschädigung *f*, spezifizierter Schadenersatz *m*

special district [*USA. School, water, highway, and sewer districts, and other units of government with power to tax and spend for particular purposes. Their boundaries are seldom identical with the political boundaries of cities, townships, or counties*] · Spezialverband *m*

special drainage charge · Entwässerungssonderabgabe *f*, Sonderentwässerungsabgabe

special encumbrance, special load, special incumbrance, special burden, special charge · Sonderbelastung *f*, Sonderlast *f*

special endorsement, full endorsement, special indorsement, full indorsement · Wechselaufschrift *f* mit Bezeichnung des Indossators

special endorsement (of claim), special indorsement (of claim) [*On a writ of summons*] · spezielle Aufschrift *f* [*Sie enthält die Natur des Anspruchs oder den Inhalt des Klageantrags*]

special equitable power of appointment · spezielles Recht *n* an einem bestimmten Vermögen Treuhand zu erklären, spezielle Befugnis *f* an einem bestimmten Vermögen Treuhand zu erklären

special executor dative [*Scotland*]; special (probate) administrator · beschränkter Nachlaßverwalter *m*, beschränkter Erb(schafts)verwalter, beschränkter erbrechtlicher Verwalter, eingeschränkter Nachlaßverwalter, eingeschränkter Erb(schafts)verwalter, eingeschränkter erbrechtlicher Verwalter, begrenzter Nachlaßverwalter, begrenzter

special fitness — special legal power of appointment

Erb(schafts)verwalter, begrenzter erbrechtlicher Verwalter, besonderer Nachlaßverwalter, besonderer erbrechtlicher Verwalter, besonderer Erb(schafts)verwalter

special fitness, suitableness, suitability, appropriateness · Zweckmäßigkeit *f*

special function · Sonderfunktion *f*

special fund · Spezialfonds *m*

special general customs (Brit.) → special customary law

special guaranty, special guarantee [*No party, other than the one to whom it is addressed, may accept it and act upon it*] · persönliche Bürgschaft *f*

special habit, local custom, special custom, local usage, local habit, special usage · örtliche Gewohnheit *f*, örtliche Gepflogenheit, örtlicher Brauch *m*, Ortsüblichkeit, Ortsgewohnheit, Ortsgepflogenheit, Ortsbrauch

special incumbrance, special burden, special charge, special encumbrance, special load · Sonderbelastung *f*, Sonderlast *f*

special indemnification, special damages, special compensation, special indemnity · spezifizierte Entschädigung *f*, spezifizierter Schadenersatz *m*

special indorsement → special endorsement

special indorsement (of claim), special endorsement (of claim) [*On a writ of summons*] · spezielle Aufschrift *f* [*Sie enthält die Natur des Anspruchs oder den Inhalt des Klageantrags*]

specialist · Sonderfachmann *m* [*Er erbringt eine Werkleistung unabhängig von der Arbeit des Architekten*]

specialist contract · Fachunternehmervertrag *m*, Spezialunternehmervertrag

specialist contractor · Fachunternehmer *m*, Spezialunternehmer

specialist enterprise, specialist undertaking · Spezialbetrieb *m*, Fachbetrieb

specialist firm · Fachfirma *f*, Fachunternehmung *f*, Fachunternehmen *n*, Spezialfirma, Spezialunternehmen, Spezialunternehmung

specialist service · Spezialdienstleistung *f*, Fachdienstleistung

specialist sub(contractor) · Fachunterunternehmer *m*, Fachnachunternehmer, Fachsubunternehmer; Fachunterakkordant *m* [*Schweiz*]

specialist supervisor · Spezialmeister *m*, Funktionsmeister [*Funktionssystem von F. W. Taylor*]

specialist's work(s) · Facharbeit(en) *f (pl)*, Fachleistung(en) *f (pl)*

specialist undertaking, specialist enterprise · Spezialbetrieb *m*, Fachbetrieb

speciality commodities, speciality goods [*Those consumers' goods on which a significant group of buyers characteristically insists and for which they are willing to make a special purchasing effort*] · Güter *npl* des speziellen Bedarfs, Waren *fpl* des speziellen Bedarfs

speciality fund · Schwerpunktfonds *m*

specialized planning, subject planning, sector planning [*Planning based on consideration of a particular type or types of development*] · fachliche Entwick(e)lungsplanung *f*, Sektorplanung, Fachplanung, sektorale Planung

specialized planning act, specialized planning law, specialized planning statute, sector planning act, sector planning law, sector planning statute, subject planning act, subject planning law, subject planning statute · Fachplanungsgesetz *n*, Sektorplanungsgesetz, sektorales Planungsgesetz, fachliches Entwick(e)lungsplanungsgesetz

specialized planning law, sector planning law, subject planning law · Fachplanungsrecht *n*, Sektorplanungsrecht, sektorales Planungsrecht, fachliches Planungsrecht

specialized planning practice, sector planning practice, subject planning practice · Fachplanungswesen *n*, Sektorplanungswesen, sektorales Planungswesen, fachliches Planungswesen

specialized pleader · Anwalt *m* auf mündliche Gerichtsverhandlung

special juror's book · besondere Geschworenenliste *f*, besonderes Geschworenenverzeichnis *n*

special knowledge, expertness, professional knowledge, expertise · berufliches Wissen *n*, Fachwissen, Fachkenntnisse *fpl*, Fachkunde *f*, Sachkenntnis, Sachkunde, Sachwissen, Spezialkenntnis, Spezialwissen, Spezialkunde

special (land) use zoning, conditional zoning, special zoning, conditional (land) use zoning · bedingte (bauliche) Nutzung *f*, bedingte Bauzonenfestlegung

special law, special act, special statute · Sondergesetz *n*

special law · Sonderrecht *n*

special legacy → specified bequest

special legal power of appointment, special legal right of appointment, special power of appointment under the statute of uses, special right of appointment under the statute of uses · spezielle Befugnis *f* an einem bestimmten Vermögen Nutzung zu erklären, spezielles Recht *n* an einem bestimmten Vermögen Nutzung zu erklären

special letter of credit, restricted letter of credit · Spezialkreditbrief *m*

special load, special incumbrance, special burden, special charge, special encumbrance · Sonderbelastung *f*, Sonderlast *f*

specially, expressly · ausdrücklicherweise

specially crossed · besonders gekreuzt [*Scheck*]

special map · Spezialkarte *f* [*Großmaßstäbliche topographische Karte (Maßstäbe etwa 1:20 000 bis 1:75 000) mit grundrißtreuer Situationszeichnung bei sparsamster Verwendung von Symbolen*]

special master · Nicht-Klassenlehrer *m*

special master (US) · Gerichtssachverständige *m* [*Er verhört unter Eid Zeugen, nimmt andere Beweise auf und gibt dem Gericht seine Schlußfolgerungen bekannt*]

special moratorium · Spezialmoratorium *n*, Spezialindult *m*, Spezialanstandsbrief *m* [*Eine obrigkeitliche Anordnung die einem einzelnen Schuldner die fälligen Schulden stundet*]

special mortgage · Spezialhypothek *f*

special occupancy · treuhänderische Besitzergreifung *f* von Leh(e)n beim Tode des Vasallen, Erbantritt *m* eines Leh(e)n(s)treuhänders

special occupant [*A person having a special right to enter upon and occupy land(s) granted pur autre vie, on the death of the tenant, and during the life of cestui que vie. Where the grant is to a man and his heirs during the life of cestui que vie, the heir succeeds as special occupant, having a special exclusive right by the terms of the original grant. This doctrine of special occupancy has been adopted in some of the United States, but is not recognized in others. Where a wife is tenant pur autre vie, and dies during the life of cestui que vie, the husband becomes the special occupant*] · Besitzergreifende *m* von Leh(e)n beim Tode des Vasallen, treuhänderisch besitzender Leh(e)n(s)erbe *m*, Sonderrechts-Besitzergreifende

special paper · Geschäftsverzeichnis *n* eines Gerichts

special partner, limited partner · Kommanditist *m*, beschränkt haftender Partner *m*, beschränkt haftender Gesellschafter; Kommanditär *m* [*Schweiz*]

special performance · besondere Leistung *f*, Sonderleistung

(special) pleader, placitator; placitans advocatus [*Latin*] [*Formerly when pleading at common law was a highly technical and difficult art, there was a class of men known as (special) pleaders not at the bar, who held a position intermediate between counsel and attorneys. The class is now extinct*] · Schriftsatzausarbeiter *m*

special policy · Sonderpolice *f* [*Versicherung*]

special power of appointment, special right of appointment, special power of disposition, special right of disposition · begrenzte Bestimmungsbefugnis *f*, begrenzte Erklärungsbefugnis, beschränkte Bestimmungsbefugnis, beschränkte Erklärungsbefugnis, eingeschränkte Erklärungsbefugnis, eingeschränkte Bestimmungsbefugnis, eingeschränktes Bestimmungsrecht *n*, eingeschränktes Erklärungsrecht, beschränktes Bestimmungsrecht, beschränktes Erklärungsrecht, begrenztes Bestimmungsrecht, begrenztes Erklärungsrecht [*Die Befugnis über ein Grundvermögen eine neue Bestimmung zu treffen, bei Gebundenheit an eine gewisse Klasse von Personen*]

special power of appointment under the statute of uses, special right of appointment under the statute of uses, special legal power of appointment, special legal right of appointment · spezielle Befugnis *f* an einem bestimmten Vermögen Nutzung zu erklären, spezielles Recht *n* an einem bestimmten Vermögen Nutzung zu erklären

special power of disposition → special power of appointment

special pre-emption → special (right of) pre-emption

special probate, limited probate, restricted probate, restrained probate · begrenzte Nachlaßbestätigung *f*, eingeschränkte Nachlaßbestätigung, beschränkte Nachlaßbestätigung, besondere Nachlaßbestätigung

special (probate) administrator; special executor dative [*Scotland*] · beschränkter Nachlaßverwalter *m*, beschränkter Erb(schafts)verwalter, beschränkter erbrechtlicher Verwalter, eingeschränkter Erb(schafts)verwalter, eingeschränkter erbrechtlicher Verwalter, begrenzter Nachlaßverwalter, begrenzter Erb(schafts)verwalter, begrenzter erbrechtlicher Verwalter, besonderer Nachlaßverwalter, besonderer erbrechtlicher Verwalter, besonderer Erb(schafts)verwalter

special property, qualified property · besitzmäßiges Eigentum, eigenartiges Eigentum *n*, eigenartiges Interesse *n* an einer Sache

special provision · Sonderbestimmung *f*

special purpose district [*USA*] · kommunale Einheit *f* mit spezifischer Aufgabenstellung

special recreation(al) area, special recreation(al) territory · Erholungssondergebiet *n*

special regional planning, regional special planning · regionale Spezialplanung *f*, spezielle Regionalplanung

special requirement · besondere Ausstattung *f* [*Fläche*]

special requirement · besondere Anforderung *f*, besondere Auflage *f*, besonderes Erfordernis *n*

special resolution · Sonderbeschluß *m*, Sonderentschließung *f*

Special Revenue Sharing for Community Development and Planning [*USA*] · Sonderverteilung *f* von Staatsmitteln für Gemeindeentwick(e)lung und -planung

special right of appointment, special power of disposition, special right of disposition, special power of appointment · begrenzte Bestimmungsbefugnis *f*, begrenzte Erklärungsbefugnis, beschränkte Bestimmungsbefugnis, beschränkte Erklärungsbefugnis, eingeschränkte Erklärungsbefugnis, eingeschränkte Bestimmungsbefugnis, eingeschränktes Bestimmungsrecht *n*, eingeschränktes Erklärungsrecht, beschränktes Bestimmungsrecht, beschränktes Erklärungsrecht, begrenztes Bestimmungsrecht, begrenztes Erklärungsrecht [*Die Befugnis über ein Grundvermögen eine neue Bestimmung zu treffen, bei Gebundenheit an eine gewisse Klasse von Personen*]

special right of appointment under the statute of uses, special legal power of appointment, special legal right of appointment, special power of appointment under the statute of uses · spezielle Befugnis *f* an einem bestimmten Vermögen Nutzung zu erklären, spezielles Recht *n* an einem bestimmten Vermögen Nutzung zu erklären

special (right of) pre-emption · besonderes Vorkaufsrecht *n*

special service · Sonderdienstleistung *f*

special session · außerordentliche Sitzung *f*

special settlement · Sonder(an)sied(e)lung *f*

special situations fund · Fonds *m* für besondere Anlage(n)werte

special statute, special law, special act · Sondergesetz *n*

special subject map, thematic map · Themakarte *f*, thematische Karte; angewandte Karte, Problemkarte [*frühere Benennungen*]

special tax funds paid by those whose property remained undamaged following the war · Lastenausgleichsmittel *f* [*Bundesrepublik Deutschland*]

special territory, distressed territory, less prosperous territory, depressed area, distressed area, special area, less prosperous area, depressed territory · Notstandsgebiet *n*, Passivgebiet, Sondergebiet, SO

special trust · Treuhand *f* mit selbständiger Tätigkeit

specialty → (contract by) specialty

specialty building contractor, specialty construction contractor · Spezialbauunternehmer *m*, Fachbauunternehmer

special(ty) contract, contract in sealed writing, sealed contract, (contract by) specialty, contract under seal, contract by seal, contract by deed, covenant in deed, covenant in fact [*Contracts under seal, such as deeds and bonds, are instruments which are not rarely in writing, but which are sealed by the party bound thereby, and delivered by him to, or for the benefit of, the person to whom the liability is thereby incurred*] · (schriftlicher) gesiegelter Vertrag *m*, gesiegelter schriftlicher Vertrag, Formalvertrag unter Siegel, Vertrag mit Siegel, förmlicher Vertrag unter Siegel

special(ty) contract section · Fach(bau)los *n*

special universal custom of the realm → special customary law

special usage, special habit, local custom, special custom, local usage, local habit · örtliche Gewohnheit *f*, örtliche Gepflogenheit, örtlicher Brauch *m*, Ortsüblichkeit, Ortsgewohnheit, Ortsgepflogenheit, Ortsbrauch

special use · Sonderbenutzung *f*, Sondergebrauch *m*

special use interest, special use right · Sondergebrauchsrecht *n*, Sonderbenutzungsrecht, subjektives Sondergebrauchsrecht, subjektives Sonderbenutzungsrecht

special use permission · Sonderbenutzungserlaubnis *f*, Sonderbenutzungsgenehmigung *f*, Sondergebrauchserlaubnis, Sondergebrauchsgenehmigung

special use right, special use interest · Sondergebrauchsrecht *n*, Sonderbenutzungsrecht, subjektives Sondergebrauchsrecht, subjektives Sonderbenutzungsrecht

special verdict · besonderes Verdikt *n*, besonderer Geschworenenspruch *m*, besonderer Spruch der Geschworenen [*Dieser Spruch gibt nur die Aussagen der Geschworenen über tatsächliche Punkte, und dem Gericht wird überlassen die rechtlichen Folgerungen daraus zu ziehen*]

special zoning, conditional (land) use zoning, special (land) use zoning, conditional zoning · bedingte (bauliche) Nut

specific appropriation (of funds) — speed limit

zung f, bedingte Baunutzung, bedingte Bauzonenfestlegung

specific appropriation (of funds) · (Mittel)Bewilligung f für ein Objekt

spec(ification), bill of quantities · Mengenverzeichnis n

specification · Verarbeitung f, Spezifikation f

specification industry · Verarbeitungsindustrie f

spec(ification)(s), description of (the) work(s), description of work(s) (content), work(s) description · Arbeitsbeschreibung f, (Bau)Leistungsbeschreibung f, Baubeschreibung f, Darstellung f der Bauaufgabe, Darstellung f der (Bau)Leistungen, Vorschreibung f

spec(ification)(s) → (technical) spec(ification)(s)

specification; specificatio [*Latin*] [*In civil law*] · Verarbeitung f, Spezifikation f [*Die Herstellung einer Sache durch Verarbeitung eines Stoffes oder mehrerer Stoffe*]

specificator [*in civil law*] · Verarbeiter m

specific goods, ascertained goods · Spezieswaren f pl

specific legacy → specified bequest

specific location, specific site · eigentlicher Standort m

specific performance, contract completion, completion of contract · Naturalerfüllung f, Vertragserfüllung, Realerfüllung, vertragsgemäße Erfüllung

specific region, region · Region f

specific region · individueller geographischer Raum m

specific site, specific location · eigentlicher Standort m

specified completion date, specified date of completion · geforderter Fertigstellungstermin m, geforderter Fertigstellungstag m, gefordertes Fertigstellungsdatum n

specified event · bestimmtes Ereignis n

specified sub(-contractor) · bestimmter Subunternehmer m, bestimmter Nachunternehmer, bestimmter Unterunternehmer; bestimmter Unterakkordant m [*Schweiz*]

specified work(s) · geforderte (Bau)-Arbeit(en) f (pl), geforderte (Bau)Leistung(en) f (pl)

specimen notice to quit [*premises*] · Musterkündigungsschreiben n

spec(s) → (technical) spec(ification)(s)

speculation, adventure · Spekulation f

speculation control · Spekulationsbekämpfung f

speculation in (building) (land) area, speculation in (building) land, (building) (land) area speculation, (building) land speculation · (Bau)Bodenspekulation f, (Bau)Landspekulation, (Bau)Flächenspekulation

speculation in land(s), realty speculation, speculation in realty, (real) estate speculation, (real) property speculation, speculation in (real) estate, speculation in (real) property, land(s) speculation · Grund(stücks)spekulation f, Bodenspekulation, Landspekulation, Liegenschaftsspekulation, Immobiliarspekulation, Immobilienspekulation

speculation in (real) property, land(s) speculation, speculation in land(s), realty speculation, speculation in realty, (real) estate speculation, (real) property speculation, speculation in (real) estate · Grund(stücks)spekulation f, Bodenspekulation, Landspekulation, Liegenschaftsspekulation, Immobiliarspekulation, Immobilienspekulation

speculation operation, speculation transaction, speculation deal, speculative operation, speculative transaction, speculative deal · Spekulationsgeschäft n

speculation price, speculative price · Spekulationspreis m

speculative ability · Spekulationsfähigkeit f, Spekulationsvermögen n

speculative builder [*One who engages in the construction of projects for sale or lease*] · Spekulationsbauträger m

speculative building · Spekulationsgebäude n

speculative building (construction) · Spekulationshochbau m

speculative land · Spekulationsland n, Spekulationsboden m

speculative operation, speculative transaction, speculative deal, speculation operation, speculation transaction, speculation deal · Spekulationsgeschäft n

speculative (physical) development, speculative binding development, speculative binding physical development, speculative physical binding development · Spekulationsbebauung f; Spekulationsüberbauung [*Schweiz*]

speculative price, speculation price · Spekulationspreis m

speculative purchase · Spekulationskauf m

speculator, adventurer, gambler · Spekulant m

speed limit · Geschwindigkeitsgrenze f

speed of construction, rate of construction, rate of progress, construction rate, progress rate, speed of progress, progress speed, construction speed, speed rate · Baugeschwindigkeit *f*, Bautempo *n*, (Bau)Fortschrittempo, (Bau)Fortschrittgeschwindigkeit

speed of working, rate of working, working speed, working rate · Arbeitsgeschwindigkeit *f*, Ausführungsgeschwindigkeit *f*, Arbeitstempo *n*, Ausführungstempo *n*

speedy internment · Sofortbestattung *f*

spending planning, planning of spending · Ausgabenplanung *f*

spending policy · Ausgabenpolitik *f*

spending variance, controllable variance, budget variance · (Mengen)Verbrauchsabweichung *f*, Abweichung (des effektiven) vom geplanten (Mengen)Verbrauch, Budgetabweichung [*Der Unterschied zwischen den Soll- und Istkosten einer Kostenart oder Kostenstelle*]

spendthrift trust [*A trust created to provide a fund for the maintenance of a beneficiary, and at the same time to secure it against his improvidence or incapacity*] · Unterhaltstreuhand *f*

spes successionis [*Latin*]; contingent remainder (land(ed)) estate, conditional remainder (land(ed)) estate, executory remainder (land(ed)) estate, possibility of (a) future (land(ed)) estate [*The remainder is contingent if the person who is to have the remainder is not yet living or if his identity is uncertain, or if the event which is to bring the remainder into existence is uncertain. The remainder becomes vested when such person is ascertained or upon the happening of the event*] · bedingter anwartschaftlicher Bodenbesitz(stand) *m*, möglicher anwartschaftlicher Bodenbesitz(stand), ungewisser anwartschaftlicher Bodenbesitz(stand)

sphere of action, action sphere · Aufgabenbereich *m*

spillover effect, side effect · mittelbare Wirkung *f*, indirekte Wirkung, Nebenwirkung [*Stadtentwick(e)lungsplanung. Eine Wirkung die nicht in den Zielen der Wirtschaftsakteure enthalten ist*]

spiral of wages and prices, wages-prices spiral · Lohn-Preis-Spirale *f*

spiritual authority, ecclesiastic(al) authority · Kirchenbehörde *f*

spiritual authority, spiritual power; jus majestaticum circa sacra, jus in sacra, potestas ecclesiastica [*Latin*]; ecclesiastic(al) power, ecclesiastic(al) authority · Kirchengewalt *f*, Kirchenhoheit *f*, Kirchenmacht *f*, Kirchenkompetenz *f*, Kirchenregiment *n*

spiritual benefice, ecclesiastic(al) benefice · geistliche Pfründe *f*, kirchliche Pfründe, Kirchenpfründe

spiritual community, ecclesiastic(al) community · Kirchengemeinde *f*

spiritual consolidation, spiritual fusion, ecclesiastic(al) consolidation, ecclesiastic(al) fusion · kirchliche Konsolidation *f*, kirchliche Verschmelzung, kirchliche Fusion, geistliche Konsolidation, geistliche Verschmelzung, geistliche Fusion

spiritual corporation, church corporation, religious house, ecclesiastic(al) corporation · geistliche Körperschaft *f*, geistliche Korporation, kirchliche Korporation, kirchliche Körperschaft

spiritual corporation sole, ecclesiastic(al) corporation sole · Pfarre(i) *f*, Pfarramt *n*, Pfarrbezirk *m*

spiritual court, ecclesiastical court, consistorial court, church-court, court Christian, consistory court; commissary court [*Scotland*] · geistliches Gericht *n*, Kirchengericht, Konsistorialgericht, kirchliches Gericht [*Die schottischen „ecclesiastical courts" haben nur eine Jurisdiktion über Fragen der Doktrin, des Gottesdienstes, der Sakramente und der Disziplin der Geistlichen*]

spiritual culture · geistige Kultur *f*

spiritual estate, ecclesiastic(al) estate, church property, spiritual property, ecclesiastic(al) property, church estate · Kirchenvermögen *n*, Kirchengut *n*, Kirchenhabe *f*

spiritual fee, spiritual feud, spiritual feod, spiritual fief, spiritual tenancy, spiritual tenement, spiritual (feodal) tenure (of land), ecclesiastic(al) fee, ecclesiastic(al) feod, ecclesiastic(al) feud, ecclesiastic(al) fief, ecclesiastic(al) tenement, ecclesiastic(al) tenancy, ecclesiastic(al) (feodal) tenure (of land), tenure (of land) by divine service; feudum ecclesiasticum, feodum ecclesiasticum, feudum religiosum, feodum religiosum [*Latin*] · Gottesleh(e)n *n*, Kirchenleh(e)n, Klosterleh(e)n, geistliches Leh(e)n [*Die geistlichen Verrichtungen waren genau definiert*]

spiritual fusion, ecclesiastic(al) consolidation, ecclesiastic(al) fusion, spiritual consolidation · kirchliche Konsolidation *f*, kirchliche Verschmelzung, kirchliche Fusion, geistliche Konsolidation, geistliche Verschmelzung, geistliche Fusion

spiritual land, ecclesiastic(al) land, church-land · Kirchenland *n*, Kirchenboden *m*

spiritual (land(ed)) estate, ecclesiastic(al) (land(ed)) estate · kirchlicher Landbesitz *m*, kirchlicher Bodenbesitz, kirchlicher Grund(stücks)besitz

spiritual law; jus ecclesiasticum [*Latin*]; law Christian, ecclesiastic(al) law [*Not to be confused with "jus canonicum"*] ·

spiritual power — sponsoring subject

Kirchenrecht n, kirchliches Recht, geistliches Recht

spiritual power → spiritual authority

spiritual property, ecclesiastic(al) property, church estate, spiritual estate, ecclesiastic(al) estate, church property · Kirchenvermögen n, Kirchengut n, Kirchenhabe f

spiritual province, church province, ecclesiastic(al) province · Kirchenprovinz f

spiritual tithe, parochial tithe, ecclesiastic(al) tithe, parish tithe · geistlicher Zehnt m, Pfarrerzehnt, kirchlicher Zehnt, Kirchenzehnt [altdeutsch: Pfarrerzehent, Pfarrezehend]

spiritual writer, ecclesiastic(al) writer · Kirchenschriftsteller m

spite fence · Neidzaun m

spiteful, intentionally mischievous, intentionally harmful, malicious · schikanös

spite masonry wall · Neidmauer f

split assembly · Teilversammlung f

split in functions, separation of functions · Funktionstrennung f, Funktionsteilung

split lot [Lot that is divided by a zone boundary] · geteilte Parzelle f

split-off point · Teilungspunkt m zwischen Kuppel- und Nebenprodukt

split re-exportation · Teilwiederausfuhr f

splitting method · Halbierungsverfahren n [Bei der Zusammenveranlagung von Ehegatten]

splitting (up) of cost(s), cost(s) division, division of cost(s), cost(s) splitting · Kostenspaltung f, Kostentrennung

splitting (up) of house room · Wohnungszerlegung f

splitting (up) of risk(s), splitting (up) of hazard(s), hazard distribution, risk distribution, risk sharing, hazard sharing, distribution of risk(s), distribution of hazard(s), sharing of risk(s), sharing of hazard(s) · Verteilung f des Risikos, Verteilung des Wagnisses, Risikoverteilung, Wagnisverteilung

splitup (US) share bonus (Brit.) · Gewinnprämie f

spoil (deposit) area · Kippe(ngelände) f, (n), Deponie(gelände) f, (n)

spoiled landscape · zerstörte Landschaft f

spoilman · Futterkrippenpolitiker m

spoils-system · Besetzung f der bezahlten Rathausstellen durch die Wahlsiegerpartei, Patronagebürokratie f, politisches Beutesystem n der Stellenbesetzung

spoliation · Pfründenberaubung f

to sponsor, to promote · fördern

sponsor, promoter · Fördernde m, Förderer

sponsoring, promoting · Fördern n

sponsoring, promotion · Förderung f

sponsoring, sponsorship, management · Federführung f [Arge]

sponsoring area, sponsoring territory, promotion(al) territory, promotion(al) area · Förderungsgebiet n, gefördertes Gebiet

sponsoring committee, promotion(al) committee · Förderungsausschuß m

sponsoring contract, promotion(al) contract · Förderungsvertrag m

sponsor(ing firm) (US); "lead" firm, pilot firm, management sponsor · federführende Firma f

sponsoring fund, sponsoring money, promotion(al) fund, promotion(al) money · Förderungsfonds m, Förderungsmittel f, Förderungsgeld n

sponsoring hous(ebuild)ing, assisted hous(ebuild)ing, promotion(al) hous(ebuild)ing · geförderter Wohn(ungs)bau m, Wohn(ungs)bauförderung f

sponsoring hous(ebuild)ing institution, promotion(al) hous(ebuild)ing institution, assistance hous(ebuild)ing institution · Wohn(ungs)bauförderungsanstalt f

sponsoring individual system, assisting individual system, individual promotion(al) system, individual sponsoring system, individual assistance system, promotion(al) individual system · Individualförderungssystem n

sponsoring measure, promotion(al) measure · Förderungsmaßnahme f

sponsoring money, promotion(al) fund, promotion(al) money, sponsoring fund · Förderungsfonds m, Förderungsmittel f, Förderungsgeld n

sponsoring of export, export promotion, export assistance, promotion of export, assistance of export · Ausfuhrförderung f, Exportförderung

sponsoring of training, training assistance, training promotion · Ausbildungsförderung f, Schulungsförderung

sponsoring plan, promotion(al) plan · Förderungsplan m

sponsoring planner, promotion(al) planner · Förderungsplaner m

sponsoring planning, promotion(al) planning · Förderungsplanung f

sponsoring rate, promotion(al) rate · Förderungssatz m

sponsoring subject, promotion(al) subject · Förderungsgegenstand m

sponsoring system, promotion(al) system · Förderungssystem *n*

sponsoring territory, promotion(al) territory, promotion(al) area, sponsoring area · Förderungsgebiet *n*, gefördertes Gebiet

sponsorship · Trägerschaft *f*, Schirmherrschaft

sponsorship, management, sponsoring · Federführung *f* [*Arge*]

sporadic development, scattered development, dispersed development, noncompact development [*Developments occurring here and there without any co-ordinating feature to lick them or give them identity*] · Splitterbebauung *f*, Streubebauung, wilde Bebauung; Splitterüberbauung, Streuüberbauung, wilde Überbauung [*Schweiz*]

sporadic industry, city-forming industry, town-forming industry · stadtbildende Industrie *f*

sport fishing · Sportfischerei *f*

spot · per Kasse [*Käufe und Verkäufe in fremden Währungen*]

spot damage · Punktschaden *m*

spot price, cash price · Kaufpreis *m*

spot transaction, cash transaction · Kassageschäft *n*

spot zoning, exclusionary land use practice, discriminatory land use practice, snob zoning, exclusionary zoning, discriminatory zoning [*A land use restraint which has the effect of barring prospective lower income or minority residents*] · diskriminierende (Bau)Nutzung *f*, diskriminierende (bauliche) Nutzung, Ausschluß(bau)nutzung

spouse · Ehepartner *m*

sprawl area, sprawl territory · Gebiet *n* mit Bevölkerungsdichten zwischen 100 und 900 Einwohnern pro qkm

sprawl of cities, spread(ing) of towns, sprawl of towns, suburbanization, decentralization, formation of sub(urb)s, suburban process, suburban urbanization, (urban) spread, (urban) sprawl, outward spread, outward sprawl, suburban spread, suburban sprawl, spread(ing) of cities · Sied(e)lungsbrei *m*, Dezentralisation *f*, Ausufern *n*, Zersied(e)lung *f*, Überwucherung des städtischen Raumes, Dezentralisierung *f*

spread · Stallagegeschäft *n* [*Terminhandel*]

spread · Ausbreitung *f*, Zuführung [*räumliches Entwick(e)lungsgefälle*]

spread → sprawl of cities

spread and backwash effects · Ausbreitungs- und Rückschlagswirkungen *fpl* [*Regionalpolitik auf Wachstumspolen und -zentren basierend*]

spread city plan, dispersed regional city plan · Plan *m* punkthafter Verdichtungszonen in weiter Streuung über eine Stadtregion

spread effect, trickling-down effect · Ausbreitungswirkung *f* [*Regionalwirtschaft*]

spread(ing) of cities, sprawl of cities, spread(ing) of towns, sprawl of towns, suburbanization, decentralization, formation of sub(urb)s, suburban process, suburban urbanization, (urban) spread, (urban) sprawl, outward spread, outward sprawl, suburban spread, suburban sprawl · Sied(e)lungsbrei *m*, Dezentralisation *f*, Ausufern *n*, Zersied(e)lung *f*, Überwucherung des städtischen Raumes, Dezentralisierung *f*

springing devise · springendes vollziehbares (Land)Vermächtnis *n*

springing user · springendes vollziehbares dingliches Grund(stücks)recht *n* [*Es wird an jemanden künftig wirksames dingliches Recht gegeben, ohne daß gleichzeitig die Verleihungsurkunde ausdrücklich ein diesem künftig wirksamen dinglichen Recht unmittelbar vorausgehendes dingliches Recht schafft*]

spring population · Frühjahrsbevölkerung *f*

spurious correlation · vorgetäuschte Korrelation *f*

spur location · Spornlage *f*

to square · quadrieren

square, plaza · Gartenplatz *m*, Schmuckplatz

squared multiple correlation estimate · SMC-Schätzung *f*, Schätzung durch Quadrate der multiplen Korrelationskoeffizienten

square grid · Quadratraster *m*

square market place · Ring *m*

squatter · (An)Siedler *m* ohne Rechtstitel, wilder (An)Siedler *m*

squatter settlement, witch town, shanty town, (suburban) squatting colony, (suburban) squatting community · Blechhüttenvorort *m* [*Fehlbenennung: Blechhüttenstadt f*]

squatter's title [*Title acquired by one who has wrongfully occupied land without payment of rent*] · (Rechts)Titel *m* eines ehemaligen wilden (An)Siedlers

squatting community → (suburban) squatting community

squeeze of money → shortage of money

squire, landowner · Gutsbesitzer *m*, Gutsherr *m*

SRAC, average cost(s) in the short run, short-run average cost(s) · kurzfristige Durchschnittskosten *f*

stability of value · Wertbeständigkeit *f*

stadium, stade, quarentena terrae [*Latin*]; furlong; furlang [*Anglo-Saxon*]; furlongus [*Latin*]; ferlingus, ferlingum [*Low Latin*] [*A piece of land bounded or terminated by the length of a furrow*] · (Ge)Wende *(n), f,* Gewann *n,* Wande *f,* Wanne *f;* Flagge [*Ostfriesland*]

staff · Stab *m*

staff, personnel · Belegschaft *f,* Personal *n*

staff cost(s), personnel cost(s) · Personalkosten *f*

staff counsel, house counsel · Haus(rechts)anwalt *m,* Firmen(rechts)anwalt, Unternehmens(rechts)anwalt

staff department, personnel department · Personalabteilung *f*

staff incidental cost(s), staff incidentals · Personalnebenkosten *f*

staffing · Personalbesatz *m*

staff inspection, staff survey [*The examination of work to determine the number and grades of staff required*] · Personalplanung *f*

staff jurist → staff lawyer

staff lawyer, house jurist, staff jurist, lawyer employed in business, jurist employed in business, house lawyer · Hausjurist, Firmenjurist *m,* Unternehmensjurist

staff management, personnel management · Personalwirtschaft *f*

staff of teachers · Lehrerkollegium *n*

staff position [*Organization of business enterprises*] · Stabstelle *f,* Stabinstanz *f*

staff recruitment · Personalanwerbung *f*

staff shortage, personnel shortage · Personalknappheit *f,* Personalmangel *m,* Personalverknappung *f,* Personalklemme *f,* Personaldefizit *n*

staff size · Personalbestand *m*

staff standard · Stabmaßstab *m*

staff supplement, personnel supplement · Personalausbau *m*

staff survey, staff inspection [*The examination of work to determine the number and grades of staff required*] · Personalplanung *f*

to staff up · aufstocken [*Personal*]

stag · Nichtbörsenmitglied *n*

stag [*A speculator who buys a large amount of new issue of shares or stock if he thinks the price likely to rise above the offer price when dealings in it begin on the stock exchange, so that he hopes to be able to sell soon at a profit*] · Konzertzeichner *m*

stage · Abschnitt *m,* zeitlicher Abschnitt, Stadium *n,* Stufe *f*

stage-by-stage migration, step-by-step migration, migration in stages, migration in steps · stufenweise Wanderung *f,* Stufenwanderung

stage completion, completion in stages, completion in sections, completion by stages, stagewise completion, completion by sections, sectionwise completion, sectional completion · abschnittsweise Fertigstellung *f,* etappenweise Fertigstellung, stufenweise Fertigstellung

stage of bidding → stage of tendering

stage of building, stage of construction, building stage, construction stage · Baustadium *n,* Baustufe *f*

stage of planning, level of planning, planning stage, planning level · Planungsebene *f;* Planungsstufe *f* [*Fehlbenennung*]

stage of settlement and land use, settlement and land use stage · Sied(e)lungsstaffel *f*

stage of state, state stage · Zustandsstufe *f*

stage of tendering, stage of bidding, tendering stage, bidding stage [*The stage in which a suitable contractor is selected and an acceptable offer obtained*] · Ausschreibungsstadium *n,* Ausschreibungsstufe *f,* Stadium *n* der Angebotseinholung, Stufe *f* der Angebotseinholung, Stufe *f* der Ausschreibung, Stadium *n* der Ausschreibung, Angebotseinholungsstufe *f,* Angebotseinholungsstadium *n*

stage settlement · Staffel(an)sied(e)lung *f*

stage settlement association · Staffel(an)sied(e)lungsverband *m*

stage theory · Stufentheorie *f*

stagewise completion, completion by sections, sectionwise completion, sectional completion, stage completion, completion in stages, completion in sections, completion by stages · abschnittsweise Fertigstellung *f,* etappenweise Fertigstellung, stufenweise Fertigstellung

stagnation · Stillstand *m,* Stagnation *f,* Stockung *f*

stagnation of population, population stagnation, demographic stagnation · Bevölkerungsstagnation *f,* Bevölkerungsstillstand *m,* Bevölkerungsstockung *f*

stallage, boothage; bothagium [*Latin*] [*Customary dues paid to the lord of a manor or soil, for the pitching or standing of booths in fairs or markets*] · Budenzins *m,* Standgeld *n*

stamp duty · Stempelabgabe f, Stempelgebühr f, Stempelsteuer f

stamp duty law, stamp duty statute, stamp duty act · Stempelsteuergesetz n, Stempelabgabegesetz, Stempelgebührgesetz

stamp tariff · Stempeltarif m

standard · Währung f [Geld im Rechtssinn]

standard account form · Standardkontoform f

standard accounting (system) → standard (cost(s)) accounting (system)

standard amenities, standard modern conveniences, standard mod cons [The standard amenities are bath or shower, wash hand basin, sink, hot and cold water to each of these and WC] · Standardwohnkomfort m

standard arrangement · Regelvorkehrung f

standard blank (form) of contract, standard contract form, standard form of contract, standard contract blank (form) · Verbands-Vertragsformular n, Verbands-Vertragsformblatt n, Verbands-Vertragsvordruck m, Verbands-Vertragsmuster n, Verbands-Vertragsblankett n, Standard-Vertragsformblatt, Standard-Vertragsformular, Standard-Vertragsvordruck, Standard-Vertragsmuster, Standard-Vertragsblankett

standard building site, standard construction site, standard (job) site · Regelbaustelle f, Standardbaustelle

standard case, usual case · Regelfall m

standard condition · Verbandsbedingung f, Standardbedingung

standard construction site, standard (job) site, standard building site · Regelbaustelle f, Standardbaustelle

standard contract · Verbandsvertrag m, Standardvertrag

standard contract blank (form), standard blank (form) of contract, standard contract form, standard form of contract · Verbands-Vertragsformular n, Verbands-Vertragsformblatt n, Verbands-Vertragsvordruck m, Verbands-Vertragsmuster n, Verbands-Vertragsblankett n, Standard-Vertragsformblatt, Standard-Vertragsformular, Standard-Vertragsvordruck, Standard-Vertragsmuster, Standard-Vertragsblankett

standard contract law → standard (owner-contractor) contract law

standard costing (system), standard (cost(s)) accounting (system) · Standard(kosten)rechnung f, Standardkostenkalkulation f, Standardkostenermitt(e)lung, Standardkostenberechnung

standard cost(s) · Standardkosten f, Normkosten, Sollkosten je Einheit bei Planbeschäftigung [Kostenvorgaben mit Sollcharakter für eine bestimmte Betriebsleistung. In der Praxis werden Standardkosten oft mit Plankosten gleichgesetzt]

standard (cost(s)) accounting (system), standard costing (system) · Standard(kosten)rechnung f, Standardkostenkalkulation f, Standardkostenermitt(e)lung, Standardkostenberechnung

standard depth [lot] · Regeltiefe f [Parzelle]

standard deviation · Standardabweichung f

standard error · Standardfehler m

standard factory, flatted factory [A lowrise loft building] · Gebäude n mit vielen kleinen Industriebetrieben, Mietfabrik f

standard form · Standardformular n, Verbandsformular

standard form contract → (printed) standard form contract

standard form contract provisions, adhesion contract provisions, general contract provisions · allgemeine Geschäftsbestimmungen fpl

standard form map, map of standard form · Musterblattkarte f

standard form of building contract, standard form of construction contract · Verbandsformular-Bauvertrag m, Standardformular-Bauvertrag

standard form of sub-contract · Verbandsformular-Nachunternehmervertrag m, Standardformular-Nachunternehmervertrag

standardization · Normung f

to standardize · normen

standard(ized) drawing · Regelzeichnung f

standard (job) site, standard building site, standard construction site · Regelbaustelle f, Standardbaustelle

standard method of (ad)measurement · Standardaufmaßverfahren n

standard metropolitan (statistical) area, SM(S)A [Formerly called: metropolitan area. Standard metropolitan (statistical) areas with 100,000 inhabitants and more are termed "principal standard metropolitan (statistical) areas"] · (statistische) städtische Raumeinheit f, städtische statistische Raumeinheit

standard modern conveniences, standard mod cons, standard amenities [The standard amenities are bath or shower, wash hand basin, sink, hot and cold water to each of these and WC] · Standardwohnkomfort m

standard of comfort → standard of living

standard of cropping, system of cropping, system of farming, standard of farming ·

standard of farming — standing tender

Wirtschaftsart f [*Nutzung eines Ackergrundstückes*]

standard of farming, standard of cropping, system of cropping, system of farming · Wirtschaftsart f [*Nutzung eines Ackergrundstückes*]

standard of living, standard of comfort, living standard, comfort standard; level of living, living level (US) · Lebensstandard m, Lebensniveau n, Lebenshaltung f

standard (owner-contractor) contract law · Verbandsvertragsrecht n, Verbandsbauvertragsrecht, Standard(bau)vertragsrecht

standard period · Regelfrist f

standard plan · Standardplan m

standard planning · Standardplanung f

standard plot (of land) → standard (value) plot (of land)

standard price · Richtpreis m

standard procedure · Standardverfahren n, maßgebliches Verfahren

standard rate, fixed rate, unit rate, rate per unit · Einheitssatz m

standard regulations, standard prescriptions, standard rules · Regelvorschriften fpl, Regelrechtsvorschriften

standard return, normal yield, normal return, regular yield, standard yield, regular return · Normalrendite f

standard rule · Standardregel f

standard-run quantity, economic lot size · rationelle Stückzahl f

standard score · Standardpunktwert m [*Statistik*]

standard (spec(ification)) → (technical) standard (spec(ification))

standard sum, fixed sum · Einheitssumme f

standard tenancy contract · Einheitsmietvertrag m, Einheitswohnungsmietvertrag

standard (value) · Richtwert m

standard (value) plot (of land), standard (value) piece of land, standard (value) parcel (of land) · Richtwertgrundstück n

standard wage rate · Standardlohnsatz m

standard yield, regular return, standard return, normal yield, normal return, regular yield · Normalrendite f

standby cost(s) · Fixkostenbestandteil m, Festkostenbestandteil

to stand by decided cases, to uphold precedents, to maintain former adjudications; stare decisis [*Latin*] · bindend wirken [*Entscheid*]

standee · Stehplatzfahrgast m

standheight measurement · Höhenzuwachsmessung f von Waldbeständen

standing, state [*A certain civil qualification*] · Status m

standing [*USA*] · Geltendmachung f der Verletzung die persönliche Rechtssphäre betreffender Interessen

standing bid; standing (bid) proposal (US); standing offer, standing tender · konstantes Angebot n

standing conference of local planning authorities, joint local planning authorities · Planungsverband m [*In der Bauleitplanung. Zusammenschluß von Gemeinden und sonstigen Trägern öffentlich-rechtlicher Planungen mit dem Ziel, durch gemeinsame Bauleitplanung den Ausgleich der verschiedenen Belange zu erreichen. (§ 4 BBauG)*]

standing conference of planning boards, joint planning board · Planungsgemeinschaft f [*Vereinigung von Trägern öffentlich-rechtlicher Planungen zwecks gemeinsamer Raumplanung*]

standing conference of regional planning authorities, standing conference on regional planning, joint regional planning authorities · regionaler Planungsverband m, Regionalplanungsverband [*Bundesrepublik Deutschland*]; Landesplanungsverband

standing cost(s) · konstante Kosten f

standing crop · Biomasse f [*Menge der organischen Substanz in Form lebender Organismen je Flächen- und Raumeinheit zu einem bestimmten Zeitpunkt*]

standing hour · Stillstandsstunde f

standing in the family, marital status, marital condition, family relationship [*i.e. whether single, married, divorced or widowed*] · Familienstand m

standing joint committee · stehender gemeinsamer Ausschuß m

Standing Joint Committee [*England*] · Ausschuß m aus Vertretern der Bezirksstädte und der Grafschaft

standing offer, standing tender, standing bid; standing (bid) proposal (US) · konstantes Angebot n

standing order [*A written instruction to a supplier to provide a specified quantity of a product at specified time intervals until further notice*] · Dauerauftrag m

standing rate · fester Satz m, Festsatz

(standing) rules of court → rules of (court) practice

standing tender, standing bid; standing (bid) proposal (US); standing offer · konstantes Angebot n

(standing) timber → (standing) trees

standing to sue, active legitimation, capacity to sue, capability to sue, qualification to sue · Aktivlegitimation f [*Zur gerichtlichen Geltendmachung von Ansprüchen*]

standing traffic · ruhender Verkehr m

standing trees, (standing) timber, wood on the stem, timber on the stem · (an)stehendes Holz n, aufstehendes Holz, Holz auf dem Stamme, Holz auf dem Stock

standing void, becoming invalid · Ungültigwerden n

to stand void, to become invalid · ungültig werden

staple; stapula [*Latin*] [*A place where the buying and selling of wool, lead, leather and other articles, were put under certain terms*] · Stapelmarkt m, Stapelplatz m

staple court, court of the staple · Stapelmarktgericht n, Stapelplatzgericht

staple debt · Stapelschuld f

staple law, law of (the) staple · Stapelgesetz n

staple transaction · Stapelmarkt(handels)geschäft n, Stapelplatz(handels)geschäft

stapula [*Latin*]; staple [*A place where the buying and selling of wool, lead, leather and other articles, were put under certain terms*] · Stapelmarkt m, Stapelplatz m

star chamber; camera stellata [*Latin*] [*The court called by this name is commonly regarded as being the Aula Regis, sitting in the star chamber, a room at Westminster*] · Sternkammer f [*in England*]

star chart · Sternkarte f

stare decisis [*Latin*]; to stand by decided cases, to uphold precedents, to maintain former adjudications · bindend wirken [*Entscheid*]

star expansion → star(-shaped) expansion

star paging · Seitennumerierung f mit Stern

star pattern, star scheme · Sternmuster n, Oktupusmuster, Sternschema n, Oktupusschema [*Stadtstruktur*]

star pattern of growth → star(-shaped) expansion

star pattern plan, finger plan, radial corridors plan · Plan m der linearen Anordnung einer Stadtregion

star(-shaped) city, finger city, star(-shaped) town, finger town · Radialstadt f, sternförmige Stadt

star(-shaped) expansion, star(-shaped) pattern of growth [*A metropolitan growth alternative*] · sternförmige Erweiterung f

start(ing) date · Antrittsdatum n, Antrittstermin m [*Beginn eines Arbeitsverhältnisses*]

start(ing) date · Anlaufdatum n, Anlaufttermin m

starting salary, salary to start · Anfangsgehalt n

to state, to declare · erklären

to state [*case*] · formulieren [*Rechtsfall*]

state, position, mode of being, condition, nature · Beschaffenheit f

state, condition [*A particular mode of being of a thing*] · Zustand m

state, standing [*A certain civil qualification*] · Status m

state · Staat m

state → (federal) state

to state a case · zulassen einer Appellation

to state a case, to count, to declare, to recite [*To narrate the facts constituting a plaintiff's cause of action*] · vorbringen einer Klage

state act, state law, state statute · Staatsgesetz n

state administration · Staatsverwaltung f

state administrative rules and regulations · Verordnungsrecht n gliedstaatlicher Behörden [*USA*]

to state again in other words, to express again in other words, to restate, to reword, to change the wording of · umschreiben, neugestalten, neuschreiben, umgestalten [*Text*]

to state an account, to settle an account, to close an account · abschließen [*Konto*]

state area, state territory, area subject to one sovereign power, territory subject to one sovereign power · Staatsgebiet n, Hoheitsgebiet

state body · staatliches Organ n

state bond · Einzelstaatobligation f, Einzelstaatschuldverschreibung f [*USA*]

state boundary map · Staatengrenzenkarte f

state building project, state construction project · staatliches Bauvorhaben n, staatliches Bauprojekt n

state capital; Land capital [*In the Federal Republic of Germany*] · Landeshauptstadt f

state chief — statement of affairs

state chief, chief of state, head of state, state head · Staatsoberhaupt *n*

state church, established church · Staatskirche *f*

(state) citizen [*An enfranchised inhabitant of a country*] · (Staats)Bürger *m*

state comptroller, state controller · staatlicher (Bücher)Revisor *m*, staatlicher Buchprüfer, staatlicher Rechnungsprüfer, staatlicher Rechnungsrevisor

state constitution · Staatsverfassung *f*

state construction project, state building project · staatliches Bauvorhaben *n*, staatliches Bauprojekt *n*

state control → land control

state controller, state comptroller · staatlicher (Bücher)Revisor *m*, staatlicher Buchprüfer, staatlicher Rechnungsprüfer, staatlicher Rechnungsrevisor

state court · Staatengericht *n* [*USA*]

stated, settled, closed · abgeschlossen [*Konto*]

stated · formuliert

stated account, account stated [*An account (Forderungsbetrag) the balance of which, as determined by the creditor, has been accepted as correct, sometimes implicitly, by the debtor*] · Buchschuldbetrag *m*

stated capital, (authorized) capital (stock) [*The number of shares and usually the par or stated value of the capital (stock) that may be issued by a corporation under its articles of incorporation. In some instances the stockholders or directors may determine the stated value per share*] · Grundkapital *n*, Stammkapital, (genehmigtes) (Aktien)Kapital

state department of justice (US); ministry of justice (Brit.) · Justizministerium *n*

stated instal(l)ment · bestimmte Rate *f*

state domain · Staatsdomäne *f*

state enterprise, state undertaking · Staatsunternehmen *n*, Staatsbetrieb *m*, Staatsunternehmung *f*

state estate, state property · Staatsvermögen *n*, Staatshabe *f*, Staatsgut *n*

state examination · Staatsexamen *n*

to state falsely, to misstate · falsch aussagen, falsch angeben

state forest · Staatswald *m*

state government · Staatsregierung *f*

state government · Staatsverwaltung *f* [*In England sind Staatsverwaltung und Gemeindeverwaltung nicht gegenübergestellt, weil alles, was die Gemeinden tun, auch „Staatsverwaltung" ist. Der Engländer teilt vielmehr die Staatsverwaltung in „Zentralverwaltung" (central government) und „Lokalverwaltung" (local government). Der Staat als souveräne Zentralgewalt kann in England nach diesem Grundprinzip der Verfassung nur durch die Lokalverwaltung administrieren und nicht durch direkte Willensträger*]

state government employe(e) · Staatsbedienstete *m*

state head, state chief, chief of state, head of state · Staatsoberhaupt *n*

state in life, condition in life, rank in life, social rank, social state, social condition · soziale Stellung *f*

state institution · Staatsanstalt *f*

state land(s) · Staatsland *n*, Staatsländerei(en) *f (pl)*

state law, state statute, state act · Staatsgesetz *n*

state law, law of the country, national law, municipal law [*The law of a particular country as distinguished from international law*] · Nationalrecht *n*, Staatsrecht, Landesrecht

state legislation, state lawmaking · Staatsgesetzgebung *f*

stateless · staatenlos

state liability · Staatshaftung *f*, Staatshaftbarkeit *f*, Staatshaftpflicht *f*

statement, (oral) pleading, verbal pleading, pleading by word of mouth · Plädoyer *n*

statement, declaration · Erklärung *f*

statement · Aussage *f*, Angabe *f*

statement in lieu of prospectus, declaration in lieu of prospectus · Erklärung *f* an Prospektes statt

statement mistake, declaration mistake · Erklärungsirrtum *m*

statement (of account), abstract (of account), account statement, account abstract, bank statement, bank abstract · (Konto)Auszug *m*

statement of accumulated earnings, statement of retained earnings, surplus statement, statement of earned surplus · Ergebnisverwendungsrechnung *f*, Erfassung und Offenlegung von Rücklagenveränderungen

statement of affairs [*Statement to be submitted by a debtor to the official receiver within three days of the receiving order — if presented by the debtor — or seven days — if presented by the creditor. It must include details of the debtor's assets, liabilities, names and addresses of creditors, etc.*] · Vermögensaufstellung *f*, Vermögens(lage)bericht *m*, Masseverzeichnis *n*

statement of (an) account, settlement of (an) account · (Konto)Abschluß *m*, (Konto)Abrechnung *f*, Saldierung

statement of assets and liabilities → position of the company

statement of assignation, assignment declaration, cession declaration, assignment statement, cession statement, assignation statement, assignation declaration, statement of assignment, declaration of assignment, declaration of cession, statement of cession, declaration of assignation · Abtretungserklärung *f*, Zessionserklärung

statement of bankruptcy, bankruptcy statement, bankruptcy declaration, declaration of bankruptcy · Konkurserklärung *f*

statement of belief, belief statement · gutgläubige Aussage *f*, gutgläubige Angabe

statement of case · Rechtsauslegung *f*

statement of case, bill of exceptions, certificate of evidence [*A formal statement in writing of the objections or exceptions taken by a party during the trial of a cause to the decisions, rulings, or instructions of the trial judge, stating the objections, with the facts and circumstances on which it is founded, and, in order to attest its accuracy, signed and sealed by the judge; the object being to put the controverted rulings or decisions upon the record for the information of the appellate court when the ends of justice require it, the terms "bill of exceptions" and "statement of case" are regarded as synonymous*] · Niederschrift *f* der Beweisverhandlung, Aufzeichnung *f* der Beweisverhandlung

statement of cession, declaration of assignation, statement of assignation, assignment declaration, cession declaration, assignment statement, cession statement, assignation statement, assignation declaration, statement of assignment, declaration of assignment, declaration of cession · Abtretungserklärung *f*, Zessionserklärung

statement of change on net assets · Veränderungsbilanz *f*

statement of claim; declaration [*obsolete*] · Klageschrift *f* [*Zivilprozeß*]

statement of cost(s), cost(s) statement · Kostenaufstellung *f*

statement of defence (Brit.); statement of defense (US) · Verteidigungsschrift *f* [*Sie kann sowohl die Tatsachen als auch die Rechtsfolgerung bestreiten*]

statement of earned surplus, statement of accumulated earnings, statement of retained earnings, surplus statement · Ergebnisverwendungsrechnung *f*, Erfassung und Offenlegung von Rücklagenveränderungen

statement of facts · Darstellung *f* des streitigen und unstreitigen Sachverhalts und der Prozeßgeschichte

statement of financial condition → position of the company

statement of financial position → position of the company

statement of funds → statement of (sources and applications of) funds

statement of honest opinion · ehrliche Aussage *f*, ehrliche Angabe

statement of immediate execution, declaration of immediate execution · Erklärung *f* zur sofortigen Zwangsvollstreckung, Unterwerfungsklausel *f*

statement of operations, results of operations, profit and loss account, income statement, earnings and profit and loss statement · Gewinn- und Verlustrechnung *f*

statement of opinion, opinion testimony · Meinungsaussage *f*, Meinungsangabe *f*

statement of readiness, readiness statement · Ankündigung *f* der Hauptverhandlungsbereitschaft

statement of retained earnings, surplus statement, statement of earned surplus, statement of accumulated earnings · Ergebnisverwendungsrechnung *f*, Erfassung und Offenlegung von Rücklagenveränderungen

statement of (sources and applications of) funds, funds statement, summary of financial operations; capital-reconciliation statement (Brit.); accounting for the flow of funds · Kapital(zu)flußrechnung *f*, Finanzierungsrechnung, Finanz(zu)flußrechnung, Bewegungsbilanz *f*, Mittelherkunft- und -verwendungsrechnung

statement of the facts, case of the facts · Darlegung *f* eines Tatbestandes, Tatbestanddarlegung

statement of trust, trust declaration, trust statement, declaration of trust [*The act by which the person who holds the legal title to property or an estate acknowledges and declares that he holds the same in trust to the use of another person or for certain specified purposes*] · einseitige Erklärung *f*, treuhänderische Übertragung, Kundgabe *f* eines Treuhandverhältnisses

statement on the oath, affidavit, statutory declaration, statutory statement, declaration on the oath [*A written statement sworn on oath which may be used in certain cases as evidence*] · Erklärung *f* an Eidesstatt, Versicherung an Eidesstatt, eidesstattliche Erklärung, eidesstattliche Versicherung, schriftlicher Eid *m*

statements of probable construction cost(s), statements of probable building cost(s) · Angaben fpl über wahrscheinliche Baukosten

statement-wage, premium-wage, wage by results, piece-wage, efficiency-wage · Akkordlohn m, Leistungslohn

statement-wage contract, piece-wage contract, piece-work contract, job(bing) work contract, premium-wage contract, efficiency-wage contract · Akkord(lohn)vertrag m

statement-wage rate, premium-wage rate, piece-wage rate, efficiency-wage rate · Akkord(lohn)satz m

state of abeyance, abbayance, state of suspension, abeyancy, temporary nonexistence, expectancy of law, contemplation of law; abeyantia [Latin]; abeyance, condition of abeyance [In the law of real estate. Where there is no person in existence in whom an inheritance can vest, it is said to be in abeyance, that is, in expectation; the law considering is as always potentially existing, and ready to vest when ever a proper owner appears] · Schwebe(zustand) f, (m)

state of agricultural use, state of cultivation, state of farming · Anbauzustand m, Bearbeitungszustand, Kultivierungszustand [landwirtschaftlich genutztes Land]

state of an intestate, intestacy [The condition of a party who dies without having made a will] · Intestatzustand m

state of being a pupil, pupil state, ward state, state of being a ward, pupilage · Mündelstand m

state of being pendent, pendency · Anhängigkeit f

state of cultivation, state of farming, state of agricultural use · Anbauzustand m, Bearbeitungszustand, Kultivierungszustand [landwirtschaftlich genutztes Land]

state of dereliction · Herrenlosigkeit f

(state of) emergency, emergency state · Notstand m

state of exclusion, exclusionary state · Ausschließlichkeit f

state of facts, actual situation, established facts, ascertained facts, case facts, situation of facts · Sachlage f, Sachverhalt m, Tatbestand m

state of farming, state of agricultural use, state of cultivation · Anbauzustand m, Bearbeitungszustand, Kultivierungszustand [landwirtschaftlich genutztes Land]

state of law, law state · Rechtszustand m

state of location · Belegenheitsstaat m

state of martial law, state of military necessity · Ausnahmezustand m

state of matters, condition, circumstance · Umstand m, Lage f

state of prosperity [of a country] · Wohlstandszustand m, Blüte(zu)stand

state of separation, severalty · Trennungszustand m

state of (the) site, site state · Baustellenzustand m

state of transit, transit state · Durchgangsstaat m, Durchfuhrstaat

state or residence · Wohnstaat m

state-owned · staatseigen

State Paper Office · Staatsministerialarchiv n [England]

state planning, planning at national level, national planning · staatliche Planung f, Nationalplanung

state property, state estate · Staatsvermögen n, Staatshabe f, Staatsgut n

state-run (trade) union · Staatsgewerkschaft f

state servitude · Staatsdienstbarkeit f

"states" of a province, provincial diet · Landstände m (pl)

state sovereignty · Staatssouveränität f

state stage, stage of state · Zustandsstufe f

state statute, state act, state law · Staatsgesetz n

state territory, area subject to one sovereign power, territory subject to one sovereign power, state area · Staatsgebiet n, Hoheitsgebiet

state theory, theory of the state · Staatslehre f

state undertaking, state enterprise · Staatsunternehmen n, Staatsbetrieb m, Staatsunternehmung f

stating again in other words, expressing again in other words, changing the text, rewording, changing the wording · Textumschreibung f, Textumgestaltung, Textneugestaltung, Textneuschreibung

station, employment, office · Posten m

station (in life) · Stand m [Person]

station of destination, destination station · Bestimmungsstation f, Bestimmungsbahnhof m, Zielstation, Zielbahnhof

statistic · statistische Größe f, statistische Maßzahl f

statistical approach · statistische Kostenauflösung f

statistical data · statistisches Material n

statistical determination — statute of disappeared persons

statistical determination · statistische Bestimmung *f*

statistical error · statistischer Fehler *m*

statistical geography · statistische Geographie *f*

statistical inference · Schluß *m* von der Stichprobe auf die Grundgesamtheit

statistical information · statistische Angabe *f*

statistical mapping · Statistikkartographie *f*

statistical package · (statistisches) Programmpaket *n*

statistical publication · statistische Veröffentlichung *f*

statistical quality control · statistische Güteüberwachung *f*

statistics of community finances · Gemeindefinanzstatistik *f*, Kommunalfinanzstatistik

status · Abhängigkeitsverhältnis *n*

status, lawful position, legal position, lawful condition, legal condition · rechtliche Stellung *f*, Status *m*, Rechtsstellung

status activus processualis [*Latin*] · Verfahrensrechtstellung *f*

status of a citizen, condition of a citizen, rank of a citizen · Bürgerstand *m*, Bürgerstatus *m*

status of a serf, (pr(a)edial) bondage, bondage (on an estate), serfdom (on an estate), villanage, ville(i)nage; nativitas [*Latin*]; servile status, villein status, villain status [*Called by Britton "naifte"*] · Hörigenstatus *m*, Leibeigenschaft *f*, Grundhörigkeit *f*, (Grund)Untertänigkeit, Bauerndienst *m*

status of planning, planning status · Planungsstatus *m*

status striving, achievement-orientation, striving for success (in achievement) · Erfolgsstreben *n*

statutable bar, statutory bar · Gesetz(es)schranke *f*

statuta mixta [*Latin*] · Mischnormen *fpl* [*Normen, die Handlungen oder weitere Kategorien, die man nicht unter die statuta realia oder statuta personalia einordnen kann, beschreiben*]

statuta personalia [*Latin*] · Personennormen *fpl*

statuta realia [*Latin*] · Normen *fpl* unbewegliche Sachen betreffend

statute, by(e)-law · Satzung *f*, Statut *n*, autonomes Recht *n* einer Körperschaft, Rechtsnorm *f* einer Körperschaft mit Personenmehrheit [*Im internen materiellen Recht*]

statute → (local) by(e)-law

statute; statutum, actus [*Latin*]; Act of Parliament, enabling act, law made by Parliament, act · formelles Gesetz *n*, parlamentarisches Gesetz, (Parlaments)Gesetz

statute and law, act and law · Gesetz *n* und Recht *n*

statute concerning unfair competition, law concerning unfair competition, act concerning unfair competition · Gesetz *n* gegen unlauteren Wettbewerb

statute for execution, law for execution, act for execution · Ausführungsgesetz *n*

statute for public utility housing, law for public utility housing, act for public utility housing · Wohnungsgemeinnützigkeitsgesetz *n*

statute for the conservation of monuments, act for the preservation of monuments, law for the preservation of monuments, statute for the preservation of monuments, act for the conservation of monuments, law for the conservation of monuments · Denkmalpflegegesetz *n*, Denkmalerhaltungsgesetz, Denkmalschutzgesetz

statute law, written law, enacted law, statutory law, statutes; lex scripta, jus scriptum [*Latin*] [*The body of law enacted by Parliament*] · geschriebenes Recht *n*, gesetztes Recht, geschriebenes Parlamentsrecht, gesetztes Parlamentsrecht, (Parlaments)Gesetz(es)recht

statute-merchant [*In medi(a)eval English law. A security for a debt acknowledged to be due, entered into before the chief magistrate of some trading town, pursuant to the statute 13 Edw. I. De Mercatoribus, by which not only the body of the debtor might be imprisoned, and his goods seized in satisfaction of the debt, but also his land(s) might be delivered to the creditor till out of the rents and profits of them the debt be satisfied. Now fallen into disuse*] · Schuldverschreibung *f* [*Im mittelalterlichen England*]

statute number, law number, act number · Gesetz(es)nummer *f*

statute of banking, act of banking, bank(ing) law, bank(ing) statute, bank(ing) act, law of banking · Kreditwesengesetz *n*

statute of (building) (land) area replotting → act of (building) (land) area replotting

statute of building lines, building line act, building line law, building line statute, law of building lines, act of building lines · Fluchtliniengesetz *n*, Bauflucht(linien)gesetz

statute of disappeared persons, law of disappeared persons, act of disappeared persons, law of missing persons, act of missing persons, statute of missing persons · Verschollenheitsgesetz *n*

Statute of Distribution [*England*] · Gesetz *n* über die Verteilung beweglichen Nachlasses eines Intestaten

statute of fraud, act of fraud, law of fraud · Betrugsgesetz *n*

statute of inheritance, inheritance act, inheritance law, inheritance statute, law of inheritance, act of inheritance · Erb(schafts)gesetz *n*

Statute of King, Law of King, Act of King · Königsgesetz *n*

statute of land (possession) → law of land (possession)

statute of limitation, law of limitation, act of limitation, limitation statute, limitation law, limitation act · Verjährungsgesetz *n*

statute of missing persons, statute of disappeared persons, law of disappeared persons, act of disappeared persons, law of missing persons, act of missing persons · Verschollenheitsgesetz *n*

statute of possession → law of possession

statute of settlement, law of settlement, act of settlement · Ortsangehörigkeitsgesetz *n* [*In England. Die Arbeiter mußten an dem Ort wo sie heimatberechtigt waren bleiben, um zu verhüten, daß eine Gemeinde die Armen einer anderen unterstützen müßte*]

statute of the country, national act, national law, national statute, act of the country, law of the country · Landesgesetz *n*, Nationalgesetz, Staatsgesetz

statute (of the) staple [*In medi(a)eval English law. A security for a debt acknowledged to be due, so called from its being entered into before the mayor of the staple, that is so say, the grand market for the principal commodities or manufacturers of the Kingdom, formerly held by Act of Parliament in certain trading towns. In other respects it resembled the statute-merchant, but like that has now fallen into disuse*] · Stapel(platz)-Schuldverschreibung *f*, Stapelmarkt-Schuldverschreibung

statute of unearthing, law of unearthing, act of unearthing, unearthing law, unearthing statute, unearthing act · Ausgrabungsgesetz *n*

Statute of Uses 1535 [*England*] · Gesetz *n* zur Aufhebung der Spaltung [*dingliches Grund(stücks)recht*]

statute of wills, act of wills, law of wills, wills act, wills statute, wills law · Testamentsgesetz *n*

statute on inspection of insurance, law on inspection of insurance, act on inspection of insurance · Versicherungsaufsichtsgesetz *n*

statute on rights in registered ships, law on rights in registered ships, act on rights in registered ships · Schiffsrechtegesetz *n*

statute relating to protection against notice to terminate, act relating to protection against notice to terminate, law relating to protection against notice to terminate · Kündigungsschutzgesetz *n*

statute relating to protection against notice to terminate residential leases, act relating to protection against notice to terminate residential leases, law relating to protection against notice to terminate residential leases · Mieterkündigungsschutzgesetz *n*

statutes · Gesetz(es)sammlung *f*

statutes; lex scripta, jus scriptum [*Latin*]; statute law, written law, enacted law, statutory law [*The body of law enacted by Parliament*] · geschriebenes Recht *n*, gesetztes Recht, geschriebenes Parlamentsrecht, gesetztes Parlamentsrecht, (Parlaments)Gesetz(es)recht

statutes annotated, annotated statutes · annotierte Gesetzessammlung *f*

Statutes of Labourers · Arbeit- und Bettelgesetze *npl* [*Im mittelalterlichen England*]

statutes of mortmain · Gesetze *npl* die das Grundeigentum der toten Hand einschränken

statutes revised, revised statutes · Gesetz(es)sammlung *f* nach Sachsystem geordnet

statutes revised and annotated, revised statutes annotated · annotierte Gesetzessammlung *f* nach Sachsystemen geordnet

statutory, legal [*These two terms imply literal connection or conformity with statute law or its administration*] · gesetzlich

statutory acknowledg(e)ment, statutory recognizance, statutory recognition, legal acknowledg(e)ment, legal recognition, legal recognizance · gesetzliche Anerkenntnis *f*, gesetzliche Anerkennung

statutory age, legal age, full age, (age of (legal)) majority, age of consent, mature years [*The age fixed by law at which a person's consent to certain acts is valid in law*] · Majorennität *f*, Volljährigkeit(salter) *f, (n)*

statutory alien, legal alien · Ausländer *m* durch Gesetz(es)kraft

statutory announcement, legal announcement · gesetzliche öffentliche Bekanntmachung *f*, öffentliche gesetzliche Bekanntmachung, gesetzliche öffentliche Bekanntgabe f, öffentliche gesetzliche Bekanntgabe

statutory assets, legal assets [*That portion of the assets of a deceased party which by law are directly liable, in the hands of his executor or administrator, to the payment of debts and legacies. Such assets as can be reached in the hands of an executor or administrator, by a suit at law against him*] · gesetzliche Einlage f

statutory authority, statutory power, public authority, public power, legal authority, legal power · gesetzliche Gewalt f, gesetzliche Macht f, gesetzliche Hoheit f, gesetzliche Kompetenz f

statutory bar → statutable bar

statutory binding, lawbinding, legal binding · gesetzliche Bindung f, gesetzliche Gebundenheit f

statutory bond, legal bond [*A bond given to comply with the terms of a statute. Such a bond must cover whatever liability the statute imposes on the principal and the surety*] · gesetzliche Garantie f

(statutory) charge, legal charge, duty · Finanzabgabe f, gesetzliche Abgabe [*Eine Pflichtleistung in Geld oder Sachgut, die kraft öffentlicher Finanzhoheit den Bürgern auferlegt wird. Man unterscheidet 1. Generelle Abgaben (Steuern und Zölle) und 2. Spezielle Abgaben (Beiträge und Gebühren)*]

statutory charge to compensate currency depreciation losses in connection with built-on plots (of land), legal charge to compensate currency depreciation losses in connection with built-on plots (of land), duty to compensate currency depreciation losses in connection with built-on plots (of land) · Abgabe f zum Ausgleich der Geldentwertung bei bebauten Grundstücken

statutory committee, legal committee · gesetzlich vorgeschriebener Ausschuß m

statutory compulsion, legal compulsion · Gesetz(es)zwang m

statutory concept, legal concept · Gesetz(es)begriff m

statutory condition, legal condition · gesetzliche Bedingung f

statutory contribution, legal contribution · gesetzlicher Beitrag m

statutory corporation, legal corporation · gesetzliche Körperschaft f, gesetzliche Korporation

statutory corporation sole · gesetzliche Ein-Mann-Körperschaft f, gesetzliche Ein-Mann-Korporation f

statutory court · Gericht n auf Gesetz beruhend [*Im Gegensatz zum Verfassungsgericht*]

statutory declaration, statutory statement, declaration on the oath, statement on the oath, affidavit [*A written statement sworn on oath which may be used in certain cases as evidence*] · Erklärung f an Eidesstatt, Versicherung an Eidesstatt, eidesstattliche Erklärung, eidesstattliche Versicherung, schriftlicher Eid m

statutory disability, statutory incapacity, statutory incapability, non ability, legal disability, legal incapability, legal incapacity [*Want of ability to do an act in law*] · gesetzliche Unfähigkeit f, gesetzliches Unvermögen n

statutory discharge, legal release, statutory exoneration, legal dispensation, statutory dispensation, legal exemption, statutory exemption, legal discharge · gesetzlicher Dispens m, gesetzliche Freistellung f, gesetzliche Freigabe, gesetzliche Entlastung, gesetzliche Dispensierung, gesetzliche Befreiung

statutory dispensation, legal exemption, statutory exemption, legal discharge, statutory discharge, legal release, statutory release, legal exoneration, statutory exoneration, legal dispensation · gesetzlicher Dispens m, gesetzliche Freistellung f, gesetzliche Freigabe, gesetzliche Entlastung, gesetzliche Dispensierung, gesetzliche Befreiung

statutory duty, legal duty · gesetzliche Pflicht f

(statutory) duty of insurance, legal duty of insurance · Versicherungspflicht f

statutory duty to register, statutory duty to record, legal duty to register, legal duty to record · gesetzliche Eintragungspflicht f

statutory (dwelling) rent, legal (dwelling) rent, statutory residential rent, legal residential rent · gesetzliche (Wohnungs)Miete f, gesetzlicher (Wohnungs)(Miet)Zins m

statutory exception, legal exception · gesetz(esrecht)liche Ausnahme f

statutory exemption, legal discharge, statutory discharge, legal release, statutory release, legal exoneration, statutory exoneration, legal dispensation, statutory dispensation, legal exemption · gesetzlicher Dispens m, gesetzliche Freistellung f, gesetzliche Freigabe, gesetzliche Entlastung, gesetzliche Dispensierung, gesetzliche Befreiung

statutory existence, legal existence · gesetzliches Dasein n

statutory exoneration, legal dispensation, statutory dispensation, legal exemption, statutory exemption, legal discharge, statutory discharge, legal release, statutory release, legal exoneration · gesetzlicher Dispens m, gesetzliche Freistellung f, gesetzliche Freigabe, gesetzliche

Entlastung, gesetzliche Dispensierung, gesetzliche Befreiung

statutory fee, legal fee · gesetzliche Gebühr f, gesetzliches Honorar n

(statutory) fee schedule, table of (statutory) fees · Honorarordnung f, Gebührenordnung

(statutory) fee schedule for architects, table of (statutory) fees for architects · Gebührenordnung f für Architekten, Honorarordnung für Architekten, GOA

(statutory) fee schedule for architects and engineers, table of (statutory) fees for architects and engineers · Gebührenordnung f für Architekten und Ingenieure, Honorarordnung für Architekten und Ingenieure, HOAI

(statutory) fee schedule for engineers, table of (statutory) fees for engineers · Gebührenordnung f für Ingenieure, Honorarordnung für Ingenieure, GOI

statutory force, statutory strength, statutory validity, legal force, legal strength, legal validity · Gesetz(es)kraft f

statutory form, legal form · gesetzlich vorgeschriebene Form f

statutory framework, legal framework · Gesetz(es)rahmen m

statutory heir (male), heir (male) at law, right heir (male), legal heir (male), lawful heir (male), nearest kin, heir (male) general, general heir (male), heir (male) whatsoever [*One who takes the succession by relationship to the decedent and by force of law*] · Intestaterbe m, gesetzlicher Erbe

statutory holiday, legal holiday, public holiday · gesetzlicher Feiertag m

statutory incapability, non ability, legal disability, legal incapability, legal incapacity, statutory disability, statutory incapacity [*Want of ability to do an act in law*] · gesetzliche Unfähigkeit f, gesetzliches Unvermögen n

statutory income · steuerlich erfaßtes Einkommen n

statutory instrument, S.I. · Verwaltungserlaß m

statutory interest, statutory right; jus legitimum [*Latin*]; (subjective) right, (legal) interest, legal right [*A system of rights enjoyed by persons, as "subjects" or owner of rights, and by virtue of law*] · (subjektives) Recht n, Berechtigung f, Anrecht n, (Rechts)Anspruch m, gesetzliches (subjektives) Recht, subjektives (gesetzliches) Recht, dingliches Recht [*im B.G.B. auch als „Gegenstand" bezeichnet*]

statutory landlord/tenant relation(ship), legal landlord/tenant relation(ship), statutory tenancy, statutory tenure, legal tenancy, legal tenure · gesetzliches Mietverhältnis n [*Wohnungen; Geschäftsräume*]

statutory law, statutes; lex scripta, jus scriptum [*Latin*]; statute law, written law, enacted law [*The body of law enacted by Parliament*] · geschriebenes Recht n, gesetztes Recht, geschriebenes Parlamentsrecht, gesetztes Parlamentsrecht, (Parlaments)Gesetz(es)recht

statutory limit, legal limit · gesetzliche Grenze f

statutory limitation (period), legal period of limitation, statutory period of limitation, legal limitation (period) · gesetzliche Verjährungsfrist f

statutory list · schwarze Liste f

statutory (local) venue, legal (local) venue · gesetzlicher Gerichtsstand m, gesetzlicher Gerichtsort

statutory owner, statutory proprietor, legal proprietor, owner by (common) law, proprietor by (common) law, owner in (common) law, proprietor in (common) law, legal owner [*As opposed to the "equitable owner"*] · Eigentümer m nach Gemeinrecht, gesetzlicher Eigentümer [*Die Eigentumsaufspaltung nach Gemeinrecht und Billigkeitsrecht ist die Folge dieser dualistischen Entwicklung in England bis 1873/75*]

statutory ownership (of property) → legal title

statutory pecuniary charge, legal pecuniary charge · gesetzliche Geldlast f, gesetzliche Geldbelastung f

statutory period of limitation, legal limitation (period), statutory limitation (period), legal period of limitation · gesetzliche Verjährungsfrist f

statutory plan, legal plan · gesetzlicher Plan m

statutory planning, legal planning · gesetzliche Planung f

statutory position, legal position · gesetzliche Stellung f

statutory possession, legal possession · gesetzlicher Besitz m

statutory possessor, legal possessor · gesetzlicher Besitzer m

statutory power, public authority, public power, legal authority, legal power, statutory authority · gesetzliche Gewalt f, gesetzliche Macht f, gesetzliche Hoheit f, gesetzliche Kompetenz f

statutory power, legal power · gesetzliche Ermächtigung f

statutory power of appointment, statutory power of disposition, statutory right of appointment, statutory right of disposition, public power of appointment,

statutory pre-emption — statutory separate property

public power of disposition, public right of appointment, public right of disposition, legal power of appointment, legal power of disposition, legal right of appointment, legal right of disposition [*It is conferred by statute upon persons exercising the duties of a particular office, e.g. as trustee, or as tenant for life*] · gesetzliche Verfügungsbefugnis *f*, gesetzliche Bestimmungsbefugnis, gesetzliches Verfügungsrecht *n*, gesetzliches Bestimmungsrecht

statutory pre-emption → statutory (right of) pre-emption

statutory prescription, statutory regulation, legal prescription, legal regulation, statutory rule, legal rule · gesetzliche Vorschrift *f*, Gesetz(es)vorschrift

statutory prevention, legal prevention · gesetzliche Verhütung *f*

statutory price, official price, price fixed by authority, licensed price, licenced price · Taxe *f* [*Ein aufgrund eines Rechtes behördlich festgesetzter Preis*]

statutory proprietor, legal proprietor, owner by (common) law, proprietor by (common) law, owner in (common) law, proprietor in (common) law, legal owner, statutory owner [*As opposed to the "equitable owner"*] · Eigentümer *m* nach Gemeinrecht, gesetzlicher Eigentümer [*Die Eigentumsaufspaltung nach Gemeinrecht und Billigkeitsrecht ist die Folge dieser dualistischen Entwicklung in England bis 1873/75*]

statutory proprietorship → legal title

statutory protection, legal protection, relief · Gesetz(es)schutz *m*

statutory purpose, legal purpose · gesetzlicher Zweck *m*

statutory recognizance, statutory recognition, legal acknowledg(e)ment, legal recognition, legal recognizance, statutory acknowledg(e)ment · gesetzliche Anerkenntnis *f*, gesetzliche Anerkennung

statutory redemption right, legal redemption right, statutory right of redemption, legal right of redemption, statutory right to redeem, legal right to redeem · gesetzliches Ablösungsrecht *n*, gesetzliches Einlösungsrecht, gesetzliches Auslösungsrecht

statutory regulation, legal regulation · gesetzliche Regelung *f*

statutory regulation, legal prescription, legal regulation, statutory rule, legal rule, statutory prescription · gesetzliche Vorschrift *f*, Gesetz(es)vorschrift

statutory relation(ship), legal relation(ship) · gesetzliche Beziehung *f*, gesetzliches Verhältnis *n*

statutory release, legal exoneration, statutory exoneration, legal dispensation, statutory dispensation, legal exemption, statutory exemption, legal discharge, statutory discharge, legal release · gesetzlicher Dispens *m*, gesetzliche Freistellung *f*, gesetzliche Freigabe, gesetzliche Entlastung, gesetzliche Dispensierung, gesetzliche Befreiung

statutory report · Gründungsbericht *m*, Gründerbericht [*Aktiengesellschaft*]

statutory reserve → statutory (surplus) reserve

statutory residential rent, legal residential rent, statutory (dwelling) rent, legal (dwelling) rent · gesetzliche (Wohnungs)Miete *f*, gesetzlicher (Wohnungs)(Miet)Zins *m*

statutory review, legal review · Gesetzmäßigkeitskontrolle *f*

statutory right; jus legitimum [*Latin*]; (subjective) right, (legal) interest, legal right, statutory interest [*A system of rights enjoyed by persons, as "subjects" or owner of rights, and by virtue of law*] · (subjektives) Recht *n*, Berechtigung *f*, Anrecht, (Rechts)Anspruch *m*, gesetzliches (subjektives) Recht, subjektives (gesetzliches) Recht, dingliches Recht [*im B.G.B. auch als „Gegenstand" bezeichnet*]

statutory right of appointment, statutory right of disposition, public power of disposition, public right of appointment, public right of disposition, legal power of disposition, legal right of appointment, legal right of disposition, statutory power of appointment, statutory power of disposition [*It is conferred by statute upon persons exercising the duties of a particular office, e.g. as trustee, or as tenant for life*] · gesetzliche Verfügungsbefugnis *f*, gesetzliches Bestimmungsbefugnis, gesetzliches Verfügungsrecht *n*, gesetzliches Bestimmungsrecht

statutory (right of) pre-emption, statutory (right of) preëmption · gesetzliches Vorkaufsrecht *n*

statutory right of redemption, legal right of redemption, statutory right to redeem, legal right to redeem, statutory redemption right, legal redemption right · gesetzliches Ablösungsrecht *n*, gesetzliches Einlösungsrecht, gesetzliches Auslösungsrecht

statutory rule, legal rule, statutory prescription, statutory regulation, legal prescription, legal regulation · gesetzliche Vorschrift *f*, Gesetz(es)vorschrift

statutory seisin, legal seisin · gesetzliche Gewere *f*

statutory separate property, statutory separate estate, legal separate property, legal separate estate · Vorbehaltgut *n* nach Gesetz(es)recht, Sondervermögen *n* nach Gesetz(es)recht, freies Ver-

statutory signification — step lease(hold)

mögen nach Gesetz(es)recht, getrenntes Vermögen nach Gesetz(es)recht

statutory signification, legal signification · gesetzliche Bedeutung f

statutory statement, declaration on the oath, statement on the oath, affidavit, statutory declaration [*A written statement sworn on oath which may be used in certain cases as evidence*] · Erklärung f an Eidesstatt, Versicherung an Eidesstatt, eidesstattliche Erklärung, eidesstattliche Versicherung, schriftlicher Eid m

statutory strength, statutory validity, legal force, legal strength, legal validity, statutory force · Gesetz(es)kraft f

statutory (surplus) reserve, legal (surplus) reserve · gesetzliche Rücklage f

statutory tenancy, statutory tenure, legal tenancy, legal tenure, statutory landlord/tenant relation(ship), legal landlord/tenant relation(ship) · gesetzliches Mietverhältnis n [*Wohnungen; Geschäftsräume*]

statutory tenure, legal tenure · gesetzliche Dienstzeit f [*Beamte*]

statutory term · gesetzliche Frist f

statutory terminology, legal terminology · Gesetz(es)terminologie f

statutory title → legal title

statutory trust, legal trust [*Part of the property is held by a personal representative to be divided equally among issue and other classes of relatives of an intestate who are alive at the death of the intestate as soon as they attain 18, or marry*] · Nachlaß(vermögen) m, (n) in den Händen des Erbschaftsverwalters als Treuhänder

statutory undertaker (Brit.); (public) utility (US) · (öffentlicher) Versorgungsbetrieb m, (öffentliches) Versorgungsunternehmen n, (öffentliche) Versorgungsunternehmung f

statutory undertaker law (Brit.); (public) utility law (US) · Versorgungsbetriebsrecht n, Versorgungsunternehmensrecht

statutory validity, legal force, legal strength, legal validity, statutory force, statutory strength · Gesetz(es)kraft f

statutory venue → (local) venue

statutory warranty deed (US) [*It contains five warranties: 1. that the grantor is the owner of the lands and has the right to convey them; 2. that the lands are unincumbered by mortgage or other burden (unless otherwise stated); 3. that the grantee shall have quiet enjoyment, that is, shall not be put out of possession by anyone having superior title; 4. that the grantor will warrant and defend the grantee in these rights and 5. that the grantor will execute any further instrument necessary to make perfect the grantee's title to the property*], full warranty deed · volle Gewährleistungsurkunde f

staurum [*Latin*]; head of cattle [*In old records, a stock of cattle. A term of common occurrence in the accounts of monastic establishments*] · Rinderbestand m, Rindviehbestand

to stay [*execution*] · einstellen, aussetzen [*Zwangsvollstreckung*]

to stay, to stop · aussetzen, einstellen [*Verfahren*]

stay, stop · Aussetzung f, Einstellung f [*Verfahren*]

stay [*execution*] · Einstellung f, Aussetzung [*Zwangsvollstreckung*]

staying, stopping · Aussetzen n, Einstellen n [*Verfahren*]

stay(ing) the (court) proceedings · Verfahrensaussetzung f [*Einrede der Schiedsgerichtsbarkeit*]

stay-in strike · Bummelstreik m

steadily applied, active, laborious, diligent · aktiv, unermüdlich, fleißig

steady flow traffic · Immerfahrtverkehr m

stealing of cattle, larceny of cattle, cattle-stealing, cattle larceny · Rindviehdiebstahl m

steam boat company · Dampfschiffahrtsgesellschaft f

steam boiler insurance · Dampfkesselversicherung f

steam-driven urban railway (Brit.); steam-driven urban railroad (US) · dampfgetriebene Stadtbahn f

steel yard, stilyard; guildhalda teutonicorum [*Latin*] [*A place or house in London, where the fraternity of the "Easterling merchants", otherwise called "The merchants of the Hanse and Almaine", had their abode*] · Stahlhof m in London

stenographic record · Kurzschriftniederschrift f

step-by-step approach, approach in stages, stagenise approach · stufenweise Kostenauflösung f, Stufenkostenauflösung

step-by-step migration, migration in stages, migration in steps, stage-by-stage migration · stufenweise Wanderung f, Stufenwanderung

step-by-step reform, reform in stages · stufenweise Reform f, Stufenreform

step lease(hold), step demise, step tenancy, step tenure · Pacht f mit periodischem Anwachsen der Rente, Verpachtung f mit periodischem Anwachsen der

Rente, Nutzungsrechtvergabe f mit periodischem Anwachsen der Rente

to step off (a distance), to measure out by steps, to pace · abschreiten [*Behördlich messend abgehen*]

stepped-up programme; stepped-up program (US) · erhöhtes Programm n

steppe-heath · Steppenheide f

step regression · Stufenregression f

step tablet · Grau(wert)skala f, Grauwertkeil m [*Kartographie*]

step tenancy → step lease(hold)

step tenure → step lease(hold)

stereophotogrammetry · Stereophotogrammetrie f

stereoscopic perception · stereoskopische Wahrnehmung f

steward of manor, bailiff, (land) steward [*A person that has administration and charge of lands, goods and chattels to make the best benefit for the owner*] · Amtmann m, (Guts)Verwalter m, Gutsschulze m, Vogt m, Rentenmeister m, Haushofmeister

steward → (land) steward

stilyard; guildhalda teutonicorum [*Latin*]; steel yard [*A place or house in London, where the fraternity of the "Easterling merchants", otherwise called "The merchants of the Hanse and Almaine", had their abode*] · Stahlhof m in London

stimulus overload · bestmögliches Reizniveau n

stint [*In English law. Used as descriptive of a species of common*] · beschränkte Anzahl f

stinted common (of pastur(ag)e) · Angerrecht n mit einer beschränkten Anzahl von Tieren, (Vieh)Weiderecht mit einer beschränkten Anzahl von Tieren, Hütungsrecht mit einer beschränkten Anzahl von Tieren, Ätzung f mit einer beschränkten Anzahl von Tieren, Atzung mit einer beschränkten Anzahl von Tieren

stipendiary magistrate · besoldeter Friedensrichter m, berufsmäßiger Friedensrichter, bezahlter Friedensrichter, ständiger Friedensrichter, beamteter Friedensrichter, Polizeirichter, Berufsfriedensrichter

stipendiary magistrate → justice of the peace

stipendiary magistrate's court; police court [*obsolete*] [*A petty sessional court, held in London and in other cities by a magistrate*] · Polizeigericht n, Friedensgericht unter Vorsitz eines berufsmäßigen Friedensrichters

to stipulate, to condition(alize) · (aus)bedingen, konditionieren

stipulated, conditionate, conditioned · ausbedungen

stipulated sum agreement, lump-sum agreement · Pauschalabkommen n, Pauschalabmachung f, Pauschalvereinbarung

stipulated sum contract, lump-sum contract, fixed-price contract [*Under such a contract the contractor agrees to perform the entire work specified in the contract at a price agreed to and fixed at the time the contract is entered into*] · Pauschalvertrag m

stipulated sum contract with billing price and price ceiling, fixed-price contract with billing price and price ceiling, lump-sum contract with billing price and price ceiling · Pauschalvertrag m mit Kostenrechnung und Preishöchstgrenze [*Der Pauschalvertragspreis wird erst während der Vertragsdurchführung festgelegt*]

stipulated sum contract with escalation, fixed-price contract with escalation, lump-sum contract with escalation · Pauschalvertrag m mit Änderung [*Ausnahmefall. Der Pauschalpreis kann gemäß einem vorher vereinbarten Verfahren geändert werden, wenn sich die wirtschaftliche Situation ändert*]

stipulation; stipulatio [*Latin*] · Stipulation f, Ausbedingung f

stipulation clause · Stipulationsklausel f, Ausbedingungsklausel

stiura [*Latin*] → petitio

stochastic continuity · stochastische Stetigkeit f

stochastic convergence, convergence in probability · stochastische Konvergenz f

stochastic dependence · stochastische Abhängigkeit f

stochastic differentiability · stochastische Unterscheidbarkeit f

stochastic differential equation · stochastische Differentialgleichung f

stochastic differential game · stochastisches Differentialspiel n

stochastic independence · stochastische Unabhängigkeit f

stochastic model · stochastisches Modell n

stochastic process · stochastischer Vorgang m

stochastic relation(ship) · stochastische Beziehung f

stochastic variable, variate, aleatory variable, random variable · stochastische Variable f, Zufallvariable

stock [*Great Britain*]; bond [*USA*] [*The term "bond" designates in Great Britain*

stock — stockturn proceeding

short- and medium-dated stocks, that means stocks up to ten years until maturity] · Schuldverschreibung f, Obligation f [nicht von einer privaten Kapitalgesellschaft]

stock [It is one of the two main types of security dealt with on the stock exchange, the other being share. Stocks are usually quoted per 100 units of currency nominal value, but fractions may be bought or sold, whereas a share is not divisible] · Aktie f

stock → (live)stock

stock account · Warenkonto n

stock book · Lagerbuch n

stock breeder → (live)stock breeder

stock breeding → (live)stock breeding

(stock)broker · Effektenmakler m, Kommissionär, Wertpapiermakler, Börsenmakler [Er kauft und verkauft an der Börse im Auftrag und für Rechnung von nicht der Börse Angehörigen]

stock class, class of stock · Aktiengattung f

stock company (US); joint-stock company, incorporated public company · Aktiengesellschaft f, AG

stock company limited by shares → (joint stock) company limited by shares

stock control [The systematic regulation of stock levels with respect to time and quantity] · Lager(bestand)überwachung f

stock conversion, conversion of stock · Konvertierung f einer Anleihe durch Herabsetzung des Zinsfußes

stock dealer → (live)stock dealer

stock depletion cost(s) · Fehlmengenkosten f

stock dividend (US); capital bonus (Brit.) · Aktiendividende f, Dividende in Form von jungen Aktien der gleichen Art, Dividende in Aktien statt in bar, Gratisaktie f

stock exchange · Effektenbörse f, Wertpapierbörse

stock exchange gazette · Wertpapierbörsenblatt n, Effektenbörsenblatt

stock exchange turnover tax · Börsenumsatzsteuer f

stock exhaust, stock-out [The occurrence of a zero stock balance, not necessarily reflecting a shortage] · erschöpfter Lagerbestand m

stock farm → (live)stock farm

stock farmer → (live)stock farmer

stock farming → (live)stock farming

stock holder · Aktieninhaber m

stock holder → (live)stock farmer

stockholders' resolution · Hauptversammlungsbeschluß m

stock husbandry → (live)stock farming

stocking transaction · Inventarfinanzierung f

stock insurance → (live)stock insurance

stock-in-trade, trade stock [The type of goods applicable to a particular branch of trade] · Sektorgut n

stock man → (live)stock farmer

stockmapping · Vorratskartierung f [Wald]

stock market → (live)stock market

stock of cattle, cattle stock · Rindviehbestand m

stock of land(s) → resource of land

stock of space, space stock, space reserve, reserve of space · Raumvorrat m, Raumreserve f

stock order, stores order [A production order to manufacture a product to replenish stock in a store] · Lagerauftrag m

stock-out, stock exhaust [The occurrence of a zero stock balance, not necessarily reflecting a shortage] · erschöpfter Lagerbestand m

stockpiling [The accumulation of stocks of strategic raw materials and foodstuffs on the expectation of war] · Kriegsvorratswirtschaft f

stock purchase (pension) plan, stock purchase retirement plan, stock purchase benefit plan · Pensionsplan m mit Belegschaftsaktienerwerb, (Alters)Versorgungsplan mit Belegschaftsaktienerwerb

stock raising → (live)stock breeding

stock record · Lagerinventar n

stock register · Aktienbuch n

stock right · Aktienbezugsrecht n

stocks → joint-stock

stock size → (live)stock size

stock taking · Inventur f

stock taking sale · Inventurausverkauf m

stockturn, turnover · Umsatz m

stockturn decrease, turnover decrease · Umsatzrückgang m

stockturn proceeding, turnover proceeding · Besitznahme f des schuldnerischen Vermögens durch den Gläubiger, (Verfahren n zur) Inbesitznahme des schuldnerischen Vermögens durch den Gläubiger

stockturn ratio — straightening

stockturn ratio, turnover ratio · Umschlaggeschwindigkeit *f* einer Anlage von Wertpapieren innerhalb eines Jahres

stockturn tax, turnover tax · Umsatzsteuer *f*

stollo hereditarius [*Latin*] · Erbstollenrecht *n*, servitutisches Erbstollenrecht, Erbstollengerechtigkeit *f*, Erbstollendienstbarkeit, Erbstollenservitut *n*, *f* [*Unter Erbstollen versteht man Stollen, welche zum Besten fremder Gruben angelegt sind und die Bestimmung haben, neue Minerallagerstätten zu erschließen oder den fremden Gruben Wasser- und Wetterlösung zu verschaffen*]

stonemason's lodge · Bauhütte *f*

stone wall · Steinmauer *f*

to stop, to cease, to abandon · einstellen [*Arbeit(en)*]

to stop, to stay · aussetzen, einstellen [*Verfahren*]

stop, stay · Aussetzung *f*, Einstellung [*Verfahren*]

stop → (transit) stop

stopbooking · Buchungssperre *f*

stop line · Ausweitungsbegrenzung *f*

stop of construction work(s) → stop(ping) of construction work(s)

stop order · Aushändigungsverbot *n* [*Konkurs*]

stoppage in transitu, stoppage in transit right, right of stoppage in transit [*The right which a vendor, when he sells goods on credit to another, has of resuming the possession of the goods, while they are in the hands of a carrier or middle man, in their transit to the consignee or vendee, and before they arrive into his actual possession, or to the destination which he has appointed for them, on his becoming bankrupt or insolvent*] · Anhalterecht *n*, Rückkaufrecht, Verfolgungsrecht, Hemmungsrecht

stoppage of payment, payment stoppage · Zahlungssperre *f*, Opposition *f*

stopped, abandoned, ceased · eingestellt [*Arbeiten*]

stopping, staying · Aussetzen *n*, Einstellen *n* [*Verfahren*]

stop(ping) of work(s), cessation of work(s), abandonment of work(s) [*Cessation of operation and intent(ion) of owner and contractor to cease operations permanently*] · Einstellung *f* der Arbeit(en), Arbeitseinstellung

storage · Lagerung *f*

storage · Vorratshaltung *f*

storage of furniture, furniture storage · Möbellagerung *f*

storage tank ordinance · Lagerbehälterverordnung *f*

store, shop · Ladengeschäft *n*, (Verkaufs)Laden *m*

store front(age), shopping front(age) · Ladenfront *f*

storekeeper, shopkeeper · Ladenkrämer *m*

store lease, store demise, shop lease, shop demise · Ladenpacht *f*

store lessee, shop lessee · Ladenpächter *m*

store location, shop site, store site, shop location · (Verkaufs)Ladenstandort *m*, Ladengeschäftsstandort

store ownership (of property), store proprietorship, store property, shop ownership (of property), shop proprietorship, shop property · Ladeneigentum *n*

store parcel, shop plot, shop parcel, store plot · Ladengrundstück *n*

store plot, store parcel, shop plot, shop parcel · Ladengrundstück *n*

store property → shop ownership (of property)

store proprietorship → shop ownership (of property)

store quarter, shop quarter · Ladenquartier *n*, Ladengeschäftsquartier, Laden(geschäfts)viertel *n*

store rent, shop rent · Ladenmiete *f*

store site, shop location, store location, shop site · (Verkaufs)Ladenstandort *m*, Ladengeschäftsstandort

stores order, stock order [*A production order to manufacture a product to replenish stock in a store*] · Lagerauftrag *m*

(stores) purchasing committee · Beschaffungsausschuß *m*

store underlease, store underdemise, shop underdemise, shop underlease · Ladenunterpacht *f*

to store (up) · (auf)speichern

storey proper (Brit.); story proper (US) · Vollgeschoß *n*, Volletage *f*, Vollstockwerk *n*

storm damage, damage by storm · Gewitterschaden *m*

straddle · Prämiengeschäft *n* zum gleichen Kurs

straight bill of lading, not negotiable bill of lading · nicht begebbares Konnossement *n*

straight bond · regelmäßige Schuldverschreibung *f*

straightening · Begradigung *f*

straight line depreciation · g(e)radlinige Abschreibung f

straight line distance · g(e)rade Entfernung f

straight line method, age-life method · lineare Abschreibung f

straight mortgage, definite term mortgage, (de)terminable mortgage · kündbare Hypothek f

straits, narrow (sea) [*A sea which runs between two coasts not far apart. This term is sometimes applied to the English Channel*] · Meer(es)enge f, Kanal m

stranger · Fremde m

stranger · Außenstehende m

stranger's cattle · fremdes (Rind)Vieh n

strategy of decision-taking, decision-taking strategy, decision(-making) strategy, strategy of decision(-making) · Entscheidungsstrategie f

strategy of planning, planning strategy · Planungsstrategie f

stratification · Schichtung f

stratification theory, theory of stratification · Schichtungstheorie f

straw-hut village · Strohhüttendorf n

straw poll, opinion poll · Meinungsumfrage f

stream, non-tidal river · Fluß m

stream bank · Flußufer n

stream bank town, stream bank city · Flußuferstadt f

stream basin · Flußsystem n

stream bed · Flußbett n

stream bed accretion · Flußbettzulandung f, Flußbettanschwemmung

stream border, stream frontier · Flußgrenze f

stream conservancy (Brit.); stream supervision commission (US) · Flußaufsicht(samt) f, (n)

stream development · Flußausbau m

stream for rafting, floatable stream [*A stream used for floating logs, rafts, etc.*] · Flößer(ei)fluß m

stream frontier → stream border

to streamline [*e.g. a system*] · straffen

streamlot · Flußhufe f

stream of commuters, commuting stream · Pendlerstrom m

stream of income, income stream · Einkommensstrom m

stream of (migration) movement, flow of (migration) movement, (migration) movement current, (migration) movement stream, (migration) movement flow, migration flow, migration stream, current of (migration) movement · Bewegungsstrom m, Wanderungsstrom

stream supervision commission (US), stream conservancy (Brit.) · Flußaufsicht(samt) f, (n)

street · Stadtstraße f ohne Vorgarten

street · Stadtstraße f in Ost-West-Richtung [*USA*]

street · Gemeindestraße f, Kommunalstraße, Ortsstraße

street → (urban) street

street appearance · Stadtstraßenbild n

street arrangement, arrangement of streets · Stadtstraßenanordnung f

street authority · Stadtstraßenbehörde f

streetcar line, troll(e)y car line (US); tramway line (Brit.) · Straßenbahnlinie f

streetcar suburb(an place) · Straßenbahnvorort m

street classification · Stadtstraßeneinteilung f

street clean(s)ing · Stadtstraßenreinigung f

street front · Straßenfront f

street frontager · Straßenanlieger m

(street) front meter · (Straßen)Frontmeter n, m

(street) front meter scale · (Straßen)Frontmetermaßstab m

street ground · Stadtstraßengelände n

street hamlet · Straßenweiler m

street illumination contract, street lighting contract · (Stadt)Straßenbeleuchtungsvertrag m

street land · Stadtstraßenland n

street law · Gemeindestraßengesetz n, Kommunalstraßengesetz, Ortsstraßengesetz

street lighting contract, street illumination contract · (Stadt)Straßenbeleuchtungsvertrag m

street line → (front) street line

street map → (community) street map

street market · Straßenmarkt m

street network · Stadtstraßennetz n

street planning · Stadtstraßenplanung f

street playground · Spielstraße f

street refuge, saving place, resting place · Bürgersteiginsel f

street row settlement · Straßenreihen(an)sied(e)lung *f*

street sleeper [*A mobile squatter without a dwelling*] · Penner *m*

street sleeping · Pennen *n*

street trader, barrow-boy, costermonger · Straßenhändler *m*

street vendor · Straßenverkäufer *m*

street with low buildings · Flachbaustraße *f*

street work(s) · Stadtstraßenarbeit(en) *f (pl)*

street work(s) code · Stadtstraßenbauordnung *f*

to strengthen, to corroborate · bekräftigen

to strengthen ex post facto, to lend additional support, to feed [*Example: "The interest when it accrues feeds the estoppel"*] · verstärken

strengthening evidence, corroborating proof, corroborative proof, strengthening proof, confirmatory evidence, confirmatory proof, corroborating evidence, corroborative evidence · bekräftigender Beweis *m*

strength of personality, force of personality · Ausstrahlungskraft *f*

strength of title, force of title · (Rechts)Titelkraft

stretch of coast, coast(al) stretch · Küstenstreifen *m*

strict duty · Erfolgsgarantiepflicht *f*

strict liability, absolute liability · Gefährdungshaftung *f*, Gefährdungshaftpflicht *f*, Haftung ohne Verschulden, Haftpflicht ohne Verschulden, Gefährdungshaftbarkeit *f*, Haftbarkeit ohne Verschulden

strictly determined game, game with saddle point · streng bestimmtes Spiel *n*, Spiel mit Sattelpunkt, Sattelpunktspiel

strict ownership (of property), direct dominion; nuda proprietas, dominium feudi [*Latin*]; ultimate ownership (of property) [*The nominal or bare right of ownership remaining in an owner who has granted the exclusive right of enjoyment and of limited or unlimited disposition over the thing to another person*] · Obereigentum *n* (der Krone), Eigentumsrecht *n* des Leh(e)n(s)herrn, Leh(e)n(s)herrlichkeit *f* [*Das Eigentum an Land ruht in England in allen Fällen unbedingt und ausnahmslos beim Thron. Diese Tatsache ist eine der wichtigsten Unterschiede zwischen dem englischen Mobiliar- und Immobiliarsachenrecht und findet ihren Ausdruck in der Rechtsdoktrin: "Land is, and goods are not, the subject of tenure"*]

strike; walk-out [*colloquial term*] · Streik *m*

strike-breaker; blackleg (Brit.); scab (US) · Streikbrecher *m*

strike clause · Streikklausel *f*

to strike off a part, to subtract, to make an abatement from, to abate, to deduct · abstreichen, abziehen

to strike out, to dismiss, to nonsuit · abweisen [*Klage*]

to strike out, to cancel, to rule through · ausstreichen, durchstreichen

strike out as applicable · Unzutreffendes streichen

striking out, ruling through, cancelling · Durchstreichen *n*, Ausstreichen

stringency, deficiency, scarcity, shortage · Knappheit *f*, Verknappung *f*, Mangel *m*, Klemme *f*, Not *f*

stringency of credit, credit scarcity, credit stringency, credit shortage, credit deficiency, deficiency of credit, shortage of credit, scarcity of credit · Kreditknappheit *f*, Kreditklemme *f*, Kreditnot *f*, Kreditmangel *m*, Kreditverknappung *f*, Kreditdefizit *n*

stringency of housing, scarcity of housing, deficiency of housing, house-famine, housing shortage, housing deficiency, housing stringency, housing scarcity, shortage of housing · Wohnungsbedarf *m*, Wohnungsfehlbestand *m*, Wohnraumfehlbestand, Wohnungsmangel *m*, Wohnraummangel, Wohnungsknappheit *f*, Wohnraumknappheit, Wohnungsdefizit *n*, Wohnraumdefizit, Wohnungsnot *f*, Wohnungsverknappung *f*, Wohnraumverknappung, Wohnraumklemme *f*, Wohnraumnot, Wohnungsklemme, Wohnraumbedarf [*Die sich aus der zahlenmäßigen Gegenüberstellung von Haushalten und Normalwohnungen in abgegrenzten Gebieten oder Bereichen ergebende Zahl fehlender Wohnungen*]

stringency of money → shortage of money

string street development, ribbon development · Bandbebauung *f*, Straßenrandbebauung, Reihenbebauung, Perlschnurbebauung; Bandüberbauung, Straßenrandüberbauung, Reihenüberbauung, Perlschnurüberbauung [*Schweiz*]

to strip, to despoil, to lay waste, to devastate, to estrepe [*To commit waste upon a real estate, as by cutting down trees, removing buildings, etc. To injure the value of a reversionary interest by stripping the (real) estate*] · verschlechtern, verwüsten, mißbrauchen, über(be)nutzen, vernachlässigen

strip · Verbindung *f* von einer Vorprämie und zwei Rückprämien

strip cities, semicontinuous cities, linear cities, ribbon cities, corridor (of cities) · Städteband *n*

strip commercial, commercial strip · Handelszeile f [*Aufreihung von Tankstellen, Garagen, Restaurants, Läden und anderer vom Auto aus zu benutzender Einrichtungen (drive-in facilities) entlang einer städtischen Ausfallstraße*]

strip cropping · streifenförmiger Wechsel m zwischen dichter und lockerer Bepflanzung [*Dichter wachsende Pflanzen bei stärkerer Hangneigung und lokkerer wachsende Pflanzen bei geringerer Hangneigung*]

strip (estate) lot · Streifenkatastergrundstück n, Streifen(kataster)parzelle f, Streifenkartengrundstück, Streifenflurstück, Streifengrundstück (im katastertechnischen Sinne)

strip farming · Langstreifenbau m

strip field · Streifenfeld n

strip head, head of strip · Vorhaupt n

strip-like shopping center (US); strip-like shopping centre (Brit.) · langgestrecktes Einkaufszentrum n, streifenförmiges Einkaufszentrum

strip lot · Streifenparzelle f

strip lot bundle, bundle of strip lots · Streifen(parzellen)verband m

strip mining, surface mining, open mining · Tage(ab)bau m, oberirdischer Abbau

strip mining land(s), open-cut mining land(s), open pit mining land(s), open work(ing) land(s), stripping land(s), open-cast work(ing) land(s), exploitation land(s), open-cut mining area, strip mining area, surface mining area, opencast work(ing) area, surface mining land(s) · Abbauland n, Tagebauland, Abbaufläche f, Tagebaufläche [*Grundstücke, die auf Grund ihrer Beschaffenheit die oberirdische Gewinnung von Bodenschätzen ermöglichen*]

strip of (building) land, (building) land strip · (Bau)Landstreifen m, (Bau)Bodenstreifen

strip of ground, ground strip, strip of terrain, terrain strip · Geländestreifen m, Terrainstreifen

stripping, laying waste, estreping, despoiling, devastating [*Committing waste upon a real estate*] · Verwüsten m, Mißbrauchen, Über(be)nutzen, Verschlechtern, Vernachlässigen (der Instandhaltung), Deteriorieren, Depravieren

stripping land(s), open-cast work(ing) land(s), exploitation land(s), open-cut mining area, strip mining area, surface mining area, open-cast work(ing) area, surface mining land(s), strip mining land(s), open-cut mining land(s), open pit mining land(s), open work(ing) land(s) · Abbauland n, Tagebauland, Abbaufläche f, Tagebaufläche [*Grundstücke, die auf Grund ihrer Beschaffenheit die oberirdische Gewinnung von Bodenschätzen ermöglichen*]

striving for success (in achievement), status striving, achievement-orientation · Erfolgsstreben n

strong component · bilaterale Komponente f, starke Komponente [*Graphentheorie*]

strong evidence, strong proof · schwerwiegender Beweis m

stronghold · Stützpunkt m

strong law of large numbers · starkes Gesetz n der großen Zahlen [*Statistik*]

strong proof, strong evidence · schwerwiegender Beweis m

structural alteration, structural conversion, (building) alteration, (building) conversion · (Gebäude)Umbau m

structural block diagram · Felddiagramm n

structural change · Strukturwandel m, Umstellung f

structural comparison · Strukturvergleich m

structural conversion, (building) alteration, (building) conversion, structural alteration · (Gebäude)Umbau m

(structural) damage in hous(ebuild)ing, (structural) damage in residential building · Bauschaden m im Wohn(ungs)bau

structural defect, defect in a structure · Bauwerkmangel m

(structural) design, DSGN · (baulicher) Entwurf m, Bauentwurf, zeichnerische Lösung f, (bauliche) Konstruktion

structural design alteration, structural design change, variation of structural design, change of structural design, alteration of structural design, structural design variation · (Ab)Änderung f des Bauentwurfs, Umänderung des Bauentwurfs, Veränderung des Bauentwurfs, Bauentwurfs(ab)änderung, Bauentwurfsumänderung, Bauentwurfsveränderung

structural improvement · strukturelle Verbesserung f, Strukturverbesserung

structuralism, rationalistic conceptual grid · Strukturalismus m

structural level · Strukturebene f

structural planning · strukturelle Planung f

structural policy · Strukturpolitik f

structural supervision, structural superintendence · Rohbauaufsicht f, Rohbauüberwachung f

structural trade, craft, construction trade, (building) trade [*Classification or type of work done by workers who restrict themselves to this type of work, established by jurisdictional agreements*] · (Bau)Gewerk n

(structural) trades, construction trades, building (construction) trades · Bauhandwerk *n* [*Die Gesamtheit der sich mit Bauarbeiten befassenden Handwerkszweige*]

structural unemployment · strukturbedingte Arbeitslosigkeit *f*, strukturbedingte Erwerbslosigkeit

structural volume, cubic extent, cubing, walled-in space, building volume, cubage, enclosed space, space enclosed, cube, cubic(al) capacity, (cubic(al)) content [*Enclosed total volume measurements of a structure*] · Baumasse *f*, umbauter Raum *m*, Rauminhalt *m*

structural volume index → cubing ratio

structural volume ratio → cubing ratio

structural weakness · Strukturschwäche *f*

to structure · strukturieren

structure, work, physical facility · (Bau)Werk *n*, (bauliche) Anlage *f*, Baulichkeit *f*, Bau(anlage) *m*, (*f*); Baute *f* [*Schweiz*] [*Hierunter ist nach der höchstrichterlichen Rechtsprechung zu § 638 BGB „eine unbewegliche, durch Verwendung von Arbeit und Material in Verbindung mit dem Baugrund hergestellte Sache" zu verstehen, die sich auf oder unter Geländeoberkante befinden kann*]

structure, composition · Aufbau *m*, Zusammensetzung *f*, Gefüge *n*, Struktur *f*

structure along a highway, structure along a street; structure along a road · Anbau *m* [*an einer Straße*]

structure characteristic, composition characteristic · Aufbaumerkmal *n*, Gefügemerkmal *n*, Strukturmerkmal *n*, Zusammensetzungsmerkmal *n*

structure data, composition data · Strukturdaten *f*

structure (development) plan, three-dimensional master (development) plan, general (development) plan, master (development) plan, comprehensive (development) plan [*A long-range plan officially recognized as a guide for the physical growth and development of a community, together with the basic regulatory and administrative controls needed to attain the physical objectives*] · General(bebauungs)plan *m*

structure for common need, work for common need, physical facility for common need · (bauliche) Anlage *f* für Gemeinbedarf, (Bau)Werk *n* für Gemeinbedarf, Baulichkeit *f* für Gemeinbedarf, Bau(anlage) *m* (*f*) für Gemeinbedarf; Baute *f* für Gemeinbedarf [*Schweiz*]

structure of act, structure of law, structure of statute · Gesetz(es)aufbau *m*, Gesetz(es)gefüge *n*, Gesetz(es)struktur *f*

structure of business, business structure · Geschäftsaufbau *m*, Geschäftsgefüge *n*, Geschäftsstruktur *f*, Geschäftszusammensetzung *f*

structure of gross migration · Bruttowanderungsstruktur *f*

structure plan, composition plan · Strukturplan *m*

structure planning, general (development) planning, master (development) planning, comprehensive (development) planning, three-dimensional master planning · General(bebauungs)planung *f*

structure planning legislation, structure planning lawmaking, general planning legislation, general planning lawmaking, master planning legislation, master planning lawmaking, comprehensive planning legislation, comprehensive planning lawmaking, three-dimensional master legislation, three-dimensional master lawmaking · Generalplanungsgesetzgebung *f*

structure to be demolished, work to be demolished, physical facility to be demolished · Abrißbauwerk *n*, Abrißbauwerk

structuring · Strukturierung *f*

struggle for space · Auseinandersetzung *f* um (Lebens)Räume, Kampf *m* um (Lebens)Räume

stubble-field · Stoppelacker *m*, Stoppelfeld *n*

stubble pasture (ground), stubble pasture land · Stoppel(vieh)weide *f*

student of law, law student · Jurastudent *m*

study, analysis · Analyse *f*, Untersuchung *f*

study area, investigation area, study territory, investigation territory · Untersuchungsgebiet *n*

study of cost(s) variances, analysis of cost(s) variances · Kostenabweichungsanalyse *f*, Kostenabweichungsuntersuchung *f*

study of location, location(al) analysis, location(al) study, analysis of site, study of site, site analysis, site study, analysis of location [*The evaluation of the qualities of a site by comparison with those of other comparable sites*] · Standortanalyse *f*, Standortstudie *f*

study of migration, migration analysis, migration study, analysis of migration · Wanderungsuntersuchung *f*, Wanderungsanalyse *f*

study of site, site analysis, site study, analysis of location, study of location, location(al) analysis, location(al) study, analysis of site [*The evaluation of the qualities of a site by comparison with those*

study territory — subdivision

of other comparable sites] · Standortanalyse f, Standortstudie f

study territory, investigation territory, study area, investigation area · Untersuchungsgebiet n

style (US); citation form, form of citation · Zitierform f

style of life, life style · Lebensstil m

sub → sub(contractor)

sub-agent (on site), sub-supervisor (on site), site sub-agent, site sub-supervisor · Unterbauleiter m, Unterbauleitung f, örtlicher Unterbauleiter, örtliche Unterbauleitung, Unterbaustellenleiter [des Unternehmers]

sub-area · Teilgebiet n

subassembly [An assembly which is not a final assembly] · vorläufiges Verbunderzeugnis n, vorläufiges Verbundprodukt n

subbid, suboffer, subtender; sub (bid) proposal (US) · Nachunternehmerangebot n, Unterunternehmerangebot, Subunternehmerangebot; Unterakkordantenangebot [Schweiz]

subbidder, subtenderer [One who submits a bid to a prime bidder or other subcontractor] · Nachunternehmerbieter m, Subunternehmerbieter; Unterakkordantenbieter [Schweiz]

sub-boscus [Latin]; woody undergrowth, underwood, copse, coppice · Niederwald m, Holzung f, Unterholz n

sub-buyer, sub-vendee, sub-purchaser · Käufer m vom Erstkäufer

subcentre, secondary business centre (Brit.); secondary business center, subcenter (US) · Satellit-Geschäftszentrum, Stadtteilzentrum, Subzentrum, C-Zentrum, sekundäres Geschäftszentrum, Unterzentrum

subcity · Nebenzentrum n [Es entsteht innerhalb einer Stadt durch Funktionsteilung]

sub-clause · Unterklausel f

sub-column · Unterspalte f

sub-committee · Unterausschuß m

sub-contract · Nachunternehmervertrag m, Subunternehmervertrag, Unterunternehmervertrag; Unterakkordantenvertrag [Schweiz]

subcontract bond [A performance or payment bond required by general contractors from their subcontractors] · Nachunternehmergarantie f, Subunternehmergarantie; Unterakkordantengarantie [Schweiz]

sub-contract breach, breach of sub-contract · Nachunternehmervertragsbruch m, Subunternehmervertragsbruch, Unterunternehmervertragsbruch; Unterakkordantenvertragsbruch [Schweiz]

sub(contractor), separate contractor (for a portion of the work) · Nachunternehmer m, Subunternehmer, Unterunternehmer; Unterakkordant m [Schweiz] [Er führt auf Grund eines Werkvertrages mit dem Unternehmer einzelne oder alle der von diesem übernommenen Arbeiten aus]

sub(contractor) list [1. List of subcontractors whose proposals were used by a prime contractor when preparing his tender. 2. List of subcontractors proposed to be employed by the prime contractor to be submitted to the owner or his representative for approval after the contract award] · Nachunternehmerliste f, Subunternehmerliste; Unterakkordantenliste [Schweiz]

sub(contractor)('s) liability · Nachunternehmerhaftpflicht f, Subunternehmerhaftpflicht, Subunternehmerhaftung f, Nachunternehmerhaftung, Unterunternehmerhaftpflicht, Unterunternehmerhaftung; Unterakkordantenhaftpflicht, Unterakkordantenhaftung [Schweiz]

subculture · Subkultur f

subdemise → sublease(hold)

subdemise contract, sublease(hold) contract, subtenancy contract, subtenure contract · Afterpachtvertrag m, Afterverpachtungsvertrag

sub-demised, sub-leased · unterverpachtet

subdistrict, subdivision · Unterbezirk m

subdistrict inspector, subdivision(al) inspector · Unterbezirksinspektor m

(sub)divided forest, lotted forest · parzell(is)ierter Wald m

(sub)divided (general) property, (sub)divided ownership (of property), (sub)divided proprietorship · geteiltes Eigentum n [Ober- und Untereigentum]

(sub)divided (into compartments), compartmented · (auf)geteilt, zerlegt [Grund(stück)]

(sub)divided land, compartmented land · (auf)geteiltes Land n

to (sub)divide (into compartments), to compart · aufteilen, zerlegen [Grund(stück)]

to (sub)divide into lots, to lot · parzell(is)ieren

(sub)divider · Parzellierer m

(sub)dividing (into compartments), compartition, comparting · Aufteilen n, Zerlegen n [Grund(stück)]

subdivision · Unterwahlkreis m

(sub)division, breakdown, make-up ·
(Auf)Gliederung f, Aufschlüsselung

subdivision, subdistrict · Unterbezirk m

subdivision(al) inspector, subdistrict
inspector · Unterbezirksinspektor m

(sub)division into (estate) lots, (sub)division (of land(s)), lotting, (land(s))
(sub)division · Parzelli(si)erung f, Landparzelli(si)erung, Bodenparzelli(si)erung

subdivision of cost(s), cost(s) breakdown,
cost(s) make-up, cost(s) subdivision,
breakdown of cost(s), make-up of
cost(s) · Kosten(auf)gliederung f,
Kostenaufschlüsselung

(sub)division (of land) ordinance ·
(Land)Aufteilungsverordnung f, Bodenaufteilungsverordnung

(sub)division (of land) regulation,
(sub)division (of land) prescription,
(sub)division (of land) rule · (Land)Aufteilungsvorschrift f, Bodenaufteilungsvorschrift

(sub)division (of land(s)), lotting, (land(s))
(sub)division, (sub)division into (estate)
lots · Parzelli(si)erung f, Landparzelli(si)erung, Bodenparzelli(si)erung

(sub)division plan, plan of (division into)
lots, plan of (sub)division (of land(s)),
plan of lotting, lotting plan, plan of
estate lots · Parzell(is)ierungsplan m

subdominant, hinterland town, hinterland
city · Hinterlandstadt f

sub-(en)feoffment → sub-infeudation

subhastare [*Latin*]; to auction(eer), to sell
at public auction · versteigern, meistbietend verkaufen

sub-infeudation, sub-(en)feoffment f, subinfeftment, sub-infeodation, sub-investiture, private lordship over lands in fee
simple · Afterbelehnung f, Unterbelehnung, Afterleihe, Unterleihe f

sub-investiture → sub-infeudation

subject → (male) subject

subject (field), sector · Fachbereich m,
Sachbereich, Sachgebiet n,
Fach(gebiet) n, Sektor m, Sachkomplex m

subject index · Sachregister n, Sachverzeichnis n

(subjective) right, (legal) interest, legal
right, statutory interest, statutory right;
jus legitimum [*Latin*] [*A system of rights
enjoyed by persons, as "subjects" or
owner of rights, and by virtue of law*] ·
(subjektives) Recht n, Berechtigung f,
Anrecht, (Rechts)Anspruch m, gesetzliches (subjektives) Recht, subjektives
(gesetzliches) Recht, dingliches Recht
[*im B.G.B. auch als „Gegenstand"
bezeichnet*]

subject land · Bewertungsboden m,
Bewertungsland n, Taxierungsboden,
Taxierungsland, Wertermitt(e)lungsboden, Wertermitt(e)lungsland, (Ab)Schätzungsboden, (Ab)Schätzungsland

subject lot · (Ab)Schätzungsparzelle f,
Bewertungsparzelle, Taxierungsparzelle, Wertermitt(e)lungsparzelle

subject matter jurisdiction · sachliche
Zuständigkeit f

subject(-matter) of (a) contract, contract
subject(-matter) · Vertragsgegenstand m

(subject-)matter of dispute, (subject-)matter in controversy · Streitgegenstand m

subject of complaint · Beschwerdegegenstand m

subject of dispute, subject of litigation,
disputed matter, disputed subject, matter in dispute, matter in issue, matter in
litigation, subject of issue ·
(Rechts)Streitsache f

subject of issue → subject of dispute

subject of litigation → subject of dispute

subject of performance, performance subject · Leistungsgegenstand m

subject of property, property subject ·
Besitzobjekt n

subject of the trust, trust subject · Treuhandgegenstand m

subject plan, sector plan · fachlicher Entwick(e)lungsplan m, sektoraler Plan,
Fachplan, Sektorplan

subject planning, sector planning, specialized planning [*Planning based on consideration of a particular type or types
of development*] · fachliche Entwick(e)lungsplanung f, Sektorplanung,
Fachplanung, sektorale Planung

subject planning law, specialized planning
law, sector planning law · Fachplanungsrecht n, Sektorplanungsrecht, sektorales Planungsrecht, fachliches Planungsrecht

subject planning practice, specialized
planning practice, sector planning practice · Fachplanungswesen n, Sektorplanungswesen, sektorales Planungswesen, fachliches Planungswesen

subject planning statute, specialized planning act, specialized planning law, specialized planning statute, sector planning act, sector planning law, sector
planning statute, subject planning act,
subject planning law · Fachplanungsgesetz n, Sektorplanungsgesetz, sektorales Planungsgesetz, fachliches Entwick(e)lungsplanungsgesetz

subject plot (of land), subject piece of
land, subject land parcel · (Ab)Schätzungsgrundstück n, Bewertungsgrundstück, Wertermitt(e)lungsgrundstück,
Taxierungsgrundstück

subject room — submission of documents

subject room · Sonderschulzimmer n

subject to answer to law, liable to answer to law, responsible to law, answerable to law, liable to be brought before any jurisdiction, amenable · verantwortlich vor dem Gesetz, rechenschaftspflichtig vor dem Gesetz

subject to contract, contractual, persuant to contract · vertragsgemäß, vertragsmäßig, vertraglich

subject to contribution(s), contributory, liable to contribution(s) · beitragspflichtig

subject to duty, dutiable · zollpflichtig

subject to military duty · (militär)dienstpflichtig, wehrpflichtig

subject to permission, requiring permission, liable to permission · erlaubnisbedürftig, erlaubnispflichtig, genehmigungsbedürftig, genehmigungspflichtig

subject to prosecution, punishable, liable to prosecution · strafbar

subject to tax(ation), rat(e)able, assessable for tax(ation) (purposes), assessible for tax(ation) (purposes), taxable · veranlagbar, steuerlich einstufbar, besteuerbar, versteuerbar

subject value · Gegenstandswert m

sublease → sublease(hold)

sub-leased, sub-demised · unterverpachtet

sublease(hold), subtenancy, subdemise, subtenure · After(boden)pacht f, After(boden)verpachtung f

sublease(hold) contract, subtenancy contract, subtenure contract, subdemise contract · Afterpachtvertrag m, Afterverpachtungsvertrag

sub-leaseholder, sublessee, subtenant (of land), underlessee, undertenant (of land), underleaseholder, undertermor, sub-termor · After(boden)pächter m, Unter(boden)pächter, Nach(boden)pächter

sublessee, subtenant (of land), underlessee, undertenant (of land), underleaseholder, undertermor, sub-termor, sub-leaseholder · After(boden)pächter m, Unter(boden)pächter, Nach(boden)pächter

to sublet, to underlet [*premises*] · abvermieten, untervermieten, aftervermieten, nachvermieten, weitervermieten

to sublet, to award a subcontract · weitervergeben, zuschlagen an Nachunternehmer, zuschlagen an Subunternehmer

to sublet · weitervermieten

subletter, underletter · Abvermieter m, Untervermieter, Aftervermieter, Weitervermieter

subletting, underletting · Abvermieten n, Weitervermieten, Untervermieten, Aftervermieten, Untervermietung f, Abvermietung, Weitervermietung, Aftervermietung

sub-letting · Zuschlagen n an Nachunternehmer, Zuschlagen an Subunternehmer, Erteilen eines Auftrags an Nachunternehmer, Erteilen eines Auftrags an Subunternehmer

submerged contour (line) · Unterwasserhöhenlinie f

submerged land(s) · überflutetes Land n, überschwemmtes Land

sub-metropolis · Untermetropole f

submission · Schiedsabrede f

submission · Anheimgeben n [*Ansicht eines Rechtsanwalts in einer mündlichen oder schriftlichen Rechtsausführung*]

submission, presentation, filing, discovery, production · Abgabe f, Einreichung f, Vorlage f, Vorlegung, Edition f, Enthüllung [*Mitteilung von Tatsachen oder Vorlegung von Schriftstücken an den Prozeßgegner*]

submission, deposit(ing), payment · Erstattung f [*Für den Erhalt von Ausschreibungsunterlagen*]

submission → submission (of tender(s))

submission → (arbitration) submission

submission amount, payment amount, deposit(ing) amount · Erstattungsbetrag m [*Betrag für den Erhalt von Ausschreibungsunterlagen*]

submission by interrogatories, presentation by interrogatories, production by interrogatories, filing by interrogatories, discovery by interrogatories · Abgabe f von Tatsachen, Einreichung f von Tatsachen, Vorlage f von Tatsachen, Vorlegung von Tatsachen, Edition f von Tatsachen, Enthüllung von Tatsachen [*An den Prozeßgegner*]

submission code · Submissionsordnung f

submission date, date of submission, date set for the opening of tenders deadline for submission of bids, date of opening, (bid) opening date; (bid) proposal opening date (US) · (Angebots)Eröffnungstermin m, (Angebots)Eröffnungsdatum n, Submissionstermin, Submissionsdatum

submission of documents, presentation of documents, discovery of documents, filing of documents, production of documents · Abgabe f von Schriftstücken, Vorlage f von Schriftstücken, Einreichung f von Schriftstücken, Vorlegung von Schriftstücken, Enthüllung von Schriftstücken, Edition f von Schriftstücken [*An den Prozeßgegner*]

submission (of tender(s)) — subsequent order

submission (of tender(s)), submission of offer(s), submission of bid(s); submission of (bid) proposal(s) (US) · (Angebots)Abgabe f, (Angebots)Einreichung f, Submission f, Anbieten n

submission practice · Submissionswesen n

submission procedure · Submissionsverfahren n

to submit, to present, to discover, to produce, to fille · abgeben, einreichen, vorlegen, enthüllen [Mitteilen von Tatsachen oder Vorlegen von Schriftstücken an den Prozeßgegner]

to submit (a bid), to (enter a) bid; to submit a (bid) proposal, to enter a (bid) proposal (US); to offer, to tender · anbieten, submittieren, einreichen eines Angebots, abgeben eines Angebots

to submit a competitive bid, to bid competitively, to offer competitively, to tender competitively · abgeben n eines Wettbewerbsangebotes, einreichen eines Wettbewerbsangebotes, anbieten im Wettbewerb, submittieren im Wettbewerb

submitting, presenting · Einreichen n, Vorlegen

submodel · Untermodell n

suboffer → subbid

subordinate, inferior · Untergebene m

subordinate, inferior, ancillary, paravail · nachgeordnet, untergeordnet

subordinate building authority, subordinate construction authority · nachgeordnete Bau(aufsichts)behörde f

subordinate law, delegated law, subordinate act, delegated act, subordinate statute, delegate statute · Verordnungsgesetz n

subordinate law, delegated law · Verordnungsrecht n

subordinate lawmaking, delegated legislation, delegated lawmaking, subordinate legislation · Gesetzgebung f auf dem Verordnungsweg, Verordnungsgesetzgebung, nachgeordnete Gesetzgebung

subordinate office · untergeordnetes Geschäftslokal n, untergeordnete (Firmen)Niederlassung f

to subp(o)ena, to sumnon, to convene before a court of law [To require a person to be present at a specified place and time, and for a specific purpose, under a penalty for non-attendance] · (vor)laden (vor Gericht)

subproposal → subbid

sub-purchaser, sub-buyer, sub-vendee · Käufer m vom Erstkäufer

subregion · Teilregion f

subregional delineation · Bildung f von Raumeinheiten

subreption [The fraud committed to obtain a pardon, title, grant, or award, by alleging facts contrary to truth] · Erschleichen n

subrogation [Transfer of financial responsibility and right of recovery from one party to another] · Gläubigerwechsel m

subrogation [Substitution of one person for another with respect to legal rights such as a right of recovery] · Rechtsübertragung f

subs., subsection · Unterparagraph m [Gesetz]

subsample · Varianzanalysengruppe f

to subscribe, to write under [To write the name under any document. To sign is to write the name at any place, not necessarily underneath] · unterschreiben

subscriber · Zeichner m von Geschäftsanteilen

subscribing witness, attesting witness · Unterschriftszeuge m

subscription, signature underneath · Unterschrift f

subscription agreement · Zeichnungsvereinbarung f, Zeichnungsabmachung, Zeichnungsabkommen n

subscription of stocks · Aktienzeichnung f, Zeichnung von Aktien

subscription share, share of stock, instal(l)ment share, partly paid share, membership share · Raten(geschäfts)anteil m [aufhörende Bausparkasse]

subscription upon a condition precedent · Zeichnung f mit aufschiebender Bedingung [Emissionsgeschäft]

subsection, subs. · Unterparagraph m [Gesetz]

subsequent · nachträglich

subsequent acquirer · Folgeerwerber m, Nacherwerber

subsequent contract, follow-on contract, continuity contract, continuation contract · Anschlußvertrag m, Folgevertrag m

subsequent indorsement, subsequent endorsement, later indorsement, later endorsement · Nachindossament n

subsequent legacy · nachfolgendes Legat n, Nachfolgelegat

subsequent liability · Nachhaftpflicht f, Nachhaftung f, Nachhaftbarkeit f

subsequent offer → subsequent tender

subsequent order, continuity order, continuation order, follow-on order · Anschlußauftrag m, Folgeauftrag

subsequent tender, follow-on tender, continuation tender, continuity tender, subsequent offer, follow-on offer, continuation offer, continuity offer, subsequent bid, follwo-on bid, continuity bid, continuation bid; subsequent (bid) proposal, follow-on (bid) proposal, continuation (bid) proposal, continuity (bid) proposal (US) · Folgeangebot *n*, Anschlußangebot

subsequent work(s) · Nachfolgearbeit(en) *f (pl)*

subsequent year · Nachfolgejahr *n*

subsidiary · Tochtergesellschaft *f*

subsidiary clause · Subsidiaritätsklausel *f*

subsidiary goal (of policy), subsidiary target goal, subsidiary policy goal · Subsidiaritätszielnorm *f*, Subsidiaritätsoberziel *n*

subsidium, auxidium, adiutorium [*Latin*]; aid [*In feudal law. A kind of pecuniary tribute paid by a vassal to his lord, on occasions of peculiar emergency, and which was one of the incidents of tenure in chivalry, or by knight's service*] · Hilfsgeld *n*

subsidization · öffentliche Förderung *f*, Förderung durch die öffentliche Hand

to subsidize · subventionieren

to subsidize, to assist publicly · öffentlich fördern

subsidized · subventioniert

subsidized apartment → publicly-assisted dwelling unit

subsidized area, subsidized territory, publicly-assisted area, publicly-assisted territory · öffentliches Förderungsgebiet *n*, öffentlich gefördertes Gebiet

subsidized dwelling → publicly-assisted dwelling unit

subsidized house, social house, lower-income house, publicly-assisted house · Sozialhaus *n*, öffentlich gefördertes Haus, Haus der öffentlichen Hand, Haus des sozialen Wohn(ungs)baues, Zuschußhaus

subsidized hous(ebuild)ing, lower-income hous(ebuild)ing, social hous(ebuild)ing, production of public housing, public(ly-assisted) hous(ebuild)ing · Zuschußwohn(ungs)bau *m*, Sozialwohn(ungs)bau, öffentlich geförderter Wohn(ungs)bau, geförderter öffentlicher Wohn(ungs)bau, sozialer Wohn(ungs)bau, Wohn(ungs)bau der öffentlichen Hand

subsidized housing, low-rent housing, social housing, low-income housing, low-cost(s) housing, publicly(-)assisted housing, publicly(-)provided housing · Zuschußwohnungen *f pl*, Sozialwohnungen, öffentlich geförderte Wohnungen, Wohnungen des sozialen Wohn(ungs)baues, Wohnungen der öffentlichen Hand

subsidized rent · subventionierte Miete *f*

subsidized residence → publicly-assisted dwelling unit

subsidized tenement → publicly-assisted dwelling unit

subsidized territory → subsidized area

subsidizing · öffentliches Fördern *n*

subsidy [*A government grant to an enterprise, organization, or person considered of benefit to the public*] · öffentliche (Kapital)Zuwendung *f*

subsidy committee · öffentlicher Förderungsausschuß *m*

subsidy payment · (öffentliche) Förderungszahlung *f*

subsidy programme; subsidy program (US) · öffentliches Förderungsprogramm *n*

subsidy provision · (öffentliche) Förderungsbestimmung *f*

subsistence allowance, cost of living allowance (Brit.); subsistence, living allowance (US); separating allowance, separation allowance · Auslösung *f*, Trennungsgeld *n*, Trennungsentschädigung [*Ein Arbeitnehmer, der auf einer Baustelle außerhalb des Betriebssitzes arbeitet, erhält eine Auslösung, wenn die tägliche Rückkehr zum Wohnort nicht zumutbar ist*]

subsistence husbandry [*crops for own use*] · Landwirtschaft *f* für Eigengebrauch

subsistence level, minimum of subsistence, poverty line · Existenzminimum *n*

subsoil of the seabed, seabed subsoil · Meeresuntergrund *m*

subspace · Teilraum *m*

substandard · unternormal, unterwertig [*Wohnung*]

substandard, less-than-average, below average · unterdurchschnittlich

substandard quality · Güte *f* unter einer Richtlinie

substantial · wohlhabend

substantial, essential, material · wesentlich

substantial · ausreichend [*Beweis*]

substantial autonomy · echte Selbständigkeit *f*

substantial completion · eigentliche Fertigstellung *f*, wesentliche Fertigstellung

substantial evidence, substantial proof · ausreichender Beweis *m*, substantiierter

substantial execution — substitute housing

Beweis, wesentlicher Beweis, erheblicher Beweis

substantial execution, substantial compliance, substantial performance, substantial fulfilment [*The doctrine of substantial performance usually allows a contractor to recover the contract price despite the existence of minor defects or omissions in his work*] · wesentliche Erfüllung *f*, wesentliche Ausführung, wesentliche Vollziehung, wesentliche Erbringung, wesentlicher Vollzug *m*

substantial injustice · sachliches Unrecht *n*

substantially completed [*It means that the project is to the point at which it can be used for its intended purposes*] · funktionsfähig fertig(gestellt) [*Bauprojekt*]

substantial proof, substantial evidence · ausreichender Beweis *m*, substantiierter Beweis, wesentlicher Beweis, erheblicher Beweis

substantiation [*The establishment by attestation on oath of the fact that there is strong prima facie evidence in support of a claim, charge or statement*] · Glaubhaftmachung *f*

substantive arbitrability · materielle Schiedsgerichtsbarkeit *f*

substantive contract law · materielles Vertragsrecht *n*, materiell(rechtlich)es Vertragsrecht, sachliches Vertragsrecht

substantive distinctness principle, substantive principle of distinctness · materiell(rechtlich)er Bestimmtheitsgrundsatz *m*, materiell(rechtlich)er Spezialitätsgrundsatz, materiell(rechtlich)es Bestimmtheitsprinzip *n*, materiell(rechtlich)es Spezialitätsprinzip [*Grundbuchrecht*]

substantive due process of law · materiell(rechtlich)es gehöriges Rechtsverfahren *n*

substantive (land) register law, substantive (land) registry law · materiell(rechtlich)es Grundbuchrecht *n* [*Es bezieht sich auf die Regelung des dinglichen Rechts, das Gegenstand der Grundbucheintragung ist*]

substantive law [*That part of law which creates, defines, and regulates rights, as opposed to "adjective or remedial law", which prescribes methods of enforcing the rights or obtaining redress for their invasion*] · materiell(rechtlich)es Recht *n*, sachliches Recht [*Nicht verwechseln mit „Sachenrecht"*]

substantive planning · Hauptplanung *f*

substantive principle of distinctness, substantive distinctness principle · materiell(rechtlich)er Bestimmtheitsgrundsatz *m*, materiell(rechtlich)er Spezialitätsgrundsatz, materiell(rechtlich)es Bestimmtheitsprinzip *n*, materiell(rechtlich)es Spezialitätsprinzip [*Grundbuchrecht*]

substantive principle of priority, substantive priority principle · materiell(rechtlich)er Vorranggrundsatz *m*, materiell(rechtlich)er Prioritätsgrundsatz, materiell(rechtliches) Vorrangprinzip *n*, materiell(rechtlich)es Prioritätsprinzip [*Grundbuchrecht*]

substantive-procedural rule · halbmateriell(rechtlich)e Norm *f*

substantive rule, substantive executive order · materielle Verwaltungsverordnung *f*

substitional gift · Ersatzschenkung *f*

substitutability, interchangeability · Auswechselbarkeit *f*

substitute, after heir (male), second heir (male), revisionary heir (male) · Aftererbe *m*, Nacherbe *m*, Substitut *m*, Ersatzerbe [*Derjenige, der nach einem ernannten Erben als Erbe in einem Testament ernannt ist, wenn der erste Erbe die Erbschaft nicht erwerben würde*]

substitute; surrogate, surrogatum [*Scotland*] · Ersatz *m*

to substitute, to surrogate, ro replace · ersetzen

substitute afterheir female, substitute after female heir, substitute afterheiress, substitute revisionary heir female, substitute revisionary female heir, substitute revisionary heiress · Ersatznacherbin *f*, Ersatzaftererbin

substitute after heir (male), substitute revisionary heir (male) · Ersatznacherbe *m*, Ersatzaftererbe

substitute arbitrator, substitute referee; substitute arbiter [*This term is rarely used*] · Ersatzschiedsrichter *m*

substitute area · Ersatzfläche *f*

substitute area, substitute territory · Ersatzgebiet *n*, Ersatzterritorium *n*

substitute facility · Ersatzeinrichtung *f*

substitute female heir, after-heiress, substitute heiress, after female heir · Aftererbin *f*, Nacherbin, Ersatzerbin

substitute for money · Geldersatzmittel *n*, Geldsurrogat *n*

substitute habitable space, substitute shelter, substitute housing · Ersatzwohnraum *m*

substitute heiress, after female heir, substitute female heir, after-heiress · Aftererbin *f*, Nacherbin, Ersatzerbin

substitute heirship, substitute inheritance · Ersatzerbschaft *f*

substitute housing, substitute habitable space, substitute shelter · Ersatzwohnraum *m*

substitute inheritance, substitute heirship · Ersatzerbschaft *f*

substitute interest, substitute right · Ersatzrecht *n*, subjektives Ersatzrecht

substitute land · Ersatzland *n*, Ersatzboden *m*

substitute location, substitute site · Ausweichstandort *m*, Ersatzstandort

substitute mortgage · Ersatzhypothek *f*

substitute performance · Ersatzleistung *f*

substitute physical facility, substitute structure, substitute work · Ersatzbau(werk) *m, (n)*; Ersatzbaute *f* [*Schweiz*]

substitute plot, substitute parcel · Ersatzgrund(stück) *m, (n)*

substitute referee; substitute arbiter [*This term is rarely used*], substitute arbitrator · Ersatzschiedsrichter *m*

substitute revisionary heir (male), substitute after-heir (male) · Ersatznacherbe *m*, Ersatzaftererbe

substitute right, substitute interest · Ersatzrecht *n*, subjektives Ersatzrecht

substitute shelter, substitute housing, substitute habitable space · Ersatzwohnraum *m*

substitute site, substitute location · Ausweichstandort *m*, Ersatzstandort

substitute sole arbitrator · Ersatzeinzelschiedsrichter *m*

substitute space · Ersatzraum *m*

substitute structure, substitute work, substitute physical facility · Ersatzbau(werk) *m, (n)*; Ersatzbaute *f* [*Schweiz*]

substitute tenant · Ersatzmieter *m*

substitute territory, substitute area · Ersatzgebiet *n*, Ersatzterritorium *n*

substitution, replacement · Ersetzung *f*, Substitution *f*

substitution effect · Substitutionswirkung *f*

substitution equilibrium · Substitutionsgleichgewicht *n*

substitution point · Substitutionspunkt *m*

sub-supervisor (on site), site sub-agent, site sub-supervisor, sub-agent (on site) · Unterbauleiter *m*, Unterbauleitung *f*, örtlicher Unterbauleiter, örtliche Unterbauleitung, Unterbaustellenleiter [*des Unternehmers*]

sub-supplier · Unterlieferant *m*

sub's work(s) → sub(-contractor)'s work(s)

sub-syndicate → (issue) sub-syndicate

subsystem · Untersystem *n*

subtenancy, undertenancy · Untermietverhältnis *n*

subtenancy → sublease(hold)

subtenancy contract, subtenure contract, subdemise contract, sublease(hold) contract · Afterpachtvertrag *m*, Afterverpachtungsvertrag

subtenant; roomer (US) · Untermieter *m*

subtenant → underlessee

subtenant (of land), underlessee, undertenant (of land), underleaseholder, undertermor, sub-termor, sub-leaseholder, sublessee · After(boden)pächter *m*, Unter(boden)pächter, Nach(boden)pächter

subtenant's addition, subtenant's markup, subtenant's surcharge · Untermietaufschlag *m*, Untermietzuschlag

subtenant's rent · Untermiete *f*

subtender → subbid

subtenderer, subbidder [*One who submits a bid to a prime bidder or other subcontractor*] · Nachunternehmerbieter *m*, Subunternehmerbieter; Unterakkordantenbieter [*Schweiz*]

subtenente · Untervasall *m*

subtenure → sublease(hold)

subtenure contract, subdemise contract, sublease(hold) contract, subtenancy contract · Afterpachtvertrag *m*, Afterverpachtungsvertrag

sub-termor, sub-leaseholder, sublessee, subtenant (of land), underlessee, undertenant (of land), underleaseholder, undertermor · After(boden)pächter *m*, Unter(boden)pächter, Nach(boden)pächter

subterraneous earth · Erdreich *n*

sub-town, market district, market town; first order centre (Brit.); urban village [*750 to 1,000 inhabitants*] (Brit.); small town with between 1,000 and 2,000 inhabitants (Brit.); first order center, urban center (US), middle-order subcentral place · Amtsort *m* [*nach W. Christaller*]

to subtract, to make an abatement from, to abate, to deduct, to strike off a part · abstreichen, abziehen

subtropical crops belt · Gürtel *m* subtropischer Kulturen

subunit · Untereinheit *f*

suburban agriculture, suburban farming · stadtnahe Landwirtschaft *f*

suburban area, suburban territory (Brit.) · Vorortgebiet *n*

suburban area (US); peripheral area, peripheral territory, umland territory, umland area; suburban territory · Umlandgebiet *n*

suburban belt (Brit.) · Vorortgürtel *m*

suburban city, suburban town (Brit.); outer city, outer town (US) · Außenstadt *f*, Vorstadt

suburban community (Brit.) · Vorortgemeinde *f*

suburban development (Brit.) · Vorortentwick(e)lung *f*

suburban development (US); peripheral community development, umland community development · Umlandgemeindeentwick(e)lung *f*

suburban district (Brit.) · Vorortbezirk *m*

suburban district (US); peripheral community district, umland community district · Umlandgemeindebezirk *m*

suburban expansion (Brit.) · Vororterweiterung *f*

suburban expansion (US); peripheral community expansion, umland community expansion · Umlandgemeindeerweiterung *f*

suburban farming, suburban agriculture · stadtnahe Landwirtschaft *f*

suburban group (Brit.) · Vorortgruppe *f*

suburban group (US); peripheral community group, umland community group · Umlandgemeindegruppe *f*

suburban growth (Brit.) · Vorortwachstum *n*

suburban growth (US); peripheral community growth, umland community growth · Umlandgemeindewachstum *n*

suburban home (Brit.) · Vororteigenheim *n*, Vororteigenhaus *n*

suburban house (Brit.) · Vororthaus *n*

suburban house (US); peripheral community house, umland community house · Umlandgemeindehaus *n*

suburban inhabitant, suburbanite (Brit.) · Vororteinwohner *m*

suburban inhabitant (US); peripheral community inhabitant, umland community inhabitant · Umlandgemeindeeinwohner *m*

suburbanism (Brit.) · Vorortwesen *n*

suburbanism (US) · Umlandgemeindewesen *n*

suburbanite · Vorstadtbewohner *m*

suburbanite (Brit.); suburban inhabitant · Vororteinwohner *m*

suburbanization, decentralization, formation of sub(urb)s, suburban process, suburban urbanization, (urban) spread, (urban) sprawl, outward spread, outward sprawl, suburban spread, suburban sprawl, spread(ing) of cities, sprawl of cities, spread(ing) of towns, sprawl of towns · Sied(e)lungsbrei *m*, Dezentralisation *f*, Ausufern *n*, Zersied(e)lung *f*, Überwucherung des städtischen Raumes, Dezentralisierung

suburbanization, incorporation, annexation, communalization, municipalization · Einbezirkung *f*, Vereinigung, Eingemeindung, Fusion(ierung) *f*, Verschmelzung, Ausbezirkung, Umbezirkung, Einverleibung, Inkorporation *f*, Inkommunalisation *f*, Inkommunalisierung, Angemeindung, Ausgemeindung, Umgemeindung [*Der rechtliche Vorgang einer organischen Verbindung mehrerer Gemeinden oder Gemeindeteile*]

suburbanization contract, annexation contract, communalization contract, municipalization contract, incorporation contract · Angemeindungsvertrag *m*, Eingemeindungsvertrag, Einbezirkungsvertrag, Vereinigungsvertrag, Verschmelzungsvertrag, Fusion(ierung)svertrag, Ausbezirkungsvertrag, Umbezirkungsvertrag, Einverleibungsvertrag, Inkorporationsvertrag, Inkommunalisationsvertrag, Inkommunalisierungsvertrag, Ausgemeindungsvertrag, Umgemeindungsvertrag

suburban land (Brit.) · Vorortland *n*

suburban land (US); peripheral land, surrounding land, surrounding area, external service area, umland [*Sometimes, by local usage also called "landed estate" and "landed property" as distinguished from land in a city*] · äußeres Ergänzungsgebiet *n*, Vorortzone *f*, Umland *n*, Umgelände *n*

suburban land use (Brit.) · Vorortlandnutzung *f*

suburban land use (US); peripheral land use, external land use, surrounding land use, service area use, umland use · Umlandnutzung *f*

suburban migration (Brit.) · Vorortwanderung *f*

suburban migration (US); peripheral community migration, umland community migration · Umlandwanderung *f*

suburban pattern, suburban scheme (US); peripheral community pattern, umland community pattern, peripheral community scheme, umland community scheme · Umlandgemeindemuster *n*, Umlandgemeindeschema *n*

suburban pattern, suburban scheme (Brit.) · Vorortmuster *n*, Vorortschema *n*

suburb(an place) (Brit.) [*Unlike the use of the term in English, which can include residential sections within the city, the American suburb(an place) is a community on the periphery of an urban area (= Umlandgemeinde) that is politically independent and distinct from the city; it is not within the legally defined geographic limits of the larger city. Thus, when translating the German "Vorort"*

suburb(an place) (US) — successful contractor 1016

into American English, the British term should be used for clear understanding with an explanation in brackets, since there is no US word for "Vorort" in the German and British definitions] · Vorort *m*

suburb(an place) (US); peripheral community, umland community · Umlandgemeinde *f*

suburban population (Brit.) · Vorortbevölkerung *f*

suburban population (US); peripheral community population, umland community population · Umlandgemeindebevölkerung *f*

suburban process, suburban urbanization, (urban) spread, (urban) sprawl, outward spread, outward sprawl, suburban spread, suburban sprawl, spread(ing) of cities, sprawl of cities, spread(ing) of towns, sprawl of towns, suburbanization, decentralization, formation of sub(urb)s · Sied(e)lungsbrei *m*, Dezentralisation *f*, Ausufern *n*, Zersied(e)lung *f*, Überwucherung des städtischen Raumes, Dezentralisierung

suburban residential area, suburban residential territory (Brit.) · Vorortwohn(ungs)gebiet *n*

suburban residential area, suburban residential territory (US); peripheral community residential area, umland community residential area, peripheral community residential territory, umland community residential territory · Umlandgemeindewohn(ungs)gebiet *n*

suburban residential territory (US); peripheral community residential area, umland community residential area, peripheral community residential territory, umland community residential territory; suburban residential area · Umlandgemeindewohn(ungs)gebiet *n*

suburban residential territory (Brit.); suburban residential area · Vorortwohn(ungs)gebiet *n*

suburban ring (Brit.) · Vorortring *m*

suburban ring (US); peripheral community ring, umland community ring · Umlandgemeindering *m*

suburban scheme (Brit.); suburban pattern · Vorortmuster *n*, Vorortschema *n*

suburban scheme (US); peripheral community pattern, umland community pattern, peripheral community scheme, umland community scheme; suburban pattern · Umlandgemeindemuster *n*, Umlandgemeindeschema *n*

suburban school (Brit.) · Vorortschule *f*

suburban school (US); peripheral community school, umland community school · Umlandgemeindeschule *f*

suburban society (Brit.) · Vorortgesellschaft *f*

suburban society (US); peripheral community society, umland community society · Umlandgemeindegesellschaft *f*

suburban spread, suburban sprawl, spread(ing) of cities, sprawl of cities, spread(ing) of towns, sprawl of towns, suburbanization, decentralization, formation of sub(urb)s, suburban process, suburban urbanization, (urban) spread, (urban) sprawl, outward spread, outward sprawl · Sied(e)lungsbrei *m*, Dezentralisation *f*, Ausufern *n*, Zersied(e)lung *f*, Überwucherung des städtischen Raumes, Dezentralisierung *f*

(suburban) squatting community, squatter settlement, witch town, shanty town, (suburban) squatting colony · Blechhüttenvorort *m* [*Fehlbenennung: Blechhüttenstadt f*]

suburban street (Brit.) · Vorortstraße *f*

suburban territory, suburban area (US); peripheral area, peripheral territory, umland territory, umland area · Umlandgebiet *n*

suburban territory (Brit.); suburban area · Vorortgebiet *n*

suburban town (Brit.); outer city, outer town (US); suburban city · Außenstadt *f*, Vorstadt

suburban traffic (Brit.) · Vorortverkehr *m*

suburban traffic (US); peripheral community traffic, umland community traffic · Umlandgemeindeverkehr *m*

suburban urbanization → suburbanization

suburbanward (Brit.) · vorortwärts

suburbia [*obsolete*]; interurbia · Auffüllung *f* der Räume zwischen zwei Städten, aufgefüllter Raum *m* zwischen zwei Städten

sub-vendee, sub-purchaser, sub-buyer · Käufer *m* vom Erstkäufer

subvention, allowance · Beihilfe *f*, Subvention *f*

subvention plan, allowance plan · Subventionsplan *m*, Beihilfeplan

subversive · verfassungsfeindlich, staatsgefährdend

sub-zero weather day · Frosttag *m*

subzone · Unterzone *f*

succeeding generation(s), posterity, descendants · Nachkommenschaft *f*

to succeed in law · erfolgreich prozessieren

successful contractor, approved bidder, low responsible bidder, successful bidder, approved tenderer, low responsible tenderer, successful tenderer [*He is not necessarily the bidder whose bid is the lowest. "Responsible" means that the bid is taken together with the bidders*

successful party (of a (law)suit) — sufferance bill

financial ability, reputation and past performance] · Auftragnehmer *m*, AN *m*

successful party (of a (law)suit) · Prozeßgewinner *m*

successio hereditaria legitima [*Latin*] · rechtmäßige Erbfolge *f*

successio in universum jus defuncti [*Latin*]; universal succession, universal privity · Gesamt(rechts)nachfolge *f*, Universal(rechts)nachfolge

succession · Nachfolge *f*

succession → (hereditary) succession

succession → privity

succession ab intestato, intestate succession [*The succession of an heir at law to the property and estate of his ancestor when the latter has died intestate, or leaving a will which has been annulled or set aside*] · gesetzliche Erbfolge *f*, Intestaterbfolge

succession according to foreign law → (hereditary) succession according to foreign law

succession by inheritance, (hereditary) succession, (hereditary) descent, heirdom [*Succession to the ownership of an estate by inheritance*] · Erbgang *m*, Erbfolge *f*, erbrechtliche Nachfolge

succession by inheritance according to foreign law, heirdom according to foreign law, (hereditary) descent according to foreign law, (hereditary) succession according to foreign law · Erbfolge *f* nach ausländischem Recht, Erbfolge nach fremdem Recht, Erbgang *m* nach ausländischem Recht, Erbgang nach fremdem Recht, erbrechtliche Nachfolge nach ausländischem Recht, erbrechtliche Nachfolge nach fremdem Recht

succession by inheritance per capita, (hereditary) succession per capita, (hereditary) descent per capita, heirdom per capita · Erbgang *m* nach Köpfen, Erbfolge *f* nach Köpfen, erbrechtliche Nachfolge nach Köpfen

succession duty [*Abolished in England by the Finance Act, 1949, s. 28*] · Nachfolgesteuer *f* [*Sie betraf nur dasjenige Mobiliarvermögen, welches ein Rechtsnachfolger vor einem englischen, schottischen oder irischen Gericht einklagen konnte*]

succession evidence, evidence of succession · Rechtsnachfolgenachweis *m*

succession ex testamento, testamentary succession · testamentarische Erbfolge *f*

succession in possession · Vollbesitz *m*

succession in title → privity

succession in title after death, (legal) succession after death, privity after death · Rechtsnachfolge *f* von Todes wegen

succession in title inter vivos, (legal) succession inter vivos, privity inter vivos · Rechtsnachfolge *f* unter Lebenden

succession of the Crown · Thronfolge *f*

succession per capita → (hereditary) succession per capita

succession to estate → succession to property

succession to property, succession to estate · Vermögensnachfolge *f*

successor · Nachfolger *m*

successor clause · Nachfolgerklausel *f*

successor in business · Geschäftsnachfolger *m*

successor in office · Amtsnachfolger *m*

successor in possession, (ab)alienee, possessory successor · Besitznachfolger *m*, Veräußerungsbegünstigte

successor in (real) estate with the original covenantee, successor in (real) property with the original covenantee, privy in realty with the original covenantee, successor in realty with the original covenantee, privy in (real) estate with the original covenantee, privy in (real) property with the original covenantee · Rechtsnachfolger *m* in das Grundstücksrecht der ursprünglichen Vertragspartei

successor in realty, successor in (real) property, successor in (real) estate, privy in (real) estate, privy in (real) property, privy in realty · Rechtsnachfolger *m* in ein Grundstücksrecht

successor in right, representative, privy successor, legal successor · Rechtsnachfolger *m*

successors in title, privies in title · Rechtsnachfolger *m pl* die sich auf denselben Titel stützen

successor state · Nachfolgestaat *m*

to sue; actionare [*Latin*]; to bring an action (against), to file a bill, to file a (law)suit, to file an action · einreichen (einer Klage), erheben (einer Klage), klagen

to sue, to prosecute by due course of law; implacitare [*Latin*]; to implead · (privatrechtlich) verklagen, gerichtlich belangen

to sue for damages, to bring an action for damages · klagen auf Schadenersatz

sufferance, toleration; sufferentia, patientia [*Latin*] · Duldung *f*, stillschweigende Billigung

sufferance bill, bill of sufferance · Freihandelsschein *m*, Passierschein [*Erlaubnisschein Güter zollfrei zu versenden*]

sufferance warehouse, bonded warehouse · Freilager *n*, Freihafenniederlage *f*

sufficiency in law · Rechtsstaatlichkeit *f*

sufficiency of tender, sufficiency of offer, sufficiency of bid; sufficiency of (bid) proposal (US) · Hinlänglichkeit *f* des Angebots

suffrage → vote

to suit, to make suitable, to adapt [*To fit a person or thing to another, to or for a purpose*] · anpassen

suit, secta · Prozeßgefolge *n*

suitability, appropriateness, special fitness, suitableness · Zweckmäßigkeit *f*

suitable for habitation, fit for habitation, (in)habitable, fit to live in · bewohnbar, belegbar

suitableness, suitability, appropriateness, special fitness · Zweckmäßigkeit *f*

suitableness, suitability, fitness, flexibility, adaptability, adaptableness, adaptiveness, adaptedness · Anpassungsvermögen *n*, Anpassungsfähigkeit *f*

suit and grist, grinding fee, fee for grinding, toll paid for grinding, multure; molitura, multura [*Latin*]; grinding toll · Mahlgeld *n*, Mahlzins *m*, Mahlgebühr *f*

suit at common law → (law-)suit at common law

suitcase farmer · Pendlerlandwirt *m* [*Er pendelt im Sommer- und Winterweizengebiet der USA zweimal im Jahr*]

suit de bonis asportatis → (law)suit de bonis asportatis

suite of offices · Büroflucht *f*

suite of rooms · Zimmerflucht *f*

suit for an account → (law)suit for an account

suit for breach of contract → (law)suit for breach of contract

suit for delivery → (court) action for delivery

suit for exemption from liability → (law)suit for exemption from liability

suit for intrusion → (law)suit for trespass

suit for money had and received → (law)suit for money had and received

suit for payment → (law)suit for payment

suit for redemption → (law)suit for redemption

suit for refunding → (law)suit for reimbursement

suit for removal → (law)suit for removal

suit for restitution → (law)suit for reimbursement

suit for specific performance → (law)suit for specific performance

suit for tort → (law)suit for tort

suit for trespass → (law)suit for trespass

suit for unjust detainment → (law)suit for unjust detention

suit founded on tort → (law)suit founded on tort

suit in error → (law)suit in error

suiting, rendering suitable, fitting, adapting · Anpassen *n*

suiting effect, adap(ta)tion effect, adapting effect, fitting effect · Anpassungswirkung *f*

suit in tort → (law)suit in tort

suit of account → (law)suit of account

suit of advowson → (law)suit of advowson

suit of assumpsit → (court) action of assumpsit

suit of contestation → (court) action of contestation

suit of contract → cause of contract

suit of debt → (law)suit of debt

suit of deceit → (law)suit of deceit

suit of detinue → (law)suit for unjust detention

suit of devastation → (law)suit of devastation

suit of equity → (law)suit of equity

suit of estrepement → (law)suit of estrepement

suit of eviction → (law)suit of eviction

suit of injunction → (law)suit of injunction

suit of mistake → (law)suit of mistake

suit of patronage → (law)suit of patronage

suit of possessory right → (law)suit of possessory right

suit of replevin → (law)suit of replevin

suit of the fold, fold suit; seeta faldae [*Latin*], fold-soke [*The duty of a tenant to set up and move about in the fields of a manor a fold for the purpose of manuring the ground*] · (Schaf)Pferchpflicht *f*

suit of transumpt → (law)suit of transumpt

suit of trover (and conversion) → (law)suit of trover (and conversion)

suit on the case → (law)suit on the case

suitor; sectator [*Latin*]; credible witness · glaubwürdiger Zeuge *m*

suitor, litigant (party), party to a (law)suit; sectator, litigans [*Latin*]; litigator · Prozessierende *m*, Prozeßpartei *f*

suit per se — sum of the years-digit method

suit per se → (law)suit per se

suit personal → (law)suit personal

suit to gain an injunction → (law)suit to gain an injunction

suit to quiet title → (law)suit to quiet title

sum invested for home building · Bausparsumme *f*

summagium, averagium [*Latin*]; carting · Fuhrdienst *m* [*Fronhofarbeit*]

summary court, registrar's court, court of summary jurisdiction, court of request, registrary's court, court of conscience, police court, P., petty court · Bagatellgericht *n*, Friedensgericht für kleine Straf- und Zivilsachen, Polizeigericht, Ortsgericht für gering(fügig)e Schuldklagen [*in England*]

summary judg(e)ment · Urteil *n* ohne streitige Verhandlung

summary motion · summarischer Antrag *m* bei Gericht

summary of bids, summary of tenders, summary of offers, schedule of bids, schedule of tenders, schedule of offers; summary of (bid) proposals, schedule of (bid) proposals (US) · Angebotsgegenüberstellung *f*

summary offence · Übertretung *f*, kleines Vergehen *n*

summary of financial operations; capital-reconciliation statement (Brit.); accounting for the flow of funds, statement of (sources and applications of) funds, funds statement · Kapital(zu)flußrechnung *f*, Finanzierungsrechnung, Finanz(zu)flußrechnung, Bewegungsbilanz *f*, Mittelherkunft- und -verwendungsrechnung

summary probate proceeding · summarisches Nachlaßverfahren *n*, summarisches Erb(schafts)verfahren

summary proceeding · summarisches Verfahren *n*

summary proceeding on documentary evidence alone, summary proceeding on documentary proof alone · summarisches Urkundenverfahren *n*

summation · (Anwalt)Schlußrede *f*

summation appraisal, appraisal by summation [*Adding together of parts of a property separately appraised to form the whole. For example, the value of the land considered as vacant is added to the cost(s) of reproduction of the building less depreciation*] · Sachwertverfahren *n*, Sachwertberechnung *f*

sum(mation) frequency, cumulative frequency · Summenhäufigkeit *f*

(summer) holiday period (camping) site [*A caravan site occupied for the summer holiday period only*] · Sommerferiencampingplatz *m*

summer holiday resort · Sommerferienort *m*, Sommerfrische *f*

summer population · Sommerbevölkerung *f*

summer rain hour · Sommerregenstunde *f*

summing-up · Rechtsbelehrung *f* durch einen Berufsrichter

to summon → to subp(o)ena

summoned, called, cited · (vor)geladen, aufgeboten [*vor Gericht*]

summoner · Vorlader *m*

summons [*In Chambers*] · (Vor)Ladung *f* zur Verhandlung über einen mündlichen Zwischenantrag

summons for directions → (general) summons for directions

summons to appear in court, assignation · (Gerichts)Vorladung *f*

summons to stay proceeding, plea in suspension of the action · Verteidigung *f* auf zeitweise Abweisung der Klage

sum of building, sum of production, construction sum, building sum, production sum, sum of construction · Bausumme *f*, Herstellungssumme

sum of building (construction), building (construction) sum · Herstellungssumme *f*, Bausumme [*Hochbau*]

sum of complaint · Beschwerdesumme *f*

sum of construction, sum of building, sum of production, construction sum, building sum, production sum · Bausumme *f*, Herstellungssumme

sum of discharge, redemption sum, sum of redemption, discharge sum · Ablösungssumme *f*, Auslösungssumme, Einlösungssumme

sum of events · Ereignissumme *f*

sum of fine · Bußgeldsumme *f*, Strafgeldsumme, Reugeldsumme

sum of heavy construction, heavy construction sum · Herstellungssumme *f*, Bausumme [*Tiefbau*]

sum of liability, liability sum · Haftsumme *f*, Haftpflichtsumme

sum of money · Geldsumme *f*

sum of production, construction sum, building sum, production sum, sum of construction, sum of building · Bausumme *f*, Herstellungssumme

sum of redemption, discharge sum, sum of discharge, redemption sum · Ablösungssumme *f*, Auslösungssumme, Einlösungssumme

sum of the years-digit method (of depreciation) · Jahressummen(abschrei-

sum overrun — superior administrative court 1020

bungs)methode f, digitale Abschreibungsmethode

sum overrun, overrun of sum · Summenüberschreitung f

sumptuary law, law against luxury · Antiluxusgesetz n

sum recovered by judg(e)ment · Summe f durch Urteil zugesprochen

(sum) total, grand sum · Gesamtsumme f

sun city, sun town · Pensionärsstadt f, Rentnerstadt [*In einem klimatisch bevorzugten Gebiet*]

sunday observance · Sonntagsruhe f

sunday work · Sonntagsarbeit f

sunk, drowned, absorbed, extinguished, merged · untergegangen [*Wenn sich z. B. Eigentum und Pfandrecht in einer Hand vereinigen, geht das kleinere im größeren unter*]

sunk capital · fest angelegtes Kapital n, fest investiertes Kapital

to supervise, to superintend, to oversee · beaufsichtigen, überwachen

supervising, superintending, overseeing · Beaufsichtigen n, Überwachen

superblock [*A very large block within a city; frequently formed by combining or consolidating several smaller blocks through an urban renewal programme*] · Großblock m

superficiar(ius) [*Latin*]; leaseholder [*A builder (up)on another's land under a contract*] · Erbbauherr m, Superfiziar m, Erbbaurechtnehmer

superficies · Superfizies f, Platzrecht n [*Das Recht auf fremdem Boden Gebäude, Bäume und Holzungen zu haben*]

superimposed levels · übereinanderliegende Ebenen fpl

to superintend, to oversee, to supervise · beaufsichtigen, überwachen

superintendence of demolition, supervision of demolition, superintendence of wrecking, supervision of wrecking, superintendence of pulling down, supervision of pulling down, supervision of razing · Abbruchaufsicht f, Einreißaufsicht, Abrißaufsicht, Einreißüberwachung f, Abbruchüberwachung, Abrißüberwachung

superintendence of planning, planning supervision, planning superintendence, supervision of planning · Planungsaufsicht f, Planungsüberwachung f

superintendence of pulling down → superintendence of demolition

superintendence of razing, superintendence of demolition, supervision of demolition, superintendence of wrecking, supervision of wrecking, superintendence of pulling down, supervision of pulling down, supervision of razing · Abbruchaufsicht f, Einreißaufsicht, Abrißaufsicht, Einreißüberwachung f, Abbruchüberwachung, Abrißüberwachung

superintendence of site(s) → supervision of site(s)

superintendence (of (the) work(s)) · (Bau)Oberleitung f, Oberbauleitung

superintendence (of the project), supervision (of the project) · Aufsicht f, Überwachung f, Beaufsichtigung f, Bauaufsicht, Bauüberwachung, Baubeaufsichtigung, Projektaufsicht, Projektüberwachung, Projektbeaufsichtigung, Bauleitung, Projektleitung

superintendence of wrecking → superintendence of demolition

superintendent → (contractor's) superintendent

superintendent inspector · Regierungskommissar m

superintendent of pauper labour · Armenarbeitsaufseher m

superintendent registrar · Hauptstandesbeamte m

superintending, overseeing, supervising · Beaufsichtigen n, Überwachen

superintending, supervising · aufsichtsführend

superintending activity, overseeing activity, supervising activity · beaufsichtigende Tätigkeit f, überwachende Tätigkeit

superintending authority, authority of supervision, authority of superintendence, supervising authority · Aufsichtsvollmacht f, Beaufsichtigungsvollmacht, Überwachungsvollmacht, Aufsichtsvertretungsmacht, Überwachungsvertretungsmacht, Beaufsichtigungsvertretungsmacht

superintending person, supervising person · Aufsichtsperson f, Überwachungsperson f

superintending power, superintending right, right of supervision, right of superintendence, power of supervision, supervising power, supervising right, power of superintendence, right to supervise, right to superintend, power to supervise, power to superintend · Aufsichtsbefugnis f, Aufsichtsrecht n, Überwachungsbefugnis f, Überwachungsrecht n

superior · höher(stehend), übergeordnet

superior · Vorgesetzte m

superior administrative court · Oberverwaltungsgericht n, OVG

superior administrative authority · höhere Verwaltungsbehörde f, vorgesetzte Verwaltungsbehörde, obere Verwaltungsbehörde

superior authority · höhere Behörde f, obere Behörde, vorgesetzte Behörde

superior court · höheres Gericht n, oberes Gericht, vorgesetztes Gericht

superiority [*Scots law*. The dominium directum of land(s), without the profit] · abstraktes Grundstücksobereigentum n

superior knowledge · besseres Wissen n

superior legislator · übergeordneter Gesetzgeber m

superior lord → liege-lord

superior plan · übergeordneter Plan m

superior planning · übergeordnete Planung f

superior worker's cottage, superior workman's cottage · besseres Arbeiterhaus n

super metropolis (US); highest-order fully-central place · Reichs-Hauptort m [*nach W. Christaller*]

superoneratio [*Latin*]; surcharge (of common), surcharge of pastur(ag)e [*The putting by a commoner, of more beasts on the common than he has a right to*] · Überbeanspruchung f eines Weiderechts

supersonic transport(ation) · Überschallflugverkehr m

superstore · Superladen(geschäft) n

supervening event · eintretendes Ereignis n

supervising, superintending · aufsichtsführend

supervising activity, superintending activity, overseeing activity · beaufsichtigende Tätigkeit f, überwachende Tätigkeit

supervising architect, principal architect, architect-in-charge · ausführender Architekt m, (bau)leitender Architekt m

supervising authority, superintending authority, authority of supervision, authority of superintendence · Aufsichtsvollmacht f, Beaufsichtigungsvollmacht f, Überwachungsvollmacht f, Aufsichtsvertretungsmacht, Überwachungsvertretungsmacht, Beaufsichtigungsvertretungsmacht

supervising duty, duty to supervise, duty of supervision · Aufsichtspflicht f, Überwachungspflicht f

supervising hour, hour of supervision · Aufsichtsstunde f, Überwachungsstunde f

supervising person, superintending person · Aufsichtsperson f, Überwachungsperson f

supervising power, supervising right, power of superintendence, right to supervise, right to superintend, power to supervise, power to superintend, superintending power, superintending right, right of supervision, right of superintendence, power of supervision · Aufsichtsbefugnis f, Aufsichtsrecht n, Überwachungsbefugnis f, Überwachungsrecht n

supervision of demolition, superintendence of wrecking, supervision of wrecking, superintendence of pulling down, supervision of pulling down, supervision of razing, superintendence of razing, superintendence of demolition · Abbruchaufsicht f, Einreißaufsicht, Abrißaufsicht, Einreißüberwachung f, Abbruchüberwachung, Abrißüberwachung

supervision of planning, superintendence of planning, planning supervision, planning superintendence · Planungsaufsicht f, Planungsüberwachung f

supervision of razing, superintendence of razing, superintendence of demolition, supervision of demolition, superintendence of wrecking, supervision of wrecking, superintendence of pulling down, supervision of pulling down · Abbruchaufsicht f, Einreißaufsicht, Abrißaufsicht, Einreißüberwachung f, Abbruchüberwachung, Abrißüberwachung

supervision of site(s), superintendence of site(s), site supervision, site superintendence, construction site supervision, construction site superintendence, job site supervision, job site superintendence, building site superintendence, building site supervision · Bau(stellen)aufsicht f, Bau(stellen)überwachung f, Objektaufsicht, Objektüberwachung

supervision (of the project), superintendence (of the project) · Aufsicht f, Überwachung f, Beaufsichtigung f, Bauaufsicht f, Bauüberwachung f, Baubeaufsichtigung f, Projektaufsicht f, Projektüberwachung f, Projektbeaufsichtigung f, Bauleitung f, Projektleitung f

supervision of wrecking → supervision of demolition

supervisor, line position [*Organization of business enterprises*] · Linienstelle f, Linieninstanz f, Chef m

supervisor (on site), site agent, site supervisor, agent (on site) · Bauleiter m, Bauleitung f, Baustellenleiter, Baustellenleitung, örtlicher Bauleiter, örtliche Bauleitung [*des Unternehmers*]

supervisory board · Aufsichtsrat m

supervisory board member · Aufsichtsratmitglied *n*

supervisory control · Dienstaufsicht *f*

supervisory employe(e), supervisory servant · leitender Arbeitnehmer *m*

supervisory management · Immobilien-Kontrollverwaltung *f*

supervisory staff · Aufsichtspersonal *n*, Überwachungspersonal *n*

supplement, addendum [*Revised, changed, or corrected document or addition to the contract documents*] · Ergänzung *f*, Nachtrag *m*

supplemental, supplementary · ergänzend

supplemental agreement, supplementary agreement · Ergänzungsabkommen *n*, Ergänzungsabmachung *f*, Ergänzungsvereinbarung, Nachtragsabkommen, Nachtragsabmachung, Nachtragsvereinbarung

supplemental agreement, supplementary agreement · Zusatzabmachung *f*, Zusatzabkommen *n*, Zusatzvereinbarung

supplemental bid, supplemental offer, supplemental tender, supplementary bid, supplementary offer, supplementary tender; supplemental (bid) proposal, supplementary (bid) proposal (US) · Nachtragsangebot *n*, Ergänzungsangebot

supplemental general conditions, supplementary general conditions · allgemeine Ergänzungsbedingungen *fpl*, allgemeine Nachtragsbedingungen

supplemental item, supplementary item · Ergänzungsposition *f*, Nachtragsposition

supplemental obligation, supplementary obligation, accessory obligation · Zusatzverpflichtung *f*, Zusatzverbindlichkeit *f*, Zusatzgebundenheit, Zusatzbindung, Ergänzungsverpflichtung, Ergänzungsverbindlichkeit, Ergänzungsgebundenheit, Ergänzungsbindung

supplemental provision, supplementary provision · Ergänzungsbestimmung *f*, Nachtragsbestimmung

supplementary, supplemental · ergänzend

supplementary agreement, supplemental agreement · Ergänzungsabkommen *n*, Ergänzungsabmachung *f*, Ergänzungsvereinbarung, Nachtragsabkommen, Nachtragsabmachung, Nachtragsvereinbarung

supplementary condition · Zusatzbedingung *f*

supplementary contour · Zwischenhöhenlinie *f*

supplementary general conditions, supplemental general conditions · allgemeine Ergänzungsbedingungen *fpl*, allgemeine Nachtragsbedingungen

supplementary item, supplemental item · Ergänzungsposition *f*, Nachtragsposition

supplementary obligation, accessory obligation, supplemental obligation · Zusatzverpflichtung *f*, Zusatzverbindlichkeit *f*, Zusatzgebundenheit, Zusatzbindung, Ergänzungsverpflichtung, Ergänzungsverbindlichkeit, Ergänzungsgebundenheit, Ergänzungsbindung

supplementary proceeding · Offenlegung *f* des schuldnerischen Vermögens, Verfahren *n* zur Offenlegung des schuldnerischen Vermögens

supplementary provision, supplemental provision · Ergänzungsbestimmung *f*, Nachtragsbestimmung

supplementary technical rule · zusätzliche technische Vorschrift *f*

supplementation · Vervollständigung *f*, Ergänzung

supplementation of a plan · Planergänzung *f*, Plannachtrag *m*

supplement (volume) · Ergänzungsband *m*, Nachtragsband

suppletory oath [*An oath administered to a party himself in cases where a fact has been proved by only one witness, in order to supply or make up the necessary complement of witnesses; two witnesses being always required to constitute full proof*] · Erfüllungseid *m*

supplier · Lieferant *m*, Zulieferer

to supply, to furnish · beistellen [*Baustoff(e)*]

supply · (Zu)Lieferung *f*

supply, furnishing · Beistellung *f* [*Baustoff(e)*]

supply · Bedienung *f*, Bedarfsdeckung, Versorgung

supply · Angebot *n*, Bereitstellung *f*

supply and demand, supply and call, market forces, demand and supply, call and supply · Angebot *n* und Nachfrage *f*, Nachfrage und Angebot

supply area, supply territory · Versorgungsgebiet *n*

supply axis · Versorgungsband *n* [*An ihm entlang verdichtet sich die Besied(e)lung punktförmig, die Zwischenräume werden forst- und/oder landwirtschaftlich genutzt oder bleiben für die Erholung frei*]

supply by owner, supply by client, supply by promoter, supply by employer, furnishing by owner, furnishing by client, furnishing by promoter, furnishing by employer · Beistellung f durch den Bauherrn [Baustoff(e)]

supply contract · Liefer(ungs)vertrag m

supply curve · Angebotskurve f

supply curve for labour (Brit.); supply curve for labor (US) · Angebotskurve f für Arbeit, Arbeitsangebotskurve

supply date, date of supply · Liefertag m, Lieferdatum n, Liefertermin m

supply facility · Versorgungseinrichtung f

supply function · Angebotsfunktion f

supplying distant needs · fernbedarfstätig

supply installation, supply plant · Versorgungsanlage f

supply into the network · Abgabe f ins Netz

supply line, utility line · Versorgungsleitung f

supply of air, air supply · Luftversorgung f

supply of gas, gas supply · Gasversorgung f

supply of housing, housing supply · Wohnraumangebot n, Wohnungsangebot, Wohnraumbereitstellung f, Wohnungsbereitstellung, Wohnraumversorgung, Wohnungsversorgung

supply of land(s), land(s) supply · Bodenangebot n, Landangebot, Bodenbereitstellung f, Landbereitstellung

supply-orien(ta)ted industry, supply-related industry · rohstoffquellenbezogene Industrie f, rohstoffquellenorientierte Industrie

supply plan · Versorgungsplan m

supply planning · Versorgungsplanung f

supply plant, supply installation · Versorgungsanlage f

supply territory, supply area · Versorgungsgebiet n

supply to user · Direktlieferung f

to support, to set forth, to propound, to propose [To put forward for consideration] · befürworten, vorschlagen

support, maintenance · Unterhalt m [Person]

supported monorail (system) · Einschienen-Standbahn f

supported railway (Brit.); supported railroad (US) · Standbahn f

supporter, backer · Unterstützende m [z. B. Kreditgeber]

supporter, proponent · Befürworter m

support price, administered price · Stütz(ungs)preis m

supposable, conceivable, imaginable · denkbar, vorstellbar

supposed title, reputed title, putative title · Putativ(rechts)titel m

suppression of files · Aktenunterdrückung f

supra-regional location · überregionale Lage f

supremacy, authority, majesty, pre-eminence; majestas [Latin]; sovereign power, sovereign right, sovereign dominion, sovereignty, liberty · Hoheitsrecht n, Hoheitsbefugnis f, hoheitliches Recht, hoheitliche Befugnis, Souveränität f, Oberhoheit f, Hoheitsmacht f, vollziehende Gewalt f

supremacy oath, oath of supremacy · Supremat(s)eid m, Kirchentreu(e)eid [1534—1829. Eid der englischen Beamten, den König oder die Königin als obersten geistlichen Herren oder oberste geistliche Herrn anzuerkennen]

supremacy of common law · Souveränität f des gemeinen Rechtes, Oberhoheit f des gemeinen Rechtes

supremacy of law · Souveränität f des Rechtes, Oberhoheit f des Rechtes

supreme, paramount · oberst, höchst

supreme board of surveyors · oberste (Bau)Aufsichtsbehörde f, höchste (Bau)Aufsichtsbehörde

supreme court · oberstes Gericht n, höchstes Gericht

Supreme Court (of a State) · Oberstes Gliedstaatengericht n, Höchstes Gliedstaatengericht, Oberstes Einzelstaatengericht, Höchstes Einzelstaatengericht [USA]

Supreme Court of Judicature [It consists of: 1. Her (or His) Majesty's High Court of Justice and 2. Her (or His) Majesty's Court of Appeal] · Oberster Gerichtshof m in England, Höchster Gerichtshof in England

Supreme Court of New York · Gerichtshof m des Staates New York mit unbegrenzter erstinstanzlicher sachlicher Zuständigkeit [Trotz seiner Amtsbezeichnung ist dieser Gerichtshof nicht der höchste des Staates New York, das ist der Court of Appeals. Der Supreme Court verdankt den irreführenden Namen dem Umstand, daß er der einzige Gerichtshof des Staates New York mit unbegrenzter erstinstanzlicher sachlicher Zuständigkeit ist. Daneben gibt es mehrere erstinstanzliche Gerichte mit begrenzter sachlicher Zuständigkeit]

Supreme Court of Tax Appeals · Reichsfinanzhof m, RFH

Supreme Court of the United States · oberster Bundesgerichtshof m, höchster Bundesgerichtshof [USA]

supreme Land authority, oberste Landesbehörde f, höchste Landesbehörde [Bundesrepublik Deutschland]

supreme legislator, supreme lawmaker · oberster Gesetzgeber m, höchster Gesetzgeber

supreme lord (of a fee), paramount lord (of a fee), sovereign lord (of a fee), lord paramount (of a fee) [The Queen or the King are lords paramount of all the lands in the Kingdom] · oberster Leh(e)n(s)herr m, höchster Leh(e)n(s)herr, oberster Feudalherr, höchster Feudalherr

supreme owner, landlord, grantor, feoffor, feoffer, manor lord, langeman, bestower of a fee, feudal chief; dominus directus, feoffator [Latin]; (feudal) lord, chief lord, possessory lord, liege-lord, over lord, lord of (the) manor, superior lord · Leh(e)n(s)herr m, Feudalherr, (feudaler) Belehner, Leh(e)n(s)gutgeber, Obereigentümer, Landübertragende, Übertragende von Land

to surcharge, to impose · auferlegen

surcharge, addition, markup [That which is added to price(s) or cost(s)] · Zuschlag m, Aufschlag [Preis; Kosten]

surcharge for resumption of work, addition for resumption of work, markup for resumption of work · Wiederaufnahmezuschlag m, Wiederaufnahmeaufschlag

surcharge (of common), surchage of pastur(ag)e; superoneratio [Latin] [The putting by a commoner, of more beasts on the common than he has a right to] · Überbeanspruchung f eines Weiderechts

surcharge of pastur(ag)e; superoneratio [Latin]; surchage (of common) [The putting by a commoner, of more beasts on the common than he has a right to] · Überbeanspruchung f eines Weiderechts

surcharge on surtax · Sonderabgabe f im Rahmen der Einkommensteuer

surcharge rate, addition rate, markup rate · Aufschlag(s)rate f, Zuschlag(s)rate

surety, insurer of a debt, guarantor, cautioner, pledge [The party who expresses his willingness to answer for the debt, default, or obligation of another. The word "surety" is sometimes used interchangeably for the word "guarantor"; but, strictly speaking, a "surety" is one who is bound with the principal debtor upon the original contract, the same as if he had made the contract himself, while a "guarantor" is bound upon a separate contract to make good in case the principal debtor fails. The guarantor is therefore an insurer of the solvency of the debtor. A surety is held primarily liable on an instrument while a guarantor is held secondarily liable on it; that is, the surety agrees that he will pay the obligation in any event, while the guarantor merely agrees that he will pay the obligation if the principal debtor fails to pay] · Bürge m

surety bond, guaranty bond, guarantee bond, guarantie bond [Guarantee by a surety company that the contractor will either complete the work or pay all obligations or both, depending on how the bond is worded. If the bond guarantees payment of financial obligation, it is called a "payment bond". If the bond guarantees the completion of the work, it is called a "performance bond" or a "completion bond"] · Kautionsversicherung f

surety company [It engages in the business of issuing surety bonds or becoming surety for trustees, guardians, executors, administrators, employees, etc. If any of these listed should be unfaithful to his trust and make away with property, the company makes good the loss] · Kautions(versicherungs)gesellschaft f

surety law · Bürgenrecht n, objektives Bürgenrecht

surety of collection, cautioner of collection, collection surety, collection cautioner, collection guarantor, guarantor of collection · Ausfallbürge m, Rückbürge, Schad(los)bürge

surety right, guarantor right, cautioner right, right of the surety, right of the guarantor, right of the cautioner, right of the insurer of a debt · Bürgenrecht n, subjektives Bürgenrecht

surface area · Oberflächeninhalt m

surface chart, synoptic chart · synoptische (Wetter)Karte f

surface line · überirdische Leitung f, Übertageleitung, oberirdische Leitung

surface mining, open mining, strip mining · Tage(ab)bau m, oberirdischer Abbau

surface mining land(s), strip mining land(s), open-cut mining land(s), open pit mining land(s), open work(ing) land(s), stripping land(s), open-cast work(ing) land(s), exploitation land(s), open-cut mining area, strip mining area, surface mining area, open-cast work(ing) area · Abbauland n, Tagebauland, Abbaufläche f, Tagebaufläche [Grundstücke, die auf Grund ihrer Beschaffenheit die oberirdische Gewinnung von Bodenschätzen ermöglichen]

surface of (real) estate, surface of (real) property, surface of land, (real) estate surface, (real) property surface, land surface, realty surface, surface of realty · Grund(stücks)oberfläche f, Bodenoberfläche, Landoberfläche

surface parking (area), open parking (area) [As distinguished from a parking garage] · Freiparkfläche f

surface physical facility, surface work, surface structure · oberirdische (bauliche) Anlage f, oberirdisches (Bau)Werk n, oberirdischer Bau m

surface street, ground level street · ebenerdige Stadtstraße f

surface structure, surface physical facility, surface work · oberirdische (bauliche) Anlage f, oberirdisches (Bau)Werk n, oberirdischer Bau m

surface utility → (public) surface utility

surface work, surface structure, surface physical facility · oberirdische (bauliche) Anlage f, oberirdisches (Bau)Werk n, oberirdischer Bau m

surfacial geology · Oberflächengeologie f

surname, family name, last name, agnomination · Nachname m, Familienname

surplus, overplus · Mehrerlös m

surplus, excess, overplus · Überschuß m

surplusage · überflüssige Bestandteile m pl [*Rechtsschrift*]

surplus asset, excess asset; excess paid-in capital (US) [*In a balance sheet*] · überschießende Aktiva f, Überschußaktiva, Mehraktiva

surplus birth rate, surplus of births over deaths, excess birth rate · Geburtenüberschuß m

surplus call, excess call, surplus demand, excess demand · Mehrnachfrage f, Übernachfrage

surplus capacity, excess capacity · Überkapazität f, überschießende Kapazität, Mehrkapazität

surplus clause, overplus clause · Mehrerlösklausel f [*Maklervertrag*]

surplus cost(s), excess cost(s) · Mehrkosten f, Überkosten, überschießende Kosten

surplus demand, excess demand, surplus call, excess call · Mehrnachfrage f, Übernachfrage

surplus gain tax, excess profit tax, excess gain tax, surplus profit tax · Übergewinnsteuer f, Überprofitsteuer

surplus (general) property, excess (general) property, surplus proprietorship, excess proprietorship, surplus ownership (of property), excess ownership (of property) · Überschußeigentum n

surplus income, excess income · Mehreinkommen n, Überschußeinkommen, überschießendes Einkommen

surplus of births over deaths, excess birth rate, surplus birth rate · Geburtenüberschuß m

surplus ownership (of property), excess ownership (of property), surplus (general) property, excess (general) property, surplus proprietorship, excess proprietorship · Überschußeigentum n

surplus population, excess population · Überschußbevölkerung f

surplus price, excess price · Mehrpreis m, Überschußpreis, überschießender Preis

surplus price clause, excess price clause · Mehrpreisklausel f

surplus production, excess production · Überproduktion f

surplus profit capitalization · Übergewinn-Kapitalisierung f

surplus profit tax, surplus gain tax, excess profit tax, excess gain tax · Übergewinnsteuer f, Überprofitsteuer

surplus proprietorship, excess proprietorship, surplus ownership (of property), excess ownership (of property), surplus (general) property, excess (general) property · Überschußeigentum n

surplus quantity, excess quantity · Überschußmenge f, Mehrmenge

(surplus) reserve, appropriated surplus [*Earned surplus earmarked on the books of account and in financial statements for some specific or general purposes*] · Rücklage f

surplus statement, statement of earned surplus, statement of accumulated earnings, statement of retained earnings · Ergebnisverwendungsrechnung f, Erfassung und Offenlegung von Rücklagenveränderungen

surplus water, excess water · Überschußwasser n, Mehrwasser

surplus work(s) · Mehr(bau)-arbeit(en) f (pl), Mehr(bau)leistung(en) f (pl)

surrebutter [*In pleading. The plaintiff's answer of fact to the defendant's rebutter*] · fünfte Gegenschrift f, Quintuplik f

surrejoinder [*In pleading. The plaintiff's answer of fact to the defendant's rejoinder*] · dritte Gegenschrift f, Triplik f

to surrender, to re-deliver · freiwillig zurückgeben

to surrender, to deliver (up), to hand over · aushändigen, übergeben

surrender, re-delivery · freiwillige (Zu)Rückgabe f

surrender date, handover date, (de)livery date, date of handing over, date of handover, date of (de)livery, date of surrender, handing over date · Aushändigungstermin m, Übergabetermin m, Aushändigungsdatum n, Übergabedatum n

surrendered, re-delivered · freiwillig zurückgegeben

surrendered, handed over, delivered (up) · ausgehändigt, übergeben

surrendering · freiwilliges Zurückgeben n

surrendering duty, duty to surrender · Rückgabepflicht f

surrender value, cash(ing)-in value · Rückkaufwert m, Rückkaufkurs m [Versicherungsfondsanteil; Sparbrief; Police]

to surrogate, ro replace, to substitute · ersetzen

surrogate [The judicial officer who presides over a probate court for the administration of the estates of deceased persons] · Nachlaßgerichtsvorsitzende m

surrogate, surrogatum [Scotland;, substitute · Ersatz m

surrogate [One who is substituted or appointed in the room of another, as by a bishop, chancellor, judge, etc.] · Ersatzperson f

surrogate's court; orphan's court (US); probate court, court of probate [A court in which wills are probated, or proved. Called "orphans" court in a few states of the USA] · Nachlaßgericht n, Erb(schafts)gericht

surrogating · Surrogation f, Ersatzgestellung f

surrogating principle, principle of surrogating · Ersatzgrundsatz m, Ersatzprinzip n, Surrogationsgrundsatz, Surrogationsprinzip, Grundsatz der Ersatzhaftung, Prinzip der Ersatzhaftung

surrounding land, surrounding area, external service area, umland; suburban land (US); peripheral land [Sometimes, by local usage also called "landed estate" and "landed property" as distinguished from land in a city] · äußeres Ergänzungsgebiet n, Vorortzone f, Umland n, Umgelände n

surrounding land use, service area use, umland use; suburban land use (US), peripheral land use, external land use · Umlandnutzung f

surroundings, ambience · Umgebung f

surtax, additional tax, accessory tax, extra tax · Zusatzsteuer f

to survey · ausmessen, vermessen, aufnehmen

survey, advisory opinion, expertise · Gutachten n, Sachverständigenbericht m

survey [The term "survey", as used in land planning, means the collection, arrangement and interpretation of all the factors under consideration; and it involves the recording, tabulating and presentation of the material in such a manner as to be readily understood] · Enquête f

survey · Bestandsaufnahme f

survey → survey(ing)

survey and plotting of (a) structure · Bauanlageaufnahme f, Bau(werk)aufnahme; Bauteaufnahme [Schweiz] [Aufzeichnen und Aufmessen eines Bauwerkes und anschließende maßstabgetreue und bauplanmäßige Auftragung]

survey chart, general chart · Übersichtskarte f [Seegebiete]

survey committee · Enquêteausschuß m

survey design · Erhebungsplan m [Statistik]

survey document, survey report · Bestandsaufnahmebericht m

survey(ing) [The process by which a plot is measured and its area is ascertained] · Grund(stücks)festlegung f, Ausmessung, Vermessung, Aufnahme f

surveying · (Bau)Aufsicht f [durch eine Behörde]

surveying authority · Vermessungsbehörde f

surveying board · Vermessungsamt n

surveying cost(s) · Vermessungskosten f

surveying error · Vermessungsfehler m

surveying practice · Vermessungswesen n

survey map, general map · Übersichts(land)karte f

survey of lines · Linienfestlegung f

surveyor · (Bau)Aufsichtskontrolleur m [früher: Baupolizeikontrolleur]

surveyor → (land) surveyor

survey ordered by court, expertise ordered by court (Brit.); expert witness of the court (US) · Sachverständigengutachten n, unabhängiges Gutachten [Es wird von einem neutralen, vom Gericht bestellten Sachverständigen angefertigt. §§ 402ff. ZPO]

surveyor-general · Oberbaurat m

surveyor of highways, surveyor of roads, highway surveyor, road surveyor · Straßenaufseher m, Wegeaufseher

surveyor of land(s), land(s) surveyor · Domäneninspektor m

surveyor of (the) forests, forest surveyor, regarder · Forstinspektor m, Waldinspektor

survey period · Enquêtezeitraum m

survey report, survey document · Bestandsaufnahmebericht m

survey sheet, investigation sheet · Erhebungsbogen m, Untersuchungsbogen

survey year · Berichtsjahr n

to survive, to outlive, to over-live, to live beyond another · überleben

surviving dependant, surviving dependent · Hinterbliebene *m*

surviving person, longest liver, longer liver, survivor · Überlebende *m*

surviving spouse · überlebender Ehepartner *m*

survivorship [*The living of one of two or more persons after the death of the other or others*] · Überleben *n*

survivorship annuity · Hinterbliebenenrente *f*

survivorship rule, rule of survivorship · Überlebensregel *f*

suspensive and conditional discharge, conditional and suspensive discharge · bedingte und suspensive Entlastung *f*, suspensive und bedingte Entlastung

susceptibility · Anfälligkeit *f*

susceptibility analysis · Empfindlichkeitsanalyse *f*

susceptible · anfällig

susceptible of being expropriated; susceptible of being condemned (US) · enteignungsfähig

susceptible of proof · beweisbar

suspected female person · Tatverdächtige *f*

suspected male person · Tatverdächtige *m*

suspected person · tatverdächtige Person *f*

to suspend (work) · aussetzen, einstellen [*Arbeit(en)*]

suspended monorail (system) · Einschienen-Schwebebahn *f*, Einschienen-Hängebahn

suspended railway (Brit.); suspended railroad (US) · Hängebahn *f*, Schwebebahn

suspension, deferment, putting off, postponement · Aufschub *m*, Aufschiebung *f*, Hinausschiebung, Verschiebung *f*

suspension of payment · Zahlungseinstellung *f*

suspension of work(s), shutdown of work(s) · Einstellung *f* der Arbeit(en), Aussetzung der Arbeit(en), Arbeitseinstellung, Arbeitsaussetzung [*Einstellung der Arbeiten mit der Absicht der Wiederaufnahme derselben seitens Bauherr und Bauunternehmer*]

suspensive condition, precedent condition, condition precedent, condition suspensive · Anfangsbedingung *f*, Suspensivbedingung, suspensive Bedingung, aufschiebende Bedingung, hinausschiebende Bedingung, verschiebende Bedingung

suspensive discharge, precedent discharge · Anfangsentlastung *f*, Suspensiventlastung, aufschiebbare Entlastung, hinausschiebende Entlastung, aufschiebende Entlastung, suspensive Entlastung [*Sie tritt nach Ablauf einer in der gerichtlichen Entlastungsverfügung festgesetzten Frist in Wirksamkeit*]

suspensory effect, effect of suspension, effect of postponement · aufschiebende Wirkung *f*, verschiebende Wirkung *f*, hinausschiebende Wirkung *f*, Hemmungswirkung *f*, Hemmungseffekt *m*, Suspensivwirkung *f*, Suspensiveffekt *m*

suspensory right, right of postponement, right of suspension · Aufschiebungsrecht *n*, Aufschubsrecht *n*, Hinausschiebungsrecht *n*

to sustain, to incur · erleiden [*Schaden; Verlust*]

to sustain, to keep alive · aufrechterhalten, beibehalten

sustained, incurred · erlitten [*Schaden; Verlust*]

sustaining occupancy [*The point at which a project can support its own expenses with income received from rentals*] · kostendeckende Belegung *f*

sustaining (residential) rent, sustaining dwelling rent · kostendeckende (Wohnungs)Miete *f*

swale [*A flattish depression of the ground surface which conveys drainage water but offers no impediment to traffic, as do ditches or gutters*] · Entwässerungsdelle *f*

swank living · Aufschneiderei *f*

swarm-like settlement, dispersed settlement combined with small nucleated units · Schwarm(an)sied(e)lung *f*

to swear; to make faith [*old Scots law*], to make oath · schwören, beeiden

sweated industry, domestic industry, domestic system, home(-work) industry, cottage industry, financed work · Hausindustrie *f*, Verlagssystem *n*, Heim(arbeits)industrie, Verlag *m*

sweat equity · Eigenleistung *f* statt Eigenkapital *n*, Schweiß *m* statt Kapital

sweating system · Schwitzsystem *n* [*Die Kolonne wird im Zeitlohn oder im Leistungslohn, der Meister aber je nach Kolonnenleistung bezahlt. Ihm liegt also daran soviel wie möglich aus der Kolonne herauszuholen*]

swell of acreage, swell of land, addition of acreage, acreage addition, addition of land, land addition, land swell, acreage swell [*of a real estate*] · Landzuwachs *m*, Flächenzuwachs, Bodenzuwachs, Landzunahme f, Bodenzunahme, Flächenzunahme

swing · Grenzkredit m, technischer Kredit

swing plough (Brit.); wheelless plow, swing plow (US); wheelless plough (Brit.) · radloser Pflug m

swing space [*For loading and unloading vehicles*] · Schwenkraum m

switch-back design, cross-over design, change-over trial · Gruppenwechselplan m [*Statistik*]

(sworn) ranger of forests · (vereidigter) Waldaufseher m, (vereidigter) Forstaufseher

syllabus, headnote · Leitsatz m, Zusammenfassung f am Anfang eines Urteilsberichtes, Rechtsauszug m [*Er wird der veröffentlichten Entscheidung eines Gerichtes vorangestellt*]

sylvan scenery · Waldpanorama n

symbol of the peace of the city [*The statute of Roland — as at Riga and Bremen*] · Stadtfried m

symmetrical residential structures, symmetrical residential buildings · spiegelgleiche Wohnbauten f

symmetric determinant · symmetrische Determinante f

symmetric distribution · symmetrische Verteilung f

synallagmatic(al) [*That which involves mutual and reciprocal obligations and duties*] · synallagmatisch

synallagmatic contract · gegenseitig verpflichtender Vertrag m, synallagmatischer Vertrag

syndic · Syndikus m

syndicate → (issue) syndicate

syndicate loan → (issue) syndicate loan

syndic-attorney · Syndikusanwalt m

synodsman, questman, sidesman · Synodalzeuge m

synoptic chart, surface chart · synoptische (Wetter)Karte f

system approach · Systemansatz m

systematic · nicht zufällig, systematisch

to systematize [*To reduce to a general system*] · systematisieren

system based on Thünen's theory · System n der auf Thünen fußenden Lehre

system dynamics · Systemdynamik f

system headquarters · Systemzentrale f

systemic environment · Systemumwelt f

system of accounts [*The classification of accounts, and the books of account, forms, procedures, and controls by which assets, liabilities, revenues, expenses, and the results of transactions generally are recorded and controlled*] · Kontensystem n

system of a legal system · Rechtssystematik f

system of appraisal, system of appraisement, system of (e)valuation · Bewertungssystem n, Wertermitt(e)lungssystem, Taxierungssystem, (Ab)Schätzungssystem

system of central places, central place system · zentralörtliches System n, System der zentralen Orte, System zentraler Orte, Zentralortsystem, zentralörtliche Gliederung f von Gemeinden

system of citation · Zitiersystem n

system of cropping, system of farming, standard of farming, standard of cropping · Wirtschaftsart f [*Nutzung eines Ackergrundstückes*]

system of (e)valuation → system of appraisal

system of (feudal) tenure → feudal (landholding) system

system of feuing, feuing system [*Scotland*] · Landpachtsystem n

system of (general) property, system of proprietorship, system of ownership (of property) · Eigentumsverfassung f

system of land(s) use, land(s) use system · Bodennutzungssystem n, Landnutzungssystem, Flächennutzungssystem

system of land(s) use classification, land(s) use classification system · Bodennutzungsklassifizierungssystem n, Flächennutzungsklassifizierungssystem, Landnutzungsklassifizierungssystem

system of law, law system · Rechtssystem n

system of law courts · Aufbau m der Gerichte, allgemeiner Aufbau der Gerichte

system of one writ for each case · aktionenrechtliches System n, Aktionenrecht n [*In England 1873 abgeschafft*]

system of poor relief, poor relief system · Armenwesen n

system of priorities, priority system · Prioritätensystem n

system of regions · Regionssystem n

system of rules · Regelwerk n

system of tenure → feudal (landholding) system

system of uses — tacit covenant

system of uses [*The interest is split up into a legal interest and a beneficial interest*] · Spaltung *f* [*dingliches Grund(stücks)recht*]

system of valuation → system of appraisal

system pattern, system scheme · Systemmuster *n*, Systemschema *n*

system planner · Systemplaner *m*

system planning · Systemplanung *f*

systems analyst · Systemanalytiker *m*

system scheme, system pattern · Systemmuster *n*, Systemschema *n*

systems engineering · Systemtechnik *f*

system simulation · Systemsimulation *f*

system under which meadows and woods around a village community of necessity and permanently belonged to all the villagers jointly · Markgenossenschaft *f*

T

TA, technology assessment · Vorausbewertung *f* der Auswirkung technologischer Entwick(e)lungen

table demesne, home farm (of the lord of the manor), demesnial settlement; terra indominicata, terra dominica [*Latin*]; demain (land), demeyne (land), demeine (land), demesne (land), inland, land in (the lord's) demesne, bordland [*Those lands of a manor not granted out in tenancy, but reserved by the lord for his own use and occupation. The opposite of "tenemental lands"*] · Hoffeld *n*, Salland *n*, grundherrliches Eigenland, Hofländerei *f*, Hofland, grundherrschaftliches Eigenland

table of accumulation, schedule of accumulation, accumulation table, accumulation schedule · Ansammlungstabelle *f*, Anhäufungstabelle, Aufhäufungstabelle

table of (statutory) fees, (statutory) fee schedule · Honorarordnung *f*, Gebührenordnung

table of (statutory) fees for architects, (statutory) fee schedule for architects · Gebührenordnung *f* für Architekten, Honorarordnung für Architekten, GOA

table of (statutory) fees for architects and engineers, (statutory) fee schedule for architects and engineers · Gebührenordnung *f* für Architekten und Ingenieure, Honorarordnung für Architekten und Ingenieure, HOAI

table of (statutory) fees for engineers, (statutory) fee schedule for engineers · Gebührenordnung *f* für Ingenieure, Honorarordnung für Ingenieure, GOI

table rent; redditus ad mensam [*Latin*] [*In old English law. A rent paid to a bishop or religious prelate, reserved or appropriated to his table or housekeeping*] · Tafelgeld *n*

tabulation, index, registry, register, bill, list, schedule · Verzeichnis *n*, Liste *f*, Aufstellung *f*, Register *n*

tabulation · Tabellierung *f*

tabulation of architects, register of architects, registry of architects, list of architects, schedule of architects, index of architects · Architektenaufstellung *f*, Architektenliste *f*, Architektenregister *n*, Architektenverzeichnis *n*

tacit, by implication, implied · stillschweigend

tacit antichresis, implied antichresis; antichresis tacita [*Latin*]; antichresis by implication · stillschweigende Antichrese *f*

tacit appointment, appointment by implication, implied appointment · stillschweigende Benennung *f*, stillschweigende Ernennung, stillschweigende Namhaftmachung, stillschweigende Nominierung, gefolgerte Benennung, gefolgerte Ernennung, gefolgerte Namhaftmachung, gefolgerte Nominierung, konkludente Benennung, konkludente Ernennung, konkludente Namhaftmachung, konkludente Nominierung

tacit authority, authority implied, authority in law, implied authority · gefolgerte Vollmacht *f*, gefolgerte Vertretungsmacht, konkludente Vollmacht, konkludente Vertretungsmacht, stillschweigende Vollmacht, stillschweigende Vertretungsmacht

tacit choice of law, tacit election of law · stillschweigende Rechtswahl *f*

tacit condition, condition implied, implied condition · konkludente Bedingung *f*, gefolgerte Bedingung, stillschweigende Bedingung

tacit construction, implied interpretation, tacit interpretation, construction by implication, interpretation by implication, implied construction · stillschweigende Deutung *f*, stillschweigende Auslegung

tacit contract, contract by implication, implied contract · stillschweigender Vertrag *m*

tacit covenant, covenant in law, covenant by implication, implied covenant · stillschweigender Formalvertrag *m*

tacit demise [*It is inferred from a tacksman's possessing peacably after his tack is expired*], tacit tack [*Scots law*]; tacit lease · stillschweigende Wiederverpachtung *f*

tacit intention (of party), implied intention (of party) · stillschweigender Parteiwille *m*

tacit interpretation, construction by implication, interpretation by implication, implied construction, tacit construction, implied interpretation · stillschweigende Deutung *f*, stillschweigende Auslegung *f*

tacit lease, tacit demise [*It is inferred from a tacksman's possessing peacably after his tack is expired*], tacit tack [*Scots law*] · stillschweigende Wiederverpachtung *f*

tacit promise, promise implied, implied promise · gefolgertes Versprechen *n*, konkludentes Versprechen, stillschweigendes Versprechen

tacit relocation [*Scots law*]; implied reletting [*Of premises, where the tenant continues in possession after the expiration of his term*] · stillschweigende Wiedervermietung *f*

tacit renunciation, implied repudiation, tacit repudiation, implied renunciation · stillschweigende Vertragsaufsage *f*, stillschweigende Leistungsverweigerung *f*

tacit repudiation, implied renunciation, tacit renunciation, implied repudiation · stillschweigende Vertragsaufsage *f*, stillschweigende Leistungsverweigerung *f*

tacit tack [*Scots law*]; tacit lease, tacit demise [*It is inferred from a tacksman's possessing peacably after his tack is expired*] · stillschweigende Wiederverpachtung *f*

tacit trust, trust by implication, implied trust [*A trust raised or created by implication of law; a trust implied or presumed from circumstances*] · stillschweigende Treuhand *f*

tacit undertaking as to title, implied undertaking as to title · Rechtsgewährleistungspflicht *f*

tack [*Scots law*], estate less than freehold, lease(hold), tenure, leasehold estate, demise, tenancy; demissio, [*Latin*]; assedation [*Holding of real estate under a lease. Such an estate continues for a fixed or determinable period of time but not for a lifetime. It is a conveyance of land whereby the owner of landed property, called the lessor, grants the possession and use of his landed property to another party, called the lessee, in consideration of a sum of money, called the rent*] · Bodenpacht *f*, Landpacht, Bodennutzungsrechtvergabe *f*, Landnutzungsrechtvergabe, Bodenverpachtung *f*, Landverpachtung, (Boden)Nutzungsrecht

tacking · Vereinigung *f*, Zusammenrechnung [*z. B. Hypotheken*]

tacking (of) mortgages, consolidation of mortgages · Hypothekenvereinigung *f*, Hypothekenzusammenrechnung, Hypothekenzusammenschreibung [*Vereinigung einer nachstehenden (meist dritten) mit einer früheren (meist ersten) Hypothek zum Nachteil der dazwischenstehenden (meist zweiten) Hypothek, von der der Gläubiger der dritten Hypothek keine Kenntnis hatte*]

tack interest [*In Scots law*] → lease(hold) right

tack law [*In Scots law*] → law of estates less than freehold

to tack mortgages · vereinigen von Hypotheken, zusammenrechnen von Hypotheken

tack right [*Scots law*] → lease(hold) right

tacksman [*Scots law*] → (land) holder

tactual map · Blindenkarte *f*

tail → (estate in) tail

tail female → (estate in) tail female

tail general → (estate in) tail general

tail male → (estate in) tail male

tail special → (estate in) tail special

tail tenant → tenant in (fee) tail

tailzie(d fee) [*Scots law. Is that which the owner, by exercising his inherent right of disposing of his property, settles upon others than those to whom it would have descended by law*] · Ausschluß *m* der gesetzlichen Erben durch Stiftungsbildung

taking-off (of quantities), take-off (of quantities) [*From the construction drawings*] · Ausziehen *n* (der Mengen), Mengenauszug *m* [*Aus den Bauzeichnungen*]

to take a doctorate · promovieren

to take (away) (physically), to take from (physically) · wegnehmen, (körperlich) ergreifen, fortnehmen

to take back, to retake · zurücknehmen

to take chance · tragen eines Risikos, tragen eines Wagnisses

to take down · abtragen [*Ein Bauwerk so einreißen, daß das Altmaterial möglichst verwendbar bleibt*]

to take effect → to come into existence

to take from (physically), to take (away) (physically) · wegnehmen, (körperlich) ergreifen, fortnehmen

to take into avizandum, to advise [*Scots law*] · prüfen [*Urteil*]

taken · genommen [*Pfand*]

take off · selbständiges Wachstumsstadium *n*

take-off (of quantities), taking-off (of quantities) [*From the construction drawings*] · Ausziehen *n* (der Mengen), Mengenauszug *m* [*Aus den Bauzeichnungen*]

take-off sheet · (Mengen)Auszugbogen *m*

to take-off (the quantities) · ausziehen (der Mengen)

to take out probate · prüfen eines Testaments auf seine Gültigkeit durch ein Gericht und anfertigen einer Testamentsabschrift unter dem Siegel des Gerichts

take-over · Übernahme *f*

take-over bid · Übernahmeangebot *n*

to take possession · Besitz ergreifen, in Besitz nehmen

taker · Nehmer *m*

taker of profits, receiver of profits, pernor (of profits) · Berechtigte *m*, Nutzungsberechtigte

to take tithes, to addecimate · einnehmen von Zehnten

taking [*The act of a person who takes*] · Entgegennehmen *n*, Entgegennahme *f*

taking a price, collusive tendering, collusive bidding, (collusive) price fixing, bid-rigging, bid collusion, rigging bids, collusion among(st) bidders, collusion among(st) offerers, collusion among(st) tenderers, price taking, collusive agreement, combining to eliminate competition, restrictive covenant, restrictive tendering agreement [*The frequently heavy cost of tendering sometimes leads contractors to put forward tenders which are not genuine, in the sense that, rather than refuse to make a tender when invited to do so, the contractor tenders a price higher than that "taken" from another contractor who does desire to obtain the contract, thus avoiding expense and leading the employer to believe that he has had genuine competitive tenders for the work*] · Abrede *f* unter Bietern, Absprache *f* unter Bietern, Preisabrede, Preisabsprache, Submissionsabrede, Submissionsabsprache, Konkurrenzvereinbarung *f*, Verständigung *f* unter Bietern, Angebotsabsprache

taking (away) → (physical) taking (away)

taking down · Abtrag(ung) *m*, (*f*), Bau(werk)abtrag(ung) [*Abbruch eines Bauwerkes, so daß das Altmaterial möglichst verwendbar bleibt*]

taking (in) possession, entry · Besitzergreifen *n*, (In)Besitznehmen [*Grundstück*]

taking-off of work quantities procedure · Ausziehvorgang *m* [*Positionen*]

taking on demise, taking on lease · Pachten *n*

taking possession → taking (in) possession

taking sides, partisanship · Parteinahme *f*

talia [*Latin*] → petitio

tally chart · Strichliste *f*

tallyman, pedlar · Hausierer *m*

tally trade, pedlar trade · Hausieren *n*

talon, renewal warrant · Erneuerungsschein *m*, Talon *m* [*Depotgesetz*]

tangential road, tangential highway · Tangentialstraße *f*

tangible → corporeal

tangible asset, corporeal asset, physical asset [*Asset for which a value can be established, e.g. real estate, equipment, furniture, inventories, etc.*] · stoffliche Aktiva *f*, körperliche Aktiva, physische Aktiva

tangible hereditament; corporeal inheritance, tangible inheritance, corporeal hereditament [*These two terms were used in old books. "Tangible" means the same thing as "land"*] · körperliches Erbgut *n*

tangible property, choses in possession, corporeal property [*Property that by its nature is susceptible to the senses. Generally, it includes the land, fixed improvements, furnishings, merchandise, and cash*] · körperliches Vermögen *n*

tangible thing, chose, physical thing, thing corporeal, corporeal chattel (personal); res corporales, res singula [*Latin*]; corporeal thing [*A thing that affects the senses and may be seen and handled*] · (Einzel)Sache *f*, körperliches Rechtsobjekt *n*, materielles Rechtsobjekt, körperliches Ding *n*, materielles Ding, körperlicher (Rechts)Gegenstand *m*, materieller (Rechts)Gegenstand [*Ausgenommen lebender menschlicher Körper. Unter den Sachbegriff fallen nicht die Rechte, die Sachgesamtheiten, d. h. Mehrheiten von Sachen, die eine besondere Benennung haben, z. B. Bücherei, Warenlager usw. und die Inbegriffe von Sachen und Rechten, z. B. Erbschaftsvermögen usw. Im Preußischen Allgemeinen Landrecht von 1794 (A.L.R.) ist (Einzel)Sache allerdings alles, was Gegenstand eines Rechtes oder einer Verbindlichkeit sein kann (§ 1. I. 2)*]

tanker owners voluntary agreement concerning liability for oil pollution, TOVALOP · Verschuldenshaftungsabkommen *n* über das Einleiten von Öl durch Schiffseigentümer

tap bill · Geldmarktpapier n

tap stock · Staatsschuldverschreibung f laufend an Anleger ausgegeben, Staatsobligation f laufend an Anleger ausgegeben [in Großbritannien]

tap water, piped water · Leitungswasser n

tap water damage, piped water damage · Leitungswasserschaden m

tap water damage insurance, piped water damage insurance · Leitungswasserschadenversicherung f

target, attainment level, level of attainment · Programmziel n

target cost(s) · Vorgabekosten f, vorgegebene Kosten

target cost(s) contract · Auf- und Abgebotsvertrag m

target cost(s) tendering method, target cost(s) bidding method · Auf- und Abgebotsverfahren n

target date, deadline date · Endtermin m, Enddatum n [Der Zeitpunkt, bis zu dem der Auftragnehmer die vertraglich vereinbarte Bauleistung zu erbringen hat]

target goal, policy goal, goal (of policy) · Zielnorm f, Oberziel n, übergeordnetes Ziel

target goal conflict, policy goal conflict, goal (of policy) conflict · Ziel(norm)konflikt m, Oberzielkonflikt, Konflikt übergeordneter Ziele

target goal formation, policy goal formation, goal (of policy) formation · Ziel(norm)bildung f, Oberzielbildung

target goal research, goal (of policy) research, policy goal research · Ziel(norm)forschung f, Oberzielforschung

target goal system, policy goal system · Zielsystem n

target price · Vorgabepreis m, vorgegebener Preis

tariff rate · Tarifsatz m

task accomplishment · Aufgabe(n)bewältigung f, Aufgabe(n)erfüllung

task distribution, distribution of tasks · Aufgabenverteilung f

task limitation · Aufgabe(n)abgrenzung f

task of duty, duty task · Pflichtaufgabe f

task-related · aufgabenbezogen, aufgabenorientiert

task to co-ordinate, co-ordinative task, co-ordination task, co-ordinating task · Koordinationsaufgabe f, Koordinierungsaufgabe

to tax · besteuern, Erheben von Steuern

tax · Staatsabgabe f, (Staats)Steuer f [Eine vom Parlament auferlegte Abgabe]

tax abatement · Steuernachlaß m

taxable, subject to tax(ation), rat(e)able, assessable for tax(ation) (purposes), assessable for tax(ation) (purposes) · veranlagbar, steuerlich einstufbar, besteuerbar, versteuerbar

taxable value, assessed value, rated value [The value of property as appraised for taxation] · bemessener Wert m, eingestufter Wert, festgesetzter Wert, veranlagter Wert

tax adviser, tax counsel(or), tax consultant · Steuerberater m

tax-aided, tax-supported; tax-favoured (Brit.); tax-favored (US), tax-sheltered, tax-privileged · steuerbegünstigt

tax aid for land · Grund(besitz)steuervergünstigung f

tax assessment · Steuerveranlagung f, Steuereinstufung, (steuerliche) Veranlagung, steuerliche Einstufung

tax assessment committee · Steuerausschuß m, (Steuer)Veranlagungsausschuß

taxation · Besteuerung f

taxation act, taxation statute, taxation law · Besteuerungsgesetz n

taxation exemption, freedom from taxes, exemption from taxes, freedom from taxation, exemption from taxation, tax relief · Steuerbefreiung f, Steuerfreiheit f, Besteuerungsausnahme f

taxation law, taxation act, taxation statute · Besteuerungsgesetz n

taxation law, law of taxation · Besteuerungsrecht n

taxation of estate, estate taxation · Nachlaßbesteuerung f [unverteilte Erbmasse]

taxation of income(s), income taxation · Einkommensbesteuerung f

taxation of inheritance, inheritance taxation · Erb(schafts)besteuerung f

taxation of land(s), land(s) taxation · Landbesteuerung f, Bodenbesteuerung

taxation of property, property taxation · Vermögensbesteuerung f

tax(ation) reform, reform of taxation · Steuerreform f

taxation statute, taxation law, taxation act · Besteuerungsgesetz n

taxation (up)on a person in respect of (real) property · Realbesitzbesteuerung f einer Person

taxator, affeeror [A officer who was sworn by the steward of the court of a manor or hundred to assess the amerciaments imposed by the court, if the amount thereof was not fixed by custom or statute. Affeerors seem also to have been employed to assess the damages in cases brought in the inferior courts] · Geschworene *m* als Schätzer

tax attorney · Steueranwalt *m*

tax authority → tax(ing) authority

tax avoidance and evasion · Steuerhinterziehung *f*

tax balance(-sheet) · Steuerbilanz *f*

tax bearer, tax payer · Steuerträger *m*, Steuerzahler

tax book · Steuerbuch *n*

tax burden, tax charge, tax incumbrance, tax encumbrance, tax load, fiscal load, fiscal burden, fiscal encumbrance, fiscal incumbrance, fiscal charge · Steuerlast *f*, Steuerbelastung *f*

tax clause · Steuerklausel *f*

tax code · Steuerordnung *f*

tax composition, tax structure · Steueraufbau *m*, Steuerstruktur *f*, Steuergefüge *n*, Steuerzusammensetzung *f*

tax consultant, tax adviser, tax counsel(or) · Steuerberater *m*

tax cost(s) · Steuerkosten *f*

tax counsel(or), tax consultant, tax adviser, tax counsellor · Steuerberater *m*

tax court · Finanzgericht *n*, FG

tax declaration · Steuererklärung *f*

tax deduction · Steuerabzug *m*

tax encumbrance, tax load, fiscal load, fiscal burden, fiscal encumbrance, fiscal incumbrance, fiscal charge, tax burden, tax charge, tax incumbrance · Steuerlast *f*, Steuerbelastung *f*

taxes and mortgage interest on (real) estate, carrying charges, recurrent cost(s) · wiederkehrende Grundstückskosten *f*, Grundstücksspesen *f*

tax expert · Steuerfachmann *m*

tax-favoured (Brit.); tax-favored (US); tax-sheltered, tax-privileged, tax-aided, tax-supported · steuerbegünstigt

tax fluctuation · Steuerschwankung *f*

tax haven · Steueroase *f*

tax incentive · Steueranreiz *m*, steuerlicher Anreiz

tax incumbrance, tax encumbrance, tax load, fiscal load, fiscal burden, fiscal encumbrance, fiscal incumbrance, fiscal charge, tax burden, tax charge · Steuerlast *f*, Steuerbelastung *f*

tax(ing) authority · Steuerbehörde *f*

taxing authority, taxing power · Steuergewalt *f*, Steuerkompetenz *f*, Steuerhoheit *f*, Steuermacht *f*

taxing law, fiscal law · Steuerrecht *n*

taxing power, taxing authority · Steuergewalt *f*, Steuerkompetenz *f*, Steuerhoheit *f*, Steuermacht *f*

tax load, fiscal load, fiscal burden, fiscal encumbrance, fiscal incumbrance, fiscal charge, tax burden, tax charge, tax incumbrance, tax encumbrance · Steuerlast *f*, Steuerbelastung *f*

tax on amusements · Vergnügungssteuer *f*

tax on articles of consumption, excise(-duty), consumption tax · Verbrauchssteuer *f*

tax on capital earning(s), capital rent(s) tax, tax on rent(s) earned by capital · Kapitalrentensteuer *f*

tax on drinks · Getränkesteuer *f*

tax on hide (of land); hidagium [*Latin*]; hidage, hidegild, hydage [*In old English law. An extraordinary tax payable to the king of every hide of land*] · Hufengeld *n*, Hufengroschen *m*, Hufensteuer *f*

tax on housing expenditure · Wohn(ungs)aufwandsteuer *f*

tax on land(s), tax on (real) property, (real) estate tax, (real) property tax, land(s) tax; capitatio terrena [*Latin*]; realty tax, tax on realty, tax on (real) estate · Grund(besitz)steuer *f*, Grundstückssteuer

tax on land(s) held inalienably by the church, charitable institutions, etc., imposed every 20 years to compensate for the taxes which would have accrued to the state if the land(s) had been sold or had changed hands in that period · Totehandabgabe *f*, Steueräquivalent *n*

tax on mortgages, mortgage tax · Hypothekensteuer *f*

tax on objects yielding rent or profit or income · Ertragssteuer *f*

tax on personal property, personal property tax · Mobilien(vermögens)steuer *f*, Mobiliar(vermögens)steuer

tax on possession, possession tax · Besitzsteuer *f*

tax on property increase · Vermögensergänzungssteuer *f*

tax on (real) estate, tax on land(s), tax on (real) property, (real) estate tax, (real) property tax, land(s) tax; capitatio terrena [*Latin*]; realty tax, tax on realty · Grund(besitz)steuer *f*, Grundstückssteuer

tax on rent(s) earned by capital, tax on capital earning(s), capital rent(s) tax · Kapitalrentensteuer *f*

tax on return from housing property, tax on yield from housing property · Hausrenditesteuer *f*

tax on sale of land(ed property) borne by the vendor (or vender) · Grund(stücks)umsatzsteuer *f*, Landumsatzsteuer, Bodenumsatzsteuer, Liegenschaftsumsatzsteuer

tax on superflous living room · Wohn(ungs)luxussteuer *f*

tax on the area occupied by houses · Hausarealsteuer *f*

tax on the built-up area of a plot · Grundflächensteuer *f*

tax on the profit accruing to a houseowner owing to the fact that he does not pay the full pre-war interest on his mortgages but only a proportion reassessed after the inflation period · Entschuldungssteuer *f*, Gebäudeentschuldungssteuer

tax on transactions in land(s), tax on transactions in (real) estate, tax on transactions in (real) property, tax on transactions in realty · Bodenverkehrssteuer *f*, Liegenschaftsverkehrssteuer, Grundstücksverkehrssteuer, Immobiliarverkehrssteuer, Immobilienverkehrssteuer

tax on yield from housing property, tax on return from housing property · Hausrenditesteuer *f*

tax on yield of a building, building yield tax · Gebäudeertrag(s)steuer *f*, Gebäuderenditesteuer

tax on yield of land, tax on return of land · Grundrenditesteuer *f*

tax paid in kind, in-kind tax · Naturalsteuer *f*, Naturalabgabe *f*

tax payer, tax bearer · Steuerträger *m*, Steuerzahler

tax paying ability · Steuerkraft *f*

tax price · preisähnliche Steuer *f*

tax-privileged, tax-aided, tax-supported; tax-favoured (Brit.); tax-favored (US); tax-sheltered · steuerbegünstigt

tax rate, rate of tax · Steuersatz *m*

tax relief, taxation exemption, freedom from taxes, exemption from taxes, freedom from taxation, exemption from taxation · Steuerbefreiung *f*, Steuerfreiheit *f*, Besteuerungsausnahme *f*

tax return · Steuermeldung *f*

tax schedule, valuation list · Steuerrolle *f*

tax-sheltered, tax-privileged, tax-aided, tax-supported; tax-favoured (Brit.); tax-favored (US) · steuerbegünstigt

tax status · Steuerstatus *m*

tax structure, tax composition · Steueraufbau *m*, Steuerstruktur *f*, Steuergefüge *n*, Steuerzusammensetzung *f*

tax-supported; tax-favoured (Brit.); tax-favored (US); tax-sheltered, tax-privileged, tax-aided · steuerbegünstigt

tax week · Steuerwoche *f*

tax year · Steuerjahr *n*

tax zero rate, zero rate of tax · Steuernullsatz *m*

teacher of law, law teacher · Rechtslehrer *m*

teacher's certificate examination · Lehr(er)befähigungsprüfung *f*

teacher's training college, teacher's training department · Lehrerseminar *n*

teaching of comparative law, comparative law in legal education · Rechtsunterrichtsvergleichung *f*

teaching of law comparatively · rechtsvergleichender Unterricht *m*

teaching(s), view · Lehrmeinung *f*

team → (working) team

tea money, pugree, salaami [*In the Far East*]; key money [*An undercover rent payment*] · Schlüsselgeld *n*

team teaching · gemeinschaftliche Gestaltung *f* des Unterrichts durch mehrere Lehrer, gemeinsame Gestaltung des Unterrichts durch mehrere Lehrer

teamwork, groupwork · Gruppenarbeit *f*

technical and administrative general supervision · technische und geschäftliche Oberleitung *f* [*Dieser Begriff umfaßt die allgemeine Aufsicht über die technische Ausführung des Baues, Vorbereitung der erforderlichen Verträge, Überprüfung der Rechnungen, Feststellung der Rechnungsbeträge sowie der endgültigen Höhe der Herstellungskosten, falls erforderlich, auch die Aufstellung eines Zeit- und Zahlungsplanes. Auf diese Teilaufgabe entfallen 10% der Gesamtsumme*]

technical building provision, technical construction provision · technische Baubestimmung *f*

technical check · technische (Über)Prüfung *f*, technische Kontrolle *f* [*Rechnung*]

technical document, engineering document · technische Unterlage *f*

technical drawing, engineering drawing · technische Zeichnung *f*

technical force(s), engineering personnel, engineering staff, engineering force(s), technical personnel, technical staff · technisches Personal *n*

technical handicap · technische Erschwernis *f*, technische Erschwerung *f*

technical independence of source · technische Lagerfreiheit *f*

technicalities · Formalien *fpl*

technically-closed primary (election), semi-open primary (election) [*USA*] · technisch-geschlossene Vorwahl *f*, technisch-geschlossene Erstwahl, technisch-geschlossene Urwahl. halb-offene Vorwahl, halb-offene Erstwahl, halb-offene Urwahl [*Der Vorwahlteilnehmer muß seine Parteizugehörigkeit angeben*]

technically qualified arbitrator [*He is usually appointed in building and engineering disputes*] · technischer Schiedsrichter *m*

technical mortgage · formgerechte Hypothek *f*

technical officer, technical official · technischer Beamter *m*

technical orientation by production · technische Erzeugungsorientierung *f*

technical personnel, technical staff, technical force(s), engineering personnel, engineering staff, engineering force(s) · technisches Personal *n*

technical press, engineering press · technische Presse *f*

(technical) spec(ification)(s) · technische Vorschrift(en) *f (pl)*

technical staff, technical force(s), engineering personnel, engineering staff, engineering force(s), technical personnel · technisches Personal *n*

(technical) standard (spec(ification)) · (technische) Norm *f*

technological advance, technological progress · technologischer Fortschritt *m*

technological gap · Technologielücke *f*

technological planner · technologischer Planer *m*

technological planning · technologische Planung *f*

technology assessment, TA · Vorausbewertung *f* der Auswirkung technologischer Entwick(e)lungen

technology of planning, planning technology · Planungstechnologie *f*

teind [*Scots law*], tithe · Zehnt *m* [*altdeutsch: Zehent m, Zehend*]

teind court [*Scots law*], tithe court · Zehntengericht *n*

telephone tapping [*Form of electronic surveillance carried out by security services after authorization by the Home Secretary*] · Abhören *n*

teller, cashier · Kassierer *m*, Kassenführer

temple-land(s) · Tempelländerei(en) *f (pl)*

temporal authority, sovereign power · weltliche Obrigkeit *f*

temporal corporation [*obsolete*]; lay corporation · Laienkörperschaft *f*, Laienkorporation *f*

temporal court, lay court · weltliches Gericht *n*

temporal service, earthly service · weltliche Dienstleistung *f*, weltliche Verrichtung [*Leh(e)n(s)mann*]

temporary, interlocutory, provisional, interim, intermediate · einstweilig, zwischenzeitlich, vorübergehend, inzidentiell

temporary excise · zeitweilige Accise *f*, vorübergehende Accise

temporary legal protection · vorläufiger Rechtsschutz *m*, vorübergehender Rechtsschutz, zeitweiliger Rechtsschutz

temporary nonexistence, expectancy of law, contemplation of law; abeyantia [*Latin*]; abeyance, condition of abeyance, state of abeyance, abbayance, state of suspension, abeyancy [*In the law of real estate. Where there is no person in existence in whom an inheritance can vest, it is said to be in abeyance, that is, in expectation; the law considering is as always potentially existing, and ready to vest when ever a proper owner appears*] · Schwebe(zustand) *f, (m)*

temporary residence · vorübergehender Aufenthalt *m*, vorläufiger Aufenthalt, zeitweiliger Aufenthalt

temporary restraining order, TRO · vorsorgliche Maßnahme *f* [*Rechtsbehelf*]

temporary revocation · zeitweiliger Widerruf *m*, vorübergehender Widerruf, vorläufiger Widerruf

temporary settlement, seasonal settlement · jahreszeitliche Sied(e)lung *f*, Saisonsied(e)lung, temporäre Sied(e)lung

temporary structure, temporary work [*Despite important distinctions which are made between permanent work and temporary work, a definition of universal application is impossible, what is left permanently in place may be more than the permanent work (e.g. sheet piles, coffer dams, etc.); and the obligation to maintain by no means clearly excludes the temporary work. Where included in the bill of quantities, "temporary work" should, however, be defined. But there must always be items incapable of precise labelling, e.g. ground treatment which is partly to facilitate construction (and therefore of a "temporary" nature) but which is relied upon in the design of* *the "permanent" work*] · (bauliche) Hilfsanlage *f*, Hilfs(bau)werk *n*, Hilfsbau *m*

temporary unemployment, frictional unemployment · vorübergehende Arbeitslosigkeit *f*, vorläufige Arbeitslosigkeit, zeitweilige Arbeitslosigkeit

temporary work(s) · (bauliche) Hilfsarbeit(en) *f (pl)*, (bauliche) Hilfsleistung(en) *f (pl)*

tenancy; demissio, dimissio [*Latin*]; assedation, tack [*Scots law*], estate less than freehold, lease(hold), tenure, leasehold estate, demise [*Holding of real estate under a lease. Such an estate continues for a fixed or determinable period of time but not for a lifetime. It is a conveyance of land whereby the owner of landed property, called the lessor, grants the possession and use of his landed property to another party, called the lessee, in consideration of a sum of money, called the rent*] · Bodenpacht *f*, Landpacht, Bodennutzungsrechtvergabe *f*, Landnutzungsrechtvergabe, Bodenverpachtung *f*, Landverpachtung, (Boden)Nutzungsrecht *n*

tenancy, tenure land(s), feodal land(s), feudal land(s), feuda(to)ry land(s), tenemental land(s), land(s) of (a) manor, land(s) held of a lord, land(s) of tenure, outland(s) [*Land held of the lord by free tenure*] · Leh(e)n(s)land *n*, Feudalland, Außenland, Grenzland, verpachtetes Land

tenancy → fee (tenure) (of land)

tenancy, demise, lease(hold), tenure; demissio, dimissio [*Latin*] · Pacht *f*, Nutzungsrechtvergabe *f*, Verpachtung *f*

tenancy, land tenure, feud, feod, tenement, (feodal) tenure (of land), land held of a lord, land in fee; feodum, feudum, tenementum [*Latin*]; feu [*Scots law*], fee (tenure) (of land), fief · Leh(e)n *n*, Leh(e)n(s)gut *n*, Leh(e)n(s)besitz *m*, leh(e)n(s)rechtlicher (Grund)Besitz(stand) *m*, Benefizium *n*

tenancy agreement → agreement of tenancy

tenancy at sufferance, tenure at sufferance, landlord/tenant relation(ship) at sufferance · Mietverhältnis *n* auf Duldung, geduldetes Mietverhältnis [*Es liegt vor, wenn ein Mieter sein ursprünglich rechtmäßiges Mietverhältnis unrechtmäßig verlängert*]

tenancy at will, tenure at will, landlord/tenant relation(ship) at will [*It is created by any letting for a time not limited. Such a tenancy is determinable at the will of either landlord or tenant, even though it be expressed to be determinable at the will of the landlord only*] · jederzeit kündbares Mietverhältnis *n*, all(e)zeit kündbares Mietverhältnis, willkürlich kündbares Mietverhältnis, einvernehmlich geduldetes Mietverhältnis

tenancy brokerage, lease brokerage · Pachtvermitt(e)lung *f*

tenancy by elegit, interest in land(s) by elegit · Boden(besitz)recht *n* durch Einweisung, (Land)Besitzrecht durch Einweisung

tenancy by the entirety, tenancy by entireties · Miteigentumsverhältnis *n* unter Ehegatten [*Es berechtigt jeden der beiden Miteigentümer zum Anteil des verstorbenen Ehegatten*]

tenancy cession, tenancy assignment, cession of lease(hold), cession of demise, cession of tenancy, assignment of lease(hold), assignment of demise, assignment of tenancy, lease(hold) cession, lease(hold) assignment, demise cession, demise assignment · Pachtabtretung *f*, Pachtzession *f*

tenancy condition, condition of lease, condition of tenancy, lease condition · Pachtbedingung *f*

tenancy contract, tenure contract, lease(hold) contract, demise contract, contract of tenancy, contract of demise, contract of lease(hold), contract of tenure · Pachtvertrag *m*, Nutzungsrechtvertrag, Verpachtungsvertrag

tenancy for a time certain → term of years

tenancy for life, tenement for life, fee (tenure) for life, fief for life, (feodal) tenure (of land) for life · lebenslanges Leh(e)n *n*, Leh(e)n auf Lebenszeit

tenancy for life, lease(hold) for life, tenure for life, demise for life, life tenancy, life lease(hold), life tenure, life demise · Pacht *f* auf Lebensdauer, Pacht auf Lebenszeit, Nutzungsrechtvergabe *f* auf Lebensdauer, Nutzungsrechtvergabe auf Lebenszeit, Verpachtung *f* auf Lebensdauer, Verpachtung auf Lebenszeit, lebenslange Pacht, lebenslange Verpachtung, lebenslange Nutzungsrechtvergabe

tenancy for years → term of years

tenancy for 3,000 years, lease(hold) for 3,000 years, demise for 3,000 years, tenure for 3,000 years · Grund(stücks)pacht *f* auf 3000 Jahre, Grund(stücks)nutzungsrechtvergabe *f* auf 3000 Jahre, Grund(stücks)verpachtung *f* auf 3000 Jahre

tenancy from year to year, lease(hold) from year to year, demise from year to year, tenure from year to year, yearly tenancy, yearly tenure, yearly demise, yearly lease(hold) [*In very early times a general letting of land, that is, a demise without limit as to the period of holding, was held to create a tenancy strictly at the will of the parties and determinable at the pleasure of either. But in modern times this rule has long been modified; and, although even at the present day, a mere general letting or permission to* occupy creates only a tenancy at will, yet if the lessor accepts from the lessee a yearly rent or rent measured by any aliquot part of a year, the Courts will ordinarily infer from this circumstance an intention to create a tenancy from year to year] · Pacht f von Jahr zu Jahr, Verpachtung f von Jahr zu Jahr, Nutzungsrechtvergabe f von Jahr zu Jahr

tenancy in burgage, tenancy of burgage, burgage tenement, tenement in burgage; burgagium, feudum burgense, feudum urbanum, feodum burgense, feodum urbanum [*Latin*]; tenure of burgage, burgage (tenure), burgage tenancy, burgage-holding, tenure in burgage [*A tenure whereby lands or houses in cities and towns were held of the king or queen or other lord, for a certain yearly rent*] · Bürgerleh(e)n n, Stadtleh(e)n, städtischer Freibesitz m (an Häusern und Land)

tenancy in capite · direktes Kronleh(e)n n, direktes Leh(e)n der Krone

tenancy in common, collective property, collective ownership (of property), collective proprietorship, co-ownership (of property), concurrent interests, co-proprietorship, co-property [*The German terms are stronger in the sense of having less flavour of individual rights than the English terms*] · Bruchteileigentum n, Anteileigentum, Gemeineigentum, Mehrheitseigentum, Miteigentum, Vielherrlich-Eigentum, gesamthänderisches Eigentum, Gesamthandschaft f, vielherrliches Eigentum, Gesamthand(eigentum) f, (n), gemeinschaftliches Eigentum, gemeinsames Eigentum, Gesamteigentum, Quoteneigentum

tenancy in dower; doweyre, dowarie [*Norman French*]; (estate in) dower, estate of dower [*The life estate to which a married woman is entitled on death of her husband, intestate, or, in case she dissents from his will, one-third in value of all land(s) of which husband was beneficially seized in law or in fact, at any time during coverture*] · Witwengut n, Wittum(sgut) n der Ehefrau

tenancy interest → lease(hold) right

tenancy law → law of estates less than freehold

tenancy lot, lease(hold) lot, leased lot, demise(d) lot, leasing lot · Pachtflurstück n, Pachtparzelle f

tenancy matters (in general), demise matters (in general), lease(hold) practice, tenancy practice, demise practice, lease(hold) matters (in general) · Pachtwesen n

tenancy of (building) (land) area → (building) (land) area tenancy

tenancy of estate → (real) estate lease(hold)

tenancy of land → (building) (land) area tenancy

tenancy (of land(s)); immov(e)ables [*International Private Law*]; (real) estate, (real) property, realty, estate in land(s), immov(e)able estate, fixed estate, landholding, land(ed) property [*Estates in land(s) are divided into (a) freehold estates and (b) estates less than freehold*] · Bodenbesitz(stand) m, Grund(stücks)besitz(stand), Landbesitz(stand), Immobilienbesitz(stand), Immobiliarbesitz(stand), Liegenschaft(en) f(pl), Immobilie(n) f(pl), (unbeweglicher) Besitz(stand), liegendes Gut n, ungereides Gut

tenancy of land(s) at will, demise of land(s) at will, lease(hold) of land(s) at will, tenure of land(s) at will · jederzeit kündbare Landpacht f, jederzeit kündbare Landverpachtung f, jederzeit kündbare Landnutzungsrechtvergabe f, willkürlich kündbare Landpacht, willkürlich kündbare Landverpachtung, willkürlich kündbare Landnutzungsrechtvergabe, all(e)zeit kündbare Landpacht, all(e)zeit kündbare Landverpachtung, all(e)zeit kündbare Landnutzungsrechtvergabe

tenancy of property → (real) estate lease(hold)

tenancy of property without destroying its substance, lease(hold) of property without destroying its substance; jus utendi [*Latin*]; demise of property without destroying its substance · Pacht f ohne Zerstörung, Nutzungsrecht n ohne Zerstörung

tenancy of (real) estate → (real) estate lease(hold)

tenancy of (real) property → (real) estate lease(hold)

tenancy of years → term of years

tenancy option, lease(hold) option, demise option · Pachtoption f

tenancy parcel (of land) → tenancy plot (of land)

tenancy plot (of land), tenancy plot of ground, tenancy piece of land, tenancy piece of ground, tenancy parcel (of land), tenancy parcel of ground, leased plot (of land), leased plot of ground, leased piece of land, leased piece of ground, leased parcel (of land), leased parcel of ground, demise(d) plot (of land), demise(d) plot of ground, demise(d) piece of land, demise(d) piece of ground, demise(d) parcel (of land), demise(d) parcel of ground, lease(hold) plot (of land), lease(hold) plot of ground, lease(hold) piece of land, lease(hold) piece of ground, lease(hold) parcel (of land), lease(hold) parcel of ground, leasing plot (of land), leasing plot of ground, leasing piece of land, leasing piece of ground, leasing

tenancy practice — **tenant group**   1038

parcel (of land), leasing parcel of ground · Pachtgrundstück *n* (im tatsächlichen Sinne)

tenancy practice, demise practice, lease(hold) matters (in general), tenancy matters (in general), demise matters (in general), lease(hold) practice · Pachtwesen *n*

tenancy protection code, demise protection code, lease(hold) protection code · Pachtschutzordnung *f*

tenancy right, right of tenancy · (subjektives) Wohn(ungs)recht *n*

tenancy right → lease(hold) right

tenancy system → (agricultural) tenancy system

tenancy to a third party, third party lease(hold), third party tenancy, third party demise, lease(hold) to a third party, demise to a third party · Zwischenpacht *f*

tenancy value, demise(d) value, leased value, lease(hold) value · Pachtwert

tenancy with an option to purchase, tenancy with an option to buy, demise with an option to purchase, demise with an option to buy, lease(hold) with an option to purchase, lease(hold) with an option to buy · Kaufoptionspacht *f*, Pacht mit Kaufoption

tenant [*Any person in possession of real property with the owner's permission, usually according to the provisions of a lease*] · Mieter *m*

tenant · Rentschuldner *m*

tenant, user, usufructuary, beneficiary; cestui (à) que use, cestui à l'use de qui, cestui (à) que trust, cestuy que trust [*Norman French*]; usufructuarius [*Latin*]; (beneficial) occupant, (beneficial) occupier, beneficial owner [*He to whose use another is enfeoffed of lands or tenements. The substantial and beneficial owner, as distinguished from the feoffee to uses*] · Nutznießer *m*, faktischer Eigentümer, Nehmer, Empfänger eines benefiziarischen Nutzungsrechts, Benefiziar, Besitznehmer, Usufruktuar, Fruchtnießer, Nießbraucher

tenant → (land) holder

tenantable, lettable · vermietbar [*Wohnungen; Geschäftsräume*]

tenantable repair, lettable repair [*The quality of repair in a house rendering it fit for occupation by tenants*] · Vermietungsreparatur *f*

tenant and landlord · Mieter *m* und Hauswirt *m*

tenant at sufferance → (land) tenant at sufferance

tenant at will [*Where tenements are let by one person to another, to have and to hold to him at will of the landlord, by force of which lease the tenant is in possession*] · einvernehmlich geduldeter Mieter *m*

tenant by copy of court roll, tenant holding by copy of court roll, copyholder, copiholder · Hintersasse *m*, Schriftsasse, Laßbesitzer, Besitzer eines Schriftsassenleh(e)ns

tenant by custom, customary tenant, common tenant · gewohnheitsrechtlicher Leh(e)n(s)mann *m*, Werkmann [*In England im 14., 15. und 16. Jahrhundert*]

tenant by elegit · Bodenbesitzer *m* durch Einweisung, (Land)Besitzer durch Einweisung

tenant by knight service, tenant in chivalry · ritterlicher Leh(e)n(s)mann *m*, ritterlicher Leh(e)n(s)träger *m*, ritterlicher Gefolgsmann, ritterlicher Vasall

tenant by scutage, scutage tenant · Schildgeldleh(e)n(s)mann *m*

tenant by socage, tenant in socage, tenant in ancient demesne, colibert, tenant of socage-land, socage-land tenant, socage tenant, gainor, sok(e)man, socman, socheman, socager · freier weltlicher Leh(e)n(s)besitzer *m*, (weltlicher) Freigutbesitzer

tenant by statute · Gläubiger *m* im Besitz [*Pfandrecht im mittelalterlichen England*]

tenant by the verge, holder of yardland, holder of virgate, holder of verge of land, yardling, virgarius [*Latin*] [*Tenant who held copyhold after a symbolic surrender and delivery of a small rod (= verge)*] · Hüf(e)ner *m*, Hufenbauer, Huf(e)ner

tenant company · mietende Gesellschaft *f*

(tenant) farmer, leasehold farmer, tenant of a farm, farm tenant [*Die Benennung "farmer" bedeutet in England nicht nur Landwirt, sondern auch Pächter und nur wenn die Pächtereigenschaft hervorgehoben wird, heißt es tenant farmer*] · (landwirtschaftlicher) Pächter *m*, Landwirtschaftspächter, Agrarpächter

tenant for a fixed number of years · Pächter *m* für eine bestimmte Anzahl von Jahren

tenant for a fixed period · Pächter *m* für eine bestimmte Zeit

tenant for life → life (land) lessee

tenant from year to year → (land) holder from year to year

tenant garage · Mietergarage *f*

tenant garden · Mietergarten *m*

tenant group, group of tenants · Mieterinitiative *f*

tenant handbook [*Booklet or pamphlet prepared by a landlord and/or tenant explaining tenant rights and responsibilities, procedures and policies not set forth or not understandable in a lease information about services available to tenants, etc.*] · Miet(er)buch *n*

tenant holding by copy of court roll, copyholder, copiholder, tenant by copy of court roll · Hintersasse *m*, Schriftsasse, Laßbesitzer, Besitzer eines Schriftsassenleh(e)ns

tenant holding over · verharrender Besitzer *m* [*Er verharrt im Besitz über die rechtmäßige Zeit hinaus*]

tenant household · Mieterhaushalt *m*

tenant in ancient demesne → tenant by socage

tenant in capite [*Landholder who held directly of the King*] · direkter Leh(e)n(s)mann *m* der Krone, direkter Leh(e)n(s)träger der Krone, direkter Gefolgsmann der Krone, direkter Vasall der Krone, direkter Grundzinsmann der Krone

tenant in capite by knight service, tenant in capite in chivalry · ritterlicher Leh(e)n(s)mann *m* der Krone, ritterlicher Leh(e)n(s)träger der Krone, ritterlicher Gefolgsmann der Krone, ritterlicher Vasall der Krone

tenant in chivalry, tenant by knight service · ritterlicher Leh(e)n(s)mann *m*, ritterlicher Leh(e)n(s)träger, ritterlicher Gefolgsmann, ritterlicher Vasall

tenant-in-demesne · Sallandbauer *m*, Hoffeldbauer

tenant in dower [*A woman who holds the third part of the land(s) and tenement(s) of which her deceased husband was seised, for the term of her life, as her dower*] · Inhaberin *f* eines Wittums, Wittumsinhaberin

tenant in fee simple, fee simple tenant · freier Grundbesitzer *m*, uneingeschränkter Grundbesitzer, unbeschränkter Grundbesitzer, unbegrenzter Grundbesitzer

tenant in (fee) tail, (fee) tail tenant · Fideikommißbesitzer *m*, Majoratbesitzer

tenant in (fee) tail male · Fideikommißbesitzer *m* mit auf männliche Nachkommen vererblichem Pachtrecht

tenant in socage → tenant by socage

tenantless · unvermietet

tenant-like · pachtähnlich

tenant-occupied, renter-occupied · mieterbelegt

tenant of a farm, farm tenant, (tenant) farmer, leasehold farmer [*Die Benennung "farmer" bedeutet in England nicht nur Landwirt, sondern auch Pächter und nur wenn die Pächtereigenschaft hervorgehoben wird, heißt es tenant farmer*] · (landwirtschaftlicher) Pächter *m*, Landwirtschaftspächter, Agrarpächter

tenant of land, holder of land, land tenant, (real) estate possessor, (real) property possessor, realty possessor, landed estate possessor, land possessor, land(ed) property possessor, landholder, possessor of land, possessor of (real) estate, possessor of (real) property · Grund(stücks)besitzer *m*, Landbesitzer, Bodenbesitzer, Immobilienbesitzer, Immobiliarbesitzer, Liegenschaftsbesitzer

tenant of land, feeholder, holder of a fee, holder of a fief, fief-tenant, feoda(to)ry, feuda(to)ry; homo pertinens [*Latin*], beneficiary, holder of a feudal benefice, land tenant, (feudal) tenant, manorial tenant, feudal bondman, vassal [*A tenant or vassal who held his estate by feudal service*] · Leh(e)n(s)mann *m*, Leh(e)n(s)träger, Gefolgsmann, Gutszinsmann, Vasall

tenant (of land) at will → (land) holder at will

tenant (of land) for life → life (land) lessee

tenant (of land) from year to year → (land) holder from year to year

tenant of (real) property → (land) holder

tenant of socage-land, socage-land tenant, socage tenant, gainor, sok(e)man, socman, socheman, socager, tenant by socage, tenant in socage, tenant in ancient demesne, colibert · freier weltlicher Leh(e)n(s)besitzer *m*, (weltlicher) Freigutbesitzer

tenant organization · Mieterorganisation *f*

tenant paravail, lowest tenant (of a fee) [*A tenant who held land(s) in fee of another and had no tenant who held of him, as opposed to a mesne lord and a lord paramount*] · niedrigster Leh(e)n(s)mann *m*

tenant-protected flat; rent-controlled flat (Brit.) · Mieterschutzwohnung *f*

(tenant) relocation, displacement, rehousing, resettlement, transfer from congested areas [*Of persons from land acquired or appropriated for planning purposes*] · Aussied(e)lung *f*, Umsied(e)lung, Standortveränderung, Verlegung, Umsetzung, Wiederunterbringung

tenants [*Persons in possessions of real properties with the owners' permissions, usually according to the provisions of leases*] · Mieter *mpl*, Mietleute *f*

tenant's act, tenant's statute, tenant's law · Mietergesetz *n*

tenant's association, lessee's association, (land) holder's association, leaseholder's association · Pächtergenossenschaft f, Pachtgenossenschaft

tenants' committee · Mieterausschuß m

tenants' council, tenants' group · Mieterinitiative f, Mieterinteressengruppe f

tenant's family · (Wohnungs)Mieterfamilie f

tenants' group, tenants' council · Mieterinitiative f, Mieterinteressengruppe f

tenants-in-chief · Landesadel m

tenants in common, concurrent (interest(s)) community · Bruchteilgemeinschaft f

tenant-slanted · mieterfreundlich

tenant's law, tenant's act, tenant's statute · Mietergesetz n

tenant's loan · Mieterdarleh(e)n n

tenants' protection, protection of tenants, protection for the tenant, security of tenants; rent control (Brit.) · Mieterschutz m

tenants' protection law, tenants' protection act, tenants' protection statute, landlord and tenant act (Brit.) · Mieterschutzgesetz n

tenants' protection law · Mieterschutzrecht n

tenants society · Mietsgenossenschaft f [*Der Unterschied zwischen einer deutschen Baugenossenschaft mit gemeinschaftlichem Eigentum und der englischen ,,tenants society" besteht darin, daß die letztere die Wohnungen und Häuser zu ortsüblichen Preisen, also nicht billiger vermietet. Die Gewinne werden den Genossen wie bei den Konsumgenossenschaften im Verhältnis zur gezahlten Miete berechnet. Sie werden aber nur gutgeschrieben, nicht ausgezahlt*]

tenant's statute, tenant's law, tenant's act · Mietergesetz n

to tender, to submit (a bid), to (enter a) bid; to submit a (bid) proposal, to enter a (bid) proposal (US); to offer · anbieten, submittieren, einreichen eines Angebots, abgeben eines Angebots

to tender [*To offer in payment of an obligation*] · anbieten einer Zahlung

tender, offer, bid; (bid) proposal (US) · Angebot n

tender · Naturalofferte f

tender action → tender(ing) action

tender analysis, offer analysis, bid analysis; (bid) proposal analysis (US) · Angebotsanalyse f, Angebotsuntersuchung f

tender (blank) form, bid (blank) form, offer (blank) form, form of tender, form of offer, form of bid, bid(ding) form; (bid) proposal form, form of (bid) proposal, (bid) proposal blank (form) (US) · Angebotsblankett n, Angebotsformular n, Angebotsvordruck m, Angebotsblankett n

tender bond, offer bond; (bid) proposal bond (US) [*A bid guarantee by bond. The function of a bid bond is to guarantee the good faith of the bidder, so that if awarded the contract within the time stipulated, he will enter into the contract and furnish the prescribed performance and payment bonds*], bid bond · Bietungsgarantie f [*Eine Bietungssicherheit durch beurkundete Schuldforderung*]

to tender competitively, to submit a competitive bid, to bid competitively, to offer competitively · abgeben n eines Wettbewerbsangebotes, einreichen eines Wettbewerbsangebotes, anbieten im Wettbewerb, submittieren im Wettbewerb

tender conditions; conditions of the (bid) proposal, (bid) proposal conditions (US); conditions of the bid, conditions of the offer, conditions of the tender, bid conditions, offer conditions · Angebotsbedingungen fpl

tender covering letter, bid covering letter, offer covering letter; (bid) proposal covering letter (US) · Angebots(an)schreiben n, Angebotsbegleitschreiben

tender drawing, bid drawing, offer drawing; (bid) proposal drawing (US) · Angebotszeichnung f

tender(ed) figure → tender(ed) sum

tender(ed) price, offer price, bid price, tender(ed) sum, offer sum, bid sum, tender(ed) figure, offer figure, bid figure; (bid) proposal sum, (bid) proposal figure, (bid) proposal price (US) [*Amount stated in the bid as the sum for which the bidder offers to perform the work*] · Angebotspreis m, Angebotssumme f

tenderer, offeror, competitor, tendering contractor, competing contractor, bidder · (an)bietende Firma f, (An)Bieter m, Angebotsabgeber

tenderer's list, competitor's list, tendering contractor's list, competing contractor's list, bidder's list · Ausschreibungsliste f, (An)Bieterliste f

tenderer's prequalifications, bidder's prequalifications · Bietereignung f

tender estimate, offer estimate, bid estimate; (bid) proposal estimate (US) · Angebotsvoranschlag m

tender figure → tender(ed) sum

tender form — tender prescriptions

tender form → tender (blank) form

tender guarantee, tender guaranty, tender security, offer guarantee, offer guarantie, offer guaranty, offer security; (bid) proposal guarantee; (bid) proposal guarantie, (bid) proposal guaranty, (bid) proposal security (US); bid guarantee, bid guarantie, bid guaranty, bid security, tender guarantie [*Deposit for cash, check, money order, or bid bond when the bid is submitted by the bidder to guarantee that he will sign the contract and furnish the required surety if awarded*] · Bietungsbürgschaft *f*, Bietungssicherheit *f*

tender(ing) action, tendering (out), bidding (action) · Ausschreibung *f*, Angebotseinholung, Einholung *f* von Angeboten

tendering authority, bidding authority · ausschreibende Behörde *f*

tendering combination, bidding partnership, tendering partnership, bidding combination · Bietergemeinschaft *f*

tendering contractor, competing contractor, bidder, tenderer, offeror, competitor · (an)bietende Firma *f*, (An)Bieter *m*, Angebotsabgeber

tendering contractor's list, competing contractor's list, bidder's list, tenderer's list, competitor's list · Ausschreibungsliste *f*, (An)Bieterliste *f*

tendering cost(s), bidding cost(s), cost(s) of tendering, cost(s) of bidding [*The cost(s) to the contractor of preparing his tender, including any amended tender necessitated by bona fide alterations in the bill of quantities and plans*] · Bieterkosten *f*, Blankettkosten, Bietungskosten, Angebots(abgabe)kosten

tendering date, closing date (for receipt of tenders), closing time (for receipt of bids), bid(ding) date, closing date for bids, date of receipt of bids · (Angebots)Abgabedatum *n*, (Angebots)Abgabetermin *m*, Einreich(ungs)datum, Einreich(ungs)termin, Angebotstermin, Angebotsdatum

tendering document, bid(ding) document, offer document; (bid) proposal document (US) · Ausschreibungsunterlage *f*, Ausschreibungsdokument *n* [*Fehlbenennungen: Angebotsunterlage, Angebotsdokument*]

tendering error, bidding error · Angebotsfehler *m*, Bietungsfehler

tendering invitation, invitation to tender, invitation to bid, bidding invitation, invitation to (submit a) bid, request for tender, request for offer, request for bid, call for tender, call for offer, call for bid; request for (bid) proposal, call for (bid) proposal (US) · (Angebots)Aufforderung *f*, Aufforderung zur Angebotsabgabe

tendering (out), bidding (action), tender(ing) action · Ausschreibung *f*, Angebotseinholung, Einholung von Angeboten

tendering partnership, bidding combination, tendering combination, bidding partnership · Bietergemeinschaft *f*

tendering period, tendering time, bidding period, bidding time, period of tendering, time of tendering, period of bidding, time of bidding · Angebotsfrist *f*, Angebotszeitraum *m*, Ausschreibungsfrist, Ausschreibungszeitraum

tendering procedure, bidding procedure · Ausschreibungsverfahren *n*

tendering result, bidding result · Ausschreibungsergebnis *n*

tendering sheet, estimating sheet, calculation sheet, bidding sheet · Angebotsbogen *m*, Kalkulationsbogen

tendering stage, bidding stage, stage of tendering, stage of bidding [*The stage in which a suitable contractor is selected and an acceptable offer obtained*] · Ausschreibungsstadium *n*, Ausschreibungsstufe *f*, Stadium *n* der Angebotseinholung, Stufe *f* der Angebotseinholung, Stufe *f* der Ausschreibung, Stadium *n* der Ausschreibung, Angebotseinholungsstufe *f*, Angebotseinholungsstadium *n*

tendering time, bidding period, bidding time, period of tendering, time of tendering, period of bidding, time of bidding, tendering period · Angebotsfrist *f*, Angebotszeitraum *m*, Ausschreibungsfrist, Ausschreibungszeitraum

tender item, offer item; (bid) proposal item (US); bid item · Angebotsposition *f*

tendermanship · Angebotswesen *n*

tender of performance [*Expressed readiness to perform an act in accordance with an obligation*] · Erfüllungsbereitschaft *f*

tender opening, offer opening; (bid) proposal opening, opening of (bid) proposal (US), opening of tenders, opening of offers, opening of bids, bid opening · Angebotseröffnung *f*, Submission *f*

tender opening time, (bid) opening time · Submissionszeit *f*

to tender out, to invite offers, to invite bids; to invite (bid) proposals (US); to put out to tender, to go out to tender, to obtain tenders, to invite tenders · ausschreiben, (Angebote) einholen, auffordern zur Angebotsabgabe

to tender out privately · privat ausschreiben

tender prescriptions, tender regulations, offer prescriptions, offer regulations, bid prescriptions, bid regulations; (bid) proposal prescriptions, (bid) proposal regulations (US) · Angebotsvorschriften *fpl*

tender price → tender(ed) sum

tender rate, bid rate, offer rate; (bid) proposal rate (US) · Angebotssatz *m*

tender regulations → tender prescriptions

tender request, offer request, bid request; (bid) proposal request (US) · Angebotsanforderung *f*

tender request form, offer request form; (bid) proposal request form (US); bid request form · Angebotsanforderungsformular *n*

tender security → tender guarantee

tender sum → tender(ed) sum

tender system · Tenderverfahren *n*, Auflegung *f* zur Zeichnung mit beweglichen Kursen [*Emissionsgeschäft*]

tender system · Zeichnung *f* mit unbestimmtem Kurs [*Emissionsgeschäft*]

tender total, bid total, offer total; (bid) proposal total (US) [*The total of the priced bill of quantities at the date of acceptance of the contractor's tender for the works*] · Angebotsendsumme *f*, Angebotsendpreis *m*

tenement [*In its original, proper, and legal sense this term signifies everything that may be owned, provided it be of a permanent nature, whether it be of a substantial and sensible kind or of an unsubstantial, ideal kind. It is of greater extent than land, including not only land but rents, commons, and other rights and interests issuing out of or concerning lands*] · Eigentum *n* an Dauergut, Dauereigentum

tenement, residence, dwelling; dwelling unit, DU, du, living unit, LU, lu, housing unit, apartment, unit of housing (US); apartment (Brit.) [*archaic*] · Wohnung *f*

tenement → house

tenement, (feodal) tenure (of land), land held of a lord, land in fee; feodum [*Latin*]; feudum, tenementum [*Latin*]; feu [*Scots law*], fee (tenure) (of land), fief, tenancy, land tenure, feud, feod · Leh(e)n *n*, Leh(e)n(s)gut *n*, Leh(e)n(s)besitz *m*, leh(e)n(s)rechtlicher (Grund)-Besitz(stand) *m*, Benefizium *n*

tenemental land(s) → tenure land(s)

tenement factory · Fabrikkaserne *f*

tenement for life, fee (tenure) for life, fief for life, (feodal) tenure (of land) for life, tenancy for life · lebenslanges Leh(e)n *n*, Leh(e)n auf Lebenszeit

tenement (house), apartment house [*A building used as a dwelling for several families, each living separate and apart*] · Mietwohn(ungs)haus *n*, Mehrwohn(ungs)haus, Mehrfamilien-(wohn)haus, Mehrparteien(wohn)haus, Miethaus, Vielwohn(ungs)haus, Familienhaus, Vermietungshaus, Zinshaus

tenement in burgage; burgagium, feudum burgense, feudum urbanum, feodum burgense, feodum urbanum [*Latin*]; tenure of burgage, burgage (tenure), burgage tenancy, burgage-holding, tenure in burgage, tenancy in burgage, tenancy of burgage, burgage tenement [*A tenure whereby lands or houses in cities and towns were held of the king or queen or other lord, for a certain yearly rent*] · Bürgerleh(e)n *n*, Stadtleh(e)n, städtischer Freibesitz *m* (an Häusern und Land)

tenementum [*Latin*]; feu [*Scots law*], fee (tenure) (of land), fief, tenancy, land tenure, feud, feod, tenement, (feodal) tenure (of land), land held of a lord, land in fee; feodum, feudum [*Latin*] · Leh(e)n *n*, Leh(e)n(s)gut *n*,Leh(e)n(s)besitz *m*, leh(e)n(s)rechtlicher (Grund)-Besitz(stand) *m*, Benefizium *n*

tenente in capite [*Latin*]; intermediate lord, arriere lord, mesne lord, mean lord, middle lord · (feudaler) Belehner *m* von Aftervasallen, Feudalherr von Aftervasallen, Leh(e)n(s)herr von Aftervasallen, Leh(e)n(s)gutgeber von Aftervasallen, mittlerer Leh(e)n(s)herr, mittlerer Feudalherr, Vasall *m* der Krone, Kronvasall, Afterleh(e)nsherr

tenor [*The purport and affect of a document as opposed to its actual words*] · Tenor *m*, Sinn *m*

tentative decision · vorläufige Entscheidung *f*, vorläufiger Entscheid *m*

tentative (e)valuation, tentative val., tentative appraisement, tentative appraisal · Vor(ab)schätzung *f*, Vorbewertung, Vor-Wertermitt(e)lung

tentative planning, planning design · Plan(ungs)entwurf *m*

tentative working rule, rule of thumb, thumb rule · Faustregel *f*

tent camp · Zeltplatz *m* [*Freifläche zur Aufstellung von Zelten für zeitweiligen Erholungsaufenthalt*]

tenure, leasehold estate, demise, tenancy; demissio, dimissio [*Latin*]; assedation, tack [*Scots law*], estate less than freehold, lease(hold) [*Holding of real estate under a lease. Such an estate continues for a fixed or determinable period of time but not for a lifetime. It is a conveyance of land whereby the owner of landed property, called the lessor, grants the possession and use of his landed property to another party, called the lessee, in consideration of a sum of money, called the rent*] · Bodenpacht *f*, Landpacht, Bodennutzungsrechtvergabe *f*, Landnutzungsrechtvergabe,

Bodenverpachtung *f*, Landverpachtung, (Boden)Nutzungsrecht

tenure; demissio, dimissio [*Latin*]; tenancy, demise, lease(hold) · Pacht *f*, Nutzungsrechtvergabe *f*, Verpachtung *f*

tenure → fee (tenure) (of land)

tenure → interest in (real) estate

tenure agreement → agreement of tenancy

tenure at will, landlord/tenant relation(ship) at will, tenancy at will [*It is created by any letting for a time not limited. Such a tenancy is determinable at the will of either landlord or tenant, even though it be expressed to be determinable at the will of the landlord only*] · jederzeit kündbares Mietverhältnis *n*, all(e)zeit kündbares Mietverhältnis, willkürlich kündbares Mietverhältnis, einvernehmlich geduldetes Mietverhältnis

tenure by custom, customary tenure, common tenure [*Examples were gavelkind and borough English*] · gewohnheitsrechtliches Leh(e)n *n*

tenure by scutage; feudum clypei, feudum clypeare, feodum clypei, feodum clypeare [*Latin*] · Schildleh(e)n *n*

tenure contract, lease(hold) contract, demise contract, contract of tenancy, contract of demise, contract of lease(hold), contract of tenure, tenancy contract · Pachtvertrag *m*, Nutzungsrechtvertrag, Verpachtungsvertrag

tenure en Burgh Engloys [*Anglo-French*]; borough-English, borough-tenure, borough-kind [*A custom of tenure by which the youngest son inherits all the land(s) and tenement(s)*] · Vererbung *f* von Liegenschaften auf den jüngsten Sohn

tenure for life → tenancy for life

tenure for 3,000 years → tenancy for 3,000 years

tenure from year to year → tenancy from year to year

tenure in bondage → tenure in ville(i)nage

tenure in bond service → tenure in ville(i)nage

tenure in capite, tenure in chief [*The holding of land direct from the king*] · Königsleh(e)n *n*

tenure in frankalmoign(e) → (feodal) tenure (of land) in frankalmoign(e)

tenure in (socage), socage tenure; socagium [*Latin*]; free lay fief, free lay feud, free lay feod, free lay tenancy, free lay tenement, free lay fee, free lay (feodal) tenure (of land) · freies weltliches Leh(e)n *n*, weltliches Freileh(e)n

tenure in ville(i)nage, tenure in bondage, tenure in bond service, tenure of bondland, bondage tenure, ville(i)nage tenure [*A distinct sort of copyhold*] · Dienstbauernleh(e)n *n*

tenure land(s), feodal land(s), feudal land(s), feuda(to)ry land(s), tenemental land(s), land(s) of (a) manor, land(s) held of a lord, land(s) of tenure, outland(s), tenancy [*Land held of the lord by free tenure*] · Leh(e)n(s)land *n*, Feudalland, Außenland, Grenzland, verpachtetes Land

tenure law, feodal law, feuda(to)ry law, manorial law; lex feudalis [*Latin*]; law of tenure(s) (of land), law of (the) manor, law of feudary tenure, law of feudal tenure, law of feodal tenure, law of feuds, law of feudal estates, feudal law · Leh(e)n(s)recht *n*, Feudalrecht

tenure lot · Besitzparzelle *f*

tenure of an office, office tenure · Amtshaltung *f*

tenure of bond-land → tenure in villenage

tenure of burgage, burgage (tenure), burgage tenancy, burgage-holding, tenure in burgage, tenancy in burgage, tenancy of burgage, burgage tenement, tenement in burgage; burgagium, feudum burgense, feudum urbanum, feodum burgense, feodum urbanum [*Latin*] [*A tenure whereby lands or houses in cities and towns were held of the king or queen or other lord, for a certain yearly rent*] · Bürgerleh(e)n *n*, Stadtleh(e)n, städtischer Freibesitz *m* (an Häusern und Land)

tenure of gavelkind, socage tenure subject to the custom of gavelkind · weltliches Freileh(e)n *n* mit Erschaft aller Söhne zu gleichen Teilen, freies weltliches Leh(e)n mit Erbschaft aller Söhne zu gleichen Teilen

tenure (of land) at (the) will of the lord → (feodal) tenure (of land) at (the) will of the lord

tenure (of land) by divine service, tenure (of land) by religious service; feudum ecclesiasticum, feodum ecclesiasticum, feudum religiosum, feodum religiosum [*Latin*]; spiritual fee, spiritual feud, spiritual feod, spiritual fief, spiritual tenancy, spiritual tenement, spiritual (feodal) tenure (of land), ecclesiastic(al) fee, ecclesiastic(al) feod, ecclesiastic(al) feud, ecclesiastic(al) fief, ecclesiastic(al) tenement, ecclesiastic(al) tenancy, ecclesiastic(al) (feodal) tenure (of land) · Gottesleh(e)n *n*, Kirchenleh(e)n, Klosterleh(e)n, geistliches Leh(e)n *n* [*Die geistliche Verrichtungen waren genau definiert*]

tenure (of land) in frankalmoign(e) → (feodal) tenure (of land) in frankalmoign(e)

tenure of land(s) at will — term of redemption 1044

tenure of land(s) at will → tenancy of land(s) at will

(tenure of) serjeanty, great fee (tenure), great (feodal) tenure, great fief, great tenure of demesne · Kronleh(e)n *n*, Leh(e)n unmittelbar unter dem König (oder der Königin)

tenure of small holding · Kleingutpacht *f*

term, currency, life · Dauer *f*, (Lauf)Zeit *f* [*z. B. eines Vertrages*]

term → time (allowed)

term date · Fristdatum *n*, Fristtermin *m*

term for appeal → time (allowed) for appeal

terminable → (de)terminable

terminable annuity · Zeitrente *f*, abgekürzte Rente

terminable annuity, annuity for terms of years [*The payments cease after a specified number of years*] · Jahresannuität *f*

terminable at will → (de)terminable at will

terminable condition → (de)terminable condition

terminable interest → (de)terminable interest

terminable mortgage → (de)terminable mortgage

terminable right → (de)terminable interest

terminal value, final value · Endwert *m*

to terminate, to lapse, to run out, to cease; to fall in (Brit.); to expire, to end · ablaufen, verfristen

to terminate (automatically), to determine (automatically), to (come to an) end [*In a certain event*] · auslaufen [*Frist*]

terminating → (de)terminating

terminating building society (Brit.); terminating (building (and loan)) association (US); building club · Bausparkasse *f* auf Zeit gegründet, aufhörende Bausparkasse [*Sie stellt ihre Tätigkeit ein, sobald alle Mitglieder ihre Bausparsummen erhalten haben*]

terminating plan · aufhörender Plan *m* [*aufhörende Bausparkasse*]

termination, falling in, lapse (of time), expiration, expiry, running out · Ablauf *m*, Fristablauf, Zeitablauf, Verfristung *f*

termination contracting officer, termination contracting official · (Beschaffungs)Beamte *m* für die Reg(e)lung von behandelten (Beschaffungs)Verträgen mit einer Regierung

termination date, falling in date, running out date, accrual date, maturity date, expiry date, expiration date, due date · Fälligkeitsdatum *n*, Fälligkeitstag *m*, Verfalldatum, Verfalltermin *m*, (Frist)-Ablauftermin, (Frist)Ablaufdatum, Fälligkeitstermin, Verfalltag, (Frist)Ablauftag

termination for convenience (of the government) clause, convenience clause · Vertragsbeend(ig)ungsklausel *f* [*(Beschaffungs)Vertrag mit einer Regierung*]

termination for default (of government) clause, default clause · (Ver)Säumnisbeend(ig)ungsklausel *f* [*(Beschaffungs)Vertrag mit einer Regierung*]

termination of settlement, settlement termination · Festlegungsbeendigung *f* [*Land*]

termination of (the) contract, contract termination · Vertragsbeend(ig)ung *f*

term insurance, term assurance [*The term policy is one taken to cover a fixed number of days, months, or years. It is paid only if the insured dies within that time*] · Risikolebensversicherung *f*

term limit, time limit · Fristgrenze *f*

term loan · langfristiges Darleh(e)n *n*

term of a week, period of a week · Wochenfrist *f*

term of contract, (contract) term [*Not to be confused with "contract condition" which is a "fundamental (contract) term"*] · (Vertrags)Nebenbedingung *f*

term (of court), court term · Gerichtsperiode *f*

term of discharge, duration of discharge, period of redemption, term of redemption, duration of redemption, redemption period, redemption term, redemption duration, discharge period, discharge duration, discharge term, period of discharge · Auslösungsfrist *f*, Einlösungsfrist *f*, Ablösungsfrist *f*

term of dwelling lease, residential lease term, dwelling lease term, term of residential lease · Wohnungsmietvertragsfrist *f*

term of exclusion, time of exclusion, exclusion period, exclusion time, exclusion term, period of exclusion · Ausschlußfrist *f*, Ausschließungsfrist *f*

term of law, word of law, law term, law word, legal term, legal word · Rechtswort *n*, Rechtsbenennung *f*

term of lease, lease term · Mietvertragsfrist *f*

term of objection, time allowed for objection · Einspruchsfrist *f*

term of redemption, duration of redemption, redemption period, redemption term, redemption duration, discharge period, discharge duration, discharge term, period of discharge, term of discharge, duration of discharge, period of redemption · Auslösungsfrist *f*, Einlösungsfrist *f*, Ablösungsfrist *f*

term of residential lease, term of dwelling lease, residential lease term, dwelling lease term · Wohnungsmietvertragsfrist *f*

term of trade, trade term · Austauschrelation *f* [*Kleine und schwache Gewerbezweige in einem Land geraten durch ungünstige Austauschrelationen in Nachteil gegenüber der den Weltmarkt beliefernden Industrie*]

term of twelve days, twelve-day term · Zwölftagefrist *f*

term of warranty, time of warranty, period of warranty, warranty term, warranty time, warranty period · Garantiefrist *f*, Garantiezeitraum *m*

term of years, estate for years, tenancy of years, tenancy for years, (good) lease(hold) title, lease(hold) right, lease(hold) (tenure), lease(hold) interest, tenancy for a time certain [*Lease(hold) for a period of years*] · (Besitz)Recht *n* auf Zeit, (Besitz)Recht auf Jahre, Grund(stücks)besitzrecht auf Jahre, Grund(stücks)besitzrecht auf Zeit, Landbesitzrecht auf Jahre, Landbesitzrecht auf Zeit, Bodenbesitzrecht auf Jahre, Bodenbesitzrecht auf Zeit, (subjektives) (Land)Pachtrecht auf Jahre, (subjektives) (Land)Pachtrecht auf Zeit, (subjektives) Bodenpachtrecht auf Jahre, (subjektives) Bodenpachtrecht auf Zeit

termor → (land) holder

term pass book account · Dauersparkonto *n* [*kapitalistische Bausparkasse*]

term probatory [*In English ecclesiastic(al) practice. A certain time within which the plaintiff is required to prove so much of the libel as the defendant has not confessed in his personal answers*] · Klagebegründungs- und Beweisführungsfrist *f*

term sight draft · Nachsichtwechsel *m*, Zeitsichtwechsel

terra affirmata [*Latin*]; land let to a farm · landwirtschaftliches Pachtland *n*

terra boscalis [*Latin*]; woody land; woody ground · holzbestandenes Gelände *n*, holzbestandenes Land *n*, holzbestandenes Terrain

terra capitalis, caput terrae, caputium, chevitia, forlandum, versura [*Latin*]; headland, foreland, forebalk, foreherda, butt; head-rig [*Scotch*]; pen tir [*Welsh*]; forera [*Latin*] [*The slip of unploughed land left at the head or end of a ploughed field on which the plough is turned*] · Anwende *f*, Voracker *m*, Vorwart *f*, Anwänder *m*

terrace-house · (Fabrik)Arbeiter-Reihenhaus *n*

terrace location · Terrassenlage *f*

terra dominica [*Latin*]; demain (land), demeyne (land), demeine (land), demesne (land), inland, land in (the lord's) demesne, bordland, table demesne, home farm (of the lord of the manor), demesnial settlement; terra indominicata [*Latin*] [*Those lands of a manor not granted out in tenancy, but reserved by the lord for his own use and occupation. The opposite of "tenemental lands"*] · Hoffeld *n*, Salland *n*, grundherrliches Eigenland, Hofländerei *f*, Hofland, grundherrschaftliches Eigenland

terra excultabilis, terra wainabilis [*Latin*]; tillable land [*Land which may be ploughed*] · pflügbares Land *n*

terra frusca, terra frisca [*Latin*]; fresh land, fresh ground · Frischland *n*, Frischboden *m*

terra haereditaria, terra libraria [*Latin*]; bócland, bookland, bockland, charterland [*Land which, in pre-Norman Conquest time, was held by charter, handbook, or other written title*] · Buchland *n*

terra hydata, virgate terrae, hida (terrae), hyda [*Latin*]; familia [*Latin*], hide ((of) land), hyde (of land), higid, hiwise, virgate (land), verge of land, yardland, hydeland, husbandland, wista; hilda [*Scotland*] [*A quantity of land not of any certain extent, but as much as a plough can by course of husbandry plough in a year. It meant in different places anything from sixty to 120 acres. A virgate is one fourth of a hide*] · Hufe(ngut) *f*, *n*, Hufenschoß *n*, Hube *f*, Hufen(gut)land *n* [*Ältere Benennungen: Hof m, Hub m, Hu(o)ba f, und Hova f*] [*Unter gutsherrlich-bäuerlichen Verhältnissen hieß der gesamte Besitz eines Dorfgenossen "Hufe(ngut)". Diese Benennung war also keine Flächengröße, sondern eine Besitzeinheit, die zahlreiche, zerstreut liegende kleine Ackerteile im Besitz derselben Person umfaßte*]

terrain, ground · Gelände *n*, Terrain *n*

terrain area, area of terrain, ground area, area of ground · Geländefläche *f*, Terrainfläche

terra indominicata, terra dominica [*Latin*]; demain (land), demeyne (land), demeine (land), demesne (land), inland, land in (the lord's) demesne, bordland, table demesne, home farm (of the lord of the manor), demesnial settlement [*Those lands of a manor not granted out in tenancy, but reserved by the lord for his own use and occupation. The opposite of "tenemental lands"*] · Hoffeld *n*, Salland *n*, grundherrliches Eigenland, Hofländerei *f*, Hofland, grundherrschaftliches Eigenland

terrain form, form of terrain, ground form, form of ground · Geländeform *f*, Terrainform

terrain strip, strip of ground, ground strip, strip of terrain · Geländestreifen *m*, Terrainstreifen

terra libraria [*Latin*]; bócland, bookland, bockland, charter-land; terra haereditaria [*Latin*] [*Land which, in pre-Norman Conquest time, was held by charter, handbook, or other written title*] · Buchland *n*

terra lucrabilis [*Latin*] [*Land gained from the sea or enclosed out of a waste*] · gewonnenes Land *n*, Neuland

terra nova [*Latin*] [*Land newly converted from wood ground*] · gewonnenes Land *n*, Neuland

terra popularis, ager publicus [*Latin*]; land of the people, folkland, folcland, falkland [*Anglo-Saxon land law*]. Folcland was held by customary law, without written title. Inheritance depended on custom. It could not be (ab)alienated without the consent of those who had some interest in it] · Volksland *n*

terra regis [*Latin*] · Königsland *n*

terrarius [*Latin*] → (real) property owner

terra sabulosa [*Latin*],; sandy ground, sandy land · sandiges Gelände *n*, sandiges Land, sandiges Terrain *n*

terra testamentalis [*Latin*] [*Allodial land, or such gavelkind land as was disposable by will*] · testamentsfähiges Land *n*, testierfähiges Land

terra wainabilis [*Latin*]; tillable land; terra excultabilis [*Latin*], [*Land which may be ploughed*] · pflügbares Land *n*

terra warrenata [*Latin. Land which had the liberty of free-warren*] · freies königliches Jagdrechtland *n*, königliches freies Jagdrechtland

terrestrial photogrammetry · terrestrische Photogrammetrie *f*

terre-tenant [*Norman French*] → (land) holder

terrier [*Land register in the early Middle Ages*] · Landbuch *n*

territorial area · Gebietsfläche *f*, Territorialfläche

territorial bay [*A bay under national jurisdiction*] · Territorialbucht *f*

territorial boundary, area(l) boundary · Gebietsgrenze *f*, Territorialgrenze

territorial change · Gebietsänderung *f*, Territorialänderung

territorial clearance, territorial redevelopment · Gebietssanierung *f*, Territorialsanierung

territorial corporation · Gebietskörperschaft *f*, Gebietskorporation *f*

(territorial) corridor, area(l) corridor · (Gebiets)Streifen *m*, Territorialstreifen

territorial determination · Bereichserklärung *f*, Gebietsbestimmung, Gebietsfestsetzung, Gebietsfeststellung, Territorialbestimmung, Territorialfestsetzung, Territorialfeststellung [*Die förmliche Festsetzung von Gebieten durch Rechtsverordnung, Satzung oder teilweise durch Landgesetz*]

territorial development plan, area development plan · Gebietsentwick(e)lungsplan *m*, Territorialentwick(e)lungsplan

territorial division, divisional unit · Gebietsteil *m*

territorial division · Gebietsgliederung *f*, Territorialgliederung

territorial fraction of a city, borough [*in American law*] · (Stadt)Bezirk *m*, Verwaltungsbezirk

territoriality · Territorialität *f*

territorial jurisdiction · Gebietszuständigkeit *f* [*Siehe Anmerkung unter „Zuständigkeit" und „Zuständigkeitsgebiet"*]

territorial limit · Hoheitsgrenze *f* [*auf See*]

territorial network, area(l) network · Gebietsnetz *n*, Territorialnetz

territorial organization · Gliederung *f*, Aufgliederung [*Territorium*]

territorial overlapping, area(l) overlapping, overlapping of areas, overlapping of territories · Gebietsüberlagerung *f*, Gebietsüberschneidung, territoriale Überlagerung, territoriale Überschneidung

territorial pattern, territorial scheme, area(l) pattern, area(l) scheme · Gebietsmuster *n*, Gebietsschema *n*, Territorialmuster, Territorialschema

territorial planning, area planning · Gebietsplanung *f*, Territorialplanung

territorial planning commission, area planning commission · Gebietsplanungskommission *f*, Territorialplanungskommission

(territorial) reapportionment plan, (territorial) reorganization plan · Gebietsreformplan *m*, gebietlicher Neugliederungsplan, gebietlicher Neuordnungsplan, (territorialer) Neuordnungsplan, (territorialer) Neugliederungsplan, (territorialer) Neugestaltungsplan, gebietlicher Neugestaltungplan, Territorialreformplan

territorial redevelopment, territorial clearance · Gebietssanierung *f*, Territorialsanierung

(territorial) reorganization, (territorial) reapportionment · Gebietsreform *f*, Territorialreform, territoriale Verwaltungsreform, Neuordnung *f* eines Gebietsstandes, gebietliche Neugliederung, gebietliche Neugestaltung, gebietliche

(territorial) reorganization plan — testamentary (ab)alienation

Neuordnung, (territoriale) Neugliederung, (territoriale) Neugestaltung, (territoriale) Neuordnung

(territorial) reorganization plan, (territorial) reapportionment plan · Gebietsreformplan *m*, gebietlicher Neugliederungsplan, gebietlicher Neuordnungsplan, (territorialer) Neuordnungsplan, (territorialer) Neugliederungsplan, (territorialer) Neugestaltungsplan, gebietlicher Neugestaltungplan, Territorialreformplan

territorial scheme, area(l) pattern, area(l) scheme, territorial pattern · Gebietsmuster *n*, Gebietsschema *n*, Territorialmuster, Territorialschema

territorial scope · Gebietsumfang *m*

territorial sea [*In political sense*] → territorial waters

territorial subdivision · Gebietsteilung *f*

territorial system, area(l) system · Gebietssystem *n*, Territorialsystem

territorial unit, area(l) unit · Gebietseinheit *f*, Territorialeinheit

territorial waters, territorial sea, maritime belt, belt of sea, sea belt [*In political sense*]; coast(al) waters [*In geographic and nautical sense*] · Küstengewässer *n*, Küstenmeer *n*, Territorialgewässer, Hoheitsgewässer, Meeresstreifen *m*, Hoheitsmeer, Territorialmeer

territorium legis [*Latin*]; territory subject to one system of law, area subject to one system of law · Rechtsgebiet *n*

territory, area · Gebiet *n*, Territorium *n*

territory category, area category · Gebietskategorie *f*, Territorialkategorie

territory forecast, area forecast · Gebietsvorhersage *f*

territory map, area map · Gebietskarte *f*

territory of a jurisdiction, precinct of a jurisdiction · Bann(meile) *m*, *(f)* [*Rechtsprechung*]

territory of comprehensive development → comprehensive development area

territory of demolition and rebuilding, territory of wrecking and rebuilding, wrecking and rebuilding territory, razing and rebuilding territory, demolition and rebuilding area, demolition and rebuilding territory, wrecking and rebuilding area, area of demolition and rebuilding, area of wrecking and rebuilding · Abbruch- und Wiederaufbaugebiet *n*, Abriß- und Wiederaufbaugebiet, Abreiß- und Wiederaufbaugebiet

territory of depopulation, area of depopulation, depopulation area, depopulation territory · Aushöhlungsgebiet *n*, Entleerungsgebiet *n*

territory of destination, area of destination · Zielgebiet *n*, Bestimmungsgebiet

territory of jurisdiction [*The territory or geographical limits with which the judgments or orders of a court can be enforced or executed*] · Zuständigkeitsgebiet *n* [*Siehe Anmerkung unter „Zuständigkeit"*]

territory of (outstanding) natural beauty, AONB, area of (outstanding) natural beauty · Naturschönheitsgebiet *n*

territory of poverty, poverty area, poverty territory, area of poverty · Armutsgebiet *n*

territory of preference, area of preference, preference territory, preference area · Vorranggebiet *n*

territory of problems, problem area, problem territory, area of problems · Problemgebiet *n*

territory of special control, area of special control [*In an area of special control, where it is usual for no advertisements to be allowed, those that are permitted are agreed exceptions to the rule*] · reklamearmes Gebiet *n*

territory of wrecking and rebuilding → territory of demolition and rebuilding

territory protection, protection of area, protection of territory, area protection · Gebietsschutz *m*

territory-related, area-related, territory-orien(ta)ted, area-orien(ta)ted · gebietsbezogen, gebietsorientiert, territorialbezogen, territorialorientiert

territory subject to one sovereign power, state area, state territory, area subject to one sovereign power · Staatsgebiet *n*, Hoheitsgebiet

territory subject to one system of law, area subject to one system of law; territorium legis [*Latin*] · Rechtsgebiet *n*

tertenant [*Norman French*] → (land) holder

tertiary sector, non-manufacturing jobs [*admistration; service*] · Tertiärwirtschaft *f*, Teritärsektor, tertiärer Wirtschaftssektor *m*, tertiär(wirtschaftlich)er Sektor [*Er ist fernbezugstätig und nahbedarfstätig*]

tertiary (sector) settlement · Dienstleistungs(an)sied(e)lung *f*

testament; testamentum [*Latin*]; will of personal property, will of mov(e)able property, will of personal estate, will of personality · Fahrnistestament *n*, Fahrhabetestament

testamentary, by will · testamentarisch, durch Testament

testamentary (ab)alienation, testamentary disposal · testamentarische Veräußerung *f*

testamentary authority — testator of lands(s) 1048

testamentary authority, testamentary power · Testamentsgewalt *f*, Testamentshoheit *f*, Testamentsmacht *f*, Testamentskompetenz *f*

testamentary capacity, disposing capacity, disposing capability, testamentary capability, testamentary qualification, capacity of the testator, capability of the testator, qualification of the testator · Testierfähigkeit *f*, Testiereignung *f*, Testamentsfähigkeit, Testamentseignung

testamentary clause · Testamentsklausel *f*

testamentary disposal, testamentary (ab)alienation · testamentarische Veräußerung *f*

testamentary disposition [*A disposition of property by way of gift, which is not to take effect unless the grantor dies or until that event*] · letztwillige Verfügung *f*, testamentarische Verfügung [*über unbewegliches und bewegliches Vermögen*]

testamentary disposition, disposition mortis causa · Verfügung *f* von Todes wegen, Rechtsgeschäft *n* von Todes wegen, letzte Verfügung, letztes Rechtsgeschäft

(testamentary) executor; executor testamentarius [*Latin*]; testamentary trustee [*He is appointed by the will, either expressly or by necessary inference from the terms of the will (executor according to the tenor)*] · (Testaments)Vollstrecker *m*, Willensvollstrecker [*Die Benennung „Willensvollstrecker" ist treffender als die übliche „Testamentsvollstrecker", da eine Willensvollstreckung auch bei gesetzlicher Erbfolge eintreten kann, z. B. wenn ein Testament nur die Einsetzung eines Testamentsvollstreckers enthält*]

(testamentary) executor according to the tenor · testamentarisch genannter (Testaments)Vollstrecker *m*

testamentary freedom · Testamentsfreiheit *f*

testamentary gift, gift by will · testamentarische Schenkung *f*

testamentary guardianship, guardianship by statute · gesetzliche Vormundschaft *f*

testamentary incapacity, testamentary incapability · Testierunfähigkeit *f*

testamentary law, wills law, law of wills · Testamentsrecht *n*

testamentary power, testamentary authority · Testamentsgewalt *f*, Testamentshoheit *f*, Testamentsmacht *f*, Testamentskompetenz *f*

testamentary provision · Testamentsbestimmung *f*

testamentary qualification, disposing qualification, capacity of the testator, capability of the testator, qualification of the testator, testamentary capacity, disposing capacity, disposing capability, testamentary capability · Testierfähigkeit *f*, Testiereignung *f*, Testamentsfähigkeit, Testamentseignung

testamentary succession, succession ex testamento · testamentarische Erbfolge *f*

testamentary trustee, (testamentary) executor; executor testamentarius [*Latin*] [*He is appointed by the will, either expressly or by necessary inference from the terms of the will (executor according to the tenor)*] · (Testaments)Vollstrecker *m*, Willensvollstrecker [*Die Benennung „Willensvollstrecker" ist treffender als die übliche „Testamentsvollstrecker", da eine Willensvollstreckung auch bei gesetzlicher Erbfolge eintreten kann, z. B. wenn ein Testament nur die Einsetzung eines Testamentsvollstreckers enthält*]

testamentary witness · Testamentszeuge *m*

testamentum [*Latin*]; will [*The word "testament" is now seldom used, except in the heading of a formal will, which usually begins — "This is the last will and testament of me, A.B., etc."*] · Testament *n*

testamentum, carta donationis, cartula donationis, epistola donationis [*Latin*] · (dispositive) Schenkungsurkunde *f* [*Urkunde, in welcher ein Schenker erklärt die Schenkung vorzunehmen oder vorgenommen zu haben*]

testamentum correspectivum [*Latin*] · korrespektives Gesamttestament *n*, gemeinschaftliches Testament im engeren Sinne

testamentum inofficium [*Latin*]; unofficious will [*One made in disregard of natural obligations as to inheritance. It has no place in the common law*] · gesetzliche Erbrechte ausschließendes Testament *n*

testamentum mere simultaneum [*Latin*] · Doppeltestament *n*

testamentum mutuum [*Latin*]; joint will · gemeinschaftliches Testament *n*, gemeinsames Testament

testamentum reciprocum [*Latin*] · letztwillige Gesamtverfügung *f*

testator [*A deceased person from whom an estate has passed to another by operation of law, in consequence of his decease*] · Bescheider *m*, Testator, Erblasser

testator of land(s), devisor of land(s) [*A giver of land(s) by will; the maker of a will of land(s)*] · Bodenerblasser *m*, Landerblasser, Grund(stücks)erblasser

testator's debts — theory of economic space

testator's debts · Bescheiderschulden *f pl*, Testatorschulden, Erblasserschulden

testatum execution, executorship, execution of a will · (Testaments)Vollstreckung *f*

test case · Probefall *m*

test construction project · Versuchsbauvorhaben *n*, Versuchsbauprojekt *n*

test engineer for statical analysis · Prüfingenieur *m* für Baustatik

test engineer ordinance · Prüfingenieurverordnung *f*

to testify, to bear witness · bezeugen

testifying in writing, giving a certificate, attesting, attestation, certifying · Bescheinigen *n*

to testify in writing, to give a certificate, to attest; certificare [*Latin*]; to certify · bescheinigen

testimonial evidence, testimonial proof · Zeugenaussage *f*

testimonium clause · Beglaubigungsklausel *f*, Schlußklausel [*Urkunde*]

testimony · Zeugenaussage *f* unter Eid

test of acceptance (of (the) work(s)), acceptance test · Abnahmeprüfung *f*, Abnahmeprobe *f*, Abnahmeversuch *m*, Bauabnahmeprüfung, Bauabnahmeprobe, Bauabnahmeversuch

test ordinance · Prüfungsverordung *f*

test statistic · Prüfgröße *f*, Prüfmaß *n* [*Statistik*]

tethinga, tithing · Zehnerschaft *f*, Dorfschaft, Zehntschaft

text, wording · Text *m*

text-book · Lehrbuch *n*

textural comparison, collation of wordings, collation of texts [*Of different copies of a document*] · Textvergleich *m*

Thünen ring · Thünenscher Ring *m*

theatre district · Theaterviertel *n*

the canons, canonry; jus canonicum [*Latin. Formerly: law canon. It is laid down in decrees of the pope and statutes of councils. Not to be confused with "jus ecclesiasticum"*], canons collectively, canon law · kanonisches Recht *n*, geistliches Recht

thematic atlas · thematischer Atlas *m*, Themenatlas

thematic cartography · thematische Kartographie *f*, Themenkartographie

thematic map, special subject map · Themakarte *f*, thematische Karte; angewandte Karte, Problemkarte [*frühere Benennungen*]

thematic mapping · thematische Kartierung *f*, Themenkartierung

then value · augenblicklicher Wert *m*

theologian · Theologe *m*

theorem of total probability, total probability theorem · Additionssatz *m* der Wahrscheinlichkeit

theoretical approach · theoretischer Ansatz *m*

theoretical economics · Wirtschaftstheorie *f*

theoretical forecasting model · formalisiertes Voraussagemodell *n*

theoretical model · theoretisches Modell *n*

theorist · Theoretiker *m*

theory approach · Theorieansatz *m*

theory building, theory formulation, building of theory, formulation of theory · Theoriegestaltung *f*, Theorieformulierung

theory formulation, building of theory, formulation of theory, theory building · Theoriegestaltung *f*, Theorieformulierung

theory of agricultural location · landwirtschaftliche Standorttheorie *f*

theory of appraisal, theory of appraisement, theory of (e)valuation, appraisal theory, appraisement theory, (e)valuation theory · Bewertungstheorie *f*, Wertermitt(e)lungstheorie, Taxierungstheorie, (Ab)Schätzungstheorie

theory of arbitration · Schiedstheorie *f*

theory of axial development, sector(ial) theory, axial development theory · Grundsatz *m* der sektoralen Differenzierung einer Stadt, Prinzip *n* der sektoralen Differenzierung einer Stadt, Sektortheorie *f*, Sektorentheorie

theory of central places, central place theory · Theorie *f* der zentralen Orte, Theorie zentraler Orte, zentralörtliche Theorie, Zentralorttheorie, Mittelzentrumtheorie

theory of cost(s), cost(s) theory · Theorie *f* der Kostenabhängigkeiten; Kostentheorie [*Fehlbenennung*]

theory of cost(s) value, cost(s) value theory · Kostenwerttheorie *f*

theory of distribution(s), distribution theory · Verteilungstheorie *f*

theory of economic cycles, economic cycle theory · Konjunkturtheorie *f*

theory of economic space, theory of space economy · Raumwirtschaftstheorie *f*, Theorie der räumlichen Ordnung der Wirtschaft, Theorie des räumlichen Gleichgewichts

theory of (e)valuation — thing corporeal

theory of economic space → theory of space economy

theory of (e)valuation, appraisal theory, appraisement theory, (e)valuation theory, theory of appraisal, theory of appraisement · Bewertungstheorie f, Wertermitt(e)lungstheorie, Taxierungstheorie, (Ab)Schätzungstheorie

theory of games, gaming theory, game theory · Theorie f der Spiele, Spieltheorie

theory of graphs, graph theory · Graphentheorie f

theory of income, income theory · Einkommenstheorie f

theory of industrial location, theory of localization of industry · Industriestandorttheorie f, industrielle Standorttheorie

theory of integration, integration theory · Integrationslehre f

theory of interest · Zinstheorie f

theory of interest on capital, theory of rent earned by capital · Kapitalzinsentheorie f

theory of investment, investment theory · Investitionstheorie f

theory of justice · Gerechtigkeitstheorie f

theory of land use, land use theory · Bodennutzungstheorie f, Flächennutzungstheorie, Landnutzungstheorie

theory of law, law theory · Rechtstheorie f

theory of lawmaking, theory of legislation · Gesetzgebungstheorie f

theory of localization of industry, theory of industrial location · Industriestandorttheorie f, industrielle Standorttheorie

theory of location, theory of sites, location(al) theory, site theory · Standorttheorie f

theory of location for all firms · gesamtwirtschaftliche Standorttheorie f

theory of location for an individual firm, theory of site for an individual firm · einzelwirtschaftliche Standorttheorie f

theory of marginal utility, marginalism · Grenznutzentheorie f, Grenzwerttheorie

theory of planning, planning theory · Planungstheorie f

theory of population, population theory · Bevölkerungstheorie f

theory of possession · Besitztheorie f

theory of production, production theory · Erzeugungstheorie f, Produktionstheorie, Herstellungstheorie, Fertigungstheorie

theory of regional growth, regional growth theory · Regionalwachstumstheorie f, regionale Wachstumstheorie

theory of regions · Landschaftslehre f

theory of rent earned by capital, theory of interest on capital · Kapitalzinsentheorie f

theory of rents, rent theory · Rententheorie f

theory of site for an individual firm, theory of location for an individual firm · einzelwirtschaftliche Standorttheorie f

theory of sites, location(al) theory, site theory, theory of location · Standorttheorie f

theory of space economy, theory of economic space · Raumwirtschaftstheorie f, Theorie der räumlichen Ordnung der Wirtschaft, Theorie des räumlichen Gleichgewichts

theory of spread of cultural advancement from several centres · Kulturkreislehre f

theory of stratification, stratification theory · Schichtungstheorie f

theory of the state, state theory · Staatslehre f

theory of urban economy · Stadtwirtschaftstheorie f

theory of utility, utility theory · Nutzentheorie f

theory of wages, wages theory · Lohntheorie f

the place governs the act; locus regit actum [*Latin*] [*The act is governed by the law of the place where it is done*] · Ortsrecht n das ein Rechtsgeschäft beherrscht, Ortsrecht ein Rechtsgeschäft beherrscht

thermal pollution · Abwärmeverschmutzung f, Abwärmeverunreinigung

thesis · schriftliche (Studiums)Arbeit f

thicket, bosket, bosquet, boscage, boskage · Dickicht n

thickly peopled, thickly settled, densely populated, densely populated, densely peopled · dicht bevölkert, dicht besiedelt

thing; res [*Latin*] [*(subjektives) Recht is in English (subjective) right or interest*] · Gegenstand m, Rechtsobjekt n, Ding n, Sache f [*Im B.G.B. werden Sachen und (subjektive) Rechte als Gegenstände bezeichnet.* §§ *260, 434, 581*]

thing → (valuable) thing

thing claimed · beanspruchter Gegenstand m, beanspruchte Sache f, beanspruchtes Ding n

thing corporeal, corporeal chattel (personal); res corporales, res singula [*Latin*]; corporeal thing, tangible thing, chose, physical thing [*A thing that affects the senses and may be seen and*

thing from a servient land — third party tenancy

handled] · (Einzel)Sache *f*, körperliches Rechtsobjekt *n*, materielles Rechtsobjekt, körperliches Ding *n*, materielles Ding, körperlicher (Rechts)Gegenstand *m*, materieller (Rechts)Gegenstand [*Ausgenommen lebender menschlicher Körper. Unter den Sachbegriff fallen nicht die Rechte, die Sachgesamtheiten, d. h. Mehrheiten von Sachen, die eine besondere Benennung haben, z. B. Bücherei, Warenlager usw. und die Inbegriffe von Sachen und Rechten, z. B. Erbschaftsvermögen usw. Im Preußischen Allgemeinen Landrecht von 1794 (A.L.R.) ist (Einzel)Sache allerdings alles, was Gegenstand eines Rechtes oder einer Verbindlichkeit sein kann (§ 1. I. 2)*]

thing from a servient land capable of ownership · Frucht *f*

thing hired, hired thing · gemietete Sache *f*, gemieteter Gegenstand *m*, gemietetes Ding *n*

thing immov(e)able, thing real, chose local, local chose; immov(e)able [*International Private Law*]; immov(e)able thing, real thing · Immobilie *f*, unbeweglicher Gegenstand *m*, unbewegliche (Einzel)Sache *f*, unbewegliches Ding *n*, unbewegliches Rechtsobjekt *n*

thing incorporeal; res incorporales [*Latin*]; incorporeal thing, intangible thing, incorporeal chattel (personal), intangible chattel (personal) · unkörperliches Ding *n*, immaterielles Ding, nichtkörperliches Ding, unkörperliches Rechtsobjekt *n*, nichtkörperliches Rechtsobjekt, immaterielles Rechtsobjekt, immaterieller Gegenstand *m*, unkörperlicher Gegenstand, nichtkörperlicher Gegenstand

thing in esse · bestehender Gegenstand *m*, bestehende Sache *f*, bestehendes Ding *n* [*Zum Zeitpunkt des Abschlusses eines Pachtverhältnisses*]

thing in posse · nicht bestehende Sache *f*, nicht bestehender Gegenstand *m*, nicht bestehendes Ding *n* [*Zum Zeitpunkt des Abschlusses eines Pachtverhältnisses*]

thing let, let thing · vermietete Sache *f*, vermieteter Gegenstand *m*, vermietetes Ding *n*

thing of an accessory character, appurtenant, appendage, appurtenance; appertinance [*obsolete*]; pertinent, pertinance [*Scots Law*]; appenditia [*Latin*] [*A thing belonging to another thing. Things appendant can be claimed only by prescription, while things appurtenant can be claimed either by prescription or by express grant*] · Zubehör *n*, Dazugehörige *n*, Pertinenz *f*; Zugehör [*Schweiz*]

thing of usufruct, usufruct thing · (Frucht)Genußgegenstand *m*, Nießbrauchgegenstand, (Frucht)Genußsache *f*, Nießbrauchsache

thing real, chose local, local chose; immov(e)able [*International Private Law*]; immov(e)able thing, real thing, thing immov(e)able · Immobilie *f*, unbeweglicher Gegenstand *m*, unbewegliche (Einzel)Sache *f*, unbewegliches Ding *n*, unbewegliches Rechtsobjekt *n*

things immov(e)able, things real, real things, immov(e)able things, choses local, local choses; immov(e)ables [*International Private Law*] · Immobilien *fpl*, unbewegliche (Einzel)Sachen *fpl*, unbewegliche Dinge *npl*, unbewegliche Gegenstände *mpl*, unbewegliche Rechtsobjekte *npl*

thing(s) mov(e)able → personal estate

thing(s) personal → personal estate

things real → immov(e)ables

thinning out · Ausdünnen *n*

third branch of the government, third governmental branch · dritte Regierungsgewalt *f*

third defendant · Drittbeklagte *m*

third governmental branch, third branch of the government · dritte Regierungsgewalt *f*

third mortgage · dritte Hypothek *f*

third party, third person · dritte Partei *f*, Dritte *m*

third party beneficiary · begünstigte Dritte, Drittbegünstigte *m*

third party beneficiary contract, contract for the benefit of third party · Vertrag *m* zugunsten Dritter

third party contract · Drittenvertrag *m*

third party damage · Drittschaden *m*

third party demise, lease(hold) to a third party, demise to a third party, tenancy to a third party, demise to a third party, tenancy to a third party, tenancy to a third party, third party lease(hold), third party tenancy · Zwischenpacht *f*

third party insurance · Drittenversicherung *f*

third party lease(hold), third party tenancy, third party demise, lease(hold) to a third party, demise to a third party, tenancy to a third party · Zwischenpacht *f*

third party notice, third party notification · Streitverkündung *f*

third party relation(ship), external relation(ship), exterior relation(ship) · Außenverhältnis *n*

third party right; jus tertii [*Latin*], right of (a) third party · Drittenrecht *n*

third party risk, liability risk, indemnity risk · Haftpflichtwagnis *n*, Haftpflichtrisiko *n*, Haftungsrisiko, Haftungswagnis

third party tenancy, third party demise, lease(hold) to a third party, demise to a

third person — through freight

third party, tenancy to a third party, third party lease(hold) · Zwischenpacht f

third person, third party · dritte Partei f, Dritte m

third-person liability clause · Dritthaftungsklausel f

third schedule development · Entwick(e)lung f gemäß der 3. Ausführungsverordnung des T.C.P.A. 1962 [*England*]

thoroughfare, major artery · Durchgangsstraße f

thoroughfare plan (US); traffic plan · Verkehrsplan m, Plan über die Verkehrsplanung

thoughtway, consecutive thought, line of thought · Gedankenfolge f, Gedankengang m

threat · Drohung f

threatening collapse, imminent crash, threatening crash, imminent collapse · drohender Einsturz m [*Bauwerk*]

three-arbitrator board, tripartite board · Dreierbesetzung f [*Schiedsgericht*]

three-decker wooden tenement, triple-decker wooden tenement · dreigeschossiges Mehrfamilien-Holzhaus n

three-dimensional master (development) plan, general (development) plan, master (development) plan, comprehensive (development) plan, structure (development) plan [*A long-range plan officially recognized as a guide for the physical growth and development of a community, together with the basic regulatory and administrative controls needed to attain the physical objectives*] · General(bebauungs)plan m

three-dimensional master legislation, three-dimensional master lawmaking, structure planning legislation, structure planning lawmaking, general planning legislation, general planning lawmaking, master planning legislation, master planning lawmaking, comprehensive planning legislation, comprehensive planning lawmaking · Generalplanungsgesetzgebung f

three-dimensional master planning, structure planning, general (development) planning, master (development) planning, comprehensive (development) planning · General(bebauungs)planung f

three-dimensional matrix · dreidimensionale Matrix f

three-dimensional representation · dreidimensionale Darstellung f

three-field system, three-field husbandry, triple-field system, triple-field husbandry · Dreifelderwirtschaft f

threefold, triple, treble · dreifach

three-generation family, triple-generation family · Dreigenerationsfamilie f

three-level operation, triple-level operation, tri-level operation · Dreiebenenbetrieb m [*öffentliches Verkehrsmittel*]

three-mile (marginal) belt · Drei-Meilen-Zone f

three-minute lighting, three-minute illumination, triple-minute lighting, triple-minute illumination · Dreiminutenlicht n

three-mode factor analysis, triple-mode factor analysis · dreimodale Faktorenanalyse f

three-order central place hierarchy, three-order hierarchial system · Dreiklassenhierarchie f der zentralen Orte, Dreiklassenhierarchie der Zentralorte

three-order hierarchial system, three-order central place hierarchy · Dreiklassenhierarchie f der zentralen Orte, Dreiklassenhierarchie der Zentralorte

three-way fund, balanced bond, umbrella fund, managed fund, mixed bond, selective bond · gemischter Versicherungsfonds m

three-way fund certificate, managed fund certificate, mixed bond certificate, umbrella fund certificate, balanced bond certificate · gemischtes Versicherungsfondszertifikat n

three-window house, triple-window house · Dreifensterhaus n

threshold analysis · Schwellenanalyse f

threshold population · untere Bevölkerungsgrenze f [*Sie gibt die Mindestzahl von Kunden bzw. den Mindestumsatz für eine rentabel wirtschaftende Einrichtung an*]

threshold population · Mindesteinwohnerzahl f pro Angebotseinheit

threshold purchasing power, threshold sales level, threshold sales volume · Mindestmenge f des Verbrauchs, Verbrauchsmindestmenge [*Sie muß garantiert sein, damit ein zentrales Gut an einem Ort angeboten werden kann*]

threshold theory · Schwellentheorie f

threshold value · Schwellenwert m

thrift account [*Chase National Bank*]; deposit account (Brit.), saving account [*Saving banks in the USA*]; compound interest account [*National City Bank*] · Sparkonto n [*In den USA dürfen die Sparkonten nur von den „saving banks" als „saving accounts" bezeichnet werden*]

through bill of lading · Durchkonossement n

through freight · Durchfracht f

throughhouse · durchgehendes Haus n

through lot [*An interior lot having frontages on two streets*] · Durchgangsparzelle f, Durchgangsflurstück n

through movements, through traffic, external-external traffic, external-external movements · Durchgangsverkehr m [*durch eine Ortschaft*]

through-railroad-ocean-bill-of-lading · Konnossement n gültig von Bahnstation bis zum überseeischen Hafen

through traffic, external-external traffic, external-external movements, through movements · Durchgangsverkehr m [*durch eine Ortschaft*]

throwing into disorder, confusing · Verwirren n, Bestürzen

thrown away, abandoned, derelict, forsaken, cast off, derserted, cast away [*Personal property abandoned or thrown away by the owner in such manner as to indicate that he intends to make no further claim thereto*] · herrenlos, aufgegeben

thumb rule, tentative working rule, rule of thumb · Faustregel f

thumb sketch (US) [*A drawing made by eye, without measurement*], eye-draught (Brit.) · Zeichnung f nach Augenmaß

T.I.A.S.No., treaty and other international act series number · Kennziffer f eines völkerrechtlichen Vertrages

to tick, to check off [*item*] · abhaken [*Position*]

tick · Kontrollzeichen n, (Prüf)Vermerk m, Paraphe f

tick → (corner) tick

ticket-day, name-day [*A stock exchange term, it is the day when the names of buyers are transmitted to the sellers of securities*] · Skontierungstag m

ticking, checking-off [*item*] · Abhaken n [*Position*]

tidal river · Gezeitenstrom m

tidal wave of metropolitan expansion · Flutwelle f [*Sie treibt in einem Ballungsraum den Bevölkerungsschwerpunkt immer weiter nach außen*]

tied accommodation [*It usually means that once the employment comes to an end, so does the accommodation*] · betriebsgebundene Wohnung f

tied cottage · Dienst-Einfamilienhaus n [*bescheiden und klein*]

tied dwelling unit, tied living unit, tied housing unit, tied apartment (US); tied dwelling, tied tenement, tied residence · Dienstwohnung f, Betriebswohnung

tied dwelling unit of a factory, tied apartment of a factory (US); tied dwelling of a factory, tied residence of a factory, tied tenement of a factory · Werkwohnung f

tied house · Wirtshaus n durch Vertrag an einen einzigen Bierlieferanten gebunden

tied housing [*Housing owned by an employer and provided for employ(e)es*] · Dienstwohnungen fpl, Betriebswohnungen

tied housing of a factory [*Housing owned by an employer and provided for employe(e)s*] · Werkwohnungen fpl

tied licensee · gebundener Schankwirt m [*an einen Lieferanten gebunden*]

tied pub(lic house), tied house (Brit.); tied drinking shop (US) · gebundene Kneipe f, gebundene Schankwirtschaft

to tie up, to sink, to lock · festlegen [*Kapital*]

tight money, dear money · knappes Geld n, teures Geld

tight money policy, dear money policy · Politik f des knappen Geldes, Politik des teuren Geldes

tillable land; terra excultabilis, terra wainabilis [*Latin*] [*Land which may be ploughed*] · pflügbares Land n

tillage field → arable land

tillage ground → arable land

tillage land → arable land

tillage system, arable farming system, arable husbandry system · Ackerbausystem n, Betriebssystem, Wirtschaftssystem

tilled · eingepflügt

tilled field → arable land

tilled ground → arable land

tilled land → arable land

timber → standing trees

timber(-bearing) land · Nutzholzland n

timberland · hochstämmiger Nutzwald m

timber line · Baumgrenze f

timber on the stem, standing trees, (standing) timber, wood on the stem · (an)stehendes Holz n, aufstehendes Holz, Holz auf dem Stamme, Holz auf dem Stock

timber planted for ornament, ornamental timber · Schmuckgehölz n, Ziergehölz, Zierholz, Schmuckholz

timber planted for shelter · Schutzgehölz n, Schutzholz n

timber tithe, wood tithe · Holzzehnt m [*altdeutsch: Holzzehent, Holzzehend*]

timber yard · Holzlagerplatz m

time — time of execution

time → time allowed

time (allowed), time period, term, (fixed) period (of time) · Frist *f*, (bestimmte) Zeit *f*, (bestimmter) Zeitraum *m*

time (allowed) for appeal, time period fo appeal, term for appeal, (fixed) period (of time) for appeal, appeal period (of time), reclaiming days · Berufungsfrist *f*, (bestimmte) Berufungszeit *f*, (bestimmter) Berufungszeitraum *m*, Appellationsfrist

time (allowed) for complaint, time period for complaint, (fixed) period (of time) for complaint · Beschwerdefrist *f*, (bestimmter) Beschwerdezeitraum *m*

time allowed for objection, term of objection · Einspruchsfrist *f*

time beyond human memory, time out of mind, time immemorial · unvordenkliche Zeit *f*

time bill (of exchange), date draft, bill (of exchange) after date, bill (of exchange) with exact expiry · Datowechsel *m*, Zeitwechsel, Zielwechsel [*Die Zahlungszeit ist auf eine bestimmte Zeit nach dem Tage der Ausstellung festgesetzt*]

time budget · (Zeit)Haushalt *m* einer Person [*Er besteht aus der systematischen Aufzeichnung aller ihrer Tätigkeiten während einer bestimmten Zeitspanne, meist über die 24 Stunden eines Tages*]

time clock · Stechuhr *f*

time-conditioned · zeitbedingt

time content · Zeitumfang *m*

time deposit, fixed deposit · zeitgebundene Einlage *f*, Festeinlage, Termineinlage, Zeitgeld *n* [*Depositenbank*]

time draft · Nachsichttratte *f*, Zeittratte, Zieltratte

time fee [*Fee calculated according to the time needed for a transaction*] · Zeitgebühr *f*, Zeithonorar *n*

time for appeal → time (allowed) for appeal

time for complaint → time (allowed) for complaint

time for completion, construction time, building time, time of construction, time of building · Bau(fertigstellungs)zeit *f*

time for construction of (the) works → time for execution of (the) work(s)

time for execution of (the) work(s), time for performance of (the) work(s), time for construction of (the) works, period for execution of (the) work(s), period for performance of (the) work(s), period for construction of (the) works · (Arbeits)Ausführungsfrist *f*, Arbeitsausführungszeit *f*, (Bau)Ausführungszeit *f*, Bauausführungsfrist *f*

time for performance of (the) work(s) → time for execution of (the) work(s)

time fund, time loan · festes Geld *n* [*Maklerdarleh(e)n*]

time immemorial, time beyond human memory, time out of mind · unvordenkliche Zeit *f*

timekeeping · Zeitnahme *f*

time lag · Zeitverzögerung *f*

time limit, term limit · Fristgrenze *f*

time limitation, limitation of time · Befristung *f*

time loan, time fund · festes Geld *n* [*Maklerdarleh(e)n*]

timely, on schedule · fristgerecht, fristgemäß

timely completion, completion on schedule · fristgerechte Fertigstellung *f*, fristgemäße Fertigstellung

time of application, time of request · Zeitpunkt *m* der Antragstellung, Zeitpunkt der Gesuchstellung

time of bidding, tendering period, tendering time, bidding period, bidding time, period of tendering, time of tendering, period of bidding · Angebotsfrist *f*, Angebotszeitraum *m*, Ausschreibungsfrist, Ausschreibungszeitraum

time of binding, binding period, binding time, period of binding · Bindungsfrist *f*, Bindefrist [*Die Zeit, in welcher der Bieter an sein Angebot gegenüber dem Auftraggeber gebunden ist*]

time of building, time for completion, construction time, building time, time of construction · Bau(fertigstellungs)zeit *f*

time of completion, completion time [*Number of calendar or working days or the actual date by which the work is required to be completed*] · Fertigstellungsfrist *f*

time of construction, time of building, time for completion, construction time, building time · Bau(fertigstellungs)zeit *f*

time of contract, full life of contract, length of contract, contract length, contract time · Vertrags(lauf)zeit *f*, Vertragsdauer *f*

time of day · Tageszeit *n*

time of depression, period of depression, depression period, depression time · (wirtschaftliche) Notzeit *f*

time of exclusion, exclusion period, exclusion time, exclusion term, period of exclusion, term of exclusion · Ausschlußfrist *f*, Ausschließungsfrist *f*

time of execution, time of fulfilment, time of performance, time of compliance · Erfüllungszeit *f*

time of lease · Pachtzeit *f*

time of legal (human) memory · Zeit *f* bis zu welcher im Rechtssinne menschliche Erinnerung reicht

time of request, time of application · Zeitpunkt *m* der Antragstellung, Zeitpunkt der Gesuchstellung

time of respite, period of respite · Stundungsfrist *f*

time of tendering, period of bidding, time of bidding, tendering period, tendering time, bidding period, bidding time, period of tendering · Angebotsfrist *f*, Angebotszeitraum *m*, Ausschreibungsfrist, Ausschreibungszeitraum

time of warranty, period of warranty, warranty term, warranty time, warranty period, term of warranty · Garantiefrist *f*, Garantiezeitraum *m*

time-orien(ta)ted, time-related · zeitbezogen, zeitorientiert

time out of mind, time immemorial, time beyond human memory · unvordenkliche Zeit *f*

time overrun · Zeitüberschreitung *f*

time period → time (allowed)

time period for appeal → time (allowed) for appeal

time period for complaint, (fixed) period (of time) for complaint, time (allowed) for complaint · Beschwerdefrist *f*, (bestimmter) Beschwerdezeitraum *m*

time preference · Zeitvorzug *m*

time rate · Zeitlohnsatz *m*

time required for examination and evaluation of tenders, period required for examination and evaluation of tenders · Zuschlag(s)frist *f* [*Der Zeitraum, den der Auftraggeber braucht um festzustellen, welches der eingereichten Angebote für ihn das günstigste ist*]

time saving · Zeiteinsparung *f*

time-schedule, time-table · Zeitplan *m*

time-schedule for (de)termination, timetable for (de)termination · Beendigungszeitplan *m*

time series · Zeitreihe *f*

time-sharing system · Teilnehmerrechensystem *n*

timesheet · Stundenzettel *m*

time-table, time-schedule · Zeitplan *m*

time-table for (de)termination, time-schedule for (de)termination · Beendigungszeitplan *m*

time to consider · Bedenkzeit *f*

timing · zeitliche Abstimmung *f*, Zeitfestsetzung

timing of work(s), timing of operations · Zeitplanung *f*

tin bounding · Zinn-Geviertung *f*

tipping point · Kippunkt *m* [*Ablösung einer Wohnbevölkerungsgruppe durch eine andere. Beim Kippunkt schlägt die Entwick(e)lung rasch um, die bisherige Bevölkerung verläßt beschleunigt ein Viertel und die andere rückt ebenso schnell nach*]

tithe; teind [*Scots law*] · Zehnt *m* [*altdeutsch: Zehent m, Zehend*]

tith(e)able, tithed, liable to pay tithe · zehnt(en)pflichtig

tithe act, tithe statute, tithe law · Zehntengesetz *n*

tithe arising immediately from the ground, pr(a)edial tithe · Grundzehnt *m*, Prädialzehnt, Realzehnt, Feldzehnt

tithe-book · Zehnt(en)buch *n*

tithe-charge · Zehnt(en)last *f*

tithe claim · Zehnt(en)forderung *f*

tithe collector, collector of tithes, titheman, tithing-man, tithe-gatherer · Zehnt(en)mann *m*

tithe commission · Zehnt(en)kommission *f*

tithe court; teind court [*Scots law*] · Zehntengericht *n*

tithed, liable to pay tithe, tith(e)able · zehnt(en)pflichtig

tithe dispute · Zehnt(en)streit(igkeit) *m*, *(f)*

tithe-free, indecimable; indecimabilis [*Latin*]; not titheable [*Exempted from the payment of tithes*] · zehnt(en)frei

tithe-gatherer, tithe-collector, collector of tithes, tithe-man, tithing-man · Zehnt(en)mann *m*

tithe-giving, tithe-paying, tithing, payment of tithes, tithe payment · Zehnt(en)zahlung *f*, Zehntenleistung

tithe holder, tithe taker, tithe owner · Zehnt(en)herr *m*, Zehnt(en)inhaber *m*

tithe impropriate, lay tithe · Laienzehnt *m*

tithe law, law of tithes · Zehnt(en)recht *n*

tithe law, tithe act, tithe statute · Zehntengesetz *n*

tithe-man, tithing-man, tithe-gatherer, tithe-collector, collector of tithes · Zehnt(en)mann *m*

tithe of corn (Brit.); grain tithe, tithe of grain, corn tithe · Getreidezehnt *m*, Kornzehnt [*altdeutsch: Kornzehent, Kornzehend*]

tithe of the sheaf, sheaf tithe · Garbenzehnt *m*

tithe owner, tithe holder, tithe taker · Zehnt(en)herr *m*, Zehnt(en)inhaber *m*

tithe (paid) in kind — title chain

tithe (paid) in kind, in-kind tithe · Naturalzehnte *m*

tithe-payer, tither; titheman [*obsolete*] · Zehnt(en)pflichtige *m*

tithe payment, tithe-giving, tithe-paying, tithing, payment of tithes · Zehnt(en)zahlung *f*, Zehnt(en)leistung

tithe rentcharge · Zehnt(en)zins *m*

tithe right · Zehnt(en)(an)recht *n*, Zehnt(en)anspruch *m*

tithe-system, tithing · Zehnt(en)wesen *n*

tithe taker, tithe owner, tithe holder · Zehnt(en)herr *m*, Zehnt(en)inhaber *m*

tithing, township [*In Saxon times of England the land was laid out in townships for occupation by communities of men*] · Gemarkung *f*

tithing, tethinga · Zehnerschaft *f*, Dorfschaft, Zehntschaft

tithing · Zehentversammlung *f*

tithing, tithe-system · Zehnt(en)wesen *n*

tithing, payment of tithes, tithe payment, tithe-giving, tithe-paying · Zehnt(en)zahlung *f*, Zehntenleistung

tithing-man, tithe-gatherer, tithe-collector, collector of tithes, tithe-man · Zehnt(en)mann *m*

tithing-man, borough's ealder, borough's ealdor, parochial constable, borsholder, head-borough · Polizeischulze *m*

title, headline, caption, heading · Überschrift *f*

title · (Rechts)Titel *m*

title acquired by adverse possession, title acquired by wrongful possession · rechtswidriger (Land)Besitztitel *m*, entgegenstehender (Land)Besitztitel, fehlerhafter (Land)Besitztitel

title aggregation, title concentration, amalgamation of titles, concentration of titles, aggregation of titles, title amalgamation · (Rechts)Titelzusammenlegung *f*

title amalgamation, title aggregation, title concentration, amalgamation of titles, concentration of titles, aggregation of titles · (Rechts)Titelzusammenlegung *f*

title bearer, bearer of title · Titelträger *m*, Titelinhaber

title by (ab)alienation, title by disposal · (Rechts)Titel *m* durch Veräußerung, Veräußerungs(rechts)titel

title by act of law · gesetzlich erworbenes dingliches Recht *n*, (Rechts)Titel *m* auf Verfügung des Gesetzes, gesetzlicher (Rechts)Titel

title by act of the parties · (Rechts)Titel *m* auf Parteientätigkeit

title by act of the party · partnerschaftlich erworbenes dingliches Recht *n*

title by administration · (Rechts)Titel *m* der Abhandlungspflege

title by assignment · entgeltlicher (Rechts)Titel *m*

title by bankruptcy · Konkurs(rechts)titel *m*

title by common law → legal title

title by contract · (Rechts)Titel *m* durch Vertrag, Vertrags(rechts)titel

title by conveyance · (Rechts)Titel *m* durch Übertragung, Übertragungs(rechts)titel

title by descent ab intestato, title by intestate succession, title by intestate descent, title by intestacy, title by succession ab intestato · (Rechts)Titel *m* durch Intestaterbfolge

title by devise · (Rechts)Titel *m* durch letztwillige Verfügung

title by disposal, title by (ab)alienation · (Rechts)Titel *m* durch Veräußerung, Veräußerungs(rechts)titel

title by escheat, escheat title · Heimfall(rechts)titel *m*

title by estoppel · (Rechts)Titel *m* durch Hinderung [*Wenn jemand nach den Normen über einen Erwerb eines Eigentums kein Eigentum erworben hat, wohl aber tatsächlich die Stellung eines Eigentümers hat, weil der wahre Eigentümer seine Rechte wegen einer Hinderung nicht geltend machen kann*]

title by gift · (Rechts)Titel *m* durch Schenkung, Schenkungstitel, unentgeltlicher (Rechts)Titel

title by (hereditary) descent, title by (hereditary) succession · (Rechts)Titel *m* der erbrechtlichen Nachfolge

title by intestate succession, title by intestate descent, title by intestacy, title by succession ab intestato, title by descent ab intestato · (Rechts)Titel *m* durch Intestaterbfolge

title by prescription, prescription title, prescriptive title · Ersitzungs(rechts)titel *m*, ersessener (Rechts)Titel, (Rechts)Titel kraft Ersitzung

title by purchase · Kauftitel *m*, Kaufrechtstitel

title by succession ab intestato, title by descent ab intestato, title by intestate succession, title by intestate descent, title by intestacy · (Rechts)Titel *m* durch Intestaterbfolge

title certificate → title-deed

title chain, chain of title(s) to land(s) [*A term applied to the past series of trans-*

actions and documents affecting the title to a particular tract of land] · (Rechts)Titelkette f, Rechtskette, Kette von (Rechts)Titeln, Kette von Rechten [Eintragung in Landregister in den USA]

title claim, title demand, claim of title, demand of title · Titelforderung f, Titelverlangen n, Freigabeforderung, Freigabeverlangen

title company → (land) title (insurance) company

title concentration, amalgamation of titles, concentration of titles, aggregation of titles, title amalgamation, title aggregation · (Rechts)Titelzusammenlegung f

title conversion, conversion of title · (Rechts)Titelumwandlung f

title-deed, deed ot title, title certificate, evidence of title, title evidence, title document, document of title [A document establishing the title to property] · (gesiegelte) (Rechts)Titelurkunde f, (gesiegelte) Dispositionsurkunde, (gesiegelte) Besitzurkunde, Dispositionsurkunde

title demand, claim of title, demand of title, title claim · Titelforderung f, Titelverlangen n, Freigabeforderung, Freigabeverlangen

title document, document of title · (Rechts)Titeldokument n, Dispositionspapier n, Traditionspapier

title document, document of title, title-deed, deed ot title, title certificate, evidence of title, title evidence [A document establishing the title to property] · (gesiegelte) (Rechts)Titelurkunde f, (gesiegelte) Dispositionsurkunde, (gesiegelte) Besitzurkunde, Dispositionsurkunde

title document to goods, document of title to commodities, title document to commodities, document of title to goods · Warendispositionsurkunde f, Dispositionsurkunde über Ware(n), Güterdispositionsurkunde, Dispositionsurkunde über Güter

title to estate, title to property · (Rechts)Titel m zum Vermögen, Vermögens(rechts)titel

title to estate → (real) estate title

title evidence, proof of title, evidence of title, title proof · (Rechts)Titelbeweis m

title evidence → title-deed

title examination → (land) title examination

title examiner, examiner of title, title man · (Rechts)Titelprüfer m

title failure, failure of title · (Rechts)Titellosigkeit f

title in law → legal title

title insurance → (land) title insurance

title insurance company, guaranteeing company · Versicherungsgesellschaft f für Schuldner-Eigentumsrecht

title (insurance) company → (land) title (insurance) company

title law → law of things

title man, title examiner, examiner of title · (Rechts)Titelprüfer m

title objection · (Rechts)Titeleinwand m, (Rechts)Titeleinwendung f

title of honour (Brit.); title of honor (US) · Ehrentitel m

title (of right), right of ownership (of property) · (Rechts)Titel m, (subjektives) Eigentumsrecht n

title page · Titelseite f

title paramount, paramount title · besserer (Rechts)Titel m, überwiegender (Rechts)Titel

title plant · Registersammlung f

title police · (Rechts)Titelversicherungsschein m

title proof, title evidence, proof of title, evidence of title · (Rechts)Titelbeweis m

title recital, recital of (title) · Titelbericht m [Auflassung]

title recital, recital of title · Berufung f auf eine Rechtsgrundlage, (Rechts)Titelberufung

title recordation, title recording, registration of title (to land), recordation of title (to land), recording of title (to land), title registration · (Rechts)Titelbuchung f, (Rechts)Titeleintrag(ung) m, (f)

title requisition, requisition on title · (Rechts)Titelnachforschung f, Nachforschung über einen (Rechts)Titel

title reservation, reservation of title · (Rechts)Titelvorbehalt m

title root → (legal) title root

title succession → privity

title to landed estate → (real) estate title

title to land(holding) → (real) estate title

title to land(s) → interest in (real) estate

title (to possession) → possessory interest

title to possession of land → (real) estate title

title to possessory estate → (real) estate title

title to property, title to estate · (Rechts)Titel m zum Vermögen, Vermögens(rechts)titel

title to (real) estate — total

title to (real) estate → (real) estate title

title to (real) property → (real) estate title

title to realty → (real) estate title

title to settled land · (Rechts)Titel *m* auf festgelegtes Land

title (up)on trust · (Rechts)Titel *m* zur treuen Hand

title weakness, weakness of title · (Rechts)Titelschwäche *f*, Schwäche des (Rechts)Titels

titular, nominal [*Existing in name only; not real or substantial; connected with the transaction or proceeding in name only; not in interest; not real or actual; merely named, stated, or given; without reference to actual conditions*] · nominell, nur dem Namen nach

titulus [*Latin*] · Rechtsgrund *m* des Besitzerwerbs

tocher [*in Scotland*]; maritagium [*Latin*]; dowry (marriage), portion, fortune, marriage goods [*Not to be confounded with "dower". A portion given with a woman to her husband in marriage*] · Mitgift *f*, Heiratsgut *n*

toft · Hofplatz *m*

together, joint(ly), unitedly, (in) common · gemeinsam, gemeinschaftlich, miteinander, gemeinheitlich, verbunden, solidarisch, zusammen

together and individually, joint(ly) and several(ly) · gemeinsam und einzeln, gemeinsam und allein, gemeinschaftlich und einzeln, gemeinschaftlich und allein, solidarisch und jeder für sich, gemeinsam und jeder für sich, zur gesamten Hand und jeder für sich

togetherness, sense of community, community sense · Zusammengehörigkeitsbewußtsein *n*, Gemeinschaftssinn *m*

token payment · Anerkenntniszahlung *f*, Anerkennungszahlung, symbolische Zahlung

token strike · Warnstreik *m*

tolerance number of defects · tolerierte Ausschußzahl *f* [*Statistik*]

toleration; sufferentia, patientia [*Latin*]; sufferance · Duldung *f*, stillschweigende Billigung

toll · (Benutzungs)Gebühr *f*, Zoll *m*, Geld *n*; Maut *f* [*Österreich*]

toll house · Mautstation *f* [*Österreich*]; Gebührenstation, Wegegeldstation

toll paid for grinding, multure; molitura, multura [*Latin*]; grinding toll, suit and grist, grinding fee, fee for grinding · Mahlgeld *n*, Mahlzins *m*, Mahlgebühr *f*

toll-paying traffic, pedage-paying traffic · Wegegeldverkehr *m*, Wegezollverkehr

toll road, toll highway; turnpike highway (US) · Gebührenstraße *f*, Wegegeldstraße; Mautstraße [*Österreich*]

toll(-through); transitura, transversa [*Latin*] · Passiergeld *n*, Passierzoll *m*

toll-traverse, pedage [*Toll paid for passing through a place*] · Wegegeld *n*, Wegezoll *m*

toll-turn [*In English law. A toll on beasts returning from a market or fair*] · Rückkehrgeld *n*, Rückkehrzoll *m*

tonnage bill, bill of tonnage · Meßbrief *m* [*Schiff*]

tontine, annuity benefit · Leibrente *f*

topgrade · erstklassig

top man · Spitzenkraft *f*

topographic(al) · topographisch, ortsbeschreibend [*Darstellung*]

topsoil · Mutterboden *m*

topsoil protection, topsoil preservation, topsoil conservation, retention of (the) topsoil · Mutterbodenschutz *m*, Mutterbodenerhaltung *f*, Mutterbodenpflege *f*

tornado insurance · Sturmschädenversicherung *f*

Torrens certificate [*A document issued by a public authority called a "registrar" acting under provision of the Torrens Law, indicating the party in whom title resides*] · Torrenszeugnis *n*

Torrens system of land registration [*System of state insurance for land titles*] · Torrensgrundbuchsystem *n*

tort · Zivilunrecht *n*

tort → violation (of law)

tort claim, tort demand, claim in tort, demand in tort · Forderung *f* aus unerlaubter Handlung, Verlangen *n* aus unerlaubter Handlung

tort-content · Unrechtsgehalt *m*

tort (court) action, tort (law)suit, tort cause, tort plea · Klage *f* aus unerlaubter Handlung

tort damages, tort compensation, tort indemnity, tort indemnification · Deliktschadenersatz *m*, Deliktentschädigung *f*

tortfeasor, wrong-doer · Delikttäter *m*

tortious act(ion) → violation (of law)

tortious claimant · Nichtberechtigte *m*

tort of deceit · Betrugsvergehen *n*

total, unrestricted, unlimited, irrebuttable, unconditional, absolute · absolut, unbeschränkt, uneingeschränkt, unbedingt, unbegrenzt, bedingungslos

total → (sum) total

total acceptance (of (the) work(s)) · Abnahme f der Gesamt(bau)leistung(en); Kollaudierung f der Gesamt(bau)leistungen [*Schweiz*]

total acreage, aggregate acreage · Totalfläche f, Gesamtfläche

total agency, aggregate agency, total authority, aggregate authority · Gesamtvertretungsmacht f, Gesamtvollmacht

total amount, aggregate amount · Gesamtbetrag m, Totalbetrag

total area, total territory, overall area, overall territory · Gesamtgebiet n

total area of habitable rooms, living floor space · Wohnfläche f

total assets, aggregate assets, whole assets · Gesamtaktiva f, Totalaktiva

total assistance system, total promotion(al) system, total sponsoring system · Gesamtförderungssystem n

total authority, aggregate authority, total agency, aggregate agency · Gesamtvertretungsmacht f, Gesamtvollmacht

total bid; total (bid) proposal (US); total offer, total tender · Gesamtangebot n

total binding authority of precedents, unrestricted binding authority of precedents, unlimited binding authority of precedents, irrebuttable binding authority of precedents, absolute binding authority of precedents · absolute Bindungswirkung f, unbeschränkte Bindungswirkung, unbegrenzte Bindungswirkung, uneingeschränkte Bindungswirkung, unbedingte Bindungswirkung

total breach of contract, total contract breach · voller Vertragsbruch m

total building cost(s), aggregate building cost(s), whole building cost(s), total construction cost(s), aggregate construction cost(s), whole construction cost(s) · Gesamtherstellungskosten f, Gesamtbaukosten, Totalbaukosten, Totalherstellungskosten

total building work(s), total (construction) work(s) · Gesamt(bau)leistung f

total collapse, total crash · Ganzeinsturz m

total construction cost(s), aggregate construction cost(s), whole construction cost(s), total building cost(s), aggregate building cost(s), whole building cost(s) · Gesamtherstellungskosten f, Gesamtbaukosten, Totalbaukosten, Totalherstellungskosten

total (construction) work(s), total building work(s) · Gesamt(bau)leistung f

total construction zone · Gesamtbaubereich m

total contract breach, total breach of contract · voller Vertragsbruch m

total cost(s), aggregate cost(s), whole cost(s); total expired cost(s), total expense(s) [*USA*] · Totalkosten f, Gesamtkosten

total cost(s) in the long run, long-run total cost(s), LRTC · langfristige Gesamtkosten f

total crash, total collapse · Ganzeinsturz m

total credit quota · Kreditkontingent n

total currency flow · Devisenbilanz f

(total) current assets, total quick assets, (gross) working capital [*The term "working capital" has two meanings. It may refer to the total current assets or to the difference between current assets and current liabilities*] · Umlaufvermögen n, Umlaufmittel f

total damage, full damage · Vollschaden m, Totalschaden

total debt · Gesamtschuld f

total density, aggregate density, overall density · Gesamtdichte f

total design · Gesamtentwurf m

total equity (Brit.); net worth, stockholder's equity, owner's equity (US) · Eigenkapital n

total expense(s) [*USA*] → expired cost(s)

total expired cost(s), total expense(s) [*USA*]; total cost(s), aggregate cost(s), whole cost(s) · Totalkosten f, Gesamtkosten

total failure of consideration · völlige Wertlosigkeit f der Gegenleistung

total failure to perform, absolute failure to perform, unrestricted failure to perform, unlimited failure to perform, irrebuttable failure to perform · absolute Nichterfüllung f, uneingeschränkte Nichterfüllung, unbeschränkte Nichterfüllung, unbedingte Nichterfüllung, unbegrenzte Nichterfüllung

total floor area, total floor space, gross floor area, gross floor space · Bruttogeschoßfläche f, Bruttoetagenfläche, Bruttostockwerkfläche [*Summe aller Geschoßflächen ohne Boden und Keller. Wände, Flure und nichtbewohnbare Nebenräume der Vollgeschosse sind mit einbegriffen*]

total freight, whole freight, aggregate freight · Gesamtfracht f

total gain, aggregate gain, whole gain, total profit, aggregate profit, whole profit · Gesamtgewinn m, Totalgewinn, Gesamtprofit, Totalprofit m

total grossed-up amount, aggregate grossed-up amount [*An amount to be*

total hazard — total usable space

charged for carrying out the whole quantity of an item] · Gesamtbetrag m, Totalbetrag [Spalte in einem L.V.]

total hazard, aggregate risk, aggregate hazard, total risk · Gesamtrisiko n, Gesamtwagnis n, Totalrisiko, Totalwagnis

total individual audience · Zahl f von Einzelpersonen die ein Sendeprogramm teilweise hören oder sehen [Umfragetechnik]

total in-migration · Gesamtzuwanderung f

total interest rate, whole interest rate, aggregate interest rate · Gesamtzinsfuß m

totality of (the) evidence, totality of (the) proof · Gesamtbeweis m

total jurisdiction, unlimited jurisdiction, absolute jurisdiction, unrestricted jurisdiction, irrebuttable jurisdiction · absolute Gerichtsbarkeit f, uneingeschränkte Gerichtsbarkeit, unbedingte Gerichtsbarkeit, unbegrenzte Gerichtsbarkeit, absolute Rechtspflege(funktion) f, uneingeschränkte Rechtspflege(funktion), unbeschränkte Rechtspflege(funktion), unbedingte Rechtspflege(funktion), unbegrenzte Rechtspflege(funktion)

total loss, aggregate loss · Gesamtverlust m, Totalverlust

total necessity, absolute necessity, natural necessity, unlimited necessity, unrestricted necessity, irrebuttable necessity · absolute Notwendigkeit f, unbedingte Notwendigkeit, unbegrenzte Notwendigkeit, uneingeschränkte Notwendigkeit, unbeschränkte Notwendigkeit

total net shift [shift analysis] · Gesamtnettoverlagerung f, regionale Gesamtabweichung nach Gerfin

total offer, total tender, total bid; total (bid) proposal (US) · Gesamtangebot n

total of rights, property, aggregate of rights · Masse f von (subjektiven) Rechten, Menge f von (subjektiven) Rechten

total out-migration · Gesamtabwanderung f

total planning, aggregate planning, whole planning · Totalplanung f, Gesamtplanung

total population, aggregate population, whole population · Gesamtbevölkerung f

total presumption, unlimited presumption, irrebuttable presumption, absolute presumption, unrestricted presumption · absolute Rechtsvermutung f, unbeschränkte Rechtsvermutung, unbegrenzte Rechtsvermutung, uneingeschränkte Rechtsvermutung, unbedingte Rechtsvermutung

total price, extension · Gesamtpreis m [Preis pro Einheit × Menge]

total probability theorem, theorem of total probability · Additionssatz m der Wahrscheinlichkeit

total production cost(s), aggregate production cost(s), whole production cost(s) · Totalherstellungskosten, Gesamtherstellungskosten fpl

total profit, aggregate profit, whole profit, total gain, aggregate gain, whole gain · Gesamtgewinn m, Totalgewinn, Gesamtprofit, Totalprofit m

total promotion(al) system, total sponsoring system, total assistance system · Gesamtförderungssystem n

total quick assets, (gross) working capital, (total) current assets [The term "working capital" has two meanings. It may refer to the total current assets or to the difference between current assets and current liabilities] · Umlaufvermögen n, Umlaufmittel f

total region · Gesamtregion f

total reimbursement · Gesamtvergütung f

total renewal, total revival · Totalerneuerung f

total rights of building, aggregate superficies, total superficies, aggregate rights of building · Gesamtbaurecht n [Es erstreckt sich über mehrere Liegenschaften]

total risk, total hazard, aggregate risk, aggregate hazard, · Gesamtrisiko n, Gesamtwagnis n, Totalrisiko, Totalwagnis

total sponsoring system, total assistance system, total promotion(al) system · Gesamtförderungssystem n

total stock, aggregate stock · Gesamtbestand m

total superficies, aggregate rights of building, total rights of building, aggregate superficies · Gesamtbaurecht n [Es erstreckt sich über mehrere Liegenschaften]

total supply function, aggregate supply function · Gesamtangebotsfunktion f, aggregierte Angebotsfunktion, Funktion des gesamten Angebots [Nach der keynesianischen Theorie ist es eine funktionale Beziehung zwischen dem gewinnmaximalen Wert der Produktion und dem entsprechenden Einsatz an Arbeit]

total tender, total bid; total (bid) proposal (US); total offer · Gesamtangebot n

total territory, overall area, overall territory, total area · Gesamtgebiet n

total usable space, whole usable space, aggregate usable space · gesamte Nutz-

total value — town auditorium building

fläche f [Summe von Wohn- und Nutzfläche der Räume eines Gebäudes]

total value, aggregate value · Gesamtwert m

total work(s) → total (construction) work(s)

to the point → relevant

to the use(r) of → ad usum

tot lot [Special play area for children who are too small to use ordinary playground equipment or too young to play with groups of other children] · Kleinkinderspielplatz m

Totten bank trust, savings bank trust · Treuhand f zugunsten eines Dritten, Dritten-Treuhand

to touch · angreifen [Kapital]

to touch; abuttare [Latin]; to abut, to reach · angrenzen [(Grundstücks)Enden]

touching, abutting, reaching, contiguous · angrenzend [(Grundstücks)Enden]

tourist route atlas · Touristenatlas m

tourist route map · Touristenkarte f

tourist traffic · Fremdenverkehr m, Touristenverkehr

tourist (traffic) community · Fremdenverkehrsgemeinde f, Touristengemeinde

tourist (traffic) location, tourist (traffic) site · Fremdenverkehrsstandort m, Touristenstandort

tourist (traffic) resort · Fremdenverkehrsort m, Touristenort

tourist (traffic) site, tourist (traffic) location · Fremdenverkehrsstandort m, Touristenstandort

tourist (traffic) town, tourist (traffic) city · Fremdenverkehrsstadt f, Touristenstadt

TOVALOP, tanker owners voluntary agreement concerning liability for oil pollution · Verschuldenshaftungsabkommen n über das Einleiten von Öl durch Schiffseigentümer

tow-generation family · Zweigenerationenfamilie f

town, city [These terms may be generally used, especially in combinations, although they have different meanings in one or the other English-speaking country] · Stadt f [Eine räumliche Konzentration von Wohn- und Arbeitsstätten und Menschen mit vorwiegend tertiär- und sekundärwirtschaftlicher Betätigung, mit innerer Differenzierung und vielfältigen Verkehrsströmen zwischen ihren Teilräumen und solchen, die auf sie insgesamt als Verkehrsmittelpunkt gerichtet sind, deren Wachstum größenteils auf Wanderungsgewinn beruht und die einen erweiterten Bereich mit Gütern und Dienstleistungen versorgt.]

town · große Mittelstadt f

town accountant, urban accountant, city accountant · Stadtbuchhalter m

town acreage, city acreage, urban acreage · Stadtflächeninhalt m

town administrative region, city administrative region, urban administrative region · Stadtgebiet n [Die Fläche der Verwaltungseinheit „Stadt", unabhängig von städtischer Bebauung und städtischer Funktion]

town affair, urban affair, city affair · städtische Angelegenheit f

town agency, town office, city office, city agency, urban agency, urban office · städtische Dienststelle f

town air, city air, urban air · Stadtluft f

town alderman, city alderman, urban alderman · Stadtälteste m

town and country, city and country; burg and land [Scotland] · Stadt f und Land n

town and country plan, (physical) development plan, plan for (physical) development, area development plan · Bauleitplan m [Förmlicher Plan einer Gemeinde zur Ordnung ihrer gemeindlichen Entwick(e)lung (§ 1 Abs. 1 BBauG). Bauleitpläne unterscheiden sich mit unterschiedlicher Genauigkeit und Verbindlichkeit in: 1.) Flächennutzungsplan = vorbereitender Bauleitplan und 2.) Bebauungsplan = verbindlicher Bauleitplan]

town and country planning, area development planning, (physical) development planning, planning for (physical) development · Bauleitplanung f

town and country planning act, town and country planning law, town and country planning statute, area development law, area development statute, area development act · Bauleitplanungsgesetz n

town area, city area, urban area · Stadtfläche f, städtische Fläche

town area, town territory, city area, city territory, urban area, urban territory · städtisches Gebiet n [Ein Gebiet, welches im funktionalen und physiognomischen Sinne vorrangig durch städtische Funktionen geprägt ist]

town area use, urban land(s) use, city land(s) use, town land(s) use, urban area use, city area use · städtische Bodennutzung f, städtische Landnutzung, städtische Flächennutzung, Stadtbodennutzung, Stadtlandnutzung, Stadtflächennutzung

town atlas, urban atlas, city atlas · Stadtatlas m

town auditorium building, urban auditorium building, (city) auditorium building · Stadthalle f

town authority — town council

town authority, city authority, urban authority · Stadtbehörde f, städtische Behörde

town bailiff · Stadtvogt m

town block, urban block, city block · Baublock m

town board, city board, urban board · Stadtamt n, städtisches Amt

town boundary, city boundary, urban boundary · Stadtgrenze f

town builder, city builder, urban builder · Städtebauer m, Stadtbauer

town building, town construction, city building, city construction, urban building, urban construction · Städtebau m

town building board, town construction board, city building board, city construction board, urban construction board, urban building board · Stadtbauamt n

town building code, town construction code, urban building code, urban construction code, city building code, city construction code · städtische Bauordnung f, Stadtbauordnung

town building (construction), city building (construction), urban building (construction) · städtischer Hochbau m

town building project, city construction project, city building project, urban construction project, urban building project, town construction project · städtebauliches Vorhaben n, städtebauliches Projekt n

town by(e)-law, town ordinance, city statute, city by(e)-law, city ordinance, urban statute, urban by(e)-law, urban ordinance, town statute · Stadtsatzung f, Stadtstatut n, Stadtgesetz n

town cartography, city cartography, urban cartography · Stadtkartographie f

town cemetery, city cemetery, urban cemetery · Stadtfriedhof m

town centre, city centre, urban centre (Brit.); urban center, town center, city center, downtown (area) (US) · Stadtzentrum n, Innenstadt f, Stadtinnere n [im funktionalen Sinne]

town child, urban child, city child · Stadtkind n

town church, city church, urban church · Stadtkirche f

town civil engineer, urban civil engineer, city civil engineer · Stadtbauingenieur m

town (civil) engineering, city (civil) engineering, municipal (civil) engineering, urban (civil) engineering · städtischer Tiefbau m

town civilization, city civilization, urban civilization · Stadtzivilisation f, städtische Zivilisation

town classification, city classification, urban classification · Städtetypisierung f

town cleansing board, city cleansing board · Stadtreinigungsamt n

town-clearing · Abrechnung f von Schecks auf die in der Londoner City gelegenen Banken

town climate, city climate, urban climate · Stadtklima n

town code, city code, urban code · Städteordnung f

town community, city community, urban community · Stadtgemeinde f, Stadtkommune f, städtische Gemeinschaft f, städtische Kommune, städtische Gemeinde [Als Organisationsform]

town composition, urban composition, city composition, town structure, city structure, urban structure · Stadtstruktur f, Stadtzusammensetzung f, Stadtgefüge n, Stadtaufbau m, städtische Struktur, städtische Zusammensetzung, städtischer Aufbau, städtisches Gefüge

town composition planning, city structure planning, city composition planning, urban structure planning, urban composition planning, town structure planning · Stadtaufbauplanung f, Stadtstrukturplanung, Stadtgefügeplanung, Stadtzusammensetzungsplanung

town conservation, town preservation, city conservation, city preservation, urban conservation, urban preservation · Stadtpflege f, Stadterhaltung f

town constitution, city constitution, urban constitution · Stadtverfassung f

town construction, city building, city construction, urban building, urban construction, town building · Städtebau m

town construction board, city building board, city construction board, urban construction board, urban building board, town building board · Stadtbauamt n

town construction code, urban building code, urban construction code, city building code, city construction code, town building code · städtische Bauordnung f, Stadtbauordnung

town construction theory, city construction theory, urban construction theory · Städtebautheorie f

town conversion, urban conversion, city conversion · Stadtumbau m

town core, city core, core of the city, core of the town, urban core · Stadtkern m [im physiognomischen Sinn]

town council, urban council, city council · (Stadt)Rat m, Stadtvertretung f, Stadtparlament n, städtischer Gemeinderat, Stadtgemeinderat

town council committee · Deputation f [Stadtverwaltung]

town councillor, urban councilman, town councilman, city councilman, town council member, city council member, urban council member, urban councillor, city councillor · (Stadt)Verordnete m, (Stadt)Rat(smitglied) m, (n)

town-county, garden city, garden town · Gartenstadt f

town culture, urban culture, city culture · Stadtkultur f

town design, city design, urban design · dreidimensionale Stadtplanung f, räumliche Stadtplanung, Stadtgestaltung [Dieser Zweig liegt zwischen Stadtplanung und Architektur und schafft Leitbilder stadträumlicher Gestaltung]

town design team, town design group, city design team, city design group, urban design team, urban design group · Städtebau(arbeits)gruppe f

town development, city development, urban development · städtische Entwick(e)lung f, städtebauliche Entwick(e)lung, Stadtentwick(e)lung

town development area, city development area, urban development area · städtische Bebauungsfläche f

town development assistance, city development assistance, urban development assistance · Städtebauförderung f

town development corporation, city development corporation, urban development corporation · Stadtentwick(e)lungskorporation f, Stadtentwick(e)lungskörperschaft f

town development land, city development land, urban development land · städtebaulicher Entwick(e)lungsbereich m

town development measure, city development measure, urban development measure · städtebauliche Entwick(e)lungsmaßnahme f

town development plan, city development plan, urban development plan · Stadtentwick(e)lungsplan m

town development planning, city development planning, urban development planning · Stadtentwick(e)lungsplanung f

town development programme, urban development programme, city development programme; town development program, urban development program, city development program (US) · Stadtentwick(e)lungsprogramm n

town development simulation, city development simulation, urban development simulation · Stadtentwick(e)lungssimulation f

town district, city district, urban district [A densely settled area within the city or town limits] · Stadtbezirk m

town drainage scheme, city drainage scheme, urban drainage scheme · Stadtentwässerungsplan m

town dweller, city dweller, urbanite, citizen, burgess, freeman of a borough, townman; cityman [obsolete], urban resident, town resident, city resident, urban inhabitant, town inhabitant, city inhabitant, urban dweller · Stadtbewohner m, Stadteinwohner, Städter, Stadtbürger

town ecology, city ecology, ecology of the town, ecology of the city, urban ecology · Stadtökologie f

town economist, city economist, urban economist · Stadtwirtschaftler m

town economy, city economy, urban economy · Stadtwirtschaft f

town educational officer, town educational official, city educational officer, city educational official, urban educational officer, urban educational official · Stadtschulrat m

town element, urban element, city element · Stadtfliese f

town engineer, urban engineer, city engineer · Stadtingenieur m

town engineering, city engineering, urban engineering · Stadtbautechnik f, Städtebautechnik

town enlargement, town extension, city enlargement, city extension, urban enlargement, urban extension · Stadterweiterung f

town enlargement plan, town extension plan, city enlargement plan, city extension plan, urban enlargement plan, urban extension plan · Stadterweiterungsplan m

town enlargement planning → urban enlargement planning

town enlargement territory → town enlargement area

town environment, city environment, urban environment · Stadtumwelt f

town environmental factor, city environmental factor, urban environmental factor · Stadtumweltfaktor m

town exchequer, city exchequer, office of municipal finances · Stadtkämmerei f

town extension, city enlargement, city extension, urban enlargement, urban extension, town enlargement · Stadterweiterung f

town extension area, town extension territory, city extension area, city extension territory, urban extension area, urban extension territory · Stadtneubaugebiet n, Stadterweiterungsgebiet

town extension plan — town land(s) use density

town extension plan, city enlargement plan, city extension plan, urban enlargement plan, urban extension plan, town enlargement plan · Stadterweiterungsplan *m*

town extension planning → urban enlargement planning

town extension territory → town extension area

town family, city family, urban family · Stadtfamilie *f*

town father, urban father, city father · Stadtvater *m*

town filler, city filler · Städtefüller *m* [*Handwerk; Dienstleistungsbetriebe usw.*]

town forest, city forest, urban forest · Stadtwald *m*

town form, city form, urban form · Stadtform *f*

town-forming, city-forming · städtebildend

town fortification, city fortification, urban fortification · Stadtbefestigung *f*

town founder, city founder · Stadtgründer *m*, Städtegründer, Stadterbauer, Städteerbauer

town fringe, city fringe, urban fringe · Vorstadtgelände *n*, Bannmeile *f*, Stadtrandzone *f*

town function, city function, urban function · städtische Funktion *f*, Stadtfunktion

town garden, city garden, urban garden · Stadtgarten *m*

town gate, city gate, urban gate · Stadttor *n*

town geography, city geography, urban geography, geography of towns, geography of cities · Stadtgeographie *f*, Städtegeographie

town (ground)plan, city (ground)plan, urban layout, town layout, city layout, urban (ground) plan · Stadtgrundriß *m*

town growth pattern, urban growth pattern, city growth pattern · Stadtwachstumsmuster *n*, Städtewachstumsmuster

town-hall, moot-house, moot-hall, city-hall · Stadthaus *n*, Rathaus

town history research, city history research, urban history research · Stadtgeschichtsforschung *f*

town hous(ebuild)ing, city hous(ebuild)ing, urban hous(ebuild)ing · Stadtwohn(ungs)bau *m*, städtischer Wohn(ungs)bau

town hous(ebuild)ing practice, city hous(ebuild)ing practice, urban hous(ebuild)ing practice · Stadtwohn(ungs)wesen *n*, städtisches Wohn(ungs)wesen

town hous(ebuild)ing sector, city hous(ebuild)ing sector, urban hous(ebuild)ing field, town hous(ebuild)ing field, city hous(ebuild)ing field, urban hous(ebuild)ing sector · Stadtwohn(ungs)sektor *m*, städtischer Wohn(ungs)sektor [*als Tätigkeitsgebiet*]

town housing, urban housing, city housing · Stadtwohnungen *fpl*, städtische Wohnungen

town housing land (area), city residential land (area), city housing land (area), urban residential land (area), urban housing land (area), town residential land (area) · städtischer Wohn(ungs)(bau)boden *m*, städtisches Wohn(ungs)(bau)land *n*, städtische Wohn(ungs)(bau)fläche *f*

town improvement planner, city improvement planner, urban improvement planner · Stadterschließungsplaner *m*

town improvement planning, city improvement planning, urban improvement planning · Stadterschließungsplanung *f*, städtische Erschließungsplanung

town infrastructure, city infrastructure, urban infrastructure · Stadtinfrastruktur *f*

town inhabitant, city inhabitant, urban dweller, town dweller, city dweller, urbanite, citizen, burgess, freeman of a borough, townman; cityman [*obsolete*]; urban resident, town resident, city resident, urban inhabitant · Stadtbewohner *m*, Stadteinwohner, Städter, Stadtbürger

town interspersed with green areas, city interspersed with green areas · durchgrünte Stadt *f*

town land, urban land, city land · städtischer Bereich *m* [*Im planerischen Sinne*]

town land, city land, urban land · städtischer Boden *m*, städtisches Land *n*, Stadtboden, Stadtland, Stadtgrund, städtischer Grund *m*

town land rent, city land rent, urban land rent · städtische Grundrente *f*

town land(s) use, urban area use, city area use, town area use, urban land(s) use, city land(s) use · städtische Bodennutzung *f*, städtische Landnutzung, Stadtbodennutzung, Stadtlandnutzung, Stadtflächennutzung

town land(s) use density, city land use density, urban land use density · städtische Flächennutzungsdichte *f*, städtische Bodennutzungsdichte, städtische Landnutzungsdichte

town land(s) use plan, city land use plan, urban land use plan · Stadtflächennutzungsplan *m*

town land(s) use planning, city land use planning, urban land use planning · Stadtflächennutzungsplanung *f*

town land(s) value, city land value, urban land value · städtischer Landwert *m*, städtischer Bodenwert, Stadtlandwert, Stadtbodenwert

town law, city law, urban law · Stadtrecht *n* [*Das in einer Stadt geltende Recht*]

town layout, city layout, urban (ground) plan, town (ground) plan, city (ground) plan, urban layout · Stadtgrundriß *m*

townlet · Städtchen *n*

town life, city life, urban life · städtisches Leben *n*, Stadtleben [*Summe der in einer Stadt sinnfällig werdenden Tätigkeiten, Verkehrsbewegungen und Einrichtungen, die der materiellen und kulturellen Bedarfsdeckung der Stadtbewohner, gegebenenfalls auch der Bewohner eines Hinterlandes dienen*]

town location, urban site, town site, city site, urban location, city location · Stadtstandort *m*, städtischer Standort

town lot, city lot, urban lot · städtisches Katastergrundstück *n*, städtisches Grundstück (im katastertechnischen Sinne), städtisches Kartengrundstück, städtisches Flurstück, städtische (Kataster)Parzelle *f*, städtisches Grundstück (im katastertechnischen Sinne), Stadtkatastergrundstück, Stadt-Kartengrundstück, Stadt(kataster)parzelle, Stadtflurstück

townman; cityman [*obsolete*]; urban resident, town resident, city resident, urban inhabitant, town inhabitant, city inhabitant, urban dweller, town dweller, city dweller, urbanite, citizen, burgess, freeman of a borough · Stadtbewohner *m*, Stadteinwohner, Städter, Stadtbürger

town (masonry) wall, city (masonry) wall, urban (masonry) wall · Stadtmauer *f*

town master plan, city master plan, urban master plan · Stadtgeneralplan *m*

town middle class, city middle class, urban middle class · städtische Mittelschicht *f*

town migrant, city migrant, urban migrant · Stadtwanderer *m*

town moat, city moat, urban moat · Stadtgraben *m*

town model, city model, urban model · Stadtmodell *n*

town morphology, urban morphology, city morphology · Stadtmorphologie *f*

town network, city network, urban network · städtisches Netz *n*, Stadtnetz

town noise, city noise, urban noise · Stadtlärm *m*

town of bureaucracy, city of bureaucracy · Verwaltungsstadt *f*

town office, city office, city agency, urban agency, urban office, town agency · städtische Dienststelle *f*

town officer, town official, city officer, city official, urban officer, urban official · Stadtbeamte *m*, städtischer Beamter

town ordinance, city statute, city by(e)-law, city ordinance, urban statute, urban by(e)-law, urban ordinance, town statute, town by(e)-law · Stadtsatzung *f*, Stadtstatut *n*, Stadtgesetz *n*

town-owned, city-owned · stadteigen

town-owned land(s), city-owned land(s) · stadteigenes Land *n*, stadteigener Boden *m*, stadteigener Grund *m*

town parish, city parish, urban parish · städtisches Kirchspiel *n*

town park city park, urban park · Stadtpark *m*

town pattern, city pattern, urban pattern · Stadtmuster *n*, Stadtschema *n*

town plan, city plan, urban plan · städtebaulicher Plan *m*, Städtebauplan

town plan → town (ground) plan

town planner, urban planner, city planner · Stadtplaner *m*, Städteplaner

town planning, urban planning, city planning · Städte(bau)planung *f*, Stadt(bau)planung, städtebauliche Planung

town planning act → town planning law

town planning administration, urban planning administration, city planning administration · Stadtplanungsverwaltung *f*

town planning area, city planning area, urban planning area, town planning territory, city planning territory, urban planning territory · Stadtplanungsgebiet *n*

town planning authority, city planning authority, urban planning authority · Stadtplanungsbehörde *f*

town planning board, city planning board, urban planning board · Stadtplanungsamt *n*

town planning commission, city planning commission, urban planning commission · Stadtplanungsausschuß *m*

town planning consultant, city planning consultant, urban planning consultant · Stadtplanungsberater *m*

town planning data, city planning data, urban planning data · städtebauliche Planungsgrundlagen *fpl*

town planning education — town residential environment

town planning education, city planning education, urban planning education · Stadtplanerausbildung *f*

town planning ideas competition, city planning ideas competition, urban planning ideas competition · städtebaulicher Ideenwettbewerb *m*

town planning institute, city planning institute, urban planning institute · Institut für Städtebau, Städtebauinstitut *n*

town planning law, city planning law, urban planning law · Stadtplanungsrecht *n*, städtisches Planungsrecht, städtebauliches Planungsrecht

town planning law, town planning act, town planning statute, city planning law, city planning statute, city planning act, urban planning act, urban planning law, urban planning statute · Stadtplanungsgesetz *n*

town planning model, city planning model, urban planning model · städtebauliches Leitbild *n*

town planning office, city planning office, urban planning office · Stadtplanungsstelle *f*

town planning officer, urban planning officer, city planning officer · Stadtplanungsbeamte *m*

town planning organization, city planning organization, urban planning organization · Stadtplanungsorganisation *f*

town planning practice, city planning practice, urban planning practice · Stadtplanungswesen *n*

town planning science, city planning science, urban planning science · Stadtplanungswissenschaft *f*

town planning statute → town planning law

town planning survey, city planning survey, urban planning survey · städtebauliche Enquête *f*

town planning task, city planning task, urban planning task · städtebauliche Aufgabe *f*

town planning territory, city planning territory, urban planning territory, town planning area, city planning area, urban planning area · Stadtplanungsgebiet *n*

town population, city population, urban population · Stadtbevölkerung *f*, städtische Bevölkerung, Stadtvolk *n*

town population density, city population density, urban population density · Stadtbevölkerungsdichte *f*

town population structure, city population structure, urban population structure · Stadtbevölkerungsstruktur *f*, Stadtbevölkerungsgefüge *n*, Stadtbevölkerungszusammensetzung *f*, Stadtbevölkerungsaufbau *m*

town preservation, city conservation, city preservation, urban conservation, urban preservation, town conservation · Stadtpflege *f*, Stadterhaltung *f*

town prison, city prison, urban prison · Stadtgefängnis *n*

town protection, urban protection, city protection · Stadtschutz *m*

town quarter, city quarter, local community, urban quarter · Stadtviertel *n*, Stadtteil *m, n*, Stadtquartier *n*

town railway, city railway, (Brit.); urban railroad, town railroad, city railroad (US), urban railway · Stadtbahn *f*

town rate, urban rate, city rate · städtische Steuer *f*, Stadtsteuer

town (real) estate, town (real) property, town realty, city (real) estate, city (real) property, city realty, urban (real) estate, urban realty, urban (real) property · städtischer Bodenbesitz *m*, städtischer Grund(stücks)besitz, städtischer Landbesitz, Stadtbodenbesitz, Stadtlandbesitz, Stadt-Grund(stücks)besitz, Grund(stücks)besitz in der Stadt, städtischer Besitz, Besitz in der Stadt

town reconstruction, town rebuilding, urban reconstruction, urban rebuilding, city reconstruction, city rebuilding · Stadtwiederaufbau *m*

town recorder, urban recorder, (city) recorder · (Stadt)Syndikus *m*

town renewal, city renewal, urban renewal [*The adjustment of obsolete parts of the urban structure to meet anticipated future demand*] · Stadterneuerung *f*

town renewal area, town revival area, city renewal area, city revival area, urban renewal area, urban revival area · Stadterneuerungsfläche *f*

town renewal legislation, town renewal lawmaking, urban renewal legislation, urban renewal lawmaking, city renewal legislation, city renewal lawmaking · Stadterneuerungsgesetzgebung *f*

town renewal specialist, town revival specialist, city renewal specialist, city revival specialist, urban renewal specialist, urban revival specialist · Stadterneuerungsfachmann *m*

town re-planning, city re-planning, urban re-planning · Stadtumplanung *f*

town resident, city resident, urban inhabitant, town inhabitant, city inhabitant, urban dweller, town dweller, city dweller, urbanite, citizen, burgess, freeman of a borough, townman; cityman [*obsolete*]; urban resident · Stadtbewohner *m*, Stadteinwohner, Städter, Stadtbürger

town residential environment, city residential environment, urban residential environment · städtische Wohnumwelt *f*

1066

town residential land (area), town housing land (area), city residential land (area), city housing land (area), urban residential land (area), urban housing land (area) · städtischer Wohn(ungs)(bau)boden *m*, städtisches Wohn(ungs)(bau)land *n*, städtische Wohn(ungs)(bau)fläche *f*

town revival area, city renewal area, city revival area, urban renewal area, urban revival area, town renewal area · Stadterneuerungsfläche *f*

townscape, urban agglomeration; conurbation (Brit); urban tract [*According to Dickinson*]; urban(ized) landscape, civicized landscape, cityscape [*An area occupied by a continuous series of dwellings, factories and other buildings, harbour and docks, urban parks and playing fields, etc., which are not separated from each other by rural land; though in many cases such an urban area includes enclaves of rural land which is still in agricultural occupation*] · Stadtlandschaft *f*, Städtelandschaft, verstädterte Landschaft, Städteschar *f*, Städteagglomeration *f*, Zusammenstädterung *f*

town scene, city scene, urban scene · Stadtprofil *n*

town selection, urban selection, city selection · Stadtauslese *f*

town service, city service, urban service · städtische Dienstleistung *f*

town serving industry → city serving industry

town setting, city setting, urban setting · städtische Umgebung *f*

town settlement, city settlement, urban settlement · Stadt(an)sied(e)lung *f*, städtische (An)Sied(e)lung

town sewage, city sewage, urban sewage · städtisches Abwasser *n*, Stadtabwasser

township, tithing [*In Saxon times of England the land was laid out in townships for occupation by communities of men*] · Gemarkung *f*

township [*USA. Territorial subdivision, 6 miles long, 6 miles wide, and containing 36 sections, each 1 mile square*] · Ortsgemeinde *f*

town site, city site, urban location, city location, town location, urban site · Stadtstandort *m*, städtischer Standort

town size, city size · Stadtgröße *f*

town size distribution, city size distribution, distribution of town size, distribution of city size · Stadtgrößenverteilung *f*

townsmen's church, market church; ecclesia forensis in civitate [*Latin*] · Marktkirche *f*

town social system, city social system, urban social system · städtisches Sozialsystem *n*

town sociologist, city sociologist, urban sociologist · Stadtsoziologe *m*

town sociology, city sociology, urban sociology · Stadtsoziologie *f*, städtische Soziologie

town space, city space, urban space · Stadtraum *m*, städtischer Raum

town space organization → town spatial organization

town space structure, urban spatial structure, urban space structure, city spatial structure, city space structure, town spatial structure · städtische Raumstruktur *f*, städtische Raumzusammensetzung *f*, städtisches Raumgefüge *n*, städtischer Raumaufbau *m*

town state, urban state, city state · Stadtstaat *m*

town statistics, urban statistics, city statistics · Städtestatistik *f*

town store, urban store, city store · Zentral(laden)geschäft *n*, zentripetales (Laden)Geschäft

town street grid → urban street grid

town structure, city structure, urban structure, town composition, urban composition, city composition · Stadtstruktur *f*, Stadtzusammensetzung *f*, Stadtgefüge *n*, Stadtaufbau *m*, städtische Struktur, städtische Zusammensetzung, städtischer Aufbau, städtisches Gefüge

town structure planning, town composition planning, city structure planning, city composition planning, urban structure planning, urban composition planning · Stadtaufbauplanung *f*, Stadtstrukturplanung, Stadtgefügeplanung, Stadtzusammensetzungsplanung

town surface, city surface, urban surface · Stadtoberfläche *f*

town surveyor, city surveyor, urban surveyor · Stadtbaumeister *m*

town surveyor-general, city surveyor-general, urban surveyor-general · Stadtoberbaurat *m*

town territory, city area, city territory, urban area, urban territory, town area · städtisches Gebiet *n* [*Ein Gebiet, welches im funktionalen und physiognomischen Sinne vorrangig durch städtische Funktionen geprägt ist*]

town trade, city trade, urban trade · Stadtgewerbe *n*, städtisches Gewerbe

town trade area, city trade area, urban trade area · Stadtgewerbegebiet *n*

town traffic, urban traffic, city traffic · Stadtverkehr *m*

town transit network → town transport(ation) network

town transport(ation) network, city transit network, city transport(ation) network, urban transport(ation) network, urban transit network, town transit network · städtisches (Massen)Verkehrsnetz *n*

town transport(ation) planning, city transit planning, city transport(ation) planning, urban transport(ation) planning, urban transit planning, town transit planning · städtische (Massen)Verkehrsplanung *f*

town treasurer, city treasurer, urban treasurer · Stadtkämmerer *m*

town treasury, municipal treasury, city treasury · Stadtkasse *f*

town uglification, urban uglification, city uglification · Stadtverschandelung *f*

town umland, city umland, urban umland · Stadtumland *n*

town-village, city-village, urban village [*According to Dickinson*], mere urban tract [*According to Wooldridge and East*] · Pseudostadt *f,* unechte Stadt, Stadtdorf *n*

townward migration, cityward migration · Stadt(zu)wanderung *f*

townward(s), cityward(s) [*Toward, or in the direction of, the city. Also capable of being used attributively or as adjective, as in "the cityward view, course, route, etc."*] · stadtwärts

town with magistrate appointed by the Crown · Stadt *f* mit geordnetem Magistrat

town with municipal charter, city with municipal charter · Stadt *f* mit Municipium

tracer · Abtastgerät *n,* Abtaster *m*

track · Seeschiffahrtsstraße *f*

track chart, ocean chart, sailing chart · Segelkarte *f,* Übersegler *m*

trackless, untrodden, pathless · unwegsam [*Gelände*]

tracklessness, pathlessness · Unwegsamkeit *f* [*Gelände*]

tract-indexing system · Realfolium *n,* Realindex *m* [*Die Fundstellen aller Grundstücksurkunden — gleich ob innerhalb oder außerhalb der Titelkette — werden auf einem Indexblatt gesammelt*]

tract of country, countryside, tract of land, land tract, country tract [*It has a kind of natural unity*] · Landtrakt *m,* Landstrich *m*

tract of fallow (land), waste, uncultivated land; novale, frusca terra [*Latin*]; fallow land, idle land · Brachflur *f,* Brachland *n,* Brachacker *m,* Brachfeld *n*

tract of land, land tract, country tract, tract of country, countryside [*It has a kind of natural unity*] · Landtrakt *m,* Landstrich *m*

trade · Gewerbe *n*

trade → (building) trade

trade balance, visible balance, balance of payments, balance of trade, balance of accounts · Zahlungsbilanz *f,* Handelsbilanz

Trade Board · Lohnfestlegungsamt *n,* Einigungsamt [*1909 in England für die Heimindustrie und Bergarbeiter geschaffen*]

trade category · Gewerbeklasse *f*

trade club, trade society · Gewerkverein *m*

trade community · Gewerbegemeinde *f*

trade credit · Lieferantenkredit *m*

trade directory, buyers' guide · Bezugsquellennachweis *m*

Trade Disputes Act [*England*] · Gesetz *n* über gewerbliche Streitigkeiten

trade enterprise · Gewerbebetrieb *m*

trade in ideas · Gedankenaustausch *m*

trade inspection · Gewerbeaufsicht *f,* Gewerbeinspektion *f*

trade licence, trade license · Konzessionierungsbefugnis *f* [*Gewerbe*]

trade licence certificate, trade license certificate · Gewerbeschein *m*

trademark law, trademark act, trademark statute · Warenzeichengesetz *n,* WZG

trade premises · Gewerberäume *m pl,* gewerblich genutzte Räume

trade protection society · kaufmännisches Auskunftsbüro *n*

trader [*One who makes trading his habitual profession*] · Kaufmann *m*

trade real estate investment project · Gewerbeobjekt *n*

trade route, commercial route · Handelsweg *m*

trades → structural trades

tradesman · Gewerbetreibende *m*

trade society, trade club · Gewerkverein *m*

tradespeople · Gewerbetreibende *m pl*

trade stock, stock-in-trade [*The type of goods applicable to a particular branch of trade*] · Sektorgut *n*

trade tax · Gewerbesteuer *f*

trade union, labour union (Brit.); labor union (US) · Gewerkschaft *f*

(trade) unionism · Gewerkschaftswesen *n*

(trade) unionist; labor skate (US) · Gewerkschaftler *m*

trade-weighted average depreciation · durchschnittlicher Kursverlust *m* gewichtet nach dem Handelsumfang

trade zone · Gewerbegebiet *n*, GE

trade zone land · gewerbliche Baufläche *f*, Gewerbegebietsfläche

trading · Handelsverkehr *m*

trading certificate · Geschäftsfähigkeitsbescheinigung *f*, Rechtsfähigkeitsbescheinigung

trading corporation · Handelsgewerbekorporation *f*, Handelsgewerbekörperschaft *f*

trading fund, working fund [*Cash advanced for working-capital or expense purposes, and replenished from time to time as needed*] · Betriebsfonds *m*

trading net gain, net profit from trading, net gain from trading, trading net profit · Handelsnettogewinn *m*, Handelsnettoprofit *m*

trading on the equity, favo(u)rable financial leverage · positive Hebelwirkung *f* [*Der Grenzsachzins liegt über dem Grenzmarktzins*]

trading stamp · Rabattmarke *f*

trading undertaking → (municipal) trading undertaking

trading with the enemy act, trading with the enemy law, trading with the enemy statute · Feindvermögensgesetz *n*

trading with the enemy law · Feindvermögensrecht *n*

traditio, sala [*Latin*] · dingliche Einigung *f* [*nach deutschem Recht*]

traditio brevi manu [*Latin*] · Besitzauflassung *f*, Übergabe *f* kurzer Hand, Aushändigung kurzer Hand, Tradition *f* kurzer Hand, Aushändigen kurzer Hand, Übergeben kurzer Hand

traditio longa manu, traditio per visum [*Latin*] · Besitzzuweisung *f*, Übergabe *f* langer Hand, Aushändigung langer Hand, Tradition *f* langer Hand, Aushändigen langer Hand, Übergeben langer Hand

tradition; traditio [*Latin*], handing over, handover, (de)livery · Aushändigung *f*, Übergabe *f*, Aushändigen *n*, Übergeben, Tradition *f*

traditional (direction) commuter traffic · Stadteinwärtspendlerverkehr *m*

traditional (direction) peak movement of (public) transit, traditional (direction) peak movement of (public) transport(ation), traditional (direction) peak movement of mass transport(ation), traditional (direction) peak movement of mass transit · Spitzenmassenverkehr *m* stadteinwärts, Spitzenmassenbeförderung *f* stadteinwärts, Massenspitzenverkehr stadteinwärts, Massenspitzenbeförderung stadteinwärts

traditional (direction) trip (to work), traditional (direction) travel (to work), traditional (direction) journey (to work) · Stadteinwärtsberufsfahrt *f*

tradition-minded · traditionsbewußt

traditio per visum [*Latin*] → traditio longa manu

traffic · Verkehr *m*

traffic architecture · Zusammenhang *m* zwischen Grundstücksnutzung und Verkehrsaufkommen

traffic area · Verkehrsfläche *f*

traffic authority · Verkehrsbehörde *f*

traffic call, traffic demand · Verkehrsnachfrage *f*

traffic catchment area · Verkehrseinzugsgebiet *n*

traffic code · Verkehrsordnung *f*

traffic data collection · Verkehrsdatenerfassung *f*

traffic demand, traffic call · Verkehrsnachfrage *f*

traffic density, density of traffic · Verkehrsdichte *f*

traffic destination, destination of traffic · Verkehrsziel *n*

traffic development · Verkehrserschließung *f*

traffic easing · Verkehrsentlastung *f*

traffic-endangering advertisement, advertisement dangerous to traffic · verkehrsgefährdende Werbung *f*, verkehrsgefährdende Reklame *f*

traffic engineer, transport(ation) engineer · Verkehrsingenieur *m*

traffic engineering · Verkehrstechnik *f*

traffic expert · Verkehrsfachmann *m*

traffic generation model · Verkehrserzeugungsmodell *n*

traffic generator, generator of movement · Verkehrserzeuger *m*

traffic green · Verkehrsgrün *n*

traffic in transit, transit traffic · Durchfuhrverkehr *m*, Durchgangsverkehr [*durch einen Staat*]

traffic management, management of traffic · Verkehrsabwick(e)lung *f*, Verkehrsführung

traffic movement · Verkehrsbewegung *f*

traffic network · Verkehrsnetz *n*

traffic noise, transport(ation) noise · Verkehrslärm *m*

traffic nuisance · Verkehrsemission f

traffic nuisance effect · Verkehrsimmission f

traffic origin, origion of traffic · Verkehrsausgang m, Verkehrsursprung m

traffic paralysis · Verkehrslähmung f

traffic peak, traffic rush · Verkehrsspitze f

(traffic) peak hour, (traffic) rush hour · Spitzen(verkehrs)stunde f, Verkehrsspitzenstunde

traffic plan; thoroughfare plan (US) · Verkehrsplan m, Plan über die Verkehrsplanung

traffic planner · Verkehrsplaner m

traffic planning · Verkehrsplanung f

traffic planning board · Verkehrsplanungsamt n

traffic policy · Verkehrspolitik f

traffic region, transport(ation) region · Verkehrsregion f

traffic regulation, regulation of traffic · Verkehrsregelung f

traffic restriction · Verkehrseinschränkung f, Verkehrsbeschränkung, Verkehrsbegrenzung

traffic route plan · Verkehrswegeplan m

traffic route planning · Verkehrswegeplanung f

traffic rush, traffic peak · Verkehrsspitze f

(traffic) rush hour, (traffic) peak hour · Spitzen(verkehrs)stunde f, Verkehrsspitzenstunde

traffic safety · Verkehrssicherheit f

traffic segregation · Verkehrsentflechtung f, Verkehrsentmischung

traffic separation · Verkehrsteilung f, Verkehrstrennung

traffic settlement · Verkehrs(an)sied(e)lung f

traffic study · Verkehrsuntersuchung f

traffic survey · Verkehrsenquête f

traffic system · Verkehrssystem n

traffic valley · Verkehrstal n

traffic volume · Verkehrsvolumen n

trailer → (travel) trailer

trailer court → (housing-type) trailer development

trailer insurance · Anhängerversicherung f

trailer park → (travel) trailer park

trailer standing → (travel) trailer standing

training · Ausbildung f, Schulung

training assistance, training promotion, sponsoring of training · Ausbildungsförderung f, Schulungsförderung

training centre (Brit.); training center (US) · Ausbildungsstätte f, Schulungsstätte

training college · Seminar n

training level, level of training · Ausbildungsstand m, Schulungsstand

training of apprentices, apprentice training, apprenticeship · Lehrlingsausbildung f, Lehre f

training of planners, planning education · Planerausbildung f, Planverfasserausbildung

training personnel, training staff · Ausbildungspersonal n, Schulungspersonal

training staff, training personnel · Ausbildungspersonal n, Schulungspersonal

training (work)shop · Lehrwerkstatt f

tramway line (Brit.); streetcar line, troll(e)y car line (US) · Straßenbahnlinie f

transaction in land(s) → (real) estate business

transaction in (real) estate → (real) estate business

transaction witness · Handlungzeuge m

transcript [*An official copy of a court record; as, a transcript, or certified copy, of a judg(e)ment*] · Gerichtsabschrift f

to transfer, to turn over, to attorn [*To another money or goods*] · übertragen

transfer · Übertragung f

transferable, attornable · übertragbar

transferable by endorsement, transferable by indorsement, negotiable · begebbar, umlaufbar, umlauffähig, indossabel

transferable quality, negotiability (of instrument) · Begebbarkeit f, Umlauffähigkeit, Umlaufbarkeit [*handelsrechtliches Wertpapier*]

to transfer a mineral right · abgewähren [*Die berggerichtliche Besitzumschreibung im Bergbuch an den neuen Erwerber*]

to transfer by will · testamentarisch übertragen

transfer clause → (voluntary) transfer clause

transferee · Übertragungsempfänger m

transfer(ence) book · Übertragungsbuch n

transfer(ence) of a mineral right, turning over of a mineral right · Abgewährung f

transfer(ence) of legal title · Übertragung f des formellen Eigentums

transfer(ence) of licence, transfer(ence) of license, turning over of licence, turning over of license, licence transfer(ence), license transfer(ence) · Lizenzübertragung f

transfer(ence) of ownership (of property), transfer(ence) of (general) property, transfer(ence) of proprietorship, turning over of ownership (of property), turning over of (general) property, turning over of proprietorship · Eigentumsübertragung f

transfer(ence) of possession, bailment · Besitzübertragung f

transfer(ence) of rights, transfer(ence) of interests, turning over of rights, turning over of interests · Übertragung f von Rechten

transfer entry · Umschreibung f

to transfer from congested areas, to decentralize, to disperse, to resite, to relocate, to resettle, to displace · aussiedeln, umsiedeln, verlegen, verändern des Standortes, umsetzen

transfer from congested areas, (tenant) relocation, displacement, rehousing, resettlement [Of persons from land acquired or appropriated for planning purposes] · Aussied(e)lung f, Umsied(e)lung, Standortveränderung, Verlegung, Umsetzung, Wiederunterbringung

transfer law → law of conveyances (of land)

transfer of industry, relocation of industry, industrial resettlement, industrial relocation, industrial shifting, resettlement of industry, displacement of industry · Industrieaussied(e)lung f, Industrieumsied(e)lung, Industrieumsetzung, Industrieverlegung, industrielle Standortveränderung, Industrieverlagerung

transfer of (real) estate, transfer of (real) property, transfer of realty · Grund(stücks)übertragung f, Liegenschaftsübertragung, Immobilienübertragung

transfer of rights in rem · Übertragung f dinglicher Rechte

transfer of shares · Aktienübertragung f

transfer of technology · Technologietransfer m

transferred, turned over, attorned · übertragen

transferring, turning over · Übertragen n

transferring authority · übertragende Behörde f

transferring voluntarily, conveyancing · freiwilliges Übertragen n

transfer stamp · Übertragungsgebühr f, Umschreibegebühr [beim Kauf englischer Aktien]

transfer tax · Wertpapierumsatzsteuer f

to transfer voluntarily, to convey · freiwillig übertragen

transformation [It may also be called "conversion" in definite cases] · sachliche Surrogation f

transfrontier, border-crossing · grenzüberschreitend, grenzüberquerend

transgressio super casum [Latin]; trespass on the case · indirekte Schadenshandlung f

transgressive trust [A trust which transgresses or violates the rule against perpetuities] · verletzende Treuhand f

transhumance [This French word denotes the periodical migrations of sheep and cattle from certain regions to others, for instance, during summer from valleys to highly situated pasture lands in the mountains] · Viehtrieb m

transit → (public) transport(ation)

transit business → (public) transit business

transit by rail → (rapid) transit by rail

transit camp · Durchgangslager n

transit duty · Durchfuhrzoll m, Durchgangszoll

transit enterprise → public transit enterprise

transit fare, transport(ation) fare · Fahrpreis m, Beförderungspreis

transit fare → (public) transit fare

transit fare submodel, transport(ation) fare submodel · Beförderungskosten-Untermodell n, Fahrtkosten-Untermodell, Untermodell über die Beförderungskosten, Untermodell über die Fahrtkosten, Untermodell über den Fahrpreis, Fahrpreis-Untermodell

transit field, transport(ation) sector, transit sector, transport(ation) field · Massenverkehrssektor m, Transportsektor, Beförderungssektor

transition · Überleitung f

transition(al) fund · Übergangsfonds m, Überleitungsfonds

transition(al) ordinance · Übergangsverordnung f, Überleitungsverordnung

transition(al) phase · Übergangsphase f, Überleitungsphase

transition(al) prescription, transition(al) regulation, transition(al) rule · Übergangsvorschrift f, Überleitungsvorschrift

transition(al) proceeding [For the purpose of effecting the transition from an existing law to a new law of the same subject] · Übergangsverfahren n, Überleitungsverfahren

transition(al) provision — transport(ation) fare submodel

transition(al) provision, transitory provision · Übergangsbestimmung *f*, Überleitungsbestimmung

transitional statute, transitional act, transitional law · Überleitungsgesetz *n*

transition zone, central belt (area), CBD frame · innenstadtnahe Wohn- und Gewerbeviertel *npl*, Ergänzungsraum *m* der Innenstadt

transit land · Durchfuhrland *n*, Durchgangsland

transit length, transport(ation) length · Beförderungslänge *f*, Transportlänge

transit line → (public) transit line

transit network, transport(ation) network · Beförderungsverkehrsnetz *n*, Transportverkehrsnetz, Massenverkehrsnetz

transit of uncleared goods · Zollgutversand *m*

transit operator → public transit operator

transitory cause, transitory (law)suit, transitory (court) action, transitory plea · Klage *f* wenn die Rechtsverletzung an jedem beliebigen Ort möglich war [*Vertragsbruch; Körperverletzung usw.*]

transitory provision, transition(al) provision · Übergangsbestimmung *f*, Überleitungsbestimmung

transitory residence · Zwischenaufenthalt *m*

transit pattern, transit scheme, transport(ation) scheme, transport(ation) pattern · Beförderungsmuster *n*, Transportmuster, Massenverkehrsmuster, Massenverkehrsschema *n*, Beförderungsschema, Transportschema

transit peak travel → transit (vehicle) peak travel

transit plan, transport(ation) plan · Beförderungsplan *m*, Transportplan, Massenverkehrsplan

transit planning, transport(ation) planning · Beförderungsplanung *f*, Transportplanung, Massenverkehrsplanung

transit practice, transport(ation) practice · Massenverkehrswesen *n*, Transportwesen, Beförderungswesen

transit rider → (public) transit rider

transit right, right of transit · Durchfuhrrecht *n*, Durchgangsrecht

transit scheme, transport(ation) scheme, transport(ation) pattern, transit pattern · Beförderungsmuster *n*, Transportmuster, Massenverkehrsmuster, Massenverkehrsschema *n*, Beförderungsschema, Transportschema

transit sector, transport(ation) field, transit field, transport(ation) sector · Massenverkehrssektor *m*, Transportsektor, Beförderungssektor

transit state, state of transit · Durchgangsstaat *m*, Durchfuhrstaat

transit station → (rapid) transit station

(transit) stop · Haltestelle *f*

transit traffic, traffic in transit · Durchfuhrverkehr *m*, Durchgangsverkehr [*durch einen Staat*]

transitura, transversa [*Latin*]; toll(-through) · Passiergeld *n*, Passierzoll *m*

transit validation · Kostenersatz *m* für die Benutzung kollektiver Verkehrsmittel

transit vehicle → (public) transit vehicle

transit (vehicle) peak travel, transit (vehicle) peak journey, transit (vehicle) peak trip · Spitzenfahrt *f* eines öffentlichen Verkehrsmittels, Spitzenfahrt eines öffentlichen Beförderungsmittels

transmission · Weiterverweisung *f* [*Internationales Privatrecht*]

transmission of the file · Aktenversendung *f*

transmittal [*Form used to transmit items of a standard nature between the parties on the project*] · Positionsaufteilung *f*

transmitter · Quelle *f* [*Graphentheorie*]

transmutation of possession at common law · Wechsel *m* des gemeinrechtlichen Besitzes

transnational law · Recht *n* des internationalen Handels, Völkerhandelsrecht, transnationales Handelsrecht

transparently artificial · sichtlich gekünstelt [*z. B. die Auslegung eines Gesetzes*]

transport → (public) transit

transport(ation) → (public) transport(ation)

transportational · transportmäßig

transport(ation) business → (public) transit business

transport(ation) company → (public) transit company

transport(ation) engineer, traffic engineer · Verkehrsingenieur *m*

transport(ation) enterprise → (public) transit enterprise

transport(ation) fare, transit fare · Fahrpreis *m*, Beförderungspreis

transport(ation) fare → (public) transit fare

transport(ation) fare submodel, transit fare submodel · Beförderungskosten-Untermodell *n*, Fahrtkosten-Untermodell, Untermodell über die Beförderungskosten, Untermodell über die Fahrtkosten, Untermodell über den Fahrpreis, Fahrpreis-Untermodell

transport(ation) field, transit field, transport(ation) sector, transit sector · Massenverkehrssektor m, Transportsektor, Beförderungssektor

transport(ation) gap · innerstädtische Verkehrsnetzlücke f

transport(ation) geography, geography of transport(ation) · Verkehrsgeographie f

transport(ation) length, transit length · Beförderungslänge f, Transportlänge

transport(ation) line → (public) transit enterprise

transport(ation) network, transit network · Beförderungsverkehrsnetz n, Transportverkehrsnetz, Massenverkehrsnetz

transport(ation) noise, traffic noise · Verkehrslärm m

transport(ation) operator → (public) transit operator

transport(ation) pattern, transit pattern, transit scheme, transport(ation) scheme · Beförderungsmuster n, Transportmuster, Massenverkehrsmuster, Massenverkehrsschema n, Beförderungsschema, Transportschema

transport(ation) plan, transit plan · Beförderungsplan m, Transportplan, Massenverkehrsplan

transport(ation) planning, transit planning · Beförderungsplanung f, Transportplanung, Massenverkehrsplanung

transport(ation) practice, transit practice · Massenverkehrswesen n, Transportwesen, Beförderungswesen

transport(ation) rate, line-haul rate · Verkehrstarif m, Fahrtarif

transport(ation) region, traffic region · Verkehrsregion f

transport(ation) rider → (public) transit rider

transport(ation) scheme, transport(ation) pattern, transit pattern, transit scheme · Beförderungsmuster n, Transportmuster, Massenverkehrsmuster, Massenverkehrsschema n, Beförderungsschema, Transportschema

transport(ation) sector, transit sector, transport(ation) field, transit field · Massenverkehrssektor m, Transportsektor, Beförderungssektor

transport(ation) system → (public) transit system

transportation to parts beyond the seas · Deportation f [*aus England*]

transport(ation) vehicle → (public) transit vehicle

transport business → (public) transit business

transport company → (public) transit company

transport distance · Verwendungsweite f [*Wabenmuster nach Lösch*]

transport fare → transport(ation) fare

transport operator → (public) transport(ation) operator

transport orientation · Transportorientierung f

transport system → (public) transit system

transumpt, (court) action of transumpt, plea of transumpt, cause of transumpt, (law)suit of transumpt [*Scots law. An action brought for the purpose of obtaining transumpt(s)*] · Klage f auf Schriftstückabschrift

transumpt [*Scots law. A judicial transcript of a writing; an authorized authentic copy, as of the evidences of title to land(s)*] · Schriftstückabschrift f

transversa [*Latin*]; toll(-through); transitura · Passiergeld n, Passierzoll m

transverse building · Quergebäude n

travel, journey, trip · Fahrt f

travel assignation, journey assignation, trip assignation · Fahrtzuweisung f (auf Verkehrsnetze)

travel attraction, trip atraction, journey attraction [*That which gives motivation, specific direction, and destination of a trip, e.g. going downtown*] · Fahrtanziehungskraft f

travel cost(s) · Fahrkosten f, Fahrgelder npl, Reisekosten, Reisegelder

travel destination-end, journey destination-end, (trip) destination-end · (Fahrt)Endpunkt m

travel distribution, journey distribution, trip distribution · Fahrt(en)verteilung f

travel distribution model, journey distribution model, trip distribution model · Fahrt(en)verteilungsmodell n

travel from work, trip from work, journey from work · Fahrt f vom Arbeitsplatz

travel generation, journey generation, trip generation · Fahrt(en)erzeugung f

travel guide · Reiseführer m

travel-maker, journey-maker, trip-maker · Fahrtteilnehmer m

travel matrix, journey matrix, trip matrix · Fahrt(en)matrix f

travel origin-end, journey origin-end, (trip) origin-end · (Fahrt)Startpunkt m

travel pattern, travel scheme, journey pattern, journey scheme, trip pattern, trip scheme · Fahrt(en)muster n, Fahrt(en)schema n

travel production — trespasser

travel production, trip production, journey production [*The motivation to make a trip, e.g. going to work*] · Fahrterzeugung *f*

travel-time survey, trip-time survey, journey-time survey · Fahrzeitenenquête *f*

travel to work, trip to work, journey to work · Fahrt *f* zum Arbeitsplatz

(travel) trailer, mobile home, caravan, housing-type trailer · Wohnwagen *m*, Wagenheim *n*

to traverse, to deny [*in pleading*] · bestreiten, leugnen

traverse, denial [*in pleading*] · Leugnung *f*, Bestreitung, Verneinung, negative Litiskontestation *f*

traverser [*in pleading*] · Leugner *m*

traversing an indictment · Unschuldbeteuerung *f*

treason · Hochverrat *m*

treasure of the earth, mineral treasure · Bodenschatz *m*, Bodenreichtum *m*

treasurer, receiver · Rendant *m*

treasurer [*England*] · (königlicher) Schatzmeister *m*

treasure-trove · Schatz(fund) *m* [*Eine entdeckte bewegliche Sache, die solange verborgen war, daß der Eigentümer nicht mehr zu ermitteln ist*]

treasure-trove right, right to treasure-trove · Schatz(fund)recht *n*, Recht auf Schatzfund(e)

treasury · Staatskasse *f*

treasury · Kämmerei *f*

Treasury Bench · Schatzbank *f* [*England*]

Treasury bill · (britischer) Schatzwechsel *m*

Treasury bond · (britische) Schatzanweisung *f*

treasury roll · Schatzamtrolle *f*

treasury solicitor, solicitor to the treasury · Generalfiskalat *n*

treasury stock transactions · Handel *m* mit eigenen Aktien

treasury warrant [*England*] · Zahlungsrescript *n* [*(königliches) Schatzamt*]

to treat [*subject*] · abhandeln [*Thema*]

to treat, to process [*application*] · bearbeiten [*Antrag*]

treatise, paper · Abhandlung *f* [*Thema*]

treatment, processing · Bearbeitung *f*, Behandlung [*Bauantrag; Angebot*]

treatment centre for alcoholics, treatment centre for drunkards (Brit.); treatment center for alcoholics, treatment center for drunkards (US) · Trinkerheilanstalt *f*

treatment of (legal) case(s) · Fallbearbeitung *f*, Rechtsfallbearbeitung

treaty; foedus [*Latin*] · völkerrechtlicher Vertrag *m*, Staatsvertrag

treaty and other international act series number, T.I.A.S.No. · Kennziffer *f* eines völkerrechtlichen Vertrages

treble, threefold, triple · dreifach

tree and standheight measurement · Holzmassenbestimmung *f*, Holzvorratsermitt(e)lung

tree belt, belt of trees · Baumgürtel *m*

tree cluster, cluster of trees · Baumgruppe *f*

tree conservation → tree retention

tree cover · Baumbestand *m*, Baumdecke *f*, Baumbewuchs *m*

tree garden · Baumgarten *m*

tree method · Baumverfahren *n* [*Netzwerktheorie*]

(tree) nursery · Baumschule *f*

tree plantation · Baumpflanzung *f*

tree planted strip · Baumstreifen *m*

tree preservation → tree retention

tree protection, protection of trees · Baumschutz *m*

tree row, row of trees · Baumreihe *f*

tref [*Welsh*], ker [*Brittanic*]; clachan [*Galic*]; bally [*Irish*]; balley [*Manx*] · Drubbel *m*; Eschdorf *n* [*nach Rothert 1924*]; Eschweiler *m* [*nach Helbok 1938*]

trend · allgemeine Entwick(e)lungslinie *f*, Linie der allgemeinen Entwick(e)lung [*Konjunkturtheorie*]

trend of prices · Preisentwick(e)lung *f*

to trespass, to encroach, to intrude, to incroach · beeinträchtigen, verletzen, stören, eindringen

trespass, incroaching, encroachment, encroaching [*Invasion of private rights by persons or economic forces*] · Störung *f*, Beeinträchtigung

trespass, intrusion, incroaching, encroachment, adverse occupation, incroachment, incroaching · (Beeinträchtigung *f* durch) Eindringen *n*, Verletzung durch Eindringen, Störung durch Eindringen, Besitzverletzung durch Eindringen, Besitzstörung durch Eindringen, Besitzbeeinträchtigung durch Eindringen

trespass → violation (of law)

trespass ab initio · rückwirkende (Besitz)Störung *f*

trespasser, intruder, invader · Beeinträchtigende *m*, Störer, Verletzer, Eindring-

trespasser from the beginning — tribesman

ling, Besitzbeeinträchtigende, Besitzstörer, Besitzverletzer, Besitzeindringling, unbefugter Betreter

trespasser from the beginning, trespasser from the first act(ion), trespasser ab initio, intruder ab initio, intruder from the beginning, intruder from the first act(ion) [*A person who, after lawfully entering on another's premises, commits some wrongful act, which in law is construed to affect and have relation back to his first entry so as to make the whole a trespass*] · rückwirkender Eindringling *m*, rückwirkender (Besitz)Störer, rückwirkender (Besitz)Beeinträchtigender, rückwirkender (Besitz)Verletzer, (Besitz)Verletzer von Anfang an, (Besitz)Störer von Anfang an, (Besitz)Beeinträchtigende von Anfang an, Eindringling von Anfang an

trespasser to land(s) · Landbesitzstörer *m*, Bodenbesitzstörer

trespass on building lines · Fluchtlinienüberschreitung *f*, Baufluchtlinienüberschreitung

trespass on the case; transgressio super casum [*Latin*] · indirekte Schadenshandlung *f*

trespass quare clausum fregit, forcible entry [*Entry by breaking open doors, windows, or other parts of a house, or by any kind of violence or circumstance of terror*] · Hausfriedensbruch *m*

trespass to chattels · (Besitz)Störung *f* beweglicher Sachen

trespass to land(s) · Landbesitzstörung *f*, Bodenbesitzstörung

trespass to the person, bodily injury, bodily harm, personal harm, personal injury · Körperverletzung *f* [*Jeder äußere Eingriff in die körperliche Unversehrtheit*]

trespass (up)on land · Landfrevel *m*

trespass (up)on property, property trespass · Eigentumsfrevel *m*, Eigentumsrechtsverletzung *f*

trespass vi et armis · gewaltsame Rechtsverletzung *f*, gewaltsamer Rechtsbruch *m*

trial · Beweisverfahren *n*, Beweisabnahme *f*

trial and error · zufällig

trial at bar, bar trial [*A trial which takes place before all the judges, at the bar of the court in which the action is brought*] · (Haupt)Verhandlung *f* vor allen Richtern, Gerichtsverhandlung vor allen Richtern, Prozeß vor versammeltem Gericht, (Haupt)Verhandlung vor einem Gericht(shof) [*Anstatt vor einem Assisenrichter*]

trial at nisi prius [*The ordinary kind of trial which takes place at the sittings, assizes or circuit, before a single judge*] · Einzelrichter(haupt)verhandlung *f*, Einzelrichtergerichtsverhandlung, (Haupt)Verhandlung vor einem delegierten Richter

trial brief · Gerichtsverhandlungsschriftsatz *f*, (Haupt)Verhandlungsschriftsatz

trial by certificate · Beweisabnahme *f* durch Bescheinigung

trial by examination, trial by inspection · Beweisabnahme *f* durch Augenschein

trial by inspection, trial by examination · Beweisabnahme *f* durch Augenschein

trial by jury, assize, jury trial [*A trial in which sworn assessors or jurymen decide questions of fact*] · Gerichtsverhandlung *f* vor Geschworenen, (Haupt)Verhandlung vor Geschworenen, Geschworenen(haupt)verhandlung, Geschworenengerichtsverhandlung, Schwurgerichtsverfahren *n*, Geschworenenverfahren, Schwurgerichtsverhandlung

trial by record · Beweisabnahme *f* durch Gerichtsprotokoll, Beweisabnahme durch Aktenlage

trial by witnesses · Beweisabnahme *f* durch Zeugen

trial court · Prozeßgericht *n*

trial court, first instance · erste Instanz *f*, Tatsacheninstanz

trial entry, entry of trial · Eintrag(ung) *m, (f)* des Termins bei Gericht, Termineintrag(ung) bei Gericht, Eintrag(ung) des Verhandlungstermins

trial examiner · Verfahrensprüfer *m*, halbrichterlicher Verfahrensbeamter

trial lawyer · Prozeßjurist *m*

trial level · Instanzebene *f*

trial notice, notice of trial · Terminanzeige *f* an die Gegenpartei, Anzeige des Termins an die Gegenpartei

trial of issue of fact [*In a stricter sense. The examination before a competent tribunal, according to the laws of the land, of the facts put in issue in a cause, for the purpose of determining such issue*] · Verhandlung *f* über tatsächliche Fragen

trial of the issue by recognition · Klagebeantwortung *f* durch Anerkenntnis

triangular distribution · Dreiecksverteilung *f* [*Statistik*]

triangular green village, triangular plaza village · Dreieckangerdorf *n*, Dreieckplatzdorf

tribe settlement · Stammes(an)sied(e)lung *f*

tribesman · männliches Stammesmitglied *n*

tribunal · Tribunal n

tribunal for matters in public administration, administrative court, administrative tribunal, court for matters in public administration · Verwaltungsgericht n, VG

Tribunal of The Hague, Hague Tribunal · Haager Gerichtshof m

tributary, affluent; branch (US) · Nebenfluß m

tributary area, tributary territory, tributary land, outlay territory, hinterland, catchment land, catchment area, catchment territory · Hinterland n, Einzugsgebiet n, Einzugsbereich m

trickling-down effect, spread effect · Ausbreitungswirkung f [Regionalwirtschaft]

tried → adjudiented

tri-level operation, three-level operation, triple-level operation · Dreiebenenbetrieb m [öffentliches Verkehrsmittel]

trim mark · Beschneidemarke f, Beschnittmarke [Kartographie]

trim size · Beschneideformat n, Beschnittformat [Kartographie]

trip, travel, journey · Fahrt f

tripartite, of three parts; tripartitus [Latin] · dreiteilig

tripartite agreement, agreement tripartite · Dreiecksabkommen n, Dreiecksabmachung f, Dreiecksvereinbarung

tripartite board, three-arbitrator board · Dreierbesetzung f [Schiedsgericht]

tripartition · Dreiteilung f

trip assignation, travel assignation, journey assignation · Fahrtzuweisung f (auf Verkehrsnetze)

trip atraction, journey attraction, travel attraction [That which gives motivation, specific direction, and destination of a trip, e.g. going downtown] · Fahrtanziehungskraft f

(trip) destination-end, travel destination-end, journey destination-end · (Fahrt)Endpunkt m

trip distribution, travel distribution, journey distribution · Fahrt(en)verteilung f

trip distribution model, travel distribution model, journey distribution model · Fahrt(en)verteilungsmodell n

trip from work, journey from work, travel from work · Fahrt f vom Arbeitsplatz

trip generation, travel generation, journey generation · Fahrt(en)erzeugung f

trip-interchange-modal split · Verkehrsmittelaufteilung f des Personenfernverkehrs nach gleichartigen Quell-Ziel-Beziehungen und Analyse der Verkehrsmittelwahl

triple, treble, threefold · dreifach

triple corner · Dreiländereck n

triple-decker wooden tenement, three-decker wooden tenement · dreigeschossiges Mehrfamilien-Holzhaus n

triple-field system, triple-field husbandry, three-field system, three-field husbandry · Dreifelderwirtschaft f

triple-generation family, three-generation family · Dreigenerationsfamilie f

triple-level operation, tri-level operation, three-level operation · Dreiebenenbetrieb m [öffentliches Verkehrsmittel]

triple-minute lighting, triple-minute illumination, three-minute lighting, three-minute illumination · Dreiminutenlicht n

triple-mode factor analysis, three-mode factor analysis · dreimodale Faktorenanalyse f, dreidimensionale Faktorenuntersuchung f

triplets · Drillinge m pl

triple-window house, three-window house · Dreifensterhaus n

trip-maker, travel-maker, journey-maker · Fahrtteilnehmer m

trip matrix, travel matrix, journey matrix · Fahrt(en)matrix f

(trip) origin-end, travel origin-end, journey origin-end · (Fahrt)Startpunkt m

trip pattern, trip scheme, travel pattern, travel scheme, journey pattern, journey scheme · Fahrt(en)muster n, Fahrt(en)schema n

trip production, journey production, travel production [The motivation to make a trip, e.g. going to work] · Fahrterzeugung f

trip-time survey, journey-time survey, travel-time survey · Fahrzeitenenquête f

trip to work, journey to work, travel to work · Fahrt f zum Arbeitsplatz

TRO, temporary restraining order · vorsorgliche Maßnahme f [Rechtsbehelf]

troll(e)y car line (US); tramway line (Brit.); streetcar line · Straßenbahnlinie f

trolley vehicle service · Oberleitungsfahrzeugbetrieb m

troops' exercise ground · Truppenübungsplatz m

trouble shooter · Krisenmanager m

trove · Fund m

trover · Deliktklage f wegen Verletzung des klägerischen Eigentums

truck farm (US); market garden, commercial garden (Brit.); truck garden · Garten(bau)betrieb *m*, Handelsgärtnerei *f*, (Erwerbs)Gärtnerei, gärtnerischer Betrieb

truck farm area (US); market garden area, commercial garden area (Brit.); truck garden area · gartenbaulich genutzte Fläche *f*, Gartenbaufläche

truck farmer (US); market gardener, commercial gardener (Brit.) · Erwerbsgärtner *m*, Handelsgärtner

truck farming (US); market gardening, commercial gardening (Brit.) · Erwerbsgartenbau *m*, Handelsgartenbau

truck garden, truck farm (US); market garden, commercial garden (Brit.) · Garten(bau)betrieb *m*, Handelsgärtnerei *f*, (Erwerbs)Gärtnerei, gärtnerischer Betrieb

truck garden area, truck farm area (US); market garden area, commercial garden area (Brit.) · gartenbaulich genutzte Fläche *f*, Gartenbaufläche

truck garden produce (US); market garden produce, commercial garden produce (Brit.) · Garten(bau)erzeugnisse *npl*

trucking belt · Gemüse(an)baugürtel *m*

trucking industry (US) · Fuhrwesen *n*

truck owner (US); lorry owner (Brit.) · LKW-Halter *m*

truck survey (US); lorry survey (Brit.) · LKW-Enquête *f*, Last(kraft)wagenenquête

truck system [*Under that system employers were in the practice of paying the wages of their workpeople in goods, or of requiring them to purchase goods at certain shops, which led to labourers being compelled to take goods of inferior quality at high prices*] · Zahlung *f* von Arbeitslöhnen in Waren

true (cash) value, fair (cash) value, capital value [*The value of land imputed from the annual rent. Determined by dividing the annual rent specified in the lease agreement by the previously concurred-in current annual rate of rent. The capital value must be not less than the fair value of the land in fee at the time of the lease. The capital value of the annual rent determined in this way provides a valid basis for comparing the proposed lease with offers to purchase*] · Kapitalwert *m*

true cost(s), correct cost(s) · Plankosten *f*, geplante Kosten, planmäßige Kosten [*Die auf dem Planbeschäftigungsgrad basierenden Normkosten mit Konstanz für längere Zeit, deren mengen- als auch wertmäßiger Faktor durch wissenschaftliche Analyse ermittelt wird und volle Maßstäblichkeit in sich trägt. In der Praxis werden Plankosten oft mit Standardkosten gleichgesetzt*]

true fact · wahre Tatsache *f*

true (general) property, true ownership (of property), true proprietorship · wahres Eigentum *n*, wirkliches Eigentum

true owner, true proprietor · wahrer Eigentümer *m*, wirklicher Eigentümer, wirkliches Eigentumssubjekt *n*, wahres Eigentumssubjekt, wahrer Eigner, wirklicher Eigner

true ownership (of property), true proprietorship, true (general) property · wahres Eigentum *n*, wirkliches Eigentum

true possessor · wahrer Besitzer *m*, wirklicher Besitzer

true proprietor, true owner · wahrer Eigentümer *m*, wirklicher Eigentümer, wirkliches Eigentumssubjekt *n*, wahres Eigentumssubjekt, wahrer Eigner, wirklicher Eigner

true proprietorship, true (general) property, true ownership (of property) · wahres Eigentum *n*, wirkliches Eigentum

(true) recovery [*In the restoration or vindication of a right existing in a person, by the formal judg(e)ment or decree of a competent court, at his instance and suit, or the obtaining, by such judg(e)ment, of some right or property which has been taken or withheld from him*] · Prozeßgewinn *m*

true regression · fehlerfreie Regression *f*

(true) rent of land(s), (true) rent of ground, land(s) rent, ground rent [*It issues out of the land, as a compensation for the possession during the term*] · Bodenrente *f*, Landrente, Grund(stücks)rente

true rule [*obsolete*]; unformulated rule · unausgesprochene Regel *f* [*Sie ist einer Entscheidung durch Auslegung zu entnehmen*]

true usufruct; usus fructus verus [*Latin*] · wahrer (Frucht)Genuß *m*, wahrer Nießbrauch

true value · wahrer Wert *m*

truncated distribution · abgeschnittene Verteilung *f* [*Statistik*]

trunk highway (Brit.); long-distance road, long-distance highway; trunk road · Fernstraße *f*

trust, affiliated group of enterprises, affiliated group of undertakings · Konzern *m*

trust, confidence · Vertrauen *n*

trust [*A right of property, real or personal, held by one party for the benefit of another*] · Treuhand *f*

trust account, fiduciary account, escrow account · Treuhandkonto *n*, Notar-Anderkonto

trust agency · Treuhandstelle f

trust bequest, trust legacy · Treuhand(fahrnis)vermächtnis n, Treuhandfahrhabevermächtnis

trust breach, breach of trust · Pflichtverletzung f eines Treuhänders, Treubruch m [*Abweichung von den Bestimmungen der Treuhand*]

trust by act of a party · Treuhandverhältnis n kraft Parteihandlung

trust by equitable construction · unechte Treuhand f

trust by implication, implied trust, tacit trust [*A trust raised or created by implication of law; a trust implied or presumed from circumstances*] · stillschweigende Treuhand f

trust by operation of law · Treuhand f kraft gesetzlichen Tatbestandes, Treuhand kraft gesetzlichem Rechtssatz

trust company · Treuhandgesellschaft f

trust composition · Treuhandvergleich m

trust declaration, trust statement, declaration of trust, statement of trust [*The act by which the person who holds the legal title to property or an estate acknowledges and declares that he holds the same in trust to the use of another person or for certain specified purposes*] · einseitige Erklärung f, treuhänderische Übertragung, Kundgabe f eines Treuhandverhältnisses

trust deed, deed of trust [*A deed that establishes a trust*] · Treuhanderrichtungsurkunde f

trust department · Treuhandabteilung f [*einer Bank*]

(trust) donor → (trust) settlor

trustee, factor [*In a strict sense, a "trustee" is one who holds the legal title to property for the benefit of another, while, in a broad sense, the term is sometimes applied to anyone standing in a fiduciary or confidential relation to another, such as agent, attorney, bailee, etc.*] · Treuhänder m, Treuhandverwalter

trustee act, trustee law, trustee statute · Treuhändergesetz n

trustee appointment act, trustee appointment law, trustee appointment statute · Treuhänderernennungsgesetz n

trustee bank · Depotbank f

trustee in bankruptcy, commissioner in bankruptcy, accountant in bankruptcy, assignee in bankruptcy, referee in bankruptcy · (Konkurs)Masse(n)kurator m, Konkursverwalter m, Kurator

trustee law, trustee statute, trustee act · Treuhändergesetz n

trustee law · Treuhänderrecht n

trustee of a charity, charitable trustee · Stiftungstreuhänder m

trustee owner, trustee proprietor · Treuhandeigentümer m, Treuhandeigentumssubjekt n

trustee proprietor, trustee owner · Treuhandeigentümer m, Treuhandeigentumssubjekt n

trustee savings bank [*In Great Britain*] · gemeinnützige Sparkasse f

trusteeship, office of trustee · Treuhänderamt n, Treuhänderstellung f, Treuhänderschaft f

trustee(ship) contract, fiduciary contract, fiducial contract, contract in trust, contract on trust, contract under trusteeship · Treuhandvertrag m, Treuhändervertrag

trustees' savings bank · Privatsparkasse f

trustee statute, trustee act, trustee law · Treuhändergesetz n

trust establishment, establishment of a trust · Treuhanderrichtung f

trust estate, trust property [*The corpus of the property which is the subject of the trust*] · anvertrautes Gut n, anvertrautes Vermögen n, fiduziarisch gebundenes Gut, fiduziarisch gebundenes Vermögen, Treu(hand)gut, Treu(hand)vermögen, Treuhändervermögen, Treuhändergut

trust estate → trust (real) estate

trust for sale (of land) [*An immediate binding trust for sale, whether or not exercisable at the request or with the consent of any person, and with or without a power at discretion to postpone the sale*] · treuhänderischer Verkauf m von Land

trust fund · Sicherungsfonds m

trust income · Stiftungseinkommen n

trust instrument → (legal) trust instrument

trust land(s), (real) estate held in trust, (real) property held in trust, land(s) held in trust, trust (real) estate, trust (real) property · Treuhandgrund(stück) m, (n), Treuhandboden m, Treuhandland n, Treuhandimmobilie f

trust legacy, trust bequest · Treuhand(fahrnis)vermächtnis n, Treuhandfahrhabevermächtnis

trust of personality, personalty trust · Fahrnistreuhand f, Fahrhabetreuhand

trustor, (trust) donor, (trust) settlor [*He supplies the property or consideration for the trust*] · (Treuhand)Begründer m, Treu(hand)geber, Treuhandstifter, (Treuhand)Errichter

trust ownership (of property), trust proprietorship, trust (general) property, fiduciary ownership (of property), fiduciary proprietorship, fiduciary (general) property · fiduziarisches Eigentum *n*, Treuhandeigentum, Treuhändereigentum

trust position, position of trust · Vertrauensstellung *f*

trust property, trust estate [*The corpus of the property which is the subject of the trust*] · anvertrautes Gut *n*, anvertrautes Vermögen *n*, fiduziarisch gebundenes Gut, fiduziarisch gebundenes Vermögen, Treu(hand)gut, Treu(hand)vermögen, Treuhändervermögen, Treuhändergut

trust property → trust ownership (of property)

trust property administration, administration for trust property · Erb(schafts)verwaltung *f* für Treuhandvermögen, Nachlaßverwaltung für Treuhandvermögen

trust (property) for separate use · Treu(hand)gut *n* dessen Früchte an eine bestimmte verheiratete Frau fallen sollen, Treu(hand)vermögen *n* dessen Früchte an eine bestimmte verheiratete Frau fallen sollen

trust proprietorship, trust ownership (of property), trust (general) property · Treuhandeigentum *n*

trust (real) estate, trust (real) property, trust land(s), (real) estate held in trust, (real) property held in trust, land(s) held in trust · Treuhandgrund(stück) *m, (n)*, Treuhandboden *m*, Treuhandland *n*, Treuhandimmobilie *f*

trust receipt · Treuhandquittung *f*

trust relation(ship) · Treuhandverhältnis *n*

trust-res · Treugutgegenstände *m pl*, Treuhandgutgegenstände

trust(s) administration, administration of trust(s) · Treuhandverwaltung *f*

(trust) settlor, trustor, (trust) donor [*He supplies the property or consideration for the trust*] · (Treuhand)Begründer *m*, Treu(hand)geber, Treuhandstifter, (Treuhand)Errichter

trust statement, declaration of trust, statement of trust, trust declaration [*The act by which the person who holds the legal title to property or an estate acknowledges and declares that he holds the same in trust to the use of another person or for certain specified purposes*] · einseitige Erklärung *f*, treuhänderische Übertragung, Kundgabe *f* eines Treuhandverhältnisses

trust subject, subject of the trust · Treuhandgegenstand *m*

trustworthiness → capacity to pay

trust(worth)y, solvent, financially able, sound, capable to pay, able to pay · zahlungsfähig, flüssig, kreditfähig, kreditwürdig

trust(worth)y, credible, faithful · glaubwürdig, glaubhaft, vertrauenswürdig

truthful · wahrheitsgemäß

truth in substance, authenticity · Echtheit *f*, Authentie *f*, Authentizität *f*

truth of the matter · wahrer Sachverhalt *m*

truth value · Wahrheitswert *m*

to try, to rule, to decide [*To settle by authoritative sentence*] · entscheiden [*Rechtsstreit*]

tunnel(l)ing easement, easement of tunnel(l)ing · Tunnelgrunddienstbarkeit *f*

turf area, lawn area · Rasenfläche *f*

to turn a tenant out of his farm, to evict a tenant from his farm, to dispossess · abmei(g)ern

to turn back, to return to, to revert [*With respect to property to go back to and lodge in former owner, who parted with it by creating estate in another which has expired, or to his heirs*] · rückfallen, zurückkehren

turncock · Wasserröhrenwärter *m*

turned over, attorned, transferred · übertragen

turning a tenant out of his farm, evicting a tenant from his farm, dispossession, expulsion from a farm, distraint · Abmei(g)erung *f* [*In den Zeiten der feudalen Grund- und Gutsherrschaft das Recht des Grundherren, einem Bauern die Bauernstelle wegen Pflichtverletzung zu entziehen*]

turning over, transferring · Übertragen *n*

turning over of a mineral right, transfer(ence) of a mineral right · Abgewährung *f*

turning over of licence, turning over of license, licence transfer(ence), license transfer(ence) of licence, transfer(ence) of license · Lizenzübertragung *f*

turning over of ownership (of property), turning over of (general) property, turning over of proprietorship, transfer(ence) of ownership (of property), transfer(ence) of (general) property, transfer(ence) of proprietorship · Eigentumsübertragung *f*

turning over of rights, turning over of interests, transfer(ence) of rights, transfer(ence) of interests · Übertragung *f* von Rechten

turnkey bid, turnkey offer, turnkey tender; all-in (bid) proposal, turnkey (bid) proposal (US), all-in bid, all-in offer, all-in tender · Angebot *n* für Entwurf und Bau

turnkey contract — type of farming (Brit.) 1080

turnkey contract, all-in service contract [*The contractor carries out design and construction*] · Vertrag *m* für schlüsselfertige Erstellung

turnover, stockturn · Umsatz *m*

to turn over, to attorn, to convey, to transfer [*To another money or goods*] · übertragen

turnover decrease, stockturn decrease · Umsatzrückgang *m*

turnover proceeding, stockturn proceeding · Besitznahme *f* des schuldnerischen Vermögens durch den Gläubiger, (Verfahren *n* zur) Inbesitznahme des schuldnerischen Vermögens durch den Gläubiger

turnover ratio, stockturn ratio · Umschlaggeschwindigkeit *f* einer Anlage von Wertpapieren innerhalb eines Jahres

turnover tax, stockturn tax · Umsatzsteuer *f*

turnpike(-gate) · Drehkreuz *n*

turnpike highway (US); toll road, toll highway · Gebührenstraße *f*, Wegegeldstraße; Mautstraße [*Österreich*]

turnpike theorem · Verhältnis *n* zwischen von-Neumannschem Wachstumspfad und optimalen Wachstum

turnpike toll (US); motorway toll (Brit.) · Autobahngebühr *f*

turnpike trust · Chausseeverwaltung *f* [*englisches Grundsteuersystem*]

tutela usufructuaria [*Latin*] · Nutzungsvormundschaft *f*

twelve-day term, term of twelve days · Zwölftagefrist *f*

twenty-eight days, lunar month · Mondmonat *m*

twin cities, twin towns · Doppelstädte *fpl*, Zwillingsstädte, Städtepaar *n*

twin citizenship, dual nationality, dual citizenship, double nationality, double citizenship, twin nationality · Doppelstaatsangehörigkeit *f*, Doppelnationalität *f*

twin core, double core, dual core · Doppelkern *m*

twin effect, dual effect, double effect · Doppelwirkung *f*

twin farm, double settlement, double farm, twin settlement · Doppel(an)sied(e)lung *f*, Doppelhof *m*, Zwiehof *m*

twin-level street → two-level street

twin nationality, twin citizenship, dual nationality, dual citizenship, double nationality, double citizenship · Doppelstaatsangehörigkeit *f*, Doppelnationalität *f*

twinning of cities, twinning of towns, affiliation · Verschwisterung *f*

twins · Zwillinge *mpl*

twin settlement, twin farm, double settlement, double farm · Doppel(an)sied(e)lung *f*, Doppelhof *m*, Zwiehof *m*

twin towns, twin cities · Doppelstädte *fpl*, Zwillingsstädte, Städtepaar *n*

twin-unit caravan · Doppelwohnwagen *m*

twin working shift, double working shift, dual working shift · Doppel(arbeits)schicht *f*

two-column account · zweispaltiges Konto *n*

two-dwelling family house; cottage-flat (Brit.); two-family house · Zweifamilienhaus *n*, Zweiwohnungshaus, Doppelfamilienhaus, Doppelwohnungshaus

two-dwelling row house, two-family row house · Zweifamilienreihenhaus *n*, Zweiwohnungsreihenhaus

two-family house, two-dwelling family house; cottage-flat (Brit.) · Zweifamilienhaus *n*, Zweiwohnungshaus, Doppelfamilienhaus, Doppelwohnungshaus

two-family row house, two-dwelling row house · Zweifamilienreihenhaus *n*, Zweiwohnungsreihenhaus

two-field husbandry, two-field farming, two-field system · Zweifelderwirtschaft *f*

twofold · zweifach

two-generation household · Zweigenerationenhaushalt *m*

two-level street, dual-level street, double-level street, twin-level street · Stadtstraße *f* mit zwei Ebenen

two-month period (of time) · Zweimonatsfrist *f*

two-person game · Zwei-Personen-Spiel *n*

two-person household · Zweipersonenhaushalt *m*

type of construction, type of building · Bauart *f* [*Die Art in der Baustoffe und/ oder Bauteile zusammengefügt sind*]

type of coverage, coverage type · Bauweise *f*, Bebauungsart *f*, Bebauungsweise; Überbauungsweise, Überbauungsart [*Schweiz*] [*Benennung einer Bebauung nach Größe und Form der Baukörper. „Bauweise" ist eine planungsrechtliche, nicht dem Bauordnungsrecht zugehörige Benennung*]

type of damages, type of compensation, type of indemnity, type of indemnification · Entschädigungsart *f*, Schadenersatzart

type of farming (Brit.); agricultural system (US) · Landwirtschaftssystem *n*, Agrarsystem

type of (land) use zoning, type of zoning · (bauliche) Nutzungsart *f,* Baunutzungsart

type of settlement (of accounts) · Abrechnungsart *f*

type of use · Benutzungsart *f,* Gebrauchsart

type of zoning, type of (land) use zoning · (bauliche) Nutzungsart *f,* Baunutzungsart

typical acknowledged experience, usual factum, customary factum · typischer Sachverhalt *m*

U

UATP, universal air travel plan · Flugreisekreditverfahren *n*

ubiquitous industry, city serving industry, town serving industry · stadtführende Industrie *f*

ubiquity through delivery · Ubiquität *f* durch Versand

ultimate cluster · Klumpen *m* letzter Ordnung [*Statistik*]

ultimate court of appeal, last resort · höchste Instanz *f,* letzte Instanz

ultimate fact, ultimate situation · Tatbestandmerkmal *n,* Sachverhaltmerkmal, Sachlagemerkmal

ultimate ownership (of property), strict ownership (of property), direct dominion; nuda proprietas, dominium feudi [*Latin*] [*The nominal or bare right of ownership remaining in an owner who has granted the exclusive right of enjoyment and of limited or unlimited disposition over the thing to another person*] · Obereigentum *n* (der Krone), Eigentumsrecht *n* des Leh(e)n(s)herrn, Leh(e)n(s)herrlichkeit *f* [*Das Eigentum an Land ruht in England in allen Fällen unbedingt und ausnahmslos beim Thron. Diese Tatsache ist eine der wichtigsten Unterschiede zwischen dem englischen Mobiliar- und Immobiliarsachenrecht und findet ihren Ausdruck in der Rechtsdoktrin: "Land is, and goods are not, the subject of tenure"*]

ultimate situation, ultimate fact · Tatbestandmerkmal *n,* Sachverhaltmerkmal, Sachlagemerkmal

ultra vires [*Latin*]; beyond the power(s), beyond the capacity, beyond the capacities · gewaltüberschreitend, hoheit(s)überschreitend, kompetenzüberschreitend, machtüberschreitend

ultra-vires principle, principle of ultra vires · Ultravires-Grundsatz *m,* Ultravires-Prinzip *n*

umbrella fund, managed fund, mixed bond, selective bond, three-way fund, balanced bond · gemischter Versicherungsfonds *m*

umbrella fund certificate, balanced bond certificate, three-way fund certificate, managed fund certificate, mixed bond certificate · gemischtes Versicherungsfondszertifikat *n*

umland; suburban land (US); peripheral land, surrounding land, surrounding area, external service area [*Sometimes, by local usage also called "landed estate" and "landed property" as distinguished from land in a city*] · äußeres Ergänzungsgebiet *n,* Vorortzone *f,* Umland *n,* Umgelände *n*

umland area; suburban territory, suburban area (US); peripheral area, peripheral territory, umland territory · Umlandgebiet *n*

umland city, peripheral town, peripheral city, umland town · Umlandstadt *f*

umland community; suburb(an place) (US), peripheral community · Umlandgemeinde *f*

umland community development; suburban development (US); peripheral community development · Umlandgemeindeentwick(e)lung *f*

umland community district; suburban district (US); peripheral community district · Umlandgemeindebezirk *m*

umland community expansion; suburban expansion (US); peripheral community expansion · Umlandgemeindeerweiterung *f*

umland community group; suburban group (US); peripheral community group · Umlandgemeindegruppe *f*

umland community growth; suburban growth (US); peripheral community growth · Umlandgemeindewachstum *n*

umland community house; suburban house (US); peripheral community house · Umlandgemeindehaus *n*

umland community inhabitant; suburban inhabitant (US); peripheral community inhabitant · Umlandgemeindeeinwohner *m*

umland community migration; suburban migration (US); peripheral community migration · Umlandwanderung *f*

umland community pattern, peripheral community scheme, umland community scheme; suburban pattern, suburban scheme (US); peripheral community pattern · Umlandgemeindemuster *n,* Umlandgemeindeschema *n*

umland community population; suburban population (US); peripheral community population · Umlandgemeindebevölkerung f

umland community residential territory; suburban residential area, suburban residential territory (US); peripheral community residential area, umland community residential area, peripheral community residential territory · Umlandgemeindewohn(ungs)gebiet n

umland community ring; suburban ring (US); peripheral community ring · Umlandgemeindering m

umland community scheme; suburban pattern, suburban scheme (US); peripheral community pattern, umland community pattern, peripheral community scheme · Umlandgemeindemuster n, Umlandgemeindeschema n

umland community school; suburban school (US); peripheral community school · Umlandgemeindeschule f

umland community society; suburban society (US); peripheral community society · Umlandgemeindegesellschaft f

umland community traffic; suburban traffic (US); peripheral community traffic · Umlandgemeindeverkehr m

umland population · Umlandbevölkerung f

umland territory, umland area; suburban territory, suburban area (US); peripheral area, peripheral territory · Umlandgebiet n

umland town, umland city, peripheral town, peripheral city · Umlandstadt f

umland use; suburban land use (US); peripheral land use, external land use, surrounding land use, service area use · Umlandnutzung f

umpire; oversman [Scots law]; imperator [Latin]; presiding arbiter [This term is rarely used], presiding arbitrator, presiding referee, impier · dritter Schiedsrichter m, Obmann [Bei einer Dreierbesetzung des Schiedsgerichts]

un(ab)alienable possession, nondisposable possession, possession held in mortmain · Tothandbesitz m, unveräußerlicher Besitz, unveräußerbarer Besitz

unable, incapable, uncapable · unfähig, nicht fähig

unable of acting, uncapable of acting, incapable of acting · handlungsunfähig, nicht handlungsfähig

unaccompanied with the possession of anything corporeal · nicht mit dem Besitz irgendeines körperlichen Gegenstandes verbunden

unacquainted with, miscognizant, ignorant of · nichtwissend, unwissend

unaddressed printed papers, direct-mail shot · Postwurfsendung f

unadvanced member, investing member, (share) investor [A member having not obtained advances from the building society but simply participating in the profits arising from the interest paid by the borrower] · nichtborgendes Mitglied n [Bausparkasse]

unallocated land project, white land project · Außen(bereich)vorhaben n

unallocated land(s), site without notation, white land(s) [Land in agricultural or other mainly open use on which, for the period of the plan, the present uses are to remain for the most part undisturbed] · Außenbereich m

unanimity, consension, consensus of opinion, unity of opinion, agreement of opinion, consent of opinion · Meinungsgleichheit f, Einstimmigkeit

unapproachable, approachless · nicht ansatzfähig

unascertained · unausgesucht [Güter]

unascertained goods · Gattungswaren fpl, Genuswaren

unassisted, nonsubsidized · nichtgefördert, frei [Wohn(ungs)bau]

unattached man, noncollegiate man [College] · Nichtangeschlossene m

unauthorized · unbefugt

unauthorized female person, nonauthorized female person · Unbefugte f

unauthorized male person, nonauthorized male person · Unbefugte m

unauthorized person, nonauthorized person · unbefugte Person f

unavoidable · unabwendbar, unvermeidlich

unbalanced (building land) improvement · ungleichgewichtige Baureifmachung f, ungleichgewichtige Erschließung, unausgewogene Baureifmachung, unausgewogene Erschließung

unbalanced growth · unausgewogenes Wachstum n, ungleichgewichtiges Wachstum

unbiassed · erwartungstreu, nichtverzerrend, frei von systematischen Fehlern, tendenzfrei [Statistik]

unbiassed estimating equation · nichtverzerrende Schätzgleichung f, erwartungstreue Schätzgleichung, tendenzfreie Schätzgleichung

unbiassed estimator · nichtverzerrende Schätzfunktion f, erwartungstreue Schätzfunktion, tendenzfreie Schätzfunktion [Statistik]

unbroken, continuous, uninterrupted · laufend, ständig, ununterbrochen, stetig

unbroken right of redemption, unbroken right to redeem, uninterrupted right to redeem, uninterrupted right of redemption, continuous right of redemption, continuous right to redeem · laufendes Auslösungsrecht *n*, laufendes Einlösungsrecht, ständiges Auslösungsrecht, ständiges Einlösungsrecht, stetiges Auslösungsrecht, stetiges Einlösungsrecht, ununterbrochenes Auslösungsrecht, ununterbrochenes Einlösungsrecht

unbuilt, not built (up)on, non built-up, open, uncovered · frei, nichtbebaut, unbebaut; unüberbaut, nicht überbaut [*Schweiz*]

unbuilt land, open land, uncovered land, land not built upon · freier Boden *m*, freier Grund, unbebauter Boden, nichtbebauter Boden, unbebautes Land *n*, freies Land, nichtbebautes Land, unbebauter Grund, nichtbebauter Grund

unbuilt plot, open plot, uncovered (land) parcel, unbuilt (land) parcel, open (land) parcel, uncovered parcel of land, unbuilt parcel of land, open parcel of land, (land) parcel not built upon, parcel of land not built upon, uncovered plot · Feldgrundstück *n*, freies Grundstück, nichtbenutztes Grundstück, unbebautes Grundstück

unburdened, unencumbered, unincumbered, clear, perfect, free from load(s), unloaded, not imperfect, without a burden, without a load, burdenless, free from encumbrance(s), free from charge(s), free from incumbrance(s), free from burden(s), uncharged · entschuldet, lastenfrei, (dinglich) unbelastet, (dinglich) nicht belastet

to unbury, to disinter, to exhume · exhumieren

unburying, exhumation, disinterment · Exhumierung *f*

uncalled capital · nicht eingefordertes Gesellschaftskapital *n*

uncapable, unable, incapable · unfähig, nicht fähig

uncapable of acting, incapable of acting, unable of acting · handlungsunfähig, nicht handlungsfähig

uncertain contract, aleatory contract, risky contract · zufallabhängiger Vertrag *m*, ungewisser Vertrag, riskanter Vertrag

uncertain meaning, doubtful meaning, ambiguity, obscure meaning, doubtfulness of meaning, uncertainty of meaning, obscurity of meaning · unklare Bedeutung *f*, Zweideutigkeit *f*

uncertainty effect · Ungewißheitswirkung *f*

uncertainty (of law) · Rechtsunsicherheit *f*

uncertainty of meaning, obscurity of meaning, uncertain meaning, doubtful meaning, ambiguity, obscure meaning, doubtfulness of meaning · unklare Bedeutung *f*, Zweideutigkeit *f*

uncertificated bankrupt · Gemeinschuldner *m* ohne Entlastungsschein, Gemeinschuldner ohne Entlastungsattest, Gemeinschuldner ohne Entlastungsbescheinigung

uncharged, unburdened, unencumbered, unincumbered, clear, perfect, free from load(s), unloaded, not imperfect, without a burden, without a load, burdenless, free from encumbrance(s), free from charge(s), free from incumbrance(s), free from burden(s) · entschuldet, lastenfrei, (dinglich) unbelastet, (dinglich) nicht belastet

unclaimed land · unbeanspruchtes Land *n*

unclaimed wreck, derelict, ship deserted at sea · herrenloses Wrack *n*

uncollectible, bad, irrecoverable, unobtainable, desparate, hopeless, non collectable, noncollectible, nonrecoverable, nonobtainable, uncollectable, unrecoverable · nicht beitreibbar, nicht einziehbar, nicht eintreibbar, uneinziehbar, uneintreibbar, uneinbringlich, unbeitreibbar [*Schuld*]

unconditional, absolute, total, unrestricted, unlimited, irrebuttable · absolut, unbeschränkt, uneingeschränkt, unbedingt, unbegrenzt, bedingungslos

unconditional, absolute, complete · bedingungslos, absolut, vollständig

unconditional discharge · nicht bedingte Entlastung *f*

unconfirmed · unbestätigt

unconfirmed letter of credit, revocable letter of credit, revokable letter of credit, letter of credit at will · Akkreditiv *n* auf Widerruf, Kreditbrief *m* auf Widerruf, widerruflicher Kreditbrief, widerrufliches Akkreditiv

unconstitutional · verfassungswidrig

unconstitutionality · Verfassungswidrigkeit *f*

un-co-ordinated (physical) development, un-co-ordinated binding development, un-co-ordinated binding physical development, un-co-ordinated physical binding development · ungeordnete Bebauung *f*, ungeordnetes Bebauen *n* (einer Fläche); ungeordnete Überbauung, ungeordnetes Überbauen (einer Fläche) [*Schweiz*]

uncorrected · ausbesserungsbedürftig

to uncover [*opening*] · aufdecken [*Öffnung*]

uncovered, unbuilt, not built (up)on, non built-up, open · frei, nichtbebaut, unbebaut; unüberbaut [*Schweiz*]

uncovered area · Freifläche f [bebautes Grundstück]

uncovered land, land not built upon, unbuilt land, open land · freier Boden m, freier Grund, unbebauter Boden, nichtbebauter Boden, unbebautes Land n, freies Land, nichtbebautes Land, unbebauter Grund, nichtbebauter Grund m

uncovered (land) parcel, uncovered parcel of land, (land) parcel not built upon, parcel of land not built upon, uncovered plot, unbuilt plot, open plot · nichtbebautes Grundstück n, unbebautes Grundstück, freies Grundstück, nichtbenutztes Grundstück, Feldgrundstück

uncovered pound, not covered pound, pound-overt, open pound · nicht eingefriedetes Grundstück n, uneingefriedetes Grundstück [Es wird der Vollstreckung unterworfen]

uncovering [opening] · Aufdecken n [Öffnung]

uncrossed cheque, open cheque (Brit.); open check, uncrossed check (US) · Barscheck m, Inhaberscheck, offener Scheck

uncultivated land; novale, frusca terra [Latin]; fallow land, idle land, tract of fallow (land), waste · Brachflur f, Brachland n, Brachacker m, Brachfeld n

undated and unstamped transfer · Blankotransfer m

undecided, contentious, unsettled, controversial, moot, adversary, contested [Litigated between adverse parties] · streitig, strittig

un(der)absorbed burden · Fixkostenunterdeckung f, Festkostenunterdeckung

under age, within age · unmündig

to underbid, to undercut, to undersell · unterbieten

underbidding, undercutting, underselling · Unterbieten n

to undercut, to undersell, to underbid · unterbieten

undercutting, underselling, underbidding · Unterbieten n

underemployed · unterbeschäftigt

under-feudatory, vassal of a vassal, arriere vassal · Aftervasall m

undergraduate · Junior m [Collegemitglied]

underground cavity · unterirdischer Hohlraum m

underground line · unterirdische Leitung f

underhand will · privatschriftliches Testament n

underimprovement (of building land) [Improvement that is not the highest and best use for the site on which it is placed by reason of being smaller in size or cost(s) that one that would bring the site to its highest and best use] · Unterbaureifmachung f, Untererschließung

to underlease · unterverpachten, afterverpachten, nachverpachten

underleaseholder, undertermor, subtermor, sub-leaseholder, sublessee, subtenant (of land), underlessee, undertenant (of land) · After(boden)pächter m, Unter(boden)pächter, Nach(boden)pächter

to underlet, to sublet [premises] · abvermieten, untervermieten, aftervermieten, nachvermieten, weitervermieten

underletter, subletter · Abvermieter m, Untervermieter, Aftervermieter, Weitervermieter

underletting, subletting · Abvermieten n, Weitervermieten, Untervermieten, Aftervermieten, Untervermietung f, Abvermietung, Weitervermietung, Aftervermietung

under oath · unter Eid

under-occupation · Unterbelegung f [Wohnung]

underpayment · Unterbezahlung f

underpopulated · unterbevölkert

underpopulation · Unterbevölkerung f

underresearched · untererforscht

underrun · Unterschreitung f

underrun of building sum, underrun of construction sum, underrun of production sum · Bausummenunterschreitung f, Herstellungssummenunterschreitung

underrun of minimum rate · Mindestsatz-Unterschreitung f

under seal gesiegelt

to undersell, to underbid, to undercut · unterbieten

underselling, underbidding, undercutting · Unterbieten n

under special law · sondergesetzlich

understanding · Abrede f, Absprache f, gemeinsame Auffassung f

understanding · Begriffsvermögen n

understeward (of manor), deputy steward (of manor) · Unteramtmann m, Untervogt, Unter-(Guts)Verwalter, Unter-Gutsschulze

under study [area] · beplant [Gebiet]

to undertake, to promise · versprechen

undertaker · Unternehmer m

undertaker — unduly influenced

undertaker · Begräbnisbesorger m, Bestatter

undertaker causing nuisance [e.g. a public utility]; person causing nuisance · Beeinträchtigende m, Störer, Schädiger

undertaking; assumpsit [Latin] [obsolete]; promise · (Leistungs)Versprechen n, Naturalversprechen

undertaking, enterprise · Betrieb m, Unternehmen n, Unternehmung f

undertaking [The act of one who undertakes some task] · Vorhaben n [Nicht im Sinne zur Errichung eines Bauwerkes]

undertaking contract, enterprise contract · Unternehmensvertrag m

undertaking financing, enterprise financing · Unternehmensfinanzierung f

undertaking value, enterprise value · Unternehmenswert m

undertenancy, subtenancy · Untermietverhältnis n

under the parental roof · im elterlichen Hause

under trusteeship, on trust, fiduciary, in trust, fiducial · zur treuen Hand, treuhänderisch

undervaluation · Unterbewertung f

undervalue · Unterwert m

under-wed(d) lecgan [Anglo-Saxon]; vadium ponere · Pfandbestellung f wegen Schuld [Englisches Pfandrecht im Mittelalter]

underwood, copse, coppice; sub-boscus [Latin]; woody undergrowth · Niederwald m, Holzung f, Unterholz n

to underwrite · übernehmen von Aktien zu einem festen Preis

underwriter · Übernehmer m

underwriter · Assekuradeur m in der Seeversicherung

underwriting · Versicherung f der Aktiengesellschaftsgründer über die Eventualität des Nichtunterbringens der Aktien

underwriting syndicate, (issue) syndicate · (Emissions)Konsortium n, (Emissions)Syndikat n

underwriting syndicate loan, (issue) syndicate loan · (Emissions)Konsortiumsanleihe f, (Emissions)Syndikatanleihe

underwriting system · Emissionsmethode f mit Garantieübernahme für den Erfolg

to underzone · (baulich) mindernutzen

underzoned · (baulich) mindergenutzt

underzoning · (bauliche) Mindernutzung f

undeveloped · nicht entwickelt, unterentwickelt

undeveloped land, raw land [Land in parcels sufficiently large enough for the planning of subdivisions, presently used for agriculture or woodland] · Bauerwartungsland n, Rohbauland, unerschlossenes Baugelände n

undischarged · unentlastet

undisclosed agency, secret agency · mittelbare Vertretung f, verdeckte Vertretung, unerkannte Vertretung

undisclosed agent, secret agent · mittelbarer Vertreter m, verdeckter Vertreter, unerkannter Vertreter [Er ist im eigenen Namen tätig ohne daß ihm die Rechte des Vertretenen fiduziarisch übertragen sind]

undisclosed partner, secret partner [Is one whose connection with the firm is not disclosed. He may be active in the conduct of the business, and if his connection with the firm becomes disclosed, third parties may hold him liable, like and any other general partner] · mittelbarer Gesellschafter m, verdeckter Gesellschafter, mittelbarer Teilhaber m, verdeckter Teilhaber, unerkannter Gesellschafter, unerkannter Teilhaber

undisguised, open, notorious · offenkundig

undistinguishable confusion, undistinguishable commixture, undistinguishable intermixture · untrennbare Vermischung f

undistinguishableness · Untrennbarkeit f [Vermengung; Vermischung]

undistinguishably (inter)mixed · untrennbar vermischt

undistrainable, priveleged against distress, privileged against distraint · unpfändbar

undistributed cost(s), accumulated cost(s) · angesammelte Kosten f, unverteilte Kosten, aufgelaufene Kosten

undistributed interest, accrued interest, run up interest, accumulated interest · aufgelaufene Zinsen f, Stückzinsen f, angehäufte Zinsen, angewachsene Zinsen, aufgelaufte Zinsen, zugewachsene Zinsen, Vorzugszinsen

undivided · ungeteilt

undivided right · unteilbares Recht n

undue, inequitable, unjust, unfair · unbillig, ungerecht(fertigt), unlauter

undue hardship · große Härte f

undue influence · ungehörige Beeinflussung f

undulation (of the ground), accidement · Bodenwelle f, (Gelände)Welle

unduly influenced, unfair influenced, biassed · voreingenommen, parteiisch, befangen

unearned betterment → unearned increment

unearned gain, unearned profit · unverdienter Profit *m*, unverdienter Gewinn *m*

unearned income, income from possession, investment income · Besitzrente *f*, Besitzeinkommen *n*, Zuwachsrente, fundiertes Einkommen

unearned increment, unearned betterment, unearned increase in value, unearned value increase [*1. Addition or increase in value said to be "unearned" because it results from population increases, community expansions, greater desirability, and more active market in real estate, development of land, and so forth." 2. Increase in value of real estate due to no effort on the part of the owner but often due to increase in population*] · unverdiente Wertsteigerung *f*, unverdiente Werterhöhung, unverdienter Wertzuwachs *m*

unearned profit, unearned gain · unverdienter Profit *m*, unverdienter Gewinn *m*

unearthing law, law of unearthing, · Ausgrabungsrecht *n* [*Zur Erhaltung völkischen Geschichts- und Überlieferungsgutes*]

unearthing law, unearthing statute, unearthing act, statute of unearthing, law of unearthing, act of unearthing · Ausgrabungsgesetz *n*

uneconomical · überhöht [*Angebotspreis; Vertragspreis*]

uneconomical, unprofitable · gewinnlos, nicht rentabel, profitlos, unwirtschaftlich, nicht gewinnbringend

uneffectiveness · Unwirksamkeit *f*

unemployed, jobless · arbeitslos

unemployed female person, jobless female person · Erwerbslose *f*, Arbeitslose

unemployed male person, jobless male person · Erwerbsloser *m*, Arbeitsloser

unemployed person, jobless person · erwerbslose Person *f*, arbeitslose Person

unemployment · Arbeitslosigkeit *f*, Erwerbslosigkeit *f*

unemployment area, unemployment territory · Erwerbslosengebiet *n*, Arbeitslosengebiet

unemployment assistance · Arbeitslosenhilfe *f*, Erwerbslosenhilfe

unemployment compensation tax · Arbeitslosenversicherungsabgabe *f*, Erwerbslosenversicherungsabgabe

unemployment insurance · Arbeitslosenversicherung *f*, Erwerbslosenversicherung *f*

unemployment rate, rate of unemployment · Arbeitslosenzahl *f*, Erwerbslosenzahl *f* [*Fehlbenennungen: Arbeitslosenziffer f, Erwerbslosenziffer*]

unemployment relief, unemployment benefit, donation money, idle money, unemployment compensation, compensation of unemployment, relief of unemployment, out-of-work-pay, out-of-work-benefit · Arbeitslosengeld *n*, Arbeitslosenunterstützung *f*, Erwerbslosengeld *n*, Erwerbslosenunterstützung

unemployment territory, unemployment area · Erwerbslosengebiet *n*, Arbeitslosengebiet

unenacted law · ungesetztes Recht *n*

unencumbered, unincumbered, clear, perfect, free from load(s), unloaded, not imperfect, without a burden, without a load, burdenless, free from encumbrance(s), free from charge(s), free from incumbrance(s), free from burden(s), uncharged, unburdened · entschuldet, lastenfrei, (dinglich) unbelastet, (dinglich) nicht belastet

unenforceable · (prozessual) unerzwingbar, unklagbar

unenforceable contract, agreement of imperfect obligation · materiell unantastbarer Vertrag *m*

unequal probability axiom, axiom of unequal probability · Axiom *n* der ungleichen Wahrscheinlichkeit, ungleiches Wahrscheinlichkeitsaxiom

unexecutable · unvollstreckbar

unexpected balance of established development value · nicht ausgeglichener Betrag *m* an festgesetztem Entwick(e)lungswert

unexpired cost(s) [*Those cost(s) which are applicable to the production of future revenues*] · Aufwand *m* aber noch nicht Kosten

unexplored region · unerforschte Region *f*

unexposed person · nichtausgesetzte Person *f* [*Eine einer Werbung nicht ausgesetzte Person*]

unfair, undue, inequitable, unjust · unbillig, ungerecht(fertigt), unlauter

unfair competition, unlawful dealing, unlawful competition, passing off, unfair dealing · unlauterer Wettbewerb *m*

unfair dealing, unfair competition, unlawful dealing, unlawful competition, passing off · unlauterer Wettbewerb *m*

unfair influenced, biassed, unduly influenced · voreingenommen, parteiisch, befangen

unfair trade practices · unlautere Handelspraktiken *fpl*, unlautere Wettbewerbspraktiken

unfavorable (financial) leverage · negative Hebelwirkung *f* [*Der Grenzsachzins ist kleiner als der Grenzmarktzins*]

unfenced · uneingezäunt

unfit · nicht geeignet, ungeeignet

unfit dwelling unit, insanitary dwelling unit, insanitary living unit, unfit living unit, insanitary housing unit, unfit housing unit (US); insanitary dwelling, unfit dwelling · Verfallswohnung *f*

unfit for work, disable (for work), incapable of working · arbeitsunfähig

unfit house, insanitary house · Verfallshaus *n*

unfit to live in, unfit for (human) habitation, unfit for (human) occupation, unsuitable for (human) habitation, unsuitable for (human) occupation, un(in)habitable, not (in)habitable · unbewohnbar, unbelegbar

unfitness · Nichteignung *f*

unfitness notice, unfitness notification · Nichteignungsbescheid *m*

unfixed · nicht eingebaut [*Baustoff*]

unforeseen, occasional, accidental, by chance, fortuitous · unvorhergesehen

unforeseen site accident · unvorhergesehener Bauunfall *m*

unforested, nonforested · unbewaldet, waldlos

unformulated rule; true rule [*obsolete*] · unausgesprochene Regel *f* [*Sie ist einer Entscheidung durch Auslegung zu entnehmen*]

unfortunate necessity; necessitas culpabilis [*Latin*]; culpable necessity [*A necessity which, while it excuses the act done under its compulsion, does not leave the doer entirely free from blame*] · schuldhafter Aggressivnotstand *m*

unfounded · unbegründet

unfree, customary, at (the) will (of the lord), non-free · unfrei, nichtfrei, zugestanden, prekarisch, auf Ruf und Widerruf, willkürlich aufkündbar [*Leh(e)n*]

unfree fee (tenure) → copyhold

unfree (feodal) tenement → copyhold

unfree (feodal) tenure → copyhold

unfree fief → copyhold

unfree tenancy → copyhold

unfree tenement → copyhold

unfree tenure → copyhold

unfulfilled, unperformed · unerfüllt, ungeleistet

unfunded · nicht ewig [*Anleihe*]

ungeared (assurance) fund · fremdmittelloser Versicherungsfonds *m*

ungoverned violence · rohe Gewalt *f*

unhealthy, insanitary · ungesund [*z. B. Wohnung*]

unification · Vereinheitlichung *f*

unification of law(s), law unification · Rechtsvereinheitlichung *f*

unified mortgage · Einheitshypothek *f*

uniform act, uniform statute, uniform law · Mustergesetz *n*, Einheitsgesetz, vereinheitlichtes Gesetz, Modellgesetz

uniform building code, uniform construction code · Einheitsbauordnung *f*

uniform cultivation of land, compulsory crop-raising under the common field system, community-regulated cultivation, community-regulated work [*Compulsion on all the members of a village community to raise the same crops, so that all should sow and reap at the same time*] · Flurzwang *m*

uniform distribution, rectangular distribution · Rechteckverteilung *f*, gleichförmige Verteilung, Gleichverteilung [*Statistik*]

uniformity of process act, uniformity of process law, uniformity of process statute · Gesetz *n* über Verfahrensgleichförmigkeit

uniform law, uniform act, uniform statute · Mustergesetz *n*, Einheitsgesetz, vereinheitlichtes Gesetz, Modellgesetz

uniform lawmaking, uniform legislation · vereinheitlichte Gesetzgebung *f*

uniform private law · Einheitsprivatrecht *n*

uniform region · homogene Region *f*

uniform sales act · Gesetz *n* zur Vereinheitlichung des Güterkaufrechts

uniform statute, uniform law, uniform act · Mustergesetz *n*, Einheitsgesetz, vereinheitlichtes Gesetz, Modellgesetz

uniform wills act-foreign probated · Gesetz *n* über außerhalb des Staates bestätigte Testamente

to unify · vereinheitlichen

unilateral, one-way · einseitig

unilateral contract, contract of benevolence, deed poll, contract without consideration, gratuitous contract, nude contract, one-sided contract · einseitiger Vertrag *m*, Vertrag ohne Gegenleistung

unilateral error, one-way error · einseitiger Fehler *m*

unilateral exchange, one-way exchange [*A gives something exchangeable to B, but B gives nothing exchangeable to A*] · einseitige Übertragung *f*

unilateral mistake, one-way mistake · einseitiger Irrtum m

unilateral obligation, one-sided obligation, requirement · Auflage f, einseitige Verpflichtung f

unilateral promise, gratuitous promise, promise of benevolence, promise without consideration, one-sided promise, nude promise · einseitiges (Leistungs)Versprechen n, einseitiges Naturalversprechen, (Leistungs)Versprechen ohne Gegenleistung, Naturalversprechen ohne Gegenleistung

unimodal · eingipf(e)lig [*Statistik*]

unimpeachable of equitable waste, unimpeachable for equitable waste · nicht pflichtig für unbillige Substanz(ver)änderung

unimpeachable of waste, unimpeachable for waste · nicht substanz(ver)änderungspflichtig

unimproved, not improved, raw · unfertig, (bau)unreif, unerschlossen, roh, unverbessert, nicht baureif

unincorporated area · ausmärkisches Gebiet n, gemeindefreies Gebiet n

unincorporated community · nicht inkorporierte Gemeinde f, nicht inkorporierte Kommune f [*Gemeinde ohne Status einer Gebietskörperschaft*]

unincorporated place · (An)Sied(e)lung f nicht mit Stadtrecht versehen, (An)Sied(e)lung ohne Stadtrecht, stadtrechtlose (An)Sied(e)lung

unincumbered, clear, perfect, free from load(s), unloaded, not imperfect, without a burden, without a load, burdenless, free from encumbrance(s), free from charge(s), free from incumbrance(s), free from burden(s), uncharged, unburdened, unencumbered · entschuldet, lastenfrei, (dinglich) unbelastet, (dinglich) nicht belastet

un(in)habitable, not (in)habitable, unfit to live in, unfit for (human) habitation, unfit for (human) occupation, unsuitable for (human) habitation, unsuitable for (human) occupation · unbewohnbar, unbelegbar

uninsurable · unversicherbar

uninsured · nicht versichert, unversichert

uninterrupted, unbroken, continuous · laufend, ständig, ununterbrochen, stetig

uninterrupted enjoyment · ununterbrochener Genuß m

uninterrupted right to redeem, uninterrupted right of redemption, continuous right of redemption, continuous right to redeem, unbroken right of redemption, unbroken right to redeem · laufendes Auslösungsrecht n, laufendes Einlösungsrecht, ständiges Auslösungsrecht, ständiges Einlösungsrecht, stetiges Auslösungsrecht, stetiges Einlösungsrecht, ununterbrochenes Auslösungsrecht, ununterbrochenes Einlösungsrecht

union · Verband m

union → (poor law) union

union assessment committee → (poor law) union assessment committee

union contract · Tarifvertrag m

unionized · gewerkschaftlich

union of communities, common · Kommunalverband m, Gemeindeverband

union of engineers, engineering union · Ingenieurverband m

union of heavy construction contractors · Tiefbauunternehmerverband m

union of isolated farms, union of single farms · Einzelhofverband m

union of single farms, union of isolated farms · Einzelhofverband m

union of workers, workers' union, union of workmen, workmen's union · Arbeiterverband m

union-set rate · Gewerkschaftssatz m

union station · gemeinsamer Bahnhof m, gemeinschaftlicher Bahnhof [*In den USA. Ein von mehreren Eisenbahngesellschaften gemeinsam benutzter Bahnhof*]

union territory · Verbandsgebiet n

union wage bond [*Bond given by the contractor to a union, guaranteeing that he will pay union scale wages to employees and remit to the union any welfare funds withheld*] · Lohngarantie f

uniqueness · Einzigartigkeit f

unit [*USA*] · Referat n

unit area [*The smallest homogeneous geographic unit that can be used for measuring and recording the data of land use*] · Raumschaft f, Großraum m

unit area act, unit area statute, unit area law · Großraumgesetz n, Raumschaftgesetz

unitary domicil(e), unitary settlement, unitary (place of) abode, unitary place of residence, unitary permanent residence, unitary legal home · gemeinsamer Wohnsitz m, gemeinsamer Wohnort, gemeinschaftlicher Wohnsitz, gemeinschaftlicher Wohnort, gemeinsamer (gesetzlicher) Aufenthaltsort m, gemeinschaftlicher (gesetzlicher) Aufenthaltsort [*beider Ehepartner*]

unit bank · Einzelbank f [*Eine Bank ohne Zweigstellen*]

unit-community input-output exchange · Einsatz-Ausstoß-Austausch *m* zwischen Gemeinde und Gemeindeeinheit

unit cost(s) theory · Theorie *f* der minimalen Nutzleistungskosten

unit defined on the basis of cultural criteria, unit defined on the basis of human criteria, cultural area · Kulturraum *m*

unit defined on the basis of physical criteria, natural area · Naturraum *m*

united-area method of land classification · Einheitsflächenmethode *f*

unitedly, (in) common, together, joint(ly) · gemeinsam, gemeinschaftlich, miteinander, gemeinheitlich, verbunden, solidarisch, zusammen

United States Code [*USA*] · Bundesgesetzblatt *n* Teil III [*Bundesrepublik Deutschland*]

United States League of Local Building and Loan Associations · Verband *m* amerikanischer örtlicher Bausparkassen

United States Statutes at Large [*USA*] · Bundesgesetzblatt *n* Teil I [*Bundesrepublik Deutschland*]

United States Supreme Court · Oberstes Bundesgericht *n* der USA, Höchstes Bundesgericht der USA

united workshop · Mietwerkstatt *f*

unit imprint · Druckvermerk *m* [*Kartographie*]

uniting, consolidating, fusioning · Konsolidieren *n*, Fusionieren, Verschmelzen

unit investment trust, unit investment company · Investmentgesellschaft *f* mit einheitlicher Kapitalanlage, Investmentfonds *m* mit einheitlicher Kapitalanlage

unitized pension scheme · fondsgebundener Pensionsversicherungsplan *m*, fondsgebundener (Alters)Versorgungsplan

unit-linked assurance · fondsgebundene Versicherung *f*

unit of appraisement, unit of appraisal, unit of (e)valuation · Bewertungseinheit *f*, Wertermitt(e)lungseinheit, (Ab)Schätzungseinheit, Taxierungseinheit

unit of comparison, comparison unit · Vergleichseinheit *f*

unit of housing (US); apartment (Brit.) [*archaic*]; tenement, residence, dwelling; dwelling unit, DU, du, living unit, LU, lu, housing unit, apartment (US) · Wohnung *f*

unit of landscape, landscape unit, landscape region · Landschaftsindividuum *n*

unit of measurement, measurement unit · Maßeinheit *f*

unit of settlement, settlement unit · (An)Sied(e)lungseinheit *f*, (An)Sied(e)lungszelle *f*

unit of work, work unit · Arbeitseinheit *f*, Leistungseinheit *f*

unit price, (unit) rate, rate per unit, fixed price (for a unit of specific work) · Einheitspreis *m*, EP

unit-price contract, measurement contract, measured contract, measure-and-value contract, bill contract, contract for measure and value · Einheits(preis)vertrag *m* [*Ein Vertrag zu Einheitspreisen für technisch und wirtschaftlich einheitliche Teilleistungen, deren Menge nach Maß, Gewicht oder Stückzahl vom Auftraggeber in den Verdingungsunterlagen angegeben ist*]

unit price tender, unit price offer, unit price bid; unit price (bid) proposal (US) · Einheitspreisangebot *n*

(unit) rate, rate per unit, fixed price (for a unit of specific work), unit price · Einheitspreis *m*, EP

unit rate, rate per unit, standard rate, fixed rate · Einheitssatz *m*

unit ticket · Einheitsfahrschein *m*

unity of interest, unity of right [*joint tenancy*] · Rechtsgleichzeitigkeit *f*

unity of opinion, agreement of opinion, consent of opinion, unanimity, consension, consensus of opinion · Meinungsgleichheit *f*, Einstimmigkeit

unity of possession; consolidatio fructus et proprietatis [*Latin*] [*The joint possession of two rights by several titles*] · Besitzeinheit *f*, gleiches Besitzrecht *n*, Einheit des Besitzes, Gleichzeitigkeit *f* des Besitzes

unity of right, unity of interest [*joint tenancy*] · Rechtsgleichzeitigkeit *f*

unity of time [*One of the essential properties of a joint estate; the estates of the tenants being vested at one and the same period*] · gleichzeitiger Erhalt *m* der Rechte, Einheit *f* der Zeit, Gleichzeitigkeit *f* der Zeit

unity of title [*One of the essential properties of a joint estate; the estate of all the tenants being created by one and the same act, whether legal or illegal*] · gleicher (Rechts)Titel *m*, Gleichzeitigkeit *f* des (Rechts)Titels, Einheit *f* des (Rechts)Titels

univariate · eindimensional [*Statistik*]

univariate linear model · eindimensionales lineares Modell *n*

universal agent · Generalbevollmächtigte *m*

universal air travel plan, UATP · Flugreisekreditverfahren *n*

universal bequest, universal legacy [*A testamentary disposition by which the testator gives to one or to several persons the whole of the property he leaves at his death*] · Gesamtlegat *n*, Universallegat

universal custom of the realm, custom which runs through the whole land (Brit.); ius commune [*Latin*]; common (law), general customs, customary law, (common) custom · gemeines Recht *n*, objektives gemeines Recht, (objektives) Gemeinrecht, Präjudizienrecht, (gemeines) Gewohnheitsrecht [*England. Das gemeine Recht, das von reisenden Richtern ("itinerant justices" oder "justices in eyre") des königlichen Gerichts zu Westminster gebildet wurde. Neben der Gegenüberstellung "common law" (oder "law") — "equity" (= „strenges Recht — Billigkeitsrecht") wird "common law" noch stellvertretend für das gesamte case law und das anglo-amerikanische Rechtssystem verwandt:* "common law — statute law" (= „Richterrecht — Gesetzesrecht"), *bzw.* "common law — civil law" *(anglo-amerikanisches Recht im Gegensatz zum kontinentaleuropäischen Recht)*]

universal law principle, principle of universal law · allgemeingültiger Grundsatz *m*, allgemeingültiges Prinzip *n*

universal legacy, universal bequest [*A testamentary disposition by which the testator gives to one or to several persons the whole of the property he leaves at his death*] · Gesamtlegat *n*, Universallegat

universal legatee, legatee by general title · Gesamtlegatnehmer *m*, Universallegatnehmer

universally accepted rules of building and construction, (generally accepted) rules of building and construction · (allgemein) anerkannte Regeln *fpl* der Baukunst, (allgemein) anerkannte Regeln der Bautechnik

universally accepted rules of engineering, (generally accepted) rules of engineering · (allgemein) anerkannte Regeln *fpl* der Technik

Universal Postal Union, International Postal Union [*Established in 1875*] · Weltpostverein *m*

universal privity; successio in universum ius defuncti [*Latin*]; universal succession · Gesamt(rechts)nachfolge *f*, Universal(rechts)nachfolge

universal privy, universal successor · Gesamt(rechts)nachfolger *m*, Universal(rechts)nachfolger

universal provider, department store · Warenhaus *n*

universal provider plot, department store plot · Warenhausgrundstück *n*

universal succession, universal privity; successio in universum ius defuncti [*Latin*] · Gesamt(rechts)nachfolge *f*, Universal(rechts)nachfolge

universal successor, universal privy · Gesamt(rechts)nachfolger *m*, Universal(rechts)nachfolger

universe, (parent) population · Ausgangsgesamtheit *f*, Grundgesamtheit [*Statistik*]

universitas iuris [*Latin*] · rechtliche Einheit *f*

universitates facti [*Latin*] · Sachgesamtheiten *fpl*

universitates iuris [*Latin*] · Gegenstände *mpl*, Sachen *fpl* und Rechte *npl* [*B.G.B.*]

university of the air [*Great Britain*] · offene Universität *f*

university quarter, campus · Universitätsviertel *n*

university town, university city · Universitätsstadt *f*

unjust, unfair, undue, inequitable · unbillig, ungerecht(fertigt), unlauter

unjust enrichment · ungerecht(fertigt)e Bereicherung *f*

unknown, dormant · unbekannt

unlawful → nonlegal

unlawful and malicious arson · ungesetzliche und dolose Brandstiftung *f*

unlawful assembly, mobbing [*Combination against peace and good order for an illegal purpose of an assemblage of people*] · Zusammenrottung *f*

unlawful competition, passing off, unfair dealing, unfair competition, unlawful dealing · unlauterer Wettbewerb *m*

unlawful condition · unrechtmäßige Bedingung *f*, gesetz(es)widrige Bedingung

unlawful conversion, diversion · rechtswidrige Verwendung *f* oder Verfügung ohne bestimmten eigenen Vorteil, unrechtmäßige Verwendung oder Verfügung ohne bestimmten eigenen Vorteil [*einer einer Gesellschaft gehörenden Sache*]

unlawful dealing, unlawful competition, passing off, unfair dealing, unfair competition · unlauterer Wettbewerb *m*

unlawful detainer [*Statutory proceedings by which a landlord removes a tenant who holds over after his lease has expired, after his tenancy is terminated by notice, or after default in payment of rent or other obligations*] · (Zwangs)Räumungsverfahren *n*

unlawful game · verbotenes Glücksspiel *n*

unlawfulness → violation (of law)

unlawful requisition · wilde Requisition *f* [*volkstümlich "Organisieren"*]

unlawful use for private benefit · unerlaubter eigennütziger Gebrauch *m*, unerlaubte eigennützige Benutzung *f*

unless; nisi [*Latin*] · falls nicht

unlettered · schreib- und leseunkundig, lese- und schreibunkundig

unlimited, irrebuttable, unconditional, absolute, total, unrestricted · absolut, unbeschränkt, uneingeschränkt, unbedingt, unbegrenzt, bedingungslos

unlimited administration of estate(s), general administration of estate(s) · allgemeine Nachlaßverwaltung *f*, unbeschränkte Nachlaßverwaltung, allgemeine erbrechtliche Verwaltung, unbeschränkte erbrechtliche Verwaltung, allgemeine Erb(schafts)verwaltung, unbeschränkte Erb(schafts)verwaltung

unlimited authority · Blankovollmacht *f*, Blankovertretungsmacht

unlimited binding authority of precedents → absolute binding authority of precedents

unlimited company · (Kapital)Gesellschaft *f* mit unbeschränkter Haftung der Gesellschafter, unbeschränkt haftende (Kapital)Gesellschaft

unlimited failure to perform, irrebuttable failure to perform, total failure to perform, absolute failure to perform, unrestricted failure to perform · absolute Nichterfüllung *f*, uneingeschränkte Nichterfüllung, unbeschränkte Nichterfüllung, unbedingte Nichterfüllung, unbegrenzte Nichterfüllung

unlimited jurisdiction, absolute jurisdiction, unrestricted jurisdiction, irrebuttable jurisdiction, total jurisdiction · absolute Gerichtsbarkeit *f*, uneingeschränkte Gerichtsbarkeit, unbeschränkte Gerichtsbarkeit, unbedingte Gerichtsbarkeit, unbegrenzte Gerichtsbarkeit, absolute Rechtspflege(funktion) *f*, uneingeschränkte Rechtspflege(funktion), unbeschränkte Rechtspflege(funktion), unbedingte Rechtspflege(funktion), unbegrenzte Rechtspflege(funktion)

unlimited liability · unbeschränkte Haftung *f*

unlimited necessity, unrestricted necessity, irrebuttable necessity, total necessity, absolute necessity, natural necessity · absolute Notwendigkeit *f*, unbedingte Notwendigkeit, unbegrenzte Notwendigkeit, uneingeschränkte Notwendigkeit, unbeschränkte Notwendigkeit

unlimited ownership (of property); dominium plenum, dominium perpetuum [*Latin*]; absolute ownership (of property), absolute interest, exclusive interest, sole interest, exclusive ownership (of property), sole ownership (of property), sole property, sole proprietorship [*In English law absolute ownership can only exist in chattels, as all land is subject theoretically to the obligations of tenure; but practically the fee simple in land gives absolute ownership*] · absolutes Eigentum *n*, uneingeschränktes Eigentum, unbeschränktes Eigentum, unbegrenztes Eigentum, ausschließliches Eigentum, unbedingtes Eigentum, Alleineigentum

unlimited presumption, irrebuttable presumption, absolute presumption, unrestricted presumption, total presumption · absolute Rechtsvermutung *f*, unbeschränkte Rechtsvermutung, unbegrenzte Rechtsvermutung, uneingeschränkte Rechtsvermutung, unbedingte Rechtsvermutung

unliquidated, unpaid, not paid · nichtbezahlt, offenstehend, unbezahlt

unliquidated damages, ordinary damages, unliquidated compensation, ordinary compensation, unliquidated indemnification, ordinary indemnification, unliquidated indemnity, ordinary indemnity · nicht festgestellte Entschädigung *f*, nicht festgestellter Schadenersatz *m*

unloaded, not imperfect, without a burden, without a load, burdenless, free from encumbrance(s), free from charge(s), free from incumbrance(s), free from burden(s), uncharged, unburdened, unencumbered, unincumbered, clear, perfect, free from load(s) · entschuldet, lastenfrei, (dinglich) unbelastet, (dinglich) nicht belastet

unloader · Ablader *m*, Auslader

unloading · Abladung *f*, Ausladung

unmarried woman, feme sole, feme discovert, single woman, sole woman · alleinstehende Frau *f*, unverheiratete Frau, ledige Frau

unmerchantable, unsal(e)able · nicht verkäuflich, unverkäuflich

unmetered parking lot · zählerloser Parkplatz *m*, parkuhrloser Parkplatz

unmortgaged, without mortgage(s) · hypothekenfrei

unnamed · ungenannt

unnatural growth, planned growth · geplantes Wachstum *n*

unnatural state, nonnatural state · veränderter Zustand *m* [*Land*]

unnegotiable, nonnegotiable, not negotiable, nontransferable by endorsement · nicht umlaufbar, nicht begebbar, nicht umlauffähig

unnegotiable warehouse receipt, not negotiable warehouse receipt, warehouse receipt nontransferable by endorsement, nonnegotiable warehouse receipt · Lagerempfangsschein m

unobstructed view · freie Aussicht f

unobtainable, desperate, hopeless, non collectable, noncollectible, nonrecoverable, nonobtainable, uncollectable, unrecoverable, uncollectible, bad, irrecoverable · nicht beitreibbar, nicht einziehbar, nicht eintreibbar, uneinziehbar, uneintreibbar, uneinbringlich, unbeitreibbar [Schuld]

unoccupied, empty, vacant · frei, leer(stehend), unbesetzt, unbelegt, nicht belegt [Raum]

unofficious will; testamentum inofficium [Latin] [One made in disregard of natural obligations as to inheritance. It has no place in the common law] · gesetzliche Erbrechte ausschließendes Testament n

unopposed, not subject to dispute · unwidersprochen

unpackaged cargo, bulk cargo · Massengutladung f

unpaid, not paid, unliquidated · nichtbezahlt, offenstehend, unbezahlt

unperformed, unfulfilled · unerfüllt, ungeleistet

unplanned · nicht beplant, unbeplant, nichtverplant [Gebiet]

unplanned growth, natural growth · natürliches Wachstum n

unploughed (Brit.); unplowed (US); untilled · unbeackert, ungepflügt, unbestellt

unploughed (turf) balk, ridge, green balk of unploughed turf, untilled green strip of land · Rainbalken m

unpopulated · unbevölkert

unpriced [bill of quantities] · unausgefüllt [L.V.]

unprivileged, non-privileged · nichtprivilegiert, unprivilegiert

unprivileged commercial lay corporation, non-privileged commercial lay corporation · nichtprivilegierte wirtschaftliche Laienkörperschaft f, unprivilegierte wirtschaftliche Laienkörperschaft, unprivilegierte wirtschaftliche Laienkorporation f

unprofitability · Unwirtschaftlichkeit f, Profitlosigkeit, Gewinnlosigkeit, Unrentabilität f

unprofitable, uneconomical · gewinnlos, nicht rentabel, profitlos, unwirtschaftlich, nicht gewinnbringend

unprofitable reduction of land · unwirtschaftliche Verkleinerung f [Flurbereinigung]

unpropertied, destitute · vermögenslos, ohne Vermögen

unproportionately, disproportionately · unverhältnismäßig

unreal, not according to realty, false, not real · unwirklich, falsch

unreal fact, fact not according to reality, false fact · falsche Tatsache f, unwirkliche Tatsache

unreasonable · unangemessen

unreasonable, opposed to sound reason, absurd · sinnwidrig, unvernünftig

unreasonable sense, absurdity, absurdness · Sinnwidrigkeit f, Unvernunft f

unrecoverable, uncollectible, bad, irrecoverable, unobtainable, desparate, hopeless, non collectable, noncollectible, nonrecoverable, nonobtainable, uncollectable · nicht beitreibbar, nicht einziehbar, nicht eintreibbar, uneinziehbar, uneintreibbar, uneinbringlich, unbeitreibbar [Schuld]

unregistered · nicht eingetragen, nicht registriert, nicht gebucht, unregistriert, ungebucht

unregistered trademark, presentation of merchandise · Ausstattung f

unregistrable, not capable of registration · nicht eintragungsfähig, nicht eintragungsreif, nicht buchungsfähig, nicht buchungsreif, nicht registrierfähig, nicht registrierreif, unregistrierbar

unregulated village with houses arranged around an inner common · unregelmäßiges Angerdorf n, unregelmäßiges Platzdorf

unremedied [defect] · nichtbeseitigt, nichtnachgebessert [Baumangel]

unrestricted, unlimited, irrebuttable, unconditional, absolute, total · absolut, unbeschränkt, uneingeschränkt, unbedingt, unbegrenzt, bedingungslos

unrestricted agglomeration of locations (or sites) · freie Häufung f von Standorten, freie Standorthäufung

unrestricted binding authority of precedents, unlimited binding authority of precedents, irrebuttable binding authority of precedents, absolute binding authority of precedents, total binding authority of precedents · absolute Bindungswirkung f, unbeschränkte Bindungswirkung, unbegrenzte Bindungswirkung, uneingeschränkte Bindungswirkung, unbedingte Bindungswirkung

unrestricted divisibility (of land(s)) · Freiteilbarkeit f

unrestricted failure to perform, unlimited failure to perform, irrebuttable failure to perform, total failure to perform, absolute failure to perform · absolute Nichterfüllung f, uneingeschränkte Nichterfüllung, unbeschränkte Nichterfüllung, unbedingte Nichterfüllung, unbegrenzte Nichterfüllung

unrestricted jurisdiction, irrebuttable jurisdiction, total jurisdiction, unlimited jurisdiction, absolute jurisdiction · absolute Gerichtsbarkeit f, uneingeschränkte Gerichtsbarkeit, unbeschränkte Gerichtsbarkeit, unbedingte Gerichtsbarkeit, unbegrenzte Gerichtsbarkeit, absolute Rechtspflege(funktion) f, uneingeschränkte Rechtspflege(funktion), unbeschränkte Rechtspflege(funktion), unbedingte Rechtspflege(funktion), unbegrenzte Rechtspflege(funktion)

unrestricted necessity, irrebuttable necessity, total necessity, absolute necessity, natural necessity, unlimited necessity · absolute Notwendigkeit f, unbedingte Notwendigkeit, unbegrenzte Notwendigkeit, uneingeschränkte Notwendigkeit, unbeschränkte Notwendigkeit

unrestricted presumption, total presumption, unlimited presumption, irrebuttable presumption, absolute presumption · absolute Rechtsvermutung f, unbeschränkte Rechtsvermutung, unbegrenzte Rechtsvermutung, uneingeschränkte Rechtsvermutung, unbedingte Rechtsvermutung

unrestricted value · Grund(stücks)wert m wenn Town and Country Planning Act mit Entwick(e)lungsverbot nicht erlassen worden wäre

unrightful possession · unrechtmäßiger Besitz m, Besitz ohne Recht zum Besitz, gesetz(es)widriger Besitz

unsal(e)able, unmerchantable · nicht verkäuflich, unverkäuflich

unsanitary, prejudicial to health, detrimental to health, offensive · gesundheitsschädlich, gesundheitsgefährdend

unsealed, simple, not under seal · nicht gesiegelt, siegellos, ungesiegelt, ohne Siegel

unsealed contract, parol contract, (written) contract not under seal, (written) contract without seal, contract by unsealed writing, simple contract [*A simple contract made by writing without seal. By a strange misuse of language, both kinds of simple contract (1. The simple contract made by word of mouth and 2. The simple contract made by writing without seal) are frequently spoken of in English law as parol contracts notwithstanding that the term "parol", both etymologically and in general parlance, means "by word of mouth"*] · nicht gesiegelter (schriftlicher) Vertrag m, ungesiegelter (schriftlicher) Vertrag, nicht formeller Vertrag, nicht notarieller Vertrag, (schriftlicher) Vertrag ohne Siegel, schriftlicher ungesiegelter Vertrag

unseated, unused · ungenutzt, nicht genutzt [*Grundstück*]

unsecured creditor, unsecural debtee · ungesicherter Gläubiger m

unsecured debenture [*Great Britain*]; unsecured corporate bond, debenture (corporate) bond, plain corporate bond [*USA*]; naked debenture, simple debenture [*Great Britain*] · ungesicherte Schuldverschreibung f, ungesicherte Obligation f [*private Kapitalgesellschaft*]

unselective, nonselective · ausleseindifferent

unsettled · ungebunden [*Land*]

unsettled, controversial, moot, adversary, contested, undecided, contentious [*Litigated between adverse parties*] · streitig, strittig

unseverable, inseparable, entire, indivisible · ganz, unteilbar, untrennbar

unsound in mind, disordered in mind, diseased in mind, of unsound mind, nonsane, insane, deranged; insanus [*Latin*] · geistesgestört, geisteskrank

unsoundness of mind, madness, derangement of intellect, mental unsoundness, mental alienation, mental disorder, mental derangement, insanity [*Lunacy is properly a species of insanity, although the terms are frequently used as synonyms*] · Geisteskrankheit f, Geistesgestörtheit

unspecialized hunting and gathering settlement · Wildbeuter(an)sied(e)lung f

unsteady · nichtkonstant

unsuitable for (human) occupation, un(in)habitable, not (in)habitable, unfit to live in, unfit for (human) habitation, unfit for (human) occupation, unsuitable for (human) habitation · unbewohnbar, unbelegbar

unsurveyed · unvermessen

unsworn · unbeeidet

untenanted land · unverpachtetes Land n

untilled; unploughed (Brit.); **unplowed** (US) · unbeackert, ungepflügt, unbestellt

untilled green strip of land, ridge, unploughed (turf) balk, green balk of unploughed turf (Brit.) · Rainbalken m

untransferable, nontransferable · unübertragbar, nicht übertragbar

untrodden, pathless, trackless · unwegsam [*Gelände*]

untrue, false, not true, not truly, not according to truth · falsch, unwahr

untrue fact, fact not true, fact not according to truth · unwahre Tatsache f

untruth — urban administrative region

untruth · Unwahrheit f

unused, unseated · ungenutzt, nicht genutzt [Grundstück]

unwarrantable · unverantwortlich

unweighted land(s) · unbewerteter Grund m, unbewertetes Land n

unwillingness to act, refusal to act · Handlungsverweigerung f

unworked [mineral] · noch nicht gewonnen

unworthiness of inheriting · Erbuntüchtigkeit f, Erbunwürdigkeit

unworthy of inheriting · erbunwürdig, erbuntüchtig

unwritten law, juristic law, law of the forum; lex non scripta [Latin] [It comprises both, judge-made law and jurist-made law] · Gerichtsrecht n; ungeschriebenes Recht [Fehlbenennung, weil Gerichtsentscheide wegen ihrer bindenden Kraft für die Zukunft geschrieben sind]

up-and-down method · Pendelmethode f [Statistik]

up-cross · Niveauschnitt m nach oben [Statistik]

updating · Laufendhaltung f

updating of map(s) · Kartenrevision f

to upgrade → to redo

upgrade · Nachfolgegeschäft n

upgrading guide-line, (physical) improvement guide line, modernization guide line, rehabilitation guide line · (bauliche) Verbesserungsrichtlinie f, Modernisierungsrichtlinie

upgrading loan, rehabilitation loan, (physical) improvement loan, modernization loan · (bauliche) Verbesserungsanleihe f, Modernisierungsanleihe

upgrading order, order to improve, order to modernize, order to rehabilitate, (physical) improvement order, rehabilitation order, modernization order · Modernisierungsverfügung f, Modernisierungsanordnung, Modernisierungsgebot n, Modernisierungsbefehl m, (baulicher) Verbesserungsbefehl

upgrading ordinance, rehabilitation ordinance, (physical) improvement ordinance, modernization ordinance · Modernisierungsverordnung f, (bauliche) Verbesserungsverordnung

upgrading plan, (physical) improvement plan, modernization plan, rehabilitation plan · Modernisierungsplan m, (baulicher) Verbesserungsplan

upgrading work(s), (physical) improvement work(s), modernization work(s), rehabilitation work(s) · (bauliche) Verbesserungsarbeit(en) f(pl), Modernisierungsarbeit(en)

upgrading zone, (physical) improvement zone, rehabilitation zone, modernization zone · Modernisierungsschwerpunkt m, (baulicher) Verbesserungsschwerpunkt [früher: Modernisierungszone f]

to uphold · bestätigen [Urteil eines niederen Gerichtes durch ein höheres]

to uphold precedents, to maintain former adjudications; stare decisis [Latin]; to stand by decided cases · bindend wirken [Entscheid]

upland · Hochland n

uplifted hand · erhobene Hand f

(up)on condition; conditionary [obsolete]; conditional · bedingt, unter Vorbehalt, mit Vorbedingung

(up)on discretion · ermessensmäßig, nach Ermessen

upper class · Oberschicht f

Upper House of Parliament · Bundesrat m [Bundesrepublik Deutschland]

upper limit, ceiling, maximum limit · Höchstgrenze f, Obergrenze

upper middle class · obere Mittelschicht f

upper price limit, price ceiling · Preishöchstgrenze f, Preisobergrenze

upper riparian owner, upstream riparian owner, upper riparian proprietor, upstream riparian proprietor · Oberwasser-Ufereigentümer, oberwasserseitiger Ufereigentümer m

upper riparian possessor, upstream riparian possessor · Oberwasser-Uferbesitzer m, oberwasserseitiger Uferbesitzer

uprooted, rootless · entwurzelt, wurzellos

upstream resident · Oberlieger m [Vorflut]

upstream riparian owner, upper riparian proprietor, upstream riparian proprietor, upper riparian owner · Oberwasser-Ufereigentümer, oberwasserseitiger Ufereigentümer m

upstream riparian possessor, upper riparian possessor · Oberwasser-Uferbesitzer m, oberwasserseitiger Uferbesitzer

up zoning · Heraufzonung f, heraufstufende Baunutzung, heraufstufende bauliche Nutzung

urban · städtebaulich

urban · städtisch

urban accountant, city accountant, town accountant · Stadtbuchhalter m

urban acquaintance field · städtisches Kontaktfeld n

urban acreage, town acreage, city acreage · Stadtflächeninhalt m

urban administrative region, town administrative region, city administrative region · Stadtgebiet n [Die Fläche der Verwal-

tungseinheit „Stadt", unabhängig von städtischer Bebauung und städtischer Funktion]

urban affair, city affair, town affair · städtische Angelegenheit *f*

urban agency, urban office, town agency, town office, city office, city agency · städtische Dienststelle *f*

urban agglomeration; conurbation (Brit); urban tract [*According to Dickinson*]; urban(ized) landscape, civicized landscape, cityscape, townscape [*An area occupied by a continuous series of dwellings, factories and other buildings, harbour and docks, urban parks and playing fields, etc., which are not separated from each other by rural land; though in many cases such an urban area includes enclaves of rural land which is still in agricultural occupation*] · Stadtlandschaft *f*, Städtelandschaft, verstädterte Landschaft, Städteschar *f*, Städteagglomeration *f*, Zusammenstädterung *f*

urban air, town air, city air · Stadtluft *f*

urban alderman, town alderman, city alderman · Stadtälteste *m*

urban architecture · Stadtarchitektur *f*, Stadtbaukunst *f*

urban area, town area, city area · Stadtfläche *f*, städtische Fläche

urban area, urban territory, town area, town territory, city area, city territory · städtisches Gebiet *n* [*Ein Gebiet, welches im funktionalen und physiognomischen Sinne vorrangig durch städtische Funktionen geprägt ist*]

urban area → urban(ized) area

urban area pattern, urban area scheme · städtisches Flächenmuster *n*, städtisches Flächenschema *n*

urban area use, city area use, town area use, urban land(s) use, city land(s) use, town land(s) use · städtische Bodennutzung *f*, städtische Landnutzung, städtische Flächennutzung, Stadtbodennutzung, Stadtlandnutzung, Stadtflächennutzung

urban atlas, city atlas, town atlas · Stadtatlas *m*

urban auditorium building, (city) auditorium building, town auditorium building · Stadthalle *f*

urban authority, town authority, city authority · Stadtbehörde *f*, städtische Behörde

urban block, city block, town block · Baublock *m*

urban board, town board, city board · Stadtamt *n*, städtisches Amt

urban boundary, town boundary, city boundary · Stadtgrenze *f*

urban builder, town builder, city builder · Städtebauer *m*, Stadtbauer

urban building, urban construction, town building, town construction, city building, city construction · Städtebau *m*

urban building board, town building board, town construction board, city building board, city construction board, urban construction board · Stadtbauamt *n*

urban building code, urban construction code, city building code, city construction code, town building code, town construction code · städtische Bauordnung *f*, Stadtbauordnung

urban building (construction), town building (construction), city building (construction) · städtischer Hochbau *m*

urban (building) land market, market in urban (building) land(s), urban (real) estate market, urban (real) property market · städtischer (Bau)Bodenmarkt *m*, städtischer (Bau)Landmarkt, städtischer (Bau)Grund(stücks)markt

urban building project, town construction project, town building project, city construction project, city building project, urban construction project · städtebauliches Vorhaben *n*, städtebauliches Projekt *n*

urban by(e)-law, urban ordinance, town statute, town by(e)-law, town ordinance, city statute, city by(e)-law, city ordinance, urban statute · Stadtsatzung *f*, Stadtstatut *n*, Stadtgesetz *n*

urban cartography, town cartography, city cartography · Stadtkartographie *f*

urban cemetery, town cemetery, city cemetery · Stadtfriedhof *m*

urban center (US); middle-order sub-central place, sub-town, market district, market town; first order centre (Brit.); urban village [*750 to 1,000 inhabitants*] (Brit.); small town with between 1,000 and 2,000 inhabitants (Brit.); first order center · Amtsort *m* [*nach W. Christaller*]

urban centre, town centre, city centre (Brit.); urban center, town center, city center, downtown (area) (US) · Stadtzentrum *f*, Stadtinnere *n* [*im funktionalen Sinne*]

urban child, city child, town child · Stadtkind *n*

urban church, town church, city church · Stadtkirche *f*

urban civil engineer, city civil engineer, town civil engineer · Stadtbauingenieur *m*

urban (civil) engineering, town (civil) engineering, city (civil) engineering,

urban civilization — urban development land

municipal (civil) engineering · städtischer Tiefbau *m*

urban civilization, town civilization, city civilization · Stadtzivilisation *f,* städtische Zivilisation

urban classification, town classification, city classification · Städtetypisierung *f*

urban climate, town climate, city climate · Stadtklima *n*

urban coalition · städtische Interessengemeinschaft *f*

urban code, town code, city code · Städteordnung *f*

urban common (land), common city land, common town land · Stadtgemarkung *f,* Stadtal(l)mend(e) *f*

urban community, town community, city community · Stadtgemeinde *f,* Stadtkommune *f,* städtische Gemeinschaft *f,* städtische Kommune, städtische Gemeinde [*Als Organisationsform*]

urban community → (human) urban community

urban community organization (for social welfare), urban community welfare organization · städtische Wohlfahrtsarbeit *f*

urban complex · Städtekomplex *m,* Stadtgebilde *n*

urban composition, city composition, town structure, city structure, urban structure, town composition · Stadtstruktur *f,* Stadtzusammensetzung *f,* Stadtgefüge *n,* Stadtaufbau *m,* städtische Struktur, städtische Zusammensetzung, städtischer Aufbau, städtisches Gefüge

urban composition planning, town structure planning, town composition planning, city structure planning, city composition planning, urban structure planning · Stadtaufbauplanung *f,* Stadtstrukturplanung, Stadtgefügeplanung, Stadtzusammensetzungsplanung

urban conservation, urban preservation, town conservation, town preservation, city conservation, city preservation · Stadtpflege *f,* Stadterhaltung *f*

urban constitution, town constitution, city constitution · Stadtverfassung *f*

urban construction, town building, town construction, city building, city construction, urban building · Städtebau *m*

urban construction board, urban building board, town building board, town construction board, city building board, city construction board · Stadtbauamt *n*

urban construction code, city building code, city construction code, town building code, town construction code, urban building code · städtische Bauordnung *f,* Stadtbauordnung

urban construction project, urban building project, town construction project, town building project, city construction project, city building project · städtebauliches Vorhaben *n,* städtebauliches Projekt *n*

urban construction research · städtebauliche Forschung *f,* Städtebauforschung

urban construction theory, town construction theory, city construction theory · Städtebautheorie *f*

urban conversion, city conversion, town conversion · Stadtumbau *m*

urban core, town core, city core, core of the city, core of the town · Stadtkern *m* [*im physiognomischen Sinn*]

urban council, city council, town council · (Stadt)Rat *m,* Stadtvertretung *f,* Stadtparlament *n,* städtischer Gemeinderat, Stadtgemeinderat

urban councillor, city councillor, town councillor, urban councilman, town councilman, city councilman, town council member, city council member, urban council member · (Stadt)Verordnete *m,* (Stadt)Rat(smitglied) *m, (n)*

urban cultural life · städtisches Kulturleben *n*

urban culture, city culture, town culture · Stadtkultur *f*

urban density · städtische Bevölkerungsdichte *f*

urban density function · städtische Bevölkerungsdichtefunktion *f*

urban design, town design, city design · dreidimensionale Stadtplanung *f,* räumliche Stadtplanung, Stadtgestaltung [*Dieser Zweig liegt zwischen Stadtplanung und Architektur und schafft Leitbilder stadträumlicher Gestaltung*]

urban design team, urban design group, town design team, town design group, city design team, city design group · Städtebau(arbeits)gruppe *f*

urban development, town development, city development · städtische Entwick(e)lung *f,* städtebauliche Entwick(e)lung, Stadtentwick(e)lung

urban development area, town development area, city development area · städtische Bebauungsfläche *f*

urban development assistance, town development assistance, city development assistance · Städtebauförderung *f*

urban development corporation, town development corporation, city development corporation · Stadtentwick(e)lungskorporation *f,* Stadtentwick(e)lungskörperschaft *f*

urban development land, town development land, city development land · städtebaulicher Entwick(e)lungsbereich *m*

urban development measure — urban extension territory

urban development measure, town development measure, city development measure · städtebauliche Entwick(e)lungsmaßnahme *f*

urban development plan, town development plan, city development plan · Stadtentwick(e)lungsplan *m*

urban development planning, town development planning, city development planning · Stadtentwick(e)lungsplanung *f*

urban development programme, city development programme; town development program, urban development program, city development program (US); town development programme · Stadtentwick(e)lungsprogramm *n*

urban development simulation, town development simulation, city development simulation · Stadtentwick(e)lungssimulation *f*

urban district · Distriktstadt *f*, Distriktgemeinde *f*, Stadtgemeinde zweiter Klasse, städtischer (Sanitäts)Distrikt *m*, städtische Distriktgemeinde, Zusammenschluß *m* städtischer Kirchspiele [*In England. Eine durch das Recht als Stadt anerkannte, d. h. aus der Kirchspielorganisation herausgehobene Ortschaft*]

urban district → city district

urban district council, urban sanitary authority · städtische Sanitätsbehörde *f*

urban dominant factor · städtebauliche Dominante *f*

urban drainage scheme, town drainage scheme, city drainage scheme · Stadtentwässerungsplan *m*

urban dweller, town dweller, city dweller, urbanite, citizen, burgess, freeman of a borough, townman; cityman [*obsolete*]; urban resident, town resident, city resident, urban inhabitant, town inhabitant, city inhabitant · Stadtbewohner *m*, Stadteinwohner, Städter, Stadtbürger

urban ecology, town ecology, city ecology, ecology of the town, ecology of the city · Stadtökologie *f*

urban economic function · Stadtwirtschaftsfunktion *f*

urban economic growth · Stadtwirtschaftswachstum *n*

urban economist, town economist, city economist · Stadtwirtschaftler *m*

urban economy, town economy, city economy · Stadtwirtschaft *f*

urban educational officer, urban educational official, town educational officer, town educational official, city educational officer, city educational official · Stadtschulrat *m*

urban element, city element, town element · Stadtfliese *f*

urban engineer, city engineer, town engineer · Stadtingenieur *m*

urban engineering, town engineering, city engineering · Stadtbautechnik *f*, Städtebautechnik

urban enlargement, urban extension, town enlargement, town extension, city enlargement, city extension · Stadterweiterung *f*

urban enlargement plan, urban extension plan, town enlargement plan, town extension plan, city enlargement plan, city extension plan · Stadterweiterungsplan *m*

urban enlargement planning, urban extension planning, town enlargement planning, town extension planning, city enlargement planning, city extension planning, subdivision control · Stadterweiterungsplanung *f*

urban enterprise, municipal enterprise [*An enterprise which is essentially a business organization, but is owned by a city government. Utilities such as electric companies are often this type of enterprise*] · städtisches Unternehmen *n*, städtischer Betrieb *m*

urban environment, town environment, city environment · Stadtumwelt *f*

urban environmental factor, town environmental factor, city environmental factor · Stadtumweltfaktor *m*

urban estate market → urban (real) estate market

urban exhibition · Städtebauausstellung *f*

urban exodus, flight from the town, movement of population from town to country, urban-rural migration, urban-rural drift, urban-to-rural movement · Stadtflucht *f*, Stadtexodus *m*, Stadt-Land-Wanderung *f*

urban extension, town enlargement, town extension, city enlargement, city extension, urban enlargement · Stadterweiterung *f*

urban extension area, urban extension territory, town extension area, town extension territory, city extension area, city extension territory · Stadtneubaugebiet *n*, Stadterweiterungsgebiet

urban extension plan, town enlargement plan, town extension plan, city enlargement plan, city extension plan, urban enlargement plan · Stadterweiterungsplan *m*

urban extension planning → urban enlargement planning

urban extension territory → urban extension area

urban family, town family, city family · Stadtfamilie f

urban father, city father, town father · Stadtvater m

urban fee (tenure) → urban tenancy

urban (feodal) tenure (of land) → urban tenancy

urban fief → urban tenancy

urban field · Stadtfeld n, funktionale Einheit f aus zentralem Ort und Einzugsbereich [Es basiert auf räumlichen Verflechtungen innerhalb von Kerngebieten die jeweils eine Mindesteinwohnerzahl von 300 000 haben und deren Fläche sich etwa 160 km oder rund 2 Autostunden nach außen ausdehnt]

urban field · städtischer Wohn- und Lebenskomplex m

urban forest, town forest, city forest · Stadtwald m

urban form, town form, city form · Stadtform f

urban fortification, town fortification, city fortification · Stadtbefestigung f

urban framework · Städtesystem n

urban fringe, town fringe, city fringe · Vorstadtgelände n, Bannmeile f, Stadtrandzone f

urban function, town function, city function · städtische Funktion f, Stadtfunktion

urban garden, town garden, city garden · Stadtgarten m

urban gate, town gate, city gate · Stadttor n

urban geography, geography of towns, geography of cities, town geography, city geography · Stadtgeographie f, Städtegeographie

urban (ground) plan, town (ground) plan, city (ground) plan, urban layout, town layout, city layout · Stadtgrundriß m

urban growth · Stadtwachstum n, Städtewachstum

urban growth pattern, city growth pattern, town growth pattern · Stadtwachstumsmuster n, Städtewachstumsmuster

urban growth policy · Städtewachstumspolitik f, Stadtwachstumspolitik

urban health officer, urban health official, urban medical officer, urban medical official, urban officer of health, urban official of health · Stadtarzt m, (Stadt)Physikus m

urban hierarchy · Städtehierarchie f, Stadthierarchie

urban history research, town history research, city history research · Stadtgeschichtsforschung f

urban home · Stadteigenheim n, Stadteigenhaus n

urban homestead · städtische Heimstätte f

urban homesteading · städtische Heimstättenbildung f

urban hous(ebuild)ing, town hous(ebuild)ing, city hous(ebuild)ing · Stadtwohn(ungs)bau m, städtischer Wohn(ungs)bau

urban hous(ebuild)ing practice, town hous(ebuild)ing practice, city hous(ebuild)ing practice · Stadtwohn(ungs)wesen n, städtisches Wohn(ungs)wesen

urban hous(ebuild)ing sector, town hous(ebuild)ing sector, city hous(ebuild)ing sector, urban hous(ebuild)ing field, town hous(ebuild)ing field, city hous(ebuild)ing field · Stadtwohn(ungs)sektor m, städtischer Wohn(ungs)sektor [als Tätigkeitsgebiet]

urban house possession · städtischer Hausbesitz m

urban house possessor · städtischer Hausbesitzer m

urban housing, city housing, town housing · Stadtwohnungen fpl, städtische Wohnungen

urban housing · städtisches Wohnungswesen n

urban housing land (area), town residential land (area), town housing land (area), city residential land (area), city housing land (area), urban residential land (area) · städtischer Wohn(ungs)(bau)boden m, städtisches Wohn(ungs)(bau)land n, städtische Wohn(ungs)(bau)fläche f

urban (immov(e)able) property · städtisches Grund(stücks)vermögen n, städtisches Liegenschaftsvermögen, städtisches Immobiliarvermögen, städtisches Immobilienvermögen, städtisches Bodenvermögen

urban improvement planner, town improvement planner, city improvement planner · Stadterschließungsplaner m

urban improvement planning, town improvement planning, city improvement planning · Stadterschließungsplanung f, städtische Erschließungsplanung

urban incorporation · Stadtwerdung f

urban individual traffic · städtischer Individualverkehr m

urban infrastructure, town infrastructure, city infrastructure · Stadtinfrastruktur f

urban inhabitant, town inhabitant, city inhabitant, urban dweller, town dweller, city dweller, urbanite, citizen, burgess, freeman of a borough, townman; cityman [*obsolete*]; urban resident, town resident, city resident · Stadtbewohner *m*, Stadteinwohner, Städter, Stadtbürger

urbanite, citizen, burgess, freeman of a borough, townman; cityman [*obsolete*]; urban resident, town resident, city resident, urban inhabitant, town inhabitant, city inhabitant, urban dweller, town dweller, city dweller · Stadtbewohner *m*, Stadteinwohner, Städter, Stadtbürger

urbanity, urbanness · städtischer Charakter *m*

urbanization · Verstädterung *f*

urbanization economies · Branchenstruktur *f* am selben Ort, Vorhandensein *n* mehrere Betriebe verschiedener Branchen am selben Ort, Verstädterungsvorteile *mpl*, branchenexterne Agglomerationsvorteile, Konzentration *f* verschiedener Branchen

urbanization pattern, urbanization scheme · Verstädterungsschema *n*, Verstädterungsmuster *n*

urbanization plan · Verstädterungsplan *m*

urbanization policy · Verstädterungspolitik *f*

urbanization scheme, urbanization pattern · Verstädterungsschema *n*, Verstädterungsmuster *n*

to urbanize, to civicize, to make urban · verstädtern

urbanized, cited, civicized [*Made into or like a city*] · verstädtert

urban(ized) area, urban(ized) tract, urban(ized) territory · verstädtertes Gebiet *n*

urban(ized) landscape, civicized landscape, cityscape, townscape, urban agglomeration; conurbation (Brit); urban tract [*According to Dickinson*] [*An area occupied by a continuous series of dwellings, factories and other buildings, harbour and docks, urban parks and playing fields, etc., which are not separated from each other by rural land; though in many cases such an urban area includes enclaves of rural land which is still in agricultural occupation*] · Stadtlandschaft *f*, Städtelandschaft, verstädterte Landschaft, Städteschar *f*, Städteagglomeration *f*, Zusammenstädterung *f*

urbanizing · verstädternd

urban land, city land, town land · städtischer Bereich *m* [*Im planerischen Sinne*]

urban land, town land, city land · städtischer Boden *m*, städtisches Land *n*, Stadtboden, Stadtland, Stadtgrund, städtischer Grund *m*

urban land allocation, allocation of urban land · Stadtlandzuweisung *f*

urban land law · städtisches Landrecht *n*, städtisches Bodenrecht

urban landlordism · Landverpächtertum *n* in der Stadt

urban land market → urban (real) estate market

urban landowners' association, association of urban landowners [*They procure money on the security of their estates*] · Stadtschaft *f*, Genossenschaft von städtischen Grundeigentümern, städtische Grundeigentümergenossenschaft

urban land reform · städtische Landreform *f*, städtische Bodenreform

urban land rent, town land rent, city land rent · städtische Grundrente *f*

urban landscape → urban(ized) landscape

urban land(s) use, city land(s) use, town land(s) use, urban area use, city area use, town area use · städtische Bodennutzung *f*, städtische Landnutzung, städtische Flächennutzung, Stadtbodennutzung, Stadtlandnutzung, Stadtflächennutzung

urban land(s) use density, town land use density, city land use density · städtische Flächennutzungsdichte *f*, städtische Bodennutzungsdichte, städtische Landnutzungsdichte

urban land(s) use plan, town land use plan, city land use plan · Stadtflächennutzungsplan *m*

urban land(s) use planning, town land use planning, city land use planning · Stadtflächennutzungsplanung *f*

urban land(s) use studies · Bestandsaufnahme *f* der städtischen Flächennutzung, Bestandsaufnahme der städtischen Bodennutzung, Bestandsaufnahme der städtischen Landnutzung

urban land(s) value, town land value, city land value · städtischer Landwert *m*, städtischer Bodenwert, Stadtlandwert, Stadtbodenwert

urban law, town law, city law · Stadtrecht *n* [*Das in einer Stadt geltende Recht*]

urban layout, town layout, city layout, urban (ground) plan, town (ground) plan, city (ground) plan · Stadtgrundriß *m*

urban life, town life, city life · städtisches Leben *n*, Stadtleben [*Summe der in einer Stadt sinnfällig werdenden Tätigkeiten, Verkehrsbewegungen und Einrichtungen, die der materiellen und kulturellen Bedarfsdeckung der Stadtbe-*

urban life style — urban planning assistance

wohner, gegebenenfalls auch der Bewohner eines Hinterlandes dienen]

urban life style, urban style of life · städtischer Lebensstil *m*

urban location, city location, town location, urban site, town site, city site · Stadtstandort *m*, städtischer Standort

urban lot, town lot, city lot · städtisches Katastergrundstück *n*, städtisches Grundstück (im katastertechnischenen Sinne), städtisches Kartengrundstück, städtisches Flurstück, städtische (Kataster)Parzelle *f*, Stadtgrundstück (im katastertechnischen Sinne), Stadtkatastergrundstück, Stadt-Kartengrundstück, Stadt(kataster)parzelle, Stadtflurstück

urban (masonry) wall, town (masonry) wall, city (masonry) wall · Stadtmauer *f*

urban master plan, town master plan, city master plan · Stadtgeneralplan *m*

urban medical officer, urban medical official, urban officer of healths, urban official of healths, urban healths officer, urban healths official · Stadtarzt *m*, (Stadt)Physikus *m*

urban mesh density, density of the urban mesh, density of towns, density of cities · Städtedichte *f*

urban middle class, town middle class, city middle class · städtische Mittelschicht *f*

urban migrant, town migrant, city migrant · Stadtwanderer *m*

urban moat, town moat, city moat · Stadtgraben *m*

urban model, town model, city model · Stadtmodell *n*

urban morphology, city morphology, town morphology · Stadtmorphologie *f*

urban mortgage · städtische Hypothek *f*

urban mortgage lending · städtische Hypothekenleihe *f*

urban nebula · Städtegruppe *f*

urbanness, urbanity · städtischer Charakter *m*

urban network, town network, city network · städtisches Netz *n*, Stadtnetz

urban noise, town noise, city noise · Stadtlärm *m*

urban office, town office, city office, city agency, urban agency · städtische Dienststelle *f*

urban officer, urban official, town officer, town official, city officer, city official · Stadtbeamte *m*, städtische Beamte

urban officer of health, urban official of health, urban health officer, urban health official, urban medical officer, urban medical official · Stadtarzt *m*, (Stadt)Physikus *m*

urban open area policy, urban open land policy, urban open space policy, vacant urban land policy, vacant urban space policy, vacant urban area policy · städtische Freiflächenpolitik *f*, städtische Freiraumpolitik, städtische Freilandpolitik

urban open space · städtischer Freiraum *m*

urban orientation · Stadtbezogenheit *f*, Stadtorientierung *f*

urban outward migration, urban outmigration, migration from an urban area · Stadtabwanderung *f*

urban parish, town parish, city parish · städtisches Kirchspiel *n*

urban park, town park city park · Stadtpark *m*

urban pattern, town pattern, city pattern · Stadtmuster *n*, Stadtschema *n*

urban pedestrian traffic · städtischer Fußgängerverkehr *m*

urban place of work, urban place of employment · städtischer Arbeitsort *m*

urban plan, town plan, city plan · städtebaulicher Plan *m*, Städtebauplan, Stadtbauplan

urban plan → urban (ground) plan

urban planner, city planner, town planner · Stadtplaner *m*, Städteplaner, Stadtbauplaner, Städtebauplaner

urban planning [*obsolete*]; urban policy · städtische Raumordnung *f*, Stadtraumordnung

urban planning, city planning, town planning · Städte(bau)planung *f*, Stadt(bau)planung, städtebauliche Planung

urban planning act, urban planning law, urban planning statute, town planning law, town planning act, town planning statute, city planning law, city planning statute, city planning act · Stadtplanungsgesetz *n*

urban planning administration, city planning administration, town planning administration · Stadtplanungsverwaltung *f*

urban planning (advisory) panel, urban planning (advisory) council · Stadtplanungsbeirat *m*

urban planning area, town planning territory, city planning territory, urban planning territory, town planning area, city planning area · Stadtplanungsgebiet *n*

urban planning assistance · städtische Planungsförderung *f*

urban planning authority, town planning authority, city planning authority · Stadtplanungsbehörde *f*

urban planning authority, urban planning power · städtebauliche Planungshoheit *f*, städtebauliche Planungsgewalt *f*, städtebauliche Planungsmacht *f*, städtebauliche Planungskompetenz *f*

urban planning board, town planning board, city planning board · Stadtplanungsamt *n*

urban planning commission, town planning commission, city planning commission · Stadtplanungsausschuß *m*

urban planning consultant, town planning consultant, city planning consultant · Stadtplanungsberater *m*

urban planning data, town planning data, city planning data · städtebauliche Planungsgrundlagen *f pl*

urban planning education, town planning education, city planning education · Stadtplanerausbildung *f*

urban planning ideas competition, town planning ideas competition, city planning ideas competition · städtebaulicher Ideenwettbewerb *m*

urban planning institute, town planning institute, city planning institute · Institut für Städtebau, Städtebauinstitut *n*

urban planning law, town planning law, city planning law · Stadtplanungsrecht *n*, städtisches Planungsrecht, städtebauliches Planungsrecht

urban planning law → urban planning act

urban planning model, town planning model, city planning model · städtebauliches Leitbild *n*

urban planning office, town planning office, city planning office · Stadtplanungsstelle *f*

urban planning officer, city planning officer, town planning officer · Stadtplanungsbeamter *m*

urban planning organization, town planning organization, city planning organization · Stadtplanungsorganisation *f*

urban planning power, urban planning authority · städtebauliche Planungshoheit *f*, städtebauliche Planungsgewalt *f*, städtebauliche Planungsmacht *f*, städtebauliche Planungskompetenz *f*

urban planning practice, town planning practice, city planning practice · Stadtplanungswesen *n*

urban planning science, town planning science, city planning science · Stadtplanungswissenschaft *f*

urban planning statute → urban planning act

urban planning survey, town planning survey, city planning survey · städtebauliche Enquête *f*

urban planning task, town planning task, city planning task · städtebauliche Aufgabe *f*

urban planning territory, town planning area, city planning area, urban planning area, town planning territory, city planning territory · Stadtplanungsgebiet *n*

urban plot (of land) · städtisches Grundstück *n* [*Einer Stadt gehörendes Grundstück*]

urban policy · Stadtbaupolitik *f*, Städtebaupolitik

urban policy; urban planning [*obsolete*] · städtische Raumordnung *f*, Stadtraumordnung

urban population, town population, city population · Stadtbevölkerung *f*, städtische Bevölkerung, Stadtvolk *n*

urban population density, town population density, city population density · Stadtbevölkerungsdichte *f*

urban population structure, town population structure, city population structure · Stadtbevölkerungsstruktur *f*, Stadtbevölkerungsgefüge *n*, Stadtbevölkerungszusammensetzung *f*, Stadtbevölkerungsaufbau *m*

urban poverty · Armut *f* in der Stadt, Stadtarmut

urban power index · Verhältnis *n* der Beschäftigtenzahl im tertiären Sektor zur Gesamtbevölkerung des Einzugsbereiches

urban preservation, town conservation, town preservation, city conservation, city preservation, urban conservation · Stadtpflege *f*, Stadterhaltung *f*

urban prison, town prison, city prison · Stadtgefängnis *n*

urban property market → urban (real) estate market

urban property transactions → urban (real) property transactions

urban protection, city protection, town protection · Stadtschutz *m*

urban psychology · Stadtpsychologie *f*, Tektopsychologie

urban quarter, town quarter, city quarter, local community · Stadtviertel *n*, Stadtteil *m*, Stadtquartier *n*

urban/race game · Spiel *n* über die Auswirkungen rassischer Vorurteile auf die Stadtentwick(e)lung

urban railway, town railway, city railway, (Brit.); urban railroad, town railroad, city railroad (US) · Stadtbahn *f*

urban rate, city rate, town rate · städtische Steuer *f*, Stadtsteuer

urban (real) estate, urban realty, urban (real) property, town (real) estate, town (real) property, town realty, city (real) estate, city (real) property, city realty · städtischer Bodenbesitz *m*, städtischer Grund(stücks)besitz, städtischer Landbesitz, Stadtbodenbesitz, Stadtlandbesitz, Stadt-Grund(stücks)besitz, Grund(stücks)besitz in der Stadt, städtischer Besitz, Besitz in der Stadt

urban (real) estate market, urban (real) property market, urban (building) land market, market in urban (building) land(s) · städtischer (Bau)Bodenmarkt *m*, städtischer (Bau)Landmarkt, städtischer (Bau)Grund(stücks)markt

urban (real) estate transactions, urban land(s) transactions, dealing with urban land(s), urban (real) property transactions · städtischer Grundstücksverkehr *m*, städtischer Bodenverkehr, städtischer Immobiliarverkehr, städtischer Immobilienverkehr, städtischer Liegenschaftsverkehr

urban (real) property market, urban (building) land market, market in urban (building) land(s), urban (real) estate market · städtischer (Bau)Bodenmarkt *m*, städtischer (Bau)Landmarkt, städtischer (Bau)Grund(stücks)markt

urban (real) property transactions, urban (real) estate transactions, urban land(s) transactions, dealing with urban land(s) · städtischer Grundstücksverkehr *m*, städtischer Bodenverkehr, städtischer Immobiliarverkehr, städtischer Immobilienverkehr, städtischer Liegenschaftsverkehr

urban rebuilding, city reconstruction, city rebuilding, town reconstruction, town rebuilding, urban reconstruction · Stadtwiederaufbau *m*

urban reconstruction, urban rebuilding, city reconstruction, city rebuilding, town reconstruction, town rebuilding · Stadtwiederaufbau *m*

urban recorder, (city) recorder, town recorder · (Stadt)Syndikus *m*

urban recreation facility · städtische Erholungseinrichtung *f*

(urban) recreation hinterland · Erholungshinterland *n*, städtisches Erholungshinterland

urban relocation, urban resettlement · Umsied(e)lung *f* städtischer Bevölkerung, Aussied(e)lung städtischer Bevölkerung, Verlegung städtischer Bevölkerung, Umsetzung städtischer Bevölkerung

urban renewal, town renewal, city renewal [*The adjustment of obsolete parts of the urban structure to meet anticipated future demand*] · Stadterneuerung *f*

urban renewal and town development act · Städtebauförderungsgesetz *n*, StBauFG

urban renewal area, urban revival area, town renewal area, town revival area, city renewal area, city revival area · Stadterneuerungsfläche *f*

urban renewal legislation, urban renewal law-making, city renewal legislation, city renewal lawmaking, town renewal legislation, town renewal lawmaking · Stadterneuerungsgesetzgebung *f*

urban renewal plan · Stadterneuerungsplan *m*

urban renewal planning · Stadterneuerungsplanung *f*

urban renewal project · Stadterneuerungsvorhaben *n*

urban renewal project land, urban revival project land · Stadterneuerungsland *n*, Stadterneuerungsboden *m*

urban renewal simulation model, urban revival simulation model · Stadterneuerungssimulationsmodell *n*

urban renewal specialist, urban revival specialist, town renewal specialist, town revival specialist, city renewal specialist, city revival specialist · Stadterneuerungsfachmann *m*

urban re-planning, town re-planning, city re-planning · Stadtumplanung *f*

urban research · Stadtforschung *f*, Stadtentwick(e)lungsforschung

urban resettlement, urban relocation · Umsied(e)lung *f* städtischer Bevölkerung, Aussied(e)lung städtischer Bevölkerung, Verlegung städtischer Bevölkerung, Umsetzung städtischer Bevölkerung

urban resident, town resident, city resident, urban inhabitant, town inhabitant, city inhabitant, urban dweller, town dweller, city dweller, urbanite, citizen, burgess, freeman of a borough, townman; cityman [*obsolete*] · Stadtbewohner *m*, Stadteinwohner, Städter, Stadtbürger

urban residential area, urban residential territory · städtisches Wohn(ungs)gebiet *n*

urban residential environment, town residential environment, city residential environment · städtische Wohnumwelt *f*

urban residential housing market · Stadtwohn(ungs)markt *m*

urban residential land (area), urban housing land (area), town residential land (area), town housing land (area), city residential land (area), city housing land (area) · städtischer Wohn(ungs)(bau)boden *m*, städtisches Wohn(ungs)(bau)land *n*, städtische Wohn(ungs)(bau)fläche *f*

urban residential land use, urban residential use of land · städtische Wohnflächennutzung f

urban residential pattern, urban residential scheme · städtisches Wohnmuster n, städtisches Wohnschema n

urban residential place · städtischer Wohnplatz m

urban residential scheme, urban residential pattern · städtisches Wohnmuster n, städtisches Wohnschema n

urban residential territory, urban residential area · städtisches Wohn(ungs)gebiet n

urban residential use of land, urban residential land use · städtische Wohnflächennutzung f

urban revival area, town renewal area, town revival area, city renewal area, city revival area, urban renewal area · Stadterneuerungsfläche f

urban-rural dichotomy · städtisch-ländliche Zwiefalt f

urban-rural disparity · Stadt-Land-Disparität f

urban-rural drift, urban-to-rural movement, urban exodus, flight from the town, movement of population from town to country, urban-rural migration · Stadtflucht f, Stadtexodus m, Stadt-Land-Wanderung f

urban-rural gradient · Stadt-Land-Gefälle n

urban-rural migration, urban-rural drift, urban-to-rural movement, urban exodus, flight from the town, movement of population from town to country · Stadtflucht f, Stadtexodus m, Stadt-Land-Wanderung f

urban-rural relation(ship) · Stadt-Land-Beziehung f

urban sanitary authority, urban district council · städtische Sanitätsbehörde f

urban (sanitary) district · Verwaltungsbereich m einer städtischen Sanitätsbehörde [England]

urban scene, town scene, city scene · Stadtprofil n

urban science · Stadtwissenschaft f

urban selection, city selection, town selection · Stadtauslese f

urban service, town service, city service · städtische Dienstleistung f

urban servitude; servitus praediorum urbanorum [Latin] · städtisches Realservitut n, städtisches Prädialservitut n, städtisches (servitutisches) Realrecht n, städtisches (servitutisches) Prädialrecht, städtische Prädialdienstbarkeit f, städtische Realgerechtigkeit, städtische Realdienstbarkeit, städtische Realservitut f, städtische Prädialservitut f

urban setting, town setting, city setting · städtische Umgebung f

urban settlement, town settlement, city settlement · Stadt(an)sied(e)lung f, städtische (An)Sied(e)lung

urban sewage, town sewage, city sewage · städtisches Abwasser n, Stadtabwasser

urban site, town site, city site, urban location, city location, town location · Stadtstandort m, städtischer Standort

urban skeleton · Städtereihe f

urban social segregation · soziale städtische Ungleichverteilung f, städtische soziale Ungleichverteilung

urban social system, town social system, city social system · städtisches Sozialsystem n

urban society · städtische Gesellschaft f, Stadtgesellschaft

urban sociologist, town sociologist, city sociologist · Stadtsoziologe m

urban sociology, town sociology, city sociology · Stadtsoziologie f, städtische Soziologie

urban space, town space, city space · Stadtraum m, städtischer Raum

urban space organization → urban spatial organization

urban spatial structure, urban space structure, city spatial structure, city space structure, town spatial structure, town space structure · städtische Raumstruktur f, städtische Raumzusammensetzung f, städtisches Raumgefüge n, städtischer Raumaufbau m

(urban) spread, (urban) sprawl, outward spread, outward sprawl, suburban spread, suburban sprawl, spread(ing) of cities, sprawl of cities, spread(ing) of towns, sprawl of towns, suburbanization, decentralization, formation of sub(urb)s, suburban process, suburban urbanization · Sied(e)lungsbrei m, Dezentralisation f, Ausufern n, Zersied(e)lung f, Überuferung des städtischen Raumes, Dezentralisierung f

urban state, city state, town state · Stadtstaat m

urban statistic(s), city statistic(s), town statistic(s) · Städtestatistik f

urban statute, urban by(e)-law, urban ordinance, town statute, town by(e)-law, town ordinance, city statute, city by(e)-law, city ordinance · Stadtsatzung f, Stadtstatut n, Stadtgesetz n

urban store, city store, town store · Zentral(laden)geschäft n, zentripetales (Laden)Geschäft

urban structure — usage

urban structure, town composition, urban composition, city composition, town structure, city structure · Stadtstruktur f, Stadtzusammensetzung f, Stadtgefüge n, Stadtaufbau m, städtische Struktur, städtische Zusammensetzung, städtischer Aufbau, städtisches Gefüge

urban structure planning, urban composition planning, town structure planning, town composition planning, city structure planning, city composition planning · Stadtaufbauplanung f, Stadtstrukturplanung, Stadtgefügeplanung, Stadtzusammensetzungsplanung

urban style of life, urban life style · städtischer Lebensstil m

urban surface, town surface, city surface · Stadtoberfläche f

urban surveyor, town surveyor, city surveyor · Stadtbaumeister m

urban surveyor-general, town surveyor-general, city surveyor-general · Stadtoberbaurat m

urban system · System n von Städten [*Nicht verwechseln mit „urbanem System" als das System einer Stadt*]

urban taxation law · städtisches Besteuerungsrecht n

urban tenancy, urban tenement, urban fief, urban fee (tenure), urban (feodal) tenure (of land) · städtisches Leh(e)n n, städtisches Leh(e)n(s)gut, städtisches Leh(e)n(s)besitz m [*Ein dem Erbbaurecht ähnliches Recht im deutschen Recht des Mittelalters. Die Bodenleihe geschah durch die Grundherren, die ihre städtischen Grundstücke an die zuwandernden Bauern abgaben. Als Entgelt wurde eine ewige, unablösbare Rente an den Grundherrn entrichtet*]

urban territory, town area, town territory, city area, city territory, urban area · städtisches Gebiet n [*Ein Gebiet, welches im funktionalen und physiognomischen Sinne vorrangig durch städtische Funktionen geprägt ist*]

urban territory → urban(ized) area

urban threshold theory · städtische Schwellentheorie f

urban-to-rural movement, urban exodus, flight from the town, movement of population from town to country, urban-rural migration, urban-rural drift · Stadtflucht f, Stadtexodus m, Stadt-Land-Wanderung f

urban tract [*According to Dickinson*] → urban agglomeration

urban trade, town trade, city trade · Stadtgewerbe n, städtisches Gewerbe

urban trade area, town trade area, city trade area · Stadtgewerbegebiet n

urban traffic, city traffic, town traffic · Stadtverkehr m

urban transit model choice · Schnellverkehrsalternative f zum Autoverkehr

urban transport(ation) network, urban transit network, town transit network, town transport(ation) network, city transit network, city transport(ation) network · städtisches (Massen)Verkehrsnetz n

urban transport(ation) planning, urban transit planning, town transit planning, town transport(ation) planning, city transit planning, city transport(ation) planning · städtische (Massen)Verkehrsplanung f

urban transport network → urban transport(ation) network

urban treasurer, town treasurer, city treasurer · Stadtkämmerer m

urban uglification, city uglification, town uglification · Stadtverschandelung f

urban umland, town umland, city umland · Stadtumland n

urban unit · städtische Sied(e)lungseinheit f, städtische Sied(e)lungszelle f

urban usable space · städtische Nutzfläche f

(urban) village [*USA*] → village

urban village [*According to Dickinson*]; mere urban tract [*According to Wooldridge and East*]; town-village, city-village · Pseudostadt f, unechte Stadt, Stadtdorf n

urban village [*750 to 1,000 inhabitants*], small town with between 1,000 and 2,000 inhabitants (Brit.); first order center, urban center (US), middle-order sub-central place, sub-town, market district, market town; first order centre · Amtsort m [*nach W. Christaller*]

urban villager [*USA*] · Bewohner m einer städtischen (An)Sied(e)lung von geringerem Status als Gebietskörperschaft gegenüber city und town

urgency of public need · Dringlichkeit f der öffentlichen Notwendigkeit

urgent case · Eilfall m

urgent instruction · Dringlichkeitshinweis m

urgent order, rush order, priority order [*An order which is identified as taking precedence over other orders to ensure its completion in the minimum time*] · Vorzugsauftrag m, Dringlichkeitsauftrag

urgent repair · Dringlichkeitsreparatur f, Notreparatur

urgent work · dringliche Arbeit f

usable space · Nutzfläche f [*Geschäftsraum*]

usage, practice long continued · Sitte f

usage, habit, mode, custom [*Uniform course of dealing in a particular trade*] · Brauch *m*, Üblichkeit *f*, Gepflogenheit *f*, Gewohnheit

usance [*French*]; special custom · Verkehrssitte *f*, Handelsbrauch *m* [*Maßstab für eine Vertragsauslegung. Ein Vertrag ist so auszulegen, wie es Treu und Glauben mit Rücksicht auf die Verkehrssitte erfordern*]

use · Nutzung *f*, Gebrauchsvorteil *m*

use · Benutzung *f*, Gebrauch *m*

use [*England. "Use" war ein bis an die Grenze des Eigentums erweitertes Nutzungsrecht, vererblich und später auch veräußerlich, dessen Bestellung und Übertragung nicht durch die Formalitäten der Tradition nach gemeinem Recht erschwert war. Da ein derartiges Nutzungsrecht auch vor der Einziehung durch die Krone sicher war, so wurde es zur Gewohnheit, statt des Eigentums das Nutzungsrecht zu erwerben. An einem solchen Grundstück waren stets zwei Personen berechtigt: Der juristische Eigentümer (feoffee to the use) und der faktische Eigentümer (cestui que use). Das Institut "use" erinnert einigermaßen an das Salmann-Institut des deutschen Rechts*] · Nutzungsrecht *n* bis an die Grenze des Eigentums erweitert

use → (beneficial) use

us(e)ability · Benutzbarkeit *f*, Benutzungsfähigkeit, Benutzungsvermögen *n*

use charge, use duty, duty for use, charge for use · Benutzungsgebühr *f*, Gebrauchsgebühr

use compulsion, compulsion of use · Nutzungszwang *m*, Gebrauchszwang, Benutzungszwang [*Durch Ortsstatut auferlegte Verpflichtung zur Benutzung einer bestimmten öffentlichen, in der Regel kommunalen Einrichtung, unter Umständen verbunden mit Anschlußzwang*]

use contract, contract of use · Benutzungsvertrag *m*, Gebrauchsvertrag

used, seated [*plot*] · genutzt [*Grundstück*]

use duty, duty for use, charge for use, use charge · Benutzungsgebühr *f*, Gebrauchsgebühr

useful to the public, of public utility, of public usefulness, nonprofit · gemeinnützig, gemeinnötig

use interest, right of use, interest of use, right to use, interest to use, use right · Gebrauchsrecht *n*, Benutzungsrecht, subjektives Gebrauchsrecht, subjektives Benutzungsrecht

use of an institution · Anstaltsnutzung *f*

use of capital, capital use · Kapitalnutzung *f*

use of land, use of (land) area, (land) area use, land use · Bodennutzung *f*, Flächennutzung, Landnutzung [*Die Inanspruchnahme einer Fläche durch den Menschen für bestimmte Zwecke*]

use of reason, argumentation · Argumentation *f*

use of rural land(s), use of country land(s), rural land(s) use, country land(s) use · ländliche Landnutzung *f*, ländliche Bodennutzung, ländliche Flächennutzung

use of (the) law, adjudication of disputes, declaration of the law; iurisdictio [*Latin*]; administration of justice, jurisdiction · Rechtsprechung *f*, Entscheidung von Einzelfällen, Justizausübung, Rechtspflege

use of the whole jointly, joint use · Gesamtgebrauch *m*, Gesamtbenutzung *f*

use permission, permission of use, permission to use · Gebrauchsgenehmigung *f*, Benutzungsgenehmigung, Benutzungserlaubnis *f*, Gebrauchserlaubnis

use plaintiff [*One for whose use (= benefit) an action is brought in the name of another*] · Interessent *m* einer Klage, Klageinteressent

user, usufructuary, beneficiary; cestui (à) que use, cestui à l'use de qui, cestui (à) que trust, cestuy que trust [*Norman French*]; usufructarius [*Latin*]; (beneficial) occupant, (beneficial) occupier, beneficial owner, tenant [*He to whose use another is enfeoffed of lands or tenements. The substantial and beneficial owner, as distinguished from the feoffee to uses*] · Nutznießer *m*, faktischer Eigentümer, Nehmer, Empfänger eines benefiziarischen Nutzungsrechts, Benefiziar, Besitznehmer, Usufruktuar, Fruchtnießer, Nießbraucher

user · Benutzer *m*

user [*A right of use based on long use*] · Benutzungsrecht *n* durch lange Benutzung erworben, Gebrauchsrecht durch langen Gebrauch erworben

user [*The exercise of a right of use*] · Benutzungsrechtausübung *f*, Gebrauchsrechtausübung

user-benefit approach, Clawson approach · Clawson-Ansatz *m* [*Zum Messen des primären Nutzens aus einem Erholungsakt über die Schätzung einer Erholungsnachfragekurve*]

use right, use interest, right of use, interest of use, right to use, interest to use · Gebrauchsrecht *n*, Benutzungsrecht, subjektives Gebrauchsrecht, subjektives Benutzungsrecht

user of an institution · Anstaltsbenutzer *m*

user of structure, user of work, user of physical facility · Bauanlagebenutzer *m*, Bau(werk)benutzer; Bautebenutzer [*Schweiz*]

user-orien(ta)ted, user-related · benutzerbezogen, benutzerorientiert

use to charity · Treuhandverhältnis *n* [*englisches Recht des Mittelalters*]

use (up)on the use · Treuhand *f* an der Treuhand

use value, value of use [*Value in money computed on the basis of the amount paid for the use of property*] · Benutzungswert *m*

use zoning → (land) use zoning

use zoning degree → (land) use zoning degree

use zoning mix(ture) → (land) use zoning mix(ture)

use zoning order → (land) use zoning order

use zoning prohibition → (land) use zoning prohibition

use zoning separation → (land) use zoning separation

US Government bond · Staatsschuldverschreibung *f*, Staatsobligation *f* [*Ein fest verzinsliches Wertpapier der Regierung der USA*]

usual, customary, ordinary, common · herkömmlich, üblich

usual case, standard case · Regelfall *m*

usual factum, customary factum, typical acknowledged experience · typischer Sachverhalt *m*

usual in the place, customary in the place · ortsüblich

usufruct; usus fructus [*Latin*] · (Frucht)Genuß *m*, Nießbrauch *m*, Nutzgewalt *f*, Nutz(ungs)recht *n* [*durch Rechtsgeschäft begründet*] [*Das dingliche Recht, einen Gegenstand in der Gesamtheit seiner Beziehungen zu nutzen, ohne Verfügung über seine Substanz. Gegenstände des Nießbrauches sind Grundstücke, bewegliche Sachen, Sachbruchteile und übertragbare Rechte*]

usufruct devise, devise of usufruct · Nießbrauchlegat *n*, Nießbrauchvermächtnis *n*, (Frucht)Genußlegat, (Frucht)Genußvermächtnis, Nutzgewaltlegat, Nutzgewaltvermächtnis [*Liegenschaft*]

usufruct donor, donor of usufruct · (Frucht)Genußbesteller *m*, Nießbrauchbesteller

usufruct for life, life usufruct · lebenslänglicher Nießbrauch *m*, lebenslänglicher (Frucht)Genuß *m*, lebenslängliche Nutzgewalt *f*

usufruct-gage · Nutzpfand *n*

usufruct heir (male), heir (male) of usufruct · Nießbraucherbe *m*, (Frucht)-Genußerbe, Nutzgewalterbe

usufruct inheritance, inheritance of usufruct · Nießbraucherbschaft *f*, Nießbraucherbe *n*, (Frucht)Genußerbschaft, (Frucht)Genußerbe, Nutzgewalterbschaft, Nutzgewalterbe

usufruct legatee · Nießbrauchlegatar *m*, Nutzgewaltlegatar, (Frucht)Genußlegatar [*Ihm steht der Nießbrauch am Nachlaß bis zum Eintritt des vom Erblasser bestimmten Falles zu*]

usufruct of disposition, disposition usufruct · Dispositionsnießbrauch *m*, Nießbrauch der freien Verfügung

usufruct of estate, usufruct of property, property usufruct, estate usufruct · Nießbrauch *m* an einem Vermögen, Nießbrauch an einem Gut, (Frucht)Genuß *m* an einem Vermögen, (Frucht)Genuß an einem Gut, Nutzgewalt *f* an einem Gut, Nutzgewalt an einem Vermögen

usufruct of rights · Nießbrauch *m* an Rechten, (Frucht)Genuß *m* an Rechten, Nutzgewalt *f* an Rechten

usufruct of the father · väterlicher Nießbrauch *m*, väterlicher (Frucht)Genuß, väterliche Nutzgewalt *f*

usufruct of the mother · mütterlicher Nießbrauch *m*, mütterlicher (Frucht)-Genuß *m*, mütterliche Nutzgewalt *f*

usufruct of things · Nießbrauch *m* an Sachen, Nießbrauch an Gegenständen, (Frucht)Genuß *m* an Sachen, (Frucht)Genuß an Gegenständen, Nutzgewalt *f* an Sachen, Nutzgewalt an Gegenständen

usufruct prescription, prescription of usufruct · Ersitzung *f* des Nießbrauchs, Nießbrauchersitzung

usufruct thing, thing of usufruct · (Frucht)Genußgegenstand *m*, Nießbrauchgegenstand, (Frucht)Genußsache *f*, Nießbrauchsache

usufructuary, beneficiary; cestui (à) que use, cestui à l'use de qui, cestui (à) que trust, cestuy que trust [*Norman French*]; usufructarius [*Latin*]; (beneficial) occupant, (beneficial) occupier, beneficial owner, tenant, user [*He to whose use another is enfeoffed of lands or tenements. The substantial and beneficial owner, as distinguished from the feoffee to uses*] · Nutznießer *m*, faktischer Eigentümer, Nehmer, Empfänger eines benefiziarischen Nutzungsrechts, Benefiziar, Besitznehmer, Usufruktuar, Fruchtnießer, Nießbraucher

usurious contract, exorbitant contract [*A contract if interest contracted to be paid exceeds the rate established by statute*] · Wuchervertrag *m*

usurious interest — vacant land percentage

usurious interest · Wucherzins *m*

usurious price, exorbitant price · Wucherpreis *m*

usurious rent, exorbitant rent · Wuchermiete *f*

usury, feneration; faeneratio [*Latin*] · Wucher *m*, Schacher

usury law, usury act, usury statute · Wuchergesetz *n*

usus fructus verus [*Latin*]; true usufruct · wahrer (Frucht)Genuß *m*, wahrer Nießbrauch

utilitarianism · Utilitarismus *m*

utilitarian point of view · Nützlichkeitsstandpunkt *m*

utility · Nützlichkeit *f*

utility → (final degree of) utility

utility analysis, worth analysis, benefit analysis · Nutz(ungs)wertanalyse *f*, NWA

utility area, area for a public utility · Versorgungsfläche *f*, Fläche für Versorgungsanlage [*Eine Grundstücksfläche für die öffentliche Versorgung; z. B. für Wasserwerk, Gaswerk, E-Werk, Trafohaus usw.*]

utility business · Versorgungswirtschaft *f*

utility index, index of utility · Nutzenindex *m*

utility law → (public) utility law

utility level, level of utility · Nutzenniveau *n*

utility line, supply line · Versorgungsleitung *f*

utility maximization, maximization of utility · Nutzenmaximierung *f*

utility measure, measure of utility · Nutzenmaß *n*

utility model, registered design · Gebrauchsmuster *n*

utility revenue · Leistungsentgelt *n* [*Versorgungsbetrieb*]

utility theory, theory of utility · Nutzentheorie *f*

utilizable · ausnutzbar

utilizable capacity · Ausnutzbarkeit *f*

utilization → (plot) utilization

utilization of land(s), utilization of land area(s), land(s) utilization · Bodenverwertung *f*, Landverwertung, Flächenverwertung

utilization of sewage, sewage utilization · Abwasserverwertung *f*

utilization of space, employment of space · Raumausnutzung *f*

utlagatus [*Latin*]; outlaw, lawless man; exlex · Geächtete *m*

utla(w)ry [*old forms*]; utlagaria [*Latin*]; outlawry · Acht *f*, Geächtetsein *n*, Außergesetzlichkeit *f*

utmost good faith · äußerste Vertragstreue *f*

utopia of escape · Fluchtutopie *f* [*Nach Lewis Mumford Abwehrverhalten gegen die als unlösbar bewerteten gesellschaftlichen Konflikte, denen der Utopist mittels Idealstadtkonzeption zu entrinnen sucht*]

utopia of reconstruction, reconstruction utopia · konstruktive Utopie *f* [*Nach Lewis Mumford die Vision einer wiederhergestellten Umwelt, die der Natur und den Zielen des Menschen besser als die derzeitige angepaßt ist*]

uttering (a) forged instrument · Benutzen *n* einer unechten Urkunde, Benutzen einer gefälschten Urkunde, Benutzen einer verfälschten Urkunde

V

vacancy · Nichtbelegung *f* [*Wohnung*]

vacancy · Brachliegen *n* [*Nutzfläche*]

vacancy loss, collection loss · Mietausfall *m*, Mietverlust *m*

vacancy (loss) decline, collection loss decline · Mietausfallrückgang *m*, Mietverlustrückgang

vacancy (loss) risk, vacancy (loss) hazard, collection loss risk, collection loss hazard · Mietausfallwagnis *n*, Mietausfallrisiko *n*, Mietverlustwagnis, Mietverlustrisiko

vacant · brachliegen [*Nutzfläche*]

vacant, unoccupied, empty · frei, leer(stehend), unbesetzt, unbelegt, nicht belegt [*Raum*]

vacant area percentage, percentage of open space, percentage of open land, percentage of open area, vacant land percentage, vacant space percentage · Freiflächenanteil *m*, Freiraumanteil, Freilandanteil

vacant (land) parcel, gap (land) parcel, vacant parcel of land, gap parcel of land, vacant site, gap site, vacant plot, gap plot · Baulücke *f*, Bebauungslücke, unbebautes Grundstück *n* in einem bebauten Gebiet, nichtbebautes Grundstück in einem bebauten Gebiet, freies Grundstück in einem bebauten Gebiet

vacant land percentage, vacant space percentage, vacant area percentage, per-

vacant site — validity of concept

centage of open space, percentage of open land, percentage of open area · Freiflächenanteil m, Freiraumanteil, Freilandanteil

vacant site, gap site, vacant plot, gap plot, vacant (land) parcel, gap (land) parcel, vacant parcel of land, gap parcel of land · Baulücke f, Bebauungslücke, unbebautes Grundstück n in einem bebauten Gebiet, nichtbebautes Grundstück in einem bebauten Gebiet, freies Grundstück in einem bebauten Gebiet

vacant space · Leerraum m

vacant space percentage, vacant area percentage, percentage of open space, percentage of open land, percentage of open area, vacant land percentage · Freiflächenanteil m, Freiraumanteil, Freilandanteil

vacant urban land policy, vacant urban space policy, vacant urban area policy, urban open area policy, urban open land policy, urban open space policy · städtische Freiflächenpolitik f, städtische Freiraumpolitik, städtische Freilandpolitik

to vacate, to evacuate [*premises; dwelling; occupied country*] · freigeben, räumen, freimachen

vacation house · Ferienhaus n

vacation house area, vacation house territory · Ferienhausgebiet n

vacation house settlement · Ferienhaussied(e)lung f, Ferienkolonie f

vacationist · Urlauber m

vacation pay · Urlaubsgeld n

vacation time of (a) court, non term; justitium, non terminus [*Latin*] · Gerichtsferien f

vaccination officer · Impfinspektor m

vaccinator → (public) vaccinator

vadium, pledge(d article), pledged object, pawned article, pawned object, article pawned, article pledged, object pawned, object pledged, pawn · Pfand n, Pfandstück n, verpfändeter Gegenstand m, gegebenes (Mobiliar)Pfand, Pfandsache f

vadium · gesetztes Pfand n, Vertragspfand, Wette f

vadium mortuum, mortuum vadium; mort gage [*in France*]; mortgage [*A pledge of land(s) of which the mortgagee did not necessarily receive the possession or have the rents and profits in reduction of the demand. In the time of Glanville this form of security was looked upon with much disfavour as a species of usury*] · Lebendsatzung f, Zinssatzung, ewige Satzung, Ewigsatzung [*Immobiliarpfandrecht. Die Nutzung diente als Zins der Forderung*]

vadium ponere, under-wed(d) lecgan [*Anglo-Saxon*] · Pfandbestellung f wegen Schuld [*Englisches Pfandrecht im Mittelalter*]

vadium (recti) dare; wed(d) syllan [*Anglo-Saxon*], wed(d) sellan [*Anglo-Saxon*] · Pfandbestellung f im Prozeß [*Englisches Pfandrecht im Mittelalter*]

vadium vivum, vivum vadium; vifgage [*In France*]; living pledge [*When a person borrowed money of another, and granted to him an estate to hold till the rents and profits repaid the sum borrowed with interest. The estate was conditioned to be void as soon as the sum was realited*] · Totsatzung f, Todsatzung

vagabondage, vagrancy · Landstreicherei f

vagrant act, vagrant law, vagrant statute · Bettelpolizeigesetz n

vagrant census book · Obdachlosenbuch n

val., appraisal (of value), appraisement (of value), assessment (of value), (e)valuation [*The determined or estimated value or price*] · (Ab)Schätzung f, Taxierung, Wertermitt(e)lung f, Bewertung

valiant beggar; beggar able to labour (Brit.); beggar able to labor (US) · arbeitsfähiger Bettler m

valid · geltend, gültig, wirksam

validating statute, curative statute · Formmängelgesetz n [*Es berichtigt Formmängel in Verfügungsurkunden (deeds of conveyance) um älteren, wegen Verstoßes gegen Formvorschriften nichtigen Verfügungen nachträglich zur Wirksamkeit zu verhelfen*]

validation, validity · Gültigkeit f

validation, validity · Bekräftigung f [*Statistik*]

validation certificate · Anerkennungsbescheinigung f [*An den Börsen der USA sind nach dem Bereinigungsgesetz für deutsche Auslandsbonds bereinigte Dollarbonds nur lieferbar, wenn sie mit einer Anerkennungsbescheinigung verbunden sind*]

valid custom(ary law) · gültiges Gewohnheitsrecht n

valid in equity, equitable [*In accordance with rules of equity*] · billigkeitsrechtlich, billig, gültig nach Billigkeit(srecht)

valid in law, good · rechtsgültig

validity, validation · Gültigkeit f

validity, validation · Bekräftigung f [*Statistik*]

validity of a contract, contract validity · Vertragsgültigkeit f

validity of concept · Begriffsgültigkeit f

validity range, range of validity, scope, of validity, validity scope · Geltungsbereich *m*

valid law, law in force · gültiges Gesetz *n*

valid until rescinded · gültig bis auf Widerruf, wirksam bis auf Widerruf

valid version · gültige Fassung *f*

valley hamlet · Talweiler *m*

valley land · Talland *n*

valley settlement · Tal(an)sied(e)lung *f*

valley village · Taldorf *n*

val. of land(s) → (real) property (e)valuation

val. of (real) estate → (real) property (e)valuation

valorization · Wertgebung *f*

valuable · geldwert

valuable · brauchbar [*Baustoff*]

valuable consideration · Kausalgeschäft *n*, Kausalverhältnis *n*, Grundgeschäft, Verpflichtungsgeschäft, kausales Rechtsgeschäft

valuable interest, proprietary right, right in property, right of property, property right, valuable right · (subjektives) Vermögensrecht *n*, vermögenswertes Recht

valuable property · Sache *f* von Wert

valuable thing, property, asset · geldwerter Gegenstand *m*, Vermögensgegenstand, Vermögenssache *f*, geldwerte Sache, Vermögensding *n*, geldwertes Ding, Vermögensrechtsobjekt *n*, geldwertes Rechtsobjekt

valuating → (e)valuating

valuation, (act of) fixing the value date · Valutierung *f*, Wertstellung

valuation → (e)valuation

valuation allowance, (valuation) reserve · Wertberichtigung *f*

valuation basis → (e)valuation basis

valuation clause → (e)valuation clause

valuation council → (e)valuation council

valuation factor → factor of (e)valuation

valuation for condemnation purposes (US) → (e)valuation for condemnation purposes

valuation for court purposes → (e)valuation for court purposes

valuation for expropriation purposes → (e)valuation for expropriation purposes

valuation for mortgage purposes → (e)valuation for mortgage purposes

valuation for private purposes → (e)valuation for private purposes

valuation guide lines → (e)valuation guide lines

valuation index → weighting index

valuation list, tax schedule · Steuerrolle *f*

valuation method → (e)valuation method

valuation of bids → (e)valuation of tenders

valuation of (building) land → (e)valuation of (building) land

valuation of estate → (real) property (e)valuation

valuation officer → (e)valuation officer

valuation of land(s) → (real) property (e)valuation

valuation of offers → (e)valuation of tenders

valuation of property → (real) property (e)valuation

valuation of proposals (US) → (e)valuation of tenders

valuation of (real) estate → (real) property (e)valuation

valuation of (real) property → (real) property (e)valuation

valuation of tenders → (e)valuation of tenders

valuation ordinance → (e)valuation ordinance

valuation panel → (e)valuation council

valuation planning → evaluative planning

valuation prescription → (e)valuation regulation

(valuation) reserve, valuation allowance · Wertberichtigung *f*

valuation scheme → (e)valuation scheme

to value, to appraise, to evaluate [*To estimate the value or amount of; to determine the worth of*] · (ab)schätzen, (be)werten, taxieren, ermitteln eines Wertes

value · Wert *m*

value added · Wertschöpfung *f*

value added by manufacture · Formwert *m*

value added by manufacture · Nettoproduktionswert *m* [*Bestimmung der Verlängerung in der Standortverteilung der Industrie*]

value added tax, VAT · Mehrwertsteuer *f*

value adjustment clause · Wertgleitklausel *f*

value approach · Wertansatz *m*

value as new · Neuwert *m*

"value as security", "value as pledge" · „zur Verpfändung" [*Pfandindossament*]

value change, change of value · Wertveränderung *f*

value control · Wertanalyse *f* für die Überwachung der Realisierungsphase der erarbeiteten Lösung

valued policy · taxierte Police *f*

value figure · Wertzahl *f*

value increase, (prospective) development value, betterment, (capital) appreciation, increase of value [*An improvement which adds to the cost(s) of a property. Distinguished from a repair or replacement*] · Wertverbesserung *f*, Wertzuwachs *m*, Wertsteigerung, Wertzunahme *f*, Werterhöhung

value increase clause, (prospective) development value clause, increase of value clause, (capital) appreciation clause, betterment clause · Werterhöhungsklausel *f*, Wertsteigerungsklausel, Wertzuwachsklausel, Wertzunahmeklausel, Wertverbesserungsklausel

value-increasing · wertsteigernd

value in dispute, disputed value; jurisdictional amount (US), amount in controversy, amount in dispute · Streitwert *m*

value in exchange, exchange(able) value · Tauschwert *m*

value in kind, in-kind value · Naturalwert *m*

value judg(e)ment · Werturteil *n*

value of complaint · Beschwerdewert *m*

value of joint lives · Rente *f* auf das Zusammenleben, Wert *m* der Koexistenz

value of possession, possessory value · Besitzwert *m*

value of previous lots · Einlagenwert *m*

value of production, production value · Erzeugungswert *m*, Herstellungswert, Produktionswert, Fertigungswert

value of property, property value · Vermögenswert *m*

value of use, use value [*Value in money computed on the basis of the amount paid for the use of property*] · Benutzungswert *m*

value parity, parity of value · Wertparität *f*

valuer, appraiser, certifier, quasi-arbitrator [*A person given authority to decide the value of goods, property, etc.*] · Schätzer *m*, Abschätzer, Taxator *m*, Wertgutachter, Schätzungssachverständige

value rate · Werttarif *m*

value-reducing · wertherabsetzend, wertverschlechternd, wertmindernd, wertverringernd

value unit · Werteinheit *f*

vapour nuisance (Brit.); vapor nuisance (US) · Dämpfeemission *f*

vapour nuisance effect (Brit.); vapor nuisance effect (US) · Dämpfeimmission *f*

variability, changeability · (Ab)Änderungsfähigkeit *f*, Umänderungsfähigkeit, (Ab)Änderungsvermögen *n*, Umänderungsvermögen

variable · Veränderliche *f*

variable, alterable, changeable · (ab)änderungsfähig, umänderungsfähig

variable · heterogrades Merkmal *n*, quantitatives Merkmal, Mengenmerkmal [*Statistik*]

variable annuity plan · variabler Pensionsplan *m*, variabler Leistungsplan

variable benefit · ungleicher Pensionsbetrag *m* für jeden Arbeitnehmer

variable costing, operating costing, variable cost(s) accounting, operating cost(s) accounting · variable Kostenrechnung *f*

variable cost(s), operating cost(s) [*Cost tending to vary directly with volume of output, e.g. the additional cost incurred in producing and marketing goods once the organization has been set up*] · variable Kosten *f*

variable gross margin, profit contribution, contribution margin, marginal revenue, marginal balance, marginal income · Deckungsbeitrag *m*, Beitragsüberschuß *m*, Überschußsaldo *m*, Erfolgsbeitrag, variabler Bruttoüberschuß, Grenzerfolg *m*, (Kosten)Deckungszuschlag *m*

variable (management) fee · veränderlicher Zuschlag *m* [*Selbstkostenerstattungsvertrag*]

variable overhead cost(s), variable overhead(s) · variable Gemeinkosten *f*

variables inspection · Abnahmeprüfung *f* mittels quantitativer Merkmale [*Statistik*]

variance · Abweichung *f* [*Kostenrechnung*]

variance of cost(s), cost(s) variance · Kostenabweichung *f*

variance ratio distribution, *F*-distribution · F-Verteilung *f* [*Statistik*]

variance-ratio test, F-test · F-Prüfung *f* [*Statistik*]

variate, aleatory variable, random variable, stochastic variable · stochastische Variable *f*, Zufallsvariable

variation, change, alteration · (Ab)Änderung *f*, Umänderung, Veränderung

variation — vendee's market

variation, divergence, deviation [*from a norm*] · Abweichung *f*

variation by equity, change by equity, alteration by equity · Umänderung *f* durch Billigkeit, (Ab)Änderung durch Billigkeit

variation clause, change clause, alteration clause · (Ab)Änderungsklausel *f*, Umänderungsklausel, Veränderungsklausel

variation contract, alteration contract, contract of variation, contract of alteration, contract of change, change contract · (Ab)Änderungsvertrag *m*, Umänderungsvertrag, Veränderungsvertrag

variation list, variation register, variation registry, alteration list, alteration register, alteration registry, change list, change register, change registry · Veränderungsliste *f*, Veränderungsverzeichnis *n*, (Ab)Änderungsliste, (Ab)Änderungsverzeichnis, Umänderungsliste, Umänderungsverzeichnis

variation of building lines, change of building lines, alteration of building lines · (Bau)Fluchtlinien(ab)änderung *f*

variation of law, alteration of law, law change, law variation, law alteration, change of law · Rechts(ab)änderung *f*, Rechtsumänderung, Rechtsveränderung

variation of structural design, change of structural design, alteration of structural design, structural design variation, structural design alteration, structural design change · (Ab)Änderung *f* des Bauentwurfs, Umänderung des Bauentwurfs, Veränderung des Bauentwurfs, Bauentwurfs(ab)änderung, Bauentwurfsumänderung, Bauentwurfsveränderung

variation of (the) design, alteration of (the) design, change of (the) design, design change, design alteration, design variation · Entwurfs(ab)änderung *f*, Entwurfsveränderung, Entwurfsumänderung, (Ab)Änderung des Entwurfs, Umänderung des Entwurfs, Veränderung des Entwurfs

variation register, variation registry, alteration list, alteration register, alteration registry, change list, change register, change registry, variation list · Veränderungsliste *f*, Veränderungsverzeichnis *n*, (Ab)Änderungsliste, (Ab)Änderungsverzeichnis, Umänderungsliste, Umänderungsverzeichnis

varied, changed, altered · (ab)geändert, umgeändert

to vary, to change, to alterate · (ab)ändern, umändern, verändern

to vary, to deviate, to diverge [*from a norm*] · abweichen

to vary slightly, to modify, to alter slightly, to change slightly · geringfügig (ab)ändern, geringfügig umändern, geringfügig verändern

vasallage · Vasallität *f*

vassal, tenant of land, feeholder, holder of a fee, holder of a fief, fief-tenant, feoda(to)ry, feuda(to)ry; homo pertinens [*Latin*]; beneficiary, holder of a feudal benefice, land tenant, (feudal) tenant, manorial tenant, feudal bondman [*A tenant or vassal who held his estate by feudal service*] · Leh(e)n(s)mann *m*, Leh(e)n(s)träger *m*, Gefolgsmann, Gutszinsmann, Vasall *m*

vassalage · Vasallentum *n*

vassal of a vassal, arriere vassal, underfeudatory · Aftervasall *m*

vast · ausgedehnt [*Grundstück*]

VAT, value added tax · Mehrwertsteuer *f*

vector diagram map · Vektordiagrammkarte *f*

vector map · Vektorkarte *f*

vegetable cultivation · Gemüse(an)bau *m*

vegetable farm · Gemüsegut *n*

vegetable-farming · Handelsgemüse(an)bau *m*, Erwerbsgemüse(an)bau

vegetation geography · Vegetationsgeographie *f*

vegetation map · Vegetationskarte *f*

vegetation mapping · Vegetationskartierung *f*

vehicle fleet · Fahrzeugbestand *m*

vehicle owner, vehicle proprietor · Fahrzeugeigentümer *m*

vehicle possessor · Fahrzeugbesitzer *m*

vehicle proprietor, vehicle owner · Fahrzeugeigentümer *m*

vehicle traffic, vehicular traffic · Fahr(zeug)verkehr *m*

vehicular access to site, drive to site · Baustellenzufahrt *f*

vehicular drive, access · Zufahrt *f*

vehicular exit · Ausfahrt *f*

vehicular traffic, vehicle traffic · Fahr(zeug)verkehr *m*

vendee, buyer, purchaser · Käufer *m*

vendee of (real) estate, vendee of (real) property, purchaser of realty, vendee of realty, buyer of realty, land buyer, purchaser, purchaser of (real) estate, purchaser of (real) property, buyer of (real) estate, buyer of (real) property · Grund(stücks)käufer *m*, Bodenkäufer *m*, Liegenschaftskäufer, Landkäufer, Immobilienkäufer, Immobilienkäufer

vendee's market, buyer's market, purchaser's market · Käufermarkt *m*

venire — vertical privity

venire → (writ of) venire

venue · örtliche Zweigzuständigkeit f, Zweigzuständigkeit nach common law

venue (of court) → (local) venue (of court)

verbal, oral, parol, by word of mouth [*In early times few persons could write, and therefore when a document was required to record a transaction the parties put their seals to it and made it a deed. Transactions of less importance were testified by word of mouth or by parol, and this use of "parol", to signify the absence of a deed, remained after simple writing without sealing had come into use*] · mündlich

verbal agreement, oral agreement, agreement by word of mouth, agreement by parol, parol agreement · mündliches Abkommen n, mündliche Vereinbarung f, mündliche Abmachung

verbal deposition, oral deposition · mündliche Vernehmung f

verbal evidence, verbal proof, oral evidence, oral proof [*That which is given by word of mouth; the ordinary kind of evidence, given by witness in court*] · mündlicher Beweis m

verbal evidence rule, oral evidence rule · Ausschließung f mündlicher Beweise wenn schriftliche vorliegen, Ausschluß m mündlicher Beweise wenn schriftliche vorliegen

verbal instruction, parol instruction, oral instruction · mündliche Anweisung f

verbal pleading, pleading by word of mouth, statement, (oral) pleading · Plädoyer n

verbal promise, oral promise · mündliches Versprechen n

verbal proof, oral evidence, oral proof, verbal evidence [*That which is given by word of mouth; the ordinary kind of evidence, given by witness in court*] · mündlicher Beweis m

verbal testimony, oral testimony · mündliche Zeugenaussage f unter Eid

verbal tradition, oral tradition · mündliche Überlieferung f

verbal will, oral will, nuncupative will · mündliches Testament n

verderor · Forstmeister m

verdict, finding (of the issue) [*From the Latin "vere dictum", a true declaration*] · Wahrspruch m, Verdikt n

verdict of guilty · Schuldspruch m

verdict of not guilty · Nichtschuldspruch m

verdict subject to special case · Geschworenenspruch m bei dem die Parteien vor Richterentscheid zuerst die Rechtsfragen formulieren müssen

verge of land, yardland, hydeland, husbandland, wista; hilda [*Scotland*]; terra hydata, virgate terrae. hida (terrae), hyda, familia [*Latin*]; hide ((of) land), hyde (of land), higid, hiwise, virgate (land) [*A quantity of land not of any certain extent, but as much as a plough can by course of husbandry plough in a year. It meant in different places anything from sixty to 120 acres. A virgate is one fourth of a hide*] · Hufe(ngut) f,(n), Hufenschoß n, Hube f, Hufen(gut)land n [*Ältere Benennungen: Hof m, Hub m, Hu(o)ba f, und Hova f*] [*Unter gutsherrlich-bäuerlichen Verhältnissen hieß der gesamte Besitz eines Dorfgenossen "Hufe(ngut)". Diese Benennung war also keine Flächengröße, sondern eine Besitzeinheit, die zahlreiche, zerstreut liegende kleine Ackerteile im Besitz derselben Person umfaßte*]

verificare [*Latin*]; to verify, to prove, to make out to be true · beweisen

verification [*An oath at the end of a pleading or petition to the effect that the statements in it are true*] · eidliche Beglaubigung f

verification · Bewahrheitung f, Wahrheitsbeweis m, Richtigbefund m

to verify, to prove, to make out to be true; verificare [*Latin*] · beweisen

versed in the law, learned in the law, skilled in the law · rechtsbeflissen, rechtsgelehrt, rechtsbeschlagen

versimilitude · Realitätsnähe f, Wirklichkeitsnähe

version · Fassung f

version of law, version of statute, version of act · Gesetzesfassung f

vertical (aerial) photograph · Senkrechtaufnahme f, Senkrechtluftbild n

vertical form, report form · Staffelform f [*Bilanz*]

vertical garden city · senkrechte Gartenstadt f, vertikale Gartenstadt

vertical interval, contour interval · Äquidistanz f

vertical mobility, social rise and fall · senkrechte Mobilität f, sozialer Aufstieg m und Niedergang m

vertical pattern, vertical scheme · senkrechtes Muster n, senkrechtes Schema

vertical photograph → vertical (aerial) photograph

vertical (plot) utilization, vertical utilization of (a) plot · senkrechte (Grundstücks)Ausnutzung f, vertikale (Grundstücks)Ausnutzung

vertical privity · Beziehung f zwischen Hersteller und Letztabnehmer

vertical scheme, vertical pattern · senkrechtes Muster *n*, senkrechtes Schema

vertical stratification of different settlement types, settlement stratification · Sied(e)lungsschichtung *f*

vertical utilization of (a) plot, vertical (plot) utilization · senkrechte (Grundstücks)Ausnutzung *f*, vertikale (Grundstücks)Ausnutzung

very common · sehr verbreitet

to vest → to instal

vested [*Which should be maintained*] · althergebracht, verbrieft, wohlerworben

vested remainder [*A fixed interest in land(s) or tenement(s) to take effect in possession, after a particular estate is spent*] · bestalltes Anwartschaftsrecht *n*, eingesetztes Anwartschaftsrecht, unbedingtes Anwartschaftsrecht

vested remainder (land(ed)) estate, vested remainder [*The remainder becomes vested if the person who ist to have it is ascertained or upon the happening of the event which is to bring the remainder into existence*] · gewisser anwartschaftlicher Landbesitz(stand) *m*, gewisser anwartschaftlicher Grund(stücks)besitz(stand), gewisser anwartschaftlicher (Boden)Besitz(stand)

vested right · wohlerworbenes Recht *n*

vested rights theory · Theorie *f* des Rechtsschutzes im eigenen Land für im fremden Land nach dortigem Recht entstandene Rechte

vesting, admission, commission, order, installation · (Amts)Einsetzung *f*, (Amts)Bestallung

vesting · Verfügung *f* über erworbene Pensionsansprüche, Anrechnung über erworbene Pensionsansprüche

vesting (created) by will · testamentarische Einsetzung *f*, testamentarische Bestallung

vesting declaration · Bestallungserklärung *f*, Einsetzungserklärung

vesting deed · Bestallungsurkunde *f*, Einsetzungsurkunde

vesting instrument · Bestallungsdokument *n*, Einsetzungsdokument

vestitor [*Latin*] · Einweiser *m* [*Erwerbung einer Gewere*]

vest-pocket park [*A park built on a vacant parcel in a built-up area of towns. It frequently serves only as playground or tot lot*] · Kleinstpark *m*

vestry · Pfarrgemeinde *f*

vestry · Pfarrgemeindeversammlung *f*

vestry-clerk · Kirchengemeindesekretär *m*, Zivilstandsbeamte einer Pfarrgemeinde

vesture, profit of land(s), land(s) profit [*In old English law. The value of the vesture of the land(s)*] · Wert *m* der Grundstücksbewachsung außer Bäumen

vesture of the land(s); vestura terrae [*Latin*] [*In old English law. The corn, grass, underwood, sweepage and the like*] · Grundstücksbewachsung *f* außer Bäumen

veteran · Kriegsteilnehmer *m*

veto · Zustimmungsverweigerung *f*, Veto *n*

veto power · Vetorecht *n*

vetus patrimonium domini [*Latin*]; customary freehold, ancient demesne, copyhold tenure by custom of ancient demesne; dominicum antiquum, antiquum dominicum [*Latin*] [*Such land(s) as were entered by William I., in Doomesday-book, under the title "De Terra Regis"; and which were held later by a species of copyhold tenure*] · altes Krongut(leh(e)n) *n*

vexation · unzulässige Rechtsausübung *f*

viability · Lebensfähigkeit *f*

vibration nuisance · Erschütterungsemission *f*

vibration nuisance effect · Erschütterungsimmission *f*

vicar · Vikar *m*

vicar-general · Generalvikar *m*

vicarial tithe · Vikarzehnt *m*

vicarious agent · Erfüllungsgehilfe *m*

vicarious immunity · Ausschluß *m* zugunsten Dritter, Ausschließung *f* zugunsten Dritter, Freizeichnung *f* zugunsten Dritter, Haftungsausschluß *m* zugunsten Dritter, Haftungsausschließung *f* zugunsten Dritter, Haftungsfreizeichnung *f* zugunsten Dritter

vicarious liability, vicarious responsibility [*The liability which arises because of one person's relation(ship) to another*] · Fremdverschuldenhaftung *f*, Fremdverschuldenhaftpflicht *f*, Fremdverschuldenhaftbarkeit *f*, stellvertretende Haftung, stellvertretende Haftbarkeit, stellvertretende Haftpflicht

vicarious liability of a master, vicarious responsibility of a master [*In tort, a master is generally liable for the acts of his servant performanced in the course of his employment. In criminal law a master may be held liable for a servant's offences performed in the course of his employment*] · Haftung *f* für einen Gehilfen, Haftpflicht *f* für einen Gehilfen, Haftbarkeit *f* für einen Gehilfen

vicariously liable, vicariously responsible · stellvertretend haftbar, stellvertretend haftpflichtig

vicariously responsible — village renewal

vicariously responsible, vicariously liable · stellvertretend haftbar, stellvertretend haftpflichtig

vicarious performance (of (the) work(s)), vicarious execution (of (the) work(s)), vicarious construction (of (the) work(s)) · stellvertretende Bauausführung f, delegierte Bauausführung

vicarious responsibility · Erfüllungsgehilfenverpflichtung f

vicarious responsibility of a master, vicarious liability of a master [*In tort, a master is generally liable for the acts of his servant performanced in the course of his employment. In criminal law a master may be held liable for a servant's offences performed in the course of his employment*] · Haftung f für einen Gehilfen, Haftpflicht f für einen Gehilfen, Haftbarkeit f für einen Gehilfen

vice chairman · stellvertretender Vorsitzender m

vicecomes · normannischer Landvogt m

vice-consul · Vizekonsul m

vice-consular officer, vice-consular official · Vizekonsularbeamte m

vicinage, adjacent area; neighbouring area (Brit.); neighboring area (US) · Nachbarfläche f, benachbarte Fläche

victim pay · Gemaßregeltenunterstützung f

viduity, widowhood · Witwenschaft f

to view · besichtigen [*Wohnung*]

view, teaching(s) · Lehrmeinung f

view · Augenscheinnahme f

view of frankpledge · Freipflegeschau f

vifgage [*In France*]; living pledge, vadium vivum, vivum vadium [*When a person borrowed money of another, and granted to him an estate to hold till the rents and profits repaid the sum borrowed with interest. The estate was conditioned to be void as soon as the sum was realized*] · Totsatzung f, Todsatzung

vigilant activity, diligence, prudence · Wachsamkeit f

vilicus [*Latin*]; Roman manorial officer, general steward of a (Roman) villa · römischer Herrengutverwalter m, römischer Frongutverwalter

villa → (Roman) villa

village · Dorf n

village, urban village [*USA*] · städtische (An)Sied(e)lung f von geringerem Status als Gebietskörperschaft gegenüber city und town [*Das Wort „village" in den USA hat nichts mit dem deutschen Wort „Dorf" zu tun. Wir dürfen es also auf keinen Fall mit diesem gleichsetzen. Die typische ländliche Siedlungsweise in den größten Teilen der Vereinigten Staaten und Kanada ist seit Beginn der weißen Besiedlung der Einzelhof gewesen, mit einer Blockflur in Besitzeinheit, als Familienbetrieb konzipiert, von der quadratischen Vermessung des Landes gefördert und auch seitens der Politik der Regierung mit der Heimstättengesetzgebung in den Vereinigten Staaten seit 1862 deutlich in den Vordergrund gestellt. Das Dorf im deutschen Sinne dagegen ist in Angloamerika die Ausnahme. Wir finden es nur in den frühesten Siedlungsgebieten der Engländer in den Neuenglandstaaten, im Siedlungsgebiet der sogenannten Pennsylvania Dutch, in dem von Angehörigen der Church of Jesus Christ of Latter-day Saints (Mormonen) Mitte des vorigen Jahrhunderts besiedelten Tale des Großen Salzsees in Utah und im Gebiete der Pueblo-Indianer des Südwestens der Union*]

village artisan · Dorfhandwerker m

village core, core of village · Dorfkern m

village desertion · Dorfwüstung f

village directly dependent on the emperor · Reichsdorf n

village economy · Dorfwirtschaft f

village forest, village wood · Dorfwald m

village (general) property, village ownership (of property), village proprietorship · Dorfeigentum n

(village) green, common, (village) plaza · Anger m, Dorfplatz m, Dorfplan m, Platz (eines Dorfes)

village head, re(e)ve, head of a village · Schultheiß m, Schulze

village herdsman · Dorfhirte m

village house · Dorfhaus n

village land(s) · Dorfland n, Dorfländerei(en) f (pl)

village location, village site · Dorfstandort m, Dorflage f

village of recent settlers · Neusiedlerdorf n

village of weavers · Weberdorf n

village pasture · Dorfweide f

(village) plaza, (village) green, common · Anger m, Dorfplatz m, Dorfplan m, Platz (eines Dorfes)

village population · Dorfbevölkerung f

village priest · Dorfpriester m

villager · Dorfbewohner m, Dorfeinwohner, Dörfler

village reform · Dorfreform f

village renewal, village revival · Dorferneuerung f

village school — violation (of law)

village school, rural school · Dorfschule *f*, Landschule

village site, village location · Dorfstandort *m*, Dorflage *f*

village street · Dorfstraße *f*

village structure · Dorfstruktur *f*

village waste · Dorfödland *n*

village with a rectangular street green · Straßenangerdorf *n*, Straßenplatzdorf

village wood, village forest · Dorfwald *m*

villain rent → labour rent

villain status → villein status

villain tenancy → copyhold

villain (tenant), villein (tenant), bondager, bond(s)man, culvert, serf; villarus [*Latin*]; regardant (to the manor), bond tenant [*Strictly a man of servile condition holding usually one virgate of land, this is the fourth part of a hide, in the common fields of a manor by base services; but the term is sometimes applied to one of free status who holds land by servile tenure*] · Leibeigene, unfreier Bauer, Dienstbauer *m*, Hörige, Unfreie, Knechtsleh(e)n(s)mann

villain tenement → copyhold

villain tenure → copyhold

villanage, ville(i)nage; culvertagium [*Latin*]; culvertage · Leibeigentum *n*

villanage land, land in ville(i)nage, ville(i)nage land, land in villanage [*It was in the occupation of tenants, but held in villanage, at the will of the lord, and at customary services*] · Hörigenland *n*, Leibeigenschaftsland, höriges Land

villanagium [*Latin*] → copyhold

villa residential quarter · Villenviertel *n*

villarus [*Latin*]; regardant (to the manor), bond tenant, villain (tenant), villein (tenant), bondager, bond(s)man, culvert, serf [*Strictly a man of servile condition holding usually one virgate of land, this is the fourth part of a hide, in the common fields of a manor by base services; but the term is sometimes applied to one of free status who holds land by servile tenure*] · Leibeigene, unfreier Bauer, Dienstbauer *m*, Hörige, Unfreie, Knechtsleh(e)n(s)mann

villein → villain (tenant)

ville(i)nage → villein status

ville(i)nage service, bondage service · Dienstbauernleistung *f*

ville(i)nage tenure, tenure in villenage, tenure in bondage, tenure in bond service, tenure of bond-land, bondage tenure [*A distinct sort of copyhold*] · Dienstbauernleh(e)n *n*

villeinage → villanage

ville(i)nage; culvertagium [*Latin*]; culvertage, villanage · Leibeigentum *n*

ville(i)nage land, land in villanage, villanage land, land in ville(i)nage [*It was in the occupation of tenants, but held in villanage, at the will of the lord, and at customary services*] · Hörigenland *n*, Leibeigenschaftsland, höriges Land

villein rent → labour rent

villein status, villain status, status of a serf, (pr(a)edial) bondage, bondage (on an estate), serfdom (on an estate), villanage, ville(i)nage; nativitas [*Latin*]; servile status [*Called by Britton "naifte"*] · Hörigenstatus *m*, Leibeigenschaft *f*, Grundhörigkeit *f*, (Grund)Untertänigkeit, Bauerndienst *m*

villein tenancy → copyhold

villein (tenant) → villain (tenant)

villein tenement → copyhold

villein tenure → copyhold

to vindicate · herausverlangen, vindizieren

vindication gregis [*Latin*] · Klage *f* auf eine Tierherde

vindication; vindicatio [*Latin*] · Herausgabeklage *f*, Rückgabeklage, Wiedererlangungsklage, Eigentumsklage, Klage auf Wiedererlangung, Klage auf Rückgabe, Klage auf Herausgabe, sachenrechtliche Klage, Sachklage, Vindikationsklage

vindictive compensation → vindictive damages

vindictive damages, vindictive compensation, vindictive indemnity, vindictive indemnification, exemplary damages, exemplary compensation, exemplary indemnification, exemplary indemnity, punitive damages, punitive compensation, punitive indemnification, punitive indemnity · Extraentschädigung(sleistung) *f*, Extraschadenersatz(leistung) *m*, (*f*)

vindictive indemnification → vindictive damages

vine-growers' village · Winzerdorf *n*, Weindorf

vintage · Jahrgang *m* [*Bei der zeitlichen Zerlegung des Faktors Kapital im einsektoralen Wachstumsmodell*]

to violate · zuwiderhandeln

violation of a duty, breach · Pflichtvergehen *n*

violation of boundaries · Grenzverletzung *f*

violation (of law), law violation, (act(ion) of) contravention, (legal) irregularity, infringement, default, disobedience, tort, (civil) wrong, tortious act(ion), illegality, trespass, unlawfulness, offence

violator — vocational instruction

(Brit.); offense, offence (US); delictum [*Latin*] · Delikt *n*, (Rechts)Verletzung *f*, (Rechts)Verstoß *m*, unerlaubte (Begehungs)Handlung, Ordnungswidrigkeit *f*, Zuwiderhandlung, (Rechts)Widrigkeit, schädigendes Verhalten *n*, deliktische (Begehungs)Handlung, Gesetz(es)übertretung, Delikthandlung, Widerrechtlichkeit, Gesetzwidrigkeit, Rechtsübertretung, Ungesetzlichkeit

violator, offender · Gesetz(es)übertreter *m*, Zuwiderhandelnde

violence · Gewalttätigkeit *f*

violent felony · Gewaltdelikt *n*

virgarius [*Latin*]; tenant by the verge, holder of yardland, holder of virgate, holder of verge of land, yardling [*Tenant who held copyhold after a symbolic surrender and delivery of a small rod (= verge)*] · Hüf(e)ner *m*, Hufenbauer, Huf(e)ner

virgate (land), verge of land, yardland, hydeland, husbandland, wista; hilda [*Scotland*]; terra hydata, virgate terrae, hida (terrae), hyda, familia [*Latin*]; hide ((of) land), hyde (of land), higid, hiwise [*A quantity of land not of any certain extent, but as much as a plough can by course of husbandry plough in a year. It meant in different places anything from sixty to 120 acres. A virgate is one fourth of a hide*] · Hufe(ngut) *f*,(*n*), Hufenschoß *n*, Hube *f*, Hufen(gut)land *n* [*Ältere Benennungen: Hof m, Hub m, Hu(o)ba f, und Hova f*] [*Unter gutsherrlich-bäuerlichen Verhältnissen hieß der gesamte Besitz eines Dorfgenossen „Hufe(ngut)". Diese Benennung war also keine Flächengröße, sondern eine Besitzeinheit, die zahlreiche, zerstreut liegende kleine Ackerteile im Besitz derselben Person umfaßte*]

virgin land, land in its natural state · jungfräuliches Land *n*

virgin soil, soil in its natural state · jungfräulicher Boden *m*

viscount · Vizegraf *m*

visible balance, balance of payments, balance of trade, balance of accounts, trade balance · Zahlungsbilanz *f*, Handelsbilanz

visible history · Geschichte *f* in Baudenkmälern

visible profitable property · nutzbarer Realbesitz *m*

visible property · sichtbares Vermögen *n*

visible property in the parish · sichtbares Vermögen *n* in der Kirchengemeinde

visionary speculation · phantastische Spekulation *f*

visit, inspection · Besichtigung *f* [*Baustelle vor Angebotsabgabe*]

to visit a site, to inspect a site · besichtigen [*Baustelle vor Angebotsabgabe*]

visitatio hemorum [*Latin*]; regard · Waldbereinigung *f* [*Zur Feststellung von Forstfrevlern*]

visit of site, inspection of site, site inspection, site visit, site examination, construction site visit, construction site examination, construction site inspection, building site visit, building site inspection, building site examination, examination of site · Baustellenbesichtigung *f*, (Baustellen)Begehung, Ortsbesichtigung [*Vor Abgabe eines Angebotes*]

visitor · Aufsichtsbehörde *f* einer Körperschaft, Aufsichtsbehörde einer Korporation

Visitors in Lunacy · Obervormundschaftskommission *f* [*England. Für vom Kanzleigericht für wahnsinnig erklärte Personen*]

visual corridor, visual opening · Durchblick *m*

visual environment · sichtbare Umwelt *f*

visual impact of a landscape · bildlicher Eindruck *m* einer Landschaft

visual opening, visual corridor · Durchblick *m*

visual pollution by billboards on highways · Verunstaltung *f* durch Straßenreklameschilder

visual privacy · Sichtabgeschlossenheit *f*

vital rate · Bevölkerungsziffer *f*

vital statistics [*Statistics related to births, deaths, ages, race, marriages, health, and similar characteristics of a population group*] · Personenstatistik *f*

vivum vadium; vifgage [*In France*]; living pledge, vadium vivum [*When a person borrowed money of another, and granted to him an estate to hold till the rents and profits repaid the sum borrowed with interest. The estate was conditioned to be void as soon as the sum was realized*] · Totsatzung *f*, Todsatzung

vocational education, vocational training, occupational training, occupational education · Berufsausbildung *f*

vocational guidance, occupational guidance, careers guidance, occupational consulting service, vocational consulting service, occupational (guidance) service, occupational advisory service, vocational (guidance) service · Berufsberatung *f*

vocational instruction · berufsorientierter Unterricht *m*, berufsbezogene Weisung *f*, berufsbezogener Unterricht, berufsorientierte Weisung

vocational test · Berufseignungsprüfung f

vocational training, occupational training, occupational education, vocational education · Berufsausbildung f

vocational training facility, occupational training facility, vocational education facility, occupational education facility · Berufsausbildungseinrichtung f

voice given → vote

void, null, invalid [*"Void" in the strict sense means that an instrument or transaction is negatory and ineffectual so that nothing can cure it. But frequently "void" is used and construed as having the meaning of "voidable"*] · ungültig, nichtig, unwirksam

voidable [*An agreement or other act is said to be voidable when one of the parties is entitled to rescind it, while until that happens is has the legal effect which it was intended to have*] · anfechtbar

voidable contract [*It has legal effect until avoided*] · anfechtbarer Vertrag m

voidable pricing mistake · externer Kalkulationsirrtum m, externer Preisgestaltungsirrtum [*Gemäß VOB ist er zur Anfechtung berechtigt, weil er voraussetzt, daß der Irrende die dem Angebot zugrunde liegende Kalkulation ausdrücklich zum Gegenstand der entscheidenden Vertragsverhandlungen gemacht hat*]

voidable transaction · anfechtbare Handlung f

voided → repealed

void marriage · Nicht-Ehe f

volition, exercise of the will, act(ion) of the will · Willensakt m, Willensausübung f, Willenshandlung, Wollen n

volume calculation, volume computation · Raumberechnung f

volume estimate [*Forecast of probable project construction cost(s) based on unit cost(s) per cubic foot*] · Kostenschätzung f nach umbautem Raum

volume variance, capacity variance, activity variance · Beschäftigungsabweichung f (im engeren Sinne) [*Diese Abweichung wird von der Kapazitätsabweichung nicht streng unterschieden*]

volume variance, capacity variance, activity variance · Kapazitätsabweichung f, Produktions(volumen)grad m, Volumenabweichung bei Kapazitätsplanung, Produktionshöhenabweichung [*Sie stellt die nicht gedeckten Plankosten dar*]

voluntarily transferable · freiwillig übertragbar

voluntarily transferred, conveyed · freiwillig übertragen

voluntary accumulation plan · unabhängiger Ansammlungsplan m

voluntary aim · Almosen m, milde Gabe f

voluntary conveyance · Schenkungsauflassung f

voluntary dissolution · freiwillige Auflösung f

voluntary insurance · freiwillige Versicherung f

voluntary land transfer, land conveyance, conveyance (of land), voluntary transfer (of land) · freiwillige Übertragung (von Land), freiwillige Landübertragung, freiwillige Bodenübertragung f

voluntary property settlement, voluntary settlement (of property) · Vermögensbindung f ohne geldwerte Gegenleistung

voluntary settlement, post-nuptial settlement [*A settlement made after marriage upon a wife or children*] · erbvertragliche Regelung f nach der Eheschließung

voluntary transfer, conveyance · freiwillige Übertragung f

voluntary transfer clause, conveyance clause · freiwillige Übertragungsklausel f

voluntary transfer law, conveyance law, land conveyance law, law of conveyances (of land), law of land conveyances, law of voluntary transfer · Auflassungsrecht n, freiwilliges Übertragungsrecht n

voluntary transfer (of land), voluntary land transfer, land conveyance, conveyance (of land) · freiwillige Übertragung (von Land), freiwillige Landübertragung, freiwillige Bodenübertragung

voluntary transfer practice, conveyancing practice · freiwilliges Übertragungswesen n

voluntary winding up · freiwillige Liquidation f

volunteer · unentgeltlicher Erwerber m

volunteer · Volontär m

volunteer · Freiwillige m

volunteer army · Freiwilligenarmee f

vote · Stimmabgabe f

vote, suffrage, voice given · Stimme f, Wahlstimme

voter, elector · Wähler m

voter apathy, elector apathy · Wahlmüdigkeit f

voter approval, elector approval · Wählerzustimmung f

voter response, elector response · Wählerreaktion f

voting age · Wahlalter n

**voting by mail, ** postal voting, voting by post · Briefwahl f

voting district · Wahlbezirk m

voting paper, ballot paper [*Used in secret voting*] · Wahlzettel, Stimmzettel m

voting place, place of voting · Wahlsprengel m

voting right, right of vote, right to vote · Wahlrecht n, Wahlberechtigung f

voting right on behalf of shareholders · Depotstimmrecht n

voting security · stimmberechtigtes Wertpapier n

voting share · Stimmaktie f

voucher · Beleg(schein) m

voucher system · Originalbelegverfahren n, Belegbuchhaltung f

vulgar law · Vulgärrecht n

W

wafer · Oblate f [*zum Siegeln*]

wage, hire [*Compensation for labo(u)r and services*] · (Arbeits)Lohn m

wage allowance system · Lohnzuschußsystem n

wage by results, piece-wage, efficiency-wage, statement-wage, premium-wage · Akkordlohn m, Leistungslohn

wage cost(s) → wage(s) cost(s)

wage earner · Lohnempfänger m

wage freeze · Lohnstop m

wage in products of the soil, wage in kind, in-kind wage · Deputat n, Naturallohn m

wage intensive, high-wage · lohnstark, lohnintensiv

wage labour (Brit.); wage labor (US) · Lohnarbeitskräfte fpl

wage level · Lohnniveau n, Lohnhöhe f

wage negotiation · Lohnverhandlung f

wage of production, production wage · Fertigungslohn m, Produktionslohn, Herstellungslohn, Erzeugungslohn

wage-orien(ta)ted, wage-related · lohnbezogen, lohnorientiert

wage rate variance · Lohnsatzabweichung f

wage-related, wage-orien(ta)ted · lohnbezogen, lohnorientiert

wager of battle · Beweisabnahme f durch Zweikampf

wager of law, law wager · Beweisabnahme f durch Eideshelfer, Prozeßaustrag m durch Eideshelfer, Reinigungseid m

wage(s) agreement · Lohnabkommen n, Lohnabmachung f, Lohnvereinbarung

wage(s) alteration, wage(s) variation, wage(s) change · Lohn(ab)änderung f

wage(s)-bill tax · Lohnsummensteuer f

wage(s) board · Lohnamt n

wage(s) change, wage(s) alteration, wage(s) variation · Lohn(ab)änderung f

wages committee · Lohnausschuß m

wage(s) cost(s), payroll cost(s) · Lohnkosten f

wage(s) distress · Lohnpfändung f

wage(s) fluctuation clause · Lohngleitklausel f

wage(s) law, law of wage(s) · Lohnrecht n

wage(s) percentage · Lohnprozentsatz m

wages-prices spiral, spiral of wages and prices · Lohn-Preis-Spirale f

wages question, wages problem · Lohnfrage f

wage(s) rate, rate of wage(s) · Lohnsatz m

wage(s) reduction · Lohnabbau m

wage(s) roll, payroll · Lohnliste f

wage(s) tax · Lohnsteuer f

wages theory, theory of wages · Lohntheorie f

wage(s) variation, wage(s) change, wage(s) alteration · Lohn(ab)änderung f

wage to start · Anfangslohn m

wage-wage spiral · Lohn-Lohn-Spirale f

waif · weggeworfenes Diebesgut n

waiting-bay, lay-by [*deprecated*] · Ausbuchtung f, Straßenausbuchtung

waiting-line theory · Warteschlangentheorie f

waiting-list · Warteliste f

waiting list for admission, admission waiting list · Anwartschaftsliste f [*z. B. für den Bezug einer Wohnung*]

to waive · erlassen [*Scheckprotest*]

waived, disclaimed, abandoned, relinquished, renounced, remised, forsaken, given up · aufgegeben, preisgegeben, Verzicht geleistet, verzichtet, ausgeschlagen, entsagt, derelinquiert

waiver, abandonment, relinquishment, renunciation, renouncement, disclaimer

[*It includes the intention, and also the external act(ion) by which it is carried into effect*] · Aufgabe *f*, Preisgabe *f*, Verzicht(leistung) *m*, *(f)*, Entsagung, Ausschlagung

walker [*Forester having the care of a certain space of ground*] · (Wald)Begeher *m*

walking city, walking town · Stadt *f* mit ortsveränderlichen Teilen

walking city, walking town, pedestrian(-prone) city, pedestrian(-prone) town · Fußgängerstadt *f*, fußgängergerechte Stadt

walking distance · Gehentfernung *f*, Gehweite *f*

walking map · Wanderkarte *f*

walking right · Gehrecht *n* [*Das Recht zum Gehen über ein fremdes Grundstück*]

walking town, walking city · Stadt *f* mit ortsveränderlichen Teilen

walking town, pedestrian(-prone) city, pedestrian(-prone) town, walking city · Fußgängerstadt *f*, fußgängergerechte Stadt

walk-out [*colloquial term*]; strike · Streik *m*

walk-up building · fahrstuhlloses Gebäude *n*

walkway, footpath · Fußweg *m*

walled-in space, building volume, cubage, enclosed space, space enclosed, cube, cubic(al) capacity, (cubic(al)) content, structural volume, cubic extent, cubing [*Enclosed total volume measurements of a structure*] · Baumasse *f*, umbauter Raum *m*, Rauminhalt *m*

walled town, walled city, fortress town, fortified town, fortified city · Festungsstadt *f*, befestigte Stadt

wall map · Wandkarte *f*

wall-work; murorum opertio [*Latin*] [*The service of work and labour done by inhabitants and adjoining tenants, in building or repairing the walls of a town or castle*] · Mauerbaudienst *m*

to wander at large · herumschweifen

wandering beast, estray, animal that has strayed away [*Any beast, not wild, found within any lordship, and not owned by any man*] · herrenloses Tier *n*, verlaufenes Tier

wandering cattle, cattle that has strayed away, estray · herrenloses Rindvieh *n*, verlaufenes Rindvieh, eingeschüttetes Rindvieh

want constitution · Bedarfsstruktur *f* [*Haushalt(ung)*]

want of consideration · Fehlen *n* einer Gegenleistung

want of due execution · Nichteinhaltung *f* der gesetzlichen Formvorschriften

want of knowledge; ignorantia [*Latin*]; ignorance · Unkenntnis *f*

want of (legal) form, formal defect, informality, irregularity in matter of form, defect of (legal) form · Formfehler *m*, Formmangel *m*

want of mutuality · Gegenseitigkeitsmangel *m*, mangelnde Gegenseitigkeit *f*

want of prosecution · mangelnde Prozeßverfolgung *f*, Prozeßverschleppung

wanton · mutwillig

wapentake · Gau *m* [*In England zur Zeit der normannischen Eroberung*]

war against poverty · Bekämpfung *f* der Armut, Armutbekämpfung

war chest · Parteifonds *m* [*in England*]

war clause · Kriegsklausel *f*

ward · Stadtbezirk *m* [*in London*]

ward, pupil · Mündel *m*

ward · Wahlkreis *m* [*Munizipalstadt*]

warda · Vormundschaftsfall *m* [*Lehensfall*]

war damage · Kriegsschaden *m*

war damage claim · Kriegsschadenforderung *f*

war damage compensation · Kriegsschadenausgleich *m*

war-damaged · kriegsbeschädigt

war-damaged site, blitzed site · (Kriegs)Trümmergrundstück *n*, (Kriegs-)Schuttgrundstück

war damage (physical) redevelopment · Kriegsschädenwiederbebauung *f*

war damages law · Kriegsfolgenrecht *n*, Kriegsschädenrecht

war debt settlement · Kriegsschuldenregelung *f*

warden · Schöffe *m*, (Zunft)Vorsteher

warden, church warden; church reeve, church master [*obsolete*] [*In England. A lay honorary officer of a parish or district church, elected to assist the incumbent in the discharge of his administrative duties, to manage such various parochial offices as by custom or legislation devolve upon him, and generally to act as the lay representative of the parish in matters of church-organization*] · Kirchenvorsteher *m*

warden · Vorsteher *m*

warden substitute · beigeordneter Schöffe *m*, beigeordneter (Zunft)Vorsteher

war destruction · Kriegszerstörung f

ward in Chancery · Erbe m vor der Erlangung der Volljährigkeit [*in England*]

ward in Chancery · Erbin f vor der Erlangung der Volljährigkeit [*in England*]

ward money, ward trust money, money held in trust for a ward, pupil money · Mündelgeld n

ward mortgage, pupil mortgage · Mündelhypothek f

wardmote · Bezirksrat m [*Stadtverwaltung von London*]

ward of court, court ward · Gerichtsmündel m

ward roll · Wählerliste f [*Munizipalstadt mit Wahlkreisen*]

ward state, state of being a ward, pupilage, state of being a pupil, pupil state · Mündelstand m

ward trust money, money held in trust for a ward, pupil money, ward money · Mündelgeld n

ward within (the walls) · Stadtbezirk m innerhalb [*in London*]

ward without (the walls) · Stadtbezirk m außerhalb [*in London*]

warehouse for foodstuffs, foodstuff warehouse · Lebensmittellager n, Lebensmittelspeicher m

warehouse-man, warehouse-keeper · Lagerhalter m, Lagerist

warehouse receipt, warrant · Lagerschein m

warehouse receipt nontransferable by endorsement, nonnegotiable warehouse receipt, unnegotiable warehouse receipt, not negotiable warehouse receipt · Lagerempfangsschein m

warehousing · Lagerhaltung f

warehousing cost(s) · Lagerkosten f

war loan [*Great Britain*]; liberty loan [*USA*] · Kriegsanleihe f

war memorial · Kriegerdenkmal n

warm zeal · pflichtschuldiger Eifer m [*Eine Pflicht des (Rechts)Anwalts gegenüber seinem Mandanten*]

warning duty, duty to warn · Anzeigepflicht f, Mitteilungspflicht, Benachrichtigungspflicht [*Des Auftragnehmers bei Behinderung*]

warning notice, warning notification · Voranzeige f, Vormitteilung f, Vorbenachrichtigung

war profiteer · Kriegsgewinnler m

to warrant [*In contracts, to engage or promise that a certain fact or set of facts, in relation to the subject matter, is, or shall be, as it is represented to be*] · gewährleisten, Gewähr leisten, Gewähr geben

to warrant [*In conveyancing, to assure the title to the property sold by an express covenant to that effect in the deed of conveyance*] · auflassen

to warrant [*To stipulate by an express covenant that the title of a grantee shall be good, and his possession undisturbed*] · bestätigen [*(Rechts)Titel*]

warrant, (writ of) capias, writ of committal, writ of commitment, writ of confinement, committal writ, commitment writ, confinement writ [*A writ commanding the officer to take the body of the person named in that, that is, to arrest him*] · Haftbefehl m

warrant, warehouse receipt · Lagerschein m

warrant [*An authority to do some judicial act(ion)*] · Auftrag m, Order f, Vollziehungsdekret n

warrant · Lagerpfandschein m

warrant book, mittimus book · Buch n der Haftbefehle

warranted price [*A price established for a property which is deemed fair and just by both the seller and the buyer*] · garantierter Preis m

warrantee [*A person to whom a warranty is made*] · Garantieempfänger m

warrant of apprehension, apprehension warrant · Vorführungsorder f, Vorführungsauftrag m, Vorführungsdekret n

warrant of attorney, attorney warrant · (Rechts)Anwaltsvollmacht f [*Unwiderrufliche Prozeßvollmacht durch welche ein Anwalt von seinem Mandanten zur Erklärung eines Anerkenntnisses vor Gericht ermächtigt wird*]

warrant of discount · Mandat n [*(königliches) Schatzamt*]

warrantor [*The heir of one's husband*] · Erbe m des Ehemanns

warrantor · Gewährleistende m, Garantiegeber

warranty, guarantee, guarantie, guaranty [*Contractor's or manufacturer's guarantee of the quality, workmanship, and performance of his work or equipment or product*] · Gewähr(leistung) f, Garantie f

warranty · Nebenpflicht f [*Liefervertrag*]

warranty bond [*This bond guarantees to the owner that all equipment under warranty from a manufacturer will be maintained in accordance with the contractual guarantees and for the stipulated time*] · Gerätegewährleistung f [*Bauwesen*]

warranty breach, breach of warranty · Garantiebruch m

warranty contract, contract of warranty · Garantievertrag *m*

warranty deed, deed of warranty · Garantieurkunde *f*

warranty exclusion, exclusion of warranty · Garantieausschluß *m*

warranty ex post facto, condition reduced to a mere warranty · Bedingung *f* mit Verzicht auf die Rechtsfolgen eines Bedingungsbruches

warranty obligation · Garantieverpflichtung *f*

warranty of goods · Gütergarantie *f*, Warengarantie

warranty period, term of warranty, time of warranty, period of warranty, warranty term, warranty time · Garantiefrist *f*, Garantiezeitraum *m*

warranty service, service of warranty · Garantieleistung *f*

warranty term, warranty time, warranty period, term of warranty, time of warranty, period of warranty · Garantiefrist *f*, Garantiezeitraum *m*

warranty time, warranty period, term of warranty, time of warranty, period of warranty, warranty term · Garantiefrist *f*, Garantiezeitraum *m*

war savings certificate · Kriegssparschein *m*

wartime housing · Kriegswohn(ungs)bau *m*

to wash ashore, to drift ashore · anschwemmen, antreiben [*Teile eines untergegangenen Schiffes*]

washing ashore, drifting ashore · Anschwemmen *n*, Antreiben [*Teile eines untergegangenen Schiffes*]

wasta boscorum [*Latin*] · Holzdiebstahl *m*

waste → waste (of the manor)

waste [*It consists of any act which alters the nature of the land whether for the better or for the worse, e.g., the conversion of arable land into woodland or vice versa*] · Substanz(ver)änderung *f*

waste, uncultivated land; novale, frusca terra [*Latin*]; fallow land, idle land, tract of fallow (land) · Brachflur *f*, Brachland *n*, Brachacker *m*, Brachfeld *n*

waste [*Any spoil or destruction in buildings, gardens, trees, etc., by a tenant*] · Vernachlässigung *f*

waste collection, refuse collection · Abfallabfuhr *f*, Müllabfuhr

waste disposal, refuse disposal · Abfallbeseitigung *f*, Müllbeseitigung

waste disposal area, refuse tip, waste tip, refuse disposal area · Abfallhalde *f*, Abfalldeponie *f*, Abfallkippe *f*, Müllhalde, Mülldeponie, Müllkippe

waste disposal law, refuse disposal law · Abfallbeseitigungsrecht *n*, Müllbeseitigungsrecht

waste gas impact · Abgaseinwirkung *f*

waste impeachment; impetitio vasti [*Latin*]; impeachment of waste [*Liability to be proceeded against or sued for committing waste upon land(s) or tenement(s)*] · Grund(stücks)veränderungshaftung *f*, Veränderungshaftung am Grundstück, Haftung für Substanzveränderung

waste limit, limit of waste · Wertminderungsgrenze *f*, Depravierungsgrenze, Verwüstungsgrenze, Schwundgrenze, Übernutzungsgrenze, Verschlechterungsgrenze, Vernachlässigungsgrenze, Mißbrauchgrenze, Deteriorierungsgrenze

waste of the manor, (manorial) waste [*obsolete*]; common (land), corporate land, allmend, commonfield, commonable land, commonable field, public land, community land, communal land, mark; county (US) · Al(l)mend(e) *f*, Allmeind *f*, Allmid *f*, Allmein(i) *f*, Allmen *f*, Allmig *f*, Allmand(e) *f*, Allmat *f*, All(ge)meinde *f*, Allmandgut *n*, Allmente *f*, (Feld)Mark *f*, Gemarkung *f*, Kommunalboden *m*, Gemeindeboden *m*, Bürgerland *n*, bürgerliches Nutzungsland *n*, Gemeindeland *n*, Gemeinheit(sland) *f*, *(n)*, Kommunalland *n*, unverteilter Gemeindegrund *m*, ländliches Gemeingut, Gemein(de)anger *m*, Gemeindeimmobilien *fpl*; Korporationsland *n* [*Schweiz*]

waste rate, rate of waste · Wertminderungssatz *m*, Verwüstungssatz, Übernutzungssatz, Verschlechterungssatz, Vernachlässigungssatz, Mißbrauchsatz, Deteriorierungssatz, Depravierungssatz, Schwundsatz

waste removal facility, refuse removal facility · Abfallbeseitigungseinrichtung *f*, Müllbeseitigungseinrichtung

waste tip, refuse disposal area, waste disposal area, refuse tip · Abfallhalde *f*, Abfalldeponie *f*, Abfallkippe *f*, Müllhalde *f*, Mülldeponie, Müllkippe

waste utilization plant, refuse utilization plant · Müllverwertungsanlage *f*, Abfallverwertungsanlage

wasting assets · wertabnehmende Aktiva *f*, wertabnehmendes Guthaben *n*

wasting property · Vermögen *n* dessen Substanz durch Fruchtentziehung schwindet

watch committee · Polizeiverwaltungsausschuß *m*

watching [*site*] · Bewachung *f* [*Baustelle*]

watchman service — water right

watchman service · Wachdienst *m*

watch rate, police-rate · (örtliche) Polizeisteuer *f*, lokale Polizeisteuer, gemeindliche Polizeisteuer, kommunale Polizeisteuer

to water · tränken [*Vieh*]

water act, water statute, water law · Wassergesetz *n*

water allotment, water apportionment, allotment of water, apportionment of water · Wasserzuteilung *f*

water area, area of water · Wasserfläche *f*

water authority · Wasserwirtschaftsbehörde *f*

water availability · Wasserdargebot *n*

water-bailiff [*An official entrusted with the enforcement of the Acts for the preservation of salmon and freshwater fish (Salmon and Freshwater Fisheries Act, 1923)*] · Fischvogt *m*

water balance · Wasserhaushalt *m*

waterborne traffic · Schiffsverkehr *m*

water code · Wasserordnung *f*

water committee · Wasserwirtschaftsausschuß *m*

water company, water undertaker · Wasserwerkgesellschaft *f*

water consumption · Wasserverbrauch *m*

watercourse; aquage, aquagium [*Latin*] · Wasserlauf *m*

watercourse easement, easement of watercourse [*The right of receiving or discharging water through another person's land, the tenement for the benefit of which the watercourse exists being the dominant tenement*] · Wasserlauf-Grunddienstbarkeit *f*

watercourse owner, watercourse proprietor · Wasserlaufeigentümer *m*

watercourse possessor · Wasserlaufbesitzer *m*

water-distributing company · Wasserversorgungsgesellschaft *f*

water easement, easement of water · Wassergrunddienstbarkeit *f*

water economy, water resources management · Wasserwirtschaft *f*

water field · Wasserwesen *n*

water for domestic purposes, household water · Haushalt(s)wasser *n*

watering-place · Quellenkurort *m*

water law, water act, water statute · Wassergesetz *n*

water main · Wasserhauptleitung *f*

water money · Wassergeld *n*

water of compensation, compensation water [*Water which any water authority or statutory water company are under an obligation to discharge into a river, stream, brook or other running water or into a canal as a condition of carrying on their undertaking*] · Ausgleichswasser *n*

water ordinance · Wasserverordnung *f*

water-orien(ta)ted recreation, water-related recreation, water(-based) recreation · Wassererholung *f*

water ownership (of property), property in water, proprietorship in water, ownership (of property) in water, water property, water proprietorship · Wassereigentum *n*

water policy · Wasser(wirtschafts)politik *f*

water pollution · Wasserverschmutzung *f*

water pollution control, water pollution prevention · Wasserreinhaltung *f*

water pollution control act, water pollution control law, water pollution control statute · Wasserreinhaltungsgesetz *n*

water pollution control legislation, water pollution control lawmaking · Wasserreinhaltungsgesetzgebung *f*

water pollution control law · Wasserreinhaltungsrecht *n*

water pollution prevention, water pollution control · Wasserreinhaltung *f*

water property, water proprietorship, water ownership (of property), property in water, proprietorship in water, ownership (of property) in water · Wassereigentum *n*

water quality control · Wassergüteüberwachung *f*

water rate · Wassertarif *m*

water recreational facility · Wassererholungseinrichtung

water resource · Wasserreserve *f*

water resource project · Projekt *n* zur Wasserreservennutzung, Vorhaben *n* zur Wasserreservennutzung

water resources · Wasservorräte *mpl*

water (resources) board, river (resources) board · Wasserwirtschaftsamt *n*

water resources framework planning, water resources skeleton planning · wasserwirtschaftliche Rahmenplanung *f*

water resources law · Wasserreservenrecht *n*

water resources management, water economy · Wasserwirtschaft *f*

water right, right of water, aquatic right [*Right to the use of sea, rivers, streams, lakes, ponds and canals, for the pur-*

water (rights) law — weather conditions

pose of fishing and navigation, and also to the soil of them] · (subjektives) Wasserrecht *n*

water (rights) law, law of water (rights) · (objektives) Wasserrecht *n*

water running off outside a bed · wild abfließendes Wasser *n*

water shortage, shortage of water · Wassermangel *m*, Wasserknappheit *f*, Wasserverknappung *f*

"water snake" · frei schwankende europäische Währungsschlange *f*, frei schwankender europäischer Währungsverbund *m*

water(s) not in the form of a watercourse · Nichtwasserlauf *m* [*Nichtwasserläufe sind: a) oberirdische Quellen, die nicht sogleich in einem sichtbaren Gerinne abfließen; b) Seen, die keinen oder nur künstlichen Abfluß haben; c) Gräben, die nicht der Vorflut von Grundstücken verschiedener Eigentümer dienen; d) oberirdisch wild abfließendes Wasser von Regen, Schneeschmelze und dgl.; e) unterirdische Gewässer, die nicht Teile eines Wasserlaufes sind; f) Grundwasser*]

water statute, water law, water act · Wassergesetz *n*

water supply · Wasserversorgung *f*

water supply area · Versorgungsfläche *f* für öffentliche Wasserversorgung, Wasserversorgungsfläche

water (supply) committee · Wasserversorgungsausschuß *m*

water supply enterprise, water utility enterprise, water utility undertaking, water supply undertaking · Wasserversorgungsbetrieb *m*, Wasserversorgungsunternehmen *n*, Wasserversorgungsunternehmung *f*

water surplus area, water surplus territory, flood plane · Wasserüberschußgebiet *n*

water undertaker, water company · Wasserwerkgesellschaft *f*

water use · Wassernutzung *f*

water utility enterprise, water utility undertaking, water supply undertaking, water supply enterprise · Wasserversorgungsbetrieb *m*, Wasserversorgungsunternehmen *n*, Wasserversorgungsunternehmung *f*

water winning facility · Wassergewinnungseinrichtung *f*

water winning plant · Wassergewinnungsanlage *f*

wave of innovation, innovation wave · Innovationswelle *f*

way · Weg *m*

way easement → (right of) way easement

wayleave, ingress, access, right to enter and leave over the land(s) of another, way right, right-of-way · Durchgangsrecht *n*, Wegerecht

wayleave for vehicles, ingress for vehicles, access for vehicles, way right for vehicles, right-of-way for vehicles · Fahrzeugwegerecht *n*

way of necessity · Notweg *m* [*Fehlt einem Grundstück die zur ordnungsmäßigen Benutzung notwendige Verbindung mit einem öffentlichen Weg, so kann der Eigentümer von den Nachbarn verlangen, daß sie bis zur Behebung dieses Mangels die Benutzung ihrer Grundstücke zur Herstellung der erforderlichen Verbindung dulden. Die Richtung des Notweges und der Umfang des Benutzungsrechts werden erforderlichenfalls durch Urteil bestimmt*]

way right, right-of-way, wayleave, ingress, access, right to enter and leave over the land(s) of another · Durchgangsrecht *n*, Wegerecht

way right for vehicles, right-of-way for vehicles, wayleave for vehicles, ingress for vehicles, access for vehicles · Fahrzeugwegerecht *n*

way ticket · Wanderschein *m*

waywarden [*Waywardens disappeared in England when the local authority was made the highway authority by the Local Government Act, 1894, S.25 (1)*] · Wegekurator *m*

weakness of title, title weakness · (Rechts)Titelschwäche *f*, Schwäche des (Rechts)Titels

wealth concentration, concentration of wealth · Reichtumsballung *f*

wealth of nations, national wealth · Volksreichtum *m*, Nationalreichtum

wealth tax, property tax [*In English law, this is understood to be an income tax payable in respect to landed property. In America, it is a tax imposed on property, whether real or personal, as distinguished from poll taxes, and taxes on successions, transfers, and occupations, and from license taxes*] · Vermögenssteuer *f*

wear (and tear) · Abnutzung *f*, Verschleiß *m*

wear (and tear) by contractual use · Abnutzung *f* durch vertraglichen Gebrauch

weariness of life on the land, land-weariness · Landmüdigkeit *f*

weather chart · Wetterkarte *f*

weather conditions · Wetterbedingungen *fpl*, Wetterverhältnisse *f*, Witterungsbedingungen, Witterungsverhältnisse

weather damage · Witterungsschaden *m*

weather influences · Witterungseinflüsse *mpl*

web of life · Allzusammenhang *m* des Lebens

wed(d) sellan [*Anglo-Saxon*]; vadium (recti) dare [*Latin*]; wed(d) syllan [*Anglo-Saxon*] · Pfandbestellung *f* im Prozeß [*Englisches Pfandrecht im Mittelalter*]

weed control · Unkrautbekämpfung *f*

week-end commuter · Wochenendpendler *m*

week-end home journey, week-end home trip, week-end home travel · Wochenendheimfahrt *f*

week-end house area, week-end house territory · SW *n*, Wochenendhausgebiet *n*

week-end house parcel, week-end house plot · Wochenendhausgrundstück *n*

week-end house zone · Wochenendhauszone *f*

week-end in-commuter · Wochenendeinpendler *m*, Wochenendzupendler

week-end out-commuter · Wochenendauspendler *m*, Wochenendwegpendler

week-end recreation · Wochenenderholung *f*

weekly commuting · Wochenpendeln *n*

weekly commutor · Wochenpendler *m*

weekly in-commuter · Wocheneinpendler *m*, Wochenzupendler

weekly market · Wochenmarkt *m*

weekly out-commuter · Wochenauspendler *m*, Wochenwegpendler

weekly rent [*premises*] · Wochenmiete *f*, Wochen(miet)zins *m*

weekly tender [*Great Britain*] · wöchentliche Schatzwechselauktion *f*

week order · Börsenauftrag *m* für eine Woche gültig

weighage [*A toll or duty paid for weighing merchandise*] · Wiegeabgabe *f*

weighing the facts, facts weighing · Abwägen *n* der Tatsachen, Tatsachenabwägen

weight bias, load bias, weight error, load error · Gewichtungsfehler *m*, Bewertungsfehler [*Statistik*]

weighted average, weighted mean · gewogenes Mittel *n*, gewogener Durchschnitt *m*

weight error, load error, weight bias, load bias · Gewichtungsfehler *m*, Bewertungsfehler [*Statistik*]

weighting, loading · Gewichtung *f*, Bewertung [*Statistik*]

weighting clause, (e)valuation clause, appraisal clause, appraisement clause, evaluative clause · (Ab)Schätzungsklausel *f*, Bewertungsklausel, Taxierungsklausel, Wertermitt(e)lungsklausel

weighting guide lines, (e)valuation guide lines, appraisal guide lines, appraisement guide lines, evaluative guide lines · (Ab)Schätzungsrichtlinien *f pl*, Wertermitt(e)lungsrichtlinien, Bewertungsrichtlinien, Taxierungsrichtlinien

weighting of votes · Stimmengewicht *n*

weighting ordinance, appraisement ordinance, (e)valuation ordinance, appraisal ordinance · Bewertungsverordnung *f*, (Ab)Schätzungsverordnung, Taxierungsverordnung, Wertermitt(e)lungsverordnung

weighting prescription, weighting regulation, appraisal regulation, (e)valuation regulation, appraisement regulation, evaluative regulation, (e)valuation prescription, appraisal prescription, appraisement prescription, evaluative prescription · (Ab)Schätzungsvorschrift *f*, Bewertungsvorschrift, Wertermitt(e)lungsvorschrift, Taxierungsvorschrift

weighting scheme, (e)valuation scheme, appraisal scheme, appraisement scheme, evaluative scheme · (Ab)Schätzungsrahmen *m*, Bewertungsrahmen, Taxierungsrahmen, Wertermitt(e)lungsrahmen

weight mistake, load mistake · Bewertungsirrtum *m*, Gewichtungsirrtum [*Statistik*]

weight restriction · Gewichtsbeschränkung *f*, Gewichtseinschränkung

weights and measures board, board of weights and measures · Eichamt *n*

weighty · gewichtig *f*

welfare body · Wohlfahrtsorgan *n*

welfare centre (Brit.); welfare center (US) · Wohlfahrtszentrum *n*

welfare council, council of social agencies · Planungsgemeinschaft *f* des sozialen Dienstes, soziale Planungsgemeinschaft

welfare economics · Verteilung *f* der Einkommen, Verteilungsgerechtigkeit *f*

welfare function · Wohlfahrtsfunktion *f*

welfare growth · Wohlfahrtswachstum *n*

welfare lawmaking, welfare legislation · Sozialgesetzgebung *f*

welfare level · Wohlfahrtsniveau *n*

welfare measure, measure of welfare · Wohlstandsindikator *m* [*Sozialprodukt*]

welfare of old people, old peoples' welfare · Altersfürsorge *f*

welfare organization · Wohlfahrtsorganisation *f*

welfare recipient · Wohlfahrtsempfänger *m*

welfare rent · Wohlfahrtsrente *f*

welfare state, social service state · Sozialstaat *m*, Wohlfahrtsstaat

welfare work for the poor, pauper relief, poor relief · Armenpflege *f*, Armenwohlfahrt *f*, Armenfürsorge *f*, Armenversorgung *f*

well-being, prosperity · Wohlstand *m*

well-being level, prosperity level, level of well-being, level of prosperity · Wohlstandsniveau *n*

well location · Brunnenlage *f*

well-maintained · guterhalten

well settled · wohlgeregelt

(Welsh) gwestva, food rent · Lebensmittelrente *f*

Welsh law, law of Wales; lex Wallensica [*Latin*] · walisisches Recht *n*

wet point-settlement · (An)Sied(e)lung *f* auf nassem Grund

wet rice cultivation, irrigated rice cultivation · Naßreisanbau *m*

W.F.T.U., World Federation of Trade Unions · Weltgewerkschaftsbund *m*

wheat belt · Weizengürtel *m*

wheel(ed) plough (Brit.); wheel(ed) plow (US); caruca [*Name given by the Gauls*] · Radpflug *m*

wheeled traffic · Rad(fahrzeug)verkehr *m*

wheelless plough, swing plough (Brit.); wheelless plow, swing plow (US) · radloser Pflug *m*

when due · bei Fälligkeit

while litigation is pending; pendente lite [*Latin*] · schwebend [*Verfahren*]

whip · Parteieinpeitscher *m* [*Parteiorganisation im englischen Parlament*]

whisky money [*In England*] · Abgabe *f* für den Kleinhandel mit Tabak und Bier und Alkohol

white collar crime · Wirtschaftsverbrechen *n*

white collar worker (US) · Kopfarbeiter *m*

white farm → blanch farm

white land project, unallocated land project · Außen(bereich)vorhaben *n*

white land(s), unallocated land(s), site without notation [*Land in agricultural or other mainly open use on which, for the period of the plan, the present uses are to remain for the most part undisturbed*] · Außenbereich *m*

white population · weiße Bevölkerung *f*

whole assets, total assets, aggregate assets · Gesamtaktiva *f*, Totalaktiva

whole body (of the corporators), whole corporation, body at large · Gesamtkörperschaft *f*, Gesamtkorporation *f*, Gesamtheit *f* der Korporationsgenossen, Körperschaft im ganzen, Korporation im ganzen

whole building cost(s), total construction cost(s), aggregate construction cost(s), whole construction cost(s), total building cost(s), aggregate building cost(s) · Gesamtherstellungskosten *f*, Gesamtbaukosten, Totalbaukosten, Totalherstellungskosten

whole cost(s); total expired cost(s), total expense(s) [*USA*]; total cost(s), aggregate cost(s) · Totalkosten *f*, Gesamtkosten

whole freight, aggregate freight, total freight · Gesamtfracht *f*

whole interest rate, aggregate interest rate, total interest rate · Gesamtzinsfuß *m*

whole planning, total planning, aggregate planning · Totalplanung *f*, Gesamtplanung

whole population, total population, aggregate population · Gesamtbevölkerung *f*

whole production cost(s), total production cost(s), aggregate production cost(s) · Totalherstellungskosten, Gesamtherstellungskosten

whole profit, total gain, aggregate gain, whole gain, total profit, aggregate profit · Gesamtgewinn *m*, Totalgewinn, Gesamtprofit, Totalprofit *m*

wholesale area, wholesaling area, wholesale territory, wholesaling territory · Großhandelsgebiet *n*

wholesale city, wholesale town, wholesaling city, wholesaling town · Großhandelsstadt *f*

wholesale dealer · Großhändler *m*

wholesale district, wholesaling district · Großhandelsbezirk *m*

wholesale purchase [*Purchase by management of water and energy for an entire project; consumption is recorded and billed to the project on the basis of master meter readings. distinguished from retail purchase*] · Gemeinschaftsbezug *m*

wholesaling · Großhandel *m*

whole society · Gesamtgesellschaft *f*

whole usable space, aggregate usable space, total usable space · gesamte Nutzfläche f [*Summe von Wohn- und Nutzfläche der Räume eines Gebäudes*]

wholly-owned subsidiary · Tochtergesellschaft f im Volleigentum (stehend)

to whom it may concern, on account of whom it may concern · wen es angeht

wide-open primary (election), blanket primary (election) [*USA*] · weit-offene Vorwahl f, weit-offene Erstwahl, weit-offene Urwahl [*Der Vorwahlteilnehmer kann für jedes Wahlamt seinen Kandidaten benennen ohne daß alle Kandidaten derselben Partei angehören müssen*]

widespread · weitgestreut

wide strip lot · Breitstreifenparzelle f

widowhood, viduity · Witwenschaft f

widow's portion · Witwenanteil m

width of lot, lot width · Parzellenbreite f, Flurstücksbreite

wife → feme covert

(wild) beasts of the chase, chase beasts, game, wild animals · (Jagd)Wild n, jagdbare Tiere npl

wilderness zone on water and wilderness zone on land · Wasser-Ökozone f [*Sie erhält das Ökosystem eines Sees*]

wild fowl · Wildgeflügel n

wild landscape · Urlandschaft f

wildlife area, game area · Wildgebiet n

wildlife preserve, game preserve, wildlife refuge, game refuge · Wildreservat n, Wildschutzgebiet n, Wildschongebiet

wildlife resources · Fauna f

wildlife wetland habitat management · Betreuung f von Feuchtgebieten [*Naturschutz*]

wilful and malicious arson · dolose Brandstiftung f

will; testamentum [*Latin*] [*The word "testament" is now seldom used, except in the heading of a formal will, which usually begins — "This is the last will and testament of me, A.B., etc."*] · Testament n

will, intent(ion) [*A somewhat formal term connecting more deliberation than intention*] · feste Absicht f, Wille m

willingness · Willigkeit f

willingness to pay · Zahlungswilligkeit f

willingness to work · Arbeitswilligkeit f

will memorial, memorial of will · Testamentsauszug m zum Registrieren

will of fixed property, will of immov(e)able property, will of (real) property, will of (real) estate, will of land(s), will of realty [*It is not called a testament*] · Bodentestament n, Grundstückstestament, Liegenschaftstestament, Landtestament, Immobilientestament

will of land signed by three witnesses · Dreizeugen-Landtestament n, Not-Landtestament vor drei Zeugen

will of party · Parteiwille m

will of personal property, will of mov(e)able property, will of personal estate, will of personalty, testament; testamentum [*Latin*] · Fahrnistestament n, Fahrhabetestament

will of possessing → will of possession

will of the state · Staatswille m

wills act, wills statute, wills law, statute of wills, act of wills, law of wills · Testamentsgesetz n

Wills and Estates Service · Loseblattsammlung f über die erbrechtlichen und erbschaftssteuerrechtlichen Bestimmungen der Gliedstaaten [*USA*]

will signed by three witnesses · Dreizeugentestament n, Testament vor drei Zeugen

wills law, law of wills, testamentary law · Testamentsrecht n

wills law → wills act

wills statute → wills act

will theory · subjektive Theorie f

will to exercise a right · Rechtsausübungswille m

to win, to extract, to get, to work · abbauen [*Mineralien*]

to win back, to regain, to collect, to get renewed possession of, to get again, to obtain again, to recover · zurückerhalten, wiedererlangen, wiedererhalten, zurückgewinnen, zurückbekommen

winding(-)up by court, liquidation by court · Abwick(e)lung f durch ein Gericht, Liquidation f durch ein Gericht, gerichtliche Liquidation, gerichtliche Abwick(e)lung [*Konkurs*]

windbreak, wind shelter · Windschutz m

windbreak action, wind shelter action · Windschutzwirkung f

windbreak planting, wind shelter planting · Windschutz(an)pflanzung f

windfall gain tax, windfall profit tax · (Abschöpfungs)Steuer f auf überhöhten Gewinn, (Abschöpfungs)Steuer auf überhöhten Profit

windfall profit, windfall gain · überhöhter Gewinn m, überhöher Profit

windfall(-wood), wind-fallen wood, cablish · Windbruchholz n, Windfallholz

winding(-)up, liquidation · Abwick(e)lung f, Liquidation f [Konkurs]

winding(-)up law, liquidation law · Liquidationsrecht n, Abwick(e)lungsrecht

winding(-)up of arrangement, liquidation of arrangement · außergerichtliche Abwick(e)lung f, außergerichtliche Liquidation f

winding(-)up (of business), handling (of business) · Abwick(e)lung f, Geschäftsabwick(e)lung

winding(-)up order, liquidation order, order for winding(-)up, order for liquidation · Liquidationsbefehl m

winding(-)up petition, liquidation petition, petition for winding(-)up, petition for liquidation · Liquidationsantrag m

windmill, kite (Brit.); accommodation bill, fictitious bill, feint bill, faint bill, feigned bill, pretended bill · Freundschaftswechsel m, Gefälligkeitswechsel, Kellerwechsel, Reitwechsel, Schornsteinwechsel, Scheinwechsel

windmill mortgage · Schornsteinhypothek f

window dressing · Bilanzfrisur f, Bilanzverschönerung f, Bilanzverschleierung

window duty, window tax · Fenstersteuer f

window envelope · Fenster(brief)umschlag m

window law · (objektives) Fensterrecht n [Meistens zivilrechtliche Bestimmungen, die das Recht des Eigentümers oder Besitzers zur Anlage von Fenstern und deren Ausgestaltung sowie die Abwehrrechte des Nachbarn regeln]

window right · Fensterrecht n, subjektives Fensterrecht

window-shopping · Schaufensterbummel m

window tax, window duty · Fenstersteuer f

wind shelter, windbreak · Windschutz m

wind shelter action, windbreak action · Windschutzwirkung f

wind shelter planting, windbreak planting · Windschutz(an)pflanzung f

to wind up, to liquidate · abwickeln, liquidieren [Konkurs]

to wind up, to handle · abwickeln [Geschäft]

winning bid, winning tender, winning offer; winning (bid) proposal (US) · Auftrag(s)angebot n, Zuschlag(s)angebot

winning facility · Gewinnungseinrichtung f

winning installation, winning plant · Gewinnungsanlage f

winning location, site of winning, location of winning, winning site · Gewinnungsstelle f, Gewinnungsstandort m

winning (of soil constituents), mineral working, mineral getting, working of minerals, getting of minerals, mineral winning, winning of minerals, extraction of minerals, mineral extraction, getting (of soil constituents), working (of soil constituents), extraction (of soil constituents) · Abbau(en) m, (n) von Bodenbestandteilen, Abbau(en) von Mineralien, Mineralienabbau, Mineralienausbeuten, Ausbeuten (von Mineralien), Ausbeuten von Bodenbestandteilen, Ausbeutung f (von Mineralien), Ausbeutung von Bodenbestandteilen, Mineralienausbeutung, Mineraliengewinnung, Gewinnung (von Mineralien), Gewinnung von Bodenbestandteilen [Die planmäßige Inangriffnahme einer Lagerstätte bei der Gewinnung von Lehm, Sand, Kies usw.]

winning plant, winning installation · Gewinnungsanlage f

winning right, exploitation right, mineral right, mineral interest, interest in minerals in land(s), right to take minerals, right to win minerals, right of exploitation, right to exploit minerals, right of taking minerals, right of winning · (Mineral(ien))Abbaurecht n, (Mineral(ien)-)Ausbeutungsrecht, (subjektives) Berg(bau)recht, (Mineral(ien))Abbaugerechtigkeit f

winning site, winning location, site of winning, location of winning · Gewinnungsstelle f, Gewinnungsstandort m

winter construction, winter building · Winterbau m

winter holiday resort · Winterferienort m, Winterfrische f

winter population · Winterbevölkerung f

winter shutdown (of work(s)), winter suspension (of work(s)) · Einstellung f der (Bau)Arbeiten im Winter, Aussetzung der (Bau)Arbeiten im Winter

winter sports area, winter sports territory · Wintersportgebiet n

wista; hilda [Scotland]; terra hydata, virgate terrae, hida (terrae), hyda, familia [Latin]; hide ((of) land), hyde (of land), higid, hiwise, virgate (land), verge of land, yardland, hydeland, husbandland [A quantity of land not of any certain extent, but as much as a plough can by course of husbandry plough in a year. It meant in different places anything from sixty to 120 acres. A virgate is one fourth of a hide] · Hufe(ngut) f, (n), Hufenschoß n, Hube f, Hufen(gut)land n [Ältere Benennungen: Hof m, Hub m, Hu(o)ba f, und Hova f] [Unter gutsherrlich-bäuerlichen Verhältnissen hieß der gesamte Besitz eines Dorfgenossen „Hufe(ngut)". Diese Benennung war also keine Flächengröße, sondern eine Besitzeinheit, die zahlreiche, zerstreut liegende kleine Ackerteile im Besitz derselben Person umfaßte]

witch town — without due process of law

witch town, shanty town, (suburban) squatting colony, (suburban) squatting community, squatter settlement · Blechhüttenvorort *m* [*Fehlbenennung: Blechhüttenstadt f*]

with dividend, cum dividend · mit Dividende, einschließlich Dividende

to withdraw, to draw (up)on · abheben [*Guthaben*]

to withdraw · zurücktreten [*von einem Vertrag*]

to withdraw · zurückziehen

to withdraw · rückfordern (vor (der) Fälligkeit) [*Durch ein ausscheidendes Mitglied einer Bausparkasse*]

to withdraw a juror · zurücknehmen einer Klage [*Geschworenenprozeß*]

withdrawal · Entzug *m*

withdrawal · Abhebung *f* [*Guthaben*]

withdrawal · Rückforderung *f* (vor (der) Fälligkeit) [*Durch ein ausscheidendes Mitglied einer Bausparkasse*]

withdrawal, rescission · Rücktritt *m*

withdrawal clause, rescission clause · Rücktrittsklausel *f*

withdrawal fee, fee of withdrawal · Rückforderungsgebühr *f* [*Bausparkasse*]

withdrawal from a case, rescission from a case · Rücktritt *m* von einem (Rechts)Fall

withdrawal from contract, rescission of contract · Vertragsrücktritt *m*

withdrawal from membership · Austritt *m*

withdrawal of ground-water, ground-water withdrawal · Grundwasserentzug *m*

withdrawal of manpower from the site · Abziehen *n* der Arbeitskräfte von der Baustelle

withdrawal of money, drawing of money · (Geld)Entnahme *f*

withdrawal of order · Auftragsentziehung *f*, Auftragsrücknahme *f*

withdrawal value · Rückforderungswert *m* [*Bausparkasse*]

to withdraw from membership · austreten

withdrawing, drawing (up)on · Abheben *n* [*Guthaben*]

withdrawing · Zurücktreten *n* [*von einem Vertrag*]

withdrawing · Zurückziehen *n*

withdrawing · Rückfordern *n* (vor (der) Fälligkeit) [*Durch ein ausscheidendes Mitglied einer Bausparkasse*]

withdrawing a juror · Zurücknehmen *n* der Klage, Klagezurücknahme *f* [*Geschworenenprozeß.* Wenn der Kläger im Laufe der Verhandlung sich mit dem Beklagten einigt, so kann dieselbe sofort beendet werden. Es wird dann fingiert, daß ein Geschworener sich zurückzieht, da dies ein Grund für eine Beendigung der Verhandlung ist*]

withdrawing shareholder · rückforderndes Mitglied *n* [*Bausparkasse*]

withdrawn · zurückgefordert [*Bausparkassenanteil*]

to withdraw (oneself) from an enterprise, to back out · zurückziehen, sich zurückziehen

withernam, reprisal · Gegenpfändung *f*

to withhold, to detain, to retain · einbehalten, zurück(be)halten, vorenthalten

withholding, detaining, retaining · Einbehalten *n*, Zurück(be)halten, Vorenthalten

withholding of food · Vorenthalten *n* von Nahrungsmitteln

withholding possession · Besitzvorenthalten *n*

within age, under age · unmündig

within group variance · Binnengruppenvarianz *f* [*Statistik*]

within judicial knowledge · gerichtskundig

without a burden, without a load, burdenless, free from encumbrance(s), free from charge(s), free from incumbrance(s), free from burden(s), uncharged, unburdened, unencumbered, unincumbered, clear, perfect, free from load(s), unloaded, not imperfect · entschuldet, lastenfrei, (dinglich) unbelastet, (dinglich) nicht belastet

without access, accessless, inaccessible · ohne Zugang, unzugänglich, zuganglos

without a load → without a burden

without a term · auf unbestimmte Zeit, ohne Festsetzung einer bestimmten Frist

without a will; intestato [*Latin*]; intestate · testamentlos, ohne Testament

without care, careless, reckless, negligent [*With an indifference whether anything is true or false*] · leichtsinnig, fahrlässig, nachlässig, leichtfertig

without cash, cashless · bargeldlos, ohne Bargeld

without child(ren), issueless, childless, without issue · kinderlos, ohne Nachkommen(schaft), ohne Kinder

without comparison; compareless [*obsolete*], incomparable · unvergleichbar

without due process of law · ohne Gerichtsverfahren *n*

without fraud; bona fide [*Latin*]; in good faith, of good faith, innocent, honestly · aufrichtig, in gutem Glauben, ehrlich, gutgläubig

without heir(s), heirless · erbenlos, ohne Erben

without impeachment of waste; absque impetitione vasti [*Latin*] · ohne Haftung f für Substanzveränderung, ohne Haftpflicht f für Substanzveränderung, ohne Haftbarkeit f, für Substanzveränderung

without issue, without child(ren), issueless, childless · kinderlos, ohne Nachkommenschaft

without mortgage(s), unmortgaged · hypothekenfrei

without notice · ohne Kenntnisnahme

without preference; parie passu [*French*]; equal(ly) · vorzugsfrei

without prejudice, nonauthoritative, nonbinding, nonobligatory, not binding · nicht bindend, nicht verpflichtend, nicht verbindlich, unverbindlich

without property, without ownership (of (general) property), without proprietorship · eigentumslos, ohne Eigentum

without recourse [*Words used in endorsing a negotiable instrument to denote that the endorser will not be liable to a future holder in the event of nonpayment*] · ohne Regreß, ohne Obligo

without regularity, irregular · unregelmäßig

without reserve · ohne Vorbehalt, vorbehaltlos

to witness → to (bear) witness

witness; deponent (US) · Zeuge m

witness-box · Zeugenstand m

witnesseth · hiermit wird vereinbart

witness for the prosecution · Belastungszeuge m

witness oath, oath of a witness · Zeugeneid m

woman juror, female juror, jurywoman · Geschworene f

woman of independent means, lady of private means, lady of independent means, woman of private means · Rentnerin f

woman of private means, woman of independent means, lady of private means, lady of independent means · Rentnerin f

wood allowance, allowance of wood, wood right, wood interest · Holzberechtigung f, Holz(bezugs)recht n

wooded landscape · holzbewachsene Landschaft f

wood fowl · Waldgeflügel n

woodland, forestry land · Waldland n, Forstland

woodland belt, belt of woodland · Waldgürtel m, Waldparkgürtel

woodland not pastured · nicht beweidetes Waldland n, unbeweidetes Waldland

woodland pasture · bewaldetes Weideland n

wood on the stem, timber on the stem, standing trees, (standing) timber · (an)stehendes Holz n, aufstehendes Holz, Holz auf dem Stamme, Holz auf dem Stock

wood tithe, timber tithe · Holzzehnt m [*altdeutsch:* Holzzehent, Holzzehend]

woodward · Holzwart m

woody land, woody ground; terra boscalis [*Latin*] · holzbestandenes Gelände n, holzbestandenes Land n, holzbestandenes Terrain

woody undergrowth, underwood, copse, coppice; sub-boscus [*Latin*] · Niederwald m, Holzung f, Unterholz n

woody vegetation · Holzbewuchs m

to word, to form, to draft, to construct, to draw up, to set up, to construe, to phrase [*To arrange or marshal words*] · abfassen, gestalten, entwerfen, ausarbeiten, formulieren

wording, formulation, formation, drafting, construction, drawing-up, setting up, construing, phrasing [*Arranging or marshalling words*] · Abfassung f, Entwurf m, Gestaltung, Ausarbeitung, Formulierung

wording, text · Text m

wording (or text) of tendering documents and (tender) covering letter · Ausschreibungstext m

word of law, law term, law word, legal term, legal word, term of law · Rechtswort n, Rechtsbenennung f

word of mouth · gesprochenes Wort n

to work, to win, to extract, to get · abbauen [*Mineralien*]

work, physical facility, structure · (Bau)Werk n, (bauliche) Anlage f, Baulichkeit f, Bau(anlage) m, (f); Baute f [*Schweiz*] [*Hierunter ist nach der höchstrichterlichen Rechtsprechung zu § 638 BGB „eine unbewegliche, durch Verwendung von Arbeit und Material in Verbindung mit dem Baugrund hergestellte Sache" zu verstehen, die sich auf oder unter Geländeoberkante befinden kann*]

work, occupation, employment · Arbeit f, Beschäftigung f

workability, practicability, feasibility · Ausführbarkeit f, Durchführbarkeit f

workability analysis, workability study, practicability analysis, practicability study, feasibility analysis, feasibility study · Ausführbarkeitsstudie *f*, Durchführbarkeitsstudie *f*, Durchführbarkeitsanalyse *f*, Ausführbarkeitsanalyse *f*

workability survey, practicability survey, feasibility survey · Ausführbarkeitsenquête *f*, Durchführbarkeitsenquête

workable, feasible, practicable · ausführbar, durchführbar

workable deposit, profitable deposit, paying deposit · Fundstätte *f*, Vorkommen *n*, Lager(stätte) *n*, *(f) [Fehlbenennung: Vorkommnis n]*

work accident · Arbeitsunfall *m* [*Ein körperlich schädigendes, zeitlich begrenztes und von außen auf den Körper einwirkendes Ereignis, wobei der Unfall mit der Tätigkeit in einem inneren ursächlichen Zusammenhang steht*]

'work as executed' drawing, as-completed drawing, as-built drawing, as-constructed drawing · (Bau)Bestandsplan *m*, (Bau)Bestandszeichnung *f*

"work as executed" state, as-constructed state, as-built state, as-completed state · Ausbauzustand *m*, Bestandszustand *m*

work camp · Arbeitslager *n*

work contract, contract of service, contract of employment, contract of job, contract of work, service contract, employment contract, job contract · Arbeitsvertrag *m*

work creation, employment creation, creation of work, creation of jobs, creation of employment, job creation · Arbeitsbeschaffung *f*

work day → work(ing) day

work density, employment density, density of employment, density of work · Arbeitsdichte *f*, Beschäftigungsdichte

work distribution chart · Arbeitsverteilungskarte *f*

work documents → work(ing) documents

worked-out pit, excavated pit · ausgebaggerte Grube *f*

work environment · Arbeitsumwelt *f*

worker, workman, operative; labourer (Brit.); blue collar worker, laborer (US) [*A wage-earning worker, skilled or semi-skilled, whose work is characterized largely by physical exertion*] · Arbeiter *m*

worker peasant village; labourer-farmer village (Brit.); laborer-farmer village (US) · Arbeiter-Bauern-Dorf *n*

worker's bank; labour bank (Brit.); labor bank (US) · Arbeitnehmerbank *f* [*Fehlbenennung: Arbeiterbank*]

workers' club, workmen's club · Arbeiterklub *m*

workers' co-operative, workmen's co-operative · Arbeitergenossenschaft *f*

workers' community, workmen's community, working-class community · Arbeitergemeinde *f*

workers' council, workmen's council, works council · Betriebsrat *m*

workers' deficiency → workers' scarcity

worker's household, workman's household, working-class household · Arbeiterhaushalt *m*

workers' (housing) colony, workers' residential colony, workmen's (housing) colony, workmen's residential colony, industrial housing estate, workers' housing estate, workmen's housing estate, industrial residential estate, workers' residential estate, workmen's residential estate, industrial settlement, workers' settlement, workmen's settlement, working class settlement, industrial (housing) colony, industrial residential colony · Arbeiter(wohn)kolonie *f*, Arbeiter(wohn)(an)sied(e)lung *f*, Industrie(wohn)(an)sied(e)lung, Industrie(wohn)kolonie

workers' housing law, workmen's housing law · Arbeiterwohn(ungs)recht *n*

workers' lodging, workmen's lodging; labouring classes lodging (Brit.); laboring classes lodging (US) · Arbeiterlogierhaus *n*

worker's mobility, workman's mobility · Arbeiterbeweglichkeit *f*, Arbeitermobilität *f*

workers' movement · Arbeiterbewegung *f*

workers' overspill, overspill of workers, overspill of labour (Brit.); overspill of labor (US) · Arbeiterüberschuß *m*, Arbeiterüberhang *m*

workers' quarter, workmen's quarter, working-class quarter · Arbeiter(wohn)viertel *n*, Arbeiter(wohn)quartier *n*

workers' residential community, workmen's residential community · Arbeiterwohngemeinde *f* [*Ein Ort in dem ein Arbeiter wohnt, der an einem anderen Ort, der Betriebsgemeinde, arbeitet*]

workers' (return) ticket, workmen's (return) ticket · Arbeiterrückfahrkarte *f*

workers' scarcity, workers' stringency, workers' shortage, workers' deficiency, workmen's shortage, workmen's scarcity, workmen's stringency, workmen's deficiency · Arbeiterknappheit *f*, Arbeiterverknappung *f*, Arbeiternot, Arbeiterklemme, Arbeitermangel *m*, Arbeiterdefizit

workers' shortage → workers' scarcity

worker's social policy, workmen's social policy · Arbeitersozialpolitik *f*

workers' stringency → workers' scarcity

workers' train, workmen's train · Arbeiterzug *m*

workers' union, union of workmen, workmen's union, union of workers · Arbeiterverband *m*

worker's wage, workman's wage · Arbeiterlohn *m*

work for common need, physical facility for common need, structure for common need · (bauliche) Anlage *f* für Gemeinbedarf, (Bau)Werk *n* für Gemeinbedarf, Baulichkeit *f* für Gemeinbedarf, Bau(anlage) *m*, *(f)* für Gemeinbedarf; Baute *f* für Gemeinbedarf [*Schweiz*]

work hour → work(ing) hour

workhouse, house of correction, reformatory (school), reform school · Arbeitshaus *n*, Besserungsanstalt *f*, Erziehungsanstalt *f*, Besserungshaus *n* [*Für jugendliche Straftäter*]

workhouse master, master of the workhouse · Arbeitshausinspektor *m*

workhouse school · Arbeitshausschule *f*

working → working (of soil constituents)

working age · arbeitsfähiges Alter *n*

working asset · Betriebsvermögen *n*

working assumption, working hypothesis · Arbeitsannahme *f*, Arbeitshypothese *f*

working capacity, operating capacity · Betriebskapazität *f*

working capital, floating capital, circulating capital [*Capital available for the purpose of meeting current expenditure*] · Betriebskapital *n*

working capital → (gross) working capital

working capital → (net) working capital

working chart, working schedule, building chart, building schedule, construction chart, construction schedule, outline of construction procedure, (contractor's) completion schedule [*Written or graphically explained, the procedure of construction prepared by the contractor, usually by a bar chart of scheduled dates by trades or a critical path chart*] · (Ausführungs)Fristenplan *m*, Baufristenplan

working-class community, workers' community, workmen's community · Arbeitergemeinde *f*

working-class household, worker's household, workman's household · Arbeiterhaushalt *m*

working-class population · Arbeiterbevölkerung *f*

working-class quarter, workers' quarter, workmen's quarter · Arbeiter(wohn)viertel *n*, Arbeiter(wohn)quartier *n*

working-class suburb(an place); labour-class suburb(an place) (Brit.); labor-class suburb(an place) (US) · Arbeitervorort *m*

working committee · Arbeitsausschuß *m*

work(ing) day · Arbeitstag *m*

work(ing) documents, building documents, construction documents · Arbeitsunterlagen *f pl*, Bauunterlagen *f pl*, (Bau)Ausführungsunterlagen *f pl*

working farmer · (mit)arbeitender Landwirt *m*

working fee · Arbeitserlaubnisgeld *n*

working fund, trading fund [*Cash advanced for working-capital or expense purposes, and replenished from time to time as needed*] · Betriebsfonds *m*

work(ing) hour, hour of work · Arbeitsstunde *f*

working hypothesis, working assumption · Arbeitsannahme *f*, Arbeitshypothese *f*

work(ing) income, income from work(ing) · Arbeiteinkommen *n*

working in-commuter · Berufseinpendler *m*, Berufszupendler

working lot · Arbeitsparzelle *f*

working member (of the population), employed person, working person, contributing person · erwerbstätige Person *f*, beschäftigte Person, arbeitende Person, berufstätige Person

working method, method of working · Arbeitsweise *f*, Ausführungsweise

working month · Arbeitsmonat *m*

working of a business, running of a business · Geschäftsbetrieb *m*

working (of soil constituents), extraction (of soil constituents), winning (of soil constituents), mineral working, mineral getting, working of minerals, getting of minerals, mineral winning, winning of minerals, extraction of minerals, mineral extraction, getting (of soil constituents) · Abbau(en) *m*, *(n)* von Bodenbestandteilen, Abbau(en) von Mineralien, Mineralienabbau, Mineralienausbeuten, Ausbeuten (von Mineralien), Ausbeuten von Bodenbestandteilen, Ausbeutung *f* (von Mineralien), Ausbeutung von Bodenstandteilen, Mineralienausbeutung, Mineraliengewinnung, Gewinnung (von Mineralien), Gewinnung von Bodenbestandteilen [*Die planmäßige Inangriffnahme einer Lagerstätte bei der Gewinnung von Lehm, Sand, Kies usw.*]

working out-commuter · Berufsauspendler *m*, Berufswegpendler

working person, contributing person, working member (of the population), employed person · erwerbstätige Person f, beschäftigte Person, arbeitende Person, berufstätige Person

work(ing) place, employment place, job place, place of employment, place of work(ing) · Arbeitsort m, Arbeitsplatz m, Beschäftigungsort m, Beschäftigungsplatz m

work(ing) point, employment point, job point, point of employment, point of work(ing) · Arbeitsstätte f, Beschäftigungsstätte f [Fehlbenennung: Arbeitsplatz m]

working population, contributing population, employed population · erwerbstätige Bevölkerung f, beschäftigte Bevölkerung, arbeitende Bevölkerung, berufstätige Bevölkerung

working progress chart, working progress schedule, progress of the work(s) chart, progress of the work(s) schedule, (job) progress chart, (job) progress schedule · Arbeitsfortschrittplan m, (Bau)Fortschrittplan m, Bauzeit(en)plan m [vom Auftraggeber aufgestellt]

working rate, speed of working, rate of working, working speed · Arbeitsgeschwindigkeit f, Ausführungsgeschwindigkeit f, Arbeitstempo n, Ausführungstempo n

working regulation, working rule, working prescription · Arbeitsvorschrift f

working/residential settlement, residential working stettlement · Arbeitsstätten-Wohn-(An)Sied(e)lung f, Wohn-Arbeitsstätten-(An)Siedelung

working room · Arbeitsraum m

working schedule → working chart

(working) shift, work shift · (Arbeits)Schicht f

working speed, working rate, speed of working, rate of working · Arbeitsgeschwindigkeit f, Ausführungsgeschwindigkeit f, Arbeitstempo n, Ausführungstempo n

working time · Arbeitszeit f

working time agreement · Arbeitszeitabmachung f, Arbeitszeitvereinbarung f, Arbeitszeitabkommen n

working to rule, go-slow [A form of industrial action by workers taking the form of working more slowly than usual, i.e., reducing output by paying exaggerated attention to rules relating to working conditions] · Dienst m nach Vorschrift

working week · Arbeitswoche f

working without contract · auftragloses Arbeiten n

working year · Arbeitsjahr n

work item, performance item, pay item · (kosten)vergütete Position f, Leistungsposition, Arbeitsposition

(work) item quantity · Positionsmenge f

work journey, work travel, work trip · Berufsfahrt f

workland, land at work · dienstpflichtiges Land n

workload · Arbeitslast f, Arbeitspensum n

workman, operative; labourer (Brit.); blue collar worker, laborer (US); worker [A wage-earning worker, skilled or semi-skilled, whose work is characterized largely by physical exertion] · Arbeiter m

workmanship · Arbeitsgüte f

workmanship quality, quality of workmanship · Güte f der Arbeitsausführung

workman's household, working-class household, worker's household · Arbeiterhaushalt m

workman's mobility, worker's mobility · Arbeiterbeweglichkeit f, Arbeitermobilität f

workman's wage, worker's wage · Arbeiterlohn m

workmen's club, workers' club · Arbeiterklub m

workmen's community, working-class community, workers' community · Arbeitergemeinde f

workmen's compensation · Arbeiter-Unfallentschädigung f

workmen's co-operative, workers' co-operative · Arbeitergenossenschaft f

workmen's council, works council, workers' council · Betriebsrat m

workmen's deficiency → workers' scarcity

workmen's housing; labour housing (Brit.); labor housing (US); workers' housing · Arbeiterwohnungen fpl, Arbeiterwohnstätten fpl

workmen's housing law, workers' housing law · Arbeiterwohn(ungs)recht n

workmen's lodging; labouring classes lodging (Brit.); laboring classes lodging (US); workers' lodging · Arbeiterlogierhaus n

workmen's quarter, working-class quarter, workers' quarter · Arbeiter(wohn)viertel n, Arbeiter(wohn)quartier n

workmen's residential community, workers' residential community · Arbeiterwohngemeinde f [Ein Ort in dem ein Arbeiter wohnt, der an einem anderen Ort, der Betriebsgemeinde, arbeitet]

workmen's (return) ticket, workers' (return) ticket · Arbeiterrückfahrkarte f

workmen's scarcity → workers' scarcity

workmen's shanty, change room · Bauarbeiterbude f

workmen's shortage → workers' scarcity

workmen's stringency → workers' scarcity

workmen's train, workers' train · Arbeiterzug *m*

workmen's union, union of workers, workers' union, union of workmen · Arbeiterverband *m*

work mobility, occupational mobility, employment mobility · Arbeitsbeweglichkeit *f,* Arbeitsmobilität *f,* Beschäftigungsmobilität *f,* Beschäftigungsbeweglichkeit *f*

work of charity, charity work · mildtätiges Werk *n*

work of improvement, improvement work · Verbesserungsarbeiten *f pl*

work order · Arbeitsauftrag *m*

to work out, to form, to draft, to construct, to construe, to draw up, to set up · ausarbeiten, abfassen, gestalten, entwerfen [*Schriftstück*]

work pattern, employment scheme, work scheme, employment pattern · Arbeitsmuster *n,* Arbeitsschema *n,* Beschäftigungsmuster *n,* Beschäftigungsschema *n*

work place → work(ing) place

work-place population · Bevölkerung *f* nach Wohn- und Arbeitsplatz

work point → work(ing) point

work product privilege · Schutz *m* des anwaltlichen Arbeitgebergeheimnisses

work quantity → (project) work quantity

work-related death · Tod *m* durch Berufsausübung

work(s) · (Arbeits)Leistung(en) *f(pl),* Werkleistung(en) *f(pl),* Arbeit(en) *f(pl)*

work(s) → (construction) work(s)

works assembly · Betriebsversammlung *f*

work scheme, employment pattern, work pattern, employment scheme · Arbeitsmuster *n,* Arbeitsschema *n,* Beschäftigungsmuster *n,* Beschäftigungsschema *n*

works council, workers' council, workmen's council · Betriebsrat *m*

works council member, workers' council member, workmen's council member · Betriebsratsmitglied *n*

works council membership, workers' council membership, workmen's council membership · Betriebsratssitz *m*

works department → (public) works department

work(s) description, spec(ification)(s), description of (the) work(s), description of work(s) (content) · Arbeitsbeschreibung *f,* (Bau)Leistungsbeschreibung *f,* Baubeschreibung *f,* Darstellung *f* der Bauaufgabe, Darstellung *f* der (Bau)Leistungen, Vorschreibung *f*

work(s) falling outside the contract, work(s) outside contract · außervertragliche Arbeit(en) *f (pl),* außervertragliche Werkleistung(en), außervertragliche (Arbeits)Leistung(en) *f (pl)*

works-hamlet · Werksweiler *m*

work shift, (working) shift · (Arbeits)Schicht *f*

(work)shop drawing · Werkstattzeichnung *f*

(work)shop wage · Werkstattlohn *m*

work(s) insurance, insurance of (the) work(s) · (Bau)Leistungsversicherung *f*

work site → work(ing) site

work(s) (of construction) on a plot · Baubestand *m* [*Gesamtheit der in einem Gebiet oder auf einem Grundstück vorhandenen baulichen Anlagen*]

work(s) of management, organizational work(s) · organisatorische Arbeit(en) *f(pl)*

work(s) of necessity · Notstandsarbeit(en) *f (pl)*

work(s) of repair, repair work(s) · Reparaturarbeit(en) *f (pl)*

work(s) phasing by the contractor, phasing of the work(s) by the contractor · (Ausführungs)Fristenplanung *f,* Baufristenplanung *f*

work(s) phasing by the owner, work(s) phasing by the client, phasing of work(s) by the owner, phasing of work(s) by the client · Arbeitsfortschrittplanung *f,* Bauzeit(en)planung *f,* (Bau)Fortschrittplanung *f*

work(s) range, range of work(s) · (Bau)Arbeitsbereich *m,* (Bau)Leistungsbereich

work(s) report, site report, job report, construction report · Arbeitsbericht *m,* Bau(stellen)bericht *m*

work(s) resources · Arbeitsmittel *npl*

work station · Digitalisierplatz *m*

work to be demolished, physical facility to be demolished, structure to be demolished · Abrißbauwerk *n,* Abreißbauwerk, Einreißbauwerk

work(s) to be (ad)measured · aufzumessende Arbeit(en) *f(pl),* aufzumessende Leistung(en) *f(pl)*

work ticket, operation card, job card [*A document which authorizes an operation and is fed back after its completion to record any relevant information* —

time, quantity, operator, etc. — for such purposes as monitoring progress, wage payments, etc] · Arbeitskarte *f*

work to help households in distress, domestic relief work · Haushalt(s)fürsorge *f*

work to the workers' policy · aktive Sanierung *f* [*Die Politik Arbeitsplätze zu den verfügbaren Arbeitskräften zu bringen*]

work travel, work trip, work journey · Berufsfahrt *f*

work unit, unit of work · Arbeitseinheit *f*, Leistungseinheit *f*

to work up [*construction material*] · aufbrauchen [*Baustoff*]

world atlas of agriculture · Weltlandwirtschaftsatlas *m*

world atlas of petroleum · Erdölweltatlas *m*

World Bank, International Bank for Reconstruction and Development · Weltbank *f*

world centre (Brit.); world center (US); world city, world town · Weltstadt *f*

World Federation of Trade Unions, W.F.T.U. · Weltgewerkschaftsbund *m*

world map, map of the world · Weltkarte *f*

world's great regional belt, major natural region, higher unit, major world region · Landschaftsgürtel *m*

world war debt(s) settlement · Weltkriegsschuldenregelung *f*

worth analysis, benefit analysis, utility analysis · Nutz(ungs)wertanalyse *f*, NWA

worthiness of approval, ability to be approved, approvable quality, approbativeness, quality of being approbative, approvableness · Zulassungswürdigkeit *f*, Zustimm(ungs)würdigkeit, Zulassungsfähigkeit, Zustimm(ungs)fähigkeit

worthy of comparison, worthy to be compared · vergleichswürdig

wreath-like hamlet · Kranzweiler *m*

to wreck, to pull down, to raze, to demolish · abbrechen, abreißen, einreißen [*Bauwerk*]

wrecking, pulling down, razing, demolishing · Abbrechen *n*, Abreißen, Einreißen, Niederreißen

wrecking, pulling down, razing, demolition · Abbruch *m*, Abriß *m*, Bauabbruch, Bauabriß

wrecking and rebuilding area, area of demolition and rebuilding, area of wrecking and rebuilding, territory of demolition and rebuilding, territory of wrecking and rebuilding, wrecking and rebuilding territory, razing and rebuilding territory, demolition and rebuilding area, demolition and rebuilding territory · Abbruch- und Wiederaufbaugebiet *n*, Abriß- und Wiederaufbaugebiet, Abreiß- und Wiederaufbaugebiet

wrecking area, wrecking territory, pulling down area, pulling down territory, razing territory, demolition area, demolition territory · Abbruchgebiet *n*, Einreißgebiet, Abrißgebiet

wrecking certificate, pulling down certificate, razing certificate, demolition certificate · Abbruchbescheinigung *f*, Abbruchschein *m*, Einreißschein, Abreißschein, Abrißschein, Einreißbescheinigung, Abreißbescheinigung, Abrißbescheinigung

wrecking contract, pulling down contract, razing contract, demolition contract · Abbruchvertrag *m*, Abrißvertrag, Einreißvertrag, Abreißvertrag

wrecking contractor, pulling down contractor, razing contractor, demolition contractor · Abbruchunternehmer *m*

wrecking cost(s), pulling down cost(s), razing cost(s), demolition cost(s) · Abbruchkosten *f*, Abreißkosten, Einreißkosten, Abrißkosten

wrecking operation, pulling down operation, razing operation, demolition operation · Abbruchvorgang *m*, Abrißvorgang, Einreißvorgang, Abreißvorgang

wrecking operations → wrecking work(s)

wrecking order, pulling down order, demolition order · (Bau)Abbruchanordnung *f*, (Bau)Abbruchverfügung, (Bau)Abbruchgebot *n*, (Bau)Abbruchbefehl *m*, (Bau)Einreißverfügung, (Bau)Einreißanordnung, (Bau)Einreißbefehl, (Bau)Einreißgebot, (Bau)Abrißanordnung, (Bau)Abrißverfügung, (Bau)Abrißbefehl, (Bau)Abrißgebot [*In den Landesbauordnungen einiger Länder der Bundesrepublik Deutschland und in § 19 des Städtebauförderungsgesetzes*]

wrecking ordinance, pulling down ordinance, demolition ordinance · (Bau)Abbruchverordnung *f*, (Bau)Einreißverordnung, (Bau)Abrißverordnung, (Bau)Abreißverordnung

wrecking parcel → wrecking plot

wrecking permission, pulling down permission, razing permission, demolition permission · Abbrucherlaubnis *f*, Abbruchgenehmigung *f*, Einreißerlaubnis, Einreißgenehmigung, Abrißerlaubnis, Abrißgenehmigung, Abreißerlaubnis, Abreißgenehmigung

wrecking plot, pulling down plot, demolition parcel, pulling down parcel, wrecking parcel, razing parcel, demolition plot · Abbruchgrundstück *n*, Einreißgrundstück, Abreißgrundstück, Abrißgrundstück

wrecking stop, pulling down stop, razing stop, prohibition of demolition, prohibition of wrecking, prohibition of pulling down, demolition stop · Abbruchverbot *n*, Abrißverbot, Einreißverbot, Abreißverbot

wrecking territory, pulling down area, pulling down territory, razing territory, demolition area, demolition territory, wrecking area · Abbruchgebiet *n*, Einreißgebiet, Abrißgebiet, Abreißgebiet

wrecking work(s), wrecking operations, pulling down work(s), pulling down operations, razing operations, razing work(s), demolition work(s), demolition operations · Abbrucharbeit(en) *f (pl)*, Abrißarbeit(en), Einreißarbeit(en), Abreißarbeit(en)

wreck-master, receiver of wrecks · Strandhauptmann *m*, Strandvogt *m*

writ · Prozeßeinleitungsdekret *n*, Prozeßformular *n*, prozeßeinleitende Schrift *f*, einleitende Prozeßschrift

writ, (court) action, (law)suit, plea, cause [*In old English law, "writ" is used as equivalent to "action", hence writs are sometimes divided into real, personal, and mixed. It is not uncommon to call a proceeding in a common law court an action(-at-law), and one in an equity court a (law-)suit, but this is not a necessary distinction*] · (Gerichts)Klage *f*

writ, order of (the) court, court order [*A mandatory precept issuing from court of justice*] · Gerichtsverfügung *f*, Gerichtsgebot *n*, Gerichtsanordnung, Gerichtsbefehl *m*, (gerichtliche) Verfügung, gerichtliche Anordnung, gerichtliches Gebot, gerichtlicher Befehl, Mandat *n*

writ; breve [*Latin*] [*A document under the seal of the Crown, a court or an officer of the Crown, commanding the person to whom it is addressed to do or forbear from doing some act*] · Dekret *n*, (Hof)Rescript *n*

writ [*Scots law*]; instrument in writing, written instrument · schriftliches Rechtsinstitut *n*, schriftliches rechtliches Institut

writ department · Zustellungsgerichtsschreiberei *f*

write-in method [*USA*] · Einschreibverfahren *n* [*Die Wähler können bei der allgemeinen Wahl jede qualifizierte Person wählen, indem sie ihren Namen in eine auf dem Stimmzettel freigelassene Zeile einschreiben*]

writer · Schreiber *m*

writer · Schriftsteller *m*

writer on planning · Planungsschriftsteller *m*

to write under, to subscribe [*To write the name under any document. To sign is to write the name at any place, not necessarily underneath*] · unterschreiben

writing [*Obligation that a transaction shall be confirmed in writing or by the signature of one or both contracting parties*] · Schriftform *f*, Schriftlichkeit *f*

writing, document · Dokument *n*, Unterlage *f*, Schriftstück *n*

writing error, clerical error · Schreibfehler *m*

writing error correction, clerical error correction · Schreibfehlerberichtigung *f*

writing error made in good faith, clerical error made in good faith · unabsichtlicher Schreibfehler *m*, unbeabsichtigter Schreibfehler

writing mistake, clerical mistake · Schreibirrtum *m*

writ not closed, patent writ, open writ, writ not sealed up · unverschlossenes Dekret *n*, offenes Dekret, unversiegeltes Dekret

writ not sealed up, writ not closed, patent writ, open writ · unverschlossenes Dekret *n*, offenes Dekret, unversiegeltes Dekret

writ of appeal · Berufungsschrift *f*, Appellationsschrift

writ of assistance · Gerichtsbefehl *m* an einen Sheriff dem erfolgreichen Kläger zu seinem Landbesitz zu verhelfen

writ of (assize of) novel disseisin; breve de nova desaisina [*Latin*] · Klage *f* zur Wiedererlangung entzogenen Grundbesitzes, Klage zum Schutz vor eigenmächtiger Entwerung

writ of attachment, attachment writ · Personalarrestdekret *n*, Arrestdekret

(writ of) capias, writ of committal, writ of commitment, writ of confinement, committal writ, commitment writ, confinement writ, warrant [*A writ commanding the officer to take the body of the person named in that, that is, to arrest him*] · Haftbefehl *m*

(writ of) capias ad satisfaciendum [*A writ to imprison the defendant after judgment until the plaintiff's claim is satisfied*] · Schuldhaftdekret *n*, Schuldhaftbefehl *m*, Schuldhaftschreiben *n*

(writ of) capias in witheram [*A writ to seize the cattle or goods of anyone who has made an unlawful distraint*] · Gegenpfändungsbefehl *m*

(writ of) capias utlagatum [*A writ to arrest an outlawed person*] · Geächtetenhaftbefehl *m*

writ of certiorari; certiorari [*Latin*] [*An original writ which issued out of the Crown side of the Queen's Bench Division addressed to judges or officers of inferior courts, commanding them to certify or to return the records of a cause depending before them, to the end that justice might be done. By the Administration of Justice (Miscellaneous Provisions) Act, 1938, S. 7, the writ of certior-*

writ of delivery (of possession) — written instrument

ari was abolished, but the High Court now has the power to make an order of certiorari] · Abberufungsdekret *n*, Abberufungsschreiben *n*

writ of delivery (of possession), delivery writ · (Besitz)Ableitungsdekret *n*, (Besitz)Übergangsdekret [*bewegliche Sachen*]

writ of dower → writ of (right of) dower

writ of elegit [*English law*] · Immobiliarbeschlagnahmebefehl *m*, Immobilienbeschlagnahmebefehl, Liegenschaftsbeschlagnahmebefehl [*Er befiehlt die Beschlagnahme des in der Grafschaft belegenen, dem Schuldner gehörenden Immobiliarvermögens. Dieser Befehl wurde durch ein unter Eduard I. erlassenes Gesetz eingeführt (Stat. Westminster II, c. 185)*]

writ of error; breve de errore [*Latin*]; motion in arrest of judg(e)ment [*In criminal cases the accused may at any time between conviction and sentence move an arrest of judg(e)ment — that is to say, move that judg(e)ment be not pronounced — because of some defect in the indictment which is more than a mere formal defect and which has not been amended or used by verdict*] · Formfehlergesuch *n*, Gesuch daß ein Urteil nicht auf einen Geschworenenspruch gegründet wird

writ of execution, court order of execution · (Zwangs)Vollstreckungsmandat *n*, (Zwangs)Vollstreckungsbefehl *m*, (Zwangs)Vollstreckungsverfügung *f*, (Zwangs)Vollstreckungsanordnung, (Zwangs)Vollstreckungsgebot *n*

writ of fieri facias · Mobilienpfändungsbefehl *m*, Mobiliarpfändungsbefehl, Fahrnispfändungsbefehl, Fahrhabepfändungsbefehl

writ of inquiry, writ of enquiry, inquiring writ, enquiring writ · Ermitt(e)lungsverfügung *f*

(writ of) mandamus, prerogative order of mandamus [*It is issued from a court of superior jurisdiction and directed to a private or municipal corporation, or any of its officers, or to an executive, administrative or judicial officer, or to an inferior court, commanding the performance of a particular act therein specified, and belonging to his or their public, official, or ministerial duty, or directing the restoration of the complainant to rights or privileges of which he has been illegally deprived*] · Erfüllungsdekret *n*, Erfüllungsbefehl *m*, Vornahmedekret, Vornahmebefehl

writ of possession, possession writ · Besitzergreifungsdekret *n*, gerichtliche Besitzeinweisungsverfügung *f*, gerichtliches Besitzeinweisungsmandat *n*, gerichtlicher Besitzeinweisungsbefehl *m* [*Einweisung in ein Grundstück*]

writ of prohibition · Abwehrdekret *n* [*Zur Abwehr von Übergriffen unterer richterlicher Instanzen über ihre Kompetenz hinaus und zur Verhinderung einer Behörde ihre Kompetenz in ungesetzlicher Weise auf Kosten der ordentlichen Gerichte zu erweitern*]

writ of restitution · Wiedereinweisungsdekret *n*

writ of right; breve de recto [*Latin*] · Eigentumsklage *f* [*Liegenschaft. Formell beseitigt durch 3 und 4 W.IV. c 77*]

writ of (right of) dower · Wittumsklage *f*

writ of strict right · gewöhnliche Klag(e)formel *f*

writ (of summons) (to appear) · Erscheinungsbefehl *m*, Erscheinungsschreiben *n*, Erscheinungsmandat *n*, (Vor)Ladungsbefehl, (Vor)Ladungsschreiben, (Vor)Ladungsmandat, (Prozeß)Ladung *f*

(writ of) venire · Geschworenenvorladung *f*

written, in writing · schriftlich

written assent, written approval, written consent, written sanction, consent in writing, assent in writing, sanction in writing, approval in writing · schriftliche Billigung *f*, schriftliche Einwilligung, schriftliche Zustimmung

written contract, contract in writing, contract evidenced by writing · schriftlicher Vertrag *m*, schriftlich abgefaßter Vertrag

(written) contract not under seal, (written) contract without seal, contract by unsealed writing, simple contract, unsealed contract, parol contract [*A simple contract made by writing without seal. By a strange misuse of language, both kinds of simple contract (1. The simple contract made by word of mouth and 2. The simple contract made by writing without seal) are frequently spoken of in English law as parol contracts notwithstanding that the term "parol", both etymologically and in general parlance, means "by word of mouth"*] · nicht gesiegelter (schriftlicher) Vertrag *m*, ungesiegelter (schriftlicher) Vertrag, nicht formeller Vertrag, nicht notarieller Vertrag, (schriftlicher) Vertrag ohne Siegel, schriftlicher ungesiegelter Vertrag

written decision · schriftliche Entscheidung *f*, schriftlicher Entscheid *m*

written defamation, defamation by writing; libellus [*Latin*]; libel · schriftliche Ehrenkränkung *f*, Schmähschrift *f*

written down value · Abschreibungswert *m*

written instrument; writ [*Scots law*]; instrument in writing · schriftliches Rechtsinstitut *n*, schriftliches rechtliches Institut

written law, enacted law, statutory law, statutes; lex scripta [*Latin*]; jus scriptum [*Latin*], statute law [*The body of law enacted by Parliament*] · geschriebenes Recht *n*, gesetztes Recht, geschriebenes Parlamentsrecht, gesetztes Parlamentsrecht, (Parlaments)Gesetz(es)recht

written notice, written notification, notice in writing, notification in writing · schriftliche Anzeige *f*, schriftliche Benachrichtigung *f*, schriftliche Mitteilung

written sanction → written assent

wrong, mistaken(ly), false(ly), erroneous(ly) · irrig(erweise), rechtsirrtümlich, irrtümlich(erweise), falsch

wrong → violation (of law)

wrong-doer · Vertragsbrüchige *m*

wrong-doer; malefactor [*Latin*] · Übeltäter *m*

wrong-doer, tortfeasor · Delikttäter *m*

wrong-doing; maleficium [*Latin*], mischief · Übeltat *f*

wronged [*contract party*] · benachteiligt [*Vertragspartner*]

wrongful, inconsistent with possessory right, adverse · entgegenstehend, fehlerhaft, entgegen dem Recht, rechtswidrig [*(subjektives) Besitzrecht*]

wrongful → nonlegal

wrongful-death statute, wrongful-death law, wrongful-death act · Gesetz *n* über widerrechtliche Tötung, Tötungsgesetz

wrongful dismissal · ungerecht(fertigt)e Entlassung *f*

wrongful possession, adverse possession [*An occupation of realty inconsistent with the right of the true owner*] · entgegenstehender (Land)Besitz *m*, entgegenstehender Bodenbesitz, entgegenstehender Grund(stücks)besitz, fehlerhafter (Land)Besitz, fehlerhafter Grund(stücks)besitz, fehlerhafter Bodenbesitz, rechtswidriger Bodenbesitz, rechtswidriger (Land)Besitz, rechtswidriger Grund(stücks)besitz

wrongful taking of personal chattels; amotio [*Latin*]; amotion · widerrechtliche Fahrnisentziehung *f*, widerrechtliche Fahrhabeentziehung, widerrechtlicher Fahrnisentzug, widerrechtlicher Fahrhabeentzug *m*

wrongness, faultiness [*Want of correctness or exactness*] · Fehlerhaftigkeit *f*

wrongous [*Scotland*] → nonlegal

Y

yardland, hydeland, husbandland, wista; hilda [*Scotland*]; terra hydata, virgate terrae, hida (terrae), hyda, familia [*Latin*]; hide ((of) land), hyde (of land), higid, hiwise, virgate (land), verge of land [*A quantity of land not of any certain extent, but as much as a plough can by course of husbandry plough in a year. It meant in different places anything from sixty to 120 acres. A virgate is one fourth of a hide*] · Hufe(ngut) *f*, *(n)*, Hufenschoß *n*, Hube *f*, Hufen(gut)land *n* [*Ältere Benennungen: Hof m, Hub m, Hu(o)ba f, und Hova f*] [*Unter gutsherrlich-bäuerlichen Verhältnissen hieß der gesamte Besitz eines Dorfgenossen „Hufe(ngut)". Diese Benennung war also keine Flächengröße, sondern eine Besitzeinheit, die zahlreiche, zerstreut liegende kleine Ackerteile im Besitz derselben Person umfaßte*]

yardling; virgarius [*Latin*]; tenant by the verge, holder of yardland, holder of virgate, holder of verge of land [*Tenant who held copyhold after a symbolic surrender and delivery of a small rod (= verge)*] · Hüf(e)ner *m*, Hufenbauer, Huf(e)ner

yardstick · Maßstab *m* [*Im übertragenen Sinne*]

yearly, annual, from year to year · auf unbestimmte Zeit, von Jahr zu Jahr [*Land(besitz)recht*]

yearly accounts → yearly (statement of) accounts

yearly amount, annual amount · Jahresbetrag *m*

yearly average, annual average · Jahresdurchschnitt *m*, Jahresmittel *n*

yearly balance(-sheet), annual balance(-sheet) · Jahresbilanz *f*

yearly cost(s) of operation, annual operating cost(s), yearly operating cost(s), annual cost(s) of operation · Jahresbetriebskosten *f*

yearly demise → tenancy from year to year

yearly gain, annual profit, annual gain, yearly profit · Jahresgewinn *m*

yearly general meeting, A.G.M., (annual) general meeting · (Jahres)Hauptversammlung *f*

yearly gross income, gross annual income, gross yearly income, annual gross

yearly gross value — yield on investment 1138

yearly gross value, gross annual value, gross yearly value, annual gross value · Bruttoertragswert *m* [*Liegenschaft*]

yearly holder → (land) holder from year to year

yearly instal(l)ment of redemption, annual instal(l)ment of redemption, amount usually put to sinking fund · jährliche Tilgungsrate *f*, jährliche Tilgungsquote, jährliche Amortisationsrate, jährliche Amortisationsquote

yearly insurance, annual insurance · Jahresversicherung *f*

yearly (land) holder → (land) holder from year to year

yearly lease(hold) → tenancy from year to year

yearly lessee → (land) holder from year to year

yearly net income, net annual income, net yearly income, annual net income · Jahresnettoeinkommen *n*, Nettojahreseinkommen

yearly occupier → (land) holder from year to year

yearly operating cost(s), annual cost(s) of operation, yearly cost(s) of operation, annual operating cost(s) · Jahresbetriebskosten *f*

yearly payment, annual payment · Jahreszahlung *f*, jährliche Zahlung

yearly production, annual production · Jahresleistung *f*

yearly profit, yearly gain, annual profit, annual gain · Jahresgewinn *m*

yearly rent, annual rent · Jahresmiete *f*

yearly rent, annual rent · Jahresrente *f*

yearly rent, annual rent [*Yearly interest on a loan of money*] · jährlich abgerechnete Darleh(e)nszinsen *f*

yearly report, yearly return, annual report, annual return · Jahresbericht *m*

yearly running cost(s), annual running cost(s) · jährliche laufende Kosten *f*, laufende jährliche Kosten

yearly (statement of) accounts, annual (statement of) accounts · Jahresabschluß *m*

yearly stockturn, annual turnover, annual stockturn, yearly turnover · Jahresumsatz *m*

yearly sum, annual sum · Jahressumme *f*

yearly tenancy → tenancy from year to year

yearly tenant → (land) holder from year to year

yearly tenure → tenancy from year to year

yearly turnover, yearly stockturn, annual turnover, annual stockturn · Jahresumsatz *m*

yearly value, annual value · Jahreswert *m*

yearly wage, annual wage · Jahreslohn *m*

year of construction, year of building, construction year, building year · Baujahr *m*

year of mining, mining year · Nutzungsjahr *n* [*Abbau einer Lagerstätte*]

year of settlement, settlement year · Abrechnungsjahr *n*

years purchase · Rückkauf *m* der Meliorationsrente zu einer bestimmten Anzahl von Jahreszinsen

yellow dog contract (US) · Vertrag *m* mit Verzicht auf Gewerkschaftsbeitritt

yellowed drawing · vergilbte Zeichnung *f*

y(e)oman, journeyman · Geselle *m*

ye(o)man(-farmer), ceorl, churl [*An old English freeman of the lowest class, opposed on one side to a thane or nobleman, on the other to the servile classes*] · Gemeinfreie *m*

y(e)oman farming · (Boden)Kultivierung *f* durch Gemeinfreie, Anbau *m* durch Gemeinfreie

y(e)oman(-peasant)ry · Gemeinfreientum *n*

y(e)omanry · Gesellenverband *m*

to yield, to show a profit, to show a gain · abwerfen, Gewinn abwerfen

yield, return · Ertrag *m*, Rendite *f*

yield from housing property, return from housing property · Hausrendite *f*

yielding of interests, bearing of interests, interest yield(ing), interest bearing, interest return, returning of interests · Verzinsung *f*

yield law, law of return, law of yield, return law · Renditegesetz *n*, Ertragsgesetz

yield maximization, maximization of return, maximization of yield, return maximization · Renditemaximierung *f*

yield mortgage, mortgage on yield [*Not on real estate*] · Revenü(en)hypothek *f*, Revenu(en)hypothek [*Nur die Grundstückserträge haften*]

yield of building, building yield · Gebäudeertrag *m*

yield on investment, return on capital, yield on capital, capital yield, capital return, investment yield, investment return, ROI, return on investment · Kapitalrendite *f* [*Verhältnis von erzieltem Gewinn zum eingesetzten Kapital*]

young settled (agricultural) land, late settled (agricultural) land · Jungsiedelland *n*

young settlement, late settlement · Jung(an)sied(e)lung *f*

youthful offender · jugendlicher Straftäter *m*

youth hostel · Jugendherberge *f*

youth recreation · Jugenderholung *f*

youth representation · Jugendvertretung *f*

Z

zero covariance · Nullkovarianz *f*

zero growth, no-growth · Nullwachstum *n*

zero growth rate, growth rate of zero, no-growth rate · Nullwachstumsrate *f*

zero population growth · Nullbevölkerungswachstum *n*

zero rate · Nullsatz *m*

zero rate of tax, tax zero rate · Steuernullsatz *m*

zero-sum game · Null-Summen-Spiel *n* [*Statistik*]

zonal arrangement · Zonenanordnung *f*

zonal border, zonal frontier, zone border, zone frontier · Zonengrenze *f*

zonal border area, zonal border territory · Zonenrandgebiet *n*

zonal data · Zonendaten *f*

zonal frontier, zone border, zone frontier, zonal border · Zonengrenze *f*

to zone · (baulich) nutzen [*Land*]

zone [*An area set off by a governing body for specific use, such as residential, commercial, or industrial use*] · Zone *f*

zone border, zone frontier, zonal border, zonal frontier · Zonengrenze *f*

zoned · (baulich) genutzt

zoned area, zoned land(s) · (baulich) genutztes Land *n*, (baulich) genutzter Boden *m*, (baulich) genutzte Fläche *f*

zoned community; zoned commune [*obsolete*] · (baulich) genutzte Gemeinde *f*

zoned for residential use · genutzt für Wohnzwecke

zoned land(s), zoned area · (baulich) genutztes Land *n*, (baulich) genutzter Boden *m*, (baulich) genutzte Fläche *f*

zone frontier, zonal border, zonal frontier, zone border · Zonengrenze *f*

zone of administration, administration zone · Verwaltungszone *f*

zone of discard, discard zone · heruntergekommene Randzone *f* eines Geschäftsviertels

zone of mixed functions, all-purpose zone · Mischgebiet *n*, Mischbaugebiet, gemischte Baufläche *f* [*Es dient dem Wohnen und der Unterbringung von Gewerbebetrieben, die das Wohnen nicht wesentlich stören*]

zone of occupation, occupation(al) zone · Besatzungszone *f*

zone of origin · Quellzone *f*

zone of passage, passage zone · Übergangszone *f*

zone size, size of zone · Zonengröße *f*

zoning, (land) use zoning · (bauliche) Nutzung *f*, Baunutzung, Bauzonenfestlegung

zoning allotment, zoning apportionment · Baunutzungszuteilung *f*

zoning approval, zoning approbation, zoning assent, zoning consent, zoning consensus · Baunutzungszustimmung *f*, Baunutzungsbilligung, Baunutzungseinwilligung, Baunutzungskonsens *m*

zoning board · Baunutzungsamt *n*

(zoning) classification, classification of zoning · (Auf)Gliederung *f* [*Baunutzungsverordnung*]

zoning code · Baunutzungsordnung *f*

zoning concession · Baunutzungskonzession *f*

zoning enabling law · Baunutzungsermächtigungsrecht *n*

zoning field, zoning sector · Baunutzungssektor *m* [*als Tätigkeitssektor*]

zoning law, law of zoning · Baunutzungsrecht *n*

zoning lawmaking, zoning legislation · Baunutzungsgesetzgebung *f*

zoning lawyer · Baunutzungs(rechts)anwalt *m*

zoning map · Baunutzungskarte *f*

zoning mix(ture), (land) use zoning mix(ture) · (bauliche) Nutzungsmischung *f*, Baunutzungsmischung

zoning order, (land) use zoning order · (bauliche) Nutzungsanordnung *f*, (bauliche) Nutzungsverfügung, Baunutzungsanordnung, Baunutzungsverfügung, (bauliches) Nutzungsgebot *n*, Baunutzungsgebot, (baulicher) Nutzungsbefehl *m*, Baunutzungsbefehl

zoning ordinance · Baunutzungsverordnung *f*, BauNVO, BNutzVO, Verordnung über die bauliche Nutzung [*Die Verordnung über die bauliche Nutzung der Grundstücke in der Fassung vom 26. 11. 1968 (BGBl. 1968 I, 1237) regelt den Inhalt der in § 1 des Bundesbaugesetzes vom 23. 6. 1960 vorgesehenen Flächennutzungspläne und -bebauungspläne im einzelnen. So ist z. B. geregelt die Aufgliederung der für die Bebauung vorgesehenen Flächen im Flächennutzungsplan in Bauflächen (Wohnbauflächen, gewerbliche Bauflächen usw.) und in Baugebiete (z. B. Kleinsiedlungsgebiete, Dorfgebiete, Gewerbegebiete, Wochenendhausgebiete usw.). Ferner enthält die BNutzVO Bestimmungen über die bauliche Nutzung von Grundstücken durch Geschoßflächenzahl, Grundflächenzahl und Zahl der Vollgeschosse (§§ 16ff.)*]

zoning plan · Baustufenplan *m*, Baustaffelplan, Baugebietsplan, (Bau)Nutzungsplan [*Plan, der vor dem Inkrafttreten des Bundesbaugesetzes vom 23. 6. 1960 (BGBl. I S. 341) für ein größeres Baugebiet, meist für das gesamte Gemeindegebiet, Art und Maße der baulichen Nutzung verbindlich regelte. Das Bundesbaugesetz verwendet diesen Begriff nicht mehr. Art und Maß der baulichen Nutzung wird nach dem Inkrafttreten des Bundesbaugesetzes nur noch verbindlich durch den Bebauungsplan geregelt (vgl. § 9 BBauG)*]

zoning policy · Baunutzungspolitik *f*

zoning power, zoning right · Baunutzungsrecht *n*, Baunutzungsbefugnis *f*

zoning practice · Baunutzungswesen *n*

zoning prescription, prescription of zoning, zoning regulation, zoning rule, rule of zoning, regulation of zoning · (bauliche) Nutzungsvorschrift *f*, Baunutzungsvorschrift

zoning prohibition, (land) use zoning prohibition · (bauliches) Nutzungsverbot *n*, Baunutzungsverbot

(zoning) reclassification · Umgliederung *f* [*Baunutzungsverordnung*]

zoning reduction · verminderter Grundstückswert *m* [*Eigentum in einem Sanierungsgebiet wird zu einem verminderten Grundstückswert gekauft*]

zoning regulation · Baunutzungsregelung *f*

zoning restriction · Baunutzungsbeschränkung *f*, Baunutzungseinschränkung

zoning right, zoning power · Baunutzungsrecht *n*, Baunutzungsbefugnis *f*

zoning sector, zoning field · Baunutzungssektor *m* [*als Tätigkeitssektor*]

zoning separation, (land(s)) use zoning separation · (bauliche) Nutzungstrennung *f*, Baunutzungstrennung

zoning variance [*A modification of or variation from the provisions of existing zoning regulations — as distinguished from a change in zoning*] · Baunutzungsänderung *f*

Bauverlag-Sprachlehrbücher

Englisch für Baufachleute
L'anglais dans le bâtiment
Von Prof. Dipl.-Ing. G. Wallnig und H. Evered F.C.S.I.
Format 17 x 24 cm. Kartoniert.
Band 1: 127 S. mit zahlreichen Abbildungen. DM 22,—
Band 2: VIII, 192 S. mit Abbildungen. DM 38,—
Band 3: 211 S. mit Abbildungen. DM 45,—

Englische und französische Fachsprache im Auslandsbau
von der Voranfrage bis zur Bauausführung
International Construction Contracts Terminology in French and English with German Vocabularies
L'anglais dans la terminologie de la construction et du bâtiment dans le monde avec des glossaires allemands
Von Prof. Dipl.-Ing. K. Lange, Dipl.-Ing. L. Ferval und Dipl.-Ing. Arch. K. Kellmann. 131 S. DIN A 5. Kart. DM 24,—

Bautechnisches Englisch im Bild
Illustrated Technical German for Builders
Von W. K. Killer. 183 S. mit zahlreichen Abbildungen.
Texte zweisprachig in Deutsch und Englisch. Format 17 x 24 cm.
Kart. DM 24,—

Englische Rechtssprache
Mustertexte und Fachausdrücke unter Einbeziehung von Amerikanismen
Von G. Glass. 87 S. DIN A 5. Kart. DM 24,—

Physik-Fachsprache
Englisch — Französisch — Deutsch
Textbeispiele und Übersetzungen
Physics Terminology French-German-English
Selected Texts for Scientists and Engineers
Terminologie de la physique anglais-allemand-français
Recueil d'articles et aide à la traduction
Von Dr.-Ing. Dipl.-Phys. A. Jesse. 129 S. Format 21 x 20 cm.
Kart. DM 28,—

Bauverlag GmbH · Wiesbaden und Berlin

Bauverlag-Wörterbücher

Holz-Wörterbuch
Dictionary of Wood and Woodworking Practice
Von H. Bucksch. Format 13,5 × 20,5 cm. Plastik.
Band 1: Deutsch-Englisch. 461 Seiten. Rund 20 000 Stichwörter. DM 85,—
Band 2: Englisch-Deutsch. 536 Seiten. Rund 20 000 Stichwörter. DM 95,—

Getriebe-Wörterbuch
Dictionary of Mechanisms
Von H. Bucksch. Deutsch-Englisch/Englisch-Deutsch in einem Band. 286 Seiten mit zahlreichen Zeichnungen. Zusammen rund 16 000 Stichwörter.
Format 13,5 × 20,5 cm. Plastik DM 165,—

Zement-Wörterbuch
Dictionary of Cement

Herstellung und Technologie
Manufacture and Technology

Von Dipl.-Ing. C. van Amerongen. Deutsch-Englisch/Englisch-Deutsch. Ca. 350 Seiten.
Format 13,5 × 20,5 cm. Gebunden ca. DM 150,—

Gips-Wörterbuch
Gypsum and Plaster Dictionary
Dictionnaire du gypse et du plâtre

Deutsch — Englisch — Französisch

Von Dipl.-Ing. K.-H. Volkart. 176 Seiten. Rund 3000 Stichwörter. Format 17 × 24 cm. Gebunden DM 85,—

Bauverlag GmbH · Wiesbaden und Berlin

Bauverlag-Wörterbücher

Wörterbuch für Baurecht, Grundstücksrecht und Raumordnung
Dictionary of Construction Law, Land Law and Regional Policy
Von H. Bucksch. Format 13,5 × 20,5 cm. Gebunden.
Band 2: Englisch-Deutsch. Etwa 1300 Seiten mit rund 70 000 Stichwörtern. DM 390,—

Die internationale Zusammenarbeit hat in den letzten Jahren vor allem auch im Baubetrieb einen beträchtlichen Umfang angenommen. Eine einwandfreie sprachliche Verständigung ist ganz entscheidend abhängig von der exakten Kenntnis der Fachbegriffe. Sicherheit bei der Wahl bzw. Übersetzung selbst des speziellsten Fachbegriffes vermittelt der 2. Band dieses umfassendsten baurechtlichen Wörterbuches.

Wörterbuch für Architektur, Hochbau und Baustoffe
Dictionary of Architecture, Building Construction and Materials
Von H. Bucksch. Format 13,5 × 20,5 cm. Plastik.
Band 1: Deutsch-Englisch. 942 Seiten. Rund 65 000 Stichwörter. DM 240,—
Band 2: Englisch-Deutsch. 1137 Seiten. Rund 75 000 Stichwörter. DM 240,—

Diese Bände beinhalten nicht nur die alphabetische Folge aller Fachbegriffe, sondern darüber hinaus in allen notwendigen Fällen kurze bis ausführliche Erläuterungen zu den Termini. So erhält das Wörterbuch den zusätzlichen Wert eines Baufachlexikons.

Wörterbuch für Bautechnik und Baumaschinen
Dictionary of Civil Engineering and Construction Machinery and Equipment
Von H. Bucksch. Format 12,5 × 17 cm.
Band 1: Deutsch-Englisch. 1184 Seiten. Rund 68 000 Stichwörter. Plastik DM 180,—
Band 2: Englisch-Deutsch. 1219 Seiten. Rund 71 000 Stichwörter. Plastik DM 180,—

Bauverlag GmbH · Wiesbaden und Berlin